UK
GAAP

Sixth Edition

00330444

Sixth Edition

UK
GAAP

Gen ...ce
in t...

Mik ...*Wilson*

Toll...

...OUNG

Sixth edition published 1999 by
Butterworths Tolley
2 Addiscombe Road
Croydon Surrey CR9 5AF

http://www.gaap.co.uk

ISBN 0 7545 0388 7

A catalogue record for this book is available from the British Library.

No responsibility for loss occasioned to any person acting or refraining from action as a result of the material in this publication can be accepted by the authors or the publishers.

Index typeset by Letterpart Limited, Reigate, Surrey.
Printed and bound in Great Britain by William Clowes Limited, Beccles and London.

℟ **A member of the Reed Elsevier plc group**

Foreword to the sixth edition

UK GAAP: Generally Accepted Accounting Practice in the United Kingdom, now in its sixth edition, continues to be an impressive work. As both a handbook for experts in the field and a primer or textbook for those who seek a grounding in the field, it is without peer.

The authors display a deep understanding of financial reporting and the standard-setting and regulatory environments in the UK as well as of those in North America, Europe and Australia and New Zealand. At a time when financial reporting in the UK and throughout the world is increasingly responding to demands for international comparability, a work with the broad sweep of UK GAAP is an indispensable guide.

The authors have succeeded in making their book accessible to non-specialists without sacrificing its value as a technical reference work for auditors, company accountants and finance directors. UK accounting standards are clearly explained and are richly illustrated with extracts from company annual reports. In each chapter, the authors make useful comparisons with US GAAP and the standards issued by the International Accounting Standards Committee.

The authors also explain how the current standards have evolved, and their criticisms of standard setters' positions are always instructive to the reader. It is especially helpful that the authors examine the implications for financial reporting of the revised draft of the Accounting Standards Board's Statement of Principles.

Through this foreword, I am pleased to commend the sixth edition to a wide audience.

August 1999

Stephen A. Zeff

Herbert S. Autrey Professor of Accounting

Rice University

Preface to the sixth edition

The sixth edition of **UK GAAP** marks the tenth year of the book's publication. In that time, financial reporting has changed significantly both in the UK and internationally. This is reflected in the size of the book itself, which has more than doubled in length since the first edition. Much of the change can be attributed to the impact of the Accounting Standards Board, which has been in office for most of the life of this book, and has now published fifteen standards, seven of them in the two years since we published the fifth edition.

In the Preface to the first edition in 1989, we promised to be forthright in our views about how accounting practice could be improved. It is well known that since then we have often disagreed with proposals put forward by the ASB, and in particular that we have profound reservations about its draft *Statement of Principles*. The reason for this is not doctrinaire; we simply do not think that this framework provides a good foundation for practical standards that will generate understandable accounts, and this book includes many examples which explain why that is the case. However, we also compliment the Board on some of its other achievements in enhancing the annual reporting package.

In our 1989 Preface we also commended the IASC on its initiative of seeking to narrow the areas of difference between the GAAP of different countries. Since that time, International Accounting Standards have done a great deal both to improve and harmonise financial reporting around the world. More importantly, though, the outcome of the IASC's core standards project which it is carrying out in co-operation with the International Organisation of Securities Commissions (IOSCO), will largely determine the course of world harmonisation of accounting and the future role of the IASC. We support the IASC in its bid to develop its standards to a level at which they will be accepted throughout the world's capital markets. We also call for the recognition of International Accounting Standards in UK law, on the grounds that this is a competitive issue for international companies registered in the UK. Above all, though, we see this as an issue of European harmonisation and pan-European comparability in financial reporting; the more so as reporting under IAS is already widely accepted in some of the major economies of Continental Europe, is practised by some of the largest European multinational groups and accepted by their respective capital markets. These developments will, in turn, have a major influence on the future direction of UK GAAP.

For all these reasons, this sixth edition of **UK GAAP** includes substantially enhanced analysis and commentary on the requirements of International Accounting Standards.

As with all previous editions, we are indebted to a number of our colleagues in Ernst & Young for their help with the publication of this book, most notably Paul Bircher, Joanne Brundish, Matthew Curtis, Tim Denton, Trevor Pijper and Gregory Wilkinson-Riddle, but also all the other members of the Technical Services Department, who contributed both directly and indirectly to the book's creation. We are also indebted to Angus McIntrye and Ben Weller of Ernst & Young's tax department who provided invaluable assistance with Chapter 21. As authors, however, we continue to take responsibility for all the opinions expressed in the book and the blame for all its faults.

August 1999

Mike Davies
Ron Paterson
Allister Wilson

List of chapters

Detailed contents

CHAPTER 2   THE QUEST FOR A CONCEPTUAL FRAMEWORK
FOR FINANCIAL REPORTING   53

CHAPTER 4   CORPORATE GOVERNANCE AND THE OFR   223

CHAPTER 5   CONSOLIDATED ACCOUNTS   267

CHAPTER 6   BUSINESS COMBINATIONS AND DISPOSALS   313

CHAPTER 8   FOREIGN CURRENCIES   527

CHAPTER 9   FINANCIAL INSTRUMENTS   651

CHAPTER 10   FIXED ASSETS   725

CHAPTER 13   CAPITALISATION OF FINANCE COSTS   921

CHAPTER 15   CAPITAL INSTRUMENTS   1011

CHAPTER 16   OFF BALANCE SHEET TRANSACTIONS   1091

CHAPTER 17   LEASES AND HIRE PURCHASE CONTRACTS   1159

CHAPTER 19   SEGMENTAL REPORTING   1243

CHAPTER 20   PENSION COSTS   1287

CHAPTER 22   REPORTING FINANCIAL PERFORMANCE   1477

CHAPTER 24   POST BALANCE SHEET EVENTS   1617

CHAPTER 26   CASH FLOW STATEMENTS   1721

CHAPTER 27   RELATED PARTIES   1787

CHAPTER 28   DIRECTORS' AND OFFICERS' LOANS AND TRANSACTIONS   1841

CHAPTER 30   INTERIM REPORTS AND PRELIMINARY
                 ANNOUNCEMENTS   1975

Abbreviations

The following abbreviations are used in this book:

Professional and regulatory bodies:

AICPA   American Institute of Certified Public Accountants
APB   Accounting Principles Board (of the AICPA, predecessor of the FASB)
         The Auditing Practices Board (in the UK)
ASB   Accounting Standards Board (the standard-setting arm of the FRC)
ASC   Accounting Standards Committee (the predecessor of the ASB)
CCAB   Consultative Committee of Accountancy Bodies
CICA   The Canadian Institute of Chartered Accountants
DTI   Department of Trade and Industry
FASB   Financial Accounting Standards Board (in the US)
FRC   Financial Reporting Council (in the UK, oversees the ASB, FRRP and UITF)
FRRP   The Financial Reporting Review Panel (the policing arm of the FRC)
IASC   International Accounting Standards Committee
ICAEW   The Institute of Chartered Accountants in England and Wales
ICAS   The Institute of Chartered Accountants of Scotland
IOSCO   The International Organisation of Securities Commissions
SEC   Securities and Exchange Commission (the USA securities regulator)
SIC   The Standing Interpretations Committee of the IASC
UITF   The Urgent Issues Task Force (a subsidiary committee of the ASB)

Accounting related terms:

CA 85   The Companies Act 1985, as amended by the Companies Act 1989
CCA   Current cost accounting
CIS   Comprehensive income statement, as developed by the G4+1 group of accounting standard-setters, and published in June 1999 in the ASB Discussion Paper *Reporting Financial Performance: Proposals for Change*
E   Exposure Draft (of an IAS)
ED   Exposure Draft (of a SSAP)
EPS   Earnings per share
FIFO   The first-in, first-out basis of valuation
FRED   Financial Reporting Exposure Draft (of a UK FRS)

FRS   Financial Reporting Standard (issued by the ASB)

GAAP   Generally accepted accounting practice (as it applies to the UK), or generally accepted accounting principles (as it applies to the US)

IAS   International Accounting Standard (issued by the IASC)

LIFO   The last-in, first-out basis of valuation

NRV   Net realisable value

OFR   Operating and financial review

R&D   Research and development

SFAC   Statement of Financial Accounting Concepts (issued by the FASB as part of its conceptual framework project)

SFAS   Statement of Financial Accounting Standards (issued by the FASB)

SOP1   The Draft *Statement of Principles for Financial Reporting* issued by the ASB in November 1995

SOP2   The revised Draft *Statement of Principles for Financial Reporting* issued by the ASB in March 1999

SORP   Statement of Recommended Practice

SSAP   Statement of Standard Accounting Practice (issued by the ASC)

STRGL Statement of Total Recognised Gains and Losses, the primary financial statement introduced by the ASB in FRS 3.

TR   Technical Release (issued by the ICAEW)

Authoritative literature

The content of this Sixth Edition takes into account all accounting standards and other relevant rules issued by 31 August 1999. Consequently, it covers all authoritative literature up to and including the following:

■ FRS 15 and UITF 22 in the UK, together with all exposure drafts up to FRED 19 published on 26 August 1999.

■ The ASB's revised Draft *Statement of Principles*, published in March 1999, and the ASB's Discussion Paper *Reporting Financial Performance: Proposals for Change*, developed in association with the other members of the G4+1 group of accounting standard-setters, published in June 1999.

■ The Companies Act 1985, as amended by the Companies Act 1989.

■ SFAS 137 and SFAC No. 6, issued by the FASB.

■ IAS 39 and E65 issued by the IASC. It also covers all amendments to pre-existing standards, including IASs 10, 12, 17, 19 and 22.

■ SIC - 16 issued by the Standing Interpretations Committee of the IASC.

Chapter 1
The development of UK GAAP

1 DEFINITION OF 'UK GAAP'

1.1 'Principles' or 'practice'

In the UK, the expression 'GAAP' is used more loosely than in most other countries; the reason for this is that GAAP does not have any statutory or regulatory authority or definition, as is the case in, for example, the US, Canada and New Zealand. Consequently, references to GAAP are rarely found in the literature in the UK, and where the expression is used, it is not adequately explained or defined.

There are two instances where the term is used in the Companies Act. In order for a business combination to be treated as a merger, one of the qualifying criteria is that the method 'accords with generally accepted accounting principles or practice'.[1] This is usually taken to mean that the transaction qualifies to be so treated under the relevant accounting standard, but the use of the alternative words 'principles or practice' suggests some doubt on the part of the legislators as to which phrase has general currency. The other arises in the context of realised profits and losses; the Act states that they are 'such profits or losses of the company as fall to be treated as realised in accordance with principles generally accepted, at the time when the accounts are prepared, with respect to the determination for accounting purposes of realised profits or losses'.[2] Although the legislation does not define the term 'principles generally accepted', the Consultative Committee of Accountancy Bodies (CCAB) issued a Technical Release (TR 481) in September 1982 which gave guidance on the determination of realised profits.[3] TR 481 stated that 'principles generally accepted' for the determination of realised profits 'should be considered in conjunction with, inter alia, the legal principles laid down in the new Schedule 8 [now Schedule 4], statements of standard accounting practice ("SSAPs"), and in particular the fundamental accounting concepts referred to in SSAP 2'.[4] This interpretation, however, applies purely to the determination of realised profits; as will be seen below, it is our view that GAAP should be more widely interpreted.

In one of their Joint Opinions referred to in 2.2 below, Hoffmann and Arden cited the decision in *Odeon Associated Theatres Ltd v Jones (Inspector of Taxes)*[5] as an illustration of the relationship between 'generally accepted accounting principles' and the legal concept of true and fair, and in so doing reached the conclusion that 'the function of the ASC is to formulate what it considers should be generally accepted accounting principles'.[6] Nevertheless, whilst most would agree that the accounting standards represent 'generally accepted accounting principles', what about those areas of accounting which are not addressed in the standards? Furthermore, what about the accounting and disclosure requirements of the Companies Act and Stock Exchange – do they constitute 'generally accepted accounting principles'?

Our view is that GAAP is a dynamic concept which requires constant review, adaptation and reaction to changing circumstances. We believe that use of the term 'principle' gives GAAP an unjustified and inappropriate degree of permanence. GAAP changes in response to changing business and economic needs and developments. As circumstances alter, accounting practices are modified or developed accordingly. The UK's Accounting Standards Board (ASB) recognises this in its *Statement of Aims*, which discusses the Board's ongoing need to issue new accounting standards, or amend existing ones, 'in response to evolving business practices, new economic developments and deficiencies being identified in current practice'.[7] We believe that GAAP goes far beyond mere rules and principles, and encompasses contemporary permissible accounting *practice*.

This is consistent with a description of GAAP laid down by the Auditing Standards Board in the United States in Statement on Auditing Standards No. 69 (SAS 69) – *The Meaning of 'Present Fairly in Conformity with Generally Accepted Accounting Principles' in the Independent Auditor's Report*. SAS 69 states that 'the phrase "generally accepted accounting principles" is a technical accounting term that encompasses the conventions, rules and procedures necessary to define accepted accounting practice at a particular time. It includes not only broad guidelines of general application, but also detailed practices and procedures ... Those conventions, rules, and procedures provide a standard by which to measure financial presentations.'[8] A similar definition of the term 'generally accepted accounting practice' has been incorporated in New Zealand's Financial Reporting Act, which came into effect in 1994.[9]

Accordingly, the boundaries of GAAP extend far beyond the accounting principles contained in accounting standards; UK GAAP includes the requirements of the Companies Act and of the Stock Exchange, as well as any other acceptable accounting treatments not incorporated in the official literature.

1.2   What is 'generally accepted'?

It is often argued that the term 'generally accepted' implies that there must exist a high degree of practical application of a particular accounting practice. However, this interpretation raises certain practical difficulties. For example, what about new areas of accounting which have not, as yet, been generally applied? What about different accounting treatments for similar items – are they all generally accepted?

It is our view that 'generally accepted' does *not* mean 'generally adopted or used'. We believe that, in the UK context, GAAP refers to accounting practices which are regarded as permissible by the accounting profession as a whole. The extent to which a particular practice has been adopted is, in our opinion, not the overriding consideration. Any accounting practice which is legitimate in the circumstances under which it has been applied should be regarded as GAAP. The decision as to whether or not a particular practice is permissible or legitimate would depend on one or more of the following factors:

- Is the practice addressed either in the accounting standards, statute or other official pronouncements?

- If the practice is not addressed in UK accounting standards, is it dealt with in International Accounting Standards, or the standards of other countries such as the US?

- Is the practice consistent with the needs of users and the objectives of financial reporting? At the time of writing (August 1999), the UK did not have an agreed conceptual framework (see Chapter 2); however, in the event that one was to be adopted it may provide the necessary frame of reference for the development of GAAP.

- Does the practice have authoritative support in the accounting literature?

- Is the practice being generally applied by other companies in similar situations?

- Is the practice consistent with the fundamental concept of 'true and fair'?

The aim of this book is to analyse existing UK GAAP on the basis of the above six criteria. In so doing, we have compared and contrasted UK GAAP with the equivalent requirements under International Accounting Standards and US GAAP.

2   ACCOUNTING STANDARDS AND THE CONCEPT OF 'TRUE AND FAIR'

2.1   The introduction of the true and fair concept

The requirement that all financial statements which are prepared for the purpose of compliance with the Companies Act should 'give a true and fair view' was first introduced in the Companies Act 1947.[10] This amended the former requirement of 'true and correct', a change considered necessary on the grounds that there was no clear distinction between the two adjectives when used to describe financial statements. Was it possible for financial statements to be 'true' yet 'incorrect'; or 'untrue' yet 'correct'?

The concept of true and fair was adopted by the EC Council in its Fourth Directive.[11] In terms of the Directive, annual accounts are defined as a 'composite whole' comprising a balance sheet, profit and loss account and notes; the accounts should be drawn up in accordance with the Directive's detailed provisions and 'give a true and fair view of the company's assets, liabilities, financial position and profit or loss'.[12] However, to obviate a potential conflict between its detailed provisions and the achievement of truth and fairness, the Directive declared the obligation to give a true and fair view to be overriding. Consequently, where the application of the provisions of the Directive would not be sufficient to give a true and fair view, additional information must be given, and where the application of a provision of the Directive is incompatible with the presentation of a true and fair view, that provision must be departed from (with appropriate disclosure in the notes of the departure).[13]

The provisions of the Fourth Directive were implemented in the UK through the enactment of the Companies Act 1981. Following the consolidation of the various Companies Acts 1948–1983 into the Companies Act 1985, and the subsequent implementation of the Seventh Directive in the 1989 Act, the detailed requirements of the Directive are contained in Schedules 4 and 4A to the 1985 Act, and the requirement that financial statements should give a true and fair view is contained in section 226 for individual companies and section 227 for group financial statements. It is therefore clear that the concept of true and fair is a legal one, and the question as to whether or not a particular company's financial statements comply with sections 226 or 227 can ultimately only be decided by the courts.

2.2   Fair presentation and compliance with International Accounting Standards

It is interesting to note that the International Accounting Standards Committee (IASC) has now also adopted the concept of an override in its own accounting standards, after considerable debate. The revised version of IAS 1 – *Presentation of Financial Statements* – now permits an enterprise to depart from another international standard if this is necessary in order to achieve a fair presentation, where compliance with that other standard would have been misleading.[14]

In dealing with the issue of fair presentation and compliance with International Accounting Standards (IAS), the IASC has tackled the so-called problem of 'IAS-lite' reporting head on. 'IAS-lite' reporting is the term that has been used to describe situations where accounts purport to have been prepared in accordance with IAS, but which seem to indulge some notable aspects of non-compliance.

Nestlé is an example of a company that, in the past, may have been less than comprehensive in its compliance with IAS. Its accounting convention note in its 1994 Management Report stated the following:

Extract 1.1: Nestlé S.A. (1994)

Annex to the consolidated accounts

Accounting policies for the consolidated accounts

Accounting convention and accounting standards[extract]

The accounting policies adopted by the Group are in accordance with International Accounting Standards issued by the International Accounting Standards Committee (IASC). Some items required to be disclosed under IAS, in particular assets by segment and depreciation by tangible fixed assets category, are not shown. IAS standards, recently revised but not yet effective, have not been applied.

The accounts have been prepared under the historical cost convention, except that tangible fixed assets are shown at their net replacement value.

Apart from the fact that Nestlé clearly elected not to provide certain disclosures (some of which were not specified), it is a moot point whether IAS permits the measurement of fixed assets at net replacement value, since IAS 16 only recognises measurement at either cost or fair value. The group was perhaps confused between IAS 16's allowed alternative treatment of measuring tangible fixed assets at their revalued amount (i.e., fair value) and inflation accounting.

It is also worth noting that Nestlé's auditors stated in the opinion paragraph of their audit report that 'In our opinion, the consolidated accounts give a true and fair view of the state of affairs of the Nestlé Group at 31st December 1994 and of its profit and cash flows for the year then ended in accordance with Swiss law and in accordance with the Group's accounting policies, which comply with International Accounting Standards.' It seems that the subtlety of this opinion was that by certifying that the *accounting policies* were in compliance with IAS, the issue of non-compliance with the disclosures was glossed over.

It is therefore encouraging to note that Nestlé upgraded its segmental reporting in 1997 by implementing the revised IAS 14 a year ahead of schedule, and in 1998 the group decided to abandon the practice of using net replacement values for tangible fixed assets and reverted to historical cost accounting.

In any event, there can be little doubt that IAS compliance involves compliance with all the recognition, measurement *and* disclosure provisions of the standards. For this reason, IAS 1 now states that 'financial statements should not be described as complying with International Accounting Standards unless they comply with all the requirements of each applicable Standard and each applicable interpretation of the Standing Interpretations Committee.'[15] The IASC has therefore established unambiguously the principle that full application of its standards and related interpretations is a necessary prerequisite for a company to assert that its financial statements comply with International Accounting Standards.

Paragraph 10 of IAS 1 requires that 'financial statements should present fairly the financial position, financial performance and cash flows of an enterprise.' It goes on to state that the appropriate application of International Accounting Standards, with additional disclosure when necessary, results, in virtually all circumstances, in financial statements that achieve a fair presentation, and that inappropriate accounting treatments are not rectified either by disclosure of the accounting policies used or by notes or explanatory material.[16]

Paragraph 13 of IAS 1 provides for those exceptional circumstances where a company's management concludes that compliance with a requirement in an IAS would be misleading. The standard requires that in those circumstances where departure from a requirement is necessary in order to achieve fair presentation, management should depart from a requirement in a standard and explain such departure by giving the following disclosures:[17]

'(a)   that management has concluded that the financial statements fairly present the enterprise's financial position, financial performance and cash flows;

(b)   that it has complied in all material respects with applicable International Accounting Standards except that it has departed from a Standard in order to achieve a fair presentation;

(c)   the Standard from which the enterprise has departed, the nature of the departure, including the treatment that the Standard would require, the reason why that treatment would be misleading in the circumstances and the treatment adopted; and

(d)   the financial impact of the departure on the enterprise's net profit or loss, assets, liabilities, equity and cash flows for each period presented.'

These requirements clearly establish the pervasive nature of the fair presentation concept, whilst being a necessary complement to paragraph 10. It is now absolutely clear that accounts that hold themselves out as being drawn up in compliance with IAS must comply with all the requirements of each applicable Standard and SIC Interpretation. At the same time, though, it is also clear that the achievement of fair presentation goes beyond mere compliance with the rules.

It is worth noting that the fair presentation override is a requirement (not an option) of IAS 1 to be applied in the extremely rare circumstances when management concludes that compliance with a requirement in a Standard would be misleading. IAS 1 confirms that 'the existence of conflicting national requirements is not, in itself, sufficient to justify a departure in financial statements prepared using International Accounting Standards.'[18] It goes on to state that it will be the case only if the application of a specific requirement in an International Accounting Standard might result in misleading financial statements 'when the treatment required by the Standard is clearly inappropriate and thus a fair presentation cannot be achieved either by applying the Standard or through additional disclosure alone. Departure is not appropriate simply because another treatment would also give a fair presentation.'[19]

The question that arises is whether a company that uses the override will still be able to claim compliance with IAS under paragraph 11 of IAS 1. However, it is clear that since the override is itself an IAS requirement, companies that invoke it will still be able to claim compliance with IAS – provided that the requirements of paragraph 13 are complied with in full.

2.3   The interaction of accounting standards and the law

The Companies Act 1989 gave, for the first time in the UK, statutory recognition to the existence of accounting standards. This recognition was achieved through the inclusion of a new section (section 256) in the Companies Act 1985 and of a new disclosure requirement in Schedule 4 to that Act. The first two sub-sections of section 256 read as follows:

'(1)   In this Part "accounting standards" means statements of standard accounting practice issued by such body or bodies as may be prescribed by regulations.

(2)   References in this Part to accounting standards applicable to a company's annual accounts are to such standards as are, in accordance with their terms, relevant to the company's circumstances and to the accounts.'

In addition, the insertion of paragraph 36A of Schedule 4 to the Companies Act 1985 resulted in the new requirement for companies to state by way of note to their accounts 'whether the accounts have been prepared in accordance with applicable accounting standards and particulars of any material departure from those standards and the reasons for it shall be given'. (There is an exemption from this requirement for small and medium-sized companies and for certain small and medium-sized groups.)

For twenty years until 1990, the responsibility for developing accounting standards was discharged by the Accounting Standards Committee (ASC). Since then, that function has been fulfilled by the Accounting Standards Board (ASB), having been prescribed by Statutory Regulation as the standard-setting body for the purposes of section 256(1) of the Companies Act with effect from 20 August 1990.

The ASB's Foreword to Accounting Standards explains the relationship between compliance with the accounting standards and the concept of true and fair. This says that: 'Accounting standards are authoritative statements of how particular types of transaction and other events should be reflected in financial statements and accordingly compliance with accounting standards will normally be necessary for financial statements to give a true and fair view.'[20] It goes on to say that 'because accounting standards are formulated with the objective of ensuring that the information resulting from their application faithfully represents the underlying commercial activity, the Board envisages that only in exceptional circumstances will departure from the requirements of an accounting standard be necessary in order for financial statements to give a true and fair view'.[21]

The meaning of the true and fair requirement, including the legal relationship between accounting standards and the Companies Act, was discussed in two Joint Opinions obtained by the ASC in 1983 and 1984 from Leonard Hoffmann QC (now the Rt. Hon. Lord Justice Hoffmann) and Miss Mary Arden (now The Hon. Mrs Justice Arden). The 1983 opinion states that 'the courts will treat compliance with accepted accounting principles as prima facie evidence that the accounts are true and fair. Equally, deviation from accepted principles will be prima facie evidence that they are not. ... The function of the ASC is to formulate what it considers should be generally accepted accounting principles. Thus the value of a SSAP to a court which has to decide whether accounts are true and fair is two-fold. First, it represents an important statement of professional opinion about the standards which readers may reasonably expect in accounts which are intended to be true and fair. ... Secondly, because accountants are professionally obliged to comply with a SSAP, it creates in the readers an expectation that the accounts will be in conformity with the prescribed standards. This is in itself a reason why accounts which depart from the standard without adequate justification or explanation may be held not to be true and fair.'[22]

This view is supported in the judgement given by Woolf J in *Lloyd Cheyham & Co Ltd v Littlejohn & Co,* in which he stated that 'while they [accounting standards] are not conclusive, ... and they are not as the explanatory foreword makes clear, rigid rules, they are very strong evidence as to what is the proper standard which should be adopted'.[23]

Following statutory recognition of the existence of accounting standards, the ASB requested Miss Mary Arden QC to write a further Opinion which addressed the legal relationship between accounting standards and the true and fair view. The Opinion was issued in April 1993 and published by the ASB as an Appendix to its *Foreword to Accounting Standards.*[24] Whilst this Opinion has been given in the context of the changes in the law discussed above, it is essentially a reiteration of the two previous Joint Opinions. It again explains that 'the immediate effect of the issue of an accounting standard is to create a likelihood that the court will hold that compliance with that standard is necessary to meet the true and fair requirement. That likelihood is strengthened by the degree to which a standard is subsequently accepted in practice. Thus if a particular standard is generally followed, the court is very likely to find that the accounts must comply with it in order to show a true and fair view. The converse of that proposition, that non-acceptance of a standard in practice would almost inevitably lead a court to the conclusion that compliance with it was not necessary to meet the true and fair requirement, is not however the case. Whenever a standard is issued by the Board, then, irrespective of the lack in some quarters of support for it, the court would be bound to give special weight to the opinion of the Board in view of its status as the standard-setting body, the process of investigation, discussion and consultation that it will have undertaken before adopting the standard and the evolving nature of accounting standards.'[25]

Clearly, therefore, although accounting standards have no direct legal authority or effect, it appears highly probable that they will have a very persuasive effect in the courts' interpretation as to whether or not a company's accounts present a true and fair view. This status is further reinforced by the Schedule 4 requirement, described above, that any departures from accounting standards be explained in the financial statements.

Nevertheless, one question that is becoming increasingly relevant in the determination of GAAP surrounds the promulgation of increasingly complex accounting standards. If the ASB introduces a complex standard (such as FRS 11 – *Impairment of fixed assets and goodwill*) so that a significant number of preparers do not fully understand how to apply the standard in practice, can the standard be said to be GAAP? We have the strong impression that the application of FRS 11 is somewhat variable, even amongst sophisticated companies, and the standard certainly lacks adequate explanation in important areas (see Chapter 10 at 4.4). Thus, whilst we know that GAAP means more than mere compliance with the standards, the question is whether GAAP sometimes can imply less than rigorous compliance with a particular standard? It would be interesting to know what view the Courts would take when faced with expert evidence attesting to the lack of understandability of a particular standard, particularly if it was not being applied uniformly in practice.

In any event, although the legal standing of accounting standards has grown over the years, it is also true that the influence of the law has increasingly encroached on UK GAAP. Prior to the 1981 Companies Act, the accounting requirements laid down by statute were relatively limited; they comprised the general rules on the scope of accounts for companies and groups, the requirement to give a true and fair view, and a range of disclosure requirements, but they did not concern themselves with the detailed mechanics of accounting or the measurement of assets and liabilities. However, the 1981 Act, and subsequently the 1989 Act, introduced the Fourth and Seventh EC Directives which now specify the format of accounts to be presented and the accounting rules to be followed in considerable detail. Consequently, both standard setters and preparers of accounts increasingly find their freedom of action constrained by the law.

The ASB has expressed its intention to consider accounting principles first and the law as a secondary matter, in the following terms: 'In its debates on any accounting topic the Board initially develops its views by considering how its principles of accounting apply to the possible accounting options available for that topic. However, in deciding what is the most appropriate treatment the Board must also consider the environment in which its standards are to be applied. The legislation with which reporting entities must comply forms an important part of that environment. Accordingly, FRSs are drafted in the context of current ... legislation and European Community Directives with the aim of ensuring consistency between accounting standards and the law.'[26]

Nevertheless, it is evident that the risk of having its proposals exposed to legal challenge does weigh heavily with the Board. In a sense, the increased legal authority that standards have gained in recent years is proving a two-edged sword, because it makes it more likely that the standards will be subject to judicial interpretation and must therefore be drafted in terms which stand up to that analysis. Increasingly, this has provoked territorial disputes between the accounting and legal professions on who has the right to opine on the interpretation of accounting rules. This rivalry has been described by the Rt. Hon. Lord Justice Hoffmann in the following terms:

'Like many rival tribes, accountants and lawyers have opinions of each other which are largely based on ignorance. The undigested gobbets of company and tax law which most accountants have to learn during training only serve to convince them that lawyers are pedants who try to confine the realities of commerce within an artificial construction of arbitrary rules. Lawyers, curiously enough, tend to think that this is a fair description of accountants. Reading financial statements makes them regard accountants as sophisters, economists and calculators, operating within a closed system capable of producing any desired result and bearing little relationship to the realities of commerce. ... In fact, both professions are deeply engaged in the intolerable wrestle with words and meanings, which give rise to philosophical problems having much in common with each other.'[27]

2.4   The role of International Accounting Standards

2.4.1   *Introduction to the IASC*

The International Accounting Standards Committee (IASC) is an independent private sector body that came into existence in 1973 as a result of an agreement by various accountancy bodies around the world. Currently, the IASC has members in 103 countries, and its business is conducted by a Board comprising representatives of up to 13 countries appointed by the Council of the International Federation of Accountants (IFAC), and up to four other organisations having an interest in financial reporting.[28]

The IASC was founded to formulate and publish, in the public interest, International Accounting Standards (IAS) to be observed in the presentation of published financial statements and to promote their worldwide acceptance and

observance.   It was envisaged that IAS should be capable of worldwide
acceptance and contribute to a significant improvement in the quality and
comparability of corporate disclosure.[29]

The objectives of the IASC as set out in its constitution are:

'(a)   to formulate and publish in the public interest accounting standards to be
       observed in the presentation of financial statements and to promote their
       worldwide acceptance and observance; and

(b)   to work generally for the improvement and harmonisation of regulations,
       accounting standards and procedures relating to the presentation of
       financial statements.'[30]

International Accounting Standards have done a great deal both to improve and
harmonise financial reporting around the world.   IAS are adopted in some
countries as the basis for national accounting standards and are used in other
countries as the international benchmark in the development of their own
standards.   A significant number of Stock Exchanges (including the London
Stock Exchange) allow foreign companies to present financial statements in
conformity with IAS in fulfilment of their listing obligations.

The Accounting Standards Board's stated approach to International Accounting
Standards is as follows: 'FRSs are formulated with due regard to international
developments. The Board supports the International Accounting Standards
Committee in its aim to harmonise international financial reporting. As part of
this support an FRS contains a section explaining how it relates to the
International Accounting Standard (IAS) dealing with the same topic. In most
cases, compliance with an FRS automatically ensures compliance with the
relevant IAS. Where the requirements of an accounting standard and an IAS
differ, the accounting standard should be followed by entities reporting within
the area of application of the Board's accounting standards.'[31]

When International Accounting Standards were first issued, they permitted
several alternative accounting treatments. The principal reason for this was that
the IASC viewed its initial function as prohibiting undesirable accounting
practices, whilst acknowledging that there might be more than one acceptable
solution to a specific accounting issue. However, in recent years, international
accounting standards have been tightened up considerably.

In 1993 the Board of the IASC completed a major project (known as the
comparability/improvements project) which had set out to reduce many of the
permitted alternative accounting options. This project took four years and
culminated in the publication of a package of ten revised international standards
which become operative for accounting periods beginning on or after 1 January
1995. Unfortunately, this project was less successful than everyone had hoped it
would be, and although the number of permitted alternative options was
reduced, they were not eliminated; this means that international standards still

incorporate 'benchmark' treatments and 'allowed alternative' treatments. However, the IASC is now making a concerted effort to reduce the options in its standards.

2.4.2   The IASC/IOSCO agreement

A much more significant initiative is now in progress, the outcome of which will largely determine the course of world harmonisation of accounting and the future role of the IASC; this, in turn, will have a major influence on the future direction of UK GAAP. In 1995, the IASC reached an agreement with the International Organisation of Securities Commissions (IOSCO) that, provided the IASC could complete a core set of upgraded standards to IOSCO's satisfaction by 1999, IOSCO would consider recommending that its members accept financial statements prepared on the basis of the resulting standards in documents used for cross-border securities issues and listings.

The IASC Board essentially completed its revised core set of standards at its December 1998 meeting at which IAS 39 – *Financial Instruments: Recognition and Measurement* – was approved for issue. The only issue that still remains outstanding relates to accounting for investment properties, which is the subject of an exposure draft, E64 – *Investment Property*, and which is expected to be converted to a final accounting standard at the Board's December 1999 meeting.

Although the final outcome of the IASC/IOSCO project cannot be predicted with any degree of certainty, it raises the stakes considerably for domestic standard-setters. If an accepted international set of standards does emerge, it will inevitably put domestic standards under considerable strain. This may be felt particularly keenly in the US, where foreign registrants are presently required to file accounts reconciled to US GAAP; if this regime were relaxed, allowing IASC rules to be used instead, the FASB and the SEC might experience considerable pressure from US companies reluctant to comply with US standards that they perceive to be more demanding; such an attitude is likely to have been reinforced by a FASB publication that claims to have identified 255 differences between US GAAP and IASC standards.[32] Partly for that reason, many observers feel that the SEC is unlikely to allow IOSCO to endorse IASC standards unconditionally unless they correspond closely to existing US standards. A more likely scenario is that some or all of the IASC standards will only be accepted by the SEC on the basis of additional disclosures or other conditions.

2.4.3   International harmonisation: the great divide

The FASB attitude towards IAS is in sharp contrast to that of the American investment bank, Morgan Stanley Dean Witter. In their study on global investing, they posed the question 'How close are IAS and U.S. GAAP?'.[33] Perhaps surprisingly to many they gave the following response: 'The answer depends on what benchmark you use; spelling out all the differences would require a textbook. FASB has identified 255 differences, although many investors would find most of them meaningless. For reflecting economic substance in most industries, IAS is easily of comparable quality to U.S. GAAP, if auditors do their jobs. Yet as a rulebook, IAS is definitely less detailed than U.S. GAAP.'[34]

This answer highlights a fundamental philosophical difference in approach to accounting harmonisation between the US and Europe and which seems to have been overlooked by FASB in preparing its publication on the differences between US GAAP and IAS. It seems clear that the present US approach to accounting harmonisation indicates a desire for all companies participating in the same capital markets to provide users with uniform information based on uniform rules.

Conversely, Europeans, for example, would argue that whilst there may be perceived benefits of international standardisation of accounting principles based on a system of uniform reporting, it also has its pitfalls. Essentially, these are that uniform financial reporting may delude the unsophisticated into thinking that genuine harmonisation has been achieved, when in fact some differences may be healthy because they emphasise real underlying commercial differences.

This is because financial reporting is, to a large extent, a product of the environment in which the reporting entity operates. For one thing, it is difficult to imagine uniformity in financial reporting without uniformity in taxation systems, since taxation considerations have considerable influence over management decisions. Similarly, political, cultural and environmental considerations are all important components of the diversity of international accounting. Any attempt to standardise international financial reporting on the basis of some uniform system will result in an over-simplification of the complexities underlying the financial statements concerned, and will create a false impression of harmonisation. In other words, if reporting entities are operating in completely different environments, and are being managed, taxed and regulated on completely different bases, then the effect of uniform reporting might mislead users by treating unlike items as if they were alike.

In contrast to the US preference for uniform reporting, the European approach is based on the notions of equivalence and mutual recognition. Equivalence means being of equal value; that is, the co-existence of two systems of financial reporting which produce similar but equally relevant and reliable information for use by the capital markets and other users. Equivalence also requires a number of common ingredients. These include: transparency, due process, high quality standards and, above all, proper independent regulation of the capital markets.

Moreover, equivalence demands from both sides a willingness to sacrifice and compromise. This means that, in order to achieve the convergence of the US and European systems of reporting under the IASC umbrella, Europe will have both to compromise on some of its existing practices and to embrace a common system of securities regulation. Similarly, IOSCO will have to be persuaded that the accommodation of different, though equally valid, reporting systems is appropriate. This means that IOSCO will have to weigh up the need to embrace a system based on the principle of equivalence instead of uniformity against the practical reality that absolute comparability in international reporting based on a uniform system is not attainable in the foreseeable future.

2.4.4   Impact on UK GAAP

At the same time, however, the UK's ASB clearly would not want international standards to be markedly different from UK standards either. As a result, the process of finalising the IASC's core standards became a highly political one, with the major standard-setters of the world all seeking to pull the international consensus in their own direction, knowing that, if they failed, they may be put under pressure to close the gap by amending their domestic standards instead.

In fact, the ASB was very successful in influencing several of the IASC's revised core standards, with the result that they incorporate many of the ASB's own ideas on subjects such as provisions and contingencies, goodwill and intangible assets, and impairment of fixed assets. In the meantime, as part of a wider review of UK Company Law, the Company Law Review Steering Group has raised the question as to whether the UK should allow the use of International Accounting Standards by quoted UK companies.[35] IAS are already recognised for listing particulars by the Stock Exchange Listing Rules for companies registered overseas.[36]

We support the recognition of International Accounting Standards in UK law, on the grounds that this is a competitive issue for international companies registered in the UK. More importantly, though, we see this as an issue of European harmonisation and pan-European comparability in financial reporting. The more so as reporting under IAS is already widely accepted in some of the major economies of Continental Europe, is practised by some of the largest European multinational groups and accepted by the respective capital markets.

Given both the desirability and likely development of a single European capital market, we can see no convincing argument for the UK to remain outside a system of EU harmonised financial reporting, particularly in the case of listed companies. The completion by the IASC of its programme of core standards has resulted in a system of high quality and transparent IAS financial reporting that is at least the equivalent in quality and robustness of UK GAAP. The only real issue outstanding for the IASC is that of enforcement, which we discuss at 2.4.5 below.

2.4.5   Shaping IASC for the future

Few would disagree that over the past 26 years the IASC has achieved a great deal within its current structure. However, with the globalisation of the world's capital markets, the increasing complexity of business transactions and the growing pressure for a single set of internationally harmonised accounting standards, the IASC believes that structural changes are needed for it to anticipate and meet effectively the new challenges that it faces.

Consequently, the IASC Board saw the completion of its programme of core standards as an appropriate moment to undertake a review of its strategy. As a result, in 1998 the IASC Board appointed a Strategy Working Party to conduct a general review of the strategy of the IASC.

The Working Party published its proposals in December 1998 in a Discussion Paper entitled 'Shaping IASC for the future'.[37] The Working Party's proposals were fairly radical, but were framed within the rather nebulous notion of a 'partnership with national standard setters'.[38] The rationale behind this was that the IASC should enter into a partnership with national standard setters enabling the IASC to work with them to accelerate convergence between national standards and International Accounting Standards. However, in order to form this 'partnership', the Working Party proposed the abolition of the current IASC Board structure and the establishment of a bicameral system in its place. Under this system, a disproportionate amount of power would be concentrated in a Standards Development Committee (SDC), comprising a small group of select full-time standard setters. It was also proposed that the SDC would replace the IASC's existing Steering Committee system, under which Standards are currently developed. The Working Party's recommendations covered a number of other areas, including the IASC's system of due process, implementation, education, enforcement and funding.

Perhaps not surprisingly, the Working Party's proposals met with considerable opposition, both from within the IASC Board and outside. The principal criticisms of the proposals centred around the bicameral system, the concept of the SDC and the issue of legitimacy. Our general perception is that the Discussion Paper was aimed at further entrenching the position of the group of accounting standard setters known as the G4+1.[39] The future role for the majority of national standard setters would, under the proposed strategy, appear to be very much reduced in comparison with their current role.

However, in our view, the biggest single failing of the Working Party's proposals was that they did not address adequately the key issue of legitimacy among the IASC's constituencies. So whilst we agree with the objectives identified by the Working Party, we do not agree with the structure that was proposed in order to achieve them, since the proposed structure would not have ensured legitimacy. The Discussion Paper contained little elaboration on the details of the proposed 'partnership with national standard setters' and other key constituencies, with the result that their role under the proposed structure was unclear. It is imperative that the future IASC should incorporate closer involvement of national standard setters and other key constituencies. However, if the proposed SDC was to become the means by which this should be achieved, then the effect would be to alienate many national standard setters and other key constituencies in favour of a chosen few.

We also agree that there should be wider participation on the Board, but again not in the way envisaged by the Working Party. In our view, the expansion of the Board and greater involvement of national standard setters and other key constituencies should be viewed together. There should be an appropriate balancing of the need for representation by various constituencies while ensuring that the Board is kept to a manageable size. Basing membership on a country representation system is outdated given the important constituencies that are supranational, regional and international in nature (i.e., the European Union, IOSCO, World Bank, etc.).

We also believe that there should be greater representation of users and preparers of accounts. Ultimately, the long-term credibility of International Accounting Standards will depend on their acceptance by the preparer and user communities as well as the international capital markets. There therefore has to be full participation by all the key players in the marketplace in order to secure the future of IAS.

Although the Discussion Paper addresses briefly the matter of enforcement, it contains no new thinking on the issue. We believe that greater representation and legitimacy will create the conditions for better enforcement to emerge. We acknowledge that the IASC should not and, in fact, cannot be responsible for the enforcement of its standards. Nevertheless, it cannot afford to be unconcerned about the issue because the absence of any enforcement mechanism severely limits the credibility and authority of IAS. Consequently, we believe that the Working Party should devote some effort to considering the options available to the IASC to promote and support enforcement at the national level. In our view the IASC has no option but to play a pro-active role in the area of enforcement. An essential element of the new structure should be the establishment by the IASC of, for example, a Compliance Monitoring Unit that would establish links or 'regulatory partnerships' with national regulators. The unit would monitor the application of IAS in practice and would alert the regulators to cases of apparent non-compliance. This would require commitment on the part of regulators to take seriously their responsibilities of enforcement and, in so doing, would establish a credible deterrent against non-compliance with IAS.

The IASC Board had a joint meeting on 30 June 1999 with the Strategy Working Party to discuss the comments received on the Discussion Paper. The discussion indicated that the proposed bicameral/SDC system should be abandoned in favour of a single Board structure. There was a general consensus that this single Board should comprise a blend of full and part-time members, although the overall size of the Board and precise proportion of full and part-timers was not agreed.

The Strategy Working Party met again during July 1999, and will continue to develop a new proposal along the lines of its June 1999 discussions with the IASC Board.

2.5 The experience of other countries

2.5.1 US

To understand the regulation of financial reporting in the US is to understand the workings of the Securities and Exchange Commission (SEC) and it relationship with the US Financial Accounting Standards Board (FASB). Before the 1930s, there were no authoritative or enforceable US standards governing corporate financial reports. Because of the lack of any statutory underpinning, the accounting profession had no authority to establish ground rules which corporations had to follow in their financial statements. However, the abuses in stock exchange practices, the financing of securities and corporate reporting which were revealed after the 1929 stock market crash, led the US Congress to enact the Securities Act of 1933, the Securities Exchange Act of 1934, and several other securities laws. Under this legislation, companies offering new issues of securities for inter-state sale, other than for certain exempted issuers and certain exempted securities, and all companies whose securities are traded publicly, must register and file periodic reports with the Securities and Exchange Commission (SEC). These laws, taken together, emphasise full disclosure by issuers of securities and others acting in the US securities markets and are intended to provide investors with information about the issuer of a security as well as the terms of the security being offered, so that informed decisions on the investment merits of securities can be made and to ensure that fair trading practices prevail in the primary and secondary markets. The SEC, though given wide power to require that full disclosures are made, was not empowered to pass judgement on the quality or merit of an investment.

The SEC was created under the 1934 Act to enforce and administer the federal securities laws subject to the oversight of Congress. Securities involved solely in intrastate transactions are subject to the separate securities laws of the state concerned, but not ordinarily to the federal securities laws. The SEC is composed of five commissioners who are nominated by the President for five-year terms (the persons nominated must be confirmed by Congress in open proceedings), one of whom serves as the chairman. It has a staff of lawyers, accountants, engineers, and financial analysts. Despite its relatively small size (by US federal standards) the SEC has earned a reputation as one of the most ably administered federal regulatory agencies. Its small size has been achieved, in part, through transferring the burden of monitoring compliance with its regulations on to securities issuers and their professional advisers, through severe legal liabilities backed up by vigorous enforcement activities, and through various discretionary powers – principally the sole right to 'accelerate' the effective date of a registration statement – granted by Congress. Though many other federal regulatory agencies are involved in various aspects of financial reporting, particularly in the financial services sector of the US economy, none has the pervasive influence of the SEC.

The US equivalent of a 'true and fair view' is 'fair presentation in conformity with GAAP'. However, the ASC and ASB in the UK and the IASC have taken rather different approaches to accounting standard setting from that of the FASB in the US. The UK and International bodies have adopted a broad fundamental approach that lays down accounting standards on the basis of principles, with a minimum of accounting rules. As a result, financial reporting under either UK GAAP or IAS requires a considerable measure of judgement to be exercised in the application of many of the standards. Conversely, some commentators have stated that the FASB has generated a plethora of highly detailed legalistic rules which have, to a large extent, obscured the concept of fair presentation.

A further significant difference between the UK and US is that for more than 50 years, the standard form audit report in the US has referred to fair presentation in accordance with 'generally accepted accounting principles'. The SEC was given statutory power to set US generally accepted accounting principles (US GAAP) for companies subject to the federal securities laws; however, with limited exceptions, it has allowed the private sector (for example, at present, the FASB) to establish financial accounting standards and has viewed generally accepted accounting principles as those which have 'substantial authoritative support'. This term was first introduced in the SEC's Accounting Series Release (ASR) No. 4, which was issued in 1938 and stated that 'in cases where financial statements filed with the Commission ... are prepared in accordance with accounting principles for which there is no substantial authoritative support, such financial statements will be presumed to be misleading or inaccurate despite disclosures contained in the certificate of the accountant or in footnotes to the statements provided the matters involved are material'.

In 1964, the Council of the AICPA adopted a Special Bulletin entitled *Disclosure of Departures From Opinions of Accounting Principles Board*, which contained, inter alia, the following recommendations:

(a) 'Generally accepted accounting principles' are those principles which have substantial authoritative support.

(b) Opinions of the Accounting Principles Board constitute 'substantial authoritative support'.

(c) 'Substantial authoritative support' can exist for accounting principles that differ from Opinions of the Accounting Principles Board.[40]

In 1973, the SEC updated ASR 4 to recognise the establishment of the FASB by stating that 'principles, standards and practices promulgated by the FASB in its Statements and Interpretations will be considered by the Commission as having substantial authoritative support, and those contrary to such FASB promulgations will be considered to have no such support'.[41] This ties in with the AICPA's Code of Professional Conduct, which states that 'a member shall not (1) express an opinion or state affirmatively that the financial statements or other financial data of an entity are presented in conformity with generally accepted accounting principles or (2) state that he or she is not aware of any material modifications that should be made to such statements or data in order for them to be in conformity with generally accepted accounting principles, if such statements or data contain any departure from an accounting principle promulgated by bodies designated by Council to establish such principles that has a material effect on the statements or data taken as a whole'.[42]

This requirement may be seen to have been influenced by decision in the famous Continental Vending case of the 1960s.[43] The defendants in this case were two partners and a manger in a firm of accountants which was the independent auditor of Continental Vending Machine Corporation. The charge was that the company's balance sheet (on which the auditors had expressed the usual unqualified opinion) was false and misleading in various respects and that the defendants had schemed and conspired with the president and major shareholder of the company to make it so. The defendants were convicted and fined and, as a result, the case was an important milestone in what it said about the obligations, over and above those imposed by the standards themselves, which the law imposes on accountants in the course of their professional work. This may be summed up in what both the Trial Judge and the Court of Appeals referred to as the 'critical test' of fair presentation. This was the test as to whether the financial statements fairly presented the financial condition of the company, and that, whilst proof of compliance with GAAP was persuasive evidence that this was the case, it was not necessarily conclusive.

The separate accounting rules and regulations of the SEC have for the most part dealt with disclosure and classification standards rather than with the establishment of basic measurement principles and, in many areas, have required accounting disclosure by registrants beyond that specified for general purpose US GAAP financial statements. The SEC has stated that disclosures required by US GAAP set a minimum standard of disclosure to which should be added such further material information as is necessary to make financial statements filed with the SEC, in the light of the circumstances under which they are prepared, not misleading. The SEC has nevertheless exerted significant influence on the development of measurement principles whenever it has believed that accounting principles were not being addressed by the private sector in a timely or appropriate manner. Apart from audited issuer financial statements, the SEC rules can also necessitate the presentation of other financial statements in defined circumstances. Such other financial statements, which must also be audited, are most frequently encountered when the security offered is guaranteed by another party, when the issuer has acquired other businesses and when investees of the issuer accounted for under the equity method are significant to its consolidated financial statements.

The content of US financial statements is designed for the general use of investors, creditors and regulators. Accordingly, they do not include financial information not considered necessary for a fair presentation of financial position and results of operations. For the most part, the SEC's proxy and other rules cover financial data not included in the basic US GAAP financial statements and this can be quite extensive in many cases. The SEC has always considered consolidated financial statements to be the most meaningful and parent-company financial statements to be relatively unimportant – unless there are contractual or other restrictions on a parent's ability to receive funds by dividend, loan, or otherwise from its subsidiaries. In general, US GAAP is applicable to all legal forms of an entity and this approach is followed also by the SEC. Financial statements are widely used, distributed and understood in the US and the litigious US environment has resulted in numerous court cases and legal opinions regarding their content and purpose. Releases following an SEC enforcement investigation and activities of the SEC practice section of the AICPA (e.g. Peer Reviews and other quality control procedures) additionally support the objectives of fair and consistent financial reporting in the US. It is essential that any inconsistency in applying accounting principles or other lack of comparability between accounting periods be clearly disclosed.

The scope of the company laws of each of the US states is generally limited to non-financial reporting matters. In short, state company law is not a factor in US financial reporting. Other than for some federally chartered banks there is no such thing as a US federal company law. Moreover, virtually none of the federal, state and local taxing authorities in the US use general purpose US GAAP financial statements for tax assessment or reporting purposes nor do the tax laws usually directly influence the manner in which such financial statements are prepared. Instead, each taxing jurisdiction requires tax returns to be prepared and filed using tax accounting principles. The main exceptions to this general approach relate to the permitted use of the LIFO method for determining the cost of inventory and to the use of book net income for "alternative minimum" tax computations.

Until the early 1980s, the SEC's focus was principally domestic. However, since 1982 a body of rules, generally running in tandem with, but in certain respects less onerous than, the domestic regime has been developed for so-called "foreign private issuers." The term "foreign private issuer" means any foreign issuer (other than a foreign governmental issuer), unless (1) more than 50 percent of the outstanding voting securities of such issuer are held of record either directly or through voting trust certificates or depositary receipts by residents of the US *and* (2) (i) the majority of the executive officers or directors of the issuer are US citizens or residents or (ii) more than 50 percent of the assets of the issuer are located in the US or (iii) the business of the issuer is administered principally in the US.

Failure to meet the foreign private issuer definition results in an entity, though incorporated or located outside the US, still being subject to the SEC's domestic rules. Special rules apply to an entity which is wholly-owned by a foreign government or agency thereof and these are not described herein because of their narrow application. Non-US and non-government owned companies meeting the foreign private issuer definition who offer debt or equity securities in a US public distribution or wish to list on a US stock exchange are required to register with the SEC beforehand and subsequently to file periodic disclosure reports. At present, such registrations and annual disclosure reports must include audited consolidated financial statements for the latest three fiscal years. The auditor for this purpose is usually the company's incumbent auditor, though the SEC's auditor independence standards must be met and the audit must be performed under US auditing standards. The consolidated financial statements can be in accordance with the registrant's home-country accounting practices provided that, if equity securities are offered, all the disclosures required by US GAAP are added and provided that a reconciliation of reported net income and shareholders' equity to their approximate amounts had US GAAP been applied is presented. When non-convertible debt is offered, certain reliefs from the full gamut of US GAAP disclosure are permitted – though no relief from the reconciliation to US GAAP is available.

2.5.2 *Canada*

In Canada, in addition to there being a federal corporations act (the Canada Business Corporations Act), the individual provinces each have their own separate corporations acts. Consequently, Canadian companies have the option of incorporating either under the legislation of the province in which they are based, or under the federal Act, although in practice most of the larger Canadian corporations are federally incorporated.

Canadian accounting standards have evolved from merely representing guidance as to good practice, through to becoming standards with full statutory backing. The landmarks in this evolutionary process are as follows:[44]

- In 1953, when the Ontario Business Corporations Act was completely revised, the profession persuaded the government of the day to incorporate into the Act virtually all of the provisions of the first CICA bulletin on financial disclosure. As a result of the companies acts of other provinces and in the federal jurisdiction picking up these provisions, the legal impact of the CICA recommendations spread throughout the country.

- In 1968, when the CICA *Handbook* was adopted, the committee followed the precedent set by the AICPA and established a requirement that 'where the accounting treatment or statement presentation does not follow the recommendations in this Handbook, the practice used should be explained in notes to the financial statements with an indication of the reason why the recommendation concerned was not followed'.[45]

- In 1972, the securities administrators of several Canadian provinces announced that they would regard the CICA *Handbook* pronouncements as 'generally accepted accounting principles'. As a result of this, the CICA *Handbook* took on quasi-legal status with respect to most filings under the jurisdiction of provincial securities acts. In 1975, as a result of the inclusion of a reference to the CICA *Handbook* in the regulations to the Canada Business Corporations Act, the same result was brought about in respect of the financial statements of companies which were under federal jurisdiction. Several provinces have also amended their companies legislation to this effect.

- In December 1988, the CICA published *Handbook* Section 1000 which, inter alia, defines 'generally accepted accounting principles' as the term used to describe the basis on which financial statements are normally prepared; this encompasses not only specific rules, practices and procedures relating to particular circumstances but also broad principles and conventions of general application, including the underlying financial statement concepts described in Section 1000. More specifically, generally accepted accounting principles comprise the Accounting Recommendations in the *Handbook*; however, for matters not covered by them, the principles that apply are either generally accepted by virtue of their use in similar circumstances by a significant number of entities in Canada, or are consistent with the Recommendations and developed through the exercise of professional judgement, by consulting other informed accountants, where appropriate, and by applying the concepts outlined in Section 1000.[46]

From time to time, the question has been raised as to whether or not the UK should follow the Canadian model of giving accounting standards increased legal backing by incorporating them in the law. As discussed at 3.1.6 below, there has been some movement in that direction as a result of measures included in the Companies Act 1989, but this fell short of the recommendations made by the Dearing Committee.

2.5.3   Germany

The incorporation of the EC Fourth Directive (Accounting Directive), the Seventh Directive (Consolidated Accounts Directive) and the Eighth Directive (Auditor Directive) was achieved in Germany through the enactment on 1 January 1986 of the Accounting Directives Law. One of the most important aspects of this modification of German law was the revision of the Commercial Code, which included the addition of a Third Book containing accounting rules applicable to all businesses.

In terms of the Commercial Code, company financial statements must, in compliance with *required accounting principles* (GoB), present a true and fair view of the net worth, financial position and results of the company.[47] GoB has been interpreted as meaning 'those principles which are not comprehensively codified but which, by application in specific cases, lead to a correct accounting treatment by reference to the objectives of financial statements. They can be determined deductively by making full use of statute and case law, accounting theory, pronouncements of the Institute of German Qualified Accountants as well as accounting practice.'[48] Since the concept of true and fair is relatively new to Germany's Commercial Code, its relationship to GoB is not entirely clear; however, it would appear that the general GoB rule would only be brought into play if, in the preparation of company financial statements, uncertainties in the interpretation and application of the specific rules of the laws and ordinances need to be resolved. Therefore, it seems that GoB will not impose any disclosure requirements additional to those contained in the law, unless the financial statements would otherwise not show a true and fair view.

It is well known that in Germany there is a close inter-relationship between the calculation of profit in the financial statements of individual companies and the calculation of taxable profit. This means that financial statements prepared in accordance with GoB form the basis for the tax computation, resulting in tax-driven balance sheet values. However, this rule need not necessarily apply in the case of group financial statements, where it is permitted for group accounting policies to be different to those followed in individual accounts. Nevertheless, practice shows that many German groups also use tax-driven values in their group financial statements – presumably because of convenience.

However, in February 1998 new legislation was enacted in Germany to the effect that International Accounting Standards (or indeed other 'internationally recognised accounting principles' such as US GAAP) may be used in the consolidated financial statements of listed groups instead of German law and accounting principles. There is an added proviso that the financial statements must also be 'consistent with' the European Accounting Directives.

Similar amended legislation was enacted in France in April 1998, allowing French companies whose securities are traded on a regulated market to use IAS or another body of international standards as the sole basis for their consolidated accounts. A number of other European countries (for example, Italy, Austria, Belgium and Spain) have either followed suit, or are in process of doing so. These are revolutionary changes, and demonstrate the influence of Anglo-American accounting philosophies, at least on those companies wishing either to seek access to the international capital markets, or merely achieve greater transparency in their financial reporting.

Lufthansa is an example of a company that has taken advantage of the new legislation in Germany, preparing its 1998 consolidated accounts in accordance with IAS. The Group's 1998 Annual Report included the following explanation of the impact of adopting IAS:

Extract 1.2: Deutsche Lufthansa AG (1998)

Adoption of IAS enhances transparency

This year the consolidated financial statements have been drawn up for the first time on the basis of the International Accounting Standards (IAS) in accordance with the option provided under the new Section 292a of the German Commercial Code. This obviates the need to compile a separate set of certified consolidated financial statements based on the German Commercial Code.

Lufthansa is also applying many provisions of the IAS standards – the use of which is not yet compulsory in German accounting – in order to improve the comprehensiveness and transparency of the information it publishes. However, a direct comparison of the year-on-year figures is possible only with the specially recompiled consolidated financial statements for 1997 (which are likewise based on IAS) but not with the financial statements of earlier years. The adoption of IAS has effects both on the consolidated balance sheet and the consolidated income statement.

Effects on the balance sheet

The consolidated balance sheet under IAS is affected in particular by the different treatment of leasing agreements and the adjustment of retirement benefit obligations. Thus the capitalisation of leased aircraft, which hitherto were not included in the balance sheet, substantially increases fixed assets. The associated financial obligations are now shown as liabilities. On the other hand, the provisions for anticipated losses in respect of leasing agreements and the inclusion under prepaid expenses of prepaid leasing instalments, which were shown previously in the consolidated balance sheet drawn up in line with German commercial law, are superfluous under IAS.

The use of a more dynamic accounting rule for pension obligations required by IAS has led to a sharp increase in retirement benefit obligations.

IAS adjustments affecting earnings in past years were shown net of offsetting deferred taxes and charged directly against retained earnings. On the other hand, the portion of earnings retained from last year's net profit partly counterbalances this effect.

Impact of IAS on income statement

The use of IAS accounting standards also has an impact on the consolidated income statement. The increase in the profit from operating activities and the concurrent deterioration in the financial result are caused by several factors. Firstly, the transfers to retirement benefit obligations, which in the past were recorded in total as staff costs, are now split into current service costs (under staff costs) and interest expense. Secondly, obligations arising from financial leasing agreements are now included in the balance sheet. Hence the interest component of the leasing instalments, which was formerly included under operating expenses, is now allocated to the financial result. Leasing expenses are no longer included under the cost of materials; however, depreciation and amortisation now also include the depreciation on aircraft acquired under finance leasing agreements.

Revenue increases. This is because under IAS the pro rata revenue earned from partly completed customer orders, including the proportional contribution to earnings, has to be shown, too.

Changes in the Group of consolidated companies

Important changes in the group of companies consolidated compared with the consolidated financial statements published in 1997 according to the German Commercial Code concern the deconsolidation of Condor Flugdienst GmbH and the Delvos companies. By contrast, START was consolidated for the first time.

Lufthansa's statement of accounting policies included the following:

Extract 1.3: Deutsche Lufthansa AG (1998)

Notes to the Consolidated Financial Statements of Deutsche Lufthansa AG 1998

1) Fundamentals and methods

The consolidated financial statements of Deutsche Lufthansa AG and its subsidiaries have been prepared in accordance with the International Accounting Standards (IAS) and the interpretations of the Standing Interpretations Committee (SIC). The provisions set out in SIC-8 concerning the first-time application of IAS have been observed whereby the following new or revised Standards have been voluntarily applied before their effective date: IAS 1 (Presentation of Financial Statements), IAS 14 (Segment Reporting), IAS 17 (Accounting for Leases), IAS 19 (Employee Benefits) and IAS 36 (Impairment of Assets). Standards relevant for the first time in the 1998 financial year have also been applied for 1997.

The following accounting and valuation methods in the present consolidated financial statements deviate from German law:

– Translation of foreign currency receivables and liabilities as at the closing rate

– Accounting for internally generated intangible assets in the balance sheet

– Revenue recognition by reference to the stage of completion of long-term customer orders

– Valuation of long-term provisions and accruals and of high or low interest-bearing liabilities at present value

– No recognition of other provisions if the probability of the outflow of resources is below 50 per cent

– Recognition of deferred tax assets and liabilities in accordance with the balance sheet liability method

– Recognition of assets and of corresponding liabilities resulting from finance lease agreements according to IAS 17

– Valuation of retirement benefit obligations according to the projected unit credit method.

The valuation of some items changed as a result of the transition to IAS at January 1, 1997. The respective changes were treated as adjustments to the opening balance of retained earnings of the earliest period presented.

Capital and Reserves	DM000
Equity according to HGB as at 31.12.1996 (without minority interest)	**5,339,322**
Changes in consolidated group	133,848
Valuation using the equity method	11,545
Finance leases on aircraft and buildings	-722,148
Retirement benefit obligations	-1,088,805
Other provisions and accruals	202,413
Other accounting and valuation differences	51,983
Deferred taxes	568,127
Equity according to IAS as at 1.1.1997	**4,496,285**

The requirements set out in section 292a, German Commercial Code (HGB) are met; thus the consolidated financial statements prepared in accordance with International Accounting Standards have an exempting effect. The assessment as to whether group accounting is consistent with the 7th EU Directive was based on the interpretation of the contact committee for accounting of the European Commission effective at the time of preparation of financial statements.

3   THE DEVELOPMENT OF ACCOUNTING STANDARDS

3.1   The Accounting Standards Committee

Prior to 1970, there were no mandatory requirements in the UK outside company law governing the presentation of financial statements of companies; and even those company law provisions which did exist comprised only the basic minimum, which was inadequate for the purpose of achieving a satisfactory standard of financial reporting. Consequently, accounting practices were varied, inconsistent and sometimes inappropriate; inter-firm and inter-period comparisons were difficult as companies altered accounting treatments and resorted to such practices as 'window-dressing' and 'reserve accounting' to achieve desired results in order to present a picture of profitability and growth. Certain professional accounting bodies (such as the ICAEW) had issued a series of recommendations on accounting principles – but these recommendations were not mandatory.

3.1.1   *The creation of the ASC*

By 1969 it had become apparent that the basic accounting requirements contained in company law needed the support of more authoritative pronouncements than the recommendations that were being issued. Consequently, the Council of the ICAEW issued a 'Statement of intent on accounting standards in the 1970s',[49] wherein they set out their strategy for the development of accounting standards.

As a result, the ICAEW set up the Accounting Standards Steering Committee in 1970 as the means of implementing this strategy. The Institute of Chartered Accountants of Scotland and the Institute of Chartered Accountants in Ireland became co-sponsors of the Committee almost immediately afterwards; the Chartered Association of Certified Accountants and the Chartered Institute of Management Accountants[50] joined subsequently in 1971 and the Chartered Institute of Public Finance and Accountancy in 1976. With effect from 1 February 1976, the Committee became the Accounting Standards Committee and was reconstituted as a joint committee of these six accountancy bodies who now comprise the Consultative Committee of Accountancy Bodies (CCAB).

3.1.2   *The objects and terms of reference of the ASC*

The objects of the ASC were 'to define accounting concepts, to narrow differences of financial accounting and reporting treatment, and to codify generally accepted best practice in the public interest. In order to achieve these objects, the ASC was given the following terms of reference:

(a)   to keep under review standards of financial accounting and reporting;

(b)   to propose to the Councils of each of the CCAB members statements of standard accounting practice and interpretations of such statements;

(c) to publish consultative documents, discussion papers and exposure drafts and submit to the Councils of each of the CCAB members non-mandatory guidance notes with the object of maintaining and advancing accounting standards;

(d) to consult, as appropriate, with representatives of finance, commerce, industry and government, and other bodies and persons concerned with financial reporting; and

(e) to maintain close links with the International Accounting Standards Committee and the accountancy profession in Europe and throughout the world.[51]

3.1.3   The Watts Report

In the light of the eight years' experience gained since its formation, a Review Group was set up in 1978 by the ASC, under the chairmanship of Mr T. R. Watts, to review the standard-setting process and to consider what improvements in that process could be effected. The Review Group submitted a draft consultative document to the ASC in May 1978. The document was adopted by the ASC and published as a basis for public discussion and comment.[52] Following extensive public consultations and debate, the ASC made a number of recommendations in a report to the CCAB which was published in 1981 (the Watts Report).[53] Many of the recommendations of the Watts Report concern fundamental issues which remained unresolved and were consequently revisited by the Dearing Committee (see 3.1.5 below). These included such issues as the need for a conceptual framework; the establishment of a supervisory body to ensure compliance with accounting standards; the application of certain standards only to large companies; a full-time paid ASC Chairman; and the need for more resources.

3.1.4   The McKinnon Report

A further review of the standard-setting process was carried out by an ASC working party in 1983. The reasons for the review were:

(a) to develop certain recommendations contained in the Watts Report;

(b) to seek ways by which the standard-setting process could be shortened; and

(c) to consider whether there was a need for alternative or new types of pronouncement.

The findings of this working party were published in a report entitled 'Review of the Standard Setting Process' (the McKinnon Report). However, the report did not address the more fundamental issues raised in the Watts Report, and instead focused on the procedural aspects relating to the development of SSAPs. The report did, nevertheless, recommend that a new category of final pronouncement be introduced, namely the Statement of Recommended Practice (SORP).

3.1.5 The Dearing Report

As the complexities of accounting issues and requirements for more sophisticated levels of financial reporting mounted, the increased demands placed on the ASC clearly indicated that it was unable to fulfil satisfactorily the standard-setting role that it was expected to perform. The ASC had to endure mounting criticism for being unable either to respond quickly to changing needs or deal adequately with fundamental issues such as inflation accounting, off balance sheet transactions and goodwill. However, when one considers that the ASC essentially comprised a voluntary part-time committee, it had achieved a great deal. Nevertheless, as companies are required to report in a fast-moving and increasingly complex environment, it was becoming apparent that the existing standard-setting process was no longer appropriate.

Consequently, in November 1987 the CCAB appointed a Review Committee, under the chairmanship of Sir Ronald Dearing, to review and make recommendations on the standard-setting process.[54]

Probably not surprisingly, the Review Committee addressed many of the issues discussed in the Watts Report, and reached very similar conclusions. The principal recommendations, which were published in a report issued in November 1988 (the Dearing Report), were as follows:[55]

A   The need for a conceptual framework

The Committee concluded that the lack of a conceptual framework was a handicap to those setting accounting standards as well as to those applying them. It recommended that further work on a conceptual framework should be undertaken on a modest scale, building on the work already done by the FASB and IASC on their respective conceptual framework projects. However, the Committee further recommended that, whether or not a conceptual framework was successfully developed, when accounting standards were issued they should be accompanied by a statement of the principles underlying them and the reasons why alternatives were rejected. (See Chapter 2 for a detailed discussion of the need for a conceptual framework.)

B   Quality of accounting standards versus quantity

The report emphasised that the purpose of accounting standards was to provide authoritative but not mandatory guidance on the interpretation of what constituted a true and fair view. Consequently, the Committee recommended that the revised standard-setting framework should concentrate on quality, timeliness, reducing the permitted options and promoting compliance – as opposed to attempting to produce a large volume of standards which attempt to cover every option.

C *Application of standards to small companies*

The Committee was clearly influenced by the approach taken latterly by the ASC in exempting small companies from the requirements of certain standards (see 4.2 below). Consequently, it recommended that, on the basis of a cost/benefit test, it should be decided whether or not the accounting and/or disclosure requirements of a particular standard should apply to small companies.

D *Public sector bodies*

The report discussed the application of standards to public sector bodies at some length. It concluded that there should be an underlying unity of approach to accounting standards across the public and private sectors, and that, therefore, public sector bodies should come within the framework of the proposals contained in the report, but with support for compliance with standards coming from the responsible Secretary of State.

E *The role of the law*

The suggestion that accounting standards should be given legal effect is one which had been mooted from time to time, and was considered by the Committee – particularly in the light of developments in other countries where there had been a trend in giving accounting standards increased legal backing.

However, the Committee stated that it did not recommend the incorporation of standards into law 'because this inescapably requires a legalistic approach and a reduction in the ability of the financial community to respond quickly to new developments'.[56] Nevertheless, whilst attempting to avoid a legalistic approach, the Committee made the following recommendations in order to help provide a sound base for the development and implementation of standards:

(a) in the case of all 'large companies', the directors should be required to state in the notes to the financial statements whether or not they had been prepared in accordance with applicable accounting standards, drawing attention to material departures and explaining the reasons for such departures;

(b) there should be a statutory power for certain authorised bodies or the Secretary of State to apply to the courts for an order requiring the revision of accounts which do not give a true and fair view;

(c) if there was a material departure from an accounting standard, then the onus of proof should be on the party who contended that the financial statements did give a true and fair view to show that this was the case. This should similarly apply in the case of auditors who had given an unqualified opinion on financial statements which contained departures; and

(d) there should be a general presumption in any legal proceedings that all accounting standards would have the support of the courts – unless it could be demonstrated that, despite a material departure, the financial statements gave a true and fair view.

F   *A Financial Reporting Council*

The Committee addressed the need for the involvement of a wide constituency of interests in the development of accounting standards. Consequently, it recommended that 'the institutional arrangements for developing accounting standards should reflect the need to involve the whole community of interests in financial reporting at the policy level, while providing for a separate professional capability to translate policy into accounting standards'.[57] Therefore, in order to achieve this, the Committee recommended that a Financial Reporting Council should be created, covering at high level a wide constituency of interests. The Council's chairman would be appointed jointly by the Secretary of State for Trade and Industry and the Governor of the Bank of England, and the objectives of the Council would be to guide the standard-setting body on work programmes and issues of public concern; to see that the work on accounting standards is properly financed; and to act as a powerful proactive public influence for securing good accounting practice.[58]

It was recommended that the Council would meet three to four times a year, and have approximately 20 members who would include accountants in practice, as well as in industry, commerce and the public sector. There would be an equal number of members drawn from all other relevant areas of interest, and the UK and Irish Governments would be invited to nominate members or observers.[59]

G   *An Accounting Standards Board*

The Committee recommended that the ASC should be reconstituted into an Accounting Standards Board (ASB) which would be able to issue accounting standards on its own authority, instead of needing the approval of the Councils of all the six accountancy bodies which make up the CCAB. The ASB would have a full-time Chairman and Technical Director and its total membership would not exceed nine. A majority of two-thirds would be required for the approval of an accounting standard. Furthermore, in order to provide an immediate and authoritative response to emerging issues the Committee recommended that the ASB should establish a capability of publishing authoritative, though non-mandatory, guidance on emerging issues.[60]

H   *A Review Panel*

The Committee addressed the difficult question of securing compliance with accounting standards in support of the 'true and fair' requirement. It was therefore recommended that, with the objective of achieving 'good financial reporting',[61] a Review Panel (possibly modelled on the Panel on Take-overs and Mergers) should be established to examine any identified or alleged material departures from accounting standards. The findings of the Review Panel should spell out what revisions to the financial statements or what additional information it considered should be made available to users to provide an acceptable set of financial statements giving a true and fair view.[62]

3.1.6 The implementation of the Dearing proposals

The recommendations of the Dearing Committee were greeted favourably, and although there was an initial hiatus during which it was feared that they might suffer the same fate as those of the Watts Committee, the Accounting Standards Board was set up in August 1990, and the Review Panel soon thereafter, as discussed under 3.2 below. The Financial Reporting Council was established initially under the chairmanship of Sir Ronald Dearing himself, with Sir Sydney Lipworth taking over the position from 1 January 1994.

The ASC remained in operation until the ASB was formed, when it was disbanded. During the 20 years of its existence it had published 25 accounting standards, three of which it later withdrew, and a total of 55 exposure drafts, nine of which were issued in the last six months of its life. In retrospect, its achievements were considerable, given the modest resources available to it, and although some of its standards can be criticised, collectively they improved UK GAAP beyond recognition from the state of financial reporting practice at the time of its creation, in 1970.

Two of the more significant changes to company law which had been recommended by the Dearing Committee were taken up in the Companies Act 1989. In particular:

(a)   the accounts of large companies have to state whether they have been prepared in accordance with applicable accounting standards and give details of, and the reasons for, any material departures.[63] Small and medium-sized companies and certain small and medium-sized groups are exempt from this disclosure requirement;[64] and

(b)   the Act took up the Dearing Committee recommendation that the Secretary of State or other authorised persons should be able to apply to the court for an order requiring the revision of defective accounts.[65] It also enables accounts to be revised without the necessity for court action, by providing procedures both for the voluntary revision of accounts[66] and for the Secretary of State to notify directors of apparent defects in accounts, thus giving them the opportunity to revise the accounts or explain why they believe no revision is required.[67]

The two other proposed changes to the law, described at (c) and (d) of 3.1.5 E above, were not taken up.

3.2   The Accounting Standards Board

The Accounting Standards Board succeeded the ASC on 1 August 1990, with Sir David Tweedie as its Chairman, Allan Cook as its Technical Director and seven other members.   The total membership of the Board has since been increased to ten. To date (August 1999), the Board has published fifteen Financial Reporting Standards (FRSs) in final form, an Interim Statement which preceded one of these standards, amendments to a number of existing standards including its own FRSs 1, 3 and 5, various non-mandatory Statements, two Draft versions of its proposed *Statement of Principles* and a large number of other exposure drafts and discussion papers. All of these are discussed under the relevant subject headings in this book.

The Board has also implemented another part of the Dearing proposals by establishing the Urgent Issues Task Force. The purpose of this group is to assist the ASB in areas where an accounting standard or a Companies Act provision exists, but where unsatisfactory or conflicting interpretations have developed or seem likely to develop. In such cases, the Task Force will consider the issue put to it, and if it is able to achieve agreement on the appropriate solution, will publish an Abstract setting out its consensus view. Such Abstracts do not constitute 'applicable accounting standards' in terms of the Companies Act, but nonetheless are meant to be observed unless it can be shown that to do so would not give a true and fair view. This view is supported by The Hon Mrs Justice Arden in her Opinion of the true and fair view referred to above, which states that 'the Court is likely to treat UITF abstracts as of considerable standing even though they are not envisaged by the Companies Acts. This will lead to a readiness on the part of the Court to accept that compliance with abstracts of the UITF is also necessary to meet the true and fair requirement.'[68]

Although it did not do so initially, the UITF now publicises its agenda, and often gives an opportunity to comment on Abstracts which it publishes in draft. This change in policy came about as a result of public criticism of the Task Force, which was accused of springing Abstracts on the business community without due notice or public debate. In any event, though, the UITF can make a ruling only if a high majority of its members agree to it. The Task Force can have up to 16 members, and it can only publish an Abstract on any issue if no more than two members vote against it. So far, it has published twenty two Abstracts, all of which are dealt with in this book. A number of further proposed Abstracts have, as a result of public opposition or a lack of majority support, not been issued in final form.

Also in accordance with the Dearing proposals, the Financial Reporting Review Panel (FRRP) was set up, initially under the chairmanship of Simon Tuckey QC. The current Chairman of the FRRP is Peter Goldsmith QC. This body is empowered to consider apparent defects in published accounts, and determine what action to take. So far approximately 50 cases have been publicised, and such action has almost exclusively been confined to obtaining the agreement of the companies concerned to amending the practice complained of in subsequent years. However, in appropriate cases the Panel might ask that the accounts be reissued, and if necessary institute court proceedings to require the company concerned to do so.

No very clear pattern can be discerned from the Panel's decisions to date. Many of them have involved relatively minor misdemeanours by companies who are not household names, and this has led some commentators to express the concern that the Panel has yet to establish its credibility in policing the more difficult areas of UK GAAP. However, there have been exceptions, where the Panel has successfully challenged major companies on important matters. A number of the more interesting decisions of the Review Panel are discussed in this book.

The following diagram illustrates the structure of the present standard-setting regime in the UK:

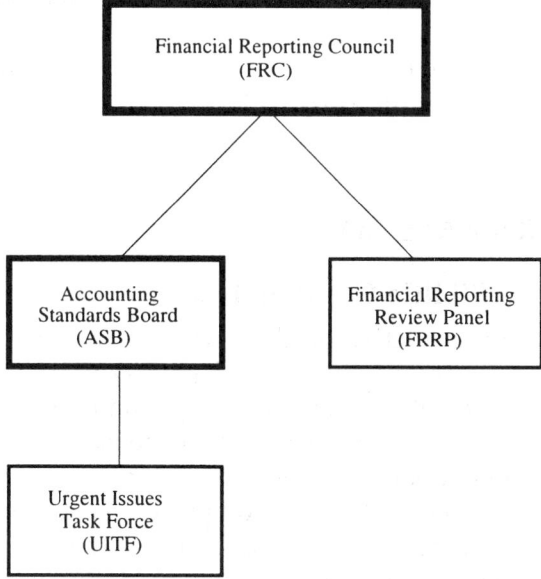

3.3   Statements of Recommended Practice (SORPs)

As stated above, the idea of SORPs was first mooted by the McKinnon Report and adopted by the ASC. SORPs are issued on subjects on which it is not considered appropriate to issue an accounting standard at the time, and usually relate to industry-specific areas of accounting where differences and varieties of accounting treatments exist. Most are issued by industry groups which are representative of the industries concerned (for example, the British Bankers' Association), and do not have any mandatory status – although they are indicative of current best practice.

The ASC had developed a system of 'franking', whereby it would give SORPs its 'stamp of approval', having followed a review and approval procedure of its own. The ASC issued two SORPs of its own, and franked a number of SORPs developed by various industry groups – most notably the Oil Industry Accounting Committee.

In coming into office, the ASB stated that it would neither issue its own SORPs nor continue the ASC procedure of franking. Instead, the ASB said that it would issue a 'negative assurance statement' on SORPs submitted to it where it is satisfied that the SORP had been properly developed and did not appear to conflict with existing or proposed accounting standards or contain any fundamental points of principle that were unacceptable to the Board in the context of current accounting practice.

However, the ASB's internal procedures for the approval of industry groups and the issuance of negative assurance statements proved rather unwieldy, with the result that in June 1994, the ASB announced the establishment of two specialist committees to advise it on proposals for SORPs: the Financial Sector and other Special Industries Committee, and the Public Sector and Not-for-Profit Committee. By enlisting the expertise of those appointed to the committees, the ASB hopes to improve the scrutiny of such proposals in a way that makes fewer demands on its resources.

4   GAAP FOR SMALL COMPANIES

4.1   The Big GAAP/Little GAAP debate

The administrative and legislative burdens which have been imposed on small businesses have been a controversial issue for many years. In particular, issues such as the retention of the small company audit and the application of accounting standards to small companies have been the subject of numerous studies in the UK and around the world.[69] With the increasing number of accounting standards, owners of small companies have complained about the cost and inconvenience of applying accounting requirements which were designed for large public companies. Some hold the view that accounting standards should apply equally to all financial statements which purport to present a true and fair view; others believe that small companies should be exempted from the requirements of certain standards which are unduly burdensome; whilst there is yet a further contention that small companies should have a completely different set of accounting standards altogether.

Whilst it is beyond the scope of this book to discuss all the issues surrounding differential reporting for small companies, it is noteworthy that there has until recently been a general reluctance to pursue the development of two GAAPs. This is reflected, for example, in a Report to the Council of the Institute of Chartered Accountants of British Columbia, wherein the Task Force on Big GAAP/Little GAAP concluded that 'any attempt to develop two separate sets of generally accepted accounting principles ... raises insurmountable difficulties'.[70] Amongst the reasons offered for these difficulties was that 'defining in a meaningful fashion Big GAAP/Little GAAP principles would appear to be unattainable given that the accounting profession has been unable to adequately define generally accepted accounting principles'.[71]

In a research study carried out in 1985 by Professor B. V. Carsberg *et al.* on small company financial reporting in the UK, the conclusion was reached that 'the burden imposed by accounting standards and other reporting requirements does not seem to be a matter for primary concern among people in small companies'.[72] In attempting to explain this finding, the report suggested that 'perhaps small company managers have little awareness of what is involved in complying with standards because they leave this aspect of their accounting to their professional advisers'.[73]

4.2 The ASC's initiative on 'small companies'

In October 1986, the ASC commissioned a working party to investigate the application of accounting standards to small companies. The findings of the working party, which were set out in TR 690,[74] were that 'there is no evidence to suggest that, in general, small companies find compliance with accounting standards unduly burdensome, given that they have to prepare financial statements that give a true and fair view'.[75] TR 690 did, however, indicate that the ASC would consider exempting small companies from certain future standards.[76]

This announcement was later followed up by TR 706, which outlined the basis on which the ASC intended to judge whether exemptions would be appropriate, defined the class of entities to which any exemption would normally apply and indicated the way in which the exemption would be formulated.[77] In TR 706, the ASC stated that it 'accepts that there is a case, in specific circumstances, for exempting small entities from certain provisions of accounting standards'; however, 'such exemptions are likely to relate more often to disclosure requirements, rather than to recognition or measurement rules'.[78] Where the ASC was satisfied that exemption was merited in a specific instance, it proposed a relaxation for a class of entities which excludes:

(a) public limited companies (plcs);

(b) companies that had a plc as a subsidiary; and

(c) other reporting entities, required to prepare true and fair accounts, which exceeded ten times the qualifying conditions for a company to be treated as a medium-sized company under section 247 of the Companies Act 1985.[79]

The effect of this proposal was that, in terms of the current thresholds (in August 1999) contained in section 247, a company would only be able to take advantage of the exemptions specified in a particular accounting standard if it was neither a plc, nor had a plc as a subsidiary, and it met two or more of the following criteria:

(a) its turnover did not exceed £112m;

(b) its balance sheet total did not exceed £56m;

(c) the average number of persons employed in the year did not exceed 2,500.

Clearly, these criteria can hardly be regarded as relating to 'small companies', and it is apparent that they were designed to apply to companies other than very large ones. It is our view, however, that the ASC introduced an unnecessary complication by including the size criteria in the exemption. It would have been more sensible if the ASC had merely distinguished between public and private companies in its exemption proposals.

This exemption has been applied (in slightly modified form) in relation to certain aspects of SSAP 13 (Revised) – *Accounting for research and development* and SSAP 25 – *Segmental reporting*. On the other hand FRS 1 – *Cash flow statements* – contains an exemption for small companies as defined by the Act, which are very much smaller than those exempted under the other two standards.

4.3   The Financial Reporting Standard for Smaller Entities (FRSSE)

4.3.1   *Introduction to the FRSSE*

In 1994, a working party of the CCAB that had been set up at the ASB's request carried out a consultation exercise on the application of accounting standards to smaller entities,[80] and issued a further paper for comment at the end of 1995.[81] After analysing the responses, the working party passed over the project to the ASB, which published an exposure draft in December 1996. This is known as the *Financial Reporting Standard for Smaller Entities* (or FRSSE), and was originally issued as an FRS in November 1997, with the first revision being issued in December 1998. It comprises a compendium standard for smaller entities, based on a simplified summary of the whole corpus of existing standards. Amendments have been made to these other standards so as to exempt entities that fall under the FRSSE.

The publication of the FRSSE in November 1997 introduced a new concept into financial reporting – that of a complete, distinct accounting standard specifically for smaller entities. The FRSSE prescribes the basis, for those entities within its scope that have chosen to adopt it, for preparing and presenting their financial statements. The definitions and accounting treatments are consistent with the requirements of companies legislation and, for the generality of small entities, are the same as those required by other accounting standards or a simplified version of those requirements. The disclosure requirements exclude a number of those stipulated in other accounting standards.

Reporting entities that apply the FRSSE are exempt from complying with other accounting standards (SSAPs and FRSs) and Urgent Issues Task Force (UITF) Abstracts, unless preparing consolidated financial statements, in which case certain other accounting standards apply (namely, FRSs 2, 6 and 7 and, as they apply in respect of consolidated financial statements, FRSs 5, 9, 10 and 11).

Financial statements will generally be prepared using accepted practice and, accordingly, for transactions or events not dealt with in the FRSSE, smaller entities should have regard to other accounting standards and UITF Abstracts, not as mandatory documents, but as a means of establishing current practice.

In issuing differential reporting standards for entities that may nonetheless be required by law to present a true and fair view in the same way as larger entities, the ASB has been mindful of the need to explain the apparent contradiction that this involves, without diluting the concept of 'true and fair'. The ASB states that it has obtained legal advice that exemptions or differing treatments can be justified provided there are rational grounds, and says that in developing the proposals it has had regard to the following considerations in relation to each requirement:

(a) The standard or requirement is likely to be regarded as having general application and as an essential element of generally accepted accounting practice for all entities.

(b) The standard or requirement is likely to lead to a transaction being treated in a way that would be readily recognised by the proprietor or manager of the business as corresponding to his or her understanding of the transaction.

(c) The standard or requirement is likely to meet the information needs and legitimate expectations of a user of a small entity's accounts.

(d) The standard or requirement results in disclosures that are likely to be meaningful and comprehensive to such a user. Where disclosures are aimed at a particular group of users, that group would be likely to receive the information, given that they may have access only to abbreviated accounts.

(e) The requirements of the standard significantly augment the treatment prescribed by legislation.

(f) The treatment prescribed by the standard or requirement is compatible with that already used, or expected to be used, by the Inland Revenue in computing taxable profits.

(g) The standard or requirement provides the least cumbersome method of achieving the desired accounting treatment and/or disclosure for an entity that is not complex.

(h) The standard provides guidance that is expected to be widely relevant to the transactions of small entities and is written in terms that can be understood by such businesses.

(i) The measurement methods prescribed in the standard are likely to be reasonably practical for small entities.[82]

The ASB believes that satisfaction of a majority of the above criteria would suggest that the standard or requirement under consideration may also be appropriate for application to smaller entities, whereas failure to satisfy a majority of the above criteria would suggest that exemption, or differing treatment, from the standard, or a specific requirement within that standard, may be more appropriate.

In fact, many of these considerations would seem to be appropriate to the Board's decisions on the development of accounting standards in general, and are not particularly specific to the circumstances of small businesses. Be that as it may, the actual effect of the FRSSE is simply to excuse smaller entities from complying with a number of the disclosure requirements that would otherwise have applied. There is no substantive amendment to the measurement rules contained in other standards, although their explanation has been simplified to some degree. Essentially, therefore, this represents a pragmatic relaxation of disclosure rules rather than any new form of financial reporting tailored to the needs of small businesses.[83] This is nonetheless welcome, because there is no doubt that the panoply of disclosure requirements imposed on UK companies is onerous, but it should not be seen as a development based on any great principle.

4.3.2   Scope of the FRSSE

The FRSSE may be applied to all financial statements intended to give a true and fair view of the financial position and profit or loss (or income and expenditure) of all entities that are:

(a)   companies incorporated under companies legislation and entitled to the exemptions available in the legislation for small companies when filing accounts with the Registrar of Companies; or

(b)   entities that would have come into category (a) above had they been companies incorporated under companies legislation, excluding building societies. Such entities should have regard to the accounting principles, presentation and disclosure requirements in companies legislation (or other equivalent legislation) that, taking into account the FRSSE, are necessary to present a true and fair view.[84]

The FRSSE therefore applies to small companies and groups as defined in the Companies Act 1985 and to other entities that meet the same size limits. As at August 1999, this means companies that satisfy at least two of the following criteria:

- Turnover not more than £2.8 million
- Balance sheet total not more than £1.4 million
- No more than 50 employees.

Accordingly, the FRSSE does not apply to:

(i)   large or medium-sized companies, groups and other entities;

(ii)   public companies;

(iii) banks, building societies or insurance companies;

(iv)   authorised persons under the Financial Services Act 1986 (in the UK) or the Investment Intermediaries Act 1995 (in the Republic of Ireland); or

(v)   members of groups that contain companies falling under (ii)-(iv) above.

Reporting entities that are entitled to adopt the FRSSE, but choose not to do so, should apply SSAPs, other FRSs and UITF Abstracts when preparing financial statements intended to give a true and fair view of the financial position and profit or loss of the entity.

4.3.3   True and fair view

Financial statements prepared under the FRSSE should present a true and fair view of the results for the period and of the state of affairs at the end of the period. To achieve such a view, regard should be had to the substance of any arrangement or transaction, or series of such, into which the entity has entered. To determine the substance of a transaction it is necessary to identify whether the transaction has given rise to new assets or liabilities for the reporting entity and whether it has changed the entity's existing assets or liabilities.[85]

Where there is doubt whether applying provisions of the FRSSE would be sufficient to give a true and fair view, adequate explanation should be given in the notes to the accounts of the transaction or arrangement concerned and the treatment adopted.[86]

4.3.4   Accounting principles and policies

FRSSE financial statements should state that they have been prepared in accordance with the Financial Reporting Standard for Smaller Entities (effective March 1999).

If the financial statements are prepared on the basis of assumptions that differ in material respects from any of the accounting principles set out in paragraphs 10 to 14 of Schedule 4 to the Companies Act, the facts should be explained.[87]   In the absence of a clear statement to the contrary, there is a presumption that the accounting principles have been observed.

The accounting policies followed for dealing with items that are judged material or critical in determining profit or loss for the period and in stating the financial position should be disclosed by way of note to the accounts. The explanations should be clear, fair and as brief as possible.[88]

A change in accounting policy may be made only if it can be justified on the grounds that the new policy is preferable to the one it replaces because it will give a fairer presentation of the result and financial position of a reporting entity.[89] Following a change in accounting policy, the amounts for the current and corresponding periods should be restated on the basis of the new policies. The disclosures necessary when a change of accounting policy is made should include, in addition to those for prior period adjustments, an indication of the effect on the current period's results. In those cases where the effect on the current period is immaterial, or similar to the quantified effect on the prior period, a simple statement saying this suffices. Where it is not practicable to give the effect on the current period, that fact, together with the reasons, should be stated.[90]

4.3.5 Future review of the FRSSE as a whole

Changing financial reporting practice, in the form of new FRSs and UITF Abstracts, will necessitate periodic revisions to the FRSSE to ensure that it is kept up to date. As a result, in July 1999 the ASB issued an Exposure Draft that proposes amendments to the FRSSE in order to take account of the four new FRSs that had been issued since July 1998 (namely, FRSs 12 to 15).[91]

In publishing the Exposure Draft, the ASB has acknowledged that in the course of the FRSSE's development conflicting views were put forward, ranging from those who believed smaller entities should be exempt from all accounting standards to those who favoured retaining virtually the status quo. Given this divergence of views, the ASB believes that it is particularly important that the FRSSE should be monitored carefully. Therefore, the ASB has announced that it intends to review how the FRSSE, as a whole, is working in practice after two full years of effective operation (i.e. in the year 2000) and to propose amendments as necessary.[92]

In the meantime, as part of a wider review of UK Company Law mentioned at 2.4.4 above, the Company Law Review Steering Group has raised a number of questions concerning the needs of small and closely-held companies.[93] The Steering Group acknowledges that a wide variety of approaches is possible and notes that various models have been proposed and adopted in other jurisdictions. The Steering Group has broken these down into two broad kinds of approach, which it has termed the 'free standing' and the 'integrated' approaches.[94]

The 'free standing' approach involves creating a separate, free-standing, limited liability vehicle for small companies, probably involving separate legislation. Eligibility criteria would be based on the economically small, closely held, company where the shape of regulation could be tailored and would be relatively light when compared with the full Companies Act provisions. Such companies would need to revert to the Companies Act regime should they develop beyond these limits. The 'integrated' approach involves a number of different options, ranging from the retention of the status quo to a totally reformulated SME-centric Companies Act.

The Steering Group has reached the provisional conclusion that it favours a variant of the 'integrated' approach involving both changes in form and changes in substance to the existing legislation. It believes that companies legislation should be reframed so that the basic model is the private company, and private company provisions should be presented as a single integrated whole. Provisions relating to public and listed companies would then be drafted so that they are separated out and dealt with as an additional set, perhaps in a separate Act or part of the Act.[95]

The Steering Group has proposed further that work on accounting and reporting would be covered in the next phase of its review, and that this would consider the value of Companies Act accounts for internal and external purposes and possible substitutes or supplements. Presumably this review will be timed to coincide with the ASB's fundamental review of the FRSSE as a whole.

4.3.6 *Does the FRSSE provide a long-term solution to differential financial reporting?*

In our view, the ASB has not really penetrated very deeply into any consideration of the objectives of differential company financial reporting for smaller entities; perhaps it concluded that such an exercise would have been futile in any case, given the inflexible and universal requirement for UK companies to prepare accounts that give a true and fair view. However, the launch of a fundamental review of the framework of core company law now provides the ASB with a unique opportunity for innovation.

Clearly, small companies do need standards; nor can it be disputed that the application of GAAP assists in the implementation of the Companies Act reporting requirements through, inter alia, the imposition of some form of accounting and reporting discipline. However, the perennial discussion of whether or not small companies find accounting standards burdensome is spurious, since this is not the real issue. This is whether existing standards provide small businessmen with a reporting framework that generates information that is useful, relevant and reliable for decision making purposes. The question, therefore, is not whether standards impose a burden on small companies, but whether they are of any value. It is therefore first necessary to establish a sensible definition of a small company for financial reporting purposes, in contrast to the definitions based on arbitrary size criteria that have been used to date.

The criteria contained in section 247 of the Companies Act are clearly not suitable for the purposes of determining whether or not a company should be subject to alternative reporting requirements. To assume that, in the application of standards, small companies are merely simpler versions of large companies is to make the same mistake inherent in company law. Modern company law focuses on the large public company, and the Companies Act, with its 747 sections and 25 Schedules, is not appropriate for the small owner-managed company. Even if standards do not impose more burdens than the law, perhaps it is time to consider seriously the development of a new limited liability vehicle for the small proprietary company. We therefore do not support the Company Law Review Steering Group's provisional conclusion that it favours a variant of the 'integrated' approach in preference to the 'free standing' approach.

The fundamental criteria that distinguish a small company from others are the compositions of its membership and management. Companies with a limited number of members, all involved in the day to day operations, should be able to incorporate under a different and specially designed limited liability regime. It is within this structure that a better financial reporting framework can be developed.

If this structure is adopted, the question of small company compliance with existing standards will involve three distinct accounting issues – those of recognition, measurement, and disclosure. The question, therefore, is not merely whether or not the application of existing standards should be relaxed, but whether alternative standards of recognition, measurement, and/or disclosure would better achieve the objectives of financial reporting for small companies.

General purpose financial statements are prepared on the assumption that there are no basic differences in the needs of those who will use them. However, as discussed in Chapter 2, the users of public companies' financial statements include existing and potential shareholders, loan creditors, financial analysts and advisers, the financial press, employees, etc. Small companies' accounts, on the other hand, are prepared primarily for the benefit of owner-managers, their bankers, and the Revenue authorities, who have little interest in the kind of information aimed at the broad spectrum of users of public companies' statements.

Furthermore, the owners of public companies are not generally involved in the management of the business. For this reason, a relationship of accountability is developed between owners and managers. Clearly, since a characteristic of a small proprietary company is that it is owner-managed, this accountability – together with the related reporting obligation – falls away, illustrating a major distinction between the objectives of financial reporting for the two types of company. If it is accepted that the needs of users of financial statements should determine the objectives of financial reporting, their needs must ultimately govern the form and content of financial statements. Although this general principle is becoming widely acknowledged, the precise uses of small companies' accounts need to be adequately identified in order that appropriate reporting practice for them can be developed.

5   SUMMARY FINANCIAL STATEMENTS

5.1   The required form of a summary financial statement

In a new departure for UK corporate reporting, the Companies Act 1989 amended the 1985 Act to allow listed companies to send a summary financial statement to shareholders who do not wish to receive the full accounts.[96] The form of the statement is specified by statutory instrument[97] as requiring the following minimum information, extracted from the full accounts:

(a) from the directors' report:

  ■ the whole, or a summary, of the 'fair review of the development of the business of the company and its subsidiary undertakings during the financial year and of their position at the end of it';

  ■ the amount recommended to be paid by way of dividend, if not disclosed in the summary profit and loss account;

  ■ the whole, or a summary, of the details of 'any important events affecting the company or any of its subsidiary undertakings which have occurred since the end of the financial year';

  ■ the whole, or a summary, of the 'indication of future likely developments in the business of the company and of its subsidiary undertakings'; and

  ■ the names of all the directors who served during the financial year;[98]

(b) from the profit and loss account, the information against these headings:

  ■ turnover;

  ■ income from shares in associated undertakings;

  ■ other interest receivable and similar income less interest payable and similar charges;

  ■ profit or loss on ordinary activities before taxation;

  ■ tax on profit or loss on ordinary activities;

  ■ profit or loss on ordinary activities after tax;

  ■ minority interests;

  ■ extraordinary items;

  ■ profit or loss for the financial year;

  ■ dividends paid and proposed; and

  ■ directors' emoluments;[99]

(c) from the balance sheet, the information against these headings:

  ■ fixed assets;

  ■ current assets;

  ■ prepayments and accrued income (if not shown within current assets in the full accounts);

  ■ creditors: amounts falling due within one year;

  ■ net current assets (liabilities);

  ■ total assets less current liabilities;

  ■ creditors: amounts falling due after more than one year;

  ■ provisions for liabilities and charges;

  ■ capital and reserves; and

  ■ minority interests.[100]

Slightly different requirements are specified for banks and insurance companies which do not produce their full accounts under the formats of Schedule 4 to the Companies Act.[101]

As well as including the information specified above, the summary financial statement must include 'any other information necessary to ensure that [it] is consistent with the full accounts'.[102] The interpretation of the word 'consistent' is problematical. At one extreme, it might simply require that the information in the summary is the same as that which is included in the full accounts; at the other, it might be thought to require that the reader of the summary will gain the same impression of the company as he would from reading the full accounts, although if that were possible, the full accounts would be redundant. Probably what is intended is some notion of fairness of summarisation, so that the statement is not unduly selective or biased, but the requirement remains an elusive one.

In addition, the summary financial statement must explain that it is only a summary of the full accounts,[103] remind readers that they are entitled to the full accounts if they want them, and include a warning (in specified form) that it does not contain enough information to allow a full understanding of the results and state of affairs of the company or group concerned.[104] It must also say whether or not the full accounts bore a qualified audit report, and reproduce it if it did,[105] and the auditors must also report whether, in their opinion, the summary is consistent with the full accounts and complies with the legal requirements.[106] Barclays is a company that prepares summary financial statements, giving the above disclosures in its Annual Review and Summary Financial Statement 1998 as follows:

Extract 1.4: Barclays PLC (1998)

SHAREHOLDERS PLEASE NOTE

This annual review and summary financial statement does not contain sufficient information to allow for a full understanding of the results of the Group and state of affairs of the Company or of the Group.

For further information, the full annual report of the Company and the related financial review, the auditors' report on those accounts and the Directors' report should be consulted.

Any shareholders who wish to receive the annual report free of charge in addition to the annual review and summary financial statement for this year or future years, should contact the Registrars at the address shown on the inside back cover. The annual report contains the full report of the Directors and audited accounts.

......

The auditors' report on the full annual accounts of the Group for the year ended 31st December 1998 was unqualified and did not contain a statement under either section 237(2) (accounting records or returns inadequate or accounts not agreeing with records and returns) or 237(3) (failure to obtain necessary information and explanations) of the Companies Act 1985.

5.2 The ICAEW survey

In 1996, a working party of the ICAEW reviewed the experience of the use of summary financial statements to date and published a survey of its findings.[107] This noted that a relatively small number of companies had taken up the opportunity to use the format. The authors of the report presented this as something of a missed opportunity, because a number of those companies who did use them had reported that they had been favourably received by shareholders. Of course, this can be seen as much as a criticism of the full report and accounts as a commendation of the shorter format. The chairman of the working party, Mr David Allvey, had this to say in introducing the 1995 summary financial statement of his now former company:

Extract 1.5: B.A.T Industries p.l.c. (1995)

Finance Director's review [extract]

It has to be acknowledged that the various new accounting regulations which came into force during 1995 have made our full Report and Accounts even harder to understand than hitherto. This Summary Financial Statement is therefore even more important in helping us meet our objective of communicating clearly with our shareholders to explain our businesses and their performance during the year.

The Group will always support the proposition that the quality of the information provided is much more important than its sheer quantity. This is especially true when much of the additional bulk (more pages to our Accounts this year) often adds little to the key information with which the Directors actually manage the business. ...

We will continue to argue for clarity, relevance and common sense in statutory accounts. This year, for example, we have lobbied hard and successfully for changes to the presentation of cash inflow information. As a result, it is likely that the statutory version will be more in line with the simplified information presented, which meets our key test of more accurately reflecting the way we actually run the business.

In view of Mr Allvey's membership of the ASB, which is responsible for some of the regulation complained of, it might be thought that this was a little self-critical. However, the ASB itself clearly shares his concern about the indigestible nature of accounts, and has taken on a project to consider the use of summary financial statements as part of a wider study of the financial reporting package as a whole, including the relationship of the report and accounts to the preliminary announcements made by listed companies.[108] Mr Allvey alluded to this in his 1996 report:

Extract 1.6: B.A.T Industries p.l.c. (1996)

Finance Director's review [extract]

It is important that financial reporting should not be regarded as an end in itself but always judged by whether it helps companies to communicate clearly with shareholders. In this context, we were one of the first to use Summary Financial Statements to improve communication, seeking to provide quality rather than quantity.

While we welcome the legislative changes in 1996, which are certainly aimed at encouraging wider use of such statements, we are concerned by emerging adverse pressures. Specifically, the changing accounting regime resulting in greater complexity and rigidity in published accounts is spilling into Summary Financial Statements, partly defeating the purpose for which they were designed.

While some of the developments have been essential to improve the quality of published financial information, we regard as timely the current debate over the objectives of financial reporting and the growing recognition that no single document can meet the needs of all users. The whole purpose of financial accounts and the relationship between the different reports needs to be reviewed.

We will, of course, continue to seek to influence the development of national and international accounting standards, both as a company and through various lobbying groups and through membership of organisations such as the Accounting Standards Board and the International Accounting Standards Committee.

He is certainly right to observe that summary financial statements are themselves growing in complexity. Initially, those companies who used them often published them in the minimal form dictated by the regulations. However, increasingly, they have been incorporated in larger documents that may contain significant amounts of narrative, such as the Operating and Financial Review, or extensive corporate governance disclosures, such as the remuneration committee report. The problem of distinguishing the wood from the trees persists.

5.3   Commentary on the summary financial statement regime

It would be encouraging to believe that the Government's initiative in introducing summarised financial statements was motivated by a desire to make financial statements more understandable to the reader. However, the reality is that it was intended as a cost-saving measure, of particular benefit to those companies who, following privatisation, had a very large number of small shareholders in respect of whom the preparation of full annual reports is a considerable expense. The form of summary financial statements dictated by the law is not particularly imaginative; it amounts to little more than the primary financial statements without the notes. Although the use of such statements has now become a feature of UK GAAP, it is difficult to see it as either a real advance in the quality of financial reporting or much of a cost saving. Instead, this approach could merely exacerbate the common misunderstanding that the results and financial position of a highly complex organisation can be encapsulated in simple headline measures such as EPS and gearing.

For all the faults of the full accounts, a great deal of careful thought has gone into the development of the existing accounting and disclosure rules which are embodied in the Companies Act 1985 and the SSAPs and FRSs. These rules are based on the principle of necessary disclosure, rather than on maximum or superfluous disclosure. It is difficult to see how, under the existing accounting framework, it is possible for companies to make their accounts more understandable or relevant by reducing them to the form specified for summary financial statements.

In 1978, the FASB's first Statement of Financial Accounting Concepts (SFAC No. 1) stated that the information provided by financial reporting should be comprehensible to those who have a reasonable understanding of business and economic activities and are willing to study the information with reasonable diligence. Information, whilst it may be relevant, will be wasted if it is provided in a form which cannot be understood by the users for whom it was intended. SFAC No. 1 elaborated on the relationship between useful information and understandability as follows: 'financial information is a tool and, like most tools, cannot be of much direct help to those who are unable or unwilling to use it or who misuse it. Its use can be learned, however, and financial reporting should provide information that can be used by all – nonprofessionals as well as professionals – who are willing to learn to use it properly. Efforts may be needed to increase the understandability of financial information. Cost-benefit considerations may indicate that information understood or used by only a few should not be provided. Conversely, financial reporting should not exclude relevant information merely because it is difficult for some to understand or because some investors or creditors choose not to use it.'[109]

We therefore consider the introduction of summary financial statements to be something of a diversion in relation to the development of better forms of financial reporting. This is because the prime motivation behind their introduction was to save costs for companies and not to provide information in a form which was more readily understood by the small shareholder. We hope that the ASB's initiative in exploring a more meaningful form of simplified reporting will be successful.

6   CONCLUSION

UK GAAP incorporates the requirements of accounting standards and UITF Abstracts, of the Companies Act and of the Stock Exchange, together with other accounting practices which are generally accepted by the accounting profession to be permissible. However, as circumstances and environments change, accounting practices require development and adaptation. GAAP, therefore, is a dynamic concept, which is not restricted to the requirements of accounting standards and the law, and is continually undergoing change as circumstances alter.

A major preoccupation for the ASB at present is the international dimension. UK GAAP cannot and should not be left to develop in isolation from accounting practice in the rest of the world. If the IASC's present endeavour to forge standards that are acceptable to the world's securities regulators proves successful, it may prove to be the most significant influence on UK GAAP (and that of many other countries) for many years to come.

No doubt, now that IOSCO has begun its assessment of the IASC's core standards, there will ensue much speculation as to how good a job the IASC has done. Unfortunately, though, it is likely that a great deal of this will involve political jockeying rather than intellectual debate. The fact of the matter is that, when it comes to a body of GAAP suitable for presenting fairly the economic substance of an entity's financial performance and position, International Accounting Standards can hold their ground against the best in the world.

Nonetheless there is likely to be a considerable degree of such politicking over the question whether or not the US SEC will endorse the IASC package. For us in Europe, however, the issue is largely irrelevant. For a start, the SEC will probably take some time over its deliberations and in the end is unlikely to issue an unqualified endorsement of IAS. More importantly, though, circumstances are very different now to those of four years ago.

Prior to the IOSCO agreement, there was always the danger that Europe's capital markets would fragment and thereby drive individual countries and companies into ad hoc alliances with the US and other international capital markets. However, as the balance in the international harmonisation debate moves away from US dominance, circumstances have changed considerably. With European Monetary Union now in place and alliances being formed between European Stock Exchanges, the capital markets in Europe will inevitably come much closer together and will, therefore, provide a significant alternative to the US capital markets. The world's largest companies will be able to have more of their capital needs satisfied in Europe at the same cost of capital as the US. For some companies already tempted to go down the US GAAP route, this means holding their nerve a little longer until the full effects of a consolidated European capital market are felt.

In the mean time, individual European countries are taking a much more active role in the harmonisation movement. For example, in Germany legislation has been passed to the effect that 'internationally accepted accounting principles' may be used in the consolidated financial statements of listed companies instead of the national law. France, Italy, Belgium, Spain and Austria have passed similar measures. For Europe, these are revolutionary changes.

More to the point, though, they also raise interesting questions about the position of the UK Accounting Standards Board and UK GAAP generally. If the European capital markets accept financial reporting by European multinational companies under the IASC umbrella, how much longer can the DTI insist that

UK companies may only report under UK GAAP? For example, one can envisage German and French multinational companies, with Euro-denominated share capital and share prices, trading freely on the London, Paris and Frankfurt exchanges, while preparing a single set of consolidated accounts under IAS. Given that the London Stock Exchange has for many years accepted foreign companies reporting under IAS GAAP, it seems unsustainable that UK companies should continue to be compelled to prepare UK GAAP accounts.

Consequently, there seems even less of a case for the UK to continue in European financial reporting isolation. If IAS GAAP is considered to be suitable for the largest multinational companies in Germany, France, Italy and elsewhere, surely it must be good enough for UK companies. The UK Government's fundamental review of the framework of core company law provides a timely opportunity for the UK to get in step with the rest of Europe on the matter of financial reporting.

With the task of balancing all these considerations, and with many conflicting political pressures in the background, the ASB has a crucial role in charting the future direction of GAAP in the United Kingdom.

References

1 CA 85, Sch. 4A, para. 10(1)(d).
2 *Ibid.*, s 262(3).
3 CCAB, TR 481: *The determination of realised profits and disclosure of distributable profits in the context of the Companies Acts 1948 to 1981*, September 1982.
4 *Ibid.*, para. 4.
5 *Odeon Associated Theatres Ltd v Jones (Inspector of Taxes)* [1971] 1 WLR 442.
6 Leonard Hoffmann QC and Mary H. Arden, The Accounting Standards Committee Joint Opinion, *Legal Opinion on 'True and Fair'*, paras. 9 and 10.
7 *Statement of Aims*, ASB, 1993, para. 2.
8 SAS 69, *The Meaning of 'Present Fairly in Conformity With Generally Accepted Accounting Principles' in the Independent Auditor's Report*, AICPA, January 1992, para. 2.
9 New Zealand: The Financial Reporting Act 1993, s 3.
10 CA 47, s 13(1), re-enacted as CA 48, s 149(1).
11 EC Fourth Directive, Article 2.
12 *Ibid.*, paras. 1 to 3.
13 *Ibid.*, paras. 4 and 5.
14 IAS 1, *Presentation of financial statements*, IASC, Revised 1997, para. 13.
15 *Ibid.*, para. 11.
16 *Ibid.*, paras. 10 and 12.
17 *Ibid.*, para. 13.
18 *Ibid.*, para. 14.
19 *Ibid.*, para. 16.
20 *Foreword to Accounting Standards*, ASB, 1993, para. 16.
21 *Ibid.*, para 18.
22 Leonard Hoffmann QC and Mary H. Arden, *op. cit.*, paras. 9 and 10.
23 *Lloyd Cheyham & Co Ltd v Littlejohn & Co* [1987] BCLC 303 at 313.

24 Miss Mary Arden QC, *Accounting Standards Board, The True and Fair Requirement, Opinion,* 21 April 1993.
25 *Ibid.*, para. 10.
26 *Foreword to Accounting Standards*, para. 34.
27 Hoffmann J., Foreword to *Law and Accountancy: Conflict and Co-operation in the 1990s,* Freedman and Power (eds.), 1992.
28 IASC, *Preface to Statements of International Accounting Standards,* para. 1. As at August 1999, the IASC Board members were: Australia, Canada, France, Germany, India, Japan, Malaysia, Mexico, Netherlands, Nordic Federation of Public Accountants, South Africa, United Kingdom, United States of America and representatives of the International Council of Investment Associations (ICIA), the Federation of Swiss Industrial Holding Companies and the International Association of Financial Executives Institutes (IAFEI). The Indian delegation includes a representative from Sri Lanka and the South African delegation includes a representative from Zimbabwe. Representatives of the European Commission, the United States Financial Accounting Standards Board (FASB), the International Organisation of Securities Commissions (IOSCO), and the People's Republic of China attend Board meetings as observers.
29 IASC, *Shaping IASC for the future: A Discussion Paper issued for comment by the Strategy Working Party of the International Accounting Standards Committee*, IASC, 7 December 1998, para. 2.
30 IASC, *Preface to Statements of International Accounting Standards*, para. 2.
31 *Foreword to Accounting Standards*, para. 36.
32 *The IASC-U.S. Comparison Project: A Report on the Similarities and Differences between IASC Standards and U.S. GAAP*, FASB, November 1996.
33 Morgan Stanley Dean Witter, *Apples to Apples.   Overcoming Accounting Differences: A Stockpicker's Guide to the Numbers that Count*, February 1998.
34 *Ibid.*
35 The Company Law Review Steering Group, Consultation Document, *Modern Company Law for a Competitive Economy: The Strategic Framework*, February 1999, para. 6.13.
36 Stock Exchange Listing Rules, paras. 6.E.2 and 12.14(d).
37 IASC, *Shaping IASC for the future: A Discussion Paper issued for comment by the Strategy Working Party of the International Accounting Standards Committee*, IASC, 7 December 1998, para. 2.
38 *Ibid.*, para. 115 *et seq.*
39 The G4+1 is an informal grouping of staff members of the standard-setting bodies of Australia, Canada, New Zealand, the United Kingdom, the United States of America and the IASC. From time to time, the G4+1 publishes position papers on accounting topics of current interest. These papers do not necessarily reflect the official views of any of the standard-setting bodies represented.
40 APB Opinion No. 6, *Status of Accounting Research Bulletins*, Appendix A, paras. 1–3.
41 SEC, Accounting Series Release No. 150.
42 AICPA, *Code of Professional Conduct*, Rule 203–Accounting principles.
43 United States v. Simon, 425 F.2d 796 (2d Cir. 1969), *certiorari* denied 397 U.S. 1006 (1970).
44 See Ross M. Skinner, *Accounting Standards in Evolution*, Holt, Rinehart and Winston, Toronto, 1986, pp. 35–36.
45 CICA, *Handbook*, Volume 1, Section 1500.06.
46 *Ibid.*, Section 1000, paras. .59 to .61, *passim.*
47 Commercial Code, Third Book, Second Section, *Supplementary Regulations for Companies*, § 264(2).
48 Jermyn Paul Brooks and Dietz Mertin, *Neues deutsches Bilanzrecht/New German Accounting Legislation*, Düsseldorf: IDW-Verlag GmbH, 1986.
49 The Institute of Chartered Accountants in England and Wales, Occasional Council and Other Pronouncements, *Statement of intent on accounting standards in the 1970s*.
50 At that stage, the Association of Certified Accountants and the Institute of Cost and Management Accountants respectively.
51 ICAEW, *Statement of intent on accounting standards in the 1970s*, p. 1.4.
52 Accounting Standards Committee, *Setting Accounting Standards: A consultative document*.
53 Accounting Standards Committee, *Setting Accounting Standards*.
54 Report of the Review Committee under the chairmanship of Sir Ronald Dearing, *The Making of Accounting Standards*, September 1988, p. ix.

55 This summary of the recommendations has been extracted from the Dearing Report, *ibid.*, pp. 17–45, *passim.*

56 *Ibid.*, para. 10.2.

57 *Ibid.*, para. 11.1.

58 *Ibid.*, p. 44.

59 *Ibid.*, para. 11.3.

60 *Ibid.*, pp. 27–29.

61 *Ibid.*, p. 31.

62 *Ibid.*, p. 33.

63 CA 85, Sch. 4, para. 36A.

64 *Ibid.*, s 246(1)(a).

65 *Ibid.*, s 245B.

66 *Ibid.*, s 245.

67 *Ibid.*, s 245A.

68 Miss Mary Arden QC, *Accounting Standards Board, The True and Fair Requirement, Opinion,* 21 April 1993, para. 12.

69 See, for example: Department of Trade and Industry, *Accounting and Audit Requirements for Small Firms,* London: DTI, 1985; Department of Trade and Industry, *Burdens on Business, Report of a Scrutiny of Administrative and Legislative Requirements,* London: HMSO, March 1985; B. V. Carsberg *et al., Small Company Financial Reporting,* London: Prentice-Hall International, 1985; AICPA, Accounting Standards Division, Committee on Generally Accepted Accounting Principles for Smaller and/or Closely Held Businesses, *Report of the Committee on Generally Accepted Accounting Principles for Smaller and/or Closely Held Businesses,* New York: AICPA, August 1976; Institute of Chartered Accountants of British Columbia, *Task Force on Big GAAP/Little GAAP,* Report to Council, Submitted 30 July 1981.

70 Institute of Chartered Accountants of British Columbia, *op. cit.*, p. 3.

71 *Ibid.*, p. 4.

72 B. V. Carsberg *et al., op. cit.*, p. 83.

73 *Ibid.*, pp. 83–84.

74 TR 690: *Statement by the Accounting Standards Committee on the application of accounting standards,* February 1988.

75 *Ibid.*, para. 5.

76 *Ibid.*, para. 17.

77 TR 706: *Statement by the Accounting Standards Committee on the definition of 'small company' for the purpose of applying accounting standards,* July 1988, para. 1.1.

78 *Ibid.*, para. 5.1.

79 *Ibid.*, para. 5.2.

80 Consultative Document, *Exemptions from Standards on Grounds of Size or Public Interest,* CCAB, November 1994.

81 *Designed to fit – A Financial Reporting Standard for Smaller Entities,* CCAB, December 1995.

82 *Financial Reporting Standard for Smaller Entities,* ASB, December 1998, pp. 4 to 6.

83 In a similar way, company law has reduced disclosure requirements for small companies, which are now set out in Schedule 8 to the Companies Act, as inserted by *The Companies Act 1985 (Accounts of Small and Medium-sized Companies and Minor Accounting Amendments) Regulations 1997.*

84 *Financial Reporting Standard for Smaller Entities,* para. 1.1.

85 *Ibid.*, para. 2.1.

86 *Ibid.*, para. 2.2.

87 *Ibid.*, paras. 2.3 and 2.4. Schedule 4 sets out the following five accounting principles: going concern, consistency, prudence, accruals/matching and non-aggregation.

88 *Ibid.*, para. 2.5.

89 *Ibid.*, para. 2.6.

90 *Ibid.*, para. 2.8.

91 Exposure Draft, *Amendment to Financial Reporting Standard for Smaller Entities,* ASB, July 1999.

92 *Ibid.*, p. 6.

93 The Company Law Review Steering Group, Consultation Document, *Modern Company Law for a Competitive Economy: The Strategic Framework,* Chapter 5.2.

94 *Ibid.*, para. 5.2.23.
95 *Ibid.*, para. 5.2.33.
96 CA 85, s 251.
97 *The Companies (Summary Financial Statement) Regulations 1995* (SI 1995/2092).
98 *Ibid.*, Sch 1, para. 2.
99 *Ibid.*, Sch 1, para. 3.
100 *Ibid.*, Sch 1, para. 4.
101 *Ibid.*, Schedules 2 and 3.
102 *Ibid.*, Sch 1, para. 1(1).
103 CA 85, s 251(4) (a).
104 *The Companies (Summary Financial Statement) Regulations 1995* (SI 1995/2092), para. 7 (3) and (4).
105 CA 85, s 251(4) (c) and (d).
106 *Ibid.*, s 251(4) (b).
107 *Summary Financial Statements – The Way Forward*, ICAEW, 1996.
108 As reported in *Inside Track*, ASB, July 1997.
109 SFAC No. 1, *Objectives of Financial Reporting by Business Enterprises*, FASB, November 1978, para. 36.

Chapter 2   The quest for a conceptual framework for financial reporting

1   INTRODUCTION

1.1   What is a conceptual framework?

In general terms, a conceptual framework is a statement of generally accepted theoretical principles which form the frame of reference for a particular field of enquiry. In terms of financial reporting, these theoretical principles provide the basis for both the development of new reporting practices and the evaluation of existing ones. Since the financial reporting process is concerned with the provision of information that is useful in making business and economic decisions, a conceptual framework will form the theoretical basis for determining which events should be accounted for, how they should be measured and how they should be communicated to the user. Therefore, although it is theoretical in nature, a conceptual framework for financial reporting has a highly practical end in view.

1.2   Why is a conceptual framework necessary?

A conceptual framework for financial reporting should therefore be a theory of accounting against which practical problems can be tested objectively, the utility of which is decided by the adequacy of the practical solutions it provides. However, the various standard-setting bodies around the world have too often attempted to resolve practical accounting and reporting problems through the development of accounting standards, without such an accepted theoretical frame of reference. The end result is that the standard-setters have determined the form and content of external financial reports, without resolving such fundamental issues as:

- what are the objectives of these reports?
- who are the users of these reports?
- what are the informational needs of these users?
- what types of report will best satisfy their needs?

Consequently, standards have tended to be produced on a haphazard and 'fire-fighting' approach; evidence of this in the UK may be seen in the way in which the (now defunct) ASC attempted to deal with issues such as off balance sheet finance and the capitalisation of brand names. On the other hand, if an agreed framework existed, the role of the standard-setters would be changed from that of fireman to that of architect, by being able to design external financial reports on the basis of the needs of the user.

Furthermore, in the absence of an agreed conceptual framework, the same theoretical issues are revisited on numerous occasions by different standard-setting working parties, sometimes resulting in the development of standards which are inconsistent with each other, or which are founded on incompatible concepts. For example, inconsistencies exist in UK accounting standards as a result of conflicts between substance versus form; matching versus prudence; and whether earnings should be determined through balance sheet measurements or by matching costs and revenue. Some of the present UK standards permit two or more methods of accounting for the same set of circumstances, whilst others permit certain accounting practices to be followed on an arbitrary and unspecified basis. This apparent ambiguity is perhaps indicative of the difficulty involved in determining what is 'true and fair'.

In the US, on the other hand, the FASB has produced a large number of highly detailed accounting rules. Clearly, the proliferation of accounting standards in the US stems from many factors; however, a satisfactory conceptual framework might reduce the need for such a large number of highly detailed standards, since more emphasis could be placed on general principles rather than specific rules.

Nevertheless, it is not only the lack of a conceptual framework that inhibits standard-setters around the world; they must also contend with the politicisation of accounting caused by the conflicting interests of the various groups of users, preparers and auditors. Where proposed accounting standards are thought likely to affect the economic interests of a particular interested party, it is possible that the quality of the accounting standard will suffer. There are several instances where this is evident in the UK. For example, lobbying by the property industry led to the temporary exemption for investment properties from the requirements of SSAP 12; this temporary exemption was originally intended to last for one year, but was extended first for a further year and subsequently for a further 18 months before SSAP 19 became effective, and SSAP 12 was then amended to make the exemption for investment properties permanent. Even in its recently published standard FRS 15 – *Tangible Fixed Assets* – on the measurement of tangible fixed assets, the ASB has specifically exempted investment properties[1] – despite the fact that the ASB had conceded in its preceding discussion paper that there was no conceptual justification for such an exemption.[2]

The only defence that standard-setters can have against such political interference in the standard-setting process is to be able to demonstrate that a proposed accounting practice is derived from a sound theoretical foundation. Otherwise, how does one persuade, for example, an industry lobby that a particular accounting treatment which they perceive as adversely affecting their economic interests is better than one which does not?[3]

An agreed framework is not the panacea for all accounting problems. Nor does it obviate the need for judgement to be exercised in the process of resolving accounting issues. Nevertheless, what it can provide is a framework within which those judgements can be made.

1.3   Early attempts to establish a framework

There have been numerous attempts over the years to define the purpose and nature of accounting. These are to be found in various writings on accounting theory, the authors of which have considered many of the conceptual issues which require resolution in the development of a conceptual framework for financial reporting. Perhaps not surprisingly, most of the earlier studies were carried out by either individual academics or academic committees in the US; for example, the writings in 1940 of Paton and Littleton[4] were intended to present a framework of accounting theory which would be regarded as a coherent and consistent foundation for the development of accounting standards, whilst the studies carried out over the years by various committees of the American Accounting Association have made a significant contribution to accounting theory.[5] In addition to the research carried out by individuals and academic committees, professional accounting bodies around the world have also, from time to time, issued statements which deal with various aspects of accounting theory. These can be seen as the first attempts at developing some form of conceptual framework, some of which are discussed later in this Chapter.

However, there was no corresponding interest in the UK at that time in developing statements on accounting theory. This fact was explained by Professor David Solomons in a lecture given by him in 1980, as follows: 'The difference between the ferment in America over accounting principles and the relative apathy that has persisted in Britain until quite recently cannot be explained by any difference in the economic environment. It can only be explained by the difference in the scale of business education there and here, and in particular by the sheer weight of numbers of accounting academics. The American Accounting Association has about 6,000 academic members. In Britain, the Association of University Teachers of Accounting has about 175.

Perhaps more importantly, most American practitioners have a university degree in accounting. They have met professors face to face and they do not think of them as troglodytes. Moreover, they know there is a subject called accounting theory; and they think of accounting academics as a distinct branch of the profession with their own contribution to make. It is more a question of quantity than quality. British accounting academics are simply not yet numerous enough to constitute a critical mass.'[6]

The question of the desirability of developing an 'agreed conceptual framework' apparently first received serious consideration by the ASC in 1978 through the publication of its consultative document entitled 'Setting Accounting Standards'[7] (see Chapter 1 at 3.1.3). In that document, the ASC conceded that it had been frequently criticised for failing to develop a conceptual framework, but defended its position by claiming that 'while such a foundation would be a great advantage, it is unavailable at present'.[8] The reasons put forward for this view were based essentially on the premise that since the users of financial statements have different objectives, it would not be possible to develop an acceptable foundation which would be universally accepted.[9] Following this argument, the ASC went on to conclude that 'if an "agreed conceptual framework" is equated with a single undisputed "model", then this is a luxury which evades us at the moment'.[10] Nevertheless, as part of the consultative process, the ASC raised the following two questions on the subject:

1.   'Is it accepted that there is at present no single "model" or "agreed conceptual framework" which can be used as the touchstone for accounting standards?'[11]

2.   'Should the ASC encourage research into the possibility of finding an acceptable "model"?'[12]

Not surprisingly, the written submissions[13] on the consultative document indicated a unanimous 'Yes' in answer to the first question. However, what probably did surprise the ASC was that the second question also received an overwhelming 'Yes'; in fact, a significant number of respondents indicated that they saw the development of a conceptual framework as a matter of great urgency. For example, the Accounting Standards Review Committee of the ICAS stated in its submission that 'it is imperative that work should begin immediately on a conceptual framework rather than that the present practice of producing standards with no theoretical underpinning should continue'.[14]

The ASC's argument that a conceptual framework would not be attainable because the users of financial statements have different objectives was clearly regarded as spurious. This Chapter will highlight the fact that different users should be furnished with different information appropriate to their various objectives, even if it means that in order to achieve this the conceptual framework should incorporate more than one accounting model. Consequently, there is no reason for ruling out an 'agreed conceptual model' by equating it with the unattainable 'single undisputed model'.

2 THE AICPA'S EARLY INITIATIVES IN THE UNITED STATES

2.1 Accounting Research Studies

The Accounting Principles Board (APB) of the American Institute of Certified Public Accountants (AICPA) was formed in 1959 to replace the former Committee on Accounting Procedure and the Committee on Terminology. During its existence, the Committee on Accounting Procedure had issued a series of Accounting Research Bulletins (ARBs). In 1953, the first 42 ARBs (eight of which dealt solely with terminology) were revised and restated as a consolidated ARB No. 43 and Accounting Terminology Bulletin No. 1; thereafter, a further eight ARBs were issued. The ARBs were supposedly aimed at the development of generally accepted accounting principles; however, the Committee met with considerable criticism over its failure to deal with contemporary accounting issues (such as leasing and business combinations), which could not be solved from precedents and required the development of accounting principles through pure accounting research.

As a direct response to this, the President of the AICPA set up the Special Committee on Research Program in 1957; in 1958 the Committee recommended the formation of the APB, and the appointment of a director of research with a permanent research staff. The Special Committee also recommended that 'an immediate project of the accounting research staff should be a study of the basic postulates underlying accounting principles generally, and the preparation of a brief statement thereof. There should be also a study of the broad principles of accounting. ... The results of these, as adopted by the [Accounting Principles] Board, should serve as the foundation for the entire body of future pronouncements by the Institute on accounting matters, to which each new release should be related.'[15]

This, therefore, was probably the first mandate given by a professional body for the development of a conceptual framework. The AICPA appointed Maurice Moonitz as its first Director of Accounting Research; Moonitz started work on the postulates study, and appointed Robert Sprouse to work with him on the study of broad accounting principles. The products of the research were contained in Accounting Research Study No. 1 – *The Basic Postulates of Accounting*[16] – and Accounting Research Study No. 3 – *A Tentative Set of Broad Accounting Principles for Business Enterprises* – which were published in 1961 and 1962 respectively.[17]

These studies, however, caused a storm of controversy. Instead of establishing a sound foundation of accounting theory through rigorous argument based on deductive reasoning, Moonitz and Sprouse attempted to persuade the accounting profession to accept a new system of financial reporting based on current values. Furthermore, the realisation principle was discarded on the basis of the assertion that 'profit is attributable to the whole process of business activity, not just to the moment of sale'.[18] This was reflected, for example, in the statement that 'inventories which are readily saleable at known prices with negligible costs of disposal, or with known or readily predictable costs of disposal, should be measured at net realizable value'.[19]

However, the criticism which was levelled at these studies appeared to be based more on the fear of the unknown, rather than on any intellectual shortcomings. Consequently, they were viewed as being too radically different from contemporary generally accepted accounting practice to be accepted, and were rejected by the APB. This resulted in the commissioning of Grady's Accounting Research Study No. 7 – *Inventory of Generally Accepted Accounting Principles for Business Enterprises* – which was published in 1965 and which catalogued the various accounting methods which had been approved by ARBs, APB Opinions or some other precedent.

In all, 15 Accounting Research Studies were published during the life of the APB. However, following the rejection of ARS Nos. 1 and 3, the studies tended to be carried out on an ad hoc basis and without the support of a common foundation. Furthermore, the recommendations contained in the research studies appeared to have been largely ignored in the drafting of the 31 Opinions which the APB issued between 1962 and 1973. Consequently, generally accepted accounting principles in the US were continuing to be formulated without the benefit of research or the foundation of an agreed theoretical framework and, for all intents and purposes, the APB slowly resorted to the position of its predecessor, the Committee on Accounting Procedure.

2.2   APB Statement No. 4

In 1965 the APB made a further attempt to provide a basis for guiding the future development of accounting by establishing a committee to carry out a study which could be used as a basis for understanding the broad fundamentals of accounting. In 1970, the APB approved Statement No. 4 – *Basic Concepts and Accounting Principles Underlying Financial Statements of Business Enterprises*.[20] The statement contained a description of (1) the environment of financial accounting, (2) the objectives of financial statements, (3) the basic features and basic elements of financial accounting and (4) a summary of existing generally accepted accounting principles.

Therefore, it was (on its own admission)[21] a descriptive statement, not prescriptive. For example, assets and liabilities were defined as economic resources and obligations 'that are recognised and measured in conformity with generally accepted accounting principles',[22] which meant that the definitions failed to provide a theoretical basis for the development of generally accepted principles. As a result APB No. 4 was deficient as a theory of accounting and did not respond to the problems which were facing the profession at the time and which had been brought about by the inconsistencies and inadequacies of financial reporting practice.

2.3   The Wheat and Trueblood Committees

In 1971, in response to continued criticism from both within the profession and from the SEC about its inability to establish sound accounting principles, the AICPA announced the formation of two study groups: the *Study Group on Establishment of Accounting Principles*, to be chaired by Francis Wheat, and the *Study Group on Objectives of Financial Statements*, to be chaired by Robert Trueblood. The Wheat Committee published its report in 1972, resulting in the establishment of the Financial Accounting Standards Board (FASB) in 1973 as the successor to the APB. This had the effect of taking the responsibility for setting accounting standards away from the accounting profession and placing it in the hands of an independent body in the private sector. The FASB comprises seven members appointed by the Financial Accounting Foundation (FAF), and is funded by the sale of publications and from contributions made to the FAF. The Board of Trustees of the FAF is appointed by its eight sponsoring organisations, which include, inter alia, the American Accounting Association, the AICPA and two organisations which represent government.

The study carried out by the Trueblood Committee represents the next significant step in the attempt to develop a conceptual framework. In setting the terms of reference of the study group, the Board of Directors of the AICPA stated that the main purpose of the study was 'to refine the objectives of financial statements'.[23] They went on to suggest that APB Statement No. 4 would be a logical starting point for the study, whilst at the same time noting that APB 4 'contains objectives in terms of what is considered acceptable today rather than in terms of what is needed and what is attainable to meet these needs'.[24] The study group was asked to consider at least the following questions:

- ■   Who needs financial statements?
- ■   What information do they need?
- ■   How much of the needed information can be provided by accounting?
- ■   What framework is required to provide the needed information?[25]

The Trueblood Report[26] was published in October 1973 and developed twelve objectives of financial statements. The principal objective was stated in the following terms: 'the basic objective of financial statements is to provide information useful for making economic decisions'.[27] Having established its twelve objectives of financial statements, the report then discussed seven qualitative characteristics which information contained in financial statements should possess in order to satisfy the needs of users.[28] As will be seen below, the Trueblood Report's objectives of financial statements formed the basis for the development of the FASB's first concepts statement, whilst the qualitative characteristics identified were amongst those discussed in the second concepts statement.

3   THE FASB CONCEPTUAL FRAMEWORK

3.1   Introduction

The Trueblood Committee was at work on its report when the FASB came into existence. Consequently, the Trueblood Report was effectively passed on to the FASB for consideration, thus signalling the beginnings of the FASB's Conceptual Framework Project. The FASB duly considered the report and in June 1974 published a Discussion Memorandum – *Conceptual Framework for Accounting and Reporting: Consideration of the Report of the Study Group on the Objectives of Financial Statements* – which asked for comments on the issues raised.[29] A public hearing was held during September 1974, and in December 1976 the FASB published its *Tentative Conclusions on Objectives of Financial Statements of Business Enterprises.* In December 1976 the FASB also published a paper – *Scope and Implications of the Conceptual Framework Project* – which summarised its aims for the project, the expected benefits to be derived and the main areas which were expected to be covered.[30]

Following the criticism and eventual replacement of first the Committee on Accounting Procedure, followed by the APB, the FASB was seen by many commentators to be the last opportunity of keeping accounting standard-setting in the private sector. The FASB was clearly aware that accounting standards had to regain the credibility of public opinion which had been lost as a result of the many perceived abuses of financial reporting during the 1960s. The FASB referred to this lack of public confidence, and the possible consequences thereof, as follows: 'skepticism about financial reporting has adverse effects on businesses, on business leaders, and on the public at large. One of these effects is the risk of imposition of government reporting and other regulatory requirements that are not justified – requirements that are not in the public interest because the perceived benefits do not exist or are more than offset by costly interference with the orderly operation of the economy. Skepticism creates adverse public opinion, which may be the antecedent of unjustified government regulation. Every company, every industry stands to suffer because of skepticism about financial reporting.'[31] The FASB, therefore, saw its conceptual framework project as the means of enhancing the credibility of financial statements in the eyes of the public.

The FASB also recognised that although there had been many attempts by individuals and organisations (such as the American Accounting Association) to develop a theory of accounting, none of these individual theories had become universally accepted or relied on in practice. They therefore expressed a need for a '*constitution,* a coherent system of interrelated objectives and fundamentals that can lead to consistent standards and that prescribes the nature, function, and limits of financial accounting and financial statements'.[32] The conceptual framework was expected to:

(a)   guide the body responsible for establishing standards;

(b)   provide a frame of reference for resolving accounting questions in the absence of a specific promulgated standard;

(c)   determine bounds for judgement in preparing financial statements;

(d)   increase financial statement users' understanding of and confidence in financial statements; and

(e)   enhance comparability.[33]

To date the FASB has issued six concepts statements, of which one (SFAC No. 4) deals with the objectives of financial reporting by non-business organisations and is beyond the scope of this book, whilst another (SFAC No. 3) dealt with elements of financial statements by business enterprises, and was superseded by SFAC No. 6, which expanded the scope of SFAC No. 3 to encompass not-for-profit organisations. The remaining four are discussed in the sections which follow.

In June 1997 the FASB issued an exposure draft of a further concepts statement which proposes general principles aimed at governing the use of discounting in accounting measurement.[34] The draft was revised and reissued in March 1999; both versions are discussed at 3.7 below.

3.2   The objectives of financial reporting

The first phase of the FASB's conceptual framework project was to develop a statement of the objectives of financial reporting. Clearly, some pioneering work in this area had been done by the Trueblood Committee (see 2.3 above), and this formed the basis of the FASB's first concepts statement. Nevertheless, it was not until 1978 that the FASB finally published this statement.

SFAC No. 1 – *Objectives of Financial Reporting by Business Enterprises* – starts off by making the point that financial reporting includes not only financial statements, but also incorporates other means of communicating financial and non-financial information; this may be achieved, for example, through the medium of stock exchange documents, news releases, management forecasts etc.[35] Having said this, the statement stresses that 'financial reporting is not an end in itself but is intended to provide information that is useful in making business and economic decisions'.[36] This, however, is no new revelation; it is the type of broad generalisation that has characterised numerous previous attempts at establishing a conceptual framework. On the other hand, what it does do is raise all the same issues which the Trueblood Committee had been asked to consider seven years previously, such as: For whom is this information intended? What types of 'business and economic decisions' do they make? What information do they need to enable them to make these decisions? What framework is required to provide this needed information?

The statement details an extensive list of potential users, distinguishing between those with a direct interest and those with an indirect interest in the information provided by financial reporting.[37] The groups of user which have a direct interest include owners, management, creditors and employees; whilst user groups such as financial analysts and advisers, journalists, regulatory authorities and trade unions are deemed to have an indirect interest, since they advise or represent those who have a direct interest. However, having identified this wide range of users, the statement focuses on the information needs of investors and creditors. These are encompassed in the first of three primary objectives identified in the statement: 'financial reporting should provide information that is useful to present and potential investors and creditors and other users in making rational investment, credit, and similar decisions'.[38]

This objective leads to the first of the two most significant and far-reaching conclusions in the statement, namely that 'financial reporting should provide information to help investors, creditors, and others assess the amounts, timing, and uncertainty of prospective net cash inflows to the related enterprise'.[39] The statement articulated its reasoning behind this conclusion as follows: 'Potential users of financial information most directly concerned with a particular business enterprise are generally interested in its ability to generate favourable cash flows, because their decisions relate to amounts, timing, and uncertainties of expected cash flows. To investors, lenders, suppliers, and employees, a business enterprise is a source of cash in the form of dividends or interest and perhaps appreciated market prices, repayment of borrowing, payment for goods or services, or salaries and wages. They invest cash, goods, or services in an enterprise and expect to obtain sufficient cash in return to make the investment worthwhile. They are directly concerned with the ability of the enterprise to generate favourable cash flows and may also be concerned with how the market's perception of that ability affects the relative prices of its securities. To customers, a business enterprise is a source of goods or services, but only by obtaining sufficient cash to pay for the resources it uses and to meet its other obligations can the enterprise provide those goods or services. To managers, the cash flows of a business enterprise are a significant part of their management responsibilities, including their accountability to directors and owners. Many, if not most, of their decisions have cash flow consequences for the enterprise. Thus, investors, creditors, employees, customers, and managers significantly share a common interest in an enterprise's ability to generate favourable cash flows. Other potential users of financial information share the same interest, derived from investors, creditors, employees, customers, or managers whom they advise or represent or derived from an interest in how those groups (and especially stockholders) are faring.'[40]

In reaching this conclusion, the FASB was aware of the fact that it might precipitate an adverse reaction leading to the possible rejection of the statement through what might have been seen as an objective which would ultimately result in companies being required to present cash flow, management forecast or current value information. The FASB pre-empted this potential adverse reaction by stating that 'the objective focuses on the purpose for which information provided should be useful ... rather than the kinds of information that may be useful for that purpose. The objective neither requires nor prohibits "cash flow information", "current value information", "management forecast information", or any other specific information. Conclusions about "current value information" and "management forecast information" are beyond the scope of this Statement. Paragraphs 42–44 [of SFAC No. 1] note that information about cash receipts and disbursements is not usually considered to be the most useful information for the purposes described in this objective.'[41]

However, in examining this objective, it is important to take cognisance of empirical research which has been conducted in this area. In 1979, Chang and Most investigated the views of individual investors, institutional investors and financial analysts in the USA, UK and New Zealand as part of a study into the importance of financial statements for investment decisions.[42] Their study included an investigation into the investment objectives of individual and institutional investors, and reached the conclusion that 'the most important investment objective for both individual and institutional investors is long-term capital gains. This, and a combination of dividend income and capital gains, are considerably more important than short-term capital gains. It would appear that prediction of short-term cash flows would not be one of the more important investor uses of financial statements, and this calls in question the conventional assumption that a principal objective of financial statements is to assist users to predict future cash flows in terms of timing, as distinct from amount and relative uncertainty.'[43] On the other hand, it is, of course, possible that institutional investors are much more influenced by short-term expectations today than they were eighteen years ago; consequently, the findings of Chang and Most may no longer be valid.

The second fundamental conclusion reached in SFAC No. 1 which has far-reaching implications for the future development of accounting standards is concerned with the primary focus of financial reporting. During the early stages of the development of accounting rules in the first half of this century, the primary focus of financial statements was based on the principle of 'stewardship'. This arose from the fact that the management of an enterprise were primarily seen to be accountable to the owners for safeguarding the assets which had been entrusted to them, leading to a balance sheet emphasis in financial reporting. However, the focus has gradually shifted away from the notion of the balance sheet reporting on the custodianship of assets, to an earnings emphasis based on the principle that the income statement should present 'decision-useful' information. This is encapsulated in the statement in SFAC No. 1 that 'the primary focus of financial reporting is information about an enterprise's performance provided by measures of earnings and its components. Investors, creditors, and others who are concerned with assessing the prospects for enterprise net cash inflows are especially interested in that information.'[44]

SFAC No. 1 still recognises the fact that financial reporting should provide information about how the management of an enterprise has discharged its stewardship responsibility.[45] However, it goes on to say that 'earnings information is commonly the focus for assessing management's stewardship or accountability. Management, owners, and others emphasize enterprise performance or profitability in describing how management has discharged its stewardship accountability.'[46]

In other words, the statement is asserting that the measurement of earnings in the income statement should take precedence over the measurement of assets and liabilities in the balance sheet. This is an important principle which should have had an important impact on the principles laid down in the development of future accounting standards. However, as will be seen below, the FASB's subsequent concepts statements have essentially avoided the issue of how to determine net income. Furthermore, more recent statements issued by the FASB tend to suggest an uncertainty as to whether an earnings or balance sheet approach should be followed (for example, SFAS 109 – *Accounting for Income Taxes* – would appear to view the balance sheet as the primary statement).

Interestingly enough, the Accounting Standards Board in the UK is proceeding down a similar road of balance sheet primacy in developing its *Statement of Principles*. As is more fully described at 5 below, both the initial (published in 1995) and revised (published in 1999) versions of the ASB's Draft *Statement of Principles* adopt a balance sheet approach to recognition, whereby all the elements of financial statements are defined in terms of assets and liabilities, and income recognition is a function of increases and decreases in net assets rather than the completion of acts of performance.

Consequently, despite the general acceptance of the fact that financial reporting should be primarily focused on performance measurement, the conceptual underpinning for financial reporting on both sides of the Atlantic appears to be focusing more and more on the recognition and derecognition of assets and liabilities.

3.3   The qualitative characteristics of accounting information

The FASB's second Concepts Statement – *Qualitative Characteristics of Accounting Information* – examines the characteristics that make accounting information useful to the users of that information. The statement views these characteristics as 'a hierarchy of accounting qualities', which then form the basis for selecting and evaluating information for inclusion in financial reports. The hierarchy is represented in Figure 1 below:[47]

Figure 1

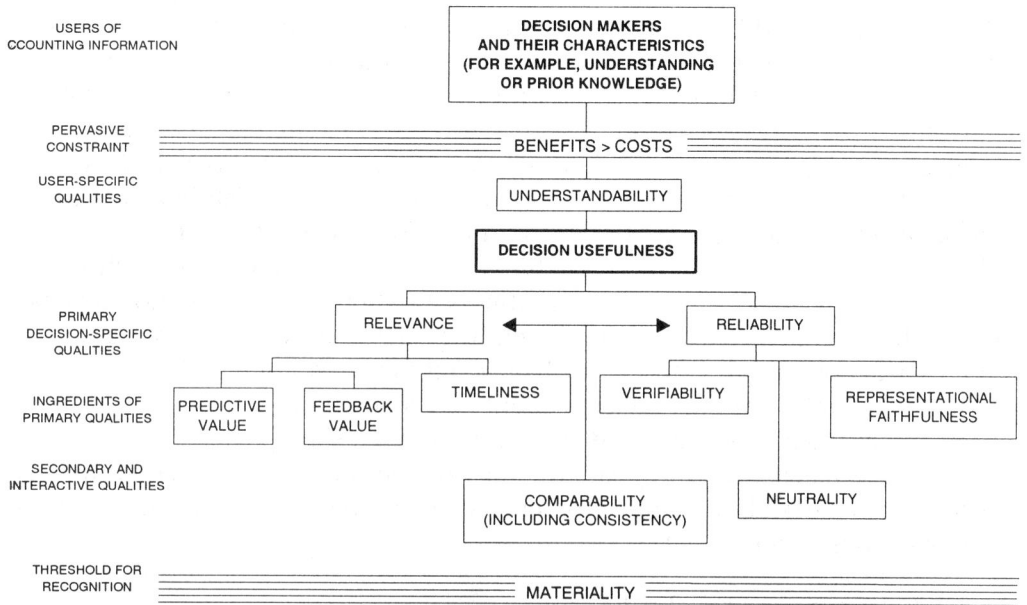

A HIERARCHY OF ACCOUNTING QUALITIES

3.3.1 The decision-makers

The decision-makers (users) appear at the top of the hierarchy against the background of their own specific characteristics. Whilst usefulness for decision-making is the most important quality that accounting information should possess, each decision-maker has to judge what information is useful for a specific decision. This judgement would be based on such factors as the nature of the decision to be made, the information already in the individual's possession or available from other sources, the decision-making process employed and the decision maker's capacity to process all the information obtained.

3.3.2 The cost/benefit constraint

Since information should be provided only if the benefits to be derived from that information outweigh the costs of providing it, the cost/benefit constraint pervades the hierarchy. However, the application of this constraint may cause a certain amount of difficulty, since the costs of providing financial information are normally borne by the enterprise (and ultimately passed on to its customers), whilst the benefits are reaped by the users. For this reason, the normal forces of demand and supply will not prevail in the market of financial information, since the external user will almost always view the benefits of additional information as outweighing the costs.

3.3.3   Understandability

The hierarchy depicts understandability as being the key quality for accounting information to achieve 'decision usefulness'. SFAC No. 1 stated that the information provided by financial reporting 'should be comprehensible to those who have a reasonable understanding of business and economic activities and are willing to study the information with reasonable diligence'.[48] Information, whilst it may be relevant, will be wasted if it is provided in a form which cannot be understood by the users for whom it was intended. SFAC No. 1 elaborated on the relationship between useful information and understandability as follows: 'financial information is a tool and, like most tools, cannot be of much direct help to those who are unable or unwilling to use it or who misuse it. Its use can be learned, however, and financial reporting should provide information that can be used by all – nonprofessionals as well as professionals – who are willing to learn to use it properly. Efforts may be needed to increase the understandability of financial information. Cost-benefit considerations may indicate that information understood or used by only a few should not be provided. Conversely, financial reporting should not exclude relevant information merely because it is difficult for some to understand or because some investors or creditors choose not to use it.'[49]

3.3.4   Relevance and reliability

The qualities that distinguish 'better' (more useful) information from 'inferior' (less useful) information are primarily the qualities of relevance and reliability, with some other characteristics that those qualities imply. SFAC No. 2 identifies relevance and reliability as 'the two primary qualities that make accounting information useful for decision making. Subject to constraints imposed by cost and materiality, increased relevance and increased reliability are the characteristics that make information a more desirable commodity – that is, one useful in making decisions.'[50] However, all this is not new – the qualitative characteristics of relevance and reliability have been discussed in several preceding studies (such as the Trueblood and Corporate Reports). What is new (and probably the most significant aspect of SFAC No. 2), is the recognition of the fact that 'reliability and relevance often impinge on each other'.[51] Consequently, whenever accounting standards are set, decisions have to be made concerning the relative importance of these two characteristics, often resulting in trade-offs being made between them.

For example, one of the most common criticisms made about the various systems of value accounting which have been proposed over the years concerns the high degree of subjectivity involved in assigning values to assets and liabilities. Consequently, for any standard-setting body to propose that the historical cost system be replaced by an income and measurement system based on current values, a decision would have to be made as to the relative weights which should be attributed to presenting information which is both relevant and reliable. The perceived gain in the relevance of the information to the user would have to outweigh the uncertainties concerning the reliability of the current value information.

A   *Relevance*

The statement defines relevant accounting information as being information which is 'capable of making a difference in a decision by helping users to form predictions about the outcomes of past, present, and future events or to confirm or correct prior expectations'.[52] The statement further describes 'timeliness' as an 'ancillary aspect of relevance. If information is not available when it is needed or becomes available only so long after the reported events that it has no value for future action, it lacks relevance and is of little or no use.'[53] Therefore, in the context of financial reporting, the characteristic of timeliness means that information must be made available to users before it loses its capacity to influence their decisions. However, timeliness alone cannot make information relevant, but a lack of timeliness can result in information losing a degree of relevance which it once had.[54] On the other hand, in many instances there also has to be a trade-off between timeliness and reliability, since generally the more timely the information the less reliable it is.

The hierarchy identifies 'predictive value' and 'feedback value' as the other components of relevance on the basis that 'information can make a difference to decisions by improving decision makers' capacities to predict or by confirming or correcting their earlier expectations'.[55] Predictive value is defined as 'the quality of information that helps users to increase the likelihood of correctly forecasting the outcome of past or present events',[56] whilst feedback value is defined as 'the quality of information that enables users to confirm or correct prior expectations'.[57] Clearly, however, in saying that accounting information has predictive value, it is not suggesting that it is itself a prediction.

B   *Reliability*

Reliability is the second of the primary qualities, and is ascribed three attributes in the hierarchy. The statement asserts that the 'reliability of a measure rests on the faithfulness with which it represents what it purports to represent, coupled with an assurance for the user, which comes through verification, that it has that representational quality'.[58] This definition gives rise to the three subsidiary qualities of 'representational faithfulness', 'verifiability', and 'neutrality'. Representational faithfulness is an unnecessary piece of jargon introduced into accounting terminology by SFAC No. 2; what it essentially means is that information included in financial reports should represent what it purports to represent. In other words, financial reporting should be truthful. For example, if a group's consolidated balance sheet discloses cash and bank balances, users would be justified in assuming that, in the absence of any statement to the contrary, the financial statements were truthful, and that these represented cash resources freely available to the group; however, if the reality of the situation was that the cash resources were situated in countries which had severe exchange control restrictions, and were, therefore, not available to the group, some might hold the view that the financial statements were not entirely 'representationally faithful'.

It should be noted, however, that there are degrees of representational faithfulness. Because the financial reporting process involves allocations, estimations and subjective judgements, it cannot produce an 'exact' result; consequently, the trade-off between relevance and reliability will often apply, resulting in the presentation of information which is assigned a high degree of relevance, but which sacrifices representational faithfulness. An example of where this might apply is in the context of fair value accounting, where fair values have to be assigned to the separable net assets acquired.

Reliable information should also be verifiable and neutral so that neither measurement nor measurer bias results in the information being presented in such a way that it influences the particular decision being made. Verifiability is a quality of representational faithfulness in that it excludes the possibility of measurement bias, whilst neutrality implies the provision of all relevant and reliable information – irrespective of the effects that the information will have on the entity or a particular user group.

3.3.5   *Comparability*

The hierarchy lists comparability as an additional quality that financial information should possess in order to achieve relevance and reliability. The quality of comparability includes the fundamental accounting concept of consistency, since the usefulness of information is greatly enhanced if it is prepared on a consistent basis from one period to the next, and can be compared with corresponding information of the same enterprise for some other period, or with similar information about some other enterprise.

3.3.6   *Materiality*

All the qualitative criteria discussed in SFAC No. 2 are subject to a materiality threshold, since only material information will have an impact on the decision-making process. However, the statement provides no quantitative guidelines for materiality, and it will be a matter of judgement for the providers of information to determine whether or not an item of information has crossed the materiality threshold for recognition. Materiality is closely related to the characteristic of relevance, since both are defined in terms of what influences or makes a difference to an investor or other decision-maker. On the other hand, the two concepts can be distinguished; a decision by management not to disclose certain information may be made because users have no interest in that kind of information (i.e. it is not relevant to their specific needs), or because the amounts involved are too small to make a difference to the users' decisions (i.e. they are not material).

However, if the preparers of financial statements are to decide on what to include in their reporting package, they must have a clear understanding of the users of their reports and their specific information and decision-making needs. In so doing, they should be aware of the types of information likely to influence their decisions (i.e. relevance) as well as the associated magnitude of this information (i.e. materiality). Consequently, financial reporting will focus generally on information which is regarded as relevant, and specifically on that which is material. The principal difficulty with this, however, is that the materiality decisions of users vary from class to class and amongst individual users in the same class (see 5.3 below for further discussion of the concept of materiality).

There is an element of rationalisation of practice, rather than revelation of principle, about the entire relevance-reliability-materiality discussion, which has also pervaded many subsequent conceptual framework attempts (see 5.3 below for the ASB's version). It is becoming increasingly fashionable for standard setters to introduce new accounting standards that are seemingly heavily biased towards relevance at the expense of reliability. For example, in introducing fair value accounting for most financial assets in IAS 39 – *Financial Instruments: Recognition and Measurement*, the IASC has effectively codified the assumption that 'fair value can be reliably determined for most financial assets classified as available for sale or held for trading'.[59] Under the standard, the reliability of measurement presumption can only be rebutted under very limited circumstances, with the result that the fair value measurement attribute has to be applied even in circumstances where it might be deemed to produce relatively unreliable results.

The standard setters rationalise this by asserting (perhaps rather pejoratively) that it is better to have financial statements that are approximately right rather than precisely wrong. By this they imply that historical cost information is *ipso facto* irrelevant, and it is preferable to have financial statements that are prepared on a fair value basis that are, in the view of the standard setters, considerably more relevant, if not as reliable. As a result, as the use of fair values is introduced more and more into the measurement of assets and liabilities, the trade-off between relevance and reliability has become increasingly less even-handed.

3.3.7 *Conservatism*

SFAC No. 2 includes an interesting discussion on the convention of 'conservatism' (i.e. prudence).[60] In so doing, it draws a distinction between the 'deliberate, consistent understatement of net assets and profits',[61] and the practice of ensuring that 'uncertainties and risks inherent in business situations are adequately considered'.[62] The statement recognised the fact that, in the eyes of bankers and other lenders, deliberate understatement of assets was desirable, since it increased their margin of safety on assets pledged as security for debts.

On the other hand, it was also recognised that consistent understatement was difficult to maintain over a period of any length, and that understated assets would clearly lead to overstated income in later periods when the assets were ultimately realised. Consequently, unwarranted and deliberate conservatism in financial reporting would lead to a contravention of certain of the qualitative characteristics, such as neutrality and representational faithfulness.

3.4   The elements of financial statements

SFAC No. 6 – *Elements of Financial Statements* – was issued in 1985 as a replacement to SFAC No. 3 – *Elements of Financial Statements of Business Enterprises* – having expanded its scope to encompass non-profit organisations. The statement defines ten 'elements' of financial statements that are directly related to the measurement of performance and financial status of an entity. However, the elements are very much interrelated, as six of them are arithmetically derived from the definitions of assets and liabilities.

3.4.1   Assets

Assets are defined as being 'probable future economic benefits obtained or controlled by a particular entity as a result of past transactions or events'.[63] However, the statement then goes on to say that the kinds of items that qualify as assets under this definition are also commonly called 'economic resources'. They are the scarce means that are useful for carrying out economic activities, such as consumption, production and exchange.[64] The common characteristic possessed by all assets is 'service potential' or 'future economic benefit' which eventually results in net cash inflows to the enterprise.[65]

The adequacy of this definition, which is used almost unchanged in the ASB's own *Statement of Principles* exposure drafts, is discussed in more detail at 5.15.1 below. However, in the context of historical cost accounting, a non-monetary asset is no more than a deferred cost; a cost which has been incurred before the balance sheet date and, in terms of the accruals concept, relates to future periods beyond the balance sheet date, thereby justifying it being carried forward as an asset. This applies to all non-monetary assets which are recognised in a historical cost balance sheet – whether they be tangible fixed assets, stock, prepayments or deferred development expenditure.

Consequently, there are certain occasions when items will be recognised as assets under the traditional historical cost system, but which will not fit the SFAC No. 6 definition of an asset. For example, if a company had to top up its pension fund to meet an experience deficiency but, in accordance with SSAP 24 (see Chapter 20), spreads the variation from regular pension cost forward, this will give rise to an asset in the balance sheet. Whilst this asset meets the 'deferred cost' criteria described above, it does not fall within the statement's definition, since it cannot be said to be an economic resource with future economic benefit; it is merely a cost awaiting recognition in the profit and loss account of future years. The same argument would apply to certain other deferred costs.

This difficulty highlights a deep-rooted problem with the FASB's conceptual framework project. First, as far as SFAC No. 6 is concerned, since most of the elements defined in the statement are derived from the definition of an asset, any inadequacy in this definition inevitably affects the validity of the definitions of certain of the other elements. Second, in identifying the elements of financial statements before addressing the fundamental issues of how they are to be measured and on what basis of capital maintenance profit is to be determined, the FASB seriously limited its ability to address the issues of recognition and measurement properly. The result of this is that SFAC No. 5 – *Recognition and Measurement in Financial Statements of Business Enterprises* – has serious shortcomings (see 3.5 below).

3.4.2   Liabilities

Liabilities are defined as 'probable future sacrifices of economic benefits arising from present obligations of a particular entity to transfer assets or provide services to other entities in the future as a result of past transactions or events'.[66] The statement goes on to say that a liability has three essential characteristics:

(a)   it embodies a present duty or responsibility to one or more other entities that entails settlement by probable future transfer or use of assets at a specified or determinable date, on occurrence of a specified event, or on demand;

(b)   the duty or responsibility obligates the entity, leaving it little or no discretion to avoid the future sacrifice; and

(c)   the transaction or other event obligating the entity has already happened.[67]

Thus, in terms of this definition, liabilities represent the amounts of obligations – giving rise to a problem similar to that outlined above in respect of the definition of assets. There are certain items which are currently recognised as liabilities, but which do not meet the statement's definition; the reason being that they are merely deferred credits awaiting recognition in the profit and loss account, rather than representing obligations to other entities. Examples of such items might include deferred government grants, and the deferred effects of favourable variations from regular pension cost.

3.4.3   Equity

Equity is defined as 'the residual interest in the assets of an entity that remains after deducting its liabilities'.[68] This is a somewhat tautological definition arising from the accounting equation that assets minus liabilities equals equity. Equity is, in fact, the sum of the equity investments made by the entity's owners, and the entity's earnings retained from its profit-making activities. Because of the way in which the definitions of the various elements are interrelated, it might appear to some that the FASB have taken the easy route in defining equity as net assets, rather than in terms of capital contributions plus retained earnings; a possible explanation for this might be that it enabled the FASB to define income in terms of changes in equity. Interestingly, and underlining the fundamental similarity of many of the framework attempts, both of the ASB's *Statement of Principles* documents (see section 5 below) have taken exactly this route to defining equity.

3.4.4   Investments by owners

Investments by owners are defined as being 'increases in equity of a particular business enterprise resulting from transfers to it from other entities of something valuable to obtain or increase ownership interests (or equity) in it'.[69] The statement goes on to say that although investments by owners are most commonly made in the form of assets, the investments can also be represented by services, or the settlement or conversion of liabilities of the enterprise.[70]

3.4.5   Distributions to owners

Distributions to owners are defined as 'decreases in equity of a particular business enterprise resulting from transferring assets, rendering services, or incurring liabilities by the enterprise to owners'.[71] Distributions to owners, therefore, incorporate all forms of capital distributions which result in a decrease in net assets.

3.4.6   Comprehensive income

Comprehensive income is defined as 'the change in equity of a business enterprise during a period from transactions and other events and circumstances from nonowner sources. It includes all changes in equity during a period except those resulting from investments by owners and distributions to owners.'[72]   On its own, the term 'comprehensive income' is somewhat meaningless; for example, how does it tie in with the statement in SFAC No. 1[73] that 'the primary focus of financial reporting is information about an enterprise's performance provided by measures of earnings and its components'? Clearly, the FASB was keeping its options open by not defining earnings; in fact, it explained (in a footnote to SFAC No. 6) that whilst 'comprehensive income' is the term used in the statement for the concept that was called 'earnings' in SFAC No. 1, SFAC No. 5 had described earnings for a period as excluding certain cumulative accounting adjustments and other non-owner changes in equity that are included in comprehensive income for a period.[74]

The FASB issued a standard on this topic in June 1997, SFAS 130 – *Reporting Comprehensive Income* – which is further discussed in Chapter 22 of this book.

3.4.7   Revenues, expenses, gains and losses

SFAC No. 6 identifies the remaining four elements as those which constitute the basic components of 'comprehensive income':

Revenues, which are 'inflows or other enhancements of assets of an entity or settlements of its liabilities (or a combination of both) from delivering or producing goods, rendering services, or other activities that constitute the entity's ongoing major central operations'.[75]

Expenses, which are 'outflows or other using up of assets or incurrences of liabilities (or a combination of both) from delivering or producing goods, rendering services, or carrying out other activities that constitute the entity's ongoing major or central operations'.[76]

Gains, which are 'increases in equity (net assets) from peripheral or incidental transactions of an entity and from all other transactions and other events and circumstances affecting the entity except those that result from revenues or investments by owners'.[77]

Losses, which are 'decreases in equity (net assets) from peripheral or incidental transactions of an entity and from all other transactions and other events and circumstances affecting the entity except those that result from expenses or distributions to owners'.[78]

Therefore, comprehensive income equals revenues minus expenses plus gains minus losses; however, although the statement states that revenues, expenses, gains and losses can be combined in various ways to obtain various measures of enterprise performance,[79] it fails to define net income.

The difficulty surrounding the FASB's definitions of the ten elements is that they are so interrelated, that in attempting to piece them together into a meaningful accounting framework, one gets caught up in a tautology of terms which all lead back to the definitions of assets and liabilities. However, if the primary focus of financial reporting is the measurement of earnings, then surely the starting point should be definitions of earnings and its components, with assets and liabilities being the residuals – rather than the other way around? Essentially, what the FASB is saying is that assets minus liabilities equals equity and comprehensive income equals changes in equity (excluding transactions with owners), therefore comprehensive income equals the change in net assets. Consequently, the definition of comprehensive income would incorporate items such as capital contributions from non-owners, government grants for capital expenditure and unrealised holding gains. This is all very well, provided that the issues of measurement and capital maintenance have already been settled. However, this is clearly not the case, with the result that the FASB is either restricting itself in the future development of different accounting models for different purposes, or it might have to develop different definitions of the elements of financial statements as different models are developed.

3.5   Recognition and measurement

Throughout the framework project, the FASB had avoided dealing with certain fundamental issues on the basis that they were the 'subject of another project'.[80]

The result was the publication in December 1984 of SFAC No. 5 – *Recognition and Measurement in Financial Statements of Business Enterprises* – which attempted to deal with all the previously unresolved issues. However, the statement was somewhat inconclusive – possibly as a consequence of both its self-imposed restrictions discussed above, and the need to reach compromises in order to complete this phase of the project. The statement tends to describe current practices, rather than indicate preferences or propose improvements; for example, in dealing with the issue of measurement attributes, the statement merely states that 'items currently reported in financial statements are measured by different attributes, depending on the nature of the item and the relevance and reliability of the attribute measured'.[81] Then, instead of either prescribing a particular measurement attribute, or discussing the circumstances under which particular attributes should apply, the statement discusses five different attributes which 'are used in present practice' – historical cost, current cost, current market value, net realisable value and present value of future cash flows – and concludes that 'the use of different attributes will continue'.[82] Furthermore, the statement fails to prescribe a particular concept of capital maintenance that should be adopted by an entity, although the FASB bases its discussions on the concept of financial capital maintenance.[83]

The statement defines recognition as 'the process of formally recording or incorporating an item into the financial statements of an entity as an asset, liability, revenue, expense, or the like'.[84] It goes on to discuss four 'fundamental recognition criteria' which any item should meet in order for it to be recognised in the financial statements of an entity. These criteria, which are subject to a cost-benefit constraint and a materiality threshold, are described as follows:

Definitions – the item meets the definition of an element of financial statements.

Measurability – the item has a relevant attribute measurable with sufficient reliability.

Relevance – the information about the item is capable of making a difference in user decisions.

Reliability – the information is representationally faithful, verifiable and neutral.[85]

Although it was probably worth setting out these criteria, they are no more than an encapsulation of certain criteria contained in Concepts Statements 2 and 6.

SFAC No. 5 does make some progress in distinguishing between comprehensive income, earnings and net income. It states that the concept of earnings is similar to net income in present practice, and that a statement of earnings will be much like a present income statement, although 'earnings' does not include the cumulative effect of certain accounting adjustments of earlier periods that are recognised in the current period.[86] However, the statement goes on to say that the FASB 'expects the concept of earnings to be subject to the process of gradual change or evolution that has characterised the development of net income'.[87] Whilst many would agree with the principle that gradual change is the best approach towards gaining general acceptance, one of the problems with SFAC No. 5 is that the FASB does not indicate what it considers to be the desirable direction for this gradual change to follow. Furthermore, the FASB seems to be saying that concepts will evolve as accounting standards are developed – instead of the other way around.

In an evaluation of the FASB's conceptual framework, Professor David Solomons (who, incidentally, was the principal author of SFAC No. 2) took a distinctly critical view of this 'evolutionary' view of the emergence of concepts, stating the following: 'These appeals to evolution should be seen as what they are – a cop-out. If all that is needed to improve our accounting model is reliance on evolution ... why was an expensive and protracted conceptual framework project necessary in the first place? ... And, for that matter, if progress is simply a matter of waiting for evolution, who needs the FASB?'[88] Professor Solomons came to the following conclusions about SFAC No. 5: 'Under a rigorous grading system I would give Concepts Statement No. 5 an F and require the board to take the course over again – that is, to scrap the statement and start afresh.'[89] This led Solomons to conclude ultimately that 'my judgment of the project as a whole must be that it has failed'.[90]

Interestingly, the FASB's own special report on its conceptual framework (see 3.6 below) makes the point that although SFAC No. 5's name implies that it gives conceptual guidance on recognition and measurement, its conceptual contributions to financial reporting are not really in those areas.[91] The report goes on to say that 'as a result of compromises necessary to issue it, much of Concepts Statement 5 merely describes present practice and some of the reasons that have been used to support or explain it but provides little or no conceptual basis for analyzing and attempting to resolve the controversial issues of recognition and measurement about which accountants have disagreed for years.'[92] The concluding sentence of the FASB's report sums up elegantly the views that have long been expressed by critics of SFAC No. 5: 'Concepts Statement 5 does make some noteworthy conceptual contributions—they are just not on recognition and measurement.'[93]

3.6 The FASB's Special Report

In January 1998 the FASB published a Special Report entitled *The Framework of Financial Accounting Concepts and Standards*, written by Reed K. Storey and Sylvia Storey. By its own admission this book is 'more of a generous introduction to the FASB's conceptual framework than a comprehensive description or analysis of it'.[94] The main content of the book was first written in 1990 and has been variously updated since that time; but it does not deal with the most recent exposure draft of a proposed SFAC concerning the use of discounted cash flow information, dealt with in section 3.7 below.

It does contain a useful historical overview of the subject, including a critique of some of the earlier (pre-conceptual framework project) attempts to define such terms as assets and liabilities. In the main, such early attempts are characterised as unsatisfactory for reasons of either their circularity or their inability to filter out unwanted asset categories, or both. For example, concerning the definitions within APB Statement 4, the authors note: 'Those definitions were circular and open ended'[95] and 'Definitions of that type provide no effective limits or restraints on the matching of costs and revenues'.[96] The report makes explicit that a main aim of the concepts project was to ensure definitions of assets and liabilities were found that would bolster 'the conceptual and practical superiority of definitions of assets and liabilities based on resources and obligations that exist in the real world rather than on deferred charges and credits that result only from bookkeeping entries'.[97] The authors indicate that the circular definitions of APB 4 were of 'little help to the Board in deciding whether results of research and development expenditures qualified as assets'.[98]

Whether it is fair to characterise (for instance) the intellectual property gained from research and development as resulting only from bookkeeping entries is not discussed.   However, the circularity of a definition is, quite correctly, characterised as fatal to its acceptance and in our view this has consequences for the ASB's *Statement of Principles* projects which are discussed at 5.15.1 of this Chapter.

The special report contains an interesting section discussing the 'conceptual primacy' of either the asset and liability view or the revenue and expense view of income measurement – already outlined in section 3.4 above.   This discussion, like much of the debate concerning this topic, contains a number of assertions for which no evidence is offered. The reluctance of the majority of practitioners to endorse the FASB's balance sheet view is referred to in terms that seem condescending when describing professional accountants who have serious reservations about the practical implications of the FASB's pronouncements. For example, 'The revenue and expense view is still deeply ingrained in many accountants' minds and their first reaction to an accounting problem is to think about "proper matching of costs and revenues". Time will be needed for them to become accustomed to thinking first about effects of transactions ... on assets or liabilities ... and then about how [this] has affected revenues, expenses, gains or losses. Many will be able to make the adjustment only with difficulty'.[99]

In our view the main utility of the Special Report is that it provides a clear summary of the FASB's position and reasons for its adoption of the balance sheet view. While the report does refer to dissenting views, these are mainly in the form of short quotations from the dissenters, in contrast to the main body of the text, where the authors' own opinions clearly coincide with those of the FASB.

3.7 Using cash flow information in accounting measurements (discounting)

In June 1997 the FASB issued an exposure draft of a proposed new Statement of Financial Accounting Concepts. A revised exposure draft of this proposed new SFAC – *Using cash flow information and present value in accounting measurements* – was issued in March 1999. The 1999 proposal was the result of considering the comment received on the 1997 draft and embodies a number of changes. The purpose of the proposed statement is to provide a framework for using future cash flows as the basis for accounting measurement. It aims to provide general principles governing the use of present value, especially when the amounts of future cash flows and/or their timing are uncertain. The proposals are limited to issues of measurement and do not address recognition questions.

Present values are used to incorporate the time value of money in a measurement. In their simplest form, present value techniques capture the amount that an entity demands (or that others demand from it) for money that it will receive (or pay) in the future.[100] The FASB's objective of using present value in an accounting measurement is to capture, to the extent that it is possible, the economic difference between sets of estimated future cash flows, taking into account their uncertainty as well as their timing differences. For example, normal discounting distinguishes between a riskless cash flow of £1,000 due in one day and a risky cash flow of £1,000 due in ten years; although both have an undiscounted measurement of £1,000. In addition, the revised draft seeks to distinguish between two identical inflows due in ten years time, based upon the relative uncertainties of receiving them. Consequently, the FASB asserts that a present value measurement which incorporates the uncertainty in estimated future cash flows always provides more relevant information than a measurement based on the undiscounted sum of those cash flows or a discounted measurement that ignores uncertainty.[101]

Any combination of cash flows and interest rates could be used to compute a present value, at least in the broadest sense of the term. However, present value is not an end in itself. Simply applying an arbitrary interest rate to a series of cash flows provides limited information to financial statement users and may mislead rather than assist. To provide relevant information in financial reporting, present value must represent some observable measurement attribute of assets or liabilities. The original exposure draft identified two situations which, in the opinion of the FASB, satisfy that requirement. When used in accounting measurements on initial recognition or re-measurement, present value techniques may be used either to estimate fair value or to develop entity-specific measurements:[102]

- the fair value of an asset (or liability) is the amount at which that asset (or liability) could be bought or incurred or sold (or settled) in a current transaction between willing parties – that is, other than in a forced or liquidation sale;

■   the entity-specific measurement of an asset (or liability) is the present value of the future cash flows that the entity expects to realise (or pay) through the use (or settlement) and eventual disposition of the item over its economic life. Conceptually, the entity-specific value is that amount at which independent willing parties that share the same information and assumptions about the entity's estimated future cash flows would agree to a transaction. Stated differently, entity-specific value is that amount at which the market would value the cash flows expected by the entity. The assumptions used in an entity-specific measurement reflect the entity's expected use of an asset or settlement of a liability and the role of the entity's proprietary skills in that use or settlement. The FASB's notion of entity-specific measurement is similar to what the ASB refers to as 'value in use' (see 5 below).[103]

However, one of the most significant changes in the revised draft is the abandonment of the entity-specific measurement of an asset or liability as an allowed measurement option, leaving fair value as the sole measurement attribute. This represents a significant point of departure from the ASB which is further discussed in section 5 below. In rejecting entity specific (value in use) measurement the FASB also considered and rejected two other possibilities:

■   'Effective settlement' measurements representing the current amounts of assets that if invested today at a stipulated interest rate will provide future cash flows that match the cash outflows for a particular liability.

■   'Cost accumulation' measurements which attempt to capture the (usually incremental) costs that an entity anticipates it will incur in acquiring an asset or satisfying a liability over its expected term.

The FASB holds that each of the rejected measurement attributes (a) adds factors that are not contemplated in the price of a market transaction for the asset or liability in question, (b) inserts assumptions made by the entity's management in the place of those the market would make, and/or (c) excludes factors that would be contemplated in the price of a market transaction. Consequently fair value represents a price and, as such, provides an unambiguous objective for the development of the cash flows and interest rates used in present value measurement.[104]

The exposure draft sets out the following four general principles that, in the opinion of the FASB, govern any application of present value techniques in measuring assets:[105]

■   To the extent possible, estimated cash flows and interest rates should reflect assumptions about all future events and uncertainties that would be considered in deciding whether to acquire an asset or group of assets in an arm's-length transaction for cash.

- Interest rates used to discount cash flows should reflect assumptions that are consistent with those inherent in the estimated cash flows. Otherwise, the effect of some assumptions will be double counted or ignored. For example, an interest rate of 12 per cent might be applied to contractual cash flows of a loan. That rate reflects expectations about future defaults from loans with particular characteristics. That same 12 per cent rate should not be used to discount expected cash flows because those cash flows already reflect assumptions about future defaults.

- Estimated cash flows and interest rates should be free from both bias and factors unrelated to the asset or group of assets in question. For example, deliberately understating estimated net cash flows to enhance the apparent future profitability of an asset introduces a bias into the measurement.

- Estimated cash flows or interest rates should reflect the range of possible outcomes rather than a single most likely, minimum, or maximum possible amount.

The 1999 revised draft alters the stance of the FASB on the measurement of liabilities. The 1997 draft included the possibility of three different liability measurement objectives:[106]

- fair value as assets – the recorded amount of some liabilities is the price at which other entities are willing to hold the entity's liabilities as assets;

- fair value in settlement – the recorded amount of some liabilities represents the amount that the entity would have to pay a third party to assume the liability; and

- value in settlement by the entity – the recorded amount of some liabilities represents the amount that the entity expects to pay in settling the obligation (the entity-specific measurement of a liability).

The revised draft opts for consistency with its conclusion on assets, and the FASB therefore decided that fair value is the single measurement objective when present value is to be used in measuring liabilities, although the draft is not particularly specific as to how fair value is to be determined, stating that the measurement of liabilities 'may require different techniques in arriving at fair value'.[107] The draft describes various techniques for estimating the fair value of liabilities, including fair value in settlement (which is the estimated price that the entity would have to pay a third party to assume the liability) and expected value (which is a technique applied to liabilities without contractual cash flows and is based on expected cash flows).[108]

However, perhaps the most significant difference between the 1997 exposure draft and this one centres around the entity's own credit standing. Fair value in settlement as described in the 1997 draft would have excluded the effects of an entity's credit standing in measuring its liabilities, whilst the FASB now asserts that the most relevant measurement of a liability always includes the credit standing of the entity obliged to pay.[109] As a result, the revised draft indicates that the credit standing of the entity must be taken into account in arriving at the fair value of its liabilities and that, accordingly, the fair value in settlement of an entity's liability should assume settlement with an entity of comparable, rather than superior, credit standing.[110] Consequently, as the entity's credit standing affects the interest rate at which it borrows in the market place it therefore affects the fair value (as defined above) of its liabilities.

This view entails the FASB adopting a quite complex form of discounting in its draft, to facilitate which it has defined for its purposes a number of terms that are not necessarily used in their normal everyday sense. Instead of discounting the best estimate of any future cash flow (i.e. the most likely amount), the draft insists that the 'expected' cash flows should be discounted. The 'expected' cash flow to be used is defined as the sum of probability-weighted amounts in a range of possible estimated amounts.[111] Therefore, the draft would require the estimation of the likelihood of a range of outcomes (for example, for the repayment of a debt); the probability weighting of each; the calculation of each probability weighted amount; their summation and finally the calculation of the present value of that derived total. The draft does not define the rate to be used in any discounting but appears to indicate that a risk free rate is often the appropriate rate to use.

The revised draft implies a number of practical results which many will find odd. For instance the fair valuation of warranty obligations, if not calculated on a cost accumulation (incremental) basis, could result in the liability being overstated. It is probable that the market's rate for performing warranty work would involve overhead costs not incurred by the entity itself, which would incur only incremental costs. This could result in the understatement of current profits and the overstatement of subsequent ones, as the extra cost factored into the (market price based) fair value warranty obligations and charged as an expense at the time of sale, was subsequently written back (usually referred to as 'unwound').

The inclusion of the credit standing of entities in the calculations can produce unwanted results. The lower the credit rating of a business, the higher interest rate it will have to pay. Therefore, the discounting of a future obligation of such a firm (using the higher discount rate its higher interest rate implies) will produce a lower net present value than that of a firm with an identical obligation and a better credit rating. This produces the extraordinary result whereby a poorer credit rated, less safe firm, shows a significantly lower liability than a higher rated, safer firm; in spite of the fact they both have a settlement payment to make which is identical.

All in all, the draft comes across as no more than an overview of the issues surrounding the use of present values in accounting measurement. In so doing, it leaves the door open to a fairly wide range of practices which can be applied as and when the FASB so decides. It is unfortunate that the draft contains no explanation in plain English of what its practical ramifications are and where, if it were to be adopted, financial reporting would be heading. It is therefore possible that the FASB may be looking to convert this exposure draft into an SFAC in a way that will seemingly provide conceptual support for an ever widening variety of discounting practices. In view of the manner in which the ASB has followed the FASB's lead throughout much of its own *Statement of Principles* project (see 5 below) this draft may have implications for the UK in the future.

3.8   Conclusion

In order to be able to assess the success or failure of the FASB's conceptual framework project, one must refer back to the originally perceived benefits of the project and evaluate whether or not any of them has been achieved (see 3.1 above). Perhaps the acid test may be found in analysing the extent to which the FASB has used the framework in the development of accounting standards. Possibly the best example of where the framework has been used as the basis for an accounting standard is in the development of SFAS 95 – *Statement of Cash Flows*; however, this is clearly the exception. An analysis of the Appendices headed 'Basis for Conclusions' in the more recently issued SFASs, reveals few references to the fact that the members of the FASB have used the concepts statements to guide their thinking – and where reference is made it is generally to broad objectives or qualitative characteristics. On the other hand, it might be argued that the concepts statements have guided the thinking of FASB members without it being expressly stated; however, if this were the case, why is it that the FASB has, for example, issued a statement on reporting comprehensive income (SFAS 130) which seemingly lacks any conceptual integrity and is in conflict with the framework?   (See Chapter 22 for further discussion of SFAS 130.)

The weakness of the FASB's conceptual framework project may be attributed to a number of factors; however, the most significant reason will probably be shown to be the Board's failure to deal with the fundamental issues of recognition and measurement. To a certain extent, the FASB has fallen into the same trap as the AICPA did in APB Statement No. 4, in that SFAC No. 5 is a descriptive rather than a prescriptive statement; a statement of accounting concepts should provide a frame of reference for the formulation of financial reporting practice, and not be a description of what current reporting practices are. In the words of Professor Stephen Zeff, 'the FASB's conceptual framework failed to fulfil expectations that it might constitute a powerful intellectual force for improving financial reporting'.[112]

Underlying the entire issue of developing a conceptual framework is the unspoken yet pervasive view of the project's authors that the logical structure for the framework should be a highly deductive one whereby the entire schema follows from a number of definitional assertions. To the practically minded accountant it seems the problem of (for instance) ensuring worthless research and development expenditure is not carried forward, is one of empirically determining whether the expenditure in question is likely to result in profitable sales. By contrast, this precise problem is cited in the FASB special report as a prime reason for adopting a definition that excludes all deferred charges. This desire for an entirely deductive system amounts to a view of what accounting is that may not coincide with reality. Accounting is an activity born out of the needs of society (principally the needs of industrialised nations) that responds to those needs as and when conditions alter. The fact that the framework project has not obviously impinged upon the thinking behind a number of standards seems to be evidence for this view. It may not be a fault that accounting lacks a set of principles that accurately and inescapably predict the future in the way that scientific laws do; rather it may be a necessary attribute of accounting continuing to be useful to society.

This is not to say that the FASB's project should be rejected out of hand; it contains some outstanding work, particularly in the area of qualitative characteristics. However, a way must be found to address the fundamental issues, which does not involve both attempting to maintain the truth of the framework's definitions while quietly compromising them when events require it. Perhaps more importantly, a method of implementation will have to be developed which will make whatever transition is necessary acceptable to both the preparers and users of financial reports.

4   UK INITIATIVES

4.1   SSAP 2: Disclosure of accounting policies

SSAP 2[113] does not really set out to form part of a conceptual framework, but its content covers some of the same ground. It was issued in 1971, and although it was not the first accounting standard to be published, it is probably the most fundamental, since its principles pervade financial reporting practice in the UK. The overall objectives of SSAP 2 are to assist in user understanding and interpretation of financial statements by promoting the improvement in the quality of information disclosed. It seeks to achieve this by establishing as generally accepted accounting practice the disclosure in financial statements of clear explanations of the accounting policies followed in the preparation of the financial statements, in so far as these are significant for the purpose of giving a true and fair view.

SSAP 2 develops the standard accounting practice for the disclosure of accounting policies in three stages: first, it describes the four fundamental accounting concepts, it then relates these to the development of accounting bases, and finally it deals with the selection of accounting policies.

4.1.1   Fundamental accounting concepts

Fundamental accounting concepts are the broad basic assumptions which underlie the periodic financial statements of business entities. They are practical rules rather than theoretical ideals and are capable of variation and evolution as accounting thought and practice develop.[114]

A   The going concern concept

This concept is applied on the basis that the reporting entity will continue in operational existence for the foreseeable future. This means in particular that the balance sheet and profit and loss account assume no intention or necessity to liquidate or curtail significantly the scale of business operations.[115]

B   The accruals (or matching) concept

In the presentation of the profit and loss account, revenue and profits recognised are matched with the associated costs and expenses incurred in earning them. In order to achieve this, revenues, profits, costs and expenses are accrued (i.e. recognised as they are earned or incurred, not as cash is received or paid), matched with one another in so far as their relationship can be established or justifiably assumed, and dealt with in the profit and loss account for the period to which they relate. However, where the accruals concept is inconsistent with the prudence concept (described below), the latter prevails.[116]

C   The consistency concept

There should be consistency of accounting treatment of like items within each accounting period and from one period to the next.

D   The prudence concept

Under the prudence concept, revenue and profits are not anticipated but are recognised by inclusion in the profit and loss account only when realised in the form of cash or of other assets the ultimate cash realisation of which can be assessed with reasonable certainty. On the other hand, provision is made for all known liabilities whether the amount of these is known with certainty or is a best estimate in the light of the information available.

These four fundamental accounting concepts, together with a fifth concept, have broadly been adopted by the Companies Act 1985 as the accounting principles which should be used in the determination of all items shown in a company's financial statements, although the terms in which they are described are not identical.[117] The fifth principle introduced by the Companies Act is that of 'non-aggregation'. This principle states that 'in determining the aggregate amount of any item the amount of each individual asset or liability that falls to be taken into account shall be determined separately'.[118] For example, compensating inaccuracies in individual amounts should not be lost in one large total, and a group of assets should be valued on an individual asset basis, as opposed to a portfolio basis.

At the same time, though, it is important to recognise that whilst the fundamental accounting concepts are, in theory, firmly entrenched in SSAP 2 and the Companies Act, they are being undermined by recent ASB initiatives. For example, FRS 12 – *Provisions, Contingent Liabilities and Contingent Assets* – specifically prohibits businesses from making a provision in certain circumstances: for instance where a company's Board has made a decision to close a division but has not communicated this to the outside world. A similar line is taken by the IASC in its standard IAS 37 – *Provisions, Contingent Liabilities and Contingent Assets*. Both standards appear to contradict the requirements of European Accounting Directives: the Fourth Directive Article 31.1(c)(bb) requires businesses to take account of 'all foreseeable liabilities and potential losses arising in the course of the financial year concerned or of a previous one even if such liabilities or losses become apparent only between the date of the balance sheet and the date on which it is drawn up'.[119]

This amounts to a fundamental reinterpretation of the prudence concept, as does the suggestion that unrealised gains on financial instruments should be taken to income, particularly when there is no active or liquid market in those instruments and they are not held for trading purposes. Indeed, the general downgrading of the importance of realisation in the reporting of income is explicit in a number of recent ASB publications. The matching concept is similarly under threat, given that the ASB's revised Draft *Statement of Principles* does not recognise items of deferred expense and income which have traditionally been recognised in the balance sheet as deferred debits and credits (see 5.4.1 below). Even the going concern concept is in question. It is not that the ASB is suggesting that it should formally be abandoned, but the going concern concept allows a long-term perspective to be applied to the measurement of long-term assets and liabilities, whereas standards like FRS 12 – *Provisions, Contingent Assets and Contingent Liabilities* – focus instead on what the entity would rationally pay to settle its liabilities today.

4.1.2   Accounting bases

Accounting bases are 'the methods developed for applying fundamental concepts to financial transactions and items, for the purpose of financial accounts, and in particular:

(a)   for determining the accounting periods in which revenue and costs should be recognised in the profit and loss account; and

(b)   for determining the amounts at which material items should be stated in the balance sheet'.[120]

Accounting bases, therefore, are accounting treatments which have evolved in response to the necessity of having to apply the fundamental concepts to areas of practice. However, because of the variety and complexity of types of business and business transactions, there may exist more than one legitimate accounting basis for dealing with a particular item; for example, there are several acceptable accounting bases for the depreciation of fixed assets, each of which is suited to particular types of assets and business circumstances.

4.1.3   Accounting policies

Having established that there exist several recognised accounting bases in respect of individual accounting issues, it is necessary for the management of an entity to select those bases which are most appropriate for their own particular circumstances; those bases selected then become the entity's accounting policies. Consequently, accounting policies are defined as 'the specific accounting bases selected and consistently followed by a business enterprise as being, in the opinion of management, appropriate to its circumstances and best suited to present fairly its results and financial position'.[121] Thereafter, the accounting policies selected for dealing with items which are judged material in determining financial position and profit or loss for the year should be disclosed by way of note to the financial statements.[122]

This means, for example, that management should select those bases of depreciating fixed assets which are most appropriate to the types of assets and their use in the business so as to allocate depreciation as fairly as possible to the periods expected to benefit from the use of the assets, and these bases selected should be set out in an accounting policy note to the financial statements. However, this highlights an interesting conflict between SSAP 2 and FRS 15 – *Tangible Fixed Assets*. Under SSAP 2, for example, the sum-of-digits and straight-line methods of depreciation are two acceptable accounting bases, each of which is appropriate to a particular pattern of asset use; in the event of management deciding that it would be more appropriate to depreciate an asset using a the sum-of-digits, rather than a straight-line method, this would constitute a change in accounting basis, and therefore a change in accounting policy. FRS 15, however, states that a change from one method of providing depreciation to another does not constitute a change of accounting policy;[123] furthermore, no explanation is given in FRS 15 for this departure from the principles laid down in SSAP 2.

4.2   The Corporate Report

The first real attempt by the accounting profession in the UK to develop a conceptual framework is to be found in a discussion paper which was issued in 1975 by the then-styled Accounting Standards Steering Committee (later the ASC) and entitled *The Corporate Report*.[124]

The discussion paper deals with 'the fundamental aims of published financial reports and the means by which these aims can be achieved'[125] and uses the term 'corporate report' to mean 'the comprehensive package of information of all kinds which most completely describes an organisation's economic activity'.[126] It was suggested that this 'comprehensive package' should include more than the 'basic financial statements' (i.e. the balance sheet, profit and loss account and funds statement), and should incorporate additional narrative and descriptive statements.[127] The discussion paper centres around three main elements: 'the types of organisation which should be expected to publish regular financial information; the main users of such information and their needs; and the form of report which will best meet those needs'.[128]

The discussion paper followed the basic approach that corporate reports should seek to satisfy, as far as possible, the information needs of users.[129] The Committee argued that every economic entity of significant size has an implicit responsibility to report publicly, and concluded that general purpose reports designed for general purpose use are the primary means by which this public accountability is fulfilled. Users were defined 'as those having a reasonable right to information concerning the reporting entity',[130] a right which arises from the entity's public accountability.

The paper identifies seven user groups[131] as having a reasonable right to information, and discusses the basis of the rights of each group and their information needs. Not surprisingly, the Committee identified a considerable overlap of interest between each of the user groups, including items such as 'evaluating the performance of the entity', 'estimating the future prospects of the entity', 'evaluating managerial performance', 'assessing the liquidity of the entity, its present or future requirements for additional fixed or working capital, and its ability to raise long and short term finance'.[132]

On this basis the Committee concluded that 'the fundamental objective of corporate reports is to communicate economic measurements of and information about the resources and performance of the reporting entity useful to those having reasonable rights to such information'.[133] They went on to say that in order to fulfil this objective and be useful, corporate reports should be relevant, understandable, reliable, complete, objective, timely and comparable[134] (these qualitative characteristics identified were similar to those discussed in the Trueblood Report).

The discussion paper then reviewed the conventional thinking on the aim of published reports together with the then-existing features of published financial statements of UK companies. The Committee also conducted a survey of corporate objectives amongst the chairmen of 300 of the largest UK listed companies, and concluded that 'distributable profit can no longer be regarded as the sole or premier indicator of performance'.[135] Consequently, it was suggested that there was a need for additional indicators of performance in the corporate reports of all entities.[136]

Part II of the study considers the 'measurement and method' of achieving the above aims. This includes a discussion of the improvement of communication and publication methods of corporate report information, as well as consideration of the frequency and distribution of reports. Since the Committee had concluded that current reporting practices did not fully satisfy the needs of users, it was suggested that the following additional statements should be published in the corporate report: a statement of value added, an employment report, a statement of money exchanges with government, a statement of transactions in foreign currency, a statement of future prospects and a statement of corporate objectives.[137]   In addition, the Committee recommended further study into methods of social accounting as well as the disaggregation of certain financial information.[138]

Finally, the Committee discussed the concepts and measurements employed in the 'basic financial statements'.   In considering the purpose of profit measurement, it concluded that income statements 'should be concerned with the measurement of performance although they may also be used in the measurement of capital maintenance and income distributability'.[139]   It was, however, recognised that this dual purpose of income statements often gives rise to conflict in the application of accounting concepts – particularly the fundamental concepts of prudence and matching. Various measurement bases were then discussed in the context of the inadequacies of the historical cost system. The Committee stated that 'the usefulness of financial statements in fulfilling user needs is restricted at the present time because of the defects of the basis of measurement generally used. Historical cost accounting fails, in times of rapidly changing prices and values, to ensure that sufficient provision is made for capital maintenance. When reported figures are not related to current values there may be over- or understatement of performance as measured by profits and return on assets.'[140]

The committee then briefly surveyed several bases of measurement, including historical cost, current purchasing power (CPP) and various current value bases such as replacement cost and net realisable value. The conclusion reached was that no one system of measurement is capable of satisfying the user needs identified in the study, and that, therefore, research should be undertaken into the feasibility of multi-column reporting, as well as into the development of a standardised system of current value accounting.[141]

The publication of the Corporate Report, however, closely coincided with the release of the Sandilands Report on inflation accounting,[142] (discussed at 4.3 below) resulting in the Corporate Report being very much overshadowed. This was probably to the relief of the business community who were concerned about the possibility of their reporting responsibility being extended beyond that of the existing requirements, through the development of the Committee's concept of public accountability. In any event, the Corporate Report fell short of making a significant contribution towards the development of a conceptual framework by virtue of its failure to select the accounting models appropriate to the informational needs of the individual user groups which it had identified. It was quite clear from the conclusions reached by the Committee that a single set of generalised external financial reports could not meet the informational needs of all the user groups identified in the report, and, in any event, financial information presented on the historical cost basis alone was clearly shown to be inadequate. The logical progression, therefore, would have been to suggest the presentation of specific supplementary information according to the measurement bases appropriate to meeting the needs of particular groups of users.

4.3   The Sandilands Report

Through most of the 1970s and early 1980s, inflation was an intractable problem in the UK, with rates of inflation well above 10% common, and on occasion over 20%. Consequently, it was within this context that, on 21 January 1974, the announcement of the membership and terms of reference of the government's Inflation Accounting Committee was made to the House of Commons by the Secretary of State for Trade and Industry. The Sandilands Committee's principal term of reference was 'to consider whether, and if so how, company accounts should allow for changes (including relative changes) in costs and prices'.[143] The Sandilands Report followed a similar approach to that of the Corporate Report to the extent that it focused on the information needs of users. The report stated that 'the requirements of users of accounts should be the fundamental consideration in deciding the information to be disclosed in company accounts'.[144]

The report proposed that the development of accounting for inflation should be an evolutionary process towards a system of current cost accounting, the essential features of which are:

(a)   money is the unit of measurement (as opposed to the 'current purchasing power' basis of expressing financial information in terms of a unit of measurement of constant value when prices change);

(b)   assets and liabilities should be shown in the balance sheet at their 'value to the business'; and

(c)   operating profit (to be known as 'current cost profit') is calculated after charging the 'value to the business' of the assets consumed during the period, thereby excluding holding gains and showing them separately.[145]

The concept of 'value to the business' is first promulgated here as a panacea to accounting measurement difficulties. In fact, although it is an intellectually appealing concept, it is difficult to determine whether or not it has any practical meaning – as will be seen in later discussions of the ASB's Draft *Statement of Principles*.

4.3.1   *Current Purchasing Power accounting*

In formulating its system of current cost accounting, the Committee examined three alternative accounting systems which had been developed in an attempt to overcome the deficiencies of historical cost accounting. The first of these systems studied was the 'current purchasing power' (CPP) method of inflation accounting recommended in the Provisional SSAP, PSSAP 7, which was published in May 1974.[146] Under PSSAP 7, companies were expected to supplement their conventional historical cost financial statements with a statement which illustrated the effects of changes in the purchasing power of money on these statements. The main features of PSSAP 7 were set out in the standard as follows:

'(a) companies will continue to keep their records and present their basic annual accounts in historical pounds, ie in terms of the value of the pound at the time of each transaction or revaluation;

(b) in addition, all listed companies should present to their shareholders a supplementary statement in terms of the value of the pound at the end of the period to which the accounts relate;

(c) the conversion of the figures in the basic accounts into the figures in the supplementary statement should be by means of a general index of the purchasing power of the pound;[147] and

(d) the standard requires the directors to provide in a note to the supplementary statement an explanation of the basis on which it has been prepared and it is desirable that directors should comment on the significance of the figures.'[148]

The Committee concluded that the CPP method 'does not remedy the main deficiencies of historic cost accounting during a time of changing costs and prices and we do not recommend it as the best long-term solution to the problem of accounting for inflation'.[149] Numerous arguments were put forward to support this conclusion, for example:

■   since, during a period of changing prices, historical cost figures expressed in terms of monetary units do not show the 'value to the business' of assets, a CPP supplementary statement will show the historic cost figures restated in units of current purchasing power, not the 'value to the business' of assets.[150] Thus, a major deficiency of historical cost accounts would not be overcome;

■   since companies were required to express their CPP supplementary statements in terms of the current purchasing power of the pound at the closing balance sheet date, the unit of measurement in the supplementary statement would change from year to year. This was likely to cause confusion, compounded by the fact that companies which had different accounting dates would be preparing supplementary statements in terms of different units, resulting in a lack of comparability;[151] and

■   since a unit of measurement with an absolute value through time is unattainable, there is no advantage in preparing financial statements in CPP units rather than in units of money.[152]

4.3.2   *Value accounting*

The Committee then examined three forms of 'value accounting' – a term used to describe a wide range of different accounting systems which measure net assets by reference to their 'value' rather than their cost. The three value accounting systems examined were replacement cost accounting, present value accounting and continuously contemporary accounting.

A   *Replacement cost accounting based on current entry values*

'Replacement cost' is the price which will have to be paid to replace an asset used or given up in exchange for another asset. Consequently, the basic principle underlying replacement cost accounting is that, since a business has to replace its assets over time in order to continue in operational existence, charges for the consumption or exchange of an asset should be based on the cost of replacing it. Consequently, assets are valued at the balance sheet date by reference to the price which would have to be paid at that date to purchase a similar asset in a similar condition – i.e. the replacement cost of the assets. This system, therefore, adopts a method of income determination which reflects changes in capital both at the point of realisation of assets and, before realisation, while holding assets.

The pioneers of an income and value model based on replacement costs (entry values) were Edwards and Bell,[153] who attempted to interpret accounting concepts in terms of economic concepts. Their theory abandoned both the realisation principle and the idea of the 'unitary income statement' which does not separate operating profit from holding gains. They introduced a new concept of 'business profit', which was made up of current operating profit of the current period, realised holding gains of the same period and unrealised holding gains.

A major disadvantage of the replacement cost model is difficulty and subjectivity in assigning replacement costs; for example, are replacement costs based on identical or equivalent replacement, and how is technological obsolescence dealt with? However, this disadvantage is far outweighed by the usefulness of the information provided by the system in the form of meaningful balance sheet values and a segregated business profit figure. The Sandilands Committee concluded that the replacement cost accounting system 'comes close to meeting the dominant requirements of users of accounts and the Committee's own proposals have many similarities with certain forms of this system of accounting'.[154]

B   *Present value accounting*

Present value accounting is based on the economic concept of income, and values an asset on the basis of the present value of the cash flows which are expected to be derived from that asset. In order to maintain the capital of the entity, an amount at least equal to the original investment should be reinvested, whilst the remaining cash flows are treated as realised. For example, if the discounted net present value of all expected future cash flows of an entity are £100,000 at the beginning of the year and £115,000 at the end of the year, and if the net cash flows arising during the year were £10,000, then the profit for the year will be £25,000, since this amount could be distributed whilst maintaining the original capital base of £100,000.

Whilst this approach might have some degree of theoretical soundness, it is totally impracticable. Issues such as risk, the determination of discount rates, changes in interest rates and the uncertainty of future cash flows present virtually insurmountable problems. The Sandilands Committee rejected present value accounting on the grounds that use of economic value as the basis of valuation of an asset would not meet the needs of users, as it would only be in comparatively few cases that this would represent the value of an asset to a business.[155]

C   Continuously Contemporary Accounting (CoCoA)

The current value income model based on exit prices or realisable market values was first advocated by MacNeal in a book published by him in 1939 which dealt, inter alia, with the ethical issue of 'truth' in accounting.[156] MacNeal maintained that financial statements could only present the 'truth' if assets were stated at their current value and the profit and losses accruing from the changes in these values are included in income, and classified as either realised or unrealised. MacNeal did, however, concede that under certain circumstances the use of net realisable values was not appropriate, and that in such cases current replacement costs should be used.

The system known as continuously contemporary accounting (CoCoA) was formally introduced by Chambers in a book which he published in 1966,[157] and the case for exit value accounting was further developed by Sterling.[158] Chambers' theory is based on the premise that entities must be able to choose between alternative courses of action and, because resources are limited, they need to know what resources are available to enable them to engage in exchanges. Consequently, Chambers asserts that this capacity to engage in exchanges is measured by the opportunity cost of holding assets in their existing form, and that this opportunity cost is represented by the current cash equivalent of assets – which Chambers defines as being their current sales value. Initially, Chambers did not apply this principle rigorously and proposed that stocks should be valued at current replacement cost. However, he subsequently amended his view and advocated that exit values should be applied to the valuation of all assets. A difference in the theories of Chambers and Sterling is, for example, that Chambers believes that net realisable values should be based on the assumption that assets are realised in an orderly manner based on sensible adaptations to changing circumstances; Sterling, on the other hand, believes that net realisable values should be based on immediate liquidation prices.

The capital maintenance concept adopted by CoCoA is based on the preservation of the purchasing power of shareholders' equity (using the monetary unit as the unit of measurement, and not the current purchasing power unit used in CPP accounting). Consequently, since all assets (both monetary and non-monetary) are measured at net realisable value, income is defined as the difference between opening and closing equity after maintaining the purchasing power or cash equivalent of such equity. Income for the year, therefore, will comprise (1) the net profit/loss on business operations, (2) the accrued profit/loss arising from the change in the current cash equivalent of assets and (3) the effect on the capital of the entity brought about by the change in the purchasing power of money.

However, despite the widespread publication of his theories, Chambers failed to gain any measure of support for CoCoA outside academic circles. Chambers believed that one of the reasons for this was the lack of empirical evidence that the users of financial statements needed financial information based on net realisable values. Consequently, he set about obtaining this evidence through an empirical survey which he published in 1980.[159] Through carefully designed (but somewhat simplistic) questions, Chambers was able to conclude that his empirical evidence justified the use of net realisable values as the primary basis of measurement.

Chambers' principal survey did, however, produce some anomalous and inconsistent answers, resulting in his having to conduct a supplementary survey of four questions. This highlighted several weaknesses in the formulation of his questions, and cast doubt about the validity of the survey as a whole. These doubts are expressed, for example, in an article by Edward Stamp[160] who stated that 'his questionnaire was inadequate and failed to include necessary questions on valuation, performance measures, and liabilities, that would not have been difficult to frame, even with the constraints imposed by Chambers'.[161] Consequently, these omissions and the style of his research undermine Chambers' claim that his empirical evidence demonstrates that CoCoA provides the best basis for financial reporting.

There is no doubt that there are some compelling theoretical arguments for the presentation of financial statements based on net realisable values; for example, they provide useful information in the assessment of liquidity and financial flexibility. However, net realisable value is unlikely to reflect an asset's 'value to the business', since, for instance, an item of plant might have negligible net realisable value but substantial use value. Therefore, whilst the disclosure of net realisable values might provide useful supplementary information, the arguments in favour of CoCoA as the primary basis of accounting are unconvincing. CoCoA was rejected by the Sandilands Committee on the basis that, as a whole, it did not satisfy the information needs of users which they had identified.[162] It is, however, noteworthy that in its discussion document – *Making Corporate*

Reports Valuable – the Research Committee of the ICAS advocated a reporting system based on net realisable values[163] (see 4.6 below).

4.3.3   Cash flow accounting

The principal proponents of cash flow reporting are Lee[164] and Lawson,[165] although there are several other advocates of various approaches to cash flow reporting. Lee's system of cash flow reporting relies heavily on exit value theory and aims to report both actual and potential cash flows. Assets are classified according to their realisability, based on Chambers' principle of orderly liquidation. If a sale price does not exist, assets are to be accounted for as having a zero cash equivalent.[166] Lee has suggested the following four asset classifications for his statement of financial position:

1. realised assets (e.g. bank balances);

2. readily-realisable assets (i.e. assets which have a ready market and sale price, such as listed securities, debtors and stocks of finished goods);

3. non-readily-realisable assets (i.e. assets which do have a market and sale price, but which would not be quickly realised because of the limited nature of the market, such as certain items of plant and work-in-progress); and

4. not-realisable assets (i.e. assets which have no known sales price and no market, and would therefore be ascribed a zero value, such as highly specialised or obsolete plant).[167]

Liabilities are classified according to maturity, in line with conventional accounting practice.

Lee proposes that, in addition to a 'statement of financial position', the cash flow reporting system should present a 'statement of realised cash flow', a 'statement of realisable earnings' and a 'statement of changes in financial position'.[168] The statement of realised cash flow reports an entity's actual cash inflows and outflows during a particular period; it is noteworthy that the information contained in this statement would be broadly equivalent to that which would be presented in a statement of cash flows under FRS 1 or SFAS 95 (see Chapter 26). The statement of realisable earnings reports periodic profit similar to that provided by a net realisable value accounting system, except that it is described in terms of realised and realisable cash flows. The statement provides an analysis of realised earnings (derived from the entity's operating cash flow), and unrealised earnings (which represent potential cash flows that have accrued during the period as a result of changes in the realisable values of assets, net of the changes in liabilities). The statement of changes in financial position is effectively a conventional funds statement presented on an exit value basis.

Although there are a number of practical accounting and disclosure problems in cash flow reporting, it does have considerable merit. Furthermore, a number of the problems are not unique to cash flow reporting, with equivalent issues remaining unsolved in historical cost accounting. However, one difficulty which does exist is caused by the artificial 12 month reporting period and the necessity to measure 'profitability' over that period and from one period to the next. The principal reason for the development of the accrual basis of accounting was that financial statements prepared on a cash basis (which was probably the oldest form of presentation) provided distorted profit figures from one period to the next. Although the Sandilands Committee stated that there was 'much of value in the cash flow accounting principle',[169] it was felt that cash flow accounting would rekindle all the 'old difficulties of assessing the profit or loss for the year when the accounting system does not match revenues against costs incurred in their generation'.[170] The Committee therefore concluded that the abandonment of the existing concept of the profit and loss account in favour of a cash flow statement would result in the information needs of users not being met. Clearly, however, the Committee had not considered the possibility of the presentation of a 'statement of realisable earnings' as advocated by Lee, which would provide a more stable basis for reporting profit than the statement of receipts and payments envisaged by the Committee. Lee, however, recognised the problems created by the traditional 12 month reporting period, and suggested that a solution might be found in the use of multi-period aggregates for analysis purposes.

4.3.4   *Current cost accounting (CCA)*

The Sandilands Committee recommended the development of a system of current cost accounting which used the monetary unit as the unit of measurement and dealt with the effects of specific price changes (as opposed to changes in the general purchasing power of money) on individual businesses. The Committee recommended that the balance sheet should present the 'value to the business' of the company's assets, which was equated with the amount of the loss which would be suffered by an entity if the asset were to be lost or destroyed. Whilst it was stated that the 'value to the business' of an asset might, under certain circumstances, be its net realisable value or economic value, it would normally be based on its replacement cost. Because the Committee recommended that financial statements be drawn up in terms of the monetary unit, no adjustment would be made for monetary items.[171] However, it is arguable that current cost accounting does not produce a balance sheet which seeks to be a statement of values of the resources of the company; it simply updates the costs at which they are recorded. This distinction can be illustrated by looking at the financial statements of an oil and gas exploration company. Even on a current cost basis, the carrying value of its principal assets is still based on the (backward-looking) cost of exploration expenditure incurred, not the (forward-looking) value of the oil and gas it has found.

Under the Sandilands system, an entity's 'current cost profit' for a period would be calculated by charging against income 'the value to the business' of assets consumed during the year. In simple terms, therefore, the current cost profit could be derived from the historical cost profit by means of an adjustment to depreciation and a cost of sales adjustment. The Committee also recommended the presentation of a summary statement of total gains or losses for the period, which would present the entity's total gains/losses in terms of three classifications: operating gains/losses (i.e. current cost profit/loss), extraordinary gains/losses and holding gains/losses. An interesting observation regarding these two statements recommended by the Committee is that each is based on different capital maintenance concepts. The calculation of current cost profit was based on the concept of physical capital maintenance, whilst the summary statement of total gains was concerned with the maintenance of financial capital. However, because the calculation of current cost profit subsequently received greater prominence than the summary of total gains, it is generally thought that the Sandilands proposals were based on the concept of physical capital maintenance.[172]

The Committee recommended that current cost accounting should replace historical cost accounting, and that its proposals should be incorporated in an accounting standard. Consequently, the ASC established the Inflation Accounting Steering Group, giving them the task of preparing a proposal for an exposure draft based on the Sandilands proposals, resulting in the publication in November 1976 of ED 18 – *Current cost accounting*. ED 18, however, met with little support, as did the Sandilands recommendations. The ASC attributed this to the fact that there was considerable objection to the replacement of historical cost accounting by a new untested system; the proposals were considered too complicated; and the profit figure was considered misleading without adjustment for monetary items.[173]

Nevertheless, the ASC perceived an urgent need for companies to disclose how their historical cost financial statements were affected by changing prices. Therefore, in order to find an immediate solution to this problem, the ASC published an interim recommendation in November 1977 which outlined a simplified version of current cost accounting (known as the 'Hyde Guidelines').[174] These guidelines recommended that the published financial statements of companies listed on the Stock Exchange should include a prominent separate statement which showed the profit/loss calculated on a current cost basis.[175] The Hyde Guidelines recommended that three adjustments should be made to the historical cost results: in addition to the depreciation and cost of sales adjustments proposed by Sandilands, it was recommended that a 'gearing adjustment' be made as an interim solution to dealing with monetary items in inflation-adjusted financial statements. Since no account of the existence of borrowings was taken in calculating current cost operating profit, the implication was that operating capability had to be maintained entirely out of the generation of revenues. However, the reality is clearly that this could be partly financed by borrowings; consequently, the gearing adjustment was designed to take account of the extent to which fixed assets and working capital were financed by borrowings.

According to the ASC, the response of the larger companies to the Hyde Guidelines was 'encouraging'.[176] However, the ASC stated that it was evident from comments made in annual reports and submitted directly to them, that many companies were reluctant to include price level information in their annual financial statements until an acceptable accounting method was proposed as a standard, and until more detailed guidance was available on problem areas.[177] Consequently, in April 1979 the ASC issued ED 24 – *Current Cost Accounting* – which was developed from the Hyde Guidelines, taking into account comments received on both the Guidelines and ED 18.

ED 24 followed the Hyde proposal that a separate statement be presented which disclosed the current cost adjustments made to the historical cost profit in respect of depreciation, cost of sales and gearing. However, the ED went further than the guidelines by:

(a)   introducing a further adjustment, called the 'monetary working capital adjustment', which effectively extended the cost of sales adjustment (which allowed for increases in the investment needed to maintain stocks when prices were increasing) to the other working capital items. Consequently, the monetary working capital adjustment represented an estimate of the extra investment in debtors, creditors and liquid resources required to maintain operations when prices were increasing;

(b)   proposing the presentation of a current cost balance sheet, in which fixed assets and stock would be measured on a current cost basis; and

(c)   proposing that listed companies disclose current cost earnings per share.[178]

ED 24 subsequently became SSAP 16,[179] which was issued in March 1980. SSAP 16 gave companies the choice as to how they could present their current cost information. They could present historical cost accounts as their main accounts with supplementary current cost accounts, or they could present current cost accounts as the main accounts with supplementary historical cost accounts, or they could present current cost accounts as the only accounts 'accompanied by adequate historical cost information'.[180]

SSAP 16 perpetuated the concept of current cost operating profit based on the maintenance of physical capital, which had been extended to monetary working capital through the monetary working capital adjustment. The associated gearing adjustment probably arose as a result of the ASC's need to compromise with its critics in order to find an acceptable solution – as opposed to having any theoretically sound justification. On the other hand, in the US SFAS 33 – *Financial Reporting and Changing Prices* – which was issued in September 1979, required the disclosure of real holding gains and losses on net monetary items and physical assets (inventory and property, plant and equipment) after eliminating the effects of general inflation.[181] In December 1986, SFAS 33 was superseded by SFAS 89 – *Financial Reporting and Changing Prices* – which encourages (but does not require) the disclosure of supplementary information on the effects of changing prices, suggesting similar disclosures to those of SFAS 33 in respect of holding gains and losses.[182] Clearly, therefore, the FASB has adopted the concept of financial capital maintenance, and its commitment to this concept is borne out in Concepts Statement No. 5[183] (see 3.5 above). However, this is not to say that the FASB has found the solution to accounting for the effects of changing prices; SFAS 89 is, in several other respects, a somewhat nebulous and inconclusive standard.

At the time that SSAP 16 was issued, the ASC stated that it was its intention, as far as possible, 'to make no change to SSAP 16 for three years so as to enable producers and users to gain experience in dealing with practical problems and interpreting the information'. However, this statement probably contributed to the eventual demise of the standard, because it was taken as an intention that it would inevitably be revised at the end of the three year period and allowed SSAP 16 to be characterised as 'experimental' or 'provisional'.[184] Over the next few years, there was a continuing decline in the level of compliance with the standard.

In July 1984, the ASC issued a further exposure draft ED 35 – *Accounting for the effects of changing prices*. This restricted the scope of the proposals to public companies which were neither value-based enterprises nor wholly owned subsidiaries, but in respect of these it sought to make CCA a mandatory feature of the primary financial statements (rather than in supplementary statements), declaring that the inclusion of this information was essential to a true and fair view. However, it soon became clear that these proposals could not command general acceptance, and the exposure draft was withdrawn in early 1985.

Soon afterwards, in the face of increasing opposition to the standard, the CCAB bodies voted to make SSAP 16 non-mandatory, and it was later completely withdrawn. The ASC persisted for some months to try to find a viable successor, seeking a more flexible approach and abandoning the proposition that it was essential to a true and fair view in the primary financial statements, but eventually gave up the search. Instead, it published *Accounting for the effects of changing prices: a Handbook*,[185] which was based on various of its earlier pronouncements on the subject together with some of its more recent, hitherto unpublished material. This was its last publication on accounting for changing prices, and although it never completely took the topic off its agenda, there were no further moves to develop a fresh statement on the subject. Interest in the topic among companies in the private sector also remains low; few companies now offer any CCA information to readers of their financial statements.

It might be argued that activities described in this section provide evidence for the view that accounting standard setting is a process of establishing convention in response to the needs of the times. The high inflation rates of the late 1970s and early 1980s drove both practitioners and academics to undertake various studies and produce a number of recommendations. Since inflation has ceased to be a concern, interest in this problem has noticeably waned.

4.4   The Macve Report

As a consequence of the written submissions received in response to its consultative document 'Setting Accounting Standards' (see 1.3 above), the ASC commissioned Professor Richard Macve to 'review critically current literature and opinion in the UK, US and elsewhere with a view to forming preliminary conclusions as to the possibilities of developing an agreed conceptual framework for setting accounting standards and the nature of such a framework; and to identify areas for further research'.[186]

Macve's report – *A Conceptual Framework for Financial Accounting and Reporting: the possibilities for an agreed structure* – was published in August 1981. As would be expected from his terms of reference, Macve concentrated his efforts on evaluating selected conceptual framework projects and studies, focusing in particular on the Corporate Report and the FASB's conceptual framework project. His discussions centred around the problems that arise in determining profit and net assets, and these he related to the difficulties involved in establishing what constitutes useful accounting information. He further highlighted the fact that the variety of user needs and conflicts of interest between different parties were likely to cause disagreement as to what information financial statements should provide.[187] On this issue, he came to the conclusion that 'recognition of the variety of user needs and of conflicts between different interests and different rights leads to the view that reaching agreement on the form and content of financial statements is as much a "political" process, a search for compromise between different parties, as it is a search for the methods which are "technically" best'.[188]

As far as the FASB's conceptual project was concerned, Macve concluded his review by saying that 'given the difficulties experienced in arriving at "useful" definitions of the elements of profit and loss accounts and balance sheets, it seems to me likely that the continuing attempts to develop "recognition criteria" and "measurement rules", that can both command general acceptance and have an impact on individual accounting disputes in relation to profit and net asset calculation, will be similarly unsuccessful'.[189] Bearing in mind that this comment was made prior to the FASB's publication in December 1984 of SFAC No. 5 – *Recognition and Measurement in Financial Statements of Business Enterprises* – his fears were later to be proved well founded. However, the FASB's failure to deal effectively with the recognition and measurement issues can be largely attributed to the fact that they were limited by the definitions of the elements of financial statements given in SFAC No. 3. On the other hand, SFAC No. 3 shows clear evidence of the compromise as a result of the 'political process' referred to by Macve.

Macve concluded his study by putting forward several suggestions for further research. As might have been expected, these centred around the need for further empirical study in various areas – such as the economic significance of accounting measures and the ways in which financial statements are used by the various classes of user – all of which might lead to a better understanding of the form and content of financial statements. However, what was probably the most practical suggestion was for the study of the process of introducing changes in accounting practice.[190] Clearly, no matter how theoretically sound proposed changes in reporting practice might be, standard-setting bodies will be faced with resistance not only from those groups who believe that their economic interests will be prejudiced by the changes, but also from those who resist change in whatever form it might take.

However, the ASC did not demonstrate any apparent inclination to pursue Macve's proposals for further research with noticeable fervour, and allowed his report to fade slowly into the background. It was not until the publication in January 1989 of the Solomons Report[191] that the ASC displayed any evidence that they were actively seeking conceptual guidelines to assist them in the standard-setting process (see 4.7 below).

4.5   The Stamp Report

In 1980, Professor Edward Stamp produced a research study primarily for the Canadian Institute of Chartered Accountants which was 'intended to provide a Canadian solution to the problem of improving the quality of corporate financial reporting standards'.[192] Stamp adopted a similar approach to that of other studies (such as the Corporate Report and Trueblood) by looking at users, their needs, their rights to information and the qualitative characteristics of that information. Stamp identified a more detailed list of users (15 in all) than did, for example, the Corporate or Sandilands Reports. However, to a large extent his list merely broke down broad categories of users into smaller groups; for example, the Corporate Report identifies the 'business contact group' as a single user group (which includes suppliers, customers, competitors and business rivals),[193] whilst Stamp lists 'customers, suppliers, industry groups, and other companies' as individual groups.[194]

Stamp then developed a set of 20 qualitative criteria which could be used as yardsticks whereby standard-setters, as well as the preparers and users of published financial statements, can decide whether or not the financial statements are meeting the objectives of financial reporting and the needs of users. An interesting rider to this aspect of Stamp's study was that he subsequently used his list of qualitative criteria as the basis of an empirical study of the ASC members' assessment of the relative importance of each of the criteria.[195] Stamp supplied each member of the ASC with a copy of Chapter 7 of his CICA research study in which the significance and meaning of each of the 20 criteria were discussed. He also gave them each a questionnaire in which they were asked to rank the 20 criteria in order of importance.[196]   Although the ranking revealed 'relevance' as the most important criterion and 'conservatism' as the least important this, in itself, was not the most significant aspect of Stamp's study; what was significant was the fact that he was able to demonstrate that it would be possible to establish rankings of characteristics of accounting information for each category of user.   Such information, if combined with research into the objectives and information needs of the same groups of user, would provide a basis for determining whether or not differential standards of reporting should be developed for different categories of user.

In his CICA research study, Stamp also devoted a considerable amount of effort towards discussing certain fundamental conceptual issues; these included the problems of allocation, income measurement, capital maintenance, as well as the issue of the proprietary versus the entity theory and the question of which attribute accounting should measure.[197]   On certain of the problems which he discussed, Stamp concluded by saying that they were 'irresolvable'; for example, the goodwill problem associated with using the balance sheet as a measure of the current worth of an enterprise.   These issues are all fundamental to the development of a conceptual framework for financial reporting; however, as was seen at 3 above, none was unequivocally resolved by the FASB in its framework project.

Stamp concluded his study by recommending that further research be carried out in various areas of user needs and decision-making processes, including (as did the Corporate Report) the investigation of and experimentation with multi-column reporting.[198]

4.6   The ICAS discussion document: 'Making Corporate Reports Valuable'

4.6.1   Background to the study

This discussion document, which was issued in 1988, was the product of a major research project undertaken by the Research Committee of the ICAS. However, it is vital that it is seen and evaluated taking into account the spirit in which it had been prepared; namely, for the purpose of stimulating discussion and experimentation.[199]   The reason why this paper was so refreshing revolved principally around the fact that the research committee started from the basis of a 'clean sheet'. In other words, the members were able to ignore existing laws, accounting rules, terminology and all other constraints in order to try and achieve what they believed to be the best result.   Clearly, this approach had widespread practical implications for the ultimate implementation of any proposals made.   This was recognised by the committee, and the document noted some of the implications of its suggestions.[200]

The Committee started off by explaining what motivated it to reconsider the nature of corporate reporting. The reasons which were given included the following basic conclusions:

- all financial reports ought to reflect economic reality;

- the information which investors need is the same in kind, but not in volume, as the information which managements need to run their entities;

- some of the information that management has but does not normally communicate comes out into the open when management wants something – such as additional capital or to be able to defend a hostile take-over bid;

- present-day financial reports are deficient in that they are based on legal form rather than economic substance, on cost rather than value, on the past rather than the future, and on 'profit' rather than 'wealth';

- there is no consistent conceptual basis underlying the production of either the profit and loss account or the balance sheet, and some of the concepts used appear to defy normal understanding of financial affairs;

- corporate reports are not made public sufficiently speedily; and

- the audit report is insufficiently informative and is often incomprehensible to non-auditors.[201]

4.6.2   *Users and their needs*

The committee then considered who are the users of financial reports and what are their informational needs. In so doing, it referred to the Corporate Report, concluding that corporate reporting should aim to communicate directly to only four of the groups identified in that report. These were identified as:

(a)   the equity investor group;

(b)   the loan creditor group;

(c)   the employee group; and

(d)   the business contact group (which includes ordinary creditors).[202]

Having identified these four groups of users, the committee listed the following five fundamental information needs of these groups which external corporate reports should be able to contribute to meeting:

(a)   knowledge of the corporate objectives of the entity, and information which would enable users to evaluate the entity's performance against these objectives;

(b)   a comparison of the total wealth of the entity now as against what it was at the time of the last corporate report, together with an explanation of the reasons for change;

(c)   the ability to judge where the entity is going in the future and whether it has the necessary financial and other resources to do so;

(d)   adequate information about the economic environment within which the entity has been and will be operating; and

(e)   knowledge of the ownership and control of the entity and the experience and background of its directors and officials.[203]

As the Committee pointed out, these proposals were a digest of the information needs of the equity investor group identified in the Corporate Report.[204] The Committee suggested further that, in order to enable users to judge the reliability of management's planning based on past period performance, they should also be given information on:

(a)   the entity's actual performance for the accounting period just past as compared with its previously published plan for that period;

(b)   management's explanations of any significant variances between the two; and

(c)   management's financial plan for the current and future accounting periods, together with explanations of the major assumptions used in preparing it.[205]

Clearly, these additional proposals were designed to provide information on how management of an entity had discharged its stewardship responsibility to owners and, as the Committee suggested, this assessment should be based on earnings information and entity performance.

4.6.3   *Valuation of assets and liabilities*

The Committee then discussed various bases for applying values to assets, focusing on historical cost, current replacement cost, current net realisable values and economic values. It is necessary to read the full text of the discussion document in order to appreciate properly the basis for the Committee's conclusions; however, having discussed what it saw as the deficiencies of historical cost and economic value, the Committee noted that current replacement cost and net realisable value both met its criteria of economic reality and 'additivity' (i.e. the total number in a statement should not mean something different in kind from its constituent numbers). Nevertheless, the Committee expressed a preference for net realisable value as the basis for applying values to assets, 'principally because it is value-based whereas replacement cost is cost-based',[206] and it was felt that 'value rather than cost is important in assessing financial wealth'.[207]

It is in this area that the paper is most open to criticism and debate. For example, the Committee dismissed replacement cost accounting by citing the problems associated with it, without giving equal consideration to the problems associated with net realisable value accounting. The problems attributed to the use of replacement costs were as follows:

'(a)   there is an assumption that assets will be replaced, which is frequently not the case;

(b) there are significant practical problems in assessing replacement values if there have been improvements in technology; and

(c) arbitrary depreciation allocations are still required.'[208]

Whilst there can be no dispute that these are valid points, there are equally several practical and theoretical problems surrounding net realisable value accounting (see 4.3.2 above for a more detailed discussion of both models). For example, should net realisable values be based on the assumption that assets are realised in an orderly manner, or should they be based on immediate liquidation prices? Furthermore, there is the whole question of whether or not net realisable values do, in fact, necessarily measure the financial wealth of a going concern; for example, what about the case of plant which has negligible realisable value but significant use value? This also raises the further issue of how compatible are net realisable values with the qualitative characteristics of accounting information – particularly with respect to the primary quality of relevance.

In addition, it is noteworthy that the literature surveys,[209] which were commissioned by the ICAS Research Committee in order to identify key issues for consideration in the production of the discussion paper, reached the following conclusion on using net realisable values (NRVs) as the main basis for financial accounting: 'generally, the literature suggests that there is a strong case for the publication of NRV based figures as supplementary accounting information, as important information on liquidity, and on the adaptability of entities, is given which is not provided by the competing valuation bases. ... However, the arguments for the adoption of NRVs as the main valuation base of financial reports are uncompelling. The arguments against this, and in particular the lack of relevance of NRVs for many assets in most situations, are substantial. The income statement is likely to be misleading. One development which may be worthy of consideration is the publication of, possible supplementary, balance sheets based on net realisable values and income statements based on replacement costs or some other valuation base.'[210]

4.6.4   *The proposed new information package*

Despite the conclusions reached in the literature surveys, the Committee proposed an entirely new information package, using net realisable values as the basis of valuation. In order to present the financial wealth of an entity, the Committee proposed that the following four basic statements should replace the existing financial statements:

(a) *Assets and Liabilities Statement*, which would present the assets and liabilities of the entity at the reporting date, each stated at its net realisable value. Net realisable values would normally be determined according to the principle of orderly disposal, unless the entity is in financial trouble, in which case 'a more appropriate method' (such as break-up values) should be used;[211]

(b)   *Operations Statement*, which calculates the financial wealth added to the entity by trading and by its operations generally. It differs from the present form of profit and loss account in that:

   (i)   there would be no depreciation charge,

   (ii)   the stock would be accounted for at net realisable value, and

   (iii) the only exceptional or extraordinary items would be those arising out of unusual events of a revenue nature; exceptional or extraordinary gains or losses on fixed assets would be dealt with in the Statement of Changes in Financial Wealth outlined at (c) below;[212]

(c)   *Statement of Changes in Financial Wealth*, which shows the change in the worth of the business for the period under consideration, such change being split into its main components with an indication of how each of these arose. The Committee proposed that the change in wealth would be measured in terms of year-end pounds, although 'in times of significant inflation it may be helpful if investors can be given an indication of the real change in financial wealth over the period concerned by applying the retail price index';[213] and

(d)   *Distributions Statement*, which reflects the distributable change in financial wealth for the period plus any surpluses retained from previous periods, less dividends paid and proposed. In times of rising prices the 'real value' of capital should be maintained by an inflation adjustment which should be shown in the distributions statement and might be computed by applying the retail price index to the value of shareholders' contributed capital as at the start of the period. The paper went on to say that entities wishing to maintain their operating capability in physical terms could make a further appropriation to maintain the asset portfolio or to provide for the replacement of the services which these assets have been supplying.[214]

4.6.5 Additional information

In addition to the four basic statements and the information relating to corporate objectives and future financial plans discussed under 4.6.2 above, the Committee suggested the inclusion of the following additional information in the reporting package:

(a)   a Cash Flow Statement showing the inflow and outflow of cash broken down into its main components, dealing with the current period and going three years forward.[215] This proposal was, for obvious reasons, somewhat controversial – particularly in the light of the recommendation that management should explain forecast variances (see 4.6.2 above);

(b)   segmental information split by product, by manufacturing location, geographically and by currency;[216]

(c)   information on related parties;

(d)   information on accounting areas subject to uncertainty, for example management's view on the margin of error in accounting estimates;

(e)   a statement on relative innovation which would illustrate the stance that the company is adopting in relation to innovation. In other words, the statement will show the proportion of production that is new and conceived internally or self-generated, and will compare this with that of its competitors;

(f)   information on effectiveness and lead-time of research and development;

(g)   information on the economic environment within which the entity operates, including an analysis of facts such as market share, market strength, market size, the activities of competitors etc.;

(h)   comparative operational statistics 'culled from similar statements by its competitors or other entities in similar markets';[217]

(i)   information on staff resources; and

(j)   information on ownership, management and their responsibilities.

The Committee also made the interesting suggestion that reports should be arranged on the basis of 'layering'.[218] In other words, each statement would start with the simplest possible presentation of the main factors, and as the user works through the information, it can be called down in layers of increasing complexity and detail.

4.6.6   *Conclusion*

This was one of the boldest, most innovative and refreshing discussion documents to be published by a professional body for a long time, exposing the several weaknesses of present day financial reporting practice. Of course it has flaws and can be criticised for either failing to address or inadequately addressing certain issues; however, it should be seen for what it was – a document designed to stimulate discussion, experimentation and further research. Nevertheless, there was always the danger that the document would be regarded as too revolutionary in its approach, and be dismissed as being an amusing intellectual exercise.

The ICAS Research Committee countered this criticism by undertaking a number of case studies in which the principles of *Making Corporate Reports Valuable* (MCRV) were put into practice by live companies, one of which has been published using the code name 'Melody plc'.[219] This was followed by a feasibility study involving the Post Office, which was carried out in order to demonstrate that the MCRV proposals for the reform of corporate reporting would be relevant to any commercial enterprise, operating in either the private or public sector.[220] However, as might be expected, the exercise brought to light some problems of implementing MCRV recommendations, particularly in respect of identifying the potential users of financial statements published by a public sector enterprise.

The ICAS research committee has also collaborated with its counterpart in the ICAEW to develop further proposals on the basis of both MCRV and the Solomons Report (see 4.7 and 4.8 below).

More importantly, though, it is now becoming increasingly clear that the ASB's current agenda of accounting reform is drawing heavily on MCRV for its inspiration and guidance. It is no coincidence that Sir David Tweedie was a member of the MCRV Committee, and it is not difficult to find similarities between the MCRV conclusions and the ASB's current proposals. One obvious example being the Statement of Changes in Financial Wealth, which has been effectively adopted in FRS 3 as the Statement of Total Recognised Gains and Losses.

4.7   The Solomons Report

In May 1987, the Research Board of the ICAEW announced that it had decided to sponsor a project to address the need for guidelines for decisions in financial reporting; the project had been originally inspired by Professor Bryan Carsberg when he was the ICAEW's Director of Research, and Professor David Solomons, a recently retired academic, agreed to carry out the study. One of the reasons for commissioning the work was that respondents to ASC exposure drafts had frequently commented that, until an agreed conceptual framework had been developed, it would be difficult to achieve either consistency in approach towards setting accounting standards, or resolution of certain of the fundamental accounting issues which were being encountered in practice. This was later echoed by the Dearing Committee, which concluded that 'the lack of a conceptual framework is a handicap to those involved in setting accounting standards as well as to those applying them'.[221]

Solomons followed what has become an almost traditional approach to a study of this nature; perhaps not surprisingly considering that he acted as consultant to the FASB on its conceptual framework project and was principal author of SFAC No. 2. He started by examining the purposes of financial reporting, identifying users and how their needs were at present being met. His report then discussed the elements of financial statements and decided upon the asset and liability rather than the revenue and expense approach to financial accounting. The report stated that although 'there is no prospect of proving that one of these views is right and the other wrong, it is possible to find reasons for preferring one view to the other, and these Guidelines will be uncompromisingly based on the asset and liability view'.[222]

Solomons' principal argument against the revenue and expense view of income determination was that it 'opens the door to all kinds of income smoothing'[223] and that it 'threatens the integrity of the balance sheet and its value as a useful financial statement. Its value is maximized if it can be seen as a statement of financial position; but it can only be that if all the items in it are truly assets, liabilities, and equity, and not other bits left over from the profit and loss account, and if all such items that are capable of being recognised are included in it.'[224]

Having established that he would be following an asset and liability approach, Solomons then set about defining the elements of financial statements on much the same basis as was done in SFAC No. 6 (see 3.4 above). Assets are defined as 'resources or rights incontestably controlled by an entity at the accounting date that are expected to yield it future economic benefits',[225] whilst liabilities are defined as 'obligations of an entity at the accounting date to make future transfers of assets or services (sometimes uncertain as to timing and amount) to other entities'.[226] All the other elements are then derived from these basic definitions; for example, owners' equity comprises net assets and income is the change in net assets.[227]

The Report then ran quickly through the qualitative characteristics of accounting information, giving what might be viewed as a summarised version of SFAC No. 2 (see 3.3 above). Thereafter he focused his attention on the issues of recognition and measurement and the choice of an accounting model for use in preparing general purpose financial statements. In view of the fact that Solomons' guidelines are based on the asset and liability view, it is not surprising that his recognition criteria concentrate on these two elements. Consequently, under Solomons' approach, an item should only be recognised in financial statements if:

'(a)   it conforms to the definition of an asset or liability or of one of the sub-elements derived therefrom; and

(b)   its magnitude as specified by the accounting model being used can be measured and verified with reasonable certainty; and

(c)   the magnitude so arrived at is material in amount'.[228]

Solomons then examined the present historical cost accounting model which is generally accepted in the UK, listing its deficiencies and pointing out that it is not a true historical cost model (as a result, for example, of asset revaluations and the translation of monetary assets and liabilities designated in foreign currencies at closing rates). Thereafter, he set about devising an improved model for general purpose financial reporting, and listed the following five criteria that such an improved model should possess:

(a)   the balance sheet should be a true and fair statement of an entity's financial condition, showing all its assets and liabilities that satisfy the above recognition criteria and conform with the asset and liability definitions;

(b)   the entity's assets and liabilities should be carried in the balance sheet at their value to a going concern at the balance sheet date;

(c)   profits or losses should mean increases or decreases of real financial capital as compared with the amount at the beginning of the year;

(d)   the results shown by the financial statements should be measured consistently and should therefore be comparable from year to year, both in periods of fluctuating prices and stable prices; and

(e)   all the information given by the financial statements should be verifiable and cost-effective.[229]

(In a subsequent posthumous publication entitled *Commentary: criteria for choosing an accounting model*[230] the number of criteria is expanded to seven, the extra two being essentially clarifications of the meanings of the original five.)

Solomons then attempted to prove that the model which best satisfies these requirements rests on two concepts: value to the business (as espoused by the Corporate Report and Sandilands Committee) and the maintenance of real financial capital.   Although these may have some intellectual appeal, it is difficult to see whether either of them has any practical meaning. Solomons sees an asset's value to the business as being the loss that the business would suffer if it were deprived of the asset; since, if deprived of an asset, the business would normally seek to replace it, replacement cost would determine value to the business.   However, Solomons recognises that circumstances exist where an asset's value to the business might be less than its replacement cost; for example, in the case of a plant asset which is technologically inferior to an equivalent new asset, the current cost of replacing the services rendered by the existing asset should be used.   Furthermore, where an asset would not be replaced by a business if it were lost, its value to the business would be its recoverable amount, which is the higher of the asset's present value and its net realisable value.   Therefore, Solomons' final formula for value to the business is that it is equal to 'current cost or recoverable amount, if that is lower'.[231]

In the case of liabilities, the equivalent to an asset's deprival value is a liability's relief value.   In other words, liabilities would be valued at the amount that the entity 'could currently raise by the issue of a precisely similar debt security or the cost of discharging the liability by the most economical means, whichever is the higher'.[232]

Solomons ended his discussion on 'value to the business' by referring to the ICAS discussion document – *Making Corporate Reports Valuable* – and explains why he believes net realisable values to be irrelevant, resulting in net realisable value accounting being unsuitable for general purpose financial statements.

As mentioned above, Solomons' model is based on the maintenance of real financial capital, with income being defined in terms of the change in net worth. However, because of the uncertainty surrounding the measurement and verification of intangible assets, the changes in such assets cannot be recognised in financial statements; consequently, income will only include changes in recognised tangible assets minus changes in recognised liabilities.[233]   Solomons describes his income model as a 'current-cost-constant-purchasing-power model', differing in a number of respects from the SSAP 16 model. First, it recognises both changes in the general level of prices and changes in specific prices and, second, it is based on the maintenance of real financial capital, not operating capacity.[234] It therefore does not require SSAP 16's unpopular gearing and monetary working capital adjustments. The following pro forma profit and loss account illustrates how Solomons' version of real income is derived:[235]

Pro forma profit and loss account as proposed by Solomons

			£
Sales revenue			xxx
Current cost (or lower recoverable amount) of goods sold			xxx
			xxx
Depreciation at current cost		xxx	
Other expenses		xxx	
			xxx
Current operating profit			xxx
Add:			
Holding gains less losses on non-monetary assets (net of inflation)		xxx	
Purchasing power gains on monetary liabilities less purchasing power losses on monetary assets		xxx	
			xxx
Real income			xxx

In an appendix to his report, Solomons discusses five specific accounting issues: deferred tax, pensions, financial commitments, goodwill and the recognition of the time value of money. Although it is beyond the scope of this Chapter to discuss the contents of the appendix in detail, there are one or two interesting points worth noting. In the case of deferred tax, Solomons builds up an argument against both the partial approach adopted by SSAP 15 and the non-recognition of deferred tax assets. Using accounts payable as an illustration of liabilities which are continually being paid off and replaced, he argues that non-replacement should not be the criterion for recognition of deferred tax liabilities. Similarly, in respect of deferred tax assets he asserts that, as is the case with accounts receivable and depreciable assets, deferred tax benefits, if expected to be recovered, with or without replacement, should be recognised as assets.[236]

As has been mentioned above, one of the consequences of the asset and liability approach proposed, for example, by both the IASC (see 6.1 below) and

Solomons results in a conflict with the generally accepted accounting practice of accounting for pensions under SSAP 24. It is therefore not surprising that this is one of the specific areas discussed by Solomons in the appendix to his report, in which he lays down a number of principles that deviate significantly from SSAP 24's approach. For example, if all or most of the assets of a pension plan can be freely moved back to the employer from the plan by a vote of the trustees, then the affairs of the plan should be consolidated with those of the employer. This approach is based on the view that a pension fund is, in effect, an off balance sheet vehicle set up to meet a company's future obligations.

Whilst this view might have considerable theoretical merit, the practical implications make Solomons' proposal completely unworkable; the reason being that each time the pension fund has an actuarial valuation, the slightest variation in the assumptions (which, by their nature, are highly volatile and imprecise) will have an unacceptable impact on the profit and loss account, the effect of which has no real bearing on operating performance or current wealth. Interestingly enough, though, Solomons' proposal is close to what has recently been adopted by the IASC in IAS 19 (Revised) – *Employee Benefits*. The only differences are that: (a) IAS 19 has introduced a smoothing mechanism, whereby actuarial gains and losses only need to be reflected in the profit and loss account if they fall outside a 10% 'corridor', and (b) the pension fund assets and employee obligations are shown in the balance sheet in net terms.

On the subject of goodwill, Solomons states that non-purchased goodwill should not be recognised; his reason for this being that 'determining the value of goodwill where it is not the subject of a purchase and sale transaction and in the presence of a highly imperfect market is too subjective to yield a reliable measure for the purpose of recognition'.[237] What he is saying, is that since non-purchased goodwill does not have an historical cost, it is not possible to update an unknown cost in order to determine its current cost. The same argument applies to all internally generated intangibles, such as brand names.

The Research Board of the ICAEW thereafter worked along with its ICAS counterpart to see what practical initiatives might be developed on the basis of both the Guidelines and the ICAS project 'Making Corporate Reports Valuable' (see 4.6 above), and this resulted in the publication of a joint paper, *The Future Shape of Financial Reports* which is discussed below.

4.8   The Future Shape of Financial Reports

In 1991, the ICAS Research Committee and the ICAEW Research Board jointly published a discussion paper with the above title. This was essentially an amalgam of the ideas in MCRV and the Solomons Report which they had previously published separately and which are discussed at 4.6 and 4.7 above. The main points covered in *The Future Shape of Financial Reports* are summarised below.

The authors of the paper start by identifying two purposes of financial reporting: (a) to provide information to shareholders, lenders and others to appraise past performance in order to form expectations about an organisation's future performance and hence, to inform their decisions concerning their relationships with the organisation; and (b) to enable the enforcement of contracts, the terms of which include reference to accounting information. The paper identified the first of these as their primary concern.[238]

Next, the paper identified what it considered to be five main defects of existing reporting practice:

- the predominant use of historical costs;
- excessive emphasis on earnings per share;
- insufficient emphasis on cash and liquidity;
- too much focus on the past rather than the future; and
- too much emphasis on legal form rather than economic substance.[239]

The paper went on to suggest that an improved reporting package would comprise the following elements:

- a statement of objectives and related strategic plan;
- a statement of assets and liabilities;
- an income statement;
- a gains statement;
- a cash flow statement; and
- information on future prospects.

The key to how some of these statements were to be assembled lies in the measurement basis suggested. Here, the authors of the paper clearly had some difficulty, because the predecessor papers had proposed different valuation approaches; MCRV had favoured exit-values, while Solomons had favoured current cost. The rather unsatisfactory result was that the paper advocated an 'eclectic' approach, choosing different approaches for different assets according to their particular characteristics, perhaps on the basis that *any* basis of current valuation is better than historical cost, but neglecting to recognise that the different methods have quite different purposes. The inherent vagueness of this idea then spread to the discussion of where gains and losses should be recorded; the paper says that 'in considering the change in value of assets carried at current values, changes due to the consumption of the asset should be shown as depreciation in the income statement. Other causes of changes in value should be charged or credited to the statement of gains.'[240] However, this rather glib suggestion does not begin to explore the issues involved or the purpose of the various statements presented.

While the paper's exhortations to challenge conventional wisdom are of some value, it has not in our view made a coherent contribution to the future development of financial statements. In particular, the appeal to an 'eclectic' approach to measurement seems more like a compromise than an attempt to devise a consistent principle on which accounts should be based.

5   THE ASB'S STATEMENT OF PRINCIPLES

5.1   Introduction

In contrast to its predecessor, the ASB made it clear from the outset that it intended to pursue the idea of a conceptual framework to underpin its standards, although it avoided the use of the term, preferring the less daunting phrase 'Statement of Principles'. In its *Foreword to Accounting Standards*, the ASB stated that 'FRSs are based on the Statement of Principles for Financial Reporting currently in issue, which addresses the concepts underlying the information presented in financial statements. The objective of this *Statement of Principles* is to provide a framework for the consistent and logical formulation of individual accounting standards. The framework also provides a basis on which others can exercise judgement in resolving accounting issues.'[241]

As it turns out, such claims concerning the *Statement of Principles* have been made somewhat prematurely. The ASB issued its *Statement of Principles for Financial Reporting* in exposure draft form in November 1995[242] and then effectively withdrew it in July 1996 following overwhelming criticism from commentators, stating that 'the Board has concluded that it would not be appropriate to proceed directly to the development of a final document'.[243] A revised exposure draft in 1997 was promised, but was actually published in March 1999.[244] The two drafts espouse similar principles, though the revised draft has been careful to attempt to settle some of the anxieties raised by the first, particularly those concerning current values. There is a noticeable change in tone between the two drafts which is further discussed below. Because of the potential impact of the ASB's conceptual framework project on GAAP, both drafts are dealt with, in some detail, in chronological order, referring to the first draft *Statement of Principles* as SoP1 and the second as SoP2.

The SoP1 comprised a compendium of seven chapters, all of which had previously been issued by the ASB in draft form on a piecemeal basis. The seven chapters are as follows, and are discussed at 5.2 to 5.8 below:

1.   The objective of financial statements
2.   The qualitative characteristics of financial information
3.   The elements of financial statements
4.   Recognition in financial statements
5.   Measurement in financial statements
6.   Presentation of financial information
7.   The reporting entity.

5.2   SoP1 Chapter 1: The objective of financial statements

The ASB acknowledged that, in drafting the *Statement of Principles*, it was drawing heavily on the work of previous projects in other countries, notably the FASB concept statements discussed at 3 above and the IASC Framework discussed at 6.1 below. This is particularly true of the early chapters of the ASB's work. Chapter 1, therefore, starts with the familiar statement that 'the objective of financial statements is to provide information about the financial position, performance and financial adaptability of an enterprise that is useful to a wide range of users for assessing the stewardship of management and for making economic decisions'.[245]

The term 'financial adaptability' is one which is used by a number of standard-setters in this context. It is described by the ASB as being 'the ability of an enterprise to take effective action to alter the amount and timing of its cash flows so that it can respond to unexpected events and opportunities.'[246] As an objective of financial reporting it seems both desirable and commendable that enterprises should strive to provide the information necessary for users to assess 'financial adaptability'. However, the question is whether it is really feasible for enterprises to do so in practice and, if it is, what this information would comprise. The chapter goes on to state, somewhat obviously, that 'All the primary financial statements provide information that is useful in evaluating the financial adaptability of the enterprise'.[247]

A familiar list of possible users is also identified, comprising investors, employees, lenders, suppliers and other creditors, customers, government and their agencies and the public.[248] However, the chapter then narrows down the focus by saying that all users 'have some interest in the financial position, performance and financial adaptability of the enterprise as a whole. Financial statements that meet the needs of providers of risk capital to the enterprise will also meet most of the needs of other users that financial statements can satisfy.'[249]

In essence, therefore, the investor's perspective is chosen as the one most likely to be useful in the preparation of what will remain general purpose financial statements. Having established this generalisation, the chapter then goes on to assert that 'the economic decisions that are taken by users of financial statements require an evaluation of the enterprise's ability to generate cash and the timing and certainty of its generation', and that the 'evaluation of the ability to generate cash is assisted by focusing on the enterprise's financial position, performance and cash flows and using these in predicting expected cash flows and assessing financial adaptability'.[250]

5.3   SoP1 Chapter 2: The qualitative characteristics of financial information

In this chapter, the ASB has again adhered closely to the work of earlier framework projects, all of which have been heavily influenced by the FASB's SFAC No. 2. As did the FASB, the ASB has presented the inter-relationship of its qualitative characteristics in diagrammatic form. This diagram is repeated with slight adjustments in the revised draft, though timeliness disappears as a constraint upon qualitative characteristics. It is shown in section 5.14 below.

The ASB confirms relevance and reliability as the two primary characteristics of accounting information, and again recognises that they are sometimes in conflict, so as to require a trade-off between them. Relevant information is that which influences 'the decisions of users by helping them evaluate past, present or future events or confirming, or correcting, their past evaluations'.[251] Reliable information is that which is 'free from material error and bias and can be depended upon by users to represent faithfully what it either purports to represent or could reasonably be expected to represent'.[252]

The primary characteristics are supported by two main secondary characteristics: comparability and understandability. Comparability embraces notions of consistent application of accounting methods throughout an enterprise and through time, as well as the ability to compare one enterprise with another, which implies adequate disclosure of accounting policies – together with changes in policies and the effects of such changes – as well as adherence to accounting standards.[253] Understandability requires clear presentation of the information, but the chapter comments that it would not be appropriate to omit important but complex information from accounts merely on the grounds that it may be too difficult for certain users to understand.[254] This way of looking at understandability arguably confuses the ability to interpret a set of accounts with the ability to understand its implications.

The chapter also refers to materiality as a 'threshold quality', i.e. one that needs to be considered first, because if information is immaterial, the other characteristics do not matter. Material information is information whose omission or mis-statement could influence the economic decisions of users taken on the basis of the financial statements.[255] The important question, however, is against which yardstick information should be judged to be material or immaterial.

The difficulty which arises is that the many different users of the financial statements cannot be consulted by the preparer to discover what is material to them; the preparer must make that assessment on their behalf. Moreover, some users might have unreasonable expectations of the accuracy of financial statements, and it would not be possible to set materiality at a level which could accommodate their wishes. According to the ASB, 'aspects of the nature of the item that affect a judgement about its materiality include the events and transactions giving rise to it and the particular financial statement headings and disclosures that are affected. Circumstances that are considered include other elements of the financial statements taken as a whole and other information available to users that would affect their evaluation of the financial statements: this involves, for example, a consideration of the implications of the item for the evaluation of trends. Where there are two or more similar items, the materiality of the aggregate as well as the individual items needs to be considered.'[256]

5.4 SoP1 Chapter 3: The elements of financial statements

The following seven elements are defined in the chapter: Assets, Liabilities, Ownership Interest, Gains, Losses, Contributions from Owners, Distributions to Owners.

5.4.1 Assets

Assets are defined as 'rights or other access to future economic benefits controlled by an entity as a result of past transactions or events'.[257] This is obviously based on the equivalent definition in SFAC 6 (see 3.4.1 above), except that the US statement refers to *probable* future economic benefits rather than *rights or other access to* future economic benefits. By using the phrase 'rights or other access', the ASB is emphasising that what constitutes an asset is not a particular item of property itself, but rather the rights deriving from ownership or other rights of occupation and use.[258] This definition, seeking as it does to alter the natural meaning of the word 'asset' (which does indeed refer to the item itself) presents serious logical difficulties that are discussed at 5.15.1 below. This definition also implies that the ability to enjoy benefits does not necessarily require an ownership interest, and the phrase 'rights or other access' is also broad enough to imply that the benefits may be uncertain, so the word 'probable' is not needed.

'Control' in the context of the definition of an asset means the ability to obtain the economic benefits and to restrict the access of others.[259] The chapter goes on to explain that 'items that cannot be separately identified from the business as a whole cannot be individually controlled by the entity and hence are not assets'.[260] It is for this reason that certain items of deferred expenditure – such as pre-opening, advertising and staff training costs – which could, under existing GAAP, be carried forward in the balance sheet under the matching concept would not be regarded by the ASB as meeting the definition of an asset and would be required to be expensed immediately.

5.4.2 Liabilities

Liabilities are defined as 'obligations of an entity to transfer economic benefits as a result of past transactions or events'.[261] Here, the wording is much shorter than the US equivalent (see 3.4.2 above) but the main features of the definition appear to be the same. Again, it is the application of this definition which is already having a fundamental impact on UK GAAP. For example, FRS 12 –

Provisions, Contingent Liabilities and Contingent Assets – published in September 1998 relies heavily on this definition to severely restrict the circumstances under which provisions can be recognised. This is because provisions are not seen as a separate element of financial statements and, instead, are defined as being a subset of liabilities (see Chapter 25). Similarly, FRS 7's strict criteria for the recognition of provisions, as part of the determination of the fair values of the assets and liabilities in an acquisition, stem from this definition.

5.4.3   Ownership interest

Ownership interest is defined as being 'the residual amount found by deducting all the entity's liabilities from all the entity's assets'.[262] Again the wording is similar to that used in SFAC 6. The logic of the definition is identical, and follows from the equation that assets minus liabilities equals equity.

5.4.4   Gains

Gains are defined as 'increases in ownership interest, other than those relating to contributions by owners'.[263] Here the ASB has adopted a simpler approach than the FASB, because it uses a single element to cover what SFAC 6 describes separately as revenues and gains (see 3.4.7 above). The distinction is that the US definitions differentiate between gains arising from central operations and those which do not, whereas the ASB uses a single definition for both. One awkward feature of the word chosen, however, is that 'gains' are conventionally thought of as the net result of income less expenditure relating to an item, whereas the term seems to be intended to mean gross income alone.

5.4.5   Losses

Losses are defined as 'decreases in ownership interest, other than those relating to distributions to owners'.[264] Again, this embraces both expenses and losses as the terms are used in SFAC 6 (see 3.4.7 above). The term 'losses', even more than gains, implies a *net* result, not simply an expense, so again there is a linguistic difficulty with the word chosen.

5.4.6   Contributions from owners

These are defined as 'increases in ownership interest resulting from investments made by owners in their capacity as owners'.[265] This is a straightforward definition, and is needed in order to exclude capital injections from being included within the definition of gains.

5.4.7   Distributions to owners

These are defined as the mirror image: 'decreases in ownership interest resulting from transfers made to owners in their capacity as owners'.[266] Again, this prevents dividends and capital repayments being categorised as losses.

5.4.8 *The overall approach*

The approach taken by Chapter 3 is therefore very similar to that used by SFAC No. 6. It employs only seven elements, rather than the US statement's ten, having combined two pairs of the American terms into two single elements, and not sought to use the further term 'comprehensive income' (which would equate to gains minus losses as the terms are used by the ASB).

This approach is also, therefore, open to some of the same challenges as its American counterpart, because all the other elements are dependent on the definitions of the first two: those of assets and liabilities. This might be acceptable providing the definitions are meaningful and as long as workable recognition and measurement rules for assets and liabilities can be devised. However, as discussed later, there is room for doubt on both counts. It will be recalled from 3.5 above that it was over recognition and measurement that the US Framework project also ran into difficulty.

5.5 SoP1 Chapter 4: Recognition in financial statements

'Recognition' is described as involving 'depiction of the element both in words and by a monetary amount, and the inclusion of that amount in the statement totals'.[267] The chapter describes the recognition of assets and liabilities as falling into three stages: initial recognition, subsequent remeasurement and derecognition.[268]

The proposed criteria for initial recognition are that an item should be incorporated in the financial statements for the first time if:

(a)   there is sufficient evidence that the change in assets or liabilities inherent in the element has occurred (including, where appropriate, evidence that a future inflow or outflow of benefit will occur); and

(b)   it can be measured at a monetary amount with sufficient reliability.[269]

A change in the amount at which an asset or liability is recorded (subsequent remeasurement) should be recorded if:

(a)   there is sufficient evidence that the amount of an asset or liability has changed; and

(b)   the new amount of the asset or liability can be measured with sufficient reliability.[270]

An asset or liability should cease to be recognised (derecognition) if there is no longer sufficient evidence that the entity has access to future economic benefits or an obligation to transfer economic benefits (including, where appropriate, evidence that a future inflow or outflow of benefit will occur).[271]

This means that whenever a change in an entity's total assets is not offset by an equal change in total liabilities or ownership interest, a gain or loss will arise.

The chapter explains that 'recognition is triggered where a past event gives rise to a measurable change in the assets and liabilities of the entity'.[272] The chapter identifies two broad classes of past events that may involve a measurable change in assets or liabilities and hence that may trigger recognition: 'transactions' and 'events other than transactions'.

The subsequent discussion of the recognition process under these two broad headings reveals that it would radically alter conventional financial reporting practices if applied rigorously. In particular it becomes clear that the rules would require assets and liabilities under certain contracts for future performance to be recognised immediately unless it was possible to cancel the contract without incurring a significant penalty. As an example of the practical application of this principle, assets obtained under *operating* leases would be liable to appear on the balance sheet of the lessee, as well as those obtained under finance leases.

As stated above, whenever a change in an entity's total assets is not offset by an equal change in total liabilities or ownership interest, a gain or loss will arise. The recognition of a gain/loss involves consideration of whether there is sufficient evidence that an increase/decrease in net assets (i.e. ownership interest) had occurred before the end of the reporting period.[273] The chapter states that what constitutes 'sufficient evidence' is a matter of judgement in the particular circumstances of each case: the evidence must be adequate, but need not be (and usually cannot be) conclusive.[274]

The recognition criteria state that a necessary condition for initial recognition or subsequent remeasurement is that an element or a change in an element can be measured with sufficient reliability. The chapter states that reliability of measurement is affected by three factors:[275]

1. the ability to measure the benefits inherent in the item in monetary terms;
2. the variability of the size of these benefits (both the spread of possible levels of benefit and the chance of any particular level of benefit occurring); and
3. the existence of a minimum amount.

Although it is not defined in any pronouncement, the recognition process which currently takes place in practice starts at the other end of the spectrum, and is based on the recording and analysis of transactions, not on the identification of assets and liabilities in a balance sheet. Under this approach, the balance sheet is not the primary statement but a derivative one; it is the result of the process which eventually converts transactions into a profit and loss account. This process reallocates transactions from the period in which they occur into the periods in which they 'belong', on the basis of accruals, matching and prudence concepts. The other side of the double entry gives rise to assets and liabilities in the balance sheet.

Formal recognition rules developed on the basis of transactions would be rather different from, and more straightforward than, the rules proposed by the ASB, and would only involve the following decisions:

(a) when is a transaction recognised in the accounting records – for example, should it be at the time a contractual commitment is created, or (more usually) at the earlier of the time that the transaction is performed or that consideration passes? Also, what events, other than transactions, give rise to entries in the accounting records?

(b) which of the debits and credits recorded in the accounting records as a result of (a) above represent assets or liabilities rather than items of current expense or income? These will be of two types:

- monetary assets and liabilities;

- amounts which should be carried forward under the matching concept (as limited by the prudence concept) because they belong in the profit and loss account of future periods – either deferred costs (such as stock, fixed assets, prepayments) or deferred revenues (such as advances received in respect of future sales, deferred government grants); and

(c) under the prudence concept, what other losses (and corresponding liabilities) have to be accrued in respect of future transactions not yet recognised in the accounting records? Examples might include contingent losses under litigation, or provisions for onerous contractual commitments. (These are relevant to the second part of (a) above, because they provide examples of events that merit recognition in advance of a transaction being carried out.)

Nevertheless, it is now clear that the ASB's proposals for the recognition of gains and losses are very similar to those in the ICAS study *Making Corporate Reports Valuable* (see 4.6 above). The idea that gains and losses arise whenever there is a change in net assets which is not offset by a transaction with owners reflects MCRV's notion of changes in financial wealth. This is borne out by the fact that the ASB states in SoP1 that 'where an asset changes in value or is disposed of, the gain or loss that is reported is the difference between the new value or the sale proceeds and the value previously reported'.[276] The added implication of this statement is that the ASB's proposed model does not distinguish between realised and unrealised gains and losses. All changes in balance sheet assets and liabilities (excluding transactions with shareholders) are recognised as gains and losses – irrespective of whether or not they are realised. This is justified by the ASB as follows: 'A more useful analysis of the quality of profits than that into realised and unrealised profits is an analysis into those gains and losses that derive from operating activities and those that result from changes in the value of those assets and liabilities that are held on a continuing basis for use in the entity's business.'[277] No evidence is offered for this assertion.

A balance sheet-centred approach would, indeed, make a good deal of sense if measurement principles based on an exit-value approach were to be advocated (as in CoCoA and MCRV as discussed at 4.3.2 C and 4.6 above respectively). However, an examination of the measurement chapter of the SoP1 reveals that this is not the view of the ASB.

5.6   SoP1 Chapter 5: Measurement in financial statements

This chapter provides a brief summary of the main features of various theoretical measurement approaches. It starts by discussing the features of historical cost accounting, commenting on the way that it has been modified in practice to incorporate asset revaluations. The chapter then contrasts the use of historical costs with the conventional current value systems – namely, entry value (replacement cost), exit value (net realisable value) and value in use (discounted present value of the cash flows expected from continuing use and ultimate sale by the present owner). In so doing, the chapter actively promotes a measurement system based on current values as being superior to historical cost accounting, and concludes that 'practice should develop by evolving in the direction of greater use of current values to the extent that this is consistent with the constraints of reliability and cost'.[278]

However, there are more difficulties associated with current values than merely reliability and cost. The most obvious of these is that current value accounting deals with current opportunities that, by definition, have not yet been realised, whereas historical cost has a grounding in actual events (past transactions). Thus, current values are regarded as particularly subjective items of information. The subjectivity increases as the opportunity moves further into the future, with value in use (requiring estimates of discount rates and the amount and timing of future cash flows) usually considered to be the most subjective of all current value measures. The ASB even acknowledges that there are particular problems of subjectivity and reliability in the case of 'assets that are not regularly dealt with in active markets and when assets are stated at value in use, since the calculation of value in use depends upon expected future returns which may be subject to error and may depend upon subjective judgements'.[279]

Paradoxically, this highlights the most significant advantage of historical cost accounting over current value accounting – namely, that it is based on the actual transactions which the company has undertaken and the cash flows which it has generated. This can be seen as an advantage not just in terms of reliability, but also in terms of relevance, because transactions and their consequent cash flows are the underlying reality of business about which accounts seek to provide information. In contrast, valuation information can be said to lack relevance (as well as reliability) because it does not relate to transactions which the company has undertaken, nor even usually to transactions that it will undertake in the future.   There is no reason why current value information (together with underlying assumptions) should not be provided on a supplementary basis (as envisaged in previous studies); however, for financial reporting purposes, the prudent view is that it is neither sufficiently reliable nor relevant to be adopted as the primary basis for measurement.

This view is supported by the findings of an empirical study on the information needs of investors and creditors, published in 1994 by the AICPA Special Committee on Financial Reporting.[280] The study shows that while many users support disclosures of fair value information, they are generally opposed to replacing today's historical cost-based accounting model with a fair value accounting model. This is because users believe that the historical cost-based model provides them with a stable and consistent benchmark that they can rely on to establish historical trends. The study highlighted concern about the subjectivity and potential volatility in reported results of a model based on fair value.

Nevertheless, despite acknowledging the fundamental shortcomings of a measurement system based on current values, the chapter supports the ASB's own perspective about the focus of financial reporting, and ultimately advocates (albeit rather hesitantly) the 'value to the business' measurement model, as advocated by the Solomons Report (see 4.7 above). The ASB describes value to the business as a 'bringing up to date of historical cost, adopting the traditional "cost or less" rule: replacement cost is reduced to net realisable value or value in use where these are lower'.[281] However, despite the ASB's attempt at defining the concept 'value to the business', its real meaning remains as opaque as it did when it was first mentioned in the Sandilands Report, and later in the Solomons Report.

This may be illustrated as follows:[282]

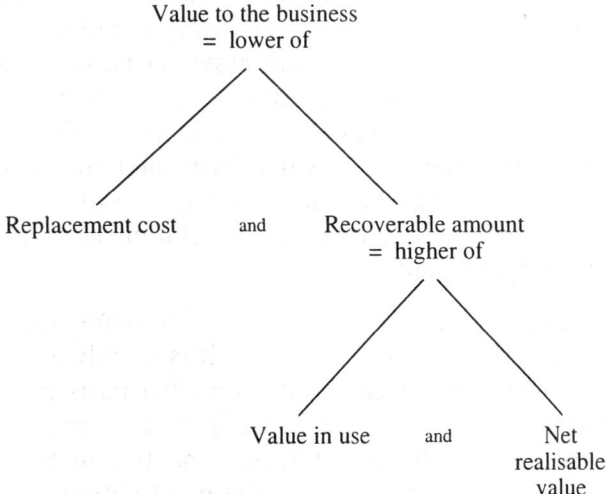

The ASB goes on to say that 'value to the business can be justified as a value that is relevant to economic decision-making',[283] although the chapter is not altogether clear as to why this is so or why it is appropriate for external financial reporting purposes. It is more probable that value to the business is a fundamentally false premise on which to base accounting measurement, and that the ASB is glossing over the most significant weakness in the concept. In reality, the value to the business formula measures deprival value, but not future benefits. What it would cost to replace an asset is irrelevant to measuring its future benefits, and therefore replacement cost cannot be relevant in this context.

Interestingly enough, though, value to the business was the fundamental valuation basis which was promulgated by SSAP 16 – *Current cost accounting* – although SSAP 16 defined recoverable amount as the greater of the net realisable value of an asset and 'the amount recoverable from its further use',[284] without explicitly referring to 'value in use'. The inclusion of 'value in use' as part of the measurement technique recommended in the draft has been somewhat undermined by its recent rejection by the FASB. As referred to in section 3.7 above, in their 1999 exposure draft of a proposed new SFAC – *Using cash flow information and present value in accounting measurements* – the FASB changed its view on value in use (entity specific measurement). It has decided the notion is flawed and opted for fair value as the only allowable measurement attribute. However, the ASB is already too far down the track to abandon the concept of value in use now, given that the fixed asset impairment calculation that is embodied in FRS 11 – *Impairment of Fixed Assets and Goodwill* – is entirely dependent on that concept.

In the case of liabilities, the discussion draft of Chapter 5 which preceded the omnibus version of the Draft *Statement of Principles* devoted considerable space to discussing the concept of 'relief value', which the ASB sees as being the mirror-image equivalent of the value to the business principle. However, this discussion was omitted from the Exposure Draft, with the ASB merely stating that the concept of relief value is an 'unnecessary complication' and that 'the same considerations that support reporting assets at current value suggest that liabilities should also be measured on that basis'.[285] The implication of this statement is that the ASB clearly believes that liabilities should be stated in an entity's balance sheet on some current value basis, and not on the basis of what the entity believes it will ultimately have to pay to settle the liability. This approach has had a significant impact on the measurement of both liabilities and provisions, as discussed in Chapter 25.

Surprisingly, the ASB devotes little space to discussing the issue of capital maintenance. Presumably, this is because profit is merely a product of balance sheet changes, and once it has been decided on what basis assets and liabilities are to be measured (i.e. 'value to the business'), profit is merely an arithmetical consequence thereof. The ASB does, however, mention in passing a 'real terms capital maintenance system', which is aimed at highlighting 'the extent to which holding gains and losses reflect the effect of general inflation' in situations where general inflation is a material factor.[286]

5.7   SoP1 Chapter 6: Presentation of financial information

Chapter 6 discusses the way in which information should be presented in financial statements in order to meet the objective of providing information about the financial position, performance and financial adaptability of an enterprise that is useful to a wide range of users for assessing the stewardship of management and for making economic decisions.

The chapter identifies the profit and loss account, the statement of total recognised gains and losses, the balance sheet and the cash flow statement as being the four primary financial statements. The important feature of this list is that it is now clear that the ASB views the statement of total recognised gains and losses as a primary statement of performance, and not just a reconciling statement. This is backed up by the statement that 'the gains and losses that are recognised in respect of a period are reported in one of the statements of financial performance, ie the profit and loss account and the statement of total recognised gains and losses'.[287] The chapter goes on to say that 'in assessing the overall financial performance of an entity during a period, all gains and losses need to be considered' and that 'the statements of financial performance report only the gains and losses that arise in the period'.[288]

As stated above, the ASB does not regard the distinction between realised and unrealised gains and losses as being relevant, stating that a more useful analysis of the quality of profits 'is an analysis into those gains and losses that derive from operating activities and those that result from changes in the value of those assets and liabilities that are held on a continuing basis for use in the entity's business'.[289] Consequently, the ASB believes that gains and losses on those assets and liabilities that are held on a continuing basis primarily in order to enable the entity's operations to be carried out, should be reported in the statement of total recognised gains and losses, and not in the profit and loss account, and all other gains and losses are reported in the profit and loss account.

SoP1 would measure total financial performance by reference to changes in balance sheet net assets (other than those which relate to transactions with owners), and the profit and loss account would become a subsidiary analysis of gains and losses that derive from operating activities. This interpretation has been strengthened by the ASB's publication in 1999 of a discussion paper entitled: *Reporting Financial Performance: Proposals for Change*, in which a single statement of financial performance is promulgated. This paper together with its implications for the realisation principle is discussed below at 5.23.

5.8   SoP1 Chapter 7: The reporting entity

Chapter 7 defines the reporting entity as being 'the entity that is the subject of a given set of financial statements'.[290] Whether or not an entity falls under this requirement depends on what the chapter terms 'the demand condition' and 'the supply condition'. The 'demand condition' exists 'if there are potential users with a legitimate interest who rely on such statements as a major source of financial information about the entity', whilst to be able to supply useful financial statements, 'an entity must be a cohesive economic unit, usually resulting from a unified control structure' (the supply condition).[291]

The chapter explores the effect on an entity of its interests in other entities and how this is reflected to give relevant information to users of both its individual and consolidated financial statements. In so doing, it discusses different kinds of investments (from the passive investment to the subsidiary) in the context of the range of different relationships that can exist between the investor and investee (from limited influence to total influence).

The chapter describes control as being 'the highest degree of influence that an investor can have over its investee'[292] and defines control as being 'the power to direct'.[293] It goes on to say that 'to have control, whether of assets or of other entities, an entity must have both of the following abilities:

(a)   the ability to deploy the economic resources, or direct the entities; and

(b)   the ability to ensure that any resulting benefits accrue to itself (with corresponding exposure to losses) and to restrict the access of others to those benefits'.[294]

Chapter 7 then focuses its attention on consolidated financial statements and discusses the main two opposing perspectives for accounting for subsidiaries, namely the proprietary approach and the entity approach. It then looks at changes in the reporting entity in the context of mergers and acquisitions, and ends with a discussion of the inclusion of associates and joint ventures in consolidated financial statements. In so doing, it compares equity accounting with proportional consolidation and rejects proportional consolidation as an acceptable method of incorporating associates into consolidated financial statements.[295]

In the case of joint ventures, the chapter suggests that proportional consolidation is acceptable only in cases where 'each venturer has its own separate interest in the risks and rewards that derive either from its particular share of the fixed assets of the venture, or by its having a distinct share of the output or service of the joint venture and, in many cases, of its financing'.[296] This approach was subsequently codified in FRS 9 – *Associates and Joint Ventures* – which only permits proportional consolidation in the very limited circumstances described above.

5.9   The reaction of respondents to SoP1

The ASB's first draft of its *Statement of Principles* attracted an unusually large response and considerable criticism when it was published for comment in November 1995. Discussion and debate was stimulated by Ernst and Young's paper – *The ASB's Framework: Time to Decide* – published in February 1996 (which was severely criticised in its turn by the ASB Chairman). There was a substantial amount of coverage of the issues in the national and trade press. However, given that the Draft sought to alter the most fundamental of accounting methods and reporting practices, the record 175 responses sent to the ASB should not have been surprising. As a consequence of the responses received, SoP1 was withdrawn for further work by the ASB and the second draft was promised, eventually being published in March 1999 (see below at 5.11).

A detailed analysis of the responses to SoP1 has been carried out by two UK academics, Professor G. J. Wilkinson-Riddle and Ms L. Holland of De Montfort University.[297] Their paper analyses the responses quantitatively and also includes a qualitative review of them in the light of the common themes that emerged. It concludes that, far from being complacent about accounting regulation, those involved with UK financial reporting are aware that principles are necessary; but are concerned that changes of a fundamental nature do not take place without being practical, coherent, justified and with the informed consent of all those concerned with preparing, auditing and using accounting information.[298]

The following table summarises the 175 respondents' views:[299]

Response Type:	**All responses**	Number of respondents expressing this view	% of 175 respondents
1	A statement is in principle a good idea	68	39%
2	This SOP is acceptable	12	7%
3	This SOP is not acceptable	134	77%
4	Current values/discounting not acceptable	125	71%
5	Current values/discounting acceptable	9	5%
6	Cash aspects not adequate	12	7%
7	Presentation of SOP inadequate	46	26%
8	Information overload for users	10	6%
9	New concepts not acceptable	12	7%
10	Do not abandon established concepts	82	47%
11	STRGL not viable	51	29%
12	Goodwill treatment inadequate	16	9%
13	Overwhelming practical problems	60	34%
14	Downgrading of P&L not acceptable	71	41%
15	New definitions inadequate	39	22%
16	Recognition/realisation criteria inadequate	39	22%
Total no. of summarised points recorded		786	

It is immediately clear from this table that the vast majority of respondents to the Draft expressed an essentially critical view of the ASB proposals, and it was for this reason that the ASB announced that its next step would be 'to issue a revised draft of the *Statement of Principles* that addresses the substantive points raised by the comment letters'.[300]

5.10   The ASB's response to the criticism

Having received such an overwhelmingly negative response to its proposals, the ASB faced a dilemma: it wished to pursue its agenda, yet it did not have a mandate to do so on the basis of SoP1. Consequently, in July 1996, the ASB published a paper in an attempt to counter the widespread criticism that it had received.[301] In this paper – *Statement of Principles for Financial Reporting: the way ahead* – the ASB attempted to redeem its position by asserting that criticism of the Draft stemmed largely from 'serious misunderstandings', some of which had been 'expressed by those who apparently had not actually read the draft itself'.[302]

Unfortunately, though, the ASB's paper was not a satisfactory response to the many criticisms which had been levelled at the Draft. It trivialised some of the concerns which had been expressed and, in so doing, avoided dealing with them in any satisfactory way. For example, the Board dismissed the criticism of its proposed balance sheet approach by stating that its intention 'is simply to add a measure of discipline to the recording of transactions'.[303] Similarly, the Board side-stepped the criticism that had been levelled at the practical issues surrounding the statement of total recognised gains and losses (STRGL), by merely stating that 'the Board accepts that there should be fuller discussion of the role of the STRGL'.[304]

The document concluded that it would 'not be appropriate to proceed directly to the development of a final document',[305] and stated that it planned to issue a revised exposure draft in 1997. In fact SoP2 was issued in March 1999. In the interim period, though, a number of standards were issued which to varying degrees reflected the conceptual approach embodied in the withdrawn SoP1.

5.11   SoP2: The Revised Draft Statement of Principles

As already stated the first draft of the *Statement of Principles* was withdrawn in July 1996 following substantial and overwhelmingly critical responses to it, which are discussed at 5.9 above. This resulted in the eventual publication of a revised draft (referred to hereafter as SoP2) in March 1999.[306] Throughout the considerable debate following the publication of SoP1, the ASB maintained it had been misunderstood by its critics. In the preface to SoP2 the Board acknowledges that SoP1 'attracted more letters of comment than any other document published by the Board. Many expressed misgivings about the draft Statement and, indeed, about the direction of the Board's work generally. However, from a careful analysis of the comments it was clear that certain aspects of that draft had not been well understood and that had partially obscured the debate'.[307] The structure of SoP2 reflected the Board's determination to ensure a proper understanding was gained of the second attempt, by being split into three separate booklets variously entitled in order of size:

1.   Statement of Principles Exposure Draft, *Statement of Principles for Financial Reporting*, Revised Exposure Draft;

2.   Draft Statement of Principles Supplement, *Statement of Principles for Financial Reporting, A Technical Supplement to the Revised Exposure Draft*; and

3.   Draft Statement of Principles Introductory Booklet, *Statement of Principles for Financial Reporting: Some Questions Answered*.

The first of these booklets largely contained the equivalent of the entire SoP1 while the third, Some Questions Answered, was 'prepared to reinforce some of [the] clarifications'[308] contained in the first. The Board asserted that the Technical Supplement contains 'explanations of the rationale for some of the approaches adopted in the draft to help [readers] take into account the factors that have influenced the Board's thinking'.[309]

The first booklet, the main draft itself, contains the following eight chapters, each of which is discussed below bearing in mind the comments already made above concerning SoP1:

1.   The objective of financial statements

2.   The reporting entity

3.   The qualitative characteristics of financial information

4.   The elements of financial statements

5.   Recognition in financial statements

6.   Measurement in financial statements

7.   Presentation of financial information

8.   Accounting for interests in other entities.

It can be seen by referring to section 5.1 above that these chapter headings are almost identical to those in SoP1. There is an introduction to the document, largely unchanged in import from SoP1, which makes it clear that 'the statement of principles is intended to be relevant to the financial statements of profit-oriented reporting entities, including profit-oriented public sector entities, regardless of their size'.[310] However unlike the first draft it is stated that a separate paper dealing with 'not-for-profit entities and the Statement of Principles' will be issued in due course.[311] The main difference in the actual texts of SoP1 and SoP2 is the splitting of each chapter into two major parts: Principles and Explanation, whereas in SoP1 these were not clearly separated.

5.12   SoP2 Chapter 1: The Objective of Financial Statements

The principles set out in this chapter are that:

■   the objective of financial statements is to provide information about the reporting entity's financial performance;

■   it can be presumed that investors are the defining class of user;

■   investors need information to enable evaluation of an entity's cash generating ability and financial adaptability.[312]

These are almost identical to its SoP1 counterpart, although the explanation section contains a new part devoted to clarifying the notion of 'financial adaptability', as follows:

'Financial adaptability comes from several sources, including the ability to:

(a)   Raise new capital, perhaps by issuing debt securities, at short notice;

(b)   Repay capital or debt at short notice;

(c)   Obtain cash by selling assets without disrupting continuing operations; and

(d)   Achieve a rapid improvement in the net cash inflows generated by operations'.[313]

Thus, it turns out that financial adaptability refers to the fact that it is desirable to have plenty of cash, readily realisable assets and a good credit rating.

5.13   SoP2 Chapter 2: The Reporting Entity

This chapter is considerably shorter than its identically titled counterpart, Chapter 7 of SoP1, partly because those aspects dealing with consolidation are discussed separately in Chapter 8 of SoP2. The principles set out are:

■   An entity should prepare and publish financial statements if there is a legitimate demand for the information that its financial statements would provide and it is a cohesive economic unit.

■   The boundary of the reporting entity is determined by the scope of its control. For this purpose, first direct control and, secondly, direct plus indirect control are taken into account.[314]

The first principle raises so many definitional problems that it seems valueless; for instance 'legitimate demand' is not a clear idea and neither is 'cohesive economic unit'. However, the second principle clearly rests upon the meaning of 'control' which the explanation section attempts to clarify. Control has two aspects: 'the ability to deploy the economic resources involved and to benefit (or suffer) from their deployment'.[315] This is further sub-divided into direct control and indirect control in a way that does not sit easily with the above and other definitions. Direct control seems to mean the business owns the asset while indirect control seems to mean the business owns, or has some sort of interest in, another business which owns the asset.

This direct/indirect control distinction is actually the familiar legal one of ownership and it makes no sense without that background understanding. What these explanations of control really amount to is the truism that businesses are in charge of the things they own and are indirectly in charge of things belonging to other businesses they own. Essentially the chapter is saying that, if one business owns or has a serious financial or economic exposure to another it should prepare consolidated accounts.

5.14 SoP2 Chapter 3: The Qualitative Characteristics of Financial Information

As with the equivalent chapter of SoP1 this chapter follows the familiar path of relevance, reliability and understandability. The definition of reliability used in SoP1 is retained, as is its circularity: 'information is reliable if it can be depended upon ... to represent what it purports to represent'.[316] Put another way, information is reliable if it is reliable. However, the diagrammatic representation of these qualities has been simplified since SoP1 and the spurious distinction between the questions: 'what makes financial information useful' and 'what qualities make the presentation of financial information useful'[317] included in the SoP1 diagram has been removed. Timeliness has disappeared as a limit on the desirable qualitative characteristics between the two diagrams, despite the fact that timeliness is becoming an ever more important factor in real-life corporate reporting, especially given the likely advance towards real time reporting and the use of the Internet as a primary means of communication. The diagrammatic representation of the qualitative characteristics is reproduced below.[318]

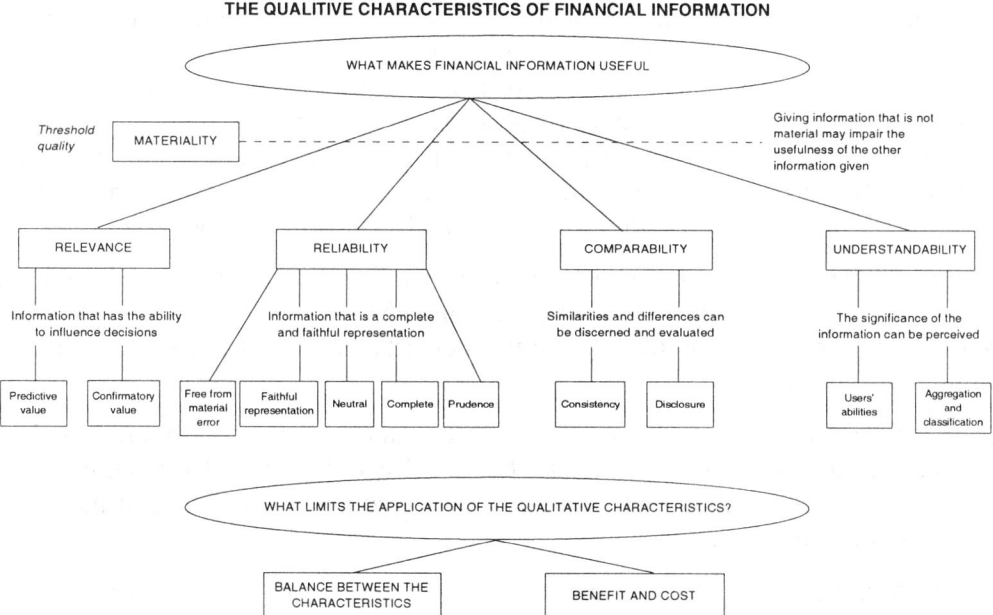

One of the factors that all framework attempts have paid lip-service to is understandability. This chapter advances as a principle the notion that 'information provided by financial statements needs to be comparable and understandable';[319] however, this is significantly different from being understood. In the explanation section relating to understandability, when identifying the required capabilities of users, the Board asserts: 'Those preparing financial statements are entitled to assume that users have a reasonable knowledge of business and economic activities and accounting and a willingness to study with reasonable diligence the information provided'.[320] This assertion, whilst similar to those in other frameworks, similarly avoids the understandability problem. The required capabilities would probably reduce the 'allowable' users to a small set of professional analysts, accountants and the odd graduate of the subject. When this constituency is contrasted with the many types of people who actually own shares, it becomes apparent that the issue of understandability is considerable and cannot be comfortably defined away. This point is, perhaps inadvertently, reinforced by the draft itself in view of the final paragraph of this chapter which warns 'it may not always be possible ... to present information in a way that can be understood by all users with the capabilities described in paragraph 3.25(b)'.[321]

5.15   SoP2 Chapter 4: The Elements of Financial Statements

The seven elements listed in section 5.4 above, which deals with the equivalent chapter in SoP1, are reproduced unchanged as are their definitions.

5.15.1 Assets

The fundamental definition is that of the asset. It is the attempts made in the revised draft to explain and make sense of the definition that highlight its unsatisfactory nature. First, the Board insists that an asset is actually 'not the item of property itself'.[322] In plain English the Board is saying that, for example, an item of stock or a vehicle is not an asset. It holds that an asset actually is 'the rights or other access to some or all of the future economic benefits derived from that item of property'.[323] Further, even cash and cash flows are not assets:

'Future economic benefits eventually result in net cash inflows to the entity. Assets are, however, not mere representations of the cash flows: they are rights and other access to the future economic benefits that can be used to generate future cash flows.

(a) Cash (including bank deposits) can be exchanged for virtually any good or service that is available or it can be saved and exchanged for them in the future. The command that cash gives over resources is the basis of its future economic benefits'.[324]

It is in trying to make sense of these startlingly counter-intuitive claims that the Board's difficulties become apparent; indeed these are difficulties inherent in the FASB's and other similar framework attempts that adopt similar definitions.

SoP2 has to deal with the problem that future economic benefits may not materialise. Consequently it allows that 'this future economic benefit need not, however, be certain'.[325] Thus, the Board maintains that cash is not an asset, fixed and current assets are not assets, but the uncertain future economic benefits they may bring are. However, the question may legitimately be asked: what is a future economic benefit? It cannot be a car or a machine or cash in the bank. If it were, the definition would be self-contradictory, as it expressly states an asset is *not* an item of property or cash. What then is a future economic benefit, if not an item of property or cash?

It is not possible to ascribe meaning to 'future economic benefits' except in terms of items of property or cash; consequently the ASB has a meaningless definition at the heart of the *Statement of Principles*. If the definition of assets is meaningless the entire logical structure derived from it is too, including all the remaining definitions of the elements of financial statements the SoP contains.

Nevertheless, what the ASB seems to be driving at in its definition is that an asset is not the physical property, but the rights that the property bestows on the entity. In other words, if a retailer owns a shop, it is not the shop that is the asset, it is the right to use the shop in order to derive cash inflows that is the asset. This approach is inextricably linked to the concept of value in use. The value in use of an asset is the present value of the cash flows that will be derived from the asset through its use in the business. Thus the ASB seems to be saying that an asset is the right to these cash flows.

That is why it is necessary to include the notion of control within the definition of an asset. SoP2 states that 'the definition of an asset requires that ... the future economic benefits are controlled by the reporting entity'.[326] How the future can be controlled is not dealt with; however, SoP2 seems to be saying that in order to recognise a right on the balance sheet as an asset, it is necessary to control the right so that future cash inflows that are going to be derived from those rights are also controlled.

The notion of control also avoids an unwanted side-effect of the Board's asset definition. There are various expenditures, such as those incurred in staff training or developing market share, that the Board does not want to allow into the balance sheet, even though they bring future benefits. Therefore a further definitional refinement is added, namely that for a future economic benefit to be an asset it must also be 'controlled independently of the business as a whole'.[327] This new concept of independence from the business as a whole is only illustrated, not defined. However, to take the Board's own example, it asserts that 'market share, superior management or good labour relations ... cannot be controlled independently of the business as a whole'.[328] In this way, the ASB believes that it is able to prevent expenditure that is being deferred in order to smooth profits from being carried forward in the balance sheet as an asset.

5.15.2 *Liabilities*

The definition of liabilities, as noted above, remains unchanged: liabilities are 'obligations of an entity to transfer economic benefits as a result of past transactions or events'.[329] However, further attempts are made in SoP2 to square the definition with the ASB's desire to prevent 'big-bath' provisions as now extant in FRS 12 – *Provisions, Contingent Liabilities and Contingent Assets.* The concept of the 'constructive obligation'[330] is introduced as a device to prevent the directors of a company creating a liability unless certain other conditions are fulfilled. In particular, 'where the event that gave rise to the obligation was communicating a decision to transfer economic benefits, the liability will have existed at the balance sheet date only if the communication took place before that date'.[331]

It seems untenable that the existence of a liability really does rest upon whether the directors have told anyone about it. We believe that the ASB is wrong to exclude the effect of management decisions in portraying the financial performance of an entity, particularly as it is not being applied consistently by the Board. For instance, while a business is precluded by FRS 12 from recognising the direct costs of a large scale restructuring announced just after the balance sheet date, FRS 11 – *Impairment of Fixed Assets and Goodwill* – requires that business to make provision for any impairment to the carrying value of the fixed assets involved.

Assets and liabilities are therefore characterised as rights and obligations – rights to receive future economic benefits in the form of cash inflows and obligations to transfer out economic benefits in the form of cash outflows. The remaining definitions are derived from the definitions of assets and liabilities: ownership interest is the residual amount found by deducting an entity's assets from its liabilities; gains and losses are increases and decreases in ownership interest not resulting from contributions from or distributions to owners. As a result, the entire accounting process as articulated in SoP2 is focused on the recognition, initial measurement, remeasurement and derecognition of assets and liabilities.

5.16   SoP2 Chapter 5: Recognition in Financial Statements

The principles set out are similar to those espoused in SoP1. The revised version sets out these conditions for recognition of assets and liabilities:

'If a transaction or other event has created a new asset or liability or added to an existing asset or liability, that event will be recognised if:

(a) Sufficient evidence exists that the new asset or liability has been created or that there has been an addition to an existing asset or liability; and

(b) The new asset or liability or the addition to the existing asset or liability can be measured at a monetary amount with sufficient reliability.'[332]

As in SoP1, these conditions have a degree of circularity about them and add little to the definitions of assets and liabilities themselves.

Revenue recognition (which is not characterised as such) is referred to in the principles section of Chapter 5 as follows:

'In a transaction involving the provision of services or goods for a net gain, the recognition criteria described above [i.e. the asset/liability criteria above] will be met on the occurrence of the critical event in the operating cycle involved'.[333]

By including this paragraph, the ASB seems to be fending off any potential criticism of its asset/liability approach to revenue recognition. In defending the approach that gains and losses are merely increases and decreases in net assets, other than those resulting from transactions with shareholders, the ASB is attempting to assert that both an asset/liability approach and a critical event approach to revenue recognition end up with the same answer. What the above paragraph is saying is that a net gain that is recognised on the basis of the critical event approach will necessarily result in an increase in net assets, with the result that the asset/liability recognition criteria will also be met.

However, while this is so, the ASB has missed the point. The ASB is trying to assert that irrespective of whether one follows a balance sheet approach to income recognition or a transactions-based income statement approach, one will always get to the same end-result. This is patently not true. Just because all revenue recognised under an income statement based transactions system will satisfy the asset/liability recognition criteria, it does not follow that the reverse will apply. Revenue recognition criteria are more demanding than those for recognising assets and liabilities, since they should embody the concept of the revenue having been earned, based on performance by the reporting company. The entire topic of revenue recognition, including the adequacy of SoP2 in this area, is discussed in detail in section 4.1 of Chapter 3 of this book.

Many of the implications of the recognition criteria for assets and liabilities have already been set out in 5.5 above, including one particularly imprudent implication concerning unperformed contracts. This caused some disquiet in the responses to SoP1 and has been further referred to in SoP2. In brief, the problem is that the balance sheet recognition criteria in SoP2 seem to require the recognition of a sale, and hence profit, where a contract has been agreed, but nothing else has happened. Certainly rights to future benefits exist at this point.

This difficulty is glossed over by the statement that 'the right and obligation will be in balance'.[334] However, assuming a profitable sale has been contracted, this cannot be the case. A footnote to para. 5.19 states: 'At present most types of unperformed ... contracts are not recognised. That is because the historical cost basis of measurement is being used and, on such a basis, the carrying amount will be the cost of entering into the agreement, which is invariably nil'. The words 'at present' seem to envisage the possibility that in the future unperformed contracts might generally be recognised. In our view this would be a grave mistake, the possibility of which the Board should specifically renounce. The matter does provide a further example of the manner in which the inadequate definitions chosen by the ASB lead to unworkable results in practice.

The remainder of the chapter mentions matching and prudence, somewhat as afterthoughts. No mention is made of the imprudence of recognising profit on unperformed contracts, however. Prudence is largely discussed in the mechanical context of whether there is sufficient evidence for an asset to be recognised; rather than whether it is prudent to recognise it at all, a subtle downgrading of the concept. However, this is perhaps not surprising, given that the ASB rather pejoratively characterises prudence and matching as mere manifestations of profit smoothing.

5.17   SoP2 Chapter 6: Measurement in Financial Statements

This chapter sets out clearly, in a much less biased way than its SoP1 counterpart (see 5.6 above), the three realistic alternatives the historical cost/current value measurement options provide:

'These measurement bases could be used in financial statements in one of several ways:

(a) all assets and liabilities could be measured at historical cost. This is known as the historical cost system.

(b) all assets and liabilities could be measured at current value. This is known as the current value system.

(c) some categories of assets or liabilities could be measured on a historical cost basis and some on a current value basis. This is known as the mixed measurement system.'[335]

SoP2 goes on to state that it 'envisages that the latter approach (the mixed measurement system) will be adopted'[336] noting that this means the same as the term 'modified historical cost' frequently used in company reports. This most sensible approach does much to reassure the critics of SoP1, which took a stance clearly favouring the use of current values.

The chapter then proceeds to discuss the alternatives and how they apply to initial measurement and subsequent remeasurement. Although curiously it states that the purpose under modified historical cost of remeasurement is to 'ensure that assets are not reported at greater than their recoverable amount'[337] when in practice under this system, revaluations are mainly to ensure users appreciate the true market value of a company's property assets; that is, to ensure property assets are not reported at substantially *less* than their recoverable amount.

There is a section which discusses the relative reliability of current value and historical cost systems claiming, somewhat disingenuously, that current values are not that much less reliable than historical cost. For instance, that under historical cost 'adjustments made to the carrying value of debtors ... for bad and doubtful debts involve a degree of estimation that is not dissimilar to that involved in estimating current values not derived from an active market'.[338] In our view, this is an enormous oversimplification of the issue that seems to ignore the fact that bad debt estimations are frequently made on the basis of both historical bad debt collection experience and actual post balance sheet date collections. There is a vast difference between, for example, a retailer estimating a provision for doubtful debts on trade receivables and a bank determining the fair value of a portfolio of loans and advances for which there is no observable market value. It should also be borne in mind that doubtful debt provisions can only involve losses, whereas fair valuations can result in reporting unrealised gains.

The chapter contains a discussion of how current values should be determined, which (as in SoP1) centres round the concept of 'value in use' now rejected by the FASB (see sections 3.7 and 5.5 above). Discounting and capital maintenance are briefly alluded to; but overall the chapter sensibly acknowledges the modified historical cost approach to measurement will continue. Whether this represents a true ASB conviction, or whether it has just been included as a tactical ploy in order to forestall any potential criticism is a moot point. If one bears in mind the ASB's active participation in an international project on the accounting for financial instruments (known as the Joint Working Group on Financial Instruments, see Chapter 9 of this book) that is aimed at developing a comprehensive system of fair value accounting for all financial assets and liabilities, it is clear that there will not be much of the mixed model left.

The ASB has gone to great lengths in SoP2 to make it clear that the introduction of a system of current cost accounting has never been on its agenda and that there are no plans to put it on the agenda.[339] Whilst this is clearly a true statement, the ASB's use of the term 'current cost accounting' is very precise. Since current cost accounting is merely historical cost accounting updated for current prices, there is no question of the ASB going down that road. What is not in doubt, however, is the fact that the ASB is clearly advancing rapidly down the road of current *value* accounting, as evidenced by its penchant for fair values and the notion of value in use.

5.18 SoP2 Chapter 7: Presentation of Financial Information

In contrast to the SoP1 there are now only three primary financial statements, '(a) financial performance ... (b) financial position (the balance sheet); and (c) cash inflows and outflows (the cash flow statement)'.[340] The Board has decided that, after all, there is no need for the statement of total recognised gains and losses (STRGL) as a separate statement; but this is almost certainly because the Board is in favour of merging the profit and loss account and STRGL into a single statement of comprehensive income. The ASB's separate publication on this matter is discussed in section 5.23 below. There is no attempt in this chapter of SoP2, unlike its SoP1 counterpart, to discuss the wisdom of edging the performance statement away from the realisation principle, although it is more fully discussed in the Technical Supplement (see 5.20.1 below and sections 3 and 4 of Chapter 3 of this book).

5.19   SoP2 Chapter 8: Accounting for Interests in other Entities

This is a very short chapter, the contents of which were incorporated in Chapter 7, the Reporting Entity, of SoP1. It mentions rather than clarifies some of the issues surrounding consolidation and accounting for business combinations. The chapter identifies: 'Control, Joint control, Significant influence and Lesser or no influence',[341] as the principle cases covering when consolidation accounting should be used and the form it should take.

One of the difficulties the Board has is that its definition of assets excludes goodwill, which poses a particular problem for the presentation of consolidated accounts. Chapter 8 acknowledges this intrusion of reality and seeks to justify the departure from the ASB's principles as follows:

'Purchased goodwill … is not an asset in itself [but] if the parent's investment is to be fully reflected in the group's financial statements and the parent is to be held accountable for its investment … purchased goodwill needs to be recognised as if it were an asset'.[342]

5.20   SoP2: 'The Technical Supplement' and 'Some Questions Answered' booklets

5.20.1   The Technical Supplement

This booklet represents a useful indication of the Board's background thinking and also a helpful amplification of the explanation sections of each chapter of the SoP2 draft itself. Its main value lies for those who wish to make detailed responses to SoP2 as part of the exposure process. In response to the critical outcry that followed SoP1, the booklet takes some pains to explain how and why the draft departs from accepted practice, particularly concerning prudence, which the text confuses with 'smoothing' profits.[343]

Interestingly, given the logical failings of the Board's definition of assets set out in section 5.15.1 above, the supplement contains the robust assertion that 'definitions that seem to promise only circularity, vagueness and reliance on intent' do 'not provide a proper basis on which to develop a Statement of Principles'.[344]

There is a useful further discussion of realised gains and the suitability or not of focusing on them in financial statements. This is discussed in detail in Chapter 3 of this book, although it is worth noting here that the ASB has adopted the position that the realisation principle is 'irrelevant', with the result that all gains and losses will be recognised in a performance statement without any distinction being made between realised profits and unrealised profits.[345] We also note that while the ASB considers a gain should only be recorded if there is a reasonable certainty that it exists,[346] one of the major problems with unrealised gains is their ability to suddenly 'unexist'. There have been numerous examples of such occurrences, particularly whenever a period of economic growth slows down, such as in the late 1980s in the UK. This represents an inherent danger in the Board's proposals to report realised and unrealised gains together.

5.20.2 The 'Some Questions Answered' booklet

This booklet represents a somewhat novel approach on the part of the ASB of posing and then answering a number of questions that it thinks will arise in the minds of readers of the revised Draft *Statement of Principles*. If one was to be charitable towards the ASB, one could conclude that the booklet represents a sensible method of quickly informing interested parties about the main thrust of the revised draft, whilst also allaying some of the fears raised by SoP1. It deals with such topics as the effect on practice of SoP2 and provides some reassurance that the fundamental concepts of SSAP 2 are not being abandoned.

However, the booklet comes across as rather condescending, stating that the main text of SoP2 is a 'long, and at times, complex document', and implying that most people would find it easier to read the booklet. Furthermore, some of the questions that the Board has chosen to answer are somewhat disingenuous. Our view is that the booklet fails on two counts: it does not ask many important questions that should be asked – for example, what capital maintenance concept is being advocated? – and, second, the answers to many of the questions are simplistic and often misleading, conveying a false sense of security to the reader.

5.21   Overall assessment of the ASB's Statement of Principles Drafts

The aim of the ASB in trying to articulate clearly the principles inherent in financial reporting is laudable, but our overall view is that neither of its *Statement of Principles* Exposure Drafts achieves this aim and that the project therefore cannot claim to have succeeded. This is not to say that the two drafts are identical; there has quite clearly been a shift in the ASB's position between the publication of the two, which we welcome. The three most contentious aspects of SoP1 were its attempts to:

- supplant the established accounting process, whereby transactions are allocated to accounting periods by reference to the matching and prudence concepts, with recognition tests based on assets and liabilities;
- phase out historical costs in favour of current values; and

- elevate the statement of total recognised gains and losses as a performance statement and correspondingly diminish the importance of the profit and loss account.

On paper at least, SoP2 represents a major shift in the ASB's position on current values, to the extent that it specifically accepts modified historical cost will remain the norm for the foreseeable future. This appears to be a considerable shift compared with such SoP1 statements as 'the Board therefore believes that practice should develop by evolving in the direction of greater use of current values',[347] although as stated at 5.17 above we are not convinced that the ASB has really abandoned this ambition. Also, although discussion of the STRGL has been quietly dropped from SoP2, any celebration of this fact would have been short-lived. The Board has subsequently published a paper on the future of the income statement, discussed at 5.23 below, indicating it still intends substantially to alter current practice.

Essentially unchanged between the two drafts is the view of balance sheet primacy, with gains defined in balance sheet terms and recognition tests equally dependent upon asset and liability definitions. SoP2 does nevertheless go to some lengths to reassure readers that the true and fair view, prudence, matching and SSAP 2 generally remain absolutely fundamental to financial reporting. Of course, only time will tell whether the ASB really believes these reassurances, or whether they have been included in the revised draft in order to head off potential criticism. Interestingly, substantial discussion of the going concern concept is absent from either draft, which seems a fundamental omission in a framework document.

One consequence of this amelioration of the ASB's views between the two drafts is that the intended outcomes of the entire project remain unclear: it is neither a convincing description of the principles that presently underlie accounting practice, nor is it a persuasive manifesto for change.

5.21.1 Recognition tests

The *Statement of Principles*, in both its drafts, seeks to build accounting around its new definitions of assets and liabilities and the proposed criteria for recognising them in the balance sheet. This approach would replace the long-established accounting process in use throughout the world, whereby transactions are allocated to accounting periods by reference to the matching and prudence concepts. It is most unlikely to work well in practice.

The fundamental problem is the way in which the Draft *Statement of Principles* views the accounting process. Assets and liabilities do not form the natural starting point for devising recognition rules; the real building blocks which underlie accounting practice are transactions, to which are applied criteria for revenue and expense recognition, the balance sheet being a result of this process, not the starting point. The balance sheet provides only a snapshot which artificially 'freezes' the action of a business which is in fact continuous. Under the going concern concept, the items in the balance sheet should reflect a long-term perspective of what are long-term activities, which demands an allocative approach — this is relevant to topics such as depreciation, pension cost accounting and so on. Furthermore, the balance sheet can never hope to capture all the aspects of a company's value: it is simply beyond the reach of financial reporting to do so. A more realistic ambition is to analyse the company's transactions so as to measure the further instalment of profit or loss that it should fairly report as a result of a further year of activity. Empirically, this is the reality of the accounting process as it has developed to date.

Even though equivalent frameworks elsewhere in the world also suggest a balance sheet approach, these documents do not correspond to the reality of the accounting process in those countries either. Moreover they all suffer from the same logical failing identified in 5.15.1 above. If the (equivalent) approach in the FASB's concepts were actually applied in the US, for example, the extensive literature on revenue recognition in that country would be redundant.

To summarise, we consider that the recognition criteria proposed in the Draft *Statement of Principles* appear to be a distortion of the real recognition rules which accountants throughout the world and the ASB itself actually use and which are in fact transaction based. Devising rules for accounting based on what assets and liabilities materialise from the transaction may be conceptually 'clean' but in practice, in anything but the most straightforward cases, it simply does not provide the concepts with which to address practical situations. Accounting in real life is essentially an allocative process in which transactions are allocated to appropriate accounting periods. Although the conventions for doing so may need to be developed further, it seems likely that this will remain a more workable approach than recognition criteria based on assets and liabilities.

5.21.2 *Historical cost replaced by current values*

The SoP1 proposals concerning current values appeared to be a somewhat self-contradictory mix of ideas drawn from various systems. SoP1 defines a gain as an increase in the excess of assets over liabilities. This means that if the assets and liabilities are measured at current values any increases in these values are gains. This is somewhat odd, for the document advocates replacement cost as the usual current value to be adopted, but an increase in the cost of replacement of assets is not usually perceived as a gain in developed current cost accounting systems. Under such systems it would be an adjustment to maintain the capital of the reporting entity, not a gain.

This aspect of SoP1 has been greatly watered down in SoP2. While SoP2 indicates current values should be used in appropriate cases, and financial instruments might well be a suitable candidate, the draft no longer recommends it as a general development target for measuring all classes of assets and liabilities. The considerable opposition expressed by the UK accounting establishment in their responses to SoP1 indicate there is no great demand for such a change.

It is unlikely that the usefulness of accounts will be improved by removing the fundamental bedrock of historical cost. There is no great user demand for such a move; historical cost accounts are intelligible to users and have an entirely legitimate claim to relevance. There are circumstances where current values may have their uses and might assist users by being given as supplementary information. For example, such disclosures might be particularly suited to the Operating and Financial Review, which would also give the opportunity to put the valuations in context and explain their inherent subjectivity, perhaps by presenting the valuation information with ranges of outcomes, sensitivities and assumptions.

5.21.3 *The Statement of Financial Performance and the Statement of Total Recognised Gains and Losses (STRGL)*

After the publication of SoP1 it was the view of many commentators that the proposals for the STRGL would damage the integrity and usefulness of the profit and loss account, to the detriment of financial reporting. It appeared that the Board intended the STRGL to assume major significance at the expense of the profit and loss account. The importance of the STRGL was justified in SoP1 by the following two assertions:

- that the importance of the distinction between realised and unrealised profits can and should be discarded;

- that a meaningful split can be made between those gains and losses relating to long-term assets and liabilities and operating gains and losses, and these should be dealt with in different (and exclusive) performance statements.

The abandonment by the ASB of the STRGL in SoP2, while welcome, does not necessarily reassure. This is because the subsequent publication of a Discussion Paper – *Reporting Financial Performance* – discussed at 5.23 below, indicates the underlying thinking that led to the STRGL has not been abandoned.

5.21.4 *The overall purpose of the Statement of Principles*

Apart from specific reservations about the matters discussed above, there are also more general concerns about the Draft *Statement of Principles* itself and the approach that it has taken, since it does not adequately acknowledge the legal and business context in which accounting is practised and the constraints thereby placed on it. The objective of financial statements is said to be to provide information about the financial position, performance and financial adaptability of an enterprise that is useful to a wide range of users for assessing the stewardship of management and for making economic decisions. But this definition is then gradually narrowed. Assessing the stewardship of management as an objective is quickly defined out of existence, because it too is apparently only done to make economic decisions; the wide range of users is collapsed down to the providers of risk capital – shareholders; and the economic decisions to be taken are based on an evaluation of cash generation. The objective of financial statements, therefore, becomes to predict future cash flows.

This tenet is the fundamental assumption in an established branch of academic thought. As an aid to academic thought and research it is a helpful simplification. As the basis for regulatory endeavour, however, it is not appropriate. Accounts do not, in fact, exist primarily to predict cash flows for investment decisions; they form a report by the stewards of an enterprise to its owners, and they sit within a legal and social context that cannot simply be ignored. They also fulfil a variety of other roles, including the identification of profits available for dividend; a starting point for the assessment of taxation (particularly in the light of recent tax cases that have enhanced the importance of accounting rules); a reference point that can be used for conditions in contracts with lenders and other parties; the calculation of executive directors' performance bonuses, and so on.

This means that the ASB will not be able to follow the implications of the Draft *Statement of Principles* in practice since there are a variety of other factors, practical and theoretical (such as company law), which it will have to consider in drafting its regulatory proposals. The utility of the draft is therefore unclear. It is not an agenda and not all of the guiding influences over the Board's work are discussed, while it is undermined by a number of the ASB's subsequent publications (for instance FRS 9 and FRS 10) which are at variance with it.

SoP1 was criticised for the number of controversial assertions it made, for which no evidence was offered. An absolutely central failing of SoP1 was the complete lack of evidence it offered for its view that the most important advantage of current values is their relevance to users. However, another assertion for which no evidence is offered remains in SoP2. It is stated that what matters is future cash flow prediction, yet the draft ignores this crucial test by repeatedly claiming only that things are, or are not, 'relevant' to users. Within the context of the framework what this must mean is whether or not these things have predictive value; but this is not put to the test.

Whereas the subliminal message of SoP1 is that there are certain fundamental accounting truths which are at present unacceptable to the business community, but which through an evolutionary or educational process will become so, the style and tone of SoP2 is much less condescending. The regulatory tradition in the UK has long been that of codifying best practice, one which has many safety features, even if it is not as revolutionary as some would like. Many support this tradition and, in their responses to the SoP1 urged the Board not to regard accounts as inherently unsatisfactory because they do not measure up to an abstract and rather theoretical benchmark. To the Board's credit, SoP2 shows the influence of these responses.

At the same time, the revised draft continues to ignore the transaction-based reality of accounting, perseveres with its empirically unsupported view of an accounting based on unsatisfactory asset and liability definitions, and the recognition of gains defined solely in these terms. It appears that the need for consistency with this stance has forced the ASB to persist in SoP2 with its dismissal of the importance of realised profits.

Existing accounting practice focuses on measuring the further instalment of profit or loss that a company should report as a result of a further year of activity. The concept of realisation has an important function in that task, because it establishes a qualitative threshold that profit must satisfy before it can be reported. This concept should not be abandoned lightly.

Of course, the definition of what is a realised profit is sometimes problematic. In particular, many would agree that literal interpretations of words such as 'readily convertible into cash', have become outmoded and that a broader definition is needed, especially to take account of the development of markets in financial instruments.

Draft guidance on the determination of realised profits under the Companies Act was issued for comment in July 1999 by the Institute of Chartered Accountants in England and Wales. This is discussed in Chapter 3 of this book.

5.22   Discounting in Financial Reporting

In April 1997 the ASB issued a 'Working Paper' on discounting in financial reporting. The ASB pointed out that the Working Paper was not a prelude to a future FRS on the topic, and that the decision on whether discounting will be prescribed in any particular circumstance will form part of the development of the relevant Standard. As a result, the Working Paper is described as being 'for the Board's own reference as the Board considers discounting within various projects'.[348]

The ASB states that, in preparing the paper, it has drawn extensively on the research of the FASB in this area. However, since the publication of the ASB's working paper the FASB has issued a further draft SFAC on this subject which contains significant changes. The FASB's latest proposals (see 3.7 above) contain substantial extra complication which may end up being recommended by the ASB, in view of the remarkable degree of commonality that exists between their framework projects. The IASC also currently has a project in progress on this topic.

The problem is that the Board has not examined the issue of discounting at a fundamental level. Before looking at specific cases, there is the need to address more general issues. For example, where do finance costs fit into the overall framework of financial reporting? This affects matters such as the capitalisation of finance costs and imputed interest, dividends and the distinction between different stakeholders.

Instead, the paper starts with no particular objectives, meanders around the subject of discounting and comes to its conclusions rather abruptly. In fact, the only real conclusion that the paper reaches is that it 'has shown that discounting future cash flows to reflect the time value of money and the effect of the variability of the cash flows is consistent with both historical cost and current value bases of accounting'.[349] However, this comes to the reader of the paper as a bolt from the blue, since there has been no real indication that this was where the paper was leading. This is because the paper was really just a rationalisation of what the ASB wanted to do on some of its current projects, such as impairment, provisions and pension liabilities. As a result, the paper includes statements such as: 'discounting is, therefore, a useful tool in accounting measurements'.[350] The paper does devote some time to discussing the issue of risk, but it does so in the context of specific projects such as pensions and provisions.

Moreover, what the paper does not adequately consider is that discounting is not just a balance sheet issue, it affects profit and loss measurement and classification as well whenever cash flows are separated from accruals of income or expenses – for example, the measurement of profit where assets are sold on deferred terms. Furthermore, even in addressing discounting in the context of accounting for environmental liabilities, the paper does not deal with issues such as accounting for abandonment costs, or explain why the balance sheet approach of recognising a discounted liability is preferable to the generally accepted unit of production approach. It is therefore not clear why the ASB believes that entities should be required to record interest on the accretion of a liability in circumstances where no cash is borrowed.

All in all, the ASB's paper adds little to existing knowledge and seems more of a rationalisation of the ASB's current agenda.

5.23　Discussion paper: Reporting Financial Performance

This paper was developed by the G4+1 group of accounting standard setters and 'reflects an agreed approach to reporting financial performance that each body ... intends to develop in its own constituency'.[351] The G4+1 paper represents the views of the staff of the standard setters from the USA, UK, Canada, Australia, New Zealand and the IASC. It is intended that there should be convergence between the constituent member's standards and this paper is published in order to foster this result in the area of reporting financial performance. The discussion paper has nine chapters, of which Chapter 2: Proposed model for reporting financial performance, Chapter 3: The contents of 'other gains and losses'; and Chapter 4: Recycling, contain the core of the proposals.

The paper takes the view that there should be only one statement of performance in which should be reported all recognised gains and losses, this single statement usually being called a 'comprehensive income statement' (CIS). It is acknowledged in the foreword that this approach represents 'substantial changes to the income statement formats used by most reporting entities'.[352] It is clear from Chapter 2 of the paper that the method of recognising and defining gains and losses is that adopted by the Board in its controversial Draft *Statement of Principles*, which is discussed above.

The paper reiterates the ASB's assertions in its Draft *Statement of Principles* that the 'key objective of financial reporting is to provide information that is useful in making predictions ... of the amount, probability and timing of future cash flows'.[353] It states that the profit and loss account and similar summary measures of financial performance have little predictive value in their current form,[354] without offering any evidence, and in the face of substantial evidence to the contrary. A list of problems with current performance reporting is included, which seem to be: the treatment of foreign currency translation adjustments; the inclusion of proposed dividends in the profit and loss account; and the assertion that basing the profit and loss account on realised profits permits the 'management of reported profits'.[355] The last of these seems out of touch with reality, given that the most notorious examples of profit 'management' usually involve unrealised gains.

The paper therefore suggests that there should be one single statement of financial performance, divided 'in three major components:

(a) the results of operating (or trading) activities;

(b) the results of financing and other treasury activities; and

(c) other gains and losses'.[356]

The following illustration is given to show what is intended.[357]

STATEMENT OF FINANCIAL PERFORMANCE

OPERATING (TRADING) ACTIVITIES

Revenues	775
Cost of sales	(620)
Other expenses	(104)
Operating income	**51**

FINANCING AND OTHER TREASURY ACTIVITIES

Interest on debt	(26)	
Gains and losses on financial instruments	8	
Financing income		**(18)**
Operating and financing income before taxation		33
Taxation on income		(12)
Operating and financing income after taxation		21

OTHER GAINS AND LOSSES

Profit on disposal of discontinued operations	3	
Profit on sale of properties in continuing operations	6	
Revaluation of long-term assets	4	
Exchange translation differences on foreign currency net investments	(2)	
Other gains and losses before taxation	11	
Taxation on other gains and losses	(4)	
Other gains and losses after taxation		7
Total		28

It is clear the above is driven by the ASB's balance sheet based recognition of gains and losses, and its consequent dismissal of the importance of realisation. The 'Financing and other Treasury Activities' section in particular seems to exist in order to facilitate an, as yet, only indirectly stated intention of the G4+1 to alter radically the manner in which liabilities are recorded.

The FASB paper on discounting, discussed at 3.7 above, envisages the recognition of borrowings in the balance sheet at their net present value (NPV). A simple example of this would be a fixed rate loan of £1m at 8% for 5 years. At the end of the first year, interest rates fall to 4% and remain at that level for the rest of the term of the loan.

Following an historical cost approach, the balance sheet would show a liability of £1m throughout the term of the loan, while the profit and loss account would show a finance cost of £80,000 for each of the five years. Applying the CIS discussion paper's ideas would introduce current values in place of historical costs and produce a very different accounting treatment. In year 1 the interest payment of £80,000 would all be charged to the profit & loss account as before. However, the loan would then be revalued to £1,145,200 (reflecting the NPV of the future cash payments discounted at 4%). The increase so produced of £145,200 would be charged to the CIS. As this procedure gives a liability in the balance sheet at the end of year 1 substantially greater than the actual repayment of principal to be made at the end of the term, it presents a difficulty. This difficulty is then fixed by allocating the subsequent interest payments in two separate ways: that part of the payment that represents interest at the market rate of 4% is charged to the CIS as a finance cost, while the remainder is debited to the loan account to begin the process of reducing it to the actual repayable principal by the end of the fifth year.

However counter-intuitive it would seem that a loss of £145,200 can result solely from borrowing £1m at a fixed interest rate, in reality things can become substantially more complex, for example where interest rates fluctuate in subsequent years. This results in a significant disconnect between the CIS and the balance sheet on the one hand and the cash payment reality on the other. This is because the CIS will reflect a charge of £145,200 which is neither a year 1 cash payment nor a loss at all, while the balance sheet shows a liability which is overstated by the same amount. The consequences of this added complication for understandability, a key objective of financial reporting, are considerable.

This complication is brought a significant step nearer by the discussion paper's promotion of a CIS with a section designed to accept just such adjustments. The procedure explained above is discussed in both the ASB's and the FASB's discounting publications (see 3.7 and 5.22 above) and it remains quite clearly part of their agendas for changing financial reporting. Indeed the ASB was unequivocal in its statement on this matter in SoP1: 'where monetary items will not give rise to cash flows in the near future, those cash flows need to be discounted in order to obtain their value at the balance sheet date'.[358]

Chapter 2 of the paper then briefly surveys some of the difficulties of defining into which of the three income statement categories the various gains it identifies should go, indicating a standard would be required on this topic. Chapter 3 discusses in more detail what should be included in the 'other gains and losses' section of the CIS. The discussion is complex and opaque with depreciation and impairment being reported in one section, while revaluations, devaluations and reversals of impairments are reported in another, depending upon the valuation bases adopted.[359]

Chapter 3 reiterates the ASB's attempts to decouple realisation from profit reporting, making the statement that 'a realised gain on a fixed asset reflects the same economic event, i.e. a rise in value, as an unrealised gain, albeit that the realised gain is confirmed by a transaction'.[360] This claim is self-contradictory, because what is termed 'confirmed by a transaction' is of course the subsequent 'economic event' that makes the two so entirely different. Moreover, any person with commercial experience will confirm that making a sale (euphemistically called 'confirmed by a transaction' by the ASB) is *the* most vital and important 'economic event' of all. There is a substantial difference between revaluing a property and actually selling it, particularly in times of economic downturn. To put the two events on the same level from a financial reporting point of view is trivialising economic reality.

The discussion paper returns to this topic in Chapter 4: Recycling. The term refers to a difficulty stemming from the balance sheet view of profit recognition, which requires the CIS to include all gains whether realised or not. However, many accounting bodies and many countries' legislation, including all EU member states, require a clear distinction to be made between realised and unrealised profits. Therefore the proponents of the CIS have to decide whether, once a gain is realised, it should be 'recycled' by reversing the previously reported 'gain' in order to report it once more as a realised one.

The discussion paper declares recycling to be unnecessary and without conceptual justification by repeating the spurious grounds, referred to above, that 'realisation merely represents confirmation of a gain'.[361] However, the FASB, which published SFAS 130 – *Reporting Comprehensive Income* – in June 1997 requires recycling. In spite of the paper's attempts to gloss over it,[362] this represents a major difference between the ASB and the FASB. Furthermore, the FASB gives so many layout options that, in reality, it allows US companies not to have a CIS at all. It would seem that the FASB takes an altogether more relaxed view of the utility of the CIS than the ASB, SFAS 130 allowing that: 'A single focus on total comprehensive income is likely to result in a limited understanding of an enterprise's activities'.[363] The IASC, in its publication on this subject IAS 1 – *Presentation of Financial Statements* – is silent on both realisation and recycling.[364]

6   OTHER INTERNATIONAL FRAMEWORK PROJECTS

The last ten years have seen what might be viewed as a renewed vigour amongst various standard-setting bodies around the world towards seeking an acceptable framework for financial reporting. Each body might have its own reason for doing so, but it is clear that the accounting profession world-wide has come under increasing pressure both as a result of the imprecision of existing accounting standards, and through not being able to respond promptly and effectively to emerging issues, such as off balance sheet finance and asset revaluations. However, as shown throughout this chapter, these recent attempts at developing a framework largely restate the same broad principles that have been repeated over the years, often comprising no more than a précis of previous studies, particularly those of the FASB. The only radically different approach is found in the discussion document issued by the ICAS[365] (see 4.6 above).

6.1   The IASC conceptual framework

In May 1988, the IASC issued an exposure draft – *Framework for the Preparation and Presentation of Financial Statements* – which set out its understanding of 'the conceptual framework that underlies the preparation and presentation of financial statements'.[366] This was converted without major change into a final statement in September 1989, although it is stressed within the statement that it will be revised from time to time in the light of the Board's experience in working with it.[367] The statement is not an accounting standard and does not override any specific IAS;[368] it therefore has much the same status as the FASB's concepts statements.

On first reading the IASC Framework statement, one might be forgiven for thinking that it is merely an encapsulation of the FASB's six concepts statements; indeed, it is likely that the IASC, quite understandably, used the FASB project as a basis for its study. This might explain why it contains very much the same basic flaws as there are in the FASB's framework and which are discussed at 3 above. Furthermore, the impression that the statement creates is that the IASC has attempted to justify the status quo; in other words, it appears to have tried to make the proposed framework consistent with current external financial reporting practice. This is evidenced, for example, by the statement in the introduction to the effect that financial statements normally include a balance sheet, a profit and loss statement, a statement of changes in financial position and notes;[369] the statement is then devoted to applying its 'framework' to this traditional financial reporting package, without, for example, following the ICAS approach of considering the possibility of an entirely new package.

The Framework statement begins well, with a lucid exposition of the nature and purposes of financial statements and their qualitative characteristics. However, it then moves into describing the various elements of financial statements and the criteria for their recognition; although this is clearly a difficult area, it has not been dealt with convincingly. Thereafter, the statement loses its impetus altogether and deals with the measurement of these elements in a mere three paragraphs, only noting that a number of possibilities exist, including historical cost, current cost, realisable value and present value.[370]

The fundamental problem with this framework (as with the FASB's framework) is that we do not believe that it is possible to develop general purpose rules on the recognition of elements of financial statements, whilst simultaneously leaving open the questions of how they are to be measured and against what capital maintenance yardstick profit is to be determined. Furthermore, the statement has similar problems to SFAC No. 6 in its definitions of assets and liabilities, with the result that certain traditionally recognised assets and liabilities would be disqualified from appearing in the balance sheet. The statement specifically says that 'the application of the matching concept under this framework does not allow the recognition of items in the balance sheet which do not meet the definition of assets and liabilities';[371] consequent practical effects could include the immediate recognition in income of government grants as they are received, pension cost variations as soon as they are identified, and so on. The effect of this would be to change fundamentally the relationship between the profit and loss account and the balance sheet in the same manner that the ASB has attempted to do in its conceptual framework project.

We do not suggest that any one system is necessarily superior to another, but it is not possible to fit all possible systems of accounting into one framework of rules on the elements of financial statements and their recognition. We believe that lack of clarity on this point has led to constant confusion on accounting concepts, where ideas which belong in discrete methodologies are used interchangeably and lead to a mish-mash that lacks any cohesion. It should be the role of a conceptual framework study to unravel this tangle, but in this respect at least we believe that this document simply compounds the confusion by failing to distinguish the essential features which make different approaches mutually incompatible. We therefore hope that, in considering the applicability of the statement in the course of its future work, the IASC finds it possible to differentiate the features of alternative approaches which require the development of distinct rules on identification and recognition of the individual elements.

6.2   The CICA financial statement concepts

In December 1988, the CICA *Handbook* Section 1000 – *Financial Statement Concepts* – was issued, describing the concepts underlying the development and use of accounting principles in the general purpose financial statements.[372] It is anticipated that the concepts will be used 'by preparers of financial statements and accounting practitioners in exercising their professional judgement as to the application of generally accepted accounting principles and in establishing accounting policies in areas in which accounting principles are developing'.[373] However, nothing in Section 1000 overrides any specific recommendation in any other Section of the CICA *Handbook*, or any other accounting principle considered to be generally accepted.[374]

In fact, both the form and content of Section 1000 are very similar to the IASC's framework, dealing with the objective of financial statements, qualitative characteristics, elements of financial statements, recognition criteria and measurement in much the same way. The definitions of assets and liabilities are almost identical in the two pronouncements and, although it discusses various measurement bases, Section 1000 also does not establish standards for particular measurement or disclosure issues.[375]

6.3   The New Zealand framework

The 'Framework for Financial Reporting in New Zealand' consists of the Statement of Concepts for General Purpose Financial Reporting, the Framework for Differential Reporting, the Explanatory Foreword to General Purpose Financial Reporting and FRS 2 – *Presentation of Financial Reports*. The Statement of Concepts became operative for periods commencing on or after 1 January 1995, the Framework for Differential Reporting was effective from

1 February 1994 (and was revised in April 1997), and the Explanatory Foreword became operative in January 1995. The purpose of FRS 2 is to build on the Statement of Concepts by establishing a framework for the information to be presented in general purpose financial reports.

The key elements of this framework that are relevant to this Chapter are as follows:

6.3.1   Statement of Concepts

The heart of the framework lies in the Statement of Concepts. It covers the objectives of general purpose financial reporting, the qualitative characteristics by which the usefulness of financial reports should be measured, the assumptions underlying the preparation of financial reports, the influences on the preparation of financial reports, the definition and recognition of the elements of financial statements and the measurement of the elements.

In discussing the objectives of financial reporting, the Statement acknowledges that they lie balanced between two roles: an accountability role (providing information to external parties on the entity's financial and service performance and its compliance with relevant legal requirements) as well as the more familiar informative/decision-usefulness role (providing information to external parties to assist them in making decisions about providing resources to or doing business with the reporting entity).

The Statement then goes on to describe the qualitative characteristics for general purpose financial reports in much the same terms as other frameworks – particularly that of the US, SFAC No. 2 – focusing on relevance, understandability, reliability and comparability as the primary characteristics. As do other frameworks, the Statement also acknowledges the trade-offs which exist between qualitative characteristics. It also discusses the cost/benefit issue, noting that the benefits derived from information should exceed the cost of providing it.

The Statement defines the elements of financial statements in essentially the same way as in most other framework documents, with the definitions of assets and liabilities providing the building blocks on which the other definitions are based. Assets are defined as service potential or future economic benefits controlled by the entity as a result of past transactions or other past events, and an asset is recognised when it is probable that the service potential or future economic benefits embodied in the asset will eventuate and the asset possesses a cost or other value that can be measured with reliability. Liabilities are defined as present obligations to sacrifice future service potential or future economic benefits to other entities as result of past transactions or other past events, and a liability is recognised when it is probable that the future sacrifice of service potential or future economic benefits will be required and the liability can be measured with reliability.

A significant point in relation to these recognition criteria is that the term 'probable' is defined as an event being more likely than less likely to occur. Therefore, if there is more than a 50% chance of future economic benefits eventuating, and it can be reliably measured, the financial element (e.g. asset or liability) should be recognised.

Like the IASC framework, the Statement only lists the range of possible approaches to the measurement of elements and the choice of capital maintenance concepts. What is noteworthy, though, is that the original Exposure Draft advocated the introduction of a new financial statement – to be termed a Statement of Changes in Financial Wealth – which was not too dissimilar to the statement of total recognised gains and losses found in the UK. However, this proposal has been toned down in the Statement, which now requires that all valuations be recognised in either the statement of financial performance or a new statement of movements in equity.

6.3.2 *Differential Reporting*

The other aspect of the framework most worthy of comment here is the Framework for Differential Reporting. The purpose of differential reporting is to allow entities which meet specified criteria (defined as 'qualifying entities') to be exempted, in part or in full, from specific financial reporting standards. The Framework sets out the criteria by which entities qualify for differential reporting exemptions. In so doing, it implicitly provides a guide to standard-setters on establishing differential reporting exemptions in respect of future financial reporting standards. Perhaps not surprisingly, the Framework applies only to general purpose financial reports, since special purpose financial reports are tailored to meet the specific information needs of particular users.

An entity is defined as a qualifying entity and will therefore qualify for differential reporting exemptions when it does not have public accountability and:

■ at balance sheet date all of its owners are members of the entity's governing body; or

■ the entity is not large.

The Framework regards an entity as large if it exceeds any two of the following:

■ total revenue of $5.0 million;

■ total assets of $2.5 million;

■ 20 full time equivalent, paid employees.

These size criteria were last amended in April 1997.

Whilst the Institute of Chartered Accountants of New Zealand's work on differential reporting is to be commended, it is unfortunate that a size test has been introduced as one of the qualifying criteria. In our view, the heart of differential reporting lies in the relationship between owners and managers, since the information needs of owner/managers are entirely different from those of external owners, irrespective of the size of the entity. Consequently, there can be little conceptual justification for differential reporting to be governed by size of entity.

6.3.3 *Explanatory Foreword*

The Explanatory Foreword sets out the context for the statements which follow, explaining the relationship between general purpose financial reports, the Statement of Concepts and Financial Reporting Standards (FRSs). It explains that general purpose financial reports are financial reports which are intended to provide information to meet the needs of external users who are unable to require, or contract for, the preparation of special reports to meet their specific information needs. Again, the distinction between general purpose financial reports and special purpose financial reports is important in a reporting environment which recognises differential reporting.

7   CONCLUSION

The aims of this Chapter have been twofold: first, we have attempted to provide an outline of the immense amount of energy that has been expended (both on the part of individuals and on the part of specifically constituted committees) in attempting to establish an agreed conceptual framework for financial reporting; second, in so doing, we have highlighted the irreconcilable differences and logical difficulties that exist in the various accounting theories that have developed over the years. We see little prospect of general agreement ever being reached on issues such as entry values versus exit values or the primacy of the balance sheet versus the profit and loss account. The fact that these differences are irreconcilable is the very reason why we believe that it will not be possible to develop a single generally accepted general purpose accounting model.

However, this does not mean that the search should be abandoned; what it does mean is that an agreed conceptual framework might have to incorporate more than one accounting model so that different users can be furnished with different information appropriate to their various objectives and information needs. This would not necessarily involve supplying less financial information to individual user groups; rather it would mean making sure that each user group has all the information it needs for its investment and other decisions.

That having been said, we believe that historical cost accounting should continue to be the primary basis for UK financial reporting, as it will continue to be in the US. Therefore we hope the ASB is true to its word, and that it intends to honour its commitment to retain the modified historical cost model as the basis for UK financial reporting.[376] Whilst we do not dispute that some users might find current value information about certain assets and liabilities useful, we think that such information should be provided in supplementary form in the operating and financial review, where users could be provided with detailed assumptions, sensitivities and ranges of values. This is because the subjectivity and potential volatility which would necessarily be inherent in the widespread use of current values would seriously undermine the reliability of the financial statements.

We are far from ignorant of the views of analysts and other users regarding the usefulness of current values. However, we are also aware of the fact that users wish to retain the historical cost model since it provides information that is reliable, because the amounts are based on market transactions and borrowings are shown at the amounts that will actually have to be repaid. Extra disclosure, therefore, would be a sounder method of offering a specialised sub-set of users current value estimates.

We are also well aware of the international dimension to the capital markets and the demand for accounting harmonisation; this is an important aspect of the globalisation of the world economy but it does not necessitate radical change to the accepted basis of financial reporting. Rather, it underlines the fact that markets, not accountants, value companies. Users want a stable, reliable and consistent platform to establish historical trends, based upon which they may, if they wish, make their own calculations and predictions about the future.

References

1 FRS 15, *Tangible Fixed Assets*, ASB, February 1999, para. 4.
2 Discussion Paper, *Measurement of tangible fixed assets*, ASB, October 1996, para. 6.6.
3 For a full discussion on the politicisation of accounting see: David Solomons, 'The Politicization of Accounting', *Journal of Accountancy*, November 1978, p. 71.
4 W. A. Paton and A. C. Littleton, *An Introduction to Corporate Accounting Standards*, Monograph No. 3, American Accounting Association, 1940.
5 See, for example: American Accounting Association, Executive Committee, 'A Tentative Statement of Accounting Principles Affecting Corporate Reports', *Accounting Review*, June 1936, pp. 187–191; American Accounting Association, Executive Committee, 'Accounting Principles Underlying Corporate Financial Statements', *Accounting Review*, June 1941, pp. 133–139; American Accounting Association, Committee to Prepare a Statement of Basic Accounting Theory, *A Statement of Basic Accounting Theory*, 1966; American Accounting Association, Committee on Concepts and Standards for External Financial Reports, *Statement on Accounting Theory and Theory Acceptance*, 1977. The 1977 report concluded that closure on the debate was not feasible, which is perhaps indicative of the complexity of the problem.
6 David Solomons, 'The Political Implications of Accounting and Accounting Standard Setting', *Being the third Arthur Young Lecture delivered within the University of Glasgow on 22nd October, 1980*, p. 9.
7 ASC, *Setting Accounting Standards: A Consultative document*.
8 *Ibid.*, para. 7.2.
9 *Ibid.*
10 *Ibid.*, para. 7.7.
11 *Ibid.*, p. 47.
12 *Ibid.*
13 ASC, *Submissions on the Accounting Standards Committee's Consultative Document: Setting Accounting Standards*, in two volumes, ASC, 1979.
14 *Ibid.*, Volume I, p. 270.
15 Maurice Moonitz, *The Basic Postulates of Accounting*, Accounting Research Study No. 1, AICPA, 1961, Preface.
16 *Ibid.*
17 Robert T. Sprouse and Maurice Moonitz, *A Tentative Set of Broad Accounting Principles for Business Enterprises*, Accounting Research Study No. 3, AICPA, 1962.
18 *Ibid.*, p. 14.
19 *Ibid.*, p. 27.
20 APB Statement No. 4, *Basic Concepts and Accounting Principles Underlying Financial Statements of Business Enterprises*, AICPA, October 1970.
21 *Ibid.*, para. 3.
22 *Ibid.*, para. 132.
23 Report of the Study Group on the Objectives of Financial Statements, *Objectives of Financial Statements*, AICPA, October 1973, p. 65.
24 *Ibid.*
25 *Ibid.*
26 Report of the Study Group on the Objectives of Financial Statements, *Objectives of Financial Statements*, AICPA, October 1973.
27 *Ibid.*, p. 13.
28 *Ibid.*, pp. 57–60.
29 FASB Discussion Memorandum, *Conceptual Framework for Accounting and Reporting: Consideration of the Report of the Study Group on the Objectives of Financial Statements*, FASB, June 6, 1974.
30 FASB, *Scope and Implications of the Conceptual Framework Project*, FASB, December 2, 1976.
31 *Ibid.*, p. 5.
32 *Ibid.*, p. 2.
33 *Ibid.*, pp. 5 and 6.

34 Proposed Statement of Financial Accounting Concepts, *Using Cash Flow Information in Accounting Measurements*, FASB, June 11, 1997.
35 SFAC No. 1, *Objectives of Financial Reporting by Business Enterprises*, FASB, November 1978, para. 7.
36 *Ibid.*, para. 9.
37 *Ibid.*, para. 24.
38 *Ibid.*, para. 34.
39 *Ibid.*, para. 37.
40 *Ibid.*, para. 24.
41 *Ibid.*, footnote 6.
42 Lucia S. Chang and Kenneth S. Most, *Financial Statements and Investment Decisions*, Miami: Florida International University, 1979.
43 *Ibid.*, p. 33.
44 SFAC 1, para. 43.
45 *Ibid.*, para. 50.
46 *Ibid.*, para. 51.
47 SFAC No. 2, *Qualitative Characteristics of Accounting Information*, FASB, May 1980, Figure 1.
48 SFAC 1, para. 34.
49 SFAC 2, para. 36.
50 *Ibid.*, p. x.
51 *Ibid.*, para. 90.
52 *Ibid.*, p. xi.
53 *Ibid.*, para. 56.
54 *Ibid.*
55 *Ibid.*, para. 51.
56 *Ibid.*, p. xvi.
57 *Ibid.*
58 *Ibid.*, para. 59.
59 IAS 39, *Financial Instruments: Recognition and Measurement*, IASC, December 1998, para. 70.
60 SFAC 2, paras. 91–97.
61 *Ibid.*, para. 93.
62 *Ibid.*, para. 95.
63 SFAC No. 6, *Elements of Financial Statements*, a replacement of FASB Concepts Statement No. 3, FASB, December 1985, para. 25.
64 *Ibid.*, para. 27.
65 *Ibid.*, para. 28.
66 *Ibid.*, para. 35.
67 *Ibid.*, para. 36.
68 *Ibid.*, para. 49.
69 *Ibid.*, para. 66.
70 *Ibid.*
71 *Ibid.*, para. 67.
72 *Ibid.*, para. 70.
73 SFAC 1, para. 43.
74 SFAC 6, p. 1, footnote 1.
75 *Ibid.*, para. 78.
76 *Ibid.*, para. 80.
77 *Ibid.*, para. 82.
78 *Ibid.*, para. 83.
79 *Ibid.*, para. 77.
80 See, for example, SFAC No. 3, *Elements of Financial Statements of Business Enterprises*, FASB, December 1980, para. 58.
81 SFAC No. 5, *Recognition and Measurement in Financial Statements of Business Enterprises*, FASB, December 1984, para. 66.
82 *Ibid.*, paras. 66–70.
83 *Ibid.*, paras. 45–48.

84 *Ibid.*, para. 58.
85 *Ibid.*, para. 63.
86 *Ibid.*, paras. 33 and 34.
87 *Ibid.*, para. 35.
88 David Solomons, 'The FASB's Conceptual Framework: An evaluation', *Journal of Accountancy*, June 1986, pp. 114–124, at p. 122.
89 *Ibid.*, p. 124.
90 *Ibid.*
91 Reed K. Storey and Sylvia Storey, *Special Report: The Framework of Financial Accounting Concepts and Standards*, FASB, January 1998, p. 158.
92 *Ibid.*
93 *Ibid.*, p. 160.
94 *Ibid.*, p. 161.
95 *Ibid.*, p. 74.
96 *Ibid.*, p. 75.
97 *Ibid.*, p. 74.
98 *Ibid.*, p. 74.
99 *Ibid.*, p. 83.
100 Proposed Statement of Financial Accounting Concepts (revised), *Using Cash Flow Information and Present Value in Accounting Measurements*, FASB, March 1999, para. 15.
101 *Ibid.*, para. 17.
102 Proposed Statement of Financial Accounting Concepts, *Using Cash Flow Information in Accounting Measurements*, FASB, June 11, 1997, para. 16
103 *Ibid.*, paras. 40 to 48.
104 Proposed Statement of Financial Accounting Concepts (revised), *Using Cash Flow Information and Present Value in Accounting Measurements*, paras. 24 and 25.
105 *Ibid.*, para. 29.
106 Proposed Statement of Financial Accounting Concepts, *Using Cash Flow Information in Accounting Measurements*, paras. 51 to 54.
107 Proposed Statement of Financial Accounting Concepts (revised), *Using Cash Flow Information and Present Value in Accounting Measurements*, para. 59.
108 *Ibid.*, para. 61 and 102.
109 *Ibid.*, para. 62.
110 *Ibid.*, para. 117.
111 *Ibid.*, Glossary of terms.
112 Stephen A. Zeff, *Accounting Horizons*, 'A Perspective on the U.S. Public/Private-Sector Approach to the Regulation of Financial Reporting', Vol. 9 No. 1, March 1995, p. 60.
113 SSAP 2, *Disclosure of accounting policies*, November 1971.
114 *Ibid.*, para. 2.
115 *Ibid.*, para. 14.
116 *Ibid.*
117 CA 85, Sch. 4. paras. 9–13.
118 *Ibid.*, para. 14.
119 This conflict has been noted by the European Commission in a document published by the Contact Committee on the Accounting Directives, stating that 'IAS 37's definition of a provision as it is applied to the specific case of restructuring provisions is inconsistent with the Fourth Directive because it will prevent provision being made for items for which provision is required by Articles 31.1(c)(bb) and 31(d) of the Directive.' See *Examination of the conformity between IAS 37 and the European Accounting Directives*, XV/6010/99 EN, Brussels, 27 April 1999.
120 SSAP 2, para. 15.
121 *Ibid.*, para. 16.
122 *Ibid.*, para. 18.
123 FRS 15, para. 82.
124 *The Corporate Report*, A discussion paper published for comment by the Accounting Standards Steering Committee, London, 1975.
125 *Ibid.*, para. 0.1.

126 *Ibid.*, para. 0.2.
127 The committee's recommended package of information which should be contained in the annual corporate reports of business enterprises is listed in Appendix 2 of the discussion paper.
128 *The Corporate Report*, para. 0.3.
129 *Ibid.*, para. 1.1.
130 *Ibid.*, para. 1.8.
131 *Ibid.*, para. 1.9. The seven user groups identified were: (a) the equity investor group, (b) the loan creditor group, (c) the employee group, (d) the analyst-adviser group, (e) the business contact group, (f) the government and (g) the public.
132 *Ibid.*, paras. 2.1–2.40.
133 *Ibid.*, para. 3.2.
134 *Ibid.*, para. 3.3.
135 *Ibid.*, para. 4.30.
136 *Ibid.*, para. 4.40.
137 *Ibid.*, para. 6.56.
138 *Ibid.*, paras. 6.56 and 6.57.
139 *Ibid.*, para. 7.4.
140 *Ibid.*, para. 7.15.
141 *Ibid.*, paras. 7.40 and 7.43.
142 Report of the Inflation Accounting Committee, *Inflation Accounting*, Cmnd. 6225, London: HMSO, 1975, (the Sandilands Report).
143 *Ibid.*, p. iv.
144 *Ibid.*, para. 144.
145 *Ibid.*, Chapter 12.
146 SSAP 7 (Provisional), *Accounting for changes in the purchasing power of money*, May 1974.
147 SSAP 7 recommended that the RPI should be used for this purpose.
148 SSAP 7, para. 12.
149 The Sandilands Report, para. 20.
150 *Ibid.*, para. 422.
151 *Ibid.*, paras. 411 and 412.
152 *Ibid.*, para. 415.
153 Edwards and Bell have made significant contributions in the areas of income determination and value measurement — however, it is beyond the scope of this book to provide a detailed analysis of their theories. Their case for income and value measurement based on replacement costs may be found in their classic work: E. O. Edwards and P. W. Bell, *The Theory and Measurement of Business Income*, University of California Press, 1961.
154 The Sandilands Report, para. 453.
155 *Ibid.*, para. 499.
156 Kenneth MacNeal, *Truth in Accounting*, Philadelphia: University of Pennsylvania Press, 1939.
157 R. J. Chambers, *Accounting, Evaluation and Economic Behaviour*, Prentice-Hall, 1966.
158 R. R. Sterling, *Theory of the Measurement of Enterprise Income*, University of Kansas Press, 1970.
159 R. J. Chambers, *The Design of Accounting Standards*, University of Sydney Accounting Research Centre, Monograph No. 1, 1980.
160 Edward Stamp, 'Does the Chambers' Evidence Support the CoCoA System', *Accounting and Business Research*, Spring 1983, pp. 119–127.
161 *Ibid.*, p. 127.
162 The Sandilands Report, para. 510.
163 The Institute of Chartered Accountants of Scotland, *Making Corporate Reports Valuable*, London: Kogan Page, 1988, paras. 6.20–6.23.
164 Lee has published numerous papers on the subject of cash flow accounting, the ideas of which have been drawn together in his book: Tom Lee, *Cash Flow Accounting*, Wokingham, Van Nostrand Reinhold (UK), 1984.
165 Lawson has published widely on the subject of cash flow accounting — see, for example: G. H. Lawson, 'Cash-flow Accounting', *The Accountant*, October 28th, 1971, pp. 586–589; G. H. Lawson, 'The Measurement of Corporate Profitability on a Cash-flow Basis', *The International Journal of Accounting Education and Research*, Vol. 16, No. 1, pp. 11–46.

166 Tom Lee, *op. cit.*, p. 51.

167 *Ibid.*, pp. 51–52.

168 Lee presents a quantified example of his proposed cash flow reporting system, *Ibid.*, pp. 57–72.

169 The Sandilands Report, para. 518.

170 *Ibid.*, para. 517.

171 *Ibid.*, para. 537.

172 For a detailed discussion of the capital maintenance concepts which apply in the Sandilands proposals, see: H. C. Edey, 'Sandilands and the Logic of Current Cost', *Accounting and Business Research*, Volume 9, No. 35, Summer 1979, pp. 191–200.

173 ASC, ED 24, *Current cost accounting*, para. 6.

174 ASC, *Inflation accounting — an interim recommendation by the Accounting Standards Committee*, November 1977.

175 *Ibid.*, para. 4.

176 ED 24, para. 8.

177 *Ibid.*

178 *Ibid.*, para. 9.

179 SSAP 16, *Current cost accounting*, March 1980.

180 *Ibid.*, para. 48.

181 SFAS No. 33, *Financial Reporting and Changing Prices*, paras. 47–56, *passim*.

182 SFAS No. 89, *Financial Reporting and Changing Prices*, paras. 34, 35 and 40–43, *passim*.

183 SFAC 5, paras. 45–48.

184 In January 1983, the Research Board of the ICAEW initiated a research project into the usefulness of current cost accounting. The research was divided into a number of studies designed to investigate the uses made by different interest groups, the benefits and the costs of current cost accounting; the whole project was undertaken under the control of the ICAEW's then Director of Research, Professor Bryan Carsberg. The project was completed in September 1983 and the results were made available to the ASC to assist with its review of SSAP 16. See: Bryan Carsberg and Michael Page (Joint Editors), *Current Cost Accounting: The Benefits and the Costs*, ICAEW, 1984.

185 Accounting Standards Committee, *Accounting for the effects of changing prices: a Handbook*, ASC, 1986.

186 Richard Macve, *A Conceptual Framework for Financial Accounting and Reporting: the possibilities for an agreed structure*, A report prepared at the request of the Accounting Standards Committee, ICAEW, 1981, Preface, p. 3.

187 *Ibid.*, Chapter 6, *passim*.

188 *Ibid.*, p. 52.

189 *Ibid.*, p. 64.

190 *Ibid.*, p. 91.

191 David Solomons, *Guidelines for Financial Reporting Standards*, A Paper Prepared for The Research Board of the Institute of Chartered Accountants in England and Wales and addressed to the Accounting Standards Committee, ICAEW, 1989, (the Solomons Report).

192 Edward Stamp, *Corporate Reporting: Its Future Evolution*, a research study published by the Canadian Institute of Chartered Accountants, 1980, (the Stamp Report), Ch. 1, para. 3.

193 The Corporate Report, paras. 2.22–2.31.

194 Stamp's proposed user groups were as follows: shareholders, management, long- and short-term creditors, analysts and advisers, employees, non-executive directors, customers, suppliers, industry groups, labour unions, government departments and ministers, the public, regulatory agencies, other companies, standard setters and academic researchers. See the Stamp Report, Table 1, p. 44.

195 Edward Stamp, 'First steps towards a British conceptual framework', *Accountancy*, March 1982, pp. 123–130.

196 Stamp's qualitative criteria were ranked (from most important to least important) by the ASC members as follows (*Ibid.*, Figure 2, p. 126): relevance, clarity, substance over form, timeliness, comparability, materiality, freedom from bias, objectivity, rationality, full disclosure, consistency, isomorphism, verifiability, cost/benefit effectiveness, non-arbitrariness, data availability, flexibility, uniformity, precision, conservatism.

197 The Stamp Report, Chapter 2.

198 *Ibid.*, Chapter 12.

199 ICAS, *Making Corporate Reports Valuable*, para. 0.2.
200 *Ibid.*, Chapter 8.
201 *Ibid.*, paras. 1.1–1.20, *passim*.
202 *Ibid.*, para. 3.6.
203 *Ibid.*, para. 3.11.
204 The Corporate Report, paras. 2.2–2.8.
205 ICAS, *Making Corporate Reports Valuable*, para. 3.12.
206 *Ibid.*, para. 6.36.
207 *Ibid.*
208 *Ibid.*, para. 6.24.
209 The Institute of Chartered Accountants of Scotland, *Making Corporate Reports Valuable — The Literature Surveys*, ICAS, 1988.
210 *Ibid.*, p. 301.
211 ICAS, *Making Corporate Reports Valuable*, paras. 7.12–7.20, *passim*.
212 *Ibid.*, para. 7.21.
213 *Ibid.*, paras. 7.23–7.26, *passim*.
214 *Ibid.*, paras. 7.27–7.32, *passim*.
215 *Ibid.*, para. 7.35.
216 *Ibid.*, para. 7.39.
217 *Ibid.*, para. 5.44.
218 *Ibid.*, para. 7.54.
219 'Melody plc', ICAS, September 1990.
220 The Institute of Chartered Accountants of Scotland, *Making Corporate Reports Valuable, A Feasibility Study: The Post Office*, Stuart MacDonald (Researcher), Pauline Weetman (Editor), ICAS, November 1993.
221 Report of the Review Committee under the chairmanship of Sir Ronald Dearing, *The Making of Accounting Standards*, September 1988, para. 7.2.
222 David Solomons, *Guidelines for Financial Reporting Standards*, p. 17.
223 *Ibid.*, p. 18.
224 *Ibid.*
225 *Ibid.*, p. 20.
226 *Ibid.*, p. 21.
227 *Ibid.*, pp. 23–28.
228 *Ibid.*, p. 43.
229 *Ibid.*, pp. 51–52.
230 Accounting Horizons, vol. 9 no.1, pages 42-51
231 David Solomons, *Guidelines for Financial Reporting Standards*, p. 53.
232 *Ibid.*
233 *Ibid.*, p. 54.
234 *Ibid.*, p. 55.
235 *Ibid.*, p. 56.
236 *Ibid.*, p. 63.
237 *Ibid.*, p. 69.
238 *The Future Shape of Financial Reports*, ICAEW/ICAS, 1991, para. 1-2.
239 *Ibid.*, paras. 3-1 to 3-5.
240 *Ibid.*, para. 4-3.
241 *Foreword to Accounting Standards*, ASB, June 1993, para. 4.
242 Statement of Principles Exposure Draft, *Statement of Principles for Financial Reporting*, ASB, November 1995.
243 *Statement of Principles for Financial Reporting – the way ahead, progress paper on the exposure draft*, ASB, July 1996.
244 Statement of Principles Revised Exposure Draft, *Statement of Principles for Financial Reporting*, ASB, March 1999.
245 Statement of Principles Exposure Draft, *Statement of Principles for Financial Reporting*, para. 1.1.
246 *Ibid.*, para. 1.13.
247 *Ibid.*, para. 1.13.

248 *Ibid.*, paras. 1.5 – 1.7.
249 *Ibid.*, para. 1.6.
250 *Ibid.*, para. 1.9
251 *Ibid.*, para. 2.8.
252 *Ibid.*, para. 2.13.
253 *Ibid.*, paras. 2.23 – 2.29.
254 *Ibid.*, paras. 2.30 – 2.33.
255 *Ibid.*, paras. 2.6 – 2.7.
256 *Ibid.*, para. 2.7.
257 *Ibid.*, para. 3.5.
258 *Ibid.*, para. 3.6.
259 *Ibid.*, para. 3.16.
260 *Ibid.*, para. 3.18.
261 *Ibid.*, para. 3.21.
262 *Ibid.*, para. 3.39.
263 *Ibid.*, para. 3.47.
264 *Ibid.*
265 *Ibid.*, para. 3.49.
266 *Ibid.*
267 *Ibid.*, para. 4.1.
268 *Ibid.*, para. 4.5.
269 *Ibid.*, para. 4.6.
270 *Ibid.*, para. 4.7.
271 *Ibid.*, para. 4.8.
272 *Ibid.*, para. 4.11.
273 *Ibid.*, paras. 4.29 and 4.32.
274 *Ibid.*, para. 4.39.
275 *Ibid.*, para. 4.43.
276 *Ibid.*, para. 6.25.
277 *Ibid.*, para. 6.26.
278 *Ibid.*, para. 5.38.
279 *Ibid.*, para. 5.28.
280 The AICPA Special Committee on Financial Reporting, *Meeting the Information Needs of Investors and Creditors*, AICPA, 1994.
281 Exposure Draft, *Statement of Principles for Financial Reporting*, para. 5.22.
282 *Ibid.*, para. 5.23.
283 *Ibid.*, para. 5.22.
284 SSAP 16, *Current cost accounting*, March 1980, para. 43.
285 Exposure Draft, *Statement of Principles for Financial Reporting*, paras. 5.26 – 5.27.
286 *Ibid.*, para. 5.37.
287 *Ibid.*, para. 6.18.
288 *Ibid.*, paras. 6.20 and 6.25.
289 *Ibid.*, para. 6.25.
290 *Ibid.*, para. 7.1.
291 *Ibid.*, para. 7.2.
292 *Ibid.*, para. 7.9.
293 *Ibid.*, para. 7.10.
294 *Ibid.*
295 *Ibid.*, para. 7.38.
296 *Ibid.*, para. 7.41.
297 G. J. Wilkinson-Riddle and L. Holland, *An analysis and discussion of the responses to the ASB's Statement of Principles for Financial Reporting*, Occasional Paper published by The Journal of Applied Accounting Research, July 1997.
298 *Ibid.*, p. 1.
299 *Ibid.*, p. 6.

300 *Statement of Principles for Financial Reporting – the way ahead, progress paper on the exposure draft*, ASB.
301 *Ibid.*
302 *Ibid.*, p. 1.
303 *Ibid.*, p. 6.
304 *Ibid.*, p. 7.
305 *Ibid.*, p. 2.
306 Statement of Principles Revised Exposure Draft, *Statement of Principles for Financial Reporting*, ASB, March 1999.
307 *Ibid.*, preface, p. 10.
308 *Ibid.*, preface, p. 10.
309 *Ibid.*, preface, p. 11.
310 *Ibid.*, introduction, para. 10.
311 *Ibid.*, introduction, para. 11.
312 *Ibid.*, Chapter 1, p. 20.
313 *Ibid.*, Chapter 1, para. 1.19.
314 *Ibid.*, Chapter 2, p. 29.
315 *Ibid.*, Chapter 2, para. 2.4.
316 *Ibid.*, Chapter 3, Principles.
317 Exposure Draft, *Statement of Principles for Financial Reporting*, p. 41.
318 Statement of Principles Revised Exposure Draft, *Statement of Principles for Financial Reporting*, Chapter 2, p. 37.
319 *Ibid.*, Chapter 3, Principles.
320 *Ibid.*, Chapter 3, para. 3.25(b).
321 *Ibid.*, Chapter 3, para. 3.35.
322 *Ibid.*, Chapter 4, para. 4.9.
323 *Ibid.*, Chapter 4, para. 4.9.
324 *Ibid.*, Chapter 4, para. 4.16.
325 *Ibid.*, Chapter 4, para. 4.15.
326 *Ibid.*, Chapter 4, para. 4.18.
327 *Ibid.*, Chapter 4, para. 4.22.
328 *Ibid.*, Chapter 4, para. 4.22.
329 *Ibid.*, Chapter 4, para. 4.24.
330 *Ibid.*, Chapter 4, para. 4.27.
331 *Ibid.*, Chapter 4, para. 4.31.
332 *Ibid.*, Chapter 5, principles p. 62.
333 *Ibid.*, Chapter 5, principles p. 62.
334 *Ibid.*, Chapter 5, para. 5.18.
335 *Ibid.*, Chapter 6, para. 6.2.
336 *Ibid.*, Chapter 6, para. 6.4.
337 *Ibid.*, Chapter 6, para. 6.13.
338 *Ibid.*, Chapter 6, para. 6.23.
339 Revised Draft Statement of Principles, *Some Questions Answered*, ASB, March 1999, Question 8.
340 Statement of Principles Revised Exposure Draft, *Statement of Principles for Financial Reporting*, Chapter 7, para. 7.4.
341 *Ibid.*, Chapter 8, para. 8.4.
342 *Ibid.*, Chapter 8, para. 8.13.
343 Revised Draft Statement of Principles, *Technical Supplement*, ASB March 1999, para. B3.7.
344 *Ibid.*, para. B4.14.
345 *Ibid.*, paras. B5.4 to B5.13.
346 *Ibid.*, para. B5.13.
347 Exposure Draft, *Statement of Principles for Financial Reporting* para. 5.38.
348 Accounting Standards Board Working Paper, *Discounting in Financial Reporting*, ASB, April 1997, p. 3.
349 *Ibid.*, para. 9.1.
350 *Ibid.*, para 1.6.

351 Discussion paper, *Reporting Financial Performance; Proposals for Change* , ASB, June 1999, p. 1.
352 *Ibid.*, p. 20.
353 *Ibid.*, para. 1.6.
354 *Ibid.*, para. 1.7.
355 *Ibid.*, para. 1.14.
356 *Ibid.*, para. 2.6.
357 *Ibid.*, para. 2.7.
358 Exposure Draft, *Statement of Principles for Financial Reporting,* para. 4.44.
359 Discussion paper, *Reporting Financial Performance; Proposals for Change* , paras. 3.6 – 3.17.
360 *Ibid.*, para. 3.17(d).
361 *Ibid.*, para. 4.12.
362 *Ibid.*, para. 4.16.
363 SFAS 130, *Reporting Comprehensive Income*, FASB, June 1997, para. 13.
364 IAS 1, para. 86.
365 The Institute of Chartered Accountants of Scotland, *Making Corporate Reports Valuable*, Kogan Page, 1988.
366 Exposure Draft, *Framework for the Preparation and Presentation of Financial Statements*, IASC, May 1988.
367 *Framework for the Preparation and Presentation of Financial Statements*, IASC, September 1989, para. 4.
368 *Ibid.*, para. 2.
369 *Ibid.*, para. 7.
370 *Ibid.*, paras. 99–101.
371 *Ibid.*, para. 95.
372 CICA Handbook, General Accounting, Section 1000, *Financial Statement Concepts*, para. .01.
373 *Ibid.*, para. .02.
374 *Ibid.*, para. .03.
375 *Ibid.*, paras. .53–.58.
376 Statement of Principles Revised Exposure Draft, *Statement of Principles for Financial Reporting*, Chapter 6, para. 6.4 and Revised Draft Statement of Principles, *Some Questions Answered*, Q.8 and Q.9.

Chapter 3   Revenue recognition

1   THE NATURE OF REVENUE

Revenue is generally discussed in accounting literature in terms of inflows of assets to an enterprise which occur as a result of outflows of goods and services from the enterprise. For this reason, the concept of revenue has normally been associated with specific accounting procedures which were primarily directed towards determining the timing and measurement of revenue in the context of the historical cost double-entry system. For example, APB Statement No. 4 defined revenue as the 'gross increases in assets or gross decreases in liabilities recognized and measured in conformity with generally accepted accounting principles that result from those types of profit-directed activities of an enterprise that can change owners' equity'.[1] Consequently, the accounting principles which evolved focused on determining when transactions should be recognised in the financial statements, what amounts were involved in each transaction, how these amounts should be classified and how they should be allocated between accounting periods.

Historical cost accounting in its pure form avoids having to take a valuation approach to financial reporting by virtue of the fact that it is transactions-based; in other words, it relies on transactions to determine the recognition and measurement of assets, liabilities, revenues and expenses. Over the life of an enterprise, its total income will be represented by net cash flows generated; however, because of the requirement to prepare periodic financial statements, it is necessary to break up the enterprise's operating cycle into artificial periods. The effect of this is that at each reporting date the enterprise will have entered into a number of transactions which are incomplete; for example, it might have delivered a product or service to a customer for which payment has not been received, or it might have received payment in respect of a product or service yet to be delivered. Alternatively, it might have expended cash on costs which relate to future exchange transactions, or it might have received goods and services which it has not yet paid for in cash. Consequently, the most important accounting questions which have to be answered revolve around how to allocate the effects of these incomplete transactions between periods for reporting purposes, as opposed to simply letting them fall into the periods in which cash is either received or paid. This allocation process is based on two, sometimes conflicting, fundamental accounting concepts: accruals (or matching), which attempts to move the costs associated with earning revenues to the periods in which the related revenues will be reported; and prudence, under which revenue and profits are not anticipated, whilst anticipated losses are provided for as soon as they are foreseen, with the result that costs are not deferred to the future if there is doubt as to their recoverability.

As a result, the pure historical cost balance sheet contains items of two types: cash (and similar monetary items), and debits and credits which arise as a result of shifting the effects of transactions between reporting periods by applying the accruals and prudence concepts; in other words, the balance sheet simply reflects the balances which result from the enterprise preparing an accruals-based profit and loss account rather than a receipts and payments account. A non-monetary asset under the historical cost system is purely a deferred cost; a cost which has been incurred before the balance sheet date and, by applying the accruals concept, is expected (provided it passes the prudence test) to benefit periods beyond the balance sheet date, so as to justify its being carried forward. Similarly, the balance sheet incorporates non-monetary credit balances which are awaiting recognition in the profit and loss account but, as a result of the application of the prudence concept, have been deferred to future reporting periods.

It is the aim of this Chapter to suggest broad principles under the existing historical cost accounting system for the recognition of revenues earned from operations. At the same time, though, we are mindful of the fact that the ASB is attempting, through its conceptual framework project to introduce a balance sheet approach to income recognition which would alter radically the basis on which gains and losses are recognised. This is discussed at 4.1 below. Nevertheless, until such time as the ASB has secured some measure of acceptance of its conceptual framework as a whole, the traditional approach to revenue recognition prevails.

Meanwhile, the IASC has moved even more rapidly towards an accounting model based on fair values, with the result that gains and losses are determined by reference to the change in fair value that has occurred over the financial reporting period. This approach has already been adopted in IAS 39 – *Financial Instruments: Recognition and Measurement* – as it applies to certain financial instruments (see Chapter 9 at 5.1), and is being explored in the IASC's current projects on investment properties (see Chapter 10 at 7.1.2) and agriculture (see 3.2.3 below).

2   REALISED PROFITS

The term 'realised profits' was introduced into UK company legislation in the Companies Act 1980 as a result of the implementation of the Second EC Directive on company law, which provided the basic framework for the co-ordination of national provisions dealing with the maintenance, increase and reduction of the capital of public limited companies.[2] The Directive stated that the amount of a distribution to shareholders may not exceed the amount of the profits at the end of the last financial year plus any profits brought forward and sums drawn from reserves available for this purpose, less any losses brought forward and sums placed to reserve in accordance with the law or the statutes.[3]

As a result, the 1980 Act restricted a company's profits available for distribution to its accumulated realised profits less accumulated realised losses, and in so doing reversed the principle which had been laid down in a number of legal cases which permitted companies to make distributions out of current profits without making good past losses. Nevertheless, it is clear that profit for this purpose is discussed in the context of individual companies and not of groups, and that intra-group transactions are sometimes capable of generating realised and, therefore, distributable profits.

The 1980 Act did not define 'realised profits', although a definition was subsequently provided as a result of the implementation of the Fourth EC Directive in the Companies Act 1981. This definition, which was later incorporated into Schedule 4 to the Companies Act 1985, has been amended by the Companies Act 1989, and is now contained in section 262(3) of the Act; it reads as follows: 'References in this Part to "realised profits" and "realised losses", in relation to a company's accounts, are to such profits or losses of the company as fall to be treated as realised in accordance with principles generally accepted, at the time when the accounts are prepared, with respect to the determination for accounting purposes of realised profits or losses.

'This is without prejudice to—

(a)   the construction of any other expression (where appropriate) by reference to accepted accounting principles or practice, or

(b)   any specific provision for the treatment of profits or losses of any description as realised.'

Whilst the Part of the Act referred to in the above definition is Part VII – Accounts and Audit – the definition is given a slightly wider application through section 742(2) which states that 'references in this Act to "realised profits" and "realised losses", in relation to a company's accounts, shall be construed in accordance with section 262(3)'.

This definition is clearly not concerned with GAAP in its broad sense, but with generally accepted accounting principles for determining realised profits for accounting purposes only. In any event, it might be argued that such principles do not necessarily exist, since UK accounting principles are directed towards the recognition and disclosure of items in the financial statements of entities in order to present a true and fair view, and not towards the determination of realised profits. Nevertheless, in its technical release on the subject (TR 481), the CCAB indicated that the term 'principles generally accepted' incorporates the legal principles laid down in Schedule 4 of the Companies Act 1985 and the requirements of the SSAPs (particularly the fundamental accounting concepts of prudence and accruals as set out in SSAP 2).[4] TR 481 concluded that 'a profit which is required by statements of standard accounting practice to be recognised in the profit and loss account should normally be treated as a realised profit, unless the SSAP specifically indicates that it should be treated as unrealised'.[5]

The difficulty that arises from this interpretation is that there are a number of areas of profit recognition which are not, as yet, dealt with in accounting standards; furthermore, certain areas which are covered by accounting standards incorporate inconsistencies in approach. For this reason, it is necessary to establish broad principles for the purpose of determining 'realised profit'. Some might hold the view that SSAP 2's definition of the prudence concept does, in fact, provide a basis for recognising realised profits in that it states that 'revenue and profits are not anticipated, but are recognised by inclusion in the profit and loss account when realised in the form either of cash or of other assets the ultimate cash realisation of which can be assessed with reasonable certainty'.[6] However, some hold the view that this definition may be flawed, since the emphasis on 'cash' and 'ultimate cash realisation' would appear to rule out the recognition of barter transactions or even the accrual of investment income on a time basis.

This view has been similarly expressed in the conclusions to a research study on the reporting of profits and the concept of realisation which was carried out by Sir Bryan Carsberg and Christopher Noke.[7] They felt that the concept of realisation should be equated with 'reliability of measurement' – i.e. to ensure that profits are recognised only when they can be said to have occurred with reasonable certainty – and not with 'convertibility to cash'.[8]

2.1   ICAEW draft guidance

In July 1999 the Company Law Committee of the Institute of Chartered Accountants in England and Wales (ICAEW) published a draft statement of guidance on the determination of realised profits and distributable profits. The aim is for this document ultimately to replace Technical Releases 481 and 482 which were issued in 1992.

The draft guidance starts of by making the statement that 'the concept of what is a realised profit or loss may change over time. This is recognised in the requirement in section 262(3) that realised profits or losses should be determined in accordance with principles generally accepted at the time when the accounts are prepared.'[9] It goes on to explain this by stating that 'SSAP 2's requirements on prudence are now not the only basis for the recognition of realised profits. Changes in the financial and economic environment since SSAP 2 was issued have led to the acceptance of the principle that, in certain circumstances, marked to market gains may constitute realised profits.'[10] It goes on to say that 'realised profits and losses are those recorded under the historical cost convention or by marking to market where used in accordance with generally accepted accounting principles.'[11]

However, since the document does not define the term 'generally accepted accounting principles', this approach could have interesting implications. The ICAEW could conceivably be saying that as long as an accounting standard stipulates the use of mark to market (i.e. fair value) accounting, the result leads to a realised profit. In any event, the document then seems to limit this general assertion by stating that a realised profit only arises when:[12]

'(a) the company concerned has recorded a change in its assets or liabilities in accordance with generally accepted accounting principles and the change arises as a result of:

(i)   a sale or other disposal of an asset or goodwill, or the provision of goods or services, for which the consideration received is 'qualifying consideration'; that is:

- cash, or

- a current asset for which there is a liquid market, or

- a total or partial release (or settlement or assumption by a third party) of a liability of the company, or

- an amount receivable which is expected to be settled within a reasonable period of time by any of the above three forms of consideration; or

(ii) the total or partial release (or settlement or assumption by a third party) of a liability of the company; or

(iii) the use of the mark to market method of accounting for current assets and liabilities; or

(iv) the translation of a monetary asset or liability denominated in a foreign currency; or

(v)   the receipt or accrual of investment or other income receivable in the form of qualifying consideration; or

(vi) a return of capital on an investment where the return is in the form of qualifying consideration; or

(vii) a gift received in the form of qualifying consideration; or

(viii) the release of a provision for a liability or loss which was treated as a realised loss; or

(ix) the reversal of a write-down or provision for depreciation, amortisation, diminution in value or impairment of an asset which was treated as a realised loss; or

(b) the company records

(i) a write-down or provision for depreciation, amortisation, diminution in value or impairment, or

(ii) a disposal for qualifying consideration

of an asset in respect of which an unrealised profit has previously been recognised in revaluation reserve, merger reserve or other similar reserve, in which case the appropriate proportion of the related profit becomes a realised profit; or

(c) the company undertakes a reduction of capital (ie, share capital, share premium or capital redemption reserve) which is credited to reserves, in which case the amount so credited represents a realised profit to the extent that:

(i) the amount was originally raised in qualifying consideration; or

(ii) the consideration received has subsequently become qualifying consideration; or

(iii) the consideration received has been written off and treated as a realised loss (ie, by way of a write-down or provision for depreciation, amortisation, diminution in value or impairment); or

(iv) the capital was originally paid up either by a capitalisation of realised profits or by a capitalisation of unrealised profits or reserves (ie, share premium or capital redemption reserve) which would subsequently have become realised in accordance with the principles set out above.

Where, in the case of a reduction of capital, after making all reasonable enquiries it is not possible to determine whether criteria (i) to (iv) above are met, the profit may be treated as realised.'

On examination, it seems that the ICAEW is attempting to reconcile its view of realised profits with the ASB's balance sheet approach to revenue recognition (see 4.1 below). Under the ASB's revised Draft *Statement of Principles*, gains are defined as being increases in balance sheet net assets other than those resulting from contributions from owners. Consequently, it seems that sub-paragraph (a) above has been designed to reflect this definition, or at least to use similar language in expressing its proposals.

However, this is where the similarity ends. Whilst the ICAEW then sets down a number of conditions that attempt to implement the realisation principle embodied in the law, the ASB has instead stated that it regards the realisation principle as being irrelevant. So whilst the ASB is content to report realised and unrealised profits alongside each other in the income statement,[13] the ICAEW is not.

This point is evident from the ICAEW's draft guidance making it clear that a realised profit only arises through the use of mark to market accounting for *current* assets and liabilities (see condition (a)(iii) above). This means, for example, that according to the draft guidance the recognition of fixed assets at fair value does not give rise to a realised profit. Conversely, because the ASB has adopted the stance that the distinction between realised and unrealised profits is irrelevant, it avoids the issue.

Once the ICAEW's draft guidance is converted into a Technical Release, it will be interesting to see the ASB's reaction thereto, since the ICAEW clearly still believes that the distinction between realised and unrealised profits is important. As a result, the ASB's vision of a single statement of performance showing all gains and losses does not sit very comfortably with the ICAEW's proposed realisation principles, which in turn reflect its understanding of the law.

2.2   Influence of the ASB

In conclusion, therefore, it is not altogether clear whether or not there exists at present a set of principles generally accepted with respect to the determination for accounting purposes of realised profits or losses, as is suggested by the Companies Act. The ASB is having an influence of its own on this matter through Chapter 5 (Recognition in financial statements) of its revised Draft *Statement of Principles*, by creating a direct link between revenue recognition and changes in balance sheet assets and liabilities.[14] This approach is discussed at 4.1 below although, as noted above, the ASB views the realisation principle as 'irrelevant', with the result that all gains and losses will be recognised in a performance statement without any distinction being made between realised profits and unrealised profits.[15] In the view of the ASB, the revenue recognition objective is to recognise a gain only if there is reasonable certainty that it exists and if it can be measured reliably.[16] Consequently, the effect of the ASB's approach is to establish a system of revenue recognition that is based on the initial recognition, subsequent measurement and derecognition of assets and liabilities.

As discussed more fully at 4.2 below, this proposed approach is directly linked with FRS 5's rules on asset recognition and derecognition. FRS 5's rules have a direct impact on the timing of revenue recognition in respect of sales of assets (fixed or current) that are recognised in the balance sheet. Again, these rules are not based on any principles of 'convertibility to cash', but instead are dependent on the transferral of all the significant benefits and risks relating to an asset disposed of, and the reliability of the measurement of the monetary amount of the asset received in exchange. It seems on the face of it, therefore, that there is the potential for conflict between SSAP 2 and FRS 5 in this area.

3   THE TIMING OF REVENUE RECOGNITION

Under the historical cost system, revenues are the inflows of assets to an enterprise as a result of the transfer of products and services by the enterprise to its customers during a period of time, and are recorded at the cash amount received or expected to be received (or, in the case of non-monetary exchanges, at their cash equivalent) as the result of these exchange transactions. However, because of the system of periodic financial reporting, it is necessary to determine the point (or points) in time when revenue should be measured and reported. This is governed by what is known as the 'realisation principle', which acknowledges the fact that for revenue to be recognised it is not sufficient merely for a sale to have been made – there has to be a certain degree of performance by the vendor as well. In the US, this principle was formally codified in 1970 in APB Statement No. 4 as follows: 'revenue is generally recognised when both of the following conditions are met: (1) the earning process is complete or virtually complete, and (2) an exchange has taken place'.[17]

The accounting practice which had developed under this principle was essentially as follows:

(a)   revenue from the sale of goods was recognised at the date of delivery to customers;

(b)   revenue from services was recognised when the services had been performed and were billable;

(c)   revenue derived from permitting others to use enterprise resources (e.g. rental, interest and royalty income) was recognised either on a time basis or as the resources were used; and

(d)   revenue from the sale of assets other than products of the enterprise was recognised at the date of sale.[18]

As stated above, revenue is recognised at the amount received or expected to be received as a consequence of the exchange transaction.

Although APB Statement No. 4 did acknowledge that there were certain exceptions to the sales basis of revenue recognition established under the realisation principle (for example, in the case of long-term construction contracts and the mining of precious metals with assured sales prices),[19] many more exceptions have developed in recent years. As a result, no common basis of revenue recognition exists in contemporary financial accounting for all types of exchange transaction; different (and sometimes inconsistent) rules exist for different circumstances. Nevertheless, these rules have been derived from three broad approaches to the recognition of revenue: the critical event, accretion and revenue allocation approaches, each of which is appropriate under particular circumstances. Each of the three approaches is discussed in turn below.

3.1 The critical event approach

In general terms, the operating cycle of an enterprise involves the acquisition of merchandise or raw materials, the production of goods, the sale of goods or services to customers, the delivery of the goods or performance of the services and the ultimate collection of cash; in some cases it might even extend beyond the cash collection stage, for example, if there are on-going after-sales service obligations. The critical event approach is based on the belief that revenue is earned at the point in the operating cycle when the most critical decision is made or the most critical act is performed.[20] It is therefore necessary to identify the event which is considered to be critical to the revenue earning process. In theory, the critical event could occur at various stages during the operating cycle; for example, at the completion of production, at the time of sale, at the time of delivery or at the time of cash collection.

Revenue recognition is subject to a number of uncertainties; these include the estimation of the production cost of the asset, the selling price, the additional selling costs and the ultimate cash collection. However, since these uncertainties fall away at various stages throughout the operating cycle, it is necessary to identify a point in the cycle at which the remaining uncertainties can be estimated with sufficient accuracy to enable revenue to be recognised. In other words, the critical event should not be judged to occur at a point when the prudence concept would preclude recognition by virtue of the uncertainties which still remain.

3.1.1 The recognition of revenue at the completion of production

Clearly, the uncertainty surrounding the cost of production is removed when the product is completed; it is therefore necessary to evaluate the remaining uncertainties in order to determine whether or not the completion of production can be used as the critical event for revenue recognition. Where the enterprise has entered into a firm contract for the production and delivery of a product, the sales price will have been determined and the selling costs will have already been incurred. Consequently, provided that both the delivery expenses and the bad debt risk can be satisfactorily assessed, it may be appropriate to report revenue on this basis. An application of this practice is the completed contract method of recognising revenue on construction contracts, in terms of which revenue is recognised only when the contract is completed or substantially completed.

It has also become accepted practice in certain industries to recognise revenue at the completion of production, even though a sales contract may not have been entered into. Normally, this practice would only be adopted in the case of the production of certain precious metals and agricultural commodities, provided that the following criteria are met:

(a)   there should be a ready market for the commodity;

(b)   the market price should be determinable;

(c)   the market price should be stable; and

(d)   selling should not be a major activity of the enterprise and there should be no substantial cost of marketing.

SFAC No. 5 refers to such assets as being 'readily realisable' (since they are saleable at readily determinable prices without significant effort), and acknowledges that revenue may be recognised on the completion of production of such assets, provided that they consist of interchangeable units and quoted prices are available in an active market that can rapidly absorb the quantity held by the enterprise without significantly affecting the price.[21] The accounting treatment for this basis would be to value closing stock at net realisable value (i.e. sales price less estimated selling costs), and write off the related production costs.

An extension of this approach is to be found in the generally accepted accounting practice adopted by many UK securities dealers and commodity traders of including commodities, futures and options in their financial statements at market value.

This has now been taken a step further by both the IASC (in IAS 39) and the FASB (in SFAS 133), in terms of which all derivative financial instruments and financial assets held for trading are remeasured at fair value at each balance sheet date, with the changes in fair value being recognised in net profit or loss for the period. IAS 39 goes further than SFAS 133 in that it requires unquoted equity securities that are not held for trading to be carried at fair value, although the standard gives companies the choice of showing the changes in fair value either in net profit or loss for the period or in the statement of changes in equity.[22] Under US GAAP, all unquoted equity instruments are reported at cost, even if fair value can be measured reliably by means other than a quotation in an active market.[23]

The important point to note is that IAS 39's fair value model for certain financial assets is predicated on the assumption that 'fair value can be reliably determined for most financial assets classified as available for sale or held for trading'.[24] The standard goes on to state that the presumption of reliability of measurement can be overcome for an investment in an equity instrument that does not have a quoted market price in an active market and for which other methods of reasonably estimating fair value are clearly inappropriate or unworkable.[25] This means that the reliability of measurement presumption can only be rebutted under very limited circumstances, with the result that for virtually all trading financial assets, revenue is recognised in the income statement on the basis of changes in fair value. By removing the reliably measurable requirement for all trading assets (apart from unquoted equity instruments, and only then in very specific circumstances) the IASC is effectively designating the assets to be 'readily realisable'—whether or not they in fact are.

A major point of departure between the FASB on the one hand and the ASB and IASC on the other is on the issue of realisation. The FASB still does regard the distinction between realised and unrealised profits as being important, and this is evidenced by the FASB approach to 'reclassification adjustments' (otherwise known as recycling) when reporting comprehensive income. Under this approach certain unrealised gains are reported in comprehensive income, and later recycled through the income statement when realised. Under UK GAAP, recycling is prohibited and, as stated above, the ASB regards the realisation principle as being irrelevant.

It is also worth noting that at present (August 1999), the fair value model laid down by IAS 39 does not conform with the European Union's Accounting Directives, with the result that EU companies are currently not able to apply IAS 39 in their statutory accounts. However, the European Commission's declared policy is to keep the European Accounting Directives in line with International Accounting Standards; as a result, the Commission has already put forward proposals for the amendment of the Accounting Directives in order to conform them with the provisions of IAS 39. It is expected that the amendment of the European Accounting Directives will be approved in time for the implementation of IAS 39 in January 2001, thus permitting EU companies to recognise certain financial assets and liabilities in their balance sheets at fair value, with the corresponding unrealised gains and losses being shown in the profit and loss account.

3.1.2   *The recognition of revenue at the time of sale*

The time of sale is probably the most widely used basis of recognising revenue from transactions involving the sale of goods. The reason is that, in most cases, the sale is the critical point in the earning process when most of the significant uncertainties are eliminated; the only uncertainties which are likely to remain are those of possible return of the goods (where the customer has the right to do so, thereby cancelling the sale), the failure to collect the sales price (in the case of a credit sale), and any future liabilities in terms of any express or implied customer warranties. However, under normal circumstances, these uncertainties will be both minimal and estimable to a reasonable degree of accuracy, based, inter alia, on past experience.

Nevertheless, the time of sale basis of revenue recognition is not always straightforward. In a large number of cases, a contract for the sale of goods would be entered into after the goods have been acquired or produced by the seller, and delivery takes place either at the same time as the contract, or soon thereafter. However, should revenues be recognised at the time of sale if the sale takes place before production, or if delivery only takes place at some significantly distant time in the future?

From a legal point of view, delivery does not necessarily have to have occurred for a sale to take place. Under the Sale of Goods Act 1979, 'a contract of sale of goods is a contract by which the seller transfers or agrees to transfer the property in goods to the buyer for a money consideration, called the price'.[26] Where, under a contract of sale, title to the goods is transferred from the seller to the buyer the contract is called a sale;[27] where the contract specifies that title to the goods will be transferred at some future date or transfer of title is subject to conditions to be fulfilled in the future, the contract is called an agreement to sell.[28] Consequently, the 'critical event' which determines whether a contract of sale is a 'sale' or whether it is an 'agreement to sell' is the passing of title.

Where the contract of sale contains no conditions as to the passing of title, and the goods are physically capable of immediate delivery to the purchaser, title will pass as soon as the contract is entered into (i.e. at the time of sale), regardless of the time fixed for payment or delivery.[29] However, where the seller is bound to do something to the goods before the purchaser is obliged to take delivery, title will pass as soon as that thing is done and the purchaser has been notified.[30] The passing of title, therefore, is a legal issue (and may be of crucial importance to the parties in certain circumstances, such as liquidation), which is governed by the terms of the contract and can occur at various stages along the earning process. As a result, for revenue recognition purposes, the time of sale is generally taken to be the point of delivery. This, in fact, would appear to be the principle implicit in the conditions for recognition set out in APB Statement No. 4 (see 3 above), where it is stated that revenue from the sales of products is recognised 'at the date of sale, usually interpreted to mean the date of delivery to customers'.[31]

This principle was reinforced by SFAC No. 5 as follows: 'Revenues are not recognized until earned. An entity's revenue-earning activities involve delivering or producing goods, rendering services, or other activities that constitute its ongoing major or central operations, and revenues are considered to have been earned when the entity has substantially accomplished what it must do to be entitled to the benefits represented by the revenues. ... If sale or cash receipt (or both) precedes production and delivery (for example, magazine subscriptions), revenues may be recognised as earned by production and delivery.'[32]

However, the use of the words 'substantially accomplished' in SFAC No. 5 suggests that delivery does not necessarily have to have taken place for revenue to be recognised. Where, for example, delivery is a relatively insignificant part of the earning process, the goods are on hand and available for delivery and there is every expectation that delivery will be made, it may be appropriate to recognise the sale as revenue before delivery takes place. (See 4.4.2 below for discussion of the principles laid down by IAS 18 for determining when to recognise revenue from a transaction involving the sale of goods.)

3.1.3   *The recognition of revenue subsequent to delivery*

Under certain circumstances, the uncertainties which exist after delivery are of such significance that recognition should be delayed beyond the normal recognition point. Where the principal uncertainty concerns collectibility, a possible approach would be to record the sale and defer recognition of the profit until cash is received; alternatively, it might be appropriate to defer recognition of the whole sale (and not just the profit) until collection is reasonably assured.

A further example of where it might be appropriate to defer the recognition of revenue beyond the date of delivery is where the enterprise sells its product but gives the customer the right to return the goods (for example, in the case of a mail order business where the customer is given an approval period of, say, 14 days). In such circumstances, revenue should be recognised only on delivery if future returns can be reasonably predicted; if this is not possible, then revenue should be recognised only on receipt of payment for the goods, or on customer acceptance of the goods and express or implied acknowledgement of the liability for payment, or after the 14 days have elapsed – whichever is considered to be the most appropriate under the circumstances.

This area of uncertainty is dealt with in the US under SFAS 48 – *Revenue Recognition When Right of Return Exists* – which states that if an enterprise sells its product but gives the buyer the right to return the product, revenue from the sales transaction is recognised at time of sale only if *all* of the following conditions are met:

(a)   the seller's price to the buyer is substantially fixed or determinable at the date of sale;

(b)   the buyer has paid the seller, or the buyer is obligated to pay the seller and the obligation is not contingent on resale of the product;

(c)   the buyer's obligation to the seller would not be changed in the event of theft or physical destruction or damage of the product;

(d)   the buyer acquiring the product for resale has economic substance apart from that provided by the seller (i.e. the buyer does not merely exist 'on paper' with little or no physical facilities, having been established by the seller primarily for the purpose of recognising revenue);

(e)   the seller does not have significant obligations for future performance to directly bring about resale of the product by the buyer; and

(f)   the amount of future returns can be reasonably estimated.[33]

Revenue which was not recognised at the time of sale because the above conditions were not met, should be recognised either when the return privilege has 'substantially expired', or when all the above conditions are met, whichever occurs first.[34]

The ability to make a reasonable estimate of future returns depends on many factors and will vary from one case to the next. Furthermore, SFAS 48 lists the following factors as being those which might impair a seller's ability to make such an estimate:

(a) the susceptibility of the product to significant external factors, such as technological obsolescence or changes in demand;

(b) relatively long periods in which a particular product may be returned;

(c) absence of historical experience with similar types of sales of similar products, or inability to apply such experience because of changing circumstances; for example, changes in the selling enterprise's marketing policies or its relationships with its customers; and

(d) absence of a large volume of relatively homogeneous transactions.[35]

These rules should be seen against the background of APB Statement No. 4's requirement that revenue should generally be recognised only when the 'earning process is complete or virtually complete'.[36] The right of return is, therefore, viewed as a significant uncertainty which would preclude recognition under certain circumstances.

3.1.4   The critical event approach and the ASB's revised Draft Statement of Principles

As discussed above, the ASB's revised Draft *Statement of Principles* is attempting to create a direct link between revenue recognition and changes in balance sheet assets and liabilities.[37] Under the ASB's approach, gains and losses are defined as being increases and decreases in net assets, other than those resulting from transactions with owners.[38] However, perhaps in order to respond to the extensive criticism that it received in respect of its first Draft *Statement of Principles*, the ASB has attempted to relate its revenue recognition proposals back to critical event theory. It does so by asserting that in a transaction involving the provision of services or goods for a net gain, the general asset/liability recognition principles will be met on the occurrence of the critical event in the operating cycle involved.[39] The ASB then goes on to suggest that it 'can be much easier to identify the appropriate moment at which to recognise gains arising from the provision of services or goods by focusing on the operating cycle of the reporting entity and, in particular, on the critical event in that cycle. This approach enables the gains arising to be identified and, as a consequence, the effect on the entity's assets and liabilities to be established.'[40]

This is explained further in the revised Draft as follows: 'on the occurrence of the critical event, there will usually be sufficient evidence that the gain exists and it will usually be possible to measure the gain with sufficient reliability; in other words, the recognition criteria set out earlier will be met and the gain and related change to assets and liabilities will be recognised.

'For many types of transaction, the critical event in the operating cycle is synonymous with full performance. In such cases the gain will be recognised when the entity providing the service or goods has fully performed. That need not, however, be the case: the critical event could occur at other times in the cycle and there could be more than one critical event in the cycle.'[41]

The ASB goes on to suggest that 'the identity of the critical event or events of an operating cycle will depend on the particular circumstances involved. For example:

(a) if the reporting entity has carried out all its obligations under an agreement except for a few minor acts of performance, the critical event will have occurred.

(b) if a sale is contingent upon acceptance by the buyer, whether the critical event has occurred will depend on whether the act of acceptance creates substantial uncertainty as to whether the contractual obligations will be met. The critical event will not have occurred if the likelihood of the goods or services not being accepted is significant.

(c) the operating cycle might involve the entity in performing a series of significant acts of performance over a period of time and, as a result, might best be viewed as involving a series of critical events. (Contracts to build large buildings are usually an example of such an operating cycle.) In such circumstances, the gain that is expected to be earned on the contract as a whole will need to be allocated among the critical events.'[42]

We find it somewhat surprising that the ASB believes that the application of the percentage-of-completion method of profit recognition in the case of long-term construction contracts is an example of the critical event approach. As explained at 3.2.2 below, this is clearly an application of the accretion approach, and the ASB's confusion on this matter seems to illustrate further its inability to devise a theoretically coherent conceptual framework.

In any event, whilst we understand the ASB's motives for attempting to link its approach to the recognition of gains and losses with the critical event approach, we do not think that the two approaches sit together very easily. This is because, in our view, the critical event approach is closely aligned with the realisation principle, which the ASB views as being irrelevant. The ASB admits that probably the most significant inconsistency between its proposals set out in its revised Draft *Statement of Principles* and the Companies Act relates to the recognition of gains: the Act requires that only profits realised at the balance sheet date are to be recognised in the profit and loss account, whilst the draft Statement adopts an alternative approach not based on the notion of realisation.[43] We therefore do not see how the ASB can imply that its proposed system of reporting realised and unrealised profits alongside each other in the income statement is consistent with the critical event approach. In our view, any alignment of the two approaches will occur purely by chance.

3.2   The accretion approach

The accretion approach involves the recognition of revenue during the process of 'production', rather than at the end of a contract or when production is complete. There are three broad areas of enterprise activity where the application of the accretion approach might be appropriate.

3.2.1   *The use by others of enterprise resources*

The traditional accrual basis of accounting recognises revenue as enterprise resources are used by others; this approach is followed, for example, in the case of recognising rental, royalty or interest income. However, the question of uncertainty of collection should always be considered (for example, in the case of accrual of interest on third world debt), in which case it might be appropriate to delay recognition until cash is received or where ultimate collection is assured beyond all reasonable doubt.

3.2.2   *Long-term contracts*

The second accepted application of the accretion approach to revenue reporting may be found in the accounting practice for long-term construction contracts. Under certain circumstances, the amount of revenue to be recognised on construction contracts is determined according to the 'percentage-of-completion method', whereby revenue is estimated by reference to the stage of completion of the contract activity at the end of each accounting period. Normally, the main uncertainty which presents difficulty in the application of this approach is the estimation of the total costs, particularly in the early stages of the contract, or where factors such as excavation and the weather may cause added uncertainty. However, the selling price is sometimes uncertain as well, owing to contract modifications which give rise to revenue from 'extras'. (Accounting for long-term contacts is dealt with in detail in Chapter 14.)

3.2.3   *Natural growth and 'biological transformation'*

Where an enterprise's activity involves production through natural growth or ageing, the accretion approach would suggest that revenue should be recognised at identifiable stages during this process. For example, in the case of livestock, there would be market prices available at the various stages of growth; revenue could, therefore, be recognised throughout the production process by making comparative stock valuations and reporting the accretions at each accounting date.

This is, in fact, an area that is currently being explored by the IASC in its project on accounting in the agricultural industry. In an Exposure Draft, E65 – *Agriculture* – which the IASC issued in August 1999, the IASC Board is proposing that there should be a blanket application of fair value accounting to all 'biological assets' throughout their period of growth, which the Board refers to as 'biological transformation'. E65 defines agricultural activity as 'the management by an enterprise of the biological transformation of biological assets into agricultural produce for sale, processing, or consumption or into additional biological assets', whilst biological assets are 'living animals and plants that are controlled by an enterprise as a result of past events'. Biological transformation 'comprises the processes of growth, degeneration, production, and procreation that cause qualitative and quantitative changes in a living animal or plant and generation of new assets in the form of agricultural produce or additional biological assets of the same class (offspring)'.[44]

E65 is proposing that all enterprises that undertake agricultural activity should measure all biological assets at fair value,[45] whilst all agricultural produce should be measured at fair value at the point of harvest, and thereafter inventory accounting (IAS 2) should be applied.[46] Fair value is defined as 'the amount for which an asset could be exchanged or a liability settled between knowledgeable, willing parties in an arm's length transaction',[47] which, in practical terms, means that it is the highest price obtainable, net of costs, in any available market.

The change in fair value of biological assets during a period is to be reported in net profit or loss from operating activities.[48] The Exposure Draft acknowledges that the change in fair value of biological assets is part physical change (growth, etc.) and part unit price change. However, separate disclosure of the two components is only encouraged by E65, not required.[49] As stated above, fair value measurement stops at harvest, and IAS 2 – *Inventories* – applies after harvest. E65 also draws a distinction between biological assets and agricultural land, requiring agricultural land to be accounted for under IAS 16 – *Property, Plant and Equipment*.[50]

Whilst we see the accretion approach as having some merit for certain agricultural activities (for example, the farming of livestock), we do not see any merit in applying a blanket approach to all agricultural activities. However, in taking this approach in E65, it seems that the IASC has formulated its ideas on a number of unproved assumptions which cast doubt as to the validity of its proposals. These are that:

- it is assumed that efficient markets exist for all biological assets;

- it is assumed that there exist active and liquid markets for all biological assets, at all stages of growth;

- it is assumed that biological transformation can be measured with a degree of reliability which is sufficient for recognition in the accounts; and

- it is assumed that all sectors of agriculture are sufficiently similar as to be accounted for on the same basis.

We question the validity of these assumptions. For instance, it seems unlikely that there exist active liquid markets for all intermediate agricultural products, such as forests and unripened fruit. In any event, even if active and liquid markets do exist, it is doubtful that the risks and volatilities of the markets justify recognising revenue on the basis envisaged by the IASC. This is not to disagree that fair value information concerning biological assets is both relevant and useful, but we question whether fair valuations will be sufficiently reliable to be incorporated in the accounts. To do so might be imprudent and, in some cases, may even be misleading. It is also likely that the fair value approach proposed by the IASC would place an unnecessary burden on the preparers of accounts to the extent that the costs (including audit costs) would outweigh the benefits.

In any event, under the present historical cost accounting system (including IAS 18), this approach would not be appropriate, since the earning process would be too incomplete, too many significant uncertainties would remain, and a profit could not be regarded as having been realised.

3.3   The revenue allocation approach

The revenue allocation approach is essentially a combination of the critical event and accretion approaches. One of the difficulties in adopting, for example, the time of sale as the critical event for revenue recognition, is the existence of the uncertainty surrounding after-sale costs (such as customer support service and warranty costs). One way of dealing with these costs could be to make a provision for the future costs to be incurred on the basis of best estimate; alternatively, an approach could be followed whereby revenue is apportioned on the basis of two or more critical events. Consequently, part of the sale price could be treated as revenue at the point of sale, and the balance could either be recognised on an accretion basis over a warranty period or on the expiration of the warranty. The recognition of profit by manufacturer/dealer lessors is an example of such an application (see Chapter 17 at 7.6).

4   THE IMPACT OF THE ASB, IASC AND FASB ON REVENUE RECOGNITION

It is a requirement of the Companies Act 1985 that 'only profits realised at the balance sheet date shall be included in the profit and loss account';[51] in establishing whether or not profits of a company should be treated as 'realised profits', reference should be made to 'principles generally accepted, at the time when the accounts are prepared, with respect to the determination for accounting purposes of realised profits or losses'.[52] It is unclear as to whether or not generally accepted accounting principles exist for the purposes of determining realised profits for accounting purposes. The only direct reference to realisation in a UK accounting standard is to be found in SSAP 2's definition of prudence;

however, this definition would appear to be inadequate, as existing practice indicates that a wider interpretation is being placed on the concept of 'realisation' (see 2 above). For this reason, revenue recognition issues tend to be dealt with on an ad hoc basis, without either a clear definition of the concept of realisation or generally accepted recognition criteria.

The ASB is attempting to address this through Chapter 5 of its Draft *Statement of Principles*, which was issued in March 1999 in the form of a revised exposure draft following the public rejection of an earlier draft issued in November 1995. As explained at 4.1 below, the effect of the ASB's proposals, if accepted, would alter radically the basis on which revenue would be recognised.

Nevertheless, until such time as the ASB has established clear recognition principles in final form, it is helpful also to examine the authoritative literature which exists internationally. Although this literature has no authority to dictate accounting practice in the UK, it may provide a basis for achieving some consistency in approach towards dealing with practical revenue recognition issues.

4.1   ASB Revised Draft Statement of Principles for Financial Reporting, Chapter 5: Recognition in financial statements[53]

Chapter 4 of the ASB's revised Draft *Statement of Principles* identifies seven elements of financial statements: these are, assets, liabilities, ownership interest, gains, losses, contributions from owners and distributions to owners.[54] However, because the revised Draft follows a balance sheet-centred approach, the definitions of the last five elements are dependent on the first two. This means that once assets and liabilities have been defined, the definitions of gains and losses are derived as follows: assets minus liabilities equals ownership interest; gains and losses are increases and decreases in ownership interest, other than those relating to contributions from and distributions to owners. In principle, it does not matter that the definitions of the various elements are so interdependent – as long as workable recognition and measurement rules for assets and liabilities can be devised. However, there is room for doubt on this matter, particularly in the light of the fact that this is where the US FASB's conceptual framework project ran into considerable difficulty.

4.1.1   The recognition process

Chapter 5 of the ASB's revised Draft *Statement of Principles* sets out three stages of the recognition process, all of which are focused on assets and liabilities. These are: initial recognition (which is where an item is depicted in the primary financial statements for the first time), subsequent remeasurement (which involves changing the amount at which an already recognised asset or liability is stated in the primary financial statements) and derecognition (which is where an item that was until then recognised ceases to be recognised).[55]

The introduction of 'subsequent remeasurement' in the recognition process provides the first hint of the ASB's balance sheet-focused approach to current value income recognition. This is because the ASB is proposing that the recognition process requires that all events that may have an effect on elements of the financial statements are, as far as is possible, identified and reflected in an appropriate manner in the financial statements. Thus, whilst existing accounting practice is to record gains and losses that occur as a result of transactions and other events (such as an adverse court judgement or damage to property as a result of a fire), it is now clear that the ASB envisages that changes in the fair value of assets and liabilities will also be recorded as gains and losses in the profit and loss account.

Since gains and losses are defined as being increases and decreases in net assets, other than those resulting from transactions with owners, the ASB develops its approach to revenue recognition by first establishing the following general recognition principles for assets and liabilities:

■   If a transaction or other event has created a new asset or liability or added to an existing asset or liability, that effect will be recognised if:

   (a)   sufficient evidence exists that the new asset or liability has been created or that there has been an addition to an existing asset or liability; and

   (b)   the new asset or liability or the addition to the existing asset or liability can be measured at a monetary amount with sufficient reliability.

■   In a transaction involving the provision of services or goods for a net gain, the recognition criteria described above will be met on the occurrence of the critical event in the operating cycle involved. (This aspect is discussed in more detail at 3.1.4 above.)

■   An asset or liability will be wholly or partly derecognised if:

   (a)   sufficient evidence exists that a transaction or other past event has eliminated a previously recognised asset or liability; or

   (b)   although the item continues to be an asset or a liability, the criteria for recognition are no longer met.[56]

By applying these principles to the process of revenue recognition, it means that if the effect of the transaction or other event is to increase the entity's recognised net assets, a gain will be recognised. A loss will be recognised if, and to the extent that, previously recognised assets have been reduced or eliminated or cease to qualify for recognition as assets without a commensurate increase in other assets or reduction in liabilities. Similarly, a loss will be recognised when and to the extent that a liability is incurred or increased without a commensurate increase in recognised assets or a reduction in other liabilities.[57] In other words, whenever a change in an entity's total assets is not offset by an equal change in total liabilities or ownership interest, a gain or loss will arise.

4.1.2 The recognition of gains

Following the ASB's approach to recognition to its logical conclusion, we are led to conclude that a gain should be recognised if there is sufficient evidence that the gain exists and it is possible to measure the gain with sufficient reliability. In other words, when the asset/liability recognition criteria are met, the related change to assets and liabilities will be recognised together with the resultant gain.

The implications of this are highly significant when combined with the ASB's vision of a current value measurement system: all increases in net assets (including those brought about by increases in current values) should be recognised as gains (provided that there is sufficient evidence that the change has occurred and it can be measured reliably).

However, a fundamental issue with this is the way in which the revised Draft *Statement of Principles* views the accounting process. Assets and liabilities do not form the natural starting point for devising recognition rules; the real building blocks which underlie accounting practice are transactions to which are applied criteria for revenue and expense recognition, the balance sheet being a result of this process, not the starting point. Revenue recognition criteria are more demanding than those for recognising assets and liabilities, since they should embody the concept of the revenue having been earned, based on performance by the reporting company.

Many would, therefore, consider these proposed criteria to be a distortion of the real recognition rules which accountants throughout the world, and the ASB itself, use and which are in fact transactions-based. Devising rules for accounting based on what assets and liabilities materialise from the transaction may be conceptually 'clean' but in practice, in anything but the most straightforward cases, it simply does not provide the concepts with which to address practical situations. Business activity is, in the main, directed towards accomplishing sales transactions, not measuring asset values; therefore it would be appropriate to devise rules that reflect this reality of commercial life. For this reason, accounting in real life is essentially an allocative process in which transactions are allocated to appropriate accounting periods. Although the conventions for doing so need to be developed further, it seems more likely that this will remain a more workable approach than recognition criteria based on determining whether or not there is sufficient evidence that a change in net assets has occurred.

4.2   FRS 5: Reporting the substance of transactions

FRS 5 – *Reporting the substance of transactions* – is a manifestation of the balance sheet approach which the ASB is promulgating in its revised Draft *Statement of Principles*. Since FRS 5 is concerned with the recognition and derecognition of assets and liabilities, it will necessarily have an impact on the recognition of gains and losses. However, it is unclear as to whether the ASB intended that FRS 5 should alter existing accounting practice in the area of revenue recognition.

FRS 5's rules on asset derecognition deal with the issue of when to remove from the balance sheet assets which have previously been recognised. The rules are designed to determine one of three possible outcomes, and essentially involve a process of determining whether or not a transaction transfers to another party all the significant benefits and risks relating to an asset. FRS 5 anticipates that in the case of most transactions affecting items recognised as assets the situation will be that either the benefits and risks will not be transferred – in which case the asset will continue to be recognised and no sale or disposal will be recorded – or the benefits and risks will be transferred – in which case the asset will cease to be recognised (i.e. a sale or disposal together with the resulting gain or loss will be recorded).

The third possible outcome envisaged by FRS 5 occurs where, although not all of the benefits and risks have been transferred, the transaction is more than a mere financing and has transferred enough of both the benefits and risks to warrant at least some derecognition of the asset. These cases arise where the transaction takes one or more of the following forms:

(a)   where the asset has been subdivided and part of it transferred;

(b)   where the asset is sold for less than its full life; and

(c)   where an asset is transferred for all of its life but some risk or benefit is retained.

FRS 5 states that in these special cases, where the amount of any resulting gain or loss is uncertain, full provision should be made for any probable loss but recognition of any gain, to the extent that it is in doubt, should be deferred.

However, the transfer of the risks and rewards of ownership associated with an asset is not sufficient for revenue to be recognised. It is also necessary to complete the other side of the transaction – namely the recognition of the asset received in exchange for the asset disposed of. The principal rule for recognition of an item as an asset under FRS 5 is that the item can be measured at a monetary amount with sufficient reliability – seemingly irrespective of whether or not the item is readily convertible into known amounts of cash or cash equivalents.

4.3   FRS 12: Provisions, contingent liabilities and contingent assets

The ASB published its original Discussion Paper on accounting for provisions on the same day as it published the first version of its Draft *Statement of Principles*. There was therefore no doubt as to the ASB's intention to link the definition and recognition of provisions with its balance sheet approach generally, and with the definition and recognition of liabilities specifically. As it turned out, FRS 12 defines a provision as 'a liability of uncertain timing or amount',[58] which means that an entity may only recognise a provision if it has a present obligation that arose as a result of a past event (i.e., a liability) and it is probable that a transfer of economic benefits will be required to settle the obligation'.[59]

The question that arises, therefore, is whether FRS 12 has any impact on generally accepted accounting practice with respect to revenue recognition, given that the UK does not have an accounting standard that deals specifically with the subject. Nevertheless, the application of the matching concept, together with the realisation principle means that, on occasion, it will be appropriate for entities to recognise an item of deferred income in the balance sheet. This will arise for example, in the case of income received but not yet earned or realised, and which is deferred and matched against future expenditure incurred to earn the income, or until significant acts of performance are completed.

However, the ASB's proposed *Statement of Principles* does not recognise deferred income as an element of financial statements. Thus, the only way that deferred income could be recognised in the balance sheet under the ASB's proposed *Statement of Principles* would be as a liability. Consequently, it is arguable that under FRS 12 it is no longer permitted to recognise deferred income on the balance sheet if it does not meet the definition of a 'liability', i.e. an obligation to transfer economic benefits as a result of past transactions or events. This means, for example, that if an entity receives income in advance that is non-refundable, even though it is still to be earned, it follows that the entity has no alternative but to recognise the advance as revenue immediately and in full. It seems that to defer recognition of the income until it is earned would be in conflict with FRS 12, since the deferred income does not represent a present obligation for which it is probable that a transfer of economic benefits will be required to settle the obligation.

However, all that having been said, we do not believe that this approach is generally applied by UK companies in these situations. It is our view that, despite murmurings from the ASB to the contrary, the principles of matching, prudence and realisation still prevail and that revenue should be recognised only once it is earned and realised. At the same time, the ASB has indicated informally that it is proposing to undertake a project on revenue recognition, and it will be interesting to see how this project develops in the light of FRS 12 and the ASB's proposed *Statement of Principles*.

4.4   IAS 18: Revenue

The original version of IAS 18 – *Revenue Recognition* – was issued in 1982 and defined revenue as the 'gross inflow of cash, receivables or other consideration arising in the course of the ordinary activities of an enterprise from the sale of goods, from the rendering of services, and from the use by others of enterprise resources yielding interest, royalties and dividends'.[60] In revising IAS 18 in

1993, the IASC attempted to retain the approach of the original standard, whilst at the same time create a link between the revised standard and the IASC's conceptual framework.

Consequently, the revised IAS 18 – *Revenue* – now includes the definition of income from the IASC's conceptual framework and states that revenue is income that arises in the course of ordinary activities of an enterprise and is referred to by a variety of different names including sales, fees, interest, dividends and royalties.[61] It goes on to explain that the objective of the revised standard is to prescribe the accounting treatment of revenue arising from the following types of transactions and events:

(a)   the sale of goods;

(b)   the rendering of services; and

(c)   the use by others of enterprise assets yielding interest, royalties and dividends.[62]

The standard then defines 'revenue' as 'the gross inflow of economic benefits during the period arising in the course of the ordinary activities of an enterprise when those inflows result in increases in ownership interest, other than increases relating to contributions from equity participants'.[63] This, in fact, is not too dissimilar from the ASB's revised Draft *Statement of Principles* which defines 'gains' and 'losses' as increases and decreases in ownership interest other than those resulting from contributions from and distributions to owners.[64] However, in distinguishing between 'gains' and 'revenue' in its definition of income, the IASC is able to exclude 'gains' from the scope of IAS 18, thereby avoiding the issue of the recognition of gains that are earned but unrealised.

In any event, though, having established the link between the *Framework* and IAS 18, the IASC then abandons the *Framework* and reverts to the old IAS 18 transactions-based critical event approach for the recognition of revenues derived from the sale of goods and the rendering of services, and an accretion approach in respect of revenues derived from the use by others of enterprise resources.

4.4.1   Measurement of revenue

IAS 18 states that the amount of revenue arising on a transaction is usually determined by agreement between the enterprise and the buyer or user of the asset. This means that it is measured at the fair value of the consideration received or receivable taking into account the amount of any trade discounts and volume rebates allowed by the enterprise.[65] The standard defines fair value as 'the amount for which an asset could be exchanged, or a liability settled, between knowledgeable, willing parties in an arm's length transaction'.[66]

Usually, this will present little difficulty as the consideration will normally be in the form of cash or cash equivalents and the amount of revenue will be the amount of cash or cash equivalents received or receivable. However, an issue does arise when the inflow of cash or cash equivalents is deferred, since the fair value of the consideration will then be less than the nominal amount of cash received or receivable. IAS 18 attempts to deal with this by introducing a requirement for the discounting of receivables under these circumstances. Consequently, when an arrangement effectively constitutes a financing transaction, the fair value of the consideration is determined by discounting all future receipts using an imputed rate of interest. The difference between the fair value and the nominal amount of the consideration is recognised as interest revenue.[67]

Although the revised IAS 18 has retained the existing requirement that an exchange of assets or services of a similar nature and value does not give rise to revenue, it has introduced new requirements for exchanges of dissimilar assets or services. As a result, when goods are sold or services are rendered in exchange for dissimilar goods or services, the exchange is regarded as a transaction which generates revenue. The revenue is measured at the fair value of the goods or services received, adjusted by the amount of any cash or cash equivalents transferred. When the fair value of the goods or services received cannot be measured reliably, the revenue is measured at the fair value of the goods or services given up, adjusted by the amount of any cash or cash equivalents transferred.[68]

4.4.2   The sale of goods

IAS 18 lays down the following five criteria which must be satisfied in order to recognise revenue from the sale of goods:

(a)   the enterprise has transferred to the buyer the significant risks and rewards of ownership of the goods;

(b)   the enterprise retains neither continuing managerial involvement to the degree usually associated with ownership nor effective control over the goods sold;

(c)   the amount of revenue can be measured reliably;

(d)   it is probable that the economic benefits associated with the transaction will flow to the enterprise; and

(e)   the costs incurred or to be incurred in respect of the transaction can be measured reliably.[69]

It is clear that IAS 18 views the passing of risks and rewards as the most crucial of the five criteria, giving the following four examples of situations in which an enterprise may retain the significant risks and rewards of ownership:

(a)   when the enterprise retains an obligation for unsatisfactory performance not covered by normal warranty provisions;

(b) when the receipt of the revenue from a particular sale is contingent on the derivation of revenue by the buyer from its sale of the goods;

(c) when the goods are shipped subject to installation and the installation is a significant part of the contract which has not yet been completed by the enterprise; and

(d) when the buyer has the right to rescind the purchase for a reason specified in the sales contract and the enterprise is uncertain about the probability of return.[70]

On closer examination of these examples, though, it is clear that the standard still advocates a critical event approach – despite its attempt to create a link with the IASC's *Framework*. This is further borne out by the statement in IAS 18 that 'in most cases, the transfer of risks and rewards of ownership coincides with the transfer of legal title or the passing of possession to the buyer'.[71]

It is, therefore, necessary to establish at which point in the earnings process both the significant risks and rewards of ownership are transferred from the seller to the buyer and any significant uncertainties (which would otherwise delay recognition) are removed. For example, the responsibilities of each party during the period between sale and delivery should be established, possibly by examination of the customer agreements. If the goods have merely to be uplifted by the buyer, and the seller has performed all his associated responsibilities, then the sale may be recognised immediately. However, if the substance of the sale is merely that an order has been placed, and the stock has still to be acquired by the seller, then the sale should not be recognised.

IAS 18 does also recognise that under certain circumstances goods are sold subject to reservation of title in order to protect the collectibility of the amount due; in such circumstances, provided that the seller has transferred the significant risks and rewards of ownership, the transaction can be treated as a sale and revenue can be recognised.[72] This issue is discussed more fully at 5.2 below.

4.4.3 The rendering of services

The principal purpose of the IASC's revision of IAS 18 was to remove the option of being able to use the completed contract method for recognising revenue arising from transactions involving the rendering of services, in the same way as the revision of IAS 11 saw the removal of the completed contract method as an allowed method of accounting for construction contracts. As a result, IAS 18 now requires that when the outcome of a transaction involving the rendering of services can be estimated reliably, revenue is recognised 'by reference to the stage of completion of the transaction at the balance sheet date'[73] (in other words, using the percentage-of-completion method). When the outcome cannot be estimated reliably, revenue is recognised only to the extent of the expenses recognised that are recoverable.[74]

According to IAS 18, the outcome of a transaction can be estimated reliably when all the following conditions are satisfied:

(a)   the amount of revenue can be measured reliably;

(b)   it is probable that the economic benefits associated with the transaction will flow to the enterprise;

(c)   the stage of completion of the transaction at the balance sheet date can be measured reliably; and

(d)   the costs incurred for the transaction and the costs to complete the transaction can be measured reliably.[75]

However, whilst the IASC is to be commended for attempting to relate these criteria back to its Framework's fundamental recognition criterion of reliability of measurement, it is clear that they provide little practical guidance. This fact is borne out by the illustrative examples in the Appendix to IAS 18 which show that, in the case of a transaction involving the rendering of services, the performance of the service is the critical event for revenue recognition.

When it comes to determining the stage of completion of a transaction, IAS 18 suggests three methods that may be used:

(a)   surveys of work performed;

(b)   services performed to date as a percentage of total services to be performed; or

(c)   the proportion that costs incurred to date bear to the estimated total costs of the transaction. Only costs that reflect services performed to date are included in costs incurred to date. Only costs that reflect services performed or to be performed are included in the estimated total costs of the transaction.[76]

For practical purposes, though, when services are performed by an indeterminate number of acts over a specified period of time, the standard permits revenue to be recognised on a straight-line basis over the specified period unless there is evidence that some other method better represents the stage of completion. However, when a specific act is much more significant than any other acts, the standard again reverts to critical event theory requiring that the recognition of revenue be postponed until the significant act is executed.[77]

4.4.4   *Interest, royalties and dividends*

When it is probable that the economic benefits associated with the transaction will flow to the enterprise and that the amount of revenue can be measured reliably, IAS 18 requires that the revenue arising from the use by others of enterprise assets yielding interest, royalties and dividends should be recognised as follows:

(a)   *Interest:* on a time proportion basis that takes into account the effective yield on the asset;

(b)   *Royalties:* on an accrual basis in accordance with the substance of the relevant agreement; and

(c)   *Dividends:* when the shareholder's right to receive payment is established.

The application of the accretion approach under these circumstances would not necessarily be in line with the principle of realised profits as contained in SSAP 2's definition of prudence, since it would sometimes result in the recognition of revenue before it is either 'realised in the form of cash or of other assets the ultimate cash realisation of which can be assessed with reasonable certainty'; nevertheless, such an approach is generally accepted accounting practice in the UK.

4.4.5   *Disclosure*

The revised IAS 18 requires a greater level of disclosure regarding revenue than is generally found in the accounts of UK companies. The new disclosures relate to both revenue recognition policies and amounts of revenue included in the accounts under the different categories of revenue, and are laid down in the standard as follows:

An enterprise should disclose:

(a)   the accounting policies adopted for the recognition of revenue including the methods adopted to determine the stage of completion of transactions involving the rendering of services;

(b)   the amount of each significant category of revenue recognised during the period including revenue arising from:

    (i)   the sale of goods;

    (ii)   the rendering of services;

    (iii) interest;

    (iv)   royalties;

    (v)   dividends; and

(c)   the amount of revenue arising from exchanges of goods or services included in each significant category of revenue.[78]

4.5   The US

4.5.1   *'The general rule'*

Chapter 1 of Accounting Research Bulletin No. 43 (issued in 1953) reprinted the six rules which had been adopted by the membership of the AICPA in 1934. The first of these rules stated that 'profit is deemed to be realized when a sale in the ordinary course of business is effected, unless the circumstances are such that the collection of the sale price is not reasonably assured'.[79] The rule then goes on to state that 'an exception to the general rule may be made in respect of inventories in industries (such as the packing-house industry) in which owing to the impossibility of determining costs it is a trade custom to take inventories at net selling prices, which may exceed cost'.[80] However, it is not entirely clear as to what the 'general rule' actually is. Does the term 'effected' mean that profit is realised when the sale takes place, when delivery takes place, or when title passes?

In addition, a number of further exceptions are created by other authoritative pronouncements. For example, Chapter 11 of ARB 43 (which deals with cost-plus-fixed-fee government contracts) states that 'delivery of goods sold under contract is normally regarded as the test of realization of profit or loss'.[81] Nevertheless, it then goes on to say that 'it is, however, a generally accepted accounting procedure to accrue revenues under certain types of contracts and thereby recognize profits, on the basis of partial performance, where the circumstances are such that total profit can be estimated with reasonable accuracy and ultimate realization is reasonably assured'.[82]

The percentage-of-completion method of recognising revenue on long-term construction contracts is another example of 'an exception to the general rule'. ARB 45 – *Long-Term Construction-Type Contracts* – recognises both the percentage-of-completion and completed contract methods of accounting for long-term contracts. The Bulletin states that: 'in general when estimates of costs to complete and extent of progress toward completion of long-term contracts are reasonably dependable, the percentage-of-completion method is preferable. When lack of dependable estimates or inherent hazards cause forecasts to be doubtful, the completed-contract method is preferable'.[83] It would appear that the criteria to be applied in the selection of method are only broadly similar to those which should be applied in the case of cost-plus-fixed-fee contracts.

APB Statement No. 4 views these practices as exceptions to the realisation principle's exchange rule (see 3 above). However, as will be seen below, there exists a number of other variations to both the general rule laid down in ARB 43 and the realisation principle.

4.5.2   SFAC No. 5

As discussed in Chapter 2 of this book, the FASB's Concepts Statement No. 5 – *Recognition and Measurement in Financial Statements of Business Enterprises* – has primarily dealt with recognition issues from the angle of providing reliability of measurement. However, the broad principle for revenue recognition laid down by SFAC No. 5 is that revenues are not recognised until they are (a) realised or realisable and (b) earned.[84] According to the Statement, revenues are realised 'when products (goods or services), merchandise, or other assets are exchanged for cash or claims to cash', and are realisable 'when related assets received or held are readily convertible to known amounts of cash or claims to cash'.[85] The characteristics of 'readily convertible assets' are that they have '(i) interchangeable (fungible) units and (ii) quoted prices available in an active market that can rapidly absorb the quantity held by the entity without significantly affecting the price'.[86] Revenues are considered to have been 'earned' when the entity 'has substantially accomplished what it must do to be entitled to the benefits represented by the revenues'.[87]

The most significant difference between the recognition principles laid down in SFAC No. 5 as opposed to APB Statement No. 4 is that whilst the APB interpreted recognition and realisation as being broadly synonymous, SFAC No. 5 uses the terms 'realized' and 'realizability' to focus on conversion and convertibility of non-cash assets into cash or claims to cash. However, it is doubtful whether SFAC No. 5's revised interpretation of the realisation principle has made any significant progress towards providing a rigorous theory of recognition and measurement. This is highlighted by the fact that SFAC No. 5 provides guidance for applying its recognition criteria and, in so doing, goes on to condone certain existing revenue practices (for example, the percentage-of-completion method and the accrual of certain revenues on a time basis) which clearly are not in accordance with the basic principles laid down in the Statement, since an exchange for cash or claims to cash may not necessarily have occurred.

Interestingly, the FASB's own special report on its conceptual framework makes the point that although SFAC No. 5's name implies that it gives conceptual guidance on recognition and measurement, its conceptual contributions to financial reporting are not really in those areas.[88] The report goes on to say that 'as a result of compromises necessary to issue it, much of Concepts Statement 5 merely describes present practice and some of the reasons that have been used to support or explain it but provides little or no conceptual basis for analyzing and attempting to resolve the controversial issues of recognition and measurement about which accountants have disagreed for years.'[89] The concluding sentence of the FASB's report sums up elegantly the views that have long been expressed by critics of SFAC No. 5: 'Concepts Statement 5 does make some noteworthy conceptual contributions—they are just not on recognition and measurement.'[90]

4.5.3   *FASB Statements and AICPA Statements of Position*

There exist a number of FASB Statements and AICPA Statements of Position which deal with either the recognition of certain forms of revenue, or the recognition of revenue in certain specific industries. These are dealt with under 5 below.

4.6   Summary of broad approaches to revenue recognition

In theory, FRS 5 has had the effect of introducing a balance sheet approach to revenue recognition. However, to date we see no evidence that this has had any significant effect on the general principles of revenue recognition which are currently enshrined in UK GAAP: namely that the buyer must assume from the seller the significant risks and rewards of ownership of the assets sold and that the amount of revenue must be reliably measurable. The theoretical possibility exists that FRS 12 might also have (perhaps inadvertently) changed the rules on revenue recognition. Nevertheless, there is also no clear evidence that this is the case, and we therefore await the outcome of the ASB's project on revenue recognition to see whether there are going to be any fundamental changes to existing practice. However, until then, existing GAAP prevails.

The following table summarises the broad approaches to revenue reporting that would appear to have achieved general acceptance through existing reporting practice. The table indicates the circumstances under which it might be appropriate to apply each of the approaches; nevertheless, it is essential that each situation is considered on its individual merits, with particular attention being paid to the risks and uncertainties that remain at each stage of the earning process and the extent to which the amount of revenue can be measured reliably.

The timing of recognition	Criteria	Examples of practical application
During production (accretion)	Revenues accrue over time, and no significant uncertainty exists as to measurability or collectibility. A contract of sale has been entered into and future costs can be estimated with reasonable accuracy.	The accrual of interest, royalty and dividend income. Accounting for biological transformation in the agricultural industry. Accounting for long-term construction contracts using the percentage-of-completion method.
At the completion of production	There should exist a ready market for the commodity which could rapidly absorb the quantity held by the entity; the commodity should comprise interchangeable units; the market price should be determinable and stable; there should be insignificant marketing costs involved.	Certain precious metals and commodities.
At the time of sale (but before delivery)	Goods must have already been acquired or manufactured; goods must be capable of immediate delivery to the customer; selling price has been established; all material related expenses (including delivery) have been ascertained; no significant uncertainties remain (e.g. ultimate cash collection, returns).	Certain sales of goods (e.g. 'bill and hold' sales). Property sales where there is an irrevocable contract.
On delivery	Criteria for recognition before delivery were not satisfied and no significant uncertainties remain.	Most sales of goods and services. Property sales where there is doubt that the sale will be completed.
Subsequent to delivery	Significant uncertainty regarding collectibility existed at the time of delivery; at the time of sale it was not possible to value the consideration with sufficient accuracy.	Certain sales of goods and services (e.g. where the right of return exists). Goods shipped subject to conditions (e.g. installation and inspection/performance).
On an apportionment basis (the revenue allocation approach)	Where revenue represents the supply of initial and subsequent goods/services.	Franchise fees. Sale of goods with after sales service.

5 PROBLEM AREAS

Because of the lack of established generally accepted principles for revenue recognition, coupled with the fact that minimal specific guidance is given in UK accounting standards as to the timing of revenue reporting, it is necessary to examine specific areas in practice which might be open to inconsistent, controversial or varied accounting practices. Many of the issues discussed below relate to specific industries which pose their own particular revenue recognition problems; in fact, much of the accounting literature on the subject has been developed (predominantly in the US) in the context of these industries.

5.1 Receipt of initial fees

The practice which has developed in certain industries of charging an initial fee at the inception of a service, followed by subsequent service fees, can present revenue allocation problems. The reason for this is that it is not always altogether clear what the initial fee represents; consequently, it is necessary to determine what proportion (if any) of the initial fee has been earned on receipt, and how much relates to the provision of future services. In some cases, large initial fees are paid for the provision of a service, whilst continuing fees are relatively small in relation to future services to be provided; if it is probable that the continuing fees will not cover the cost of the continuing services to be provided, then a portion of the initial fee should be deferred over the period of the service contract such that a reasonable profit is earned throughout the service period.

5.1.1 Franchise fees

The franchise agreements which form the basis of the relationships between franchisors and franchisees can vary widely both in their complexity and in the extent to which various rights, duties and obligations are dealt with in the agreements. For this reason, no standard form franchise agreement exists which would dictate standard accounting practice for the recognition of all franchise fee revenue. Consequently, only a full understanding of the franchise agreement will reveal the substance of a particular arrangement so that the most appropriate accounting treatment can be determined; nevertheless, the following are the more common areas which are likely to be addressed in any franchise agreement and which would be relevant to franchise fee revenue reporting:[91]

(a) *Rights transferred by the franchisor:* the agreement would give the franchisee the right to use the trade name, processes, know-how of the franchisor for a specified period of time or in perpetuity.

(b) *The amount and terms of payment of initial fees:* payment of initial fees (where applicable) may be fully or partially due in cash, and may be payable immediately, over a specified period or on the fulfilment of certain obligations by the franchisor.

(c)   *Amount and terms of payment of continuing franchise fees:* the franchisee will normally be required to pay a continuing fee to the franchisor – usually on the basis of a percentage of gross revenues.

(d)   *Services to be provided by the franchisor initially and on a continuing basis:* the franchisor will usually agree to provide a variety of services and advice to the franchisee, such as:

- site selection;
- the procurement of fixed assets and equipment – these may be either purchased by the franchisee, leased from the franchisor or leased from a third party (possibly with the franchisor guaranteeing the lease payments);
- advertising;
- training of franchisee's personnel;
- inspecting, testing and other quality control programmes; and
- bookkeeping services.

(e)   *Acquisition of equipment, stock, supplies etc.:* the franchisee may be required to purchase these items either from the franchisor or from designated suppliers. Some franchisors manufacture products for sale to their franchisees, whilst others act as wholesalers.

In the US, SFAS 45 – *Accounting for Franchise Fee Revenue* – states that franchise fee revenue should be recognised 'when all material services or conditions relating to the sale have been substantially performed or satisfied by the franchisor'.[92] Substantial performance for the franchisor means that:

(a)   the franchisor has no remaining obligation or intent (in terms of the franchise agreement, the law or trade practice) to refund any cash received or waive any debts receivable;

(b)   substantially all of the initial services of the franchisor required by the franchise agreement have been performed; and

(c)   no other material conditions or obligations related to the determination of substantial performance exist.[93]

SFAS 45 also deals with the issue of mixed revenue – i.e. where the initial franchise fee incorporates not only the consideration for the franchise rights and the initial services to be provided by the franchisor, but also tangible assets such as equipment, signs etc. In such cases, the portion of the initial fee which is 'applicable to the tangible assets shall be based on the fair value of the assets and may be recognized before or after recognizing the portion applicable to the initial services. For example, when the portion of the fee relating to the sale of specific tangible assets is objectively determinable, it would be appropriate to recognize that portion when their titles pass, even though the balance of the fee relating to services is recognized when the remaining services or conditions in the franchise agreement have been substantially performed or satisfied.'[94]

In revising IAS 18, the IASC has expanded the Appendix thereto in order to better illustrate the application of the standard in commercial situations. Included in the Appendix is a broad discussion of the receipt of franchise fees, where it is stated that they 'are recognised as revenue on a basis that reflects the purpose for which the fees were charged'.[95] For example, franchise fees for the provision of continuing services, whether part of the initial fee or a separate fee, are recognised as revenue as the services are rendered. When the separate fee does not cover the cost of continuing services together with a reasonable profit, part of the initial fee, sufficient to cover the costs of continuing services and to provide a reasonable profit on those services, is deferred and recognised as revenue as the services are rendered.[96]

In summary, therefore, we suggest that the following basic principles may be applied for the recognition of initial franchise fees:

(a) first, it is necessary to break down the fee into its various components; for example, fee for franchise rights, fee for initial services to be performed by the franchisor, fair value of tangible assets sold etc. The reason for this is that the individual components may be recognised at different stages; the portion that relates to the franchise rights may be recognised in full immediately, or part of it may have to be deferred (see (b) below); the fee for initial services to be performed should only be recognised when the services have been 'substantially performed' (it is unlikely that substantial performance will have been completed before the franchisee opens for business); and the portion of the fee which relates to tangible assets may be recognised when title passes;

(b) next, it should be considered whether or not the continuing fee will cover the cost of continuing services to be provided by the franchisor. If not, then a portion of the initial fee should be deferred and amortised over the life of the franchise;

(c) if the collection period for the initial fees is extended and there is doubt as to the ultimate collectibility, revenue should be recognised on a cash received basis; and

(d) in the event of the franchisor having the option to buy out the franchisee, and there is considered to be a significant probability that he will do so, initial franchise fee revenue should be deferred in full and credited against the cost of the investment when the buy-out occurs.

5.1.2   *Advance royalty/licence receipts*

Under normal circumstances, the accounting treatment of advance royalty/licence receipts is straightforward; under the accruals concept of SSAP 2, the advance should be treated as deferred income when received, and released to the profit and loss account when earned under the royalty/licence agreement. However, there are certain industries where the forms of agreement entered into are such that advance receipts comprise a number of components, each requiring different accounting treatments.

For example, in the record and music industry, a record company will normally enter into a contractual arrangement with either a recording artist or a production company to deliver finished recording masters over a specified period of time. The albums are then manufactured and shipped to retailers for ultimate sale to the customer. The recording artist will normally be compensated through participating in the record company's sales and licence fee income (i.e. a royalty), although he may receive a non-refundable fixed fee on delivery of the master to the record company.

Example 3.1   Revenue recognition for licensors in the record and music industry

For each recording master delivered by a pop group, THRAG, the group (which operates through a service company) receives a payment of £1,000,000. This amount comprises a non-returnable, non-recoupable payment of £200,000, a non-returnable but recoupable advance of £600,000 and a returnable, recoupable advance of £200,000. The recoupable advances can be recouped against royalties on net sales earned both on the album concerned and on earlier and subsequent albums. This is achieved by computing the total royalties on net sales on all albums delivered under THRAG's service company's agreement with its recording company, and applying against this total the advances and royalties previously paid on those albums.

It is clear that the non-recoupable advance should be recognised in income when received, since it is not related to any future performance; at the other end of the spectrum, recognition of the refundable advance should be deferred and recognised only when recouped. However, the question arises as to whether the non-refundable but recoupable advance on royalties should be recognised immediately or deferred. If one accepts that revenue may be recognised when it is absolutely assured, there is an argument to justify the immediate recognition of the recoupable advance, since it is non-refundable; furthermore, it might be argued that, as far as THRAG is concerned, the earning process is complete, since the group does not have any further performance obligations. Conversely, some might argue that although the advance is non-refundable, it is not earned until it is recouped; furthermore, immediate recognition of royalty advances is likely to lead to a significant distortion of reported income, resulting in there being little correlation between reported income and album sales.

Clearly, therefore, there is no clear-cut answer, and it is our view that either approach is acceptable – i.e. the non-refundable but recoupable advance may be recognised in full as soon as the master is delivered to the recording company or, alternatively, it may be treated as deferred income when received and matched to subsequent album sales, being released to the profit and loss account in the period in which the sales are made. The most important point is that, whichever method is adopted, it is applied consistently. Of course, if the ASB's revised Draft *Statement of Principles* was to be adopted, its asset/liability approach to the recognition of gains would dictate that all non-returnable advances – whether recoupable or not – would be recognised in income immediately. This is because the ASB's proposed conceptual framework does not recognise deferred income as an element of financial statements. Indeed, it is even arguable that under FRS 12 – *Provisions, Contingent Liabilities and Contingent Assets* – it is no longer permitted to recognise deferred income on the balance sheet if it does not meet the definition of a 'liability', i.e. an obligation to transfer economic benefits as a result of past transactions or events. Consequently, since there is no obligation to repay the non-refundable advance, it may be argued that there is no alternative but to recognise it as revenue as soon as it becomes payable (see 4.3 above).

It is, perhaps, noteworthy that the deferral approach is supported by the US accounting requirement contained in SFAS 50 – *Financial Reporting in the Record and Music Industry* – which states that where an amount is paid in advance by a licensee to a licensor for the right to sell or distribute records or music, 'the licensor shall report such a minimum guarantee as a liability initially and recognize the guarantee as revenue as the license fee is earned under the agreement. If the licensor cannot otherwise determine the amount of the license fee earned, the guarantee shall be recognized as revenue equally over the remaining performance period, which is generally the period covered by the license agreement.'[97]

Chrysalis is an example of a company that has adopted this approach of deferring the recognition of non-returnable advances against royalties, as illustrated by the following extract:

Extract 3.1: Chrysalis Group PLC (1998)

Notes to the Accounts For the year ended 31st August 1998

1   Accounting policies

Record royalties (excluding record producer services and music publishing royalties) [extract]

Royalty income is included on a receivable basis calculated on sales of records arising during each accounting period as reported by licensees, any unrecouped advances being included in the period in which the licence agreement expires.

Similar recognition principles should be applied in the case of advance fees paid on the sale of film/TV rights. Receipts that are non-refundable and non-recoupable should be recognised immediately, whilst any non-refundable but recoupable royalty advances may either be recognised immediately, or be deferred and recognised as earned; again, the accounting policy selected should be applied consistently.

5.1.3   Loan arrangement fees

The practice of recognising loan arrangement fees as income in the year that the loans are arranged was outlawed in the US through the publication of SFAS 91 – *Accounting for Nonrefundable Fees and Costs Associated with Originating or Acquiring Loans and Initial Direct Costs of Leases* – which requires loan origination fees to be deferred and recognised over the life of the related loan as an adjustment of interest income.[98] Similarly, direct loan origination costs should be deferred and recognised as a reduction in the yield of the loan.[99]

Since there is no corresponding requirement in the UK, the recognition of arrangement fees on receipt may be regarded as acceptable; however, our preferred approach is that the principles contained in SFAS 91 should equally be applied in the UK. Nevertheless, situations may exist where the lending institution is providing other financial services which are, in themselves, valuable to the borrower and which are covered by the arrangement fee. If this is the case, then it may be argued that the portion of the initial fee that relates to those services should be recognised as income immediately, provided that the interest rate to be charged on the loan is fair and reasonable in relation to the risk involved and that the arrangement fee is not merely an interest prepayment.

The Appendix to IAS 18 includes a series of illustrative examples which relate to financial service fees, pointing out that the recognition of revenue for financial service fees depends on the purposes for which the fees are assessed and the basis of accounting for any associated financial instrument. The examples in the Appendix divide up the types of fees which arise into three categories, distinguishing between:

(a) those which are an integral part of the effective yield of a financial instrument – in which case the fees are generally treated as an adjustment to the effective yield;

(b) those which are earned as services are provided – in which case the fees are recognised as revenue either as the services are provided or on a time proportion basis; and

(c) those which are earned on the execution of a significant act – in which case the fees are recognised as revenue when the significant act has been completed.[100]

Consequently, provided that the arrangement fee is not an integral part of the effective yield of a loan, the fee can be recognised as revenue when the loan has been arranged.

5.1.4   Commitment fees

Commitment fees are fees paid by potential borrowers for a commitment to originate or purchase a loan or group of loans within a particular period of time. According to the ICAEW Industry Accounting and Auditing Guide on banks, 'the fact that a commitment fee may be legally payable at the commencement of a facility should not be allowed to detract from the fact that the fee relates to the provision of a service over a future period of time. Consequently it should usually be accounted for on a time apportionment basis.'[101] This contrasts with the accounting treatment prescribed by SFAS 91, namely that the fee should be deferred until either the commitment is exercised or it expires. If the commitment is exercised, it should normally be recognised over the life of the loan as an adjustment to interest income, and if it expires unexercised it should be recognised in income on expiration.[102]

SFAS 91 does, however, allow the following two exceptions to this general rule:

(a) if the enterprise's experience with similar arrangements indicates that the likelihood that the commitment will be exercised is remote (i.e. the likelihood is slight that a loan commitment will be exercised prior to its expiration), the commitment fee should be recognised over the commitment period on a straight-line basis as service fee income. If the commitment is subsequently exercised during the commitment period, the remaining unamortised commitment fee at the time of exercise should be recognised over the life of the loan as an adjustment to interest income;[103]

(b)   if the amount of the commitment fee is determined retrospectively as a percentage of the line of credit available but unused in a previous period, then the fee should be recognised as service fee income as of the determination date, provided that:

(i)   the percentage applied is nominal in relation to the stated interest rate on any related borrowing; and

(ii)   the borrowing will bear a market interest rate at the date the loan is made.[104]

Applying the criteria set out in the Appendix to IAS 18 (see 5.1.3 above), if it is unlikely that a specific lending arrangement will be entered into, the commitment fee will be recognised as revenue on a time proportion basis over the commitment period.

5.1.5   Credit card fees

It is common practice in the UK for credit card companies to levy a charge, payable in advance, on its cardholders. Although such charges may be seen as commitment fees for the credit facilities offered by the card, they clearly cover the many other services available to cardholders as well. Accordingly, we would suggest that the fees which are periodically charged to cardholders should be deferred and recognised on a straight-line basis over the period the fee entitles the cardholder to use the card.[105]

5.2   Goods sold subject to reservation of title

The Romalpa case,[106] which was decided in 1976, focused attention on the terms of a particular form of sale whereby the seller retains title to the goods sold and, in some cases, the right to other goods produced from them and the ultimate sale proceeds. The appropriate accounting treatment of such sales will depend on the commercial substance of the transaction, rather than its legal form. For example, it may be that the reservation of title is of no economic relevance to either party, except in the event of the insolvency of the purchaser; in other words, the goods are supplied and payment is due on an identical basis to other goods which are sold without reservation of title. In such circumstances, provided there is no significant uncertainty regarding the collectibility of the amount due, the sale should be recognised as revenue.

However, the circumstances surrounding the sale might be such that the parties view it as a consignment sale; for example, the purchaser may retain the right to return unsold goods to the seller, and the obligation to pay for the goods might be deferred until such time as the goods are sold to a third party. In such a case it would be inappropriate for the seller to recognise the sale until such time as the purchaser sells the goods and is liable for payment. However, situations of this nature fall within the scope of FRS 5 generally and Application Note A thereof in particular – the details of which are discussed in Chapter 16 of this book at 3.1.

The accounting treatment of goods sold subject to reservation of title is discussed in a statement of guidance issued by the ICAEW in July 1976 and, although rather out of date, it has never been superseded by a more authoritative document.[107]

5.3   Subscriptions to publications

Publication subscriptions are generally paid in advance and are non-refundable. Nevertheless, since the publications will still have to be produced and delivered to the subscriber, the subscription revenue cannot be regarded as having been earned until production and delivery takes place. Consequently, we recommend that revenue should be deferred and recognised either on a straight-line basis over the subscription period or, where the publications vary in value, revenue should be based on the proportion of the sales value that each publication bears to the total sales value of all publications covered by the subscription. Metal Bulletin is an example of a company which follows such an approach:

Extract 3.2: Metal Bulletin plc (1998)

Statement of Accounting Policies

A)   TURNOVER [extract]

Turnover comprises the value of goods and services supplied during the year, excluding value added tax and intra group sales.

(i)   Subscription revenue is allocated to accounting periods in proportion to the number of issues covered by the subscription published before and after the accounting date. Unappropriated subscription revenue is included within current liabilities.

This accounting policy is a perfect illustration of the difference between the ASB's balance sheet approach to the recognition of gains (as espoused in its revised Draft *Statement of Principles*), and conventional transactions-based accounting. Metal Bulletin is, quite appropriately, applying the accruals and prudence concepts to allocate the subscription revenue to its profit and loss account as it is earned. Subscriptions received in advance of being earned are carried in the balance sheet as deferred income.

However, the ASB's revised Draft *Statement of Principles* implicitly denies that such a separate category exists, since it is not acknowledged as one of the elements of financial statements. The ASB, in its original Draft *Statement of Principles*, tried to reconcile this anomaly by using the example of a magazine subscription that had been received in advance by a publisher, asserting that what is in reality deferred income can be embraced satisfactorily within the definition of a liability.[108]

It does not take much to show that this argument does not stand up. If one was to accept that a balance sheet approach should be followed in accounting for this situation, it would be necessary to consider the nature of the 'liability' involved and measure it appropriately. The publisher's contractual obligation is to provide the magazine, and it would be appropriate to measure such liability at the cost of doing so, not the amount of advance subscriptions received. This would therefore mean recording the profit in the year in which the cash happened to be received, not when the sale was performed, which would be quite inappropriate. It would also mean, for example, that the publisher could boost its immediate reported profits by inducing customers to take out subscriptions for longer periods in advance, such as a five-year subscription at a reduced rate.

It is therefore perhaps not surprising that, in revising its Draft *Statement of Principles*, the ASB has deleted the magazine subscription example referred to above, and instead has made the general (and unsubstantiated) assertion that 'although the starting point for the recognition process may be the effect on assets and liabilities, the notions of matching and the critical event in the operating cycle will often help in identifying these effects'.[109] As explained immediately above, this too is complete nonsense, since by applying matching and the critical event approach you would end up with an entirely different outcome to that which would result from applying the ASB's asset/liability approach.

5.4 Advertising revenue

The examples in the Appendix to IAS 18 adopt the performance of the service as the critical event for the recognition of revenue derived from the rendering of services. Consequently, media commissions are recognised when the related advertisement or commercial appears before the public. Production commissions are recognised by reference to the stage of completion of the project.[110] We concur with this broad approach which, as illustrated by the following extracts, appears to have been enshrined in UK GAAP:

Extract 3.3: Metal Bulletin plc (1998)

Statement of Accounting Policies

A)   TURNOVER [extract]

Turnover comprises the value of goods and services supplied during the year, excluding value added tax and intra group sales.

....

(ii)   Advertisement revenue is brought into account on publication date. All publication expenses are written off at that date.

Extending this principle to media commissions would mean that such revenue should be recognised when the related advertisement or commercial appears before the public. Similarly, production commissions should generally be recognised by reference to stage of completion of the project. This is, in fact, the approach adopted by media group Aegis:

Extract 3.4: Aegis Group plc (1998)

1. Principal accounting policies

Turnover [extract]

Turnover is recognised when charges are made to clients, principally when advertisements appear in the media. Fees are recognised over the period of the relevant assignments or agreements.

5.5   Software revenue recognition

There are a number of issues relating to the timing of revenue recognition in the software services industry. The issues that arise surround the question of when to recognise revenue from contracts to develop software, software licensing fees, customer support services and data services. However, few of these issues have been addressed in the authoritative literature and, because of the nature of the products and services involved, applying the general revenue recognition principles to software transactions can sometimes be difficult. The result of this has been that in practice software companies have used a variety of methods to recognise revenue, often producing significantly different financial results for similar transactions.

This problem was recognised in the US by the FASB and SEC who encouraged the AICPA to provide guidance on software revenue recognition methods. This culminated in AICPA Statement of Position (SOP) 91–1, which was issued in December 1991. The SOP applied to all entities that earned revenue from licensing, selling, leasing or otherwise marketing computer software, although it did not apply to revenue from the sale or licensing of a product containing software that is incidental to the product as a whole, such as software sold as part of a telephone system.

However, it was found that certain provisions of SOP 91–1 were being applied inconsistently, thereby leading to diversity in practice. As a result, in October 1997 the AICPA issued SOP 97–2,[111] entitled *Software Revenue Recognition,* which superseded SOP 91–1. In 1998 two further SOPs were issued amending SOP 97–2: SOP 98–4 (which merely deferred the effective date of a provision of SOP 97–2), and SOP 98–9 (which modified SOP 97-2 with respect to certain transactions, adding a further example of revenue recognition in the case of the sale of software product which included post-contract customer support).

Whilst SOP 97–2 has no direct bearing on companies reporting under UK GAAP, many such companies tend to adopt the US requirements in the absence of a comparable UK pronouncement, particularly if they have long-term ambitions of a NASDAQ listing. We therefore encourage companies to adopt the provisions of the SOP in all appropriate circumstances, as we consider that at present it probably represents best practice.

5.5.1 *The basic principles of SOP 97–2*

Software arrangements range from those that simply provide a licence for a single software product, to those that require significant production, modification or customisation of the software. Arrangements also may include multiple products or services. SOP 97–2 states that if the arrangement does not require significant production, modification or customisation of existing software (i.e. contract accounting does not apply – see 5.5.2 below), revenue should be recognised when all of the following criteria are met:[112]

■ persuasive evidence of an arrangement exists (e.g., signed contract, purchase authorisation, on-line authorisation);

■ delivery has occurred (and no future elements to be delivered are essential to the functionality of the delivered element);

■ the vendor's fee is fixed or determinable (for arrangements with multiple elements, the threshold for meeting the 'determinable' criterion is 'vendor-specific objective evidence of fair value'); and

■ collectibility is probable (fee is not subject to forfeiture, refund or other concessions if the undelivered elements are not delivered).

These criteria are similar in many respects to those previously required by SOP 91–1, but SOP 91–1 also required that there be no remaining significant vendor obligations (such as installation, testing and data conversion) in order to recognise revenue. Under SOP 97–2, it is no longer necessary or appropriate to differentiate between significant and insignificant vendor obligations. The licence fee under an arrangement with multiple elements should be allocated to the elements according to the 'vendor-specific objective evidence of fair value'.

In addition, SOP 97–2 requires a company to allocate a portion of the licence fee from a software arrangement to elements that are deliverable on a when-and-if-available basis, whereby a vendor agrees to deliver software only when or if it becomes deliverable while the agreement is in effect. Furthermore, SOP 97–2 requires that if a vendor has a customary practice of obtaining written contracts, revenues should not be recognised until the contract is signed by both parties. Therefore, in the absence of a signed contract, revenue should not be recognised even if the software has been delivered and payment made.

5.5.2 *Accounting for arrangements which require significant production, modification or customisation of software*

Where companies are running well-established computer installations with systems and configurations which they do not wish to change, off-the-shelf software packages are generally not suitable for their purposes. For this reason, some software companies will enter into a customer contract whereby they agree to customise a generalised software product to meet the customer's specific processing needs. A simple form of customisation would be to modify the system's output reports so that they integrate with the customer's existing management reporting system. However, customisation will often entail more involved obligations; for example, having to translate the software so that it is able to run on the customer's specific hardware configuration, data conversion, system integration, installation and testing.

The question that arises, therefore, is on what basis should a software company be recognising revenue where it enters into this type of contract which involves significant contractual obligations? It is our view that the principles laid down in SSAP 9 – *Stocks and long-term contracts* – should be applied in this situation.[113] SSAP 9 defines a long-term contract as 'a contract entered into for the design, manufacture or construction of a single substantial asset or the provision of a service (or of a combination of assets or services which together constitute a single product) where the time taken substantially to complete the contract is such that the contract activity falls into different accounting periods'.[114] The standard requires that 'long-term contracts should be assessed on a contract by contract basis and reflected in the profit and loss account by recording turnover and related costs as contract activity progresses. Turnover is ascertained in a manner appropriate to the stage of completion of the contract, the business and the industry in which it operates. Where it is considered that the outcome of a long-term contract can be assessed with reasonable certainty before its conclusion, the prudently calculated attributable profit should be recognised in the profit and loss account as the difference between the reported turnover and related costs for that contract.'[115]

Consequently, where the software company is able to make reliable estimates as to the extent of progress toward completion of a contract, related revenues and related costs, and where the outcome of the contract can be assessed with reasonable certainty, the percentage-of-completion method of profit recognition should be applied. One company which follows this approach is Logica, a company whose principal activities include the marketing, design, production, integration and maintenance of custom built software and associated hardware systems:

Extract 3.5: Logica plc (1998)

Accounting policies

4   Recognition of profits [extract]

Profit is taken on fixed price contracts while the contract is in progress, having regard to the proportion of the total contract which has been completed at the balance sheet date. Provision is made for all foreseeable future losses.

5   Amounts recoverable on contracts

Amounts recoverable on contracts represent turnover which has not yet been invoiced to clients. Such amounts are separately disclosed within Debtors.

The valuation of amounts recoverable on fixed price contracts is adjusted to take up profit to date or foreseeable losses in accordance with the accounting policy for recognition of profits.

Other amounts recoverable on contracts are valued at the lower of cost or estimated net realisable value.

Cost comprises:

- professional amounts recoverable valued at the cost of salaries and associated payroll expenses of employees engaged on assignments and a proportion of attributable overheads

- unbilled expenses incurred and equipment purchased for clients in connection with specific contracts.

On the other hand, where the uncertainties are such that prudence would preclude the accrual of profit, or where the contracts are of a relatively short duration, the completed contract method of accounting should be applied.

Under SOP 97-2, if an arrangement to deliver software or a software system, either alone or together with other products or services, requires significant production, modification or customisation of software, the entire arrangement should be accounted for in accordance with Accounting Research Bulletin (ARB) No. 45 – *Long-Term Construction-Type Contracts* – and SOP 81–1 – *Accounting for Performance of Construction-Type and Certain Production-Type Contracts.*[116]

Similarly, the Appendix to IAS 18 suggests that fees from the development of customised software are recognised as revenue by reference to the stage of completion of the development, including completion of services provided for post delivery service support.[117]

5.5.3   *Accounting for arrangements with multiple elements*

Software arrangements may provide licences for multiple software products or for multiple software products and services (referred to in SOP 97–2 as 'multiple elements') such as: additional software products, upgrades/enhancements, rights to exchange or return software, post-contract customer support (PCS) or other services including elements deliverable only on a when-and-if-available basis. The SOP states that if contract accounting does not apply (because significant customisation is not needed), revenue recognition should be based on an allocation of the total fee to the individual elements based on 'vendor-specific objective evidence of fair value' of each of the elements. This requirement (explained at 5.5.4 below) could have a significant impact on income if elements are recognised as revenue in different periods. If sufficient vendor-specific objective evidence of fair value does not exist for each element, revenue from the arrangement should be deferred until such sufficient evidence exists, or until all elements have been delivered.[118]

If a discount is offered in a multiple element arrangement, a proportionate amount of that discount should be applied to each element included in the arrangement based on each element's fair value without regard to the discount.[119]

5.5.4   *Determining fair value based on vendor-specific objective evidence*

SOP 97–2 states that if an arrangement includes multiple elements, the fee should be allocated to the various elements based on vendor-specific objective evidence of fair value, regardless of any separate prices stated within the contract for each element.[120] Under the SOP, vendor-specific objective evidence of fair value is limited to the following:

- the price charged when the same element is sold separately; and

- for an element not yet being sold separately, the price established by management having the relevant authority; it must be probable that the price, once established, will not change before the separate introduction of the element into the marketplace.[121]

With the exception of changes in the estimated percentage of customers not expected to exercise an upgrade right, the amount allocated to undelivered elements is not subject to later adjustment.[122] However, if it becomes probable that the amount allocated to an undelivered element will result in a loss on that element of the arrangement, the loss should be recognised.[123]

If a multiple-element arrangement includes an upgrade right, the fee should be allocated between the elements based on vendor-specific objective evidence of fair value. The fee allocated to the upgrade right is the price for the upgrade/enhancement that would be charged to existing users of the software product being updated. If the upgrade right is included in a multiple-element arrangement on which a discount has been offered, no portion of the discount should be allocated to the upgrade right. If sufficient vendor-specific evidence exists to reasonably estimate the percentage of customers that are not expected to exercise the upgrade right, the fee allocated to the upgrade right should be reduced to reflect that percentage. SOP 97–2 goes on to state that this estimated percentage should be reviewed periodically, and that the effect of any change in that percentage should be accounted for as a change in accounting estimate.

As stated above, if sufficient vendor-specific objective evidence does not exist for the allocation of revenue to the various elements of the arrangement, the SOP provides that all revenue from the arrangement should be deferred until the earlier of the dates at which:

(a)   such sufficient vendor-specific objective evidence does exist; or

(b)   all elements of the arrangement have been delivered.[124]

However, the SOP provides for the following exceptions to this principle:

▪   if the only undelivered element is post-contract customer support (PCS), the entire fee is recognised on a pro-rata basis;[125]

▪   if the only undelivered element is services that do not involve significant production, modification or customisation of software, the entire fee should be recognised over the period during which the services are expected to be performed;[126]

▪   if the arrangement is in substance a subscription, the entire fee should be recognised on a pro-rata basis;[127] and

▪   if the fee is based on the number of copies, the revenue should be accounted for on an allocation basis, as specified in the SOP.[128] For example, some fixed fee licence arrangements provide customers with the right to reproduce or obtain copies at a specified price per copy of two or more software products up to the total amount of the fixed fee. A number of the products covered by the arrangement may not be deliverable or specified at the inception of the arrangement. In such cases, the revenue allocated to the delivered products should be recognised when the product master or first copy is delivered. If during the term of the arrangement, the customer reproduces or receives enough copies of these delivered products so that revenue allocable to the delivered products exceeds the revenue previously recognised, such additional revenue should be recognised as the copies are reproduced or delivered. The revenue allocated to the undeliverable product(s) should be reduced by a corresponding amount.[129]

5.5.5   *Upgrades, enhancements and post-contract customer support (PCS)*

Under SOP 97–2, the right to receive specified upgrades or enhancements (even on a when-and-if-available basis) under a PCS arrangement is considered a separate element of licensing arrangement. However, rights to receive unspecified upgrades/enhancements on a when-and-if-available basis are PCS services and generally should be recognised as revenue on a pro rata basis over the term of the PCS arrangement. SOP 97–2 defines PCS to exclude rights to specific upgrades/enhancements. For a specific upgrade, a portion of the total licensing fee should be allocated to the elements using the 'vendor-specific objective evidence of fair value' criteria. The fee allocated to the upgrade right is the price for the upgrade/enhancement that would be charged to existing users of the software product being updated.[130]

If a multiple-element software arrangement includes explicit or implicit rights to PCS, the total fees from the arrangement should be allocated among the elements based on vendor-specific objective evidence of fair value. The fair value of the PCS should be determined by reference to the price the customer will be required to pay when it is sold separately (that is, the renewal rate). The portion of the fee allocated to PCS should be recognised as revenue on a pro rata basis over the term of the PCS arrangement, because PCS services are assumed to be provided on a pro rata basis. However, revenue should be recognised over the period of the PCS arrangement in proportion to the amounts expected to be charged to expense for the PCS services rendered during the period if:

- sufficient vendor-specific historical evidence exists demonstrating that costs to provide PCS are incurred on other than a straight-line basis; and

- the vendor believes that it is probable that the costs incurred in performing under the current arrangement will follow a similar pattern.[131]

The following extract illustrates what we consider to be an appropriate policy:

Extract 3.6: Total Systems plc (1999)

1.   Accounting policies

Software maintenance

For software covered by maintenance contracts income is credited to the profit and loss account over the period to which the contract relates. Costs associated with these contracts are expensed as incurred.

5.5.6   *Evaluation of whether a fee is fixed or determinable and arrangements that include extended payment terms*

One of the SOP's basic criteria for software revenue recognition is determining whether the fee under the arrangement is fixed or determinable. The SOP states that any extended payment terms in a software licensing arrangement may indicate that the fee is not fixed or determinable.[132] Furthermore, it goes on to state that a software licensing fee should be presumed not to be fixed if payment of a significant portion of the fee is not due until after expiration of the licence or more than twelve months after delivery of the software. However, this presumption may be overcome by evidence that the vendor has a standard business practice of using long-term or instalment contracts and a history of successfully collecting under the original payment terms without making concessions.[133]

If it cannot be concluded that the fee is fixed or determinable at the outset of the arrangement, revenue should be recognised as payments from customers become due (assuming, of course, that the other revenue recognition criteria have been met).[134]

5.5.7   *Rights to return or exchange software*

As part of a software licensing arrangement, a software vendor may provide a customer with the right to return or exchange software. Depending on the circumstances, the customer might exchange software for a product with minimal or more than minimal differences in price, functionality and features.

Consistent with SFAS 48 – *Revenue Recognition When Right of Return Exists*, SOP 97–2 requires a software vendor to establish a reserve for estimated returns; however, no amounts should be reserved for the right to exchange because exchange rights do not affect revenue recognition, although any estimated costs for such exchanges should be accrued. SOP 97–2 also provides that exchanges of software products for different software products or for similar software products with more than minimal differences in price, functionality or features are considered returns and are accounted for in conformity with SFAS 48.[135]

5.5.8 Services

Many software arrangements include both software and service elements (services). Services may include training, installation or consulting (but do not include PCS-related services). Consulting services often include implementation support, software design or development or the customisation or modification of the licensed software.[136]

According to the SOP, if an arrangement includes such services, a determination must be made as to whether the service element can be accounted for separately as the services are performed.[137] The SOP lays down the following criteria that must be met in order to account separately for the service element of an arrangement that includes both software and services:

■ sufficient vendor-specific objective evidence of fair value must exist to permit allocation of the revenue to the various elements of the arrangements (see 5.5.4 above);

■ the services must not be essential to the functionality of any other element of the transaction; and

■ the services must be described in the contract such that the total price of the arrangement would be expected to vary as the result of the inclusion or exclusion of the services.[138]

If these criteria are met, revenue should be allocated between the service and software elements of the contract. This allocation should be based on vendor-specific objective evidence of fair value. Revenue from the service element should be recognised as the services are performed or on a straight-line basis over the service period if no pattern of performance is discernible.[139]

5.5.9 Disclosures in practice

The following extracts illustrate software revenue recognition policies that are to be found in practice in the UK and which, in our view, provide examples of good practice:

Extract 3.7: Misys plc (1998)

ACCOUNTING POLICIES

REVENUE RECOGNITION

Turnover represents amounts invoiced to customers (net of value added tax) for goods and services. Revenue from systems are recognised upon delivery to a customer when there are no significant vendor obligations remaining and the collection of the resulting receivable is considered probable. In instances where a significant vendor obligation exists, revenue recognition is delayed until the obligation has been satisfied. Service revenue comprise revenues for maintenance, transaction processing and professional; services. Maintenance and support contracts are recognised rateably over the period of the contract. Electronic data interchange and remote processing services are recognised monthly as the work is performed. Professional services, such as implementation, training and consultancy, are recognised when the services are performed.

Extract 3.8: MDIS Group plc (1998)

RECOGNITION OF REVENUE

Revenue on the outright sale of equipment and standard software, where no significant vendor obligations exist, is recognised on despatch. Revenue on non-standard software or where significant vendor obligations exist, is recognised on customer acceptance.

Revenue from professional services (project management, implementation and training) is recognised as the services are performed. Revenue from software support and hardware maintenance agreements is recognised rateably over the term of the agreement.

On contracts involving a combination of products and services, revenue is recognised separately on each deliverable in accordance with the above policy, unless all deliverables are considered to be interdependent when revenue is recognised on final acceptance.

On major contracts extending over more than one period, revenue is taken based on the stage of completion when the outcome of the contract can be foreseen with reasonable certainty and after allowing a contingency for unforeseen costs to completion.

Where equipment is leased or software is licensed under certain long term contracts for the greater part of their economic life, the contracts are classified as sales-type (finance) leases and the present value of future lease rentals, after calculating a deduction for maintenance, is recognised as revenue at the inception of the lease. Interest is included in turnover over the period of the contract so as to produce a constant rate of return on the net investment in the lease.

Where equipment in an equipment lease or the interest in a software licence is sold to a finance company which then leases the equipment or licences the software to a customer, revenue is taken on the sales value after deferral of income for future maintenance, where applicable.

Provision for maintenance on equipment or software licences sold to finance companies as described above is released to revenue over the period of the contract. The related interest is charged to profit over the same period and represents a constant proportion of the balance outstanding.

Where the Group leases equipment or licences software under contracts which do not have the characteristics of a sales-type lease, the rentals are taken to revenue on an accruals basis.

5.6   Film exhibition rights

Revenue received from the licensing of films for exhibition at cinemas and on television should be recognised in accordance with the general recognition principles discussed in this Chapter. Contracts for the television broadcast rights of films normally allow for multiple showings within a specific period; these contracts usually expire either on the date of the last authorised telecast, or on a specified date, whichever occurs first. It is our view that the revenue from the sale of broadcast or exhibition rights may be recognised in full (irrespective of when the licence period begins), provided the following conditions are met:

(a)   a contract has been entered into;

(b)   the film is complete and available for delivery;

(c)   there are no outstanding performance obligations, other than having to make a copy of the film and deliver it to the licensee; and

(d)   collectibility is reasonably assured.

Rights for the exhibition of films at cinemas are generally sold either on the basis of a percentage of the box office receipts or for a flat fee. In the case of the percentage basis, revenue should be recognised as it accrues through the showing of the film. Where a non-refundable flat fee is received, we suggest that revenue be recognised on the same basis as described above for television broadcast rights.

In the US, under SFAS 53 – *Financial Reporting by Producers and Distributors of Motion Picture Films* – revenue from a television broadcast contract should be recognised in full only when the licence period begins, and all of the following conditions have been met:

(a)   the licence fee for each film is known;

(b)   the cost of each film is known or reasonably determinable;

(c)   collectibility of the full licence fee is reasonably assured;

(d)   the film has been accepted by the licensee in accordance with the conditions of the licence agreement; and

(e)   the film is available for its first telecast.[140]

5.7   The disposal of land and buildings

Unlike the US, there are no laid down rules in the UK for the recognition of the proceeds on disposal of land and buildings. Consequently, the general principles of revenue recognition should be applied in order to determine the point in time at which property sales should be recognised in the profit and loss account. There are two significant points in the earning process which could, depending on the circumstances of the sale, be considered to be the critical event for recognition. The first point is on exchange of contracts, at which time the vendor and purchaser are both bound by a legally enforceable contract of sale; whilst the second possible point of recognition is on completion of the contract. The following extracts illustrate the fact that both approaches are followed in practice:

Extract 3.9: Crest Nicholson Plc (1998)

Accounting Policies

    (d) Income recognition

        Profit is recognised on houses when contracts are exchanged and building is substantially complete. Profit is recognised on commercial property developments or units of development when they are substantially complete and subject to binding and unconditional contracts of sale and where legal completion has occurred shortly thereafter. Where the sale price is conditional upon letting, profit is restricted by reference to the space unlet. Profit in respect of construction is recognised when the contract is complete.

        In the case of contracts that are regarded as long term, profit is recognised during execution provided a binding contract for sale exists and the outcome can be foreseen with reasonable certainty.

Extract 3.10: Hammerson plc (1998)

1. ACCOUNTING POLICIES

    Profits on Sale of Properties [extract]

    Profits on sale of properties are taken into account on the completion of contract and receipt of cash.

Extract 3.11: Countryside Properties PLC (1998)

1 Accounting policies

Profit Profit is taken on legal completion of sale of each property, except in the case of long-term building contracts where attributable profit is taken having regard to the proportion of the contract completed at the Balance Sheet date.

Although legal title and beneficial ownership do not pass until the contract is completed and the transfer is registered, it is likely that the earnings process is sufficiently complete to permit recognition to take place on exchange of contracts. The reason for this is that the selling price would have been established, all material related expenses would have been ascertained and, usually, no significant uncertainties would remain. If, however, on exchange of contracts there exists doubt that the sale will be ultimately completed, recognition should take place on the receipt of sales proceeds at legal completion.

Since both approaches appear to be widely used in practice, they should both be regarded as being acceptable accounting practice. Nevertheless, it is important to ensure that, whichever policy is adopted, it is applied consistently, although recognition should always be delayed until completion if significant uncertainties still exist on exchange of contracts. The income recognition policy of Crest Nicholson reproduced above is a good example of the application of this principle.

The illustrative example in the Appendix to IAS 18 states that revenue is normally recognised when legal title passes to the buyer; however, at the same time, it acknowledges that recognition might take place before legal title passes, provided that the seller has no further substantial acts to complete under the contract.[141]

In the US, SFAS 66 – *Accounting for Sales of Real Estate* – lays down rigid rules for the recognition of profit on real estate transactions, and distinguishes between retail land sales (i.e. sales under a property development project) and other sales of real estate. The statement contains extensive provisions which have been developed to deal with complex transactions which are beyond the scope of this book. However, the general requirements for recognising all of the profit on a non-retail land sale are as follows:

Profit should not be recognised in full until all of the following criteria are met:
(a) the sale is consummated;
(b) the purchaser's initial and continuing investments are adequate to demonstrate a commitment to pay for the property;
(c) the vendor's receivable is not subject to future subordination; and
(d) the vendor has transferred to the purchaser the usual risks and rewards of ownership in a transaction that is in substance a sale and does not have a substantial continuing involvement with the property.[142]

A sale is not considered to be consummated until:
(a) the parties are bound by the terms of the contract;
(b) all consideration has been exchanged (i.e. either all monies have been received, or all necessary contractual arrangements have been entered into for the ultimate payment of monies – such as notes supported by irrevocable letters of credit from an independent lending institution);
(c) any permanent financing for which the vendor is responsible has been arranged; and
(d) all conditions precedent to closing the contract have been performed.[143]

SFAS 66 states that these four conditions are usually met 'at the time of closing or after closing, not when an agreement to sell is signed or at a preclosing'.[144]

5.8 Sale and leaseback transactions

A sale and leaseback transaction takes place when an owner sells an asset and immediately reacquires the right to use the asset by entering into a lease with the purchaser. The accounting treatment of any apparent profit arising on the sale of the asset will depend on whether the leaseback is an operating or finance lease. In general terms, if the leaseback is an operating lease, the seller-lessee has disposed of substantially all the risks and rewards of ownership of the asset, and so has realised a profit on disposal. Conversely, if the leaseback is a finance lease, the seller-lessee is, in effect, reacquiring substantially all the risks and rewards of ownership of the asset; consequently, it would be inappropriate to recognise a profit on an asset which, in substance, was never disposed of.[145]

The accounting treatment of the profit arising on sale and leaseback transactions is discussed in Chapter 17 at 7.4.

5.9   Non-monetary/barter transactions

There is currently no authoritative guidance in the UK that deals directly with the accounting for non-monetary transactions. Under IAS 18, when goods or services are exchanged for goods or services that are of a similar nature and value, the exchange is not regarded as a transaction that generates revenue.[146] This is often the case, for example, with exchanges of licence interests in the oil and gas industry.

However, when goods or services are exchanged for dissimilar goods or services, the exchange is regarded as a transaction which generates revenue. The revenue is measured at the fair value of the goods or services received, adjusted by the amount of any cash or cash equivalents transferred. When the fair value of the goods or services received cannot be measured reliably, the revenue is measured at the fair value of the goods or services given up, adjusted by the amount of any cash or cash equivalents transferred.[147]

IAS 16 deals also with exchanges of fixed assets. An item of property, plant and equipment may be acquired in exchange for a similar asset that has a similar use in the same line of business and which has a similar fair value. An item of property, plant and equipment may also be sold in exchange for an equity interest in a similar asset. IAS 16 states that in both cases, since the earnings process is incomplete, no gain or loss is recognised on the transaction. Instead, the cost of the new asset is the carrying amount of the asset given up.[148] However, the fair value of the of the asset received may provide evidence of an impairment in the asset given up. Under these circumstances the asset given up is written down and this written down value assigned to the new asset.[149]

Where an item of property, plant and equipment is acquired in exchange or part exchange for a dissimilar item of property, plant and equipment or other asset, IAS 16 states that the cost of the item received is measured at its fair value, which is equivalent to the fair value of the asset given up adjusted by the amount of any cash or cash equivalents transferred.[150] IAS 16 is silent on the matter of whether the difference between the book value and the fair value of the asset given up represents a gain, although it would seem to imply that it does. For example, if an enterprise owns a machine with a book value of 100 and a fair value of 120 and it exchanges it for a vehicle, then the cost of the vehicle acquired is measured at 120, resulting in an apparent gain of 20 on the disposal of the machine. However, in our view, this does not constitute a realised gain and the 20 should be transferred to an unrealised reserve until such time as the vehicle acquired is, itself, realised.

The general principles under US GAAP are similar to IAS 18 and are addressed in APB Opinion No. 29 – *Accounting for Nonmonetary Transactions*. APB 29 states that the basis of accounting for non-monetary transactions is the same as for monetary transactions – i.e. fair values – and a gain or loss is recognised when the book value of the asset given up differs from the fair value recorded for the asset received.[151] However, APB 29 recognises that when neither the fair value of the non-monetary asset received nor the fair value of the non-monetary asset given up can be determined within reasonable limits, the recorded amount of the asset transferred from the enterprise may be the only available measure of the transaction.[152] Furthermore, where the exchange involves 'similar productive assets' – i.e. assets that are of the same general type, that perform the same function or that are in the same line of business – a gain is not recognised.[153]

APB 29 also recognises that the exchange of non-monetary assets may include an amount of monetary consideration. In such cases, the recipient of the monetary consideration has realised a gain on the exchange to the extent that the amount of the monetary receipt exceeds a proportionate share of the recorded amount of the asset surrendered. The portion of the cost applicable to the realised amount should be based on the ratio of the monetary consideration to the total consideration received (i.e. monetary consideration plus the estimated fair value of the non-monetary asset received) or, if more clearly evident, the fair value of the non-monetary asset transferred.

6   CONCLUSION

The growing complexity and diversity of business activity have given birth to a variety of forms of revenue-earning transactions which were never contemplated when the point of sale was established several decades ago as the general rule for revenue recognition. Added to this, the gradual move away from strict adherence to the realisation concept has resulted in contemporary generally accepted practice for the recognition of revenue becoming haphazard. Whilst there appears to be a growing practice of recognising revenue during the course of productive activity, it is generally done on the basis of exception, rather than in terms of an established principle.

At the same time, though, instead of bringing order to existing practice, the ASB has proposed a radical new approach to revenue recognition based on changes in balance sheet net assets. This approach, if implemented, would replace the long-established accounting process in use throughout the world, whereby transactions are allocated to accounting periods by reference to the matching and prudence concepts. However, it is most unlikely to work well in practice. Revenue recognition criteria are more demanding than those for recognising assets and liabilities, since they should embody the concept of the revenue having been earned, based on performance by the reporting company. Although the conventions for applying this transactions-based approach need to be developed further, it seems more likely that it will remain a more workable system than recognition criteria based on determining whether or not there is sufficient evidence that a change in net assets has occurred.

Nevertheless, the ASB appears to be moving inexorably towards a system of performance reporting that is based on increases and decreases in net assets, other than those resulting from transactions with owners. This approach, which has been advocated in its two versions of its Draft *Statement of Principles* has now been reinforced by the publication in June 1999 of its Discussion Paper entitled *Reporting Financial Performance: Proposals for Change*. This paper, too, is founded on the preconception that all the non-owner movements from one balance sheet to the next represent 'performance', and takes FRS 3 one step further by proposing that the profit and loss account and statement of total recognised gains and losses be combined into one statement of 'total financial performance'.

Rather than assuming that all its balance sheet-orientated measurement rules contribute inexorably to an assessment of performance, we think the ASB needs to start at the other end. It should first consider what deserves to be regarded as performance and then devise a framework of accounting rules that fits that definition.

References

1 APB Statement No. 4, *Basic Concepts and Accounting Principles Underlying Financial Statements of Business Enterprises*, AICPA, October 1970, para. 134.
2 The Council of the European Communities, *The Second Council Directive on Company Law*, 77/91/EEC.
3 *Ibid.*, Article 15.1(c).
4 CCAB, *The determination of realised profits and disclosure of distributable profits in the context of the Companies Acts 1948 to 1981 (TR 481)*, September 1982, paras. 4–6, passim.
5 *Ibid.*, para. 10.
6 SSAP 2, *Disclosure of accounting policies*, ASC, November 1971, para. 14.
7 Professor Sir Bryan Carsberg and Christopher Noke, *The reporting of profits and the concept of realisation: A report prepared for the Research Board of the Institute of Chartered Accountants in England and Wales*, London, 1989, p. 41.
8 *Ibid.*, p. 42.
9 Draft Technical Release, *The determination of realised profits and distributable profits in the context of the companies act 1985*, ICAEW, 23 July 1999, para. 6.
10 *Ibid.*, para. 8.
11 *Ibid.*, para. 9.
12 *Ibid.*, para. 10.
13 Revised Exposure Draft, *Statement of Principles for Financial Reporting: A Technical Supplement to the Revised Exposure Draft*, ASB, March 1999, para. B5.4.
14 Revised Exposure Draft, *Statement of Principles for Financial Reporting*, ASB, March 1999, para. 5.24.
15 Revised Exposure Draft, *Statement of Principles for Financial Reporting: A Technical Supplement to the Revised Exposure Draft*, paras. B5.4 to B5.13.
16 *Ibid.*, para. B5.13.
17 APB Statement No. 4, para. 150.
18 *Ibid.*, para. 151.
19 *Ibid.*, para. 152.
20 John H. Myers, 'The Critical Event and Recognition of Net Profit', *Accounting Review 34*, October 1959, pp. 528–532.
21 SFAC No. 5, *Recognition and Measurement in Financial Statements of Business Enterprises*, FASB, December 1984, paras. 83 and 84.
22 IAS 39, *Financial Instruments: Recognition and Measurement*, IASC, December 1998, para. 103.
23 US GAAP requires fair value measurement for all derivatives, including those linked to unquoted equity instruments if they are to be settled in cash but not those to be settled by delivery, which are outside the scope of SFAS 133.
24 IAS 39, para. 70.
25 *Ibid.*
26 Sale of Goods Act 1979, s 2(1).
27 *Ibid.*, s 2(4).
28 *Ibid.*, s 2(5).
29 *Ibid.*, s 18, Rule 1.
30 *Ibid.*, s 18, Rule 2.
31 APB Statement No. 4, para. 151.
32 SFAC No. 5, paras. 83 and 84.
33 SFAS 48, *Revenue Recognition When Right of Return Exists*, FASB, June 1981, para. 6.
34 *Ibid.*
35 *Ibid.*, para. 8.
36 APB Statement No. 4, para. 150.
37 Revised Exposure Draft, *Statement of Principles for Financial Reporting*, ASB, para. 5.24.
38 *Ibid.*, para. 4.40.
39 *Ibid.*, p. 62.
40 *Ibid.*, para. 5.32.
41 *Ibid.*, paras. 5.33 to 5.34.

42 *Ibid.*, para. 5.35.
43 Revised Exposure Draft, *Statement of Principles for Financial Reporting: A Technical Supplement to the Revised Exposure Draft*, para. C15.
44 E65, *Agriculture*, IASC, July 1999, para. 9.
45 *Ibid.*, para. 21.
46 *Ibid.*, para. 36.
47 *Ibid.*, para. 10.
48 *Ibid.*, para. 22.
49 *Ibid.*, para. 55.
50 *Ibid.*, para. 38.
51 CA 85, Sch. 4, para. 12(a).
52 *Ibid.*, s 262(3).
53 For a full analysis of the ASB's attempt to develop a statement of principles for financial reporting (conceptual framework), see Chapter 2 of this book.
54 Revised Exposure Draft, *Statement of Principles for Financial Reporting*, p. 47.
55 *Ibid.*, para. 5.1.
56 *Ibid.*, pp. 62 and 63.
57 *Ibid.*, para. 5.24.
58 FRS 12, *Provisions, Contingent Liabilities and Contingent Assets*, ASB, September 1998, para. 2.
59 *Ibid.*, para. 14.
60 IAS 18 (Original), *Revenue Recognition*, IASC, December 1982, para. 4.
61 IAS 18 (revised 1993), *Revenue*, IASC, 1993, Objective.
62 *Ibid.*, para. 1.
63 *Ibid.*, para. 7.
64 Revised Exposure Draft, *Statement of Principles for Financial Reporting*, ASB, para. 4.40.
65 IAS 18, para. 10.
66 *Ibid.*, para. 7.
67 *Ibid.*, para. 11.
68 *Ibid.*, para. 12.
69 *Ibid.*, para. 14.
70 *Ibid.*, para. 16.
71 *Ibid.*, para. 15.
72 *Ibid.*, para. 17.
73 *Ibid.*, para. 20.
74 *Ibid.*, para. 26.
75 *Ibid.*, para. 20.
76 *Ibid.*, para. 24.
77 *Ibid.*, para. 25.
78 *Ibid.*, para. 35.
79 ARB 43, *Restatement and Revision of Accounting Research Bulletins*, AICPA, June 1953, Chapter 1, Section A, para. 1.
80 *Ibid.*
81 *Ibid.*, Chapter 11, Section A, para. 11.
82 *Ibid.*, para. 13.
83 ARB No. 45, *Long-Term Construction-Type Contracts*, AICPA, October 1955, para. 15.
84 SFAC No. 5, para. 83.
85 *Ibid.*
86 *Ibid.*
87 *Ibid.*
88 Reed K. Storey and Sylvia Storey, *Special Report: The Framework of Financial Accounting Concepts and Standards*, FASB, January 1998, p. 158.
89 *Ibid.*
90 *Ibid.*, p. 160.
91 Based on the AICPA Industry Accounting Guide, *Accounting for Franchise Fee Revenue*, AICPA, 1973.
92 SFAS 45, *Accounting for Franchise Fee Revenue*, FASB, March 1981, para. 5.

93 *Ibid.*
94 *Ibid.*, para 12.
95 IAS 18, Appendix, para. 18.
96 *Ibid.*, Appendix, para. 18(b).
97 SFAS 50, *Financial Reporting in the Record and Music Industry*, FASB, November 1981, para. 8.
98 SFAS 91, *Accounting for Nonrefundable Fees and Costs Associated with Originating or Acquiring Loans and Initial Direct Costs of Leases*, FASB, December 1986, para. 5.
99 *Ibid.*
100 IAS 18, Appendix, para. 14.
101 C. I. Brown, D. J. Mallett and M. G. Taylor, *Banks: An Accounting and Auditing Guide*, Industry Accounting and Auditing Guide published by the ICAEW, 1983, para. 20.2.
102 SFAS 91, para. 8.
103 *Ibid.*, para. 8a.
104 *Ibid.*, para. 8b.
105 This is also the view taken in the US; see SFAS 91 at para. 10.
106 Aluminium Industrie Vaassen B.V. v Romalpa Aluminium Limited [1976] WLR 676.
107 Accounting Recommendation 2.207, *Accounting for goods sold subject to reservation of title*, ICAEW, July 1976.
108 Exposure Draft, *Statement of Principles for Financial Reporting*, ASB, November 1995, para. 4.30.
109 Revised Exposure Draft, *Statement of Principles for Financial Reporting*, ASB, para. 5.25.
110 IAS 18, Appendix, para. 12.
111 Statement of Position 97–2, *Software Revenue Recognition*, Accounting Standards Executive Committee, American Institute of Certified Public Accountants, October 27, 1997. It became effective for transactions entered into in fiscal years beginning after December 15, 1997.
112 *Ibid.*, para. 8.
113 Companies reporting under US GAAP would apply Accounting Research Bulletin (ARB) No. 45, *Long-Term Construction-Type Contracts*, and SOP 81–1, *Accounting for Performance of Construction-Type and Certain Production-Type Contracts*.
114 SSAP 9, *Stocks and long-term contracts*, Revised September 1988, para. 22.
115 *Ibid.*, paras. 28 and 29.
116 SOP 97–2, para. 7.
117 IAS 18, Appendix, para. 19.
118 SOP 97–2, para. 12.
119 *Ibid.*, para. 11.
120 *Ibid.*, para. 10.
121 *Ibid.*
122 *Ibid.*
123 *Ibid.* Companies reporting under UK GAAP would recognise the loss in accordance with FRS 12, *Provisions, Contingent Liabilities and Contingent Assets*, whilst companies reporting under US GAAP would apply SFAS 5, *Accounting for Contingencies*.
124 *Ibid.*, para. 12.
125 *Ibid.*, paras. 56 to 62.
126 *Ibid.*, paras. 63 to 71.
127 *Ibid.*, paras. 48 and 49.
128 *Ibid.*, paras. 43 to 47.
129 *Ibid.*, paras. 43 and 47.
130 *Ibid.*, para. 37.
131 *Ibid.*, para. 57.
132 *Ibid.*, para. 28.
133 *Ibid.*
134 *Ibid.*, para. 29.
135 *Ibid.*, para. 51.
136 *Ibid.*, para. 63.
137 *Ibid.*, para. 64.
138 *Ibid.*, para. 65.
139 *Ibid.*, para. 66.

140 SFAS 53, *Financial Reporting by Producers and Distributors of Motion Picture Films*, FASB, December 1981, para. 6.
141 IAS 18, Appendix, para. 9.
142 SFAS 66, *Accounting for Sales of Real Estate*, FASB, October 1982, para. 5.
143 *Ibid.*, para. 6.
144 *Ibid.*
145 ASC, *Guidance Notes on SSAP 21: Accounting for Leases and Hire Purchase Contracts*, August 1984, paras. 150–156, passim.
146 IAS 18, para. 12.
147 *Ibid.*
148 IAS 16, *Property, Plant and Equipment*, IASC, Revised 1998, para. 22.
149 *Ibid.*
150 *Ibid.*, para. 21.
151 APB Opinion No. 29, *Accounting for Nonmonetary Transactions*, Accounting Principles Board, May 1973, para. 18.
152 *Ibid.*, para. 26.
153 *Ibid.*, paras. 3e and 21b.

Chapter 4   Corporate governance and the OFR

1   THE NEED FOR CORPORATE GOVERNANCE REFORM

A series of spectacular corporate failures and financial scandals in the late 1980s, including BCCI, Polly Peck and Maxwell, heightened concerns about the standard of financial reporting and accountability. These concerns centred around an apparent low level of confidence both in financial reporting and in the ability of auditors to provide the safeguards which the users of company annual reports sought and expected. The factors underlying these were seen as the looseness of accounting standards, the absence of a clear framework for ensuring that directors kept under review the controls in their businesses, and competitive pressures both on companies and on auditors which made it difficult for auditors to stand up to demanding boards.[1] These concerns were heightened by criticisms of the seeming lack of effective board accountability for such matters as directors' remuneration – particularly in the light of an increasing trend in directors being appointed on lucrative rolling contracts, as well as certain well-publicised large compensation payments for loss of office.

1.1   The Cadbury Committee

In response to these concerns, the Committee on the Financial Aspects of Corporate Governance (the Cadbury Committee) was set up in May 1991 by the Financial Reporting Council, the London Stock Exchange and the accountancy profession, under the chairmanship of Sir Adrian Cadbury. The terms of reference of the Committee were to consider the following issues in relation to financial reporting and accountability and to make recommendations on good practice:[2]

(a)   the responsibilities of executive and non-executive directors for reviewing and reporting on performance to shareholders and other financially interested parties; and the frequency, clarity and form in which information should be provided;

(b)   the case for audit committees of the board, including their composition and role;

(c)   the principal responsibilities of auditors and the extent and value of the audit;

(d)   the links between shareholders, boards and auditors; and

(e)   any other relevant matters.

The Committee's approach was to provide a framework for establishing good corporate governance and accountability. This was done through its Code of Best Practice (the Cadbury Code), which it put forward as a benchmark against which companies could be assessed. The Code embodied underlying principles of openness, integrity and accountability which, according to the Committee, went together.

Although compliance with the Code was recommended, the Committee stressed that it was voluntary and directed at establishing best practice. The Committee was also of the view that companies should be allowed some flexibility in implementing the Code; this was necessary in order to encourage companies to comply with the spirit of the recommendations. The Code provided a target to which companies could aspire, rather than a straitjacket of rules and regulations.

In response to the Committee's recommendations, the London Stock Exchange adopted as part of its Listing Rules the requirement for UK incorporated listed companies to include in their annual report and accounts a statement as to whether or not they had complied throughout the accounting period with the Code. This was supplemented by the requirement to report details of, and reasons for, any non-compliance during the period and to have the directors' statement reviewed by the auditors insofar as it related to objectively verifiable matters in the Code.[3]

Two aspects of the Code could not initially be complied with as they were the subject of continuing debate. These were the requirements for directors to report on the effectiveness of internal control and that the business was a going concern. The Committee noted that companies would not be able to comply with these points until the necessary guidance had been developed. It recommended that such guidance be developed by the accountancy profession together with representatives of preparers of accounts. Two working parties were set up under the auspices of the Hundred Group of Finance Directors, the ICAEW and the ICAS: the Going Concern Working Group, under the chairmanship of Mr Rodney Baker-Bates and the Internal Control Working Group, under the chairmanship of Mr Paul Rutteman. However, the development of the guidance proved to be a difficult task and it was to be about two years after the issue of the Cadbury Report before the working parties produced the necessary guidance to enable the Cadbury jigsaw to be completed.

1.2   The Greenbury Committee

The remit of the Cadbury Committee had been corporate governance as a whole, of which executive remuneration was only a part. The comprehensive review of directors' pay as a single issue fell to the Study Group on Directors' Remuneration, commonly known as the Greenbury Committee after its chairman Sir Richard Greenbury, chairman of Marks and Spencer. This Committee was established in January 1995 at the initiative of (but independent from) the CBI, with the remit of identifying good practice in determining directors' remuneration and preparing a Code of such practice for use by UK PLCs.

The Greenbury Committee issued its report in July 1995,[4] which contained a Code of Best Practice. In October 1995 and June 1996 the London Stock Exchange gave effect to certain of these recommendations by amending its *Listing Rules*.

1.3   The Hampel Committee

In the Cadbury Report, the Committee stated that it would 'remain responsible for reviewing the implementation of the proposals until a successor body is appointed in two years' time, to examine the progress and to continue the ongoing governance review. It will be for our sponsors to agree the remit of the new body and to establish the basis of its support. In the meantime, a programme of research will be undertaken to assist the future monitoring of the Code.'[5]

In fulfilling that latter responsibility the Cadbury Committee:

(a)   set up a Monitoring Sub-Committee;

(b)   encouraged research into a number of projects related to corporate governance; and

(c)   collaborated with the Association of British Insurers in a project to monitor best practice.

In the event, it was to be almost three years before a successor body was formed, in November 1995, under the chairmanship of Sir Ronald Hampel, Chairman of ICI. The remit of this Committee was to seek to promote high standards of corporate governance in the interests of investor protection and in order to preserve and enhance the standing of companies listed on the Stock Exchange. The Committee's remit was to extend to listed companies only. Against this background the Committee was to:

(a)   conduct a review of the Cadbury Code and its implementation to ensure that the original purpose was being achieved, proposing amendments to and deletions from the Code as necessary;

(b)   keep under review the role of directors, executive and non-executive, recognising the need for board cohesion and the common legal responsibilities of all directors;

(c)   be prepared to pursue any relevant matters arising from the report of the Study Group on Directors' Remuneration chaired by Sir Richard Greenbury;

(d)   address as necessary the role of shareholders in corporate governance issues;

(e)   address as necessary the role of auditors in corporate governance issues; and

(f)   deal with any other relevant matters.

Without impairing investor protection the Committee was always to keep in mind the need to restrict the regulatory burden on companies, e.g. by substituting principles for detail wherever possible.[6]

The Hampel Committee began its work early in 1996, and published a preliminary report in August 1997. In January 1998 it published its final report, taking into account comments on the earlier document.

As can be seen from its remit, the work of the Hampel Committee was in large part one of review of the findings of earlier committees, the overwhelming majority of which it endorsed in its final report.[7]

The Hampel Report accepted the Cadbury Committee's definition of corporate governance[8] being 'the system by which companies are directed and controlled'.[9] Hampel then notes that this 'puts the directors of a company at the centre of any discussion on corporate governance, linked to the role of shareholders, since they appoint the directors.'[10] The report emphasises that how companies are run cannot be prescribed, saying: 'Good corporate governance is not just a matter of prescribing particular corporate structures and complying with a number of hard and fast rules. There is a need for broad principles. All concerned should then apply these flexibly and with common sense to the varying circumstances of individual companies.'[11] More generally still, it states that 'The true safeguard for good corporate governance lies in the application of informed and independent judgement by experienced and qualified individuals - executive and non-executive directors, shareholders and auditors.'[12] Having reached broad conclusions on the nature and purpose of corporate governance, the Committee identified some broad principles which it hoped would command general support.[13] These were supplemented with a number of detailed Code provisions. The objective of the principles and Code, like those of the Cadbury and Greenbury Codes, is not to prescribe corporate behaviour in detail but to secure sufficient disclosure so that investors and others can assess companies' performance and governance practice and respond in an informed way.[14] In a sensible evolution from Cadbury and Greenbury, Hampel recommends that companies describe how they have applied these general principles as well as stating whether or not they have complied with the detailed provisions.[15]

The final task of the Hampel Committee was to pass on this set of principles and Code of good corporate governance practice embracing Cadbury, Greenbury and its own work to the London Stock Exchange with the intention that it would be incorporated into the listing rules.[16] In June 1998, the London Stock Exchange published the final version of the Principles of Good Governance and Code of Best Practice (the 'Combined Code'), together with revisions to the *Listing Rules*. The content of the Combined Code is discussed at 2 below.

In this chapter we review the recommendations of the Hampel Committee in so far as they impact on the company annual report and accounts. The impact of the Cadbury Report on interim reporting is discussed at 2.2 in Chapter 30.

2 REPORTING UNDER THE COMBINED CODE

The Combined Code is presented in two sections. Section 1 relates to companies whereas Section 2 relates to institutional investors and is outside the scope of this book. As stated above, we are primarily concerned in this chapter with the impact that the Combined Code has on the company annual report and accounts. This is governed by the rules of the London Stock Exchange as follows:

'In the case of a company incorporated in the United Kingdom, the following additional items must be included in its report and accounts:

(a) a narrative statement of how it has applied the principles set out in Section 1 of the Combined Code, providing explanation which enables its shareholders to evaluate how the principles have been applied;

(b) a statement as to whether or not it has complied throughout the accounting period with the Code provisions set out in Section 1 of the Combined Code. A company that has not complied with the Code provisions, or complied with only some of the Code provisions or (in the case of provisions whose requirements are of a continuing nature) complied for only part of an accounting period, must specify the Code provisions with which it has not complied, and (where relevant) for what part of the period such non-compliance continued, and give reasons for any non-compliance;'[17]

The most significant change from the previous regime is part (a) above. Rather than making a simple statement of compliance, or otherwise, with the detailed provisions of a code, boards must now also describe, in their own words, how they apply the general principles of corporate governance. We believe this to be a much more meaningful requirement, although to give a reasoned and considered description of their governance procedures represents a significant challenge for boards. The detailed Combined Code provisions set out some basic elements of the governance process, and it is likely that some may be reproduced by companies in these discussions. It is to be hoped, however, that this be kept to a minimum to prevent the disclosures degenerating into general boilerplate.

Section 1 of the Combined Code is divided into four parts as follows:

A   Directors;

B   Directors' remuneration;

C   Relations with shareholders; and

D   Accountability and audit.

Set out below is a discussion of the points under A, C and D. Some of the detailed provisions are of a factual nature and hence self explanatory. The principles are shown in bold text, followed by the related Code provisions. The provisions which must be covered by the auditors' review are marked with an asterisk, although auditors' review procedures are not discussed. The requirements of part B are discussed at 4.3 in Chapter 29. It should be noted that the Hampel Report did not seek to reproduce all the discussions of Cadbury and Greenbury with which it agreed, and accordingly much of these earlier reports remains relevant. For this reason many of the footnote references that follow are to the Cadbury Report as well as the Hampel Report.

Some examples of corporate governance disclosures from company accounts are shown in the Appendix at the end of this chapter.

2.1   Directors

A.1   The Board

Every listed company should be headed by an effective board which should lead and control the company.

A.1.1 The board should meet regularly.

A.1.2* The board should have a formal schedule of matters specifically reserved to it for decision.

A.1.3* There should be a procedure agreed by the board for directors in the furtherance of their duties to take independent professional advice if necessary, at the company's expense.

A.1.4 All directors should have access to the advice and services of the company secretary, who is responsible to the board for ensuring that board procedures are followed and that applicable rules and regulations are complied with. Any question of the removal of the company secretary should be a matter for the board as a whole.

> A.1.5 All directors should bring an independent judgement to bear on issues of strategy, performance, resources, (including key appointments) and standards of conduct.
>
> A.1.6 Every director should receive appropriate training on the first occasion that he or she is appointed to the board of a listed company, and subsequently as necessary.

Every public company should be headed by an effective board which can both lead and control the business. Within the context of the UK unitary board system, this means a board made up of a combination of executive directors, with their intimate knowledge of the business, and of non-executive directors, who can bring a broader view to the company's activities, under a chairman who accepts the duties and responsibilities which the position entails.[18]

The arrangements whereby boards ensure effective leadership and control will differ greatly between companies. The level of direct involvement with management below board level will depend on the extent of empowerment of executive management, and the amount of monitoring required will vary accordingly.

Provision A.1.1

The prime responsibility of the board of directors is to determine the broad strategy of the company and to ensure its implementation. To do this successfully requires high quality leadership. It also requires that the directors have sufficient freedom of action to exercise their leadership. The board can only fulfil its responsibilities if it meets regularly and reasonably often.[19]

The frequency of board meetings may also vary considerably between companies, depending, inter alia, on the role of its sub-committees and executive management.

Provision A.1.2

Some companies have policies and procedures manuals which specifically cover this point, while others have prepared a list of items to be considered, if appropriate, at each board meeting. Irrespective of the form of such a schedule, it is important that it is formally adopted by the board, that it is circulated to directors and, at least, to executive management and that it is kept up to date.

The schedule might include:

- approval of material acquisitions, disposals, investments, capital projects and other significant transactions;
- authority levels, including the definition of transactions which require multiple board signatures;

- procedures to be followed when decisions are required between board meetings;
- corporate business plan and strategy;
- treasury and risk management policy;
- selection and appointment of non-executive directors and company secretary;
- selection and appointment of senior executives;
- approval of accounts and other reports to shareholders; and
- the establishment of codes of conduct regarding compliance with laws and ethical standards of behaviour.

The existence of a formal schedule will meet the basic requirement of the Combined Code provision. However, as part of effective leadership and control, the directors should consider the procedures to ensure that all relevant matters are referred to the board together with adequate information on which to base decisions, and the sanctions available to them where, for example, authority levels are exceeded.

Provision A.1.3

This requirement is in addition to any procedures that enable the directors to consult the company's advisers, and recognises that there may be situations in which a director might wish to take independent advice.

The procedures should be formalised, for example, by board resolution, in the company's articles or in a director's letter of appointment.[20]

Provision A.1.4

The company secretary has a key role to play in ensuring that board procedures are both followed and regularly reviewed. The chairman and the board will look to the company secretary for guidance on what their responsibilities are under the rules and regulations to which they are subject and on how those responsibilities should be discharged. All directors should have access to the advice and services of the company secretary and should recognise that the chairman is entitled to the strong and positive support of the company secretary in ensuring the effective functioning of the board.[21] Although the procedures allowing such access may be clearly understood, they should be acknowledged by the board by way of minute or in the letter of appointment for each director.

Provision A.1.5

The basic legal duties of directors are to act in good faith in the interests of the company and for a proper purpose; and to exercise care and skill. These are derived from common law and are common to all directors. The duties are owed to the company, meaning generally the shareholders collectively, both present and future, not the shareholders at a given point in time.[22] The Cadbury Committee clearly saw independence of judgement as the essential quality which non-executive directors should bring to the board's deliberations,[23] the Combined Code makes clear that this is a duty of all directors. Hampel also notes that there is a view that non-executive directors should face less onerous duties than executive directors. However, it supports the retention of common duties in the interests of the unity and cohesion of the board.[24]

A.2   Chairman and CEO

There are two key tasks at the top of every public company - the running of the board and the executive responsibility for the running of the company's business. There should be a clear division of responsibilities at the head of the company which will ensure a balance of power and authority, such that no one individual has unfettered powers of decision.

A.2.1   A decision to combine the posts of chairman and chief executive officer in one person should be publicly justified. Whether the posts are held by different people or by the same person, there should be a strong and independent non-executive element on the board, with a recognised senior member other than the chairman to whom concerns can be conveyed. The chairman, chief executive and senior independent director should be identified in the annual report.

Cadbury saw the chairman's role in securing good corporate governance as being crucial and described it as follows: 'Chairmen are primarily responsible for the working of the board, for the balance of its membership subject to board and shareholders' approval, and for ensuring that all directors, executive and non-executive alike, are enabled to play their full part in its activities'.[25] Hampel endorsed this description, subject to its view on the role of the nomination committee (see later), and added: 'The chief executive officer's task is to run the business and to implement the policies and strategies adopted by the board. There are thus two distinct roles.'[26]

Accordingly, both committees came to the view that the roles of chairman and chief executive should in principle be separate. Hampel further noted that a number of companies have combined the two roles successfully, either permanently or for a time.[27] Where the roles are combined the board should explain and justify the fact.

Whether or not the roles are combined, the Combined Code now requires a senior non-executive director to be identified, to cater for occasions when there is a need to convey concerns to the board other than through the chairman or chief executive.[28] The Cadbury Code only required this when these two posts were held by the same individual.

A.3   Board Balance

The board should include a balance of executive and non-executive directors (including independent non-executives) such that no individual or small group of individuals can dominate the board's decision taking.

A.3.1 The board should include non-executive directors of sufficient calibre and number for their views to carry significant weight in the board's decisions. Non-executive directors should comprise not less than one third of the board.

A.3.2 The majority of non-executive directors should be independent of management and free from any business or other relationship which could materially interfere with the exercise of their independent judgement. Non-executive directors considered by the board to be independent in this sense should be identified in the annual report.

As a consequence of its remit, precipitated largely by corporate failures, Cadbury emphasised the control function of non-executive directors. Hampel sought to rebalance the debate by stressing that non-executives should have a strategic as well as a monitoring function.[29]

Provision A.3.1

Non-executive directors can bring to boards both breadth of experience and specialist knowledge and contribute to business prosperity, as well as independently monitoring the governance of the company. For non-executives to be effective, Hampel considered that they should comprise at least one third of the board.

Provision A.3.2

Cadbury recommended that a majority of non-executive directors should be independent, and defined this as 'independent of management and free from any business or other relationship which could materially interfere with the exercise of their independent judgement'.[30] Hampel agreed with this definition, and did not consider it practicable to lay down more precise criteria for independence.[31] The Committee made it clear that it is for the board to decide in particular cases whether this definition of independence is met. The corollary is that boards should disclose in the annual report which of the directors are considered to be independent and be prepared to justify their view if challenged.[32] An example of a company confirming the independence of non-executives by specific reference to provision A.3.2 is United Assurance (Extract 4.3 in the Appendix to this chapter). Hampel recognised, however, that non-executive directors who are not in this sense 'independent' may nonetheless make a useful contribution to the board.[33] Laura Ashley (Extract 4.4 in the Appendix to this chapter) is an example of a company disclosing non-executives who are not independent in this sense.

A.4   Supply of information

The board should be supplied in a timely manner with information in a form and of a quality appropriate to enable it to discharge its duties.

A.4.1   Management has an obligation to provide the board with appropriate and timely information, but information volunteered by management is unlikely to be enough in all circumstances and directors should make further enquiries where necessary. The chairman should ensure that all directors are properly briefed on issues arising at board meetings.

Hampel endorsed the view of the Cadbury Committee that the effectiveness of non-executive directors (indeed, of all directors) turns, to a considerable extent, on the quality of the information they receive.[34]

A.5   Appointments to the Board

There should be a formal and transparent procedure for the appointment of new directors to the board.

A.5.1   Unless the board is small, a nomination committee should be established to make recommendations to the board on all new board appointments. A majority of the members of this committee should be non-executive directors and the chairman should be either the chairman of the board or a non-executive director. The chairman and members of the nomination committee should be identified in the annual report.

Appointment to the board should be a transparent process, with decisions taken, in reality as well as in form, by the whole board. To assist in this process Hampel recommends that the use of a nomination committee should be accepted as best practice, with the proviso that smaller boards may prefer to fulfil the function themselves.[35]

Hampel also considered the practice of appointment of directors to represent outside interests, for example a major creditor or a major shareholder. It concluded that this practice is, other than in exceptional cases, incompatible with board cohesion.[36]

A.6   Re-election

All directors should be required to submit themselves for re-election at regular intervals and at least every three years.

A.6.1* Non-executive directors should be appointed for specified terms subject to re-election and to Companies Act provisions relating to the removal of a director, and reappointment should not be automatic.

A.6.2* All directors should be subject to election by shareholders at the first opportunity after their appointment, and to re-election thereafter at intervals of no more than three years. The names of directors submitted for election or re-election should be accompanied by sufficient biographical details to enable shareholders to take an informed decision on their election.

Directors of listed companies are required by the Listing Rules to submit themselves for election at the first AGM after their appointment. The National Association of Pension Funds (NAPF) and the Association of British Insurers (ABI) expect all directors to submit themselves for re-election at intervals of no more than three years. Hampel endorsed this latter view and recommended that those companies who do not as yet conform with it should make the necessary changes in their Articles of Association as soon as possible. Hampel also recommended that all names submitted for election or re-election as directors should be accompanied by biographical details indicating their relevant qualifications and experience. As a result of this provision the previous Stock Exchange requirement for the annual report to give a short biographical note on each of the independent non-executive directors has been repealed.

2.2   Relations with shareholders

C.1   Dialogue with Institutional Shareholders

Companies should be ready, where practicable, to enter into dialogue with institutional shareholders based on the mutual understanding of objectives.

C.2   Constructive use of the AGM

Boards should use the AGM to communicate with private investors and encourage their participation.

C.2.1 Companies should count all proxy votes and, except where a poll is called, should indicate the level of proxies lodged on each resolution, and the balance for and against the resolution, after it has been dealt with on a show of hands.

C.2.2   Companies should propose a separate resolution at the AGM on each substantially separate issue and should in particular propose a resolution at the AGM relating to the report and accounts.

C.2.3   The chairman of the board should arrange for the chairmen of the audit, remuneration and nomination committees to be available to answer questions at the AGM.

C.2.4   Companies should arrange for the Notice of the AGM and related papers to be sent to shareholders at least 20 working days before the meeting.

The recommendation of Cadbury, reiterated by Hampel, was that 'Institutional investors should encourage regular, systematic contact at senior executive level to exchange views and information on strategy, performance, board membership and quality of management'.[37] The idea of greater contact between companies and institutions was developed in 1995 in the report of a joint City/Industry working group chaired by Mr Paul Myners and titled Developing a Winning Partnership. The main recommendations of this report included:

■   investors to articulate their investment objectives to management;

■   investors to be more open with managements in giving feedback on companies' strategies and performance;

■   improved training for fund managers on industrial and commercial awareness;

■   improved training for company managers involved in investor relations;

■   meetings between companies and institutional investors to be properly prepared, with a clear and agreed agenda.[38]

Principle C.1 now requires boards to describe how they conduct such dialogue with their institutional investors.

Provision C.2.1

Hampel considered recommending that companies should put all resolutions to a postal vote, and announce the results of the ballot at the beginning of the meeting. However, it concluded that this might be seen as a move to stifle debate, and that the time was not ripe for a radical change of this kind.[39]

Provision C.2.2

The practice of 'bundling' different proposals in a single resolution has been widely criticised. Hampel considered that shareholders should have an opportunity to vote separately on each substantially separate proposal.[40] The directors must lay before the AGM the annual accounts and the directors' report.[41] Whilst many boards propose a resolution relating to the report and accounts, this is not a legal requirement. Hampel recommended this as best practice, to allow a general discussion of the performance and prospects of the business, and provide an opportunity for the shareholders in effect to give – or withhold – approval of the directors' policies and conduct of the company.[42]

Provision C.2.3

Cadbury had recommended that the chairman of the audit committee should be available to answer questions about its work at the AGM,[43] and Greenbury had made a similar recommendation relating to the chairman of the remuneration committee. Hampel extended this requirement to the chairman of the nomination committee, although noted that it should be for the chairman of the meeting to decide which questions to answer himself and which to refer to a colleague.[44]

As well as allowing reasonable time for discussion at the meeting, Hampel also recommended that the chairman should, if appropriate, also undertake to provide the questioner with a written answer to any significant question which cannot be answered on the spot.[45]

Provision C.2.4

The requirement to give 20 working days (i.e. excluding weekends and Bank Holidays) notice of the AGM is a lengthening of the notice currently required by law of 21 days.[46] The reason given by Hampel is that this longer period will help institutions to consult their clients before deciding how to vote.

2.3   Accountability and audit

D.1   Financial reporting
The board should present a balanced and understandable assessment of the company's position and prospects.
D.1.1* The directors should explain their responsibility for preparing the accounts and there should be a statement by the auditors about their reporting responsibilities.
D.1.2 The board's responsibility to present a balanced and understandable assessment extends to interim and other price-sensitive public reports and reports to regulators as well as to information required to be presented by statutory requirements.
D.1.3 The directors should report that the business is a going concern, with supporting assumptions or qualifications as necessary.

It is well known that both the flexibility allowed to directors through the selection of accounting policies, and the degree of judgement and estimation which underlies the financial reporting process, are significant elements of the expectation gap. The fact that different accounting treatments could be applied to essentially the same facts, means that a company could theoretically report several materially different results of operations and financial positions, each of which could comply with the overriding requirement to show a true and fair view.

Consequently, in order to obviate as far as possible the effects of alternative accounting treatments and presentational techniques, Cadbury placed considerable emphasis on the need for shareholders to receive a coherent narrative, supported by figures, of a company's performance and prospects. The Cadbury Committee recommended that boards should pay particular attention to their duty to present a balanced and understandable assessment of their companies' position, stressing that balance requires that setbacks should be dealt with as well as successes.[47]

With this in mind, and with a view to providing a framework within which directors can discuss the main factors underlying their companies' financial performance and position, the ASB issued in July 1993 a statement of best practice entitled *Operating and Financial Review*. The Operating and Financial Review (OFR) is discussed in detail at 5 below.

Provision D.1.1

(a) Directors' responsibilities

The requirement for such an explanation of responsibilities is included in the auditing standard *Auditors' Reports on Financial Statements* (SAS 600), which requires auditors to provide such an explanation in their audit report if directors have not done so in the accounts. SAS 600 provides example wording for the statement of directors' responsibilities in respect of the accounts as set out below. As it is phrased in terms of a single company a group will need to amend it accordingly.[48]

Company law requires the directors to prepare financial statements for each financial year which give a true and fair view of the state of affairs of the company and of the profit or loss of the company for that period. In preparing those financial statements, the directors are required to

- select suitable accounting policies and then apply them consistently;
- make judgements and estimates that are reasonable and prudent;
- state whether applicable accounting standards have been followed, subject to any material departures disclosed and explained in the financial statements;[6]
- prepare the financial statements on the going concern basis unless it is inappropriate to presume that the company will continue in business.[7]

The directors are responsible for keeping proper accounting records which disclose with reasonable accuracy at any time the financial position of the company and to enable them to ensure that the financial statements comply with the Companies Act 1985. They are also responsible for safeguarding the assets of the company and hence for taking reasonable steps for the prevention and detection of fraud and other irregularities.

[6] Large companies only.

[7] If no separate statement on going concern is made by the directors.

It is no longer necessary for the final bullet point to be included since listed companies are required to make a specific statement about going concern (discussed under provision D.1.3 below).

An article on directors' responsibilities statements appeared in the 3 November 1993 issue of the Law Society *Gazette*.[49] The article (which emanated from the Law Society's Committee on Company Law) expressed concern that companies could, if they did not take legal advice on the contents of the statement of responsibilities, run the risk of extending the legal liability of directors 'unnecessarily'. It is, however, difficult to understand how the example statement in SAS 600 could give rise to an extension of directors' liability as it merely summarises the responsibilities imposed on directors by the Companies Act together with their fiduciary duty to safeguard the company's assets.

The article implied that there is some element of shared responsibility between the directors and auditors for the preparation of financial statements, whereas the legal position is that the directors have sole responsibility in this regard. Further, it was implied that the directors are responsible for instructing the auditors to take whatever steps and undertake whatever inspections they consider necessary. In fact, the auditors' responsibilities in company law already require them to perform whatever work they consider necessary; this legal responsibility may neither be added to nor diminished by the directors.

The Cadbury Committee recommended the inclusion in the report and accounts of a statement of directors' responsibilities 'so that shareholders are clear where the boundaries between the duties of directors and auditors lie'.[50] Unfortunately, the wording suggested in the *Gazette* appeared to confuse rather than clarify in this regard.

It is probably for this reason that a further article on the matter appeared in the 17 December 1993 issue of the *Gazette* which, following discussions between the Auditing Practices Board and the Law Society's Committee on Company Law, took a more measured view of the issue, concluding that 'the directors' responsibility statement and the wording describing the auditors' responsibilities and the basis of their opinion should, in all cases, be considered together so as to avoid inconsistency and yet correctly reflect the legal and factual position'.[51]

(b)   Auditors' responsibilities

The requirement for such an explanation of responsibilities was also included in SAS 600. Following the publication of the Combined Code, and the resultant changes in the *Listing Rules*, the APB considered it appropriate to revisit auditors' responsibilities in relation to corporate governance and to reconsider the way in which these, and the broader responsibilities of auditors, are communicated to users of the annual report.[52] As a result of this exercise the APB published Bulletin 1998/10, *Corporate Governance Reporting and Auditors' Responsibilities Statements*. This bulletin provides example wording for the statement of auditors' responsibilities as follows:

Respective responsibilities of directors and auditors

The directors are responsible for preparing the Annual Report, including as described on page ... the financial statements. Our responsibilities, as independent auditors, are established by statute, the Auditing Practices Board, the Listing Rules of the London Stock Exchange and by our profession's ethical guidance.

We report to you our opinion as to whether the financial statements give a true and fair view and are properly prepared in accordance with the Companies Act. We also report to you if, in our opinion, the directors' report is not consistent with the financial statements, if the company has not kept proper accounting records, if we have not received all the information and explanations we require for our audit, or if the information specified by law or the Listing Rules regarding directors' remuneration and transactions with the company is not disclosed.

We review whether the statement on page ... reflects the company's compliance with those provisions of the Combined Code specified for our review by the Stock Exchange, and we report if it does not. We are not required to form an opinion on the effectiveness of the company's corporate governance procedures or its internal controls.

We read the other information contained in the Annual Report and consider whether it is consistent with the audited financial statements. We consider the implications for our report if we become aware of any apparent misstatements or material inconsistencies with the financial statements. ...

The directors' review of internal controls is discussed under Provision D.1.4 below, while the auditors' review of corporate governance disclosures is discussed at 3 below.

Provision D.1.3

As noted at 1.1 above, this was one of the aspects of the Cadbury Code that companies could not initially comply with until guidance became available. A working party comprising representatives of the Hundred Group of Finance Directors, the ICAEW and the ICAS finally issued its guidance in November 1994.[53] At the same time, the APB issued guidance for auditors reviewing directors' statements on going concern[54] and also issued an auditing standard, SAS 130,[55] which provides guidance to auditors considering, as part of their work in forming their audit opinion, the appropriateness of the going concern basis.

Since the necessary guidance was now available, in August 1995 the Stock Exchange introduced a separate requirement for listed companies to include in their annual report a statement by the directors that the business is a going concern with supporting assumptions or qualifications as necessary, as interpreted by the guidance for directors. Such a statement was to be reviewed by the auditors before publication.[56] The Hampel report did not recommend changing the current practice, saying 'We understand that directors in preparing 'going concern' statements and auditors in reporting on them have found the guidance satisfactory, and we see no need for legislation.'[57]

The guidance for directors recommends a number of procedures relevant to considering going concern under the following categories:[58]

- forecasts and budgets
- borrowing requirements
- liability management
- contingent liabilities
- products and markets
- financial risk management
- other factors
- financial adaptability.

An appendix suggests more detailed procedures under these categories.

When the directors have weighed up the results of the procedures that they have undertaken in order to establish the appropriateness of the going concern basis, there are three basic conclusions that they can reach:

- they have a reasonable expectation that the company will continue in operational existence for the foreseeable future and have therefore used the going concern basis in preparing the financial statements;

- they have identified factors which cast some doubt on the ability of the company to continue in operational existence in the foreseeable future but they have used the going concern basis in preparing the financial statements; or

- they consider that the company is unlikely to continue in operational existence in the foreseeable future and therefore the going concern concept is not an appropriate basis on which to draw up the financial statements.[59]

The guidance envisages that in normal circumstances where the going concern presumption is appropriate the following statement should be made:[60]

> After making enquiries, the directors have a reasonable expectation that the company has adequate resources to continue in operational existence for the foreseeable future. For this reason, they continue to adopt the going concern basis in preparing the accounts.

The guidance recommends that the statement on going concern should be included in the company's Operating and Financial Review (see 5 below). However, some companies include the statement with the rest of the corporate governance disclosures. An example of a company making this 'normal' disclosure is United Assurance (Extract 4.3 in the Appendix to this chapter). Laura Ashley (Extract 4.4) on the other hand includes more extensive supporting assumptions.

The guidance also illustrates the form of statement where the going concern basis is used despite doubts about going concern.[61]

The Cadbury Report emphasised that the directors are not expected to give a guarantee about their company's prospects because there can never be complete certainty about future trading. Therefore the directors are required to state only that they have a 'reasonable expectation' that the company will continue in operation for the foreseeable future. However, the principal area of controversy concerned the meaning of the phrase 'foreseeable future'.

The draft guidance issued by the working party had proposed that the directors should consider at least the period to the next balance sheet date. However, the guidance then went on to state that 'the foreseeable future should extend beyond the next balance sheet date to the extent that the directors are aware of circumstances which could affect the validity of the going concern basis for the company'.[62]

It seems that this guidance was drafted on the basis that most companies would prepare detailed budgets covering the 12 months after the balance sheet date. An alternative would have been to require the directors to look at a period of at least one year from the date that the accounts are signed, but this approach would have been more difficult for some companies as detailed budgets will not always be available. This was the approach taken by the APB when drafting a new auditing standard on the subject. It was clear that a compromise position had to be found.

The final guidance produced for directors by the working party discusses 'foreseeable future' and now concludes that it is not possible to specify a minimum period to which directors should pay particular attention in assessing going concern. Stipulating a minimum period would, the working party believes, be artificial and arbitrary. Instead of inventing a 'cut-off point' after which there would be a sudden change in the approach adopted, the working party believes that directors should take account of all information of which they are aware at the time.

However, the working party goes on to state that 'where the period considered by the directors has been limited, for example, to a period of less than one year from the date of approval of the financial statements, the directors should determine whether, in their opinion, the financial statements require any additional disclosure to explain adequately the assumptions that underlie the adoption of the going concern basis'.[63]

In its guidance to auditors reporting on whether the financial statements give a true and fair view, SAS 130 requires that 'if the period to which the directors have paid particular attention in assessing going concern is less than one year from the date of approval of the financial statements, and the directors have not disclosed that fact, the auditors should do so within the section of their report setting out the basis of their opinion, unless the fact is clear from any other references in their report'.[64]

It would therefore appear that one year from the date of approval of financial statements is a reasonable working definition of 'foreseeable future', although information beyond that period cannot be ignored. However, this does not necessarily mean that cash flow forecasts and budgets are needed for the whole of this period – SAS 130 says that it will depend on the circumstances.[65]

D.2 Internal control

The board should maintain a sound system of internal control to safeguard shareholders' investment and the company's assets.

D.2.1* The directors should, at least annually, conduct a review of the effectiveness of the group's system of internal control and should report to shareholders that they have done so. The review should cover all controls, including financial, operational and compliance controls and risk management.

D.2.2 Companies which do not have an internal audit function should from time to time review the need for one.

Provision D.2.1

This provision stems from the earlier Cadbury recommendation that 'The directors should report on the effectiveness of the company's system of internal control.'[66] Of all the suggestions in the Cadbury Code, this proved the most problematic and it was the one that took the longest time to bring into force. The trouble is that it is much harder than it sounds. Superficially, it seems entirely sensible that the directors of a company should be able to comment on how good their control systems are. But on reflection, it soon becomes apparent that this is fraught with difficulty, because there can be no objective yardstick against which to judge the adequacy of internal controls. For one thing, the need for controls depends upon perceived risks, and accordingly their adequacy can only be judged in that context; there is no all-purpose standard of controls that is accepted as necessary in all circumstances. For another, there is a cost/benefit judgement to be made in relation to any system of controls, which means that some managements will legitimately decide to spend more than others on control mechanisms. And since the people who are being asked to report on the adequacy of controls are also those who have had the responsibility of installing them, the requirement is always in danger of becoming a self-fulfilling one – it seems implausible that any board would ever determine that the system they themselves had established was in fact ineffective, unless it had demonstrably broken down to a material degree. Thus the undoubtedly well-intentioned requirement in the Cadbury Code proved difficult to deliver in practice.

Initially, the requirement was inoperative pending the issue of guidance for directors on how to implement it, and a working party was established to prepare such guidance. Its terms of reference were drawn from the Cadbury Report, which had recommended that the accountancy profession, in conjunction with representatives of preparers of accounts, should take the lead in:

(a)   developing a set of criteria for assessing the effectiveness of systems of internal control; and

(b)   developing guidance for companies on the form in which directors should report.[67]

In October 1993, the working party, in order to stimulate public debate, published draft guidance for directors in a document entitled *Internal Control and Financial Reporting*.[68] However, the document (which ran to nearly 70 pages) met with widespread opposition and criticism. This led to the working party issuing in August 1994 a revised exposure draft of only seven pages,[69] adopting a much more simplified high level approach than in the first draft. This was converted into a final version (the Guidance)[70] in December 1994, and took effect for financial years beginning on or after 1 January 1995.

As a matter of fact, it did not contain much guidance at all; rather, it watered down the requirements of the Cadbury Code. Whereas that Code unequivocally called upon the directors to report on the effectiveness of the company's system of internal control, the Guidance demoted this to an optional extra and required instead that the directors make a statement covering these four points:

■   acknowledgement by the directors that they are responsible for the company's system of internal financial control;

■   explanation that such a system can provide only reasonable and not absolute assurance against material misstatement or loss;

■   description of the key procedures that the directors have established and which are designed to provide effective internal financial control; and

■   confirmation that the directors (or a board committee) have reviewed the effectiveness of the system of internal financial control.[71]

Although the last of these sounds like the requirement of the Code, it was in fact subtly designed to fall imperceptibly short of it. The distinction is that although the directors had to say that they had reviewed the effectiveness of the system, they did not necessarily have to report the results of that review. Whereas the Guidance did go on to say that 'directors may also wish to state their opinion on the effectiveness of their system of internal financial control'[72] (i.e. the actual requirement of the Cadbury Code), the wording had been constructed to make that actual requirement non-mandatory. Clearly, there was a feeling within the working party that a meaningful report on effectiveness was not deliverable, and this awkward compromise was the result.

However, despite the fact that the Guidance had fallen slightly short of the target, the Cadbury Committee contributed a foreword to the Guidance document which accepted that this diluted version would be sufficient to constitute compliance with the Code, at least for the time being. As a result, the requirement was changed de facto into the statement containing the four points listed above.

The Guidance also narrowed down the requirement in a second way. The Cadbury Code called for a statement on the effectiveness of internal control, but as can be seen from the four point requirement listed above the working party interpreted that as meaning internal *financial* control, a rather narrower term. Again, however, there was some equivocation on this issue, reflecting a possible lack of consensus in the working party; the Guidance says that 'Directors may wish to and are encouraged to extend the scope of their statement to cover their responsibility for the wider aspects of internal control (rather than just internal financial control) ...'.[73]

Thus, when Hampel came to review this area, the original Cadbury proposal that directors report on the effectiveness of internal controls had been attenuated in two ways. First, the requirement to report on the effectiveness of controls was replaced by a requirement to say that the effectiveness of the controls had been reviewed, without the need to say what that review had revealed. Second, the internal controls in question were restricted from all internal controls to only internal financial controls.

Regarding the first of these restrictions, Hampel concurred by saying 'It has been suggested that point 4.5 of the Cadbury Code should be amended to read 'The directors should report on the company's system of internal control' – i.e dropping the word 'effectiveness'. This would not require any change to the minimum requirements of the working group's guidance – the directors would still need to review the system's effectiveness. This would recognise what is happening in practice and seems eminently sensible.'[74]

As regards the second dilution of the original Cadbury recommendations, Hampel did not agree, saying 'We are not concerned only with the financial aspects of corporate governance and we fully endorse the Cadbury comment that internal control is a key aspect of efficient management. Directors should therefore maintain and review controls addressing all relevant control objectives. These should include business risk assessment and response, financial management, compliance with laws and regulations and the safeguarding of assets, including minimising the risk of fraud.[75]

Following publication of the Combined Code, the Institute of Chartered Accountants in England and Wales (ICAEW) agreed with the Stock Exchange to convene a working party to produce guidance for directors on the scope, extent, nature and review of internal controls to which Code principle D.2 and provision D.2.1 refer. The working party, under the chairmanship of Mr Nigel Turnbull, published consultative guidance in April 1999[76] (the Draft Turnbull Guidance), with the aim of producing final guidance by the end of 1999. Pending the development of this guidance, the London Stock Exchange introduced a limited relaxation of the disclosure requirements. This was communicated in a letter to listed companies on 10 December 1998 saying 'Until the guidance has been published, a company's statement of compliance will, in our view, satisfy the requirements of paragraph 12.43A(b) in respect of Code provision D.2.1 if a company complies with the existing arrangements on internal controls, by reporting on their internal financial controls pursuant to the guidance for directors on internal controls and financial reporting that was issued by the Rutteman Working Group in December 1994. A company which has adopted this approach should indicate in its statement of compliance that it has done so. Companies may wish also to reflect this approach as part of their narrative statement under paragraph 12.43A(a) in relation to internal controls (Code principle D.2).'

The Draft Turnbull Guidance

Much of the guidance addresses the aim of internal control and the principle characteristics of, and processes for reviewing, a sound system of internal control, which is outside the scope of this book. The guidance also covers the content of the statement on internal control required by the Listing Rules as follows.

'The board's disclosures should be aimed at providing users of the annual report with meaningful high-level information. The board should ensure its disclosures do not give a misleading impression. In explaining how the company has maintained a sound system of internal control and in reporting to shareholders that it has reviewed the effectiveness of the system, the board should, as a minimum, disclose where applicable:

- that there is an on-going process for identifying, evaluating and managing the company's key risks that is regularly reviewed by the board and accords with this guidance; and

- how the board has reviewed the effectiveness of the process (e.g. the role of the audit committee and other relevant committee(s), management reviews, and how it has had regard to the work of its internal audit function).

Where a company is not able to make one or other of the disclosures in this paragraph, the board should state this fact and explain what it is doing to rectify the situation.'[77]

Whatever the merits of public reporting in relation to internal control, we believe that the debate initiated by Cadbury has achieved a useful objective; that of raising the profile of internal controls on board agendas, and providing a framework in which they can be discussed, which has provided a mechanism through which companies' systems can be assessed and improved. However, no controls are, or are intended to be, foolproof and failures will occur. The inevitable outcome is that really meaningful disclosure is probably always going to come only after a control failure, as illustrated by Powerscreen:

Extract 4.1: Powerscreen International PLC (1998)

Internal financial control [extract]

The directors have overall responsibility for the group's system of internal financial control and had established a framework designed to provide reasonable but not absolute assurance against material mis-statement or loss. Over a period of time, the control system was over-ridden and there were no compensating mechanisms in place to detect, report on, control and eliminate this abuse. Eventually, the group's systems, primarily based on cash forecasting, detected the Matbro losses.

Any framework supporting internal financial controls is designed to provide reasonable but not absolute assurance against material misstatement or loss. This framework has been fundamentally reviewed since 31 March 1998. The key procedures are being critically assessed and strengthened.

Unlike under the previous structure, the group financial function is now completely independent of operations. It will also have its own full time, permanent staff under the newly appointed Group Finance Director, Mr JFW Kennerley. The appointment of other group financial staff will follow shortly.

D.3   Audit Committee and Auditors

The board should establish formal and transparent arrangements for considering how they should apply the financial reporting and internal control principles and for maintaining an appropriate relationship with the company's auditors.

D.3.1*The board should establish an audit committee of at least three directors, all non-executive, with written terms of reference which deal clearly with its authority and duties. The members of the committee, a majority of whom should be independent non-executive directors, should be named in the report and accounts.

D.3.2 The duties of the audit committee should include keeping under review the scope and results of the audit and its cost effectiveness and the independence and objectivity of the auditors. Where the auditors also supply a substantial volume of non-audit services to the company, the committee should keep the nature and extent of such services under review, seeking to balance the maintenance of objectivity and value for money.

Provision D.3.1

Cadbury recommended that 'The Board should establish an audit committee of at least three non-executive directors with written terms of reference which deal clearly with its authority and duties'.[78] The notes to the Code further recommended that a majority of the non-executive directors on the committee should be independent of management. Both recommendations were endorsed by Hampel, saying 'Larger companies have implemented the recommendations almost universally, and we believe that the results have been beneficial. Audit committees have strengthened the independence of the auditors by giving them an effective link to the board; and the explicit remit of the audit committee has strengthened its members in questioning the executive directors.'[79]

The original Cadbury paragraph was supported by detailed recommendations in the notes to the Code on the working of audit committees. These remain relevant and should be considered by directors when describing the application of principle D.3. These recommendations are outlined below.

The audit committee should be a formally constituted sub-committee reporting to the board and should meet at least twice a year. It should have written terms of reference dealing with membership, authority and duties. It should have full support to carry out its duties both from within the company and, if necessary, from external advisers. Membership of the committee should be confined to non-executive directors, the majority of whom should be independent. The internal and external auditors and finance director should normally attend audit committee meetings, whilst other members of the board should have the right to attend. The Cadbury Report also included specimen terms of reference for an audit committee including such matters as constitution, membership, frequency of meetings, authority, duties and reporting procedures.

This was the main area of the Cadbury Code where companies, particularly smaller companies, reported non-compliance. Whilst this was noted by Hampel, it saw no justification for relaxing the rules, saying: 'We recognise that smaller companies may find it difficult to recruit a sufficient number of non-executive directors to meet Cadbury's preferred composition of the audit committee. We recommend shareholders to examine such cases carefully on their merits. But we do not favour relaxing the guidelines on this point by size of company.'[80]

Provision D.3.2

Cadbury identified the central issue with regard to the audit as being how to ensure its objectivity and effectiveness. The responsibility for maintaining an appropriate relationship rests with both the board and the auditors. Hampel added that 'The audit committee is an essential safeguard of auditor independence and objectivity; we suggest that it should keep under review the overall financial relationship between the company and the auditors.' An audit committee can play an important part in maintaining such a relationship by providing a forum dedicated to the review of matters within the purview of audit, such as financial statements and internal control.

An audit committee gives the non-executive directors the opportunity to consider, in more detail than is generally possible at board meetings, the important financial aspects of the approach to, and system of, corporate governance. A specific step in the process is for the audit committee to hold a separate meeting with the auditors at least once a year, without executive board members present. This allows discussion to ensure that there are no unresolved issues of concern. Cadbury included this process in its recommendations on audit committees in the notes to the Cadbury Code.

3   THE ROLE OF AUDITORS IN CORPORATE GOVERNANCE

The Stock Exchange requires the directors' statement on compliance with the provisions of the Combined Code to be reviewed by the auditors insofar as it relates to seven of the forty five provisions.[81] The Stock Exchange rules are silent on whether the auditors should report on their review and whether any report should be made public. Cadbury recommended that auditors should not be required formally to report a satisfactory review, but rather mention any non-disclosed non-compliance in their report on the accounts; and this was not changed by Hampel.

Guidance for auditors in this area is contained in APB Bulletin 1995/1, as supplemented by APB Bulletin 1996/3, and APB Bulletin 1998/10. The last of these was published in response to the Combined Code and related *Listing Rules* changes, and significantly amends, but does not supersede the earlier Bulletins. One of the most notable changes introduced by Bulletin 1998/10 relates to the issue and publication of a formal report on the review of corporate governance disclosures. Notwithstanding the Cadbury recommendation mentioned above, Bulletin 1995/1 originally stated that auditors should always issue a report to the company and that the APB 'strongly recommends that such reports be included in the annual report'.[82] In light of the changes brought about by the Combined Code the APB reassessed this recommendation, and concluded as follows: 'The APB is of the view that a description of the auditors' responsibilities in relation to the whole annual report would be helpful to users of annual reports. Since such a description will encompass the auditors' review of the company's compliance with the specified provisions of the Combined Code it will remove the need for a separate auditors' report on this aspect. In view of the narrow scope of the auditors' review and the introduction of a statement of auditors' responsibilities, the APB believes that it is no longer appropriate for auditors' reports on the directors' compliance statement to be published in the annual report. For listed companies this supersedes the APB's recommendation in paragraph 46 of Bulletin 1995/1 and is expected to result in the discontinuance of published auditors' reports on corporate governance matters in the annual reports of listed companies.'[83]

The statement of auditors' responsibilities is discussed under Provision D.1.1 at 2.3 above.

4   SMALLER QUOTED COMPANIES

Cadbury made no distinction in its recommendations between larger and smaller listed companies. Hampel considered whether such a distinction should be drawn, and concluded that it should not, saying: 'For the most part, the larger listed companies have implemented both codes fully. Smaller companies have also implemented most provisions, but there are some aspects with which they find it harder to comply. We considered carefully whether we should distinguish between the governance standards expected of larger and smaller companies. We concluded that this would be a mistake. Any distinction by size would be arbitrary; more importantly, we consider that high standards of governance are as important for smaller listed companies as for larger ones. But we would urge those considering the governance arrangements of smaller listed companies to do so with flexibility and a proper regard to individual circumstances.'[84]

In our view this is sensible; it is for the board to determine its corporate governance procedures in the best interests of the company. Whilst the provisions of the Combined Code form a basic framework in which to do this they are not, and should not be, prescriptive. If the board determines that a particular provision is not appropriate to them it is perfectly proper for them to disapply it, as long as they can clearly communicate the fact and the reasons for it to shareholders. Shareholders can then consider the decisions and performance of the board in an informed way, based on the individual circumstances of the company.

In considering any Combined Code provisions that the board has not complied with, shareholders may want to consider the guidance prepared by The City Group for Smaller Companies (CISCO).

Early in 1994, in response to Cadbury, CISCO published guidance for smaller quoted companies which was aimed at identifying those areas of the Cadbury Code which may, initially, prove difficult for smaller companies to implement and, wherever possible, suggesting alternative recommendations which are believed feasible and appropriate.[85] The idea behind this was to provide a guide to the measures that all companies (without exception) could reasonably be expected to implement, which is preferable to the option of companies doing nothing. In response to the publication of the Combined Code, CISCO published revised guidance in March 1999, which is discussed below.[86]

The areas where alternative recommendations are given mainly relate to the number of non-executive directors and the constitution of audit committees. However, it should be noted that these recommendations do not represent an alternative code, and therefore a listed company that has complied with CISCO's recommendations but not the full Combined Code is still required to report such non-compliance (with reasons) in its annual accounts.

CISCO's principal alternative recommendations and other refinements are as follows:

- provision A.3.1 of the Combined Code requires companies to appoint non-executives of sufficient calibre and number for their views to carry significant weight in the board's decisions, and that they should comprise not less than one third of the board. To meet the recommendation on the composition of the audit committee, boards will require a minimum of three non-executives, a majority of whom should be independent. CISCO has recommended that there should be at least two independent non-executives, as more than two may be excessive in some companies. Where companies have only two non-executives CISCO considers it sufficient for those directors to constitute the audit committee;

■   in line with the Combined Code requirement that boards should meet regularly, and effectively lead and control the company, CISCO suggests that boards should normally meet monthly, and not less than six times a year and that the agenda of regular board meetings should always include a report of management accounts from the finance director. It also suggests that whilst it is accepted that any system of corporate governance should not fetter entrepreneurial talent, systems can nevertheless be established where, in relation to certain areas of management, the entrepreneur must always consult the board as a whole before implementing a decision taken in principle;

■   CISCO recommends that companies should seek to define the role each non-executive director is expected to fulfil, and the specific objectives of that role, as they should for any other senior appointment, in order to ensure that they receive optimum benefit from the appointment. This should be done before starting the selection or reselection procedure;

■   provision A.2.1 of the Combined Code recommends that all boards recognise a senior independent non-executive, who is identified in the annual report. CISCO disagreed and, seemingly going beyond its remit of small companies, said 'This requirement should not be necessary on a properly run Board, is possibly excessive (particularly in companies which have only two non-executive directors) and may be divisive.' The guidance does, however, reiterate that companies not identifying a senior non-executive will need to explain why in their annual reports.

It must again be emphasised that CISCO's refined code is not, for Stock Exchange reporting purposes, to be seen as an alternative option to the Combined Code. All UK incorporated quoted companies (irrespective of size) are required by the Stock Exchange to include in their annual report and accounts a statement as to whether or not they have complied throughout the accounting period with the Combined Code, and to report details of, and reasons for, any non-compliance.

5   THE OPERATING AND FINANCIAL REVIEW (OFR)

In considering the responsibility of boards with respect to financial reports, the Cadbury Committee concluded that what shareholders need from the report and accounts is a coherent narrative, supported by figures, of the company's performance and prospects. As a result, the Committee recommended that boards should pay particular attention to their duty to present a balanced and understandable assessment of their company's position. It went on to say that balance requires that setbacks should be dealt with as well as successes, while the need for the report to be readily understood emphasises that words are as important as figures.[87] The Committee further recognised the advantage to users of accounts of being provided with some explanation of the factors likely to influence their company's future progress, and concluded that the inclusion of an essentially forward-looking Operating and Financial Review (OFR), along the lines of that which was being developed by the ASB, would serve this purpose.[88] The Hampel Committee did not add further guidance on this topic, but incorporated the Cadbury recommendation as follows: 'The board should present a balanced and understandable assessment of the company's position and prospects.'[89] The report makes clear that this principle is not limited to annual reports to shareholders, but also covers interim and other price-sensitive public reports and reports to regulators.[90]

The ASB document to which the Cadbury Committee referred was ultimately published in July 1993 as a Statement of best practice. It has persuasive rather than mandatory force and is not an accounting standard. It is intended that the OFR should be a discussion of the business as a whole and should give insights into the facts which underlie the figures in the accounts; it should not just repeat these figures in narrative form with no amplification. It should discuss individual aspects of the business in the context of explaining the performance of the business as a whole. The statement requires a consideration of the factors that will affect future performance as well as the year under review. Consequently, although the OFR is a report on the year under review, not a forecast of future results, it should nevertheless draw out those aspects of the year under review that are relevant to an assessment of future prospects.

The essential features of an OFR are as follows:[91]

- it should be written in a clear style and as succinctly as possible, to be readily understandable by the general reader of annual reports, and should include only matters that are likely to be significant to investors;

- it should be balanced and objective, dealing even-handedly with both good and bad aspects;

- it should refer to comments made in previous statements where these have not been borne out by events;

- it should contain analytical discussion rather than merely numerical analysis;

- it should follow a 'top-down' structure, discussing individual aspects of the business in the context of a discussion of the business as a whole;

- it should explain the reason for, and effect of, any changes in accounting policies;

- it should make it clear how any ratios or other numerical information given relate to the financial statements; and
- it should include discussion of:
  - trends and factors underlying the business that have affected the results but are not expected to continue in the future; and
  - known events, trends and uncertainties that are expected to have an impact on the business in the future.

In discussing trends and uncertainties, the OFR should explain their significance to the business, but it is not intended that the OFR should necessarily include a forecast of the outcome of such uncertainties; nor is it suggested that the OFR should contain anything of the nature of a profit forecast.[92] Furthermore, the directors may conclude that, in some cases, a proper discussion of some aspects of the business would require disclosure of confidential or commercially sensitive information. Where the directors decide not to disclose such information, the OFR should ensure that the user is not misled by a discussion that is no longer complete and balanced.[93]

As its title suggests, the OFR consists of two sections: the operating review and the financial review. These are discussed below.

5.1   The operating review

The principal aim of the operating review is to enable the user to understand the dynamics of the various lines of business undertaken – that is, the main influences on the overall results, and how these inter-relate. Thus the OFR needs to identify and explain the main factors that underlie the business, and in particular those which either have varied in the past or are expected to change in the future.[94] It should include a discussion of:[95]

- the significant features of the operating performance for the period. This should cover changes in the industry or the environment in which the business operates, developments within the business, and their effect on results. Examples of such changes given by the Statement are as follows:
  - changes in market conditions;
  - new products and services introduced or announced;
  - changes in market share or position;
  - changes in turnover and margins;
  - changes in exchange rates and inflation rates; and
  - new activities, discontinued activities and other acquisitions and disposals;
- the dynamics of the business, discussing the main factors and influences that may have a major effect on future results, whether or not they were significant in the period under review; for example, dependence on major

suppliers or customers. The Statement lists the following additional examples of matters that may be relevant:

- scarcity of raw materials;
- skill shortages and expertise of uncertain supply;
- patents, licences or franchises;
- product liability;
- health and safety;
- environmental protection costs and potential environmental liabilities;
- self insurance;
- exchange rate fluctuations; and
- rates of inflation differing between costs and revenues, or between different markets;

■ the extent to which the directors have sought to maintain and enhance future income or profits by investment in, for example, capital expenditure, marketing and advertising campaigns and pure and applied research. The Statement lists the following additional examples of activities and expenditure for the enhancement of future profits that may be relevant:

- training programmes;
- refurbishment and maintenance programmes;
- development of new products and services; and
- technical support to customers;

■ the overall return attributable to shareholders, in terms of dividends and increases in shareholders' funds, commenting on the contributions from the operating performance of the various business units and on other items reported as part of total recognised gains and losses;

■ a comparison between profit for the financial year and dividends, both in total and per share terms, indicating the directors' overall dividend policy. Other measures of earnings per share reported should also be discussed; and

■ any subjective judgements to which the financial statements are particularly sensitive.

5.2   The financial review

The principal aim of the financial review is to explain the capital structure of the business, its treasury policy and the dynamics of its financial position – i.e. its sources of liquidity and their application, including the implications of the financing requirements arising from its capital expenditure plans.[96] It should include a discussion of:[97]

■ the capital structure of the business, in terms of maturity profile of debt, type of capital instruments used, currency and interest rate structure. This should include comments on relevant ratios such as interest cover and debt/equity ratios;

■   the capital funding and treasury policies and objectives. These will cover the management of interest rate risk, the maturity profile of borrowings and the management of exchange rate risk. The Statement suggests that the OFR should also discuss the implementation of these policies in the period under review in terms of:

   –   the manner in which treasury activities are controlled;

   –   the currencies in which borrowings are made and in which cash and cash equivalents are held;

   –   the extent to which borrowings are at fixed interest rates;

   –   the use of financial instruments for hedging purposes; and

   –   the extent to which foreign currency net investments are hedged by currency borrowings and other hedging instruments;

■   the main components of the reconciliation between the actual and standard tax charges where the overall tax charge is different from the standard charge (i.e. the normal UK tax rate applied to the profit before taxation);

■   the cash generated from operations and other cash inflows during the period, commenting on any special factors that influenced these. Where segmental cash flows are significantly out of line with segmental profits, this should be indicated and explained;

■   the business's liquidity at the end of the period, including comment on the level of borrowings at the end of the period, the seasonality of borrowing requirements and the maturity profile of both borrowings and committed borrowing facilities;

■   any restrictions on the ability to transfer funds from one part of the group to meet the obligations of another part of the group where they represent, or might foreseeably come to represent, a significant constraint on the group;

■   debt covenants which could have the effect of restricting the use of credit facilities, and where a breach of a covenant has occurred or is expected to occur, the OFR should give details of the measures taken or proposed to remedy the situation;

■   the business's ability to remain a going concern as recommended by the Cadbury Committee [now superseded by the Combined Code as discussed under provision D.1.3 at 2.3 above]; and

■   the strengths and resources of the business whose value is not fully reflected in the balance sheet – for example, as is the case with intangible assets which have not been capitalised.

Much of the information in the first two points above is now mandatory for listed companies as it is required by FRS 13, which is discussed in Chapter 9.

5.3   Statement of compliance

As the OFR Statement represents voluntary best practice, directors are not expected to include in the annual report any formal confirmation that they have complied with the principles set out in the Statement – although, clearly, the inclusion of some comment on the extent to which the Statement has been followed may be helpful to the user. However, the Statement suggests that where it is implied, through the use of the words 'operating and financial review' or otherwise, that the directors have endeavoured to follow the principles laid down in the Statement, they should signal any fundamental departure therefrom.[98]

6   CONCLUSION

We believe that great strides have been made in Corporate Governance over recent years and welcome the development of the Combined Code. In our view such matters are better dealt with in this relatively informal manner, rather than, as is sometimes suggested, by way of statute which would be necessarily more detailed and would be open to all the difficulties of statutory interpretation. Furthermore a code of practice is much better able to respond quickly to the changing market place and the changing expectations of shareholders and other interested parties. The latest changes to the Listing Rules now require boards to describe in their own words how they apply the general principles of corporate governance as well as making a statement of compliance, or otherwise, with the detailed provisions of the Combined Code. We believe this to be a much more meaningful requirement, although to give a reasoned and considered description of their governance procedures represents a significant challenge for boards. The detailed Code provisions set out some basic elements of the governance process, and it is likely that some may be reproduced by companies in these discussions. However, we hope that this be kept to a minimum to prevent the disclosures degenerating into general boilerplate.

We think that the OFR should be regarded as one of the ASB's most successful innovations. By providing a well-considered framework but allowing scope for experimentation, the Board has encouraged companies to approach the task imaginatively and constructively. Inevitably, some have carried it out better than others, but as the capital markets become more demanding and directors become more aware of their corporate governance responsibilities, balanced, objective and understandable OFRs are increasingly becoming a standard feature of UK GAAP.

APPENDIX: EXAMPLES OF CORPORATE GOVERNANCE DISCLOSURES

The following extracts reproduce the corporate governance disclosures of three different companies, and illustrate the variety of approaches seen in practice.

Extract 4.2: Imperial Chemical Industries PLC (1998)

Corporate governance [extract]

Corporate governance

The Group is committed to high standards of corporate governance. The Board is accountable to the Company's shareholders for good governance and this statement describes how the relevant principles of governance are applied to the Company. Throughout the year the Company has been in compliance with the provisions set out in the Combined Code for Corporate Governance issued by the London Stock Exchange.

The ICI Board currently comprises the Chairman, the Chief Executive, four other Executive Directors and five independent Non-Executive Directors. Their biographies appear on page 36. These demonstrate a range of business, financial and global experience, which is vital to the successful direction of a multi-national company. Two additional Executive Directors have been appointed with effect from 1 March 1999. The Board is balanced both numerically and in experience.

All Directors are equally accountable under the law for the proper stewardship of the Company's affairs. The Non-Executive Directors have a particular responsibility to ensure that the strategies proposed by Executive Directors are fully discussed and critically examined, not only against the best long-term interests of shareholders, but also to ensure that they take proper account of the interests of employees, customers, suppliers and the many communities within which ICI is represented. The Non-Executive Directors also test fully the operational performance of the whole Group. The Board has prescribed reserved powers which reinforce its control of the Company.

To enable them to do this all Directors have full and timely access to all relevant information. The Board meets at least eight times a year and there is frequent contact between meetings to progress the Company's business.

The Non-Executive Directors fulfil a vital role in corporate accountability. The remits and memberships of the three relevant Board Committees are set out opposite. The Remuneration and Nomination Committee and the Audit Committee comprise solely Non-Executive Directors.

Remuneration and Nomination Committee

Executive Directors are in attendance at the Remuneration and Nomination Committee for appropriate items but are always excluded when their own performance and remuneration are under review. The Company Chairman is not a member of the Remuneration and Nomination Committee except when it meets as the Nomination Committee. He attends all remuneration discussions except when his own position is being discussed. The Company Chairman from time to time promotes discussion with the Executive Directors about Non-Executive Directors' remuneration based on full external comparisons. Any recommendations are laid before the full Board. Non-Executive Directors have the option of taking part of their remuneration in the Company's shares.

The Remuneration report, on pages 41 to 44, includes details on remuneration policy and procedures, and on the remuneration of Directors.

The Chairman of the Remuneration and Nomination Committee, currently Sir Roger Hurn, acts as the Company's lead Non-Executive Director. In this position he promotes discussion at appropriate times about the Company's chairmanship and succession to it.

The Non-Executive Directors normally meet twice a year with the Chairman and Chief Executive to discuss Board and individual Directors' performance and succession plans. At appropriate times the Chief Executive and then the Chairman absent themselves so their performance can be assessed. The final discussion is led by the Chairman of the Remuneration and Nomination Committee and there is feedback to individuals.

Appointments to Executive Director are fully discussed by the Chairman and Chief Executive with the Remuneration and Nomination Committee before a proposal is formally made to the Board by the Chairman of that Committee. Possible new Non-Executive Directors are suggested by all members of the Board against the requirements of the Company's business and the need to have a balanced Board. In appropriate cases recruitment consultants are used to assist the process. Possible candidates are discussed with all Directors before any approach is made to them. All Directors are subject to re-election at least every three years.

Audit and internal control

The Combined Code introduced a requirement, that directors review the effectiveness of the Group's system of internal controls. This requirement extends the Directors' review to cover all controls including operational compliance and risk management as well as financial. Formal guidance on the review of non-financial internal control has still to be developed by the Task Force established by the Institute of Chartered Accountants of England and Wales (ICAEW). The Directors will seek to ensure that the Group is compliant with such guidance when it is issued. Despite the absence of such detailed guidance, the Directors consider that they have nevertheless observed the principles of the Combined Code in 1998. The key components of the Group's system of internal controls and the process by which the Directors have reviewed the effectiveness of the system of such controls are described in the following paragraphs.

The Board is responsible for the effectiveness of the Group's system of internal controls. The internal control systems are designed to meet the Group's particular needs and the risks to which it is exposed, and by their nature can only provide reasonable but not absolute assurance against misstatement or loss.

The Group's strategic direction is regularly reviewed by the Board, and the Executive Management Team considers the strategy for the individual businesses through an integrated disciplined process on a biannual basis. Annual plans and performance targets for each business are set by the Executive Management Team and reviewed in total by the Board in the light of the Group's overall objectives.

The processes to manage the key risks to the success of the Group are reviewed and improved as necessary. Such processes include strategic planning, the appointment of senior managers, control over capital expenditure and the setting of high standards and targets for safety, health and environmental performance.

Within the financial and overall objectives for the Group, agreed by the Board, the management of the Group as a whole is delegated to the Chief Executive and the Executive Directors. The conduct of ICI's individual businesses is delegated to the Executive Vice Presidents and Chief Executive Officers of the International Businesses, the Chief Executives of major subsidiaries and the Vice Presidents for Western Hemisphere and for Asia. They are accountable for the conduct and performance of their businesses within the agreed business strategy. They have full authority to act subject to the reserved powers and sanctioning limits laid down by the Board and to Group policies and guidelines.

Businesses are responsible for meeting the defined reporting timetables and compliance with Group accounting manuals which set out accounting policies, controls and definitions.

The Executive Management Team receives a monthly summary of financial results from each business, and the Group's published quarterly financial information is based on a standardised reporting process. On completion of all major investments, post event reviews are carried out by the relevant businesses and reviewed by the Executive Management Team. This process helps improve the quality of business judgements through the understanding and experience gained.

Responsibility for ensuring compliance with certain Group policies and guidelines has been delegated by the Board to nominated senior functional managers. These nominated managers receive annual compliance reports from Executive Vice Presidents, Chief Executive Officers of Businesses and from other senior managers. In turn, the nominated managers provide annually separate reports to the Audit Committee, on behalf of the Board, on the degree of compliance with Group policies and guidelines. Corrections to any weaknesses found are monitored and controls are developed to match changing circumstances.

The Audit Committee receives reports from the internal and external auditors on a regular basis. The internal audit function reviews internal controls in all key activities of the ICI Group, typically over a three year cycle. It acts as a service to the Businesses by assisting with the continuous improvement of controls and procedures. Actions are agreed in response to its recommendations and these are followed up to ensure that satisfactory control is maintained. Annual reviews are also conducted between internal audit management and the senior management of Businesses and major functions to assess their current control status and to identify and address any areas of concern.

Communications

Communications with shareholders are given a high priority. There is a succinct Annual Review and a separate Safety, Health and Environment Performance Report both of which are sent to shareholders; a full Annual Report and Accounts and Form 20-F is available on request. At the half year, an interim report is published. There is a regular dialogue with individual institutional shareholders as well as general presentations after the quarterly results. There is also an opportunity for individual shareholders to question the Chairman at the AGM. As an alternative, shareholders can leave written questions for the Company to respond. Directors meet informally with shareholders after the meeting. The Company responds throughout the year to numerous letters from individual shareholders on a wide range of issues.

...

Directors' report [extract]

Going concern

The operation of the Group's control procedures gives the Directors a reasonable expectation that the Group has adequate resources to continue in operation for the foreseeable future. Accordingly they continue to adopt the going concern basis in preparing the Group accounts.

Extract 4.3: United Assurance Group plc (1998)

STATEMENT OF DIRECTORS' RESPONSIBILITIES AND CORPORATE GOVERNANCE

STATEMENT IN RESPECT OF THE APPLICATION OF THE PRINCIPLES IN THE COMBINED CODE

Relevant sections in this report with reference to the board of directors, directors' remuneration, internal financial control and relations with shareholders explain the application by the Group of the requirements of the Principles in the Combined Code.

THE BOARD OF DIRECTORS

The board of directors comprises a balance of executive and non-executive directors. All non-executive directors are considered by the board to be independent within the meaning of code provision A.3.2. Mr A J S Ewen is the senior independent non-executive director within the meaning of code provision A.2.1. The roles of Chairman and Group Chief Executive are separated.

The selection and appointment of non-executive directors is a matter for consideration by the nomination committee.

It is a requirement of the Company's articles of association that one third of the directors retire by rotation at every annual general meeting with the opportunity to stand for re-election. All new directors must stand for election at the first annual general meeting following their appointment.

A schedule of matters reserved for decision of the board has been prepared which is supported by detailed board reports, where appropriate. A procedure exists for directors to take independent professional advice at the Company's expense in the furtherance of their duties.

The procedures in place to determine the policy on directors' remuneration and details of the remuneration of each director are set out in the Report on Directors' Remuneration on pages 20 to 25.

STATEMENT OF DIRECTORS' RESPONSIBILITIES

The directors are required by the Companies Act 1985 to prepare financial statements for each financial year which give a true and fair view of the state of affairs of the Company and the Group as at the end of the financial year and of the profit and loss of the Group for that period.

In preparing those financial statements, the directors are required to adopt suitable accounting policies and apply them on a consistent basis, make judgements and estimates which they consider prudent and reasonable, and to state whether appropriate accounting standards have been followed.

The directors have responsibility for ensuring that the Group keeps accounting records which disclose with reasonable accuracy the financial position of the Group and which enable them to ensure that the financial statements comply with the provisions of the Companies Act 1985.

The directors have a general responsibility for taking such steps as are reasonably open to them to safeguard the assets of the Group and to prevent and detect fraud and other irregularities.

INTERNAL FINANCIAL CONTROL

The directors are responsible for, and have reviewed, the Group's system of internal financial control. Such systems can only provide reasonable and not absolute assurance against material misstatement or loss.

The principal features of the Group's internal control framework are as follows:

- Appropriate division of responsibilities and diversity of experience of directors and management.
- Procedures for the evaluation of key business risks and effective policies for their management, where appropriate.
- Regular reporting of appropriate management information and monitoring of performance against business plans.
- Internal audit of the Group's system of internal control and operational control procedures.
- Consideration of significant control issues by the audit committee of the board of directors.

The audit committee, comprising non-executive directors, reviews, on behalf of the board, matters concerning the internal financial controls of the Group and receives reports from the internal and external auditors on a regular basis.

An assessment of the Group's position and prospects are given in the Operating and Financial Review on pages 9 to 12.

STATEMENT OF COMPLIANCE WITH THE CODE PROVISIONS IN THE COMBINED CODE

Throughout the year ended 31 December 1998, the Group has been in compliance with the Code provisions set out in Section 1 of the Combined Code on Corporate Governance issued by the London Stock Exchange, with the following exceptions. The Group has not complied with code provisions B.1.7 and B.1.8 on directors' service contracts. Details of actions taken since the balance sheet date to comply with those provisions are given in the Report on Directors' Remuneration on pages 20 to 25. The Group did not comply with code provisions B.3.5, C.2.1 and C.2.4 in respect of the conduct of the 1998 annual general meeting as these were not requirements at that time. As permitted by the London Stock Exchange, the Group has complied with Code provision D.2.1 on internal control by reporting on internal financial control in accordance with the guidance for directors on internal control and financial reporting which was issued in December 1994.

RELATIONS WITH SHAREHOLDERS

The directors meet periodically with institutional shareholders and, where practicable, enter into a dialogue on areas of interest to those investors.

The board views the annual general meeting as a key method of communicating with private investors and welcomes their participation.

GOING CONCERN

After making enquiries, the directors have a reasonable expectation that the Company and the Group have adequate resources to continue in operational existence for the foreseeable future. For this reason, the going concern basis has been adopted in the preparation of the financial statements.

DERIVATIVE INSTRUMENTS

Derivative instruments (including futures, options and forward contracts) are used in portfolio management as a quick and effective method of obtaining or reducing exposure to underlying assets. In particular, they can usefully insulate funds from falling markets and enable portfolios to be managed more efficiently. The Group makes only limited use of derivatives, principally for hedging and efficiency purposes. These instruments are not used for speculation and strict controls apply to staff empowered to enter into derivative transactions. At the balance sheet date, no derivative instruments were held.

VOTING POLICY

As an institutional investor, the Group acknowledges that it has a responsibility to encourage improved performance by the companies in which it invests. Voting on all company resolutions (whenever practicable) is an important element in the relationship between a company and its investors. It is also an opportunity for the Group to demonstrate that it fully recognises the fiduciary issues involved with voting rights and that it is acting as a responsible investor. It is the policy of the Group to exercise its ownership rights by voting on all company resolutions whenever practicable.

Extract 4.4: Laura Ashley Holdings plc (1999)

Directors Report [extract]

Corporate governance

The Board endorses the Combined Code of Best Practice ('the Code'), which was issued by the Hampel Committee in June 1998. During the financial year the Company has complied with the provisions set out in the Combined Code, except to the extent disclosed in the statement of appliance set out below.

The Board meets regularly, at least six times a year, and has full and timely access to all relevant information to enable it to carry out its duties. Furthermore, the Board has regular contact with the Company Secretary for his services and advice. The Secretary provides an induction and briefing pack to all Directors, on their appointment and is responsible for ensuring that Board procedures are followed and that applicable rules and regulations are complied with. The appointment and removal of the Secretary is a matter reserved for the Board.

The Company did not, during the year, have a Nomination Committee for the appointment of Directors, as required by the Code. The appointment of Directors was a matter reserved for the full Board which was receptive to nomination suggestions from all Directors.

Going forward, however, the Directors will form a Nominations Committee the quorum of which will be a majority of non-MUI nominated Directors. The Nominations Committee will meet on a six monthly basis to decide and give recommendations to the Board on all matters relating to the selection, number, appointment and removal of independent directors to the Board. The Company will also make arrangements with the auditors of the Company whereby, on a six monthly basis, the auditors will report to the audit committee of the Board on the arm's length nature and normal commercial basis of the relationship between the North American business and the remainder of the Group. The Nominations Committee will receive copies of the reports of auditors sent to the audit committee of the Board. This will enable the trading relationship between the North American business and the remainder of the Group to be independently monitored.

A formal schedule of matters specifically reserved for the Board is in place and is incorporated into the Company's Manual on Corporate Governance, together with details of the procedures that Directors may follow for taking independent professional advice, at the Company's expense, if necessary. No such advice was sought during the year.

The Company is fortunate in having the services of its non-Executive Directors, who make up over two-thirds of the Board and who provide an important contribution to the strategic development of the Group.

In reviewing the Code's requirements for the independence of non-Executive Directors, the Board is of the view that the majority of the current non-Executive Directors do not strictly meet the criteria for independence; in particular, Dr. Khoo and Messrs. Okada and Walton Masters, as they are representative directors of the Company's major shareholders. However, the Board considers that the current non-Executive Directors have the appropriate range of experience and skills.

Whilst the Company does not recognise a senior independent Director of the Board, a provision of the Code, Mr. Walton Masters was appointed Deputy Chairman, on 9 March 1999, to whom concerns can be conveyed.

The Board has delegated specific responsibilities to the Audit and Remuneration Committees, membership of which is detailed on the inside front cover. None of the three non-Executive Directors who make up each Committee are considered by the Board to fulfil the strict criteria to be independent Directors. The Board, however, considers that all members of the Committees have the appropriate experience and none of them have interests which conflict with their positions on either of the Committees.

The Audit Committee meets at least three times a year. It assists the Board in observing its responsibility for ensuring that the Group's financial systems provide accurate information on its financial position and that its published financial statements represent a true and fair reflection of this position. It also assists the Board in ensuring that appropriate accounting policies, internal financial controls and compliance procedures are in place and in assessing the cost effectiveness, independence and objectiveness of the Auditors.

The Remuneration Committee meets on average three times a year and is responsible for advising on remuneration policy for Executive Directors and senior executives.

Previously, only non-Executive Directors were subject to retirement by rotation and therefore the Company did not comply with the provision that all Directors should submit themselves for re-election at regular intervals and at least every three years. The Company addressed this issue prior to the publication of the Code and amended its Articles of Association so that both Executive and non-Executive Directors are subject to retirement by rotation. However, under the current provisions in the Articles, it is still possible that a small number of Directors could remain in office for more than three years without submitting themselves for re-election. In order to comply with the Code, it is the Company's policy that every Director should submit themselves for re-election at least every three years.

Details of the level and composition of the Directors' remuneration packages are disclosed in the Remuneration Report on pages 18 to 22.

The Board considers the AGM to be an opportunity to meet and communicate with private investors, giving shareholders the opportunity to raise with the Board any issues or concerns they may have. Both the Chairmen of the Audit and Remuneration Committees are available at the AGM to answer any queries raised. The Company has not previously provided an indication of the level of proxies lodged on each resolution, but it is the Company's intention to comply with this Code provision at the forthcoming AGM and in the future.

Internal Financial Control

As permitted by the London Stock Exchange, the Company has complied with Code provision D.2.1. on internal control by reporting on internal financial control in accordance with the guidance for directors on internal control and financial reporting that was issued in December 1994.

The Directors are responsible for the Group's system of internal control. Any such system can, however, only provide reasonable and not absolute assurance against material mis-statement or loss. The Directors have sought to establish clear operating procedures, lines of responsibility and delegated authority. In particular, procedures exist for:

- the appraisal and authorisation of capital investment
- the authorisation and implementation of interest rate and foreign currency hedging instruments
- monthly financial reporting, within an annual budgeting and ongoing forecasting process
- maintaining day to day financial control of operations within a framework of defined policies and procedures
- regular reviews by the internal audit function of the Group's operations and the systems of internal control.

The system of internal financial control has been reviewed through a system of structured self-assessment. This process, which has been co-ordinated by the Internal Audit Manager, involved senior managers identifying the risks facing the Group and assessing the significance of those risks within their area of responsibility; existing controls have been reviewed against those risks.

In addition, guidelines have been introduced setting out the required level of internal controls needed at each operating subsidiary. The Directors, through the Audit Committee, confirm that they have reviewed the effectiveness of the Group's system of internal financial control.

Going Concern

The Group has reported a loss after tax of £33.0 million. Trading performance since the year end has continued to be weak, particularly in North America. The Company's banking syndicate has agreed, subject to certain conditions, to provide a revised facility for the period to 30 April 2000. The principal conditions to be met for the revised facility are that the Company must raise equity and either sell its North American retail business by 31 July 1999 or commence closure proceedings if a sale is not completed by that date.

The Board has announced that it proposes to raise approximately £24.6 million, net of expenses, by way of an underwritten rights issue of new ordinary shares and has also announced the intended sale of the North American retail business to its management. Both transactions are subject to shareholders' approval to be obtained at the Extraordinary General Meeting to be held on 3 June 1999, as well as completion of a number of technical and procedural matters. The Directors have unanimously recommended that shareholders vote in favour of these transactions.

The Directors are of the opinion that, on the assumption that the transactions proceed as planned, the Group will have sufficient funding to meet its working capital needs and obligations to the banks for the foreseeable future. As a result, the Directors consider it appropriate to prepare the financial statements on an ongoing basis.

References

1 The Committee on the Financial Aspects of Corporate Governance, *The Financial Aspects of Corporate Governance*, (The Cadbury Report), December 1992, para. 2.1.
2 *Ibid.*, Appendix 1.
3 *The Listing Rules*, London Stock Exchange, Chapter 12, para. 12.43(j).
4 The Study Group on Directors' Remuneration, *Directors' Remuneration: Report of a Study Group chaired by Sir Richard Greenbury*, (The Greenbury Report), July 1995.
5 The Cadbury Report, para. 1.4.
6 Committee on Corporate Governance: *Final Report* (Hampel Report), January 1998, annex B
7 *Ibid.*, para. 1.7.
8 *Ibid.*, para. 1.15.
9 The Cadbury Report, para. 2.5.
10 Hampel Report, para. 1.15
11 *Ibid.*, para. 1.11.
12 *Ibid.*, para. 1.14.
13 *Ibid.*, para. 1.20.
14 *Ibid.*, para. 1.25.
15 *Ibid.*, para. 1.24.
16 *Ibid.*, para. 1.25.
17 *The Listing Rules*, London Stock Exchange, Chapter 12, para. 12.43A.
18 The Cadbury Report, para. 4.1.
19 Hampel Report, para. 3.11.
20 The Cadbury Report, para. 4.18.
21 *Ibid.*, para. 4.25.
22 Hampel Report, para. 3.2
23 The Cadbury Report, para. 4.12.
24 Hampel Report, para. 3.3.
25 The Cadbury Report, para. 4.7.
26 Hampel Report, para. 3.16.
27 *Ibid.*, para. 3.17.
28 *Ibid.*, para. 3.18.
29 *Ibid.*, para. 3.8.
30 The Cadbury Report, para. 4.12.
31 Hampel Report, para. 3.9.
32 *Ibid.*, para. 3.9.
33 *Ibid.*, para. 3.9.
34 *Ibid.*, para. 2.6.
35 *Ibid.*, para. 3.19.
36 *Ibid.*, para. 3.20.
37 The Cadbury Report, para. 6.11.
38 Hampel Report, para. 5.10.
39 *Ibid.*, para. 5.14.
40 *Ibid.*, para. 5.17.
41 Companies Act 1985, s.241.
42 Hampel Report, para. 5.20.
43 The Cadbury Report, Appendix 4, para. 6(f).
44 Hampel Report, para. 5.19
45 *Ibid.*, para. 5.18
46 Companies Act 1985, s.369.
47 The Cadbury Report, para. 4.50.
48 SAS 600, *Auditors' reports* on *financial statements*, APB, May 1993, Appendix 3.
49 *Gazette*, 'Directors Responsibilities', Gazette 90/40, 3 November 1993.
50 The Cadbury Report, para. 4.28.
51 *Gazette*, 'Directors responsibilities for financial statements', Gazette 90/46, 17 December 1993.

52 Bulletin 1998/10, *Corporate Governance Reporting and Auditors' Responsibilities Statements*, APB, December 1998.

53 Going Concern Working Group, *Going Concern and Financial Reporting: Guidance for directors of listed companies registered in the UK*, November 1994.

54 Bulletin 1994/1, *Disclosures relating to corporate governance (revised)*, APB, November 1994.

55 SAS 130, *The going concern basis in financial statements*, APB, November 1994.

56 *The Listing Rules*, London Stock Exchange, Chapter 12, para. 12.43(v).

57 Hampel Report, para. 6.17.

58 Going Concern Working Group, *Going Concern and Financial Reporting: Guidance for directors of listed companies registered in the UK*, paras. 24–40.

59 *Ibid.*, para. 47.

60 *Ibid.*, para. 49.

61 *Ibid.*, paras. 51 and 52.

62 Going Concern Working Group, *Going Concern and Financial Reporting: Draft guidance for directors of listed companies developed in response to the recommendations of the Cadbury Committee*, May 1993, para. 2.14.

63 Going Concern Working Group, *Going Concern and Financial Reporting: Guidance for directors of listed companies registered in the UK*, para. 20.

64 SAS 130, para. 45.

65 *Ibid.*, para. 47.

66 The Cadbury Code, para. 4.5.

67 *Ibid.*, para. 5.16.

68 Internal Control Working Group, *Internal Control and Financial Reporting: Draft guidance for directors of listed companies developed in response to the recommendations of the Cadbury Committee*, October 1993.

69 Internal Control Working Group, *Internal Control and Financial Reporting: Draft guidance for directors of listed companies developed in response to the recommendations of the Cadbury Committee*, August 1994.

70 Internal Control Working Group, *Internal Control and Financial Reporting: Guidance for directors of listed companies registered in the UK*, December 1994.

71 *Ibid.*, para. 8.

72 *Ibid.*

73 *Ibid.*, para. 14.

74 Hampel Report, para. 6.12.

75 *Ibid.*, para. 6.13.

76 Internal Control Working Party, *Internal Control: Guidance for directors of listed companies incorporated in the United Kingdom*, April 1999.

77 *Ibid.*, paras 32 and 33.

78 The Cadbury code, para. 4.3.

79 Hampel Report, para. 6.3.

80 *Ibid.*, para. 6.4.

81 *The Listing Rules*, London Stock Exchange, Chapter 12, para. 12.43A.

82 Bulletin 1995/1, *Disclosures relating to corporate governance (revised)*, APB, February 1995, para. 46.

83 Bulletin 1998/10, *Corporate Governance Reporting and Auditors' Responsibilities Statements*, APB, December 1998, paras. 16 and 17.

84 Hampel Report, para. 1.10.

85 The City Group for Smaller Companies, *The Financial Aspects of Corporate Governance: Guidance for Smaller Companies*, CISCO, London, 1994.

86 The City Group for Smaller Companies, *The Committee on Corporate Governance Report and The Combined Code: Guidance for Smaller Quoted Companies*, CISCO, 1999.

87 The Cadbury Report, para. 4.50.

88 *Ibid.*, para. 4.53.

89 Hampel Report, para. 2. D. I.

90 *Ibid.*, para. 2.19

91 ASB Statement, *Operating and Financial Review*, ASB, July 1993, para. 3.

92   *Ibid.*, para. 4.
93   *Ibid.*, para. 5.
94   *Ibid.*, para. 8.
95   *Ibid.*, paras. 9–22.
96   *Ibid.*, para. 23.
97   *Ibid.*, paras. 25–37.
98   *Ibid.*, para. 38.

Chapter 5   Consolidated accounts

1   THE CONCEPT OF A GROUP

1.1   The objectives of group accounts

Group accounts are designed to extend the reporting entity to embrace other entities which are subject to its control or influence. They involve treating the net assets and activities of subsidiaries held by the holding company as if they were part of the holding company's own net assets and activities; the overall aim ·is to present the results and state of affairs of the group as if they were those of a single entity.

The basic legal framework for group accounts is to be found in the Companies Act 1985, as amended by the Companies Act 1989. This requires that group accounts are to be in the form of consolidated accounts which 'give a true and fair view of the state of affairs as at the end of the financial year, and the profit or loss for the financial year, of the undertakings included in the consolidation as a whole, so far as concerns members of the company',[1] and that they should comply with the provisions of Schedule 4A with respect to their form and content.[2]

The relevant accounting standard on the subject is FRS 2 – *Accounting for subsidiary undertakings*. This explains that the purpose of consolidated financial statements is to present financial information about a parent undertaking and its subsidiary undertakings as a single economic entity to show the economic resources controlled by the group, the obligations of the group and the results it achieves with those resources.[3] FRS 2 is drafted in terms of the Companies Act, but it applies to all parent undertakings that prepare consolidated financial statements intended to give a true and fair view of the group.[4]

1.2   What is a subsidiary?

The question of the definition of a subsidiary is fundamental to any discussion of group accounts because otherwise it is impossible to say what constitutes the entity which is the subject of the report. The question is also related to the subject of off balance sheet financing, because frequently this hinges on whether the group balance sheet should embrace the accounts of an entity which holds certain assets and liabilities which management may not wish to include in the group accounts (see Chapter 16).

The term used in the legislation is 'subsidiary undertaking'. The definition of this (see 1.2.2 below) is based on the EC Seventh Directive and the same definition has also been adopted by FRS 2.

1.2.1   The EC Seventh Directive

Article 1 of the EC Seventh Directive on Company Law sets out six sets of circumstances under which a parent/subsidiary relationship will be regarded as existing, so as to require the parent to present consolidated accounts, and one further situation requiring consolidation even though such a relationship does not exist. Five of the six sets of circumstances have been incorporated in the UK legislation through the enactment of the Companies Act 1989 and these are discussed at 1.2.2 below. The other two situations contained in the Directive, which were optional and have not been incorporated, are as follows:

(a)   De facto control over appointment of the board

The parent shall consolidate its subsidiary if it is a shareholder or member of it and a majority of the members of the board who have held office throughout the year, the previous year, and up to the time of the issue of the consolidated accounts have *in fact* been appointed solely as a result of the exercise of the parent's voting rights.[5] This is to cater for the situation where, due to the fact that the majority of the shares are widely dispersed, a minority shareholder can exercise de facto control. The Directive allows member states not to implement this part of the definition, or to make it conditional on the holding of at least 20% of the voting rights; the UK government was opposed to this part of the definition at the time of the negotiation of the terms of the directive, and they decided to take advantage of the first of these exemptions.

(b)   Horizontal groups

Consolidated accounts must be prepared for companies which have no shareholding relationship in either of two sets of circumstances. The first is if they are managed on a unified basis under the terms of a contract or provisions in their memorandum or articles of association; the second is if the same people form the majority of the members of the board of both companies during the year and for the period up to the preparation of the accounts.[6] Although the thinking behind the second set of circumstances is easy to understand, it would appear to result occasionally in the consolidation of separate enterprises which were associated with each other only by coincidence and whose combined accounts would have neither meaning nor relevance to anyone. Neither of these provisions has been incorporated in the Companies Act.

1.2.2   The Companies Act

In implementing the Directive, the Companies Act 1989 introduced the term 'subsidiary undertaking' and moved the definition from one based strictly on the form of the shareholding relationship between the companies, nearer to one which reflects the substance of the commercial relationship and in particular who exercises de facto control. The use of the term 'undertaking' also extended the types of entity which may have to be consolidated, in that it not only includes companies or bodies corporate, but also unincorporated associations and partnerships.[7]

Under the Act, a subsidiary undertaking is one in which the parent:

(a)   has a majority of the voting rights; or

(b)   is a member and can appoint or remove a majority of the board; or

(c)   is a member and controls alone a majority of the voting rights by agreement with other members; or

(d)   has the right to exercise a dominant influence through the Memorandum and Articles or a control contract; or

(e)   has a participating interest and either

  (i)   actually exercises a dominant influence over it, or

  (ii)   manages both on a unified basis.[8]

These are discussed further below.

A   Majority of voting rights

This is the main definition based on the power of one entity to control another through the exercise of shareholder voting control. Unlike the old definition of a subsidiary,[9] it concentrates on those shares which can exercise voting power rather than those which are defined in terms of their rights to participate beyond a specified amount in a distribution.

'Voting rights' are defined as 'rights conferred on shareholders in respect of their shares or, in the case of an undertaking not having a share capital, on members, to vote at general meetings of the undertaking on all (or substantially all) matters'.[10]

There are a number of detailed provisions for determining whether or not certain rights are to be taken into account.[11] Paragraph 21 of ED 50, the forerunner of FRS 2, summarised these as follows:

'One example is where rights are only exercisable under certain circumstances; in this case those rights should be taken into account for as long as the particular circumstances continue, or the circumstances are within the control of the holder of the rights. Rights which are normally exercisable but which are temporarily interrupted should continue to be taken into account. Rights should be treated as held by the enterprise on whose behalf a nominee holds them or whose instruction, consent or concurrence is required for their exercise. Fiduciary interests are not taken into account and rights given as security remain the rights of the provider of the security, if the rights are mainly exercisable only in accordance with his instructions or in his interests. Rights of any of its subsidiaries are to be treated as the rights of the parent but rights of a parent should not be attributed to its subsidiaries. The voting rights in an enterprise are to be reduced by any rights held by the enterprise itself.'

B   Control of the board of directors

Essentially this is an anti-avoidance measure, which extends the control concept from control of the company in general meeting to control of the board, to cover situations where the latter exists but not the former.

Whereas previously the right to control the composition of the board only meant the right to appoint or remove a majority in number of the directors, the Companies Act 1989 extended it to mean the right to appoint or remove members of the board entitled to a majority of the voting rights on all (or substantially all) matters at board meetings.[12] This was a further anti-avoidance measure, to cope with the situation where control of the board's decisions is achieved either through the exercise of differential voting rights or a casting vote without having a majority in number of the membership of the board.

However, this change to the criterion could have implications for 'true' 50:50 joint ventures. Where the shareholders in such a joint venture, in order to prevent a deadlock, take it in turns each year to appoint the chairman (with the casting vote), this will mean that the joint venture will be a subsidiary undertaking of each shareholder company every second year. The question then arises, should the undertaking be consolidated, then equity accounted, in alternate years? (Depending on the timing, this could actually mean the undertaking is consolidated for the first part of the shareholding company's year and equity accounted for the remainder, and vice versa in alternate years!) In our view this would clearly be a nonsense and we believe that the appropriate treatment would be not to consolidate on the grounds that there are long-term restrictions which hinder control (see 5.3 below), but to equity account throughout.

One company which discloses the fact that it has a subsidiary by virtue of board control is Rio Tinto, as shown below:

Extract 5.1: Rio Tinto plc and Rio Tinto Limited (1998)

30 PRINCIPAL SUBSIDIARY COMPANIES [extract]

Company and country of incorporation	Principal activities	Class of shares held	Proportion of class held %	Group interest %
Namibia				
Rossing Uranium Limited (note c)	Uranium mining	'B'N$1	71.16)	68.58
		'C'N10c	70.59)	

(c)   The Group holding of shares in Rossing Uranium Limited carries 35.54 per cent of the total voting rights. Rossing is consolidated by virtue of Board control.

Another company which has had a subsidiary due to board control is Sema Group, as shown below:

Extract 5.2: Sema Group plc (1996)

11. GROUP UNDERTAKINGS [extract]

The principal Group undertakings at 31 December 1996, all of which are engaged in the provision of information technology services, were as follows (all holdings were in ordinary shares):

	Immediate holding company (%)	Country of registration and operation
DIRECT GROUP UNDERTAKINGS		
BAeSEMA Limited	50	England
Sema Group SA	99.8	France
OWNED BY BAeSEMA LIMITED		
Aerosystems International Limited	50	England
OWNED BY SEMA GROUP SA		
TS FM Holdings	40	France

BAeSEMA Limited and TS FM Holdings have been fully consolidated as Group undertakings as defined by the Companies Act 1985. BAeSEMA is consolidated on the basis of a shareholders' agreement which gives the Group control of the Board of directors. TS FM Holdings is consolidated on the basis that it is managed on a unified basis with Sema Group SA.

BAeSEMA's 50% holding in Aerosystems International Limited has been fully consolidated from 1 January 1996 since it is managed on a unified basis with BAeSEMA.

C   Control by contract

Such a contract, which is a feature of German business organisations, is not usually possible under general principles of UK company law, because it would conflict with the directors' fiduciary duty to conduct the affairs of the company in accordance with its own best interests, and is allowed only where the Memorandum and Articles specifically permit it. The Directive provides that this part of the definition applies only where it is consistent with the company law of the country concerned, and for this reason it has been enacted in the UK in a fairly restricted way; it will apply only in cases where the parent company has the right to give directions with respect to the operating and financial policies of the other undertaking which its directors are obliged to comply with whether or not they are for the benefit of that other undertaking, where the undertaking's domestic law and its Memorandum and Articles permit a dominant influence to be exerted through such a contract, and where the contract in question is in writing.[13] This criterion is therefore likely to be of relevance only where a company has a business operation in Germany or another country which adopts the German model.

One company which has disclosed the fact that it had a subsidiary by virtue of a control contract is Sema Group, as shown below:

Extract 5.3: Sema Group plc (1993)

11. GROUP UNDERTAKINGS [extract]

The Group's 50% holding in BAeSEMA Limited, its 50% holding in Sema Group Télécom SA and its 49% holding in Tibet SA have been fully consolidated as Group undertakings as defined by the Companies Act 1989.

BAeSEMA is consolidated on the basis of a shareholders' agreement which gives the Group control of the board of directors. Tibet SA is consolidated on the basis of actual dominant influence exercised by the Group by virtue of a control contract.

D   Control by agreement

This is a more stringent application of the concept of de facto control by a minority investor (see 1.2.1 (a) above), requiring agreement with other shareholders rather than merely their tacit acceptance that control can be exercised. The Directive provides that the member states may introduce more particular requirements for the form and content of such agreements, and the Department of Trade and Industry announced that it intended to draft the legislation so that the agreement must be legally binding but need not be in writing, and that it should include agreements *not* to exercise voting rights as well as those to exercise them in a particular way.[14] Neither of these issues is, in fact, specifically dealt with in the Act; it may, therefore, be that in their absence, oral agreements and agreements not to exercise voting rights are intended to come within the scope of the legislation.

E   Participating interest with dominant influence or unified management

This criterion is one of the member state options contained in the Directive which has been introduced into the legislation in addition to the mandatory definitions set out in A to D above. This part of the Directive has been introduced in a very broad form which is based on a wide definition of 'participating interest', with the clear intention of preventing artificial structures designed to achieve the purposes of off balance sheet finance schemes.

A participating interest in an undertaking is deemed to mean an interest in the shares of the undertaking which is held for the long term for the purpose of securing a contribution to the activities of the investing company by the exercise of control or influence arising from that interest.[15] This is similar to the definition of a related company previously contained in the Companies Act 1985, but is wider in that it includes interests in partnerships and unincorporated associations; it also includes interests which are convertible into interests in shares, such as convertible loan stock, and options to acquire an interest in shares.[16] There is a rebuttable presumption that a holding of 20% or more is a participating interest.[17]

Although 'participating interest' is defined in the Act, there is no further definition of the concept of either 'actually exercises a dominant influence' or 'managed on a unified basis' (both are concepts derived from German law); the reason being that the DTI did not want to elaborate on these definitions, since it regarded this as an area to be more appropriately dealt with by means of accounting standards, although ultimately it is a matter of law to be interpreted by the courts. The Act does state, however, that although 'a right to exercise a dominant influence' over another undertaking is defined as 'a right to give directions with respect to the operating and financial policies of that other undertaking which its directors are obliged to comply with whether or not they are for the benefit of that other undertaking' (see D above), this is not to be read as affecting the construction of 'actually exercises a dominant influence'.[18]

In FRS 2, 'dominant influence' is defined as 'influence that can be exercised to achieve the operating and financial policies desired by the holder of the influence, notwithstanding the rights or influence of any other party' and the 'actual exercise of dominant influence' is defined as being 'the exercise of an influence that achieves the result that the operating and financial policies of the undertaking influenced are set in accordance with the wishes of the holder of the influence and for the holder's benefit whether or not those wishes are explicit. The actual exercise of dominant influence is identified by its effect in practice rather than by the way in which it is exercised.'[19]

As explained in FRS 2, 'the effect of the exercise of dominant influence is that the undertaking under influence implements the operating and financial policies that the holder of the influence desires. Thus a power of veto or any other reserve power that has the necessary effect in practice can form the basis whereby one undertaking actually exercises a dominant influence over another. However, such powers are likely to lead to the holder actually exercising a dominant influence over an undertaking only if they are held in conjunction with other rights or powers or if they relate to the day-to-day activities of that undertaking and no similar veto is held by other parties unconnected to the holder.'[20]

Clearly, it will be a matter of judgement and interpretation as to whether these definitions apply to any particular set of circumstances. As FRS 2 explains, 'the full circumstances of each case should be considered, including the effect of any formal or informal agreements between the undertakings, to decide whether or not one undertaking actually exercises a dominant influence over another. Commercial relationships such as that of supplier, customer or lender do not of themselves constitute dominant influence.'[21]

The standard also states that dominant influence can be exercised 'in an interventionist or non-interventionist way. For example, a parent undertaking may set directly and in detail the operating and financial policies of its subsidiary undertaking or it may prefer to influence these by setting out in outline the kind of results it wants achieved without being involved regularly or on a day-to-day basis. Because of the variety of ways that dominant influence may be exercised evidence of continuous intervention is not necessary to support the view that dominant influence is actually exercised. Sufficient evidence might be provided by a rare intervention on a critical matter. Once there has been evidence that one undertaking has exercised a dominant influence over another, then the dominant undertaking should be assumed to continue to exercise its influence until there is evidence to the contrary.'[22]

Where a subsidiary undertaking is so only by virtue of this criterion then FRS 2 requires disclosure of the basis of the parent company's dominant influence.[23] Examples of companies which consolidate subsidiary undertakings which qualify under this criterion are shown in the following extracts:

Extract 5.4: Rentokil Initial plc (1998)

PRINCIPAL SUBSIDIARY AND ASSOCIATED UNDERTAKINGS [extract]

South Korea   Yu Yu Calmic Co Ltd (50%)

The group's 50% interest in Yu Yu Calmic Co Ltd is consolidated as a subsidiary to reflect the group's dominant influence exercised over this company because of its shareholding and its involvement in the management and because the business is conducted under licence from the group.

Extract 5.5: Glaxo Wellcome plc (1998)

GROUP COMPANIES [extract]

Subsidiary undertaking	%
Glaxo Saudi Arabia Ltd.	49[a]
Glaxo-Sankyo Co., Ltd.	50[a]

[a] Consolidated as subsidiary undertaking in accordance with section 258(4)(a) of the Companies Act 1985 on the grounds of influence over marketing strategy.

One interesting example is that of Booker which in its 1995 accounts consolidated a subsidiary under this criterion, as indicated below:

Extract 5.6: Booker plc (1995)

Subsidiary and associated undertakings [extract]

Recheio Distribuição SA (40%)5

5   Recheio Distribuição SA is treated as subsidiary on the grounds of Booker plc exercising a dominant influence over the operating and financial policies of that company.

However in the following year the position would appear to have changed:

Extract 5.7: Booker plc (1996)

13.   Fixed asset investments [extract]

Recheio Distribuição SA, in which the group holds a 40% equity interest and which has been consolidated hitherto on the basis of the group exercising dominant control, has been deconsolidated and treated as an associated undertaking effective from 28 December 1996. The change in the status of the investment in Recheio reflects the group's loss of dominant control over the operating and financial policies of that company.

One difficulty which this definition can give rise to is the apportionment of the results and net assets of the subsidiary undertaking between the parent and the minority interests, particularly where the participating interest is in the form of convertible loan stock or options to acquire an interest in shares. This is discussed at 1.3.4 below.

The ASB has defined 'managed on a unified basis' in FRS 2 as being where 'two or more undertakings are managed on a unified basis if the whole of the operations of the undertakings are integrated and they are managed as a single unit. Unified management does not arise solely because one undertaking manages another.'[24]

One company which consolidates subsidiary undertakings which qualify under this criterion is Unilever, as indicated below:

Extract 5.8: Unilever PLC (1998)

Unilever [extract]

The two parent companies, NV and PLC, operate as nearly as is practicable as a single entity (the Unilever Group, also referred to as Unilever or the Group). NV and PLC have the same directors and are linked by a series of agreements, including an Equalisation Agreement, which is designed so that the position of the shareholders of both companies is as nearly as possible the same as if they held shares in a single company.

Basis of consolidation [extract]

By reason of the operational and contractual arrangements referred to above and the internal participating interests ... , NV and PLC and their group companies constitute a single group under Netherlands and United Kingdom legislation for the purposes of presenting consolidated accounts. Accordingly the accounts of the Unilever Group are presented by both NV and PLC as their respective consolidated accounts.

Another example can be seen in Extract 5.2 above.

Questions which have arisen include that of whether more than one party can exercise dominant influence over a single undertaking. We believe that logically, there can only be one *dominant* influence, but there is a more general question of whether an undertaking can be the subsidiary of more than one parent, given that there are five alternative definitions of a subsidiary undertaking relationship, and if it is possible for an undertaking to have two parent companies, should both companies consolidate the undertaking?

On this question, FRS 2 states that 'where more than one undertaking is ... identified as a parent of one subsidiary undertaking, not more than one of those parents can have control as defined in paragraph 6 [of the standard]'.[25] It then suggests that such anomalies might be resolved by taking into account:

(a)   the existence of a quasi subsidiary (see Chapter 16);

(b)   the existence of severe long-term restrictions on the rights of the parent undertaking (see 5.3 below); or

(c)   the existence of a joint venture agreement, whether formal or informal.[26]

In relation to the last of these, the standard states that 'where the tests of the Act identify more than one undertaking as the parent of one subsidiary undertaking it is likely that they have shared control and, therefore, their interests in the subsidiary undertaking are in effect interests in a joint venture and should be treated accordingly (see Chapter 7). Alternatively, one or more of the undertakings identified under the Act as a parent undertaking may exercise a non-controlling but significant influence over its subsidiary undertaking, in which case it would be more appropriate to treat that subsidiary undertaking in the same way as an associated undertaking rather than to include it in the consolidation.'[27]

1.3   Consolidating partly owned subsidiaries

Various alternative ways of looking at a group become relevant when there are subsidiary companies which are not wholly owned by the holding company; the particular matters which are affected are the elimination of the effects of inter-company transactions, the calculation of minority interests and the treatment of changes in stake in the subsidiary. There are two widely accepted concepts, referred to respectively as the entity concept and the proprietary concept, but the latter has a number of further variants. These are described in turn below.

1.3.1   The entity concept

The entity concept focuses on the existence of the group as an economic unit, rather than looking at it only through the eyes of the dominant shareholder group. It concentrates on the resources controlled by the entity, and regards the identity of owners with claims on these resources as being of secondary importance. It therefore makes no distinction between the treatment given to different classes of shareholders, whether majority or minority, and transactions between the shareholders are regarded as internal to the group.

1.3.2 The proprietary concept

The proprietary concept emphasises ownership through a controlling shareholding interest, and regards the purpose of the production of the consolidated financial statements as being primarily for the information of the shareholders of the holding company. Correspondingly, it makes no attempt to present financial statements which are relevant to the minority shareholders. This is achieved either by treating the minority shareholders as 'outsiders' and reflecting their interests as quasi-liabilities or by leaving them out of the group financial statements entirely, thereby only consolidating the parent's percentage interest in the assets and liabilities of the subsidiary (the 'proportional consolidation' method). This latter version of the concept is the one described in ED 50.[28] The proprietary concept is sometimes referred to as the 'parent company' concept, and there is a variant of it known as the 'parent company extension' concept, which leans more towards the entity concept described above.

1.3.3 Comparison between the different concepts of a group

The distinction between the different methods in practice can best be illustrated by an example:

Example 5.1: Comparison between the different concepts of a group

Assume that company A buys 75% of company B for £1,200 when company B has total net assets with a fair value of £1,000 and a book value of £800. Under the concepts described above, the consolidated balance sheet of company A would incorporate the effects of the acquisition calculated as follows:

	Entity concept £	Proprietary concept £	Parent coy. extension concept £
Net assets of B	1,000	950	1,000
Goodwill	600	450	450
	1,600	1,400	1,450
Minority interest	400	200	250
Investor interest	1,200	1,200	1,200

Under the entity concept, both the tangible net assets and goodwill are reported in the balance sheet at the full amount of their fair value as determined by the transaction involving the majority shareholder. These amounts are then apportioned between the majority and minority shareholders. By way of contrast, the proprietary concept leaves the minority interest unaffected by the transaction of the majority shareholder; it is shown simply as their proportionate share of the book values of the assets of the company. This means that the goodwill is stated at a figure which represents the difference between the cost of the 75% investment (£1,200) and 75% of the fair value of the assets (£750). Perhaps more disturbingly, the assets are carried on a mixed basis which represents 75% of their fair value and 25% of their book value. This feature is eliminated if proportional consolidation is adopted; the minority interest is disregarded altogether, being set against the assets and liabilities of the subsidiary on a line by line basis, so that only the majority investor's share of the subsidiary's assets are consolidated. This would result in consolidation of assets of £750 and goodwill of £450, representing the total of the investment of £1,200. However, the Companies Act does not allow the proportional consolidation approach to be adopted for subsidiary undertakings. The feature is also avoided in the parent company extension concept, which includes the assets at the whole amount of their fair value and apportions that between the majority and minority interests, but includes goodwill only as it relates to the majority investor.

The rules contained in the legislation do not permit the use of the entity concept as set out above, because they require that goodwill be calculated by comparing the acquisition cost with the investor's proportionate share of the investee's capital and reserves (after adjusting for fair values); by requiring the assets and liabilities to be included at their fair values, they would also appear to rule out the proprietary concept (although the rules on minority interests do not refer to *adjusted* capital and reserves).[29] The entity method is also ruled out by the international standard on business combinations, IAS 22. This permits either of the other two methods, with the proprietary concept being the preferred approach and the parent company extension method a permitted alternative.[30]

The different concepts are also relevant to the calculation of the adjustments made to eliminate the effects of inter-company transactions. If company A in the above example sold an item of stock to company B for a profit of £100, and company B still held the asset in stock at the year end, it would be necessary to make an adjustment on consolidation to eliminate what was an unrealised profit from the group point of view. Under the proprietary concept, the minority shareholders are regarded as outsiders, and therefore there is a case for saying that 25% of the profit *has* been realised; this would be done by limiting the write-down of stock to £75, all of which is taken off the balance on the group profit and loss account. Under the proportional consolidation method, only 75% of the stock would appear in the consolidated balance sheet in the first place, so the adjustment would simply be to deduct £75 from both the group profit and loss account and from the stock. If the entity concept is followed, as it is the parent which has made the sale, the whole write down of stock of £100 would be charged against the group profit and loss account; no amount would be attributed to the minority interest. Under another approach, the separate entities approach,[31] the adjustment would be effected by apportioning the £100 between the group profit and loss account and the minority interest in the ratio 75:25. In this case the rules in the Companies Act permit inter-company profit eliminations to be made either at their gross amounts or in proportion to the investor's stake in the investee.[32]

A further practical situation where differences between the concepts emerge is when the partly owned subsidiary makes losses which put it into overall deficit. Under the entity concept, the consolidated financial statements would continue to account for these losses and apportion them between the majority and minority interests in proportion to their holdings, even if these created a debit balance for the minority interest in the balance sheet. A proprietary viewpoint would not normally permit the minority interest to be shown as a debit balance, because it could not usually be regarded as a recoverable asset from the point of view of the majority interest, which is the orientation of the financial statements under the proprietary concept. This was the position taken by SSAP 14, which said that 'debit balances should be recognised only if there is a binding obligation on minority shareholders to make good losses incurred which they are able to meet'.[33] FRS 2, on the other hand, has adopted an entity perspective and requires that losses are attributable to the minority interests according to their holdings in loss making subsidiaries, regardless of whether or not this leads to a debit balance or not. Such a debit balance is not regarded as an asset, but the minority share of net liabilities. However, the standard does require the group to make provision to the extent that it has 'any commercial or legal obligation (whether formal or implied) to provide finance that may not be recoverable in respect of the accumulated losses attributable to the minority interest'.[34]

1.3.4 ED 50 and FRS 2

ED 50 discussed these conceptual issues and developed a new concept, called the 'control/ownership concept', which is effectively a variant of the parent company extension concept described above. Under this concept, it is argued that the shareholders of the holding company need information not only on the group as a whole but also on the distinction between what they own and what others own.[35] In deciding how to deal with the particular matters which are affected by the existence of the minority shareholders, the concept looks at whether 'control' or 'ownership' is the most relevant issue. In respect of questions where control is the most relevant issue, minorities are considered to be within the group, similar in nature to equity, because they are part of the controlled entity. Where ownership is considered to be most important, the minorities are treated as external to the group and regarded as being a liability.[36]

FRS 2 does not contain a detailed discussion of the concepts described above, leaving the conceptual basis of consolidated accounts to be dealt with eventually in the ASB's Statement of Principles (see 5.8, 5.13 and 5.19 of Chapter 2). However, apart from the treatment of debit balances relating to minority interests (see 1.3.3 above), FRS 2 adopts an approach in respect of minority interests similar to that proposed by ED 50. The practical effects of this approach are as follows.

Where a company becomes a parent of another entity, then as it controls that entity as a whole, all of the net assets of the subsidiary should be restated at fair values and included in the consolidated accounts, not just the proportion owned. Consequently, a minority interest should be recognised at the date of the acquisition based on those fair values. The amount for the minority should not include any share of goodwill arising on the acquisition.[37] In Example 5.1 above, this would result in the same treatment as shown under the parent company extension concept. Thereafter, any profits or losses of the subsidiary are consolidated in full, with an allocation made to the minority interest based on the proportion held by the minority shareholders. As indicated at 1.3.3 above losses continue to be allocated to minority interests even if this leads to a debit balance, although provision should be made to the extent that the parent has any commercial or legal obligation to provide finance that may not be recoverable.[38]

Where dealings in the shares of the subsidiary subsequently take place between the parent company and the minority interests, then as these are ownership issues, they are to be considered as external to the group and accounted for as such. Where the parent is increasing its stake in the subsidiary, then any difference between the consideration paid and the appropriate proportion of the net assets (based on fair values if necessary), i.e. the amount of the minority interest therein, should be treated as goodwill.[39] Where the parent reduces its stake in the subsidiary then a profit or loss should be recorded.[40] These issues are discussed further at 2.5 and 3.4 in Chapter 6 respectively.

The other main area is the elimination of the effects of inter-company transactions. This is regarded as a control issue as transactions between two companies under common control may be arranged without reference to any external party. The minority is, therefore, internal to the group for the calculation of these adjustments and it is not sufficient to adjust only for that part of the transaction which relates to the parent's interest; adjustment for the whole transaction and thus the full amount of any unrealised profit or loss must be made, with a suitable allocation made between the parent and the minority.[41] This is discussed further at 3.4 below.

FRS 2 emphasises that despite the title 'minority interests', there is in principle no upper limit to the proportion of shares in a subsidiary undertaking which may be held as a minority interest while the parent undertaking still qualifies as such under the Companies Act (and the standard).[42] This is due to the fact that the parent/subsidiary relationship is based on the parent having a 'controlling interest', whereas the apportionment of the results and net assets of the subsidiary between the parent and the minority interests is effectively based on their respective equity interests. This will be particularly relevant where the parent/subsidiary relationship is due to the parent having a participating interest and exercising a dominant influence over the subsidiary (see 1.2.2 E above). For example, a company may only have a 45% interest in the ordinary shares of another company but be in a position to exercise dominant influence over it, in which case 55% of the results and net assets of the subsidiary would be attributable to the minority interests.

One area which the standard does not deal with is are those unusual situations which can arise because control and ownership are divorced. There may be difficulties in determining the relevant apportionment particularly where the parent's participating interest is in the form of convertible loan stock or an option to acquire an interest in the shares of the subsidiary. An extreme example of this would be 'the 0% subsidiary' where the participating interest is in the form of an option over all the shares. In our view the apportionment to the minority interests will depend on the particular circumstances. On the one hand, it may be that the minority interests should be attributed 100%; for example, where the option price is yet to be determined or it is based on future results/net assets of the subsidiary, or where it has been agreed between the parties that prior to the exercise of the option all retained profits of the subsidiary are to be distributed to the existing shareholders. On the other hand, it may be that there is a put and call option over the shares, the option price is fixed and it is agreed between the parties that no dividends will be paid to the existing shareholders, in which case no amounts should be attributed to the minority interests; the minority interests should be included at an amount equivalent to the exercise price under the option.

2 HISTORICAL DEVELOPMENT OF RULES ON GROUP ACCOUNTS

2.1 Origins of group accounts

The idea of using a holding company to own further investments in subsidiaries evolved in the US more than 150 years ago, but the preparation of consolidated accounts to portray the results of the group did not become widely established until the early part of this century.

In the UK, groups of companies only became a significant form of business structure around the time of the First World War, and the first time that a company drew up a consolidated balance sheet for its members was when Nobel Industries presented such a statement as at December 1920. At that time there was no reporting requirement for any profit and loss account (even unconsolidated) to be presented, and the first group profit and loss account was not published until 1933, when the Dunlop Rubber Co. included one in its annual accounts. The Stock Exchange made the publication of consolidated accounts a requirement for new issuers in 1939, and the ICAEW published recommendations in 1944[43] which made such accounts best practice for all groups.

2.2 The UK legislative background

The first requirement for group accounts was introduced into the legislation by the Companies Act 1947, which was consolidated soon thereafter into the Companies Act 1948. These basic requirements, having been again consolidated into the Companies Act 1985, remained unchanged until the incorporation into UK law of the EC Seventh Directive on company law, which was one of the principal purposes of the Companies Act 1989. This Directive was issued by the Council of the European Communities in 1983, to establish a financial reporting framework for groups in all member states. The most significant changes were in the definition of a subsidiary, discussed at 1.2.2 above, and in the qualifying conditions for merger accounting, which are covered at 2.1.5 in Chapter 6. Apart from these changes, the impact of the 1989 Act on most groups was relatively minor as, to a large extent, the new rules codified existing practice.

2.3   Accounting standards in the UK

The first general accounting standard on group accounts in the UK was SSAP 14
– *Group accounts* – issued in September 1978. This provided the broad
framework to support the basic legal requirements, and dealt in particular with
the form which group accounts should take and various miscellaneous matters in
relation to the mechanics of the consolidation process. The standard eventually
required revision to reflect the new provisions of the Companies Act 1989 and,
accordingly, an exposure draft, ED 50 – *Consolidated accounts* – was issued in
June 1990. Following the demise of the ASC, the ASB issued its Interim
Statement: Consolidated Accounts in December 1990 as a stop-gap measure,
and in July 1992 issued FRS 2, *Accounting for Subsidiary Undertakings*, to
replace SSAP 14.

There are other standards which deal in more detail with business combinations.
These are mainly discussed in Chapter 6.

3   CONSOLIDATION OF SUBSIDIARIES

3.1   Basic principles

It is beyond the scope of this chapter to discuss the detailed mechanics of the
consolidation process; there are a number of basic texts which give a full
exposition of this subject. The Companies Act 1989 introduced into the
legislation some rules relating to the consolidation of subsidiaries,[44] but until
then there were no authoritative rules on the subject at a detailed level; SSAP 14
merely stated that 'the method of preparation of consolidated financial
statements on an item-by-item basis, eliminating intra-group balances and
transactions and unrealised intra-group profit, is well understood ...'.[45]

FRS 2 now defines consolidation as 'the process of adjusting and combining
financial information from the individual financial statements of a parent
undertaking and its subsidiary undertakings to prepare consolidated financial
statements that present financial information for the group as a single economic
entity'.[46] This is not as explicit as the definition contained in ED 50 which stated
that consolidation was 'a method of accounting under which the information
contained in the separate financial statements of a parent and its subsidiaries is
presented as though for a single entity. Investments in subsidiaries are eliminated
against the subsidiaries' share capital and reserves in accordance with the
method of accounting adopted for the business combination. After any necessary
consolidation adjustments for such matters as minority interests, intra-group
transactions and to obtain consistency of accounting policies, the amounts for
assets and liabilities, revenue and expenses in the individual financial statements
are added together on a line-by-line basis to form the consolidated accounts.'[47]
(Arguably, this was more of a description rather than a definition of a

consolidation.) FRS 2 introduces authoritative rules relating to some of these consolidation adjustments and these are referred to below.

One interesting example is that of Photo-Me International which in its 1997 accounts did not eliminate intra-group sales by invoking the true and fair override as shown below.

Extract 5.9: Photo-Me International Plc (1997)

1   Accounting policies [extract]

(k)   Turnover

Turnover comprises the net invoiced value of sales and the revenue arising from cash takings in operating companies, stated net of value added tax. Turnover includes sales, by the Group's manufacturing divisions to Group undertakings, of equipment which is then capitalised within the accounts of the Group's undertakings. It is the opinion of the directors that excluding sales from turnover would understate the Group's activities and as such would fail to give a true and fair view. Inter-company profit arising on such sales is excluded from the Group's profit.

2   Turnover [extract]

Turnover was contributed as follows:

Area of activity	1997 £'000	%	1996 £'000	%
Manufacturing:				
Sales to Group undertakings	10,788	6.3	15,552	7.8
Sales to third parties	35,307	20.8	43,327	21.8
	46,095	27.1	58,879	29.6
Operating	123,864	72.9	139,813	70.4
	169,959	100.0	198,692	100.0

This highly unusual treatment attracted the attention of the Review Panel who were not persuaded by the company's arguments for departing from the basic principles contained in the Companies Act as regards intra-group sales.[48] Accordingly, Photo-Me International changed its policy in this regard in the following year as shown below.

Extract 5.10: Photo-Me International Plc (1998)

1   Accounting policies [extract]

(b)   Changes in accounting policy

(i) Following discussion with the Financial Reporting Review Panel the Group has this year decided to change the method of accounting for sales of operating equipment, manufactured by Group undertakings, sold to other Group undertakings, and then capitalised. The Group now shows the removal of these from turnover (Note 2) and reflects a corresponding reduction in cost of sales (Note 3) by inclusion of the same value (which excludes intra-group profit) as "own work capitalised". The turnover shown in the profit and loss account now excludes any intra-group turnover.

The comparative figures for the year to 30 April 1997 have been adjusted to reflect the new policy.

The effect of this change is shown in Notes 1(l), 2 and 3.

3.2   Uniform accounting policies

It is axiomatic that the figures being aggregated in the consolidation process must have been compiled on a consistent basis and therefore that uniform accounting policies should have been adopted by all the members of the group. Of course, local reporting requirements for each subsidiary might dictate that different policies must be used for domestic purposes; the only necessity where this occurs is that appropriate adjustments are made in the course of the consolidation process to eliminate the effects of such differences. FRS 2 endorses this general principle.[49]

The Companies Act does not refer to accounting policies as such in this context, but says that 'where assets and liabilities ... have been valued or otherwise determined by undertakings according to accounting rules differing from those used for the group accounts, the values or amounts shall be adjusted so as to accord with the rules used for the group accounts'.[50] However, this need not be done if the effect is immaterial,[51] or if there are 'special reasons' for leaving them unchanged (in which case disclosure of particulars of the departure, the reasons for it and its effect are to be given).[52] FRS 2 also acknowledges that this may be appropriate in exceptional cases.[53]

Notwithstanding these apparent loopholes in FRS 2 and the Act, the accounts must still give a true and fair view of the group as a whole and it is difficult to imagine that this could be achieved by adding together material figures which have been compiled using profoundly different policies. In practice, however, the relaxation allowed does not seem to be relied on in many cases and groups generally do exert themselves to achieve consistency of policies unless the effect is insignificant.

Although there is no requirement to do so, some companies disclose the fact that adjustments are made to achieve uniform accounting policies, as illustrated below:

Extract 5.11: Allied Domecq PLC (1998)

CONSOLIDATION [extract]

In cases where the statutory accounts of overseas undertakings are prepared on bases inconsistent with group accounting policies, appropriate adjustments are made to conform with the bases adopted in the UK.

Extract 5.12: British Telecommunications plc (1999)

I   Basis of preparation of the financial statements [extract]

Where the financial statements of subsidiary undertakings, associates and joint ventures do not conform with the group's accounting policies, appropriate adjustments are made on consolidation in order to present the group financial statements on a consistent basis.

3.3   Coterminous accounting periods

Since the group is seen as an extension of the parent company in UK law, it is necessary that the period covered by the group accounts corresponds to the accounting reference period of the parent, both in terms of duration and balance sheet date. Once again, this requirement is implicit in the objective that the group accounts should be prepared as if the group were a single entity.

The Companies Act places an onus on the directors of the parent company to ensure that the financial year of each subsidiary is the same as the parent. However, it does acknowledge that there can be good reasons why the individual subsidiaries' own accounts might be drawn up to a different date;[54] for example, in certain countries their year end might be dictated by law, they might choose to adopt a particular accounting period for tax purposes or their trade may be seasonal and have a natural cycle which makes it appropriate to choose a particular reporting date. Another reason could be that they deliberately prepare their accounts to a date shortly before that of the parent (as a materially accurate approximation to the period of the parent) so as to facilitate speedy reporting by the parent of the group results.

Where the period covered by the accounts of an individual member of the group does not correspond to that of the parent, two solutions are possible. The first is for the subsidiary to prepare special accounts solely for the purpose of the consolidation for a period which does match that of the parent. Under the provisions of the Act, such special statements (termed interim accounts) *must* be used if the subsidiary's year end is more than three months before that of the parent; their use is only optional if the year end is no more than three months before that of the parent.[55] One company which has had to use interim accounts is HSBC Holdings, as shown below:

Extract 5.13: HSBC Holdings plc (1998)

1   Basis of preparation [extract]

Accounts of subsidiary undertakings are made up to 31 December, including those of Hongkong Bank of Canada, which in previous years has had a 31 October year-end. For Hongkong Bank of Canada, accounts for a period of 14 months have been used in the 1998 consolidated accounts. In the case of the principal banking and insurance subsidiaries of HSBC Roberts, whose accounts are made up to 30 June annually to comply with local regulations, the Group uses audited interim accounts, drawn up to 31 December annually.

Although, under the Companies Act, the use of interim accounts is only optional if the year end is no more than three months before that of the parent, FRS 2 requires interim accounts to be used in such circumstances unless it is impracticable to do so, in which case the second solution should be adopted.[56] This solution is to use the statutory accounts of the subsidiary for the period last ending before that of the parent. As indicated above such an approach is only possible where the subsidiary's year end is no more than three months before that of the parent. FRS 2 then requires that any changes that have taken place in the intervening period that materially affect the view given by the group's accounts should be taken into account by adjustments in the preparation of the consolidated accounts.[57] In effect, therefore, this means that the group accounts must present (within limits of materiality) the same position as if coterminous year ends had been adopted.

One company which has used interim accounts when statutory accounts made up to within three months of the parent's year end were available is Johnson Fry Holdings, as shown below:

Extract 5.14: Johnson Fry Holdings plc (1996)

Basis of preparation [extract]

The financial statements include the financial statements of the Company and all its subsidiary undertakings made up to 31 December 1996, with the exception of the Pinnacle businesses which changed their year end to 31 October so that audited figures would be available prior to the anticipated sale which was completed on 15 January 1997. In respect of these subsidiary undertakings, audited financial statements to 31 October, together with management accounts covering the remaining two months have been used to draw up these financial statements.

Notwithstanding the preference in FRS 2 for interim accounts to be used, some companies appear to regard the use of such accounts as impracticable as they use the accounts of some of their subsidiaries made up to earlier dates in order to avoid undue delay in the presentation of the group's accounts, as illustrated in the extracts below:

Extract 5.15: Imperial Chemical Industries PLC (1998)

1 **Basis of presentation of financial information** [extract]

Owing to local conditions and to avoid undue delay in the presentation of the Group accounts, five companies made up their accounts to dates earlier than 31 December, but not earlier than 30 September; five subsidiaries made up their accounts prior to 30 September but interim accounts to 31 December were drawn up for consolidation purposes.

Extract 5.16: National Westminster Bank Plc (1998)

(ii) **Basis of consolidation** [extract]

To avoid undue delay in the presentation of the Group's accounts, the accounts of certain subsidiary undertakings have been made up to 30 November. There have been no changes in respect of these subsidiary undertakings, in the period from their balance sheet dates to 31 December, that materially affect the view given by the Group's accounts.

FRS 2 requires that, where coterminous year ends are *not* used in respect of any of the group's subsidiaries, there should be disclosure of the name of the subsidiaries involved, the year ends used (and duration of accounting periods, if different from that of the parent) and the reasons for the use of the different dates.[58] The Act contains similar requirements.[59] Given that, as discussed above, the accounts must in any event present materially the same picture as if coterminous years had been used, these requirements seem irrelevant.

The use of the accounts of foreign subsidiaries with non-coterminous year ends also raises the question of what exchange rate should be used for translation purposes. This point is covered in 3.4.1 of Chapter 8.

3.4 Elimination of unrealised profits/losses on inter-company transactions

The reasons for making such an elimination are straightforward; 'no man can make a profit by trading with himself', and when a group is trying to present its results as if it were a single entity, it clearly must not regard internal transactions as giving rise to a realised profit.

In most cases the treatment is uncontentious and entails writing down the value of items of stock (if that is what is involved) held by one group company at the year end which have been purchased from another group company which has made a profit on the deal; the adjusting entry is simply to remove the profit element from the stock valuation and from the balance on the group profit and loss account (net of a deferred tax adjustment if appropriate; the elimination of this profit can be regarded as giving rise to a timing difference, because the group will still be taxed on the profit which is eliminated). This will result in the assets being stated at their cost to the group. Similar adjustments should normally be made where a loss arises on the transfer. However, as indicated in

ED 50, where a loss arises on the transfer, this may be indicative of a permanent impairment in value of the asset (or a reduction to net realisable value) and therefore no adjustment should be made. The cost (or written down value) of the asset to the group is then used in calculating the profit or loss with anyone outside the group, so that the full profit or loss to the group is reflected at the point at which the asset is sold to the outside party.[60]

Complications can arise when either the selling or the purchasing company (or both) is not a wholly owned subsidiary, or when one of the parties to the transaction is a subsidiary which is not consolidated. There are essentially two questions: (a) what proportion of the profit in the stock is to be eliminated, and (b) whether, and if so how, to make the elimination against minority interests as well as group shareholders' funds (which has already been discussed to some extent at 1.3.3 above). FRS 2 requires that the whole amount of the profit be eliminated, and that the adjustment be apportioned between the majority and minority interests in proportion to their holdings in the selling company, even if the subsidiary is equity accounted.[61] In Example 5.1 at 1.3.3 above, the parent company was the selling company and therefore *no* amount would be attributed to the minority shareholders; if, on the other hand, the subsidiary had made the profit on selling to the parent, 25% would have been attributed to the minority shareholders.

The Companies Act also contains provisions requiring intra-group profits (and losses) included in the book value of assets to be eliminated in preparing the consolidated accounts. However, where a partly owned subsidiary is involved the Act allows the elimination to be either the whole of the profit (or loss) or the group's interest thereof. These rules do not extend to transactions with subsidiaries which are equity accounted in the group accounts; for example, subsidiaries excluded from consolidation on grounds of different activities.[62] Nevertheless, as indicated above, FRS 2 requires the whole of the profit (or loss) to be eliminated and clarifies that this also applies to transactions with subsidiaries excluded from consolidation on grounds of different activities.[63] It also says that profits and losses arising on transactions with subsidiaries which are excluded for other reasons need not be eliminated except to the extent appropriate if they are equity accounted because significant influence is retained.[64]

The foreign currency complications which can arise from inter-company transactions are dealt with in 3.7.2 of Chapter 8.

4   EXEMPTIONS FROM PREPARING GROUP ACCOUNTS

As well as various rules on exclusion of particular subsidiaries, there are a number of provisions which exempt parent companies from having to present consolidated accounts at all. Previously both SSAP 14[65] and the Companies Act[66] contained provisions that group accounts need not be produced if the reporting company was itself a wholly owned subsidiary, although the Companies Act exemption applied only if it was owned by another British company. This exemption in the legislation was extended by the Companies Act 1989 to companies owned by parents incorporated elsewhere in the EEC, and is not limited to subsidiaries which were wholly owned, although there are provisions which allow minority shareholders to demand the preparation of consolidated accounts.[67] As a result of the creation of the European Economic Area with effect from 1994, the exemption was further extended.[68] The Companies Act also contains provisions to exempt parent companies from having to prepare consolidated accounts if the group falls within certain size limits.[69] FRS 2 repeats the exemptions contained in the legislation.[70] These exemptions are discussed below.

4.1 Intermediate holding companies

As indicated above, intermediate holding companies whose immediate parent undertaking is established in a member state of the European Economic Area (EEA) are exempt from preparing group accounts. The exemption is not confined to wholly owned subsidiaries, but is available where the immediate parent holds more than 50% of the shares in a company. However, minority shareholders have the right to request the preparation of consolidated accounts for a financial year by serving a notice on the company within six months of the end of the previous financial year. The minority in question must hold more than half of the shares in the company not held by the immediate parent or more than 5% of the total shares of the company.[71] The exemption does not apply to companies having shares or debentures listed on a stock exchange in a member state[72] and is subject to the following conditions:

(a)   the company must be included in audited consolidated accounts of a parent undertaking established under the law of a member state of the EEA and which comply with the Seventh Directive. The consolidated accounts must be drawn up to the same date as the company's accounts or an earlier date during the same financial year;[73]

(b)   the following disclosures must be given in the accounts of the company:

(i)   the fact that the company is exempt from preparing group accounts;[74] and

(ii)   the name of the parent undertaking which drew up the accounts referred to in (a) above; and

■   its country of incorporation, if incorporated outside Great Britain; or

■   if it is unincorporated, the address of its principal place of business;[75] and

(c)   the accounts referred to in (a) above must be delivered by the company to the registrar together with (if they are not in English) a certified English translation.[76]

This exemption can result in the same set of group accounts being filed by a number of different companies and an example will show that it has some rather surprising effects.

Example 5.2:   Exemption for intermediate parents

The Company A group has the following structure:

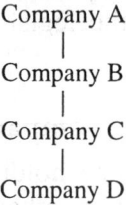

Company A
|
Company B
|
Company C
|
Company D

All the subsidiary undertakings of Company A are 100% owned and all companies prepare their accounts up to the same year end. The effect of the exemption on several different sets of circumstances will be considered as shown by the columns in the following table:

Company	Incorporated in		
	(a)	(b)	(c)
Company A	Great Britain	Netherlands	Netherlands
Company B	United States of America	France	Great Britain
Company C	Great Britain	Great Britain	Great Britain
Company D	Great Britain	Great Britain	Great Britain

(a)   Company A and Company C must both prepare group accounts. In the case of Company C, this is because its immediate parent is not incorporated in a member state of the EEA. This structure is, however, unlikely to arise frequently in practice as Company A would not be in the same UK tax group as Company C and Company D.

It would make no difference to the above if Company B were incorporated in the Channel Islands or the Isle of Man as these are not member states of the EEA. Northern Ireland is part of a member state so if Company B were incorporated there, only Company A would have to prepare group accounts.

(b)   Company C is exempt from preparing group accounts. If Company B as well as Company A chose to prepare consolidated accounts complying with the Seventh Directive, then Company C could choose to file an English translation of either Company A or Company B's group accounts.

(c)   Company B and Company C are exempt from preparing group accounts but both companies must file an English translation of Company A's group accounts. If the Company B (or Company C) group were small or medium-sized (see 4.2 below) it could claim exemption on grounds of size without having to file Company A's accounts. This could reduce duplication of filing to an extent, but it means obtaining a report that in the auditor's opinion the group is entitled to the exemption claimed. Often this will be less costly and time-consuming than translating documents into English. However, this would not be of any assistance if the Company A group contained a public company, a bank or an insurance or financial services company. There is also the drawback that the disclosure requirements are more onerous where the exemption is claimed on grounds of size rather than as an intermediate parent company.

One situation where the exemption may not be available is when a holding company becomes a subsidiary of another EEA company. Under the legislation, the exemption will not be available if the company has not been included in a set of consolidated accounts of the new parent made up to a date which is coterminous or earlier than its own year end. It should be noted that the requirement is not that the *particular accounts* of the company will be included in a set of consolidated accounts of the parent, but that the *company* is included in accounts made up to a date which is coterminous or *earlier* than its own year end.

One other problem with the particular requirements is that other member states may not have actually implemented the Seventh Directive, in which case the UK intermediate holding company will not be able to avail itself of the exemption. Most of the major countries in the EEA have now implemented the Seventh Directive so this will now be less of a problem. However, if the EEA is expanded to encompass other European countries, then it may become more of an issue. It will be necessary, therefore, to check whether a particular member state has embodied the Seventh Directive into its local legislation and, if so, whether there are any transitional provisions delaying the application of the provisions.

Even where the year ends of the UK intermediate holding company and the parent company are the same, problems can arise. The directors of the intermediate holding company have to state in the company's accounts that they are exempt from the obligation to prepare group accounts. However, some of the conditions which have to be met may not have taken place by the time the directors approve their accounts. For example, the consolidated accounts, in which the company is to be included, may not have been prepared and audited; this will be the case if the parent company has a timetable which requires audited accounts of the company to be submitted prior to the audit report on the consolidated accounts being signed. Certainly, the company will still have to file with the registrar the consolidated accounts of the parent. In order to get round these logistical problems, it may be possible for the directors to anticipate these conditions in preparing their accounts, in which case they should only release one set of their audited accounts to the parent company and only file those accounts once they have received the consolidated accounts of the parent. Another possibility would be to submit only an audited consolidation package to the parent company and only prepare their statutory accounts once they have received the consolidated accounts of the parent.

4.2   Small and medium-sized groups

The Companies Act contains provisions such that small and medium-sized groups are exempt from the requirement to prepare consolidated accounts. Where advantage is taken of this exemption, certain disclosures are required in the parent company's accounts concerning its subsidiary undertakings.[77]

To qualify as small or medium-sized, a group must satisfy certain criteria based on the statutory accounts of companies within the group and on the number of employees of the group. The provisions actually include criteria for both small and medium-sized groups although those relating to small groups are redundant for the purposes of the exemption, since any group satisfying them will also satisfy the medium-sized group criteria.

Certain groups may not claim exemption even if they satisfy the criteria. These are groups which contain:

(a)   a public company or a body corporate other than a company (this would include foreign companies) whose constitution allows it to offer its shares or debentures to the public;

(b)   an authorised institution under the Banking Act 1987;

(c)   an insurance company to which Part II of the Insurance Companies Act 1982 applies; or

(d)   an authorised person under the Financial Services Act 1986.[78]

A group qualifies for this exemption if it satisfies at least two of the following three tests:

(a)   its aggregate turnover is not more than £11.2 million net (or £13.44 million gross);

(b)   its aggregate balance sheet total is not more than £5.6 million net (or £6.72 million gross);

(c)   its aggregate number of employees is not more than 250.[79]

It can be seen that there are two sets of financial limits for small or medium-sized groups, one based on aggregate figures from the accounts of group companies before making consolidation set-offs ('gross') and the other on aggregate figures after consolidation set-offs ('net'). If a group satisfies the criteria on either basis, it is exempt from preparing consolidated accounts. The bases can be mixed, i.e. one limit satisfied on a net basis, the other on a gross basis.[80] These financial limits are subject to periodic revision.[81]

The use of the gross basis allows groups to claim exemption from preparing group accounts without having to perform a consolidation exercise to prove their entitlement. Some groups with a significant amount of intra-group trading are likely to have to use the net basis as they may not meet the gross limits.

Unlike the provisions for individual companies filing abbreviated accounts, there is no requirement to adjust the turnover limit in respect of a financial year which is less than or more than 12 months in length.

The Act explains how the aggregate figures should be determined and defines 'balance sheet total' as the total of items A to D if Format 1 is used and the total under the heading 'Assets' if Format 2 is used.[82] All the figures must be taken from statutory accounts.[83] Management accounts are not allowed to be used for this purpose but are permitted, and in some cases required, as a basis for consolidated accounts (see 3.3 above). Some groups may find that, because of the different periods the accounts may cover, consolidated accounts prepared using management accounts give the impression that the group qualifies for the new exemption when this is not in fact the case. In deciding whether the criteria are satisfied, all subsidiary undertakings must be taken into account even if the group is entitled to exclude some of them from consolidation.

The rules for changing an existing status as a small, medium-sized or large group are the same as those for individual companies. This means that an existing status will only change in the second consecutive year in which a group fails to meet (or meets) two out of the three criteria.[84] In the first accounting reference period of the parent company, the group qualifies if it satisfies two out of the three criteria in that year.[85]

4.3 Exemptions contained in FRS 2

As indicated above, FRS 2 repeats the exemptions contained in the Act. Where these exemptions are taken the standard requires that certain disclosures are made in addition to those required by the Act. It requires that the parent's accounts should contain a statement that they present information about it as an individual undertaking and not about its group. The statement should also include or refer to a note giving the grounds on which the parent is exempt from preparing consolidated financial information.[86]

ED 50 had stated that 'in certain circumstances where a parent has made use of an exemption from preparing consolidated accounts, the accounts of the exempt parent alone will not be sufficient to give a true and fair view of the financial position and profit and loss for that period of that parent. Sufficient additional disclosures should be made to enable the parent's accounts to show a true and fair view of its activities and financial position. In some cases such information may best be presented by providing consolidated accounts for the whole group.'[87] This controversial proposal attracted adverse criticism and was omitted from the standard.

5   EXCLUSION OF SUBSIDIARIES FROM GROUP ACCOUNTS

5.1   Sources of rules on exclusion of particular subsidiaries

Where group accounts are required, there are various circumstances under which it is considered appropriate not to consolidate particular subsidiaries, but instead either to deal with them in some other manner or to exclude them from the group accounts altogether.

Under the Companies Act subsidiaries may be excluded from the consolidated accounts where:

(a)   their activities are sufficiently different from those of the rest of the group;

(b)   there are severe long-term restrictions over the parent's rights;

(c)   they are held with a view to subsequent resale;

(d)   obtaining the information needed would involve disproportionate expense or undue delay; or

(e)   they are immaterial (in aggregate).[88]

FRS 2 only permits subsidiaries to be excluded from consolidation on grounds of criteria (a) to (c) above,[89] although as the standard does not apply to immaterial items exclusion under criterion (e) is also permissible. The ASB took the view that criterion (d) was not an appropriate reason for excluding material subsidiaries.[90] The circumstances under which the three permissible criteria might be applied are discussed in turn below.

5.2   Different activities

The specific rules on this in the Companies Act read as follows:

'Where the activities of one or more subsidiary undertakings are so different from those of other undertakings to be included in the consolidation that their inclusion would be incompatible with the obligation to give a true and fair view, those undertakings shall be excluded from consolidation.

'This ... does not apply merely because some of the undertakings are industrial, some commercial and some provide services, or because they carry on industrial or commercial activities involving different products or provide different services.'[91] In the case of banking and insurance groups, undertakings may not be excluded under the Companies Act on these grounds if their activities are a direct extension of, or ancillary to, the banking or insurance business.[92]

FRS 2 adopts the same approach, stressing that the exclusion is to be applied only in very exceptional cases. It explains that 'the key feature of this exclusion is that it refers only to a subsidiary undertaking whose activities are so different from those of other undertakings included in the consolidation that to include that subsidiary undertaking in the consolidation would be incompatible with the obligation to give a true and fair view. Cases of this sort are so exceptional that it would be misleading to link them in general to any particular contrast of activities. For example, the contrast between Schedule 9 and 9A companies (banking and insurance companies and groups) and other companies or between profit and not-for-profit undertakings is not sufficient of itself to justify non-consolidation. The different activities of undertakings included in the consolidation can better be shown by presenting segmental information rather than by excluding from consolidation the subsidiary undertakings with different activities.'[93]

Where a subsidiary is excluded from consolidation on these grounds, both the Act[94] and FRS 2 require it to be equity accounted.[95] Unlike some of the other exclusions, therefore, this is in essence a different manner of incorporating the company concerned in the group accounts, rather than excluding it altogether.

The previous rules in both UK law and SSAP 14 were not drafted in such a restrictive way. Subsidiaries were frequently not consolidated on the grounds that their accounts were prepared on entirely different bases of accounting from the rest of the group. An obvious example would be a group which owned a subsidiary in the banking or insurance sector which applied substantially different accounting policies from the rest of the group. In fact, there were a number of companies which took a broader view than this, and excluded subsidiaries which they viewed as being in different businesses in less extreme circumstances than those mentioned above; a common example was companies with finance subsidiaries.[96]

FRS 2 and the Companies Act require various general disclosures in respect of subsidiaries excluded from consolidation, which are discussed at 5.6 below. In addition to these general disclosures, the standard requires that, where subsidiaries have been excluded from consolidation because of different activities, their separate accounts should be included in the consolidated accounts. These can be presented in summary form unless the excluded undertakings account for more than 20% of any of the following: the group's operating profits; or its turnover; or its net assets. These amounts should be measured by including the excluded subsidiary undertakings.[97]

Where an excluded subsidiary undertaking is either:

(a)   a body corporate incorporated outside Great Britain which does not have an established place of business in Great Britain; or

(b)   an unincorporated undertaking

the Act requires its latest accounts (or group accounts) to be appended to the accounts delivered to the registrar. However, this does not require the preparation of accounts which would otherwise not be prepared; neither does it require the publication of accounts which would not otherwise be required to be published, but the reason for such accounts not being appended must be explained.[98] For example, a partnership excluded on these grounds might prepare accounts for its own purposes; however, these would not need to be appended provided the accounts delivered to the registrar contained a note to the effect that the partnership accounts were not appended as they were not required to be published. In the case of foreign companies, this means that, for example, the accounts of a Canadian company would have to be appended but not those of most US companies (since US companies, other than those with a SEC listing, are not required to publish their accounts).

5.3   Operating under severe restrictions

The provisions of the Companies Act which deal with this exclusion state that 'a subsidiary undertaking may be excluded from consolidation where ... severe long-term restrictions substantially hinder the exercise of the rights of the parent company over the assets or management of that undertaking'.[99] The Act specifies that the rights which are restricted must be rights in the absence of which the company would not be the parent company.

FRS 2 goes further and *requires* subsidiaries to be excluded from consolidation when these circumstances apply. The standard explains that this ground for exclusion ties in with its underlying concept of control as the basis for consolidation. Thus, where the restrictions amount to a loss of control, it would be misleading to continue to include the subsidiary in the consolidation. However, it emphasises that the exclusion should not be applied where only the prospect of restrictions exists, or if the restrictions are minor. The standard refers to the need for them to have 'a severe and restricting effect in practice in the long-term on the rights of the parent undertaking'. It quotes the case of a subsidiary undertaking which is subject to an insolvency procedure in the UK such that control over that undertaking may have passed to a designated official, e.g. an administrator, administrative receiver or liquidator, with the effect that severe long-term restrictions are in force. However, it states that a company voluntary arrangement does not necessarily lead to loss of control. Similarly, in some overseas jurisdictions even formal insolvency procedures may not amount to loss of control.[100]

Two companies which have not consolidated subsidiaries due to insolvency proceedings are Huntingdon Life Sciences and Creston Land and Estates, as shown below:

Extract 5.17: Huntingdon Life Sciences Group plc (1998)

Basis of consolidation [extract]

The consolidated accounts incorporate the accounts of the Company and each of its subsidiaries for the 12 months ended December 31, 1998. The Travers Morgan Group of Companies has not traded since February 1995 and although these companies are 100% owned by the Group, their assets have not been included since control of these companies is exercised by an administrator.

Extract 5.18: Creston Land and Estates plc (1996)

BASIS OF CONSOLIDATION [extract]

The group accounts consolidate the accounts of the company and all of its subsidiaries except those where severe long term restrictions substantially hinder the exercise of rights over the assets or management of the subsidiary undertaking. Where such restrictions exist a subsidiary undertaking is treated as a fixed asset investment in accordance with Financial Reporting Standard 2.

9   INVESTMENTS HELD AS FIXED ASSETS [extract]

During the year Co-ordinated Land and Estates Limited ("CLE") and its subsidiaries were put into creditors' voluntary liquidation. In addition, British Patent Glazing Limited was put, during the year, into administrative receivership.

Two companies which have invoked this rule in circumstances where insolvency procedures would not appear to have been in progress are shown in the following extracts:

Extract 5.19: London and Metropolitan plc (1997)

b)   BASIS OF CONSOLIDATION [extract]

The Company and other Group companies have been released from any financial liability in respect of certain subsidiaries' liabilities and borrowings. As a result of this, the Group has ceased to have any financial interest in the losses of these subsidiaries. As the prospect of the relevant subsidiaries ever making profits is extremely remote and as there are severe long term restrictions on the Group's interest in these subsidiaries, their results have not been consolidated.

34.   GROUP COMPANIES [extract]

During the year the Group disposed of its 99% subsidiary undertaking, Pont Royal SA, a company incorporated in France, with net liabilities of £19,300,000 for nil consideration.

For the reasons detailed in the Accounting Policies (Note 2b), the results of The Bicester Park Development Company Limited and Bettertrade Limited are not consolidated in the Group financial statements. For the same reasons, the results of Pont Royal SA had not been consolidated.

Summary financial information in respect of subsidiary undertakings not consolidated in the Group accounts is set out below.

	Capital and reserves as at 31 December 1997 £'000	Profit/(loss) for the year ended 31 December 1997 £'000
The Bicester Park Development Company Limited	(15,984)	312
Bettertrade Limited	—	—

During the year ended 31 December 1997 the Group received £120,000 from The Bicester Park Development Company Limited for the provision of development and project management services to that company. As at 31 December 1997 there were no balances outstanding between the Group and either of the above companies.

Extract 5.20: Regal Hotel Group PLC (1996)

BASIS OF CONSOLIDATION [extract]

The consolidated financial statements incorporate the financial statements of the Company and all of its subsidiaries, with the exception of Bramhope Limited.

11. INVESTMENTS IN SUBSIDIARIES [extract]

Bramhope Limited ceased to be treated as a consolidated subsidiary undertaking on 25th March 1993 in accordance with Financial Reporting Standard 2.

This was as a result of the severe long term restrictions placed on the Company's control over Bramhope Limited in having to accommodate the wishes of Bramhope's bankers.

Other circumstances which may justify non-consolidation on these grounds involve political unrest in the country in which the subsidiary is based. An example of this was to be found in the 1991 accounts of Booker set out below:

Extract 5.21: Booker plc (1991)

11 FIXED ASSET INVESTMENTS [extract]

	1991 £m	1990 £m
Attributable net asset value of subsidiary companies not consolidated at 31 December 1991	3.7	3.2
Reduction required under stated accounting policy	1.1	0.9
Balance sheet value 31 December 1991	2.6	2.3
Profit on ordinary activities before taxation attributable to parent company	1.6	1.7
Attributable profit after extraordinary items	1.4	1.2

Consolidation [extract]

Certain subsidiary undertakings operate in countries overseas where the amount of profit that may be remitted is restricted or where freedom of action may be limited. In the opinion of the directors, it would be misleading to consolidate these subsidiaries and the group share of their results is therefore included in profit only to the extent of remittances received. The group's total investment in these subsidiaries is shown as an asset at attributable net asset value either at the date from which this accounting policy was adopted for such companies adjusted for capital subsequently invested or withdrawn, or attributable net asset value at the balance sheet date, whichever is the lower amount.

The reduction to net asset value at the balance sheet date was presumably to recognise an impairment in value.

Another example was in the 1991 accounts of Low & Bonar in respect of its African subsidiaries shown below:

Extract 5.22: Low & Bonar PLC (1991)

(ii) Basis of consolidation [extract]

(b) The accounts of Group companies in Africa are not consolidated as the Directors consider the control of those companies by Low & Bonar PLC significantly impaired by severe long term restrictions.

6. Income from Fixed Asset Investments

	1991 **£000**	1990 £000
Income from shares in group companies not consolidated	**1,355**	683

13. Fixed Asset Investments [extract]

	£000
African interests: At 30 November 1990 and 30 November 1991 — Directors' valuation	**2,230**

29. Subsidiaries and Associates not Consolidated

	Accounting period	**% Owned**	**Profit after tax £000**	**1991** **Net assets £000**	Profit after tax £000	1990 Net assets £000
Subsidiaries						
Bonar Industries (Pty) Ltd	12 months to 30/11/91	**100**	**332**	**1,769**	483	2,253
Bonar (EA) Ltd	12 months to 31/08/91	**75**	**(142)**	**439**	(235)	570
Bonar Colwyn Ltd	12 months to 30/09/91	**90**	**172**	**1,390**	471	1,052
Bonar Plastics Ltd	12 months to 30/09/91	**72**	**41**	**183**	97	169
Bonar Industries (Pyt) Ltd	12 months to 31/08/91	**100**	**203**	**969**	285	1,551
Associate						
Tarpaulin Industries (WA) Ltd	12 months to 30/11/91	**40**	**(9)**	**254**	(13)	274

The required accounting treatment under FRS 2 in these circumstances is to 'freeze' the carrying value of the subsidiary at its equity amount at the time the restrictions came into force, and to carry it as a fixed asset investment. It should not accrue for any trading results thereafter as long as the restrictions remain, unless it is still able to exercise significant influence, in which case it should equity account for the subsidiary as if it were an associate. A provision for impairment in the value of the investment and any inter-company balances may also be needed.[101]

If the restrictions are subsequently removed, the trading results of the subsidiary which accrued during the period when the investment was carried at a frozen amount will need to be accounted for. FRS 2 requires that they be dealt with as a separately disclosed item in the profit and loss account in the year in which control is resumed, along with the release of any previous provision for impairment.[102]

The disclosures required in respect of subsidiaries excluded from consolidation on these grounds are discussed at 5.6 below.

5.4   Held for subsequent resale

The Companies Act allows a subsidiary undertaking to be excluded from the consolidated accounts when 'the interest of the parent company is held exclusively with a view to subsequent resale and the undertaking has not previously been included in consolidated group accounts of the parent company'.[103] This reason cannot be used to justify exclusion of a subsidiary which the parent company has previously consolidated and decides to sell some years after its acquisition; it should be used only for those cases where a group acquires a subsidiary with the intention of selling it on soon thereafter. The Act, however, does not define what is meant by 'held exclusively for subsequent resale'.

FRS 2 supplies such a definition, saying that it is

(a)   an interest for which a purchaser has been identified or is being sought, and which is reasonably expected to be disposed of within approximately one year of its date of acquisition; or

(b)   an interest that was acquired as a result of the enforcement of a security, unless the interest has become part of the continuing activities of the group or the holder acts as if it intends the interest to become so.[104]

As with subsidiaries subject to severe restrictions, FRS 2 goes further than the Act by *requiring* subsidiaries to be excluded when these circumstances apply.[105] Instead, the standard requires that the investment should be carried in the group balance sheet as a current asset, at the lower of cost and net realisable value.[106]

Examples of situations where subsidiaries have been excluded from consolidation as they are held for subsequent resale are shown in the following extracts:

Extract 5.23: Fine Art Developments p.l.c. (1996)

13   INVESTMENTS HELD FOR RESALE

The group owns the whole of the issued share capital of Greeting Card House Limited (formerly Flaxcase Limited), a holding company which in turn owns the whole of the issued share capital of Flaxcase Limited (formerly Macsel Greetings Limited), a greeting card wholesaler. Greeting Card House Limited and Flaxcase are both registered in England and Wales.

The group assumed management control of Greeting Card House and Flaxcase on 7 March 1996. Those companies have been excluded from consolidation as the group's interest is held exclusively with a view to subsequent resale and accordingly the investment has been accounted for as a current asset, at cost. No material trading transactions with other group companies took place during the period from acquisition to 31 March 1996.

Flaxcase and Greeting Card House prepare accounts to 31 January although audited accounts to 31 January 1996 are not yet available. The unaudited management accounts of Flaxcase show a deficit on capital and reserves of £1.4m at 31 January 1996 and a loss for the year then ended of £0.7m. The unaudited management accounts of Greeting Card House show capital and reserves of £0.2m at 31 January 1996 and a loss for the year then ended of £nil.

Extract 5.24: Barclays PLC (1997)

46   Principal subsidiary undertakings [extract]

In 1992, the Group acquired a 100% interest in Imry Holdings Limited (Imry), a company registered in England, as a result of enforcing security against a loan to Chester Holdings (UK) Limited, the parent company of Imry. The interest was held exclusively with a view to subsequent resale and therefore was not consolidated. The assets of Imry Holdings have been sold in two parts. The first resulted in a provision release of £25m in March 1997, which was reported in the first half results. A second sale was agreed in December 1997 and is due to be completed in February 1998. This transfers Imry's remaining significant assets to a joint venture in which the Group has a 50% interest. This transaction resulted in a provision release of £19m in December 1997. The companies which own the assets were still within the ownership of the Group at 31st December 1997 but have not been consolidated pending disposal or liquidation. Had Imry been consolidated in 1996 or 1997, there would have been no material effect on total assets, shareholders' funds or profit before tax of the Group.

Imry's accounts are made up to 31st March. At 31st December 1997, the unaudited consolidated capital and reserves of Imry (including the Imry Jersey Limited preference shares held by the Group) amounted to £71m (1996 £81m) and its total assets amounted to £74m (1996 £326m). The unaudited loss before taxation of Imry for the 12 months ended 31st December was £15m (1996 loss £8m, 1995 profit £8m). There were outstandings of £nil (1996 £94m) due to the Group, secured by a fixed and floating charge on the assets of Imry. Interest payments by Imry to the Bank in the year amounted to £3m (1996 £7m). Except as noted above, there were no other material transactions between Imry and the Group during the year.

One question which can be significant in some circumstances is how to account for the interest cost of financing a temporary investment in a subsidiary; if no profits are consolidated during the period of ownership then the financing cost will result in the group reporting a loss. Where the subsidiary to be sold has been acquired as part of a group then this should not cause a problem because FRS 7 requires that the fair value to be attributed to the subsidiary should be based on the estimated sales proceeds, discounted to obtain the net present value at date of acquisition, if material (see 2.4.3 G of Chapter 6). This does not offend the requirement of FRS 2 to carry such investments at cost, because in this case cost is derived from an allocation of the total purchase price on the basis of their fair value to the acquiring company. The subsequent unwinding of the discount will be credited to the profit and loss account thereby offsetting any interest cost of financing such a temporary investment.

An example of this can be seen in the 1996 accounts of De La Rue:

Extract 5.25: De La Rue plc (1996)

Basis of consolidation [extract]

A number of subsidiaries which were acquired as part of the acquisition of Portals Group plc in the year ended 31 March 1995 were excluded from consolidation because they were held exclusively with a view to subsequent resale. These subsidiaries were recorded as assets held for disposal within current assets. In the year, the Group has disposed of virtually all of its investments in these businesses.

13 Assets held for disposal [extract]

Group	**£m**
At 1 April 1995	**160.0**
Unwinding of discounted value of expected proceeds of assets held for disposal	**4.0**
Cash inflow from disposals	**(141.7)**
Cash payments to businesses held for resale	**15.4**
Retained interests in businesses sold	**(6.6)**
Further goodwill arising on the acquisition of Portals Group plc	**(21.3)**
At 31 March 1996	**9.8**

Assets held for disposal at 1 April 1995 included the Group's investment in businesses and properties, all of which were owned by Portals Group plc or its subsidiaries when the Group acquired Portals Group plc, and were held exclusively with a view to resale. In the year, the Group has disposed of its investment in these businesses and certain properties. Assets held for disposal at 31 March 1996 include properties, which following consultation with professional advisers, are held at the directors' valuation of anticipated sales proceeds.

5.5   Immateriality

As indicated above, the Companies Act allows subsidiaries to be excluded from consolidation where they are immaterial in aggregate. FRS 2 does not contain a specific ground for exclusion on this basis because the standard only deals with material items.[107]

One company which had excluded a subsidiary for this reason was Alliance Trust in its 1994 accounts, as shown below:

> *Extract 5.26: The Alliance Trust PLC (1994)*
>
> **1.**   **ACCOUNTING POLICIES** [extract]
>
> f.   The accounts of Alliance Trust (Finance) Limited have not been consolidated with those of the Company as the directors consider that the amounts involved are not material and that their inclusion would detract from the clarity of the accounts in respect of the principal activity of the Company as an authorised investment trust. A separate statement of affairs of Alliance Trust (Finance) limited is on page 23.

The value attributable to the subsidiary amounted to £23,028m out of total investments of £1,042,252m and this was presumably why the directors considered the subsidiary not to be material (although it seems odd that a summarised profit and loss account and summarised balance sheet should be given for something that is considered to be not material). However, this treatment attracted the attention of the Review Panel following the company's approach to the Stock Exchange for guidance on the question of consolidation. Although not explicitly stated by the Review Panel it would appear that it was of the view that the subsidiary was material and therefore should have been consolidated. The Review Panel ruling does not state why it thought it was material but it may have been because of the impact on the revenue account or on particular assets and liabilities. Accordingly, the 1995 accounts were prepared on this basis, as shown below:

> *Extract 5.27: The Alliance Trust PLC (1995)*
>
> **REPORT OF THE DIRECTORS** [extract]
>
> The consolidated accounts, which are provided for the first time this year, include the results of our banking and savings subsidiary, Alliance Trust (Finance) Limited. These have been produced in the light of developing accounting standards, which will lead shortly to adoption of a Statement of Recommended Practice for investment trusts, and after discussion with the Financial Reporting Review Panel, the Company having raised the issue of consolidation with the Stock Exchange. Full information on the subsidiary had previously been included separately within the accounts. Relevant information continues to be given in note 12.

Clearly whether a subsidiary is material or not is a matter of judgement and companies should therefore consider carefully whether a subsidiary is immaterial or not before excluding it from the consolidated accounts.

5.6   General disclosure requirements in respect of excluded subsidiaries

The Companies Act requires the following information to be given in respect of each subsidiary excluded from the consolidated accounts:

(a)   its name;[108]

(b)   the reasons for excluding it;[109] and

(c)   the aggregate amount of its share capital and reserves as at the end of its financial year and of its profit or loss for that year.[110]

The information described in (c) above is not required if the subsidiary is equity accounted or if less than 50% of its nominal value of shares is held and it does not publish its balance sheet anywhere in the world.[111]

FRS 2 requires that in addition to the information required by the Companies Act the following information should be disclosed:

(a)   particulars of the balances between the excluded subsidiary undertakings and the rest of the group;

(b)   the nature and extent of transactions of the excluded subsidiary undertakings with the rest of the group; and

(c)   unless the excluded subsidiary is equity accounted, any amounts included in the consolidated accounts in respect of:

  (i)   dividends received and receivable from that undertaking;

  (ii) any write-down in the period in respect of the investment in that undertaking or amounts due from that undertaking.[112]

These disclosures should be given for each excluded subsidiary. However, the standard states that 'if the information about excluded subsidiary undertakings is more appropriately presented for a sub-unit of the group comprising more than one excluded subsidiary undertaking, the disclosures may be made on an aggregate basis. Any individual sub-unit for these disclosures is to include only subsidiary undertakings excluded under the same sub-section of section 229 [of the Act]. Individual disclosures should be made for any excluded subsidiary undertaking, including its sub-group where relevant, that alone accounts for more than 20% of any one or more of operating profits, turnover or net assets of the group. The group amounts should be measured by including all excluded subsidiary undertakings.'[113]

6   COMPARISON WITH IASC AND US PRONOUNCEMENTS

6.1   IASC

The relevant international accounting standard is IAS 27 – *Consolidated Financial Statements and Accounting for Investments in Subsidiaries*. This simply defines a subsidiary as 'an enterprise which is controlled by another enterprise (known as the parent)'. Control is defined as 'the power to govern the financial and operating policies of an enterprise so as to obtain benefits from its activities'.[114]

Control is presumed to exist if the parent owns, directly or indirectly, a majority of the voting rights in the enterprise unless, in exceptional circumstances, it can be clearly demonstrated that such ownership does not constitute control. Control is also considered to exist even when the parent does not own a majority of the voting rights when there is:

(a)   power over more than one half of the voting rights by virtue of an agreement with other investors;

(b)   power to govern the financial and operating policies of the enterprise under a statute or an agreement;

(c)   power to appoint or remove the majority of the members of the board of directors or equivalent governing body; or

(d)   power to cast the majority of votes at meetings of the board of directors or equivalent governing body.[115]

The only exemption in IAS 27 from producing consolidated accounts is for intermediate holding companies. A parent that is a wholly owned subsidiary need not produce consolidated accounts. The exemption is also available to a parent which is virtually wholly owned (it is suggested in the standard that this will often mean that the parent owns 90% or more of the voting power) provided that it obtains the approval of the owners of the minority interest.[116] A parent which uses this exemption should disclose the reasons why consolidated accounts have not been presented together with the bases on which subsidiaries are accounted for in its separate financial statements. The name and registered office of its parent that publishes consolidates accounts should also be disclosed.[117]

The grounds for non-consolidation of subsidiaries are similar to those in the UK. It is not possible to exclude from consolidation those subsidiaries which undertake dissimilar activities;[118] a subsidiary should only be excluded for consolidation when:

(a)   control is intended to be temporary because the subsidiary is acquired and held exclusively with a view to its subsequent disposal in the near future; or

(b)   it operates under severe long-term restrictions which significantly impair its ability to transfer funds to the parent.[119]

The consolidation procedures required by IAS 27 are principally similar to those required in the UK. The consolidated accounts should be prepared using uniform accounting policies for like transactions and other events in similar circumstances. If it is not practicable to use uniform accounting policies in preparing the consolidated accounts, that fact should be disclosed together with the proportions of the items in the consolidated financial statements to which the different accounting policies have been applied.[120]

When the accounts used in the consolidation are drawn up to different reporting dates, adjustments should be made for the effects of significant transactions or other events that occur between those dates and the date of the parent's accounts. In any case the difference between reporting dates should be no more than three months.[121] Unlike FRS 2, IAS 27 does not require any disclosure where coterminous year ends are not used.

Intragroup balances and intragroup transactions and resulting unrealised profits should be eliminated in full. Unrealised losses resulting from intragroup transactions should be eliminated unless cost cannot be recovered.[122]

Minority interests should be presented in the consolidated balance sheet separately from liabilities and the parent shareholders' equity. Minority interests in the income of the group should also be separately presented.[123] One difference from FRS 2 is where there are losses applicable to the minority which exceeds the minority interest in the equity of the subsidiary. IAS 27 indicates that the excess should be charged against the majority interest except to the extent that the minority has a binding obligation to, and is able to, make good the losses,[124] which was the position taken by SSAP 14 (see 1.3.3 above). Another difference is that IAS 22 – *Business Combinations* adopts as its benchmark treatment that any minority interest arising on an acquisition should be calculated based on the pre-acquisition carrying amounts of the net assets of the subsidiary, although it does allow the use of fair values as an alternative.[125] As discussed at 1.3.4 above, FRS 2 requires the minority interest to be based on the fair values attributed to the net assets of the subsidiary.

In addition to the specific disclosures mentioned earlier above, IAS 27 requires the following disclosures to be made in consolidated accounts:[126]

(a)   a listing of significant subsidiaries including the name, country of incorporation or residence, proportion of ownership interest and, if different, proportion of voting power held;

(b)   where applicable:

     (i)   the reasons for not consolidating a subsidiary;

     (ii)   the nature of the relationship between the parent and a subsidiary of which the parent does not own, directly or indirectly through subsidiaries, more than one half of the voting power;

     (iii)   the name of an enterprise in which more than one half of the voting power is owned, directly or indirectly through subsidiaries, but which, because of the absence of control, is not a subsidiary; and

     (iv)   the effect of the acquisition and disposal of subsidiaries on the financial position at the reporting date, the results for the reporting period and on the corresponding amounts for the preceding period.

6.2   US

The basic statement which outlines the US approach to the consolidation of subsidiaries is ARB 51 – *Consolidated financial statements* – which was issued in 1959. The basic criterion on which the definition of a subsidiary rests is the holding of a controlling financial interest in it. Paragraph 2 of ARB 51 (as amended by SFAS 94) goes on: 'The usual condition for a controlling financial interest is ownership of a majority voting interest, and, therefore, as a general rule ownership by one company, directly or indirectly, of over fifty percent of the outstanding voting shares of another company is a condition pointing towards consolidation.'

A subsidiary is also described in APB 18 (which deals with equity accounting) as 'a corporation which is controlled, directly or indirectly, by another corporation. The usual condition for control is ownership of a majority (over 50%) of the outstanding voting stock. The power to control may also exist with a lesser degree of ownership, for example, by contract, lease, agreement with other stockholders or by court decree.'[127]

This definition excludes entities which are controlled through significant minority ownership. Hence, entities which qualify as 'subsidiary undertakings' due to a participating interest with dominant influence or unified management (see 1.2.2 E above) would not always be regarded as subsidiaries in the US.

The SEC has a definition of subsidiary, based on control and risk, which is applicable to its registrants. Although the SEC has not developed a list of criteria that provides definitive guidance for determining when an entity should be consolidated, the SEC staff will look to the substance of a parent–subsidiary relationship rather than the legal form of an equity holding. They have cited cases where consolidation of a less-than majority-owned subsidiary has been required when the parent essentially has the ability to control the subsidiary.

The US has also moved towards full consolidation with segmental disclosure as a response to diversified activities. SFAS 94 was issued in October 1987, making it no longer possible to avoid consolidating a subsidiary because of 'nonhomogeneous' operations. The statement explains its reasoning as follows:

'The managerial, operational and financial ties that bind an enterprise into a single economic unit are stronger than the differences between its lines of business. ... Similarly, differences between the varied operations of a group of affiliated corporations that constitutes an economic and financial whole do not preclude including them all in consolidated accounts. Those differences also do not make the equity method a valid substitute for consolidation of majority owned subsidiaries.'[128]

Accordingly, the only grounds for non-consolidation of subsidiaries are where control is likely to be temporary, control does not rest with the majority shareholder or if the subsidiary operates under foreign exchange restrictions, controls or other governmental imposed uncertainties which cast significant doubt on the parent's ability to control the subsidiary.

The FASB is currently undertaking a project involving several groups of issues, one of which is concerned with developing a concept of reporting entity and related conceptual matters and applying these to reach conclusions on the broad issue of consolidation policy and on specific issues of consolidation techniques. In October 1995 it issued an exposure draft – *Consolidated Financial Statements: Policy and Procedures* which proposed that a parent should consolidate all entities that it controls unless control is temporary at the time the entity becomes a subsidiary. For purposes of that requirement, control of another entity was to be represented by the power to use or direct the use of the individual assets of another entity in essentially the same ways as the controlling entity can use its own assets. Subsequent to public hearings and redeliberations, the FASB decided to retain most of the basic provisions of the exposure draft but continued to deliberate issues relating to transition, definition of control and special purpose entities.

In August 1997, the FASB reconsidered its priorities and decided to focus first on completing the consolidation policy portion of the project, including the definition of control of an entity. As a result, in February 1999 it issued a revised exposure draft with the same title as before, but this statement does not consider issues about consolidation procedures that were addressed in the initial exposure draft. Like before, under the revised proposals, a parent is required to consolidate all entities that it controls unless control is temporary at the time the entity becomes a subsidiary. However, for purposes of that requirement, control of an entity is now a non-shared decision-making ability of an entity to direct the policies and management that guide the ongoing activities of another entity, so as to increase its benefits and limit its losses from that other entity's activities. The proposed statement would preclude consolidation of a new subsidiary if a parent's control is temporary at the date that control is obtained. Control of a newly acquired subsidiary would be considered temporary if at the date of acquisition the parent either had committed to a plan to relinquish control of that subsidiary or was obligated to do so and it was likely that loss of control would occur within one year. However, control would also be considered temporary if at the date of acquisition circumstances beyond management's control were likely to require more than one year to complete the ultimate disposition.

The exposure draft provides guidance for applying its definition of control. That guidance includes certain situations, which are identified in paragraphs 18 and 21 of this proposed statement, that would lead to rebuttable presumptions of control. They are those circumstances in which an entity:

(a) has a majority voting interest in the election of a corporation's governing body or a right to appoint a majority of the members of its governing body;

(b) has a large minority voting interest in the election of a corporation's governing body and no other party or organised group of parties has a significant voting interest;

(c) has a unilateral ability to (1) obtain a majority voting interest in the election of a corporation's governing body or (2) obtain a right to appoint a majority of the corporation's governing body through the present ownership of convertible securities or other rights that are currently exercisable at the option of the holder and the expected benefit from converting those securities or exercising that right exceeds its expected cost; or

(d)   is the only general partner in a limited partnership and no other partner or
organised group of partners has the current ability to dissolve the limited
partnership or otherwise remove the general partner.

Appendix A to the exposure draft contains implementation guidance, including a
number of illustrative examples of the application of the definition and
description of control of an entity.

The proposed statement is intended to be effective for financial statements for
annual periods beginning after 15 December 1999 and all interim periods in the
year of adoption.

References

1   CA 85, s 227(2)–(3).
2   *Ibid.*, s 227(4).
3   FRS 2, *Accounting for subsidiary undertakings*, ASB, July 1992, para. 1.
4   *Ibid.*, para. 18.
5   EC Seventh Directive, Article 1(1)(d)(aa).
6   *Ibid.*, Article 12.
7   CA 85, s 259(1).
8   *Ibid.*, s 258(1)–(2).
9   CA 85 (original), s 736(1).
10 CA 85, Sch. 10A, para. 2(1).
11 *Ibid.*, paras. 5–8.
12 *Ibid.*, para. 3(1).
13 *Ibid.*, para. 4(1)–(2).
14 Companies Bill, Clause 19, s 258(2).
15 CA 85, s 260(1).
16 *Ibid.*, s 260(3).
17 *Ibid.*, s 260(2).
18 *Ibid.*, Sch. 10A, para. 4(1), (3).
19 FRS 2, para. 7.
20 *Ibid.*, paras. 69–73.
21 *Ibid.*, para. 72.
22 *Ibid.*, para. 73.
23 *Ibid.*, para. 34.
24 *Ibid.*, para. 12.
25 *Ibid.*, para. 62.
26 *Ibid.*, para. 63.
27 *Ibid.*, para. 67.
28 ED 50, *Consolidated accounts*, ASC, June 1990, para. 26.
29 CA 85, Sch. 4A, paras. 9(2) and 17(2).
30 IAS 22, *Business Combinations*, IASC, September 1998, paras. 32–35.
31 R. M. Wilkins, *Group Accounts*, Second edition, London: ICAEW, 1979, p.170.
32 CA 85, Sch. 4A, para. 6(3).
33 SSAP 14, *Group accounts*, ASC, September 1978, para. 34.
34 FRS 2, para. 37.
35 ED 50, para. 28.
36 *Ibid.*, para. 33.
37 FRS 2, paras. 38 and 82.
38 *Ibid.*, paras. 37 and 81.
39 *Ibid.*, paras. 51 and 90.
40 *Ibid.*, paras. 52 and 91.
41 *Ibid.*, paras. 39 and 83.
42 *Ibid.*, para. 80.
43 ICAEW, *Recommendation VII*.
44 CA 85, Sch. 4A.
45 SSAP 14, para. 3.
46 FRS 2, para. 5.
47 ED 50, para. 85.
48 FRRP PN 54, 2 September 1998.
49 FRS 2, para. 40.
50 CA 85, Sch. 4A, para. 3(1).
51 *Ibid.*, para. 3(3).
52 *Ibid.*, para. 3(2).
53 FRS 2, para. 41.
54 CA 85, s 223(5).

55 *Ibid.*, Sch. 4A, para. 2(2).
56 FRS 2, para. 43.
57 *Ibid.*
58 *Ibid.*, para. 44.
59 CA 85, Sch. 5, para. 19
60 ED 50, para. 36.
61 FRS 2, paras. 39 and 83.
62 CA 85, Sch. 4A, para. 6
63 FRS 2, para. 39.
64 *Ibid.*, para. 83.
65 SSAP 14, para. 19.
66 CA 85 (original), s 229(2).
67 CA 85, s 228.
68 European Economic Area Act 1993, s 2, states that references to the European Economic Community in earlier legislation, such as the Companies Act 1985, is to be interpreted as being to a reference to the European Economic Area.
69 CA 85, ss. 248–249.
70 FRS 2, para. 21.
71 CA 85, s 228(1).
72 *Ibid.*, s 228(3).
73 *Ibid.*, s 228(2)(a).
74 *Ibid.*, s 228(2)(c).
75 *Ibid.*, s 228(2)(d).
76 *Ibid.*, s 228(2)(e)–(f).
77 *Ibid.*, Sch. 5, paras. (1)–(6).
78 CA 85, s 248(4).
79 *Ibid.*, s 249(3).
80 *Ibid.*, s 249(4)
81 In March 1999, the DTI issued a Consultative Document, *Raising the Threshold Levels for SMEs*, outlining proposals to raise the financial limits up to the level permitted by EC law. There is also a proposal that the limits under the EC Accounting Directives should be increased by 25%. If that is adopted the new UK financial limits would be increased to those higher levels. This would mean that the limits would be, for turnover, £19.2m net (or £23.04m gross) and, for the balance sheet total, £9.6m net (or £11.52m gross).
82 CA 85, s 247(5).
83 *Ibid.*, s 249(5).
84 *Ibid.*, s 249(1)–(2).
85 *Ibid.*, s 249(1)(a).
86 FRS 2, para. 22.
87 ED 50, para. 91.
88 CA 85, s 229(2)–(4).
89 FRS 2, para. 25.
90 *Ibid.*, para. 78(b).
91 CA 85, s 229(4).
92 *Ibid.*, Sch. 9, Part II, para. 1.
93 FRS 2, para. 78(e).
94 CA 85, Sch. 4A, para. 18.
95 FRS 2, para. 30.
96 See earlier editions of the book for examples of companies adopting such a practice.
97 FRS 2, para. 31(d).
98 CA 85, s 243.
99 *Ibid.*, s 229(3)(a).
100 FRS 2, para. 78(c).
101 *Ibid.*, para. 27.
102 *Ibid.*, para. 28.
103 CA 85 s 229(3)(c).

104 FRS 2, para. 11.
105 *Ibid.*, para. 25(b).
106 *Ibid.*, para. 29.
107 *Ibid.*, para. 78(a).
108 CA 85, Sch. 5, para. 15(2).
109 *Ibid.*, para. 15(4).
110 *Ibid.*, para. 17.
111 *Ibid.*, para. 17(2).
112 FRS 2, para. 31.
113 *Ibid.*, para. 32.
114 IAS 27, *Consolidated Financial Statements and Accounting for Investments in Subsidiaries*, IASC, Reformatted November 1994, para. 6.
115 *Ibid.*, para. 12.
116 *Ibid.*, paras. 8 and 10.
117 *Ibid.*, para. 8.
118 *Ibid.*, para. 14.
119 *Ibid.*, para. 13.
120 *Ibid.*, para. 21.
121 *Ibid.*, para. 19.
122 *Ibid.*, para. 17.
123 *Ibid.*, para. 26.
124 *Ibid.*, para. 27.
125 IAS 22, paras. 32–35.
126 IAS 27, para. 32.
127 APB 18, *The Equity Method of Accounting for Investments in Common Stock*, AICPA, March 1971, para. 3.
128 SFAS 94, *Consolidation of All Majority-owned Subsidiaries*, FASB, October 1987, paras. 30 and 31.

Chapter 6   Business combinations and disposals

1   INTRODUCTION

Chapter 5 deals with the preparation of consolidated accounts by a parent undertaking, but is restricted to issues such as when such accounts should be prepared, what entities should be considered to be part of the group for the purposes of inclusion therein, and how such entities should be dealt with in the consolidated accounts. This chapter deals with those situations where the group structure changes, through entities either joining or leaving the group.

Business combinations is the generic term for the transactions which result in one company joining a group by becoming the subsidiary of another. In accounting terms there are two distinctly different forms of reporting the effects of such an event, referred to in the UK as acquisition accounting and merger accounting respectively.

The two methods of accounting look at business combinations through quite different eyes. An acquisition is seen as the absorption of the target into the clutches of the predator; there is continuity only of the holding company, in the sense that only the post-acquisition results of the target are reported as earnings of the group, and the comparative figures remain those of the holding company (and any previously held subsidiaries). In contrast, a merger is seen as the uniting of the interests of two formerly distinct shareholder groups, and in order to present continuity of both entities there is retrospective restatement to show the group as if the companies had always been together, by combining the results of both companies pre- and post-combination and also by restatement of the comparatives. The difficulty for accountants, however, has been how to translate this difference in philosophy into criteria which permit particular transactions to be categorised as being of one type or the other.

There have been several successive attempts to distinguish between the circumstances when each of these methods is appropriate, culminating in the issue of FRS 6 – *Acquisitions and mergers* – in September 1994. In addition, the Companies Act, which incorporates the requirements of the EC Seventh Directive, also sets forth qualifying conditions for merger accounting. In December 1998 the ASB published for public comment a Discussion Paper – *Business Combinations*. This paper was not developed by the ASB but merely reprinted a Position Paper prepared by G4+1, the international group of representatives of the standard-setting bodies of Australia, Canada, New Zealand, the UK and the USA, together with the IASC. This paper proposes that there should only be one method of accounting for business combinations, acquisitions accounting, and that merger accounting should be banned. Although the ASB has acknowledged that there is no general demand for a revision of FRS 6, it has indicated that if other countries ban merger accounting, then the subject would be very likely to come under review. We disagree with the proposals in the paper and think it would be a retrograde step if the ASB were to amend FRS 6 to prohibit the adoption of merger accounting.

FRS 2 – *Accounting for subsidiary undertakings* – which is the general accounting standard on consolidated accounts in the UK, also deals with some aspects which are relevant to business combinations, and there are currently two further accounting standards which deal in detail with business combinations. FRS 7 – *Fair values in acquisition accounting* – was published in September 1994 and FRS 10 – *Goodwill and intangible assets* – was issued in December 1997. This latter standard is dealt with in Chapter 10 at 3.4. The other standards, and their predecessors, are all explained in this chapter at 2 below.

The other possible change in the composition of a group involves the disposal of a group company. There is no specific accounting standard in the UK dealing with this issue. It is generally covered in FRS 2, although FRS 10 is also of some relevance. Again, the changes to the Companies Act as a result of the EC Seventh Directive also had some implications. The issues relating to disposals are dealt with at 3 below.

The chapter also deals with some issues relating to group reorganisations at 4 below. These involve the restructuring of the relationships between companies in a group by, for example, setting up a new holding company, changing the direct ownership of a subsidiary within the group, or transferring businesses from one company to another because of a process of divisionalisation. In principle, most of such changes should have no impact on the consolidated financial statements (provided there are no minority interests affected), because they are purely internal and cannot affect the group when it is being portrayed as a single entity. However, all such transactions can have a significant impact on the financial statements of the individual companies in the group.

2 BUSINESS COMBINATIONS

2.1 Historical development of rules on the criteria for mergers and acquisitions

2.1.1 ED 3

In the UK, the first pronouncement on the subject was ED 3, issued by the ASC in 1971. In the event, ED 3 was never proceeded with, and was eventually withdrawn nearly ten years later. One of the reasons why the ASC did not persist with it was that there was a school of thought which held that merger accounting was in fact contrary to company law; this is because the mechanics of the method require the shares issued by the holding company as consideration for the shares of the subsidiary to be recorded at their nominal value rather than their fair value, and this was thought to be in possible contravention of the Companies Act rules on share premium account. This legal doubt was eventually confirmed in a tax case, *Shearer v Bercain*,[1] in 1980, and this prevented any further progress towards an accounting standard until the law was amended to facilitate merger accounting by introducing variations to the rules on share premium account (described as 'merger relief').

2.1.2 Merger relief

In order to be able to record shares issued at their nominal value, and the cost of an investment in a subsidiary acquired in exchange for these shares at the same amount, it is necessary to satisfy the requirements of what is now section 131 of the Companies Act 1985. This is the part in the Act which was originally introduced in the Companies Act 1981 to remove the obstacle to merger accounting which was revealed in the case of *Shearer v Bercain*, as discussed above.

The section broadly relieves companies from the basic requirement to set up a share premium account in respect of equity shares issued in exchange for shares in another company in the course of a transaction which results in the issuing company securing at least a 90% holding in the equity shares of the other company. (This paraphrases the words in the Act, and the precise wording should be referred to in order to ensure that any particular transaction falls within its terms.) In addition there are further provisions with a similar purpose which apply to shares issued in the course of a group reconstruction.

The rules on merger relief and those on merger accounting are frequently confused with each other. However, not only are they based on the satisfaction of different criteria, they in fact have quite distinct purposes. Merger accounting is a form of financial reporting which applies to business combinations, but although the merger relief provisions were brought in to facilitate it, merger relief is purely a legal matter to do with the maintenance of capital for the protection of creditors and has very little to do with accounting per se. Moreover, merger relief may be available under transactions which are accounted for as acquisitions, rather than mergers, and the two are not interdependent in that sense.

There are some differences of legal opinion as to whether merger relief is in fact *compulsory* when the conditions of section 131 are met, or whether it is optional. The Act says that where the conditions are met, then section 130 does not apply to the premiums on the shares issued. Section 130 is the basic requirement to set up a share premium account where shares are issued at a premium and therefore some people argue that the effect of this relief is simply to make section 130 optional rather than mandatory, but others take the view that it makes it illegal to set up a share premium account. The most common treatment adopted by those who qualify for merger relief but account for the transaction as an acquisition has in fact been to regard the issue as having taken place at fair value, but to record a 'merger reserve' rather than a share premium account.

On the other hand, some companies record the transaction in their individual company financial statements based on the nominal value of the shares issued, the merger reserve only arising in the consolidated financial statements where it is used for writing off the goodwill on the acquisition. One company which adopts such a treatment is Glynwed International, as indicated below:

Extract 6.1: Glynwed International plc (1998)

1.   Accounting policies

Acquisitions [extract]

In the Company accounts, where advantage can be taken of the merger relief rules, shares issued as consideration for acquisitions are accounted for at nominal value.

On the face of it, such a treatment is not allowed since paragraphs 11 and 45 of FRS 4 – *Capital instruments* –require the net proceeds received on the issue of shares to be credited to shareholders' funds, based on the fair value of the consideration. This appears to remove the 'nominal value' option except where the shares have been issued as part of a business combination that is accounted for as a merger, although paragraph 3 of Appendix I to the standard which deals with legal requirements might suggest otherwise as it states that nothing in the standard affects the availability of merger relief under section 131 of the Act. Similarly, Appendix I to FRS 6 states that the requirements of that standard do 'not deal with the form of accounting to be used in the acquiring or issuing company's own accounts and in particular does not restrict the reliefs available under sections 131–133 of the Companies Act'.[2] We therefore do not consider that the ASB can have intended to ban this practice, and in our view it remains acceptable.

2.1.3   ED 31

Once the legal obstacle was removed, the ASC was able to continue the development of an accounting standard to distinguish between the two types of business combination, and ED 31 – *Accounting for acquisitions and mergers* – was issued in October 1982. The exposure draft put forward a new concept as the guiding principle as to what was a merger – that no material resources should leave the group.[3] This contrasted with the philosophy pursued by ED 3, which was based on a notion of 'continuing ownership in a continuing business'.[4]

2.1.4   SSAP 23

ED 31 was eventually converted into a standard – SSAP 23 – issued by the ASC in April 1985. It continued to use the principle of 'no material resources leaving the group' as its central point of reference for defining a merger, and laid down the following detailed criteria for permitting a business combination to be treated as a merger:

(a)   the business combination results from an offer to the holders of all equity shares and the holders of all voting shares which are not already held by the offeror; and

(b)   the offeror has secured, as a result of the offer, a holding of (i) at least 90% of all equity shares (taking each class of equity separately) and (ii) the shares carrying at least 90% of the votes of the offeree; and

(c)   immediately prior to the offer, the offeror does not hold (i) 20% or more of all equity shares of the offeree (taking each class of equity separately), or (ii) shares carrying 20% or more of the votes of the offeree; and

(d)   not less than 90% of the fair value of the total consideration given for the equity share capital (including that given for shares already held) is in the form of equity share capital; not less than 90% of the fair value of the total consideration given for voting non-equity share capital (including that given for shares already held) is in the form of equity and/or voting non-equity share capital.[5]

The standard made merger accounting *optional* when the criteria were met, whereas under ED 31, satisfaction of the criteria was expressed as leading to the *mandatory* use of merger accounting.

The SSAP 23 rules, therefore, depended very much on the form of the transaction being undertaken, and many of its critics were concerned about the ease with which it was possible to vary the form in order to bring a transaction within these rules. For example, the '20% prior holding' rule could be circumvented by selling any holding in excess of that limit to a third party (such as a merchant bank) immediately before making the offer and then acquiring it again in the course of the general offer. Also, cash consideration could, in theory at least, be disguised as equity by issuing redeemable preference shares (which could be brought within the equity definition by giving them theoretical rights to participate beyond a specified amount in a distribution) as part of the consideration and then redeeming them a short time later, so that in substance the consideration was in cash.

A more widespread ploy was the use of 'vendor rights' or 'vendor placings' as a means of coming within the merger criteria although still offering cash to the vendors. This involved offering shares to the vendor in exchange for his shares in the company being acquired, but with a side arrangement where, if the vendor preferred to receive cash, the shares would be placed either with the acquirer's own shareholders (vendor rights) or with third parties (vendor placings) and the proceeds passed on to the vendors.

2.1.5 Companies Act 1989

The implementation of the EC Seventh Directive on Company Law in the Companies Act 1989 to some extent restricted the ability of UK companies to apply merger accounting. Article 20 of the Directive sets out the qualifying conditions for merger accounting, and this disqualifies transactions where the consideration includes a cash payment exceeding 10% of the nominal value of the shares issued to effect the business combination. Although this looked superficially similar to the rule in SSAP 23 that at least 90% of the fair value of the consideration must be in the form of equity share capital, there were two important differences.

The first is that the Seventh Directive refers to the *nominal* value of the shares issued, rather than their *fair* value in setting the 10% limit. Since shares cannot be issued at a discount, this limit would never be wider than the SSAP 23 equivalent, and would often be much narrower; the extent of this restriction depended on how much higher was the fair value of the predator's shares compared with their nominal value.

The other difference is that the Seventh Directive rule is expressed in terms of the 10%, and refers to cash, whereas the SSAP 23 equivalent required at least 90% to be in the form of equity. Other forms of consideration, such as loan stock, are not addressed directly by either rule and would be dealt with differently as a result. Thus it would have been possible for a substantial part of the consideration to be in the form of loan stock without breaching the Seventh Directive limit, whereas this would have breached the SSAP 23 rule if it exceeded 10% in value of the total consideration. However, in drafting the Companies Act, the DTI extended the restriction on cash to cover any form of consideration other than equity, so that loan stock will not qualify.

The conditions laid down in the Act which have to be met before merger accounting can be applied are as follows:

'(a) that at least 90% of the nominal value of the relevant shares in the undertaking acquired is held by or on behalf of the parent company and its subsidiary undertakings,

 (b) that the proportion referred to in (a) was attained pursuant to an arrangement providing for the issue of equity shares by the parent company or one or more of its subsidiary undertakings,

(c)   that the fair value of any consideration other than the issue of equity shares given pursuant to the arrangement by the parent company and its subsidiary undertakings did not exceed 10% of the nominal value of the equity shares issued, and

(d)   that adoption of the merger method of accounting accords with generally accepted accounting principles or practice.'[6]

'Relevant shares' are defined as being those carrying unrestricted rights to participate both in distributions and in surplus assets on a winding up.[7]

2.1.6   ED 48

In answering some of the criticisms made against SSAP 23 (see 2.1.4 above), the ASC in February 1990 issued ED 48 – *Accounting for acquisitions and mergers* – which abandoned the principle of 'no material resources leaving the group' for determining what is a merger and when merger or acquisition accounting should be used. Instead, the ASC proposed a series of subjective tests designed to identify whether or not a merger had taken place in substance. These were very similar to those eventually proposed by the ASB in FRED 6 and subsequently converted into FRS 6.

2.1.7   FRED 6

The ASB replaced the ASC six months later and the subject was not progressed for some time. However, in May 1993 the ASB published FRED 6 – *Acquisitions and mergers*. As mentioned above, the proposals of this exposure draft were developed from those in ED 48 and, although no major changes were proposed, the ASB sought to remove some of the subjectivity which would have been required in applying ED 48. The overall approach of FRED 6, therefore, was based on the belief that merger accounting should only be applied to those rare business combinations that can properly be regarded as mergers in substance, and that, except for such rare cases, business combinations are more appropriately accounted for as acquisitions.

2.1.8   FRS 6

FRED 6 was converted into a standard in September 1994. The accounting practices set out in FRS 6 were to be adopted in respect of business combinations first accounted for in accounts relating to periods beginning on or after 23 December 1994.[8] Since it would clearly be impracticable to restate accounts for previous business combinations that had taken place in earlier years, the standard did not require retrospective application for previous periods.

A 'business combination' is defined in FRS 6 as 'the bringing together of separate entities into one economic entity as a result of one entity uniting with, or obtaining control over the net assets and operations of, another'.[9] The standard applies not only when an entity becomes a subsidiary undertaking of a parent company but also where an individual company or other reporting entity combines with a business other than a subsidiary undertaking.[10]

FRS 6 defines a merger as 'a business combination that results in the creation of a new reporting entity formed from the combining parties, in which the shareholders of the combining entities come together in a partnership for the mutual sharing of the risks and benefits of the combined entity, and in which no party to the combination in substance obtains control over any other, or is otherwise seen to be dominant, whether by virtue of the proportion of its shareholders' rights in the combined entity, the influence of its directors or otherwise'.[11] It is thus regarded not as the augmentation of one entity by the addition of another, but as the creation of a new reporting entity from the parties to the combination. An acquisition is defined as any other business combination that is not a merger.

The standard sets out the following five criteria that a business combination must meet for it to be accounted for as a merger, at the same time emphasising that merger accounting must also be allowed by companies' legislation (see 2.1.5 above). In aggregate, these criteria are very restrictive and in interpreting them the parties to the merger are considered to be not just the business of each entity that is combining but also the management of the entity and the body of its shareholders. Merger accounting is considered by the ASB not to be appropriate where any of the parties does not have an established independent track record as a result of it being a recent divestment from a larger entity.[12] It is unclear why this should be the case.

(a) no party to the combination is portrayed as either acquirer or acquired, either by its own board or management or by that of another party to the combination.[13]

If the terms of a share for share exchange indicate that one party has paid a premium over the market value of the shares acquired, this is evidence that that party has taken the role of acquirer unless there is a clear explanation for this apparent premium other than its being a premium paid to acquire control.[14]

It is necessary to consider all the circumstances surrounding the transaction in interpreting the nature of the combination.[15]

(b) all parties to the combination, as represented by the boards of directors or their appointees, participate in establishing the management structure for the combined entity and in selecting the management personnel, and such decisions are made on the basis of a consensus between the parties to the combination rather than purely by exercise of voting rights;[16]

It is necessary to consider not only the formal management structure of the combined entity but also the identity of all persons involved in the main financial and operating decisions and the way in which the decision making process operates in practice within the combined entity.[17]

Also, although it is only necessary to consider the decisions made in the period of initial integration and restructuring at the time of the combination, both the short term and long term consequences of decisions made in this period need to be considered.[18]

(c) the relative sizes of the combining entities are not so disparate that one party dominates the combined entity by virtue of its relative size;[19]

A party would be presumed to dominate if its ownership interest in the combined entity is more than 50% larger than that of each of the other parties to the combination (although this presumption is rebuttable).[20] This means that if any party obtains a 60% interest in the combined entity, the combination probably cannot be accounted for as a merger.

(d) under the terms of the combination or related arrangements, the consideration received by equity shareholders of each party to the combination, in relation to their equity shareholding, comprises primarily equity shares in the combined entity, and any non-equity consideration, or equity shares carrying substantially reduced voting or distribution rights, represents an immaterial proportion of the fair value of the consideration received by the shareholders of that party. Where one of the combining entities has, within the period of two years before the combination, acquired equity shares in another of the combining entities, the consideration for this acquisition should be taken into account in determining whether this criterion has been met.[21]

For the purpose of this criterion, the consideration should not be taken to include the distribution to shareholders of:

(i) an interest in a peripheral part of the business of the entity in which they were shareholders and which does not form part of the combined entity; or

(ii) the proceeds of the sale of such a business, or loan stock representing such proceeds.

A peripheral part of the business is one that can be disposed of without having a material effect on the nature and focus of the entity's operations.[22] However, interpretation of what is a peripheral part of an entity would necessarily be a fairly subjective judgement.

(e) no equity shareholders of any of the combining entities retain any material interest in the future performance of only part of the combined entity.[23] In particular, therefore, any earn-out arrangements or similar performance related schemes would mean the combination could not be interpreted as a merger.[24]

For the purposes of these criteria, any convertible shares or loan stock should be regarded as equity to the extent that they are converted into equity as a result of the business combination.[25] Equity and non-equity shares are defined in identical terms to those set out in FRS 4 (see 2.2.2 of Chapter 15).

FRS 6 states that in applying these criteria, it is necessary to consider the substance and not just the form of the arrangements, and to take account of all relevant information related to the combination.[26] It also discusses each of the criteria in more detail, providing examples of situations which might indicate whether or not the particular criterion is met.[27] Failure to meet any of the five criteria is to be regarded as meaning that the definition of a merger has not been met and thus merger accounting is not to be used for the business combination. Conversely, where a business combination meets these criteria, acquisition accounting is not permitted. In reality, however, merger accounting remains voluntary in the sense that it would be very easy for any company not wishing to use the method to 'fail' one of the very restrictive criteria.

Since the issue of FRS 6, merger accounting has become a much more rare occurrence as most business combinations have to be regarded as acquisitions. When it exposed FRED 6, the ASB also suggested an alternative approach of prohibiting the use of merger accounting entirely other than for certain group reconstructions, but did not, in the event, take this more extreme step. It may be just as well that they did not do so because since the standard was issued there have been a number of instances where merger accounting has been applied.[28] The main use of merger accounting nowadays, however, is for combinations made within a group, i.e. group reconstructions (see 4 below).

2.2   Acquisitions: basic principles

When Company A acquires Company B, it has to consolidate B's trading results from the effective date of acquisition onwards. Similarly, it thereafter includes B's assets and liabilities in its consolidated balance sheet, eliminating the share capital and reserves of B at the acquisition date against the cost of A's investment in B's shares. In contrast to merger accounting, the pre-acquisition results and reserves of B are completely eliminated from the consolidated financial statements, rather than brought in retrospectively. The Companies Act 1989 has enshrined this principle in the law.[29]

FRS 2 defines the date of acquisition in terms of when control passes; it states that 'the date for accounting for an undertaking becoming a subsidiary undertaking is the date on which control of that undertaking passes to its new parent undertaking'.[30] This is a matter of fact and cannot be artificially backdated or otherwise altered. It then explains when such a date might be under various circumstances: 'Where control is transferred by a public offer, the date control is transferred is the date the offer becomes unconditional, usually as a result of a sufficient number of acceptances being received. For private treaties, the date control is transferred is generally the date an unconditional offer is accepted. Where an undertaking becomes ... a subsidiary undertaking as a result of the issue or cancellation of shares, the date control is transferred is the date of issue or cancellation. The date that control passes may be indicated by the acquiring party commencing its direction of the operating and financial policies of the acquired undertaking or by changes in the flow of economic benefits.' It also states that 'the date on which the consideration for the transfer of control is paid is often an important indication of the date on which a subsidiary undertaking is acquired or disposed of. However, the date the consideration passes is not conclusive evidence of the date of the transfer of control because this date can be set to fall on a date other than that on which control is transferred, with compensation for any lead or lag included in the consideration. Consideration may also be paid in instalments.'[31]

In order to account for the acquisition, the acquiring company must first measure the cost of what it is accounting for, which will normally represent both the cost of the investment in its own balance sheet and the amount to be allocated between the identifiable net assets of the subsidiary and goodwill in the consolidated financial statements. This issue is considered at 2.3 below.

Secondly, in allocating the cost of the acquisition, the acquiring company then needs to identify the assets and liabilities of the subsidiary and attribute fair values to them, rather then merely relying on the book values in the subsidiary's accounts. This is discussed at 2.4 below.

Once the fair values of both the consideration given and the net assets acquired have been measured, the difference between the two represents purchased goodwill which remains to be accounted for. How to account for it is a subject on which widely differing opinions are held, and this is evidenced both by the time which it originally took the ASC to develop a standard on the subject and by the fact that the eventual standard, SSAP 22, permitted a choice between two alternative methods: amortisation through the profit and loss account and immediate write-off direct to reserves. Most companies adopted the latter approach. This standard was superseded when the ASB issued FRS 10 in December 1997 which radically changed the way companies account for goodwill. No longer can companies write off goodwill immediately to reserves but they must now capitalise it as an asset. The subsequent accounting for goodwill is dealt with in Chapter 10 at 3.4.

2.3 Acquisitions: measuring the fair value of the consideration

Both the law and accounting standards have for some time specified that the cost is to be based on the fair value of the consideration given if acquisition accounting is used, but until the publication of FRS 7, there was no standard which elaborated on how this was to be determined, although there had been a number of previous initiatives to produce one.

In July 1990, the ASC issued an exposure draft, ED 53 – *Fair value in the context of acquisition accounting* – having published a Discussion Paper two years earlier on the topic;[32] the main proposals of the exposure draft dealt with monetary items, securities and other non-monetary assets given as consideration together with deferred and contingent consideration.[33]

In April 1993 the ASB published a Discussion Paper – *Fair values in acquisition accounting* – which limited its discussion on the fair value of purchase consideration to deferred and contingent consideration in terms which were more consistent with the ASB's draft Statement of Principles, as most commentators had been supportive of the proposals in ED 53 relating to ascertaining the fair values of other elements of the purchase consideration. An exposure draft, FRED 7,[34] was published in December 1993 and its proposals in respect of determining the cost of acquisition were similar to those contained in ED 53. This was converted into FRS 7 nine months later, without substantial change. The accounting practices set out in FRS 7 were to be adopted in respect of business combinations first accounted for in accounts relating to periods beginning on or after 23 December 1994.[35] Since it would clearly have been impracticable to restate accounts for previous business combinations that had taken place in earlier years, the standard did not require retrospective application for previous periods.

The basic requirement of FRS 7 is that 'the cost of acquisition is the amount of cash paid and the fair value of other purchase consideration given by the acquirer, together with the expenses of the acquisition … . Where a subsidiary undertaking is acquired in stages, the cost of acquisition is the total of the costs of the interests acquired, determined as at the date of each transaction.'[36] This latter aspect of acquiring a subsidiary in stages is discussed further at 2.5 below. Issues relating to the first part of the requirement are discussed at 2.3.1 to 2.3.6 below.

2.3.1 Cash and other monetary consideration

The purchase consideration may comprise cash or other monetary items, including the assumption of liabilities by the acquirer. FRS 7 states that the fair value of such items 'is normally readily determinable as the amount paid or payable in respect of the item'.[37] However, when settlement is deferred, fair values are to be obtained by discounting to their present value the amounts expected to be payable in the future, using an appropriate discount rate (see 2.3.4 below).

The effect of discounting future obligations is to reduce the amount of goodwill recognised on the acquisition (or increase the amount of any negative goodwill). This is because the amount of consideration given is deemed to be smaller. It is then augmented by notional interest charges in the post-acquisition profit and loss account to bring the carrying value of the obligation up to the settlement value by the due date.

2.3.2 Capital instruments

The purchase consideration may comprise capital instruments issued by the acquirer, including shares, debentures, loans and debt instruments, share warrants and other options relating to the securities of the acquirer.

Where such instruments are quoted on a ready market, FRS 7 states that 'the market price on the date of acquisition would normally provide the most reliable measure of fair value'. Where the acquisition arises out of a public offer, 'the relevant date is the date on which the offer or, where there is a series of revised offers, the successful offer becomes unconditional, usually as a result of a sufficient number of acceptances being received'. However, 'where, owing to unusual fluctuations, the market price on one particular date is an unreliable measure of fair value, market prices for a reasonable period before the date of acquisition, during which acceptances could be made, would need to be considered'.[38] Unfortunately, unlike ED 53, FRS 7 gives no guidance as to what a reasonable period might be. ED 53 observed that the period chosen would depend on both specific conditions and also general market conditions.[39] However, it advised that usually a period of 10 dealing days prior to the date of acquisition would be appropriate. It may be that in the absence of anything more specific in FRS 7, this could be taken as a guide, although obviously the specific circumstances would have to be taken into account. The purpose of this is to take some sort of average price so that the value of the consideration given is not distorted by a transient fluctuation.

For other securities, a suitable market price might not exist; this might be due to the fact that the securities are not quoted, or if they are quoted, the market price is unreliable owing, for example, to the lack of an active market in the quantities involved. Where this is the case, the fair value should be estimated by taking into account items such as:

(a) the value of similar securities that are quoted;

(b) the present value of the future cash flows of the instrument issued;

(c) any cash alternative to the issue of securities; and

(d) the value of any underlying security into which there is an option to convert.[40]

Where it is not possible to value the consideration given by any of the above methods, the best estimate of its value may be given by valuing the entity acquired.[41]

Many British companies have always used the price ruling at the date at which the offer became unconditional; one company which explicitly says that this is its policy is Travis Perkins, as shown below:

Extract 6.2: Travis Perkins plc (1998)

Accounting Policies

(b) **Basis of preparation** [extract]

The cost of acquisition represents the cash value of the consideration and/or the market value of the shares issued on the date the offer became unconditional, plus expenses.

One company which did not use the market price of its shares at the date of acquisition was Harveys Furnishing (then named Cantors) in respect of its acquisition of Harveys Holdings. The company took the view that its market price at that date (£1.65) was unreliable so instead adopted the share valuation (£1) ruling at the date four months earlier when the transaction had been negotiated. This treatment was challenged by the Review Panel[42] and as a result the company issued a supplementary note in respect of its 1997 accounts (as part of its 1998 Annual Report) which contained the following explanation of the issue.

Extract 6.3: Harveys Furnishings plc (1998)

SUPPLEMENTARY NOTE TO THE FINANCIAL STATEMENTS
for the 52 weeks ended 26 April 1997 [extract]

The company has held discussions with the Financial Reporting Review Panel ("the Panel") regarding the value of the consideration given by Cantors for Harveys following the acquisition by Cantors, as stated in the financial statements for the 52 weeks ended 26 April 1997 and as to the way that certain other financial information has been presented in those financial statements. As a result of these discussions, the directors have decided to revise the financial statements in accordance with Statutory Instrument 2570(1990), which permits revision by way of Supplementary Note.

The issue concerning the valuation of Harveys relates to a complex accounting matter. At the point at which the acquisition of Harveys was negotiated in March 1996, the Cantors' share price was in the region of £1. This formed the basis for the valuation of Harveys by both parties and the basis of the share exchange ratio. At the date of the shareholder approval for the transaction in July 1996, the price had moved to £1.65. As this was a reverse take-over the directors considered that the Cantors' share price had reacted in a similar way as a target in a bid would normally react; anticipating the benefits that an acquisition would bring to the existing Cantors' shareholders. The situation was exacerbated by the existence of a thin market in which a small transaction could move the price dramatically. Trading in Cantors' shares was suspended in June 1996 and the dealings in this period were the subject of a Stock Exchange enquiry.

Both the Directors and Coopers & Lybrand were concerned that if a price of £1.65 were used to determine the carrying value of the investment in Harveys the carrying value would be approximately £55 million, which in the context of expected after tax profits for the year ended 31 August 1996 of approximately £2.3 million inputed an inflated earnings multiple. After considering the above factors and taking into account the abnormal circumstances of a reverse takeover, the Directors and Coopers & Lybrand deemed the share price of £1.65 to be unreliable for the purposes of attributing a value to Harveys as at the date of the merger. We consequently adopted an alternative valuation of £1, since this had formed the basis of the negotiations for the merger. However, the Panel considered that the price of £1.65 formed the appropriate basis for the fair value of the consideration as required by FRS 7, which the directors have decided to accept.

Interestingly, the auditors in their report on the revised accounts still maintained that valuing the cost of the acquisition on the basis of £1 per share was acceptable, but conceded in the circumstances that the revised basis now adopted by the directors was also acceptable.

Perhaps mindful of this Review Panel ruling, Brown & Jackson, who had similarly negotiated a deal based on the company's share price at the date of the acquisition agreement, used the market price at the date the acquisition became unconditional following shareholder approval as shown below.

Extract 6.4: Brown & Jackson plc (1998)

18 Notes to the cash flow statement [extract]

   (d) Acquisitions of Your More Store Ltd and WEW Group Plc (see note 19)

On 27 September 1997 two new wholly owned subsidiaries, Your More Store Ltd (YMS) and WEW Group Plc (WEW) were acquired. WEW was acquired for £6.543 million in cash plus expenses of £539,000.

The agreement for the purchase of the shares in YMS dated 27 August 1997 provided for a consideration of £7.651 million to be settled by the issue of 34,242,424 10p ordinary shares at 16.5p (which was the closing mid-market share price on the date of the agreement) and the payment of £2 million in cash. The agreement was conditional upon the subsequent approval in General Meeting by the independent shareholders and this approval was obtained on 27 September 1997.

Financial Reporting Standard 7 'Fair values in acquisition accounting' requires the fair value of the share consideration for accounting purposes to be determined at the date that the acquisition became unconditional. At 27 September 1997, the date the agreement became unconditional, the mid-market price of the shares in the Company was 21.5p. Accordingly the fair value of the share consideration for these purposes was £7.363 million as shown below.

The fair values of the identifiable assets and liabilities of the new subsidiaries at the date of acquisition are provisional subject to the agreement of certain tax computations and were as follows:

	Book value at acquisition YMS £'000	Fair value adjustments YMS £'000	Fair value YMS £'000	Book value at acquisition WEW £'000	Accounting policy alignment WEW £'000	Fair value WEW £'000
Net assets acquired						
Fixed assets	8,614	–	8,614	21,983	–	21,983
Stocks	7,725	–	7,725	16,717	–	16,717
Debtors	1,977	–	1,977	6,874	–	6,874
Cash at bank and in hand	78	–	78	812	–	812
Creditors and provisions	(6,618)	13	(6,605)	(19,444)	(793)	(20,237)
Reorganisation provision previously created in the accounts to 2 August 1997	–	–	–	(3,117)	–	(3,117)
Bank overdrafts	(2,771)	–	(2,771)	(8,506)	–	(8,506)
Loans and finance leases	(2,500)	–	(2,500)	(2,424)	–	(2,424)
Less minority interests	–	–	–	(2,178)	–	(2,178)
	6,505	13	6,518	10,717	(793)	9,924
Goodwill/(negative goodwill)			3,229			(2,842)
			9,747			7,082
Satisfied by						
34,242,424 shares at 16.5p per agreement			5,651			–
Increase in share price between 27 August and 27 September 1997			1,712			–
Fair value of share consideration for these purposes			7,363			–
Cash to ordinary shareholders			2,000			6,543
Expenses of acquisition			384			539
			9,747			7,082

Sometimes, shares are issued by the acquirer which rank fully for dividends which are to be paid in respect of a period before the acquisition took place. In these circumstances, some companies apportion the subsequent dividend into two components when it is paid, with a 'pre-acquisition' element added to the cost of the investment in the subsidiary (and therefore increasing the goodwill) and leaving only the post-acquisition element to be taken out of the profit and loss account. FRS 7 does not deal with this specific issue. In our view such a treatment is inappropriate where the cost of the investment in the acquired subsidiary is recorded at the (cum div) fair value of the securities issued as consideration; this is because the fair value of the securities will already reflect the fact that the shareholders are entitled to the dividend and therefore the dividend cost is double-counted. This is not the case where merger relief has been taken (see 2.1.2 above) and the cost of the investment is recorded at the nominal value of the shares issued as consideration. One example of this is to be found in the 1989 financial statements of BICC, as shown in the following extract:

Extract 6.5: BICC plc (1989)

11   ORDINARY DIVIDENDS

	1989		1988	
	Per share p	**Amount £m**	Per share p	Amount £m
Interim payable	**5.75**	**15.1**	4.75	11.2
Final proposed	**13.25**	**36.0**	11.25	26.7
	19.00	**51.1**	16.00	37.9
Pre-acquisition proportion relating to shares issued for acquisitions		**(2.2)**		(0.9)
		48.9		37.0

15   INVESTMENTS [extract]

BICC plc issued 7.6m ordinary shares in 1988 and 2.6m ordinary shares in 1989 for the share capital of Ceat Cavi Industrie Srl. 22.1m were also issued in 1989 to acquire Manshine Ltd, a company formed in connection with the acquisition of BRIntic Corporation, and 0.7m ordinary shares were issued for the share capital of Syntek Ltd and Cruickshank and Partners Ltd.

...

Having taken advantage of the merger relief provisions under s 131, Companies Act 1985, the investment in these companies is recorded at the nominal value of the shares issued as consideration, plus costs, including the pre-acquisition proportion of dividend and related advance corporation tax in respect of the shares issued in the year.

2.3.3   Non-monetary assets

The purchase consideration may comprise non-monetary assets, including securities of another entity. FRS 7 states that for such consideration 'fair values would be determined by reference to market prices, estimated realisable values, independent valuations, or other available evidence'.[43] This is not as specific as the proposal in ED 53 which focused on the value of the sacrifice made by the acquirer by giving up such assets, and invoked a concept similar to that of 'deprival value' which was used as the basis of valuations in current cost accounting. The loss suffered by the acquirer was the alternative proceeds he could have received for the asset, unless he could make good his loss by replacing the asset, in which case it was the cost of such replacement. In the absence of anything more specific in FRS 7, the deprival value principle seems a sensible one to adopt.

Two companies which had to address this issue are George Wimpey and Tarmac when they swapped their respective construction and housing businesses in

1996. George Wimpey regarded the consideration given as being the equivalent of the book values of the net assets of the construction business, as seen below:

Extract 6.6: George Wimpey PLC (1996)

26   Asset Exchange with Tarmac plc

On 1 March 1996, George Wimpey PLC acquired Tarmac's Housing division, McLean Homes, by exchange of Wimpey's Construction and Minerals divisions. The Group has used acquisition accounting to account for the acquisition. Goodwill arising on consolidation has been written off direct to reserves. The impact of this acquisition on the consolidated net assets was as follows:

	Book Cost of Assets Acquired	Revaluation	Provisions	Reassessment of Fair Values of Net Current Assets	Fair Value of Assets Acquired
Net assets acquired from Tarmac:					
Tangible assets and fixed asset investments	6.1	0.3	–	–	6.4
Net current assets	316.7	–	–	(14.1)	302.6
Provisions	–	–	(1.2)	–	(1.2)
Cash at bank and in hand	2.2	–	–	–	2.2
Borrowings and inter-company debt	(51.1)	–	–	–	(51.1)
Total net assets	273.9	0.3	(1.2)	(14.1)	258.9

Consideration:	
Net assets of Construction and Minerals divisions	
Tangible assets and fixed asset investments	335.7
Net current assets	(7.1)
Cash at bank and in hand	43.9
Borrowings and inter-company debt	(35.3)
Provisions	(27.0)
Minority interests	(13.6)
Total net assets	296.6
Professional fees and other costs of the transaction	4.2
Goodwill arising on asset exchange	41.9

Provisions acquired from Tarmac relate mainly to rental provisions for void property which existed at the date of acquisition. Of this provision, £0.2 million had been utilised at 31 December 1996. The fair value adjustment to net current assets mainly results from a reassessment of the net realisable value of work in progress and land.

This can be contrasted with Tarmac which regarded the consideration given for the Wimpey business acquired as being an estimate of the fair value of the housing division given in return as shown below:

Extract 6.7: Tarmac plc (1996)

29   Acquisitions and divestments [extract]

Exchange of businesses with George Wimpey PLC

On 1st March 1996 the Group's UK and US private sector housing business ('the Housing Division') was exchanged for the world-wide minerals and construction businesses of George Wimpey PLC ('Wimpey'). The effects of this exchange on the net assets of the Group are summarised below:

| | **Wimpey businesses acquired** | | | | |
	Book value £m	Revaluation of assets acquired £m	Accounting policy alignment £m	Fair value £m	Housing Division divested £m
Tangible assets	334.6	13.3	–	347.9	6.1
Associated undertakings	1.1	(1.1)	–	–	–
Stocks	30.9	(0.4)	–	30.5	397.4
Debtors	183.2	(38.6)	–	144.6	58.8
Cash, less overdrafts	36.5	–	–	36.5	(53.5)
Creditors, deferred liabilities and provisions	(249.2)	(18.8)	(9.5)	(277.5)	(130.1)
Inter-group loans	(29.2)	–	–	(29.2)	4.5
Equity minority interests	(13.6)	(5.3)	–	(18.9)	–
Net assets	294.3	(50.9)	(9.5)		
Fair value of assets exchanged				233.9	283.2
Professional fees and other costs of transaction				(7.5)	7.1
				226.4	290.3
Directors' estimate of fair value of Housing Division, as divested			291.0	291.0	
Goodwill arising on acquisition of Wimpey businesses, written off directly to reserves				64.6	
Unrealised profit on disposal of Housing Division					0.7

The £9.5 million accounting policy alignment adjustment represents additional environmental and restoration provisions, which remain substantially unutilised at the year end.

The revaluation of assets acquired within the above table incorporates the adjustment of book values to those achieved on subsequent divestments of US businesses, an independent valuation of mineral reserves (note 12) and a reassessment of the realisable values of amounts recoverable on contracts and other net current assets.

It is interesting to note from the above extracts that both parties to the transaction considered that the fair value of the assets acquired was less than the corresponding book value. Indeed, they also disagreed as to what the book values were.

Another company which acquired a subsidiary in return for non-monetary consideration is Kingfisher as shown below:

Extract 6.8: Kingfisher plc (1999)

37 Acquisitions [extract]

(a) Merger of B&Q and Castorama

On 18 December 1998, the effective date of acquisition, the Group completed the combination of B&Q plc with Castorama Dubois Investissements S.C.A. (Castorama). The transaction has been treated as an acquisition and was effected by the transfer by the Group of its 100% interest in B&Q in exchange for a 57.9% interest (54.6% on a fully diluted basis) in the consequently enlarged Castorama group. The transaction was effected by an exchange of shares, being new shares in Castorama for the Group's shares in B&Q and the book value of the 42.1% of the assets of B&Q at the date of acquisition has been treated as the cost of that investment. The difference between the consideration and the fair value of the Castorama net assets received has been treated as a non-distributable reserve.

The details of the transaction adjustments are set out below. The fair value adjustments are of a provisional nature, because the timing of the acquisition has meant that it has not been possible to complete the investigation for determining fair values. The exercise will be completed in 1999 and any further fair value adjustments will be made in next year's accounts.

£ millions	Book value	Fair value adjustments: Revaluations	Accounting policy alignments	Fair value to the Group
Tangible fixed assets	614.3	–	84.8	699.1
Investments	1.6	–	–	1.6
Stocks	400.6	–	–	400.6
Other current assets	312.7	–	1.2	313.9
Creditors	(862.8)	–	(23.5)	(886.3)
Castorama net assets	466.4	–	62.5	528.9
B&Q net assets on completion				325.5

£ millions	Reserve arising
Share of Castorama net assets acquired (57.9% of £528.9m)	306.2
Share of B&Q net assets given up (42.1% of £325.5m)	(137.0)
Transaction expenses	(22.9)
Non-distributable reserve arising	146.3

Accounting policy alignments have been made to the books of Castorama as at 31 December 1998 principally comprising the reversal of depreciation on freehold buildings and the restatement of deferred tax from a full provision basis to a partial provision basis. Deferred tax assets arising on unutilised tax losses and charges to the consolidated profit and loss account on which tax relief will be available in future years have been eliminated.

As the Castorama merger was completed very close to the Group's year end, an exercise to revalue land and buildings has not been undertaken. A full valuation exercise will be undertaken during 1999 for reflection next year. Land and buildings are shown at cost in the above provisional fair value table.

The book values of the assets and liabilities have been translated at the actual exchange rate as at 31 December 1998 of £1:FF 9.241.

It can be seen that, like Wimpey, Kingfisher has regarded the consideration as being the equivalent of its share of the book value of the B&Q net assets given up. However, rather than treating the difference of £146.3m between this consideration and the fair value of the assets (after allowing for the transaction expenses) as negative goodwill under FRS 10, it has taken it to a non-distributable reserve. This seems to treat the transaction more like a disposal, but regarding the gain as unrealised.

2.3.4 Deferred consideration

The term 'deferred consideration' is not used in FRS 7 but was stated in the ASB's Discussion Paper to denote consideration, payable in cash, shares or other securities, which is determined precisely at the time of the acquisition either in value or as a number of shares, but where the payment is delayed for a defined period.

The standard only discusses the situation where settlement of cash consideration is deferred, in which case 'fair values are obtained by discounting to their present value the amounts expected to be payable in the future. The appropriate discount rate is the rate at which the acquirer could obtain a similar borrowing, taking into account its credit standing and any security given.'[44]

Deferred consideration in a form other than cash is not discussed in FRS 7; it is unclear why this should be the case. However, it may be that where such consideration is payable in shares, or other securities, then the acquirer is regarded as having issued a capital instrument as part of the consideration at the time of the acquisition and therefore the fair value should be determined following the principles set out for capital instruments discussed at 2.3.2 above. The standard also does not deal with how deferred consideration payable in shares should be dealt with, but in our view it should be dealt with in a similar manner to contingent consideration which is to be satisfied by shares (see 2.3.5 below).

Although many companies refer to deferred consideration in their accounts, such consideration usually is in reality contingent consideration under FRS 7.

2.3.5   *Contingent consideration*

The terms of an acquisition may provide that the value of the purchase consideration, which may be payable in cash, shares or other securities at a future date, depends on uncertain future events, such as the future performance of the acquired company. FRS 7 quotes the example of an 'earn out', 'where consideration payable to the vendor takes the form of an initial payment, together with further payments based on a multiple of future profits of the acquired company. By its nature, the fair value of such contingent consideration cannot be determined precisely at the date of acquisition.'[45]

The standard requires that 'where the amount of purchase consideration is contingent on one or more future events, the cost of acquisition should include a reasonable estimate of the fair value of amounts expected to be payable in the future. The cost of acquisition should be adjusted when revised estimates are made, with consequential corresponding adjustments continuing to be made to goodwill until the ultimate outcome is known.'[46]

For this calculation, therefore, goodwill can remain open for several periods after the acquisition. This is in contrast to the normal rule that fair values and thus goodwill should not be adjusted after the first full period following the one in which the acquisition took place (see 2.4.2 below).

Although the ASB's Discussion Paper proposed that if such amounts were to be payable in cash or by the issue of a debt instrument, they were to be discounted to their present value,[47] FRS 7 does not specifically state this to be the case. However, it is arguable that such amounts by their nature are 'deferred' and therefore any amount payable in cash should be discounted, and if payable by the issue of a loan instrument, the fair value of such an instrument would reflect a discounted value. Similarly, the ASB Discussion Paper proposed that if such amounts were payable in shares, then the fair value of contingent consideration should be based on its expected value.[48] Again, FRS 7 is silent on this issue.

Although, as the standard comments, by its nature the fair value of contingent consideration cannot be determined precisely at the date of acquisition, acquiring companies should provide for a reasonable estimate of the outcome. Usually, an indication of the likely amounts payable should be available since in drawing up the terms of the agreement the parties will have had to consider closely the likely outcomes.

In some cases it will be clear that at least a certain amount is very likely to be payable, and in these circumstances it would seem appropriate to provide for that amount. This is more likely to be the case in those situations where the contingent consideration is based on the target company maintaining a level of profits which it is currently earning (either for a particular period or as an average over a set period) or achieving profits which it is currently budgeting.

One company which has made full provision for contingent consideration is Logica as shown below:

Extract 6.9: Logica plc (1998)

26 Acquisitions [extract]

Aldiscon Limited

The acquisition of Aldiscon Limited, a company registered in Ireland, was completed on 1 August 1997.

The consideration paid or payable is as follows:

(i) a fixed amount of IR£52.4 million (£47.0 million) excluding costs of the acquisition

(ii) an amount contingent upon Logica Aldiscon achieving certain performance criteria in the period to 30 June 1998, the maximum amount payable being IR£4.5 million (£3.8 million). This is expected to be paid subject only to the continued employment of certain of the vendors.

The provisional fair value to the group of net assets acquired is shown below:

	Book value of assets acquired £'000	Revaluation adjustments £'000	Accounting policy adjustments £'000	Provisional fair value £'000
Intangible fixed assets	35	–	(35)	–
Tangible fixed assets	2,074	–	422	2,496
Debtors/work in progress	12,939	(937)	1,365	13,367
Cash at bank and in hand	2,712	–	–	2,712
Creditors	(8,748)	(886)	–	(9,634)
Taxation	(334)	(622)	–	(956)
Borrowings	(853)	–	–	(853)
Net assets acquired	7,825	(2,445)	1,752	7,132
Goodwill				44,065
				51,197

Satisfied by:	
Cash (including costs of the acquisition of £831,000)	47,831
Contingent consideration (discounted)	3,366
	51,197

The main adjustments are:

Intangible fixed assets
Capitalised patents of £35,000 have been written off to bring Aldiscon into line with Logica's accounting policy on intangible assets.

Tangible fixed assets
The net book value of fixed assets was adjusted to realign Aldiscon fixed asset depreciation policies with those of Logica.

Debtors/work in progress
Reversal of general work in progress provision of £90,000 to confirm with Logica accounting policy. Logica revenue recognition policy was applied against Aldiscon's open projects as at 1 August 1997 resulting in an acceleration of revenue recognition compared to Aldiscon's existing policy. The impact was an increase in debtors of £2.9 million and an increase in accrued costs associated with those revenues of £1.4 million. Specific provisions of £937,000 were made for all debts more than 12 months old at the date of acquisition. There has been no movement in this provision to 30 June 1998.

Creditors
Provisions were established in respect of a planned US office relocation entered into prior to the acquisition date (£246,000) and identified social security expenditure (£640,000).

Taxation
Provisions were established to cover specific tax exposures identified.

Movements on fair value provisions
An amount of £123,000 of the provision for the US office relocation has been utilised in the period since acquisition to cover the rent on the property for the period since it was vacated and other costs of relocation.

It can be seen from the above extract that Logica has discounted the contingent consideration. Another company that does likewise and has an accounting policy on the matter is Daily Mail and General Trust as illustrated below:

Extract 6.10: Daily Mail and General Trust plc (1998)

Accounting Policies [extract]

2   Basis of Consolidation

(d)   In calculating the goodwill, the total consideration, both actual and deferred, is taken into account. Where the deferred consideration is payable in cash, the liability is discounted to its present value. Where the deferred consideration is contingent and dependent upon future trading performance, an estimate of the present value of the likely consideration payable is made. This contingent consideration is re-assessed annually. The difference between the present value and the total amount payable at a future date gives rise to a finance charge which is charged to the profit and loss account and credited to the liability over the period in which the consideration is deferred. The discount used approximates to market rates.

Notes to the Profit and Loss Account [extract]

8 Other Finance Charges	Note	1998 £m	1997 £m
Premium on repurchase of Exchangeable Bonds		**(1.1)**	(15.5)
Premium on repurchase of US $ Loan Notes		**(2.6)**	–
		(3.7)	(15.5)
Finance charge on discounting of deferred consideration	32	**(2.3)**	–
		(6.0)	(15.5)

Notes to the Balance Sheets [extract]

32 Summary of the Effects of Acquisitions and Disposals

The principal acquisitions completed during the year and the dates of acquisition were:

Regional Broadcasters Australia Pty Limited	October 1997
Teletext Holdings Limited (15%)	December 1997
Risk Management Solutions, Inc	February 1998
Essex Radio plc	February 1998
Study Group International Limited (60%)	June 1998
Alderton Limited	July 1998

The aggregate consideration for these and other businesses was £250.1 million, of which £151.7 million was paid during the year, £6.6 million issued by a subsidiary in the form of shares and an estimated amount of £91.8 million payable in the form of deferred consideration over the next few years, dependent upon trading results. This deferred consideration has been discounted back to current values in accordance with FRS 7, giving rise to a finance charge of £2.3 million (Note 8). A further £10.7 million of loans were taken on in the form of debt. In each case, the Group has used acquisition accounting to account for the purchase.

Clearly, Logica had to provide in full for the contingent consideration in respect of its acquisition as the profit target related to the year just past (it effectively was no longer contingent). Daily Mail and General Trust on the other hand appears to have provided in full on the basis that it was the current best estimate of the amount payable. Another company which has made provision on the basis of its current expectations is Rebus Group, as shown below:

Extract 6.11: Rebus Group PLC (1998)

22 Financial commitments [extract]

Deferred consideration

In connection with the acquisition of certain subsidiaries, the Group has entered into arrangements which provide for the minority shareholders of the subsidiaries to sell their remaining interests to the Group, where the amount of the future consideration is dependent upon the future performance of the relevant subsidiary. Provision for such future consideration is only made where the consideration can be estimated with reasonable certainty. The amount provided at 31 March 1998 was £153,000 (1997 – nil) and the aggregate unprovided consideration, based upon current contributions to the Group's earnings by the relevant subsidiaries, is estimated to amount to approximately £500,000 (1997 – £820,000).

As there is an element of uncertainty about the ultimate amount payable occasionally it will be necessary to revise the liability originally recognised. One company which has had to reverse out its provision was Cobham as shown below.

Extract 6.12: Cobham plc (1998)

21   Reserves [extract]

	Profit and Loss Account £m
Group	
At 1 January 1998	76.2
Goodwill written back on sale of a subsidiary (note 3)	2.6
Contingent consideration provision, no longer required (note below)	3.9
Profit retained for the year	28.5
Foreign exchange	(0.1)
At 31 December 1998	111.1

£3.9m has been added to reserves as a result of the release from provisions of this sum which was deferred consideration potentially due to certain vendors of Westwind which is now no longer payable.

The cumulative goodwill written off on acquisition net of disposals totals £182.0m from 1954 to 31 December 1998 (1997 – £188.5m) after writing back £6.5m in 1998 (1997 – nil).

It can be seen from the above that in line with FRS 7 the corresponding adjustment has been made against goodwill.

Occasionally the terms of the agreement may be such that it is impossible to say whether, and if so how much, additional consideration will be paid, and in that case companies may have no option but to deal with the matter by disclosure, rather than by provision. Where consideration is only payable on profits which are in excess of those currently being earned or budgeted for by the target company, then it may be more appropriate to disclose only the contingent consideration. FRS 7 is clear, however, that even 'where it is not possible to estimate the total amounts payable with any degree of certainty, at least those amounts that are reasonably expected to be payable would be recognised'.[49]

Examples of companies which have not made any provision for contingent consideration but merely give disclosure of its existence are shown below.

Extract 6.13: Frogmore Estates plc (1998)

25   Contingent liabilities [extract]

Additional consideration, up to a maximum of £2,000,000 in cash, may become payable for the acquisition of the business of White Druce & Brown, which completed in April 1995, dependent on the financial performance of the Frogmore group relative to a number of comparable companies over the five year period ending on 30th June 2000.

Extract 6.14: Tibbett & Britten Group plc (1995)

24 DEFERRED CONSIDERATION ON ACQUISITION

Under the terms of the agreement for the acquisition of Metra Media Transport BV a further consideration of up to £1,005,000 may be payable to the vendors in 2000, subject to the continuance of an agreed minimum level of business during the five years starting 2 July 2000.

Under the terms of the acquisition of Transportes y Distribuciones Martinez, SA (Tradismasa) a further consideration of up to £133,000 may be payable to the vendors in the years to 1997. Such payments are contingent upon the levels of profits achieved by Tradismasa in 1996.

Due to the degree of uncertainty, the directors consider a provision for these amounts to be inappropriate.

Under the terms of the acquisition of Eskimo-Iglo Tiefkühllogistik AG ("TKL") in Austria further consideration of up to £7,995,000 (ATS 125 million) may be payable to the vendors for the remaining 30% of the shareholding in TKL in instalments on 1 January 1997, 1998, 1999 and 2000. Such payments are contingent upon the cumulative levels of profit achieved by TKL in the five years 1995 to 1999.

The 1996 accounts showed that the company was correct not to provide any consideration in respect of the Tradismasa acquisition as no amount was paid, and in the 1998 accounts provision is still not made in respect of the others.

Where contingent consideration is to be satisfied by the issue of shares, then as FRS 7 explains 'there is no obligation to transfer economic benefits and, accordingly, amounts recognised would be reported as part of shareholders' funds, for example as a separate caption representing shares to be issued. In the analysis of shareholders' funds, amounts would be attributed to equity and non-equity interests depending on the nature of the shares to be issued, in accordance with FRS 4 "Capital Instruments". When the shares are issued, appropriate transfers would be necessary between any amounts then held in shareholders' funds in respect of their issue and called up share capital and share premium.'[50]

In some situations the acquirer has an option to issue either shares or cash; because there is no obligation to transfer economic benefits then this future consideration is not a liability. Accordingly, the standard states that the expected future consideration should be accounted for as a credit to shareholders' funds (as explained above) until an irrevocable decision regarding the form of consideration has been taken. Where the vendor has the choice, then the expected future consideration represents an obligation to the vendor and should be accounted for as a liability until the shares are issued or the cash is paid.[51] One company which includes contingent consideration within shareholders' funds is Dorling Kindersley as shown below:

Extract 6.15: Dorling Kindersley Holdings plc (1998)

Group and Company Balance Sheets as at 30 June 1998 [extract]

	Note	Group 1998 £'000	Group 1997 As restated £'000	Company 1998 £'000	Company 1997 £'000
Capital and reserves					
Called-up share capital	17	**3,584**	3,520	**3,584**	3,520
Share premium account	18	**36,770**	34,854	**36,770**	34,854
Profit and loss account	18	**12,313**	12,460	**2,017**	1,992
Shares to be issued after year end	18	**770**	1,541	**770**	1,541
Equity shareholders' funds		**53,437**	52,375	**43,141**	41,907

Notes to the Financial Statements [extract]

9.   FIXED ASSET INVESTMENTS

In respect of the acquisition of Funfax Limited reported in the 1995 financial statements, deferred consideration of up to a maximum of £0.8 million is potentially payable, in new shares or loan notes at the Company's option, on 30 September 1998. The first two tranches of consideration were settled by the issue of shares on 30 September 1996 and 1997 (see note 17).

17.   SHARE CAPITAL

During the year, the Company allotted 1,285,831 new ordinary shares. The aggregate nominal value of these shares and the consideration received was as follows:

	Number of shares	Nominal value £'000	Consideration £'000
Shares options exercised	985,326	49	1,209
Deferred consideration	300,505	15	771
	1,285,831	64	1,980

On 30 September 1996, the Company issued 128,895 shares as the first tranche of deferred consideration on the acquisition of Funfax Limited, and on 30 September a further 300,505 shares were issued in the second tranche of deferred consideration (see note 9).

FRS 7 also discusses the situation where acquisition agreements may require payments to be made in various forms, for example as non-competition payments or as bonuses to the vendors who continue to work for the acquired company. The standard states that 'in such circumstances, it is necessary to determine whether the substance of the agreement is payment for the business acquired, or an expense such as compensation for services or profit sharing. In the first case the expected payments would be accounted for as contingent purchase consideration; in the other case the payments would be treated as expenses of the period to which they relate.'[52]

2.3.6 Acquisition expenses

FRS 7 takes a deliberately restrictive view as to what acquisition expenses should be treated as part of the cost of the acquisition in order to avoid the danger of overstating the cost of acquisition. The standard requires that only 'fees and similar incremental costs incurred directly in making an acquisition should, except for the issue costs of shares and other securities that are required by FRS 4 "Capital Instruments" to be accounted for as a reduction in the proceeds of a capital instrument, be included in the cost of acquisition. Internal costs and other expenses that cannot be directly attributed to the acquisition should be charged to the profit and loss account.'[53] Costs which may be capitalised include 'incremental costs such as professional fees paid to merchant banks, accountants, legal advisers, valuers and other consultants'; they do not include 'any allocation of costs that would still have been incurred had the acquisition not been entered into – for example, the costs of maintaining an acquisitions department or management remuneration'.[54]

The Companies Act also allows 'such amount (if any) in respect of fees and other expenses of the acquisition as the company may determine' to be included in arriving at the cost of the acquisition.[55]

2.3.7 Pre-acquisition dividends

Although it has no bearing on the determination of the fair value of the consideration given under FRS 7, one question which sometimes arises is how the acquiring company should account for dividends received from the subsidiary out of its pre-acquisition profits. The rules on this are less than clear. The traditional view was that this was, in effect, a return of the capital paid to acquire the company and was not in any sense a profit, and that accordingly it should be applied to reduce the cost of the investment in the acquiring company's balance sheet. This view was supported by some rather arcane wording that used to be in paragraph 15(5) of Schedule 8 to the Companies Act 1948, but this was changed in the Companies Act 1981.[56]

The more widely accepted view of the law is now that the question of whether or not pre-acquisition dividends have to be written off against the cost of the investment has to be subdivided into two sub-questions:

(a)   does the receipt of the dividend constitute a realised profit in the financial statements of the holding company? and

(b)   does provision for impairment have to be made against the cost of the investment?

Of the two questions set out above, (a) is the more straightforward, provided it can be accepted that the receipt of the dividend can properly be described as a profit at all; the issue of whether it is realised is generally not in question. However, the one which really requires interpretation is (b).

Appendix I to FRS 6 does address the topic but does not come out with a firm conclusion. It states that 'where a dividend is paid to the acquiring or issuing company out of pre-combination profits, it would appear that it need not necessarily be applied as a reduction in the carrying value of the investment in the subsidiary undertaking. Such a dividend received should be applied to reduce the carrying value of the investment to the extent necessary to provide for a diminution in value of the investment in the subsidiary undertaking as stated in the accounts of the parent company. To the extent that this is not necessary, it appears that the amount received will be realised profit in the hands of the parent company.'[57]

The Companies Act requires provision to be made only for *permanent* diminution in the value of a fixed asset. It is possible to advance the view that, provided the investment will eventually recover the value which has been removed from it by making the distribution (by earning further profits, say) then it is unnecessary to write it down and hence the dividend to the holding company can be passed on to its own shareholders.

Following this approach would allow an acquiring company to distribute immediately all the pre-acquisition profits shown in the subsidiary's balance sheet provided that it could foresee that the subsidiary would earn an equivalent amount of profits in the future. Even if this is good law, it is questionable whether it is good accounting. There is a strong argument that the receipt of a pre-acquisition dividend *is* a partial return of the purchase price and the true and fair way to account for it is to deduct it from the cost of the investment rather than to call it a profit, which was the conclusion favoured by Accountants Digest No. 189 on SSAP 23.[58]

The answer to question (b) above could also be affected by FRS 11 – *Impairment of Fixed Assets and Goodwill* (see 4.4 of Chapter 10). That standard requires companies to carry out an impairment review of fixed assets, including investments in subsidiaries, if events or circumstances indicate that the carrying amount of the asset may not be recoverable. Although FRS 11 includes a list of examples of such indicators of impairment, the receipt of a pre-acquisition dividend from a subsidiary is not one of them. However, FRS 11 indicates that these are only examples and there have to be no other indications that an investment in a subsidiary has become impaired. It could be argued that if the subsidiary has paid a significant dividend out of pre-acquisition profits then the investment in the subsidiary *may* have become impaired, so an impairment test should be carried out. As such a test involves discounting future cash flows it may well be that an impairment loss needs to be recognised.

It should of course be pointed out that the above discussion is based on the premise that the cost of the investment in the holding company's books does represent the fair value of the subsidiary. There may be circumstances where it does not, such as when merger relief has been taken or if the subsidiary was not purchased in an arm's-length transaction, and obviously this could require a different view to be taken. In such a case there would seem to be no reason to write down the value of the investment unless the effect of the dividend was to reduce the underlying value of the subsidiary below its carrying amount in the financial statements of the holding company.

2.4 Acquisitions: measuring the fair value of the net assets acquired

2.4.1 Basic principles

The central requirement to bring in the assets of the subsidiary in the group accounts at their fair value rather than their book value in the subsidiary's accounts has been laid down in accounting standards for many years. However, until FRS 7, no standard elaborated in much detail on how this should be done.

The Companies Act takes a similar approach; it states that 'the identifiable assets and liabilities of the undertaking acquired shall be included in the consolidated balance sheet at their fair values at the date of the acquisition'.[59] The Act defines such assets and liabilities as those which are capable of being disposed of or discharged separately without necessarily disposing of a business of the undertaking.

The purpose of the fair value allocation is simply to establish a realistic starting point for the consolidation of the subsidiary's assets and results. The book values in the subsidiary's own financial statements are of no direct relevance for this purpose, because they do not stem from transactions of the reporting entity (the acquiring group), and in effect they are based on the original cost of what are second-hand assets from the group's point of view. The fair value exercise is an attempt to account fairly for the acquisition transaction by asking what the acquiring group has spent, and what it has got for its money.

Of course, the purchase price for most acquisitions is not settled on the basis of an analysis of the individual assets and liabilities of the target company; it is based instead on factors such as the earnings and cash flows which can be brought to the acquiring group. In that sense the purchase allocation exercise is an artificial one rather than portraying the results of a real analysis which has formed part of a business decision. Nevertheless such an allocation has to take place if the group is to be able to present consolidated financial statements, and the hypothetical nature of the allocation does not render it invalid.

The two basic questions which need to be answered in carrying out such an exercise are:

(a)   what assets and liabilities have been acquired? and

(b)   what values should be placed on them?

The answers to these questions depend on whether the exercise should be carried out based on the perspective of the acquiring company or not.

A   Acquirer's perspective – ED 53

ED 53 proposed that 'the fair values of the identifiable assets and liabilities should represent estimates, based on the perspective of the acquiring company, of the amount it would have cost that company had there been direct acquisition of those items individually in their current location and condition'.[60] This meant that the acquirer's intentions regarding the future use of assets or the incurring of future costs were allowed to be taken into account. This was a key point because it was on the basis of this perspective that provision could be made in the fair value exercise for, for example, reorganisation costs. FRS 7 has not retained this 'acquirer's perspective'.

B   Neutral perspective – FRS 7

The key to the approach adopted by the ASB in FRS 7 is that 'the identifiable assets and liabilities to be recognised should be those of the acquired entity that existed at the date of the acquisition'.[61] The standard defines identifiable assets and liabilities as those 'that are capable of being disposed of or settled separately, without disposing of a business of the entity'.[62] It indicates that these may include items that were not previously recognised in the accounts of the acquired company, such as pension surpluses or deficiencies and contingent assets.[63] It also indicates that identifiable liabilities include items such as onerous contracts or commitments that existed at the time of acquisition, whether or not the corresponding obligations were recognised as liabilities in the accounts of the acquired company.[64] Although these items were not recognised in the accounts of the acquired company, the ASB would nevertheless see them as assets and liabilities. The key point is that they existed at the date of the acquisition; they merely had not been recognised.

However, items such as provisions for reorganisation costs expected to be incurred as a result of the acquisition are not permitted; this is because they are not liabilities of the acquired company at the date of acquisition.[65] The perspective of the acquirer, the acquiring company management's intention to undertake a programme of reorganisation, is not relevant. In the acquired company at the time of acquisition there is no such programme contemplated which would justify provision – only if the acquired entity was already committed to the reorganisation, and unable realistically to withdraw from it, would it be regarded as pre-acquisition.

In Appendix III to FRS 7, the ASB explains that it takes the view that 'under its draft Statement of Principles, management intent is not a sufficient basis for recognising changes to an entity's assets or liabilities. It is events, not intentions for future actions, that increase or decrease an entity's assets and liabilities. When intentions are translated into actions that commit the entity to particular courses of action, the accounting should then reflect any obligations or changes in assets that arise from those actions. In relation to acquisition accounting, the Board concluded that events of a post-acquisition period that resulted in the recognition of additional liabilities or the impairment of existing assets of an acquired entity should be reported as events of that period rather than of the pre-acquisition period.'[66]

FRS 7 says that its general principles will result in the following being treated as post-acquisition items:

(a)   changes resulting from the acquirer's intentions or future actions;

(b)   impairments, or other changes, resulting from events subsequent to the acquisition; and

(c)   provisions or accruals for future operating losses or for reorganisation and integration costs expected to be incurred as a result of the acquisition, whether they relate to the acquired entity or to the acquirer.[67]

The recognised assets and liabilities are to be measured at fair values that reflect the conditions at the date of the acquisition.[68]

The requirements of FRS 7 for attributing fair values to particular categories of assets and liabilities are discussed at 2.4.3 below. FRS 7 defines 'fair value' as 'the amount at which an asset or liability could be exchanged in a transaction in an arm's length transaction between informed and willing parties, other than in a forced or liquidation sale'.[69]

Although most of the detailed rules are based on the perspective outlined above, there are occasions (for example, deferred tax) where they do not seem to be in accordance with the principle that they should not be affected by the acquirer's intentions.

One area where the judgement of the acquirer is still specifically important is in the choice of accounting policies to be used in recognising and measuring the assets and liabilities which have been acquired. Although FRS 7 sets out the general principles already discussed and sets out further specific rules which are discussed below, it allows that subject to these, fair values should be determined in accordance with the acquirer's accounting policies for similar assets and liabilities. One particular area where this will be important is in the discretion allowed to reporting entities in the calculation of cost. For example, a property development company which does not capitalise interest into the cost of its developments may acquire a company which does. (Rather surprisingly, the standard appears to imply that the fair value of development stocks should be calculated with reference to cost rather than market value.) In that case, the fair value of the acquired company's developments should be calculated according to the acquirer's policies i.e. excluding interest. The post-acquisition profit shown on disposal of the developments will therefore be higher in the hands of the acquirer than it would have been in the hands of the acquired company. Fair values are thus not independent of the acquirer's choices.

2.4.2   *The use of hindsight*

The fact that the fair value process is inevitably, to some degree, a rationalisation of the price paid after the event means that an accounting issue arises: how much hindsight can the acquirer impute into the values assigned, or must the allocation be based solely on the information which he had at the time when he was making his bid? There is a theoretical argument for the latter, which is that if he was unaware of a particular matter, such as the fact that there was a deficiency in the pension fund of the target, then it cannot have influenced the acquisition price and thus should not feature in any allocation of that price.

Whatever the merits of that view in theory, however, it cannot be used in practice. If the acquirer was only able to assign values to items that he knew about at the time of the acquisition, the exercise would in many cases be completely impossible, because, as noted above, most acquisitions are not primarily based on an assessment of the value of the assets and liabilities of the target company. It is therefore necessary to allow the acquirer a reasonable period of time in which to investigate the assets and liabilities which have been acquired and make a reasoned allocation of values to them. The remaining question is, how much time should be allowed?

The ASC originally suggested that, as a practical matter, the date to be used as the limit of the hindsight period should in fact be the date on which the acquiring company has to present the first consolidated financial statements which incorporate the acquired subsidiary. However, many commentators viewed this as an unrealistically tight deadline. ED 53, therefore, relaxed this proposal to say that if accounts are approved within the first six months after the date of the acquisition, and if there has been insufficient time to complete the fair value exercise, then a provisional allocation should be made for the purpose of these accounts which may be amended (with an adjustment to goodwill) in the next accounts if any of the valuations is found to be inaccurate.

In its Discussion Paper the ASB noted that 'several of those who commented on ED 53 argued that the time limit proposed by ED 53 was too inflexible for groups to be able to deal adequately with major and complex acquisitions. Concern was also expressed that, for listed companies, it was inappropriate to define this limit by reference to the publication of subsequent interim accounts.'[70] Accordingly, the ASB proposed to extend the period even further, notwithstanding the fact that its proposed restrictions on fair value adjustments were designed to simplify the exercise.

FRS 7 now requires that adjustments to the fair values of assets and liabilities should be fixed, if possible, by the date at which the accounts for the first full financial year following the acquisition are approved by the directors. If that is not possible, however, provisional valuations should be made. These should be amended, if necessary, in the next financial statements for the first full financial year following the acquisition, with a corresponding adjustment to goodwill.[71]

Thereafter, adjustments should be recognised as profits or losses when identified. The only circumstances in which a retrospective adjustment to the goodwill calculation could be regarded as appropriate would be if the original allocation was regarded as a fundamental error which required to be dealt with as a prior year adjustment under FRS 3.[72] This would probably be the case only if the original allocation was based on a complete misinterpretation of the facts which were available at the time; it would not apply simply because new information had come to light which changed the acquiring management's view of the value of the item in question.

As indicated at 2.4.1 B above, the recognised assets and liabilities are to be measured at fair values that reflect the conditions at the date of the acquisition. So whatever period of hindsight is used, therefore, it is important that the allocation reflects conditions as they existed at the date of the acquisition, rather than being affected by subsequent events. There is a parallel to be drawn here with the accounting treatment of post-balance sheet events; only those events which provide further evidence of conditions as they existed at the acquisition date should be taken into account.

A number of extracts in this chapter make it clear that the fair value assessment is provisional and therefore it may be that further adjustments will be required in the following year. One company which made further adjustments was Reckitt & Colman as illustrated in Extracts 6.43 to 6.45 at 2.8.2 below.

2.4.3 Requirements for individual assets and liabilities

The requirements of FRS 7 for each class of asset or liability are set out below.

A   Non-monetary assets

FRS 7 states that, 'where similar assets are bought and sold on a readily accessible market, the market price will represent the fair value. Where quoted market prices are not available, market prices can often be estimated, either by independent valuations, or valuation techniques such as discounting estimated future cash flows to their present values. In some cases, where quoted market prices are not available, subsequent sales of acquired assets may provide the most reliable evidence of fair value at the time of the acquisition.'[73]

An important factor which this fails to address is whether the market price is intended to be a buying price or a selling price, and this confusion pervades much of the standard. Also, although the passage cited above might suggest that market values, if available, are to be used for all non-monetary assets, it is clear that this is not always to be the case. For example, it is not envisaged that stocks of finished goods are included at their sales value, but on the other hand, the discussion of investments implies that a sales price is being discussed. In contrast, FRED 7 contained a more understandable general rule, which was not carried through to the standard, that non-monetary assets were to be measured at the lower of replacement cost and recoverable amount.[74] It is not clear what the ASB intended by making that change, particularly since some of the more detailed discussion continues to reflect the terms of the exposure draft.

Where the value of an asset is impaired due, for example, to lack of profitability, underutilisation or obsolescence, such that the replacement cost is not recoverable in full, the fair value is the estimated recoverable amount.[75] 'Recoverable amount' is described as 'the greater of the net realisable value of an asset and, where appropriate, the value in use', which is in turn defined as 'the present value of the future cash flows obtainable as a result of an asset's continued use, including those resulting from the ultimate disposal of the asset'.[76] This is similar to the 'value to the business' rule for valuing assets advocated in the ASB's draft Statement of Principles (see 5.6 and 5.17 of Chapter 2) and now incorporated within FRS 11 (see 4.4 of Chapter 10). The recoverable amount should reflect the condition of the asset on acquisition but not any impairments resulting from subsequent events.[77] FRS 7 emphasises that where acquired assets that had not been impaired before acquisition are subsequently disposed of for a reduced price (for example, as part of a post-acquisition reorganisation of the enlarged group), any losses resulting from their disposal are to be treated as post-acquisition losses, not as adjustments to the fair values as at the acquisition date.[78]

FRS 7 contains more detailed provisions for particular types of non-monetary asset as follows:

■   Tangible fixed assets

'The fair value of a tangible fixed asset should be based on:

(a)   market value, if assets similar in type and condition are bought and sold on an open market; or

(b)   depreciated replacement cost, reflecting the acquired business's normal buying process and the sources of supply and prices available to it.'

The fair value should not exceed the recoverable amount of the asset.[79]

The standard also suggests that in some circumstances, the historical cost of an asset updated by the use of price indices may be the most reliable means of estimating replacement cost. Where prices have not changed materially, or where no relevant price indices are available, it would be acceptable to use a carrying value based on historical cost as a reasonable proxy for fair value.[80]

Examples of fair value adjustments in respect of tangible fixed assets are illustrated in the following extracts:

Extract 6.16: BAA plc (1998)

1   Acquisitions [extract]

Acquisitions during the period consist of Duty Free International, Inc (DFI) and Societa Gestione Servizi Aeroporti Campani SpA (GESAC). On 23 March 1998 DFI changed its name to World Duty Free Americas, Inc.

The acquisition method of accounting has been adopted for both acquisitions and the goodwill arising on the purchases has been capitalised and is being amortised through the profit and loss account over a period of 20 years in accordance with BAA's accounting policy.

Duty Free International, Inc

On 6 August 1997 BAA acquired 99% of the common stock of DFI. The remaining shares were acquired through a merger of a wholly owned subsidiary into DFI. The total consideration paid was £423 million and acquisition costs of £6 million were incurred. The estimated fair value of DFI's net assets was £76 million and the resultant goodwill of £353 million has been capitalised.

The goodwill arising on the acquisition of DFI is provisional pending the resolution and final settlement of certain claims and liabilities for which provision has been made in the table below.

The assets and liabilities of DFI at the date of acquisition and the fair value adjustments made are set out below.

	Book values at 6 August 1997 £m	Fair value adjustments Revaluations £m	Accounting policies £m	Other £m	Fair values at 6 August 1997 £m
Intangible fixed assets	51	–	–	(51)	–
Tangible fixed assets	59	15	(7)	–	67
Short term investments	13	–	–	–	13
Stocks	69	–	–	(2)	67
Debtors	45	–	–	(6)	39
Subsidiaries held for resale	6	–	–	(6)	–
Cash at bank and in hand	27	–	–	(1)	26
Creditors and provisions	(49)	–	–	(13)	(62)
Borrowings	(74)	–	–	–	(74)
	147	15	(7)	(79)	76

The material fair value adjustments to the net assets of DFI were determined as follows:

(a)   Intangible fixed assets

In accordance with FRS 7, fair values have been attributed only to the separable net assets of DFI at the date of acquisition. As a result, £51 million of purchased goodwill within DFI has been written off as a fair value adjustment.

(b)   Tangible fixed assets

DFI's land and buildings have been revalued to open market value. This resulted in an increase in net book value of £15 million. The accounting policy adjustments have been made so as to be consistent with the Group's accounting policies and bases.

(c)   Creditors and provisions

A number of additional provisions have been established to reflect DFI's assets at their fair value at the date of acquisition.

→ A £7 million provision has been made for liabilities arising from litigation against DFI arising from a previous acquisition.

→ A £6 million provision has been made to reduce the carrying value of certain DFI subsidiary companies to their estimated net realisable value following decisions made to sell these entities. These entities are now accounted for as subsidiaries held for resale.

→ Other provisions have been established against stocks, to reduce them to the lower of cost and net realisable value and debtors, to reduce them to their recoverable amount.

Extract 6.17: Scottish Television plc (1996)

29 ACQUISITIONS [extract]

On 18 October 1996, the Company declared its offer for Caledonian unconditional and the results of Caledonian have been consolidated from this date using the acquisition method.

The book values of the assets and liabilities of Caledonian immediately prior to the acquisition and the fair value adjustments required in recognition of the change of ownership are as follows:

	Book value prior to acquisition £m	Revaluations £m	Accounting policy alignment £m	Fair value £m
Intangible assets	64.5	(8.5)(a)	–	56.0
Tangible assets	18.5	(7.3)(b)	–	11.2
Stocks	0.6	–	(0.2)(c)	0.4
Debtors	11.5	(0.2)(d)	–	11.3
Cash	1.4	–	–	1.4
Creditors	(12.2)	(1.3)(e)	–	(13.5)
Net assets acquired	**84.3**	**(17.3)**	**(0.2)**	**66.8**

Consideration	
Cash	53.4
Assumption of liabilities	67.6
Loan notes	0.8
Total consideration	**121.8**
Fair value of net assets acquired above	(66.8)
Goodwill	**55.0**

Fair value adjustments

a)   The directors have derived the value of the intangible assets owned by Caledonian using discounted cash flow valuations and are supported by a comparative view of the transaction values of similar properties within the newspaper industry. The main intangible assets together with the values attributed may be summarised as follows:

	Book value £m	Fair value £m	Adjustment £m
The Herald	60.5	50.0	(10.5)
Evening Times	–	6.0	6.0
Scottish Farmer	4.0	–	4.0
Totals	**64.5**	**56.0**	**(8.5)**

b)   Caledonian's freehold land and buildings have been adjusted to open market value. The open market value has been assessed by Fuller Peiser Property Consultants. This resulted in a reduction of book value by £5.4 million. Caledonian's plant and machinery has been adjusted to market value in accordance with information received from manufacturers. This has resulted in a reduction in book value of £1.7 million. Obsolete equipment has been written down by £0.2 million. Tangible fixed assets have therefore been written down by £7.3 million in aggregate.

c)   Group policy is not to recognise a value for stocks of engineering and electrical stores. Stocks have been written down by £0.2 million to align the Caledonian accounting policy with that of the Group.

d)   The fair value of debtors has been reduced by £0.2 million in respect of potential bad debts not previously provided and credit notes issued post acquisition in respect of pre acquisition sales.

e)   The fair value of creditors falling due within one year has been increased by £1.3 million to reflect the estimated costs of repairing the buildings to meet minimum health and safety standards, to allow for a number of contractual arrangements entered into by previous management which are regarded as onerous and for additional taxation liabilities.

f)   The actuarial value of liabilities arising under the pension arrangements committed to by Caledonian has been reassessed in accordance with assumptions generally used by the Group in determining such liabilities. This valuation indicated that the assets of the Caledonian pension funds exceeded the actuarial liabilities by £0.9 million at the date of acquisition. In accordance with accounting standards, this excess has been recognised as an asset on acquisition and is included in Caledonian's book value prior to fair value adjustments.

It can be seen from the above extract that Scottish Television has incorporated plant and machinery at valuation as well as properties. It is fair to say that although most companies will make adjustments to include properties at a valuation, for example BAA above, very few companies appear to make similar adjustments for plant and machinery. However, that is not to say that no fair value adjustments are made in respect of such assets. It can be seen from Extract 6.16 above BAA has an adjustment to align the depreciation policy in line with that of the group. Another example is Logica, as shown in Extract 6.9 above.

Arguably such adjustments to reflect the acquirer's depreciation methods or lives are not necessary to align the accounting policies of the two companies as they both had policies to depreciate the assets over their useful service lives. If the target company were to change its depreciation methods or asset lives to those adopted by its new parent, then FRS 15 would not allow these to be dealt with by way of prior year adjustment as a change in accounting policy (see Chapter 10 at 3.3.4 and 3.3.6).

Other companies which have made adjustments to reflect their own accounting policies are Oxford Instruments and Kingfisher, as shown below:

Extract 6.18: Oxford Instruments plc (1999)

17   Acquisitions [extract]

Vickers Medical Neurology Business

As reported last year on 18 December 1997 the Group acquired the entire share capital of all the companies comprising the neurology business of Vickers PLC Medical Division. The total cash consideration previously indicated as £12.9 million has now been finalised and settled at £11.0 million, including costs of acquisition.

The fair values attributed to the business at the date of the acquisition have now been finalised and were:

	Book value £000	Accounting policy alignment £000	Fair value adjustments £000	Fair value to the Group £000
Tangible fixed assets	3,434	(64)	(206)	3,164
Stocks	6,854	(463)	(1,133)	5,258
Debtors	11,715	–	(668)	11,047
Cash at bank and in hand	4,106	–	–	4,106
Bank overdrafts and loans	(2,349)	–	–	(2,349)
Creditors	(17,197)	(182)	(863)	(18,242)
Taxation	466	286	(293)	459
Net assets	7,029	(423)	(3,163)	3,443
Negative goodwill				(2,057)
Cash consideration				1,386
Cash at bank and in hand acquired				(4,106)
Bank overdrafts and loans acquired				13,725
Net outflow of cash in respect of the purchase				11,005

The fair value adjustments for the alignment of accounting policies reflect the adoption of Group accounting policies in respect of fixed asset capitalisation, stock provisioning including accelerated depreciation of demonstration stocks, stock overhead absorption, warranty and holiday pay entitlements.

The revaluation adjustments in respect of tangible fixed assets include the write off of obsolete plant, machinery and computers. The revaluation of stocks reflect the write down to estimated realisable value. The revaluation of debtors relates wholly to bad debt provisioning to reflect the estimated recoverable value. The revaluation of creditors relates to liabilities which were not fully reflected in the balance sheet on acquisition. These include provisions for reorganisation which relate to the following areas:

	£000
Provision for the transfer of needle manufacturing operation from the US to UK	183
Provision for the reduction in the headcount in Northern Europe	275
Provision for the reorganisation of manufacturing in the UK	170

All the reorganisation provisions relate to commitments made prior to the date of acquisition. Net deferred tax assets have not been recognised.

Extract 6.19: Kingfisher plc (1999)

37   Acquisitions [extract]

(c) Acquisition of Wegert

On 29 June 1998 the Group acquired a 60% interest in Wegert-Verwaltungs GmbH & Co Beteiligungs-KG (Wegert), a German electrical retailer. Simultaneously, Wegert purchased the entire share capital of the German electrical ProMarkt Holding GmbH (ProMarkt) using cash from its own resources for the equivalent of £14.5m. These transactions have been accounted for using acquisition accounting.

Details of these transactions showing fair value adjustments are set out in the table below:

£ millions	Book value	Fair value adjustments: Revaluations	Fair value adjustments: Accounting policy alignments	Fair value to the Group
Intangible fixed assets	8.6	–	(8.6)	–
Tangible fixed assets	17.7	–	7.4	25.1
Investments	3.5	–	–	3.5
Stocks	67.5	(2.6)	–	64.9
Other current assets	24.0	–	(0.7)	23.3
Creditors	(101.9)	–	(8.3)	(110.2)
	19.4	(2.6)	(10.2)	6.6

£ millions	Goodwill arising
Consideration	54.7
Net assets acquired (60% of £6.6m)	(4.1)
Goodwill	50.6

Consideration satisfied by:	
Cash (including £2.7m acquisition expenses)	54.7

The fair value revaluation adjustment was made in the books of Wegert at acquisition in respect of unprovided risks relating to slow moving stocks and stocks with decreasing sales prices.

Accounting policy alignments have been made in the books of Wegert to eliminate internally generated goodwill, to eliminate historical acquisition goodwill, to apply UK finance lease accounting to a property asset, to write off pre-opening expenses capitalised on loss making stores and to apply UK pension accounting.

The book values of the assets and liabilities have been translated using the exchange rate at the date of acquisition of £1: DM 2.910.

It can be seen that in these situations the difference in accounting policy for fixed assets was not in respect of differences in depreciation policy but, in the case of Oxford Instruments, whether or not the policy was to capitalise the particular type of asset and, in the case of Kingfisher, to align the policy with UK GAAP.

One company which made no fair value adjustment in respect of tangible fixed assets, but possibly should have, was Wace Group:

Extract 6.20: Wace Group PLC (1996)

22. ACQUISITION [extract]

On 31 January 1996 the Group completed the purchase of the trade, assets and goodwill of Hallmark Cards Inc.'s greetings cards manufacturing facility in Rathfarnham. Dublin. On the same date the Group and Hallmark also entered into a five year supply agreement for the manufacture of greetings cards for Hallmark brands in the UK and Eire. The acquisition has been accounted for using acquisition accounting and has been consolidated into the Group balance sheet as follows:

	Book value at acquisition	Fair value adjustments: Revaluation	Fair value at acquisition
	£000	£000	£000
Tangible fixed assets	4,576	–	4,576
Stock	1,207	(108)	1,099
Pension surplus	–	1,396	1,396
Deferred taxation	–	(823)	(823)
Pre-acquisition reorganisation provision	(661)	–	(661)
Net assets	5,122	465	5,587
Goodwill arising			351
Total cost of acquisition			5,938
Satisfied by			
Cash consideration			5,783
Cash costs			155
			5,938

The principal adjustments reflect the Group's estimate of the net realisable value of certain work in progress and the recognition of the surplus on the pension scheme. The provision for deferred tax relates to the pension surplus and the freehold property included in tangible fixed assets.

The value of the surplus as at 31 January 1996 of I£1,346,000 was advised by the scheme's actuaries, Mercer Limited, based on their last actuarial valuation performed as at 1 January 1996 which reported a surplus of I£1,220,400. The valuation used the projected unit cost method and the principal assumptions used were that investment returns would be 2.5 per cent higher than the growth in annual salaries and 3.5 per cent higher than the growth in state pensions: no allowance was made for increases in pensions in the course of payment which were valued using a yield of 8.5 per cent. The actuarial value of the assets at 31 January 1996 I£6,706,400 which on a continuance basis represented 125 per cent of the benefits accrued to the members of the scheme. The surplus will be amortised over the expected working lives of the members.

25. POST BALANCE SHEET EVENTS [extract]

On 21 February 1997 the Group exchanged contracts to sell and lease back the land and buildings at Rathfarnham Dublin acquired with the purchase from Hallmark. Completion is scheduled to take place on 30 June 1997. The contractual consideration is I£6.5m which compares with an anticipated carrying value at the date of disposal of I£3.4m. The Group also completed the disposal of a property at Market Road London on 14 February 1997 for a consideration of £1.85m which is the carrying value within properties for resale at 31 December 1996.

It can be seen that the consideration for the property under the sale and leaseback arrangement is approximately double the carrying value of the property acquired as part of the acquisition which might suggest that the value at the date of acquisition was also greater than the book value at that date.

■ Intangible assets

FRED 7 said that intangible assets, such as patent rights and licences, that are permitted by other accounting standards to be recognised separately from purchased goodwill should be valued at current replacement cost, which is normally their estimated value in the market. The exposure draft gave no further indication as to how this proposal was to apply in practice. It was unclear whether it meant that unless other accounting standards specifically permitted their recognition (such as SSAP 13 on research and development) then no fair values could be attributed – although that would not have been consistent with its reference to patent rights and licences. FRS 7 is even more abbreviated saying only that, 'where an intangible asset is recognised, its fair value should be based on its replacement cost, which is normally its estimated market value'.[81] In other words, FRS 7 does not mandate the recognition of intangible assets, it only requires them to be accounted for in a certain way *if* the decision is made to recognise them.

The main issue is to what extent assets such as brand names or newspaper titles can be regarded as part of the identifiable assets as defined. The recognition of such assets has become more frequent in recent years.

One company which recognises such intangible assets (and makes fair value adjustments to the items already recognised) is Emap as shown below.

Extract 6.21: Emap plc (1999)

25   Acquisitions [extract]

(a)   Businesses acquired

During the year the Group has made a number of acquisitions, *Melody FM* in the Radio division and in the Business Communications division; *Register Information Services, 'Shots'* and *Automotive Management*. On 15 January 1999 Emap acquired The Petersen Companies, Inc. in the USA, all of which have been accounted for using acquisition accounting principles.

The impact of all of the acquisitions in the year on the consolidated balance sheet and the Group cash flow statement was:

	Net book value £m	Fair value adjustments £m	Fair value to Group £m
Intangible fixed assets[1]	341.8	497.1	838.9
Tangible fixed assets	4.9	(1.0)	3.9
Investments	2.5	0.1	2.6
Current assets	75.3	(25.4)	49.9
Current liabilities[2]	(71.0)	(5.0)	(76.0)
Net debt	(192.2)	–	(192.2)
Provisions	(6.1)	(5.4)	(11.5)
	155.2	460.4	615.6
Costs associated with the acquisitions			(19.7)
Goodwill			187.1
Total consideration			**783.0**
Less: Contingent deferred consideration			(1.7)
Add: Transaction costs associated with acquisitions			19.7
Add: payments against acquisition provisions			0.6
Total cash outflow on acquisitions			**801.6**

(1) Following the acquisitions, the Publishing Rights acquired were revalued on a discounted future cash flow basis, and capitalised in accordance with the Group's accounting policies. There were no other significant fair value adjustments, other than for Petersen, see Note 25(b).
(2) Net book value includes £1.0m of reorganisation provisions within Petersen.

(b) Acquisition of Petersen

On 15 January 1999 the Group acquired the entire share capital of The Petersen Companies, Inc. for a consideration of US$34 per share. The impact of the acquisition on the consolidated net assets using an exchange rate of £1=US$1.66 was:

	Net book value [1] £m	Revaluation adjustments £m	Accounting Policy adjustments [2] £m	Fair value to the Group £m
Intangible fixed assets	341.8	467.9 [3]	–	809.7
Tangible fixed assets	4.8	(0.9) [4]	–	3.9
Investments	2.5	–	–	2.5
Current assets	75.3	(10.2) [5]	(15.2)	48.1
Current liabilities	(69.2)	(3.8) [6]	–	(73.0)
Net debt	(192.2)	–	–	(192.2)
Provisions	(6.1)	(5.4) [7]	–	(11.5)
Net assets acquired	155.2	447.6	(15.2)	597.5
Costs associated with the acquisition				(18.4)
Goodwill				154.2
Total discharged by way of cash				723.3

(1) The book values of the assets and liabilities have been taken from the management accounts of Petersen. The fair value adjustments are provisional figures which will be finalised in the 1999/2000 financial statements on final review of judgement areas.

(2) Accounting policy alignments relate to the revision of accounting policy for deferring subscription promotion costs of £9.8m, £3.5m being the income recognition policy for minimum guaranteed licensing revenues which are now spread over the life of the contract, £1.5m spreading of rebates over the life of the relevant contracts, and the write off of retail racking costs of £0.4m. Of these total adjustments approximately £12.2m relates to the year ended 31 December 1998, and £3.0m to the year ended 31 December 1997.

(3) Elimination of goodwill and other intangible assets of £341.8m, and replacement with the Directors' valuation of titles of £809.7m.

(4) The write off of fixed assets relating to sublet space.

(5) £5.3m write off of deferred financing costs and £4.9m write off of debtors and prepayments.

(6) Further accruals mainly for deferred subscription promotion costs.

(7) Provision for onerous property contracts.

Another example is Scottish Television (see Extract 6.17 above).

The distinction between such items and goodwill probably rests on whether or not they can be regarded as identifiable assets, i.e. assets which can be identified and sold without necessarily disposing of the business as a whole. There is no doubt that such assets can be very valuable; the real test is whether the business would remain if they were disposed of. This might depend on the facts of each individual case, because in some cases the right to sell particular brands might be the very essence of a business, while in others the ownership of such rights might be more incidental to the main activities.

The ASB's Discussion Paper on goodwill had proposed that intangible assets arising on an acquisition should be subsumed within purchased goodwill rather than being accounted for separately. However, most commentators disagreed with that approach, so FRS 10 requires that such intangible assets should be recognised separately as long as a reliable value can be placed on such assets. The option of not recognising such intangible assets is no longer available under FRS 10. The intangible assets must be recognised if they meet the 'measured reliably' criterion of FRS 10. However, this may be somewhat illusory since it would still be possible for the acquiror to take the view that some acquired intangible assets could not be measured reliably. This is discussed further in Chapter 10 at 1.3.

One other change that FRS 10 has made is that any value that is attributed to such intangible assets is to be limited to such an amount that neither creates nor increases negative goodwill arising on the acquisition.[82]

An example of a company which has made a fair value adjustment on the basis of aligning accounting policies, to eliminate intangible assets previously recognised by the target company, is Vodafone, as shown below:

Extract 6.22: Vodafone Group Plc (1999)

20   Acquisitions and disposals [extract]

Acquisition of subsidiary undertakings

Vodafone New Zealand

	Balance sheet acquisition £m	Fair value adjustments (2), (3) £m	Accounting policy conformity (4) £m	Fair value balance sheet £m
Tangible fixed assets	94.8	–	–	94.8
Intangible fixed assets	136.5	–	(134.8)	1.7
Other net current assets/(liabilities)	1.0	(0.8)	(1.7)	(1.5)
	232.3	(0.8)	(136.5)	95.0
Goodwill				139.6
Cash consideration paid				234.6

Notes

1. The table above sets out details of the acquisition of the New Zealand GSM cellular network and related assets, radio communication rights and licences.
   The transaction was completed on 30 October 1998.

2. Adjustments to net current assets primarily comprise stock provisions and other accruals.

3. Due to the proximity of the acquisition to the year end, fair value adjustments are provisional.

4. Under UK GAAP, the intangible fixed assets acquired have been included within goodwill on consolidation. Deferred payments for licences have been accrued and capitalised in accordance with Group policy.

It is not clear from the above extract what the intangible assets actually were, but it would appear from Note 1 that they may have been radio communications rights and licences. If that is the case it seems strange that under UK GAAP they have been included within goodwill rather than being recognised separately.

These rules introduced by FRS 10 only apply to those intangibles within its scope. They therefore do not apply to:

(a)   oil and gas exploration and development costs; and

(b)   research and development costs.

This raises one further area of interest which is the interplay between the acquiring company's own accounting policy for development costs and the requirements of FRS 7. For example, a computer software development company may base its own accounting policy on the treatments permitted by SFAS 86 (the US standard on the topic). This is very much more prescriptive, and restrictive, about the capitalisation of software development costs than the more general rules in SSAP 13. In particular, all expenditures are written off until technological feasibility, strictly evidenced by a working model, has been established. If such a company buys another software company, the target may have several valuable products on the brink of commercial realisation – this may indeed be the reason for the acquisition. However, despite the value of such products, there would appear to be no requirement for the acquiring company to attempt to ascribe a fair value to them. FRS 7 refers only to situations where an intangible is recognised – if the accounting policies of the acquirer do not call for recognition, there is no need to include any amount in respect of the software products in the fair value exercise. This is likely to enhance post-acquisition profits since the amortisation, if any, of the enhanced figure for goodwill may be over a longer period than any amortisation of the development costs if they had been recognised separately. This is an area which has recently been the focus of attention in the US (see 5.2.6 C below).

■   Stocks and work in progress

FRS 7 requires that 'stocks including commodity stocks, that the acquired entity trades on a market in which it participates as both a buyer and a seller should be valued at current market prices'.[83]

However, 'other stocks, and work-in-progress, should be valued at the lower of replacement cost and net realisable value. Replacement cost is for this purpose the cost at which the stocks would have been replaced by the acquired entity, reflecting its normal buying process and the sources of supply and prices available to it – that is, the current cost of bringing the stocks to their present location and condition.'[84] For example, for a business purchasing in wholesale markets the replacement cost would be the wholesale price.

On the other hand, the replacement cost of manufactured stocks and work-in-progress would normally be the current cost of manufacturing based, for example, on current standard costs where these are employed. The standard does indicate that in practice, where there is a short manufacturing cycle, replacement cost may not be materially different from historical cost.[85]

This aspect of the standard is significantly different from the proposal in ED 53 whereby such stock was to be valued including profit earned to date, which would thus have been pre-acquisition from the point of view of the acquiring group and hence would not appear in its results when the stock was subsequently sold; FRS 7 is only taking account of input price changes during the period the stock is held.

For long-term maturing stocks, replacement cost would be based on market values if stocks at similar stages are regularly traded in the market. In other situations, a surrogate for replacement cost may be the historical cost of bringing such stock to its present location and condition, including an amount representing an interest cost in respect of holding the stock.[86] For long-term contracts, the standard envisages that no fair value adjustments will be made, other than those that would normally result from assessing the outcome of the contract under SSAP 9, or reflecting the changeover to the acquirer's accounting policies.[87]

Another issue which FRS 7 addresses is the effect of incorporating stocks at their net realisable value. The standard states that where an acquirer reaches a judgement about the value of slow-moving or redundant stocks that differs from that of the management of the acquired company, any material write-down of the carrying value of stocks in the acquired company's books before or at the time of the acquisition needs to be justified by the circumstances of the acquired company before acquisition. If exceptional profits appear to have been earned on the realisation of stocks after the date of the acquisition, the fair values should be re-examined and, if necessary, an adjustment made to these values and a corresponding adjustment to goodwill.[88] This is clearly aimed at ensuring that acquirers do not make excessive provisions against the carrying value of stock, but then sell the stock at prices which give rise to a profit.

Although the standard appears to be very strict about write-downs, it is nevertheless the case that the acquirer can genuinely have a view about the value of slow moving or redundant stocks that differs from that of the management of the acquired entity. Existing management, particularly if the company has been going through a hard time with poor profitability, may have actively resisted write-downs in the value of the stock. The acquiring management may feel less accountable for the levels of such stock and feel able to take a much more critical look at its value.

One company which would appear to have had a significantly different view of the value of stock compared to that of the existing management is Kingfisher in relation to its acquisition of part of Norweb Retail in 1996, as indicated below:

Extract 6.23: Kingfisher plc (1997)

28 Acquisitions [extract]

On 24 November 1996, Comet Group PLC completed the purchase of a substantial part of Norweb Retail, a division of Norweb plc. Details of the net assets acquired are given in the following table:

£ millions	Book value at acquisition	Revaluation adjustments	Fair value to the Group
Tangible fixed assets	23.2	(3.2)	20.0
Stocks	55.2	(25.2)	30.0
Provision for reorganisation	(22.0)	–	(22.0)
Warranty provision	(4.2)	–	(4.2)
	52.2	(28.4)	23.8
Goodwill written off to reserves			1.2
Net cost of acquisition satisfied wholly in cash			25.0

The revaluation adjustments are made to reflect the fair value of the net assets acquired.

The provision for reorganisation of £22.0m relates to the closure of the Norweb high street stores which had been a commitment prior to acquisition. A further post acquisition provision has been charged in this year's profit and loss account of £8.7m relating to the reorganisation of the combined portfolio of out of town stores.

Although there are other examples of companies making fair value write-downs in respect of the net realisable values of stocks acquired the impact is not as great as that in the extract above. It is also fair to say that there do not appear to be many examples whereby adjustments are made to increase book values of stocks, although this may be due to the fact that replacement cost is not materially different from book values given the current low levels of inflation.

Where adjustments have been made to reduce the carrying value of stocks, an interesting question which then arises is where the new management turns the company around and generates a profit on the now written-down stock. Such a profit would be disclosable (see 2.8.2 below) but as discussed, FRS 7 also entertains the idea that the profit should not be taken, but that the fair values should be re-opened and the goodwill figure adjusted instead. It appears necessary, therefore, to assess what would have been the value of the stock in the target company, with the old management and prospects. The acquiring management may feel that the value of the stock was low, justifying its fair value exercise write-down. If the profits on the disposal of the stock have then been generated because of the new management's efforts in finding new outlets or uses for that stock then it is consistent with the philosophy of FRS 7 that those profits should be taken post-acquisition.

A further issue which arises in the context of the fair value of stocks is the calculation of cost. The accounting policy adopted for the identification of stock cost can legitimately differ as between the acquirer and the acquired company. Mention has already been made of the choice as to whether interest is capitalised into cost. In the context of stocks, issues such as the level of overheads to be costed into stocks are legitimate bases of difference as between companies. Application of the costing basis adopted by the acquiring company may result in quite legitimately lower stock carrying values being adopted by the acquiring company, and thus higher post-acquisition profits being reported. Thus, although the standard quite rightly directs attention to unusual post-acquisition profits being made on acquired stock, there can be acceptable reasons why such profits are not inappropriate.

One company which has made fair value adjustments due to different policies in respect of determining the cost of stocks is Persimmon as shown in the following extract:

Extract 6.24: Persimmon plc (1996)

15 Acquisitions [extract]

On 26 February 1996 the company acquired the whole of the issued share capital of Ideal Homes Holdings Limited for a total consideration of £177,572,000. The consideration was satisfied by cash and the acquisition expenses amounted to £2,373,000. The acquisition has been accounted for by the acquisition method of accounting.

The consolidated assets and liabilities of Ideal Homes Holdings Limited acquired are set out below:

	Book value £'000	Revaluations £'000	Other adjustments £'000	Accounting policy alignment £'000	Fair value £'000
Tangible fixed assets	1,627	(480)	(336)	–	811
Investments	9,546	–	(1,000)	–	8,546
Stock	173,380	–	(3,917)	(3,437)	166,026
Debtors	13,217	–	(510)	–	12,707
Deferred tax	–	–	7,000	–	7,000
Total assets	197,770	(480)	1,237	(3,437)	195,090
Creditors	(41,733)	–	(1,307)	–	(43,040)
Net assets	156,037	(480)	(70)	(3,437)	152,050
Goodwill					27,895
Total cost of assets acquired					179,945

The book value of the assets and liabilities shown above have been taken from the management accounts of the acquired business at the date of acquisition.

The fair value adjustments above principally arise for the following reasons:

a.   Revaluations representing the restatement of certain of the long leasehold properties acquired to their estimated market values.

b.   Other adjustments principally representing the:

- write down of fixed assets following a physical verification exercise and assessment of the realisable value of certain assets

- write down of investments following a review of the underlying net assets and assessment of their realisable value

- write down of stock following an assessment of the realisable value of work in progress and strategic land

- write down of debtors following an assessment of the estimated recoverable value

- recognition of unprovided amounts in respect of onerous contracts and other liabilities

- recognition of a deferred tax asset in respect of trading losses acquired

c.   Accounting policy realignments, which align the accounting policies of the acquired group with those adopted by Persimmon. being principally the write-off of capitalised selling costs and ground rents which were both carried in stocks.

Another example, but in respect of work in progress, is Logica as shown in Extract 6.9 above.

One interesting fair value adjustment made in respect of stocks was that made by FKI in respect of its acquisition of Bridon. As shown in Extract 6.27 below, an adjustment has been made to eliminate intercompany profit in stocks for the element which existed in Bridon in relation to stocks sold by other FKI companies prior to acquisition, amounting to £523,000. This would appear to have been made so that the stocks are reflected at 'cost' to the group. However, we do not believe this to be appropriate because FRS 7 regards replacement cost to be the cost at which the stocks would have been replaced by the acquired entity, rather than reflecting their value to the acquiring company.

■ Investments

FRS 7 says that 'quoted investments should be valued at market price, adjusted if necessary for unusual price fluctuations or for the size of the holding'.[89]

Little guidance is given as to how these values, or adjustments to them, are to be determined. As noted above, it is not clear whether the market price is that for a purchase or a sale and thus whether the adjustment for an unmarketable size of holding is intended to be made upwards or downwards. Rather confusingly, the standard comments that the adjustments for large holdings may be to reflect either a lower realisable value representing the difficulties of disposal or a higher value for a holding representing a substantial voting block.[90]

No specific guidance is given on the treatment of unquoted investments which therefore fall to be valued at the amount they could be exchanged at in an arm's length transaction between informed and willing parties. The standard does briefly discuss the valuation of unquoted instruments in the context of valuing capital instruments given as part of the consideration (see 2.3.2 above). Similar considerations would apply in the valuation of unquoted investments acquired.

One company which made a significant adjustment in respect of investments was Granada Group:

Extract 6.25: Granada Group PLC (1996)

25   Acquisition of businesses [extract]

	Book value	Fair value adjustment	Fair value to Group
a Summary of the effect of the acquisition of Forte			
Tangible fixed assets	3,908.3	4.7	3,913.0
Investments	177.9	117.2	295.1
Stocks	29.6	(1.4)	28.2
Debtors	182.7	(8.1)	174.6
Creditors	(439.3)	(173.2)	(612.5)
Cash and cash equivalents	228.0	–	228.0
Corporation tax	(61.5)	–	(61.5)
Deferred taxation	(49.7)	–	(49.7)
Finance lease obligations	(517.6)	–	(517.6)
Borrowings	(981.8)	–	(981.8)
Minority interests	(63.5)	–	(63.5)
Net assets acquired	2,413.1	(60.8)	2,352.3
Shares issued			1,911.9
Cash paid (excluding share issue costs)			2,084.0
Fair value of consideration			3,995.9
Goodwill			(1,643.6)
			2,352.3

No indication is given in the accounts as to what the fair value adjustment was. However, the major investments held by Forte were its associates, The Savoy Hotel and ALPHA Airports Group, both of which were quoted.

An example of a company making adjustments in respect of unquoted investments is United Utilities, as shown below:

Extract 6.26: United Utilities PLC (1996)

Financial review [extract]

Acquisition of Norweb [extract]

The consideration was offset by the realisation of £300 million in cash on the disposal of Norweb's investments in the National Grid and the Pumped Storage Business. These proceeds exceeded our expectations at the time of the acquisition.

The investments in the National Grid and Pumped Storage Business were revalued upward by £199.6 million, net of £48 million tax provisions, reflecting the net proceeds received on disposal.

It can be seen that the investments have been valued at amounts subsequently realised, rather than the values which were expected to be realised at the time of the acquisition. This is consistent with the guidance in the standard in respect of businesses held for resale (see G below).

B   Monetary assets and liabilities

The standard states that 'the fair value of monetary assets and liabilities, including accruals and provisions, should take into account the amounts expected to be received or paid and their timing. Fair value should be determined by reference to market prices, where available, by reference to the current price at which the business could acquire similar assets or enter into similar obligations, or by discounting to present value.'[91]

Short-term monetary items, such as trade debtors and creditors, will be recognised at the amount expected to be received or paid on settlement or redemption. It is unlikely that these will require to be discounted. However, the fair values of certain long-term monetary items may be materially different from their book values. This is designed to deal with the situation, say, where the acquired company has long-term debt with a fixed rate of interest that no longer reflects current rates. Another example is a material long-term debtor where the delay in settlement is not compensated for by an interest charge reflecting current rates.

FRS 7 does not specify a discount rate which is appropriate for all situations. It states that 'the choice of interest rate to be applied to long-term borrowings would be affected by current lending rates for an equivalent term, the credit standing of the issuer and the nature of any security'. (The reference to the issuer suggests that the interest rate is to be specific to the acquired company, not that of the acquirer, which is consistent with the standard's general approach.) 'For long-term debtors (after any necessary provisions had been made) the interest rate would be based on current lending rates.'[92]

The differences between fair values arrived at by discounting and the total amounts receivable or payable in respect of the relevant items represent discounts or premiums on acquisition and are dealt with as interest income or expense by allocation to accounting periods over the term of the monetary amounts at a constant rate based on their carrying amounts, along the lines of FRS 4.[93]

Example 6.1:   Effect of discounting long-term loans

A company, X plc, acquires another, Y plc on 1 January 1999. Y has a fixed rate bank loan of £10,000 taken out when interest rates were higher. It is committed to a rate of 10% pa on this borrowing which is due for repayment in two years. Interest is payable annually in one year and two years' time and the principal is to be repaid with the final interest payment. If it took a two year loan out at the time of the acquisition, it would be able to obtain a rate of only 6%.

Under FRS 7 the fair value of the loan is :

$$[£1,000 \div 1.06] + [£11,000 \div (1.06 \times 1.06)]$$
$$= £10,733$$

The acquired loan would therefore be recorded at this figure.

The accounting should therefore be as follows. The profit and loss account charge for the first period will be £1,000, the coupon, reduced by a debit to the carrying value of the loan of £356. This gives a 'correct' charge of £644 for the period being £10,733 x 6%. The carrying value of the loan is then £10,377.

The charge for the second period will be £1,000, the coupon, reduced by a debit to the carrying value of the loan of £377. This gives a 'correct' charge of £623 for the period, being £10,377 x 6%. The carrying value of the loan is then the amount repayable.

	Cash flows £	Interest charge £	Carrying value in the balance sheet £
At 1 January 1999			10,733
At 31 December 1999	(1,000)	644	10,377
At 31 December 2000	(11,000)	623	0

Where debt instruments are quoted, market values at the date of acquisition will be used instead of present values. However, the standard states that where a reduced pre-acquisition market value on an acquired company's debt reflected the market's perception that it was at risk of being unable to fulfil its repayment obligations, the reduction would not be recognised in the fair value allocation if the debt was expected to be repaid at its full amount[94] (presumably as a result of having been acquired). In contrast to the choice of interest rate discussed above in this case it seems that the credit rating of the *acquiring* company is to be reflected in the value attached to such items, which seems to depart from the standard's general approach on this occasion.

One possible difficulty with this requirement is the extent to which the principle of discounting should be applied to some of the other requirements for attributing fair values of particular assets or liabilities. For example, if provisions are to be made in respect of deferred taxation or for environmental liabilities should these be discounted? Clearly, any provision, such as one for environmental liabilities, which is now covered by FRS 12 – *Provisions, Contingent Liabilities and Contingent Assets* – should be discounted where the effect is material. Although there may be a theoretical argument for doing the same for any provision for deferred tax, we do not believe that this was intended by the ASB. It would clearly be anomalous for the deferred tax relating to the acquired company to be discounted, but the rest of the group's deferred tax not to be discounted.

Examples of companies making fair value adjustments for monetary assets or liabilities based on market values or by discounting amounts receivable or payable are few and far between. This could be due to the fact that companies have floating rate debt and therefore the existing book value will be equivalent to the fair value, or any adjustments may not be material. However, FKI and Cable & Wireless have made fair value adjustments in respect of loan capital, as shown in the following extracts.

Extract 6.27: FKI plc (1998)

28 Acquisitions during the year [extract]

During the year the Group made the following acquisitions, to which were applied the acquisition method of accounting:

Bridon plc on 1 August 1997 and

CMP Corporation on 1 October 1997.

The acquisition of Bridon plc represents a substantial acquisition and the following table sets out the book values of the identifiable assets and liabilities acquired as a result of the acquisition and their fair value to the Group.

	Book value £'000	Accounting policy alignments £'000	Fair value adjustments £'000	Fair value to Group £'000
Fixed assets				
Tangible assets	75,565	–	(7,064)	68,501
Investments	590	–	–	590
Current assets				
Assets held for resale	8,599	–	1,649	10,248
Stocks	57,313	–	(523)	56,790
Debtors	72,539	–	–	72,539
Short-term deposits	1,285	–	–	1,285
Cash	13,524	–	–	13,524
Total assets	229,415	–	(5,938)	223,477
Liabilities				
Loans, overdrafts and finance leases	(63,482)	–	(1,250)	(64,732)
Other creditors	(63,902)	(1,500)	(2,147)	(67,549)
Deferred tax	(577)	(3,763)	–	(4,340)
Minority interest	(1,156)	–	–	(1,156)
Net assets acquired	100,298	(5,263)	(9,335)	85,700
Total consideration				137,488
Goodwill				51,788

The accounting policy alignments were to:

a) provide for known environmental obligations amounting to £1,500,000 and

b) provide for deferred taxation in accordance with the Group's accounting policy for deferred taxation whereby provision is made for deferred taxation using the liability method to take account of timing differences between the incidence of income and expenditure for taxation and accounting purposes.

The principal fair value adjustments were made to:

a) Revalue land and buildings based upon valuations prepared by independent professionally qualified valuers. The effect of these valuations was to reduce the value of land and buildings by £6,193,000.

b) Adjust the book value of business assets acquired which were disposed of shortly after acquisition to their net realisable value. The effect of these adjustments was to increase the value of assets held for resale by £1,649,000.

c) Eliminate intercompany profit in stocks for the element which existed in Bridon in relation to stocks sold by other FKI companies prior to acquisition, amounting to £523,000.

d) Provide for the loss on sale of businesses and assets acquired which are planned to be disposed of amounting to £3,018,000.

e) Adjust the fair value of the US dollar fixed rate guaranteed senior notes which existed in Bridon plc to reflect the market rate of interest prevailing at the date of acquisition by FKI plc. The effect of this was to increase the value of the obligation by £1,250,000.

Extract 6.28: Cable and Wireless plc (1998)

36   ACQUISITIONS [extract]

The following major acquisitions were made by the Group during the year:

Between 25 and 28 April, Cable & Wireless Communications plc ('CWC') acquired 100% of the issued share capital of the NYNEX CableComms Group plc and NYNEX CableComms Group, Inc. (together 'NYNEX'), 100% of the issued share capital of Bell Cablemania plc ('Bell Cablemania') and 100% of the issued share capital of Mercury Communications Limited in exchange for shares in CWC. The group transferred its 85.17% interest in Mercury Communications Limited and 32.5% interest in Bell Cablemania in exchange for 52.9% of CWC;

These have been accounted for using acquisition accounting principles and goodwill arising has been written off to reserves. Details of the book value and the fair value of the assets and liabilities at the dates of acquisition, after making the necessary adjustments, are summarised in the tables below:

NYNEX and Bell Cablemania	Book values		Adjustments		Fair values
	NYNEX £m	Bell Cablemania £m	Revaluations £m	Aligning accounting policies £m	£m
Goodwill	–	517	–	(517)	–
Tangible fixed assets	1,158	1,214	(193)	–	**2,179**
Debtors	66	78	(36)	–	**108**
Cash	5	132	–	–	**137**
Borrowings	(615)	(1,385)	(197)	–	**(2,197)**
Other creditors	(28)	(111)	(26)	–	**(165)**
Provisions	–		(49)	–	**(49)**
Minority interests	–	(13)	–	–	**(13)**
Net assets	586	432	(501)	(517)	–
Share already held	–	(140)	125	168	**153**
	586	292	(376)	(349)	**153**

Goodwill
Bell Cablemania held £517m of goodwill in its balance sheet arising principally on its acquisition of Videotron Holdings plc. This amount has been written off directly to reserves in accordance with Group policy.

Fixed assets
A provision of £129m has been made to reduce the value of analogue set-top boxes and head-end equipment included in fixed assets in Bell Cablemania. The provision was made because the analogue set-top boxes and head-end equipment had no value over their expected life. The balance relates to the write down of £31m of property and information technology systems and £33m for other fixed assets.

Borrowings
The borrowings in Bell Cablemania were revalued increasing the book value of these borrowings by £164m. The revaluation was made to restate the high yield debt obligations of Bell Cablemania at their fair value to reflect the difference between a market rate at the date of acquisition, adjusted to take account of the credit rating of the Cable Companies as subsidiaries of CWC, and the fixed rates applicable to the debt. An adjustment to write off deferred financing costs and arrangement fees of £58m, £25m of which was classified in debtors and £33m in borrowings.

Provisions
An adjustment has been made to provide for onerous contracts of £49m, principally relating to programming costs and commitments to purchase analogue set top boxes.

Another example is shown in Extract 6.32 below.

Most fair value adjustments relating to monetary assets, such as debtors, are due to reassessments of their recoverable amount or to align accounting policies for bad debt provisions; for example, see Extracts 6.16, 6.17 and 6.18 above.

C   Contingencies

Both contingent assets and liabilities should be measured at fair values where these can be determined. For this purpose reasonable estimates of the expected outcome may be used.[95] The treatment of contingent assets is an example of the situation whereby assets are recognised as part of the fair value exercise when they are not normally recognised in accounts when no acquisition is involved;

FRS 12 does not allow any contingent assets to be recognised as this could give rise to recognition of a profit that may never be realised. However, where the realisation is virtually certain, then the related asset is not contingent and should therefore be recognised as an asset.[96] SSAP 18 had a similar criterion, but used the phrase 'reasonably certain', which in practice was the same as the high threshold level now required by FRS 12. The level of probability under FRS 7 is lower than in FRS 12, and although the treatment in FRS 7 seems imprudent at first sight, it is in fact designed to *exclude* from post-acquisition profits any windfall gains from transactions or events which took place before the acquisition was made. In effect, the acquirer has made an investment in a speculative asset.

On a practical note, acquiring managements will often be reluctant to recognise contingent assets. The details surrounding them will often be hazy and managements will be reluctant to threaten post-acquisition profits with the possibility of a write down of the contingent asset if the gain does not in the event materialise – from their point of view there is downside but no upside. An example of a contingent asset, however, would be the need to reflect expected receipts under an 'earn-out' arrangement in respect of a company previously disposed of from the acquired group.

Certain contingent assets and liabilities that crystallise as a result of the acquisition are also to be recognised as part of the fair value exercise, provided that the underlying contingency was in existence before the acquisition. An example is where the acquired company has previously entered into a contract that contains a clause under which obligations are triggered in the event of a change in ownership.[97]

One company which made a fair value adjustment in respect of a contingent asset was GKN in its 1994 accounts, as shown below:

Extract 6.29: GKN plc (1994)

23   ACQUISITIONS [extract]

The fair value adjustments made include:

(c)   a debtor for the net cash received in June 1994 amounting to £112 million arising from an arbitration award against the Arab Organisation for Industrialisation (AOI) following the termination of a joint venture between AOI and Westland Helicopters Limited to manufacture Lynx helicopters under licence. This receipt was secured as a result of actions initiated by Westland prior to acquisition and has accordingly been referred back to 31st March 1994. A further final net receipt of £51 million was negotiated in August 1994 and has been treated as a post acquisition exceptional profit (see note 4). These items, taken together with the net £15 million received by Westland in December 1993, give a total net receipt of £178 million from the reward.

Examples of companies providing for contingent liabilities are BAA in Extract 6.16 above and TI Group in Extract 6.32 below.

D   Pensions and other post-retirement benefits

FRS 7 requires that the fair value of a deficiency in a funded pension or other post-retirement benefits scheme, or accrued obligations in an unfunded scheme, should be recognised as a liability of the acquiring group. To the extent that it is reasonably expected to be realised, a surplus in a funded scheme should be recognised as an asset.[98] The assets or liabilities which are recognised are in substitution for any existing prepayments or provisions that have accumulated in the accounts of the acquired company under the requirements of SSAP 24 or UITF 6.

This is another example where assets or liabilities are to be recognised as part of the fair value exercise which would otherwise not be allowed in the absence of an acquisition; in most situations SSAP 24 does not allow the immediate recognition of surpluses or deficiencies of pension schemes, but requires them to be recognised systematically over the average remaining service lives of the employees. Essentially this requirement is based on the fact that a pension fund represents an off balance sheet resource (which may be positive or negative, depending on the solvency of the fund), and that post-acquisition results will be distorted unless recognition is given to the existence of this asset or liability at the time of the acquisition.

A change from the exposure draft was the introduction of the proviso regarding the recognition of assets through use of the phrase 'to the extent that it is reasonably expected to be realised'. As was indicated when FRED 7 was published, this was an area which the ASB could not agree upon. A minority of the members disagreed with giving instant recognition to a pension surplus and would have preferred to spread it forward over the average service lives of the employees.[99] The wording above appears to have been the compromise reached, but like many compromises it is far from satisfactory, because it is unclear what it means.

The explanation section of FRS 7 states that 'the fair value attributed to a surplus in a funded scheme would be determined taking into account not only the actuarial surplus of the fund, but also the extent to which the surplus could be realised in cash terms, by way of reduction of future contributions or otherwise, and the time-scale of such potential realisations',[100] but this still does not clarify the issue, because it introduces a vague test of recoverability that has no equivalent in SSAP 24 itself. It further states that 'a pension asset ... would be recognised only insofar as the acquired entity or the acquirer was able to benefit from the existing surplus',[101] but it remains unclear in what circumstances the acquired entity or acquirer will not benefit from such a surplus.

FRS 7 says that changes in pension or other post-retirement arrangements following an acquisition should be accounted for as post-acquisition items.[102] An example is the cost of improvements to benefits granted to members of an acquired scheme as part of harmonising remuneration packages in the enlarged group. This is consistent with accounting for any changes affecting the pension arrangements of the acquirer's own workforce. The cost of these changes should therefore be dealt with in accordance with SSAP 24 or UITF 6 by being spread forward over average service lives.

BICC made an adjustment to incorporate a pension surplus in its 1996 accounts, as shown below:

Extract 6.30: BICC plc (1996)

19   Acquisitions [extract]

	Consideration and costs £m	Fair value of assets acquired £m	Goodwill £m
British Rail Infrastructure companies	53	30	23
BTCC Phillips Inc minority interest	7	1	6
	60	31	29

On 3 April 1996 the Group acquired three British Rail Infrastructure companies The total consideration including expenses was £33m of which £32m was paid on completion. On 29 March 1996 the Group acquired the outstanding minority interest in its Canadian subsidiary BICC Phillips Inc for £7m. The Group has used acquisition accounting to account for these purchases. Adjustments have been made to reflect the fair value of assets of the British Rail Infrastructure companies acquired as follows:

	Net tangible assets acquired £m	Fair value adjustments £m	Fair value of assets acquired £m
Fixed assets	16	–	16
Stocks	8	–	8
Debtors	79	31	110
Creditors	(70)	–	(70)
Provisions, including deferred taxation	(2)	(20)	(22)
Net borrowings	(12)	–	(12)
	19	11	30

Fair value adjustments, which include, principally, recognition of the pension fund surplus, related deferred taxation and provisions for known liabilities, are provisional estimates which will be revised if necessary in 1997.

Another example is shown in Extract 6.17 above, although interestingly in that case, the adjustment is included as part of the book values rather than as a fair value adjustment.

One company which did not appear to have made any fair value adjustment in respect of a pension surplus was United Utilities in its 1996 accounts. No reference is made to pensions in the discussion of fair value adjustments yet the pensions note disclosed the following:

Extract 6.31: United Utilities PLC (1996)

23   Pensions [extract]

Most employees of NORWEB plc who joined prior to 1 October 1991 are members of the ESPS, a defined benefit scheme. This scheme is now closed to new employees.

The latest full actuarial valuation of NORWEB's section of the ESPS was carried out by Bacon & Woodrow, consulting actuaries, as at 31 March 1995. The attained age method was used for the valuation and the principal actuarial assumptions adopted for average annual growth rates were investment returns 9 per cent, salary increases (exclusive of merit awards) 6.5 per cent and pensions increases 5 per cent.

The total market value of NORWEB's share of the net assets of the ESPS at 31 March 1995 was £662.3 million.

The valuation showed that the actuarial value of the assets of NORWEB's section of the ESPS as at 31 March 1995 represented 112.8 per cent of the actuarial value of the accrued benefits. This is within the statutory maximum. The accrued benefits include all benefits for pensioners and other former members as well as benefits based on service completed to date for active members, allowing for future salary rises. In deriving the pension cost, the surplus remaining after benefit improvements is being spread over the future working lifetime of the members.

It would seem from the above that there may have been a pension surplus at the date of acquisition. Although the fair values in respect of Norweb were reassessed in the following year, pensions was not one of the areas adjusted.[103]

TI Group made an adjustment to reflect a pension deficit in respect of its acquisition of EIS Group, as shown below.

Extract 6.32: TI Group plc (1998)

23.   ACQUISITIONS AND DISPOSALS [extract]

Provisional fair value of net assets – EIS Group

	Book values prior to acquisition £m	Transfer to assets held for disposal £m	Conformity with TI accounting policies £m	Pensions & other liabilities £m	Onerous contracts £m	Provisional fair values to TI Group £m
		Provisional fair value adjustments				
Fixed tangible assets	93.7	(16.8)	(3.4)	–	(1.9)	**71.6**
Investments	0.7	–	–	–	–	**0.7**
Stocks	113.5	(45.1)	(3.1)	–	(0.2)	**65.1**
Assets held for disposal	–	35.6	–	–	–	**35.6**
Debtors	130.0	(31.5)	(3.0)	–	–	**95.5**
Creditors	(110.5)	25.1	(0.3)	–	(1.2)	**(86.9)**
Pensions and other post-retirement obligations	(6.4)	0.6	–	(20.7)	–	**(26.5)**
Other provisions	(4.3)	–	–	(14.5)	(9.0)	**(27.8)**
Deferred taxation	6.5	(0.1)	(6.5)	6.0	–	**5.9**
Minority interests	(1.3)	–	–	–	–	**(1.3)**
Net debt	(63.4)	–	–	–	–	**(63.4)**
Net assets	158.5	(32.2)	(16.3)	(29.2)	(12.3)	**68.5**

Provisional fair value adjustments comprise the following:

Transfers to assets held for disposal: Businesses identified at acquisition as being held for disposal in the short term were valued at their actual or estimated disposal proceeds, discounted to their present values as at the date of the transaction of EIS Group.

Conformity with TI accounting policies: Adjustments were made to align accounting policies principally affecting tooling capitalisation, and stock, debtor and deferred taxation provisions.

Pensions and other liabilities: As anticipated at the time of acquisition an adjustment of £21.0m was made to recognise the initial estimate of a deficit in the principal EIS Group UK pension schemes, which will be the subject of a full actuarial valuation during 1999. Provisions of £14.5m were made for the estimated costs of disputes and claims, actual and potential, principally related to businesses discontinued by EIS Group prior to its acquisition by TI Group.

Onerous contracts: Provisions of £9.0m and asset write downs of £2.1m were made for expected future losses on specific customer contracts. Fixed rate borrowings were revalued to their fair values, based on market rates at the date of acquisition, resulting in an increase in creditors of £1.2m.

All fair value adjustments will be reviewed during 1999; any revisions made will be adjustments to goodwill.

The carrying value of land and buildings at acquisition was reviewed and no material adjustment was required to restate to open market existing use value.

E   Taxation

FRS 7 says that deferred tax assets and liabilities recognised in the fair value exercise should be determined by considering the enlarged group as a whole.[104]

Although no specific guidance is given by the standard, the recognition of deferred tax in the context of a fair value exercise falls into two areas. First of all there will be existing timing differences within the acquired company which will give rise to a potential liability to deferred tax which will need to be considered. In addition, the adjustments made as a result of the fair value exercise may lead to quasi-timing differences which will also require provision for deferred tax. The difference between the fair values assigned and the tax base values of the assets and liabilities acquired are in fact not strictly timing differences within the SSAP 15 definition; however, differences between accounting profits and taxable profits will arise in subsequent periods as items pass through the profit and loss account and therefore it is necessary to treat them as such in order to avoid distorting post-acquisition earnings. Arguably, however, not all fair value adjustments are to be regarded as timing differences; as FRED 7 proposed, it is only those that would be timing differences under SSAP 15 if reflected in the accounts of the acquired company.

Although not specifically addressed by FRS 7, where assets or liabilities are recognised in respect of pension schemes and post-retirement benefits, then the deferred tax implications should be accounted for in accordance with SSAP 15 (as amended in December 1992) - see Chapter 21 at 1.2.8. This should obviously be based on the accounting policy of the acquirer for such differences. One company which made full provision in respect of the tax implications of incorporating a pension surplus as part of a fair value exercise was Premier Farnell in its 1996 accounts, as shown below.

Extract 6.33: Premier Farnell plc (1996)

23.   ACQUISITIONS AND DISPOSALS [extract]

(i)   **Acquisition of Premier**

On 11th April 1996 the Group acquired Premier Industrial Corporation ("Premier") for a consideration of £1,877.2 million. Details of the acquisition, including the fair value adjustments made to the assets and liabilities acquired are set out below:

	Book value at acquisition £m	Accounting policy alignment £m	Other £m	Fair value £m
Tangible fixed assets	43.2	(2.0)	4.9[a]	46.1
Intangible assets	8.5	(8.5)[1]	–	–
Investments	2.0	–	(2.0)	–
Stock	127.3	(20.8)[2]	–	106.5
Debtors - due within one year	92.5	(3.4)	(1.2)	87.9
- due after one year	13.7	–	40.4[b]	54.1
Creditors	(57.7)	(2.1)	(2.7)	(62.5)
Corporate and deferred taxes	(7.1)	(3.7)[3]	(18.0)[b]	(28.8)
Provisions	–	–	(4.6)[c]	(4.6)
Net cash	82.0	–	–	82.0
	304.4	(40.5)	16.8	280.7

Consideration	
Shares	923.7
Cash including costs	953.5
	1,877.2

Goodwill written off (note 21)	1,596.5

Accounting policy alignment

[1]write-off of goodwill.

[2]adjustments required to reflect UK GAAP eliminate overheads from stock valuation and adopt stock provisioning in accordance with Group accounting practice.

[3]write-off of deferred tax assets in accordance with UK GAAP.

Accounting policy alignments also reflect the adoption of Group policies in respect of fixed asset capitalisation, catalogue costs, sales returns and holiday pay.

Other

[a]revaluation of land and buildings.

[b] actuarial valuation of pension surplus in accordance with FRS7 and SSAP24 and recognition of corresponding deferred tax provision.

[c] actuarial valuation of post-retirement obligation.

Other adjustments also reflect the write-down of investments to net realisable value and the recognition of liabilities existing at the acquisition date.

The standard also requires that the benefit to the group of any tax losses attributable to an acquired entity at the date of acquisition should be recognised in accordance with the requirements of SSAP 15.[105] Again, application of this principle may result in deferred tax assets being recognised on acquisition that were previously unrecognised in the acquired company's accounts because SSAP 15 did not allow it. One company which has made a fair value adjustment to reflect a deferred tax asset in respect of losses is Persimmon, as shown in Extract 6.24 above.

It can be seen that FRS 7 requires that the deferred tax to be recognised should be determined on an overall group basis; similarly, losses can be recognised if they benefit the group. This seems to be at odds with the standard's general approach that assets and liabilities recognised as part of the fair value exercise should not reflect increases or decreases resulting from the acquirer's intentions or future actions. The ASB's Discussion Paper had proposed an approach for deferred tax which did not take account of the acquirer's different plans for capital expenditure or post-acquisition group relief arrangements, but reflected only the acquired company's plans etc. However, the ASB has recognised that it would be extremely difficult, if not impossible, for such an approach to work in practice. The partial provision approach of SSAP 15 has to be based on future intentions and these can only be those of the reporting entity, therefore it has to be done on an overall group basis.

F   Provisions

The most significant impact of FRS 7 has been on the area of provisions, particularly reorganisation or rationalisation provisions and provisions for future trading losses of the acquired companies.

■   Reorganisation or rationalisation provisions

As indicated at 2.4.1 B above, FRS 7 states that the assets and liabilities that are to be fair valued are to be those of the acquired company and should not include 'provisions or accruals ... for reorganisation and integration costs expected to be incurred as a result of the acquisition, whether they relate to the acquired entity or to the acquirer'.[106] Only if the acquired entity was already committed to the course of action in question, and unable realistically to withdraw from it would it be regarded as pre-acquisition.

In practice this had been one of the areas of fair value accounting which prior to FRS 7 had given rise to a great deal of controversy, and alleged abuse. The ability to provide for costs of reorganisation programmes without having to charge these costs in the profit and loss account was a very attractive opportunity, and one which understandably tempted some companies to be enthusiastic in their estimation of these provisions.

The ASB adopted a restrictive approach, with the costs of any such reorganisations or rationalisation being treated as post-acquisition costs. By doing this the ASB really only moved the goalposts so far, because although provisions for such costs could no longer bypass the profit and loss account as part of the goodwill calculation, such one-off provisions were still being made but highlighted in the profit and loss account as exceptional items. The ASB has now taken this a stage further by issuing FRS 12 which restricts the ability of companies to create such big bath provisions (see Chapter 25 at 4.1).

It might be thought that it is possible to get around the FRS 7 rules by getting the vendor to commit itself, prior to the formal acquisition date, to a particular course of action to reorganise or restructure the business so that the costs can be regarded as being pre-acquisition costs. However, the standard emphasises that where provisions for future costs were made by the acquired company shortly before the acquisition took place, particular attention has to be paid to the circumstances in order to determine whether obligations were incurred by the acquired company before the acquisition. Only if the acquired company was demonstrably committed to the expenditure whether or not the acquisition was completed would it have a liability at the date of acquisition. If obligations were incurred as a result of the influence of the acquirer, it would be necessary to consider whether control had passed to the acquirer at an earlier date and, consequently, whether the date of acquisition pre-dated such commitments.[107] The ASB's earlier Discussion Paper had, in fact, proposed an anti-avoidance measure whereby decisions taken before the date of acquisition either at the request of, or during negotiations with, the acquirer would be deemed to be post-acquisition.[108] These proposals were not well supported, so the standard does not include such prescriptive anti-avoidance measures.

One company which disregarded these rules in FRS 7 by invoking the true and fair override was Aim Group as shown below.

Extract 6.34: Aim Group plc (1998)

24   Purchase of undertaking

On 16th February 1998 the Group acquired the assets and business of Hunting Aviation Interiors Division from Hunting plc.

Details of the acquisition are as follows:

	£'000
Net assets acquired	
Tangible fixed assets	137
Stocks and work in progress	2,482
Provisions for onerous contracts	(410)
Provisions for closure costs	(951)
	1,258
Goodwill arising on acquisition	2,189
	3,447
Analysis of consideration:	
Cash (including expenses of acquisition)	2,847
Deferred consideration	600
	3,447

The deferred consideration is payable over three years commencing in May 1999 and is based on sales of the division.

True and fair override on determination of goodwill arising on acquisition

The net assets acquired include a provision for the costs associated with the closure of the operational facility at Biggin Hill. Financial Reporting Standard 7 only allows these costs to be included in the fair value adjustment to goodwill where the vendor was already committed to the closure. Although the closure decision was taken by the Group, the Directors consider that these closure costs were an integral part of the overall decision to purchase the business, and their inclusion is necessary to give a true and fair view of the goodwill on acquisition. The effect on the Group's financial statements of this departure from the requirements of Financial Reporting Standard 7 is to increase the goodwill capitalised on acquisition by £951,000. These costs would otherwise have been charged to the profit and loss account as an exceptional item increasing the loss for the year by £951,000.

This treatment was challenged by the Review Panel which did not accept the directors' justification for invoking the true and fair override and since Aim Group had taken the closure decision, it was therefore a post-acquisition event.[109] As a result, the company revised its 1998 accounts by way of supplementary note published the same day as the ruling by the Review Panel. The directors also amended the accounts to give more disclosures in respect of the fair value table to meet the requirements of FRS 6 and the Companies Act (see 2.8 below).

Examples of companies who have reflected pre-acquisition reorganisation provisions as part of the book values of the net assets acquired without making any adjustments thereto are Kingfisher and Wace Group, as shown in Extracts 6.23 and 6.20 above. In the former example, the note discloses that a further post-acquisition provision has been charged to the profit and loss account. Oxford Instruments in Extract 6.18 above provides an example of a company making a fair value adjustment for a reorganisation provision which was not fully reflected in the book values. Rentokil Initial at Extract 6.36 below is another example of a company making a fair value adjustment to an existing pre-acquisition reorganisation provision. However, there were also further reorganisation costs in respect of the acquisition charged to the profit and loss account.

■   Provisions for future operating losses

For the same reasons as for reorganisation provisions, FRS 7 requires that the assets and liabilities that are to be fair valued are to be those of the acquired company and should not include provisions for future operating losses.[110] The future trading results of the subsidiary do not represent one of its identifiable assets or liabilities, and they must be consolidated with those of the rest of the group from the date of acquisition. Thus the effect on the acquisition price of whatever future results were anticipated will fall to be dealt with as part of goodwill, positive or negative.

■   Other provisions

Although FRS 7 takes a restrictive view in setting up provisions for reorganisation costs or for future losses, this does not mean that it does not allow any provisions to be set up as part of the fair value exercise. An acquired company may have certain commitments which are not reflected as liabilities in its own accounts which nevertheless should form part of the identifiable liabilities to be recognised as part of the acquisition. Paragraph 38 of the standard states that 'identifiable liabilities include items such as onerous contracts and commitments that existed at the time of acquisition, whether or not the corresponding obligations were recognised as liabilities in the financial statements of the acquired entity'.

It is clear that the possibility under the FRS of recognising as liabilities of the acquired entity such items as onerous contracts and commitments, and thus bringing them into the fair value exercise, will provide some scope for reflecting the affairs of an acquired company more fully than if the fair value exercise were limited to items just recognised by the acquired company. FRS 7 does not define what it regards as an onerous contract, nor does it give any examples. Although FRS 12 defines an onerous contract as 'a contract in which the unavoidable costs of meeting the obligations exceed the economic benefits expected to be received under it',[111] in our view this is not necessarily the same as an onerous contract for the purposes of FRS 7. The only example of an onerous contract quoted in FRS 12 is vacant leasehold property. An example of a company making provision in respect of onerous property contracts as part of the fair value exercise is Emap, as shown in Extract 6.21 above.

Some might argue that examples of onerous contracts could include leases at an unfavourable rental or for an excessive amount of space; and contracts to provide services in an area of business which is uneconomic. It has been argued by some commentators that provision for leases, the rentals for which at the date of acquisition are above present market rents, should not be made as part of the fair value exercise. This is because under SSAP 21 such operating leases are not reflected as liabilities.[112] However, the counter argument to this is that FRS 7 requires fair value adjustments to be made for other items such as contingencies and pensions which would not otherwise be allowed by the relevant accounting standards in these areas (see C and D above). Also, much of the guidance in other areas in the standard require fair values to be based on market conditions at the acquisition date. In our view such leases can be regarded as onerous leases under FRS 7 and provision made for the excess over market rates.

An interesting example of a company making provision for onerous contracts was United Utilities in respect of its acquisition of Norweb in its 1996 accounts, as shown below:

Extract 6.35: United Utilities PLC (1996)

Financial review [extract]

Acquisition of Norweb [extract]

Provision was made for gas and electricity contracts of £173.2 million mainly in relation to long term power purchase agreements, where the recent collapse in gas prices and reduced capacity costs resulted in onerous conditions compared to prices available in November 1995, the date the fair valuation was made. The provisions are of a long term nature and, in any event, will not be utilised prior to 1998. Also included is a small element relating to short term take or pay gas purchase contracts.

The fair value adjustments will be reviewed again during the course of 1996/97 and amended as necessary in the light of subsequent events.

This seems to suggest that the contracts only became onerous after the acquisition, in which case it is questionable as to whether such an adjustment should have been made. As can be seen from the above extract, the fair value adjustments were to be reviewed the following year and although subsequent adjustments were made, none of them related to these contracts.[113]

Other examples of companies making provisions for onerous contracts are shown in Extracts 6.28 and 6.32 above.

One company which made significant fair value adjustments to reflect various provisions was Rentokil Initial in respect of its acquisition of BET in 1996, as can be seen from the following extract.

Extract 6.36: Rentokil Initial plc (1996)

29   Acquisitions [extract]

The group purchased 15 companies and businesses during the year as set out on page 63 for a total consideration of £2,230.3m of which £2,221.7m was in respect of the acquisition on 29th April 1996 of BET Public Limited Company. The total adjustments required to the balance sheet figures of companies and businesses acquired in order to present the net assets of those companies and businesses at fair values in accordance with group accounting principles were £260.8m, of which £259.7m related to BET, details of which are set out on pages 58 and 59 together with the matching adjustment to goodwill. All of these businesses have been accounted for as acquisitions.

BET acquisition

	Book value	Revaluations	Consistency of accounting policy	Other	Fair value
	£m	£m	£m	£m	£m
Tangible fixed assets	609.2	(24.1)	(22.9)	–	562.2
Investments	33.0	(3.4)	(18.3)	(1.0)	10.3
Stock	35.0	(3.3)	–	–	31.7
Debtors	372.5	12.4	(0.6)	–	384.3
Creditors	(472.1)	(61.4)	(6.0)	–	(539.5)
Provisions					
– Vacant property	(20.7)	–	–	(47.5)	(68.2)
– Environmental	(4.4)	–	–	(49.9)	(54.3)
– Subsidiary	–	–	–	(33.0)	(33.0)
– Pre-acquisition restructuring	(1.8)	–	–	(5.0)	(6.8)
Taxation	(108.2)	3.5	–	–	(104.7)
Net debt	(130.5)	–	–	–	(130.5)
	312.0	(76.3)	(47.8)	(136.4)	51.5
Minority interests	(1.7)	0.8	–	–	(0.9)
Net assets acquired	310.3	(75.5)	(47.8)	(136.4)	50.6
Special dividend to BET shareholders					38.2
Adjusted assets					88.8
Goodwill					2,132.9
Consideration					2,221.7

Satisfied by	
Shares issued	1,653.2
Cash (including special dividend paid of £38.2m and deducting cash received from exercise of share options of £18.0m)	568.5
	2,221.7

The book values of the assets and liabilities shown on page 58 have been taken from the management accounts of BET at the date of acquisition (at actual exchange rates at that date). The fair value adjustments set out on page 58 are provisional figures which will be finalised in the 1997 financial statements following professional property valuations as at the date of acquisition and on final review of judgemental areas.

Revaluation adjustments in respect of tangible fixed assets comprise the revaluation of certain freehold properties and the write-off of obsolete or impaired plant and machinery and fixtures and fittings.

Revaluations of investments and stock reflect the write-down to estimated realisable value. The adjustment to debtors includes establishing an asset (£16.9m) to reflect the pension fund surplus arising from actuarial valuations, offset by various write-downs to reflect estimated realisable value.

The revaluations of creditors relate to liabilities which were not fully reflected in the balance sheet of BET's business on acquisition. These include adjustments to provisions for insurance claims, liabilities under onerous contracts and the reassessment of legal claims. An adjustment of £5.6m has been made in order to reflect a market coupon on the BET US $ bond.

A net deferred tax asset of £10.7m for expected tax relief on fair value adjustments has been recognised partially offset by tax liabilities of £7.2m.

The book values acquired included provisions for reorganisation and restructuring costs amounting to £1.8m. These provisions related to reorganisations established by BET in the year prior to acquisition, which were reviewed and increased by £5.0m. This increase relates to irrevocable reorganisations commenced by BET management before the acquisition.

The fair value adjustments for alignment of accounting policies reflect the restatement of assets and liabilities in accordance with the policies of the group including the removal of capitalised security alarm installation costs (£14.3m), the write-off of capitalised container and vehicle refurbishment costs in distribution companies, provision for the group's share of deferred consideration payable by an associated company for the acquisition of a business (£18.3m), provision for outstanding holiday pay entitlements of employees and the alignment of general bad debt provisioning policy.

Additional provision has also been made for vacant property costs relating to future net rental outgoings of the substantial number of vacant and sub-let properties owned and leased by BET. Environmental provisions were also made for the estimated costs of remediation on BET sites. Provision has also been made for major regulatory and taxation problems in a subsidiary.

It can be seen from the above that most of the adjustments made by Rentokil Initial are not to reflect new liabilities, but are reassessments of provisions and creditors which were already recorded within the books of BET. In the previous edition of this book we stated that it would be 'interesting to see when these provisional fair values are reviewed in 1997 as to whether the company has been over-enthusiastic in making these provisions'. As it turned out the company had to increase the amounts of creditors and provisions as shown below.

Extract 6.37: Rentokil Initial plc (1997)

30 Acquisitions and disposals [extract]

As indicated in the 1996 financial statements the provisional fair value adjustments recorded in relation to the acquisition of BET PLC have been finalised during the year, following professional property valuations and final reviews of judgemental areas. As a result, further adjustments of £41.5m were made in 1997. Details of these adjustments are set out below.

BET PLC fair value adjustments

	Fair value as stated in the 1996 financial statements	Revaluations	Consistency of accounting policy	Other	Fair value as now restated
	£m	£m	£m	£m	£m
Tangible fixed assets	562.2	(1.5)			560.7
Investments	10.3				10.3
Stock	31.7				31.7
Debtors	384.3				384.3
Creditors	(539.5)	(12.0)	(0.4)		(551.9)
Provisions					
– Vacant property	(68.2)			(17.3)	85.5
– Environmental	(54.3)			(6.2)	(60.5)
– Subsidiary	(33.0)				(33.0)
– Pre-acquisition restructuring	(6.8)				(6.8)
Taxation	(104.7)	(4.1)			(108.8)
Net debt	(130.5)				(130.5)
	51.5	(17.6)	(0.4)	(23.5)	10.0
Minority interests	(0.9)				(0.9)
Net assets acquired	50.6	(17.6)	(0.4)	(23.5)	9.1

The further adjustments above comprise the following items:

Professional property valuations performed in the year as at the date of acquisitions resulted in £1.5m reduction in value.

The increase in creditors principally relates to the reassessment of legal claims as a result of additional information being obtained subsequent to the original fair value exercise concerning the circumstances relating to the claims made against BET PLC and its subsidiaries.

The increase in taxation provisions principally arises from a further review of the taxation affairs of the BET PLC group both in the UK and overseas. The taxation liabilities of a number of group companies had not been agreed with the appropriate revenue authorities for many years and the adjustment made arises from detailed reviews of certain tax computations since the original fair value exercise, including some for companies which BET PLC had sold prior to the date of acquisition, with indemnities relating to taxation liabilities.

Additional provisions of £17.3m have been made for future net rental and outgoings on a sublet property leased by BET to reflect contractual arrangements separate from the sub-lease agreement which enabled the sub-tenant to terminate the sub-lease. These arrangements had not been identified at the time of the original fair value exercise.

The additional environmental provision (£6.2m) in respect of cost of remediation arises from further knowledge gained on one of the former BET PLC operational sites in the US as a result of further reports by environmental and legal specialists provided during the course of the year.

G   *Businesses held exclusively with a view to subsequent resale*

This is another area where the detailed rules of the standard seem to be at odds with its general approach that the fair value exercise should not reflect the acquirer's intentions for future actions. It requires that 'where an interest in a separate business of the acquired entity is sold as a single unit within approximately one year of the date of acquisition, the investment in that business should be treated as a single asset for the purposes of determining fair values. Its fair value should be based on the net proceeds of the sale, adjusted for the fair value of any assets or liabilities transferred into or out of the business, unless such adjusted net proceeds are demonstrably different from the fair value at the date of acquisition as a result of a post-acquisition event. This treatment should be applied to any business operation, whether a separate subsidiary undertaking or not, provided that its assets, liabilities, results of operations and activities are clearly distinguishable, physically, operationally and for financial reporting purposes, from the other assets, liabilities, results of operations and activities of the acquired entity.'[114]

Where the business has not yet been sold by the time of approval of the first set of accounts after the date of acquisition, the fair value of the interest in the business is based on the estimated net proceeds of sale and carried as a current asset, provided that:

'(a)   a purchaser has been identified or is being sought; and

(b)   the disposal is reasonably expected to occur within approximately one year of the date of acquisition.'[115]

This is based on the requirement of FRS 2, that a subsidiary which is reasonably expected to be disposed of with approximately one year of acquisition is to be included in the consolidated balance sheet as a current asset at the lower of cost and net realisable value; its results and assets and liabilities should not be consolidated (see 5.4 of Chapter 5). However, the principle has been extended to other business operations that are not subsidiaries.

The fair value to be attributed will normally be the actual realised amount as this is considered to be the most reliable evidence of fair value at the date of acquisition (or if the sale has not yet been completed, at the estimated sales proceeds). The net proceeds, which should take into account any costs of disposal (including incremental costs such as professional fees), should be discounted to obtain the net present value at date of acquisition, if material.[116]

This appears inconsistent with the general approach of FRS 7, as it depends on the acquirer's intentions for the business operation. However, in an appendix to FRED 7 the ASB said that it 'rejects that interpretation because it believes that the resale value of a business in an arm's length transaction would normally provide the most reliable evidence of its fair value, and should be used unless specific post-acquisition events occur during the holding period that require a profit or loss on disposal to be recorded'.[117]

The overall objective is therefore to produce a neutral impact on the group's results (apart from any interest effect, if discounting is applied). Accordingly, any initial estimate of fair value should normally be adjusted to actual net realised value within the period allowed for completing the investigation of fair values (see 2.4.4 below). However, it will be appropriate for a post-acquisition profit or loss on disposal to be recognised and for the fair values at acquisition to be different from the net realised value where:

(a) the acquirer has made a material change to the acquired business before disposal;

(b) specific post-acquisition events occur during the holding period that materially change the fair value of the business from the fair value estimated at the date of acquisition; or

(c) the disposal is completed at a reduced price for a quick sale.[118]

Examples of companies making fair value adjustments to reflect businesses held for resale at their estimated realisable value are BAA, FKI and TI Group as shown in Extracts 6.16, 6.27 and 6.32 above.

One company which included businesses held for resale as part of the net assets acquired (and having provisionally revalued them upwards in the year of acquisition reduced the values the following year) was Reckitt & Colman, as illustrated in Extracts 6.43, 6.44 and 6.45 at 2.8.2 below.

2.4.4   *Subsequent amendments to fair value*

FRS 7 says that the fair value exercise should be completed, if possible, by the date on which the first post-acquisition accounts of the acquirer are approved by the directors, although if this is not possible, a provisional allocation of fair values is allowed which must be finalised in the next year (see 2.4.2 above). Otherwise, the only circumstances in which a retrospective adjustment to the goodwill calculation could be regarded as appropriate would be if the original allocation was regarded as a fundamental error which required to be dealt with as a prior year adjustment under FRS 3. This would probably be the case only if the original allocation was based on a complete misinterpretation of the facts which were available at the time; it would not apply simply because new information had come to light which changed the acquiring management's view of the value of the item in question.

2.4.5   *'Push-down accounting'*

The term 'push-down accounting' relates to the practice of incorporating, or 'pushing-down', the fair value adjustments which have been made by the acquiring company into the financial statements of the acquired subsidiary, including the goodwill arising on the acquisition. Such a practice is used in the US, where it has been required in certain situations by the Securities and Exchange Commission.[119] It is argued that the acquisition, being an independently bargained transaction, provides better evidence of the values of the assets and liabilities of the subsidiary than those previously contained within its financial statements, and therefore represents an improved basis of accounting.

There are, however, contrary views, which hold that the transaction in question was one to which the reporting entity was not a party, and there is no reason why it should intrude into the entity's own accounting records.

Whatever the theoretical arguments, it is certainly true that push-down accounting can be an expedient practice, because it obviates the need to make extensive consolidation adjustments in each subsequent year, based on parallel accounting records. But in fact most of the adjustments which push-down accounting would entail would fall foul of the Companies Act valuation rules or of other accounting standards. It is possible, by using the alternative valuation rules, to revalue fixed assets directly in the subsidiary's financial statements, and where this constitutes a major part of the fair value adjustments then this can be a worthwhile move; however, most of the other adjustments discussed in 2.4.3 above could not be made directly in the subsidiary's financial statements.

2.5   Step-by-step acquisitions

2.5.1   Background

So far, this chapter has discussed acquisitions which result from a single purchase transaction, or at least a series of related transactions which occur over a relatively short period of time. However, in practice some subsidiaries are acquired in a series of steps which take place over an extended period, during which the underlying value of the subsidiary is likely to change, both because of the trading profits (or losses) which it retains and because of other movements in the fair values of its assets and liabilities. The accounting problems which this creates are therefore how to establish the fair values of the net assets acquired, and how to measure its pre-acquisition reserves.

2.5.2   Example

The problem can be illustrated by the following example, which is based on that in the ASC Discussion Paper on fair value accounting.[120]

Example 6.2:   Step-by-step acquisitions

Company A acquires an 80% holding in Company B as a result of four separate transactions over a number of years, as set out in the table below. At the time of these transactions, the fair values of the net assets of B were as shown, and for the purpose of this illustration, the consideration paid was exactly proportionate to the share of the net assets, at fair value, which was thereby being acquired.

Transaction number	Holding acquired %	Total value of investee £m	Price paid £m	Cumulative holding %	Cumulative price paid £m
1	10	10	1.00	10	1.00
2	20	13	2.60	30	3.60
3	21	15	3.15	51	6.75
4	29	20	5.80	80	12.55
	80		12.55		

As the above table shows, Company B was merely an unconsolidated investment after transaction 1, became an associate as a result of transaction 2 and a subsidiary as a result of transaction 3, while transaction 4 resulted in the minority interest being reduced from 49% to 20%.

The accounting choices which are available are of two sorts; when to make the initial calculation of fair values for the purposes of determining goodwill, and whether to make a revised calculation when each successive change in the size of the holding takes place. As stated at 4.1 of Chapter 7, FRS 9 requires that the investment in an associate should be analysed at the time of acquisition between the investor's share of the underlying separable net assets (at fair value, if possible) and goodwill, so the answer to the first question above is that this calculation should be made after transaction 2; however, if Company A is unable to get the information on fair values which is required for that exercise, it may be possible to carry it out only after transaction 3. The more significant question is whether each further purchase of shares thereafter should lead to a recalculation of the goodwill equation.

If the exercise were first carried out after transaction 2, and reperformed after each subsequent increase in the shareholding, the calculations would be as follows:

After transaction 2	£m
Cost of investment	3.60
Share of assets at fair value (30% of £13m)	3.90
Negative goodwill on consolidation	0.30

Note that, in this particular example (because all purchases take place at the underlying asset value), the negative goodwill in fact represents the increase in reserves attributable to the 10% stake held by Company A during the period when its value grew from £10m to £13m. However, it has been beyond the scope of normal consolidation accounting entries to treat this as part of the group's post-acquisition reserves.

After transaction 3	£m
Cost of investment	6.75
Share of assets at fair value (51% of £15m)	7.65
	0.90
Less: post-acquisition share of reserves of associate (30% of (£15m – £13m))	0.60
Negative goodwill on consolidation	0.30

After transaction 4	£m	£m
Cost of investment		12.55
Share of assets at fair value (80% of £20m)		16.00
		3.45
Less: post-acquisition share of reserves		
of associate (30% of (£15m – £13m))	0.60	
of subsidiary (51% of (£20m – £15m))	2.55	
		3.15
Negative goodwill on consolidation		0.30

Although the accounting set out above may be appropriate in principle, it can give rise to difficulties in practice. One of these is that, once the shareholding crosses the 50% threshold, the assets of the investee will be consolidated on a line-by-line basis and it is thereafter difficult (and arguably inappropriate) to ascribe new fair values to them when further shares have been acquired, so as to reduce the size of the minority interest. If, in the above example, Company B owned a single investment property (and nothing else) which was appreciating in value throughout the period during which Company A's stake was changing, the accounting consequences would be as follows:

*Example 6.3:	Step-by-step acquisitions: consolidating the assets concerned*

After transaction 2	£m
Cost of investment as before	3.60
Represented by:	
Share of associate's assets at fair value (30% of £13m)	3.90
Negative goodwill on consolidation	(0.30)
	3.60

After transaction 3	£m
Cost of investment as before	6.75
Represented by:	
Investment property	15.00
Minority interest (49% of £15m)	(7.35)
	7.65
Negative goodwill on consolidation	(0.30)
Post-acquisition reserves (as before)	(0.60)
	6.75

The post-acquisition reserves would in fact represent Company A's 30% share of the revaluation reserve arising from the uplift in the value of the property from £13m to £15m.

After transaction 4	£m
Cost of investment as before	12.55
Represented by:	
Investment property	20.00
Minority interest (20% of £20m)	(4.00)
	16.00
Negative goodwill on consolidation	(0.30)
Post-acquisition reserves (as before)	(3.15)
	12.55

In order to achieve this accounting, it is necessary to revalue the investment property in the consolidated accounts following transaction 4. (This also takes place implicitly following transaction 3, but is not obvious because an investment property appears in the consolidated balance sheet in substitution for an investment in an associate.) The ASC Discussion Paper on fair value had mentioned two other possibilities, which are discussed below:

The first of these is that the asset remains at £15m, in which case the consolidated financial statements after transaction 4 will show the following:

	£m
Cost of investment (as before)	12.55
Represented by:	
Property	15.00
Minority interest (20% of £15m)	(3.00)
	12.00
Goodwill on consolidation[*]	1.15
Post-acquisition reserves (as after transaction 3)	(0.60)
	12.55

[*]This can be analysed as follows:

Cost of 29% acquired	5.80
Minority interest: 29% of £15m	(4.35)
	1.45
Negative goodwill existing after transaction 3	(0.30)
	1.15

The defect with this treatment is that it overstates goodwill by attributing to it an amount which is in reality attributable to the property. Conversely, the cost of the property to the group is understated and gains on any subsequent valuation or on disposal which are measured by reference to that cost will be overstated.

The ASC Discussion Paper therefore offered a further alternative which involved accounting for the property on a 'mixed' basis that takes account of the cost of the different transactions. Applying this approach to transaction 4 would give the following result:

	£m
Cost of investment (as before)	12.55

Represented by:	
Property	16.45
Minority interest (20% of £15m)	(3.00)
	13.45
Negative goodwill on consolidation	(0.30)
Post-acquisition reserves (as after transaction 3)	(0.60)
	12.55

This is achieved by applying the cost of the transaction 4 investment of £5.8m to increase the asset by 29% of £5m (the increase in the stake of the uplift in value since the previous transaction) and applying the remainder to reduce the minority interest. Whatever the theoretical case for this treatment, it seems to produce figures which have little meaning or usefulness.

2.5.3 FRS 2 requirements

There is no ideal solution to this problem of accounting for step-by-step acquisitions; each of the approaches shown in the above example would appear to have some defects. In theory, the best treatment (and the one recommended in the ASC Discussion Paper) would appear to be to recalculate fair values whenever there has been a significant change of stake as shown in the first of the treatments in the example. However, in practice companies seldom made any further adjustments to the fair values of the net assets of their subsidiaries after majority control has been secured. The 'mixed' treatment shown above is also unlikely to have been applied in practice.

The ASB reconsidered this issue in FRS 2 and effectively adopted the treatment recommended by the ASC Discussion Paper, although there are some differences due to the implications of the Companies Act provisions on acquisition accounting.

A   Investment becoming a subsidiary

The standard states that the Companies Act requires that 'the identifiable assets and liabilities of a subsidiary undertaking should be included in the consolidation at fair value at the date of its acquisition, that is the date it becomes a subsidiary undertaking. This requirement is also applicable where the group's interest in the undertaking that becomes a subsidiary undertaking is acquired in stages.'[121] As explained by the standard, 'the effect of the Schedule 4A paragraph 9 method of acquisition accounting is to treat as goodwill, or negative goodwill, the whole of the difference between, on the one hand, the fair value, at the date of its identifiable assets and liabilities and, on the other hand, the total acquisition cost of the interests held by the group in that subsidiary undertaking. This applies even where part of the acquisition cost arises from purchases of interests at earlier dates.'[122]

The effect of this on Example 6.3 above would appear to be as follows:

Example 6.4:   Step-by-step acquisitions: consolidating the assets concerned

After transaction 3

In consolidating the subsidiary there is a difference between the fair value of the net assets at the date of becoming a subsidiary and the aggregate cost of the investment, being:

	£m
Investment property	15.00
Minority interest (49% of £15m)	(7.35)
	7.65
Cost of investment	6.75
Difference	0.90

FRS 2 indicates that this difference is negative goodwill in terms of the Companies Act. However, as the consideration paid was exactly proportionate to the share of net assets, at fair value, which was thereby being acquired, there was in fact no goodwill. This difference is equivalent to:

	£m
Post-acquisition reserves of associate (as before)	0.60
Negative goodwill on consolidation (as before)	0.30
	0.90

The post-acquisition reserves represent Company A's 30% share of the revaluation reserve arising from the uplift in the value of the property from £13m to £15m which will be reflected in the group's reserves. However, in other situations these post-acquisition reserves may have been reflected in the group retained profits. Such reserves have now effectively become part of goodwill, in this case negative goodwill (which under FRS 10 is treated as a negative asset).

However, FRS 2 indicates that, in special circumstances (such as an associate becoming a subsidiary), 'not using fair values at the dates of earlier purchases, while using an acquisition cost part of which relates to earlier purchases, may result in accounting that is inconsistent with the way the investment has been treated previously and, for that reason, may fail to give a true and fair view. ... In the rare cases where the Schedule 4A paragraph 9 calculation of goodwill would be misleading, goodwill should be calculated as the sum of the goodwill arising from each purchase of an interest in the relevant undertaking adjusted as necessary for any subsequent diminution in value. Goodwill arising on each purchase should be calculated as the difference between the cost of that purchase and the fair value at the date of that purchase of the identifiable assets and liabilities attributable to the interest purchased. The difference between the goodwill calculated on this method and that calculated on the method provided by the Act is shown in reserves.'[123] When such a 'true and fair override' is used, it will be necessary to disclose the particulars of the departure, the reasons for it and its effect as required by the Act.[124]

An example of a company using the 'true and fair override' is Cable and Wireless, as shown below:

Extract 6.38: Cable and Wireless plc (1999)

31   Acquisitions [extract]

On 24 November 1998, Cable & Wireless Optus was listed on the Australian Stock Exchange. The listing involved the issue by Cable & Wireless Optus of 1,402 shares for a cash consideration of Aus$2,917m including 556.4 shares to Cable and Wireless plc for a cash consideration of Aus$1,105m, the exercise by Cable and Wireless plc of its option to subscribe for 332.9 shares for a cash consideration of Aus$583m and the conversion of loan notes held by third parties for 130m shares. In addition, Aus$209m was paid up on the outstanding partly paid shares. Of this amount Aus$105m was paid by Cable and Wireless plc. Following the listing, Cable and Wireless plc's interest in Cable & Wireless Optus increased from 49.1% to 52.8%.

Prior to becoming a subsidiary undertaking, Cable & Wireless Optus was accounted for as an associated undertaking. In accordance with FRS 2 – 'Accounting for Subsidiary Undertakings', and in order to give a true and fair view, purchased goodwill has been calculated as the sum of the goodwill arising on each purchase of shares in Cable & Wireless Optus, being the difference at the date of each purchase between the fair value of the consideration paid and the fair value of the identifiable assets and liabilities attributable to the interest purchased. This represents a departure from the statutory method, under which goodwill is calculated as the difference between cost and fair value on the date that Cable & Wireless Optus became a subsidiary undertaking.

FRS 2 recognises that, where an investment in an associated undertaking is increased and it becomes a subsidiary undertaking, in order to show a true and fair view goodwill should be calculated on each purchase as the difference between the cost of that purchase and the fair value at the date of that purchase. The statutory method would not give a true and fair view because it would result in the Group's share of Cable & Wireless Optus' retained reserves, during the period that it was an associated undertaking, being recharacterised as goodwill. The effect of this departure is to increase retained profits by £80m, and to increase purchased goodwill by £80m.

A number of other companies have adopted a similar method to calculate goodwill but have not given the 'true and fair override' disclosures, presumably on the basis that the effect was not material.

B   Increased investment in existing subsidiary

Where a group increases its holding in the equity of a subsidiary undertaking, the standard requires that the net identifiable assets and liabilities of that subsidiary undertaking should be revalued to fair value and goodwill arising on the increase in interest should be calculated by reference to those fair values. This revaluation is not required if the difference between net fair values and carrying amounts of the assets and liabilities is not material.[125] Companies which have normally adopted the practice of comparing the consideration paid with the carrying value of the minority interest acquired and regarded the difference as goodwill, will need to reconsider their treatment.

Although the legislation contains certain detailed acquisition accounting rules which refer to fair values,[126] it does state that they apply 'where an undertaking becomes a subsidiary undertaking of the parent company';[127] they would, therefore, appear not to apply to acquisitions of shares in a company after it has become a subsidiary.

An example of a company making fair value adjustments in these circumstances was Glaxo Wellcome in its 1996 accounts, as shown in the following extract:

Extract 6.39: Glaxo Wellcome plc (1996)

23 Acquisitions and Disposals [extract]

Acquisitions

Nippon Glaxo Limited

In December 1996 the Group redeemed the 50 per cent equity interest in Nippon Glaxo Limited previously held by its joint venture partner, Shin Nihon Jitsugyo Co. Ltd. ("SNJ"), thereby increasing the Group's interest to 100 per cent. SNJ is the family company of the then president and vice-president of Nippon Glaxo Limited, who relinquished these positions on the redemption. The cost of the redemption was Yen 68 billion (£343 million) comprising consideration of Yen 67 billion (£339 million) and redemption expenses of Yen 1 billion (£4 million). The consideration was paid in cash, Yen 54 billion on 25th December 1996 and Yen 13 billion on 10th January 1997.

Previously Nippon Glaxo Limited had been consolidated as a subsidiary undertaking in accordance with Section 258(4)(a) of the Companies Act 1985 and a minority interest of 50 per cent had been accounted for. The redemption eliminates the minority interest.

The fair value of the net assets of Nippon Glaxo Limited at the date of redemption exceeded the book value by £39 million, comprising adjustments of £42 million in respect of the value of land and £3 million for additional liabilities. Consolidated Group net assets have therefore been increased by £39 million, with the 50 per cent attributable to the Group's pre-existing interest added to reserves and 50 per cent added to minority interests. Goodwill on consolidation is calculated as the difference between the cost of redemption and the adjusted value of the minority interest.

Burroughs Wellcome (India) Limited

In February 1996 the Group purchased an additional 19 per cent equity interest in Burroughs Wellcome (India) Limited, increasing its holding to 51 per cent. From that point Burroughs Wellcome (India) Limited has been consolidated as a subsidiary undertaking, having previously been accounted for as an associated undertaking.

Goodwill arising on acquisitions in the year

	Book values £m	Fair value adjustments £m	Net assets acquired £m	Cost of acquisition £m	Goodwill £m
Nippon Glaxo Limited	85	20	105	343	238
Burroughs Wellcome (India) Limited	7	–	7	15	8
	92	20	112	358	246

It is unclear why there should have been a fair value adjustment to reflect additional liabilities, because as the company was an existing subsidiary all liabilities would normally already have been provided.

Although it may be possible to incorporate fair value adjustments for valuation of fixed assets, some of the fair value adjustments required by FRS 7 discussed at 2.4.3 above would fall foul of the Companies Act valuation rules or of other accounting standards. For example, one fair value adjustment might be to incorporate a pension scheme surplus, but this would not be allowed by SSAP 24, so clearly there are limitations as to the fair value adjustments which can be made in this sort of situation.

2.6   Reverse acquisitions

A reverse acquisition, or reverse takeover, occurs when the owners of a company being 'acquired' (Company B) receive as consideration sufficient voting shares of the 'acquiring company' (Company A) so as to obtain control over the new combined entity. The acquisition is 'reverse' because from an economic point of view the acquiror (Company A) is, in economic terms, being taken over by the acquiree (Company B). This could arise, for example, in the case where a smaller listed company takes over a larger unlisted company in exchange for voting shares and, as a result, the owners of the unlisted company gain control over the majority of the voting shares of the new combined entity.

The Companies Act 1985, however, regards Company A as being the parent undertaking of Company B and therefore it is Company A which is required to prepare consolidated accounts. In preparing those accounts, Company A is required by the Act to acquisition account for the acquisition of its subsidiary undertaking, Company B.[128] FRS 6 is framed in terms of an entity becoming a subsidiary of a parent company and does not address reverse acquisitions.

As noted at 5.1.3 below, in these circumstances IAS 22 requires that the entity issuing the shares is deemed to be acquired by the other, i.e. Company A in preparing its consolidated accounts should regard itself as having been acquired by Company B. Fair values would be attributed to the net assets of Company A rather than those of Company B. However, IAS 22 is then silent as to how its requirements should be applied in practice in such situations. As indicated earlier FRS 6 does not address reverse acquisitions. However, Appendix II notes that the accounting in IAS 22 is incompatible with companies legislation in the UK and the Republic of Ireland.[129] It had been suggested, that in the light of this reference in FRS 6, it was not possible to apply reverse acquisition accounting by invoking the true and fair override in such cases.

This issue was considered by the UITF and in its Information Sheet no 17 issued in July 1996 it was stated that the UITF 'concluded that, whilst each case should be considered on its merits, there are some instances where it would be right and proper to invoke the true and fair override and apply reverse acquisition accounting. It also agreed that, as this is simply an application of the general requirement that the true and fair override may be invoked in the circumstances prescribed by companies legislation, and the point could be clarified by this announcement, no useful purpose would be served by issuing an Abstract on this issue.'

2.7   Mergers

2.7.1   *Basic principles*

In contrast to acquisition accounting, merger accounting involves retrospective restatement of the consolidated financial statements to show the reporting entity as if the combining companies had always been members of the group.[130] This means that the effective date of the combination has no significance other than for the purposes of various disclosures; both pre- and post-combination results of the subsidiary are combined with those of the holding company in showing the results for the period of the combination, and it is therefore of little significance whether it took place at the beginning or the end of the year. Similarly, the comparative figures and any historical summaries should be restated to consolidate the results of the new subsidiary retrospectively, which will usually mean that the earnings trend will be significantly different from what it would have been had acquisition accounting been applied.

In the balance sheet, the assets and liabilities of both companies are combined on the basis of their book values, with adjustments made only to eliminate any differences in accounting policies between the two.[131] Thus, there is no equivalent of the requirement under acquisition accounting to attribute fair values to the net assets of the subsidiary so as to reflect their cost to the group; merger accounting seeks to portray continuity of both of the combining entities, not that of the holding company, and therefore makes no amendment to the values at which the assets of either are included other than to harmonise accounting policies.

These basic principles are also embodied in the legislation following changes made by the Companies Act 1989.[132]

2.7.2   *Equity eliminations*

The cost of the investment will normally be carried at the nominal value of the shares of the holding company which have been issued to effect the combination, together with the fair value of any other consideration given. (The ability to record these shares at nominal rather than fair values on issue depends on qualifying for merger relief under section 131 of the Companies Act 1985, which is discussed under 2.1.2 above.)

As well as combining the assets and liabilities of the companies concerned, it will be necessary to eliminate the share capital of the subsidiary against the cost of the investment as stated in the balance sheet of the holding company. This is in principle a straightforward exercise, but when the two amounts do not equate to each other, the question arises of what to do with the difference, positive or negative.

FRS 6 requires the difference to be shown as a movement on other reserves in the consolidated accounts and also to be shown in the reconciliation of shareholders' funds.[133] It also emphasises that such a difference is not goodwill.[134] The Companies Act also requires such difference to be shown as a movement in consolidated reserves.[135] However, neither the standard nor the legislation specify any particular reserve.

Where the cost of the investment is less than the nominal value of the share capital of the subsidiary, the elimination of these two amounts will leave a residual credit in shareholders' funds in the consolidated balance sheet; this is generally classified as some form of capital reserve.

Where the reverse situation applies, the net debit has to be eliminated against consolidated reserves in some way and choices have to be made as to the order in which the group's reserves should be applied for this purpose. There are no particular rules on the matter in any authoritative document, but the normal practice is to apply these first against the most restricted categories of reserves,[136] and subsequently if any excess remains, against the group's retained earnings. Where the reserves are in the subsidiary concerned then, in effect, this is equivalent to the partial capitalisation of the reserves of the subsidiary; if they had had a bonus issue out of their own reserves prior to the merger, to make their share capital equal to the consideration shares offered by the new holding company, no consolidation difference would have emerged.

Apart from the effects of dealing with any imbalance as discussed above, there is no other elimination of the reserves of the subsidiary, which are combined with those of the holding company, in contrast to the treatment under acquisition accounting. However, some of the subsidiary's reserves may need to be reclassified in order to make sense in the context of the group financial statements.

FRS 6 requires that any existing balance on the share premium account or capital redemption reserve of the new subsidiary undertaking should be brought in by being shown as a movement on other reserves.[137] This is because they do not relate to the share capital of the reporting entity. Again, this difference should be shown in the reconciliation of movements in shareholders' funds.[138] Such a difference should probably be taken to the same reserve as that on the elimination of the share capital of the subsidiary, because in reality the distinction between share capital and share premium can be seen to be somewhat arbitrary in this context.

2.7.3   *Expenses of the merger*

One other question which sometimes arises in this context is how to account for the expenses of the merger. Although in the past there may have been good arguments for various treatments, FRS 6 requires that *all* merger costs should be charged through the profit and loss account at the effective date of the merger as costs of a fundamental reorganisation or restructuring under FRS 3 (see Chapter 22 at 2.6.3).[139]

However, some of these costs may be regarded as share issue expenses and therefore qualify to be written off against the share premium account of the holding company (if such an account exists). FRS 6 does not prohibit the subsequent charging of such costs to the share premium account by means of a transfer between reserves.[140]

2.7.4   Non-coterminous accounting periods

Particular practical problems in accounting for the merger can arise in the frequent circumstances that the accounting periods of the combining companies do not match each other. Although this can also create problems when acquisition accounting is used, the requirement in merger accounting to restate the consolidated financial statements retrospectively makes the difficulties particularly severe.

Company law dictates that the financial statements of the group must give a true and fair view in respect of the accounting period of the holding company, so this will require the period used by the subsidiary to be made to conform to that of its parent rather than the other way round. Naturally, the parent can change its own accounting reference date, but this can only be done for the future, not retrospectively. It will therefore be necessary to try to draw up financial statements for the subsidiary at each of the relevant balance sheet dates of the holding company.

The easiest part of the process will be to make sure that the subsidiary prepares a balance sheet at the next balance sheet date of the holding company, to allow a consolidated balance sheet at that date to be prepared. The difficult part will be to recreate balance sheets at the dates previously used by the parent, which will be necessary not only for the purposes of comparative figures for the balance sheet but also in order to allow the profit and loss account and cash flow statement of the current and comparative periods (together with any historical periods disclosed) to be drawn up.

Quite often it might prove impossible to draw up financial statements at these earlier dates with the same degree of accuracy that would be attainable in normal circumstances, because it is not possible after the event to institute normal year-end procedures such as stock counts and so on. It may therefore be necessary to make estimates of what such financial statements would have shown if they had been drawn up at that time, by relying on management information or by extrapolation between the reporting dates which were used (with allowance for seasonal or other relevant factors).

Another treatment which may be found appropriate would be to use non-coterminous years for the comparative figures, with the result that there will be the need to deal with the effects of either a 'gap' or an overlapping period as an adjustment to reserves. This was the solution chosen by Belhaven when it merger accounted for its acquisition of Garfunkels Restaurants, as explained in the following extract:

Extract 6.40: Belhaven plc (1987)

BASIS OF CONSOLIDATION [extract]

The accounting year end of Belhaven plc has been changed and the results are therefore presented for a nine-month period to December 31, 1987. The comparative figures combine the results of Belhaven plc for the year to March 31, 1987 and the audited results of Garfunkels Restaurants plc for the year to December 28, 1986, and the Balance Sheets of the two Groups as at these dates. The results for Garfunkels for the three months to March 31, 1987 are dealt with as a movement in reserves (Note 21).

The use of such non-coterminous accounts is only appropriate if the consolidated accounts present materially the same picture as if coterminous years had been used (see 3.3 of Chapter 5).

A particular problem can arise when a company is incorporated specially for the purpose of acting as the new holding company of a merging group. Because, as noted above, the accounting reference period of the group must by law be that of the holding company, this may result in the inadvertent creation of an accounting period which is not the one which the group would have preferred. Moreover, unless the company has been in existence for two years, arguably its statutory accounts should not be able to deal with the results of the group for the current and comparative periods, because strictly they should only go as far back as the date of incorporation of the holding company. One solution to this might be to present the information for the more relevant chosen period in supplementary pro-forma form. However, it appears that in practice, particularly in situations where a new holding company is set up as part of a group reconstruction, some companies do not go to such trouble and just produce accounts for the period they wish, as if the company had always been in existence. This was the approach adopted in the 1996 accounts of Securicor Group.

The best solution to the problem, however, would be to ensure that the new holding company has an accounting reference date which suits that of the group, and has been in existence long enough to allow a full set of group accounts for the chosen period to be presented. This was the approach adopted by PIC (see Extract 6.52 at 4.2 below).

2.7.5   *Dividends of the subsidiary*

Since the profit and loss accounts of both the combining companies will be aggregated retrospectively, it will be necessary to consider how to deal with the dividends of the subsidiary paid before the date of the combination. Essentially, the pre-merger dividends of both the parent and the subsidiary will be combined and shown as distributions in the consolidated profit and loss account, although it would be helpful to distinguish them either on the face of the profit and loss account or in a note. However, after the date of the merger, the only dividends shown will be those of the parent (those of the subsidiary will by then be inter-company payments and will thus be eliminated on consolidation).

2.8 Disclosure requirements relating to business combinations

Most disclosures relating to business combinations in group accounts arise from the requirements of FRS 6. These are considered at 2.8.1 to 2.8.3 below.

The Companies Act contains a number of detailed disclosure requirements. Many of these duplicate those contained in the standards, but there are a few additional matters in the legislation and these are considered at 2.8.4 below.

2.8.1 All business combinations

The following information should be disclosed in respect of all business combinations occurring in the financial year, whether they be acquisitions or mergers:

(a)   the names of the combining entities (other than the reporting entity);

(b)   whether the combination has been accounted for as an acquisition or a merger;

(c)   the date of the combination.[141]

Taking both the requirements of the Companies Act (see 2.8.4 below) and the standard together, details must be given for all combinations, even small ones. There is no explicit materiality limitation – all entities must be named and the date of acquisition given.

FRS 2 requires that where an undertaking becomes a subsidiary undertaking other than as a result of a purchase or exchange of shares then the circumstances should be disclosed.[142]

2.8.2 Acquisitions

FRS 6 requires the disclosures set out below in (a) to (k) to be given for each material acquisition, and in aggregate for other acquisitions that are material in total but not individually.[143]

(a)   the composition and fair value of the consideration given by the acquiring company and its subsidiary undertakings should be disclosed. The nature of any deferred or contingent consideration should be stated. For contingent consideration, the range of possible outcomes and principal factors affecting the outcome should be given.[144]

Examples of disclosures in respect of contingent consideration are given at 2.3.5 above.

(b)   a table should be provided showing, for each class of assets and liabilities of the acquired entity:

(i)   the book values recorded in the acquired entity's books immediately before the acquisition and before any fair value adjustments;

(ii)   the fair value adjustments, analysed into

■   revaluations,

■   adjustments to harmonise accounting policies, and

■   any other significant adjustments.

The reasons for the adjustments must be given; and

(iii)   the fair values at date of acquisition.

The table should include a statement of the amount of goodwill (positive or negative) arising on the acquisition.[145]

It may be necessary to modify the disclosures given in the fair value table where a business is acquired, rather than a company, because the acquiring company may be unable to give all the required information as it may not have access to the book values of the assets and liabilities recorded by the previous owner. However, we would recommend that where a business is acquired a full fair value table should be provided if at all possible. Extracts 6.20 and 6.23 above show examples of companies giving full fair value tables in respect of businesses acquired.

Stratagem Group gave the following disclosures about an acquisition in its 1996 accounts.

Extract 6.41: Stratagem Group plc (1996)

2.   Companies consolidated for the first time during the year[extract]

On 3rd January 1996 the Group purchased the whole of the issued share capital of NRC Refrigeration Ltd (formerly Northampton Refrigeration Co Limited) for an initial consideration of £4,000,000, plus acquisition costs of £353,000.

NRC Refrigeration Ltd has been accounted for under the acquisition method of accounting. The assets and liabilities of NRC Refrigeration Ltd which were acquired are set out below:

	Book Value £'000	Adjustments £'000	Fair Value £'000
Fixed assets	11,098	(1,883)	9,215
Current assets			
Stock	8,480	(1,405)	7,075
Debtors	8,933	(338)	8,595
Cash	922	–	922
	18,335	(1,743)	16,592
Current liabilities			
Creditors	(19,031)	(1,256)	(20,287)
Bank overdrafts	(5,828)	–	(5,828)
	(24,859)	(1,256)	(26,115)
Due to Stratagem Group PLC	(3,400)	–	(3,400)
Creditors due > 1 year	(2,426)	–	(2,426)
	(5,826)	–	(5,826)
Net liabilities	(1,252)	(4,882)	(6,134)
Goodwill			10,487
Consideration (including acquisition costs)			4,353

However, this disclosure was considered inadequate by the Review Panel as it did not analyse the fair value adjustments into revaluations, adjustments to achieve consistency of accounting policies, and other significant adjustments, and the table did not include an explanation for the adjustments.[146] As a result the company had to include the following note in its 1997 accounts.

Extract 6.42: Stratagem Group plc (1997)

35.   Companies consolidated in the financial year ended 31st August 1996

Last year a table was provided of the fair value adjustments made to the assets and liabilities of NRC Refrigeration Ltd at the time of its acquisition on 3rd January 1996. The Financial Reporting Review Panel considered that certain additional analysis and information should be provided to explain those adjustments. This is provided below:

NRC Refrigeration Ltd has been accounted for under the acquisition method of accounting. The assets and liabilities of NRC Refrigeration Ltd which were acquired are set out below:-

	£'000	Revaluations £'000	Accounting policy alignment £'000	Increase in provisions £'000	Total £'000
Fixed assets	11,098	(253)	(1,630)	–	9,215
Stock	8,480	(1,405)	–	–	7,075
Debtors	8,933	–	–	(338)	8,595
Cash	922	–	–	–	922
Creditors and provisions	(19,031)	–	–	(1,256)	(20,287)
Bank overdrafts	(5,828)	–	–	–	(5,828)
Stratagem Group PLC	(3,400)	–	–	–	(3,400)
Creditors due after one year	(2,426)	–	–	–	(2,426)
Net liabilities	(1,252)	(1,658)	(1,630)	(1,594)	(6,134)
Goodwill					10,487
Consideration (including acquisition costs)					4,353

Explanatory notes:

Fixed assets

The figure for revaluations reflects a third party valuation of freehold properties. The accounting policy alignment reflects the application of the depreciation policies of Stratagem Group PLC.

Stock

The adjustment to stock reflects the result of a review of the net realisable values of the stock.

Debtors

Bad debt provisions have been reviewed and adjusted as appropriate.

Creditors and provisions

Of the total figure of £1,256,000, £600,000 relates to increases in the provision for disposal of surplus properties. The balance reflects the outcome of an examination of the accounts on acquisition which identified a number of items that had not been adequately provided.

Stratagem Group is not alone in having incurred the wrath of the Review Panel in this area. The Panel has also issued a ruling on the 1997 accounts of Concentric which did not include any fair value table in its accounts, yet the Chairman's statement had referred to an acquisition.[147] As indicated at 2.4.3 F above, it also required Aim Group to give extra disclosures in this area.

(c)   also in the table above, there must be separately identified any provisions for reorganisation and restructuring costs included in the liabilities of the acquired entity (and any related asset write downs) made in the twelve months up to the date of acquisition.[148]

As already discussed at 2.4.3 F above, the creation of reorganisation provisions has been made much more difficult by FRS 7. However, there may still be circumstances where they can be made and will feature in the liabilities recognised for the acquired entity. Although, strictly speaking, this requirement does not call for separate disclosure of reorganisation and similar provisions set up in the context of the fair value exercise rather than by the management of the acquired entity within the twelve months prior to the date of acquisition, there appears to be no reason why the disclosure of the two elements of any provisions should be different. It may be best therefore to disclose all such provisions in the fair value table required, whenever made. Extracts 6.20, 6.23 and 6.36 show examples of companies giving disclosure of pre-acquisition reorganisation provisions.

(d)   where fair values are determined on a provisional basis only, that fact has to be stated and the reasons given. Subsequent material adjustments to these provisional fair values (and corresponding adjustments to goodwill) should be disclosed and explained.[149]

Many of the extracts at 2.4.3 above show examples of companies giving disclosure in respect of provisional fair values. One company which made subsequent adjustments to provisional fair values was Reckitt & Colman. In its 1994 accounts Reckitt & Colman gave the following disclosures in respect of its acquisition of the L&F household products business:

Extract 6.43: Reckitt & Colman plc (1994)

27   ACQUISITION OF BUSINESSES [extract]

On 31 December 1994 the group purchased the L&F household products business ('L&F Household') of Eastman Kodak Company ('Kodak'). The purchase consideration, including fees and costs of £8.40m associated with the acquisition, amounted to £1,001.90m, payable in cash, of which £1.25m was paid in 1994 and $989.50m on 3 January 1995. The remaining cost of acquisition has been or will be paid during 1994. The value of these assets and the consequent adjustment to the consideration is subject to agreement with Kodak. The net assets of all acquisitions were:

	Book value	Revaluation of assets/ (liabilities)	Other	Fair value of assets/ (liabilities) acquired
	£m	£m	£m	£m
L&F Household:				
Intangible fixed assets	–	635.99	–	635.99
Tangible fixed assets	59.45	44.04	–	103.49
Current assets/(liabilities)				
Stocks	31.99	–	–	31.99
Debtors	40.20	–	13.00	53.20
Businesses and brands held for				
disposal	11.60	77.10	(8.80)	79.90
Creditors	(44.39)	–	(2.46)	(46.85)
Provisions for liabilities and charges/				
liabilities due after more than one year	(41.86)	(4.40)	(4.01)	(50.27)
	56.99	752.73	(2.27)	807.45
Other businesses acquired	1.09	–	–	1.09
All acquisitions	58.08	752.73	(2.27)	808.54

Subsequent adjustments were made the following year and the 1995 accounts contained the following disclosure in respect of these adjustments:

Extract 6.44: Reckitt & Colman plc (1995)

25 ACQUISITION OF BUSINESSES [extract]

On 31 December 1994 the group purchased the L&F household products business (L&F Products) which was provisionally valued in the 1994 accounts. In accordance with FRS 7, an adjustment has been made in the 1995 accounts for amendments to that provisional fair value, now that the investigation for determining such a value has been completed. The difference has been taken as an adjustment to goodwill on acquisition. Amended and provisional values of net assets acquired are as follows:

	Amended value 1995 £m	Provisional value 1994 £m
L&F Products:		
Intangible fixed assets	**636.0**	636.0
Tangible fixed assets	**72.6**	103.5
Current assets/(liabilities)		
Stocks	**29.4**	32.0
Debtors	**53.2**	53.2
Businesses and brands held for disposal	**31.9**	79.9
Creditors	**(49.8)**	(46.9)
Provisions for liabilities and charges/liabilities		
due after more than one year	**(47.1)**	(50.3)
	726.2	807.4
Goodwill	**279.9**	194.5
Cost of acquisition	**1,006.1**	1,001.9
L&F Products: amount paid in year	**1,004.8**	1.3
Other businesses acquired: amounts paid relating to prior year		
acquisitions	**1.6**	10.8
Effect on cash flow	**1,006.4**	12.1

The company obviously felt that this gave adequate disclosure and explanation of the adjustments that were made. However, the matter was brought to the attention of the Financial Reporting Review Panel and it concluded that the disclosure was insufficient. In the Panel's view this second stage of disclosure requires a similar level of disclosure and explanation as is given in the year of acquisition under (b) above and should include an analysis of the adjustments and an explanation of the reasons for them. Accordingly, Reckitt & Colman included the following disclosure in its 1996 accounts:

Extract 6.45: Reckitt & Colman plc (1996)

24.   Acquisition of businesses

a)   Fair value adjustments in 1995 Annual Accounts (see Note 25 of the 1995 Annual Accounts)

As a result of an enquiry by the Financial Reporting Review Panel, the note on the fair value adjustments that were made in the 1995 accounts has been reissued in order to give full disclosure and reason for these adjustments. The figures themselves are unchanged.

On 31 December 1994 the group purchased the L&F household products business (L&F Products) which was provisionally valued in the 1994 accounts. In the initial period post acquisition communications between the acquired L&F business and Reckitt & Colman were specifically prohibited by a "hold separate" decree issued by the Federal Trade Commission (FTC). This gave rise to one of the issues referred to in Note i). The acquisition was also conditional on the disposal of certain businesses in the US as required by the FTC.

In accordance with FRS 7 an adjustment was made in the 1995 accounts for amendments to that provisional fair value.

The difference was taken as an adjustment to goodwill on acquisition. Amended and provisional values of net assets acquired were as follows and the explanations for those changes are given in the notes below:

	Amended value 1995 £m	Adjustments Total	Adjustments Revaluation	Adjustments Other	Provisional value 1994 £m
L&F Products					
Intangible fixed assets	636.0				636.0
Tangible fixed assets	72.6	(30.9)	(30.9)i		103.5
Current assets/(liabilities):					
Stocks	29.4	(2.6)		(2.6)ii	32.0
Debtors	53.2				53.2
Businesses and brands held for disposal	31.9	(48.0)	(48.0)iii		79.9
Creditors	(49.8)	(2.9)		(2.9)ii	(46.9)
Provisions for liabilities and charges due after more than one year	(47.1)	3.2		3.2ii	(50.3)
	726.2	(81.2)	(78.9)	(2.3)	807.4
Goodwill	279.9iv	85.4			194.5
Cost of Acquisition	1,006.1	4.2			1,001.9

Note i) - The adjustments to the provisional fair values of the tangible assets arose because the initial calculations, carried out by external appraisal consultants, were based on US fair value accounting and included inappropriate elements of future cash flow as a basis of their valuation. As some of these cash flows were brand-related the plant was inappropriately overvalued. This anomaly was not identified until later in 1995 when full control and access to the business was gained (see introductory paragraph for an explanation of this).

Note ii) - Small adjustments in drawing up the definitive disposal balance sheet.

Note iii) - A more detailed investigation into the businesses held for disposal was completed subsequent to the date of signing the annual accounts. The businesses and brands held for disposal comprised parts of the acquired operation in both the US and Germany, and these were immediately placed for sale following the acquisition. As a result of the tight timetable for the completion of the 1994 accounts, the value of the businesses held for disposal had not been fully evaluated when the 1994 accounts were completed and this meant that the provisional fair value of the businesses held for disposal had been overstated by some £48m in the 1994 accounts against their estimated worth as at the end of 1995.

Note iv) - The goodwill adjustment is a reflection of the amended fair values mentioned above.

It can be seen that not only does this give more explanation about the adjustments, it also gives more detailed explanation as to why the fair value adjustments were provisional in the first place.

(e)   any exceptional post-acquisition profit or loss that is determined using the fair values recognised on acquisition should be disclosed in accordance with FRS 3, and identified as relating to the acquisition.[150] The explanatory note in the standard gives three examples:

> (i)   profits or losses on the disposal of acquired stocks where the fair values of stocks sold lead to abnormal trading margins after the acquisition;

> (ii)   the release of provisions in respect of an acquired loss making long-term contract that the acquirer makes profitable; and

> (iii)   the realisation of contingent assets or liabilities at amounts materially different from their attributed fair values.[151]

This is potentially a rather onerous disclosure requirement but it is not clear what it was intended to achieve or that it adds much of use to the existing FRS 3 disclosures about exceptional items. It would seem that it is necessary to ascertain whether any exceptional items arising in the period are calculated using fair values that were ascribed in a fair value exercise (regardless of how far in the past those fair values were ascribed). If so, the identification of the exceptional items must be given, as for the rest of these disclosures, separately for each material acquisition and in aggregate for the rest. It is fair to say that such disclosure is rarely seen.

(f)   movements on provisions or accruals for costs related to acquisitions should be disclosed and analysed between the amounts used for the specific purpose for which they were created and amounts released unused.[152]

The ASB probably intended this to mean that provisions should not be used for anything other than the purpose for which they were established (although this is not actually stated). It is again worth stressing that this disclosure must be given for each material acquisition separately. It is therefore necessary that any provisions maintained must be analysed by acquisition, so that any individually material movement relating to an acquisition provision established in a material acquisition can be disclosed separately.

(g)   as required by FRS 3, in the period of acquisition the post-acquisition results of the acquired entity should be shown as a component of continuing operations in the profit and loss account (other than those which are also discontinued in the same period). Where an acquisition has a material impact on a major business segment, this should be disclosed and explained.[153]

(h)   where it is not practicable to determine the post-acquisition results of an operation, an indication of its contribution to turnover and operating profit should be given, or, if even that is not possible, that fact and the reasons for it should be explained.[154]

Although (g) and (h) appear to duplicate FRS 3 requirements, the information is now required for each material acquisition separately and only in aggregate for others. The requirements of FRS 3 are discussed further at 2.5 of Chapter 22.

One way of giving this disclosure is for the material acquisition to be identified on the face of the profit and loss account, as shown below:

Extract 6.46: Granada Group PLC (1996)

Consolidated profit and loss account [extract]

Note	For the 52 weeks ended 28 September 1996	Total before exceptional items £m	Exceptional items (note 7) £m	Total after exceptional items 1996 £m	1995 £m
1	Turnover:				
	Continuing operations	**2,611.7**	–	**2,611.7**	2,381.2
	Acquisitions - Forte	**1,205.2**	–	**1,205.2**	–
		3,816.9	–	**3,816.9**	2,381.2
	Depreciation on tangible assets	**184.6**	–	**184.6**	132.3
2	Staff costs	**884.8**	**43.8**	**928.6**	528.4
3	Net other operating costs	**2,070.6**	**33.4**	**2,104.0**	1,332.4
		3,140.0	**77.2**	**3,217.2**	1,993.1
	Operating profit:				
	Continuing operations	**444.4**	**(3.6)**	**440.8**	388.1
	Acquisitions - Forte	**232.5**	**(73.6)**	**158.9**	–
1	Total operating profit	**676.9**	**(77.2)**	**599.7**	388.1

Alternatively the information can be disclosed by way of note, as shown below:

Extract 6.47: BTP plc (1999)

28   Purchase of businesses and subsidiary undertakings[extract]

Archimica

During the year, the Archimica businesses contributed turnover of £47.1 million and operating profit of £12.9 million to the results of the Fine Chemicals Division. The net assets of the Archimica businesses at 31 March 1999 were £30.5 million.

Hexachimie

During the year, Hexachimie contributed turnover of £21.3 million and operating profit of £4.4 million to the results of the Fine Chemicals Division. The net assets of Hexachimie at 31 March 1999 were £31.9 million.

(i)   in accordance with FRS 1, the cash flow statement should show the amount of cash paid in respect of the consideration, showing separately any balances of cash and overdrafts acquired. In addition, a note to the cash flow statement should show a summary of the effects of acquisitions indicating how much of the consideration comprised cash.[155]

(j)   in accordance with FRS 1, material effects on amounts reported under each of the standard headings reflecting the cash flows of the acquired entity in the period should be disclosed, as far as is practicable.[156]

Although (i) and (j) appear to duplicate FRS 1 requirements, the disclosures must be given for each material acquisition and in aggregate for the remainder. The requirements of FRS 1 are discussed further at 2.4.7 and 2.7.1 of Chapter 26.

(k)   in financial statements following the acquisition, the costs incurred in the period in reorganising, restructuring and integrating the acquisition should be shown. Such costs are those that:

(i)   would not have been incurred had the acquisition not taken place; and

(ii)   relate to a project identified and controlled by management as part of a reorganisation or integration programme set up at the time of acquisition or as a direct consequence of an immediate post-acquisition review.[157]

These costs, whether relating to a fundamental restructuring or not, are to be disclosed separately from other exceptional items.[158] The point of this disclosure requirement appears to be to ensure that the costs of reorganisation are still disclosed even though they do not feature any longer in the fair value exercise. The disclosure, however, appears to be voluntary since it will be easy for managements who feel burdened by the disclosure requirements to 'fail' the test of having set up the programme of reorganisation at the time of acquisition or in an immediate post-acquisition review. Nevertheless, where reorganisation or restructuring costs are incurred most companies are giving disclosure (see for example Extract 6.23 above).

As these costs may extend over more than one period, it is suggested in the explanation section of the standard that 'for major acquisitions, therefore, management may wish to state in the notes to the financial statements the nature and amount of such costs expected to be incurred in relation to the acquisition (including asset write-downs), indicating the extent to which they have been charged to the profit and loss account'.[159] An illustrative example of how such information might be shown is included in Appendix IV to the standard. As this is not a requirement of the standard, companies do not appear to be bothering with such disclosure other than giving disclosure under (k) above.

It should be emphasised again that the disclosures discussed in (a) to (k) above are to be given for each material acquisition, and in aggregate for other acquisitions that are material in total but not individually. Most of the extracts to which reference has been made generally have been in situations when there has been only one material acquisition. Where a company is acquisitive, then it may be that separate disclosures will need to be given for a number of acquisitions in the year. Indeed, Kingfisher in its 1999 accounts has given disclosures in respect of 4 separate acquisitions plus 3 others in aggregate.[160]

The disclosure requirements discussed at (d), (e), (f) and (k) above do not necessarily apply to the period in which the acquisition is made, but in future accounting periods following the acquisition.

FRS 6 clarified and extended the disclosures to be given in respect of pre-acquisition performance (which used to be required under paragraph 13(4) of Schedule 4A to the Companies Act 1985). For each material acquisition the profit after taxation and minority interests of the acquired entity should be given for:

(a)   the period from the beginning of the acquired entity's financial year to the date of acquisition, giving the date on which this period began; and

(b)   its previous period.

There is no requirement to give this information in aggregate for other acquisitions.[161] The information is not only required when a material subsidiary is acquired but also if a material unincorporated business has been acquired.

The standard also extended the pre-acquisition information to be given in the context of substantial acquisitions, i.e. those where:

(a)   for listed companies, the combination is a Class I or Super Class I transaction under the Stock Exchange listing rules; or

(b)   for other entities, either

   (i)   the net assets or operating profits of the acquired entity exceed 15 per cent of those of the acquiring entity, or

   (ii)   the fair value of the consideration given exceeds 15 per cent of the net assets of the acquiring entity;

and in any other exceptional cases where disclosure is necessary to give a true and fair view. For the purposes of (b) above, net assets and profits should be those shown in the accounts for the last financial year before the date of the acquisition; and the net assets should be augmented by any purchased goodwill eliminated against reserves as a matter of accounting policy and not charged to the profit and loss account.[162] About a year after the standard was issued the Stock Exchange Listing Rules were amended deleting all reference to Class 1 transactions. In order to maintain the status quo, the UITF issued Abstract 15 - *Disclosure of substantial acquisitions.* In February 1999, the UITF had to revise its abstract because the Stock Exchange Listing Rules were again amended so that they no longer refer to Super Class 1 transactions but Class 1 transactions. The revised abstract again maintains the status quo. Accordingly, for the purposes of (a) above, the reference to Class 1 transactions should be interpreted as meaning those business combinations in which any of the ratios set out in the

Stock Exchange Listing Rules for the classification of transactions exceeds 15%.[163] The required information is:

(a)   the summarised profit and loss account and statement of total recognised gains and losses of the acquired entity for the period from the beginning of its financial year to the effective date of acquisition, giving the date on which this period began. The summarised profit and loss account should show, as a minimum, the analysis of turnover, operating profit and those exceptional items falling under paragraph 20 of FRS 3; profit before taxation; taxation and minority interests; and extraordinary items; and

(b)   the profit after tax and minority interests for the acquired entity's previous financial year.

This information should be shown on the basis of the acquired entity's accounting policies prior to the acquisition.[164] An example of such disclosure is shown below:

Extract 6.48: FKI plc (1998)

28   Acquisitions during the year [extract]

The summarised profit and loss account and statement of total recognised gains and losses of Bridon plc for the period 1 January 1997 to 31 July 1997, being the period from the beginning of its financial year to the effective date of acquisition, are disclosed below.

Also disclosed below is the summarised profit and loss account for the financial year ended 31 December 1996.

	Period 1 January 1997 to 31 July 1997 £'000	Year ended 31 December 1996 £'000
Turnover	204,186	361,818
(Loss)/profit before interest and exceptional item	(436)	11,379
Exceptional item (see below)	(2,005)	–
(Loss)/profit before interest	(2,441)	11,379
Net interest payable	(2,147)	(4,107)
(Loss)/profit before tax	(4,588)	7,272
Tax	(4,146)	(2,247)
(Loss)/profit after tax	(8,734)	5,025
Equity minority interests	125	(84)
(Loss)/profit for the financial period	(8,609)	4,941

The exceptional item comprises mainly bid costs associated with the takeover by FKI plc.

Statement of total recognised gains and losses	Period 1 January 1997 to 31 July 1997 £'000
Loss for the financial period	(8,609)
Currency translation differences (net)	(544)
Total recognised losses relating to the period	(9,153)

As noted above, this disclosure requirement is effectively an extension of the now repealed Companies Act requirement to disclose information about the pre-acquisition results of acquired subsidiaries. It seems of questionable relevance, as it is to be based on pre-acquisition accounting policies and values which do not reflect the terms of the acquisition transaction.

2.8.3   Mergers

FRS 6 requires that for each business combination accounted for as a merger (other than group reconstructions), the following information should be disclosed:[165]

(a)   an analysis of the principal components of the current year's profit and loss account and statement of total recognised gains and losses into:

   (i)   amounts relating to the merged entity for the period after the effective date of the merger, and

   (ii)   for each party to the merger, amounts relating to that party for the period up to the date of the merger;

(b)   an analysis similar to (a) (ii) for the previous year;

(c)   the composition and fair value of the consideration given by the issuing company and its subsidiary undertakings;

(d)   the aggregate book value of the net assets of each party to the merger at the date of the merger; and

(e)   the nature and amount of significant accounting adjustments made to the net assets of any party to the merger to achieve consistency of accounting policies, and an explanation of any other significant adjustments made to the net assets of any party to the merger as a consequence of the merger; and

(f)   a statement of the adjustments to consolidated reserves.

The analysis of the profit and loss account in (a) and (b) above should show as a minimum the turnover, operating profit and exceptional items, split between continuing operations, discontinued operations and acquisitions; taxation and minority interests; and extraordinary items.

An example of these disclosures is shown below:

Extract 6.49: United News & Media plc (1996)

29. **Business merger** As explained in the accounting policies, on 8 February 1996, United and MAI announced plans for the merging of their respective businesses. The merger was to be effected by way of offers made by United for the whole of the issued share capital of MAI, being 332,718,123 ordinary shares of 5 pence each and 120,956.330 preference shares of 5 pence each, for a consideration of 242,090,550 ordinary shares of 25 pence each, the fair value of which amounted to £1,560.3 million. These offers became unconditional on 2 April 1996. The merger has been accounted for using the merger accounting principles set out in Financial Reporting Standard 6. Accordingly the financial information for the current period has been presented, and that for the prior periods restated, as if MAI had been owned by United throughout the current and prior accounting periods.

The book value of net assets at the time of the merger together with adjustments arising from the alignment of accounting policies were

	£m
United	
Book value of net assets at time of merger	238.0
Merger adjustment (note 24)	(73.0)
Restated net assets at time of merger	165.0
MAI	
Book value of net assets at time of merger	224.6
Merger adjustment (note 24)	(27.7)
Restated net assets at time of merger	196.9

An analysis of contribution to the profit attributable to shareholders made by the combining groups in the period prior to the merger date on 2 April 1996, the principal components of the profit and loss accounts and statements or total recognised gains and losses is as follows:

Profit and loss account	United pre merger £m	MAI pre merger £m	Combined post merger £m	Total £m
Turnover				
Continuing operations	268.8	196.9	1,451.8	1,917.5
Acquisitions	2.7	–	18.3	21.0
Discontinued operations	6.8	14.6	30.8	52.2
	278.3	211.5	1,500.9	1,990.7
Operating profit				
Continuing operations	21.4	23.5	129.6	174.5
Acquisitions	0.7	–	(18.1)	(17.4)
Discontinued operations	0.2	4.0	6.9	11.1
	22.3	27.5	118.4	168.2
Income from interests in associated undertakings	1.9	3.9	(47.1)	(41.3)
Income from other fixed asset investments	0.6	–	1.6	2.2
Total operating profit	24.8	31.4	72.9	129.1
Merger expenses	–	–	(31.0)	(31.0)
Profit on the disposal of fixed asset investments	–	11.6	–	11.6
Profit on sales and closure of businesses	–	–	138.0	138.0
Profit on ordinary activities before interest	24.8	43.0	179.9	247.7
Net interest expense	(4.0)	(1.0)	(8.9)	(13.9)
Profit before tax	20.8	42.0	171.0	233.8
Tax	(6.8)	(14.0)	(55.1)	(75.9)
Profit after tax	14.0	28.0	115.9	157.9
Minority interest	–	(0.2)	(5.3)	(5.5)
Profit for the year	14.0	27.8	110.6	152.4
Total recognised gains and losses				
Profit for the year	14.0	27.8	110.6	152.4
Exchange gains	–	–	1.4	1.4
	14.0	27.8	112.0	153.8

The equivalent analysis for the year ended 31 December 1995 is as follows

Profit and loss account	United £m	MAI £m	Total £m
Turnover			
Continuing operations	1,032.9	768.2	1,801.1
Discontinued operations	37.7	52.6	90.3
	1,070.6	820.8	1,891.4
Operating profit			
Continuing operations	111.2	89.1	200.3
Discontinued operations	3.9	12.8	16.7
	115.1	101.9	217.0
Income from interests in associated undertakings	0.9	12.9	13.8
Income from other fixed asset investments	3.3	–	3.3
Total operating profit	119.3	114.8	234.1
Loss on sales and closure of businesses	(2.9)	–	(2.9)
Profit on ordinary activities before interest	116.4	114.8	231.2
Net interest expense	(11.9)	(4.0)	(15.9)
Profit before tax	104.5	110.8	215.3
Tax	(34.3)	(36.0)	(70.3)
Profit after tax	70.2	74.8	145.0
Minority interest	(1.5)	1.4	(0.1)
Profit for the year	68.7	76.2	144.9

Total recognised gains and losses			
Profit for the year	68.7	76.2	144.9
Exchange losses	(0.5)	–	(0.5)
	68.2	76.2	144.4

24.   Merger adjustments The merger adjustments reflect the alignment of accounting policies following the merger:

(a)   Intangible assets - in previous periods publishing rights and titles had been stated at directors' valuation. These are now stated at fair value on acquisition and are not revalued. The effect of this restatement is a debit adjustment to the revaluation reserve of £73 million. The comparative figures for 1995 have been restated.

(b)   Consolidation - on acquisition of subsidiary undertakings, businesses or associated undertakings the purchase consideration is allocated between underlying assets on a fair value basis. Any goodwill arising is written off direct to reserves. Previously in MAI the goodwill relating to certain associates was amortised over its expected economic life. The effect of this restatement is a debit adjustment to goodwill of £27.7 million. The comparative figures for 1995 have been restated.

23. Share premium account and reserves[extract]

Group	Share premium account £m	Merger reserve £m	Revaluation reserve £m	Other reserves £m	Goodwill reserve £m	Profit and loss account £m	Total £m
At 1 January 1996 as previously reported:							
United	205.6	–	80.2	467.3	(826.5)	236.3	162.9
MAI	60.7	–	–	30.2	(237.4)	340.2	193.7
Consolidation adjustment	–	(37.1)	–	–	–	–	(37.1)
Merger adjustment	(60.7)	60.7	(73.0)	–	(27.7)	–	(100.7)
As restated	205.6	23.6	7.2	497.5	(1,091.6)	576.5	218.8

The consolidation adjustment represents the difference between the nominal value of 25 pence of the shares issued to former MAI shareholders and the nominal value of 5 pence of the MAI shares acquired.

Many of these disclosures have their origin in the previous disclosure requirements in SSAP 23, updated for the impact of FRS 3. In our view, these original disclosure requirements were needed to compensate for the fact that merger accounting was very easily available under SSAP 23 for business combinations which, in substance, were acquisitions. This information would seem to be irrelevant in the context of a true merger.

Group reconstructions that are accounted for by using merger accounting are exempted from the disclosure requirements in the FRS, but must still give the information required by companies legislation.

2.8.4   Companies Act

As indicated at 2.8.1 above, some of the above disclosure requirements which are contained in FRS 6 are duplicated in the Companies Act,[166] but in many cases the standard has extended the information required by the legislation.

However, the Act requires the names of subsidiaries acquired, and whether they have been accounted for as acquisitions or mergers, even if they do not significantly affect the figures shown in the group accounts.[167] This was an issue noted by the Financial Reporting Review Panel in its findings in respect of the 1990 financial statements of Williams Holdings.[168]

Any information required by the Companies Act need not be given in respect of an undertaking established under the law of a country outside the UK or an undertaking which carries on business outside the UK if the directors consider it would be prejudicial to the business of the undertaking or any other group member. However, this is subject to the agreement of the Secretary of State.[169]

As indicated at 2.8.3 above, group reconstructions that are accounted for by using merger accounting are exempted from the disclosure requirements in

FRS 6, but must still give (in addition to the information outlined at 2.8.1 above) the following information which is required by companies legislation:

(a) the composition and fair value of the consideration given by the issuing company and its subsidiary undertakings;[170] and

(b) an explanation of any significant adjustments made to the assets and liabilities of the undertaking acquired, together with a statement of any resulting adjustment to the consolidated reserves (including the re-statement of the opening consolidated reserves).[171]

3 DISPOSALS

3.1 Basic principles

The other possible change in the composition of a group involves the disposal of a group company. In principle the results of the company being disposed of should continue to be consolidated as part of the group results until the effective date of disposal, and the gain or loss on disposal should be determined by comparing the carrying value of the subsidiary's net assets at that date with the sales proceeds obtained. There are, however, a number of aspects which need to be considered, which are discussed more fully below.

3.2 Effective date of disposal

FRS 2 defines the date of disposal in terms of when control passes; it states that 'the date for accounting for an undertaking ceasing to be a subsidiary undertaking is the date on which its former parent undertaking relinquishes its control over that undertaking'.[172] These provisions are discussed further at 2.2 above.

One complication which can arise is when a decision has been taken before a year-end to dispose of a subsidiary after the year-end and a loss is expected to emerge. Under FRS 3, if a decision has been made to sell an operation, any consequential provision should reflect the extent to which obligations have been incurred that are not expected to be covered by the future profits of the operation. Such a provision can only be made in respect of a proposed sale if the company is demonstrably committed to the sale; this should be evidenced by a binding sale agreement. In these circumstances, provision should be made for the loss which is anticipated, and this should also take account of the trading results which are expected to arise up to the date of disposal, which will either be trading losses which increase the amount of the loss on disposal or trading profits which go to mitigate it. The effective date of 'deconsolidation' will be the balance sheet date in the sense that the group financial statements for the following period will not be impacted by the results of the subsidiary being disposed of, except to the extent of any difference between the amount provided and the actual results until the date of disposal.

This then gives rise to questions of presentation of the 'deconsolidated'. subsidiary, both in the balance sheet and in the profit and loss account. In the balance sheet, the straightforward treatment would be to continue to consolidate the company on a line-by-line basis as normal. However, an alternative treatment sometimes adopted in the past was to show the net assets as one line in the balance sheet, possibly with a summarised balance sheet shown by way of note. Arguably, the former treatment is the one required by the Companies Act; at the balance sheet date it is still a subsidiary which must be consolidated (none of the grounds for non-consolidation applies) and the Act requires line-by-line consolidation. This is also reinforced by the fact that FRS 2 requires consolidation up to the date of disposal.

In the profit and loss account, similarly, it is possible to continue to consolidate the results of the subsidiary in question as normal. Again, this is arguably what is required by the Companies Act. Where a provision for losses up to the date of actual disposal has been made at the balance sheet date, the question arises of whether, and if so how, to show the actual results in the consolidated financial statements of the following year. Frequently companies used to show only the net effect of any over or under provision. However, a strict application of the rules on the effective date of disposal would require the results to continue to be consolidated until that date as normal, and to show an offsetting release of the provision made at the previous year-end.

FRS 2 requires that the consolidated profit and loss account should include the results of a subsidiary undertaking up to the date of its disposal.[173] In addition, FRS 3 indicates that the results of discontinued operations should be shown under the statutory format headings with the utilisation of the provision analysed as necessary between the operating loss and the loss on sale.[174] It would seem therefore that a strict application of the rules is required and the alternative treatment is no longer possible.

3.3   Goodwill of subsidiaries disposed of

Where a subsidiary has been acquired and then disposed of (particularly if the period of ownership was relatively short), it is necessary to keep sight of what has happened to any goodwill, positive or negative, which arose on the acquisition. If it has been taken to reserves (which was by far the predominant practice under SSAP 22), then there is a danger that it will bypass the profit and loss account altogether and result in a mis-statement of the gain or loss on disposal because the goodwill has not been taken into account.

This matter was first considered by the UITF when in December 1991 it issued Abstract 3 – *Treatment of Goodwill on Disposal of a Business*. The UITF determined that goodwill should be taken into account in the calculation of the gain or loss on disposal. The ruling made by the UITF in Abstract 3 was then reinforced by FRS 2. The standard requires that where a subsidiary undertaking is disposed of, the gain or loss should be calculated 'by comparing the carrying amount of the net assets of that subsidiary undertaking attributable to the group's interest before the cessation with any remaining carrying amount attributable to the group's interest after the cessation together with any proceeds received. The net assets compared should include any related goodwill that has not previously been written-off through the profit and loss account or attributed to prior period amortisation or impairment on applying paragraph 70 of FRS 10.'[175] Although UITF 3 has since been superseded, FRS 10 retains the regime. This issue is discussed more fully in Chapter 10 at 3.4.5.

3.4 Partial disposals

When part of the investment in a subsidiary is sold, but a sufficient number of the shares are held for it to retain subsidiary or associate status, it is necessary to consider how to account for the disposal in the consolidated financial statements. When more than 50% of the shares are retained, all the assets and liabilities remain consolidated on a line-by-line basis, so the accounting entries affect only the consolidated reserves and the minority interest. The calculation of the gain or loss on sale will be achieved by comparing the sale proceeds with the consolidated net asset value (including any related goodwill) attributable to the shares sold at the date of the disposal, as in the following example:

Example 6.5:   Partial disposal of shares in a subsidiary

Company A has a 100% investment in Company B, based on an original investment of £4,000. No goodwill arose on this transaction. Company B has subsequently earned profits of £6,000 which it has retained. The balance sheets of the companies and of the group show the following immediately before the sale:

	Company A £000	Company B £000	Consolidated £000
Investment in B	4		
Other net assets	20	10	30
	24	10	30
Share capital	10	4	10
Reserves	14	6	20
	24	10	30

Company A sells 40% of its shares in Company B to a third party for £7,000. It will compute its gain on this transaction (ignoring any taxation payable on the gain), in its own profit and loss account and in that of the group, thus:

	Own accounts £000	Group accounts £000
Sale proceeds	7.0	7.0
40% of investment/net assets	1.6	4.0
Gain on sale	5.4	3.0

The balance sheets will now show the following:

	Company A £000	Company B £000	Consolidated £000
Investment in B	2.4		
Other net assets	27.0	10.0	37.0
	29.4	10.0	37.0
Minority interest			4.0
Share capital	10.0	4.0	10.0
Reserves	19.4	6.0	23.0
	29.4	10.0	37.0

The same basic principles apply where only an associate holding is retained, the only difference being that the balance sheet will carry the underlying assets of Company B on one line. If Company A had sold 60% of its holding for £11,000, the effect on the profit and loss accounts and balance sheets (again ignoring the effects of any taxation payable) would have been as follows:

	Own accounts £000	Group accounts £000
Sale proceeds	11.0	11.0
60% of investment/net assets	2.4	6.0
Gain on sale	8.6	5.0

The balance sheets would now show the following:

	Company A £000	Company B £000	Consolidated £000
Investment in B	1.6		4.0
Other net assets	31.0	10.0	31.0
	32.6	10.0	35.0
Share capital	10.0	4.0	10.0
Reserves	22.6	6.0	25.0
	32.6	10.0	35.0

The above approach is that which is required by FRS 2.[176] It might be thought that such an approach is inconsistent with the treatment of intra-group transactions under the standard (see 3.4 of Chapter 5). However, as explained by the ASB, 'where the group disposes of part of its interest in a subsidiary undertaking it transacts directly with third parties and a profit or loss for the group is reported in the consolidated financial statements. This can be contrasted with the treatment of intra-group transactions where no profit or loss arises for the group as a whole because the transaction involves only undertakings included in the consolidation and under common control and does not directly involve any third party.'[177]

3.5 Deemed disposals

An undertaking may cease to be a subsidiary undertaking, or the group may reduce its proportional interest in that undertaking, other than by actual disposal. These deemed disposals may arise for a number of reasons:

(a) the group does not take up its full allocation in a rights issue;

(b) the subsidiary undertaking declares special scrip dividends which are not taken up by the parent so that its proportional interest is diminished;

(c) another party exercises its options or warrants; or

(d) the subsidiary undertaking issues shares to third parties.

FRS 2 says that the accounting for deemed disposals and direct disposals should be the same; in respect of both, the profit or loss should be calculated as described in 3.3 above.[178]

Example 6.6:   Dilution in the holding of an investment in a subsidiary undertaking

Company H owns 800,000 £1 shares in Company S which has a share capital of £1,000,000 and net assets of £2,500,000, the balance of £1,500,000 being retained profits. Company H has owned its investment since the formation of Company S, and therefore has consolidated 80% of its profits (£1,200,000). Its share of Company S's net assets is therefore £2,000,000.

Company S issues 1,000,000 shares to third parties for cash of £3,000,000 thereby increasing its net assets to £5,500,000. The share capital and reserves of Company S and the amounts attributable to Company H (40%) are now as follows:

	Company S	Attributable to Company H
	£	£
Share capital	2,000,000	800,000
Share premium account	2,000,000	800,000
Profit and loss account	1,500,000	600,000
Total	5,500,000	2,200,000

Company H has increased its share of net assets from £2,000,000 to £2,200,000. On the face of it, FRS 2 would seem to require this gain of £200,000 to be included in Company H's consolidated profit and loss account. However, it could be argued that this does not represent a realised profit and therefore under the Companies Act it should be included not in the profit and loss account,[179] but in the statement of total recognised gains and losses. Also, Company H's share of Company S's distributable reserves has actually declined from £1,200,000 to £600,000. It could also be argued that Company H should reclassify its group reserves by making a transfer of £800,000 from retained profits to some other reserve, reflecting the fact that these profits have been replaced by a share of Company S's share premium account, which is not distributable. This may be the preferable route particularly if Company S is now to be treated as an associate of Company H. However, FRS 2 does not give any guidance on this issue.

An example of a company recognising a profit through the profit and loss account in respect of a deemed disposal is shown in the following extract from the 1995 accounts of Courts:

Extract 6.50: Courts Plc (1995)

5   Exceptional credit

	1995 £'000	1994 £'000
Profit on deemed disposal of interest in Courts (Mauritius) Ltd	550	–
Profit arising on sale of shares in Courts (Singapore) Ltd	–	9,428
	550	9,428

On the other hand, South African Breweries has reflected the gain through its statement of total recognised gains and losses, as illustrated below:

Extract 6.51: South African Breweries plc (1999)

29.   Acquisitions [extract]

The Suncrush business was purchased through the Group's subsidiary undertaking, ABI, which issued shares to Suncrush Limited as part of the purchase consideration. The immediate effect of this was to dilute the Group's holding in ABI from 68 per cent to 53 per cent. At the same time, the Group repurchased from Suncrush Limited a portion of the shares issued by ABI issuing shares of SAB Limited as consideration. This resulted in the Group's holding in ABI being increased to 65 per cent. On consolidation, the reduction in the Group's holding in ABI from 68 per cent to 65 per cent has resulted in a deemed disposal of 3 per cent of ABI. The profit of US$52 million (R290 million) arising on this deemed disposal has not been realised and has been accounted for as a movement through the consolidated statement of total recognised gains and losses.

3.6   Disposals or swap transactions?

As noted at 3.3 above, FRS 2 requires that where a subsidiary undertaking is disposed of, the gain or loss should be calculated 'by comparing the carrying amount of the net assets of that subsidiary undertaking attributable to the group's interest before the cessation with any remaining carrying amount attributable to the group's interest after the cessation together with any proceeds received. The net assets compared should include any related goodwill that has not previously been written-off through the profit and loss account or attributed to prior period amortisation or impairment on applying paragraph 70 of FRS 10.'[180]

However, a parent may sell a subsidiary, or a business, in return for receiving shares in an entity whereby that entity becomes either an associate or a joint venture or even a subsidiary. The issue then is whether such a transaction should be accounted for as a disposal of a subsidiary (with a gain or loss being recognised) together with an acquisition of an associate, joint venture or subsidiary (with fair values being attributed to the net assets acquired and goodwill being recognised on the acquisition) or whether it should be accounted for in some other way. UK literature on this subject is lacking. At 4.2 of Chapter 7, we discuss this issue in Example 7.6 in the context of a creation of a joint venture where we conclude that in our view no gain should be recognised for accounting purposes because it does not satisfy the criteria for being treated as a realised profit.

In that example, the selling company was contributing a 100% subsidiary for a 40% stake in a joint venture. What if it was receiving an interest such that the combined entity was a subsidiary?

Example 6.7:   Creation of larger subsidiary by contribution of existing subsidiary

Group A has a subsidiary, Subsidiary C, which originally cost £55m, of which £35m was represented by the fair value of net assets. The remaining £20m was taken to reserves as goodwill in accordance with SSAP 22 and remains there in accordance with the transitional provisions of FRS 10. Since then it has earned and retained profits of £5m, as a result of which the book value of its net assets is now £40m. However, the value of Subsidiary C is now reckoned to be £90m, implying goodwill of £50m.

It has now agreed with Group B that Group A will sell subsidiary C to Group B in exchange for shares resulting in a 60% stake in the enlarged Group B. The value of Group B before the transaction is £60m. The fair value of its net assets is £35m.

How should this be accounted for by Group A?

(a)   As a sale of Subsidiary C giving rise to an accounting gain for Group A together with the acquisition of a new subsidiary, Group B?

(b)   As for (a) but eliminating the gain on sale as a consolidation adjustment?

(c)   As for (a) but not recognising the gain in the profit and loss account?

(d)   As an asset exchange?

(a)   Sale of Subsidiary C and acquisition of enlarged Group B

As noted above, FRS 2 requires the gain or loss on disposal of a subsidiary to be calculated as the difference between the carrying amount of the net assets of the subsidiary attributable to the group before the disposal, including any goodwill not previously written off to the profit and loss account, and the proceeds received.

	£m
Value of 60% stake in enlarged Group B	90
Assets disposed of	(40)
Goodwill previously taken to reserves	(20)
Gain on disposal	30

Correspondingly, the acquisition of the enlarged Group B would give rise to goodwill as follows:

	£m
Consideration given, being value of Subsidiary C	90
60% of the enlarged Group B net assets at fair value	
(being 60% of (40 + 35))	(45)
Goodwill	45

(b) Sale of Subsidiary C, but eliminating gain on disposal, and acquisition of enlarged Group B

It could be argued that as Group A has sold Subsidiary C to Group B which has become a subsidiary, then any gain on disposal should be eliminated on consolidation. Although FRS 2 does not deal with such a situation, an analogy can be drawn with FRS 9 whereby consolidation adjustments are made not only in respect of transactions with associates and joint ventures but also on setting up such entities. However, as Group A is the selling company then all of the gain should be eliminated even although Subsidiary C has been sold to a 60% subsidiary.

In this instance, the gain should be eliminated against the assets which gave rise to the gain. This could either be the net tangible assets or the goodwill. Our preference would be to eliminate it against the goodwill.

(c) Sale of Subsidiary C, but not recognising the gain on disposal in the profit and loss account, and acquisition of enlarged Group B

One reason for concluding that no gain can be reported is that it is not a realised profit. UK company law permits only realised profits to be included in the profit and loss account.[181] As noted in Example 7.6 at 4.2 of Chapter 7, it is very doubtful that the exchange of the subsidiary for a 40% stake in an unquoted joint venture can be regarded as realising a profit, in either the entity or the group accounts of A. Interestingly, the Financial Reporting Review Panel took a similar view in its adverse ruling on the accounts of Butte Mining PLC.[182] the same would hold true for a 60% stake. In this case the gain would be taken to the statement of total recognised gains and losses.

The goodwill on the acquisition of the enlarged Group B would be as calculated under (a) above.

(d) As an asset swap

Another reason for not recognising a gain on disposal is that this is simply an asset swap transaction rather than a true disposal and therefore does not qualify for gain recognition. On this basis, Group A has exchanged a 40% share of Subsidiary C in return for a 60% stake in the existing Group B. Accordingly no gain is recognised, but the goodwill on the acquisition of Group B is calculated as follows:

	£m
Consideration given, being 40% of Subsidiary C's net assets	16
60% of the existing Group B net assets at fair value	(21)
Negative goodwill	(5)

This is an area which is under consideration in the US. The EITF has discussed this at a number of meetings. Some EITF members have expressed the view that a business exchanged for another business can be accounted for at historical cost, and that gain recognition would not be appropriate. On the other hand, the SEC staff hold the view that the swapping of consolidated businesses, even if in the same line of business, must be accounted for as a fair value transaction.[183]

It is our view that no gain should be recognised for accounting purposes because it does not satisfy the criteria for being treated as a realised profit. However, this can be achieved by either of methods (b), (c) or (d) above.

Not surprisingly this is an area where practice is diverse. At 2.3.3 above, we discussed the treatments of George Wimpey and Tarmac when they swapped their respective construction and housing businesses in 1996. Neither company recognised any gain or loss in their profit and loss account. As can be seen in Extracts 6.6 and 6.7, George Wimpey followed method (d) while Tarmac followed method (c). Also, as noted at 2.3.3 above, Kingfisher has treated its exchange of its 100% interest in B&Q for a 57.9% interest in Castorama as if it were an asset swap under (d) above, but rather than recognising negative goodwill has regarded the difference as an unrealised gain through the statement of total recognised gains and losses.

3.7 Disclosure requirements relating to disposals

FRS 10 requires disclosure of the profit or loss on each material disposal of a previously acquired business or business segment.[184] Any amount of goodwill which remained eliminated against reserves on implementation of that standard which is included within the calculation of the profit or loss should also be disclosed.[185]

For businesses which were acquired before 1 January 1989, if it is impossible or impracticable to ascertain the attributable goodwill, then this fact should be stated and the reason for non-disclosure given.[186]

In addition, the Companies Act requires that where there has been a disposal of a material subsidiary during the financial year, disclosure should be made of the name of the subsidiary and of its results up to the date of disposal.[187] However, a similar exemption to that in respect of business combinations indicated at 2.8.4 above applies if disclosure is thought to be prejudicial.

FRS 2 has repeated the requirements of the Act, but has extended them such that the name of each material undertaking which ceases to be a subsidiary undertaking, together with any ownership interest retained, should be disclosed. Where this arises other than by way of disposal of at least part of the interest held by the group, the circumstances in which the undertaking ceased to be a subsidiary undertaking should be explained.[188]

In addition, FRS 1 requires disclosure of the effects of disposals of subsidiaries on the cash flow statement and FRS 3 requires separate disclosure of the aggregate results of discontinued operations during the period. These are discussed at 2.7.1 of Chapter 26 and 2.3 of Chapter 22 respectively.

4 GROUP REORGANISATIONS

4.1 Introduction

Group reorganisations involve the restructuring of the relationships between companies in a group by, for example, setting up a new holding company, changing the direct ownership of a subsidiary within the group, or transferring businesses from one company to another because of a process of divisionalisation. In principle, most of such changes should have no impact on the consolidated financial statements (provided there are no minority interests affected), because they are purely internal and cannot affect the group when it is being portrayed as a single entity. However, all such transactions can have a significant impact on the financial statements of the individual companies in the group, and this is described for each of the main types of transaction in the sections which follow. All the examples given assume that all the subsidiaries are owned 100% by the parent company.

4.2 Setting up a new top holding company

Reorganisations of this type may take place, for example, to introduce a public company over the top of an existing group as a vehicle for flotation, or to improve the co-ordination of diverse businesses. It involves H becoming the new holding company of A, as shown in the diagram below, and this may be achieved either by the shareholders subscribing for shares in H and then H paying cash for A or, more usually, by H issuing its own shares to the shareholders of A in exchange for the shares in A.

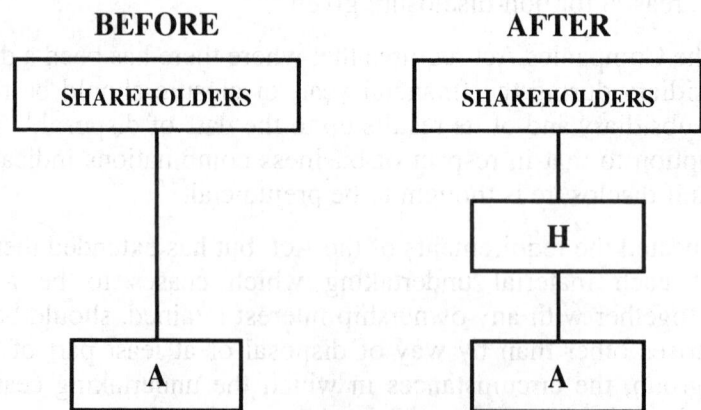

This type of reorganisation will qualify as a 'group reconstruction' under FRS 6 which is defined as any of the following arrangements:

(a) the transfer of a shareholding in a subsidiary undertaking from one group company to another;

(b) the addition of a new parent company to a group;

(c)   the transfer of shares in one or more subsidiary undertakings of a group to a new company that is not a group company but whose shareholders are the same as those of the group's parent; and

(d)   the combination into a group of two or more companies that before the combination had the same shareholders.[189]

FRS 6 has not exempted group reconstructions from its provisions but states that merger accounting may be used for group reconstructions, even though there is no business combination meeting the definition of a merger, provided:

(a)   the requirements of the Companies Act for merger accounting are met (see 2.1.5 above);

(b)   the ultimate shareholders remain the same, and the rights of each such shareholder, relative to the others, are unchanged; and

(c)   no minority's interest in the net assets of the group is altered by the transfer.[190]

It can be seen that under FRS 6 the use of merger accounting for group reconstructions is to be optional. However, because of condition (a) above, if the new holding company pays cash for the subsidiary, then merger accounting will not be possible as the Companies Act provisions will not be met. Merger accounting is only permitted under the legislation where the shares are acquired by means of a share for share exchange and the fair value of any consideration other than equity shares does not exceed 10% of the nominal value of the equity shares issued.[191]

Therefore if H pays cash for A, it should (in theory at least) account for the transaction as an acquisition, which involves attributing fair values to A's assets, consolidating only the post-acquisition results of A and possibly freezing A's pre-acquisition reserves from being distributed to H's shareholders in the future (see 2.3.7 above for a discussion of the treatment of pre-acquisition dividends). All these consequences are usually undesirable when the sole intention is to insert a new holding company at the top of the group, and it is relatively unlikely that this means of effecting the transaction will be chosen. In any event, H could have difficulty in financing such a transaction, and A could not provide the necessary finance (e.g. by any kind of loan or guarantee) because UK company law does not permit a company to provide financial assistance for the purchase of its own shares.[192]

It is therefore more likely that the transaction will be effected by the exchange of shares. In this case the transaction will qualify for merger accounting (subject to all the provisos in FRS 6 set out above) and hence the consolidated financial statements may continue to carry the assets and liabilities of A at their previous book values and all profits before and after the merger can continue to be consolidated (although there are possible problems if H does not have the same accounting period and has not been in existence long enough – see 2.7.4 above). Also, the transaction will qualify for merger relief under section 131 of the

Companies Act, so the investment in A can be recorded by H at the nominal value of the shares issued by H (although as indicated at 2.1.2 above, this may only be possible under FRS 4 if merger accounting is adopted); the reserves of A will be 'frozen' as a result of the transaction only to the extent that the nominal value of H's shares exceeds that of A's shares.

Where the option of using merger accounting is not taken, or cannot be taken because cash is involved, it would seem that acquisition accounting needs to be used, although as FRS 6 states 'acquisition accounting would require the restatement at fair value of the assets and liabilities of the company transferred, and the recognising of goodwill, which is likely to be inappropriate in the case of a transaction that does not alter the relative rights of the ultimate shareholders'.[193] (In the US, the basic rules on acquisition accounting do not apply to a transfer of assets or an exchange of shares between companies under common control.)[194]

In recent years a number of companies have created a new holding company as part of an arrangement to return capital to the shareholders. This generally involves the new company issuing shares to the members of the existing company together with cash and/or loan notes in exchange for their existing shares. However, the value of the non-share element generally exceeds 10% of the nominal value of the share element of the consideration which means that not all of the requirements of the Companies Act are met. Nevertheless, such companies have adopted merger accounting by invoking the true and fair override,[195] as illustrated in the extract below.

Extract 6.52: PIC International Group PLC (1998)

1   ACCOUNTING POLICIES [extract]

a)   Basis of preparation

The accounts are prepared on historical cost accounting principles modified to incorporate the revaluation of certain tangible fixed assets. The accounts are prepared in accordance with applicable UK accounting standards except for the adoption of merger accounting referred to below.

The consolidated profit and loss account, balance sheet and cash flow statement include the Company and its subsidiaries, together with the Group's share of the profits and retained post acquisition reserves of joint ventures and associates, which have been accounted for under the gross equity method and equity method of consolidation respectively. Except as noted below, the profits or losses of subsidiaries, joint ventures and associates acquired or sold during the year are included as from or up to their respective dates of acquisition or disposal.

The Company was incorporated on 24 June 1996 as Joyce Café Limited, changed its name to PIC International Group PLC and re-registered as a public limited company on 3 April 1998. Up to 3 April 1998, the Company's assets and paid up capital amounted to only £2, and it did not trade or declare or pay any dividends or make any other distributions.

Effective from 22 June 1998, the Company acquired 100% of the issued share capital of Dalgety Limited (formerly Dalgety PLC) following implementation of a Scheme of Arrangement under section 425 of the Companies Act 1985.

The Scheme of Arrangement involved the cancellation of the issued share capital of Dalgety Limited amounting to £292,015,716; the issuance of £292,015,716 of share capital of Dalgety Limited to the Company; and for each share cancelled the issuance of the following consideration by the Company to the former shareholders of Dalgety Limited:

- one 10 pence ordinary share in the Company;
- one convertible loan note redeemed for 138.0 pence;
- cash of 94.5 pence.

The Scheme of Arrangement has been accounted for in accordance with the principles of merger accounting, although it does not satisfy all the conditions required (see below). The consolidated accounts are presented as if the Scheme of Arrangement had been effected on 24 June 1996, except for the effect of the issue of the redeemable convertible loan notes which took place on 22 June 1998 and the redemption payment under the loan notes and the return of cash to shareholders which took place on 26 June 1998. The consolidated profit and loss account combines the results of the Company with those of the Dalgety Limited Group for the year ended 30 June 1998. The comparative figures combine the results of the Company from incorporation to 30 June 1997 with those of the Dalgety Limited Group for the year ended 30 June 1997. The comparative consolidated balance sheet as at 30 June 1997 combines the balance sheet of the Company and that of the Dalgety Limited Group as at that date.

Schedule 4A to the Companies Act 1985 and FRS 6 "Acquisitions and Mergers" require acquisition accounting to be adopted where all the conditions laid down for merger accounting are not satisfied. The Scheme of Arrangement does not satisfy the condition that the fair value of the non-share element of the consideration given by the Company for the shares in Dalgety Limited should not exceed 10% of the nominal value of the share element of the consideration.

However, in the opinion of the directors, the Scheme of Arrangement is a Group reconstruction rather than an acquisition, since the shareholders of the Company are the same as the former shareholders in Dalgety Limited and the rights of each shareholder, relative to the others, are unchanged and no minority interest in the net assets of the Group is altered. Hence the shareholders have a continuing interest in the businesses of Dalgety Limited, both before and after the Scheme of Arrangement. Consequently, the directors consider that to record the Scheme of Arrangement as an acquisition by the Company, to attribute fair values to the assets and liabilities of the Group and to reflect only the post-Scheme of Arrangement results within these accounts would fail to give a true and fair view of the Group's results and financial position.

Accordingly, having regard to the overriding requirement under section 227(6) of the Companies Act 1985 for the accounts to give a true and fair view of the Group's results and financial position, the directors have adopted merger accounting principles in drawing up these accounts. The directors consider that it is not practicable to quantify the effect of this departure from the Companies Act 1985 requirements.

4.3 Changing direct ownership of a company within a group

4.3.1 *Subsidiary moved 'up'*

This involves a 'grandson' subsidiary being moved up to become a 'son', as shown in the diagram below. Such a change might be made say, to allow B to be disposed of while C is retained, or because B and C are in different businesses and the group wishes to restructure itself so that the different businesses are conducted through directly owned subsidiaries.

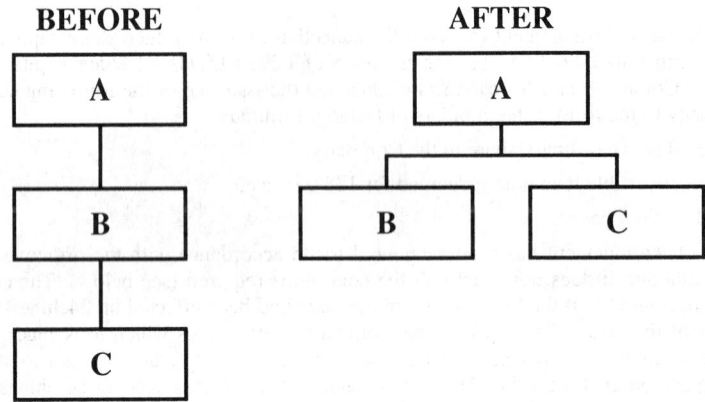

This result could be achieved either by B transferring its investment in C to A as a dividend in specie, or by A paying cash (or a cash equivalent) to B for the investment in C. It is not possible to effect this transaction by a share for share exchange, because an allotment by a holding company (A) to its subsidiary (B) is void.[196]

If the mechanism used is to be a dividend in specie then B must have sufficient distributable profits. If B has previously revalued its investment in C then the amount of that revaluation may be treated as a realised profit in deciding whether the dividend is legal and in accounting for the dividend; for example, if B's balance sheet is as follows:

	£
Investment in C (cost £100)	900
Other net assets	100
	1,000
Share capital	100
Revaluation reserve	800
Profit and loss account	100
	1,000

On the face of it, B cannot make a distribution of more than £100. However, if it makes a distribution in kind of its investment in C, the revaluation reserve can be treated as realised.[197]

Where the transaction is effected as a dividend in specie then the problem of how A accounts for it also arises. It will need to reflect its new investment in C at a value, but two questions then arise; what value to place on it, and whether the transaction gives rise to a realised profit. The legal position on both of these points is unclear. On the first question, a range of possible values would appear to be possible – the value might for example be agreed between the parties, it could be at current fair value, it could be the carrying value previously recorded in B's financial statements or it might even be nil. In practice, it might be convenient to use B's carrying value, but it cannot be said with certainty that this is the right answer. On the second issue, it may appear that A has realised a profit by being given a valuable asset (subject to the need to write down its investment in B), but it might be contended with some justification that this is not realised, since in substance nothing has changed – A still owns the same two subsidiaries as it did before. Where it is sufficiently significant (e.g. in relation to a proposed distribution), it may be advisable to seek legal advice on these points.

If A pays cash to B in exchange for its investment in C, the transaction is on the face of it straightforward. B will have to record a gain or loss on sale if the purchase price differs from the value at which it carried its investment in C, although frequently the transfer may be made on such terms that no gain or loss is recorded. However, there is a danger that a transfer at a price which does not fully reflect the true value of C (i.e. made at less than an arm's-length price) will be regarded as having given rise to a distribution, and if the transaction is made to facilitate B's leaving the group, it could also be regarded as financial assistance which may be illegal – there are therefore various possible legal pitfalls which must be borne in mind.

Regardless of the value at which these transactions take place, there should be no effect on the group financial statements, because the group as a whole is in no different position from before; it has made neither an acquisition nor a disposal.

4.3.2 Subsidiary moved 'down'

This involves a 'son' becoming a 'grandson' as shown in the diagram below. Such a change might be made, say, if A is a foreign holding company but B and C are UK companies who will form a UK tax group as a result of the reorganisation.

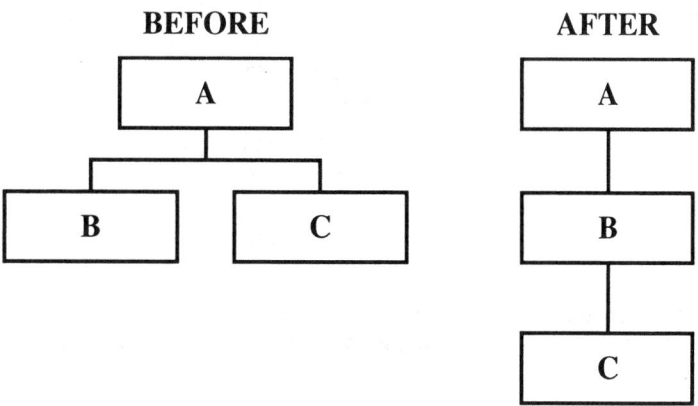

This reorganisation could be achieved either by B paying cash to A or by B issuing its shares to A in exchange for the shares in C. As in the previous two examples, there should be no effect on the group financial statements as a result of the reorganisation.

The accounting in the case of a cash transaction is relatively straightforward, following the principles described above in 4.3.1. However, if C is sold at an amount greater or smaller than its carrying value, the issue of whether A should recognise a gain or loss will again arise; as with the question discussed in 4.3.1 above, the law on this is unclear. The question of whether B has effectively made a distribution is again unlikely to arise; in the context of this transaction it could arise only if the transfer were made at a price which was in excess of the fair value of C, which is in practice unlikely.

In the case of a share-for-share exchange, the provisions of section 132 of the Companies Act 1985 become relevant. This section is designed to give partial relief from the requirement to set up a share premium account in the circumstances of a group reconstruction involving the issue of shares. It requires a share premium account of the 'minimum premium value' to be established; this is the amount by which the book value of the investment (or cost, if lower) exceeds the nominal value of the shares issued. The effect of this is to preserve the book value of the investment (any amount by which the investment had been revalued would effectively be reversed, but the investment could also be revalued again). The operation of the section is illustrated in the following example:

Example 6.8

The balance sheets of A and its direct subsidiaries B and C are as follows:

	A £	B £	C £	Group £
Investment in B	200			
Investment in C	100			
Other net assets	300	275	300	875
	600	275	300	875
Share capital	500	200	100	500
Profit and loss account	100	75	200	375
	600	275	300	875

B then issues 50 £1 shares to A in exchange for A's investment in C, which is shown in A's balance sheet at a cost of £100. The minimum premium value is therefore £50. The resultant balance sheets would be:

	A £	B £	C £	Group £
Investment in B	300			
Investment in C		100		
Other net assets	300	275	300	875
	600	375	300	875
Share capital	500	250	100	500
Share premium		50		
Profit and loss account	100	75	200	375
	600	375	300	875

Care must be taken in this situation to avoid issuing shares at a discount; this means that it must be possible to demonstrate that C is worth at least the nominal value of the shares issued by B.

If B were to prepare group accounts then the accounting considerations are similar to those discussed at 4.2 above.

4.3.3   Subsidiary moved 'along'

This involves a 'grandson' subsidiary being moved along to become another 'grandson' but under a different 'son', as shown in the diagram below. It would be achieved by C paying cash or other assets to B rather than issuing shares, because otherwise the resulting holding of B in C would probably negate the desired effect of the transaction.

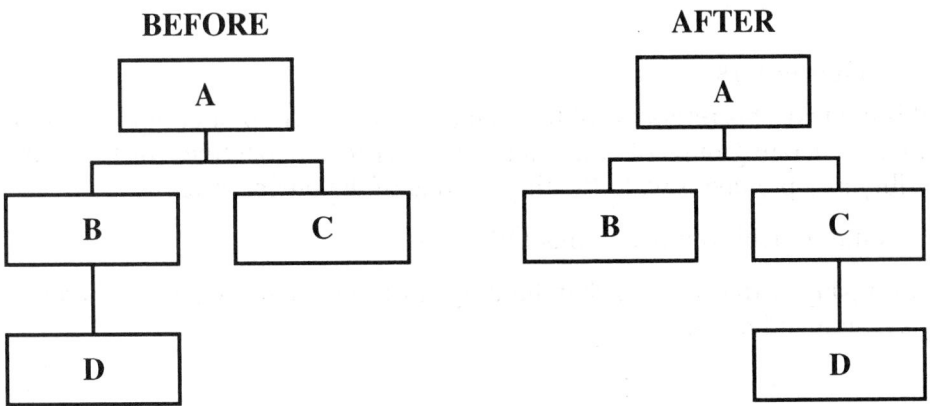

The accounting considerations are similar to those under 4.3.1 above, and once again there can be no effect on the group financial statements, because when the group is looked upon as a single entity there has been no change. The question of an effective distribution cannot arise because the purchaser is not the holding company. As above, if the transaction is a prelude to B leaving the group, or is intended to facilitate it, and C pays less than fair value then problems of financial assistance can arise. If C were to prepare group accounts then the accounting considerations are similar to those discussed at 4.2 above where the new holding company pays cash.

Although C cannot issue shares directly to B as it might negate the desired effect of the transaction, it may, however, be possible to achieve the same effect by utilising a combination of the reorganisations outlined at 4.3.1 and 4.3.2 above.

4.4   Divisionalisation of an existing group

The term 'divisionalisation' in this context is used to signify the transfer of the assets and trades of a number of subsidiaries into one company so that the businesses are brought together. It is a means of rationalising and simplifying the group and can result in a saving of administration costs. Transactions of this type are usually effected for a cash consideration, which is often left outstanding on inter-company account as the shell company has no requirement for cash.

In principle the accounting treatment is straightforward. However, one complication which can arise is that there might be an apparent need to write down the investment in the shell company to reflect an impairment in its value, depending on the price at which the assets were transferred. This will typically arise where the shell company was originally purchased at a price which included goodwill, but the business is then transferred to another company at a price which reflects only the value of the net tangible assets; this will mean that, although the goodwill still exists, the business to which it relates is now in another company, and although the group as a whole is unaffected, the value of the investment in the shell company now falls short of its cost. This issue is discussed in Chapter 11 at 2.2.1.

4.5   Demergers

In this context, this refers to splitting up an existing group of companies into two or more separate groups of companies, in order to separate their different trades, possibly as a prelude, say, to floating off one of the businesses.

This could be achieved in a number of ways:

(a) Company A transfers its shareholdings in a subsidiary, B, to its shareholders as a dividend in specie.

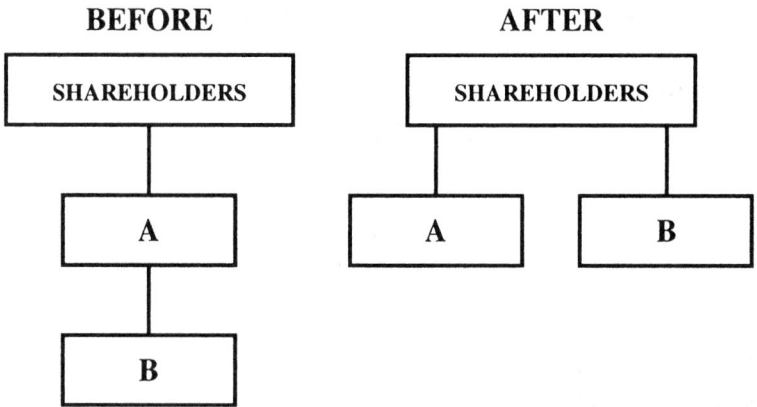

(b) Company A transfers a trade to another company, C (usually formed for the purposes of the demerger) and in exchange C issues shares to the shareholders of A.

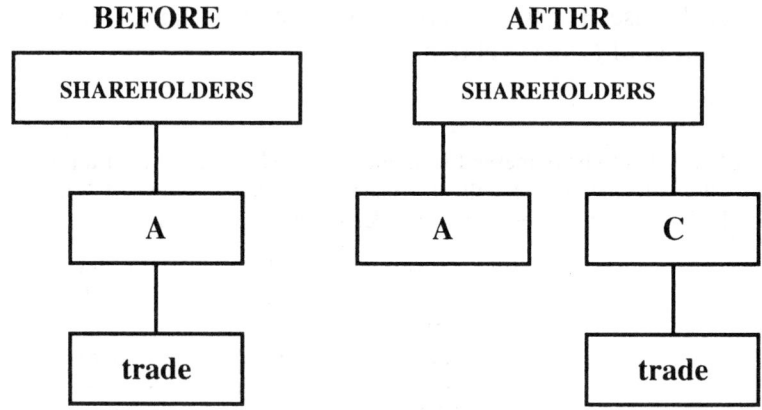

(c) Company A transfers its shareholding in a subsidiary, B, to another company, C; in return, shares in C are issued to some or all of the shareholders in A.

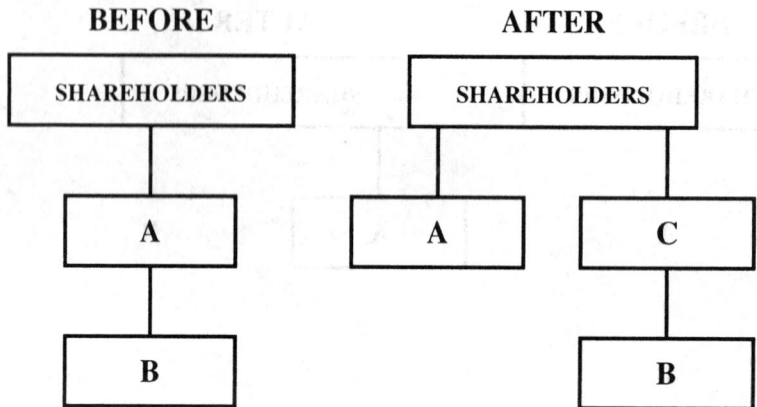

Whichever route is adopted, the transaction involves a distribution by A to its shareholders. This is less obvious in the second and third examples outlined above, but it is as though A had distributed the assets or shares in question to its own shareholders, which they then exchange for shares in C. Similar accounting issues arise in each case; for the purposes of illustration, an example is shown below of a transaction of type (c) above.

Example 6.9

B is a subsidiary of A and is to be demerged from the group. The form of the transaction is that a new company, C, is to be formed which will issue shares to the shareholders of A in exchange for A's investment in B. The balance sheets before the demerger are as follows:

	A £	B £	A group £
Investment in B	500		
Other net assets	1,200	800	2,000
	1,700	800	2,000
Share capital	1,000	500	1,000
Profit and loss account	700	300	1,000
	1,700	800	2,000

C is to issue 500 £1 ordinary shares to the shareholders of A in exchange for the shares in B held by A. In effect this amounts to a distribution of £500 by A to its shareholders so that, in the A group financial statements the company's net assets are reduced by £500 and the group's net assets by £800 (i.e. the net asset value of B). In the financial statements, the usual treatment is to disclose these amounts as movements on retained earnings, along the following lines:

Profit and loss account	Group	Company
	£	£
Balance at 1 January 1999	1,000	700
Demerger of B	(800)	(500)
Profit for the year	350	350
Balance at 31 December 1999	550	550

From C's point of view, the questions which arise are whether its shares are being issued at a premium and if so whether share premium relief should be taken. As this part of the transaction amounts to a merger of C with B, the answers to both questions are yes. However, if the demerger was of an unincorporated business, then merger relief would not be available, since it applies only to share exchanges and not to issues of shares in exchange for assets; this contrasts with group reconstruction relief, which is available for both – see 4.3.2 above. The same point applies to a transaction of type (b) above.

It also seems logical to use merger accounting for this kind of transaction and it is likely to be a 'group reconstruction' under FRS 6; merger accounting can therefore be adopted provided all the conditions are met. Although this is likely to be the case for the demerger transaction itself, in many cases it is likely to have been preceded by a number of other internal transactions involving transfers of subsidiaries or businesses around the group some of which may have been for shares and others for cash or on inter-company account.

One example of a demerger was ICI's bioscience interests to Zeneca in 1993. However, as disclosed in Zeneca's 1993 accounts merger accounting was applied even though all the conditions laid down for merger accounting were not met, the 'true and fair override' being used:

Extract 6.53: Zeneca Group PLC (1993)

2 BASIS OF CONSOLIDATION AND PRESENTATION OF FINANCIAL INFORMATION [extract]

The transfer of ZENECA Limited to the Company has been accounted for in accordance with the principles of merger accounting set out in Statement of Standard Accounting Practice No. 23 (SSAP 23) and Schedule 4(A) to the Companies Act 1985. The financial statements are therefore presented as if ZENECA Limited and its subsidiaries had been owned and controlled by the Company throughout.

ZENECA Limited was created through an internal reorganisation within ICI which resulted in the transfer to it of ICI's bioscience activities with effect from 1 January 1993. The bioscience interests included both subsidiaries, some of which were themselves subject to reorganisation prior to transfer, and certain unincorporated business activities of ICI. These transactions have been accounted for in these group accounts using the principles of merger accounting as if ZENECA Limited had been in existence throughout. This is not in accordance with SSAP 23 and Schedule 4(A) to the Companies Act 1985 as the transfer of the unincorporated business activities and the reorganisation of certain subsidiaries prior to transfer to ZENECA Limited do not meet all the conditions laid down for merger accounting.

> The directors consider that to apply acquisition accounting to any part of the reorganisation of the Zeneca businesses, with consequent adjustments to the fair values of the related assets and liabilities and the reflection of post reorganisation results only within ZENECA Group PLC's accounts, would fail to give a true and fair view of the Group's state of affairs and results for the shareholders since they have had a continuing interest in the Zeneca businesses both before and after the demerger. Due to the number and complexity of transactions involved, it is not practicable to quantify the effect of this departure.

Although this demerger preceded FRS 6, such preliminary transactions would also not have met the conditions laid down in FRS 6 (given that one of the conditions for group reconstructions is that it is allowed by the Companies Act).

As far as ICI's accounts are concerned, the businesses transferred to Zeneca were consolidated up to the date of demerger and shown as discontinued operations. As indicated above, a demerger involves a distribution to the shareholders. ICI dealt with this as follows:

Extract 6.54: Imperial Chemical Industries PLC (1993)

10   DIVIDENDS

	1993	1992	1993	1992
	pence per £1 share		£m	£m
Interim, paid 4 October 1993	10.5p	21p	76	150
Second interim, to be confirmed as final, payable 28 April 1994	17.0p	34p	123	243
	27.5p	55p	199	393
Demerger dividend – This comprises the net assets of Zeneca at date of demerger. The resolution to give effect to the demerger, which was passed at the Extraordinary General Meeting of the Company on 28 May 1993, approved a dividend of £464,566,941 on the Ordinary Shares of £1 each in the Company: this was the holding value of Zeneca Limited by the Company.			363	
			562	393

23 RESERVES [extract]

The cumulative amount of goodwill resulting from acquisitions during 1993 and prior years, net of goodwill attributable to subsidiary undertakings or businesses demerged or disposed of prior to 31 December 1993, amounted to £609m (1992 £1,700m, reduced by £69m following a detailed review to identify all such goodwill). Goodwill in respect of Zeneca businesses which were demerged totalled £1,011m.

It can be seen that ICI has charged as the demerger dividend in the consolidated profit and loss account the amount of the net assets of businesses demerged, although noting the dividend approved by the shareholders which was based on the carrying amount of the investment in the parent's books. Although not a disposal or closure of a business, it is arguable that the demerger dividend should also have included the goodwill attributable to the businesses demerged based on the requirements of UITF 3 (see 3.3 above). Such an approach was adopted by Fine Art Developments in respect of its demerger of Creative Publishing in 1998, as shown below:

Extract 6.55: Fine Art Developments p.l.c. (1998)

8   DEMERGER DIVIDEND

	Group	
The demerger dividend represents the net assets and attributable goodwill of the Creative Publishing business and is calculated as follows:	1998 £'000	1997 £'000
Tangible fixed assets	30,901	–
Investments	562	–
Stocks	62,550	–
Debtors	74,233	–
Net borrowings	(68,961)	–
Creditors and provisions	(44,509)	–
Net assets on demerger	60,776	–
Goodwill previously written off	14,070	–
Demerger dividend	74,846	–

4.6   Capital contributions

One form of transaction which is sometimes made within a group is a 'capital contribution', where one company injects funds in another (usually its subsidiary) in the form of a non-returnable gift. Whenever capital contributions are made, complex tax considerations can arise and should be addressed.

Capital contributions have no legal status in the UK – certainly the term is not used anywhere in the Companies Acts. This has led to uncertainty over the appropriate accounting treatment in the financial statements of both the giver and the receiver of the capital contribution.

Until recently there has been no reference to capital contributions in accounting standards. However, the Application Notes in FRS 4 – *Capital instruments* – deal with the treatment from the standpoint of a subsidiary receiving the contribution.

4.6.1   *Treatment in the financial statements of the paying company*

In the most common situation, where the contribution is made by a company to one of its subsidiaries, the treatment is relatively straightforward; the amount of the contribution should be added to the cost of the investment in the subsidiary. However, it will not be possible to regard it as part of the purchase price of shares in the subsidiary, so it should be classified as a separate item when the cost of the investment is analysed. As with any fixed asset, it will be necessary to write down the investment whenever it is recognised that its value has been permanently impaired; this should be considered when subsequent dividends are received from the subsidiary which could be regarded as having been met out of the capital contribution and hence representing a return of it.

Where the contribution is made to a fellow-subsidiary, it will not be possible to regard it as an asset of any kind; it is neither an investment in the other company, nor can it be treated as a monetary receivable, since by definition there is no obligation on the part of the recipient to return it. Accordingly, the only available treatment to the paying company in these circumstances will be to write it off in the profit and loss account of the period in which the payment is made.

4.6.2   *Treatment in the financial statements of the receiving company*

The Application Notes in FRS 4 state that a subsidiary should include capital contributions received from its parent within shareholders' funds, and in the year in which a contribution is received, it should be reported in the reconciliation of movements in shareholders' funds. No indication is given as to where in shareholders' funds it is to be included, but the most common treatment would appear to be to credit the amount received to a separate reserve with a suitable title, such as 'capital contribution', or 'capital reserve'.

Notwithstanding this, it is generally considered that the contribution can be regarded for distribution purposes as a realised profit, and accordingly is available to be paid out by way of dividend. However, where the contribution received is in the form of a non-monetary asset it is doubtful whether this should be the case. Where a contribution is regarded for distribution purposes as a realised profit, it may be appropriate to reclassify the reserve to which the contribution was originally taken as part of the profit and loss account balance.

Where the contribution is received from a fellow-subsidiary, then it could be argued the contribution should be credited to the profit and loss account in the year of receipt as it is not a transaction with the company's shareholder.

There is no compelling reason why there need be symmetry of treatment between the accounting used by the giving and receiving companies, although this will usually be the case; it would, for example, be theoretically possible for the giving company to charge the contribution made to the profit and loss account, while the recipient credited the contribution directly to shareholders' funds. Whatever treatment is adopted, the whole effect of the transaction will be eliminated from the consolidated financial statements.

5 COMPARISON WITH IASC AND US PRONOUNCEMENTS

5.1 IASC

The relevant international standard is IAS 22 – *Business Combinations*. The original standard was issued in November 1983, but was revised in 1993. This covers not only those areas dealt with in FRSs 6 and 7 but also the accounting for goodwill. Some consequential changes were made following the issue of a revised version of IAS 12 – *Income Taxes* – in October 1996 (see Chapter 21 at 5.1). These changes prohibited discounting of deferred tax assets and liabilities resulting from business combinations and conformed the guidance in IAS 22 re taxation balances to the guidance in IAS 12. These changes became operative for accounting periods beginning on or after 1 January 1998.

In 1998 IAS 22 was revised yet again, the main changes being in relation to accounting for goodwill (including negative goodwill) and restricting the recognition of restructuring provisions at the date of acquisition. The revised standard becomes operative for annual accounts covering periods beginning on or after 1 July 1999. Earlier implementation is encouraged, but that fact should be disclosed and the enterprise also needs to adopt IAS 36 – *Impairment of assets*, IAS 37 – *Provisions, Contingent Liabilities and Contingent Assets* – and IAS 38 – *Intangible Assets* – at the same time.

The requirements of IAS 22 relating to goodwill are dealt with at 7.1.2 of Chapter 10. The main differences between the IASC requirements and those in the UK are dealt with below.

5.1.1 Uniting of interests

As in the UK, IAS 22 draws a distinction between an acquisition and a uniting of interests (merger). A uniting of interests is defined as 'a business combination in which the shareholders of the combining enterprises combine control over the whole, or effectively the whole, of their net assets and operations to achieve a continuing mutual sharing in the risks and benefits attaching to the combined entity such that neither party can be identified as the acquirer'.[198]

The criteria to be satisfied before a combination can be accounted for as a uniting of interests are similar to the criteria in FRS 6, although they are not phrased quite as prescriptively. IAS 22 states that in order to achieve a mutual sharing of the risks and benefits of the combined entity:[199]

(a)   the substantial majority, if not all, of the voting common shares of the combining enterprises must be exchanged or pooled;

(b)   the fair value of one enterprise is not significantly different from that of the other enterprise; and

(c)   the shareholders of each enterprise maintain substantially the same voting rights and interest in the combined entity, relative to each other, after the combination as before.

However, IAS 22 comments that the likelihood of a mutual sharing of the risks and benefits of the combined entity diminishes and the likelihood that an acquirer can be identified increases when:[200]

(a)   the relative equality in fair values of the combining enterprises is reduced and the percentage of voting common shares exchanged decreases;

(b)   financial arrangements provide a relative advantage to one group of shareholders over the other shareholders; and

(c)   one party's share of the equity in the combined entity depends on how the business which it previously controlled performs subsequent to the business combination.

If the combination is one of the exceptional cases in which an acquirer cannot be identified then it should be accounted for as a uniting of interests ('merger' or 'pooling-of-interests'). The way in which such accounting should be done is consistent with the method required by FRS 6.[201]

5.1.2   Acquisitions

The prescribed treatments under IAS 22 are in general very similar to those specified by FRS 7. The cost of acquisition is thus defined as 'the amount of cash or cash equivalents paid or the fair value, at the date of exchange, of the other purchase consideration given by the acquirer in exchange for control over the net assets of the other enterprise, plus any costs directly attributable to the acquisition'.[202]

One difference between the UK and the International standard is in the treatment of contingent consideration. IAS 22 states that where the acquisition agreement provides for an adjustment to the purchase consideration contingent on one or more future events, the amount of the adjustment should be included in the cost of acquisition as at the date of acquisition if the adjustment is probable and the amount can be measured reliably.[203] This is less prescriptive than FRS 7.

IAS 22 no longer allows the fair values of identifiable assets and liabilities to be determined by reference to their intended use by the acquirer, which was the case under the previous version of the standard.[204] Like FRS 7, liabilities should not be recognised at the date of acquisition if they result from the acquirer's intentions or actions. Liabilities should also not be recognised for future losses or other costs expected to be incurred as a result of the acquisition, whether they relate to the acquirer or the acquiree.[205] However, IAS 22 contains one specific exception to this general principle, and that is if the acquirer has developed plans that relate to the acquiree's business and an obligation comes into existence as a direct consequence of the acquisition. In that instance, IAS 22 requires that, at the date of acquisition, the acquirer should recognise a provision that was not a liability of the acquiree at that date if, and only if, the acquirer has:

(a) at, or before, the date of acquisition, developed the main features of a plan that involves terminating or reducing the activities of the acquiree and that relates to:

(i) compensating employees of the acquiree for termination of their employment;

(ii) closing facilities of the acquiree;

(iii) eliminating product lines of the acquiree; or

(iv) terminating contracts of the acquiree that have become onerous because the acquirer has communicated to the other party at, or before, the date of acquisition that the contract will be terminated;

(b) by announcing the main features of the plan at, or before, the date of acquisition, raised a valid expectation in those affected by the plan that it will implement the plan; and

(c) by the earlier of three months after the date of acquisition and the date when the annual financial statements are approved, developed those main features into a detailed formal plan identifying at least:

(i) the business or part of a business concerned;

(ii) the principal locations affected;

(iii) the location, function, and approximate number of employees who will be compensated for terminating their services;

(iv) the expenditures that will be undertaken; and

(v) when the plan will be implemented.

Any provision recognised under this paragraph should cover only the costs of the items listed in (a)(i) to (iv) above.[206] Such provisions are limited to costs of restructuring the operations of the acquiree; they cannot include costs of the acquirer.

Many of the guidelines contained in IAS 22 for determining the fair values of particular assets and liabilities[207] are similar to those in FRS 7, although inventories are to be fair valued on a similar basis to that used in the US (see 5.2.6 D below).

5.1.3 *Reverse acquisitions*

IAS 22 defines an acquisition as 'a business combination in which one of the enterprises, the acquirer, obtains control over the net assets and operations of another enterprise, the acquiree, in exchange for the transfer of assets, incurrence of a liability or issue of equity'.[208] The standard recognises that occasionally an enterprise obtains ownership of the shares of another enterprise but as part of the exchange transaction issues enough voting shares, as consideration, such that control of the combined enterprise passes to the owners of the enterprise whose shares have been acquired. This situation is described as a reverse acquisition. Although legally the enterprise issuing the shares may be regarded as the parent or continuing enterprise, the enterprise whose shareholders now control the combined enterprise is the acquirer for the purposes of IAS 22. The enterprise issuing the shares is deemed to have been acquired by the other enterprise; the latter enterprise is deemed to be the acquirer and applies the purchase method to the assets and liabilities of the enterprise issuing the shares.[209] However, the standard is then silent as to how its requirements should be applied in practice in such situations. FRS 6 makes no reference to reverse acquisitions, other than to state that the provision in the previous version of IAS 22 is incompatible with companies legislation in the UK and the Republic of Ireland.[210]

5.1.4   Disclosures

For uniting of interests the disclosure requirements are similar to those for mergers under FRS 6.[211] For acquisitions, like the US, the disclosure requirements of IAS 22 are less onerous than those in FRS 6.[212]

5.2   US

The main standard in the US in this area is APB Opinion 16 – *Business Combinations*– which was issued by the AICPA in 1970. In addition there are several interpretations issued by the AICPA and the FASB, a number of EITF consensuses and various SEC rulings dealing with the topic.

Notwithstanding the volume of literature in the US and the fact that the original standards are nearly 30 years old, the requirements in respect of business combinations are broadly similar to those of FRSs 6 and 7; the more significant differences are noted in the discussions below.

5.2.1   The pooling-of-interests method

As in the UK, the purchase method (acquisition accounting) and the pooling-of-interests method are both acceptable in accounting for business combinations, although not as alternatives in accounting for the same business combination. As in the UK, a business combination either qualifies for the pooling-of-interests method or must be accounted for as a purchase.[213]

A 'pooling-of-interests' is a business combination where two or more previously independent common shareholder groups exchange voting common stock and combine their resources, talents and risks to form a new entity to carry on in combination the previous businesses and to continue their earnings streams. Neither shareholder group withdraws nor invests resources but, in effect, they mutually exchange risks and benefits.[214]

The general concept of a pooling is supported by a series of detailed rules in APB 16 designed to prevent what is really a purchase from qualifying for pooling accounting. A business combination must meet all of the following criteria to be accounted for as a pooling of interests:

A   *Attributes of the combining companies*

(a)   Each of the combining companies is autonomous and has not been a subsidiary or division of another company within two years before the plan of combination is initiated.

(b)   Each of the combining companies is independent of the others, and in particular does not hold investments in the others.[215]

B   *Manner of the combination*

(a)   The combination is effected in a single transaction, or in accordance with a specific plan, within one year after the plan is initiated.[216]

(b)   The issuing company offers and issues only common stock with rights identical to those of the majority of its outstanding voting common stock in exchange for substantially all (90% or more) of the voting common stock interest of the other company.[217]

(c)   No change in the equity interests of the voting common stock of any combining company may be made in contemplation of a pooling-of-interests either within the two years prior to the merger being initiated or between the dates the merger is initiated and consummated.[218]

(d)   The ratio of the interest of an individual common stockholder to those of other common stockholders in a combining company remains the same as a result of the exchange of stock.[219]

(e)   The voting rights to which the common stock ownership interests in the resulting combined entity are entitled are exercisable by the stockholders; the stockholders are neither deprived of nor restricted in exercising those rights.[220]

(f)   The entire plan of combination must be resolved by the consummation date. Thus, the combined entity may not agree to contingently issue additional shares or distribute other consideration at a later date to the former owners of the combining company.[221]

C   *Absence of planned transactions*

(a)   Stock issued in a pooling must remain outstanding outside the combined entity without arrangements for any of the entities involved to use their financial resources to buy out former stockholders or induce others to do so.[222]

(b)   The combined company must not enter into other financial arrangements for the benefit of the former stockholders of a combining company, such as the guarantee of loans secured by stock issued in the combination, which in effect negates the exchange of equity securities.[223]

(c)   The combined company may not intend or plan to dispose of a significant part of the assets of the combining companies within two years after the combination other than disposals in the ordinary course of business.[224]

Although these conditions were intended to limit the use of the pooling-of-interests method, it continues to be used widely today in the US.[225] As discussed at 5.2.9 below, in April 1999 the FASB tentatively agreed to eliminate the pooling-of-interests method and is expected to issue an exposure draft during the third or fourth quarter of 1999.

5.2.2   Application of pooling-of-interests method

When applying the pooling-of-interests method, the recorded assets and liabilities of the separate companies should be combined in the financial statements. Adjustments may have to be made to eliminate differences in accounting policies adopted by the separate enterprises. The consolidated financial statements should report results of operations for the period in which the combination occurs as though the companies had been combined as of the beginning of the period.[226]

Notes to the financial statements should disclose details of the effects of a business combination which is to be accounted for by the pooling method consummated before the issuance of but after the date of the financial statements. The details including revenue, net income and earnings per share should be disclosed as if the consummation had occurred at the date of the financial statements.[227]

5.2.3   The purchase method

As in the UK, if a business combination does not meet the pooling-of-interests criteria, it must be accounted for under the purchase method. The purchase method under APB 16 is very similar in outline to acquisition accounting under UK GAAP.[228] However, some differences do exist between them.

The purchase method follows principles normally applicable under historical cost accounting when recording acquisitions of assets for cash, by exchanging other assets, or by issuing shares. Acquiring assets in a group requires ascertaining the cost of the assets as a group and then allocating the cost to the individual assets that comprise the group. Like FRS 7 in the UK, APB 16 provides guidance on determining the cost of a group of assets and on assigning a portion of the total cost to each individual asset acquired on the basis of its fair value. A difference between the sum of the assigned costs of the tangible and identifiable intangible assets acquired less liabilities assumed and the cost of the group is evidence of unspecified intangible values – i.e. goodwill.

5.2.4   Acquisition date

In the US, the normal date of acquisition is the date on which assets are received and other assets are given or securities are issued – in other words, when consideration passes. FRS 2 regards the acquisition date as being when control passes, which may or may not be the same time as when consideration passes. Also in the US, the parties are allowed to designate the end of an accounting period as being the effective date, provided it is between the dates on which the business combination is initiated and consummated. However, where the effective date is before the date on which the consideration passes, US GAAP requires that the purchase price be adjusted for imputed interest on the amount of the consideration outstanding between these dates.[229] This is to prevent what would in effect be double counting during this period, because the acquiring company would be both recognising the profits from the new subsidiary and also continuing to enjoy the use of the funds which were to be paid to the vendors.

5.2.5   *The cost of the acquired enterprise*

Cash and other assets distributed, securities issued unconditionally and amounts of contingent consideration that are determinable (i.e. where the outcome of the contingency is determinable beyond reasonable doubt) at the date of acquisition should be included in determining the cost of an acquired enterprise and recorded at that date.[230]

Contingent consideration is usually recorded when the contingency is resolved and consideration is issued or becomes issuable.[231] As noted above it is only recorded at the date of acquisition if the outcome of the contingency is determined beyond reasonable doubt.

The cost of an acquired company is measured by the fair values of assets distributed (e.g. marketable securities). In the case of quoted equity securities, the market price for a reasonable period before and after the date the terms of the acquisition are agreed to and announced should be considered in determining the fair value of securities issued.[232] In other words, the date of measurement of the value of the shares should not be influenced by the need to obtain shareholder or regulatory approval.[233]

The fair value of a debt security is its present value. A premium or discount should be recorded for a debt security issued with an interest rate fixed materially above or below the effective rate or current yield for an otherwise comparable security.[234]

The issue of additional securities or other consideration at the resolution of contingencies based on earnings results in an addition to the cost of an acquired company and consequently to the goodwill also. This additional element should be amortised over the remaining life of the goodwill.[235]

5.2.6   *Recording fair values of identifiable assets and liabilities*

A   *General approach*

APB 16 requires an acquiring company to allocate the cost of an acquired company to all identifiable assets acquired and liabilities assumed in a business combination by reference to their fair values at date of acquisition.[236] The concept of fair value differs from that in FRS 7. Under APB 16, it is appropriate to take account of the acquirer's intentions when identifying and allocating fair values to the assets acquired and liabilities assumed. For example, it is appropriate to recognise as liabilities the costs of a plan to exit an activity of an acquired company or to terminate the employment, or relocate, employees of an acquired company provided certain conditions are met.

The rules for attributing fair values to specific assets and liabilities are set out below.

B   Tangible fixed assets

The fair values of tangible fixed assets should be determined as follows:

(a)   Assets such as land and natural resources at appraised values;[237]

(b)   Plant and equipment that is to be:

- used, at current replacement cost for similar capacity unless the expected future use of the assets indicates a lower value to the acquirer. Replacement cost may be determined directly if a used asset market exists for the assets acquired. Otherwise, it should be approximated from replacement cost new less estimated accumulated depreciation;

- sold, at fair value less cost to sell.[238]

C   Intangible assets

Identifiable intangible assets (except goodwill) that can be identified and named, including contracts, patents, franchises, customer and supplier lists, and favourable leases should be included at appraised values.[239]

These will include in-process research and development costs which are then required to be written off immediately.[240] The FASB was planning to issue an exposure draft proposing that such capitalised assets would no longer be written off immediately but would be amortised over their service lives. However, faced with complaints from technology companies and investment bankers, in July 1999 the FASB decided to put off the issue until a later date (see 5.2.1 of Chapter 12).

D   Inventories

The fair values of inventories should be determined as follows:[241]

(a)   Finished goods at estimated selling price less any future anticipated costs and less a reasonable profit allowance for the selling effort of the acquiring company;

(b)   Work in progress at estimated selling price less any future costs to completion and less a reasonable profit allowance for the completing and selling effort of the acquiring company;

(c)   Raw materials at current replacement costs.

E   *Investments*

Marketable securities at current net realisable values.[242] Non-marketable securities at appraised values.[243]

F   *Monetary assets and liabilities*

Receivables at their present values based on appropriate current interest rates and after making provisions for bad debts.[244]

All liabilities (including notes and accounts payable, long-term debt), and accruals (e.g. accruals for warranties, vacation pay, deferred compensation) at their present value determined at appropriate current interest rates. Similarly, other liabilities and commitments (including unfavourable leases, contracts and commitments and plant closing expense incident to the acquisition) at present values of amounts to be paid determined at appropriate current interest rates.[245]

G   *Businesses sold or held exclusively with a view to subsequent resale*

The allocation of purchase price to assets to be sold is addressed in EITF 87-11. The guidance is more detailed but consistent with the approach used in FRS 7 in the UK.

H   *Pre-acquisition contingencies*

Amounts that can be reasonably estimated for contingencies in existence at the date of acquisition that are probable should be recorded as part of the fair value exercise.[246]

I   *Pensions and OPEBs*

The requirements in SFAS 87 and SFAS 106 are similar to those in FRS 7. However, the measurement of such assets or liabilities should reflect the effect of:

(a)   any changes in assumptions based on the purchaser's assessment of relevant future events;

(b)   changes to benefit plans of the acquired entity in compliance with the conditions of the business combination. If improvements were not a condition of the combination, credit granted for prior service should be treated as a plan amendment (i.e. impacting post-acquisition earnings).

(c)   terminating or curtailing the acquired entity's benefit plans, if those actions are expected.[247]

J   Deferred taxation

Under SFAS 109, a deferred tax liability or asset should be recognised for differences between the assigned values and the tax bases of the assets and liabilities recognised in a purchase business combination except, inter alia, goodwill.

If the tax benefits of an acquired entity's operating loss or tax credit carryforward for financial reporting are not recognised at the acquisition date (i.e. a valuation allowance is made under SFAS 109), subsequent recognition should:

(a)   first be applied to eliminate any goodwill and other non current intangible assets related to the acquisition; and

(b)   next be recognised as a reduction of the tax expense.[248]

K   Provisions for reorganisations and future losses

APB 16 permits consideration of the acquirer's intentions when identifying and allocating fair values to the assets acquired and liabilities assumed. For example, it is appropriate to recognise as liabilities the costs of a plan to exit an activity of an acquired company or to terminate the employment, or relocate, employees of an acquired company provided the following conditions are met:

(a)   as of the acquisition date, management begins to assess and formulate a plan;

(b)   as soon as possible after the acquisition date, management completes its assessment of which activities are to be ceased or which employees are to be affected and commits itself to the plan;

(c)   the plan identifies the actions to be taken to complete the plan, including the method of disposition and location of activities or the number, function and location of employees who are to be made redundant or relocated; and

(d)   actions required by the plan will begin as soon as possible after the plan is finalised and the period of time to complete the plan indicates that significant changes are unlikely.[249]

5.2.7   The allocation period

An allocation period is permitted for the management of the acquiring company to conduct an investigation of the assets and liabilities which have been acquired. The duration of this is not an absolute period of time, although it should usually not extend beyond one year from the acquisition date; the period in fact ends 'when the acquiring enterprise is no longer waiting for information which it has arranged to obtain and which is known to be available and obtainable'. Adjustments should be made to fair values (if necessary) when uncertainties existing at the date of acquisition have been resolved prior to the close of the 'allocation' period. The exceptions to this rule are adjustments resulting from economic events that clearly occurred subsequent to the acquisition date and adjustments to deferred tax, which should be accounted for in accordance with SFAS 109 and EITF 93-7.[250]

5.2.8 Disclosures in respect of acquisitions

The disclosure requirements in the US are less onerous than those in the UK. The disclosures required are:[251]

(a) name and brief description of the acquired entity:

(b) method of accounting;

(c) period for which results of operations of the acquired entity are included in the income statement of the acquiring company;

(d) cost of the acquired entity and, if applicable, the number of shares of stock issued or issuable, and the amount assigned to the issued and issuable shares;

(e) description of the plan for amortisation of acquired goodwill, the amortisation method, and the period;

(f) contingent payments, options, or commitments specified in the acquisition agreement; and

(g) the results of the period (unless the acquisition was at or near the beginning of the period) and of the immediately preceding period on a pro forma basis as though the companies had been combined throughout those periods. Such pro forma information should be given after taking account of fair value adjustments.

5.2.9 Future developments

These differences may become fewer in the future because in August 1996 the FASB added to its agenda a project to reconsider APB 16. This was because there was a continued need for interpretation on the part of the EITF and the FASB (notwithstanding the volume of existing interpretative literature) and because of the opportunity it presents for further international harmonisation, particularly in view of the work being carried out by the ASB and the IASC.

The project is focusing on what constitutes a business combination, the determination of when the pooling-of-interests method (merger accounting) and the purchase method (acquisition accounting) should be applied (including issues such as the need for two separate and distinct methods of accounting for business combinations, or whether to narrow the differences in accounting results between those methods), the income statement recognition and timing of purchase accounting (fair value) adjustments, and the accounting for goodwill and other intangible assets.[252] In June 1997 the FASB issued a Special Report – *Issues Associated with the FASB Project on Business Combinations* – which sought comments on a number of questions posed about the project.

The FASB's initial discussions focused primarily on accounting for goodwill, so it wasn't until July 1998 that it embarked on the phase of the project dealing with the methods of accounting for business combinations. As noted in the introduction to this chapter, G4+1 issued a Position Paper proposing that there should only be one method of accounting for business combinations, acquisition accounting, and that the pooling-of-interests method should be banned. Like the ASB, the FASB sought comments on this paper. Notwithstanding the fact that approximately 40% of the respondents did not support the proposal and approximately 25% expressed only qualified support provided that the FASB change the accounting for goodwill and retain the pooling-of-interests method for those rare 'true' mergers, in April 1999 the FASB tentatively agreed to eliminate the pooling-of-interests method. All business combinations initiated after the issuance of the final standard would have to be accounted for under the purchase method. There is clearly a lot of opposition in the US to such a proposal. The percentages quoted above in fact understate the opposition, because the analysis excluded 40 letters from high tech companies and investment bankers on the basis that they did not address the specific questions, but only expressed support for the pooling-of-interests method. The FASB has since agreed to hold a rare public hearing on the issue in early 2000, but it would seem that despite the opposition it is unlikely to change its position.

In June 1999 the FASB also tentatively agreed that the project should include both incorporated and unincorporated entities that are involved in a purchase business combination and on certain disclosures that would be required in the year of acquisition for material business combinations. The proposed disclosures are very similar to those required in the UK. However, these disclosures would also be required for any material business combination which was completed after the balance sheet date but before the date of the issue of the accounts.

6   CONCLUSION

By issuing FRSs 6 and 7, the ASB narrowed down some of the contentious issues relating to business combinations. Merger accounting is now rare, and therefore all the attention is now focused on acquisition accounting. Although the Board has acknowledged that there is no general demand for a revision of FRS 6, it has indicated that if other countries ban merger accounting, then the subject would be very likely to come under review. As noted at 1 above, we disagree with the proposals put forward in the G4+1 paper and think it would be a retrograde step if the ASB were to amend FRS 6 to prohibit the adoption of merger accounting.

FRS 7 has certainly reduced some of the more significant abuses in fair value accounting, but it has to be said that it is not a very convincing standard at a conceptual level and shows signs of the haste with which it was finalised. Although the general approach within the standard that fair values should not reflect increases or decreases from the acquirer's intentions or future actions effectively removed the opportunity for including reorganisation provisions as part of the fair value exercise, the guidance within the standard on areas such as taxation and businesses held for resale seem to be at odds with that approach.

It also has to be said that there still seems to be a tendency for fair value adjustments to reduce the book values of the net assets acquired, generally on the basis of alignment of accounting policies; adjustments reflecting increased values of tangible fixed assets, other than land and buildings, or pension scheme surpluses, are rarely seen. We therefore think that the ASB may have to revisit the subject before long.

References

1 *Shearer (Inspector of Taxes) v. Bercain (Ltd.)*, (1980) 3 All E.R. 295.
2 FRS 6, *Acquisitions and mergers*, ASB, September 1994, Appendix I, para. 15.
3 ED 31, *Accounting for acquisitions and mergers*, ASC, October 1982, para. 3.
4 ED 3, *Accounting for acquisitions and mergers*, ASC, January 1971, para. 1.
5 SSAP 23, *Accounting for acquisitions and mergers*, ASC, April 1985, para. 17.
6 CA 85, Sch. 4A, para. 10.
7 *Ibid.*, para. 10(2).
8 FRS 6, para. 38.
9 *Ibid.*, para. 2.
10 *Ibid.*, para. 4.
11 *Ibid.*, para. 2.
12 *Ibid.*, para. 58.
13 *Ibid.*, para. 6.
14 *Ibid.*, para. 61.
15 *Ibid.*, para. 62.
16 *Ibid.*, para. 7.
17 *Ibid.*, para. 64.
18 *Ibid.*, para. 66.
19 *Ibid.*, para. 8.
20 *Ibid.*, para. 68.
21 *Ibid.*, para. 9.
22 *Ibid.*, para. 10.
23 *Ibid.*, para. 11.
24 *Ibid.*, para. 76.
25 *Ibid.*, para. 12.
26 *Ibid.*, para. 56.
27 *Ibid.*, paras. 60–77.
28 For example, BP Amoco and Diageo.
29 CA 85, Sch. 4A, para. 9.
30 FRS 2, *Accounting for subsidiary undertakings*, ASB, July 1992, para. 45.
31 *Ibid.*, para. 85.
32 ASC Discussion Paper, *Fair value in the context of acquisition accounting*.
33 ED 53, *Fair value in the context of acquisition accounting*, ASC, July 1990, paras. 58-65.
34 FRED 7, *Fair values in acquisition accounting*, ASB, December 1993.
35 FRS 7, *Fair Values in Acquisition Accounting*, ASB, September 1994, para. 30.
36 *Ibid.*, para. 26.
37 *Ibid.*, para. 77.
38 *Ibid.*, para. 78.
39 ED 53, para. 58.
40 FRS 7, para. 79.
41 *Ibid.*
42 FRRP PN 53, 7 August 1998.
43 FRS 7, para. 80.
44 *Ibid.*, para. 77.
45 *Ibid.*, para. 81.
46 *Ibid.*, para. 27.
47 ASB Discussion Paper, *Fair values in acquisition accounting*, ASB, April 1993, para. 12.4.
48 *Ibid.*
49 FRS 7, para. 81.
50 *Ibid.*, para. 82.
51 *Ibid.*, para. 83.
52 *Ibid.*, para. 84.
53 *Ibid.*, para. 28.
54 *Ibid.*, para. 85.

55 CA 85, Sch. 4A, para. 9(4).
56 CA 81, s 40(3).
57 FRS 6, Appendix I, para. 16.
58 Accountants Digest No. 189, *A Guide to Accounting Standards – SSAP 23 Accounting for acquisitions and mergers*, Summer 1986.
59 CA 85, Sch. 4A, para. 9(2).
60 ED 53, para. 68.
61 FRS 7, para. 5.
62 *Ibid.*, para. 2.
63 *Ibid.*, para. 35.
64 *Ibid.*, para. 38.
65 *Ibid.*, para. 39.
66 *Ibid.*, Appendix III, para. 14.
67 FRS 7, para. 7.
68 *Ibid.*, para. 6.
69 *Ibid.*, para. 2.
70 ASB Discussion Paper, *Fair values in acquisition accounting*, para. 5.5.
71 FRS 7, paras. 23–24.
72 *Ibid.*, para. 25.
73 *Ibid.*, para. 43.
74 FRED 7, para. 13.
75 FRS 7, para. 47.
76 *Ibid.*, para. 2.
77 *Ibid.*, para. 47.
78 *Ibid.*, para. 48.
79 *Ibid.*, para. 9.
80 *Ibid.*, para. 51.
81 *Ibid.*, para. 10.
82 FRS 10, para. 10.
83 FRS 7, para. 11.
84 *Ibid.*, para. 12.
85 *Ibid.*, paras. 53 and 54.
86 *Ibid.*, para. 55.
87 *Ibid.*, para. 56.
88 *Ibid.*, para. 57.
89 *Ibid.*, para. 13.
90 *Ibid.*, para. 58.
91 *Ibid.*, para. 14.
92 *Ibid.*, para. 61.
93 *Ibid.*, para. 62.
94 *Ibid.*, para. 63.
95 *Ibid.*, para. 15.
96 FRS 12, paras. 31–33.
97 FRS 7, para. 37.
98 *Ibid.*, para. 19.
99 FRED 7, Appendix III, para. 35.
100 FRS 7, para. 71.
101 *Ibid.*, para. 72.
102 *Ibid.*, para. 20.
103 United Utilities PLC, Annual Report & Accounts 1997, p. 48.
104 FRS 7, para. 21.
105 *Ibid.*, para. 22.
106 *Ibid.*, para. 7.
107 *Ibid.*, para. 40.

108 ASB Discussion Paper, *Fair values in acquisition accounting*, paras. 2.10–2.12. It was also suggested that there should be a rebuttable presumption that a decision taken within six months before the acquisition should be deemed to be post-acquisition.
109 FRRP PN 56, 24 February 1999.
110 FRS 7, para. 7.
111 FRS 12, para. 2.
112 A. Lennard and S. Peerless, Accountancy, January 1995, p.129.
113 United Utilities PLC, Annual Report & Accounts 1997, p. 48.
114 FRS 7, para. 16.
115 *Ibid.*, para. 17.
116 *Ibid.*, paras. 65 and 66.
117 FRED 7, Appendix III, para. 33.
118 FRS 7, para. 69.
119 Staff Accounting Bulletin No. 54, SEC, Washington, 1983.
120 ASC Discussion Paper, *Fair value in the context of acquisition accounting*.
121 FRS 2, para. 50.
122 *Ibid.*, para. 89.
123 *Ibid.*
124 CA 85, s 228(6).
125 FRS 2, para. 51.
126 CA 85, Sch. 4A, para. 9.
127 *Ibid.*, para. 7(1).
128 *Ibid.*, paras. 7–9.
129 FRS 6, Appendix II.
130 FRS 6, paras. 16 and 17.
131 *Ibid.*, para. 17.
132 CA 85, Sch. 4A, para. 11.
133 FRS 6, para. 18.
134 *Ibid.*, para. 41.
135 CA 85, Sch. 4A, paras. 11(5)–(6).
136 However, it is probably not permissible to use reserve categories which would not have been available as a destination for goodwill if acquisition accounting had been applied; see the discussion on this topic at 2.5.2 in the previous edition of this book.
137 FRS 6, para.18.
138 *Ibid.*
139 *Ibid.*, para. 19.
140 *Ibid.*, para. 51.
141 *Ibid.*, para. 21.
142 FRS 2, para. 49.
143 FRS 6, para. 23.
144 *Ibid.*, para. 24.
145 *Ibid.*, para. 25.
146 FRRP PN 48, 10 November 1997.
147 FRRP PN 55, 20 October 1998.
148 FRS 6, para. 26.
149 *Ibid.*, para. 27.
150 *Ibid.*, para. 30.
151 *Ibid.*, para. 85.
152 *Ibid.*, para. 32.
153 *Ibid.*, para. 28.
154 *Ibid.*, para. 29.
155 *Ibid.*, para. 33. The requirement of FRS 6 is based on the original FRS 1 and has been interpreted in a way which is consistent with FRS 1 (Revised 1996).
156 *Ibid.*, para. 34. Again, the requirement of FRS 6 is based on the original FRS 1 and has been interpreted in a way which is consistent with FRS 1 (Revised 1996).
157 *Ibid.*, para. 31.

158 *Ibid.*, para. 86.
159 *Ibid.*, para. 87.
160 Kingfisher plc, Report and Accounts 1999, pp. 83–88.
161 FRS 6, para. 35.
162 *Ibid.*, para. 37.
163 UITF 15 (revised 1999), para. 5.
164 FRS 6, para. 36.
165 *Ibid.*, para. 22.
166 CA 85, Sch. 4A, para. 13.
167 *Ibid.*, para. 13(2).
168 FRRP PN 5, 28 January 1992.
169 CA 85, Sch. 4A, para. 16.
170 *Ibid.*, para. 13(3).
171 *Ibid.*, para. 13(6).
172 FRS 2, para. 45.
173 *Ibid.*, para. xxii.
174 FRS 3, *Reporting financial performance*, ASB, October 1992, para. 18.
175 FRS 2, para. 47.
176 *Ibid.*, para. 52.
177 *Ibid.*, para. 91.
178 *Ibid.*, para. 87.
179 CA 1985, Schedule 4, para. 12(a).
180 FRS 2, para. 47.
181 CA 1985, Schedule 4, para. 12(a).
182 FRRP PN 43, October 1996.
183 EITF 98–3, *Determining Whether a Transaction is an Exchange of Similar Productive Assets or a Business Combination*.
184 FRS 10, para. 54.
185 *Ibid.*, para. 71(c).
186 *Ibid.*
187 CA 85, Sch. 4A, para. 15.
188 FRS 2, para. 48. Para. 49 appears to contain a similar requirement.
189 FRS 6, para. 2.
190 *Ibid.*, para. 13.
191 CA 85, Sch. 4A, para. 10(c).
192 *Ibid.*, s 151 et seq.
193 FRS 6, para. 78.
194 APB 16, *Business Combinations*, AICPA, August 1970, para. 5 and AIN–APB 16, *Business Combinations: Accounting Interpretations of APB Opinion No. 16*, AICPA, March 1973, para. 39.
195 See also Reuters Group PLC, Report and Accounts 1998, p. 51 and Viridian Group PLC, Report and Accounts 1998, p.27.
196 CA 85, s 23.
197 *Ibid.*, s 276.
198 IAS 22, para. 8.
199 *Ibid.*, para. 15.
200 *Ibid.*, para. 16.
201 *Ibid.*, paras. 77-83.
202 *Ibid.*, para. 21.
203 *Ibid.*, para. 65.
204 IAS 22 (Original), para. 38.
205 IAS 22, para. 29.
206 *Ibid.*, para. 31.
207 *Ibid.*, para. 39.
208 *Ibid.*, para.8.
209 *Ibid.*, para. 12.
210 FRS 6, Appendix II.

211 IAS 22, paras. 86 and 94.
212 *Ibid.*, paras. 86, 87, 92 and 93.
213 APB 16, paras. 42 and 43.
214 *Ibid.*, para. 45.
215 *Ibid.*, para. 46.
216 *Ibid.*, para. 47a.
217 *Ibid.*, para. 47b.
218 *Ibid.*, para. 47c.
219 *Ibid.*, para. 47e.
220 *Ibid.*, para. 47f.
221 *Ibid.*, para. 47g.
222 *Ibid.*, para. 48.
223 *Ibid.*, para. 48b.
224 *Ibid.*, para. 48c.
225 FASB Special Report, *Issues Associated with the FASB Project on Business Combinations*, FASB, June 1997, p. 2.
226 APB 16, paras. 51-56.
227 *Ibid.*, para. 65.
228 *Ibid.*, paras. 66-68.
229 *Ibid.*, para. 93.
230 *Ibid.*, para. 78.
231 *Ibid.*, para. 79.
232 *Ibid.*, para. 74.
233 EITF 95-19, *Determination of the Measurement Date for the Market Price of Securities Issued in a Purchase Business Combination*.
234 APB 16, para. 72.
235 *Ibid.*, para. 80.
236 *Ibid.*, para. 68.
237 *Ibid.*, para. 88f.
238 *Ibid.*, para. 88d.
239 *Ibid.*, para. 88e.
240 FIN 4, *Applicability of FASB Statement No. 2 to Business Combinations Accounted for by the Purchase Method*, FASB, February 1975, paras. 4 and 5.
241 APB 16, para. 88c.
242 *Ibid.*, para. 88a.
243 *Ibid.*, para. 88f.
244 *Ibid.*, para. 88b.
245 *Ibid.*, paras. 88g, h and i.
246 SFAS 38, *Accounting for Preacquisition Contingencies of Purchased Enterprises*, FASB, September 1980, para. 5.
247 SFAS 87, *Employers' Accounting for Pensions*, FASB, December 1985, para. 74 and SFAS 106, *Employers' Accounting for Postretirement Benefits Other than Pensions*, FASB, December 1990, paras. 86 and 87.
248 SFAS 109, *Accounting for Income Taxes*, FASB, February 1992, para. 30.
249 EITF 95-3, *Recognition of Liabilities in Connection with a Purchase Business Combination*.
250 SFAS 38, paras. 4 and 5.
251 APB 16, paras. 95 and 96.
252 FASB Status Report No. 287, FASB, 22 April 1997, p. 3.

Chapter 7 — Associates, joint ventures and JANEs

1 INTRODUCTION

Traditionally, investments in companies which did not satisfy the criteria for classification as subsidiaries were carried at cost, and the revenue from them was recognised only on the basis of dividends received. However, during the 1960s it was recognised that there was a case for an intermediate form of accounting, since there was a growing tendency for groups to conduct part of their activities by taking substantial minority stakes in other companies and exercising a degree of influence over their business which fell short of complete control. Mere recognition of dividends was seen to be an inadequate measure of the results of this activity (and one which could be manipulated by the investor, where it could influence the investee's distribution policy). Moreover, since it was unlikely that the investee would fully distribute its earnings, the cost of the investment would give an increasingly unrealistic indication of its underlying value.

This intermediate form of accounting, equity accounting, was first used by the Royal Dutch Shell group in 1964. It involves a modified form of consolidation of the results and assets of investees in the investor's financial statements when the investor exercises 'significant influence', but not control, over the management of the investee. The essence of equity accounting is that, rather than full scale consolidation on a line by line basis, it requires incorporation of the investor's share of net assets of the investee in one line in the investor's consolidated balance sheet and the share of its results at only some levels of the profit and loss account.

Another form of 'intermediate consolidation' used by some entities, particularly in certain industries, was proportional consolidation. As its name implies, this involves bringing in the results and assets and liabilities of an investment on a line-by-line basis, but only to the extent of the investor's share, rather than, as under normal consolidation, in full with credit given for any minority interest.

Equity accounting was first formally recognised in UK accounting literature by the issue of SSAP 1 – *Accounting for associated companies* – by the ASC in 1971. SSAP 1 was revised a number of times without fundamental change, until being finally superseded by FRS 9, issued by the ASB in November 1997. Whilst this made changes more far-reaching than the previous revisions to SSAP 1, the fundamentals of equity accounting remain much the same as when it first appeared in the 1960s.

The main changes made by FRS 9 were to restrict the circumstances in which equity accounting can be applied and to provide, for the first time in UK GAAP, detailed rules on accounting for joint ventures. Given that these changes were hardly radical, FRS 9 took a surprisingly long time to develop.

The initial impetus for change came in 1989 with the incorporation into UK law of the EU Seventh Accounting Law Directive on consolidated accounts. This changed the law so as to require associated undertakings (see 2.1.2 below) to be equity accounted (previously the Companies Act only permitted such treatment),[1] and to permit unincorporated joint ventures to be proportionally consolidated (see 2.2.2 below). In June 1990 the ASC issued ED 50 *Consolidated accounts*, which proposed changing the definition of associate in SSAP 1 to bring it more in line with the then new legislation. With the winding up of the ASC, this document was not formally progressed further, although many of its ideas can be seen in the ASB's later work.

Later in 1990 the newly-formed ASB issued *Interim statement: Consolidated accounts* as a stop-gap measure which (inter alia) made such changes to SSAP 1 and SSAP 14 – *Group accounts* – as were required to make them consistent with the new legislation. The replacement for SSAP 14 followed relatively quickly in the form of FRS 2 – *Accounting for subsidiary undertakings*, issued in July 1992, which is discussed in Chapters 5 and 6. However, it was not until July 1994 that the ASB published a discussion paper setting out its initial proposals for accounting for associates and joint ventures, which was followed in March 1996 by the exposure draft FRED 11 – *Associates and joint ventures*. The main reasons for the delay were that the ASB wished to formalise the accounting treatment for joint ventures, and was concerned that equity accounting was being applied in situations where it was not really appropriate.

The most radical aspect of the 1994 discussion paper was a proposal to prohibit proportional consolidation for joint ventures,[2] which would have represented a major change for some companies, particularly those with interests in mineral exploration or property. The ASB sought to justify this proposal on the grounds that it was in many cases difficult to distinguish between such entities as were then being proportionally consolidated and associated undertakings accounted for under the equity method.[3] On this basis, it was argued, joint ventures and associates should be dealt with in the same way, and equity accounting was proposed as the common method – ostensibly because it was conceptually superior, but in reality as a necessity, given the Companies Act's prohibition of proportional consolidation of corporate entities.[4]

In the light of strong representations received, however, the ASB softened its stance on proportional consolidation and, in FRED 11, proposed it for those joint ventures where each investor has a separate interest in the activities of the venture rather than a share in its activities as a whole.[5] This is in substance the position in FRS 9, even though the final standard reverted to the general prohibition of proportional consolidation proposed in the 1994 discussion paper. This apparently impossible reconciliation was achieved by introducing the concept of the 'joint arrangement that is not an entity', which requires the reporting entity to account for certain activities carried on through another entity to be accounted for as if the reporting entity carried them out directly. Whilst this is not technically 'proportional consolidation', it is often arithmetically identical (see 2.3 below).

The other main proposal of the 1994 discussion paper was that the definition of associated undertaking should be tightened.[6] Despite some criticism, this proposal emerged largely unscathed in the final FRS, with the result that, in principle, it is less easy to equity account for an investment under FRS 9 than it was under SSAP 1.

FRS 9 indicates that the ASB had been concerned about equity accounting being applied in situations where it may not have been appropriate, such as where the reporting entity holds a significant stake in another company as the result of a failed take-over bid, but is unable to exercise any real influence over it.[7] In our view, however, such abuse as there had been of equity accounting under SSAP 1 tended to be at the other end of the spectrum; in other words, where a company *failed* to equity account for an investment (usually loss-making!) on the assertion that it did not have significant influence over it. There must be a concern that FRS 9 may have made such abuse rather easier, although we have not seen any evidence of this in practice.

Despite its title *Associates and Joint Ventures*, FRS 9 in fact deals with three types of vehicle:

(a) associates;

(b) joint ventures; and

(c) joint arrangements that are not entities. The UK accounting profession was quick to reduce this phrase to the acronym 'JANE', which is now in such common use that, although it is not used in FRS 9, we shall adopt it in the remainder of this chapter.

2   THE DEFINITIONS OF ASSOCIATE, JOINT VENTURE AND JANE

As noted in above, FRS 9 distinguishes between associates, joint ventures and JANEs. The definitions of each of these are set out and discussed below. The FRS does not make it clear what is to be done when an investment falls within more than one definition — for example, almost any 'joint venture' as defined will also be an 'associate' (but not vice-versa). We presume that in such cases the more exclusive definition (i.e. joint venture) is intended to apply.

2.1   Definition of associate

2.1.1   FRS 9

An associate is defined as 'an entity (other than a subsidiary[8]) in which another entity (the investor) has a *participating interest* and over whose operating and financial policies the investor *exercises a significant influence*'.[9] The phrases in italics are further defined, and are discussed below.

There is something of an ambiguity in the phrase '(other than a subsidiary)' since it begs the question 'A subsidiary of what?'. We believe that it means a subsidiary in the reporting group. In other words the phrase is simply for the avoidance of doubt, since any subsidiary will also meet the definition of associate. This is because a subsidiary is an investment subject to the 'control' of the group; any investment under the 'control' of the group must inevitably be subject to its 'significant influence' as well. However, a respectable case could be made that the phrase in fact means a subsidiary of anything, such that no investment could be both a subsidiary of one entity and an associate of another. This latter interpretation is supported by the overall thrust of FRS 9 (that the burden of proof is on the investor to show that it has significant influence over any purported associate).

The wording of the equivalent definition of 'associated undertaking' in the Companies Act states unambiguously that an associate cannot be a subsidiary 'of the parent company'.[10] The omission of these words in the FRS could be argued to be deliberate so as to admit a wider interpretation. More plausibly, it could be said that the Companies Act definition was clearly the inspiration for that in the FRS and the two should, therefore, be construed in the same way.

A   Participating interest

A 'participating interest' is an interest in the shares (or equivalent ownership rights) of an entity held on a long term basis for the purpose of securing a contribution to the investor's activities by the exercise of control or influence arising from or related to that interest.[11] This definition is essentially the same as that in section 260 of the Companies Act and, as in the Act, there is a presumption that a holding of 20% or more is a participating interest.[12]

An interest 'held on a long-term basis' is one held other than exclusively with a view to subsequent resale. An interest is held with a view to subsequent resale if either:

(a)   a purchaser is being actively sought and disposal of the interest is reasonably expected to occur within approximately one year of its acquisition; or

(b)   the interest was acquired as the result of enforcement of a security, and has not subsequently become part of the continuing activities of the group.[13]

The FRS clarifies that the issue of whether an investment is held for the long-term is to be determined by reference to the time at which the investment is first acquired, rather than at each balance sheet date. Thus, once an investment has been treated as held on a long-term basis, it should continue to be so treated, even if the investor intends to dispose of it.[14]

The FRS contains a reminder that, as is the case under the Companies Act, a 'participating interest' includes an interest convertible into shares or an option to acquire shares.[15] This means that entities (such as start-up ventures) in which the reporting entity currently has only a small, or no, equity stake, but has an option to increase it later, may still qualify as associates if the other necessary conditions are met.

B   Exercise of significant influence

FRS 9's definition of 'exercise of significant influence' was intended to restrict the number of entities that qualified as associates compared to those so treated by SSAP 1. SSAP 1 defined an associate as an investee over which the investor was 'in a position to exercise significant influence'.[16] By contrast, FRS 9 requires the investor actually to exercise influence.

The introduction of FRS 9 did indeed result in some companies ceasing to regard as associates certain investments which had been so treated under SSAP 1. Examples included Norcros and William Baird, which dealt with the change in different ways. As the extracts below show, Norcros chose to restate its former associate at cost, whereas William Baird revalued it to net asset value under the alternative accounting rules (with the result that the carrying amount of the investment remained unchanged, but the previously equity accounted profits were transferred to revaluation reserve).

Extract 7.1: Norcros p.l.c. (1998)

23   PRIOR YEAR ADJUSTMENT

H&R Johnson (India) Ltd. has, for the year ended 31st March 1998, been accounted for as a trade investment rather than as an associate as, in the opinion of the directors, the Group does not exercise significant influence over the company as required under the new definition of associate in FRS 9.

The investment has been written down as a prior year adjustment by £3.4m, from £6.1m to its original cost of £2.7m. Had the previous accounting policy applied, then the Group's profit before tax would have been £0.2m higher in 1997/8.

The effect of the change on the profit and loss account for the year ended 31st March 1997 was not material.

Extract 7.2: William Baird PLC (1997)

Change in accounting policy

The Group has adopted Financial Reporting Standard 9 "Associates and Joint Ventures". The Group's investment in Micropore International Limited was previously treated as an associated undertaking in accordance with SSAP1. The Group's investment does not meet the definition of an associate under the new standard since the Group has not participated in the direction of the investment. The investment is now treated as a fixed asset investment and valued by the directors to give a fairer reflection of the value of the investment. The 1996 figures have been restated accordingly.

The effect of this change in accounting policy on the results for 1996 and 1997 is not material.

18   Reserves [extract]

	Share Premium Account £'000	Revaluation Reserve £'000	Profit and Loss Account £'000
Group			
At 1 January 1997	31,015	1,036	37,665
Prior year adjustment			
– elimination of post acquisition reserves	–	–	(11,732)
– revaluation	–	11,732	–
As restated	31,015	12,768	25,933
...			

An investor 'exercises significant influence' when it 'is actively involved and is influential in the direction of the investee through its participation in policy decisions covering aspects of policy relevant to the investor, including decisions on strategic issues such as:

(a)   the expansion or contraction of the business, participation in other entities or changes in products, markets and activities of its investee; and

(b)   determining the balance between dividend and reinvestment.'[17]

FRS 9 notes that in the Companies Act there is a presumption that control of 20% or more of the voting rights of an investee gives rise to significant influence over it,[18] but gives a strong hint that rebuttal of this presumption will be quite frequent. As the FRS puts it, a holding of 20% or more 'suggests but does not ensure' that the investor exercises significant influence.[19]

Examples of companies which rebut the presumed exercise of significant influence over an investment of more than 20% are RMC Group and Arjo Wiggins Appleton.

Extract 7.3: RMC Group p.l.c. (1998)

13d) Other investments [extract]

At 31st December 1998, RMC Group p.l.c. held 25.72% of the issued Ordinary share capital of Alexander Russell PLC, a company registered and principally operating in Scotland as listed in the United Kingdom. ... This company is not regarded as an associated undertaking as RMC Group p.l.c. is not in a position to exercise significant influence in management.

Extract 7.4: Arjo Wiggins Appleton p.l.c. (1998)

12.   Other investments [extract]

The Group has a 33.43% investment in La Salvadora S.A., which operates a small paper mill in Spain. However, this company has not been accounted for as an associate as, in the opinion of the directors, the Group is not in a position to exercise significant influence over its operations or policies. ...

However, the converse situation of a holding of less than 20% being regarded as an associate is still to be found. Examples occur in the 1998 accounts of the Royal Bank of Scotland (12.8%) and Daily Mail and General Trust (19%).[20]

What principally distinguishes an associate from an ordinary fixed asset investment, in the ASB's view, is that in the case of an ordinary fixed asset investment the investor takes a relatively passive role, whereas an associate is a medium through which the investor conducts part of its business. An associate is therefore expected to implement policies that are consistent with, or complementary to, those of the investor.[21]

The FRS also suggests that the investor's attitude towards the investee's dividend policy may indicate the status of the investment. In the case of an ordinary fixed asset investment, the investor may often press for the highest dividend possible. In the case of an associate, however, 'the investor's long-term interest in the future cash flows of its investee is compatible with a policy of reinvestment', so that the investor will tend not to be so concerned with a high dividend.[22] In practical terms, the FRS indicates that associate status is 'usually achieved' when the investor has board representation (or other active participation in the decision-making process) combined with at least 20% of the voting rights.[23]

The somewhat surprising implication of this is that the ASB envisages 'significant influence' over an investee as requiring more active involvement by the investor than 'control' may entail. 'Control' is defined in FRS 9 as the 'ability' to direct the operating and financial policies of the investee;[24] the same definition is also used in FRS 2 – *Accounting for subsidiary undertakings*, FRS 5 – *Reporting the substance of transactions* and FRS 8 – *Related party disclosures*. By contrast, the mere 'ability' to exercise significant influence is not enough; the investor must actively exercise it. Rather confusingly, however, in FRS 8 the mere ability to exercise influence may be enough to create a related party relationship – see Chapter 27 at 2.2.1 B.[25]

As we noted in 1 above, FRS 9's emphasis on the actual exercise of influence might provide a loop-hole for those seeking to avoid equity accounting for an investment, particularly when it is making losses, as may be the case in a start-up company. The ASB clearly shares this concern. The FRS emphasises that, once an investee has qualified as an associate or joint venture, this relationship is not disturbed by minor or temporary changes in it. In particular, whether the investment is profitable or loss-making does not, in itself, alter the relationship.

Accordingly, the FRS provides that, once an investor has exercised significant influence over an entity, it should be presumed to continue to do so until some specific event or transaction occurs that removes the investor's ability to exercise such influence.[26] An example of a company ceasing to treat an investment as an associate on these grounds is Hanson.

Extract 7.5: Hanson PLC (1998)

12   Investments [extract]

The group's investment in Westralian Sands Limited (formerly RGC Limited) was previously treated as an associate. The group's investment does not now meet the definition of an associate since the group has not exercised significant influence since January 1, 1998 because Hanson no longer has appropriate board representation. The investment is now treated as a fixed asset investment. As the investment was no longer regarded as being an associate the carrying amount was restated by adjusting for goodwill of £184.0m previously written off to reserves on acquisition. The directors consider that the resultant investment was permanently impaired and therefore the investment was written down based on market value and the charge of £155.8m taken through the profit and loss account as an exceptional item.

Whilst we understand the need for such a provision as an anti-avoidance measure, it does rather stand the underlying rationale of FRS 9 on its head, in that, whilst *actual* exercise of significant influence is necessary to create an associate relationship, to maintain that relationship requires merely the *ability* to exercise significant influence. This opens up at least the possibility that an investor may at the balance sheet date have two similar investments over which it could (but does not) exercise significant influence, of which one is equity accounted for because of an actual exercise of influence five years ago, but the other treated as a fixed asset investment because influence has yet to be positively exercised.

On the whole, we do not regard FRS 9 as an improvement on SSAP 1 in this respect. Any instances of companies equity accounting for investments over which they had no real influence in our view indicated a failure to comply with, rather than an inherent deficiency in, SSAP 1.

2.1.2 Companies Act 1985

The Act defines associated undertakings in similar terms to FRS 9, as an undertaking in which a participating interest is held and over which significant influence is exercised.[27] A participating interest in an undertaking is an interest in the shares of the undertaking which is held for the long term for the purpose of securing a contribution to the activities of the investing company by the exercise of control or influence arising from that interest.[28] This includes interests in partnerships and unincorporated associations; it also includes interests which are convertible into interests in shares, such as convertible loan stock, and options to acquire an interest in shares.[29] The Act also asserts that a holding of 20% of the shareholders' or members' voting rights is presumed to confer significant influence.

2.2 Definition of joint venture

2.2.1 FRS 9

A joint venture is 'an entity in which the reporting entity holds an interest on a long-term basis and is jointly controlled by the reporting entity and one or more other venturers under a contractual arrangement.' A reporting entity jointly controls a venture with one or more other entities when 'none of the [investing] entities alone can control that entity but all together can do so and decisions on financial and operating policy essential to the activities, economic performance and financial position of that venture require each venturer's consent'.[30]

Key to this definition is the fact that a 'joint *venture*' must be an 'entity', whereas a 'joint *arrangement*', or JANE, (discussed in 2.3 below) is not. FRS 9 defines an entity as a 'body corporate, partnership or incorporated association carrying on a trade or business with or without a view to profit',[31] which is essentially the same as the definition of 'undertaking' in the Companies Act.[32] The FRS, however, goes on to clarify that the reference to the entity's 'carrying on a trade or business' means a trade or business of its own, and not just part of the trades or businesses of the entities that have interests in it (as is the case with a JANE).[33] FRS 9 does not envisage a formal agreement between the venturers as necessary to create joint control, provided that in practice each venturer's consent is required for high-level strategic decisions.[34]

This seems straightforward enough, but it raises a number of issues. Most importantly, this definition has the effect that all 50/50 companies, typically accounted for as associates under SSAP 1, are now joint ventures as, in the nature of things, mutual consent of the shareholders is required for all major decisions. The significance of this is that FRS 9 imposes slightly more extensive accounting, presentational and disclosure requirements on joint ventures than on associates (see 3.2 and 5 below).

It could be argued that because the definition refers to joint control 'under a contractual arrangement', a 50/50 shareholding structure does not, of itself, create a joint venture in the absence of a separate shareholders' agreement. It is our view, however, that in a 50/50 company there is inevitably de facto joint control and it seems perverse that the accounting treatment should depend on whether or not there is a shareholders' agreement. In practice, the norm for such companies, particularly where they are specific vehicles for a single venture, is to have shareholders' agreements, in which case it is beyond doubt that they are joint ventures under FRS 9.

In other shareholding structures (assuming that all shares have equal rights), a shareholders' agreement will clearly be needed to assure joint control. The FRS allows for control by some but not all shareholders, as the following example shows.

Example 7.1: Joint control of joint venture by some, but not all, shareholders

A company has three shareholders holding shares in the proportions 45/45/10 and there is an agreement between the two 45% shareholders requiring their agreement on all major issues. They clearly control the company between them, even though the minority shareholder is not party to the agreement. This is quite common in companies which have a 'sleeping' minority shareholder, perhaps for tax or local regulatory reasons. In this case the 45% shareholders would account for their interests as a joint venture, but the 10% shareholder would account for its interest as an ordinary investment.[35]

Somewhat controversially, in our view, FRS 9 provides that a partly-owned subsidiary of the reporting entity should not be consolidated, but treated as a joint venture, where there is a contractual arrangement with the minority shareholder(s) that has the effect of giving the reporting entity joint, rather than sole, control. The FRS argues that such an arrangement amounts to 'severe long term restrictions' within the meaning of paragraph 25 of FRS 2 and, by implication, section 229 of the Companies Act.[36]

This is, in our view, a rather free interpretation of FRS 2 and the law, both of which make it clear that the 'severe long-term restrictions' referred to are restrictions only over those rights 'by reason of which the parent undertaking is defined as such ... and in the absence of which it would not be the parent undertaking'.[37] To put this in more plain English, the most usual reason why an undertaking is a subsidiary of its parent is that the parent has the majority of the voting rights (i.e. as a shareholder at general meetings) in the subsidiary. The law and FRS 2 therefore require non-consolidation only where there are real restrictions over the parent's rights as a member, and these may well be unaffected by shareholders' agreements (see Chapter 5 at 5.3).

Suppose, for example, that a parent company enters into a shareholders' agreement with a minority shareholder of a subsidiary that the subsidiary, absent mutual consent for change, must not operate outside the UK, diversify its product range, spend more than £1 million on new plant, or declare a dividend beyond a certain level. Whilst such an agreement clearly puts significant commercial restrictions on the parent's freedom of action with respect to the subsidiary, it does not affect its voting rights in a shareholders' meeting (i.e. the rights by virtue of which it is the parent). It should also be borne in mind that any restrictions imposed by a shareholders' agreement are presumably entered into voluntarily by the parent.

It is therefore, in our view, questionable whether such an agreement amounts to 'significant long-term restrictions' as defined in the law and FRS 2. If, however, the shareholders' agreement required mutual consent on matters normally decided by the shareholders in general meeting (e.g. appointment of directors and auditors), then it would impose significant restrictions as defined by FRS 2 and the Companies Act. We presume that the ASB has had the benefit of legal advice that its wider interpretation is sustainable.

Apart from these admittedly rather technical concerns on this aspect of FRS 9, the more real risk is that it may have created an unintended opportunity for off-balance sheet financing. Suppose, for example, that a company sets up a 99%-owned subsidiary with the 1% held by a 'friendly' third party. It then puts in place a shareholders' agreement requiring unanimity on all issues, which the parent is certain will in practice be obtained. On the face of it FRS 9 requires that, as the parent has only joint, rather than sole, control in these circumstances, the subsidiary should not be consolidated, so that its borrowings (for example) do not appear as such on the consolidated balance sheet!

We realise that in practice companies are unlikely to establish, or their auditors to accept, as blatant a scheme as this. The provisions of the Companies Act relating to nominee shareholdings might also be relevant. However, there are bound to be cases that are more on the borderline. It appears that FRS 9 has readmitted at least the possibility of some of the abuses that the Companies Act 1989, and FRSs 2 and 5, were aimed at eradicating.

2.2.2 *Companies Act 1985*

Although FRS 9 prohibits proportional consolidation, the Companies Act 1985 contains provisions which permit proportional consolidation in group accounts for certain joint ventures[38] and the following points are worth noting:

(a)   the Act restricts proportional consolidation to unincorporated joint ventures. Incorporated joint ventures will therefore generally be equity accounted;

(b)   the Act requires that the joint venture should be managed 'jointly with one or more undertakings not included in the consolidation' but otherwise places no restriction on the type of non-corporate joint venture which may be proportionally consolidated; and

(c)   the Act contains no detailed description of the proportional consolidation method, stating merely that 'the provisions of this Part relating to the preparation of consolidated accounts apply, with any necessary modifications, to proportional consolidation under this paragraph'.

A number of companies availed themselves of these provisions before FRS 9 came into force. Now such companies must demonstrate that an investee for which it wishes to 'proportionally consolidate' is in fact a JANE (see 2.3 below). An example of a company which had to equity account for a previously proportionally consolidated venture on implementing FRS 9 is Lasmo.

Extract 7.6: Lasmo plc (1998)

Basis of consolidation [extract]

The consolidated accounts include the accounts of the Company and all its subsidiary undertakings for the year ended 31 December 1998. All these undertakings are companies, and hereafter are identified as such, except for a 50 per cent interest in a general partnership (Unimar Company). This interest has been accounted for using the gross equity method in accordance with FRS 9. Previously the Group's interest in Unimar Company was consolidated on a proportionate basis. Prior year figures have been restated to conform to the current year's presentation. This change is presentational only and has no effect on the (loss)/profit before tax or the net assets of the current or the prior year.

2.3   Definition of joint arrangement that is not an entity (JANE)

A 'joint arrangement that is not an entity' is defined by FRS 9 as 'a contractual arrangement under which the participants engage in joint activities that do not create an entity because it would not be carrying on a trade or business of its own. A contractual arrangement where all significant matters of operating and financial policy are predetermined does not create an entity because the policies are those of its participants, not of a separate entity.'[39] This is one of the more difficult aspects of FRS 9, which can be understood only by considering the background to it.

As noted in 1 above, it had been a long-standing practice in certain industries (in particular oil exploration, engineering and property) to account for certain types of joint venture using proportional consolidation, and it is no secret that during the development of FRS 9 those industries vigorously lobbied the ASB not to change this practice. However, the ASB is strongly opposed to proportional consolidation. The grounds for this, set out in Appendix III to FRS 9, are that proportional consolidation misleadingly presents the reporting entity's shares of the assets and liabilities, profits and losses and cash flows of jointly controlled entities as equivalent to the completely controlled assets and liabilities, profits and losses and cash flows of subsidiaries.[40]

The ASB approached this problem in effect by, in effect, challenging whether the practice in these industries really was 'proportional consolidation'. In the oil industry, for example, several companies may agree to explore a particular site. Whilst the detail of such arrangements may vary quite considerably, typical features are that all the companies contribute to the cost of exploration and take an agreed share of the output (which is sold separately by each of them), but one of the companies actually operates the site, earning a fee from the other partners for doing so.

While such arrangements can create the illusion of a separate entity, closer examination may reveal this not to be the case. The test of whether or not a business arrangement is a separate entity or a JANE is whether it is carrying on a trade of its own or is merely an extension of the individual businesses of the participants in the arrangement. FRS 9 states that the following are indicators that a joint arrangement is not an entity:

(a)   the participants derive their benefit from product or services taken in kind rather than by receiving a share in the results of trading; or

(b)   each participant's share of the output or result of the joint activity is determined by its supply of key inputs to the process producing that output or result.[41]

It seems that under FRS 9 a JANE is an arrangement involving full control of a part of an operation, whereas proportional consolidation of the sort criticised in Appendix III to FRS 9 implies partial control of the whole operation.

Unfortunately, matters are complicated by the fact that sometimes these joint arrangements may actually be conducted through separate legal entities. FRS 9 notes that in some cases there may be 'structures with the form but not the substance of a joint venture', which should be accounted for in exactly the same way as JANEs.[42] Examples of such structures might include agency or distribution companies. Similarly, joint interests in pipelines and other plant may, for regulatory or other legal reasons, actually be held through a legal entity rather than directly by the participants.

Appendix I to FRS 9 (which discusses the interaction of FRS 9 with the provisions of the Companies Act) makes it clear that there will be cases where a JANE will be 'contained' within a legal entity, such as a company or partnership.[43]   In such cases, FRS 9 argues (in effect) that the *form* of the arrangement is that each participant in the venture has an investment in another entity, but the *substance* is that each is carrying on its own business through that entity, and that the accounting should be driven by the substance, not the form.

What this means in practice can be illustrated with the following simple example.

Example 7.2   Distinction between joint venture and JANE

Property X and Property Y are identical blocks containing 50 high quality residential flats. Legal title to the properties is held by two management companies, X Limited and Y Limited, in both of which two property companies, A plc and B plc, each own 50% of the shares. However, in the case of property Y there is a shareholders' agreement to the effect that A plc is entitled to the net income relating to Flats 1 to 25 and B plc to the net income relating to Flats 26 to 50.

Under FRS 9, A plc and B plc would account for their interests in X Limited as a joint venture, but their interests in Y Limited as a JANE. This is because in the case of Property X, A plc and B plc bear all risks and rewards of the whole block of flats equally. Thus, if the rent for, say, Flat 10 falls into arrears, A plc and B plc both suffer 50% of the bad debt. In Property Y, however, the effect of the shareholders' agreement is such that the bad debt risk on Flat 10 would fall entirely on A plc, rather than on A plc and B plc equally.

Examples of companies that conduct business through both joint ventures and JANEs, and distinguish between the two in their accounting policies are BP Amoco, Rolls Royce and Billiton.

Extract 7.7: BP Amoco p.l.c. (1998)

Accounting policies [extract]

A joint venture is an entity in which the group has a long-term interest and shares control with one or more co-venturers. The consolidated financial statements include the group proportion of turnover, operating profit or loss, exceptional items, stock holding gains or losses, interest expense, taxation, gross assets and gross liabilities of the joint venture (the gross equity method).

Certain of the group's activities are conducted through joint arrangements and are included in the consolidated financial statements in proportion to the group's interest in the income, expenses, assets and liabilities of these joint arrangements.

Extract 7.8: Rolls-Royce plc (1998)

Basis of consolidation [extract]

The Group financial statements include the financial statements of the Company and all of its subsidiary undertakings made up to December 31, together with the Group's share of the results up to December 31 of:

i)   joint ventures

    A joint venture is an entity in which the Group holds a long-term interest and which is jointly controlled by the Group and one or more other venturers under a contractual arrangement. The results of joint ventures are accounted for using the gross equity method of accounting.

ii)   joint arrangements that are not entities

    The Group has certain contractual arrangements with other participants to engage in joint activities that do not create an entity carrying on a trade or business of its own. The Group includes its share of assets, liabilities and cash flows in such joint arrangements, measured in accordance with the terms of each arrangement, which is usually pro-rata to the Group's risk interest in the joint arrangement.

Extract 7.9: Billiton Plc (1998)

Accounting Policies [extract]

Joint ventures

A joint venture is an entity in which the Group holds a long term interest and which is jointly controlled by the Group and one or more venturers under a contractual arrangement. The results of joint ventures are accounted for using the gross equity method of accounting.

Joint arrangements

The Group has certain contractual arrangements with other participants to engage in joint activities that do not create an entity carrying on a trade or business of its own. The Group includes its share of the assets, liabilities and cash flows in such joint arrangements measured in accordance with the terms of each arrangement, which is usually pro-rata to the Group's interest in the joint arrangement.

Interestingly, all these extracts refer to 'interests in' or 'share of' the joint arrangements, which could imply that the arrangements concerned are entities and therefore not JANEs. It is our view that the arrangements as described are JANEs as defined in FRS 9, but that the wording used to describe the accounting treatment reveals the tension (referred to above) between the companies' perception that this is a form of proportional consolidation and the view in FRS 9 that they are in fact accounting directly for 'their own' activities that happen to be carried on through an arrangement involving other parties.

An example of an interest in a JANE held through a separate legal entity is given by Hammerson.

Extract 7.10: Hammerson plc (1998)

1.   ACCOUNTING POLICIES [extract]

Basis of Consolidation

The group financial statements consolidate the financial statements of the Company and all its subsidiaries, together with the group's share of assets, liabilities and cash flows arising from joint arrangements. Following the adoption of Financial Reporting Standard 9 Associates and Joint Ventures, the group's investment in Essen Shopping Centre BV has been reclassified as a joint arrangement. Comparative figures have been reclassified. The value of shareholders' funds and the profit for the year are not affected by this reclassification. In addition, certain UK shopping centres have been reclassified as joint arrangements and gross rental income and rents payable adjusted accordingly.

All in all, we consider the JANE concept as one of the weaker aspects of FRS 9. It appears to have been developed in order to avoid disturbing established practice in specific industries. Significantly, much of FRS 9's discussion of JANEs refers to, or uses examples specific to, the oil, property and engineering industries,[44] which have also provided all of the extracts relating to JANEs included above. The problem, in our view, is that in attempting to rationalise practice in those industries, FRS 9 has introduced a definition of a JANE which could include certain entities which (we assume) are not meant to be accounted for as JANEs.

For example, many groups have companies whose sole function is to act as a distributor, hold properties, raise finance or perform some other function on behalf of the group, such that it is not 'carrying on a trade or business of its own'. It seems clear to us that the ASB had no intention that such companies should be regarded as JANEs.

At the other end of the spectrum, one sees arrangements with many characteristics of JANEs which do not fall within the definition in FRS 9. This is because the discussion of the JANE in FRS 9 relies on a clearly-defined distinction (that often does not exist in the real world) between an entity carrying on a business of its own and one that is simply a conduit for the businesses of the participants. In the pharmaceutical industry, for example, two drug companies may set up a company to market two products (or groups of products), one from each company. Often, there is some sharing of results up to, (or beyond) a certain threshold, but with each company receiving only the profits from its own product before (or after) the threshold point. It is our view that, whilst such 'hybrid' arrangements have many of the characteristics of JANEs, FRS 9 requires them to be accounted for as associates or joint ventures as appropriate.

FRS 9 adds to the confusion by noting that sometimes the nature of a JANE changes over time and it may begin to trade as an entity in its own right. In such circumstances the accounting treatment must be modified accordingly (i.e. it should be treated as a joint venture, associate or ordinary investment as appropriate).[45]

We suggest that the confusion surrounding the JANE concept illustrates that it is generally unwise to elevate to a general accounting principle what is in reality a solution to a specific problem (i.e. in this case, the fact that influential sectors of British industry would not have accepted a prohibition on proportional consolidation without a strong fight). An earlier example of this was the 'linked presentation' in FRS 5 (see Chapter 16 at 2.6).

3   THE ACCOUNTING TREATMENT OF ASSOCIATES, JOINT VENTURES AND JANEs

As discussed in 2 above, the ASB distinguishes in FRS 9 between associates, joint ventures and joint arrangements that are not entities. Not surprisingly, therefore, the FRS requires different accounting treatments for each, which are discussed in detail below. In practice, however, the accounting for associates and joint ventures differs only in detail, whereas that for JANEs is substantially different. The discussion below concentrates on only the basic treatments required. More complicated aspects of equity accounting are dealt with in 4 below.

3.1 Accounting for associates

3.1.1 Consolidated accounts

In the investor's consolidated accounts associates are to be accounted for using the equity method, which FRS 9 defines (or more correctly describes) as follows:

'A method of accounting that brings an investment into its investor's financial statements initially at its cost, identifying any goodwill arising. The carrying amount of the investment is adjusted in each period by the investor's share of the results of its investee less any amortisation or write-off for goodwill, the investor's share of any relevant gains or losses, and any other changes in the investee's net assets including distributions to its owners, for example by dividend. The investor's share of its investee's results is recognised in its profit and loss account. The investor's cash flow statement includes the cash flows between the investor and its investee, for example relating to dividends and loans.'[46]

The FRS then deals with the requirements for each of the primary statements in more detail, as set out below.

A Consolidated profit and loss account

In spite of the fact that FRS 9 ostensibly prohibits proportional consolidation, it requires the share of associates' results to be shown at more levels of the group profit and loss account than was the case under SSAP 1 (and remains the case under international practice generally). Indeed, what is required is in reality proportional consolidation at every level except turnover and operating costs. A comprehensive example of the presentation required by FRS 9 is given by Cable and Wireless (see Extract 7.11 below).

At the turnover level, the share of associates' sales is not included. However, FRS 9 goes on to provide that, where it is helpful to give an indication of the size of the business as a whole, the total of group turnover plus the share of associates' turnover may be included as a memorandum item on the face of the profit and loss account. The share of associates' turnover must be clearly distinguished from group turnover, and it is the latter that must form the starting point for the group profit and loss account. This effectively sanctioned what had, before the issue of FRS 9, been a long-standing practice by a number of companies, and is the approach adopted by Cable and Wireless in Extract 7.11. Where segmental analysis of turnover is given, any amounts relating to associates also should be clearly distinguished from those relating to the group.[47]

The share of associates' operating results should be included after the group operating result and, where applicable, after and separately from the share of the operating results of joint ventures[48] (see Extract 7.11). We presume that this approach is to be followed at each level of the profit and loss account where the share of associates' and joint ventures' results is to be included. This is implied by the illustrative examples in Appendix IV to the FRS, but not explicitly stated.

Extract 7.11: Cable and Wireless plc (1999)

CONSOLIDATED PROFIT AND LOSS ACCOUNT [extract]†

FOR THE YEAR ENDED 31 MARCH

	Acquisitions £m	Other continuing operations £m	1999 £m	1998 £m
Turnover of the group including its				
share of joint ventures and associates	736	8,384	**9,120**	8,302
Share of turnover of – joint ventures	–	(1,064)	**(1,064)**	(1,141)
– associates	–	(112)	**(112)**	(160)
Group turnover	736	7,208	**7,944**	7,001
Operating costs before depreciation, amortisation				
and exceptional items	(596)	(4,662)	**(5,258)**	(4,517)
Exceptional items	–	46	**46**	(92)
Operating costs before depreciation and amortisation	(596)	(4,616)	**(5,212)**	(4,609)
EBITDA	140	2,592	**2,732**	2,392
Depreciation before exceptional items	(111)	(912)	**(1,023)**	(833)
Exceptional items	–	–	–	(158)
Depreciation	(111)	(912)	**(1,023)**	(991)
Amortisation of capitalised goodwill	(61)	–	**(61)**	–
Group operating profit	(32)	1,680	**1,648**	1,401
Share of operating profits in joint ventures	–	103	**103**	37
Share of operating profits/(losses) in associates	–	20	**20**	(4)
Total operating profit	(32)	1,803	**1,771**	1,434
Profits less (losses) on sale and termination of				
operations before exceptional items			–	6
Exceptional items			–	519
Profits less (losses) on sale and termination of operations			–	525
Exceptional costs of a fundamental reorganisation			–	(200)
Profits less (losses) on disposal of fixed assets before				
exceptional items			170	85
Exceptional items			198	518
Profits less (losses) on disposal of fixed assets			368	603
Net interest and other similar income – Group			(232)	(100)
– joint ventures			(85)	(78)
Profit on ordinary activities before taxation			**1,822**	2,184
...				

---

† This extract is also relevant to the discussion of accounting for joint ventures in section 3.2.

Any amortisation or write-off of goodwill relating to associates must be 'charged at this point and disclosed'.[49] This implies (but without specifically requiring or permitting it) that the amount shown on the face of the profit and loss account can be the aggregate of the share of profit and the amortisation of goodwill, provided that these are shown separately in the notes. We consider that this is the most appropriate treatment given the requirement of FRS 10, reinforced by the ruling of the Financial Reporting Review Panel on the 1997 accounts of Reuters, that amortisation of goodwill is an integral part of operating profit (see Chapter 10 at 3.4). Accounting for such goodwill is considered in more detail in 4.6 below.

It is not clear how FRS 9 interacts with the provision of FRS 3 that, whilst income from associates and other participating interests does not normally form part of operating profit, it may do so in certain cases.[50] FRS 9 is explicit that the share of associates' operating profit must never be included in group operating profit. It also provides that any segmental analysis of operating profit should clearly distinguish amounts relating to associates from those relating to the group.[51] This implies that the group's share of its associates' operating profit (like that of turnover) is not to be considered as part of the true group result. Moreover, FRS 9 amended or deleted those paragraphs of FRS 1 (Revised) that referred to the investor's share of the operating results of associates being included in operating profit.[52] All this leads us to conclude that the lack of a consequential amendment to FRS 3 was an oversight.

That said, however, the requirement to exclude the operating results of associates from those of the group seems inconsistent with the definition of associate in FRS 9, which, with its emphasis on the active exercise of influence, should arguably mean associates are more likely to form part of the reporting entity's main operations than was the case under SSAP 1. Example 2 in Appendix IV to FRS 9 gives the name 'Total operating profit' to profit including the results of associates and joint ventures, a pragmatic description that has been adopted by many companies, including Cable and Wireless in Extract 7.11 above, even when using the more normal presentation in Example 1 in the same Appendix.

The group's share of its associates' post-operating exceptional items and interest must be separately given. At the levels of profit before tax and below, the associates' share of each item should be aggregated with that of the group, but must be separately disclosed.[53] The requirement to give the share of associates' interest is somewhat curious, since the related borrowings are not included within liabilities in the consolidated balance sheet. This means that, where associates have material borrowings, the effective interest rate shown in the accounts (i.e. interest charge in the profit and loss account divided by borrowings in the balance sheet) will be seriously overstated. We do not regard this as a satisfactory result.

Also unsatisfactory is the lack of clarity in FRS 9 as to whether the group's share of its associates' post-operating exceptional items and interest is to be given on the face of the profit and loss account or in a note. The (somewhat loose) wording of paragraph 27 of the standard is that:

(a)   the share of operating results must be 'included' in the profit and loss account. We take this to mean that it must be presented on the face of the profit and loss account;

(b)   the share of post-operating exceptional items and interest should be '*shown* separately from the amounts for the group'. We believe that this should be taken to mean that the portion of such items relating to associates can be aggregated with the amounts for the group on the face of the accounts and shown separately in the notes. However, the wording here could also suggest that these amounts must be given on the face of the profit and loss account. This view is supported both by the examples in Appendix IV to the FRS and by the contrasting wording ('should be *disclosed*') in respect of profit before tax and items below it (see following). This is the interpretation adopted by Cable and Wireless in Extract 7.11 above;

(c)   the share of profit before tax and items below it 'should be included within the amounts for the group, although for items below this level, such as taxation, the amounts relating to associates should be disclosed.' This clearly envisages aggregation on the face of the accounts and analysis in the notes. An example of the disclosure of the share of tax of associates and joint ventures is given in Extracts 21.5 and 21.6 in Chapter 21 at 3.1.4. Bizarrely, if the FRS is read literally, it seems:

(i)   not to require the group's share of its associates' profit before tax to be disclosed, since this applies only to items 'below' that point; and

(ii)   to prohibit companies from presenting the shares of these items on the face of the profit and loss account if they so wish.

We do not believe that either of these consequences was intended.

All in all, the FRS's precise requirements on these straightforward issues could, and should, have been much clearer. Our analysis above is not intended as some form of pedantic point-scoring; rather it is made against the background of a number of adverse findings by the Financial Reporting Review Panel against companies for failure to comply with the detailed presentational requirements of standards. It is surely not unreasonable to expect the ASB to draft standards with the attention to detail applied by the Panel in enforcing them.

B   *Consolidated statement of total recognised gains and losses*

In the statement of total recognised gains and losses (STRGL), the amount relating to associates should be 'shown separately under each heading' where material, although there are no 'headings' in the STRGL specified as such by FRS 3. The FRS is apparently indifferent as to whether this is done on the face of the STRGL or in an accompanying note, which must be cross-referred to in the STRGL.[54]

In practice, this requirement, at least if interpreted strictly, is more honoured in the breach than in the observance. The one component of the STRGL of a group with associates in which there will always be an amount relating to associates is the profit or loss for the period, but companies do not normally disclose this. Indeed, a recent survey of published accounts noted that only 9% of companies surveyed with associates mention them at all in the STRGL.[55]

We presume that the real intention is that where another item in the STRGL (e.g. foreign exchange movements, revaluation gains) contains a material amount relating to associates, that amount should be shown separately. A comprehensive example is given by BOC.

Extract 7.12:The BOC Group plc (1998)

Total recognised gains and losses [extract]

Years ended 30 September

	1998 £ million	1997 £ million	1996 £ million
Parent	482.8	365.9	38.8
Subsidiary undertakings	(213.7)	(95.3)	235.6
Joint ventures	2.4	13.2	21.2
Associates	0.7	3.8	3.6
Goodwill written off on disposal of subsidiary undertakings	(100.0)	–	(20.9)
Goodwill written off on impairment	(51.8)	–	–
Profit for the financial year	120.4	287.6	278.3
Unrealised surplus/(deficit) on revaluations	1.0	–	(0.7)
Exchange translation effect on:			
– results for the year of subsidiaries	(5.0)	(2.3)	(2.7)
– results for the year of joint ventures	(1.3)	(0.6)	(0.5)
– results for the year of associates	–	(1.1)	–
– foreign currency net investments in subsidiaries	(130.8)	(74.6)	(14.2)
– foreign currency net investments in joint ventures	(17.5)	(10.1)	0.1
– foreign currency net investments in associates	(4.8)	(5.1)	0.4
Total recognised gains and losses for the financial year	(38.0)	193.8	260.7

A rare example of a STRGL where the only item relating to associates and joint ventures is profit for the year that gives the full disclosure strictly required by FRS 9 is that of Severn Trent.

Extract 7.13: Severn Trent Plc (1998)

Statement of total recognised gains and losses [extract]

		1998 £m	1997 £m
Profit for the financial year	- group	**13.4**	315.1
	- joint ventures	-	(0.2)
	- associates	**1.5**	1.8
Total profit for the financial year		**14.9**	316.7
Currency translation differences		**(4.3)**	(8.8)
Total recognised gains and losses for the year		**10.6**	307.9

C   Consolidated balance sheet

The consolidated balance sheet should include the reporting entity's share of the net assets (or liabilities) of associates and the amount of goodwill arising on acquisition, less any amounts amortised or written off. The investment in associates must be shown separately on the face of the balance sheet. It cannot be aggregated with other investments on the face and disclosed separately in the notes (as would be permitted under the Companies Act 1985). The amount of goodwill included in the carrying amount must be separately disclosed.[56] Presumably this disclosure can be made in the notes rather than on the face of the balance sheet, although the FRS does not contain explicit guidance on this.

D   Consolidated cash flow statement

FRS 9 amended FRS 1 so as to require dividends received from associates and joint ventures to be included in the cash flow statement under a separate main heading 'Dividends from joint ventures and associates' immediately after cash flow from operating activities. Further discussion of this will be found in Chapter 26 at 2.4.3.

3.1.2   Single entity accounts

In the investor's single entity accounts, associates are treated as fixed asset investments and carried at cost (less any amounts written off) or valuation. FRS 9 gives no specific guidance on the treatment in the other primary statements (i.e. to include only transactions between the investor and the associate), presumably because these are assumed to be sufficiently well understood as not to warrant guidance.

A company which has no subsidiaries, but which has an investment in an associate, has a particular problem because of the requirements of the Companies Act that only realised profits can be included in the profit and loss account.[57] Since it does not produce group financial statements, its profit and loss account will be a company profit and loss account, and the only income 'realised' from the associate in that context will be dividends received and receivable.

FRS 9 therefore requires investors that do not prepare consolidated accounts (other than those that are exempt from preparing them, or would be exempt if they had subsidiaries) to give the amounts for associates that would be given in the consolidated financial statements. This can be done either by preparing pro-forma 'consolidated' accounts including the associates' results and net assets, or by simply disclosing the relevant amounts for associates and the effect of including them.[58]

There is a certain amount of confusion as to the treatment of associates in the cash flow statements of the single entity, since FRS 9, if read literally, amended FRS 1 so as to require the caption 'Dividends from joint ventures and associates' in both consolidated and single entity cash flow statements. However, this would mean that, whilst dividends from subsidiaries are simply included in the main heading 'Returns on investments and servicing of finance', those from associates and joint ventures are given under a separate heading. We do not believe that this can have been the ASB's intention. In practice, fortunately, the company with investments in associates that is required to prepare a single entity cash flow statement is so rare that this does not cause any real difficulty.

3.2   Accounting for joint ventures

The accounting treatment for joint ventures is the same as that for associates as set out in 3.1 above, except that in the consolidated profit and loss account and balance sheet the reporting entity must apply the 'gross equity method', a term introduced by FRS 9 and defined as follows:

'A form of equity method under which the investor's share of the aggregate gross assets and liabilities underlying the net amount included for the investment is shown on the face of the balance sheet and, in the profit and loss account, the investor's share of the investee's turnover is noted.'[59]

The effect of this treatment in practice is discussed in more detail below.

3.2.1   *The gross equity method*

A   Consolidated profit and loss account

Under the gross equity method, the reporting entity must present its share of the turnover of joint ventures on the face of the profit and loss account and in the segmental analysis of turnover, whereas under the equity method applicable to associates this presentation is optional. However, as under the equity method, this does not form part of the group turnover, and must be clearly distinguished from it.[60] An example of this can be seen in the accounts of Cable and Wireless (Extract 7.12 at 3.1.1 A above).

For most companies, which prepare their accounts in accordance with Schedule 4 to the Companies Act 1985, this disclosure is relatively straightforward since turnover is the first item in the profit and loss account formats. However, it poses something of a practical difficulty for banking and insurance companies, which prepare their accounts under Schedule 9 and Schedule 9A, respectively, of the Act. The issue is partly that those formats do not contain an item 'turnover', but more substantially that the amount that is generally agreed within each of those industries to comprise the equivalent of 'turnover' is in fact the aggregate of a number of items required by the Companies Act to be shown under separate headings.

B   *Consolidated balance sheet*

In the consolidated balance sheet, the gross equity method requires the share of net assets shown under the equity method to be analysed into the share of total assets and total liabilities on the face of the balance sheet. The analysis is to be given in the form of a linked presentation[61] (rather than by including the shares of assets and liabilities separately in the relevant sections of the balance sheet), which the ASB believes 'emphasises the special nature of joint control'.[62] The FRS in fact avoids using the phrase 'linked presentation', possibly because the amounts shown linked under the gross equity method would not meet the criteria for linked presentation in FRS 5! An example of the required disclosure is given by TI Group.

Extract 7.14: TI Group (1997)		
BALANCE SHEETS [extract]		
		The Group
	1997	1996
	£m	£m
Fixed assets		
Tangible assets	361.6	342.7
Investments		
– joint venture	28.0	29.8
share of gross assets	*112.9*	*112.9*
share of gross liabilities	*(84.9)*	*(83.1)*
– associates	3.7	9.9
– other	6.7	3.6
	400.0	386.0

Although the FRS is not explicit on this point, the share of total assets must include any unamortised acquisition goodwill relating to a joint venture;

otherwise, the analysis would not total to the carrying value of the joint venture. For the same reason, the share of total liabilities must include provisions.

A complication not explicitly anticipated by FRS 9 is that the carrying amount of an investment in a joint venture may often not in fact be the share of the underlying assets and liabilities, such that the disclosure required by FRS 9 is not actually possible. For example, there could be loans between the reporting entity and the joint venture, or provisions against the joint venture in the reporting entity's accounts that are not included in the underlying accounts of the venture. Examples of companies that have had to address this issue are Clydeport and Billiton, both of which have distinguished between the share of net assets of, and loans to, joint ventures on the face of the group balance sheet.

Extract 7.15: Clydeport plc (1998)

Group Balance Sheet [extract]
as at 31 December 1998

	£000	1998 £000	1997 £000
Fixed assets			
Tangible assets		38,198	38,139
Investment in joint venture:			
Share of gross assets	3,815		1,577
Share of gross liabilities	3,757		1,541
	58		36
Loans to joint venture	1,074		433
Investments		1,132	469
		39,330	38,608

Extract 7.16: Billiton Plc (1998)

Group Balance Sheet [extract]
as at 30 June 1998

	1998 US$m	1997 US$m
Fixed assets		
Tangible assets	**4,681**	4,587
Investments – joint ventures	**162**	248
– joint ventures share of gross assets	**670**	824
– joint ventures share of gross liabilities	**(508)**	(576)
– loans to joint ventures and other investments	**330**	373
	5,173	5,208

Cable and Wireless has also had to address this issue, but with the additional complication that its total net investment in joint ventures comprised a mixture of investments in net assets, shown within fixed assets, and investments in net liabilities, shown within liabilities. (The accounting treatment of an interest in net liabilities is discussed in more detail in 4.8 below). Its solution is to provide a short narrative footnote on the face of the balance sheet and a more detailed analysis in the notes to the accounts.

The 'Share of net assets' in note 16 in the extract below reconciles to the net of the two figures shown in the balance sheet (e.g. for 1999, interest in net assets of £310m less interest in net liabilities £187m gives £123m, the figure in note 16). We presume that Cable and Wireless included the narrative footnote at the bottom of the balance sheet so as comply with the requirement of FRS 9 that the share of gross assets and liabilities be shown 'on the face' of the balance sheet. It is slightly curious that the £1,336m described as the group's 'share of gross liabilities' in the balance sheet footnote includes the loan from the group, but the £1,173m so described in note 16 excludes it. In our view, the £1,336m (i.e. including the loan) is the amount that more correctly meets this description.

Extract 7.17: Cable and Wireless plc (1999)

[GROUP] BALANCE SHEET [extract]

		1999 £m	1998 £m
Fixed assets			
...			
Interest in net assets of joint ventures	16	**310**	570
...			
Interest in net liabilities of joint ventures	16	**187**	78
...			

[Footnote to balance sheet]

Interests in the net assets and net liabilities of joint ventures include the Group's share of gross assets of joint ventures of £1,292m (1998 – £2,255m) and the Group's share of gross liabilities of joint ventures of £1,336m (1998 – £2,070m).

16   Fixed asset investments [extract]

Joint ventures ...: Group share of net assets

	1999 £m	1998 £m
Fixed assets	816	1,764
Current assets	476	491
Share of gross assets	1,292	2,255
Current borrowings	(48)	(86)
Other current liabilities	(342)	(420)
Long term borrowings	(936)	(1,430)
Other long term liabilities	(10)	(134)
Share of gross liabilities	(1,336)	(2,070)
Less: Loans from Group companies	163	307
Group share of gross liabilities	(1,173)	(1,763)
Add: Goodwill capitalised	4	–
Share of net assets	123	492

3.2.2   *Voluntary additional disclosure of amounts relating to joint ventures*

FRS 9 permits (and indeed encourages through an example in Appendix IV) separate disclosure on the face of the consolidated profit and loss account and balance sheet of amounts relating to the group's investments in joint ventures where these represent a significant part of the business of the reporting entity.[63]

Where this is done, however, all amounts relating to joint ventures (other than those included in profit and loss account captions below profit before tax) must be clearly distinguished from amounts relating to the group.[64] The exemption for items below profit before tax is presumably because the equity method requires the share of these items applicable to joint ventures to be aggregated with the corresponding group figures and disclosed separately (see 3.1.1 A above).

The presentation suggested in Appendix IV to the FRS is to give two additional columns: one for the reporting entity's share of its joint ventures' results, assets and liabilities and another for the total of group and joint ventures. The total column thus represents proportional consolidation of the reporting group's share of its interests in joint ventures. It seems inconsistent that the FRS, while rejecting proportional consolidation as a method of accounting because it 'can be misleading',[65] states that as a method of disclosure it may be appropriate 'because an investor's joint control of a joint venture is a more direct form of influence than the significant influence exercised over associates'.[66]

An example of a company that has adopted this approach is Henlys Group.

Extract 7.18: Henlys Group plc (1998)
Group Profit and Loss Account [extract]

	Group 1998 £000	Interest in Joint Ventures 1998 £000	Total 1998 £000
Turnover			
...			
Total turnover	157,290	186,877	344,167
Cost of sales	(131,336)	(157,559)	(288,895)
Gross Profit	25,954	29,318	55,272
Other operating expenses (net)	(8,943)	(12,557)	(21,500)
Operating Profit			
Continuing operations	17,011	16,761	33,772
Amortisation of goodwill	(8)	(774)	(782)
Bid costs	(2,557)	—	(2,557)
	14,446	15,987	30,433
Share of operating profit in joint ventures	15,987		
Total Operating Profit	30,433		
...			

It will be seen that the share of the operating profit of joint ventures is carried across into the total operating profit, and the rest of the group profit and loss account is presented as a single column. Whilst this form of presentation works well enough in the relatively straightforward circumstances of the example above, we have some reservations as to whether it would add clarity to the accounts of most large groups. When it is combined with the requirement of FRS 3 to distinguish the results of continuing, acquired and discontinued operations[67] (not to mention the so-called 'railway timetable' multi-columnar profit and loss accounts used by many companies as a method of excluding various items from what they consider their 'true' results), the overall result could be a bewildering matrix of figures.

What happens in such a case if, for example, the joint ventures themselves have acquired or discontinued operations or exceptional items? In fact, in the accounts from which the Extract 7.18 is taken, the joint venture made a significant acquisition, and note 12 to the accounts gives an analysis of the components of the operating profit of the joint venture between acquisitions and other continuing operations. However, the analysis given is of the total results of the joint venture, rather than of Henlys' share of them.

Henlys also gave a full memorandum analysis of the group balance sheet as shown below.

Extract 7.19: Henlys Group plc (1998)

Balance sheets [extract]

	Group 1998 £000	Interest in Joint Ventures 1998 £000	Total 1998 £000
Fixed Assets			
Intangible assets	178	17,565	17,743
Tangible assets	34,578	15,669	50,247
Investments	44,141	(44,141)	—
	78,897	(10,907)	67,990
Current Assets			
Pension fund prepayment	3,294	—	3,294
Stocks	46,461	42,987	89,448
Debtors	11,030	13,664	24,694
Cash at bank and in hand	40,260	6,376	46,636
	101,045	63,027	164,072
Creditors			
Amounts falling due within one year	59,336	49,249	108,585
Net Current Assets	41,709	13,778	55,487
Total Assets less Current Liabilities	120,606	2,871	123,477
Creditors			
Amounts falling due after more than one year	6,287	2,279	8,566
Provision for Liabilities and Charges	2,615	592	3,207
	111,704	—	111,704

3.3 Investment funds

Investment funds, such as investment trusts or venture capitalists, are not required to equity account for associates or joint ventures that are held as part of their investment portfolios. For this purpose, investments are held as part of an investment portfolio if their value to the investor is through their marketable value as part of a basket of investments rather than as media through which the investor carries out its business.[68] This effectively sanctions long-standing practice in at least some sections of the investment trust and venture capital industries.

The grounds given for what amounts almost to an exemption from FRS 9 are that it is important for all portfolio investments to be accounted for consistently whether or not the investor has significant influence or joint control.[69] However, it is perhaps more realistic to see the prescribed treatment as a concession to established industry practice. One consequence of FRS 9 is an inconsistency between the treatment of subsidiaries held as portfolio investments, which both the law and FRS 2 still require to be fully consolidated, and that of associates or joint ventures similarly held, which are to be accounted for as ordinary investments.

3.4   Accounting for JANEs

The requirements for JANEs, compared to those for associates and joint ventures, are relatively straightforward. As indicated in the discussion in 2.3 above, the distinguishing feature of a JANE is that it has no activity of its own and is simply a conduit through which the participants conduct their own business. On this basis, the participants are simply required to account for their own 'assets, liabilities and cash flows' (and presumably results as well!) within the arrangement, measured according to the terms of the agreement governing the arrangement.[70]

As noted in 2.3 above, in many cases this will generate the same numbers in the accounts that would have been obtained using proportional consolidation, particularly where the arrangement is structured as a legal entity. However, it is important to be clear that, according to FRS 9, this is *not* proportional consolidation, but the reporting entity recording its own transactions. Therefore FRS 9 requires JANEs to be accounted for at the individual entity level as well as on consolidation. Examples of companies accounting for JANEs are given in Extracts 7.7 to 7.10 at 2.3 above, the wording of which indicates that to some extent at least, the companies concerned regard accounting for a JANE as little more than proportional consolidation under another name.

4   APPLYING THE EQUITY AND GROSS EQUITY METHODS

FRS 9 provides some detailed guidance on a number of aspects of the application of the equity and gross equity methods, which are discussed below. In four of these, FRS 9 can be seen as conforming the consolidation requirements for associates and joint ventures to those for subsidiaries in FRS 2:

- fair values and goodwill;

- transactions between associates and joint ventures and the reporting entity;

- accounting policies; and

■ non-coterminous accounting periods.

Other issues covered by the FRS are:

■ goodwill (in periods after the acquisition);

■ calculation of the share of net assets to be accounted for;

■ non-corporate associates and joint ventures;

■ losses and deficiencies of assets; and

■ commencement or cessation of a joint venture or associate relationship.

We discuss all these issues in turn below.

4.1 Fair values and goodwill

When an associate or joint venture is first acquired, the share of its underlying net assets included in the reporting entity's consolidated balance sheet should be stated at fair value using the reporting entity's accounting policies.[71] Presumably, such fair values are to be calculated in accordance with FRS 7 – *Fair values in acquisition accounting*, although neither FRS 9 nor FRS 7 is explicit on the matter.

The following example illustrates why such fair value adjustments are necessary:

Example 7.3:   Attributing fair values to the assets of associates

Company A buys a 40% stake in Company B for £2,000,000. Company B is an investment company and its only asset is a portfolio of investments with a book value of £3,000,000 but a fair value of £5,000,000.

If Company A did not apply fair value accounting to the analysis of its stake in Company B, it would record its share of the net assets of B at £1,200,000 and goodwill of £800,000. The proper treatment in this particular case would be to attribute all of its investment in B to the underlying portfolio of investments and to recognise no goodwill. (Tax effects have been ignored in this example for the sake of simplicity.)

If one year later, Company B sells its portfolio for £6,000,000, it will report a pre-tax profit of £3,000,000, of which Company A's share will be £1,200,000. However, A must make an adjustment to this figure to eliminate the £800,000 fair value adjustment which reflected the pre-acquisition gain made by B, but not recorded in its own books at that time, and therefore record a profit of only £400,000. That this is the appropriate answer is easily proved as follows:

	£
A's share of net assets of B (40% of £6,000,000)	2,400,000
Cost of investment in B	2,000,000
Gain	400,000

The attribution of fair values can be problematical in practice because the investor has only influence, not control, over the investee and therefore cannot insist on receiving the same degree of information that could be demanded from a subsidiary. It may therefore be that the fair value exercise will have to be confined to the most significant items, such as the revaluation of major property assets, and this will often be acceptable on grounds of materiality.

FRS 9 provides that, where access by the investor to information on fair values (or on other items necessary in order to apply the equity or gross equity methods) is 'limited', estimates may be used instead. Where information is 'extremely limited', however, this may call into question whether the investor in fact exercises the significant influence, or joint control, necessary for the investment to be treated as an associate or joint venture.[72]

The investor's share of depreciation of fixed assets held by the associate or joint venture at acquisition should be based on their fair value rather than their cost to the associate or joint venture.[73] Similar adjustments apply to the profit and loss account treatment of all other assets and liabilities whose fair value differs from their carrying amount in the associate's own accounts.

Any goodwill included in the accounts of an associate or joint venture at the date of acquisition by the investor is ignored in calculating the investor's share of its net assets.[74] The arithmetical effect of this is to increase the portion of the reporting entity's carrying value for its investment represented by goodwill. It also has the questionable result that, in effect, the investor's share of any existing goodwill of an associate or joint venture will be written off over the period appropriate to the premium paid by the investor rather than the period applicable to the underlying goodwill of the associate or joint venture.

Somewhat inconsistently, this appears to apply only to any goodwill recognised by the associate or joint venture at the date of acquisition. Any goodwill arising on a post-acquisition transaction of the associate or joint venture will apparently fall to be included in the share of net assets. Conversely, if the associate or joint venture converts goodwill recognised at the date of acquisition into cash through disposal, the reporting entity must, on the face of it, continue to account for its share of this cash as 'goodwill'. In practice, however, we believe that, where the effect is material, it will be appropriate to adjust the allocation of the carrying value of the investee as between share of net assets and goodwill.

Where an associate or joint venture is itself a parent undertaking, FRS 9 provides that the share of net assets included in the reporting entity's balance sheet should be based on the associate's or joint venture's consolidated balance sheet.[75] The FRS is silent on what is to be done where such an associate or joint venture does not prepare group accounts. Presumably, the share of net assets should still be based on notional group accounts. Otherwise the overall carrying value of the investment could include a huge amount for 'goodwill' that is in reality a share of the investee group's underlying net assets, particularly if the investee is a thinly capitalised holding company.

4.2 Transactions between associates and joint ventures and the reporting entity

Where an investor transacts with an associate or joint venture, the investor's share of any profit arising should be eliminated in the consolidated accounts.[76] FRS 9 requires that 'where profits and losses resulting from transactions between the investor and its associate or joint venture are included in the carrying amount of assets in either entity, the part relating to the investor's share should be eliminated'.

This treatment should be contrasted with that required when an inter-company transaction takes place involving a company which is not a wholly owned subsidiary. In such a situation, FRS 2 requires elimination of *all* of the profit or loss.[77] Therefore, if a parent sells an asset to a 51% subsidiary all of the profit will be eliminated and no amount would be attributed to the minority shareholders. However, if the parent sold the asset to a 50% associate or joint venture, under FRS 9 only 50% has to be eliminated.

It is, to put it mildly, extremely unfortunate that FRS 9 provides no further guidance as to what precisely is intended by this requirement, since the elimination of such profits sounds much more straightforward than it actually is. We believe that what is intended is the treatment originally proposed, and more clearly explained, by the ASC in ED 50 *Consolidated Accounts*, i.e.:

■ In the consolidated profit and loss account the adjustment should be taken against either the group profit or the share of the associate's (or joint venture's) profit, according to whether the group or the associate (or joint venture) recorded the profit on the transaction.

■ In the consolidated balance sheet the adjustment should be made against the asset which was the subject of the transaction if it is held by the group or against the carrying amount for the associate (or joint venture) if the asset is held by the associate (or joint venture).[78]

Our interpretation of this treatment is illustrated by Examples 7.4 and 7.5 below. Both examples deal with H plc and its 50% joint venture JV Limited. The journal entries are based on the premise that the consolidation is initially prepared as a simple aggregation of each member of the group and the relevant share of its associates and joint ventures. The entries below would then be applied to the numbers at that stage of the process.

Example 7.4   Elimination of profit on sale by group to joint venture

On 1 December 1999 H plc sells goods costing £750,000 to JV Limited for £1 million. On 10 January 2000, JV sells the goods to a third party for £1.2 million. What adjustments are made in the group accounts of H plc at 31 December 1999 and 31 December 2000?

In the year to 31 December 1999, the group has recorded turnover of £1m and cost of sales of £0.75m. However, at the balance sheet date, since the stock is still held by JV Limited, only half this transaction is regarded by FRS 9 as having taken place (in effect with the other 50% shareholder of JV Limited). This is reflected by the consolidation entry:

	£	£
Turnover	500,000	
Cost of sales		375,000
Investment in JV Limited		125,000

This effectively defers recognition of half the sale and offsets the deferred profit against the carrying amount of JV Limited.

During 2000, when the stock is sold by the joint venture, this deferred profit can be released to the group P&L account, reflected by the following accounting entry.

	£	£
Opening reserves	125,000	
Cost of sales	375,000	
Turnover		500,000

Opening reserves are adjusted because the consolidation runners (if prepared as assumed above) will already include this profit in opening reserves, since it forms part of H plc's opening reserves.

Example 7.5   Elimination of profit on sale by joint venture to group

This is the mirror image of the transaction in Example 7.4 above. On 1 December 1999 JV Limited sells goods costing £750,000 to H plc for £1 million. On 10 January 2000, H plc sells the goods to a third party for £1.2 million. What adjustments are made in the group accounts of H plc at 31 December 1999 and 31 December 2000?

H plc's share of the profit of JV Limited as included on the consolidation runners at 31 December 1999 will include a profit of £125,000, being 50% of (£1,000,000 – £750,000), which is regarded by FRS 9 as unrealised by the group, and is therefore deferred and offset against closing stock of the group:

	£	£
Share of profit of JV (P&L)	125,000	
Stock		125,000

In the following period when the stock is sold H plc's single entity accounts will record a profit of £200,000, which must be increased on consolidation by the £125,000 deferred from the previous period. The entry is:

	£	£
Opening reserves	125,000	
Share of profit of JV (P&L)		125,000

Again, opening reserves are adjusted because the consolidation runners (if prepared as assumed above) will already include this profit in opening reserves, this time, however, as part of H plc's share of the opening reserves of JV Limited.

A slightly counter-intuitive consequence of this treatment is that at the end of 1999 the investment in JV Limited in the balance sheet has increased by £125,000 more than the share of profit of joint ventures as reported in the group profit and loss account (and in 2000 by £125,000 less). This is because the balance sheet adjustment at the end of 1999 is made against stock rather than carrying value of the investment in JV Limited. It might therefore be necessary to indicate in the fixed asset note that part of the profit made by JV Limited is regarded as unrealised by the group in 1999 and has therefore been deferred until 2000 by offsetting it against stock.

An example of a company that has consistently adopted this treatment (even before FRS 9 was issued) is Tesco.

Extract 7.20: Tesco PLC (1998)

Note 12   Fixed asset investments [extract]

	Group	
	Associated undertakings (b) £m	Other investments £m
At 22 February 1997	21	2
Additions	179	–
Share of loss of associated undertakings	(15)	–
Disposals	–	(2)
At 28 February 1998	**185**	**–**

b) ...

An amount of £3m representing the unrealised 50% element of the profit on sale of properties to the Tesco British Land Property Partnership has been offset against the cost of the investment of £179m shown above.

An issue related to the examples above is whether similar adjustments should be made to the amount required by FRS 9 to be disclosed as the group's share of the turnover of associates or joint ventures (see 3.1.1A and 3.2.1A above). If, in the circumstances of Examples 7.4 and 7.5, H plc were to show both its own turnover as stated in its individual accounts and 50% of the turnover of JV Limited as stated in that entity's accounts, there would clearly be an element of double counting. Whilst FRS 9 does not address this directly, we believe that some adjustment should be made to compensate for this, as is done by GKN.

Extract 7.21: GKN plc (1998)

2.   Sales [extract]

In the ordinary course of business, sales and purchases of goods and services take place between subsidiaries, joint ventures and associates priced on an 'arms-length basis'. These transactions are not significant except for amounts charged by GKN Westland Helicopters Ltd to EH Industries Ltd (jointly owned by the Group and Finmeccanica SpA) of £148 million (1997 – £100 million) and, conversely, charges made by EH Industries to GKN Westland Helicopters Ltd of £48 million (1997 – £31 million) under the terms of contracts in connection with the manufacture and sale of EH101 helicopters. To avoid duplication, the Group's share of EH Industries Ltd sales is excluded from joint venture sales.

Rolls-Royce deals with the same issue in a slightly different way, by disclosing what appears to be the full amount of sales to joint ventures and the group's share of sales by joint ventures.

Extract 7.22: Rolls-Royce plc (1998)

Group profit and loss account [extract]

	Continuing operations £m	Discontinued operations £m	1998 £m	Restated 1997 £m
Turnover: Group and share of joint ventures	**4,517**	170	**4,687**	4,552
Sales to joint ventures	**701**	–	**701**	629
Less share of joint ventures' turnover	**(892)**	–	**(892)**	(833)
Group turnover	**4,326**	170	**4,496**	4,348

...

The requirement to eliminate partially unrealised profits or losses on transactions with associates or joint ventures applies only to transactions involving such profits, such as trading transactions or asset disposals. It would not apply in the case of items such as interest paid on loans between associates or joint ventures and the reporting entity.

The requirement to eliminate unrealised profits applies not only to transactions with an existing associate or joint venture, but also to those undertaken in order to set up an associate or joint venture.[79] In this case the mechanics of elimination, and the further accounting issues raised, become far more complicated, as the following example illustrates.

Example 7.6   Creation of joint venture by contribution of non-cash assets

Group A has a subsidiary which originally cost £55m, of which £35m was represented by the fair value of net assets. The remaining £20m was taken to reserves as goodwill in accordance with SSAP 22 and remains there in accordance with the transitional provisions of FRS 10. Since then it has earned and retained profits of £5m, as a result of which the book value of its net assets is now £40m. However, the value of the business as a whole is now reckoned to be £90m, implying goodwill of £50m.

It has now agreed with Group B to form a joint venture whereby Group A will contribute its subsidiary to a new joint venture company (JVCo) in exchange for 40% of the shares, and Group B will do likewise with one of its own businesses for the other 60%. The value of the respective businesses contributed is agreed to be £90m and £135m.

Two accounting issues arise, which are discussed below:

(a)   whether the transaction gives rise to an accounting gain for Group A; and

(b)   whether the answer depends on whether the transaction is varied to include a cash element.

1.   Does the transaction give rise to an accounting gain for Group A?

Applying FRS 9 paragraph 41 (which applies to associates and joint ventures the provisions of FRS 2 applicable to partial disposals) suggests that it does, but other considerations would suggest the opposite. FRS 2, paragraph 47, requires the gain or loss on disposal of a subsidiary to be calculated as the difference between the carrying amount of the net assets of the subsidiary attributable to the group before and after the disposal, less any goodwill not previously written off to the profit and loss account (see Chapter 6 at 3.3).

Taken together, paragraphs 31(b) and 41 of FRS 9 would suggest that Group A has made a gain on the disposal, calculated thus:

	£m
Value of 40% stake in JVCo	90
Assets disposed of	(40)
Goodwill previously taken to reserves	(20)
Gain on disposal	30
Less element attributable to 40% stake retained	(12)
Gain on effective disposal of 60%	18

Correspondingly, the carrying value of the investment in JVCo would be £78m, which could be considered as representing either:

	£m
40% of Newco's assets	90
Less unrealised profit on sale	(12)
	78

or

	£m
40% of B's former assets (£135m x 0.4) at fair value	54
40% of A's former assets and goodwill at their former book value	24
	78

The £12m that is eliminated because of A's continuing stake in JVCo should feed back through the profit and loss account in the form of enhanced profits from the joint venture. This is because the profits as reported by JVCo in its own accounts will be derived *after* charging £90m in respect of A's former assets and goodwill, whereas as shown by the table above, A is accounting for its share of JVCo at an amount that reflects A's share of these assets at their cost to it of £60m. Thus, in principle at least, the amounts taken up in the accounts of the investor may bear little relation to its share of the underlying financial statements of the investee, and it may be necessary to keep a 'memorandum' set of books for consolidation purposes. In practice, however, this may be easier said than done, and a fairly broad brush approach may be needed.

However, there are also a number of reasons why A should *not* recognise any gain on the initial transaction. The first is that this is simply an asset swap transaction rather than a true disposal and therefore does not qualify for gain recognition.

UK literature on this subject is lacking, but the IASC's SIC 13 prohibits gain recognition on transactions of this sort where (*inter alia*) they are exchanges of similar non-monetary assets.[80] It is not obvious how to interpret this restriction. Clearly the assets exchanged are similar in the sense that they are shares in another company, but is that the relevant test? Is it relevant that A has swapped a controlling interest in a subsidiary for a jointly controlled JV, and does that distinction make them dissimilar? What if the residual investment were an associate, involving influence rather than control, or even a trade investment involving neither? Is it relevant to consider whether the business of JVCo is dissimilar from that of A's former subsidiary (because the injection of B's business has changed its character)? The reference to similar or dissimilar assets has been drawn from other literature on barter transactions that discuss swaps of assets such as oil reserves or tangible assets, but it is rather harder to apply to this kind of transaction.

A more understandable consideration, also mentioned in SIC 13, is that no gain can be recognised unless the values of the assets exchanged are reliably measurable.[81] It may seem from the transaction discussed here that this criterion is met, because A and B have agreed to form the joint venture on the basis of the assets being worth £90m and £135m. But the more likely economic reality is that they have agreed not the absolute, but the relative, values of the contributed businesses, because the transaction would be identical if they had agreed that the respective values of the two businesses were £40m and £60m, or for that matter £400m and £600m! It is therefore right to have regard to this criterion.

A more particular reason for concluding that no gain can be reported is that it is not a realised profit. UK company law permits only realised profits to be included in the profit and loss account.[82] It is very doubtful that the exchange of the subsidiary for a 40% stake in an unquoted joint venture can be regarded as realising a profit, in either the entity or the group accounts of A. Interestingly, the Financial Reporting Review Panel took the same view in its adverse ruling on the accounts of Butte Mining PLC.[83]

It is our view that no gain should be recognised for accounting purposes because it does not satisfy the criteria for being treated as a realised profit. This would mean that Group A's investment in JVCo should initially be recorded at £40m, based on the book value of the assets of the subsidiary disposed of, or perhaps £60m by including also the goodwill attributable to it. Depending on the fair value of JVCo's identifiable assets, this would then give rise to negative goodwill, or reduced positive goodwill, which would be accounted for as appropriate thereafter.

2.   *What if the deal were varied to include a cash element?*

Assume that, instead of the original transaction, Group A received shares representing only 36% of JVCo together with cash of £9m (which Group B had contributed in order to lift its own stake to 64%). Whether this changes the answer to question 1 depends on the reasoning behind that answer.

If no gain was recognised because the deal was simply an asset swap transaction, then it may depend on whether the new cash element is significant enough to shift that perception. In this example it might be argued that the receipt of only 10% of the consideration in cash does not materially change the character of the transaction, and that the £9m that has been received should be credited to the carrying value of the investment in JVCo. However, there must come a point

point where enough of the consideration is in cash to warrant at least some element of gain recognition. If the original objection was that the values exchanged were not reliably measurable, the inclusion of a cash component may help to dispel that concern (although not necessarily entirely). If the original objection was that no profit had been realised, the receipt of cash goes some way to alleviate that concern.

If it is now concluded that some element of the gain can be recognised, the amount still has to be calculated and this is also problematic, as shown below.

	£m
Value of 36% stake in JVCo	81.0
Cash	9.0
Assets disposed of	(40.0)
Goodwill previously taken to reserves	(20.0)
Profit on disposal	30.0
Less element attributable to 36% stake retained	(10.8)
Gain from effective disposal of 64%	19.2

However, of this gain of £19.2m, only £9m has been received in cash. How much can be reported as a realised profit in the profit and loss account? The possible answers would seem to be:

(i)   £9m (i.e. that part of the total gain that is backed by cash); or

(ii)   £1.92m? (i.e. 9/90 x £19.2m, representing the proportion of the gain attributable to the cash element of the total consideration).

We believe that (i) is the more appropriate answer. In either case, however, there remains the issue of the treatment of the gain not recognised (either £10.2m or £17.28m). Should it simply be deducted from the cost of the investment in JVCo as before (our preferred treatment) and therefore fed into the calculation of goodwill, or should it be deferred in some other way pending realisation?

An example of a company that has to account for a transaction of this type is EMI. In March 1998 it sold its investment in HMV to the newly-floated HMV Media Group, in which it immediately acquired a 45.2% equity interest. As explained in the extract below, EMI did not recognise 45.2% of the profit on disposal as a profit, but credited it to reserves.

Extract 7.23 :EMI Group (1998)

29. Disposal of business [extract]

The only disposal in the current year is HMV, which was substantially disposed of on 28 March 1998. ...

In order to determine the profit on disposal recognised in the profit and loss account for the year, in accordance with UK GAAP, the disposal of HMV to HMV Media Group plc has been considered in conjunction with the Group's subsequent acquisition of an initial 45.2% equity investment in HMV Media Group plc. Looking at both of these transactions together results in 45.2% of the gross profit on disposal being deemed intercompany. This intercompany element of the profit, together with the associated taxation charge, has been eliminated on consolidation and treated as a reserves movement netting against the goodwill on acquisition of the investment in HMV Media Group plc. The estimated goodwill arising on the acquisition of the associated

> undertaking HMV Media Group plc is £184.7m, £278.1m on acquisition (based on estimated net
> liabilities: see Note 13(ii)) less a net £93.4m intercompany elimination (gross profit: £120.5m less
> taxation charge £27.1m).

FRS 9 goes on to say that, where a transaction between an investor and its associate or joint venture provides evidence of the impairment of the asset transferred, 'this should be taken into account'.[84] Again, exactly what is envisaged here is not clear, but the suggestion seems to be that, where a transaction between the investor and an associate or joint venture generates a loss, the loss should not necessarily be adjusted out on consolidation.

In the consolidated cash flow statement no adjustment is made in respect of transactions with associates and joint ventures (whereas cash flows between members of the group are eliminated in the same way as intra-group profits).

Whilst we generally support the ASB's view that standards should not be unduly detailed, we do see the lack of any detailed guidance on this issue in FRS 9 as a serious omission that should be rectified as soon as practicable, as the creation of joint ventures by contributions of assets from the parties is becoming an increasingly common form of business structure in the UK.

4.3   Conformity of accounting policies

FRS 9 requires the investor to account for its share of the results and net assets of an associate or joint venture, by adjusting them where necessary so as to conform them to its own accounting policies. Similar considerations in respect of the availability of information apply to such adjustments as to fair value adjustments (see 4.1 above).[85] This may mean that, in more complex cases, such as the arrangements assumed in Example 7.6 above, the amounts taken up in the accounts of the investor may bear little relation to its share of the underlying financial statements of the investee, and it may be necessary to keep a 'memorandum' set of books for consolidation purposes. An example of a company disclosing that consolidation adjustments have been made in respect of equity accounted investments is United News and Media.

> *Extract 7.24: United News & Media plc (1998)*
>
> **Group accounting policies** [extract]
> **INVESTMENTS**
> ...
> Where the accounting policies of associates and/or joint ventures do not conform in all material
> respects to those of the group, adjustments are made on consolidation.

4.5   Non-coterminous accounting periods

Where possible, FRS 9 requires the investor's share of an associate or joint venture to be included on the basis of financial statements prepared to the investor's period end. Where this is not practicable, the investor may use financial statements prepared to a date preceding its own period end by not more than three months.[86]

This period can be extended up to six months if use of financial statements for an earlier period would entail publication of restricted, price-sensitive information.[87] In amplifying this requirement, the FRS emphasises the need to have regard to any relevant 'regulations' on the dissemination of price-sensitive information.[88] The implication seems to be that the exemption for 'price-sensitive' information applies only in respect of information that is treated as such by applicable regulations rather than to any information considered as such by the investor or investee. This is consistent with the requirements of the law and FRS 2 in respect of the consolidation of subsidiaries with non-coterminous year ends.[89]

FRS 9 requires that, where the investor's equity accounting is based on the accounts of an associate or joint venture for a period ending before its own, adjustments should be made in respect of any material event that has occurred in the interim.[90]

FRS 9 recognises that it can be difficult to ensure that the associate provides up-to-date information. A holding company can usually secure that a subsidiary has a coterminous year end, but the various investors in an associate or joint venture may all have different year ends. None of them has the control needed in order to dictate the year end of the investee, nor can they necessarily demand the production of interim accounts for their own purposes (although this can sometimes give an indication of whether or not they do, in fact, exercise significant influence or joint control).[91]

An example of a company disclosing that interim accounts of associates have been used for consolidation purposes is Pearson, even though this is technically no longer required, as it was under SSAP 1.

Extract 7.25: Pearson plc (1998)

B) BASIS OF CONSOLIDATION [extract]

The profit of the Group includes the Group's share of the profit of partnerships and associated undertakings, and the consolidated balance sheet includes the Group's interest in partnerships and associated undertakings at the book value of attributable net tangible assets. The figures included in the financial statements have been based on audited accounts, adjusted where necessary by reference to unaudited management accounts for the subsequent period to 31 December.

4.6   Goodwill

FRS 9 provides that the element of the carrying value of an investment in an associate or joint venture represented by goodwill must be accounted for in accordance with FRS 10,[92] the detailed requirements of which are discussed in Chapter 10. This means that, for any associate or joint venture acquired in a period to which FRS 10 applied, any goodwill arising on acquisition must be included in the carrying value of the investment and either:

(a)   amortised over twenty years (or less); or

(b)   amortised over more than twenty years or not amortised, subject in either case to an annual impairment review.

Neither FRS 9 nor FRS 10 gives any guidance as to how to undertake an annual impairment review of an investment in an associate or joint venture. The basic principle is to compare the carrying value of the investment with the higher of its net realisable value (if known) or value in use (effectively, discounted future cash flows from the investment).

Unless the associate or joint venture is a listed company it may be difficult to estimate a net realisable value for it. So far as estimating a value in use is concerned, however, this is a difficult enough exercise at the best of times as we discuss more fully in Chapter 10.

At least where the investment concerned is a subsidiary, the parent can usually ensure full distribution of profits if it so wishes. This means that the future profits of that investment form a starting point for estimating future cash flows from it. In the case of an investment in an associate or joint venture, however, the only cash flows are normally dividends received together with the proceeds of any eventual realisation of the investment. Both the amount and the timing of such cash flows will in many cases be very difficult to determine.

The difficulties of assessing either net realisable value or value in use for investments in associates and joint ventures are such that we doubt whether any goodwill in the carrying value of such investments is, except in very rare circumstances, 'capable of continued measurement' within the terms of FRS 10.[93] This means that it must be amortised over twenty years or less, and a longer (or indefinite) life cannot be used.

There may, however, be cases where the cash flows are sufficiently predictable to enable an impairment review to be undertaken. This might be the case, for example, where cash flows from the associate or joint venture are expected to be generated through sales to it by the reporting entity, or where the investee has been set up for a specific, and relatively short-term, project. There are companies that have taken the view that goodwill relating to associates is capable of continued measurement, an example being Cadbury Schweppes (see Chapter 10 at 3.4.1).

There may also be a more general argument that, in the case of a joint venture, the investor's joint control gives it more power to convert profits into cash flows than is the case with an associate. On this basis, the forecast future profits of a joint venture may form a more valid basis than those of an associate for predicting future cash flows.

Where an impairment review identifies any impairment in the value of goodwill arising on acquisition of an associate or joint venture, FRS 9 requires the goodwill to be written down and the amount written off to be disclosed.[94] The FRS notes that any impairment in the assets of the associate or joint venture will 'normally' be reflected in its own accounts with the result that further adjustments should not 'usually' be necessary in the investor's financial statements.[95]

The use of the words 'normally' and 'usually', combined with the requirement to adjust the underlying accounts of an associate or joint venture to reflect the investor's accounting policies (see above), implies that, where an investee does not make adjustments for impairment of assets in its own accounts (e.g. because it is not subject to UK GAAP), the investor should do so on consolidation. However, we simply do not see how this can be practicable. If, as we suggest above, the investor would be hard-pressed to undertake an impairment review of its entire investment in an associate or joint venture, it could hardly do so in respect of the underlying assets of the associate or joint venture.

4.7 Calculation of the share of an associate or joint venture to be accounted for

FRS 9 provides some guidance on the calculation of the share of net assets to be accounted for under the equity and gross equity methods. It first clarifies that the group's effective interest in an associate or joint venture is the aggregate of the interests held by the parent and its subsidiaries, and that any interests held by its associates or joint ventures are to be ignored.[96] No specific guidance is provided in respect of cross-holdings (i.e. where the reporting entity and an associate (or joint venture) have shares in each other). However, the requirement (discussed above) partially to eliminate profits of transactions between the group and its associates and joint ventures clearly suggests that cross-holdings should be adjusted for.

FRS 9 notes that in most cases the investor's effective interest will be determined by the proportion of equity shares held.[97] However, matters may be complicated when the investee has two or more classes of share, with differing rights, in issue, or where the investor holds non-equity shares, convertibles or options in the investee. FRS 9 states that in some cases the rights attaching to options, convertibles, or non-equity shares are such that the investor should take them into account.[98]

FRS 9 does not elaborate on the circumstances in which such rights should be adjusted for. The implication is that where an investor has a contingent right to acquire equity shares in an associate or joint venture (e.g. through an option or convertible security), and that right is likely to be exercised, the investor should equity account for the share of its investment that it would have if those rights were exercised. Where this is done, however, the costs of exercising such rights should be taken into account, and care must be taken not to double count such interests. For example, an investor should not increase its equity accounted interest in an investment on the basis that some contingent right will be exercised whilst simultaneously marking that right to market.[99] It would also be necessary to have regard to the dividend rights of other shareholders, since it would clearly be wrong to equity account for profits that were in reality more likely to be paid as dividend to other shareholders than to the reporting entity.

FRS 9 deals only with rights held by the reporting entity. It is of course quite possible that other investors in an associate or joint venture may have a contingent right to acquire shares in it which, if exercised, would dilute the effective interest of the reporting entity. We believe that, in assessing the interest of the reporting entity, regard should be had to such rights and interests of other investors.

FRS 9 also notes that the arrangements for sharing dividends and other distributions may be more complicated and may depend on the type of distribution or the nature of the underlying cash flows of the investee. In such cases, it is necessary for the substance of the arrangements to be taken into account in establishing the most appropriate measure of the investor's share.[100]

4.8   Losses and deficiencies of assets

FRS 9 requires an investor to account for the appropriate share of a loss-making associate or joint venture, even where this results in the investor showing a share of net liabilities rather than net assets. Where this occurs, the resulting balance is shown as a provision or liability rather than as a negative fixed asset. The only exception is where there is sufficient evidence that there has been an irrevocable change in the relationship between the parties marking the 'irreversible withdrawal' of the investor. The FRS implies that in such cases it is necessary that either:

(a)   the investor makes a public statement of its intention to walk away from its investment combined with a demonstrable commitment to the process of withdrawal; or

(b)   there is evidence that the operating and financing policies of the investee are to become the responsibility of its creditors rather than the shareholders (e.g. the appointment of a receiver).[101]

Examples of companies disclosing such a deficit are Cable and Wireless (see Extract 7.17 above), and Cordiant Communications Group (see Extract 7.26 below). Both companies present it as a separate balance sheet format heading, after 'Provisions for liabilities and charges' in the case of Cable and Wireless, but before it in the case of Cordiant, which also analyses the deficit between the underlying share of gross assets and gross liabilities. It is noteworthy that neither Cable and Wireless nor Cordiant strictly includes the share of net deficit *within* provisions, as suggested by FRS 9. It may be that the companies share our view that FRS 9's required treatment is not altogether appropriate since the investor's share of such deficits does not meet the definition either of 'provision' in FRS 12 (see Chapter 25), or of 'liability' in the ASB's draft *Statement of Principles* (see Chapter 2).

Extract 7.26: Cordiant Communications Group plc (1998)

CONSOLIDATED BALANCE SHEET [extract]

	Notes	1998 £m	1997 £m
...			
Total assets less current liabilities		**73.0**	**46.3**
Creditors: amounts falling due after more than one year	18	(73.8)	(53.8)
Provision for joint venture deficit			
Share of gross assets		83.6	51.6
Share of gross liabilities		(98.3)	(65.9)
	21	(14.7)	(14.3)
Provisions for liabilities and charges	21	(53.4)	(57.8)
Net liabilities		**(68.9)**	**(79.6)**
...			

An example of an entity that does not provide for its share of net liabilities of joint ventures and associates, on the grounds that there is no obligation to make good such deficits, is the BBC. Whilst this may well fairly represent the substance of the arrangements, it is not clear that FRS 9's very demanding conditions for this treatment (as set out in (a) and (b) above) have strictly been satisfied.

Extract 7.27: British Broadcasting Corporation (1999)

10c Accounting for entities within the Flextech and Discovery agreements [extract]

The Group, through its subsidiary BBC Worldwide Limited, has major partnership deals with Flextech plc ('Flextech') for the production and marketing of subscription channels in the UK, and with Discovery Communications Inc. ('Discovery') for incorporating and operating new channels around the world and providing new co-production funding for programmes. These alliances operate under a number of statutory entities, listed below.

...

Under the terms of the agreements with Flextech and Discovery, the Group has no obligation to fund losses incurred by the entities nor to make good their net liabilities. As a result, the Group does not share in the losses of the relevant entities and accordingly no share of losses is included in the financial statements for the year ended 31 March 1999 (1998 nil).

10d Interests in joint ventures [extract]

The Group's proportionate share of the joint ventures' assets and liabilities, based on its equity interest, adjusted to reflect the agreements referred to in note 10c above, is as follows:

Group interests in joint ventures	1999 £m	1998 £m
Share of turnover	**26.0**	13.1
Share of fixed assets	**4.3**	0.1
Share of current assets	**23.5**	21.4
Share of liabilities due within one year	**(18.7)**	(12.0)
Share of liabilities due after more than year	**(77.6)**	(65.1)
Adjustment to reflect effective obligation	**68.5**	55.6
	–	–

4.9   Non-corporate associates and joint ventures

The issue here is related to the last. Where the investor has an interest in an unincorporated associate or joint venture it may have liabilities greater than the amount that results from taking into account only its share of net assets. This may be the case, for example, where the investors in the entity concerned have joint and several liability for its debts and one of the other investors gets into financial difficulties. In such cases, the FRS requires the reporting investor to disclose any such additional obligation as a contingent liability or, in more extreme cases, to recognise it in the financial statements.[102]

Whilst this provision of FRS 9 appears under the heading 'Non-corporate associates and joint ventures' the same principles will apply to an investment in an incorporated entity where the shareholders have joint and several liability (e.g. where the shareholders of a company jointly guarantee a bank loan).

4.10   Commencement or cessation of an associate or joint venture relationship

An investment becomes an associate on the date that the investor first holds a participating interest in it *and* exercises significant influence over it. It therefore ceases to be one when the investor ceases *either* to hold a participating interest *or* exercise significant influence.[103]

As noted in the discussion in 2.1.1 B above, there is a presumption in FRS 9 that once an investor has exercised significant influence over an investment, it carries on doing so until some transaction or event occurs to remove this influence. Moreover, once an investment is considered to be long-term (one of the key elements of a 'participating interest'), FRS 9 requires that it continue to be treated as such until disposal. Taken together, this all means that, in practice, it will be relatively rare that an investment ceases to be an associate, other than by disposal or dilution of the reporting entity's interest, or loss of board representation.

An investment becomes a joint venture on the day on which the investor first exercises joint control over it, and ceases to be one when the investor ceases to exercise joint control.[104] These dates may not be as clear-cut as might appear at first sight, given that FRS 9 provides that joint control can be established through habitual behaviour as well as through a formal agreement.

Where an associate or joint venture is disposed of, in whole or in part, the profit or loss should be calculated as the sales proceeds less:

(a) share of net assets (i.e. the amount at which the investment would have been stated under the equity method on the date on which it ceased to qualify as an associate or joint venture); and

(b) any goodwill that arose on acquisition (to the extent not already charged to the profit and loss account, or charged as a prior year adjustment under the transitional rules in FRS 10).[105]

If an investment ceases to be an associate or joint venture other than through disposal, it should be carried in the consolidated balance sheet at an amount comprising the share of net assets plus goodwill (calculated as in (a) and (b) above).[106] This carrying amount should be reviewed for impairment and adjusted, if necessary, to reflect dividend payments and other distributions to shareholders.

It has to said that FRS 9 could be clearer as to whether unamortised goodwill is to be included in the carrying amount, but it is our view that this is the intention of paragraphs 40-43 of the standard when read as a whole. It is also not clear, if goodwill is included in the carrying value of a former associate or joint venture in this way, whether it is meant to be separately identified and treated as such, or simply added to the cost of investment.

We believe FRS 9 intends the latter treatment, because it refers to the resulting figure as a 'surrogate cost'.[107] On this view, the 'cost' of a former associate or joint venture is the amount originally paid (i.e. including goodwill) plus the share of profits 'foregone' as a result of the loss of influence (or joint control). If this interpretation is correct, it has the effect that, where an associate or joint venture loses its status as such, any goodwill that arose on acquisition and was eliminated against reserves under SSAP 22 must under FRS 9 be added to the carrying value. This was the treatment adopted by Hanson in these circumstances (see Extract 7.5 at 2.1.1 B above).

In fact, this treatment of former associates and joint ventures may be relatively short-lived, since they will be carried at market value if the proposals in the

ASB's 1996 discussion paper *Derivatives and other financial instruments* are given effect in a future FRS.[108]

Where an associate or joint venture is acquired or disposed of piecemeal, processes similar to those required by FRS 2 for piecemeal acquisition or disposals of subsidiaries should be applied.[109] These are discussed more fully in sections 2.5, 3.4 and 3.5 of Chapter 6.

5   DISCLOSURE REQUIREMENTS FOR ASSOCIATES AND JOINT VENTURES

In addition to the disclosures that directly amplify the primary statements (discussed in 3 above), FRS 9 requires further disclosures in respect of associates and joint ventures. Most of these are duplicated by the requirements of the Companies Act, but there are a few additional ones in the legislation. Where a company has acquired or disposed of an associate during the year, certain disclosures may also be required by FRS 10 – *Goodwill and intangible assets*.

There are, broadly, two tiers of disclosure in FRS 9. Some items, mostly of a narrative nature, are required in respect of all associates and joint ventures, irrespective of size. Where, however, associates and joint ventures form a particularly large part of the reporting entity's business, additional financial information must be given.

5.1   Scope of disclosures

There is some lack of clarity in FRS 9 as to exactly what entities are required to give these disclosures. Because paragraph 51 of the FRS states that they should be given 'in addition to the amounts required on the face of the primary financial statements under the equity or the gross equity method', it is our view that:

■   They are required in consolidated accounts (because these include equity accounted amounts on the face of the profit and loss account and balance sheet).

■   They are not required in single entity accounts of investors that are not required to give supplementary information on associates or joint ventures (see 3.1.2 above). This is because disclosure is required only 'in addition' to equity accounted amounts, and no such information appears on the face of the primary statements. Moreover, most of the disclosures would be of no relevance to the accounts of such a company. However, it must be remembered that some information, similar to that which would otherwise be required by FRS 9, is required under the Companies Act (see 5.3 below and Chapter 27 at 3.1.3).

- They are probably required in (and are certainly relevant to) single entity accounts of investors that are required to give supplementary information on associates or joint ventures (see 3.1.2 above). There is room for debate here, however, as to whether the supplementary equity accounted information given by such companies appears 'on the face of the primary statements' (a necessary condition for triggering the disclosure requirement). The information does not, obviously, appear on the face of the primary financial statements of the *company*, but it does appear on the face of the *supplementary* primary financial statements. The position is even less clear when the supplementary information is given by way of note, rather than in pro-forma accounts.

If this is the intended position, however, it is slightly confusing that the disclosures required by paragraph 52 (but no other paragraph) are specifically restricted to the group accounts. If our interpretation of paragraph 51 is correct, it is not necessary to restrict the scope of paragraph 52 in this way.

5.2 Disclosures required for all associates and joint ventures

5.2.1 *Name, shareholding, accounting date etc.*

In group accounts only, an investor should give for each principal associate and joint venture:

(a)   its name;

(b)   the proportion of shares held, together with any special rights or restrictions attaching to the shares;

(c)   the accounting period or date of the financial statements used, if different from that of the reporting group; and

(d)   an indication of the nature of its business.[110]

5.2.2 *Matters material to understanding the effect of associates and joint ventures*

FRS 9 requires an investor to disclose matters that are disclosed in the accounts of its associates or joint ventures (or would have been noted had the associate or joint venture applied the investor's accounting policies), and which are material to understanding the effect on the investor of its investments. FRS 9 particularly highlights the investor's share of contingent liabilities and capital commitments as being relevant to this requirement.[111]

5.2.3 *Restrictions on distribution*

The investor should indicate the extent of any significant statutory, contractual or exchange restrictions on the distribution of the reserves of an associate or joint venture (other than those shown as non-distributable).[112] This corresponds to the similar requirement in respect of investments in subsidiaries in FRS 2.[113]

5.2.4   Balances with associates and joint ventures

FRS 9 requires balances between the investor and its associates or joint ventures to be analysed between loans and trading balances,[114] as do the balance sheet formats in the Companies Act 1985.[115] FRS 9 notes that these disclosures overlap somewhat with those required by FRS 8 – *Related party disclosures* – which are discussed in Chapter 27, and permits the disclosures made under the two standards to be combined.[116]

5.2.5   Rebuttal of presumptions relating to interests of 20% or more

FRS 9 requires the reporting entity to disclose why the facts in any particular case rebut the presumption that control of 20% or more of the voting rights in an investment gives rise to significant influence over it. It also requires similar disclosure where the presumption that a 20% (or greater) shareholding gives rise to a participating interest has been rebutted.[117] See Extracts 7.3 and 7.4 at 2.1.1 B above for examples of disclosure under this requirement.

In SSAP 1 there had been a converse requirement to disclose why the facts in any particular case rebutted the presumption (in SSAP 1) that control of less than 20% of the voting rights in an investment did not give rise to significant influence.[118] This presumption (and therefore the disclosure relating to it) was not reproduced in FRS 9, which was somewhat surprising, given that it is now arguably even more relevant, given the stricter definition of 'associate' in FRS 9.

5.3   Disclosures required for material associates or joint ventures

FRS 9 requires disclosure of supplementary financial information in respect of associates and joint ventures where these represent a material part of the group's activities. Broadly speaking, this information must be given in respect of:

(a)   total associates (and/or joint ventures) where these comprise more than 15% of the group; and

(b)   each individual associate (or joint venture) that represents more than 25% of the group.

The precise rules for calculating whether these thresholds have been reached are slightly complicated.

5.3.1   Determining whether disclosure is required

In order to determine whether the additional disclosures are required, the reporting group must first calculate its own:

(a)   turnover;

(b)   average operating profit for the current and previous two periods;

(c)   gross assets; and

(d)   gross liabilities.

Somewhat inconsistently, whilst profit is calculated using a rolling three-year average, turnover is simply the figure for the year. Each of these adjusted group figures is then compared with the corresponding figures for the group's share of:

(a)   associates in total;

(b)   joint ventures in total; and

(c)   each individual associate or joint venture.

The disclosure thresholds are reached when any one of the figures for total associates or total joint ventures is more than 15%, or any of the figures for an individual associate or joint venture is more than 25%, of the corresponding adjusted group figure.[119] The disclosures required are set out in 5.2.2 and 5.2.3 below.

In undertaking the calculations in each case the reporting entity must exclude from the 'group' numbers (for reasons that are not entirely clear) any amounts arising from equity accounting for associates or joint ventures. This raises the issue of how to treat goodwill included in the carrying amount of associates or joint ventures. We consider that, because it represents part of the group's equity accounted interest in associates or joint ventures, it should be treated as a gross asset of the associate or joint venture rather than of the group. However, it could be argued that, at least to the extent that it represents a premium paid on acquisition rather than underlying goodwill of the associate or joint venture, it should be treated as an asset of the group.

5.3.2   The '15%' disclosures

A   Associates

Where the 15% threshold is reached in respect of total associates, the group should disclose its share, in total, of its associates':

(a)   turnover (unless shown already as a memorandum item);

(b)   fixed assets;

(c)   current assets;

(d)   liabilities due within one year; and

(e)   liabilities due after one year or more.[120]

B   Joint ventures

Where the 15% threshold is reached in respect of total joint ventures, the group should disclose its share, in total, of its joint ventures':

(a)   fixed assets;

(b)   current assets;

(c)   liabilities due within one year; and

(d)   liabilities due after one year or more.[121]

5.3.3　The '25%' disclosures

Where the 25% threshold is reached in respect of any individual associate or joint venture, the accounts should name the entity concerned and disclose the group's share of its:

(a)　turnover;

(b)　profit before tax;

(c)　taxation;

(d)　profit after tax;

(e)　fixed assets;

(f)　current assets;

(g)　liabilities due within one year; and

(h)　liabilities due after one year or more.[122]

If a single associate or joint venture falling within the 25% threshold represents nearly all the total amount included for associates or joint ventures respectively, these disclosures may be given in respect of total associates (and/or joint ventures) rather than for the individual investment concerned. The accounts must disclose that this approach has been adopted, and name the main associate or joint venture concerned.[123]

Further analysis of any amounts disclosed under these requirements should be given where this is necessary to understand the total amount involved. The FRS suggests that it may be important to give more information on the size and maturity profile of liabilities.[124] An example of a company which adopts this approach is Reed International, virtually all of whose activities are, due to the Reed Elsevier group structure, carried out through joint ventures. It therefore includes in the notes to the accounts what virtually amounts to a full set of primary statements for the joint ventures, which are too voluminous to quote in full here.[125] A similar approach is adopted by Henlys Group (see also 3.2.2 above).

5.4　Companies Act 1985

5.4.1　Associated undertakings

The following information must be given in group accounts in respect of each associated undertaking:

(a)　its name;

(b)　its country of incorporation (if outside Great Britain);

(c)　if it is unincorporated, the address of its principal place of business; and

(d)　the identity of each class of shares held and the proportion of the nominal value of the shares of that class represented by those shares. If applicable, the holdings should be split between those held directly by the parent company, and those held indirectly via other group companies.[126]

Equivalent disclosures must be given in respect of joint ventures accounted for under the gross equity method, by virtue of the fact that they will typically fall within the Companies Act definitions of 'associated undertaking' and/or 'significant holding'.[127]

5.4.2   *Proportionally consolidated joint ventures*

As noted above, FRS 9 no longer permits proportional consolidation of joint ventures. However, as noted in 2.2.2 above, the Companies Act permits proportional consolidation of unincorporated joint ventures and, where this is done, requires certain disclosures to be made in respect of each such venture, as follows:

(a)   its name;

(b)   its principal place of business;

(c)   the factors on which joint management is based;

(d)   the proportion of the capital of the joint venture held by the group; and

(e)   where the financial year end of the joint venture did not coincide with that of the parent company of the reporting group, the date of its last year end (ending before the financial year end of the parent company).[128]

At present these requirements are of no practical effect and we include them only for the sake of completeness.

5.5   The disclosures in practice

A comprehensive example of most of the disclosures required by FRS 9 and the Companies Act is that given by Pilkington (see Extract 7.28 below)

Extract 7.28: Pilkington plc (1999)

	1999 Group £m	1998 Group £m
19 Investments – joint ventures		
Cost or valuation		
At beginning of year	44	52
Exchange rate adjustments	2	(2)
Disposals	–	(3)
Transfer to subsidiary undertakings	–	(2)
Transfer to trade investments	–	(1)
	46	44
Share of post-acquisition profits less losses		
At beginning of year	31	32
Exchange rate adjustments	1	–
Disposals	–	(6)
Retained profits	6	5
	38	31
At end of the year	84	75

The Group's principal joint ventures are as follows:

	Proportion of issued shares held	Accounting date	Activity	Country of operation and incorporation
Cebrace Cristal Plano Limitada	50%	31.3.99	Glass manufacturing	Brazil
Flovetro SpA	50%	31.12.98	Glass manufacturing	Italy

In addition, there are three further joint ventures at 31st March 1999.

No significant additional taxation would be payable if the joint ventures were sold at the carrying value.

At 31st March 1999 the share of profits less losses retained by joint ventures included within the Group's profit and loss account balance amounted to £38 million (1998 £31 million) of which £5 million (1998 £2 million) is considered to be distributable, the remainder being subject to restriction within the countries in which the joint ventures operate.

The Group's share of the net assets of joint ventures comprises:

	1999 £m	1998 £m
Fixed assets	99	97
Current assets	20	22
Liabilities due within one year	(20)	(29)
Liabilities due after more than one year	(15)	(15)
	84	75

Additional disclosures are given in respect of the Group's share of Cebrace which exceeds certain thresholds under FRS 9, as follows:

	1999 £m	1998 £m
Turnover	40	44
Profit before taxation	10	13
Taxation	(2)	(4)
Profit after taxation	8	9
Fixed assets	94	91
Current assets	13	16
Liabilities due within one year	(17)	(26)
Liabilities due after more than one year	(14)	(13)
Net assets	76	68

		1999 Group £m	1998 Group £m
20	**Investments – associates**		
	Cost or valuation		
	At beginning of year	76	23
	Exchange rate adjustments	2	(7)
	Additions	4	1
	Disposals	–	(3)
	Transfer to subsidiary undertakings	–	(19)
	Transfer from trade investments	–	48
	Other movements	–	33
		82	76

Share of post-acquisition profits less losses

At beginning of year	2	2
Exchange rate adjustments	(1)	(1)
Disposals	–	(2)
Retained profits less losses	1	3
	2	2
At end of the year	**84**	78

The Group's principal associates are as follows:

	Proportion of issued shares held	Accounting date	Activity	Country of operation and incorporation
Vitro Plan SA de CV+	35%	31.12.98	Glass manufacturing and processing	Mexico
Wuhan Yaohua Pilkington Safety Glass Co Limited+	46%	31.12.98	Glass processing	China
Holding Concorde SA+	49%	31.12.98	Glass manufacturing	Colombia

+Audited by a firm other than PricewaterhouseCoopers.

No additional taxation would be payable if the investments were sold at the carrying value.

At 31st March 1999 the share of profit less losses retained by associates included within the Group's profit and loss account balance amounted to £2 million (1998 £2 million), of which £4 million of the profits (1998 £2 million) are considered to be distributable.

The Group's share of the net assets of associates comprises:

	1999 £m	1998 £m
Fixed assets	**122**	116
Current assets	**50**	48
Liabilities due within one year	**(43)**	(32)
Liabilities due after more than one year	**(45)**	(54)
	84	78

Additional disclosures are given in respect of the Group's share of Vitro Plan SA de CV which exceeds certain thresholds under FRS 9, as follows:

	1999 £m	1998 £m
Turnover	**192**	171
Profit before taxation	**28**	27
Taxation	**(10)**	(11)
Profit after taxation	**18**	16

Fixed assets	**115**	114
Current assets	**50**	47
Liabilities due within one year	**(43)**	(32)
Liabilities due after more than one year	**(45)**	(54)
Net assets	**77**	75

6 COMPARISON WITH IASC AND US PRONOUNCEMENTS

6.1 IASC

One of the more striking features of FRS 9 at the time of its issue was that it took the UK further away from international accounting practice than had been the case under SSAP 1. This seemed particularly ironic given the ASB's strong support for, and involvement in the IASC's harmonisation project (see Chapter 1).

6.1.1 Associates

The relevant international pronouncement is IAS 28 – *Accounting for Investments in Associates*. IAS 28 defines an associate as 'an enterprise in which the investor has significant influence and which is neither a subsidiary nor a joint venture of the investor.'[129] Significant influence is defined as 'the power to participate in the financial and operating policy decisions of the investee but is not control over those policies'. The IAS states that this will usually be evidenced in one or more of the following ways:

(a) representation on the board of directors or equivalent governing body of the investee;

(b) participation in policy-making processes;

(c) material transactions between the investor and the investee;

(d) interchange of managerial personnel; or

(e) provision of essential technical information.[130]

This wording is based on the equivalent requirement in the US.[131]

There are a number of differences between FRS 9 and IAS 28, which FRS 9 seeks, not altogether convincingly, to portray as 'minor',[132] as follows:

- Under FRS 9, an investor has actually to exercise significant influence over an investment for it to be treated as an associate. Under IAS 28, it is sufficient to be in a position to exercise such influence. FRS 9 seeks to play down this important difference of emphasis with the argument that 'the best evidence of an entity's ability to exercise significant influence is the fact that it is exercising such influence'.[133]

- Under IAS 28, a holding of 20% or more of the voting rights is presumed to give rise to significant influence. Whilst this is also true under FRS 9, the FRS suggests that this presumption may be rebutted relatively frequently.

- IAS 28 excludes from equity accounting any investment that is acquired and held exclusively for subsequent disposal in the near future.[134] FRS 9 does not have a specific exclusion for such investments, although it notes that the definition of 'participating interest' (see 2.1.1 A above) will produce much the same result.[135]

- IAS 28 also excludes from equity accounting any investment that operates under severe long-term restrictions that significantly impair its ability to transfer funds to the investor. FRS 9 has no such specific exclusion. However, Appendix II to the FRS states that the definition of 'exercise of significant influence' (see 2.1.1 B above) is unlikely to be fulfilled in respect of such an investment, such that the overall effect is the same. It is not entirely clear how this statement can be reconciled to FRS 9's requirement to disclose details of 'significant' restrictions on the ability of an associate or joint venture to distribute its profits (see 5.1.3 above). The implication seems to be that an investor can exercise significant influence over an investee subject to 'significant', but not 'severe', restrictions.

- Where an investor does not have any subsidiaries, IAS 28 permits associates either to be equity accounted for or to be carried at cost (or valuation).[136] FRS 9 (and the Companies Act) requires them to be carried at cost (or valuation).

- IAS 28 simply requires that 'the income statement reflects the share of the results of the operations of the investee'.[137] FRS 9 is much more specific, requiring the investing group's share of the results is included at every main level of the profit and loss account except turnover and other components of operating profit. However, IAS 28 requires that the net investment in associates should be included as a separate item in the balance sheet and the share of profits should be separately disclosed in the income statement, with disclosure of the investor's share of any extraordinary or prior period items.[138]

- There is no equivalent in IAS 28 for the additional disclosures required by FRS 9 where total associates represent more than 15% (or an individual associate represents more than 25%) of the group.

- Under FRS 9, losses of associates must continue to be accounted for until some event occurs that marks the investor's irreversible withdrawal. Under IAS 28, the treatment is to account for losses only until the investment is reduced to zero unless the investor has an obligation to make good those losses.[139]

It is not surprising, given the relative lack of prescription in IAS 28, that practice varies considerably between companies. For example, Nestlé includes the post-tax results of its associates as the final item in its consolidated profit and loss account. It also discloses that it makes no adjustments to conform the results of associates to its own accounting policies, which would be required under UK GAAP.

Extract 7.30: Nestlé S.A. (1998)

Consolidated income statement [extract]

In millions of Swiss francs	Notes	**1998**	1997
...			
Profit before taxation		**6,121**	5,938
Taxation		**(2,002)**	(1,842)
Net profit of consolidated companies		**4,119**	4,096
Share of profit attributable to minority interests		**(128)**	(170)
Share of results of associated companies	6	**300**	256
Net profit for the year		**4,291**	4,182

Accounting policies [extract]

Associated companies

Companies where the Group has a participation of 20% or more but does not exercise management control are accounted for by the equity method. The net assets and results are recognised on the basis of the associates' own accounting policies which may differ from those of the Group.

6. Share of results of associated companies

In millions of Swiss francs	**1998**	1997
Share of profit before taxation	**499**	430
Less share of taxation	**(199)**	(174)
Share of profit after taxation	**300**	256

12. Investments in associated companies

This item includes substantially our share of the equity of the indirect participation in L'Oréal, Paris for Fr. 1367 million (1997: Fr. 1206 million). Its market value at 31st December 1998 amounts to Fr. 17 609 million (1997: Fr. 10 224 million).

Roche includes the net results of its associates within other operating income, as disclosed in the extract below. However, it does not disclose the amount included or provide an analysis of the movement in the carrying amount.

Extract 7.30: Roche Holding Ltd (1998)

10.   Investments in associated companies

The Group has investments in associated companies as listed below. These have been accounted for using the equity method. The Group's share of net income is recorded as part of other operating income (expense), net.

Laboratory Corporation of America Holdings

The Group has a 48.95% interest in Laboratory Corporation of America Holdings (LabCorp), which operates clinical laboratories in the United States. During 1997 Roche Holdings, Inc. increased its investment by purchasing from LabCorp non-voting, convertible 8.5% preferred stock for 249 million US dollars (361 million Swiss francs).

Investments in other associated companies

The Group has investments in other associated companies with a combined carrying value on the balance sheet of 17 million Swiss francs (1997: 16 million Swiss francs).

Nokia shows its share of the results of associates on the face of the profit and loss account immediately after the group operating profit, as would be required by FRS 9, although it is not clear whether the amounts included at this level correspond entirely to those that would be included at this level under FRS 9.

Extract 7.31: Nokia Corporation (1998)

Consolidated Profit and Loss Account, IAS [extract]

Financial year ended December 31	1998 MFIM	1997 MFIM
Net sales	**79,231**	52,612
Cost of goods sold	**-49,342**	-33,999
Research and development expenses	**-6,838**	-4,560
Selling, general and administrative expenses	**-8,252**	-5,599
Operating profit	**14,799**	8,454
Share of results of associated companies	**38**	54
Financial income and expenses	**-234**	-137
Profit before tax and minority interests	**14,603**	8,371
...		

6.1.2   Joint ventures

The differences between FRS 9 and International Accounting Standards in respect of joint ventures are even more marked than those relating to associates. The relevant international standard is IAS 31 – *Financial Reporting of Interests in Joint Ventures*. The standard defines a joint venture as 'a contractual arrangement whereby two or more parties ('venturers') undertake an economic activity which is subject to joint control'. Joint control is the 'contractually agreed sharing of control' over an economic activity', control being defined as 'the power to govern the financial and operating policies of an economic activity so as to obtain benefits from it)'.[140]

Under IAS 31 the accounting for interests in joint ventures depends on whether they are interests in:

(a)   jointly controlled operations;

(b)   jointly controlled assets; or

(c)   jointly controlled entities.

A jointly controlled operation is one which involves the use of assets and other resources of the venturers, rather than the establishment of an entity separate from the venturers themselves.[141] In respect of its interest in a jointly controlled operation, a venturer should recognise in both its own and its consolidated financial statements:

(a)   the assets that it controls and the liabilities that it incurs; and

(b)   the expenses that it incurs and its share of the income that it earns from the sale of goods or services by the joint venture.[142]

Some joint ventures involve the joint control and/or ownership of assets, but without the establishment of an entity separate from the venturers themselves. Joint ventures of this type are particularly common in extractive industries. For example, a number of oil companies may jointly control and operate an oil pipeline.[143]

In respect of its interest in jointly controlled assets, a venturer should recognise in both its own and its consolidated financial statements:

(a)   its share of the jointly controlled assets, classified according to the nature of the assets;

(b)   any liabilities which it has incurred; and

(c)   its share of any liabilities incurred jointly with the other venturers.[144]

A jointly controlled entity, as its name implies, is a separate legal entity in which each venturer has an interest.[145] In its consolidated financial statements, a venturer should include its interest in a joint venture entity by means of proportional consolidation.[146] This should be carried out either:

(a)   on a line-by-line basis (i.e. the venturer includes its share of the assets, liabilities, income and expenditure of the entity in the similar items in its own consolidated accounts); or

(b)   on an aggregated basis (i.e. the venturer includes separate line items for its share of the total assets, liabilities, income and expenditure of the entity in its own consolidated accounts).[147]

This is irrespective of whether the entity is a corporate body or not. IAS 31 also permits, but strongly discourages, the use of equity accounting for jointly controlled entities in consolidated financial statements.[148] It expresses no preference for the treatment of jointly controlled entities in a venturer's individual financial statements.[149]

To summarise, the above requirements of IAS 31 principally differ from FRS 9 in the following respects:

■   Of the three types of joint venture in IAS 31 only 'jointly controlled entities' meet the definition of joint venture in FRS 9. 'Jointly controlled operations' and 'jointly controlled assets' as defined in IAS 31 will normally meet the definition of a JANE under FRS 9.

■   Crucially, FRS 9 requires joint ventures to be equity accounted, whereas under IAS 31, the benchmark treatment is proportional consolidation, with equity accounting being merely an allowed (and strongly discouraged) alternative.

6.1.3   *Possible future developments*

The whole question of equity accounting is currently being debated by the so-called G4+1 group. The Group comprises members of the national standard-setting bodies of Australia, Canada, New Zealand, the UK and the USA, with members of the IASC attending as observers. Whilst the group has no official status, it has become an increasingly important influence on the thinking both of the IASC and of the national standard setters represented on it.

At a meeting in March 1999, the G4+1 discussed a preliminary paper on the underlying rationale for equity accounting. As a result of those discussions it was agreed to explore limiting the use of equity accounting to jointly controlled entities, with full consolidation being used for controlled entities and other investments being marked to market.[150]

Whilst this would be a radical change from current practice, we are far from convinced that it would represent an improvement. The great majority of investments that are currently equity accounted for as associates are large holdings in unquoted companies, the valuation of which is difficult and often subjective. On the whole, we believe that equity accounting is a more reliable and objective method of capturing changes in the value of such investments than use of a 'market value' where there is no real market.

There was further discussion on these issues at a further meeting in June 1999, after which it was announced that the group was shortly to publish a paper on accounting for joint ventures.[151]

6.2   US

The principal pronouncement in the US which deals with this topic is APB 18 – *The Equity Method of Accounting for Investments in Common Stock*. This requires equity accounting to be followed by an investor whose investment in voting stock gives it the ability to exercise significant influence over the operating and financial policies of an investee,[152] including investments in corporate joint ventures.[153] Equity accounting will also be appropriate in accounting for investments in unincorporated joint ventures and partnerships; however, circumstances and industry practice may determine that the investor accounts on a pro-rata basis for its share of the assets, liabilities, revenues and expenses.[154]

The main differences between APB 18 and FRS 9 are as follows:

- Under FRS 9, an investor has actually to exercise significant influence over an investment for it to be treated as an associate. Under APB 18, it is sufficient to have the ability to exercise such influence.

- Under APB 18, a holding of 20% or more of the voting rights is presumed to give rise to significant influence. Whilst this is also true under FRS 9, the FRS suggests that this presumption may be rebutted relatively frequently. APB 18 also states that a holding of less than 20% should lead to a presumption that the investor does not have significant influence.[155]

- APB 18 applies (mandatorily) only to corporate joint ventures, whereas FRS 9 applies to all joint ventures. APB 18 requires joint ventures to be accounted for under the equity method; FRS 9 requires the gross equity method to be applied.

- Where an investor does not prepare group accounts, APB 18 requires associates and joint ventures to be equity accounted in the single entity accounts.[156] FRS 9 (and the Companies Act) requires them to be carried at cost (or valuation).

- Under APB 18, the share of post-tax profits or losses is normally included as a single line item.[157] Under FRS 9, the investing group's share of the results is included at every main level of the profit and loss account except turnover and cost of sales.

- FRS 9 requires disclosure of supplementary financial information where total associates represent more than 15% (or an individual associate represents more than 25%) of the group. APB 18 requires various disclosures to be made in respect of all associates where they are material.[158]

- Under APB 18, an investor is required to disclose the potential effect on its reported earnings of the exercise of any outstanding options, convertibles etc. of the investee.[159] FRS 9 does not require disclosure of such outstanding rights, but does require them to be taken into account when calculating the investor's share to be equity accounted.

■   Under FRS 9 losses of associates must continue to be accounted for until
      some event occurs that marks the investor's irreversible withdrawal. Under
      APB 18, the basic treatment is to account for losses only until the
      investment is reduced to zero unless either (a) the investor has an
      obligation to make good those losses or (b) the loss is expected to be
      reversed in the near future.[160]

7   CONCLUSION

Equity accounting for associates has been a feature of UK accounting since the
issue of SSAP 1 in 1971. Although SSAP 1 was revised a number of times since
then, the basic rules remained little changed until the issue of FRS 9 in 1997.
Overall, however, we find FRS 9 a somewhat disappointing standard,
particularly when the time taken to develop it is taken into account.

The underlying rationale appears to have been a concern that some companies,
particularly following a failed takeover bid, were unjustifiably taking credit for
their share of profits of investees without subsequently being able to gain access
to them. Although we agree that it is inappropriate to equity account in such
cases, we think that SSAP 1, if properly applied, already precluded it. A more
frequent abuse of the standard actually lay in the other direction where
companies, particularly in start-up situations, sometimes argued that they should
not equity account for an investment (which was often loss-making) on the
grounds that they did not have significant influence. By restricting the criteria to
active and actual influence, the ASB has run the risk of lending support to such
arguments.

The one major issue that FRS 9, in our view, should have addressed, but did not,
is the treatment of contributions of non-cash assets to form a new joint venture
with another party. This is becoming an increasingly common way of setting up
new business arrangements in the UK and it is a cause of concern that FRS 9
apparently allows such contributions to be accounted for in a number of ways,
with materially different accounting results.

Also, we are not convinced by FRS 9's requirements in respect of accounting for
joint ventures and JANEs. The ASB's conceptual objection to proportional
consolidation appears to hang mainly on an assertion that it is misleading to
aggregate controlled with jointly controlled operations. This might be more
convincing if FRS 9 did not require what is, in effect, almost complete
proportional consolidation in the profit and loss account, and did not encourage
disclosure of other information on a proportional consolidation basis.

We hope that the ASB will consider these two aspects of FRS 9 when it comes
to review it. We also urge the ASB not to go down the road currently under
discussion by the G4+1 Group, whereby only joint ventures would be equity
accounted and other non-controlled investments (including associates) would be

marked to market (see 6.1.3 above). With all its faults, equity accounting for associates has generally served its purpose very well for nearly thirty years. It would, in our view, be a mistake to abandon it in the pursuit of what many will see as a somewhat esoteric conceptual purity, particularly when the proposed alternative will be generally perceived as a less robust method of accounting, given the absence of reliable market values for large holdings of unquoted securities, which currently comprise the great majority of equity accounted investments.

References

1 CA 85, Sch. 4A, para. 22.
2 Discussion Paper, *Associates and Joint Ventures*, ASB, July 1994, paras. 4.12-4.13.
3 *Ibid.*, para. 2.11.
4 CA 85, Sch. 4A, para. 19(1)(a).
5 FRED 11, *Associates and Joint Ventures*, ASB, March 1996, para. 9
6 *Ibid.*, para. 3.7.
7 FRS 9, *Associates and Joint Ventures*, ASB, November 1997, Appendix III, para. 3.
8 Throughout FRS 9 and this Chapter, 'subsidiary' means 'subsidiary undertaking' as defined in FRS 2 and the Companies Act 1985 (see Chapter 5).
9 FRS 9, para 4.
10 CA 85, Schedule 4A, para. 20(1)(a).
11 FRS 9, para. 4.
12 *Ibid*
13 *Ibid.*
14 FRS 9, para. 43.
15 *Ibid.*, para. 13.
16 SSAP 1, *Accounting for associated companies*, ASC, 1971, amended 1982 and 1990, para. 13.
17 FRS 9, para. 4.
18 *Ibid.*
19 *Ibid.*, para. 16.
20 Royal Bank of Scotland plc, Annual Report and Accounts 1998, p. 57; Daily Mail and General Trust plc, Annual Report and Accounts 1998, p. 52.
21 FRS 9, para. 14.
22 *Ibid.*, para. 15.
23 *Ibid.*, para. 16.
24 *Ibid.*, para. 4.
25 FRS 8, *Related party disclosures*, ASB, October 1995, para. 2.5(a)(iii).
26 FRS 9, para. 17.
27 CA 85, Sch. 4A, para. 20.
28 *Ibid.*, s 260(1).
29 *Ibid.*, s 260(3).
30 FRS 9, para. 4.
31 *Ibid.*
32 CA 85, s 258.
33 FRS 9, para. 4.
34 *Ibid.*, para. 12.
35 *Ibid.*, para. 10.
36 *Ibid.*, para. 11.

37 CA 85 s 229(3); FRS 2, *Accounting for subsidiary undertakings*, ASB, July 1992, para. 25a.
38 CA 85, Sch. 4A, para. 19.
39 FRS 9, para. 4
40 *Ibid.*, Appendix III, para. 13
41 *Ibid.*, para. 8.
42 *Ibid.*, paras. 24 and 25.
43 *Ibid.*, Appendix I, para. 6.
44 FRS 9, paras. 8 and 9.
45 *Ibid.*, para. 9.
46 FRS 9, para. 4
47 *Ibid.*, para. 27
48 *Ibid.*
49 *Ibid.*
50 FRS 3, *Reporting financial performance*, ASB, October 1992, para. 39.
51 FRS 9, para. 27.
52 *Ibid.*, para. 61.
53 *Ibid.*, para. 27.
54 *Ibid.*, para. 28.
55 *Company Reporting*, No. 108, June 1999, p. 5.
56 *Ibid.*, para. 29.
57 CA 85, Sch. 4, para. 12(a).
58 *Ibid.*, para. 26.
59 *Ibid.*, para. 4.
60 *Ibid.*, para. 21.
61 *Ibid.*
62 *Ibid.*, Appendix III, para. 7(b).
63 FRS 9, para. 23.
64 *Ibid.*, para. 22.
65 *Ibid.*, Appendix III, para. 13.
66 FRS 9, para. 23.
67 FRS 3, para. 14.
68 FRS 9, para 49.
69 *Ibid.*
70 *Ibid.*, paras. 18 and 24.
71 FRS 9, para. 31(a).
72 *Ibid.*, para. 35.
73 *Ibid.*, para. 31(a).
74 *Ibid.*
75 *Ibid.*, para. 32.
76 *Ibid.*, para. 31(b).
77 FRS 2, para. 39.
78 ED 50, *Consolidated accounts*, ASC, June 1990, para. 115.
79 FRS 9, para. 36.
80 SIC-13, *Jointly Controlled Entities – Non-monetary Contributions by Venturers*, IASC, June 1998, para. 5(c).
81 *Ibid.*, para. 5(b).
82 CA 1985, Schedule 4, para. 12(a)
83 FRRP PN 43, Financial Reporting Review Panel, October 1996.
84 FRS 9, para. 31(b).
85 *Ibid.*, paras. 31(c) and 35.
86 *Ibid.*, para. 31(d).
87 *Ibid.*
88 *Ibid.*, para. 37.
89 CA 85, Schedule 4A, para. 2(2); FRS 2, para. 43
90 FRS 9, para. 31(d).
91 *Ibid*, para. 35.

92 *Ibid.*, paras. 31(a).
93 FRS 10, *Goodwill and Intangible Assets*, ASB, December 1997, para. 19(b).
94 FRS 9, para. 38.
95 *Ibid.*, para. 39.
96 *Ibid.*, para. 32.
97 *Ibid.*, para. 34.
98 *Ibid.*, para. 33.
99 *Ibid.*
100 *Ibid.*, para. 34.
101 *Ibid.*, paras. 44-45.
102 *Ibid.*, paras. 46-47.
103 *Ibid.*, para. 40.
104 *Ibid.*
105 *Ibid.*
106 *Ibid.*, para. 42.
107 *Ibid.*, para. 43.
108 Discussion paper, *Derivatives and other financial instruments*, ASB, July 1996, paras. 1.4.1 and 2.5.1.
109 FRS 9, para. 41.
110 *Ibid.*, para. 52.
111 *Ibid.*, para. 53.
112 *Ibid.*, para. 54.
113 FRS 2, para. 53.
114 FRS 9, para. 55.
115 CA 1985, Schs. 4, 9 and 9A, Balance sheet formats, Sch 4A para. 21, Sch 9, Pt. II, para. 3, Sch 9A Pt. II, paras. 3 and 4.
116 FRS 9 para. 55.
117 *Ibid.*, para. 56.
118 SSAP 1, paras. 15, 38.
119 FRS 9, para. 57.
120 *Ibid.*, para. 58(a).
121 *Ibid.*, para. 58(b).
122 *Ibid.*, para. 58(c).
123 *Ibid.*
124 *Ibid.*, para. 58.
125 Reed International P.L.C, Report and Accounts 1998, pp. 27-31.
126 CA 85, Sch. 5, Part II, para. 22.
127 *Ibid.*, Sch. 4A, para. 21; Sch. 5, Part II, para. 23
128 *Ibid.*, Sch. 5, Part II, para. 21.
129 IAS 28, *Accounting for investments in associates*, IASC, reformatted 1994, para. 3.
130 *Ibid.*, para. 5.
131 APB 18, *The Equity Method of Accounting for Investments in Common Stock*, AICPA, March 1971, para. 17.
132 FRS 9, Appendix II, para. 2.
133 *Ibid.*
134 IAS 28, para. 8.
135 FRS 9, Appendix II, para. 2.
136 IAS 28, para. 12.
137 *Ibid.*, para. 3.
138 *Ibid.*, para. 28.
139 *Ibid.*, para. 22.
140 IAS 31, *Financial Reporting of Interests in Joint Ventures*, IASC, Reformatted 1994, para. 2.
141 *Ibid.*, para. 8.
142 *Ibid.*, para. 10.
143 *Ibid.*, paras. 13–15.
144 *Ibid.*, para. 16.

145 *Ibid.*, para. 19.
146 *Ibid.*, para. 25.
147 *Ibid.*, para. 28.
148 *Ibid.*, paras. 32–33.
149 *Ibid.*, para. 41.
150 ASB PN 136, ASB, April 1999.
151 ASB PN 144, ASB, July 1999
152 APB 18, *The Equity Method of Accounting for Investments in Common Stock*, AICPA, March 1971, para. 17.
153 *Ibid.*, para. 16.
154 AIN-APB 18, *The Equity Method of Accounting for Investments in Common Stock: Accounting Interpretations of APB Opinion No. 18*, AICPA, November 1971–February 1972, para. 2.
155 APB 18, para. 17.
156 *Ibid.*, para. 16.
157 *Ibid.*, para. 19c.
158 *Ibid.*, para. 20d.
159 *Ibid.*, para. 20e.
160 *Ibid.*, para. 19i.

Chapter 8 Foreign currencies

1 THE DEVELOPMENT OF AN ACCOUNTING STANDARD IN THE UK

1.1 Background

A company can engage in foreign currency operations in two ways. It may enter directly into transactions which are denominated in foreign currencies, the results of which need to be translated into the currency in which the company reports. Alternatively, it may conduct foreign operations through a foreign enterprise, normally a subsidiary or associated company, which keeps its accounting records in a foreign currency and, in order to prepare consolidated financial statements, will need to translate the financial statements of the foreign enterprise into its own reporting currency.[1] Accounting for these translation processes has been one of the most significant problem areas in financial reporting in recent years.

Before the present UK standard was developed, there were four distinct methods which could be used in the translation process:

(a) *current rate method* – all assets and liabilities are translated at the current rate of exchange, i.e. the exchange rate at the balance sheet date;

(b) *temporal method* – assets and liabilities carried at current prices are translated at the current rate of exchange, e.g. cash, debtors, creditors, investments at market value. Assets and liabilities carried at past prices, e.g. property, investments at cost, prepayments, are translated at the rate of exchange in effect at the dates to which the prices pertain;

(c) *current/non-current method* – all current assets and current liabilities are translated at the current rate of exchange. Non-current assets and liabilities are translated at historical rates, i.e. the exchange rate in effect at the time the asset was acquired or the liability incurred; and

(d) *monetary/non-monetary method* – monetary assets and liabilities, i.e. items which represent the right to receive or the obligation to pay a fixed amount of money, are translated at the current rate of exchange. Non-monetary assets and liabilities are translated at the historical rate.

There was no consensus either in the UK or internationally on the best theoretical approach to adopt. In essence, the arguments surround the choice of exchange rates to be used in the translation process and the subsequent treatment of the exchange differences which arise. The fact that foreign exchange rates had become increasingly volatile only magnified the effects of using different approaches. As a result of these problems, the subject of foreign currency translation had been on the agenda of the ASC since the early 1970s.

1.2 SSAP 6

When SSAP 6[2] was issued in April 1974, although dealing mainly with extraordinary items and prior year adjustments, it gave recognition to the problem by stating: 'At a time of frequent movement of foreign currency exchange rates, the accounting treatment of foreign currency transactions and conversions and the distinguishing of items that are extraordinary present many problems. These problems are currently under study with a view to the issue of a separate accounting standard. In the meantime, the accounting policies adopted should be disclosed and explained in accordance with Statement of Standard Accounting Practice No. 2 Disclosure of accounting policies.'[3]

1.3 ED 16

The first pronouncement by the ASC on the treatment of the problems was in ED 16[4] issued in September 1975. This did not require any particular method of translation to be adopted other than to require foreign currency borrowings to be translated at closing rates of exchange.[5] It mainly set out how exchange differences were to be dealt with; namely, in the profit and loss account as part of the ordinary activities of the business except:

(a) differences arising from extraordinary items, which were themselves to be treated as extraordinary items;

(b) differences arising on translation of fixed assets, which were to be treated as if they were revaluations of fixed assets, i.e. taken direct to reserves unless they represented losses not covered by gains on the same items held in reserves or gains on items where losses had previously been taken to profit and loss account; and

(c) exchange losses arising on the translation of foreign currency net borrowings, which could be taken to reserves to offset gains arising in (b) above which had also been taken to reserves.[6]

The ASC acknowledged that this was just a temporary measure by stating: 'The subject is one in which conflicting opinions are strongly held and it must be expected that some time will elapse before a standard is issued which will describe the method or methods of accounting to be applied.'[7]

1.4   ED 21

The next step by the ASC was to issue ED 21[8] in September 1977. This limited the options of accounting methods by permitting the use of either the closing rate or temporal methods.[9]

If the closing rate method were to be used, exchange differences would be treated in the same way as required by ED 16, except that the differences which were to be dealt with in the profit and loss account as part of the ordinary activities of the business were now to be treated as a quasi-extraordinary item, i.e. as a separate item after the profit for the year from ordinary operations.[10]

If the temporal method were to be used, then all exchange differences would be reported as part of the profit from ordinary operations unless they arose from items which would themselves be treated as extraordinary.[11]

The main comments received on ED 21 were that:[12]

(a)   there was a lack of clarity in the distinction between the treatment of exchange differences in individual companies and differences arising on consolidation;

(b)   two methods of translation should not be allowed when the closing rate was so widely adopted in the UK;

(c)   the occasions when the cover concept could be applied were not clear;

(d)   the different treatment given to current assets as opposed to fixed assets was not supported;

(e)   support for the use of the closing rate and the average rate for translating the profit and loss account was evenly divided;

(f)   the net investment concept in ED 21 was inadequately developed;

(g)   there was strong support for keeping exchange differences out of operating profit but little support for displaying them as quasi-extraordinary items; and

(h)   the global concept for offsetting gains and losses on exchange was thought to be imprudent.

1.5   ED 27

The reason why ED 16 and ED 21 permitted the use of either the closing rate or the temporal method was that the latter method was the only method which could be used in the USA. Following the implementation of SFAS 8 in the USA it gradually became evident that when consolidated accounts are drawn up in a relatively weak currency, such a method produces results which do not seem to make commercial and economic sense. As a result the FASB decided to review its existing standard, SFAS 8.[13] In Canada, the Canadian Institute of Chartered Accountants (CICA), which had published its standard on foreign currencies in 1978,[14] advocating the use of the temporal method, suspended it in 1979 pending further study. Conscious of the need for international harmonisation in this field, there then followed a long period of consultation between the ASC, the FASB and the CICA.

So it was that the ASC issued ED 27 in October 1980. This was based on the closing rate/net investment concept and proposed an approach to translation which is related to the cash flow consequences of exchange movements. Exchange differences which give rise to cash flows, i.e. those resulting from business transactions, are reported as part of the profit or loss for the period. Other exchange differences which do not give rise to cash flows, because they result from retranslations of the holding company's long-term investment in the foreign subsidiary, are reported as reserve movements. ED 27 also introduced another version of the cover concept where a foreign currency loan has been used to finance the purchase of an investment in a foreign subsidiary.

1.6   SSAP 20

The majority of commentators supported the principles set out in ED 27 and so it eventually formed the basis of SSAP 20. However, since the exposure draft was issued the Companies Act 1981 had been enacted. The accounting rules contained in the Act had certain ramifications on the treatment of exchange differences and these had to be resolved. It was not, therefore, until April 1983 that SSAP 20 was finally issued. Its requirements are discussed at 2 below.

1.7   UITF Abstracts

Over the years the UITF has issued a number of abstracts dealing with aspects relating to foreign currencies.

In June 1993 it issued Abstract 9 – *Accounting for Operations in Hyper-inflationary Economies* – which became effective for accounting periods ending on or after 23 August 1993. This is discussed at 3.4.9 A below.

Following the introduction of a new tax regime for foreign exchange differences in 1995 whereby exchange gains and losses on foreign currency borrowings can now be taxable, the UITF considered how the tax effect on such borrowings should be reported and also whether taxation should be taken into account in applying the cover method under SSAP 20. Accordingly, in February 1998 the UITF issued Abstract 19 – *Tax on gains and losses on foreign currency borrowings that hedge an investment in a foreign enterprise,* which became effective for accounting periods ending on or after 23 March 1998. The requirements of this abstract are dealt with at 2.5.2 and 3.5 below.

In addition, as a result of some concerns over the advent of the introduction of the euro, in March 1998 the UITF issued Abstract 21 – *Accounting issues arising from the proposed introduction of the euro,* again effective for accounting periods ending on or after 23 March 1998. This was supplemented in August 1998 by an Appendix to the abstract dealing with some further accounting issues. These are discussed at 3.8 below.

1.8　The ASB's financial instruments project

The ASB has embarked on a project dealing with financial instruments which impinges on many of the areas covered by this chapter, particularly in relation to forward currency contracts, currency swaps and currency options as well as extending the disclosures in respect of foreign currencies. In September 1998 the ASB issued the first instalment of its rules on financial instruments, FRS 13 – *Derivatives and Other Financial Instruments: Disclosures*. The requirements of FRS 13 and a discussion of the ASB's other proposals for financial instruments are covered in Chapter 9.

The exposure draft which preceded FRS 13 had proposed currency disclosures which were aimed at showing the currency exposures which gave rise to exchange differences taken directly to reserves under SSAP 20 (see 2.3.7 below). It tried to do this by suggesting disclosure of a currency analysis of net assets compared to borrowings.[15] This proposed requirement was dropped from the final standard for non-financial entities, although a variant of the requirement was retained for banks. In February 1999 the ASB resurrected this idea by issuing an exposure draft to amend SSAP 20 calling for such disclosures. However, many commentators raised other concerns about SSAP 20 and proposed further amendments or even a full-scale review of SSAP 20. In the light of these comments in May 1999 the ASB withdrew this proposal but indicated that it plans to review SSAP 20 in its entirety and that an exposure draft will be developed as soon as its project on financial instruments has settled some key issues that are fundamental to foreign currency translation.

2　REQUIREMENTS OF SSAP 20

2.1　Objectives of translation

SSAP 20 states that 'the translation of foreign currency transactions and financial statements should produce results which are generally compatible with the effects of rate changes on a company's cash flows and its equity and should ensure that the financial statements present a true and fair view of the results of management actions. Consolidated statements should reflect the financial results and relationships as measured in the foreign currency financial statements prior to translation.'[16] It will be seen when looking at the requirements of the standard that in certain situations these objectives conflict.

2.2　Definitions of terms

The main definitions of terms which are contained in SSAP 20 are as follows:[17]

A *foreign enterprise* is a subsidiary, associated company or branch whose operations are based in a country other than that of the investing company or whose assets and liabilities are denominated mainly in a foreign currency.

A *foreign branch* is either a legally constituted enterprise located overseas or a group of assets and liabilities which are accounted for in foreign currencies.

Translation is the process whereby financial data denominated in one currency are expressed in terms of another currency. It includes both the expression of individual transactions in terms of another currency and the expression of a complete set of financial statements prepared in one currency in terms of another currency.

A company's *local currency* is the currency of the primary economic environment in which it operates and generates net cash flows.

An *exchange rate* is a rate at which two currencies may be exchanged for each other at a particular point in time; different rates apply for spot and forward transactions.

The *closing rate* is the exchange rate for spot transactions ruling at the balance sheet date and is the mean of the buying and selling rates at the close of business on the day for which the rate is to be ascertained.

A *forward contract* is an agreement to exchange different currencies at a specified rate. The difference between the specified rate and the spot rate ruling on the date the contract was entered into is the discount or premium on the forward contract.

The *net investment* which a company has in a foreign enterprise is its effective equity stake and comprises its proportion of such foreign enterprise's net assets; in appropriate circumstances, intra-group loans and other deferred balances may be regarded as part of the effective equity stake.

Monetary items are money held and amounts to be received or paid in money and, where a company is not an exempt company, should be categorised as either short-term or long-term. Short-term monetary items are those which fall due within one year of the balance sheet date. (An exempt company is essentially a bank or an insurance company.)

2.3   Individual companies

As indicated in 1.1 above, a company can either enter directly into foreign currency transactions or it may conduct foreign operations through a foreign enterprise. The standard therefore requires that the procedures to be adopted when accounting for foreign operations should be considered in two stages, namely the preparation of the financial statements of the individual company and the preparation of the consolidated financial statements.

The first stage to be considered is the preparation of the financial statements of an individual company. The procedures to be followed should be applied to each company within a group prior to the preparation of the consolidated accounts. The general requirements of SSAP 20 are as follows.

2.3.1 Recording of transactions

Generally, all foreign currency transactions entered into by a company should be translated into its local currency at the exchange rate ruling on the date the transaction occurs. An average rate for a period is acceptable if rates do not fluctuate significantly during the relevant period. Where the transaction is to be settled at a contracted rate then that rate should be used.[18]

2.3.2 Retranslation of monetary/non-monetary assets and liabilities at balance sheet date

At the balance sheet date, monetary assets and liabilities denominated in foreign currencies resulting from unsettled transactions should be translated using the closing rate. Again, where the transaction is to be settled at a contracted rate then that rate should be used.[19]

Non-monetary assets should not be retranslated but should remain translated at the rate ruling when they were originally recorded.[20]

2.3.3 Treatment of exchange differences

Exchange differences will arise when transactions are settled at exchange rates which are different from those used when the transactions were previously recorded. They will also arise on any unsettled transactions at the balance sheet date if the closing rate differs from those used previously.[21] All exchange differences should be included as part of the profit or loss for the period from ordinary activities, unless they arise as a result of events which themselves are treated as extraordinary, in which case they should be included as part of such items. This treatment should be adopted for all monetary items irrespective of whether they are short-term or long-term and irrespective of whether the exchange differences are gains or losses.[22]

The rationale for the above treatment is that the exchange differences have already been reflected in cash flows, in the case of settled transactions, or will be in the future in the case of unsettled transactions.[23] This is consistent with the accruals concept; it results in reporting the effect of a rate change that will have cash flow effects when the event causing the effect takes place. As paragraph 10 of SSAP 20 explains, 'exchange gains on unsettled transactions can be determined at the balance sheet date no less objectively than exchange losses; deferring the gains whilst recognising the losses would not only be illogical by denying in effect that any favourable movement had occurred but would also inhibit fair measurement of the performance of the enterprise in the year. In particular, this symmetry of treatment recognises that there will probably be some interaction between currency movements and interest rates and reflects more accurately in the profit and loss account the true results of currency involvement.'

2.3.4   Worked examples

The above general requirements can be illustrated in the following examples:

Example 8.1

A UK company purchases plant and machinery on credit from a US company for US$328,000 in January 1999 when the exchange rate is £1=US$1.64. The company records the asset at a cost of £200,000. At the UK company's year end at 31 March 1999 the account has not yet been settled. The closing rate is £1=US$1.61. The creditor would be retranslated at £203,727 in the balance sheet and an exchange loss of £3,727 would be reported as part of the profit or loss for the period from ordinary operations. The cost of the asset would remain as £200,000.

Example 8.2

A UK company sells goods to a German company for €87,000 on 28 February 1999 when the exchange rate is £1=€1.45. It receives payment on 31 March 1999 when the exchange rate is £1=€1.50. On 28 February the company will record a sale and corresponding debtor of £60,000. When payment is received on 31 March the actual amount received is only £58,000. The loss on exchange of £2,000 would be reported as part of the profit or loss for the period from ordinary operations.

2.3.5   Examples of accounting policies

> *Extract 8.1: United Biscuits (Holdings) plc (1998)*
>
> **Foreign currency translation** [extract]
>
> **Company:**   Monetary assets and liabilities denominated in foreign currencies are translated at the rate of exchange ruling at the balance sheet date. Transactions in foreign currencies are recorded at the rate ruling at the date of the transaction, all differences being taken to the profit and loss account.

> *Extract 8.2: Safeway plc (1999)*
>
> **Foreign Currency** [extract]
>
> Transactions in foreign currencies are translated into sterling at the rates of exchange current at the dates of the transactions. Foreign currency monetary assets and liabilities in the balance sheet are translated into sterling at the rates of exchange ruling at the end of the year. Resulting exchange gains and losses are taken to the profit and loss account.

2.3.6   Exchange gains where there are doubts as to convertibility or marketability

As indicated in 2.3.3 above SSAP 20 requires both exchange gains and losses on long-term monetary items to be recognised in the profit and loss account. However, paragraphs 11 and 50 of the standard indicate that where there are doubts as to the convertibility or marketability of the currency in question then it may be necessary to consider on the grounds of prudence whether the amount of any exchange gain, or the amount by which exchange gains exceed past exchange losses on the same items, to be recognised in the profit and loss account should be restricted.

2.3.7 Foreign equity investments financed by borrowings

One exception to the rule that non-monetary items are not retranslated is where foreign equity investments have been financed by foreign currency borrowings, or where the borrowings have been taken out to hedge the exchange risks associated with existing equity investments. Application of the procedures set out in 2.3.1 to 2.3.3 above would cause exchange differences on loans to pass through the profit and loss account while no exchange differences would arise on the equity investments. The standard recognises that in such situations a company may be covered in economic terms against any movement in exchange rates and states that it would be inappropriate in such cases to record an accounting profit or loss when exchange rates change.[24]

Paragraph 51 of the standard therefore allows companies in such situations, subject to the conditions set out below, to treat the cost of the investments as being denominated in the appropriate foreign currencies and retranslating them at the closing rates each year. Where this is done the resulting exchange differences should be taken to reserves. The exchange differences arising on the related foreign currency borrowings should also be taken to reserves and should not be reported as part of the profit or loss for the period.

The conditions to be fulfilled are:

(a)   exchange gains or losses arising on the borrowings may be offset only to the extent of exchange differences arising on the equity investments in that particular period;

(b)   the foreign currency borrowings should not exceed the total amount of cash that the investments are expected to generate, whether from profits or otherwise; and

(c)   the accounting treatment should be applied consistently from period to period.

Example 8.3

A UK company purchases equity shares in a Canadian company for C\$1,200,000 on 31 January 1999 when the exchange rate is £1=C\$2.48. It partially finances the investment by borrowing C\$1,000,000 on the same date. The investment would therefore be recorded as £483,871 and the loan as £403,226. At the UK company's year end of 30 April 1999 the closing rate is £1=C\$2.34. The loan would be retranslated as £427,350 resulting in an exchange loss of £24,124. The investment would be translated as £512,821 resulting in an exchange gain of £28,950. Both the exchange gain and the exchange loss would be taken to reserves.

If the UK company did not wish to adopt the treatment contained in paragraph 51 of the standard then the exchange loss of £24,124 would have to be reported as part of the profit or loss for the period and the investment would have been retained at its original cost of £483,871 with no exchange gain being recognised.

Examples of accounting policies of companies which have adopted such a treatment are illustrated below:

Extract 8.3: Ladbroke Group PLC (1998)

Foreign currencies [extract]

Gains or losses arising on the translation of the net assets of overseas subsidiaries and associates are taken to reserves, net of exchange differences arising on related foreign currency borrowings, as are differences arising on equity investments denominated in foreign currencies in the holding company's accounts.

Extract 8.4: Imperial Chemical Industries PLC (1998)

Foreign currencies [extract]

In the Group accounts, exchange differences arising on consolidation of the net investments in overseas subsidiary undertakings and associated undertakings are taken to reserves, as are differences arising on equity investments denominated in foreign currencies in the Company accounts. Differences on relevant foreign currency loans are taken to reserves and offset against the differences on net investments in both Group and Company accounts.

2.3.8   Forward contracts

The standard recognises that where a company has covered a foreign currency transaction by entering into a related or matching forward contract it may not be appropriate to record the transaction using the spot rate ruling at the date of the transaction or to retranslate the monetary asset or liability at the closing rate. Accordingly, paragraphs 46 and 48 allow companies to use the rate of exchange specified in the related or matching forward contract instead.

Example 8.4

A UK company sells goods to a Swiss company for SFr100,000 on 30 April 1999 at which date the exchange rate is £1=SFr2.45. As payment is not due until 31 July 1999, the company decides to hedge its exposure to exchange risk by entering into a forward contract to sell SFr100,000 in three months time at a rate of £1=SFr2.425. As a result the company has fixed the amount of sterling it will realise from the sale at £41,237. The standard allows the company to record the sale and corresponding debtor at that amount and not at £40,816 using the rate ruling at the date of the transaction. If at its year end of 30 June 1999 the exchange rate is £1=SFr2.50 there is no need for the company to retranslate the debtor at £40,000 and record a loss on exchange, but it retains it at £41,237. This treatment recognises the fact that as a result of entering into the forward contract the company is no longer susceptible to exchange rate movements and therefore there should be no effect on its profit or loss if exchange rates do change.

An example of an accounting policy of a company which adopts such a treatment is illustrated below:

Extract 8.5: Reckitt & Colman plc (1998)

Foreign currency translation [extract]

Transactions denominated in foreign currencies are translated at the rate of exchange on the day the transaction occurs or at the contracted rate if the transaction is covered by a forward exchange contract.

Assets and liabilities denominated in a foreign currency are translated at the exchange rate ruling on the balance sheet date or, if appropriate, at a forward contract at a forward contract rate.

2.4   Consolidated accounts

The second stage to be considered is the preparation of consolidated financial statements.

2.4.1   Scope

The procedures to be adopted apply not only to the inclusion of subsidiaries but also to the incorporation of the results of associated companies. They also apply when the results of a foreign branch are to be incorporated into the accounts of an individual company.[25]

2.4.2   Choice of method

The standard requires that the method to be used for translating the financial statements of a foreign enterprise should reflect the financial and other operational relationship which exists between the holding company and its foreign enterprise.[26] It recognises that in most cases this means that the consolidated accounts will be prepared using the closing rate/net investment method as described in 2.4.3 below. However, as explained in 2.4.4 below, in certain circumstances the standard requires the temporal method to be used.

The method used for translating the financial statements of a foreign enterprise should only be changed when the financial and other operational relationship changes and renders the method used inappropriate.[27]

2.4.3   Closing rate/net investment method

For most investing companies in the UK where foreign operations are carried out by foreign enterprises it is normally the case that the foreign enterprises operate as separate or quasi-independent entities.[28] The day to day operations of the foreign enterprise will be based in its local currency, are likely to be financed wholly or partly in its own currency, and will not be dependent on the reporting currency of the holding company. The foreign enterprise will be managed so as to maximise the local currency profits attributable to the holding company. Consequently, the financial statements of the foreign enterprise expressed in its local currency will be the best available indicator of its performance and value to the group. In order to preserve the inherent relationships included in these local currency financial statements it is therefore necessary to use a single rate of exchange when translating the financial statements in the preparation of the consolidated financial statements.[29]

A   Balance sheet

The standard therefore requires that under the closing rate/net investment method the balance sheet of the foreign enterprise should be translated into the reporting currency of the investing company using the rate of exchange at the balance sheet date, i.e. the closing rate.[30]

B   Profit and loss account

The profit and loss account of the foreign enterprise under this method should be translated at the closing rate or at an average rate for the period.[31] In our view the use of the closing rate is preferable as this will achieve the objective of translation of reflecting the financial results and relationships as measured in the foreign currency financial statements prior to translation.[32] The use of an average rate is justified by SSAP 20 on the grounds that it reflects more fairly the profits or losses and cash flows as they arise to the group throughout an accounting period.[33] Although the standard allows a choice as to which rate is used it does require that the one selected is applied consistently from period to period.[34]

C   Treatment of exchange differences

Exchange differences will arise under the closing rate/net investment method if the exchange rate used for translating the balance sheet differs from that ruling at the previous balance sheet date or at the date of any subsequent capital injection or reduction.[35] Exchange differences will also arise where an average rate is used for translating the profit and loss account and this differs from the closing rate.[36] The standard requires that both such exchange differences should be recorded as a movement on reserves.[37] As paragraph 19 of SSAP 20 explains: 'If exchange differences arising from the retranslation of a company's net investment in its foreign enterprise were introduced into the profit and loss account, the results from trading operations, as shown in the local currency financial statements would be distorted. Such differences may result from many factors unrelated to the trading performance or financing operations of the foreign enterprise; in particular, they do not represent or measure changes in actual or prospective cash flows. It is therefore inappropriate to regard them as profits or losses and they should be dealt with as adjustments to reserves.'

Example 8.5

A UK company owns 100% of the share capital of a foreign company which was set up ten years ago in 1988 when the exchange rate was £1=FC4. It uses the closing rate method for incorporating the accounts of the subsidiary in its consolidated accounts for the year ended 31 December 1998. The exchange rate at the year end is £1=FC2 (1997: £1=FC3). The profit and loss account of the subsidiary for that year and its balance sheet at the beginning and end of the year in local currency and translated into sterling are as follows:

Profit and loss account

	FC	£
Sales	35,000	17,500
Cost of sales	(33,190)	(16,595)
Depreciation	(500)	(250)
Interest	(350)	(175)
Profit before taxation	960	480
Taxation	(460)	(230)
Profit after taxation	500	250

Balance sheets	1997 FC	1998 FC	1997 £	1998 £
Fixed assets	6,000	5,500	2,000	2,750
Current assets				
Stocks	2,700	3,000	900	1,500
Debtors	4,800	4,000	1,600	2,000
Cash	200	600	67	300
	7,700	7,600	2,567	3,800
Current liabilities				
Creditors	4,530	3,840	1,510	1,920
Taxation	870	460	290	230
	5,400	4,300	1,800	2,150
Net current assets	2,300	3,300	767	1,650
	8,300	8,800	2,767	4,400
Long-term loans	3,600	3,600	1,200	1,800
	4,700	5,200	1,567	2,600
Share capital	1,000	1,000	250	250
Retained profits	3,700	4,200	1,317	2,350
	4,700	5,200	1,567	2,600

The movement in retained profits is as follows:

	£
Balance brought forward	1,317
Profit for year	250
Exchange difference	783
	2,350

The exchange difference of £783 is the exchange difference on the opening net investment in the subsidiary and is calculated as follows:

Opening net assets at opening rate	– FC4,700 at FC3=£1 =	£1,567
Opening net assets at closing rate	– FC4,700 at FC2=£1 =	£2,350
Exchange gain on net investment		£ 783

This exchange gain should be shown as a movement on reserves and should not be reflected in the profit and loss account.

If the company were to have adopted a policy of translating the profit and loss account at an average rate of exchange and the appropriate weighted average rate was FC2.5=£1 then the profit and loss account would have been as follows:

	FC	£
Sales	35,000	14,000
Cost of sales	(33,190)	(13,276)
Depreciation	(500)	(200)
Interest	(350)	(140)
Profit before taxation	960	384
Taxation	(460)	(184)
Profit after taxation	500	200

The difference between the profit and loss account translated at an average rate, i.e. £200, and at the closing rate, i.e. £250, would be recorded as a movement in reserves.

Examples of accounting policies of companies using this method of translation are illustrated below:

Extract 8.6: Racal Electronics Plc (1999)

4   Foreign currencies [extract]

The accounts of overseas subsidiary companies, associated companies and joint ventures, and assets and liabilities denominated in foreign currencies held by United Kingdom companies, have been translated at the rates ruling on 31 March 1999. Exchange differences arising on the retranslation of these accounts at the beginning of the year, and differences on long term foreign currency loans which relate to investments in overseas companies, are dealt with as a movement in reserves.

> *Extract 8.7: BP Amoco p.l.c. (1998)*
>
> **Foreign currencies** [extract]
>
> On consolidation, assets and liabilities of subsidiary undertakings are translated into US dollars at closing rates of exchange. Income and cash flow statements are translated at average rates of exchange.
>
> Exchange differences resulting from the retranslation of net investments in subsidiary and associated undertakings at closing rates, together with differences between income statements translated at average rates and at closing rates, are dealt with in reserves.

2.4.4   Temporal method

As already indicated in 2.4.2 above, the standard recognises that in certain circumstances it would be inappropriate to use the closing rate/net investment method for translating the financial statements of a foreign enterprise and requires the temporal method to be used.

Such a method is to be used where the trade of the foreign enterprise is more dependent on the economic environment of the investing company's currency than that of its own reporting currency. By using the temporal method the consolidated accounts reflect the transactions of the foreign enterprise as if they had been carried out by the investing company itself.[38]

A   Determination of dominant currency

It is impossible to specify any one factor which would indicate when the temporal method should be used. The standard indicates that the following factors should be taken into account:[39]

(a)   'the extent to which the cash flows of the enterprise have a direct impact upon those of the investing company' (e.g. whether there is a regular and frequent movement of cash between the holding company and the foreign enterprise or whether there are only occasional remittances of, for example, dividends);

(b)   'the extent to which the functioning of the enterprise is dependent directly upon the investing company' (e.g. whether management is based locally or at head office and whether pricing decisions are based on local competition and costs or are part of a worldwide decision process);

(c)   'the currency in which the majority of the trading transactions are denominated' (e.g. whether the foreign currency is used for both invoicing goods and paying expenses, or whether the majority of such items are denominated in the currency of the investing company);

(d)   'the major currency to which the operation is exposed in its financing structure' (e.g. whether the company is dependent on local financing or whether the majority of the financing is in the currency of the investing company and possibly obtained through, or guaranteed by, that company).[40]

B   Example of situations

Situations where the temporal method may be appropriate are where the foreign enterprise:

(a)   'acts as a selling agency receiving stocks of goods from the investing company and remitting the proceeds back to the company';

(b)   'produces a raw material or manufactures parts or sub-assemblies which are then shipped to the investing company for inclusion in its own products';

(c)   'is located overseas for tax, exchange control or similar reasons to act as a means of raising finance for other companies in the group'.[41]

C   Method

The mechanics of the temporal method are essentially the same as those procedures used in preparing the accounts of an individual company[42] discussed in 2.3 above. In theory, this means translating each transaction of the foreign enterprise at the rates ruling at the date of each transaction. In order to simplify the translation process, however, average rates may be used as an approximation.

Example 8.6

Using the same basic facts as Example 8.5 above, i.e. a UK company owns 100% of the share capital of a foreign company which was set up ten years ago in 1988 when the exchange rate was £1=FC4. It uses the temporal method for incorporating the accounts of the subsidiary in its consolidated accounts for the year ended 31 December 1998. The exchange rate at the year end is £1=FC2 (1997: £1=FC3) and the average exchange rate for the year is £1=FC2.5.

Details of fixed assets are as follows:

Date of acquisition	1 January 1994	1 July 1995
	FC	FC
Cost	2,500	5,000
Aggregate depreciation – 31/12/97	668	832
Depreciation charge for year	167	333
Aggregate depreciation – 31/12/98	835	1,165
Net book value – 31/12/97	1,832	4,168
Net book value – 31/12/98	1,665	3,835

The relevant exchange rates at the dates of acquisition are £1=FC3.8 and £1=FC3.4 respectively. The average rates of exchange relating to opening and closing stocks are £1=FC3.3 and £1=FC2.4.

The profit and loss account of the subsidiary for that year and its balance sheet at the beginning and end of the year in local currency and translated into sterling using the temporal method are as follows:

Profit and loss account

	FC	Exchange rate	£
Sales	35,000	Average – FC2.5	14,000
Opening stock	2,700	Historical – FC3.3	818
Purchases	33,490	Average – FC2.5	13,396
Closing stock	(3,000)	Historical – FC2.4	(1,250)
Cost of sales	(33,190)		(12,964)
Gross profit	1,810		1,036
Depreciation	(500)	Historical – FC3.8/3.4	(142)
Interest	(350)	Average – FC2.5	(140)
Translation loss		Balance	(596)
Profit before taxation	960		158
Taxation	(460)	Average – FC2.5	(185)
Profit after taxation	500		(27)

Balance sheets	1997 FC	Exchange rate	1997 £	1998 FC	Exchange rate	1998 £
Fixed assets	6,000	FC3.8/3.4	1,708	5,500	FC3.8/3.4	1,566
Current assets						
Stocks	2,700	FC3.3	818	3,000	FC2.4	1,250
Debtors	4,800	FC3	1,600	4,000	FC2	2,000
Cash	200	FC3	67	600	FC2	300
	7,700		2,485	7,600		3,550
Current liabilities						
Creditors	4,530	FC3	1,510	3,840	FC2	1,920
Taxation	870	FC3	290	460	FC2	230
	5,400		1,800	4,300		2,150
Net current assets	2,300		685	3,300		1,400
	8,300		2,393	8,800		2,966
Long-term loans	3,600	FC3	1,200	3,600	FC2	1,800
	4,700		1,193	5,200		1,166
Share capital	1,000	FC4	250	1,000	FC4	250
Retained profits	3,700	Balance	943	4,200	Balance	916
	4,700		1,193	5,200		1,166

The translation loss of £596 which is shown in the profit and loss account represents the exchange loss on monetary items during the year and is calculated as follows:

	Opening monetary items	Closing monetary items
	FC	FC
Debtors	4,800	4,000
Cash	200	600
Creditors	(4,530)	(3,840)
Taxation	(870)	(460)
Long-term loans	(3,600)	(3,600)
	(4,000)	(3,300)

			£	£
Opening monetary items at opening rate	– FC(4,000) at FC3	=	(1,334)	
Opening monetary items at closing rate	– FC(4,000) at FC2	=	(2,000)	
				(666)
Change in monetary items at average rate	– FC700 at FC2.5	=	280	
Change in monetary items at closing rate	– FC700 at FC2	=	350	
				70
Total exchange loss				(596)

Examples of accounting policies of companies using this method of translation are illustrated below:

Extract 8.8: Reuters Group PLC (1998)

Foreign currency translation [extract]

Where it is considered that the functional currency of an operation is sterling the financial statements are expressed in sterling on the following basis:

a. Fixed assets are translated into sterling at the rates ruling on the date of acquisition as adjusted for any profits or losses from related financial instruments.

b. Monetary assets and liabilities denominated in a foreign currency are translated into sterling at the foreign exchange rates ruling at the balance sheet date.

c. Revenue and expenses in foreign currencies are recorded in sterling at the rates ruling for the month of the transactions.

d. Any gains or losses arising on translation are reported as part of profit.

Extract 8.9: Babcock International Group PLC (1999)

Foreign currencies [extract]

Where it is considered that the results of an overseas undertaking is more dependent on sterling than its own reporting currency, the Financial Statements of the undertaking are consolidated using the temporal method, thereby treating all transactions as though they had been entered into by the undertaking itself in sterling.

2.4.5 Foreign equity investments financed by borrowings

We have already seen in 2.3.7 above that where a company has used foreign currency borrowings to finance, or provide a hedge against, its foreign equity investments the standard allows the exchange differences on the borrowings to be taken to reserves rather than the profit and loss account.

A similar provision for consolidated accounts is contained in paragraph 57 of the standard. This is because under the closing rate method exchange differences on the net investment in foreign enterprises are taken to reserves and not reflected in the profit for the year. It would therefore be inappropriate for exchange differences on group borrowings which have been used to finance the investments or provide a hedge against the exchange risk associated with the investments to be taken to the profit and loss account. As the group is covered in economic terms against any movement in exchange rates then the exchange differences on the borrowings should be taken to reserves to offset the exchange differences on the net investments in the foreign enterprises.[43]

Where foreign currency borrowings of the group, therefore, have been used to finance, or provide a hedge against group equity investments then, subject to the conditions set out below, the exchange differences arising on the related foreign currency borrowings may be offset against the exchange differences arising on the retranslation of the net investments as a movement on reserves so that they are not reported as part of the profit or loss for the period.[44]

The conditions to be fulfilled are:

(a)   the relationships between the investing company and the foreign enterprises concerned justify the use of the closing rate method for consolidation purposes;

(b)   exchange gains or losses arising on foreign currency borrowings are offset only to the extent of the exchange differences arising on the net investments in foreign enterprises in that particular period;

(c)   the foreign currency borrowings should not exceed the total amount of cash that the net investments are expected to generate, whether from profits or otherwise; and

(d)   the accounting treatment should be applied consistently from period to period.[45]

The last three conditions are similar to those contained in paragraph 51 of the standard relating to the offset procedures for individual companies. The first condition is necessary as it is only when the closing rate method is used that the financial statements would not otherwise reflect the fact that the group is covered in economic terms against movements in exchange differences. Where a foreign enterprise is consolidated using the temporal method then, as all exchange differences are taken to the profit and loss account, any exchange differences on related borrowings should also be taken to the profit and loss account.

Although the general principles of paragraph 57 of the standard are the same as those used in the offset procedures for individual companies there are a number of differences in detail. These will normally require the calculations used in the individual companies' financial statements to be reversed on consolidation and the amount recalculated for the purposes of the consolidated financial statements:

(a)   in the individual companies' financial statements *all* equity investments are included in the calculation, whereas for the consolidated financial statements investments which are consolidated using the temporal method are excluded;

(b)   in the individual companies' financial statements it is the exchange difference on the carrying value of the investment which is included in the calculation, whereas for the consolidated financial statements it is the exchange difference on the underlying net assets which is included; and

(c)   in the individual companies' financial statements only borrowings of the company can be included in the calculation, whereas in the consolidated financial statements borrowings of any group company can be included.

The only situation in which there will be no need to recalculate the amount of the offset is where the provisions of paragraph 51 of the standard have been applied in the investing company's financial statements to a foreign equity investment which is neither a subsidiary nor an associated company. This is because paragraph 58 of the standard allows the amount of the offset in the individual company's financial statements to be carried forward to the consolidated financial statements, since the exchange risk is hedged in both the company and the group. It should be borne in mind, however, that this does not mean that all such equity investments throughout the group can be retranslated at closing rates and the resulting exchange differences used in the offset process.

Example 8.7

A UK company is preparing its financial statements for the year ended 31 December 1998. It has two wholly owned subsidiaries:

(i) A Japanese company which it acquired a number of years ago at a cost of ¥500m. It incorporates the financial statements of the subsidiary in its consolidated financial statements using the closing rate method. During 1997 the company borrowed ¥1,000m repayable in ten years' time in 2007, to provide a hedge against the investment, which was then considered to be worth in excess of ¥1,500m. The net assets of the subsidiary at 31 December 1997 were ¥1,200m.

(ii) A Canadian company which it set up on 1 February 1998 at a cost of C$5m. It is going to incorporate this subsidiary in its consolidated financial statements using the temporal method. The exchange loss for the period is £38,925. It partially financed the acquisition of the shares by borrowing C$4m repayable in 2003.

In addition, the UK company has a 10% investment in a US company which it acquired in 1997 at a cost of US$2m, financed by means of a US dollar loan of the same amount. At 31 December 1998 none of the loan has been repaid.

The relevant exchange rates are:

	£1=¥	£1=C$	£1=US$
31/12/97	207		1.64
1/2/98		2.39	
31/12/98	188	2.56	1.66

Using the provisions of paragraphs 51, 57 and 58 of the standard the treatment in the company and consolidated financial statements would be as follows:

Company financial statements			Profit/loss for year £	Reserves £
Investment in Japanese company				
31/12/97 – ¥500m	@ 207	= £2,415,459		
31/12/98 – ¥500m	@ 188	= £2,659,574		
Exchange gain		£ 244,115		244,115
¥1,000m Loan				
31/12/97 – ¥1,000m	@ 207	= £4,830,918		
31/12/98 – ¥1,000m	@ 188	= £5,319,149		
Exchange loss		£ (488,231)	(244,116)	(244,115)
Investment in Canadian company				
1/2/98 – C$5m	@ 2.39	= £2,092,050		
31/12/98 – C$5m	@ 2.56	= £1,953,125		
Exchange loss		£ (138,925)		(138,925)
C$4m Loan				
1/2/98 – C$4m	@ 2.39	= £1,673,640		
31/12/98 – C$4m	@ 2.56	= £1,562,500		
Exchange gain		£ 111,140		111,140
Investment in US company				
31/12/97 – US$2m	@ 1.64	= £1,219,512		
31/12/98 – US$2m	@ 1.66	= £1,204,819		
Exchange loss		£ (14,693)		(14,693)
US$2m Loan				
31/12/97 – US$2m	@ 1.64	= £1,219,512		
31/12/98 – US$2m	@ 1.66	= £1,204,819		
Exchange gain		£ 14,693		14,693
Net exchange loss			(244,116)	(27,785)

The exchange loss on the ¥1,000m loan taken to reserves has had to be restricted as a result of condition (a) of paragraph 51 of the standard.

It can be seen that where an exchange gain arises on a foreign loan and it is taken to reserves under paragraph 51 then it is possible to have a net exchange loss being taken to reserves as the exchange loss on the investment can exceed the exchange gain on the related loan.

Consolidated financial statements	Profit/loss for year £	Reserves £
Net investment in Japanese company		
31/12/97 – ¥1,200m @ 207 = £5,797,101		
31/12/98 – ¥1,200m @ 188 = £6,382,979		
Exchange gain	£ 585,878	585,878
¥1,000m Loan		
31/12/97 – ¥1,000m @ 207 = £4,830,918		
31/12/98 – ¥1,000m @ 188 = £5,319,149		
Exchange loss	£ (488,231)	(488,231)
Investment in Canadian company		
Exchange loss (as given)	(38,925)	
C$4m Loan		
1/2/98 – C$4m @ 2.39 = £1,673,640		
31/12/98 – C$4m @ 2.56 = £1,562,500		
Exchange gain	£ 111,140	111,140
Investment in US company		
31/12/97 – US$2m @ 1.64 = £1,219,512		
31/12/98 – US$2m @ 1.66 = £1,204,819		
Exchange loss	£ (14,693)	(14,693)
US$2m Loan		
31/12/97 – US$2m @ 1.64 = £1,219,512		
31/12/98 – US$2m @ 1.66 = £1,204,819		
Exchange gain	£ 14,693	14,693
Net exchange gain	72,215	97,647

In the consolidated financial statements all of the exchange loss on the ¥1,000m loan can be taken to reserves as it is less than the exchange gain on the net investment in the Japanese subsidiary. The exchange gain on the C$4m loan has to be taken to the profit/loss for the year as the temporal method is used and therefore condition (a) of paragraph 57 of the standard is not met. It can be seen that the same treatment is adopted for the US$ investment and loan as in the company financial statements as a result of paragraph 58.

2.4.6   Associates and joint ventures

As indicated in 2.4.1 above, the provisions of the standard relating to consolidated financial statements apply to the incorporation of the results of all foreign enterprises, including associates and joint ventures. The definition of associates and joint ventures and the required accounting treatment are dealt with in FRS 9[46] and are discussed in Chapter 7.

When incorporating the results of foreign associates or joint ventures, therefore, the closing rate/net investment method should normally be used. In view of the fact that the investing company only has significant influence over an associate and does not control it, and only has joint control over a joint venture, it is unlikely that the affairs of such entities are so closely linked with those of the investing company that the use of the temporal method will be appropriate. The requirements of the closing rate/net investment method have been explained in 2.4.3 above.

2.4.7   Foreign branches

The provisions of the standard relating to consolidated financial statements also apply to the incorporation of the results of foreign branches, not only in the consolidated financial statements but also in the financial statements of an individual company.[47] The definition of a foreign branch contained in the standard is such that it includes not just a legally constituted enterprise located overseas but also a group of assets and liabilities which are accounted for in foreign currencies.[48]

The reason for this wide definition was to cater for the situation where a company had international assets such as ships or aircraft which earn revenues in a foreign currency, normally US dollars, financed by borrowings in the same currency and to allow the use of the closing rate/net investment method. If this had not been done, then under the provisions of the standard it would have been necessary for such assets to be translated at historical rates, the borrowings to be translated at closing rates and any exchange difference thereon taken to the profit or loss for the year. The cover method contained in paragraphs 51 and 57 of the standard would not have applied as these provisions only deal with borrowings which finance equity investments and not other types of non-monetary assets.

A   Possible situations

In addition to the situation referred to above, the statement issued by the ASC on the publication of the standard also quoted the following as being examples of situations where a group of assets and liabilities should be accounted for under the closing rate/net investment method:

(a)   a hotel in France financed by borrowings in French francs;

(b)   a foreign currency insurance operation where the liabilities are substantially covered by the holding of foreign currency assets.[49]

B   Treatment

The results of a foreign branch should be incorporated in the financial statements in the same way as foreign subsidiaries are included in the consolidated financial statements, i.e. the closing rate/net investment method should normally be used.[50] The use of this method is explained in 2.4.3 above.

However, in many cases the operations of a branch are a direct extension of the trade of the investing company and its cash flows have a direct impact upon those of the investing company in which case the temporal method is required to be used. It should not automatically be assumed, therefore, that the closing rate/net investment method is the correct method to use and careful consideration should be given to the factors referred to in 2.4.4 above.

British Airways effectively regards its aircraft and related financing as a foreign branch as illustrated in its accounting policy below:

Extract 8.10: British Airways Plc (1999)

Foreign currency translation

Foreign currency balances are translated into sterling at the rates ruling at the balance sheet date, except for certain loan repayment instalments which are translated at the forward contract rates where instalments have been covered forward at the balance sheet date. Aircraft that generate substantial foreign currency revenues are accounted for as foreign currency assets and are translated into sterling at rates ruling at the balance sheet date. Changes in the sterling value of outstanding foreign currency loans, finance leases and hire purchase commitments which finance certain fixed assets are taken to reserves together with the differences arising on the translation of the related foreign currency denominated assets. Exchange differences arising on the translation of overseas subsidiary undertakings and associated undertakings are taken to reserves. Profits and losses of such undertakings are translated into sterling at average rates of exchange during the year. All other profits or losses arising on translation are dealt with through the profit and loss account.

2.5 Disclosures

2.5.1 Requirements of SSAP 20

The standard requires the following disclosures to be made in the financial statements:

(a) the methods used in the translation of the financial statements of foreign enterprises, i.e. closing rate method or temporal method. Where the closing rate method is used it should also be stated whether the closing rate or an average rate has been used to translate the profit and loss account;[51]

(b) the net amount of exchange gains and losses on foreign currency borrowings less deposits charged or credited to the profit and loss account.[52] It should be noted that exchange differences on deposits have to be taken into account; it is not just the exchange differences on borrowings;

(c) the net amount of exchange gains and losses on foreign currency borrowings less deposits offset in reserves under the provisions of paragraphs 51, 57 and 58 of the standard;[53]

(d) the net movement on reserves arising from exchange differences.[54] This will normally be the exchange differences on the net investments of those subsidiaries translated using the closing rate method.

There is no requirement for exchange differences taken to profit and loss account, other than those referred to in (b) above, to be disclosed. This is because the ASC considered 'that such disclosure is not necessarily helpful since it is influenced by the extent to which the company's trade is conducted in foreign currencies and the extent to which the company covers its exchange risk by entering into forward exchange contracts. Moreover, an agreement to settle a transaction in a foreign currency reflects only one aspect of the pricing or purchasing decision involved in normal trading. In any case a small difference may disguise a significant gain and significant loss and disclosure of the net figure will not indicate the risks inherent in trading in foreign currencies.'[55]

2.5.2 *Examples of disclosures*

Examples of disclosures of the methods used have been illustrated earlier in the chapter in giving extracts of accounting policies used. A good example of an accounting policy for foreign currencies which covers most of the various aspects is that of Reckitt & Colman:

Extract 8.11: Reckitt & Colman plc (1998)

Foreign currency translation

Transactions denominated in foreign currencies are translated at the rate of exchange on the day the transaction occurs or at the contracted rate if the transaction is covered by a forward exchange contract.

Assets and liabilities denominated in a foreign currency are translated at the exchange rate ruling on the balance sheet date or, if appropriate, at a forward contract rate. Exchange differences arising in the accounts of individual undertakings are included in the profit and loss account except that, where foreign currency borrowings have been used to finance equity investments in foreign currencies, exchange differences arising on the borrowings are dealt with through reserves to the extent that they are covered by exchange differences arising on the net assets represented by the equity investments.

The accounts of overseas subsidiary and associated undertakings are translated into Sterling on the following basis:

Assets and liabilities are at the rate of exchange ruling at the year-end date except for tangible fixed assets of undertakings operating in countries where hyper-inflation exists, which are translated at historical rates of exchange.

Profit and loss account items at the average rate of exchange for the financial year. An inflation adjustment is charged in arriving at local currency profits of undertakings operating in hyper-inflation countries before they are translated to reflect the impact of the hyper-inflation on the undertakings' working capital requirements.

Exchange differences arising on the translation of accounts into Sterling are recorded as movements on reserves. Where foreign currency borrowings have been used to finance equity investments in foreign currencies, exchange differences arising on the borrowings are dealt with through reserves to the extent that they are covered by exchange differences arising on the net assets represented by the equity investments.

(The particular problem of hyper-inflation is discussed in 3.4.9 below.)

The requirements to disclose those exchange differences taken to reserves are usually met in one of two ways:

(a)   Show both types of exchange difference separately.

Extract 8.12: Reckitt & Colman plc (1998)

22.   Reserves [extract]

	Group Profit and loss £m	Parent Profit and loss £m
Net exchange gain on foreign currency borrowings*	3.7	4.8
Exchange differences arising on translation of net investments in overseas subsidiary undertakings	(17.0)	(4.8)

*Net exchange gain on foreign currency borrowings is stated after deducting UK corporation tax of £1.5m (1997, £8.0m) in accordance with current accounting practice.

(b)   Show a net figure but disclose that relating to borrowings by way of a note.

Extract 8.13: Bunzl plc (1998)

20   Movements on reserves [extract]

	Share premium account £m	Revaluation reserve £m	Profit and loss account £m
Currency translation movement	–	–	(5.0)

Currency gains/(losses) of £0.2m (1997: £(2.7)m) relating to foreign currency exchange contracts and borrowings to finance investment overseas have been included within the currency translation movement in the profit and loss account.

Such exchange differences have to be reported in the statement of total recognised gains and losses and UITF 19 requires that the amount of any tax charges and credits that are also taken to that statement should be disclosed, in addition to the gross amount of the exchange differences on the borrowings.[56]

2.5.3   FRS 13

As mentioned earlier, in September 1998 the ASB issued FRS 13 which requires disclosures relating to the foreign currency aspects of a company's financial instruments (see 3 of Chapter 9).

3   PROBLEM AREAS

3.1   Individual companies

3.1.1   *Date of transaction*

The basic requirement of paragraph 46 of SSAP 20 is that transactions should be recorded at the rate ruling at the date the transaction occurred. No guidance is given in the standard as to what that date should be. SFAS 52 gives some help by defining the transaction date as being the date at which a transaction is recorded in accounting records in conformity with generally accepted accounting principles.[57] The following example illustrates the difficulty in determining the transaction date:

Example 8.8: Establishing the transaction date

A UK company buys an item of stock from a German company. The dates relating to the transaction, and the relevant exchange rates, are as follows:

Date	Event	£1=€
14 April 1999	Goods are ordered	1.50
5 May 1999	Goods are shipped from Germany and invoice dated that day	1.53
7 May 1999	Invoice is received	1.52
10 May 1999	Goods are received	1.51
14 May 1999	Invoice is recorded	1.52
28 May 1999	Invoice is paid	1.53

In our view the date of the transaction should be when the company should recognise an asset and liability as a result of the transaction. This will normally be when the risks and rewards of ownership of the goods have passed to the UK company.

It is unlikely at the date the goods are ordered that all the risks and rewards of ownership of the goods have passed to the UK company and therefore this date should not be used as the date of the transaction.

If the goods are shipped free on board (f.o.b.) then as the risks and rewards of ownership pass on shipment then this date should be used.

If, however, the goods are not shipped f.o.b. then the risks and rewards of ownership normally pass on delivery and therefore the date the goods are received should be treated as the date of the transaction.

The dates on which the invoice is received and is recorded are irrelevant to when the risks and rewards of ownership pass and therefore should not be considered to be the date of the transaction. In practice, it may be acceptable that as a matter of administrative convenience that the exchange rate at the date the invoice is recorded is used, particularly if there is no undue delay in processing the invoice. If this is done then care should be taken to ensure that the exchange rate used is not significantly different from that ruling on the 'true' date of the transaction.

It is clear from SSAP 20 that the date the invoice is paid is not the date of the transaction because if it were then no exchange differences would arise on unsettled transactions.

Most companies do not indicate in their accounting policies what is meant by the date of transaction. One company which does is Racal Electronics:

Extract 8.14: Racal Electronics Plc (1999)

4   Foreign currencies [extract]

United Kingdom exports in foreign currencies are converted at the rates relative to the period of shipment.

3.1.2 Use of average rate

As indicated in 2.3.1 above, rather than using the actual rate ruling at the date of the transaction 'if the rates do not fluctuate significantly, an average rate for the period may be used as an approximation'.[58] For companies which engage in a large number of foreign currency transactions it will be more convenient for them to use an average rate rather than using the exact rate for each transaction. If an average rate is to be used, what guidance can be given in choosing and using such a rate?

(a) Length of period
     As an average rate should only be used as an approximation of actual rates then care has to be taken that significant fluctuations in the day to day exchange rates do not arise in the period selected. For this reason the period chosen should not be too long. We believe that the maximum length of period should be one month and where there is volatility of exchange rates it will be better to set rates on a more frequent basis, say, a weekly basis, especially where the value of transactions is significant.

(b) Estimate of average rate
     The estimation of the appropriate average rate will depend on whether the rate is to be applied to transactions which have already occurred or to transactions which will occur after setting the rate. Obviously, if the transactions have already occurred then the average rate used should relate to the period during which those transactions occurred; e.g. purchase transactions for the previous week should be translated using the average rate for that week, not an average rate for the week the invoices are being recorded.
     If there is no time delay between the date of the transaction and the date of recording and the rate is therefore being set for the following period then the rate selected should be a reasonable estimate of the expected exchange rate during that period. This could be done by using the closing rate at the end of the previous period or by using the actual average rate for the previous period. We would suggest that the former be used. Although a forward rate could be used, it should be remembered that forward rates are *not* estimates of future exchange rates but are a function of the spot rate adjusted by reference to interest differentials (see 3.3.1 A below). Whatever means is used to estimate the average rate, the actual rates during the period should be monitored and if there is a significant move in the exchange rate away from the average rate then the rate being applied should be revised.

(c) Application of average rate
     We believe that average rates should only be used as a matter of convenience where there are a large number of transactions. Even where an average rate is used we would recommend that for large one-off transactions the actual rate should be used; e.g. purchase of a fixed asset or

an overseas investment or taking out a foreign loan. Where the number of foreign currency transactions is small it will probably not be worthwhile setting and monitoring average rates and therefore actual rates should be used.

3.1.3   Dual rates or suspension of rates

One practical difficulty in translating foreign currency amounts is where there is more than one exchange rate for that particular currency depending on the nature of the transaction. In some cases the difference between the exchange rates can be small and therefore it probably does not matter which rate is actually used. However, in other situations, such as was the case with the South African rand, the difference can be quite significant. In these circumstances, what rate should be used? SSAP 20 is silent on this matter, but some guidance can be found in SFAS 52. It states that 'the applicable rate at which a particular transaction could be settled at the transaction date shall be used to translate and record the transaction. At a subsequent balance sheet date, the current rate (closing rate) is that rate at which the related receivable or payable could be settled at that date.'[59] Companies should therefore look at the nature of the transaction and apply the appropriate exchange rate. If there are doubts as to whether funds will be receivable at the more favourable rate then it may be necessary on the grounds of prudence to use the less favourable rate.

Another practical difficulty which could arise is where for some reason exchangeability between two currencies is temporarily lacking at the transaction date or at the subsequent balance sheet date. Again SSAP 20 makes no comment on this matter but SFAS 52 requires that the first subsequent rate at which exchanges could be made shall be used.[60]

3.1.4   Monetary or non-monetary

As discussed in 2.3.2 above, SSAP 20 generally requires that monetary items denominated in foreign currencies be retranslated using closing rates at each balance sheet date and non-monetary items should not be retranslated. Monetary items are defined as 'money held and amounts to be received or paid in money'.[61] The only examples of such items given in the standard are the obvious ones such as 'cash and bank balances, loans and amounts receivable and payable'.[62] Examples of non-monetary items given are equally obvious: 'plant, machinery and equity investments'.[63] Further examples of non-monetary items are those items listed in SFAS 52 as accounts to be remeasured using historical exchange rates when the temporal method is being applied.[64] Even with this guidance there are a number of particular items where the distinction may not be that clear.

A   Deposits or progress payments paid against fixed assets or stocks

Companies may be required to pay deposits or progress payments when acquiring fixed assets or stocks from overseas. The question then arises as to whether such payments should be retranslated as monetary items or not.

Example 8.9

A UK company contracts to purchase an item of plant and machinery for C$10,000 on the following terms:

Payable on signing contract (1 April 1999)   – 10%
Payable on delivery (19 April 1999)   – 40%
Payable on installation (3 May 1999)   – 50%

At 30 April 1999 the company has paid the first two amounts on the due dates when the respective exchange rates were £1=C$2.46 and £1=C$2.41. The closing rate at its balance sheet date, 30 April 1999, is £1=C$2.34.

	(i)	(ii)
	£	£
First payment – C$1,000	407	427
Second payment – C$4,000	1,660	1,709
	2,067	2,136

(i) If the payments made are regarded as progress payments then the amounts should be treated as non-monetary items and included in the balance sheet at £2,067. This would appear to be consistent with SFAS 52 which in defining 'transaction date' states: 'A long-term commitment may have more than one transaction date (for example, the due date of each progress payment under a construction contract is an anticipated transaction date).'[65]

(ii) If the payments made are regarded as deposits, and are refundable, then the amounts should probably be treated as monetary items and included in the balance sheet at £2,136 and an exchange gain of £69 recorded in the profit and loss account.

In practice, it will often be necessary to consider the terms of the contract to ascertain the nature of the payments made in order to determine the appropriate accounting treatment.

B   Debt securities held as investments

Companies may acquire or invest in overseas debt securities which have a fixed term of redemption, e.g. a US treasury bond or loan stock of an American company.

Example 8.10

A UK company invests in US$1m 6% Treasury bonds at a cost of US$950,000 on 30 September 1998 when the exchange rate was £1=US$1.70. The bonds are redeemable at par on 30 September 2003. At the company's year end, 31 March 1999, the closing rate of exchange is US$1.61.

In our view whether the investment is regarded as a monetary item or not depends on how the company is accounting for the investment.

(i)   At lower of cost or market value

If the company is accounting for the investment at lower of cost or market value, then the investment should be regarded as a non-monetary item and recorded at a cost of £558,824 and no exchange difference taken to profit and loss account. If the investment is written down because the market value at the year end is lower than cost, then the investment should be translated using the rate of £1=US$1.61 as this is the rate relevant to the measurement date of the item.

(ii)   At amortised cost

If the company intends holding the investment to the redemption date and is amortising the difference between cost and redemption value over the period to redemption we believe that the carrying amount is in the nature of a monetary item and therefore should be retranslated at the closing rate:

Cost	$950,000		
Amortisation – $50,000 ÷ 10	5,000		
	$955,000	@ £1=US$1.61	= £593,168

(iii)   Marking to market

If the company is accounting for the investment by marking it to market then the investment should be translated using the rate of £1=US$1.61 as this is the rate relevant to the measurement date of the item.

C   Foreign currency loans convertible into equity shares

Occasionally companies in the UK have issued bonds (or debentures), expressed in a foreign currency (usually US dollars), which are convertible into a fixed number of ordinary shares of the UK company at the holder's option. The terms of the bonds normally require the company to redeem the bonds at a fixed amount (expressed in the foreign currency) at the end of their term. The holders and/or the company may also have the option of redeeming the bonds at an agreed amount (expressed in the foreign currency). The question then arises – do the bonds represent a monetary liability to be translated at closing rates or, because they may never be repaid in cash if they are converted for shares, do they represent a non-monetary item which should not be retranslated at closing rates?

Example 8.11

A UK company issues US$100m 6% convertible bonds on 31 March 1997 when the exchange rate was £1=US$1.64. The share price at that date was £2.75 per share and the conversion terms are based on a share price of £3.05. The bonds are expressed as being convertible into shares at a share price of £3.05 per share and at a fixed exchange rate of £1=US$1.64. Assuming full conversion, therefore, the maximum number of shares which would be issued would be 19,999,200. (The conversion terms could have been expressed as 'convertible into shares at a fixed price of US$5.00' or as 'convertible into 1,000 shares for each US$5,000 of bonds held'; the number of shares to be issued would effectively be the same.) The bonds are only redeemable in 20 years' time on 31 March 2017.

How should the company account for these bonds in its accounts for the year ended 30 September 1997 and the year ended 30 September 1998? The exchange rates at the balance sheet dates are £1=US$1.61 and £1=US$1.70 respectively. No bonds have been converted by 30 September 1998.

	Option 1 £m	Option 2 £m	Option 3 £m	Option 4 £m
Accounts for 30 September 1997				
Issue price	61.0	61.0	61.0	61.0
Exchange loss taken to p/l account	1.1	–	1.1	1.1
Balance sheet liability	62.1	61.0	62.1	62.1
Accounts for 30 September 1998				
Exchange gain taken to p/l account	(3.3)	–	(1.1)	(1.1)
Exchange gain deferred	–	–	–	(2.2)
Balance sheet liability	58.8	61.0	61.0	58.8

Option 1

It could be argued that until such time as the bonds have been converted they are monetary liabilities of the company and therefore should be retranslated at the closing rate of exchange at each year end. The fact that the company may never actually pay any cash if all the bondholders exercise their right of conversion is irrelevant. At the time of conversion the bondholder will assess whether it is beneficial to convert his holding into shares with regard to the then sterling amount of the bond using the exchange rate at that time. It is therefore this value which the company should treat as having received in return for the issue of shares.

Option 2

It could be argued that as the terms are likely to be set so that it is probable that conversion will take place during the term of the bond then as no cash will actually be paid by the company the bonds should not be treated as a monetary liability. They should, therefore, not be retranslated at closing rates of exchange at each balance sheet date but should be translated at the historical rate of US$1.64. The company should treat the amount received on the issue of the bonds as being the amount received on the issue of the shares.

Option 3

This is a variation of option 2 above. The difference is that until conversion has taken place some recognition should be given to the fact that the bonds may be redeemed and if the bonds translated at closing rate gives a greater liability than that using the historical rate then, on the grounds of prudence, a loss should be recognised. Gains would only be recognised to the extent that they matched losses previously taken to profit and loss account.

Option 4

This is a variation of option 1 above. The difference is that as the bonds may be converted into shares and not repaid in cash it is considered that they may not ultimately be a monetary item and therefore some recognition of this fact should be given. This is done by not recognising any gains in the profit and loss account except to the extent that they offset previously recognised losses. On the grounds of prudence any excess gains would be treated as a deferred credit as they may not ultimately be realised if the bonds are converted.

Under FRS 4, convertible bonds should be accounted for by reference to their current form, i.e. as liabilities; the finance cost should be calculated on the assumption that the debt will never be converted (see Chapter 15 at 2.2.2). Accordingly, it would be inconsistent, if for translation purposes, any allowance were made for the possible conversion of the bond. In our view, convertible bonds should now be treated no differently from normal borrowings for translation purposes and therefore option 1 should be adopted.

It would appear that such bonds are commonly treated as monetary items as they are retranslated at closing rates of exchange. However, frequently the cover method (see 2.3.7 and 2.4.5 above) is applied and the exchange differences on the bonds are taken to reserves and not reflected in the profit or loss for the year. LASMO in fact used to translate its convertible bonds at the fixed rate of exchange but changed its accounting policy in 1987:

Extract 8.15: London & Scottish Marine Oil PLC (1987)

1 Restatement of prior years

In the past, the liability under the 9¼ per cent Convertible Bonds Due 1999 (which are denominated in US dollars, and are convertible into ordinary shares at the option of the bond holders) was translated into sterling at the fixed exchange rate contained in the conditions of the Bonds. To reflect more accurately the liability prior to conversion, the liability has been translated at the exchange rate current at the balance sheet date. Prior years have been restated to reflect the above.

3.1.5 Treatment of exchange differences

The general rule of SSAP 20 is that all exchange differences on monetary items should be recognised as part of the profit or loss for the year.[66] Apart from the possible treatment of gains on long-term monetary items (see 2.3.6 above) and the treatment of exchange differences on borrowings financing, or hedging against, foreign equity investments (see 2.3.7 above), are there any other circumstances where it is possible for exchange differences not to be taken as part of the profit or loss for the year?

A Capitalisation of exchange differences

On many occasions where a UK company is acquiring an asset (other than an equity investment) from overseas it finances the acquisition by means of a foreign loan. The general rules of SSAP 20 require the asset to be translated at historical rates and for the loan to be translated at closing rates.[67] Consequently, exchange differences on the loan are taken to profit and loss account with no offsetting exchange difference on the asset. One means of avoiding this situation is if the asset and liability can be regarded as a foreign branch, as discussed in 2.4.7 above. However, it will not always be possible to regard them as such and therefore consideration has to be given to any other way in which the exchange differences on the loan need not be taken to the profit or loss for the year.

In our view the only other possible circumstance is where the asset is still in the course of production. The Companies Act 1985 requires assets to be included at their purchase price or production cost.[68] Under the Act, production cost can include indirect overheads attributable to the production of the asset to the extent that they relate to the period of production[69] One of the overheads that the Companies Act 1985 specifically allows to be included is interest on borrowings.[70]

However, FRS 15 – *Tangible Fixed Assets* – only allows directly attributable costs to be capitalised as part of the cost of an asset (see 2 of Chapter 10 for a fuller discussion of these requirements). This might suggest that exchange differences can no longer be included. Nevertheless, it is often argued that exchange differences on foreign borrowings are really part of the interest cost of the foreign borrowing. A UK company may take out a borrowing in a 'hard' currency, e.g. Swiss francs, rather than in sterling so as to benefit from the low interest rate. However, as this lower interest charge is likely to be offset by exchange losses on the borrowing then these losses should be treated as part of the interest cost of the borrowing. Indeed, paragraph 68 of SSAP 20 suggests that exchange differences on borrowings should be disclosed as part of 'other interest receivable/payable and similar income/expense' in the profit and loss account.

FRS 15 allows companies to adopt a policy of capitalising finance costs that are directly attributable to the construction of a fixed asset as part of the cost of the asset. The standard is silent on whether exchange differences are 'finance costs'; however, IAS 23, the international standard on the capitalisation of borrowing costs, specifically allows exchange differences to be included within borrowing costs. We therefore believe that exchange differences on foreign currency loans can be capitalised as part of the cost of the asset when interest costs on the same borrowings are being capitalised. Capitalisation of borrowing costs is discussed more fully in Chapter 13. Where such a treatment is being adopted then similar disclosure to that of the interest costs shown in 2.3.6 of that chapter should be given for the exchange differences on the borrowings.

B   *Hedging transactions – deferment of exchange differences*

The only specific reference which SSAP 20 makes to hedging is in respect of foreign currency borrowings providing a hedge against its foreign currency equity investments.[71] It also allows transactions to be recorded at the rate specified in a related forward contract,[72] which is another way of hedging. A further method by which companies may hedge against a foreign currency exposure is by matching foreign currency debtors in one currency with creditors in the same currency. By requiring the exchange differences on both these items to be taken to profit and loss account then SSAP 20 recognises this matching. However, what happens if one of the items is only a commitment (e.g. an agreement to purchase a fixed asset) and is still to be recognised in the accounts?

Example 8.12

A UK company has a debtor of US$1m resulting from a sale on 1 March 1999 and expects to receive payment on 31 March 1999. On 15 March 1999 the company signs a contract for the purchase of a fixed asset for US$1m from a US company. The asset is due to be delivered on 15 April 1999 with payment due on 31 May 1999. Rather than entering into a forward contract for the purchase of the US$1m to fix the sterling cost of the asset the company decides on 15 March 1999 that it will retain the US$1m once it is received from the debtor in a US$ bank account as a hedge against the cost of the fixed asset. Is it possible for the company to freeze the debtor at the rate ruling on 15 March 1999 and record the asset at the same amount? If not, can the exchange differences on the debtor and the bank balance be deferred and included in recording the cost of the asset?

It would appear that under SSAP 20 the answer to both questions is no. The debtor and bank balance are monetary items requiring to be translated at closing rates and the exchange differences on the settlement of the debtor and the bank balance taken to profit and loss account. The fixed asset should be recorded at the rate ruling at the date of the transaction, i.e. the date of delivery. It could be argued that this is illogical as the company could have entered into two forward contracts on 15 March 1999, one to buy US$1m to fix the cost of the fixed asset and one to sell US$1m to fix the amount to be received, and therefore have achieved what it wished.

SFAS 52 recognises this illogicality by requiring not only exchange gains and losses on a forward contract that is intended to hedge an identifiable foreign currency commitment to be deferred and included in the cost of the related foreign currency transaction, but also those which arise on other foreign currency transactions, e.g. cash balances, which are intended to hedge an identifiable foreign currency commitment.[73] This is because the accounting for the transaction should reflect the economic hedge of the foreign currency commitment.[74] Losses should not be deferred, however, if it is estimated that deferral would lead to recognising losses in later periods.[75] The requirements of SFAS 52 relating to forward contracts are more fully discussed in 3.3 below. SFAS 133 also allows a non-derivative financial instrument that gives rise to exchange differences to be designated as hedging changes in the fair value of an unrecognised firm commitment.[76] If all of the criteria are met, although the accounting is different under SFAS 133 in that exchange differences on both are taken to net income, the overall effect is the same as the exchange differences will offset each other.

3.2 Exchange gains on long-term monetary items

Paragraphs 11 and 50 of SSAP 20 indicate that where there are doubts as to the convertibility or marketability of the currency in question then it may be necessary to consider on the grounds of prudence whether the amount of any exchange gain, or the amount by which exchange gains exceed past exchange losses on the same items, to be recognised in the profit and loss account should be restricted.

3.2.1 In what circumstances do 'doubts as to convertibility or marketability' arise?

Such circumstances do not include normal currency fluctuations after the year end or even devaluations of a foreign currency after the year end.[77] It is thought that such circumstances will be rare and would only arise when there is political upheaval or very stringent exchange control regulations in the country whose currency is being considered.[78]

Such events will probably only arise in those countries whose currencies are weakest and therefore UK companies are unlikely to have liabilities expressed in the foreign currency on which exchange gains would arise. Even if a UK company did have a liability expressed in such a currency why should it not recognise the gain? It is unlikely that the UK company would have to pay more than the foreign currency amount at the closing rate and if anything is likely to pay less as the foreign currency will probably continue to weaken.

It is more likely that UK companies will have amounts receivable in these foreign currencies and therefore exchange losses are likely to arise. If for some reason such a currency were to strengthen against sterling so that exchange gains did arise on the amounts receivable the restriction of exchange gains suggested by SSAP 20 is irrelevant in these circumstances. If these circumstances did apply then it will probably be necessary for a UK company to make provision against all amounts receivable in that currency, whether short-term or long-term, to reduce them to their expected recoverable amounts.

If it is considered that the restriction of exchange gains contained in SSAP 20 is sufficient to deal with the situation, there are a number of problem areas relating to the accounting for the restriction.

3.2.2 Past exchange losses

Paragraph 50 of the standard states that 'the amount of the gain, or the amount by which exchange gains exceed past exchange losses on the same items to be recognised in the profit and loss account should be restricted'. It is unclear whether this means that where there have been past exchange losses on the same item a company has the option of restricting either the whole amount of the gain arising in the year or only the excess over the past losses. In our view the proper interpretation of this paragraph is that past losses are to be taken into account in determining the amount to be restricted.

3.2.3 Settled or unsettled transactions

The part of paragraph 50 quoted above refers to past exchange losses on the 'same items'. This is clearly meant to stop companies taking into account past exchange losses on unrelated items. However, what if part of a transaction has been settled and only part of it remains unsettled? If a realised loss arose on the part that was settled can this be taken into account in determining the amount of the gain on the unsettled portion to be restricted? In our view as the gain only relates to the unsettled portion then only past exchange losses on that portion should be taken into account in determining the amount to be restricted.

3.2.4 *Current portion of long-term item*

Paragraph 50 of the standard only relates to long-term items. What happens, therefore, where a company has an amount receivable part of which is due within one year of the balance sheet date and part which does not? It could be argued that all of the item should be regarded as a long-term item and therefore all of the exchange gain is to be restricted. However, this would mean that the current portion would be treated differently from any other amount receivable in that same currency within one year. It could therefore be argued that the current portion should be excluded and it is only the non-current portion which is the long-term item. It is only the exchange gain on that part which is restricted and the exchange gain on the current portion has to be taken to the profit or loss for the year. In our view it is illogical to treat the gains differently and, if it is necessary in the circumstances envisaged by the standard for exchange gains on long-term items expressed in one currency to be excluded from the profit and loss account on the grounds of prudence, then a similar treatment should be adopted for short-term items in the same currency.

3.2.5 *Restriction of gain*

It is not clear from the standard how gains in these circumstances should be restricted. Three possible treatments would be:

(a)   subtract the gain from the monetary item, i.e. effectively translate it at the historical rate; or

(b)   credit the gain to a deferral account; or

(c)   credit the gain directly to reserves.

In our opinion, treatment (b) is to be preferred as it treats the item as a monetary amount and excludes the gain from the net equity of the company. However, we consider that the other treatments are acceptable as they achieve the objective of paragraph 50 of the standard by excluding gains which ultimately may not be realised from the profit or loss for the year.

3.3   Forward contracts, currency swaps and currency options

In view of the volatility of exchange rates nowadays many companies are entering into such transactions to protect themselves from the potentially adverse effects of foreign currency rate movements. As indicated in 2.3.8 above, SSAP 20 only mentions forward contracts very briefly and does not say anything about currency swaps or currency options. The accounting for such items could be affected in the future as a result of the ASB's proposals on financial instruments (see 2 of Chapter 9), particularly in relation to whether any form of hedge accounting is allowed. In the meantime, however, how should companies account for such items?

Much of the guidance given below is based on the rules contained in SFAS 52. It should be borne in mind that SFAS 133 has introduced new requirements which supersede these provisions. However, as the hedging rules in SFAS 133 are based on measuring the financial instruments within its scope at fair values, then we believe that until such time as the ASB has finalised its own proposals for financial instruments, SFAS 52 is still appropriate as an aid to the interpretation of SSAP 20.

3.3.1   Forward contracts

A   What are forward contracts?

A forward contract is an agreement to exchange different currencies at a specified future date and at a specified rate.[79] A contract will normally be for a fixed period; e.g. one month, three months, six months, from the date of entering the contract. The rate under the contract is not an estimate of what the exchange rate will be at the end of the contract but is essentially a function of:

(a)   the spot rate at the date the contract is taken out; and

(b)   the interest rate differential between the two countries.

This is illustrated in the following example:

Example 8.13

On 31 March 1999 a UK company wishes to enter into a forward contract to buy €1m in six months' time. Ignoring any profit which the bank would take on the transaction the rate under contract would be calculated as if the bank had on 31 March 1999:

(i)   sold the company an amount of euros at the spot rate on that date, which would yield a total of €1m in six months' time;

(ii)   placed the amount of euros in (i) above on deposit for the company; and

(iii)   lent the company the amount of sterling in (i) above repayable, with interest, in six months' time.

At 31 March 1999 the spot rate is £1=€1.50 and the euro and sterling interest rates are 2.5% p.a. and 5.25% p.a. respectively.

The amount of euros which the bank would 'sell' to the company would be €987,654. Interest on the 'deposit' at 2.5% p.a. for six months would be €12,346 which would mean that the company would be entitled to €1m in six months' time.

The amount of sterling 'lent' to the company would be £658,436 (i.e. €987,654 @ €1.50=£1). Interest on this loan at 5.25% p.a. for the six months would be £17,284 and therefore the company would have to pay £675,720 at the end of the six months.

This cost of £675,720 for the €1m gives an exchange rate of £1=€1.48.

Sometimes forward contract rates are not quoted as single figures but are quoted as being either at a discount or premium on the spot rate. To arrive at the contract rate a discount is *added* to the spot rate and a premium is *deducted* from the spot rate.

B Reasons for companies taking out forward contracts

In most situations companies enter into a forward contract to protect themselves from the risks of exchange rate variations. This will normally be done to hedge:

(a) a future commitment or an expected transaction which will require the purchase or sale of foreign currency; or

(b) an existing foreign currency monetary asset or liability; or

(c) an investment in a foreign enterprise, such as an overseas subsidiary; or

(d) the results of a foreign enterprise.

In the first two situations a company is hedging the transaction to fix the amount of cash in sterling terms which will be required, whereas in the other two situations a company is hedging to offset the effect of translating the investment or results of the foreign enterprise.

In addition, companies may also enter into a forward contract by way of speculation in the hope that they can make a profit out of doing so.

In our view the accounting for forward contracts should be based on the economic rationale for the company entering into the contract in the first place and therefore will be different in each of these situations. We will now look at how this can be done by considering examples of each of these situations.

C Forward contracts taken out to hedge future commitments or transactions

Example 8.14

On 30 September 1998 a UK company contracts to buy an item of plant and machinery from a US company for US$500,000, with delivery on 31 January 1999 and payment due on 31 March 1999. In order to hedge against the movements in exchange rates it enters into a forward contract on 30 September 1998 to buy US$500,000 in six months' time. The premium on such a contract is US$0.02 and based on the spot rate of £1=US$1.70 gives a contracted rate of £1=US$1.68.

The relevant spot rates are:

	£1=US$
31 December 1998	1.66
31 January 1999	1.64
31 March 1999	1.61

How should the company account for these transactions in its financial statements for the years ended 31 December 1998 and 31 December 1999?

There are two basic methods:

(i) Record the asset and the liability at 31 January 1999 at £297,619 being US$500,000 translated at the contracted rate of £1=US$1.68. No exchange loss would be recognised on the forward contract in either year and no exchange gain on the liability to the supplier would be recognised in the year ended 31 December 1999. This treatment is straightforward and reflects the fact that the company has eliminated all currency risks by entering into the forward contract.

It could however be argued that such a treatment is not allowed by SSAP 20. Paragraph 46 of the standard only refers to *trading* transactions being translated at rates specified in related forward contracts. Trading transactions are not defined in SSAP 20 and a narrow interpretation would preclude capital transactions, such as the purchase of fixed assets, from being so treated. However, it would appear that some companies adopt a wider interpretation, as indicated in 3.3.1 D below. We concur with such an interpretation.

(ii) The forward contract and the acquisition of the asset are accounted for as two separate transactions. The asset and the liability to the supplier are initially recorded at 31 January 1999 at £304,878 (US$500,000 @ 1.64). An exchange loss on the amount due to the supplier up to the date of payment of £5,681, being £310,559 (US$500,000 @ 1.61) less £304,878, is recognised in the profit and loss account for the year ended 31 December 1999.

The exchange difference on the forward contract up to the transaction date is not recognised in the profit and loss account but is deferred and included in the recorded amount of the asset. Thereafter, any exchange difference on the contract is matched against the exchange difference on the liability to the supplier. Accordingly, although there is an exchange gain on the contract at 31 December 1998 of £7,087, being £301,205 (US$500,000 @ 1.66) less £294,118 (US$500,000 @ 1.70) this is not recognised in the profit and loss account but is deferred. In 1999 there is an exchange gain on the contract up to the date of the transaction on 31 January 1999 of £3,673, being £304,878 (US$500,000 @ 1.64) less £301,205. Again, this is not recognised in the profit and loss account. This gain together with the gain previously deferred is included in recording the asset. Accordingly, the asset is recorded at £294,118 (£304,878 - £7,087 - £3,673). This is equivalent to the asset being recorded at the spot rate ruling when the forward contract was entered into.

Following the transaction date there is an exchange gain on the forward contract of £5,681 which should be taken to the profit and loss account. It can be seen that this will offset the exchange loss on the amount due to the supplier in the same period and therefore reflects the fact that the company had hedged its exposure to exchange differences.

In addition to the exchange difference on the forward contract, recognition has to be given to the premium on the contract, i.e. the difference between the contracted amount translated at the contracted rate and translated at the spot rate when the contract was taken out. In this case the premium is £3,501 being £297,619 (US$500,000 @ 1.68) less £294,118 (US$500,000 @ 1.70). As this premium essentially represents an interest cost (see Example 8.13 above) over the period of the contract then this should be amortised over that period as a finance charge. Accordingly, £1,750 would be charged to the profit and loss account in the year ended 31 December 1999 and £1,751 in the following year. This second method is that suggested by SFAS 52.[80]

We believe that both of these methods are acceptable but would recommend that companies adopt the approach suggested in SFAS 52 as outlined in (ii) above. However, it should be borne in mind that where an exchange loss on the forward contract arises it should not be deferred if it would lead to recognising losses in later periods.[81] An alternative treatment allowed by SFAS 52 for the premium or discount on a contract which hedges a future commitment or transaction is to include that proportion of the premium or discount which relates to the commitment period, i.e. up to the date of the transaction, as part of the transaction.[82]

It should be noted that the treatment discussed in the second method in the above example is only allowed by SFAS 52 if the contract is designated as a hedge and the foreign currency commitment is firm.[83] Accordingly, if in the above example the company had not contracted for the plant and machinery at 30 September 1999 but it was only their intention at that date to enter into such contract then the US standard would not have allowed deferral of any of the exchange differences on the forward contract prior to contracting for the plant. We believe that in the UK it is unnecessary for such a stringent test to be applied and the treatment can be applied where a company has a reasonable expectation of entering into the transaction.

One company which refers to forward contracts taken out to hedge future transactions is Diageo, as shown in the extract below:

Extract 8.16: Diageo plc (1998)

Financial instruments [extract]

Gains and losses on contracts hedging forecast transactional cashflows, and on option instruments hedging the sterling value of foreign currency denominated income, are recognised in the hedged periods.

D   *Forward contracts taken out to hedge an existing foreign currency monetary asset or liability*

Example 8.15

Suppose the UK company in the previous example enters into the same forward contract. However, this time it does so because it has an existing loan of US$500,000 which is due for repayment on 31 March 1999 and wishes to hedge against any further exchange risk.

How should the forward contract and the loan be treated in the financial statements for the years ended 31 December 1998 and 31 December 1999?

There are three basic methods:

(i) Translate the loan at the contracted rate of £1=US$1.68, i.e. £297,619. The difference between this amount and the recorded amount at 30 September 1998 based on the spot rate at that date, i.e. £294,118, is written off in the profit and loss account for the year ended 31 December 1998 along with the previous exchange differences on the loan. No amounts are recorded in the profit and loss account for the year ended 31 December 1999.

(ii) Again, translate the loan at the contracted rate. However, as the difference of £3,501 (£297,619 less £294,118) represents the premium on the contract then it is deferred and amortised over the period of the contract. Accordingly, £1,750 is charged in the profit and loss account for the year ended 31 December 1998 and £1,751 in the following year.

It has been suggested that the treatment of the loans in each of these methods is not allowed by SSAP 20 as loans are not trading transactions.[84] However, we believe this to be a narrow interpretation of the standard and it would appear that companies do translate loans at rates specified in forward contracts (see Extract 8.17 below).

(iii) Treat the loan and the forward contract as two separate transactions. The loan is translated at the closing rate at 31 December 1998 and the exchange difference thereon is taken to profit and loss account. This exchange difference will include an exchange loss of £7,087 for the period from 30 September 1998 to 31 December 1998, being £301,205 (US$500,000 @ 1.66) less £294,118 (US$500,000 @ 1.70). The forward contract should also be regarded as a foreign currency transaction on which an exchange difference arises. SSAP 20 does not make this clear. However, it is clear from SFAS 52 that a forward contract is a foreign currency transaction.[85] Accordingly, an exchange gain of £7,087 on the contract should be recognised in the profit and loss account for the year ended 31 December 1998. This will offset the loss on the loan and therefore the results will not be affected by exchange differences from 30 September 1998, which was the purpose of taking out the contract. In the profit and loss account for the year ended 31 December 1999 a further exchange loss of £9,354, being £310,559 (US$500,000 @ 1.61) less £301,205 will be recognised on the loan offset by an equivalent exchange gain on the forward contract. As in method (ii) the premium on the contract would be amortised over the period of the contract. This method is that required by SFAS 52.[86]

We believe that all three methods are acceptable but would recommend that companies adopt method (iii). However, it would appear that at least some companies are translating loans at contracted rates, as the following extract shows:

Extract 8.17: British Airways Plc (1999)

Foreign currency translation [extract]

Foreign currency balances are translated into sterling at the rates ruling at the balance sheet date, except for certain loan repayment instalments which are translated at the forward contract rates where instalments have been covered forward at the balance sheet date.

E   Forward contracts taken out to hedge a foreign currency investment

Example 8.16

A UK company has a US subsidiary which had net assets of US$1m at 31 December 1997. On that date the UK company enters into a forward contract to sell US$400,000 in six months' time as a means of partially hedging against the investment in the subsidiary. The premium on such a contract is US$0.02 and based on the spot rate of £1=US$1.65 gives a contracted rate of £1=US$1.63. On maturity of the contract the company buys US$400,000 at the spot rate in order to fulfil the contract. At that time it decides not to enter into another forward contract.

The relevant spot rates are:

	£1=US$
30 June 1998	1.67
31 December 1998	1.66

The exchange difference on the net investment in the subsidiary taken to reserves in the consolidated financial statements for the year ended 31 December 1998 will be a loss of £3,651, being £606,061 (US$1m @ 1.65) less £602,410 (US$1m @ 1.66), of which £7,259 relates to the six months to 30 June 1998.

The overall gain which the company has made on the contract is £5,878 being £245,399 (US$400,000 @ 1.63) less £239,521 (US$400,000 @ 1.67). This gain represents the exchange gain on the contract of £2,903, being £242,424 (US$400,000 @ 1.65) less £239,521, and the premium of £2,975 (£245,399 less £242,424).

How should the forward contract be accounted for in the consolidated financial statements for the year ended 31 December 1998?

(i) It could be argued that all of the gain of £5,878 should be reflected in the profit and loss account. This is based on the fact that SSAP 20 only refers to forward contracts in the context of recording related transactions or monetary items. In this case there is no corresponding transaction or monetary item. However, this fails to recognise the rationale for entering into the contract which was to hedge against exchange rate movements on the investment in the subsidiary.

(ii) In order to recognise the rationale for entering into the contract, the exchange gain of £2,903 should be taken to reserves to be offset against the exchange loss on the investment. This will reflect the fact that the exchange loss on the investment for the six months to 30 June 1998 of £7,259 was hedged to the extent of 40%. The premium of £2,975 should be reflected in the profit and loss account.

The effect of such a treatment is similar to that which would have arisen if the company had decided to hedge the investment by borrowing US$400,000 for six months and investing the proceeds in a sterling deposit for the same period.

This second method is essentially that required by SFAS 52.[87] An alternative treatment for the premium would be to take it to reserves in addition to the exchange gain on the contract which is an option allowed by SFAS 52.[88]

In the absence of specific requirements in SSAP 20, we believe that both methods are acceptable although we would recommend that companies adopt the second method as it more fairly recognises the rationale for entering into the contract.

Where at its year end a company has an open forward contract which is intended as a hedge against a foreign currency investment, similar principles should be applied. We recommend that this is achieved by translating the assets and liabilities of the foreign enterprise at the relevant closing rate and by recording an exchange difference on the related forward contract.

An alternative approach may be to translate the assets and liabilities at the contracted rate, although it could be argued that this method is not allowed by SSAP 20 as it is only *transactions* of individual companies which can be translated at rates specified in forward contracts and the translation of the net assets of foreign investments for the purposes of consolidation is not a transaction. Another argument for not adopting such an approach is that the contract may not necessarily be for the same amount of currency as the net assets represent.

F   *Forward contracts taken out to hedge the results of a foreign currency investment*

Example 8.17

Suppose in the previous example the company took out the forward contract not as a hedge against the net investment in the subsidiary but against the expected profits of the subsidiary for the year ended 31 December 1998. The company normally translates the results of the subsidiary at closing rates. The actual profits of the subsidiary were US$500,000, all of which were retained by the subsidiary.

How should the company account for the results of the subsidiary and the forward contract?

(i) The profits of the subsidiary should be translated at the closing rate and, therefore, included as £301,205 (US$500,000 @ 1.66). The total gain on the contract of £5,878 should also be included in the profit and loss account. This will, therefore, reflect the fact that the company hedged against the effects of movements in the exchange rate up to 30 June 1998 on the results but not for exchange rate movements after that date.

(ii) That part of the profits covered by the forward contract should be translated at the contracted rate and the balance translated at the closing rate. This would mean that the profits included would be as follows:

	£
US$400,000 @ 1.63 =	245,399
US$100,000 @ 1.66 =	60,241
	305,640

It can be seen that this is lower than the total profits arrived at under (i) above by £1,443. It will therefore be necessary to credit a gain of a similar amount as a movement in reserves. This amount represents the gain on exchange on the US$400,000, which has been translated at the contracted rate, as a result of retaining those profits in the subsidiary from 30 June 1998 until 31 December 1998, being £240,964 (US$400,000 @ 1.66) less £239,521 (US$400,000 @ 1.67).

It could be argued that this method is not allowed by SSAP 20 as it is only *transactions* of individual companies which can be translated at rates specified in forward contracts and the translation of the results of subsidiaries for the purposes of consolidation is not a transaction. Another argument against this method is that it is effectively translating some of the results at an 'average' rate and some at the closing rate.

For these reasons we believe method (i) to be more appropriate, particularly where companies normally translate results of foreign subsidiaries at closing rates and the forward contract only covers part of the period. We also consider it preferable that the exchange difference on the forward contract is treated as a finance cost within the profit and loss account, rather than being absorbed within the operating results.

Where companies translate the results of subsidiaries at an average rate or the contract covers the full period of the results then using method (ii) will be acceptable. If in the above example the contract had been for the full year then the overall gain on the contract would have been £4,435, being £245,399 less £240,964 (US$400,000 @ 1.66). Accordingly, both methods would have yielded the same overall profit of £305,640, although as noted above the classification within the profit and loss account would be different.

Where a forward contract is taken out towards a year end with the intention of hedging the remainder of a subsidiary's results for the current year and its expected results for the following year then that part of the exchange difference on the contract which relates to the current year's results should be taken to the profit and loss account and the remainder deferred until the following year. The premium should preferably be amortised over the period of the contract.

It can be seen from Examples 8.16 and 8.17 above that different treatments for the contract arise depending on what the contract is supposed to be hedging; the net investment or the results of the investment. For this reason it is particularly important that the company recognises at the time of taking out the contract the reason for doing so.

One company which translates the results of subsidiaries at contracted rates is Rolls-Royce, as the following extract from its accounting policy indicates:

Extract 8.18: Rolls-Royce plc (1998)

Foreign currencies [extract]

The trading results of overseas undertakings are translated at the average exchange rates for the year or, where applicable, at the estimated sterling equivalent, taking account of future foreign exchange and similar contracts.

G   *Speculative forward contracts*

Example 8.18

A UK company enters into a forward contract on 30 September 1998 to sell US$500,000 in six months' time in the hope that it will make a profit out of doing so. It has no monetary liabilities in US dollars and is not planning to enter into any transaction which requires US dollars.

The relevant spot rates are:

	£1=US$
30 September 1998	1.70
31 December 1998	1.66

The premium on the contract is US$0.02, giving a contracted rate of £1=US$1.68. At 31 December 1998 the company still has the contract. The premium on three month contracts at that date is US$0.01 giving a contract rate of £=US$1.65.

How should the company account for the contract in its financial statements for the year ended 31 December 1998?

There are three possible methods:

(i) Record an exchange loss of £7,087, being £301,205 (US$500,000 @1.66) less £294,118 (US$500,000 @ 1.70). In addition, recognise the proportion of the premium of £3,501, being £297,619 (US$500,000 @ 1.68) less £294,118 which relates to the period up to December, 1998, i.e. £1,750. This is the same treatment which has been recommended if the contract had been taken out to hedge an amount of US$500,000 receivable on 30 March 1999. However, as in this case the reason for taking out the contract was speculative then it is likely that a company will 'close' such a contract at such time either when it considers that it has made the maximum profit it will make or to cut its losses. Rather than deferring the premium to a period where the contract may be closed out, an alternative approach is not to give any separate recognition to the premium but to recognise the gain or loss on the contract based on its 'realisable value'.

(ii) One method of doing this would be to record a loss of £3,586 being £301,205 less £297,619 (US$500,000 @1.68). This represents the difference between the sterling amount receivable under the contract and the dollar amount translated at the spot rate. This effectively assumes that the company could buy the required amount of foreign currency at the spot rate on the balance sheet date and therefore fix the loss at that amount. However, this ignores the cost of holding the currency until the contract matures.

(iii) The method which overcomes the deficiencies in the other two methods is to record a loss of £5,411, being £303,030 (US$500,000 @ 1.65) less £297,619. This effectively represents the difference between the sterling amount receivable under the contract less the amount it would cost to take out an equal and opposite forward contract to buy US$500,000 on the date the existing contract matures. This method is that required by SFAS 52.[89]

In the absence of detailed requirements in SSAP 20 we believe that all three methods are acceptable although we would recommend that companies adopt method (iii) above.

H   Conclusion

It can be seen from the above examples that different treatments of a forward contract are possible depending on the reason for entering into the contract in the first place. It is therefore important that companies should establish the reason for so doing prior to or at the same time as entering into the contract. As mentioned previously, the accounting for such items could be affected in the future as a result of the ASB's proposals on financial instruments (see 2 of Chapter 9), particularly in relation to whether any form of hedge accounting is allowed.

The methods recommended, and the other suggested possibilities, in each of the above examples follow the general principle in SSAP 20 that there should be symmetry of treatment of exchange gains and losses and should meet the objectives of translation contained in the standard. However, as there are no specific requirements relating to forward contracts in the standard then it may be possible that other treatments such as recognising losses but not profits on such contracts or treating them as 'commitments' are acceptable. Where such alternative treatments are adopted then the policy adopted should be disclosed and details of the financial commitments under the contracts will probably be required to meet the requirements of the Companies Act.[90]

3.3.2   *Currency swaps*

Another way in which companies can hedge against the risk of exchange rate movements is by entering into currency swaps. SSAP 20 makes no reference to such agreements and therefore the question arises as to how these should be accounted for. As currency swaps are essentially similar in nature to forward contracts then we believe that they should be accounted for in the same way as we have suggested for forward contracts above. Indeed, SFAS 52 states that 'agreements that are, in substance, essentially the same as forward contracts, for example, currency swaps, shall be accounted for in a manner similar to the accounting for forward contracts'.[91]

Most companies who have entered into currency swaps appear to do so to hedge against foreign currency borrowings and translate their borrowings at the swap rate. For example:

Extract 8.19: BP Amoco p.l.c. (1998)

23 Finance debt [extract]

Where the liability for any borrowing is swapped into another currency, the borrowing is accounted in the swap currency and not in the original currency of denomination.

One company which uses currency swaps to hedge its foreign currency investments is Boots, as shown below:

Extract 8.20: The Boots Company PLC (1999)

Foreign currencies [extract]

Exchange differences arising from the translation of the results and net assets of overseas subsidiaries, less offsetting exchange differences on foreign currency borrowings and currency swaps hedging those assets (net of any related tax effects) are dealt with through reserves.

3.3.3 Currency options

Where companies use forward contracts and currency swaps to hedge against exchange risks they eliminate not only the risk of exchange losses but also the possibility of exchange gains. One way that companies can eliminate the 'downside' of exchange losses but still participate in the 'upside' of exchange gains is to enter into currency options. As the name suggests these give companies the *right* to buy or sell foreign currency on or by a certain date in the future at a specified rate, but they are not *obliged* to do so. A company which purchases an option will have to pay a premium at the outset. The amount of the premium will depend on:

(a)   the current spot rate;

(b)   the specified rate (generally referred to as the strike price);

(c)   the period to the expiry of the option; and

(d)   the volatility of the exchange rate.

How should companies account for currency options?

SSAP 20 makes no reference to currency options at all. Due to the nature of currency options it is not really possible to translate transactions or monetary items in foreign currencies at the rates ruling under related currency options as they may never be exercised. Accordingly, it will be necessary to account for the currency option and any related transaction, asset or liability separately.

In accounting for the currency option it must be remembered that the maximum loss that the company can make is the cost of the premium. There are essentially two ways of calculating the gain or loss on a currency option:

(i)   The premium paid for the option should initially be recorded as an asset. At a subsequent balance sheet date this should be revalued to the current premium for the currency option, known as 'marking to market'. If the exchange rate has moved such that it is likely that the currency option will be exercised then the premium will have increased. This increase will represent the gain that the company can make by closing out the option. If the exchange rate has moved such that it is unlikely that the currency option will be exercised then the premium will have decreased. If the time remaining to the expiry date is short then the premium is likely to be a nominal sum. This decrease will represent the loss on the option.

(ii)   Again the premium is initially recorded as an asset. At a subsequent balance sheet date the currency amount under the option is translated at the current rate. If this shows an exchange gain when compared to the rate under the option then this gain is recognised. However, it will then be necessary to offset against this gain the cost of the option. If the comparison with the spot rate shows a loss exceeding the amount of the premium then the premium paid should be written off. If the loss is less than the premium paid then the premium should be written off to the extent of the loss.

These methods can be illustrated in the following example:

Example 8.19

On 30 April 1999 a UK company records a creditor of US$503,125 which it is due to pay on 31 July 1999. The exchange rate at 30 April 1999 is £1=US$1.61 and the creditor is recorded at £312,500. The company decides to take out some July put option contracts at a strike price of US$1.60 in order to provide a hedge against the creditor. Accordingly, it takes out 10 contracts of £31,250 on the Philadelphia Stock Exchange at a premium of US$0.0171 per £1. The total premium paid is £3,319 (being 10 x £31,250 x US$0.0171 = US$5,344 @ £1=US$1.61).

At 30 June 1999, the company's balance sheet date, the creditor is translated at the exchange rate ruling on that date of £1=US$1.576 at £319,242, thereby recording an exchange loss of £6,742.

At 30 June 1999 the premium on July put option contracts at a strike price of US$1.60 is now US$0.0241 per £1. Accordingly, under method (i) above, the gain on the option contracts is as follows:

Premium at 30 June 1999 – 10 x £31,250 x US$0.0241 = US$7,531 @ 1.576 =	£4,779
Less premium paid	3,319
Gain on option contracts	£1,460

Under method (ii) above the gain is as follows:

Currency amount of contracts = 10 x £31,250 x US$1.60 =   US$500,000

Amount payable at option rate –	US$500,000 @ 1.60 = £312,500
Amount payable at current rate –	US$500,000 @ 1.576 = £317,259

Exchange gain on option contracts	£ 4,759
Less premium paid	3,319

Gain on option contracts	£ 1,440

In the absence of detailed guidance in SSAP 20, we believe either method of calculation is acceptable, although we would recommend that the first method be adopted if possible as the gain or loss recognises the 'time value' contained in the premium.

The accounting for such gains or losses on the currency options should essentially follow the same principles as those outlined for forward contracts in 3.3.1 above and will again depend on the reason for taking out the currency option.

This is an area which has been under much discussion in the US because currency options are not specifically identified in SFAS 52. The Emerging Issues Task Force has issued a consensus dealing with hedging foreign currency risks with purchased options.[92] However, this only deals with a purchased option with little or no intrinsic value at the time it is designated as a hedge. The main issue dealt with by the Task Force was under what circumstances, if any, hedge accounting (i.e. deferral of unrealised or realised gains on the option) was appropriate for options used to hedge anticipated transactions. The Task Force considered that it was appropriate provided that the conditions of paragraphs 4 and 9 of SFAS 80 are met.[93] More specifically:

(a)   the item to be hedged must expose the transacting enterprise to foreign currency risk;

(b)   the option purchased must be designated as a hedge and must reduce the enterprise's exposure to risk;

(c)   the significant characteristics and expected terms of the anticipated transaction must be identified; and

(d)   it is probable that the transaction will occur.

In addition, the Task Force also considered whether hedge accounting using foreign currency options would be appropriate in the following circumstances:

(a)   hedging foreign export sales;

(b)   hedging foreign subsidiary sales;

(c)   hedging identifiable anticipated transactions;

(d)   hedging anticipated transactions with no enterprise risk;

(e)   hedging anticipated sales for several years;

(f)   hedging net income; and

(g)   hedging competitive risk.

It concluded that hedge accounting would be appropriate for (a) and (c), but not for (b), (d), (f) and (g); for (e) it would depend on an assessment using the criteria described above.

Having reached the above consensus in respect of purchased options with little or no intrinsic value, the Task Force began discussing the use of complex options (e.g. deep-in-the-money purchased options, written options, options purchased and written as a unit) and similar transactions (e.g. synthetic forwards, range forwards and participating forwards). However, no consensus as to how they should be accounted for was reached and no further discussion is planned.[94]

As mentioned previously, the accounting for such items could be affected in the future as a result of the ASB's proposals on financial instruments (see 2 of Chapter 9), particularly in relation to whether any form of hedge accounting is allowed.

3.4   Consolidated accounts – closing rate/net investment method

3.4.1   *Subsidiary with non-coterminous year end*

It is sometimes the case that UK companies consolidate the financial statements of foreign subsidiaries made up to a date which is not coterminous with the year end of the parent company. Where the results of the subsidiary are consolidated using the closing rate/net investment method the question then arises – which closing rate is to be used? The rate applying to the subsidiary's balance sheet date or the one applying to the parent company's balance sheet date?

SSAP 20 makes no reference to which one it should be. However, guidance can be drawn from SFAS 52 which states that the rate to be used is the one in effect at the date of the subsidiary's balance sheet.[95] The reason for this is that this presents the functional currency performance of the subsidiary during the subsidiary's financial year and its position at the end of that period in terms of the parent company's reporting currency.[96] The subsidiary may have entered into transactions in other currencies, including sterling, and monetary items in these currencies will have been translated using rates ruling at the subsidiary's balance sheet date. The profit and loss account of the subsidiary will reflect the economic consequences of carrying out these transactions during the period ended on that date. In order that the effects of these transactions in the subsidiary's financial statements are not distorted, the financial statements should be translated using the closing rate at the subsidiary's balance sheet date.

An alternative argument can be advanced for using the closing rate ruling at the parent company's balance sheet date. All subsidiaries within a group should normally prepare financial statements up to the same date as the parent company so that the parent company can prepare consolidated accounts which show a true and fair view of the state of affairs of the group at the parent company's balance sheet date and of the results of the group for the period then ended. The use of financial statements of a subsidiary made up to a date earlier than that of the parent is only an administrative convenience and must be recognised as being a surrogate for financial statements made up to the proper date. In view of this the closing rate which should be used is that which would have been used if the financial statements were made up to the proper date, i.e. that ruling at the date of the balance sheet date of the parent company. Another reason for using this rate is that there may be subsidiaries who have the same functional currency who make up their financial statements to the same date as the parent company and therefore in order to be consistent it is necessary for the same rate to be used.

We believe that both treatments are acceptable. In many cases where companies have such subsidiaries it is unclear from their accounting policies which treatment is adopted as they just refer to the financial statements being translated at the 'closing rate'. However, it would appear that where companies do make it clear which treatment is adopted, the use of the rate ruling at the parent company's balance sheet date is favoured. Two companies which have subsidiaries with non-coterminous year ends and would appear to use such a rate are Blue Circle and ICI. Extracts from their accounting policies are illustrated below:

Extract 8.21: Blue Circle Industries PLC (1998)

4   Foreign currency [extract]

Profit and loss accounts of foreign entities in foreign currencies are translated into sterling at average rates for the year. Assets and liabilities denominated in foreign currencies are translated into sterling at the rates of exchange ruling at 31 December.

Extract 8.22: Imperial Chemical Industries PLC (1998)

Foreign currencies [extract]

Profit and loss accounts in foreign currencies are translated into sterling at average rates for the relevant accounting periods. Assets and liabilities are translated at exchange rates ruling at the date of the Group balance sheet.

3.4.2   *Dual rates or suspension of rates*

The problems of dual rates and suspension of rates in relation to the accounts of an individual company have already been discussed in 3.1.3 above and many of the points made in that section apply equally to the consolidated accounts.

SSAP 20 makes no reference to what should happen when applying the closing rate/net investment method when there is more than one exchange rate for a particular currency. Again, guidance can be sought from SFAS 52 which states that the rate to be used to translate foreign statements should be, in the absence of unusual circumstances, the rate applicable to dividend remittances.[97] The reason for this is that the use of that rate is more meaningful than any other rate because cash flows to the parent company from the foreign enterprise can be converted only at that rate, and realisation of a net investment in the foreign enterprise will ultimately be in the form of cash flows from that enterprise.[98]

As mentioned in 3.1.3 above one currency where there used to be dual rates was the South African rand. It would appear that companies generally used the commercial rand, which was applicable to dividend remittances, for translating the financial statements of their South African subsidiaries.

3.4.3   Calculation of average rate

Paragraph 54 of SSAP 20 allows the profit and loss account of foreign enterprises to be translated at an average rate for the period. No definitive method of calculating the average rate has been prescribed and all the standard says is that 'the average rate used should be calculated by the method considered most appropriate for the circumstances of the foreign enterprise'. It does, however, give some guidance on the factors to be taken into account in determining what is most appropriate – 'Factors that will need to be considered include the company's internal accounting procedures and the extent of seasonal trade variations; the use of a weighting procedure will in most cases be desirable.'[99] What methods are, therefore, available to companies to use? Possible methods might be:

(a)   mid-year rate;

(b)   average of opening and closing rates;

(c)   average of month end/quarter end rates;

(d)   average of monthly average rates;

(e)   monthly/quarterly results at month end/quarter end rates; or

(f)   monthly/quarterly results at monthly/quarterly averages.

Example 8.20

A UK company has a US subsidiary and is preparing its consolidated accounts for the year ended 30 April 1999. It intends to use an average rate for translating the results of the subsidiary. The relevant exchange rates for £1=US$ (rounded to two decimal places) are as follows:

Month	Month end	Average for month	Average for quarter	Average for year
April 1998	1.67			
May 1998	1.63	1.67		
June 1998	1.67	1.64		
July 1998	1.64	1.65	1.65	
August 1998	1.67	1.64		
September 1998	1.70	1.63		
October 1998	1.67	1.68	1.65	
November 1998	1.65	1.70		
December 1998	1.66	1.66		
January 1999	1.64	1.67	1.68	
February 1999	1.60	1.65		
March 1999	1.61	1.63		
April 1999	1.61	1.62	1.63	1.65

Average of month end rates – 1.65
Average of quarter end rates – 1.64

The results of the subsidiary for each of the 12 months to 30 April 1999 and the translation thereof under each of the above methods (using monthly figures where appropriate) are shown below:

Month	US$	(e) quarterly £	(e) monthly £	(f) quarterly £	(f) monthly £
May 1998	1,000		613		599
June 1998	1,100		659		671
July 1998	1,200	2,012	732	2,000	727
August 1998	1,300		778		793
September 1998	1,300		765		798
October 1998	1,350	2,365	808	2,394	804
November 1998	1,400		848		824
December 1998	1,400		843		843
January 1999	2,000	2,927	1,220	2,857	1,198
February 1999	5,000		3,125		3,030
March 1999	10,000		6,211		6,135
April 1999	4,000	11,801	2,484	11,656	2,469
Total	31,050	19,105	19,086	18,907	18,891

Method (a)	US$31,050 @ 1.67= £18,593
Method (b)	US$31,050 @ 1.64= £18,933
Method (c) – monthly	US$31,050 @ 1.65= £18,818
Method (c) – quarterly	US$31,050 @ 1.64= £18,933
Method (d)	US$31,050 @ 1.65= £18,818

It can be seen that by far the simplest methods to use are the methods (a) to (d).

In our view methods (a) and (b) should not be used as it is unlikely in times of volatile exchange rates that they give appropriate weighting to the exchange rates which have been in existence throughout the period in question. They are only likely to give an acceptable answer if the exchange rate has been static or steadily increasing or decreasing throughout the period.

Method (c) based on quarter end rates has similar drawbacks and therefore should not normally be used.

Method (c) based on month end rates and method (d) are better than the previous methods as they do take into account more exchange rates which have applied throughout the year with method (d) being preferable as this will have taken account of daily exchange rates. Average monthly rates for most major currencies are likely to be given in publications issued by the government, banks and other sources and therefore it is unnecessary for companies to calculate their own. The work involved in calculating an average for the year, therefore, is not very onerous. Method (d) will normally give reasonable and acceptable results when there are no seasonal variations in items of income and expenditure.

Where there are seasonal variations in items of income and expenditure then this may not be the case. In these situations appropriate exchange rates should be applied to the appropriate items. This can be done by using either of methods (e) or (f) preferably using figures and rates for each month. Where such a method is being used care should be taken to ensure that the periodic accounts are accurate and that cut-off procedures have been adequate, otherwise significant items may be translated at the wrong average rate.

Where there are significant one-off transactions then it is likely that actual rates at the date of the transaction should be used to give a more accurate weighting. Indeed, SFAS 52 requires that for revenues, expenses, gains, and losses the exchange rate at the date on which these elements are recognised should be used or an appropriately weighted average.[100]

Most companies do not indicate how they have applied an average rate, but merely state that the results are translated at average rates or weighted average rates. Two companies which are more specific in their accounting policies on the use of average rates are Allied Domecq and Boots, as illustrated below:

Extract 8.23: Allied Domecq PLC (1998)

FOREIGN CURRENCIES [extract]

The profits of overseas undertakings are translated at weighted average exchange rates each month.

Extract 8.24: The Boots Company PLC (1999)

Foreign currencies [extract]

The results and cash flows of overseas subsidiaries are translated into sterling on an average exchange rate basis, weighted by the actual results of each month.

3.4.4 Change from closing rate to average rate or vice versa

By allowing companies the choice of using either the closing rate or an average rate for the period in translating the results of foreign enterprises, the question then arises – can a company change the method used by switching from closing rate to an average rate or vice versa?

Paragraph 17 of the standard states that the use of either method is permitted 'provided that the one selected is applied consistently from period to period'. It could be argued that this means that once a company has chosen a particular method no change should be made on the grounds of consistency. However, in view of the arguments expressed in paragraph 17 about the use of each of the methods it would seem possible that a company could justify changing from one method to the other on the grounds that it was adopting a better method.

If a change is made, it could be argued either that it is a change in accounting policy needing a prior year adjustment under FRS 3[101] and therefore the previous year's profit and loss account changed to the new basis, or that it is only a refinement of the existing policy which would not require a prior year adjustment. A refinement of an accounting policy is normally one that seeks to give a more accurate estimation in pursuit of the same basis of measurement; for example, a provision for stock obsolescence. This is not the case here, and in view of the conceptual differences of each method discussed in paragraph 17 of SSAP 20 we believe that this suggests a change in accounting policy. This would also appear to be required by paragraph 17 when it says that the method should be applied consistently from period to period.

A number of companies did change from the closing rate method to the average rate method in 1985/86. This was probably due to the dramatic weakening of the US dollar from January/February 1985 to the autumn of that year. In particular, the exchange rate moved from £1=US$1.08 at the end of February to £1=US$1.24 at the end of March. Companies were finding that, in addition to depressing their reported results, they were having to reassess their expected results due to the change in the exchange rate. They were also finding that figures previously reported in their interim announcements could be remarkably different when the annual figures were being translated at the closing rate. This particular problem is discussed in 3.4.11 below.

Since then more companies have changed to using average rates. Most major companies now use the average rate method.

3.4.5 To which reserve should exchange differences be taken?

SSAP 20 requires that exchange differences arising from the retranslation of the net investment at the closing rate should be recorded as a movement on reserves; however, it does not specify the category of reserves to which they should be taken. A number of companies take them to retained profits. Many companies in addition to showing such exchange differences as movements on retained profits also show them as movements on other reserves such as revaluation reserves and capital reserves. However, this is likely to be as a result of items dealt with in 3.4.6 below.

One company which has taken the exchange differences to a separate currency translation reserve is Low & Bonar, as shown below:

Extract 8.25: Low & Bonar PLC (1998)

19   Reserves [extract]

	Group £000
Exchange reserve	
At 30 November 1997	(12,336)
Adjustment on translation of currency loans to fund overseas investments	(451)
Adjustment on translation of net assets and results of overseas subsidiaries	(363)
At 30 November 1998	(110,271)

3.4.6   Post-acquisition capital or revaluation reserves

As indicated above, SSAP 20 does not specify the reserve to which the exchange difference arising from the retranslation of the net investment at the closing rate should be taken. Normally, they should be taken to only one category of reserve. However, the foreign enterprise may have a non-distributable capital reserve which arose after the company was acquired by the investing company. Alternatively, it may have revalued some assets since it was acquired and therefore has a revaluation reserve. As these reserves will not be reported as part of retained profits in the consolidated financial statements the question then arises – if exchange differences are normally taken to retained profits, should part of the exchange difference be taken to these other categories of reserves so that they are effectively translated at the closing rate?

Example 8.21

A UK company has a German subsidiary which was set up on 1 January 1997 with a share capital of DM500,000. In the year to 31 December 1997 the subsidiary made a post-tax profit of DM100,000 and at its year end transferred 5% thereof to a non-distributable legal reserve. In the following year the subsidiary made no profit or loss and therefore made no further transfer to the legal reserve. In the consolidated financial statements at 31 December 1997 the legal reserve was treated as a capital reserve and the exchange difference on the net investment was taken to retained profits. How should the capital reserve and the current year's exchange difference be treated in the consolidated financial statements at 31 December 1998?

The relevant exchange rates are:

	£1=DM
1 January 1997	2.64
31 December 1997	2.96
31 December 1998	2.77

	31 December 1998 DM	31 December 1997 £	(i) 31 December 1998 £	(ii) 31 December 1998 £
Net assets	600,000	202,703	216,606	216,606
Share capital	500,000	189,394	189,394	189,394
Opening retained profits	90,000	–	9,931	9,931
Profit for year	–	33,784	–	–
Transfer to capital reserve	–	(3,378)	–	–
Exchange difference	–	(20,475)	13,903	13,671
Closing retained profits	90,000	9,931	23,834	23,602
Opening capital reserve	10,000	–	3,378	3,378
Transfer from retained profits	–	3,378	–	–
Exchange difference	–	–	–	232
Closing capital reserve	10,000	3,378	3,378	3,610
	600,000	202,703	216,606	216,606

(i) This method has continued to take the exchange difference on the opening net investment to retained profits. The capital reserve has been retained at the rate ruling at which the reserve was created.

(ii) This method has taken that part of the exchange difference which relates to the net investment which is not distributable to the capital reserve so that the reserve represents the amount which is non-distributable at the closing rate. It should be borne in mind, however, that the split of consolidated reserves between distributable and non-distributable amounts are really irrelevant as it is the parent company's reserves which are important in determining whether a company can legally make a distribution. In any case, the figure for retained profits does not represent the amount that the subsidiary could distribute translated at the closing rate.

In our view either of these treatments is acceptable.

Example 8.22

A UK company has a Swiss subsidiary which was set up on 1 August 1997 with a share capital of SFr1m. The main asset of the subsidiary is an investment property which it acquired on the same day that the company was set up at a cost of SFr800,000. The subsidiary made a profit after tax of SFr50,000 for the six months to 31 January 1998 and a profit after tax of SFr100,000 in the following year. The property was revalued at 31 January 1998 at SFr950,000 which was incorporated in its financial statements. The valuation was updated at 31 January 1999 to SFr1.2m. The exchange difference on the net investment was taken to a separate exchange reserve in the 1998 financial statements. How should the revaluation reserve and the current year's exchange difference be treated in the consolidated financial statements at 31 January 1999?

The relevant exchange rates are:

	£1=SFr
1 August 1997	2.48
31 January 1998	2.41
31 January 1999	2.33

	31/1/98 SFr	31/1/98 £	31/1/99 SFr	(i) 31/1/99 £	(ii) 31/1/99 £
Investment property	950,000	394,191	1,200,000	515,021	515,021
Other assets	250,000	103,734	350,000	150,215	150,215
	1,200,000	497,925	1,550,000	665,236	665,236
Share capital	1,000,000	403,226	1,000,000	403,226	403,226
Opening retained profits			50,000	20,747	20,747
Profit for year	50,000	20,747	100,000	42,919	42,919
Closing retained profits	50,000	20,747	150,000	63,666	63,666
Opening revaluation reserve			150,000	62,241	62,241
Surplus for year	150,000	62,241	250,000	107,296	107,296
Exchange difference					2,137
Closing revaluation reserve	150,000	62,241	400,000	169,537	171,674
Opening exchange reserve				11,711	11,711
Exchange difference		11,711		17,096	14,959
Closing exchange reserve		11,711		28,807	26,670
Total capital and reserves	1,200,000	497,925	1,550,000	665,236	665,236

(i) This method has continued to take the exchange difference on the opening net investment to the separate exchange reserve. Surpluses credited to the revaluation reserve are retained at the rates ruling at the date the surpluses arise.

(ii) This method has taken that part of the exchange difference on the opening net investment which arises only because of the fact that the investment property has been revalued to the revaluation reserve. If the property had been retained at cost then that exchange difference would not have arisen in the consolidated financial statements. This treatment means that the revaluation reserve in the consolidated financial statements represents the revaluation reserve expressed in the foreign currency translated at the closing rate. It also represents the difference between the carrying amount of the asset in the consolidated financial statements and the historical cost of the asset translated at the closing rate which should be included in the historical cost information required by the Companies Act 1985 in respect of assets affected by revaluations[102] (see 6.7 of Chapter 10); i.e.

	£
Carrying value at 31 January 1999	515,021
Historical cost at 31 January 1999	
SFr800,000 @ £1=SFr2.33 =	343,347
	171,674

Although we believe both methods to be acceptable, in our view method (ii) is preferable for the reasons stated above. It would appear that this is the method adopted by a number of companies, as indicated in 3.4.5 above.

3.4.7 Treatment of exchange differences on disposal of subsidiary

The issues relating to the calculation of the gain/loss on disposal of subsidiaries are discussed at 3 in Chapter 6. In relation to foreign subsidiaries there is one further issue – what should happen to the cumulative exchange differences on the net investment in a foreign subsidiary when all or part of it is sold? SSAP 20 does not specifically deal with this.

Example 8.23

A UK company has a US subsidiary which was set up on 1 January 1996 with a share capital of US$200,000 when the exchange rate was £1=US$1.55. The subsidiary is included at its original cost of £129,032. The profits of the subsidiary, all of which have been retained by the subsidiary, for each of the three years ended 31 December 1998 were US$40,000, US$50,000 and US$60,000 respectively. In the consolidated financial statements the results of the subsidiary have been translated at the respective closing rates of £1=US$1.71, £1=US$1.65 and £1=US$1.66. All exchange differences have been taken to a separate exchange reserve. The consolidated reserves have therefore included the following amounts in respect of the subsidiary:

	Retained profit £	Exchange reserve £
1 January 1996	–	–
Movement during 1996	23,392	(12,073)
31 December 1996	23,392	(12,073)
Movement during 1997	30,303	(5,104)
31 December 1997	53,695	(6,969)
Movement during 1998	36,144	(1,059)
31 December 1998	89,839	(8,028)

The net assets at 31 December 1998 of US$350,000 are included in the consolidated financial statements at £210,843.

On 1 January 1999 the subsidiary is sold for US$400,000 (£240,964), thus resulting in a gain on sale in the parent company's books of £111,932, i.e. £240,964 less £129,032. On consolidation the gain on sale is reduced to £30,121, being the difference between the proceeds of £240,964 and net asset value of £210,843. How should the cumulative exchange difference of £(8,028) be treated in the consolidated financial statements for 1999?

Option (i) – Leave it as a negative exchange reserve.

In our view this is illogical as the consolidated financial statements will include in retained profits a different amount in respect of the subsidiary than has actually been realised by the parent company and included in its own retained profits. In addition, a consolidation entry will be required forever more in respect of the former subsidiary.

Option (ii) – Transfer it to retained profits as a reserve movement.

This is based on the view that the consolidated retained profits should reflect the same amount of retained profits that the parent company has realised and recorded in its own financial statements. This treatment, therefore, overcomes the criticism made above in respect of the previous option. It also means that the retained profits position is now the same as it would have been if the company had adopted the policy of taking the exchange differences to retained profits as they arose rather than taking them to a separate reserve.

Option (iii) – Transfer it to the profit and loss account for the year and treat it in a similar way as the gain on sale.

This is based on the view that one of the objectives of SSAP 20 is to produce results which are compatible with the effects of rate changes on a company's cash flow; that is why exchange differences on monetary items are normally recognised as part of the profit or loss for the year. Exchange rate changes in this instance have ultimately caused the company to receive less cash and therefore should be reflected at some time in arriving at the profit or loss for the year. It could also be argued in this particular case that not to do so would mean that the company has reported more profits in the consolidated profit and loss account than has actually been realised, contrary to the requirements of the Companies Act 1985.[103]

The treatment suggested in option (iii) above is that which is required by SFAS 52 upon the sale or upon complete or substantially complete liquidation of an investment in a foreign entity.[104] Indeed, under US GAAP if a partial sale takes place then the relevant proportion of the accumulated exchange difference should be included in the gain/loss on sale.[105] Similar requirements are contained in the international standard, IAS 21.[106] In the above example if 25% of the shares in the subsidiary had been sold then £(2,007) would have been included in the calculation of the gain/loss on sale.

However, under FRS 3, as the original exchange differences would have been reflected in the statement of total recognised gains and losses when they arose then they should not be recognised again in the year of disposal in either the profit and loss account or the statement of recognised gains and losses (see Chapter 22 at 2.9.1). Accordingly, option (iii) is unacceptable and in our view option (ii) is preferable to option (i).

3.4.8 *Change from closing rate/net investment method to temporal method or vice versa*

As indicated in 2.4.2 above, the method used for translating the financial statements of a foreign enterprise should normally only be changed when the financial and other operational relationship changes and renders the method used inappropriate. Where this is the case, therefore, it must be remembered that, as it is a change in the circumstances which has given rise to the change in method, this is not a change in accounting policy and therefore a prior year adjustment under FRS 3 is inappropriate. How should the change, therefore, be accounted for?

SSAP 20 does not deal with this situation; however, guidance can be sought from SFAS 52.

A   *Change from closing rate/net investment method to temporal method*

SFAS 52 states that the translated amounts of non-monetary assets at the end of the period prior to the change should become the accounting basis for those assets for the current and future periods.[107] There is therefore no need to translate these assets at the historical rates that applied when the assets were acquired. The cumulative exchange differences that have been taken to reserves in prior periods should not be taken to the profit and loss account in the year of change but should remain in reserves. SFAS 52 actually requires these exchange differences to remain in equity.[108]

B   *Change from temporal method to closing rate/net investment method*

SFAS 52 states that the adjustment attributable to restating non-monetary assets, previously translated at historical rates, at closing rates should be reported in the cumulative translation adjustments component of equity.[109] This adjustment should, therefore, be treated as a reserve movement.

3.4.9 *Hyper-inflation*

One particular problem with the use of the closing rate/net investment method is when it is applied to a foreign enterprise which operates in a country where a very high rate of inflation exists. Consider the following example:

Example 8.24

On 30 June 1990 a UK company sets up a subsidiary overseas. On that date the subsidiary acquires property for HC100,000. Ignoring depreciation on the property, this asset would be included in the group financial statements at 30 June 1990 and 30 June 1999, as follows:

	HC	Exchange rate	£
30 June 1990	100,000	£1=HC1	100,000
30 June 1999	100,000	£1=HC200	500

This example illustrates the 'disappearing assets' problem and it is for this reason that SSAP 20 says that in these circumstances 'it may not be possible to present fairly in historical cost accounts the financial position of a foreign enterprise simply by a translation process'.[110] The other impact is that profits may be inflated (either from high interest income on deposits in a rapidly depreciating currency or from trading operations at unrealistic levels of profitability) whilst a significant exchange loss is taken direct to reserves. The standard suggests, therefore, that the local currency financial statements should be adjusted where possible to reflect current price levels before the translation process is undertaken. No indication is given as to whether this restatement should be done based on specific price changes (current cost principles) or general price changes (current purchasing power principles), so either would appear to be acceptable.

SSAP 20 does not define what 'a very high rate of inflation' is; in addition, it is not that clear as to when and how the guidance in the standard should be applied in practice.

A   UITF 9

As a result of this uncertainty the UITF considered the matter and in June 1993 issued Abstract 9 – *Accounting for Operations in Hyper-inflationary Economies* – which became effective for accounting periods ending on or after 23 August 1993.

The UITF agreed that adjustments are required where the cumulative inflation rate over three years is approaching, or exceeds, 100% and the operations in the hyper-inflationary economies are material.[111] Although this sounds high, this is equivalent to an annual inflation rate of 26% compounded over that period. This is similar to what SFAS 52 regards as a highly inflationary economy.[112]

Countries which have recently had three-year cumulative inflation of 100% or more include:[113]

Afghanistan	Congo	Malawi	Sudan
Angola	Ecuador	Mongolia	Turkey
Armenia	Ghana	Mozambique	Ukraine
Azerbaijan	Guinea-Bissau	Myanmar	Uruguay
Belarus	Indonesia	Nigeria	Venezuela
Bulgaria	Iran	Romania	Zambia
Burundi	Kazakhstan	Russia	

Information on inflation rates in various countries is available in *International Financial Statistics*, published monthly by the International Monetary Fund.

Although SSAP 20 suggests that the local currency financial statements should be adjusted to reflect current price levels, the UITF recognised that the lack of reliable and timely inflation indices can pose a major practical problem. Accordingly the UITF regards two methods as being acceptable to eliminate the distortion caused by hyper-inflation:

(a)   adjust the local currency financial statements to reflect current price levels before the translation process (as suggested by SSAP 20). This includes taking any gain or loss on the net monetary position through the profit and loss account. This is the same treatment as required by IAS 21;[114] or

(b)   use a relatively stable currency (not necessarily sterling) as the functional currency of the foreign operations. If the transactions of the operation are not recorded initially in that stable currency, then they must be remeasured into the stable currency by applying the temporal method (see 2.4.4 above). These remeasured financial statements are then translated into sterling using the closing rate method.[115] This is effectively the same treatment as required by SFAS 52 which regards the reporting currency of the investing company (the US dollar) as if it were the functional currency of the foreign enterprise.[116]

We can see the effect of using these two methods on the 'disappearing assets' problem illustrated above in the following example:

Example 8.25

(a)   Adjusting for current price levels

The relevant consumer price indices at 30 June 1990 and 30 June 1999 are 100 and 23,000 respectively. The asset would therefore be included in the group financial statements at 30 June 1999 as follows:

HC100,000 x 23,000/100 = HC23,000,000 @ £1=HC200 = £115,000.

(b)   Remeasuring using a stable currency

The US dollar is regarded as the relevant stable currency. The asset is remeasured using a historical rate of exchange for US dollars at 30 June 1990 of US$1=HC0.60. This produces a cost for the asset of US$166,667. This is then translated into sterling at the US dollar exchange rate at 30 June 1999 of £1=US$1.58 which gives an amount of £105,485.

Two companies which follow the former method are Lonrho and Unilever, as illustrated in the following extracts:

Extract 8.26: Lonrho Plc (1998)

Consolidation of Group companies [extract]

Results of subsidiaries and associates operating in hyper-inflationary economies are adjusted to reflect current price levels in those countries concerned.

Extract 8.27: Unilever PLC (1998)

Foreign currencies [extract]

In preparing the consolidated accounts, the profit and loss account, the cash flow statement and all movements in assets and liabilities are translated at annual average rates of exchange. The balance sheet, other than the ordinary share capital of NV and PLC, is translated at year-end rates of exchange. In the case of hyper-inflation economies, the accounts are adjusted to remove the influences of inflation before being translated.

On the other hand, two companies which adopt the latter method are Courtaulds and GKN, as shown below:

Extract 8.28: Diageo plc (1998)

Foreign currencies [extract]

The results, assets and liabilities of operations in hyper-inflationary economies are determined using an appropriate relatively stable currency as the functional currency. The exchange differences arising from this process are taken to the profit and loss account.

Extract 8.29: GKN plc (1998)

FOREIGN CURRENCIES [extract]

The accounts of operations in countries where hyper-inflationary conditions have existed, are prepared using a stable currency before translation into sterling.

Although UITF 9 considers that either of its two methods should be used for dealing with this problem of hyper-inflation, it does state that if neither of them is appropriate, then the reasons should be stated and alternative methods to eliminate the distortions should be adopted.[117]

Where group operations in areas of hyper-inflation are material, the accounting policy adopted to eliminate the distortions of such inflation should be disclosed.[118]

3.4.10 Goodwill on consolidation

FRS 10 – *Goodwill and Intangible Assets* – now requires goodwill on consolidation to be capitalised and classified as an asset on the balance sheet.[119] (This was also one of the options allowed by SSAP 22 – *Accounting for goodwill*.)[120] Where goodwill is capitalised on the purchase of a foreign enterprise, the question then arises as to whether or not such goodwill should be retranslated at closing rates.

Example 8.26

A UK company acquires all of the share capital of an Australian company on 31 January 1999 at a cost of A\$3m. The fair value of the net assets of the Australian company at that date was A\$2.1m. In the consolidated financial statements at 30 April 1999 the goodwill is capitalised as an intangible asset and amortised over its useful economic life. (For the purposes of this example, amortisation for the three months to 30 April 1999 is ignored.) The relevant exchange rates at 31 January 1999 and 30 April 1999 are £1=A\$2.61 and £1=A\$2.43 respectively. At what amount should the goodwill on consolidation be included in the balance sheet?

	A\$	(i) £	(ii) £
Goodwill	900,000	344,828	370,370

(i) This method regards goodwill as being the excess of (a) the sterling price paid over (b) the fair value of the net assets of the subsidiary expressed in the foreign currency translated into sterling at the date of acquisition; i.e. a sterling asset which does not fluctuate with changes in the exchange rate. Although not specifically covered by SSAP 20 this would appear to be the method adopted by the standard.

Paragraph 53 of the standard only refers to the exchange difference on the net investment being taken to reserves and the definition of the net investment contained in the standard refers to the net assets of the foreign enterprise.[121] As the goodwill only arises on consolidation and is not included in the balance sheet of the foreign enterprise then it could be argued that the goodwill is not part of the net assets of the foreign enterprise. This view is supported by the statement issued by the ASC on the publication of SSAP 20 which indicated that any goodwill element contained in the carrying amount of the investment in the investing company's financial statements would not be available for offset on consolidation when applying the cover method provisions of paragraph 57 of the standard.[122]

(ii) This method regards goodwill as being the excess of (a) the foreign currency price paid or the sterling price paid translated into the foreign currency at the date of acquisition over (b) the fair value of the net assets of the subsidiary expressed in the foreign currency, i.e. a currency asset which is retranslated at closing rates.

This treatment is required by SFAS 52[123] and is, in our view, more logical as the value of the foreign company as a whole is likely to be based on the expected future earnings stream expressed in the foreign currency and the goodwill relates to a business which operates in the economic environment of that currency.

For these reasons we believe method (ii) to be preferable.

3.4.11 Inter-period comparisons

As indicated in 2.4.3 above the use of the closing rate/net investment method is intended to reflect in the consolidated financial statements the financial results and relationships as measured in the foreign currency financial statements of the foreign enterprise prior to translation. This is likely to be the case for amounts within the profit and loss account for the year; amounts within the balance sheet; and the relationship of the profit or loss for the year to the balance sheet, particularly where the closing rate is used for translating the results of the foreign enterprise. However, this will not be the case when a comparison is made between figures for the current year and figures for the previous year or, alternatively, figures for the first half of the year and figures for the second half. This is normally more important when looking at a comparison of the results for the respective periods.

Example 8.27

A UK company has a wholly owned Canadian subsidiary. In preparing its consolidated financial statements the company translates the results of the subsidiary using the closing rate. The profits of the subsidiary for the four six-month periods ended 31 December 1998 and the rate of exchange at the end of each period are as follows:

Six-month period ended	C$	£1=C$
30 June 1997	100,000	2.30
31 December 1997	110,000	2.35
30 June 1998	121,000	2.45
31 December 1998	133,100	2.56

The two interim financial statements ended 30 June and the two annual financial statements ended 31 December for the group therefore include the profits of the subsidiary as follows:

	C$	£1=C$	£
Six months ended 30 June 1997	100,000	2.30	43,478
Six months ended 31 December 1997	110,000	Balance	45,884
Year ended 31 December 1997	210,000	2.35	89,362
Six months ended 30 June 1998	121,000	2.45	49,388
Six months ended 31 December 1998	133,100	Balance	48,870
Year ended 31 December 1998	254,100	2.56	99,258

It can be seen from the above that the reported sterling figures do not show the 10% increase each period that the Canadian dollar figures show. In 1998, the annual profit shows an increase of approximately 11% compared to the 1997 profit whereas in Canadian dollar terms the profit has increased by 21% and the second half results appear to show a decrease of approximately 1% compared to the results of the first half instead of the 10% increase. This latter effect is caused by the second half results effectively including the exchange adjustment resulting from restating the first half's results at the year-end exchange rate. The results of the first half translated at the year-end rate are £47,266 and therefore a loss of £2,122 is effectively included in the second half's results. This restatement of previously reported figures is one of the reasons why some companies have changed to using average rates when translating profit and loss accounts. Even where this is done this problem will still arise if each period's results are not translated at the average rate for that period, i.e. if the annual results are translated at an average rate for the year, although the effect is unlikely to be particularly significant.

If average rates had been used in the above example the figures would have been as follows:

Example 8.28

	Method (i)			Method (ii)	
	C$	£1=C$	£	£1=C$	£
Six months ended 30 June 1977	100,000	2.24	44,643	2.24	44,643
Six months ended 31 December 1977	110,000	Balance	47,868	2.30	47,826
Year ended 31 December 1977	210,000	2.27	92,511	Balance	92,469
Six months ended 30 June 1998	121,000	2.37	51,055	2.37	51,055
Six months ended 31 December 1998	133,100	Balance	50,993	2.54	52,402
Year ended 31 December 1998	254,100	2.49	102,048	Balance	103,457

Method (i) translates the results for the year at the average rate for the year and method (ii) translates each six-month period at the average rate for the respective period. It can be seen that under method (i) the second half results for 1998 still show a decrease compared to the first half. Method (ii) shows an increase but nothing like the 10% shown by the Canadian dollar figures.

In order to try to overcome this, some companies have disclosed the effect of using different exchange rates. For example, Fisons in its 1993 accounts disclosed the following:

Extract 8.30: Fisons plc (1993)

1   Analysis of results [extract]

	1993 £m	1992 £m
Group turnover – continuing operations		
At 1992 average exchange rates	**1,143.8**	1,139.7
Translation effect of exchange rate movements	**118.3**	–
At average exchange rates for the year	**1,262.1**	1,139.7

An alternative treatment is to express the figures for the comparative year in terms of the current exchange rates, as illustrated below:

Extract 8.31: Guinness PLC (1996)

1.   SEGMENTAL ANALYSIS OF TURNOVER AND PROFIT

(F)   Exchange rates [extract]

If the trading results of overseas companies for 1995 had been translated at the average exchange rates ruling during 1996 and if the rates achieved in 1995 for transaction receipts under hedging arrangements had been the same as those achieved in 1996, turnover for 1995 would have been £33m lower and profit before interest and taxation (excluding MH) for 1995 would have been £13m higher.

Some companies go further than Guinness in that they, in giving their segmental disclosures, restate all the comparative figures based on the current year's exchange rates.[124]

Although this extra disclosure can only help a user of financial statements it must be remembered that this mathematical effect of different exchange rates ignores the economic effect of the changes in the exchange rates on the actual trading results of the foreign enterprises. SFAS 52 states that the Financial Accounting Standards Board when preparing the standard 'considered a proposal for financial statement disclosure that would describe and possibly quantify the effects of rate changes on reported revenue and earnings. This type of disclosure might have included the mathematical effect of translating revenue and expenses at rates that are different from those used in a preceding period as well as the economic effects of rate changes, such as the effects on selling prices, sales volume, and cost structures.' The Board rejected requiring such disclosures 'primarily because of the wide variety of potential effects, the perceived difficulties of developing the information, and the impracticality of providing meaningful guidelines'. However, the Board encouraged management to give extra disclosure of 'an analysis and discussion of the effects of rate changes on the reported results of operations. The purpose is to assist financial report users in understanding the broader economic implications of rate changes and to compare recent results with those of prior periods.'[125]

3.4.12 Branches

We have discussed previously the application of the provisions of SSAP 20 in relation to branches and we have seen that the definition of a foreign branch is a very wide one in that it includes a group of assets and liabilities which are accounted for in foreign currencies. This was mainly to cater for international assets which are financed by foreign borrowings, since the cover method could not be used as it is only applicable to equity investments. In many cases, therefore, the reason for regarding assets and liabilities as a foreign branch will be to allow exchange differences on the related borrowing to be taken to reserves rather than to the profit and loss account.

Once a company has decided that a particular category of assets and liabilities should be regarded as a foreign branch consideration should be given as to which assets and liabilities should be included. In our view the minimum which can be included is the international asset itself, e.g. aircraft, ship or oil and gas interest, and the related borrowing. However, we recommend that, in addition, any trading balances, e.g. debtors and creditors, should also be included. In particular, as the branch should not be an integral part of the company's business and its cash flows should not have an impact upon those of the rest of the company in order to justify the use of the closing rate/net investment method, the bank account through which most of the cash flows of the branch will flow should be considered to be part of the branch assets and liabilities.

It should be borne in mind that the exchange difference which is taken to reserves is on the net investment in the branch. As such this amount can be a net exchange gain or loss and the exchange difference on the borrowings included in the branch can exceed the corresponding exchange difference on the branch assets. There is, therefore, no restriction on the exchange differences on the borrowings taken to reserves as there would be if the provisions of the cover method applied.

3.5   Cover method

We have looked at the basic requirements of the cover method in 2.3.7 above and 2.4.5 above as it is applied in individual companies' financial statements and consolidated financial statements respectively. There are, however, a number of problem areas resulting from the provisions of the standard which we believe have to be addressed. Many of these problem areas are relevant to both sets of financial statements. Until recently, the main focus of attention in this area has generally been in relation to the external financial reporting aspects of the consolidated financial statements. However, due to the introduction of a new tax regime for foreign exchange differences in 1995 the focus has shifted to the position in individual companies since taxation is assessed on individual companies not groups. All of the examples used in the rest of this section to illustrate these problem areas assume that a matching election has been made and therefore no taxation arises on any of the exchange differences. Where taxation does arise then UITF 19 requires that the provisions of the cover method should be applied after taking into account any tax charge or credit directly or solely attributable to the borrowings. It also requires that in considering the amount of cash that the investment is expected to generate, consideration should be in after-tax terms.[126]

3.5.1 What are 'foreign currency borrowings'?

By adopting the cover method companies can take some, if not all, of the exchange differences arising on the foreign currency borrowings to reserves. Borrowings are not defined in the standard, so what should be regarded as borrowings?

The statement issued by the ASC on the publication of the standard in commenting on these provisions referred to 'loans'[127] but even then we do not believe that this term should be interpreted too literally.

The Stock Exchange, in requiring disclosure of indebtedness in listing particulars of listed companies, includes within this category loan capital, term loans, bank overdrafts, liabilities under acceptances (other than normal trade bills), acceptance credits, hire purchase commitments and obligations under finance leases.[128] In our view all of these items can be regarded as borrowings for the purpose of the standard although it is unlikely that liabilities under hire purchase contracts, or finance leases, will have been taken out with a view to providing a hedge against foreign equity investments. Normal trade creditors and trade bills should not be regarded as borrowings, although it has been suggested that extended credit from a supplier could be included as the economic effects are the same as for a straightforward loan.[129]

3.5.2 Borrowings taken out before or after the investment

The provisions of the standard apply to borrowings which have been used to finance, or provide a hedge against, its foreign equity investments. Accordingly, the provisions not only apply to borrowings taken out at the same time as the investment is made but also to borrowings which have been taken out before the investment is made and to borrowings which are taken out after the investment is made. How should the provisions be applied, therefore, in the first accounting period when the investment holding period has been different from the period for which the borrowing has been in place?

A   *Borrowings taken out before the investment*

Example 8.29

A UK company is intending to invest in a US company so on 1 December 1998 it borrows US$500,000, repayable in five years' time, which it places in a US$ deposit account in the meantime. On 31 December 1998 it purchases all of the shares of the US company at a cost of US$800,000 using the US$500,000 in the deposit account and the balance paid out of its sterling bank account. How should the company apply the cover method in its financial statements for the period to 30 April 1999?

The relevant exchange rates are:

	£1=US$
1 December 1998	1.69
31 December 1998	1.66
30 April 1999	1.61

		Option (i)		Option (ii)	
		P/L account	Reserves	P/L account	Reserves
Exchange differences		£	£	£	£
Investment					
US$800,000	@ 1.66 = £481,928				
	@ 1.61 = £496,894				
			14,966		14,966
Deposit					
US$500,000	@ 1.69 = £295,858				
	@ 1.66 = £301,205				
		5,347		5,347	
Borrowing					
US$500,000	@ 1.69 = £295,858				
	@ 1.66 = £301,205				
			(5,347)	(5,347)	
	@ 1.61 = £310,559		(9,354)		(9,354)
		5,347	265	nil	5,612

Option (i) is based on the view that as the borrowings were used to finance the purchase of the investment all of the exchange difference on the borrowings can be offset against the exchange differences as long as the criteria of the standard are met. However, in our view this ignores the fact that for the period prior to purchasing the investment the borrowing was effectively matched against the deposit. Therefore our preference would be for the exchange difference on the borrowing for the period up to purchasing the investment to be taken to profit and loss to offset the exchange difference on the deposit as shown in option (ii).

We also believe that such a treatment should be adopted if the proceeds of the borrowings had been placed in a sterling deposit account as the company would have been uncovered during that period. The effect of exchange differences would have impacted on the cash flow of the company as it would have been required to pay an extra £5,347 out of its sterling bank account to purchase the investment. Accordingly, the exchange difference should be taken to profit and loss account.

Problems also arise when borrowings are taken out as a hedge against existing foreign investments.

B Borrowings taken out after the investment

Example 8.30

A UK company has an equity investment in a Swiss company which it acquired a number of years ago at a cost of SFr500,000 when the exchange rate was £1=SFr5.00. Up until 1998 the UK company has had no foreign borrowings so the investment has been carried in the company's financial statements at its historical sterling cost of £100,000. On 30 June 1998 the company considered the investment to be worth SFr1,000,000 and in order to provide a hedge against the investment borrowed SFr1,000,000, repayable in three years' time, and used the proceeds to reduce its sterling overdraft. How should the company apply the cover method in its financial statements for the year ended 31 December 1988?

The relevant exchange rates are:

	£1=SFr
31 December 1997	2.40
30 June 1998	2.53
31 December 1998	2.29

		P/L £	Reserves £
Option (i)			
Exchange differences			
Investment – SFr500,000	@ 5.00 = £100,000		
	@ 2.29 = £218,341		
			118,341
Borrowing – SFr1,000,000	@ 2.53 = £395,257		
	@ 2.29 = £436,681		
			(41,424)
			76,917

		P/L £	Reserves £
Option (ii)			
Exchange differences			
Investment – SFr500,000	@ 5.00 = £100,000		
	@ 2.40 = £208,333		
			108,333
	@ 2.29 = £218,341		10,008
Borrowing – SFr1,000,000	@ 2.53 = £395,297		
	@ 2.29 = £436,681		
		(31,416)	(10,008)
		(31,416)	108,333

Option (iii)
Exchange differences
Investment – SFr500,000   @ 5.00 = £100,000
                             @ 2.53 = £197,629

                             ————————   97,629
                             @ 2.29 = £218,341   20,712
Borrowing – SFr1,000,000   @ 2.53 = £395,257
                             @ 2.29 = £436,681

                             ————————   (20,712)   (20,712)

                                             (20,712)   97,629

Option (i) regards all of the exchange gain on the investment which is recognised in this accounting period as being available for offset against the exchange loss on the total borrowing. This would appear to meet the conditions laid down in paragraphs 51 and 57 of the standard.

Option (ii) regards only the exchange difference arising on the investment during the year as being available for offset. As there is only a gain of £10,008, then under the conditions of the above paragraphs the exchange loss on the borrowings taken to reserves is restricted to £10,008, with the balance of £20,712 being taken to profit and loss for the year.

Neither of these options, although acceptable under the standard, reflects the rationale for taking out the borrowings in the first place which was to hedge the exchange risk on the investment from the date it was decided to do so, i.e. 30 June 1998. To achieve this, the exchange differences on the investment available for offset should be those which arise during the same period as the borrowing has been in existence.

Option (iii) is done on this basis and it can be seen that only half of the exchange loss on the borrowings can be offset against the exchange difference on the investment. This is due to the fact that the investment is recorded at the original cost of SFr500,000 whereas the borrowing is twice that amount. In order for the company to reflect fully the rationale behind their decision they should incorporate the investment at its valuation of SFr1,000,000. If this were done, then all of the exchange loss on the borrowing could be taken to reserves.

It can be seen from option (iii) in the above example that the carrying amount of the investment can have implications for the amount of exchange differences on the borrowings which can be taken to reserves under the cover method. Under the recently introduced tax regime, individual companies may make an election to match a foreign currency borrowing against shares in a foreign currency subsidiary, so that no taxable loss or gain on the borrowing results. However, to achieve such a result it is necessary that the translation of the carrying amount of the subsidiary gives rise to exchange differences which exceed those on the borrowings. Thus in the above example, the UK company would need to incorporate the investment at its valuation at 30 June 1998 to ensure such a result on an ongoing basis (assuming all the conditions of paragraph 51 of SSAP 20 are met). If under its hedging strategy the company were to increase the amount of foreign currency borrowings because the underlying value of the subsidiary had increased, then it would be necessary to incorporate further valuations at the time the borrowings were increased in order to ensure that no exchange differences on the borrowings have to be taken to the profit and loss account.

3.5.3 Repayment of borrowings

Similar problems also arise when a company repays a foreign currency borrowing which has provided a hedge against a foreign equity investment.

A   Treatment of exchange differences

Example 8.31

A UK company has an equity investment in a Canadian company which it acquired for a cost of C$3m when the exchange rate was £1=C$2.00. It financed the acquisition by borrowing C$3m. In the financial statements up to 31 December 1997 the cover method has been applied. On 30 August 1998 the company took advantage of the strong pound and decided to repay the borrowings in full. The company has no other foreign borrowings. How should the company apply the cover method in its financial statements for the year ended 31 December 1998?

The relevant exchange rates are:

	£1=C$
31 December 1997	2.35
30 August 1998	2.62
31 December 1998	2.56

		Option (i)		Option (ii)	
		P/L	Reserves	P/L	Reserves
		£	£	£	£
Exchange differences					
Investment					
C$3,000,000	@ 2.35 = £1,276,596				
	@ 2.62 = £1,145,038				
			(131,558)		(131,558)
Borrowing					
C$3,000,000	@ 2.35 = £1,276,596				
	@ 2.62 = £1,145,038				
		131,558			131,558
		131,558	(131,558)	nil	nil

Option (i) is based on the view that as there are no borrowings at the year end then the cover method does not apply and the matching should be considered as having ceased at the beginning of the accounting period. As the exchange gain on the loan has arisen on a settled transaction it should be reported as part of the profit or loss for the year. However, it could be argued that this does not comply with condition (c) of paragraph 51 of the standard which requires the accounting treatment adopted to be applied consistently. Again, such a treatment does not reflect the fact that the company had hedged its investment up to 30 August 1998 and it is only after that date that it has not been covered. Accordingly, we believe that option (ii) should be followed.

Another problem which arises when such borrowings are repaid is – how should the related investment which is no longer hedged subsequently be accounted for in the financial statements of the investing company?

B   *Subsequent treatment of investment*

Example 8.32

In the above example, how should the investment be included in the balance sheet at 31 December 1998 and at subsequent year ends?

Option (i) – The investment should be retained at the exchange rate ruling at the final date of repaying the loan, i.e. £1,145,038 (£1=C$2.62). No further retranslation should take place until another borrowing is taken out to provide a hedge. This method regards the investment as being a currency asset only during the period there are related currency borrowings. This would appear to be the method suggested by other commentators.[130] It does mean, however, that the figure for the investment in future periods is rather meaningless as it represents neither the historical cost in sterling terms nor the currency amount at closing rates. It does not even necessarily represent the actual sterling cost of the investment, as not all of the investment may have been financed by borrowings and the borrowings may have been repaid at different dates.

Option (ii) – The investment is translated at the closing rate of £1=C$2.56 and included at £1,171,875 and is retranslated each year at closing rates. This is based on the view that the company *has* used foreign currency borrowings to finance the investment and therefore the provisions of paragraph 51 can still be applied. It also means that the accounting treatment for this investment is being applied consistently from period to period. Even if it were considered that such a policy was not in accordance with the standard then it would be possible for the company to adopt such a treatment by retaining a nominal borrowing in the foreign currency!

Option (iii) – The investment is retained at the rate ruling at the beginning of the period, i.e. £1,276,596 (£1=C$2.35). This is based on the same premise as option (i) in the previous example.

Option (iv) – The investment should be restated at the historical rate ruling at the date of purchase, i.e. £1,500,000 (£1=C$2.00). This is based on the view that the company no longer has a hedge against its investment and should account for it as if this had always been the case. The financial statements will, therefore, reflect the effect on net equity of choosing to finance the investment for the period it was so financed only by including the net exchange difference on the borrowing in reserves.

In our view all of the above options are acceptable, but the one chosen should be consistently applied.

3.5.4   Goodwill on consolidation

We have already discussed in 3.4.10 above the question of whether or not goodwill on consolidation, which arises on the acquisition of a foreign enterprise and is capitalised and amortised, is a currency asset. We indicated that our preference was to treat it as such. Where the investment is financed by foreign currency borrowings the question then arises, can the exchange differences arising on the goodwill be used in the offset process under the provisions of paragraph 57 of the standard? Indeed, where the company has chosen to write off goodwill on consolidation immediately to reserves under SSAP 22 (and under FRS 10 has not reinstated such goodwill as an asset), can any of the exchange differences on the related borrowing be taken to reserves in the consolidated financial statements?

Example 8.33

A UK company acquired all the equity share capital of an Australian company for A$3m on 31 January 1999. The acquisition was financed by taking out a loan of A$3m which is repayable over ten years commencing 31 March 1999. As the net assets of the Australian company are negligible, all of the purchase price is represented by goodwill. The company has applied the cover method in its own financial statements for the period ended 30 April 1999. The relevant exchange rates at 31 January 1999 and 30 April 1999 are £1=A$2.61 and £1=A$2.43 respectively.

Accordingly, the investment and the loan are both included in the company's financial statements at £1,234,568 and an exchange gain on the investment of £85,143 and a corresponding exchange loss on the loan are taken to reserves.

The company capitalises the goodwill on consolidation and treats it as a currency asset and translates it at closing rate then, ignoring any amortisation of the goodwill for the three months to 30 April 1999, an exchange gain of £85,143 on the goodwill will arise and be taken to reserves in the consolidated financial statements. Can the company apply the cover method under paragraph 57 of the standard and take the exchange loss on the loan to reserves?

Paragraph 57 of the standard only allows the exchange difference on the borrowing to be taken to reserves to the extent that it is offset by the exchange difference on the net investment which is taken to reserves and the definition of the net investment contained in the standard refers to the net assets of the foreign enterprise.[131] As the goodwill only arises on consolidation and is not included in the balance sheet of the foreign enterprise then it could be argued that the goodwill is not part of the net assets of the foreign enterprise. (However, the same could also be said about any fair value adjustments made in respect of the net assets.) This view is supported by the statement issued by the ASC on the publication of SSAP 20 which indicated that any goodwill element contained in the carrying amount of the investment in the investing company's financial statements would not be available for offset on consolidation when applying the cover method provisions of paragraph 57 of the standard.[132] Based on these arguments it would appear that the answer to this question is no.

However, we believe that in such circumstances the company should be able to apply the cover method provided that condition (c) of paragraph 57 is met.

The goodwill is being regarded as a currency asset which is retranslated at closing rates. This treatment is required by SFAS 52[133] and, in our view, more logical as the value of the foreign company as a whole is likely to be based on the expected future earnings stream expressed in the foreign currency and the goodwill relates to a business which operates in the economic environment of that currency. Not to take into account the exchange differences arising on the goodwill in applying the cover method ignores the economic reality that the group is covered against movements in exchange rates.

What if the acquisition in the above example had taken place in an earlier year when SSAP 22 applied and under that standard the company had chosen to write off the goodwill to reserves immediately?

Again, it could be argued that the cover method cannot be applied. No asset is being recognised in the financial statements and therefore there can be no exchange differences arising thereon against which the exchange difference on the loan can be offset. However, most companies who chose a policy of writing off goodwill immediately did so as a matter of policy, not because of the fact that the goodwill had suddenly become worthless and it could be argued that the treatment of exchange differences on borrowings should not be affected by the choice of accounting policy for goodwill. We believe, therefore, there is a case to say that such goodwill, which would have been included in the consolidated balance sheet had a policy of capitalisation and amortisation been followed, can be taken into account when applying the cover method.

Examples of companies which take goodwill into account when applying the cover method are TI Group and United News & Media, as illustrated below:

Extract 8.32: TI Group plc (1998)

24   RESERVES [extract]

Exchange translation included within total recognised gains and losses comprised positive movements in respect of overseas investments of £0.5m (1997 £36.5m negative, inclusive of goodwill) and negative movements of £3.0m (1997 £2.0m positive) in respect of foreign currency financing of those investments.

Extract 8.33: United News & Media plc (1998)

FOREIGN CURRENCIES [extract]

Differences arising on the restatement of investments, including goodwill, in foreign subsidiary undertakings and related net foreign currency borrowings, and from the translation of the results of those companies at average rate, are taken to reserves, and are reported in the statement of total recognised gains and losses.

3.5.5   All investments/borrowings?

Companies may have more than one foreign currency investment which have been financed, or are hedged by, more than one foreign currency borrowing. The question may then arise, can a company apply the cover method for some investments/borrowings and not apply it for others?

Example 8.34

On 31 January 1999 a UK company acquires all the equity share capital of two foreign companies as follows:

(i) A US company at a cost of US$1,640,000 financed by a loan of US$1,640,000 repayable in five years' time.

(ii) A German company at a cost of €1,450,000 financed by a loan of €1,450,000 repayable in five years' time.

The company wishes to apply the cover method to the US investment and related loan but not to apply it to the German investment and related loan in its financial statements for the year ended 30 April 1999. Is such a treatment possible under SSAP 20?

The relevant exchange rates are:

	£1=€	£1=US$
31 January 1999	1.45	1.64
30 April 1999	1.52	1.61

The effect of such a treatment is as follows:

		P/L account £	Reserves £
Exchange differences			
Investments			
– US$1,640,000	@ US$1.64 = £1,000,000		
	@ US$1.61 = £1,018,634		
			18,634
– €1,450,000	@ €1.45 = £1,000,000		
	@ €1.45 = £1,000,000		
			–
Loans			
– US$1,640,000	@ US$1.63 = £1,000,000		
	@ US$1.61 = £1,018,634		
			(18,634)
– €1,450,000	@ €1.45 = £1,000,000		
	@ €1.52 = £ 953,947		
		46,053	
		46,053	–

It can be seen that by applying the cover method to the US investment/loan only the exchange gain on the Euro loan has been taken to profit and loss account whereas the exchange loss on the US$ loan has been taken to reserves offset by a corresponding exchange gain on the net investment. It would appear that this is allowed by SSAP 20, as paragraph 51 states that the equity investments *may* be denominated in foreign currencies. It must be emphasised, however, that where exchange losses on the investments are arising but are not being recognised consideration has to be given as to whether a provision for impairment is necessary. Paragraph 57 in dealing with the consolidated financial statements is equally permissive as it states that the exchange differences on the borrowings *may* be offset as reserve movements. If in the above example the net assets of the German company at the date of acquisition were equivalent to the price paid then although an exchange loss of £46,053 would be taken to group reserves, the company could continue to take the exchange gain on the loan to the profit and loss account.

It has been suggested that the final condition of paragraphs 51 and 57 requires companies to apply the cover method to all matched investments.[134] The final condition requires companies to apply the same accounting policy from *period to period* and therefore this suggestion seems to be a rather broad interpretation of the provisions. Nevertheless, we believe it is preferable for companies to adopt the same policy for all matched investments.

3.5.6   *Must currencies be the same?*

All of the previous examples which we have considered have been based on situations where the investment and the related borrowing have been expressed in the same foreign currency. The provisions of the standard actually make no reference to the currencies of the borrowings or the investments, and consequently it is not necessary for this to be the case. ED 27 included such a restriction but this was removed 'since a number of commentators considered it to be unacceptably rigid, particularly having regard to the wide variety of loan arrangements available and to the multi-currency nature of many of them. Since the alternative of a complete offset of currencies would allow too much freedom and carry the risk of imprudent accounting, a compromise solution has been adopted. The offset is now permitted only to the extent that the underlying foreign currency borrowings do not exceed the amount of cash expected to be generated by the net investments, either from profits or otherwise. ASC considers that this restriction should ensure that offset is permitted only when there is genuine cover for the related exchange gains and losses, whilst at the same time recognising the realities of treasury management.'[135] Specific problems relating to this compromise solution are addressed at 3.5.8 and 3.5.9 below.

An illustration of the cover method provisions where the currencies are not the same can be seen in the following example:

Example 8.35

On 1 January 1993 a UK company acquires an equity investment in a Swiss company at a cost of SFr2,270,000 and finances the acquisition by borrowing DM2,470,000 repayable in seven years' time. Based on the exchange rates at that date both amounts are equivalent to £1,000,000. By applying the cover method in SSAP 20 the amounts of the investment and the borrowing in the financial statements for each of the years ended 31 December up until 1998 would be as follows:

	Investment		Borrowing	
	£1=SFr	£	£1=DM	£
31 December 1993	2.20	1,031,818	2.57	961,089
31 December 1994	2.05	1,107,317	2.45	1,008,163
31 December 1995	1.79	1,268,156	2.22	1,112,613
31 December 1996	2.30	986,957	2.64	935,606
31 December 1997	2.40	945,833	2.96	834,459
31 December 1998	2.29	991,266	2.77	891,697

The treatment of exchange differences under the cover method would be as follows:

	Investment Reserves	Borrowing Reserves	P/L account
	£	£	£
31 December 1993	31,818	–	38,911
31 December 1994	75,499	(47,074)	–
31 December 1995	160,839	(104,450)	–
31 December 1996	(281,199)	177,007	–
31 December 1997	(41,124)	41,124	60,023
31 December 1998	45,433	(45,433)	(11,805)
	(8,734)	21,174	87,129

In 1993 as both the investment and the borrowing are showing exchange gains then none of the exchange gain in the borrowing can be offset in reserves and therefore all of the gain must be taken to the profit and loss account.

In 1994 and 1995 all of the exchange loss on the borrowing can be offset in reserves. Similarly, in 1996 all of the exchange gain on the borrowing can be offset in reserves.

In 1997 although there is a total exchange gain on the borrowing of £101,147, only £41,124 can be offset in reserves as that is the extent of the exchange loss on the investment. The balance of £60,023 has to be taken to the profit and loss account. No account can be taken of the previous exchange losses on the investment which are sitting in reserves. It is only the exchange difference arising in the year which can be used in the offset process.

Similarly, in 1998 the exchange loss which is capable of being offset is limited. It can be seen from the figures for 1997 and 1998 that this applies whether or not the exchange difference on the borrowing is a gain or a loss.

It can be seen from the above example that when the cover method contained in SSAP 20 is used in circumstances where the investment and borrowings are in different currencies it can lead to inconsistent treatment of the exchange differences on the borrowing. In the above example in two of the years part of the exchange difference is taken to reserves and part to the profit and loss account. In three of the years all of the difference is taken to reserves and in the other year all of the difference is taken to profit and loss account. In our view this makes a nonsense of the consistency concept.

Another weakness of the cover method when different currencies are involved can be illustrated by the following example:

Example 8.36

A UK company has a Canadian subsidiary. At 30 April 1998 the net assets of the subsidiary are C$2,390,000. On 1 May 1998 the company decides to double its investment in the Canadian company by investing a further C$2,390,000 and borrows US$1,670,000 repayable in five years' time.

The relevant exchange rates are as follows:

	£1=C$	£1=US$
30 April 1998 and 1 May 1998	2.39	1.67
30 April 1999	2.34	1.61

Using the cover method, the financial statements would reflect the following treatment for the resulting exchange differences:

Exchange gain on investment
      C$4,780,000   @ 2.39 = £2,000,000
                          @ 2.34 = £2,042,735

                                           £42,735

Exchange loss on borrowing
      US$1,670,000   @ 1.67 = £1,000,000
                          @ 1.61 = £1,037,267

                                         (37,267)

Net gain taken to reserves   £ 5,468

The cover method allows all of the exchange difference on the investment to be used in the offset process. However, the result of the decision to finance the extra investment by the US$ loan has been:

Gain on increased investment of C$2,390,000   £21,367
Loss on US$ loan   (37,267)

                                         £(15,900)

Although a net loss has arisen as a result of the decision no loss is reflected in the profit and loss account.

The above examples demonstrate that the cover method of SSAP 20 does not produce sensible results which reflect the economic substance of the transactions when different currencies are involved.

In our view proper cover can only exist if the risk of exposure to currency movements is removed. This can only happen if the borrowings, which are providing the hedge, are in the same currency as the investment. One of the arguments put forward by the ASC for removing the restriction of having the same currency was that it was too rigid 'particularly having regard to the wide variety of loan arrangements available and to the multi-currency nature of many of them'.[136] We consider the fact that companies can borrow in most of the major foreign currencies means that having a requirement for the same currency would not be too rigid because they can arrange to have the borrowings in the currency they want in order to provide effective cover against their investments.

Another criticism of the cover method in SSAP 20 is that 'the position taken by the ASC is that if there is a gain on a net investment and a loss on borrowings, then ex-post facto there has been cover; if there has been a gain on both or a loss on both, then there has been no cover. The basic flaw here is that cover by its very nature – to remove the risk – is a matter of premeditated intent. Evidence of this intent is a key feature of SFAS 52's approach to cover.'[137]

SFAS 52 requires that exchange gains and losses on transactions that are designated as, and are effective as, economic hedges of a net investment in a foreign entity shall not be included in the profit and loss account but shall be reported in the same manner as the translation adjustments relating to the net investment.[138] Ordinarily, a transaction that hedges a net investment should be denominated in the same currency as the net investment. SFAS 52 recognises that it may not be practical or feasible for this to be the case and, therefore, in these situations allows the hedging transaction to be in a currency which generally moves in tandem with the currency of the net investment.[139]

3.5.7   Pooled basis?

Where companies have a number of investments financed by a number of borrowings, how should the cover method be applied? Should it be applied on a pooled basis, i.e. by aggregating all the investments and all the borrowings and comparing the net exchange difference on each; or should it be done on an individual basis if specific borrowings can be identified or on a currency by currency basis?

Depending on how it is done different treatments are likely to arise. We can see this from the following example:

Example 8.37

A UK company has two wholly owned foreign subsidiaries, a Norwegian company and a Danish company. The net investments in these subsidiaries at 30 April 1998 are NKr50m and DKr15m respectively. The original investments in these companies were financed by borrowings of NKr45m and DKr18m respectively. How should the company apply the cover method in its consolidated financial statements for the year ended 31 April 1999?

The relevant exchange rates are:

	£1=NKr	£1=DKr
30 April 1998	12.47	11.44
30 April 1999	12.54	11.30

	P/L account £	(i) Reserves £	(ii) Reserves £
Exchange difference on investments			
Norwegian company			
– NKr50m @ 12.47 = £4,009,623			
@ 12.54 = £3,987,241			
		(22,382)	(22,382)
Danish company			
– DKr15m @ 11.44 = £1,311,189			
@ 11.30 = £1,327,434			
		16,245	16,245
			(6,137)
Exchange difference on borrowings			
Norwegian kroner loan			
– NKr45m @ 12.47 = £3,608,661			
@ 12.54 = £3,588,517			
		20,144	20,144
Danish kroner loan			
– DKr18m @ 11.44 = £1,573,426			
@ 11.30 = £1,592,920			
	(3,249)	(16,245)	(19,494)
			650
	(3,249)	(2,238)	(5,487)

Method (i) has applied the cover method by regarding the investments/borrowings as being in two separate pools of currencies. As a result, that part of the loss on the DKr loan which has not been covered by exchange gain on the DKr investment has been taken to the profit and loss account.

Method (ii) has taken a global approach and as there are sufficient net losses on the investments to offset the net gains on the borrowings then all of the exchange differences can be offset to reserves.

It has been suggested that SSAP 20 requires an aggregate basis as illustrated in method (ii). The reason is that companies usually manage their treasuries on a pool basis and finance groups of investments with the basket of loans, often in different currencies.[140] In our view companies are permitted to apply the cover method on an individual basis or a currency by currency pool basis, as illustrated in method (i) above. We believe that such a basis is preferable as it is only when the currencies are the same that proper cover exists.

The global approach will have the same effect where all the investments in each particular currency exceed the amount of the borrowings in each particular currency. However, where there may be a shortfall of investments in any particular currency when compared to borrowings in the same currency, the global approach has the effect of regarding the excess borrowings as providing a hedge against investments in different currencies.

Whichever method is used it should be applied consistently from period to period.

3.5.8 *What is meant by condition (b) of paragraph 51 and condition (c) of paragraph 57?*

These conditions require that the foreign currency borrowings used in the offset process should not exceed the total amount of cash that the investments are expected to be able to generate, whether from profits or otherwise. As explained in 3.5.6 above the reason for this condition was to allow the cover method to be used when different currencies were involved. No guidance is given in the standard as to how such amount of cash should be determined. UITF 19, however, requires that the comparison with the total amount of cash that the investments are expected to be able to generate and the exposure created by the borrowings should be considered in after-tax terms.[141]

How should these conditions therefore be applied? For the purposes of illustration, the examples below assume that there is no taxation relating to the borrowings and the cash expected to be generated is in after-tax terms.

Example 8.38

A UK company acquires an equity investment in a Japanese company at a cost of ¥225m on 1 May 1998. During 1997 the company had taken out a loan of US$2m repayable in five years' time with a view to investing in a US company. However, this investment was never made and the company was left with the loan. In preparing its financial statements for the year ended 30 April 1999 the company wishes to regard the US$ loan as providing a hedge against the Japanese investment and apply the cover method. How should this be done?

The relevant exchange rates are:

	£1=¥	£1=US$
30 April 1998		1.67
1 May 1998	221	
30 April 1999	192	1.61

Exchange differences		
Investment – ¥225m	@ 221 = £1,018,100	
	@ 192 = £1,171,875	
Exchange gain	————	£153,775
Loan – US$2m	@ 1.67 = £1,197,605	
	@ 1.61 = £1,242,236	
Exchange loss	————	£(44,631)

By just applying condition (a) of paragraph 51 of the standard it would seem that all of the exchange loss on the loan can be taken to reserves as there are sufficient exchange gains on the investment available for offset.

However, what about condition (b)? How should the amount of cash which the investment is expected to generate be determined?

(i) It could be argued that it should be calculated as being the amount that would be raised if the investment were sold immediately.

If this is equivalent to its book value at the year end, i.e. £1,171,875, then as the loan exceeds this amount it could be argued that the cover method cannot be applied and therefore all of the exchange loss on the loan of £44,631 should be taken to the profit and loss account and the investment should be recorded at the historical rate; i.e. £1,018,100. Alternatively, it could be argued that a proportion of the loan can be used in the offset process to the extent that it is covered by the value of the investment. This means that US$1,886,719 (£1,171,875 @ £1=US$1.61) can be used in the process. The exchange loss on this amount is £42,103 and it is this amount which can be taken to reserves. The remainder of the exchange loss on the loan of £2,528 would be taken to the profit and loss account. We believe the latter approach is the more appropriate treatment.

What if the amount at which the investment could be sold is in excess of its book value? It may be that the investment is now worth ¥250m which is equivalent to £1,302,083. It would appear that in these circumstances all of the exchange loss on the borrowing can be offset in reserves, even although the financial statements do not reflect the fact that the borrowings are covered. On the grounds of prudence, we believe it would be preferable to use the carrying value of the investment.

(ii) It could be argued that it is not necessary to consider an immediate sale of the investment, particularly as it is unlikely that such a course of action is the intention of the investing company, but that regard should be given to future profits which will result in further dividends being received or an increase in the amount ultimately received when the investment is sold. No guidance is given at all in the standard as to the period over which profits are to be taken into account. In view of the impracticalities of forecasting future dividend streams and ultimate sale proceeds, we believe that companies in applying these provisions should consider the cash proceeds which would be received from the immediate sale of the investment as in (i) above. If a future sale and future dividends have to be taken into account then consideration should also be given to the future interest expense which will be incurred on the borrowing.

Where the currencies are the same, in most situations condition (b) of paragraph 51 and condition (c) of paragraph 57 are irrelevant. This is because of the requirement that exchange differences on the borrowings can only be offset in reserves to the extent that there are corresponding exchange differences on the related investment. This ensures that full cover will only arise if the carrying value of the investment is at least equivalent to the amount of the borrowings. If the investment will not generate cash equivalent to the amount of the borrowings then provision should be made against the carrying value of the investment. This means that the amount of exchange differences on the net investment will correspondingly be less and therefore the exchange differences on the borrowings which exceed that amount will have to be taken to the profit and loss account.

However, even where the currencies are the same, problems can arise in the year the conditions are not met.

3.5.9   What should happen in the year of change of the above conditions not being met?

A   Investment making losses

Example 8.39

A UK company has a wholly owned Japanese subsidiary which it set up several years ago at a cost of ¥1,000m. Up until 1996 the subsidiary was profitable and on 1 January 1977 the company borrowed ¥1,000m repayable in four years' time to provide a hedge against its investment. During 1997 the subsidiary began to make losses such that at 31 December 1997 the net assets of the subsidiary had been reduced to ¥1,000m. In its financial statements for the year ended 31 December 1997 the company applied the cover method and exchange gains of £455,308 were offset in reserves. At that date, exchange gains on the investment included in the company and consolidated reserves were £1,175,000 and £1,500,000 respectively. In the year to 31 December 1998 the subsidiary has made further losses of ¥400m but it is now considered that the losses have been stemmed and that the subsidiary will break even in the next three years. The results of the subsidiary are translated using closing rates. Assuming that the net asset value at 31 December 1998 is considered to be the cash expected to be generated by the investment, how should the cover method be applied in the financial statements for the year ended 31 December 1998?

The relevant exchange rates are:

	£1=¥
31 December 1997	214
31 December 1998	188

Exchange differences		
Investment – ¥1,000m	@ 214 = £4,672,897	
	@ 188 = £5,319,149	
		£646,252
Loan – ¥1,000m	@ 214 = £4,672,897	
	@ 188 = £5,319,149	
		£(646,252)

As the exchange loss on the loan is matched by the exchange gain on the investment it would appear that none of the exchange loss on the loan need be taken to profit and loss account. However, as the cash expected to be generated from the investment is only ¥600m then this condition has to be considered. The possible effects of this on the cover method are as follows:

(a) Abandon the cover method with retrospective effect.

It could be argued that as the amount of the loan exceeds the cash expected to be generated then the cover method cannot be applied and therefore this year's exchange loss on the loan should be reflected in the profit and loss account for the year. The previous exchange gains on the loan cannot be taken through the profit or loss account for the year as a result of FRS 3, but if necessary should be transferred to retained profits. In the company financial statements the investment should be translated at historical rates and the exchange gains of £1,175,000 on the investment reversed. This reflects the position which would have been shown if the cover method had not been applied. A prior year adjustment is inappropriate as it is a change in circumstances which has given rise to the cover method not being used.

(b) Abandon the cover method for the current year and thereafter.

As in (a), this year's exchange loss on the loan should be reflected in the profit and loss account. However, as the company was hedged last year, the company's financial statements should still reflect that fact. The investment would not be restated at historical rates but a provision of £1,481,408 would be made against last year's carrying value for the investment to reduce it to ¥600m @ £1=188, i.e. £3,191,489.

(c) Apply the cover method for the current year but abandon it thereafter.

The calculation of exchange differences is based on opening figures for the investment and the loan. At that time the cash expected from the investment was sufficient to meet the loan, and accordingly the cover method can still be applied and therefore all of the exchange loss on the loan can be taken to reserves. However, provision would have to made in the company's financial statements to reduce the retranslated cost of investment of £5,319,149 to its recoverable amount of £3,191,489.

(d) Apply the cover method to the amount recoverable.

This treatment considers that in applying the cash restriction the loan is effectively split into two parts: (i) an amount equivalent to the cash expected to be generated and (ii) the excess over this amount. The first part is still considered to hedge the investment and the cover method can still be applied to that part. The second part is no longer providing a hedge against any investment and therefore any exchange differences relating to this part must be taken to profit and loss account. In this example, therefore, the treatment would be as follows:

```
Exchange gain on investment (as above)£646,252
Exchange loss on restricted loan
¥600m              @ 214 = £2,803,738
                   @ 188 = £3,191,489
                   ───────────
                                        (387,751)
                                        ─────────
Net exchange gain taken to reserves     £258,501
                                        ─────────
```

The exchange loss on the remainder of the loan, of £258,501, would be taken to the profit and loss account. In the company's financial statements a provision of £2,127,660 would be made to reduce the retranslated cost of investment to its recoverable amount as in (c) above.

In our view all of these treatments are acceptable under the standard but we believe that method (d) is preferable as this recognises that the company is still hedged to a certain extent.

B   Respective currency movements

We indicated earlier that the reason for condition (b) of paragraph 51 and condition (c) of paragraph 57 of the standard was to allow the cover method to be used when different currencies were involved. Although companies may decide to invest in one currency and borrow in another with the expectation or hope that they will generally move in tandem in relation to sterling, this will not always be the case. In any period some currencies will strengthen in relation to sterling and others will weaken and of those that move in the same direction the extent to which they strengthen or weaken can be markedly different. As a result, the cash restriction conditions may become relevant where they have not been before.

Example 8.40

On 1 May 1998 a UK company invests in an Australian company at a cost of A$2,560,000. How should the company apply the cover method in its financial statements for the year ended 30 April 1999 if it financed the investment with (a) a loan of 1,670,000 US dollars or (b) a loan of 2,510,000 Swiss francs ?

The relevant exchange rates are:

	£1=A$	£1=US$	£1=SFr
1 May 1998	2.56	1.67	2.51
30 April 1999	2.43	1.61	2.45

	(a) £	(b) £
Exchange gain on investment		
A$2,560,000 @ 2.56 = £1,000,000		
@ 2.43 = £1,053,498		
	53,498	53,498
Exchange loss on loan		
(a) US$1,670,000 @ 1.67 = £1,000,000		
@ 1.61 = £1,037,267		
	(37,267)	
(b) SFr2,510,000 @ 2.51 = £1,000,000		
@ 2.45 = £1,024,490		
		(24,490)
	16,231	29,008

It can be seen that in both cases the hedging has been successful and the cover method can be applied.

We now look at the position in the financial statements for the following year, 30 April 2000. Assuming the relevant exchange rates at the year end are £1=A$2.50=US$1.62=SFr2.40.

	(a) £	(b) £
Exchange loss on investment		
A$2,560,000 @ 2.43 = £1,053,498		
@ 2.50 = £1,024,000		
	(29,498)	(29,498)
Exchange difference on loan		
(a) US$1,670,000 @ 1.61 = £1,037,267		
@ 1.62 = £1,030,864		
	6,403	
(b) SFr2,510,000 @ 2.45 = £1,024,490		
@ 2.40 = £1,045,833		
		(21,343)

It can be seen that in the case of the US$ loan condition (a) of paragraph 51 of the standard is met and therefore it would appear that the cover method can be applied. However, if the book value of the investment is considered to be the recoverable amount of the investment then condition (b) has to be considered as the book value of £1,024,000 is less than the amount of the loan which is £1,030,864.

This is due to the fact that although both currencies have weakened in relation to sterling the Australian dollar has weakened more than the US dollar.

In the case of the Swiss franc loan the cover method cannot be applied as there are exchange losses on both the investment and the loan. This is because the currencies have moved in opposite directions in relation to sterling with the Swiss franc continuing to strengthen. Again, consideration has to be given to the effect of condition (b) as this loan is even more clearly not covered by the amount of the investment.

The possible treatments of condition (b) are those which were considered in the previous example. In the case of the US$ loan in this example, adopting either of methods (a), (b) or (d) will have the curious effect of actually improving the results shown in the profit and loss account as all or part of the exchange gain on the loan will be reflected therein.

3.6   Intra-group long-term loans and deferred trading balances

3.6.1   General requirement

SSAP 20 requires that all monetary items are translated at closing rates[142] and the resulting exchange differences are taken to profit and loss account.[143] This requirement is equally valid for amounts due to or from other companies within the group.[144] Any exchange differences on these inter-company accounts would be reflected, initially, in the profit and loss account of the group company which was exposed to the currency risk. On consolidation, such exchange differences would normally remain in the profit and loss account in the same way as exchange differences on monetary items resulting from transactions with third parties.

In certain circumstances, however, a holding company may decide to finance a subsidiary with loan capital rather than equity share capital with the intention of providing long-term capital for the subsidiary. This may be done for a variety of reasons: there may be tax advantages in so doing; the subsidiary may be restricted in paying dividends but not interest payments; or it may be easier to recover loans rather than equity in the event of nationalisation of the subsidiary.

Whatever the reason, the substance of the transaction is to provide long-term finance for the subsidiary and therefore the question arises of why the financial statements should show a different result by including exchange differences on the loan in the profit and loss account when exchange differences relating to the equity finance would be taken to reserves.

3.6.2   Paragraphs 20 and 43

Paragraph 20 of SSAP 20 recognises this and the fact that companies may finance subsidiaries by deferring trading balances as follows: 'Although equity investments in foreign enterprises will normally be made by the purchase of shares, investments may also be made by means of long-term loans and inter-company deferred trading balances. Where financing by such means is intended to be, for all practical purposes, as permanent as equity, such loans and inter-company balances should be treated as part of the investing company's net investment in the foreign enterprise; hence exchange differences arising on such loans and inter-company balances should be dealt with as adjustments to reserves.'

The definition of 'net investment' in paragraph 43 of the standard states that 'in appropriate circumstances, intra-group loans and other deferred balances may be regarded as part of the effective equity stake'.

3.6.3　How permanent is permanent?

It can be seen from the above that this treatment for the exchange differences should be applied where such inter-company accounts are intended to be, for all practical purposes, as permanent as equity. How should this be interpreted?

It could be argued that if it is planned or intended to repay the inter-company amount at any time while the company is a subsidiary then it is not as permanent as equity and the exchange differences should be taken to the profit and loss account. The amount should only be considered as permanent as equity if it will be repaid only when the holding company disinvests entirely from the subsidiary. This would mean that even if a company had financed a subsidiary by providing it with a loan which was due to be repaid in twenty or thirty years' time and the intention was that this would be repaid at that time then the exchange differences on the loan during that period should be recorded in the profit and loss account. This is because the exchange differences will ultimately be reflected in cash flows.

However, it is recognised that in such circumstances this would be unrealistic and therefore a shorter timespan should be considered. It has been suggested by other writers that if there is no intention to repay the amount within the foreseeable future then the inter-company account can be regarded as permanent as equity.[145]

The term 'foreseeable future' is used in paragraph 12 of SSAP 15 – *Accounting for deferred taxation* – and, although not defined, is often taken to mean a period of approximately three to five years.[146] It has been suggested that this same criterion is used in considering whether an inter-company account is as permanent as equity.[147]

It is probably easier to regard a long-term loan which is not repayable until twenty or thirty years as being as permanent as equity. What if the loan is a short-term one which is continually rolled over? In our view, if the intention is that the loan will continue to be rolled over so that it is effectively a long-term one which is not repayable in the foreseeable future, then the loan can be regarded as permanent as equity. However, we believe that if the intention is that the loan will only be rolled over until such time as the subsidiary can repay the loan, then the loan should not be regarded as permanent as equity.

The standard also allows deferred trading balances to be regarded as permanent as equity.[148] As well as including balances arising from purchase and sale of goods and services these could also include interest payments and dividend payments which have not been paid for in cash but are accumulated in the inter-company account.

In our view, such balances should only be regarded as permanent if cash settlement is not made or planned to be made in the foreseeable future. If a subsidiary makes payment for purchases from its parent company, but is continually indebted to the parent company as a result of new purchases, then in these circumstances, as individual transactions are settled, no part of the inter-company balance should be regarded as permanent. Accordingly, such exchange differences should be taken to profit and loss account.

3.6.4 What happens in year of change?

It may happen that a company will decide that its subsidiary requires to be refinanced and instead of investing more equity capital in the subsidiary decides that an existing inter-company account, which has previously been regarded as a normal monetary item, should become a long-term deferred trading balance and no repayment of such amount will be requested within the foreseeable future. How should the company treat the exchange differences relating to the inter-company account in the consolidated financial statements in the year it was so designated?

Example 8.41

A UK company has a wholly owned Canadian subsidiary whose net assets at 31 December 1997 were C$2,000,000. These net assets were arrived at after taking account of a liability to the UK parent of £250,000. Using the closing exchange rate of £1=C$2.35 this liability was included in the Canadian company's balance sheet at that date at C$587,500. On 30 June 1998 the company decided that in order to refinance the Canadian subsidiary it would regard the liability of £250,000 as a long-term liability which would not be called for repayment in the foreseeable future. Consequently, the company thereafter regarded such loan as being part of its net investment in the subsidiary. In the year ended 31 December 1998 the Canadian company made no profit or loss other than any exchange difference to be recognised on its liability to its parent company. The relevant exchange rate at that date was £1=C$2.56.

The financial statements of the subsidiary in C$ and translated using the closing rate are as follows:

Balance sheet	31 December 1998		31 December 1997	
	C$	£	C$	£
Assets	2,587,500	1,010,742	2,587,500	1,101,064
Amount due to parent	640,000	250,000	587,500	250,000
Net assets	1,947,500	760,742	2,000,000	851,064

Profit and loss account		
Exchange difference	(52,500)	

The normal treatment would be for this exchange loss to be translated at the closing rate and included in the consolidated profit and loss account as £20,508. As the net investment was C$2,000,000 then there would have been an exchange loss taken to reserves of £69,814, i.e. £851,064 less £781,250 (C$2,000,000 @ £1=C$2.56).

However, as the company now regards the amount due as being as permanent as equity it has to be included in the net investment. The question then arises as to when this should be regarded as having happened and how the exchange difference on it should be calculated. The only guidance given in SSAP 20 is in paragraph 16 which states that when applying the closing rate/net investment method, exchange differences arise if the rate ruling at the balance sheet date differs from the rate ruling at the date of subsequent capital injection. In this case there has been no capital injection as such, merely a 'redesignation' of a previous inter-company balance.

One treatment would be to regard the 'capital injection' as having taken place at the beginning of the accounting period and, therefore, the net investment increased at that date to C$2,587,500. The exchange loss on this amount is £90,322, i.e. £1,101,064 less £1,010,742, and this amount should be taken to reserves. Accordingly, all of the exchange loss included in the subsidiary's profit and loss account would be taken to reserves on consolidation. This has the merit of treating all of the exchange loss for this year consistently in the same way and it could be argued that this treatment is necessary as none of the exchange loss has any impact on the prospective cash flows of the group.

An alternative treatment would be to regard the 'capital injection' as having occurred when it was decided to redesignate the inter-company account and to take the exchange difference arising on the account up to that date to the profit and loss account. Only the exchange difference arising thereafter would be taken to reserves. At 30 June 1998 the subsidiary would have translated the inter-company account as C$612,500 (£250,000 @ £1=C$2.45) and therefore the exchange loss up to that date was C$25,000. Translated at the closing rate this amount would be included in the consolidated profit and loss account as £9,766. Accordingly, £10,742 (£20,508 less £9,766) would be taken to reserves.

This amount represents the exchange loss on the 'capital injection' of C$612,500. Translated at the closing rate this amounts to £239,258 which is £10,742 less than the original £250,000. This treatment has the merit of treating the inter-company account up to the date of redesignation consistently with previous years and taking the same exchange difference to reserves which would have been taken if a capital injection had taken place at 30 June 1988. For these reasons we believe that this treatment is preferable to the former treatment although both treatments are acceptable.

Suppose, instead of the inter-company account being £250,000, it was denominated in dollars at C$587,500. In this case the parent company would be exposed to the exchange risk; what would be the position?

The subsidiary's net assets at both 31 December 1997 and 1998 would be:

Assets	US$2,587,500
Amount due to parent company	587,500
Net assets	US$2,000,000

As the inter-company account is expressed in Canadian dollars, there will be no exchange difference thereon in the subsidiary's profit and loss account.

There will, however, be an exchange loss in the parent company as follows:

C$587,500   @ 2.35 = £250,000
                   @ 2.56 = £229,492
                   _____

                   £20,508
                   _____

Again, in the consolidated financial statements as the inter-company account is now regarded as part of the equity investment some or all of this amount can be taken to reserves. If the treatment of regarding this as happening at the beginning of the period is adopted then all of the exchange loss would be taken to reserves. This gives the same result as when the account was expressed in sterling.

If the alternative treatment is adopted then the position would be:

C$587,500   @ 2.35 = £250,000
                   @ 2.45 = £239,796
                   _____   £10,204

                   @ 2.45 = £239,796
                   @ 2.56 = £229,492
                   _____   £10,304

The exchange loss up to 30 June 1998 of £10,204 would be taken to the profit and loss account and the exchange loss thereafter of £10,304 would be taken to reserves. This is different from when the account was expressed in sterling because the 'capital injection' in this case is C$587,500 whereas before it was effectively C$612,500.

3.6.5   *Is such a treatment allowed in the company financial statements?*

We saw in the above example that when the inter-company account was expressed in Canadian dollars an exchange difference arose in the parent company and how this would be treated in the consolidated financial statements. What about the parent company financial statements? Is a similar approach allowed?

Some people take the view that SSAP 20 does not permit exchange differences on loans and deferred trading balances which are considered to be as permanent as equity to be taken to reserves in the parent company's own financial statements.[149] This is because the standard only refers to such treatment when discussing the closing rate/net investment method and in defining the net investment in the foreign enterprise.[150] As a result, it is only relevant to consolidated financial statements. No allowance is made in the provisions of SSAP 20 dealing with the financial statements of individual companies for such a treatment. These provisions require all exchange differences on monetary items to be taken to the profit and loss account (except in circumstances which are not relevant here).[151] The parent company's financial statements should therefore reflect in the results the effect of the parent company being exposed to exchange risk on its inter-company account as it is a monetary item.

Another view is that the parent company's financial statements should reflect the fact that in substance the inter-company account is not a monetary item.[152] If the account is intended to be as permanent as equity then the financial statements of the parent company should effectively show the same results and financial position as if it were an equity investment. One of the objectives of SSAP 20 is to produce results which are compatible with the effects of exchange rate changes on a company's cash flows.[153] As there is no intention for the inter-company account to be repaid until disinvestment or at least in the foreseeable future then there will be no effect on the company's cash flows as no repayments are being made. Accordingly, no exchange differences relating to the inter-company account should be reflected in the profit and loss account. We believe that this is the approach which companies should be adopting.

3.6.6 If so, how should loans be translated?

Example 8.42

Suppose in the previous example the inter-company account of C$587,500 initially arose when the exchange rate was £1=C$2.00. The possible treatments would be:

(a) Translate at closing rate

The reason for this treatment is to reflect the fact that the inter-company account is a monetary item and as such should be retranslated at closing rate. However, as the exchange differences will not impact on cash flows they should not all be taken to the profit and loss account for the year but some or all of them should be taken to reserves as explained in 3.6.4 above. It could be argued that as paragraph 20 of the standard refers to exchange differences being taken to reserves that this is the treatment required by the standard.

(b) Translate at historical rate ruling when account originally arose

As the account is considered to be as permanent as equity then it should be translated as such. Equity investments should be included at the historical rate of exchange (unless they have been financed or hedged by foreign borrowings). The account would therefore be included in the parent company balance sheet at £293,750, i.e. C$587,500 @ £1=C$2.00. The difference between this and the previously recorded amount of £250,000, or the amount when it was regarded as permanent, of £239,796, should be treated as a reserve movement.

(c) Retain at the rate ruling when the account was considered to be permanent

The reason for this treatment is that the decision during the year is a change in circumstance. Accordingly, the nature of the account only changed on 30 June 1998 and it is this date which is relevant for determining the historical rate of exchange. The account would therefore be translated as £239,796 and no further exchange difference would be recorded. (If the former treatment referred to in 3.6.4 above is adopted on consolidation then a consistent treatment in the parent company's financial statements would be to retain the account at the amount included in the previous balance sheet, i.e. £250,000.)

All previous exchange differences relating to the account should not be reversed as they arose when the inter-company account was considered to be a monetary amount.

In our view method (c) is preferable as this would be the amount included if it were an equity investment; however, all three methods are probably acceptable.

3.6.7   *UK subsidiary with loan from overseas parent company*

The previous sections have dealt with a UK parent considering that an amount due by a foreign subsidiary is as permanent as equity. What about the opposite situation where an amount is owed by a UK company to its overseas parent company, expressed in the foreign currency? Can similar treatments be adopted where the overseas parent company considers the amount due by the UK company as permanent as equity so that exchange differences on the inter-company account do not need to be reflected in the UK company's profit or loss for the year in its own financial statements?

SSAP 20 does not deal with this specific point. It could be argued that if there is no intention that such an amount will be repaid then any exchange differences will have no effect on the cash flows of the UK company and, therefore, they should not be reflected in the profit and loss account. To adopt similar treatments to those referred to above would reflect the substance of the transaction.

We believe, however, that the UK company has to translate the inter-company account at closing rate and take the exchange differences arising thereon to the profit and loss account. This is because the amount will be shown as a liability in the balance sheet and cannot be shown as equity until such time as shares are issued to the parent company or the parent company writes off the inter-company account as a capital contribution.

3.7   Other intra-group transactions

As indicated in 3.6.1 above, exchange differences on intra-group transactions should normally be treated in the same way as if they arose on transactions with third parties. However, there are two further problem areas which arise when preparing the consolidated financial statements.

3.7.1   *Dividends*

The first area relates to dividends payable by a foreign subsidiary to its UK parent company.

If a subsidiary pays a dividend to the parent company during the year the UK company should record the dividend at the rate ruling when the dividend was declared. An exchange difference will arise in the parent company's own financial statements if the exchange rate moves between the declaration date and the date the dividend is actually received. This exchange difference requires to be taken to profit and loss account and will remain there on consolidation. However, on consolidation another exchange difference is likely to arise as the dividend paid by the subsidiary will be translated at closing rate (or average rate) and this is likely to be different from the dividend received recorded by the parent company.

Example 8.43

A UK company has a wholly owned US subsidiary. On 30 September 1998 the subsidiary declares a dividend of US$0.10 per share and is due to pay a dividend of US$100,000 to the UK parent company. In preparing the consolidated financial statements for the year ended 31 March 1999 the UK company uses the closing rate/net investment method and translates the results of the US subsidiary at the closing rate. The relevant exchange rates at 30 September 1998 and 31 March 1999 are £1=US$1.70 and £1=US$1.61 respectively. Accordingly, the dividend received is recorded at £58,824 and the dividend paid in the translated profit and loss account is £62,112. What should happen to the difference of £3,288 when the inter-company dividends are eliminated on consolidation?

One treatment would be to take it to the profit and loss account as an adjustment of the subsidiary's profit or loss, as suggested by Westwick.[154] This has the effect of including in the consolidated profit and loss account the profits of the subsidiary which were distributed at the sterling amount received and the profits retained by the subsidiary translated at the closing rate.

An alternative treatment would be to treat it as a movement on reserves as the consolidated profit and loss account should reflect the profits of the subsidiary translated at the closing rate. This method will therefore retain the same financial relationships shown in the subsidiary's own financial statements in the consolidated financial statements. Consequently, we consider this treatment to be preferable.

We believe that such a treatment should also be adopted even if the dividend was unpaid at the year end. In the above example, if this had been the case, by the year end the parent company would have recorded an exchange gain of £3,288 on the dividend receivable in its own profit and loss account. We consider that this gain should remain in the profit and loss account and the difference on consolidation taken to reserves even although it is a loss of the same amount.

Another situation concerning intra-group dividends is when a dividend is proposed by the subsidiary company and this is recorded at the year end in both companies' financial statements. There is no problem in that year as both the intercompany accounts and the dividends will eliminate on consolidation with no exchange differences arising. However, as the dividend will not be received until the following year an exchange difference will arise in the parent company's financial statements in that year.

Example 8.44

A UK company has a wholly owned French subsidiary. When preparing the financial statements for the year ended 31 December 1998 it was decided that the French company would propose a dividend of FFr0.20 per share for the year then ended payable on 30 April 1999, resulting in a dividend due to the parent company of FFr200,000. The parent company, therefore, recorded in its financial statements for the year ended 31 December 1998 a dividend receivable of FFr200,000, which translated at the exchange rate ruling on that date of £1=FFr9.29, amounted to £21,529. As the subsidiary was consolidated using the closing rate/net investment method then the dividend receivable and the dividend payable cancelled each other out on consolidation. On 30 April 1999 the dividend was paid and as the exchange rate was then £1=€1.52=FFr9.98 the amount actually received was £20,040 and, therefore, the parent company recorded an exchange loss of £1,489. How should this exchange difference be dealt with in the consolidated financial statements for the year ended 31 December 1999?

This exchange difference should remain in the profit and loss account as it is no different from any other exchange difference arising on inter-company accounts resulting from other types of inter-company transactions. It should not be taken to reserves.

It may seem odd that the consolidated results can be affected by exchange differences on inter-company dividends. In order to minimise the effect of exchange rate movements companies should, therefore, arrange for inter-company dividends to be paid on the same day the dividend is declared, or as soon after the dividend is declared as possible. In addition, they should consider not booking proposed dividends in the year to which they relate but when they are actually declared unless there are commercial reasons for doing so, e.g. in order to maximise the distributable profits of the parent company shown in the year end financial statements.

One company which discloses the fact that exchange differences on payment of inter-company dividends impact on the group's results is British American Tobacco:

Extract 8.34: British American Tobacco p.l.c. (1998)

4   Foreign currencies [extract]

The differences between retained profits of overseas subsidiaries and associated undertakings translated at average and closing rates of exchange are taken to reserves, as are differences arising on the retranslation to sterling (using closing rates of exchange) of overseas net assets at the beginning of the year, after taking into account related foreign currency borrowings. Other exchange differences, including those on remittances, are reflected in profit.

3.7.2   Unrealised profits

The other problem area is the elimination of unrealised profits resulting from inter-company transactions when one of the parties to the transaction is a foreign subsidiary whose results are incorporated into the consolidated financial statements using the closing rate/net investment method.

Example 8.45

A UK company has a wholly owned German subsidiary. On 28 February 1999 the subsidiary sold goods to the parent company for €1,000. The cost of the goods to the subsidiary was €700. The goods were recorded by the parent company at £685 based on the exchange rate ruling on

28 February 1999 of £1=€1.46. All of the goods are unsold by the year end, 30 April 1999. The exchange rate at that date was £1=€1.52. How should the inter-company profit be eliminated?

SSAP 20 contains no guidance on this matter and it has been suggested that it would be logical to use the rate ruling at the date of the transaction.[155]

The profit shown by the subsidiary is €300 which translated at the rate ruling on the transaction of £1=€1.46 equals £205. Consequently, the goods will be included in the balance sheet at:

Per parent company balance sheet	£685
Less unrealised profit eliminated	205
	£480

It can be seen that the resulting figure for stock is equivalent to the original euro cost translated at the rate ruling on the date of the transaction. This is the treatment required by SFAS 52.[156] However, it should be remembered that SFAS 52 requires the results of foreign enterprises to be translated using actual or weighted average rates[157] and, therefore, is to be recommended when a weighted average is being used. Where the closing rate is being used then such an approach does not eliminate the profit from the profit and loss account. In this example, the profit of the subsidiary includes €300 which translated at €1.52 equals £197 and the amount eliminated is £205. We believe it is the former amount which should be eliminated even though this will not result in a balance sheet figure for the goods equivalent to the original cost of the goods to the group.

Consequently, where the closing rate is used to translate the results of foreign subsidiaries then we would recommend that any adjustment made to eliminate any of those profits which are unrealised as far as the group is concerned should be calculated using that closing rate. If a weighted average rate is used then the rate ruling on the date of the transaction should be used.

If in the above example the goods had been sold by the UK company to the US subsidiary then we believe the amount to be eliminated is the amount of profit shown in the UK company's financial statements. Again, this will not necessarily result in the goods being carried in the consolidated financial statements at their original cost to the group.

3.8   Introduction of the euro

The advent of the introduction of the euro raised a number of concerns and in June 1997 the European Commission published a paper – *Accounting for the introduction of the euro.* Most of the areas addressed in that paper were really of relevance to those countries who were going to participate in the first phase of Economic and Monetary Union from 1 January 1999. Nevertheless, there were some issues which were relevant in the UK and in March 1998 the UITF issued Abstract 21 – *Accounting issues arising from the proposed introduction of the euro,* effective for accounting periods ending on or after 23 March 1998. This was supplemented in August 1998 by an Appendix to the abstract dealing with some further accounting issues.

3.8.1   UITF 21

UITF 21 deals with, firstly, the treatment of costs incurred in connection with the introduction of the euro and, secondly, potential accounting implications.

A   Treatment and disclosure of costs incurred

The expenditures that may be incurred in preparation for the euro not only relate to modifications to computer software; UITF 21 also cites such examples as staff training, providing information to customers and the modification of cash handling equipment such as vending machines or cash registers.[158] The impact of the euro will clearly be greatest for companies that operate in those EU member states that have joined the system (which may include subsidiaries of UK companies), but there may be some effect on UK domestic companies as well.

Most of the expenditure mentioned above is of a revenue nature and will be expensed as incurred. However, the Abstract indicates that capitalisation of expenditure necessary to modify assets will be allowed where an entity already has an accounting policy to capitalise assets of the relevant type, but only to the extent that the expenditure clearly results in an enhancement of an asset beyond that originally assessed rather than merely maintaining its service potential.[159]

The Abstract requires that any expenditure incurred in preparing for the changeover to the euro and regarded as exceptional should be disclosed in accordance with FRS 3. Particulars of commitments at the balance sheet date in respect of costs to be incurred (whether to be treated as capital or revenue) should be disclosed where they are regarded as relevant to assessing the entity's state of affairs. However, it takes a much softer line on narrative disclosures than UITF 20 did on Year 2000 disclosures, imposing no mandatory requirement but simply recommending that some discussion should be made of the impact of the euro where it is expected to be significant, including an indication of the total costs likely to be incurred. Such disclosure may be more appropriately located in the directors' report or any operating and financial review or other statement included in the annual report published by the entity.[160]

B   Foreign currency translation effects

The foreign currency issues dealt with are likely to be relevant only to those companies that account in a currency that has become linked to the euro. The first deals with those companies that have taken exchange differences in respect of their investment in foreign subsidiaries to reserves under SSAP 20, and now find that the two currencies are irrevocably locked to the euro (and therefore to each other), so that no future exchange differences can arise. The question is whether the cumulative exchange difference in reserves should now be regarded as 'realised' and recycled through the profit and loss account. However, there is no such concept of recycling in SSAP 20, and UITF 21 makes it clear that it would be contrary to FRS 3; so the answer is that such differences should remain in reserves.[161]

The second foreign currency issue concerns anticipatory hedges of future transactions (see 3.3.1 C above). Where a company has taken out a hedge against a future transaction in a foreign currency, and once again the two currencies become linked by joining the euro, so that there will be no further exchange movements between them and no need for any hedge to be continued, should any deferred gain or loss on the hedge now be recognised in the profit and loss account? Again, UITF 21 says that the answer is no: the deferred gain or loss should continue to be carried forward and matched with the income or expense that it was originally designed to hedge.[162]

These foreign currency issues discussed are unlikely to be relevant to UK companies until sterling is linked to the euro, and by that time some of the guidance given in UITF 21, notably on hedging, may have been superseded by the ASB's conclusions on financial instruments.

3.8.2 UITF 21 - Appendix

The Appendix to UITF 21 deals primarily with issues arising for companies whose functional currency is participating in monetary union. The document itself makes clear that it is not presenting any new concepts, but rather setting out how the existing rules in SSAP 20 should be applied to some of the issues raised by the euro. The issues addressed and answers given by the UITF are summarised below:[163]

(a) What translation rate should be used where an entity chooses to provide a convenience translation of its financial statements, including comparative amounts in respect of accounting periods before the introduction of the euro?

The original reporting currency amounts should be translated at that currency's conversion rate to the euro established at 1 January 1999. It is not appropriate to rework the translations underlying the preparation of the original financial statements in the relevant national currency of the Member State.

(b) What exchange rate should be used for financial statements with year-ends other than 31 December (for example, should the fixed conversion rates be anticipated in respect of balances at dates earlier than the date of introduction of the euro)?

The normal rules in SSAPs 17 and 20 should apply. If, for example, a company with a September 1998 year-end includes in its assets and liabilities foreign currency amounts with participating Member States (amounts that may not be settled until after 1 January 1999) it would not be appropriate to record the balances at other than the closing rate at the end of September 1998.

(c) Is any special treatment needed for apparent differences arising from the use of the temporal method as, for example, the same asset may be reported at a different euro figure in a subsidiary's own accounts and in the group accounts?

The temporal method is described in paragraphs 21-24 of SSAP 20 (see 2.4.4 above). It is possible that there could be a different euro figure for the same asset (acquired before 1 January 1999) in a subsidiary's own accounts and in the group accounts, but this is a natural consequence of the temporal method, which preserves in group accounts the historical rates of exchange at which transactions were undertaken.

(d)   Does the introduction of the euro and the fixing of exchange rates mean that exchange gains on unsettled items (in respect of currencies of countries in participating Member States) become realised?

The UITF notes that the European Commission's paper concludes that such gains should be treated as realised. However, SSAP 20 requires continuous recognition of gains and losses on all monetary items, even long-term ones, whether realised or not. There is no cause to recognise any further gain or loss when realisation takes place.

4   MAIN CRITICISMS OF SSAP 20 AND SUGGESTED SOLUTIONS

We believe that SSAP 20 provides a reasonably sound basis for the reporting of foreign currency transactions in financial statements. However, in our view a number of criticisms can be made against the standard and further improvements could be made to ensure greater comparability between companies both within the UK and internationally. The ASB's proposals on financial instruments may provide the impetus for changes to be made to the standard.

4.1   Forward contracts and similar hedging contracts

4.1.1   Criticisms

We have looked at the many problem areas which arise in accounting for these types of transactions in 3.3 above. In our view there are two main criticisms of the approach taken by SSAP 20 in relation to forward contracts and other similar hedging contracts, such as options and currency swaps.

A   Insufficient guidance

First, there is insufficient guidance on the accounting for such contracts. Forward contracts are only mentioned by stating that the contract rate may be used to record transactions and monetary assets and liabilities.[164] Although reference is made to the discount or premium on the forward contract when defining what a forward contract is,[165] no further guidance is given as to how to account for the discount or premium. As indicated in 3.3.1 above, a forward contract can be taken out as a hedge against an investment in a foreign enterprise, the results of a foreign enterprise, an existing monetary asset or liability position, or a future commitment, or it may be taken out as a speculative transaction. In each case the accounting for the contract is not necessarily the same.

No mention is made of currency swaps and other agreements which are essentially the same as forward contracts or of currency options.

B   *Use of forward rates is optional*

Second, by stating that the rates included in forward contracts *may* be used to record transactions or translate monetary assets or liabilities has meant that the accounting for the forward contracts has become optional. Companies can choose to ignore a related forward contract if they wish. As a result consistency of treatment between different companies is unlikely to be achieved.

4.1.2   *Solution*

We believe that SSAP 20 should be amended to deal with the topic of forward contracts and similar agreements, such as currency swaps, in a similar way to SFAS 52 as suggested in 3.3 above, except that companies should be able to account for forward contracts which are designated as a hedge against anticipated future transactions rather than just those which are the subject of a firm commitment.

4.2   Cover method

4.2.1   *Criticisms*

We have looked at a number of problem areas relating to the use of the cover method in 3.5 above. In our view there are three main criticisms which can be made against the provisions of SSAP 20 in respect of borrowings which have been used to finance, or provide a hedge against, equity investments.

A   *Use is optional*

First, by stating that the equity investments *may* be denominated in foreign currencies [166] the standard allows companies to choose whether or not they wish to apply the cover method provisions. As a result comparability between different companies is unlikely to be achieved. This also applies to the provisions relating to consolidated financial statements as exchange differences *may* be offset as reserve movements.[167]

B   *Cover may not exist when borrowings are in different currencies*

Second, the absence of a requirement that borrowings be in the same currency as the investment means that cover may not exist. Different currencies may move in different directions in relation to sterling or to a different extent in the same direction in relation to sterling. Accordingly, companies cannot be assured that they will always be covered. In order to eliminate the exchange risk completely it is necessary for the borrowings to be in the same currency as the investment.

C   *It can lead to inconsistent treatment from period to period*

Third, by allowing borrowings to be in different currencies from the investments then the exchange differences on the borrowings will not necessarily be treated the same way each year. In those periods in which the criteria contained in SSAP 20 are met exchange differences will be taken to reserves, and in periods in which they are not met exchange differences will either all be taken to profit and loss account or some will be taken to reserves and the rest to profit and loss account.

4.2.2   Solution

We believe that SSAP 20 should be amended along similar lines to that contained in SFAS 52.[168]

A   *Designation requirement*

Exchange differences on transactions (including borrowings) that are designated, and are effective, as economic hedges of an equity investment or the net investment in a foreign enterprise should be taken to reserves and should not be taken to the profit and loss account, commencing from the designation date. Such treatment will ensure that the accounting for the exchange differences reflect the economic rationale of the decision taken by the company.

B   *Same currency requirement with exception for use of tandem currency*

The transaction which hedges the equity investment or the net investment in the foreign enterprise should be denominated in the same currency as the investment. Where it is not practical or feasible for the currency to be the same then the hedging transaction may be in a currency which generally moves in tandem with the currency of the hedged investment. Such a requirement will recognise that an effective hedge can only arise where the currencies are the same.

5   RELATED COMPANIES ACT REQUIREMENTS

There are a number of requirements of the Companies Act 1985 which have to be considered when accounting for foreign exchange transactions. The main implications are considered below.

5.1   Realised profits

Most companies in the UK when preparing their financial statements have to comply with the accounting requirements of Schedule 4 of the Companies Act 1985.

5.1.1 Schedule 4, paragraph 12

Paragraph 12 of Schedule 4 requires that items in a company's financial statements shall be determined on a prudent basis and only profits which are realised at the balance sheet date can be included in the profit and loss account. However, what is meant by realised profits?

5.1.2 Section 262(3)

Section 262(3) of the Companies Act 1985 states that realised profits should be interpreted as 'such profits of the company as fall to be treated as realised profits for the purposes of those accounts in accordance with principles generally accepted with respect to the determination for accounting purposes of realised profits at the time when those accounts are prepared'.

The main reference to realised profits by the accountancy profession in the UK is in SSAP 2 when defining the concept of prudence. This states 'revenue and profits are not anticipated, but are recognised by inclusion in the profit and loss account only when realised in the form either of cash or of other assets the ultimate cash realisation of which can be assessed with reasonable certainty'.[169]

The normal requirement for exchange differences in the financial statements of a company is that they are taken to the profit and loss account. As a result the ASC in considering this treatment for exchange differences had to give some guidance as to whether exchange gains were to be regarded as realised or not and whether the treatment of such gains required by the standard was consistent with the provisions of paragraph 12.

SSAP 20 identifies three categories of exchange gains which have to be considered.

5.1.3 Settled transactions

First, those arising on settled transactions. As such exchange gains have already impacted on the cash flows of the company then they are clearly realised in cash terms and, therefore, their inclusion in the profit and loss account does not conflict with paragraph 12.

5.1.4 Short-term monetary items

Second, those arising on short-term monetary items. A short-term monetary item is defined in SSAP 20 as one which falls due within one year of the balance sheet date.[170] The statement issued by the ASC at the time the standard was issued said that such exchange gains could be regarded as realised in accordance with the prudence concept contained in SSAP 2, as their ultimate cash realisation can normally be assessed with reasonable certainty. Accordingly, their inclusion in the profit and loss account is not considered to be in conflict with paragraph 12.[171]

5.1.5   Long-term monetary items

Third, those arising on long-term monetary items. It is generally considered that such gains are probably unrealised. The ASC recognised this potential conflict with paragraph 12 but still decided that exchange gains on such items should be taken to the profit and loss account. It considered that a symmetrical treatment of exchange gains and losses was necessary to show a true and fair view of the results of a company involved in foreign currency operations. This treatment acknowledges that exchange gains can be determined no less objectively than exchange losses and it would be illogical to deny that favourable movements in exchange rates had occurred whilst accounting for adverse movements. As there will probably be some interaction between currency movements and interest rates then the profit and loss account will reflect the full impact of the currency involvement.[172] So how was the conflict resolved?

One way would have been to invoke the true and fair view override allowed by what is now section 226 of the Companies Act 1985. However, as the problem was with one of the accounting principles contained in Schedule 4 it was decided to invoke paragraph 15 of that schedule.[173]

This paragraph specifically permits a departure from the accounting principles where there are special reasons and it is considered that the need for a symmetrical treatment constitutes a special reason. As a result, companies which have taken exchange gains on long-term monetary items need to disclose the particulars of the departure, the reasons for it and its effect in a note to the financial statements. An example of such disclosure is as follows:

The profit and loss account includes gains on translation of long-term monetary items. The inclusion of these gains represents a departure from the statutory requirement that only realised profit may be included in the profit and loss account. The directors consider that this accounting treatment, which is in accordance with SSAP 20, is necessary in order to give a true and fair view. The unrealised gains included for the year amounted to £10,000 (1998–£5,000) and the cumulative amount included at 31 December 1999 is £15,000.

A   Problem areas

In 3.2 above we considered a number of problem areas in relation to exchange gains on long-term monetary items which will also be relevant in deciding whether it is necessary to invoke paragraph 15 and give the necessary disclosures, in particular the amount of the exchange gains which are involved.

(a)   Past exchange losses

It could be argued that past exchange losses on a long-term monetary item should be ignored and that all of the exchange gain in the current year is unrealised and therefore disclosure is required of the full amount. This would appear to be an ultra cautious view.[174]

Our view is that past exchange losses should be taken into account and that disclosure is only required to the extent that the exchange gain exceeds the net losses previously recognised. Any exchange gain up to the amount of the past losses is effectively a reversal of a provision for losses no longer required. This would appear to be the approach taken by other writers.[175]

Accordingly, if the exchange gain is less than the past exchange losses no disclosure is required under paragraph 15.

(b)   Settled or unsettled transactions

As the exchange gain in question relates to an unsettled long-term monetary item then in considering the effect of past exchange losses we believe that it is only the past exchange losses which relate to the proportion that is still outstanding which should be taken into account. Past exchange losses and any current year's exchange losses which relate to amounts that have already been settled should be ignored.

(c)   Current portion of long-term monetary items

As any current portion at the end of the financial year will be reflected in cash flows within one year then any exchange gains relating thereto should be regarded as realised. Accordingly, if a long-term item at the end of the previous period has all become due within one year at the end of the current period then no disclosure is required under paragraph 15.

In view of these problem areas we would recommend that companies keep a detailed record of the exchange differences which have arisen on all long-term monetary items since origination.

5.2   Distributable profits

5.2.1   Section 263(3)

Under section 263(3) of the Companies Act 1985, dividends can only be paid by a company out of cumulative realised profits less realised losses and, therefore, the question of whether exchange gains are realised or not, or indeed whether exchange losses are realised or not, has an important bearing on the distributable profits of a company. The distributable profits of a public company are further restricted to the extent that unrealised losses exceed unrealised profits.[176]

The statement issued by the ASC at the time the standard was published made it clear that the statement only set out the standard accounting practice for foreign currency translation and was not intended to deal with the determination of distributable profits. It emphasised that the question of distributability depends upon the interpretation of company legislation and should be resolved by individual companies, with legal advice where necessary.[177] It did, however, comment on two possible problem areas.

5.2.2   Long-term monetary items

The first area was in relation to exchange gains on long-term monetary items. In the previous section we considered whether such gains were realised or not. Where the exchange gains are unrealised, then even although they can be taken to the profit and loss account, they cannot be included in arriving at the distributable profits of a company.[178] This makes it even more important for companies to keep a detailed record of exchange differences on such items.

5.2.3   *Section 275 and Schedule 4, paragraph 89*

So much for exchange gains, what about exchange losses?

Section 275 of the Companies Act 1985 requires that for the purposes of determining distributable profits a provision of any kind mentioned in paragraph 89 of Schedule 4 is to be treated as a realised loss.

Paragraph 89 states that 'references to provisions for liabilities or charges are to any amount retained as reasonably necessary for the purpose of providing for any liability or loss which is either likely to be incurred, or certain to be incurred but uncertain as to amount or as to the date on which it will arise'.

It is generally recognised that exchange losses on settled transactions and on unsettled short-term monetary items should be regarded as realised losses. It is also considered, on the grounds of prudence, that exchange losses on long-term monetary items should also be regarded as realised. However, this brings us to the second possible problem area – the cover method.

5.2.4   *Cover method*

As the cover method can be applied in individual companies' financial statements, this will result in exchange gains and losses on borrowings being taken to reserves to be offset against exchange differences on related equity investments. If exchange losses have arisen on the borrowings should these be regarded as realised?

A   *TR 504 – paragraph 33(b)*

It could be argued that any exchange loss on a borrowing should be regarded as a provision under paragraph 89 of Schedule 4 and therefore a realised loss which would have to be deducted before arriving at distributable profits, whereas the compensating exchange gain on the investment would be unrealised and not available for distribution. However, as stated by the ASC 'this does not reflect the economic realities of hedging which is designed to avoid the creation of any loss' and it can therefore be argued that the exchange 'loss' on the borrowing is not a provision (nor a realised loss) 'either likely to be incurred, or certain to be incurred but uncertain as to amount or as to the date on which it will arise'.

B   *Problem of timing – income required before payment of loan*

We believe that one possible approach to this problem is to consider the timing of the cash flows relating to the investment and the borrowings. The statement by the ASC makes no reference to the fact that some of the exchange losses which have been offset in reserves may relate to borrowings which have already been repaid. We believe that such losses should be regarded as realised as they have been reflected in the cash flows of the company. If the company has regarded the borrowing as a hedge against its investment it is likely to have received dividends from the investment to enable it to repay the borrowings. As the dividends will be recorded at the rate ruling when the dividends were due these will reflect an element of exchange difference since the investment was made. The inherent exchange gain will offset the realised exchange loss on the borrowings which have been repaid.

In considering whether any exchange losses on the borrowings which are still outstanding should be regarded as realised or not, regard should be had to the timing of the income to be received from the investment. If sufficient dividends will be received from the investment prior to each instalment on the borrowings being repaid then it could be argued that there will be no loss on the borrowings. Although any exchange loss will become realised at the time the instalment is paid this will be offset by the inherent exchange gain in the dividend. Accordingly, any exchange losses on the borrowings do not represent a provision for a loss and therefore do not have to be regarded as a realised loss under section 275. We believe that this approach recognises the economic reality that the company is hedged.

If insufficient dividends will be received prior to an instalment of the borrowing being repaid then to the extent that the borrowing is uncovered the exchange loss relating to that portion should be regarded as a realised loss.

Although we believe such an approach to be a sensible one it is unclear as to whether the courts would take a similar view. Accordingly it is important to emphasise the advice given by the ASC in its statement that where the existence of an economic hedge would have to be taken into account in order to make a distribution, it may be appropriate for the directors of the company to seek legal advice.[179]

5.2.5   *Branch accounting*

Another area, which the ASC did not deal with in its statement, is where an individual company has a foreign branch. As we have already seen the definition of a foreign branch is a wide one and can include a group of assets and liabilities which are accounted for in foreign currencies.[180] The standard requires the exchange difference on the net investment in the foreign branch to be taken to reserves.[181] The question then arises, is this one net exchange difference which has to be regarded as a realised or unrealised item, or is it an amalgamation of a number of exchange differences some of which may be realised and some of which may be not?

It could be argued that the former treatment is the more correct, particularly as the closing rate/net investment method should only be used if there is no cash flow impact on the rest of the company. If all of the net cash flows of the branch are retained in the foreign currency and not converted into sterling then why should any of the exchange difference be regarded as realised?

In our view it is likely that this former treatment can only be applied where the branch is a legally constituted branch overseas. Where the branch is a group of assets and liabilities then it is likely that the latter approach will have to be applied as the legal entity is the company. This, therefore, gives rise to a couple of problems.

A   Similar to cover method

First, the main asset is likely to be a non-monetary item and the main liability is likely to be a long-term monetary item. This gives rise to a similar problem as that discussed in relation to the cover method above in that the exchange differences on the asset will be unrealised and the exchange differences on the borrowing could be regarded as realised. We believe, however, that it would be sensible to adopt a similar approach to that suggested in relation to borrowings under the cover method above.

B   Short-term monetary items

Second, it is likely that part of the branch will be represented by trading balances i.e. debtors, creditors, and bank balances. As these are all short-term monetary items then any exchange gains or losses should be regarded as realised.

As a result of the above it is recommended that detailed records are kept of the breakdown of exchange differences on the net investment in the foreign branch. The cumulative exchange difference at each year end should be split into:

(a)   the cumulative exchange difference on the non-monetary assets.

   This will be the difference between the net book value in currency terms translated at closing rate and translated at historical rates applying at the date of purchase. This difference should be regarded as an unrealised difference;

(b)   the cumulative exchange difference on the borrowings.

   This will be the difference between the amount outstanding in currency terms translated at closing rate and translated at historical rate when the borrowing originated. This difference should then be determined to be realised or unrealised as recommended above, i.e. consider whether sufficient net income will be received from the asset prior to paying each instalment of the borrowing;

(c)   the remainder.

   This should represent the exchange differences on assets which have been depreciated or sold, borrowings which have been repaid, and on the monetary trading balances. All of this amount should be regarded as realised.

We would emphasise that although we believe such an approach to be a sensible one the courts may take a different view. Therefore, if it is necessary in order to make a distribution to regard some of the exchange differences on the borrowings as unrealised because they are covered by foreign currency assets, then it may be appropriate for the directors of the company to seek legal advice.

5.3   Disclosure

There are a number of provisions of the Companies Act which have to be considered in relation to disclosure within a company's financial statements.

5.3.1   *Basis of translation*

A   Schedule 4, paragraph 58(1)

Paragraph 58(1) of Schedule 4 requires that 'where sums originally denominated in foreign currencies have been brought into account under any items shown in the balance sheet or profit or loss account, the basis on which those sums have been translated into sterling shall be stated'.

B   SSAP 20, paragraph 59

This effectively extends the requirement of paragraph 59 of the standard so that disclosure of the method of translating monetary and non-monetary items by individual companies is given. Paragraph 59 only requires the method used in translating the financial statements of foreign enterprises to be disclosed.

5.3.2   *Treatment of exchange differences in profit and loss account*

A   Formats

The profit and loss formats contained in Schedule 4 set out the headings of income and expenditure which a company should use in preparing its profit and loss account. It will therefore be necessary for companies to consider under which heading exchange differences reported as part of the profit or loss for the year should be included. Distinction is effectively made in the formats between operating income and expenditure and other income and expenditure. Accordingly, the nature of each exchange difference will have to be considered.

B   SSAP 20, paragraph 68

Guidance is given in paragraph 68 of the standard. Gains or losses arising from trading transactions should normally be shown as 'other operating income or expense' while those arising from arrangements which may be considered as financing should be disclosed separately as part of 'other interest receivable/payable and similar income/expense'. The amounts included do not have to be separately disclosed; however, it should be borne in mind that the standard requires the net exchange difference on foreign currency borrowings less deposits to be disclosed.

5.3.3 Reserve movements

A   Schedule 4, paragraph 46

Paragraph 46 of Schedule 4 requires the following information to be disclosed about movements on any reserve:

(a)   the amount of the reserve at the date of the beginning of the financial year and as at the balance sheet date respectively;

(b)   any amounts transferred to or from the reserve during that year; and

(c)   the source and application respectively of any amounts so transferred.

B   SSAP 20, paragraph 60

These requirements are unlikely to have any major impact as paragraph 60 of the standard requires the net movement on reserves arising from exchange differences to be disclosed.

5.3.4 Movements on provisions for liabilities and charges

A   Schedule 4, paragraph 46

The requirements referred to above in respect of reserve movements apply equally to movements on provisions for liabilities and charges, e.g. a provision for deferred tax. Accordingly, it will be necessary to disclose separately the net movement on the provision which arises from exchange differences.

5.3.5 Movements on fixed assets

A   Schedule 4, paragraph 42

Paragraph 42 of Schedule 4 requires, inter alia, disclosure of movements on fixed assets resulting from:

(a)   acquisitions of any assets during the year;

(b)   disposals of any assets during the year; and

(c)   any transfer of assets of the company to and from another category of asset during the year.

Similarly, movements on provisions for depreciation or diminution in value have to be shown.

As a result of these requirements, where fixed assets are translated at closing rates it will be necessary to disclose separately the net movements arising on the cost or valuation of the fixed assets and on any related provision resulting from exchange differences.

5.4   Alternative accounting rules

5.4.1   Schedule 4, Part II, section C

Section C of Part II of Schedule 4 allows companies to include assets in the balance sheet at amounts based on valuations or current costs rather than being included at amounts based on historical costs. Where this is done there are a number of requirements which have to be followed, e.g. disclosure of comparable figures based on historical costs.

The question then arises – does the process of translating assets at closing rates constitute a departure from the normal historical cost rules and the requirements of Section C apply?

It could be argued, particularly where the cover method is being used and investments are translated at closing rates or where a tangible asset is regarded as part of a branch and translated at closing rates, that items do have a sterling historical cost and if they are included at an amount other than that cost then it must be a departure.

5.4.2   SSAP 20, paragraph 66

Paragraph 66 of SSAP 20, however, makes it clear that this is not the view taken by the standard. The translation process by itself merely translates the historical cost expressed in foreign currency at a closing rate of exchange. It does not result in a valuation of the asset or express it at its current cost. Accordingly, if it is thought that the provisions of SSAP 20 do result in a departure from the historical cost rules then it would appear that the provisions of the Companies Act are being breached. This is because the alternative accounting rules only allow assets to be included at a valuation, normally a market value, or at current cost.

6   COMPARISON WITH IASC AND US PRONOUNCEMENTS

6.1   IASC

6.1.1   General comment

The principal international standard dealing with this topic is IAS 21 – *The Effects of Changes in Foreign Exchange Rates*. The original standard was issued in July 1983, but a revised version was published in December 1993. Although the revised standard follows the same general approach as SSAP 20, nevertheless there are a number of differences, of which the main ones are outlined below.

In addition, derivative instruments such as forward currency contracts, swaps and options are covered by IAS 39 – *Financial Instruments: Recognition and Measurement* – which has detailed rules on hedging (see Chapter 9 at 5.1.3).

The Standing Interpretations Committee of the IASC has issued ·two interpretations of IAS 21. In October 1997 it issued SIC 7 which deals with how the provisions of IAS 21 should be applied as a result of the changeover from the national currencies of participating Member States of the European Union to the euro. In January 1998 it also issued SIC 11 – *Foreign Exchange - Capitalisation of Losses Resulting from Severe Currency Devaluations* – which is discussed at 6.1.2 A below.

6.1.2   Main differences

A   Treatment of exchange differences

Like SSAP 20, IAS 21 requires exchange differences on the settlement or retranslation of monetary items to be recognised as income or as expenses in the period in which they arise, with the exception of:

(a)   those arising on a monetary item that, in substance, forms part of an enterprise's net investment in a foreign entity; and

(b)   those arising on a foreign currency liability accounted for as a hedge of an enterprise's net investment in a foreign entity.

In these situations the exchange differences should be classified as equity.[182]

However, IAS 21 allows an alternative treatment for exchange differences which result from a severe devaluation or depreciation of a currency against which there is no practical means of hedging and that affects liabilities which cannot be settled and which arise directly on the recent acquisition of an asset invoiced in a foreign currency. Such exchange differences can be included in the carrying amount of the related asset, provided that the adjusted carrying amount does not exceed the lower of the replacement cost and the amount recoverable from the sale or use of the asset.[183] This treatment requires several conditions to be met cumulatively before an enterprise can include exchange losses on foreign currency liabilities in the carrying amount of related assets. SIC 11 deals with how the conditions should be interpreted that the liability 'cannot be settled' and that there is 'no practical means of hedging' against the foreign currency exchange risk and that the liability should arise on the 'recent acquisition' of an asset.[184] The SIC agreed that foreign exchange losses on liabilities that result from the recent acquisition of assets should only be included in the carrying amount of the assets if those liabilities could not have been settled or if it was not practically feasible to hedge the foreign currency exposure before the severe devaluation or depreciation occurred.[185] Only in these cases foreign exchange losses are unavoidable and therefore part of the asset's acquisition costs. Recent acquisitions of assets are acquisitions within twelve months prior to the severe devaluation or depreciation of the reporting currency.[186] SSAP 20 has no similar rules.

B   Translation of foreign enterprises

Like SSAP 20, IAS 21 requires the closing rate/net investment method to be used,[187] unless the foreign enterprise is integral to the operations of the reporting enterprise in which case the temporal method should be used.[188]

When there is a change in the classification of a foreign operation, IAS 21 requires that the translation procedures applicable to the revised classification should be applied from the date of the change in the classification.[189] When a foreign operation that is integral to the operations of the reporting enterprise is reclassified as a foreign entity, exchange differences arising on the translation of non-monetary assets at the date of the reclassification are classified as equity. When a foreign entity is reclassified as a foreign operation that is integral to the operation of the reporting enterprise, the translated amounts for non-monetary items at the date of the change are treated as the historical cost for those items in the period of change and subsequent periods.[190] SSAP 20 does not deal with such situations.

C   Results of foreign enterprises

Where the closing rate/net investment method is being used, IAS 21 requires the income and expense items of foreign enterprises (except those reporting in a currency of a hyperinflationary economy as discussed at G below) to be translated at the exchange rates ruling at the dates of the transactions (or at an average rate that approximates the actual rate).[191]

SSAP 20, on the other hand, allows a choice of translating the results of the foreign enterprise either at the closing rate of exchange or at an average rate for the period.[192]

D   Disposal of investment

IAS 21 requires that on the disposal of a foreign entity, the cumulative amount of the exchange differences which have been deferred or taken to equity and which relate to that foreign entity are to be included as part of the gain or loss on disposal.[193]

SSAP 20 contains no provisions as to what should happen to the cumulative exchange differences when the investment is sold or liquidated. However, under FRS 3, as the original exchange differences would have been reflected in the statement of total recognised gains and losses when they arose, then they should not be recognised again in the year of disposal in either the profit and loss account or the statement of recognised gains and losses (see Chapter 22 at 2.9.1).

E   Cover method

IAS 21 does not deal with hedge accounting for foreign currency items, other than the requirement for exchange differences arising on a foreign currency liability accounted for as a hedge of a net investment in a foreign entity to be taken to reserves as part of equity.[194] Other aspects of hedge accounting, including the criteria for the use of hedge accounting, are no longer covered in IAS 21 as they are now dealt with in IAS 39 (see Chapter 9 at 5.1.3).[195]

F   Forward exchange contracts

IAS 21 regards an unperformed foreign exchange contract as being like any other type of foreign currency transaction.[196] However, again it no longer deals with forward contracts in any detail as they are now covered by IAS 39.

SSAP 20 contains very little guidance on accounting for forward exchange contracts. It allows, but does not require, companies to record transactions and monetary assets and liabilities using the forward rate specified in any related or matching forward contract.[197]

G   Hyper-inflation

IAS 21 requires the financial statements of an enterprise that reports in the currency of a hyper-inflationary economy to be restated in accordance with the international standard, IAS 29 – *Financial Reporting in Hyperinflationary Economies* – before the translation process is undertaken.[198] It also requires the income and expense items of such enterprises to be translated at the closing rate of exchange.[199]

IAS 29 does not establish an absolute rate at which hyper-inflation is deemed to arise, but lists a number of characteristics of such an economy, one of which is that the cumulative inflation rate over three years is approaching, or exceeds, 100%.[200] Under IAS 29 the financial statements of an enterprise that reports in the currency of a hyper-inflationary economy, whether they are based on a historical cost approach or a current cost approach, should be stated in terms of the measuring unit current at the balance sheet date.[201]

SSAP 20 gives no guidance as to what it means by 'a very high rate of inflation'. It suggests that where a company has an investment in a foreign enterprise which operates in a country with a high rate of inflation then the financial statements should be adjusted where possible to reflect current price levels before the translation process takes place.[202] However, UITF 9 effectively defines hyper-inflation by using the characteristic in IAS 29 described above, but requires the financial statements of the foreign enterprise either to be adjusted for inflation first or to be prepared using a strong currency (not necessarily the reporting currency) as the functional currency.

Under IAS 21 when the economy ceases to be hyper-inflationary and the foreign entity discontinues the preparation of its financial statements under IAS 29, it should use the amounts expressed in the measuring unit current at the date of discontinuation as the historical costs for translation into the reporting currency of the reporting enterprise.[203]

H   Disclosure

IAS 21 requires the amount of exchange difference taken to profit and loss account to be disclosed. It also requires the exchange adjustments which result from translating the foreign enterprise's financial statements to be classified as a separate component of equity and for a reconciliation of the amount of such exchange differences at the beginning and end of the period to be disclosed.[204] Accordingly, the cumulative exchange differences will be disclosed.[204]

SSAP 20 does not require the net exchange gain or loss included in net profit to be disclosed. It does, however, require the net exchange gain or loss on borrowings less deposits included in net profit to be disclosed.[205]

SSAP 20 only requires the translation adjustments which result from translating the foreign enterprise's financial statements to be taken to reserves and for the movement in reserves during the period to be disclosed.[206] They do not have to be taken to a separate reserve and therefore the cumulative exchange differences will not be apparent from the financial statements.

IAS 21 also requires disclosure of the following:

(a)   The amount of exchange differences arising during the period which is included in the carrying amount of an asset in accordance with the allowed alternative treatment discussed at A above.[207]

(b)   When the reporting currency is different from that of the country in which the enterprise is domiciled the reason for using that different currency. The reason for any change in reporting currency should also be disclosed.[208]

(c)   When there is a change from using the temporal method to the closing rate method or vice versa:

   (i)   the nature of the change in classification;

   (ii)   the reason for the change;

   (iii)   the impact of the change in classification on shareholders' equity; and

   (iv)   the impact on net profit or loss for each prior period had the change in classification occurred at the beginning of the earliest period presented.[209]

(d)   The method selected to translate goodwill and fair value adjustments arising on the acquisition of a foreign entity.[210]

6.2   US

6.2.1   *General comment*

The equivalent standard in the US is SFAS 52 – *Foreign Currency Translation*. Prior to the issue of the respective exposure drafts of both SSAP 20 and SFAS 52 there was a long period of consultation between the standard setting bodies of the two countries, together with that of Canada.

Accordingly, the requirements of SSAP 20 and SFAS 52 are both based on the same conceptual theory in that they both advocate the use of the closing rate/net investment method when dealing with the financial statements of foreign enterprises whose functional currency is different from that of the reporting currency of the holding company. Nevertheless, there are a number of differences between the two standards, of which the main ones are outlined at 6.2.2 below.

In June 1998 the FASB issued SFAS 133 – *Accounting for Derivative Instruments and Hedging Activities*. This standard requires derivatives, such as forward exchange contracts, swaps or options, to be carried at fair value. It allows 'special accounting' for three different categories of hedging transaction provided certain criteria are met. The requirements of this standard are discussed in Chapter 9 at 5.2.3. SFAS 133 had originally been intended to be mandatory for accounting periods beginning after 15 June 1999 but this has now been deferred for an extra year. However, some companies may implement the standard earlier because it allows hedging of anticipated transactions which was not the case under SFAS 52. As a result of SFAS 133, SFAS 52 no longer deals with forward exchange contracts or swaps and most of the hedging rules have been superseded by those contained in SFAS 133. Nevertheless until SFAS 133 is applied, the rules in SFAS 52 continue to be relevant.

6.2.2   Main differences

A   Translation of foreign enterprises

Like SSAP 20, SFAS 52 requires the closing rate/net investment method to be used,[211] unless the functional currency of the foreign enterprise is the same as that of the reporting enterprise in which case the temporal method should be used.[212]

If significant changes in economic facts and circumstances indicate clearly that the functional currency has changed, SFAS 52 gives similar guidance to that in IAS 21 as to how this should be dealt with. As indicated at 6.1.2 B above, SSAP 20 does not deal with such situations.

B   Results of foreign enterprises

Where the closing rate/net investment method is being used, SFAS 52 requires the revenues, expenses, gains, and losses of foreign enterprises to be translated at the exchange rates ruling when those elements are recognised or at an appropriate weighted average rate for the period.[213]

As indicated in 6.1.2 C above SSAP 20 allows a choice of translating the results of foreign enterprises either at the closing rate or at an average rate for the period.

C   Disposal of investment

SFAS 52 and FASB Interpretation 37 require that where all or part of an investment in a foreign enterprise is sold, or it is substantially liquidated, then the cumulative exchange differences included within other comprehensive income relating to the part which is sold or liquidated shall be included in the net profit for the period as part of the gain or loss on sale or liquidation.[214]

SSAP 20 contains no provisions as to what should happen to the cumulative exchange differences when the investment is sold or liquidated. However, under FRS 3, as the original exchange differences would have been reflected in the statement of total recognised gains and losses when they arose, then they should not be recognised again in the year of disposal in either the profit and loss account or the statement of recognised gains and losses (see Chapter 22 at 2.9.1).

D   Cover method

The cover method in SFAS 52 can only be applied where the investment which is being hedged is consolidated or equity accounted.[215] However, the hedging transaction is not restricted to being a foreign currency borrowing but can be any foreign currency transaction which provides a hedge.[216] SFAS 52 requires such a transaction to be designated as, and effective as, an economic hedge of the net investment in the foreign enterprise. If a transaction is designated a hedge then all exchange differences until such time as it is no longer designated must be taken to reserves.[217] In order that the hedge is effective the transaction has to be in the same foreign currency as the investment or, if this is impossible to arrange, in a foreign currency which moves in tandem with that of the investment.[218]

The cover method in SSAP 20 can be applied in individual companies' financial statements to investments which are carried at cost. However, the cover method only applies to foreign currency borrowings. The method may or may not be applied to such borrowings which provide a hedge as long as the treatment is applied consistently from period to period. The borrowings need not be in the same foreign currency as the investment, but the exchange difference taken to reserves is restricted to the offsetting exchange difference on the investment.[219]

E   Forward exchange contracts

Until superseded by SFAS 133, SFAS 52 contains detailed requirements in respect of forward exchange contracts, including agreements that are essentially the same as forward exchange contracts.[220] The accounting for such contracts depends on whether they are taken out as a hedge against a foreign currency exposure or are merely speculative. Where the contract is a hedge then any exchange gain or loss on the contract is accounted for separately from the discount or premium on the contract. The accounting for these amounts will depend on whether the contract is a hedge against:

(a)   a net investment in a foreign enterprise; or

(b)   a foreign currency commitment; or

(c)   other foreign currency exposures.

Where the forward contract is speculative then no separate accounting recognition is given to the discount or premium on the contract.

The requirements of SFAS 52 in respect of such contracts are dealt with in 3.3.1 above.

As indicated earlier in 6.1.2 F above SSAP 20 contains little guidance in this area and allows companies to use the forward rate in recording transactions and translating monetary items, including long-term items.

F   *Hyper-inflation*

SFAS 52 defines a highly inflationary economy as one that has cumulative inflation of approximately 100% or more over a three year period. Where a company has an investment in a foreign enterprise in a highly inflationary economy, then the financial statements of the enterprise have to be remeasured as if its functional currency were the reporting currency, i.e. effectively translated using the temporal method.[221]

SSAP 20 only recommends that a similar approach is adopted 'where possible', although as indicated at 6.1.2 G above, UITF 9 requires the financial statements of the foreign enterprise either to be adjusted for inflation first or to be prepared using a strong currency (not necessarily the reporting currency) as the functional currency.

G   *Disclosure*

SFAS 52 requires the net exchange gain or loss included in net profit to be disclosed.[222] It also requires the translation adjustments which result from translating the foreign enterprise's financial statements to be classified separately within other comprehensive income. Accordingly, the cumulative exchange differences will be disclosed.[223]

SSAP 20 does not require the net exchange gain or loss included in net profit to be disclosed. It does, however, require the net exchange gain or loss on borrowings less deposits included in net profit to be disclosed.[224]

SSAP 20 only requires the translation adjustments which result from translating the foreign enterprise's financial statements to be taken to reserves and for the movement in reserves during the period to be disclosed.[225] They do not have to be taken to a separate reserve and therefore the cumulative exchange differences will not be apparent from the financial statements.

7 CONCLUSION

Ever since the first edition of this book in 1989 we have criticised SSAP 20 and suggested improvements (see 4 above). We continue to believe that the reporting of foreign currency transactions would be significantly improved if SSAP 20 were amended as suggested in 4 above and greater comparability of results between companies within the UK and internationally would be achieved. As all of the suggestions are compatible with the existing provisions of SSAP 20 we would recommend that companies adopt such treatments presently.

We therefore welcome the ASB's announcement that it plans to review SSAP 20 in its entirety and that an exposure draft is to be developed. However, this is tempered by the fact that this is only to be as soon as its project on financial instruments has settled some key issues that are fundamental to foreign currency translation and, as indicated in our conclusion to Chapter 9, we have significant concerns about the way that project is heading. We are therefore not confident that any improvements to SSAP 20 will be achieved in the near term.

References

1 SSAP 20, *Foreign currency translation*, ASC, April 1983, para. 1.
2 SSAP 6, *Extraordinary items and prior year adjustments*, ASC, April 1974.
3 *Ibid.*, para. 6.
4 ED 16, *Supplement to extraordinary items and prior year adjustments*, ASC, September 1975.
5 *Ibid.*, para. 17.
6 *Ibid.*, paras. 15 and 16.
7 *Ibid.*, para. 5.
8 ED 21, *Accounting for foreign currency transactions*, ASC, September 1977.
9 *Ibid.*, para. 30.
10 *Ibid.*, paras. 32–34.
11 *Ibid.*, para. 35.
12 ED 27, *Accounting for foreign currency translations*, ASC, October 1980, para. 92.
13 SFAS 8, *Accounting for the translation of foreign currency transactions and foreign currency financial statements*, FASB, October 1975.
14 CICA Handbook, Section 1650, *Translation of foreign currency transactions and foreign currency financial statements*.
15 FRED 13, *Derivatives and other financial instruments: Disclosures*, ASB, April 1997, para. 15.
16 SSAP 20, para. 2.
17 *Ibid.*, paras. 36–44.
18 *Ibid.*, para. 46.
19 *Ibid.*, para. 48.
20 *Ibid.*, para. 47.
21 *Ibid.*, para. 7.
22 *Ibid.*, paras. 49 and 50.
23 *Ibid.*, para. 8.
24 *Ibid.*, para. 28.
25 *Ibid.*, para. 52.
26 *Ibid.*, para. 13.
27 *Ibid.*, para. 14.
28 *Ibid.*, para. 21.
29 ED 27, para. 98.
30 SSAP 20, para. 16.
31 *Ibid.*, para. 54.
32 *Ibid.*, para. 2.
33 *Ibid.*, para. 17.
34 *Ibid.*
35 *Ibid.*, para. 16.
36 *Ibid.*, para. 54.
37 *Ibid.*, paras. 53 and 54.
38 *Ibid.*, para. 22.
39 *Ibid.*, para. 23.
40 Accountants Digest No. 150, *A guide to accounting standards – foreign currency translation*, Winter 1983/84, p. 9.
41 SSAP 20, para. 24.
42 *Ibid.*, para. 22.
43 *Ibid.*, para. 30.
44 *Ibid.*, para. 51.
45 *Ibid.*.
46 FRS 9, *Associates and Joint Ventures*, ASB, November 1997.
47 SSAP 20, para. 52.
48 *Ibid.*, para. 37.
49 Technical Release 504, *Statement by the Accounting Standards Committee on the publication of SSAP 20: Foreign currency translation*, April 1983, para. 24.
50 SSAP 20, para. 52.

51   *Ibid.*, para. 59.
52   *Ibid.*, para. 60.
53   *Ibid.*
54   *Ibid.*
55   TR 504, para. 28.
56   UITF 19, *Tax on gains and losses on foreign currency borrowings that hedge an investment in a foreign enterprise*, February 1998, para. 9.
57   SFAS 52, *Foreign currency translation*, FASB, December 1981, para. 162.
58   SSAP 20, para. 46.
59   SFAS 52, para. 27.
60   *Ibid.*, para. 26.
61   SSAP 20, para. 44.
62   *Ibid.*, para. 6.
63   *Ibid.*, para. 5.
64   SFAS 52, para. 48.
65   *Ibid.*, para. 162.
66   SSAP 20, para. 49.
67   *Ibid.*, paras. 46 and 47.
68   CA 85, Sch. 4, paras. 17 and 22.
69   *Ibid.*, para. 26(3).
70   *Ibid.*, para. 26(3).
71   SSAP 20, para. 51.
72   *Ibid.*, para. 46.
73   SFAS 52, paras. 21 and 132.
74   *Ibid.*, para. 133.
75   *Ibid.*, para. 21.
76   SFAS 133, *Accounting for Derivative Instruments and Hedging Activities*, FASB, June 1998, para. 37.
77   Accountants Digest No. 150, p. 6.
78   C. A. Westwick, *Accounting for Overseas Operations*, Aldershot: Gower, 1986, p. 18.
79   SSAP 20, para. 42.
80   SFAS 52, paras. 17, 18 and 21.
81   *Ibid.*, para. 21.
82   *Ibid.*, para. 18.
83   *Ibid.*, para. 21.
84   Accountants Digest No. 150, p. 5.
85   SFAS 52, para. 17.
86   *Ibid.*, paras. 17 and 18.
87   *Ibid.*, paras. 18 and 20.
88   *Ibid.*, para. 20.
89   *Ibid.*, para. 19.
90   CA 85, Sch. 4, para. 50(5).
91   SFAS 52, para. 17.
92   Issue No. 90-17, *Hedging Foreign Currency Risks with Purchased Options*, EITF.
93   SFAS 80, *Accounting for Futures Contracts*, FASB, August 1984.
94   See Issue No. 91-4, *Hedging Foreign Currency Risks with Complex Options and Similar Transactions*, EITF.
95   SFAS 52, para. 28.
96   *Ibid.*, para. 139.
97   *Ibid.*, para. 27.
98   *Ibid.*, para. 138.
99   SSAP 20, para. 18.
100   SFAS 52, para. 12.
101   FRS 3, *Reporting financial performance*, ASB, October 1992, paras. 29 and 62.
102   CA 85, Sch. 4, para. 33.
103   *Ibid.*, para. 12.

104 SFAS 52, para. 14.
105 FASB Interpretation No. 37, *Accounting for Translation Adjustments upon Sale of Part of an Investment in a Foreign Entity*, FASB, July 1983, para. 2.
106 IAS 21, *The Effects of Changes in Foreign Exchange Rates*, IASC, Revised 1993, para. 37.
107 SFAS 52, para. 46.
108 *Ibid.*
109 *Ibid.*
110 SSAP 20, para. 26.
111 UITF 9, *Accounting for Operations in Hyper-inflationary Economies*, June 1993, para. 5.
112 SFAS 52, para. 11.
113 Based on information published by the International Monetary Fund, *International Financial Statistics*, Volume LII, Number 1, January 1999. Countries which are close to the highly inflationary criteria are Albania, Algeria, Colombia, Haiti, Kyrgyz Republic, Sierra Leone and Zimbabwe. There may be additional countries with cumulative inflation of 100% or more because the cited source only includes inflation data for approximately 93 countries and not all those countries have reported data for 1998 so it may be that other countries need to be considered as having a hyper-inflationary economy.
114 IAS 21, para. 36.
115 UITF 9, para. 6.
116 SFAS 52, para. 11.
117 UITF 9, para. 7.
118 *Ibid.*, para. 8.
119 FRS 10, Goodwill and Intangible Assets, December 1997, para.
120 SSAP 22, *Accounting for goodwill*, Revised July 1989, para. 41.
121 SSAP 20, para. 43.
122 TR 504, para. 21.
123 SFAS 52, para. 101.
124 See, for example, The Weir Group PLC, Report & Accounts 1998, p. 38.
125 SFAS 52, para. 144.
126 UITF 19, para. 9.
127 TR 504, paras. 18 and 19.
128 The London Stock Exchange, *The Listing Rules*, Chapter 6, para. 6.E.15(a).
129 Westwick, *op. cit.*, p. 22.
130 Touche Ross & Co., *Financial Reporting and Accounting Manual*, Fourth Edition, London, Dublin and Edinburgh: Butterworths, 1994, p. 339, and N. Spinney, *The Accountant's Magazine*, May 1983, p. 178.
131 SSAP 20, para. 43.
132 TR 504, para. 21.
133 SFAS 52, para. 101.
134 Accountants Digest No. 150, p. 7.
135 TR 504, para. 18.
136 *Ibid.*
137 D. Hegarty, *Accountancy*, November 1983, p. 147.
138 SFAS 52, para. 20.
139 *Ibid.*, para. 130.
140 Accountants Digest No. 150, p. 7.
141 UITF 19, para. 8.
142 SSAP 20, para. 48.
143 *Ibid.*, para. 49.
144 *Ibid.*, para. 12.
145 See Westwick, *op. cit.*, p. 99 and J. Carty, *Foreign Currency Accounting – A practical guide for 1982 financial statements*, pp. 21 and 22.
146 SSAP 15, *Accounting for deferred tax*, ASC, Amended December 1992, appendix, para. 4.
147 Carty, *op. cit.*, pp. 21 and 22.
148 SSAP 20, para. 20.
149 See Accountants Digest No. 150, p. 16 and Westwick, *op. cit.*, p. 99.

150 SSAP 20, paras. 20 and 43.
151 *Ibid.*, paras. 46–51.
152 Touche Ross, *op. cit.*, p. 333.
153 SSAP 20, para. 2.
154 Westwick, *op. cit.*, p. 101.
155 Accountants Digest No. 150, p. 15.
156 SFAS 52, para. 25.
157 *Ibid.*, para. 12.
158 UITF 21, *Accounting issues arising from the proposed introduction of the euro*, March 1998, para. 2.
159 *Ibid.*, para. 17.
160 *Ibid.*, para. 18.
161 *Ibid.*, para. 19.
162 *Ibid.*, para. 20.
163 *Ibid.*, Appendix.
164 SSAP 20, paras. 46 and 48.
165 *Ibid.*, para. 42.
166 *Ibid.*, para. 51.
167 *Ibid.*, para. 57.
168 SFAS 52, paras. 20, 128 and 130.
169 SSAP 2, para. 14(d).
170 SSAP 20, para. 44.
171 TR 504, para. 10.
172 *Ibid.*, para. 11.
173 *Ibid.*, para. 12.
174 Westwick, *op. cit.*, p. 77.
175 *Ibid.* and Accountants Digest No. 150, p. 32.
176 CA 85, s 264.
177 TR 504, para. 32.
178 *Ibid.*, para. 33(a).
179 *Ibid.*, para. 32.
180 SSAP 20, para. 36.
181 *Ibid.*, para. 53.
182 IAS 21, paras. 15–19.
183 *Ibid.*, para. 21.
184 SIC 11, *Foreign Exchange - Capitalisation of Losses Resulting from Severe Currency Devaluations*, para. 2.
185 *Ibid.*, para. 3.
186 *Ibid.*, para. 6.
187 IAS 21, para. 30.
188 *Ibid.*, para. 27.
189 *Ibid.*, para. 39.
190 *Ibid.*, para. 40.
191 *Ibid.*, para. 30(b).
192 SSAP 20, para. 54.
193 IAS 21, para. 37.
194 *Ibid.*, para. 19.
195 *Ibid.*, para. 2.
196 *Ibid.*, para. 8(c).
197 SSAP 20, paras. 46 and 48.
198 IAS 21, para. 36.
199 *Ibid*, para. 30(b).
200 IAS 29, *Financial Reporting in Hyperinflationary Economies*, IASC, Reformatted 1994, para. 3.
201 *Ibid*,
202 SSAP 20, para. 26.
203 IAS 21, para. 36.
204 *Ibid*, para. 42(a) and (b).

205 SSAP 20, para. 60(a).
206 *Ibid*, paras. 54 and 60(b).
207 IAS 21, para. 42(c).
208 *Ibid*, para. 43.
209 *Ibid*, para. 44.
210 *Ibid*, para. 45.
211 SFAS 52, para. 12.
212 *Ibid*, para. 10.
213 *Ibid*, para. 12.
214 *Ibid*, para. 14 and FASB Interpretation No. 37, para. 2.
215 This is due to the definition of 'foreign entity' in SFAS 52, para. 162.
216 SFAS 52, para. 20(a).
217 *Ibid*
218 *Ibid*, para. 130.
219 SSAP 20, paras. 51 and 58.
220 SFAS 52, paras. 17–20.
221 *Ibid*, para. 11.
222 *Ibid*, para. 30.
223 *Ibid*, paras. 13 and 31.
224 SSAP 20, para. 60(a).
225 *Ibid*, paras. 54 and 60(b).

Chapter 9   Financial instruments

1   INTRODUCTION

1.1   Background

The development of sophisticated financial markets, which permit companies to trade in previously uninvented contracts and thereby transform their risk profile, is perhaps the new factor in business life that poses the most searching challenge to traditional financial reporting practices. The IASC, in its newsletter of December 1996, commented on the issue in these terms:

'At the roots of the need for change in accounting for financial instruments are fundamental changes in international financial markets. ... An enterprise can substantially change its financial risk profile instantaneously, requiring careful and continuous monitoring. ... Alternatively, an enterprise may use derivatives as speculative tools to multiply the effects of changes in interest, foreign exchange or security or commodity prices, thus multiplying the gains if prices move advantageously or, alternatively, multiplying the losses if they move adversely. ... Accounting for financial instruments has not kept pace with information needs of financial market participants.

'Existing accounting practices are founded on principles developed when the primary focus of accounting was on manufacturing companies that combine inputs (materials, labour, plant and equipment, and various types of overheads) and transform them into outputs (goods or services) for sale. Accounting for these revenue-generating processes is concerned primarily with accruing costs to be matched with revenues. A key point in this process is the point of revenue realisation – the point at which a company is considered to have transformed its inputs into cash or claims to cash (i.e., financial instruments).

'These traditional realisation and cost-based measurement concepts are not adequate for the recognition and measurement of financial instruments. Recognising this, many countries have moved part way to embrace fair value accounting for some financial instruments. ...'[1]

This was the forerunner of the IASC Discussion Paper published in March 1997 (see 5.1.1 below) and it lays down the challenge very cogently. Do we need a new approach to accounting if we are to cope with the particular characteristics of financial instruments? And indeed, does this approach in turn imply that we should now abandon traditional accounting methods for other areas of business activity as well? The IASC authors felt able to distinguish the two issues, but in the UK some of the thinking behind the financial instruments proposals has had a profound effect on the ASB's work in other areas. However, putting these broader ramifications to one side, the subject matter of this chapter is the improvement of the recognition, measurement and disclosure of financial instruments themselves.

The ASB is addressing the subject in two stages, by developing first a disclosure standard and then a standard that deals with recognition and measurement issues. It published a comprehensive Discussion Paper[2] on the topic in July 1996, which set out its long-term aims for both stages of the project, and in April 1997 it issued FRED 13, a proposed standard on disclosure.[3] This was later modified, in July 1997, by a further exposure draft proposing a different regime for banks and similar institutions.[4] The Discussion Paper envisaged that although the recognition and measurement rules would apply only to listed companies and other public interest entities, most of the disclosure requirements would apply to all entities. However, by the time FRED 13 had been developed the scope of the proposed disclosure requirements had been limited to publicly traded companies, banks and insurance companies. The final standard, FRS 13,[5] was published in September 1998 and represents the culmination of the ASB's efforts as far as the disclosure aspects of financial instruments are concerned. Although most of the disclosures proposed in FRED 13 remain in FRS 13, the scope was amended again to exclude insurance companies. The next task for the ASB is the recognition and measurement side. The Board's rules on disclosure are covered in 3 and 4 below and its ideas so far on recognition and measurement are dealt with in 2 below.

1.2   What is a financial instrument?

1.2.1   Definition

The ASB has adopted the same definitions as have been used by the IASC in its equivalent project. The main terms used are defined as follows:

A *financial instrument* is any contract that gives rise to both a financial asset of one entity and a financial liability or equity instrument of another entity.

A *financial asset* is any asset that is:

(a)   cash;

(b)   a contractual right to receive cash or another financial asset from another entity;

(c)   a contractual right to exchange financial instruments with another entity under conditions that are potentially favourable; or

(d)   an equity instrument of another entity.

A *financial liability* is any liability that is a contractual obligation:

(a)   to deliver cash or another financial asset to another entity; or

(b)   to exchange financial instruments with another entity under conditions that are potentially unfavourable.

An *equity instrument* is any contract that evidences an ownership interest in an entity, i.e. a residual interest in the assets of the entity after deducting all of its liabilities.[6]

Appendix II to FRS 13[7] states that the terms 'contract', 'contractual right' and 'contractual obligation' are fundamental to the above definitions. The reference to a contract is 'to an agreement between two or more parties that has clear economic consequences and which the parties have little, if any, discretion to avoid, usually because the agreement is enforceable at law.' Such contracts need not be in writing.

Contractual rights and contractual obligations are rights and obligations that arise out of a contract. It is also noted that most contracts give rise to a variety of rights and obligations and these will change as the contract is performed. The Appendix goes on to say 'some of these rights and obligations may fall within the definition of a financial instrument and some may not. For example, an unperformed contract for the purchase or sale of a tangible asset usually gives rise to rights and obligations to exchange a physical asset for a financial asset (although it is possible that, if the contract is breached, the exchange will involve the payment of compensation). These rights and obligations do not represent a financial instrument. Under the same contract, once the physical asset has been delivered, a debtor or creditor will usually arise and this will be a financial instrument.' Contractual rights and contractual obligations encompass rights and obligations that are contingent on the occurrence of a future event, e.g. those arising under a financial guarantee.

Assets and liabilities which are not contractual in nature are not financial assets or financial liabilities. It is for this reason that tax liabilities are not financial liabilities, as such liabilities arise from statutory requirements, not from a contract.

'Equity instruments' has a wider meaning than 'equity shares' (as defined in FRS 4) because it includes some non-equity shares, as well as warrants and options to subscribe for or purchase equity shares in the issuing entity. It presumably also includes warrants and options to subscribe for or purchase such non-equity shares.

1.2.2   *Examples of financial instruments*

Appendix II to FRS 13 cites the following as examples of financial instruments:[8]

(a)   deposits, debtors, creditors, notes, loans, bonds, and debentures to be settled in cash;

(b)   unconditional lease obligations;

(c)   shares including ordinary shares, preference shares and deferred shares;

(d)   warrants or options to subscribe for shares of, or purchase shares from, the issuing entity;

(e)   obligations of an entity to issue or deliver its own shares, such as a share option or warrant;

(f)   derivative instruments such as forward contracts, futures, swaps and options that will be settled in cash or another financial instrument. An example of the latter is an option to purchase shares; and

(g)   contingent liabilities that arise from contracts and, if they crystallise, will be settled in cash – an example is a financial guarantee.

In fact, in terms of the definitions quoted at 1.2.1 above, many of these are actually examples of financial *assets* or *liabilities*, not financial *instruments*; for example, debtors cannot be described as contracts, which is an essential element of the definition, although they may arise from such contracts. The ASB had originally asserted in the Discussion Paper that even 'cash' was a financial instrument but Appendix II now says that 'cash, including foreign currency, is a financial asset because it represents the medium of exchange and is the basis on which all transactions are measured and reported in financial statements'. FRS 13 tends to use the terms loosely rather than strictly as they are defined, which sometimes makes its requirements difficult to interpret.

Appendix II to FRS 13 does make it clear that the following are *not* financial instruments:[9]

(a)   physical assets, such as stock, property, plant and equipment;

(b)   intangible assets, such as patents and trademarks;

(c)   prepayments for goods or services, since these will not be settled in cash or another financial instrument;

(d)   obligations to be settled by the delivery of goods or the rendering of services, such as most warranty obligations;

(e)   income taxes (including deferred tax), since these are statutory rather than contractual obligations;

(f)   forwards, swaps and options to be settled by the delivery of goods or the rendering of services;

(g)   contingent items that do not arise from contracts, for example a contingent liability for a tort judgement; and

(h)   the minority interest that arises on consolidating a subsidiary that is not wholly-owned.

The overall scope of the financial instruments project therefore seems to embrace the following:

■   cash;

■   other monetary assets and liabilities, insofar as they have arisen as a result of a contract rather than by some other means;

■   derivatives to be settled by the exchange of monetary assets or liabilities, but not those to be settled by the delivery of commodities or other physical assets;[10] and

■   shares, both in the reporting entity and in other entities, and derivatives giving rights over such shares.

2   THE ASB'S MEASUREMENT PROPOSALS

2.1   Current values

2.1.1   *The Board's view*

The ASB has taken the view that all financial instruments held by listed and other public interest entities should be carried in the balance sheet at current values, with one minor exception. This is that movements in the value of the reporting entity's own liabilities that are attributable to changes in its own creditworthiness should be ignored. The Board intends eventually to develop an accounting standard which reflects that conclusion, but in the meantime wishes to improve the disclosure given about financial instruments, as discussed in 3 and 4 below.

The Board sees it as necessary to use current values for *all* financial instruments because any more restricted application of current values would result in asymmetries and anomalies. In its Discussion Paper, it explicitly considered four 'half-way house' options but rejected them all. These were:

■   To require current values to be used only by more sophisticated companies which actively managed their treasury exposures. This was rejected as an untenable distinction for several reasons,[11] although at the same time it is noteworthy that the Board has implicitly made a similar proposal by saying that the eventual measurement rules should apply only to listed and other large companies.

■   To distinguish between different instruments based on management's intent for holding them. The ASB has always been suspicious of management intent as the basis for any accounting distinction, and was quick to reject it in this context.[12] Again, however, the distinction does resurface elsewhere in the Discussion Paper; for example, at least one of the categories of gains and losses taken to the statement of total recognised gains and losses rather than to the profit and loss account (see 2.2 below) depends on management intent.

■ To require current value accounting to be used only for derivatives and not for other financial instruments. The Board also dismissed this because it did not represent a meaningful distinction in the context of modern treasury management practices – it is often possible to construct the same exposure from a synthesis of various financial instruments, which may involve either derivatives or non-derivatives, and it does not seem sensible that the accounting treatment should differ depending on which particular cocktail is employed.[13]

■ To limit current value accounting to derivatives and those other instruments that they are designed to hedge. This is essentially the basis adopted by the FASB (see 5.2 below), and is less easy to dismiss. It adopts the point of view that conventional accounting still works adequately for traditional forms of finance, and it is only necessary to accommodate the impact of the newly burgeoning derivatives industry. However, in the end the ASB has rejected this as well because it considers that it introduces at least as many difficulties as it resolves.[14]

2.1.2   *How to determine current values*

Any requirement to use current values presupposes that reliable valuations can be obtained. The Board is optimistic on this point, perhaps excessively so in relation to certain instruments such as non-marketable securities or those for which the market is thin. It puts forward the following principles for guidance:

'(a)   For short-term financial instruments, such as trade debtors and creditors, and for instruments, such as floating rate borrowings, whose payments are reset to market rates at frequent intervals, historical cost (i.e. the principal amount due adjusted, in the case of assets, for bad debts) will normally approximate to current value and can be used as a surrogate.

(b)   The current value of a deposit without a specified maturity is the amount payable on demand at the balance sheet date.

(c)   In other cases, where a quoted price is available, it should be used (bid price for an asset and offer price for a liability, although active market participants may use mid-market price where this reflects the price that they can achieve). Where more than one quoted price is available, the price in the most active market for transactions of the relevant size should be used.

(d)   Otherwise the entity should estimate current value based on either the quoted price of a similar instrument (adjusted to take account of the differences) or valuation techniques such as discounted cash flow analysis and accepted option pricing models. The rate used to discount future cash flows should be a risk-adjusted rate, where practicable the prevailing market rate of interest for an instrument with substantially the same terms and characteristics including remaining term, currency, time for which the interest rate is fixed, prepayment risk and, for an asset, creditworthiness of the debtor. Alternatively, an entity may discount at a rate that reflects only some of these factors and make a separate adjustment to reflect the others (particularly changes in the creditworthiness of a debtor). Changes in the entity's own creditworthiness should not be taken into account.

(e)   The method chosen should be applied consistently from year to year.

(f)   The method and assumptions used should not generally produce a gain or loss on issue/acquisition of the instrument.'[15]

Further guidance on how to identify fair values is now given in Appendix IV of FRS 13 (see 3.8 below).

2.2   The disposition of gains and losses

The Discussion Paper states that 'the Board believes that resolving the ... issue of where the gains and losses are reported is essential to measuring all instruments at current value'.[16] The ASB's tentative solution to this issue is that all gains and losses should be reported in the profit and loss account with the exception of the following, which should go to the statement of total recognised gains and losses:

(a)   Changes in the value of the reporting entity's long-term fixed rate debt and non-equity shares (except to the extent that it reflects a change in the entity's creditworthiness). Similarly, any gain or loss on early redemption of the borrowing is to be reported in the statement of total recognised gains and losses, not the profit and loss account.[17]

It should be noted that the interest cost on fixed rate debt in the profit and loss account is to remain unaffected by this valuation, which is anomalous and contrary to the ASB's general philosophy on the treatment of revalued items. For example, it contrasts with the treatment of a revalued fixed asset, where the subsequent depreciation charge is based on the revalued amount, not on the historical cost.[18] The difference can be illustrated in the following example:

Example 9.1   Treatment of interest on fixed rate borrowing

A company borrows £1m at a fixed rate of 12% for five years. At the end of the first year, interest rates fall to 8% and remain at that level for the rest of the five year term.

Following the ASB's proposals, the profit and loss account would show a finance cost of £120,000 for each of the five years whereas the balance sheet would show the liability at each year end of the remaining cash flows discounted at 8%, giving rise to the figures in the table below. As this shows, the gains and losses in the statement of total recognised gains and losses net out to zero over the term of the loan (all figures in £000s).

Year	P&L charge	STRGL movement	Total charge	Opening loan balance	Closing loan balance
1	120	132	252	1,000	1,132
2	120	(29)	91	1,132	1,103
3	120	(32)	88	1,103	1,071
4	120	(34)	86	1,071	1,037
5	120	(37)	83	1,037	1,000
Total	600	–	600		

If, on the other hand, the treatment was consistent with that used for depreciating a revalued fixed asset, the accounting treatment would be rather different. In year 1, the interest payment of £120,000 would again all be charged to the profit and loss account and, the loan would again be revalued to £1,132,000 with the increase of £132,000 being charged to the STRGL. In years 2 to 5, the interest payment of £120,000 would be divided between the profit and loss account (based on 8% of the outstanding balance) and a 'repayment' element that would reduce the balance sheet amount of the loan (the remainder). The latter element would bring the balance back to £1m at the end of the 5 year term. This is summarised below.

Year	P&L charge	STRGL charge	Total charge	Opening balance	'Repayment' element	Closing balance
1	120	132	252	1,000		1,132
2	91		91	1,132	29	1,103
3	88		88	1,103	32	1,071
4	86		86	1,071	34	1,037
5	83		83	1,037	37	1,000
Total	468	132	600			

The result this time would therefore be that only £468,000 of the £600,000 interest paid would be charged in the profit and loss account, with the remaining £132,000 charged to the STRGL. The treatment proposed in the Discussion Paper effectively 'recycles' this charge back through the profit and loss account so as to restore the interest expense to a historical cost basis.

The ASB notes that this latter treatment may be more conceptually attractive but also that it may be regarded as counter-intuitive, since it portrays the company as having a variable interest loan whereas in fact it is contracted to pay a fixed rate. Accordingly, it has opted for the former treatment for the time being. This, however, is a fundamental issue which is not confined to the revaluation of debt. If the profit and loss account consequences of fair valuing all instruments are too disturbing for even the Board to accept, then it must call into question whether the proposal is well founded.

(b)   Changes in the value of interest rate derivatives, to the extent that they serve to 'convert' a borrowing from fixed to floating or vice versa.[19]

(c)   Changes in the value of fixed interest rate debt investments to the extent that they 'match-fund' a borrowing (i.e. that they are in the same currency and have a similar maturity and interest basis as the borrowing).[20]

(d)   Differences arising on the retranslation of a net investment in an overseas operation (as already required by SSAP 20 – see Chapter 8 at 2.4.5), and, to the extent that a derivative or borrowing serves to mitigate the translation risk on the investment, exchange differences on that derivative or borrowing.[21]

(e) Changes in the value of long-term strategic investments.[22]

It should be noted that items (b) to (d) all require judgments to be made as to the effectiveness or otherwise of a hedge, and therefore introduce some of the issues that the ASB considered that it was avoiding by proposing that all financial instruments be carried at current values rather than adopting one of the approaches it dismissed as 'halfway houses'. Furthermore, item (e), in requiring some investments to be designated as long-term strategic investments, depends on an expression of management intent which the Board was again anxious to avoid. We agree with the Board that resolving the issue of where to report gains and losses is critical to the whole fair value basis of the future standard, but these proposals are far from convincing and must call the whole approach into question.

One further issue to note is that at present (August 1999) EU companies are not permitted (by the European Union's Accounting Directives) to fair value financial assets and liabilities and take the resulting unrealised gains and losses to the profit and loss account in their statutory accounts. However, the European Commission has put forward proposals for the amendment of the Accounting Directives in order to allow such a treatment.

2.3   Hedging issues

The most difficult issue that remains to be resolved is whether some form of hedge accounting should be allowed and if so what it should be. Hedge accounting can be described as an exception routine whereby separate transactions are linked with each other for accounting purposes because one of them is designed to offset exposures arising on the other. This might take a number of forms:

■   it may link transactions that would otherwise fall in different accounting periods; for example, a company that has ordered a fixed asset from a foreign supplier for delivery in the next financial year might take out a forward contract this year to buy the required amount of foreign currency so as to fix the sterling cost of the asset;

■   it may link items that might in any case have been reported within the same period but in a way that affects their classification in the accounts, such as items taken to the statement of total recognised gains and losses rather than the profit and loss account as discussed under 2.2 above.

The ASB's discussion of hedging implicitly accepts the second of these as legitimate and focuses on the first. Some ASB members take the view that inter-period hedge accounting should not be allowed at all, but others believe that at least some manifestations of it should be permitted. Possible scenarios in which this might be applied are illustrated below:

Example 9.2   Hedging of contracted but unrecognised items

A company has an obligation to buy a certain minimum quantity of raw materials in the following financial year for a price denominated in US dollars under a take-or-pay contract. In order to fix the sterling cost of the materials it takes out a forward contract to buy dollars at the requisite time.

If no hedge accounting were permitted, the ASB's proposals would require the forward contract to be valued at the year end and the resulting gain or loss to be recognised in the profit and loss account for the period which had ended. Furthermore, in the following financial year, the purchase of the raw materials would be recorded at the spot rate for dollars ruling at the date of purchase and that amount would be recorded as the cost of the stock; any further gain or loss on closing out the forward contract would be taken to the profit and loss account. This distinction affects both the timing of recognition of the gain or loss (when the stock is purchased or when it is sold) and its classification (as a financial item or as part of cost of sales). Obviously, if the hedged item were a fixed asset rather than stock these differences would be accentuated.

Alternatively, if hedge accounting were permitted, the gain or loss on valuing the forward contract at the year end would be deferred to be matched with the transaction in the next period which it was designed to hedge. This would be consistent with SSAP 20, which presently (if rather vaguely) allows purchases to be recorded at the rate specified in a matching forward contract. Some members of the ASB would continue to permit such a treatment, whereas others would not.

Example 9.3   Hedging of future transactions

The scenario is the same as in the previous example, except that no contract exists at the year end which requires the reporting entity to purchase the minimum quantity of raw materials. However, it fully expects to make the purchase and indeed these raw materials are essential to its business. The raw materials are only available from the US, so there is an inevitable currency risk involved in the purchase.

Some of those who would have permitted hedge accounting in the first set of circumstances would not permit it in this case. In the previous scenario, the obligation was a contractual one and would have been recognised in the balance sheet and revalued to its current value were it not for what the ASB regards as a present accounting 'anomaly' in that future firm commitments are not necessarily recognised in the balance sheet. However, under this new scenario there is no contractual obligation at the balance sheet date, so this argument does not apply.

Others, however, would still permit hedge accounting so long as the requirement to purchase the raw materials could be regarded as a 'commercial commitment'. This is a notoriously difficult concept to pin down. The Discussion Paper talks of it in terms of the need for a business to continue in business for at least the short term because the costs of immediate shut-down would be prohibitive, and would therefore permit necessary purchases to support continued operations for that short term period as falling within the meaning of the expression 'commercial commitment'. This is clearly a far-fetched way of looking at healthy businesses in real life, although it is possible to sympathise with the ASB's objective in trying to limit the future period during which forecast transactions could be hedged; otherwise, there would be little to stop the company saying that it will hedge its expected dollar purchases of the next five years and rolling forward the gains and losses on forward contracts that cover the whole of that period.

The Discussion Paper also considered the possibility of hedging of existing assets or liabilities that were not carried at current value; however, if the ASB succeeds in its broader objective of requiring all financial instruments to be fair valued, then the relevance of this category will largely fall away.

3   THE ASB'S DISCLOSURE REQUIREMENTS

3.1   Introduction

As noted earlier in this chapter, although the ASB's long term objective is to resolve the measurement issues that arise on financial instruments, its more immediate aim has been to improve their disclosure. The Discussion Paper contained a number of recommended disclosures which were to be regarded as best practice pending the development of a standard on the subject. This was superseded in April 1997 by the publication of FRED 13, and then in September 1998 the final standard, FRS 13, was published the requirements of which are set out below.

The disclosures required by FRS 13 fall into two categories: narrative disclosures, which may be either included in the accounts or relegated, with an appropriate cross reference, to the Operating and Financial Review (or equivalent statement); and numerical disclosures to be included in the notes to the accounts. In the ASB's earlier Discussion Paper, the narrative disclosures were to be separate from the accounts and non-mandatory, but FRED 13 proposed to make them compulsory. Notwithstanding concerns raised about this proposal, FRS 13 makes the narrative disclosures mandatory. Accordingly, they are subject to audit. These narrative disclosures apply to all entities included within the scope of FRS 13 and are discussed at 3.2 below.

As mentioned at 1.1 above, FRED 13 was modified in relation to banks and similar institutions by the publication in July 1997 of a further exposure draft. This disapplied most of the numerical disclosure requirements in the original exposure draft so far as banks were concerned and substituted a different set of proposals. Most significantly, it acknowledged the need for different disclosures as between banks' trading and non-trading activities – a distinction that had until then been largely rejected in other recent proposals.

It was to be expected that other financial institutions which were not banks would argue that a similar distinction was appropriate to them and this has proved to be the case. However, given the wide range of different types of financial institution and the difficulty of deciding which disclosures were most relevant to which type of financial institution, FRS 13 effectively allows such entities to decide (with a couple of exceptions) which body of numerical disclosures best suits their circumstances.

Accordingly, FRS 13 has different numerical disclosure requirements for:

662 Generally Accepted Accounting Practice in the United Kingdom

- entities other than financial institutions

- banks and similar institutions

- other financial institutions.

For the purposes of FRS 13, a bank or similar institution is defined in such a way as to include building societies and credit unions. The definition of 'financial institution' is very broad and encompasses entities such as leasing companies, stockbrokers and money brokers, investment dealing companies, investment managers, corporate finance companies and investment vehicles, such as investment trusts and unit trusts.

Although FRS 13 is structured in such a way that all of the requirements (and related definitions) for each of these 3 types of entity are set out in separate parts of the standard, it is only the numerical disclosures which are different. The numerical disclosures required by entities other than financial institutions are discussed in this section below. Although there is a different regime for banks and similar institutions, some of the disclosures are the same as for other entities. Those disclosures which are specific to banks and similar institutions are discussed at 4.1 below. The disclosures by other financial institutions are discussed at 4.2 below.

In view of the wide-ranging nature of the definition of a financial instrument, steps are taken within the standard to exclude certain items which fall within the definition from the disclosure requirements. The first category of items which are excluded are those which are the subject of other standards or statutory rules that the ASB does not wish to disturb at this stage. These are:

(a) interests in subsidiary and quasi-subsidiary undertakings which are consolidated under FRS 2 and FRS 5 respectively;

(b) interests in associated undertakings, partnerships and joint ventures accounted for under FRS 9;

(c) obligations to employees under employee share option and employee share schemes, and any shares held in order to fulfil these obligations;

(d) assets and liabilities relating to pensions and other post-retirement benefits that fall within SSAP 24 and UITF Abstract 6;

(e) rights and obligations arising under operating leases, as defined by SSAP 21. (This makes it clear that assets and liabilities under finance leases are to be so included.);

(f) equity shares of the reporting entity, and warrants and options over such shares, other than those that are held exclusively with a view to a subsequent resale. (However, non-equity shares are to be included.);

(g) financial assets, financial liabilities and cash-settled commodity contracts of an insurance company or group.

The above items are to be excluded from all of the disclosure requirements, except for the currency risk disclosures set out in 3.6 and 4.1.2 below.[23]

Interests in subsidiary, quasi-subsidiary and associated undertakings, partnerships and joint ventures which are held exclusively with a view to subsequent resale do fall within the disclosure requirements because they are really like any other current asset investment. The same would also appear to apply to interests held by a reporting entity in its own equity shares (including warrants and options) which are held exclusively with a view to a subsequent resale.

The next category of items which *may* be excluded from the disclosures (except for the currency risk disclosures set out in 3.6 and 4.1.2 below) are short-term debtors and creditors.[24] These are defined in the standard as being:

'Financial assets and financial liabilities that meet all of the following criteria:

(a) they would be included in the balance sheet under one of the following headings if the entity was preparing its financial statements in accordance with Schedule 4 to the Companies Act 1985:

   (i)   debtors;

   (ii)   prepayments and accrued income;

   (iii) creditors: amounts falling due within one year, other than items that would be included under the 'debenture loans' and 'bank loans and overdrafts' sub-headings;

   (iv)   provisions for liabilities and charges; and

   (v)   accruals and deferred income;

(b) they mature or become payable within 12 months of the balance sheet date; and

(c) they are not a derivative financial instrument.'[25]

The reason why such items can be excluded is that they are not regarded by the ASB as being the main focus of the standard. We agree that such items should be excluded, because in our view they do not give rise to significant financial risks of the nature which the standard is trying to address. However, as a result of (b) above, any debtors which are not due within 12 months have to be included within the disclosures as would any provisions (if they meet the definition of a financial liability) which are expected to be payable after more than one year. Similarly, all creditors due after more than one year are also to be included within the disclosures. We would also have excluded such items from the disclosures.

We would recommend that reporting entities take advantage of this optional exemption for short-term debtors and creditors. If the exemption is not taken, then *all* such debtors and creditors need to be included in *all* of the disclosures.

The term 'short-term debtors and creditors' is restricted for banks and other financial institutions as indicated in 4.1 and 4.2 below.

In summary, the standard effectively requires the following items to be included within the disclosures:

- fixed asset investments (other than associated undertakings, partnerships and joint ventures accounted for under FRS 9 and investments in own shares held in respect of employee share schemes);

- current asset investments (including interests in subsidiary, quasi-subsidiary and associated undertakings, partnerships and joint ventures held exclusively with a view to subsequent resale);

- debtors which are receivable after one year (other than non-contractual debtors such as tax recoverable);

- cash and bank deposits;

- bank overdrafts;

- bank loans and debenture loans;

- other loans, creditors and provisions which are payable after one year (other than non-contractual items such as tax liabilities or provisions that are not financial liabilities);

- non-equity shares issued by the reporting entity; and

- derivative instruments.

In addition, although commodity contracts requiring settlement by physical delivery are not financial instruments, the standard requires cash-settled commodity contracts (including those for the delivery of gold) nevertheless to be included within certain of the disclosures (see 3.11 below). Banks and other financial institutions also have to treat all other contracts for the delivery of gold as if they were financial instruments (see 4.1 and 4.2 below).

3.2 Narrative disclosures

FRS 13 requires entities to include narrative disclosures which discuss their objectives, policies and strategies in using financial instruments. The intention of these disclosures is to put in context the numerical disclosures required by the standard. It is emphasised that the primary focus of the narrative disclosures is the risks that arise in connection with financial instruments and how they have been managed. These risks, which are discussed in more detail in Appendix I to FRS 13, include credit risk, liquidity risk, cash flow risk, interest rate risk, currency risk and other types of market price risk.[26]

It is envisaged that the information provided in respect of these risks will be presented in the context of a discussion of the entity's activities, structure and financing and that the discussion will consider the financial risk profile of the entity as a whole, before focusing specifically on financial instruments.[27]

First of all, an explanation should be provided of the role that financial instruments have had during the period in creating or changing the risks that an entity faces in its activities. This should include an explanation of the objectives and policies for holding or issuing financial instruments and similar contracts, and the strategies for achieving those objectives that have been followed during the period.[28]

This disclosure is intended to include a discussion of the nature of the main types of financial instruments and similar contracts and the purposes for which they are held or issued, with separate disclosure of instruments used for financing, risk management or hedging, and trading or speculation.[29]

The disclosure would also normally include a description of the financial risk management and treasury policies agreed by the board of directors, including its main policies, with quantification where appropriate, on:

(a)   the fixed/floating split, maturity profile and currency profile of financial assets and liabilities;

(b)   the extent to which foreign currency debtors and creditors are hedged to the functional currency of the business unit concerned;

(c)   the extent to which foreign currency borrowings and other instruments are used to hedge foreign currency net investments; and

(d)   any other hedging.[30]

As far as hedging is concerned, the standard also calls for specific disclosure of a description of:

(a)   the transactions and risks that have been hedged, including the period of time until they are expected to occur; and

(b)   the instruments used for hedging purposes, distinguishing between those that have been accounted for using hedge accounting and those that have not.[31]

In this context, a 'hedge' is 'an instrument that individually, or with other instruments, has a value or cash flow that is expected, wholly or partly, to move inversely with changes in the value or cash flows of the position being hedged'.[32]

The above explanation of the role of financial instruments is intended to put in context the numerical disclosures required by the standard. Accordingly, an explanation of how the year end figures reflect the agreed objectives, policies and strategies is also required. If the year end position is unrepresentative of the position during the year or of the agreed objectives, policies and strategies, an explanation of the extent to which it is regarded as unrepresentative should be provided.[33]

If the explanation about the role of financial instruments reflects a significant change from that stated in the previous year, that fact should be disclosed and the reasons for the change explained. This is intended to encompass both changes in the risks faced by the entity and changes in the way the exposures to such risks are managed.[34]

The standard also says that if by the date of approving the accounts, the directors have agreed to make a significant change in the role of financial instruments, then that change should be explained.[35]

As indicated at 3.1 above, these narrative disclosures are to be either included in the accounts or relegated, with an appropriate cross reference, to the Operating and Financial Review (or equivalent statement).[36]

Appendix III to FRS 13 provides illustrations of the disclosures required by the standard. The first 2 illustrations include examples of those narrative disclosures which would be relevant for companies which are not financial institutions. Examples of the sort of disclosures which companies are giving in practice are shown in the following extracts:

Extract 9.1: Cable and Wireless plc (1999)

Operating and Financial Review (extract)

Treasury and funding activities

The Group's principal treasury and funding operations are carried out by the London based Group Treasury operation according to objectives, policies and authorities approved by the Board. The Company's internal treasury policies and strategies are regularly reviewed and have not changed significantly since the last financial year. Hongkong Telecom, Cable & Wireless Communications and Cable & Wireless Optus also operate treasury and funding operations whose policies and authorities are adopted by their individual boards but are consistent with the Group's. The Group uses financial instruments including foreign exchange contracts, interest rate swaps and cross currency swaps in its management of exchange and interest rate exposures. Although these instruments are subject to the risk of loss, these losses are offset by gains in the related exposures. The Group does not speculate in derivative financial instruments. Counterparty credit risk is closely monitored and derivatives activity is tightly controlled. Both UK and overseas treasury activities are subject to close supervision and internal audit reviews.

Funding

The funding policy of the Group continues to be one of maintaining a broad portfolio of debt, diversified by source and maturity.

The majority of the Group's short term deposits are held in Hongkong Telecom. Hongkong Telecom at 31 March 1999, managed a sterling equivalent of £1,310 million. The cash is invested in US dollar and Hong Kong dollar money market instruments for periods ranging between one and twelve months.

In May 1998 Cable & Wireless Communications redeemed Senior Discount Notes 2004 previously issued by Videotron for $340 million (£210 million). The repurchase was financed by drawing down under the Cable & Wireless Communications £2 billion bank facilities. This was the last step in completing the refinancing of Cable & Wireless Communications after its formation in the previous year.

In November 1998 Cable & Wireless Communications returned to the US bond market and issued a ten year $700 million bond. In March 1998 Cable & Wireless Communications issued $1.8

billion of US bonds spread over three maturities. The US dollar proceeds were hedged into sterling since Cable & Wireless Communications is a sterling-based company.

During the year Cable & Wireless Communications increased its receivables securitisation programme from £250 million to £375 million. This enabled Cable & Wireless Communications to reduce the use of its bank facility further. At the end of the year borrowings were £775 million under the £1 billion, five year facility. £500 million of the £1 billion 364 day facility was cancelled.

At 31 March 1999 the Group had net debt of £3,984 million and gross debt of £5,903 million. The principal components of gross debt were £2,972 million in Cable & Wireless Communications, £1,293 million in Cable & Wireless plc, £593 million in Cable & Wireless International Finance BV and £375 million in Cable & Wireless Optus.

Interest rate risk management

The Group assesses the exposure of its overall financial position on a net basis, after considering the extent to which variable rate liabilities can be offset with variable rate assets, typically short term deposits and cash. The Group's policy is to minimise interest expense. In order to achieve this policy, the Group targets a ratio of fixed to variable rate debt which is approved by the Board, based on an assessment of interest rate trends. To obtain this ratio in a cost efficient manner, the Group mainly uses interest rate swaps and forward rate agreements (FRAs) that have the effect of converting specific debt obligations of the Group from fixed to variable rate, or vice versa, as required.

Approximately 76% of the Group's borrowings is currently at fixed rates of interest. Long term and short term interest rate instruments are used to manage the impact of interest rates on the total Group borrowings.

Approximately three quarters of the Cable & Wireless Communications $700 million bond issued in November 1998 was swapped into fixed sterling borrowings and the rest was swapped into floating sterling debt.

Cable & Wireless Communications took action on interest rate hedging to take advantage of falling interest rates by executing £700 million of three year collars from July 1999. 96% of Cable & Wireless Communications' debt is at fixed rates.

Hongkong Telecom uses FRAs, caps and interest rate swaps to manage interest rate risk on its short term deposits. At the year end, the equivalent of £489 million sterling of such instruments was outstanding.

All medium and long term debt held by Cable & Wireless Optus has been fixed using interest rate swaps.

Exchange rate risk management

The Group's debt has an average maturity of approximately six years with about 75% being denominated in sterling, 14% in US dollars and 11% in other currencies. A proportion of the overseas asset base is matched by foreign currency borrowings.

The Group carries out foreign exchange hedging operations, mainly using forward rate contracts and currency options, to manage its exposures in respect of material transactions. Hedging strategies are regularly reviewed to ensure that the most effective and efficient methods are being used. Although the Group trades in over 70 countries, much of its revenue is from international traffic flows and is settled in major currencies on a regular basis. For this reason, the Group is not unreasonably exposed to localised currency fluctuations or exchange controls.

Credit risk management

The counterparties to the Group's financial instruments are major international financial institutions. Credit risk represents the loss that would be recognised at the reporting date if counterparties failed completely to perform as contracted. It is the Group's policy to monitor the financial standing of these counterparties on an ongoing basis. The Group does not have a significant exposure to any individual counterparty.

Borrowing facilities

The total amount of the Group's undrawn committed facilities available as at 31 March 1999 is £2,396 million. Cable & Wireless Communications had £725 million, Hongkong Telecom £688 million and Cable & Wireless Optus £653 million of this total. As at 31 March 1999, Cable and Wireless plc had undrawn committed medium term bank facilities of £330 million with maturities ranging from 1999 though to 2003. These facilities are provided by a number of banks and can be used either to support the Group's sterling, Eurodollar and US dollar domestic commercial paper programmes or as direct bank lending. During the year, additional bi-lateral facilities of £500 million were agreed, £350 million were cancelled and £55 million expired. The £500 million facility is 364 days and is split between five banks. None of the Company's covenants relating to loans and other financing are expected to restrict normal business activities.

Extract 9.2: Meyer International PLC (1999)

Financial Review (extract)

Treasury Activities and Policies

Treasury activities are managed under policies and procedures approved and monitored by the Board. These are designed to reduce the financial risks faced by the Group, which primarily relate to funding and liquidity, interest rate exposures and currency rate exposures.

The central Treasury Department provides a service to the Group and operates as a cost centre, not a profit centre. All transactions in derivatives (principally foreign exchange swaps, forward foreign currency contracts, interest rate swaps and interest rate options) are undertaken to manage the risks arising from underlying business activities and no transactions of a speculative nature are undertaken. Further details of derivatives are provided in note 19 to the accounts.

Funding and liquidity

The Group always ensures that it has committed borrowing facilities in place in excess of its peak forecast gross borrowings for at least the next 12 months. At 31st March 1999, the Group's principal committed bank borrowing facility, which is in place until November 2002, totalled £275.0 million, of which £180.0 million was undrawn. In addition, it is the Group's policy to maintain uncommitted facilities for use in its daily treasury management. At the year end the undrawn amount of such facilities totalled £40.9 million.

Interest rate risk

The Group borrows at both fixed and floating interest rates and then uses interest rate swaps and interest rate options (caps and collars) to manage its exposure to interest rate fluctuations. The Group's policy is to keep approximately 50% of gross borrowings at fixed or capped rates. At 31st March 1999, the proportion of the Group's borrowings at fixed rates was 15%, fixed for an average period of 4.7 years. 33% of the Group's borrowings were at floating rates covered by interest rate options for an average period of 1.6 years.

Net interest costs increased by £5.8 million to £13.7 million for the year, again due largely to the Group's average borrowings for the year being higher than last year following the acquisition of Harcros. Interest was covered 5.5 times by profit on ordinary activities before interest.

Currency rate risk

The Group mitigates the effect on its balance sheet of structural currency exposures (due to its investments in overseas operations) by borrowing in the same currencies as its various operations and by using currency swaps to match the currency of some of its other borrowings to its various functional currencies. The policy is for between 80% and 95% of the Group's investment in the US to be hedged into Sterling and for between 50% and 75% of its investment in the Netherlands to be hedged. At 31st March 1999, 61% of non-Sterling assets were covered by currency borrowings.

The Group also has transactional currency exposures as it imports large quantities of timber and other building materials. Where these are purchased in foreign currency, in general the Group does not fix their price in local currency until arrival in the UK unless a matched sale has been arranged. Overseas earnings are not fixed in Sterling.

The disclosures are intended to be a summary of the facts specific to the reporting company, and not either subjective statements or a forecast of what might happen in the future. The ASB expects that the disclosures will be drawn from documented policies and decisions and be about transactions and exposures that have occurred.[37] Some companies may need to determine what their objectives, policies and strategies in respect of financial instruments actually are, before considering the disclosures to be made in the accounts.

The illustrations of these narrative disclosures in Appendix III and the above extracts are relevant to companies which are not financial institutions. Banking companies and other financial institutions also have to give narrative disclosures, but although the requirements of the standard are the same, their discussion needs to reflect the nature of their business. This is likely to involve more discussion on credit risk and other market price risk, particularly in relation to their financial assets.

3.3 Disclosure of accounting policies

FRS 13 also includes a reminder that SSAP 2 requires disclosure of all significant accounting policies, and suggests this extensive list of matters that might require to be disclosed in relation to financial instruments:

(a) the methods used to account for derivative financial instruments, the types of derivative financial instruments accounted for under each method and the criteria that determine the method used;

(b) the basis for recognising, measuring (both on initial recognition and subsequently), and ceasing to recognise financial assets and liabilities;

(c) how income and expenses (and other gains and losses) are recognised and measured;

(d) the treatment of financial assets and financial liabilities not recognised, including an explanation of how provisions for losses on such items are recognised; and

(e) policies on offsetting.[38]

It is also suggested that these further policies may be relevant where financial instruments are carried on a historical cost basis:

(a) the treatment of premiums and discounts on financial assets;

(b) the treatment of changes in the estimated amount of determinable future cash flows associated with a financial instrument, such as a debenture indexed to a commodity price;

(c) the treatment of a fall in the fair value of a financial asset below its carrying amount; and

(d)   the treatment of restructured financial liabilities.[39]

Where hedge accounting has been applied, yet more detailed policies are suggested:

(a)   the circumstances in which a financial instrument is accounted for as a hedge;

(b)   the recognition and measurement treatment applied to the instrument;

(c)   the method used to account for an instrument that ceases to be accounted for as a hedge;

(d)   the method used to account for the hedge when the underlying item or position matures, is sold, extinguished or terminated; and

(e)   the method used to account for the hedge of a future transaction when that transaction is no longer likely to occur.[40]

The above list goes far beyond the level of detail which has in the past been disclosed by most companies, although it should be emphasised that the standard is only suggesting that they should be included where the choice of policy has had a material impact on the accounts. Indeed many companies have not had an accounting policy note devoted to financial instruments or derivatives at all. Examples of the sort of accounting policies which companies are now disclosing in this area are shown in the following extracts:

Extract 9.3: Johnson Matthey plc (1999)

Accounting Policies (extract)

Financial instruments: In this year's accounts the group has adopted Financial Reporting Standard (FRS) 13 – 'Derivatives and Other Financial Instruments: Disclosures'. The group uses financial instruments, in particular forward currency contracts and currency swaps, to manage the financial risks associated with the group's underlying business activities and the financing of those activities. The group does not undertake any trading activity in financial instruments.

A discussion of how the group manages its financial risks is included in the Financial Review on page 10. Financial instruments are accounted for as follows:

*   Forward exchange contracts are used to hedge foreign exchange exposures arising on forecast receipts and payments in foreign currencies. These forward contracts are revalued to the rates of exchange at the balance sheet date and any aggregate unrealised gains and losses arising on revaluation are included in other debtors / other creditors. At maturity, or when the contract ceases to be a hedge, gains and losses are taken to the profit and loss account.

*   Currency options are occasionally used to hedge foreign exchange exposures, usually when the forecast receipt or payment amounts are uncertain. Option premia are recognised at their historic cost in the group balance sheet as prepayments. At maturity, or upon exercise, the option premia net of any realised gains on exercise are taken to the profit and loss account.

*   Interest rate swaps are occasionally used to hedge the group's exposure to movements on interest rates. The interest payable or receivable on such swaps is accrued in the same way as interest arising on deposits or borrowings. Interest rate swaps are not revalued to fair value

prior to maturity.

- Currency swaps are used as balance sheet hedging instruments to hedge foreign currency assets and borrowings. Currency swaps are used to reduce costs and credit exposure where the group would otherwise have cash deposits and borrowings in different currencies. The difference between spot and forward rate for these contracts is recognised as part of the net interest payable over the period of the contract. These swaps are revalued to the rates of exchange at the balance sheet date and any aggregate unrealised gains or losses arising on revaluation are included in other debtors / other creditors. Realised gains and losses on these currency swaps are taken to reserves in the same way as for the foreign investments and borrowings to which the swaps relate.

The aggregate fair values at the balance sheet date of the hedging instruments described above are disclosed as a note on the accounts.

The group has taken advantage of the exemption available for short term debtors and creditors.

Extract 9.4: Cable and Wireless plc (1999)

Accounting Policies (extract)

Derivatives

Swaps and forward rate agreements

The net interest paid or received under interest rate and cross currency swaps and forward rate agreements (FRAs) is recorded on an accruals basis and included within net interest in the profit and loss account.

The notional amounts of interest rate swaps and FRAs are recorded off balance sheet. Cross currency swaps are used to hedge the initial draw down and final repayment of currency denominated debt, as well as the currency interest flows, and are recorded on the balance sheet. This has the effect of restating the underlying currency denominated debt in the swapped currency.

Forward exchange contracts

Forward exchange contracts are carried on balance sheet at the difference between the amounts of the payable and receivable currency revalued at the closing exchange rate. The interest differential, being the difference between the contract rate and the spot rate on the date of entering into the forward exchange contract, is charged to the profit and loss account as interest over the life of the contract.

Exchange gains and losses

Exchange gains and losses on revaluation and maturity of forward exchange contracts are treated differently depending on the underlying exposure they hedge:

- for contracts which hedge firm third party commitments the exchange gains and losses are recognised in the profit and loss account in the same period as the underlying transaction;

- for contracts over underlying currency assets or liabilities exchange gains and losses are off-set against the equal and opposite exchange gains or losses arising on the retranslation of the underlying assets or liabilities;

- for contracts taken out to hedge overseas equity investments the exchange gains and losses are taken to reserves to off-set against the exchange differences arising on the retranslation of the net assets of the investments on consolidation;

- for contracts which hedge general trading flows the exchange gains or losses are taken to the profit and loss account in the period they arise.

Where the underlying exposure changes, or ceases to exist, the contract would be terminated and the exchange gain or loss arising taken to the profit and loss account.

Extract 9.5: British Telecommunications plc (1999)

Accounting Policies (extract)

XIII Financial instruments

(a) Debt instruments

Debt instruments are stated at the amount of net proceeds adjusted to amortise any discount evenly over the term of the debt.

(b) Derivative financial instruments

The group uses derivative financial instruments to reduce exposure to foreign exchange risks and interest rate movements. The group does not hold or issue derivative financial instruments for financial trading purposes.

Criteria to qualify for hedge accounting

The group considers its derivative financial instruments to be hedges when certain criteria are met. For foreign currency derivatives, the instrument must be related to actual foreign currency assets or liabilities or a probable commitment and whose characteristics have been identified. It must involve the same currency or similar currencies as the hedged item and must also reduce the risk of foreign currency exchange movements on the group's operations. For interest rate derivatives, the instrument must be related to assets or liabilities or a probable commitment and must also change the nature of the interest rate by converting a fixed rate to a variable rate or vice versa.

Accounting for derivative financial instruments

Principal amounts underlying currency swaps are revalued at exchange rates ruling at the date of the group balance sheet and are included in debtors or creditors.

Interest differentials, under interest rate swap agreements used to vary the amounts and periods for which interest rates on borrowings are fixed, are recognised by adjustment of interest payable.

The forward exchange contracts used to change the currency mix of net debt are revalued to balance sheet rates with net unrealised gains and losses being shown as part of debtors or creditors. The difference between spot and forward rate for these contracts is recognised as part of net interest payable over the term of the contract.

The forward exchange contracts hedging transaction exposures are revalued at the prevailing forward rate on the balance sheet date with net unrealised gains and losses being shown as debtors and creditors.

3.4 Numerical disclosures by entities that are not financial institutions

FRS 13 requires various numerical disclosures which are to be given in the accounts. These disclosures are intended to be highly summarised. One effect of this is that it may not be possible for the components to be traced back to their respective balance sheet captions. Where this is the case, the standard encourages provision of additional detail to enable the figures to be traced back unless it would unduly complicate the disclosure.[41]

The following are the main numerical disclosures required by the standard:

■ interest rate risk disclosures;

■ currency risk disclosures;

■ liquidity disclosures; and

■ fair value disclosures.

There are also further numerical disclosures for particular types of financial instruments:

■ those used as hedges;

■ those held or used for trading; and

■ commodity contracts treated as financial instruments.

Each of these requirements is discussed below.

3.5   Interest rate risk disclosures

The standard requires information on interest rate risks for both financial liabilities (not just borrowings) and financial assets. Information is only required for the latter where an entity has a significant holding of financial assets.[42] For most companies, information will only be necessary for their financial liabilities. The specific information which is called for is as follows:

(a)   An analysis of the aggregate carrying amount of financial liabilities by principal currency, further subdivided between:

(i)   those at fixed interest rates,

(ii)   those at floating interest rates, and

(iii) those on which no interest is paid.[43]

For the purpose of this analysis, floating rate financial liabilities are those that attract an interest charge and have their interest reset at least once a year.[44] Those that are reset less frequently are to be treated as fixed rate financial liabilities. It is unclear how the third category is to be interpreted. Is it to include items which involve no interest payments, but into which interest is imputed for accounting purposes? The standard states that finance lease obligations, and deep discounted bonds and similar liabilities whose finance costs are allocated in accordance with FRS 4, do not fall within this category.[45] However, it is silent on other items such as deferred consideration or long-term monetary provisions wherever they are discounted. One interpretation is that where the financial liability stems from a transaction that will implicitly have considered the time value of money (such as deferred consideration) the liability should be classified as fixed rate, along with deep discounted bonds and finance lease obligations. But in other cases, such as a provision for the onerous rentals on a vacant property where there is no implicit interest in the rentals, the provision should be treated as one on which no interest is paid.

This analysis is after taking account of interest rate swaps, currency swaps, forward contracts and other derivatives whose effect is to 'alter' the interest basis or currency of the financial liabilities (it is noteworthy that the ASB has chosen to avoid the word 'hedge' in this context).[46] For example, if a company has taken out a currency swap in respect of US$ borrowings to effectively convert the liability into sterling, then for the purposes of this analysis the borrowing should be treated as a sterling liability.

The analysis is to be shown on a gross basis (i.e. without netting off cash and liquid resources or similar items). However, if entities wish to provide the information on a net basis they can do so as long as the gross position is also shown.[47]

(b)   The above analysis should exclude the effect of financial liabilities and other derivative instruments that cannot be adequately reflected in it. These are likely to include interest rate caps, collars and floors and instruments that incorporate an option to exercise. Instead, a summary should be provided of the main effects of such instruments. This might include such elements as the notional principal amounts involved, the rates of interest, the period for which the instrument is operative and the terms of any options contained within the instrument.[48]

(c)   For the fixed rate liabilities, the weighted average interest rate and weighted average period for which rates are fixed are both to be disclosed, again analysed by principal currency.

(d)   For the floating rate liabilities, the benchmark rate (such as LIBOR) for determining interest payments is to be given, again by principal currency. Although the standard does not require disclosure of the particular margin over that rate that is payable, it emphasises that it may need to be given in order to comply with companies legislation.

(e)   For the liabilities on which no interest is paid, the weighted average period until maturity, again analysed by currency.[49]

The first 2 illustrations within Appendix III to the standard provide examples of these disclosures. Examples of how companies are presenting the required information are given in the extracts below:

Extract 9.6: Johnson Matthey plc (1999)

19 Financial risk management [extract]

19a Interest rate risk

	At fixed interest rates £ million	At floating interest rates £ million	Total £ million	Fixed rate financial liabilities Weighted average interest rates %	Fixed rate financial liabilities Weighted average period for which rates are fixed Years
Financial liabilities					
Sterling (preference shares)	0.3	–	0.3	3.50	*
US dollar	62.0	168.2	230.2	6.36	7
Euro	–	22.8	22.8	–	–
Australian dollar	–	14.7	14.7	–	–
Japanese yen	–	14.6	14.6	–	–
Other currencies	–	6.0	6.0	–	–
	62.3	226.3	288.6		

* There is no redemption date on the preference shares, but a resolution is being put at the Annual General Meeting on 21st July 1999 to cancel them and repay the nominal value (plus any arrears of dividend) to the shareholders.

The financial liabilities of the group comprised:	1999
	£ million
Total borrowings and finance leases	280.2
Borrowings generated by swaps	7.0
Other creditors falling due after more than one year	1.1
Cumulative preference shares	0.3
	288.6

Floating rate financial liabilities comprise bank borrowings and overdrafts bearing interest at commercial rates.

	At floating interest rates £ million	Interest free £ million	Total £ million
Financial assets			
Sterling	16.4	–	16.4
US dollar	11.3	–	11.3
Euro	9.1	–	9.1
Australian dollar	0.8	–	0.8
Japanese yen	5.3	–	5.3
Hong Kong dollar	13.4	–	13.4
Other Currencies	10.8	3.0	13.8
	67.1	3.0	70.1

The financial assets of the group comprised:	1999 £ million
Cash and deposits	58.6
Deposits generated by swaps	7.0
Debtors due after one year (excluding prepaid pensions)	1.5
Other short term investments	3.0
	70.1

Floating rate financial assets comprise bank deposits bearing interest at commercial rates and finance leases to an associate bearing interest based on the US Prime rate plus 1.5%. Interest free financial assets are shares held in two publicly quoted companies, Ballard Power Systems, Inc. and AnorMed Inc.

Extract 9.7: British Telecommunications plc (1999)

33. Financial instruments and risk management[extract]

The following information is provided in accordance with the requirements of FRS 13 – "Derivatives and other financial instruments: disclosures". As permitted by the FRS, comparative figures are not provided since this is the first accounting period in which the FRS has come into effect. Except for disclosures under *currency exposures* below, the financial information excludes all of the group's short-term debtors and creditors.

Financial liabilities

After taking into account the various interest rate swaps and forward foreign currency contracts entered into by the group, the interest rate profile of the group's financial liabilities at 31 March 1999 was:

Currency:	Fixed rate financial liabilities	Floating rate financial liabilities	Financial liabilities on which no interest is paid	Total
	£m	£m	£m	£m
Sterling	2,395	1,592	–	3,987
US dollar	1,662	(1,654)	–	8
Euro	303	2	24	329
Other	–	9	–	9
Total	**4,360**	**(51)**	**24**	**4,333**

For the fixed rate financial liabilities, the average interest rates and the average periods for which the rates are fixed are:

Currency:	Weighted average interest rate %	Weighted average period for which rate is fixed Years
Sterling	9.5	9
US dollar	7.2	5
Euro	5.6	8
Total	**8.4**	**7**

The floating rate financial liabilities bear interest at rates fixed in advance for periods ranging from one day to six months by reference to LIBOR. The financial liabilities on which no interest is paid are due to mature within two months of the balance sheet date.

The maturity profile of financial liabilities is as given in *note 22*.

Financial assets

After taking into account the various interest rate swaps and forward foreign currency contracts entered into by the group, the interest rate profile of the group's financial assets at 31 March 1999 was:

	Fixed rate financial assets £m	Floating rate financial assets £m	Total £m
Currency:			
Sterling	273	2,651	2,924
US dollar	–	369	369
Euro	–	57	57
Other	–	30	30
Total	**273**	**3,107**	**3,380**

The sterling fixed rate financial assets yield interest at a weighted average of 5.5% for a weighted average period of 15 months.

The floating rate financial assets bear interest at rates fixed in advance for periods up to one year by reference to LIBOR

Extract 9.8 Pilkington plc (1999)

			Fixed rate financial liabilities		
	Total	Floating rate financial liabilities	Fixed rate financial liabilities	Weighted average interest rate	Weighted average period for which rate is fixed
28 Analysis of the financial liabilities shown in notes 26 and 27	£m	£m	£m	%	Months
Currency					
Sterling	162	150	12	7.06	32
US dollar	159	146	13	8.64	62
Deutschmark	101	78	23	7.21	49
Australian dollar	39	35	4	6.74	64
Italian lira	129	104	25	7.09	52
Swedish kroner	40	31	9	5.42	12
Finnish marks	34	15	19	4.16	12
Euro	9	1	8	10.58	57
Other currencies	50	16	34	17.10	12
Financial liabilities excluding non-equity shares	723	576	147	9.26	35
Non-equity minority shares	219	–	219	6.22	47
	942	576	366	7.44	41

> The disclosures made in notes 28 and 29 should be read in conjunction with the finance and liquidity, treasury and hedging policies and currency risk sections of the Financial Review on pages 14 and 15.
>
> The weighted average interest rate on the other currencies' fixed rate financial liabilities has been affected by a short term working capital Brazilian real loan with an interest rate of 35.16 per cent, taken out for a two week period.
>
> The Group has two financial liabilities on which no interest is payable, an Australian dollar loan of $20,000 and a United States dollar loan of $251,000.
>
> The financial liabilities, as defined by FRS 13, include the non-equity minority interests of £191 million, which relate to the preference shareholders in Pilkington Channel Islands Limited, who have a right to a fixed dividend of 6.55 per cent per annum, fixed for 47 months. In addition, any proceeds obtained by Pilkington Channel Islands Limited on repayment of a Eurobond of $369 million (£228 million, 1998 £221 million) issued by Pilkington Finance Limited to Pilkington Channel Islands Limited will be used, inter alia, to redeem these preference shares for $369 million (£228 million) after 4th March 2003. The remaining non-equity minority shares of £28 million relate to Flachglas AG and Dahlbusch AG, who have a right to a dividend of 3.65 per cent and 3.09 per cent respectively. These rates remain fixed in perpetuity and, in consequence, the average periods for which the rates are fixed are excluded from the figures noted in the above table.

As indicated earlier, if an entity has significant holdings of financial assets it should give similar analyses to those described above in relation to financial liabilities. Included within such financial assets may be investments in equity shares and other instruments that neither pay interest nor have a maturity rate. The standard therefore indicates that the disclosures will typically be limited to information about the currency exposures involved.[50] Although this is of some relevance, the major risks of equity shares and similar investments are more likely to be attributable to the businesses they are in than their currency exposure.

3.6   Currency risk disclosures

The next analysis required by FRS 13 is an analysis of the net monetary assets and liabilities at the balance sheet date, by reference to the principal functional currency of operations, showing the amount denominated in each principal currency.[51] The purpose of this analysis is to explain the currency exposures that give rise to exchange gains or losses which are taken to the profit and loss account under SSAP 20.[52] Accordingly, assets and liabilities denominated in the same currency as the functional currency of operations are excluded from the analysis, as are any foreign currency borrowings that are treated as a hedge against foreign net investments under SSAP 20.[53]

Like the interest rate risk disclosures discussed above, this analysis is also after taking account of currency swaps, forward contracts and other derivative financial instruments that contribute to the matching of the foreign currency exposures (again, it is noteworthy that the ASB has chosen to avoid the word 'hedge' in this context).[54] For example, if a company has taken out a forward contract in respect of DM debtors to effectively convert the amounts receivable into sterling, then for the purposes of this analysis the debtors should be treated as a sterling asset.

Although not specifically mentioned in the standard, it would seem that derivatives such as currency options should be excluded from the analysis. This is because the standard also requires disclosure of a summary of the main effect of any derivative financial instruments that are not so included.

Clearly, in order to meet this disclosure requirement reporting entities have to collate the underlying information, which may be no easy task. This is the sort of information which prior to FRS 13 companies had not usually disclosed.

Illustration 2 in Appendix III to the standard provides an example of this disclosure. Some examples of what companies are reporting in practice are given in the extracts below:

Extract 9.9: Volex Group p.l.c. (1999)

23 Derivatives and other financial instruments [extract]

b. Currency exposures

As explained on page 19 of the Financial Review, the Group's objectives in managing its structural currency exposures arising from its net investment overseas are to maintain a low cost of borrowings whilst partially hedging against currency depreciation. Gains and losses arising from these structural currency exposures are recognised in the statement of total recognised gains and losses.

The table below shows the Group's currency exposures; in other words, those transactional exposures that give rise to the net currency gains and losses recognised in the profit and loss account. Such exposures comprise the monetary assets and monetary liabilities of the Group that are not denominated in the operating currency of the operating unit involved, other than certain non-sterling borrowings treated as hedges of net investment in overseas operations. As at 31 March 1999 these exposures were as follows:

Functional currency of Group operation	Net foreign currency monetary assets (liabilities)*			
	Sterling £'000	US dollar £'000	HK dollar £'000	Total £'000
Sterling	–	957	–	957
Irish punt	(417)	1,112	–	695
Singapore dollar	(518)	997	(477)	2
Total	(935)	3,066	(477)	1,654

The exposures at 31 March 1998 for comparison purposes were as follows:

Functional currency of Group operation   Net foreign currency monetary assets (liabilities)*

	Sterling £'000	US dollar £'000	HK dollar £'000	Total £'000
Sterling	–	660	–	660
Irish punt	(603)	2,334	–	1,731
Singapore dollar	(551)	1,433	407	1,289
Total	(1,154)	4,427	407	3,680

The amounts shown in the tables above take into account the effect of any derivatives (including forward contracts) entered into to manage these currency exposures.

* comprising net trade debtors and creditors.

Extract 9.10: Cable and Wireless plc (1999)

24 Financial instruments [extract]

Exchange risk management

The table below shows the Group's currency exposures at 31 March 1999; being exposures on currency transactions that give rise to the net currency gains and losses recognised in the profit and loss account. Such exposures comprise the monetary assets and liabilities of the Group that are not denominated in the functional currency of the operating company involved, other than certain non-sterling borrowings treated as hedges of net investments in overseas investments.

Net foreign currency monetary assets/(liabilities) in £m

Functional currency of the operating company	Sterling	US$	HK$	Aus$	Other	Total
Sterling	–	55	–	(59)	(6)	**(10)**
HK$	–	628	–	–	–	**628**
Aus$	1	38	–	–	–	**39**
Other	–	(298)	–	–	–	**(298)**
	1	423	–	(59)	(6)	**359**

The amounts shown in the table take into account the effect of any cross currency swaps, forward contracts and other derivatives entered into to manage these currency exposures.

FRED 13 originally proposed further currency disclosures which were aimed at showing the currency exposures which gave rise to exchange differences taken directly to reserves under SSAP 20. It tried to do this by suggesting disclosure of a currency analysis of net assets compared to borrowings. This proposed requirement has been dropped in the standard for non-financial entities, although a variant of the requirement has been retained for banks (see 4.1.2 below). In February 1999 the ASB released an Exposure Draft[55] which was intended to introduce the disclosure as a modification to SSAP 20. However, in May 1999 it announced that it would not be proceeding with the amendment in advance of a review of SSAP 20 as a whole.[56]

3.7   Liquidity disclosures

The next category of numerical disclosures relates to liquidity risk. First, the standard requires entities to disclose a maturity profile of the carrying amount of financial liabilities, showing the amounts falling due:

- in 1 year or less, or on demand;

- in more than 1 year but not more than 2 years;

- in more than 2 years but not more than 5 years; and

- in more than 5 years.

This maturity profile is to be determined by reference to the earliest date on which payment can be required or on which the liability falls due.[57] This is the same as the equivalent rule within FRS 4 and the companies legislation in relation to loans.

This disclosure is similar to the existing requirement of FRS 4 to give a maturity analysis of debt and that of SSAP 21 in relation to finance lease obligations, but it is not quite the same.

The time bands are slightly different from those in FRS 4, therefore a corresponding amendment has been made to that standard.[58] The effect of this amendment is that any amount which is due exactly 5 years after the balance sheet date now falls within the third band rather than the fourth band. Also, amounts due exactly 2 years after the balance sheet date now fall within the second band, whereas before the amendment it was possible for such an amount to be included in the third band.

It is noted in FRS 13 that in order to provide the disclosures required, the maturity analyses already provided in FRS 4 and SSAP 21 could be brought together. However, if this is done the information needs to be extended to provide further analysis of finance lease obligations showing the split between the second and third bands. Also it will be necessary for the disclosures to include any financial liabilities, other than debt and finance lease obligations; this would include any creditors due after more than one year and any monetary provisions which are expected to be paid after more than one year.[59]

The standard also notes that the analysis of debt and finance lease obligations for this purpose needs to be based on the carrying amount, not on the amounts to be paid on maturity.[60] Accordingly, if companies have traditionally given the maturity analysis of their finance lease obligations by showing the rentals payable in each of the relevant periods and then deducting the aggregate finance charges to reconcile to the carrying amounts of the obligations in the balance sheet, they will need to revise their treatment if they wish to combine all of the disclosures within one table.

In addition, FRS 13 asks for disclosure of a maturity analysis of any material committed but undrawn borrowing facilities. This is similar to the maturity analysis described above, but only requires a distinction between those expiring:

■   in 1 year or less;

■   in more than 1 year but not more than 2 years; and

■   in more than 2 years.

Facilities should only be included in the above analysis if all conditions precedent attached to the facility were satisfied at the balance sheet date.[61]

The standard suggests that this disclosure might also go on to explain the purpose and period for which the facilities are committed and whether they are subject to annual review.[62]

Paragraph 41 of the standard indicates that where the maturity analysis of debt under FRS 4 takes into account committed borrowing facilities, then to avoid double-counting, such facilities should not be included within this disclosure. This could be interpreted as meaning none of the facilities are to be disclosed. However, we believe the excess of the facilities over the amount taken into account should be disclosed.

An example of the disclosure is given in the extract below:

Extract 9.11: Pilkington plc (1999)

29 Financial instrument disclosures

(c) Borrowing facilities

The Group has various available borrowing facilities. The undrawn committed facilities available at 31st March 1999 in respect of which all conditions precedent had been met at that date, were as follows:

	£m
Expiring in one year or less	57
Expiring in more than one year but not more than two years	137
Expiring in more than two years	132
	326

On 20th April 1999 the Group completed arrangements to borrow $250 million (£154 million) redeemable on fixed dates between April 2006 and April 2014 with an average life of 11 years from the balance sheet date at 31st March 1999. This has not been reflected in these financial statements.

The standard also suggests that some companies might wish to produce a maturity analysis of financial assets.

3.8   Fair values

As with some of the other disclosure requirements of FRS 13, this requirement reflects the ASB's views as to the eventual measurement rules for financial instruments. Although those who do not necessarily agree that it is appropriate to carry all instruments at fair value may not be persuaded about the relevance of disclosing such values, nevertheless such information must now be given.

The requirement is for an entity to group its financial assets and liabilities, including amounts not recognised in the balance sheet, into appropriate categories and for each category to disclose either:

- the aggregate fair value at the balance sheet date compared to the aggregate book value; or

- the aggregate fair value of those financial instruments at the balance sheet date with a positive fair value and, separately, those with a negative fair value, compared to the book amounts.[63]

FRED 13 only proposed the former type of disclosure, but a number of commentators suggested the latter form of disclosure and as the ASB believed that the arguments involved were evenly balanced, the standard permits a choice. However, the standard warns that if a subsequent FRS requires most or all financial instruments to be carried on the balance sheet at fair value, systems capable of producing the latter type of disclosure would then be required.[64]

The exposure draft had also proposed that those financial assets and liabilities that are not traded on organised markets in a standard form were to be shown separately, but this has been dropped from the standard.

The first stage in giving these disclosures is to determine the appropriate categories. The standard is not prescriptive about how this should be done, but suggests that the classification should take account of the nature of the item and the purpose for which it is held. This should tie in with the discussion of the use of these instruments given in the narrative disclosures (see section 3.2 above). One categorisation might be between items used for financing, risk management or hedging, and trading or speculation. However, the standard then suggests that these categories should be analysed in more detail; for example, with interest rate swaps shown separately from currency swaps, and separate disclosure of optional derivatives, such as currency options and interest collars and caps. It is also suggested that financial assets would not be included in the same sub-category as financial liabilities.[65] (This would be necessary if entities wished the components to be traced back to the respective balance sheet captions as discussed at 3.4 above.)   It may be that for this purpose similar derivative financial instruments held or issued for the same purpose would be grouped together, regardless of whether their fair value was positive or negative, although clearly this could only be done if the former method of disclosure was being followed.

The next stage in the process is to determine the fair values to be disclosed. Fair value is defined in the usual manner as 'the amount at which an asset or liability could be exchanged in an arm's length transaction between informed and willing parties, other than in a forced or liquidation sale'.[66] Guidance on procedures for estimating the fair value of financial assets and financial liabilities is set out in Appendix IV to the standard. Where quoted market prices are available, these should generally be used. Where quoted market prices are not available or may not be indicative of the fair value due to infrequent activity in a market, then fair values might be estimated by using discounted cash flow techniques or option-pricing models.

For some financial assets and liabilities the estimated difference between the carrying amount and its fair value may not be material, in which case the carrying amount may be used as the fair value for the purposes of the disclosure.[67] This is likely to be the case with any floating rate debt and could also apply to cash on short-term deposit. Where an entity decides to include short-term debtors and creditors within its disclosures, then this also likely to be appropriate for such items.

The methods and any significant assumptions used in determining the fair values have to be disclosed.[68] This applies in all cases, not just in those situations where fair values have had to be estimated in the absence of quoted market prices, or such prices were not considered indicative of fair value.

If it is not practicable to estimate with sufficient reliability the fair values of items that are not traded on an organised market in a standard form, it will be permissible instead to disclose a description of such items, their book values, the reasons why estimating their value is impracticable, and information about the main characteristics that affect their value and the market for such instruments. If the directors consider the disclosure of this last item would be seriously prejudicial, then it can be omitted but that fact and the reasons for doing so need to be stated. However, disclosure of all of this information is not meant to be an easy loophole to avoid disclosure of the fair value – FRS 13 makes it clear that this alternative is only available in rather extreme circumstances and that the entity should have exhausted all viable methods of estimating and disclosing the information, e.g. by disclosing a range of values.[69]

Some examples of the disclosures companies are giving in practice are set out below:

Extract 9.12: The National Grid Group plc (1999)

19 Financial instruments [extract]

Fair values of financial instruments at 31 March 1999	Book value £m	Fair value £m
Cash and deposits	1,524.5	1,524.5
Total borrowings	(2,227.9)	(2,334.2)
Net borrowings	(703.4)	(809.7)
Other financial liabilities*	(43.6)	(43.6)
Net investment in finance lease	52.3	62.0
Assets held for exchange	16.6	248.8
Net financial liabilities*	(678.1)	(542.5)
Financial instruments held to manage interest rate and currency profile:		
Interest rate swaps	–	(4.8)
Interest rate swap options	–	(0.3)
Forward currency contracts and cross currency swaps	(0.3)	(68.4)

*Excluding forward currency contracts (book value: £0.3m).

Market values, where available, have been used to determine fair values. Where market values are not available, fair values, with the exception of assets held for exchange, have been calculated by discounting cash flows at prevailing interest rates. The fair value of the assets held for exchange is deemed to be the fair value attributed to the 6% mandatorily exchangeable bonds 2003 to which the assets relate (see note 15).

Extract 9.13: Cable and Wireless plc (1999)

24 Financial instruments [extract]

Fair value

The estimated fair value of the Group's financial instruments are summarised below:

	1999		1998	
	Carrying amount £m	Estimated fair value £m	Carrying amount £m	Estimated fair value £m
Primary financial instruments held or issued to finance the Group's operations				
Trade investments	**498**	**925**	187	219
Cash	**319**	**319**	332	332
Short term deposits	**1,600**	**1,600**	1,355	1,355
Current asset investments	**60**	**60**	–	–
Net investment in finance lease receivables	**39**	**39**	39	39
Loans and obligations under finance leases due within one year	**(1,102)**	**(1,102)**	(471)	(471)
Convertible bonds	**(71)**	**(263)**	(84)	(299)
Other loans and obligations under finance leases due after more than one year	**(4,370)**	**(4,915)**	(4,092)	(4,193)
Provisions for onerous contracts	**(59)**	**(59)**	–	–
Derivative financial instruments held to manage interest rate and currency exposure				
Interest rate swaps – assets	–	**10**	–	9
– (liabilities)	–	**(96)**	–	(4)
Cross currency swaps – assets	–	**38**	–	7
– (liabilities)	–	**(33)**	–	(54)
Forward foreign exchange contracts	**(5)**	**(5)**	–	–

Trade investments
Trade investments above are detailed in note 16 but exclude ESOP shares carried at £17m (1998 – £10m). The fair value is based on year end quoted prices for listed investments and estimates of likely sales proceeds for other investments.

Current asset investments
The fair value is based on market value or estimates of likely sales proceeds.

Cash at bank and in hand, short term deposits and short term borrowings
The carrying value approximates to fair value either because of the short maturity of the instruments or because the interest rate on investments is reset after periods not greater than six months.

Convertible bonds and other long term debt
The fair value is based on quoted market prices or, where these are not available, on the quoted market prices of comparable debt issued by other companies.

Interest rate and cross currency swaps
The fair value of interest rate and cross currency swaps is the estimated amount which the Group would expect to pay or receive were it to terminate the swaps at the balance sheet date. This is based on quotations from counterparties and takes into consideration current interest rates, current exchange rates and the current creditworthiness of the counterparties. The nominal value of the interest rate and currency swaps at 31 March 1999 was £4,526m (1998 – £2,732m).

Forward exchange contracts

The value of these contracts is the estimated amount which the Group would expect to pay or receive on the termination of the contracts. At 31 March 1999 the Group had £578m of such contracts outstanding (1998 – £307m).

Extract 9.14: Raglan Properties plc (1999)

18. Financial instruments [extract]

A comparison of book values and fair values of the group's financial assets and liabilities is set out below:

	Book value £000	Fair* value £000	Fair value adjustment £000
Fixed rate borrowings	(74,579)	(92,159)	(17,580)
Variable rate borrowings	(2,965)	(2,965)	–
Cash and short term deposits	22,110	22,110	–
Interest rate cap	287	2	(285)
Total adjustment			**(17,865)**

*Net of tax.

The fair value of fixed rate borrowings and interest rate caps has been assessed by calculating the cash flows which would arise if the commitments at 31 March 1999 had been entered into at market rates at that date.

The expiry profile of the fair value adjustment is as follows:

	Fair value adjustment £000
2000	(285)
2012	(17,580)
	(17,865)

The fair value adjustment represents approximately 23.1% of group borrowings and has a notional adverse effect on net asset value per share of 12.1 pence per share at 31 March 1999. Comparatives have not been provided due to the impractical nature of obtaining the information. The fair value adjustment of other financial assets and liabilities is, in the opinion of the Directors, not material to the balance sheet.

Extract 9.15: The British Land Company PLC (1999)

14. Net Debt [extract]

Comparison of market values and book values at 31st March, 1999

	Book Value £m	Market Value £m	**Difference £m**
Long term fixed rate debt	986.1	1,354.6	**368.5**
Bank debt (net)	1,259.7	1,259.7	
Convertible debt	462.4	541.8	**79.4**
Continuing derivatives		(28.3)	**(28.3)**
Net debt	2,708.2	3,127.8	**419.6**
Derivatives provision – closed out derivatives	68.0	68.0	

The market value and difference are shown before any tax relief. The difference between book value and market value on the convertibles arises principally from the British Land share price.

In accordance with accounting standards book value of the debt is par value net of amortised issue costs. The valuation of 135 Bishopsgate Securitisation 2018 has been undertaken by Greenwich NatWest. The valuation of other long term fixed rate debt and convertible debt has been undertaken by Warburg Dillon Read. The bank debt has been valued assuming the bank debt and could be renegotiated at contracted margins. The derivatives have been valued by the independent treasury adviser Record Treasury Management.

Extract 9.16: Scottish and Southern Energy plc (1999)

23. Derivatives and financial instruments [extract]

Contracts for differences

The electricity trading mechanism in England and Wales requires all physical delivery and initial settlement for electricity to be via the Pool which sets prices on a half hourly basis. In order to fix purchase costs and sale prices, Contracts for Differences (CfDs) are entered between generators and public electricity suppliers and take the form of a difference payment from the pool price back to the underlying terms agreed. These derivative financial instruments are necessary to produce the same economic effect as a straightforward fixed price contract and are not used as a vehicle for speculating against pool prices.

In the majority of cases there is neither an organised visible market nor standard form for these instruments. Therefore any estimate of fair value of the CfDs outstanding at the balance sheet date must necessarily be based on internal assumptions on the future level of pool prices and, if available, prices being quoted in private bilateral transactions for similar contracts. Having regard to current contract prices for similar short-term CfDs (i.e. between 6 months and 1 year), the Directors believe that the fair value of these contracts outstanding at the year end is not material to the Group's Accounts.

The Group has a number of longer term CfDs extending up to 12 years from the balance sheet date. The Directors do not believe it is practicable to estimate with sufficient reliability a fair value for such longer term CfDs as there are no directly comparable contract prices. In addition, assumptions on the future level of pool prices are highly subjective due to the influence of such factors as future market structure, projected supply and demand, generating plant constructed and plant availability. Other information on these long-term CfDs has not been provided as the Directors believe such information is commercially confidential.

Trading CfDs does involve a degree of credit risk in that the counterparty may default on settlement. The Group controls credit risk arising from entering into the CfDs through credit approvals, limits and monitoring procedures.

3.9 Hedges

Many entities use financial assets and liabilities as hedges to manage their risk profile. A 'hedge' is not defined in FRS 13, but in the discussion of the narrative disclosures within the standard it regards a 'hedge' as 'an instrument that individually, or with other instruments, has a value or cash flow that is expected, wholly or partly, to move inversely with changes in the value or cash flows of the position being hedged'.[70] As explained in paragraph 58 of FRS 13, when instruments are used for hedging purposes, they are usually accounted for using hedge accounting whereby 'changes in fair values of the hedge (referred to hereafter as "the gain or loss on the hedge") are not recognised in the profit and loss account immediately they arise. Instead, they either are not recognised at all or are recognised and carried forward in the balance sheet; then, when the hedged transaction occurs, the gain or loss on the hedge is usually either used to adjust the amount at which the hedged item is dealt with in the financial statements or recognised in the profit and loss account at the same time as the hedged item.'

The ASB's distrust of hedge accounting is evident from the extent of the required disclosures where instruments have been accounted for as hedges. FRED 13 had proposed that these disclosures should only be in respect of hedges of future transactions, but they have now been extended to all hedges. However, the proposal in FRED 13 for separate disclosure of hedges of firm contracts and other hedges has been dropped.

The standard calls for disclosure of the following information about gains and losses on financial assets and financial liabilities for which hedge accounting has been used:

(a)   the cumulative aggregate gains and cumulative aggregate losses that are unrecognised at the balance sheet date. If an item's fair value is not disclosed under the standard (see 3.8 above), any gain or loss on the item need not be included within this disclosure;

(b)   the cumulative aggregate gains and losses carried forward in the balance sheet pending their recognition in the profit and loss account;

(c)   the extent to which the gains and losses disclosed under (a) and (b) above are expected to be recognised in the profit and loss account of the following year; and

(d)   the amount of gains and losses included in the current year's profit and loss account that arose in previous years but were brought forward to the current year as a hedge.[71]

The amounts disclosed under (b), (c) and (d) above should exclude any amounts which have been accounted for by adjusting the carrying amount of a fixed asset recognised in the balance sheet.[72] This exception has been allowed as a pragmatic response to the practical difficulties of keeping track of such gain and losses and their recognition in the profit and loss account as part of the depreciation charge on those assets.[73] However, the exception does not seem to apply to instruments taken out to hedge future purchases of fixed assets as these assets are not yet 'recognised on the balance sheet'. Thus, any 'gain or loss' on the instrument which is carried forward in the balance sheet should be included in the disclosures under (b). Any 'gain or loss' which is unrecognised at the balance sheet will need to be included under (a) since no exemption is given in respect of the disclosures under that sub-paragraph. As far as disclosure under (c) is concerned, arguably the impact of any such 'gains or losses' on the following year's depreciation charge should be included. We do not think that is appropriate because once the asset is purchased and included in the balance sheet, the 'gain or loss' is not to be included within the disclosures. However, we do not believe that is the only problem. If the 'gain or loss' is excluded from the disclosure under (c), users of the accounts might infer that the excess of the amounts disclosed under (a) and (b) over the amount shown under (c) are to be recognised in the profit and loss in later years. This problem will be exacerbated if entities follow the illustrations of these disclosures contained in Appendix III to the standard, which include a line for the gains and losses to be recognised in later years. We would therefore suggest that entities should indicate how much of the gains and losses disclosed under (a) and (b) relate to future fixed asset purchases.

As the exception is only made in respect of fixed assets, it would seem that where gains and losses have been recognised and have been accounted for as part of the cost of stock, then such gains and losses need to be included within the disclosures, even although there may be similar practical difficulties.

These requirements are worded in language that reflects the ASB's views on hedge accounting; in particular, they ask for the disclosure of 'gains' and 'losses' on financial assets and financial liabilities for which hedge accounting has been used. From the point of view of the companies who use them, however, these are not gains and losses at all, but simply constitute an element of the cost of the item being hedged, and there is a significant risk that the disclosures will be misinterpreted as a result.

The wording of the standard is also unclear as to whether what is required to be disclosed is the gains and losses on both hedging instrument and hedged item (where both are financial assets or financial liabilities for which hedge accounting has been used) or just those gains and losses on the hedging instrument. The UITF has subsequently clarified that it is just the gains and losses on the hedging instrument which have to be disclosed.[74]

Occasionally an entity may reclassify an instrument previously accounted for as a hedge. Where, as a consequence of such a reclassification during the year, gains or losses that arose in previous years and were deferred in the balance sheet or not recognised are now recognised in the current year's profit and loss account, then the amount of such gains and losses should be disclosed.[75] This should not be taken to mean that this is the most appropriate way that gains or losses should be dealt with. As the standard says, such reclassifications can be accounted for in different ways. We believe that in most circumstances the gains or losses up to the point of reclassification should continue to be deferred or not recognised, and recognised when the transaction it was originally intended to hedge takes place (see Chapter 15 at 2.2.6). Although the standard does not call for any specific disclosure where such gains and losses continue to be deferred or not recognised, we believe that they should continue to be incorporated within the disclosures set out above.

Examples of disclosures in respect of hedges are illustrated below:

Extract 9.17: Scottish Power plc (1999)

20 Loans and other borrowings [extract]

(g) Hedges

The group's policy is to hedge the following exposures:

– interest rate risk using interest swaps, both sterling and cross currency, caps, collars, and forward foreign currency contracts;

– currency exposures on foreign denominated debt and future purchases/sales using currency swaps and forwards and spot foreign currency contracts.

Gains and losses on instruments used for hedging are not recognised until the exposure that is being hedged is itself recognised. Unrecognised gains and losses on instruments used for hedging, and the movements therein, are as follows:

	Gains £m	Losses £m	Total net gains/losses £m
Unrecognised (losses) on hedges at 1 April 1998	(1.6)	(60.2)	(61.8)
Losses arising in previous years that were recognised in 1998-99	9.7	6.5	16.2
Gains and (losses) arising before 1 April 1998 that were not recognised in 1998-99	8.1	(53.7)	(45.6)
Gains and (losses) arising in 1998-99 that were not recognised in 1998-99	2.6	(38.0)	(35.4)
Unrecognised gains and (losses) on hedges at 31 March 1999	10.7	(91.7)	(81.0)
Gains and (losses) expected to be recognised in 1999-00	(4.6)	(23.6)	(28.2)
Gains and (losses) expected to be recognised in 2000-01 or later	15.3	(68.1)	(52.8)

The total net unrecognised loss of £81.0 million principally represents the opportunity cost of protecting the group's interest charge against movements in interest rates at a time when interest rates were higher than at 31 March 1999.

The analyses of financial instruments in this Note do not include short-term debtors and creditors as permitted by FRS 13.

Extract 9.18: Cable and Wireless plc (1999)

24 Financial instruments [extract]

Hedges

Gains and losses on instruments used for hedging are not recognised until the exposure that is being hedged is itself recognised. Unrecognised gains and losses on instruments used for hedging (excluding hedges that have been accounted for by adjusting the carrying value of a fixed asset recognised on the balance sheet), and the underlying asset or liability are as follows:

	Gains £m	(Losses) £m	Net gains/ (losses) £m
Unrecognised gains and losses on hedges			
At 1 April 1998	16	(159)	(143)
Gains/(losses) arising in the previous year that were recognised during the year	–	–	–
Gains/(losses) arising before 1 April 1998 that were not recognised during the year	16	(159)	(143)
Gains/(losses) arising in the year that were not recognised during the year	32	(155)	(123)
At 31 March 1999	**48**	**(314)**	**(266)**
Of which:			
Gains and losses expected to be recognised in less than one year	–	–	–
Gains and losses expected to be recognised after more than one year	48	(314)	(266)

As highlighted in the interest rate management table on page 66, 76% of the Group's financial liabilities have fixed interest rates. The above net unrecognised loss is a reflection of different market interest rates ruling at 31 March 1999.

It should be noted that the illustration of these disclosures in Appendix III to the standard goes beyond that which is required. In the table below, which is taken from Illustration 2, it is only the lines which are shaded which are required to be disclosed, although the amounts in the first line would be disclosed as part of the comparatives.

	Gains £ millions	Losses £ millions	Total net gains/(losses) £ millions
Unrecognised gains and losses on hedges at 1.1.X1	53	28	25
Gains and losses arising in previous years that were recognised in 19X1	22	21	1
Gains and losses arising before 1.1.X1 that were not recognised in 19X1	31	7	24
Gains and losses arising in 19X1 that were not recognised in 19X1	66	41	25
Unrecognised gains and losses on hedges at 31.12.X1	97	48	49
Of which:			
Gains and losses expected to be recognised in 19X2	71	40	31
Gains and losses expected to be recognised in 19X3 or later	26	8	18

3.10 Instruments held or issued for trading

It might be thought that this requirement would only be applicable to banks and other financial institutions. However, for the purposes of the standard, trading in financial assets and financial liabilities is defined as 'buying, selling, issuing or holding financial assets and financial liabilities in order to take advantage of short-term changes in market prices or rates ...'[76] Arguably, this could embrace financial instruments taken out for hedging purposes, so the standard clarifies that items taken out to hedge the risks associated with another transaction or position are deemed to be trading only if that other transaction or position involves such trading.

It would seem therefore that these disclosures would embrace current asset investments, derivatives which are not regarded as hedges, and any derivatives which hedge such items.

Where an entity trades in financial assets and financial liabilities, the following information should be disclosed:

- The net gain or loss included in the profit and loss account from trading such assets and liabilities during the period. This is to be analysed by type of financial instrument, business activity, risk or 'in such other way as is consistent with the entity's management of this activity'. If the analysis provided is other than by type of financial instrument, then a description of the types of financial instruments involved should be given for each item in the analysis. However, there is no need to quantify the net gain or loss for each type of instrument involved.

■ The fair values at the balance sheet date of financial assets and, separately, financial liabilities that are held or issued for trading. This information may already be disclosed as part of the fair value disclosures discussed in 3.8 above. However, since information has to be given for financial assets and financial liabilities separately, then it may be necessary to give additional disclosure to meet this requirement. This is likely to be the case where derivative financial instruments have been grouped together for the purposes of the fair value disclosures regardless of whether the fair values were positive or negative. If the year-end position is considered to be materially unrepresentative of the entity's use of such instruments during the year, then average amounts for the year are also to be disclosed. Ideally, these average amounts should be calculated using daily figures, but if this is not the case, then the entity should use the most frequent interval that its systems generate for management, regulatory or other reasons.[77]

3.11 Commodity contracts treated as financial instruments

As noted earlier at 3.1 above, although commodity contracts requiring settlement by physical delivery are not financial instruments, the standard requires some such contracts nevertheless to be included within certain of the disclosures. The contracts to be included are cash-settled commodity contracts which are commodity contracts (including contracts for the delivery of gold) which, though having contract terms that require settlement by physical delivery only, are of a type that is normally extinguished other than by physical delivery in accordance with general market practice.[78]

Such contracts are to be included within the following disclosures:

■ the narrative disclosures (see 3.2 above);

■ the fair value disclosures (see 3.8 above);

■ the disclosures about hedges (see 3.9 above); and

■ the disclosures about instruments held or issued for trading (see 3.10 above).[79]

However there is a 'commercially prejudicial' exemption which allows some or all of the numerical disclosures to be omitted in exceptional cases. This applies where the market in the commodity is illiquid and dominated by very few participants, and if disclosure of the information at the time the financial statements become publicly available would be likely to move the market significantly and, in the directors' opinion, would be seriously prejudicial to the reporting entity's interests. If this exemption is taken, this fact must be disclosed, with an explanation of the reasons.[80]

3.12 Market price risk

The standard's final set of disclosures is non-mandatory, to encourage experimentation in an admittedly difficult area. It calls for additional numerical disclosures to explain the magnitude of market price risk for all financial instruments, cash-settled commodity contracts and, if significant, all other items that carry market price risk. The manner in which this is done should reflect the way (or ways) in which the entity manages its risk exposures.[81] This disclosure should be accompanied by narrative explanation that puts the figures in context.

This disclosure should also be supplemented by:

(a)   an explanation of the method used and the main parameters and assumptions underlying the data provided;

(b)   an explanation of the objective of the method used and of the limitations that may result in the information not fully reflecting the market price risk; and

(c)   reasons for any material changes in the amount of reported market price risk when compared with that reported for the previous period.[82]

If material changes are made to the method, or main assumptions and parameters, used in providing this disclosure, the reasons for the change should be given and the comparative information restated using the basis adopted in the current year.[83]

Paragraph 68 of FRS 13 gives a number of suggestions as to how market price risk might be evaluated and presented, but notes that each has its shortcomings and thus a combination of approaches might be more helpful.

This seems a very ambitious suggestion given the already far-reaching nature of the mandatory disclosures, and it seems unlikely that many companies will respond to this particular challenge. Nevertheless some companies have been providing some sensitivity analysis information as illustrated below:

Extract 9.19: Johnson Matthey plc (1999)

19 Financial risk management [extract]

19g Market price risk

The group monitors its interest rate and currency risks and other market price risks to which it is exposed primarily through a process known as 'sensitivity analysis'. This involves estimating the effect on profit before tax over various periods of possible changes in interest rates and exchange rates.

Most of the group's borrowings and deposits are at floating rates. A 1% change on all interest rates would have a 1.2% impact on group profit before tax. This is well within the range the group regards as acceptable.

> The main impact of movements in exchange rates on the group's results arises on translation of overseas subsidiaries' profits into sterling. The group's largest exposure is to the US dollar since Johnson Matthey's largest single overseas investment is in the USA. A 5 cent (3%) movement in the average exchange rate for the US dollar against sterling has a 1.8% impact on group profit before tax. This exposure is part of the group's economic risk of operating globally which is essential to remain competitive in the markets in which the group operates.

One company which gives value at risk disclosures is Reuters, as shown below in an extract prior to the mandatory implementation date of FRS 13:

Extract 9.20: Reuters Group PLC (1998)

Operating and financial review [extract]

The company has adopted value at risk (VAR) analysis as a means of quantifying the potential impact of exchange rate volatility on reported earnings. VAR is a measure of the potential loss on a portfolio within a specified time horizon, at a specified confidence interval. Loss is defined, in this instance, as the diminution in value of rolling 12 month forecast group profits denominated in sterling. Due to the approximations used in determining VAR, the theory provides order of magnitude estimates only but these are useful for comparison purposes.

Reuters estimates that there is currently a 5% chance that profits forecast for the coming 12 months will deteriorate by more than £70 million as a result of currency fluctuations before hedging and £37 million after taking into account hedging at 31 December 1998 (1997: £74 million before hedging and £42 million after hedging). These figures represent the value at risk and are illustrated graphically opposite.

During 1998 the average value at risk before hedging on forecast profits for the coming 12 months varied between £55 million and £76 million and averaged £64 million (1997: £72 million) and after hedging varied between £30 million and £43 million, averaging £35 million (1997: £36 million).

---

4 DISCLOSURE REQUIREMENTS FOR FINANCIAL INSTITUTIONS

4.1 Banks and similar institutions

The requirements for banks and similar institutions are contained within Part B of FRS 13. FRS 13 defines a bank or similar institution as 'an entity that:

(a)   is authorised under the Banking Act 1987 (in the UK) or the Central Bank Acts 1942-1989 (in the Republic of Ireland); or

(b)   whose business is to receive deposits or other repayable funds from the public and to grant credits for its own account.'[84]

As a result of paragraph (b) above, entities such as building societies and credit unions are brought within the scope of this alternative regime. This regime is also to be followed by banking or similar groups, i.e. groups where:

(a)   the parent company is a bank or similar institution; or

(b)   the parent company:

   (i)   does not carry on any material business apart from the acquisition, management and disposal of interests in subsidiary undertakings; and

  (ii)   its principal subsidiary undertakings are wholly or mainly entities that are banks or similar institutions.[85]

The instruments to be included within the disclosures by banks and similar institutions are effectively the same as for non-financial institutions. However, it should be noted that banks and similar institutions cannot exclude financial assets and financial liabilities arising from traditional lending activities and deposit-making activities from the disclosures, since they cannot be treated as falling within the term 'short-term debtors and creditors' (see 3.1 above).[86] Also, for the purposes of the disclosures in respect of commodity contracts, all contracts for the delivery of gold are to be treated as if they were financial instruments (see 4.1.5 below).[87]

Like non-financial institutions, banks and similar financial institutions have to provide narrative disclosures of objectives, policies and strategies (see 3.2 above).[88] This discussion will need to reflect the nature of their business and is likely to involve more discussion on credit risk and market price risk, particularly in relation to financial assets. The recommendations in FRS 13 for disclosures in respect of accounting policies also apply to banks and financial institutions (see 3.3 above).[89]

As mentioned at 3.1 above, the main impact of the different regime in FRS 13 is in respect of the numerical disclosures to be given by banks and similar institutions. The requirements for banks and similar institutions reflect the fact that financial instruments play an integral part in generating such an entity's net income, which arises from the management of the mismatches in the exposures arising from such instruments and the margins earned thereon. Also, a distinction is made between the trading and non-trading activities of such entities by requiring different disclosures in respect of the 'trading book' and the 'non-trading book'.

The trading book comprise those assets and liabilities arising from the trading activity of the entity which includes:

- providing financial instruments to clients (other than through traditional lending and deposit-taking activities or by granting finance leases) – i.e. customer facilitation;

- providing liquidity to the market – i.e. market making;

- acting as a connecting link between different markets – i.e. arbitrage;

- taking proprietary positions; and

- related hedges.

The non-trading book comprises all the entity's other assets and liabilities which arise from non-trading activities which include:

- traditional lending and deposit-taking;

- granting of finance leases;

- asset/liability and liquidity management;

- investment activity, including activity of a strategic nature; and

- related hedges.

The standard indicates that this categorisation is not exactly the same as for capital adequacy purposes.[90] However, in practice, there is likely to be little difference and it will be in the bank's interest for it to be the same.

4.1.1 Interest rate risk disclosures

The interest rate risk disclosures reflect the fact that the net income of banks and similar institutions is generated by mismatches in the exposures arising from such instruments and the margins earned thereon. Accordingly, an interest rate sensitivity gap analysis (sometimes referred to as an 'interest rate repricing table') is to be provided showing the aggregate carrying amounts of assets and liabilities in the non-trading book, analysed by major category of asset and liability and, within those categories, into time bands. In preparing this analysis:

(a) items should be allocated to time bands by reference to whichever is the earlier of the period to the next interest rate repricing date and the maturity date;

(b) the time bands used should include at least the following:
   (i) not more than the next three months;
   (ii) more than three months but not more than six months;
   (iii) more than six months but not more than one year;
   (iv) more than one year but not more than five years; and
   (v) more than five years; and

(c) the analysis should show the net position for each time band.[91]

The analysis is also to be after taking account of derivatives whose effect is to alter the interest basis of the assets and liabilities. Where any derivatives have not been included within the analysis, a summary should be provided of the main effects of such instruments.[92] This might include such elements as the notional principal amounts involved, the period for which the instruments are operative, the main potential effect of the instruments on information provided in the analysis and the terms of any options contained within the instrument. The aim of this information should be to ensure that the risks associated with such instruments are adequately disclosed.[93]

One aspect of interest rate risk is the currency in which the assets and liabilities are denominated. It may be that a bank has a financial asset in one currency funded by a liability in another currency, both repricing within the same time band. The analysis would therefore suggest there is no interest rate risk exposure. However, it may be that the asset is in a currency of a country with high and volatile interest rates whereas the liability is in a currency of a country with low and stable interest rates, giving rise to potentially significant interest rate risk in the future. Nevertheless, the standard only encourages, but does not require, incorporation of the currency in which assets and liabilities within the table are denominated where this is of significance.[94]

The third illustration in Appendix III to the standard provides an example of the disclosures required. This example includes all assets and liabilities including shareholders' funds and non-financial assets, whether interest bearing or not. Arguably this is not strictly necessary but it does provide a reconciliation to the balance sheet. One company which gives such disclosures is Bank of Ireland as shown in the extract below.

As discussed at 4.1.4 below, similar interest rate risk disclosures may be provided in respect of the trading book, but such disclosures should be shown separately from those for the non-trading book.

4.1.2   Currency risk disclosures

FRS 13 states that the currency risk exposure of banks and similar institutions comprises 3 elements:

(a)   the structural currency exposures that arise from the entity's foreign equity investments as mitigated by the foreign currency borrowings taken out to finance or hedge such investments;

(b)   the currency exposures arising on the monetary assets and liabilities in the non-trading book; and

(c)   the currency exposures that arise on the monetary assets and liabilities in the trading book.[95]

The disclosures required by the standard in respect of the trading book are dealt with in 4.1.4 below. The other disclosures are intended to be constructed to reflect the entity's application of SSAP 20.[96]

First, the entity's foreign net investments should be analysed according to its main functional currencies and these amounts compared with the currencies of its borrowings which qualify as a hedge under the cover method of SSAP 20.[97]

In preparing this analysis, account should be taken of the effect of currency swaps, forward contracts and other derivatives that contribute to the matching or hedging. Derivatives whose effect is variable or conditional (e.g. options) should be excluded from the analysis and disclosed separately.[98]

The second analysis which is required is one that shows the currency exposures on the non-trading book by principal functional currencies of the operations involved. Again, account should be taken of the effect of currency swaps, etc. that contribute to the matching or hedging of the foreign currency exposures, with separate disclosure of derivatives whose effect is variable or conditional.[99]

The standard recognises that many banks and similar institutions transfer all their currency risk arising from the commercial banking/lending activities to their trading book. If, as a result, there are no remaining currency exposures in the non-trading book, or if any remaining exposures are not material, the standard suggests that it would be helpful to explain why no disclosures have been provided.[100]

As discussed at 4.1.4 below, similar currency risk disclosures may be provided in respect of the trading book, but such disclosures should be shown separately from those for the non-trading book.

4.1.3 Fair value disclosures

FRS 13 requires banks and similar institutions to provide fair value disclosures in respect of certain of their financial assets and financial liabilities. The items to be included are:

(a) all financial assets and financial liabilities held in the trading book; and

(b) the following financial assets and liabilities held in the non-trading book:

    (i) all derivatives;

    (ii) all listed and/or publicly traded securities; and

    (iii) any other financial asset or financial liability for which a liquid and active market exists for the asset or liability or for its component parts.

These items are included regardless of whether they are recognised or unrecognised.[101]

A market is liquid and active if all of the following apply:

■ Assets (or liabilities) of the same type are regularly traded on the market.

■ The price determined from the market (by reference to, for example, quoted prices or last traded prices) is a reliable indicator of the price that would be obtained if some or all of the asset (or liability) was actually sold in the market at the time in normal market conditions.

■ There are willing buyers and sellers in the market at all times during normal business hours at the price determined from the market.[102]

Although there may be markets for certain types of financial assets (or liabilities), such as unlisted bonds, commercial debt, distressed debt and trade finance paper, determining whether they fall within this definition of a liquid and active market is a matter of judgement and will depend on the particular circumstances.

The standard indicates that because markets are evolving rapidly, the fact that a liquid and active market does not exist at present does not mean that such a market will not exist in the future.[103] Banks will therefore need to keep the status of markets under frequent review.

The requirement is for an entity to group the relevant financial assets and liabilities, including amounts not recognised in the balance sheet, into appropriate categories of trading book and non-trading book items and for each category to disclose either:

■ the aggregate fair value at the balance sheet date compared to the aggregate book value; or

■ the aggregate fair value of those financial instruments with a positive fair value and, separately, those with a negative fair value, compared to the book amounts.[104]

This requirement is similar to that for other entities (see 3.8 above).

As with other entities, for some financial assets and liabilities the estimated difference between the carrying amount and its fair value may not be material, in which case the carrying amount may be used as the fair value for the purposes of the disclosure.

Similarly, the methods and any significant assumptions used in determining the fair values have to be disclosed.

4.1.4   Trading book disclosures

Banks and similar institutions have to provide the same disclosures as that given by other entities in respect of financial assets and financial liabilities held or issued for trading (see 3.10 above).[105] However, the standard also requires them to provide additional disclosures relating to the risks arising on the trading book but, in recognition of the fact that different entities manage their trading book in different ways, allows some flexibility in how this information is provided.

The entity should disclose the highest, lowest and average exposure of its trading book to market price risk during the reporting period together with the exposure at the balance sheet date, using at least one of the following methods:

(a)   The value at risk of the trading book as a whole.

(b)   Sensitivity analysis showing the potential effect on earnings or net assets of selected hypothetical changes in market prices and rates on the trading book. In this analysis:

    (i)   separate disclosures should be provided for each type of market price risk; and

(ii)   the hypothetical changes used should be reasonably possible during the twelve months following the date of approval of the financial statements. One of the hypothetical changes should be an adverse change of at least 10% in the period-end market prices or rates unless such a fall can be shown to be not reasonably possible.

(c)   Some other market price risk measure, but only if it is used by the management for the purpose of managing the market price risk of the trading book; and the model used has been approved by the entity's regulator for the purpose of providing that regulator with capital adequacy returns.[106]

Paragraph (c) has been included to allow for the possibility of more sophisticated risk management being developed.

If an entity does not use one of the above methodologies for managing the market price risk of its trading book, then instead of providing one of the disclosures above, it can provide the interest rate risk disclosures and currency risk disclosures discussed at 4.1.1 and 4.1.2 above in respect of its trading book.[107]

The above disclosure should also be accompanied by:

(a)   an explanation of the method used and the key parameters and assumptions underlying the data provided;

(b)   an explanation of the objective of the method used and of the limitations that may result in the information not fully reflecting the market price risk;

(c)   the frequency with which the figures were calculated when determining the highest, lowest and average figures for the period. This should, as a minimum, be the frequency at which the figures are calculated for risk management purposes. However, if figures are calculated more frequently than daily, then it will be sufficient to use daily figures for the purposes of the disclosure; and

(d)   reasons for any material changes in the amount of reported market price risk when compared with that reported for the previous period.[108]

An example of the disclosure is given in the extract from the financial statements of Bank of Ireland below:

Extract 9.21: Bank of Ireland (1999)

Financial Review [extract]

MARKET RISK

Market risk is the potential adverse change in Group income or the value of Group net worth arising from movements in interest rates, exchange rates or other market prices. Market risk arises from the structure of the balance sheet, the execution of customer and interbank business and proprietary trading. The Group recognises that the effective management of market risk is essential to the maintenance of stable earnings, the preservation of stockholder value and the achievement of the Group's corporate objectives.

The Group's exposure to market risk is governed by policy approved by the Court of Directors. This policy sets out the nature of risk which may be taken, the types of financial instruments which may be used to increase or reduce risk and the way in which risk is controlled. In line with this policy, the Court approves aggregate risk limits and receives a quarterly report of compliance with these limits.

Based on these aggregate limits, the Group Asset and Liability Committee (ALCO) assigns risk limits to all Group businesses and compliance with these limits is monitored by the Committee. Material exposure to market risk is permitted only in specifically designated business units. In other units market risk is eliminated by way of appropriate hedging arrangements with Group Treasury which is responsible for the centralised management of Group market risk.

Market risk throughout the Group is subject to independent measurement, reporting and control.

INTEREST RATE RISK

TRADING BOOK

The interest rate trading book consists of Group Treasury's mark to market interest rate book and small bond positions which may arise in J & E Davy through the execution of client business. During the course of the year, trading book risk was predominately concentrated in the euro constituent currencies and in sterling, though positions were also taken in a number of other developed country markets.

The instruments in which interest rate risk was taken in the trading book include Government securities, interest rate futures, options on interest rate futures, FRAs, forward foreign exchange, swaps and interest rate caps. Foreign exchange risk was taken almost exclusively in the spot market.

Value at Risk (VaR) is used to measure and set limits on interest rate risk in the Group's trading books. VaR provides an estimate of the potential mark-to-market loss on a set of exposures over a specified time horizon at a defined level of statistical confidence. This time horizon is 1 day and the confidence level is 97.5%. This implies that, on any given day, the VaR figure provides an estimate of the potential loss over a 1 day period which has no more than a 2.5% probability of being exceeded.

The VaR system uses the variance–covariance matrix approach. Interest rate risk positions are represented in terms of exposure to 14 key points on the relevant currency yield curve. For the purpose of measuring exposure against limits, VaR is calculated using a variance–covariance matrix which has been estimated on the preceding 6 months daily data using simple unweighted estimation.

Management recognises that VaR is subject to certain inherent limitations. The past will not always be a reliable guide to the future and the statistical assumptions employed may understate the probability of very large market moves. For this reason, VaR limits are supplemented by a range of controls which include position limits and loss tolerances. The Group backtests the VaR model using historic simulation of hypothetical positions which are representative of the trading risks actually taken. The results of these backtests have been very supportive of the reliability of the Group's VaR methodology.

During the financial year ended 31 March 1999, the average VaR of the Group's interest rate trading book was IR£0.9m. The maximum VaR was IR£1.4m, the minimum VaR IR£0.5m and the VaR on 31 March was IR£0.5m.

The interest rate VaR of the Group's combined trading books at 31 March 1998 was IR£0.8m.

NON TRADING BOOK

The Group's non trading book consist of its retail and corporate deposit and loan books, as well as Group Treasury's interbank cash books and its investment portfolio. In the non Treasury areas interest rate risk arises primarily from the Group's fixed rate mortgage business in Ireland and the UK. The exposure in these books is managed using interest rate swaps and other conventional hedging instruments.

For analytical and control purposes, VaR is applied to Group Treasury's non trading books and is also used in Bristol & West, although these are accrual accounted for financial reporting purposes. In the other non-Treasury businesses, sensitivity analysis is used to measure and control interest rate risk. This analysis involves calculating exposure in net present value terms to a 1% parallel shift of interest rate curves. This is supplemented by estimates of the maturity distribution of this exposure using a methodology which provides estimates of the sensitivity of positions to selected points on the yield curve.

In calculating exposures, undated assets and liabilities (principally non-interest bearing current accounts, capital and fixed assets) are assigned a duration equivalent to that of a portfolio of coupon-bearing bonds with an average life of 4 years. The analysis then proceeds as though these items were constant-maturity dated liabilities.

All of the Group's material non-trading exposure is in euro and sterling. At end March, the Group's exposure to a parallel upward shift in the euro and sterling yield curves (including exposure on Treasury's non-trading books which is not reflected in the VaR quoted above) was IR£4.8m (1998: IR£8.8m) and IR£22.7m (1998: IR£24.7m) respectively.

The tables below provide an indication of the repricing mismatch in the Group's euro and sterling banking books at 31 March 1999. For the major categories of assets and liabilities, these 'gap' tables show the volumes maturing in selected maturity bands, taking account of any amortisation of principal. Items are allocated to time bands by reference to the earlier of the next interest rate repricing date and the maturity date. A net asset position in a particular time period indicates an exposure to a rise in interest rates when these net volumes are re-financed.

The tables show actual on-balance sheet volumes and net off-balance sheet amounts. In the case of undrawn fixed rate lending where the Group is effectively committed in price terms and there is a high degree of predictability in relation to the expected drawdown – notably in relation to the mortgage pipeline - the expected drawn volumes have been included in the table. These tables exclude trading assets of the Group and assets and liabilities denominated in currencies other than euro and sterling. The Group has no material prepayment or option like exposure in its non trading book.

Interest Rate Repricing – Euro

	Not more than three months	Over three months but not more than six months	Over six months but not more than one year	Over one year but not more than five years	Over five years	Non interest bearing	Total
	IR£m	IR£m	IR£m	IR£m	IR£m	IR£m	IR£m
Assets							
Central Government bills and other eligible bills	60	–	–	–	–	–	60
Loans and advances to banks	842	573	20	–	–	3	1,438
Loans and advances to customers	5,432	704	592	1,931	620	312	9,591
Debt securities and equity shares	415	86	–	278	52	–	831
Other assets	4	21	16	75	–	1,628	1,744
Total assets	6,753	1,384	628	2,284	672	1,943	13,664
Liabilities							
Deposits by banks	1,748	328	–	–	–	106	2,182
Customer accounts	8,313	225	273	383	181	1,795	11,170
Debt securities in issue	10	–	–	3	–	–	13
Other liabilities	115	28	1	–	–	522	666
Minority interests and shareholders' funds	–	–	–	–	–	1,137	1,137
Total liabilities	(10,186)	(581)	(274)	(386)	(181)	(3,560)	(15,168)
Net amounts due from / to Group units	1,088	131	12	(19)	(139)	544	1,617
Off balance sheet items	(307)	30	116	80	81	–	–
Interest rate repricing gap	(2,652)	964	482	1,959	433	(1,073)	–
Cumulative interest rate repricing gap	(2,652)	(1,688)	(1,206)	753	1,186	113	–

Interest Rate Repricing – Sterling

	Not more than three months	Over three months but not more than six months	Over six months but not more than one year	Over one year but not more than five years	Over five years	Non interest bearing	Total
	IR£m	IR£m	IR£m	IR£m	IR£m	IR£m	IR£m
Assets							
Treasury bills and other eligible bills	457	–	–	–	–	–	457
Loans and advances to banks	272	2	–	–	–	19	293
Loans and advances to customers	10,388	464	1,085	6,000	292	–	18,229
Debt securities and equity shares	464	116	76	360	–	–	1,016
Other assets	169	9	1	–	–	433	612
Total assets	11,750	591	1,162	6,360	292	452	20,607

Liabilities							
Deposits by banks	1,856	109	228	–	–	–	2,193
Customer accounts	12,319	698	620	468	123	294	14,522
Debt securities in issue	305	35	6	–	–	–	346
Other liabilities	–	3	1	–	–	842	846
Loan capital	307	–	–	–	352	–	659
Minority interests and shareholders' funds	–	–	–	–	–	1,141	1,141
Total liabilities	(14,787)	(845)	(855)	(468)	(475)	(2,277)	(19,707)
Net amounts due to / from Group units	(616)	191	(12)	(289)	141	1,175	590
Off balance sheet items	3,839	(239)	(206)	(3,335)	(59)	–	–
Interest rate repricing gap	186	(302)	89	2,268	(101)	(650)	–
Cumulative interest rate repricing gap	186	(116)	(27)	2,241	2,140	1,490	–

TRADING RISK

Traded foreign exchange risk is almost entirely confined to Group Treasury and arises from normal commercial and interbank foreign exchange business and from proprietary trading. It is controlled by way of limits on open positions where the limits take account of the volatility of the exchange rates in question. The Group's open position (the sum of all long or short positions) was IR£11.4m at 31 March 1999. The peak position during the year was IR£327m. This reflected a DM/Irish pound position created by the repatriation, via DMs of the proceeds of the Group's divestment from Citizens Financial Group.

At 31 March 1999 the Group's traded foreign exchange position was as follows:

	IR£m
EUR / GBP	2.6
EUR / USD	–
Other	8.8
Total open position	11.4

Looked at in terms of exchange rate sensitivity, the impact of a 10% appreciation of the euro against all other currencies at 31 March would generate a profit of IR£0.4m (1998: IR£0.6m).

STRUCTURAL RISK

Structural foreign exchange risk is defined as the Group's non trading net asset position in foreign currencies. Structural risk arises almost entirely from the Group's net investments in its sterling based subsidiaries.

A structural open position in a particular currency can also be considered to be a measure of that part of the Group's capital which is denominated in that currency. In considering the most appropriate structural foreign exchange position, the Group takes account of the currency composition of its risk weighted assets and the desirability of maintaining a similar currency distribution of capital. Doing so will ensure that capital ratios are not excessively exposed to changes in exchange rates. The divestment from Citizens Financial Group and the associated repatriation of capital led to an imbalance in the currency composition of capital. To address this capital imbalance, IR£200m was converted from Irish Pounds to Sterling, thereby increasing the Group's structural open position in Sterling.

At 31 March 1999, the Group's structural foreign exchange position was as follows:

	IR£m
GBP	1,141
USD	33
Total structural FX position	1,174

The positions indicate that a 10% movement in the value of the euro against all other currencies at 31 March would result in an amount taken to reserves of IR£117m (1998: IR£78m).

At year end the currency composition of capital and risk weighted assets is broadly in line and, as a result, exchange rate movements can be expected to have a non material impact on capital ratios. However, such movements will have an impact on reserves.

TRANSLATION HEDGING OF OVERSEAS EARNINGS

The Group may choose to hedge all or part of its overseas earnings in a particular year, thereby fixing a translation rate for the amount hedged. In the year ended 31 March 1999, the Group sold forward Stg£128.5m at an average exchange rate of 0.861 against the Irish Pound. It also sold forward US$55.5m at 1.3886 against the Irish Pound. These dollar hedges were cancelled at market in the context of the divestment from Citizens Financial Group.

If an entity makes material changes to the method used, or to the main assumptions and parameters used, in providing these market price risk disclosures, then the reasons for the change should be given and the previous period's balance sheet date information should be restated using the basis adopted for the current period. In addition, entities are encouraged to restate the highest, lowest and average information.[109]

4.1.5   Other numerical disclosures

In addition to the disclosures discussed in 4.1.1 to 4.1.4 above, as mentioned earlier, banks and similar institutions are required to give the numerical disclosures discussed in 3.9 – 3.12 above. However, for the purposes of the disclosures in respect of commodity contracts which are to be treated as financial instruments (3.11 above), banks and similar institutions are required to include all contracts for the delivery of gold held or issued within the disclosures. The fair value disclosures in respect of commodity contracts which are to be treated as financial instruments are those outlined in 4.1.3 above rather than those in 3.8 above.

4.2   Other financial institutions

The requirements for financial institutions, other than banks and similar institutions, are contained within Part C of FRS 13.

As noted earlier the definition of 'financial institution'[110] is very broad and encompasses entities such as leasing companies, stockbrokers and money brokers, investment dealing companies, investment managers, corporate finance companies and investment vehicles, such as investment trusts and unit trusts.

The instruments to be included within the disclosures by such institutions are the same as for banks and similar institutions. Therefore, they cannot exclude financial assets and financial liabilities arising from traditional lending activities and deposit-making activities from the disclosures as they cannot be treated as falling within the term 'short-term debtors and creditors' (see 3.1 above).[111] Also, for the purposes of the disclosures in respect of commodity contracts, all contracts for the delivery of gold are to treated as if they were financial instruments.[112]

Like other entities, such financial institutions have to provide narrative disclosures of objectives, policies and strategies (see 3.2 above).[113] This discussion will need to reflect the nature of their business and is likely to involve more discussion on credit risk and other market price risk, particularly in relation to financial assets. The recommendations in FRS 13 for disclosures in respect of accounting policies also apply to such financial institutions (see 3.3 above).[114]

The main impact of this different regime for such financial institutions is in respect of the numerical disclosures. As mentioned in 3.1 above, financial institutions (other than banks or similar institutions) effectively have a choice as to which requirements to follow in respect of their numerical disclosures. They can give the disclosures required by those entities that are not financial institutions discussed in 3 above. Alternatively, they can omit the interest rate risk and currency risk disclosures for such entities (3.5 and 3.6 above) and give the corresponding disclosures for banks and similar institutions together with the trading book disclosures required by such entities (4.1.1, 4.1.2 and 4.1.4 above).[115]

In view of the wide range of entities which fall within this category it is impossible to suggest a rule of thumb for deciding which types of entity should follow which route. It may be that leasing companies and investment dealing companies see the bank-type disclosures as more relevant to their business, but on the other hand such disclosures are more onerous. For the other types of financial institutions, it may be that the non-bank regime is more appropriate, although for investment vehicles the emphasis is more likely to be in respect of their financial assets rather than their financial liabilities.

5   COMPARISON WITH IASC AND US PRONOUNCEMENTS

5.1   IASC comparison

5.1.1   Introduction

The IASC has been conducting a project on financial instruments for several years in conjunction with the Canadian Institute of Chartered Accountants. Two attempts were made to deal comprehensively with the issue, in two successive exposure drafts (E40 in 1991 and E48 in 1994). However, the IASC then decided to lower its sights in the same way as other standard setters and converted E48 into a standard dealing with disclosure issues alone; IAS 32 was published in March 1995, and is summarised in 5.1.2 below. Two years later, the Steering Group published a Discussion Paper dealing extensively with the measurement and recognition issues and making proposals for a comprehensive standard on financial assets and liabilities. In concept, its main proposals were very simple: all financial assets and liabilities should be recognised as soon as the reporting entity becomes a party to the contractual provisions that they entail;[116] thereafter they should be stated at fair value in the balance sheet;[117] and all movements in fair value thereafter should be reported in income.[118] The Discussion Paper also took a very restrictive view of hedge accounting. With two minor exceptions, it proposed that no special treatment should be accorded to financial instruments that are designated as hedges of other exposures; they should all still be carried at fair value and gains or losses reported in income.

However, later in 1997 the IASC recognised that completion of such a comprehensive standard in 1998 was not a realistic possibility. It therefore decided that it should join with national standard setters (including the UK) to develop an integrated and harmonised standard on financial instruments, building on its own Discussion Paper, existing and emerging national standards, and the best thinking and research on the subject world-wide. This work is being carried out by the Joint Working Group (JWG) and early indications are that it has remained strongly committed to the theoretical approach of the Discussion Paper. At the same time, the IASC committed to completing an interim international standard on recognition and measurement in 1998. Accordingly, in May 1998 the IASC issued an exposure draft, E62,[119] and in December 1998 converted it into IAS 39[120], its interim standard. This is summarised in 5.1.3 below.

5.1.2   IAS 32 – Financial Instruments: Disclosure and Presentation

IAS 32 came into force for accounting periods beginning on or after 1 January 1996. It is intended to be applied by all companies, whereas FRS 13 is mandatory only for companies that have capital instruments which are listed or publicly traded (other than insurance companies) and for banks and similar institutions. Its main definitions are the same as those subsequently used by the ASB (see 1.2.1 above). Like FRS 13, IAS 32 does not apply to interests in subsidiaries, associates or joint ventures, or to obligations arising under post-employment benefits, employee stock option or purchase plans. However, all interests in subsidiaries, associates or joint ventures are excluded by IAS 32, whereas FRS 13 still includes any such interests that are held exclusively with a view to subsequent resale. IAS 32 has no similar exemptions to those in FRS 13 in respect of certain equity shares (and warrants and options over such shares) of the reporting company. It also does not permit short-term debtors and creditors to be excluded from its provisions. Unlike FRS 13, IAS 32 does not require certain types of commodity contracts to be dealt with in the disclosures.[121]

The disclosure requirements of IAS 32 generally are not as specific as those in FRS 13. However, for each class of financial asset, financial liability and equity instrument (whether recognised on the balance sheet or not) IAS 32 requires enterprises to disclose:

(a)   information about the extent and nature of the financial instruments, including significant terms and conditions that may affect the amount, timing and certainty of future cash flows; and

(b)   the accounting policies and methods adopted, including the criteria for recognition and the basis of measurement applied.[122]

FRS 13 does not specifically require the disclosure under (a) above and only contains a reminder that SSAP 2 requires disclosure of all significant accounting policies with a suggested list of the matters which might be covered by such policies.

For financial assets and liabilities, enterprises should also disclose information about their exposure to interest rate risk, including contractual repricing or maturity dates, whichever dates are earlier, and their effective interest rates where applicable.[123] Estimates of fair values for each class of financial asset and liability must also be given, unless this is impracticable, in which case that fact must be disclosed together with information about the principal characteristics of the item that are relevant to its fair value.[124]

IAS 32 requires, in relation to assets, information about credit risk to be disclosed, including the maximum exposure to credit risk (ignoring any collateral) if other parties fail to perform their obligations under financial instruments, together with any significant concentrations of credit risk.[125] Also, where any asset is carried at an amount above its fair value, the enterprise must disclose both its fair value and book value and the reason for management's belief that the latter will be recovered.[126] FRS 13 does not require such disclosure.

Where the reporting enterprise has used financial instruments to hedge anticipated future transactions IAS 32 also requires disclosures to be made, although they are not quite the same as those in FRS 13. In such a case, companies must disclose details of both the hedging instruments and the anticipated transactions, including details of when they are expected to occur, and the amount of any deferred or unrecognised gains or losses and when they are likely to be recognised in the profit and loss account.[127]

IAS 32 deals not only with disclosures but also with presentational aspects; these features are not dealt with in FRS 13 but are effectively covered by other standards in the UK, principally FRS 4 and FRS 5.

IAS 32's distinction between debt and equity depends on whether or not the issuer has a contractual obligation to deliver cash or another financial asset to the holder of the instrument (or to exchange another financial instrument with him on potential unfavourable terms), regardless of the legal form of the instrument.[128] On this analysis, redeemable preference shares are regarded as liabilities rather than equity instruments. The classification of finance costs between interest and dividends in the income statement is consistent with the analysis of the instruments in the balance sheet.[129] While there is obvious conceptual merit in such an approach, it runs into conflict with the law in the UK; accordingly, while FRS 13 requires that redeemable preference shares be treated as financial liabilities for the purposes of the various analyses it requires, they remain classified as non-equity shares for balance sheet purposes.

The standard also differs from UK practice by requiring 'split accounting' (as described in 2.2.2 of Chapter 15) for hybrid instruments such as convertible bonds. In other words, the proceeds of issue of such a bond have to be allocated between the amount that represents a straight financial liability and the element which represents an equity instrument.[130]

In presenting related amounts in the balance sheet, IAS 32 requires the reporting entity to net off a financial asset against a financial liability only when it has a legally enforceable right of set-off and intends to settle the two amounts either on a net basis or simultaneously.[131] FRS 5 contains provisions dealing with offsetting of debit and credit balances and certain types of financial assets and financial liabilities, but otherwise does not permit assets and liabilities to be offset in any circumstances and management intent is regarded as irrelevant to such questions.

5.1.3   IAS 39 – Financial Instruments: Recognition and Measurement

As indicated above, in December 1998 the IASC issued IAS 39, its interim standard dealing with recognition and measurement of financial instruments, including rules on hedging. It is effective for periods beginning on or after 1 January 2001. It applies to all enterprises and all financial instruments except that certain financial instruments are then excluded from its scope.[132]

Some of these are similar to those listed for exemption from FRS 13 (see 3.1 above), but exemption is also proposed for rights and obligations under insurance contracts, certain financial guarantee contracts, contracts for contingent consideration in a business combination and contracts that require a payment based on climatic, geological or other physical variables. Like FRS 13, certain commodity based contracts that give either party the right to settle are also brought within the scope of the standard.[133]

All financial assets and liabilities are to be recognised on the balance sheet of the reporting enterprise as soon as it becomes a party to the contractual provisions of the instrument (using consistently one of either the trade date or the settlement date where the assets are acquired in a 'regular way' purchase).[134] There are extensive rules as to when the enterprise should derecognise such assets and liabilities (or part thereof). The difference between the carrying amount of such items and the proceeds or payment is to be recognised in the net profit or loss for the period (together with, in the case of an asset, any prior adjustment to reflect the fair value of that asset that had been reported in equity).[135]

Most financial assets, including derivatives, are to be included at fair values; the exceptions being 'held-to-maturity' investments, loans and receivables originated by the enterprise and not held for trading and any financial asset whose fair value cannot be reliably measured[136] (although there is a presumption that fair value can be reliably determined for most financial assets).[137] Such items are to be measured at amortised cost (or cost if there is no fixed maturity) and are to be subject to an impairment test.[138] There are detailed conditions which have to be met in determining 'held-to-maturity' investments. Most financial liabilities are to be included at amortised cost, the exceptions being liabilities held for trading purposes and derivatives (other than certain derivatives settled by delivery of an unquoted equity instrument for which there is no reliable fair value). Such items are to be measured at fair value.[139]

The treatment of gains or losses arising on the remeasurement of financial assets and liabilities at fair value depends on the function of the particular asset or liability. Gains or losses on items held for trading purposes are to be taken to the profit and loss account. This applies to all derivatives which are not used for hedging.[140] The rules in the standard for derivatives also apply to certain derivatives embedded in a host contract. If the risks and economic characteristics of the embedded derivative are not closely related to those of the host, and if a separate instrument with the characteristics of the embedded derivative would itself meet the definition of a derivative, and if the embedded derivative and the host contract are not together measured at fair value with changes in the fair value being taken to the profit and loss account, then the embedded derivative should be separated out and accounted for as a derivative under the standard.[141] Gains or losses on financial assets not held for trading and that are not part of a hedging relationship can either be included in the profit and loss account or taken to equity and recycled through the profit and loss account when the asset is derecognised or impaired. Whichever policy is adopted is to be applied consistently.[142]

For financial assets and liabilities that are part of a hedging relationship (for which purpose a number of conditions need to be met),[143] the treatment will depend on whether the hedge is a fair value hedge, a cash flow hedge or a hedge of a net investment in a foreign entity.

- For fair value hedges, the gain or loss on the hedging instrument should be taken to the profit and loss account together with the gain or loss on the hedged item. This applies even if the hedged item is otherwise measured at fair value with changes in fair value taken to equity or at cost.[144]

- For cash flow hedges (which are stated to include hedges of unrecognised firm commitments to buy an asset at a fixed price in the reporting currency),[145] the portion of the gain or loss on the hedging instrument that is determined to be an effective hedge is to be taken to equity.[146] These amounts are then to be channelled back through the profit and loss account as the hedged firm commitment or forecasted transaction affects net profit or loss.[147] However, where the hedged firm commitment or forecasted transaction results in recognition of an asset or liability then at the time the asset or liability is recognised, the associated gains or losses recognised directly in equity should be recycled into the initial measurement of the asset or liability.[148] Any ineffective portion of a cash flow hedge is to be accounted for in the profit and loss account if the hedging instrument is a derivative or,[149] in the limited cases where not a derivative (only allowed when it is being used as a hedge of foreign currency risk)[150], in the profit and loss account or in equity depending on the policy adopted;[151]

■   For a hedge of a net investment in a foreign entity, any gain or loss should be accounted for similarly to cash flow hedges above. The gain or loss on the hedging instrument relating to the effective portion of the hedge should be classified in the same manner as the foreign currency translation gain or loss.[152]

IAS 39 requires that the disclosures required by IAS 32 should continue to be given, except that the fair value disclosures are not applicable to those financial assets and liabilities that are included in the balance sheet at fair value.[153] It also proposes that the accounting policies disclosed under IAS 32 should specifically deal with the methods and assumptions applied in estimating fair values for those items carried at fair value, what its policy is for those gains or losses on available for sale financial assets that can either be taken to equity or included in the profit and loss account and whether trade date or settlement date is used in accounting for 'regular way' purchases of financial assets.[154] The standard also calls for a number of additional disclosures, including:

■   a description of the financial risk management objectives and policies, including the policy for each major type of forecasted transaction;[155]

■   details of fair value hedges, cash flow hedges and hedges of a net investment in a foreign entity including a description of the hedge and the hedging instruments, the fair value of the hedging instruments, the nature of the risks hedged, and for hedges of forecasted transactions the periods in which forecasted transactions are expected to occur and when they are expected to impact on net profit or loss;[156]

■   for gains and losses on hedging instruments in cash flow hedges which have been recognised directly in equity, the amount recognised in equity in the period and the amounts removed either to net profit or loss or to the initial measurement of an asset or liability;[157]

■ the amounts of gains and losses in the period arising from remeasuring available for sale financial assets to fair value which have been taken to equity and which have been recycled back to the profit and loss account;[158]

■ details of available for sale or held for trading financial assets which have been measured at amortised cost;[159]

■ significant items of income, expense, and gains and losses resulting from financial assets and liabilities, whether in the profit and loss account or taken to equity;[160]

■ details of securitisation or repurchase agreements;[161]

■ the reason for the change where financial assets have been reclassified so as to be carried at amortised cost rather than fair value;[162] and

■ details of any impairment loss or reversal thereof in respect of a financial asset.[163]

5.2   US COMPARISON

In the United States, the FASB has been working on a complex project on financial instruments since 1986. Several pronouncements have been issued to date. Initially, SFAS 105, SFAS 107 and SFAS 119 dealt with disclosure issues. However, in June 1998 the FASB issued SFAS 133 which principally deals with matters of recognition and measurement of derivatives. As a result, SFAS 105 and SFAS 119 have been superseded and SFAS 107 amended to include some of the disclosure requirements originally in SFAS 105. SFAS 133 was due to be effective for accounting periods beginning after 15 June 1999. Earlier adoption was encouraged, but only for periods beginning after the date of issue of the standard. However, in June 1999 the FASB issued SFAS 137 delaying implementation of the standard so that it is now mandatory only for periods beginning after 15 June 2000. The requirements of these standards are described briefly in 5.2.2 and 5.2.3 below.

5.2.1   Definition of financial instrument

The FASB's definition of financial instrument is rather different from that used by the ASB and IASC. It defines a financial instrument as:

■ cash;

■ evidence of an ownership interest in an entity; or

■ a contract that both:

   (a)   imposes on one entity a contractual obligation:

      (i)   to deliver cash or another financial instrument to a second entity; or

(ii) to exchange financial instruments on potentially unfavourable terms with the second entity; [and]

(b) conveys to that second entity a contractual right:

(i) to receive cash or another financial instrument from the first entity; or

(ii) to exchange other financial instruments on potentially favourable terms with the first entity.[164]

This is a complex definition, but in fact it seems to describe the intended subject matter of the standard rather more successfully than the ASB/IASC definition does.

As the standard notes, the definition is recursive but not circular, because although it contains the term being defined (financial instrument) itself, it requires a chain of contractual obligations that ultimately ends in the delivery of cash or an ownership interest in an entity. The standard also emphasises that, when it talks about contractual rights and obligations, it includes conditional as well as unconditional rights and obligations.[165]

5.2.2   Disclosure requirements pre-implementation of SFAS 133

SFAS 105 requires note disclosure of the details of instruments that expose the entity to off balance sheet risk of accounting loss – that is, those where the potential for loss exceeds the amount of assets on the balance sheet or goes beyond the amount of disclosed liabilities. The standard requires quantification of credit risk – the worst-case position that would result if the counterparty to each such instrument completely failed to honour its contractual obligations – together with details of security held to mitigate such risks.[166] On the other hand, market risk – the risk of loss through movements in market prices – is dealt with by narrative discussion rather than any attempt to quantify such loss; no worst-case can generally be measured in respect of such risks.[167] The standard also requires disclosure of all significant concentrations of credit risk arising from all financial instruments, whether from an individual counterparty or groups of counterparties.[168]

SFAS 107 requires disclosure to be made of the fair value of financial instruments, except for any where it is impracticable to do so.[169] In the latter case, entities must say why it is impracticable and also give other information relevant to an assessment of the instrument's value, such as its carrying amount, effective interest rate and maturity.[170]

The FASB's third disclosure standard, SFAS 119, extends the scope of the previous two (mainly to require more disaggregation) and focuses primarily on derivatives, in particular futures, forward, swap and option contracts. It requires a distinction to be made between derivatives held or issued for trading purposes and those used for other purposes, with different disclosure requirements for each.

Where an entity uses derivatives for trading purposes, the standard requires it to disclose not just their fair value at the end of the year, but also their average fair value during the year. In addition, detailed disaggregated disclosure is to be given of the net gains and losses arising from trading in derivatives during the year.[171]

Entities that use derivatives for purposes other than trading must describe their objectives for holding or issuing them and their strategies for pursuing these objectives, explaining the classes of derivatives used. They must also give a full description of the accounting policy used in respect of these derivatives. Where the derivatives are used to hedge anticipated transactions, they must also disclose details of these transactions, the classes of derivatives used to hedge them, the amounts of hedging gains and losses deferred, and the transactions or events that will lead to these deferred gains or losses being recognised in earnings.[172]

5.2.3 SFAS 133

As indicated above, in June 1998, the FASB issued a standard, SFAS 133, which contains rules for the recognition and measurement of derivatives (including embedded derivatives), and also for hedging activities.

SFAS 133 requires that all derivatives should be measured and included in the balance sheet at fair value.[173] However, the change in value is to be reported differently in the accounts depending on the function that the derivative fulfils:

■ If the derivative is designated as a hedge of a net investment in a foreign entity, the change in value of the derivative is reported in comprehensive income (broadly equivalent to the UK concept of total recognised gains and losses) to the extent it is effective as a hedge.

■ If the derivative is designated as a hedge of an existing asset, liability or firm commitment (referred to as a fair value hedge), the change in value of the derivative is reported in the profit and loss account together with the gain or loss on the hedged item to the extent that it offsets the change in value of the derivative.

■ If the derivative is designated as a hedge of the cash flows of a forecasted transaction (referred to as a cash flow hedge), the effective portion of the change in value is again included in comprehensive income, but then channelled through the profit and loss account in the period when the forecasted transaction affects earnings. Any remaining gain or loss is reflected immediately in the profit and loss account.

■ Otherwise the change in fair value of the derivative is to be reported in the profit and loss account.[174]

The standard precludes non-derivative financial instruments from being designated as hedges, except that a non-derivative instrument denominated in a foreign currency may be designated as a hedge of a foreign currency exposure of an unrecognised firm commitment denominated in a foreign currency or a net investment in a foreign entity. In such cases, the accounting is the same as when derivatives are used.[175]

As a result of these new requirements, many of the existing disclosure requirements of the previous US standards are no longer necessary so SFAS 105 and SFAS 119 have been superseded.[176] However, the disclosures required by SFAS 107 remain in place and now incorporate the disclosures in respect of concentration of credit risk originally required by SFAS 105, but with the additional requirement to disclose the policy for entering into master netting arrangements to mitigate the credit risk of financial instruments and a brief description of the terms of those arrangements. SFAS 107 has also been amended to encourage, but not require, entities to disclose quantitative information about the market risks of financial instruments.[177]

In addition, SFAS 133 requires an entity that uses derivatives (or non-derivatives that qualify for hedging) to disclose its objectives for using them, the context needed to understand those objectives and its strategies for achieving those objectives. This description distinguishes between instruments used as fair value hedges, cash flow hedges, hedges of net investments in foreign entities and all other derivatives. The entity's risk management policy for each type of hedge is to be indicated, including a description of the items or transaction being hedged. The entity is encouraged, but not required, to describe these objectives and strategies in the context of its overall risk management profile.[178]

The standard also requires entities to give the following quantitative disclosures:

- For instruments used as hedges of net investments in foreign entities, the net gain or loss reported in comprehensive income.

- For instruments used as fair value hedges and the related items, the net gain or loss included in earnings that represents the amount of the ineffectiveness of the hedge (including any component of the gain or loss on the derivative excluded from the assessment of effectiveness of the hedge), together with a description of where this net gain or loss is reported. Where a hedged firm commitment no longer qualifies as a fair value hedge, the amount of the net gain or loss included in earnings.

- For derivatives used as cash flow hedges and the related transactions, similar information as for fair value hedges. In addition, a description of the transactions or other events that will result in reclassification into earnings from comprehensive income, together with the net amount of gains or losses expected to be so reclassified in the next 12 months. The maximum length of time over which the entity is hedging its exposures for forecasted transactions is also to be disclosed, but excluding those related to the payment of variable interest on existing financial instruments.

Entities are encouraged, but not required, to present a more complete picture of their activities by disclosing similar information about other financial instruments or non-financial assets and liabilities to which the derivative instruments are related by activity.[179]

In addition, the net gain or loss on derivative instruments used as cash flow hedges are to be reported separately in comprehensive income[180] and, as part of the disclosures of accumulated other comprehensive income, entities must disclose the opening and closing accumulated derivative gain or loss, the related net change associated with current period hedging transactions, and the net amount of any reclassification into earnings.[181]

6 CONCLUSION

It is clear that the subject of accounting for financial instruments is likely to remain one of the most difficult regulatory challenges for the next few years. Perhaps surprisingly, there seems to be a high degree of consensus among the major standard-setters and their representatives on the Joint Working Group that fair valuing all financial instruments can be the only ultimate solution. This is a controversial view that may yet meet with considerable resistance, as the response to the IASC Discussion Paper showed. Standard setters in this area appear to have moved considerably ahead of current practice since the proposed solution has not yet commanded acceptance in any country. This is a bold step since the traditional role of accounting regulators has been to codify accepted best practice rather than, as now, to invent new practice.

The arguments for fair value accounting seem cogent, and the IASC has assembled them very persuasively in its Discussion Paper. But they are nonetheless revolutionary; by the authors' own admission, they require the adoption of a new capital maintenance concept ('current-market-rate-of-return') for measuring financial instruments.[182] And this will simply introduce a new inconsistency, unless it is applied to the measurement of other items in the accounts as well, which would be an even more radical proposal. Although elegant, the proposals do not sit well with widespread perceptions of the role and meaning of accounts.

The disclosure requirements in FRS 13, by contrast, are somewhat less controversial, and do in some respects make companies' treasury activity more transparent. However, even these requirements are ambitious and sometimes contentious. They require significant interpretation and some of them (particularly those on hedging) are not as well crafted as they might be. They are, however, certainly voluminous.

References

1   *IASC Update*, IASC, December 1996.
2   Discussion Paper, *Derivatives and other financial instruments*, ASB, July 1996.
3   FRED 13, *Derivatives and other financial instruments: Disclosures*, ASB, April 1997.
4   FRED 13 Supplement – *Derivatives and other financial instruments: Disclosures by banks and similar institutions*, ASB, July 1997.
5   FRS 13, *Derivatives and other financial instruments: Disclosures*, ASB, September 1998
6   *Ibid.*, para. 2.
7   *Ibid.*, Appendix II, para. 5.
8   *Ibid.*, Appendix II, para. 3.
9   *Ibid.*, Appendix II, para. 4.
10 *Ibid.*, paras. 2, 10 and 64.
11 *Derivatives and other financial instruments*, Summary of issues and the Board's initial conclusions, paras. 14 and 15.
12 *Ibid.*, paras. 16 and 17.
13 *Ibid.*, paras. 18–21.
14 *Ibid.*, paras. 22–25.
15 *Ibid.*, Appendix, para. A6.
16 *Ibid.*, para. 2.5.3.
17 *Ibid.*, para. 3.5.1(b) and (c).
18 SSAP 12, *Accounting for Depreciation*, ASC, December 1977, para. 16.
19 *Derivatives and other financial instruments*, para. 3.5.1(d).
20 *Ibid.*
21 *Ibid.*, para. 3.3.21.
22 *Ibid.*, para. 3.5.1(b) and (c).
23 FRS 13, para. 5.
24 *Ibid.*, para. 6.
25 *Ibid.*, para. 2.
26 *Ibid.*, para. 11.
27 *Ibid.*, para. 12.
28 *Ibid.*, para. 13.
29 *Ibid.*, para. 14.
30 *Ibid.*, para. 15.
31 *Ibid.*, para. 21.
32 *Ibid.*, para. 22.
33 *Ibid.*, para. 20.
34 *Ibid.*, paras. 16 and 17.
35 *Ibid.*, para. 18.
36 *Ibid.*, para. 23.
37 *Ibid.*, Appendix VII, para. 26.
38 *Ibid.*, para. 74.
39 *Ibid.*, para. 75.
40 *Ibid.*, para. 76.
41 *Ibid.*, paras. 24 and 25.
42 *Ibid.*, para. 32.
43 *Ibid.*, para. 26.
44 *Ibid.*, para. 2.
45 *Ibid.*, para. 27.
46 *Ibid.*, para. 26(a).
47 *Ibid.*, para. 31.
48 *Ibid.*, paras. 26(b) and 29.
49 *Ibid.*, para. 30.
50 *Ibid.*, para. 33.
51 *Ibid.*, para. 34.
52 *Ibid.*, para. 35.
53 *Ibid.*, para. 34(b) and (c).

54 *Ibid.*, para. 34(d).
55 ASB Exposure Draft, *Amendment to SSAP 20 'Foreign Currency Translation': Disclosure*.
56 ASB Press Notice number 138.
57 FRS 13, para. 38.
58 *Ibid.*, para. 77.
59 *Ibid.*, para. 39.
60 *Ibid.*
61 *Ibid.*, para. 40.
62 *Ibid.*, para. 42.
63 *Ibid.*, para. 44.
64 *Ibid.*, para. 45.
65 *Ibid.*, para. 46.
66 *Ibid.*, para. 2.
67 *Ibid.*, para. 48.
68 *Ibid.*, para. 51.
69 *Ibid.*, paras. 53 and 54.
70 *Ibid.*, para. 22.
71 *Ibid.*, para. 59.
72 *Ibid.*, para. 60.
73 *Ibid.*, para. 61.
74 UITF Information Sheet No. 33.
75 FRS 13, para. 62.
76 *Ibid.*, para. 2.
77 *Ibid.*, para. 57.
78 *Ibid.*, para. 2.
79 *Ibid.*, para. 64.
80 *Ibid.*, para. 65.
81 *Ibid.*, para. 66. .
82 *Ibid.*, para. 69.
83 *Ibid.*, para. 71.
84 *Ibid.*, para. 81.
85 *Ibid.*
86 *Ibid.*, para. 83(c).
87 *Ibid.*, para. 113.
88 *Ibid.*, para. 84.
89 *Ibid.*, para. 116.
90 *Ibid.*, para. 81.
91 *Ibid.*, para. 87.
92 *Ibid.*
93 *Ibid.*, para. 89.
94 *Ibid.*, para. 88.
95 *Ibid.*, para. 90.
96 *Ibid.*, para. 91.
97 *Ibid.*, para. 92.
98 *Ibid.*, para. 97.
99 *Ibid.*, para. 95.
100 *Ibid.*, para. 96.
101 *Ibid.*, para. 98.
102 *Ibid.*, para. 99.
103 *Ibid.*, para. 100.
104 *Ibid.*, para. 101.
105 *Ibid.*, para. 103.
106 *Ibid.*, para. 104.
107 *Ibid.*, para. 111.
108 *Ibid.*, para. 107.
109 *Ibid.*, paras. 108 and 109.

110 *Ibid.*, para. 119.
111 *Ibid.*, para. 121.
112 *Ibid.*, para. 130.
113 *Ibid.*, para. 122.
114 *Ibid.*, para. 133.
115 *Ibid.*, para. 124.
116 Discussion Paper, *Accounting for Financial Assets and Financial Liabilities*, Chapter 3, para. 3.1.
117 *Ibid.*, Chapter 4, para. 2.1 and Chapter 5, para. 3.1.
118 *Ibid.*, Chapter 6, para. 5.1.
119 E62, *Financial Instruments: Recognition and Measurement,* IASC, June 1998.
120 IAS 39, *Financial Instruments: Recognition and Measurement*, IASC 3, December 1998.
121 *Ibid.*, para. 1.
122 *Ibid.*, para. 47.
123 *Ibid.*, para. 56.
124 *Ibid.*, para. 77.
125 *Ibid.*, para. 66.
126 *Ibid.*, para. 88.
127 *Ibid.*, para. 91.
128 *Ibid.*, para. 18.
129 *Ibid.*, para. 30.
130 *Ibid.*, para. 23.
131 *Ibid.*, para. 33.
132 IAS 39, *Financial Instruments: Recognition and Measurement*, para. 1.
133 *Ibid.*, para. 6.
134 *Ibid.*, paras. 27 and 30.
135 *Ibid.*, paras. 43 and 63.
136 *Ibid.*, para. 69.
137 *Ibid.*, para. 70.
138 *Ibid.*, para. 73.
139 *Ibid.*, para. 93.
140 *Ibid.*, para. 103(a).
141 *Ibid.*, para. 23.
142 *Ibid.*, paras. 103(b) and 104.
143 *Ibid.*, para. 142.
144 *Ibid.*, para. 153.
145 *Ibid.*, para. 137(b).
146 *Ibid.*, para. 158(a).
147 *Ibid.*, para. 162.
148 *Ibid.*, para. 160.
149 *Ibid.*, para. 158(b)(i).
150 *Ibid.*, para. 122.
151 *Ibid.*, para. 158(b)(ii).
152 *Ibid.*, para. 164.
153 *Ibid.*, para. 166.
154 *Ibid.*, para. 167.
155 *Ibid.*, para. 169.
156 *Ibid.*
157 *Ibid.*
158 *Ibid.*, para. 170.
159 *Ibid.*
160 *Ibid.*
161 *Ibid.*
162 *Ibid.*
163 *Ibid.*
164 SFAS 105, *Disclosure of Information about Financial Instruments with Off-Balance-Sheet Risk and Financial Instruments with Concentrations of Credit Risk*, FASB, March 1990, para.6.

165 *Ibid.*, footnote 1.
166 *Ibid.*, para. 18.
167 *Ibid.*, para. 17.
168 *Ibid.*, para. 20.
169 SFAS 107, *Disclosures about Fair Value of Financial Instruments*, FASB, December 1991, para. 10.
170 *Ibid.*, para. 14.
171 SFAS 119, *Disclosure about Derivative Financial Instruments and Fair Value of Financial Instruments,* FASB, October 1994, para. 10.
172 *Ibid.*, para. 11.
173 SFAS 133, *Accounting for Derivative Instruments and Hedging Activities,* FASB, June 1998, para. 17.
174 *Ibid.*, para. 18.
175 *Ibid.*, paras. 37 and 42.
176 *Ibid.*, para. 525.
177 *Ibid.*, para. 531.
178 *Ibid.*, para. 44.
179 *Ibid.*, para. 45.
180 *Ibid.*, para. 46.
181 *Ibid.*, para. 47.
182 Discussion Paper, *Accounting for Financial Assets and Financial Liabilities*, Chapter 6, para. 2.4.

Chapter 10   Fixed assets

1 INTRODUCTION

1.1 Background

The broad principles for accounting for fixed assets are generally well understood in the UK. The cost of fixed assets is capitalised when they are acquired, subsequently depreciated through the profit and loss account over their working lives, and written down if at any time the carrying value is seen not to be fully recoverable. When a fixed asset is sold or scrapped, the difference between the written down value and any proceeds is recorded as the gain or loss on disposal. But there are many complications in applying these simple principles in practice. When should a fixed asset initially be recognised? How should its cost be measured? How should it be depreciated? When should it be regarded as not fully recoverable? Worse, a new and confusing dimension is added to these and other problems if management decides to revalue the asset rather than continuing to carry it on the basis of its historical cost.

Some of the issues mentioned above are addressed by company law. The statutory requirements cover depreciation, diminutions in value, the components of the cost of an asset, whether purchased or self-constructed, and the bases of valuation of fixed assets. However, although these set out some basic rules to reinforce the broad principles described above, they do not go very far, and the development of more detailed requirements has been left to accounting standards.

There are several accounting standards on fixed assets and together they form something of a patchwork quilt. One reason is the wide range of fixed assets that exists: there are separate standards for tangible fixed assets (FRS 15),[1] goodwill and intangible assets (FRS 10),[2] investment properties (SSAP 19)[3] and capitalised research and development (SSAP 13).[4] But also, different aspects of the subject have been addressed at different times and in different standards. For example, impairment of fixed assets is dealt with in a separate standard

(FRS 11)[5] from depreciation, which was originally governed by SSAP 12[6] and now by FRS 15, while the measurement and classification of a disposal of a fixed asset is addressed by FRS 3.[7]

Of the more recent standards, FRS 10 and FRS 11 both came into force for accounting periods ending on or after 23 December 1998, whereas FRS 15 only becomes mandatory for periods ending on or after 23 March 2000, although earlier application is encouraged.

1.2 The meaning of fixed assets

The Companies Act 1985 defines fixed assets as those which are intended for use on a continuing basis in the company's activities and any assets which are not intended for such use are taken to be current assets.[8]

The statutory balance sheet formats give further information as to what is intended as a fixed asset: intangible assets including development costs and goodwill, tangible fixed assets and investments, including shares in subsidiary and associated undertakings. The full formats for fixed assets are given in 6.3 below.

This chapter confines itself to tangible and intangible fixed assets. Investment properties are dealt with in this chapter, but other investments, both fixed and current, are discussed in Chapter 11, while the particular issue of capitalisation of interest (which is not confined to fixed assets) is covered by Chapter 13. The initial recognition of goodwill is considered in Chapter 6, but its subsequent accounting treatment is dealt with in this chapter, while capitalised development expenditure is discussed in Chapter 12.

The distinction between fixed and current assets is usually clear, but in 1995, Brammer fell foul of the Financial Reporting Review Panel because it had been carrying a pool of instruments that were rented out to customers as stock in its balance sheet rather than as fixed assets. The 1994 accounts read as follows:

Extract 10.1: Brammer plc (1994)

Accounting Policies

Stock

Stock of rental instruments is valued at the lower of amortised cost and net realisable value, net realisable value being the present value of the net anticipated future rental income.

This policy was amended in the 1995 accounts as explained here:

Extract 10.2: Brammer plc (1995)

Accounting Policies

Change of accounting policy – rental inventory

... the company has agreed with the Financial Reporting Review Panel that rental inventory, previously classified as current assets, should be reclassified as fixed assets. As a result of effecting this change:

- proceeds from the disposal of previously rented instruments is excluded from turnover and included in profit on sale of fixed assets in the profit and loss account.

- rental inventory is classified as fixed assets and is valued at cost less depreciation on a straight line basis over the expected economic lives of the assets (generally 2 to 6 years) taking account of estimated residual values, less any necessary provision for permanent diminution in value.

- the depreciation charge for the year on rental inventory is added back to operating profit in arriving at net cash inflow from operating activities in the cash flow statement.

The accounts carrying value of rental inventory is unchanged and, accordingly, the change of classification does not affect the profit for the year in any year or the shareholders' equity at the end of any year. The figures in the 1994 consolidated profit and loss account, balance sheet and cash flow statement have been reclassified as a result of this change.

The Act's definition says that fixed assets must be intended for use on a continuing basis, but this is not normally interpreted to mean that individual items should be transferred out of fixed assets when a decision to dispose of them has been made; the definition refers more to the nature of the item and its original function when it was acquired. Nevertheless, one or two companies have a policy of making such a transfer, such as that appearing in the accounts of Wolseley.

Extract 10.3: Wolseley plc (1998)

Accounting policies

Real property awaiting disposal

Real property awaiting disposal is transferred to current assets at the lower of book written down value and estimated net realisable value. Depreciation is not applied to real property awaiting disposal, but the carrying value is reviewed annually and written down through the profit and loss account to current estimated net realisable value if lower.

The practices of property companies in moving properties between fixed and current categories are discussed further in 5.3.5 below.

The ASB defines tangible fixed assets as:

'Assets that have physical substance and are held for use in the production or supply of goods and services, for rental to others, or for administrative purposes on a continuing basis in the reporting entity's activities.'[9]

This builds upon the Companies Act definition but is much more specific. Its use of the wording 'held for use' is somewhat stronger than the statutory 'intended for use', and could again encourage the view that it would be appropriate to reclassify fixed assets that were intended to be sold as current assets. However, we do not consider that this interpretation was intended, and thus it remains appropriate to keep assets held for disposal within fixed assets.

In contrast to its definition of tangible assets, the Board defines intangible assets as:

'Non-financial fixed assets that do not have physical substance but are identifiable and are controlled by the entity through custody or legal rights.'[10]

'Identifiable' assets and liabilities are further defined as those 'that are capable of being disposed of or settled separately, without disposing of a business of the entity'.[11] This therefore really means 'separable', rather than identifiable, although the wording is similar to that in the Companies Act.[12]

The notion of maintaining custody over something that has no physical substance may seem rather strange, but FRS 10 explains that it means such things as keeping technical or intellectual knowledge secret. The requirement to maintain control through legal rights or custody, however, means that pseudo-assets such as portfolios of clients or a team of skilled staff could not be recognised as assets.

1.3   What intangibles qualify to be treated as assets?

The whole question of what intangible assets can and cannot be recognised in accounting terms has been a difficult one for standard setters, and it remains a controversial subject. No one doubts that intangibles are of real economic value to businesses, and in certain industry sectors they are of overwhelming importance to the success of the enterprise. The debate is not on that issue; it is on whether it is within the compass of our present accounting model to capture and convey useful information about such assets.

FRS 10 uses this three part approach to set different rules for the various circumstances in which intangible assets can be included in the balance sheet:

(a)   Intangible assets bought separately should be capitalised at cost.[13]

This may seem straightforward and obvious, but it has changed previous practice in certain areas. For example, football clubs now capitalise transfer fees, whereas previously they were often expensed as incurred.

Extract 10.4: Nottingham Forest plc (1998)

1. Accounting policies

Transfer fees and signing on fees

Amounts paid to third parties (including league levies) on acquisition of players' registrations are capitalised as intangible assets and amortised over the period of players' initial contracts. This represents a change of accounting policy. In previous years transfer fees payable were taken to the profit and loss account in the year of purchase or sale of the respective player. This change has been made in accordance with the early adoption of Financial Reporting Standard Number 10.

The effect of this change in accounting policy is to decrease the loss for the year by £4,947,000 (1997: £3,725,000) and to increase the profit and loss account reserve and net assets by £3,725,000 at 31 May 1997.

(b)   Intangible assets obtained in the course of acquiring a business should be recognised separately from goodwill if their value can be measured reliably on initial recognition.[14] The standard explains that this does not necessarily require there to be a market value, but also allows the use of valuation methods based on factors such as notional royalties or multiples of turnover.[15] The standard also caps the amount that can be attributed to intangible assets by saying that the fair value must be limited to an amount that does not create or increase any negative goodwill that arises on the acquisition.[16]

The requirement that acquired intangibles must be capable of being measured reliably is not meant to be a major obstacle. The test is often likely to be met by such assets as brands, publishing rights and titles, concessions, patents, licences, trade marks and similar rights and assets.

Diageo, Cadbury Schweppes and WPP all provide examples of acquired brands that have been capitalised:

Extract 10.5: Diageo plc (1998)

Accounting policies

Brands

Brands acquired which have a value which is substantial and long term are recorded at cost, less appropriate provisions. Acquired brands are only recognised where title is clear, brand earnings are separately identifiable and the brand could be sold separately from the rest of the business.

No annual amortisation is provided except where the end of the useful economic life of the acquired brand can be foreseen. The useful economic lives of brands and their carrying value are subject to annual review and any amortisation or provision for permanent impairment charged against the profit for the period.

Notes

12. Fixed assets - intangible assets

The brands are stated at fair value on acquisition, denominated in the currencies of their principal markets. An annual review is carried out by the directors to consider whether any brand has suffered permanent diminution in value.

The principal brands included above are Johnnie Walker, Smirnoff, Pillsbury, Old El Paso, Progresso and Burger King.

Extract 10.6: Cadbury Schweppes p.l.c. (1998)

1. Nature of Operations and Accounting Policies

(o) Intangibles

Intangibles represent significant owned brands acquired since 1985 valued at historical cost. No amortisation is charged as the annual results reflect significant expenditure in support of these brands. For the 1998 financial statements, the Group has adopted FRS 10 "Goodwill and Intangible Assets" and FRS 11 "Impairment of Fixed Assets and Goodwill". As permitted by FRS 10 and FRS 11, the Group will continue its policy of capitalising acquired intangible assets (brands) and reviewing the carrying values on an annual basis for any impairment in value.

12 Intangible Assets and Goodwill	1998	1997
	£m	£m
Cost at beginning of year	1,575	1,547
Exchange rate adjustments	(14)	28
Goodwill arising on acquisition of subsidiaries	46	–
	1,607	1,575

The only goodwill included in the £1,607 million total was the £46 million arising in the year, which is presumably why Cadbury Schweppes did not believe it necessary to disclose the split between goodwill and other intangibles more fully.

Extract 10.7: WPP Group plc (1998)

Accounting policies

3   Goodwill and intangible fixed assets

Intangible fixed assets comprise goodwill and certain acquired separable corporate brand names.

...

The directors are of the opinion that the goodwill and intangible assets of the Group have an infinite economic life because of the institutional nature of the corporate brand names, their proven ability to maintain market leadership and profitable operations over long periods of time and WPP's commitment to develop and enhance their value. The carrying value of intangible assets will continue to be reviewed annually for impairment and adjusted to the recoverable amount if required.

...

The initial recognition of the J. Walter Thompson corporate brand was credited to the revaluation reserve. Following the implementation of FRS 10 this amount of £175.0 million has been transferred to the profit and loss account reserve. ...

Notes to the accounts

12 Intangible fixed assets

	1998 **£m**	1997 £m	1996 £m
Corporate brand names	**350.0**	350.0	350.0

Corporate brand names represent J. Walter Thompson, Hill and Knowlton and Ogilvy & Mather Worldwide. These assets are carried at historical cost in accordance with the Group's accounting policy for intangible assets as stated on page 52.

It is interesting that these amounts are now described as being at historical cost, because in previous years the same amounts were said to represent directors' valuations of the brands, which in terms of the Act had to represent their current cost and thus be updated each year. This change is related to the rather odd reference in the policy note above to a transfer of £175 million from revaluation reserve to profit and loss account reserve. The explanation for this is that no value was attributed to the J Walter Thompson and the Hill and Knowlton brands when they were originally acquired, but they were revalued in 1988 at £175 million – the same amount as was attributed to the Ogilvy & Mather brand when it was acquired in 1989. Technically, therefore, the latter was carried at cost and the former at a valuation, which under FRS 10 would have had to be reversed because intangibles of this kind cannot be revalued. But the directors have instead decided to reopen the fair value accounting for J Walter Thompson and Hill and Knowlton, more than a decade after the acquisition, so as to reclassify goodwill of £175 million (which had been deducted from profit and loss account reserve) as the cost of these brands. Critics of brand accounting, however, might be forgiven for questioning the informational content of these numbers in the accounts. It seems a remarkable coincidence that not only did both sets of brands have the same value of £175 million when they were acquired, but also that they both remained at these same values in each of the last ten years, when they were said to be stated at a directors' valuation that reflected their current cost.

(c)   Internally developed intangible assets should be recognised only if they have a readily ascertainable market value.[17] Here the rule is much more restrictive, because it requires there to be an active market, evidenced by frequent transactions, in that particular asset; it says that the item must belong to a homogeneous population of assets that are equivalent in all material respects, such as certain operating licences, franchises and quotas. This therefore rules out the possibility of recognising unique intangibles such as brands, publishing titles, and patented inventions if they are home-grown rather than acquired.

A prominent but isolated example of recognition of 'homegrown' brand names (which would not now permitted since it falls within (c) above), was Ranks Hovis McDougall:

Extract 10.8: Ranks Hovis McDougall PLC (1991)

ACCOUNTING POLICIES

Intangible assets   The accounting treatment for additions to goodwill is considered on an individual basis and elimination against reserves has been selected as appropriate for the current year.

Brands, both acquired and created within the Group, are included at their 'current cost'. Such cost, which is reviewed annually, is not subject to amortisation.

NOTES TO THE ACCOUNTS

13   Intangible assets

	The Group £m	The Company £m
Brands		
At 1 September 1990	588.0	–
Revaluation	20.0	–
At 31 August 1991	608.0	–

The Group has valued its brands at their 'current use value to the Group' in conjunction with Interbrand Group plc, branding consultants.

This basis of valuation ignores any possible alternative use of a brand, any possible extension to the range of products currently marketed under a brand, any element of hope value and any possible increase in value of a brand due to either a special investment or a financial transaction (e.g. licensing) which would leave the Group with a different interest from the one being valued.

In 1992 the company was acquired by Tomkins. Interestingly, however, Tomkins decided not to attribute any value to the brands in allocating the purchase price to the assets acquired.

Although the valuation of internally developed brands was rare, it was not uncommon for publishers to put a value on titles that they had established. Mirror Group carried its home-grown newspaper titles at a valuation, but has been forced by FRS 10 to remove these from the balance sheet, as shown in this extract:

Extract 10.9: Mirror Group PLC (1998)

1. Basis of preparation and principal accounting policies

GOODWILL AND INTANGIBLE ASSETS [extract]

The Group has changed its accounting policy with regard to the accounting for the value of certain newspaper titles in order to comply with FRS 10 – Goodwill and Intangible Assets. In previous years a value of £625m was attributed to the national and Scottish titles in the balance sheet but FRS 10 does not permit the value of internally generated intangible assets which do not have readily ascertainable market values to be reflected in the balance sheet. Accordingly the revaluation has been reversed as a prior year adjustment against opening shareholders' funds. This accounting adjustment does not reflect any change in the directors' opinion of the value of these titles and has no impact on the profit and loss account or on the Company's ability to pay dividends.

11. Intangible fixed assets

Movements in intangible fixed assets are as follows:

	Titles £m	Goodwill £m	Total £m
Balance at 28 December 1997 as previously reported	810	–	810
FRS 10 prior year adjustment (note 1)	(625)	–	(625)
Balance at 28 December 1997 as restated for FRS 10	185	–	185
Acquisitions (note 13)	14	6	20
Balance at 3 January 1999	199	6	205

The £625m FRS 10 prior year adjustment is in respect of the value previously attributed to the Group's national and Scottish titles. The £199m in respect of titles comprises the amounts attributed to the value of the MIN and other acquired regional titles. The £6m of goodwill, which is being amortised over 20 years, relates to the acquisition in 1998 of The Derry Journal Limited and a number of magazines and exhibitions.

It now seems clear that home grown brands and newspaper titles cannot be recognised, but there is less clarity about the treatment of some other intangible assets that are created by the reporting entity rather than purchased externally.

In its 1997 accounts, Orange disclosed that it had two categories of intangible assets, as shown in the following extract.

Extract 10.10: Orange plc (1997)

2 Accounting policies

g) Intangible fixed assets

Subscriber acquisition costs:

The difference between the cost of Orange handsets to the Group and the lower amount recoverable from sales to intermediaries, if any, together with any additional commission payments, are recorded as subscriber acquisition costs. These costs are capitalised and amortised over twelve months, consistent with the duration of the subscriber contract. Costs of acquiring subscribers who return handsets within the 14 days refund period are written off when the handsets are returned.

Costs of obtaining new subscribers for the Group's service providers are charged against the profit and loss account as incurred as the Group does not control the third party mobile network by which the service is accessed by the subscriber.

Pre-launch network development costs:

Costs incurred during the construction phase of the mobile digital cellular network prior to launch date are accounted for as follows: Information technology services costs incurred prior to launch were capitalised and are amortised over five years using the straight line method commencing at launch. Other network related costs incurred prior to launch in April 1994 were capitalised and are amortised over ten years commencing at launch at the rates specified in Note 2 (e) above. Post-launch network operating costs are expensed as incurred.

Operating and overhead costs incurred during the construction phase of other Group networks prior to launch date were capitalised and are amortised over ten years using the straight line method.

12. Intangible fixed assets

Group	Subscriber acquisition costs £m	Network development costs £m	Total £m
Cost			
1 January 1997	268.9	44.5	313.4
Expenditure during the period	164.7	–	164.7
31 December 1997	433.6	44.5	478.1
Amortisation			
1 January 1997	192.4	16.1	208.5
Charged in period	156.0	4.6	160.6
31 December 1997	348.4	20.7	369.1
Net book amount			
31 December 1997	85.2	23.8	109.0
31 December 1996	76.5	28.4	104.9

In 1998 the company implemented FRS 10, as a result of which it reclassified these two categories of intangible assets as debtors and tangible fixed assets respectively, as shown below.

Extract 10.11: Orange plc (1998)

2 Accounting policies

The accounting policies adopted by the Group, as set out below, reflect the requirements of Financial Reporting Standards ('FRS') adopted in the year including FRS 9: Associates and Joint Ventures; FRS 10: Goodwill and Intangible Assets; FRS 11: Impairment of Fixed Assets and Goodwill; FRS 13: Derivatives and Other Financial Instruments: Disclosures and FRS 14: Earnings Per Share. ...

The adoption of these standards has no effect on the net operating results and net liabilities for prior years or the current year. Comparative figures within the financial statements have been restated where appropriate.

(f) Tangible fixed assets

Tangible fixed assets are stated at historical cost less depreciation.

The cost of the Orange network comprises network assets purchased at cost, together with direct construction costs of the network. Information technology services costs incurred prior to launch were capitalised and are amortised over five years using the straight line method commencing at launch. Costs incurred during, and attributable to, the construction phase of the Orange wirefree digital cellular network and other Group networks prior to launch date are included within tangible fixed assets - networks, and are depreciated in accordance with the Group's depreciation policy for such assets.

Depreciation of the Orange network commenced from the date of launch of the network in April 1994. Depreciation rates have been established to amortise the network over ten years. For assets placed in service prior to 1995, the depreciation rates applied in the first five years are based upon the level of subscriber usage, while a constant rate is applied in the second five years. Assets placed in service after 31 December 1994 are depreciated at a constant rate from the date they become operational.

Costs of maintaining the network are charged to the profit and loss account as incurred. ...

(g) Subscriber acquisition costs

The difference between the cost of Orange handsets to the Group and the lower amount recoverable from sales to intermediaries, if any, together with any additional commission payments, are recorded as subscriber acquisition costs, included within debtors and released to the profit and loss account over 12 months. Costs of acquiring subscribers who return handsets within the 14 day refund period are written off when the handsets are returned. Costs of obtaining new subscribers through the Group's service providers are charged against the profit and loss account as incurred, as the Group does not control the third party mobile networks by which the service is accessed by such subscribers.

The accounting treatment is therefore the same as before, even though the assets are now included elsewhere (and less transparently) in the balance sheet. Had they been left in intangibles they would have been regarded as internally developed assets, and failed to satisfy FRS 10's stringent tests for capitalisation of that category; they do not belong to a homogeneous population of assets that are traded on an active market.

Some companies have used a different route to escape an inappropriate outcome under FRS 10 – invoking SSAP 13 as the relevant standard. Great Universal Stores disclosed this policy in relation to its databases in its 1999 accounts:

Extract 10.12: The Great Universal Stores P.L.C. (1999)

1. Accounting policies

(f) other intangible fixed assets and depreciation [extract]

Intangible fixed assets other than goodwill comprise the data purchase and data capture costs of internally developed databases and are capitalised so that the costs thereof are recognised over the period of their commercial use. These costs are treated as development costs and capitalised under SSAP 13. Depreciation is provided by equal annual instalments on the cost of the assets at rates ranging from 20% to 33$\frac{1}{3}$%.

14. OTHER INTANGIBLE ASSETS	Databases
The Group	£m
Cost	
At 31 March 1998	285.5
Movements in year:	
Difference on exchange	10.7
Additions	61.4
Sales	(10.2)
At 31 March 1999	347.4
Depreciation	
At 31 March 1998	178.8
Movements in year:	
Difference on exchange	7.2
Provided in year	44.9
Sales	(6.9)
At 31 March 1999	224.0
Net Book Value at 31 March 1999	123.4
Net Book Value at 31 March 1998	106.7

Again, the treatment of these costs had not changed from the previous year, but the middle sentence of the policy note quoted above is new; in the 1998 accounts the company neither described these as development costs nor made any reference to SSAP 13. We agree that such costs should be capitalised and amortised over the period that they benefit, but whether they properly fall under SSAP 13 is more questionable. That standard addresses only a narrow class of expenditure that relates to scientific or technical knowledge, and does not really embrace costs of this kind. On the other hand, since this expenditure would not qualify to be capitalised under FRS 10, we entirely understand why it is desirable to assert that SSAP 13 is the more relevant standard.

We think FRS 10's rules on non-purchased intangibles are too restrictive and should be changed. We are not surprised to see companies arguing that certain items of expenditure fall outside the scope of the standard so that they may be capitalised when it manifestly makes sense to do so.

Critics of FRS 10 have questioned why the same intangible asset should sensibly pass or fail tests for inclusion on the balance sheet according solely to the manner in which it was acquired or created. However, by their nature, intangible assets have certain characteristics which cause unusual accounting difficulty, and this is what has led to these seemingly inconsistent rules. Some of these characteristics are described below.

A   Separability

As noted above, one element of the definition of intangible assets in FRS 10 is that they must be identifiable, meaning that they must be capable of separate disposal without disposing of the business to which they relate. This notion first emerged in SSAP 22 – *Accounting for goodwill*. Paragraph 13 of that standard read as follows:

'In deciding whether a particular asset falls into the category of separable net assets, the test is whether that asset could be identified and sold separately without disposing of the business as a whole. For example an asset may be an essential part of a company's manufacturing operations, and it may be that the asset would be of very little value other than in its present use; but it could be sold separately or bought from its manufacturers, whereas goodwill could not be – it could only be either acquired or sold as part of the process of acquiring or selling the business as a whole. Separable net assets may include identifiable intangibles such as those specifically mentioned in the balance sheet formats in the Companies Act 1985, i.e. "concessions, patents, licences, trade marks and similar rights and assets"; other examples include publishing titles, franchise rights and customer lists. (This list of examples is not intended to be comprehensive.) Identifiable intangibles such as these form part of the separable net assets which are recorded in an acquiring company's accounts at fair value, even if they were not recorded in the acquired company's accounts.'

SSAP 22 went on to define separable net assets as 'those assets (and liabilities) which can be identified and sold (or discharged) without necessarily disposing of the business as a whole. They include identifiable intangibles.'[18]

The Companies Act[19] and FRS 10[20] contain a similar concept, but use the word 'identifiable' rather than 'separable', otherwise retaining the same definition.

However, the characteristic of 'separability' is not generally seen as a criterion for recognition of an asset. Moreover, the above definition is not a very illuminating one and causes confusion in practice; for example, some might argue that the brand of a one-brand company was not separable because without it there would be no business left, whereas if it belonged to a company with a hundred brands then it would be separable – however, this may not be logical because the same asset is involved in each case.

Possibly what SSAP 22 really meant by its definition of separability is that the asset must be distinguishable from goodwill. It may not have intended to establish a general principle of separability as a characteristic of an asset; it simply sought to disqualify assets which are too much like goodwill, by setting a test which goodwill itself could not satisfy. Unfortunately it did so in terms which permitted differences of opinion on whether certain assets, such as brands, are truly separable. However, it seems that the ASB considers that assets such as brands *can* be separately recognised if they are obtained as part of an acquisition (under (b) above), even though questions might be raised as to whether they are really 'identifiable' in the sense of being capable of disposal while retaining the business to which they relate.

There is, however, a broader aspect of separability which may be relevant to the debate; this is the question of whether the asset is a discrete asset, in the sense that the boundaries between it and other assets can be clearly and unequivocally drawn. In the case of intangible assets, discreteness is particularly hard to establish because of the essential woolliness of an intangible asset. It is possible to establish it in some individual cases, if it represents a right to a particular stream of income which is independent of any other asset; an example would be a copyright giving rise to a stream of royalty income. However, where it is something which is used in combination with other assets to achieve income for the business, then it is very hard to say where the boundaries of the asset lie. Thus brands, which may be an important asset of a business, are used in combination with both the tangible assets of the business and the other intangible assets, such as a skilled workforce, an established distribution network, customer lists and so on. It is very difficult, if not impossible, to put a value on any of these intangible elements individually in a meaningful way. Moreover, if elements are valued individually there is a danger that their joint contribution to the profitability of the business will be arbitrarily assigned to one of these individual elements or even double-counted by being assigned to more than one element; furthermore, if the value of the elements is derived from the value of the business as a whole it would appear that all that is being done in reality is a valuation of goodwill.

B   Maintenance or substitution?

A related difficulty in accounting for such intangibles is that it is often difficult to determine whether the asset originally recorded is being maintained or whether a new asset is being gradually substituted for it. This enters into the question of how to account for the asset in subsequent years; must the original asset be written down as it erodes, even if a very similar asset grows up to replace it at the same time as a result of management's efforts in nurturing the valuable aspects of the business? The question of whether the asset is the same one or a different one can take on a metaphysical air. For example, if a customer list is bought, does it have to be written off if the customers on the list change, even if the new ones are as valuable as the old ones? That is a relatively concrete example; it may be even more difficult to determine whether a brand remains the same asset over time as it is subtly reshaped to meet new market opportunities.

Until the ASB introduced FRS 10 and FRS 11, this was seen as a significant problem. Conventional accounting has always required disaggregated assets and liabilities to be reflected in accounts and measured individually, not as part of a shifting portfolio of varying components. However, in these standards the Board has taken a much more pragmatic view, that substitution does not matter so long as overall value is maintained. (Curiously, it has dismissed the same argument in relation to tangible assets; it has often been claimed that continual refurbishment restores the fabric of certain assets and removes the need to record any depreciation, but the Board has resisted this idea in FRS 15 (see 3.3 below).

C   *Uncertainty of cost of creation*

A third difficulty, again on the same theme, is that when assets of the nature under discussion are created, it is generally not as the result of specific expenditure on that particular asset but as the by-product of expenditures made in the general conduct of the business. A well-trained workforce is built up over a period, not just as a result of expenditure on training, but because successful management and employment strategies of all kinds are in operation. The value of a brand is made not simply by inventing a desirable product with a consumer-seductive name, but by building market share by the skilful exploitation of the product in a whole host of ways. Joint or by-product costing is not a new technique for accountants, but it would be tested beyond the limit if it had to address how to determine the cost of intangible assets developed as a result of the general operations of the business.

These are just a few of the issues that make it very difficult to accommodate a comprehensive range of intangible assets within our familiar accounting framework. This view was supported by a 1989 research study from the London Business School. The authors concluded that 'the present flexible position, far from being neutral, is potentially corrosive to the whole basis of financial reporting and that to allow brands – whether acquired or homegrown – to continue to be included in the balance sheet would be highly unwise'.[21]

A major complicating factor in this debate has been a widespread disagreement and misunderstanding of what a balance sheet is intended to portray. To those people who see the balance sheet as trying to give an indication of the value of the company's assets, the inclusion of brands at a current value makes eminent sense. However, since the balance sheet is derived from the transactions of the company, and is still primarily a repository of unexpired costs and revenues, then it is hard to argue that the valuation of brands fits in to this framework. If the balance sheet were to become a statement of value, many more changes would be needed to the historical cost system than the mere valuation of brands.

At a conceptual level, the debate has not really advanced very much in recent years. FRS 7 rather ducked the issue in relation to acquired brands, saying only that '*where* [emphasis added] an intangible asset is recognised, its fair value should be based on its replacement cost, which is normally its estimated market value', but did not resolve the question of when such assets should be recognised. FRS 10 is more positive on the subject, by saying that 'an intangible asset acquired as part of the acquisition of a business should be capitalised separately from goodwill if its value can be measured reliably on initial recognition',[22] but it rather glosses over the problem that brands do not qualify to be counted as intangible assets in terms of the definition unless they are regarded as separable. In respect of homegrown brands, however, FRS 10 is much clearer: they should not be recognised. But altogether, the topic of brand accounting, and indeed the wider question of what intangible assets deserve to be recognised in balance sheets, remains an area of some controversy.[23]

2   COST

2.1   Introduction

The Companies Act requires that, subject to any provision for depreciation or diminution in value, the amount to be included in respect of any fixed asset shall be its purchase price or production cost.[24] (The alternative of carrying assets at a valuation is discussed in 5 below.) FRS 10 does not elaborate on how cost is to be determined for intangibles, whereas FRS 15 does so for tangible fixed assets, and at some length, as discussed below. It lays down a slightly different principle from the statutory one, saying that a tangible fixed asset should be initially measured at its cost,[25] and this should include 'costs, but only those costs, that are directly attributable to bringing the asset into working condition for its intended use'.[26] In practice, these two different principles substantially overlap, as discussed below.

FRS 15 does not deal with donated assets other than in connection with charities, for whom it says that the initial carrying amount of tangible fixed assets should be the current value of the assets at the date they are received.[27]

2.2   Purchase price

The Companies Act defines 'purchase price' as to include any consideration, whether in cash or otherwise, given by the company in respect of that asset.[28] In addition, according to the Act, 'the purchase price of an asset shall be determined by adding to the actual price paid any expenses incidental to its acquisition'.[29]

'Purchase price' has been interpreted by some as prohibiting the deduction of capital grants received from the cost of the asset, one of the treatments permitted by SSAP 4[30] (this is discussed more fully in Chapter 18 at 3.1.1).

'Expenses incidental to its acquisition' are those costs which have been incurred as a direct consequence of the purchase of the asset and are necessary in order to make it available for use.

2.3 Production cost

The definition in the Act of the production cost of any asset (fixed or current) says that it:

'shall be determined by adding to the purchase price of the raw materials and consumables used the amount of the costs incurred by the company which are directly attributable to the production of that asset.

In addition there may be included in the production cost of an asset –

(a) a reasonable proportion of the costs incurred by the company which are only indirectly attributable to the production of that asset, but only to the extent that they relate to the period of production; and

(b) interest on capital borrowed to finance the production of that asset, to the extent that it accrues in respect of the period of production.'[31]

As noted in 2.1 above, FRS 15 now only permits *directly* attributable costs to be included in tangible assets, so the standard effectively removes the possibility of including indirectly attributable costs as well.

Some of the elements of these definitions require further interpretation, notably the meanings of 'attributable costs' and 'period of production', and these are discussed further below. Capitalisation of interest is dealt with in Chapter 13.

2.4 Attributable costs

FRS 15 defines directly attributable costs as:

'(a) the labour costs of own employees (eg site workers, in-house architects and surveyors) arising directly from the construction, or acquisition, of the specific tangible fixed asset; and

(b) the incremental costs to the entity that would have been avoided only if the tangible fixed asset had not been constructed or acquired.'[32]

The standard includes the following examples:

■ acquisition costs such as stamp duty, import duties and non-refundable purchase taxes;

■ the costs of site preparation and clearance;

■ initial delivery and handling costs;

■ installation costs; and

■ professional fees such as legal, architects' and engineers' fees.[33]

FRS 15 goes on to say that administration and other general overheads fall outside the definition (these would be what the Act regards as indirectly attributable costs). It also stresses that employee costs not related to a specific asset, such as site selection activities, do not qualify for capitalisation.[34] The capitalisation of management time is thus unlikely to be permitted under FRS 15.

The standard goes on to say that any 'abnormal costs' are not directly attributable either. Examples of these are 'those relating to design errors, industrial disputes, idle capacity, wasted materials, labour or other resources and other production delays', and 'costs such as operating losses that occur because a revenue activity has been suspended during the construction of a tangible fixed asset'.[35]

Deciding what is an abnormal cost and is thus to be excluded may not always be straightforward, however. In the discussion paper that preceded FRS 15, the ASB distinguished abnormal costs from scenarios where 'the technical difficulties encountered in construction may be greater than foreseen, or estimates of the construction time may have been over-optimistic',[36] saying that cost overruns arising from the latter events should still be capitalised. The difference, as the ASB saw it, was that these costs were necessary to the asset's construction, whereas cost inefficiencies were not. Although this discussion has not been carried forward into FRS 15, it nevertheless gives an indication of how difficult the distinction will be to make in practice.

Taken together, the rules on what may be capitalised are therefore quite restrictive. They are much narrower than the equivalent rules on what may be carried forward in the cost of stock. SSAP 9 excludes from stock neither abnormal costs that arise from inefficiencies nor costs that are not incremental, and it does require an appropriate allocation of relevant overheads to be included. FRS 15 essentially restricts the costs that may be included to those that are essential to the creation of the asset and that would not otherwise have been incurred.

There is one further curiosity in the definition of directly attributable costs, which can only be described as a contradiction in terms. FRS 15 requires inclusion of 'the estimated cost of dismantling and removing an asset and restoring the site, to the extent that it is recognised as a provision under FRS 12.'[37] This is a direct breach of the principle of including only these costs that are directly attributable to bringing the asset *into* working condition. The reason for this absurdity is that FRS 12 requires the full estimated cost of decommissioning assets, such as oil rigs, to be set up as soon as the obligation arises, often at the start of the asset's life, rather than being gradually built up over that life (see Chapter 25 at 4.5). The ASB has then sought to neutralise the profit and loss account effect of this change in practice by allowing the provision to be capitalised as an asset rather than expensed as a cost, even though it breaches its own principle on what may be treated as the cost of an asset.

2.5   The period of production

As indicated in 2.3 above, the Act allows certain costs to be included in production cost to the extent that they relate to the period of production. However, there is no guidance in the Act to help determine when the period of production either commences or finishes. This is of most significance in relation to the capitalisation of borrowing costs (see Chapter 13), but there are some implications for other costs as well.

FRS 15 requires capitalisation of directly attributable costs to cease when substantially all the activities (i.e. its physical construction) that are necessary to get the tangible fixed asset ready for use are complete, even if it has not yet been brought into use.[38] It therefore prohibits the practice of extending the production period beyond the date of practical completion of the physical asset. This applies particularly to sectors where this period may be prolonged, such as property investment, where capitalisation of finance costs is the major issue. The argument in the past has been that the asset being constructed is not simply the physical structure of the building but a fully tenanted investment property, and the production period correspondingly includes not simply the construction period but also the letting period. Examples of such policies appear in these extracts from the accounts of MEPC, British Land and Hammerson, all of which predate FRS 15:

Extract 10.13: MEPC plc (1998)

1   Accounting policies

Properties [extract]

A property ceases to be treated as being in the course of development at the earliest of:

(1) the date when the development becomes fully let and income producing

(2) the date when income exceeds outgoings

(3) a date up to three years after completion to allow for letting.

Extract 10.14: British Land plc (1999)

Accounting policies

Properties [extract]

A property ceases to be treated as a development either nine months after practical completion or when two-thirds of the anticipated gross income becomes receivable, whichever is the earlier.

Extract 10.15: Hammerson plc (1998)

1   ACCOUNTING POLICIES

Cost of Properties [extract]

A property is regarded as being in the course of development until substantially let and income producing or until income exceeds outgoings.

As can be seen, these interpretations vary substantially. However, for the future, FRS 15 appears to prohibit extending the production period beyond the date of practical completion of the physical asset. Although FRS 15 exempts investment properties from its scope, the definition of such properties includes the requirement that any construction work and development has been completed (see 3.5 below); accordingly, properties which are in the course of construction or development fall within the scope of FRS 15.

FRS 15 endorses the practice of continuing to capitalise costs during an initial commissioning period, but only where 'the asset is available for use but incapable of operating at normal levels without such a start-up or commissioning period'.[39] This would allow capitalisation of, for example, the costs of a commissioning period that is necessary for running in machinery or testing equipment. It distinguishes this from the case where the asset is fully operational but is not yet achieving its targeted profitability because demand is still building up, for example in a new hotel or bookstore. In this case, the production period has finished and no further costs should be capitalised; these do not meet the definition of 'directly attributable' because they have been incurred after physical completion and they are not necessary in order to use the asset.

2.6   Subsequent expenditure

It can often be difficult to decide whether expenditure on improvements and repairs is capital or revenue in nature and, if it is capital, whether it should be treated as part of the original asset or as a separate category of fixed asset. These issues have not been greatly clarified by FRS 15. However, the standard does attempt to differentiate between revenue and capital expenditure.

Subsequent expenditure is *revenue* and should be expensed as incurred if it is for repairs and maintenance, that 'maintains the previously assessed standard of performance', or is necessary in order to prevent the useful life or residual value of the asset from decreasing.[40] Examples include the costs of servicing or overhauling plant or repainting buildings.

Subsequent expenditure is *capital* and should be included in the carrying value of the assets only if it falls within one of the following three circumstances:

(a)   where it provides an enhancement of economic benefits in excess of the previously assessed standard of performance; or

(b)   where a component of the tangible fixed asset that has been treated as a separate asset and depreciated over its individual useful life is replaced or restored; or

(c)   where the subsequent expenditure relates to a major inspection or overhaul and the asset has already been depreciated to reflect the consumption of economic benefits of the asset that led to the need for the expenditure.[41]

Criterion (a) is based on the equivalent suggestions contained in IAS 16. Examples of the enhancement of benefits given by the IAS include:

- an extension in the asset's estimated useful life or an increase in its capacity;
- a substantial improvement in the quality of output; or
- a substantial reduction in previously assessed operating costs.[42]

Criterion (b) has been added to prevent the capitalisation criteria being unnecessarily restrictive. Repairs would otherwise almost always have been excluded from being capitalised as they rarely extend the life of the asset beyond that previously assessed (and indeed expenditure on replacing components would almost undoubtedly have been taken into account in the previous assessment, whether this was made at the point of purchase or occasioned by subsequent capital expenditure).

The principle is straightforward. If, for example, a property's roof or lift system has been separately identified and depreciated, its replacement can be capitalised, subject, of course, to writing off the remaining carrying amount of the old asset. This is simply straightforward asset accounting but with the existing asset reclassified as a series of separate assets with separate lives. However, by no means all organisations have records that would allow suitable asset components to be identified and it would not necessarily be to their advantage to do so; the costs could well outweigh the benefits.

This would appear to mean that expenditure that does not enhance the benefits and has not been separately identified and depreciated will be deemed to be repairs and maintenance expenditure and expensed when incurred, unless it falls within criterion (c).

Criterion (c) is another consequence of FRS 12. One of the examples in the application notes to that standard deals with those entities that make major periodic repairs to large assets and have accounted for these by setting up provisions to meet the costs. This has been a common practice in the airline and oil refining industries, although it has never been universally applied in either sector; some companies either accounted for the expenditure when incurred or capitalised the cost and depreciated it over the period until the next major overhaul. Similar policies are followed by utilities that apply 'asset maintenance plans'.

FRS 12 explicitly disallows setting up provisions for such periodic overhauls on the basis that there is no obligation to carry out the expenditure independently of the entity's future actions. However, FRS 12 suggests that the entity's results can be largely insulated from the effects of any change in the policy of providing for repair costs over time by adjusting the asset's carrying value and depreciation charge. Extract 10.20 at 3.3.2 below from Anglian Water's accounts shows the change it has made in response to FRSs 12 and 15.

FRS 15 argues that this is similar to treating a major component of an asset as a separate asset and depreciating it over its useful life, i.e. as a variation of category (b) above. Under (b), a company may choose to account separately for major components such as furnace linings; these linings would be capitalised and depreciated over the period until they are replaced, whereupon the replacement lining is capitalised in its place. Major inspections and overhauls could be treated in the same way. The depreciation of the asset could reflect an amount equivalent to the expected overhaul costs over the period until the next overhaul, when those costs would be capitalised and the cycle repeated.

There are a number of shortcomings in these rules. The costs themselves are not necessarily tangible – they may comprise inspection costs rather than tangible assets like a furnace lining. Nothing is being made or added at the periodic overhaul; it is not the same as replacing a tangible part of the asset whose cost could be established and written off over its useful life. The depreciation over the period until the first overhaul would have to be an estimate. It would be neither an allocation of the asset's cost over its life, nor an allocation of value consumed.

As this treatment only applies where there is no separately identifiable asset being depreciated and replaced, this could result in some rather odd depreciation charges. An asset that is not otherwise distinguished into separate parts would be regarded as having more than one life and be depreciated at different rates.

The ASB does not really seem very keen on category (c). It suggests that the decision to identify separate components or overhauls for depreciation over a shorter economic life would depend on a number of factors, including:

■   whether the useful economic lives of the components or the period until the next overhaul is substantially different from the useful economic life of the rest of the asset;

■   the degree of irregularity in the levels of expenditure required to restate the component or asset in different accounting periods; and

■   their materiality.[43]

Ultimately, therefore, the ASB appears to accept that it may often be preferable to expense subsequent expenditure that does not enhance the economic benefits in excess of the previously assessed standard of performance. It may be neither practicable nor desirable to record each individual asset as several different assets nor to depreciate part of the asset over a different timescale to the rest of the asset.

3   DEPRECIATION AND AMORTISATION

3.1   Introduction

This section deals with the general principles of depreciation and in particular with how it applies to assets carried at historical cost. The specific problems of depreciation of assets carried at valuation are dealt with in 5.3.3 below.

3.1.1 The meaning of depreciation

Depreciation is defined by FRS 15 as 'the measure of the cost or revalued amount of the economic benefits of the tangible fixed asset that have been consumed during the period.'[44] This wording is mildly different from that in SSAP 12, but the meaning is effectively the same. It is explained that consumption includes the wearing out, using up or other reduction in the useful economic life of a tangible fixed asset whether arising from use, effluxion of time or obsolescence through either changes in technology or demand for the goods and services produced by the asset. Depreciation is the term usually applied to tangible assets while 'amortisation' is the equivalent term for intangible assets; however, the two are the same in concept. There is no formal definition of 'amortisation' in FRS 10.

Depreciation should therefore be seen as a measure of consumption, not a means of valuation. Fixed assets involve costs that will be consumed over an extended period and which should therefore be matched to the periods expected to benefit from their use. However, depreciation is sometimes misconstrued as a measure of loss of value,[45] which would therefore only be charged if the value of an asset at the end of an accounting period was less than the carrying value at the beginning of the period. The purpose of depreciation is sometimes also thought of as being to provide a fund for replacement, but this aim is not supported by FRS 15 and was specifically considered and rejected in the US.[46]

Ever since SSAP 12 was first published, there has been some resistance to the requirement to apply depreciation to particular types of asset. Often, the arguments rely at least to some extent on the view that it makes no sense to apply depreciation to an asset whose value is not currently declining, taking the position that depreciation is a valuation technique rather than a measure of consumption. Other arguments often depend on the assertion that the asset in question has an unlimited life. FRS 15 and FRS 10 have now addressed these various arguments, as discussed in 3.3 and 3.4 below. However, one specific category of assets – investment properties – has been exempted from depreciation as discussed at 3.5 below.

3.2 The requirements of the Companies Act

The Companies Act requires any fixed asset, whether tangible or intangible, that has a limited useful economic life to be depreciated over that life, on a systematic basis, down to its residual value (if any).[47] The Act does not permit goodwill to be accorded an indefinite life,[48] which has caused the ASB some difficulty in relation to FRS 10, which does contemplate such a possibility (see 3.4 below). Depreciation is to be based on the carrying value; on the purchase price or production cost under the historical cost rules,[49] and on the revalued amount if the alternative accounting rules are being followed.[50] Depreciation of revalued assets is dealt with in 5.3.3 below.

3.3   Depreciation of tangible assets

Until recently, the accounting standard that governed this subject was SSAP 12, originally published in 1977 (following ED 15, which was published in January 1975). Subsequently, in 1982 the ASC issued a Discussion Paper dealing with a number of new issues including the effect of revaluations on depreciation, supplementary depreciation and the estimation of useful lives.[51] This was followed by ED 37 in April 1985 and finally by a revised version of SSAP 12 in January 1987. In February 1999, however, it was superseded by FRS 15, which is effective for accounting periods ending on or after 23 March 2000.

FRS 15 itself has had a long gestation period. It is largely based on ED 51[52] – an exposure draft published by the ASC nine years earlier but which the ASB did not progress when it took office. It was only in 1996 that the Board published its own Discussion Paper,[53] followed by FRED 17[54] a year later. Despite this delay, FRS 15 has made relatively few changes either to the principles of depreciation established by SSAP 12 or the ASC's wider proposals in ED 51.

FRS 15 covers all tangible fixed assets except for investment properties[55] (see 3.5 below). Intangible assets and goodwill are addressed by FRS 10 (see 3.4 below). The main requirements of FRS 15 in relation to depreciation are discussed below.

3.3.1   Definitions relating to depreciation

Depreciation is the measure of the cost or revalued amount of the economic benefits of the tangible fixed asset that have been consumed during the period.

Depreciable amount is the cost of a tangible fixed asset (or, where an asset is revalued, the revalued amount) less its residual value.

Residual value is the net realisable value of an asset at the end of its useful economic life. Residual values are based on prices prevailing at the date of acquisition (or revaluation) of the asset and do not take account of expected future price changes.

The *useful economic life* of a tangible fixed asset is the period over which the entity expects to derive economic benefits from that asset.[56]

3.3.2   Requirement to depreciate

FRS 15's basic requirement is that the depreciable amount of a tangible fixed asset is to be allocated on a systematic basis over its useful economic life, using a method that reflects as fairly as possible the pattern in which its economic benefits are consumed.[57] It is emphasised that this is done in order to charge operating profits with the consumption of the asset; in other words the treatment has a profit and loss account objective not a balance sheet one, and depreciation must be charged whether or not the asset has declined in value in the period.[58]

Unless the asset's residual value at the end of its useful economic life is at least going to equal its present book value in real terms, then depreciation is required.

This emphasis of the purpose of depreciation is designed to forestall the arguments that some companies have made in the past to justify non-depreciation of certain properties. This has been a source of continual argument ever since SSAP 12 was originally published in 1977. Resistance began with the brewers, but it was later extended to several other industries. In 1978 the finance directors of some of the major brewers met with members of the ASC in order to present their case that licensed premises did not have to be depreciated. Their argument rested on a number of points, of which the most important was that brewers have to maintain their premises to high standards in order to attract and retain custom. Every year a proportion of the premises would be refurbished and the costs charged to revenue.

However, the brewers did not succeed in gaining an exemption from the requirements of SSAP 12. Instead, it was acknowledged that the combination of very long life and high residual value meant that there was not a significant amount of depreciation to be charged. When SSAP 12 first came to be revised, this argument had become so well established that it was incorporated into the exposure draft of the proposed new standard.[59] It was not included in the revised standard because, as the ASC statement accompanying the revised version of SSAP 12 stated,[60] 'a significant number of commentators expressed concern that the proposal could be open to misinterpretation or misuse. It was believed that it might represent a loophole in the standard, permitting non-depreciation of many types of property, in addition to freehold land and investment properties.' The statement went on to point out that the general principle of SSAP 12 should be applied in all cases but that there may be circumstances where it would not be appropriate to charge depreciation.

Notwithstanding this, the practice remained widely adopted by brewers and then spread to hotels, High Street retailers and banks, among others. Examples of each of these follow (all of which pre-date FRS 15):

Extract 10.16: Allied Domecq PLC (1998)

Accounting Policies

DEPRECIATION [extract]

No depreciation is provided on land, or on licensed and certain other properties, which are freehold or held on lease for a term exceeding 100 years unexpired. It is the group's policy to maintain the licensed estate in such condition that the value of the estate is not impaired by the passage of time. As a consequence, any element of depreciation would, in the opinion of the directors, be immaterial. Deficits arising on the revaluation of the properties below cost are charged to the profit and loss account.

Extract 10.17: Friendly Hotels plc (1998)

1. Accounting policies

Depreciation – tangible fixed assets

It is group policy not to provide depreciation on freehold and long leasehold premises. The premises are maintained to a high standard and the directors consider that the lives of the premises are so long and their residual value so great that depreciation is not necessary except for short leasehold premises under 21 years unexpired.

Where any permanent diminution of property value is incurred, a provision is made in the profit and loss account. The directors' estimate of residual values is based on prices prevailing at the time of acquisition or subsequent independent valuation.

Arcadia is one among a number of retailers with a similar policy in respect of its High Street shops:

Extract 10.18: Arcadia Group plc (1998)

1 Accounting policies

d Depreciation

Depreciation is calculated so as to allocate the cost of tangible fixed assets over their estimated useful economic lives. No depreciation is charged on non-industrial freehold and long leasehold properties, other than rack-rented properties, because the directors consider that the economic lives of these properties and their residual values, excluding inflation, are such that their depreciation is not significant. The residual values of the properties are regularly reviewed in order to identify any permanent diminution in value which would be charged to the profit and loss account. Rack-rented long leasehold properties are those held on leases providing for full market rent reviews every five years. ...

Lloyds TSB is typical of the clearing banks in not depreciating its branch properties:

Extract 10.19: Lloyds TSB Group plc (1998)

1 Accounting policies

i Tangible fixed assets [extract]

Land is not depreciated. Leasehold premises with unexpired lease terms of 50 years or less are depreciated by equal annual instalments over the remaining period of the lease. Freehold and long leasehold buildings are maintained in a state of good repair and it is considered that residual values, based on prices prevailing at the time of acquisition or subsequent valuation, are such that depreciation is not significant. ...

For a number of years most of the major supermarket operators followed a practice of non-depreciation in respect of their stores. However, in 1994 falling values of their stores brought the realisation that these assets were not really of the same character as pubs and hotels, and it has since become normal in that sector to follow a traditional approach to depreciation. A similar trend has become evident in the leisure industry – see for example First Leisure, quoted in Extract 10.50 at 5.1.1 below.

The ASB clearly regarded the arguments for non-depreciation as spurious, and in 1997 it sought to stamp out the practice by including the following paragraph in FRED 17, which unfortunately was equally spurious:

'It is often argued that the residual value of a well maintained tangible fixed asset is not materially different from the cost of the asset. However, the physical life of a tangible fixed asset (other than land) cannot be indefinite. Therefore if the asset is held for its entire life its residual value must be zero (assuming zero scrap value) whatever maintenance has been carried out. Where an entity intends to hold the asset for only a short period of time the residual value of the asset (given appropriate maintenance) may not be materially different from cost; where an asset is held for longer periods of time such an assumption is not appropriate. Therefore, an entity should assume that the residual value of an asset will be materially different from its cost unless it intends to dispose of the asset shortly after purchasing it and it is reasonably expected that the asset can be disposed of within approximately one year of its date of acquisition.'[61]

The problem with this was that it neglected the Board's own definition of an asset's economic useful life, which focuses on the period for which the entity will retain the asset rather than the whole of its natural life. FRED 17 assumed that businesses will tend to sell their fixed assets either soon after they buy them or not at all, neither of which seems very likely.

In FRS 15, the Board has adopted a more reasonable stance. It has accepted that there will be some assets whose lives are so long and/or residual values so high that depreciation would genuinely be immaterial, in which case it need not be charged. However, it has required such assets, as well as any with a remaining useful economic life of over 50 years, to be subject to an annual impairment test (see 4.4 below).[62] It also suggests that it will only be plausible to assume a high residual value where all of the following apply:

- the entity has a policy of regular repair to keep its assets to their previously assessed standard of performance;
- the asset is not prone to obsolescence;
- the entity habitually sells such assets well before the end of their economic lives; and
- such sales do not give rise to material losses (after excluding the effects of price changes).[63]

It remains to be seen how companies in the industries affected will react to the new standard. It would appear to be incumbent on them to examine the components of their asset portfolios more critically so as to determine which individual assets really meet these criteria. Although there may still be a case for non-depreciation of some assets, it is likely to be applied less widely than before.

Another category of assets which in the past was generally not depreciated is the infrastructure assets of certain public utilities. The ASB acknowledges that assets of this kind may need special consideration, and sees the issue as similar to subsequent expenditure as described in 2.6 above. The issue arises because FRS 12 now prohibits provision being made for rolling programmes for the maintenance of such infrastructure assets, as discussed in Chapter 25 at 4.6. However, FRS 15 says that in certain circumstances it may still be acceptable to make a charge to the profit and loss account based on estimated annual expenditure (so-called 'renewals accounting') but the charge must be treated as depreciation and deducted from the carrying value of the asset, while actual expenditure is capitalised as incurred. The conditions are:

(a)　the infrastructure asset is a system or network that as a whole is intended to be maintained at a specified level of service potential by the continuing replacement and refurbishment of its components;

(b)　the level of annual expenditure required to maintain the operating capacity (or service capability) of the infrastructure asset is calculated from an asset management plan that is certified by a person who is appropriately qualified and independent; and

(c)　the system or network is in a mature or steady state.[64]

The most difficult of these criteria to meet is (c) — that the network is in a mature or steady state. Any entity that is intending to expand its infrastructure may find it difficult to satisfy this condition.

Anglian Water's 1999 accounts show the change that it made in order to comply with FRS 12.

Extract 10.20: Anglian Water Plc (1999)

1. Accounting policies

a) changes in preparation of financial statements [extract]

It has been necessary to change the method of accounting for infrastructure maintenance expenditure following the introduction of FRS 12 'Provisions, contingent liabilities and contingent assets' as it is no longer possible to account for the difference between planned and actual expenditure on infrastructure renewals as a provision or prepayment. As a consequence the balance sheet has been restated to take account of necessary changes in the year to 31 March 1989, when renewal accounting was first adopted in the accounts, and any previous provisions or prepayments have been subsumed into fixed assets. This had the effect of removing the provision for infrastructure renewals of £67.7 million at 31 March 1998 and reducing fixed assets by the same amount. This change of accounting disclosure has no effect on the profit and loss account other than to reclassify the renewal charge of £17.8 million (1998–£18.9 million) as depreciation. The comparative amounts have been restated.

e) tangible fixed assets and depreciation [extract]

Infrastructure assets (being mains and sewers, impounding and pumped raw water storage reservoirs, dams, sludge pipelines and sea outfalls) comprise a network of systems. Investment expenditure on infrastructure assets relating to increases in capacity or enhancements of the network and on maintaining the operating capability of the network, in accordance with defined standards of service, is treated as an addition and included at cost after deducting grants and contributions. The depreciation charge for infrastructure assets is the estimated average level of expenditure required to maintain the operating capability of the network which is based on the company's independently-certified asset management plan.

15. tangible fixed assets [extract]	Infrastructure assets £m
Cost	
At 31 March 1998	
As previously reported	1,362.1
Adjustment for change in method of accounting	183.8
As restated	1,545.9
Additions	117.5
Disposals	(0.6)
At 31 March 1999	**1,662.8**
Grants and contributions	
At 31 March 1998	110.8
Additions	12.0
At 31 March 1999	**122.8**
Depreciation	
At 31 March 1998	
As previously reported	–
Adjustment for change in method of accounting	251.5
As restated	251.5
Charge for the year	17.8
Disposals	(0.6)
At 31 March 1999	**268.7**
Net book amount	
At 31 March 1999	**1,271.3**
At 31 March 1998 as restated	1,183.6

Following a change in accounting disclosure (as stated in note 1) infrastructure assets are now depreciated and the figures for prior years have been restated accordingly. Although a provision is made for depreciation of infrastructure assets, these assets have no finite economic life and hence no basis exists to amortise the related grants and contributions.

It is difficult to see this change as an improvement, and certainly the comments made by Anglian, such as in the last sentence of the above extract, suggest that it does not regard it as one either. All that seems to have been accomplished is that the former provision has been hidden by netting it off against the assets in order to satisfy the ASB's conceptual difficulty in accepting it as a liability, but without any real change of substance in the accounting treatment of these costs.

A slightly different practice which has grown up among companies which exploit mineral deposits is to depreciate their deposits only over the last portion of the life of the minerals being extracted. An example is to be found in the accounts of Tarmac:

Extract 10.21: Tarmac plc (1998)

Principal Accounting Policies

Depreciation [extract]

Depreciation is based on historic cost or revaluation, less the estimated residual values, and the estimated economic lives of the assets concerned. Freehold land is not depreciated. Mineral reserves are amortised over their estimated commercial life where this is less than ten years. Other tangible assets are depreciated in equal annual instalments over the period of their estimated economic lives …

Similar policies are followed by several other companies in the same industry. The argument advanced to support such a treatment is generally that the value of the deposits does not tend to diminish appreciably until the deposits are nearly exhausted – again a valuation perspective of depreciation rather than a consumption view. In some respects this is similar to the SSAP 19 rule, that leasehold properties should be depreciated at least over the last 20 years of their lives, presumably on the same argument that the value does not decline significantly until then.

An ICAEW report to the ASB on SSAP 12 commented on this practice as follows: 'Because mineral reserves are valued on a net present value basis, in practice there would be little difference between the values of a mine with, say, 20 years' reserves as compared with a mine with 60 years' reserves of the same mineral. Consequently, it is argued that any loss in value of a mine occurs in the last 20 (or 15 or 10) years of its life, and therefore no depreciation is necessary until that point. Some people express this slightly differently (but achieve the same result) by asserting that they are using the annuity method of depreciation [see 3.3.6 D below] and that accordingly depreciation is weighted heavily towards the final years of the life of the mine. This again highlights the need to reassess the role of depreciation – i.e. is it an allocation of cost or recognition of decline in value?'[65] The report concluded that the ASB should consult with companies in the industry and consider giving specific guidance on this matter.

In the event, FRS 15 does not discuss it specifically, but nonetheless seems to have dealt with it in passing, by saying that the depreciation method 'should result in a depreciation charge throughout the asset's useful economic life and not just towards the end of its useful economic life or when the asset is falling in value.'[66] It therefore seems that companies who have adopted such a practice will have to change it when they first apply FRS 15.

Another version of the same argument is to be found in Granada's accounts in relation to motorway service areas:

Extract 10.22: Granada Group PLC (1998)

Accounting policies

5 Depreciation [extract]

... Motorway service areas held subject to short leaseholds are not depreciated whilst their value is
maintained or increased. Depreciation thereafter is provided on a straight line basis over the
residual period of the lease.

It is also sometimes argued that assets not currently in use, for example ships
that have been laid up, do not need to be depreciated. However, depreciation is
viewed as an allocation of the cost of an asset over its useful life, so it should
normally continue to be charged while the asset is not used. The lack of use may
affect the asset's estimated useful life or be symptomatic of circumstances that
affect its residual value (for example, it may be caused by a major slump in the
world shipping markets), either of which may affect the amount of depreciation
being charged. It might be argued that where an asset has not been used in a
particular year its useful economic life has effectively been extended; but in that
case depreciation will still need to be charged, albeit at a reduced rate.

3.3.3   What to depreciate

FRS 15 states that an asset may need to be analysed for depreciation purposes
into any subcomponents that have substantially different useful economic lives;[67]
some subcomponents will have indefinite lives and will not need to be
depreciated at all. The most obvious example is a freehold property; the element
of the carrying value that relates to the land should not be depreciated but the
building has a finite useful life and should be depreciated over that life. This is
the position that SSAP 12 has always taken, and FRS 15 similarly stresses that
increases in land values do not affect the residual value of the building or its
useful economic life.[68]

The Royal Institution of Chartered Surveyors (RICS) gives guidance to its
members on how to apportion the cost or valuation of a property between the
depreciable amount and the land element.[69] This, it argues, may be done in either
of the following ways:

(a)   by valuing the land in its existing use and deducting this from the total. It
        is argued that this may be appropriate where there is suitable evidence of
        land values; or

(b)   by assessing the net current replacement cost of the asset, in which case
        the value of the land is the balancing figure.[70]

This is relatively straightforward where the analysis is only between land and
buildings, and when assets are recorded on the basis of cost, although even then
the apportionments may be somewhat arbitrary. However, the issue quickly
becomes more complicated if additional subcomponents are identified, as
FRS 15 now suggests, or if the asset is revalued, because the property as a whole

may be valued on a basis that is not readily disaggregated into component parts in any meaningful way.

The value of such properties may include fixtures or plant that are now to be separately depreciated under FRS 15. However, a further level of complexity is added if the property is valued on the basis of its earning potential, e.g. as a pub or hotel. This basis is described in more detail at 5.2.2 B below. One major problem is what to do with the 'trading potential', which reflects the goodwill attaching to the business and represents the difference between the underlying separable fixed assets and the total valuation, and whether it should be added to the land value (which does not depreciate) or carried with the buildings. FRS 15 states that it would be inappropriate to treat the trading potential as a separate component, where the value and life of any such trading potential is inseparable from that of the property.[71] The reasoning behind this is not explained, but it is unlikely to mean that the property (meaning land and buildings and any other assets) should not be disaggregated into its various components. It is our view that, however the trading potential is allocated, it is similar to goodwill and its useful life should be considered in that light.

This need to identify depreciable components within a previously aggregated whole gives rise to a difficult transitional issue on first application of FRS 15. As discussed in 3.3.2 above, a substantial number of companies in the retail sector have not charged depreciation in the past, but may now do so for at least some of the components of their assets. Frequently, their properties have been carried at a valuation based on their trading potential. Allocating the value of a business unit measured on this basis to components of the asset to be depreciated presents difficult problems in both theory and practice. The essential difficulty is that the valuation is unrelated to the individual underlying assets, which makes any attempt to apportion it somewhat theoretical.

FRS 15 sets rules on how any transitional changes should be dealt with in accounting terms. Its basic rule is that revisions to economic lives or residual values that are made on the first implementation of the standard are not changes of policy and accordingly should not give rise to a prior year adjustment. Instead, they should be accounted for prospectively.[72] But there is an exception to this rule where assets are divided into components with significantly different economic lives; these are to be treated as the result of a change of policy and dealt with as a prior year adjustment.[73]

On the face of it, this seems to permit prior year adjustments in the circumstances of companies who now start to depreciate components of their property. However, Marks & Spencer has chosen to implement the standard in a hybrid way, with a prior year adjustment relating to its shop fittings, but a prospective approach to the depreciation of its buildings, as shown in this extract.

Extract 10.23: Marks and Spencer p.l.c. (1999)

11. Tangible fixed assets [extract]

B CHANGE OF ACCOUNTING POLICY

The Group has adopted FRS15, 'Tangible Fixed Assets' and has followed the transitional provisions to retain the book value of land and buildings, certain of which were revalued in 1988.

Adoption has resulted in two key changes:

(i) The FRS encourages the separation of assets into components where they have very different useful economic lives and states that these changes should be dealt with as prior year adjustments. The cost of fitting out properties, which has up to now been included within the cost of buildings, has been separately identified and disclosed together with fixtures, fittings and equipment. Fit out has previously been accounted for on a replacement basis but under this policy will be depreciated evenly over periods ranging from 10-25 years depending on its nature. As a result, £53.2m of fit out which had been expensed in previous years has now been capitalised as at 31 March 1998. In addition, £264.1m of accumulated depreciation has also been recognised as at that date, being the depreciation on fit out which would have been recognised had the new policy been in place in previous years. As a consequence of the prior year adjustment, the net book value of Group tangible fixed assets as at 31 March 1998 has been reduced by £210.9m with a corresponding reduction in the profit and loss account reserve. The effect of this on reported profits has been an additional Group depreciation charge in the current year of £28.6m (last year £23.5m) and a reduction in the charge for repairs and renewals of £18.3m (last year £10.5m).

(ii) In previous years the Group has stated that the useful economic lives of its freehold and long leasehold properties are so long and the residual values are so high that any depreciation charge was immaterial. The Group agrees with the theory of 'consumption' and has charged depreciation against the book value of its properties this year amounting to £10.8m. There is no corresponding prior year adjustment since the previous policy was to depreciate properties at 1% or nil.

This distinction may stem from a view that the prior year adjustment treatment can only be applied to sub-divisions of the building, and not the building itself; it has always been a requirement to separate buildings from land for depreciation purposes, so if they were not depreciated before it can only be because they were thought to have sufficiently long lives or high residual values to render depreciation immaterial, and if this is no longer the case then depreciation of the building should now be charged prospectively. We see some merit in this view where, as in Marks & Spencer's case, the properties are carried at cost or at outdated valuations. However, the arguments become more complex when properties are carried at current values based on trading potential, because moving from what is essentially a business valuation model to an exercise of depreciating sub-components has more of the character of a change of policy than a change of estimate. Extract 10.53 below shows that UA Group has changed its policy from one of revaluation to one of cost and also started to depreciate its properties, and the prior year adjustment included an element of backlog depreciation. Furthermore, where a policy of revaluation is to be continued, a change of policy on depreciation in these circumstances would not change the balance sheet figures, but only the analysis of reserves and the amount of depreciation in the profit and loss account that would be charged in the future. The issues are therefore quite complex, and a variety of treatments may emerge in practice.

3.3.4   *Useful economic life*

One of the critical assumptions on which the depreciation charge depends is the useful economic life of the asset. As noted above, this is the period over which the present owner will benefit and not the total potential life of the asset; the two will often not be the same. For example, a company may have a policy of replacing all of its cars after three years, so this will be their estimated useful life for depreciation purposes.

FRS 15 says that the following factors should be considered in assessing the useful life, residual value and depreciation method to be used for an asset:

■   the expected usage of the asset by the entity, assessed by reference to the asset's expected capacity or physical output;

■   the expected physical deterioration of the asset through use or effluxion of time; this will depend upon the repair and maintenance programme of the entity both when the asset is in use and when it is idle;

■   economic or technological obsolescence, for example arising from changes or improvements in production, or a change in the market demand for the product or service output of that asset;

■   legal or similar limits on the use of the asset, such as the expiry dates of related leases.[74]

The standard requires asset lives to be estimated on a realistic basis and reviewed at the end of each reporting period.[75] This is a slight tightening of the equivalent requirement in SSAP 12, which said only that the lives should be 'reviewed regularly'. The effects of changes in the estimated life are to be recognised prospectively, over the remaining life of the asset.[76] This is similar to SSAP 12, except that the latter also allowed a cumulative catch-up, disclosed as an exceptional charge, in the year in which the asset's life was revised if not to do so would result in a material distortion of future results.[77]

First Leisure provides an example of this cumulative catch-up adjustment when it started to depreciate its properties:

Extract 10.24: First Leisure Corporation PLC (1998)

Principal accounting policies

Tangible fixed assets and depreciation

In prior years, no depreciation was provided on freehold and long leasehold buildings as the Director's estimates of useful life were so long, and residual values were so high, that any depreciation would have been insignificant. Following the publication of FRED 17, the Directors believe that best accounting practice has moved towards depreciating buildings and have therefore revised their estimates of useful economic lives and residual values. Buildings are now analysed into their primary components which are depreciated on a straight line basis over periods of between 15 to 50 years. Additionally, the disposal of the Group's Resorts division has significantly reduced the useful life of its amusement machines as this division could utilise older machines than the Group's other divisions. The Directors consider that accounting for the entire impact of these changes in estimate over the remaining lives of these assets would materially distort its future results and, to the extent that the additional depreciation relates to the change in assets lives, a backlog depreciation charge of £17.4m has been included as an exceptional item in the current year's profit and loss account as required by SSAP 12.

Such a treatment would no longer be allowed under FRS 15.

J D Wetherspoon provides an example of a change in asset lives being accounted for prospectively:

Extract 10.25: J D Wetherspoon plc (1996)

2 Accounting adjustments

The Directors decided that, with effect from 1 August 1995, all freehold buildings would be depreciated to residual value over a life of fifty years and leasehold buildings over the lease term (or fifty years or less). In prior periods, such properties were not depreciated. Additionally, it was decided that major renovations to trading properties would henceforward be depreciated over six years, whereas previously they were depreciated over three years. UK generally accepted accounting principles do not allow the previous years' figures to be restated and hence the comparative figures have not been adjusted. Had they been, the depreciation charge in 1995 would have been £1.6 million greater than the figure shown in Note 7.

In practice, many companies tend to use quite a broad brush in estimating asset lives, often based on perceived norms rather than a close analysis of their own expectations. As a result, companies often have a material proportion of assets still in use but fully depreciated. In the 1980s, this became so commonplace that ED 37 proposed a requirement that fully depreciated assets be reinstated if it was considered necessary in order for the accounts to give a true and fair view.[78] However, it was not clear what kind of circumstances were envisaged and the requirement was dropped from the revised version of SSAP 12.

One company which discloses the amount of its fully depreciated assets is British Steel, as shown in the following extract:

Extract 10.26: British Steel plc (1999)

10. Tangible fixed assets [extract]

(i) Included above are fully depreciated assets with an original cost of £1,332m (1998: £1,127m) which are still in use. In addition, there are fully depreciated assets with an original cost of £139m (1998: £101m) which are permanently out of use and pending disposal, demolition or reapplication elsewhere in the business.

An example of a company that explicitly states that it regularly reviews asset lives is ICI. As a result the accounting policy note cannot give the period over which the assets are depreciated, except as global averages, as illustrated below:

Extract 10.27: Imperial Chemical Industries PLC (1998)

Accounting policies

Depreciation

The Group's policy is to write-off the book value of each tangible fixed asset evenly to its residual value over its estimated remaining life. Reviews are made annually of the estimated remaining lives of individual productive assets, taking account of commercial and technological obsolescence as well as normal wear and tear. Under this policy it becomes impracticable to calculate average asset lives exactly; however, the total lives approximate to 31 years for buildings and 18 years for plant and equipment. Depreciation of assets qualifying for grants is calculated on their full cost.

Companies often charge a full year's depreciation in the year of acquisition, regardless of when the assets were acquired, but many also depreciate their assets on a monthly basis for management accounts purposes and carry the same figures into their annual accounts. At the opposite extreme, one or two commence depreciation only in the following year; GKN is an example, as shown in the following extract:

Extract 10.28: GKN plc (1998)

3 Operating Profit [extract]

Depreciation is not provided on freehold land. In the case of buildings and computers, depreciation is provided on valuation or original cost. For all other categories of asset, depreciation is provided on the written down value at the beginning of the financial year. Except in special cases, depreciation is not charged on fixed assets capitalised during the year and available for use but a full year's depreciation is charged on fixed assets sold or scrapped during the year.

In fact, charging a full year's depreciation in the year of disposal only affects the classification of the profit and loss account, because it changes the gain or loss reported on sale by an equal and opposite amount. GKN's practice of providing no depreciation in the first year is probably convenient, and is unlikely to create a material distortion in practice, but in principle depreciation should be charged from the date the asset is brought into use.

3.3.5   *Residual values*

Both FRS 15 and the Act require residual values to be taken into account when calculating depreciation on an asset. The original SSAP 12 stated in its explanatory note that where residual value was likely to be small in relation to cost it was convenient to regard it as nil.[79] As noted at 3.3.2 above, the ASB proposed a similar assertion in FRED 17 as a means of combating the arguments of some companies who were resisting the need to depreciate, but later retreated from that stance.

The residual value must be based on prices prevailing at the time of purchase or subsequent revaluation. For example, if an asset has an estimated useful life of six years, the company should look at the net realisable value of a six year old equivalent asset as at the date of purchase rather than considering how much the asset can be sold for in six years' time. Other factors to be taken into account will include location (in the case of property), the risk of obsolescence and the planned maintenance policy. This obviously makes an accurate assessment of residual value difficult.

Basing residual values on prices prevailing at the time of purchase means that it is not permitted to anticipate inflationary holding gains. During periods of price increases, and other things being equal, a company that has calculated the residual value in accordance with the requirements of the standard will provide more depreciation than is necessary to reduce the carrying value to the actual sales proceeds, which will result in a profit on disposal of the asset being reported.

SSAP 12 was silent on adjustments to residual values but FRS 15 requires material residual values to be reassessed at the end of each reporting period to take account of the effects of technological changes (if possible, still at price levels consistent with the date of acquisition or revaluation). Changes to the residual value should result in a prospective write off over the remaining useful life unless they indicate that the asset has been impaired at the balance sheet date.[80]

Technological change affects many assets, not only high technology plant and equipment such as computers. Many buildings, including those purpose-built as offices in the post-war period, have become technologically obsolete long before their fabric has been impaired, perhaps because it is not possible to introduce modern computer technology or air conditioning. Contemporary buildings may be affected in the same way because they may not be capable of being adapted to new technologies that may become commonplace over the next decades.

3.3.6   *Depreciation methods*

There is little discussion of depreciation methods in either FRS 15 or SSAP 12. FRS 15 simply says that 'the depreciation method should reflect as fairly as possible the pattern in which the asset's economic benefits are consumed'.[81] The standard describes only two depreciation methods, straight line and reducing balance.

A change from one method of providing depreciation to another is permitted only if the new method will more fairly present the enterprise's results and financial position. A change of method is not a change in accounting policy, and should accordingly be accounted for prospectively.[82]

Some of the possible methods of charging depreciation are explained below.

A   Straight line method

The asset is written off in equal instalments over its estimated useful life. The method is easy to apply, and also allows revisions to estimates to be made easily. FRS 15 suggests that this method is usually adopted as a default, where the pattern of consumption of economic benefits is uncertain.[83]

Example 10.1   Straight line depreciation

An asset costs £8,000 and has a residual value of nil. Depreciation is to be provided at 25% on a straight line basis.

		£
Year 1	Cost	8,000
	Depreciation at 25% of £8,000	2,000
	Net book value	6,000
Year 2	Depreciation at 25% of £8,000	2,000
	Net book value	4,000
Year 3	Depreciation at 25% of £8,000	2,000
	Net book value	2,000
Year 4	Depreciation at 25% of £8,000	2,000
	Net book value	–

B   Reducing balance method

The same percentage of the asset's net book value is written off annually. FRS 15 suggests that this method more closely reflects the pattern of consumption of the economic benefits of assets that provide greater benefits when new than when they become older, perhaps because the asset has become more prone to breakdown or because the asset will become relatively disadvantaged by technological advances.[84] It is also frequently argued in favour of this method that the depreciation charge complements the costs of maintaining and running the asset. In the early years these costs are low and the depreciation charge is high, while in later years this is reversed.

Example 10.2   Reducing balance depreciation

An asset costs £8,000. Depreciation is to be provided at 25% on the reducing balance.

		£
Year 1	Cost	8,000
	Depreciation at 25% of £8,000	2,000
	Net book value	6,000
Year 2	Depreciation at 25% of £6,000	1,500
	Net book value	4,500
Year 3	Depreciation at 25% of £4,500	1,125
	Net book value	3,375

Under this method, the carrying value of the asset is never completely written off.

C   *Other reducing balance methods*

(a)   *Double declining balance*

This method is sometimes applied in the US, where it has corresponded to tax allowances on assets. The method involves determining the asset's depreciation on a straight line basis over its useful life. This annual amount is multiplied by an appropriate factor (it does not have to be doubled) to give the first year's charge and depreciation at the same percentage rate is charged on the reducing balance in subsequent years.

Example 10.3   Double declining balance depreciation

An asset costs £6,000 and has a life of ten years, which means that, calculated on the straight line basis, the annual depreciation charge would be £600. On the double declining balance method (assuming a factor of two), the depreciation charge for the first year would be £1,200 and depreciation would continue to be charged at 20% on the reducing balance thereafter.

(b)   *Sum of digits*

This is another form of reducing balance method, but one that is based on the estimated life of the asset and which can therefore easily be applied if the asset has a residual value. If an asset has an estimated useful life of four years then the digits 1, 2, 3, and 4 are added together, giving a total of 10. Depreciation of four-tenths, three-tenths and so on, of the cost of the asset, less any residual value, will be charged in the respective years. The method is sometimes called the 'rule of 78', 78 being the sum of the digits 1 to 12.

Example 10.4   Sum of the digits depreciation

An asset costs £10,000 and is expected to be sold for £2,000 after four years. Depreciation is to be provided over four years using the sum of the digits method.

		£
Year 1	Cost	10,000
	Depreciation at $^4/_{10}$ of £8,000	3,200
	Net book value	6,800
Year 2	Depreciation at $^3/_{10}$ of £8,000	2,400
	Net book value	4,400
Year 3	Depreciation at $^2/_{10}$ of £8,000	1,600
	Net book value	2,800
Year 4	Depreciation at $^1/_{10}$ of £8,000	800
	Net book value	2,000

(c)   Reducing percentage

Another method which is sometimes used, and may represent an approximation to one of the previous methods, is to set predetermined proportions of the asset which are to be written off in each year of the asset's life. An example of a company using this method for certain of its assets in 1996 was RMC Group.

Extract 10.29: RMC Group p.l.c. (1996)

Accounting Policies
DEPRECIATION AND DEPLETION

Depreciation is calculated to write off the cost of tangible fixed assets over their expected useful lives using the straight line basis, except as referred to below. ...

Commercial vehicles in the United Kingdom are depreciated over a period of 5 to 8 years on a reducing percentage basis, which reflects value consumed. ...

D   Annuity method

This is a method where account is taken of the cost of capital notionally invested in the asset. Notional interest and depreciation combined will give an approximately constant charge to revenue: depreciation is therefore low in the early years when the capital invested is high.

BOC applies this method to certain of its production plants, as illustrated below:

Extract 10.30: The BOC Group plc (1998)

Accounting policies
Tangible fixed assets [extract]

No depreciation is charged on freehold land or construction in progress. Depreciation is charged on all other fixed assets on the straight line basis over the effective lives except for certain tonnage plants where depreciation is calculated on an annuity basis over the life of the contract.

These 'tonnage plants' are built to supply specific long-term fixed contract customers.

As mentioned at 3.3.2 above, some argue that such a method is appropriate for assets such as mineral reserves, because it reflects the fact that the value of the asset (on a net present value basis) tends to decline only as the end of its life approaches. Perhaps a more powerful way of expressing the argument would be that, if the asset generates cash flows evenly over a long period, it is in that respect analogous to a lease receivable, and the annuity method of depreciation mirrors the accounting treatment which SSAP 21 requires in relation to leases, where a growing proportion of the revenue stream is allocated to write off the capital balance over the life of the lease. There is some merit in that argument, but to apply it consistently it would be necessary to consider all the items in the balance sheet and see how the cost of capital should influence their accounting treatment, not just certain selected assets.

It might be thought that this method is no longer permitted by FRS 15, on the argument that it does not seek to charge the cost of the asset in line with its consumption. However, what really differentiates the annuity method from other approaches is that it also takes account of the cost of capital invested in the fixed asset (in a similar way to the ASB's own impairment test, see 4.4 below). Given that, it would be surprising if the ASB had really wished to ban it, and even more surprising that they did not say so, if that had indeed been their intention.

E   *Unit of production method*

Under this method, the asset is written off in line with its estimated total output. By relating depreciation to productive capacity it reflects the fact that the useful economic life of certain assets, principally machinery, is more closely linked to its usage and output than to time. This method is normally used in extractive industries, for example, to amortise the costs of development of productive oil and gas facilities,[85] as shown in the following extract:

Extract 10.31: BP Amoco p.l.c. (1998)

Accounting policies

Depreciation

Oil and gas production assets are depreciated using a unit-of-production method based upon estimated proved reserves. ...

Each of the various methods of calculating depreciation has its adherents who believe that conceptually it gives the 'best' answer in a given accounting context. In most circumstances the straight line method will give perfectly acceptable results. For certain assets where economic life is more linked to usage than to time, the unit of production method is preferable. As well as the extractive industries mentioned above, this could also apply to vehicles and aircraft. However, a complicating factor here, particularly in the case of aircraft, is that there may be many component parts, each of which has a separate life which may be measured by mileage or hours of service. As discussed at 2.6 above, these may be accounted for individually.

3.3.7 Treatment of minor items

Some types of business may have a very large number of minor fixed assets such as tools, cutlery, containers or sheets and towels. There are practical problems in recording them on an asset-by-asset basis in an asset register; they are difficult to control and frequently lost. The main consequence is that it becomes very difficult to provide depreciation on them.

There are a number of ways in which companies attempt to deal with the problems of depreciating minor assets. The items may be written off to the profit and loss account (the company will probably have a minimum value for capitalising assets), they may be capitalised at a fixed amount, a treatment which is permitted in the Act, or the company may have some other form of policy that writes them off when they are used up but without having to identify them individually.

Some companies capitalise their minor items at a fixed amount, for example, when they are originally provided, as a form of capital 'base stock'; additions are not capitalised and depreciation is not charged. This is permitted under the accounting rules in the Companies Act, which state that tangible fixed assets may be included at a fixed amount provided that their overall value is not material to assessing the company's state of affairs and their quantity, value and composition are not subject to material variation.[86]

Although this is a recognised accounting practice, it does not strictly conform to the requirements of SSAP 12 or FRS 15 that all assets be depreciated, and companies that do apply such a policy do so on the basis that the constant loss and replacement of stock items does lead to a materially constant amount. It is only acceptable as an accounting policy on the grounds of materiality. In periods of inflation the difference between the carrying value of these assets and their actual cost could quickly become very marked, in which case the policy may have to be modified.

3.4   Amortisation of goodwill and intangible assets

The accounting treatment of goodwill and intangible assets is governed by FRS 10. This standard adopts a combination of amortisation and impairment review in attempting to ensure that its objective 'that capitalised goodwill and intangible assets are charged in the profit and loss account in the periods in which they are depleted'[87] is achieved. A flowchart which depicts how the combination of amortisation and impairment review applies to different circumstances is shown below.

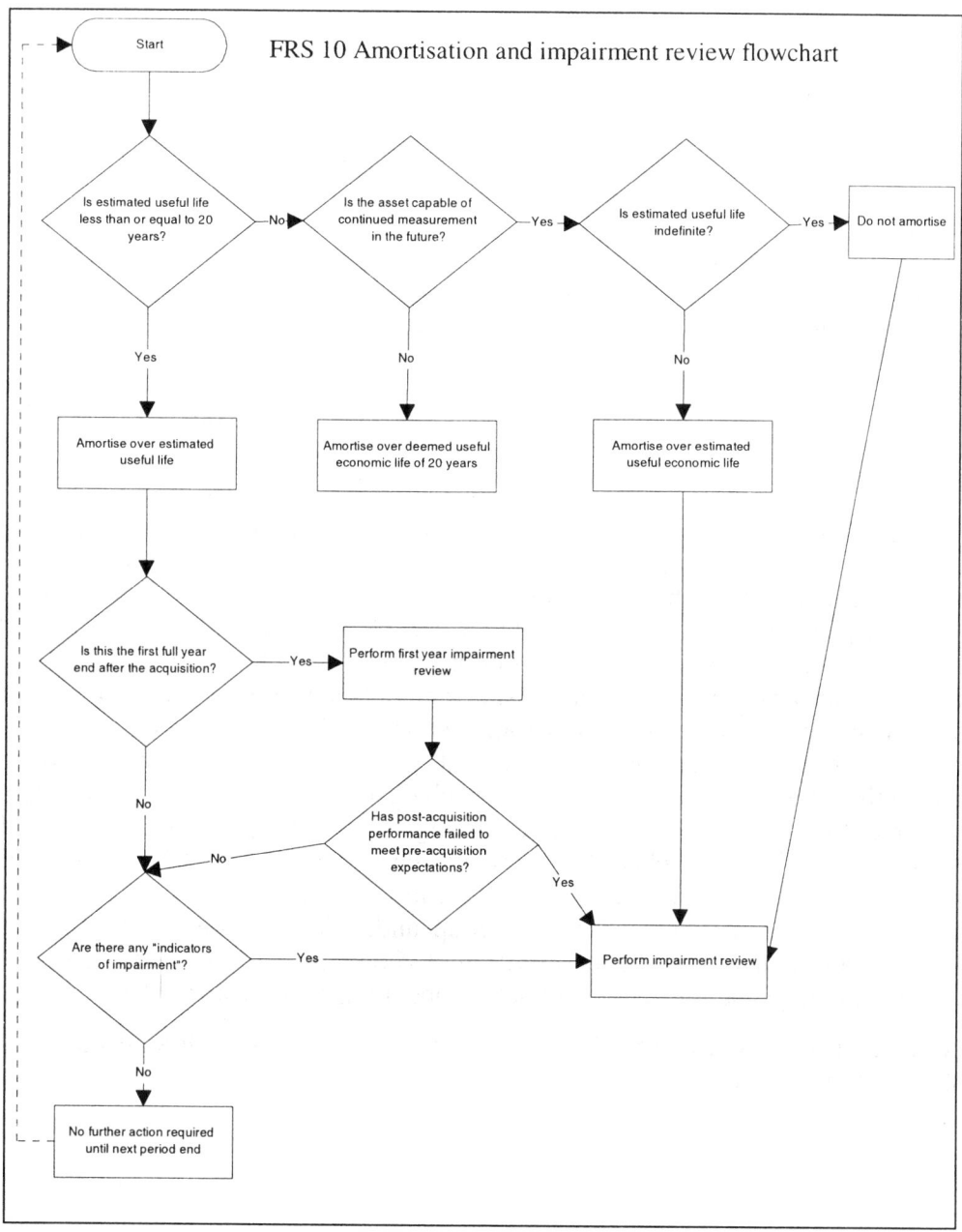

Except for those cases where the useful life of goodwill or an intangible asset is believed to be indefinite, goodwill and intangible assets should be amortised over their estimated useful lives. FRS 10 makes it clear that amortisation of goodwill and intangible assets should be charged to the profit and loss account but it does not explicitly state that it should be charged in arriving at operating profit. Reuters applied the standard early, in its 1997 accounts, but adopted a presentation that excluded the amortisation charge from operating profit as shown below:

Extract 10.32: Reuters Group PLC (1997)

CONSOLIDATED PROFIT AND LOSS ACCOUNT FOR THE YEAR ENDED 31 DECEMBER [extract]

	1997	1996	1995
	£M	£M	£M
Revenue	**2,882**	2,914	2,703
Operating costs	**(2,290)**	(2,273)	(2,152)
Operating profit	**592**	641	551
Goodwill amortisation	**(51)**	(49)	(41)
	541	592	510

...

This attracted the attention of the Financial Reporting Review Panel,[88] who raised the matter with the company. The Panel's view was that 'the formats set out in Schedule 4 to the Companies Act 1985 prescribe the headings under which depreciation and other amounts written off tangible and intangible fixed assets – ie including goodwill amortisation – are to be included in the profit and loss account. Under formats 1 and 3 such amounts are to be included in cost of sales, distribution costs and administrative expenses. Under formats 2 and 4 they are to be shown as a separate heading. In all four formats the headings to which goodwill amortisation is required to be charged appear before the line item 'income from shares in group undertakings'. Operating profit is not itself referred to within the Schedule 4 formats. Paragraph 39 of FRS 3, however, indicates that for non-financial reporting entities, operating profit is normally profit before income from shares in group undertakings. Consequently in the Panel's view a charge for the amortisation of goodwill should be classified as an operating charge and thus deducted before operating profit is arrived at.'[89]

As a result of this, Reuters changed its presentation in the 1998 accounts, as shown in this extract:

Extract 10.33: Reuters Group PLC (1998)

Consolidated profit and loss account for the year ended 31 December [extract]

	1998 £M	1997 £M	1996 £M
Revenue	**3,032**	2,882	2,914
Operating costs	**(2,482)**	(2,341)	(2,322)
Operating profit	**550**	541	592

3.4.1 Useful economic life

The standard includes a rebuttable presumption that the useful economic lives of purchased goodwill and intangible assets are limited and do not exceed 20 years. This is consistent with the IASC standard,[90] which is surprising because the two have a quite different philosophy. FRS 10 defines the useful economic life very broadly, as 'the period over which the value of the underlying business acquired is expected to exceed the values of its identifiable net assets',[91] whereas IAS 22 focuses more conventionally on the benefits that flow from the particular goodwill that exists at the time of the acquisition.

The implication of the ASB's definition encourages the view that the life is normally indefinite, and not just in exceptional cases; when will an acquirer ever predict that the value of the business it is buying will not be maintained at a level in excess of the identifiable assets? This definition really highlights a major change in thinking in FRS 10 compared to previous approaches; it ignores the formerly accepted wisdom, which still underlies the international standard, that purchased goodwill tends to diminish over time and be replaced by internally generated goodwill. This also has important implications for the impairment review which is discussed at 4 below.

In practice, most preparers seem to have ignored the strict definition of the useful economic life of goodwill within FRS 10 and adopted an approach more consistent with that in IAS 22. The predominant practice has been to apply an amortisation approach rather than relying on the view that the value of the goodwill will be maintained indefinitely. In practice, the impairment test has been seen to be very onerous, and this has been a powerful disincentive for companies to argue that the life of the goodwill will exceed 20 years.

Tesco provides a typical example of the goodwill policy disclosed by companies on the adoption of FRS 10.

Extract 10.34: Tesco PLC (1999)

Accounting policies

Goodwill

The Group has adopted Financial Reporting Standard 10, 'Goodwill and Intangible Assets' in its accounts this year. The standard does not require restatement for goodwill arising and taken to reserves in previous years. All goodwill which arose in previous years has been written off through reserves.

Goodwill arising on consolidation as a result of the acquisitions of subsidiaries or joint ventures after 1 March 1998 is capitalised under the heading Intangible Fixed Assets and amortised on a straight line basis over its useful economic life up to a maximum of 20 years.

There are, however, a number of companies who have chosen not to amortise goodwill, including WPP and Cadbury Schweppes as illustrated in Extracts 10.7 at 1.3 above and 10.36 below. Companies who follow this route have to invoke the true and fair override to surmount the Companies Act rule that goodwill be amortised.

FRS 10 defines the useful life of an intangible asset differently from that of goodwill, reflecting a more conventional approach. It is defined as 'the period over which the entity expects to derive economic benefit from that asset'.[92]

The standard goes on to stress that where the economic benefits are achieved through legal rights that have been granted for a finite period, the economic life of the intangible asset may only be assessed as longer than that period if the legal rights are renewable and renewal is assured.[93]

The presumption that the useful life of both goodwill and intangible assets will not exceed 20 years can be rebutted only where:

(a)   the durability of the acquired business or intangible asset can be demonstrated and justifies estimating the useful economic life to exceed 20 years; and

(b)   the goodwill or intangible asset is capable of continued measurement (so that the annual impairment reviews will be feasible).[94]

Durability depends on a number of factors such as:

- the nature of the business
- the stability of the industry in which the acquired business operates
- typical lifespans of the products to which the goodwill attaches
- the extent to which the acquisition overcomes market entry barriers that will continue to exist
- the anticipated future impact of competition on the business.[95]

As shown in the extracts in 1.3 above relating to Diageo, Cadbury Schweppes, WPP and Mirror Group, several companies regard their intangible assets as having an indefinite life and do not amortise them. A further example is Daily Mail, as shown below.

Extract 10.35: Daily Mail and General Trust plc (1998)

Accounting Policies

4. Intangible fixed assets

Publishing rights, titles and certain other intangible assets are stated at fair value as explained in note 18 to the accounts. These assets are valued by management on the basis of cashflow projections, and the values attributed represent the economic value of the assets to the Group at the date of acquisition. Since these assets have no finite life, amortisation is not provided unless there is a permanent diminution in their values, which are re-assessed annually.

Where goodwill or intangible assets have an estimated useful economic life of more than 20 years or the useful economic life is indefinite, but the goodwill or intangibles are not expected to be capable of continued measurement, then, by definition, it is not possible to perform an impairment review as envisaged by the standard. The standard implies that, in such circumstances, the goodwill or intangible asset should be amortised over a deemed useful life of 20 years.

This raises the question as to what 'capable of continued measurement' means. The standard states that 'Goodwill and intangible assets will not be capable of continued measurement if the cost of such measurement is considered to be unjustifiably high. This may be the case when, for example:

- acquired businesses are merged with existing businesses to such an extent that the goodwill associated with the acquired business cannot readily be tracked thereafter; or

- the management information systems used by the entity cannot identify and allocate cash flows at a detailed income-generating unit level; or

- the amounts involved are not sufficiently material to justify undertaking the detailed procedures of annual impairment reviews.'[96]

It is far from clear how the first bullet point fits into the rules for the impairment review where an acquired business is merged with an existing business. This scenario is the subject of detailed procedures, as set out in FRS 11 (and discussed at 4.4.7 below).

The second bullet point appears to be a permission for less sophisticated companies to avoid the impairment test. However, such companies would then have to apply a maximum economic life of 20 years to their goodwill and intangible assets.

One scenario where goodwill may not be capable of continued measurement is where it arises on the acquisition of an associate. Most investors are unlikely to be able to obtain detailed cash flows of their associates in order to perform an impairment review. Accordingly, in most cases, goodwill on associates will be written off over a maximum of 20 years. However, there will be exceptions: Cadbury Schweppes provides an example.

Extract 10.36: Cadbury Schweppes p.l.c. (1998)

1 Nature of Operations and Accounting Policies

In accordance with FRS 10 the Group has concluded that goodwill arising in 1998 on its associates, The American Bottling Company ("ABC") and Amalgamated Beverage Industries Ltd ("ABI"), should not be amortised as it has an indefinite useful economic life. Both of these investments are considered to have indefinite durability that can be demonstrated, and the value of both investments can be readily measured.

ABC operates in a longstanding and profitable market sector; the US soft drinks bottling industry has over 100 years of history. The sector has high market entry barriers due to the nature of licence agreements with soft drink concentrate owners (including the Group's subsidiary Dr Pepper/Seven Up, Inc. ("DPSU")) and the capital required to operate as a bottler and distributor. As an associate, the company is managed separately from the Group and can be valued on a discounted cash flow basis.

ABI operates in the South African soft drinks bottling industry with similar high market entry barriers and has valuable licence agreements (including with the Group's subsidiary, Cadbury Schweppes (South Africa) Ltd) which give it market leadership in significant regions of the country, including Johannesburg. ABI is a listed company and the value of the Group's investment can be determined by reference to the share price.

The Group has not amortised this goodwill, a departure from the Companies Act 1985 Paragraph 21 of Schedule 4, for the over-riding purpose of giving a true and fair view of the Group's results, for the reasons outlined above. If the goodwill arising on ABC and ABI had been amortised over a period of 20 years, operating profit and investment in associates would have decreased by £5m in 1998.

Even where goodwill or intangible assets are believed to have useful economic lives of 20 years or less, the impairment review might still have to be performed. What must be done, in these circumstances, if the goodwill or intangible asset is not 'capable of continued measurement'? FRS 10 is silent on this point. However, it seems to follow that if continued measurement is not possible then the impairment review cannot be performed. Therefore, in these circumstances, the asset would be subject to an annual amortisation charge but, apparently, not to an impairment test. Again, it is far from clear how this apparent exemption in FRS 10 correlates to the requirements of FRS 11 which, explicitly at least, gives no similar exemption.

Although the useful economic life of goodwill and intangibles is often uncertain, the standard makes it clear that this uncertainty should not be grounds for regarding the useful economic life to be indefinite or for adopting a 20 year period by default.[97]

By the same token, while the useful economic life should be estimated on a prudent basis, this does not imply that an unrealistically short period should be selected (for example, one year).[98] Nor can it be argued that goodwill or an intangible asset should be written off because it has been impaired, unless that impairment can be justified by reference to an impairment test.

The useful lives of goodwill and intangible assets should also be reviewed where an impairment review has been triggered by an indicator of impairment, even if that impairment review did not identify an impairment loss.[99]

As is the case with tangible fixed assets, it is necessary to review the estimated useful lives of goodwill and intangible assets at the end of each reporting period and revise them as necessary. If the useful economic life is revised (either extended or shortened), then the carrying value of the goodwill or intangible assets at the date of revision should be amortised over their remaining useful lives. If the estimated useful economic life is extended such that the effect is to extend the useful economic life to more than 20 years *from the date of acquisition*, the additional requirements of the standard which apply to goodwill and intangible assets that are amortised over periods of more than 20 years, or are not amortised, then become applicable. This means that an impairment review will be required at the end of each financial year.[100]

3.4.2 Residual values

In amortising goodwill, no residual value may be attributed to it.[101] (This corresponds to the requirements of the Companies Act 1985). In contrast, a residual value may be assigned to an intangible asset, but only if such residual value can be 'measured reliably'.[102] FRS 10 suggests that, in most cases, the residual value of an intangible asset may be insignificant and will be capable of being measured reliably only when:

(a)   there is a legal or contractual right to receive a certain sum at the end of the period of use of the intangible asset; or

(b)   there is a readily ascertainable market value for the residual asset.[103]

This is a different use of the term 'measured reliably' from that adopted in the recognition rules within the standard (as discussed at 1.3 above).

3.4.3 Amortisation methods

Having established the original carrying value of the goodwill or intangible asset, its estimated useful economic life and the amount of its residual value (if applicable), the only remaining question as regards amortisation is how to spread the difference between the original carrying value and the residual value (if any) over the estimated useful economic life. The standard states that 'the method of amortisation should be chosen to reflect the expected pattern of depletion of the goodwill or intangible asset. A straight line method should be chosen unless another method can be demonstrated to be more appropriate'.[104] The straight line basis is an obvious pragmatic response to the need to allocate what is a derived figure over different accounting periods. An example of where an intangible asset can be amortised other than on a straight line basis would be where a licence entitles the holder to produce a finite quantity of a product. The method of amortisation could be, in those circumstances, on a unit-of-production basis.

FRS 10 appears to frown on methods of amortisation for goodwill which are less conservative than a straight line basis, but without explicitly prohibiting them.[105] There is no equivalent view expressed in relation to intangible assets. However, the standard does prohibit methods of amortisation of goodwill which aim to produce a constant rate of return on the carrying value of an investment.[106] Hence an annuity approach (see 3.3.6 D above) is ruled out. This is somewhat ironic given that the impairment review will normally involve a discounted cash flow test which has the effect of producing a carrying value for goodwill which, assuming perfect knowledge of the future, could lead to a constant rate of return on the carrying value of assets!

In any event, such methods have always been rare for goodwill. One example of a rising amortisation profile, now ten years old, was seen in the accounts of Charterhall for 1989.

Extract 10.37: Charterhall PLC (1989)

INTANGIBLE ASSETS [extract]
Goodwill

On the acquisition of subsidiaries and businesses, the purchase consideration is allocated over the underlying net tangible assets, significant intangible assets and goodwill. Goodwill arising on the acquisition of subsidiaries has been capitalised and is amortised (after taking account of the anticipated impact of inflation on future earnings) through the Profit and Loss Account over a period not exceeding 40 years, estimated by the Directors to be the useful economic life.

On the acquisition of associated companies which are deemed non-core activities, goodwill is written off to Reserves.

3.4.4   Negative goodwill

Negative goodwill arises in accounting for an acquisition where the amount paid for a business is less than the fair value of the net assets acquired. FRS 10 requires, somewhat surprisingly, that it should be shown as a negative asset in the balance sheet immediately after any positive goodwill, with a sub-total of the net amount of positive and negative goodwill also shown.[107] The ASB argues that the requirement to include negative goodwill within the 'assets' section of the balance sheet ensures consistency with the treatment of positive goodwill. Some standards internationally require negative goodwill to be offset against the fair value of fixed assets acquired. The ASB rejected this argument on the grounds that it would mean that these assets would be valued at something other than their fair value, contrary to the requirements of FRS 7. What is not so clear is why the ASB did not recommend that negative goodwill be included as a deferred credit in the balance sheet. It may be because it is demonstrably not a liability under the Board's draft *Statement of principles*, but that hardly justifies showing it as a negative asset.

FRS 10 requires that negative goodwill is subsequently released to the profit and loss account on one of two bases discussed below. This represents a change from

FRED 12, which had said that releases of negative goodwill should be credited to the statement of total recognised gains and losses.[108] The ASB dropped this proposal in the light of responses received from a number of commentators who argued that such treatment would be inconsistent with the treatment of positive goodwill.

The primary basis on which negative goodwill is to be released to the profit and loss account is over the periods in which the non-monetary assets are recovered, whether through depreciation or sale.[109] This was probably intended to mirror the effect, in profit and loss account terms, of applying the goodwill to reduce the amounts attributed to fixed assets, as discussed above. However, whether by design or accident, the ASB has widened the scope of this by referring to 'non-monetary assets', which includes items such as stocks. Since stocks usually turn over relatively quickly, any negative goodwill up to the fair value of the stocks is capable of being released to the profit and loss account over a short period following the acquisition.

Any negative goodwill in excess of the fair values of non-monetary assets acquired should be released to the profit and loss account 'in the periods expected to be benefited'.[110] This wording would make sense in relation to the amortisation of an asset, but it is incomprehensible in relation to the release of a pseudo-liability. Any reasonable interpretation is likely to be acceptable. Hopefully, this particular rule will only be relevant in rare circumstances, when the negative goodwill exceeds the non-monetary assets acquired. Where it does apply, the amount of negative goodwill being released in this way is to be disclosed, together with an explanation of where it came from and the period over which it is being released.[111]

Although the positioning is not specifically dealt with in the standard, we believe that releases of negative goodwill should be credited in arriving at operating profit, in the same way as positive goodwill is charged there.

Babcock has a significant amount of negative goodwill, which in fact exceeds its positive goodwill and gives rise to a net credit in its profit and loss account when both these amounts are amortised, as shown in this extract.

Extract 10.38: Babcock International Group PLC (1999)

1) Accounting policies

Goodwill

When the fair value of the consideration for an acquired undertaking exceeds the fair value of its separable net assets the difference is treated as purchased goodwill and is capitalised and amortised through the profit and loss account over its estimated economic life. The estimated economic life of goodwill is between ten and twenty years.

Where the fair value of the separable net assets exceeds the fair value of the consideration for an acquired undertaking the difference is treated as negative goodwill and is capitalised and amortised through the profit and loss account in the period in which the non-monetary assets acquired are recovered. In the case of fixed assets this is the period over which they are depreciated and in the case of current assets, the period over which they are sold or otherwise realised.

12) Fixed assets – intangible assets

	Goodwill £'000	Negative goodwill £'000	Development costs £'000	Total £'000
Cost				
At 1 April 1998	27,064	(34,406)	3,255	**(4,087)**
Additions	–	–	17	**17**
On acquisition of subsidiaries	4,488	–	–	**4,488**
Reduction in deferred consideration	(465)	–	–	**(465)**
Exchange adjustment	–	–	95	**95**
On disposal of subsidiaries	(164)	–	–	**(164)**
At 31 March 1999	30,923	(34,406)	3,367	**(116)**
Accumulated amortisation				
At 1 April 1998	(7,544)	7,846	(2,833)	**(2,531)**
Exchange adjustment	–	–	(81)	**(81)**
Charge for the year	(1,630)	3,967	(270)	**2,067**
On disposal of subsidiaries	93	–	–	**93**
At 31 March 1999	(9,081)	11,813	(3,184)	**(452)**
Net book value at 31 March 1999	21,842	(22,593)	183	**(568)**
Net book value at 31 March 1998	19,520	(26,560)	422	**(6,618)**

The standard states quite clearly that purchased goodwill arising on a single transaction should not be divided into positive and negative components.[112] It is unclear whether this rule relates purely to presentation or whether it relates to subsequent measurement generally. If the standard is referring to the latter, then some counter-intuitive results may ensue.

For example, there may be a number of different income-generating units acquired as a result of one transaction. Since the impairment tests are required to be performed for each income-generating unit, the net goodwill has to be allocated across each of the income-generating units. If the net goodwill cannot be allocated into negative and positive components, the allocation of goodwill across the income-generating units will not necessarily reflect the 'true' positive and negative goodwill attaching to each income-generating unit. The impairment review would, accordingly, be distorted as a result.

Also, if part of an acquired business is subsequently disposed of, the gain or loss on disposal of that business should reflect its share of the original goodwill. If no splitting of positive and negative goodwill is allowed, the allocation of the goodwill to the business disposed of will not necessarily reflect its proper share of the original goodwill.

3.4.5   *Goodwill arising before FRS 10*

FRS 10 does not apply mandatorily to goodwill that arose in periods before the standard was first applied. Although it is permitted to bring this old goodwill on to the same basis as the new goodwill, the ASB has acknowledged that this will often be impracticable. Consequently, old goodwill may continue to be accounted for under the previously existing accounting rules.

These previous rules had a long and chequered history. The ASC first considered the matter in a Discussion Paper published in 1980.[113] This recommended that goodwill should be carried as a fixed asset in the balance sheet and subjected to annual amortisation, and written down to its recoverable amount to recognise any permanent impairment in value which became evident. It rejected the notion that it could be carried as a permanent asset without amortisation.

Two years later, however, when the Committee issued an exposure draft (ED 30) on the subject, it had retreated from the attempt to mandate a single treatment; either amortisation through the profit and loss account or immediate elimination through reserves was to be permitted, provided the policy was applied consistently.[114] This choice was maintained in the eventual accounting standard, SSAP 22, which was issued at the end of 1984, but by now the direct write-off treatment had become the preferred one.[115]

As well as permitting two different treatments, which were based on different philosophical views on the nature of goodwill, SSAP 22 (unlike ED 30) even allowed the same company to choose between the different methods to be applied in relation to different acquisitions. One company which adopted such a policy is Chloride Group, as shown below:

Extract 10.39: Chloride Group PLC (1999)

1 Accounting policies

Goodwill [extract]

Goodwill arising on consolidation represents the excess of fair value of the consideration given over the fair value of the separable net assets acquired. Goodwill in respect of acquisitions made prior to 1 April 1998 was either written off directly against reserves or, alternatively, was capitalised and amortised over an appropriate period. Goodwill in respect of acquisitions made since 1 April 1998 is shown as an asset (in accordance with FRS 10) and each acquisition is assessed to determine the useful economic life of the business and goodwill.

There were also instances of companies who started accounting for goodwill under one policy and changed to the alternative policy soon thereafter; most commonly this involved changing from amortisation to direct write-off (perhaps after adequate reserves had been built up to absorb the write-off), but there were also some instances of companies who moved in the opposite direction.

This extreme form of flexibility of approach led to substantial criticism of the standard, whose only real effect had therefore been to outlaw the practice of carrying goodwill as a permanent asset without amortisation.

In view of the criticism received, the ASC reconsidered its stance in relation to goodwill and in 1990 it issued ED 47 – *Accounting for goodwill* – which proposed that goodwill should be recognised as a fixed asset and should be amortised through the profit and loss account; the option of writing it off immediately to reserves was not to be allowed. The ASC had therefore turned full circle since issuing its initial views on the matter in the Discussion Paper published ten years before. However, the ASB did not pick up ED 47 when it took office later that year and did not issue a revised standard until seven years later.

By far the predominant practice under SSAP 22, therefore, was to take goodwill to reserves and leave it there. The only further embellishment that later emerged was a requirement to channel it through the profit and loss account if the business it related to was subsequently sold, as part of the gain or loss on sale. The UITF ruled on this matter in December 1991 by issuing Abstract 3 – *Treatment of Goodwill on Disposal of a Business*. This states that 'the amount included in the consolidated profit and loss account in respect of the profit or loss on disposal of a previously acquired business, subsidiary or associated undertaking should be determined by including, if material, the attributable goodwill where it has previously been eliminated against reserves as a matter of accounting policy and has not previously been charged in the profit and loss account'.[116]

It can be seen that it was not only on the disposal of a subsidiary that any goodwill had to be taken into account, but also on the disposal of a business or an associate. In addition, the principle also applied to closures of businesses and to negative goodwill.[117] UITF 3 required the amount of the goodwill included in the calculation to be separately disclosed as a component of the profit or loss on disposal, either on the face of the profit and loss account or in a note to the financial statements.[118]

A supplementary issue which the UITF considered was whether the amount of the goodwill brought into the calculation should be the gross amount that has been eliminated against reserves or whether some allowance should be made for any notional amortisation during the period of ownership. The UITF concluded that, 'if there has been no charge in the profit and loss account in respect of the premium paid on acquisition, the gross attributable amount should be brought into the calculation'.[119] This was to ensure that none of the goodwill bypasses the profit and loss account.

Although UITF 3 only dealt with the treatment of goodwill on the disposal and closure of businesses, some companies extended the principle to situations where goodwill had become permanently impaired, as illustrated below:

Extract 10.40: Saatchi & Saatchi Company PLC (1993)

GOODWILL

Goodwill, including any additional goodwill arising from the contingent capital payments disclosed in Note 22, is written off directly to reserves in the year in which it arises. A charge is recognised in the Group's profit and loss account in respect of any permanent diminution in value of acquisition goodwill.

CONSOLIDATED PROFIT AND LOSS ACCOUNT [extract]

	Note:	Total Year ended 31 Dec 1993 £ million	Total Year ended 31 Dec 1992 £ million
TRADING PROFIT		36.8	34.2
Write down of goodwill reserves	4	–	(600.0)
OPERATING PROFIT (LOSS)		36.8	(565.8)

4. EXCEPTIONAL ITEMS [extract]

The write down of goodwill reserves in 1992 arose from a review of the cost of acquired goodwill and assessment of permanent diminution in value.

The ruling made by the UITF in Abstract 3 was later reinforced by FRS 2 in relation to subsidiaries. This standard requires that where a subsidiary undertaking is disposed of, the gain or loss should be calculated 'by comparing the carrying amount of the net assets of that subsidiary undertaking attributable to the group's interest before the cessation with any remaining carrying amount attributable to the group's interest after the cessation together with any proceeds received. The net assets compared should include any related goodwill not previously written-off through the profit and loss account.'[120] Since FRS 2 only addressed consolidated accounts, UITF 3 was left in force to deal with associates and unincorporated businesses, but it has now been superseded by FRS 10[121] although without any change to the principle involved.

For companies that elect not to resurrect old goodwill from reserves on implementing FRS 10, therefore, this remains the regime. Goodwill remains in reserves unless and until the business concerned is disposed of, at which point it is recycled through the profit and loss account. By far the majority of companies have decided to follow this route. Williams is one example.

Extract 10.41: Williams Holdings PLC (1998)

1 Accounting policies

Basis of preparation

The financial statements have been prepared in accordance with applicable accounting standards using the historical cost convention adjusted for revaluations of certain tangible fixed assets. FRS 10 "Goodwill and Intangible Assets" has been adopted in 1998. Goodwill arising on 1998 acquisitions has been capitalised in intangible fixed assets and amortised over expected useful economic lives. Goodwill arising in earlier years has remained offset against other reserves. As required by FRS 10, the negative balance on other reserves at 1st January 1998, arising from goodwill offset, has been transferred to the profit and loss account reserve.

NatWest, however, is an example of a company that has chosen to reinstate old goodwill, as shown below.

Extract 10.42: National Westminster Bank Plc (1998)

1 Principal accounting policies

Change of accounting policy and presentation

The Group's accounting policy for goodwill has been changed in line with FRS 10 'Goodwill and Intangible Assets'. Purchased goodwill is capitalised, classified as an asset and amortised over its useful economic life. The gain or loss on the disposal of a subsidiary or associated undertaking is calculated by comparing the carrying value of the net assets sold (including any unamortised goodwill) with the proceeds received. Previously the Group's policy was for goodwill to be either deducted from profit and loss account reserves or capitalised. Goodwill eliminated from reserves in prior periods has been reinstated by means of a prior year adjustment and comparatives restated. The effects of this change of policy on the Group's profit and loss account and balance sheet are set out in note 26 on page 97.

26 Intangible fixed assets [extract]

Effect of change of accounting policy for goodwill		Year ended 31 December	
	1998 **£m**	1997 £m	1996 £m
Profit and loss account			
Profit before tax on previous basis	**2,113**	1,011	1,122
Additional goodwill amortisation	**(32)**	(42)	(56)
Decrease in loss on disposal or termination of businesses	**61**	6	271
Profit before tax on new basis	**2,142**	975	1,337

Perhaps rather surprisingly, the effect on NatWest's profit for 1998 was to increase it. Although it now has to bear an extra amortisation charge, the amount of goodwill that has to be accounted for in the profit and loss account on disposal of a business is reduced. This is because most of the goodwill that was formerly offset in reserves (£278 million) would have been amortised by now if the new policy had always been in force. Accordingly, only £90 million (i.e. the £278 million net of £188 million amortisation attributed to earlier years) has been reinstated as an asset, and the £188 million no longer has to be dealt with in subsequent profit and loss accounts when businesses are disposed of.

Where companies do leave old goodwill in reserves, FRS 10 says that it must be offset against the profit and loss account or another appropriate reserve, which explains why Williams made the transfer mentioned in Extract 10.41 above. In addition, the amount by which the reserve has been reduced by this offset must not be disclosed on the face of the balance sheet.[122] This curious prohibition relates to a practice which developed under SSAP 22 of taking the goodwill, not to any particular reserve, but to a special 'goodwill write-off reserve', which therefore often had a debit balance equal to the amount of the goodwill, although there were many other combinations and variants of this treatment. The ASB clearly regarded this as an undesirable practice and no longer permits it, although it remains possible to show the goodwill element separately in a note, as in this extract from Cookson's accounts. Cookson's balance sheet shows a negative balance of £355.8 million on its profit and loss account reserve, but the reserves note explodes that amount into two columns to show that a goodwill element of £532.5 million is offset by retained earnings of £176.7 million, thus:

Extract 10.43: Cookson Group plc (1998)

26 Reserves

Group	Profit and loss account			Other reserves	Other reserves
	Pre-1998 goodwill £m	Other £m	Total £m	£m	£m
At 1 January 1998	–	191.7	191.7	(294.4)	(102.7)
Exchange adjustments	–	(5.6)	(5.6)	–	(5.6)
Transfer of goodwill	(587.2)	–	(587.2)	587.2	–
Other transfers	–	75.3	75.3	(75.3)	–
Goodwill written back on disposals	54.7	–	54.7	–	54.7
Net loss transferred from profit and loss account	–	(84.7)	(84.7)	–	(84.7)
At 31 December 1998	(532.5)	176.7	(355.8)	217.5	(138.3)

Cookson is slightly unusual in dealing with this change as a reserve transfer within the year, whereas most companies have done it by a prior year adjustment involving the reclassification of previously reported figures. However, this is not really an important difference.

3.5   Investment properties

When SSAP 12 was being developed, the property industry was quick to campaign against it, as a result of which they gained a temporary exemption for investment properties when SSAP 12[123] was published in December 1977. This was originally intended to last for one year, but was progressively extended. ED 26[124] was issued by the ASC in September 1980, with the objective that it should form the basis of an additional section to SSAP 12, dealing specifically with the accounting for investment properties, but in fact it led ultimately to the publication of a separate standard. The ASC published a statement together with ED 26 setting out this reasoning for a special accounting treatment for investment properties:

'It is ... persuasively argued that a different treatment is required for a fixed asset which is not held for "consumption" in the business operations of an enterprise but is held as a disposable investment. In such a case the current value of the investment, and changes in that current value, are of prime importance rather than a calculation of systematic annual depreciation.

'The argument therefore proceeds:

(a) the financial statements of enterprises holding investments are more helpful to users of financial statements if the investments are accounted for at current values rather than on the basis of a cost or valuation established some time in the past; and

(b) depreciation is only one element which enters into the annual change in the value of a property and as the use of a current value places the prime emphasis on the values of the assets, it is not generally useful to attempt to distinguish, estimate and account separately for the element of depreciation; and

(c) depreciation, although not separately identified, will be taken into account in dealing with changes in current values.'[125]

ED 26 led to SSAP 19, which was published in 1981 and requires investment properties to be carried at the current market valuation without provision for depreciation, except in the case of leasehold properties where the lease has fewer than 20 years remaining. An investment property is defined as an interest in land and/or buildings:

(a) in respect of which construction work and development have been completed; and

(b) which is held for its investment potential, any rental income being negotiated at arm's length.[126]

Excluded from this definition are properties owned and occupied by a company for its own purposes and properties let to and occupied by other companies in the same group.[127] It should also be noted that this definition is not confined to properties held by property companies. Charities were originally exempted from SSAP 19,[128] but FRS 15 has now removed this exemption.[129]

While the position of the property industry was being considered, it was necessary also to consider the EU Fourth Directive, enacted in the UK in 1981, which made depreciation a legal requirement. A compromise was eventually reached based on the proposition that to depreciate investment properties would lead to the accounts not giving a true and fair view, and it was therefore necessary to invoke the 'true and fair override'.[130] This remains a controversial use of the override, however, and the European Commission has questioned it from time to time.

Although the standard was issued shortly after the Fourth Directive was enacted in the UK, the rules in SSAP 19 relating to revaluation deficits were inconsistent with those in the Companies Act (see 5.3.2 below) until the ASB made a limited amendment to the standard in July 1994 to bring it into line with the Act.[131]

In its 1996 Discussion Paper, the Board considered the whole issue more fully, and examined a number of arguments that it said had frequently been advanced to justify non-depreciation of investment properties:

■ the tenant is required to maintain the property to a specified standard

- the valuation of an investment property takes account of depreciation
- depreciation reduces distributable reserves
- there are practical difficulties in measuring depreciation
- investment properties play a fundamentally different role from owner-occupied properties and for this reason it is appropriate to adopt a different accounting treatment.

The paper dismissed the first four of these, but the Board was divided on the merits of the last issue. In the event, however, no change to the existing exemption from depreciation has been made, and FRS 15 scopes out investment properties,[132] with the result that SSAP 19 remains intact for the time being.

4   IMPAIRMENT

4.1   Introduction

The requirement to write-down fixed assets whose carrying value, even after depreciation, cannot be justified has long been a feature of UK accounting practice. Until recently, there was little detailed guidance to support this broad principle; however, in 1998 the ASB published FRS 11, and this now contains extensive and complex rules on how impairment is to be determined. FRS 11 is described in detail in 4.4 below.

This section covers impairment both in general and as it applies to assets carried at historical cost. The specific problems relating to assets carried at valuation are dealt with in 5.3.4 below.

4.2   Companies Act requirements

The Act requires provisions for diminution in value to be made in respect of any fixed asset if the reduction in value is expected to be permanent.

The provisions are to be made through the profit and loss account.[133] Provisions no longer required are to be written back, again through the profit and loss account.[134] In either case, amounts not shown in the profit and loss account must be disclosed in the notes to the accounts.[135] It should also be noted that, except in the circumstances of a revaluation of all assets (see 5.3.6 below), the Act requires any provision to be treated as a realised loss for distribution purposes whether it is considered to be permanent or temporary.

4.3   SSAP 12 and permanent diminutions

Although primarily concerned with depreciation, SSAP 12 made some passing comments on the treatment of permanent diminutions in value of assets carried at cost. (It specifically excluded revalued assets from this discussion.)[136] SSAP 12 required provisions to be made, if at any time there was a permanent diminution in value, to write the net book amount of the asset down to its estimated recoverable amount. This was then to be written off over the remaining useful life of the asset. If the reasons for making the provision ceased to apply it was to be written back to the profit and loss account.[137]

4.4   FRS 11

4.4.1   *Background*

In April 1996 the ASB published a Discussion Paper on *Impairment of tangible fixed assets*[138] and subsequently broadened its scope, to cover goodwill and intangible assets as well, in an exposure draft, FRED 15, issued in June 1997.[139] This was converted into a standard on 2 July 1998, when the ASB published FRS 11, to become mandatory in respect of financial statements relating to accounting periods ending on or after 23 December 1998.[140]

The objective of the standard is stated as being to ensure that:

(a)   fixed assets and goodwill are recorded in the financial statements at no more than their recoverable amount;

(b)   any resulting impairment loss is measured and recognised on a consistent basis; and

(c)   sufficient information is disclosed in the financial statements to enable users to understand the impact of the impairment on the financial position and performance of the reporting entity.[141]

Fixed assets had previously been written down if they had suffered a permanent diminution in value. However, the FRS explicitly notes[142] that it is concerned with impairments rather than permanent diminutions in value. As discussed below, an impairment is in some cases rather different from a permanent diminution in value and practice has changed accordingly.

However, the ASB argued that it was not actually breaking with accepted practice since it had long been accepted that a fixed asset should not be carried at more than its recoverable amount. What had been lacking was guidance on how recoverable amount should be calculated, and when impairment losses (to write assets down to their recoverable amount) should be recognised. The standard sought to provide this guidance.

Based on this view, FRS 11 stressed that write-downs that become necessary when its rules were applied for the first time were not to be shown as a prior year adjustments[143] – a rather questionable position, since the standard's methodology is quite different from previous practice. As a result, a number of companies have recorded impairment write-downs in the year of implementation of the standard.

Rio Tinto wrote down certain mining assets on implementing FRS 11 in its 1998 accounts, as shown in this extract:

Extract 10.44: Rio Tinto plc and Rio Tinto Limited (1998)

1 PRINCIPAL ACCOUNTING POLICIES

h Depreciation and carrying values of fixed assets [extract]

Tangible fixed assets and goodwill are reviewed for impairment if events or changes in circumstances indicate that the carrying amount may not be recoverable. In addition, goodwill is reviewed for impairment at the end of the first complete financial year after the relevant acquisition and, where the goodwill is being amortised over a period exceeding 20 years, annually thereafter. When a review for impairment is conducted, the recoverable amount is assessed by reference to the net present value of expected future cash flows of the relevant income generating unit or disposal value if higher. The discount rate applied is based upon the Group's weighted average cost of capital with appropriate adjustment for the risks associated with the relevant unit.

3 EXCEPTIONAL ASSET WRITE-DOWNS

The exceptional charge, analysed at the foot of the profit and loss account, comprises provisions for impairment of the carrying values of fixed assets. These are added back in arriving at adjusted earnings and adjusted earnings per share. To calculate these impairment provisions, forecast cash flows have been expressed in US dollars and discounted using a nominal rate of approximately 13 per cent when grossed up at the Group's 1998 average tax rate (before exceptional items) of 34 per cent. The 13 per cent included 2.5 percentage points to allow for the effect of inflation. The discount rate applied is based upon the Group's weighted average cost of capital with appropriate adjustment for the risks associated with the relevant unit. The provisions made in 1998 are predominantly the result of the implementation of Financial Reporting Standard 11 (see Principal Accounting Policies – paragraph h).

Similarly, Rank recognised an impairment loss of £98m as an operating exceptional item in its 1998 accounts, as disclosed in this extract:

Extract 10.45: Rank Group plc (1998)

Accounting Policies

Changes in accounting policy [extract]

FRS 11 requires fixed assets to be written down where their recoverable amount falls below their carrying value. The standard defines the recoverable amount of an asset as the higher of value in use to the business and net realisable value. The standard does not allow consideration of whether the deficit is temporary or permanent. Previously, the Group's policy was to book permanent diminutions only, as required by the Companies Act. In defining its income generating units as required by the standard, the Group has taken into account its separate lines of business and the economic areas in which they operate. A pre-tax discount rate of 16% has been applied in the value in use calculations.

Operating and Financial Review

Exceptional items include a £98m impairment charge under the new Accounting Standard FRS 11 which relates mainly to the Oasis Lakeland Holiday village, the former Butlins sites at Ayr and Pwllheli (being redeveloped as Haven sites), and Tom Cobleigh pub restaurants within Leisure.

4.4.2 Scope

FRS 11 is a general impairment standard, designed to be applied to all fixed assets as well as to purchased goodwill recognised in the balance sheet. However, there are some exceptions to this general rule[144] and in particular the standard does not apply to the following:

(a)   fixed assets within the scope of FRS 13, the standard on financial instrument disclosures.[145]

The definition of financial instruments in FRS 13 is very broad and encompasses things such as investments and loans. There are, however, some financial assets that are excluded from its scope and therefore *do* fall within the scope of FRS 11. This includes interests in subsidiaries, associates, partnerships and joint ventures (unless those interests are held exclusively for resale). The effect of this standard on parent company accounts is therefore very significant. If goodwill on consolidation has been subject to an impairment review which revealed an impairment loss, the investment in the subsidiary, as recorded in the parent's accounts, should also be reviewed for impairment. However, this issue must be considered even if there has been no impairment of group assets. In the past, most consolidation goodwill has been written off under SSAP 22 and thereby escapes FRS 11, but it will usually still be represented in the carrying value of the parent's investments, rendering them more vulnerable to the need for a write-down. This can be a serious issue, because any write-down will directly affect the parent's profit and loss account and hence the group's ability to pay dividends.

(b)   investment properties

This exemption for investment properties is a change from FRED 15, which included no such exemption. However, since investment properties are carried at market value under SSAP 19 anyway, the exemption is unlikely to have much effect.

(c)   an entity's own shares held by an ESOP and shown as a fixed asset in the entity's balance sheet under UITF Abstract 13 – *Accounting for ESOP Trusts*.

This is also a change from FRED 15, which gave no such exemption. Appendix IV to the standard explained that the Board now intended these to be accounted for in the same way as other investments and that they would be considered under the financial instruments project.

(d)   costs capitalised pending determination (i.e. while a field is still being appraised) under the Oil Industry Accounting Committee SORP, *Accounting for oil and gas exploration and development activities.*

This fourth exemption is for oil companies in respect of exploration and development costs carried forward before the viability of the field has been determined. This is clearly a necessary exemption as the standard could otherwise require forecasts of the cash flows to be generated from the field (among other things) and by definition these will not be available. However, the standard does apply to such costs after the viability of the field has been established.

The standard also makes it clear that it does not apply to goodwill already written off to reserves (under SSAP 22) and not subsequently resurrected on the implementation of FRS 10.[146] As a consequence, goodwill previously written off to reserves still has to be passed through the profit and loss account only when the related business is sold or terminated.

4.4.3   The theory behind the review

The purpose of the review is to ensure that fixed assets and goodwill are not carried at a figure greater than their recoverable amount. The definition of recoverable amount, therefore, is a key issue. The standard defines it as the higher of net realisable value and value in use,[147] which has an intuitive appeal – the underlying concept is that an asset should not be carried at more than the amount you are going to get from it, either from sale proceeds or from using it.

The two elements of this definition are themselves further defined. Net realisable value (NRV) is 'the amount at which an asset could be disposed of, less any direct selling costs'.[148] This is a familiar definition. The standard does briefly discuss the calculation of NRV by noting that it should be calculated by reference to market value where an active market exists. If there is no active market, the question then is whether a reliable estimate can be made – if not, then the recoverable amount will have to be determined by reference to value in use alone.

Value in use (VIU), however, is not defined in so familiar a way. It is 'the present value of the future cash flows obtainable as a result of an asset's continued use, including those resulting from its ultimate disposal'.[149] The new element is that the recoverable amount is to be calculated in present value rather than actual terms. Discounting is a central feature of the impairment test.

Diagramatically, this comparison of carrying value and recoverable amount can be portrayed as follows:

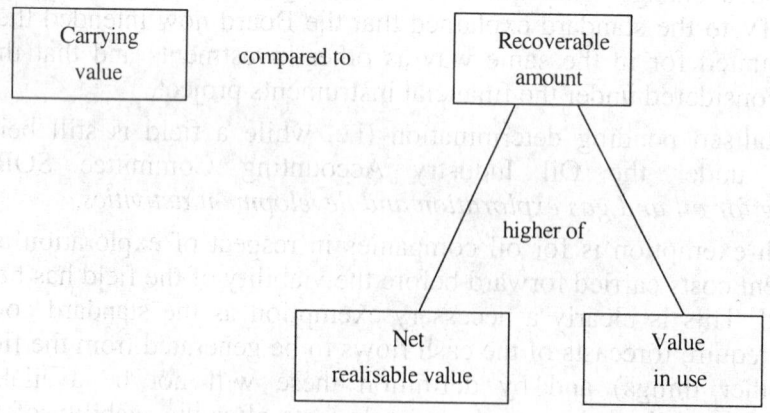

A further complication is that the standard requires deferred tax to be taken into account in deciding whether net realisable value or value in use is the higher figure. Thus, it says that if NRV is £100 and would give rise to a deferred tax liability of £30, while VIU is £110 and would give rise to a deferred tax liability of £45, recoverable amount should be based on NRV and not on VIU.[150]

FRS 11 emphasises that it will not always be necessary to calculate both VIU and NRV. If *either* VIU *or* NRV is higher than the carrying amount then there is no impairment and no write-down is necessary.[151] Thus, if NRV is greater than the carrying amount then no further consideration need be given to VIU, or to the need for a write-down. But even if VIU does have to be calculated, the standard notes that in many cases it will not be difficult to do so. A detailed calculation of VIU may not be necessary as a simple estimate might be sufficient to demonstrate that it is above the carrying amount.[152] However, if both VIU and NRV are below carrying amount, a write-down is necessary.

Ideally, the review for impairment should be done at the level of the individual asset. The carrying amount of the fixed asset or goodwill should be compared with its recoverable amount (the higher of NRV, if known, and VIU). To the extent that the carrying amount exceeds the recoverable amount, the fixed asset or goodwill is impaired and should be written down.

An impairment review might theoretically be conducted by looking only at the NRVs of individual fixed assets. In practice this is likely to be a rare occurrence for a number of reasons. It may not be possible to obtain reliable estimates for all fixed assets and some, such as goodwill or certain intangible assets, may not have an NRV at all. Furthermore, some assets may have an NRV below their carrying amount. In these cases, VIUs will have to be calculated and although NRVs can often be obtained for individual fixed assets, estimates of VIUs usually cannot be. This is because the cash flows necessary for the VIU calculation are not usually generated by single assets, but by groups of assets being used together. In this case, therefore, the impairment review cannot be done at the level of the individual asset and it must be done at the level of what the standard defines as an income-generating unit (IGU). This is 'a group of assets, liabilities and associated goodwill that generates income that is largely independent of the reporting entity's other income streams. The assets and liabilities include those directly involved in generating the income and an appropriate portion of those used to generate more than one income stream'.[153]

The shift of focus from individual asset to IGU is fundamental to the impairment review required by FRS 11. As is discussed further below, it has the effect of making the review a business value test (so that the assets of the business unit cannot usually be carried at an amount greater than the value of that business unit). This is somewhat different from the way in which the carrying amount of fixed assets had been assessed before FRS 11 was introduced.

The standard notes that it would be unduly onerous for all fixed assets and goodwill to be reviewed for impairment every year.[154] In general, therefore, fixed assets and goodwill need be reviewed for impairment only if there is some indication that impairment may have occurred. If events or changes in circumstances indicate that the carrying amount of the fixed asset may not be recoverable, a review for impairment should be carried out. These events or changes in circumstances may affect either the fixed assets themselves or the economic environment in which they are operated.

To make the concept more concrete, the standard gives a number of examples of such indicators which would trigger a review:[155]

- A current period operating loss in the business in which the fixed asset or goodwill is involved or net cash outflow from the operating activities of that business, combined with either past operating losses or net cash outflows from such operating activities or an expectation of continuing operating losses or net cash outflows from such operating activities.

It is interesting to note that this indicator operates at a less stringent level than the impairment review itself. This may be because it is borrowed from the equivalent US standard without regard for the fact that the condition it is designed to test is different. Under SFAS 121, an impairment review is triggered only if *undiscounted* future cash flows are insufficient to cover the carrying value of the assets. In contrast, FRS 11's use of discounting means that a write-down is made, not just when losses are expected but also when sub-standard profits are foreseen. But unless actual losses are experienced, the company may not have to undertake a full impairment review in the first place, at least under this particular test.

A single period's operating loss or net cash outflow from operations would not by itself be enough to trigger an impairment review. However, if this is combined with past losses then the review is triggered. The standard does not discuss when these past losses need have happened, but it would be unreasonable to count them if they were in the distant past. Recent losses, such as those of the previous year, would however trigger the review.

If there are expectations of continuing future losses alongside the current losses or outflows, the review is also triggered. The question arises of what the standard means by 'continuing' losses – however, we suggest that if losses are expected in the next period (as reflected in the latest budgets) that should trigger the review.

If losses (or net cash outflows) have not yet occurred but are expected to do so in the future, then as drafted the standard would require the review to be triggered only when they do materialise. However, it may be prudent to address the matter in advance if the losses are reasonably certain.

This indicator of impairment is primarily concerned with impairment at a higher level than that of the individual fixed asset. It is concerned with losses or net cash outflows at the business or IGU level. If the losses or outflows are occurring only in one part of the business then that part alone need be reviewed for impairment. The rest of the business has not experienced an indication of impairment and thus can be left alone.

■   A significant decline in a fixed asset's market value during the period

■   Evidence of obsolescence or physical damage to the fixed asset

These two examples appear to be aimed primarily at individual fixed assets (rather than IGUs). However, they may also spill over into a wider review of the business or IGU. For example, if there is a property slump, and the value of the entity's new head office falls below its cost this would constitute an indicator of impairment and trigger a review. At the level of the individual asset, NRV is below carrying amount and this might indicate that a write-down is necessary. However, the standard is clear that if NRV is lower than the carrying amount of the fixed asset, it is necessary, before writing down the asset to net realisable value, to establish whether value in use is higher than NRV. If it is, the recoverable amount will be based on value in use, not NRV.[156] Accordingly, the option of just writing fixed assets down to their market value does not appear to be available, although some reporting entities may well be tempted to do this as a simpler way of giving effect to an apparent impairment than carrying out a full review. Strictly, however, FRS 11 allows no fast track option to recognising an impairment loss just because NRV is lower than the carrying amount.

Other examples of indicators of impairment are:

■   A significant adverse change in:

     ■   either the business or the market in which the fixed asset or goodwill is involved, such as the entrance of a major competitor

     ■   the statutory or other regulatory environment in which the business operates

     ■   any 'indicator of value' (for example turnover) used to measure the fair value of a fixed asset on acquisition

■   A commitment by management to undertake a significant reorganisation (a mere intention to do so is apparently not enough)

■   A major loss of key employees

■   A significant increase in market interest rates or other market rates of return that are likely to affect materially the fixed asset's recoverable amount[157]

The last of these is particularly noteworthy, because it highlights how radically FRS 11 changed previous practice. Assets are now judged to be impaired if they are no longer expected to earn a current market rate of return. This means that an upward move in general interest rates may give rise to a write-down in fixed assets even though they will generate the same cash flows as before and, correspondingly, a decline in interest rates will lead to the reversal of any such write-down. Implicitly, therefore, this imports the 'current-market-rate-of-return' capital maintenance concept that has been controversially proposed by the IASC for financial instruments (see Chapter 9 at 5).

The standard makes it clear, however, that these are examples only and, therefore, not a comprehensive list. It states that if none of the events or changes in circumstances are identified, *and there are no other indications* that a tangible fixed asset, investment in subsidiary, associate or joint venture has become impaired, there is no requirement for an impairment review.[158] The ASB drew a distinction between those types of fixed asset on the one hand and goodwill and intangible assets on the other, since it envisaged circumstances when, even if there were no indicators of impairment, goodwill and intangible assets would still have to be reviewed for impairment. These are primarily when it has been assumed that they have an economic life of greater than 20 years and thus under FRS 10 an annual impairment review has to be carried out.[159] Also, at the end of the first full year following an acquisition, a review must be carried out to compare the post-acquisition performance of the acquired business with the pre-acquisition forecasts used to support its purchase price.[160] If the performance falls short of that expected, this triggers a full impairment review. This is to make sure that goodwill and intangibles are not carried in the balance sheet at amounts which reflect a bad purchase, even where the goodwill and intangible assets are being amortised over a fairly short period.

The standard states that if an impairment is identified at the time of the first year impairment review, this impairment reflects:

(a)   an overpayment,

(b)   an event that occurred between the acquisition and the first year review; or

(c)   depletion of the acquired goodwill or intangible asset between the acquisition and the first year review that exceeds the amount recognised through amortisation.[161]

It is necessary to interpret the requirement that a comparison should be made of the post-acquisition performance with the pre-acquisition forecasts used to support the purchase price. Presumably, this is not a simple comparison of post-acquisition profit with pre-acquisition forecast profit. Instead, it appears open to preparers to consider the whole gamut of performance measures that they apply to the business. For example, a poorer than expected profit may be offset by a better than expected market share. Perhaps order books, product development and many other performance measures can be taken into account. If so, how does one weight the various over and under-achievements that the acquired business may have experienced since its acquisition (compared to pre-acquisition expectations)? There is no easy answer to this. It is likely that, in practice, it will only be in those cases where it is particularly evident that the purchase has been a 'bad' one that the preparers of the reporting entity's accounts will feel moved to perform a full impairment review.

Subsequently, the Board has introduced a further rule that requires certain tangible assets to be annually tested for impairment, even in the absence of any indicator of impairment. This applies to any intangible asset (other than non-depreciable land) that is not being depreciated on grounds of immateriality or has a remaining useful economic life that is estimated for depreciation purposes to exceed 50 years.[162]

One further indicator of impairment that might be considered is where the carrying value of a listed company's net assets exceeds its market capitalisation. This is one of the indicators cited in the equivalent international standard (IAS 36).[163] There are in fact hundreds of UK companies in this position. Friendly Hotels provides one example, as shown in this extract:

Extract 10.46: Friendly Hotels plc (1998)

Financial Review

Net Asset Value

The net asset value (NAV) on a diluted basis is £2.92 per share, treating the redeemable preference shares as debt the NAV increases marginally. The ordinary share price of £1.40p as at 14 May 1999 represented a considerable discount to the group's net asset value.

This seems to imply that the return sought by investors in the company is significantly higher than the yields used by the valuers in assessing the values of its hotels for accounts purposes. However, in the absence of an indicator of impairment, there appears to be no need for the company to undertake an impairment review which might have highlighted this issue.

Interpretation of whether or not there is an indication of impairment, therefore, is likely to be important. As discussed below, once triggered, an impairment review can become a complicated process with serious implications for the financial statements of an entity. Many will therefore wish to avoid performing such a process and thus may wish to argue that there has not been an indication of impairment of sufficient consequence. Much may turn on whether there has been a *significant* adverse change in the market or just an adverse change, or whether any loss of key employees constitutes a *major* one!

4.4.4 Carrying out the review in practice

If an impairment review has to be carried out then it will frequently be necessary to calculate the value in use of the impaired asset or, more likely, income-generating unit. This is because:

■ if a single asset appears to be impaired because NRV is below carrying value, it will be necessary to calculate its value in use (assuming the cash flows arising from it can be separately identified) to ensure that the value in use is not higher.[164]

■   where an IGU is being reviewed for impairment, this will involve calculation of the value in use of the IGU as a whole unless a reliable estimate of the IGU's NRV can be made. If no such NRV is identifiable, or if it is below the total of the IGU's net assets, value in use will have to be calculated.

Value in use calculations at the level of the IGU will thus crop up when:

■   goodwill is suspected of being impaired;

■   an IGU itself is suspected of being impaired (and no satisfactory NRV is available); or

■   intangible assets or other fixed assets are suspected of being impaired, individual future cash flows cannot be identified for them and either no reliable NRV is available or the NRV is below carrying amount.

Much of the complexity of the new regime is associated with the value in use concept. The process of carrying out an impairment review, and the role of the value in use concept in it, is portrayed below.

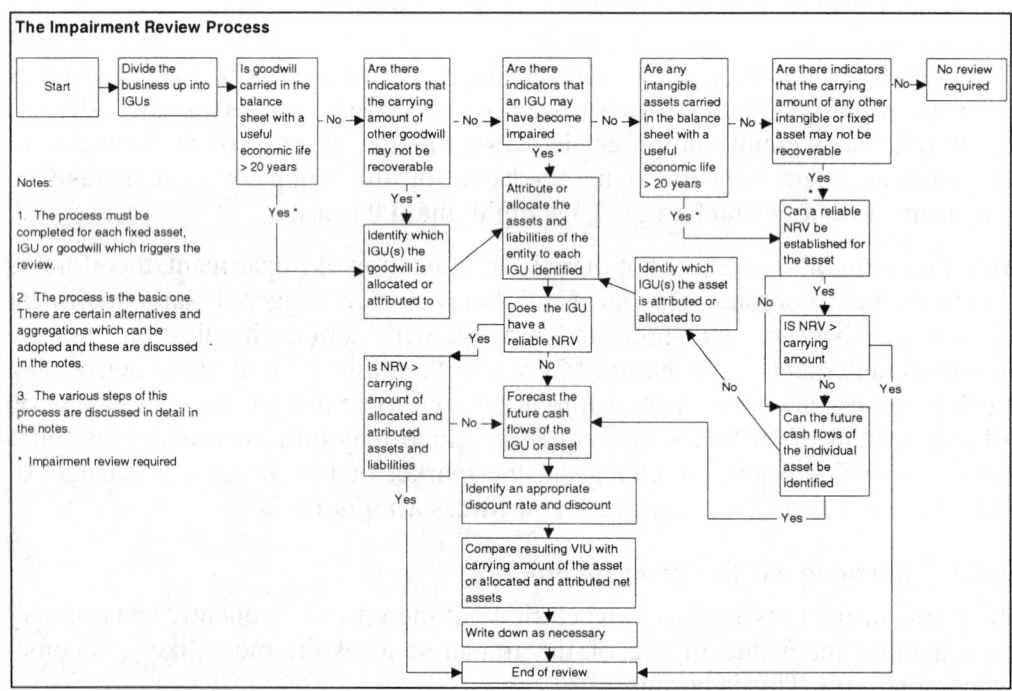

The point of the test is to value the business unit by reference to its ability to earn an acceptable return on capital and ascertain that the net assets allocated or attributed to it are not greater than that value. To the extent that they are greater, they have to be written down. The methodology falls into five steps, described below:

Step 1   Dividing the enterprise into income-generating units (IGUs)

If an impairment review is called for, one of the early tasks will be to divide the entity into IGUs. The group of assets and liabilities that are considered together should be as small as is reasonably practicable, i.e. the entity should be divided into as many IGUs as possible.[165] That said, the division should not go beyond the level at which each income stream is capable of being separately monitored and not beyond the point at which it would become necessary to start allocating direct costs between IGUs.

Nevertheless, the degree of flexibility as to what constitutes an IGU is obvious. The key guidance which the standard offers is that 'the income streams identified are likely to follow the way in which management monitors and makes decisions about continuing or closing the different lines of business of the entity'.[166] In the same way that the reporting of segmental information ultimately has to be left to the discretion of the directors, so too does the division of the entity into IGUs. The standard does, however, further discuss the issue, saying for example that unique intangible assets will often have their own income stream and associated IGU. It also gives four examples[167] which are intended to assist the process of identifying other income streams by reference to major products or services. These examples deal with the following scenarios :

■   Supporting routes operated by a transport company are to be treated as part of the income stream represented by the trunk routes (as these onward routes are operated to contribute to the trunk routes rather than being maintained for their own sake). The key justifications for this are that the decision to continue or close the supporting routes is made with reference to the contribution they make to the trunk routes. Also, the income from the supporting routes is not deemed to be independent from the trunk routes. Accordingly, the two are deemed to be part of one income stream.

■   If a product can be manufactured at one of several manufacturing sites and in total those sites are utilised at less than 100%, the sites should all be considered one IGU. The logic is that the cash inflows of each site are not independent from each other since they depend on an allocation of the production.

■   In a restaurant chain each restaurant should be considered an IGU if its cash flows can be monitored and sensible allocations of costs made to it. However, the standard allows a grouping of restaurants to be treated as the IGU if they are affected by the 'same economic factors', which presumably means that they tend to either rise or fall in value together.

■   In a sequential production process (growing and felling of trees, creating parts of wooden furniture and assembling the parts into finished goods) the IGUs are determined by reference to the test of whether there is an external market for the output of each stage. Thus, since there is an external market for timber this creates an IGU of the first stage but the second and third stages are to be considered together as one IGU. In any impairment review, the deemed cash flows of the two IGUs are to be based on the market price of the timber (rather than the internal transfer price) to give their notional cash inflows from sales and cash outflows for purchases respectively.

In practice, however, different entities have varying approaches to determining their IGUs. There is substantial judgement to be exercised in determining an income stream and in determining whether it is largely independent of other streams. There is also substantial judgement to be exercised in analysing the managerial process to determine how monitoring and closure/continuation decisions are taken.

As can be seen from Extract 10.45 at 4.4.1 above, Rank has written down two former Butlins sites, but not its Haven sites, and pub restaurants under its Tom Cobleigh brand, which suggests a fairly discriminating approach. Marks & Spencer has written down its European stores to the tune of £64 million, as shown in this extract:

Extract 10.47: Marks and Spencer p.l.c. (1999)

11. Tangible fixed assets [extract]

The Group has adopted FRS11, 'Impairment of Fixed Assets and Goodwill'. Included within the Group depreciation charge for fit out, fixtures, fittings and equipment for the year of £280.0m is an impairment loss of £64.0m relating to European properties. Further details are given in note 3.

3. Operating profit [extract]

(2) Following the recent deterioration in results, we reviewed the carrying value of fixed assets in accordance with FRS11, 'Impairment of Fixed Assets and Goodwill'. This review indicated that it would be appropriate to adjust the carrying value of European fixed assets. Accordingly, a provision of £64.0m was made in the first half of this year to adjust those fixed assets to their estimated recoverable amount.

The retail sector, of course, is likely to be able to identify separate cash flows for its trading outlets more readily than, say, a manufacturing concern could for its factories and warehouses, and there is still likely to be a reasonable degree of flexibility in most organisations. Given this, therefore, entities may tend towards larger rather than smaller IGUs so as to keep the complexity of the process within reasonable bounds. One incidental effect of this may be to reduce the incidence of write-downs. The larger the IGU, the more likely that an impairment loss can be avoided, due to the ability to offset impairments in value of some assets with unrecognised valuation surpluses in other assets.

An inevitable result of the IGU-based approach to impairment is that the impairment of assets is being assessed on some sort of portfolio basis. It is debatable whether this in fact complies with company law, which strictly requires impairment to be assessed on an individual asset by asset basis.[168]

Step 2   Allocating the assets and liabilities of the enterprise to the IGUs

Once the IGUs have been determined, FRS 11 requires that all the assets and liabilities of the entity be allocated to them.[169] This is done either by attributing them to an IGU that they are directly involved with or apportioning them over several IGUs. The only things not to be allocated in this way are financing and tax items. Other than these, the IGUs should be complete and non-overlapping, so that the sum of the carrying amounts of the IGUs equals the carrying amount of the net assets of the entity as a whole. There are, however, some exceptions to this basic rule which are discussed below.

Financing items are likely to include interest-bearing debt, interest payable, dividends payable, finance lease obligations and interest-bearing deposits. The reason for not allocating them is explained by the future cash flows that are to be identified and discounted. The cash flows that will be forecast are the cash flows before interest and dividends (i.e. the cash flows which will be available to service the debt and share capital of the entity). The higher levels of cash flow (i.e. before interest deduction) should therefore be related to the higher level of net assets of the IGU (i.e. before deduction of debt and other financing items).

Tax items are also to be excluded. FRED 15 had in fact proposed that the whole exercise was to be done on a post-tax basis, but this was changed to a pre-tax basis in the final version of the standard. Accordingly, the allocation of assets and liabilities should exclude tax assets and liabilities as well. In fact, the standard does not explicitly say this, referring only to the exclusion of *deferred* tax balances. However, the logic would appear to require that all tax balances be excluded from the allocation.

Central assets also have to be allocated. The allocation of central assets to the various IGUs is often referred to as the 'head office issue' – the head office being a prime example of an asset that relates to more than one IGU. The standard requires that such central assets should be allocated on a 'logical and systematic basis' across the units. This obviously affords some flexibility; any reasonable basis of allocation would appear to be acceptable.

However (in another change from FRED 15), FRS 11 says that if it is not possible to apportion central assets such as the head office, then a two tier approach may be adopted.[170] This first requires the calculation of any impairment without allocation of the central assets. Next, it is necessary to compare the value in use of all the IGUs to which the central assets contribute against the carrying amounts of those IGUs (after any initial write-down) plus the central assets. Any impairment revealed at this stage goes against the central assets.

Similarly, capitalised goodwill is also to be attributed to or apportioned between IGUs in the same way as are other assets and liabilities of the entity.[171] However, where similar IGUs were acquired together in one investment, these units may be combined to assess the recoverability of the goodwill.

Example 10.5   Two-tier impairment test

A company acquires a business comprising three IGUs, X, Y and Z. Each IGU contains an intangible asset which is not being amortised. After five years the carrying amount of the net assets in the three IGUs and the purchased goodwill compares with the value in use as follows:

Income generating unit	X	Y	Z	Goodwill	Total
Carrying amount	£120m	£180m	£210m	£75m	£585m
Value in use	£150m	£210m	£180m		£540m

An impairment loss of £30m is recognised in respect of IGU Z, reducing its carrying value to £180m and the total carrying value to £555m. A further impairment loss of £15m is then recognised in respect of the goodwill.

In a further change from FRED 15, FRS 11 says that 'if there is any working capital in the balance sheet that will generate cash flows equal to its carrying amount, the carrying amount of the working capital may be excluded from the income-generating units and the cash flows arising from its realisation/settlement excluded from the value in use calculation.'[172] It is not entirely clear why this extra twist was thought necessary. Obviously, it will make no net difference to the calculation, but since cash flow forecasts are unlikely to distinguish the settlement of existing working capital items separately it seems an unhelpful elaboration.

The steps above lead to the identification of the IGUs of the reporting entity and the allocation of the net assets to them. This is the 'carrying value' half of the exercise. The other half of the exercise is to compute the value in use. This is dealt with below.

Step 3   Estimating the future pre-tax cash flows of the IGU under review

This step need be performed only for those IGUs that are actually being reviewed for impairment. The expected future cash flows of the IGU which is being assessed for impairment should be estimated, based on reasonable and supportable assumptions.[173]

These cash flows should be those that relate to the net assets attributed to the IGU, and accordingly should exclude flows relating to financing and tax. Additionally, depending on the treatment of central assets and working capital items as discussed above, they may also exclude the cash flows associated with such items. More usually, however, they are likely to include a share of central overheads. As with the allocation of central assets, there may be some flexibility in how overhead cash flows are allocated to the various IGUs, although obviously the two should be consistent.

Cash flows should be consistent with the most up-to-date budgets and plans that have been formally approved by management. Cash flows for the period beyond that covered by formal budgets and plans should normally assume a steady or declining growth rate that does not exceed the long-term average for the country or countries in which the business operates. (The standard explains that the UK average post-war growth in gross domestic product, expressed in real terms, is 2.25% per annum).

Only in exceptional circumstances should a higher growth rate be used, or should the period before a steady or declining growth rate is assumed extend to more than five years.[174] The reason for this five year rule is that, based on general economic theory, the ASB believes that any returns of above-average growth rates will only be achievable in the short-term, because such returns from a business will lead to competitors entering the market. This will, over time, lead to a reduction of returns towards the average for the economy as a whole.

It is, however, this stage of the impairment review that really brings home the point that it is not just fixed assets that are being assessed. The future cash flow to be forecast is all cash flows – receipts from sales, purchases, administrative expenses, etc. It is akin to a free cash flow valuation of a business with the resulting valuation then being compared to the carrying value of the assets in the IGU. It is not at all straightforward in practice.

The standard includes a further change from FRED 15 which adds another complication, if not a contradiction. This is that the future cash flows should be forecast for IGUs or assets in their *current* condition, and should not take account of either:

(a)   future cash outflows or related cost savings (for example reductions in staff costs) or benefits that are expected to arise from a future reorganisation for which provision has not yet been made; or

(b)   future capital expenditure that will improve or enhance the income-generating units or assets in excess of their originally assessed standard of performance or the related future benefits of this future expenditure.[175]

While this may be understandable in theory, it adds a further layer of unreality to the process, and it is hard to reconcile it with the standard's discussion of growth rate assumptions; how is it possible to assume growth while denying the possibility of enhancing the capacity of the assets beyond their original standard of performance? The formally approved budgets that the standard requires to be the foundation of the forecast will obviously be based on the business as it is actually expected to develop in the future. No one produces forecasts that assume a static business unless that is the actual expectation. Nor will it necessarily be easy to produce such a forecast on such unrealistic assumptions, even for this limited purpose, and it will probably be impossible to check it with hindsight (as FRS 11 also requires – see 4.4.5 below).

The point of this restriction is presumably to stop optimistic forecasts that depend on vaguely specified improvements. But an assumption as to new capital investment is actually intrinsic to the value in use test. As we have seen, what has to be assessed is the future cash flows of a productive unit, such as a factory. The cash flows, out into the far future, will include the sales of product, cost of sales, administrative expenses, etc. They must necessarily include capital expenditure as well. This is the whole point of the test – it is a business valuation test, not a cash from certain specific fixed assets test. Accordingly, capital expenditure cash flows must be built into the forecast cash flows. FRS 11 appears to require that improving capital expenditure is not recognised, while routine or replacement capital expenditure is. This is a difficult distinction to draw in practice.

There is one exception to this restriction, although it is hard to see the conceptual distinction. Where a new income-generating unit is acquired and the purchaser has planned certain reorganisation or investment expenditure in order to obtain the benefits from its investment, these planned actions and their benefits can be included in the forecast.[176]

As well as estimating the future cash flows from the IGU, the forecast cash flows of course have to be allocated to different periods for the purpose of the discounting exercise below.

Step 4   *Identifying an appropriate discount rate and discounting the future cash flows*

When the future cash flows have been estimated and allocated to different periods, the present value of these cash flows should then be calculated by discounting them. The discount rate to be applied should be an estimate of the rate that the market would expect on an equally risky investment, and should be calculated on a pre-tax basis.[177]

These discounting provisions highlight how radical these rules are compared to previous practice. Assets are judged to be impaired if they are no longer expected to earn a current market rate of return. This also means that an upward movement in general interest rates may give rise to a write-down in assets even though they may generate the same cash flows as before and, correspondingly, a decline in interest rates may lead to the reversal of any such write-down. The standard emphasises, however, that there may be less volatility of this sort than one might think; even though short term interest rates may fluctuate, the discount rates that are relevant for assessing impairment are longer term rates which are likely to be more stable.[178]

The 'discount rate that the market would expect on an equally risky investment' may be estimated in a variety of ways and in particular by reference to:

- the rate implicit in market transactions of similar assets; or
- the current weighted average cost of capital (WACC) of a listed company whose cash flows have similar risk profiles to those of the IGU; or
- the WACC for the entity as a whole but only if adjusted for the particular risks associated with the IGU.[179]

In the case of the last bullet point above, the standard makes two caveats. The first is that where the cash flows assume a growth rate that exceeds the long-term average for more than five years, it is likely that the discount rate used will be increased to reflect a higher risk. The second is that the discount rates applied to individual IGUs must always be such that, if they were to be calculated for every unit, the weighted average rate would equal the entity's overall WACC.[180]

It is likely that an estimate of the appropriate discount rate will have to be made using the concept of the WACC underlying the second and third bullet points. The first bullet point is really applicable to traded assets (such as properties) rather than to IGUs. Since most value in use calculations are done in the context of an IGU, and only rarely is there likely to be a market in similar IGUs, it will not usually be possible to calculate the discount rate in this way.

The second and third bullet points both refer to the WACC; one for a listed company with 'similar risk profiles' to the IGU, and the other for the IGU directly (albeit arrived at by adjusting the entity's WACC for the particular risks of the IGU).

The appropriate discount rate to use is an extremely technical subject, and one which has spawned a vast and complicated academic literature. The standard provides no guidance on how to calculate the required rate. This is likely to prove a demanding part of the impairment testing process and in practice it will probably not be possible to obtain a rate which is theoretically perfect – the task is just too intractable for that. The objective, therefore, will be to obtain a rate which is sensible and justifiable.

There are likely to be a number of acceptable methods of arriving at the appropriate rate. One method which may be acceptable is set out below. While this illustration may appear to be quite complex, it has been written at a fairly general level. In practice, the calculation of the appropriate discount rate will be extremely complex and specialist advice may be needed.[181]

Example 10.6   Calculating a discount rate

This example is based on determining the WACC for a listed company with a similar risk profile to the IGU in question. Because it is highly unlikely that such a company will exist, it will usually have to be simulated by looking at a hypothetical company with a similar risk profile.

The following three elements need to be estimated for the hypothetical listed company with a similar risk profile:

■   gearing, i.e., the ratio of market value of debt to market value of equity

■   cost of debt; and

■   cost of equity.

Gearing can best be obtained by reviewing quoted companies operating predominantly in the same industry as the IGU and identifying an average level of gearing for such companies. The companies need to be quoted so that the market value of equity can be readily determined.

Where companies in the sector typically have quoted debt, the cost of such debt can be determined directly. In order to calculate the cost of debt for bank loans and borrowings more generally, one method is to take the rate implicit in gilt-edged bonds – with a period to maturity similar to the expected life of the assets being reviewed for impairment – and to add to this rate a bank's margin, i.e., the commercial premium that would be added to the bond rate by a bank lending to the hypothetical listed company. In some cases, the margin being charged on existing borrowings to the company in question will provide evidence to help with establishing the bank's margin. Obviously, the appropriateness of this will depend upon the extent to which the risks facing the IGU being tested are similar to the risks facing the company or group as a whole.

If goodwill or fixed assets being reviewed for impairment were expected to have an indefinitely long life, the appropriate gilt-edged bond rate to use would be that for irredeemable bonds. The additional bank's margin to add would be a matter for judgement but would vary according to the ease with which the sector under review was generally able to obtain bank finance and, as noted above, there might be evidence from the borrowings actually in place of the likely margin that would be chargeable. Sectors that invest significantly in tangible assets such as properties that are readily available as security for borrowings, would require a lower margin than other sectors where such security could not be found so easily. Some sectors typically have no bank finance, for instance the biotechnology sector where bank financing is hardly ever seen.

Cost of equity is the hardest component of the cost of capital to determine. One technique frequently used in practice and written up in numerous textbooks is the 'Capital asset pricing model' (CAPM). The theory underlying this model is that the cost of equity is equal to the risk-free rate plus a multiple, known as the beta, of the market risk premium.

The risk-free rate is the same as that used to determine the nominal cost of debt and described above as being obtainable from gilt-edged bond yields with an appropriate period to redemption.

The market risk premium is the premium that investors require for investing in equities rather than government bonds. Significant amounts of research have been carried out to determine what the market risk premium is; a figure of 7.4% is often used but papers are regularly published showing much lower rates. There are also reasons why this rate may be loaded in certain cases, for instance to take account of specific risks in the IGU in question that are not reflected in its market sector generally. Loadings are typically made when determining the cost of equity for a small company.

The beta for a quoted company is a number that is greater or less than one according to whether market movements generally are reflected in a proportionately greater (beta more than one) or smaller (beta less than one) movement in the particular stock in question. Most betas fall into the range 0.4 to 1.5.

Various bodies, such as The London Business School, publish betas on a regular basis both for individual stocks and for industry sectors in general. Published betas are levered, i.e., they reflect the level of gearing in the company or sector concerned.

The cost of equity for the hypothetical company having a similar risk profile to the IGU is:

Cost of equity = risk-free rate + (levered beta x market risk premium)

Having determined the component costs of debt and equity and the appropriate level of gearing, the WACC for the hypothetical company having a similar risk profile to the IGU in question is:

WACC = (1-t) x D x{g/(1+g)} + E x [1-{g/(1+g)}]

where:

D is the cost of debt;

E is the cost of equity

g is the gearing level (i.e. the ratio of debt to equity) for the sector; and

t is the rate of tax relief available on the debt servicing payments.

All that remains to be done is to multiply by 1/(1-t) to obtain an estimate of the pre-tax WACC. (As noted below, Appendix I to FRS 11 says that this simple gross-up may sometimes be unduly simplistic, but it should be acceptable in most circumstances.)

The standard requires that the forecast cash flows be before tax and finance costs. It is, perhaps, more common in discounted cash flow valuations to use cash flows after tax. However, as pre-tax cash flows are being used, the standard requires a pre-tax discount rate to be used.[182] This will involve discounting higher future cash flows (before deduction of tax) with a higher discount rate. In principle, this is the rate of return that, after deduction of tax, gives the required post-tax rate of return.

The standard is more than a little confusing on this subject, but for most purposes we suggest that a simple grossing-up calculation will suffice. Once the WACC has been calculated, the pre-tax WACC can be calculated by applying the fraction 1/(1-t). Thus, if the WACC comes out at, say, 12% the pre-tax WACC will be 12% divided by 0.7 (given a current corporation tax rate of 30% and assuming that that is the appropriate rate in the context of the reporting entity) which would give a rate of 17.1%. (Note, however, that Appendix I to the standard[183] warns that this simple grossing-up method may not be sufficiently accurate where the various cash flows involve disparate tax consequences, although we believe that this will seldom make a material difference.)

Finally, on the subject of discount rates, the standard introduces two variants which can be chosen.[184] Firstly, the standard allows the cash flows to be forecast in terms of either current or expected future prices (with a real or nominal discount rate as appropriate). Secondly, although the risk associated with the cash flows is usually reflected in the chosen discount rate, the standard introduces the possibility of adjusting the cash flows for risk and then discounting them using a risk free rate (such as the return on a government bond).[185] This no doubt can be made (mathematically) to give the same answer but the way of adjusting the cash flows for risk is not discussed. In theory it should not be just a matter of taking the expected values of the cash flows (or even very prudent estimates of them) since risk in the context of investment capital is a highly technical issue that is measured against the yardstick of other alternative investments. The forecast cash flows should strictly be adjusted for their riskiness in that sense. Once again, the standard throws in a difficult concept and does not explain how it is to be implemented.

The selection of discount rates has proved immensely difficult in the absence of clearer guidance, and it is likely that many very different approaches have been applied in practice, even though this may not always be evident from the accounts. A number of companies have, however, given good disclosure of their methodology and assumptions. LASMO reported a major impairment loss in relation to its oil and gas assets, using a 10% nominal interest rate which equated to its cost of capital, as shown in this extract:

Extract 10.48: LASMO plc (1998)

3 Exceptional items	1998 £ million	1997 £ million
Operating items:		
Write-down of tangible oil and gas assets (a)	(307)	–
Write-off of intangible exploration and appraisal assets (a)	(19)	–
Write-down of tangible non-oil and gas assets (b)	(6)	–
	(332)	–
Non-operating items:		
Share of joint venture's exceptional item (a)	(34)	–
Profit on disposal of oil and gas assets (c)	40	–
Restructuring costs (d)	(34)	–
	(360)	–

(a) Write-down of tangible oil and gas assets includes £146 million for fields in production and under development in the North Sea, £111 million for fields in production in Indonesia (of which £34 million is dealt with through the Group's interest in the Unimar joint venture) and £84 million for fields under development in Venezuela. Write-off of intangible exploration and appraisal assets of £19 million relates to the Mariner project in the North Sea. Further information on the write-downs is set out as shown ... in the Annual Review and Financial Summary.

Financial Review

In 1998 exceptional provisions were made in respect of tangible oil and gas assets amounting to £341 million (1997 nil), including £34 million in respect of assets held by Unimar Company. These provisions followed an assessment of the balance sheet carrying value of the Group's oil and gas assets and the recoverable amount of those assets against the background of low oil prices.

In assessing the appropriate level of write-downs the directors consider that oil prices will continue to remain weak during 1999, with Brent averaging below $11.50 per barrel for the year, before recovering to average approximately $13 per barrel in 2000, $15 per barrel in 2001, and $15.50 per barrel in 2002 and no growth in real terms thereafter. Projected cash flows have been discounted using the Group's weighted average cost of capital (10 per cent nominal) adjusted for the particular risks associated with the assets.

The write-downs have been made against the Group's assets in the North Sea (£146 million), Indonesia (£111 million) and Venezuela (£84 million).

As shown in Extracts 10.44 and 10.45 in 4.4.1 above, Rio Tinto and Rank have referred respectively to their use of 13% and 16% discount rates.

One company that has been very explicit about its difficulties in this area is Eurotunnel, which is in an unusual position both because of the nature of its activities and the difficult economic position it has found itself in. As described in the following extract, it has not felt able to use a market-based discount rate and has made no write-down as a result.

Extract 10.49: Eurotunnel P.L.C. (1999)

1 – Accounting policies

f   Tangible fixed assets and depreciation [extract]

During 1998, Financial Reporting Standard 11 "Impairment of fixed assets and goodwill" (FRS11) was issued. FRS 11 requires that any impairment be identified and measured by comparing the carrying value of fixed assets to the present value of projected cash flows using a market-based discount rate. Eurotunnel PLC is currently in a "stabilisation period" after the Financial Restructuring in 1998.

During this period Eurotunnel does not have access to capital markets in the usual way; and interest which cannot be paid in cash may be settled by issuing Stabilisation Notes, which do not bear interest until 2006. In addition, Eurotunnel, being a single service concession company with highly dedicated fixed assets, is not able to reinvest its existing capital in alternative assets or services in order to improve stakeholder returns. In these circumstances, the Directors consider that identifying and applying a market-based discount rate is inappropriate and would not give a true and fair view of the state of affairs of the Eurotunnel PLC Group. Instead, the Directors think that the discount rate to be applied in any year should be the internal rate of return for that year implicit in the lower case financial projections used in the Financial Restructuring and published in the May 1997 prospectus.

In reviewing the potential impairment of fixed assets at the 31 December 1998, the Directors have considered the current and future cash flow positions of the Eurotunnel PLC Group. No long term cash flow projections has been formally approved by the Directors since those approved for the purposes of the Financial Restructuring (lower and base cases).

However, having considered recent experiences (including the fact that the cash flows projected for the first two years have been exceeded) and reviewed the assumptions underlying the base case projection, the Directors are satisfied that the Base Case projection remains reasonable. This projection covers the entire period of the concession (up to 2052) and assumes a steady underlying growth rate in GDP of 2% in both the UK and France from 2004 onwards. This is the basic assumption upon which more detailed assumptions of market size, market share and yields were made for each of the sources of revenue, resulting in overall growth rates for a number of areas which exceed the underlying rate. The projections as a whole reflect the start up position of Eurotunnel in a market which has exhibited strong growth over a sustained period.

The discount rate (determined as referred to above) applied to the base case projections is 7.5%. On this basis there is no impairment at 31 December 1998. Application of a discount rate of 8.7% to this projection would yield a present value approximately equal to book value. Increasing the discount rate by a further 1% from this level would give an impairment of £1.4 billion; because it is not practicable to identify a market-based discount rate, it is not otherwise possible to quantify the effect of this departure from FRS 11.

Step 5   Compare the carrying value of the IGU with its value in use and allocate the impairment loss (if any)

Where the carrying value of the IGU is less than (or equal to) its calculated value in use, there is no impairment. Where, on the other hand, the carrying value of the IGU is greater than its value in use, an impairment write-down should be recognised.

Unless there is an obvious impairment of specific assets within an IGU, the impairment should be allocated as follows:

■   firstly, to any capitalised goodwill in the unit;

■   secondly, to any capitalised intangible in the unit; and

■   finally, to the tangible assets in the unit on a pro rata or more appropriate basis.[186]

The clear intention of this hierarchy of allocation is to write down the assets with the less reliable measures before those with more reliable measures.

There are a couple of qualifications to this allocation process. Firstly, no *intangible* asset which has a 'readily ascertainable market value' should be written down below its net realisable value.[187] 'Readily ascertainable market value' is defined as 'the value of an intangible asset that is established by reference to a market where (a) the asset belongs to a homogeneous population of assets that are equivalent in all material respects; and (b) an active market, evidenced by frequent transactions, exists for that population of assets'.[188] Secondly, no *tangible* asset with a net realisable value that can be measured reliably should be written down below that value.[189] These qualifications, however, do not mean that the full impairment loss should not be recognised. Rather they act as a restraint on an arbitrary allocation process which could lead to some anomalous results.

This process, then, writes down the fixed assets and goodwill attributed or allocated to an IGU until the carrying value of the net assets is not more than the computed value in use. In certain cases, however, even if all fixed assets and goodwill are either written off or down to their NRV, the carrying value of the assets may still be higher than the computed value in use. There is no suggestion that their net assets should be reduced any further (e.g. by making provisions for future losses). Indeed, this is explicitly prohibited by FRS 12, the standard on provisions (see Chapter 25 at 4.3).

If an impairment is indicated for an IGU, the write-down will eat into both the assets directly attributed to it and the share of central assets allocated to it. Accordingly, for the latter it may be worthwhile just writing down the specific assets and then doing the two-stage test (as discussed above) to see if the central assets do need to be written down.

Once the write-down has been made, however, the entity will be returned to making the level of returns on its assets which the providers of its capital are looking to see on their funds invested. The return on capital employed ratio will improve accordingly. The effect of the standard, therefore, is that no UK companies should report sub-standard returns on an ongoing basis. If the profitability of the company is such that it is not earning the rate of return on its capital employed that investors would require to invest in it now, the capital employed must be written down so that the rate of return rises. This is achieved by writing the fixed assets and shareholders' funds down until capital employed is sufficiently low.

4.4.5 Subsequent monitoring of cash flows

Where an impairment review has been performed, and recoverable amount been based on value in use, the standard requires that the future cash flows incorporated in the review be monitored. This is to be done, for five years following the original review, by comparing the forecast cash flows with the actual out-turn.[190] Where the actual cash flows are 'so much less' than those forecast that the use of the actual cash flows could have resulted in an impairment loss being recognised in previous periods, the original impairment calculations should be reperformed, this time using the actual cash flows. Any impairment identified as a result of this later calculation should be recognised in the current period and not as a prior year adjustment.

This subsequent monitoring of cash flows is necessary even where a 'new' impairment review is not required to be performed for the current period. In theory, therefore, once an IGU undergoes a value in use test, it will need to be reassessed in each of the next five years. This appears quite an onerous task although in practice it is likely to be achieved by the process of updating previous forecasts. In any event, a recalculation is only triggered when the actual cash flows are 'so much less' than forecast that an impairment might have been triggered.

In reperforming the original impairment review, all the actual cash flows for the intervening period (of up to five years) have to be incorporated, but the cash flows which are still in the future have to be the ones forecast in the original test. The test is thus just a straight reperformance, using the same assumptions (e.g. as to what constitutes the various IGUs) but adjusted for actual events. The only changes that can be made to the future cash flows are ones that result directly from the actual cash flows.[191] For example, if the reperformance is being done after three years and cash flows originally expected in the fourth year have already been received, they should not still be included in the fourth year as well as shown as a current receipt.

If an impairment is revealed by the reperformance, it will have to be recognised in the current period unless the impairment has reversed (and this reversal is permitted to be recognised as discussed below). In order to test whether it has reversed, however, a new impairment review, as at the current date, with revised forecasts will now have to be performed.

4.4.6 Restoration of past losses

The restoration of past losses is another part of FRS 11 which can prove problematic in practice. If an impairment loss has been recognised and that loss has now reversed, whether or not the reversal can be recognised depends on the nature of both the asset and the reversing event. Tangible fixed assets and investments are subject to one regime; goodwill and intangible assets to another.

A   Tangible fixed assets and investments

If an impairment has been recognised in respect of a tangible fixed asset or investment, and a change in economic conditions or in the expected use of an asset reverses that loss, the carrying value of the relevant asset can be written back up. The credit is taken through the profit and loss account (in the same way that reversal of permanent diminutions has always been treated). However, the reversal should not be recognised in full, but only enough to write the asset back up to the amount it would now be carried at if the original impairment had not been recognised. For example, if the asset was being depreciated when the impairment took place it will only be reinstated to its original value minus the depreciation appropriate to the intervening period.[192]

However, there are a number of caveats. The reversal must take place as a consequence of a change in economic conditions or in the expected use of the asset[193] and indicators of the increase in value will tend to be the reverse of those indicators of impairment discussed above. If recoverable amount is based on value in use and this increases for reasons other than a change in economic conditions, the rise in recoverable amount cannot be recognised. The standard gives two examples of such increases – the passage of time (the present value of future cash flows increases as they come closer) and the occurrence of forecast cash outflows.[194] However, this inability to recognise the rise in value can give rise to some illogical results:

Example 10.7   Double counted losses

At the end of 1999, a company with a single IGU is carrying out an impairment review. The discounted forecast cash flows for years 2001 and onwards are just enough to support the carrying value of the firm's assets. However, 2000 is forecast to produce a loss and net cash outflow. The discounted value of this amount is accordingly written off the carrying value of the fixed assets in 1999 as an exceptional impairment loss. It is then suffered again in 2000 (at a slightly higher amount being now undiscounted) as the actual loss. Once that loss is past, the future cash flows are sufficient to support the original unimpaired value of the fixed assets. Nevertheless, the assets cannot be written back up through the P&L to counter the double counting effect as the increase in value does not derive from a change in economic conditions or in the expected use of an asset.

The treatment above is tantamount to providing for certain costs in advance but then charging the ensuing costs to the profit and loss account without releasing the provision, which would be absurd. In fact, a number of the aspects of FRS 11 raise the suspicion that its logic is not entirely consistent with that of FRS 12. The ASB took great pains in that other standard to stamp out provisions for future losses. However, as can be seen, FRS 11 requires equivalent provisions against the carrying value of fixed assets, and indeed goes beyond mere losses so that provision is made for inadequate profits as well.

B   *Goodwill and intangible assets*

An impairment review may identify that an impairment loss recognised in an earlier accounting period appears to have been reversed in the current period. However, the standard does not allow such reversals to be recognised for goodwill and intangibles unless 'an external event caused the recognition of the impairment loss in previous periods and subsequent external events clearly and demonstrably reverse the effects of that event in a way that was not foreseen in the original impairment calculations'. There is also the possibility of recognising reversals of write-downs in the carrying value of intangibles with readily ascertainable market values when their net realisable values rise, but as such assets are rare, such reversals will seldom be recognised.[195]

Example 10.8   Impairment of goodwill

Company A has an income-generating unit which has a carrying value of £2,000,000 at 31 December 1999. This carrying value comprises £500,000 relating to goodwill and £1,500,000 relating to net tangible assets. The goodwill is not being amortised as its useful life is believed to be indefinite.

In 2000, as a result of losses, net tangible assets have decreased to £1,400,000 reducing the total carrying value of the unit to £1,900,000. Changes in the regulatory framework surrounding its business mean that the income-generating unit has a value in use of £1,600,000 and has thus suffered an impairment loss of £300,000. This is charged to the profit and loss account. The carrying value of goodwill is reduced to £200,000.

In 2001 the company develops a new product with the result that the value in use of the income-generating unit rises to £1,700,000. Net tangible assets have remained at £1,400,000. Despite the value in use of the business unit now being £1,700,000 compared to its carrying value of £1,600,000, it is not possible to reverse £100,000 of the prior year's impairment loss of £300,000 since the reason for the increase in value of the business unit (the launch of the new product) is not the same as the reason for the original impairment loss (the change in the regulatory environment in which the business operates).

The logic of this rule within the standard is quite clear. If the reason for the recovery in value is not the same as the reason for the original loss, then recognising a reversal of the impairment loss would be tantamount to giving credit for internally generated goodwill. However, this ignores two points. Firstly, the existence of sufficient internally generated goodwill can be used, implicitly, to justify the belief that no impairment write-down is required in the first place. Secondly, while the above example seems clear-cut, in practice the 'reasons' quoted may be much wider than those used in that example. For instance, if a company argues that the reason for its impairment loss is the economic recession within the country in which the business operates, it would be reasonably easy to argue that the reason for the recovery in value of the business is the improvement in the general economy. While this may be an extreme example, there may be a number of variations where it is difficult to counter a general reason for an impairment having occurred ('a lack of demand for our products', 'a lack of confidence in the market place', etc.).

The reason for an impairment loss and its reversal would need to be credible however, because disclosure of the reason for the reversal of a past impairment loss is required by the standard.[196]

As before, the reversal of the impairment loss should be recognised to the extent that it increases the carrying amount of the goodwill or intangible asset up to the amount that it would have been had the original impairment not occurred.[197] What makes this a bit tricky is having to make some assumptions about what the amortisation of the goodwill or intangible asset would have been if the impairment had not occurred. In practice it is likely that most entities will simply assume the continuation of their amortisation policy which existed prior to the impairment loss being recognised.

4.4.7   Allocation of impairment when an acquired business is merged with an existing business

One particularly convoluted aspect of the standard is the discussion of how an impairment is to be recognised where an acquired business has been merged with an existing business to form a larger IGU.[198] This unit will include both purchased and internally generated goodwill and the problem to be guarded against is that the internally generated goodwill of the existing unit can be used to shield the assets of an underperforming acquired business.

In these circumstances it is necessary to value the goodwill of the existing business (which will be internally generated goodwill or any purchased goodwill previously written off to reserves under SSAP 22) at the date of the merging of the businesses.[199] The standard explains that the goodwill is estimated by deducting the fair values of the assets and the carrying value of any purchased goodwill within the existing IGU from its estimated value in use (on a pre-merger basis). The calculation of this notional internally generated goodwill does not mean that it will be recognised as an asset. It is merely a notional figure to be used in determining how an impairment loss in respect of assets which *are* recognised on the balance sheet should be accounted for. The effect of this exercise means that any previous impairment in the goodwill relating to the existing business will be notionally recognised for this purpose before the acquisition takes place.

The notional goodwill on the existing business is then added to the actual carrying amount of the new enlarged IGU, purely for the purposes of the impairment review.

Once the merger of operations does take place, the value in use test may or may not give rise to an impairment loss in the new enlarged business. If an impairment arises on the merging of the businesses, this must be attributable to the newly acquired business (since the existing business has already been 'tested' for impairment). Accordingly, the purchased goodwill within the newly acquired business (and, if necessary, any intangible assets and tangible assets) would be written down by the amount of the impairment loss.

If a value in use test is performed in a subsequent period, it will not be possible to attribute the impairment directly to either the newly acquired business or the existing business. Therefore, in these circumstances, the impairment is allocated, on a pro rata basis, between the recognised goodwill on the acquisition of the acquired business and the notional internally generated goodwill relating to the 'old' business. The impairment loss attributed to the recognised goodwill should be recognised in the profit and loss account. The impairment loss attributed to the notional goodwill is not recognised in the financial statements since it is a loss in value of notional goodwill which itself is not recognised in the accounts.

The notional goodwill is to be amortised on the same basis as the recognised goodwill.[200]

Rather counter-intuitively, therefore, a value in use impairment review can result in a write-down even when the value in use is greater than the carrying value of the net assets. This is because the net assets are to be inflated by the notional internally generated goodwill.

4.4.8 Presentation

The standard says that impairment losses that are recognised in the profit and loss account should be included within operating profit under the appropriate statutory heading, and disclosed as an exceptional item if appropriate.[201] For tangible and intangible assets, the choice of 'appropriate statutory heading' will depend on which of the Companies Act profit and loss account formats is being used. Under Format 2 of Schedule 4, it will be 'depreciation and other amounts written off tangible and intangible fixed assets', but under Format 1 it may have to be analysed among cost of sales, distribution costs and administrative expenses, according to the nature of the assets being written down. For investments, the two formats contain the same heading – 'amounts written off investments' – which incidentally means that such an impairment will be shown after operating profit, despite FRS 11's requirement that it be included within operating profit. The Companies Act formats used by banks and insurance companies are different again.

Impairment losses that are recognised in the statement of total recognised gains and losses (those that are the reversal of revaluation gains and that do not represent the consumption of economic benefits) should be disclosed separately on the face of that statement.[202]

One issue that FRS 11 addresses is whether amounts written off a fixed asset should be regarded as a reduction of the gross amount (cost or valuation) of the asset in question or as an increase in the cumulative depreciation charged against it. This will affect the presentation of the amounts in the fixed assets note. The standard concludes that the answer to this question depends on how the amount at which the asset is carried is determined.[203] Thus:

- if the asset is carried on a historical cost basis, the impairment loss should be included within cumulative depreciation;

- if the asset is carried at market value, the impairment loss should be included within the revalued carrying amount.

So far so good; but if the asset is carried at a valuation based on depreciated replacement cost, the classification of the impairment for this purpose depends on where the write-down has been charged. If it has been taken to the profit and loss account the impairment should be added to cumulative depreciation, but if it has been charged to the statement of total recognised gains and losses the impairment should be deducted from the gross amount of the asset. This makes some sense as a pragmatic rule, although it is not easy to see any very obvious principle behind it. However, this is simply an aspect of the ambiguities created by including such valuations within historical cost accounts.

5   REVALUATIONS

5.1   Introduction

5.1.1   *Background*

The incorporation of revalued assets into historical cost accounts was widespread during the 1970s when the United Kingdom was suffering from high levels of inflation. Since then, there has been a gradual drift away from the use of valuations, although it remains a requirement for investment properties and it is still common practice in certain industries, such as hotels and brewers. For industrial companies, the present low rates of inflation have made it something of an irrelevance.

First Leisure provides an example of a company that has reverted to a historical cost basis:

Extract 10.50: First Leisure Corporation PLC (1998)

Principal accounting policies

Changes to accounting policies [extract]

Freehold and long leasehold land and buildings have been restated to historical cost. Previously they were stated at valuation. The effect of this change, which has been shown as a prior year adjustment, has been to increase the exceptional write-down of the Bingo division in the year ended 31st October 1997 by £2.3m and to reduce shareholders' funds at that date by £59.8m (1996: £52.1m). Of the £59.8m reduction in shareholders' funds, £57.1m relates to the tangible fixed assets of the Company and its subsidiary undertakings, and £2.7m relates to associated undertakings included within investments. Had the previous policy been applied in the year ended 31st October 1998, the profit on sale of discontinued operations and fixed assets would have been £19.1m lower and the fixed asset impairment would have been £5.0m lower. The impact of restating to historical cost on the backlog depreciation charge, as referred to below, is not meaningful and cannot readily be calculated. The directors believe that this change facilitates a more objective and meaningful basis for assessing shareholder returns.

Although this change was attributed to a desire to clarify shareholder returns, it is noteworthy that it also had a beneficial effect on current year earnings. Marks and Spencer has also signalled its intention to cease to revalue its properties, but this time because it disagrees with the basis of valuation required by FRS 15, as shown in this extract.

Extract 10.51: Marks and Spencer p.l.c. (1999)

FINANCIAL REVIEW

ACCOUNTING DEVELOPMENTS [extract]

We held discussions with the ASB during the development of FRS 15 and expressed our concern that the existing use value (EUV) basis for the valuation of properties is not appropriate to our circumstances. There is usually a 'special interest' in the sites we seek because of their size and scarcity, and the cost is therefore in excess of EUV. Our investment in these properties is justified by the cash flow they generate. We have therefore adopted the transitional arrangement under FRS 15 and will retain the current book values for our existing properties and record all future additions at cost. We do not intend to adopt a policy of revaluation in the future.

Until the advent of FRS 15, UK practice on valuations was extremely flexible. SSAP 12 encouraged revaluations of tangible fixed assets on the grounds that they give 'useful and relevant information to users of accounts', and this paragraph went on: 'This statement does not prescribe how frequently assets should be revalued but, where a policy of revaluing assets is adopted, the valuations should be kept up to date.'[204] In spite of this wording (which was in the explanatory notes and so did not form part of the standard itself), the valuations of property in many companies' accounts tended to be undertaken at infrequent intervals and often would be some years out of date. Valuations were permitted on an asset-by-asset basis; they did not have to cover all of the assets in a particular class and in practice seldom did so. Companies usually did not disclose a policy on revaluations and the tolerance of ad hoc valuations meant that in fact they often did not have one; they had to give no reasons as to why certain assets had been revalued and others left at historical cost. Finally, it was rarely clear as to exactly which basis of valuation has been used. The Companies Act is vague; 'market value' and 'current cost', the two permitted bases for the valuation of tangible fixed assets, would permit a number of different interpretations (see 5.2 below).

Under this regime, many accounts included valuations of some tangible assets, almost always confined to land and buildings, but there was no overall rationale for the inclusion of revalued assets in the first place. This has made it very difficult to develop a systematic and consistent approach to the accounting problems which result from their inclusion: how to account for impairments in value, depreciation and disposals. As the discussion below will show, although FRS 15 has sensibly imposed a requirement for consistency on the use of valuations, it has not resolved these other conceptual problems very convincingly.

5.1.2   ED 51

In May 1990, the ASC published ED 51 – *Accounting for fixed assets and revaluations* – which sought to impose some order on the diversity of practice described above. As well as dealing with the issues of how to account for revaluations once the decision has been made to incorporate them (described in more detail at 5.3 below), it addressed the basic question of whether assets should be revalued at all and what restrictions should be placed on a company's freedom to incorporate valuations in its accounts.

The stance taken by the exposure draft was essentially a pragmatic one. It accepted that the incorporation of valuations in historical cost accounts has little, if any, conceptual validity. Nevertheless, it acknowledged that the practice had become widespread, and that there was little purpose in trying either to prohibit it or to make it compulsory. Accordingly, ED 51 proposed certain ground rules to impose greater consistency on the practice where companies had chosen to adopt it.

The exposure draft proposed, first of all, that a decision should be made in relation to each class of assets as to whether that class was to be carried at historical cost or at a valuation.[205] In other words, it sought to prohibit piecemeal valuations where some assets within a class are carried at cost while others are carried at a valuation. For this purpose, a class of assets was defined as a category 'having a similar nature or function in the business of the enterprise and which comprises one or more items each of which is shown in the financial statements as a single item without further subdivision. For the purpose of this definition, subdivision by reference to the geographical location of fixed assets should be ignored.'[206]

As well as restricting piecemeal valuations, ED 51 proposed to require valuations to be kept up to date. It did not specifically call for annual valuations, but proposed that valuations that were more than five years old should not be used.[207] In addition, however, it required more frequent valuations if values had moved significantly since the date of the previous valuation. A continuous 'rolling' basis of valuation was also permissible.[208] The purpose of these proposals was clear; irrelevant, outdated valuations should not be presented in company accounts.

Although the ASB did not progress ED 51 when it succeeded the ASC in August 1990, it can be seen that the proposals described above eventually provided the core of FRS 15.

5.1.3   ASB Discussion Paper on valuations

In March 1993, the ASB published a Discussion Paper entitled *The role of valuation in financial reporting*. This put forward a different set of possibilities and invited comment. The scope of the paper was not confined to fixed assets, but extended to other items in the balance sheet as well. It suggested that current values should be used for the following categories of assets, only the first of which is relevant to this chapter:

- properties, excluding fixed assets specific to the business;
- quoted investments; and
- stock of a commodity nature and long-term stock where a market of sufficient depth exists.[209]

However, these proposals were not really explored in any depth. The question of what made fixed assets 'specific to the business', was not adequately explained. More importantly, it was not established why it would be appropriate to revalue some fixed assets and not others; the paper discussed valuations only in nebulous terms and without any clarity of purpose. It did not even discuss where the other side of the revaluation entry should go, saying only that 'the Board will need to consider how gains and losses should be allocated between the profit and loss account and the statement of total recognised gains and losses'.[210]

5.1.4   ASB Discussion Paper on the Measurement of tangible fixed assets

The ASB's Discussion Paper of October 1996 picked up where ED 51 had left off more than six years before. Like that earlier draft, it did not propose to make valuations compulsory, but sought to ban out of date valuations from the balance sheet and to require any policy of valuation to be applied to a whole class of assets rather than on a selective basis. A class, however, was defined in a more accommodating way than was proposed in ED 51; the proposed definition was 'a category of tangible fixed assets having a similar nature or function in the business of the entity. Assets used within different geographical segments and classes of business may be treated as separate classes of asset.' This therefore allowed quite small classifications to be used, which would have imposed less consistency on valuation policy than was originally intended.

Like ED 51, these proposals also required valuations to be kept up to date, suggesting a full external valuation every three to five years, with less formal interim valuations in the intervening years. A 'rolling' basis would again be permitted.

Unlike the ASB's earlier Discussion Paper on valuations, this paper tried to explain the benefits of using a valuation approach, at least for non-specialised properties. It asserted that:

(a) the demand from potential users tends to cause the current value of non-specialised property to diverge from historical cost to a greater extent than that of most specialised assets. Balance sheets with up-to-date non-specialised property values therefore provide useful information on a company's asset base;

(b) non-specialised properties represent a store of value affecting the financial position and adaptability of an entity and therefore up-to-date values give more relevant information than historical values about the assets available as security for borrowings and the asset base used to generate earnings. They also make possible the calculation of a more realistic gearing ratio;

(c) changes in value of non-specialised properties can have potentially major effects on profit measurement on disposal. However, where values are kept up-to-date, gains and losses are recognised in the year in which they occur rather than when they are realised. One potential effect is that the opportunity for purchasers to make profits from understated values is much reduced:

(d) an established market normally exists for non-specialised property and therefore, in the majority of cases when compared with more specialised assets, a reliable market value can be obtained at a reasonable cost.[211]

These are rather unconvincing arguments. Taking them one by one,

(a) no evidence was summoned to support the paper's assertion that the values of non-specialised assets diverge more from historical cost than those of specialised assets. Common sense suggests that the reverse is more likely to be true.

(b) relevance was said to follow from the fact that non-specialised properties represent a 'store of value' affecting the financial position and adaptability of an entity. Yet most such assets are properties such as factory units, warehouses, offices and retail outlets. They are actually a necessary input for production that must be paid for, not items which can be disposed of to realise that value without disrupting the business. This 'store of value' appears to boil down to the assets' potential use as security for borrowings, hardly a major argument in favour of the inclusion of valuations in accounts.

(c) current values were thought to be superior because they alter reported profits on disposal by dealing with revaluation movements through the statement of total recognised gains and losses. This obviously depends entirely on one's point of view on the merits of historical cost accounting, and it does not acknowledge the difference in quality between revaluation surpluses and realised profits. In addition, this argument is expressed solely in relation to non-specialised assets carried at valuation. Carrying specialised assets at depreciated replacement cost was also to be permitted, whereas an increase in the cost of replacing an asset cannot realistically be seen as an economic gain for the reporting entity.

(d)   it was said to be an advantage of valuations of non-specialised assets that there are usually established markets in which reliable market values can be obtained at reasonable cost. However, this is not always true. During the worst of the property slump, in 1990 to 1992, valuers were not always able to provide reasonably accurate valuations because of the thinness of the property market. At times the only valuations which could be obtained were 'deathbed' valuations which could hardly have been regarded as being relevant. Moreover, many non-specialised properties are actually sold as businesses, not as assets, and the problems (and unreliability) of these valuations were not addressed in the Discussion Paper at all – see the discussion of Queens Moat Houses at 5.2.2 below. In any case, the cheapness of these valuations is not an argument for their relevance, but an admission of the difficulties and obstacles of obtaining reliable valuations of specialised assets.

Altogether, the supposed advantages of valuations that were advanced in this paper were less than compelling.

5.1.5   FRED 17

The ASB's 1996 Discussion Paper was followed in October 1997 by FRED 17. This contained a new and radical suggestion in relation to the disposal of tangible fixed assets: immediately prior to disposal they were to be 'adjusted' (i.e. revalued) to the disposal proceeds.[212] The purpose of this odd entry was to move the reported gain or loss on disposal out of the profit and loss account and into the statement of total recognised gains and losses, although losses below cost and those that were 'clearly due to the consumption of economic benefits' were to remain in the profit and loss account.

The thinking behind these so-called 'deathbed' valuations was that it was anomalous to report in the statement of total recognised gains and losses all the movements in value on a property that was regularly revalued, but then take the final movement to the profit and loss account in the year of disposal (the difference between the last revalued amount and the proceeds of sale). However, the treatment proposed by the ASB was to apply to all tangible fixed assets, not just those that were revalued,[213] excluding only the gains or losses that represented 'marginal adjustments to depreciation previously charged', which were to be left in the profit and loss account.[214]

This proposal was slated by commentators. The ASB's apparent view of the purpose of the statement of total recognised gains and losses, and its relationship with the profit and loss account found little support. Respondents particularly disliked the lopsided effect of the proposal – gains would be excluded from earnings, but losses would often remain there. In consequence, the ASB recognised that this was, at best, an idea whose time had not yet come, and they did not carry it through to the final standard.

Most of the other valuation aspects of FRED 17 were supported and are now reflected in the standard, which is described below.

5.1.6   FRS 15

FRS 15 was published in February 1999, to take effect for accounting periods ending on or after 23 March 2000. Like the two ASB documents that led up to it, it neither prohibits valuations nor makes them compulsory but contents itself with codifying existing practice and imposing a requirement for consistency of policy. Rather unexpectedly, also, the ASB gives no reasons for its pragmatic approach. The standard contains no arguments for or against valuations and no rationale for incorporating them in accounts.

The standard seeks to prohibit piecemeal valuations by requiring a consistent policy to be applied to all assets within a class; a decision must be made in relation to each class as to whether it is to be carried at historical cost or at a valuation.[215] However, the effectiveness of this requirement is somewhat reduced because the definition of 'class' is not rigorous. It is defined as 'a category of tangible fixed assets having a similar nature, function or use in the business of the entity'.[216]

The standard implies that identification of classes of assets should start from the broad classifications in the Companies Act 1985:

> II Tangible assets
>   1. Land and buildings
>   2. Plant and machinery
>   3. Fixtures, fittings, tools and equipment
>   4. Payments on account and assets in
>   course of construction

Entities are 'within reason' permitted to adopt other, narrower classes that meet the definition and are appropriate to their business. This is expanded: land and buildings may be split between specialised and non-specialised categories, or analysed by business segment.[217] There is no indication that 'business segments' need be those disclosed in the entity's segmental information, nor would this necessarily be appropriate. The only limitation is that detailed disclosures have to be made for each class of revalued asset. The disclosure requirements are dealt with in 6 below.

Under FRS 15, valuations must be kept up to date. Where a tangible fixed asset is revalued its carrying amount should be its current value at the balance sheet date.[218] The standard does not require valuations to be carried out annually but has detailed rules on frequency and nature of the valuations that are needed to meet its requirements, as discussed below. Charities and other not-for-profit and public sector organisations are exempted from the detailed requirements.[219]

The FRS requires properties to have a full valuation at least every five years and an interim valuation in the third year. Interim valuations should also be carried out in the remaining years 'where it is likely that there has been a material change in value'.[220] This is defined as meaning a change in value that would reasonably influence the decisions of a user of the accounts.[221]

There are detailed requirements for full and interim valuations. Full valuations must either be performed by qualified external valuers or by suitably qualified employees. If it is an internal valuation it must be reviewed by an external valuer, who is required to value a sample of the entity's properties for comparison purposes and express an opinion on the overall accuracy of the valuation based on this sample. The external valuer must be satisfied that the sample is representative of the entity's portfolio.[222]

Interim valuations are to be performed by qualified external or internal valuers.

A full valuation is to include the following procedures:

(a)   detailed inspection of the interior and exterior of the property (on an initial valuation this will involve detailed measurement of floor space etc, but this would need to be reperformed in future full valuations only if there was evidence of a physical change to the buildings);

(b)   inspection of the locality;

(c)   enquiries of the local planning and similar authorities;

(d)   enquiries of the entity or its solicitors; and

(e)   research into market transactions in similar properties, identification of market trends, and the application of these to determine the value of the property under consideration.[223]

Interim valuations include the same processes as in (e) above but, in addition, the valuer is required to confirm that there have been no significant changes to the physical buildings, the legal rights or local planning considerations. The property need only be physically inspected to the extent that this is considered professionally necessary.[224]

The standard explicitly allows rolling valuations of portfolios of non-specialised properties. Entities will be required to carry out a full valuation over a five-year cycle with interim valuations of the remaining four fifths of the portfolio if it is likely that there has been a material change in value. Rolling valuations will only be appropriate where either all properties are of broadly similar types or they can be stratified so that each year's revalued properties form a reasonable cross-section of the total portfolio.[225]

Regal Hotel Group discloses this policy of rolling revaluations for its hotels.

Extract 10.52: Regal Hotel Group PLC (1998)

Principal Accounting Policies

Hotel Properties [extract]

Hotel properties are maintained to the highest standard. All hotel properties are externally valued on an existing use basis on acquisition. One third of the hotel properties pledged as security for the debenture stock are externally valued annually. All other properties are externally valued at least every five years subsequent to acquisition. In the period between external valuations the Directors review the value of the properties. Any impairment in value of a property is recognised in the profit and loss account.

Assets other than properties are not subject to the same revaluation regime of full and interim valuations described above, where either:

- there is an active second-hand market (e.g. company cars); or

- there are appropriate indices on which the company's directors may rely.[226] These indices must not only be appropriate to the asset's class, location and condition but also take technological change into account. They must also have a proven record of regular publication and use that is expected to continue for the foreseeable future.[227]

In such cases the directors will be required to update the assets' values annually. If this information is not available, revaluations will need to be made by valuers and full and interim valuations performed using the same rules as those for properties outlined above.

If an entity has previously revalued any of its fixed assets, it will need to decide what its future policy will be when it first implements FRS 15. If it does not wish to tie itself into a consistent revaluation policy for all assets of a certain class, it has the following options:

(a) restate the assets at depreciated historical cost, as a change in accounting policy; or

(b) continue to carry the assets at the revalued book amounts, subject to any indications of impairment that require the carrying value to be reviewed in accordance with FRS 11. The entity should disclose:

   - the fact that the transitional arrangements are being followed and that the valuation has not been updated; and

   - the date of the last revaluation.

This transitional arrangement is only available when the standard is first introduced. The standard does not specify whether these disclosures need to be made in subsequent years, although the second one is in any case required by the Companies Act.[228]

UA Group has opted for the first of these choices: restating its assets at historical cost.

Extract 10.53: UA Group plc (1999)

2. PRIOR PERIOD ADJUSTMENT

The prior period adjustment represents the effect of a change in accounting policy in respect of land and buildings following the issue, in February 1999, of FRS 15 Tangible Fixed Assets by the Accounting Standards Board.

Land and buildings have previously been shown at revalued amounts. This policy has been changed and these assets are now shown at cost. As a consequence of this change, gains or losses on disposal of these assets are calculated by reference to cost instead of revalued amount. In previous years buildings with an estimated life of more than 50 years were not depreciated. This policy has been changed and all buildings are depreciated over their estimated useful lives.

The amounts for the previous year have been restated in accordance with the new policies. This gives rise to a cumulative adjustment to reserves of £3,926,610 and a decrease in profit before tax and profit for the previous financial year of £213,917. Had the new policy not been adopted the profit before tax in the current year would have been £137,971 lower and the profit for the financial year £130,971 lower than that reported in the profit and loss account.

Marks & Spencer, on the other hand, has chosen to freeze its assets at their existing valuations (option (b) above).

Extract 10.54: Marks and Spencer p.l.c. (1999)

ACCOUNTING POLICIES
FIXED ASSETS
c Land and buildings

The Company's freehold and leasehold properties in the United Kingdom were valued on the basis of open market value for existing use in 1982. At 31 March 1988 those same properties (excluding subsequent additions and adjusted for disposals) were revalued. On adoption of FRS 15, the Group has followed the transitional provisions to retain the book value of land and buildings which were revalued in 1988, but not to adopt a policy of revaluation in the future.

These values are retained subject to the requirement to test assets for impairment in accordance with FRS 11.

FRS 15's rules on how to account for revalued properties are described in 5.3 below.

5.1.7   SSAP 19

FRS 15 scopes out investment properties,[229] which therefore continue to be governed by SSAP 19. This standard requires investment properties to be included in the balance sheet at their open market value. They should not be depreciated, except for leasehold property which should be depreciated at least over the last twenty years of the lease period.[230]

The standard does not require the valuations to be carried out by qualified or independent valuers, but recommends that 'where investment properties represent a substantial proportion of the total assets of a major enterprise (e.g. a listed company) the valuation thereof would normally be carried out:

(a)   annually by persons holding a recognised professional qualification and having recent post-qualification experience in the location and category of the properties concerned; and

(b)   at least every five years by an external valuer'.[231]

Some property companies have no stated policy on the frequency of independent valuations; however, most have regular valuations. Examples of companies having a stated policy on the subject are shown below.

Extract 10.55: Raglan Property Trust plc (1997)

(c) Investment properties [extract]

Investment properties are shown at their open market value based on annual valuations. Such valuations are undertaken by independent valuers at least once every three years and by the directors in consultation with independent valuers in the interim periods.

Since then, Raglan has changed its policy and it now values its properties every year in the same way as Liberty International does.

Extract 10.56: Liberty International Holdings PLC (1998)

Principal accounting policies

Investment properties [extract]

Completed investment properties are professionally valued on an open market basis by external valuers at the end of each financial year. Surpluses and deficits arising during the year are reflected in the revaluation reserve. Permanent diminutions in the value of an investment property are charged in the profit and loss account.

Some property companies have annual external valuations and include a copy of the valuer's report in their annual report and accounts.[232]

5.2   Bases of valuation

5.2.1   General principles

The legal rules that specify what basis of valuation can be used in company accounts is to be found in the Companies Act 1985, and in particular in the Alternative Accounting Rules in Part C of Schedule 4 of the Act. In addition to historical cost, the Act recognises the following bases of valuation for the various classes of fixed asset:

(a)   tangible fixed assets may be included at market value or current cost;[233]

(b)   intangibles, except goodwill, may be included at current cost;[234]

(c)   investments may be included at market value or at directors' valuation.[235]

In each case 'market value' is at the date of the asset's last valuation; in other words, the Act does not require the value to be as of the date of the accounts. Current cost, however, implies a value as at the balance sheet date.

The three bases listed above (current cost, market value and directors' valuation) are not explained further in the Act and they are discussed further below. It is important to appreciate, however, that these are not three distinct and mutually exclusive valuation bases: on the contrary, they overlap with each other.

Current cost as used in the Act is really a broader valuation *concept* developed in relation to current cost accounting, and is generally defined as shown in this diagram:[236]

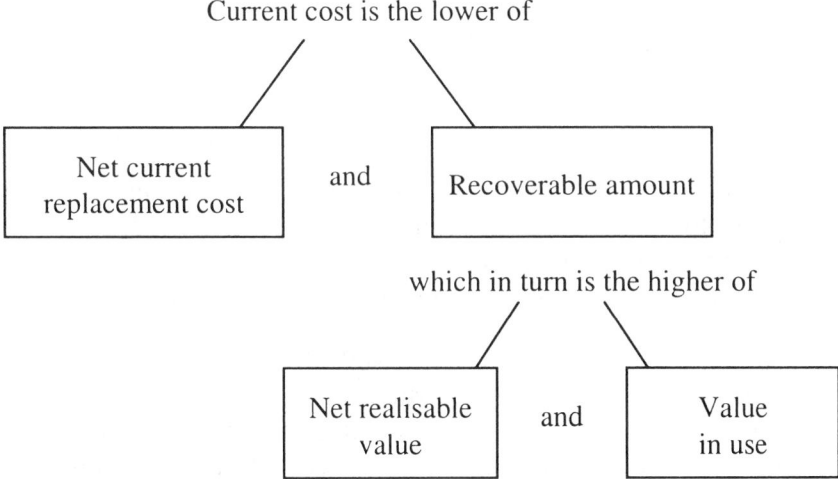

Current cost is the lower of

| Net current replacement cost | and | Recoverable amount |

which in turn is the higher of

| Net realisable value | and | Value in use |

Each of these three elements still requires a *method* of valuation to measure what the relevant amount is. 'Market value' may be appropriate in determining replacement cost and/or net realisable value, depending on the manner in which the enterprise would replace and/or dispose of the asset in question, and there are a number of different valuation methods which are designed to arrive at some form of market value. Similarly, 'directors' valuation' is not a basis as such, but simply permits the directors to adopt whatever basis seems to them appropriate in the circumstances of the company, subject to disclosure of the basis used and the reasons for choosing it. Accordingly, in exercising that judgement, they may be trying to assess the replacement cost of the asset in question and they may be aiming to estimate its market value for that purpose. It can therefore be seen that the three apparently different 'bases' are in fact pitched at different levels of description and the application of all three is substantially intertwined.

FRS 15 uses the model shown in the above diagram as its conceptual basis for valuation, although calling the resulting amount 'current value to the business' rather than 'current cost'. In fact, it can be argued that *neither* term properly describes the model; 'current cost' really only refers to the net current replacement cost leg of the diagram, whereas 'current value to the business', in any normal meaning of the words, would address the amount the entity expected to recoup from its existing asset; that is, its recoverable amount. The true significance of the model is that it reflects the greatest loss the entity could suffer if, hypothetically, it were to be deprived of the asset. This 'deprival value' is the foundation of current cost accounting, in which its function is to measure the cost of replacing resources as they are consumed in the profit and loss account, not the value of those that remain in the balance sheet.

This is a fundamental distinction, but one which has never been properly unravelled by UK standard setters. Measuring consumption in the profit and loss account is a backwards-looking exercise, designed to match costs (albeit current costs in this context) against revenues. Replacement cost is an entry value, and movements in it are not gains and losses but rather adjustments to the (physical) capital that must be maintained before any profit can be achieved. If the desire is to measure value in the balance sheet it is necessary to concentrate on forward-looking measures – exit values – and forget about cost-based measures. Under this approach, movements in value can be regarded as gains and losses.

Modified historical cost accounting, the ad hoc mixture of costs and valuations that has grown up in the UK, is a muddle of the two approaches. In seeking to rationalise it, the ASB Discussion Paper on the *Measurement of tangible fixed assets* invoked the 'value to the business' model and asserted that it was relevant because it 'considers an asset in terms of the opportunities available to the owner in relation to the asset, ie to replace, hold or sell'.[237] However, this statement does not bear much scrutiny. The only opportunities an owner has in relation to an existing asset are to hold it or sell it. The possibility of buying another asset, whether as a replacement or not, does not add to these two choices in relation to the existing asset, and consequently it cannot affect its value. The truth is that the model properly belongs only in a current cost system.

FRS 15's requirements for the measurement of assets carried at a valuation are discussed below.

5.2.2   FRS 15's rules on the bases of valuation

As discussed above, 'market value' is not defined further in the Act, and it can have many different meanings. In 1974 a joint working party of members of the ICAEW and the Royal Institution of Chartered Surveyors (RICS) was set up; this resulted in the issuance by the RICS of guidance notes on the valuation of properties for the purposes of company accounts. At this time the ICAEW issued an accounting recommendation[238] which stated that these notes contained the acceptable bases for valuation and the circumstances in which they should be used. The RICS guidance notes have been regularly updated and were reissued in 1990 as 'Statements of Asset Valuation Practice' (SAVPs) and more recently embodied in the RICS *Appraisal and Valuation Manual*, but the ICAEW never revised its original statement. However, the RICS's guidance forms the basis of the rules that FRS 15 now imposes.

From time to time, there have been concerns about the reliability of valuations in company accounts, fuelled most notably in 1993 by the publication of a succession of valuations of the hotels operated by Queens Moat Houses. The *Financial Times* summarised the salient facts in an article in November of that year:

'The two firms of chartered surveyors under scrutiny for valuing Queens Moat Houses' assets at figures that differed by nearly £500m used the same basis to prepare their figures, the company said yesterday. Both Weatherall Green & Smith and Jones Lang Wootton compiled their valuations on an open market, willing seller basis ... Weatherall produced a final valuation of £1.35bn for the 1992 accounts. Within four months, Jones had submitted an alternative figure of £861m based on the same financial information.'

The article also went on to describe earlier valuations: 'QMH ... said Weatherall had prepared a 1991 valuation of £2bn and a draft valuation for 1992 of £1.86bn. The latter was presented to banks in April this year and did not take into account the changed circumstances of the group. At the board's request, Weatherall supplied a revised figure in May of £1.35bn, qualified because it was based on unaudited financial information.'

When the accounts were eventually issued, the properties were included at a valuation of £732 million, which meant that £1,342 million had to be written off the previous year's valuation. The fixed assets note contained the following footnote:

Extract 10.57: Queens Moat Houses P.L.C. (1992)

12 Tangible fixed assets [extract]

The group's properties were valued as at 31st December 1992 by Jones Lang Wootton, Chartered Surveyors, on an open market existing use basis as fully operational business units. The valuations were carried out in accordance with the Statements of Asset Valuation Practice and Guidance Notes published by the Royal Institution of Chartered Surveyors. The group has revalued its property assets as at 31 December 1992 on the basis of these independent professional valuations.

As explained in the directors' report, the current directors consider that they do not have a sufficient understanding of the 1991 property valuation to enable them to provide a full explanation for the decline in the property values from 31 December 1991 to 31 December 1992 of £1,341.5 million, of which £537.6 million has been charged to revaluation reserve (note 21) and £803.9 million charged as an exceptional item in the profit and loss account (note 6).

In March 1994, the Royal Institution of Chartered Surveyors published the report of a working party (the Mallinson Report) responding to recent criticisms of its profession. This said that 'valuers need to be able to demonstrate to clients that, although there are many valuers who will make different judgements, all work within a common body of knowledge, application and expression. Differences will therefore be as narrow as possible, and where they occur they will be reasonable and explicable, not perverse or chaotic.'[239] The report went on to make 43 detailed recommendations aimed at improving the practices of the valuation profession, which have also contributed to its present guidance.

A   *Valuation of land and buildings*

FRS 15 requires the following bases for the valuation of properties:

(a) non-specialised properties should be valued on the basis of existing use value (EUV), with the addition of notional directly attributable acquisition costs where material;

(b) specialised properties should be valued on the basis of depreciated replacement cost; and

(c) properties surplus to an entity's requirements should be valued on the basis of open market value (OMV), with expected directly attributable selling costs deducted where material.[240]

For the purpose of the standard, specialised properties have the same meaning as given by the RICS in its Appraisal and Valuation Manual, as follows:

'Specialised properties are those which, due to their specialised nature, are rarely, if ever, sold on the open market for single occupation for a continuation of their existing use, except as part of a sale of the business in occupation. Their specialised nature may arise from the construction, arrangement, size or location of the property, or a combination of these factors, or may be due to the nature of the plant and machinery and items of equipment which the buildings are designed to house, or the function, or the purpose for which the buildings are provided.'

Examples given by the RICS are shown in D below. All other properties are non-specialised. They are those for which there is a general demand and for which there is an open market in their existing or similar use. The RICS's examples of properties to which this definition applies include residential properties, shops, offices, standard industrial and warehouse buildings, public houses and petrol filling stations.

Although many specialised buildings are built for their specific purpose, what really distinguishes them is the lack of market. A building that might be specialised by virtue of its size and location, e.g. a large administrative centre put up in a remote location because of the nature of the entity's business, could be non-specialised if it had been built in a town centre. A number of non-specialised buildings (public houses, petrol filling stations) are usually sold with regard to their trading potential, i.e. as businesses, but unlike the specialised properties they are frequently bought and sold on the open market.

Notional directly attributable acquisition costs include professional fees and non-recoverable taxes and duties (e.g. stamp duty) but exclude any conversion or enhancement costs. The standard accepts that these, and directly attributable selling costs, may well not be material and can thus be ignored.[241]

B   *Valuation bases for non-specialised properties*

The valuation bases Open Market Value (OMV) and Existing Use Value (EUV) have been developed by the RICS in conjunction with the accounting profession for use in company accounts.

OMV is 'an opinion of the best price at which the sale of an interest in property would have been completed unconditionally for cash consideration on the date of valuation, assuming:

(a)   a willing seller;

(b)   that, prior to the date of valuation, there had been a reasonable period (having regard to the nature of the property and the state of the market) for the proper marketing of the interest, for the agreement of the price and terms and for the completion of the sale;

(c)   that the state of the market, level of values and other circumstances were, on any earlier assumed date of exchange of contracts, the same as on the date of valuation;

(d)   that no account is taken of any additional bid by a prospective purchaser with a special interest; and

(e)   that both parties to the transaction had acted knowledgeably, prudently and without compulsion.'[242]

EUV is open market value with two extra conditions:

(f)   the property can be used for the foreseeable future only for the existing use; and

(g)   that vacant possession is provided on completion of the sale of all parts of the property occupied by the business.[243]

The RICS Manual explains that, where a property is fully developed for its most beneficial use, its EUV is likely to be the same as its OMV with vacant possession.[244] However, there will be occasions where the two diverge. On the one hand, OMV may exceed EUV because the latter does not admit the possibility of putting a higher value on a property because it could be redeployed to a more valuable use. Less usually, OMV may fall short of EUV, for example because the present owner enjoys some benefits that could not be passed on in a sale, such as planning consents that are personal to the present occupier. Where the OMV is materially different from EUV, the OMV and the reasons for the difference should be disclosed in the notes to the accounts.[245]

The RICS manual also explains that EUV has been developed specifically for financial reporting purposes. The concept behind it is that of net current replacement cost, i.e. 'the cost of purchasing, at the least cost, the remaining service potential of the asset at the balance sheet date'.[246]

There is one particular variant of EUV that is customarily applied to certain types of property – valuations that include trading potential. This approach is based upon the earning capacity of the properties, essentially valuing them more as businesses than physical assets. Such properties, which can include hotels, public houses, cinemas, theatres, petrol stations, betting shops or specialised leisure and sporting facilities, are sold on the open market as fully operational business units at prices based directly on trading potential. The valuation will therefore include all of the assets of the business as a going concern, including fixtures and fittings and the value of the trading potential. The report may not distinguish between the various elements that make up the valuation.

FRS 15 allows such valuations but requires specific disclosures (see 6.7 below). Otherwise it says surprisingly little about this issue; its only comment is as follows:

'The EUV of a property valued as an operational entity is determined by having regard to trading potential, but excludes personal goodwill that has been created in the business by the present owner or management and is not expected to remain with the business in the event of the property being sold.'[247]

However, this is an entirely different basis of valuation to a straightforward EUV, as it is a value of a business and not a building. These units are valued according to the business they can generate by examining the 'fair maintainable level of trade'[248] and the valuer is concerned with factors such as hotel occupancy rates or sales of alcoholic drinks. It is not actually possible to disaggregate such a valuation into separate parts without having one (or more) balancing figures. The implication in the FRS is that the 'trading potential' is a balancing figure, the difference between the value of the unit taken as a whole and the value of the underlying assets.

SSAP 22 discussed the issue in these terms: 'this trading potential is sometimes thought of as goodwill, but such a basis of valuation would normally exclude any goodwill which is personal to the present owner or management and which would not pass with the property on a sale with vacant possession. This practice is acceptable in certain limited categories of business. Where it is followed, the assets concerned should be disclosed separately and the notes to the accounts should make clear that this practice has been followed and that the amount at which the assets concerned are stated does not exceed their open market value, having regard to the trading potential of the business.'[249]

It is arguable that such intangible assets *should* be split out from the valuation and accounted for separately. Even if they are not capable of being disposed of separately from the land and buildings they may well have a different useful life from the bricks and mortar and hence justify a different period of amortisation from the life attributed to the building for depreciation purposes. After all, the trading potential would appear to comprise at least part of the 'goodwill' that would have been accounted for under a fair value exercise if the separate assets were valued; it may even include other separate intangibles such as the value of the licence. However, the Board does not accept this argument or allow this allocation. FRS 15 states that it would not be appropriate to treat the trading potential associated with a property as a separate component (i.e. as a separate asset) because the value and life of any such trading potential is inherently inseparable from that of the property.[250]

Trading potential valuations can also cause problems in respect of fixtures and fittings. The trading potential valuation will include those fixtures and fittings that are necessary for the business to function. For example, a hotel's valuation would have to include beds, bed linen and other necessary furnishings. A valuation may also be performed on the hotel in its current condition, i.e. including fixtures and fittings that have been added by the existing owner over and above this basic level. However, part or all of either category of fixtures and fittings may have been purchased by the current owner and included in the accounts, probably at cost, as a separate category of fixed asset.

C   *Valuation basis for specialised properties*

Some specialised buildings do not have a readily obtainable market value because they are usually sold only as part of the businesses in which they are used. If they are to be revalued it will be necessary for them to be incorporated on the basis of their depreciated replacement cost (DRC).

The RICS Manual gives the following examples of specialised properties:

- oil refineries and chemical works where, usually, the buildings are no more than housings or cladding for highly specialised plant;

- power stations and dock installations where the building and site engineering works are related directly to the business of the owner, it being highly unlikely that they would have a value to anyone other than a company acquiring the undertaking;

- properties of such construction, arrangement, size or specification that there would be no market (for a sale to a single owner occupier for the continuation of existing use) for those buildings;

- standard properties in particular geographical areas and remote from main business centres, located there for operational or business reasons, which are of such an abnormal size for that district that there would be no market for such buildings there;

- schools, colleges, universities and research establishments where there is no competing market demand from other organisations using these types of property in the locality;

- hospitals, other specialised health care premises and leisure centres where there is no competing market demand from other organisations wishing to use these types of property in the locality; and

- museums, libraries, and other similar premises provided by the public sector.[251]

Depreciated replacement cost is defined as 'the aggregate amount of the value of the land for the existing use or a notional replacement site in the same locality, and the gross replacement cost of the buildings and other site works, from which appropriate deductions may then be made to allow for the age, condition, economic or functional obsolescence and environmental factors etc; all of these might result in the existing property being worth less to the undertaking in occupation than would a new replacement.'[252]

The standard suggests that the objective of depreciated replacement cost is to 'make a realistic estimate of the current cost of constructing an asset that has the same service potential as the existing asset'.[253] Whatever the merits of this argument, it is noticeable that the FRS does not make such claims on behalf of EUV as a basis for valuing non-specialised properties (and, indeed, leaves it to the RICS to explain that the concept behind EUV is that of net current replacement cost).

However, DRC is inevitably a rather unsatisfactory basis; it is represented as a valuation of property, but in circumstances where, by definition, the asset has no market value. It has obvious relevance within the context of current cost accounting, where the objective is to measure profit against the current cost of resources consumed, but much less relevance outside that context. It is particularly odd that increases in the cost of replacing assets should be regarded as gains, to be reported in measuring the company's performance in the statement of total recognised gains and losses. Moreover, a DRC valuation is often likely to give a higher valuation than one done on an open market basis. For this reason, it is necessary to ensure that the property really is so specialised that an open market value cannot be obtained. The RICS also points out that it is necessary to be satisfied that the potential profitability of the business is adequate to support the value derived on a depreciated replacement cost basis, failing which a lower figure should be adopted.[254]

Diageo and BOC value their specialised properties at depreciated replacement cost, as illustrated below:

Extract 10.58: Diageo plc (1998)

13 Fixed assets – tangible assets [extract]

... The professional valuations were made on an open market existing use basis except for specialised properties which were valued on a depreciated replacement cost basis.

Extract 10.59: The BOC Group plc (1998)

Accounting Policies

Tangible fixed assets [extract]

Land and buildings are revalued periodically. The basis of valuation for non-specialised property is existing use value, and for specialised property is depreciated replacement cost.

D   *Adaptation works*

The standard notes that structural changes or special fittings may comprise adaptation works that have a low or nil market value owing to their specialised nature. The standard suggests that the adaptation works and shell of the building should be separately valued, the former using DRC and the latter at EUV.[255]

This is another example of a constant theme in the standard: assets may actually comprise various components that behave, in accounting terms, in different ways, and that they should be disaggregated into these separate components.

E   *Valuations of other assets*

Assets other than properties are rarely revalued. However, should it be the entity's policy to revalue such assets, the FRS requires them to be valued using market value where possible. If market value is not obtainable, assets should be valued on the basis of depreciated replacement cost. The FRS states that such assets should be valued in accordance with the RICS guidance and refers to the RICS's definition of the value of plant and machinery to the business.[256]

'An opinion of the price at which an interest in the plant and machinery utilised in a business would have been transferred at the date of valuation assuming:

(a)   that the plant and machinery will continue in its present use in the business;

(b)   adequate potential profitability of the business, or continuing viability of the undertaking, both having due regard to the value of the total assets employed and the nature of the operation; and

(c)   that the transfer is part of an arm's length sale of the business wherein both parties acted knowledgeably, prudently and without compulsion.'[257]

This is similar to the definition of EUV for properties.

5.3   Accounting for revaluations

When an asset is revalued the Companies Act states that the 'profit or loss' on revaluation must go to a separate reserve, the revaluation reserve.[258] Under FRS 3 and FRS 12, this also means that the revaluation surplus or deficit is reported in the statement of total recognised gains and losses.[259]

Under the Act, the revaluation reserve has to be reduced if amounts standing to its credit are, in the opinion of the directors, 'no longer necessary for the purposes of the valuation method used'.[260] Amounts may be released to the profit and loss account only if they were previously charged to that account or if they represent realised profits.[261] This permits transfers from revaluation reserve for the depreciation which has been charged through the profit and loss account on the revaluation surplus and for the surplus realised on the sale of a revalued asset. It also allows a company to change its policy from one where assets are revalued and to write back the reduction in the carrying value against the surplus. The Act also states that the revaluation reserve can be capitalised in a bonus issue, but apart from all these specified uses, the balance on the reserve shall not be reduced.[262] The use of the word 'reduced' is not ideal, given that the Act permits the balance on the reserve to be either a debit or a credit, but presumably the intention is that credits should not be released from the reserve except in one of the ways permitted by the Act.

5.3.1   Accounting for revaluation gains

The accounting treatment of a gain arising on the revaluation of a fixed asset is uncontroversial. The whole of the revaluation surplus is credited to the revaluation reserve. There is no adjustment to the profit and loss account balance, even though any depreciation that was originally charged there has now been reversed; it was correct to charge depreciation in previous years.

The treatment is based on the view that the revaluation establishes a new base of a used asset and, accordingly, the surplus to be taken to the revaluation reserve is the difference between the valuation and the net book value at the date of the valuation. This is consistent with the Companies Act, which states that the amount of the profit to be credited to the revaluation reserve is to be 'after allowing, where appropriate, for any provisions for depreciation or diminution in value made otherwise than by reference to the value so determined'.

5.3.2   Accounting for revaluation losses

The rules become more complex when there are revaluation losses and subsequent reversals thereof. The main question that has to be addressed is whether these movements belong in the profit and loss account or the statement of total recognised gains and losses, or some combination of the two. What makes this question difficult to answer is the inevitable confusion between downward revaluations and impairments.

In addressing this, the ASB has laid down three overlapping rules, which are described below:

(a)   First of all, FRS 15 says that a revaluation loss is to be recognised wholly in the profit and loss account if it is caused by 'a clear consumption of economic benefits';[263] as examples, the standard cites physical damage or a deterioration in the quality of the service provided by the asset. This is equated to an impairment, and accordingly the whole deficit should be charged in the profit and loss account as an operating charge analogous to depreciation.[264] This applies even if the asset was previously valued upwards and is still worth more than its depreciated historical cost. If the deficit against carrying value is charged to the profit and loss account any corresponding credit balance in the revaluation reserve relating to that asset will be transferred to the profit and loss account as a reserve movement.

(b) Failing evidence of a clear consumption of economic benefits, the loss will be recognised in the statement of total recognised gains and losses until the carrying amount reaches the asset's depreciated historical cost – in other words if the asset was previously revalued upwards, the deficit is first applied to cancel the previous surplus. The standard then imposes an arbitrary but understandable rule that any falls in value below depreciated historical cost are presumed to be due to a 'consumption of economic value' and taken through the profit and loss account.[265]

(c) As an exception to (b), if it can be demonstrated that the asset's recoverable amount is greater than its revalued amount, the loss can be recognised in the statement of total recognised gains and losses and taken to the revaluation reserve. This means that even if the value of the asset now falls below depreciated cost, the deficit does not have to be charged in the profit and loss account.[266] However, this rule seems to ignore the aggregation problem discussed in 4.4 above; under this approach, it would seem that even definite losses on individual assets need not be charged to the profit and loss account if the assets belong to a segment that remains unimpaired in overall terms. This seems a dubious outcome.

Recoverable amount is calculated in accordance with FRS 11 and is the higher of net realisable value (NRV) and value in use. Usually companies will have to demonstrate that the asset's value in use is higher than the revalued amount. In some cases, however, the asset may have a net realisable value that exceeds its EUV, usually because of the value of the site in alternative use. The difference between NRV and EUV need not, therefore, be an impairment loss under FRS 11. While in principle the asset may continue to be carried at EUV, with the deficit being carried forward in the revaluation reserve, it will be necessary to consider whether the asset is still part of the class of assets being revalued. EUV may not be the appropriate basis of valuation if the asset is being held for resale.

The operation of these rules is illustrated by this example, which is partly based on an example in the standard:

Example 10.9 Reporting revaluation gains and losses

A non-specialised property costs £1 million and has a useful life of 10 years and no residual value. It is depreciated on a straight-line basis and revalued annually. The entity has a policy of calculating depreciation based on the opening book amount. At the end of years 1 and 2 the asset has an EUV of £1,080,000 and £700,000 respectively. At the end of year 2, the recoverable amount of the asset is £760,000 and its depreciated historical cost is £800,000.

There is no obvious consumption of economic benefits in year 2, other than that accounted for through the depreciation charge.

Accounting treatment under modified historical cost

	Year 1 £000	Year 2 £000
Opening book amount	1,000	1,080
Depreciation	(100)	(120)
Depreciated book amount	900	960
Revaluation gain (loss)		
• recognised in the STRGL	180	(220)
• recognised in the profit and loss account	–	(40)
Closing book amount	1,080	700

In year 1, after depreciation of £100,000, a revaluation gain of £180,000 is recognised in the statement of total recognised gains and losses.

In year 2, depreciation of £120,000 is charged. At the beginning of year 2, as the remaining useful economic life of the asset is nine years, the depreciation charge in year 2 is 1/9th of the opening book amount. The book value of the building at the end of year 2, before taking account of the year end valuation, is £960,000. The EUV of the property at the end of the year is £700,000 so the asset has to be written down by £260,000. If there is not a clear consumption of economic benefits, revaluation losses should be recognised in the statement of total recognised gains and losses until the carrying amount reaches its depreciated historical cost. Therefore, the fall in value from the adjusted book amount (£960,000) to depreciated historical cost (£800,000) of £160,000 is recognised in the statement of total recognised gains and losses.

The rest of the revaluation loss, £100,000 (i.e. the fall in value from depreciated historical cost (£800,000) to the revalued amount (£700,000)), should be recognised in the profit and loss account, unless it can be demonstrated that recoverable amount is greater than the revalued amount. In this case, recoverable amount of £760,000 is greater than the revalued amount of £700,000 by £60,000. Therefore £60,000 of the revaluation loss is recognised in the statement of total recognised gains and losses, rather than the profit and loss account – giving rise to a total revaluation loss of £220,000 (£60,000+£160,000) that is recognised in the statement of total recognised gains and losses. The remaining loss (representing the fall in value from depreciated historical cost of £800,000 to recoverable amount of £760,000) of £40,000 is recognised in the profit and loss account.

The entity would reflect these transactions in its accounts as follows:

	Year 1 £000	Year 2 £000
Profit and loss account (extract)		
Depreciation	100	120
Impairment in value		40
Statement of total recognised gains and losses		
Surplus/deficit on revaluation of properties	180	(220)

Fixed assets
Cost or valuation

At beginning of year	1,000	1,080
Surplus/deficit on revaluation	80	(380)
At end of year	1,080	700
Depreciation		
Charge for the year	(100)	(120)
Depreciation written back on revaluation	100	120
At end of year	–	–
Net book value	1,080	700
Revaluation reserve		
At beginning of year	–	180
Surplus/deficit on revaluation	180	(220)
At end of year	180	(40)

In practice, it seems likely that a clear consumption of economic benefits of the assets concerned will seldom be evident, so in most cases any remaining valuation surplus will be reversed before making any charge to the profit and loss account.

The Companies Act also requires that any permanent diminution in value of a revalued asset should be measured by reference to the asset's revalued amount rather than its historical cost.[267] However, this again depends on a determination that a provision for permanent diminution has been made, rather than a downward revaluation, which should be debited to the revaluation reserve in terms of the Act.

The problems are compounded further when revaluation deficits are themselves later reversed. FRS 15 says that revaluation gains are only taken to the profit and loss account if they are the reversal of losses previously recognised there,[268] and if the revalued asset is being depreciated, the credit to the profit and loss account must take account of the depreciation that would have been charged on the previously higher book value.[269] The latter requirement is not easy to follow, because it is not clear what it is trying to achieve. The credit must be split between the profit and loss account and the statement of total recognised gains and losses, and the following example demonstrates a way in which the requirements may be interpreted:

Example 10.10 Reversal of downward valuations

An asset has a cost of £1,000,000 and a life of 10 years. At the end of year 3, when the asset's NBV is £700,000, it is written down to £350,000. This write down below historical cost is taken through the profit and loss account.

The entity will now depreciate its asset by £50,000 per annum, so as to write off the carrying value of £350,000 over the remaining 7 years.

At the end of year 6, the asset is revalued to £500,000. The effect on the entity's fixed asset is as follows:

Fixed assets	
Valuation	*£000*
At beginning of year	350
Surplus on revaluation	150
At end of year	500
Depreciation at beginning of year*	100
Charge for the year	50
Depreciation written back on revaluation	(150)
At end of year	–
Net book value at the end of the year	500
Net book value at the beginning of the year	250

* Two year's depreciation (years 4 and 5) at £50,000 per annum. The asset will be written off over the remaining four years at £125,000 per annum.

The total credit is £300,000. The standard says that only £200,000 may be taken to the profit and loss account as £100,000 represents depreciation that would otherwise have been charged to the profit and loss account in years 4 and 5. This will be taken to the revaluation reserve via the statement of total recognised gains and losses.

In the example the amount of the revaluation that is credited to the revaluation reserve represents the difference between the net book value on a historical cost basis (£400,000) and on a revalued basis (£500,000).

The standard says that the charge to the profit and loss account is restricted in order to achieve the same overall effect that would have been reached had the original downward revaluation reflected in the profit and loss account not occurred.[270] This is perhaps understandable when dealing with impairments of assets but the underlying logic is not clear when the assets are being held at valuation. There may be major practical difficulties for any entity that finds itself in the position of reversing revaluation deficits on depreciating assets. It will need to continue to maintain asset registers on the original, pre-write down basis.

FRS 15 does not apply to investment properties, so it is necessary to look to SSAP 19 to discover how deficits are to be accounted for in relation to such assets. The original SSAP 19 effectively adopted a portfolio approach and required only overall deficits on revaluation to be charged to profit and loss account, as opposed to deficits on individual properties. The Companies Act, on the other hand, requires permanent deficits below historical cost on individual properties to be charged to profit and loss account but permits temporary valuation deficits to be included in revaluation reserve even if this results in a negative reserve.[271] The original SSAP 19 made no reference to the distinction between temporary and permanent deficits.

As a result, the ASB took steps to amend SSAP 19 in July 1994 so as to bring it into line with the Companies Act. SSAP 19 as amended now requires companies to consider their properties individually and record permanent impairments in the profit and loss account, but downward valuations that do not reflect permanent impairment can give rise to a deficit on investment property revaluation reserve.[272]

5.3.3   *Depreciation of revalued assets*

FRS 15 unambiguously requires depreciation even if an asset has risen in value or been revalued.[273] Depreciation is based on the revalued amount and the remaining life of the asset at the time of the valuation. The estimated residual value to be taken into account should be based on prices prevailing at the date of the valuation.

If the asset has been revalued the standard suggests that ideally the depreciation charge should be based on the average carrying value during the year, or else on the opening or closing balance.[274] In practice the depreciation charge is generally based on the opening value and the written down asset is revalued as at the end of the accounting period.

FRS 15 requires the whole of the depreciation charge to be passed through the profit and loss account. This was also a requirement of SSAP 12.[275] The original SSAP was amended in order to outlaw the practice of 'split depreciation', whereby depreciation in the balance sheet was based on the asset's carrying amount but only the portion that related to depreciation on historical cost was passed through the profit and loss account, the balance being charged directly to the revaluation reserve.

The ASB Discussion Paper on *Measurement of tangible fixed assets* dismissed the case for split depreciation, saying that 'the purpose of charging depreciation to the profit and loss account is to show the cost of the economic benefits consumed during the period. Depreciation based on current value reflects the cost that the entity would have avoided if it had not used the asset. Hence depreciation measured at current prices represents the best measure of the operating cost of using the asset in question.'[276] Curiously, this argument strongly *supports* split depreciation if 'cost' in the three sentences quoted above is taken to mean historical cost! Obviously, however, the Board's mindset throughout the above passage was rooted in current cost, so much so that it did not appear to have noticed that the word 'current' was implied rather than explicitly stated.

The accounting treatment for a depreciable asset that is revalued is shown in the following example:

Example 10.11 Effect of depreciation on revaluation reserve

On 1 January 1997 a company acquires an asset for £1,000. The asset has an economic life of ten years and is depreciated on a straight line basis. The residual value is assumed to be £nil. At 31 December 2000 the asset is valued at £1,200. The company accounts for the revaluation by crediting £600 to the revaluation reserve. At 31 December 2000 the economic life of the asset is considered to be the remainder of its original life, i.e. six years, and its residual value is still considered to be £nil. In the year ended 31 December 2001 and later years, depreciation charged to the profit and loss account is £200 p.a.

The usual treatment thereafter is to transfer £100 p.a. from the revaluation reserve to retained profits within the reserves note. This avoids the revaluation reserve being maintained indefinitely even after the asset ceases to exist, which does not seem sensible. The transfer is to retained earnings and not to the profit and loss account for the year; the latter treatment would be tantamount to allowing split depreciation and would also fall foul of FRS 3, which does not permit amounts which have previously been reported in the statement of total recognised gains and losses to pass subsequently through the profit and loss account.[277] The treatment is also sanctioned by para. 34(3) of Schedule 4 to the Companies Act which allows amounts to be transferred to the profit and loss account if the amount has previously been charged there or is a realised profit. A transfer is possible because the amount of £100 is a realised profit in terms of s 275(2) of the Companies Act.

Where the revaluation reserve has been capitalised by making a bonus issue, further problems arise. To the extent that the revaluation reserve no longer exists, it could be argued that such amount can no longer be used for making any transfers which a company normally makes between revaluation reserve and retained profits, or for writing off that part of a permanent diminution in the value of an asset which the company could have charged to revaluation reserve. If all of the revaluation reserve has been capitalised then no such transfers or write-offs could be made. In most situations only some of the reserve will have been capitalised and, therefore, under this approach it will be necessary to:

(a) decide that specific revaluation surpluses have been capitalised and, therefore, no transfers or write-offs can be made in respect of the assets to which the surpluses related. However, transfers and write-offs in respect of other assets can continue; or

(b) decide that a proportion of each revaluation surplus has been capitalised and, therefore, a proportion still remains. Accordingly, a proportion of the amount of the transfers or write-offs which would have been made can be made; or

(c) continue to make the transfers or write-offs until the remaining surplus has been extinguished.

All three methods are probably acceptable.

On this subject, a footnote in the ASB's earlier Discussion Paper on the *Impairment of tangible fixed assets* confirmed that the question of whether impairments of revalued assets can be charged to the statement of total recognised gains and losses rather than the profit and loss account is unaffected by whether or not the revaluation reserve has already been used for some other purpose.[278]

5.3.4 Disposal of revalued assets

The measurement of profit when a revalued asset is disposed of was a subject that the ASC wrestled with in five different sets of proposals during its life,[279] always without resolution. The issue was whether it should be based on the carrying amount in the balance sheet, with the revaluation surplus on that asset transferred as a reserve movement to realised reserves, or on the depreciated historical cost, in which case the revaluation surplus would be treated as part of the calculation of profit on disposal. The ASB finally resolved the matter in favour of the former treatment with the issue of FRS 3.

FRS 15 does not change the treatment of profits and losses required by FRS 3. The profit or loss is the difference between the net sale proceeds and the carrying value of the asset, whether carried at historical cost or at valuation. This is disclosed in accordance with the requirements of FRS 3 which means that the profit or loss, or provision for loss on disposal, may be shown as an exceptional item below operating profit. However, losses or provisions for losses are *prima facie* evidence that the asset had been impaired in value before sale, so care will have to be taken with the requirements of FRS 11 as, under that standard, impairment write downs are to be reflected in operating profit.[280]

A proposal in FRED 17[281] that assets be revalued immediately prior to disposal (so as to make profits on disposal consistent with revaluation gains) was not carried forward into the FRS, the ASB noting that this would have 'raised anomalies' when assets were carried at historical cost. However, in June 1999 this idea was resurrected in a different form in the Board's discussion paper *Reporting Financial Performance: Proposals for change*. This proposed that the profit and loss account and the statement of total recognised gains and losses should be combined into a single performance statement, divided into three sections: operating (trading) activities; financing and other treasury activities; and other gains and losses.

The discussion paper as a whole is described in detail in Chapter 22 at 5, but the aspect that is relevant to this chapter is the proposed disposition of gains and losses that relate to fixed assets between the 'operating' and 'other' sections of the statement. The ASB proposes the analysis shown in this matrix:[282]

Component of performance	Gains and losses
Operating/ trading	**Depreciation** based on carrying value All **impairment losses** and their reversal **Disposal gains/losses** representing adjustments to depreciation **Disposal losses** that are impairments
Other gains and losses	**Revaluation gains** **Disposal gains** that do not represent adjustments to depreciation or reversals of impairment **Revaluation and disposal losses**: extent to which there has been no impairment or adjustment to depreciation

The conceptual basis that lies behind this proposed split is rather woolly. What it seems to boil down to is a desire that the operating section should be charged with the consumption of the assets employed in the activities of the business, but should be insulated from the effects of holding gains and losses that reflect price change; those should be reported as 'other gains and losses' instead. But such a goal could not be accomplished without mandating some form of current cost accounting that requires the price changes of all fixed assets to be systematically tracked and accounted for separately. And under a system of current cost accounting, price changes do not represent gains and losses at all, but capital maintenance adjustments that should not be included in any statement purporting to reflect the company's performance.

In the absence of such a system, furthermore, it is difficult to answer some of the questions that the allocation requires with any degree of assurance. For example, unless it is clear that consumption has to be measured on a current cost basis, it is impossible to say to what extent a disposal loss should be treated as an adjustment to depreciation or impairment. As a result, any allocation based on this distinction is likely to be rather arbitrary.

5.3.5   *Transfers of properties between current assets and fixed assets*

A   Reclassifications from investment property to trading property

Property companies sometimes transfer properties from their investment portfolio to their trading portfolio. The question then arises as to what should happen to the revaluation surplus/deficit which had previously been recognised when the property was regarded as an investment property. A few companies reflect these reclassifications in their group accounts as if they were transactions with third parties, and treat them as having become realised. This is an issue which the UITF briefly considered in 1992 but did not pursue.

There may be an argument for saying that the property has realised its investment potential on becoming a trading property. Also, such transfers are usually between two distinct companies (i.e. an investment and a trading company) so the profit is realised in the transferor company. However, it is difficult to reconcile treating gains as realised in the group accounts, as opposed to an individual company's accounts, with the notion that consolidation is intended to represent the group as a single economic entity. Nevertheless, such profits at least do not distort the profit and loss account in the year of transfer since they are dealt with as a realisation of the revaluation reserve by a transfer between reserves.

An alternative treatment is to leave the property at its valuation on transfer but not to treat the accumulated valuation surplus as realised. If this treatment is adopted, interest capitalised on any subsequent development should be based on cost.

Another approach is to reverse any revaluation surplus/deficit relating to a property transferred and include it in trading property at the lower of cost and net realisable value; this will ensure consistency in the accounting treatment of all trading properties. For example:

Extract 10.60: Daejan Holdings PLC (1991)

(g) **Properties** [extract]

(ii) Trading and Development Properties

These properties are stated at the lower of cost and net realisable value. In the case of properties acquired from other Group companies any profit in the transferor company is eliminated on consolidation until realised by the Group.

B   *Reclassifications from trading property to investment property*

On a reclassification from trading property to investment property, the basis of valuation in the accounts will change from the lower of cost and net realisable value to open market value. As discussed in A above, such transfers are usually between two separate companies, but any intra-group profit should be eliminated on consolidation, to avoid distorting the profit and loss account.

At the time of the slump in the property market at the end of the 1980s, the question became not so much one of whether any profit should be recognised or eliminated, but whether a transfer should be recorded at the carrying amount in the previous balance sheet or at an amount equivalent to the lower of cost and net realisable value at the date of the transfer. Trafalgar House adopted the former treatment in its 1991 accounts, as shown in the following extract:

Extract 10.61: Trafalgar House Public Limited Company (1991)

12 Tangible fixed assets [extract]

	Properties			
		Leaseholds		
	Freeholds	Long	Short	Total
Reclassification from current assets	111.4	44.0	–	155.4
Deficit on valuation	(50.5)	(17.5)	–	(68.0)

Properties reclassified from current assets were valued on 30th September 1991 on the basis of open market value by independent firms of chartered surveyors (£78.1), and by internal qualified surveyors (£9.3m).

14 Developments for sale [extract]

On 1st October 1990 certain commercial properties in the UK were transferred to tangible fixed assets (Note 12).

The deficit on revaluation of £68.0 million was taken to revaluation reserve.

This issue is one which the UITF did take up. In July 1992 it issued Abstract 5 – *Transfers from Current Assets to Fixed Assets*. The UITF was concerned, particularly in the economic climate of the time, that there was a 'possibility that companies could avoid charging the profit and loss account with write-downs to net realisable value arising on unsold trading assets. This could be done by transferring the relevant assets from current assets to fixed assets at above net realisable value, as a result of which any later write down might be debited to revaluation reserve.'[283]

The UITF agreed that in respect of such transfers, the current asset accounting rules should be applied up to the effective date of transfer, which is the date of management's change of intent. Consequently, the transfer should be made at the lower of cost and net realisable value, and accordingly an assessment should be made of the net realisable value at the date of transfer. If this is less than its previous carrying value the diminution should be charged in the profit and loss account, reflecting the loss to the company while the asset was held as a current asset.[284]

Further to the issue of UITF 5 (and after the intervention of the Financial Reporting Review Panel), Trafalgar House adopted the requirements of the abstract in its 1992 accounts and restated its 1991 comparatives accordingly.

5.3.6 Distributable profits and revaluations of fixed assets

The Companies Act states that a revaluation surplus is not a realised profit and may only be transferred to the profit and loss account on realisation.[285] It is not available for distribution.[286]

Provisions made against fixed assets are normally to be treated as realised losses.[287] These are defined in paragraph 88 of Schedule 4 to the Companies Act. The definition include provisions for depreciation, except to the extent that the charge has been increased because of a previous upward revaluation of the asset, in which case the surplus over depreciation based on historical cost is a realised profit[288] and should be transferred from the revaluation reserve. Amounts provided for 'diminution in value of assets' are also to be treated as realised losses. The wording of this part of the legislation is particularly obscure. It would make some sense if it was referring only to provisions for diminution in value made under the historical cost accounting rules and taken through the profit and loss account,[289] and not to downward valuations when assets are carried at revalued amounts under the alternative accounting rules, but it is far from certain that this is the proper interpretation of the actual wording of the Act.

An exception to the rule that provisions for diminution in value are regarded as realised losses is made for such a provision if it appears on a revaluation of *all* of the fixed assets other than goodwill of the company. For this purpose, the directors do not have to formally revalue all fixed assets and incorporate these revaluations into the accounts in order to take advantage of the exception; the value only has to be 'considered', and this does not imply that the book amount of the asset has to be altered. The Act states that fixed assets that have not actually been revalued are to be treated as if they had, if the directors are satisfied that the aggregate value of all fixed assets is not less than the amount at which they are currently stated in the company's accounts.[290] Thus a downward valuation of a fixed asset need not be treated as a realised loss if the directors are satisfied that the company's fixed assets are worth, in total, not less than their net book value.

This exception can only be taken if the following note disclosure is made:[291]

(a) that the directors have considered the value of some of the fixed assets of the company, without actually revaluing those assets;

(b) that they are satisfied that the aggregate value of those assets at the time in question is or was not less than the aggregate amount at which they are being stated in the company's accounts; and

(c) that the relevant items are accordingly stated in the relevant accounts on the basis that a revaluation of all of the company's fixed assets which was deemed to have taken place included the assets that have suffered a diminution in value.

An example of such a note is to be found in the accounts of Berisford:

Extract 10.62: Berisford plc (1998)

Accounting policies

Investments

a) Subsidiary entities

In the accounts of the Company investments in subsidiary entities are valued at cost plus post-acquisition retained profits, unless there is evidence of a permanent diminution in value in which case the lower value is adopted.

21 Reserves [extract]

a The Directors have revalued the Company's investments in subsidiary entities at 26 September 1998 in the manner set out in the accounting policies note [quoted above]. The Directors have considered the value of the remaining fixed assets and are satisfied that these are worth, in total, not less than the aggregate amount at which they are stated in the Company's accounts. Accordingly, in accordance with Section 275 of the Companies Act 1985 the aggregate provision does not fall to be classified as a realised loss and therefore distributable reserves of the Company are £106.9m (1997 £52.9m) as analysed [below]:

	1998 £m	1997 £m
Profit and loss account	**(2.8)**	(54.0)
Provisions against investments in subsidiary entities	**158.2**	215.9
Excess of provisions over surpluses on revaluation of investments in subsidiary entities	**(48.5)**	(84.1)
Gain arising on purchase of CULS	–	(24.9)
Distributable reserves	**106.9**	52.9

The note must be repeated in subsequent accounts for as long as advantage is to be taken of the exemption as these may become 'relevant accounts', i.e. those on which a distribution is to be based.[292]

6   DISCLOSURE

6.1   Introduction

There are extensive disclosure requirements for fixed assets in both the Companies Act and accounting standards. These requirements are dealt with here in the order in which they are usually encountered in a company's annual report: directors' report, balance sheet and profit and loss account, accounting policies and notes to the accounts. The additional disclosure requirements relating to impairments and revaluations are dealt with in 6.6 and 6.7 below, and those for investment properties are dealt with in 6.8.

6.2   Directors' report

The market value of 'interests in land' (taken to mean land and buildings)[293] should also be disclosed if it differs substantially from the amount at which the assets are carried in the balance sheet and if, in the directors' opinion, the difference is of such significance that it should be brought to the attention of the members or debenture holders. The difference should be quantified 'with such degree of precision as is practicable'.[294]

This disclosure is seldom seen in practice, except perhaps when the property market has moved significantly up or down. An example of it was seen in the 1993 accounts of Lloyds Bank:

Extract 10.63: Lloyds Bank Plc (1993)

Directors' Report [extract]

PREMISES

The directors have reviewed the current value of premises and are of the opinion that, compared with the balance sheet amount, there is a shortfall of £162 million, of which £155 million relates to UK premises and £7 million to overseas premises. The directors are of the opinion that this shortfall, an average of some 13 per cent, will not prove to be permanent and no adjustment has been made in the balance sheet.

6.3 Balance sheet and profit and loss account

There are various statutory disclosures with regard to the balance sheet and profit and loss account.

The statutory formats require that fixed assets be disclosed under the headings shown here.[295] Companies' accounts usually include only the net book amounts of intangible and tangible assets and investments on the face of the balance sheet, with the information required by the Arabic numerals relegated to the notes.

As is permitted by the Act, the format categories with Arabic numerals are frequently modified to suit the

---

I   Intangible assets
    1. Development costs
    2. Concessions, patents, licences, trademarks, and similar rights and assets
    3. Goodwill
    4. Payments on account

II Tangible assets
    1. Land and buildings
    2. Plant and machinery
    3. Fixtures, fittings, tools and equipment
    4. Payments on account and assets in course of construction

III Investments
    [with various sub-classifications]

---

circumstances of the business. Allied-Domecq, for example, has two main categories of 'Production and other properties' and 'Licensed properties'. The former is analysed between 'properties' of various kinds, 'plant and machinery' and 'vehicles, casks and sundry equipment'; the latter between 'properties' and 'furniture, fittings and equipment'.[296]

If profit and loss account Formats 2 or 4 are chosen, then 'depreciation and other amounts written off tangible and intangible fixed assets' must be shown, either on the face of the profit and loss account or in the notes.[297] If Formats 1 or 3 are chosen, the equivalent information must be given in the notes to the accounts.[298]

If a provision for permanent diminution in value of any fixed asset has been made then it must be disclosed in the notes to the accounts if it is not shown in the profit and loss account.[299]

As discussed in Chapter 22 at 2.6.3, the gain or loss on sale of fixed assets is one of the three specified exceptional items which is required to be shown after operating profit in the profit and loss account.[300]

6.4   Accounting policies

FRS 15, like SSAP 12 before it, requires that disclosure be made, for each class of tangible fixed asset, of the depreciation methods used and the useful economic lives or the depreciation rates used.[301] FRS 10 has a similar requirement for intangible assets and goodwill,[302] and for negative goodwill.[303] This information is usually given in the accounting policies note.

Certain categories of asset, for example plant and machinery, will probably include items depreciated at a variety of rates. It is usual to disclose a range of lives and/or rates in order to satisfy the disclosure requirements.

The following disclosures are also required in respect of amortisation of positive goodwill and intangible assets:

(a)   where an amortisation period is shortened or extended following a review of the remaining useful lives of goodwill and intangible assets, the reason and the effect, if material, should be disclosed in the year of change;[304]

(b)   where there has been a change in the amortisation method used, the reason and the effect, if material, should be disclosed in the year of change;[305]

(c)   where goodwill or an intangible asset is amortised over a period that exceeds 20 years from the date of acquisition or is not amortised, the grounds for rebutting the 20 year presumption should be given. This should be a reasoned explanation based on the specific factors contributing to the durability of the acquired business or intangible asset.[306]

FRS 10 also requires disclosure of the method used to 'value' intangible assets.[307] This disclosure comes under the heading 'Recognition and measurement' and therefore is not intended to cover the rare case of intangible assets that are being revalued, for which there are separate requirements. Instead, the word 'valued' refers to the initial measurement of the intangible asset when it is first recognised in the financial statements.

Bass gives a comprehensive description of its accounting policies on fixed assets and depreciation, as shown in the following extract:

Extract 10.64: Bass PLC (1998)

accounting policies

Fixed assets and depreciation

i) Intangible assets

On acquisition of a business, no value is attributed to intangible assets which cannot be separately identified or reliably measured. No value is attributed to internally generated intangible assets.

ii) Tangible assets

Freehold and leasehold properties are stated at cost or valuation less depreciation where relevant. All other fixed assets are stated at cost.

iii) Revaluation reserve

Surpluses and deficits arising from the professional valuations of properties are taken direct to the revaluation reserve. Where a diminution in the value of an asset is identified, the deficit is eliminated first against any revaluation reserve in respect of that asset with any excess being charged to the profit and loss account. Surpluses or deficits realised on the disposal of an asset are transferred from the revaluation reserve to the profit and loss account reserve.

iv) Depreciation

Freehold land is not depreciated.

Hotels and public houses held as freehold or with a leasehold interest in excess of 50 years are maintained, as a matter of policy, by a programme of repair and refurbishment such that their residual values are at least equal to book values. Having regard to this, it is the opinion of the directors that depreciation on any such property, as required by the Companies Act 1985 and accounting standards, would not be material.

Hotels and public houses held under a leasehold interest of 50 years or less are amortised over the unexpired term of the lease.

Other freehold and leasehold properties are depreciated over 50 years, with the exception of breweries and maltings which are depreciated over 25 years, from the later of the date of acquisition and latest valuation.

Other tangible fixed assets are depreciated over their estimated useful lives, namely:

Plant and machinery	4-20 years
Information technology equipment	3-5 years
Equipment in hotels and leisure retail outlets	3-10 years
Vehicles	3-10 years

All depreciation is charged on a straight line basis.

6.5   Notes to the accounts

The note disclosures with regard to cost and depreciation of fixed assets are based on the requirements of the Companies Act and FRSs 10, 11 and 15. The requirements of the Act cover all fixed assets, and are duplicated to some extent by these accounting standards.

For each of the categories of fixed asset shown in the statutory formats (see 6.3 above) the Companies Act requires the following to be disclosed:

(a)   the appropriate amounts at the beginning of the financial year and as at the balance sheet date, based either on historical cost (purchase price or production cost) or alternative accounting rules;[308]

(b)   all movements during the year, including revaluation surpluses and deficits, acquisitions, disposals and transfers.[309] Other movements that might also be reflected in the carrying value of the asset, such as exchange differences, will also be disclosed in the note; and

(c)   the cumulative amount of depreciation as at the beginning and end of the financial year on the appropriate basis of cost or valuation, the depreciation charge for the period and adjustments in respect of disposals or for other reasons.[310]

For the most part, FRS 15's rules for tangible assets repeat those of the Act. It requires that, for each major class of depreciable asset, the following is disclosed:

- total depreciation charged for the period;

- where material, the financial effect of a change during the period in either the estimate of useful economic lives or the estimate of residual values;

- the cost or revalued amount at the beginning of the financial period and at the balance sheet date;

- the cumulative amount of provisions for depreciation or impairment at the beginning of the financial period and at the balance sheet date;

- a reconciliation of the movements, separately disclosing additions, disposals, revaluations, transfers, depreciation, impairment losses, and reversals of past impairment losses written back in the financial period; and

- the net carrying amount at the beginning of the financial period and at the balance sheet date.[311]

In addition, where there has been a change in depreciation method any material effect and the reason for the change should be disclosed in the year of change.[312]

These are not new requirements; the standard simply consolidated the various disclosure requirements previously contained in accounting standards and statute. However, the rules on revaluations may lead to this information being separately given for more classes of assets (see 5.1.6 above).

Similarly, FRS 10 requires the following information to be disclosed separately for positive goodwill, negative goodwill and each class of capitalised intangible asset:

(a)   the cost or revalued amount at the beginning of the financial period and at the balance sheet date;

(b)   the cumulative amount of provisions for amortisation or impairment at the beginning of the financial period and at the balance sheet date;

(c)   a reconciliation of the movements, separately disclosing additions, disposals, revaluations, transfers, amortisation, impairment losses, reversals of past impairment losses and amounts of negative goodwill written back in the financial period; and

(d)   the net carrying amount at the balance sheet date.[313]

For negative goodwill, these further disclosures are required:

(a)   the period in which it is being written back in the profit and loss account;[314] and

(b)   where the negative goodwill exceeds the fair values of the non-monetary assets, an explanation of the amount and source of this excess and the period in which it is being written back.[315]

In the event that a company chooses to carry goodwill as a permanent asset subject to the impairment test, it has to invoke the 'true and fair override' to justify departing from the statutory requirement to amortise goodwill. This brings with it a further set of disclosure requirements: the Companies Act requires disclosure of 'particulars of the departure, the reasons for it and its effect' in a note to the accounts.[316] In December 1992 the UITF issued Abstract 7 – *True and fair override disclosures* – which interprets the Companies Act disclosure requirement as follows:[317]

(a)   'Particulars of any such departure' – a statement of the treatment which the Act would normally require in the circumstances and a description of the treatment actually adopted;

(b)   'the reasons for it' – a statement as to why the treatment prescribed would not give a true and fair view;

(c)   'its effect' – a description of how the position shown in the accounts is different as a result of the departure, normally with quantification except:

    (i)   where quantification is already evident in the accounts themselves; or

    (ii)   whenever the effect cannot reasonably be quantified, in which case the directors should explain the circumstances.

The disclosure required by UITF 7 should either be included, or cross-referenced, in the note stating compliance with accounting standards (as required by the Companies Act).[318]

Extract 10.36 above provides an example of this disclosure in the accounts of Cadbury Schweppes.

Companies will generally comply with these requirements by including separate notes for each major category of fixed asset: i.e. intangible fixed assets, tangible fixed assets and investments. An example of such a note for tangible fixed assets is illustrated below:

Extract 10.65: Reckitt & Colman plc (1998)

10. Fixed assets – tangible assets [extract]

	Freehold land £m	Properties £m	Plant and equipment £m	Total £m
Cost:				
At 4 January 1998	27.6	180.0	496.2	703.8
Additions during the year	–	9.7	68.5	78.2
Disposals during the year	(5.1)	(8.9)	(18.3)	(32.3)
Exchange adjustments	(0.9)	(3.4)	(8.7)	(13.0)
At 2 January 1999	21.6	177.4	537.7	736.7
Accumulated depreciation:				
At 4 January 1998	–	(50.8)	(248.5)	(299.3)
Provided during the year	–	(5.7)	(41.8)	(47.5)
Disposals during the year	–	3.2	4.3	7.5
Exchange adjustments	–	0.5	3.3	3.8
At 2 January 1999	–	(52.8)	(282.7)	(335.5)
Net book amounts:				
At 4 January 1998	27.6	129.2	247.7	404.5
At 2 January 1999	21.6	124.6	255.0	401.2

	1998 £m	1997 £m
The net book amount of properties comprise:		
Freehold buildings	119.6	126.3
Long leaseholds	4.3	2.3
Short leaseholds	0.7	0.6
	124.6	129.2

It can be seen from the above extract that separate disclosure is given of the gross amount of depreciable assets by distinguishing freehold land from 'properties'. This is a disclosure requirement under SSAP 12,[319] but not under FRS 15. An alternative is to show these as a single amount of freehold property and to disclose the amount of freehold land included, so that the depreciable amount (that relating to the buildings) can be deduced, as illustrated below:

Extract 10.66: The Weir Group PLC (1998)

8 Tangible Assets [extract]

The value of freehold land included in freehold land and buildings amounted to £7,157,000 at cost and £923,000 at valuation (1997 £7,838,000 at cost and £946,000 at valuation).

Gleeson discloses the depreciable amount of its fixed assets more directly, as a footnote to the fixed assets note, as shown below:

Extract 10.67: M J Gleeson Group plc (1998)

11 Tangible fixed assets [extract]

	Owner occupied property £000	Investment property £000	Plant and machinery £000	Total £000
Cost or valuation at 30th June 1998:				
At cost			18,727	18,727
At Directors' valuation	458	7,104	–	7,562
At professional valuation in 1997	9,165	38,775	–	47,940
At professional valuation in 1998	–	19,825	–	19,825
	9,623	65,704	18,727	94,054
Depreciable amount thereof	6,159	–	18,727	24,886

FRS 15 also requires that where there has been a change in the depreciation method used, the effect, if material, should be disclosed in the year of change. The reasons for the change should also be disclosed.[320]

The Companies Act requires the carrying amount of 'land and buildings' to be analysed between that held under freehold and long and short leaseholds.[321] Long leases are those with more than 50 years unexpired as at the balance sheet date.[322] This is normally achieved either by splitting the 'land and buildings' category in the fixed asset note into the three sub-categories or by making separate note disclosure as illustrated in the extract of Reckitt & Colman shown above.

6.6   Additional disclosures about impairment

The presentational aspects of impairment losses were discussed at 4.4.8 above. However, FRS 11 requires a number of additional disclosures about impairment, as set out below.

Where a value in use calculation has given rise to an impairment loss, the discount rate applied to the cash flows should be disclosed.[323] The extracts from the accounts of Rio Tinto and Rank in 4.4.1 above illustrate this disclosure. The standard appears to require this disclosure only when a loss has in fact been recognised, although arguably this information might be more significant where the calculation has been performed without giving rise to such a loss. FRS 11 also says that, if the discount rate used has been a risk-free rate, 'some indication' of the risk adjustments made to the cash flows should be given. It is not clear, however, exactly what kind of description the drafters had in mind, and there is a danger that any such disclosures will tend to be anodyne.

If an impairment loss that was recognised in a previous year is reversed in the current year, the reason for the reversal must be disclosed, stating any changes in the assumptions upon which the calculation of recoverable amount is based.[324] Rather more controversially, however, FRS 11 also requires that, where an impairment loss would have been recognised in a previous period had the forecasts of future cash flows been more accurate, but fortuitously the impairment has reversed and the reversal of the loss is permitted to be recognised, the impairment now identified and its subsequent reversal should be disclosed.[325]

The standard also contains two disclosure requirements designed to expose unusually optimistic growth assumptions within cash flow forecasts used to measure value in use. These are:

- where, the period before a steady or declining long-term growth rate has been assumed extends beyond five years, the length of the longer period and the circumstances justifying it should be disclosed;[326] and

- where the long-term growth rate used is more than the long-term average growth rate for the country or countries in which the business operates, the growth rate assumed and the circumstances that justify it should be disclosed.[327]

6.7   Additional disclosures for items carried at valuation

The Companies Act requires that where assets have been included in the accounts at amounts based on a valuation then the items affected and the basis of valuation adopted should be disclosed in a note to the accounts.[328] The revaluation reserve itself should be included as a separate sub-heading in the position shown in the formats, but need not be so called.[329] The treatment for tax purposes of amounts credited or debited to the revaluation reserve must be disclosed in a note to the accounts.[330]

In the case of each balance sheet item affected, disclosure should be made of either:

(a)   the comparable amounts based on historical costs; or

(b)   the differences between the amounts in (a) above and the amounts actually included in the balance sheet.[331]

The comparable amounts are the gross amounts and cumulative provisions for depreciation or diminution in values and should relate to *all* of the assets covered by the balance sheet item.[332]

Most major companies would appear to adopt the former method of disclosure. A good example of disclosure is that of Blue Circle, as illustrated below:

Extract 10.68: Blue Circle Industries PLC (1998)

14 Tangible assets [extract]

| | Land and buildings | | | | | |
	Freehold £m	Long lease £m	Short lease £m	Plant and machinery £m	Assets under construction £m	Total £m
Group						
Net book value at 31 December 1998	107.5	0.6	1.0	158.3	63.3	330.7
Net book value at 31 December 1997	109.2	0.6	1.2	180.3	33.0	324.3
Historical cost at 31 December 1998	156.0	0.6	1.8	410.3	63.3	632.0
Accumulated historical depreciation	55.6	0.1	1.2	255.9	–	312.8
Net historical cost at 31 December 1998	100.4	0.5	0.6	154.4	63.3	319.2

It can be seen from the above extract that almost all of the categories of tangible fixed assets have been affected by valuations and Blue Circle has, therefore, included the disclosure as part of its fixed asset table; in most situations, it will only be land and buildings which are affected by valuations and disclosure will generally be given by way of footnote.

Although the Act requires the amounts to be disclosed to deal with all the assets included in the balance sheet item affected by valuations, some companies disclose the comparable historical cost information for only the assets which have been revalued. Where such an approach is taken then it is necessary to disclose the gross amount and accumulated depreciation for the revalued assets which are included in the balance sheet so that the total figures, in historical cost terms, can be deduced. This is shown in the following extract.

Extract 10.69: Associated British Foods plc (1998)

11   FIXED TANGIBLE ASSETS [extract]

	1998	1997
	£m	£m
Analysis of land and buildings at net book value		
Freehold	450	442
Long leasehold	42	39
Short leasehold	8	8
	500	489

Land and buildings stated at valuation had a net book value at 12 September 1998 of £17 million (1997 – £21 million) based on valuations carried out principally in 1981/82. On a historical cost basis the net book value of these assets at 12 September 1998 would have been £13 million (1997 – £16 million).

For all items (other than listed investments) that are carried at valuation, the Companies Act also requires the years in which the assets were valued and the amounts at which they were valued to be disclosed.[333] An example of this disclosure is given by the following extract from the notes to Delta's accounts:

Extract 10.70: Delta plc (1998)

12 Tangible assets [extract]

	£ million
Analysis of cost or valuation of land and buildings at professional valuation in:	
1996 and earlier years	18.6
1997	17.8
1998 (iv)	34.2
At cost	67.0
At 2 January 1999	**137.6**

(iv) The revaluations which were made in 1998 comprise: UK £22.3 million valued on an existing use basis, these valuations having been carried out by HBSV Ltd Chartered Surveyors, in accordance with the RICS Appraisal and Valuation Manual and £11.9m overseas valued on an existing use basis by independent surveyors.

The information in this extract is often the only information given by companies in respect of past valuations, despite the fact that, as mentioned earlier, the Companies Act also strictly requires the basis of valuation to be disclosed.[334] However, some companies do give more information than the statutory minimum, for example by disclosing the names and professional qualifications of valuers in respect of valuations that took place in previous years, as illustrated in the following extract:

Extract 10.71: Sears plc (1997)

9. Fixed tangible assets [extract]

The majority of the Group's properties were professionally valued by Messrs Healey & Baker, Chesterton and Jones Land Wootton as at 31st January 1993. The basis for valuation was open market value for existing use or, for those properties not occupied by the Group, open market value. Freeholds and leaseholds which expire more than 25 years after the date of valuation are included at 31st January 1993 valuations amounting to £392.5 million. The remaining properties are included at cost or at their previous valuation less depreciation if the period to expiry had fallen to less than 25 years by 31st January 1997.

Where fixed assets (other than investments) have been revalued during the year, then the Companies Act also requires disclosure of the names or qualifications of the persons making the valuation and the bases used by them.[335] An excellent example of such disclosure is shown below:

Extract 10.72: Taylor Woodrow plc (1998)

9 Investment properties [extract]

The investment properties of the group were valued at £397.1m as at 31 December 1998 by the following valuers, on an open market basis:

Canada – Stewart, Young Hillesheim & Atlin Limited	C$168.0m equivalent £65.6m
Gibraltar – a team member who is a Fellow of the Royal Institution of Chartered Surveyors	£1.1m
United Kingdom – Knight Frank	£328.8m
United Kingdom – a team member who is an Associate of the Royal Institution of Chartered Surveyors	£1.6m

Investment property valuations in Gibraltar and the United Kingdom were undertaken by Chartered Surveyors (external unless noted as team members) in accordance with the Appraisal and Valuation Manual of the Royal Institution of Chartered Surveyors.

10 Other tangible assets [extract]

The valuations of fixed asset properties as at 31 December 1997 were made by the following valuers, on an existing use value basis, and those valuations, as adjusted for sales, amounted to £45.3m:

		Equivalent
Australia – J L W Advisory Services Pty. Limited	A$5.3m	£2.0m
Canada – Stewart, Young, Hillesheim & Atlin Limited	C$3.8m	£1.5m
Denmark –ADBO Ejendomsmaeglerfirma MDE	DKr15.8m	£1.5m
Gibraltar – Vail Williams	£0.5m	£0.5m
Ireland – Gunne Property Consultants	IR£0.7m	£0.6m
United Kingdom – Knight Frank	£38.3m	£38.3m
United States of America – Edward R. Thatcher	US$1.5m	£0.9m

Fixed asset property valuations in Gibraltar and the United Kingdom were undertaken by external Chartered Surveyors in accordance with the Appraisal and Valuation Manual of the Royal Institution of Chartered Surveyors.

FRS 15 requires the following disclosures for every class of tangible fixed assets that has been revalued. The information is required in each reporting period:[336]

(a)   the valuer's name and qualifications or the valuer's organisation and a description of its nature;

(b)   the basis or bases of valuation. This should include whether the valuation has reflected notional directly attributable acquisition costs or expected selling costs;

(c)   the date and amounts of the valuations;

(d)   the carrying amount that would have been included in the accounts if the assets had been carried at historical cost less depreciation. This is only required where historical cost records are available;

(e)   whether the valuer is internal or external to the entity;

(f)   a statement by the directors if the valuations have not been updated because they are not aware of any material change in value; and

(g)   the date of the last full valuation where it is an interim valuation or the valuation has not been updated.

In addition, the standard requires the following additional disclosure for revalued properties:[337]

(a)   a statement where properties have been valued having regard to their trading potential and the amount of such properties; and

(b)   the total amount of notional directly attributable acquisition costs or expected selling costs reflected in the carrying amount, where material.

Where the open market value (OMV) is materially different from existing use value (EUV), the OMV and the reasons for the difference should be disclosed in the notes to the accounts.[338]

If it has not proved possible to obtain a reliable valuation of an asset held outside the UK or the Republic of Ireland, the carrying amount of the tangible fixed asset and the fact that it has not been revalued must be stated.[339]

In the unusual event of any class of intangible assets being revalued, FRS 10 requires disclosures to be given that are essentially the same as those already required by the Act.[340]

6.8   Disclosures for investment properties

6.8.1   *Disclosures required by SSAP 19*

The carrying value of investment properties and the investment revaluation reserve should be shown prominently in the financial statements.[341] The following details concerning the valuation should also be given:

(a)   the basis of the valuation;

(b)   the names or qualifications of the valuers; and

(c) if the valuation was made by an officer or employee of the company or group owning the property, the financial statements should disclose this fact.[342]

SSAP 19 refers to an 'investment revaluation reserve'[343] but in practice this term is seldom used in property company accounts. Most companies prefer just 'revaluation reserve', although some take advantage of the freedom allowed by the Companies Act to change this particular heading[344] with headings such as 'property revaluation reserve' and 'unrealised capital account'.

SSAP 19 requires that the carrying value of investment properties and the investment revaluation reserve be 'displayed prominently in the accounts'.[345] This means that if assets other than investment properties are revalued, the revaluation reserve should be split to show the amount relating to investment properties as opposed to other revalued assets. In practice, such splits are seldom seen.

6.8.2 Balance sheet classification

Many companies with investment properties adapt the Companies Act balance sheet headings, often by splitting tangible fixed assets into two categories, one for investment properties and one for other tangible fixed assets. Where appropriate, the former figure should be analysed between completed investment properties and properties under development, since investment properties by definition do not include properties in the course of development. Some companies give this analysis on the face of the balance sheet, others in the notes to the accounts. The latter figure is usually analysed in the notes to the accounts between the headings shown above, although this is not strictly necessary where the total of other tangible fixed assets is immaterial.[346]

6.8.3 Disclosure on use of 'true and fair override'

The company law requirement to depart from the usual legal rules if to follow them would lead to the accounts not showing a true and fair view (the 'true and fair override') was referred to in 3.2.1 above, as was the reliance on this requirement as a basis for SSAP 19. This means that the further disclosures required by the Act and referred to in 6.5 above must be given. Examples of such disclosures are illustrated below:

Extract 10.73: Hammerson plc (1998)

1   ACCOUNTING POLICIES

Basis of accounting

The financial statements are prepared under the historical cost convention as modified by the revaluation of investment properties and in accordance with all applicable accounting standards. The financial statements are in compliance with the Companies Act 1985 except that, as explained below, investment properties are not depreciated.

Depreciation [extract]

In accordance with Statement of Standard Accounting Practice No. 19, no depreciation is provided in respect of freehold properties or leasehold properties with over 20 years to expiry. This is a departure from the requirements of the Companies Act 1985 which requires all properties to be depreciated. Such properties are not held for consumption but for investment and the directors consider that to depreciate them would not give a true and fair view. Depreciation is only one of many factors reflected in the annual valuation of properties and accordingly the amount of depreciation which might otherwise have been charged cannot be separately identified or quantified. The directors consider that this policy results in the accounts giving a true and fair view.

Extract 10.74: Land Securities PLC (1999)

1   Accounting Policies

The financial statements have been prepared under the historical cost convention modified by the revaluation of properties and in accordance with applicable accounting standards. Compliance with SSAP 19 "Accounting for Investment Properties" requires a departure from the requirements of the Companies Act 1985 relating to depreciation and amortisation and an explanation of this departure is given in (e) below.

(e)   DEPRECIATION AND AMORTISATION [extract]

In accordance with SSAP 19, no depreciation or amortisation is provided in respect of freehold or leasehold properties held on leases having more than 20 years unexpired. This departure from the requirements of the Companies Act 1985, for all properties to be depreciated, is, in the opinion of the Directors, necessary for the financial statements to give a true and fair view in accordance with applicable accounting standards, as properties are included in the financial statements at their open market value.

The effect of depreciation and amortisation on value is already reflected annually in the valuation of properties, and the amount attributed to this factor by the valuers cannot reasonably be separately identified or quantified. Had the provisions of the Act been followed, net assets would not have been affected but revenue profits would have been reduced for this and earlier years.

The above extracts can be contrasted with the disclosure which is given by MEPC, as shown below:

> *Extract 10.75: MEPC plc (1998)*
>
> **Depreciation and amortisation** [extract]
>
> In accordance with Statement of Standard Accounting Practice No 19 investment properties are revalued annually and the aggregate surplus or deficit is transferred to a revaluation reserve, and no depreciation or amortisation is provided in respect of freehold investment properties and leasehold investment properties with over 20 years to expiry. This treatment may be a departure from the requirements of the Companies Act concerning the depreciation of fixed assets. However, these properties are not held for consumption but for investment and the Directors consider that systematic annual depreciation would be inappropriate. The accounting policy adopted is therefore necessary for the accounts to give a true and fair view. Depreciation or amortisation is only one of many factors reflected in the annual valuation and the amount which might otherwise have been shown cannot be separately identified or quantified.

It can be seen that MEPC has not said that there is a departure from the Companies Act requirement but that there *may* be a departure. It is unclear why this should be the case, but it may be because the depreciation would not have been sufficiently material to involve a departure from the Act. Another company which has not categorically stated that there is a departure is Slough Estates.[347]

The extracts shown above say that the effect of the departure cannot reasonably be quantified, which is what most property companies say.

7 COMPARISON WITH IASC AND US PRONOUNCEMENTS

7.1 IASC

7.1.1 IAS 16

IAS 16 – *Accounting for property, plant and equipment* – like FRS 15, addresses only tangible fixed assets and it deals with the same issues as its UK equivalent. The original version of the standard was issued in 1982, and its most recent revision was in September 1998, taking effect for accounting periods beginning on or after 1 July 1999.

The benchmark treatment under IAS 16 is to carry fixed assets at historical cost.[348] However, it also permits them to be carried at fair values as an allowed alternative, so long as the valuations are kept materially up to date.[349] Like FRS 15, it also requires that an entire class of assets be revalued, where the valuation approach is followed, rather than allowing piecemeal valuations of individual assets.[350] However, it is much less detailed than the UK standard on the bases of valuation to be applied.

The gain or loss on disposal of revalued assets is to be measured by reference to the revalued amount of the asset, not its original cost,[351] but write-downs of revalued assets are to be charged against the revaluation reserve to the extent that there is a surplus held there in relation to the asset in question, and only thereafter charged as an expense.[352] FRS 15 has a similar approach, but also requires losses to be taken to the profit and loss account when they are 'clearly caused by the consumption of economic benefits'; there is no equivalent to this rule in IAS 16. On the other hand, IAS 16 allows revaluation losses to be recognised in the statement of total recognised gains and losses rather than the profit and loss account only if they are the reversal of revaluation gains, whereas FRS 15 also allows this treatment to the extent that the asset's recoverable amount exceeds its revalued amount.

IAS 16 also contains requirements on depreciation that broadly correspond to those in FRS 15. However, it has no equivalent to the UK requirement that an annual impairment review be carried out when depreciation has not been charged because it would be immaterial, or when the remaining life of an asset is assumed to exceed 50 years.

7.1.2   IAS 22

This standard was first published in 1983, and like IAS 16 it was last revised in September 1998 to take effect for accounting periods beginning on or after 1 July 1999. It deals with all aspects of business combinations, but its treatment of goodwill and negative goodwill are the only aspects that are relevant to this chapter.

Under IAS 22, goodwill must be amortised over its useful life, with a rebuttable presumption that the life will not exceed 20 years.[353] The straight line method is favoured unless another method better reflects the pattern of consumption of benefits.[354] Consistent with the requirements for intangible assets in IAS 38 (see 7.1.5 below), if the life is taken to exceed 20 years, the company should amortise the goodwill over that longer life and:

(a)   test it for impairment at least annually in accordance with IAS 36, (see 7.1.4 below); and

(b)   disclose why the presumption of a 20 year life is rebutted and what were the factors that played a significant role in determining the useful life.

This regime is therefore very similar to that now prevailing in the UK, with the significant difference that it is not possible under IAS 22 to assume an indefinite life so as to avoid an amortisation charge altogether. The IASC rejects the principle that underpins FRS 10, that internally generated goodwill can replace purchased goodwill so as to justify an infinite life.[355]

Negative goodwill is measured as the excess of the acquirer's interest in the fair values of the identifiable assets and liabilities acquired over the cost of its acquisition. The previous treatment of allocating the negative goodwill to reduce the fair values of identifiable assets acquired which was the benchmark treatment before the 1998 revision is no longer permitted.

As in the UK, IAS 22 requires negative goodwill to be presented in the balance sheet as a deduction from positive goodwill.[356] It should thereafter be recognised as income as follows:

(a)   to the extent that it relates to expectations of future losses and expenses that are identified in the acquirer's plan for the acquisition and can be measured reliably, it should be recognised as income when the identified future losses and expenses occur;[357] and otherwise

(b)   negative goodwill not exceeding the fair values of the non-monetary assets acquired should be recognised as income over the remaining weighted average useful life of the depreciable/amortisable non-monetary assets acquired.[358] Negative goodwill in excess of the fair values of the non-monetary assets acquired should be recognised as income immediately.[359]

These last rules differ from FRS 10 in a few detailed respects. The release of negative goodwill to offset losses and expenses ((a) above) is not permitted in the UK, although it had been suggested in FRED 12.[360] The amortisation over the lives of non-monetary assets sounds similar to UK GAAP, but IAS 22's reference to '*depreciable/amortisable* non-monetary assets' appears to restrict it to fixed assets, which may be what FRS 10 intended but is not what it achieved. In the rare case that the negative goodwill exceeds such assets, IAS 22 requires it to be released to income immediately, whereas FRS 10 has a more vague requirement to recognise it in the periods expected to be benefited' (see 3.4.4 above).

7.1.3   IAS 25

IAS 25 on accounting for investments permits investment properties to be classified either as property or as long-term investments.[361] If classified as property, they must be depreciated in accordance with IAS 16.[362] If classified as long-term investments they may be either revalued or retained at cost.[363]

Other requirements of IAS 25 which are relevant to investment properties are:

(a)   if revaluations are used, a policy for the frequency of revaluations should be adopted and an entire category of long-term investments should be revalued at the same time;[364]

(b)   provision must be made for permanent diminutions in the value of long-term investments. This must be done for each investment individually;[365]

(c)   increases in value on a revaluation should be credited to revaluation reserve. Any reduction below cost on an individual investment should be charged to profit and loss account. A subsequent reversal of such a decrease should be credited to profit and loss account;[366]

(d)   if short-term investments are carried at the lower of cost and market value, revaluations should be reversed on a reclassification from long-term to short-term;[367]

(e)   the accounts should disclose:

(i)   the accounting policies for determining the carrying amount of investments and the treatment of revaluation surpluses on the disposal of revalued investments;

(ii)   the fair value of investment properties if treated as long-term investments and not revalued;

(iii)   for long-term investments carried at valuation:

■   the policy for the frequency of revaluations;

■   the date of the latest revaluation; and

■   the basis of revaluation, stating whether an external valuer was used;

(iv)   movements on revaluation surplus and the nature of such movements; and

(v)   for enterprises whose main business is the holding of investments, an analysis of the portfolio of investments.[368]

In 1989, the IASC issued an exposure draft, E32 – *Comparability of Financial Statements* – which proposed to amend, inter alia, the requirements of IAS 25. The main change proposed was to make the preferred treatment for investment properties that they should be measured at cost and depreciated as normal. However, the alternative treatment of dealing with such assets as long-term investments carried at valuation was still to be allowed, provided additional information was given.[369] The only change to the provisions dealing with the accounting for revaluations of such assets was that on disposal of a revalued asset any revaluation surplus remaining in the revaluation reserve relating to the disposed asset should be transferred to retained earnings (and not to income as presently allowed).[370] These proposals were endorsed in a statement of intent published by the IASC in July 1990,[371] but were never implemented.

In July 1999, the IASC issued a further exposure draft, E64, which proposes that investment properties should be carried at fair value, but with the controversial twist that all movements in value would be reported in the income statement[372] (rather than in the statement of total recognised gains and losses as is required under SSAP 19). If this becomes a standard, the IASC intends to withdraw IAS 25.

E64 defines an investment property as property that meets the following conditions:

(a)   it is held to earn rentals or for capital appreciation or both rather than for:

(i)   use in the production or supply of goods or services or for administrative purposes; or

(ii)   sale in the ordinary course of business; and

(b) when the enterprise acquired or constructed the property (or first held the property to earn rentals or for capital appreciation), it expected that it would be able to determine its fair value reliably on a continuing basis.[373]

There is a hint of an opt-out in part (b) of the definition. There is a rebuttable presumption that this condition will be met, but if it is rebutted the accounting treatment for the property defaults to IAS 16. The draft also says that a property is not an investment property if the owner provides significant ancillary services to the occupants (such as a hotel),[374] nor is a lessee's interest in a property held under an operating lease able to be classified as an investment property.[375]

7.1.4 IAS 36

The IASC issued IAS 36 – *Impairment of Assets* – in June 1998, and it is mandatory for periods beginning on or after 1 July 1999. It is very similar to FRS 11 in its approach, having been developed in parallel with it, but nonetheless there are a number of detailed differences between the two, notably the following:

- In principle, IAS 36 applies to assets in general rather than only to fixed assets, although it then scopes out most financial assets, inventories, assets arising from construction contracts, deferred tax assets, and assets arising from employee benefits, all of which bring it back towards FRS 11. However, it does not exempt investment properties, oil exploration costs or an entity's own shares held by an ESOP, all of which are scoped out of FRS 11;

- The indicators of impairment that IAS 36 uses are similar to those in FRS 11, but IAS 36 also mentions the case where a listed company's market capitalisation is less than the book value of its net assets;[376]

- FRS 11 requires the impairment losses in an income-generating unit to be charged (after writing off goodwill) against intangible assets in priority to tangible assets, whereas IAS 36 treats these two categories equally;[377]

- Like FRS 11 (although unlike SFAS 121), IAS 36 requires impairment provisions that are subsequently found to be unnecessary to be reversed.[378] However, it applies the same rules to intangible assets (other than goodwill) as it does to tangible assets and investments, whereas FRS 11 imposes additional restrictions on intangibles as well as goodwill. Furthermore, FRS 11 does not permit impairment to be reversed when the cash outflows that caused the write-down have passed, whereas IAS 36 contains no such restriction;

- IAS 36 is as unspecific as FRS 11 on how to determine an appropriate discount rate, but it also hints that the use of the entity's incremental borrowing rate might be an appropriate starting point as an alternative to the weighted average cost of capital;[379]

- IAS 36 is slightly less restrictive as to the assumptions that may be made about future growth rates;

■ Unlike FRS 11, IAS 36 does not require an impairment loss identified in an operation in which an existing business has been combined with an acquired one to be allocated between the goodwill relating to the latter and the notional goodwill existing in the former;

■ IAS 36 does not include FRS 11's requirements for companies to continue to review value in use tests retrospectively for the next five years and make write-downs that are revealed by hindsight to have been necessary. Similarly, it does not require disclosure of an impairment write-down that is still unnecessary but would have been recorded in earlier years if forecasts at that time had been more accurate; and

■ IAS 36 requires more detailed disclosures about write-downs and their reversal.

7.1.5   IAS 38

IAS 38 – *Intangible Assets* – was issued in September 1998 and applies to periods beginning on or after 1 July 1999. This follows a similar approach to FRS 10 in most respects; in particular, it sets fairly restrictive criteria for the recognition of intangible assets. The IASC's benchmark treatment is to carry intangibles on the basis of historical cost, but like FRS 10 it allows revaluation as an alternative, provided there is an ascertainable market value for the intangible in question. There are, however, a number of differences, the most significant of which are discussed below:

■ The definition of intangible assets in both IAS 38 and FRS 10 requires them to be 'identifiable'. However, in the UK standard this term is defined in a special way to mean 'capable of being disposed of or settled separately, without disposing of a business of the entity', whereas in the IASC version it has its natural meaning;[380]

■ The IASC version embraces research and development expenditure within its scope, whereas FRS 10 leaves that issue to SSAP 13. This is because the IASC rejects a 'deferred cost' perspective for including items in the balance sheet, although it has to use rather tortuously worded recognition criteria to continue to allow the same expenditure to be capitalised from a balance sheet perspective; and

■ IAS 38 is consistent with FRS 10 in imposing a presumption that intangibles have a maximum life of 20 years, and allowing it to be rebutted if adequate evidence to support a longer life exists, subject to an annual impairment test being required. However, the possibility of an indefinite life is not acknowledged.

7.2   US

As in the UK, there is no accounting standard in the US that covers all aspects of accounting for fixed assets, but a number of standards cover different parts of the subject. An important item in the cost of assets constructed for a business's own use or resale, the capitalisation of interest, is covered by SFAS 34.[381] There are also industry-specific standards such as SFAS 67[382] which deals with the costs of constructing buildings for real estate developers.

There is no general standard on depreciation in the US equivalent to FRS 15, although some aspects are covered in ARBs 43 and 44 (revised).[383] There are, however, a number of standards that deal with detailed aspects of the subject.[384] Disclosure is dealt with by paragraphs 4 and 5 of APB 12.

Depreciation is defined in ARB 43 as follows:

'A system of accounting which aims to distribute the cost or other basic value of tangible capital assets, less salvage (if any), over the estimated useful life of the unit (which may be a group of assets) in a systematic and rational manner. It is a process of allocation, not of valuation.'[385]

Under US GAAP, positive goodwill must be amortised on a straight line basis over its estimated useful life not exceeding 40 years. In most cases the useful life will be less than 40 years. An accelerated method of amortisation should be used for goodwill when the amount assigned to goodwill includes costs for identifiable intangibles whose fair values are not determinable and the benefits expected to be received from those intangibles decline over the expected life of the factors which are the basis for those intangibles. It is generally inappropriate to lengthen the period of amortisation once established at acquisition.[386]

Negative goodwill should be allocated to reduce proportionately the values assigned to non-current assets in determining their fair values. Any remainder should be classified as a deferred credit and amortised to income over a period estimated to be benefited but not in excess of 40 years.[387]

The FASB is presently engaged in a major project to review the whole approach to business combinations, and this may affect the rules on both positive and negative goodwill. It plans to reduce the amortisation period for positive goodwill from 40 to 20 years, but to move the charge further down the profit and loss account, to be shown as a separate line item on a net-of-tax basis. Negative goodwill would be applied to reduce depreciable or amortisable non-monetary assets on a pro rata basis, but any amount that remained thereafter would be reported immediately as an extraordinary gain, rather than amortised over a period.

In 1995 the FASB issued its statement on the impairment of fixed assets, SFAS 121.[388] This is similar in some respects to the ASB proposals (which were to some extent modelled on it), but there are also some important differences.

Like FRS 11 (discussed at 4.4 above), SFAS 121 first requires companies to consider whether there are 'indications of impairment'. However, unlike the UK standard, the US approach assesses this on the basis of the *un*discounted future cash flows of the business segment concerned; if this test shows no shortfall, nothing further requires to be done. If there is a shortfall on this test, then the asset has to be written down to its fair value, which may be either an externally determined market value or an internal calculation based on *discounted* future cash flows. This switch from an undiscounted basis for triggering the recognition of impairment to a discounted basis for measuring it can obviously produce some anomalous results.

Another important difference between the two approaches is that once an impairment write-down has been recorded under the US standard, it cannot subsequently be reversed even if conditions improve.[389] In contrast, an impairment provision made in the UK is reversed if the need for it has gone away.

Revaluations of fixed assets are not generally permitted in US accounts. In APB 6 it is stated: 'Property, plant and equipment should not be written up by an entity to reflect appraisal, market or current values which are above cost to the entity.'[390]

The US position on accounting for investment properties contrasts starkly with that in the UK. No special treatment is allowed for investment properties and, as indicated above, revaluations are generally not permitted.[391] Real estate companies tend to have unclassified balance sheets with all properties shown under the same heading. Some give supplementary current value information.

8   CONCLUSION

In principle, accounting for fixed assets should not pose many conceptual difficulties. The essential purpose is to allocate the cost of assets which provide enduring benefits against the revenues of the periods which enjoy these benefits. However, that straightforward objective does not always prove easy to achieve.

One of the main factors which complicates the issue is the permitted practice of incorporating revaluations in what are otherwise historical cost accounts. This immediately poses accounting questions about how to treat the revaluation surplus subsequently, but it also tends to confuse the objectives of traditional accounting for fixed assets; it lends some support to the view that the balance sheet is intended to portray the value of the assets employed and therefore that depreciation should also be designed to meet that end, or at least that the maintenance of value can justify the absence of depreciation.

Unfortunately, we do not believe that the ASB's standards have succeeded in unravelling these issues very convincingly. The approach for intangible assets and goodwill that FRS 10 has adopted does depend on the view that maintenance of value can justify non-amortisation, and this can include the implicit substitution of internally generated intangibles for purchased intangibles. At the same time, however the Board has rejected such an approach in relation to tangible assets under FRS 15 and accepted it only on pragmatic grounds for investment properties. It has also been unable to develop a consistent approach for revalued assets as between depreciation and disposals on the one hand and impairment on the other. And by requiring impaired assets to be measured on a discounted basis under FRS 11, the Board has introduced a new inconsistency, since depreciation methods typically do not take account of the time value of money. Although these standards have successfully eliminated some undesirable practices, therefore, we regret that they have not managed to achieve greater conceptual consistency in the accounting treatment of fixed assets.

References

1   FRS 15, *Tangible Fixed Assets*, ASB, February 1999.
2   FRS 10, *Goodwill and Intangible Fixed Assets*, ASB, December 1997.
3   SSAP 19, *Accounting for investment properties*, ASC, November 1981.
4   SSAP 13, *Accounting for research and development*, ASC, revised 1989.
5   FRS 11, *Impairment of Fixed Assets and Goodwill*, ASB, May 1998.
6   SSAP 12, *Accounting for depreciation*, ASC, revised January 1987.
7   FRS 3, *Reporting Financial Performance*, ASB, October 1992, paras. 20 and 21.
8   CA 85, s 262(1).
9   FRS 15, para. 2.
10   FRS 10, para. 2.
11   *Ibid.*
12   CA 85, Sch 4A, para. 9(2).
13   FRS 10, para. 9.
14   *Ibid.*, para. 10.
15   *Ibid.*, para. 12.
16   *Ibid.*, para. 10.
17   *Ibid.*, para. 14.
18   SSAP 22, *Accounting for goodwill*, ASC, Revised July 1989, para. 27.
19   CA 85, Sch 4A, para. 9(2).
20   FRS 10, para. 2.
21   Barwise, Higson, Likierman and Marsh, *Accounting for Brands*, 1989, p. 8.
22   FRS 10, para. 10.
23   On 2 July 1999, the G4+1 issued a communiqué which announced, inter alia, that it had identified accounting for internally developed intangible assets as a potential project for further study.
24   CA 85, Sch. 4, para. 17.
25   FRS 15, para. 6.
26   *Ibid.*, para. 7.
27   *Ibid.*, para. 17.
28   CA 85, s 262(1).
29   *Ibid.*, Sch. 4, para. 26(1).
30   SSAP 4, *Accounting for government grants*, ASC, Revised July 1990, para. 25.
31   CA 85, Sch. 4, paras. 26(2) and 26(3).
32   FRS 15, para. 9.
33   *Ibid.*, para. 10.
34   *Ibid.*, para. 9.
35   *Ibid.*, para. 11.
36   Discussion paper, *Measurement of Tangible Fixed Assets*, ASB, October 1996, para. 1.6.
37   FRS 12, para. 10.

38 FRS 15, paras. 12, 13.
39 *Ibid.*, para. 14.
40 *Ibid.*, para. 35.
41 *Ibid.*, para. 36.
42 IAS 16, *Property, Plant and Equipment*, IASC, Revised 1998, para. 24.
43 FRS 15, para. 40.
44 *Ibid.*, para. 2.
45 This view was to an extent supported by the definition in the original version of SSAP 12, at para. 15 which ran (in part): 'depreciation is the measure of the wearing out, consumption or other loss of value of a fixed asset…'.
46 ARB 43, para. 7. Note that this consolidates the earlier ARB 33 that dates from 1947, but has not been superseded.
47 CA 85, Sch. 4, para. 18.
48 *Ibid.*, para. 21.
49 *Ibid.*
50 *Ibid.*, para. 32.
51 ASC, *A review of SSAP 12 – Accounting for depreciation*, paras. 3.1–3.4, 6.1–6.2 and 4.1–4.6.
52 ED 51, *Accounting for fixed assets and revaluations*, ASC, May 1990.
53 *Measurement of Tangible Fixed Assets*.
54 FRED 17, *Measurement of Tangible Fixed Assets*, ASB, October 1997.
55 FRS 15, para. 4.
56 *Ibid.*, para. 2.
57 *Ibid.*, para. 77.
58 *Ibid.*, para. 78.
59 ED 37, *Accounting for depreciation*, ASC, March 1985, para. 25, stated, 'In certain very restricted instances it may not be appropriate to charge depreciation in respect of what would normally be a depreciable asset. This would arise only where the asset is maintained to such a standard that:
    a) the estimated residual value is equal to or greater than its net book amount, or
    b) its estimated useful economic life is either infinite or such that any depreciation charge would be insignificant.'
60 Technical Release 648, *Statement on the publication of SSAP 12 (Revised) Accounting for depreciation*, para. 10.
61 FRED 17, para. 78.
62 FRS 15, para. 89.
63 *Ibid.*, para. 91.
64 *Ibid.*, para. 97.
65 FRAG 2/92, ICAEW, 1992, para. 47.
66 FRS 15, para. 81.
67 *Ibid.*, para. 83.
68 *Ibid.*, para. 84.
69 RICS Guidance Note 5, para. 5.3.4
70 *Ibid.*, para. 5.3.5
71 FRS 15, para. 85
72 *Ibid.*, para. 106.
73 *Ibid.*, para. 108.
74 *Ibid.*, para. 80.
75 *Ibid.*, para. 93.
76 *Ibid.*
77 SSAP 12, para. 18.
78 ED 37, para. 20.
79 Original SSAP 12, para. 4.
80 FRS 15, para. 95.
81 *Ibid.*, para. 77.
82 *Ibid.*, para. 82.
83 *Ibid.*
84 *Ibid.*, para. 81.

85   See the SORP on *Accounting for oil and gas exploration and development activities*, Oil Industry Accounting Committee, December 1987, paras. 62–65 and 84–87.

86   CA 85, Sch. 4, para. 25.

87   FRS 10, para. 1.

88   FRRP PN 52, 22 July 1998.

89   *Ibid.*, Notes to Editors, para. 3.

90   IAS 22, *Business Combinations*, IASC, Revised September 1998, para. 44.

91   FRS 10, para. 2.

92   *Ibid.*

93   *Ibid.*, para. 24.

94   *Ibid.*, para. 19.

95   *Ibid.*, para. 20.

96   *Ibid.*, para. 23.

97   *Ibid.*, para. 21.

98   *Ibid.*, para. 22.

99   FRS 11, para. 12.

100 FRS 10, para. 33.

101 *Ibid.*, para. 28.

102 *Ibid.*

103 *Ibid.*, para. 29.

104 *Ibid.*, para. 30.

105 *Ibid.*, para. 31.

106 *Ibid.*, para. 32.

107 *Ibid.*, para. 48.

108 FRED 12, *Goodwill and Intangible Assets*, ASB, June 1996, para. 96.

109 FRS 10, para. 49.

110 *Ibid.*, para. 50.

111 *Ibid.*, para. 64.

112 *Ibid.*, para. 51.

113 ASC Discussion Paper, Accounting for goodwill, 1980.

114 ED 30, Accounting for Goodwill, October 1982, para. 56.

115 SSAP 22, paras. 39 and 41.

116 UITF 3, Treatment of Goodwill on Disposal of a Business, December 1991, para. 7.

117 *Ibid.*, para. 12.

118 *Ibid.*, para. 10.

119 *Ibid.*, para. 9.

120 FRS 2, para. 47.

121 FRS 10, para 77.

122 *Ibid.*, para. 71(b)

123 SSAP 12, para. 22.

124 ED 26, *Accounting for investment properties – an addition to SSAP 12 'Accounting for depreciation'*, ASC, September 1980.

125 *Statement by the Accounting Standards Committee on the publication of ED 26 'Accounting for investment properties'*, paras. 7 and 8.

126 SSAP 19, para. 7.

127 *Ibid.*, para. 8.

128 *Ibid.*, para. 9.

129 FRS 15, para 109.

130 CA 85, s 228(5).

131 *Amendment to SSAP 19 'Accounting for investment properties'*, ASB, July 1994, para. 7.

132 FRS 15, para. 4.

133 CA 85, Sch. 4, para. 19(2).

134 *Ibid.*, para. 19(3).

135 *Ibid.*, paras. 19(1) and (2). The use of the word 'shown' makes the wording ambiguous, but it is generally considered to mean that the provisions must be made through the profit and loss account and either disclosed on the face of the profit and loss account or in the notes to the accounts.

136 SSAP 12, para. 20.
137 *Ibid.*, para. 19.
138 *Impairment of Tangible Fixed Assets*, ASB, April 1996.
139 FRED 15, *Impairment of Fixed Assets and Goodwill*, ASB, June 1997.
140 FRS 11, para. 74.
141 *Ibid.*, para. 1.
142 FRS 11, Appendix II, para. 5.
143 FRS 11, para. 75.
144 *Ibid.*, para. 5.
145 FRS 13, *Derivatives and other financial instruments: Disclosures*, ASB, September 1998, para. 5.
146 FRS 11, para. 7.
147 *Ibid.*, para. 2.
148 *Ibid.*
149 *Ibid.*
150 *Ibid.*, para. 19.
151 *Ibid.*, para. 15.
152 *Ibid.*, para. 18.
153 *Ibid.*, para. 2.
154 *Ibid.*, Appendix IV, para. 4.
155 FRS 11, para. 10.
156 *Ibid.*, para. 17.
157 *Ibid.*, para. 10.
158 *Ibid.*, para. 13.
159 FRS 10, para. 34.
160 *Ibid.*, para. 34(a).
161 *Ibid.*, para. 35.
162 FRS 15, para. 89.
163 IAS 36, para. 9(d).
164 FRS 11, para. 17.
165 *Ibid.*, para. 27.
166 *Ibid.*, para. 29.
167 *Ibid.*, Examples 1-4.
168 CA85, Sch 4, para. 14.
169 FRS 11, para. 30.
170 *Ibid.*, para. 32.
171 *Ibid.*, para. 34.
172 *Ibid.*, para. 33.
173 *Ibid.* para. 36.
174 *Ibid.* para. 37.
175 *Ibid.* para. 38.
176 *Ibid.* para. 39.
177 *Ibid.* para. 41.
178 *Ibid.* para. 11.
179 *Ibid.* para. 42.
180 *Ibid.* para. 43.
181 One source of reference which may prove useful is a Digest issued by the Corporate Finance Faculty of the ICAEW – *The Cost of Capital*, Simon Pallett, ICAEW, 1999.
182 *Ibid.* para. 44.
183 *Ibid.* Appendix I.
184 FRS 11, para. 46.
185 *Ibid.* para. 45.
186 *Ibid.* para. 48.
187 *Ibid.* para. 49.
188 *Ibid.* para. 2.
189 *Ibid.* para. 49.
190 *Ibid.* para. 54.

191 *Ibid.* para. 55.
192 *Ibid.* para. 56.
193 *Ibid.* para. 57.
194 *Ibid.* para. 58.
195 *Ibid.* para. 60.
196 *Ibid.* para. 70.
197 *Ibid.* para. 61.
198 *Ibid.* para. 50.
199 *Ibid.* para. 52.
200 *Ibid.*
201 *Ibid.* para. 67.
202 *Ibid.*
203 *Ibid.* para. 68.
204 SSAP 12, para. 5.
205 *Ibid.*, para. 81.
206 *Ibid.*, para. 53.
207 ED 51, para. 84.
208 *Ibid.*, para. 86.
209 Discussion paper, *The Role of Valuation in Financial Reporting*, ASB, March 1993, para. 34.
210 *Ibid.*, para. 10.
211 *Measurement of Tangible Fixed Assets*, ASB, October 1996, para. 2.5.
212 FRED 17, para. 60.
213 *Ibid.*, para 62.
214 *Ibid.*, para 61.
215 FRS 15, para. 42.
216 *Ibid.*, para. 2.
217 *Ibid.*, para. 62.
218 *Ibid.*, para. 43.
219 *Ibid.*, para. 44.
220 *Ibid.*, para. 45.
221 *Ibid.*, para. 52.
222 *Ibid.*, para. 48.
223 *Ibid.*, para. 47.
224 *Ibid.*, para. 49.
225 *Ibid.*, para. 46.
226 *Ibid.*, para. 50.
227 *Ibid.*, para. 51.
228 *Ibid.*, paras. 104 and 105.
229 *Ibid.*, para. 4. This was a change from FRED 17, which had proposed to embrace investment properties within its scope and repeal SSAP 19.
230 SSAP 19, paras. 10 and 11.
231 *Ibid.*, para. 6.
232 See for example Land Securities PLC, Report and Financial Statements 1999, p. 43.
233 CA 85, Sch. 4, para. 31(2).
234 *Ibid.*, para. 31(1).
235 *Ibid.*, para. 31(3).
236 *Accounting for the effects of changing prices: a Handbook*, ASC, 1986, paras. A1.3 and A1.4. In fact, the same diagram is often used to describe the alternative term 'value to the business'.
237 *Measurement of tangible fixed assets*, para. 4.11.
238 (S20) 2.205, *Valuation of company property assets and their disclosure in directors' reports or accounts of companies*.
239 *Report of the President's Working Party on Commercial Property Valuations*, Foreword.
240 FRS 15, para. 53.
241 *Ibid.*, para. 55.
242 RICS Appraisal and Valuations Manual Practice Statement 4, para. 4.2.
243 *Ibid.*, para. 4.3.1.

244 *Ibid.*, para. 4.3.10.
245 FRS 15, para. 53(a).
246 RICS Appraisal and Valuations Manual Practice Statement 4 para. 4.3.2.
247 FRS 15 para. 56.
248 RICS Guidance Note 7, para. 7.2.8.
249 SSAP 22, para. 15.
250 FRS 15 para. 85.
251 RICS, Definitions.
252 *Ibid.*, Practice Statement 4, para. 4.8.1.
253 FRS 15, para. 58.
254 RICS, Practice Statement 4, para. 4.8.5.
255 FRS 15, para. 57.
256 *Ibid.*, para. 60 and RICS Practice Statement 4, para. 4.17.
257 RICS Practice Statement 4, para. 4.17.
258 CA 85, Sch. 4, para. 34(1).
259 FRS 3, para. 13, and FRS 12, para. 63.
260 CA 85, Sch. 4, para. 34(3). Until amended by the CA 89, this read '... for the purpose of the accounting policies adopted by the company', which was capable of wider interpretation.
261 *Ibid.*, para. 34(3)(a).
262 *Ibid.*, paras. 34(3A) and (3B).
263 *Ibid.*, para. 65.
264 *Ibid.*, para. 68.
265 *Ibid.*, para. 69.
266 *Ibid.*, para. 70.
267 *Ibid.*, para. 32.
268 FRS 15, para. 63.
269 *Ibid.*, para. 64.
270 *Ibid.*
271 CA 85, Sch. 4, paras. 19 and 34.
272 SSAP 19, Investment properties, ASC, Revised July 1994, para. 13. There are also some variations of treatment available to companies in particular industries.
273 FRS 15, para. 78.
274 *Ibid.*, para. 79.
275 SSAP 12, para. 16.
276 *Measurement of Tangible Fixed Assets*, para. 5.41.
277 FRS 3, para. 56.
278 *Impairment of Tangible Fixed Assets*, footnote to para. 5.10. This issue was not addressed specifically in the subsequent standard.
279 ASC Discussion Paper, *A review of SSAP 6 – Extraordinary items and prior year adjustments*, para. 2.11, ASC Discussion Paper, *A review of SSAP 12 – Accounting for depreciation*, paras. 7.2 and 7.3, ED 16, *Supplement to 'Extraordinary items and prior year adjustments'*, ASC, September 1975, para. 14, ED 36, *Extraordinary items and prior year adjustments*, ASC, January 1985, para. 26 and ED 51, para. 80.
280 FRS 11, para. 67.
281 FRED 17, para. 60.
282 *Reporting Financial Performance: Proposals for change*, ASB, June 1999, Foreword para. 19.
283 UITF 5, *Transfers from Current Assets to Fixed Assets*, July 1992, para. 2.
284 *Ibid.*, para. 5.
285 CA 85, Sch. 4, para. 34(3).
286 *Ibid.*, s 263(3).
287 *Ibid.*, s275(1).
288 *Ibid.*, s275(2).
289 *Ibid.*, Sch. 4, para. 19.
290 CA 85, s 275(5).
291 *Ibid.*, s 275(6).
292 'Relevant accounts' are defined in *Ibid.*, ss. 270–273.

293 Interpretation Act 1978, Sch. 1.
294 CA 85, Sch. 7, para. 1(2).
295 *Ibid.*, Sch. 4, para. 8, balance sheet formats.
296 Allied Domecq PLC, Report & Accounts 1998, p. 25.
297 CA 85, Sch. 4, para. 8, profit and loss account formats.
298 *Ibid.*, note (17) on the profit and loss account formats.
299 *Ibid.*, paras. 19(1) and 19(2).
300 FRS 3, para. 20.
301 FRS 15, para. 100.
302 FRS 10, para. 55.
303 *Ibid.*, para. 63.
304 *Ibid.*, para. 56.
305 *Ibid.*, para. 57.
306 *Ibid.*, para. 58.
307 *Ibid.*, para. 52.
308 CA 85, Sch. 4, paras. 42(1)(a) and 42(2).
309 *Ibid.*, para. 42(1)(b).
310 *Ibid.*, para. 42(3).
311 FRS 15, para. 100.
312 *Ibid.*, para. 102.
313 FRS 10, para. 53.
314 *Ibid.*, para. 63.
315 *Ibid.*, para. 64.
316 CA 85, s 228(6).
317 UITF 7, *True and fair override disclosures*, December 1992, para. 4.
318 *Ibid.*, para. 7.
319 SSAP 12, para. 25(d)
320 FRS 15, para. 102.
321 CA 85, Sch. 4, para. 44.
322 *Ibid.*, para. 83(1).
323 FRS 11, para. 69.
324 *Ibid.*, para. 70.
325 *Ibid.*, para. 71.
326 *Ibid.*,, para. 72.
327 *Ibid.*, para. 73.
328 CA 85, Sch. 4, paras. 33(1) and (2).
329 *Ibid.*, para. 34(2).
330 *Ibid.*, para. 34(4).
331 *Ibid.*, para. 33(3).
332 *Ibid.*, para. 33(4).
333 *Ibid.*, para. 43(a).
334 *Ibid.*, para. 33(2).
335 *Ibid.*, para. 43(b).
336 FRS 15, para. 74.
337 *Ibid.*
338 *Ibid.*, para.53(a).
339 *Ibid.*, para. 61.
340 FRS 10, paras 61 and 62.
341 SSAP 19 (amended), para. 15.
342 *Ibid.*, para. 12.
343 *Ibid.*, para. 13.
344 CA 85, Sch. 4, para. 34(2).
345 SSAP 19 (amended), para. 15.
346 CA 85, Sch. 4, para. 3(4).
347 See Slough Estates plc, Annual Report 1998, p. 63.
348 IAS 16, para. 28.

349 *Ibid.*, para. 29.
350 *Ibid.*, para. 34.
351 *Ibid.*, para. 56.
352 *Ibid.*, para. 38.
353 IAS 22, *Business Combinations*, IASC, Revised 1998, para. 44.
354 *Ibid.*, para. 45.
355 *Ibid.*, para. 47.
356 *Ibid.*, para. 64.
357 *Ibid.*, para. 61.
358 *Ibid.*, para. 62(a).
359 *Ibid.*, para. 62(b).
360 FRED 12, para. 98.
361 IAS 25, para. 45.
362 IAS 16, para. 5.
363 IAS 25, para. 47.
364 *Ibid.*
365 *Ibid.*
366 *Ibid.*, para. 48.
367 *Ibid.*, para. 51(a).
368 *Ibid.*, para. 55.
369 E32, *Comparability of Financial Statements*, IASC, January 1989, para. 203.
370 *Ibid.*, para. 220.
371 Statement of Intent, *Comparability of Financial Statements*, IASC, July 1990.
372 E64, *Investment Property*, IASC, July 1999, para. 26
373 *Ibid.*, para. 3.
374 *Ibid.*, para. 9.
375 *Ibid.*, para. 11.
376 IAS 36, para. 9(d).
377 *Ibid.*, para. 88.
378 *Ibid.*, para. 99.
379 *Ibid.*, para. 51.
380 IAS 38, paras. 10-12.
381 SFAS 34, *Capitalization of Interest Cost*, FASB, October 1979.
382 SFAS 67, *Accounting for Costs and Initial Rental Operations of Real Estate Projects*, FASB, October 1982.
383 ARB No. 43, *Restatement and Revision of Accounting Research Bulletins*, Chapter 9 and ARB No. 44 (Revised), *Declining-balance Depreciation*.
384 These include ARB 43, Chapter 9A which discusses whether assets should be depreciated more quickly to compensate for inflation and rejects the idea, and a number of statements that deal with depreciation methods approved by the Internal Revenue and the timing differences that may result, including ARB 44 (Revised) – *Declining Balance Depreciation* and APB 1 – *New Depreciation Guidelines and Rules*.
385 ARB 43, Chapter 9, para. 5.
386 APB 17, para. 30.
387 APB 16, para. 91.
388 SFAS 121, *Accounting for the Impairment of Long-Lived Assets and for Long-Lived Assets to Be Disposed Of*, FASB, March 1995.
389 *Ibid.*, para. 11.
390 APB 6, para. 17. This continues: 'This section is not intended to change accounting practices followed in connection with quasi-reorganizations or reorganizations. This section may not apply to foreign operations under unusual conditions such as serious inflation or currency devaluation. However, when the accounts of an enterprise with foreign operations are translated into US currency for consolidation, such write-ups normally are eliminated. Whenever appreciation has been recorded in the books, income shall be charged with depreciation computed on the written-up amounts.'
391 APB Opinion No. 6, *Status of Accounting Research Bulletins*, October 1965, para. 17.

Chapter 11   Investments

1   INTRODUCTION

Investments come in so many different forms, and may be held for such different purposes, that it can be difficult to formulate a precise definition of them. Although not directly relevant to financial reporting, the Financial Services Act 1986 includes the following in its definition of an investment:

- shares and stock in the share capital of a company;

- debentures, including debenture stock, loan stock, bonds, certificates of deposit and other instruments creating or acknowledging indebtedness including those issued by public bodies;

- warrants or other instruments entitling the holder to subscribe for any of the above;

- certificates or other instruments which confer property rights in respect of the above, rights to acquire, dispose of, underwrite or convert an investment, and rights (other than options) to acquire investments other than by subscription;

- units in collective investment schemes including shares in or securities of an open-ended investment company;

- options to acquire or dispose of currency, gold or silver, or any investment as defined in the Act, including other options;

- futures;

- contracts for differences and similar instruments;

- long-term insurance contracts; and

- rights and interests in any of the above.[1]

Each of these is further described in some detail by the Act.

In 1990, the ASC published an exposure draft on the subject, ED 55 – *Accounting for investments*, but it has never been progressed further. Its definition of investments was at the other end of the spectrum; whereas the

Financial Services Act is highly specific, ED 55's definition was very general. It defined an investment simply as 'an asset that is characterised by its ability to generate economic benefits in the form of distributions and/or appreciation in value'.[2] This was a slight variant of the equivalent in the international accounting standard on the subject, which says that 'an investment is an asset held by an enterprise for the accretion of wealth through distribution (such as interest, royalties, dividends and rentals), for capital appreciation or for other benefits to the investing enterprise such as those obtained through trading relationships'.[3]

Although they would otherwise fall within the above definition, investment properties were excluded from the scope of ED 55 because they are dealt with in a separate accounting standard, SSAP 19. They are similarly excluded from the scope of this chapter, but are discussed in Chapter 10.

As mentioned above, enterprises may hold investments for a variety of different purposes. For example, an investment may be held:

- as a short-term store of wealth, perhaps by a seasonal business during the part of the year when its stocks are low, or by any enterprise for a period pending investment in operational assets;

- as a trading asset, by an enterprise whose business entails dealing in investments for profit;

- as a means of exercising control or influence over another enterprise which becomes its subsidiary or associated undertaking as a result;

- as a trade investment, to form a long-term but less influential relationship with another enterprise in a similar line of business;

- as a means of building up resources to meet long-term obligations, as in the case of a pension fund or an insurance company;

- as a means of hedging against some obligation of the enterprise, where the investment and the obligation have certain risk-related characteristics in common;

- as part of a managed portfolio of investments, in order to allow members of the enterprise to spread their risk without having to invest directly in the underlying components of the portfolio, as in the case of investment trusts and unit trusts.

Schedule 4 to the Companies Act addresses accounting for investments at a general level, but does not apply to banking and insurance companies, which are governed by separate schedules of their own. There are also some particular provisions for investment companies in Schedule 4 itself.[4] It is beyond the scope of this book to discuss detailed requirements for companies in specialised industries, and accordingly this chapter will confine itself to the general requirements for accounting for investments.[5]

In the absence of any accounting standard,[6] the Companies Act remains the only source of rules on accounting for investments. As indicated above, the ASB has never progressed ED 55; however, its current project on financial instruments (which is dealt with in Chapter 9) is broad enough to embrace almost all investments within its scope and this is likely to form the basis of accounting for investments in the future. The present statutory requirements are discussed in 2 below, together with an indication of how these might change in the future.

2 REQUIREMENTS FOR ACCOUNTING FOR INVESTMENTS

2.1 Classification

The formats in Schedule 4 to the Companies Act 1985 indicate that investments may be classified as either fixed asset investments or current asset investments. The available categories within each are shown opposite:[7]

The Act does not have a particular rule for distinguishing between fixed and current asset *investments*. It is necessary to apply the general rule that a fixed asset is one which is intended for use on a continuing basis in the company's activities and a current asset is one not intended for such use.[8] However, this is an unhelpful distinction for investments which, by their nature, are not intended for *use* in a company's activities at all, whether on a continuing basis or otherwise.

B	Fixed assets
III	Investments
	1. Shares in group undertakings
	2. Loans to group undertakings
	3. Participating interests
	4. Loans to undertakings in which the group has a participating interest
	5. Other investments other than loans
	6. Other loans
	7. Own shares
C	**Current assets**
III	Investments
	1. Shares in group undertakings
	2. Own shares
	3. Other investments

ED 55 proposed a more practical test for distinguishing between fixed and current asset investments. It defined a fixed asset investment as one 'which is intended to be held for use on a continuing basis in the activities of the enterprise. An investment should be classified as a fixed asset only where an intention to hold the investment for the long term can clearly be demonstrated or where there are restrictions as to the investor's ability to dispose of the investment.'[9] A current asset investment was the 'default' category; in other words it was defined, as in the Companies Act, as one which fails to meet the criteria for classification as a fixed asset investment.[10]

ED 55's definition therefore built on the Companies Act definition, but tried to make more sense of it. It elaborated on its own definition by saying that the category of fixed asset investments would comprise:

(a)   equity shareholdings in or loans to subsidiaries and associates;

(b)   investments arising from other trading relationships;

(c)   investments that either cannot be disposed of or cannot be disposed of without a significant effect on the operations of the enterprise; and

(d)   investments that are intended to be held for use on a continuing basis by enterprises whose objective is to hold a portfolio of investments to provide income and/or capital growth for their members.[11]

It emphasised that the fact that an investment is held for a lengthy period does not mean that it is to be accounted for as a fixed asset investment; it must be held for reasons which bring it within the definition.

This approach contrasts with that used in IAS 25, which defines a current investment as 'an investment which is by its nature readily realisable and is intended to be held for not more than one year',[12] and leaves all other investments to be classified as long-term investments. However, the international standard is not constrained by the terms of the Companies Act, which in distinguishing between a current and a fixed asset places emphasis on the purpose for which the asset is held rather than its liquidity.

2.2   Accounting rules

2.2.1   *Fixed asset investments*

The general statutory rule for the valuation of a fixed asset applies, namely that it should be included at its purchase price (production cost is an irrelevant alternative for an investment).[13] Purchase price includes any expenses incidental to its acquisition,[14] which will normally only include relatively minor dealing costs and stamp duty, but in the context of a contested takeover of a public company, the incidental costs may be very significant indeed.

Where the alternative accounting rules are invoked, fixed asset investments may be carried either at their market value determined at the date of their last valuation or at a directors' valuation.[15] The latter may be on any basis which appears to the directors to be appropriate in the circumstances of the company, so long as details of the basis and the reasons for adopting it are disclosed in a note to the accounts. One common practice is to include investments in subsidiary and/or associated undertakings in the balance sheet of the parent company at their net asset value, as shown in this extract:

Extract 11.1: Kwik-Fit Holdings plc (1999)

Statement of Accounting Policies

Investment in Subsidiary Undertakings

The Company accounts for its investments in subsidiary undertakings by the equity method, whereby the original cost of the investments is adjusted for the movement in underlying net assets applicable to the investments since their date of acquisition with an adjustment to the Company's revaluation reserve.

ED 55 proposed to tighten up the basic requirements of the Companies Act by removing the possibility of using a historical valuation which is neither the original purchase price nor the current value of the asset. Unless a company wished to carry its investments at historical cost, ED 55 required annual valuations.[16] Moreover, it proposed that the revalued amount should be treated as if it were cost for all subsequent purposes. This meant that if any decline in value was expected to be a permanent one, then the whole amount of the write-down (compared to its previously revalued amount) was to be charged to the profit and loss account.[17]

This proposal was inconsistent with the requirements of IAS 25, which requires that amounts written off revalued assets should first be charged against any revaluation surplus existing in respect of the asset, and only thereafter should any remaining write-off be charged to the profit and loss account.[18] The logic of the ED 55 proposal was not really explained. More recently, the ASB has issued FRS 11 – *Impairment of Fixed Assets and Goodwill* – which adopts the IAS 25 treatment described above except where the impairment loss 'is caused by a clear consumption of economic benefits' in which case the loss should be charged to the profit and loss account.[19] However, most investments are scoped out of FRS 11; these rules thus apply only to investments in subsidiaries, associates and similar entities as shown in the accounts of the parent company, whose unconsolidated profit and loss account is seldom published in any case.

Where a revalued investment is subsequently sold, ED 55 again required the gain or loss on disposal to be calculated as the difference between the proceeds and the (revalued) carrying amount prior to disposal. Any net surplus previously credited to and retained in the revaluation reserve was to be released to the profit and loss account as a reserve transfer.[20] The gain or loss on disposal was normally to be dealt with in the profit and loss account, but an exemption from this requirement was proposed for investment companies as defined in the Companies Act,[21] since their articles prohibit them from distributing gains on disposal of such investments and as a result they customarily deal with both gains and losses in reserves.[22] These proposals have since been adopted in FRS 3, which requires the gain or loss on the sale of all revalued assets to be measured by reference to their revalued amount rather than their historical cost, and also allows the exemption for investment companies described above.[23]

Investments are not excluded from the depreciation rules of the Act (although they are outside the scope of FRS 15, which deals only with tangible fixed assets), but these usually do not apply because most investments have an indefinite life. However, for investments such as dated gilts, bonds or redeemable preference shares that are to be held to maturity it is common to amortise the premium or discount to redemption over their term; this treatment was proposed by ED 55.[24] The amortisation should be systematic and designed to recognise the constant yield earned on the investment or an approximation to it, although in practice a straight line basis may meet this requirement within bounds of materiality.[25]

The Post Office discloses such a policy, as shown in this extract:

Extract 11.2: The Post Office (1999)

Accounting policies and general notes

H   Investments [extract]

(ii) Financial investments held as fixed assets are stated in the balance sheet on the basis of cost adjusted so as to amortise to redemption value over the period to maturity. If sold before maturity, the difference between the proceeds and the amortised value is taken to the profit and loss account in the year of realisation.

Glaxo Wellcome discloses a policy of recognising income on this basis for such investments if they are to be held to redemption, although it is not entirely clear why such a condition should apply to investments held as current assets, as shown in this policy:

Extract 11.3: Glaxo Wellcome plc (1998)

2 Accounting policies

Current asset investments [extract]

... In the case of securities acquired at a significant premium or discount to maturity value, and intended to be held to redemption, cost is adjusted to amortise the premium or discount over the life to maturity of the security. ...

A policy of amortising premiums or discounts is most frequently applied to gilts, but is equally relevant to other types of redeemable security, such as deep discounted bonds. In the case of more complex securities which have a number of redemption options at different dates and different prices it will be appropriate to exercise prudence in determining the amount of income to be recognised in order to avoid the danger of reporting income which is not subsequently received.

Fixed asset investments are also subject to the statutory requirement to write them down to reflect any permanent diminution in their value. Such a provision is to be charged in the profit and loss account and is to be released if it is subsequently found to be unnecessary, with disclosure of the amounts in each case.[26] As well as these requirements, which apply to all fixed assets, the Act specifically allows provision to be made against the value of fixed asset investments even where their fall in value is not expected to be permanent.[27] As noted above, FRS 11 contains further rules on the impairment of fixed assets, but scopes out most investments (essentially, those that are covered by the ASB's project on financial instruments)[28] which means that it addresses only investments in subsidiaries, associates and the like.

One particular issue which frequently arises is how a holding company should deal with investments in subsidiaries whose value has been impaired, either as a result of trading losses or following a group reconstruction.

If a subsidiary company has made losses then the amount at which the investment is stated in the parent company's balance sheet may exceed its 'recoverable amount' as defined in FRS 11 (See Chapter 10), in which case the parent must recognise a loss in its own accounts. As described above, it is quite common for holding companies to carry investments in subsidiaries at their consolidated net asset value, taking movements to revaluation reserve. Any fall in net asset value as a result of losses does not necessarily mean that the investment is not recoverable in terms of FRS 11 – the test is still whether the carrying amount of the investment can be recouped, whether through future dividend streams or proceeds of sale, albeit using a discounting methodology. However, where an impairment of this kind is identified, then it should be charged to the profit and loss account.

Kinta Kellas is an example of a company that has recognised an impairment in value of one of its subsidiaries:

Extract 11.4: Kinta Kellas Public Limited Company (1998)

PRINCIPAL ACCOUNTING POLICIES

VI Subsidiary Undertakings

Investments in subsidiary undertakings are initially stated at cost in the balance sheet of the Company and reviewed for impairment at the end of the first full financial year following their acquisition and in other periods if events or changes in circumstances indicate that the carrying value may not be recoverable.

NOTES TO THE ACCOUNTS

11 FIXED ASSET INVESTMENTS [extract]

(a) The Directors have performed an impairment review on the carrying amount of the subsidiary undertakings in accordance with FRS 11 and as a result an amount of RM44,800,000 has been provided in the profit and loss account of the Company during the year. For the purpose of calculating the impairment provisions, forecast cash flows in respect of a unit have been discounted using a rate of 7%, which takes account of the risk associated with that relevant unit, resulting in a provision of RM44 million. ...

A common form of group reconstruction involves the transfer to another group company of the tangible assets and trade of a subsidiary. If the original purchase price included an element of goodwill, the remaining shell may have a carrying value in the parent company's balance sheet in excess of its net worth. It could be argued that as the subsidiary is now a shell company a provision should be made against the carrying value to reduce it to its net worth. However, in such a reorganisation there has been no real loss either to the holding company or to the group, and as a result companies frequently conclude that it would be inappropriate to make a provision. Nevertheless, the impairment in carrying value should always be recognised if the assets and/or the trade transferred are themselves sold outside the group. It is only possible to argue that the loss need not be recognised as long as there is a matching gain elsewhere in the group which has also not been recognised.

Signet Group has taken a different approach to this problem, applying a true and fair override and transferring the excess amount to goodwill, as shown in this extract:

Extract 11.5: Signet Group plc (1999)

31 Company balance sheet

(l) Intangible assets and investments (held as fixed assets) [extract]

True and fair override on divisionalisation of subsidiary undertakings As part of a rationalisation of the Group in previous years, the trade and net assets of a subsidiary undertaking were transferred to the Company at their book value. The cost of the Company's investment in that subsidiary undertaking reflected the underlying fair value of its net assets and goodwill at the time of its acquisition. As a result of this transfer, the value of the Company's investment in that subsidiary undertaking fell below the amount at which it was stated in the Company's accounting records. Schedule 4 to the Companies Act 1985 requires that the investment be written down accordingly and that the amount be charged as a loss in the Company's profit and loss account. However, the directors consider that, as there had been no overall loss to the Group, it would fail to give a true and fair view to charge the diminution to the Company's profit and loss account and it should instead be re-allocated to goodwill and the identifiable net assets transferred, so as to recognise in the Company's individual balance sheet the effective cost to the Company of those net assets and goodwill. The effect on the Company's balance sheet of this departure is to recognise goodwill of £60,320,000 (1998: £62,205,000), net of amortisation of £15,080,000 (1998: £13,195,000).

Given that the business concerned operates in a generally stable market, the directors have concluded that the estimated economic life of the resulting intangible asset was 40 years at the date the transfer took place.

The asset is reviewed annually for impairment. The review at 30 January 1999 indicated that no such impairment had arisen.

As discussed more fully in Chapter 9, in 1996 the ASB issued a discussion paper on financial instruments that proposed valuing all investments at market value, without differentiating between fixed and current asset investments[29] (but excluding shares in subsidiaries and associates[30]). Movements in value would normally be dealt with in the profit and loss account, but two exceptions were proposed, for which the movements would be reported in the statement of total recognised gains and losses. These were:

- 'Long-term, strategic holdings of shares'.[31] This category was not defined further but was distinguished from 'shares that are held for trading in the short term or as a readily disposable store of value'. This therefore carried overtones of a fixed/current split.

■ 'Debt investments that match-fund a borrowing'.[32] These were holdings of fixed interest securities that had similar maturities and interest bases to fixed interest rate debt. The implicit argument was that, since they provided a hedge to the interest rate exposure on the debt, and since movements in the value of the debt were taken to the statement of total recognised gains and losses, the offsetting gains and losses on the investments were to be taken there as well.

2.2.2 Current asset investments

The valuation rules for current asset investments in the Companies Act again dictate that the investment should initially be recorded at its purchase price, including any incidental expenses.[33] A current asset investment must be written down to its net realisable value if it is less than its purchase price, but that write-down should again be reversed if the reasons for it cease to apply.[34] If the alternative accounting rules are adopted, a current asset investment may be revalued to its current cost.[35]

ED 55 proposed to distinguish between 'readily marketable' investments and others. An investment was to be regarded as readily marketable if it was one 'for which an active market exists, which is both open and accessible, and for which a market value (or some other indicator from which a value may be calculated) is quoted openly'.[36] The purpose of the distinction was to ensure that those investments thus classified were capable of being readily disposed of at the stated value. The exposure draft proposed that such investments, if they were held as current assets, should be marked to market; in other words, they should be carried in the balance sheet at their current market value and all movements in that value between one balance sheet date and the next should be included in the profit and loss account as a component of income from investments.[37] Current asset investments that were not readily marketable were to be valued in accordance with the Companies Act rules as set out above.

Marking to market is commonly applied by companies whose business involves dealing in investments, but is not generally used by most other companies. The Post Office discloses such a policy in relation to gilts, as shown in this extract:

Extract 11.6: The Post Office (1999)

Accounting policies and general notes

H   Investments [extract]

(iv) Investments held as current assets are stated at market value at the balance sheet date and the difference between cost and market value is taken to the profit and loss account. This treatment is a departure from UK accounting rules which stipulate that unrealised profits be credited to a revaluation reserve. In the opinion of the Board Members, the treatment adopted is necessary to present a true and fair view. All such investments are readily marketable Government securities. The accounting treatment adopted represents a fairer reflection of the investment return.

ED 55 argued that this treatment is the most appropriate for measuring the results of the enterprise because it reflects the success or failure of the decision to invest in all its readily marketable current asset investments during the year – not simply those which management has chosen to sell before the year end. An analogy was drawn between this treatment and that required by SSAP 20 in respect of foreign currency balances, where profits are recognised on all such balances, not simply those converted into sterling at the end of the year. It is argued that gains arising on marking to market can be regarded as realised profits, because, as with the foreign currency balances, they could readily have been converted into cash at the end of the year had management chosen to do so. However, the exposure draft limited the proposal to those investments which are readily marketable, because only they are capable of being readily disposed of at their stated value, and to those which are current assets, because fixed assets are by definition not intended to be disposed of at all.

Where the holding in an otherwise readily marketable investment is so large that it could not be disposed of without a material effect on the quoted market price, the exposure draft said that the price used should be adjusted to reflect the proceeds that could realistically be expected from gradual disposal of the investment in the ordinary course of business.[38] This was seen as a controversial suggestion, because it may be argued that the practice of marking to market is only justified where the investment in question could have been instantaneously liquidated at a reliable market price, and that if this could not be done because the holding is a very large one, then the practice should not be applied. ED 55 asked for specific comment on this issue.

The ASB's proposals on financial instruments go much further. They say that *all* investments should be marked to market, even those held as fixed assets, those which are not readily marketable, and those which are large holdings (except that certain gains and losses are proposed to be dealt with in the statement of total recognised gains and losses rather than the profit and loss account, as explained in 2.2.1 above). The implicit logic is not that these gains and losses could have been instantaneously realised, but simply that it is necessary to use market values for financial assets in order to reflect the performance of the company for the period.

Marking to market involves a departure from the requirements of the Companies Act as discussed above. The difficulty is not so much that any appreciation in value does not represent a realised profit – the determination of realised profits allows some room for interpretation by accounting rules – but rather that the balance sheet valuation rules in Schedule 4 do not allow valuations unless the other side of the entry is taken to a revaluation reserve under the alternative accounting rules. ED 55 sought to justify this departure on the basis that it was necessary to depart from these rules in order to give a true and fair view, but this was a controversial proposition, because the true and fair override can only be invoked in 'special circumstances' and it may be argued that the mere decision to hold readily marketable investments as a current asset does not give rise to circumstances which are sufficiently special to warrant the departure. This legal difficulty was probably one of the factors that prevented the ASB from picking up the project and turning ED 55 into a standard. However, there now appears to be a good prospect of amendment to the EU Fourth Directive which will allow UK law to accommodate this treatment in the future.

Companies which are not required to prepare their accounts under Schedule 4 to the Act are not subject to this legal obstacle. This category includes banks, which are also among those most likely to be engaging in investment dealing activities where marking to market is most appropriate. Schedule 9 to the Companies Act explicitly recognises the practice.[39]

Coats Viyella discloses accounting policies for fixed and current asset investments which follow the orthodox measurement rules described above:

Extract 11.7: Coats Viyella Plc (1998)

Statement of accounting policies

Investments

Fixed asset investments are stated at cost unless, in the opinion of the Directors, there has been an impairment, in which case an appropriate adjustment is made.

Listed current asset investments are stated at the lower of cost or market value, and other current asset investments are stated at the lower of cost and estimated net realisable value.

2.2.3 Other matters relevant to all investments

One issue which sometimes arises is the treatment of reclassifications of investments from current assets to fixed assets or vice versa, since the rules governing their measurement are not the same. Under UITF 5, current assets which are transferred to fixed assets should continue to be accounted for under the appropriate rules for current assets up to the date of transfer, and therefore transferred at the amount that is appropriate under these rules.[40] This rule was devised to prevent companies avoiding a write-down of current assets to net realisable value by redesignating them as fixed assets. The Abstract does not deal with transfers in the opposite direction, from fixed to current assets.

Where a company has an investment holding that results from a number of purchases and sales at different prices, it is not necessary for the actual purchase price to be assigned to the specific securities acquired in each transaction; instead it is permissible to use one of the methods suggested by the Act for 'fungible assets' (which are most commonly used for valuing stock – see 3.1 and 3.2 of Chapter 14). These allow costs to be assigned on the basis of FIFO, LIFO, weighted average or any other similar method rather than using the actual cost, but with the proviso that the replacement cost or most recent purchase price of the holding should be disclosed if it is materially different from the balance sheet amount.[41] ED 55 sought to narrow this down by requiring the average purchase price to be used for the purposes of accounting for any subsequent partial disposals.[42] ED 55 also said that each investment within a category should be accounted for separately, rather than on a portfolio basis.[43] This is in any event a Companies Act requirement.[44]

ED 55 proposed that an investment transaction should be accounted for as of the date on which the risks and rewards of ownership pass from the seller to the purchaser.[45] This will generally be the date on which the trade was made, rather than the subsequent settlement date (a view supported by the ASB in its financial instruments project, whereas IAS 39[46] allows either approach). It also said that if an investment was acquired with an accrued entitlement to interest or a fixed dividend, its cost should be based on its purchase price excluding the amount of the accrued interest or dividend.[47] There is no equivalent discussion in the law.

2.2.4   Income recognition

ED 55 proposed that all income from investments should be recognised in the profit and loss account when it became receivable.[48] This implies a normal accruals basis for interest and fixed rate dividends, while in the case of dividends on equity securities the amount due should be recognised when it is declared or, in the case of quoted securities, on the ex-dividend date; in practice, a cash basis of accounting for such income may produce materially the same results. However, it suggested an exception for the case of intra-group dividends, where frequently decisions on such dividends are made after the year end but before the accounts are finalised; it said that the parent company could recognise such dividends from subsidiary undertakings provided they were declared before the date of approval of its own financial statements.[49]

This approach is common, and is symmetrical with the present accepted practice of accruing outgoing dividends that are proposed after the year end and before the date of approval of the accounts. However, the ASB has voiced its doubts as to the appropriateness of such accruals on the basis that they do not reflect liabilities that existed at the balance sheet date, and the IASC has banned the practice in its recent revision to IAS 10.[50] It is therefore possible that accruing incoming dividends from subsidiaries may be similarly challenged at some time in the future.

2.2.5   *Investments held for hedging purposes*

ED 55 did not purport to set rules to govern the accounting treatment of investments held to hedge obligations of the enterprise, since this is a highly complex matter. However, it avoided inadvertently frustrating the aims of hedging by giving an exemption from its requirements where to apply them 'would not properly reflect the economic substance of the hedge'.[51] As explained in Chapter 9, the ASB means to address this issue in its current project on financial instruments, but has not so far determined its position.

2.3   Disclosure requirements

The Act requires various disclosures to be made in relation to investments. In respect of fixed asset investments, the following must be shown:

(a)   the appropriate amounts at the beginning of the financial year and as at the balance sheet date, based either on historical cost or alternative accounting rules.[52] Where investments are carried at valuation, equivalent historical cost information must be disclosed;[53]

(b)   all movements during the year, including revaluation surpluses and deficits, acquisitions, disposals and transfers.[54] Such movements would also include exchange differences; and

(c)   the cumulative amount of provisions for depreciation or diminution in value as at the beginning and end of the financial year on the appropriate basis of cost or valuation, the provision for the period and adjustments in respect of disposals or for other reasons.[55] Systematic depreciation will not apply to most investments since they will not have a finite life and hence will not be depreciated: however, it will apply to dated securities where they are being amortised to their eventual redemption price. The need to provide for permanent diminution in value can of course apply to any investment.

This information has to be disclosed in respect of each type of investment included in the balance sheet formats (see 2.1 above). The following extract shows the investments note relating to the consolidated accounts of Tate & Lyle.

Extract 11.8: Tate & Lyle Public Limited Company (1998)

10 Fixed Asset Investments [extract]	**1998** **£ million**	1997 £ million
Group		
Joint ventures – unlisted	**132.9**	127.3
Associates – unlisted	**14.0**	13.7
Other fixed asset investments:		
Listed – at cost[1]	**8.2**	18.1
Unlisted – at cost less amounts provided of £1.2 million (1997 – £3.4 million)[2]	**11.0**	14.0
Loans	**18.9**	14.9
	185.0	188.0

[1]Market value £9.5 million (1997 – £39.5 million)
[2]Directors' valuation £11.2 million (1997 – £14.3 million)

Movement in book value	Joint ventures £ million	Associates £ million	Other equity investments £ million	Loans £ million	Group £ million
At 27 September 1997	127.3	13.7	32.1	14.9	**188.0**
Differences on exchange	(18.9)	(2.4)	(1.7)	(0.7)	**(23.7)**
Additions	38.7	3.4	1.5	0.1	**43.7**
Goodwill	(14.3)	–	–	–	**(14.3)**
Reclassification	0.9	(0.9)	(2.7)	4.6	**1.9**
Disposals	–	(0.1)	(10.0)	–	**(10.1)**
Retained profits of joint ventures and associates	0.6	0.3	–	–	**0.9**
Movement in provisions	(1.4)	–	–	–	**(1.4)**
At 26 September 1998	132.9	14.0	19.2	18.9	**185.0**

The Act also requires these disclosures in respect of both fixed and current asset investments:

(a) the amount relating to listed investments;[56]

(b) the aggregate market value of listed investments, if different from the book value, and the stock exchange value if it is less than the market value thus disclosed;[57]

(c) various details where the investment is 'significant', i.e. where it is either 20% or more of the nominal value of the shares of that class in the investee, or it represents more than 20% of the investor's own assets. The details to be disclosed are:

   (i)   the name of the investee;

   (ii) its country of incorporation (if outside Great Britain). For unincorporated investees the address of the principal place of business has to be disclosed; and

   (iii) a description and the proportion of each class of shares held.[58]

In addition, the statutory formats for the profit and loss account contain separate headings for the following:

- Income from shares in group undertakings
- Income from participating interests
- Income from other fixed asset investments
- Other interest receivable and similar income
- Amounts written off investments.

There are also various statutory disclosure requirements concerning investments in subsidiary and associated undertakings when group accounts are not prepared, which are beyond the scope of this chapter but are listed in Chapter 27 at 3.1.3.

Two examples of balance sheet notes are shown below: on fixed asset investments in an extract from the accounts of TI Group, and on current asset investments in an extract from the accounts of Pearson:

Extract 11.9: TI Group plc (1998)

13 INVESTMENTS

	Joint Venture £m	Associated Undertakings £m	Other Participating Interests £m	Own Shares £m	Total £m
The Group					
Shares at valuation					
At 31st December 1997	28.0	3.7	1.0	5.7	38.4
Exchange rate adjustments	(0.8)	1.0	–	–	0.2
Acquisitions	–	1.1	(0.4)	1.9	2.6
Disposals	(25.6)	–	–	(1.8)	(27.4)
Movement during year	(1.6)	1.0	–	(2.1)	(2.7)
At 31st December 1998	**–**	**6.8**	**0.6**	**3.7**	**11.1**

Joint venture

The Group's only joint venture, the 50% stake in Messier-Dowty, was sold to Snecma on 30th June 1988.

Associated undertakings

The principal associated undertakings are:

	Country of operation	% held	Class of Share
John Crane (Japan) Inc	Japan	49	Ordinary
Korea Bundy Corp	South Korea	39	Ordinary

The interest in associated undertakings is shown in the Group balance sheet at a valuation being the proportion of net assets attributable to TI Group at the date of acquisition, plus TI Group's share of post-acquisition earnings which at 31st December 1998 amounted to £1.0m (1997 £0.2m losses).

Lips United has 50% owned associated undertakings in France, Greece, Italy, Portugal and Spain. EIS Group has 50% owned associates in Argentina, Canada and India and a 40% owned associate in the USA.

The financial year end of John Crane (Japan) Inc is 31st March; the Group's share of its results is for the calendar year using management accounts for the unaudited period.

Sales by the Group to its associates in 1998 amounted to £2.0m (1997 £2.2m). Sales by the associates to TI Group were not material to either party in either year.

Other participating interests

The principal other participating interest is Tube Investments of India Ltd of which the Group holds 3% of the ordinary shares. Participating interests are all listed companies stated at Directors' valuation with a market value at 31st December 1998 of £0.8m (1997 £0.8m).

Own shares

The TI Group Employee Share Ownership Trust was established in 1995 with the purpose of holding shares in the Company for subsequent transfer to employees under various incentive schemes. In accordance with UITF 13 the Trust's accounts are incorporated into the Company and Group accounts.

At 31st December 1998 the Trust held 1,134,355 shares in the Company (1997 1,079,210) with a market value of £3.7m (199 £5.0m). Costs of administration are included in the profit and loss account as they accrue. The Trust retains dividend income for reinvestment.

The Company	£m
Shares in subsidiaries at cost and own shares	
At 31st December 1997	**1,174.4**
Acquisitions	**310.7**
Disposals	**(158.4)**
Other movements	**(2.1)**
At 31st December 1998	**1,324.6**

Provisions for diminution in value included in the above at 31st December 1998 amounted to £67.5m (1997 £65.4m).

A list of the Group's principal subsidiaries, associated undertakings and other participating interests is set out on pages 84 and 85.

Extract 11.10: Pearson plc (1998)

17 Current asset investments [extract]

	1998		1997	
ALL FIGURES IN £ MILLIONS	VALUATIONS	BOOK VALUES	VALUATIONS	BOOK VALUES
Unlisted	5	5	8	8
Businesses held for resale	148	148	–	–
	153	153	8	8

NOTE: *Investments are at directors' valuations. If all investments were realised at valuation there would be no liability for taxation.*

Insofar as marking to market invokes the 'true and fair override' (see 2.2.2 above), it will also be necessary to disclose particulars of the departure from the valuation rules of Schedule 4 to the Companies Act, the reasons for the departure and its effect on the financial statements.[59]

3   COMPARISON WITH IASC AND US PRONOUNCEMENTS

3.1   IASC

3.1.1   IAS 25

The international standard IAS 25 – *Accounting for Investments* – was issued in 1986 and is fairly accommodating in its requirements. It permits current asset investments to be carried either at market value or at the lower of cost and market value, and in the former case it permits movements in value to be taken either to the profit and loss account or to owners' equity. Long-term investments may similarly be carried at either cost or valuation, and gains and losses on disposal of revalued assets can be measured against either their original cost or their revalued amount.[60]

IAS 25 remains in force for non-financial investments such as investment properties, but in relation to financial assets it has been superseded by IAS 39, which is discussed at 3.1.5 below. However, since IAS 39 does not become mandatory until 2001, IAS 25 may still be applied for the time being.

3.1.2   E32

In 1989, the IASC issued E32, which proposed changes to reduce the options available in a large number of its standards, including IAS 25. The main changes proposed were that it would be the preferred treatment to carry current asset investments at market value, with the lower of cost and market basis as the allowed alternative, and to carry long-term investments at cost, with revalued amounts as the allowed alternative. However, the IASC then embarked on a wide-ranging project on financial instruments, and since this bore heavily on the subject of investments the Committee decided not to implement the proposals on investments in E32.

3.1.3   E48

The IASC published E48 – *Financial Instruments* – in January 1994, replacing an earlier exposure draft, E40, which had been issued over two years earlier. The exposure draft was a long and complex one and its scope was very wide. It sought to establish a comprehensive framework of accounting rules for financial assets and liabilities from the point of view of both the issuer and the holder. Accordingly, it dealt with accounting for investments, since these represented financial assets from the point of view of the holder, but its coverage was much wider.

Different measurement rules were proposed for financial assets depending on whether they were held (a) for the long term or to maturity, (b) as hedges or (c) for other purposes, and a 'Benchmark' treatment for each was proposed as described below.

Financial assets held for the long term or to maturity were to be carried at the amount initially recognised (i.e. cost), or recoverable amount if lower.[61] If the asset was to be settled through scheduled payments of fixed or determinable amounts, it was to be remeasured at each balance sheet date at the amount of the scheduled future payments discounted at the rate of interest inherent in the initially recognised amount.[62] Gains and losses in the fair value of a financial asset accounted for as a hedge were to be recognised in income at the same time as the corresponding loss or gain from a change in the fair value of the hedged position was recognised in income.[63] Financial assets held for other purposes were to be marked to market.[64]

Again, however, E48 was not progressed, but was overtaken by a further discussion paper, which is discussed below.

3.1.4 Accounting for Financial Assets and Financial Liabilities

This discussion paper was published by the IASC's Steering Committee on Financial Instruments in March 1997. It took the most simple, but also radical, approach to investments that could be imagined; they should all be marked to market and all gains and losses recognised in the profit and loss account. No variations in treatment were proposed for investments held for different purposes, nor was there any differential approach for unmarketable securities.

As more fully discussed in Chapter 9 at 5.1.1, the proposals aroused considerable controversy. The result was the project changed direction yet again and was split in two. These ambitious proposals were to be developed further, but at a more modest pace, while in the meantime a less radical standard – IAS 39 – was developed as a stop-gap measure.

3.1.5 IAS 39

IAS 39 – *Financial Instruments: Recognition and Measurement* – was finalised in December 1998 and issued in March 1999. It comes into force for periods beginning on or after 1 January 2001.

The standard requires investments (as a subset of financial assets) to be analysed into the following categories:

(a) fixed maturity investments that the enterprise both intends and is able to keep to maturity. (There are obsessively detailed rules that set conditions to constrain that apparently straightforward definition). These are to be measured at amortised cost;[65]

(b) investments that do not have a quoted market price in an active market and whose fair value cannot be reliably estimated. It is emphasised that this category is expected to be rarely necessary. Such investments are carried at cost;[66]

(c) investments held for trading purposes. These are to be marked to market, with the differences going to the profit and loss account;[67]

(d) investments that are available for sale (the rest). These are also to be carried at market value, but the enterprise must decide, as a matter of policy, whether movements in value also go to the profit and loss account or whether they are taken to equity initially and only recycled into the profit and loss account when the investment is subsequently disposed of or judged to be impaired.[68]

3.2 US

In the US, SFAS 107, *Disclosures about Fair Value of Financial Instruments*, was issued in 1991. It requires all entities to disclose the fair value of financial instruments where practicable. The definition of financial instruments will include most investments, although equity investments in consolidated subsidiaries are specifically exempted. Where disclosure of the fair value is impracticable, the reason for this has to be disclosed, together with information pertinent to estimating the fair value, such as the carrying amount, effective interest rate and maturity of the financial instrument.

The question of how to account for marketable equity investments and all debt securities is addressed by SFAS 115 – *Accounting for Certain Investments in Debt and Equity Securities* – issued in 1993 to supersede SFAS 12.[69] Rather like IAS 39 (for which it provided the basis), this requires that such investments be classified as falling into one of three categories and accounted for as follows:

(a) *Held-to-maturity securities* (debt securities whose owner has both the positive intent and the ability to hold them to maturity) are carried at amortised cost.

(b) *Trading securities* (debt and equity securities that are bought and held principally for resale in the near term) are carried at fair value and the resulting gains and losses included in earnings.

(c) *Available-for-sale securities* (the rest) are also carried at fair value but the gains and losses included in a separate component of shareholders' equity, not in earnings.

The statement also adds several further disclosure requirements.

SFAS 115 does not apply to investments in associates and subsidiaries, nor to securities whose fair value is not readily determinable, broadly those that are not quoted on an exchange. There are also certain exemptions for companies in industries which have specialised accounting practices relating to investments.

4 CONCLUSION

ED 55 has never been progressed, largely because of the legal obstacles within the EU Fourth Directive that appear to rule out mark-to-market accounting for most UK companies. However, there is now a clear trend among standard setters internationally towards the increased use of this treatment, and if this gains widespread acceptance there may well be some relaxation of these legal prohibitions. The issue may then become how far to take the approach. Both the ASB and the IASC wish to move towards a fairly complete version of it, but this remains controversial, particularly when it involves reporting in the profit and loss account unrealised gains on the revaluation of unmarketable securities that are held for the long term. The future direction of this subject, therefore, is likely to depend on the degree to which such an approach commands international acceptance.

References

1   Financial Services Act 1986, Sch. 1, Part 1.
2   ED 55, *Accounting for investments*, ASC, July 1990, para. 54.
3   IAS 25, *Accounting for Investments*, IASC, March 1986, para. 3.
4   CA 85, Sch. 4, Part V.
5   For recommendations on accounting by Investment Trusts, see the SORP on *Financial Statements of Investment Trust Companies*, The Association of Investment Trust Companies, December 1995. For recommendations on accounting for securities in the financial statements of banks, see the SORP on *Securities*, British Bankers Association and Irish Bankers' Federation, September 1990.
6   Other than FRS 9, which deals with associates, joint ventures and JANEs: see Chapter 7.
7   CA 85, Sch. 4, para. 8, balance sheet formats.
8   *Ibid.*, s 262(1).
9   ED 55, para. 55.
10 *Ibid.*, para. 56.
11 *Ibid.*, para. 24.
12 IAS 25, para. 3.
13 CA 85, Sch. 4, para. 17.
14 *Ibid.*, para. 26(1).
15 *Ibid.*, para. 31(3).
16 ED 55, para. 63.
17 *Ibid.*, para. 68.
18 IAS 25, para. 48.
19 FRS 11, *Impairment of Fixed Assets and Goodwill*, ASB, July 1998, para. 63.
20 ED 55, para. 69.
21 CA 85, s 266 and Sch. 4, para. 73.
22 ED 55, para. 70.
23 FRS 3, *Reporting financial performance*, ASB, December 1992, paras. 21 and 31.
24 ED 55, para. 74.
25 *Ibid.*, para. 42.
26 CA 85, Sch 4, paras. 19(2) and (3).
27 *Ibid.*, para. 19(1).
28 FRS 11, para. 5(a).
29 ASB Discussion Paper, *Derivatives and other financial instruments*, ASB, July 1996, para. 3.5.1(a).
30 *Ibid.*, para. 1.4.1(c).
31 *Ibid.*, para. 3.3.21.
32 *Ibid.*, para. 3.5.1(d).
33 CA 85, Sch 4, para. 22.
34 *Ibid.*, para. 23.
35 *Ibid.*, para. 31(5).
36 ED 55, para. 57.
37 *Ibid.*, paras. 60 and 66.
38 *Ibid.*, para. 61.
39 CA 85, Sch. 9, Part 1, paras. 33 and 34.
40 UITF 5, *Transfers from current assets to fixed assets*, UITF, July 1992, para. 5.
41 *Ibid.*, para. 27.
42 ED 55, para. 71.
43 *Ibid.*, para. 65.
44 CA 85, Sch. 4, para. 14.
45 ED 55, para. 76.
46 IAS 39, para. 30.
47 ED 55, para. 64.
48 *Ibid.*, para. 73.
49 *Ibid.*, para. 41.
50 IAS 10, *Events After the Balance Sheet Date*, IASC, Revised May 1999, para. 11.
51 ED 55, para. 59.

52   CA 85, Sch. 4, paras. 42(1)(a) and 42(2).
53   *Ibid.*, para. 33(3).
54   *Ibid.*, para. 42(1)(b).
55   *Ibid.*, para. 42(3).
56   *Ibid.*, para. 45(1).
57   *Ibid.*, para. 45(2).
58   *Ibid.*, Sch. 5, paras. 7 and 8.
59   CA 85, ss 226(5) and 227(6).
60   IAS 25, paras. 46–50.
61   *Ibid.*, paras. 85, 100 and 113.
62   *Ibid.*, para. 92.
63   *Ibid.*, para. 150
64   *Ibid.*, paras. 162 and 163.
65   IAS 39, *Financial Instruments: Recognition and Measurement*, IASC, December 1998, para. 73.
66   *Ibid.*
67   *Ibid.*, para. 103(a).
68   *Ibid.*, para. 103(b).
69   SFAS 12, *Accounting for Certain Marketable Securities*, FASB, December 1975.

Chapter 12

Research and development

1 INTRODUCTION

1.1 Possible accounting treatments of research and development expenditure

Theoretically, there are essentially four possible methods of accounting for research and development expenditure. These are as follows:

(a) charge all costs to expense when incurred; or

(b) capitalise all costs when incurred; or

(c) capitalise costs when incurred providing specified conditions are fulfilled and charge all others to expense; or

(d) accumulate all costs in a special category distinct from assets and expenses until the existence of future benefits can be determined.

Each of the above is considered in turn.

1.1.1 Charge all costs to expense when incurred

This is the required treatment in the US (see 5.2 below). The five factors offered by the FASB as support for its requirements to expense all expenditure immediately were as follows:[1]

(a) uncertainty of future benefits

The primary reason offered by the FASB for expensing research and development costs was the uncertainty associated with such costs. It was argued that research and development projects have considerable risk, i.e. a large probability of failure and consequently all such costs should be expensed. As support for this argument, the FASB cited one study of a number of industries which found that an average of less than 2% of new product ideas and less than 15% of product development projects were commercially successful.

(b)   *lack of causal relationship between expenditure and benefits*

The FASB cited in its statement three research studies that generally failed to find a significant connection between research and development expenditure and increased future benefits by subsequent sales, earnings or share of industry sales. However, the fact that the three studies cited failed to find a causal relationship between expenditure and benefits does not mean that such a relationship does not exist. If this was the case, then companies would be much more reluctant to incur such expenditure.

(c)   *research and development does not meet the accounting concept of an asset*

The FASB argued that to be an asset the expenditure would need to be subject to reasonable measurement. They stated that 'the criterion of measurability would require that a resource not be recognised as an asset for accounting purposes unless at the time it is acquired or developed its future economic benefits can be identified and objectively measured'.[2] However, this could be argued in relation to practically any asset at the time it is acquired.

(d)   *matching of revenues and expenses*

The FASB argued that because of the uncertainty of future benefits of research and development expenditure there was an insufficient cause and effect relationship to justify the carrying forward of research and development expenditure to future periods.

(e)   *relevance of resulting information for investment and credit decisions*

The FASB stated that APB Statement No. 4 indicates that certain costs are immediately recognised as expenses because allocating them to several accounting periods is considered to serve no useful purpose. The FASB went on to state that 'the relationship between current research and development costs and the amount of resultant future benefits to an enterprise is so uncertain that capitalisation of any research and development costs is not useful in assessing the earnings potential of the enterprise'.[3]

1.1.2   Capitalise all costs when incurred

Enterprises undertake research and development expenditure in the hope of future benefits. Hence, it could be argued that if future benefits were unlikely then the expenditure would not be incurred. Whilst this may be the case for some projects, it is undoubtedly not so for all such expenditure. One could, however, perhaps argue that since future benefits will be gained from some of the expenditure, then an enterprise should capitalise all such costs and match the total costs to the future benefits derived from some of them.

However, a meaningful method of amortisation would be impossible to achieve since the expenditure would be carried out at different points in time and also the period of benefit would be extremely difficult to determine.

1.1.3 Capitalise costs when incurred if certain conditions are met

A prerequisite of this treatment is the establishment of conditions that must be fulfilled before research and development costs may be capitalised. Furthermore, once such conditions are established they must be capable of being applied by all enterprises. If the specified conditions are not met, then costs are to be expensed.

1.1.4 Accumulation of costs in a special category

At a future date such costs could then be either transferred to assets if future benefits could reasonably be established or written off if it were reasonably established that no significant future benefits would arise. This is analogous to the full cost method of accounting for oil and gas exploration expenditure.

This treatment would draw attention to the uncertainty surrounding the expenditure and would also delay the decision of whether to capitalise or expense. However, such accumulated costs would arguably serve little purpose insofar as analysts and other users are concerned.

1.1.5 Which treatment should be adopted?

SSAP 13 – *Accounting for research and development* – states that the choice of an appropriate accounting treatment for research and development centres around the application of fundamental accounting concepts 'including the "accruals" concept by which revenue and costs are accrued, matched and dealt with in the period to which they relate and the "prudence" concept by which revenue and profits are not anticipated but are recognised only when realised in the form either of cash or of other assets the ultimate cash realisation of which can be established with reasonable certainty. It is a corollary of the prudence concept that expenditure should be written off in the period in which it arises unless its relationship to the revenue of a future period can be assessed with reasonable certainty.'[4]

It was on the basis of this argument that the existing UK practice was formulated although, as is explained below, SSAP 13 has adopted an approach which is somewhat of a hybrid of the various options available.

1.2 Development of accounting standards in the UK

1.2.1 ED 14

As a result of the different accounting treatments that were being adopted by companies in practice, the ASC issued ED 14 – *Accounting for Research and Development* – in January 1975. Although the exposure draft made a distinction between pure and applied research and development expenditure, it proposed that all research and development expenditure should be written off as incurred to the profit and loss account, with very minor exceptions. The exposure draft received widespread criticism, particularly from the aerospace industry, with the bulk of such criticism being concerned with the treatment of development expenditure. It was pointed out that the design and development stage of a new aircraft took at least five years prior to the delivery of the first production aircraft to a customer, and that sales of a successful aircraft then continued for at least ten years with delivery of spares continuing well beyond that point.[5]

1.2.2   ED 17

Owing to the criticism received, ED 14 was withdrawn and replaced by ED 17 – *Accounting for research and development–revised* – which was issued in April 1976. Whilst still proposing that pure and applied research expenditure be expensed in the year in which it was incurred, it recognised that some development expenditure could be clearly matched to future benefits which were reasonably certain. Consequently, the exposure draft concluded that such expenditure should be capitalised provided certain criteria were met. This exposure draft was more favourably received. However, a number of commentators made the point that 'where companies wished to write off development expenditure, even though the projects fulfilled the conditions in ED 17 which would justify carrying forward the expenditure, they should be permitted to do so provided the treatment was disclosed in notes to the accounts'.[6]

1.2.3   SSAP 13

Consequently, when SSAP 13 was issued in December 1977, although the standard contained essentially the same requirements as those of ED 17, it did not *require* companies to defer development expenditure but, where certain criteria were fulfilled, *allowed them the choice* between immediate write off or capitalisation.[7]

1.2.4   ED 41

Since the issue of SSAP 13, the Fourth EC Company Law Directive was enacted in UK company law, following which the ASC embarked on a policy of reviewing its existing accounting standards. (The relevant requirements of the Companies Act which relate to research and development expenditure are discussed at 3 below.) As a result, ED 41 – *Accounting for research and development* – was issued in June 1987. The principal change to SSAP 13 proposed by ED 41 related to the disclosure of the amount of research and development costs charged to the profit and loss account in the current period.

The exposure draft also proposed that deferred research and development expenditure be disclosed under intangible fixed assets in the balance sheet, rather than deferred expenditure, as it was classified under the original SSAP 13.[8] The exposure draft also intended to continue the requirement of SSAP 13 that development expenditure once written off should not be reinstated even though the uncertainties which led to its being written off no longer applied.[9] However, such a treatment arguably conflicts with the Companies Act requirements relating to fixed assets. Paragraph 19(3) of Schedule 4 to the Companies Act requires any provisions against the value of a fixed asset to be released when the reasons for its creation cease to apply.

1.2.5 SSAP 13 (Revised)

SSAP 13 (Revised) – *Accounting for research and development* – was issued in January 1989, following essentially the line taken by ED 41. The main changes between the standard and the exposure draft were as follows:

(a) although the standard requires the amount of research and development costs charged to the profit and loss account to be disclosed, certain enterprises are exempt from this disclosure; and

(b) the requirement that development expenditure once written off should not be reinstated even though the uncertainties which led to its being written off no longer apply, was deleted in the revised standard, presumably in view of the apparent conflict with the Companies Act referred to at 1.2.4 above.

2 REQUIREMENTS OF SSAP 13

2.1 Definitions

Research and development expenditure is defined in SSAP 13 as 'expenditure falling into one or more of the following broad categories (except to the extent that it relates to locating or exploiting oil, gas or mineral deposits or is reimbursable by third parties either directly or under the terms of a firm contract to develop and manufacture at an agreed price calculated to reimburse both elements of expenditure):

(a) *pure (or basic) research:* experimental or theoretical work undertaken primarily to acquire new scientific or technical knowledge for its own sake rather than directed towards any specific aim or application;

(b) *applied research:* original or critical investigation undertaken in order to gain new scientific or technical knowledge and directed towards a specific practical aim or objective;

(c) *development:* use of scientific or technical knowledge in order to produce new or substantially improved materials, devices, products or services, to install new processes or systems prior to the commencement of commercial production or commercial applications, or to improving substantially those already produced or installed.'[10]

The definitions of the different types of research and development used in the standard are based on those used by the Organisation for Economic Co-operation and Development (OECD).[11]

However, as paragraph 4 of the standard states, 'the dividing line between these categories is often indistinct and particular expenditure may have characteristics of more than one category. This is especially so when new products or services are developed through research and development to production, when the activities may have characteristics of both development and production.' For example, a project may start out as basic research, the results of which may lead to the development of new products or systems, particularly in, say, the pharmaceutical industry.

It can be seen that the standard specifically excludes from the definition:

(a)   expenditure incurred in locating and exploiting oil, gas and mineral deposits. However, development of new surveying methods and techniques as an integral part of research on geographical phenomena should be included in research and development;[12] and

(b)   research and development expenditure which is reimbursed by a third party. Any such expenditure which has not been reimbursed at the balance sheet date should be dealt with as contract work in progress.[13]

2.2   Accounting

The accounting treatment of research and development prescribed by SSAP 13 is as follows:

2.2.1   Fixed assets

The cost of fixed assets acquired or constructed in order to provide facilities for research and development activities over a number of accounting periods should be capitalised and written off over their useful life through the profit and loss account.[14] The depreciation so written off should be included as part of the expenditure on research and development.[15] Where an asset is used in the course of the development activities, however, the depreciation thereon can be regarded as part of the overhead costs to be included as part of development costs, if such costs are to be deferred (see 2.2.3 below).

2.2.2   Pure and applied research

Expenditure on pure and applied research (other than the cost of fixed assets used for the purpose of research activities) should be written off in the year of expenditure through the profit and loss account.[16] SSAP 13 states the reason for this as being because such expenditure can be regarded as part of a continuing operation required to maintain a company's business and its competitive position; in general, no one particular period rather than any other will be expected to benefit and therefore it is appropriate that these costs should be written off as they are incurred.[17] In any event, the Companies Act does not allow pure or applied research to be treated as an asset (see 3.1 below).

2.2.3 *Development expenditure*

The standard proposes a different treatment for development expenditure, the reason being that the development of new products or services is distinguishable from pure and applied research. Expenditure on such development is normally undertaken with a reasonable expectation of specific commercial success and of future benefits arising from the work, either from increased revenue and related profits or from reduced costs. On these grounds it may be argued that such expenditure, to the extent that it is recoverable, should be deferred to be matched against the future revenue.[18] Consequently, the standard allows such expenditure to be deferred, but only if certain conditions are met.

The standard requires that development expenditure should be written off in the year of expenditure except in the following circumstances when it *may* be deferred to future periods:

(a)   there is a clearly defined project; and

(b)   the related expenditure is separately identifiable; and

(c)   the outcome of such a project has been assessed with reasonable certainty as to:

    (i)   its technical feasibility, and

    (ii)   its ultimate commercial viability considered in the light of factors such as likely market conditions (including competing products), public opinion, consumer and environmental legislation; and

(d)   the aggregate of the deferred development costs, any further development costs, and related production, selling and administration costs is reasonably expected to be exceeded by related future sales or other revenues; and

(e)   adequate resources exist, or are reasonably expected to be available, to enable the project to be completed and to provide any consequential increases in working capital.[19]

Where these circumstances exist, the standard permits (but does not require) development expenditure to be deferred to the extent that its recovery can reasonably be regarded as assured.[20] However, if a policy of deferral is adopted, it should be consistently applied to all development projects that meet the above criteria.[21]

The development costs should be amortised and the amortisation should commence with the commercial production or application of the product, service, process or system and should be allocated on a systematic basis to each accounting period, by reference to either the sale or use of the product, service, process or system or the period over which these are expected to be sold or used.[22]

The deferred development expenditure should be reviewed at the end of each accounting period and, where the circumstances that justified the deferral no longer apply, or are considered doubtful, the expenditure, to the extent that it is considered irrecoverable, should be written off immediately. This should be done on a project by project basis.[23]

2.3   Disclosure

The disclosure requirements of SSAP 13 are as follows:

(a)   the accounting policy on research and development expenditure should be stated and explained (as, in any event, required by SSAP 2);[24]

(b)   the total amount of research and development expenditure charged in the profit and loss account should be disclosed, analysed between the current year's expenditure and amounts amortised from deferred expenditure.[25] It is emphasised that the amounts disclosed should include any amortisation of fixed assets used in the research and development activity;

(c)   movements on deferred development expenditure and the amount carried forward at the beginning and the end of the period should be disclosed;[26] and

(d)   deferred development expenditure should be disclosed under intangible fixed assets in the balance sheet.[27]

However, the information contained in (b) above need only be given by:[28]

(a)   public companies (as defined in section 1 of the Companies Act 1985) or holding companies that have one or more public companies as a subsidiary;

(b)   banking and insurance companies (as defined in section 744 of the Companies Act), and preparing accounts in accordance with Schedules 9 or 9A thereto, or holding companies that have one or more banking and insurance companies as a subsidiary; and

(c)   private companies (and other enterprises) which do not satisfy the criteria, multiplied in each case by ten, for defining a medium-sized company under section 247 of the Companies Act.

At present, this means that enterprises with any two of the following fall outside the exemption and will have to give the additional disclosures:

(i)   turnover exceeding £112m,

(ii)   total assets exceeding £56m,

(iii) average number of employees exceeding 2,500.[29]

2.4   Current reporting practice

Most major companies which incur research and development costs adopt a policy of writing off the expenditure as it is incurred.[30] One company which adopts such a policy is SmithKline Beecham, as illustrated below:

Extract 12.1: SmithKline Beecham plc (1998)

Accounting Policies [extract]

Research and Development expenditure

Laboratory buildings and equipment used for Research and Development are included as tangible fixed assets and written off in accordance with the Group's depreciation policy. Other Research and Development expenditure is written off in the year in which it is incurred.

Consolidated profit and loss account [extract]

	1998 **Total** **£m**	1997 Total £m
Sales	**8,082**	7,795
Cost of goods sold	**(2,432)**	(2,328)
Gross profit	**5,650**	5,467
Selling, general and administrative expenses	**(3,122)**	(2,933)
Research and development expenditure	**(910)**	(841)
Trading profit	**1,618**	1,693

It is noteworthy that SmithKline Beecham has disclosed the research and development charge for the year as a separate item in the body of its profit and loss account, as opposed to disclosing the amount in the notes, which is the route which most companies have taken. Furthermore, it can be seen that, in compliance with SSAP 13, the company treats its fixed assets which are used in research and development activities in the same way as any other fixed asset.

One company which adopts the policy of deferring certain development costs is FKI, as illustrated below:

Extract 12.2: FKI plc (1998)

1   Accounting policies [extract]

Research and development

Development expenditure on clearly defined projects whose outcome can be assessed with reasonable certainty is capitalised and amortisation is commenced in the year the expenditure is incurred by reference to the lesser of the life of the project or three years. All other research and development expenditure is written off in the year in which it is incurred.

4   Profit on ordinary activities before taxation [extract]

Profit on ordinary activities before taxation is stated after charging (crediting):

	1998	1997
	£000	£000
Research and development costs	**6,274**	7,035

13   Intangible fixed assets - Group

	Development Costs £'000
Cost:	
1 April 1997	7,884
Exchange adjustments	(136)
On disposal of subsidiary undertakings	(550)
Additions	167
31 March 1998	**7,365**
Amortisation:	
1 April 1997	6,628
Exchange adjustments	(129)
On disposal of subsidiary undertakings	(533)
Provided during the year	565
31 March 1998	**6,531**
Net book value 31 March 1998	**834**
Net book value 31 March 1997	1,256

---

3   REQUIREMENTS OF THE COMPANIES ACT 1985

3.1   Accounting

The accounting treatment for research and development costs required by SSAP 13 is in effect backed up by the requirements of the Companies Act 1985. The Act permits a company's balance sheet or profit and loss account to include an item representing or covering the amount of any asset or liability, income or expenditure not otherwise covered by any of the items listed in the formats set out in Schedule 4 to the Act, but prohibits the treatment of costs of research as an asset.[31] Paragraph 20(1) of Schedule 4, however, states that development costs which are included under fixed assets in the balance sheet formats may only be included in a company's balance sheet in 'special circumstances'. There is no explanation in the Act as to what the 'special circumstances' might be, but it is reasonable to assume that the circumstances under which development expenditure may be deferred in accordance with SSAP 13 satisfy the requirements for 'special circumstances' for Companies Act purposes; this is because ED 41 stated that the DTI had confirmed that the recommended practice concerning deferral of development expenditure satisfied the term.[32]

As deferred development costs are to be treated as fixed assets, then all of the Companies Act requirements relating to fixed assets apply to such costs (see Chapter 10).

3.2 Disclosure

3.2.1 Financial statements

Where an amount is included in a company's balance sheet in respect of development costs the following information must be given in a note to the accounts:

(a) the period over which the amount of those costs originally capitalised is being written off; and

(b) the reasons for capitalising the development costs in question.[33]

The disclosure requirements relating to fixed assets generally will also apply.

3.2.2 Directors' report

The directors' report should contain an indication of the activities (if any) of the company and its subsidiary undertakings in the field of research and development.[34] However, in practice this frequently results in a fairly minimal statement on the subject being given, for example:

Extract 12.3: Halma p.l.c. (1999)

Report of the Directors [extract]

Research and development

Group companies have continuous research and development programmes established with the objective of the improvement of their product ranges and increasing the profitability of their operations.

Extract 12.4: British American Tobacco p.l.c. (1998)

Directors' report [extract]

Research and development

The Group's research and development activities are concentrated on the development of new products, new processes, quality improvement of existing products and cost reduction programmes in the tobacco industry.

Research is also undertaken into various aspects of the science and behavioural science related to smoking, including continued significant funding of independent studies.

A good example of disclosure is that of Glaxo Wellcome, which devotes four pages of its annual report to meeting the requirement.[35] However, this is only to be expected from a company which states in its mission statement that it 'is a research-based company whose people are committed to fighting disease by bringing innovative medicines and services to patients throughout the world and to the healthcare providers who serve them'.[36]

3.3   Distributable profits

The Companies Act only allows distributions to be made out of a company's net realised profits.[37] In determining such net realised profits, any amount shown in respect of development costs, which is included as an asset in the balance sheet, is to be treated as a realised loss.[38] However, this will not apply if:

(a)   there are special circumstances in the company's case justifying the directors in deciding that the amount shown in respect of development costs is not to be treated as a realised loss; and

(b)   the note to the accounts required by paragraph 20 of Schedule 4 to the Companies Act (reasons for showing development costs as an asset) states that the amount is not to be so treated and explains the circumstances relied upon to justify the decision of the directors to that effect.[39]

In September 1982 the CCAB issued a technical release on distributable profits which states that development costs carried forward in accordance with SSAP 13 will not normally affect distributable profits. It went on to indicate that directors will normally be able to justify the amount carried forward as not being treated as a realised loss if the costs are carried forward in accordance with SSAP 13. However, it emphasised that such justification must be included in the note on capitalised development costs required under (b) above.[40]

4   PROBLEM AREAS

4.1   What activities should be included within research and development?

Although the definition of research and development is very broad, there are difficulties in determining what types of activity constitute 'research and development'. SSAP 13 states that research and development activity is distinguished from non-research based activity by the presence or absence of an element of innovation. If the activity departs from routine and breaks new ground it should normally be included; if it follows an established pattern it should normally be excluded.[41]

Examples of activities that would normally be included in research and development are as follows:[42]

(a) experimental, theoretical or other work aimed at the discovery of new knowledge, or the advancement of existing knowledge;

(b) searching for applications of that knowledge;

(c) formulation and design of possible applications for such work;

(d) testing in search for, or evaluation of, product, service or process alternatives;

(e) design, construction and testing of pre-production prototypes and models and development batches;

(f) design of products, services, processes or systems involving new technology or substantially improving those already produced or installed; and

(g) construction and operation of pilot plants.

Examples of activities which should not be included are as follows:[43]

(a) testing and analysis either of equipment or product for purposes of quality or quantity control;

(b) periodic alterations to existing products, services or processes even though these may represent some improvement;

(c) operational research not tied to a specific research and development activity;

(d) cost of corrective action in connection with break-downs during commercial production;

(e) legal and administrative work in connection with patent applications, records and litigation and the sale or licensing of patents;

(f) activity, including design and construction engineering, relating to the construction, relocation, rearrangement or start-up of facilities or equipment other than facilities or equipment whose sole use is for a particular research and development project; and

(g) market research.

Although the above items are not normally to be included within 'research and development' and accounted for as such under SSAP 13, this does not mean that all costs of such activities will invariably be charged to the profit and loss account as incurred. This may be appropriate for certain of the costs (such as (a) or (b) above), but for some of the other costs it may be possible to regard them as part of the cost of a fixed asset (such as (f) above).

4.2   What costs should be included within the category of research and development?

Having decided which activities are to be included as research and development it is then necessary to determine what costs are to be included as the cost of those activities. SSAP 13 does not give guidance on the types of costs which can be included. However, guidance can be sought from both SFAS 2 in the US and IAS 9 as these identify the elements of costs which should be included (see 5.1.1 and 5.2 below). It must be remembered, however, that where development expenditure is to be deferred as an intangible asset, the accounting rules for fixed assets under Schedule 4 to the Companies Act must be taken into account.

4.3   Availability of choice between immediate write off and capitalisation of development expenditure

As indicated at 2.2.3 above, it is possible for a company to choose a policy of either writing off, or deferring and amortising, development expenditure which fulfils all the conditions laid down in paragraph 25 of SSAP 13. In view of this choice, is it possible for a company to change from a policy of writing off such expenditure to one of deferring and amortising or vice versa? We believe that a change of policy will normally be acceptable; furthermore, it will be necessary to restate comparative figures to reflect the new policy in accordance with FRS 3 (see Chapter 22 at 2.14). However, where a change from a policy of writing off such expenditure to one of deferring and amortising is contemplated, care should be taken to ensure that all the conditions which require to be fulfilled were applicable at the time the expenditure was incurred. If the conditions were not met at that time, then the costs should not be capitalised under the new policy but should remain written off; this is because such costs would not have been capitalised if the new policy had been in force at the time the expenditure was incurred.

One company which has recently changed its policy from one of deferring and amortising to one of writing off is Network Technology as shown below.

Extract 12.5: Network Technology plc (1998)

Financial Review [extract]

Accounting Policies

At the year end the Group changed its accounting policy for research and development expenditure. The impact of this has been included in Note 1 to the accounts. The Group will now write off research and development expenditure as it is incurred. This is a more prudent policy and is adopted by most other companies.

1.   Accounting Policies [extract]

Research and development

At the year end the Company changed its accounting policy with regard to research and development. Previously expenditure on pure and applied research was charged to the profit and loss account in the year in which it was incurred. Development costs were also charged to the profit and loss account in the year of expenditure, unless individual projects satisfied the following criteria:

- The project was clearly defined and related expenditure was separately identifiable;
- The project was technically feasible and commercially viable;
- Current and future costs were expected to be exceeded by future sales; and
- Adequate resources exist for the project to be completed.

In such circumstances the costs were carried forward and amortised over a period not exceeding 5 years commencing in the year the Group starts to benefit from expenditure. The new accounting policy is to charge all expenditure on pure and applied research and development expenditure to the profit and loss account in the year in which it is incurred.

Prior year adjustment

The changes to the accounting policy for research and development and for office set up costs has resulted in a prior year adjustment, the effects of which are as follows:

	Year to 30.9.98 £'000	Year to 30.9.97 £'000
Profit before tax for the year under the old policy	2,286	4,170
Taxation for the year under the old policy	(979)	(1,406)
Profit for the year after tax under the old policy	1,307	2,764
Less expenditure on intangible developments previously capitalised	(1,915)	(1,084)
Less expenditure on office set up costs previously capitalised	–	(9)
Add amortisation on development expenditure previously capitalised	535	107
Add amortisation on office set up costs no longer charged	106	107
Add taxation	337	313
Profit for the year after tax	370	2,198

The effect of this adjustment on the net assets of the group are as follows:

	30.9.97	30.9.96
Net assets under old policy	11,869	4,742
Net assets under new policy	10,933	4,372

4.4   Elimination of uncertainty in respect of development expenditure

4.4.1   *Expenditure previously not capitalised*

The last three conditions for deferral laid down in paragraph 25 of SSAP 13 effectively mean that development expenditure should only be deferred if it can be shown to be recoverable with sufficient certainty (see 2.2.3 above). However, what happens if a company has not capitalised development expenditure because the conditions were not met, but at a later date the uncertainties which led to its write-off no longer apply?

The original SSAP 13 (and ED 41) made it clear that such expenditure could not be reinstated as an asset; however, the revised SSAP 13 is silent on the matter. Nevertheless, we believe that in such circumstances the expenditure should not be reinstated as an asset.

4.4.2   *Deferred expenditure previously capitalised and subsequently written down*

Paragraph 29 of SSAP 13 requires deferred development expenditure to be reviewed annually and to be written down to its recoverable amount (see 2.2.3 above). What happens if at a later date the uncertainties which gave rise to that write-down no longer apply?

Again, SSAP 13 is silent on this issue; however, consideration in this instance has to be given to the requirements of the Companies Act relating to provisions for diminutions in value of fixed assets. These require that where the reasons for which any provision was made have ceased to apply to any extent, then the provision shall be written back to the extent that it is no longer necessary.[44] These requirements of the Companies Act do not apply to the situation discussed at 4.4.1 above as no asset was recorded in the first instance.

5   COMPARISON WITH IASC AND US PRONOUNCEMENTS

5.1   IASC

Until recently, the relevant international standard was IAS 9 – *Research and Development Costs*. However, as discussed in Chapter 10 at 7.1.5, the IASC has issued a standard on intangible assets, IAS 38 – *Intangible Assets*. It was originally intended to scope out research and development from this standard;[45] however, in 1997 the IASC changed its mind and IAS 38 now embraces research and development expenditure within its scope. This is because the IASC rejects a 'deferred cost' perspective for including items in the balance sheet although it has to use rather tortuously worded recognition criteria to continue to allow the same expenditure to be capitalised from a balance sheet perspective. IAS 38 is operative for annual financial statements covering periods beginning on or after

1 July 1999. IAS 9 can continue to be used for financial statements before that date, but thereafter will be withdrawn.

5.1.1   IAS 9

IAS 9 was issued originally in July 1978, but a revised version was published in December 1993. The requirements of this revised standard are broadly similar to those of SSAP 13, with one exception; IAS 9 specifically requires that development costs *must* be recognised as an asset when they meet the criteria in paragraph 17 of IAS 9 and it is probable that these costs will be recovered.

The definitions of 'research' and 'development' contained in IAS 9 are as follows:[46]

'*Research* is original and planned investigation undertaken with the prospect of gaining new scientific or technical knowledge and understanding.'

'*Development* is the application of research findings or other knowledge to a plan or design for the production of new or substantially improved materials, devices, products, processes, systems or services prior to the commencement of commercial production or use.'

No distinction is made between 'pure' and 'applied' research.

Whereas SSAP 13 provides examples of the activities that would normally be included within research and development, IAS 9 provides examples of the activities that would normally be 'research' and those that would normally be 'development'.

Examples of activities typically included in research are:[47]

(a)   activities aimed at obtaining new knowledge;

(b)   the search for applications of research findings or other knowledge;

(c)   the search for product or process alternatives; and

(d)   the formulation and design of possible new or improved product or process alternatives.

These are equivalent to items (a) to (c) within SSAP 13 (see 4.1 above).

Examples of activities typically included in development are:[48]

(a)   the evaluation of product or process alternatives;

(b)   the design, construction and testing of pre-production prototypes and models;

(c)   the design of tools, jigs, moulds and dies involving new technology; and

(d)   the design, construction and operation of a pilot plant that is not of a scale economically feasible for commercial production.

These are equivalent to items (d) to (g) within SSAP 13 (see 4.1 above).

Like SSAP 13, IAS 9 then provides the following examples of activities that may be closely associated with research and development activities but are neither research nor development:[49]

(a) engineering follow-through in an early phase of commercial production;

(b) quality control during commercial production, including routine testing of products;

(c) trouble-shooting in connection with breakdowns during commercial production;

(d) routine efforts to refine, enrich or otherwise improve upon the qualities of an existing product;

(e) adaptation of an existing capability to a particular requirement or customer's need as part of a continuing commercial activity;

(f) seasonal or other periodic design changes to existing products;

(g) routine design of tools, jigs, moulds and dies; and

(h) activities, including design and construction engineering, related to the construction, relocation, rearrangement, or start-up of facilities or equipment other than facilities or equipment used solely for a particular research and development project.

IAS 9 also identifies the costs which should be included within research and development costs as follows:[50]

(a) the salaries, wages and other related costs of personnel engaged in research and development activities;

(b) the costs of material and services consumed in such activities;

(c) the depreciation of property, plant and equipment to the extent that they are used for such activities;

(d) a reasonable allocation of overhead costs, other than general overheads, related to such activities; and

(e) other costs, such as the amortisation of patents and licences, to the extent that they are used for such activities.

The standard provides that research costs should be expensed in the period in which they are incurred. Development costs should also be charged as an expense of the period in which they are incurred unless certain criteria are met (similar to those conditions laid down in SSAP 13), in which case they should be capitalised as an asset and accounted for in the same manner as required by SSAP 13.[51]

IAS 9 requires all enterprises to disclose the amount of research and development expenditure charged as an expense to be disclosed, whereas SSAP 13 exempts certain enterprises from disclosing such information (see 2.3 above).

5.1.2 IAS 38

As indicated above, IAS 38 now embraces research and development expenditure within its scope, but has had to use rather tortuously worded recognition criteria to continue to allow the same expenditure to be capitalised from a balance sheet perspective.

The definitions of 'research' and 'development' contained in IAS 38[52] are exactly the same as those in IAS 9. However, the examples of research activities and development activities are slightly different.

Examples of research activities given in IAS 38 are:[53]

(a) activities aimed at obtaining new knowledge;

(b) the search for, evaluation and final selection of, applications of research findings or other knowledge;

(c) the search for alternatives for materials, devices, products, processes, systems or services; and

(d) the formulation, design, evaluation and final selection of possible alternatives for new or improved materials, devices, products, processes, systems or services.

Examples of development activities are:[54]

(a) the design, construction and testing of pre-production or pre-use prototypes and models;

(b) the design of tools, jigs, moulds and dies involving new technology;

(c) the design, construction and operation of a pilot plant that is not of a scale economically feasible for commercial production; and

(d) the design, construction and testing of a chosen alternative for new or improved materials, devices, products, processes, systems or services.

Notwithstanding that these are slightly different from those in IAS 9, and IAS 38 does not provide any specific examples of activities closely related (but which are neither research nor development), it is thought unlikely that there will be any practical effect.

Although research and development has been brought within the scope of IAS 38 and is therefore covered by the general recognition and measurement rules dealing with intangible assets,[55] the standard contains more specific rules for research and development.

No intangible asset arising from research (or from the research phase of an internal project) should be recognised. Expenditure on research (or on the research phase of an internal project) should be recognised as an expense when it is incurred.[56]

An intangible asset arising from development (or from the development phase of an internal project) should be recognised if, and only if, an enterprise can demonstrate all of the following:[57]

(a) the technical feasibility of completing the intangible asset so that it will be available for use or sale;

(b) its intention to complete the intangible asset and use or sell it;

(c) its ability to use or sell the intangible asset;

(d) how the intangible asset will generate probable future economic benefits. Among other things, the enterprise should demonstrate the existence of a market for the output of the intangible asset or the intangible asset itself or, if it is to be used internally, the usefulness of the intangible asset;

(e) the availability of adequate technical, financial and other resources to complete the development and to use or sell the intangible asset; and

(f) its ability to measure the expenditure attributable to the intangible asset during its development reliably.

Although similar to the criteria in SSAP 13 (and IAS 9), these are more restrictive because in order to demonstrate to fulfil criterion (d) above an enterprise needs to assess the future economic benefits to be received from the asset using the principles in IAS 36 – *Impairment of Assets*, i.e. using discounted cash flows. If the asset will generate economic benefits only in combination with other assets, the enterprise applies the concept of cash-generating units as set out in IAS 36. The requirements of that standard are discussed in Chapter 10 at 7.1.4. Like IAS 9, IAS 38 identifies the costs which would be included in arriving at the cost of such an asset, and those that would not, although the discussion is in terms of internally generated intangible assets rather than being specifically related to development activities.[58]

As with SSAP 13 and IAS 9, such capitalised development costs should be amortised and tested for recoverability. However, the wording of the requirements of IAS 38 are designed for all intangible assets, not just development costs. Accordingly, the depreciable amount should be allocated on a systematic basis over the best estimate of its useful life. There is a rebuttable presumption that the useful life of an intangible asset will not exceed twenty years from the date when the asset is available for use. Amortisation should commence when the asset is available for use.[59] It is unlikely that this maximum life of 20 years will be appropriate for development costs.

The amortisation method used should reflect the pattern in which the asset's economic benefits are consumed by the enterprise. If that pattern cannot be determined reliably, the straight-line method should be used.[60] Paragraph 89 of IAS 38 also states that 'there will rarely, if ever, be persuasive evidence to support an amortisation method for intangible assets that results in a lower amount of accumulated amortisation than under the straight-line method.'

An enterprise should estimate the recoverable amount of the following intangible assets at least at each financial year end, even if there is no indication that the asset is impaired:

(a)   an intangible asset that is not yet available for use; and

(b)   an intangible asset that is amortised over a period exceeding twenty years from the date when the asset is available for use.

The recoverable amount should be determined under IAS 36 and impairment losses recognised accordingly.

As a result of (a) above, any development costs which are not yet being amortised will therefore need to be tested for recoverability on an annual basis. However, where the asset is being used and is being amortised it would only be tested for impairment as required by IAS 36 (see Chapter 10 at 7.1.4). SSAP 13 requires the development expenditure to be reviewed annually to see whether it is still recoverable.

In addition to the general disclosures required for intangible assets,[61] IAS 38 requires disclosure of the aggregate amount of research and development expenditure recognised as an expense during the period,[62] whereas SSAP 13 exempts certain enterprises from disclosing such information (see 2.3 above).

5.2   US

The principal standard in the US which deals with this issue is SFAS 2 – *Accounting for Research and Development Costs* – which was issued in October 1974.[63] The statement defines 'research' and 'development' as follows:

'*Research* is planned search or critical investigation aimed at discovery of new knowledge with the hope that such knowledge will be useful in developing a new product or service (hereinafter "product") or a new process or technique (hereinafter "process") or in bringing about a significant improvement to an existing product or process.'

'*Development* is the translation of research findings or other knowledge into a plan or design for a new product or process or for a significant improvement to an existing product or process whether intended for sale or use. It includes the conceptual formulation, design, and testing of product alternatives, construction of prototypes and operation of pilot plants. It does not include routine or periodic alterations to existing products, production lines, manufacturing process, and other on-going operations even though those alterations may represent improvements and it does not include market research or market testing activities.'[64]

It can be seen that no distinction is made between 'pure' and 'applied' research as is done in SSAP 13, and that a more detailed definition of 'development' is given.

Like SSAP 13, SFAS 2 provides examples of those activities that would normally be included in research and development and those that would not.[65] In addition, however, SFAS 2 identifies elements of costs which are identified with the research and development activities; these are as follows:

(a)   materials, equipment and facilities;

(b)   personnel;

(c)   intangibles purchased from others;

(d)   contract services; and

(e)   indirect costs.[66]

The main difference between SSAP 13 and SFAS 2 is that SFAS 2 requires that all research and development costs encompassed by the statement should be charged to expense when incurred, for the reasons discussed at 1.1.1 above. Like IAS 38, SFAS 2 requires all enterprises to disclose the amount expensed whereas SSAP 13 exempts certain enterprises from disclosing such information (see 2.3 above).

It should be noted that SFAS 2 encompasses research and development costs incurred in the process of creating a software product. SFAS 86 – *Accounting for the Costs of Computer Software to be Sold, Leased, or Otherwise Marketed* – specifically states that 'all costs incurred to establish the technological feasibility of a computer software product to be sold, leased or otherwise marketed are research and development costs'. Those costs are charged to expense when incurred as required by SFAS 2.[67] Technical feasibility is established upon completion of a detailed program design or, in its absence, completion of a working model.[68]

5.2.1   In-process research and development

This treatment of writing off research and development costs also applies to such projects acquired in business combinations. As discussed at 5.2.6 C of Chapter 6, fair values have to be attributed to such in-process research and development costs which are then required to be written off immediately.[69] Recently, however, financial analysts in the US have questioned the rationale under which companies are writing off large amounts of the purchase price right after an arms-length transaction has taken place, and how such treatment correlates with investor expectations. As a result, the FASB was planning to issue an exposure draft which would amend SFAS 2, proposing that such capitalised assets would no longer be written off immediately but amortised over their service lives. Any subsequent costs to complete purchased in-process research and development projects would also be capitalised. The costs of other research and development projects which were started after the business combination would continue to be governed by SFAS 2 and therefore would be written off as incurred. However, faced with complaints from technology companies and investment bankers that this would make mergers and acquisitions far less attractive, in July 1999 the FASB decided to put off the issue until a later date, indicating that it would probably undertake a comprehensive review of the accounting for research and development costs when it had the necessary resources.

References

1   SFAS 2, *Accounting for Research and Development Costs*, FASB, October 1974, paras. 39–50.
2   *Ibid.*, para. 44.
3   *Ibid.*, para. 50.
4   SSAP 13, *Accounting for research and development*, ASC, Issued December 1977, Revised January 1989, para. 1.
5   Letter dated 15 August 1975 from the Society of British Aerospace Companies Ltd to the Technical Director of ICAEW.
6   Technical Release 264, *Statement by the Accounting Standards Committee on the publication of SSAP 13 Accounting for research and development*.
7   Original SSAP 13, para. 21.
8   ED 41, *Accounting for Research and Development*, ASC, June 1987, para. 33; Original SSAP 13, para. 28.
9   ED 41, para. 29.
10 SSAP 13, para. 21.
11 *Ibid.*, para. 2.
12 *Ibid.*, para. 18.
13 *Ibid.*, para. 17.
14 *Ibid.*, para. 23.
15 *Ibid.*, para. 16.
16 *Ibid.*, para. 24.
17 *Ibid.*, para. 8.
18 *Ibid.*, para. 9.
19 *Ibid.*, para. 25.
20 *Ibid.*, para. 26.
21 *Ibid.*, para. 27.
22 *Ibid.*, para. 28.
23 *Ibid.*, para. 29.
24 *Ibid.*, para. 30.
25 *Ibid.*, para. 31.
26 *Ibid.*, para. 32.
27 *Ibid.*
28 *Ibid.*, para. 22.
29 In March 1999, the DTI issued a Consultative Document, *Raising the Threshold Levels for SMEs*, outlining proposals to raise the financial limits up to the level permitted by EC law. There is also a proposal that the limits under the EC Accounting Directives should be increased by 25%. If that is adopted the new UK financial limits would be increased to those higher levels. This would mean that the limits under SSAP 13 would be £192m for turnover and £96m for total assets.
30 It was reported in *Company Reporting No. 104*, Company Reporting Limited, February 1999, p. 10 that its database shows that, of companies with evidence of research and development spend, 73% write it off as incurred.
31 CA 85, Sch. 4, para. 3(2).
32 ED 41, Preface, para. 1.5.
33 CA 85, Sch. 4, para. 20(2).
34 *Ibid.*, Sch. 7, para. 6(c).

35 Glaxo Wellcome plc, Annual Report & Accounts and Form 20-F 1998, pp. 13–16.
36 *Ibid.*, p. 7.
37 CA 85, s 263.
38 *Ibid.*, s 269(1).
39 *Ibid.*, s 269(2).
40 CCAB, *The determination of distributable profits in the context of the Companies Act (TR 482)*, September 1982, para. 23.
41 SSAP 13, para. 5.
42 *Ibid.*, para. 6.
43 *Ibid.*, para. 7.
44 CA 85, Sch. 4, para. 19(3).
45 E50, *Intangible Assets*, IASC, June 1995, para. 2.
46 IAS 9, *Research and Development Costs*, IASC, December 1993, para. 6.
47 *Ibid.*, para. 8.
48 *Ibid.*, para. 9.
49 *Ibid.*, para. 10.
50 *Ibid.*, para. 12.
51 *Ibid.*, paras. 16–29.
52 IAS 38, *Intangible Assets*, IASC, September 1998, para. 7.
53 *Ibid.*, para. 44.
54 *Ibid.*, para. 47.
55 *Ibid.*, paras. 19–21.
56 *Ibid.*, para. 42.
57 *Ibid.*, para. 45.
58 *Ibid.*, paras. 54 and 55.
59 *Ibid.*, para. 79.
60 *Ibid.*, para. 88.
61 *Ibid.*, para. 107.
62 *Ibid.*, para. 115.
63 See also, for example, SFAS 7, *Accounting and Reporting by Development Stage Enterprises*, FASB, June 1975 and SFAS 68, *Research and Development Arrangements*, FASB, October 1982.
64 SFAS 2, para. 8.
65 *Ibid.*, paras. 9 and 10.
66 *Ibid.*, para. 11.
67 SFAS 86, *Accounting for the Costs of Computer Software to be Sold, Leased, or Otherwise Marketed*, FASB, August 1985, para. 3.
68 *Ibid.*, summary.
69 FIN 4, *Applicability of FASB Statement No. 2 to Business Combinations Accounted for by the Purchase Method*, FASB, February 1975, paras. 4 and 5.

Chapter 13   Capitalisation of finance costs

1   INTRODUCTION

1.1   The development of the practice of capitalisation

A point of contention in determining the initial measurement of a tangible fixed asset is whether finance costs incurred during the period of construction of an asset should or should not be capitalised. This issue was referred to in company law for the first time in 1981, with the Companies Act 1981 permitting the inclusion of interest in the production cost of an asset.[1]

Since then, the practice of capitalising finance costs has become increasingly common in the UK in industries that have major fixed asset developments, such as property, retail and hotels. However, the issue had not been dealt with in any UK accounting standard until the ASB published FRS 15 – *Tangible Fixed Assets* – in February 1999, and only then on the basis that the capitalisation of finance costs is optional.

In the US, the capitalisation of finance costs received renewed attention in the early 1970s, following the increased use of borrowed funds to finance business operations, coupled with a sharp rise in interest rates. Prior to that, it was predominantly the public utility companies that capitalised finance costs, with most other companies accounting for interest cost as a current period expense. In 1971, the Accounting Principles Board set up a committee to consider the subject; however, although the committee prepared a comprehensive working paper setting out the principal issues to be considered, its activities were terminated before a pronouncement could be issued.

In 1974, the SEC became concerned about the growing popularity of interest capitalisation, when it noted an increase in the number of non-utility registrants that were adopting a policy of capitalising interest as part of the cost of certain assets. This was causing inconsistency between those companies whose earnings were boosted by capitalisation and others which expensed finance costs as incurred. In 1974, the SEC imposed a moratorium[2] on companies adopting or extending a policy of interest capitalisation (public utilities[3] and registrants covered by AICPA Guides *Accounting for Retail Land Sales* and *Audits of Savings and Loan Associations* were excluded from the moratorium). Shortly thereafter, the FASB agreed to consider the subject, and added the project to its technical agenda. This ultimately led to the publication in 1979 of SFAS 34 – *Capitalisation of Interest Cost* – which made capitalisation of interest compulsory for certain assets requiring a period of time to get them ready for their intended use.[4]

In March 1984, the IASC published IAS 23 – *Capitalisation of Borrowing Costs* – which provided a more flexible approach to the issue than does SFAS 34. Under this original version of IAS 23, capitalisation was optional, but certain rules were laid down if a policy of capitalisation was adopted.[5] However, as part of its Improvements Project, the IASC proposed that the flexibility contained in IAS 23 should be reduced and that borrowing costs that meet certain specified criteria should be recognised as an asset. These proposals were set out in Exposure Draft E39 – *Capitalisation of Borrowing Costs* – and bore a number of close similarities to the underlying principles and requirements of SFAS 34. Nevertheless, an eleventh hour change of heart on the part of the Board of the IASC saw the revised version of IAS 23 – *Borrowing Costs* – issued in 1993 with an entirely different approach. Under the revised IAS 23 the 'benchmark treatment' for borrowing costs is that they should be recognised as an expense in the period in which they are incurred regardless of how the borrowings are applied.[6] However, the IASC did not go so far as to ban the capitalisation of borrowing costs altogether, and the revised IAS 23 incorporates capitalisation as an 'allowed alternative treatment'.

Thus, there is currently a major difference in approach between the UK and IAS on the one hand, and the US on the other. In the UK, capitalisation is permitted under the Companies Act and FRS 15 but is entirely optional, whilst IAS 23 prefers interest to be expensed but allows capitalisation within a framework of rules; on the other hand, in the US, capitalisation is mandatory under certain prescribed conditions, subject to certain exemptions.

1.2   Arguments for and against capitalisation

The arguments for and against capitalisation are evenly balanced, and this was clearly evidenced by the fact that SFAS 34 was only adopted by a margin of four votes to three,[7] and that both FRS 15 and IAS 23 allow companies a free choice. Proponents of the view that finance costs should be capitalised under prescribed conditions usually advance the following arguments:[8]

(a)   finance costs incurred as a consequence of a decision to acquire an asset are not intrinsically different from other costs that are commonly capitalised. If an asset requires a period of time to bring it to the condition and location necessary for its intended use, the finance costs incurred during that period as a result of expenditures on the asset are a part of the cost of acquiring the asset;

(b) a better matching of income and expenditure is achieved, in that interest incurred with a view to future benefit is carried forward to be expensed in the period or periods expected to benefit. Consequently, the failure to capitalise the finance costs associated with the acquisition of assets will reduce current earnings as a consequence of the acquisition of assets;

(c) this method results in greater comparability between companies constructing assets and other companies buying similar completed assets, as well as between the costs of those assets paid for in stages and those paid for on completion within an individual company. Treating the finance costs as an expense distorts the choice between purchasing and constructing a tangible fixed asset. This is because the purchase price of completed assets acquired will normally include interest, as the vendor needs to take into account all his costs, including interest, in pricing the asset; and

(d) although tangible fixed asset costs are higher as a result of capitalising interest, and therefore are more likely to exceed the recoverable amount of the asset, the accounts are more likely to reflect the true success or failure of the project. If interest costs are not capitalised, the recoverable amount of the asset may exceed its book value and the fact that the initial decision to proceed with the project was poor would not become apparent from the accounts.

On the other hand, proponents of the view that finance costs should always be charged to income, regardless of how the borrowings are applied, generally advance the following arguments to support their view:[9]

(a) it is illogical to treat financing costs as a period expense in normal circumstances, then to treat them as a direct cost of an asset during its period of construction and to revert to treating them as a period expense once the asset is complete even though financing costs are probably continuing to be incurred in respect of the asset. This is because the nature of interest does not change because of the use to which the funds are put; it remains a period cost of financing the business, and its treatment should not change merely as a result of the completion of a tangible fixed asset;

(b) finance costs are incurred in support of the whole of the activities of the enterprise. Any attempt to associate finance costs with a particular asset is necessarily arbitrary;

(c) capitalisation of finance costs results in the same type of asset having a different carrying amount, depending on the method of financing adopted by the enterprise. Limiting capitalised interest to interest on borrowings would preclude the equity-funded enterprise from capitalising interest, even though it incurs an economic cost of the same order as an enterprise that has borrowed funds. In other words, it is inconsistent to allow debt funded entities to include interest costs in the cost of an asset, whilst prohibiting equity funded entities from reflecting similarly the cost of capital in the cost of an asset;

(d)   treating finance costs as a charge against income results in financial statements giving more comparable results from period to period, thus providing a better indication of the future cash flows of an enterprise. Finance costs fluctuate with the borrowing levels and rates which give rise to them, not with asset acquisition; and

(e)   capitalisation leads to higher tangible fixed asset costs, which are more likely to exceed the recoverable amount of the asset. Although the impairment reviews established by the ASB in FRS 11 and IASC in IAS 36 may identify such irrecoverable amounts, these reviews will be applied to business units that will usually be much wider than individual tangible fixed assets, and it may be argued that they should be regarded as a 'long stop' rather than as the principal means of ensuring that individual assets are not overstated.

In the Discussion Paper that preceded FRS 15, the ASB stated that it believed that the capitalisation of interest should be either mandatory or prohibited, and that the present position that is optional could not be regarded as satisfactory.[10] However, this was not to be the final outcome. In the Appendix on the development of FRS 15, the ASB acknowledges that it would have preferred either to prohibit or to require the capitalisation of finance costs.[11] It states that the ASB believes that, conceptually, there are strong arguments in favour of the capitalisation of directly attributable finance costs. However, the Board was influenced by the argument that if capitalisation is to become mandatory, in theory notional interest should also be capitalised.[12] Otherwise, as stated above, capitalisation of finance costs results in the same type of asset having a different carrying amount, depending on the method of financing adopted by the enterprise.

Consequently, until an international consensus is established, the ASB has decided to take a pragmatic approach and one which is consistent with IAS 23 in its effects, although the international standard prefers interest to be expensed but allows capitalisation within a framework of rules. Under FRS 15, capitalisation of interest is neither required nor forbidden; instead it is to be a matter of accounting policy.

1.3   The accounting alternatives

There are essentially three possible methods of accounting for finance costs; these are as follows:[13]

(a)   account for finance costs as an expense of the period in which they are incurred;

(b)   capitalise finance costs as part of the cost of an asset when prescribed conditions are met; and

(c)   capitalise finance costs and imputed interest on shareholders' equity as part of the cost of an asset when prescribed conditions are met.

In drafting SFAS 34, the FASB considered these three methods and concluded that alternative (b) should be adopted, whilst in its revision of IAS 23 the Board of the IASC opted for alternative (a) as the 'benchmark treatment' and alternative (b) as an 'allowed alternative treatment'. In the UK, the ASB has taken the view in FRS 15 that, in the absence of international consensus on the issue, companies should have the option of whether to capitalise or expense finance costs. The standard does not express a preference for either of the approaches.

In arriving at its conclusions on SFAS 34, the FASB considered the possibility of capitalising interest, not just as a cost of acquiring assets, but also as a cost of holding assets. However, this idea was rejected on the grounds that under the present accounting model, costs are not added to assets subsequent to their readiness for use; therefore, consideration of such a proposal would require a comprehensive re-examination of this fundamental principle.[14]

No standard setter has taken the step of allowing the capitalisation of notional interest, although there is a conceptual argument for measuring the cost of financing the acquisition of certain assets on the basis of the enterprise's cost of capital, which would include imputed interest on equity capital.

1.3.1   *Account for finance costs as an expense of the period in which they are incurred*

This is the benchmark treatment under IAS 23, and was the approach favoured by the three dissenting FASB members, who held the view that 'interest cost, like dividends, is more directly associable with the period during which the capital giving rise to it is outstanding than the material, labor, and other resources into which capital is converted'.[15] It was therefore being suggested that interest should not be allocated to assets in the way that other costs are; the reasoning being that the financing structure of an enterprise is used to finance all its activities, and any allocation of particular sources of finance to particular assets is arbitrary. A decision to discontinue a particular project will not usually result in immediate repayment of any borrowings allocated as financing it, since the borrowings will normally continue to finance the remaining activities. As a cost of obtaining finance, interest should be expensed as incurred over the period of availability of the finance. The dissenting FASB members also held the view that capitalisation misstated the calculation of the return on a company's total capital employed – a computation often made by users of financial statements.

Conversely, the majority members of the FASB argued that an enterprise which is funded wholly by equity capital is not the same as one which has borrowed funds; and, similarly, an enterprise that is making substantial expenditures for asset construction differs from one which is not. They therefore maintained that 'those who assert that comparability among enterprises would be greater if all interest cost were expensed would create an illusion of comparability that may disguise the differences in facts'.[16]

1.3.2   *Capitalise finance costs as part of the cost of an asset when prescribed conditions are met*

This alternative was both adopted by SFAS 34 and sanctioned by IAS 23 as an 'allowed alternative treatment'. The FASB experienced some difficulty in reconciling capitalisation based on cost of capital (see 1.3.3 below) with the historical cost convention, and it was this that led to their conclusion that the capitalisation rate should be based on rates of interest on outstanding borrowings. In arriving at this conclusion, the FASB put forward the following argument:

'In the present accounting framework, the cost of a resource is generally measured by the historical exchange price paid to acquire it. However, funds are an unusual kind of resource in that, although an enterprise obtains funds from various sources, only borrowed funds give rise to a cost that can be described as a historical exchange price. Although a historical exchange transaction may occur when equity securities are issued, that transaction is not the basis generally advocated for measuring the cost of equity capital. It is generally agreed that the use of equity capital entails an economic cost, but in the absence of a historical exchange price, the cost of equity capital is not reliably determinable. The Board concluded, therefore, that the cost of financing expenditures for a qualifying asset should be measured by assigning to the asset an appropriate proportion of the interest cost incurred on borrowings during the period of its acquisition.'[17]

It then remained to be determined exactly which borrowings should be used as a basis for the capitalisation rate. The FASB adopted the concept of borrowings which could have been avoided in the absence of expenditure on the asset as being most consistent with the arguments quoted above. It also concluded that interest capitalised should not exceed interest incurred for similar reasons.

1.3.3 Capitalise finance costs and imputed interest on owners' equity in respect of qualifying assets during their production period

This method is based on the premise that an asset must be financed during its production period and that finance has an associated cost. The FASB developed the argument as follows:

'Financing has a cost. The cost may take the form of explicit interest on borrowed funds, or it may take the form of a return foregone on an alternative use of funds, but regardless of the form it takes, a financing cost is necessarily incurred. On the premise that the historical cost of acquiring an asset should include all costs necessarily incurred to bring it to the condition and location necessary for its intended use, the Board concluded that, in principle, the cost incurred in financing expenditures for an asset during a required construction or development period is itself a part of the asset's historical acquisition cost.'[18]

Some FASB members were of the opinion, therefore, that there is a valid conceptual argument for measuring the cost of financing the acquisition of certain assets on the basis of the enterprise's cost of capital, which would include imputed interest on equity capital, as well as interest on borrowed capital. Nevertheless, in view of the fact that, in the present accounting framework, the cost of a resource is generally measured by the historical exchange price paid to acquire it, all the FASB members agreed that recognition of the cost of equity capital does not conform to this framework.[19] Perhaps fortunately, this obviated the necessity of having to resolve the issue of how to account for the credit corresponding to the imputed interest.

2 THE CURRENT POSITION UNDER UK GAAP

2.1 The Companies Act

The Companies Act 1985 permits the inclusion in the production cost of an asset of:

'(a) a reasonable proportion of the costs incurred by the company which are only indirectly attributable to the production of that asset; and

(b) interest on capital borrowed to finance the production of that asset, to the extent that it accrues in respect of the period of production;

provided, however, in a case within paragraph (b) above, that the inclusion of the interest in determining the cost of that asset and the amount of the interest so included is disclosed in a note to the accounts'.[20]

The wording of (b) above raises the question as to whether or not capitalisation can only take place where there have been specific borrowings made for the financing of a specific asset. For example, if a company has held a vacant piece of land for several years, and then begins to develop it using internally generated financial resources without incurring any additional borrowings, can it, nevertheless, capitalise other unrelated borrowing costs despite the absence of 'capital borrowed to finance the production of that asset'? Whatever the answer, it seems that in practice companies have applied a liberal interpretation to this provision, and capitalise interest costs irrespective of whether or not they relate to incremental or specific borrowings.

It is worth noting that FRS 15 is itself liberal on this point. On the one hand, the standard states that only finance costs that are 'directly attributable to the construction of a tangible fixed asset ... should be capitalised',[21] but then, on the other hand, it allows capitalisation in cases where 'the funds used to finance the construction of a tangible fixed asset form part of the entity's general borrowings'.[22] It is hard to see how the construction of a fixed asset can be funded out of general group borrowings (including those of subsidiaries), whilst at the same time the finance costs are deemed to be 'directly attributable' to the construction. The standard squares the circle by defining 'directly attributable' finance costs as those that would have been avoided if the expenditure had not taken place. This means that the company must be able to identify avoidable borrowings.

In any event, the words 'interest on capital borrowed ...' in the Companies Act clearly indicate that actual borrowings must have been incurred before capitalisation can take place. This rules out the capitalisation of 'notional interest', a point now reinforced by FRS 15.[23]

2.2   SSAP 9

In the case of long-term contracts, interest is referred to in Appendix 1 to SSAP 9 – *Stocks and long-term contracts* – in the following terms:

'In ascertaining costs of long-term contracts it is not normally appropriate to include interest payable on borrowed money. However, in circumstances where sums borrowed can be identified as financing specific long-term contracts, it may be appropriate to include such related interest in cost, in which circumstances the inclusion of interest and the amount of interest so included should be disclosed in a note to the financial statements.'[24]

Whilst this paragraph would appear to discourage rather than encourage capitalisation, it is nevertheless clear that, provided that the Companies Act criteria for capitalisation of interest costs are met, it is perfectly acceptable to do so. This is, in fact, the position adopted by IAS 11 – *Construction Contracts* – which states that costs that may be attributable to contract activity in general and can be allocated to specific contracts also include borrowing costs when the contractor adopts the allowed alternative treatment in IAS 23.[25]

2.3   FRS 15

2.3.1   *The development of FRS 15*

In October 1996 the ASB published a Discussion Paper entitled *Measurement of tangible fixed assets* in which it indicated that it did not support the situation where interest capitalisation was optional.[26] However, at the time of publishing the Discussion Paper there was no agreement amongst Board members as to whether capitalisation should be mandatory or prohibited. For this reason, as part of the ASB consultative process, respondents to the Discussion Paper were asked to give their views on which option they preferred.[27]

A year later, the ASB published the exposure draft FRED 17 – *Measurement of Tangible Fixed Assets* – in which the Board advocated that 'the capitalisation of borrowing costs should remain optional'.[28] The reason that the ASB gave for its climbdown was that there was little support amongst respondents to the Discussion Paper for prohibiting capitalisation, and that if capitalisation was to become mandatory, notional interest should also be capitalised.[29] Hence, this was the position that was followed through to FRS 15. It should be remembered, though, that FRS 15 deals with the entire subject of accounting for tangible fixed assets, with the result that it devotes relatively little attention to the issue of the capitalisation of finance costs. Nevertheless, the provisions in FRS 15 on the capitalisation of finance costs appeared to have been modelled on IAS 23, and it seems that compliance with FRS 15 will ensure compliance with the international standard.

2.3.2   *Definition of finance costs*

FRS 15 defines finance costs as being 'the difference between the net proceeds of an instrument and the total amount of payments (or other transfers of economic benefits) that the issuer may be required to make in respect of the instrument.'[30] This definition is taken from FRS 4 – *Capital Instruments* – and means that all finance costs are to be capitalised, including:

(a)   interest on bank overdrafts and short-term and long-term debt;

(b)   amortisation of discounts or premiums relating to debt; and

(c)   amortisation of ancillary costs incurred in connection with the arrangement of debt.[31]

Consequently, the scope for capitalisation extends beyond interest alone.

2.3.3   *Accounting policy*

As already mentioned, under FRS 15 – *Tangible Fixed Assets* – capitalisation of finance costs is neither required nor prohibited, but is a matter of accounting policy for companies. However, if a policy of capitalisation is adopted it must be applied consistently to all finance costs directly attributable to the construction of tangible assets.[32]

It is noteworthy that British Land is an example of a company that has a policy of interest capitalisation in respect of development properties, but which only applies the policy when the directors consider it prudent to do so:

Extract 13.1: The British Land Company PLC (1999)

Accounting Policies

Properties [extract]

(III) DEVELOPMENT PROPERTIES are stated at the lower of cost and net realisable value. The cost of properties in course of development includes attributable interest and other outgoings net of rental income provided the directors consider it prudent having regard to the development potential of the property.

Since FRS 15 applies to accounting periods ending on or after 23 March 2000, it would seem that British Land will now have to refine its policy in order to bring it in line with the standard's requirements.

FRS 15 requires further that the total amount of finance costs capitalised during a period should not exceed the total amount of finance costs incurred during that period,[33] which means that notional interest may not be capitalised. Furthermore, only finance costs that are directly attributable to the construction of a tangible fixed asset, or the financing of progress payments in respect of the construction of a tangible fixed asset by others for the entity, should be capitalised. Directly attributable finance costs are those that would have been avoided (for example by avoiding additional borrowings or by using the funds expended for the asset to repay existing borrowings) if there had been no expenditure on the asset. Finance costs are to be capitalised on a gross basis, that is, before the deduction of any attributable tax relief.[34]

This last requirement will necessitate a change in accounting policy for many entities; Sainsbury, who adopted FRS 15 early, fell into this category:

Extract 13.2: J Sainsbury plc (1999)

Accounting policies

Capitalisation of interest

Following the implementation of FRS 15, interest incurred on borrowings financing specific property developments is capitalised gross of tax relief. In prior years, interest has been capitalised net of tax relief. Prior year figures have not been adjusted to reflected this accounting policy change as the amounts are not material.

2.3.4   *Capitalisation rate*

If an entity has borrowed funds specifically to construct the asset, the costs capitalised are to be the actual finance costs during the period.[35]

If a project has been financed from the entity's general borrowings, the standard imposes a detailed calculation method, applying a capitalisation rate calculated as follows:

(a)   the expenditure is the weighted average carrying amount of the asset during the period, including finance costs previously capitalised;

(b)   the capitalisation rate is the weighted average of rates applicable to general borrowings outstanding in the period; and

(c)   general borrowings exclude loans for other specific purposes including constructing other fixed assets, finance leases and loans held to hedge foreign investments.[36]

The standard acknowledges that determining general borrowings will not always be straightforward. It will be necessary to exercise judgement to meet the main objective – a reasonable measure of the directly attributable finance costs. The particular problem of groups is alluded to; the standard suggests that sometimes all group borrowings will have to be taken into account while in other cases only the individual subsidiaries' borrowings will be applicable.[37] Presumably this will be largely determined by the extent to which borrowings are made centrally (and, perhaps, expenses met in the same way) and passed through to individual group companies via intercompany accounts.

It is not entirely clear why the standard requires that, in the case of general borrowings, a weighted average capitalisation rate be used. Given that the standard only allows the capitalisation of directly attributable finance costs that would have been avoided if the expenditure had not taken place, then surely the capitalisation rate should be based on the cost of the most expensive general borrowings that would have been capable of being repaid had the asset not been constructed? Nevertheless, as stated above, the standard lays down a clear and detailed weighted average calculation method that should be applied.

While it has been generally accepted that interest capitalised should not exceed the total interest charged in the period, practice in relation to other aspects of the calculation has probably varied quite widely. Few companies disclose their method of calculating interest to be capitalised, although exceptions to this include Safeway and MEPC:

Extract 13.3: Safeway plc (1999)

Notes to the accounts

5.0   Net interest payable [extract]

Interest costs relating to the financing of freehold and long leasehold developments are capitalised at the weighted average cost of the related borrowings up to the date of completion of the project.

Extract 13.4: MEPC plc (1998)

Accounting policies

Properties [extract]

An amount equivalent to interest and other outgoings less rental income attributable to properties in course of development is transferred to the cost of properties. For this purpose, the interest rate applied to funds provided for property development is arrived at by reference, where appropriate, to the actual rate payable on borrowings for development purposes and, in regard to that part of the development cost financed out of general funds, to the average rate paid on funding the assets employed by the Group.

The standard makes no recommendations regarding the treatment of interest income where borrowed funds are invested until they are needed to meet expenditure. We consider that in this specific situation the investment income earned should be deducted from the finance costs eligible to be capitalised. However, the more general point as to whether the amount of borrowing costs which may be capitalised is the gross amount of borrowing costs incurred, or whether this amount should be reduced by interest income earned, is discussed more fully at 3.2.2 and 4.1.1 B below.

2.3.5 Capitalisation period

Problems are frequently encountered in defining the capitalisation period – when to start, when to suspend and when to stop capitalising. Many companies give no indication of their interpretation of the capitalisation period despite the fact that difficulties can arise at virtually every stage in the production period.

This should now be made easier with FRS 15, which stipulates that where finance costs are capitalised, capitalisation should begin when:

(a) finance costs are being incurred; and

(b) expenditures for the asset are being incurred; and

(c) activities that are necessary to get the asset ready for use are in progress.[38]

These conditions are identical to those to be found in IAS 23.[39] Necessary activities can start before the physical construction of the asset, for example technical and administrative work such as obtaining permits.[40] However, it is not likely that finance costs on specific borrowings would be incurred for any significant period before the asset is actually acquired.

Land awaiting development often causes difficulties. Given that there must be a period of production, the standard states that finance costs incurred while land acquired for building purposes is held without any associated development activity do not qualify for capitalisation.[41] In theory at least, this causes no change to current practice as there is no 'period of production' under the Companies Act. However, in the light of this, it is noteworthy that Slough Estates appears to have a policy of interest capitalisation in respect of land held for development, but which is not actually *under* development, although its reference to the period of development makes the policy less than entirely clear.

Extract 13.5: Slough Estates plc (1998)

Accounting Policies

Capitalisation of interest [extract]

Interests costs incurred in funding land for or under development and construction work in progress are capitalised during the period of development.

It is sometimes argued that capitalisation of interest should be suspended when interruptions or delays occur during development, since interest incurred during an interruption or delay does not add to the value of the development. Whilst this is true, it is also true that delays and interruptions add to the *cost* of a development. It therefore seems more appropriate to continue to capitalise interest even though a write down may be necessary.

Nevertheless, FRS 15 states that capitalisation of borrowing costs should cease during 'extended periods in which active development is interrupted'; such costs are costs of holding partially completed assets and do not qualify for capitalisation under the standard.[42] In practice, however, it may be difficult to distinguish 'extended periods' from other production delays, other than in circumstances in which the development has clearly been mothballed.

Both IAS 23 and SFAS 34 specifically state that capitalisation should be suspended during extended periods in which active development is interrupted.[43] However, neither standard requires suspension of capitalisation where there are brief interruptions in activities, interruptions that are externally imposed, and delays that are inherent in the asset acquisition process.[44]

The rules regarding the end of the capitalisation period is the aspect of FRS 15 that is most likely to affect current accounting practices. The standard says that capitalisation of finance costs should cease when substantially all the activities that are necessary to get the asset ready for use are complete. Furthermore, when construction of a tangible fixed asset is completed in parts and each part is capable of being used while construction continues on other parts, capitalisation of finance costs relating to a part should cease when substantially all the activities that are necessary to get that part ready for use are completed. A business park comprising several buildings, each of which can be used individually, is an example of an asset of which parts are usable while construction continues on other parts.[45]

In the property construction industry it is common to continue to capitalise costs, of which interest and letting costs are the most significant, on properties which have been constructed but are not yet fully let. The argument has been that the asset being constructed is not simply the physical structure of the building but a fully tenanted investment property, and the production period correspondingly includes not simply the construction period but also the letting period. Such policies also allow for the costs of letting to be capitalised.

The following are examples of companies that have an accounting policy which refers to the end of the capitalisation period:

Extract 13.6: Slough Estates plc (1998)

Accounting Policies

Capitalisation of interest

Interest costs incurred in funding land for or under development and construction work in progress are capitalised during the period of development. A property is regarded as being in the course of development until substantially let or the expiration of a period varying from 6 months to 2 years from the issue of the Architect's certificate of practical completion, whichever is the earlier.

Extract 13.7: MEPC plc (1998)

Accounting policies

Properties [extract]

A property ceases to be treated as being in course of development at the earliest of:

(1)   the date when the development becomes fully let and income producing

(2)   the date when income exceeds outgoings

(3)   a date up to three years after completion to allow for letting.

The standard does not appear to permit policies such as these. In our view it is likely that capitalisation will have to cease when the building is physically complete, not at the later dates when the development is deemed to be complete. Certainly, under US GAAP, capitalisation would have to cease on each part of the development as it became substantially complete and ready for use.[46]

2.3.6   Disclosure

FRS 15 requires that where an enterprise adopts a policy of capitalisation of finance costs, the financial statements should disclose:

(a)   the accounting policy adopted;

(b)   the aggregate amount of finance costs included in the cost of tangible fixed assets;

(c)   the amount of finance costs capitalised during the period;

(d)   the amount of finance costs recognised in the profit and loss account during the period; and

(e)   the capitalisation rate used to determine the amount of finance costs capitalised during the period.

However, since FRS 15 only applies to tangible fixed assets, companies that capitalise finance costs in respect of current assets will need to comply only with the related disclosure requirements in the Companies Act. These are that the company should disclose that its accounting policy is to include interest in determining the cost of the asset, identifying the asset(s) to which the policy applies and the amount of interest so included.[47]

Where interest is being capitalised on tangible fixed assets (which must by definition be in a period of production) it is likely that the assets to which it relates will have to be disclosed separately from other tangible fixed assets as the balance sheet formats require 'payments on account and assets in course of construction' to be disclosed.[48]

Companies listed on The Stock Exchange must also disclose the amount of interest capitalised during the year and give an indication of the amount and treatment of any related tax relief.[49]

In practice, finance costs capitalised are usually shown as a deduction from gross finance costs, for example:

Extract 13.8: MEPC plc (1998)

1998 Notes to the accounts

10 Cost of finance (net)	1998 £m	1997 £m
On loans not wholly repayable within 5 years	**75.2**	91.0
On loans repayable wholly within 5 years	**63.7**	62.5
On bank overdrafts	**0.2**	0.1
	139.1	153.6
Transfer to cost of properties	**(12.1)**	(6.1)
	127.0	147.5
Interest income	**(28.4)**	(36.5)
Cost of finance (net)	**98.6**	111.0

2.3.7 Transitional provisions

FRS 15 does not set down any transitional provisions that deal specifically with the capitalisation of finance costs. Nevertheless, there are potentially some transitional issues surrounding the capitalisation of finance costs that could affect fixed asset measurement. For example some entities that currently capitalise finance costs might do so on a basis that does not comply with FRS 15. In principle, measurement issues such as this should be dealt with by way of a prior year adjustment under FRS 3. Also, on implementing FRS 15, an entity may wish to change its accounting policy with respect to the capitalisation of finance costs. Again, any such change would be dealt with by way of a prior year adjustment.

3   ISSUES ARISING IN PRACTICE

As already stated, FRS 15 deals with the entire subject of accounting for tangible fixed assets, and therefore devotes relatively little attention to the issue of the capitalisation of finance costs. As a result, for those companies that adopt a policy of capitalising finance costs, there are a number of practical issues that need to be considered.

3.1   Qualifying assets

In the UK, the range of assets on which companies have capitalised interest covers both fixed assets and stock. Although FRS 15 is confined to tangible fixed assets, the Companies Act permits capitalisation with respect to a broader spectrum of assets (see 2.1 above). Specific examples of the types of assets included are property developments, ships, aircraft, maturing whisky stocks and tobacco, allowing the policy of capitalising interest to be fairly widespread in the UK – particularly in the case of the property industry. One notable exception, however, is Land Securities, which makes it clear in its accounting policies that all interest is expensed:

Extract 13.9: Land Securities PLC (1999)

Notes to the Financial Statements

1   Accounting Policies

(d)   PROPERTIES [extract]

Additions to properties include costs of a capital nature only; interest and other costs in respect of developments and refurbishments are treated as revenue expenditure and written off as incurred.

Guinness is an example of a company which had in the past adopted the policy of capitalising financing costs in respect of its whisky and other spirit stocks:

Extract 13.10: Guinness PLC (1996)

Accounting policies

Stocks

Stocks are stated at the lower of cost and net realisable value. Cost includes raw materials, duties where applicable, direct labour and expenses and the appropriate proportion of production and other overheads, including financing costs in respect of whisky and other spirit stocks during their normal maturation period.

However, following its merger with GrandMet to form Diageo plc, this policy was changed:

Extract 13.11: Diageo plc (1998)

Notes

27   Merger accounting [extract]

Balance sheet

...

(b) Stocks: The cost of stocks on the balance sheet no longer includes financing costs on maturing whisky and other spirit stocks. This has resulted in a reduction of £563 million in the combined stocks at 31 December 1997.

Given that Diageo's stocks of maturing whisky at 30 June 1998 were £1,372 million, this illustrates the very material amounts of finance costs that can be capitalised within balance sheet assets.

Tilbury Douglas is an example of a company that capitalises interest in respect of its property developments held within stocks and work in progress:

Extract 13.12: Tilbury Douglas Plc (1998)

Notes on the accounts

1   ACCOUNTING POLICIES

(h)   Stocks and work in progress

...

(iii) In the case of long term property development projects, interest on borrowings related to individual projects is included as a cost of these projects.

The Companies Act is drawn sufficiently widely to permit interest to be included in the production cost of any fixed or current asset,[50] but in practice capitalisation only takes place where the production period is sufficiently long for borrowing costs to be significant in relation to the total production cost.

On the other hand, as described at 4.2.1 below, the US definition of qualifying assets is narrower than this. In particular, capitalisation of interest on stocks which are routinely manufactured or otherwise produced in large quantities on a repetitive basis, is not permitted in the US. The reason given by the FASB for this was that they considered that 'the informational benefit does not justify the cost of so doing'.[51] This principle could also be applied to maturing whisky or tobacco stocks, on the basis that, although an individual batch of whisky or tobacco may be held in stock for a significant period, there is a constant flow of product into and out of stock; hence, the effect on earnings of capitalising interest on such items usually would not be significant in the long run. In addition, some commentators argued that the ageing of such stocks is not part of the production process.[52] However, interpretational difficulties of the phrase 'routinely manufactured or otherwise produced in large quantities on a repetitive basis'[53] may lead companies to capitalise interest in these situations.

IAS 23, on the other hand, specifically includes 'inventories that require a substantial period of time to bring them to a saleable condition' amongst its examples of qualifying assets, whilst inventories that are routinely manufactured or otherwise produced in large quantities on a repetitive basis over a short period of time are not qualifying assets.[54]

In the case of equity accounted investments, SFAS 34 regards them as being qualifying assets as long as the investee has activities in progress necessary to commence its planned principal operations and provided that the investee's activities include the use of funds to acquire qualifying assets for its operations. Conversely, the IASC has taken the view that capitalising interest in respect of investments could involve an element of double-counting, since the investee itself would apply the standard. Consequently, investments fall outside the IAS 23 definition of qualifying assets.

In the light of these differing requirements, it is noteworthy that Rio Tinto capitalises interest on investments in mining joint ventures and associates during the development period of the mines, and whilst this clearly complies with SFAS 34 it is unclear as to whether or not it follows a strict application of the Companies Act:

Extract 13.13: Rio Tinto plc and Rio Tinto Limited (1998)

Notes to the 1998 accounts

11   FIXED ASSET INVESTMENTS [extract]

(a) The Group's investments in joint ventures and associates include, where appropriate, entry premiums on acquisition plus interest capitalised by the Group during the development period of the relevant mines. At December 31, 1998, this capitalised interest less accumulated amortisation amounted to US$20 million (1997 – US$46 million).

3.2   Determination of amount to be capitalised

3.2.1   Borrowings and capitalisation rate

Few companies give any indication of their method of calculating interest to be capitalised, and it seems likely that there is a wide divergence in methods used. However, the situation should now change as companies adopt FRS 15, which requires that the costs capitalised are to be the actual finance costs during the period.

If a project has been financed from the entity's general borrowings, the standard imposes a detailed calculation method, applying a capitalisation rate calculated as follows:

(a)   the expenditure is the weighted average carrying amount of the asset during the period, including finance costs previously capitalised;

(b)   the capitalisation rate is the weighted average of rates applicable to general borrowings outstanding in the period; and

(c)   general borrowings exclude loans for other specific purposes including constructing other fixed assets, finance leases and loans held to hedge foreign investments.

The standard acknowledges that determining general borrowings will not always be straightforward. It will be necessary to exercise judgement to meet the main objective – a reasonable measure of the directly attributable finance costs.

The following example illustrates the practical application of FRS 15's method of calculating the amount of finance costs to be capitalised:

Example 13.1: Calculation of capitalisation rate

On 1 April 2001 a company engages in the development of a property which is expected to take five years to complete, at a cost of £6,000,000. The balance sheets at 31 December 2000 and 31 December 2001, prior to capitalisation of interest, are as follows:

	31 December 2000 £	31 December 2001 £
Development property	–	1,200,000
Other assets	6,000,000	6,800,000
	6,000,000	8,000,000
Loans		
8% debenture stock	2,500,000	2,500,000
Bank loan at 10% p.a.	–	2,000,000
Bank loan at 12% p.a.	1,000,000	1,000,000
	3,500,000	5,500,000
Shareholders' equity	2,500,000	2,500,000

The bank loan at 10% was taken out on 31 March 2001 and the total interest charge for the year ended 31 December 2001 was as follows:

	£
£2,500,000 x 8%	200,000
£2,000,000 x 10% x 9/12	150,000
£1,000,000 x 12%	120,000
	470,000

Expenditure was incurred on the development as follows:

	£
1 April 2001	600,000
1 July 2001	400,000
1 October 2001	200,000
	1,200,000

(a) If the bank loan at 10% p.a. is a new borrowing taken out specifically to finance the development, then the amount of interest to be capitalised is:

	£
£600,000 x 10% x 9/12	45,000
£400,000 x 10% x 6/12	20,000
£200,000 x 10% x 3/12	5,000
	70,000

(b) If all the borrowings would have been avoided but for the development then the amount of interest to be capitalised is:

$$\frac{\text{Total interest expense for period}}{\text{Weighted average total borrowings}} \quad x \quad \text{Development expenditure}$$

i.e.

$$\frac{470,000}{3,500,000 + (2,000,000 \times 9/12)} = 9.4\%$$

	£
£600,000 x 9.4% x 9/12	42,300
£400,000 x 9.4% x 6/12	18,800
£200,000 x 9.4% x 3/12	4,700
	65,800

If the 8% debenture stock was irredeemable then as the borrowings could not have been avoided the above calculation would be done using the figures for the bank loans and their related interest costs only.

3.2.2   Limitation on interest capitalised

As already stated, FRS 15 requires that the amount of borrowing costs capitalised during a period should not exceed the total amount of borrowing costs incurred by the enterprise in that period. However, the standard makes no recommendations regarding the treatment of interest income where borrowed funds are invested until they are needed to meet expenditure. We consider that in this specific situation the investment income earned should be deducted from the finance costs eligible to be capitalised. This would be consistent with IAS 23, which states that to the extent that funds are borrowed specifically for the purpose of obtaining a qualifying asset, the amount of borrowing costs eligible for capitalisation on that asset should be determined as the actual borrowing costs incurred on that borrowing during the period less any investment income on the temporary investment of those borrowings.[55] However, the more general question arises as to whether the amount of borrowing costs which may be capitalised is the gross amount of borrowing costs incurred, or whether this amount should be reduced by interest income earned.

One can only assume that the reason why FRS 15 does not address this issue specifically is that the underlying principle in FRS 15 for capitalisation is that only directly attributable finance costs that would have been avoided if there had been no expenditure on the asset can be capitalised. Nevertheless, the standard also contemplates the capitalisation of finance costs incurred in respect of an entity's general borrowings, and this muddies the waters somewhat. Consequently, in our view companies applying FRS 15 should adopt the following approach:

(a) in cases where specific borrowed funds are invested until they are needed to meet expenditure on a specific asset, the investment income earned should be deducted from the finance costs eligible to be capitalised; and

(b) in cases where funds are borrowed generally, the amount of borrowing costs which may be capitalised is limited to the gross amount of borrowing costs incurred, and this amount is not reduced by interest income earned. In our view this is the correct approach, since to deduct interest income in determining the amount to be capitalised would, in these circumstances, produce illogical results.

In the US, interest earned is not offset against interest cost in determining either capitalisation rates or limitations on the amount of interest cost to be capitalised, except in situations involving the acquisition of qualifying assets financed by the proceeds of tax-exempt borrowings if those funds are externally restricted to finance the acquisition of specified qualifying assets or to service the related debt.[56] The provisions in SFAS 34 for determining the amount of interest cost to be capitalised deal solely with the interest cost incurred and the rates applicable to borrowings outstanding. Temporary or short-term investment decisions are not related to the determination of the acquisition cost of the asset or to the allocation of that cost against revenues of the periods benefited by the asset.

3.2.3 Accrued costs

In principle, costs of a qualifying asset which have only been accrued but have not yet been paid in cash should be excluded from the amount on which interest is capitalised. It should be noted that the effect of applying this principle is often merely to delay the capitalisation of interest since the costs will be included once they have been paid in cash. In most cases it is unlikely that the effect will be material as the time between accrual and payment of the cost will not be that great. However, the effect is potentially material where a significant part of the amount capitalised relates to costs which have been financed interest-free by third parties for a long period. An example of this is retention money which is not generally payable until the asset is completed.

3.2.4   Asset carried in the balance sheet below cost

An asset may be recognised in the financial statements during the period of production on a basis other than cost, i.e. it may have been written down below cost as a result of being impaired. The question then arises as to whether the calculation of interest to be capitalised should be based on cost or book value. In these circumstances, cost should be used as this is the amount that the company or group has had to finance.

3.3   Group financial statements

3.3.1   Borrowings in one company and development in another

A question which often arises in practice is whether it is appropriate to capitalise interest in the group financial statements on borrowings where the borrowings appear in the financial statements of a different group company from that carrying out the development. Based on the underlying philosophy of FRS 15, capitalisation in such circumstances would only be appropriate if the amount capitalised fairly reflected the interest cost of the group on borrowings from third parties which could theoretically have been avoided if the expenditure on the qualifying asset were not made.

Although it may be appropriate to capitalise interest in the group financial statements, the company carrying out the development should not capitalise any interest in its own financial statements as it has no borrowings. If, however, the company has intra-group borrowings then interest on such borrowings may be capitalised.

3.3.2   Qualifying assets held by joint ventures

In the UK, property developments are often carried out through the medium of joint ventures. In such cases, the joint venture may be financed principally by equity and the joint venture partners may have financed their participating interests by borrowings. It is not appropriate to capitalise interest in the joint venture on the borrowings of the partners as the interest charge is not a cost of the joint venture. Neither would it be appropriate to capitalise interest in the individual (as opposed to group) financial statements of the investing companies because the qualifying asset does not belong to them. The asset which the investing companies have is a participating interest, which is not in the course of production. However, the question does arise whether an adjustment may be made in the investor's group financial statements to capitalise interest on the borrowings financing the participating interest when the joint venture is equity accounted.

Example 13.2

A company has a 50% investment in a joint venture whose balance sheet is as follows:

	£'000	£'000
Expenditure on development	1,600	
Capitalised interest	100 *	
		1,700
Cash		300
		2,000
Share capital		100
Share premium		900
		1,000
Borrowings: 10% loan		1,000
		2,000

* £1,600,000 x 10% restricted to actual interest incurred of £100,000.

The cost of the investment was £500,000 which was financed by a borrowing at 9% p.a. The investing company could, therefore, capitalise additional interest of £27,000 (being (1,600,000 - 1,000,000) x 50% x 9%) in its group financial statements (recognising that only 50% of the development expenditure not funded by borrowings is funded by the investing company).

Capitalisation in these circumstances appears to be justified on the basis that the borrowings are effectively financing the company's share of the development. It would have been possible for a similar result to be shown if the investing companies had decided to finance the joint venture with borrowings and only a nominal amount of equity. As shown in Extract 13.13 above, Rio Tinto capitalises interest on investments in mining joint ventures and associates during the development period of the mines, and therefore appears to be applying this principle in practice. Nevertheless, it is worth noting that, in revising IAS 23, the IASC decided that investments in enterprises should not be qualifying assets.

Where the qualifying assets are held by an investment which is not effectively an interest in a joint venture it is unlikely that an adjustment should be made in the group financial statements. This is because the interest in the investing company would probably not have been avoided if the investee had not incurred the costs on the qualifying asset.

The circumstances under which capitalisation would be permitted in the US for such assets are described in 4.2.1 below.

3.4   Other issues

3.4.1   *Change of policy*

When interest is capitalised for the first time, FRS 3 requires that a prior year adjustment be made as this is a change of accounting policy. In theory, the adjustment should be made in respect of all assets still held which would, during their period of production, have satisfied the criteria adopted for capitalisation. However, this can create considerable difficulty in the case of fixed assets that were produced many years ago; accordingly, some compromises may have to be made in calculating the prior year adjustment; nevertheless it should be possible to produce a materially accurate figure.

Interestingly enough though, in revising IAS 23 the IASC appears to have anticipated this potential difficulty by introducing the following transitional provisions: 'When the adoption of this Standard constitutes a change in accounting policy, an enterprise is encouraged to adjust its financial statements in accordance with International Accounting Standard IAS 8, Net Profit or Loss for the period, Fundamental Errors and Changes in Accounting Policies. Alternatively, enterprises following the allowed alternative treatment should capitalise only those borrowing costs incurred after the effective date of the Standard which meet the criteria for capitalisation.'[57]

During the property slump of the late 80s/early 90s a number of UK property companies changed their borrowing costs' policy from one of capitalisation to one of annual expense. In a number of cases this resulted in substantial asset write-downs by way of prior year adjustment. Trafalgar House is an example of a company that made such a change:

Extract 13.14: Trafalgar House Public Limited Company (1991)

NOTES TO THE ACCOUNTS

1   Accounting policies

Comparative figures have been restated to reflect the changes in accounting policies for fixed asset investments and developments for sale and for changes in presentation.

14   Developments for sale [extract]

From 1st October 1990 the Group's policy in regard to the inclusion of financing charges in the costs of residential developments was changed so as to include interest only in respect of certain long term developments; the amount of such interest at 30th September 1991 was nil.

24   Reserves [extract]

Developments for sale include financing charges on commercial developments and certain long-term residential developments. This is a change from the previous accounting policy of including financing charges on all developments. Adjustments to the Group's reserves as at 30th September 1990 have been made in respect of finance charges of £41.7m previously included in residential developments for sale.

It is interesting to note that Trafalgar House's change in policy was effected in two stages, thereby affording the company a second opportunity of reducing the impact of property write-downs on the profit and loss account – as revealed by the following extract from the company's 1993 accounts:

Extract 13.15: Trafalgar House Public Limited Company (1993)

Notes to the Accounts

---

1 **Changes in accounting policies and in presentation** [extract]

Changes in accounting policies

Financing charges on developments are now charged to the profit and loss account as incurred except where these relate to major long term commercial developments. Previously, related financing charges were included in the cost of commercial developments and certain long term residential developments. The accounting policy has been changed because the directors consider that the new policy reflects the current trend of accounting practice in the property industry.

The effect of the change of accounting policy for financing charges on developments has been to reduce the opening carrying value of development properties and therefore to decrease the amount of the required write down. Accordingly, the loss for the current year has been reduced by £21.2 million.

BAA provides an example of a company that refined its policy on interest capitalisation so that interest is now only capitalised once planning permission has been obtained and a firm decision to proceed has been taken. In previous years, BAA's accounting policy was stated rather loosely as applying when 'the borrowing finances tangible fixed assets in the course of construction'. This is now more tightly described, as shown in the following extract:

Extract 13.16: BAA plc (1997)

Financial review [extract]

Interest capitalisation policy

For many years, BAA has followed a policy of capitalising interest on borrowings which finance its capital projects. The announcement of further delays to the Terminal 5 enquiry at Heathrow has led the Board to reconsider the application of its policy on interest capitalisation. Following a detailed review, the Board has refined its definition of the period of production to commence only when planning permission has been obtained and a firm decision to proceed has been taken.

As a result, interest of £40m, representing interest in the pre-production phase which was capitalised in earlier years, has been charged as an exceptional interest charge. If the previous method of calculating interest to be capitalised had been applied in 1996/97, then a further £13m would have been capitalised, which would have represented an increase in earnings per share of 1.2 pence. Even if the old basis had been used, the directors confirm that there would be no need, at today's date, to write down any fixed assets as a result of impairment in value.

Accounting policies

Interest [extract]

Interest payable is charged as incurred except where the borrowing finances tangible fixed assets in the course of construction. Such interest is capitalised once planning permission has been obtained and a firm decision to proceed has been taken until the asset is complete and income producing and is then written off by way of depreciation of the relevant asset.

BAA's disclosures are to be commended on two counts: first, the company was not being selective in refining its policy – that is, it did not just apply the refined policy to the Terminal 5 project, and keep the old policy for everything else and, second, the company is to be commended for clarifying that the policy refinement was not being used as a surrogate for an impairment problem.

3.5.3 *Exchange differences as a borrowing cost*

Borrowings in one currency may have been used to finance a development the costs of which are incurred primarily in another currency, e.g. a Swiss franc loan financing a sterling development. This may have been done on the basis that, over the period of the development, the interest cost, after allowing for exchange differences, was expected to be less than the interest cost of an equivalent sterling loan. In these circumstances, there is a good argument for capitalising the interest cost and the exchange difference. In fact, SSAP 20 – *Foreign currency translation* – suggests that gains or losses arising from arrangements which may be considered as financing should be disclosed separately as part of 'Other interest receivable/payable and similar income/expense'.[58] This approach would also be consistent with IAS 23, which defines borrowing costs as including exchange differences arising from foreign currency borrowings to the extent that they are regarded as an adjustment to interest costs.[59]

On the other hand, accounting practice in the US would be different. This is because US GAAP focuses more narrowly on interest costs, rather than on the broader concept of total borrowing costs; consequently, whilst SFAS 34 does not address the issue directly, in practice items such as foreign currency differences relating to borrowed funds would not be included in the total amount of interest cost incurred available for capitalisation.

3.5.4 *Assets produced by others*

According to the Companies Act 1985, the production cost of an asset 'shall be determined by adding to the purchase price of the raw materials and consumables used the amount of the costs incurred by the company which are directly attributable to the production of that asset'.[60] Similarly, under FRS 15, the cost of a fixed asset comprises those costs that are directly attributable to bringing the asset into working condition for its intended use. Consequently, although finance costs may of course be included in cost, this could be interpreted as meaning that finance costs may only be capitalised on assets produced by the company itself rather than assets produced by others for the company. This is because, if the assets are produced entirely by others, the production costs are not incurred by the company.

However, this interpretation would rule out capitalisation on most development and construction projects, which hardly seems logical given that the rationale for capitalising interest is strongly dependent on the view that it is an integral part of cost. Not surprisingly, therefore, a wider interpretation of the Companies Act is currently used in practice, and we do not see that FRS 15 introduces anything new to change such practice. The following extract illustrates the application of this approach:

Extract 13.17: The Peninsular and Oriental Steam Navigation Company (1998)

Accounting policies

Ships and other fixed assets [extract]

Interest incurred in respect of payments on account of assets under construction is capitalised to the cost of the asset concerned.

SFAS 34 does, in fact, make it clear that qualifying assets include 'assets constructed or produced for the enterprise by others for which deposits or progress payments have been made',[61] although both FRS 15 and IAS 23 are silent on this point. FRS 15 does, however, talk about capitalising finance costs 'in respect of expenditures to date on the tangible fixed asset',[62] which would seem to imply that finance costs that relate to deposits and progress payments can be capitalised.

3.5.5 Depreciation

It is sometimes argued that capitalised interest should be written off faster than the depreciation rate of other costs of a development on the basis that it is less tangible. Certainly this is a conservative approach, but it is not a rational one. The basis for capitalising interest in the first place depends strongly on the view that it is an integral part of cost so there is no reason to treat it separately for depreciation purposes.

3.5.6 Interest capitalisation and 'creative accounting'

Critics of the standard of UK corporate reporting have, from time to time, stated that interest capitalisation is not a prudent policy. It has even been suggested, or at least implied, that it was a contributing factor to the financial difficulties that many companies within the property sector experienced in the late 80s and early 90s. Apparently, it was felt by some that the capitalisation, rather than the expensing, of interest had in some way hidden the high debt service costs within the property sector.

Many such comments can be rebutted quite simply. Certainly, it should always be possible to determine the extent of the interest capitalised, and this is required to be shown in UK accounts by law. This does require a reader of the accounts to look at the notes as well as the primary statements, but this should be done anyway to obtain a full view of the reported results and financial position of a company.

Some would argue that the combination of capitalisation and the need to consider the end value of the properties concerned will actually produce a worse, and arguably more prudent, result than if interest had been expensed. The reasons for this are twofold:

(a) First, capitalisation clearly increases the risk that project costs will exceed value, particularly if the market falls. However, this does no more than reflect the real financial success or failure of a project as measured against the original assessment of the development's viability, which will always have an interest cost factored into it.

(b) Second, if interest is regarded as an intrinsic cost of the project, future interest to the end of the production period should be taken into account in determining whether any accounting provision is necessary. If interest is not capitalised, such future interest will normally be expensed in future periods and will therefore be recognised later.

Thus, although both policies will produce the same aggregate result over the life of a development, a policy of capitalisation should actually accelerate the recognition of losses. One would have thought that such a result was entirely in keeping with the overriding concept of accounting prudence; perhaps the opponents of capitalisation have not quite grasped this point. Certainly, from the point of view of a company's bankers, the proper application of capitalisation is likely to give an earlier warning of covenant and cash flow problems.

4 COMPARISON WITH THE IASC AND US REQUIREMENTS

4.1 The position under IAS

In common with many of the other earlier international standards, the original version of IAS 23 issued in 1984 allowed a choice of treatments. In this case, the choice was between adopting a policy of capitalising or of not capitalising borrowing costs in respect of 'assets that take a substantial period of time to get them ready for their intended use or sale'.[63] This meant that capitalisation was optional – even if the criteria for capitalisation were met. However, for those enterprises that did adopt a policy of capitalisation, the standard was broadly similar to the US position discussed in 4.2 below, although IAS 23 was somewhat less specific.

E32, which was issued by the IASC in January 1989 under its improvements project, proposed to amend, inter alia, the requirements of IAS 23. The main change proposed was that the benchmark treatment for borrowing costs would be that they should be recognised as an expense when incurred, although the alternative treatment of capitalising such costs would still be allowed when certain criteria were met, and provided certain information was given.[64]

However, in July 1990 the IASC published a Statement of Intent[65] which set out its decisions following its review of the comments received on E32. One of the issues on which the IASC agreed to make substantive changes to the proposals in E32 related to IAS 23. These proposed changes were subsequently published in Exposure Draft E39 – *Capitalisation of Borrowing Costs*.[66]

E39 followed a substantially US GAAP approach, proposing that borrowing costs had to be recognised as part of the cost of an asset if it took a substantial period of time to get the asset ready for its intended use or sale; in all other circumstances they were to be recognised as an expense.[67] However, in the ultimate revision of IAS 23, the Board of the IASC had a last minute change of heart and reverted to the approach that had originally been proposed in E32.

4.1.1 The revised IAS 23

The revised IAS 23 was issued in December 1993 with the 'benchmark treatment' that borrowing costs should be recognised as an expense in the period in which they are incurred regardless of how the borrowings are applied.[68] However, the IASC did not go so far as to prohibit the capitalisation of borrowing costs altogether, and the revised standard incorporates capitalisation as an 'allowed alternative treatment'.[69] Under the allowed treatment, borrowing costs that are directly attributable to the acquisition, construction or production of a qualifying asset are included in the cost of that asset. Such borrowing costs are capitalised when it is probable that they will result in future economic benefits to the enterprise and the costs can be measured reliably. In the case of enterprises which follow this treatment, the requirements of the revised standard are as follows:

A   Qualifying assets

IAS 23 defines a qualifying asset as 'an asset that necessarily takes a substantial period of time to get ready for its intended use or sale'.[70] Examples of qualifying assets are stocks that require a substantial period of time to bring them to a saleable condition, manufacturing plants, power generation facilities and investment properties. Stocks that are routinely manufactured, or otherwise produced in large quantities on a repetitive basis over a short period of time, and assets that are ready for their intended use or sale when acquired are not qualifying assets. In the case of equity accounted investments, the IASC considered whether or not the investor should look through to the investee's activities when applying the proposed revised Standard. However, it decided that this could involve an element of double-counting, since the investee itself would apply the Standard.[71] Accordingly, in contrast to the original IAS 23, the revised standard states that 'other investments' should not be qualifying assets.[72]

It is noteworthy that the revised standard also reflects a change in thinking in the case of routinely manufactured stocks. Unlike the original IAS 23, distinction is now made between stocks that require a substantial period of time to bring them to a saleable condition (such as whisky and plantations), and stocks that are routinely manufactured or otherwise produced in large quantities on a repetitive basis over a short period of time. Previously, the original standard implied that borrowing costs should not be capitalised on stocks which take a long time to mature.

B   Borrowing costs eligible for capitalisation

Borrowing costs are interest and other costs incurred by an enterprise in connection with the borrowing of funds.[73] These may include:

(a)   interest on bank overdrafts and short-term and long-term borrowings;

(b)   amortisation of discounts or premiums relating to borrowings;

(c)   amortisation of ancillary costs incurred in connection with the arrangement of borrowings;

(d)   finance charges in respect of finance leases; and

(e)   exchange differences arising from foreign currency borrowings to the extent that they are regarded as an adjustment to interest costs.[74]

However, the fundamental requirement for capitalisation under IAS 23 is that the borrowing costs must be 'directly attributable to the acquisition, construction or production of a qualifying asset'.[75] In determining which costs satisfy this criterion, the standard starts from the premise that directly attributable borrowing costs are those that would have been avoided if the expenditure on the qualifying asset had not been made – which is very much in line with the strict interpretation of the requirements in the UK as laid down in the Companies Act and FRS 15. Nevertheless, IAS 23 concedes that practical difficulties arise in identifying a direct relationship between particular borrowings and a qualifying asset and in determining the borrowings which could otherwise have been avoided; for example, in the case of an enterprise with a group treasury function that uses a range of debt instruments to borrow funds at varying rates of interest and lends those funds on various bases to other enterprises in the group. (Some might argue that it is for this very reason that capitalisation of borrowing costs should always be recognised as an expense when incurred.)

In any event, though, the standard makes allowance for the difficulties that arise in practice and concedes that the exercise of judgement is required. Consequently, to the extent that funds are borrowed specifically for the purpose of obtaining a qualifying asset, the amount of borrowing costs eligible for capitalisation on that asset should be determined as the actual borrowing costs incurred on that borrowing during the period, less any investment income on the temporary investment of those borrowings.[76]

On the other hand, to the extent that funds are borrowed generally and used for the purpose of obtaining a qualifying asset, the amount of borrowing costs eligible for capitalisation should be determined by applying a capitalisation rate to the expenditures on that asset. The capitalisation rate should be the weighted average of the borrowing costs applicable to the borrowings of the enterprise that are outstanding during the period, other than borrowings made specifically for the purpose of obtaining a qualifying asset. The amount of borrowing costs capitalised during a period should not exceed the amount of borrowing costs incurred during that period.[77]

It is noteworthy that, where funds are borrowed generally, the amount of borrowing costs which may be capitalised is limited to the gross amount of borrowing costs incurred, and that this amount is not reduced by interest income earned. In our view this is the correct approach, since to deduct interest income in determining the amount to be capitalised would, in these circumstances, produce illogical results. For example, retail groups are likely to have substantial amounts of excess cash available for short-term investment, and to attempt to establish a relationship between the interest earned on these funds and the interest paid on project finance would seem to be a misapplication of the principles of interest capitalisation.

C   Commencement of capitalisation

IAS 23 requires that capitalisation should commence when:

(a)   expenditures for the asset are being incurred;

(b)   borrowing costs are being incurred; and

(c)   activities that are necessary to prepare the asset for its intended use or sale are in progress.[78]

The standard goes on to state that the activities necessary to prepare an asset for its intended use or sale encompass more than the physical construction of the asset. They also include technical and administrative work (such as activities associated with obtaining permits) prior to the commencement of physical construction. However, such activities exclude the holding of an asset when no production or development that changes the asset's condition is taking place. For example, borrowing costs incurred while land is under development are capitalised during the period in which activities related to the development are being undertaken. However, borrowing costs incurred while land acquired for building purposes is held without any associated development activity do not qualify for capitalisation.[79]

D   Suspension of capitalisation

IAS 23 states that capitalisation should be suspended during extended periods in which active development is interrupted. However, the standard distinguishes between extended periods of interruption (when capitalisation would be suspended) and periods of temporary delay (when capitalisation is not normally suspended).[80]

E   *Cessation of capitalisation*

The standard requires that capitalisation should cease when substantially all the activities necessary to prepare the qualifying asset for its intended use or sale are complete.[81] An asset is normally ready for its intended use or sale when the physical construction of the asset is complete even though routine administrative work might still continue. If minor modifications, such as the decoration of a property to the purchaser's specification, are all that are outstanding, this indicates that substantially all the activities are complete.

Furthermore, when the construction of a qualifying asset is completed in parts and each part is capable of being used while construction continues on other parts, capitalisation should cease when substantially all the activities necessary to prepare that part for its intended use or sale are completed.[82] An example of this might be a business park comprising several buildings, each of which is capable of being fully utilised while construction continues on other parts.

F   *Disclosure*

Under IAS 23 the following disclosures are required to be made:

(a)   the accounting policy adopted for borrowing costs;

(b)   the amount of borrowing costs capitalised during the period; and

(c)   the capitalisation rate used to determine the amount of borrowing costs eligible for capitalisation.[83]

4.1.2   *SIC – 2: Consistency*

An area of apparent uncertainty surrounding IAS 23 was whether an enterprise that has chosen a policy of capitalising borrowing costs should apply this policy to all qualifying assets or whether the enterprise could choose to capitalise borrowing costs for certain qualifying assets and not for others. In other words, is a policy of 'selective' capitalisation (as apparently adopted by British Land, see Extract 13.1 above) permitted under IAS? This issue was referred to the IASC's Standing Interpretations Committee (SIC), who issued the following consensus in interpretation SIC – 2 entitled *Consistency - Capitalisation of Borrowing Costs*:

'Where an enterprise adopts the Allowed Alternative Treatment, that treatment should be applied consistently to all borrowing costs that are directly attributable to the acquisition, construction or production of all qualifying assets of the enterprise. If all the conditions laid down in IAS 23.11 are met, an enterprise should continue to capitalise such borrowing costs even if the carrying amount of the asset exceeds its recoverable amount. However, IAS 23.19 explains that the carrying amount of the asset should be written down to recognise impairment losses in such cases.'[84]

This interpretation is consistent with FRS 15's requirement that if an entity adopts a policy of capitalisation of finance costs, then it should be applied consistently to all tangible assets where finance costs fall to be capitalised.[85]

4.2   The position under US GAAP

SFAS 34's stated objectives of capitalising interest are: '(a) to obtain a measure of acquisition cost that more closely reflects the enterprise's total investment in the asset and (b) to charge a cost that relates to the acquisition of a resource that will benefit future periods against the revenues of the periods benefited.'[86] The standard makes capitalisation of interest compulsory for certain assets requiring a period of time to get them ready for their intended use. These are referred to as 'qualifying assets'. Since its introduction, SFAS 34 has been amended by two subsequent standards: SFAS 58[87] and SFAS 62.[88]

4.2.1   *Qualifying and non-qualifying assets*

Qualifying assets are defined as follows:

(a)   assets that are constructed or otherwise produced for an enterprise's own use (including assets constructed or produced for the enterprise by others for which deposits or progress payments have been made);[89]

(b)   assets intended for sale or lease that are constructed or otherwise produced as discrete projects (e.g. ships or real estate developments);[90] and

(c)   investments accounted for by the equity method 'while the investee has activities in progress necessary to commence its planned principal operations provided that the investee's activities include the use of funds to acquire qualifying assets for its operations'.[91]

The following are non-qualifying assets:

(a)   inventories that are 'routinely manufactured or otherwise produced in large quantities on a repetitive basis';[92]

(b)   assets that are in use or ready for their intended use;[93]

(c)   assets not in use which are not being prepared for use;[94]

(d)   assets that are not included in the consolidated balance sheet of the parent company and consolidated subsidiaries;[95] and

(e)   investments accounted for by the equity method after the planned principal operations of the investee begin.[96]

Land that is not undergoing activities necessary to get it ready for its intended use is not a qualifying asset. If activities are undertaken for the purpose of developing land for a particular use, the expenditures to acquire the land qualify for interest capitalisation while those activities are in progress.[97]

4.2.2   Capitalisation rate

The amount to be capitalised is the interest cost which could theoretically have been avoided if the expenditure on the qualifying asset were not made. This is determined by applying an interest rate (the 'capitalisation rate') to the average amount of accumulated expenditure for the asset during the financial year. The capitalisation rate must be based on borrowings outstanding during the year. The borrowings used may be specific borrowings used to finance the qualifying asset. Alternatively, a weighted average rate of interest on other borrowings may be used, provided that the borrowings are selected with the objective in mind of capitalising that part of the interest cost which could theoretically have been avoided in the absence of expenditure on the qualifying asset. Also, with this objective in mind, it follows that interest capitalised must not exceed the interest cost incurred by the enterprise.[98]   In consolidated financial statements, this limitation would be based on the total borrowing costs incurred by the parent company and its consolidated subsidiaries.[99]

The expenditure to which the capitalisation rate is applied is not necessarily the same as the amount capitalised for the asset in question. If a significant part of the amount capitalised relates to costs which have effectively been financed interest-free by third parties (e.g. retention money) that part must be excluded from the expenditure on which interest is capitalised.[100]

4.2.3   Capitalisation period

Generally, the period during which interest should be capitalised is defined in terms of the following three conditions:

(a)   expenditures for the asset must have been made;

(b)   activities that are necessary to get the asset ready for its intended use are in progress; and

(c)   interest cost is being incurred (including the imputation of interest on certain types of payables in accordance with APB Opinion No. 21 –*Interest on Receivables and Payables*).

The capitalisation period begins when all three conditions are present and continues as long as they all remain present. The capitalisation period ends when the asset is substantially complete and ready for its intended use.[101]

If an asset is completed in parts and each part is capable of being used independently while work continues on the other parts, then capitalisation should cease on each part when it is substantially complete and ready for use.[102]

Interest capitalisation is not discontinued merely because it is necessary to write the asset down to a value below cost. In that case, the provision is increased to take account of the capitalised interest.[103]

4.2.4   Disclosure

The financial statements must disclose the total interest cost incurred and the amount capitalised during the financial year.[104]

5   CONCLUSION

Although the ASB has now issued an accounting standard that addresses the capitalisation of finance costs, it only applies to tangible fixed assets and capitalisation remains optional. The ASB has, to a certain extent, thus adopted a holding position until there is international consensus on the issue. However, there is no reason why the ASB should not take a lead on this, as it has done on many other issues. The capitalisation of finance costs is an important part of the wider issue of accounting for interest effects. Given the zeal with which the ASB is seeking to introduce discounting under other standards, it is surprising that it is taking such an equivocal stance on the capitalisation of finance costs.

However, in our view, no decision should have been taken on whether or not to capitalise interest without a discussion of the nature of finance costs and how they fit within the structure of financial reporting by a company to its stakeholders. The ASB needs to consider whether or not the capitalisation of finance costs is a conceptually sound basis of accounting.

In so doing, the ASB will need to take cognisance of the fact that there is a valid conceptual argument for measuring the cost of financing the acquisition of qualifying assets on the basis of the entity's cost of capital, including imputed interest on equity capital as well as interest on borrowings. At the same time it must be recognised that the capitalisation of the cost of equity capital does not conform to the present historical cost accounting framework, under which the cost of a resource is measured by reference to historical exchange prices. Nevertheless, to only permit the capitalisation of interest on borrowed capital is an incomplete approach.

Conversely, it may be argued that the capitalisation of borrowing costs into most types of property development is an entirely logical and appropriate policy. Interest is a development cost and is no different in this respect to the concrete, bricks and land. The ASB will, therefore, need to decide whether or not the arguments in favour of capitalisation of borrowing costs outweigh the disadvantages of allowing an accounting practice which often produces arbitrary results. The only way to do this is to conduct a proper debate on the issue of accounting for interest effects, which would encompass both the capitalisation of finance costs and discounting.

References

1 CA 85, Sch. 4, para. 26(3)(b).
2 The moratorium was imposed on November 14, 1974 by Accounting Series Release No. 163, *Capitalisation of Interest by Companies Other Than Public Utilities*. Washington D.C.: Securities and Exchange Commission, 1974.
3 'Public utilities' was defined to include electric, gas, water, and telephone utilities.
4 SFAS 34, *Capitalisation of Interest Cost*, FASB, October 1979. For a more detailed discussion of the background to SFAS 34, see Appendix A to the statement.
5 IAS 23 (Original), *Capitalisation of Borrowing Costs*, IASC, March 1984, paras. 21–27.
6 IAS 23, *Borrowing Costs*, IASC, Revised 1993, para. 8.
7 For a full understanding of the reasons for the dissenting vote, see SFAS 34 for the text of the statement issued by the dissenting members of the FASB.
8 IAS 23 (Original), para. 6; ASB Discussion Paper, *Measurement of tangible fixed assets*, October 1996, para. 1.15; FRS 15, *Tangible Fixed Assets*, ASB, February 1999, Appendix IV, para. 10.
9 IAS 23 (Original), para. 7; ASB Discussion Paper, *Measurement of tangible fixed assets*, para. 1.16.
10 ASB Discussion Paper, *Measurement of tangible fixed assets*, para. 1.13.
11 FRS 15, *Tangible Fixed Assets*, Appendix IV, para. 10.
12 *Ibid.*, para. 11.
13 SFAS 34, para. 36.
14 *Ibid.*, para. 38.
15 *Ibid.*, text of the statement issued by the dissenting members of the FASB.
16 *Ibid.*, para. 54.
17 *Ibid.*, para. 49.
18 *Ibid.*, para. 40.
19 *Ibid.*, Appendix B, para 49.
20 CA 85, Sch. 4, para. 26(3).
21 FRS 15, para. 21.
22 *Ibid.*, para. 23.
23 *Ibid.*, para. 19.
24 SSAP 9, *Stocks and long-term contracts*, Issued May 1975, Revised September 1988, Appendix 1, para. 21.
25 IAS 11, *Construction Contracts*, IASC, Revised 1993, para. 18.
26 ASB Discussion Paper, *Measurement of tangible fixed assets*, para. 1.17.
27 *Ibid.*
28 FRED 17, *Measurement of Tangible Fixed Assets*, ASB, October 1997, Appendix IV, para. 8.
29 *Ibid.*, paras. 5 and 7.
30 FRS 15, para. 2.
31 *Ibid.*
32 *Ibid.*, paras. 19 and 20.
33 *Ibid.*, para. 19.
34 *Ibid.*, para. 21.
35 *Ibid.*, para. 22.
36 *Ibid.*, para. 23.
37 *Ibid.*, para. 24.
38 *Ibid.*, para. 25.
39 IAS 23, para. 20.
40 FRS 15, para. 26.
41 *Ibid.*
42 *Ibid.*, paras. 27 and 28.
43 IAS 23, para. 23; SFAS 34, para. 17.
44 IAS 23, para. 24; SFAS 34, para. 17.
45 FRS 15, paras. 29 and 30.
46 SFAS 34, para. 18.
47 CA 85, Sch. 4, para. 26(3).
48 *Ibid.*, para. 8.

49 *The Listing Rules*, London Stock Exchange, Chapter 12, para. 12.43(c).
50 CA 85, Sch. 4, paras. 17, 22 and 26(3).
51 SFAS 34, para. 10.
52 *Ibid.*, paras. 10, 45 and 46.
53 *Ibid.*, para. 10.
54 IAS 23, para. 6.
55 *Ibid.*, para. 15.
56 SFAS 62, para. 3.
57 IAS 23, para. 30.
58 SSAP 20, *Foreign currency translation*, ASC, April 1983, para. 68.
59 IAS 23, para. 5(e).
60 CA 85, Sch. 4, para. 26(2).
61 SFAS 34, para. 9(a).
62 FRS 15, para. 21.
63 IAS 23 (Original), para. 21.
64 E32, *Comparability of Financial Statements*, January 1989, para. 188.
65 IASC, *Statement of Intent: Comparability of Financial Statements*, July 1990.
66 E39, *Capitalisation of Borrowing Costs*, August 1991.
67 *Ibid.*, para. 6.
68 IAS 23, Revised 1993, paras. 7 and 8.
69 *Ibid.*, paras. 10–28.
70 *Ibid.*, para. 4.
71 IASC, *Insight*, October 1991, p. 10.
72 IAS 23, para. 6.
73 *Ibid.*, para. 4.
74 *Ibid.*, para. 5.
75 *Ibid.*, para. 11.
76 *Ibid.*, para. 15.
77 *Ibid.*, para. 17.
78 *Ibid.*, para. 20.
79 *Ibid.*, para. 22.
80 *Ibid.*, paras. 23 and 24.
81 *Ibid.*, para. 25.
82 *Ibid.*, para. 27.
83 *Ibid.*, para. 29.
84 SIC – 2, *Consistency - Capitalisation of Borrowing Costs*, IASC Standing Interpretations Committee, July 1997, para. 3.
85 FRS 15, para. 20.
86 SFAS 34, para. 7.
87 SFAS 58, *Capitalisation of Interest Cost in Financial Statements That Include Investments Accounted for by the Equity Method*, FASB, April 1982.
88 SFAS 62, *Capitalisation of Interest Cost in Situations Involving Certain Tax-Exempt Borrowings and Certain Gifts and Grants*, FASB, June 1982.
89 SFAS 34, para. 9.
90 *Ibid.*
91 SFAS 58, para. 5.
92 SFAS 34, para. 10.
93 *Ibid.*
94 *Ibid.*
95 SFAS 58, para. 6.
96 *Ibid.*
97 SFAS 34, para. 11.
98 *Ibid.*, paras. 12–15.
99 *Ibid.*, para. 15.
100 *Ibid.*, para. 16.
101 *Ibid.*, paras. 17 and 18.

102 *Ibid.*, para. 18.
103 *Ibid.*, para. 19.
104 *Ibid.*, para. 21.

Chapter 14 Stocks and long-term contracts

1 INTRODUCTION

1.1 The importance of stocks and long-term contracts within financial statements

Accounting for stock involves the determination of both the cost of goods sold during the period and the amount that should be carried forward in the balance sheet as stock to be matched against future revenues. This is because the determination of profit for an accounting period requires the matching of costs with related revenues. The cost of unsold or unconsumed stocks will have been incurred in the expectation of future revenue, and when this will only arise in future periods it is appropriate to carry forward this cost to be matched with the revenue when it arises; the applicable concept is the matching of cost and revenue in the year in which the revenue arises rather than in the year in which the cost of acquiring the stock is incurred.

For companies in certain industry sectors such as retail and manufacturing, stock is generally one of the most significant items in the balance sheet and, as a result, the measurement of stock can have a very material impact on reported performance and financial position. At the same time, though, it has been said that no area of accounting has produced wider differences in practice than the computation of the amount at which stocks are stated in financial statements. This is particularly the case in countries such as the US, where companies have the free choice between a number of methods of accounting for stock, some of which produce very different results and make inter-company comparisons difficult. It is perhaps therefore not surprising that some thorny conceptual and practical problems arise in the area of stock measurement, particularly in relation to the determination of the constituents of cost and the methods used in allocating costs to stocks.

1.2   What are stocks and long-term contracts?

The applicable UK accounting standard, SSAP 9 – *Stocks and long-term contracts* – defines 'stocks' in the following terms:[1]

'*Stocks* comprise the following categories:

(a)   goods or other assets purchased for resale;

(b)   consumable stores;

(c)   raw materials and components purchased for incorporation into products for sale;

(d)   products and services in intermediate stages of completion;

(e)   long-term contract balances; and

(f)   finished goods.'

The US definition of stock (or 'inventory') appears, *prima facie*, to be more restrictive than the UK definition in that it requires stock to be 'tangible'.[2] However, this anomaly is probably no more than a function of the fact that the definition was laid down more than 40 years ago at a time when it was not envisaged that items such as a service company's unbilled work would be included in inventory. In practice, though, this is not an issue since intangible current assets would be included in the balance sheet as separate line items and would not be subsumed within inventory. Nevertheless, it is noteworthy that the scope of the International Accounting Standard on inventories (IAS 2) has recently been extended to deal with the accounting treatment of work in progress of an enterprise which provides professional services, whilst at the same time the former requirement that inventories could only include tangible property has been removed from the relevant definition.[3]

SSAP 9 defines a 'long-term contract' as being 'a contract entered into for the design, manufacture or construction of a single substantial asset or the provision of a service (or of a combination of assets or services which together constitute a single project) where the time taken substantially to complete the contract is such that the contract activity falls into different accounting periods. A contract that is required to be accounted for as long-term by this accounting standard will usually extend for a period exceeding one year. However, a duration exceeding one year is not an essential feature of a long-term contract. Some contracts with a shorter duration than one year should be accounted for as long-term contracts if they are sufficiently material to the activity of the period that not to record turnover and attributable profit would lead to a distortion of the period's turnover and results such that the financial statements would not give a true and fair view, provided that the policy is applied consistently within the reporting entity and from year to year.'[4]

It is noteworthy that when SSAP 9 was revised it was considered necessary to go into enormous detail in defining long-term contracts, while, in contrast, both the US and international standards merely give a general description of them. The reason for this detailed definition in SSAP 9 is that it is attempting to meet objections raised to the arbitrariness of the definition in the original SSAP 9, in terms of which duration was the key criterion for deciding whether or not a contract was long-term. Arguably, however, whilst solving this issue, the revised definition has created further problems.

Long-term contracts are effectively a special category of stocks and all the rules and principles relating to stocks also apply to long-term contracts. Consequently, this Chapter looks at these subjects separately, but on the basis that all matters relating to stocks apply equally to long-term contracts. However, there are additional factors stemming from the time taken to complete long-term contracts, which require separate consideration; these are discussed at 7 below.

1.3 Objectives of stock measurement

It is generally accepted that, within the historical cost accounting system, the principal objective of stock measurement is the proper determination of income through the process of matching costs with related revenues.[5] In order to match costs and revenue, 'costs' of stocks should comprise that expenditure which has been incurred in the normal course of business in bringing the product or service to its present location and condition.[6] The result of this is that all costs incurred in respect of stocks should be charged as period costs, except for those which relate to those unconsumed stocks[7] which are expected to be of future benefit to the entity. These should be carried forward to be matched with the revenues that they will generate in the future. Therefore, in the income measurement process, stocks have characteristics similar to those of prepaid expenses or fixed assets such as plant and equipment.

If, however, there is expected to be no future benefit, or if the future benefit is expected to be less than the associated costs, then the prudence concept is applied, and the carrying value of those stocks must be reduced to the value of their future benefit. This gives rise to the basic rule for the balance sheet valuation of stocks, i.e. that they should be stated at the lower of cost and net realisable value.[8] Clearly, however, the application of this rule can result in stocks being reported at amounts which neither reflect the historical costs which have been incurred in bringing them to their present location or condition, nor the replacement cost of such stocks.

A second objective of stock measurement is to present a value of stock for the purpose of presentation in the balance sheet. The value at which stocks are reported in the balance sheet is governed by the interpretation that is intended to be placed on such valuation; for example, realisable value is the cash amount that the entity could receive on the sale of its stock in the ordinary course of business, whilst current replacement cost is the amount of cash that would be required if the entity did not hold the goods, but had to acquire them. However, because of the present emphasis on matching historical costs with revenues, the balance sheet 'lower of cost and net realisable value' of stock has little interpretational value. Furthermore, it should be stressed that under the historical cost framework, the amount reflected in the balance sheet represents no more than deferred costs which are yet to be matched.

A more general objective is to present users with information which will assist them in predicting the firm's future cash flows. Clearly, in the context of the historical cost framework, this objective is not easily attainable, since stock stated at the lower of cost and net realisable value will neither assist in the prediction of cash inflows from future sales, nor assist in the prediction of cash outflows required for the replacement of the stock to be sold in the next accounting period.

2   DETERMINING THE COST OF STOCK

As stated above, SSAP 9 defines cost in relation to stock as 'that expenditure which has been incurred in the normal course of business in bringing the product or service to its present location and condition'.[9] There should be included in the expenditure both cost of purchase and such costs of conversion 'as are appropriate to that location and condition'.[10] Cost of purchase comprises 'purchase price including import duties, transport and handling costs and any other directly attributable costs, less trade discounts, rebates and subsidies';[11] whilst cost of conversion comprises:

'(a)   costs which are specifically attributable to units of production, eg, direct labour, direct expenses and sub-contracted work;

(b)   production overheads (as defined in paragraph 20 [of SSAP 9]);

(c)   other overheads, if any, attributable in the particular circumstances of the business to bringing the product or service to its present location and condition'.[12]

In the past, before production processes became complex, it was common for manufactured stocks to be costed at 'prime cost' – i.e. only the cost of materials and direct labour were included. At that time, this was a justifiable basis of determining cost, since prime costs constituted a high percentage of total costs. However, as manufacturing systems became more mechanised with the advent of assembly lines, overheads grew in relative proportion to total costs until it became clear that to continue valuing stock only at prime cost resulted in a figure which did not reflect the full costs involved in manufacture. Consequently, businesses developed costing systems in order to facilitate the allocation of production overheads to the cost of stock – primarily as an aid to making product pricing decisions.

2.1 Direct costing versus full absorption costing

Although it was inevitable that individual firms would develop their own unique costing systems, the methods adopted could be classified between two broad approaches: namely, 'full absorption' and 'direct' costing. These systems differed in only one fundamental conceptual respect: the treatment of fixed overheads. Under direct costing, fixed overheads are expensed on a time basis and are therefore excluded from the cost of manufactured products, whilst under absorption costing fixed overheads are applied to the cost of the product, to be subsequently released to expense as part of cost of sales. Over the years, numerous arguments have been put forward both for and against each of the approaches. In essence, advocates of direct costing argue that fixed production overheads (e.g. rent) are more closely related to the *capacity* to produce, rather than to the production of individual products, and should therefore be expensed in the period in which they are incurred. Conversely, advocates of absorption costing maintain that fixed costs should be included in the cost of stock, since they are costs necessarily incurred to produce the goods.

A further complication arises through the conflict in the objectives of internal versus external financial reporting. Because of the importance of contribution analysis in managerial accounting and performance measurement, many businesses adopt the direct costing approach for internal reporting purposes. On the other hand, the accounting standard-setting bodies advocate at least some degree of absorption costing for external financial reporting purposes. For example, SSAP 9 states that the costs of stock 'will include all related production overheads'[13] and the definition of cost of conversion as stated above implies that at least direct fixed overheads should be allocated to the cost of stock.

IAS 2 – *Inventories* – states that 'the cost of inventories should comprise all costs of purchase, costs of conversion and other costs incurred in bringing the inventories to their present location and condition'.[14] It goes on to define costs of conversion as including 'a systematic allocation of fixed and variable production overheads that are incurred in converting materials into finished goods'.[15] Similarly in the US, ARB 43 states that 'cost means in principle the sum of the applicable expenditures and charges directly or indirectly incurred in bringing an article to its existing condition and location'.[16] Consequently, under UK, US and International standards, fixed production overheads should only be excluded from the valuation of manufactured stocks in cases where they do not relate to 'bringing the stocks to their present location and condition'.

3 DETERMINING THE COST OF SALES

As discussed above, in the historical cost framework the principal objective of accounting for stock is the matching of costs with related revenues. However, since costs are continually changing over time, this objective is difficult to achieve in practice. Consequently, accountants have found it necessary to develop systematic bases for the recognition of the cost of sales, founded on certain cost flow assumptions. Some cost flow assumptions are based on the premise that the cost of sales should be identified with the physical flow of goods; whilst others disregard the physical flow of goods and attempt to achieve a more accurate matching of current costs with current revenues.

3.1   Cost flow assumptions based on the physical flow of goods

The explanatory note to SSAP 9 states that 'the methods used in allocating costs to stocks need to be selected with a view to providing the fairest possible approximation to the expenditure actually incurred in bringing the product to its present location and condition'.[17] Consequently, SSAP 9 sees the allocation of actual costs on the basis of the physical flow of goods as the ideal.

3.1.1   *Specific identification/actual cost*

Where it is both possible and practicable to attach a specific cost to each item of stock, the costs of goods sold are specifically identified and matched with the goods physically sold.   In practice this is a relatively unusual method of valuation as the clerical effort required does not make it feasible unless there are relatively few high value items being bought or produced. Consequently, it would normally be used where the stock comprised items such as antiques, jewellery and cars in the hands of dealers. Nevertheless, there are a number of manufacturing companies which state that their stocks are valued on the basis of actual cost. For example:

Extract 14.1: Low & Bonar PLC (1998)

ACCOUNTING POLICIES

(viii)   Stock valuation [extract]

Raw materials and bought-in components are valued on the basis of actual cost including freight and handling charges, or net realisable value if lower.

3.1.2   *FIFO (first-in, first-out)*

In the vast majority of businesses it will not be practicable to keep track of stock cost on an individual unit basis; nevertheless, the objective of stock measurement is still to match costs and revenues. The FIFO method probably gives the closest approximation to actual cost flows, since it is assumed that when stocks are sold or used in a production process, the oldest are sold or used first and that, therefore, the balance of stock on hand at any point represents the most recent purchases or production. This can best be illustrated in the context of a business which deals in perishable goods, since clearly such a business will dispose of the earliest goods received before fresher goods. Therefore, by allocating the earliest costs incurred against revenue, actual cost flows are being matched with the physical flow of goods with reasonable accuracy. In any event, even in the case of businesses which do not deal in perishable goods, this would reflect what would probably be a sound management policy. Consequently, in practice where it is not possible to value stock on an actual cost basis, the FIFO method is generally used since it is most likely to approximate the physical flow of goods sold, resulting in the most accurate measurement of cost flows. For example, Laura Ashley discloses a comprehensive FIFO stock policy:

Extract 14.2: Laura Ashley Holdings plc (1999)

Accounting Policies

Stocks and work in progress

Stocks are valued at the lower of cost and net realisable value. Cost is determined on a first in, first out basis.

The cost of Group manufactured products includes all direct expenditure and attributable overheads based on a normal level of activity. Net realisable value is the price at which stocks can be sold in the normal course of business after allowing for the costs of realisation and, where appropriate, the cost of conversion from their existing state to a finished state. Provision is made where necessary for non-current and defective stocks.

3.2 Cost flow assumptions which disregard the physical flow of goods

3.2.1 Weighted average

This method, which is suitable where stock units are identical or near identical, involves the computation of an average unit cost by dividing the total cost of units by the number of units. The average unit cost then has to be revised with every receipt of stock, or alternatively at the end of predetermined periods. The justification for this approach is that 'it is illogical to distinguish between similar stock items merely because different levels of cost existed at the time they were purchased or produced'.[18] In practice, weighted average would appear to be less widely used than FIFO as it involves more clerical effort, and its results are not very different from FIFO in times of relatively low inflation, or where stock turnover is relatively quick.

Nevertheless, there are certain businesses which hold large quantities of relatively homogeneous stock for which the weighted average method of stock valuation is the most appropriate. For example:

Extract 14.3: The Rugby Group PLC (1998)

Notes on the Accounts

1 Accounting Policies

(i) Stocks

Stocks are valued at the lower of cost and net realisable value after making due allowance for obsolete and slow moving items. Cost is based upon "First in, First out" or "Weighted Average" valuation methods and includes, where appropriate, a proportion of production overheads.

However, given that the group has applied both the FIFO and weighted average bases to the valuation of its stocks, it would, perhaps, have been useful to know which basis has been applied to which stocks.

3.2.2 LIFO (last-in, first-out)

This method is, as its name suggests, the opposite to FIFO and assumes that the most recent purchases or production are disposed of first; in certain cases this could represent the physical flow of stock (e.g. if a store is filled and emptied from the top). This is in an attempt to match current costs with current revenues so that the profit and loss account excludes the effects of holding gains. Essentially, therefore, LIFO is an attempt to achieve something closer to replacement cost accounting for the profit and loss account, whilst disregarding the balance sheet. Consequently, the period-end balance of stock on hand represents the earliest purchases of the item, resulting in stocks being stated in the balance sheet at amounts which usually bear little relationship to recent cost levels. For this reason, LIFO is ordinarily not permitted to be used under SSAP 9[19] despite the fact that it is specifically allowed under the legislation.[20] However, since the balance sheet value of stock merely represents a deferred cost, and bears no relationship to the stock's worth to the firm, we do not see any conceptual difficulty in using LIFO in an historical cost accounting framework which is profit and loss oriented. The difficulty which does arise is that LIFO distorts the calculation of working capital ratios and makes inter-firm comparisons difficult. The simple solution to this would be to report current stock valuations as supplementary information (in any event, the Companies Act requires a company to disclose the difference between the replacement cost or most recent purchase price of stocks and their book value, where this difference is material).[21]

LIFO has not been widely used in the UK, principally because the Inland Revenue has never permitted its use for tax purposes. The position is different in the US, where the Internal Revenue Codes of 1938 and 1939 officially recognised LIFO as an acceptable method for the computation of tax, provided that it was used consistently for tax and financial reporting purposes. Therefore, if LIFO is used by individual companies in a group for tax purposes, it must also be used for reporting purposes in the financial statements of those companies as well as in the group financial statements.

Some companies have used LIFO as a method of attempting to solve the problem of accounting for changes in price levels, even to the extent of viewing it as a substitute for the cost of sales adjustment under SSAP 16.[22] Although this does achieve a measure of success in that the profit and loss account reflects current costs of sales, it does not fully adjust income for general price changes (although neither did the SSAP 16 cost of sales adjustment); in addition, there is the danger that the profit and loss account can be seriously distorted if stock quantities fall and cause very old costs to be included in cost of sales.

The revision in 1993 of IAS 2 had the effect of setting down the FIFO and weighted average cost formulas as the 'benchmark treatments' for determining the cost of inventories,[23] although LIFO was, at the eleventh hour, retained as an 'allowed alternative treatment'[24] (see 6.3.2 below).

3.2.3   Base stock

This is another valuation method which is permitted by the legislation[25] but not approved by SSAP 9 (using the same reasoning as for LIFO).[26]   Under this method a fixed quantity of stock is stated at a fixed price and any amount over the fixed quantity is valued using more usual methods, such as FIFO.   The philosophy behind this method is that any on-going business must hold a certain minimum quantity of stock at all times; this base level of stock is then viewed as being more in the nature of a fixed asset, rather than stock to be sold or consumed.   The fixed quantity is taken to be that level of stock which must always be held to maintain normal operating levels.   The base stock method is not permitted for tax purposes in either the UK or US, and is rarely seen in practice.   It is important to note that the use of the base stock method would only be permitted by the Companies Act 1985 in the case of 'assets of a kind which are constantly being replaced where–

(a)   their overall value is not material to assessing the company's state of affairs; and

(b)   their quantity, value and composition are not subject to material variation'.[27]

The revision in 1993 of IAS 2 saw the elimination of the base stock cost formula as a permitted method of costing (see 6.3.2 below).

3.3   Illustration of the effect of different cost flow assumptions

The following example illustrates the practical effect of the FIFO, weighted average and LIFO cost flow assumptions:

Example 14.1

Company A's stock transactions for the three months ended 31 March 2001 were as follows:

	Units	Unit cost	Unit selling price
		£	£
Stock on hand: 1 January 2001	60	30	
January purchases	90	45	
January sales	(40)		60
February purchases	55	60	
February sales	(45)		100
March purchases	60	75	
March sales	(75)		130
Stock on hand: 31 March 2001	105		

The company maintains its stock records on the perpetual system, and all purchases are made on the first day of the month.

The value of cost of sales for the three months ended 31 March 2001 and closing stock at that date under various costing methods are as follows:

	FIFO	Weighted average	LIFO
	£	£	£
Sales	16,650	16,650	16,650
Cost of sales	(6,450)	(7,805)	(9,825)
Gross profit	10,200	8,845	6,825
Stock at 31 March 2001	7,200	5,845	3,825

The above example illustrates that, under the historical cost framework, accounting for stock is merely a cost allocation process, and that stock disclosed in the balance sheet is no more than a deferred cost. Therefore, it is necessary to decide how much of the cost of goods available for sale during the period should be written off, and how much should be deferred. In this example, the total costs of £13,650 are allocated/deferred according to the three costing methods illustrated.

Clearly, the extent of the divergence in results under the three methods illustrated above is a function of the rate of price changes. In times of rising prices, FIFO tends to overstate profit because earlier and lower unit costs are matched with current prices, whilst valuing period-end stocks at the most recent costs which are the more realistic measures of current cost. Conversely, LIFO more realistically reflects profit by matching the most recent unit costs with current selling price, whilst valuing period-end stocks at the oldest and, therefore, less realistic unit costs.

An interesting example of a company which attempted to overcome this difficulty is Cookson. Until 1993, the company used the base stock and LIFO methods to value certain of its commodity stocks for profit and loss account purposes, whilst stating these stocks in the balance sheet at a FIFO valuation. The difference between the base stock/LIFO and FIFO valuations was included in reserves.

Extract 14.4: Cookson Group plc (1992)

Notes to the accounts

1   Accounting policies

Accounting convention

The accounts on pages 28 to 46 are prepared in accordance with the Companies Act 1985 and under the historical cost convention as modified by the revaluation of certain tangible fixed assets. Other than as stated below for certain of the Group's stocks, the Group accounts have been prepared in accordance with applicable accounting standards, including Financial Reporting Standard No. 3.

Stocks

All stocks are stated in the Group balance sheet at the lower of cost and net realisable value on the first in first out (FIFO) method. Cost comprises expenditure directly incurred in purchasing or manufacturing stocks together with, where appropriate, attributable overheads based on normal activity levels.

The valuation of stocks for the Group profit and loss account differs, for certain Group subsidiaries, from that required by Statement of Standard Accounting Practice No 9. An explanation and quantification of this departure from SSAP 9 is given in note 11 on page 38.

---

11   Stocks

| | 1992 | 1991 |
	£m	£m
Raw materials	**76.9**	64.5
Work in progress	**38.3**	30.3
Finished goods	**97.4**	85.2
Total stocks	**212.6**	180.0

Certain metals and minerals stocks held by Group subsidiaries are valued in the profit and loss account on the Base Stock or, for certain overseas subsidiaries, the last in first out (LIFO) method. As market prices of the materials involved can fluctuate widely over a period, and because these companies are processors and not traders, the effects of such variations in stock values are not operating profits or losses. The use of the Base Stock and LIFO methods, together with covering arrangements for quantities in excess of Base Stock levels, causes the profit and loss account to be charged with the current cost of the materials consumed. The stock valuation for the balance sheet is at the lower of cost and net realisable value on the first in first out (FIFO) method. The difference between the Base Stock or LIFO valuations, where these methods are used, and the FIFO valuation is included in reserves. This amounted to a charge of **£4.1m** in 1992 (1991: £7.5m).

The directors believe that this method of accounting is more appropriate for these stocks than that required by Statement of Standard Accounting Practice No 9.

The above approach previously followed by Cookson may be compared with that which would be followed under current cost accounting, since the difference between the base stock/LIFO and FIFO methods included in reserves is broadly similar to a current cost reserve. Nevertheless, some might argue that the company's balance sheet presentation of stocks amounts to a form of reserve accounting which is contrary to UK GAAP, and that, under existing rules, the amounts at which stocks are stated in the balance sheet and profit and loss account should be the same.

In any event, in 1993 Cookson decided to discontinue this differential approach to stock valuation and adopt a more conventional FIFO policy in conformity with SSAP 9. This change in policy was described in the company's 1993 accounts in the following terms:

Extract 14.5: Cookson Group plc (1993)

Notes to the accounts

20 PRIOR YEAR ADJUSTMENTS [extract]

(c) Stock valuation

In previous years the valuation of certain stocks for the Group profit and loss account differed from that required by Statement of Standard Accounting Practice No. 9 (SSAP 9). These stocks were valued in the profit and loss account on the Base Stock or, for certain overseas subsidiaries, the Last In First Out (LIFO) method. As the market prices of the materials in question could fluctuate widely over a period, and because these companies were processors and not traders, the effects of such variations in stock values were not operating profits or losses. The use of the Base Stock and LIFO methods, together with covering arrangements for quantities in excess of Base Stock level, caused the profit and loss account to be charged with the current costs of the materials consumed.

In recent years, as a result of the combined effects of changes in some of the products concerned, in procurement and also in the composition of the Group, the Directors believe that it is no longer warranted to apply policies for these stocks which differ from that required by SSAP 9. Accordingly all Group stocks are now valued on the basis explained in the Accounting Policies in Note 1 and in accordance with SSAP 9.

The results for 1992 have been restated in the Group profit and loss account, reducing the operating profit for that year by £3.7m. Had the previous policy been applied for 1993, the effect on the results would have been negligible.

---

4 THE DEVELOPMENT OF SSAP 9 (REVISED)

4.1 The original SSAP 9

SSAP 9 was originally issued in 1975 because, as the preamble to the standard stated, 'no area of accounting has produced wider differences in practice than the computation of the amount at which stocks and work in progress are stated in financial accounts'.[28] The standard began by stating the basic requirement that stocks and work in progress should normally be stated at the lower of cost and net realisable value.[29] It made it clear that production overheads must be included in stock by requiring that 'such costs [of stocks and work in progress] will include all related production overheads, even though these may accrue on a time basis'.[30] Furthermore, it emphasised that the approach previously taken by some companies of excluding certain overheads from stocks on the grounds of prudence was unacceptable, by stating that 'in so far as the circumstances of the business require an element of prudence in determining the amount at which stocks and work in progress are stated, this needs to be taken into account in the determination of net realisable value and not by the exclusion from cost of selected overheads'.[31]

In relation to contracting work in progress SSAP 9 required a different treatment only in respect of those contracts which extend for more than one year.[32] Any work in progress in respect of contracts lasting less than one year had to be accounted for on the normal basis, i.e. at the lower of cost and net realisable value. This immediately gave rise to a conceptual problem in that activities which are identical in nature were required to be accounted for in different ways because of an artificial distinction based on an arbitrary duration. The difference in treatment arose from the requirement to include 'attributable profit'[33] within the balance sheet figure for long-term contract work in progress. In arriving at this balance sheet figure one also had to deduct any foreseeable losses and progress payments received and receivable.[34] This latter rule ensured that for the most part long-term contract work in progress was stated at the lower of: (i) cost plus attributable profit and (ii) net realisable value.

The reason why a different treatment is required for long-term contracts is that if the basic rule of accounting for stocks was applied to them this would result in an annual profit and loss account reflecting the outcome only of contracts completed during the year, which, in a contracting company, might bear no relation to the company's actual level of activity for the year. Obviously, if a company operated at the same level of activity over the years on contracts of similar size and duration there would be no real difference in the results reported each year under the percentage of completion and the completed contracts methods. However, in practice this is not the way things happen in any contracting industry and therefore attributable profit has to be accrued on uncompleted contracts in order to present a consistent view of the results of the company's activities during the period.

4.2   The need for revision

One of the accounting rules introduced by the Companies Act 1981 in its implementation of the EC Fourth Directive was that current assets are to be stated at the lower of their cost and net realisable value. This principle has been carried through to the Companies Act 1985 via paragraphs 22 and 23 of Schedule 4, which state that 'the amount to be included in respect of any current asset shall be its purchase price or production cost. If the net realisable value of any current asset is lower than its purchase price or production cost, the amount to be included in respect of that asset shall be the net realisable value.' However, this resulted in a conflict with SSAP 9, which required long-term work in progress in the balance sheet to include attributable profit. The legislation was not outlawing the inclusion of the attributable profit in the profit and loss account, merely the inclusion of it within the value of a current asset. Nevertheless, there was scope within the legislation to depart from the detailed accounting rules if this was necessary to give a true and fair view and if full details of the departure, including its effect, were given in a note to the accounts (the 'true and fair override').[35]

In so doing, there were essentially two approaches followed by companies to fulfil the requirement to disclose the details and effect of the departure from the statutory valuation rules:

> *Extract 14.6: The Plessey Company plc (1988)*
>
> **16 Stocks** [extract]
>
> In accordance with the provisions of SSAP 9, attributable profit amounting to £36.6m (1987 – £35.0m) has been included in the value of long term contract work-in-progress. The directors are of the opinion that this departure from statutory valuation rules is necessary to enable the accounts to give a true and fair view.

> *Extract 14.7: The Peninsular and Oriental Steam Navigation Company (1987)*
>
> **18 Stocks** [extract]
>
> To enable the accounts to give a true and fair view, attributable profit is included in long term work in progress. This is a departure from the statutory valuation rules but is required by section 228 of the Companies Act 1985. Work in progress is stated net of progress payments of £1,366.2m (1986 £1,090.8m) which cannot be allocated between the related cost and profit.

Representatives of the Department of Trade and Industry (DTI) had made it clear that they were unhappy with the use of the true and fair override in such a general way as it was intended that it only be used in very rare circumstances.

4.3   SSAP 9 (Revised)

As a result of the DTI's objections, a working party was set up by the ASC to review SSAP 9. This resulted in ED 40 being published in November 1986, and ultimately in the release of SSAP 9 (Revised) in September 1988. There were effectively no changes to the accounting and disclosure requirements contained in the original standard in respect of stocks and work in progress. The changes made, therefore, were only in respect of long-term contracts and were two-fold: one concerned the presentation of long-term contract balances within the balance sheet and was designed to meet the DTI's objections, while the other was a revision to the definition of a long-term contract and was intended to remove the problems associated with the arbitrariness of the twelve month rule within the definition in the original standard.

The requirements of SSAP 9 (Revised) in respect of stocks and work in progress are dealt with in 6 below; long-term contracts are dealt with in 7 below.

5   THE REQUIREMENTS OF THE COMPANIES ACT 1985

The legal requirements of accounting for and disclosure of stocks within a company's financial statements are included along with most other legal accounting requirements in Schedule 4 to the Companies Act 1985. There is no specific mention made in the legislation of long-term contracts. This is because the legislation treats all current assets in the same way and is the principal reason why SSAP 9 was revised.

5.1   Lower of cost and net realisable value

Paragraphs 22 and 23 of Schedule 4, which apply to all current assets and not just stocks, are very similar to paragraph 26 of SSAP 9 and provide that current assets should be stated at the lower of their purchase price or production cost and net realisable value.

5.2   Stock included at a fixed amount

As discussed at 3.2.3 above in the context of the base stock method of costing stock, paragraph 25 of Schedule 4 provides that stocks of raw materials and consumables which are constantly being replaced may be included at a fixed quantity and value provided that the overall value of such stocks is not material to the company's balance sheet and that their quantity, value and composition are not subject to material variation.

5.3   Determination of purchase price or production cost

The rules that apply in determining the cost of an asset are set out in paragraph 26 of Schedule 4, as follows:

(a)   the purchase price of an asset should include any expenses incidental to the acquisition of that asset, e.g. customs duties;

(b)   the production cost of an asset should include, in addition to the cost of the raw materials and consumables, any other directly attributable production costs, e.g. direct labour costs;

(c)   in the case of current assets, distribution costs may not be included in production costs;

(d)   in addition to the costs at (b) above there may be included some costs 'which are only indirectly attributable to the production of that asset'. Most commonly these would be costs that vary with time rather than production, e.g. rent, rates and insurance; and

(e)   'Interest on capital borrowed to finance the production' may also be included in stock. Capitalisation of interest is discussed in Chapter 13.

Any costs that fall to be included under (d) and (e) above can only be included to the extent that they accrue during the period of production, and the amount of any interest included must be separately disclosed.

5.4   Costing method and replacement cost

Paragraph 27 of Schedule 4 provides that stocks may be stated using FIFO, LIFO, weighted average or any other method similar to any of those, but whichever method is chosen, it must be appropriate to the circumstances of the company. However, where any item of stock is valued by one of these methods rather than at actual cost, the difference between the amount at which it is included in the financial statements and its replacement cost or most recent actual purchase price or production cost is required to be disclosed if that difference is material. A strict interpretation of the paragraph could require some meaningless disclosures to be given. However, in practice, if an amount is disclosed it is usually the total replacement cost of stocks. For example:

Extract 14.8: BP Amoco p.l.c. (1998)

NOTES ON ACCOUNTS

20 Stocks

	$ million	
	1998	1997
Petroleum	**1,896**	3,140
Chemicals	**917**	1,043
Other	**174**	86
	2,987	4,269
Stores	**655**	654
	3,642	4,923
Replacement cost	**3,747**	4,985

In fact, BP Amoco provides considerably more replacement cost information in its 1998 accounts, thereby affording the reader the opportunity to gain a better appreciation of the group's performance. For example, in addition to a discussion in the Financial Review of the 1998 results in terms of replacement cost profits, the group prepares its profit and loss account in such a way as to show its operating profit for the year on both a replacement cost and historical cost basis, thereby illustrating the effects of stock holding gains and losses on the group results:

Extract 14.9: BP Amoco p.l.c. (1998)

Group income statement

For the year ended 31 December	Note	1998	1997
		$ million	
Turnover		**83,732**	108,564
Less: Joint ventures		**15,428**	16,804
Group turnover	1	**68,304**	91,760
Replacement cost of sales		**56,354**	73,928
Production taxes	2	**604**	1,307
Gross profit		**11,346**	16,525
Distribution and administration expenses	3	**6,044**	6,742
Exploration expense		**921**	962
		4,381	8,821
Other income	4	**709**	662
Group replacement cost operating profit	5	**5,090**	9,483
Share of profits of joint ventures	5	**825**	544
Share of profits of associated undertakings	5	**522**	556
Total replacement cost operating profit	5	**6,437**	10,583
Profit (loss) on sale of businesses	6	**395**	127
Profit (loss) on sale of fixed assets	6	**653**	313
Merger expenses	6	**(198)**	–
Refinery network rationalization	6	**–**	71
Replacement cost profit before interest and tax	5	**7,287**	11,094
Stock holding gains (losses)	5	**(1,391)**	(939)
Historical cost profit before interest and tax		**5,896**	10,155
Interest expense	7	**1,053**	908
Profit before taxation		**4,843**	9,247
Taxation	9	**1,520**	3,066
Profit after taxation		**3,323**	6,181
Minority shareholders' interest		**63**	151
Profit for the year		**3,260**	6,030
Distribution to shareholders	10	**4,121**	3,452
Retained profit (deficit) for the year		**(861)**	2,578
Earnings per ordinary share – cents			
Basic	11	**34**	63
Diluted	11	**34**	63

Replacement cost results			
Historical cost profit for the year		**3,260**	6,030
Stock holding (gains) losses		**1,391**	939
Replacement cost profit for the year		**4,651**	6,969
Exceptional items, net of tax	6	**(652)**	(320)
Replacement cost profit before exceptional items		**3,999**	6,649
Earnings per ordinary share – cents			
On replacement cost profit before exceptional items	11	**42**	69

BP Amoco then takes this further by basing the segmental information of its result on a replacement cost basis, as explained in the following accounting policy note:

Extract 14.10: BP Amoco p.l.c. (1998)

Accounting policies
Replacement cost

The results of individual businesses and geographical areas are presented on a replacement cost basis. Replacement cost operating results exclude stock holding gains or losses and reflect the average cost of supplies incurred during the year, and thus provide insight into underlying trading results. Stock holding gains or losses represent the difference between the replacement cost of sales and the historical cost of sales calculated using the first-in first-out method.

Clearly, therefore, BP Amoco provides substantially more replacement cost information than virtually any other major UK company. However, this is perhaps a function of the industry in which BP Amoco operates, since it can be strongly argued that results prepared on a replacement cost basis provide more meaningful data with which to assess the underlying performance of a company in the oil industry.

5.4.1   *Most recent actual purchase price or production cost*

It should be noted that paragraph 27(5) of Schedule 4 permits the use of the most recent actual purchase price or production cost rather than replacement cost if the former appears more appropriate to the directors of the company – although such disclosure is likely to have most relevance in the cases of companies that value their stocks on bases other than FIFO and is, therefore, rarely seen in practice.

5.5   Current cost

Paragraph 31 of Schedule 4 allows stocks to be included at their current cost. However, this treatment is rarely seen in practice, as almost all companies prepare their statutory financial statements under the historical cost convention. In past years, one notable exception to this had always been BG plc which used to prepare its primary accounts under current cost principles, and provide historical cost information on a supplementary basis. The company's auditors used to report on both sets of information, giving a 'true and fair' opinion on the current cost accounts and a 'properly prepared in accordance with the accounting policies' opinion on the supplementary historical cost information.[36]

However, in 1997 the company decided to abandon its current cost reporting regime, explaining why as follows:

Extract 14.11: BG plc (1997)

Notes to the accounts

1   Basis of preparation [extract]

During the year the Directors decided that the Group should change its accounting convention from current cost to modified historical cost. Prior year comparative information has been restated accordingly. Current cost accounting includes adjustments to reflect the impact of price changes on capital structure, stocks and monetary working capital. The Directors consider that the users of the financial statements no longer find this information useful and further, that this change enhances the relevance and comparability of the financial information. The modified historical cost convention is considered to provide an appropriate basis of accounting for the Group, given that it has long life assets, without requiring the price change adjustments described above.

Other companies which are subject to price regulation generally prepare their primary financial statements for shareholders on an historical cost basis, with the regulatory accounts being filed separately and made available on request.

6   STOCKS

6.1   The accounting and disclosure requirements of SSAP 9 (Revised)

6.1.1   Suitable analysis of stocks

Stocks should be stated in financial statements at 'the total of the lower of cost and net realisable value of the separate items of stock or of groups of similar items'.[37] (The constituents of cost are dealt with at 6.2.1 below.)

Stocks should be sub-classified on the face of the balance sheet or in the notes thereto, so as to indicate the amounts held in each of the main categories in the standard balance sheet formats contained in Schedule 4 to the Companies Act 1985.[38] These sub-headings are as follows:

- raw materials and consumables
- work in progress
- finished goods and goods for resale
- payments on account.[39]

In practice, most companies follow these classifications strictly and present stock as a note to the financial statements, as follows:

Extract 14.12: Smiths Industries plc (1998)

Notes to the accounts

	Consolidated		Company	
	1998	1997	**1998**	1997
18 Stocks	**£m**	£m	**£m**	£m
Stocks comprise:				
Raw materials and consumables	**61.4**	46.9	**1.9**	0.6
Work in progress	**61.0**	59.0	**25.2**	26.3
Finished goods	**71.5**	68.6	**9.9**	10.5
	193.9	174.5	**37.0**	37.4
Less: Payments on account	**(6.9)**	(5.3)	**(3.4)**	(2.2)
	187.0	169.2	**33.6**	35.2

The application of these classifications should, however, be done in conjunction with the requirements of Schedule 4, paragraph 3(3), which states that 'in preparing a company's balance sheet or profit and loss account the directors of the company shall adapt the arrangement and headings and sub-headings ... in any case where the special nature of the company's business requires such adaptation'.[40]

It is therefore the responsibility of the directors to ensure that the classifications used are appropriate to the nature of the company's business. Although variations are rarely found in practice, ANS presents an example of a company that has described its stock categories in more detail than is generally the norm:

Extract 14.13: Associated Nursing Services plc (1999)

Notes to the financial statements

13. Stocks and Work in Progress

	The Group		The Company	
	1999	1998	**1999**	1998
	£000's	£000's	**£000's**	£000's
Land for development	**131**	619	**130**	619
Long term contract balances	–	38	–	–
Close Care Units held for sale	**1,853**	1,067	**856**	–
	1,984	1,724	**986**	619

6.1.2   Accounting policies

SSAP 9 requires that the accounting policies that have been applied to stocks should be stated and applied consistently within the business from year to year. In practice, the degree of detail given varies quite considerably, with some policies being comprehensive and informative, and others less so. For example:

Extract 14.14: British Steel plc (1999)

Presentation of accounts and accounting policies
IX   Stocks

Stocks of raw materials are valued at cost or, if they are to be realised without processing, the lower of cost and net realisable value. Cost is determined using the 'first in first out' method. Stocks of partly processed materials, finished products and stores are individually valued at the lower of cost and net realisable value. Cost of partly processed and finished products comprises cost of production including works overheads. Net realisable value is the price at which the stocks can be realised in the normal course of business after allowing for the cost of conversion from their existing state to a finished condition and cost of disposal. Provisions are made to cover slow moving and obsolescent items.

Extract 14.15: Booker plc (1999)

Principal accounting policies
Valuation of stocks

Stocks, stores and work-in-progress are valued at the lower of cost and net realisable value. Cost includes, where appropriate, production and other direct overhead expenses.

Extract 14.16: Carpetright plc (1999)

Principal accounting policies

(d) Stock

Stock is valued at the lower of cost and net realisable value.

Nevertheless, we believe that the accounting policy for stock should at least provide the following level of detail of information (where applicable):

Stocks

> Stocks are stated at the lower of cost and net realisable value. Cost includes all costs incurred in bringing each product to its present location and condition, as follows:

Raw materials, consumables and goods for resale	– purchase cost on a first-in, first-out basis.
Work in progress and finished goods	– cost of direct materials and labour plus attributable overheads based on a normal level of activity.

> Net realisable value is based on estimated selling price less any further costs expected to be incurred to completion and disposal.

6.2   Problem areas

6.2.1   *Constituents of cost*

Both SSAP 9 and the Companies Act 1985 require that stocks should be stated in the balance sheet at the lower of cost and net realisable value. Both SSAP 9 and the Companies Act 1985 also require that the purchase price of stocks shall be determined by adding to the actual purchase price paid any incidental expenses of acquisition, together with both directly and indirectly attributable overheads.[41]

SSAP 9 states that:

'The determination of profit for an accounting year requires the matching of costs with related revenues. ...

'In order to match costs and revenue, 'costs' of stocks should comprise that expenditure which has been incurred in the normal course of business in bringing the product or service to its present location and condition. Such costs will include all related production overheads, even though these may accrue on a time basis.

'The methods used in allocating costs to stocks need to be selected with a view to providing the fairest possible approximation to the expenditure actually incurred in bringing the product to its present location and condition.'[42]

SSAP 9 at paragraph 17 defines cost as being 'that expenditure which has been incurred in the normal course of business in bringing the product or service to its present location and condition'. Paragraph 17 goes on to say that 'this expenditure should include, in addition to cost of purchase, such costs of conversion as are appropriate to that location and condition'. Cost of purchase comprises 'purchase price' and 'any other directly attributable costs', and 'cost of conversion' includes 'other overheads, if any, attributable in the particular circumstances of the business to bringing the product or service to its present location and condition'.[43]

The term 'present location and condition' is not defined or explained in SSAP 9 and is therefore a matter of interpretation and judgement depending on the particular facts and circumstances surrounding the business in question. For example, in the context of a retail company, the particular circumstances of the business are that 'present location and condition' may be interpreted to mean positioned on the stores' shelves and ready for sale – i.e. point of sale. Safeway is an example of a company that adopts this approach:

Extract 14.17: Safeway plc (1999)

Notes to the accounts

1.0 Sales and profit

Cost of sales represents the purchase cost of goods for resale and includes the cost of transfer to the point of sale.

Appendix 1 to SSAP 9 incorporates ten paragraphs that deal with further practical considerations in respect of the allocation of overheads. Paragraph 10 of the Appendix reinforces the point that the allocation of all attributable overheads to the valuation of stock is a mandatory requirement of SSAP 9, and that even the prudence argument cannot be used as a reason for omitting selected overheads from allocation. Paragraph 10 reads as follows:

'The adoption of a conservative approach to the valuation of stocks and long-term contracts has sometimes been used as one of the reasons for omitting selected production overheads. In so far as the circumstances of the business require an element of prudence in determining the amount at which stocks and long-term contracts are stated, this needs to be taken into account in the determination of net realisable value and not by the exclusion from cost of selected overheads.'

This means that overheads should be allocated to the cost of stock on a consistent basis from year to year, and should not be omitted in anticipation of a net realisable value difficulty. Once overheads have been allocated, the carrying value of stock should then be reviewed in order to ensure that it is stated at the lower of cost and net realisable value.

For the most part there are few problems over the inclusion of direct costs in stocks. Problems tend to arise, however, over certain overheads and with regard to the question of how overheads are to be incorporated into stock valuation.

A   Distribution costs

By law, distribution costs may not be included in the cost of stocks (see 5.3 above). However, SSAP 9 defines cost as 'that expenditure which has been incurred in the normal course of business in bringing the product or service to its present location and condition'.[44] As a result, a company which includes in stock the cost of transporting goods from its factory to its warehouse in accordance with the standard may not be complying with the law. In practice, however, the costs of such transport are not likely to be material and the company can take advantage of paragraph 86 of Schedule 4 to the Companies Act 1985 which provides that immaterial amounts may be disregarded for the purposes of any provision of Schedule 4. Where such costs are material it may be necessary for the company to invoke the 'true and fair override'.[45] However, an alternative and perhaps more reasonable view might be that the 'distribution costs' referred to in paragraph 26 of Schedule 4 are costs of distribution to customers, and that therefore the costs of transporting goods to a warehouse would not fall within the meaning of the prohibition.

B   Selling costs

SSAP 9 states that normally only purchase and production costs should be included in the cost of stocks. However, in certain specific circumstances the standard recognises that it might be appropriate to include other types of cost in stock:

'Where firm sales contracts have been entered into for the provision of goods or services to customer's specification, overheads relating to design, and marketing and selling costs incurred before manufacture may be included in arriving at cost.'[46]

Although ordinarily such costs should be expensed in the period in which they are incurred, the matching concept requires that, in the above circumstances, they should be deferred and matched against their related revenues.

IAS 2 specifically cites selling costs as one of the examples of costs which should be excluded from the cost of inventories and recognised as expenses in the period in which they are incurred.[47]

C   Storage costs

Storage costs are not costs which would normally be incurred in bringing a product to its present location and condition. However, where it is necessary to store raw materials or work in progress prior to a further processing or manufacturing stage, the costs of such storage should be included in production overheads. In addition, the costs of storing maturing stocks, such as whisky, should be included in the cost of production.

Storage costs were specifically addressed by the IASC in its revision of IAS 2, which now states that such costs should be excluded from the cost of stocks, unless they are necessary in the production process prior to a further production stage.[48]

D   General/administrative overheads

SSAP 9 makes it clear that the costs of general, as opposed to functional, management are not normally costs of production and should therefore be excluded from the value of stock.[49] However, the standard recognises that in smaller organisations there may not be a clear distinction of management functions and that 'in such organisations the cost of management may fairly be allocated on suitable bases to the functions of production, marketing, selling and administration'.[50] Overheads relating to service departments, such as accounts and personnel departments, should be allocated to the main functions of production, marketing, selling and administration on a basis which reflects the amount of support supplied by the service department to the particular main function. SSAP 9 states that 'problems may also arise in allocating the costs of central service departments, the allocation of which should depend on the function or functions that the department is serving. For example, the accounts department will normally support the following functions:

(a) production – by paying direct and indirect production wages and salaries, by controlling purchases and by preparing periodic financial statements for the production units;

(b) marketing and distribution – by analysing sales and by controlling the sales ledger;

(c) general administration – by preparing management accounts and annual financial statements and budgets, by controlling cash resources and by planning investments.

Only those costs of the accounts department that can be allocated to the production function fall to be included in the cost of conversion.'[51]

IAS 2 adopts a similar approach to that of SSAP 9, stating that costs other than production overheads 'are included in the cost of inventories only to the extent that they are incurred in bringing the inventories to their present location and condition'.[52] Consequently, administrative overheads which are not clearly related to production should be excluded from the cost of stocks.[53]

E   Allocation of overheads

SSAP 9 states that the overheads to be included in stock must be allocated on the basis of a company's normal level of activity.[54] Unfortunately 'normal' is not defined although the standard does give some guidance as to the factors to be considered:

'(a) the volume of production which the production facilities are intended by their designers and by management to produce under the working conditions (e.g. single or double shift) prevailing during the year;

(b) the budgeted level of activity for the year under review and for the ensuing year;

(c) the level of activity achieved both in the year under review and in previous years'.[55]

In practice, a normal level of activity is established by reference to the budgeted or expected level of activity over several years; however, during a start-up period, and until normal operating conditions are reached, the actual level of activity will generally be taken as normal. The reason for this is that it would arguably be unreasonable to expense to the profit and loss account start-up costs which are expected to result in future revenues. It has been suggested that the overhead recovery rate in a start-up period 'should be based on the level of activity which obtains when the plant is working at normal production capacity';[56] but this is unlikely to be done in practice as the first year's results will be depressed through the recognition of non-recurring costs involved in the start-up.

No matter how overheads are being allocated to stock, it is necessary to ensure that only 'normal' costs are being included and that 'abnormal' costs, e.g. excess scrap and the cost of excess facilities, are being expensed as period costs. This occurs automatically as a result of using standard costing, assuming that the standards are regularly reviewed and variances are properly analysed and appropriately dealt with. However, where a standard costing system is not in place, it is necessary for an exercise to be carried out to ensure that no such abnormal costs have been included in closing stock. It is important to bear in mind that this exercise should be carried out on all cost categories, including direct costs.

The overheads to be included based on the normal level of activity should be applied by reference to the most significant direct cost. Thus if a process is particularly capital intensive the overheads should be applied to stock by an overhead recovery rate based on direct machine hours, while if labour costs are more significant the recovery rate should be based on direct labour hours. In practice a recovery rate based on direct labour hours has often been used because, historically speaking, labour has been regarded as the key limiting factor on the level of production.

In computing the costs to be allocated via the overhead recovery rate, costs such as distribution and selling must be excluded, together with cost of storing raw materials and work in progress, unless it is necessary that these latter costs be incurred prior to further processing.

IAS 2 is more specific on this issue and states that the allocation of fixed production overheads should be based on the normal capacity of the production facilities, although the actual level of production may be used if it approximates normal capacity. 'Normal capacity' is defined as being the production expected to be achieved on average over a number of periods or seasons under normal circumstances, taking into account the loss of capacity resulting from planned maintenance. Consequently, the proportion of overhead allocated to a unit of production is not increased as a consequence of low production or idle plant, and overheads which are not allocated are recognised as an expense in the period in which they are incurred. Furthermore, in periods of abnormally high production, the proportion of overhead allocated to a unit of production is decreased so that stocks are not measured above historical cost.[57]

6.2.2 Net realisable value

As already discussed, it is the basic rule of accounting for stocks that they are stated at the lower of their cost and net realisable value. SSAP 9 defines net realisable value as follows:

'*Net realisable value:* the actual or estimated selling price (net of trade but before settlement discounts) less:

(a)   all further costs to completion; and

(b)   all costs to be incurred in marketing, selling and distributing.'[58]

Appendix 1 to SSAP 9 identifies the following situations where net realisable value might be less than cost:

'(a)   an increase in costs or a fall in selling price;

(b)   physical deterioration of stocks;

(c)   obsolescence of products;

(d)   a decision as part of a company's marketing strategy to manufacture and sell products at a loss;

(e)   errors in production or purchasing'.[59]

In addition it points out that when a company has excess stocks on hand the risk of situations (a) to (c) above occurring increases and must be considered in assessing net realisable value. A provision will also be required for losses on commitments made for both the future purchases and sales of stocks.

SSAP 9 requires that the comparison of cost and net realisable value should be done on an item by item basis or by groups of similar items.[60]   In the US, ARB 43 states that 'depending on the character and composition of the inventory, the rule of *cost or market, whichever is lower* may properly be applied either directly to each item or to the total of the inventory (or, in some cases, to the total of the components of each major category). The method should be that which most clearly reflects periodic income.'[61]   The reasoning behind allowing the comparison to be done on an overall basis in certain circumstances, is that 'the reduction of individual items to *market* may not always lead to the most useful result if the utility of the total inventory to the business is not below its cost. This might be the case if selling prices are not affected by temporary or small fluctuations in current costs of purchase or manufacture. Similarly, where more than one major product or operational category exists, the application of the *cost or market, whichever is lower* rule to the total of the items included in such major categories may result in the most useful determination of income.'[62]

This highlights an important difference in approach between the UK and US. Net realisable value, as it would be applied in the UK, depends on the ultimate selling price of a completed product. Thus, a whisky distiller, for example, would not write down his stock of grain because of a fall in the grain price, so long as he expected still to sell the whisky at a profit. However, the US definition of market is partly based on *replacement cost*, so a different result might follow unless stocks are looked at in aggregate.

The following example illustrates the different effects that can be achieved by applying the 'lower of cost and net realisable value' rule to individual items, groups of items and to the total stock:

Example 14.2: Alternative methods of applying the lower of cost and net realisable value rule

	Value of stock at:		Application of rule to:		
	Cost	Net realisable value	Individual items	Major groups	Total stock
	£	£	£	£	£
Group 1					
Item A	2,000	3,000	2,000		
Item B	4,000	2,500	2,500		
Item C	5,000	3,000	3,000		
TOTAL	11,000	8,500	7,500	8,500	
Group 2					
Item D	1,000	1,500	1,000		
Item E	8,000	16,000	8,000		
Item F	10,000	6,000	6,000		
TOTAL	19,000	23,500	15,000	19,000	
TOTAL STOCK	30,000	32,000	22,500	27,500	30,000

The valuation of £30,000 which arises from the application of the rule to the total of stock is not acceptable in the UK, as it results in what are regarded as realised losses being offset against what are regarded as unrealised gains. The valuation of £27,500 which results from the application of the rule to groups of similar items is acceptable, provided the individual items within the groups are sold together – because the stock is effectively being regarded as consisting of two major lines. The valuation of £22,500 is, of course, acceptable as it is the result of the strictest application of the rule.

The comparison of cost and net realisable value of finished goods is normally straightforward where there are established selling prices for the finished goods. Where a provision is required in respect of finished goods, the carrying value of any related raw materials, work in progress and spares must also be reviewed to see if any further provision is required.

Where the selling price of finished goods varies with the price of raw materials and there has been a fall in the price of the raw materials, then some provision may be required in respect of any stock of the finished goods (as well as possibly being required in respect of stocks of the raw materials and any forward purchase contracts).

Often raw materials are bought in order to make different product lines. In these cases it is normally not possible to arrive at a particular net realisable value for each item of raw material based on selling price. Therefore, current replacement cost might be the best guide to net realisable value in such circumstances. If current replacement cost is less than historical cost, however, a provision is only required to be made if the finished goods into which they will be made are expected to be sold at a loss. No provision should be made just because the anticipated profit will be less than normal.

6.2.3   *The valuation of high volumes of similar items of stock*

Practical problems in the valuation of stock arise in the case of businesses which have high volumes of various line items of stock. This situation occurs almost exclusively in the retail trade where similar mark-ups are applied to all stock items or groups of items, and the selling price is marked on each individual item of stock (e.g. in the case of a supermarket). In such a situation, it may be time-consuming to determine the cost of the period-end stock on a more conventional basis; consequently, the most practical method of determining period-end stock may be to record stock on hand at selling prices and then convert it to cost by removing the normal mark-up. Not surprisingly, this method of stock valuation is known as the 'retail method'.

However, a complication in applying the retail method is in determining the margin to be applied to the stock at selling price to convert it back to cost. Since different lines and different departments may have widely different margins, it is normally necessary to subdivide stock and apply the appropriate margins to each subdivision. Furthermore, where stocks have been marked down to below original selling price, adjustments have to be made to eliminate the effect of these markdowns so as to prevent any item of stock being valued at less than both its cost and its net realisable value. In practice, however, companies which use the retail method, tend to apply a gross profit margin computed on an average basis, rather than apply specific mark-up percentages. This practice is, in fact, acknowledged by IAS 2 which states that 'an average percentage for each retail department is often used'.[63]

Marks & Spencer and Safeway both apply the retail method:

Extract 14.18: Marks and Spencer p.l.c. (1999)

Accounting policies

STOCKS

Stocks are valued at the lower of cost and net realisable value using the retail method.

Extract 14.19: Safeway plc (1999)

Notes to the accounts

13.0 Stocks

Stocks are stated at the lower of cost and net realisable value. For stocks at retail stores, cost is calculated by reference to selling price less appropriate trading margins.

There is no significant difference between the balance sheet value and replacement cost of stocks.

It is noteworthy that Appendix 1 to SSAP 9 states that this method 'is acceptable only if it can be demonstrated that the method gives a reasonable approximation to the actual cost'.[64]

6.2.4 *Marking to market*

The practice has developed, principally among commodity dealing companies, of stating stock at market value and also taking into account profits and losses arising on the valuation of forward contracts ('marking to market'). This represents a departure from the statutory valuation rules in that stocks are being stated at more than cost, but this is generally justified as being necessary in order to show a true and fair view. SSAP 9 does not specifically deal with this issue; in fact it is difficult to come to any conclusion other than that the requirement in the standard that stocks should be included at the lower of cost and net realisable value has, in this instance, been dispensed with. Advocates of marking to market would argue, however, that this is a specialised development to which the generality of SSAP 9 should not apply and which was not envisaged when SSAP 9 was being originally developed. Unfortunately, the problem of marking stock at market value was not addressed when SSAP 9 was revised. However, as discussed at 6.3.1 below, there is support for this practice under US GAAP. Interestingly enough, IAS 25 – *Accounting for Investments* – recognises that enterprises might hold marketable commodities as investments (as opposed to inventory).[65] Where this is the case, and the investment is classified as a 'current investment' (i.e., it is readily realisable and is intended to be held for not more than one year), the standard allows the commodity investment to be carried in the balance sheet at market value, with changes in market value being shown in the income statement.[66]

It is our opinion that under UK GAAP, despite the departure from the standard, marking to market is acceptable in certain circumstances. We would suggest that appropriate criteria might be that:

(a) the company's principal activity is the trading of commodities and/or marketable securities;

(b) the nature of the business is such that the commodities traded do not alter significantly in character between purchase and sale;

(c) the commodities are or can be traded on an organised terminal or futures market; and

(d) the market is sufficiently liquid to allow the company to realise its stock and forward contracts at prices close to those used in their valuation.

6.3 Comparison with the US and IASC requirements

6.3.1 US

In the US, accounting for stocks is governed by Chapter 4 of Accounting Research Bulletin No. 43.[67] As with SSAP 9, ARB 43 recognises that the matching concept is the main principle underlying the accounting for stocks. The underlying principles of the bulletin are as follows:

(a) stocks should normally be stated at the lower of cost or market ('market' as used here follows a formula reflecting current replacement cost as well as net realisable value).

Depending on the character of the stock, in certain circumstances the rule of lower of cost or market may be applied to the total of stock (see 6.2.2 above); and

(b) the basis of stating stocks and the cost flow assumption used should be disclosed and should be consistently applied. The assumption made on the flow of costs should be that which most clearly reflects periodic income. As discussed at 3.2.2 above, the LIFO method of costing is permitted – seemingly on the basis of fiscal considerations.

In certain circumstances, principally where there is an organised and liquid market at fixed prices (e.g. precious metals) with little or no selling costs, stocks may be stated at market value, even where this is greater than cost.

6.3.2 IASC

IAS 2, which was revised in December 1993 (effective 1 January 1995), has similar requirements to both SSAP 9 and ARB 43, Chapter 4. The principal rule is that 'inventories should be measured at the lower of cost and net realisable value'.[68]

In January 1989, the IASC issued an exposure draft, E32 – *Comparability of Financial Statements* – which proposed to amend, inter alia, the requirements of IAS 2. The main change proposed in respect of IAS 2 was that the base stock method should no longer be permitted, although LIFO would continue to be an allowed alternative.[69]

However, many commentators on E32 argued that the use of LIFO should not be permitted because:

(a)   fiscal considerations unique to particular countries do not provide an adequate conceptual basis for selecting appropriate accounting treatments; and

(b)   it is inconsistent to retain LIFO in an historical cost context as a partial attempt to account for the effects of changing prices without introducing other changes to provide a more comprehensive method of inflation accounting.[70]

These arguments persuaded the Board of the IASC to revise its proposals with respect to LIFO. Consequently, the IASC's Exposure Draft E38 (which was ultimately converted to the revised version of IAS 2) proposed that FIFO and weighted average cost should be the only formulas permitted.[71]

At its meeting in June 1992, the IASC Board reviewed the comment letters on E38 and agreed the substance of the provisions to be included in the revised IAS on inventories. In general, it was agreed that these should follow the proposals in E38 and, in particular, the Board confirmed that the revised standard should not permit the use of the LIFO and base stock cost formulas.[72] However, despite all this, the IASC Board had a last-minute change of heart and decided to retain LIFO as an 'allowed alternative treatment', although the base stock formula was eliminated as a permitted method.

Consequently, the stated preference or 'benchmark treatment' in the revised IAS 2 is for using either FIFO or weighted average as the assumption on cost flows, with LIFO as the allowed alternative treatment.[73] However, where the LIFO cost formula is used, disclosure must be given of the difference between the amount of the stocks as disclosed in the balance sheet and either (a) the lower of the amount arrived at in accordance with either the FIFO or weighted average methods and net realisable value, or (b) the lower of current cost at the balance sheet date and net realisable value.[74] The only exception to the benchmark and allowed alternative treatments applies in the cases of stocks of items which are not ordinarily interchangeable and goods or services which are produced and segregated for specific projects; in these situations, costs should be assigned on the basis of specific identification.[75]

The remainder of the revised standard describes how to arrive at historical cost and net realisable value as well as the disclosure to be made in financial statements, and follows the principles contained in SSAP 9.

7   LONG-TERM CONTRACTS

7.1   The accounting and disclosure requirements of SSAP 9 (Revised)

As has been discussed in 4.2 above, the need for the ASC's revision in 1988 of SSAP 9 arose principally as a result of the conflict which existed between the original statement and the Companies Act regarding the balance sheet measurement of long-term contract balances. At the same time it was decided to redefine 'long-term contract' so as to remove the problems associated with the arbitrariness of the twelve month rule within the definition in the original standard.

7.1.1   Definition

The original SSAP 9 defined a long-term contract as 'a contract entered into for manufacture or building of a single substantial entity or the provision of a service where the time taken to manufacture, build or provide is such that a substantial proportion of all such contract work will extend for a period exceeding one year'.[76] This definition had an illogical practical result in that two contracts which were identical in all respects except for duration had to be accounted for differently: a 51-week contract had to be treated as short term, whilst a 53-week contract had to be treated as long term. A possible solution to this anomalous situation might have been that if a company was substantially engaged in long-term contracts, then *all* contracts should be accounted for as long term on the percentage of completion basis – even if there were some which lasted for less than a year. Conversely, if a company was substantially engaged in short-term contracts, then *all* contracts should be accounted for as short term on the completed contracts basis – even if some contracts extended for more than a year. However, such an approach would not have been in compliance with the original SSAP 9, and would probably only have been acceptable on grounds of materiality.

SSAP 9 (Revised) removed the arbitrary nature of this one-year rule whilst, at the same time, retaining one year as one criterion which might distinguish a long-term contract. The revised definition is as follows: a *long-term contract* is 'a contract entered into for the design, manufacture or construction of a single substantial asset or the provision of a service (or of a combination of assets or services which together constitute a single project) where the time taken substantially to complete the contract is such that the contract activity falls into different accounting periods. A contract that is required to be accounted for as long-term by this accounting standard will usually extend for a period exceeding one year. However, a duration exceeding one year is not an essential feature of a long-term contract. Some contracts with a shorter duration than one year should be accounted for as long-term contracts if they are sufficiently material to the activity of the period that not to record turnover and attributable profit would lead to a distortion of the period's turnover and results such that the financial statements would not give a true and fair view, provided that the policy is applied consistently within the reporting entity and from year to year.[77]

The practical impact of this revised definition is that short-term contracting businesses will probably be able to account for all their contracts as short term (even if some contracts extend for more than a year), and long-term contracting businesses will be able to account for all their contracts as long term (even if some are for less than a year). However, if a business is clearly in both the short-term and long-term contracting businesses, criteria must be established for distinguishing between such contracts, and appropriate accounting policies must be established and applied consistently.

However, it should be noted that whilst the revised definition of a long-term contract does eliminate the rigid one-year rule, it does create a new area of potential controversy with regard to the accrual of profit on short-term contracts. This is discussed at 7.2.4 below.

7.1.2 Turnover, related costs and attributable profit

Long-term contracts should be:

(a)   assessed on a contract by contract basis; and

(b)   reflected in the profit and loss account by recording turnover and related costs as contract activity progresses.[78]

The standard fails to lay down a method for determining turnover and merely states that 'turnover is ascertained in a manner appropriate to the stage of completion of the contract, the business and the industry in which it operates'.[79] SSAP 9 then states that 'where it is considered that the outcome of a long-term contract can be assessed with reasonable certainty before its conclusion, the prudently calculated attributable profit should be recognised in the profit and loss account as the difference between the reported turnover and related costs for that contract'.[80] Based on this requirement, it would appear that the attributable profit is merely the balancing figure once 'turnover' and 'related costs' have been determined. One would therefore have expected SSAP 9 to define 'related costs' and require companies to disclose an accounting policy for the determination of 'related costs'. Instead it defines 'attributable profit' and requires an accounting policy which sets out how it has been ascertained. As a result, either turnover or related costs will be the balancing figure.

'Attributable profit' is defined as 'that part of the total profit currently estimated to arise over the duration of the contract, after allowing for estimated remedial and maintenance costs and increases in costs so far as not recoverable under the terms of the contract, that fairly reflects the profit attributable to that part of the work performed at the accounting date. (There can be no attributable profit until the profitable outcome of the contract can be assessed with reasonable certainty.)'[81]

This definition, however, raises the question as to whether or not a company is required to book a loss in the early years of an overall profitable contract merely because the high cost work of the contract is being carried out in the earlier years. In our view, this was clearly not the intention of SSAP 9 – provided that the overall profitability of the contract can be assessed with reasonable certainty.

See 7.2 below for further discussion of the problems associated with determining profit and turnover.

7.1.3   Accounting policies

SSAP 9 requires that companies must disclose their accounting policies in respect of long-term contracts; in particular the method of ascertaining both turnover and attributable profit. These policies must be applied consistently within the business and from year to year.[82]

Current reporting practice reflects a wide variety in the amount of detail given by companies in their accounting policies for turnover and profit recognition. BICC discloses fairly comprehensive policies:

Extract 14.20: BICC plc (1998)

Principal accounting policies

4   Turnover

Turnover represents amounts invoiced to outside customers, except in respect of contracting activities where turnover represents the value of work carried out during the year including amounts not invoiced. Turnover is recognised on property developments when they are subject to substantially unconditional contracts for sale. Turnover excludes value added and similar sales-based taxes.

5   Profit recognition on contracting activities

Profit on individual contracts is taken only when their outcome can be foreseen with reasonable certainty, based on the lower of the percentage margin earned to date and that prudently forecast at completion, taking account of agreed claims. Full provision is made for all known or expected losses on individual contracts, taking a prudent view of future claims income, immediately such losses are foreseen. Profit for the year includes the benefit of claims settled on contracts completed in prior years.

7.1.4 The financial statement presentation of long-term contracts

In order to solve the conflict between the original SSAP 9 and the Companies Act, the revised standard requires that long-term contracts should be disclosed in the financial statements as follows:

'(a) the amount by which recorded turnover is in excess of payments on account should be classified as "amounts recoverable on contracts" and separately disclosed within debtors;

(b) the balance of payments on account (in excess of amounts (i) matched with turnover; and (ii) offset against long-term contract balances) should be classified as payments on account and separately disclosed within creditors;

(c) the amount of long-term contracts, at costs incurred, net of amounts transferred to cost of sales, after deducting foreseeable losses and payments on account not matched with turnover, should be classified as "long-term contract balances" and separately disclosed within the balance sheet heading "Stocks". The balance sheet note should disclose separately the balances of:

   (i) net cost less foreseeable losses; and

   (ii) applicable payments on account;

(d) the amount by which the provision or accrual for foreseeable losses exceeds the costs incurred (after transfers to cost of sales) should be included within either provisions for liabilities and charges or creditors as appropriate.'[83]

The 'amounts recoverable on contracts' represent the excess of the value of work carried out to the balance sheet date (which has been recorded as turnover) over cumulative payments on account. 'The amount and realisability of the balance therefore depend on the value of work carried out being ascertained appropriately. The balance arises as a derivative of this process of contract revenue recognition and is directly linked to turnover. In substance, it represents accrued revenue receivable and has the attributes of a debtor.'[84]

SSAP 9 defines 'foreseeable losses' as 'losses which are currently estimated to arise over the duration of the contract'.[85] This means that all future losses must be provided for in full as soon as they are know about, even though profits are taken over the duration of the contract. SSAP 9 is unclear as to what the circumstances are under which it would be appropriate to classify the provision or accrual for foreseeable losses within creditors, and it is our view that, under normal circumstances, these amounts should be included in the balance sheet within provisions for liabilities and charges.

7.1.5 Illustrative examples of the disclosure of long-term contracts

The following example is based on Appendix 3 to SSAP 9, and serves to illustrate the financial statement disclosure requirements of SSAP 9 as they apply to the various circumstances which might arise in respect of long-term contracts.

Example 14.3: Application of the principles of SSAP 9 to long-term contracts

The following assumptions apply to each of the contracts, and in each case the company's summarised profit and loss account for the year ended 31 October 2000 and a balance sheet as at that date is illustrated:

(1)   This is the first year of the contract.

(2)   The company has only one contract.

(3)   All payments on account have actually been received in the form of cash.

(4)   All costs incurred have been paid in cash.

(5)   All the information is as at the balance sheet date, 31 October 2000.

(6)   Share capital is minimal and is ignored.

(7)   Any necessary finance is provided by bank overdraft.

Contract 1

	£'000
Turnover	145
Cost of sales	110
Payments on account	100
Costs incurred	110

Financial statement presentation of Contract 1 (SSAP 9, para. 30):

SUMMARISED PROFIT AND LOSS ACCOUNT for the year ended 31 October 2000

	£'000
Turnover	145
Cost of sales	110
Gross profit on long-term contracts	35

SUMMARISED BALANCE SHEET as at 31 October 2000

	£'000
Current assets	
Debtors	
Amounts recoverable on contracts [145 - 100]	45
Current liabilities	
Overdraft	10
Net current assets	35
Profit and loss account	35

Contract 2

	£'000
Turnover	520
Cost of sales	450
Payments on account	600
Costs incurred	510

Financial statement presentation of Contract 2 (SSAP 9, para. 30):

SUMMARISED PROFIT AND LOSS ACCOUNT for the year ended 31 October 2000

	£'000
Turnover	520
Cost of sales	450
Gross profit on long-term contracts	70

SUMMARISED BALANCE SHEET as at 31 October 2000

	£'000
Current assets	
Stocks (Note 1)	–
Cash	90
	90
Current liabilities	
Payments on account [600 - 520 - 60]	20
Net current assets	70
Profit and loss account	70

Note 1
Long-term contract balances

	£'000
Net cost [510 - 450]	60
less: payments on account	(60)
	–

Contract 3

	£'000
Turnover	380
Cost of sales	350
Payments on account	400
Costs incurred	450

Financial statement presentation of Contract 3 (SSAP 9, para. 30):

SUMMARISED PROFIT AND LOSS ACCOUNT for the year ended 31 October 2000

	£'000
Turnover	380
Cost of sales	350
Gross profit on long-term contracts	30

SUMMARISED BALANCE SHEET as at 31 October 2000

Current assets	
Stocks	
Long-term contract balances (Note 1)	80
Current liabilities	
Overdraft	50
	30
Profit and loss account	30

Note 1
Long-term contract balances

Net cost [450 - 350]	100
less: payments on account [400 - 380]	20
	80

Contract 4

	£'000	
Turnover	200	
Cost of sales	250	
Payments on account	150	
Costs incurred	250	
Provision for foreseeable losses	40	(not included in cost of sales above)

Financial statement presentation of Contract 4 (SSAP 9, para. 30):

SUMMARISED PROFIT AND LOSS ACCOUNT for the year ended 31 October 2000

	£'000
Turnover	200
Cost of sales [250 + 40]	290
Gross (loss) on long-term contracts	(90)

SUMMARISED BALANCE SHEET as at 31 October 2000

Current assets	
Debtors	
Amounts recoverable on contracts [200 - 150]	50
Current liabilities	
Overdraft	100
Net current (liabilities)	(50)
Provisions for liabilities and charges	
Provision for foreseeable losses on contracts	(40)
	(90)
Profit and loss account	(90)

(Note that the provision for foreseeable losses of 40 is not offset against the debit balance of 50 included in debtors.)

Contract 5

	£'000	
Turnover	55	
Cost of sales	55	
Payments on account	80	
Costs incurred	100	
Provision for foreseeable losses	30	(not included in cost of sales above)

Financial statement presentation of Contract 5 (SSAP 9, para. 30):

SUMMARISED PROFIT AND LOSS ACCOUNT for the year ended 31 October 2000

	£'000
Turnover	55
Cost of sales [55 + 30]	85
Gross (loss) on long-term contracts	(30)

SUMMARISED BALANCE SHEET as at 31 October 2000

Current assets	
Stocks	
Long-term contract balances (Note 1)	–
Current liabilities	
Overdraft	20
Payments on account [80 - 55 - 15]	10
Net current (liabilities)	(30)
Profit and loss account	(30)

Note 1
Long-term contract balances

Net cost (after deducting foreseeable losses) [100 - 55 - 30]	15
less: payments on account	(15)
	–

7.2 Problem areas

7.2.1 *How much profit?*

Although SSAP 9 requires the accrual of attributable profit into long-term contract balances, it does not give adequate guidance on how the amount is actually to be computed. The following example illustrates difficulties which may arise under certain circumstances:

Example 14.4: Calculation of attributable profit

Halfway through its 2001 financial year a company starts work on a contract that will last for 24 months. The total sales value is £1,200 and this is to be invoiced in total on completion of the contract. The total expected costs are £600 and these will be incurred evenly throughout the contract. Everything goes according to plan for the rest of the financial year. During the following financial year, 2002, the company runs into problems on this contract and incurs additional costs of £100 which will not be recovered from the customer. At the end of that year the company is reasonably certain that costs to complete will still be the planned £150. Future experience bears this out.

Using the definition of attributable profit in paragraph 23 of SSAP 9, the profit taken could be calculated as follows:

	2001 £	2002 £	2003 £
Total expected profit on contract	600	500	500
Percentage of contract completed	25%	75%	100%
∴ total profit to be attributed	150	375	500
Less: profit already taken	–	150	375
Attributable profit for the period	150	225	125

Some might hold the view that the above does not reflect the results of 2002 and 2003 fairly, however, as it effectively defers inefficiencies of 2002 into 2003. The additional costs in 2002 are an unfortunate incident occurring in that year which, while impacting on the overall profitability of the contract, do not affect the costs to complete at the end of that year and should consequently be expensed in 2002. A fairer allocation of profits might be as follows:

	2001 £	2002 £	2003 £
Turnover (being sales value of work done)	300	600	300
Cost of sales	150	*400	150
Attributable profit	150	200	150

* Comprises anticipated cost of sales of £300 and the additional costs of £100.

Paragraph 9 of SSAP 9 states that 'any known inequalities of profitability in the various stages of a contract' should be taken into account in calculating the attributable profit. It then goes on to confirm the latter treatment illustrated in the above example, by detailing the procedures which should be followed in order to take the inequalities into account. The procedures are 'to include an appropriate proportion of total contract value as turnover in the profit and loss account as the contract activity progresses. The costs incurred in reaching that stage of completion are matched with this turnover, resulting in the reporting of results that can be attributed to the proportion of work completed.'[86] As the above example shows, it is in fact desirable that such inequalities be taken into account, as otherwise there may not be a proper matching of costs and revenues.

In the above example the inequality was an inefficiency which had to be taken into account by being written off as a period expense. Some inequalities have to be taken into account in a different way, however. For example, where a contract is split into various stages with each stage having a separate price established, it may be necessary to allocate the total contract price over all the stages so as to reflect the 'real' profit on each stage. Obviously, where each stage's price reflects the relative value of that particular stage, this is not a problem and no adjustment is required; however, where there has been a payment in advance (or 'front-end loading') some adjustment will be necessary or profit will be taken in advance and not over the duration of the contract as it is earned.

7.2.2   How much turnover?

SSAP 9 states that it deliberately does not define turnover because of the different methods used in practice to determine it.[87] It does require, however, that the means by which turnover is ascertained be disclosed. Although there are a wide variety of methods used, whichever is selected the amount should represent an appropriate proportion of total contract value.[88] The following example illustrates some of the more common methods of computing turnover:

Example 14.5: Determination of turnover

A company is engaged in a long-term contract with an expected sales value of £10,000. It is the end of the accounting period during which the company commenced work on this contract and it needs to compute the amount of turnover to be reflected in the profit and loss account for this contract.

Scenario (i)   An independent surveyor has certified that at the period-end the contract is 55% complete and that the company is entitled to apply for cumulative progress payments of £5,225 (after a 5% retention). In this case the company would record turnover of £5,500 being the sales value of the work done. (If it is anticipated that rectification work will have to be carried out to secure the release of the retention money then this should be taken into account in computing the attributable profit – it should have no bearing on the amount of turnover to be recorded.)

Scenario (ii)   No valuation has been done by an independent surveyor as it is not required under the terms of the contract. The company's best estimate is that the contract is 60% complete. There is no real difference here from the first scenario. The value of the work done and, therefore, the turnover to be recognised is £6,000.

Scenario (iii) The company has incurred and applied costs of £4,000. £3,000 is the best estimate of costs to complete. The company should therefore recognise turnover of £5,714, being the appropriate proportion of total contract value, and computed thus:

$$\frac{4,000}{7,000} \ \times \ 10,000 \ = \ 5,714$$

If the costs incurred to date included, say, £500 in respect of unapplied raw materials, then the turnover to be recognised falls to £5,000 being:

$$\frac{\text{costs incurred and applied}}{\text{total costs}} \qquad \frac{(4,000-500)}{7,000} \ \times \ 10,000 \ = \ 5,000$$

There are, however, other ways than cost of measuring work done, e.g. labour hours. The use of cost will tend to lead to an overstatement of progress (because materials are usually acquired up front), and the use of labour hours might lead to a more realistic basis for computing turnover.

Note that in each of the above scenarios the computation of the amount of turnover is quite independent of the question of how much (if any) profit should be taken. This is as it should be, because even if a contract is loss-making the sales price will be earned and this should be reflected by recording turnover. In the final analysis, any loss arises because costs are greater than revenue, and costs should be reflected through cost of sales. In view of the different results that can arise from the use of different methods, the importance of disclosing the particular method used is highlighted.

The above example applies only to fixed-price contracts. Where a contract is on a cost-plus basis, it is necessary to examine the costs incurred to ensure they are of the type and size envisaged in the terms of the contract. Only once this is done and the recoverable costs identified can the figure be grossed up to arrive at the appropriate turnover figure.

7.2.3   *Approved variations and claims*

Appendix 1 to SSAP 9 states that 'where approved variations have been made to a contract in the course of it and the amount to be received in respect of these variations has not yet been settled and is likely to be a material factor in the outcome, it is necessary to make a conservative estimate of the amount likely to be received and this is then treated as part of the total sales value. On the other hand, allowance needs to be made for foreseen claims or penalties payable arising out of delays in completion or from other causes.'[89]

Due to the extended periods over which contracts are carried out and sometimes to the circumstances prevailing when the work is being done or due to be done, it is quite normal for a contractor to submit claims for additional sums to a customer. Such claims arise 'from circumstances not envisaged in the contract' or 'as an indirect consequence of approved variations'[90] and their outcome can be crucial in determining whether the related contract will be profitable. Because their settlement is by negotiation (which can in practice be very protracted), they are subject to a very high level of uncertainty; consequently, no credit should be taken for them until they have been agreed at least in principle. In the absence of an agreed sum, the amount to be accrued should be prudently assessed.

In practice, few companies give any indication as to how variations and claims are dealt with in their accounts; however, those companies which do deal with this matter in their accounting policies generally state that revenues derived from claims and variations on contracts are recognised only when they have been either received in cash or certified for payment.

7.2.4   Should profits be accrued on short-term contracts?

In discussing the revised definition of a long-term contract at 7.1.1 above, it was mentioned that the new definition creates a new area of potential controversy concerning the accrual of profit on short-term contracts. This arises as a result of the last sentence of the definition, which states that 'some contracts with a shorter duration than one year should be accounted for as long-term contracts if they are sufficiently material to the activity of the period that not to record turnover and attributable profit would lead to a distortion of the period's turnover and results such that the financial statements would not give a true and fair view, provided that the policy is applied consistently within the reporting entity and from year to year'.[91]

The implication of this requirement is that even if a company is purely involved in short-term contracting work and has adopted the completed contract method, if it has a material amount of uncompleted short-term contracts at the year-end, they should be accounted for as long-term contracts – i.e. turnover should be recorded and profit accrued. Since many contracting companies are likely to be in this position, it seems that, on the face of it, most short-term contracts will have to be accounted for as long term – irrespective of the accounting policy adopted. Our view, however, is that this could hardly have been the standard's intention. Consequently, we believe that the crucial factor in applying this definition is to ensure that whatever policy is applied, it is used on a consistent basis. If contracts with a shorter duration than one year are accounted for as long-term contracts, this should be a stated accounting policy, and not applied only when it is expedient to do so.

7.2.5   *Inclusion of interest*

Paragraph 26(3)(b) of Schedule 4 to the Companies Act 1985 states that 'there may be included in the production cost of an asset interest on capital borrowed to finance the production of that asset, to the extent that it accrues in respect of the period of production'.[92] Appendix 1 to SSAP 9 deals with this issue in the context of long-term contracts, and states that 'in ascertaining costs of long-term contracts it is not normally appropriate to include interest payable on borrowed money. However, in circumstances where sums borrowed can be identified as financing specific long-term contracts, it may be appropriate to include such related interest in cost, in which circumstances the inclusion of interest and the amount of interest so included should be disclosed in a note to the financial statements.'[93]

It is our view that, provided that all the criteria for capitalisation of interest costs are met (e.g. qualifying assets, period of production, etc.), it is perfectly acceptable to do so. This is, in fact, the position adopted by IAS 11, which states that costs that may be attributable to contract activity in general and can be allocated to specific contracts also include borrowing costs when the contractor adopts the allowed alternative treatment in IAS 23.[94] (See Chapter 13 for a detailed discussion of the circumstances under which interest may be capitalised.)

7.3   Comparison with the US and IASC requirements

7.3.1   *US*

In the US, accounting for contracting activity is governed by Accounting Research Bulletin No. 45 – *Long-Term Construction-Type Contracts* – issued in 1955. ARB 45 allows both the percentage of completion and the completed contract methods of accounting for long-term contracts, although it expresses a preference for the former 'when estimates of costs to complete and extent of progress toward completion of long-term contracts are reasonably dependable'.[95] It is emphasised under both methods that full provision must be made for anticipated losses.

7.3.2   *IASC*

The 1993 revision of IAS 11 – *Construction Contracts* – saw the removal of the completed contract method as an allowed method of accounting for construction contracts. IAS 11 now requires that when the outcome of a construction contract can be reliably estimated, revenue and expenses associated with the construction contract should be recognised by reference to the stage of completion of the contract activity at the balance sheet date.[96]

The stage of completion of a contract may be determined in a variety of ways, including: the proportion that contract costs incurred for work performed to date bear to the estimated total contract costs; surveys of work performed; or completion of a physical proportion of the contract work.[97] However, IAS 11 states that when the stage of completion is determined by reference to the contract costs incurred to date, only those contract costs that reflect work performed are included in costs incurred to date. Examples of contract costs which are excluded are: contract costs that relate to future activity on the contract, such as costs of materials that have been delivered to a contract site or set aside for use in a contract but not yet installed, used or applied during contract performance, unless the materials have been made specially for the contract; and payments made to subcontractors in advance of work performed under the subcontract.[98]

In the case of a fixed price contract, the outcome of a construction contract can be estimated reliably when all the following conditions are satisfied:

(a)   total contract revenue can be measured reliably;

(b)   it is probable that the economic benefits associated with the contract will flow to the enterprise;

(c)   both the contract costs to complete the contract and the stage of contract completion at the balance sheet date can be measured reliably; and

(d)   the contract costs attributable to the contract can be clearly identified and measured reliably so that actual contract costs incurred can be compared with prior estimates.[99]

In the case of a cost plus contract, the outcome of a construction contract can be estimated reliably when the following conditions are satisfied:

(a)   it is probable that the economic benefits associated with the contract will flow to the enterprise; and

(b)   the contract costs attributable to the contract, whether or not specifically reimbursable, can be clearly identified and measured reliably.[100]

When the outcome of a construction contract cannot be measured reliably, revenue should be recognised only to the extent of recoverable costs incurred and costs should be recognised as an expense in the period when incurred.[101] In both instances, when it is probable that total contract costs will exceed total contract revenue, the expected loss should be recognised as an expense immediately.[102] The amount of the loss is determined irrespective of whether or not work has commenced on the contract, the stage of completion of the contract, or the amount of profits expected to arise on other contracts which are not treated as a single construction contract.[103]

The revised IAS 11 also introduced the following new disclosures to be given by enterprises in respect of construction contracts:

(a)   the amount of contract revenue recognised as revenue in the period;

(b)   the methods used to determine the contract revenue recognised in the period; and

(c)   the methods used to determine the stage of completion of contracts in progress.[104]

In the case of contracts in progress at the balance sheet date, an enterprise should disclose each of the following:

(a)   the aggregate amount of costs incurred and recognised profits (less recognised losses) to date;

(b)   the amount of advances received; and

(c)   the amount of retentions.[105]

In addition, an enterprise should present:

(a)   the gross amount due from customers for contract work as an asset for all contracts in progress for which costs incurred plus recognised profits (less recognised losses) exceed progress billings (i.e. the net amount of costs incurred plus recognised profits, less the sum of recognised losses and progress billings); and

(b)   the gross amount due to customers for contract work as a liability for all contracts in progress for which progress billings exceed costs incurred plus recognised profits (i.e. the net amount of costs incurred plus recognised profits, less the sum of recognised losses and progress billings).[106]

8   CONCLUSION

This is one area of financial reporting that remains fairly uncontroversial both in the UK and internationally, particularly since the IASC removed the completed contract method as an allowed method of accounting for construction contracts.

Perhaps the only remaining area of contention is the continued recognition by certain standard setters (including the FASB and IASC) of LIFO as an acceptable method for the valuation of stock. – seemingly on the basis of fiscal considerations. Nevertheless, in our view, the fiscal considerations of particular countries do not provide an adequate conceptual basis for selecting appropriate accounting treatments.

One question that will inevitably be asked sooner or later is whether the gradual move towards a system of accounting that recognises in the balance sheet an ever-broadening range of assets and liabilities at their fair values will ultimately see the measurement of stocks at fair value as well? Given the ASB's abandonment of the realisation principle and its stated ambition to report realised and unrealised profits alongside each other in the income statement,[107] this may not be as far off as many would believe.

References

1   SSAP 9, *Stocks and long-term contracts*, Revised September 1988, para. 16.
2   Accounting Research Bulletin No. 43, AICPA, June 1953, Chapter 4, *Inventory Pricing*, Statement 1.
3   IAS 2, *Inventories*, IASC, Revised 1993, paras. 4 and 16.
4   SSAP 9, para. 22.
5   See, for example, SSAP 9, para. 1; ARB 43, Chapter 4, Statement 2; and Eldon S. Hendriksen, *Accounting Theory*, p. 299.
6   SSAP 9, para. 3.
7   The term 'stocks' as used in this Chapter, includes 'manufacturing work-in-progress'.
8   This basic rule is entrenched in the UK, US and IASC pronouncements on stock: SSAP 9, para. 26; ARB 43, Chapter 4, Statement 5; IAS 2, para. 6.
9   SSAP 9, para. 17.
10 *Ibid.*
11 *Ibid.*, para. 18.
12 *Ibid.*, para. 19.
13 *Ibid.*, para. 3.
14 IAS 2, para. 7.
15 *Ibid.*, para 10.
16 ARB 43, Chapter 4, Statement 3.
17 SSAP 9, para. 4.
18 Accountants Digest No. 158, *A Guide to Accounting Standards — Valuation of Stocks and Work in Progress*, Summer 1984, p. 7.
19 SSAP 9, Appendix 1, para. 12.
20 CA 85, Sch. 4, para. 27(2)(b).
21 *Ibid.*, Sch. 4, para. 27(3). This requirement does not apply if stocks are valued at actual cost.
22 SSAP 16, *Current cost accounting*. This statement was withdrawn in April 1988.
23 IAS 2, para. 21.
24 *Ibid.*, para. 23.
25 CA 85, Sch. 4, para. 25.
26 SSAP 9, Appendix 1, para. 12.
27 CA 85, Sch. 4, para. 25(2).
28 SSAP 9 (Original), *Stocks and work in progress*, May 1975.
29 *Ibid.*, para. 1.
30 *Ibid.*, para. 3.
31 *Ibid.*, Appendix 1, para. 10.
32 *Ibid.*, para. 22.
33 *Ibid.*, para. 27.
34 *Ibid.*
35 CA 85, Sch. 4, para. 15.
36 BG plc, Annual Report and Accounts 1996, p. 36.
37 SSAP 9, para. 26.
38 *Ibid.*, para. 27.
39 *Ibid.*; CA 85, Sch. 4, Balance Sheet Formats.
40 *Ibid.*, para. 3(3).
41 CA 85, Sch. 4, para. 26; SSAP 9, paras. 17 to 19.
42 SSAP 9, paras. 1, 3 and 4.
43 *Ibid.*, paras. 18 and 19(c).
44 *Ibid.*, para. 17.
45 See CA 85, Sch. 4, para. 15. The company's directors will have to explain in the financial statements that their policy represents a departure from the statutory valuation rules, but has been applied in order to comply with SSAP 9 and is necessary to give a true and fair view. The full particulars and effects of the departure will also have to be given.
46 SSAP 9, Appendix 1, para. 2.
47 IAS 2, para. 14.
48 *Ibid.*, para. 14.
49 SSAP 9, Appendix 1, para. 5.

50 *Ibid.*, para. 6.
51 *Ibid.*, para. 7.
52 IAS 2, para. 13.
53 *Ibid.*, para. 14(c).
54 SSAP 9, Appendix 1, para. 8.
55 *Ibid.*
56 Accountants Digest No. 158, p. 12.
57 IAS 2, para. 11.
58 SSAP 9, para. 21.
59 *Ibid.*, Appendix 1, para. 20.
60 *Ibid.*, para. 26.
61 ARB 43, Chapter 4, Statement 7.
62 *Ibid.*, para. 11.
63 IAS 2, para. 18.
64 SSAP 9, Appendix 1, para. 14.
65 IAS 25, *Accounting for Investments*, IASC, 1994, para. 6.
66 *Ibid.*, para. 31.
67 ARB 43, Chapter 4, *Inventory Pricing*.
68 IAS 2, para. 6.
69 E32, *Comparability of Financial Statements*, IASC, January 1989, para. 29.
70 IASC, *Insight*, October 1991, p. 9.
71 E38, para. 19.
72 IASC, *Update*, June 1992.
73 IAS 2, paras. 21–24.
74 *Ibid.*, para. 36.
75 *Ibid.*, paras. 19 and 20.
76 SSAP 9 (Original), para. 22.
77 SSAP 9, para. 22.
78 *Ibid.*, para. 28.
79 *Ibid.*
80 *Ibid.*, para. 29.
81 *Ibid.*, para. 23.
82 *Ibid.*, para. 32.
83 *Ibid.*, para. 30.
84 *Ibid.*, Appendix 3, para. 5.
85 *Ibid.*, para. 24.
86 SSAP 9, para. 9.
87 *Ibid.*, Appendix 1, para. 23.
88 *Ibid.*, para. 9.
89 *Ibid.*, Appendix 1, para. 26.
90 *Ibid.*, Appendix 1, para. 27.
91 *Ibid.*, para. 22.
92 CA 85, Sch. 4, para. 26(3)(b).
93 SSAP 9, Appendix 1, para. 21.
94 IAS 11, para. 18.
95 Accounting Research Bulletin No. 45, *Long-Term Construction-Type Contracts*, AICPA, October 1955, para. 15.
96 IAS 11, *Construction Contracts*, IASC, Revised 1993, para. 22.
97 *Ibid.*, para. 30.
98 *Ibid.*, para. 31.
99 *Ibid.*, para. 23.
100 *Ibid.*, para. 24.
101 *Ibid.*, para. 32.
102 *Ibid.*, para. 36.
103 *Ibid.*, para. 37.
104 *Ibid.*, para. 39.

105   *Ibid.*, para. 40.
106   *Ibid.*, paras. 42 to 44.
107   Revised Draft Statement of Principles, *Technical Supplement*, ASB March 1999, para. B5.4.

Chapter 15   Capital instruments

1   INTRODUCTION

The accounting treatment of capital instruments – shares and debt securities – by their issuer was not historically regarded as presenting significant problems in the UK. However, the substantial development of innovative forms of finance during the 1980s made the accounting profession ask whether the conventional framework for distinguishing share and loan capital, together with the Companies Act disclosure requirements, remained adequate. With the further development of financial derivatives in recent years this aspect of financial reporting has become increasingly complex.

The traditional distinction between shares and debt is clear. The issue of shares creates an ownership interest in a company, remunerated by dividends, which are accounted for as a distribution of profits, not a charge made in arriving at it. Loan finance, on the other hand, is remunerated by interest, which is charged in the profit and loss account as an expense. In general, lenders will rank before shareholders in priority of claims over the assets of the company, although in practice there may also be differential rights between different categories of lenders and classes of shareholders. The two forms of finance also have different tax implications, both for the investor and the investee.

In economic terms, however, the distinction between share and loan capital can be less clear-cut than the legal categorisation would suggest. For example, a redeemable preference share could be considered to be, in substance, much more like debt than equity, while on the other hand many would argue that a bond which will be converted into ordinary shares deserves to be thought of as being more in the nature of equity than of debt, even before conversion has occurred.

The fact that instruments which are otherwise similar in substance can have different tax and accounting consequences, because of their form, has encouraged the development of a number of complex forms of finance which exhibit characteristics of both equity and debt. The accounting profession has not always found it easy to decide how to balance competing considerations of substance and form in accounting for these instruments, especially since the fundamental distinction between debt and equity is rooted in form to begin with.

Many of these questions have been answered by FRS 4 – *Accounting for Capital Instruments* – which was issued in December 1993. This standard lays down a framework for distinguishing between shares and debt, and also between sub-categories of each. In addition, it prescribes how these instruments and their associated finance costs are to be measured, and lays down detailed requirements for the disclosure of their terms. This chapter analyses the standard and explains how it is applied in practice.

As explained in Chapter 9, the ASB has embarked upon a more fundamental re-examination of this subject under the umbrella of its financial instruments project (which looks at assets as well as liabilities). In addition, the Board has adopted a separate project on accounting for equity, which will reconsider where to draw the dividing line between liabilities and equity interests. These may eventually transform the whole approach to accounting for share and loan capital, but any such changes lie some way ahead. This chapter refers to some of these longer-term proposals in passing, but otherwise confines itself to the accounting rules for capital instruments as they stand at present.

2   FRS 4

2.1   The development of FRS 4

2.1.1   TR 677

In 1987 the Technical Committee of the ICAEW published TR 677 – *Accounting for complex capital issues*. This Technical Release carried no mandatory status, but was issued as a discussion paper on which comment was invited. It was not subsequently developed into any more authoritative statement and has now been superseded by FRS 4.

TR 677 was a relatively brief document and, despite its title, dealt with relatively simple forms of financing instrument and discussed them only superficially. It put forward the following 'general principles':

(a)   When equity or loan capital is raised the amount of capital shown in the balance sheet should increase by the net proceeds of this issue after deducting proper expenditure incurred with third parties in the course of the issue. Such expenditure incurred may be allowed to be written off to share premium account.

(b)   Where the cost of repaying loan capital is greater than the proceeds of the issue the difference should be charged through the profit and loss account by instalments, calculated on an appropriate basis, over the period from the date of issue to the date of repayment.

(c)   Unless there are good economic reasons for taking another approach, the total charge to the profit and loss account in any year should be based on the effective annual rate throughout the whole period of the loan. Where the date or the amount of the repayment is uncertain, the amount of the charge in the profit and loss account should be related to best estimates available each time financial statements are prepared.

(d)   Cash proceeds received on the issue of options to subscribe for the company's own shares should be treated as capital.

(e)   Where a transaction has a number of constituent parts the accounting treatment of each should be considered separately, but having regard to the true commercial effect of the transaction taken as a whole.

(f)   The financial statements should disclose sufficient information about a complex capital issue for a reader to appreciate its nature and impact. In particular, where instruments, or parts of instruments, representing complex capital issues are quoted in the market, disclosure of market value at each balance sheet date may be useful.

An Appendix to the Technical Release discussed how these principles should be applied to various instruments.

2.1.2   UITF 1

The UITF published its first Abstract in July 1991.[1] This dealt with a relatively narrow topic: the accounting treatment of 'supplemental interest' on a convertible bond. Where a convertible bond was issued on terms which entitled the holder to receive an additional amount of backdated interest if he redeemed the bond, the UITF ruled that this supplemental interest had to be accrued from the outset. This outlawed the practice of ignoring the supplemental interest on the argument that conversion was likely to occur and hence that the supplemental interest would not become payable. The requirement was subsequently incorporated in FRS 4 and UITF 1 has been withdrawn.

2.1.3   The ASB Discussion Paper

In December 1991, the ASB published a Discussion Paper on capital instruments as the forerunner of the exposure draft of an accounting standard.[2] The paper addressed a wide range of issues, including the distinction between debt and equity and the measurement principles governing each category, together with their classification and disclosure in the balance sheet and profit and loss account.

2.1.4   FRED 3

A year later, in December 1992, the Board published the exposure draft of a standard on capital instruments, FRED 3.[3] This was based on the main proposals which had been set out in the earlier Discussion Paper, redrawn in the form of a draft standard, and it was subsequently converted into FRS 4 without substantial amendment.

There was a subsequent consultation on one additional matter: the appropriate accounting treatment when debt is renegotiated. Companies in financial difficulties sometimes reach an agreement with their lenders which allows them to reduce or defer their future payments of principal or interest under the debt. In these circumstances, the ASB proposed that the renegotiated debt should be stated at its fair value (based on discounting the rescheduled payments to their net present value) with a corresponding gain being recognised in the profit and loss account.[4] However, commentators criticised this proposal on the grounds that it was imprudent; in particular they noted that the amount of the reported gain would be inflated because the discount rate used in valuing the debt would reflect the collapse of the company's own credit rating, which seemed perverse. As a result of these comments, the matter was not dealt with in the eventual standard, although the general issue will re-emerge within the Board's financial instruments project.

2.1.5   UITF 8

In March 1993, the UITF published its eighth Abstract, dealing with the repurchase of debt.[5] This provided that, where a company has purchased its own debt at a price which differed from the carrying amount of the liability on its balance sheet, it should account for the difference as a profit or loss in the year of repurchase. As with UITF 1, this requirement was incorporated in FRS 4 and the Abstract has been withdrawn.

2.1.6   FRS 4

FRS 4 was issued in December 1993. As mentioned above, it contained only minor changes from the exposure draft, and it incorporated the requirements of UITFs 1 and 8, as a result of which these two Abstracts were withdrawn. The main features of the standard are summarised in the next section, while its application to particular types of capital instrument is dealt with in 4 below. The standard itself contains a set of Application Notes which illustrate how the rules are to be applied in practice. FRS 4 came into effect for accounting periods ending on or after 22 June 1994. Its requirements are discussed in 2.2 below.

As more fully discussed in Chapter 9, in July 1996 the ASB published a wide-ranging discussion paper on *Derivatives and other financial instruments*, proposing a radical new approach to the recognition and measurement of share and loan capital (as well as other financial items) and also suggesting substantial new disclosure requirements. This was to be progressed in two stages, with disclosure taking precedence, and in September 1998 the Board duly published FRS 13 as the standard that requires these disclosures. The recognition and measurement proposals are less immediate, and the approach in FRS 4 is likely to remain in force until at least 2001 if not beyond.

2.2 The requirements of FRS 4

2.2.1 The definition of capital instruments

The standard defines capital instruments as 'all instruments that are issued by reporting entities as a means of raising finance, including shares, debentures, loans and debt instruments, options and warrants that give the holder the right to subscribe for or obtain capital instruments. In the case of consolidated financial statements the term includes capital instruments issued by subsidiaries except those that are held by another member of the group included in the consolidation.'[6]

FRS 4 discusses the accounting treatment of capital instruments only from the issuer's point of view; it does not say how investors should account for such instruments. In addition, three particular classes of capital instrument are excluded from the scope of the standard:

(a)   warrants issued to employees under employee share schemes;

(b)   leases;

(c)   equity shares issued as part of a business combination that is accounted for as a merger.[7]

The first of these involves complex matters which the Board did not wish to address in this standard, although the UITF has since addressed certain issues concerning employee share schemes – see 4.7 below. The remaining two were already the subject of rules from other sources – see Chapters 17 and 6. FRS 4 also has a minor exemption for investment companies allowing them to charge finance costs to capital in certain circumstances,[8] the details of which are beyond the scope of this book.

2.2.2 The distinction between debt and share capital

The first main issue which the standard discusses is how to distinguish an instrument between debt and share capital (or minority interests in the case of instruments issued by a subsidiary). The ASB bases the distinction on the definition of a liability which it is developing under its *Statement of Principles*. This says that 'liabilities are obligations of an entity to transfer economic benefits as a result of past transactions or events',[9] so the Board's criterion is to classify all instruments which contain an obligation to transfer economic benefits as debt.[10] This applies equally whether the obligation is unconditional or merely contingent. This means that (for example) convertible debt has to be shown as a liability, rather than classifying it as shares on the argument that it is likely to be converted into shares in the future. It also applies to subordinated debt; even if debt is subordinated to the claims of all other creditors, that is not sufficient to make it equivalent to share capital, and it should therefore continue to be classified as debt.

On the other hand, under this approach, any obligation that the reporting entity can elect to satisfy by issuing the requisite number of new shares is regarded as an equity item rather than as debt. For instance, FRS 7 says that 'where contingent consideration is to be satisfied by the issue of shares, there is no obligation to transfer economic benefits and, accordingly, amounts recognised would be reported as part of shareholders' funds, for example as a separate caption representing shares to be issued'.[11] This applies even where the number of shares issued has to be varied to provide sufficient value to meet a fixed amount of consideration. In contrast, the IASC has determined that in these circumstances the item should be classified as a liability, since 'the holder of the obligation is not exposed to gain or loss from fluctuations in the price of the equity securities'[12] (which would be true of a holder of an equity interest in the company, but not of a creditor).

Applying the above approach might also be expected to result in redeemable preference shares being shown as debt. However, the standard does not go this far; any instrument which is part of the company's share capital must remain in the share capital section of the balance sheet. This may seem to be preferring form to substance, but the Board argues that shares should always be treated differently, because payments made under them are subject to legal restrictions and (more to the point) to classify them as liabilities would be in breach of the format requirements of the Companies Act.[13]

Nevertheless, FRS 4 does require shareholders' funds to be subdivided into equity and non-equity components, so that shares which have more of the character of debt are distinguished from pure equity shares. For this purpose, the standard has had to distinguish between these two categories and has done so by defining non-equity shares and making equity shares the residual category. The definition of non-equity shares is somewhat complex; they are defined as shares possessing any of the following characteristics:

(a) any of the rights of the shares to receive payments (whether in respect of dividends, in respect of redemption or otherwise) are for a limited amount that is not calculated by reference to the company's assets or profits or the dividends on any class of equity share;

(b) any of their rights to participate in a surplus in a winding up are limited to a specific amount that is not calculated by reference to the company's assets or profits and such limitation had a commercial effect in practice at the time the shares were issued or, if later, at the time the limitation was introduced; or

(c) the shares are redeemable either according to their terms, or because the holder, or any party other than the issuer, can require their redemption.[14]

Some aspects of the definition are not particularly intuitive. A participating preference share, whose holder receives a dividend which is both partly fixed and partly variable, might be thought to be an equity share because the overall amount of the dividend is not limited; however, the relevant Application Note to FRS 4 says that they are non-equity shares, on the argument that the fixed element of the dividend is for a limited amount. This result suggests another way of looking at non-equity shares, as those whose holders enjoy a degree of priority over the equity shareholders, in the sense that they are entitled to receive certain amounts (provided they are available) without regard to the results of the company.

The standard similarly calls for shares issued by subsidiaries, and therefore shown as minority interests in the consolidated balance sheet, to be analysed into equity and non-equity categories. Arjo Wiggins Appleton provides an example of this disclosure:

Extract 15.1: Arjo Wiggins Appleton p.l.c. (1998)

	1998	1997
21. Minority interests	**£m**	£m
Equity interests	**5.3**	2.6
Non-equity interest	**1.1**	1.0
	6.4	3.6

The non-equity minority interest relates to Arjomari-Prioux S.A.'s holding of 100,000 Class B shares of FFR 100 each, fully paid, in the capital of Arjo Wiggins S.A., which carry a right to a priority dividend. The company had an option to acquire these shares at their par value (FFR 10 million), plus accrued interest, in the event of the liquidation of Arjo Wiggins S.A., or if the total shareholding of Arjomari-Prioux S.A. in the Company fell to below 5%. However, with the change to the arrangements for paying dividends referred to in note 5, the Company has been granted a right to acquire these shares at any time after 31 December 1999 for a consideration of FFR 10 million.

The minority interests in the Group's profit and loss account relate entirely to equity interests.

FRS 4 goes further than it was able to do with shares of the reporting entity by saying that shares held by minorities are sometimes equivalent to debt from the group's point of view and should therefore be shown as such. This would apply if any member of the group had an obligation to transfer economic benefits to the minority shareholder, for example if the parent company guaranteed the redemption of these shares.[15] Arjo Wiggins Appleton was in this position in 1996:

Extract 15.2: Arjo Wiggins Appleton p.l.c. (1996)

13 Borrowings [extract]

During the year, the Group raised £364.7 million through the issue, by a subsidiary undertaking, of cumulative redeemable preference shares, denominated in sterling and French francs, to a consortium of banks. In accordance with FRS 4 'Capital instruments', these preference shares are classified as unsecured bank loans in the Group accounts, as the Company has undertaken to purchase the shares, in the event of the subsidiary failing to make the expected payments, and has, accordingly, provided guarantees. The consolidated balance sheet as at 31 December 1996 includes borrowings of £341.9 million in respect of these shares, the reduction being due to the retranslation of the French franc tranche.

Sometimes, however, such a guarantee will be subordinated to such a degree that the rights of the holder of the shares in the subsidiary are no greater than those of a preference shareholder of the parent. If this is the case, FRS 4 allows the shares to remain in minority interests.[16] Diageo shows an example of this:

Extract 15.3: Diageo plc (1998)

24 Minority interests – non-equity

Non-equity minority interests of £366m *(1996 – 360m)* comprise £333m of 9.42% and £33m of 7.973% cumulative guaranteed preferred securities issued by subsidiaries. The holders of these securities have no rights against group companies other than the issuing entity and, to the extent prescribed by the guarantee, the company. To the extent that payments due under the guarantee are not made because the company has insufficient distributable profits, the company has covenanted that it will not make any distribution on any share capital which ranks junior to these securities.

One potentially controversial matter is the classification of hybrid instruments which have characteristics of both debt and equity, such as convertible debt. As discussed in 4.2.4 below, in the years before the standard was issued some companies had developed the practice of showing certain convertible debt instruments in their balance sheet under share capital, on the argument that conversion into equity was highly probable. The standard takes a contrary view. Although it concedes that it is not certain that such instruments will result in the transfer of economic benefits, and therefore fall within the definition of a liability, it takes the view that any future conversion should not be anticipated, and that accordingly hybrid instruments should be classified according to their present form, although disclosed separately from other liabilities on the face of the balance sheet.[17]

An alternative approach would have been to split hybrid instruments into their debt and equity components. The ASB's earlier Discussion Paper invited comments on two variants of this, described in an Appendix to the Discussion Paper as 'split accounting' and the 'imputed interest approach'.[18] These attempt to recognise the substance of the convertible bond as a hybrid instrument with debt and equity elements – a combination of straight debt and an option or warrant – and account separately for each of the two components.

The steps involved in split accounting are as follows:

1   The net proceeds received from the issue of convertible debt are analysed between the amount that represents the liability and the amount in respect of the conversion rights. These two components are thereafter accounted for entirely separately.

2   The liability is accounted for as any other debt. As the amount repayable on redemption will normally exceed the amount allocated to the debt at the time of issue, a finance cost, additional to the coupon actually paid, will be accrued in each accounting period.

3   The amount of the proceeds which relates to the conversion rights is accounted for as a warrant. (See 2.2.8 below.)

4   In the event of conversion the liability is extinguished. The carrying amount of the liability is credited to called up share capital and share premium account.

The 'imputed interest' approach is similar in concept, but the accounting treatment is slightly different in its effect. It was originally proposed in TR 677, which suggested that 'an adjustment may need to be made to charge a fair interest cost in the profit and loss account and to treat the difference as a payment received for an option'.[19] In other words the proceeds of issue of the bond should be accounted for in the normal way, but thereafter the profit and loss account should be charged with a market rate of interest, with the excess charge over the actual coupon paid being credited to a capital reserve which is built up over the life of the bond to represent the equivalent of option proceeds discussed at 2.2.8 below.

An example of these two approaches is shown below:

Example 15.1: Split accounting and imputed interest

A company issues a bond for £50 million with an interest rate of 8% per annum, at a time when general interest rates indicate a rate of 12% per annum for straight borrowing. The bond is convertible into shares of the company after five years, and is otherwise redeemable at par. (Issue costs are ignored in this example.)

The 'split accounting' approach would analyse the proceeds of issue of the bond between two elements: one amount taken immediately to capital reserve to represent the value of the 'warrant' inherent in the bond, and the remainder shown as the liability under the straight borrowing element, in relation to which the coupon paid would represent a market rate of interest. The split would be made by discounting the interest payments of £4,000,000 per annum and the amount payable on redemption of £50,000,000 at 12%, to give a net present value of £42,790,000. The £7,210,000 difference between that and the proceeds of the issue is regarded as the amount attributable to the warrant and taken to reserves: in addition the £42,790,000 is built up to the redemption value of £50,000,000 by an additional finance cost charged in the profit and loss account. The mechanics would be as follows (all figures in £000s):

Year	Total finance cost	Interest paid	Amortisation of discount	Capital reserve
1	5,135	4,000	1,135	7,210
2	5,271	4,000	1,271	7,210
3	5,424	4,000	1,424	7,210
4	5,594	4,000	1,594	7,210
5	5,786	4,000	1,786	7,210
Total	27,210	20,000	7,210	

The 'imputed interest' method would calculate a finance cost of £6,000,000 per annum, being £50,000,000 at 12%. The £2,000,000 difference between that and the interest payment of £4,000,000 is credited to capital reserve each year. The mechanics would be as follows (all figures in £000s):

Year	Total finance cost	Interest paid	'Warrant element'	Capital reserve
1	6,000	4,000	2,000	2,000
2	6,000	4,000	2,000	4,000
3	6,000	4,000	2,000	6,000
4	6,000	4,000	2,000	8,000
5	6,000	4,000	2,000	10,000
Total	30,000	20,000	10,000	

The essential difference between the two approaches is that split accounting accounts for the warrant element at the time of the issue of the bonds rather than building it up over their life, and takes account of the time value of money in making the split, in effect by discounting the value applied to the option element.

Such an analysis has obvious merit in reflecting the economic substance of the arrangement, but the ASB regarded it as rather too radical for the time being, and FRS 4 rules out such an approach. It says that capital instruments should be accounted for separately only if they are capable of being transferred, cancelled or redeemed independently of each other.[20] Thus, for example, loan stock issued with detachable warrants would be accounted for as two instruments and the proceeds of the issue split between the two for accounting purposes, whereas convertible loan stock (which is very similar in substance) would be accounted for as one.

One problem with FRS 4's approach is that it continues to take hybrid instruments at face value, with the result that the finance cost is manipulable based on the terms of the instrument. In an extreme case, it could even be negative, as shown in this example:

Example 15.2: Convertible bonds with negative finance cost

A company issues convertible debt for £1,000,000 which is repayable at £900,000. The debt carries no coupon; to compensate for this, the conversion terms are extremely favourable. However, FRS 4 does not permit conversion to be assumed, and says that the finance cost must be measured on the assumption that conversion will not take place. The finance cost is negative as a result and the company can therefore *credit* £100,000 to its profit and loss account over the life of the instrument. When the conversion option is exercised at the end of that period, the apparent consideration for the shares would be £900,000. (When shares are issued by conversion of debt, FRS 4 says that the consideration for the issue is the carrying amount of the debt immediately before conversion.)[21] However, it is obviously questionable whether this could be regarded as giving a true and fair view.

In substance, this is more like a warrant than a convertible debt, because the likelihood of redemption must be very small.[22] The example could be taken to a greater extreme by reducing the putative redemption amount yet further – even down to a negligible amount. FRS 4 would continue to imply that the whole of the difference between the amount subscribed and the amount available if the bond were not converted would be credited to the profit and loss account over the life of the instrument.

Clearly, a negative overall finance cost from such an arrangement would be regarded as too ridiculous to accept. However, a very low positive cost – perhaps even down to zero – might not. This is the essential weakness of accounting for hybrid instruments as if they were straight debt, which a split accounting approach would have gone some way to remedy.

Practice in this area is mixed. Granada shows a negative component of finance cost in relation to convertible preference shares which have a redemption option at a price below their issue price, as shown in this extract:

Extract 15.4: Granada Group PLC (1998)

	1998 £m	1997 £m
9 Dividends		
Equity shares:		
Interim Dividend of 5.14p (1997: 4.66p) per share, paid 28 September 1998	**46**	40
Proposed final dividend of 11.56p (1997: 9.84p) per share, payable 1 April 1999	**105**	87
	151	127
Non-equity shares:		
Dividend of 7.5p per share, paid in two instalments on 31 January and 31 July 1998	**11**	13
Finance credit (FRS 4)	**(1)**	(1)
	10	12
	161	139

In contrast, Williams Holdings has the same kind of instrument but has not taken credit for this negative component. This may reflect its view that redemption is unlikely to occur so that the potential profit on redemption will never materialise, or it may simply be on grounds of materiality (the total premium is about £8 million, to be spread over the term of the instrument).

Extract 15.5: Williams Holdings PLC (1998)

	1998 £m	1997 £m
8 Dividends		
Ordinary – interim paid 6.25p per share (1997 6.05p)	**46.1**	47.4
final proposed 10.04p per share (1997 9.75p)	**73.2**	76.3
Total equity dividends	**119.3**	123.7
10¾% cumulative preference shares	**0.2**	0.2
8½% cumulative redeemable preference shares	**1.1**	2.1
8.0p cumulative convertible redeemable preference shares	**20.5**	21.5
Non-cumulative convertible redeemable preference B shares	**0.2**	–
Total non-equity	**22.0**	23.8
Total dividends	**141.3**	147.5

20 Share capital [extract]

Conversion and redemption details
(a) The 8.0p preference shares, which were issued at 103p, a premium over redemption value of 3p, are convertible to ordinary shares at the shareholders' option on the basis of 0.31746 ordinary shares for each 8.0p preference share, up to a maximum of 77.4m ordinary shares, in May of each year to 2008 inclusive. If not converted, the shares may be redeemed at the company's option within the period from 30th June 2008 to 30th December 2018. If not converted or redeemed by 30th December 2018, all outstanding shares will be redeemed at 100p on 31st December 2018.

2.2.3   *The accounting treatment of debt instruments*

Under FRS 4, debt should initially be recorded in the balance sheet at the fair value of the consideration received upon issue, less the amount of issue costs.[23] Usually, the consideration received is cash, and there is thus no difficulty in determining its value. Thereafter, the difference between that amount and the total payments required to be made under the debt (interest and repayment of principal together with any premium) represents the total finance cost,[24] which is accounted for over the term of the debt. Except to the extent that it may be capitalised (see Chapter 13), this finance cost should be charged to the profit and loss account over the term at a constant rate of interest on the outstanding amount of the debt.[25] The carrying value of the debt is increased annually by the amount of the finance cost relating to that period, and reduced by the amount of payments made.[26]

The measurement of the finance cost is discussed in more detail in 2.2.5 below, and the mechanics of the process are illustrated in the Examples shown in 4.1.

If debt is repurchased or settled before its maturity, the difference between the amount repaid and the carrying value should be recognised immediately in the profit and loss account.[27] The repurchase of debt is discussed further in 2.2.6 below.

2.2.4 The accounting treatment of share capital

With the exception of shares issued in a business combination which is accounted for as a merger, share issues should be recorded at the net proceeds received. These net proceeds are taken direct to shareholders' funds and reported in the reconciliation of movements in shareholders' funds.[28] As in the case of debt, 'net proceeds' is defined as the fair value of the consideration received less costs that are incurred directly in connection with the issue.[29]

In the majority of cases, shares are issued for cash and therefore the fair value of the consideration received will be easy to determine. In some circumstances, however (e.g. where shares are issued for property), the fair value of the consideration received may not be so easily determined and external valuations may be required. Although the standard focuses on the value of the consideration for the shares, sometimes it may be expedient to consider the market value of the shares issued, to provide indirect evidence of the fair value of non-cash consideration received for them.

The standard does not give guidance on how to allocate 'net proceeds' to the various elements of total shareholders' funds. However, this is dictated by company law; the amount at which share capital is recorded is determined by the nominal value of the shares issued. If the net proceeds from the issue exceed that amount, the excess is to be recorded as share premium.

Issue costs are regarded as inseparable from the consideration received, and are therefore taken straight to reserves; they should not be disclosed in either the statement of total recognised gains and losses or the profit and loss account. Provided the Companies Act conditions are satisfied, they may be set off against any share premium account.

The mechanics of a simple equity share issue are shown in the following example:

Example 15.3: Equity share issue

A company issues 1 million £1 ordinary shares at par. Issue costs of £20,000 are incurred.

If there is a share premium account in existence, the share issue may be recorded by increasing share capital by £1,000,000 and setting off the issue costs against share premium account. In the analysis of total shareholders' funds, the equity interests will have increased by £980,000.

If there is no share premium account, share capital will be increased by £1,000,000 but the issue costs would be deducted from another reserve (usually profit and loss account reserve) subject to the provisions of the company's articles. Prior to FRS 4, companies in this situation had to charge the issue costs to the profit and loss account for the year.

The accounting for non-equity shares is slightly different, because finance costs are to be measured in the same way as for debt instruments,[30] except that they are shown as an appropriation in the profit and loss account rather than as an expense. The effect of this is that, for non-equity shares with a finite term, although issue costs are initially taken to reserves in the same way as for equity shares, they are subsequently recycled through the profit and loss account as an appropriation and charged in arriving at earnings per share.

Example 15.4: Non-equity share issue

A company issues 1 million £1 redeemable preference shares at par. Issue costs of £20,000 are incurred. The shares carry a coupon of 7% and are redeemable at par in five years.

In the same way as for the equity share issue in Example 15.3 above, the non-equity interests will increase by £980,000 in the analysis of total shareholders' funds. However, thereafter the appropriation in the profit and loss account will include not only the £70,000 dividend but also an annual instalment to write off the issue costs. This has the effect of transferring £20,000 from equity shareholders' funds to non-equity shareholders' funds over the five year life of the preference shares, at the end of which the non-equity shareholders' funds will be stated at the redemption amount of £1 million.

However, where the non-equity share has no finite term, for example if it is an irredeemable preference share, it will not be appropriate to make this transfer and the issue costs will thus be dealt with in the same way as for equity shares.

2.2.5   *The allocation of finance costs*

As mentioned at 2.2.3 above, the standard requires that finance costs should be accounted for over the life of the instrument at a constant rate on the carrying amount – in other words, at the effective rate implicit in all the cash flows which are to be made.[31] This may sound complex, but it is in fact what happens automatically in the case of a simple loan on which the interest is paid over the term of the loan. However, the requirement also accommodates more complex forms of borrowing, such as where a premium is payable on redemption, or the interest is not paid evenly over the life of the loan.

Finance costs are defined by FRS 4 as 'the difference between the net proceeds of an instrument and the total amount of the payments (or other transfers of economic benefits) that the issuer may be required to make in respect of the instrument'.[32] When this definition refers to 'net proceeds', it means that the costs of issuing the instrument are to be deducted from the amount raised, with the result that such costs are to be spread over the life of the instrument as part of the finance cost. Issue costs are defined as 'the costs that are incurred directly in connection with the issue of a capital instrument, that is, those costs that would not have been incurred had the specific instrument in question not been issued'.[33] This definition is deliberately restrictive; it extends only to incremental costs, not to allocations of fixed costs, and they must be specific to the instrument in question.

It would be possible to interpret these words very narrowly indeed, by considering which of the costs would have been avoided on the hypothesis that an alternative instrument had been substituted for the actual instrument issued, and deciding that only these costs are specific to the actual instrument issued. However, we doubt if such a narrow interpretation is intended. The costs of the actual issue will generally fall within the definition, even if they are not peculiar to the particular instrument chosen.

Examples of costs that qualify as issue costs include underwriting fees, or arrangement fees to cover the administrative work involved in assessing and setting up the loan. Examples of costs that would not qualify include:

(a)   costs of ascertaining the suitability or feasibility of particular instruments;

(b)   costs of researching different sources of finance;

(c)   allocations of internal costs that would still have been incurred if the instrument had not been issued (e.g. management remuneration);

(d)   costs of viability studies commissioned by the lender which are borne by the issuer;

(e)   costs of a financial restructuring or renegotiation (as they are incurred primarily to establish whether the whole exercise is worthwhile rather than related to the issue of replacement finance which occurs later).

The principles apply not only to debt but also to non-equity shares,[34] except that dividends and transfers to reserves are to be dealt with as appropriations of profit, whereas the costs of debt will be charged in arriving at profit before taxation. Where the instrument is classified as a minority interest, the finance cost will again be calculated in the same way, but included in minority interests in the profit and loss account.[35]

Under FRS 4, the term of a debt instrument has a direct impact on the calculation and allocation of the finance costs of the instrument. Oddly enough, it does not determine the classification of debt between short term and long term nor any other analysis of the maturity of debt. Separate rules apply here – see 2.2.7 below.

The term of an instrument is defined as follows:

'The period from the date of issue of the capital instrument to the date at which it will expire, be redeemed, or be cancelled. If either party has the option to require the instrument to be redeemed or cancelled and, under the terms of the instrument, it is uncertain whether such an option will be exercised, the term should be taken to end on the earliest date at which the instrument would be redeemed or cancelled on exercise of such an option. If either party has the right to extend the period of an instrument, the term should not include the period of the extension if there is a genuine commercial possibility that the period will not be extended.'[36]

This therefore means that the term is taken to be the minimum which either party could insist upon, and since this dictates the period over which issue costs have to be written off, the definition has a conservative bias. This cautious approach to evaluating options to reduce or extend the term of debt instruments disregards the actual intentions of the option holder. The effect of this is often to produce a shorter 'term' for accounting purposes than that which will materialise in practice. Where the borrower has the ability to repay the debt at any time, as will often be the case, a literal interpretation of the standard would suggest that the issue costs should be written off immediately, because the term of the debt (as defined) is zero.

Some instruments contain terms which allow the borrower to repay early, but at a price. A strict application of FRS 4 could produce some unexpected results:

Example 15.5: Loan with issuer call option

A company issues a five year debt instrument carrying a fixed interest rate of 7%. The terms of the instrument include an 'issuer call option', permitting the company to redeem the debt early on payment of a premium.

On the face of it, the term of the instrument, as defined by FRS 4, is restricted to the period up to the first date at which the option could be exercised, as discussed above. This means that issue costs have to be written off over that period. It might also be thought to mean that the premium payable under the option would have to be accrued as part of the finance costs, whether or not the company intends to exercise the option. The effect of this would be that the company would be accounting for the redemption of the instrument regardless of whether or not it actually intended to redeem it.

In order to avoid this result, in 1994 the UITF issued an Abstract which made it clear that any payments required on the exercise of such options do not form part of the finance costs which have to be accounted for.[37] This is because they cannot be described as 'payments that the issuer may be required to make in respect of the instrument', since exercising the option, and therefore incurring the requirement to make the payment, is voluntary. However, the Abstract does not affect the determination of the term of the instrument, which remains governed by FRS 4. The result of this is that the issue costs still have to be written off over the period up to the date on which the call option could be exercised, even though it is otherwise being assumed that the option will not be exercised. The treatment of finance costs is therefore based on two mutually exclusive assumptions, which seems rather anomalous.

2.2.6 Repurchase of debt or shares

Where a company buys in its own debt (or repays it early) at a price which differs from the liability carried in the balance sheet, the difference between the two amounts is taken to the profit and loss account as an additional finance cost or credit.[38] This applies even if the debt is not cancelled. For example, a company which bought some of its own listed debentures in the market would be at liberty to sell them again at some time in the future, but would still record a gain or loss in the meantime; if it resold them, that would be treated as a new debt issue, recorded at the proceeds of that sale.

As explained at 2.1.5 above, this issue was originally addressed by UITF 8, which was replaced by FRS 4 soon after. The UITF had taken up the issue to resolve the question of whether or not companies which refinanced their fixed-rate debt should spread the resulting gain or loss over the life of the replacement debt, and it concluded that they should not, except in circumstances where either:

(a)   the replacement borrowing gives the same effective economic result as the original borrowing and thus there has been no change of substance in the debt. For this to be the case, as a minimum the following conditions should be met:

- The replacement borrowing and the original borrowing are both fixed rate;

- The replacement borrowing is of a comparable amount to the original borrowing;

- The maturity of the replacement borrowing is not materially different from the remaining maturity of the original borrowing;

- The covenants of the replacement borrowing are not materially different from those of the original borrowing.

A refinancing may fall within this exception whether or not the lender of the replacement debt is the same as the lender of the original debt; or

(b)   the overall finance costs of the replacement borrowing are significantly different from market rates.[39]

These exceptions were not repeated in FRS 4. Notwithstanding this, some companies clearly believe that they still apply. Tate and Lyle discloses this note:

Extract 15.6: Tate & Lyle Public Limited Company (1998)

16 Borrowings – due after more than one year [extract]

On 10 June 1996, £190.5 million 5¾% Guaranteed Bonds were redeemed for £163.8 million and replaced by borrowings with substantially the same terms. The premium on redemption of £23.3 million is being amortised over the life of the replacement debt and is treated as a payment of interest in the statement of cash flows. The £163.8 million 7.863% unsecured borrowings due 2001, which replaced the Guaranteed Bonds, were fully drawn by a UK subsidiary undertaking and are guaranteed on a subordinated basis by Tate & Lyle PLC. The effective rate of interest (including both coupon and accrued issue discount) on the 5¾% Guaranteed Bonds was 13.3%

Although FRS 4 dictates how to account for the gain or loss on the repayment of debt, it does not address the equivalent issue when swaps are terminated, and some companies carry forward gains or losses that arise in these circumstances. Tesco is an example, as shown in this extract:

Extract 15.7: Tesco PLC (1999)

Note 17 Creditors falling due within one year [extract]

d) A gain of £45m, realised in a prior year, on terminated interest rate swaps is being spread over the life of replacement swaps entered into at the same time for similar periods. Accruals and deferred income include £6m (1998 – £5m) attributable to these realised gains with £12m (1998 – £18m) being included in creditors falling due after more than one year (note 18).

At first sight, this may seem inconsistent with the rules on the termination of loans, but in fact the arguments are rather different, as shown in this example:

Example 15.6: Termination of a swap

A company takes out a five-year floating rate loan of £10m and then swaps it to a fixed rate of 6% by entering into an interest rate swap whereby it pays £600,000 for 5 years in exchange for receiving a floating rate on £10m. It therefore presents the loan in its accounts as a fixed rate loan at 6%. A year later, interest rates have risen and the swap has a positive value of £500,000. The company terminates the swap. Should it take the £500,000 to its profit and loss account?

In our view it should not. The original hedging decision had the economic effect of fixing the rate at 6%, and the cancellation of the swap has not changed that. The £500,000 that the company receives is simply the present value of the future cash flows expected to be received under the swap, and whether or not the swap is cashed in, the protection that it has given to the interest payable under the loan is still there. Accordingly, the most appropriate treatment would be to spread the apparent gain over the life of the loan, which will mean that it will continue to show an interest rate of 6% (apart from the effect of subsequent movements in interest rates that were not foreseen when the swap was terminated). This is the accounting treatment required in the US under EITF 84-7.

A different result follows if the underlying loan itself is repaid. Again the accounting result is the same whether or not the swap is also terminated, because any such termination is only an acceleration of the expected cash flows. Since there is nothing left to hedge, if the swap is retained it should now be treated as a speculative instrument and marked to market, giving rise to a reported profit of £500,000.

Sometimes, rather than repurchasing or repaying their debt, companies enter into arrangements which have a similar economic effect. For example, they might irrevocably deposit funds with a third party which are to be applied solely in settlement of the debt, and agree with the creditor that he can look only to those funds for repayment of the debt. Such arrangements are sometimes referred to as resulting in 'defeasance' (meaning extinguishment) of the debt. FRS 4 does not deal with this issue; it only addresses actual repayment. However, IAS 39, the IASC standard on financial instruments, does address this issue. It says that such a transaction does result in derecognition of the liability from the balance sheet provided the creditor legally releases the company from its obligation to settle the debt. But otherwise the arrangement is described as only 'in-substance defeasance', which IAS 39 says is ineffective in removing the debt from the balance sheet.[40] The standard also warns that, even though the liability may be extinguished, it is possible that the assets that have been transferred do not qualify for derecognition, in which case a new liability may have to be recognised in place of the old one.[41] This type of transaction is not directly addressed by any UK standard, but the thought processes in FRS 5 may lead to similar conclusions.[42]

Pennon's 1999 accounts show that at the beginning of the year it had reduced the disclosed amount of lease payables by £75m because it had deposited that amount with the lessor's bank group, as shown in this extract:

Extract 15.8: Pennon Group Plc (1999)

28 Loans and other borrowings [extract]

... at 31 March 1998, obligations under finance leases of £75.0 million had been offset against cash of an equal amount had been deposited with the lessor's bank group (collateralisation); South West Water Limited could insist this cash be utilised to meet the finance lease obligations as they fell due. During the year South West Water Limited withdrew the cash deposits placed with the lessor's bank group. Accordingly, a finance lease obligation of £75.0 million is included above.

It appears from the above description that Pennon was able to insist on a net settlement, even though the deposits were not with the lessor companies themselves but with other members of their group, and presumably this would still have applied in the event of the insolvency of any of the parties, otherwise the FRS 5 offset conditions would not have been satisfied.[43] However, it also seems that the deposits were not irrevocable, since they have now been withdrawn. This would suggest that they may not have met the more general FRS 5 test for derecognition of an asset, which might have been interpreted to mean that the amounts should have been shown gross.

Another kind of arrangement which has a similar economic effect to the repurchase of debt is illustrated in this extract from the 1994 accounts of Sears:

Extract 15.9: Sears plc (1994)

13. Debtors [extract]

Included within prepayments due after more than one year is a call option, which was purchased for £41.8 million on normal commercial terms and which gives the Company the right to acquire £50 million of Sears plc Bonds 1996. It is exercisable at certain dates up to January 1996 at an exercise price that is linked to the net present value of the remaining interest payable on the Bonds. Accordingly, the exercise price reduces during the period up to January 1996, resulting in an increase in the value of the call option. This increase in value is credited to interest receivable on an actuarial basis and is reflected in the carrying amount of the asset, which was £43.5 million at 31st January 1994.

£43.5 million equated to the present value of the principal of the debt (£50 million) if discounted at approximately 7.2%. From this it can be surmised that the exercise price under the option was little different from the present value of the outstanding interest payments. Subsequently, the 1996 accounts showed that the option had been sold for £50m on the same day as the debt was repaid. Interestingly, the purchase of the option was described in the 1994 accounts as 'Prepayment of 12½% bonds 1996' in the financing section of the cash flow statement, not as the purchase of an option in the investing section. It might therefore be argued that Sears had already repurchased its debt in substance, but in such a way that it did not have to write off the premium payable – instead, it was recognised over the remaining two years of the instrument as the difference between the interest payable on the debt, at 12½% and the accretion of interest on the prepayment, at 7.2%.

It is again debatable whether this should be regarded as the repurchase of debt or not. On the one hand, it achieves a similar result in economic terms, and therefore could be said to be a repurchase in substance. On the other, it would be possible to simulate a repurchase of debt in a variety of other ways, for example using derivatives without getting close to repurchasing the debt. Moreover, unless there is right of offset between the option and the debt, FRS 5 would again say that the two items should continue to be carried gross on opposite sides of the balance sheet.

The standard refers only fleetingly to the repurchase of *shares*. This subject is discussed at 3.3 below.

2.2.7   *The disclosure of debt maturities*

As discussed in 3.2 below, both the Companies Act and Stock Exchange rules require debt to be analysed in the accounts by reference to when the creditor is entitled to require repayment. The standard repeats that requirement.[44] However, in interpreting this rule, companies are to take account of committed facilities in existence at the year end that would permit short-term debt to be refinanced for a longer period, provided some exacting conditions are met. These conditions are as follows:

(a)   the debt and the facility are under a single agreement or course of dealing with the same lender or group of lenders;

(b)   the finance costs for the new debt are on a basis which is not significantly higher than that of the existing debt;

(c)   the obligations of the lender (or group of lenders) are firm: the lender is not able legally to refrain from providing funds except in circumstances the possibility of which can be demonstrated to be remote; and

(d)   the lender (or group of lenders) is expected to be able to fulfil its obligations under the facility.[45]

It is important to note that the borrower's own intentions and financial plans do not affect this reclassification; the rules require the position to be assessed only from the lenders' perspective.

An example of this classification is shown by Senior Engineering:

Extract 15.10: Senior Engineering Group plc (1998)

18 Creditors: Amounts falling due after more than one year [extract]

	Group 1998 £m	Group 1997 £m	Company 1998 £m	Company 1997 £m
Loans comprise :				
Revolving credit facility	34.8	17.0	1.5	17.0
Other bank loans	9.5	11.4	–	–
Other loans	0.2	0.2	–	–
Less – Current portion	(0.4)	(0.2)	–	–
	44.1	28.4	1.5	17.0
8.57% Private placement loan – 2004*	3.0	3.0	3.0	3.0
8.75% Private placement loan – 2007*	15.1	15.2	15.1	15.2
6.52% Private placement loan – 2008*	45.2	–	45.2	–
	63.3	18.2	63.3	18.2
Total loans falling due after more than one year	107.4	46.6	64.8	35.2

*Due for repayment (not by instalments) after more than five years.

Amounts drawn down under the revolving credit facility fall due for repayment in January, February and March 1999. However, the facility is committed for a period of five years ending in July 2000. Accordingly, under the terms of Financial Reporting Standard No. 4, the amounts drawn down have been classified as payable between one and two years.

Before FRS 4 was issued, many companies which issued commercial paper reported it as long term, by reference to back-up facilities. Commercial paper is generally a cheaper alternative to short-term direct bank borrowing for many large companies, and the maturity periods are very short – usually between 5 and 45 days. Most programmes are backed up by lines of credit from banks, but as the back-up facility is not provided by the lenders (i.e. the investors who buy the paper), condition (a) quoted above cannot be met, with the result that commercial paper borrowings will always be reported as short term.

Rio Tinto provides an example of this analysis, although their footnote suggests some irritation with the rule:

Extract 15.11: Rio Tinto plc and Rio Tinto Limited (1998)

15 SHORT TERM BORROWINGS [extract]

1998 A$m	1997 A$m	1998 £m	1997 £m		1998 US$m	1997 US$m
				Secured		
23	29	**8**	11	Bank loans repayable within 12 months	**14**	18
52	11	**19**	4	Debentures and other loans repayable within 12 months	**32**	7
75	40	**27**	15		**46**	25
				Unsecured		
207	223	**76**	88	Bank overdrafts and notes	**127**	145
375	304	**138**	120	Bank loans repayable within 12 months	**230**	198
78	548	**29**	217	Debentures and other loans repayable within 12 months	**48**	357
3,985	3,476	**1,470**	1,378	Commercial paper	**2,445**	2,266
4,645	4,551	**1,713**	1,803		**2,850**	2,966
4,720	4,591	**1,740**	1,818		**2,896**	2,991

In accordance with Financial Reporting Standard No.4, all commercial paper is classified as short term borrowings though US$1,301 million is backed by medium term facilities. Under US and Australian GAAP this amount would be classified as medium term borrowings.

Many companies also borrow on a short-term basis under multiple option funding facility agreements (MOFs). Short-term drawdowns under MOFs may be classified as long term by reference to the maturity date of the MOF provided all the four conditions above are met. Condition (a) will be satisfied even if it is not always the same banks who participate in individual financings under the MOF – they are regarded as being part of the same 'group of lenders' provided they are parties to the same agreement or course of dealing. Although the standard does not define the term 'course of dealing' which is used in condition (a), the choice of words suggests more latitude than the alternative – 'a single agreement'.

Condition (b) quoted above limits the choice of facilities even further. The drafting suggests that borrowings under the facility should be of the same type as those of the existing debt. So, for example, if the basis for determining the finance costs of the existing debt is a fixed margin over 1 month LIBOR, only facilities that allow borrowings that are priced on a similar basis should be considered. Hence it would not be possible to use a floating-rate medium-term facility to reclassify maturing fixed rate debt or vice versa.

In addition, the basis for determining the finance costs of borrowings under the facility should not be 'significantly higher'. The standard does not explain when one basis is significantly higher than another. However, in its discussion on the development of the FRS, the ASB implicitly provides an indication of how this condition should be interpreted. It discusses why commercial paper should be shown as short term notwithstanding the back-up facilities and explains that conditions (a) and (b) above are not usually met. The prices of commercial paper back-up facilities are thus considered to be 'significantly higher' than commercial paper rates.

Conditions (c) and (d) have a common goal. They seek to establish whether or not it is safe to rely on the borrowings under the facility. The conditions cover obvious escape routes that the provider of the facility (the lender) may have negotiated. Condition (d) is fairly straightforward; condition (c) focuses on the facility agreement and requires it to be both legally binding and genuinely committed. In this regard, the FRS requires that any circumstances specified in the facility agreement which permit the lender to refrain from providing new borrowings should be demonstrated to be remote, both at the balance sheet date and at the time the accounts are approved.

It will not be possible to confirm that the 'obligations of the lender are firm' if any of the circumstances in which the lender can refrain from providing new borrowings can only be interpreted subjectively. The example provided in the explanatory section of the FRS is that of a 'material adverse change' clause where that term has not been defined.[46] This is probably a stricter test than is applied for existing long-term borrowings, where the existence of a term which would entitle the lender to early repayment is disregarded provided it is reasonable to believe that the circumstances that would allow the term to be invoked will not arise.

If maturity of debt analysis has been compiled by reference to committed facilities in existence at the balance sheet date, the FRS also requires disclosure of the amounts of the debt involved, analysed by the earliest date on which the lender could demand repayment in the absence of the facilities.[47]

2.2.8   Warrants

A warrant is defined in FRS 4 as 'an instrument that requires the issuer to issue shares (whether contingently or not) and contains no obligation for the issuer to transfer economic benefits'.[48] When a warrant is issued, the standard requires the net proceeds to be credited direct to shareholders' funds;[49] the implication appears to be that it should be reported only in the reconciliation of shareholders' funds, not in the statement of total recognised gains and losses, presumably on the argument that it is a transaction with (potential) shareholders.

Thereafter the accounting depends on whether the warrant is exercised or is allowed to lapse. If it is exercised, the proceeds on the original issue of the warrant are included in the net proceeds of the shares issued;[50] if it lapses, they are included instead in the statement of total recognised gains and losses,[51] since the original issue has turned out not to have been a transaction with shareholders after all, but a gain.

These conclusions are questionable. Given that the warrant may lapse, in which case the proceeds will be shown never to have been a transaction with shareholders, there is a case for saying that it should be shown as deferred income until the outcome is known, not credited to shareholders' funds. However, the ASB's proposed definitions of the elements of financial statements (see Chapter 2) do not admit the possibility of deferred income, so presumably the Board felt that this was not a course open to them. Furthermore, if the warrant does lapse the proceeds will constitute a realised profit which arguably belongs in the profit and loss account, not the statement of total recognised gains and losses. The rule in FRS 4 seems to be based on the fact that the transaction has a 'capital' flavour.

2.2.9   Scrip dividends

Scrip dividends arise when shareholders are given the opportunity to receive further fully paid up shares in their company as an alternative to cash dividends. The standard deals with only some of the accounting issues which arise in relation to such transactions, and in a rather ambiguous way. It says that the value of the shares should be deemed to be the amount receivable under the cash alternative.[52] However, this is probably addressing only the initial recording of the dividend in the profit and loss account before the shareholders have chosen whether to take cash or shares, not the subsequent recording of the issue itself, in respect of which a later passage in the standard suggests that a different treatment might be appropriate.[53] The standard also says that the whole cash amount should be set up as a liability until the number of shareholders who will elect to receive the scrip dividend is known.[54] These various topics are discussed further at 4.6 below.

2.2.10   Disclosure requirements

A large number of disclosures are required by FRS 4. These are as follows:

(a)   The following analyses of balance sheet items:
   (i)   An analysis of shareholders' funds between equity and non-equity interests.[55] The non-equity interests should be further analysed into each class of non-equity shares and series of warrants for non-equity shares;[56]
   (ii)   An analysis of minority interests between equity and non-equity interests in subsidiaries;[57]
   (iii)   An analysis of liabilities between amounts in respect of convertible debt and other amounts.[58]

Where these analyses are given in the notes rather than on the face of the balance sheet, the balance sheet caption should indicate that non-equity interests or convertible debt is included in the amount shown.[59] The balance sheet should also disclose the amount of shareholders' funds in total.[60]

British Aerospace's balance sheet shows the following analysis:

Extract 15.12: British Aerospace Public Limited Company (1998)

Balance Sheets [extract]

	Group		Company	
	1998	1997	**1998**	1997
Capital and reserves	**£m**	£m	**£m**	£m
Called up share capital	**111**	111	**111**	111
Share premium account	**110**	59	**110**	59
Statutory reserve	**202**	202	**202**	202
Revaluation reserve	**324**	764	**192**	205
Capital reserve	**–**	–	**24**	24
Profit and loss account	**1,273**	316	**765**	576
Shareholders' funds				
Equity: ordinary shares	**1,750**	1,182	**1,134**	907
Non-equity: preference shares	**270**	270	**270**	270
	2,020	1,452	**1,404**	1,177
Equity minority interests	**6**	–	–	–
	2,026	1,452	**1,404**	1,177

A number of companies have fallen foul of the requirement to analyse shareholders' funds between equity and non-equity categories and have had to restate their accounts after intervention by the Financial Reporting Review Panel. One was Ransomes, as shown in the following note:

Extract 15.13: Ransomes plc (1996)

22. Shareholders' Funds [extract]

After discussion with the Financial Reporting Review Panel, the analysis of shareholders' funds between equity and non-equity interests at 30th September 1995 has been restated to conform with Financial Reporting Standard 4. The restatement for the Group has resulted in a £47.9m decrease in equity interests and a £47.9m increase in non-equity interests. The change relates to the inclusion of the premium arising on the issue of the 8.25p preference shares in 1989. This amount had previously been regarded as having been set-off by the write off of goodwill of £47.9m. The restatement in the Company books is £15.1m and is lower as the goodwill set-off only related to the intangible assets purchased on the acquisition of the Cushman Group in 1989. The 8.25p cumulative convertible preference shares are not redeemable. Total shareholders' funds remain unchanged. The restated analysis of shareholders' funds as at 30th September 1995 is given in the table below:

Group			
	1995 £'000	Restated 1995 £'000	Change £'000
Equity interests	6,793	(41,075)	(47,868)
Non-equity interests	9,307	57,175	47,868
Shareholders' funds	16,100	16,100	–

Company			
	1995 £'000	Restated 1995 £'000	Change £'000
Equity interests	45,663	30,590	(15,073)
Non-equity interests	42,102	57,175	15,073
Shareholders' funds	87,765	87,765	–

Alexon made a similar change, but also changed its treatment of dividends on non-equity shares, as shown in this note:

Extract 15.14: Alexon plc (1996)

24 Non equity shareholders' funds

Group and Company

	1996 £000	1995 £000
Non-equity shareholders' funds may be analysed as follows:		
Share capital	2,137	2,137
Share premium	18,219	18,220
Unamortised issue costs	(232)	(250)
Undeclared preference dividends	1,692	423
	21,816	20,530
Representing:		
6.25p (net) convertible cumulative redeemable preference shares of 10p each	21,698	20,416
5% (now 3.5% plus tax credit) cumulative preference shares of £1 each	105	101
Non-voting deferred shares of 10p each	13	13
	21,816	20,530

Following developments in the application of Financial Reporting Standard No. 4 (FRS 4) and an enquiry by the Financial Reporting Review Panel, the directors have reviewed the disclosure for equity and non-equity shareholders' funds and have restated the analysis at 28 January 1995 to accord with the method specified by FRS 4. The effect has been to reduce equity shareholders' funds by £17,970,000 and to increase non-equity shareholders' funds by the same amount, and to include the accrued preference dividends within non-equity shareholders' funds. This has resulted in an increase in total shareholders' funds by the amount of the accrued preference dividends, previously included within creditors.

As can be seen from this extract, Alexon included the accrued dividends on its preference shares (which were in arrears) within shareholders' funds rather than showing them as a liability, even though they also showed them as an appropriation in the profit and loss account as required by FRS 4. This means that the appropriation entry was a circular one. The standard is not entirely clear about the balance sheet classification of accrued dividends; it can be read to require *all* proposed dividends (not simply those in arrears, or those relating to non-equity shares) to remain in shareholders' funds, because they do not become liabilities until they are declared, but we do not believe this was intended by the ASB and it is certainly not an interpretation that is applied in practice other than in circumstances similar to Alexon (see 4.4.1 below).

The Rank Group gives this note to analyse its minority interests between equity and non-equity categories:

Extract 15.15: The Rank Group Plc (1998)

24 ANALYSIS OF MINORITY INTERESTS

	Equity £m	Non-equity £m	Total £m
Balances at 31st December 1997	2	25	27
Minority interest in the profit on ordinary activities after tax	1	2	3
Contributions from minority shareholders	9	–	9
Dividends payable to minority shareholders	–	(2)	(2)
Purchase of minority interests	–	(25)	(25)
Balances at 31st December 1998	12	–	12

The non-equity minority interest was redeemed at par during the year.

(b)   A brief summary of the rights of each class of shares, including

   (i)   the rights to dividends;

   (ii)   the dates at which they are redeemable and the amounts payable in respect of redemption;

   (iii)   their priority and the amounts receivable on a winding up; and

   (iv)   their voting rights.

If the rights vary according to circumstances, the details should be explained. The summary of rights should also be sufficient to explain why the class of shares has been classified as equity or non-equity shares.[61] The same disclosure also has to be given in respect of any shares of a new class which may have to be issued because of any existing warrants or convertible debt.[62]

The description of rights specified above need not be given for routine equity shares with all of the following features:

   (i)   no rights to dividends other than those that may be recommended by the directors;

   (ii)   no redemption rights;

(iii)   unlimited right to share in the surplus remaining on a winding up after all liabilities and participation rights of other classes of shares have been satisfied; and

(iv)   one vote per share.[63]

BBA provides a good example of the disclosure of the rights of shares:

Extract 15.16: BBA Group plc (1998)

18 CAPITAL AND RESERVES [extract]

Rights of non-equity interests

5% Cumulative preference £1 shares:

i.   entitle holders, in priority to holders of all other classes of shares, to a fixed cumulative preferential dividend at a rate of 5.0% per annum (previously 3.5% per annum) per share payable half yearly in equal amounts on 1 February and 1 August. The increase from 3.5% to 5.0% is necessitated by the forthcoming abolition of Advance Corporation Tax on 6 April 1999;

ii.   on a return of capital on a winding up, or otherwise, will carry the right to repayment of capital together with a premium of 12.5p per share and a sum equal to any arrears or deficiency of dividend; this right is in priority to the rights of the convertible preference and ordinary shareholders;

iii.   carry the right to attend and vote at a general meeting of the Company only if, at the date of the notice convening the meeting, payment of the dividend to which they are entitled is six months or more in arrears, or if a resolution is to be considered at the meeting for winding-up the company or reducing its share capital or sanctioning the sale of the undertakings of the Company or varying or abrogating any of the special rights attaching to them.

6.75% Cumulative redeemable convertible preference £1 shares

i.   entitle holders (subject to the prior rights of the 5% cumulative £1 preference shares) to a fixed cumulative preferential dividend at a rate of 6.75% per annum per share, payable half yearly in equal amounts on 31 May and 30 November;

ii.   carry the right to be converted into ordinary shares at the option of the holder on 31 May in any of the years 1997 to 2005 inclusive at the rate of 54.64 ordinary shares for every £100 nominal of convertible preference shares;

iii.   will be redeemed by the Company on 31 May 2006 at par (if not previously converted or redeemed) and any arrears of dividend will be paid;

iv.   on a return of capital on a winding up, or otherwise, will carry the right to repayment of capital and payment of accrued dividends in priority to ordinary shares but after the 5% cumulative £1 preference shares;

v.   carry the right to attend and vote at a general meeting of the Company only if, at the date of the notice convening the meeting, payment of the dividend to which they are entitled is six months or more in arrears, or if a resolution is to be considered at the meeting for winding-up the Company, or for modifying or abrogating any special rights attaching to them.

(c)   In respect of non-equity minority interests, a description of any rights of the holders against other group companies.[64]

(d)   An analysis of the maturity of debt showing amounts falling due:

(i)   in one year or less, or on demand;

(ii)   between one and two years;

(iii) between two and five years; and

(iv)   in five years or more.[65]

Where short-term debt has been reclassified as long term because the lender has granted a longer term facility, the amount of the debt which has been reclassified should be disclosed, analysed by its maturity before such reclassification.[66]

Pearson's accounts contain an example of this disclosure:

Extract 15.17: Pearson plc (1998)

19 Financial instruments [extract]

	1998		1997	
ALL FIGURES IN £ MILLIONS	GROUP	COMPANY	GROUP	COMPANY
Maturity of borrowings				
Short term				
Loans or instalments due within one year	–	–	8	–
Bank loans, overdrafts and commercial paper	72	172	305	295
Total due within one year	72	172	313	295
Medium and long term				
Loans or instalments thereof repayable:				
From one to two years	151	151	1	–
From two to five years	2,036	1,935	242	141
After five years not by instalments	365	100	366	100
Total due after more than one year	2,552	2,186	609	241
Total borrowings	2,624	2,358	922	536

NOTE: *In the absence of enforceable contracts from the relevant lenders to refinance current advances as they fall due, at 31 December 1998 £755m (1997:£141m) of debt currently classified from two to five years would be repayable within one year. The short term bank loans, overdrafts and commercial paper of the Group are lower than those of the Company because of bank offset arrangements.*

(e)   For convertible debt:

(i)   the dates of redemption and the amounts payable on redemption;

(ii)   the number and class of shares into which the debt may be converted, and the dates at or periods within which conversion may take place; and

(iii)   whether conversion is at the option of the issuer or the holder.[67]

Cookson provides an example of this disclosure:

Extract 15.18: Cookson Group plc (1998)

17 Convertible bond

On 28 September 1994, the Company issued £80.0m 7% Convertible Bonds. Interest on the bonds is payable semi-annually on 2 November and 2 May. Redemption of the bonds will take place on 2 November 2004, unless the bonds have previously been purchased, redeemed or converted. Redemption may take place at any time after 16 November 1999 at par at the option of the Company or prior to this date if 85% of the bonds have been purchased or converted. All bonds purchased by the Company or any Group company must be cancelled. Holders of the bonds may convert them into ordinary shares of the Company at a price of 288p, as adjusted for the rights issue made in March 1995, representing a premium at the date of issue of 17.55%, at any time to 26 October 2004. On 2 November 1994 bonds of a principal amount of £20.4m were swapped for a fixed term of 5 years for a principal of DM50.0m bearing interest at 5.6%.

	1998 £m	1997 £m
Capital value of bonds in issue	**80.0**	80.0
Principal amount swapped into DM50m of debt	**(20.4)**	(20.4)
Value of DM50m debt at year-end exchange rate	**18.2**	17.0
Unamortised issue costs (original total £2.2m)	**(0.5)**	(0.9)
Carrying value of bond at 31 December	**77.3**	75.7

(f)　For debt in general:

　　(i)　anything unusual about the legal nature of the debt, for example that it is subordinated or that the obligation to repay it is conditional; and

　　(ii)　the amount payable, or which could be claimed on a winding up, if it is significantly different from the carrying amount.

These disclosures may be summarised and need not be given for each individual instrument.[68]

(g)　Where the summary of the terms of an instrument (required by (b), (c), (e) and (f) above) cannot adequately convey its full commercial effect, that fact has to be stated and particulars given of where the relevant information can be obtained. The principal features of the instruments still have to be stated.[69]

(h)　Any gain or loss arising on the repurchase or early settlement of debt.[70]

(i)　The aggregate dividends for each class of shares, disclosing separately the total amounts in respect of the following:

　　(i)　dividends on equity shares;

　　(ii)　participating dividends on non-equity shares (those dividends which, under the memorandum and articles, are always equivalent to a fixed multiple of the dividend payable on an equity share);[71] and

　　(iii)　other dividends on non-equity shares.

Any additional appropriations in respect of non-equity shares should also be disclosed.

This information may be shown in the dividends note rather than on the face of the profit and loss account so long as the profit and loss account caption indicates that the distributions include amounts in respect of non-equity shares if that is the case.[72]

(j)   An analysis of the amount of the minority interest charge in the profit and loss account between equity and non-equity interests.[73]

(k)   For investment companies, the amount of any finance costs which have been allocated to capital rather than revenue (as a separately disclosed item in the statement of total recognised gains and losses), and the accounting policy on which this allocation has been based.[74]

One further disclosure was proposed in FRED 3 but did not survive as a requirement in the standard: this is the market value of the company's debt and non-equity shares.[75] However, the explanatory section of FRS 4 did suggest that this disclosure be considered where 'information on market values would assist users',[76] and it is now required for major companies by FRS 13 (see Chapter 9 at 3.8).

FRS 13 prescribes several further disclosures for financial instruments in the notes to the accounts, several of which apply to share and loan capital. These are detailed in Chapter 9 at 3).

3   COMPANIES ACT REQUIREMENTS

3.1   Share capital

3.1.1   *Measurement*

Under the Companies Act, the amount at which share capital is recorded is dictated by the nominal value of the shares issued, and if the value of the consideration received for the issue of shares exceeds that amount, the excess is recorded in the share premium account.[77] The share premium account is regarded as permanent capital of the company and only certain expenses of a capital nature may be set off against it, namely:

(a)   the company's preliminary expenses;

(b)   the expenses of, or the commission paid or discount allowed on, any issue of shares or debentures of the company; or

(c)   the premium payable on redemption of debentures of the company.[78]

Under FRS 4, the costs of issuing debentures or non-equity shares have to be accounted for as a finance cost or an appropriation in the profit and loss account over the life of the instrument. The same is also true of any discounts on the issue of debentures and any premiums on their repayment. This treatment does not prevent such costs ultimately from being deducted from the share premium account, but they will have to get there by transfer from the profit and loss account reserve after having first been taken to the profit and loss account in accordance with the standard.

The Companies Act gives relief from the requirement to set up a share premium account in certain circumstances where shares are being issued in exchange for shares in another company, and to limit the amount of the share premium account when shares are being issued to effect a group reconstruction (see 2.1.2 of Chapter 6).[79] Correspondingly, the legislation allows the consideration received to be recorded at the nominal value of the shares issued. This may have been affected to some degree by FRS 4, which requires shares to be recorded on the basis of the fair value of the consideration received,[80] exempting only instances where merger *accounting* is applied,[81] not where merger relief is taken. However, it seems that this change, if indeed it was one, was inadvertent; accounting standards do not usually seek to withdraw reliefs specifically granted by legislation. The ASB subsequently made it clear in FRS 6 that its rules on acquisition accounting were not intended to have any effect on the parent company's own accounts and in particular to the availability of merger relief,[82] and we suggest that that interpretation be extended to FRS 4 as well.

The share capital of UK companies is generally denominated in sterling, but there is no requirement for this to be the case, except that a public company must have a minimum share capital of £50,000.[83] Neither FRS 4 nor SSAP 20 addresses the treatment of translation of share capital denominated in a currency other than the reporting currency. In theory two treatments are possible: the foreign currency share capital could be maintained at a fixed sterling amount by being translated at a historical rate of exchange, or it could be retranslated annually at the closing rate as if it were a monetary amount. In the latter case a second question would arise: whether to take the difference arising on translation to the profit and loss account or deal with it within reserves. The latter treatment is probably the most appropriate for forms of share capital which are closely akin to debt; however, it might be more appropriate to use a historical exchange rate where the shares which are denominated in a foreign currency are ordinary shares.

3.1.2 Disclosure

The main disclosure requirements in the Companies Act begin with the format in which the balance sheet is to be laid out. The formats require capital and reserves to be analysed as shown in the box. [84]

The Act also requires the following note disclosures in respect of share capital:

(a)   the authorised share capital;

(b)   where there is more than one class of shares, the number and aggregate nominal value of each class of share allotted; [85]

Capital and reserves
I   Called up share capital
II   Share premium account
III   Revaluation reserve
IV   Other reserves
1.   Capital redemption reserve
2.   Reserve for own shares
3.   Reserves provided for by the articles of association
4.   Other reserves
V   Profit and loss account

(c)   these details about redeemable shares which have been allotted:

(i)   their earliest and latest redemption dates;

(ii)   whether redemption is automatic, or is at the option of either the company or the shareholder; and

(iii)   the amount of any redemption premium; [86]

(d)   in relation to the allotment of shares during the year:

(i)   the classes of shares allotted; and

(ii)   the number allotted, their aggregate nominal value and the consideration received, in respect of each class of shares; [87]

(e)   in respect of contingent rights to the allotment of further shares (such as options to subscribe), the following information:

(i)   the number, description and amount of the shares involved;

(ii)   the period during which the right is exercisable; and

(iii)   the price to be paid for the shares allotted; [88] and

(f)   the amount of any arrears of fixed cumulative dividends on any class of the company's shares, and the period for which they are in arrears. [89]

In respect of dividends, the Act requires that the total dividends paid and proposed in respect of the year are to be disclosed on the face of the profit and loss account, and the amount of proposed dividends has to be shown separately either on the face of the profit and loss account or in a note. [90] However, FRS 4 requires dividends on non-equity shares to be accounted for on an accruals basis if the entitlement to them is time-based, [91] and this may complicate the legal disclosure requirement if the accrued amount is not the same as that proposed for payment.

The Companies Act also contains various requirements for matters to be disclosed in the Directors' Report in respect of share capital. Those relating to directors' interests in shares are discussed in Chapter 27 at 3.1.1, while those in respect of the purchase by a company of its own shares are dealt with at 3.3 below. The Stock Exchange also requires listed companies to disclose details of holdings in the company's shares of 3% or more which have been notified to the company.[92]

3.2   Loan capital

In terms of the Companies Act, loan capital will fall under the general heading of creditors, which has to be analysed under the formats as shown here.[93]

Most UK companies follow Format 1 of the two formats available in the Act, and this means that they have to give two separate analyses under these headings, one for amounts falling due within one year and the other for amounts falling due after more than one year.

> Creditors
> 1. Debenture loans
> 2. Bank loans and overdrafts
> 3. Payments received on account
> 4. Trade creditors
> 5. Bills of exchange payable
> 6. Amounts owed to group undertakings
> 7. Amounts owed to undertakings in which the company has a participating interest
> 8. Other creditors including taxation and social security
> 9. Accruals and deferred income.

In distinguishing amounts between these two categories, the deciding factor is the earliest date at which the creditor could demand repayment.[94] As discussed in 2.2.7 above, FRS 4 interprets this restrictively.

In addition to the formats, the Act requires the following disclosures in respect of each item shown under creditors in the balance sheet:

(a)   the amount that is not repayable within five years of the balance sheet date and the terms of repayment and interest for such items;[95] and

(b)   the total amount in respect of which any security has been given, and an indication of the nature of the security.[96]

The Act also requires the following information to be given in relation to the issue of debentures:

(a)   the classes of debentures issued; and

(b)   the amount issued and the consideration received in respect of each class.[97]

Details must also be given of any debentures held by a nominee or a trustee for the company.[98]

A debenture is not defined in the Companies Act, except that it is said to *include* 'debenture stock, bonds and other securities of a company, whether constituting a charge on the assets of the company or not'.[99] In general legal use, it is a term applying to any document evidencing a loan, and in the context of company law it means a debt instrument issued by the company and usually giving some form of security or charge over its assets, although this is not an essential feature.

The Companies Act requires interest payable to be analysed into two categories:

(a)   that relating to bank loans and overdrafts; and

(b)   interest on all other loans.[100]

3.3   The purchase of a company's own shares

At one time, UK companies were prohibited from purchasing their own shares and could redeem only preference shares. These restrictions were eased by the Companies Act 1981, and a new regime introduced which permitted both the purchase and redemption of shares on a wider basis, subject to various conditions and safeguards.[101] The most important of these are as follows:

(a)   the capital of the company must be maintained, either by freezing up an equivalent amount of distributable profits in a 'capital redemption reserve' or by making it good from the proceeds of a fresh issue of shares made for the purposes of the redemption. However, there is a relaxation of this principle for private companies, discussed below;

(b)   the shares which are redeemed or purchased must be cancelled and may not be reissued;

(c)   the transaction must be permitted under the company's articles, and in certain cases must also be authorised by shareholder resolution; and

(d)   a transaction may not be undertaken if its effect will be that no shares remain in issue, or that the only shares in issue will be redeemable shares.

Some examples of the accounting treatment of such transactions are shown below:

Example 15.7: Redemption of own shares

A company has the following balance sheet:	£
Cash	20,000
Ordinary £1 shares	8,000
Redeemable preference £1 shares	5,000
Profit and loss account	7,000
	20,000

It decides to redeem half of its preference shares at par. The entries to effect the redemption and to maintain the original capital are as follows:

		£	£
Dr.	Redeemable preference shares	2,500	
Cr.	Cash		2,500

To redeem the shares, and

		£	£
Dr.	Profit and loss account reserve	2,500	
Cr.	Capital redemption reserve		2,500

To maintain the capital at its original amount.

As a result, the balance sheet will now be:

	£
Cash	17,500
Ordinary £1 shares	8,000
Redeemable preference £1 shares	2,500
Capital redemption reserve	2,500
Profit and loss account	4,500
	17,500

If there had been a fresh issue of shares, the second journal entry would not be needed except to the extent that the proceeds of the fresh issue fell short of £2,500.

If the redemption had been at a premium of (say) 20 pence per share, the entries and the balance sheet would have been as follows:

		£	£
Dr.	Redeemable preference shares	2,500	
Dr.	Profit and loss account reserve	500	
Cr.	Cash		3,000

To redeem the shares, and

		£	£
Dr.	Profit and loss account reserve	2,500	
Cr.	Capital redemption reserve		2,500

To maintain the capital at its original amount.

As a result, the balance sheet will now be:

	£
Cash	17,000
Ordinary £1 shares	8,000
Redeemable preference £1 shares	2,500
Capital redemption reserve	2,500
Profit and loss account	4,000
	17,000

The redemption premium of £500 must be met out of distributable profits; it cannot be met out of the proceeds of a fresh issue.

If the redeemable shares had originally been issued at a premium, and there is a fresh issue for the purposes of the redemption, then the premium on redemption can be met out of the proceeds of the fresh issue up to the limit of the lesser of:

(a)   the premium received by the company on the issue of the shares now being redeemed, or

(b)   the current balance on the share premium account including any premium on issue of the new shares.[102]

This is shown in the following example:

Example 15.8: Redemption of own shares at a premium

A company has the following balance sheet:

	£
Cash	40,000
Ordinary £1 shares	20,000
Redeemable preference £1 shares	5,000
Share premium account	3,000
Profit and loss account	12,000
	40,000

The preference shares were originally issued at a premium of 10 pence per share. The company now decides to redeem all of its preference shares, which carry a redemption premium of 30 pence per share, and at the same time have a fresh issue of 2,000 ordinary shares at an issue price of £2 per share. The entries are as follows:

		£	£
Dr.	Cash	4,000	
Cr.	Ordinary £1 shares		2,000
Cr.	Share premium account		2,000

To record the proceeds of the new issue.

		£	£
Dr.	Redeemable preference shares	5,000	
Dr.	Share premium account	500	
Dr.	Profit and loss account reserve	1,000	
Cr.	Cash		6,500

To effect the redemption, and

		£	£
Dr.	Profit and loss account reserve	1,500	
Cr.	Capital redemption reserve		1,500

To make good the capital.

The amount initially credited to share premium account in respect of the preference shares (£500) is the limiting factor on what can be released to offset the premium payable on redemption of the shares – the rest has to be met from distributable profits. The capital has to be made good because the proceeds from the new issue (£4,000) less the amount already applied towards the redemption premium (£500) fell short of the nominal value of the shares redeemed (£5,000). The amount of £2,500 charged to the profit and loss account represents the difference between the redemption cost of £6,500 and the proceeds of the fresh issue of £4,000.

As a result, the balance sheet will now be:

	£
Cash	37,500
Ordinary £1 shares	22,000
Redeemable preference £1 shares	–
Share premium account	4,500
Capital redemption reserve	1,500
Profit and loss account	9,500
	37,500

It can be seen that the aggregate of the share capital and undistributable reserves remains the same before and after the transaction, which is the objective of the rules which lie behind these journal entries.

	Before £	After £
Ordinary £1 shares	20,000	22,000
Redeemable preference £1 shares	5,000	–
Share premium account	3,000	4,500
Capital redemption reserve	–	1,500
	28,000	28,000

As mentioned above, these capital maintenance rules are relaxed for private companies which are unable to meet the cost of redemption either out of their distributable profits or from the proceeds of a fresh issue.[103] In order to be permitted to do this, various procedures have to be followed which are designed to protect the creditors of the company from the consequences of eroding its capital base. In particular, the directors must make a statutory declaration that they are of the opinion that there will be no grounds on which the company could be found to be unable to pay its debts, both immediately following the transaction and for a year thereafter, and the auditors must confirm, after enquiry, that they are not aware of anything which would indicate that the directors' opinion was unreasonable. An example of the accounting treatment in such a case is set out below:

Example 15.9: Redemption of own shares out of capital

A private company has the following balance sheet:

	£
Cash	20,000
Ordinary £1 shares	10,000
Redeemable preference £1 shares	5,000
Share premium account	3,000
Profit and loss account	2,000
	20,000

The directors decide that they wish to redeem all the preference shares at par. The distributable profits of the company are not adequate to allow this without reduction of its capital and accordingly the requirements of the Act must be followed to permit the transaction to proceed. When this has been done, the necessary entries will be as follows:

		£	£
Dr.	Redeemable preference shares	5,000	
Cr.	Cash		5,000
	To effect the redemption, and		
Dr.	Profit and loss account reserve	2,000	
Cr.	Capital redemption reserve		2,000

To make good the capital so far as the company is able to do so from its distributable profits.

As a result, the balance sheet will now be:

	£
Cash	15,000
Ordinary £1 shares	10,000
Redeemable preference £1 shares	–
Share premium account	3,000
Capital redemption reserve	2,000
Profit and loss account	–
	15,000

This time, the aggregate of the share capital and undistributable reserves is not the same before and after the transaction, because of the shortfall. The amount of the shortfall (£3,000 in this example) is referred to in the Act as the 'permissible capital payment'.

	Before	After
	£	£
Ordinary £1 shares	10,000	10,000
Redeemable preference £1 shares	5,000	–
Share premium account	3,000	3,000
Capital redemption reserve	–	2,000
	18,000	15,000

The mechanics for accounting for purchases of shares are the same as those for redemptions as shown above. Where a company has purchased some of its shares, it has to make various disclosures in the directors' report. These include the number and nominal value of the shares purchased, together with the amount of the consideration paid and the reasons for the purchase, and the percentage of the called-up share capital which it represents. These and other similar disclosures are also required in other similar circumstances, such as where a company takes a lien or charge over its shares, or provides financial assistance for the purchase of its shares and has a beneficial interest in such shares.[104]

Barclays is an example of a company which regularly purchases its own shares. The relevant disclosures from its accounts are shown below:

Extract 15.19: Barclays PLC (1998)

Directors' report

Share capital [extract]

During the year, Barclays PLC purchased in the market for cancellation 29,299,135 of its ordinary Shares at a total cost of £501 million as part of its programme of returning excess capital to shareholders. These transactions represented some 2% of the issued ordinary share capital at 1st January 1998. As at 15th February 1999, the Company has an unexpired authority to repurchase further shares up to a maximum of 195,700,865 ordinary shares.

Notes to the accounts

39 Called up share capital [extract]

	1998 £m	1997 £m
Called up share capital, allotted and fully paid		
Ordinary shares:		
At beginning of year	**1,529**	1,541
Issued to staff under the SAYE share option scheme	**9**	12
Issued under Share Dividend Scheme	**–**	5
Issued under Executive Share Option Scheme	**1**	1
Repurchase of shares	**(29)**	(30)
At end of year	**1,510**	1,529

In 1998, the Company repurchased ordinary shares with a nominal value of £29m at a total cost of £501m. In 1997, ordinary shares with a nominal value of £30m were repurchased at a total cost of £351m.

Consolidated statement of changes in reserves [extract]

	1998 £m	1997 £m
Capital redemption reserve		
At beginning of year	**150**	120
Repurchase of ordinary shares	**29**	30
At end of year	**179**	150
Profit and loss account [extract]		
At beginning of year	**4,304**	4,055
...		
Repurchase of ordinary shares	**(472)**	(321)
Transfer to capital redemption reserve	**(29)**	(30)
...		

Listed companies have to give the following disclosure requirements in relation to the purchase of their own shares:

(a) any shareholders' authority which existed at the year end for the company to purchase its own shares;

(b) the names of the sellers of any shares purchased or proposed to be purchased by the company during the year otherwise than through the market or by tender or partial offer to all shareholders; and

(c) where purchases, or options or contracts to make such purchases, have been entered into since the year end, the number, nominal value and percentage of the called up shares of the class purchased, the consideration paid and the reasons for the purchase.[105]

4   ACCOUNTING FOR PARTICULAR TYPES OF INSTRUMENT

4.1   Bonds with no rights to conversion

4.1.1   Fixed interest rate bonds

This is the most straightforward kind of borrowing to account for and the only mild complication is that the issue costs have to be deducted from the amount borrowed so as to be spread over the life of the loan.

Example 15.10: Fixed interest rate bonds

A company issues a £20 million bond for 5 years in respect of which the interest rate is 7%. The costs of the issue amount to £400,000.

FRS 4 requires the issue costs to be deducted from the proceeds of the borrowing to produce an initial net liability of £19.6 million. This is then accreted back up to the amount payable, in the following way (all figures in £000s):

Year	Total finance cost	Interest paid	Amortisation of issue costs	Balance sheet liability
0				19,600
1	1,469	1,400	69	19,669
2	1,474	1,400	74	19,743
3	1,480	1,400	80	19,823
4	1,485	1,400	85	19,908
5	1,492	1,400	92	20,000
Total	7,400	7,000	400	

The calculation of the total finance cost shown above is based on the rate inherent in all the cash flows (7.49% in this case), but in practice the amount of issue costs will usually not be material enough to require such rigour to be applied. Simplified methods of disposing of the issue costs, such as straight line amortisation or even immediate write-off will often be acceptable on materiality grounds.

4.1.2   Variable interest rate bonds

These are again simple borrowing arrangements, the only difference being that the interest cost varies in accordance with some external rate, such as LIBOR. FRS 4 does not require the finance cost to be 'equalised'; the interest is simply charged at whatever rate is in force for the period. The only mild complication is again created by any other components of finance cost (such as issue costs or premiums payable on redemption).

Example 15.11: Variable interest rate bonds

A company issues a £20 million bond for 5 years in respect of which the interest rate is LIBOR plus 1%. The cost of the issue is again £400,000. LIBOR is 6% at the outset but changes to 8% after 2 years.

Initially, this example is identical to the previous one and if LIBOR did not change, the accounting result would be exactly the same. The only variation comes when LIBOR changes. At that time, FRS 4 strictly requires a fresh calculation of the interest rate implicit in the arrangement – in other words, what is the rate needed to discount the future payments of interest (now £1.8m per annum) and principal to a present value of £19,743,000 (the amount carried in the balance sheet at the end of year 2). In this example, the rate changes from 7.49% to 9.51% and produces the following result (all figures in £000s):

Year	Total finance cost	Interest paid	Amortisation of issue costs	Balance sheet liability
0				19,600
1	1,469	1,400	69	19,669
2	1,474	1,400	74	19,743
3	1,878	1,800	78	19,821
4	1,886	1,800	86	19,907
5	1,893	1,800	93	20,000
Total	8,600	8,200	400	

Clearly in this example, the change makes a negligible difference to the pattern of amortising the non-interest component of finance costs, and the calculation need not therefore be performed in the rigorous way required by the standard. However, in some cases (for example, where the instrument is a deep discounted bond with a long life), the effect might be sufficiently material to justify making the calculation.

4.1.3   Stepped bonds

Stepped bonds are borrowing instruments whose interest rate escalates over the life of the bond in a predetermined way. This is illustrated in the following example:

Example 15.12: Stepped bonds

A company issues a £10 million bond for 10 years in respect of which the interest rate is 8% for the first three years, 10% for the next three and 13% for the final four. The annual interest payable therefore escalates from £800,000 to £1,300,000. (Issue costs are ignored in this example.)

If the company accounted for this on a cash basis it would record an artificially low finance cost in the early years and an artificially high cost towards the end of the life of the bond. FRS 4 requires that the total finance cost over the life of the bond should be calculated and charged to the profit and loss account at a constant rate on the outstanding amount rather than taking the cash payments at face value. This produces the following result (all figures in £000s):

Year	Finance cost	Interest paid	Difference	Accrued interest
1	1,006	800	206	206
2	1,027	800	227	433
3	1,050	800	250	683
4	1,075	1,000	75	758
5	1,082	1,000	82	840
6	1,091	1,000	91	931
7	1,100	1,300	(200)	731
8	1,080	1,300	(220)	511
9	1,057	1,300	(243)	268
10	1,032	1,300	(268)	0
Total	10,600	10,600		

The calculation of the interest charge shown above is again based on the rate inherent in all the cash flows, rather than simply the total interest charge (£10,600,000) divided by the period of the loan (10 years) which would give a flat annual charge of £1,060,000. Nevertheless in practice the straight line method is simpler and can often be used since it will seldom produce a material distortion.

4.1.4 Deep discounted bonds

A deep discounted bond is a bond which is issued at a discount to its par value and redemption value, and it is described as a deep discount because the proceeds on issue are considerably smaller than the par value. The instrument will normally pay either no interest (generally referred to as a zero coupon bond) or a very low annual rate of interest, so that the discount and any interest payable together represent a commercial rate of interest.

Under FRS 4, the discount forms part of the finance cost and is provided for through the profit and loss account over the life of the bond. The bond is therefore included as a liability at its issue price and thereafter accretes to the redemption value over its life, as shown in the example below:

Example 15.13: Deep discounted bonds

A company issues a bond for £47 million which is redeemable at its par value of £100 million at the end of 10 years. The interest rate is 3% per annum, and the annual interest payable is thus £3 million. The costs of issuing the bond are £2 million. Spreading the discount and the issue costs over the life of the bond in addition to the interest charge produces the following result (all figures in £000s):

Year	Finance cost	Interest paid	Amortisation of discount and issue costs	Balance sheet liability
0				45,000
1	5,953	3,000	2,953	47,953
2	6,344	3,000	3,344	51,297
3	6,785	3,000	3,785	55,082
4	7,287	3,000	4,287	59,369
5	7,854	3,000	4,854	64,223
6	8,496	3,000	5,496	69,719
7	9,223	3,000	6,223	75,942
8	10,046	3,000	7,046	82,988
9	10,978	3,000	7,978	90,966
10	12,034	3,000	9,034	100,000
Total	85,000	30,000	55,000	

Once again, the calculation of the total finance charge shown above is based on the rate inherent in all the cash flows (in this case 13.23%), rather than simply the total charge (£85,000,000) divided by the period of the loan (10 years) which would give a flat annual charge of £8,500,000. In this case, the more rigorous calculation is materially different from that which would be produced by amortising the total discount on a straight line basis, and the latter is therefore unlikely to produce an acceptable answer.

Since the balance sheet figure in the final column of the table falls substantially short of the liability ultimately payable (by the amount of finance costs to be recognised in the future, other than interest), it is necessary to disclose the full liability by way of note.[106]

4.1.5   Index-linked bonds

FRS 4 requires that, where the payments to be made under a debt instrument are contingent on future events, these events should be taken into account in the calculation of finance cost only when they have occurred.[107] This applies to variable interest loans (discussed at 4.1.2 above) but also to those whose interest or redemption values vary in accordance with a price index, such as the RPI.

A bond which is index-linked is analogous to one which is denominated in a foreign currency, and the accounting follows a similar pattern. The effect on the principal of the movement in the index is treated similarly to a translation difference; in other words the whole amount of the movement in the period is dealt with in the profit and loss account, while the interest payable in the period continues to be charged at whatever amount results from applying the index adjustment to it.

Example 15.14: Index-linked bonds

A company issues a £10 million bond for 5 years in respect of which the interest rate is 2%, but both interest and principal payments are linked to the RPI at the end of the year. Issue costs are ignored in this example. This will be accounted for in the following way (all figures in £000s):

Year	Index	Interest paid	Indexation adjustment	Total finance cost	Balance sheet liability
0	100				10,000
1	103	206	300	506	10,300
2	104	208	100	308	10,400
3	106	212	200	412	10,600
4	109	218	300	518	10,900
5	111	222	200	422	11,100
Total		1,066	1,100	2,166	

Sometimes, bonds that are linked to indexes which move in a predictable way may really only be stepped loans in disguise. These should be accounted for in accordance with their substance – by forecasting the total finance cost payable over the term of the instrument and allocating it so as to achieve a constant rate on the outstanding balance. Accordingly it is necessary to distinguish between arrangements with a genuine economic purpose and those which are contrived solely to have a particular accounting effect. Linking amounts payable under a loan to the RPI will have a commercial purpose; linking them to the age of the finance director's cat will not.

4.2 Convertible bonds

4.2.1 Traditional convertible bonds

A convertible bond is a hybrid instrument which initially has the character of a loan, bearing interest, but also entitles the bondholder to exchange the bond for shares in the company at some date in the future in accordance with specified conditions. Because of the conversion right, the coupon on the bond is set at a lower level than would be appropriate for straight borrowing. The effect from the equity shareholders' point of view is that they gain the benefits of cheap borrowing for a period but ultimately are likely to suffer a dilution in their holding in the company when the bonds are converted.

FRS 4 requires these to be accounted for as debt rather than equity and the finance cost to be measured on the assumption that the debt will never be converted. If conversion does take place, the carrying value of the instrument at that time is regarded as the consideration for the issue of the shares; no gain or loss is recorded on the conversion.[108]

4.2.2 Bonds with share warrants attached

In this case, a deep discount bond is issued together with a detachable warrant; such instruments are sometimes known as 'synthetic convertibles'. The warrant entitles the holder to obtain ordinary shares, and the further price that has to be paid for those shares on exercise of the warrant is paid out of the redemption of the bond at the end of its life.

In this case FRS 4 does take the view that the two elements should be accounted for separately, and the treatment required is therefore based on the example of 'split accounting' described at 2.2.2 above. It distinguishes the two cases on the basis that convertible debt is a single financial instrument whose various rights cannot be exercised independently, whereas bonds with warrants are really two separable instruments which should be accounted for individually. An example of this treatment can be found in the 1994 accounts of Pilkington, as shown below:

Extract 15.20: Pilkington plc (1994)

28. Called Up Share Capital [extract]

In April 1993 the company issued £80 million 7.5% bonds at an issue price of £95 million to finance the acquisition of the United Kingdom glass processing and merchanting business of Heywood Williams Group PLC. The bonds were issued with 78.2 million warrants, each warrant entitling the holder to procure up to 4 May 1998 the allotment of one share in Pilkington plc at a price of 120p.

The capital amount attributable to the warrants is £16.4 million and is included in other reserves.

4.2.3 *Convertible bonds with premium puts or enhanced interest*

A further elaboration on the convertible bond theme is to give the bondholder the option of putting his bond back to the company at a premium as an alternative to exercising his right to convert it into shares in the company. This raises a further question for the issuing company – whether to make provision for the premium over the life of the bond despite the fact that it may never become payable because the conversion option is exercised instead. A similar question arises when the interest rate on the bond is enhanced in later years if it remains unconverted; should the increased finance cost be accounted for from the outset, even though it may never be suffered?

FRS 4 requires that provision be made for such premiums or enhanced interest, and this is discussed in the Application Notes to the standard. This is consistent with an earlier ruling by the UITF[109] as well as the recommendation of TR 677. The standard requires that the finance cost on convertible debt should be calculated on the assumption that it will never be converted,[110] on the argument that this is the minimum return to which the holder is entitled, and is what he will be surrendering if he elects to convert. On the same argument, when conversion occurs, the consideration for the issue of the shares is the carrying amount of the debt, including the accrued premium.[111]

4.2.4 *Convertible capital bonds*

In the late 1980s, a number of groups issued convertible capital bonds, which are another form of hybrid instrument with features of both debt and equity. FRS 4 describes a typical example as being along the following lines: 'Convertible capital bonds are debt instruments on which interest is paid periodically, issued by a special purpose subsidiary incorporated outside the UK. Prior to maturity they may be exchanged for shares of the subsidiary which, at the option of the bondholder, are either immediately redeemed or immediately exchanged for ordinary shares of the parent. The bonds and payments in respect of the shares of the subsidiary are guaranteed by the parent. The parent has the right to issue convertible redeemable preference shares of its own in substitution for the bonds should it wish to do so.'[112]

A practice developed of showing such bonds at the end of the equity section of the balance sheet rather than within the liabilities section, on the argument that they were likely to form permanent capital of the company and that it was more realistic to include them with equity for such purposes as assessing the company's gearing. Because conversion into shares was mandatory except in a situation of default, it was argued that the liability to repay the debt was a remote contingency and could be disregarded. On this basis it was asserted that it was appropriate to treat the instrument as if it were a convertible preference share, the accounting for which is described at 4.4.2 below.

FRS 4 dismisses these arguments, because it does not permit conversion to be assumed under any circumstances. Accordingly, the relevant Application Note says that convertible capital bonds now have to be disclosed as debt in all cases.

4.2.5 *Perpetual debt*

Debt is sometimes issued on such terms that it is irredeemable, but that a coupon payment is to be made indefinitely. FRS 4 dismisses any suggestion that this means that no liability need be shown on the balance sheet, because the standard's guiding principle is to look at all the payments which the company is contractually bound to make, whether they are characterised as being capital or revenue. Where there is an obligation to pay a perpetual interest payment, the carrying value of the debt will by definition always be the original issue proceeds, because that is the figure derived from discounting the future payments at the rate implicit in the loan.

Sometimes a more artificial arrangement is devised, generally with a tax motive, whereby substantially all of the interest payments are made in the early part of the life of the debt, and the payments thereafter are negligible or even nil. The substance of such an arrangement is that the 'interest' payments are in reality a mixture of interest and capital repayments, and following the principles of FRS 4, this is how they should be accounted for. A variation on the same theme is to use very long-dated rather than perpetual debt. Often, any obligation to make payments of interest and capital beyond the initial term is transferred to another party for a small consideration, or another group company buys the right to receive such amounts from the original lender, with the result in either case that the group is left with only the liability for the significant payments during the initial term.

Examples of such instruments are disclosed in the accounts of Cadbury Schweppes:

Extract 15.21: Cadbury Schweppes p.l.c. (1998)

19 Borrowings [extract]

	1998		1997	
	Amounts due within one year	Amounts due after one year	Amounts due within one year	Amounts due after one year
Group	£m	£m	£m	£m
Secured				
Bank overdrafts	2	–	3	–
Other loans	1	–	3	–
European Bank for Reconstruction and Development Loan	3	38	4	3
Unsecured				
Floating Rate Notes 1998	–	–	250	–
5.875% Notes 1998 (US$200m)	–	–	122	–
8.5% Guaranteed Notes 1999 (A$75m)	28	–	–	30
6.25% Notes 1999 (US$300m)	181	–	–	182
8% Notes 2000 (£150m)	–	142	–	144
5.125% Guaranteed Notes 2001 (DM300m)	–	109	–	119
Obligations under perpetual loan (FFr 743m)	9	71	8	75
Obligations under fixed rate notes	18	26	17	44
Commercial paper (C$141m)	55	–	96	–
Master notes (US$250m)	151	–	152	–
Bank loans in foreign currencies	24	8	39	10
Bank overdrafts	43	–	41	–
Other loans	5	84	4	3
Obligations under finance leases	6	21	6	23
Acceptance credits	1	–	2	–
	527	499	744	673

... The obligations under the perpetual subordinated loan represent the present value of the future interest payments on the principal amount of FFr 1,600m which terminate in 2005; the interest rate is variable based on the Paris Inter-Bank Offered Rate. The obligations under the fixed rate notes represent the present value of future interest payments on £200 million of 12.55% Eurobonds up to 2001; the principal of the bonds and subsequent interest coupons have been acquired by a Group company. ...

4.3   Share options and warrants

As explained in 2.2.8, the standard requires the net proceeds of a warrant to be credited direct to shareholders' funds, and thereafter the accounting depends on whether the warrant is exercised or is allowed to lapse. If it is exercised, the proceeds on the original issue of the warrant are included in the net proceeds of the shares issued;[113] if it lapses, they are included instead in the statement of total recognised gains and losses.[114]

The question of what should be credited to share premium account is ultimately one of law.[115] It is not beyond legal doubt that warrant proceeds should be regarded subsequently as part of the consideration for the issue of shares if the warrant is exercised, which is the premise on which FRS 4's requirement is based. If this is the law, the same might be thought to apply to convertible instruments which are issued as an intermediate stage in a share issue, but this view does not always appear to be adopted in practice.

4.4   Preference shares

4.4.1   Redeemable preference shares

Redeemable preference shares can be regarded as quite similar in substance to fixed interest borrowings. There are, however, some important legal differences; for example, when they are redeemed, there is a requirement to make good the capital by a transfer to a capital redemption reserve; dividends can only be paid if there are sufficient distributable reserves; also, there are some significant differences between the treatment for both tax and accounting purposes of the dividends paid on shares compared to the interest paid on debt.

Dividends are regarded as a distribution of profits to the owners of the business rather than as an expense charged in measuring that profit. As such, prior to FRS 4 they were not generally accounted for on an accruals basis; this meant, for example, that when cumulative preference dividends were in arrears, they were not accrued in the accounts but simply noted as being in arrears. Similarly, if redeemable preference shares carried an escalating dividend rate, conventional accounting practice in the UK did not seek to 'equalise' the dividends in the way required for stepped bonds as discussed in 4.1.3 above. However, FRS 4 has changed this practice, so that appropriations are now made on an accruals basis, measured in the same way as for a debt instrument, unless ultimate payment is remote.[116] This is required even if the company currently has no distributable profits. The only normal circumstances in which dividends are not accrued are where they are non-cumulative, so that the holder permanently loses his right to a return on the shares for that period. However, Brunel Holdings has decided not to accrue for dividends on preference shares within minority interests on slightly different grounds, as shown in this extract.

Extract 15.22: Brunel Holdings plc (1999)

26. Contingent liabilities

Brunel Holdings plc or the Group have the following contingent liabilities which have not been provided in the balance sheet since no actual liability is expected to arise:

(i) *Unpaid preference dividends*

As set out in note 23, Blackwood Hodge plc has two classes of cumulative preference shares in issue. There are arrears of dividends totalling £581,000 (1997: £506,000) in respect of these shares. In the opinion of the Directors payment of the arrears and future dividends is remote in view of the substantial deficit on the distributable reserves of Blackwood Hodge plc.

Where cumulative preference dividends which are in arrears are accrued under FRS 4, it has to be considered whether the credit entry should be shown as a liability or as an element of non-equity shareholders' funds. Since they have not been declared, they do not represent a liability of the company as defined in FRS 4 and there is therefore quite a persuasive argument that they should be shown in the shareholders' funds section; the only difficulty with this argument is that it applies to *all* accrued dividends which have not yet been declared, whereas conventional UK accounting practice is to show such dividends in the liabilities section. In the light of these conflicting arguments, we believe that either classification can be justified for preference dividends in arrears.

In 1997, Signet Group showed arrears of dividends within shareholders' funds rather than within liabilities, and described the appropriation in the profit and loss account as an additional finance cost, not as a dividend, as shown in this extract:

Extract 15.23: Signet Group plc (1997)

Consolidated profit and loss account

for the 52 weeks ended 1 February 1997 [extract]

	52 weeks ended 1 February 1997 £000	53 weeks ended 3 February 1996 £000
Profit for the financial period	33,855	17,517
Dividends	–	–
Additional finance costs of non-equity shares	(26,398)	(42,075)
Retained profit/(loss) attributable to equity shareholders	7,457	(24,558)

23 Non-equity shareholders' funds

On 20 January 1992 the directors announced that payment of dividends on all of the Company's various classes of preference shares would cease until further notice. No dividends have been paid since that date. Dividends on all classes of preference shares are cumulative and payment of arrears of preference dividends would be due to be made before payments of dividends on ordinary shares recommenced. Cumulative arrears of preference dividends as at 1 February 1997 amounted to £155,281,000 (1996: £128,517,000).

In addition to the dividend arrears above, £6,221,000 (1996: £6,587,000) of preference dividends were accumulated on a time basis at 1 February 1997, but not in arrears. The increase in unpaid preference dividends in the period is stated net of £5,012,000 exchange loss (1996: £3,867,000 loss). In accordance with FRS 4, the following analysis sets out net issue proceeds plus the cumulative amount of accrued finance costs in respect of each class of the Company's preference shares.

	1997			1996
	Net issue proceeds £000	Unpaid preference dividends £000	Total non-equity shareholders' funds £000	Total non-equity shareholders' funds £000
Analysis of non-equity shareholders' funds				
6.875p convertible preference shares of 20p each	33,841	13,093	46,934	44,565
Cumulative redeemable preference shares 1997 of £10 each	30,000	16,633	46,633	43,519
Variable term preference shares of US$1 each	149,537	87,832	237,369	222,956
Convertible preference shares of US$0.01 each	104,223	43,944	148,167	141,665
Total non-equity shareholders' funds	**317,601**	**161,502**	**479,103**	452,705

Equity shareholders' funds, representing the difference between total shareholders' funds and non-equity shareholders' funds, showed a deficit of £178,358,000 (1996: £181,378,000 deficit) for the Group. In the Company's balance sheet equity shareholders' funds at 1 February 1997 amounted to £117,437,000 (1996:£152,710,000).

FRS 4 requires the full finance cost of non-equity shares to be shown as appropriated from profits, even if the Company does not have sufficient distributable reserves to pay a dividend at that time. As it is not legally possible to show dividends payable if the Company has insufficient distributable reserves to support a dividend, the appropriation has been classified as an additional finance cost in respect of non-equity shares.

Upon the capital restructuring, which was approved by shareholders on 26 June 1997, becoming effective (expected to be on 21 July 1997), all of the preference shares will be converted into new ordinary shares and all arrears and accruals of preference dividends will be cancelled.

As mentioned at the end of the above extract, the group subsequently underwent a capital reduction to eliminate these arrears, as described in the following extract from its 1999 accounts.

Extract 15.24: Signet Group plc (1999)

22 Cancellation of dividend accruals and arrears

Before the capital restructuring became effective on 21 July 1997, there were in issue various classes of preference shares. Dividends on all the classes of preference shares were cumulative and payment of arrears of preference dividends would have been due to be made before payments of dividends on ordinary shares. Since no dividends had been paid since 20 January 1992, cumulative arrears and accruals of preference dividends as at 1 February 1997 amounted to £161,502,000. As part of the capital restructuring, all preference shares were redesignated as deferred shares and all arrears and accruals of preference dividends were cancelled.

FRS 4 required the full finance cost of non-equity shares to be shown as appropriated from profits, even if the Company did not have sufficient distributable reserves to pay a dividend at that time.

As it is not legally possible to show dividends payable if the Company has insufficient distributable profits to support a dividend, the appropriation was classed as an additional finance cost in respect of non-equity shares.

The cancellation of the accumulated arrears and accruals of dividends on preference shares was credited in the profit and loss account as follows:

	1999 £000	1998 £000	1997 £000
Appropriation to preference shareholders in the period	–	(3,840)	(26,398)
Appropriation from preference shareholders arising from cancellation of dividend arrears and accruals	–	165,342	–
	–	161,502	(26,398)
Costs of share capital reorganisation	–	(6,971)	–
	–	154,531	(26,398)

The appropriations to preference shareholders in 1998 and 1997 are stated net of £6,634,000 and £5,012,000 exchange gains respectively.

Preference shares are sometimes structured so that they have a variable dividend level which depends on prevailing interest rates, which may be set at auction; the investors who make the lowest bid each month hold the instrument. The cost of this form of finance is thus similar to that of commercial paper, and it might be regarded as in substance a debt issue, but under FRS 4 they are nonetheless classified as non-equity shares.

SmithKline Beecham has subsidiaries that have issued some shares of this kind, whose terms are fully described in this extract from its financial statements:

Extract 15.25: SmithKline Beecham plc (1998)

19 PREFERENCE SHARES – NON-EQUITY INTERESTS

SB Corp, a wholly-owned subsidiary incorporated in Pennsylvania, U.S., has in issue 800 Auction Rate (ARPS) of $500,000 each, issued in ten series. The dividend rate on each series varies (predominantly with prevailing interest rates) and is set every seven weeks at an 'auction' at which the shares are also traded.

SmithKline Beecham Holdings Corp (SBH Corp), a wholly owned subsidiary incorporated in Delaware, U.S., has in issue 7,500 shares of Flexible Auction Market Preferred Stock (FAMPS) of $100,000 each issued in three series. The dividend on each series of FAMPS is fixed over a three- to seven-year period. SBH Corp also has in issue 4,000 shares of Money Market Preferred Stock (MMPS) of $100,000 each issued in five series. The dividend on each series of MMPS varies and is currently set every seven weeks at an 'auction' at which the shares are also traded.

Together, the ARPS, the FAMPS and the MMPS, constitute the 'Preference Shares'.

Payment of dividends declared on the Preference Shares is guaranteed by the Company in certain circumstances, and the Company has also agreed with SB Corp and SBH Corp that in certain circumstances it will provide support to SB Corp and SBH Corp in relation to the principal. However, any guarantee or support is limited so that in no circumstances could the holder of Preference Shares be in a more favourable position than had he been a holder of a Preference Share in SB plc. The Preference Shares represent a long-term, non-equity minority interest in the Group balance sheet in accordance with FRS 4 'Capital Instruments'.

4.4.2 Convertible preference shares

Such instruments are simply disclosed as a separate class of non-equity share capital, with details of their terms. Where the preference shares have been issued by the parent, the only available treatment is to show them as a component of shareholders' funds, but frequently such shares are issued by a subsidiary company for tax reasons. In this case they will either fall under the category of minority interest on consolidation or, if guaranteed by the parent or another group company, they will be shown as liabilities in the consolidated balance sheet.

Convertible preference share issues may be issued with a premium put, so that, in effect, if the redemption option is chosen, an enhanced dividend will be paid. As with convertible debt, FRS 4 requires this to be taken into account in measuring the finance cost of the instrument. This requires an additional annual appropriation of profits to be made, so that the total amount appropriated in respect of the shares is at a constant proportion to the total amount recognised for the shares in the balance sheet.[117]

4.5 Interest rate swaps

An interest rate swap is an agreement between two counterparties that they will exchange fixed rate interest for floating rate interest on a notional amount of principal. The principal is notional in the sense that it itself is not exchanged, only the amounts of interest determined by reference to it.

The objective of entering into an interest rate swap is effectively to convert existing finance from a fixed interest basis to a floating rate basis or vice versa.

The treatment recommended by TR 677 was therefore to incorporate the terms of the swap into those of the existing finance; for example, if a company has a floating rate loan but enters into an interest rate swap because it prefers not to have exposure to floating rates, then the accounts would portray the loan as if it were at fixed rates. The Technical Release went on to say that 'there should be full disclosure of the arrangement in the notes to the financial statements, so that the true commercial effect on the whole transaction, including any possible risk of exposure in the event of the failure of the swap-party, is clearly explained'.[118] The subject of interest rate swaps or other similar hedges is not addressed in FRS 4, but is now being addressed in the ASB's project on financial instruments (see Chapter 9).

4.6 Scrip dividends

Scrip dividends arise when a company offers its shareholders the choice of receiving further fully paid up shares in the company as an alternative to receiving a cash dividend.

The FRS requires that a scrip dividend should initially be recorded at its cash amount as an appropriation in the profit and loss account. As it is unclear at that time how many shareholders will elect to receive shares, the whole amount of the dividend should be recorded as a liability in the balance sheet. This obviously applies to final dividends, since the take-up of the scrip will not be known until after the accounts have been prepared. However, where the interim dividend has taken the form of a scrip dividend during the year it will be possible to reflect exactly what has been paid in cash and what has been issued in the form of shares. We believe, however, that FRS 4 still intends that the dividend be shown as an appropriation in the profit and loss account at its full cash amount.[119]

Once shareholders have chosen to receive shares instead of cash, two possible approaches exist, described respectively as the reinvestment approach and the bonus share approach. As the name suggests, the former takes the view that a dividend has been paid, but then reinvested in shares; accordingly, the consideration for the issue of the shares is the amount of the dividend and is divided as appropriate between share capital (to the extent of their nominal value) and share premium account. The alternative view is that the shares are issued *instead* of a dividend; accordingly, no consideration has been received and the issue is a simple bonus issue, which results in the capitalisation of a suitable reserve to the extent of the nominal value of the shares issued.

FRS 4 is rather ambiguous about the choice between these approaches. On the one hand, paragraph 48 suggests that it favours the reinvestment approach, because it says that 'the value of such shares should be deemed to be the amount receivable if the alternative of cash had been chosen', but it may be that this is discussing only the initial treatment in the profit and loss account as mentioned above. Paragraph 99, on the other hand, says that if the 'scrip dividend takes the legal form of a bonus issue of shares, the appropriation should be written back as a reserve movement, and appropriate amounts transferred between reserves and share capital to reflect the capitalisation of reserves', which is the bonus share approach.

Some lawyers maintain that no choice is available between these two methods; the right method is dictated by the form of the transaction. They would say that the question of whether the shares are issued for consideration or not is one of legal fact, not of interpretation. Accordingly, where a shareholder signs a mandate form which says that he elects to receive an allotment of shares instead of the dividend (as is typically the case), he will thereafter receive a bonus issue, which should be accounted for as such. If one accepts this view, the normal accounting treatment would be as illustrated in this example:

Example 15.15: Scrip dividend

A company declares a final dividend for the year ended 31 December 1999 of 20 pence per share, but offers shareholders the alternative of accepting 1 share for every 10 held. The issued share capital of the company is 10 million £1 shares, and their current market price is £2 per share.

When it draws up its accounts for 1999 it does not know how many shareholders will opt for the scrip dividend. Under FRS 4, it records £2 million (being the cash amount) as an appropriation in the profit and loss account and provides the same amount within creditors as 'dividends payable'.

Subsequently, the shareholders accept the cash dividend in respect of 8 million shares but opt for the further shares in respect of the remaining 2 million.

Assuming that the legal form of the scrip dividend was a bonus issue, the issue of shares to those who have opted for them is viewed as a bonus issue and accounted for at nominal value. Thus the further journal entries which have to be made are as follows:

		£000	£000
Dr.	Dividends payable	2,000	
Cr.	Cash		1,600
Cr.	Profit and loss account reserve		400

To reverse the previous entry to the extent of the scrip dividend and recognise the payment of the remainder, and

		£000	£000
Dr.	Reserves	200	
Cr.	Share capital		200

To record the bonus issue. The reserve to be used would depend on what was available, but could be, for example, a share premium account or a revaluation reserve as well as the profit and loss account reserve.

If, on the other hand, the scrip dividend did not take the legal form of a bonus issue, the share issue would have to be accounted for differently. This situation may arise if, under the mandate form, the shareholder elects to receive a cash dividend but irrevocably authorises the company to apply the cash on his behalf in subscribing for the appropriate number of new shares. As this is tantamount to an issue of shares for cash, FRS 4 would require the shares to be recorded by reference to the cash equivalent of the dividend foregone.

The guidance on scrip dividends in FRS 4 therefore remains rather ambiguous. It would seem likely that both the reinvestment approach and the bonus issue approach can continue to be used, subject to any legal advice which companies obtain as to the proper interpretation of the terms of the transaction and the particular requirements of the company's articles. However, it appears that the bonus issue approach has become the predominant method in practice; HSBC uses this approach.

Extract 15.26: HSBC Holdings plc (1998)

8 Dividends

	1998		1997	
	US$ per share	US$m	US$ per share	US$m
First interim	0.370	996	0.325	874
Second interim	0.555	1,499	0.505	1,332
	0.925	5,495	0.830	2,206

Of the first interim dividend for 1998, US$107 million (1997: US$125 million) was settled by the issue of shares. Of the final dividend for 1997, US$477 million (1996: US$212 million) was settled by the issue of shares in 1998.

32 Reserves [extract]

	Group	Company	Associated undertakings
	US$m	US$m	US$m
Share premium account:			
At 1 January 1998	489	489	–
Shares issued under option schemes	14	14	–
Shares issued in lieu of dividends and associated issue costs	(27)	(27)	–
Exchange movements	4	4	–
At 31 December 1998	480	480	–
Profit and loss account			
At 1 January 1998	18,923	4,753	163
Retained profit (deficit) for the year	1,823	(1,423)	126
Transfer of depreciation to revaluation reserve	52	–	–
Realisation on disposal of properties	13	–	–
Arising on shares issued in lieu of dividends	584	584	–
Exchange and other movements	(36)	(1)	(42)
At 31 December 1996	21,359	3,913	247

As the above extract shows, HSBC has added back US$584m to the profit and loss account within its reserves note, being the amount of dividends (US$107m and US$477m) taken in shares rather than cash. The US$27m charged to share premium is the nominal value of the shares issued by way of the bonus issue.

An example of the reinvestment approach can be found in the 1996 accounts of Hillsdown Holdings:

Extract 15.27: Hillsdown Holdings plc (1996)

	1996 £m	1995 £m
7 Dividends		
Per 10p ordinary share		
Interim – 2.2p (1995: 2.2p)	15.5	15.3
Final – 7.8p (1995: 7.3p)	55.7	51.1
	71.2	66.4
Canadian C$1,000 preference shares	–	0.7
	71.2	67.1

18 Reserves [extract]

	Share premium £m	Revaluation reserve £m	Profit and loss account £m	Total reserves £m
Group				
At 1st January 1996	63.3	51.4	453.0	567.7
Movements in year				
Profit retained	–	–	24.2	24.2
Revaluation reserve realised	–	(9.6)	9.6	–
Revaluations	–	(3.1)	–	(3.1)
Issue of ordinary shares:				
Scrip dividend election	3.8	–	–	3.8
Share option schemes	8.5	–	–	8.5
Goodwill arising from acquisitions	–	–	(115.5)	(115.5)
Exchange adjustments	–	–	(6.2)	(6.2)
At 31st December 1996	**75.6**	**38.7**	**365.1**	**479.4**

This time there is a credit rather than a debit to share premium, because the new shares are regarded as having been issued in exchange for reinvested dividends, not as a bonus issue. There is no adjustment to the dividends that have been declared, nor any add-back to retained earnings.

4.7   Employee share schemes

FRS 4 does not address questions relating to transactions in the reporting entity's own shares for the purposes of employee share schemes. However, the Urgent Issues Task Force has issued two Abstracts dealing with different problems that have arisen in relation to such schemes. These are discussed below.

4.7.1   UITF 13 – Accounting for ESOP Trusts

The subject of employee share ownership plans ('ESOPs') came to the UITF as an off balance sheet finance question, requiring interpretation under FRS 5, although arguably the more important issue concerns the recognition and measurement of the cost of such arrangements, and it would have been better addressed from that perspective. Companies frequently establish share ownership schemes for their employees, whereby the employees are given the opportunity to buy shares in the company on favourable terms or to receive them free under a profit sharing scheme. Either new or existing shares may be used for this purpose; where existing shares are used, they are generally purchased by a trust or other third party, which is financed by a loan from either the company itself or from a bank. In the latter case, the bank loan will usually be guaranteed by the company. The accounting issue that arises under FRS 5 is how to deal with the trust in the employing company's accounts.

Arrangements of this sort are not discussed directly in FRS 5, but the UITF issued guidance on the matter by publishing its thirteenth Abstract in June 1995. This rules that certain assets and liabilities of the trust should be accounted for as those of the employer company itself where the company 'has de facto control of the shares held by the ESOP trust and bears their benefits or risks'.[120] More specifically, the Abstract goes on to say that:

(a)   Until such time as the shares held by the ESOP trust vest unconditionally in employees, they should be recognised as assets of the sponsoring company. Where shares have been gifted unconditionally to specific employees, they should no longer be recognised as assets of the sponsoring company, even if they are still held by the ESOP trust.

(b)   Where the shares are held for the continuing benefit of the sponsoring company's business they should be classified as 'own shares' within fixed assets; otherwise they should be classified as 'own shares' within current assets.

(c)   Where the shares are classified as fixed assets, any permanent diminution in their value should be recognised immediately.

(d)   Where shares are conditionally gifted or put under option to employees at below the book value determined in (c) above, (i.e. for fixed assets, after taking account of any permanent diminution in value), the difference between book value and residual value should be charged as an operating cost over the period of service of the employees in respect of which the gifts or options are granted.

(e)   The sponsoring company should record as its own liability any borrowings of the ESOP trust that are guaranteed, formally or informally, by the sponsoring company.

(f)   Finance costs and any administrative expenses should be charged as they accrue and not as funding payments are made to the ESOP trust.

(g)   Any dividend income arising on the shares should be excluded in arriving at profit before tax and deducted from the aggregate of dividends paid and proposed. The deduction should be disclosed on the face of the profit and loss account, if material, or in a note. Until such time as the shares vest unconditionally in employees, the shares should also be excluded from earnings per share calculations as, under FRS 14 'Earnings per Share' they are treated as if they were cancelled.[121]

The general thrust of the above is that companies should account for the transactions of their ESOP trusts as if they had conducted them themselves; the trust is portrayed as merely an extension of the company. A possible alternative approach would have been to regard the trust as a quasi-subsidiary of the company which therefore had to be consolidated in it group accounts, but the Abstract goes further, by requiring the assets and liabilities of the trust to be treated as belonging directly to the employer company.

UITF 13 requires disclosure of sufficient information to enable readers of the accounts to understand the significance of the ESOP trust in the context of the sponsoring company, and in particular:

(a)   a description of the main features of the ESOP trust including the arrangements for distributing shares to employees;

(b)   the manner in which the costs are dealt with in the profit and loss account;

(c)   the number and market value of shares held by the ESOP trust and whether dividends on those shares have been waived; and

(d)   the extent to which these shares are under option to employees, or have been conditionally gifted to them.[122]

Appendix II to the Abstract gives a number of illustrative examples of the accounting treatment required under various scenarios.

The accounts of Enterprise Oil and BOC disclose the following information about the shares that are held in their ESOP trusts:

Extract 15.28: Enterprise Oil plc (1998)

13. Investments (held as fixed assets) [extract]

	At 1 January 1998 £m	Movements £m	At 31 December 1998 £m
Own shares held by employee share scheme trusts			
Shares (at cost)	31.0	10.3	**41.3**
Amortisation	(5.4)	1.5	**(3.9)**
	25.6	11.8	**37.4**

ii) Own shares held by employee share scheme trusts

Employee share schemes set up as trusts hold Enterprise Oil plc ordinary shares to meet potential obligations under the schemes.

Shares are held in trust until such time as they may be transferred to employees in accordance with the terms of the schemes, details of which are given on pages 41 and 42. Surplus shares may be held to satisfy future awards.

The group recognises the cost of the Enterprise Oil Long Term Performance Related Scheme through an annual amortisation charge based on management's estimate of the likely level of vesting of shares, apportioned over the period of service to which the award relates.

At 31 December 1998 the trusts held a total of 8,025,715 shares (1997: 5,725,849), which had not vested unconditionally in employees, with a market value at that date of £23.7 million (1997: £33.5 million). No provision in respect of the difference between the market value and carried value has been made since, in the opinion of the directors, there has not been a permanent impairment in the value of Enterprise shares. Dividends on these shares have been waived by the respective trustees.

Extract 15.29: The BOC Group plc (1998)

9. Fixed assets – investments [extract]

	Own shares at cost £million
a) Group	
At 1 October 1997	24.0
Acquisitions/additions	5.4
Disposals	(2.6)
At 30 September 1998	**26.8**

ii) **Own shares**

For share-based incentive schemes which do not use new issue shares, options are satisfied by the transfer of shares held in trust for the purpose. At 30 September 1998, options over 3.9 million shares were outstanding under these schemes, for which 3.8 million shares in the Company were held pending exercise.

Loans and advances for the purchase of shares in trust have been made either by the company or its subsidiaries. If the value of shares in trust is insufficient to cover the loans, the company and subsidiaries will bear any loss. The company also bears administrative costs on an accruals basis.

Deposits of £3.4 million are currently held in trust by the BOC Group Qualifying Share Ownership Trust 1997. These deposits are included as part of the Group's net borrowings in accordance with UITF Abstract 13.

Based on the Company's share price on 30 September 1998 of 728.75p, the market value of own shares held in trust was £27.8 million. This compares with the acquisition cost shown above.

Own shares are shown as fixed asset investments for accounting purposes, in accordance with FRS 5 and UITF Abstract 13. Information on share option schemes appears in the report of the management resources committee and notes 6 and 12.

In fact, these shares are carried only in BOC's group balance sheet, whereas those of Enterprise Oil appear in the balance sheets of both the group and parent company.

The economics of these arrangements are similar to those which arise under a defined benefits pension scheme. As in BOC's case, the employer generally has to meet any shortfall in value of the shares in the trust in the same way as it would have to meet the balance of cost necessary to provide final salary pensions, and it thus it has a direct economic interest in the fund even though the scheme is operated by independent trustees. However, FRS 5 does not require the assets and liabilities of pension funds to be brought on to the balance sheets of employers, saying that: 'As SSAP 24 contains the more specific provisions on accounting for pension obligations and does not require consolidation of pension funds, such funds should not be consolidated as quasi-subsidiaries.'[123]

An Appendix to the Abstract tries to reconcile its requirements with those applying to pension schemes, saying 'the substance of ESOP trusts is different from that of pension schemes ... in that pension schemes have a longer time-frame and are wider in scope with the result that the obligations imposed by trust law and statute have a much greater commercial effect in practice'.[124] However it has to be said that this distinction is not entirely convincing and some ESOP trustees have even seen this comparison as impugning their integrity in a rather offensive way.

One awkward result of the Abstract's approach is that is not entirely clear what to do in the common situation where a number of operating subsidiaries each make contributions to the trust under a group scheme. Can it be said that each of them 'has de facto control of the shares held by the ESOP trust and bears their benefits or risks'? This wording rather assumes that the employer will be a single entity which both controls the trust and is exposed to the benefits or risks of the shares held; however, in a group situation the parent company is likely to be the only entity that can claim to exercise any control, whereas the exposure to benefits and risks lies with each of the operating companies in relation to their various employees. Clearly, the consolidated accounts will still follow the accounting treatment specified by the Abstract because these various elements are united at group level, but arguably the individual entities are not within its scope.

In fact, the whole approach to this issue – based as it is on FRS 5 and the recognition of assets and liabilities – has been both narrow and somewhat oblique. As noted above, a preferable approach might have been to view the question as one of expense recognition; coming at the issue from this direction might also have achieved a treatment that is more compatible with pension scheme accounting. This would have focused on the fact that benefits have been awarded to employees in the form of shares that entail a cost which must be systematically accounted for, and buying shares through an ESOP trust is only one of the possible ways of hedging that cost – as shown below, the 1996 accounts of Grand Met show that it was hedging most of this exposure off balance sheet, through options on shares:

Extract 15.30: Grand Metropolitan Public Limited Company (1996)

15 Fixed assets – investments [extract]

Other investments include £4m *(1995 – £217m)* in respect of 1,208,084 *(1995 – 53,428,489)* ordinary shares of 25p each in Grand Metropolitan Public Limited Company with an aggregate nominal value of £0.3m *(1995 – £13m)*. The shares are held for the sole purpose of satisfying obligations under employee share option schemes operated by the group. On 1st December 1995, 51,879,015 shares were sold to an independent third party, and employee share trusts simultaneously purchased options from the third party which gave them the right to obtain the shares, as required, at the same price as the employee share options.

In March 1999, the UITF issued a proposal that sought to amend the requirements of UITF 13 in respect of the balance sheet classification of the shares held by the ESOP. Instead of being shown as an asset in the sponsoring company's accounts, the cost of the shares acquired would be shown as a separately disclosed deduction from share capital and reserves.[125] However, respondents showed limited enthusiasm for this proposal, and the UITF subsequently dropped the issue, leaving it to be picked up by the ASB as part of its project on accounting for equity.[126]

4.7.2　UITF 17 – Employee share schemes

In April 1997, the UITF published its seventeenth Abstract, *Employee share schemes*.[127] This addresses the relatively narrow issue of how companies should recognise and measure the cost of new shares issued as part of an employee share scheme, and was designed to counter arrangements that had been contrived to charge the profit and loss account with only the nominal value of such shares. The Abstract does not apply to Inland Revenue approved Save-As-You-Earn schemes and similar arrangements.

UITF 17 says that the total amount charged to the profit and loss account in such circumstances should be the fair value of the shares at the time the right to the shares is granted to the employee (less any amount payable by him or her).[128] The shares are therefore regarded as issued at whatever the market value was at the date of grant, and this holds true even though the market value at the date of issue later turns out to be higher or lower. For the purposes of the rules on share premium account, however, the Task Force was advised that the consideration for the issue of the shares could normally be taken as being only the amount of cash subscribed for the shares, which means that the difference (the excess of the market value at the date of grant over the cash subscribed) can be credited to any other reserve, including profit and loss account reserve, on issue of the shares. The total credit entry will appear in the reconciliation of shareholders' funds, not in the statement of total recognised gains and losses.[129]

The accounting treatment described above assumes that the obligation to deliver shares to the employee is indeed eventually satisfied by a new issue of shares. In the event that existing shares are bought on the market by an ESOP instead, then the price paid (less the cash to be received from the employee) will become the cost instead of the market value at the date of grant.[130]

The cost is to be recognised in the profit and loss account over the period to which the employee's performance relates, usually on a straight line basis unless some other basis better matches the services received. This may be in one year, in the case of an annual bonus, or a longer period for a long-term incentive scheme.[131] The period will not normally extend to include any secondary 'loyalty' period (for which the employee must remain in employment after meeting the performance conditions) 'unless it is clear that the effect of the scheme is to reward services over the longer period'.[132] The amount charged to the profit and loss account will continue to be adjusted during this period as estimates of the total cost are refined – this will reflect changes in assumptions such as the likelihood of the performance conditions being met, the number of employees leaving the company before qualifying for the awards, and so on.[133]

The accounting treatment described above also applies to the grant of share options, with the result that any options granted at a discount to the then ruling market price of the shares will require the discount to be charged to the profit and loss account.[134] (This will rarely apply in relation to directors, because the Stock Exchange requires shareholder approval before listed companies can grant options to directors at a discount.)

An Appendix to the Abstract contains a number of illustrative examples that show the mechanics of the required accounting treatment.

The Abstract came into force for periods ending on or after 22 June 1997, without offering any transitional relief for the costs of schemes that had arisen in earlier periods.[135]

In March 1999, the UITF proposed an amendment to the Abstract to eliminate the difference between the cost charged for schemes satisfied by existing shares and newly issued shares. The proposal was that the cost should be determined at the date of granting the options for all schemes, irrespective of how the shares were subsequently sourced. This meant that if shares were later bought on the market at different prices, that difference would no longer be reported through the profit and loss account as an element of the cost of the scheme; instead, it would be dealt with as a transaction with shareholders, within reserves. This was consistent with the perspective of the change to UITF 13 that was proposed at the same time, that such shares should be classified in the balance sheet as a deduction from equity rather than as an asset.[136] As with that other proposal, however, respondents were not convinced of the merits of the change. The UITF therefore decided to leave UITF 17 unchanged, and referred the matter to the ASB for further consideration under its project on accounting for equity.[137]

Another issue that was revisited in the course of this debate was the exemption for SAYE schemes. The UITF did not propose to remove the exemption, but did suggest that the benefit to the profit and loss account from using the exemption should be disclosed. Again, however, this proposal did not survive.

One company that has elected not to use the exemption for SAYE schemes, however, is Boots, as shown in the extract below. As a result, it has recorded a £60 million expense that it could have avoided, although this has been reported as a one-off exceptional item rather than being allocated against the years in which the employees earned their entitlement to the shares, as UITF 17 would have required if it had applied to such schemes. The Abstract says that 'where there are no performance criteria and the award is clearly unrelated to past performance, the period over which the cost is recognised should be that from the date of the award to the date at which the employee becomes unconditionally entitled to the shares'.[138]

Extract 15.31: The Boots Company PLC (1999)

Financial Review

QUEST During the year, the company established a qualifying employee share ownership trust ('QUEST') in connection with its existing SAYE share scheme, which is open to all UK employees. (The company ceased granting executive options in 1995.) The QUEST enables the company to use existing shares to satisfy options, rather than issuing new shares, in a tax-efficient way. The QUEST has bought in the market 16.9 million shares, enough to meet all existing options, at an average price of 909p per share. The cost of these purchases, which is the difference between the option price and the price paid for the shares, was charged this year against profits as an exceptional item. In addition, interest charges have been incurred for funding the shares while they are in the QUEST. However, we could have decided to issue new shares and if so the accounting treatment would have avoided charging costs to the profit and loss account. Perhaps for this reason, most other companies issue new shares.

We believe, however, that using existing shares avoids diluting the value of existing shareholdings and helps produce a more efficient capital structure. In addition it is more transparent as the cost is shown against profits.

£60 million has been charged against profits this year as a result of acquiring shares to cover all existing SAYE options. In future, it will only be necessary to acquire shares to meet new options and the charge should be much lower.

Notes relating to the Financial Statements

12 Fixed asset investments [extract]

During the year a qualifying employee share ownership trust ('the trust') was established by the company under a deed of trust dated 16th February 1999. The purpose of the trust is to acquire shares in the company as a means through which shares will be delivered to employees (including executive directors) who exercised options granted in respect of the company's shares under the Boots 1990 SAYE share option scheme. Under this scheme, options have been granted enabling employees to subscribe for ordinary shares at 80% of the average middle market price on the three days preceding the date of offer. The options may normally be exercised up to six months after they mature either three, five or seven years after grant.

At 31st March 1999 16.9m (1998 Nil) ordinary shares at a cost of £154.8m (1998 £Nil) with a market value of £150.9m (1998 Nil) had been purchased by Boots (QUEST) Trustee Limited on behalf of the trust. The company provided funds to the trust for this purpose. A provision for permanent diminution in the value of shares of £59.7m has been charged to the profit and loss account as an exceptional item. Dividends have been waived by the trust.

Outstanding options for which shares have been acquired are as follows:

Option granted	Number of shares held (millions) 1999	Number of shares held (millions) 1998	Option price (p)
1991	0.1	–	337
1992	0.4	–	352
1992	0.2	–	386
1993	0.3	–	350
1993	0.4	–	418
1994	1.1	–	421
1994	1.0	–	415
1995	1.8	–	410
1996	3.0	–	485
1997	4.6	–	588
1998	4.0	–	808

5 COMPARISON WITH IASC AND US PRONOUNCEMENTS

5.1 IASC

5.1.1 IAS 10

In May 1999, the IASC published a revised version of IAS 10 – *Events After the Balance Sheet Date*. This amended previous practice on the accrual of outgoing equity dividends, so as to prevent such dividends being provided for if they were approved or declared only after the year end.[139] Previously, the standard had permitted the UK practice of accruing dividends that were proposed to be paid in respect of the period being reported on, even though the decision as to the amount of the dividend had not been made at the balance sheet date. Consistent with its framework, the IASC does not believe that such dividends represent liabilities that can be recognised. The revised standard comes into force for accounting periods beginning on or after 1 January 2000.[140]

5.1.2 IAS 32

IAS 32 – *Financial Instruments: Disclosure and Presentation* – came into force for accounting periods beginning on or after 1 January 1996. It does not apply to obligations arising under post-employment benefits, employee stock option or purchase plans or insurance contracts, but it is intended to be applied by all companies.[141] As its title suggests, the standard is not concerned with issues of recognition and measurement, but simply with disclosure and presentational matters, although necessarily the disclosures that have to be made are influenced by some recognition and measurement issues.

The most important definitions used in the standard are as follows.

A *financial liability* is any liability that is a contractual obligation:

(a)   to deliver cash or another financial asset to another enterprise; or

(b)   to exchange financial instruments with another enterprise under conditions that are potentially unfavourable.[142]

A *financial instrument* is any contract that gives rise to both a financial asset of one enterprise and a financial liability or equity instrument of another enterprise.[143]

An *equity instrument* is any contract that evidences a residual interest in the assets of an enterprise after deducting all of its liabilities.[144] On this analysis, redeemable preference shares are regarded as liabilities rather than equity instruments, whereas in the UK such shares are included in shareholders' funds as non-equity interests.

IAS 32's distinction between debt and equity therefore depends on whether or not the issuer has a contractual obligation to deliver cash or another financial asset to the holder of the instrument (or to exchange another financial instrument with him on potential unfavourable terms), regardless of the legal form of the instrument.[145] The classification of finance costs between interest and dividends in the income statement is consistent with the analysis of the instruments in the balance sheet.[146] While there is obvious conceptual merit in such an approach, it runs into conflict with the law in the UK; accordingly, whereas FRS 13 requires that redeemable preference shares be included with debt for the purposes of its various analyses,[147] they remain classified as non-equity shares for balance sheet purposes.

In presenting related amounts in the balance sheet, IAS 32 requires the reporting entity to net off a financial asset against a financial liability only when it has a legally enforceable right of set-off and intends to settle the two amounts either on a net basis or simultaneously.[148] In the UK, the ASB regards management intent as irrelevant to such questions.

For each class of financial liability and equity instrument (whether recognised on the balance sheet or not) the standard requires enterprises to disclose:

(a)   information about the extent and nature of the financial instruments, including significant terms and conditions that may affect the amount, timing and certainty of future cash flows; and

(b)   the accounting policies and methods adopted, including the criteria for recognition and the basis of measurement applied.[149]

For financial liabilities, they should also disclose information about their exposure to interest rate risk, including contractual repricing or maturity dates, whichever dates are earlier, and their effective interest rates where applicable.[150] Estimates of their fair value must also be given, except if this is impracticable, in which case that fact must be disclosed together with information about the principal characteristics of the item that are relevant to its fair value.[151]

One particular set of disclosures is required when the reporting entity has used financial instruments to hedge anticipated future transactions. In such a case, it must disclose details of both the hedging instruments and the anticipated transactions, including details of when they are expected to occur, and the amount of any deferred or unrecognised gains or losses and when they are likely to be recognised in the profit and loss account.[152] This issue is discussed in more detail in Chapter 9 at 5.1.2.

5.1.3 IAS 39

The IASC issued IAS 39, a standard on the recognition and measurement of financial instruments, in March 1999, having approved it three months earlier. It does not come into force until periods beginning on or after 1 January 2001; the unusually long lead time is to allow an alternative, more radical standard to be developed in the mean time, on which work is continuing.

The standard deals with the accounting treatment of financial instruments in the accounts of both the issuer and the holder of the instruments, and it uses the same definitions as those quoted above in relation to IAS 32. The main requirements that are relevant to share and loan capital from the issuer's point of view are summarised below.

Under IAS 39, an enterprise should recognise a financial liability on its balance sheet 'when, and only when, it becomes a party to the contractual provisions of the instrument.'[153] The liability should be measured initially at the fair value of the consideration received, net of transaction costs.[154] Thereafter, unless it is a derivative or a liability that is held for trading, the liability should be measured at amortised cost; in other words, it should be accreted to the amount at which it will be repaid, in the same way as in the UK under FRS 4.[155] The standard also permits hedge accounting to be applied to liabilities so long as certain conditions are satisfied as more fully discussed in Chapter 9 at 5.1.3.[156] Liabilities that are either derivatives or are held for trading are to be remeasured at fair value at each balance sheet date and the difference included in the profit and loss account for the year.[157]

A financial liability should be removed from the balance sheet 'when, and only when, it is extinguished – that is, when the obligation specified in the contract has been discharged, cancelled, or expires.'[158] This can apply to parts of liabilities as well as to the whole amount, in other words liabilities may be subdivided into components (based on their relative fair values) for the purpose of determining questions of derecognition.

The most straightforward way of removing a liability is obviously by repaying the creditor, but the standard says that derecognition is also achieved when the debtor is legally released from primary responsibility for the liability, either by process of law or by the creditor. This condition may be satisfied even if the debtor has guaranteed the performance of the party that has taken over the primary obligation;[159] the debtor would simply establish a provision representing the fair value of the guarantee, which would enter into calculation of the gain or loss on extinguishment of the debt.[160] However, simply depositing money with a trust or other third party (under an 'in-substance defeasance' transaction) does not satisfy the condition in the absence of any legal release of the debtor's primary obligation to the creditor.[161]

In relation to refinancing transactions, IAS 39 says that 'an exchange between an existing borrowing and lender of debt instruments with substantially different terms is an extinguishment of the old debt that should result in derecognition of that debt and recognition of a new debt instrument.' The same applies where there is a substantial modification of the terms of an existing debt instrument.[162] The standard explains that 'substantially different terms' will be deemed to exist if the discounted present values of the cash flows under the old and new debt (including the effect of fees paid on the exchange) are at least 10 per cent different.[163] Where this applies, a gain or loss on extinguishment of the old debt will be taken to the profit and loss account, including the costs of the transaction.[164] This is similar to the treatment under UK GAAP although, as discussed in 2.2.6 above, some confusion remains in the UK as to what conditions (if any) permit the new borrowing to be regarded as a continuation of the old borrowing.

The more radical alternative standard that is under development as mentioned above is based on an earlier discussion paper published by the IASC in 1997.[165] This proposed a full fair value model for all financial assets and liabilities including the reporting company's own debt, and also espoused 'split accounting' (as described in 2.2.2 above) for hybrid instruments such as convertible bonds. It is also likely that the proposed standard will not allow any form of hedge accounting. However, such proposals are likely to prove highly controversial, and it remains to be seen whether they will be command acceptance, either in the international context or in individual countries.

5.2   US

5.2.1   *Share capital*

In the US, common stock issued by an enterprise is recorded at par value. Differences between the fair value of the proceeds of the issue and the par value are recorded as additional paid-in capital. When no-par-value stock is issued, the common stock account is credited with the entire proceeds of the issue.

The only exception to the general requirement to account for additional paid-in capital is when accounting for common stock issued to effect a business combination accounted for as a pooling.

For each class of shares, the following information is disclosed:

(a)   the number and value of shares issued or outstanding;

(b)   the title of the issue and number of shares authorised;

(c) the amount of any common shares subscribed but unissued. The amounts receivable should be presented as a deduction from stockholders' equity;

(d) for each period for which an income statement is presented, the changes in the class of common shares;

(e) the price at which preferred stock may be called or redeemed through sinking fund requirements or otherwise; and

(f) the aggregate and per share amounts of cumulative preferred dividends in arrears.

Changes in stock and the number of shares outstanding for at least the most recent year are disclosed.

5.2.2   Redeemable shares

The initial carrying amount of redeemable preferred stock is its fair value at the date of issue. The difference between the fair value at the date of issue and the mandatory redemption amount should be accounted for by making periodical charges against retained earnings (not through the profit and loss account) so that the carrying amount will equal the redemption amount at the mandatory redemption date. These charges should be deducted from earnings for earnings per share purposes.

Preferred stocks which are subject to mandatory redemption requirements or whose redemption is outside the control (no matter how remote the event might be) of the issuer are included in an intermediate category between liabilities and stockholders' equity.

These disclosures are made for redeemable shares:

(a) the title of each issue, the carrying amount and redemption amount;

(b) the dollar amounts of any shares subscribed but unissued and the deduction of subscriptions receivable therefrom;

(c) the accounting treatment of the difference between the carrying amount and the redemption amount;

(d) the number of authorised shares and the number issued or outstanding;

(e) in a separate note captioned 'Redeemable Preferred Stocks',

- a general description of each issue including its redemption features;

- the combined aggregate amount of redemption requirements for all issues each year for the five years following the date of the latest balance sheet; and

- the changes in each issue for each period for which an income statement is presented.

5.2.3   Treasury stocks

In the US, an enterprise may acquire shares of its own capital stock for purposes other than retirement subject to state laws and the requirements of listing agreements. In such situations, the status of such shares is akin to that of authorised but unissued capital stock.

When treasury stock is acquired with the intention of retiring the stock, the excess of the price paid for the treasury stock over its par value may either:

(a)   be charged entirely to retained earnings; or

(b)   be allocated between additional paid-in capital arising from the same class of stock and retained earnings.

If the price paid is less than its par value, the difference is credited to additional paid-in capital. The original capital balances relating to the shares acquired are eliminated.

Treasury stock acquired for purposes other than retirement should be separately disclosed in the balance sheet as a deduction from stockholders' equity or alternatively accounted for as retired stock.

A gain on the sale of treasury stock should be credited to paid-in capital. Losses may be charged to paid-in capital but only to the extent of available net gains from previous sales or retirements of the same class of stock. Any excess should be charged against retained earnings. The dividends on treasury stock should not be credited to income.

5.2.4   Additional paid-in capital

Additional paid-in capital is broadly equivalent to a share premium account in the United Kingdom, but is not subject to the same restrictions on its use and distribution. Any of these events may result in an entry to additional paid-in capital:

(a)   stock issued in excess of par or stated value or in a business combination;

(b)   stock dividends;

(c)   sale of treasury stock at a gain or loss;

(d)   conversion of convertible preferred stock;

(e)   issue and exercise of detachable stock warrants;

(f)   donated assets from a related party (e.g. capital contributions);

(g)   forgiveness of a debt from a stockholder; and

(h)   expenses or liabilities paid by a principal stockholder.

Occasionally, common stock is issued below par or stated value. The holder of shares issued below par may nevertheless be required to pay the discount in the event of a liquidation where creditors will sustain a loss. The enterprise may either create a 'discount on stock' account or charge such amount to additional paid-in capital to the extent available from the same class of stock.

5.2.5 Dividends

In the US, dividends are a charge to retained earnings at the point in time at which they are formally declared by the board of directors. This contrasts with the position in the UK, where equity dividends are accounted for when they are proposed, even though they have not yet been formally declared, and time-based dividends are accrued.

Disclosure is made of the aggregate dividends and dividends per share for each class of stock,[166] and the same information is given for any arrears of cumulative preferred dividends.[167] Disclosure must also be made of restrictions which limit the payment of dividends by the company.[168]

5.2.6 Debt

A   Classification

Short-term obligations that are scheduled to mature within one year after the balance sheet date (or within the enterprise's operating cycle) are classified as current liabilities, except when:

(a)   the enterprise intends to refinance the obligation on a long-term basis; and

(b)   the enterprise's ability to consummate the refinancing is demonstrated by either a post balance sheet issue of a long-term obligation or equity securities, or the execution of a financing agreement which permits the refinancing of the short-term obligation on a long-term basis prior to the issuance of the financial statements.[169] If short-term obligations are excluded from current liabilities because they are expected to be refinanced, a general description is given of the financing agreement and the terms of any new obligation incurred or equity securities issued (or expected to be incurred/issued) as a result of a refinancing.[170]

A long-term obligation that becomes callable by the creditor because of a violation of the debt agreement which is not cured within any period of grace allowed is classified as a current liability.[171] If a violation exists but a waiver has been obtained for a stated period of time, the amount of the obligation and the period of the waiver are disclosed. Details of all breaches/defaults in debt agreements, sinking fund or redemption provisions at the date of the latest balance sheet are given in the notes.

B   Disclosure

Liabilities to the following are separately disclosed:[172]

- banks for borrowings;
- factors or other financial institutions for borrowings;
- holders of commercial paper;
- trade creditors; and
- related parties.

For long-term debt such as bonds, mortgages etc, the following disclosures are given for each issue or type of obligation:[173]

- the general character of each type of debt including rate of interest;
- the date of maturity or, if maturing serially, a brief indication of the serial maturities;
- if the payment of principal or interest is contingent, an indication of such contingency;
- a brief indication of priority (i.e. whether subordinated); and
- if convertible, the basis of conversion.

For each category of short-term borrowings, the following disclosures are given, in aggregate:[174]

- the balance at the end of the period;
- the maximum amount outstanding at any month-end during the period;
- the weighted average interest rate both during and at the end of the period; and
- the average amount outstanding during the period.

The amount and terms of unused lines of credit for short-term financing are also disclosed if significant.[175]

In relation to redeemable stock and other similar liabilities, the following are disclosed for each of the 5 years following the date of the latest balance sheet:[176]

- the combined aggregate amount of maturities and sinking fund requirements for all long-term borrowings; and
- the amount of redemption requirements for all issues of capital stock that are redeemable at fixed or determinable prices on fixed or determinable dates, separately by issue or in aggregate.

5.2.7 *Convertible debt and debt issued with warrants*

The entire proceeds of issue of convertible debt are credited to a liability account. It is not permitted to allocate part of the proceeds to the conversion option since the debt and the conversion option are inseparable.[177] This is in line with FRS 4. Conversely, where debt is issued with detachable stock purchase warrants then the proceeds of issue should be allocated between the two elements on the basis of their fair values; the portion attributed to the warrants should be accounted for as paid-in capital, and whatever discount or premium on the debt that results from the allocation should be amortised to the income statement as a component of finance cost.[178] Again, this is consistent with the UK standard. The distinction turns on the detachable nature of the warrants; if the warrants are not detachable, then the accounting is the same as for convertible debt. This therefore means that the interest cost recognised in respect of these instruments depends on whether the warrants can be separated from the debt, even though their economic substance is otherwise similar.

5.2.8 Convertible bonds with a 'premium put'

Where convertible bonds are issued with a 'premium put' (a redemption option entitling the bondholder to redeem the bonds at a specified date prior to maturity at a price above the issue price), US GAAP requires provision to be made for the premium over the life of the bond by a supplementary interest accrual. This applies regardless of how probable it is that the bondholder will convert rather than exercise the redemption option. This is consistent with the treatment required under FRS 4 (see 4.2.3 above).

Subsequently, if the redemption option expires without being exercised, the accounting treatment of the provision which has been built up depends on the relationship between the put price and the market value at that date of the underlying stock into which conversion can be made. If the market value exceeds the put price, the provision should be credited to additional paid-in capital; if the reverse is true, it is to be amortised to the profit and loss account over the remaining term of the debt as a reduction of interest expense.[179]

5.2.9 Extinguishment of debt

Extinguishment is the term used in US GAAP to describe the circumstance when debt ceases to be a liability that is recognised in the balance sheet. It is not to be confused with offsetting, which deals with how recognised assets and recognised liabilities should be presented in a balance sheet.

Under SFAS 125, debt is considered extinguished for financial reporting purposes when either of the following conditions is met:

(a) the debtor pays the creditor and is relieved of its obligation for the liability. This may be done either by giving cash or other assets to the creditor or, if the debt takes the form of a security such as a bond, by reacquiring that security; or

(b) the debtor is legally released as the primary obligor under the debt, either judicially or by the creditor.[180] The debtor can still derecognise the debt even if it remains secondarily liable under a guarantee, but must recognise the guarantee instead at its fair value, with a consequential reduction to any gain (or increase in any loss) arising on the extinguishment.

The previous standard, SFAS 76, also allowed debt to be derecognised in another circumstance, known as 'in-substance defeasance'. This occurred when the debtor irrevocably placed cash or certain other assets in a trust, solely for the purpose of satisfying the interest and principal payments of the debt, in such a way that the possibility that the debtor would be required to make further payments with respect to that debt was remote. The creditor was not a party to this arrangement, and indeed may well have been unaware that it had occurred.

However, this is no longer possible under SFAS 125, and SFAS 76 has been withdrawn.

Gains and losses from all extinguishments of debt (including convertible debt) are recognised in income of the period of extinguishment and identified as a separate item. This is also true for repurchases of debt in the UK.

5.2.10 Troubled debt restructuring

A restructuring of a debt constitutes a 'troubled debt restructuring' if the borrower is experiencing financial difficulties and the lender, in an attempt to protect as much of its investment as possible, grants concessions that it would not otherwise consider. There are different ways in which a lender might grant such concessions to the borrower, which give rise to different accounting treatments:

(a)   Debt for equity swap

The borrower uses the fair value of the equity interest granted to the lender to account for the shares that are issued.[181] The difference between this and the carrying value of the debt which is thereby settled is recognised in the profit and loss account as an extraordinary item, if material.

(b)   Transfer of assets in full settlement

The borrower recognises a gain on restructuring payables where the carrying amount of the payable settled exceeds the fair value of the assets transferred.[182] Such gains are classified as extraordinary, if material. A difference between the fair value and carrying amounts of assets transferred to a creditor to settle a payable is recognised as a gain or loss on transfer of assets.[183]

(c)   Modification of debt agreement

Where the lender agrees to modify the debt agreement, the effects of the modification are generally accounted for prospectively from the time of the restructuring. If the carrying value of the debt at the time of the restructuring is lower than the total future cash payments due under the revised agreement (including contingent payments), a new effective rate of interest should be calculated and applied to determine the finance costs in the period to maturity. The concession granted by the lender is therefore spread over the term to maturity.[184]

If, however, the total future cash payments are less than the carrying value of the debt, the difference should be recognised as an extraordinary gain on restructuring. In subsequent periods, the cash payments made to the lender are applied to reduce the carrying value of the debt. No future interest cost arises under this approach.[185]

As mentioned in 2.1.4 above, the ASB at one stage intended to address the renegotiation of debt in FRS 4 but ultimately did not do so.

5.2.11 Financial instruments project

The FASB is currently engaged in a major project on the whole subject of financial instruments, which may eventually affect a number of the statements referred to above. One of the standards that has resulted from this project is SFAS 107 – *Disclosures about Fair Value of Financial Instruments* – issued in December 1991. It requires all entities to disclose the fair value of financial instruments where practicable, and this includes liabilities such as loans.[186] Trade creditors whose fair value approximates to their carrying value are exempt,[187] as are lease creditors, equity instruments issued by the company and a number of other specific items.[188] Where disclosure of the fair value is impracticable, the reason for this has to be disclosed, together with information pertinent to estimating the fair value, such as the carrying amount, effective interest rate and maturity.[189] In the UK, disclosure of the market value of loans was encouraged but not required by FRS 4, as discussed in 2.2.10 above, but is now a requirement under FRS 13 (see Chapter 9 at 3.9).

As described more fully in Chapter 9 at 5.2.3, the FASB has also issued SFAS 133 to address the recognition and measurement of financial instruments, with the primary focus on derivatives.[190] This imposes new requirements for the measurement of items (such as loans) if they are hedged by derivatives (such as swaps). These requirements are designed to achieve symmetry with the standard's rules on how to account for the hedging derivative. However, the standard does not disturb the rules for items which are not hedged.

5.2.12 Employee shares

In October 1995, the FASB issued SFAS 123 – *Accounting for Stock-Based Compensation*. This had been one of the most fiercely-resisted pronouncements ever produced by the Board, and the final terms of the standard represent something of a compromise; the Board's preferred method of accounting is not mandatory, but if not adopted, the effect of not doing so has to be disclosed.

The standard applies to arrangements whereby employees are remunerated in the form of shares in the employer or in amounts that are determined by the price of such shares. The FASB's preferred method of accounting is to measure the cost of such remuneration at the fair value of the award at the date it is granted, and to expense that over the qualifying period of service. Where share options are granted to employees, for example, this requires the use of an option pricing model to value the award, and this takes account of the time value of the option as well as its intrinsic value. Under the alternative method, which was specified by the previous standard, APB 25 (which corresponds more closely to UITF 17), only the intrinsic value is recognised, i.e. any excess of the market price of the shares at the date of grant over the amount that the employee must pay to acquire the shares. The latter method would therefore record no cost unless the options were issued at a discount to their market value, whereas the former method seeks to value the option rather more scientifically by putting a value on the opportunity to buy the shares at some time in the future at a specified price.

6   CONCLUSION

FRS 4 has been useful in developing a framework of rules on capital instruments; the requirements of the Companies Act alone were no longer adequate to deal with innovative forms of finance. The standard has created much more consistency in the classification and disclosure of companies' share and loan capital than had been displayed in the years before it was issued. Although it does give rise to certain anomalies, it has proved to be one of the Board's most successful standards to date.

In developing FRS 4, the ASB was constrained to some degree by the balance sheet formats prescribed by the Companies Act, and was inhibited from adopting an approach which focused fully on the substance of the instrument in question. However, the use of the 'non-equity' classification and the detailed disclosure requirements as to the terms of complex instruments compensates for this drawback to a large degree.

In the longer term, however, more needs to be done on the measurement issues which complex instruments give rise to, and in particular ways of subdividing them into their component parts need to be explored. The scope of this study should include the 'split accounting' idea which the ASB has not yet pursued, but may also have a wider remit. It must not be forgotten that these issues have a profit and loss account dimension as well as a balance sheet one; for example, the use of split accounting in relation to convertible bonds seeks to charge earnings with a proper finance cost, which arguably is understated under the conventional accounting approach which FRS 4 endorses.

As discussed in Chapter 9, however, the real question is whether the ASB will abandon FRS 4's whole approach in favour of the mark-to-market model that it has espoused in its financial instruments project. This would be a very radical step and would again run into considerable legal difficulties. It is also far from certain that this is what the financial community wants, and as a result the proposal is likely to encounter significant resistance. Ultimately, much will depend on how the debate on financial instruments develops internationally over the next few years.

References

1 UITF Abstract 1, *Convertible bonds – Supplemental interest/premium*, UITF, July 1991.
2 ASB Discussion Paper, *Accounting for capital instruments*, ASB, December 1991.
3 FRED 3, *Accounting for Capital Instruments*, ASB, December 1992.
4 ASB Bulletin Issue No. 39, July 1993.
5 UITF 8, *Repurchase of own debt*, UITF, March 1993.
6 FRS 4, *Capital Instruments*, ASB, December 1993, para. 2.
7 *Ibid.*, para. 21.
8 *Ibid.*, para. 52.
9 Statement of Principles Revised Exposure Draft, *Statement of Principles for Financial Reporting*, ASB, March 1999, Chapter 4, para. 4.24.
10 FRS 4, para. 24.
11 FRS 7, *Fair Values in Acquisition Accounting*, ASB, September 1994, para. 82.
12 IAS 39, *Financial Instruments: Recognition and Measurement*, IASC, December 1998, para. 11.
13 CA 85, Sch. 4, para. 8.
14 FRS 4, para. 12.
15 *Ibid.*, para. 49.
16 *Ibid.*, para. 90.
17 *Ibid.*, para. 25.
18 ASB Discussion Paper, *Accounting for Capital Instruments*, Appendix 3.
19 TR 677, Appendix para. 5(a).
20 FRS 4, para. 22.
21 *Ibid.*, para. 26.
22 In fact, this would be the effective result under US GAAP. Where convertible debt is issued at a substantial premium over its face value, the premium is accounted for as additional paid-in capital. (APB 14, *Accounting for Convertible Debt and Debt Issued with Stock Purchase Warrants*, March 1969, para. 18.)
23 FRS 4, paras. 27 and 11.
24 *Ibid.*, para. 8.
25 *Ibid.*, para. 28.
26 *Ibid.*, para. 29.
27 *Ibid.*, para. 32.
28 *Ibid.*, para. 37.
29 *Ibid.*, para. 11.
30 *Ibid.*, para. 42.
31 *Ibid.*, para. 28.
32 *Ibid.*, para. 8.
33 *Ibid.*, para. 10.
34 *Ibid.*, para. 42.
35 *Ibid.*, para. 51.
36 *Ibid.*, para. 16.
37 UITF 11, *Accounting for Issuer Call Options*, UITF, September 1994.
38 FRS 4, para. 32.
39 UITF 8, para. 7.
40 IAS 39, paras. 57-59.
41 *Ibid.*, para 60.
42 FRS 5, *Reporting the Substance of Transactions*, ASB, April 1994, para. 29.
43 *Ibid.* These rules also appear strictly to allow offset only if there are two parties involved, whereas there are at least three in this case, but we doubt if this was intended provided the offset conditions are otherwise satisfied.
44 FRS 4, para. 34.
45 *Ibid.*, para. 35.
46 *Ibid.*, para. 81.
47 *Ibid.*, para. 36.
48 *Ibid.*, para. 17.

49 *Ibid.*, para. 45.
50 *Ibid.*, para. 46.
51 *Ibid.*, para. 47.
52 *Ibid.*, para. 48.
53 *Ibid.*, para. 99.
54 *Ibid.*, para. 48.
55 *Ibid.*, para. 40.
56 *Ibid.*, para. 55.
57 *Ibid.*, para. 50.
58 *Ibid.*, para. 25.
59 *Ibid.*, para. 54.
60 *Ibid.*, para. 38.
61 *Ibid.*, para. 56.
62 *Ibid.*, para. 58.
63 *Ibid.*, para. 57.
64 *Ibid.*, para. 61.
65 *Ibid.*, para. 33.
66 *Ibid.*, para. 36.
67 *Ibid.*, para. 62.
68 *Ibid.*, para. 63.
69 *Ibid.*, para. 65.
70 *Ibid.*, para. 64.
71 *Ibid.*, para. 13.
72 *Ibid.*, para. 59.
73 *Ibid.*, para. 60.
74 *Ibid.*, para. 52.
75 FRED 3, para. 59.
76 FRS 4, para. 102.
77 CA 85, s 130(1).
78 *Ibid.*, s 130(2).
79 *Ibid.*, ss. 131 and 132.
80 FRS 4, paras. 45 and 11.
81 *Ibid.*, para. 21c.
82 FRS 6, *Accounting for Business Combinations*, ASB, September 1994, Appendix I, para. 15.
83 CA 85, ss. 117 and 118.
84 *Ibid.*, Sch. 4, para. 8.
85 *Ibid.*, para. 38(1).
86 *Ibid.*, para. 38(2).
87 *Ibid.*, para. 39.
88 *Ibid.*, para. 40.
89 *Ibid.*, para. 49.
90 *Ibid.*, para. 3(7)(b) and (c).
91 FRS 4, para. 43.
92 *The Listing Rules*, London Stock Exchange, Chapter 12, para. 12.43(l).
93 CA 85, Sch. 4, para. 8.
94 *Ibid.*, para. 85.
95 *Ibid.*, para. 48(1) and (2).
96 *Ibid.*, para. 48(4).
97 *Ibid.*, para. 41(1).
98 *Ibid.*, para. 41(3).
99 *Ibid.*, s 744.
100 *Ibid.*, Sch. 4, para. 53(2).
101 CA 85, ss. 159–181.
102 *Ibid.*, s 170.
103 *Ibid.*, s 171 *et seq.*
104 *Ibid.*, Sch. 7, paras. 8 and 9.

105 *The Listing Rules*, London Stock Exchange, Chapter 12, para. 12.43(n).
106 FRS 4, para. 63.
107 *Ibid.*, para. 31.
108 *Ibid.*, para. 26.
109 UITF 1, para. 5.
110 FRS 4, para. 25.
111 *Ibid.*, para. 26.
112 *Ibid.* – Application Notes.
113 *Ibid.*, para. 46.
114 *Ibid.*, para. 47.
115 CA 85, s 130.
116 FRS 4, para. 43.
117 *Ibid.*, paras. 42 and 28.
118 TR 677, Appendix, para. 7.
119 FRS 4, para. 99.
120 UITF 13, *Accounting for ESOP Trusts*, UITF, June 1995, para. 8.
121 *Ibid.* Sub-paragraph (g) is as amended by FRS 14, *Earnings per share*, ASB, September 1998, para. 16. Previously the earnings per share treatment depended on whether or not dividends had been waived.
122 *Ibid.*, para. 9.
123 FRS 5, para. 44.
124 UITF 13, Appendix I.
125 UITF Information Sheet No 32, 18 March 1999.
126 UITF Information Sheet No 33, 24 June 1999.
127 UITF 17, *Employee share schemes*, UITF, April 1997.
128 *Ibid.*, para. 13(c).
129 *Ibid.*, para. 16.
130 *Ibid.*, para. 13(c).
131 *Ibid.*, para. 13(a).
132 *Ibid.*, para. 13(d).
133 *Ibid.*
134 *Ibid.*, para. 15.
135 *Ibid.*, para. 17.
136 UITF Information Sheet No 32.
137 UITF Information Sheet No 33.
138 UITF 17, para. 14.
139 IAS 10 – *Events After the Balance Sheet Date*, IASC, May 1999, para. 11.
140 *Ibid.*, para. 22.
141 IAS 32, *Financial Instruments: Disclosure and Presentation*, IASC, March 1995, para. 1.
142 *Ibid.*, para. 5.
143 *Ibid.*
144 *Ibid.*
145 *Ibid.*, para. 19.
146 *Ibid.*, para. 30.
147 FRS 13, *Derivatives and other Financial Instruments: Disclosures*, ASB, September 1998, para. 8.
148 *Ibid.*, para. 33.
149 *Ibid.*, para. 47.
150 *Ibid.*, para. 56.
151 *Ibid.*, para. 77.
152 *Ibid.*, para. 91.
153 *Ibid.*, para. 27.
154 *Ibid.*, para. 66.
155 *Ibid.*, para. 93.
156 *Ibid.*, paras. 136-165.
157 *Ibid.*
158 *Ibid.*, para. 57.

159 *Ibid.*, para. 58.
160 *Ibid.*, para. 64.
161 *Ibid.*, para. 59.
162 *Ibid.*, para. 61.
163 *Ibid.*, para. 62.
164 *Ibid.*, para. 63.
165 *Accounting for Financial Assets and Financial Liabilities*, IASC, March 1997.
166 Statement S-X, SEC, para. 3-04.
167 APB 15, *Earnings per share*, para. 50, footnote 16.
168 SFAS 5, *Accounting for contingencies*, FASB, March 1975, para. 18.
169 SFAS 6, *Classification of Short-Term Obligations Expected To Be Refinanced*, FASB, May 1975, paras. 8–11.
170 *Ibid.*, para. 15.
171 SFAS 78, *Classification of Obligations That Are Callable by the Creditor*, FASB, December 1983, para. 5.
172 Statement S-X, SEC, para. 5-02.19–20.
173 *Ibid.*, para. 5-02.23.
174 *Ibid.*, para. 12-10.
175 *Ibid.*, para. 5-02.20.
176 SFAS 47, *Disclosure of Long-Term Obligations*, FASB, March 1981, para. 10.
177 APB 14, para. 12.
178 *Ibid.*, para. 16.
179 EITF Issue No. 85-29.
180 SFAS 125, *Accounting for Transfers and Servicing of Financial Assets and Extinguishment of Liabilities*, FASB, June 1996, para. 16.
181 SFAS 15, *Accounting by Debtors and Creditors for Troubled Debt Restructurings*, FASB, June 1977, para. 15.
182 *Ibid.*, para. 13.
183 *Ibid.*, para. 14.
184 *Ibid.*, para. 16.
185 *Ibid.*, para. 17.
186 SFAS 107, *Disclosures about Fair Value of Financial Instruments*, FASB, December 1991, para. 10.
187 *Ibid.*, para. 13.
188 *Ibid.*, para. 8.
189 *Ibid.*, para. 14.
190 SFAS 133, *Accounting for Derivative Instruments and Hedging Activities*, FASB, June 1998.

Chapter 16   Off balance sheet transactions

1   INTRODUCTION

1.1   Background

Off balance sheet finance can be difficult to define, and this poses the first problem in discussing the subject. The term implies that certain things belong on the balance sheet and that those which escape the net are deviations from this norm. But there are as yet no authoritative general principles which determine conclusively what should be on the balance sheet and when. As discussed in Chapter 2, the ASB is attempting to establish such principles in its *Statement of Principles* project and has used these as the basis of FRS 5 – *Reporting the substance of transactions* – which directly addresses the issue of off balance sheet finance.

The practical effect of off balance sheet transactions is that they do not result in full presentation of the underlying activity in the accounts of the reporting company. This is generally for one of two reasons. The items in question may be included in the balance sheet but presented 'net' rather than 'gross'; examples would include one-line presentation of an unconsolidated subsidiary rather than line by line consolidation, or netting off loans received against the assets they finance. Alternatively, the items might be excluded from the balance sheet altogether on the basis that they represent future commitments rather than present assets and liabilities; examples would include operating lease commitments, obligations under take-or-pay contracts or consignment stock agreements, contingent liabilities under options, and so on. The result in both cases will be that the balance sheet suggests less exposure to assets and liabilities than really exists, with a consequential flattering effect on certain ratios, such as gearing and return on assets employed.

There is usually also a profit and loss account dimension to be considered as well, perhaps because assets taken off balance sheet purport to have been sold (with a possible profit effect), and also more generally because the presentation of off balance sheet activity influences the timing or disclosure of associated revenue items. In particular, the presence or absence of items in the balance sheet usually affects whether the finance cost implicit in a transaction is reported as such or rolled up within another item of income or expense.

Depending on their roles, different people tend to react differently to the use of the term 'off balance sheet finance'. To an accounting standard setter, the expression carries the connotation of devious accounting, intended to mislead the reader of financial statements. Off balance sheet transactions are those which are designed to allow a company to avoid reflecting certain aspects of its activities in its accounts. The term is therefore a pejorative one, and the inference is that those who indulge in such transactions are up to no good and need to be stopped. From this perspective, FRS 5 is intended to be an anti-avoidance standard which seeks to prevent accounts being perverted by the effects of transactions whose primary motivation is cosmetic.

However, there is also room for a more honourable use of the term 'off balance sheet finance'. Companies may, for sound commercial reasons, wish to engage in transactions which share with other parties the risks and benefits associated with certain assets and liabilities. Increasingly sophisticated financial markets allow businesses to protect themselves from selected risks, or to take limited ownership interests which carry the entitlement to restricted rewards of particular assets. Also, off balance sheet transactions are often undertaken as an element of a company's tax planning strategy. Such transactions are not undertaken to mislead readers of their accounts, but because they are judged to be in the best commercial interests of the companies undertaking them.

Whatever the motivation behind these transactions, company accounts have to reflect them in such a way that a true and fair view is given. FRS 5 seeks to deal with transactions whose form is at variance with their economic substance. The thrust of the standard is to identify what the substance is in reality and represent the transactions in that light.

1.2 The forerunners of FRS 5

1.2.1 ICAEW Technical Release 603

In December 1985, the ICAEW issued Technical Release 603 – *Off-Balance Sheet Finance and Window Dressing* – as a preliminary document for discussion. It detailed certain points to be considered by preparers of financial statements in examining off balance sheet transactions:

'(1) In financial statements which are intended to give a true and fair view the economic substance of such transactions should be considered rather than their mere legal form when determining their true nature and thus the appropriate accounting treatment. Where items are included in the accounts on the basis of the substance of the transactions concerned and this is different from their legal form, the notes to the accounts should disclose the legal form of those transactions and the amounts of the items involved.

(2)   In the rare circumstances where accounting for a material transaction on the basis of its substance rather than its legal form would not comply with the requirements of the Companies Act, adequate disclosure should be made in order to provide a true and fair view, possibly by presenting separate pro-forma accounts prepared on the basis of the economic substance of the transactions.'[1]

The publication of this Technical Release stimulated a good deal of debate, both within the accounting profession and also with certain members of the legal profession. In particular, the Law Society stated that while agreeing with TR 603's basic objectives, they disagreed with its proposed solution. It was argued that a major purpose of financial statements was to provide comparability and consistency and this was best achieved by keeping subjectivity to a minimum. Further, the desired level of objectivity was said to be best achieved by reflecting the legal position relating to assets and liabilities in a set of financial statements. It was also pointed out that the 'true and fair override' could only be applied in narrowly limited circumstances and this did not permit widespread departure from the requirements of the Act to report the form of transactions in the course of a quest for their substance.

1.2.2   ED 42

As a result of the interest which this debate generated, the Accounting Standards Committee put the subject of off balance sheet transactions on its own agenda with a view to developing an accounting standard. In March 1988, it issued ED 42 – *Accounting for special purpose transactions*. A *special purpose transaction* was defined as one 'which combines or divides up the benefits and obligations flowing from it in such a way that they fall to be accounted for differently or in different periods depending on whether the elements are taken step by step or whether the transaction is viewed as a whole'.[2]

This exposure draft differed from most others produced by the ASC in that it addressed the issue from a conceptual angle rather than laying down a set of detailed rules. The essence of the argument it set out was as follows.

The concept of 'true and fair' demanded that transactions should be accounted for in accordance with their substance rather than their legal form; this was to be determined by examining all the aspects and implications of a transaction (or series of transactions, if they were linked), and concentrating on those which were likely to have a commercial effect in practice.[3] The substance was to be determined by identifying whether the transaction had increased or decreased the assets or liabilities which were to be recognised in the financial statements of the enterprise.[4] When it was determined that assets and liabilities should be recognised in the financial statements, they were to be accounted for individually, rather than offset against each other: a right of set-off was to alter this principle only if the items were of the same type as each other.[5]

Much of the argument within the proposed standard rested on whether or not the transaction in question was regarded as giving rise to an asset or liability. These terms were described in the exposure draft in a broadly similar way to the definitions eventually incorporated in FRS 5.

There were specific rules to deal with 'controlled non-subsidiaries' (later termed 'quasi subsidiaries'). The exposure draft asserted that such a vehicle should be consolidated as if it were a subsidiary.[6]

The explanatory note of the exposure draft examined the application of the principles of the proposed standard to a number of common transactions and arrangements, but did not develop mandatory detailed rules in relation to these specific transactions.

1.2.3   ED 49

ED 42 received a fair measure of support from those people who responded to it. Nevertheless, it was two years before the ASC issued a further document on the subject. The delay was not due to inertia on the Committee's part; rather it was because a Companies Bill was in process in 1989 which had a very significant bearing on the subject, and it was necessary to see how that was finally enacted before the project could be progressed. Most significantly, the resultant Act changed the definition of a subsidiary which had to be consolidated from one based strictly on the form of the shareholding relationship between the companies to one which reflected the substance of the commercial relationship, and in particular focused on who exercised de facto control.

When the ASC did return to the subject, it decided that the climate had changed sufficiently to require it to issue a further exposure draft rather than an accounting standard. Accordingly, ED 49 – *Reflecting the substance of transactions in assets and liabilities* – was published in May 1990. The main changes from ED 42 were to refine the definitions of assets and liabilities and to give guidance on the criteria for their recognition in accounts, to add a new section on the identification of control (in the light of the Companies Act 1989) and to introduce detailed, mandatory Application Notes to prescribe the accounting treatment of some common forms of off balance sheet finance. The exposure draft no longer referred specifically to 'special purpose transactions' and indeed the title was changed to reflect this slightly different focus of attention.

As mentioned above, the definition of a 'subsidiary undertaking' introduced by the Companies Act 1989 allowed more straightforward recognition of de facto control than was possible under the previous legislation, and accordingly there was less need than before for an accounting standard to address this issue. However, ED 49 took the view that even this new definition was not conclusive in determining what entities are to be included in consolidated accounts. It envisaged that there would be occasions where the need to give a true and fair view would require the inclusion of 'quasi subsidiaries' (defined in the same terms as ED 42 had used for 'controlled non-subsidiaries').

In publishing the exposure draft, the ASC set a relatively short period for comment, on the basis that the general principles of the proposed standard had not changed from ED 42, and that the main innovation requiring consultation was the Application Notes. Its hope was that a standard based on ED 49 could be brought into force relatively quickly, but in the event the ASB, which succeeded the ASC shortly afterwards, did not find it possible to do so.

1.2.4   FRED 4

The ASB published FRED 4 – *Reporting the substance of transactions* – nearly three years later, in February 1993 but with a consultation period running only to the end of April. Although the general thrust of the proposed standard was the same as that of ED 49, the new exposure draft was three times as long as its predecessor and much more complex. Among the innovations was a new proposition: the 'linked presentation', which was to allow liabilities to be shown on the balance sheet as a deduction from the assets which they financed, under certain closely defined circumstances. FRED 4 also borrowed much of its conceptual argument from the Board's draft *Statement of Principles* (see Chapter 2), including the definitions of assets and liabilities and rules for their recognition, and it also discussed offset and the treatment of options in greater detail than before.

The exposure draft attracted a good deal of further comment, not least because of its daunting size and complexity, but in the event it was converted into a standard a year later with relatively little alteration.

2   FRS 5

2.1   Scope and general requirements

FRS 5 – *Reporting the substance of transactions* – was published in April 1994, to take effect for accounting periods ending on or after 22 September 1994. Significantly, the standard gave no transitional relief to exempt transactions or arrangements which predated these periods, with the result that additional assets and liabilities often had to be recognised when the standard was applied for the first time.

The standard applies to all entities whose accounts are intended to give a true and fair view, but it excludes a number of transactions from its scope, unless they form part of a larger series of transactions that does fall within the scope of the standard. These exclusions are:

(a)   forward contracts and futures (such as those for foreign currencies or commodities);

(b)   foreign exchange and interest rate swaps;

(c)   contracts where a net amount will be paid or received based on the movement in a price or an index (sometimes referred to as 'contracts for differences');

(d)   expenditure commitments (such as purchase commitments) and orders placed, until the earlier of delivery or payment; and

(e)   employment contracts.[7]

The first three of these relate to financial derivatives and are presumably excluded in order that they may be addressed in the ASB's financial instruments project. However, the remaining two are more problematic. They seem to have been excluded only because the application of the recognition criteria in the standard would otherwise have some undesirable effects. Literal application of these criteria could require companies to include assets and liabilities in their accounts in respect of contracts for future performance; for example, the commitment to buy goods, or to employ staff, qualifies as a liability as the standard has defined it. Since including such liabilities in the balance sheet would be a radical and unwelcome result, the ASB has avoided the problem by scoping such transactions out of the standard altogether. This, however, seems a rather clumsy solution, when the real problem probably lies in the recognition rules themselves.

The interaction of FRS 5 with other standards and statutory requirements is also something which must be considered. Transactions which are directly addressed by other rules will sometimes also fall within the remit of FRS 5, and it is necessary to consider which set of rules takes precedence. The standard says that whichever rules are more specific should be applied.[8] A particular example quoted is the leasing standard, SSAP 21, which addresses a particular aspect of off balance sheet finance but in a more narrowly prescribed way. Straightforward leases which fall squarely within the terms of SSAP 21 should continue to be accounted for without reference to FRS 5, but where their terms are more complex, or the lease is only one element in a larger series of transactions, then FRS 5 comes into play. More generally, the standard says that its overall principle of substance over form should apply to the operation of other existing rules.[9]

FRS 5 deals with certain specific aspects of off balance sheet finance through the medium of detailed Application Notes. These cover the following topics:

■   Consignment stock

■   Sale and repurchase agreements

- Factoring of debts
- Securitised assets
- Loan transfers.
- The Private Finance Initiative and similar contracts

The first five of these were published as part of the original standard, while the last was added in 1998. They are intended to clarify and develop the methods of applying the standard to the particular transactions which they describe and to provide guidance on how to interpret it in relation to other similar transactions. They also contain specific disclosure requirements in relation to these transactions. The Application Notes are not exhaustive and they do not override the general principles of the standard itself, but they are regarded as part of the standard (i.e. they are authoritative) insofar as they assist in interpreting it. Each of these topics is discussed in 3 below.

As with the three earlier exposure drafts, the central premise of FRS 5 is that the substance and economic reality of an entity's transactions should be reported in its financial statements, and this substance should be identified by considering all the aspects and implications of a transaction, with the emphasis on those likely to have a commercial effect in practice. In determining the substance, it is necessary to consider whether the transaction has given rise to new assets and liabilities for the entity, and whether it has changed any of its existing assets and liabilities.[10]

Sometimes there will be a series of connected transactions to be evaluated, not just a single transaction. The overall substance of these transactions as a whole must be determined and accounted for, rather than accounting for each individual transaction. The standard quotes some examples of complex arrangements to which its provisions will be particularly relevant. These involve the following features:

(a) the separation of legal title to an item from rights or other access to the principal future economic benefits associated with it and exposure to the principal risks inherent in these benefits;

(b) the linking of a transaction with others in such a way that the commercial effect can be understood only by considering the series as a whole; and

(c) the inclusion of options or conditions on terms that make it highly likely that the option will be exercised or the condition fulfilled.[11]

Where transactions include options which may or may not be exercised or conditions which may or may not apply, it is necessary to form a view as to their likely outcome, by considering the motivations of all the parties to the transaction and the possible scenarios which they have contemplated in negotiating the terms of the deal. Only in this way can the commercial substance of the arrangement be identified.

2.2   Definition of assets and liabilities

For the purpose of the standard, assets and liabilities are defined as follows:

Assets are rights or other access to future economic benefits controlled by an entity as a result of past transactions or events.[12]

Liabilities are an entity's obligations to transfer economic benefits as a result of past transactions or events.[13]

These definitions are the same as those which the ASB has proposed in its draft *Statement of Principles*,[14] as discussed in Chapter 2.

2.3   Analysis of risks and rewards

The standard goes on to say that identifying the party that is exposed to variations in the benefits relating to an asset will generally indicate who has the asset itself.[15] It also says that if an entity is in certain circumstances unable to avoid an outflow of benefits, this will provide evidence that it has a liability.[16] The various risks and rewards relating to particular assets and liabilities are discussed in Application Notes which deal with different forms of off balance sheet finance.

In any consideration of where the risks and rewards lie as a result of a transaction, it is useful to remember that each of the risks and rewards relating to a particular asset or liability must lie *somewhere*. Although they may be partitioned and transferred as a result of the transactions, they cannot be increased or diminished in total. In addition, an analysis of the commercial effect of the deal can be expedited by looking at it from the point of view of each of the parties involved. By considering what risks and rewards they have acquired or disposed of, and their motivation for doing so, the substance of the transaction can be discerned more clearly than by considering the position of one of the parties alone.

2.4   Recognition

Once items which satisfy the definition of assets and liabilities have been identified, the next key question is whether they should be recognised in the balance sheet. This question, of course, is what the whole subject of off balance sheet finance is about. The standard says that 'where a transaction results in an item which meets the definition of an asset or liability, that item should be recognised in the balance sheet if:

(a)   there is sufficient evidence of the existence of the item (including, where appropriate, evidence that a future inflow or outflow of benefit will occur); and

(b)   the item can be measured at a monetary amount with sufficient reliability.'[17]

These principles are similar to those set out in the ASB's draft *Statement of Principles*.[18] They are rather abstract criteria, and are not particularly easy to understand in isolation; in particular, item (a) appears to add little but a reinforcement of the definition of an asset or liability. Critically, it does not really specify the defining event which dictates when to bring an item on to the balance sheet.

The difficulty is therefore in identifying exactly when an asset or liability is created in the terms in which they have been defined. Conventional accounting practice is to recognise most transactions only when they are performed, for example when goods are received under a purchase contract. However, an enthusiastic interpretation of the recognition criteria would say that merely entering into the contract has resulted in the creation of an asset (the right to the goods) and a liability (the amount due under the purchase contract). This is similar to the IASC's standard on financial instruments, which says that 'An enterprise should recognise a financial asset or financial liability on its balance sheet when, and only when, it becomes a party to the contractual provisions of the instrument.'[19] However this would be a radical change of practice.

This idea that the creation, rather than the execution, of a contract should be the event which triggers the recognition of assets and liabilities has an obvious theoretical appeal. However, quite apart from the difficulty of capturing the relevant information in a company's accounting system, it is debatable whether this forms a sensible basis for the preparation of a balance sheet. The difficulty with it is that every commitment under contract would become a liability; examples might include all leasing commitments (not just those for finance leases, as at present),[20] long-term supply contracts for raw materials, and even future salary payments under employment contracts (at least for the required period of notice). There could also be some difficulty in defining and describing the nature of the corresponding asset in such cases. It is presumably to avoid this result that expenditure commitments and employment contracts have been scoped out of the standard, as discussed under 2.1 above, but this does not resolve the principle behind the recognition test.

2.5   Derecognition

2.5.1   *General principles*

As the word suggests, derecognition is the opposite of recognition. It concerns the question of when to remove from the balance sheet the assets and liabilities which have previously been recognised. FRS 5 addresses this issue only in relation to assets, not liabilities, and its rules are designed to determine one of three outcomes (together with a fourth possibility, the linked presentation, which is discussed at 2.6 below). These are summarised in the following diagram:

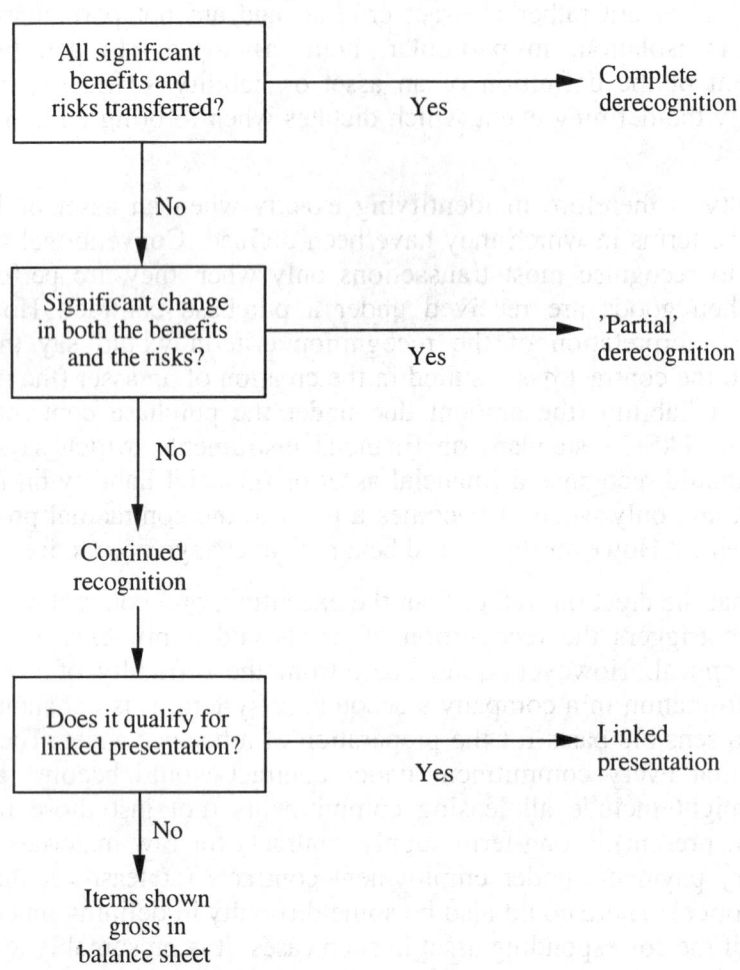

Summary of derecognition tests

2.5.2   *Complete derecognition*

In the simplest case, where a transaction transfers to another party all the significant benefits and risks relating to an asset, the standard confirms that the entire asset should cease to be recognised.[21] In this context, the word 'significant' is explained further: it should not be judged in relation to all the conceivable benefits and risks that could exist, but only in relation to those which are likely to occur in practice.[22] This means that the importance of the risk retained must be assessed in the context of the total realistic risk which existed in the first place.

Thus, if a company sold an asset and agreed to compensate the buyer for any subsequent loss in its value up to a maximum of 2% of the selling price, the significance of that retention of risk depends on how realistic it is that a fall in value of more than 2% will occur. If the asset is a portfolio of high quality receivables where the bad debt risk is very small, retaining a 2% risk may mean retaining all the realistic risk that attaches to that asset, in which case the transaction would not qualify as a sale. However, if the asset is a much more volatile one, whose value could easily fall by 20 or 30%, then the degree of risk retained is relatively small and the transaction could be treated as a sale. The seller would simply provide for any expected loss under the guarantee in measuring the profit on sale.

2.5.3 *Continued recognition*

At the other end of the spectrum, where a transaction results in no significant change to the benefits *or* to the risks relating to the asset in question, no sale can be recorded and the entire asset should continue to be recognised.[23] It should be noted that retention of *either* the benefits *or* the risks is sufficient to keep the asset on the balance sheet. This means that the elimination of risk by financing the asset on a non-recourse basis will not remove it from the balance sheet; it would be necessary to dispose of the potential benefits as well, to justify recording a sale. (A further variant, the special case of a 'linked presentation', is discussed at 2.6 below.)

The standard also says that any transaction that is 'in substance a financing' will not qualify for derecognition, with the item therefore staying on balance sheet, and the finance received being introduced as a liability. There is no explicit definition of transactions that are 'in substance a financing', but some of the discussion elsewhere in FRS 5 indicates that they are those where the reporting entity retains the significant benefits and risks of the asset while the other party earns only a lender's return on the deal. Examples of such transactions are shown in Extracts 16.17 and 16.18 at 3.2 below from the respective accounts of Barratt and Gleeson.

2.5.4 *Partial derecognition*

As can be seen, the above criteria are relatively restrictive. At a late stage in the development of the standard, a third possibility was introduced, to deal with circumstances where, although not all of the benefits and risks have been transferred, the transaction is more than a mere financing and has transferred enough of the benefits and risks to warrant at least some derecognition of the asset. The standard addresses three such cases.

(a) where an asset has been subdivided

Where an identifiable part of an asset is separated and sold off, with the remainder being retained, the asset should be split and a partial sale recorded. The examples quoted in the standard are those of the sale of a proportionate part of a loan receivable, where all future receipts are shared equally between the parties, or the stripping of interest payments from the principal of a debt instrument; other obvious examples would be the subdivision of a freehold property with part being sold off, the sale of a share in a racehorse, and so on.

For this to be permitted, the two parts must be distinct in the sense that the benefits and risks associated with the separate parts do not impact upon each other. Thus, the sale of a share of a loan qualifies for partial derecognition so long as the share sold is a proportionate one, but not if the effect of the separation results in the retention of the significant risks or rewards attaching to the whole asset. An example will illustrate this distinction:

Example 16.1:   Partial sale of a receivable

Company A has a receivable, comprising the right to receive five amounts of £20,000 each from a third party over a period, totalling £100,000 in all. It wishes to sell half of its asset to Company B.

If it sold a 50% proportionate share in each of the receipts to Company B, the two parties would thereafter be equally exposed to the risk of the third party's default, and this would qualify as a partial sale. Accordingly, Company A would divide the carrying value of the asset in two, leaving one half on the balance sheet and taking the other half to the profit and loss account to match it with the proceeds received from Company B.

If, instead, Company B bought the right to receive the first £50,000 of whatever amounts were received, the position could be different, because the bad debt risk would be unevenly shared between the parties. The answer under FRS 5 seems to depend on whether or not the total realistic bad debt risk falls within A's retained share, in other words whether there was only a remote possibility that more than half of the original receivable would prove bad. If this is the case, then from A's point of view there has been no significant change in the risks attaching to the (whole) asset, and accordingly the whole receivable has to stay on its balance sheet while the proceeds received from Company B would be shown as a liability. However, if there was a realistic risk of loss beyond the first 50%, then there has been a significant change in A's risk and it is entitled to treat the part transferred to B as a sale and remove it from the balance sheet.

In order to account for any partial sale, it is necessary to be able to apportion the previous carrying value of the asset between the part sold and the part which is retained so as to measure both the gain or loss on sale and the carrying value of the residual asset. The following example shows how this could be done in relation to an interest strip.

Example 16.2:   Interest strip

Bank A has made a £10 million loan to Company C for 5 years. The loan carries a fixed interest rate of 8%. After one year, it sells the right to receive the interest payments for the remaining four years to Bank B for £2,700,000, but retains the right to the repayment of the principal.

In order to account for this, it is necessary to apportion the £10 million asset in its balance sheet between the amount sold and the amount retained. It does this by discounting the future payments due under the loan at the interest rate implicit in the arrangement – 8% in this case. This shows that the present value of £10 million receivable in four years' time is £7,350,300, which stays in its balance sheet, whereas the similarly discounted value of four annual payments of £800,000 is £2,649,700. Comparing this to the proceeds of £2,700,000 produces a profit of £50,300.

(b)   where an item is sold for less than its full life

This exception arises where the seller retains a residual value risk by agreeing to buy the asset back (if the buyer wishes to sell it back) at a predetermined price at a later stage in the asset's life. Such an arrangement is sometimes offered in relation to commercial vehicles, aircraft, and so on. The standard says that in such cases the original asset will have been replaced by a residual interest in the asset together with a liability for its obligation to pay the repurchase price. Again, it will be necessary to put a value on this in order to measure the profit or loss on the initial sale.

The standard does not make it entirely clear whether such residual assets and liabilities should be accounted for gross or net. This may depend on how likely it is that the repurchase will take place. If it is reasonably certain that it will, then it would be appropriate to reflect both the liability expected to be paid and the residual interest in the asset as separate items on opposite sides of the balance sheet. However, if it is more in the nature of a guarantee which may never be called upon, then it could be appropriate to provide only for the net exposure under the guarantee.

As can be seen from Extract 16.12 at 3.1 below, Lookers recognises an obligation to repurchase motor vehicles under a Motability arrangement, and has a corresponding asset representing its interest in the vehicles.

FRS 5 does not explicitly say how much of the life of the asset has to be disposed of in order to justify recording a sale and derecognising the asset. It does, however, say that both the benefits and the risks retained must be significantly different from those which were held before the transaction took place, and the examples discussed in the standard envisage that the asset will be transferred for most of its life, and will be repurchased in a substantially depreciated state.[24] This means that selling an asset and buying it back after only a short time would not allow any part of the asset to be removed from the balance sheet. This may be compared with accounting by lessors, where substantially all the risks and rewards of ownership must be disposed of under the lease in order for the lessor to be able to regard it as a finance lease and therefore record a sale.

(c)   where an item is transferred for its full life but some risk or benefit is retained

The standard discusses various examples of this.[25] Some risk may be retained because a company gives a warranty or residual value guarantee in relation to the product being sold, but this should not preclude the recording of the sale so long as the exposure under the warranty or guarantee can be assessed and provided for if necessary. Companies may also sometimes retain the possibility of an upward adjustment to the sale price of an asset based on its future performance – for example, when a business is sold subject to an earn-out clause – but again this should not preclude the recognition of the sale.

Countryside Properties discloses the following information about guarantees given in relation to some of the houses that it has sold, but this has not prevented derecognition of the assets:

Extract 16.1: Countryside Properties PLC (1998)

23 Contingent liabilities

Sales of housing units amounting in aggregate to £12m benefit from the Group's Assured Value Guarantee under which any reduction in the resale prices of the units is guaranteed by the Group within predetermined time limits.

Rolls Royce and British Aerospace disclose some rather more complicated arrangements in relation to some of their sales:

Extract 16.2: Rolls-Royce plc (1998)

26 CONTINGENT LIABILITIES [extract]

In connection with the sale of its products, on some occasions the Group and Company enter into individually and collectively significant long-term contingent obligations. These can involve, inter alia, guaranteeing financing for customers, guaranteeing a proportion of the values of both engine and airframe, entering into leasing transactions, commitments to purchase aircraft and in certain circumstances could involve the Group and Company assuming certain of its customers' entitlements and related borrowing or cash flow obligations until the value of the security can be realised.

At December 31, 1998, having regard to the estimated net realisable value of the relevant security, the net contingent liabilities in respect of financing arrangements on all delivered aircraft amounted to **£63m** (1997 £68m). Sensitivity calculations are complex, but, for example, if the value of the relevant security was reduced by 20%, a net contingent liability of approximately **£237m** (1997 £156m) would result. There are also net contingent liabilities in respect of undelivered aircraft but it is not considered practicable to estimate these as deliveries can be many years in the future and the related financing will only be put in place at the appropriate time.

At the date these accounts are approved, the directors regard the possibility that there will be any significant loss arising from these contingencies, which cover a number of customers over a long period of time, as remote. In determining this, and the values above, the directors have taken account of advice, principally from Airclaims Limited, professional aircraft appraisers, who base their calculations on a current and future fair market value basis assuming an arms length transaction between a willing seller and a willing buyer.

Extract 16.3: British Aerospace Public Limited Company (1998)

1 Accounting policies

Aircraft financing

The Group is exposed to actual and contingent liabilities arising from commercial aircraft financing, both from financing arranged directly by the Group and from that arranged by third parties where the Group has provided guarantees or has other recourse obligations. Provision for these risks is made on a systematic basis, having regard to the ability to re-lease or re-sell the underlying aircraft.

20 Commercial aircraft financing

Commercial aircraft are frequently sold for cash with the manufacturer retaining some financial exposure. Aircraft financing commitments of the Group can be categorised as either direct or indirect. Direct commitments arise where the Group has sold the aircraft to a third party lessor and then leased it back under an operating lease (or occasionally a finance lease) prior to an onward lease to an operator. Indirect commitments (contingent liabilities) may arise where the Group has sold aircraft to third parties who either operate the aircraft themselves or lease the aircraft on to operators. In these cases the Group may give guarantees in respect of the residual values of the related aircraft or certain head lease and finance payments to be made by either the third parties or the operators. The Group's exposure to these commitments is offset by future lease rentals and the residual value of the related aircraft.

During 1998, an external review was commissioned of the likely income to be generated from the portfolio of aircraft to which the Group has either direct or indirect financing exposures. This review identified a most likely level of income of some £2.4 billion. Following this analysis, in September 1998, the Group entered into arrangements which have reduced its exposure from commercial aircraft financing by obtaining insurance cover from a syndicate of leading insurance companies over a significant proportion of the contracted and expected income stream from the aircraft portfolio including those aircraft where the Group has provided residual value guarantees. At the start of the insurance arrangements a minimum level of income of £2.2 billion was underwritten.

As a consequence the net exposure of the Group to aircraft financing has been reduced by the insured amount and as at 31 December 1998 was:

	1998	1997
	£m	£m
Direct operating lease commitments	854	1,012
Direct finance lease commitments	6	8
Indirect exposure through aircraft contingent liabilities	1,481	1,530
Exposure to residual value guarantees	504	420
Income guaranteed through insurance arrangements	(2,053)	–
Net exposure	792	2,970
Expected income not covered by insurance arrangements	(43)	(2,253)
Expected income on aircraft delivered post insurance arrangements	(99)	–
Adjustment to net present value	(160)	(181)
Recourse provision	490	536

Income guaranteed through insurance arrangements represents the future income stream from the aircraft assets guaranteed under the insurance arrangements after deducting the policy excess.

The external review identified likely income of £250 million above the level guaranteed under the insurance arrangements. *Expected income not covered by insurance arrangements and on aircraft delivered post insurance arrangements* represents the amount of this income assumed by management for the purpose of provisioning.

Given the long term nature of the liabilities, the Directors believe it is appropriate to state the recourse provision at its net present value. The provision covers costs to be incurred over a forecast period of 14 years from the balance sheet date. The *adjustment to net present value* reduces the expected liabilities from their outturn amounts to their anticipated net present value.

As can be seen from the above extracts, in the case of partial disposals, there may be uncertainty as to the measurement of the initial profit or loss. FRS 5 says that the normal rules of prudence should be applied, but also that the uncertainty should be explained if it could have a material effect on the accounts.[26]

It has to be said, however, that this remains a vague area of the standard, because it is not at all clear where to draw the line between recording a sale with substantial provision for attendant uncertainties and not regarding it as achieving a sale at all because of the extent of the risks retained. In contrast, SSAP 21 has a much clearer distinction (albeit one that still requires judgement) between leasing transactions that transfer substantially all the risks and rewards of the asset concerned and those that do not, and the latter do not qualify for sale recognition by the lessor. Applying such a perspective to some of the transactions illustrated above would give rise to very different accounting results.

2.6   The linked presentation

FRED 4 introduced a new idea which was not proposed in the two earlier exposure drafts – the concept of a 'linked presentation' – and this was carried through into FRS 5. This requires non-recourse finance to be shown on the face of the balance sheet as a deduction from the asset to which it relates (rather than in the liabilities section of the balance sheet), provided certain stringent criteria are met.[27] This appears to be really a question of how, rather than whether, to show the asset and liability in the balance sheet, so it is not the same as derecognition of these items, although the treatment remains a rather ambiguous one.[28]

The treatment was devised by the ASB in response to strong representations from the banks in relation to securitisation, but use of the treatment is not confined to any particular kind of asset. It is to be used when 'the commercial effect ... is that the item is being sold but the sale process is not yet complete'.[29] The object of the linked presentation is to show that the entity retains significant benefits and risks associated with the asset, and that the claim of the provider of finance is limited solely to the funds generated by it. It is therefore something of a halfway house, because it discloses the gross amount of the asset which remains a source of benefit to the entity, while simultaneously achieving a net presentation in the balance sheet totals.

The standard says that the linked presentation should be used when an asset is financed in such a way that:

(a)   the finance will be paid only from proceeds generated by the specific item it finances (or by transfer of the item itself) and there is no possibility whatsoever of a claim on the entity being established other than against funds generated by that item (or the item itself); and

(b)   there is no provision whatsoever whereby the entity may either keep the item on repayment of the finance or reacquire it at any time.[30]

There are also some more specific conditions discussed below.

Part (b) above makes it clear that the non-recourse nature of the borrowing is not sufficient to justify the linked presentation; the entity must also relinquish its grip on the asset by dedicating it to repay the loan. The requirement to include both non-recourse finance and the related asset in a balance sheet illustrates an important feature of the standard's philosophy. Financiers tend to think of the isolation of risk as being the primary consideration in relation to questions of whether items should be included in the balance sheet or not. To them, the question as to which assets are available as security for which borrowings is of great significance and they would like the accounts to focus on this criterion. However, FRS 5 approaches the matter from a different angle: it wants to identify those assets and activities which are within the control of the reporting company and are a source of benefits and risks to it, because these are the things which are relevant to an assessment of the company's performance. In this context, the question of who has claims over which asset is of lesser importance, although perhaps it is one which lends itself to note disclosure.

The detailed qualifying criteria which have to be satisfied in order to justify a linked presentation are explained in the following terms:

(a)   the finance relates to a specific item (or portfolio of similar items) and, in the case of a loan, is secured on that item but not on any other asset of the entity;

(b)   the provider of the finance has no recourse whatsoever, either explicit or implicit, to the other assets of the entity for losses and the entity has no obligation whatsoever to repay the provider of finance;

(c)   the directors of the entity state explicitly in each set of financial statements where a linked presentation is used that the entity is not obliged to support any losses, nor does it intend to do so;

(d)   the provider of the finance has agreed in writing (in the finance documentation or otherwise) that it will seek repayment of the finance, as to both principal and interest, only to the extent that sufficient funds are generated by the specific item it has financed and that it will not seek recourse in any other form, and such agreement is noted in each set of financial statements where a linked presentation is used;

(e)   if the funds generated by the item are insufficient to pay off the provider of the finance, this does not constitute an event of default for the entity; and

(f)   there is no provision whatsoever, either in the financing arrangement or otherwise, whereby the entity has a right or an obligation either to keep the item upon repayment of the finance or (where title to the item has been transferred) to reacquire it at any time. Accordingly:

(i)   where the item is one (such as a monetary receivable) that directly generates cash, the provider of finance will be repaid out of the resulting cash receipts (to the extent these are sufficient); or

(ii)   where the item is one (such as a physical asset) that does not directly generate cash, there is a definite point at which either the item will be sold to a third party and the provider of the finance repaid from the proceeds (to the extent these are sufficient) or the item will be transferred to the provider of the finance in full and final settlement.[31]

The ASB has made it clear that these highly detailed criteria are indeed meant to be interpreted restrictively, and only a narrow category of assets is likely to qualify for linked presentation. The explanation section of FRS 5 enlarges on (a) above as follows: 'A linked presentation should not be used where the finance relates to two or more items that are not part of a portfolio, or to a portfolio containing items that would otherwise be shown under different balance sheet captions. Similarly, a linked presentation should not be used where the finance relates to any kind of business unit, or for items that generate the funds required to repay the finance only by being used in conjunction with other assets of the entity. The item must generate the funds required to repay the finance either by unwinding directly into cash (as in the case of a debt), or by its sale to a third party.'[32]

A number of the other conditions concern the need for the entity to be protected from losses in respect of the item transferred. Among the forms of recourse which could breach these conditions are the following:

■   an agreement to repurchase non-performing items or to substitute good items for bad ones;

■   a guarantee given to the provider of the finance or any other party (of performance, proceeds or other support);

■   a put option under which items can be transferred back to the entity;

■   a swap of some or all of the amounts generated by the item for a separately determined payment; or

■   a penalty on cancelling an ongoing arrangement such that the entity bears the cost of any items that turn out to be bad.[33]

Under the standard, the use of the linked presentation is expressed as being mandatory whenever all the conditions listed above are met. However, because compliance with some of the conditions is itself voluntary, the treatment is in reality optional. For example, both conditions (c) and (d) above mean that the use of the linked presentation is conditional on certain disclosures being made in the accounts; it is therefore open to anyone who does not wish to use it to avoid doing so simply by failing to make the required disclosures and thus being disqualified from using the linked presentation.

An example of the use of the linked presentation is shown below:

Example 16.3: Linked presentation

Company A has a portfolio of receivables totalling £500,000. Past experience suggests that bad debts will not exceed 3%. It transfers title to the receivables to Company B in exchange for proceeds of £460,000 plus a further amount which varies according to when or whether the receivables are realised. In addition, Company B has recourse to Company A for the first £50,000 of any losses. Assuming all the conditions for a linked presentation are met, Company A's balance sheet would contain the following items:

Receivables subject to financing arrangements	£000
Gross receivables (after bad debt provision of £15,000)	485
Less: non-returnable proceeds	(410)
	75

The other £50,000 of the proceeds from Company B (i.e. the returnable portion) would be shown within creditors.

Inchcape has used a linked presentation in relation to discounted debts, as shown below:

Extract 16.4: Inchcape plc (1998)

9 Net current assets [extract]

	1998 £m	1997 £m
b Debtors		
Amounts due within one year:		
Trade debtors subject to limited recourse financing	**4.1**	4.0
less: non-returnable amounts received	**(3.6)**	(3.5)
	0.5	0.5
Other trade debtors	**318.9**	499.2
...		
Amounts due beyond one year:		
Trade debtors subject to limited recourse financing	**36.8**	36.0
less: non-returnable amounts received	**(32.5)**	(31.5)
	4.3	4.5
...		

Trade debtors subject to limited recourse financing represent hire purchase debtors discounted with banks, so that the majority of cash received by the Group on discounting is not returnable and carries interest at variable rates. The returnable element of the proceeds is recorded as bank loans and overdrafts due within and after one year as appropriate. It has been agreed with the banks that the Group is not required to make good any losses over and above the agreed recourse limit.

As can be seen above, Inchcape has set out its note so as to segregate the debtors that are subject to limited course financing from those that are not, and the standard can be read as requiring this. However, this is not the only possible interpretation, and some other companies simply deduct the non-recourse finance from the total of the relevant category, and disclose the amount involved by way of footnote. Cookson provides an example of this.

Extract 16.5: Cookson Group plc (1998)

15 Debtors [extract]

	Group	
	1998	1997
	£m	£m
Amounts falling due within one year:		
Gross trade debtors	283.5	288.1
less: non-returnable proceeds	(6.7)	–
	276.8	288.1
Amounts owed by associates	2.4	7.1
...		

During the year, the Group commenced an asset securitisation programme in respect of certain of its US trade debtors. Under the terms of this programme, an interest in a pool of trade debtors was sold to a bank in exchange for a cash advance, on which interest is payable to the bank. A security interest has been granted to the bank over this pool of trade debtors. At 31 December 1998, the pool comprised £23.1m of trade debtors, and the cash advance was £6.7m.

The Group is not obliged and does not intend to support any losses arising from the assigned debts against which cash has been advanced. The providers of the finance have confirmed in writing that in the event of default in payment by a debtor, they will seek repayment of cash advanced only from the remainder of the pool of debts in which they hold an interest, and that repayment will not be required from the Group in any other way.

Although the standard insists that gross amounts are disclosed for balance sheet purposes, it allows the corresponding revenues and costs to be dealt with net on the face of the profit and loss account and grossed up only in the notes, except if presentation of the gross figures on the face of the profit and loss account is thought necessary in order to give a true and fair view.[34] This is a rather glib statement, which does not really consider where in the profit and loss account such items may belong – for example, they may be a mixture of operating and financing items, in which case it would be inappropriate to present them on a single line. The standard offers no suggestion as to how items are to be presented in the cash flow statement.

FRS 5 says that, insofar as the non-returnable proceeds received exceed the amount of the asset being financed, the entity should regard the excess as a profit, but that otherwise profits and losses should continue to be recognised in the periods in which they arise. However, this exposes the essential ambiguity of the treatment. There are two possible interpretations of what the linked presentation is seeking to achieve, and this part of the standard seems to mix them up. The two interpretations are:

- A sale of the original asset has taken place, giving rise to a residual (net) asset, but because the entity continues to benefit from its interest in this net asset it should be grossed up within the assets section of the balance sheet to give additional information about its underlying components.

■ No sale of the original asset has taken place. Instead, non-recourse finance has been advanced to the entity in respect of the asset. However, because of its close relationship with the asset, the finance should be deducted from it within the assets section of the balance sheet.

We suspect that the second of these better reflects the ASB's thinking about the linked presentation. However, it creates a conflict with the law because moving a liability to the assets side of the balance sheet contravenes the format rules of the Companies Act. Accordingly, it has been necessary to present the argument in terms of the first description set out above.

The problem is that the rules as to profit recognition quoted above are not really consistent with either of these interpretations. If the transaction is not a sale (the second interpretation) then it would not be appropriate to recognise any profit at that stage, whether or not the non-returnable proceeds exceeded the carrying value of the asset. On the other hand, if it *is* a sale (the first interpretation) then it would be appropriate to measure the profit *or loss* based on the difference between the proceeds and that proportion of the previous carrying value which is regarded as being sold – in other words it falls directly within the rules for partial derecognition discussed in 2.5 above.

It has to be said that the linked presentation seems to be the classic result of an expedient compromise. It is a highly ambiguous treatment with shaky conceptual foundations, and whatever its pragmatic advantages, its introduction has not added to the elegance of the standard, particularly given the obsessively complex qualifying conditions which accompany it. We hope that the circumstances which led to its creation will change so as to enable it to be withdrawn at some time in the future.

2.7 Offset

FRS 5 makes it clear that assets and liabilities which qualify for recognition should be accounted for individually, rather than netted off. It is a general tenet of accounting practice that assets and liabilities should be dealt with separately in the absence of reasons for offsetting them, and this principle is also recognised in the Companies Act.[35] Netting off is allowed by the standard only where the debit and credit balances are not really separate assets and liabilities,[36] for example where they are amounts due to and from the same third party and where there is a legal right of set-off.

The detailed criteria which permit offset are set out in FRS 5 as follows:

(a) the parties owe each other determinable monetary amounts, denominated either in the same currency or in different but freely convertible currencies;

(b)   the reporting entity has the ability to insist on a net settlement, which can be enforced in all situations of default by the other party; and

(c)   the reporting entity's ability to insist on a net settlement is assured beyond doubt. This means that the debit balance must be receivable no later than the credit balance requires to be paid, otherwise the entity could be required to pay the other party and later find that it was unable to obtain payment itself. It also means that the ability to insist on a net settlement has to survive the insolvency of the other party (which may require detailed examination in group situations).[37]

The crux of the test is that the entity can enforce a right of set off so that there is no possibility of having to pay the creditor balance without recovering the debtor amount. Conditions (b) and (c) above seem only to be different elaborations of the same point.

In other ways, however, the criteria are very tightly drawn. For example, they refer only to situations involving two parties, whereas sometimes there may be three or more. This could be interpreted to mean that offset is never permitted where more than two parties are involved, but we doubt whether this was intended. In accordance with the standard's general principles, we think that offset will still be available as long as the reporting entity has enforceable rights which allow its assets to negate its liabilities even if these are with different parties.

One of the most common issues that arises in relation to these offset rules is the extent to which the various bank balances and overdrafts of various companies within a group that involve the same bank can be netted down in the consolidated accounts. Although the conditions of the banking arrangements will generally allow for a degree of offsetting, they do not always meet the demanding tests of FRS 5, and it is necessary to consider the precise contractual terms in each case.

Tesco discloses the following note in relation to its banking arrangements:

Extract 16.6: Tesco PLC (1999)

Note 17 Creditors falling due within one year

	Group		Company	
	1999	1998	**1999**	1998
	£m	£m	**£m**	£m
Bank loans and overdrafts (a)	**811**	607	**1,341**	1,263

a) Bank deposits at subsidiary undertakings of £767m (1998 – £750m) have been offset against borrowings in the parent company under a legal right of set-off.

One sector that experienced initial difficulty in applying the offset rules was the insurance broking industry. Their problems were twofold: first, it is debatable whether certain of the debtor and creditor balances in their accounting records are properly their own assets and liabilities, or whether they are only those of their principals for whom they act as agents; and second, it is not clear what the legal rights of set-off are in all cases, since conventional settlement practices are not based on the strict legal position. Because of this, the ASB deferred the application of the offset rules for two years in respect of insurance broking transactions, to allow time to consider how to apply these rules and to develop the necessary systems, but this period has now expired and no exemption now exists.

2.8   Consolidation of other entities

The question of whether or not to consolidate the accounts of another entity can also be thought of as involving an off balance sheet finance issue. If an investee company is included in consolidated accounts, its assets and liabilities are shown on a line by line basis with those of the investor, whereas if it is only equity accounted, or carried at cost, it will be shown on one line, simply as an investment.

As discussed in Chapter 5, the definition of a 'subsidiary undertaking' introduced by the Companies Act 1989 means that consolidation of other entities is now based largely on de facto control. This change curtailed one of the major areas of abuse which had been possible under the old legislation, since it was previously very easy to conduct business through another company while keeping it outside the Companies Act definition of a subsidiary. However, FRS 5 takes the view that even the present definition is not conclusive in determining what entities are to be included in consolidated accounts. It envisages that there will be occasions where the need to give a true and fair view will require the inclusion of 'quasi subsidiaries'. This means that, even if a subservient entity escapes the legal definition of a subsidiary undertaking, it will still have to be consolidated as a quasi subsidiary if that is what the substance of the relationship dictates. FRS 5 defines a quasi subsidiary in these terms:

'A quasi subsidiary of a reporting entity is a company, trust, partnership or other vehicle that, though not fulfilling the definition of a subsidiary, is directly or indirectly controlled by the reporting entity and gives rise to benefits for that entity that are in substance no different from those that would arise were the vehicle a subsidiary.'[38]

The key feature of the above definition is control, which in the context of a quasi subsidiary means the ability to direct its financial and operating policies with a view to gaining economic benefit from its activities.[39] Control is also indicated by the ability to prevent others from exercising those policies or from enjoying the benefits of the vehicle's net assets.[40]

Control can be derived from a variety of sources and may be exercised in a number of different ways, some of which may be more evident than others. Sometimes there will be little overt sign that control is being exercised, yet it may still exist, even if invisibly. For example, the mere threat of the exercise of control may persuade the quasi subsidiary to behave in accordance with the dominant party's perceived wishes, so that the actual exercise of control never becomes necessary. The standard acknowledges, however, that it can sometimes be very hard to ascertain who is exercising control.

In some cases, the allocation of the benefits and risks may be predetermined and immutable, so that the ostensible owner of the quasi subsidiary has surrendered its normal rights of ownership, and with them, control. In these cases the standard suggests that the best way of identifying the party in control might be to determine who is receiving the benefits of the quasi subsidiary's activities, since it can normally be presumed that the party entitled to the benefits will have made sure that it retains control.

If the apparent owner of the enterprise has accepted severe constraints on its normal powers of ownership it must be apparent that the real benefits of ownership lie elsewhere. For example, its share in the profits earned by the enterprise might be limited to a nominal sum or to an amount which really represents only a lending return on its investment, because all of the remaining profits will perpetually be diverted to another party in the form, say, of a fee under a contract. In such circumstances, it may be evident that the recipient of the fee is the equity owner in substance, while the ostensible owner is more in the nature of a lender or simply an intermediary with no real interest in the enterprise.

As with many complex relationships, it is often helpful to consider the position of each of the parties in turn as a means of analysing the overall substance of the arrangement. By understanding what has motivated each party to accept its own particular rights and obligations under the deal, it becomes easier to see the commercial reality of the structure as a whole.

An example of an arrangement involving the use of a quasi subsidiary is as follows:

Example 16.4: Quasi subsidiary

A hotel company, Company H, sells some of its hotels to Company B, the subsidiary of a bank. B is financed by loans from the bank at normal interest rates. H and B enter into a management contract whereby H undertakes the complete management of the hotels. It is remunerated for this service by a management charge which is set at a level which absorbs all the profits of B after paying the interest on its loan finance. There are also arrangements which give H control over the sale of any of the hotels by B, and any gain or loss on such sales also reverts to it through adjustment of the management charge.

In these circumstances, it is clear that the bank's legal ownership of B is of little relevance. All the profits of B go to H, and the bank's return is limited to that of a secured lender. In substance, H holds the equity interest in both B and the hotels that it owns. B will therefore be regarded as a quasi subsidiary of H and will be consolidated by it. As a result, all transactions between the two companies will be eliminated from the group accounts of H, and the group balance sheet will show the hotels as an asset and the bank loans as a liability. The group profit and loss account will show the full trading results of the hotels and the interest charged by the bank on its loans, while the inter-company management charge will be eliminated on consolidation.

A 'deadlock' 50:50 joint venture will still be off balance sheet for both parties, but only if the two parties concerned are genuine equals in terms of both their ability to control the venture and their interests in its underlying assets. Such a relationship will seldom exist where one of the parties is a trading company and the other is a bank, because banks are primarily in the business of financing their customers, not entering into real joint ventures with them on an equal basis.

Example 16.5: Deadlock joint venture

A retailer, Company R, transfers a number of its shops to a newly created company, Company N, which is owned 50:50 by R itself and a third party, Company T. The shops are leased back to R on operating leases on normal commercial terms.

Provided that N is a genuine 50:50 company and that the risks and rewards of ownership of the shops are henceforth to be shared equally between its two shareholders, then R will simply have an investment in a joint venture which will be accounted for under the gross equity method in its balance sheet. This means that, although N's gross assets and liabilities will be displayed as an analysis of R's net investment in the joint venture, the underlying assets (the shops) and liabilities (the finance for the shops) will no longer be shown within the tangible assets and the debt sections of R's balance sheet. However, there are many possible pitfalls, any of which might put the assets and liabilities back into these balance sheet categories.

The first of these is that if R exercises a dominant influence over N, then it will be a subsidiary undertaking rather than an associate and will have to be fully consolidated. To avoid this, control over N must be balanced evenly between R and T.

Second, the sale of the shops must have succeeded in transferring the risks and rewards of ownership to N, and there must be no mechanism whereby they are transferred back to R. This means that the lease must genuinely be an operating lease, but also that R must not participate in future gains and losses on the shops except in its capacity as a 50% investor in N. For example, it must not have the opportunity to buy the shops back other than at their then market value, nor can it provide a guarantee which protects either N or T against future falls in the value of the shops, except to the extent that it is required to do so as a tenant under a normal repairing lease.

Other factors that would cause the deal to be looked upon with suspicion would be any arrangement whereby the profits and losses of N were not borne equally by R and T. Such an arrangement might take the form of differential rights to dividends, but could include also other factors, such as management charges which had the effect of stripping out profits, or guarantees of N's borrowings which were given by R alone.

The key factor which really dictates the substance of the arrangement is the identity of the two investors in N and their objectives in entering into the arrangement. If T is another retailer, a property company or some other party which is also selling its own properties to N, and if the two investors are content to accept half of the risks and rewards of each other's properties, then off balance sheet treatment is appropriate. However, if T is a financial institution and is seeking to achieve a lender's return on the deal, then it is unlikely that the conditions for off balance sheet treatment will be met.

Since the law requires consolidated accounts to be drawn up to include subsidiary undertakings, and FRS 5 says that quasi subsidiaries (which by definition are not subsidiary undertakings) should also be so included, it is necessary to reconcile these two requirements. This is done by reference to the 'true and fair override', the section of the Companies Act which says that, where compliance with the detailed rules of the Act would not be sufficient to give a true and fair view, then the company should either give additional information in the accounts or (in special circumstances) depart from the detailed rules in order to give a true and fair view.[41] Including a quasi subsidiary in the consolidation is regarded as giving additional information in terms of this requirement. Accordingly, compliance with the standard will not result in a breach of the law even though it involves extending the definition of what has to be consolidated. FRS 5 requires that when quasi subsidiaries are included in consolidated accounts, the fact of their inclusion should be disclosed, together with a summary of their own financial statements. Where there are a number of quasi subsidiaries which fulfil a similar purpose, their accounts can be combined for the purposes of this summary.[42] Associated Nursing Services provides an example of this disclosure:

Extract 16.7: Associated Nursing Services plc (1999)

12. Investments held as Fixed Assets

b) Shares in quasi-subsidiaries [extract]

For the reasons given in note 1(b) the following companies are accounted for as quasi-subsidiaries at 31 March 1999.

Name of company	Description of shares held	Percentage shareholding	Nature of business
Ebbgate Nursing Homes Limited	Ordinary	50%	Nursing Homes
Ebbgate Nursing Homes (London) Limited	Ordinary	50%	Nursing Homes
Hornchurch VCT Limited	Ordinary	50%	Nursing Homes

A summary of the combined quasi-subsidiary financial statements is shown [in note 29 below]. These companies are all registered and operate in England and Wales.

29. Summary of Combined Quasi-subsidiaries' Financial Statements included in the Consolidated Financial Statements

a) Profit and Loss Account

For the year to 31 March	1999 £000's	Restated 1998 £000's
Turnover	7,236	11,861
Cost of services	(4,715)	(7,475)
Gross profit	2,521	4,386
Operating expenses	(1,398)	(2,754)
Operating profit	1,123	1,632
Exceptional items – profit on sale of Nursing Homes	205	–
Net interest payable	(1,286)	(2,119)
Interest receivable	168	637
Net profit before taxation	210	150
Taxation	(370)	(39)
Net profit after taxation	(160)	111
Dividends	–	(225)
Retained loss for the financial year	(160)	(114)

There are no recognised gains or losses other than those shown in the profit and loss account shown above.

b) Balance Sheet

As at 31 March	**1999** **£000's**	1998 £000's
Fixed assets		
Tangible assets	**10,740**	20,302
Long term bank deposit	**–**	–
	10,740	20,302
Current assets		
Debtors	**281**	2,291
Bank deposit	**–**	5,300
Cash at bank and in hand	**129**	464
	410	8,055
Creditors: amounts falling due within one year	**(2,979)**	(16,510)
Net current assets	**(2,569)**	(8,455)
Total assets less current liabilities	**8,171**	11,847
Creditors: amounts falling due after more than one year	**(8,051)**	(11,861)
Provisions for liabilities and charges	**(32)**	(367)
Net assets	**88**	(201)
Capital and reserves		
Called up share capital	16	12
Share premium account	736	542
Profit & loss account	(664)	(755)
	88	(201)

c) Cash flow statement

As at 31 March	1999 £000's	1999 £000's	1998 £000's	1998 £000's
Net cash inflow from operating activities		**447**		2,283
Returns on investments and servicing of finance				
Interest paid	**(975)**		(1,650)	
Dividends paid to non-equity shareholders	–		389	
Interest received	**2,214**		21	
Net cash outflow from returns on investments		**1,239**		(2,018)
Advanced Corporation Taxation	–		(72)	
Corporation tax	**(135)**		(88)	
Tax paid		**(135)**		(160)
Capital expenditure and financial investment				
Payments to acquire tangible fixed assets	**(235)**		(3,882)	
Receipts from sale of fixed assets	**8,039**		2,599	
Net cash outflow from capital expenditure and financial investment		**7,804**		(1,283)
Net cash outflow before financing		**(9,355)**		(1,178)
Management of liquid resources				
Receipt from cash placed on deposit				249
Financing				
Proceeds from share issue	367		283	
Shares redeemed	–		(400)	
Bank loan repayments	(8,558)		(3,029)	
Bank loan received	6,161		3,325	
Other loans received	490		700	
Other loans repaid	(13,610)		–	
Net cash inflow from financing		**(15,150)**		879
Decrease in cash in the financial year		**(5,795)**		(50)

In fact, these companies are treated as quasi-subsidiaries as a result of an earlier challenge from the Financial Reporting Review Panel which developed into a lengthy dispute. In its 1996 accounts the company said this:

Extract 16.8: Associated Nursing Services plc (1996)

1 Accounting Policies

Basis of consolidation [extract]

... The Panel has queried the Company's treatment in its 1995 consolidated financial statements of three companies as Associated Undertakings and of two sale and leaseback transactions. The Panel has expressed the view that, under the terms of Financial Reporting Standard No 5, the Associated Undertakings should have been consolidated as quasi-subsidiaries and the properties sold under sale and leaseback arrangements should have remained on the Balance Sheet at cost or valuation with the sales proceeds being included in borrowings.

The same treatments have been adopted in the 1996 consolidated financial statements. The Company does not and cannot alone control the Associated Undertakings and the purchaser of the properties has no access to the sales proceeds. Following consultation with its Auditors the Board does not agree with the current views of the Panel. It should be noted that if the Panel's views were implemented they would have no material impact on the profit before taxation for the year ended 31 March 1996. Having regard to these matters and following consultation with its Auditors, the Board considers that it would be inappropriate at this time to change the Company's accounting policies but it is in continuing discussions with the Panel.

As a result of these continuing discussions, however, the company was eventually persuaded to change its mind. The Panel issued a Press Notice explaining the issue and its reasoning in the following terms:

'ANS had entered into joint ventures with two partners and had treated the joint ventures as associated undertakings in the 1995 and 1996 Financial Statements.

'In one case, which involved a joint venture with a bank, the board of the joint venture company was 'deadlocked'. In the Panel's view however the financial and operating policies of that company were substantially predetermined by underlying agreements; and through its interest in the joint venture ANS gained benefits arising from the net assets of the company such that it had control. In the other case a venture capital arrangement with five venture capital funds had been set up through an intermediary. In the Panel's view the financial and operating policies of that company were again substantially predetermined by underlying agreements. Although in this case ANS held only a minority of the ordinary share capital, the investor's interests were effectively limited and the Panel took the view that ANS gained benefits arising from the net assets of the company such that it had control.

'In the Panel's view therefore the substance of the arrangements was such that the companies were quasi-subsidiaries as defined by FRS 5. Consequently they should not have been accounted for by the equity method but treated, as FRS 5 requires, as though they were subsidiaries.

'Under the accounting treatment adopted by the company and challenged by the Panel only the company's share of the net assets of the companies in question were reflected in the consolidated balance sheet. In the Panel's view, which the directors have now accepted, the substance of the transactions is such as to require that, in accordance with FRS 5, the full amount of their assets and liabilities should be included in the consolidated balance sheet with appropriate changes to the consolidated profit and loss account.'[43]

Most companies that have quasi-subsidiaries will also have actual subsidiary undertakings and be presenting consolidated accounts. However, a company that has no subsidiary undertakings as defined in the Act will ordinarily produce only entity accounts. FRS 5 deals with this issue by saying that if such a company has a quasi subsidiary then it has to present consolidated accounts incorporating the quasi subsidiary with the same prominence as is given to its unconsolidated accounts.[44]

As discussed in Chapter 5 at 5, the Companies Act permits subsidiary undertakings to be excluded from the consolidation under various circumstances. Only one of these grounds for exclusion applies to quasi subsidiaries under FRS 5 – the case where the quasi subsidiary has not previously been included in the consolidation and is held exclusively for resale.[45]

2.9 Disclosure

FRS 5 has a general requirement to disclose transactions in sufficient detail to enable the reader to understand their commercial effect, whether or not they have given rise to the recognition of assets and liabilities.[46] This means that where transactions or schemes give rise to assets and liabilities which are *not* recognised in the accounts, disclosure of their nature and effects still has to be considered in order to ensure that the accounts give a true and fair view. One company that fell foul of this requirement was Burn Stewart Distillers. In its 1996 accounts, the chairman made these remarks:

Extract 16.9: Burn Stewart Distillers PLC (1996)

Chairman's Statement [extract]

... I am dismayed to have to report sharply reduced profits for the year ended 30 June 1996. The principal reason for this decline is the application of accounting standard FRS 5, introduced in 1994. The strict application of this standard, which is technical and subjective, has had a modest effect on our turnover, cost of sales and distribution costs, but has impacted heavily and disproportionately on profit before tax. In simple terms, what has happened is that profit which was expected to feature in the year under review was deferred until a subsequent period. The effect on profit before tax is accentuated because the required adjustments leave overheads and finance costs substantially unchanged. The standard has been applied to business with one of our customers. Because of the relationship which has evolved with that customer, our auditors have judged it to be, in effect, not independent. The directors do not share this view. The business with this customer was not unusual in either scale or profitability, nor was the relationship with the customer particularly unusual in our industry. However, the combination of circumstances which led our auditors to take this view were somewhat unique and we do not foresee this problem arising again.

The chairman therefore seemed to regard this transaction as of great significance but, curiously, the accounts did not really explain what it was all about. This led to intervention by the FRRP, who reminded the company of the requirement mentioned above and persuaded it to issue a supplementary note to its accounts which explained the transaction in the following terms:

Extract 16.10: Burn Stewart Distillers PLC (1996)

SUPPLEMENTARY NOTE TO FINANCIAL STATEMENTS FOR THE YEAR ENDED 30 JUNE 1996 [extract]

1996 Material Transaction

Under the terms of a sale in December 1995, the company sold whiskies at an invoice value of £5.1m, the customer made an immediate part payment of £3.0m and the balance is receivable no later that 31 December 1996. Settlement in kind of all or part of the balance is provided for at the company's discretion. The directors have concluded in compliance with FRS 5 that this sale cannot properly be recognised in the results for 1996 since settlement of the outstanding balance is considered to be conditional upon a sale of the whiskies by the customer or by a refinancing of the customer's entire undertaking. The exclusion of the sale is further supported by the fact that the customer is regarded as financially dependent on the company since its principal source of income at the date of sale arose from a marketing consultancy agreement with the company effective from 1993. The profit and loss account therefore excludes the invoiced sale of £5.1m and the related profit of £2.3m. The balance sheets of the company and the group include (i) in stocks £2.8m (although legal title to the whiskies has transferred to the customer) – see revised note 10; and (ii) in creditors and accruals the part payment of £3.0m.

It appears from this supplementary note that the directors had come to share the auditors' views on the accounting treatment of this transaction, despite the wording of the chairman's statement, which was still attached to the same accounts. To put the transaction in context, the Review Panel noted that the purported profit on this transaction of £2.3m was to be compared with the group's total profit for the year (which excluded the effect of transaction) of £1.01m. As it turned out, this £2.3m profit was never fully realised, as explained in this note from the following year's accounts, which vindicated the decision not to recognise it in 1996.

Extract 16.11: Burn Stewart Distillers PLC (1997)

3 PROFIT ON ORDINARY ACTIVITIES BEFORE TAXATION [extract]

Profit on ordinary activities before taxation is stated after charging:

	1997	1996
	£000	£000
Provision against stocks acquired from related party (note i)	775	–

(i) HURLINGHAM INTERNATIONAL LIMITED (HIL)

HIL is a small organisation with whom the company has had a business relationship since 1993. At no time has the company had any interest in the shares of HIL. HIL is independently managed and advised.

Under an agreement entered into between the company and HIL in February 1993 and terminated in December 1996, HIL provided a marketing consultancy service to the company, principally in relation to overseas markets. HIL provided valuable assistance to the company in connection with a number of important initiatives in the Far East. The company also contracted with HIL to support HIL in the development of a range of spirit brands, with these amounts recoverable against commissions and other revenues earned by HIL from its trading activities. Over the whole course of the agreement the company has made payments totalling £419,000 and in addition funded brand

---

development expenditure totalling £95,000. As at 30 June 1996 the company had provided £336,000 against such costs and the balance has been provided against in full during the current year.

Under a subsequent agreement entered into between the company and HIL in March 1997 the company has been appointed exclusive supplier to HIL in respect of the range of spirit products which HIL sells in a number of overseas markets. During the year ended 30 June 1997, the company supplied products under this agreement to a value of £22,000, all of which remained outstanding at the year end.

In December 1995 the company contracted with HIL to sell specific maturing whiskies at a total price of £5,091,000 with a book value of £2,754,000, the terms of which required HIL to pay £3,000,000 cash upon delivery in December 1995, with the balance to be paid no later than December 1996. HIL borrowed the cash paid upon delivery from its bankers and granted them a security over the whiskies purchased. The contract provided that the objective of the sale was to put HIL into a position to sell its whole undertaking, including its brands, and allowed for early payment of the balance of the price if this objective was achieved before December 1996. The contract also provided for settlement in kind of all or part of the balance of the price at the company's discretion. In addition, the company warranted to the bank which had provided funds to HIL that on 27 December 1995 the stocks were fairly valued at £5,091,000 and that the net realisable value of the stocks was not less than £3,600,000. The directors concluded, following discussion with the auditors, that this transaction should not be recorded in last year's accounts because settlement of the outstanding balance of the purchase price was considered to be dependent upon a sale of the whiskies by HIL or by a refinancing or sale of HIL's undertaking.

The company allowed HIL an extension of time until 30 June 1997 to settle the balance of the purchase price. In March 1997, following the sale by HIL of all the stocks, the company elected under the terms of the contract to take settlement in kind by purchasing from HIL certain specified whisky stocks. In June 1997 the company negotiated and agreed with HIL the purchase of whisky stocks in an amount of £1,906,000. The company has therefore recorded £5,091,000 in turnover for the year in respect of the December 1995 transaction. A provision of £185,000 has been made in respect of the remaining balance due and still owing by HIL as at 30 June 1997. Since the company and HIL are deemed to be related parties, the company has also made a provision of £775,000 against the invoiced value of the stocks acquired so as to record them at a pro rata share of the book cost of the stock originally sold to HIL. The profit recognised in the year on the December 1995 sale amounts to £1,377,000.

A further general disclosure requirement of FRS 5 is to give an explanation where there are any assets or liabilities whose nature is different from that which the reader might expect of assets or liabilities appearing in the accounts under that description.[47] For example, disclosure might be made where an asset appears in the balance sheet but is not available for use as security for liabilities of the entity. The standard also calls for specific disclosures in relation to the use of the linked presentation and the inclusion of quasi subsidiaries in the accounts, both of which have been described above, and the various transactions dealt with in the Application Notes discussed below.

3   COMMON FORMS OF OFF BALANCE SHEET FINANCE

This section discusses some of the most common forms of off balance sheet transactions and illustrates how FRS 5 tries to deal with them.

3.1   Consignment stock

Stocks held on a consignment basis are common in certain trades, particularly in motor vehicle dealerships. Essentially, this usually involves the manufacturer retaining title to stock despatched to dealers. Whether such arrangements come within the realm of off balance sheet transactions will depend on the terms of the relevant agreement, which have to be considered in their entirety so that the overall substance of the arrangement can be judged. The basic question is whether the risks and rewards of the stock have passed to the dealer in substance, even though legal title has not been transferred; has the dealer already bought the stock, on extended credit terms, or is he merely 'borrowing' it from the manufacturer?

The principal terms of the contract which bear on this question will be:

(a)   the rights of each party to the arrangement to have the stock returned to the manufacturer. If either party has an absolute right to have the stock returned, then it would be difficult to argue that ownership had passed in substance to the dealer. However, even then there might be room for debate if (as is frequently the case) this right is never exercised in practice and is therefore not seen as an important term of the contract. In practice, neither party will usually have complete freedom to have the stock returned, but will be bound by certain contractual obligations or subject to certain penalties and it will be necessary to evaluate whether these terms are more consistent with the stock being the property of the manufacturer or the dealer. In particular, the party enforcing the return of the stock may have to compensate the other party in some way which neutralises the benefit of having the right of return.

(b)   the price at which the sale is set when ownership eventually passes to the dealer. If this is based on the manufacturer's factory price at the date of that eventual sale, it will tend to indicate that he has never relinquished the risks and rewards of ownership of the stock during the time that it has been in the dealer's possession. Conversely, if the price is based on that ruling at the date of the initial supply plus interest it will tend to indicate that ownership of the stock has passed in substance and that the dealer has received a loan from the manufacturer to finance it. The date at which title will eventually pass to the dealer is also relevant. If it will inevitably pass after a certain time period, such as 90 days, even if the dealer has not sold or used it, the transaction will have more of the character of a sale on deferred payment terms; if title does not pass until some other critical event takes place, such as the onward sale by the dealer to the end user, then it will suggest that the dealer has not yet assumed the risks and rewards of ownership. However, the interrelationship of the duration of the arrangement and the price will also be significant, because it will indicate who is financing the stock and is bearing the risk of slow movement.

(c) whether or not the dealer is required to make a deposit with the manufacturer when the stock is supplied, and the terms of that deposit. This may indicate the parties' expectations as to the eventual outcome of the transaction and the terms, taken together with the terms as to the sale price, will indicate who is bearing the cost of financing the stock while it is in the dealer's possession.

(d) whether or not the dealer has the right to use the stock. The exercise of the right to use the stock, e.g. for demonstration purposes, is likely to trigger transfer of the title to the dealer, but the mere existence of that right does not by itself mean that it is an asset of the dealer before the right is exercised.

Application Note A discusses these factors, but concludes only that the stock should be included on the dealer's balance sheet if it has access to the principal benefits and risks of the stock, emphasising that the relative importance of the various terms will depend on the circumstances of each arrangement. In practice, the benefits and risks of ownership will tend to be shared between the two parties rather more evenly than in some of the other arrangements discussed in this chapter. These other arrangements often involve transactions between a commercial enterprise and a financier where their motivations are quite distinct. In the case of consignment stock, the manufacturer and the dealer have the mutual objective of selling cars to the ultimate customer, and this can make it difficult to categorise the arrangement in the manner required by FRS 5.

The following example illustrates the thought process which FRS 5 calls for:

Example 16.6: Consignment stock

A car manufacturer, M plc, supplies cars to a dealer, D Ltd, on a consignment basis. The terms of the deal permit either party to have the cars returned or (at the option of M) transferred to another dealer. D has to pay a monthly rental charge of 1% of the cost of the car for the privilege of displaying it in its showroom and it also has to arrange its own insurance for the cars. When the car is eventually sold to a customer, D has to pay M the lower of:

(i) the factory price of the car when it was first supplied, or

(ii) the current factory price of the car, less all the monthly charges paid to date.

D also has to pay for the cars (on the same terms) if they remain unsold after three months.

This example shows that it can be difficult to interpret the substance of the deal. The available accounting choices rest on whether D is considered to have already bought the car in substance or whether it is merely borrowing it from M. In practice, these arrangements generally have some features of both, and their overall substance falls between the two; this example is a case in point, because the risks and rewards of ownership are shared between the parties to some extent. This is not a helpful answer, however; the deal can only be accounted for in one way or the other. It is not possible to show the cars 'half-on' the balance sheet.

The factors which point towards treating the cars as stock of D are:

- its obligation to pay for the cars after three months, and to pay a monthly rental in the interim, which might be regarded as a finance charge on the amount outstanding. (However, if it has an unfettered right of return, it can (theoretically) avoid the obligation to pay for the cars by returning them before three months have elapsed; also, unless the factory price has gone up by 1% per month, it is able to recoup some of the rental/finance charge.)

- the fact that it cannot be compelled to pay more for the cars than the original factory price at the date of supply

- its obligation to insure the cars. (However, it would be a simple matter to transfer that obligation to M and pay a slightly increased monthly rental without altering the substance of the deal, so this element is not very persuasive.)

The main factors which point towards treating the cars as stock of M are its ability to demand return or transfer of the cars, D's right to return them to it, and the fact that it is deriving rental income from the cars in the meantime. However, this rental income will have to be refunded to the extent that the factory price increases fall short of 1% per month.

On balance, it is likely that this deal would be regarded as a sale and the cars would therefore appear in the balance sheet of D. However, before reaching that conclusion it would be necessary to see how the deal in fact worked in practice and to identify which of the terms were of real, rather than theoretical, significance.

The balance would be fundamentally affected if the settlement price was changed to become the *higher* of the two elements. D would then have to pay at least the current factory price for the cars when they were eventually purchased. This means that it would not yet have secured the main benefits of ownership and it would therefore be inappropriate to record the cars on its balance sheet.

Since the substantive ownership of the stock is frequently difficult to agree upon, a more fruitful approach is sometimes to look at the other side of the balance sheet instead. In other words, rather than focusing on whether or not the dealer has an asset, with a corresponding obligation to pay for it, it can be more useful to consider whether it has a liability, with a corresponding right to obtain the asset.

This approach might also be more in tune with the typical form of consignment stock arrangements than the approach discussed in the application note. Deposits are often paid to manufacturers, not by the dealer, but by a finance company which then charges interest to the dealer in one form or another. Since the dealer has paid no deposit itself, it may initially consider that it has no asset to account for (leaving aside for the moment the question of whether it is the substantive owner of the cars) but if it has a clear obligation to the finance company then it will have to recognise a liability under FRS 5, and an equal and opposite asset to match it. The corresponding asset is not necessarily stock – it might be equally appropriate to regard it as a deposit.

Lookers includes deposits paid to manufacturers in its stock note, in addition to consignment stock and its interest in Motability buy-back vehicles:

Extract 16.12: Lookers plc (1998)

12 STOCKS

	Group	
	1998	1997
	£000	£000
Goods for resale	**49,074**	44,909
Bulk deposit paid for vehicles on consignment	**1,410**	915
Interest bearing consignment vehicles	**6,139**	4,323
Motability buy-back vehicles	**16,593**	17,896
	73,216	68,043

PRINCIPAL ACCOUNTING POLICIES
6. STOCKS [extract]
Deposits paid for vehicles on consignment represent bulk deposits paid to manufacturers.
Interest bearing consignment vehicles and motability buy-back vehicles are included in stocks. The related liabilities are included in trade and other creditors respectively.

Henlys shows consignment stock within its stocks note, and as with Lookers above its description seems to imply that the interest-bearing nature of the arrangement may have been a major factor that determined that it should be brought on balance sheet. The group used to disclose by way of footnote a further category of off balance sheet consignment stock whose risks and benefits remained with the supplier, but no longer does so.

Extract 16.13: Henlys Group plc (1998)

13 Stocks

	Group	Group	**Company**	Company
	1998	1997	**1998**	1997
	£000	£000	**£000**	£000
Raw materials	**8,959**	3,743	**8,959**	2,512
Work in progress	**9,255**	10,456	**9,255**	8,624
Finished goods	**22,604**	29,364	**22,604**	27,912
Consignment stocks	**3,224**	1,032	**3,224**	1,032
Properties held for sale	**2,419**	3,976	**151**	1,435
	46,461	48,571	**44,193**	41,515

Consignment stocks include interest bearing consignment vehicles and the corresponding liability has been included in creditors.

Where it is concluded that the dealer owns the stock in substance, it will appear on its balance sheet with a corresponding liability to the manufacturer (offset to the extent of any deposit). Where the liability escalates through time as a result of the application of interest, such interest will be charged to the profit and loss account as it accrues. Where it is concluded that the stock remains in the ownership of the manufacturer, the only item which the dealer will have to account for is any deposit paid, which will be shown as a debtor in its accounts. Whether or not the stock is on the balance sheet, the notes to the accounts should disclose the nature of the arrangement, the amount of consignment stock held and the main terms on which it is held, including the terms of any deposit.[48]

Signet, Cookson and Wolseley all disclose that they hold material amounts of consignment stock but that it remains off balance sheet, as shown in these extracts:

Extract 16.14: Signet Group plc (1999)

11 Stocks [extract]

Subsidiary undertakings held £55,231,000 of consignment stock as at 30 January 1999 (1998: £42,999,000) which is not recorded on the balance sheet. The principal terms of the consignment agreements, which can generally be terminated by either side, are such that the Group can return any or all of the stock to the relevant suppliers without financial or commercial penalties and the supplier can vary stock prices.

Extract 16.15: Cookson Group plc (1998)

14 Stocks [extract]

In addition to the stocks recorded in the balance sheet, the Group held precious metals on consignment terms with a total value at 31 December 1998 of £159.5m (1997: £141.3m).

The Group's Precious Metal fabrication operations utilise significant amounts of precious metals, primarily gold, held on consignment terms. The terms provide inter alia that the consignor retains title to the metal and both parties have a right of return over the metal without penalty. In the great majority of cases, when fabrication is complete the consignor sells or consigns the metal directly to the Group's customers, the Group charging customers solely for the fabrication process. In the other cases the Group purchases the metal and sells it concurrently to the customer. Under these arrangements the Group is neither liable to buy the metal nor is it at risk in relation to market fluctuations in metal prices. Accordingly the stocks are not recorded in the balance sheet. Consignment fees charged by the consignors totalled £5.2m in 1998 (1997: £4.7m).

The Group also holds precious metal on behalf of customers for processing, with a total value at 31 December 1998 of £24.8m (1997: £35.1m).

Extract 16.16: Wolseley plc (1998)

11. STOCKS [extract]

Certain subsidiary undertakings have consignment stock arrangements with suppliers in the ordinary course of business. Items drawn from consignment stock are generally invoiced to the companies concerned at the price ruling at the date of drawdown. The value of such stock, at cost, which has been excluded from the balance sheet in accordance with the application notes included in FRS 5, amounted to £6.8m (1997 £8.4m).

Application Note A does not discuss the appropriate treatment in the accounts of the manufacturer, but under general rules of revenue recognition (see Chapter 3) the manufacturer could not treat the stock as sold in most cases. It is therefore quite possible that the stock will end up being shown on the balance sheets of both parties.

3.2   Sale and repurchase agreements

This type of arrangement is addressed by Application Note B of FRS 5. Transactions of this kind can take many forms, but the essential feature which unites them is that the company which purports to have sold the asset in question has not relinquished all the risks and rewards associated with the asset in the manner which would have been expected of a normal sale. If there is no significant change in the company's access to the benefits of the asset and exposures to its risks, FRS 5 requires that the sale should not be recorded and the asset in question should remain on the company's balance sheet. A straightforward illustration of the rules is given by this example:

Example 16.7:   Sale with contract to repurchase

A whisky blending company, W plc, has several years' worth of maturing whisky in stock. It contracts to sell a certain quantity of the whisky to a bank for £5 million, and agrees to buy it back one year later for £5.5 million. The whisky remains on its own premises.

Under FRS 5, this series of transactions would be accounted for as a financing deal. W has not transferred the risks and rewards of ownership of the whisky to the bank; instead, it has merely borrowed money on the security of the whisky. The accounts will continue to include the whisky stock in the balance sheet and show the £5 million received as the proceeds of a loan, extinguished one year later by the repayment of £5.5 million (which includes an interest charge of £0.5 million which would be accrued through the year).

This is a clear-cut arrangement with no uncertainty as to its outcome. However, it would not be difficult to imagine a more complex arrangement, such as this:

Example 16.8:   Sale with options to repurchase/resell

W plc sells the same quantity of whisky as before in Example 16.7 to X Limited (another whisky company) for £5 million. The whisky is stored in a third party warehouse and responsibility for the storage costs thus passes to X. W arranges put and call options with X to purchase the same quantity of the same or equivalent whisky in one year's time for £6 million. (The factor which makes the repurchase price higher in this case is that X has to bear the cost of storing the whisky for a year.)

If one assumes that the existence of both the put and the call options makes it inevitable that one or other party will exercise the option, then there seems little difference between this case and the previous one. Even though the precise identity of the whisky might be different when it gets it back, W seems to be disposing of its whisky stock only temporarily, and on that argument, FRS 5 requires it to remain on the balance sheet, with the £1 million differential in the price being accrued as warehouse rent and interest.

The example could be complicated further by removing the put option, so that W had the right to reacquire the whisky, but not the obligation to do so. Presumably, if it could buy the equivalent whisky cheaper from another source in a year's time it would do so (assuming it wanted the whisky back at all). Effectively, W would have retained the right to increases but disposed of the risks of decreases in value of the whisky. The appropriate accounting would depend on all the circumstances of the transaction; unless it was clear that the option was very likely to be exercised, then there would be a good argument that the sale should be taken at face value and the stock removed from the balance sheet; W's only remaining asset would be its option to purchase the whisky. However, this depends on all the terms of the arrangement, as discussed below.

The principal question to be answered in all such arrangements is whether the reporting company has made a sale in substance, or whether the deal is a financing one. In approaching this question, it is instructive to consider which of the parties involved will enjoy the benefits, and be exposed to the risks, of the property in question during the period between the sale and the repurchase transactions. In the most straightforward kind of arrangement, this will generally be indicated by the prices at which the two transactions are struck; for example, if they are both at the market values current at the date of each transaction, then the risks and rewards of ownership are passed to the purchaser for this period; however, if the second selling price is linked to the first by an interest element, then these risks and rewards remain with the original owner throughout the period and the purchaser has the position only of a lender in the deal.

Another key factor in evaluating such an arrangement is the part of the agreement which permits or requires the repurchase to take place. As already illustrated, this may take the form of a contractual commitment which is binding on both parties, but it may also take the form of a put option allowing the buyer to resell the asset to the vendor, a call option allowing the vendor to repurchase the asset from the buyer, or a combination of such options.

Where there is a binding commitment, it is clear that the asset will revert to the vendor and the only remaining factor which will determine the accounting treatment of the overall deal is the price at which the transactions are struck, as discussed above. The same is likely to be true where there is both a put and a call option in force on equivalent terms; unless the option is to be exercised at the then market price of the asset in question, it must be in the interests of one or other of the parties to exercise its option so as to secure a profit or avoid a loss, and therefore the likelihood of the asset remaining the property of the buyer rather than reverting to the vendor must be remote. However, the position is less clear where there is only a put option or a call option in force rather than a combination of the two.

Where there is only a put option, the effect will be (in the absence of other factors) that the vendor has disposed of the rewards of ownership to the buyer but retained the risks. This is because the buyer will only exercise its option to put the asset back to the vendor if its value at the time is less than the repurchase price payable under the option. This means that if the asset continues to rise in value the buyer will keep it and reap the benefits of that enhanced value; conversely if the value of the asset falls, the option will be exercised and the downside on the asset will be borne by the vendor.

This analysis does not of itself answer the question of whether the deal should be treated as a sale or as a financing transaction. The overall commercial effect will still have to be evaluated, by taking account of all the terms of the arrangement and by considering the motivations of both of the parties in agreeing to the various terms of the deal; in particular it will need to be considered why they have each agreed to have this one-sided option. It may be, for example, that the downside risks of the asset value compared to the option price can be seen to be negligible, in which case the fact that they remain with the vendor is not very important to the evaluation of the whole arrangement. However, in other cases the fact that the vendor retains these risks might be very significant, and sufficient to prevent the deal being treated as a sale; if the buyer has the right to put the asset back to the vendor, and if it appears reasonably likely that this option might be exercised, then it would be difficult for the vendor to say that it had made a sale, and realised any profit, on a transaction which the other party was at liberty to reverse. In other cases again, the transaction might qualify for partial derecognition as discussed at 2.5 above – for example, where a commercial vehicle manufacturer has sold a truck and given the customer an option to put it back at a guaranteed price in 5 years' time.

Where there is only a call option, the position will be reversed. In this case, the seller has disposed of the risks, but retained the rewards to be attained if the value of the asset exceeds the repurchase price specified in the option. Once again, the overall commercial effect of the arrangement has to be evaluated in deciding how to account for the deal. Emphasis has to be given to what is likely to happen in practice, and it is instructive to look at the arrangement from the point of view of both parties to see what their expectations are and what has induced them to accept the deal on the terms which have been agreed. It may be obvious from the overall terms of the arrangement that the call option will be exercised, in which case the deal will again be a financing arrangement and should be accounted for as such – for example, the seller may continue to use the asset, and it could be obvious that its commercial need for it would compel it to exercise the option. Similarly, the financial effects of *not* exercising the option (such as continued exposure to escalating costs) may sometimes make it obvious that the option will be exercised. But in other cases, it could be quite likely that the option will not be exercised and if this is the case the transaction could be treated as a sale. The seller need not include a liability in its balance sheet for the exercise price of the option if it is quite conceivable that it would not exercise it; correspondingly, the asset in its balance sheet would simply be the call option itself, not the underlying property that is the subject of the option.

Another example is shown below:

Example 16.9: Sale at below market value with call option

A building company, B plc, sells part of its land bank to a property investment company, P plc, for £40 million at a time when its market value is £50 million. It has the right under the agreement to buy it back for the same price plus interest at any time in the next three years. Conversely, however, P has no corresponding put option to require B to buy it back.

The effect of this deal is that B is protected from a collapse in the value of the land below 80% of its former price, because it cannot be compelled to buy it back. It has therefore passed that risk to P (which has presumably charged for it accordingly in the interest rate implicit in the deal). But it has retained the rewards of ownership, because it can always benefit from an increase in value of the land by exercising its option. Moreover, at the time of entering into the deal, it must have expected that it would exercise the option – otherwise it would have sold the property for full value, not for £10 million less. FRS 5 would be likely to interpret this as a financing deal, rather than a sale.

Where the overall substance is that of a financing deal rather than a sale, neither a sale nor a profit will be recorded. Instead, the ostensible sales proceeds will be recorded as a loan, and any charges which are in substance interest on that loan will be accrued and disclosed as interest costs. (This means that they may qualify for capitalisation in appropriate circumstances – see Chapter 13.) A brief description of the arrangement and the status of the asset and the relationship between the asset and the liability should be disclosed in the notes to the financial statements.[49]

Where the seller has made a sale and has a new asset and/or liability (such as an option) it should recognise or disclose such residual items as appropriate. Any unconditional commitment to repurchase needs to be recognised in the balance sheet, not merely disclosed. Profits and losses should be recognised on a prudent basis. The notes to the accounts should disclose the main features of the arrangement including the status of the asset, the relationship between the asset and the liability and the terms of any provision for repurchase (including any options) and of any guarantees.[50]

Barratt's accounts include a note showing that they have kept on the balance sheet houses sold to BES companies subject to a guarantee:

Extract 16.17: Barratt Developments PLC (1998)

13. STOCKS

Group	1998 £m	1997 £m
Work in progress	551.3	415.4
Showhouse complexes and houses awaiting legal completion	111.3	107.5
Properties in Business Expansion Schemes	7.5	17.0
	670.1	539.9

In 1993 the group supported four Business Expansion Scheme companies to provide assured tenancy housing, all of which were fully subscribed at a total of £20.0m. A major portion of this amount was used to purchase properties at market value from various Barratt subsidiaries. The group gave guarantees that there would be sufficient cash resources available for distribution from the four BES companies in 1998 and 1999 to provide the BES investors with a guaranteed return per share. The sale of properties covered by the guarantees still in place has not been recognised in these accounts. The properties are held in the balance sheet at their original cost of £7.5m (1997 £17.0m). The sale proceeds of £8.3m (1997 £18.9m) are held in creditors and the profit attributable to the properties of £0.8m (1997 £1.9m) has not been recognised in these accounts.

Similarly, Gleeson discloses these notes in respect of properties sold to BES companies with an option to have them put back to it after five years:

Extract 16.18: M J Gleeson Group plc (1998)

1. Accounting policies [extract]

Stock and work in progress

iv) Properties sold to Cavendish Gleeson Cash Backed PLC are included in Stock and work in progress at their original cost and their sale proceeds are added to Deferred income.

22. Business Expansion Scheme Companies [extract]

The Company had previously entered into commitments in the form of put and call options with three BES companies. These commitments required the Company, on exercise of the Options, to purchase residential properties from these companies at such prices as to enable the shareholders to receive a set return on their investment. The substance of these transactions was that of secured loans and, in accordance with FRS 5, the cost of financing these debts (being the difference between the issue proceeds and the ultimate cost of exercising the options) was allocated over the periods of the loans at fixed rates. On February 19th 1998 and 2nd April 1998 the Company acquired the issued share capital of Cavendish Gleeson Guaranteed PLC and Cavendish Gleeson Second PLC respectively, two of the BES companies in settlement of the financing obligations in respect of these companies.

As at 30th June 1998 the remaining contingent liability in respect of the final BES company, Cavendish Gleeson Cash Backed PLC is £6,000,000 with an option to exercise date of 31st December 1998.

Although the policy refers to the proceeds as deferred income, the outstanding amount is included within creditors in the balance sheet, which is where it belongs.

3.3   Factoring of debts

Factoring is a long-established means of obtaining finance by selling trade debtors so as to accelerate the receipt of cash following a sale on credit. The essence of the question posed by FRS 5 (in Application Note C) is again whether the transaction is really a sale in substance or whether it is simply a borrowing transaction with the trade debtors being used as collateral. Once again, the overall terms of the arrangement have to be considered in aggregate, and there may be a number of different services that the factor provides which will feature in this evaluation. Since there is no likelihood of any upside benefit in relation to debtors (except perhaps through reduced finance cost as a result of early payment) the focus in this case is on the risks of ownership rather than the rewards.

Application Note C says there are three possible treatments: derecognition, a linked presentation and a separate presentation. It does not mention 'partial' derecognition, although this could also be appropriate in some circumstances. Derecognition will be appropriate if all the significant benefits and risks relating to the debts in question have been transferred to the factor. The standard indicates that this will normally be the case only if:

(a)   the transaction takes place at an arms' length price for an outright sale;

(b)   the transaction is for a fixed amount of consideration and there is no recourse whatsoever, either implicit or explicit, to the seller for losses from either slow payment or non-payment; and

(c)   the seller will not benefit or suffer in any way if the debts perform better or worse than expected.[51]

If the conditions for derecognition are met, the debtors transferred will be set against the proceeds received from the factor with the difference being taken to the profit and loss account. Insofar as this represents discount on the sale of the debts it would seem appropriate to treat this as a finance cost, while other factoring costs should be included in administrative expenses.

A linked presentation will be appropriate if the requirements of paragraphs 26 and 27 of FRS 5 are satisfied, as discussed in 2.6 above. In the context of debt factoring, this means that the trader may retain significant benefits and risks in relation to the factored debts, but there must be no arrangement permitting or requiring the trader to reacquire any of the debts and the trader must have limited its downside exposure to loss to a fixed monetary amount.[52]

Where a linked presentation is applied, the debtors will stay on the balance sheet but the amount of any non-returnable advance from the factor will be deducted from them rather than being shown as a separate liability. The factor's charges will be accrued, with the interest element being accounted for as interest expense, and other costs within administrative expenses, both of which are to be disclosed. The notes should also disclose the main terms of the arrangement and the gross amount of factored debts outstanding at the year end as well as the disclosures which are required by paragraph 27 of the FRS (see 2.6) whenever the linked presentation is used.[53]

If neither of these sets of conditions is satisfied, a separate presentation is required. This means that the debtors will remain on the trader's balance sheet and amounts advanced by the factor will be shown as a loan within current liabilities. As with the linked presentation, the factor's charges should be accrued and appropriately analysed between interest and administrative expenses, but in this case the standard does not require these to be separately disclosed. The only required disclosure is the amount of factored debts outstanding at the year end.[54]

The Application Note contains two examples which illustrate different scenarios which could lead to different accounting treatments. These are as follows:

Example 16.10: Debt factoring with recourse

A company (S) enters into a factoring arrangement with a factor (F) with the following principal terms:

- S will transfer all its trade debts to F, subject only to credit approval by F and a limit placed on the proportion of the total that may be due from any one debtor;

- F administers S's sales ledger and handles all aspects of collection of the debts in return for an administration charge at an annual rate of 1% payable monthly, based on the total debts factored at each month end;

- S may draw up to 70% of the gross amount of debts factored and outstanding at any time, such drawings being debited in the books of F to a factoring account operated by F for S;

- F credits collections from debtors to the factoring account, and debits the account monthly with interest calculated on the basis of the daily balances on the account using a rate of base rate plus 2%. Thus this interest charge varies with the amount of finance drawn by S under the finance facility from F, the speed of payment of the debtors and base rate;

- any debts not recovered after 90 days are resold to S for an immediate cash payment which is credited to the factoring account;

- F pays for all other debts, less any advances and interest charges made, 90 days after the date of their assignment to F, and debits the payment to the factoring account; and

- on termination of the agreement the balance on the factoring account is settled in cash.

FRS 5 concludes that in substance the effect of these terms is that the deal is a financing one rather than an outright sale of the debts, and a separate presentation should be adopted. S continues to bear both the slow payment risk (the interest charged by F varies with the speed of payment by the debtors) and the bad debt risk (it must pay F for any debts not recovered after 90 days), and its exposure to loss is therefore unlimited.

Example 16.11: Debt factoring without recourse

A company (S) sells debts to a factor (F) on the following terms:

- S will transfer to F such trade debts as S shall determine, subject only to credit approval by F and a limit placed on the proportion of the total that may be due from any one debtor. F levies a charge of 0.15% of turnover, payable monthly, for this facility;

- S continues to administer the sales ledger and handle all aspects of collection of the debts;

- S may draw up to 80% of the gross amount of debts assigned at any time, such drawings being debited in the books of F to a factoring account operated by F for S;

- weekly, S assigns and sends copy invoices to F as they are raised;

- S is required to bank the gross amounts of all payments received from debts assigned to F direct into an account in the name of F. Credit transfers made by debtors direct into S's own bank account must immediately be paid to F;

- F credits such collections from debtors to the factoring account, and debits the account monthly with interest calculated on the basis of the daily balances on the account using a rate of base rate plus 2.5%. Thus this interest charge varies with the amount of finance drawn by S under the finance facility from F, the speed of payment of the debtors and base rate;

- F provides protection from bad debts. Any debts not recovered after 90 days are credited to the factoring account, and responsibility for their collection is passed to F. A charge of 1% of the gross value of all debts factored is levied by F for this service and debited to the factoring account;

- F pays for the debts, less any advances, interest charges and credit protection charges, 90†days after the date of purchase, and debits the payment to the factoring account; and

- on either party giving 90 days' notice to the other, the arrangement will be terminated. In such an event, S will transfer no further debts to F, and the balance remaining on the factoring account at the end of the notice period will be settled in cash in the normal way.

FRS 5 concludes that the effect of these terms is that S continues to bear the slow payment risk for 90 days (the interest charged by F varies with the speed of payment by the debtors) but thereafter all risks pass to F. Since it has not disposed of all significant risks, derecognition is not appropriate, but since its exposure is limited, a linked presentation is available. This allows the non-returnable proceeds from F to be shown on S's balance sheet as a deduction from the debts factored. The amount to be deducted will be the lower of the proceeds received and the gross amount of the debts less all charges to the factor in respect of them.

3.4   Securitised assets

Securitisation is a process whereby finance can be raised from external investors by enabling them to invest in parcels of specific financial assets. Domestic mortgage loans were the first main type of assets to be securitised in the United Kingdom, but in principle the technique can readily be extended to other assets, such as credit card receivables, other consumer loans, lease receivables and so on.

A typical securitisation transaction involving a portfolio of mortgage loans would operate as follows:

The company which has initially advanced the loans in question (the originator) will sell them to another company set up for the purpose (the issuer). The issuer may be a subsidiary or associate of the originator, or it may be owned by a charitable trust or some other party friendly to the originator; in either case, its equity share capital will be small. The issuer will finance its purchase of these loans by issuing loan notes on interest terms which will be related to the rate of interest receivable on the mortgages. The originator will continue to administer the loans as before, for which it will receive a service fee.

The structure will therefore be as shown in this diagram:

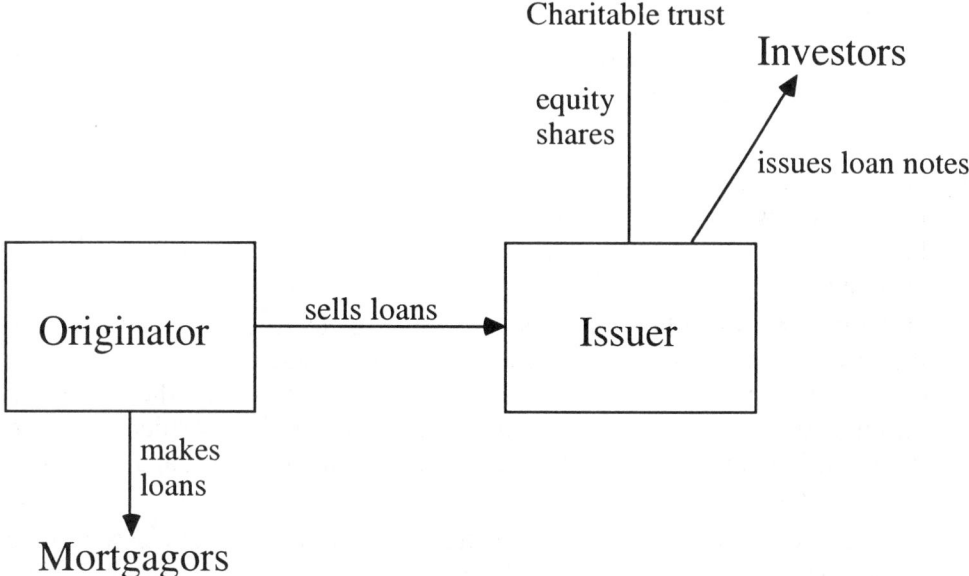

Potential investors in the mortgage-backed loan notes will want to be assured that their investment is relatively risk-free, and the issue will normally be supported by obtaining a high rating from a credit rating agency. This may be achieved by use of a range of credit enhancement techniques which will add to the security already inherent in the quality of the mortgage portfolio. Such techniques can include the following:

■   limited recourse to the originator in the event that the income from the mortgages falls short of the interest payable to the investors under the loan notes and other expenses. This may be made available in a number of ways; for example, by the provision of subordinated loan finance from the originator to the issuer; by the deferral of part of the consideration for the sale of the mortgages; or by the provision of a guarantee;

■   the provision of loan facilities from third parties to meet temporary shortfalls as a result of slow payments of mortgage interest; or

■   insurance against default on the mortgages.

The overall effect of the arrangement is that outside investors have been brought in to finance a particular portion of the originator's activities. These investors have first call on the income from the mortgages which back their investment, and earn a floating rate of interest which moves broadly in sympathy with the underlying rate paid on the mortgages. The originator is left with only the residual interest in the differential between the rates paid on the notes and earned on the mortgages, net of expenses; generally, this profit element is extracted by adjustments to the service fee or through the mechanism of interest rate swaps. He has thus limited his upside interest in the mortgages, while his remaining downside risk on the whole arrangement will depend on the extent to which he has assumed obligations under the credit enhancement measures.

The question of whether or not the mortgage loans and the loan notes should appear on the balance sheet of the originator can be subdivided into two main issues:

(a)   has the sale of the mortgages succeeded in transferring the risks and rewards of ownership from the originator to the issuer? If it has not, then the mortgages will have to remain as an asset on the originator's balance sheet and the purported sales proceeds shown as a loan received; and

(b)   is the issuer a subsidiary or quasi subsidiary of the originator? If it is, then the issuer's accounts will have to be consolidated with those of the originator, with the result that transactions between them will be eliminated on consolidation and the assets and liabilities which appear on the issuer's balance sheet will appear on the consolidated balance sheet of the originator.

When ED 49 addressed the overall question of whether to include securitised mortgages in the originator's balance sheet, it laid down a long list of qualifying conditions which were substantially based on those developed by the Bank of England for supervisory purposes in relation to loan transfers. However, a number of commentators pointed out that the criteria which might be appropriate for regulation of this kind, which focused on risk and capital adequacy, did not necessarily provide a sound basis for an accounting standard, which was designed to result in companies showing a true and fair view of their financial position and the results of their activities. They also criticised some of the detailed criteria as being inconsistent with the philosophy of the exposure draft itself.

The ASB made substantial modifications to the approach of the previous exposure draft in developing FRED 4. As a result, the previously straightforward on/off balance sheet decision became a three-way choice, and the qualifying conditions were also substantially changed. The possibilities became:

(a)   separate presentation, whereby the gross securitised assets appear on the asset side of the balance sheet, with the proceeds of the issue within creditors;

(b)   linked presentation, whereby the proceeds of the note issue are shown as a deduction from the securitised assets as a net figure within the assets section of the balance sheet; and

(c)   derecognition, whereby the securitised assets are regarded as sold and therefore removed from the balance sheet.

This basic approach was carried through into FRS 5. Application Note D does not mention the possibility of 'partial' derecognition. This would only be appropriate if some of the significant benefits and some of the significant risks relating to the securitised assets were transferred to other parties as a result of the transaction while others were retained by the originator.

As with other forms of finance, FRS 5 says that derecognition is appropriate only if all the significant benefits and risks relating to the debts in question have been disposed of, which is likely to require that:

(a)   the transaction takes place at an arms' length price for an outright sale;

(b)   the transaction is for a fixed amount of consideration and there is no recourse whatsoever, either implicit or explicit, to the originator for losses from whatever cause. Normal warranties given in respect of the condition of the assets at the time of transfer would not breach this condition, but any warranties concerning their value or performance in the future would do so; and

(c)   the originator will not benefit or suffer if the securitised assets perform better or worse than expected. This condition will not be satisfied where the originator has a right to further sums from the vehicle which vary according to the eventual value realised for the securitised assets.[55]

If all these conditions are met, the securitised assets are likely to be regarded as sold and will be removed from the balance sheet. They will be set against the proceeds received from the issue, with the difference being taken to the profit and loss account. If the conditions are not met, then either a linked presentation or a separate presentation is required.

A linked presentation will be appropriate if the requirements of paragraphs 26 and 27 of FRS 5 are satisfied, as discussed in 2.6 above. In the context of securitisation, this means that the originator may retain significant benefits and risks in relation to the securitised assets, but must have limited its downside exposure to loss to a fixed monetary amount. There must also be no arrangement under which the originator can reacquire any of the securitised assets in the future. These conditions are discussed further in paragraphs D10 to D13 of the Application Note, which make it clear that they are to be applied restrictively.

Where a linked presentation is applied, the securitised assets remain on the balance sheet but the proceeds of the issue will be shown as deducted from them on the assets side of the balance sheet rather than as a liability. Extensive disclosure requirements are called for, namely:

(a)   a description of the assets securitised;

(b)   the amount of any income or expense recognised in the period, analysed as appropriate;

(c)   the terms of any options for the originator to repurchase assets or to transfer additional assets to the issuer;

(d)   the terms of any interest rate swap or interest rate cap agreements between the issuer and the originator that meet the conditions set out in paragraph D11 of the Application Note;

(e)   a description of the priority and amount of claims on the proceeds generated by the assets, including any rights of the originator to proceeds from the assets in addition to the non-recourse amounts already received;

(f)   the ownership of the issuer; and

(g)   the disclosures required by paragraph 27(c) and (d) of the standard.[56]

The standard also says that where there are several securitisation arrangements they may be shown in aggregate if they relate to a single type of asset, but should otherwise be presented separately. Similarly, the note disclosures should only deal with the arrangements in aggregate to the extent that they relate to the same type of asset and are on similar terms.[57]

Kingfisher has used the linked presentation in respect of securitised consumer receivables, as shown in this extract:

Extract 16.19: Kingfisher plc (1999)				
Balance sheet [extract]				
£ millions	**1999**	**1999**	1998	1998
Current assets				
Development work in progress		**69.0**		49.1
Stocks		**1,465.4**		840.5
Debtors due within one year		**608.8**		447.0
Debtors due after more than one year		**144.1**		149.0
Securitised consumer receivables	**321.0**		189.9	
Less: non-recourse secured notes	**(247.4)**	**73.6**	(146.1)	43.8
Investments		**311.7**		254.7
Cash at bank and in hand		**241.2**		74.9
		2,913.8		1,859.0

Notes to the accounts

18 Securitised consumer receivables

In January 1996, the Group entered into an agreement to securitise consumer receivables (which derive principally from the provision of credit facilities by Time Retail Finance Ltd (TRF) to customers of the Group) through Time Finance Ltd (TFL). TRF sells the consumer receivables, with no impact on the profit and loss account, to TFL, who issues Notes secured on those assets. The issue terms of the Notes include provisions that their holders have no recourse to TRF or any other member of the Group. Neither TRF nor any other Group company is obliged to support any losses, nor does it intend to. Principal and interest is repayable from, and secured solely on, the consumer receivables. At 30 January 1999 the amount of consumer receivables securitised was £321.0m (1998: £189.9m) raising funds of £247.4m (1998: £146.1m) and this is shown on the balance sheet using linked presentation.

If the conditions for derecognition or a linked presentation are not satisfied, a separate presentation is required, which means that the securitised assets will remain on balance sheet and the proceeds of the issue will be shown as a loan within creditors. The gross amount of assets securitised at the year end is to be disclosed.[58]

These considerations have been discussed above in relation to the originator's accounts, but the same factors apply to the issuer's accounts as well. However, in the latter case the answer is generally clear – a separate presentation is required.[59] A question which can then arise is whether the issuer has to be consolidated by the originator, and if so, how that will affect the presentation. Where the issuer is a quasi subsidiary of the originator, the standard allows the assets and liabilities of the issuer to be included in the originator's group accounts in a linked presentation (provided the qualifying conditions are met from the point of view of the group) even if a separate presentation is required in the accounts of the issuer itself.[60]

3.5 Loan transfers

Loan transfers is the collective term used to describe various methods by which banks and other lenders seek to transfer an advance to a different lender. Such transactions often involve a gain or loss because of movements in interest rates since the original loan was taken out, so they can have a profit and loss account dimension as well as giving rise to questions of balance sheet recognition and disclosure.

Since the original loan is a contract which is personal to the parties involved, its transfer is not straightforward. It is necessary to effect the transfer of benefits and risks less directly, by one of the three following arrangements:

(a)   Novation

This is where a new contract, with a new lender, is drawn up to replace the original one, which is cancelled. This therefore extinguishes the original loan altogether from the accounts of the lender as well as removing any residual obligations it had to the borrower (such as to make further advances under a committed facility). Unless there are any side agreements, no further questions of off balance sheet finance arise once this process has been completed.

(b)   Assignment

This involves the assignment of some or all of the original lender's rights (but not obligations) to another lender, and may be done on either a statutory or an equitable basis, which have different legal requirements and effects. They are both subject to equitable reliefs; in particular, the borrower's rights under its contract with the original lender are not to be prejudiced.

In accounting terms, the effect of an assignment is less clear cut than that of a novation, because the original lender may have some residual rights and obligations to the other parties involved.

(c)   Sub-participation

This does not involve the formal transfer of the legal rights and obligations involved in the loan, but the creation of a non-recourse back-to-back agreement with another lender (the sub-participant) whereby the sub-participant deposits with the original lender an amount in respect of the whole or part of the loan in exchange for the right to receive a share of the cash flows arising from the loan from the original lender. The accounting question that arises from such a transaction is whether the deposit and the loan can be offset to show only the net position.

The Application Note in ED 49 proposed detailed criteria for determining when a loan transfer could be treated as having transferred substantially all the risks associated with the loan so as to remove it from the balance sheet. These were derived from the Bank of England's paper of February 1989 on its supervisory policy on the treatment of loan transfers involving banks, which was also used as the basis for ED 49's proposals on securitised mortgages as discussed in 3.4 above. However, as with securitisation, this approach was not adopted by the ASB when it published FRED 4 and, subsequently, FRS 5.

FRS 5 discusses the possibilities in rather different terms. As for other forms of finance, the three options which Application Note E offers are derecognition, a linked presentation and a separate presentation. However, it also refers to the possibility of splitting a loan so that some of it is transferred while the rest is retained, which constitutes 'partial' derecognition.

Derecognition is appropriate when all the significant risks and rewards pertaining to the loans have been passed from the original lender to the transferee. In the absence of side agreements, this will generally be the case where the loan has been novated, but might also apply where there has been an assignment or a sub-participation.[61] The essential test is whether there are any circumstances in which the original lender retains the possibility of any benefit from the loans (or from the part transferred),[62] or might be called upon to repay the new lender so as to bear any losses or meet any obligations; if not, derecognition is appropriate and the loan is therefore taken off the balance sheet. The tests which generally have to be satisfied in order to achieve this are that:

(a) the transaction takes place at an arms' length price for an outright sale;

(b) the transaction is for a fixed amount of consideration and there is no recourse whatsoever, either implicit or explicit, to the lender for losses from whatever cause. Normal warranties given in respect of the condition of the loans at the time of transfer would not breach this condition, but any warranties concerning their condition or performance in the future would do so; and

(c) the lender will not benefit or suffer in any way if the loans perform better or worse than expected. This condition will not be satisfied where the lender has a right to further sums which vary according to the future performance of the loans (i.e. according to whether, when or how much the borrowers pay).[63]

Derecognition also gives rise to a profit and loss account effect, because the loans are regarded as 'sold', and accordingly the difference between their carrying amount and the proceeds received is taken to the profit and loss account. Insofar as all the proceeds have been received in cash, this poses no difficulty, but otherwise the profit should be restricted to the amount realised if there is uncertainty as to its eventual amount. Losses should, however, be provided in full.[64]

As with the other examples discussed earlier in this chapter, a linked presentation is appropriate where some of the risks and rewards relating to the loans have been retained (thus rendering derecognition unavailable) but the original lender's downside risk is nonetheless definitely limited to a fixed monetary amount. This combination of circumstances is less likely to apply in the case of loan transfers; it is more likely that the risks and rewards will have been wholly disposed of or wholly retained. However, there are various possible transactions which involve a partial transfer of the loans and result in the original lender's maximum exposure being capped, and these may give rise to the use of the linked presentation.[65]

Where the conditions are met, the non-returnable proceeds received will be shown as a deduction from the loans to which they relate within the assets section of the balance sheet. Insofar as these proceeds exceed the amount of the loans, FRS 5 says that the difference should be taken to the profit and loss account, but the standard does not explicitly require the recognition of equivalent losses even if a loss is implicit in the transaction. We believe that it is appropriate to apply the same principle to both profits and losses.

Application Note E calls for the following disclosures when a linked presentation is used:

(a) the main terms of the arrangement;

(b)	the gross amount of loans transferred and outstanding at the balance sheet date;

(c)	the profit or loss recognised in the period, analysed as appropriate; and

(d)	the disclosures required by paragraph 27(c) and (d) (see 2.6 above).[66]

Where the conditions for neither derecognition nor a linked presentation are satisfied, a separate presentation is required; in other words, the original loan stays on balance sheet as an asset and the amount received from the transferee appears on the other side of the balance sheet as a loan payable. The Application Note calls for disclosure of the amount of loans outstanding at the year end which are subject to loan transfer arrangements.[67]

## 3.6	Take-or-pay contracts and throughput agreements

Take-or-pay contracts and throughput agreements are unconditional commitments to buy goods or services from a supplier in the future, generally from a new operational facility created by the supplier. From the supplier's point of view, such contracts guarantee a certain level of sales which gives assurance that the facility will be viable, and expedite the financing; from the purchaser's point of view, it secures a medium or long-term source of supply, probably at favourable prices. Sometimes the supplier is set up by a consortium of customers who wish to share a particular facility, such as a pipeline to service the needs of a number of oil companies.

Take-or-pay contracts and throughput agreements are essentially the same in concept. The only distinction between the two terms (as defined in the US standard)[68] is that throughput agreements relate to the use of a supplier's transportation facility (such as a ship or a pipeline) or processing plant, whereas take-or-pay contracts relate to the supply of goods or other services.

Under these contracts, the purchaser is obliged to pay a certain minimum amount even if, in the event, it does not take delivery of the goods or make use of the services it has contracted for. The accounting question which therefore arises is whether the purchaser has to account for a liability (its commitment under the contract) together with a corresponding asset (its right to use the facilities it has contracted for).

FRS 5 does not address these transactions specifically. Under its general principles the rights and obligations under such contracts would seem to require to be recognised in the balance sheet, which would be a radical departure from present practice, and one which the FASB shied away from (see 4.2.4 below). Indeed, a literal application of the principles might require *all* purchase obligations to be recognised on the balance sheet whenever a purchase order is accepted, rather than when the contract is fulfilled, which would be an even more radical departure. However, the ASB has avoided this consequence by scoping all such transactions out of the standard; one of the exclusions from the scope of FRS 5 is 'expenditure commitments',[69] as a result of which it would appear that take-or-pay contracts are permitted to remain off balance sheet.

This, however, is not necessarily the end of the story. Such contracts might fall within the extended definition of a lease in SSAP 21, and therefore be bound by the terms of that standard. This definition says that 'the term "lease" as used in this statement also applies to other arrangements in which one party retains ownership of an asset but conveys the right to the use of the asset to another party for an agreed period of time in return for specified payments'.[70] Where this applies, it is necessary to consider whether the contract has the character of a finance lease, in which case the asset should be recognised in the balance sheet of the user. This will be the case where substantially all the risks and rewards of ownership of the asset are transferred to the user under the contract – typically where there is only ever going to be one user for the asset.

ICI discloses the existence of a take-or-pay contract in its commitments note:

Extract 16.20: Imperial Chemical Industries PLC (1998)

42 Commitments and contingent liabilities[extract]

The only significant take-or-pay contract entered into by subsidiaries is the purchase of electric power, which commenced in the second quarter of 1998, for 15 years. The present value of this commitment at the year end is estimated at £163m.

Scottish Power discloses this extensive range of commitments:

Extract 16.21: Scottish Power plc (1999)

30 Financial commitments

(c) Other contractual commitments

Under contractual commitments, the group has rights and obligations in relation to the undernoted contracts. The annual value of the purchases and sales arising from these contracts is provided below:

	Note	Commitment entered into	Commitment expires	Purchases/sales in year under group commitments 1999 £m	1998 £m
The purchase of electricity from British Energy Generation (UK) Limited		1990	2005	**367.7**	365.8
The purchase of electricity from Scottish and Southern Energy plc	(i)	1990	see below	**78.8**	100.5
The supply of electricity to Scottish and Southern Energy plc		1990	2004	**18.2**	16.8
Revenue from the operation of the company's transmission system and access by Scottish and Southern Energy plc to the Anglo-Scottish connector		1990	No fixed date of expiry	**27.7**	26.1
Purchase of coal from the Scottish Coal Company Limited		1998	2003	**22.0**	76.9
Purchase of coal from the Scottish Coal (Deep Mine) Company Limited		1998	2004	**50.5**	–
Purchase of gas from various fields in the North Sea		1994	2010	**123.6**	81.8

(i) There are two agreements relating to the purchase of electricity from Scottish and Southern Energy plc. These expire in 2012 and 2039.

3.7 Transactions under the Private Finance Initiative

The Private Finance Initiative (PFI) is a fairly recent innovation, designed to provide a new mechanism for procuring public services. The basic idea is that, rather than having bodies in the public sector take on the whole responsibility for funding and building roads, bridges, railways, hospitals, prisons and other infrastructure assets, some of these should be contracted out to private sector operators from whom the public sector bodies would buy services. The overriding goal is to maximise value for money from the taxpayers' perspective by passing such risks to the private sector as that sector is best able to manage.

A typical PFI transaction, therefore, is a long term contract whereby a private sector entity agrees to provide services to a public sector entity in exchange for a stream of payments. The contract is likely to specify that these payments will vary according to complex formulae, involving such factors as the volume of services delivered, the level of adherence to defined quality standards, and so on.

The accounting challenge is to reflect the substance of these payments fairly in the accounts of both the contracting parties. It would be possible simply to take the contract at face value and account for the amounts paid and received as service payments; however, closer analysis may sometimes reveal that this is in reality a composite transaction whereby the public sector body is buying assets as well as services. In such a case, it will be appropriate to subdivide the contract into its components and account for the asset-related part as if it were a finance lease.

From the point of view of the public body, the main issue is whether or not to recognise an asset together with an associated borrowing, by treating some of the future contractual payments as being akin to finance lease rentals. From the private entity's point of view, a similar analysis applies in reverse, although this is a less sensitive issue in practice. A further complication is that the private sector entity is often a joint venture whose participants may include service providers, facilities managers, financial institutions, constructors or other bodies, so questions of joint venture accounting can also arise (see Chapter 7 at 4).

In September 1998 the ASB published a further Application Note to FRS 5[71] to address the treatment of such transactions, which closely followed the terms of an exposure draft that had been issued nine months earlier. This requires a thorough analysis of the contract so as to determine its substance, focusing in particular on the formula for varying the contractual payments in order to identify the reasons for these variations, so as to see whether they relate to risks associated with the ownership of the asset, or to the risks of operating it to deliver services. The purpose of this is to see whether the variations are more consistent with a hypothesis that the asset belongs in substance to the public sector body and not to its ostensible owner, the private sector entity. As far as the parties involved are concerned, the distinctions that have to be made involve determining whether:

(a)   the purchaser in a PFI contract (the public sector body) has an asset of the property used to provide the contracted services together with a corresponding liability to pay the operator for it or, alternatively, has a contract only for services; and

(b)   the operator has an asset of the property used to provide the contracted services or, alternatively, a financial asset being a debt due from the purchaser.[72]

In practice (b) is not such a difficult issue as (a). It is clear that the operator has *some* kind of asset on its balance sheet, whereas the choice in relation to the purchaser's accounts is whether or not anything at all is recognised on its balance sheet.

The Application Note goes on to say that 'In some cases the contract may be separable, i.e. the commercial effect will be that elements of the PFI payments operate independently of each other. 'Operate independently' means that the elements behave differently and can therefore be separately identified. Where this is the case, and where some elements relate only to services (such as cleaning, laundry, catering etc.) rather than to the property, any such service elements are not relevant to determining whether each party has an asset of the property and should be ignored.'[73] It will not be relevant that the contract designates the payments as 'unitary' or, indeed, what labels they are given.

The next step under the Application Note, after excluding any separable service elements, is to distinguish PFI contracts between:

'(a)   those where the only remaining elements are payments for the property. These will be akin to a lease and SSAP 21 (interpreted in the light of the FRS) should be applied.

(b)   other contracts (i.e. where the remaining elements include some services). These contracts will fall directly within the FRS rather than SSAP 21.'[74]

Most PFI contracts will fall under (b) as the 'availability' element of the payment may vary if services are not performed to the agreed standard. For such contracts, determining which party has an asset of the property involves examining the extent to which each of them would bear any variations in property profits (or losses). The Application Note identifies three important principles that are relevant to this examination:

(a)   a range of factors will be relevant and it will be necessary to look at the overall effect of these factors when taken together;

(b)   any potential variations in profits (or losses) that relate purely to services should be excluded as they are not relevant to determining whether each party has an asset of the property; and

(c)   greater weight should be given to those features that are more likely to have a commercial effect in practice. Where there is no genuine commercial possibility of a particular scenario or cash flow occurring, this scenario/cash flow should be ignored.[75]

The principle is to distinguish potential variations in costs and revenues that flow from features of the property which are relevant to determining whose asset it is. The main factors that are relevant are likely to be:

■   who carries the demand risk;

■   the presence, if any, of third-party revenues;

■   who determines the nature of the property;

■   penalties for underperformance or non-availability;

■   potential changes in relevant costs;

■   obsolescence, including the effects of changes in technology; and

■   the arrangements at the end of the contract, which will indicate who bears the residual value risk.[76]

These are discussed in further detail in the Application Note. Needless to say, such an analysis may still not produce a clear-cut answer, not least because the contract may have been deliberately designed to produce an ambiguous accounting result. However, it is helpful to try to see it through the eyes of the contracting parties, and understand what has been in their minds in negotiating these particular terms.

PFI projects necessarily enjoy a high political profile and their accounting treatment can be highly sensitive as a result, since it affects the public perception of the economic substance of these transactions. This has led the Treasury to take a particular interest in the development of this guidance, that has not always appeared to be benign. This culminated in June 1999 in the issue of the Treasury's own guidance[77] on how to interpret the Application Note, and although the ASB has not demurred, the two documents do not really seem to be in complete harmony. The consequence is that this remains an area of some confusion, but we believe that Application Note F is the more reliable source of reference and that PFI transactions should be carefully analysed according to its approach.

Arrangements that are similar in nature to PFI contracts are increasingly being formed between entities in the private sector as well. For example, a retailer may outsource its warehousing and distribution activities to a specialist distribution company, and questions might arise as to which party owns the warehouses in substance. Application Note F is also designed to be the appropriate source of guidance for interpreting such contracts.[78]

4 COMPARISON WITH IASC AND US PRONOUNCEMENTS

4.1 IASC

4.1.1 IAS 1

The IASC has not issued any pronouncements dealing specifically with off balance sheet transactions. However, IAS 1 states that '... management should develop policies to ensure that the financial statements provide information that is ... reliable in that they ... reflect the economic substance of events and transactions and not merely their legal form'.[79]

4.1.2 IAS 39

The IASC's standard on the recognition and measurement of financial instruments includes both recognition and derecognition tests for financial assets and liabilities. The recognition test states that 'an enterprise should recognise a financial asset or financial liability on its balance sheet when, and only when, it becomes a party to the contractual provisions of the instrument.'[80] This implies very early recognition of transactions, in advance of their execution, but some of the subsequent discussion in the standard suggests that it does not necessarily mean the rule to be interpreted in this way – for example, purchases of marketable securities are allowed to be recognised only on settlement date, rather than on trade date, although either practice is permitted by the standard.

The derecognition tests are slightly different as between assets and liabilities. The rule for assets is that 'an enterprise should derecognise a financial asset or a portion of a financial asset when, and only when, the enterprise loses control of the contractual rights that comprise the financial asset (or a portion of the financial asset). An enterprise loses such control if it realises the rights to benefits specified in the contract, the rights expire, or the enterprise surrenders those rights'.[81] Like SFAS 125 in the US (see 4.2.6 below), IAS 39 uses a 'financial-components' approach that allows assets to be subdivided, allowing a degree of partial derecognition. Unlike FRS 5, it allows factored debts to be taken off the balance sheet even if the transferor retains the bad debt risk; a financial liability in respect of that risk is recognised instead.[82]

The derecognition rule for liabilities is that 'an enterprise should remove a financial liability (or a part of a financial liability) from its balance sheet when, and only when, it is extinguished – that is, when the obligation specified in the contract has been discharged, cancelled, or expires.'[83] FRS 5 does not include any derecognition rules for liabilities.

4.1.3   SIC 12

In November 1998, the Standing Interpretations Committee of the IASC issued SIC 12 entitled *Consolidation – Special Purpose Entities*. This deals with the same issue as FRS 5 did when it established the need to consolidate quasi-subsidiaries as well as subsidiary undertakings as defined by the law. The Interpretation comes into force for periods beginning on or after 1 July 1999.

The concept of a special purpose entity (or 'SPE') has not been formally defined by the SIC, but it is described as an entity 'created to accomplish a narrow and well-defined objective (e.g. to effect a lease, research and development activities or a securitisation of financial assets)'.[84] The SIC agreed that an enterprise should consolidate the SPE when the substance of the relationship between them indicates that the enterprise controls the SPE.[85]

In assessing this it is appropriate to use the concept of control set down in IAS 27, which requires the ability to direct or dominate decision-making, and to consider also whether the enterprise has the aim of obtaining benefits from the SPE's activities. The Interpretation provides these examples as indications of when control may exist in the context of an SPE:

- in substance, the activities of the SPE are being conducted on behalf of the enterprise according to its specific business needs so that the enterprise obtains benefits from the SPE's operation;

- in substance, the enterprise has the decision-making powers to obtain the majority of the benefits of the activities of the SPE or, by setting up an 'autopilot' mechanism, the enterprise has delegated these decision-making powers;

■ in substance, the enterprise has rights to obtain the majority of the benefits of the SPE and therefore may be exposed to risks incident to the activities of the SPE; and

■ in substance, the enterprise retains the majority of the residual or ownership risks related to the SPE or its assets in order to obtain benefits from its activities.[86]

4.2 US

4.2.1 General

There is no one standard in the US which tries to address the whole spectrum of off balance sheet finance in a manner comparable to FRS 5. However, there are a large number of individual standards and Emerging Issues Task Force abstracts that deal with particular aspects of the subject, the chief of which are mentioned below. There is no equivalent to the idea of a linked presentation in US accounting practice.

4.2.2 Subsidiaries and quasi subsidiaries

In the US, the basic criterion which defines a subsidiary is the holding of a controlling financial interest, usually through ownership of over 50% of the outstanding voting shares. A subsidiary is described in APB 18 (which deals with equity accounting) as 'a corporation which is controlled, directly or indirectly, by another corporation. The usual condition for control is ownership of a majority (over 50%) of the outstanding voting stock. The power to control may also exist with a lesser degree of ownership, for example, by contract, lease, agreement with other stockholders or by court decree.' The US does not directly have the concept either of 'dominant influence' or of a quasi subsidiary, although the SEC has been known to require the consolidation of minority-owned investments that are subsidiaries in substance.

The FASB is currently undertaking a project which is concerned with consolidation policy and specific issues of consolidation techniques. It has been considering the implications of the 'economic unit concept' which is based primarily on control rather than the ownership of a majority voting interest. In February 1999 it issued an exposure draft on the subject, defining control as a non-shared decision-making ability of one entity to direct the policies and management that guide the ongoing activities of another entity so as to increase its benefits and limit its losses from that other entity's activities (see Chapter 5 at 6.2). If this is converted into a standard in its present form it will move practice in this area substantially closer to that in the UK.

4.2.3   Sale of assets

SFAS 49 – *Accounting for Product Financing Arrangements* – produces results similar to those which follow from Application Note B of FRS 5. A product financing arrangement is a transaction in which an enterprise sells a product to another entity and in a related transaction agrees to repurchase the product (or a substantially identical product).[87] Where the arrangement is such that the product will be repurchased at a predetermined price, which is not subject to change except for fluctuations due to finance and holding costs,[88] then the original sale will not be treated as such but, rather, as a liability.[89] Such a treatment also applies where the enterprise has an option to repurchase the product and will be subject to a significant penalty if it fails to exercise the option or where the other party has an option whereby it can require the enterprise to purchase the product.[90]

4.2.4   Long-term obligations

In 1981, the FASB issued SFAS 47 – *Disclosure of Long-Term Obligations* – in response to requests to consider accounting for project financing arrangements. These are arrangements relating to the financing of a major capital project in which the lender looks principally to the cash flows and earnings of the project as the source of funds for repayment and to the assets of the project as collateral for the loan.[91] This says that 'the particular requests related to whether the unconditional purchase obligations and indirect guarantees of indebtedness of others typical of project financing arrangements result in participants acquiring ownership interests and obligations to make future cash payments that should be recognised as assets and liabilities on their balance sheets. The Board concluded … that the accounting questions could be answered better after further progress is made on the conceptual framework for financial accounting and reporting.' The statement is, therefore, an interim measure and only requires disclosures to be made about the obligations under such arrangements. However, although the FASB completed the relevant part of its conceptual framework in 1985, SFAS 47 has never been superseded. The scope exclusion for 'expenditure commitments' in FRS 5 similarly means that such obligations need not be included in the balance sheet in the UK.

4.2.5   Sales of real estate

This is covered by SFAS 66, a highly detailed standard which lays down rigid rules for the recognition of profit on property transactions, and has consequential effects on whether or not the property is removed from the balance sheet. The basic requirements are that profit should be recognised in full only when all the following criteria are met:

(a)   the sale is consummated. This requires the following:

   (i)   the parties are bound by the terms of the contract; and

(ii) all consideration has been exchanged (i.e. either all monies have been received, or all necessary contractual arrangements have been entered into for the ultimate payment of monies – such as notes supported by irrevocable letters of credit from an independent lending institution); and

(iii) any permanent financing for which the vendor is responsible has been arranged; and

(iv) all conditions precedent to closing the contract have been performed;[92]

(b) the purchaser's initial and continuing investments are adequate to demonstrate a commitment to pay for the property;

(c) the vendor's receivable is not subject to future subordination; and

(d) the vendor has transferred to the purchaser the usual risks and rewards of ownership in a transaction that is in substance a sale and does not have a substantial continuing involvement with the property.[93]

The following are some of the examples of the circumstances specified in the standard as falling foul of the last of these requirements:

- The seller is obliged to repurchase the property, or has an option to do so.

- The seller guarantees the return of the buyer's investment or a return on that investment for an extended period.

- The seller has ongoing commitments to operate the property at his own risk.

- The seller is contractually committed to develop the property in the future, to construct facilities on the land, or to provide off-site improvements or amenities.

- The seller will participate in future profit from the property without risk of loss.

In each of these (and other) cases SFAS 66 indicates the further factors to be considered and discusses the appropriate accounting treatment. These rules appear to be more stringent than the equivalent requirements in FRS 5.

4.2.6 Transfers of receivables

The FASB issued SFAS 125 – *Accounting for Transfers and Servicing of Financial Assets and Extinguishments of Liabilities* – in 1996. This adopts a 'financial-components approach' – which permits partial derecognition because it allows assets and liabilities to be subdivided into components and accounted for separately – and it focuses on whether or not control over the items in question is maintained. It therefore takes quite a different approach from FRS 5 to questions such as debt factoring and securitisation transactions.

SFAS 125 says that transfers of financial assets (or components thereof) should be accounted for as a sale if the transferor surrenders control over the assets and in exchange receives consideration other than beneficial interests in the assets that have been transferred. To have surrendered control over the assets requires all of the following:

(a)   the transferred assets have been isolated from the transferor so that they are beyond the reach of the transferor and its creditors, even in bankruptcy or receivership;

(b)   the transferee obtains the right – free of conditions that constrain it from taking advantage of that right – to pledge or exchange the financial assets. (Where the transferee is a qualifying special purpose entity, these conditions apply to the holders of beneficial interests in that entity.); and

(c)   the transferor does not maintain effective control over the transferred assets through (1) an agreement that both entitles and obligates the transferor to repurchase or redeem them before maturity or (2) an agreement that entitles the transferor to repurchase or redeem transferred assets that are not readily obtainable.[94]

These rules are more accommodating than those in FRS 5. For example, the retention of bad debt risk by the transferor does not prevent a sale being recorded; it simply requires a liability representing that risk to be recorded.

4.2.7   Offset

The FASB has interpreted the conditions for setting off assets against liabilities in terms similar to the offset rules in FRS 5, but with one extra criterion. This is that the reporting entity must actually intend to use the right of set off in settling the amounts in question. The ASB considered this criterion in developing FRS 5, but rejected it on the view that the intended manner of settlement is a matter of administrative convenience and does not affect the economic position of the parties.

5   CONCLUSION

FRS 5 has been fairly successful in curbing the wilder excesses of creative accountants. In particular, the requirement to consolidate quasi subsidiaries, together with the general injunction to account for the substance of transactions rather than being diverted by their narrow legal form, have provided useful ammunition against contrived schemes that rely on artificial structures or improbable interpretations of events. The original five Application Notes have also been helpful in prescribing the accounting treatment of the transactions which they address; it is too early to say whether the sixth – on PFI transactions – will prove sufficiently robust in the very political climate in which it has to be applied.

Nonetheless, we believe that the standard requires substantial revision, because it is a large and impenetrable document and some of its key principles are questionable. Its recognition rules are difficult to understand and do not really underpin established practice. The derecognition rules are also insufficiently developed; in particular, the idea of partial derecognition appears in the standard as something of an afterthought and is not consistently applied even in the Application Notes. And the linked presentation is neither fish nor fowl, and would have been better strangled at birth. We hope that the ASB will take the opportunity to re-examine it before too long.

References

1   TR 603, para. 17.
2   ED 42, *Special purpose transactions*, ASC, March 1988, para. 56.
3   *Ibid.*, para. 57.
4   *Ibid.*, para. 58.
5   *Ibid.*, para. 62.
6   *Ibid.*, para. 65.
7   FRS 5, *Reporting the substance of transactions*, ASB, April 1994, para. 12.
8   *Ibid.*, para. 13.
9   *Ibid.*, para. 43.
10 *Ibid.*, para. 16.
11 *Ibid.*, para. 47.
12 *Ibid.*, para. 2.
13 *Ibid.*, para. 4.
14 Exposure Draft of *Statement of Principles for financial reporting*, ASB, March 1999, paras. 4.7 and 4.24.
15 FRS 5, para. 17.
16 *Ibid.*, para. 18.
17 *Ibid.*, para. 20.
18 Exposure Draft of *Statement of Principles for financial reporting*, Chapter 5. In fact the wording of FRS 5 is more like that used in the 1995 draft of the *Statement of Principles*.
19 IAS 39, *Financial Instruments: Recognition and Measurement*, IASC, December 1998, para. 27.
20 This, however, is a possible future development; see Chapter 17.
21 FRS 5, para. 22.
22 *Ibid.*, para. 25.
23 *Ibid.*, para. 21.
24 *Ibid.*, para. 72.
25 *Ibid.*, para. 73.
26 *Ibid.*, para. 24.
27 *Ibid.*, paras. 26 and 27.
28 The standard in fact appears to argue that the asset and liability *have* been derecognised and replaced by a new asset (i.e. the net amount) which is then grossed up again for presentation purposes. However, this tortuous argument appears to have been designed only to avoid breaching the general prohibition on offsetting assets and liabilities which would otherwise prevent the linked presentation being applied.
29 FRS 5, para. 81.
30 *Ibid.*, para. 26.
31 *Ibid.*, para. 27.
32 *Ibid.*, para. 82.
33 *Ibid.*, para. 83.
34 *Ibid.*, paras. 28 and 88.
35 CA 85, Sch. 4, para. 5.
36 FRS 5, para. 29.
37 *Ibid.*
38 *Ibid.*, para. 7.
39 *Ibid.*, para. 8.
40 *Ibid.*, para. 33.
41 CA 85, s 227(5) and (6).
42 FRS 5, para. 38.
43 FRRP PN 44, *Findings of the Financial Reporting Review Panel in respects of the accounts of Associated Nursing Services plc for the year ended 31 March 1995 and 31 March 1996*, FRRP, 17 February 1997.
44 *Ibid.*, para. 35.
45 *Ibid.*, para. 36.
46 *Ibid.*, para. 30.

47   *Ibid.*, para. 31.
48   *Ibid.*, Application Note A, paras. A11 and A12.
49   *Ibid.*, Application Note B, para. B19.
50   *Ibid.*, para. B21.
51   FRS 5, Application Note C, para. C12.
52   These conditions are discussed further in paras. C15 and C16 of the Application Note.
53   FRS 5, Application Note C, para. C19.
54   *Ibid.*, para. C20.
55   FRS 5, Application Note D, para. D8.
56   *Ibid.*, para. D22.
57   *Ibid.*, para. D23.
58   *Ibid.*, para. D24.
59   The reasons for this are explained in para. D16 of the Application Note.
60   FRS 5, Application Note D, para. D20.
61   This is explained more fully in para. E14 of Application Note E.
62   As discussed in para. 71 of FRS 5, where the proportionate share of benefits and risks of part of an
     asset has been transferred, that part can be treated as a separate asset.
63   FRS 5, Application Note E, para. E15.
64   *Ibid.*, para. E22.
65   *Ibid.*, paras. E19 and E20.
66   *Ibid.*, para. E23.
67   *Ibid.*, para. E24.
68   SFAS 47, *Disclosure of Long-Term Obligations*, FASB, March 1981, para. 23.
69   FRS 5, para. 12(d).
70   SSAP 21, *Accounting for leases and hire purchase contracts*, ASC, August 1984, para. 14.
71   *Application Note F – Private Finance Initiative and Similar Contracts*, ASB, September 1998.
72   *Ibid.*, para. F4.
73   *Ibid.*, para. F6.
74   *Ibid.*, para. F7.
75   *Ibid.*, para. F8.
76   *Ibid.*, para. F22.
77   Technical Note No. 1 (Revised), *How to Account for PFI Transactions*, H M Treasury, June 1999.
78   *Application Note F*, para. F3.
79   IAS 1, *Presentation of Financial Statements*, IASC, Revised July 1977, para. 20 (b) (ii).
80   IAS 39, para. 27.
81   *Ibid.*, para. 35.
82   *Ibid.*, paras. 51-53.
83   *Ibid.*, para. 57.
84   SIC-12, *Consolidation – Special Purpose Entities*, IASC, November 1998, para. 1.
85   *Ibid.*, para. 8.
86   *Ibid.*, para. 10.
87   SFAS 49, *Accounting for Product Financing Arrangements*, FASB, June 1981, para. 3.
88   *Ibid.*, para. 5.
89   *Ibid.*, para. 8.
90   *Ibid.*, para. 5.
91   SFAS 47, *Disclosure of Long-Term Obligations*, FASB, March 1981, para. 23(a).
92   SFAS 66, *Accounting for Sales of Real Estate*, FASB, October 1982, para. 6.
93   *Ibid.*, para. 5.
94   SFAS 125 – *Accounting for Transfers and Servicing of Financial Assets and Extinguishments of
     Liabilities*, FASB, June 1996, para. 9.

Chapter 17   Leases and hire purchase contracts

1   INTRODUCTION

SSAP 21 broke new ground in UK financial reporting in two ways: it was the first accounting standard to apply the concept of substance over form, and it was the first to incorporate the present value basis of measurement into the historical cost model. These two innovations allowed the standard to introduce the requirement for companies to capitalise assets in their balance sheets (together with the corresponding obligations) in prescribed circumstances – irrespective of the fact that legal title to those assets vested in another party.

The substance over form approach was based on the view that a lease that transfers substantially all of the risks and benefits incident to the ownership of an asset to the lessee should be accounted for as the acquisition of the asset and the assumption of an obligation by the lessee, and as a sale or financing by the lessor. Such leases were termed 'finance leases' and are equivalent to what are known as 'capital leases' in the US. In the case of leases which did not transfer substantially all the risks and rewards of ownership of an asset to the lessee, the accounting was relatively unchanged. These leases became known as 'operating leases' and do not require capitalisation in the balance sheet. Instead, operating lease rentals are charged to the profit and loss account of the lessee on a straight line basis over the lease term.

The second SSAP 21 innovation, the incorporation of the present value basis of measurement within the historical cost model, related to the amount at which the lease finance obligation and the capitalised lease itself was to be stated in the lessee's balance sheet. This is because it is the present value of the minimum lease payments that is recognised in the balance sheet as the liability under the lease, whilst the corresponding asset that is capitalised (at the same amount) represents the right to the use of the physical asset over the lease term. This means that the 'asset' capitalised under a finance lease is not the leased asset itself – although clearly the amount capitalised should approximate to the fair value of the asset.

SSAP 21, together with its equivalent standards around the world, has been in place for many years. Consequently, the distinction between finance and operating leases and the related accounting consequences are now widely accepted internationally. At the same time, though, conventional accounting in this area is currently being challenged, and some major standard-setters around the world have strongly held views that the finance/operating distinction should be removed and that all rights and obligations arising under lease contracts should be recognised as assets and liabilities in the financial statements of lessees. This proposed new approach is discussed at 1.6 below.

1.1   What are leases and hire purchase contracts?

'A *lease* is a contract between a lessor and a lessee for the hire of a specific asset. The lessor retains ownership of the asset but conveys the right to the use of the asset to the lessee for an agreed period of time in return for the payment of specified rentals.'[1] The term 'lease' is also used to refer to any arrangement with a similar result.

'A *hire purchase contract* is a contract for the hire of an asset which contains a provision giving the hirer an option to acquire legal title to the asset upon the fulfilment of certain conditions stated in the contract';[2] usually, this merely involves the payment of a specified final rental.

1.2   The tax position

The tax position for both lessees and lessors can be briefly outlined as follows:

(a)   lessees – the total rentals payable are an allowable expense (with a restriction for cars costing more than £12,000)[3] whilst no capital allowances are received;

(b)   lessors – the total rentals receivable are taxable income and capital allowances are given on the cost of the leased assets.

Under Statement of Practice SP3/91, the Inland Revenue will normally allow tax relief to a lessee for amounts charged in the accounts in respect of finance costs if these are dealt with in accordance with SSAP 21. They will also allow a deduction for depreciation charged in respect of assets held under finance leases, as long as the charge is calculated on normal commercial accounting principles. In other situations the basis of allowance may have to be negotiated.

For hire purchase contracts or leases which include a purchase option, any capital allowances are receivable by the hirer not the owner. As a result, the hirer can only claim the interest element of rentals payable as a tax deductible expense.

At the time of writing (August 1999) it is understood that the Inland Revenue believes that tax-based leasing should end and is therefore pursuing an agenda of developing an entirely new framework for the taxation of leasing, based on treating leases where allowances are not given as trading transactions, so that the lessor is taxed on the commercial profit.

1.3   SSAP 21

SSAP 21 – *Accounting for leases and hire purchase contracts* – was issued in August 1984 after a lengthy and active exposure/discussion period. ED 29,[4] which led to SSAP 21, was issued in October 1981 after approximately five years of debate. It was argued that comparability between companies would require capitalisation of finance leases by lessees; in particular, the effects of non-capitalisation on companies' gearing and rates of return on assets were said to affect comparability. It was further argued that readers of financial statements could not determine the economic substance of asset financing transactions from the financial statements. This was because, in effect, a leased fixed asset represented an asset financed by a borrowing in an identical fashion to an asset purchased with a bank loan. However, in the case of a lease, neither the asset nor the borrowing would have been recognised in the balance sheet.

One case highlighting this was that of Court Line Limited, a public company which collapsed in 1974. The group used leased aircraft to operate a package holiday business, and at 30 September 1973 had undisclosed leasing obligations relating to assets costing £40m.[5] The shareholders' funds shown in the group balance sheet at that date amounted to approximately £18m.[6] As the Inspectors stated, 'the amounts involved were material and should have been disclosed'.[7] Although this suggested that full disclosure might suffice (rather than new accounting treatments), it certainly highlighted the need for changes in financial statement presentation in order that readers could fully appreciate the financial position of a company involved in leasing.

At the time that it was issued, SSAP 21 was one of the most controversial accounting standards, as it effectively invoked a substance over form approach to give an accounting treatment possibly different from the legal ownership position. As discussed below, this is not done explicitly, however, as the lessee is required to capitalise the right to the use of an asset – not the asset itself – that corresponds to the present value of the minimum lease payments under a finance lease that constitutes the balance sheet liability. In practice, the fair value of the asset will approximate to the right that has been capitalised, and the inclusion of the latter as an asset achieves the accounting result of substance over form.

SSAP 21 essentially involves a decision as to whether or not a lease meets the given definition of a finance lease; if not, then an operating lease exists. Such decisions will be made independently by both the lessee and lessor to determine the appropriate accounting treatment and disclosures. Broad guidelines and requirements are given in SSAP 21, but many areas are not specifically covered or are discussed only in the Guidance Notes issued with it.[8]

Under SSAP 21, hire purchase contracts which are of a financing nature should be treated similarly to finance leases, whilst the others should be treated similarly to operating leases. The vast majority will be of a financing nature and were already being accounted for similarly to the finance lease treatment required by SSAP 21. This is because it is usually intended that the hirer will obtain title to the asset concerned at the end of the hire period. All references in this Chapter to leases include hire purchase contracts of the appropriate type, unless the context requires otherwise.

SSAP 21 'does not apply to lease contracts concerning the rights to explore for or to exploit natural resources such as oil, gas, timber, metals and other minerals. Nor does it apply to licensing agreements for items such as motion picture films, video recordings, plays, manuscripts, patents and copyrights'.[9] This, however, does not preclude SSAP 21 from being referred to for general guidance where it is considered appropriate.

1.4   Accounting requirements of SSAP 21

Lessees should capitalise finance leases and recognise a corresponding obligation in creditors. The capitalised asset should then be depreciated over the shorter of the leased asset's useful life or the lease term (see 2.1.5 below); capitalised hire purchase contracts should be depreciated over the hired asset's useful life. The obligation will be reduced by the element of rental payments which is calculated to relate to its repayment, as distinct from the payment of interest. Lessee accounting is discussed in detail at 3 below.

Lessors should treat finance leases to their customers as amounts receivable included in debtors, i.e. the assets which are so leased will not be included as fixed assets. The amount receivable will be reduced by the element of rental receipts which is calculated to relate to the repayment of the receivable. This involves a complex calculation of allocating the rental receipt between capital and revenue. Lessor accounting is discussed in detail at 5 below.

SSAP 21 involves no special accounting treatment of operating leases unless the rentals are payable/receivable by the lessee/lessor other than on a straight-line basis. In such a case the rentals should be taken to profit and loss account on a straight-line basis unless a more systematic basis is more appropriate. This is discussed at 3.6 and 5.2 below for lessees and lessors respectively.

SSAP 21 specifies certain disclosures to be made by lessees and lessors in addition to the adoption of the required accounting treatments above. The disclosures are outlined and examples given at 4 (lessee) and 6 (lessor) below.

1.5   ICAEW review of SSAP 21

In the Autumn of 1991 the ASB requested the technical and research committees of the various CCAB bodies to review a number of existing SSAPs with a view to submitting a report on problems that are being encountered with them in practice.   One of the SSAPs which the ICAEW was given to review was SSAP 21, and the resulting report was issued in March 1992 as a Technical Release of the Institute's Financial Reporting & Auditing Group, titled FRAG 9/92 – *Review, for major practical problems, of SSAP 21.*

FRAG 9/92 discussed a number of practical difficulties which had been experienced with SSAP 21, and in particular it focused on the distinction between finance and operating leases, accounting for sale and leaseback transactions and accounting for residual values. The recommendations of this report are referred to as the relevant topics are discussed throughout this Chapter.

1.6   The G4+1's proposed new approach to lease accounting

The development of conceptual frameworks for financial reporting by the ASB, the IASC and other standard setting bodies around the world could fundamentally change the way in which financial contracts such as leases are accounted for. Each of these conceptual frameworks identifies the elements of financial statements, including assets, liabilities, equity, gains and losses as the basic elements, and sets down recognition rules for their incorporation in financial statements. In the case of lease accounting, assets and liabilities are the most relevant elements, and the ASB's revised Draft *Statement of Principles* defines these particular elements as follows: assets are 'rights or other access to future economic benefits controlled by an entity as a result of past transactions or events',[10] whilst liabilities are 'obligations of an entity to transfer economic benefits as a result of past transactions or events'.[11]

Looking at these two definitions, it seems likely that most leases, including non-cancellable operating leases, will qualify for recognition as assets and liabilities. This is because, irrespective of whether the lease is finance or operating in nature, the lessee is likely to enjoy the future economic benefits embodied in the leased asset, and will have an unavoidable legal obligation to transfer economic benefits to the lessor.

This is the conclusion that was reached by a Working Group consisting of staff members of the standard-setting bodies of Australia, Canada, New Zealand, UK, the USA and the IASC (loosely known as the G4+1). In 1996 the Working Group published a discussion paper entitled *Accounting for leases: a new approach*, which discussed the limitations of current lease accounting standards and set out a new approach to lease accounting.[12]   Although the paper has not been officially approved by the boards of the various standard-setters involved in its preparation, it is seen to be influential.

The Working Group claimed that 'current lease accounting standards are now agreed by many observers to be unsatisfactory, at least with respect to accounting by lessees'.[13] It asserted that the 'most frequently noted concern relates to the fact that the standards do not require rights and obligations arising under operating leases to be recognised as assets and liabilities in the lessee's financial statements'.[14] According to the paper, the result has been that the standards have inadvertently promoted the structuring of financial arrangements so as to meet the conditions for classification as an operating lease, thereby avoiding recognition in lessees' balance sheets of material assets and liabilities arising from operating lease contracts. Consequently, the paper advocated a new approach to accounting for lease contracts which was aimed at overcoming these perceived concerns about the effectiveness of current lease accounting.

The Working Group's new approach to accounting for lease contracts was based on the definitions of assets and liabilities contained in the various conceptual frameworks. Under the IASC's *Framework*, an asset is defined as 'a resource controlled by the enterprise as a result of past events and from which future economic benefits are expected to flow to the enterprise', whilst a liability is defined as 'a present obligation of the enterprise arising from past events, the settlement of which is expected to result in an outflow from the enterprise of resources embodying economic benefits'. [15] According to the Working Group, the clear implication of applying the IASC *Framework* to accounting for lease contracts 'is that it can be reasoned that all finance leases and most, if not all, operating leases qualify for recognition as assets and liabilities'.[16]

The Working Group's reasoning seems to have been based on the belief that the rights and obligations established by operating leases are no different in nature to those established by finance leases. This conclusion was reached through the application of the asset and liability definitions of the IASC's *Framework*: under both finance and operating leases, the lessee acquires a contractual right to enjoy the future economic benefits embodied in the leased property and incurs a contractual obligation to compensate the lessor for the use of the leased property over the lease term.[17] However, the question which should be asked is whether the conclusion reached reflects a shortcoming in existing lease accounting or whether it exposes a flaw in the *Framework*.

Overall, the Working Group's paper was well written and thought provoking. On the other hand, though, whilst it raised a number of legitimate issues, it did not provide many solutions. For example, the paper was critical of the existing criteria laid down in accounting standards to distinguish between finance and operating leases (describing them as being 'arbitrary') and suggested a distinction based on cancellable and non-cancellable leases in its place. However, it did not resolve the problem of how to distinguish between cancellable and non-cancellable leases. In our view, it may be just as difficult to distinguish between leases on this basis as it is to distinguish between finance and operating leases.

Furthermore, the paper did not distinguish between non-cancellable leases and other commitments or executory contracts, such as electricity supply agreements, service contracts and contracted capital commitments. This was a major shortcoming of the paper and, in our view, it should not be progressed further until the uncertainty regarding the application of the paper's lease capitalisation principles to other executory contracts is resolved. In particular, existing disclosure requirements relating to executory contracts would seem currently to serve the needs of the capital markets adequately. However, the paper did not address the possibility of enhanced disclosures related to operating leases, and did not explain why – given the efficiency of the capital markets – the capitalisation of all non-cancellable leases is superior to such enhanced disclosure.

In any event, at its meeting in March 1999, the G4+1 continued its discussions of a number of the technical issues that emerged from the 1996 discussion paper. The issues discussed included:[18]

■ the scope of any revised lease accounting standards;

■ accounting for sale and leaseback transactions; and

■ identification of the appropriate discount rate to be used by the lessee in determining the present value of lease rentals.

It is reported that the Group tentatively agreed on the following proposals:[19]

■ Any revised lease accounting standards should apply to all leases, i.e. both long-term and short-term leases, and leases of both tangible and intangible assets. Perhaps in response to the above-mentioned criticism that the 1996 discussion paper failed to distinguish between non-cancellable leases and other executory contracts, the Group noted that, while leases are executory contracts at their inception, the lessor has substantially performed its responsibilities under the lease and the lease ceases to be executory when the leased property is 'delivered' to the lessee. In the view of the Group, this feature of lease contracts distinguishes them from contracts such as take or pay contracts, which are considered to be executory throughout their term. To us this seems to be a rather tenuous distinction, given that not all leases fit neatly into the Group's characterisation of the lessor substantially performing its responsibilities when the leased property is delivered. For example, how would the Group view a lease of a machine where the lessor was responsible for the on-going repairs and maintenance thereof?

■ The amount of profit to be recognised by the seller/lessee in a sale and leaseback transaction should be based on the proportion of the asset 'sold' to the purchaser/lessor rather than on the difference between the asset's carrying amount and its fair value at the date of the sale and leaseback. However, it is reported that the Group did not have a unanimous view on this issue and, as a result, any future discussion paper will discuss both approaches. It seems that this difference of opinion between some of the G4+1 members reflects the contrast between the FASB's 'components' approach to asset derecognition and ASB's 'risk and rewards' approach. This is a perennial trans-Atlantic conceptual difference that pervades a number of accounting issues, including the derecognition of financial instruments.

Lease accounting was again on the agenda of the June 1999 meeting of the G4+1, where the following issues were discussed:[20]

- the assets that should be identified separately in the lessor's balance sheet, including assets arising from future lease payments, residual values and guarantees. The Group considered the extent to which contingent rentals, price changes, cancellation and renewal options should be included in the assets arising from the lease contract. Again, this seems to involve a discussion of the components approach (this time as it applies to asset recognition) and whether or not each component meets the definition of an asset under the various conceptual frameworks;

- the measurement of the lessor's assets arising under the lease contract both at the inception of the lease and over the term of the lease;

- whether or not the lessor's gains and losses should be recognised at the inception of the lease for leases other than those entered into by manufacturers and dealers; and

- various methods of income recognition, including those where the tax effects of the lease contract are significant in relation to the total return generated under the lease.

It therefore seems clear that the next step will be for the G4+1 to issue a revised discussion paper on the subject, providing the necessary detail that was lacking in its 1996 paper. However, whatever is contained in the detail, it seems certain that the G4+1 is intent on pursuing its agenda of removing the distinction between operating and finance leases such that all non-cancellable leases (however described and defined) are recognised in the balance sheet.

2   DETERMINING THE LEASE TYPE

2.1   The 90% test

A finance lease is defined as 'a lease that transfers substantially all the risks and rewards of ownership of an asset to the lessee',[21] whilst an operating lease 'is a lease other than a finance lease'.[22]

SSAP 21 gives guidelines for deciding whether 'substantially all the risks and rewards' have passed to a lessee. It is stated that 'it should be presumed that such a transfer of risks and rewards occurs if at the inception of a lease the present value of the minimum lease payments, including any initial payment, amounts to substantially all (normally 90 per cent or more) of the fair value of the leased asset. The present value should be calculated by using the interest rate implicit in the lease ... . Notwithstanding the fact that a lease meets [these] conditions ... , the presumption that it should be classified as a finance lease may in exceptional circumstances be rebutted if it can be clearly demonstrated that the lease in question does not transfer substantially all the risks and rewards of ownership (other than legal title) to the lessee. Correspondingly, the presumption that a lease which fails to meet [these] conditions ... is not a finance lease may in exceptional circumstances be rebutted.'[23] The more important terms used in performing the 90% test in SSAP 21 are explained below.

2.1.1　*The fair value*

This 'is the price at which an asset could be exchanged in an arm's length transaction less, where applicable, any grants receivable towards the purchase or use of the asset'.[24] If this fair value cannot be determined for the purposes of the 90% test, then an estimate thereof should be used. This will not usually be required for lessors, but may be for lessees who are unaware of the cost of the leased asset.

2.1.2　*The implicit interest rate*

This 'is the discount rate that at the inception of a lease, when applied to the amounts which the lessor expects to receive and retain, produces an amount (the present value) equal to the fair value of the leased asset'.[25]

The amounts the lessor expects to receive and retain comprise the following:

(a) the minimum lease payments to the lessor (all elements (a) to (c) at 2.1.3 below); plus

(b) any unguaranteed residual value; less

(c) any part of (a) and (b) above for which the lessor will be accountable to the lessee.

If the implicit interest rate cannot be calculated due to inadequate information then an estimate may be used. This will not usually apply to the lessor, who will be likely to have all relevant information available. However, a lessee may not have access to this information and may be unable to make estimates thereof. If the interest rate implicit in the lease is not determinable, it should be estimated by reference to the rate which a lessee would be expected to pay on a similar lease.

Nevertheless, it was pointed out by the ICAEW working party that reviewed SSAP 21 that situations may arise where the lessee might also not know the rate payable on a similar lease. The working party recommended that in these circumstances the lessee's incremental borrowing rate should be used.[26]

2.1.3   The minimum lease payments[27]

There are three possible elements of this:

(a)   the minimum payments over the remaining part of the lease term;

(b)   any residual amount guaranteed by the lessee or a party related to the lessee; and

(c)   any residual amounts guaranteed by any other party.

The elements to be included depend on the intended use of the minimum lease payments calculation as follows:

(i)   all elements are used in the calculation of the implicit interest rate (for use in the 90% test);

(ii)   all elements are used in the 90% test performed by the lessor. The total of these elements plus any unguaranteed residual value will represent the lessor's gross investment in the lease (see 5.3 below);

(iii) elements (a) and (b) are used in the 90% test performed by the lessee. The present value of this minimum lease payments figure will represent both the capitalised fixed asset and the initial finance lease obligation for the lessee (see 3.2 and 3.3 below respectively).

The minimum lease payments should not include any contingent rentals, e.g. those dependent on the level of use of the equipment. However if, for example, the lessee guaranteed to use the equipment to a certain level, then that level of rental would be included.

2.1.4   An unguaranteed residual value

This is 'that portion of the residual value of the leased asset (estimated at the inception of the lease), the realisation of which by the lessor is not assured or is guaranteed solely by a party related to the lessor'.[28]

2.1.5   The lease term

This is 'the period for which the lessee has contracted to lease the asset and any further terms for which the lessee has the option to continue to lease the asset, with or without further payment, which option it is reasonably certain at the inception of the lease that the lessee will exercise'.[29]   Usually a lease can be easily divided into the primary term, during which the lessee is committed to make certain rental payments (with a termination rental payable upon termination before the end of the primary term) and a secondary term, for which the lessee can extend the lease if desired.   It is general practice that any secondary term is only included in the lease term for 90% test calculations if it is highly probable that the term will be so extended, i.e. the 'reasonably certain' criterion is generally strictly interpreted.   If a peppercorn (nominal) rental is payable in the secondary lease term period, the lease term should normally include the secondary term although the rentals can probably be ignored on materiality grounds in performing the 90% test.

2.2   90% test example

The following example illustrates the application of the 90% test:

Example 17.1

Details of a non-cancellable lease are as follows:

(i)   Fair value (per 2.1.1 above) = £10,000

(ii)   Five annual rentals payable in advance of £2,000

(iii) Total estimated residual value at end of five years = £3,000 of which £2,000 is guaranteed
       by the lessee.

The implicit interest rate in the lease (per 2.1.2 above) is that which gives a present value of
£10,000 for the five rentals plus the total estimated residual value at the end of year 5. This rate
can be calculated as 10.93%.

This rate is then used to calculate the present value of the minimum lease payments. As
explained in 2.1.3 above, this example gives rise to identical minimum lease payments from both
the lessee's and lessor's points of view. This is because there is no guarantee of any part of the
residual by a party other than the lessee and the minimum lease payments will be the five annual
rentals plus the residual guaranteed by the lessee of £2,000. The present value of these minimum
lease payments is calculated as £9,405.

This present value figure is 94.05% of the asset's fair value and a finance lease is therefore
indicated.

All of the above information will be known to the lessor as it will have been used in the pricing
decision for the lease. However, the lessee may not know either the fair value or the
unguaranteed residual value and, therefore, the implicit interest rate. If either of the first two of
these is not known, the lessee is permitted by SSAP 21 to estimate what they are and so calculate
the implicit interest rate. Alternatively, the lessee may feel that such an estimation is better made
of the implicit interest rate directly, rather than of a parameter which will then allow that rate to
be calculated.

It is important to note that the 90% test can result in different answers being
given for the lessor and lessee, e.g. it may indicate a finance lease from the
lessor but an operating lease to the lessee. There are two possible reasons for
this. First, and most commonly, the lessor may receive a guarantee of the
estimated (significant) residual of the leased asset by a party other than the
lessee and accordingly, using the 90% test, an operating lease may be indicated
for the lessee whereas a finance lease is indicated for the lessor. Second, as
shown above, the lessee may not have the full information available to the lessor
and his estimates of fair value or residual value may be so different from the
correct figures (known to the lessor) that his classification of the lease is
incorrect.

2.3   Determining the lease type – other factors

In 1987 the ICAEW published TR 664 – *Implementation of SSAP 21
'Accounting for leases and hire purchase contracts'* – in an attempt to influence

the practice of interpreting the 90% test as a firm rule. It stated that any evaluation of a lease agreement should involve an overall examination of substantial risks and rewards as follows: 'Lease agreements give rise to a set of rights, rewards, risks and obligations and can be complex. The package must be analysed with greater weight given to aspects of the agreement which are likely to have a commercial effect in practice. In this way the substance of the transaction can be identified and then reflected in the financial statements in order to give a true and fair view. ... [The 90% test] does not provide a strict mathematical definition of a finance lease. Such a narrow interpretation would be contrary to the spirit of SSAP 21 and SSAPs generally.'[30]

Consequently, although the 90% test outlined above is important, there are a number of other factors which need to be considered in deciding whether or not substantially all the risks and rewards of ownership have passed. The crucial question is whether the terms of the transaction, taken as a whole, are such that the lessor can expect to be fully compensated for his investment in the leased asset without having to enter into further transactions with other parties. Affirmative answers to the following questions would tend to indicate that a finance lease exists:

(a)   If the lessee can cancel the lease, will he bear any losses associated with the cancellation?

(b)   Will the lessee gain or lose from any fluctuations in the market value of the residual? (For example, he may receive a rental rebate equalling most of the sales proceeds at the end of the lease.)

(c)   Does the lessee have the ability to continue the lease for a secondary period at a nominal rental?

(d)   Is the expected lease term equal to substantially all of the asset's expected useful life?

(e)   Are the leased assets of a specialised nature such that only the lessee (or a limited number of other parties) can use them without major modifications being made?

One factor which is sometimes considered to be relevant in determining the lease type is whether or not the lessee is responsible for insurance, maintenance, etc. However, we do not believe that this should necessarily be a conclusive factor in determining the lease type. This is because, even if under the lease the lessor (or another party) accepts responsibility for these items, the lessee through making increased rental payments to the lessor (or the other party) is in fact bearing the responsibility for them. Consequently, the position is no different from that where the lessee owns an asset which is insured and is covered by a maintenance agreement.

In evaluating the risks and rewards, one should consider which factors are most likely to have an economic effect on the parties to the lease. The various factors are interdependent to some extent, e.g. if the lease term is for substantially all of the asset's expected useful economic life, or the asset is of a specialised nature, then the residual value is likely to be very low.

In fact, this was the approach favoured by the ICAEW working party which reviewed SSAP 21 for practical problems. In its report (see ICAEW Technical Release FRAG 9/92), the working party recommended a move away from the 90% test which, in its view, had become a mechanistically applied rule, towards an approach based on qualitative tests.

The report stated that 'any percentage test is arbitrary in that a 90% test for one asset may generate significant risks for a lessor and an 80% test for another asset may produce lower levels of risk for a lessor. ... Some [of the working party] believe that a percentage test should be retained but relegated to one of several tests. However, the majority view is that a percentage test should be abandoned; if it remains there is a fear that its status will be elevated in the same way that SSAP 21's 90% guide has become a rule. We therefore suggest that if the "substantially all risks and rewards" route is to be taken the ASB considers replacing a numerical approach, whether guide or strict rule, with an approach based on qualitative tests.'[31]

The report then listed the following six examples of qualitative tests which might be considered in deciding whether or not substantially all the risks and rewards of ownership of an asset have been transferred:[32]

■ are the lease rentals based on a market rate for use of the asset or a financing rate for use of the funds?

■ what is the nature of the lessor's business?

■ is the existence of put and call options a feature of the lease? If so, are they exercisable at a predetermined price or formula or are they exercisable at the market price at the time the option is exercised?

■ which party carries the risk of a fall in value of the asset and which party benefits from any capital appreciation?

■ does the lessee have the use of the asset for a period broadly equating to the likely useful economic life of the asset?

■ does the lessor intend to earn his total return on this transaction alone or does he intend to rely on subsequent sales or lease revenue?

However, the working party points out that in applying these qualitative tests in practice, the answers to the above questions would have to be interpreted in the context of the risks that lessors will be prepared to take. In this context, the report notes that the leasing industry has changed considerably over the last ten years and that lessors will now take on very different risks. For this reason, it is suggested that a lessor should not, on the face of it, be equated to a bank; similarly, a lessor in a banking group is not *necessarily* a finance lessor.[33]

We fully support the ICAEW working party's recommendation for the abolition of the 90% test in favour of an approach based on qualitative tests. In fact, it is our view that a qualitative approach as outlined above is inherent in SSAP 21 as currently drafted and is, to a certain extent, already followed in practice. More importantly though, such an approach is endorsed by the general principles contained in FRS 5 for reporting the substance of transactions. However, as discussed at 1.6 above, it seems that the ASB will soon be putting forward proposals for the abolition of the operating/finance lease distinction; consequently, it seems highly unlikely that the ASB will embark on an exercise to refine SSAP 21.

It is perhaps worth noting that the equivalent International Accounting Standard, IAS 17 – *Leases* – although very similar to SSAP 21, does not include the 90% test in the criteria for determining the classification of leases. Instead, the standard sets down the broad principle that a lease is classified as a finance lease if it transfers substantially all the risks and rewards incident to ownership of an asset, and then sets down a number of classification indicators to facilitate the classification process.[34]

2.4 Determining the lease type – the impact of FRS 5

Since the overriding principle of FRS 5 – *Reporting the Substance of Transactions* – is that transactions should be accounted for according to their economic substance rather than their legal form, some might suggest that FRS 5 has superseded SSAP 21 in the area of lease classification. However, FRS 5 states clearly that where the substance of a transaction or the treatment of any resulting asset or liability falls not only within the scope of FRS 5 but also directly within the scope of another FRS, SSAP or a specific statutory requirement governing the recognition of assets or liabilities, the standard or statute that contains the more specific provisions should be applied.[35]

Presumably, the purpose of this requirement is to ensure that FRS 5 does not inadvertently undermine the authority of existing standards and legislation. For example, obligations under non-cancellable operating leases which are currently off balance sheet under SSAP 21, would otherwise be caught by the FRS 5 definition of liabilities and would have to be brought on balance sheet, were it not for the requirement that the more specific provisions of (in this case) SSAP 21 should be applied.

Consequently, since SSAP 21 contains the more specific provisions governing lease accounting, one would look to that standard as the primary source of authoritative guidance in this area – despite the fact that it is stated in the explanation section of FRS 5 that 'the general principles of the FRS will also be relevant in ensuring that leases are classified as finance or operating leases in accordance with their substance'.[36] The practical reality is that unless and until SSAP 21 is superseded and the 90% test abolished, preparers should continue to look to that standard when accounting for stand-alone leases that fall wholly within its parameters. However, where FRS 5 will come more into play in the classification of leases will be in situations such as sale and leaseback transactions involving options, where FRS 5 contains more specific guidance than SSAP 21. This is discussed in more detail at 7.4 below.

3   ACCOUNTING BY LESSEES

3.1   Introduction

When it is determined that material finance leases exist for a lessee on the basis of 2 above, there are two elements of the accounting entries which must be considered – the capitalised fixed asset and the related rental obligations. Each of these is dealt with in turn below.

3.2   Capitalised fixed asset

A finance lease should be capitalised at the present value of the minimum lease payments (MLP). The MLP have already been discussed at 2.1.3 above. The elements of MLP to be included for this purpose are:

(a)   the minimum payments over the remaining part of the lease term; and

(b)   any residual amounts guaranteed by the lessee or a party related to him.

This present value will be calculated using the implicit interest rate in the lease (the calculation of which is detailed at 2.1.2 above). In most cases the fair value of the leased asset at the inception of the lease will approximate to this amount. This is because we are calculating a present value of the relevant MLP using all MLP elements also used in the calculation of implicit interest rate, other than:

(a)   any residual amounts guaranteed by a party other than the lessee (or parties related to him); and

(b)   any part of either the total MLP to the lessor or unguaranteed residual value for which the lessor will be accountable to the lessee.

In most cases, these items will be insignificant, and the fair value of leased assets will, therefore, usually approximate to the present value of the relevant MLP. Example 17.1 at 2.2 above involved a situation where the present value of minimum lease payments was 94% of the fair value. This is lower than 100% because a part of the total estimated residual value is unguaranteed, i.e. the present value of the unguaranteed residual value (of £1,000) is 6% of the fair value of the asset. In such a situation a lessee would probably be entitled to take the fair value (of £10,000) as an approximation of the present value of MLP (of £9,405).

The capitalised fixed asset is then depreciated on a similar basis to owned assets (i.e. over the asset's useful economic life). For finance leases (but not hire purchase contracts) the depreciation should be calculated over the lease term, if this is shorter than the asset's useful economic life. The lease term should include any secondary periods over which it is reasonably certain that the lessee will exercise his extension option.

3.3   Finance lease obligation

Accounting for this can be split into three stages, as follows:

(a)   the allocation of total rental payments over the lease term between finance charges and repayment of lease obligation;

(b)   the allocation of the total finance charges to accounting periods; and

(c)   the reduction of the obligation by the element of total rentals payable not allocated at (b).

In allocating total rental payments between finance charges and the repayment of lease obligation the total finance charge is calculated as the difference between the undiscounted total of MLP as per 3.2 above (i.e. including any residual amount guaranteed by the lessee), and the amount at which the lessee records the asset at the inception of the lease. This latter amount will, of course, be the discounted value of the relevant MLP (with the fair value of the leased asset usually being a close approximation to this). The discount element will, therefore, equal the total finance charges over the lease term.

The obligation under finance leases will be set up at an amount equal to the present value of relevant MLP with the other side of this accounting entry being the capitalised fixed asset described above.

3.4   Methods of allocating finance charges to accounting periods

In allocating the total finance charges over the lease term to accounting periods, SSAP 21 requires that this is done 'so as to produce a constant periodic rate of charge on the remaining balance of the obligation for each accounting period, or a reasonable approximation thereto'.[37]

The guidance notes to SSAP 21 detail three methods: actuarial, 'sum of the digits' ('rule of 78') or straight-line.[38] These are progressively easier to apply but also give progressively less accurate answers. There is, therefore, a trade-off to be made between the costs versus benefits of achieving complete accuracy. In making this trade-off, the question of materiality is important because differences between allocated finance charges under the three methods may be immaterial, such that the simplest method may be used for convenience. The following example illustrates the actuarial and sum of the digits methods of allocating finance charges to accounting periods:

Example 17.2

A five year lease of an asset commences on 1 January 2001. The rental is £2,600 p.a. payable in advance. The fair value of the asset at lease inception is £10,000 and it is expected to have a residual at the end of the lease of £2,372 (being its tax written down value at that time) which will be passed to the lessee as a refund of rentals. In addition, the lessee is responsible for all maintenance and insurance costs.

The minimum lease payments are 5 x £2,600 = £13,000 which gives finance charges of £13,000 – £10,000 = £3,000. The actuarial method attempts to calculate the finance charge in each period to give a constant periodic rate of charge on the remaining balance of the obligation for each period. This is done as follows:

Year	Capital sum at start of period £	Rental paid £	Capital sum during period £	Finance charge (15.15% per annum) £	Capital sum at end of period £
2001	10,000	2,600	7,400	1,121	8,521
2002	8,521	2,600	5,921	897	6,818
2003	6,818	2,600	4,218	639	4,857
2004	4,857	2,600	2,257	343	2,600
2005	2,600	2,600	–	–	–
		13,000		3,000	

The finance charge of 15.15% is that which results in a capital sum at the end of 2005 of zero and can be found by trial and error, using a financial calculator, computer program, mathematical formula or present value tables.

This lease involves fairly straightforward figures but it is still not easy to calculate manually. It is, therefore, possible to use the sum of the digits method to give an allocation of finance charge which is a close approximation to that given by the actuarial method.

The sum of the digits method calculations, for example, are as follows:

	number of rentals not yet due	x	total finance charge ⎯⎯⎯⎯⎯⎯⎯⎯ sum of number of rentals	=	Finance charge per annum
Year					£
2001	4 }				1,200
2002	3 }				900
2003	2 }	x	£3,000 ÷ 10	=	600
2004	1 }				300
2005	– }				–
	10 }				3,000

We can now compare the finance charges in each of the five years under the actuarial and sum of the digits methods:

	Finance charge as % of total		Finance charge	
	Actuarial	Sum of the digits	Actuarial	Sum of the digits
Year	%	%	£	£
2001	37	40	1,121	1,200
2002	30	30	897	900
2003	21	20	639	600
2004	12	10	343	300
2005	–	–	–	–
	100	100	3,000	3,000

In situations where the lease term is not very long (typically not more than seven years) and interest rates are not very high, the sum of the digits method gives an allocation of finance charges which is close enough to that under the actuarial method to allow the simpler approach to be used.

It should be noted that the expected residual of £2,372 (which will be paid to the lessee) does not affect any of the above calculations. This expected residual will merely influence the depreciation policy of the lessee as regards the capitalised asset. He will depreciate to an expected residual of £2,372 and any difference between this net book value figure and the amount received by the lessee will give rise to a gain or loss on disposal of the asset.

3.5 Carrying values

At any point during the lease term the depreciated book value of a capitalised leased fixed asset and the remaining finance lease obligation under that lease will not usually be equal. Normally, this is because the method of depreciation bears no relation to that for allocating finance charges to accounting periods, as can be seen in the following example:

Example 17.3

If the lessee in the previous example depreciates the asset to its residual value of £2,372 on a straight-line basis over its life of five years, then the net book value compared with the outstanding lease obligation (using the actuarial method) at the end of each year will be as follows:

Year	Net book value £	Outstanding lease obligation £
2001	8,474	8,521
2002	6,948	6,818
2003	5,422	4,857
2004	3,897	2,600
2005	2,372	–

3.6 Operating leases

3.6.1 Lease rentals

SSAP 21 requires that operating lease rentals are charged to the profit and loss account on a straight-line basis over the lease term irrespective of when payments are due.[39] This is logical as, for example, a large up-front payment made by the lessee should be allocated to the period over which a benefit is gained. Conversely, leases of land and buildings sometimes have a rent-free period in the early part of the lease, followed by a relatively higher rental over the remainder. Alternatively, leases are sometimes structured on the basis of stepped rentals, whereby lease rentals start at a below market rate, but are subject to pre-determined stepped increases, sometimes ending at above market rates to compensate for the lower rentals in the earlier years. In such cases, the rentals should again be charged to profit and loss account on a straight-line basis over the lease term. However, if a more systematic and rational basis is more appropriate, then that basis may be used; e.g. if the level of the use of the asset determines the level of rentals, then it would be appropriate to charge rentals when incurred.

3.6.2 Reverse premiums and similar incentives

An operating lease may include incentives for the lessee to enter into the lease. These incentives can take various forms, such as an up front cash payment to the lessee (a reverse premium), a rent-free period or a contribution to lessee costs. The question as to how such incentives should be accounted for in the accounts of lessees came to the fore following a decision of the Financial Reporting Review Panel in February 1994. The Panel was concerned about the adequacy of the information provided by Pentos plc in its 1992 accounts about the company's accounting treatment of reverse premiums received in respect of property leases. The relevant disclosures in Pentos' accounts were as follows:

Extract 17.1: Pentos plc (1992)

Accounting Policies

Reverse Premiums

Net income from reverse premiums is taken to profit over two accounting periods in order to match income received and start up costs incurred for new shops.

The amount taken to the profit and loss account in the year was included in 'Other Operating Expenses (Net)' and was not separately disclosed. The matter was resolved by the company agreeing to explain its accounting policy more fully in its 1993 accounts, and to disclose the amounts of reverse premiums received in 1993 and 1992. As a result, Pentos' 1993 accounts disclosed the following:

Extract 17.2: Pentos plc (1993)

Accounting Policies

Reverse Premia

Reverse premia arising in the period are matched with the costs of negotiating property leases and premia, and the costs of holding and maintaining unused property. The remaining balance of reverse premia is taken to profit over two accounting periods to match the initially low performance of new shops in the start up period.

Notes to the Accounts

3   Expenses [extract]

Included in other operating expenses are property costs which are reduced by gross reverse premia in the amount of £3.4m (1992 – £6.3m).

However, despite the findings of the Panel, it is not entirely clear as to exactly what it was that the Panel was querying. Perhaps Pentos' referral to the Panel was driven by the school of thought which says that lessees should account for incentive payments received on a straight line basis over the period of the lease (as is the requirement under US GAAP)[40] and should not therefore be taken to income over the first two years of the lease. Evidence for the fact that the Panel was pursuing more than a mere disclosure issue may be found in the following paragraph in the Press Notice which publicised the Panel's decision: 'The Panel noted that existing requirements in the law and accounting standards did not provide unequivocal guidance as to the correct accounting treatment of reverse premiums and is drawing this matter to the attention of the Accounting Standards Board.'

In any event, the issue ended up on the agenda of the UITF which, in December 1994, issued Abstract 12 dealing with the issue.[41] The UITF's consensus requires that all incentives, whatever form they take, should be spread by the lessee on a straight-line basis over the lease term or, if shorter than the full lease term, over the period to the review date on which the rent is first expected to be adjusted to the prevailing market rate. Where, exceptionally, the presumption can be rebutted that an incentive (however structured) is in substance part of the lessor's market return, another systematic and rational basis may be used, with the following disclosures:

(a)   an explanation of the specific circumstances that render the standard treatment specified by the Abstract misleading;

(b)   a description of the basis used and the amounts involved, and

(c)   a note of the effect on the results for the current and corresponding period of any departure from the standard treatment.[42]

If, in exceptional circumstances, another method of spreading is considered more accurately to adjust the rents paid to the prevailing market rate, UITF 12 allows that method to be used, provided the disclosures detailed in (a) to (c) above are given.[43]

UITF 12 does not deal with incentives to surrender leases; however, such incentives should be examined to determine whether in substance the incentive relates to a new lease, particularly where the offer of the incentive is linked to an arrangement to vacate a property under lease from a different lessor. Such consideration should take into account the market rentals applicable to the old and new leases. If it is determined that the incentive, or part thereof, relates in substance to the new lease, the provisions of UITF 12 should be applied.[44]

The Standing Interpretations Committee (SIC) of the IASC has also addressed the issue of operating lease incentives, resulting in the publication of SIC – 15 which takes a similar line to that taken by UITF 12. SIC – 15 is discussed at 8.1.4 below.

4   DISCLOSURE BY LESSEES

4.1   SSAP 21 requirements

The following lessee disclosures are required by SSAP 21:

(a)   policies adopted in accounting for operating and finance leases;[45]

(b)   total operating lease rentals charged, analysed between those payable in respect of hire of plant and machinery and other operating leases.[46] All hire charges should be treated as operating lease rentals including very short-term rentals and rental of property;

(c)   aggregate finance charges allocated for the period in respect of finance leases;[47]

(d)   aggregate depreciation charged in the period on assets held under finance leases and hire purchase contracts;[48]

(e)   totals of gross amount and accumulated depreciation for each major class of asset held under finance leases and hire purchase contracts. If this information is combined with owned assets then the net amount included in the overall total should be disclosed;[49]

(f)   net obligations under finance leases and hire purchase contracts split between amounts payable in the next year, in two to five years inclusive and after five years. Alternatively, this may be shown as gross obligations with future finance charges being deducted from the total. The net obligations analysis may be combined with other obligations and liabilities;[50]

(g)   payments committed to be made *in the next year* under operating leases for (1) leases of land and buildings, and (2) other leases; both amounts split between those expiring:

  (i)   within one year;

  (ii) in the second to fifth years inclusive;

  (iii) in over five years.[51]

This disclosure, which is illustrated in Extracts 17.3 and 17.6 below, is a rather incomplete requirement, since companies do not have to disclose the more useful total amount of minimum lease payments outstanding as of the balance sheet date (as is required for finance leases). In contrast, US GAAP requires that lessees with operating leases should disclose future minimum rental payments payable over each of the next five years and in aggregate thereafter; and

(h) commitments in respect of finance leases and hire purchase contracts existing at the balance sheet date when at that date neither has the asset been brought into use nor have rentals started to accrue.[52]

4.2   Related Companies Act requirements

The main disclosure requirements of the Companies Act which affect lessees are as follows:

(a) the balance sheet formats require creditors falling due within one year to be shown separately from creditors falling due after more than one year.[53] The net obligations under finance leases and hire purchase contracts will have to be split accordingly;

(b) particulars of financial commitments which:

  (i)   have not been provided for; and

  (ii) are relevant to assessing the company's state of affairs.[54]

Since finance leases are capitalised and the obligations are provided, this will normally only be relevant for operating leases. Usually, the disclosures required in (g) in 4.1 above will meet this requirement. Where, however, there are contingent rentals which have not been provided for, extra disclosure may be required.

There are a number of other disclosures required by the Companies Act which may affect lessees and these should also be considered; e.g. details of movements in fixed assets[55] and details in relation to creditors.[56]

4.3 Disclosures in practice

The following are examples of disclosures given in practice by lessees:

Extract 17.3: Haden MacLellan Holdings plc (1998)

Notes to the Accounts

1. Accounting policies

e. Leasing

Assets held under finance leases and hire purchase contracts are capitalised at the fair value of the asset at the inception of the lease, with an equivalent liability categorised as appropriate under creditors due within and after more than one year.

The interest element of the rental obligations is charged to the profit and loss account over the period of the lease and represents a constant proportion of the balance of the capital repayments outstanding.

Rentals under operating leases are charged to the profit and loss account on a straight-line basis over the lease term.

3. Operating costs [extract]

	1998 £m	1997 £m
Operating costs comprise the following charges/(credits):		
Depreciation of tangible fixed assets:		
owned	**6.6**	5.6
held under finance leases	**1.0**	1.0
Operating lease rentals:		
land and buildings	**3.7**	2.9
other	**2.5**	1.9

6. Net interest [extract]

	1998 £m	1997 £m
Interest payable on:		
Finance leases	**0.3**	0.4

11. Tangible fixed assets [extract]

a. Group

	Freehold £m	Land and buildings Long leasehold £m	Short leasehold £m	Plant, equipment and vehicles £m	Total £m
Net book value:					
As at 31st December, 1998	**10.4**	**1.6**	**1.0**	**25.0**	**38.0**
Net book value of assets held under finance leases included above:					
As at 31st December, 1998	–	**1.6**	–	**4.9**	**6.5**

15. Creditors: Amounts falling due
within one year [extract]

	The Group		Parent Company	
	1998	1997	**1998**	1997
	£m	£m	**£m**	£m
Obligations under finance leases	**1.8**	2.2	–	–

16. Creditors: Amounts falling due after
more than one year [extract]

Obligations under finance leases	**2.0**	2.2	–	–

22. Analysis of net debt [extract]

The gross debt falls due as shown in the table below:

	Within one year	Within one to two years	Within two to five years	Over five years	Total
	£m	£m	£m	£m	**£m**
Net bank overdraft	8.2	–	–	–	**8.2**
Medium term loan	–	2.1	6.5	6.5	**15.1**
Bank loans	10.0	2.0	6.0	–	**18.0**
Loan notes	–	–	1.2	–	**1.2**
Finance leases	1.8	1.1	0.9	–	**3.8**
Gross debt	**20.0**	**5.2**	**14.6**	**6.5**	**46.3**

28. Capital commitments [extract]

The Group leases a number of properties and certain items of plant and equipment under operating leases. The minimum annual rentals under these leases are as follows:

	1998		1997	
	Land and buildings	**Other**	Land and buildings	Other
	£m	**£m**	£m	£m
Operating leases which expire:				
within one year	**0.4**	**0.4**	0.2	0.2
in two to five years	**0.9**	**1.3**	0.9	1.4
over five years	**2.4**	**0.8**	2.1	0.8
	3.7	**2.5**	3.2	2.4

It can be seen from the above extract that Haden MacLellan Holdings discloses the information relating to its finance lease obligations within a note dealing with net debt. Another way is to give the information in a separate note, as illustrated below:

Extract 17.4: Racal Electronics Plc (1999)

Notes on the Financial Statements

24	**Obligations under finance leases**	**1999**	1998
			as restated
		£m	£m
	Obligations under finance leases fall due as follows:		
	(a) between one and two years	**14.5**	13.9
	(b) between two and five years	**21.5**	29.0
	(c) in more than five years	**33.1**	40.2
		69.1	83.1
	(d) in one year or less	**14.0**	13.4
		83.1	96.5

As noted at 4.1(f) above, there is an alternative permitted method of disclosure of finance lease obligations. Rather than splitting the obligations by date of payment net of the future interest charges as illustrated in Extracts 17.3 and 17.4 above, some companies show the gross obligations with the future finance charges being deducted from the total. Cadbury Schweppes adopts this form of disclosure, as illustrated below:

Extract 17.5: Cadbury Schweppes p.l.c. (1998)

Notes to the Financial Statements

24   **Leasing Commitments** [extract]

The future minimum lease payments (excluding advances pending formal commencement of leases) to which the Group is committed as at the year end were as follows:

	Finance leases		Operating leases
	1998	1997	**1998**
	£m	£m	**£m**
Within one year	**7**	7	**28**
Between one and two years	**7**	7	**21**
Between two and three years	**6**	6	**14**
Between three and four years	**5**	5	**11**
Between four and five years	**3**	5	**10**
After five years	**4**	6	**79**
	32	36	**163**
Less: Finance charges allocated to future periods	**(5)**	(7)	–
	27	29	**163**

As noted at 4.1(g) above, the requirement to disclose payments committed to be made in the next year under operating leases is, in our view, somewhat deficient. Far more useful disclosure would be that which is, for example, required under US GAAP – namely the future minimum rental payments payable over each of the next five years and in aggregate thereafter. As can be seen from Extract 17.5 above, this disclosure has been provided by Cadbury Schweppes, although this is probably due to the fact that the company is an SEC registrant and prepares its UK annual report and Form 20-F as a combined document. In any event, several other UK companies that are registered with the SEC provide this sort of information on a voluntary basis in their UK annual reports. Included amongst these are British Airways, Reuters and, as illustrated below, BT:

Extract 17.6: British Telecommunications plc (1999)

NOTES TO THE FINANCIAL STATEMENTS

	Group		Company	
27. Financial commitments and contingent liabilities [extract]	**1999 £m**	1998 £m	**1999 £m**	1998 £m
Operating lease payments payable within one year of the balance sheet date were in respect of leases expiring:				
Within one year	**3**	9	**1**	3
Between one and five years	**29**	39	**19**	21
After five years	**116**	135	**93**	94
Total payable within one year	**148**	183	**113**	118

Future minimum operating lease payments for the group at 31 March 1999 were as follows:

Payable in the year ending 31 March:	**1999 £m**
2000	148
2001	137
2002	130
2003	125
2004	120
Thereafter	1,238
Total future minimum operating lease payments	**1,898**

Operating lease commitments were mainly in respect of leases of land and buildings.

As illustrated in the above extract, SSAP 21 applies to leases of land and buildings as for any other assets. However, where property companies act as lessees of long leasehold investment properties, the commitments for ground rents under these operating leases are not usually shown. In fact, MEPC states in its accounts that 'in the opinion of the directors, the disclosure requirements of SSAP 21 to show leasing commitments in respect of ground rents are not relevant to a property investment company'.[57] The reason for this view is unclear.

One element of the disclosure requirements of SSAP 21 which is rarely seen in practice is that in respect of finance lease and hire purchase contract commitments existing at the balance sheet date when at that date neither has the asset been brought into use nor have rentals started to accrue.[58] Presumably companies are aggregating these commitments (where they exist) with their general disclosure of capital commitments contracted but not provided for.

5   ACCOUNTING BY LESSORS

5.1   Introduction

Essentially, a lessor is required to show amounts due from lessees under finance leases as amounts receivable in debtors, and assets leased out under operating leases as tangible fixed assets. The mechanics of lessor accounting for finance leases are more complex than those for a lessee, although, of course, the criteria which determine the classification of leases as either finance or operating are identical for both lessors and lessees (see 2 above).

5.2   Operating leases

Rentals receivable under an operating lease should be recognised on a straight-line basis (irrespective of when rentals are actually receivable) unless another systematic and rational basis is more representative of the time pattern in which the benefit from the leased asset is receivable.[59] This requirement of SSAP 21 is an attempt to ensure a proper matching of revenues with associated costs. A non-straight-line basis may be appropriate where, for example, operating lease rentals are dependent on the level of use of the leased asset. In this case, rentals should be recognised in the periods they become receivable.

Examples of situations where a lessor should recognise operating lease rentals on a straight-line basis, even if they are not so received, are where there is a rent-free period at the beginning of a lease of land or buildings, or where a balloon payment is to be made at the beginning or end of the lease period.

5.3   Finance leases

Broadly, there are two stages in accounting for finance lease receivables; first, the calculation of the gross earnings (finance lease income) element of total lease rentals receivable and, second, the allocation of gross earnings to accounting periods over the lease term. Gross earnings represent:[60]

(a)   the lessor's gross investment in the lease which is the total of the minimum lease payments and any unguaranteed residual value estimated as accruing to the lessor; *less*

(b)   the cost of the leased asset less any grants receivable towards purchase or use of the asset.

Gross earnings should then be allocated to accounting periods to give a constant periodic rate of return on the lessor's net cash investment.[61]   The net cash investment is the amount of funds invested in a lease by the lessor and comprises the cost of the asset plus or minus certain related payments or receipts.[62]   Tax-free grants that are available to the lessor against the purchase price of assets acquired for leasing should be spread over the period of the lease and dealt with by treating the grant as non-taxable income.[63]

The allocation of gross earnings to accounting periods is detailed at 5.4 (finance leases) and 5.5 (hire purchase contracts) below.

Having calculated the allocation of gross earnings to accounting periods, the lessor must then consider the amount at which the receivable should be shown in its balance sheet. The finance lease receivable should equal the lessor's net investment in the lease. This net investment will initially equal the cost of the asset less any grants receivable (i.e. the fair value) and will then be reduced by a portion of total rentals received. This portion will be the element of rentals receivable in a period which is not taken as gross earnings in the calculations described above.

5.4   Allocation of gross earnings – finance leases

5.4.1   Introduction

Owing to differences in tax treatments (see 1.2 above), different methods are used to allocate gross earnings to accounting periods under finance leases and hire purchase contracts.   The latter is dealt with at 5.5 below, and the justification for the different treatments of finance leases and hire purchase contracts is considered at 5.4.5 below.

For finance leases, the gross earnings allocation should be made to give a constant periodic rate of return on the lessor's net cash investment.   This involves the use of an 'after tax' method of allocation; the two most common are the actuarial after tax method and the investment period method.[64]

5.4.2   Methodology

The actuarial after tax and investment period methods allocate gross earnings on a basis which takes the tax effect on cash flows into account. This approach is used because we are attempting to match the revenue recognised under the lease with the expenses incurred (which may be partly notional) in funding the lessor's investment in the lease.

At any time during the lease, the lessor's net cash investment will represent:

(a)   the original cost of the asset; less

(b)   cumulative cash flow receipts to date (rental income, grants received, tax relieved through both capital allowances and payment of interest, together with interest receivable during any period of negative net cash investment); plus

(c)   cumulative cash flow payments to date (interest payments and tax payable on both rental receipts and any interest receivable). This should also include an adjustment in respect of the profit the lessor takes out of the lease, because part of the rental receipts represents profit to the lessor over and above any interest he is estimated to be paying.

The interest payable/receivable is likely to be a notional figure, using appropriate rates for the lessor as at lease inception, to reflect an opportunity cost of funds raised or invested. Both interest payable/receivable and profit taken out should be calculated on the average net cash investment in any period. The profit taken out will be calculated at the percentage rate which results in a net cash investment of zero at the end of the lease term.

The actuarial after tax method and the investment period method differ in their use of the calculated net cash investment at each period end to allocate gross earnings. Under the actuarial after tax method, the estimated profit taken out in each period is grossed up for tax and estimated interest costs, to give a derived apportionment of gross earnings in each period.

In contrast, under the investment period method the estimated net cash investment at each period end is divided by the total of such figures over the lease term to give the fraction of total gross earnings allocated to each period. Whereas the actuarial after tax method is more accurate, the investment period method may be preferred (if resulting differences are immaterial) since it is arithmetically simpler.

The application of the actuarial after tax and investment period methods is illustrated in the following example:

Example 17.4

The terms of a lease are as in Example 17.2 above, i.e. a five year lease of an asset commences on 1 January 2001. The rental is £2,600 p.a. payable in advance. The fair value of the asset at lease inception is £10,000 and it is expected to have a residual at the end of the lease of £2,372 (being its tax written down value at the time) which will be passed to the lessee. In addition, the lessee is responsible for all maintenance and insurance costs.

The lessor obtains writing down allowances on the leased asset at the rate of 25%. The rate of corporation tax is 35%. The lessor's accounting year-end is 31 December and he pays or recovers tax in the following year. Interest on funds borrowed is assumed to be 10% p.a., payable on 31 December.

The lessor's net cash investment in this lease can be analysed as follows:

	(a) Net cash investment at start of year	(b) Cash flows in year cost/tax	(c) Cash flows in year rentals	(d) Average net cash investment in year	(e) Interest paid	(f) Profit taken out of lease	(g) Net cash investment at end of year
Year	£	£	£	£	£	£	£
2001	—	(10,000)	2,600	(7,400)	(740)	(277)	(8,417)
2002	(8,417)	224	2,600	(5,593)	(559)	(210)	(6,362)
2003	(6,362)	(58)	2,600	(3,820)	(382)	(144)	(4,346)
2004	(4,346)	(284)	2,600	(2,030)	(203)	(76)	(2,309)
2005	(2,309)	(470)	2,600	(179)	(18)	(7)	(204)
2006	(204)	204	–	–	–	–	–
		(10,000) (384)	13,000		(1,902)	(714)	

Notes to table:

(a)   net cash investment at start of year: this is simply zero at the beginning of the lease and the previous year-end figure in later years;

(b)   cash flows in year – cost and tax: the £10,000 outflow in 2001 is the purchase of the asset which is, for simplicity, assumed to take place on the day the lease commences. All other amounts relate to tax payable/repayable.

The basis of taxation of the lessor was detailed above and tax payable/repayable relates to the previous year's rentals receivable, interest paid and writing down allowance. The tax repayable in 2006 relates to 2005's rental receivable, interest paid, writing down allowance and the deduction relating to the passing of the asset's sales proceeds of £2,372 to the lessee. This deduction should actually enter the table in 2007, as that is when the tax repayment would arise from the sale in 2006, but is included in 2006 for simplicity. The sales proceeds and payment to the lessee are not shown as their net effect on the cash flows is nil;

(c)   cash flows in year – rentals: the annual rentals received at the beginning of each year;

(d)   average net cash investment in year: this is the sum of columns (a) to (c). For the purposes of this example, all cash flows are assumed to arise on 1 January of each year;

(e)   interest paid: calculated at 10% of the average net cash investment in year shown in column (d);

(f)   profit taken out of lease: this represents the amount required by the lessor to give a return on the lease over and above tax and interest costs. It is the percentage of the average net cash investment in year shown in column (d) which results in a net cash investment at the end of the whole transaction of zero. It can be found by trial and error but computer programs are usually used to do this. In this example the annual rate is 3.75%;

(g)   net cash investment at end of year: this is the sum of columns (d) to (f). It can be seen that this is zero at the end of the whole transaction.

The above analysis is performed under both the actuarial after tax and investment period methods. However, these methods then differ in their use of the table to give gross earnings allocated to the years of the lease.

The actuarial after tax method merely grosses up the profit taken out of lease figure for each year by the tax rate of 35% and adds interest paid to give gross earnings allocated to each year as follows:

Year	Profit taken out of lease £	Tax (35/65ths) £	Profit grossed up for tax £	Interest paid £	Allocated gross earnings £
2001	277	149	426	740	1,166
2002	210	113	323	559	882
2003	144	77	221	382	603
2004	76	41	117	203	320
2005	7	4	11	18	29
	714	384	1,098	1,902	3,000

In contrast the investment period method allocates a portion of total gross earnings (of £13,000 – £10,000) to each year in the proportion of the net cash investment at the relevant year-end to the total of such net cash investments as follows:

$$\text{Net cash investment at end of year} \times \frac{\text{Total gross earnings}}{\text{Sum of net cash investments}} = \text{Allocated gross earnings}$$

Year	Net cash investment at end of year £			Allocated gross earnings £
2001	8,417 }			1,167
2002	6,362 }			882
2003	4,346 }	x	$3,000 \div 21,638$ =	603
2004	2,309 }			320
2005	204 }			28
	21,638			3,000

It can be seen that the differences between the gross earnings allocated to each year by each method in this example are negligible. Under the assumption of 35% tax and 25% writing down allowances, both methods give similar results. The reason for this is that the lease never goes into surplus. If different assumptions are made about rates of tax and allowances, cash surpluses may arise in certain periods, and in these circumstances the actuarial after tax method and the investment period method yield different results. Using the former method, the interest received on the cash surplus (the reinvestment income) is brought back and recognised in the periods when the lessor has funds invested in the lease, rather than taken to income when it arises. Thus no profit is recognised in the period when the lease is in surplus. Because of this effect, the lessor may be in an exposed position in this period in the event, for example, of early termination of the lease by the lessee. If this method is used, it may therefore be necessary to make an appropriate provision for early termination losses so that the net investment in the lease does not exceed the termination value at any time. Under the investment period method, any reinvestment income is recognised when it arises; that is, it is not brought back and recognised in the periods in which the lessor has funds invested in the lease. Thus, where cash surpluses arise, the investment period method is more conservative than the actuarial after tax method.[65]

The above example is a simplified one, in that all cash payments and receipts have been assumed to have occurred on either the first or last day of the year. In practice, the calculations would have to reflect the actual timing of the cash payments and receipts; for example, if the rentals were received monthly then the calculations would be performed at monthly rests.

5.4.3   Assumptions

Although they differ in the way gross earnings are allocated, both the actuarial after tax and investment period methods use the same assumptions and process to calculate the net cash investment at the end of each relevant period (quarter/year etc.).

The major assumptions used in this calculation of net cash investment are as follows:

(a)   sufficient taxable capacity will exist to relieve any tax deductible expenses and capital allowances in the forecast period;

(b)   borrowing and reinvestment interest rates and levels of taxation will be as predicted;

(c)   defaults or termination of the lease will not occur;

(d)   administrative costs will be negligible.

If any of these assumptions ceases to hold, and the effect on the calculated allocation of gross earnings to accounting periods is material, then the calculations should be re-performed from the date when the change in assumptions takes place.

5.4.4   Other methods

Many variations of the actuarial after tax and investment period methods are found in practice owing to differences in treatment of certain elements, e.g. reinvestment income. Further, other methods exist of allocating gross earnings, e.g. the net earnings sum of the digits method allocates gross earnings to each period using the usual sum of the digits arithmetic (i.e. the balance is allocated to a period in proportion to the number of periods remaining).

5.4.5   Net investment or net cash investment

A lessor is concerned with both his net cash investment in a lease for allocating gross earnings to accounting periods and, also, his net investment for calculating the finance lease receivable in his balance sheet. These amounts are quite different in their calculation and use. As is explained at 5.5 below, owners under hire purchase contracts use the net investment in the contract for both of the above purposes.

The difference between net cash investment and net investment can be illustrated by way of the actuarial after tax figures in Example 17.4 above. The gross earnings given are deducted from total rentals in the year to give the reduction in net investment in that year. The opening net investment is simply the cost of the asset. This is shown as follows:

Example 17.5

Year	Total rentals £	Gross earnings £	Reduction in net investment £	Net investment at year end £
2000	–	–	–	10,000
2001	2,600	1,166	1,434	8,566
2002	2,600	882	1,718	6,848
2003	2,600	603	1,997	4,851
2004	2,600	320	2,280	2,571
2005	2,600	29	2,571	–
	13,000	3,000	10,000	

The net investment at each year-end will be the finance lease debtor amount shown by the lessor in the balance sheet.

The use in SSAP 21 of both net investment and net cash investment for finance leases, but not hire purchase contracts, was explained by the less important tax effects of hire purchase contracts compared to finance leases for lessors; essentially because finance lessors receive capital allowances, but owners under hire purchase contracts do not. The Finance Act 1984 reduced the importance of these tax effects by lowering capital allowance and corporation tax rates. It is now questionable whether the extra complexity of the net cash investment approach of allocating gross earnings by finance lessors is warranted.

It is perhaps noteworthy that until recently IAS 17 – *Accounting for Leases* – allowed a free choice of methods to recognise finance lease income.[66] However, with effect from 1 January 1999, this standard has been superseded by IAS 17 (revised) – *Leases* – which only permits the net investment method to be used.[67] IAS 17 (revised) is discussed at 8.1.2 below.

5.5 Allocation of gross earnings – hire purchase contracts

5.5.1 Introduction

As discussed above, the difference between the net investment and net cash investment in a lease relates to taxation and interest payable/receivable. SSAP 21 allows the use of a net investment method to allocate total gross earnings to accounting periods under those hire purchase contracts which are treated similarly to finance leases under SSAP 21 (the vast majority of them).[68] This is justified by the fact that capital allowances on an asset subject to a hire purchase contract usually accrue to the hirer. When SSAP 21 was introduced this meant that taxation was not such a major factor in the owner's evaluation of cash flows under a hire purchase contract as it was in the lessor's evaluation under a finance lease.

5.5.2   *Methodology*

There are two usual net investment methods of allocating gross earnings – the actuarial before tax method, and the sum of the digits ('rule of 78') method.[69]

The actuarial before tax method involves an analysis of the net investment in a contract for each period. The gross earnings percentage is then calculated such that when it is applied to the net investment figure in each period (to give a gross earnings allocation for each period) the net investment at the end of the lease/hire term is zero.

The sum of the digits method simply involves an apportionment of gross earnings over the hire purchase period in proportion to the number of future rentals receivable.

These methods usually ignore notional interest payments/receipts, with the result that the calculations are performed in exactly the same way as in Example 17.2 at 3.4 above in calculating the allocation of the finance charge for a lessee.

When considering hire purchase contracts it can be seen that the net investment in the lease/hire is used for both the allocation of gross earnings to accounting periods and the calculation of the lease/hire receivable in the owner's balance sheet. This contrasts with the position for finance leases (see 5.4.5 above).

5.5.3   *Choice of method*

The actuarial before tax method is the most accurate net investment method. Alternatives (the sum of the digits method or a simpler one, e.g. straight-line over the contract term) can be used where the differences in allocated gross earnings are immaterial.

6   DISCLOSURE BY LESSORS

6.1   SSAP 21 requirements

The following lessor disclosures are required by SSAP 21:

(a)   policies adopted for accounting for operating and finance leases and, in detail, the policy for accounting for finance lease income;[70]

(b)   aggregate rentals receivable in respect of the relevant accounting period from (i) finance leases and (ii) operating leases;[71]

(c)   if the provisions of SSAP 21 have not been applied retroactively to all leases existing at 1 July 1984, disclosure of the gross earnings from the finance leases and hire purchase contracts which have arisen under each of the methods used;[72]

(d)   net investment in (i) finance leases and (ii) hire purchase contracts;[73]

(e)   costs of assets acquired for the purpose of letting under finance leases and hire purchase contracts;[74]

(f)   gross amount of fixed assets held for use under operating leases, together with the related accumulated depreciation.[75]

6.2   Related Companies Act requirements

It is suggested in the Guidance Notes on SSAP 21 that the net investment in finance leases and hire purchase contracts should be included in current assets under the heading of debtors.[76] Accordingly, lessors who have to comply with Schedule 4 of the Companies Act, will have to comply with the requirement that 'the amount falling due after more than one year shall be shown separately for each item included under debtors'.[77]

There are a number of other disclosures required by the Companies Act which may affect lessors, and these should also be considered; e.g. details of fixed assets.[78] (This is relevant to assets leased under operating leases.)

6.3   Disclosure in practice

The following are examples of disclosures given in practice by lessors:

Extract 17.7: RMC Group p.l.c. (1998)

Accounting Policies

FINANCE LEASE RECEIVABLES

Income from finance leasing contracts, being the excess of total rentals received over the cost of the net investment in finance leasing contracts, is taken to profit in accordance with the investment period method of accounting in direct relationship to the reducing capital invested during the primary leasing period.

Amounts written off the net investment in such leases are calculated to write off the cost over the primary periods of the contracts.

Extract 17.8: HSBC Holdings plc (1998)

2   Principal accounting policies

f   *Finance and operating leases*

i   Assets leased to customers under agreements which transfer substantially all the risks and rewards associated with ownership, other than legal title, are classified as finance leases. Where the Group is a lessor under finance leases the amounts due under the leases, after deduction of unearned charges, are included in 'Loans and advances to banks' or 'Loans and advances to customers'. Finance charges receivable are recognised over the periods of the leases in proportion to the funds invested.

ii   Where the Group is a lessee under finance leases the leased assets are capitalised and included in 'Equipment, fixtures and fittings' and the corresponding liability to the lessor is included in 'Other liabilities'. Finance charges payable are recognised over the periods of the leases based on the interest rates implicit in the leases.

iii   All other leases are classified as operating leases and, where the Group is the lessor, are included in 'Tangible fixed assets'. Rentals payable and receivable under operating leases are accounted for on the straight line basis over the periods of the leases and are included in 'Administrative expenses' and 'Other operating income' respectively.

Extract 17.9: Rolls-Royce plc (1998)

Notes to the financial statements

1   Accounting policies

Accounting for leases [extract]

....

ii)   As lessor

Amounts receivable under finance leases are included under debtors and represent the total amount outstanding under lease agreements less unearned income. Finance lease income, having been allocated to accounting periods to give a constant periodic rate of return on the net cash investment, is included in turnover.

Rentals receivable under operating leases are included in turnover on an accruals basis.

Extract 17.10: Cable and Wireless plc (1999)

Notes to the accounts

18 Debtors [extract]

	Group	
	1999	1998
	£m	£m
Amounts falling due within one year		
Trade debtors (excluding securitised trade debtors)	**977**	811
Amounts owed by associates and joint ventures	**12**	18
Other debtors	**191**	396
Prepayments and accrued income	**385**	168
	1,565	1,393
Net securitised debtors	**121**	54
Amounts falling due after more than one year		
Other debtors	**60**	54
Prepayments and accrued income	**312**	85
Net investment in finance leases	**39**	39
	411	178
Total debtors	**2,097**	1,625
Net investment in finance leases comprises:		
Total lease payments receivable	**39**	39
Total rentals received during the year in respect of finance leases	**–**	2

A company within the Group is a limited partner in a number of limited partnerships which own and lease assets to third parties. Non recourse finance of £251m (1998 – £247m) has been offset, under paragraph 29 of FRS 5 – 'Reporting the Substance of Transactions', against the net investment in finance leases.

7 PROBLEM AREAS

7.1 Classification of leases

7.1.1 *Current practice*

The 90% test detailed in SSAP 21 (discussed at 2.1 above) appears to have, in the past, been used in practice by some companies as a fairly definitive test instead of being only one factor in deciding whether substantially all of the risks and rewards of ownership have been transferred to the lessee under a lease. However, it would seem that more recently companies have tended to follow an approach based on qualitative tests rather than merely rely on the 90% test.

Perhaps this is as a result of FRS 5 providing guidance on factors to be considered in establishing the economic substance of a transaction and influencing current thinking and practice towards adopting a more substance based approach to accounting.

7.1.2   Leasing as an off balance sheet transaction

It goes without saying that some lessees may prefer not to capitalise leased assets. This is because capitalisation adversely affects the lessee's gearing and return on assets. As a result, instances exist where leases are structured such that an operating lease treatment is permitted by SSAP 21 but, at least on certain interpretations, the substance of the lease is to provide a source of finance to the lessee.

Methods of achieving this typically involve use of the expected residual value of the leased asset because (based on our earlier outline of lease classification criteria) if this residual is significant and is not guaranteed by the lessee or a party related to him, then the lease is likely to be classified as an operating lease. Further, a lease may be structured such that the most likely outcome of events relating to the residual value indicates that no significant risk will attach to the lessee.

Example 17.6:   A lease structured such that the most likely outcome is that the lessee has no significant residual risk

Brief details of a motor vehicle lease are:

Fair value   –   £10,000

Rentals   –   20 monthly @ £275, followed by final of £2,000

At end of lease, lessee sells vehicle as agent for lessor, and if sold for

(i)   more than £3,000, 99% of excess is repaid to lessee; or

(ii)   less than £3,000, lessee pays deficit to lessor up to maximum of 0.4 pence per mile above 25,000 miles p.a. on average that the leased vehicle has done.

Therefore, as a result of (ii) above, this lease involves a guarantee of the residual value of the leased vehicle by the lessee of £3,000. However, the guarantee will only be called upon if both:

(a)   the vehicle's actual residual value is less than £3,000; and

(b)   the vehicle has travelled more than 25,000 miles per year on average over the lease term.

Further, the lessee is only liable to pay a certain level of the residual; namely, £100 for each 2,500 miles above 25,000 miles that the vehicle has done. It is arguable whether SSAP 21 intended that this guarantee should be treated similarly to a guarantee of £3,000 with no restrictions on when it will apply. One could argue that the guarantee should be assumed not to apply if experience or expectations of the sales price and/or the mileage that vehicles have done (and the inter-relationship between these) indicate that a residual payment by the lessee will not be made. On the other hand it could be said that the guarantee exists and therefore should be taken into account.

The treatment of the guarantee would obviously affect the 90% test and the overall consideration of factors which impinge on the risks and rewards of ownership.

7.2   Termination of leases

7.2.1   *Lease classification*

The expectations of lessors and lessees regarding the timing of termination of a lease may affect the classification of a lease as either operating or finance. This is because it will affect the expected lease term, level of payments under the lease and expected residual value of the lease assets.

Termination during the primary lease term will generally not be anticipated at the lease inception because the lessee can be assumed to be using the asset for at least that period. In addition, such an early termination will be unlikely because a termination payment is usually required which will give the lessor an amount equivalent to most or all of the rental receipts which would have been received if no such termination had taken place.

7.2.2   *Operating leases*

If a lease has been classified as an operating lease at its inception, then no major difficulty arises on a termination. Any termination payment due under the lease agreement will be accounted for as income when receivable by the lessor and as an expense when due by the lessee.

7.2.3   *Finance leases – lessee*

Early termination of a finance lease results in a disposal of the capitalised asset by the lessee. Any payment made by the lessee will reduce the lease obligation which is being carried in the balance sheet. If either a part of this obligation is not eliminated or the termination payment exceeds the previously existing obligation, then the remainder or excess will be included as a gain or loss (respectively) in calculating the total gain or loss arising on the disposal of the asset.

A similar accounting treatment is required where the lease terminates at the expected date and there is a residual at least partly guaranteed by the lessee. For the lessee, a payment made under such a guarantee will reduce the obligation to the lessor under the lease as the guaranteed residual would obviously be included in the lessee's finance lease obligation. If any part of the guaranteed residual is not called upon, then the lessee would eliminate it by transferring it to the calculation of gain/loss on disposal of the leased asset. The effect on the overall gain or loss will depend on the extent to which the lessee expected to make the residual payment as this will have affected the level to which the capitalised asset has been depreciated. For example, if the total guaranteed residual was not expected to become payable by the lessee, then he would have calculated the depreciation charge to give a net book value at the end of the lease term equal to the residual element not expected to become payable. If this estimate was correct then the remaining obligation will equal (and contra out) the net book value of the relevant asset.

Example 17.7

We can consider this in the context of Example 17.6 in 7.1.2 above, where there is effectively a guarantee of a residual of £3,000 dependent on the mileage done by the leased vehicle. Assuming that the lease is capitalised as a finance lease, if the lessee considers at the lease inception that the guarantee will not be called upon, then he will depreciate the vehicle to an estimated residual value of £3,000 over the lease term. In the event that his estimate is found to be correct, then the asset written down value will simply contra out with the lease obligation of £3,000. However, if, for example, £1,000 of the guarantee was called upon, whereas the lessee had estimated that it would not be, then the net book value of £3,000 and the unused guarantee of £2,000 will both be eliminated and a loss of £1,000 will be shown on disposal of the vehicle.

7.2.4 Finance leases – lessor

Any termination payment received by a lessor upon an early termination will reduce the lessor's net investment in the lease shown as a receivable. If the termination payment is greater than the previously shown net investment, then a profit on termination of the lease will be shown by the lessee. On the other hand, if the termination payment is smaller than the net investment, a loss will be shown. Such a loss is usually deducted from finance lease income unless exceptionally large, in which case it is separately disclosed.

Any loss on termination is unlikely to arise in most situations because a finance lease is likely to have termination terms such that the lessor is compensated fully for early termination and the lessor has legal title to the asset. Because he has title, the lessor can continue to include the asset in current assets as a receivable to the extent that sales proceeds or new finance lease receivables are expected to arise. If the asset is then re-leased under an operating lease, the asset may be transferred to fixed assets and depreciated over its remaining useful life.

To some extent, these two reasons for losses on termination of a finance lease not arising (full compensation and legal title remaining with the lessor) are complementary. If the termination payment is intended to give full compensation, then the asset may be retained by the lessee and sold with any proceeds going to him. On the other hand, if the termination payment is not structured in this way then the lessor will repossess the asset and sell or re-lease it.

7.3 Tax variation clauses

7.3.1 Introduction

The level of rentals in a lease is determined using the tax regime which exists at the time the lease terms are agreed. Tax variation clauses are common in finance leases and are designed to protect the lessor from any adverse changes in the capital allowance or corporation tax rates which the lessor has assumed will exist when the level of rentals is agreed. These may also apply where any tax changes operate to the lessor's benefit.

7.3.2 Adjustments

Where a tax variation clause takes effect the rental adjustment may be made via:

(a) lump sum payments as and when the lessor pays the new higher/lower tax charge for any period; or

(b) the future rentals including stepped increases or decreases to reflect the changes; or

(c) a new fixed rental being calculated to be paid over the remainder of the primary lease term.

7.3.3 Lessee

As regards the lessee, any change in total rentals payable represents an alteration to his remaining finance charges under a lease. These alterations should be accounted for by spreading the revised finance charges over the remaining lease term using the methods detailed at 3.4 above. However, in the possibly unusual circumstances of 7.3.2 (a) above, where the calculations of lump sum payments are not made until the relevant tax calculation is made by the lessor, then the altered rentals should be accounted for in the periods in which they arise. Although a constant rate of charge on the lessee's remaining liability will not result, this approach is justified because the lessee does not know what the future rentals will actually be.

Under either approach, if any reduction in rentals exceeds the finance charges which were expected to accrue, then the excess should be deducted from the capitalised cost such that future depreciation charges are lower than they would have been.[79] Negative finance charges are not permitted.[80]

7.3.4 Lessor

Any variations in taxation and rentals (due to a tax variation clause) which materially alter the lessor's analysis of net cash investment in the lease over its remaining term will alter the total of future gross earnings and also their allocation to accounting periods. This will therefore affect the reduction in net investment in the lease (shown as a receivable in the lessor's balance sheet) over its remaining term. The specifics of such an exercise are outside the scope of this Chapter.

7.4 Sale and leaseback transactions

7.4.1 Introduction

Such transactions involve the original owner of an asset selling it (usually to a finance house or a merchant bank) and immediately leasing it back. These parties will be termed the seller/lessee and buyer/lessor respectively. Sometimes, instead of selling the asset outright, the original owner will lease the asset to the other party under a finance lease and then lease it back. Such a transaction is known as a 'lease and leaseback' and has similar effects. The term 'sale and leaseback' is taken to include such a transaction.

Sale and leaseback transactions are a fairly common feature of an number of industries (such as the retail and hotel industries), where it is as accepted a form of financing as taking out a mortgage or a bank overdraft. However, from a commercial point of view, the important point of differentiation lies between an entity which decides that it is cheaper to rent than to own – and is willing to pass on the property risk to the landlord – and an entity which decides to use the property as a means of raising finance – and will therefore retain the property risk.

7.4.2 *Finance or operating lease?*

The buyer/lessor will treat the lease in the same way as he would any other lease which was not part of a sale and leaseback transaction.[81]

For the seller/lessee there are further considerations which may apply if the transaction has certain characteristics. He must first decide whether the leaseback transaction gives rise to an operating or finance lease in the normal way, i.e. the fact that he has sold the asset to the lessor is irrelevant for this purpose. The accounting consequences depend on this categorisation.

We discussed at 2 above the issues to be considered and the factors involved in determining the classification of a lease, including the fact that the general principles of FRS 5 are relevant in ensuring that a lease is classified as either finance or operating in accordance with its substance. These factors and considerations apply equally in the case of a sale and leaseback transaction. This means that, in order to enable the seller/lessee to derecognise the asset, recognise a profit (or loss) in his profit and loss account and account for the lease as an operating lease, he needs to ensure that substantially all the risks and rewards of ownership of the asset have passed to the buyer/lessor.

The ICAEW working party which reviewed SSAP 21 highlighted sale and leaseback as one of the areas where practical problems are encountered. In its report, the working party suggested that the problems manifest themselves in the fact that an owner of an asset may realise a profit on sale and continue to use the asset without retaining it on the balance sheet.[82] The report goes on to say that 'currently the conditions for removal of an existing owned asset from the balance sheet appear to differ in practice from those applying to capitalisation of an asset not previously owned by the lessee. A company wishing to acquire, say, an oil tanker may get a different answer depending upon whether it bought the oil tanker and then entered into a sale and leaseback transaction or whether it entered into a lease agreement in the first place. We believe this is wrong; we do not believe that there should be a difference between the conditions for recognition and for derecognition.'[83]

Consequently, the working party suggests that in order to determine whether or not the transaction should be recorded as a sale, six qualitative tests should be used as a guide in order to determine whether or not substantially all the risks and rewards of ownership have passed.[84] The six tests include the same tests as discussed at 2.3 above, and are as follows:

1. is the sale at market value?

2. are the lease rentals based on a market rate for use of the asset or a financing rate for use of the funds?

3. what is the nature of the lessor's business?

4. is the existence of put and call options a feature of the lease? If so, are they exercisable at a predetermined price or formula or are they exercisable at the market price at the time the option is exercised?

5. which party carries the risk of a fall in value of the asset and which party benefits from any capital appreciation?

6. does the lessee have the use of the asset for a period broadly equating to the likely useful economic life of the asset?

It is not altogether clear which 'general principles' of FRS 5 should be applied in ensuring that leases are classified as finance or operating leases in accordance with their substance, although presumably they will include both the principle of a lender's return and the requirement to consider the position of all the parties to a transaction, including their apparent expectations and motives for agreeing to its various terms. In any event, though, the above six tests may be helpful as a starting point in the process of identifying all the aspects and implications of a transaction.

7.4.3 Leaseback under a finance lease

It follows from the discussion at 7.4.2 above that where the leaseback is of a financing nature and the sales value is greater than the written down value, then this apparent profit should not be taken to profit and loss account at the time of the sale and leaseback.[85] This is because it would be inappropriate to show a profit on disposal of an asset which has then, in substance, been reacquired under a finance lease.

However, SSAP 21 is somewhat ambivalent about the way in which the sale and leaseback transaction should be presented in the balance sheet; two alternative presentations are suggested in the standard and guidance notes:

(a) the asset is treated as sold in the normal way except that the apparent profit should be deferred and taken to the profit and loss account over the lease term. The asset and the obligation under the lease are recorded at the sales value; or (b)	the asset remains in the seller/lessee's balance sheet at its previous book value and the sales proceeds are shown as a creditor. This creditor balance represents the finance lease liability under the leaseback. When lease payments are then made, they are treated partly as a repayment of that creditor, and partly as a finance charge to the profit and loss account (in the usual way for a finance lease).

Nevertheless, FRS 5 now states that the carrying value of the asset should not be adjusted in such a transaction and, accordingly, (a) above should no longer be regarded as an option.[86] This is because treatment (b) reflects the substance of the transaction, namely the raising of finance secured on an asset that continues to be held and is not disposed of.

If the sales value is less than the written down value, the apparent loss arising on the sale should again not be taken to the profit and loss account at the time of the sale and leaseback; the transaction should be accounted for in the same way as described in (b) above. However, if the low sales value demonstrates that a permanent diminution in value has occurred, this will result in an immediate write down in the profit and loss account.

If an asset which is carried at a revalued amount is sold and leased back under a finance lease, then the relevant revaluation reserve should continue to be treated in the way it was prior to the sale and leaseback. If the revaluation reserve is being transferred to profit and loss reserve, this should now be over the shorter of the lease term and the asset's remaining useful life in order that the period of transfer matches the depreciation term of the leased asset.

### 7.4.4	Sale and leasebacks involving options

The point has already been made that since SSAP 21 contains the more specific provisions governing lease accounting, one would look to that standard as the primary source of authoritative guidance concerning lease accounting – although the general principles of FRS 5 will also be relevant in ensuring that leases are classified as finance or operating leases in accordance with their substance. However, in the case of a sale and leaseback arrangement where there is also an option for the seller/lessee to repurchase the asset, the provisions of Application Note B of FRS 5 are more specific than those of SSAP 21 and should therefore be applied in determining the appropriate accounting for such a transaction.

Sale and leaseback deals can take a variety of forms, but the essential feature which is common to all of them is that the company which purports to have sold the asset in question has not disposed of all the risks and rewards associated with the asset in the manner expected of a normal sale. If there is no significant change in the company's access to the benefits of the asset and exposures to the risks inherent in those benefits, then the substance of the deal is that of a secured loan. In such circumstances, FRS 5 requires that the sale should not be recorded and the asset in question should remain on the company's balance sheet.

Thus the principal question to be answered is whether the reporting company has made a sale in substance, or whether the deal represents the raising of finance secured on an asset. In approaching this question, FRS 5 tells us to consider the positions of both the buyer and seller, together with their apparent expectations and motives for agreeing to the various terms of the arrangement. In particular, where the substance is that of a secured loan, the buyer will require that it is assured of a lender's return on its investment and the seller will require that the buyer earns no more than this return. Conversely, if the buyer is not assured of a lender's return, this indicates that some benefit and some risk have been passed to the buyer such that the seller has not retained the original asset. Therefore, whether or not the buyer earns such a return is an important indicator of the substance of the transaction.[87]

The second key factor in determining the substance of a sale and leaseback transaction relates to an evaluation of the commercial effect of the option(s). This may take the form of a put option allowing the buyer to resell the asset to the seller, a call option allowing the seller to repurchase the asset from the buyer, or a combination of these.

Where there is both a put and a call option in force on equivalent terms, it is clear that the asset will revert to the seller. Unless the option is to be exercised at the then market price of the asset in question, it must be in the interests of one or other of the parties to exercise his option so as to secure a profit or avoid a loss, and therefore the likelihood of the asset remaining the property of the buyer rather than reverting to the seller must be remote. However, the position is less clear where there is only a put option or a call option in force rather than a combination of the two.

Where there is only a put option, the effect will be (in the absence of other factors) that the seller/lessee has disposed of the rewards of ownership to the buyer/lessor but retained the risks. This is because the buyer will only exercise his option to put the asset back to the seller if its value at the time is less than the repurchase price payable under the option. This means that if the asset continues to rise in value the buyer will keep it and reap the benefits of that enhanced value; conversely if the value of the asset falls, the option will be exercised and the downside on the asset will be borne by the seller.

This analysis does not of itself answer the question of whether the deal should be treated as a sale or as a financing transaction. The overall commercial effect will still have to be evaluated, taking account of all the terms of the arrangement and by considering the motivations of both of the parties in agreeing to the various terms of the deal; in particular it will need to be considered why they have each agreed to have this one-sided option.

Where there is only a call option, the position will be reversed. In this case, the seller has disposed of the risks, but retained the rewards to be attained if the value of the asset exceeds the repurchase price specified in the option. Once again, though, the overall commercial effect of the arrangement has to be evaluated in deciding how to account for the deal. Emphasis has to be given to what is likely to happen in practice, and it is instructive to look at the arrangement from the point of view of both parties to see what their expectations are and what has induced them to accept the deal on the terms which have been agreed. It may be obvious from the overall terms of the arrangement that the call option will be exercised, in which case the deal will again be a financing arrangement and should be accounted for as such. For example, the exercise price of the call option may be set at a significant discount to expected market value, the seller may need the asset to use on an ongoing basis in its business, or the asset may provide in effect the only source of the seller's future income.[88] Similarly, the financial effects of *not* exercising the option (such as continued exposure to escalating costs) may sometimes make it obvious that the option will be exercised. But in other cases, it could be quite likely that the option will not be exercised and if this is the case the transaction could be treated as a sale.

The following is an example of a sale and leaseback deal where the seller has a call option to repurchase the asset but has no commitment to do so:

Example 17.8: Sale and leaseback transaction involving escalating rentals and call options

Company S sells a property to Company B for £100,000,000 and leases it back on the following terms:

Rental for years 1 to 5	£3,900,000 per annum
Rental for years 6 to 10	£5,875,000 per annum
Rental for years 11 to 15	£8,830,000 per annum
Rental for years 16 to 20	£13,280,000 per annum
Rental for years 21 to 25	£19,970,000 per annum
Rental for years 26 to 30	£30,025,000 per annum
Rental for years 31 to 35	£45,150,000 per annum
Rental thereafter	open market rent

Rentals are payable annually in advance.

Company S has the right to buy back the property at the following dates and prices:

At the end of year 5	£125,000,000
At the end of year 10	£150,000,000
At the end of year 15	£168,000,000
At the end of year 20	£160,000,000
At the end of year 25	£100,000,000

Company B has no right to put the property back to Company S.

An analysis of the economics of this deal suggests that whilst Company S has no legal obligation to repurchase the property, there is no genuine commercial possibility that the option will not be exercised. This is because the rentals and option prices are structured in such a way as to give the buyer of the property a lender's return whilst, at the same time, there is no commercial logic for the seller not to exercise the option at year 25, if not earlier. Exercising the option at the end of year 25 will mean that Company S will regain ownership of the property and will have had the use of the £100,000,000 at an effective rate of approximately 8.2% per annum; failure to exercise the option will mean additional lease obligations of £375,875,000 over the ten years from years 25 to 35, followed by the obligation to pay market rents thereafter.

The 1994 accounts of Forte revealed that the group had in the past entered into sale and leaseback transactions involving escalating rentals and call options. As can be seen from the following extract, these transactions were accounted for by Forte as operating leases:

Extract 17.11: Forte Plc (1994)

Financial Review [extract]

Sale, leaseback and repurchase agreements

Details of the sale, leaseback and repurchase arrangements the Company has entered into are set out in note 29 to the Accounts. These arrangements affect a limited proportion of the properties operated by the Company. The leases are for between 20 and 30 years and may be renewed by the Company at prevailing market rates. The lessors have no rights to require repurchase.

The rentals paid under these leases currently amount to £37m per year and are approximately covered by the current earnings from the leased properties. Over the remaining periods of the leases the rental costs will not rise significantly in real terms and it can reasonably be expected that they will continue to be financed by the income from the properties concerned.

Notes to the Accounts

29 Commitments [extract]

Sale and leaseback agreements

In the normal course of its activities, the Group has entered into a number of sale and leaseback agreements, which include options for the Group to repurchase the leased properties. The current agreements were entered into during the period between 1986 and 1992 and gave rise to sale proceeds amounting to £480m. The leases have durations of between 20 and 30 years but may be renewed at the Group's option. The lessors have no rights to require repurchase by the Group. Under current accounting practice, these leases are treated as operating leases and the profit and loss account is charged with the rental payments made in each accounting period.

During the year ended 31 January 1994 the profit before rent from the properties concerned amounted to £34m and the total rental payments amounted to £37m. The present value of the average future rental payments under these leases amounts to £39m per annum (assuming the continuation of current interest rates for leases with variable rental clauses).

Although these sale and leaseback agreements were entered into prior to the implementation of FRS 5, there are one or two observations that can be made about them. First, it is noteworthy that whilst these leases were being accounted for as operating leases, the lease rentals were being charged to the profit and loss account as incurred and not, as is required by SSAP 21, on a straight-line basis. Second, taking the fact that the rental payments exceed the profit before rent from the properties together with Forte's assumption relating to current interest rates, it seems that rentals were linked to market interest rates and did not necessarily reflect market rentals. This might suggest that the leases had been structured in such a way that the lessors received no more than a lender's return, indicating that the substance of the transactions may have been that of a financing.

This, in fact, did prove to be the case as, following the implementation of FRS 5, a substantial proportion of these assets were brought back on balance sheet – as explained in Forte's 1995 accounts:

Extract 17.12: Forte Plc (1995)

Financial Review [extract]

Lease and sale and leaseback arrangements

We reported last year that the accounting authorities were introducing new procedures for accounting for sale and leaseback agreements – which have been a traditional form of financing in the hotel industry. During the year a new accounting standard, called Financial Reporting Standard No. 5 ('FRS5'), was issued which changed the basis on which leased properties are accounted for. Certain leasing arrangements which were previously accounted for as operating leases are now required to be treated as finance leases – with the lease obligations treated as a type of debt and the leased properties treated as assets in our own accounts. Following a detailed review of these accounting requirements, and the Company's leasing agreements, we have decided that certain lease and sale and leaseback agreements will now be accounted for on this basis.

The relevant assets (amounting to £415m) and the associated future obligations (amounting to £475m) have been included on the balance sheet. As required under the accounting rules, this has been done by way of a prior year adjustment and last year's figures have been restated on the new basis.

In the profit and loss account, an additional non-cash charge of £10m (1994 – £10m) has also been provided, representing the difference between rents payable under these agreements (previously accounted for as rentals charged against operating profits) and the financing cost under FRS5, accounted for as interest payable evenly over the period of the leases. The rents payable and the additional charge, amounting to £44m are now also treated as a financing cost.

This accounting will not give rise to any changes in the Company's cash flow. The leases involved generally have substantial periods to run before they expire and in practice the issue of possible repurchase will not generally arise for an average of at least fifteen years.

Notes to the Accounts

18   Lease and sale and leaseback agreements [extract]

In the normal course of its activities, in the period 1986 to 1992 the Group entered into a number of lease agreements and sale and leaseback agreements, which include options for the Group to acquire or repurchase the relevant properties.

FRS5 became effective during the current financial year and changes the basis on which leases are accounted for so that certain leases which were previously regarded as being operating leases are now required to be treated as finance leases.

Following a detailed review of the accounting requirements under FRS5 and the Group's leasing arrangements, it has been decided that certain sale and leaseback agreements will now be accounted for as finance leases. The original proceeds under these agreements were £407m. The agreements are secured on specific hotels and restaurants with a primary duration of 30 years and are renewable thereafter. The Group has options to repurchase the properties at varying intervals with the lessors having no rights to require repurchase. The relevant fixed assets, together with the associated future obligations have been included on the balance sheet by way of a prior year adjustment.

The hotel and restaurant properties under these agreements have been stated in the Group balance sheet as at 31 January 1994 at £430m, being fair market value.

It is interesting to note from these disclosures that the original proceeds which Forte received under these sale and leaseback agreements which were brought back on balance sheet were £407m – yet future lease obligations of £475m were required to be recognised on the balance sheet. This must raise at least some doubt as to whether Forte had disposed of all the risks associated with the assets at the time the original transactions were entered into.

The accounting for sale and leaseback transactions is an area where the Financial Reporting Review Panel has shown some interest. In February 1997, the Review Panel issued a Press Notice which explained that the 1995 and 1996 accounts of Associated Nursing Services plc (ANS) had been under consideration in respect of two matters – one of which related to the accounting treatment of a sale and leaseback transaction. The transaction at issue involved a 25 year lease, renewable for a further 25 years, and a call option held by ANS. The Review Panel's view (which the directors finally accepted after extended discussions with the Panel) was that the nature of the sale and leaseback transaction was such that not all the significant rights or other access to benefits relating to the asset in question and not all the significant exposure to the risk inherent in those benefits had been transferred to the purchaser. Consequently, in accordance with FRS 5, the asset should have remained on the balance sheet and the sale proceeds should have been included in borrowings. As a result of this Review Panel decision, the directors of ANS issued revised accounts. Interestingly enough, the 1999 accounts of ANS show an accounting policy for sale and leaseback arrangements:

Extract 17.13: Associated Nursing Services plc (1999)

Notes to the financial statements

1. Accounting Policies

k) Sale and Leaseback Arrangements

The Group has entered into certain sale and leaseback transactions whereby the risks and rewards of ownership of the assets concerned have not been substantially transferred to the lessor. In accordance with SSAP 21 and FRS 5 the assets subject to these sale and leaseback transactions have been retained on the Group's balance sheet and the proceeds of sale are included within creditors as liabilities under sale and leaseback arrangements. The rent payable by the Group throughout the term of the lease is apportioned first as a partial repayment of the related liabilities and, secondly, as interest charged to profits.

Any increase in rent under the terms of the lease will be charged to profit.

The fixed assets subject to the sale and leaseback arrangements are depreciated on a straight line basis over the period of the initial lease term.

7.4.5 Leaseback under an operating lease

Where a lessee enters into a sale and leaseback transaction which results in an operating lease then (1) the original asset should be treated as having been sold, and (2) the operating lease should be accounted for under the provisions of the standard (see 3.6 above).

Where the transaction is established at the fair value of the asset concerned, then any profit or loss on the sale of the asset should be recognised immediately.[89] Where the transaction is not based on the fair value of the asset, then the accounting treatment is best explained by the schedule, as shown below, which uses the following three amounts:

(a)   WDV :   the written down value of the asset prior to its sale by the seller/lessee;

(b)   SV   :   the sales value at which the asset is sold to the buyer/lessor; and

(c)   FV   :   the fair value of the asset, i.e. the price it would fetch if sold in an arm's length transaction to a third party (not as part of a sale and leaseback transaction).

Schedule of possibilities:[90]

1.   SV<WDV<FV   Loss (WDV–SV) recognised immediately unless lease rentals are below normal levels when it should be deferred and amortised.

2.   SV<FV<WDV   Loss based on fair value (WDV–FV) recognised immediately. Balance (FV–SV) should also be recognised immediately unless lease rentals are below normal levels when it should be deferred and amortised.

3.   WDV<SV<FV   Profit (SV–WDV) recognised immediately.

4.   WDV<FV<SV   Profit based on fair value (FV–WDV) recognised immediately. Balance (SV–FV) deferred and amortised.

5.   FV<WDV<SV   Loss based on fair value (WDV–FV) recognised immediately. Profit (SV–FV) deferred and amortised.

6.   FV<SV<WDV   Loss based on fair value (WDV–FV) recognised immediately. Profit (SV–FV) deferred and amortised.

Where any amounts are to be deferred and amortised, this should be done evenly over the shorter of the lease term and the period to the next lease rental review.

Transactions in categories 5 and 6 above are, essentially, dealt with in two stages. The asset is first written down to fair value because the asset is treated as having been sold for that amount; second, the excess of sales value over the fair value is treated as only an apparent profit, which is deferred and amortised.

The rationale behind the above treatments is that if the sales value is not based on fair values, then it is likely that the normal market rents will have been adjusted to compensate. Accordingly, the transaction should be recorded as if it had been based on fair values. However, this will not always be the case:

(a)   where the fair value is above the written down value of the asset it is possible for the seller/lessee to arrange for the sales value to be anywhere within that range and report a gain in the year of sale based on that sales value. Any compensation which the seller/lessee obtains by way of reduced rentals will be reflected in later years; and

(b)   where the sales value is less than fair value there may be legitimate reasons for this to be so, e.g. where the seller has had to raise cash quickly. In such situations, as the rentals under the lease have not been reduced to compensate, the profit or loss should be based on the sales value.

7.5 Income recognition by lessors

The ICAEW working party that reviewed SSAP 21 expressed particular concern about the standard's general lack of guidance concerning income recognition by lessors.[91] However, the working party believed that the basic rules for inter-period profit allocation, using the net cash investment as the key parameter, to be sound and that they were not the cause of the variety of accounting by lessors which may be found in practice. Instead, the working party believed that the problems related primarily to the definition and treatment of 'initial direct costs' which may effectively be deferred (that is, costs may be deferred or profit may be accelerated) and to the assessment and accounting treatment of residual values.[92]

7.5.1 Initial direct costs

Initial direct costs are defined in SSAP 21 as being 'those costs incurred by the lessor that are directly associated with negotiating and consummating leasing transactions, such as commissions, legal fees, costs of credit investigations and costs of preparing and processing documents for new leases acquired'.[93] The Guidance Notes on SSAP 21 make the point that this definition is not intended to exclude salespersons' costs.[94]

This means that in practice, initial direct costs may be variously interpreted as being limited to brokers' commissions or extended to encompass overhead costs sometimes tenuously attributed to the sales and new business departments of the leasing operation. The working party suggested that the definition should be drawn more restrictively so that costs that do not automatically reduce on a fall in levels of new business are excluded from the category of costs which may be effectively deferred.[95]

As far as the accounting for the initial direct costs is concerned, the Guidance Notes state that initial direct costs may be apportioned over the lease term on a systematic basis (or may be written off immediately). The same effect as apportioning the costs over the lease term may be achieved by either (a) treating the costs as a deduction from the total gross earnings before the latter are allocated to accounting periods or (b) recognising sufficient gross earnings in the first year to cover the costs. In the case of an operating lease initial direct costs may also either be written off immediately or be deferred and amortised over the lease term.[96]

In July 1990 the Equipment Leasing Association (ELA) issued guidance to its members on income recognition. As part of the guidance, the ELA stated that 'it is assumed that a lessor will enter into a lease only if the overall transaction is such as to produce a profit after allowing for all expenses in setting up the lease, the costs of carrying the asset, and the cost of collecting the rental income. The income and expenses taken together should be accounted for in such a way that the lease does not move into a loss position at any stage after Year 1 during the primary lease period, having regard to all factors such as credit risk."[97]

In the light of this, the ICAEW working party stated in its report that it believed that in addition to restricting the definition of initial direct costs, the principle referred to above should, in respect of finance leases, be reflected in a future standard on leasing.[98] We concur with this view, and believe that any revised standard on leasing should, at absolute minimum, specifically prohibit a lessor from recognising a profit in early years and losses in later years in respect of the same lease.

7.5.2   *Residual values*

The collapse in April 1990 of Atlantic Computers highlighted the fact that there are major practical problems in relation to the estimation of residual values. Whether or not these problems are entirely due to an absence of definitive guidance in accounting standards is a moot point. An alternative view might be that a number of problems have arisen as a result of lessors being less than prudent in setting residual values by not paying sufficient regard to all the commercial risks involved.   Nevertheless, the ICAEW working party recommended that a revised leasing standard 'should define residual value and provide guidance on the practical issues in accounting for residual values. It should provide guidance on the re-evaluation of residuals and how upward and downward adjustments should be respectively treated in the profit and loss account.'[99]

Whilst such guidance will be undoubtedly helpful, it may also be necessary to require lessors to provide considerably more disclosure in their accounts relating to residual values. These might include disclosures concerning assumptions, sensitivities, comparisons between aggregate residuals by category of asset compared with independently compiled statistics, etc.

7.6   Manufacturers/dealers

7.6.1   *Introduction*

A manufacturer or dealer (M/D) in assets may offer customers the option of either outright purchase or rental of the assets. Where a rental agreement is such that it comes within the definition of an operating lease, then the M/D should not recognise a selling profit.[100] Where, on the other hand, a rental agreement is such that it comes within the definition of a finance lease (as substantially all the risks and rewards of ownership have passed), then there can be seen to be two elements of the M/D's overall profit or loss on the transaction. These are:

(a)   the selling profit or loss at the inception of the lease which is equivalent to the profit or loss that would arise on an outright sale made under an arm's length transaction; and

(b)   the gross earnings received by the M/D as lessor under the finance lease.

7.6.2   *Allocating the total profit of the manufacturer/dealer*

If the M/D is in the (relatively unlikely) position of incurring an overall loss because the total rentals receivable under the finance lease are less than the cost of the asset to the M/D, then the prudence concept dictates that this loss should be taken to the profit and loss account at the inception of the lease. If an overall profit is made, then an allocation between the selling profit and lessor's gross earnings must be made.

Racal Electronics is an example of a company which discloses a manufacturer/lessor policy:

Extract 17.14: Racal Electronics Plc (1999)

Statement of Accounting Policies

3   Turnover

Turnover represents invoiced sales (net of sales related taxes) by the Group to outside customers and in the case of long term contracts an estimate of the selling value of work done. The equivalent sales value of equipment sold under a finance lease arrangement is included in turnover. Revenue from equipment leased to customers under operating leases is recorded as turnover in equal amounts over the life of the leases.

In those situations where the customer is offered the choice of paying the cash price for the asset immediately or paying for it on deferred credit terms then, as long as the credit terms are the M/D's normal terms, the cash price can be used for determining the selling profit. However, in many cases such an approach should not be followed as the terms of the lease are often influenced by the M/D's marketing considerations. For example, a car dealer may offer 0% finance deals instead of reducing the normal selling price of his cars. It would be wrong in this instance for the dealer to record a profit on the sale of the car and no finance income under the lease.

It is not appropriate to take a 'normal' level of selling profit if the gross earnings under the finance lease would then be lower than normally expected. This is because the selling profit is taken to the profit and loss account at the lease inception and, if it is partly offset by lower than normal gross earnings under the lease, prudence dictates that this be taken into account. The correct practice is, therefore, to calculate gross earnings under the finance lease at the normal level, with any remaining element of the overall profit being taken as selling profit at the lease inception.

How then should the appropriate level of gross earnings under the finance lease be estimated? This clearly depends on the estimated interest rate implicit in the lease. In some situations the M/D will have a normal implicit interest rate based on his other leasing activity. However, in other situations where the M/D does not conduct other leasing business, an estimate will have to be made of the implicit rate for such leasing activity.

7.7   Sub-leases and back-to-back leases

7.7.1   Introduction

Situations arise where there are more parties to a lease arrangement than simply one lessor and one lessee. The discussion below relates to situations involving an original lessor, an intermediate party and an ultimate lessee. The intermediate party may be acting either as both a lessee and lessor of the asset concerned or, alternatively, as an agent of the lessor in the transaction.

Both sub-leases and back-to-back leases involve the intermediate party acting as both lessor and lessee of the asset. The difference between the two arrangements is that, for a back-to-back lease, the terms of the two lease agreements match to a greater extent than would be the case for a sub-lease arrangement. This difference is really only one of degree, and the important decision to be made concerns whether the arrangement is one of agency or, rather, the intermediate party is acting as both lessee and lessor in two related but independent transactions.

7.7.2   The original lessor and the ultimate lessee

The accounting treatment adopted by these parties will not be affected by the existence of sub-leases or back-to-back leases. The original lessor has an agreement with the intermediate party which is not affected by any further leasing of the assets by the intermediate party unless the original lease agreement is thereby replaced.

Similarly, the ultimate lessee has a lease agreement with the intermediate party. He will have use of the asset under that agreement and must make a decision, in the usual way, as to whether the lease is of a finance or operating type per SSAP 21.

7.7.3   The intermediate party

The appropriate accounting treatment by the intermediate party depends on the substance of the series of transactions. This turns on whether the intermediate party is acting either as an agent/broker for the original lessor or as a principal in both transactions. In the latter case, the intermediate party will act as lessee to the original lessor and lessor to the ultimate lessee.

In determining the role of the intermediate party, the question of recourse is important. If the ultimate lessee defaults on his lease obligations (for whatever reason), does the original lessor have recourse against the intermediate party for the outstanding payments under the lease?

Another important factor in the decision of how the intermediate party should account for the transaction is what happens if the original lessor defaults, e.g. through his insolvency. If the intermediate party is merely a broker/agent, then he will suffer no loss upon such default, and the ultimate lessee would only have a claim against the original lessor.

If these factors indicate that the intermediate party is acting merely as a broker or agent for the original lessor, he should not include any asset or obligation relating to the leased asset in his balance sheet. The income received by such an intermediary should be taken to profit and loss account on a systematic and rational basis.[101]

If, on the other hand, the intermediate party is taken to be acting as both lessee and lessor in two independent although related transactions, he should recognise his assets and obligations under finance leases in the normal way.

The recognition of income as lessor will be affected by the lease from the original lessor. Clearly, if the intermediate party had purchased the asset concerned outright, then his income recognition as a lessor would be on the usual net cash investment basis explained in 5.3 above. However, as he has obtained use of the asset under a finance lease, his income recognition will be based on the net investment in the lease. This is because the intermediate party's investment in the leased asset will be shown as the present value of the minimum lease payments, as reduced throughout the lease by the capital portion of total rental payable to the original lessor. In other words, there are no major tax consequences of the lease from the original lessor. The net investment approach to income recognition used for hire purchase contracts will therefore be appropriate (see 5.5 above).

It should not be inferred from the above discussion that all situations encountered can be relatively easily allocated as one of either a broker/agent or lessee/lessor in nature. In practice this is unlikely to be the case, as the risks and rewards will probably be spread between the parties involved. This is especially likely where more than the three parties discussed above are involved. In all cases, it is a question of judgement as to whether substantially all the risks and rewards from an asset attach to any party under the leases.

An illustration of the difficulties associated with transactions involving sub-leases can be found in the 1993 accounts of British Aerospace (BAe), which revealed for the first time the full extent of the seemingly significant financial risks that the group had been taking in order to sustain its civil aircraft manufacturing operations, including those associated with its participation in Airbus Industrie.

It has now become apparent that the bulk of BAe's commercial aircraft sales made in the 1980s were to banks and not airlines. It is understood that the banks then leased the aircraft back to BAe under 15 to 20 year agreements, and BAe leased the aircraft to airlines under sub-leases of between three and five years. The result was that the group was exposing itself to the risk of substantial losses if those sub-leases were not renewed. However, with the backdrop of a highly buoyant market in second-hand aircraft in the 1980s, this risk was presumably considered to be low, and deals of this nature were apparently common practice amongst commercial aircraft manufacturers. Furthermore, even when BAe did sell aircraft directly to airlines, the group often provided guarantees on leases which the airlines themselves entered into with banks.

Consequently, when the recession hit the travel industry following the Gulf War, the demand for second-hand commercial aircraft collapsed and the risks became a reality. The result was that BAe was faced with significant exposure to third party guarantees and other recourse obligations, as was evidenced in its 1996 accounts:

Extract 17.15: British Aerospace Public Limited Company (1996)

Notes to the Accounts

1   Accounting policies [extract]

Aircraft financing

The Group is exposed to actual and contingent liabilities arising from commercial aircraft financing, both from financing arranged directly by the Group and from that arranged by third parties where the Group has provided guarantees or has other recourse obligations. Provision for these risks is made on a systematic basis at the time of sale, having regard to the ability to re-lease or re-sell the underlying aircraft.

20 Commercial aircraft financing

Commercial aircraft are frequently sold for cash with the manufacturer retaining some financial exposure either by guaranteeing a minimum residual value of the aircraft at some date in the future or through the arrangement of lease finance on extended terms, which may include guarantees back to the manufacturer in the event of default by the lessee (the operator).

The following paragraphs summarise the actual and contingent liabilities of the Group in relation to Regional Jets, Turboprops and Airbus aircraft which arise from 1996 and prior year sales involving the types of financing arrangements described above.

Regional Jets and Turboprop aircraft

Aircraft financing commitments

Aircraft finance arranged by the Group may involve selling the aircraft to a third party lessor and leasing it back under an operating lease, the head lease. The aircraft are then leased under a sub-lease to an operator (the lessee) and it is not uncommon for an aircraft to be leased to several lessees during the period of the head lease. The commitment of the Group in respect of these head lease rental payments, which relate to sales in prior years, is set out below:

	1996 £m	1995 £m
Head lease commitments on operating leases		
At 1st January	1,373	1,543
New commitments entered into	–	10
Commitments paid off	(147)	(171)
Foreign exchange and interest movements	–	(9)
Reclassified aircraft	(36)	–
At 31st December	1,190	1,373
Payments due under head leases		
In one year or less	143	143
Between one and five years	521	517
In later years	526	713
	1,190	1,373

Aircraft contingent liabilities

Aircraft finance arranged by the Group may also involve selling the aircraft to third parties who lease the aircraft to operators; again this may be to several operators during the life of the aircraft. The risks and benefits associated with the operator lease payments and the residual values of the aircraft rest with the third parties. However, the Group may give guarantees in respect of certain head lease and finance payments to be made by those third parties. Sales are also made directly to operators and this may involve the Group guaranteeing certain head lease and finance payments on behalf of those operators.

In the event of the guarantees to third parties or operators described above being called, the Group's exposure would be offset by future sub-lease rentals and the residual values of the related aircraft.

Provision for financing commitments and contingent liabilities

The following table sets out the Group's exposure to the above head lease financing commitments and contingent liabilities. Provision for these risks has been made in the accounts on a net present value basis.

	1996 £m	1995 £m
Head lease commitments, as above	1,190	1,373
Finance leases on balance sheet	20	86
Aircraft contingent liabilities	1,726	1,766
	2,936	3,225
Contracted sub-lease income	(1,051)	(1,091)
Obligations less contracted income	1,885	2,134
Expected sub-lease income and residual aircraft values	(1,203)	(1,376)
Net risk	682	758
Adjustment to reduce to net present value	(163)	(173)
Recourse provision (note 19)	519	585

Head lease commitments (£1,190 million) arise from sale and operating leaseback transactions, which were entered into in prior years, and continue to reduce as existing obligations are paid off. As described above, these represent the amounts payable by the Group under head leases in future years.

Finance leases on balance sheet (£20 million) are the liability the Group has for aircraft held under finance leases. The decrease from 1995 arises from the restructuring of certain aircraft leases.

Aircraft contingent liabilities (£1,726 million) represent the exposure arising from transactions where the head lease obligations and finance payments of third parties have been guaranteed by the Group.

Contracted sub-lease income (£1,051 million) represents the outturn value of contracted lease income and takes into account the income due on these contracts to the first contractual right of an operator to return an aircraft. In many instances customers do not exercise such rights and will continue to lease aircraft to the full contractual term. Where anticipated, this additional income has been classified within expected sub-lease income.

Expected sub-lease income and residual aircraft values (£1,203 million) represent the amounts anticipated from extensions to existing contracted sub-leases and assumed future aircraft sub-leases on aircraft where the Group has a recourse exposure, and the anticipated market values of aircraft at the expiry of their head lease term based upon independent professional advice. The level of expected income has been calculated on a systematic basis, taking into account current and expected future market conditions, remarketing and other costs.

Given the long term nature of the liabilities, the Directors believe it is appropriate to state the recourse provision at its net present value. The *adjustment to reduce to net present value (£163 million)* reduces the expected liabilities described above from their outturn amounts to their anticipated net present value.

Residual value guarantees

In addition to the above, in some cases aircraft have been sold for cash with the transaction supported by a residual value guarantee. The majority of sales in 1996 were for cash with residual values guarantees given by the Group for values at specific dates in the future. At 31st December, 1996 the Group had given residual value guarantees for 52 aircraft totalling some £360 million (1995 20 aircraft, £160 million).

Based upon independent professional advice, the Directors believe that the Group's exposure to these guarantees is covered by the residual values of the related aircraft.

Airbus

The Group is involved in similar transactions through its participation in Airbus Industrie. Provision for the net exposure is included in the accounts of Airbus Industrie and included within the Group's share of the results of Airbus Industrie.

Although not part of UK GAAP at that time, it is noteworthy that the BAe Directors considered it appropriate to state the recourse provision at its net present value. Of course, both the ASB and IASC have issued standards (FRS 12 and IAS 37 respectively) that now require provisions to be measured at the present value of the expenditures expected to be required to settle the obligation.[102]

The group's 1998 accounts still show significant financial exposures as a result of its commercial aircraft financing arrangements; however, these are greatly lessened by the group having insured against a large proportion of the risk:

Extract 17.16: British Aerospace Public Limited Company (1998)

Notes to the Accounts

20 Commercial aircraft financing [extract]

Commercial aircraft are frequently sold for cash with the manufacturer retaining some financial exposure. Aircraft financing commitments of the Group can be categorised as either direct or indirect. Direct commitments arise where the Group has sold the aircraft to a third party lessor and then leased it back under an operating lease (or occasionally a finance lease) prior to an onward lease to an operator. Indirect commitments (contingent liabilities) may arise where the Group has sold aircraft to third parties who either operate the aircraft themselves or lease the aircraft on to operators. In these cases the Group may give guarantees in respect of the residual values of the related aircraft or certain head lease and finance payments to be made by either the third parties or the operators. The Group's exposure to these commitments is offset by future lease rentals and the residual value of the related aircraft.

During 1998, an external review was commissioned of the likely income to be generated from the portfolio of aircraft to which the Group has either direct or indirect financing exposures. This review identified a most likely level of income of some £2.4 billion. Following this analysis, in September 1998, the Group entered into arrangements which have reduced its exposure from commercial aircraft financing by obtaining insurance cover from a syndicate of leading insurance companies over a significant proportion of the contracted and expected income stream from the aircraft portfolio including those aircraft where the Group has provided residual value guarantees. At the start of the insurance arrangements a minimum level of income of £2.2 billion was underwritten.

As a consequence the net exposure of the Group to aircraft financing has been reduced by the insured amount and as at 31 December 1998 was:

	1998 £m	1997 £m
Direct operating lease commitments	854	1,012
Direct finance lease commitments	6	8
Indirect exposure through aircraft contingent liabilities	1,481	1,530
Exposure to residual value guarantees	504	420
Income guaranteed through insurance arrangements	(2,053)	-
Net exposure	792	2,970
Expected income not covered by insurance arrangements	(43)	(2,253)
Expected income on aircraft delivered post insurance arrangements	(99)	-
Adjustment to net present value	(160)	(181)
Recourse provision	490	536

Income guaranteed through insurance arrangements represents the future income stream from the aircraft assets guaranteed under the insurance arrangements after deducting the policy excess.

The external review identified likely income of £250 million above the level guaranteed under the insurance arrangements. *Expected income not covered by insurance arrangements and on aircraft delivered post insurance arrangements* represents the amount of this income assumed by management for the purpose of provisioning.

Given the long term nature of the liabilities, the Directors believe it is appropriate to state the recourse provision at its net present value. The provision covers costs to be incurred over a forecast period of 14 years from the balance sheet date. The *adjustment to net present value* reduces the expected liabilities from their outturn amounts to their anticipated net present value.

8   COMPARISON WITH IASC AND US PRONOUNCEMENTS

8.1   IASC

8.1.1   *The original IAS 17*

IAS 17 – *Accounting for Leases* –was issued in September 1982 for accounting periods beginning on or after 1 January 1984.[103] Its basic requirements were similar to those of SSAP 21. A finance lease was defined as one that 'transfers substantially all the risks and rewards incident to ownership of an asset'.[104] Examples of situations where a lease would normally be classified as a finance lease were given, one of which was a 'present value test', but this did not make any reference to a specific percentage, such as the 90% mentioned in SSAP 21.

The original IAS 17 allowed lessors accounting for finance leases to recognise finance income to reflect a constant periodic rate of return on either the net investment or net cash investment in the lease. The definitions of these terms were essentially the same as those in SSAP 21.

In January 1989 the IASC issued an exposure draft, E32 – *Comparability of Financial Statements* – which proposed to amend, inter alia, the requirements of IAS 17. The main changes proposed were as follows:

(a)   for finance leases other than leveraged leases, lessors were to recognise finance income to reflect a constant periodic rate of return on the net investment in the lease; the present option of using the net cash investment in the lease (which is that required by SSAP 21) would no longer be available;[105] and

(b)   leveraged leases were to be distinguished from other finance leases, and lessors were to recognise finance income on leveraged leases to reflect a constant periodic rate of return on the net cash investment in the lease during periods in which the net cash investment is positive.[106]

However, in July 1990 the IASC published a Statement of Intent[107] which set out its decisions following its review of the comments received on E32. One of the issues on which the IASC deferred consideration pending further work related to IAS 17. At the time, the IASC stated that it 'believes that further study is required on the recognition of finance income on those leases on which the lessor's net investment outstandings is materially affected by income tax factors. It plans to develop an internationally acceptable definition of such a lease and delete the use of the term "leveraged lease".'[108]

8.1.2   *The revised IAS 17*

The IASC eventually gave the subject its attention in 1997, when it published Exposure Draft E56 entitled *Leases*. E56 proposed a very limited review of IAS 17, focusing only on those issues that the International Organization of Securities Commissions (IOSCO) considered essential for the purpose of fulfilling the IASC/IOSCO plan to complete a comprehensive set of core accounting standards that will be acceptable to all major stock exchanges for cross-border listings.

In December 1997, E56 was converted to IAS 17 (revised 1997) – *Leases* – which superseded the original IAS 17 with effect from 1 January 1999. The principal changes from the original IAS 17 are as follows:

■ The original IAS 17 defined a lease as an arrangement whereby the lessor conveys the right to use an asset in return for rent payable by a lessee. IAS 17 (revised) modifies the definition by substituting the term 'rent' with 'a payment or series of payments'. So the new definition of a lease now reads as follows: 'A lease is an agreement whereby the lessor conveys to the lessee in return for a payment or series of payments the right to use an asset for an agreed period of time.' A finance lease continues to be defined as 'a lease that transfers substantially all the risks and rewards incident to ownership of an asset', whilst an operating lease 'is a lease other than a finance lease.'[109]

■ In stipulating that the classification of leases should be based on the extent to which risks and rewards incident to ownership of a leased asset lie with the lessor or lessee, justified by the application of the principle of substance over form, the original IAS 17 provided examples of situations that indicated that a lease was a finance lease. IAS 17 (revised) has added additional classification indicators to further facilitate the classification process. The standard now lists the following examples of situations which would normally lead to a lease being classified as a finance lease:[110]

(a) the lease transfers ownership of the asset to the lessee by the end of the lease term;

(b) the lessee has the option to purchase the asset at a price which is expected to be sufficiently lower than the fair value at the date the option becomes exercisable such that, at the inception of the lease, it is reasonably certain that the option will be exercised;

(c) the lease term is for the major part of the economic life of the asset even if title is not transferred;

(d) at the inception of the lease the present value of the minimum lease payments amounts to at least substantially all of the fair value of the leased asset; and

(e) the leased assets are of a specialised nature such that only the lessee can use them without major modifications being made.

Whilst (d) above talks about the present value of the minimum lease payments being at least substantially all of the fair value of the asset, the standard does not go as far as putting a percentage to it.

The revised standard then goes on to list the following indicators of situations which individually or in combination could also lead to a lease being classified as a finance lease:

(a)   if the lessee can cancel the lease, the lessor's losses associated with the cancellation are borne by the lessee;

(b)   gains or losses from the fluctuation in the fair value of the residual fall to the lessee (for example in the form of a rent rebate equalling most of the sales proceeds at the end of the lease); and

(c)   the lessee has the ability to continue the lease for a secondary period at a rent which is substantially lower than market rent.[111]

The revised standard states further that lease classification is made at the inception of the lease. If at any time the lessee and the lessor agree to change the provisions of the lease, other than by renewing the lease, in a manner that would have resulted in a different classification of the lease under the criteria in the standard had the changed terms been in effect at the inception of the lease, the revised agreement is considered as a new agreement over its term. Changes in estimates (for example, changes in estimates of the economic life or of the residual value of the leased property) or changes in circumstances (for example, default by the lessee), however, do not give rise to a new classification of a lease for accounting purposes.[112]

■   Contingent rent is defined in the revised standard as that portion of the lease payments that is not fixed in amount but is based on a factor other than just the passage of time (e.g. percentage of sales).[113] The original IAS 17 required the disclosure of contingent rents but was silent as to whether contingent rents should be included or excluded in the computation of minimum lease payments. The revised IAS 17 requires that contingent rents be excluded from minimum lease payments.[114]

■   The original IAS 17 was silent on the accounting treatment of initial direct costs incurred by a lessee in negotiating and securing leasing arrangements. IAS 17 now provides guidance by requiring costs that are directly attributable to activities performed by a lessee for securing a finance lease to be included in the amount of the leased asset.[115]

■   The original IAS 17 provided a free choice of method in the allocation of finance income by a lessor, namely the recognition of income basing on a pattern reflecting a constant periodic rate of return based on either:

(i)   the lessor's net investment outstanding in respect of the finance lease; or

(ii)   the lessor's net cash investment outstanding in respect of the finance lease.

IAS 17 (revised) requires that the recognition of finance income should reflect a constant periodic rate of return based on the first method, namely the lessor's net investment outstanding in respect of the finance lease.[116]

It is less than clear why it is that the IASC has eliminated as an option the net cash investment method of recognising finance lease income. It is understood that IOSCO had asked the IASC to clarify the position as to when each of the two methods was appropriate – however this does not necessarily mean the elimination of one of the methods. What is clear is that in certain circumstances the net investment method is not appropriate (for example, when there are significant tax cash flows which affect the lessor) and that it does not make sense to require the net investment method to be applied in all circumstances. US GAAP requires the net investment method to be applied except in the case of leveraged leases as defined in SFAS 13, for which the net cash investment method is required. It would seem sensible for the IASC to have adopted a similar approach.

■ IAS 17 (revised) draws reference to IAS 36 – *Impairment of Assets* – in providing guidance on the need to assess the possibility of an impairment of assets.[117] The original IAS 17 did not address the matter.

■ IAS 17 (revised) mandates enhanced disclosures by both lessees and lessors for operating and finance leases compared with the disclosure items required under the original IAS 17.

New disclosures required by IAS 17 (revised) include:

(a) the total of minimum lease payments reconciled to the present values of lease liabilities in three periodic bands: not later than one year; later than one year and not later than five years; and later than five years (required of a lessee);

(b) the total gross investment in the lease reconciled to the present value of minimum lease payments receivable in three periodic bands: later than one year; later than one year and not later than five years; and later than five years (required of a lessor);

(c) the related finance charges in (a) and (b) above;

(d) the future minimum sublease payments expected to be received under non-cancellable subleases at balance sheet date;

(e) the accumulated allowance for uncollectible minimum lease payments receivable; and

(f) contingent rents recognised in income by lessors.

In addition, because leases are financial instruments, reference to the relevant IAS 32 disclosures have been incorporated in the revised standard.[118]

8.1.3   Sale and leaseback transactions

On the matter of sale and leaseback transactions, the revised IAS 17 is unchanged from the original, except that an Appendix has been added in order to provide guidance in interpreting the various permutations of facts and circumstances that are set out in the requirements.

Under the revised standard, if a sale and leaseback transaction results in a finance lease, any excess of sales proceeds over the carrying amount should not be immediately recognised as income in the financial statements of a seller-lessee. Instead, it should be deferred and amortised over the lease term.[119]

If a sale and leaseback transaction results in an operating lease, and it is clear that the transaction is established at fair value, any profit or loss should be recognised immediately. If the sale price is below fair value, any profit or loss should be recognised immediately except that, if the loss is compensated by future lease payments at below market price, it should be deferred and amortised in proportion to the lease payments over the period for which the asset is expected to be used. If the sale price is above fair value, the excess over fair value should be deferred and amortised over the period for which the asset is expected to be used.[120]

For operating leases, if the fair value at the time of a sale and leaseback transaction is less than the carrying amount of the asset, a loss equal to the amount of the difference between the carrying amount and fair value should be recognised immediately,[121] whilst for finance leases, no such adjustment is necessary unless there has been an impairment in value, in which case the carrying amount is reduced to recoverable amount in accordance with the International Accounting Standard dealing with impairment of assets.[122]

The illustrative Appendix to the revised IAS 17 includes the following tabulation of the standard's requirements concerning sale and leaseback transactions:

Sale price established at fair value (paragraph 52)	Carrying amount equal to fair value	Carrying amount less than fair value	Carrying amount above fair value
Profit	no profit	recognise profit immediately	not applicable
Loss	no loss	not applicable	recognise loss immediately

Sale price below fair value (paragraph 52)			
Profit	no profit	recognise profit immediately	no profit (note 1)
Loss not compensated by future lease payments at below market price	recognise loss immediately	recognise loss immediately	(note 1)
Loss compensated by future lease payments at below market price	defer and amortise loss	defer and amortise loss	(note 1)

Sale price above fair value (paragraph 52)			
Profit	defer and amortise profit	defer and amortise profit	defer and amortise profit (note 2)
Loss	no loss	no loss	(note 1)

Note 1   These parts of the table represent circumstances that would have been dealt with under paragraph 54 of the Standard. Paragraph 54 requires the carrying amount of an asset to be written down to fair value where it is subject to a sale and leaseback.

Note 2   The profit would be the difference between fair value and sale price as the carrying amount would have been written down to fair value in accordance with paragraph 54.

IAS 17's disclosure requirements for lessees and lessors apply equally to sale and leaseback transactions. The requirement in paragraph 23(e) of the standard for lessees to give a general description of their significant leasing arrangements will lead to the disclosure of unique or unusual provisions of the agreement or terms of the sale and leaseback transactions. Furthermore, sale and leaseback transactions may meet the separate disclosure criteria for 'exceptional items' set out in paragraph 16 of IAS 8.

8.1.4   SIC – 15: Operating lease incentives

On the matter of operating lease incentives, the Standing Interpretations Committee (SIC) of the IASC was asked to consider the accounting implications of a lessor providing incentives for a lessee to enter into a new or renewed operating lease agreement. Examples of such incentives are an up-front cash payment to the lessee or the reimbursement or assumption by the lessor of costs of the lessee (such as relocation costs, leasehold improvements and costs associated with a pre-existing lease commitment of the lessee). Alternatively, initial periods of the lease term may be agreed to be rent-free or at a reduced rent.

The consensus reached by the SIC was that all incentives for the agreement of a new or renewed operating lease should be recognised as an integral part of the net consideration agreed for the use of the leased asset, irrespective of the incentive's nature or form or the timing of payments.[123]

It was agreed further that the lessor should recognise the aggregate cost of incentives as a reduction of rental income over the lease term, on a straight-line basis unless another systematic basis is representative of the time pattern over which the benefit of the leased asset is diminished. Similarly, the lessee should recognise the aggregate benefit of incentives as a reduction of rental expense over the lease term, on a straight-line basis unless another systematic basis is representative of the time pattern of the lessee's benefit from the use of the leased asset.[124]

And finally, SIC – 15 requires that costs incurred by the lessee, including costs in connection with a pre-existing lease (for example costs for termination, relocation or leasehold improvements), should be accounted for by the lessee in accordance with the International Accounting Standards applicable to those costs, including costs which are effectively reimbursed through an incentive arrangement.[125]

8.2   US

In most situations there are not major differences between accounting for leases in the UK and the US. This is because SSAP 21 is based on the same principles as SFAS 13 – *Accounting for Leases* – which became effective for leases entered into on or after 1 January 1977.[126] There are, however, some differences in detail between the two standards.

As regards lease classification, SFAS 13 gives four classification criteria. If any of these criteria are met, then the lease is a capital lease (which is equivalent to a finance lease in the UK). A 90% test, similar to that in SSAP 21, forms one of these four criteria, which means that the 90% test is more accurately described and legalistically applied as a rule in the US. This is because if the 90% test indicates a capital lease under SFAS 13, then no other factors can change this classification. As has been discussed in this Chapter, the 90% test in SSAP 21 gives a rebuttable assumption of a particular lease classification (as finance or operating). The other three criteria are:

(a)   the lease transfers ownership of the asset to the lessee at the end of the lease;

(b)   the lease contains a bargain purchase option (i.e. a provision allowing the lessee, at his option, to purchase the asset at a price sufficiently lower than the fair value at the exercise date, such that it is reasonably assured that he will exercise the option); and

(c)   the lease term is equal to 75% or more of the estimated remaining economic life of the asset. However, if the lease term begins within the last 25% of the total economic life of the asset, then this criterion should not be used for the purpose of classifying the lease.

Under US GAAP the position with regard to accounting for operating leases with rent-free periods and/or escalating rentals is clearly set out in two FASB Technical Bulletins.[127] Essentially, the effects of rental holidays and scheduled rent increases should be recognised on a straight-line basis over the lease term. The only exception to this rule is where scheduled rent increases are designed to accommodate the lessee's projected physical use of the property being leased. In this situation, Technical Bulletin No. 88-1 makes a distinction between agreements that give the lessee the right to control the use of the leased property at the beginning of the lease term and those that do not. Escalated rents under agreements that give the lessee the right to control the use of the entire leased property at the beginning of the lease term should be included in the minimum lease payments and recognised on a straight-line basis over the lease term. However, where the agreement provides that the lessee gains control over additional leased property during the course of the agreement, rental expense should be recognised on the basis of the relative fair value of the additional property leased and the period during which the lessee has the right to control the use of the additional property.[128]

Other requirements of SFAS 13 which are different from those of SSAP 21 include the following:

(a)   lessees with operating leases should disclose future minimum rental payments payable over each of the next five years and in aggregate thereafter;

(b)   specific rules are given for the classification of leases involving real estate although once this is done, accounting and disclosure are the same as for other leases;

(c)   lessor accounting for leveraged leases is based on additional specific rules, although the basic concept is the same as for other leases. Essentially, a leveraged lease is one that involves the lessor funding a large element of the purchase of the asset by non-recourse debt under a long-term credit arrangement; and

(d)   the net investment method is used by lessors to allocate gross earnings to accounting periods. SSAP 21 uses this only for hire purchase contracts, with the net cash investment method being used for finance leases.

9   CONCLUSION

SSAP 21 has been in force for a long time, and practice under it is well established. Although FRS 5 does not override SSAP 21, it does provide additional guidance on the factors to be considered in ensuring that leases are classified as finance or operating leases in accordance with their substance. This would seem to provide further evidence of the reduced significance of the 90% test in favour of an approach based on qualitative considerations.

In any event, though, SSAP 21 should be regarded as a standard with a relatively short remaining shelf live. Reports of the proceedings at the meetings of the G4+1 group of standard setters would indicate that the Group is getting close to issuing a new discussion paper on lease accounting. By all accounts, this will move further in the direction that it took when it published its 1996 discussion paper entitled *Accounting for leases: a new approach*, which advocated the end of the distinction between operating and finance leases. Furthermore, given that all leases fall within the definition of a financial instrument, it seems only a matter of time before companies are required to recognise all leases in their balance sheets at fair value.

Similarly, the revision of IAS 17 should be seen purely as a stop-gap measure in order for the IASC to satisfy IOSCO's requirements in the short-term. Since the IASC is a constituent of the G4+1, it is clear that it, too, is intent on pursuing a fundamental review of lease accounting.

References

1 SSAP 21, *Accounting for leases and hire purchase contracts*, August 1984, para. 14.
2 *Ibid.*, para. 18.
3 Increased from £8,000 to £12,000 for contracts entered into after 10th March 1992.
4 ED 29, *Accounting for leases and hire purchase contracts*, October 1981.
5 Department of Trade, *Inspectors' Final Report on Court Line Limited*, p. 153.
6 *Ibid.*, Appendix J, p. 141.
7 *Ibid.*, p. 153.
8 ASC, *Guidance Notes on SSAP 21: Accounting for Leases and Hire Purchase Contracts*, August 1984.
9 SSAP 21, Introductory paragraph.
10 Revised Exposure Draft, *Statement of Principles for Financial Reporting*, ASB, March 1999, para. 4.7.
11 *Ibid.*, para. 4.24.
12 Warren McGregor, *Accounting for leases: a new approach: Recognition by Lessees of Assets and Liabilities Arising under Lease Contracts*, FASB, 1996.
13 *Ibid.*, p. 3.
14 *Ibid.*
15 *Framework for the Preparation and Presentation of Financial Statements*, IASC, September 1989, paras. 49(a) and (b).
16 W McGregor, *op. cit.*, p. 16.
17 *Ibid.*, p. 17.
18 ASB, *Inside Track*, Number 19, April 1999.
19 *Ibid.*
20 ASB, *Inside Track*, Number 20, July 1999.
21 SSAP 21, para. 15.
22 *Ibid.*, para. 17.
23 *Ibid.*, paras. 15 and 16.
24 *Ibid.*, para. 25.
25 *Ibid.*, para. 24.
26 ICAEW, *Financial Reporting & Auditing Group, Technical Release FRAG 9/92*, March 1992, para. 33.
27 SSAP 21, para. 20.
28 *Ibid.*, para. 26.
29 *Ibid.*, para. 19.
30 ICAEW, Technical Release 664, *Implementation of SSAP 21 'Accounting for leases and hire purchase contracts'*, July 1987, paras. 4 and 5.
31 ICAEW, FRAG 9/92, para. 35.
32 *Ibid.*
33 *Ibid.*, para. 36.
34 IAS 17 (revised 1997), *Leases*, IASC, December 1997, paras. 5 to 11.
35 FRS 5, *Reporting the Substance of Transactions*, ASB, 1994, para. 13.
36 *Ibid.*, para. 45.
37 SSAP 21, para. 35.
38 Guidance Notes on SSAP 21, para. 20.
39 SSAP 21, para. 37.
40 FASB Technical Bulletin No. 85-3, *Accounting for Operating Leases with Scheduled Rent Increases*, FASB, November 14, 1985.
41 UITF 12, *Lessee accounting for reverse premiums and similar incentives,* ASB, 5 December 1994.
42 *Ibid.*, para. 8.
43 *Ibid.*, para. 9.
44 *Ibid.*, para. 6.
45 SSAP 21, para. 57.
46 *Ibid.*, para. 55.
47 *Ibid.*, para. 53.
48 *Ibid.*, para. 50.

49 *Ibid.*
50 *Ibid.*, paras. 51 and 52.
51 *Ibid.*, para. 56.
52 *Ibid.*, para. 54.
53 CA 85, Sch. 4, para. 8.
54 *Ibid.*, para. 50(5).
55 *Ibid.*, paras. 42 to 44.
56 *Ibid.*, para. 48.
57 MEPC plc, Report and Financial Statements 1998, Note 33, p. 43.
58 SSAP 21, para. 54.
59 *Ibid.*, para. 43.
60 *Ibid.*, para. 28.
61 *Ibid.*, para. 39.
62 *Ibid.*, para. 23.
63 *Ibid.*, para. 41.
64 Guidance Notes on SSAP 21, para. 92.
65 *Ibid.*, para. 121. See *Guidance Notes on ED 29: Accounting for Leases and Hire Purchase Contracts*, ASC, October 1981, paras. 81–86 for an illustration of the difference that can arise in such circumstances.
66 IAS 17, *Accounting for Leases*, IASC, September 1982, paras. 30 to 38.
67 IAS 17 (revised 1997), para. 30.
68 SSAP 21, para. 39.
69 Guidance Notes on SSAP 21, para. 116.
70 SSAP 21, para. 60.
71 *Ibid.*
72 *Ibid.*, para. 61.
73 *Ibid.*, para. 58.
74 *Ibid.*, para. 61.
75 *Ibid.*, para. 59.
76 Guidance Notes on SSAP 21, para. 124.
77 CA 85, Sch. 4, para. 8.
78 *Ibid.*, paras. 42–44.
79 Guidance Notes on SSAP 21, para. 38.
80 SSAP 21, para. 34.
81 *Ibid.*, para. 48.
82 ICAEW, FRAG 9/92, para. 15.
83 *Ibid.*
84 *Ibid.*, para. 44.
85 SSAP 21, para. 46.
86 FRS 5, Application Note B, para. B20.
87 *Ibid.*, Application Note B, para. B6.
88 *Ibid.*, Application Note B, para. B11.
89 SSAP 21, para. 47.
90 Adapted from para. 122 of Guidance Notes on ED 29.
91 ICAEW, FRAG 9/92, para. 16.
92 *Ibid.*, para. 46.
93 SSAP 21, para. 30.
94 Guidance Notes on SSAP 21, para. 82.
95 ICAEW, FRAG 9/92, para. 47.
96 Guidance Notes on SSAP 21, para. 82.
97 ICAEW, FRAG 9/92, para. 48.
98 *Ibid.*, para. 49.
99 *Ibid.*, para. 58.
100 SSAP 21, para. 45.
101 Guidance Notes on SSAP 21, para. 165.

102 FRS 12, *Provisions, Contingent Liabilities and Contingent Assets*, ASB, September 1998, para. 45; IAS 37, *Provisions, Contingent Liabilities and Contingent Assets*, IASC, September 1998, para. 45.

103 IAS 17, *Accounting for Leases*, IASC, September 1982 (reformatted 1994).

104 *Ibid.*, para. 3.

105 E32, *Comparability of Financial Statements*, IASC, January 1989, para. 76.

106 *Ibid.*, para. 81.

107 Statement of Intent, *Comparability of Financial Statements*, IASC, July 1990.

108 *Ibid.*, Appendix 3.

109 IAS 17 (revised 1997), para. 3.

110 *Ibid.*, para. 8.

111 *Ibid.*, para. 9.

112 *Ibid.*, para. 10.

113 *Ibid.*, para. 3.

114 *Ibid.*

115 *Ibid.*, para. 16.

116 *Ibid.*, para. 30.

117 *Ibid.*, para. 46.

118 *Ibid.*, paras. 23 and 27.

119 *Ibid.*, para. 50.

120 *Ibid.*, para. 52.

121 *Ibid.*, para. 54.

122 *Ibid.*, para. 55.

123 SIC – 15, *Operating Leases - Incentives*, Standing Interpretations Committee of the IASC, June 1998, para. 3.

124 *Ibid.*, paras. 4 and 5.

125 *Ibid.*, para. 6.

126 SFAS 13, *Accounting for Leases*, FASB, November 1976. See the detailed US requirements relating to leases in FASB, *Accounting Standards as of June 1, 1996, Current Text, Volume I, General Standards*, FASB, 1996, Section L10, pp. 29141–29259.

127 FASB Technical Bulletin No. 85-3, *Accounting for Operating Leases with Scheduled Rent Increases*, FASB, November 14, 1985; FASB Technical Bulletin No. 88-1, *Issues Relating to Accounting for Leases: Time Pattern of the Physical Use of the Property in an Operating Lease, Lease Incentives in an Operating Lease, Applicability of Leveraged Lease Accounting to Existing Assets of the Lessor, Money-Over-Money Lease Transactions, Wrap Lease Transactions*, FASB, December 28, 1988.

128 FASB Technical Bulletin No. 88-1, para. 5.

Chapter 18   Government grants

1   INTRODUCTION

Government grants are defined in SSAP 4, the relevant accounting standard on the subject, as 'assistance by government in the form of cash or transfers of assets to an enterprise in return for past or future compliance with certain conditions relating to the operating activities of the enterprise'.[1] Such assistance has been available to commercial enterprises for many years, although its form and extent have undergone various changes according to the shifting economic philosophies of the government of the day.

The accounting issue which arises is how to deal with the income which the grant represents. Before the original accounting standard on the subject was developed, the treatment adopted by different companies was diverse. At that time, the grants which were available were generally of a capital nature, intended to subsidise the purchase of fixed assets. Some companies adopted the policy of crediting the grant directly to income when received; some spread it over the life of the assets involved; some took it directly to reserves as a capital receipt so that it never featured in the profit and loss account at all. SSAP 4 – *The accounting treatment of government grants* – issued in 1974, elected for the second of these three options, adopting a matching approach as its guiding principle. This matching approach is still evident in the present version of SSAP 4, which was issued in July 1990, but the current standard offers more guidance on how to apply the principle to the many different kinds of government assistance which now exist.

2   THE DEVELOPMENT OF SSAP 4

2.1   The original SSAP 4

The original version of the standard was preceded by ED 9 – *The Accounting Treatment of Grants under the Industry Act 1972* – which was published in March 1973. As the title of the exposure draft suggests, it was introduced to deal with a very specific matter – the treatment of the Regional Development Grants introduced by that Act to provide a subsidy for capital expenditure.

SSAP 4 itself was issued in April 1974 and, although it had a less specific title, it was still relatively narrow in its scope. It extended to a mere ten paragraphs, eight of which comprised the explanatory note, and of the remaining two which stated the standard accounting practice to be adopted, the second merely gave the date from which the standard was to be applied. It concentrated solely on capital grants, stating that revenue grants 'do not produce accounting problems as they clearly should be credited to revenue in the same period in which the revenue expenditure to which they relate is charged'.[2]

2.2 ED 43

The general principle underlying SSAP 4, of matching the grant with the expenditure to which it relates, has never been seriously in question since the original standard was issued. However, it became increasingly evident over the years that the standard did not give adequate guidance on how to account for the widely varying forms of government assistance which later became available. Furthermore, the terms on which certain grants were by then being made did not precisely identify the expenditure to which they related; as a result, accountants were often faced with the problem of how to ascribe grants to specific expenditure. In addition, the ASC noted that various requirements of IAS 20 – *Accounting for Government Grants and Disclosure of Government Assistance* – which was issued in 1983 were not reflected in the UK standard, and that this should therefore be considered in a revision of it.

Consequently, the ASC issued a proposed revision to the standard, ED 43, in June 1988. A significant difference between the exposure draft and the original standard was the depth in which the subject was discussed; it followed the same basic approach, but ran to 45 paragraphs rather than SSAP 4's 10, and also had an Appendix illustrating the application of the rules to the particular forms of assistance available.

2.3 SSAP 4 (Revised)

The revised version of SSAP 4 was issued in July 1990 and closely followed the proposals in ED 43, although the Appendix showing how to apply the standard to current forms of assistance was dropped. The new standard became effective for accounting periods beginning on or after 1 July 1990. Subsequent references to SSAP 4 in this Chapter are to the revised version unless the original is specified.

3   THE REQUIREMENTS OF SSAP 4

3.1   Accounting

3.1.1   Treatment of capital grants

The single rule set out in the original version of SSAP 4 was that grants which related to fixed assets were to be credited to revenue over the expected useful life of the asset concerned.[3] This was to be accomplished either:

(a)   by setting the grant directly against the cost of the asset in the balance sheet, so that depreciation was charged on the net figure; or

(b)   by carrying the grant in the balance sheet as a deferred credit, and releasing it to income over the life of the related asset to offset the depreciation charge.[4]

ED 43 followed the same matching principle as SSAP 4, namely that grants of all kinds (both capital and revenue) should be recognised in income at the same time as the expenditure which they subsidise.[5] In respect of grants towards fixed assets, however, the exposure draft sought to eliminate option (a) above, requiring instead that the deferred credit approach be adopted. It advanced three reasons for this proposed change:

■   the netting approach might be in conflict with the Companies Act rules that fixed assets should be carried at their purchase price or production cost,[6] or that amounts representing assets should not be set off against amounts representing liabilities;[7]

■   the deferred credit approach allows the amount of grant credited to income to be disclosed (which was proposed as a new disclosure requirement in the exposure draft), whereas the netting approach loses this amount within the depreciation charge;

■   if grants become repayable, and the netting approach has been adopted, then there may need to be retrospective adjustments to the cost and depreciation of the asset concerned, which may be confusing to the user of the financial statements.

However, a large number of commentators questioned the need for this change, stressing that the netting approach was a convenient practical method, and expressing doubt that a conflict with company law necessarily existed.

The revised version of the standard left the option to use either form of balance sheet presentation, since the ASC considered that both treatments were acceptable and capable of giving a true and fair view. However the Committee went on to say that it had obtained Counsel's opinion that the 'netting' approach would be illegal for enterprises governed by Schedule 4 to the Companies Act 1985, since grant-aided assets would as a result not be stated at their purchase price or production cost.[8] The Companies Act requirement comes from the EC Fourth Directive, but it is interesting to note that it is not interpreted in this way in other countries governed by the Directive. In Germany, for example, it is normal to net capital grants off against the cost of fixed assets and this is not seen as a legal problem.

Under SSAP 4, therefore, enterprises not governed by Schedule 4 remain free to use either treatment, but the remainder should adopt the 'deferred credit' approach if they wish to avoid the risk of contravening the law. The great majority of companies now use the latter form of presentation.

Under the netting method, depreciation on fixed assets is charged net of government grants, thereby releasing the grant to income over the lives of the related assets in the form of a reduced depreciation charge. As discussed in 4.2 below, this form of presentation is also popular among companies which receive grants on assets that are not subject to depreciation.

The current version of SSAP 4 contains a number of other requirements on accounting for grants which had no equivalent in the original standard. These are set out below.

3.1.2   Treatment of revenue-based grants

The general rule, that grants should be recognised in the profit and loss account so as to match them with the expenditure towards which they are intended to contribute, applies equally to revenue-based grants as it does to capital grants. In some situations, the revenue costs towards which a grant is given may already have been incurred, in which case the grant would be included in the profit and loss account as soon as it is capable of being recognised under the rules discussed in 3.1.3 below. However, where a grant has been received, but not all of the revenue costs have been incurred, it will be necessary to defer a proportion of the grant so as to match it with those costs. Railtrack is an example of a company whose accounting policy specifically refers to revenue grants:

Extract 18.1: Railtrack Group PLC (1999)

PRINCIPAL ACCOUNTING POLICIES [extract]

(g)   Grants

Grants and other contributions received towards the cost of tangible fixed assets are included in creditors as deferred income and credited to the profit and loss account over the life of the asset. Revenue grants are credited to the profit and loss account so as to match them with the expenditure to which they relate.

One of the difficulties which face companies is that grants are sometimes given to provide assistance for projects which involve both revenue and capital costs; the question then arises as to which costs the grant should be matched against. This is considered further in 4.1 below.

3.1.3   *Accounting for receipt and repayment of grants*

SSAP 4 requires that grants should not be recognised in the profit and loss account until the conditions for their receipt have been complied with and there is reasonable assurance that the grant will be received.[9] This rule sets the earliest limit for the recognition of the grant, but does not address the question of how it is to be matched against related expenditure; this is discussed at 3.1.4 below.

Grants are frequently received on terms which could result in their repayment if certain conditions are not met throughout a subsequent qualifying period. The revised version of the standard says that provision should be made for such repayment only to the extent that it is probable.[10] Again, the existence of these conditions does not directly enter into the question of when the grants should be recognised in income.

Where a grant does become repayable, the standard requires that the repayment should be accounted for by setting it off against any unamortised deferred credit relating to the grant, with any excess being charged to the profit and loss account.[11] This has the effect of minimising the impact on the profit and loss account; it means that any part of the grant which has not been retained will have been matched against depreciation of the earlier years of the asset's life (if a capital grant). An alternative approach would have been to recompute the release of grant to income as if the amount repaid had never been received, with the result that the reduced amount of the grant (if any) would be spread over the whole life of the asset involved, rather than allocated to the earlier years.

A literal interpretation of the above requirement could mean that, where the company uses the 'netting' method of presentation in the balance sheet (method (a) at 3.1.1 above), the whole amount of the repayment would have to be charged immediately to the profit and loss account because there is no deferred credit to absorb it. However, it is difficult to see the logic of this and we do not believe that such an interpretation was intended. We believe that the balance sheet treatment chosen should not influence the effect of a repayment on the profit and loss account, and that the reference to 'unamortised deferred credit' was intended to include the amount set off against the book value of the asset when the 'netting' approach is used.

3.1.4   *Matching grants against related expenditure*

In practice, this is the most significant accounting issue which arises in respect of government grants. The required approach is summarised by SSAP 4 as follows:

(a)   provided the conditions for its receipt have been complied with and there is reasonable assurance that it will be received, a grant should be recognised in the profit and loss account so as to match it with the expenditure to which it is to contribute;

(b)   the grant should be assumed to contribute to whatever expenditure is the basis for its receipt, unless there is persuasive evidence to the contrary;

(c)   where the grant is a contribution to specific expenditure on fixed assets, it should be recognised over the expected useful economic lives of the related assets;

(d)   if the grant is made in order to give immediate financial support or assistance or to reimburse costs previously incurred, it should be recognised in the profit and loss account of the period in which it becomes receivable; and

(e)   if the grant is made to finance the general activities of an enterprise over a specific period or to compensate for a loss of current or future income it should be recognised in the profit and loss account of the period in which it is paid.[12]

The application of these rules still requires a significant amount of interpretation, and this is discussed in 4.1 below.

3.2   Disclosure

The original version of SSAP 4 contained only one explicit disclosure requirement: the amount of any deferred credit in respect of grants was to be shown separately if it was material, and was not to be included in shareholders' funds.[13] In terms of the Companies Act formats, this amount will normally be shown under the heading of 'Accruals and deferred income' in one of two optional positions in the balance sheet.[14]

ICI's accounts provide an example of this disclosure:

Extract 18.2: Imperial Chemical Industries PLC (1998)

BALANCE SHEETS

at 31 December 1998 [extract]

	Group		Company	
	1998	1997	**1998**	1997
	£m	£m	**£m**	£m
Creditors due after more than one year				
Loans	2,954	2,975	360	694
Other creditors	55	67	2,784	3,262
	3,009	3,042	3,144	3,956
Provisions for liabilities and charges	1,429	1,342	210	218
Deferred income: Grants not yet credited to profit	49	79	–	–

The revised version of the standard has not retained the original disclosure requirement in such specific terms. However, it requires that the effects of government grants on the financial position of the enterprise should be shown.[15] The explanatory note to the standard makes it clear that this is to be done where the results of future periods are expected to be affected materially by the recognition in the profit and loss account of grants already received.[16] It would appear that the most straightforward way of doing this would simply be to disclose the amount of the deferred credit which is still to be released to income, so it may be taken that the previous disclosure requirement is unchanged despite the different manner in which it is expressed.

Leeds Group has an elaborate disclosure, which is in effect a mirror image of its fixed assets note. It shows the following:

Extract 18.3: Leeds Group plc (1998)

19 Accruals and deferred income – *Government grants*

Group	Buildings £000	Plant and machinery £000	Total £000
Received:			
At 1 October 1997 and 30 September 1998	**905**	**451**	**1,356**
Amortisation:			
At 1 October 1997	401	415	816
Credited in year	20	–	20
At 30 September 1998	**421**	**415**	**836**
Net amount:			
At 30 September 1998	**484**	**36**	**520**
At 30 September 1997	504	36	540

However, Leeds Group is very much an exception; few companies give such detailed analysis of the deferred credit.

The revised SSAP 4 introduced these additional disclosure requirements:

(a) the accounting policy adopted for government grants[17] (this is in any case required in general terms by SSAP 2);

An example is shown in Extract 18.1 above.

(b) the effect of government grants on the results of the period;[18]

Such a disclosure can be found in the accounts of Adwest Automotive.

Extract 18.4: Adwest Automotive PLC (1998)

3 Operating Profit [extract]	**1998 £000**	1997 £000
Group operating profit is after crediting:		
Rents receivable	**378**	127
Pension credit	**1,200**	1,050
Industrial development government grant	**36**	68

(c) any potential liability to repay grants in specified circumstances which needs to be disclosed, if necessary, in accordance with FRS 12[19] (which means that no disclosure is necessary if the possibility is remote, although consideration would have to be given to the requirements of the Companies Act).[20] Once again, this disclosure is clearly already required in terms of FRS 12 (and the Companies Act);

(d) where the results of the period are affected materially by the receipt of government assistance in a form other than grants, the nature of that assistance and an estimate of its effects on the financial statements, to the extent that these effects can be measured.[21]

In the explanatory note section of the standard, a further disclosure requirement is suggested. This is that the period or periods over which grants are released to the profit and loss account should be disclosed, insofar as it is practicable given the number and variety of grants that are being received; it is suggested that normally a broad indication of the future periods in which grants already received will be recognised in the profit and loss account will be sufficient.[22] However, this apparent requirement does not appear in the standard section of SSAP 4, so its status is unclear, and it is virtually never seen in practice. It would seem likely that most companies will regard the disclosure of fixed asset lives which they will be giving as part of their depreciation policy note as a sufficient provision of this information, assuming that the grant relates to capital expenditure. However, there may be exceptional cases where a more explicit disclosure would be helpful to an understanding of the accounts.

4 PROBLEM AREAS

4.1 Achieving the most appropriate matching

Most problems of accounting for grants fall into a single category: that of interpreting the requirement to match the grant against the expenditure towards which they are expected to contribute. This apparently simple principle can be extremely difficult to apply, because it is sometimes far from clear what the essence of the grant was, and in practice grants are sometimes given for a particular kind of expenditure which forms an element of a larger project, making the allocation a highly subjective matter. For example, government assistance which is in the form of a training grant might be:

(a) matched against direct training costs; or

(b) taken over a period of time against the salary costs of the employees being trained, for example over the estimated duration of the project; or

(c) taken over the estimated period for which the company or the employees are expected to benefit from the training; or

(d) not distinguished from other project grants received and therefore matched against total project costs; or

(e)   taken to income systematically over the life of the project, for example the total grant receivable may be allocated to revenue on a straight-line basis; or

(f)   as in (d) or (e) above, but using, instead of project life, the period over which the grant is paid; or

(g)   taken to income when received in cash.

Depending on the circumstances, any of these approaches might produce an acceptable result. However, we would comment on them individually as follows:

Under method (a), the grant could be recognised as income considerably in advance of its receipt, since often the major part of the direct training costs will be incurred at the beginning of a project and payment is usually made retrospectively. As the total grant receivable may be subject to adjustment, this may not be prudent or may lead to mismatching.

Methods (b) to (e) all rely on different interpretations of the expenditure to which the grant is expected to contribute, and could all represent an appropriate form of matching.

Method (f) has less to commend it, but the period of payment of the grant might in fact give an indication (in the absence of better evidence) of the duration of the project for which the expenditure is to be subsidised.

Similarly, method (g) is unlikely to be the most appropriate method per se, but may approximate to one of the other methods, or may, in the absence of any conclusive indication as to the expenditure intended to be subsidised by the grant, be the only practicable method which can be adopted.

Many grants are taxed as income on receipt; consequently, this is often the argument advanced for taking grants to income when received in cash. However, SSAP 4 specifically states that 'the treatment of an item for tax purposes does not necessarily determine its treatment for accounting purposes, and immediate recognition in the profit and loss account may result in an unacceptable departure from the principle that government grants should be matched with the expenditure towards which they are intended to contribute'.[23] Consequently, the recognition of a grant in the profit and loss account in a period different to that when it is taxed gives rise to a timing difference, and should be accounted for in accordance with SSAP 15 – *Accounting for deferred tax*.

In the face of the problems (described above) of attributing a grant to related expenditure, it is difficult to offer definitive guidance; companies will have to make their own judgements as to how the matching principle is to be applied. The only overriding considerations are that the method should be systematically and consistently applied, and that the policy adopted (in respect of both capital and revenue grants, if material) should be adequately disclosed. However, it is possible to offer the following points for consideration:

4.1.1 Should the grant be split into its elements?

The grant received may be part of a package, the elements of which have different costs/conditions. It may be appropriate to treat these different elements on different bases rather than accounting for the entire grant in one way.

4.1.2 What was the purpose of the grant?

As discussed in 3.1.4 above, SSAP 4 says that in the absence of persuasive evidence to the contrary, government grants should be assumed to contribute towards the expenditure which is the basis for their payment.[24] However, the method by which the amount of grant receivable is calculated does not conclusively determine its accounting treatment. For example, the amount of the grant may be based on the creation of jobs but it may be intended to contribute towards capital expenditure or other costs as well. It will be necessary to examine the full circumstances of the grant in order to determine its purpose.

4.1.3 What is the period to be benefited by the grant?

The qualifying conditions which have to be satisfied are not necessarily conclusive evidence of the period to be benefited by the grant. For example, certain grants may become repayable if assets cease to be used for a qualifying purpose within a certain period; notwithstanding this condition, the grant should be recognised over the whole life of the asset, not over the qualifying period. The same may apply to the period during which new jobs have to be maintained (although the contrary suggestion is made in the explanatory note to SSAP 4).[25]

4.1.4 Is a grant capital or revenue?

In general, we recommend that grants should be regarded as linked to capital expenditure where this is a possible interpretation and there is no clear indication to the contrary, particularly where the payment of the grant is based on capital expenditure. However, we believe that the most important consideration where there are significant questions over how the grant is to be recognised, and where the effect is material, is that the accounts should explicitly state what treatment has been chosen and disclose the financial effect of adopting that treatment.

4.2 Capital grants on non-depreciating assets

Grants are sometimes given as a contribution to assets which are not depreciated on the grounds that they do not have a finite life. In these circumstances, following the basic rule of SSAP 4, the release of the grant to the profit and loss account is also indefinitely postponed. The question which then arises is whether it makes sense to show the amount received as deferred income, given that it is likely to be there permanently.

Public utility companies, such as those in the water or electricity industries, frequently face this issue. They often receive contributions to the costs of their infrastructure assets, and although they now charge some depreciation under the convoluted 'renewals accounting' expedient devised by FRS 15 (see Chapter 10 at 3.3.2), they do not regard these assets as having a finite life. Their usual response to the problem is to revert to the 'netting' approach, crediting the contributions against the cost of the asset concerned. An example of this approach is to be found in the accounts of Severn Trent:

Extract 18.5: Severn Trent Plc (1999)

Accounting policies [extract]

f) Grants and contributions

Grants and contributions received in respect of non infrastructure assets are treated as deferred income and are transferred to the profit and loss account over the useful economic life of those assets.

Grants and contributions received relating to infrastructure assets have been deducted from the cost of fixed assets. This is not in accordance with Schedule 4 to the Act, which requires assets to be shown at their purchase price or production cost and hence grants and contributions to be presented as deferred income. This departure from the requirements of the Act is, in the opinion of the Directors, necessary to give a true and fair view as, while a provision is made for depreciation of infrastructure assets, these assets do not have determinable finite lives and therefore no basis exists on which to recognise grants and contributions as deferred income. The effect of this departure is that the net book value of fixed assets is £206.1 million lower than it would otherwise have been (1998: £177.0 million).

The last three sentences of this note give the information required by UITF 7 when the 'true and fair override' is used to depart from the detailed requirements of the Companies Act.[26] However, many companies that use this approach do not agree that it is a departure from the Act, and thus do not make the disclosure.

5 COMPARISON WITH THE IASC PRONOUNCEMENT

IAS 20 – *Accounting for Government Grants and Disclosure of Government Assistance* – was issued in 1983, and reformatted in 1994 without substantive amendment. It follows the same basic approach that is adopted in the UK, and also permits grants related to assets to be presented in the balance sheet either by setting up the grant as deferred income or by deducting the grant in arriving at the carrying amount of the asset. Inevitably, because of the international context in which it is written, it does not address specific questions which relate to particular types of grant that are available in individual countries.

In January 1998, the IASC's Standards Interpretations Committee determined that the scope of IAS 20 extended to broad forms of government assistance that did not impose conditions relating to operating activities of an enterprise but simply required it to operate in certain regions or industry sectors.[27] This ruling was to avoid any implication that such forms of assistance were not governed by the standard and could be credited directly to equity.

References

1   SSAP 4, A*ccounting for government grants*, ASC, Revised July 1990, para. 22.
2   SSAP 4 (Original), *The accounting treatment of government grants*, ASC, April 1974, para. 2.
3   *Ibid.*, para. 9.
4   *Ibid.*
5   ED 43, para. 27.
6   CA 85, Sch. 4, para. 17.
7   *Ibid.*, para. 5.
8   SSAP 4, para. 15.
9   *Ibid.*, para. 24.
10 *Ibid.*, para. 27.
11 *Ibid.*
12 *Ibid.*, para. 23.
13 SSAP 4 (Original), para. 9.
14 CA 85, Sch. 4, para. 8.
15 SSAP 4, para. 28(b).
16 *Ibid.*, para. 18.
17 *Ibid.*, para. 28(a).
18 *Ibid.*, para. 28(b).
19 *Ibid.*, para. 29. The standard in fact still refers to SSAP 18, which has been superseded by FRS 12.
20 CA 85, Sch. 4, para. 50(2).
21 SSAP 4, para. 28(c).
22 *Ibid.*, para. 17.
23 *Ibid.*, para. 7.
24 *Ibid.*, para. 23.
25 *Ibid.*, para. 9.
26 UITF 7, *True and fair view override disclosures*, UITF, December 1992, para. 4.
27 SIC - 10, *Government Assistance – No Specific Relation to Operating Activities*, IASC, January 1998, para. 3.

Chapter 19   Segmental reporting

1   INTRODUCTION

1.1   Historical background

Segmental reporting involves the reporting of disaggregated financial information, such as turnover, profits and assets, about a business entity. This information is generally analysed in two ways:

(a) by business segment. A business segment is a distinguishable component of an enterprise that is engaged in providing an individual product or service, or a group of related products or services, and that is subject to risks and returns that are different from those of other business segments;[1] and

(b) by geographical segment. A geographical segment is the distinguishable component of an enterprise that is engaged in providing products or services within a particular economic environment and that is subject to risks and returns that are different from those of components operating in other economic environments.[2]

Segmental reporting has been debated since the early 1960s, that period being significant for the rapid emergence and growth, especially in the US, of the multinational conglomerate business entity.

As enterprises became involved in a large number of distinct products and markets, even industries, the readers of their accounts found it increasingly difficult to analyse the effect of different segments' results on past performance and the likely effect on future performance. Clearly, there could be a wide range of levels of profitability, levels of growth and risk factors concealed within the consolidated accounts of a diversified multinational business enterprise. Pressures grew, mainly from the investment analyst community, for disclosure of the results and resources of the different segments which comprised the whole business. As Mautz noted, 'The progress and success of a diversified company are composites of the progress and success of its several parts. The analyst must have some knowledge about each of these parts to have a basis for forecasting the future of the company. By definition the diversified company is subject to internally varying rates of profit, degrees of risk and potential for profit.[3]

Since the early 1960s, most major industrialised countries have introduced segmental reporting requirements to varying degrees; by legislation, accounting standard and Stock Exchange pronouncement.

Despite the emergence of some more recent trends towards demerger, the growth of the diversified, multinational business entity has continued to the present day; it is a predominant feature of modern business and there is no evidence that this will change in the future. Recurring periods of merger and acquisition activity merely confirm that the justification for segmental reporting is as strong as ever.

1.2   The objectives of segmental reporting

1.2.1   Introduction

The objectives of segmental reporting derive from the fact that users need a greater level of detail of information about the results and resources of a business entity than is provided by its profit and loss account and balance sheet in order to make more informed economic decisions. There is, obviously, a vast amount of detail that could be given about a large business entity's financial activities. Nevertheless, it is presumably as a result of pressure from interested parties that this additional feature of financial reporting has developed and that there is a need, or a perceived need, for such information.

To understand the objectives of segmental reporting it is useful to discuss these in the context of a number of the user groups identified in Chapter 2. The groups most likely to benefit from segmental information are:

1.2.2   The shareholder group

Shareholders are interested in assessing the potential profits and cash flows of the company. If they are provided with disaggregated data, it is presumed that they will be able to make more informed decisions. Research undertaken, both in the US and the UK, has indicated that segmental information does improve the ability of shareholders to predict an entity's future profits.

Shareholders will also be interested in the stewardship of their funds in the past. Therefore they may regard relatively poor performance in one segment as an indication that their company has failed to use its resources in the most efficient manner.

1.2.3   The investment analyst group

The objectives of the investment analyst group are broadly similar to those of the individual shareholder. However, because they are more expert in the techniques of financial analysis, segmental information is, perhaps, even more useful to this group. This is reflected in the fact that much of the early pressure for segmental reporting came from investment analysts.

It would be likely that investment analysts would be supplied with more segmental information, if it were not for the fact that reporting entities have to bear both the costs of producing the information and the possible risk that some advantage may accrue to competitors having more detailed knowledge of their activities. Therefore, opposing pressures are likely to lead to a compromise position, although the compromise position may change over time.

1.2.4   *The lender/creditor group*

To the extent that segmental information improves the ability to predict future profits and cash flow, lenders and creditors will be similarly interested in having such information available. Improved ability to predict cash flows will assist lenders and creditors to make decisions regarding short-term liquidity and long-term solvency.

1.2.5   *Government*

Governments could be interested in segmental information for a number of reasons. It is likely that segmental information assists governmental bodies to collate statistics on macro-economic performance; for example, the investment in and the performance of various industries and products.

Geographical analysis of results and resources may be of significant interest to foreign Governments. They will be better able to assess the activities of the reporting company within their borders. This assessment may lead to a change in level of regulation, revision of tax status, adjustment to the amount of financial assistance and so on.

Government may also take the view that more detailed information will act as an aid to competition, thus resulting in benefits to the general economy.

2   THE UK POSITION

2.1   Legislative requirements

The Companies Act 1967 introduced the requirement that where a company carried on business of two or more classes which 'in the opinion of the directors, differ substantially from each other', turnover and profit before tax split into those classes should be disclosed. This disclosure was to be made in the directors' report.[4]

The 1967 Act also required the directors' report to include a statement of the value of goods exported from the UK (unless turnover did not exceed £50,000). If the directors were able to satisfy the Board of Trade that it was not in the national interest to disclose this export information the requirement could be waived.[5]

These requirements were extended by the Companies Act 1981. Firstly, the requirement to state the value of goods exported from the UK was replaced by a requirement to disclose turnover by export market.[6] Secondly, this disclosure and the disclosure of turnover and profit before tax split by class of business required by the 1967 Act were to be made in the notes to the accounts rather than in the directors' report.

The exemption from the requirement to disclose this information was also extended by the 1981 Act. Exemption was permitted 'where in the opinion of the directors, the disclosure ... would be seriously prejudicial to the interests of the company'. However, the fact that the information had not been disclosed was required to be stated.[7]

These legislative requirements were consolidated into the Companies Act 1985,[8] although the requirement to disclose pre-tax profit by class of business has since been deleted.[9]

2.2   SSAP 25

2.2.1   *The development of the standard*

The exposure draft which preceded the standard was ED 45, which was issued in November 1988.[10] The eventual accounting standard was issued in June 1990 and took effect for accounting periods beginning on or after 1 July 1990.[11] In developing SSAP 25, the ASC made relatively few changes to the proposals in the exposure draft, although one notable omission was a suggested requirement to disclose the basis of inter-segment pricing, which had attracted a good deal of adverse comment in the exposure period and was not retained.[12]

The standard has continued without amendment until the present day. The ASB did consider revisions to the standard in the light of the new standards that were developed by the IASC and by the FASB in the US (see 4.1 and 4.2 below). In May 1996 it published a discussion paper[13] explaining what was being proposed internationally and seeking comment. The responses showed little enthusiasm for change, and the Board subsequently took the matter off its agenda.

2.2.2   *General approach*

SSAP 25 is based on the principle that, unless the financial statements of an entity contain segmental information, they do not enable the reader to make judgements about the nature of the different activities or of their contribution to its overall financial result.[14]

It aims to contribute to improved segmental reporting in two ways: first, by providing guidance as to how the reportable segments should be determined and, second, by specifying the information to be disclosed.

2.2.3 Scope

The standard contains two levels of disclosure requirements: those relating to the statutory requirements contained in the UK companies legislation apply to all companies (and to other entities to whom the standard applies),[15] and a number of additional provisions relating to segmental disclosures which are not required by companies legislation. These additional provisions only apply to:[16]

(a) public limited companies (as defined in section 1 of the Companies Act 1985) or holding companies that have one or more public companies as a subsidiary;

(b) banking and insurance companies or groups as defined in section 744 of the Companies Act, and preparing accounts in accordance with Schedules 9 or 9A thereto; and

(c) private companies (and other entities) which exceed the criteria, multiplied in each case by ten, for defining a medium-sized company under section 247 of the Companies Act.

At present, this means that entities with any two of the following will have to give the extra information:

(i) turnover exceeding £112m,

(ii) total assets exceeding £56m, and

(iii) average number of employees exceeding 2,500.[17]

Entities that are not within the above categories are not subject to the full requirements of the standard, as explained in 2.2.5 below.

Where both parent entity and consolidated accounts are presented, segmental information is to be presented on the basis of the consolidated accounts.[18] Comparative figures for the previous accounting period are to be given.

The exemption remains that where, in the opinion of the directors, the disclosure of any information required would be seriously prejudicial to the interests of the company that information need not be disclosed, but the fact that any such information has not been disclosed must be stated.[19] In practice fairly few companies choose to take advantage of this exemption. One which does is Yorkshire Group, as shown in this extract:

Extract 19.1: Yorkshire Group Plc (1998)

2. TURNOVER [extract]

Yorkshire Group Plc competes internationally with specialist divisions of the world's chemical majors. Because detailed information relating to this competitor activity is not published, the directors are of the opinion that to comply fully with the requirements of SSAP 25 'Segmental Reporting' would be seriously prejudicial to the interests of the group.

2.2.4   What is a reportable segment?

Information can be segmented in two main ways – by class of business and geographically. SSAP 25 supports the provisions of the Companies Act 1985 which state that it is the directors' responsibility to determine the analysis of the segments.[20] The standard does not seek to override these provisions; instead it aims to provide guidance on factors which should influence the definition of segments.

The basic guidance of the standard is that directors should have regard to the overall purpose of presenting segmental information and the need for the readers of the financial statements to be informed if a company carries on operations in different classes of business or in different geographical areas that:

(a)   earn returns on investment that are out of line with the remainder of the business; or

(b)   are subject to different degrees of risk; or

(c)   have experienced different rates of growth; or

(d)   have different potentials for future development.[21]

In establishing segments for both classes of business and geographical areas, there is no single set of factors which is universally applicable, nor is any single factor predominant in all cases. However, the standard suggests that in order to determine whether or not a company operates in different classes of business the directors should take into account the following:

(a)   the nature of the products or services;

(b)   the nature of the production processes;

(c)   the markets in which the products or services are sold;

(d)   the distribution channels for the products;

(e)   the manner in which the entity's activities are organised; and

(f)   any separate legislative framework relating to part of the business.[22]

Similarly, in determining whether or not a company operates in different geographical segments the directors should take into account the following:

(a)   expansionist or restrictive economic climates;

(b)   stable or unstable political regimes;

(c)   exchange control regulations; and

(d)   exchange rate fluctuations.[23]

Particularly in some parts of the world, adjacent countries may not share similar characteristics of these kinds and it may be appropriate to analyse them separately. The standard emphasises that 'although geographical proximity may indicate similar economic trends and risks, this will not always be the case'.[24]

Having established that a segment is distinguishable on the basis of features such as these, it is also necessary to consider whether it is significant enough to warrant separate disclosure. A segment will normally be regarded as significant if:

(a) its third party turnover is 10% or more of the total third party turnover of the entity; or

(b) its segment result, whether profit or loss, is 10% or more of the combined result of all segments in profit or of all segments in loss, whichever combined result is the greater; or

(c) its net assets are 10% or more of the total net assets of the entity.[25]

It should be noted that the segment need satisfy only one of these three criteria in order to be regarded as significant. The criteria above are similar to those set out in the US accounting standards SFAS 14 and SFAS 131 (see 4.2 below) to determine a reportable industry segment.[26]

2.2.5 *What is to be reported?*

The company should define each of its reported classes of business and geographical segments.[27] For each separate class of business and geographical segment, those companies which are subject to the full requirements of the standard (broadly all public and large private companies, and those involved in banking or insurance – see 2.2.3 above) are required to disclose:

(a) turnover;

(b) results; and

(c) net assets.[28]

The discussion which follows is of the full requirements. The exemptions for smaller private companies are shown at the end of this section.

Turnover should be analysed between sales to external customers and sales between segments.[29]

The geographical analysis of turnover is to be given, in the first instance, with reference to its source (i.e. the geographical location from which products or services are supplied). This is consistent with the most likely basis for disclosure of geographical analyses of results and net assets. However, it is recognised that it would also be useful to readers of accounts to be provided with information on the markets which the company serves, which is the basis of the Companies Act requirement. There is, therefore, the additional requirement that turnover (but not results or net assets) be analysed between geographical segments with reference to its destination (i.e. the geographical area to which products or services are supplied). Where this amount is not materially different from turnover to third parties with reference to its source, disclosure is not required but a statement that this is the case should be made.[30]

The standard says that entities that are not required by statute to disclose turnover are not required to analyse such turnover segmentally, but this fact should be stated.[31] This referred at the time to banks, but the subsequently revised Schedule 9 to the Companies Act makes this exemption largely irrelevant. The schedule contains various segmental disclosure requirements,[32] and the banks have also published their own SORP on the subject.[33] However, the rules for specialised industries are beyond the scope of this book.

'Results' means the profit or loss before tax, minority interests and extraordinary items.[34] Profit or loss is normally taken before accounting for interest also. However, the profit or loss after interest is likely to be used in those companies where the earning of interest income or the incurring of interest expense is fundamental to the nature of the business; for example, companies in the financial sector.[35] In giving the geographical analysis of results it is considered that it will be more appropriate if it is based on the areas from which goods or services are supplied.[36] To gather the information based on destination would usually be very difficult in any event.

'Net assets' is not defined in the standard. Generally it is taken as non-interest bearing operating assets less non-interest bearing operating liabilities. However, where interest income/expense has been included in arriving at the segmental results the related interest bearing assets/liabilities should be taken into account in determining the net assets.[37] The aim should be to relate the definition of net assets to the definition of results so that a 'return on investment' type calculation can be performed. Operating assets and liabilities which are shared by more than one segment are to be allocated, as appropriate, to those segments.[38]

Because of the wide differences in their circumstances, it is inevitable that companies interpret net assets in various ways. The best that can be achieved is for companies to settle on one definition of net assets that is meaningful for themselves, and apply it consistently. This means that the value of comparison between companies of returns on assets employed may be limited, even apart from the effects of other differences of accounting policy.

The total of the information disclosed by segmental analysis should agree with the related totals in the financial statements. If they do not agree, a reconciliation between the two figures is required, with reconciling items properly identified and explained.[39]

As indicated in 2.2.3 above, certain of the disclosure requirements of SSAP 25 only apply to public companies (and groups with a public company as subsidiary), banking and insurance companies or groups and very large private companies (and other entities). Companies which are not within these categories need not disclose the following (although disclosure is still encouraged):[40]

(a)   split of turnover between external customers and other segments;

(b)   segmental analysis of results;

(c)   net assets;

(d)   share of results and net assets of significant associated undertakings; and

(e)   geographical analysis of turnover by reference to its source (analysis by destination is still required by the Companies Act).

2.2.6   *Associated undertakings*

The standard requires groups to give segmental disclosure, in their consolidated accounts, of the following information in respect of their associated undertakings:

(a)   their share of the profits or losses of associated undertakings before accounting for taxation, minority interests and extraordinary items; and

(b)   their share of the net assets of associated undertakings (including goodwill to the extent it has not been written off) stated, where possible, after attributing fair values to the net assets at the date of the acquisition of the interest in each associated undertaking.

This disclosure should be of the aggregate information for all associated undertakings and should be shown separately in the segmental report.[41] For this purpose, associated undertakings are as defined in the Companies Act, and embrace both associates and joint ventures as they are defined in FRS 9 (see Chapter 7 at 2).

The disclosure is only required if the results or assets of associated undertakings form a material part of the group's results or assets. For this purpose, associated undertakings form a material part of the reporting company's results if, in total, they account for at least 20% of the total results or at least 20% of the total net assets of the reporting group (including the group's share of the results and net assets of the associated undertakings).[42]

An example of such disclosure can be seen in the following extract from the financial statements of Chrysalis Group, even though the joint ventures in question do not seem to be material enough to require such disclosure. As well as giving details of the joint ventures' results and net assets, Chrysalis analyses its share of their turnover:

Extract 19.2: Chrysalis Group PLC (1998)

3. Analysis of joint ventures' turnover, profit/(loss) before tax and net assets/(liabilities) and total recognised gains and losses

	Third party turnover		(Loss)/profit before taxation		Share of net assets/ (liabilities)	
	1998	1997	**1998**	1997	**1998**	1997
	£'000	£'000	**£'000**	£'000	**£'000**	£'000
a Analysis by class of business						
Music	**1,285**	1,256	**(8)**	(6)	**95**	207
Export	**–**	1,186	**–**	29	**–**	2
Visual Entertainment	**1,376**	5,376	**(53)**	163	**(373)**	(168)
Other	**1,201**	989	**(17)**	(142)	**3,144**	2,671
Total	**3,862**	8,807	**(78)**	44	**2,866**	2,712
b Analysis by geographical location						
United Kingdom	**3,224**	3,950	**(70)**	(197)	**2,879**	2,564
North America	**51**	39	**(35)**	(41)	**(67)**	31
Europe	**–**	4,818	**–**	282	**156**	179
Rest of the world	**587**	–	**27**	–	**(102)**	–
Total	**3,862**	8,807	**(78)**	44	**2,866**	2,712

c Analysis of total recognised gains and losses

Total recognised losses in respect of joint venture companies were £107,000 (1997: total recognised losses of £73,000).

Another good example is to be found in the accounts of Pearson:

Extract 19.3: Pearson plc (1998)

13 Associates [extract]

ALL FIGURES IN £ MILLIONS	1998 OPERATING PROFIT	NET ASSETS	1997 OPERATING PROFIT	NET ASSETS
Analysis of partnerships and other associates				
Business sectors				
FT Group	15	6	16	(3)
Pearson Education	4	5	3	5
The Penguin Group	–	–	1	1
Pearson Television	(8)	23	(20)	49
Lazard	42	111	43	123
Continuing operations	53	145	43	175
Discontinued operations	(2)	–	4	23
	51	145	47	198
Geographical markets supplied and location of net assets				
United Kingdom	10	109	(1)	138
Continental Europe	11	13	9	11
North America	29	15	30	19
Rest of World	3	8	5	7
Continuing operations	53	145	43	175
Discontinued operations	(2)	–	4	23
	51	145	47	198

Associated undertakings themselves often do not come within the scope of the standard and therefore do not disclose segmental information in their own accounts. Where this is the case the investing company may be unable to obtain the necessary information to meet the requirement of the standard as it does not control the associated undertaking. Similarly, publication of the information may be thought to be prejudicial to the business of the associate where, for example, its competitors are not owned by an entity to which all of the provisions of SSAP 25 apply. SSAP 25 recognises these problems by providing an exemption to the effect that the segmental information requirements do not apply where the company is unable to obtain the information or where publication of the information would be prejudicial to the business of the associate. However, in these circumstances, the reason for the non-disclosure should be stated by way of note, together with a brief description of the omitted business or businesses.[43]

2.2.7 Common costs

Common costs are costs relating to more than one segment.[44] The standard merely requires that they are treated in the way that the directors deem most appropriate with regard to the objectives of segmental reporting. If the apportionment of common costs would be misleading, then they should not be apportioned but the total should be deducted from the total of the segment results.[45]

2.2.8 Disclosure in practice

Most companies present their segmental information in a separate note to the accounts while a few show it in a separate statement alongside the primary statements. Some good examples of segmental disclosures are set out below:

Extract 19.4: Imperial Chemical Industries PLC (1998)

4 Segment information [extract]

Classes of business

	Turnover			Trading profit before exceptional items			Profit before interest and taxation after exceptional items		
	1998 £m	1997 £m	1996 £m	1998* £m	1997 £m	1996 £m	1998* £m	1997 £m	1996 £m
Continuing operations									
Specialty Products									
National Starch	1,646	782		219	116		219	116	
Quest	656	321		82	32		82	8	
Industrial Specialties	1,027	831	546	84	67	28	72	31	28
	3,329	1,934	546	385	215	28	373	155	28
Coatings	2,167	2,170	2,161	132	160	147	57	166	103
Materials	1,352	1,490	1,583	114	130	158	114	134	130
Industrial Chemicals	2,466	3,020	3,399	(41)	(98)	20	(104)	(569)	(1)
Inter-class eliminations	(202)	(235)	(211)						
	9,112	8,379	7,478	590	407	353	440	(114)	260
Sales to discontinued operations	(17)	(216)	(276)						
	9,095	8,163	7,202	590	407	353	440	(114)	260
Discontinued operations									
Total	267	3,062	3,410	37	213	312	216	898	300
Sales to continuing operations	(76)	(163)	(92)						
	191	2,899	3,318	37	213	312	216	898	300
Share of profits less losses of associated undertakings							3	16	27
Amounts written off investments							(34)	–	–
	9,286	11,062	10,520	627	620	665	625	800	587

* After amortisation of goodwill of £23m (National Starch £12m; Coatings £11 m)

The Group's policy is to transfer products internally at external market prices. Inter-class turnover affected several businesses the largest being sales from Industrial Chemicals to Coatings £64m (1997 Industrial Chemicals to Discontinued operations of £194m; 1996 £252m).

	Depreciation			Capital expenditure		
	1998	1997	1996	**1998**	1997	1996
	£m	£m	£m	**£m**	£m	£m
Continuing operations						
Specialty Products						
National Starch	**51**	23		**115**	44	
Quest	**19**	12		**27**	11	
Industrial Specialties	**39**	28	14	**62**	47	20
	109	63	14	**204**	102	20
Coatings	**53**	43	45	**78**	65	83
Materials	**61**	61	74	**89**	142	192
Industrial Chemicals	**126**	415	132	**169**	212	329
	349	582	265	**540**	521	624
Discontinued operations	**14**	187	151	**14**	196	402
	363	769	416	**554**	717	1,026

Geographic areas

The information [above] is re-analysed in the table below by geographic area. The figures for each geographic area show the turnover and profit made by, and the net operating assets owned by, companies located in that area; export sales and related profits are included in the areas from which those sales were made.

	Turnover			Trading profit before exceptional items			Profit before interest and taxation after exceptional items		
Continuing operations	**1998**	1997	1996	**1998***	1997	1996	**1998***	1997	1996
United Kingdom	**£m**	£m	£m	**£m**	£m	£m	**£m**	£m	£m
Sales in the UK									
External	**1,589**	1,715	1,748						
Intra-Group	**180**	327	73						
	1,769	2,042	1,821						
Sales overseas									
External	**951**	1,009	903						
Intra-Group	**415**	470	713						
	1,366	1,479	1,616						
	3,135	3,521	3,437	**20**	(9)	54	**(50)**	(244)	37
Continental Europe									
External	**1,912**	1,423	1,180						
Intra-Group	**491**	422	475						
	2,403	1,845	1,655	**178**	49	51	**166**	(43)	45
USA									
External	**2,765**	2,227	1,928						
Intra-Group	**280**	286	253						
	3,045	2,513	2,181	**246**	199	143	**192**	87	73
Other Americas									
External	**735**	687	492						
Intra-Group	**85**	96	37						
	820	783	529	**63**	59	31	**63**	31	29
Asia Pacific									
External	**1,038**	1,005	862						
Intra-Group	**125**	99	107						
	1,163	1,104	969	**69**	87	68	**55**	40	70
Other countries									
External	**105**	97	89						
Intra-Group	**13**	9	9						
	118	106	98	**14**	22	6	**14**	15	6
	10,684	9,872	8,869	**590**	407	353	**440**	(114)	260
Inter-area eliminations	**(1,572)**	(1,493)	(1,391)						
Sales to discontinued operations	**(17)**	(216)	(276)						
	9,095	8,163	7,202	**590**	407	353	**440**	(114)	260
Discontinued operations	**191**	2,899	3,318	**37**	213	312	**216**	898	300
Share of profits less losses of associated undertakings							**3**	16	27
Amounts written off investments							**(34)**		
	9,286	11,062	10,520	**627**	620	665	**625**	800	587

* After amortisation of goodwill of £23m.

Turnover by discontinued operations is primarily in the following geographic areas:
United Kingdom £64m, USA £57m and Other Americas £53m (1997 Asia Pacific £1,537m, 1996
Asia Pacific £1,885m)

Classes of business

	Total assets less current liabilities		
	1998 **£m**	1997 £m	1996 £m
Net operating assets			
Continuing operations			
Specialty Products			
National Starch	**1,451**	961	
Quest	**336**	339	
Industrial Specialties	**674**	646	189
	2,461	1,946	189
Coatings	**1,114**	783	724
Materials	**1,002**	964	928
Industrial Chemicals	**1,457**	1,384	1,764
	6,034	5,077	3,605
Discontinued operations	–	455	2,263
Total net operating assets	**6,034**	5,532	5,868
Net non-operating (liabilities) assets	**(1,387)**	(909)	231
	4,647	4,623	6,099

	Net non-operating (liabilities) assets		
	1998 **£m**	1997 £m	1996 £m
Net non-operating (liabilities) assets			
Non-operating assets			
Fixed asset investments	**170**	254	172
Non-operating debtors	**137**	134	70
Investments and short-term deposit	**455**	935	560
Cash at bank	**367**	340	341
	1,129	1,663	1,143
Non-operating liabilities			
Short-term borrowings	**(1,445)**	(1,105)	(186)
Current instalments of loans	**(585)**	(950)	(243)
Non-operating creditors	**(486)**	(517)	(483)
	(2,516)	(2,572)	(912)
	(1,387)	(909)	231

Employees	**1998**	1997	1996
Average number of people employed by the Group			
Continuing operations			
Specialty Products			
National Starch	**9,900**	4,500	
Quest	**4,400**	2,100	
Industrial Specialties	**5,600**	4,100	2,400
	19,900	10,700	2,400
Coatings	**19,200**	18,700	17,100
Materials	**4,300**	4,700	4,700
Industrial Chemicals	**14,000**	14,900	16,500
Corporate			
Board support	**200**	200	200
Group technical resources and other shared service	**1,500**	1,700	1,500
	59,100	50,900	42,400
Discontinued operations	**1,500**	18,600	21,600
	60,600	69,500	64,000

Geographic areas

	Tangible fixed assets			Total assets less current liabilities		
	1998	1997	1996	**1998**	1997	1996
	£m	£m	£m	**£m**	£m	£m
Tangible fixed assets/Net operating assets						
Continuing operations						
United Kingdom	**880**	886	895	**1,731**	1,467	1,274
Continental Europe	**822**	712	431	**1,230**	922	588
USA	**1,260**	1,172	623	**1,880**	1,549	710
Other Americas	**179**	187	146	**310**	328	334
Asia Pacific	**656**	633	569	**848**	777	671
Other countries	**19**	19	12	**35**	34	28
	3,816	3,609	2,676	**6,034**	5,077	3,605
Discontinued operations	**–**	347	1,781	**–**	455	2,263
Total net operating assets				**6,034**	5,532	5,868
Net non-operating (liabilities) assets				**(1,387)**	(909)	231
	3,816	3,956	4,457	**4,647**	4,623	6,099

Total assets of discontinued operations are primarily in the following geographic areas:
1997 UK £140m, 1996 Asia Pacific £1,161m

Turnover by customer location

	1998 £m	1997 £m	1996 £m
Continuing operations			
United Kingdom	1,693	1,756	1,765
Continental Europe	2,330	1,981	1,723
USA	2,702	2,169	1,905
Other Americas	862	807	581
Asia Pacific	1,152	1,090	920
Other countries	356	360	308
	9,095	8,163	7,202
Discontinued operations	191	2,899	3,318
	9,286	11,062	10,520

Turnover by customer locations to discontinued operations are primarily in the following geographic areas:
Discontinued operations: United Kingdom £69m, USA £57m and Other Americas £45m (1997 Asia Pacific £1,537m, 1996 Asia Pacific £1,885m)

Employees

	Continuing operations			Total		
	1998 £m	1997 £m	1996 £m	1998 £m	1997 £m	1996 £m
Average number of people employed by the Group						
United Kingdom	16,100	14,900	14,800	16,900	18,100	17,700
Continental Europe	10,600	7,800	5,700	10,600	8,100	6,100
USA	13,100	10,700	8,400	13,300	12,200	10,100
Other Americas	7,100	6,300	3,900	7,500	8,700	6,500
Asia Pacific	11,400	10,500	9,200	11,500	18,000	19,200
Other countries	800	700	400	800	4,400	4,400
Total employees	59,100	50,900	42,400	60,600	69,500	64,000
Number of people employed by the Group at the year end						
Continuing operations				58,700	58,500	42,500
Discontinued operations				–	9,000	20,800
Total employees				58,700	67,500	63,300

Extract 19.5: Coats Viyella Plc (1998)

2 Analysis of turnover, operating profit and net assets	Turnover 1998 £m	Turnover 1997 £m	Operating profit 1998 £m	Operating profit 1997 £m	Net Assets 1998 £m	Net Assets 1997 £m
Product category:						
Industrial	556.8	640.1	40.3	49.7	373.4	389.3
Crafts	350.2	401.2	32.3	33.1	164.0	196.5
Thread	907.0	1,041.3	72.6	82.8	537.4	585.8
Precision Engineering	315.2	319.0	27.3	35.4	100.4	99.0
Other Indian Businesses	103.3	104.3	7.2	8.1	42.5	50.1
Coats Divisions	1,325.5	1,464.6	107.1	126.3	680.3	734.9
Contract Clothing	350.1	390.4	1.9	(0.9)	96.4	92.1
Fashion Retail & Branded Clothing	230.5	260.5	3.9	12.3	85.4	97.5
Home Furnishings	167.8	189.1	5.3	13.7	60.7	69.4
Viyella Divisions	748.4	840.0	11.1	25.1	242.5	259.0
Corporate	–	–	(0.8)	(7.8)	71.1	96.5
Continuing operations	2,073.9	2,304.6	117.4	143.6	993.9	1,090.4
Discontinued operations	9.0	53.9	(1.6)	(8.0)	–	–
Less: 1997 provision	–	–	1.6	–	–	–
	2,082.9	2,358.5	117.4	135.6	993.9	1,090.4
Reorganisation costs and impairment of fixed assets			(26.5)	(29.8)		
Other exceptional items			(2.4)	(18.1)		
			88.5	87.7		
Other items			(18.1)	(19.6)		
Profit before interest and associated companies			70.4	68.1		

	Turnover		Operating profit		Net Assets	
	1998	1997	**1998**	1997	**1998**	1997
Geographical analysis by location:	**£m**	£m	**£m**	£m	**£m**	£m
United Kingdom	**740.0**	816.8	**5.6**	22.4	**351.5**	383.4
Rest of Europe	**402.2**	439.5	**21.9**	22.5	**148.9**	165.3
North America	**523.9**	562.8	**58.3**	65.4	**223.3**	246.6
South America	**123.6**	153.1	**2.9**	3.0	**90.0**	102.2
Africa, Asia, Australasia	**284.2**	332.4	**28.7**	30.3	**180.2**	192.9
Continuing operations	**2,073.9**	2,304.6	**117.4**	143.6	**993.9**	1,090.4
Discontinued operations	**9.0**	53.9	**(1.6)**	(8.0)	–	–
Less: 1997 provision	–	–	**1.6**	–	–	–
	2,082.9	2,358.5	**117.4**	135.6	**993.9**	1,090.4
Reorganisation costs and impairment of fixed assets			**(26.5)**	(29.8)		
Other exceptional items			**(2.4)**	(18.1)		
			88.5	87.7		
Other items			**(18.1)**	(19.6)		
Profit before interest and associated companies			**70.4**	68.1		
Associated companies					**2.8**	3.0
					996.7	1,093.4
Net debt					**(320.8)**	(361.9)
Other fixed and current asset investments					**33.6**	24.3
Net assets per consolidated balance sheet					**709.5**	755.8

Geographical analysis of turnover by destination:		
	1998	1997
	£m	£m
United Kingdom	**715.4**	827.8
Rest of Europe	**431.7**	473.7
North America	**522.4**	571.7
South America	**131.9**	153.9
Africa, Asia, Australasia	**281.5**	331.4
	2,082.9	2,358.5

Note
Associated companies are principally Thread businesses based in Asia and Australasia.

Guidance on the form of presentation which may be followed in disclosing all of the information required by the standard is provided in the appendix to SSAP 25. During the development of the standard it was, at one point, suggested that a matrix format be encouraged. This gives additional information, because it means that each geographical segment is also analysed by activity and vice versa. However, while many commentators felt that a matrix approach had some merit, others contended that a complex matrix of segmental information may confuse readers as well as giving competitors valuable commercial advantage.

One company which does in fact present its segmental information for turnover in matrix form is BOC, as illustrated in the following extract:

Extract 19.6: The BOC Group plc (1998)

1 Segmental information [extract]

a) **Turnover**	Continuing operations						
	Gases and Related Products £ million	Vacuum Technology £ million	Distribution Services £ million	Total £ million	Discontinued operations £ million	Total by origin £ million	Total by destination £ million
1998							
Europe	**667.5**	**104.8**	**312.4**	**1,084.7**	**76.7**	**1,161.4**	**1,120.5**
Americas	**831.8**	**177.0**	–	**1,008.8**	**114.3**	**1,123.1**	**1,076.6**
Africa	**333.9**	–	–	**333.9**	–	**333.9**	**335.4**
Asia/Pacific	**864.1**	**41.3**	**1.5**	**906.9**	**24.6**	**931.5**	**1,017.4**
Turnover	**2,697.3**	**323.1**	**313.9**	**3,334.3**	**215.6**	**3,549.9**	**3,549.9**
1997							
Europe	659.3	109.4	287.9	1,056.6	161.3	1,217.9	1,058.7
Americas	805.0	202.6	–	1,007.6	262.9	1,270.5	1,484.0
Africa	341.0	–	–	341.0	–	341.0	341.0
Asia/Pacific	1,024.6	55.0	1.4	1,081.0	53.2	1,134.2	1,079.9
Turnover	2,829.9	367.0	289.3	3,486.2	477.4	3,963.6	3,963.6
1996							
Europe	642.9	122.9	282.5	1,048.3	181.0	1,229.3	1,150.3
Americas	754.7	211.1	–	965.8	259.5	1,225.3	1,217.7
Africa	354.4	–	–	354.4	–	354.4	360.5
Asia/Pacific	1,062.2	82.9	–	1,145.1	65.4	1,210.5	1,291.0
Turnover	2,814.2	416.9	282.5	3,513.6	505.9	4,019.5	4,019.5

Such a presentation is fairly rare, but it does provide a great deal of information; not only is the user given the level of turnover attributable to, say, vacuum technology (£323.1 million) and the level of turnover from continuing operations attributable to Europe (£1,084.7 million), but also the amount of turnover attributable to vacuum technology in Europe (£104.8 million). BOC does not, however, use a similar matrix approach in giving its segmental analyses of operating profit, capital employed and capital expenditure.

2.3   Voluntary segmental disclosures

A number of companies give segmental information which goes beyond present requirements. As shown in Extract 19.4 above, ICI gives segmental analyses of its depreciation charge, capital expenditure and employees. Some other examples of voluntary segmental disclosures are illustrated in the following extracts.

BP Amoco analyses its fixed assets by business segments:

Extract 19.7: BP Amoco p.l.c. (1998)

18 Tangible assets – property, plant and equipment [extract]   **$ million**

	Exploration and Production	Refining and Marketing	Chemicals	Other businesses and corporate	Total	of which Assets under construction
Cost						
At 1 January 1998	78,862	18,306	12,645	2,070	111,883	6,183
Exchange adjustments	309	(181)	169	6	303	(9)
Acquisitions	–	17	177	–	194	–
Additions	5,163	1,165	1,175	198	7,701	4,339
Transfers	455	(164)	195	99	585	(5,541)
Deletions	(1,804)	(991)	(183)	(469)	(3,447)	(827)
At 31 December 1998	**82,985**	**18,152**	**14,178**	**1,904**	**117,219**	**4,145**
Depreciation						
At 1 January 1998	43,841	8,889	5,896	994	59,620	
Exchange adjustments	334	(46)	73	2	363	
Charge for the year	3,652	789	478	112	5,031	
Transfers	127	(41)	108	48	242	
Deletions	(1,306)	(847)	(120)	(229)	(2,502)	
At 31 December 1998	**46,848**	**8,744**	**6,435**	**927**	**62,754**	
Net book amount						
At 31 December 1998	**36,337**	**9,408**	**7,743**	**977**	**54,465**	**4,145**
At 31 December 1997	35,021	8,417	6,749	1,076	52,263	6,183

Rio Tinto gives segmental analysis of its employees by geographical location, although it no longer does so by activity as well:

Extract 19.8: Rio Tinto plc and Rio Tinto Limited (1998)

25 EMPLOYEES [extract]

	Subsidiaries		Joint ventures and associates (Rio Tinto share)		Group total	
	1998	1997	**1998**	1997	**1998**	1997
The principal locations of employment were:						
North America	**7,717**	7,428	**65**	65	**7,782**	7,493
Australia and New Zealand	**8,192**	9,119	**543**	679	**8,735**	9,798
Africa	**7,109**	7,427	**508**	509	**7,617**	7,936
Europe	**2,858**	2,752	**738**	719	**3,596**	3,471
South America	**1,592**	1,474	**805**	790	**2,397**	2,264
Indonesia	**1,009**	1,026	**2,559**	2,142	**3,568**	3,168
Other countries	**151**	212	**963**	1,000	**1,114**	1,212
Total	**28,628**	29,438	**6,181**	5,904	**34,809**	35,342

3   PROBLEM AREAS

3.1   How to define the segments

SSAP 25 specifies that the definition of segments should be made by the management of the reporting company. Guidance on how such segments are defined can be given but only in very general terms (see 2.2.4 above).

The factors which provide guidance in determining an industry segment are often those which lead a company's management to organise its enterprise into divisions, branches or subsidiaries. In turn, this means that the company's own management accounts may well be prepared in this form and the information required for segmental reporting will be more readily available.

EMAP provides an unusual example because it analyses its turnover into segments of two different kinds, as shown in the following extract:

Extract 19.9: Emap plc (1999)

Group activity analysis [extract]

for the financial year ended 31 March 1999

	%	1999 £m	%	1998 £m
Turnover by category				
Advertising	**41**	**356.6**	41	318.8
Circulation	**45**	**395.8**	45	344.8
Events	**7**	**65.2**	7	55.9
Other	**7**	**62.5**	7	53.1
	100	**880.1**	100	772.6
Turnover by division				
Emap Consumer UK	**33**	**290.2**	35	271.9
Emap France	**26**	**232.3**	29	225.0
Emap Petersen	**5**	**43.2**	–	–
Emap Business Communications	**25**	**219.9**	26	196.7
Emap Radio	**9**	**77.8**	9	70.3
New Media/International	**2**	**16.7**	1	8.7
	100	**880.1**	100	772.6

The standard recommends that the directors should review their definitions annually and redefine them when appropriate, and this is now common in an environment where companies continually have to adapt to changing market conditions.[46] Where this is done, the comparative figures should be restated to reflect the change; disclosure of the nature of, the reasons for, and the effect of the change should also be made.[47] TI Group provides an example of such disclosures.

Extract 19.10: T I Group plc (1998)

2 SEGMENT ANALYSIS [extract]

	Turnover		Operating profit		Operating assets	
	1998	1997	**1998**	1997	**1998**	1997
	£m	£m	**£m**	£m	**£m**	£m
By class of business						
John Crane	**585.6**	411.1	**76.0**	65.4	**231.9**	111.5
Forsheda	**248.5**	243.8	**33.8**	33.6	**83.6**	82.0
Bundy	**794.0**	740.0	**90.9**	78.2	**279.1**	247.4
Dowty	**451.2**	275.1	**59.3**	42.0	**174.1**	74.1
Parent and other	–	–	**(3.9)**	(1.7)	**16.7**	23.0
Continuing operations	**2,079.3**	1,670.0	**256.1**	217.5	**785.4**	538.0

...

As from 1st January 1998 the polymer engineering businesses of John Crane were separated to form a fourth business segment, which trades as Forsheda. 1997 figures have been restated accordingly.

Titeflex, Lewis & Saunders and Cambridge Vacuum Engineering, three businesses previously reported as part of Bundy, were transferred to Dowty with effect from 1st January 1998, as their principal products are aerospace related and they are now managed by Dowty. Their 1997 sales and operating profit reported in Bundy in 1997 were £67.9m and £5.4m respectively, and have not been restated.

Companies who operate in global markets can have particular difficulty in analysing their operations geographically. The following extracts show the approaches of British Airways, Barclays and Reuters to this problem:

Extract 19.11: British Airways Plc (1999)

1. Accounting policies

Segmental reporting

b Geographical segments

i) *Turnover by Destination* The analysis of turnover by destination is based on the following criteria:

Scheduled and non scheduled services Turnover from domestic services within the United Kingdom is attributed to the United Kingdom. Turnover from inbound and outbound services between the United Kingdom and overseas points is attributed to the geographical area in which the relevant overseas point lies.

Other revenue Revenue from the sale of package holidays is attributed to the geographical area in which the holiday is taken, while revenue from aircraft maintenance and other miscellaneous services is attributed on the basis of where the customer resides.

ii) *Turnover by origin* The analysis of turnover by origin is derived by allocating revenue to the area in which the sale was made. Operating profit resulting from turnover generated in each geographical area according to origin of sale is not disclosed as it is neither practical nor meaningful to allocate the Group's operating expenditure on this basis.

iii) *Geographical analysis of net assets* The major revenue-earning asset of the Group is the aircraft fleet, the majority of which are registered in the United Kingdom. Since the Group's aircraft fleets are employed flexibly across its worldwide route network, there is no suitable basis of allocating such assets and related liabilities to geographical segments.

Extract 19.12: Barclays PLC (1998)

Accounting policies [extract]

Analyses by geographical segments and classes of business

The analyses by geographical segment are generally based on the location of the office recording the transaction.

In note 59, the global swaps business is included within the United Kingdom segment. Foreign UK-based comprises activities in the United Kingdom with overseas customers, including sovereign lendings, and the main foreign exchange trading business arising in the United Kingdom. Of the £14bn of assets reported under this heading in 1998, it is estimated that £7bn relates to customers domiciled in Other European Union countries and £3bn relates to customers domiciled in the United States.

United States includes business conducted through the Bahamas and the Cayman Islands.

The world-wide activities of Barclays are highly integrated and, accordingly, it is not possible to present geographical segment information without making internal allocations, some of which are necessarily subjective. Where appropriate, amounts for each geographical segment and class of business reflect the benefit of earnings on a proportion of shareholders' funds, allocated generally by reference to weighted risk assets. ...

Extract 19.13: Reuters Group PLC (1998)

Notes on the consolidated profit and loss account

2. Segmental analysis

The tables below are a segmental analysis of revenue, costs and contribution. Central costs comprise the costs of corporate administration and the centrally controlled elements of development, marketing and technical operations. The table does not purport to show geographical profitability but reflects how Reuters controls costs and monitors contribution including the worldwide activities of Instinet and TIBCO which are managed separately. Because of the interactive nature of the worldwide operations of Reuters, Instinet and TIBCO costs incurred in one location often relate to revenues earned in other locations.

	1998 £M	% CHANGE	1997 £M	% CHANGE	RESTATED 1996 £M
Revenue					
Europe, Middle East and Africa (see note below)	**1,566**	**6%**	1,484	(5%)	1,564
Asia/Pacific	**466**	**(6%)**	496	(2%)	504
The Americas	**454**	**4%**	437	(1%)	440
	2,486	**3%**	2,417	(4%)	2,508
Instinet	**446**	**16%**	383	11%	346
TIBCO (see note below)	**100**	**23%**	82	37%	60
	3,032	**5%**	2,882	(1%)	2,914
Operating costs where incurred					
Europe, Middle East and Africa	**(1,028)**	**4%**	(986)	1%	(976)
Asia/Pacific	**(289)**	**(7%)**	(312)	–	(311)
The Americas	**(429)**	**7%**	(400)	(3%)	(414)
	(1,746)	**3%**	(1,698)	–	(1,701)
Instinet	**(291)**	**25%**	(234)	11%	(211)
TIBCO	**(87)**	**31%**	(67)	40%	(48)
	(2,124)	**6%**	(1,999)	2%	(1,960)
Contribution					
Europe, Middle East and Africa	**538**	**8%**	498	(15%)	588
Asia/Pacific	**177**	**(4%)**	184	(5%)	193
The Americas	**25**	**(33%)**	37	45%	26
	740	**3%**	719	(11%)	807
Instinet	**155**	**3%**	149	11%	135
TIBCO	**13**	**(13%)**	15	23%	12
	908	**3%**	883	(7%)	954
Central costs	**(351)**	**1%**	347	7%	(324)
Net currency gain	**39**	**(29%)**	56	–	11
Goodwill amortisation	**(46)**	**(9%)**	(51)	2%	(49)
Operating profit	**550**	**2%**	541	(8%)	592

United Kingdom and Ireland revenue was £542 million (1997 – £509 million, 1996 – £477 million). Instinet's and TIBCO's operations are predominantly based in the Americas.

Revenue is normally invoiced by Reuters in the same geographical area in which the customer is located. Revenue earned, therefore, generally represents revenue both by origin and by destination. The main exception is TIBCO, where a substantial proportion of revenue billed by the Americas is from customers located elsewhere. In 1998, 38% (1997 – 42%, 1996 – 42%) of TIBCO's revenue was generated from customers in the Americas, 47% (1997 – 43%, 1996 – 42%) from customers located in Europe, Middle East and Africa and 15% (1997 – 15%, 1996 – 19%) from customers in Asia/Pacific.

Revenue by product category	1998 £M	% CHANGE	1997 £M	% CHANGE	1996 £M
Information products					
Europe, Middle East and Africa	**1,164**	**7%**	1,087	(5%)	1,145
Asia/Pacific	**342**	**(5%)**	359	(2%)	365
The Americas	**343**	**6%**	324	1%	322
TIBCO	**100**	**23%**	82	37%	60
	1,949	**5%**	1,852	(2%)	1,892
Transaction products					
Europe, Middle East and Africa	**266**	**–**	266	(7%)	286
Asia/Pacific	**97**	**(9%)**	107	(1%)	108
The Americas	**73**	**1%**	72	(1%)	73
Instinet	**446**	**16%**	383	11%	346
	882	**6%**	828	2%	813
Media and professional products					
Europe, Middle East and Africa	**136**	**3%**	131	(1%)	133
Asia/Pacific	**27**	**(9%)**	30	(3%)	31
The Americas	**38**	**(8%)**	41	(9%)	45
	201	**(1%)**	202	(3%)	209
	3,032	**5%**	2,882	(1%)	2,914

Reuters operates in a single class of business: the provision of news and financial information and related services. With the exception of Instinet and TIBCO, Reuters products are delivered and sold through a common network and geographical infrastructure.

Revenue by type	1998 £M	% CHANGE	1997 £M	% CHANGE	1996 £M
Recurring	**2,170**	**1%**	2,147	(4%)	2,232
Usage	**621**	**22%**	511	7%	478
Outright sales	**241**	**8%**	224	10%	204
	3,032	**5%**	2,882	(1%)	2,914

Recurring revenue is derived from the sale of subscription services, including maintenance contracts. Usage revenue is based on volume and primarily relates to transaction products, including Instinet and certain activities of Reuters Television. Outright sales mainly represents once-off sales of information management systems.

Notes on the Consolidated Balance Sheet

15. Segmental analysis

The tables below show net assets and total assets by location on a basis consistent with the segmental analysis of profit in note 2. For the reasons discussed in that note, the assets in any location are not matched with the revenue earned in that location.

	1998	RESTATED 1997	1996
Location of net assets	£M	£M	£M
Non-interest bearing assets/(liabilities)			
Europe, Middle East and Africa	**253**	301	295
Asia/Pacific	**96**	101	98
The Americas	**4**	53	80
Instinet	**84**	114	37
TIBCO	**28**	6	4
Central	**(70)**	(180)	(98)
Non-interest bearing net assets	**395**	395	416
Interest bearing net (liabilities)/assets	**(6)**	1,284	1,043
	389	1,679	1,459

Central non-interest bearing liabilities consist principally of dividend and taxation liabilities partially offset by unamortised goodwill. Interest bearing net assets are stated after deducting deferred consideration which has been discounted for accounting purposes.

	1998	1997	1996
Location of total assets	£M	£M	£M
Europe, Middle East and Africa	**584**	644	584
Asia/Pacific	**213**	224	206
The Americas	**158**	178	195
Instinet	**686**	500	355
TIBCO	**64**	56	33
Central	**1,000**	1,311	1,202
	2,705	2,913	2,575
Fixed assets	**1,098**	1,046	1,026
Current assets	**1,607**	1,867	1,549
	2,705	2,913	2,575

Central assets consist principally of purchased goodwill net of accumulated amortisation, short-term investments and cash.

One or two companies assert that they have only one business operation, but then go on to give some further analysis of it. Since they do not regard the sub-units as separate segments, they avoid having to give the full range of disclosures required by SSAP 25. Safeway is an example:

Extract 19.14: Safeway plc (1999)

1.0 Sales and profit [extract]

The group's sole trading activity is grocery retailing which is carried out almost entirely in the United Kingdom.

In order to provide shareholders with additional information, the group's sales and operating profit have been analysed as set out below:

	1999 **£m**	1998 £m
Sales		
Britain	**7,925.5**	7,429.8
Ireland	**145.7**	63.8
	8,071.2	7,493.6
Turnover, excluding VAT		
Britain	**7,374.2**	6,919.1
Ireland	**136.5**	59.6
	7,510.7	6,978.7
Operating profit, before the costs of the store portfolio review and redundancy programme		
Britain	**431.2**	435.3
Ireland	**(9.4)**	(8.9)
Total	**421.8**	426.4
% margin – VAT excl.	**5.6%**	6.1%
Share of BP joint venture operating profit/(loss)	**0.2**	(0.2)
Net interest payable	**(64.9)**	(51.0)
Profit after interest	**357.1**	375.2
Net property losses	**(16.5)**	(5.0)
Profit before taxation and the store portfolio review and redundancy programme	**340.6**	370.2
Store portfolio review and redundancy programme	**–**	(30.0)
Profit on ordinary activities before taxation	**340.6**	340.2

3.2   Inter-segment sales

The standard requires that the turnover disclosed for each segment be split between sales to external customers and sales to other segments. Prior to the introduction of SSAP 25 few companies disclosed all such information; they either disclosed the total turnover for each segment and deducted one figure for inter-segment sales or disclosed sales to external customers only.

While ED 45 proposed the disclosure of the basis of transfer pricing, this proposal was not reflected in SSAP 25 as many commentators felt that companies would either argue that disclosure would be prejudicial or would provide a suitably vague and unhelpful general statement. Conscious of the effect on the credibility of the standard as a whole if there was widespread avoidance of this requirement, the ASC omitted it from the eventual standard. The absence of such information can, however, limit the usefulness of the disclosure of segmental results.

Some companies do however state the basis on which inter-segment sales are conducted. One example is ICI, as shown in Extract 19.4 above. Another is Unilever, which gives this description in its accounting policies, as shown below:

Extract 19.15: Unilever PLC (1998)

Accounting policies [extract]

Transfer pricing

The preferred method for determining transfer prices for own manufactured goods is to take the market price. Where there is no market price, the companies concerned follow established transfer pricing guidelines, where available, or else engage in arm's length negotiations.

Trade marks owned by the parent companies and used by the operating companies are, where appropriate, licensed in return for royalties or a fee.

General services provided by central advisory departments, Business Groups and research laboratories are charged to operating companies on the basis of fees.

3.3 Common costs

Common costs will normally take the form of central administration overheads, but in practice there could be a wide range of categories of common costs. However, the standard emphasises that 'costs that are directly attributable to individual reportable segments are not common costs for the purposes of this accounting standard and therefore should be allocated to those segments, irrespective of the fact that they may have been borne by a different segment or by Head Office'.[48]

SSAP 25 allows common costs to be allocated to different segments on what the company's management believes is a reasonable basis (see 2.2.7 above) but where the apportionment of common costs would be misleading, the standard requires that they should not be apportioned but the total should be deducted from the total of the segment results. Notwithstanding this, one or two companies disclose that they have apportioned such costs, as shown in these extracts:

Extract 19.16: Cookson Group plc (1998)

3 Segmental analyses [extract]

In each of the following analyses, central costs and net assets have been allocated according to the relative contribution of each continuing operation segment to the total. ...

Extract 19.17: Standard Chartered PLC (1998)

40. Segmental Information [extract]

... Group central expenses have been distributed between classes of business in proportion to their direct costs. The benefit of the Group's capital has been distributed between classes of business in proportion to their risk weighted assets.

Such a practice is consistent with the ASB's rules on the assessment of impairment of assets, whereby central assets such as head offices have to be apportioned across income-generating units for the purposes of the test (see Chapter 10 at 4.4). Nevertheless, we do not believe this to be a helpful approach, because it implies a relationship where none exists and is unlikely to add to the usefulness of the segmental information disclosed.

3.4   Allocation of interest income and interest expense

SSAP 25 suggests that in the majority of companies the individual segments will be financed by interest-bearing debt and equity in varying proportions. The interest earned or incurred by the individual segments is, therefore, a result of the holding company's overall policy rather than a proper reflection of the results of the various segments. For this reason, the standard requires that in these circumstances the results should exclude interest as 'comparisons of profit between segments or between different years for the same segment are likely to be meaningless if interest is included in arriving at the result'.[49]

However, where interest is fundamental to the nature of the business, the standard suggests that interest should be included in arriving at the segment result. Such an approach would be relevant to those companies involved in the financial sector, but it can also apply to diverse groups where some divisions are cash-generative and finance the others.

3.5   Exceptional items

The results which are to be analysed in terms of SSAP 25 are those 'before accounting for taxation, minority interests and extraordinary items', and usually also before interest.[50] The standard predated FRS 3 (see Chapter 22), which has virtually abolished extraordinary items but expanded the categories of exceptional items to be disclosed instead, and it is necessary to consider how these should be dealt with for segmental reporting purposes.

Exceptional items are not specifically addressed in SSAP 25, and by implication are to be included in the analysed results. In practice, some companies analyse their results before exceptional items, and do not always fully disclose to which segments the exceptional items belong.

In its 1993 accounts, BET excluded exceptional items from its operating profit and also its segmental analysis, but after the intervention of the Financial

Reporting Review Panel, it restated the figures in its 1994 accounts, as shown below:

Extract 19.18: BET Public Limited Company (1994)

Accounting policies [extract]

The 1993 comparatives have been restated to show operating exceptional items of £76.0 million within the statutory format headings to which they relate (£60.2 million in cost of sales and £15.8 million in administrative expenses) in recognition of developing practice in the application of FRS 3 and after a recent discussion with the Financial Reporting Review Panel. The restatement of the previously disclosed operating exceptional items is highlighted in Note 1(c) on page 39.

Notes to the consolidated accounts

Note 1 Analysis of profit and loss account [extract]

(c) Adjustment to 1993 comparatives

	1993 Published £m	Adjustment £m	1993 Restated £m
BY BUSINESS SECTOR			
Business services	25.6	(11.5)	14.1
Distribution services	20.8	(11.5)	9.3
Plant services	26.5	(10.7)	15.8
Textile services	28.1	(22.5)	5.6
Trading activities	101.0	(56.2)	44.8
Associated undertakings	7.3	–	7.3
Corporate and other	(24.6)	(10.7)	(35.3)
Loss on disposal of property	(4.0)	–	(4.0)
Continuing operations	79.7	(66.9)	12.8
Discontinued operations	(5.5)	(9.1)	(14.6)
	74.2	(76.0)	(1.8)
Costs previously disclosed as operating exceptional items	(76.0)	76.0	–
Operating loss	(1.8)	–	(1.8)
BY GEOGRAPHICAL LOCATION			
Europe – UK	33.3	(51.7)	(18.4)
– Continent	20.3	(14.3)	6.0
North America	13.5	(9.4)	4.1
Rest of the World	7.1	(0.6)	6.5
	74.2	(76.0)	(1.8)
Costs previously disclosed as operating exceptional items	(76.0)	76.0	–
Operating loss	(1.8)	–	(1.8)

In our view the best approach is to analyse the profit after exceptional items, while also making it clear how much each segment has been affected by such items.

3.6   Changes in composition of the group

FRS 3 requires that 'where an acquisition, or a sale or termination, has a material impact on a major business segment this should be disclosed and explained'.[51]

Some of the companies shown earlier in this chapter have shown discontinued operations separately in their segmental analyses, including ICI (Extract 19.4), Coats Viyella (Extract 19.5) and BET (Extract 19.18). The most common form of disclosure is simply to show discontinued operations as a residual category, analysing only the continuing operations into segments (which is not strictly what FRS 3 requires). Again, however, it is often evident from the discussion elsewhere in the accounts what the discontinued businesses related to.

The requirement in FRS 3 is a rather glib one, and deserves reconsideration when the standard is revised. In fact, a more rewarding approach might be to readdress the issue in any future revision of SSAP 25, because it would be more natural to incorporate such requirements into the framework of existing segmental disclosures. Indeed, the whole topic of disclosing the effects of acquisitions and discontinuances arguably fits more comfortably in the context of segmental reporting than in a general standard on the format of the profit and loss account.

3.7   How to define net assets

Net assets are not defined in the standard although it does indicate that, in most cases, these will be the non-interest bearing operating assets less the non-interest bearing operating liabilities. Where, and to the extent that, the segment result is calculated after accounting for interest, for example by companies in the financial sector, then the corresponding interest bearing assets and liabilities should be included in the calculation of net assets.[52]

Operating assets of a segment should not normally include loans or advances to, or investments in, another segment unless interest therefrom has been included in arriving at the segment result.[53]

Operating liabilities will normally include creditors which are included in working capital but will exclude liabilities in respect of proposed dividends and corporation tax as well as interest bearing liabilities such as loans, overdrafts and debentures. In the case of a consolidated balance sheet with a minority interest, the calculation of net assets should not involve the deduction of that interest.

Non-operating assets and liabilities, as well as unallocated assets and liabilities, should therefore be shown in the segmental analysis as reconciling items between the total of the individual segments' net assets and the figure for net assets appearing in the balance sheet.

As shown in Extract 19.4 above, ICI has shown a total of net non-operating assets which reconciles the segmentally analysed net assets to the balance sheet, and has listed the items included therein. There are a number of other ways of giving this information; BP Amoco has a reconciliation to tie up the segmental figures with the balance sheet:

Extract 19.19: BP Amoco p.l.c. (1998)

30 Group balance sheet analysis   **$ million**

	Capital expenditure and acquisitions		Operating capital employed	
	1998	1997	**1998**	1997
By business				
Exploration and Production	**6,318**	7,879	**38,586**	36,184
Refining and Marketing	**1,937**	1,824	**13,091**	14,578
Chemicals	**1,606**	1,145	**10,488**	9,979
Other business and corporate	**501**	572	**(1,899)**	(1,091)
Total	**10,362**	11,420	**60,266**	59,650
By geographical area				
UK [a]	**2,463**	2,413	**14,361**	13,035
Rest of Europe	**1,248**	1,243	**5,034**	4,800
USA	**3,720**	3,315	**25,758**	25,556
Rest of World	**2,931**	4,449	**15,113**	16,259
Total	**10,362**	11,420	**60,266**	59,650

Includes the following amounts for the BP/Mobil joint venture	**620**	646

[a] UK area includes the UK-based international activities of Refining and Marketing		**1998**	1997
	Operating capital employed	**60,266**	59,650
	Liabilities for current and deferred taxation	**(3,653)**	(3,925)
	Capital employed	**56,613**	55,725
	Financed by:		
	Finance debt	**13,755**	12,877
	Minority shareholders' interest	**1,072**	1,100
	BP Amoco shareholders' interest	**41,786**	41,748
		56,613	55,725

Firth Rixson analyses the excluded items more fully, as shown below:

Extract 19.20: Firth Rixson plc (1998)

17 Net assets

Segmental analysis	United Kingdom		United States		Total	Total
	1998	1997	**1998**	1997	**1998**	1997
	£'000	£'000	**£'000**	£'000	**£'000**	£'000
Net operating assets	**59,811**	48,002	**31,083**	26,929	**90,894**	74,931
Cash and short term deposits	**7,129**	6,904	**384**	1,169	**7,513**	8,073
Taxation recoverable	**–**	–	**611**	–	**611**	–
Bank overdrafts	**(2,318)**	(3,513)	**–**	–	**(2,318)**	(3,513)
Taxation payable	**(2,745)**	(2,435)	**–**	(311)	**(2,745)**	(2,746)
Dividends payable	**(3,197)**	(2,833)	**–**	–	**(3,197)**	(2,833)
Loans	**(24,326)**	(17,750)	**–**	–	**(24,326)**	(17,750)
Deferred taxation	**(958)**	–	**–**	–	**(958)**	–
Net assets	**33,396**	28,375	**32,078**	27,787	**65,474**	56,162

---

4   COMPARISON WITH IASC AND US PRONOUNCEMENTS

4.1   IASC

The international standard on the issue of segmental reporting is IAS 14 – *Segment Reporting*. The original version was published by the IASC in August 1981[54] and reformatted in 1994, but was revised again in 1997. The original IAS 14 was similar to SSAP 25 in that the definition of reportable segments was left to the management of the reporting company and that disclosure of turnover, profits and assets analysed by industry and geographical segments was required, but the revised version contains a little more of the flavour of SFAS 131 (see 4.2.3 below). The main features of the current version, and how it compares with SSAP 25, are set out below:

4.1.1   Scope

IAS 14 applies to all enterprises whose equity or debt securities are publicly traded (or are about to be). The original version also applied to other 'economically significant entities', including subsidiaries. SSAP 25 applies to all companies to the extent that its requirements are equivalent to those contained within Schedule 4 to the Companies Act 1985 and, generally, to public companies (whether their securities are publicly traded or not), to banking and insurance companies or groups and to large private companies (and other entities). There is no exemption in IAS 14 to allow companies not to disclose segmental information on the grounds that disclosure would be seriously prejudicial to the interests of the company. SSAP 25 acknowledges that, in this respect, compliance with SSAP 25 will not ensure compliance with IAS 14.

4.1.2   Identification of segments

IAS 14 requires information to be reported for both business segments and geographical segments, but one of these is to be regarded as the primary basis and the other as the secondary basis (requiring less information to be disclosed), depending on which is regarded as providing the more meaningful analysis of the predominant source and nature of risks and returns. The segments are to be identified on the basis of the internal organisational structure and reporting systems, because they are presumed to be aligned to the same objectives. However, if the systems place equal emphasis on these two dimensions, the business segmentation is to be regarded as the primary basis for analysis and the geographical segmentation as the secondary one.

In contrast, SSAP 25 gives equal prominence to business and geographical segmental information. More generally, IAS 14's emphasis on the use of internal reporting systems as the key to identification of segments owes more to the US standard than to SSAP 25 (and the original version of IAS 14); however, it may well be that there is no substantial difference in practice, and that the same segments would often be identified under all these standards.

4.1.3   Information to be disclosed

In respect of the primary segmental analysis, IAS 14 requires the following to be disclosed:

- Segment revenue (both external and intra-segment)
- Segment result
- Total segment assets
- Segment liabilities
- Capital expenditure
- Depreciation
- Other significant non-cash expense
- Share of results of associates and joint ventures, and aggregate investment in these entities

All these amounts should be reconciled to the totals in the accounts of the reporting enterprise. These go some way beyond the equivalent requirements in the UK; in particular, SSAP 25 does not require disclosure of capital expenditure, depreciation and other non-cash expense, and it does not require segmental net assets to be grossed up to show total assets and liabilities by segment.

For the secondary analysis, the main items to be reported are the segment revenue, total assets and capital expenditure.[55]

Nestlé gives this note of segmental information.

Extract 19.21: Nestlé S.A. (1998)

1 Segmental information
By management responsibilities and geographic area

In millions of Swiss francs	Sales		Results	
	1998	1997	**1998**	1997
Food				
Europe	**26798**	25706	**2452**	2348
Americas	**22563**	22262	**2963**	2716
Africa, Asia and Oceania	**12429**	13493	**1618**	2039
Other activities	**9957**	8537	**1343**	1091
	71747	69998	**8376**	8194
Unallocated items [a]			**(1276)**	(1137)
Trading profit			**7100**	7057

(a) Mainly corporate expenses, research and development costs as well as amortisation of intangible assets.

The analysis of sales by geographic areas is stated by customer destination. Inter-segment sales are not significant.

In millions of Swiss francs	Assets		Liabilities	
	1998	1997	**1998**	1997
Food				
Europe	**14354**	13080	**5083**	4704
Americas	**9971**	10618	**2748**	2753
Africa, Asia and Oceania	**6526**	6809	**1588**	1663
Other activities	**6124**	4934	**2350**	1979
	36975	35441	**11769**	11099
Unallocated items [b]	**6828**	3619	**38**	83
Eliminations	**(587)**	(751)	**(587)**	(751)
	43216	38309	**11220**	10431

(b) Corporate and research and development assets/liabilities, including intangible assets.

In millions of Swiss francs	Capital expenditure		Depreciation of tangible fixed assets	
	1998	1997	**1998**	1997
Food				
Europe	**1026**	1041	**997**	1023
Americas	**827**	823	**728**	756
Africa, Asia and Oceania	**457**	736	**378**	414
Other activities	**629**	572	**434**	413
	2939	3172	**2537**	2606
Unallocated items [c]	**122**	89	**72**	71
	3061	3261	**2609**	2677

(c) Corporate and research and development tangible fixed assets.

By major product group

In millions of Swiss francs	Sales		Results	
	1998	1997	**1998**	1997
Beverages	**19879**	19142	**3253**	3243
Milk products, nutrition and ice cream	**19175**	19334	**1837**	1932
Prepared dishes and cooking aids				
(and miscellaneous activities)	**18765**	17660	**1617**	1525
Chocolate and confectionery	**10485**	10663	**976**	1054
Pharmaceutical products	**3443**	3199	**915**	825
	71747	69998	**8598**	8579
Unallocated items [a]			**(1498)**	(1522)
Trading profit			**7100**	7057

(a) Mainly corporate expenses, research and development costs, amortisation of intangible assets as well as restructuring costs.

In millions of Swiss francs	Assets	
	1998	1997
Beverages	**9685**	9529
Milk products, nutrition and ice cream	**10759**	11109
Prepared dishes and cooking aids		
(and miscellaneous activities)	**9316**	8624
Chocolate and confectionery	**6343**	6423
Pharmaceutical products	**1095**	910
	37198	36595

In millions of Swiss francs	Capital Expenditure	
	1998	1997
Beverages	**593**	629
Milk products, nutrition and ice cream	**576**	745
Prepared dishes and cooking aids		
(and miscellaneous activities)	**442**	445
Chocolate and confectionery	**388**	435
Pharmaceutical products	**81**	66
	2080	2320
Administration, distribution, research		
and development	**981**	941
	3061	3261

4.1.4   Basis of inter-segment pricing

IAS 14 requires the basis of inter-segment pricing to be disclosed. Although this was proposed by ED 45, it was not carried through to SSAP 25 because it was felt that the quality of compliance with this requirement was likely to be poor and could adversely affect the credibility of the standard as a whole. Again, to this extent, compliance with SSAP 25 will not ensure compliance with IAS 14.

4.2 US

4.2.1 *Introduction*

In 1969 the SEC issued requirements for reporting line-of-business information in registration statements. In 1970, those requirements were extended to annual reports filed with the SEC on Form 10-K and in 1974 they were extended to the annual report to security holders of companies filing with the SEC. The FASB responded with the issue of SFAS 14 – *Financial Reporting for Segments of a Business Enterprise* – which was issued in 1976.[56] In June 1997, however, the FASB issued SFAS 131 – *Disclosures about Segments of an Enterprise and Related Information* – and this standard became effective for periods beginning after 15 December 1997, superseding SFAS 14.

4.2.2 *SFAS 14*

The requirements of SFAS 14 were essentially the same as those of SSAP 25 in that disclosure of turnover, profits and assets analysed by industry and geographical segments was required. Like SSAP 25, SFAS 14 left the determination of the different industry and geographical segments of an enterprise to the management.[57] However, it also required a number of extra disclosures, such as the basis of inter-segment pricing and details of each segment's capital expenditure and depreciation.[58]

4.2.3 *SFAS 131*

SFAS 131 differs from SFAS 14 by adopting a 'management approach' to defining what segmental information is to be reported. This reflects the way in which the management of the business organises its operating segments for decision-making purposes. The guiding principle is that the manner in which segmental information is presented to the chief executive officer should also determine how it is reported externally; this is thought both to be the most relevant information (since it presents the business as the management itself sees it) and the easiest to produce. However the application of this principle means that the information presented may be less easy to compare with that of other enterprises; it may even be produced using different accounting policies from those used in the accounts as a whole. SFAS 131 requires any such measurement differences to be explained,[59] and also requires segmental information to be reconciled to the totals shown in the consolidated accounts.[60]

A *Scope*

SFAS 131 applies to public business enterprises, which are defined as those (a) whose debt or equity securities trade in a public market on a foreign or domestic stock exchange or in the OTC market, or (b) which are required to file financial statements with the SEC.[61]

B   *Definition of segments*

An operating segment is defined as a component of an enterprise:

(a)   that engages in business activities from which it may earn revenues and incur expenses (including revenues and expenses relating to transactions with other components of the same enterprise),

(b)   whose operating results are regularly reviewed by the enterprise's chief operating decision-maker to make decisions about resources to be allocated to the segment and assess its performance, and

(c)   for which discrete information is available.[62]

Similar segments may be reported in aggregate rather than separately if they are similar in all the following respects:

(a)   the nature of the products and services;

(b)   the nature of the production processes;

(c)   the type or class of customer for their products and services;

(d)   the methods used to distribute their products or provide for their services; and

(e)   if applicable, the nature of the regulatory environment, for example, banking, insurance, or public utilities.[63]

Separate information should be given where a segment contributes 10% or more of the enterprise's revenues, assets, profits or losses.[64] Profits and losses are to be assessed for this purpose by comparing the segment's profit with all other profitable segments or its loss with all other loss-making segments. The separately reported segments must account for at least 75% of the enterprise's revenue – in other words, no more than 25% of the total can be classified as 'other'.[65] Disclosure has to be made of the factors that have been used to identify the segments, and the types of products or services from which they derive their revenues.

C   *Information to be disclosed*

SFAS 131 requires the results and total assets of each segment to be disclosed, but whether more detail is given depends on whether it is reviewed by the chief executive officer. The following profit and loss account items should be disclosed if they meet that test:

■   External sales

■   Inter-segment sales

■   Interest receivable

■   Interest payable

■   Depreciation and amortisation, and other significant non-cash items

■   Unusual items and extraordinary items

■   Share of associates' results

■   Tax.[66]

Similarly, this information has to be given about assets if it is reviewed by the chief executive officer:

- Investments in associates
- Capital expenditure
- Long-term customer relationships of a financial institution
- Mortgage and other servicing rights
- Deferred policy acquisition costs
- Deferred tax assets.[67]

As a minimum, SFAS 131 requires segmental disclosure of external sales by product or service, and also geographical analysis of external sales and fixed assets. If the above 'management approach' has not delivered that disclosure, it has to be given in addition, this time using the same policies and bases as are used in the consolidated accounts.[68]

If sales to one customer (or a group of entities under common control) are 10% or more of the total revenue, that fact and the amount of revenue from each customer must be disclosed. The segment making the sales must be named, but the customer of the customer need not be given.[69]

5   CONCLUSION

It is clear that the general standard of segmental reporting in the UK has significantly improved in the years since SSAP 25 was introduced. As shown by some of the extracts reproduced in this chapter, large companies typically now devote a substantial amount of space in their annual reports to the description and analysis of their divisional activities. Provided it is applied constructively and with common sense, the present reporting framework gives companies the opportunity to present a good deal of useful information for the readers of accounts.

The ASB has found little enthusiasm in the UK for any amendment that would bring the present requirements under SSAP 25 closer to those of the more recent international standards. The 'management approach' relied upon by SFAS 131 and, to some extent, IAS 14 attracted few supporters when the ASB suggested it; many felt that if this rather curious approach of using internal information really had merit, it would be appropriate to extend the principle to all aspects of financial reporting, not just for segmental reporting, which would substantially reduce the need for accounting standards. But it also seems that there is little appetite among users for any significant expansion in the extent of segmentally reported information. It may be that the analyst community already receives enough information on this from sources outside the financial statements. It therefore seems that this is one area of UK financial reporting that is unlikely to undergo significant further change for the time being.

References

1   IAS 14, *Segment Reporting*, IASC, Revised 1997, para. 9.
2   *Ibid*.
3   R. K. Mautz, *Financial Reporting by Diversified Companies*, Financial Executives Research Foundation, 1968, p. 94.
4   CA 67, s 17.
5   *Ibid.*, s 20.
6   CA 81, Sch. 1, para. 55(2).
7   *Ibid.*, para. 55(5).
8   CA 85, Sch. 4, para. 55.
9   By the Companies Act 1985 (Miscellaneous Accounting Amendments) Regulations 1996 (SI96/189).
10 ED 45, *Segmental reporting*, November 1988.
11 SSAP 25, *Segmental reporting*, June 1990.
12 ED 45, para. 37(a).
13 Discussion Paper – *Segmental Reporting*, ASB, May 1996.
14 SSAP 25, para. 1.
15 *Ibid.*, paras. 3 and 40.
16 *Ibid.*, paras. 4 and 41.
17 These limits are reviewed from time to time. In March 1999, the government issued proposals to increase the limits to the maximum permitted by the EU, which in turn were subject to a proposal for upward revision. If these changes were made, the equivalent thresholds for the purposes of this test would become a turnover of £192 million and total assets of £96 million.
18 *Ibid.*, para. 35.
19 *Ibid.*, para. 43.
20 *Ibid.*, paras. 7 and 8.
21 *Ibid.*, para. 8.
22 *Ibid.*, para. 12.
23 *Ibid.*, para. 15.
24 *Ibid.*, para. 16.
25 *Ibid.*, para. 9.
26 SFAS 14, *Financial Reporting for Segments of a Business Enterprise*, FASB, December 1976, para. 15, and SFAS 131, *Disclosure about Segments of a Business and Related Information*, FASB, June 1997, para. 18.
27 SSAP 25, para. 34.
28 *Ibid*.
29 *Ibid.*, para. 34(a).
30 *Ibid.*, para. 34.
31 *Ibid.*, para. 44.
32 See CA 85, Sch. 9, Part I, para. 76.
33 *Segmental Reporting*, British Bankers' Association and Irish Bankers' Federation, January 1993.
34 SSAP 25, para. 34.
35 *Ibid.*, para. 22.
36 *Ibid.*, para. 21.
37 *Ibid.*, para. 24.
38 *Ibid.*, para. 25.
39 *Ibid.*, para. 37.
40 *Ibid.*, paras. 4 and 41.
41 *Ibid.*, para. 36.
42 *Ibid*.
43 *Ibid*.
44 *Ibid.*, para. 23.
45 *Ibid*.
46 *Ibid.*, para. 10.
47 *Ibid.*, para. 39.
48 *Ibid.*, para. 23.
49 *Ibid.*, para. 22.

50   *Ibid.*, para. 34.
51   FRS 3, *Reporting Financial Performance*, ASB, December 1992, para. 15.
52   SSAP 25, para. 24.
53   *Ibid.*, para. 25.
54   IAS 14 (original), *Reporting Financial Information by Segment*, IASC, 1981.
55   IAS 14 (revised), paras. 69 & 70.
56   There were also a number of subsequent US standards that amended SFAS 14, namely: SFAS 18, *Financial Reporting for Segments of a Business Enterprise — Interim Financial Statements*; SFAS 21, *Suspension of the Reporting of Earnings per Share and Segment Information by Nonpublic Enterprises*; SFAS 24, *Reporting Segment Information in Financial Statements That Are Presented in Another Enterprise's Financial Report*; and SFAS 30, *Disclosure of Information about Major Customers*.
57   *Ibid.*, para. 15.
58   SFAS 14, para. 27.
59   SFAS 131, *Disclosures about Segments of an Enterprise and Related Information*, FASB, June 1997, para. 31.
60   *Ibid.*, para. 32.
61   *Ibid.*, para. 9.
62   *Ibid.*, para. 10.
63   *Ibid.*, para. 17.
64   *Ibid.*, para. 18.
65   *Ibid.*, para. 20.
66   *Ibid.*, para. 27.
67   *Ibid.*, para. 28.
68   *Ibid.*, paras. 37 & 38.
69   *Ibid.*, para. 39.

Chapter 20   Pension costs

1   INTRODUCTION

1.1   Background

Accounting for the costs of pensions and similar benefits in the accounts of employer companies presents one of the most difficult challenges in the whole field of financial reporting. The amounts involved are large, the timescale is long, the estimation process is complex and involves many areas of uncertainty which have to be made the subject of assumptions; in addition the actuarial mechanisms used for matching the costs to years of employment are complicated and their selection open to debate.

Before the introduction of SSAP 24, generally accepted practice in the UK had been to charge pension costs in the profit and loss account on the basis of funding payments made to the pension scheme, which obviously meant that the reported profit of the employer company was susceptible to fluctuations because of changes in the contributions made. In addition, most companies gave only very limited information in their accounts about the obligations to pay the pensions to which they were committed, and the assets which had been built up in their pension funds to meet these obligations.

The effect of SSAP 24 was to look through the veil that lies between the employer company and its pension fund. The measure of pension cost ceased to be simply the amount of contributions paid to the fund; instead it is necessary to examine the condition of the fund itself to see what the long-term cost of providing pensions really is. Thus, pension expense is derived directly from actuarial valuations of the scheme, although the standard requires that changes in these valuations are to be recognised only gradually, by amortising them over a number of years, so as to reduce the volatility which would otherwise result.

The philosophy of the standard therefore rests on the premise that the pension fund is in substance a vehicle of the employer company and that any surplus held by the fund should be regarded as a company asset, even if it is not directly shown as such on the company's balance sheet. This follows from the argument that, in a final salary scheme, the employer has to bear whatever cost is needed to provide the pensions promised to the workforce after taking account of their own (fixed) contributions; any excess of assets which emerges in the form of a pension scheme surplus therefore belongs to the employer. However, this stance is not free from controversy. Employees and their representatives frequently assert that a pension fund surplus morally belongs to the members, and the legal position will depend on the precise terms of the scheme and the trust deed under which the fund is administered. Some recent decisions by the Pensions Ombudsman, supported by the courts, have given strength to this view.

Certainly, if a pension scheme surplus is an asset, it is not one which the company can easily get its hands on. Although there are circumstances whereby the company may take refunds from an over-funded scheme, it can only do so under penalty of tax at a rate of 40% and provided certain conditions are satisfied. However, the surplus gives the company the opportunity to reduce its future contributions to the fund below what they would otherwise be, and in these terms it may be appropriate to think of it as an asset; this is probably the main rationale for the approach adopted by the standard.

The meaning and treatment of the balance sheet figure has become the main area of controversy in the application of SSAP 24. The ASB is considering revisions to the standard and, influenced both by its draft *Statement of Principles* and by international developments, is likely to focus much more on the balance sheet than the profit and loss account in any replacement standard. Whether such a change of emphasis is really appropriate, however, given the long-term nature of pension provision, is a matter for debate.

1.2   The development of an accounting standard in the UK

1.2.1   *Napier interim report*

The first document on the subject to be published by the ASC comprised an assessment of the issues to be addressed, set out in an interim report by Christopher Napier of the London School of Economics in 1982.[1] Napier's interim report was a by-product of a research study commissioned by the Institute of Chartered Accountants in England and Wales in 1981, and his full report was finally published by the Institute in 1983.[2] This comprises a comprehensive and lucid exposition of the issues involved in accounting for pension costs, and is of particular value in explaining the mechanics of the actuarial valuation process and how they may be adapted to accounting use.

This paper identified certain key characteristics of pension schemes which subsequently formed the foundation of the ASC's thinking on the subject. These were that pensions should be seen simply as a form of deferred remuneration; that the application of the accruals concept would require that their cost should be matched against the benefits of the employees' services over their working lives; and that although the objective of funding the pension scheme was also to provide for the ultimate cost of the pensions, the pattern of funding payments depended on management decisions which were not necessarily a good basis for measuring the annual cost for accounting purposes.

The paper also drew a distinction between 'normal' costs of providing for pensions, and 'abnormal' or 'special' costs. Normal costs were described as those which would arise if (a) no credit was given by the pension scheme for service prior to the scheme's introduction, and (b) the assumptions of the actuary as to mortality, employee turnover, salary progression, investment returns etc. were borne out by subsequent events. Abnormal or special costs were therefore those costs which arose because of variations in the assumptions in (a) and (b) above. This distinction subsequently formed the basis for that used in SSAP 24 between the regular ongoing cost and the effects of variations, which are discussed in 2.5.1 and 2.5.2 below.

Napier also briefly touched on the need for disclosure of information about pension arrangements in company accounts, and listed several possible disclosures for consideration.

1.2.2 ED 32

At the time of publishing Napier's interim report, the ASC was already working on the subject of pension costs, and in 1983 they published the exposure draft of a standard on the subject, ED 32 – *The disclosure of pension information in company accounts.*[3] As the title reveals, the Committee had decided as a first stage to limit its strategy to one of ensuring better disclosure in accounts about the details of company pension schemes, before proceeding towards the more difficult question of measurement in the profit and loss account. The main thrust of the proposals of the exposure draft was contained in a single, lengthy, paragraph, which read as follows:

'Disclosure should be made in financial statements of sufficient information concerning pension arrangements to enable users of the statements to gain a broad understanding of the significance of pension costs in the accounting period and of actual and contingent liabilities and commitments at the balance sheet date. Towards this general objective, the disclosures should include at least the following, subject to any necessary modifications in the case of employees paid abroad and to summarising to a reasonable extent in the case of individual companies or groups with a number of different pension schemes:

(a) the nature of the pension schemes (e.g. defined benefit or defined contribution), whether they are externally funded or internally financed and any legal obligations of the company (e.g. undertakings to meet the balance of cost);

(b)   the accounting policy, and the funding policy if different from the accounting policy, indicating the basis used for allocating pension costs to accounting periods;

(c)   whether the pension costs and liabilities are assessed in accordance with the advice of a professionally qualified actuary and, if so, the date of the most recent actuarial valuation;

(d)   the amount charged in the profit and loss account for pension costs, distinguishing between normal charges related to employees' pay and service in the accounting period and other charges or credits (e.g. additional charges to cover the cost of post-retirement awards not covered by the normal charge, or reductions in the normal charge to take account of contribution holidays or a temporarily reduced contribution rate resulting from overfunding), with explanations of such charges or credits;

(e)   any commitments to change the rate of contributions or to make special contributions;

(f)   any provisions or prepayments in the balance sheet, resulting from a difference between the accounting policy and the funding policy;

(g)   the amount of any deficiency on a discontinuance basis actuarial valuation or on the requirements of the Occupational Pensions Board, indicating the action, if any, being taken to deal with it in future financial statements;

(h)   the amount of any material self-investment (i.e. investment by the pension fund in the employer company itself);

(i)   in the case of internally financed schemes, the amount of the provision at the balance sheet date and of any identifiable fund of assets representing the provision; and

(j)   expected significant effects on future financial statements of any changes which have occurred in the above, including the effects of any material improvements in benefits.'[4]

This list picked up a number of the requirements which Napier had suggested, but also introduced a number of new ones. The exposure draft drew attention to the Companies Act requirements to disclose pension costs and commitments (described in 5 below), but said that compliance with the ED would not necessarily ensure compliance with the legal requirements.

1.2.3   Statement of Intent

In 1984, the ASC published a further document on the subject; this time it was a consultative Statement of Intent.[5] This revealed that the Committee had altered its strategy and was now ready to address the measurement of pension costs, rather than merely proposing disclosure requirements about pension arrangements. The broad principles which it outlined were consistent with those recommended by Napier, but were discussed in rather more detail than in Napier's interim report.

1.2.4   ED 39

Having received and considered the reaction to its statement of intent, the ASC proceeded to formulate an exposure draft based on the principles which the statement had outlined, and in May 1986 it published ED 39 – *Accounting for pension costs*.[6] The exposure draft dealt both with the measurement of pension cost for profit and loss account purposes and with fairly extensive disclosure requirements. Its main proposals were as follows:

(a)   pension costs should be recognised on a systematic basis over the expected service lives of employees;

(b)   total pension cost charged in the profit and loss account should be equal to regular cost plus variations arising from experience deficiencies and surpluses, changes in assumptions, etc. This broadly corresponded to the analysis made by Napier of 'normal' and 'abnormal' costs;

(c)   for a defined benefit scheme, the regular pension cost should be a substantially level percentage of pensionable payroll. (For defined contribution schemes, the cost is simply the contribution payable, since that is the extent of the employer's commitment.);

(d)   variations from regular cost should generally be allocated over expected average remaining service lives of employees. The only exceptions would be if prudence dictated that a deficiency should be recognised over a shorter period, or if the variation were linked to an extraordinary item, in which case it would be recognised immediately as part of that item;

(e)   a liability should be provided for if the cumulative pension cost charged against profits has not been completely discharged by contributions or directly paid pensions; and

(f)   various proposals were made on how to account for the pension arrangements of an acquired company.

The exposure draft also proposed a fairly comprehensive list of disclosure requirements.

1.2.5   SSAP 24

In May 1988, the ASC finally issued SSAP 24[7] which was modelled on ED 39. The main amendments which were made from the exposure draft were to incorporate some exceptions to the basic rule that variations from regular cost should be spread over the average future working lives of the employees, to add transitional provisions, to soften the requirement to take account of expected discretionary pension increases, and to modify certain aspects of the disclosure requirements. In addition, the proposals concerned with accounting for the pension costs of an acquired company were deleted, since the subject was instead being addressed by the ASC under its project on accounting for fair values in the context of an acquisition. The standard became effective for periods beginning on or after 1 July 1988.

1.2.6　Subsequent developments

Two further relevant pronouncements have been issued since SSAP 24 came into force. In 1992, the Urgent Issues Task Force issued an Abstract that extended the principles of the standard to health care and other similar post-retirement benefits; this is dealt with in 4.8 below. Later, in 1994, the ASB addressed the question of accounting for the pension arrangements of acquired companies in FRS 7. This necessarily adopted a balance sheet focus, and it introduced a new angle that is absent from SSAP 24: the recoverability of the pension asset in the balance sheet (see Chapter 6 at 2.4.3 D).

More recently the ASB has been considering a wholesale revision of the standard, and in June 1995 it published a Discussion Paper – *Pension Costs in the Employer's Financial Statements*. This set out two possible approaches to accounting for defined benefit schemes. The approach preferred by the majority of the board was to retain SSAP 24's overall philosophy, but to limit some of the options available to preparers when applying the standard and improve the disclosure requirements. However, a minority favoured an alternative approach which required the 'market value' of the scheme to be recognised on the balance sheet each year. This is an estimate of the amount that a hypothetical third party would pay or receive in exchange for taking the future pension obligation away from the reporting entity. However, since the pension ultimately paid will be based on a future, as yet undetermined, salary, such a value is not readily available, and a calculation to approximate to this value was proposed. To limit the annual volatility to the profit and loss account it was also proposed that some movements would be taken to the statement of total recognised gains and losses.

Respondents to this Discussion Paper strongly favoured the majority view and were dismissive of the alternative. Since then, however, the IASC has revised its own standard in a way that is much more in line with the approach favoured by the minority on the ASB (see 6.1 below). The ASB followed this in July 1998 with a further Discussion Paper – *Aspects of accounting for pension costs*. This focused on four main issues:

(a)　The basis of valuation of the assets for a pension scheme

The paper concluded that assets in a pension scheme should be valued at market value, on the basis that this provided the most objective and reliable measure of scheme assets and that it was now the international approach (See 6.1 below). It acknowledged that the use of market values would inevitably lead to more volatility in asset valuations, but said that this volatility could be reduced by selecting an appropriate discount rate for the liabilities of the scheme.

(b)　The rate at which pension liabilities are discounted

The ASB proposed that the pension liability should be discounted using a rate of return on matching assets, and said it was looking to the actuarial profession to develop guidance on how to determine appropriate rates for different classes of liabilities. The suggestion was that liabilities for pensions to current and deferred pensioners would be discounted at rates of return based on fixed interest or index-linked bonds, depending on whether the pensions are fixed or index-linked. On the other hand, liabilities for pensions to current employees would be discounted at a rate that incorporates an element of equity return.

One of the reasons put forward for applying this discount rate was that it would mitigate the effect of fluctuations in asset values. This is because when confidence is high, leading to high share prices and high asset values in a pension scheme, the risk premium that investors require on equities is low and so the discount rate will be low, giving rise to a higher pension liability. However, if the market crashed and asset values fell, the equity risk premium will rise, giving a higher discount rate for the pension liability. This would result in a decreased pension liability which would mitigate the impact of the drop in asset values.

It is interesting that this was not the approach taken in IAS 19. The international standard requires pension obligations to be discounted at the market rate on high quality fixed-rate corporate or government bonds (see 6.1.3 below). This will generally result in a larger liability being recognised under the international standard. Other standard setters internationally have rejected the idea of seeking to use the rate of return on matching assets as the discount rate because they do not believe that such matching assets really exist; there is no close correlation between final salaries and equity returns.

(c)   The method of dealing in the accounts with actuarial gains and losses

The paper considered four possible options for the treatment of actuarial gains and losses and discusses the pros and cons of each:

■   Amortisation in the profit and loss account over the average service lives of employees, as is currently required under SSAP 24;

■   Charge in full to the profit and loss account, as a non-operating exceptional item;

■   Charge in full to the statement of total recognised gains and losses; and

■   Charge in full to the statement of total recognised gains and losses and amortise from there to the profit and loss account over the average remaining service lives.

The ASB used this paper to discuss the more general issue of the role of the statement of total recognised gains and losses in financial reporting, as discussed more fully in Chapter 22.

(d)   Treatment of past service costs

The paper addressed the issue of how to treat past service costs arising from an increase in benefits, and put forward three alternatives:

■   Recognise all past service costs in the profit and loss account immediately when the improved benefits are awarded;

■   Recognise past service costs of former employees immediately and spread forward those relating to current employees; and

■   Offset past service costs against any surplus funding them and recognise the excess in the profit and loss account. (The impact of this would depend on the method prescribed for the treatment of actuarial gains and losses. For example, if the surplus was being amortised in the profit and loss account, only the unamortised balance would be available for setting off past service costs.)

The paper concluded that the majority of the ASB favoured charging the costs immediately when the improved benefits are awarded.

It seems clear from this discussion paper that the Board continues to favour an approach that incorporates an annual valuation of the pension fund in the employer's balance sheet. It therefore seems likely that proposals will soon be brought forward to introduce a new standard that adopts this approach. In the meantime, however, SSAP 24 remains in force and the remainder of this chapter discusses its requirements and how they are applied in practice.

2   REQUIREMENTS OF SSAP 24

2.1   Scope

SSAP 24 is very broad in its scope. It applies to all pension arrangements, whether they arise from an explicit contractual commitment, or from custom and practice, or even if they are of an ex gratia nature; it applies to both funded and unfunded schemes; it applies to defined benefit schemes, defined contribution schemes and to those which are a hybrid mixture of the two; it applies to all schemes, whether insured or self-administered; it applies both to UK schemes and to foreign schemes (although when it is difficult to apply it to the latter, there is a hint of de facto relaxation of the requirements in the standard); and it applies to schemes of all sizes. The only specific exclusions from the scope of the standard are in respect of state social security contributions and redundancy payments.

The application of the standard to other post-retirement benefits, such as private health care, was an area of some confusion. The standard itself says that its principles may be applicable to such benefits,[8] but the ASC subsequently indicated that this was not intended to be mandatory.[9] However, in November 1992 the UITF published an Abstract requiring SSAP 24 principles to be applied to all such benefits, although with an extended period for implementation.[10] This is discussed in more detail in 4.8 below.

2.2   Accounting objective

The basic accounting objective which the standard sets is that the employer should recognise the cost of providing pensions on a systematic and rational basis over the period during which he receives benefit from the employees' services.[11] The standard explicitly distinguishes this from the funding objective, which is described as being to build up assets in a prudent and controlled manner in advance of the retirement of the members of the scheme, in order that the obligations of the scheme may be met without undue distortion of the employer's cash flow.[12] It is emphasised that the funding plan will not necessarily provide a satisfactory basis for the allocation of pension cost to accounting periods.

The standard is expressed in terms of the profit and loss account, and no explicit objective is set in relation to the balance sheet. However, it can be demonstrated that the balance sheet will reflect the underlying surplus or deficit in the pension scheme, although this figure will be combined with the amount of variations in pension cost which are being carried forward for recognition in the profit and loss account of future years. The balance sheet dimension of SSAP 24 is explored further in 2.5.4 below.

2.3   Definition of terms

There are several technical terms relating to pensions which have specific meanings laid down by the standard. These are shown below.

Accrued benefits are the benefits for service up to a given point in time, whether the rights to the benefits are vested or not. They may be calculated in relation to current earnings or projected final earnings.

An *accrued benefits method* of actuarial valuation is a valuation method in which the actuarial value of liabilities relates at a given date to:

(a)   the benefits, including future increases promised by the rules, for the current and deferred pensioners and their dependants; and

(b)   the benefits which the members assumed to be in service on the given date will receive for service up to that date only.

Allowance may be made for expected increases in earnings after the given date, and/or for additional pension increases not promised by the rules. The given date may be a current or future date. The further into the future the adopted date lies, the closer the results will be to those of a prospective benefits valuation method (which is defined below).

The *average remaining service life* is a weighted average of the expected future service of the current members of the scheme up to their normal retirement dates or expected dates of earlier withdrawal or death in service. The weightings can have regard to periods of service, salary levels of scheme members and future anticipated salary growth in a manner which the actuary considers appropriate having regard to the actuarial method and assumptions used.

A *current funding level valuation* considers whether the assets would have been sufficient at the valuation date to cover liabilities arising in respect of pensions in payment, preserved benefits for members whose pensionable service has ceased and accrued benefits for members in pensionable service, based on pensionable service to and pensionable earnings at, the date of valuation including revaluation on the statutory basis or such higher basis as has been promised. (This is sometimes called a 'discontinuance' basis, because it evaluates the scheme's ability to meet its obligations if it were to be discontinued.)

A *discretionary or ex gratia increase* in a pension or an *ex gratia pension* is one which the employer has no legal, contractual or implied commitment to provide.

A *defined benefit scheme* is a pension scheme in which the rules specify the benefits to be paid and the scheme is financed accordingly. (These are commonly referred to as 'final salary' schemes. This means that the employer promises to pay the member a pension which is related to (usually) his final salary at or near the date of retirement; a typical example might give the employee a pension which was calculated at one sixtieth of his final salary for each year in which he was an employee and a member of the scheme. Because various factors, notably the amount of the final salary, will not be known until many years have elapsed, the eventual cost of providing the pension will have to be estimated.)

A *defined contribution scheme* is a pension scheme in which the benefits are directly determined by the value of contributions paid in respect of each member. Normally the rate of contribution is specified in the rules of the scheme. (These are commonly referred to as 'money purchase' schemes. In contrast to defined benefit (final salary) schemes, the employer has no obligation to provide a pension beyond that which is earned by the contributions which are payable under the scheme, so the cost of providing the pension is fixed and known from the outset.)

An *experience surplus or deficiency* is that part of the excess or deficiency of the actuarial value of assets over the actuarial value of liabilities, on the basis of the valuation method used, which arises because events have not coincided with the actuarial assumptions made for the last valuation.

A *funding plan* is the timing of payments in an orderly fashion to meet the future cost of a given set of benefits.

A *funded scheme* is a pension scheme where the future liabilities for benefits are provided for by the accumulation of assets held externally to the employing company's business.

The *level of funding* is the proportion at a given date of the actuarial value of liabilities for pensioners' and deferred pensioners' benefits and for members' accrued benefits that is covered by the actuarial value of assets. For this purpose, the actuarial value of future contributions is excluded from the value of assets.

An *ongoing actuarial valuation* is a valuation in which it is assumed that the pension scheme will continue in existence and (where appropriate) that new members will be admitted. The liabilities allow for expected increases in earnings.

Past service is used in SSAP 24 to denote service before a given date. It is often used, however, to denote service before entry into the pension scheme.

Pensionable payroll/earnings are the earnings on which benefits and/or contributions are calculated. One or more elements of earnings (e.g. overtime) may be excluded, and/or there may be a reduction to take account of all or part of the state scheme benefits which the member is deemed to receive.

A *pension scheme* is an arrangement (other than accident insurance) to provide pension and/or other benefits for members on leaving service or retiring and, after a member's death, for his/her dependants.

A *prospective benefits method* of valuation is a valuation method in which the actuarial value of liabilities relates to:

(a)   the benefits for current and deferred pensioners and their dependants, allowing where appropriate for future pension increases; and

(b)   the benefits which active members will receive in respect of both past and future service, allowing for future increases in earnings up to their assumed exit dates, and where appropriate for pension increases thereafter.

Regular cost is the consistent ongoing cost recognised under the actuarial method used.

2.4   Defined contribution schemes

2.4.1   *Accounting*

Accounting for defined contribution ('money purchase') schemes remains straightforward under SSAP 24. Since the employer has no obligation beyond payment of the contributions which he has agreed to make, there is no difficulty in measuring the cost of providing pensions; it is simply the amount of those contributions payable in respect of the accounting period.[13] If the amount actually paid in the period is more or less than the amount payable, a prepayment or accrual will appear in the balance sheet in accordance with normal accounting practice, but otherwise the payments made will simply be charged in the profit and loss account when made.

2.4.2   *Disclosure*

A   *Requirements*

The disclosure requirements of the standard for defined contribution schemes are also very simple, and add little to the requirements of SSAP 2 and the Companies Act. They are:

(a)   the nature of the scheme (i.e. the fact that it is a defined contribution scheme);

(b)   the accounting policy (arguably required already by SSAP 2);

(c)   the pension cost charge for the period (already required by the Companies Act – see 5.2 below);

(d)   any outstanding or prepaid contributions at the balance sheet date.[14]

All these details could be given in a single note, but it is more common to deal with the different elements of the disclosure in different places. The policy and the nature of the scheme can be dealt with together as part of the statement of accounting policies, the expense for the year will be included in the statutory staff costs note, and any prepayment or accrual can readily be shown on the balance sheet or in a note analysing the relevant balance sheet figure. Unilever operates a number of defined contribution schemes, and makes these disclosures.

Extract 20.1: Unilever PLC (1998)

Accounting policies

Retirement benefits [extract]

Contributions to defined contribution schemes are charged to the profit and loss account as incurred.

Notes to the consolidated accounts

3 Staff costs and employees [extract]

	£ million	
	1998	1997
Pension costs		
Defined contribution schemes	**(11)**	(25)

30 Pension schemes [extract]

The Group also operates a number of defined contribution schemes. The assets of all the Group's defined contribution schemes are held in independently administered funds. The pension costs charged to the profit and loss account represent contributions payable by the Group to the funds. The market value of the assets of externally funded defined contribution schemes as at 31 December 1998 was £1 082 million (1997: £941 million).

2.5   Defined benefit schemes

The accounting requirements for defined benefit ('final salary') schemes are very much more complicated. In this case the employer's commitment is open-ended, and in order to achieve the accounting objective mentioned at 2.2 above it is necessary to apply actuarial valuation techniques and use a large number of assumptions. The standard seeks to achieve this by drawing a distinction between regular (ongoing) pension cost and variations from that cost. The essence of the standard's measurement rules is that the basic charge for pension cost in the profit and loss account should be the regular cost, but with adjustments for the effects of the variations from that cost which arise from time to time. In addition, there is a third element of pension cost to be recognised, although regrettably SSAP 24 does not make this sufficiently clear. This is interest,[15] and is discussed in more detail in 4.1 below.

2.5.1 Regular pension cost

As can be seen from the list of definitions in 2.3 above, regular cost is the consistent ongoing cost recognised under the actuarial method used. The standard goes on to say that 'where a stable contribution rate for regular contributions, expressed as a percentage of pensionable earnings, has been determined, that rate will provide an acceptable basis for calculating the regular cost under the stated accounting objective so long as it makes full provision for the expected benefits over the anticipated service lives of employees'.[16] The actuary will be able to inform the company of the amount of the total cost which is to be regarded as the regular cost component.

Essentially, the regular cost is that amount which the actuary would regard as a sufficient contribution to the scheme to provide the eventual pensions to be paid in respect of future service, provided present actuarial assumptions about the future were borne out in practice and there were no future changes to the terms of the scheme. Even then, this amount will depend on the particular method which the actuary is using to attribute cost to individual years. (The standard does not stipulate that a particular actuarial method be used, provided that it meets the accounting objective of recognising the cost of pensions on a systematic and rational basis over the employees' working lives. However, the ASB's 1995 Discussion Paper proposed that a future standard would require the use of the projected unit method.[17])

2.5.2 Variations from regular cost

A   Examples of variations

The standard identifies four categories of variations from regular cost.[18] The first two are to do with the actuarial process and the methods and assumptions which it entails, while the second two are to do with changes in the scope or the terms of the scheme itself. The four categories are:

(a)   experience surpluses or deficiencies. These are surpluses or deficiencies which are identified in the course of an actuarial valuation of the scheme which have arisen because the assumptions which were made at the time of the previous valuation have not been fully borne out by subsequent experience. For example, an assumption will have been made as to the rate of return to be earned on the scheme's investments. If this rate was in fact exceeded in practice, this will give rise to a surplus at the time of the next valuation, and this will be an experience surplus as the term is used in the standard. Similar variations may arise in relation to all the other main assumptions, such as those relating to salary inflation, the pattern of people joining and leaving the scheme, and so on;

(b)　the effects on the actuarial value of accrued benefits of changes in assumptions or method. Insofar as they relate to assumptions, these are similar to the previous category, except that they relate to the period beyond the date of the present valuation, rather than to the period since the previous valuation. Thus, a change in the assumption to increase the rate of predicted salary inflation in a final salary scheme would have the effect of increasing the total pension cost to be recognised and give rise to a variation. A change in actuarial method will have similar effects, in that it will give rise to a different present valuation of the scheme because of the particular way of attributing cost to particular years of service.

The wording of the standard is perhaps deficient in referring only to the effects on the value of the accrued *benefits*, which might be regarded, by implication, as excluding effects on the valuation of assets available to meet these benefits. We do not believe that any such distinction was intended, and we believe that the proper way to apply the standard is to regard changes affecting any part of the actuarial valuation of the scheme as variations and account for them as such;

(c)　retroactive changes in benefits or in conditions for membership. These might arise, for example, when the scope of a scheme is changed to include a class of employee which was previously excluded, and some credit is given for their past service with the company; alternatively, it might be an enhancement of the rights of existing members, say to give them an improvement in the terms of the formula under which their eventual pension will be calculated. These will generally entail an increase in the overall cost of pensions to the employer, and the past service element will give rise to a variation from regular cost; and

(d)　increases to pensions in payment or to deferred pensions for which provision has not previously been made. The standard takes the position that all such increases, including those of a discretionary or an ex gratia nature, should preferably be embraced within the scope of the actuarial assumptions. Where this has been the position, but the actual increases granted are not in line with those previously assumed, the difference will give rise to a variation. However, where the increases are of a discretionary or ex gratia nature and no allowance has previously been made for them in the actuarial assumptions, then they fall outside the scope of the valuation of the scheme; they are not treated as variations under the standard but are dealt with separately (see 2.5.3 below).

B　　*Normally allocated over the remaining service lives of current employees*

The basic rule set by the standard for all such variations from regular cost is that they should not be recognised immediately, but rather spread forward over the expected remaining service lives of employees in the scheme. There are, however, a number of exceptions to this basic rule, some of which in our view detract from the conceptual cohesion of the standard. These are discussed at C to F below.

The rationale for this basic rule merits some discussion. First of all it has to be looked at in the context of the standard's overall approach, which is directed towards achieving a steady charge in the profit and loss account rather than valuing the fund in the balance sheet. If actuarial surpluses and deficiencies were included directly in the balance sheet as soon as they were recognised, there would be enormous volatility in the amounts reported and, assuming the differences between the balance sheet figures were charged or credited directly in the profit and loss account, there could be a very significant effect on earnings in the years of actuarial valuation. The standard has instead opted for a smoothing approach, so that these effects are recognised in the profit and loss account gradually rather than immediately following a valuation.

Insofar as these variations arise from changes to do with the actuarial process (categories (a) and (b) above), this treatment can be justified because of the high degree of uncertainty and subjectivity inherent in actuarial valuations; it would be wholly inappropriate to give immediate recognition to such changes, which are of a very long-term nature and may easily be reversed at the time of the next valuation. However, at first sight it may seem more justifiable to give immediate recognition to the other broad class of variations – those reflecting changes in the scheme itself, described above under headings (c) and (d).

Broadly, the reason for not doing so is that such changes, even if they are expressed in terms which give credit for periods relating to the past, are made with a view to providing benefits for the future, not to meet any latent obligation which already exists. An improvement to the pension terms of an employee is only one of a range of possible improvements to his remuneration package; it may be decided on, for example, as an alternative to (or in conjunction with) a future salary increase. Accordingly, it is thought appropriate to spread such increases forward over the employee's working life.

In its 1995 Discussion Paper, the ASB recommended that experience differences should continue to be spread over the working lives of employees. However, improvements in benefits for former employees should be written off immediately, on the basis that they would render no further service and thus there was no future benefit to be matched with the cost.[19]

SSAP 24 does not specify exactly how variations are to be amortised, and there are various possible ways of doing so. This is discussed in more detail at 4.2.2. Although factors such as interest and salary inflation should be built into the amortisation pattern in practice, these have been excluded from some of the worked examples shown in the remainder of this chapter for the purposes of simplicity. These examples also use an average period to represent the working lives of members in the scheme.

SSAP 24 does not provide any worked examples of the spreading treatment, but the forerunner of the standard, ED 39, contained two such examples, the second of which[20] is reproduced below to illustrate the mechanics of the accounting process:

Example 20.1: Spreading variations from regular cost

The actuarial valuation at 31 December 1998 of the pension scheme of company B showed a surplus of £260m. The actuary recommended that B eliminate the surplus by taking a contribution holiday in 1999 and 2000 and then paying contributions of £30m p.a. for 8 years. After that the standard contribution would be £50m p.a. The average remaining service life of employees in the scheme at 31 December 1998 was 10 years. B's year end is 31 December.

Assuming no change in circumstances, the annual charge in the profit and loss account for the years 1999 to 2008 will be:

$$\text{Regular cost} - \frac{\text{surplus}}{\text{average remaining service life}} = £50m - \frac{£260m}{10} = £24m$$

The funding in these periods will be:

1999–2000	Nil
2001–2008	£30m p.a.

The difference between the amounts funded and the amounts charged in the profit and loss account will be recognised as a provision, as follows:

Year	Funded £m	Charged £m	(Provision) £m
1999	–	24	(24)
2000	–	24	(48)
2001	30	24	(42)
2002	30	24	(36)
2003	30	24	(30)
2004	30	24	(24)
2005	30	24	(18)
2006	30	24	(12)
2007	30	24	(6)
2008	30	24	–

The effect can be shown in graphical form, as follows:

Spreading variations from regular cost

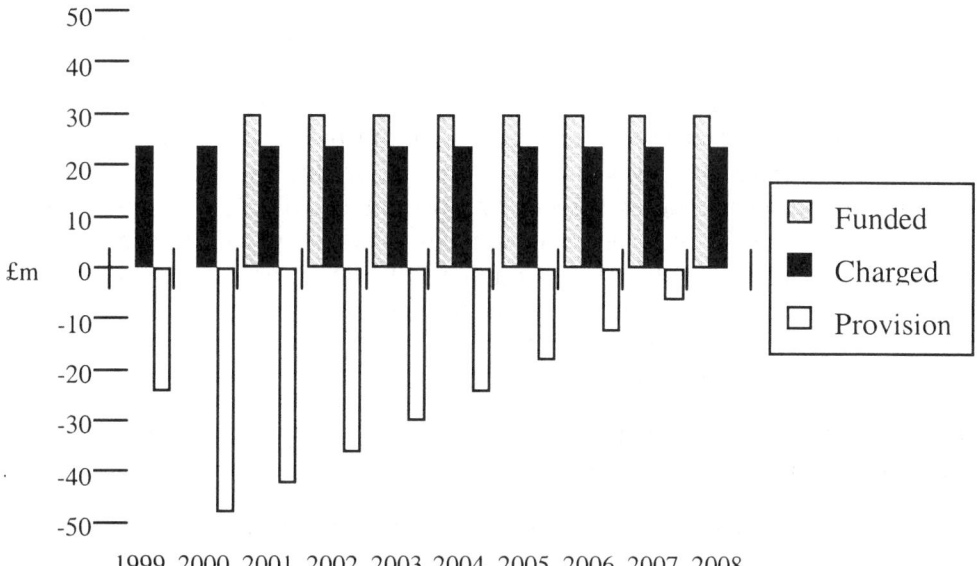

The example notes that in practice further actuarial valuations will occur, usually triennially, during the 10 year amortisation period and that these may reveal a surplus or deficiency which will require an adjustment to the charge and prepayment/provision in succeeding periods. However, it does not specify how this might be calculated. This point is considered below at 4.2.5.

C   *Reductions in employees relating to the sale or termination of an operation*

The original version of the standard said that where the variation was associated with an event which gave rise to an extraordinary item, such as the closure of a business segment, the spreading rule was overridden by the requirements of SSAP 6.[21] When FRS 3 replaced SSAP 6, extraordinary items were defined almost out of existence, and consequential amendments were made to SSAP 24. As a result, the relevant paragraph of SSAP 24 now says that where a 'significant reduction in the number of employees is related to the sale or termination of an operation, the associated pension cost or credit should be recognised immediately to the extent necessary to comply with paragraph 18 of FRS 3'.[22] It is explained that 'this is because FRS 3 requires provisions consequent on the sale or termination of an operation to be made after taking account of future profits of the operation or the disposal of its assets'.[23]

The drafting of these paragraphs is unfortunate. They link the rule to paragraph 18 of FRS 3, which deals with provisions made in anticipation of a sale or termination rather than with the sale or termination itself. The literal result is that any pension credit arising on the sale or termination should be recognised immediately only to the extent that it offsets a provision for other aspects of the sale or termination, and that any excess credit therefore falls instead into exception D, as discussed below. However, we doubt if this was intended and we do not think it produces a sensible result. We believe that a company which closes or sells a segment of its business should account for all the financial effects of that event at the same time, including the full pension cost or credit that results. Where this gives rise to an overall credit, this means that it will be reported in the year in which the sale or closure takes place; on the other hand, if it is a net debit there may be circumstances in which it will be provided for in advance, provided the rules of paragraph 18 of FRS 3 (as modified by FRS 12 – see Chapter 25 at 3.5) regarding such provisions are satisfied. In neither case, however, does it make sense to dislocate any part of the pension effect from the other consequences of the sale or closure.

The operation of this exception can be illustrated by the following example, which is based on the figures used in Example 20.1:

Example 20.2: Variations arising from the sale or closure of an operation

The actuary advises that £50m out of the £260m surplus is attributable to the redundancy programme associated with the closure of a business segment in 1999. The accounting treatment in this instance will be to deal with this variation from regular cost immediately, as a credit to the cost of the closure, and to deal with the remaining £210m by amortising it over the working lives of the employees in the scheme.The effect of this amortisation on the amount charged will be as follows:

$$\text{Regular cost} - \frac{\text{surplus}}{\text{average remaining service life}} = \text{£50m} - \frac{\text{£210m}}{10} = \text{£29m}$$

The effect on the accounts will therefore be:

Year		Funded £m	Charged (Credited) £m	Prepayment (Provision) £m
1999	ordinary charge	–	29	
	exceptional credit		(50)	
			(21)	21
2000		–	29	(8)
2001		30	29	(7)
2002		30	29	(6)
2003		30	29	(5)
2004		30	29	(4)
2005		30	29	(3)
2006		30	29	(2)
2007		30	29	(1)
2008		30	29	–

D   *Other significant reductions in the number of employees*

The next exception from the general 'spreading' rule occurs where there is a significant change in the normal level of contributions in order to eliminate a surplus or a deficiency which results from a significant reduction in the number of employees in the scheme that does not arise from the sale or termination of an operation. The standard says that where these circumstances apply, the effect of the variation in cost should not be spread over the average working lives of the remaining employees, but rather recognised when the reduction in contributions occurs.[24] An example of this rule being invoked is to be found in the following extract from the 1991 accounts of ECC Group:

Extract 20.2: ECC Group plc (1991)

3 EXCEPTIONAL ITEMS

In the fifteen months to 31st December 1990, the programme of reorganisation and cost reduction resulted in a provision of £32.0M being made which was shown as an exceptional item. As a result of this restructuring the Actuary has advised that at least £5M of the surplus within the Group's UK pension schemes is attributable to the reduction in manpower. Accordingly, the Group has reduced its contributions by £2.2M in 1991 (also shown as an exceptional item) and will take credit for a similar amount in 1992.

The rationale for this exception is probably that it makes little sense to spread this effect over the working lives of those who remain, when it arises from those who have left. An illustration of the effect of the exception is set out below, again using the same figures as for Example 20.1 above:

Example 20.3: Variations arising from a significant reduction in employees

The actuary advises that £50m out of the £260m surplus is attributable to a major redundancy programme occurring since the date of the last valuation. Accordingly the accounting treatment will be to deal with this variation from regular cost in line with the adjustments made to the funding programme, and deal with the remaining £210m by amortising it over the working lives of the employees in the scheme.

The effect of this amortisation on the amount charged will again be as follows:

$$\text{Regular cost} - \frac{\text{surplus}}{\text{average remaining service life}} = £50\text{m} - \frac{£210\text{m}}{10} = £29\text{m}$$

However it is still necessary to decide when to recognise the effect of the £50m which is attributable to the reduction of employees, because in reality the contributions have been adjusted to eliminate the whole of the £260m surplus, not just the £50m. If the whole of the contribution holiday in the first year were designated as intended to deal with this part of the surplus, the effect would be as follows:

Year	Funded £m	Charged (Credited) £m	Prepayment (Provision) £m
1999	–	(21)	21
2000	–	29	(8)
2001	30	29	(7)
2002	30	29	(6)
2003	30	29	(5)
2004	30	29	(4)
2005	30	29	(3)
2006	30	29	(2)
2007	30	29	(1)
2008	30	29	–

The credit in 1999 is calculated in the same way as in Example 20.2, although the whole effect is shown as part of the ordinary pension cost in this case. In fact, the result is the same as in that example only because the contribution holiday in 1999 is large enough to deal with the whole amount of the surplus arising from withdrawals.

Clearly, this produces a rather extreme and, some may say, unfair result. It would be possible to arrive at different results by attributing the changes in the contribution rates to their underlying reasons in a different way. For example if the allocation were made in proportion to the changes in the contribution rate, the effect would be as follows:

Year	Funded £m	Charged £m	(Provision) £m
1999	–	19.2	(19.2)
2000	–	19.2	(38.4)
2001	30	25.2	(33.6)
2002	30	25.2	(28.8)
2003	30	25.2	(24.0)
2004	30	25.2	(19.2)
2005	30	25.2	(14.4)
2006	30	25.2	(9.6)
2007	30	25.2	(4.8)
2008	30	25.2	–

(The effect on the funding rate has been to reduce it by £50m in each of the first two years and by £20m in the remaining eight. Accordingly, the total surplus of £50m attributable to the redundancy programme has been apportioned over that period in the same way, to reduce the £29m charge (calculated as shown above) by £9.8m in the first two years and by £3.8m in the remaining eight years.)

This appears to produce a more sensible and consistent charge, and may be regarded as preferable for that reason. Nevertheless either allocation, or indeed any other reasoned allocation, would appear to be acceptable under the terms of the standard. After the first year, the difference between the two approaches is not very significant in terms of the profit and loss account, but the effect on the balance sheet remains quite different for some time.

Overall, we do not believe that this exception to the general spreading rule stands up very well to closer examination. The standard requires that recognition be given to the effects of significant reductions in the number of employees in line with the consequential change in contributions, which is an uneasy compromise between the basic spreading rule described at B above and the immediate recognition required in the circumstances of C. Moreover, this leaves the timing of recognition to the whim of management, who may take it in the form of a contribution holiday, by a longer term reduction of the contribution rate, or they may even decide to make no change in the contribution rate at all. As illustrated above, even when they have amended the contribution rate they will still have to decide how to allocate the change in rate against the various factors which have given rise to it. As a result, we do not believe that this exception improves comparability and consistency in financial reporting.

In any event, the general thrust of the standard is to treat variations of all kinds in the same manner, and to look at the workforce as a whole, rather than to focus attention on particular groups of employees. We therefore think it odd to make an exception for these particular circumstances.

E   *Refunds subject to tax may be taken in the period the refund occurs*

Another exception to the normal spreading rule which is allowed by the standard is where the company receives a refund from the scheme that is subject to the deduction of tax. The standard provides that, where such refunds are taken, the company is allowed (but not required) to credit the refund to income in the year of receipt, rather than spreading forward the effects of the variations which have given rise to the surplus.[25] In other words, it allows a cash basis to be used for this transaction if desired. It is very difficult to see any conceptual merit in this exception to the basic spreading rule. The only concession to comparability made by the standard is to require full disclosure of the treatment where a refund is taken.

As is discussed at 2.5.4 below, it can be shown that the surplus or deficit in the fund is represented in the balance sheet figure, although it will usually be combined with an amount which represents deferred variations which are being released to the profit and loss account. For this reason, it seems clear that the appropriate accounting treatment should be to credit the amount of any refund to the balance sheet figure and not to the profit and loss account, otherwise a double counting effect could result. This is most obvious in the case of a company which had a surplus in its scheme at the time of first implementing SSAP 24 and chose to incorporate the surplus in its balance sheet as a pension prepayment; if it subsequently took a refund from the scheme and accounted for it in the profit and loss account, the asset would remain intact in the balance sheet even though it had been converted into cash to the extent of the refund. But the same is true even if the company did not incorporate the surplus in its balance sheet on transition, because as demonstrated in 2.5.4, the surplus is still indirectly represented in the balance sheet figure and this is where the credit should go; at the very least, if the refund is taken to the profit and loss account, the subsequent release of variations to the profit and loss account must be reduced by an equivalent amount.

We regret that the option to credit refunds direct to the profit and loss account is available, because we believe that there is no logical case for it within the framework of SSAP 24. We hope that it will be removed when the standard is revised, and are glad that the ASB has indicated its intention to do so.[26]

Unilever provides an example of a group that has received a refund from one of its pension schemes, and has taken the appropriate step of deducting it from the balance sheet prepayment rather than crediting it to the profit and loss account:

Extract 20.3: Unilever PLC (1998)

30 Pension schemes [extract]

In 1998 the Group received a cash refund of £106 million from a Netherlands fund in a surplus position. This cash refund does not directly impact the pension charge for 1998 as the surplus is amortised in accordance with accounting policies. Further refunds from this fund are expected in 1999 and 2000 and from a Finnish fund in 1999.

F   *In certain circumstances material deficits may be recognised over a shorter period*

The standard provides that, in very limited circumstances, prudence may require that recognition should be given to the costs of making good a material deficit over a period shorter than the normal amortisation period. This exception applies only where significant additional contributions have been required, and where the deficiency has been occasioned by a major event or transaction which has not been allowed for in the actuarial assumptions and is outside their normal scope.[27] An example which is quoted in the standard is that of a major mismanagement of the scheme's assets (presumably resulting in their loss for reasons other than the normal risks of investment). Although this may be a justifiable exception in certain cases, it is expected to be only very rarely applicable; however, it was applied by Mirror Group Newspapers in 1991 following the misappropriation of a large part of its pension fund.

G   *Transitional provisions*

The standard offered a choice between two methods of implementation in the year of adoption. Companies could look upon the actuarial surplus or deficiency in the scheme as equivalent to an experience surplus or deficiency which gave rise to a variation from regular pension cost, and accordingly spread it forward over the working lives of the members in the scheme. Alternatively, they could incorporate the surplus or deficiency in the balance sheet by means of a prior year adjustment, as a pension prepayment or accrual, which meant that the pension charge until the next valuation of the scheme would be solely the regular cost.[28] Where the company had a surplus in its fund, it could therefore apply it either to subsidise its future earnings, by reducing the future pension costs to be charged, or to increase its assets and reserves immediately.

In practice, the great majority of companies chose the first of these options, and indeed none of the top 100 UK companies followed the prior year adjustment route.[29]

2.5.3   *Discretionary and ex gratia pension increases and ex gratia pensions*

As mentioned in 2.5.2 A (d) above, the standard suggests that allowance should be made in the actuarial assumptions for pension increases of all kinds, even where these are not the result of any contractual obligation. Where this applies, any increases in pensions which are different from those previously assumed will be dealt with as giving rise to variations, to be treated as discussed in the previous section.

However, where no allowance has been made for such increases, different rules apply. The standard requires that the full capitalised value of these is provided for in the year in which they are made, except to the extent that they are covered by an existing surplus. This would appear to mean that if there is a surplus in the scheme at the time the increases are granted then the cost can, in effect, be spread forward (as a reduction of a variation which would otherwise have reduced future pension cost), but if there is no such surplus, or an insufficient surplus, then the cost must be charged against current profits.

It is not clear whether this applies only where it is possible in fact to use the surplus in the fund to meet this expense. This may be impossible if the provisions of the scheme do not permit the trustees to apply the funds for this purpose. It is arguable that even then the treatment may still be justifiable because the unrecognised gain in the fund provides sufficient reason to justify non-recognition of the unfunded liability for the discretionary or ex gratia award. However, we believe that the standard intended the narrower interpretation, that the offset can be applied only when the surplus in the scheme is in fact applied to meet the cost of the new award. Furthermore, we assume that the treatment is only available to the extent that the surplus has not already been recognised in the balance sheet; in other words the offset is permitted only against an *unrecognised* surplus, and even then it will be necessary to reduce the future variations being released to the profit and loss account by an equivalent amount.

The accounting policy of Wolseley makes specific reference to ex gratia payments:

Extract 20.4: Wolseley plc (1998)

Accounting policies

Pensions [extract]

… The cost of ex gratia pensions is provided in full in the year in which they are awarded.

2.5.4   Balance sheet

As explained earlier, the standard is expressed mainly in terms of the profit and loss account, and the asset or liability which appears in the balance sheet is literally the balancing figure. It is the cumulative difference between the amount which has been charged in the profit and loss account and the amount which has been paid in the form of contributions, and under SSAP 24 it is to be shown as a prepayment or an accrual, representing the extent to which contributions have been paid either ahead of or behind the recognition of cost. Since companies will generally continue to have contributions allowed for tax when they are paid, this figure will also represent the cumulative timing difference which has to be taken into account for the purposes of deferred tax.

It might be thought that this balance has no definable meaning, particularly as there are circumstances where it appears to 'go the wrong way'. For example, as is shown above in Example 20.1, a company which takes a contribution holiday because there is an underlying surplus in the fund may end up showing a liability in its accounts, which may seem incongruous. However, in reality the balance can be explained as being the combination of two figures; the most recently reported actuarial surplus or deficiency in the fund (as adjusted for subsequent contributions and regular costs), combined with the cumulative amount of unamortised variations awaiting recognition in the profit and loss account. This can be shown using the figures in that example. The balance is analysed in this chart, and explained below:

Analysis of balance sheet figure

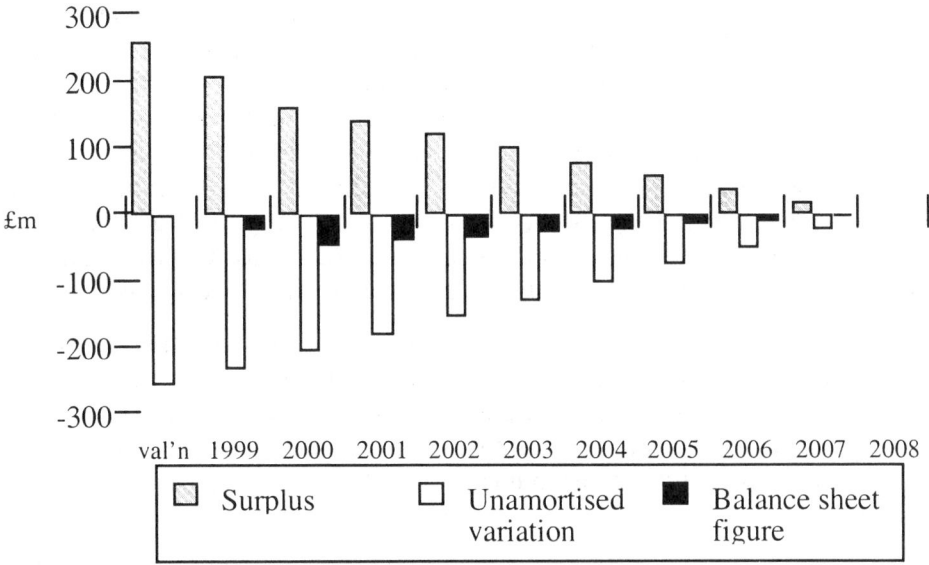

| | □ Surplus | □ Unamortised variation | ■ Balance sheet figure |

Example 20.4: *Explanation of balance sheet figure*

	Fund			Financial statements	
	1	2	3	4	5
				Unamortised	
Year	Contribution	Regular cost	Surplus	variation	Balance
	£m	£m	£m	£m	£m
Actuarial surplus/					
variation			260	(260)	–
1999	–	50	210	(234)	(24)
2000	–	50	160	(208)	(48)
2001	30	50	140	(182)	(42)
2002	30	50	120	(156)	(36)
2003	30	50	100	(130)	(30)
2004	30	50	80	(104)	(24)
2005	30	50	60	(78)	(18)
2006	30	50	40	(52)	(12)
2007	30	50	20	(26)	(6)
2008	30	50	–	–	–

Columns 1 to 3 show the theoretical movements in the fund after the valuation resulting from the effects of contributions and regular costs; for the sake of simplicity the effects of interest and the time value of money have been ignored. Column 4 is the amount of the unrecognised variation, being the variation identified in the 1998 valuation, successively reduced by annual amortisation of £26m p.a. to reduce the pension cost charged in the profit and loss account. Column 5 is the net of columns 3 and 4 and is the amount shown as a provision in the balance sheet. Although it may seem odd that a liability is shown when an underlying surplus exists, it simply reflects the fact that the effects of the surplus have been recognised more quickly in cash terms (by the contribution holiday) than for accounting purposes.

When the prepayment or accrual is explained in this way, it can be seen that the standard is more balance sheet orientated than is often recognised. In effect, it is possible to regard SSAP 24 as requiring companies to adopt a half-hearted form of equity accounting for their pension funds, particularly if they adopted the 'prior year adjustment' method of implementing the standard and recognise interest on the surplus (as discussed at 4.1 below). The treatment is 'half-hearted' in the sense that the effect of variations is recognised gradually rather than immediately, and because there is no requirement to undertake an annual actuarial valuation of the pension fund to be reflected in the accounts.

This perception of the standard has a bearing on a number of other questions of interpretation which arise, such as the treatment of interest and its relationship with the amortisation of variations, and whether it is legitimate to recognise a negative pension cost (where regular cost is outweighed by variations or interest credited to the profit and loss account). These matters are discussed at 4.1 and 4.3 below.

As mentioned above, the standard requires any excess of contributions paid over the amount of cumulative pension cost charged to be shown as a prepayment (or provision if it is a shortfall) in the balance sheet. When the balance is described in these terms, its classification as a current asset or liability seems entirely reasonable; however, when its underlying nature is examined under the analysis set out above, it can be seen that it is really a composite figure made up of two long-term items: the surplus in the fund and the amount of unamortised variations. The first of these is itself a net figure, being the excess of the investments held by the pension scheme over its obligations to pay pensions (both long-term items), while the second is a deferred credit awaiting transfer to the profit and loss account over a number of years.

To include this composite figure as a prepayment has a major effect on some conventional balance sheet ratios. Initially, the position was accentuated for the minority of companies who originally chose to implement the standard by incorporating the surplus in the balance sheet, rather than by spreading it forward to reduce pension cost over the service lives of the members, because in these circumstances there would have been no offsetting deferred credit to reduce the composite figure to manageable proportions. But even companies who did not do so have often found that a material figure can quickly build up, since the balance sheet figure will always tend towards the amount of the surplus or deficit in the scheme as the deferred element is gradually released (although, of course, new valuations will create further variations to be deferred and released in this way). As shown in this extract, the prepayment in BP Amoco's accounts at the end of 1998 stood at $2.2 billion:

Extract 20.5: BP Amoco p.l.c. (1998)

21 Debtors [extract]

				$ million Group
		1998		1997
	Within 1 year	After 1 year	Within 1 year	After 1 year
Trade	**5,778**	–	7,725	–
Joint ventures	**644**	–	905	
Associated undertakings	**153**	**7**	154	3
Prepayments and accrued income	**786**	**509**	773	164
Taxation recoverable	**248**	**165**	50	242
Pension prepayment	–	**2,213**	–	1,880
Other	**1,795**	**411**	1,776	709
	9,404	**3,305**	11,383	2.998

There is no easy solution to this problem. One approach would be to 'explode' the balance into its underlying components, so as to show the surplus within fixed asset investments and the unamortised variations within deferred income (preferably outside the current liabilities total). Alternatively, the prepayment classification could be maintained, but backed up by a note which 'explodes' it in the same way. In effect, this would provide a reconciliation between the balance sheet figure and the funded status of the scheme, which is a requirement of SFAS 87, the equivalent standard in the USA, and was proposed in the ASB's 1995 Discussion Paper.[30] Whatever approach is adopted, however, it would appear to be incumbent on the directors to provide a sufficient explanation of the balance to avoid giving a misleading impression of the liquidity of the company. As shown above, BP Amoco has correctly identified it as an amount not receivable within one year and many other companies do the same.

In July 1992, the UITF published an Abstract dealing with the general question of long-term debtors in current assets, mentioning pension assets as a possible example of such an item. This ruled that where amounts due after more than one year are very material, they should be shown separately on the face of the balance sheet (but still within current assets).[31]

2.5.5 Disclosure

A Requirements

Although the standard does deal with the calculation of pension cost, there is still a large degree of flexibility as to the measurement of the amounts to be recognised, partly because of the exceptions to the basic spreading rule mentioned above but also because there is a large degree of subjectivity inherent in the actuarial process, and because no single actuarial method has been specified. In this light, it is still possible to characterise the standard as being primarily a disclosure standard, because the disclosure requirements which it introduced are very extensive. These are as follows:[32]

(a)   the nature of the scheme (i.e. the fact that it is a defined benefit scheme);

(b)   whether it is funded or unfunded;

(c)   the accounting policy and, if different, the funding policy;

(d)   whether the pension cost and provision (or asset) are assessed in accordance with the advice of a professionally qualified actuary and, if so, the date of the most recent formal actuarial valuation or later formal review used for this purpose. If the actuary is an employee or officer of the reporting company, this fact should be disclosed;

(e)   the pension cost charge for the period together with explanations of significant changes in the charge compared to that in the previous accounting period;

(f)   any provisions or prepayments in the balance sheet resulting from a difference between the amounts recognised as cost and the amounts funded or paid directly;

(g)   the amount of any deficiency on a current funding level basis (a 'discontinuance' basis) indicating the action, if any, being taken to deal with it in the current and future accounting periods. Where there is more than one pension scheme, the standard emphasises that it is not permitted to set off a surplus of this type arising on one scheme against a deficiency on another;

(h)   an outline of the results of the most recent formal actuarial valuation or later formal review of the scheme on an ongoing basis. This should include disclosure of:

   (i)   the actuarial method used and a brief description of the main assumptions (for SSAP 24 purposes, not for funding purposes, where the two are different).[33] This should include the assumption made regarding new entrants unless it is apparent from the description of the method used.[34] If there has been a change in the method, this fact should be disclosed and the effect quantified;[35]

   (ii)   the market value of scheme assets at the date of their valuation or review. (Note that this means the actual market value of the assets, which will not generally be the same as the value on the basis used by the actuary for valuing the scheme – see 3.1.5 below);

   (iii)   the level of funding expressed in percentage terms.[36] (This, taken with the previous requirement, will allow a reasonable estimate of the actuarial surplus or deficiency to be derived. It will be only an estimate because the previous requirement calls for the market value of the assets to be shown, rather than the value put on them for the purposes of the actuarial valuation);

(iv) comments on any material actuarial surplus or deficiency indicated by (iii) above;[37] and

(v) the effects of any significant post-valuation events;[38]

(i) any commitment to make additional payments over a limited number of years;

(j) the accounting treatment adopted in respect of a refund made under deduction of tax (see 2.5.2 E above), where a credit appears in the financial statements in relation to it. (We presume that this means a credit in the profit and loss account rather than in the balance sheet, otherwise the last few words of the previous sentence add nothing to the requirement); and

(k) details of the expected effects on future costs of any material changes in the company's pension arrangements.[39]

Many of these requirements are similar to those contained in the ASC's original proposals on the disclosure of pension cost information (ED 32),[40] but SSAP 24 goes further in its requirements relating to actuarial information. Conversely, the standard does not contain the requirement to disclose any material self-investment (i.e. investment by the pension fund in the employer company itself), which was one of ED 32's suggestions.

B   Extracts illustrating disclosure requirements

Examples of comprehensive notes, taken from the accounts of Smiths Industries, BOC and SmithKline Beecham are set out below:

Extract 20.6: Smiths Industries plc (1998)

12   Post-Retirement Benefits

Smiths Industries operates a number of pension schemes throughout the world. The major schemes are located in the UK and the USA and are of the defined benefit type, with assets held in separate trustee administered funds.

Contributions to pension schemes are made on the advice of independent qualified actuaries, using in the UK the Projected Unit method and in the USA the Entry Age Normal method. The aim is for the benefits to be fully funded during the scheme members' working lives.

In both countries the regular pension cost is assessed using the Projected Unit method. The latest actuarial assessments were as at 31 March 1998 for the UK and 31 July 1998 for the USA for the major schemes.

At these dates the market value of the defined benefit schemes' assets was £729m for the UK and $273m for the USA. The aggregate funding levels of the principal schemes were 125% for the UK and 119% for the USA. The funding levels were determined by comparing the market value of the funds' assets with the value of benefits accrued to date. Allowance is made for future annual salary increases at approximately 5% and, for the UK schemes, for pension increases of approximately 3%. The future investment return assumed in assessing the present value of future benefits was 6% p.a. for UK pensioner liabilities and 7% p.a. for UK active member liabilities and 7% p.a. for the USA. The investment return assumptions were derived from prevailing yields on government stocks.

The regular pension cost is assessed at each actuarial valuation and applied until the next valuation. The variation from regular pension cost, which recognises the excess of assets over liabilities of the pension schemes, is spread over the average remaining working life of relevant employees, generally between 10 and 15 years.

A prepayment of £36.7m is included in debtors, this being the excess of the amount funded over the accumulated pension cost.

The pension costs of other countries' schemes were assessed in accordance with local practice. The Company operates a defined contribution (401K) plan for its USA employees, and provides post retirement healthcare benefit plans, principally at Grand Rapids in the USA. The cost of the post retirement healthcare benefits is assessed by independent qualified actuaries and is fully accrued (see note 23). The major assumptions used are interest rate 7.25% p.a., and medical cost inflation 7% p.a., ultimately reducing to 5% p.a.

Extract 20.7: The BOC Group plc (1998)

6.   Employees

e)   Retirement benefits

i)   Pensions – UK GAAP

The Group operates a number of pension schemes throughout the world. The majority of the schemes are self-administered and the schemes' assets are held independently of the Group's finances. Pension costs are assessed in accordance with the advice of independent professionally qualified actuaries.

The principal schemes are of the defined benefit type. The UK scheme is based on final salary, the US on annual salary and South Africa on the final 24 months' salary. With effect from 1 January 1998 the Australian scheme changed to operate primarily as a defined contribution scheme, although it retains some defined benefit guarantees. The accounting basis used is the same as the prior year. On the advice of respective actuaries, Group funding is suspended and is unlikely to be required during the next financial year for all principal funds.

The cost for the year was:

	1998 **£ million**	1997 £ million	1996 £ million
Principal schemes			
Regular pension cost	**44.8**	42.4	34.8
Variations from regular cost	**(39.9)**	(34.2)	(34.5)
Interest	**(1.8)**	(1.7)	(1.5)
Other schemes	**4.8**	4.3	12.6
Net pension cost	**7.9**	10.8	11.4

The results of the most recent valuations of the principal schemes were:

	UK[3]	US	Australia	South Africa[4]
Valuation data				
Date of latest formal valuation	31 March 1996	1 January 1997	31 December 1997	30 June 1997
Market value of investments (£ million)	961	539	114	124
Level of funding[1]	126%	133%	122%	135%
Method used	Projected Unit	Projected Unit	Projected Unit	Projected Unit
Main assumptions for UK accounting purposes				
Rate of price inflation	3.5%	3.8%	3.0%	12.5%
Overall return on investments[2]	3.6%	2.7%	3.5%	3.25%
Increase in earnings[2]	2.0%	1.7%	1.5%	1.1%
Main assumptions for US accounting purposes				
Discount rate	6.3%	6.5%	5.5%	15%
Return on assets	7.7%	9.0%	8.0%	15%
Compensation increase	5.0%	5.5%[5]	4.0%	13.8%

1. The actuarial value of assets expressed as a percentage of the accrued service liabilities.
2. Above price inflation
3. The pension cost for the year under UK GAAP is based on an interim valuation at 31 March 1998. At this interim valuation, assets were taken into account as £1,167 million representing 92 per cent of their market value. The level of funding on this basis was 133 per cent.
4. South Africa was included as a principal scheme for the first time in 1997. It was not included as a principal scheme in 1996 disclosures for either UK or US GAAP.
5. This relates to interest credits to cash accounts.

ii)   Pensions – US GAAP

The principal schemes are those described in ei). At 30 September 1998 approximately 82 per cent of plan assets of the principal schemes were held in equity securities, with the remainder primarily in fixed income securities.

The pension cost under US GAAP has been calculated for the principal schemes in accordance with SFAS 87 using the assumptions shown in ei). The difference between the net credits is shown in the reconciliation of net income between UK GAAP and US GAAP in note 16. In 1998, the Group sold its interest in its Ohmeda health care business resulting in a one-time curtailment gain of £12.8 million. The net pension costs/(credits) for the principal schemes on a US GAAP basis were as follows:

	Years ended 30 September		
	1998	1997	1996
	£ million	£ million	£ million
Service cost	**39.3**	39.5	33.5
Interest cost	**90.4**	89.1	78.5
Actual returns on assets	**(302.7)**	(270.5)	(224.1)
Net amortisation	**161.6**	144.3	106.4
Curtailment gain	**(12.8)**	–	–
Net pension cost/(credit)	**(24.2)**	2.4	(5.7)

Under US GAAP valuation methods, all of the principal schemes are overfunded. The following table shows the plans' funded status and the prepaid pension cost used to determine the adjustment required to bring the UK GAAP shareholders' funds to a US GAAP basis (see note 16):

	1998	1997
	£ million	£ million
Projected benefit obligation	**(1,332.4)**	(1,186.7)
Plan assets at fair value	**1,864.4**	1,716.1
Plan assets in excess of projected benefits obligation	**532.0**	529.4
Unrecognised net asset	**(91.8)**	119.7
Unrecognised prior service costs	**27.4**	33.3
Unrecognised net gain	**(333.9)**	(322.1)
Prepaid pension cost at 30 September	**133.7**	120.9

iii)   Other retirement costs

In the US, the Group provides post-retirement benefits to former employees. In 1998, the Group sold its interest in its Ohmeda health care business resulting in a one-time curtailment gain of £9.3 million. These costs are accounted for on a basis similar to pensions. The cost for the year was:

	1998	1997	1996
	£ million	£ million	£ million
Regular cost	**1.2**	1.3	1.4
Variations from regular cost	**(0.8)**	(1.1)	(1.0)
Interest	**2.1**	2.2	2.3
Curtailment gain	**(9.3)**	–	–
	(6.8)	2.4	2.7

As the above example shows, in 1996 BOC experienced a negative pension cost in relation to its main schemes, although the overall effect of all its schemes still produced a net charge to the profit and loss account. The question of negative pension cost is discussed further at 4.3 below.

Extract 20.8: SmithKline Beecham plc (1998)

28   RETIREMENT BENEFITS

The Group operates plans throughout the world covering the majority of employees. These plans are devised in accordance with local conditions and practices in the countries concerned and include defined contribution and benefit schemes. The assets of the plans are generally held in separately administered trusts or are insured, although in Germany the plans are not externally funded. Pension plan assets are managed by independent professional investment managers. It is the Group's policy that none of the assets of the funds are invested directly or indirectly in any Group company. The contributions to the plans are assessed in accordance with independent actuarial advice mainly using the projected unit credit method.

The total pension cost was £87 million (1997 – £94 million; 1996 – £89 million) of which £38 million (1997 – £44 million; 1996 – £59 million) relates to defined benefit plans in the UK, US and Germany which cover some 55% of total employees, and for which further disclosures are set out below.

	UK	US	Germany
Main assumptions:			
Investment return	10%	10.25%	7%
Salary increases p.a.	6.5%	5.5%	4.5%
Pension increases p.a.	3.5%	–	3%
Last valuation date	30.6.97	31.12.97	31.12.97
Level of funding, being the actuarial value of assets expressed as percentage of the accrued service liabilities	105%	92%	n/a
	£m	£m	£m
Market valuation of investment at last valuation date	735	1,006	n/a
Regular pension cost	10	27	2
Variations from regular cost	(5)	–	4
Total pension costs for 1998	5	27	6

Variations from regular cost are spread over the remaining service lives of current employees in the plans. A provision of £216 million (1997 – £189 million) is included in provisions for liabilities and charges, representing the excess of the accumulated pension cost over the amount funded (see note 16) including £54 million (1997 – £47 million) relating to Germany.

In addition to pension benefits, approximately 20,000 of SB's employees in the US become eligible for certain healthcare and life insurance benefits upon retirement. The amount charged to the profit and loss account in the year for these items was £26 million (1997 – £23 million; 1996 – £22 million). The main assumptions used in determining the required provision are an investment return of 10% and medical cost inflation of 6% reducing to 5% by the year 2003. The last valuation date was 1 January 1998.

Some of the most varied forms of disclosure have been those relating to the actuarial assumptions used. In addition to the extracts shown above, some further examples of such disclosures from accounts are set out below. A straightforward form of this disclosure is given by Cadbury Schweppes:

Extract 20.9: Cadbury Schweppes p.l.c. (1998)

18   Pension Arrangements and other Post-Retirement Benefits [extract]

The major scheme is the Cadbury Schweppes Pension Fund in the UK for which the last full valuation was made as at 5 April 1996 on the projected unit method when the market value of the assets was £990m. The level of funding on the assumptions shown below was 110%.

The principal long term assumptions used for the purposes of the actuarial valuation were as follows:

Rate of return on new investments	8.5%
Earnings increases	6.0%
Pensions increases	4.0%
Growth of dividends	4.0%

Another approach to disclosing aggregated information about a large number of different schemes is illustrated by the accounts of ICI. The company has disclosed the main assumptions by means of weighted averages, rather than simply giving ranges of assumptions used:

Extract 20.10: Imperial Chemical Industries PLC (1998)

38   Pensions and other post-retirement benefits

Group

The Company and most of its subsidiaries operate retirement plans which cover the majority of employees (including directors) in the Group. These plans are generally of the defined benefit type under which benefits are based on employees' years of service and average final remuneration and are funded through separate trustee-administered funds. Formal independent actuarial valuations of the Group's main plans are undertaken regularly, normally at least triennially and adopting the projected unit method.

The actuarial assumptions used to calculate the projected benefit obligation of the Group's pension plans vary according to the economic conditions of the country in which they are situated. The weighted average discount rate used in determining the actuarial present values of the benefit obligations was 8.3% (1997 8.2%). The weighted average expected long-term rate of return on investments was 8.4% (1997 8.3%). The weighted average rate of increase of future earnings was 5.5% (1997 5.5%).

The actuarial value of the fund assets of these plans at the date of the latest actuarial valuations was sufficient to cover 94% (1997 93%) of the benefits that had accrued to members after allowing for expected future increases in earnings; their market value was £7,770m (1997 £6,525m).

The total pension cost for the Group for 1998 was £162m (1997 £171m). Accrued pension costs amounted to £14m (1997 £38m) and are included in other creditors; provisions for the benefit obligation of a small number of unfunded plans amounted to £256m (1997 £261m) and are included in provisions for liabilities and charges – unfunded pension. Prepaid pension costs amounting to £281m (1997 £244m) are included in debtors.

ICI Pension Fund

The ICI Pension Fund accounts for approximately 85% of the Group's plans in asset valuation and projected benefit terms.

From the date of the actuarial valuation of the ICI Pension Fund as at 31 March 1994 the Company has been making payments into the fund to reflect the extra liabilities arising from early retirement as retirements occur. In addition, the Company agreed to make accelerated contributions to the Fund to reduce the deficit identified in the 1994 valuation. A Funding Review as at 31 March 1997 disclosed a solvency ratio on a current funding level basis, which assumes a cessation of operation, of 95%. The solvency ratio, on an ongoing basis, was 92%. Based on the Funding Review as at 31 March 1997, the Company agreed to make six annual payments into the Fund of £100m pa from 1998 through 2003 which are expected to eliminate the deficit on an ongoing valuation basis. The deficit, together with the prepayment, is taken into account in arriving at the employers' pension costs charged in the accounts by being amortised as a percentage of pensionable emoluments over the expected working lifetime of existing members.

Sometimes, companies are less forthcoming about the absolute amounts of the assumptions used, perhaps because they believe that the disclosure of the salary assumption might compromise their negotiating position with the unions, although this information is in any event generally given in the actuarial statement which accompanies the fund accounts. One form of disclosure which is sometimes used is to give the information by reference to an (undisclosed) inflation assumption:

Extract 20.11: BICC plc (1998)

22   Pensions [extract]

At the date of the latest valuations of the principal defined benefit schemes, the market value of the assets of those schemes amounted to £1,448m. The actuarial value of those assets exceeded the benefits which had accrued to members after allowing for expected future increases in earnings. The latest actuarial valuation of the main UK scheme was carried out by independent actuaries at 5 April 1996 using the projected unit method and disclosed a surplus of assets over past service liabilities of 16%, which is being used to reduce company contributions over a period of ten years. The principal actuarial assumptions of the main UK scheme are for new investment returns to exceed inflation by 4.5% and for dividends to grow at the rate of inflation.

Although in principle this might be a permissible way of complying with the standard, BICC does not seem to have disclosed the salary inflation assumption at all, which is important information for an assessment of the strength of the actuarial valuation.

Another way of disclosing these assumptions which is often seen in practice is simply to give their relationship to each other, without actually disclosing the absolute figures. One company which has adopted this approach is Glynwed International:

Extract 20.12: Glynwed International plc (1998)

5 Employee information [extract]

The latest full valuations of the main schemes were carried out by Watson Wyatt Partners, consulting actuaries, as at 31st March 1998 using the projected unit credit method. The principal assumptions on which these valuations were based for the purposes of establishing the Group's pension cost were that the investment return would be 2.75% greater than general salary increases, 4.25% greater than increases in future pension payments and 3.5% greater than the assumed rate of growth on United Kingdom equity dividends. The results of these valuations showed that together the schemes had a market value of £746.5m and were 109% funded. The valuations were used in assessing the expected cost of providing pensions for the remaining nine months of 1998 and for subsequent years and the surplus was spread over the expected future service of employees on a straight line basis. At 31st December 1998 the pension prepayment held in the Group's balance sheet is £8.0m (1997: £1.1m)

It is true that the relationship between the figures is generally more significant than the figures themselves, particularly the gap between the assumed investment return and the salary inflation assumption. Nevertheless the presentation of the absolute figures, as has been done in most of the extracts illustrated here, would provide the reader with this information in a more straightforward and understandable way.

General Accident is an example of a company which changed its actuarial valuation method in its 1993 accounts. The effect of the change is disclosed, as shown in the following extract:

Extract 20.13: General Accident plc (1993)

5 Pension and Other Post Retirement Benefits

(a) Staff Pension Costs

The principal pension schemes operate in the UK and North America. These schemes are of the defined benefit type and their assets are held in separate trustee administered funds. Each of the schemes has been subject to actuarial valuation or review in the last twelve months using the 'Projected Unit Credit' method. In previous years the 'Entry Age' method of actuarial valuation was applied in respect of the UK schemes. The effect of this change in method has been to reduce the annual pension cost by approximately £3.6 million. The actuarial valuation of the defined benefit scheme was carried out by a qualified actuary who is an employee of the Group.

---

3   THE ACTUARIAL ASPECTS OF SSAP 24

3.1   Actuarial valuation methods

3.1.1   Background

Actuarial methods have been developed, not with the objective of generating figures for the measurement of pension cost for accounting purposes, but with a view to valuing the fund and determining appropriate contribution rates. The focus of funding recommendations is to ensure that assets are set aside in a prudent and orderly way so as to meet the obligations of the scheme when they become due for payment; it is to do with cash flows, not with profit measurement.

Nevertheless, although the methods have been developed for funding purposes, they can provide a good basis for attributing cost to the years in which the employees render their services to the employer company. The difficulty is that, even if the actual amount of pensions which would eventually be paid to existing employees were known with precision, there is no particular method of attributing the cost of that pension to individual years of employment which is unarguably the best way of applying the matching concept. Different actuarial methods would approach this task in different ways.

To explain such differences it is helpful to draw the distinction between the two main families of methods used by actuaries – 'accrued benefits methods' and 'projected benefits methods' (or 'level contribution methods' as they are sometimes called). These terms are defined in the standard as shown in 2.3 above, but the essential difference between the two can be explained, slightly simplistically, as follows:

- the accrued benefits approach measures the cost of providing the pension by putting a value directly on each incremental year's service so that it builds up towards the final liability which will arise on retirement;

- the projected benefits approach looks directly at the expected eventual liability and seeks to provide for it evenly over the whole period of service.

The first method will tend to show a rising trend of cost over the employee's working life, while the second will tend to show a flatter charge. The methods, and some of their different versions, are described more fully in 3.1.3 and 3.1.4 below.

There are different possible accounting arguments as to why either of these might be the more desirable way of matching cost and benefits. For example, the accrued benefits method could be portrayed as an approach which tries more precisely to measure the cost of the pension which has accrued in any specific year, and therefore is a more faithful application of the matching concept than the projected benefits method, which seems to adopt more of a 'smoothing' approach. Conversely, it may be argued that the benefits from employees' services accrue over their whole working lives and that the total cost of their pensions should be recognised evenly over those lives, as is achieved by the projected benefits approach, rather than weighting it towards the later years of their employment, as happens under the accrued benefits approach. A variety of further arguments could be summoned to support either side of the debate; but suffice it to say that there is no unanswerable point which seems to make either method conclusively the best.

The distinctions between the methods are in practice blurred when one moves from considering the cost of the pension of an individual employee to looking at the cost of a scheme comprising many employees, with a range of ages. For mature schemes where the age profile of the scheme remains steady through time, there will be comparatively little difference between the total cost calculated under either approach.

3.1.2 The approach taken by the standard

As has been explained already, SSAP 24 does not prescribe a particular valuation method, and leaves it to the employer, with the benefit of actuarial advice, to ensure that the method chosen can fulfil the accounting objective set out in the standard, that the cost should be recognised on a systematic and rational basis over the working lives of the employees in the scheme. Both of the broad categories of actuarial method described above could generally be said to meet that objective, although some of their variants may not, as discussed in the two sections which follow.

The standard says comparatively little about particular actuarial methods, but discusses them briefly in the following terms: 'In practice, it is common for actuaries to aim at a level contribution rate, as a proportion of pensionable pay in respect of current service. The contribution rate thus determined depends on the particular actuarial method used and the assumptions made regarding new entrants to the scheme. In broad terms, in projecting a stable contribution rate, accrued benefits methods rely on the assumption that the flow of new entrants will be such as to preserve the existing average age of the workforce; prospective benefits methods, on the other hand, normally look only to the existing workforce and seek a contribution rate that will remain stable for that group despite its increasing age profile until the last member retires or leaves. In a mature scheme both types of method may in practice achieve stable contribution rates, but the size of the fund under a prospective benefits method will tend to be larger than under an accrued benefits method because it is intended to cover the ageing of the existing workforce.'[41]

A group of companies will often have a number of different pension schemes in operation for different subsidiaries and the question often arises as to whether they must be valued using the same actuarial methods and assumptions. On the basis that the various methods attribute pension costs to years of service in a different way, there is an argument that a single method should be used throughout the group, just as it would be desirable to use the same depreciation method consistently throughout the group. However, provided the methods chosen all achieve the standard's aim of charging pension cost as a relatively consistent percentage of payroll, then it is acceptable to use different methods. It can be seen from Extract 20.6 that uniform valuation methods are not necessarily used in practice.

It can also be seen from several of the extracts quoted in this chapter that different actuarial assumptions are commonly used for different schemes. Again this is quite legitimate provided the assumptions are appropriate for the schemes to which they are applied, and since the schemes themselves will not be uniform, there is no reason why the assumptions should be. In particular the economic assumptions used for the schemes of an international group will need to reflect the circumstances of each country, although a greater degree of consistency would be expected between schemes within the same country.

3.1.3 Possible actuarial methods – accrued benefits methods

As mentioned above, the accrued benefit approach focuses directly on the incremental liability which builds up year by year as pensionable service is recorded by the employee. It sees each year as giving rise to a further unit of pension entitlement, and values each unit separately to build up the total accrued liability.

Although the emphasis is on the benefits that have been earned to date, this does not mean that the method is incapable of looking to the future, and in particular it is not necessarily the case that it does not anticipate future pay rate inflation (which is a vital factor in a final salary scheme). Admittedly some variants of the accrued benefits approach do not take such factors into account, but the most significant version, the projected unit method, is based on estimates of final salary rather than on present rates of pay. (Confusingly, the projected unit method is in the 'accrued benefit' family of valuations, not the 'projected benefit' family.) This method is discussed below.

A   Projected unit method

A description of the main features of this method runs as follows:

'Under the projected unit method, a standard contribution rate expressed as a percentage of earnings is obtained by dividing the present value of all benefits which will accrue in the year following the valuation date (by reference to service in that year and projected final earnings) by the present value of members' earnings in that year. An actuarial liability is calculated by summing the present value of all benefits accrued at the valuation date (based on projected final earnings for members in service). The recommended contribution rate expressed as a percentage of earnings is obtained by modifying the standard contribution rate to reflect the difference between the value placed on the scheme assets for valuation purposes and this actuarial liability.'[42]

A diagrammatic representation of the valuation of the fund using the projected unit method could appear as follows:

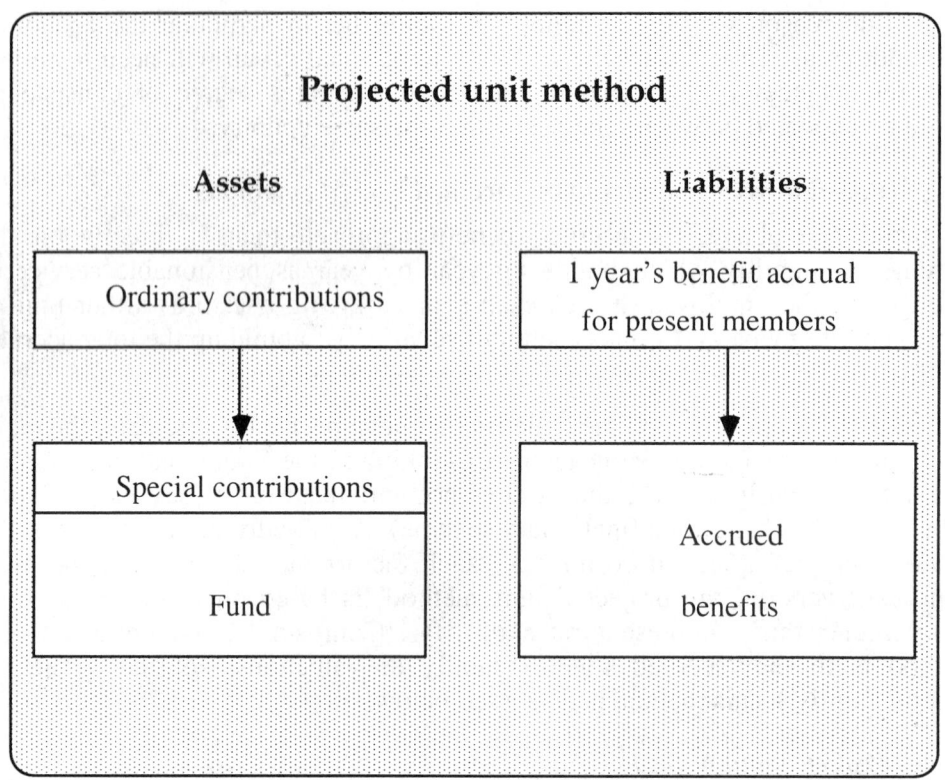

The 'special contributions' shown in the diagram are those that are needed to take account of a deficiency in the fund which may have arisen due to factors such as experience differences or benefit improvements. It is equally possible that a surplus might emerge, so that reduced contributions become an available option. In terms of SSAP 24, therefore, the 'special contributions' shown in the diagram is equivalent to variations, while the amount shown as 'ordinary contributions' represents the regular cost.

This method can result in a stable level of contributions provided the age profile of the workforce remains steady. In these circumstances it will generally form a suitable basis for the measurement of cost under SSAP 24. However, its use might have to be more critically considered if the characteristics of the scheme are likely to result in a more volatile contribution rate, and actuarial advice on this point may be necessary. Guidance Note 17 (GN 17) issued by the actuarial profession comments that the method 'is unlikely to be satisfactory if it is evident from the circumstances that the standard contribution rate is likely to change in future years. A change might for example be foreseeable because (a) the scheme is or will be closed to new entrants, or (b) new entrants are admitted on a pension scale which is materially different in cost from the scale applicable to current members.'[43]

This method has emerged as the one which commands majority support among large companies. It has also been suggested by the ASB that the method may be made mandatory in a future revision of SSAP 24.[44]

B   *Current unit method*

This method is essentially similar to the projected unit method, with the vital distinction that it looks at current, rather than projected pay rates. As a result, the effects of salary inflation have to be picked up in future years in an accelerating pattern, which means that the cost is likely to be heavily skewed towards the later years of employment. For this reason such a method does not meet the accounting objective of SSAP 24. GN 17 comes to a similar conclusion, saying that the method 'is unsatisfactory if used without a control period [see below] of adequate length, or if it is evident from the circumstances that the standard contribution rate is likely to change materially in future years. A change might for example be foreseeable (a) if the scheme is or will be closed to new entrants or if new entrants are admitted on a pension scale which is materially different in cost from the scale applicable to current members, or (b) as an effect of future pay increases upon accrued pension rights.'[45]

C   *Discontinuance method*

This method, which is described in SSAP 24 as a 'current funding level' basis, is, as its name suggests, founded on the premise that the scheme is to be wound up immediately and the assets applied to meet the existing entitlements of the members. It therefore does not form an appropriate method for valuing the scheme on a forward-looking, going concern basis. Because of the objectives of the method, contribution rates are not calculated, and for all these reasons the use of a discontinuance approach could not provide an appropriate measure of cost under SSAP 24.

A variant of the discontinuance method, which is sometimes referred to as the 'discontinuance target method', is occasionally used to determine funding rates, and is quite commonly used by insurance companies. This involves funding for the discontinuance liability which would arise if the scheme were to be wound up at some specified time, say 20 years, in the future. The period chosen is referred to as the 'control period' in actuarial parlance. In principle this method would still not follow the accounting objective of SSAP 24, because it does not look through to the final salaries on which the pensions are expected to be paid. However, the greater the length of the control period, the nearer the method will become to one which is acceptable under the standard. Where the method is used, it will be necessary to obtain actuarial advice on whether it produces results which are materially different from one which is based on projected final salaries.

GN 17 says that 'a control period can be regarded as of adequate length if (a) the resulting standard contribution rate, which is to be used as the regular cost, is not altered materially by extending the control period and (b) the calculation of the pension cost makes specific provision for future increases in earnings not materially different from a full provision for all future increases in earnings, including merit increases, and not solely those occurring up to the end of the control period'.[46]

3.1.4   Possible actuarial methods – projected benefits methods

As discussed previously, these methods try to look at the eventual amount of pensions which are expected to be paid, and establish contribution rates which are designed to remain stable over the period of the employees' service. Usually, this means that they are designed to represent a level percentage of payroll costs, not a level figure in pounds, but the latter is also theoretically possible (although not an appropriate method for SSAP 24 purposes).

A   Aggregate method

The actuaries' description of this method reads as follows:

'Under the aggregate method, a recommended contribution rate expressed as a percentage of earnings is obtained by dividing the excess of the present value of all benefits which have accrued and will accrue (based on total service and projected final earnings for members in service) over the value placed on the scheme assets for valuation purposes by the present value of total projected earnings for all members throughout their expected future membership.'[47]

A diagrammatic view of this method would show:

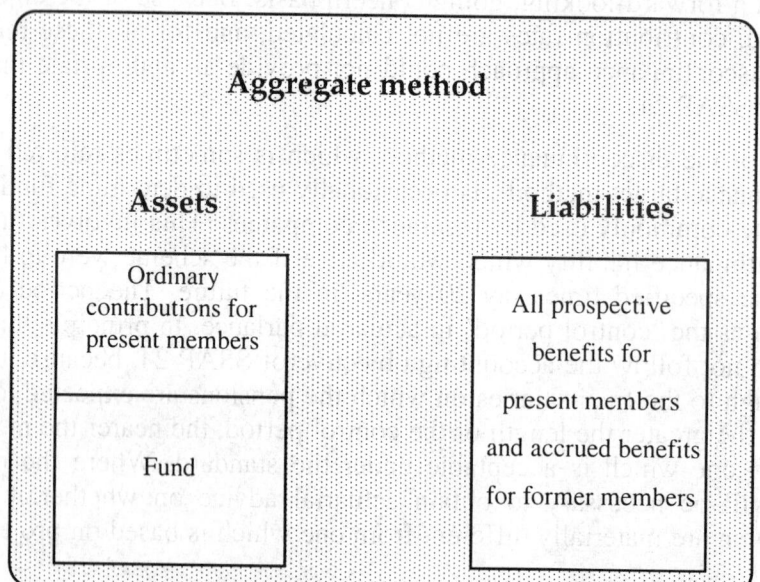

The 'Ordinary contributions' box represents the balancing figure in the valuation, and the method does not in fact identify either the surplus or deficit on the fund or the element of contributions which relates to variations from regular cost. As a result it does not provide the analysis which the standard requires and is seldom likely to be a usable method without modification. It is regarded by some as rather a simplistic method of valuation, and while it has been quite extensively used in the past in the UK, it is now much less common.

GN 17 takes a similar view, but notes that it may be seen as a variant of the Attained Age Method or the Entry Age Method (both described below). It comments that it may be suitable where the scheme is closed to new entrants, but that otherwise one of these other two methods should be used so as to distinguish regular cost from variations.[48]

B Attained age method

This method is described by the actuaries thus:

'Under the attained age method, a standard contribution rate expressed as a percentage of earnings is obtained by dividing the present value of all benefits which will accrue to present members after the valuation date (by reference to service after the valuation date and projected final earnings) by the present value of total projected earnings for all members throughout their expected future membership. An actuarial liability is calculated by summing the present value of all benefits accrued at the valuation date (based on projected final earnings for members in service). The recommended contribution rate expressed as a percentage of earnings is obtained by modifying the standard contribution rate to reflect the difference between the value placed on the scheme assets for valuation purposes and the accrued actuarial liability.'[49]

On a diagram, a valuation under this method looks like this:

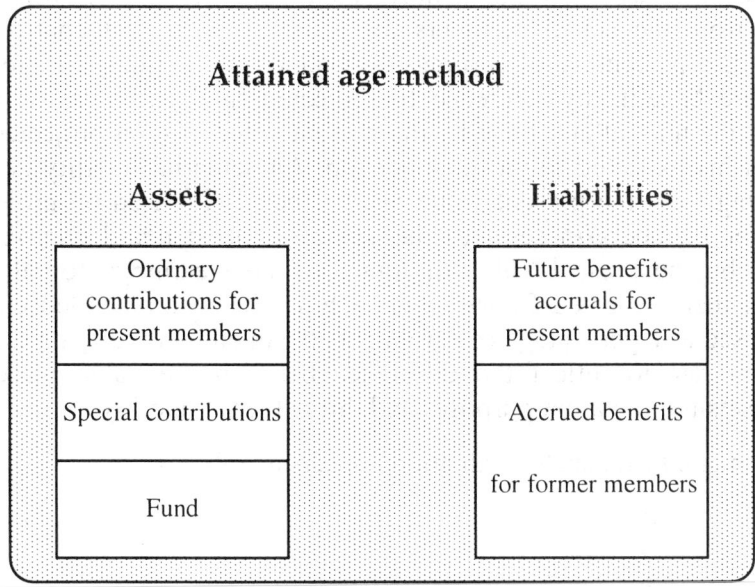

Attained age method	
Assets	**Liabilities**
Ordinary contributions for present members	Future benefits accruals for present members
Special contributions	Accrued benefits for former members
Fund	

In concept, this is not dissimilar to the aggregate method, and if the 'special contributions' are paid as well as the ordinary contributions they will produce the same total contribution as under that method. The main difference is that the liabilities are split between those benefits which have already accrued and those which are projected to accrue in the future for existing members. By splitting it in this way, the amount of 'special contributions' can be identified which represents the amount needed to redress the deficit between the value of the fund and the accrued benefits. Again, this could be a negative figure if the scheme were in surplus.

For SSAP 24 purposes, the 'ordinary contributions' shown in the diagram again equate to regular cost, and the 'special contributions' to variations from that regular cost.

GN 17 comments that the method is unlikely to be satisfactory '(a) where a scheme has a regular and significant flow of new entrants and if the payment of the standard contribution rate in respect of the new entrants is expected to create material surpluses or deficits, or (b) where a scheme is or will be closed to new entrants and the standard contribution rate is expected to increase materially at each succeeding valuation. (However the method can be satisfactory for a closed scheme where the regular cost is based throughout upon the standard contribution rate calculated in respect of the membership present at the time when the scheme was closed.)'[50]

C   *Entry age method*

This method is comparatively rare in the UK, but has been more commonly used in North America. It is described as follows:

'Under the entry age method, a normal entry age is chosen which may be estimated from the actual membership records. A standard contribution rate expressed as a percentage of earnings is obtained by dividing the present value of all future benefits by reference to projected final earnings for a member entering at the normal entry age by the present value of total projected earnings throughout his expected future membership. An actuarial liability is calculated by deducting from the present value of total benefits (based on projected final earnings for members in service) the value of the standard contribution rate multiplied by the present value of total projected earnings for all members throughout their expected future membership. The recommended contribution rate expressed as a percentage of earnings is obtained by modifying the standard contribution rate to reflect the difference between the value placed on the scheme assets for valuation purposes and this actuarial liability.'[51]

In diagrammatic form, such a valuation appears as follows:

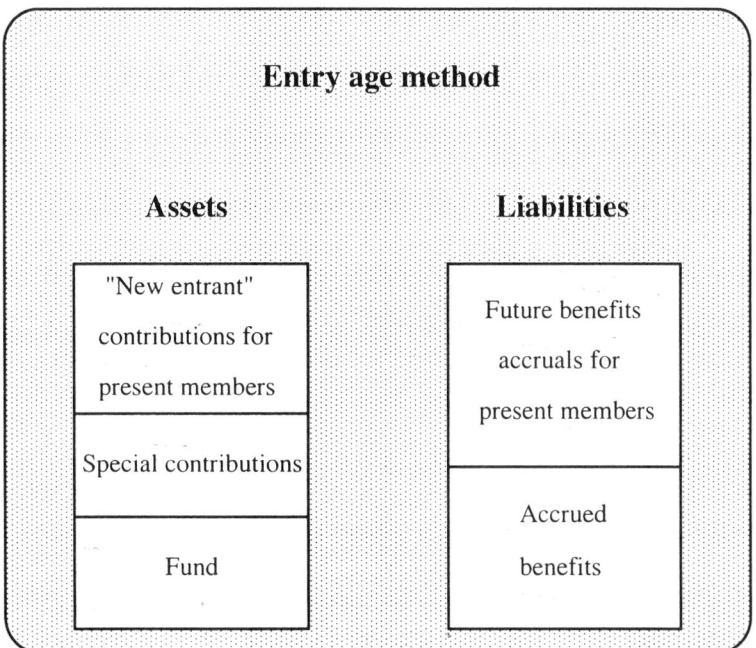

In this case the calculation of the liabilities is the same, but the amount of 'special contributions', which is the balancing figure (and could again be negative), is determined after calculating the ordinary contributions in a different way; rather than basing it on the actual contributions to be made by the existing members, it is calculated on the basis that existing members are at the age of the typical new entrant to the scheme. This creates a difficulty in theory at least, because the 'new entrant' contributions are calculated in such a way that they do not distinguish between past and future service (from the point of view of a new entrant, all service is future service). Accordingly, it might be argued that the split shown in the diagram does not follow the SSAP 24 approach that variations should deal with the past service elements of cost and the regular cost should deal with the ongoing cost related to future service. However, we expect that in practice such a split is applied and is regarded as acceptable.

According to GN 17, this method 'is unlikely to be satisfactory if the standard contribution rate is based on a weighted average of rates applicable to existing members of the scheme and the weights are likely to change in respect of future new entrants. A change might for example be foreseeable because (a) new entrants join at ages which are on average either higher or lower than the ages at which existing members joined, or (b) new entrants are admitted on a pension scale which is materially different in cost from the scale applicable to current members.'[52]

3.1.5   *Actuarial valuation of assets*

Under any of the above methods chosen for valuing the accrued benefits of the fund, the actuary will also have put a value on the fund's investments. Practice in this area differs, but generally the investments will not be valued directly at their quoted market prices on the relevant day but rather at a value which takes a longer term perspective. A common method will be to value the investments on the basis of their projected dividend income.

When this approach is applied, it provides an effective cushion against short-term fluctuations in the securities markets. Thus, the market crash which occurred in October 1987 did not have the devastating effect on the valuation of pension funds which would have resulted if the valuation had been based directly on market values. Conversely, the Budget change in July 1997 whereby pension funds lost the benefit of the tax credit on UK dividend income had a significant effect on the actuarial value of their investments, whereas there was no adverse movement in quoted share prices.[53]

3.1.6   *Conclusion*

As discussed at 3.1.2 above, the standard does not specify that a particular actuarial valuation method be used, so long as the effect is to allocate the cost rationally and systematically over the period of the employees' services. This means that the calculations must be based on the final salaries which are expected to be paid. It would seem, therefore, that the only methods discussed above which could *not* achieve this objective are those which do not try to take into account the value of the pension which will be paid on the basis of final salary – the current unit method and the discontinuance basis. As noted above, there may also be a difficulty, where the entry age method is used, in obtaining a sensible split between regular cost and variations.

For mature schemes, the remaining valuation methods seem likely in practice to produce broadly similar costs for recognition in the profit and loss account, and on that basis they are likely to be equally acceptable. In fact it is often the case that the effect of using different methods is much less significant than the effect of varying the amounts of the key actuarial assumptions. However, for schemes which are likely not to remain stable in terms of their age profile, companies should discuss the circumstances in more detail with their actuaries. We recommend that they should base their choice of method on that which can be predicted to show greatest stability of pension cost as a percentage of pensionable payroll in the future.

3.2   Actuarial assumptions and best estimates

The standard requires that the actuarial assumptions and method, taken as a whole, should be compatible and should lead to the actuary's best estimate of the cost of providing the pension benefits promised.[54] Frequently, the assumptions made by the actuary for funding purposes cannot be described as 'best estimates', because, for example, the company has consciously decided to fund the scheme strongly and has therefore asked that assumptions be made on a deliberately conservative basis. While this is entirely legitimate as the basis of funding decisions, it is necessary to reconsider the assumptions when they are to be used to measure cost for accounting purposes; if necessary it may lead to the use of two different sets of assumptions, one for accounting purposes and the other for the purposes of funding.

It is quite difficult to talk about 'best estimates' in the context of actuarial assumptions, because the matters which are the subject of estimation can be extremely uncertain and a wide range of possible estimates could be made. Nevertheless it is appropriate that, so far as possible, the choice is made sensibly around the middle of the possible range rather than at the extreme. GN 17 offers guidance to the effect that 'it is not inappropriate to adopt assumptions which, taken together, are somewhat more likely to lead to surplus rather than to deficiency at future valuations, this being in accordance with the accounting convention of prudence. However, it is not satisfactory to include significant margins which are likely to lead to future surpluses or deficits which are material … .'[55]

The standard talks about the assumptions 'taken as a whole': because of the way in which the various factors interrelate, it is possible to arrive at a similar overall result by flexing individual estimates in opposite directions so as to compensate for an optimistic estimate in one area by making a conservative assumption in another. In this way, it is also mathematically possible to make implicit allowance for factors which on the face of it are not provided for, such as increases in pensions.

In our view it is preferable that implicit offsetting allowances of this nature are not made, and that each assumption in isolation should seek to reflect a realistic view of what will happen in the future. We take this view partly because it makes the valuation process more explicit to those within the company who are involved in it, but also because the standard requires the key assumptions to be disclosed in the accounts and, unless they are meaningful on a stand-alone basis, the reader of the accounts may be misled as to the strength of the valuation on which the figures are based.

3.3   The role of the actuary

By virtue of the wording of the trust document, many actuaries are appointed by, and are responsible only to, the trustees of the pension scheme and not to the employer company. Consideration should be given in these cases to extending the actuary's duties under the trust deed to report also to the company. However, this may not always be appropriate, and in these cases the company may wish to appoint a separate and independent actuary.

The accountancy bodies have produced an Audit Brief entitled 'The work of a pension scheme actuary'[56] which auditors, and other interested parties, may find useful when reviewing the results of actuaries' work.

In carrying out his work in relation to SSAP 24, the actuary will need to ensure that the methods and assumptions which have been chosen fulfil the following requirements:

- they meet the accounting objective of recognising the expected cost of providing the benefits on a systematic and rational basis over the period during which the employer derives benefit from the employees' services;

- they make full provision for the expected benefits over the anticipated service lives of the employees;

- they take account of the circumstances of the specific employer and his workforce – for example, it would not be appropriate to use a method which assumes a steady flow of new entrants if the employer has pension arrangements which are available only to existing employees;

- they recognise the effect of expected future increases in earnings, including merit increases, up to the assumed retirement date or earlier date of leaving or dying in service;

- they take account of future increases in deferred pensions and pensions payment where the employer has expressed or implied a commitment to grant such increases;

- they enable benefit levels to be calculated based on situations most likely to be experienced and not on contingent events unlikely to occur. For example, if there has been a regular practice of enhancing pensions on early severance and this is likely to be a feature of the employer's employment policies, it would not be acceptable to assume no enhancement on early retirements;

- they are used consistently over all similar pension arrangements within the employer's business and consistently between different accounting periods except where different circumstances justify a different approach; and

- taken as a whole, they are mutually compatible and lead to the actuary's best estimate of the cost of providing the benefits.

4   PROBLEM AREAS

4.1   The treatment of interest

Where an asset or liability emerges in the balance sheet because the cost charged in the profit and loss account is not the same as the funding payments made, we recommend that notional interest should be added to this amount thereafter as a third component of pension cost. Many companies explicitly do this (see for example Extract 20.7 above), but others do not, and SSAP 24 is far from clear on the matter.[57] The standard touches on the issue in paragraph 40, but leaves it ambiguous, saying that the question of discounting is not unique to pensions but requires to be answered more generally for many different accounting issues. It says that the interest effects of short-term differences between the payment of contributions and the recognition of cost are likely to be immaterial and can therefore be ignored, but suggests that they should be recognised in relation to longer term differences, and in particular on unfunded liabilities. However, this does not really explore the meaning of the balance sheet figure, or address the purpose of applying interest to it. The issues are best illustrated by use of an example:

Example 20.5: Application of interest to balance sheet figures

A company has a pension fund with an actuarial surplus of £1.4 million at the time of the implementation of SSAP 24. The actuary has assumed that an interest rate of 9% will be earned by the surplus in the fund, and the average remaining service lives of the employees is 8 years. The regular cost of providing for pensions is 10% of pensionable payroll – this gives rise to a present figure of £360,000, which is expected to increase at an annual rate of 7%.

The table set out overleaf shows both the movements in the fund itself over the next eight years and the related accounting entries under the two different methods of implementing the standard in the first year of application. To simplify the interest calculations, it is assumed that the movements in the fund (i.e. contributions and regular cost) occur at the beginning of each year.

As a result of the surplus the actuary has recommended that the contributions for the next eight years be reduced to 4.82% of pensionable pay, which will mean that £173,000 will be contributed in year 1. As is shown in column 1 of the table, this has the effect of eliminating the surplus by the end of the eight year period, assuming everything else works out in line with the actuarial assumptions.

Where the company has chosen to implement SSAP 24 by incorporating the surplus directly in the balance sheet (rather than spreading it forward as a quasi-variation), columns 1 and 2 show the figures that will appear in its balance sheet and profit and loss account, provided that it recognises interest on the balance sheet figure. On implementing the standard, the company will set up the £1.4 million asset in its balance sheet, and in the profit and loss account for year 1 it will show a pension cost of £251,000, which represents the regular cost of £360,000 less interest of £109,000 (9% of (£1,400,000 + £173,000 - £360,000) – to simplify the calculation it is assumed that all movements in the fund are reflected at the beginning of the year) deemed to be earned on the balance sheet figure. The excess of this cost over the contributions paid of £173,000 will be applied to reduce the balance sheet figure by £78,000 to leave the closing balance sheet with an asset of £1,322,000. The same process is repeated in each year, and it can be seen that the balance sheet figure tracks the amount of the surplus in the fund throughout the period.

It is worth considering what would happen if interest on the balance sheet figure were not recognised. In this case the profit and loss account charge would simply be the regular cost of £360,000, and the balance sheet asset would be reduced by £187,000 (the difference between the profit and loss account charge and the £173,000 contribution). By the end of the eight year period this would result in the balance sheet showing a liability of £515,000, which would have no equivalent in the fund; it would simply be the amount of the interest earned in the fund over that period which the accounts had failed to recognise. Any new actuarial valuation carried out during the period would show an apparent variation (being the amount of unrecognised interest) which, in terms of SSAP 24, would be recognised prospectively, as an offset to the pension cost of the next 8 years. It would seem much more sensible to recognise this interest in the years in which it accrues rather than over a protracted future period.

Columns 3 and 4 show the figures which would appear in the balance sheet and the profit and loss account if the company adopted the other possible way of implementing the standard – treating the surplus as a quasi-variation and spreading it forward over the remaining service lives of the employees. The calculation of the pension cost is based on the regular cost of £360,000 less the release of an instalment of the £1.4 million quasi-variation which is spread in this example using the 'straight line method', and plus interest on the opening balance sheet figure in each year. There are two interest elements in this calculation. As well as the interest added on the balance sheet figure, the amortisation of the quasi-variation is done by releasing amounts which include interest so that their *present value* totals £1.4 million (see 4.2.2 below for a more detailed discussion of spreading methods). The balance sheet figure is simply the cumulative difference between the profit and loss account charge and the contributions paid.

It can be seen that, over the eight years, the total charge to the profit and loss account under the 'prospective' method (column 4) is £1.4 million less than that under the 'PYA' method (column 2). This simply reflects the fact that the surplus is being channelled through the profit and loss account under the former method but taken straight to reserves under the latter. Column 5 shows how this total difference is allocated to each of the years involved; in this example it is a level amount of one-eighth of the total surplus, because the straight line method of amortisation was used. Column 6 shows the amount of the surplus remaining to be recognised at the end of each year, in other words the amount of the initial surplus successively reduced by the figures in column 5. Column 6 also represents the difference between the balance sheet figures under each of the two methods at the end of each year. (As explained at 2.5.4 above, the balance sheet figure under SSAP 24 can be defined as the net of the surplus or deficit in the fund and the amount of unamortised variations awaiting recognition in the profit and loss account.)

Year	Movements in pension fund	PYA method Balance sheet £000	P&L account £000	Prospective method Balance sheet £000	P&L account £000	Difference £000	Unamortised variations £000
		1	2	3	4	5	6
1	Surplus	1,400					
	Contribution	173					
	Regular cost	(360)					
	Interest	109					
	P&L charge		251		76	175	
2	Balance	1,322		97			1,225
	Contribution	186					
	Regular cost	(385)					
	Interest	101					
	P&L charge		284		109	175	
3	Balance	1,224		174			1,050
	Contribution	198					
	Regular cost	(412)					
	Interest	91					
	P&L charge		321		146	175	
4	Balance	1,101		226			875
	Contribution	212					
	Regular cost	(441)					
	Interest	79					
	P&L charge		362		187	175	
5	Balance	951		251			700
	Contribution	227					
	Regular cost	(472)					
	Interest	64					
	P&L charge		408		233	175	
6	Balance	770		245			525
	Contribution	243					
	Regular cost	(505)					
	Interest	46					
	P&L charge		459		284	175	
7	Balance	554		204			350
	Contribution	260					
	Regular cost	(540)					
	Interest	25					
	P&L charge		515		340	175	
8	Balance	299		124			175
	Contribution	279					
	Regular cost	(578)					
	Interest	0					
	P&L charge		578		403	175	
9	Balance	0		0			0
	Totals		3,178		1,778	1,400	

To illustrate the application of the calculations further, another example is shown in the table on the next page which assumes the same basic facts, except that the company has chosen to eliminate the surplus more quickly by taking a contribution holiday rather than reducing its rate of contribution over a longer period.

Example 20.6   Application of interest to balance sheet figure

This example alters the facts in Example 20.5 slightly, and shows the figures which would arise if the company eliminated the surplus by taking a contribution holiday for nearly four years rather than by reducing its contributions for eight years. Once again, column 1 in the table on the next page shows the movements in the fund itself; the surplus is run off over four years as a result of the contribution holiday, and thereafter the fund is kept in equilibrium because the contributions are restored to an amount equal to the regular cost.

As before, columns 1 and 2 show the figures that will appear in the company's balance sheet and profit and loss account, provided that interest is recognised on the balance sheet figure. In this case the pension cost will be higher than in the previous example because the surplus in the fund is being reduced more sharply and as a result is earning less interest. From year 5 on, there is no surplus in the fund and the charge in the profit and loss account is simply the regular cost. Once again, the balance sheet figure tracks the amount of the surplus in the fund throughout the period, provided interest is recognised on the balance sheet figure.

Columns 3 and 4 again show the figures which appear in the balance sheet and the profit and loss account under the prospective approach. It can again be demonstrated that, over the eight years, the total charge to the profit and loss account under the prospective method is £1.4†million less than that under the PYA method.

Having given these illustrations, it is now possible to consider why the figures work out in the way that they do. Where the balance sheet figure simply represents the surplus in the fund (as it will to begin with under the PYA approach) then it is easy to see that it is necessary to recognise the interest which the fund is earning in the company accounts in order to preserve that relationship. However, where the prospective method is applied, it is harder to understand why interest should be applied to the balance sheet figure, and indeed, as in Example 20.6, it may be difficult to explain why an extra interest *charge* should be made on a balance sheet liability when the fund is still *earning* interest on a surplus.

To explain this, it is necessary to see the balance sheet figure in the light that has been discussed in 2.5.4 above, as a composite figure which is the net of the surplus in the fund and the amount of unamortised variations awaiting recognition in the profit and loss account. Thus, the liability of £91,000 at the end of year 1 under the prospective method (column 3 in Example 20.6) is the net of the surplus in the fund of £1,134,000 and the unamortised variations of £1,225,000 (columns 1 and 6). Applying interest to the £91,000 can similarly be interpreted as a credit for interest on the surplus in the fund which is more than offset by a charge on the amount of the unamortised variations.

Year	Movements in pension fund	1 PYA method Balance sheet	2 PYA method P&L account	3 Prospective method Balance sheet	4 Prospective method P&L account	5 Difference	6 Unamortised variations
		£000	£000	£000	£000	£000	£000
1	Surplus	1,400					
	Contribution	0					
	Regular cost	(360)					
	Interest	94					
	P&L charge		266		91	175	
2	Balance	1,134		(91)			1,225
	Contribution	0					
	Regular cost	(385)					
	Interest	67					
	P&L charge		318		143	175	
3	Balance	816		(234)			1,050
	Contribution	0					
	Regular cost	(412)					
	Interest	36					
	P&L charge		376		201	175	
4	Balance	440		(435)			875
	Contribution	1					
	Regular cost	(441)					
	Interest	0					
	P&L charge		441		266	175	
5	Balance	0		(700)			700
	Contribution	472					
	Regular cost	(472)					
	Interest	0					
	P&L charge		472		297	175	
6	Balance	0		(525)			525
	Contribution	505					
	Regular cost	(505)					
	Interest	0					
	P&L charge		505		330	175	
7	Balance	0		(350)			350
	Contribution	540					
	Regular cost	(540)					
	Interest	0					
	P&L charge		540		365	175	
8	Balance	0		(175)			175
	Contribution	578					
	Regular cost	(578)					
	Interest	0					
	P&L charge		578		403	175	
9	Balance	0		0			0
	Totals		3,496		2,096	1,400	

This analysis offers a different way of looking at the make-up of the pension cost charge, which may be more readily understood. The total pension cost can be explained as being made up of the regular cost less the interest on the surplus (even though it is not included in the balance sheet) and less the release of the quasi-variation into the profit and loss account. This can be illustrated as follows using the figures from Example 20.5:

Year	Regular cost	Interest in fund	Release of variations	Total
	£000	£000	£000	£000
1	360	109	175	76
2	385	101	175	109
3	412	91	175	146
4	441	79	175	187
5	472	64	175	233
6	505	46	175	284
7	540	25	175	340
8	578	0	175	403
	3,693	515	1,400	1,778

The method shown in Example 20.5 differs from this in two ways, which cancel each other out:

(a)   interest is applied to the whole balance sheet figure, not just the surplus (i.e. it is also applied to the component which represents the deferred variations awaiting recognition in the profit and loss account);

(b)   the variations are taken into the profit and loss account at amounts whose *net present value* adds up to £1.4m, not their absolute amount.

This analysis may be easier to understand in concept, but that which is given in Example 20.5 may be easier to apply in practice because it simply involves applying interest to the balance sheet figure, whatever it may be, rather than looking through it to see what the actual surplus in the fund is.

When interest is recognised in the profit and loss account, it is necessary to consider whether to include it as a component of pension cost, or as an amount of interest payable or receivable within the general classification of finance costs. Respectable arguments can be mounted for either treatment where the interest is simply that which is being earned in the fund itself (where the balance sheet figure directly represents the balance in the fund). However, where the interest is charged on a composite figure which includes an amount of unamortised variations, the interest charge or credit has no real significance by itself because it is inseparably linked to the release of these variations. For this reason, it is suggested that the preferable treatment in all cases is to include the interest as a component of pension cost. This was the tentative conclusion of the

ASB in its 1995 Discussion Paper,[58] although the contrary suggestion was made in the Board's later paper on Discounting.[59]

In conclusion, it can be seen from the illustrations given above that interest considerations pervade the calculations which underlie pension accounting, and that unless they are consistently accounted for, the accounts will not allocate them to the periods to which they belong. Despite the apparent complexity of these examples, the rules to be applied are relatively straightforward; companies should both account for imputed interest on the balance sheet figure and also spread any variations into the profit and loss account on a basis which includes the effects of interest. If they do not do so, apparent variations will arise in subsequent actuarial valuations which are simply the result of the company's failure to recognise interest in the periods in which it has accrued.

4.2 Variations from regular cost

4.2.1 Calculation of remaining service lives

The standard says that variations should normally be spread over the remaining service lives of employees currently in the scheme after making suitable allowances for future withdrawals, and that it is possible to apply this principle by using an average period relevant to the current membership if desired.[60] This issue is discussed at 2.5.2 B above. Where the average approach is taken, this will be determined by the actuary on the basis of the age profile of the workforce and the assumptions made about mortality, retirements and withdrawals. The period is usually likely to be shorter than might intuitively be assumed, and a range of 10 to 15 years might be typical.

SSAP 24 does not require the period of amortisation to be disclosed, but in practice a number of companies do so and we regard this as a helpful disclosure. Two examples are shown in Extracts 20.14 and 20.15 below.

4.2.2 How should variations be amortised?

As mentioned in 2.5.2 B and at 4.2.1 above, the standard does not specify the particular method by which variations should be amortised, saying only that they should be amortised over the expected remaining service lives of the employees in the scheme, and that an average period may be used if desired.[61] Three main methods have emerged in practice, although others may also be permissible if they meet the objective described above. These three are known as (a) the straight line method (b) the mortgage method and (c) the percentage of pay method, and they are illustrated in the following three extracts:

Extract 20.14: Rio Tinto plc and Rio Tinto Limited (1998)

1 PRINCIPAL ACCOUNTING POLICIES

l Post retirement benefits

The expected costs of post retirement benefits under defined benefit arrangements are charged to the profit and loss account so as to spread the costs over the service lives of employees entitled to those benefits. Variations from the regular cost are spread on a straight line basis over the expected average remaining service lives of relevant current employees. Costs are assessed in accordance with the advice of qualified actuaries.

37 POST RETIREMENT BENEFITS [extract]

... The expected average remaining service life in the major schemes ranges from 12 to 23 years with an overall average of 13 years. ...

Extract 20.15: Reed Elsevier plc (1998)

4 Pension schemes [extract]

... The actuarial surplus is being spread as a level amount over the average remaining service lives of current employees, which has been assessed as eight years. ...

Extract 20.16: Whitbread PLC (1999)

ACCOUNTING POLICIES

J Pension funding

Pension costs are charged to the profit and loss account over the average expected service life of current employees. Actuarial surpluses are amortised over the expected remaining service lives of current employees, using the percentage of pensionable salaries method. Differences between the amount charged in the profit and loss account and payments made to the schemes are treated as assets or liabilities in the balance sheet.

There is no explicit requirement in SSAP 24 to disclose the method used, and most companies do not do so. However, the different methods can produce answers which are materially different, and we encourage disclosure of the method chosen: this has also been recommended by the ICAEW.[62] The majority of those companies who do make this disclosure use the percentage of pay method.

The mechanics of the three methods are illustrated by the following example, which is based on the same situation as described in Example 20.5:

Example 20.7: Methods of amortisation of variations

An actuarial valuation of a company's pension scheme identifies a variation of £1,400,000 to be spread over the working lives of the employees, which is assessed to be 8 years. The company's payroll cost is expected to increase at a rate of 7% per annum and the return earned on the fund's investments will be 9%. The figures derived from the three most common methods of spreading the variation are set out below.

Year	Straight line method £000	Mortgage method £000	Percentage of pay method £000
1	277	232	186
2	262	232	200
3	247	232	213
4	233	232	229
5	218	232	244
6	204	232	262
7	189	232	280
8	175	232	300
Total	1,805	1,856	1,914

The straight line method is computed by dividing the amount to be spread (£1,400,000) by the number of years (8) to achieve a level capital amount of £175,000. Interest is added to the balance which remains unamortised in each year to give the total charge.

The mortgage method involves calculating the annuity for 8 years which equates, at an interest rate of 9%, to a capital value of £1,400,000. The resulting annual figure can be regarded, as with the repayments under a mortgage, as comprising a relatively small capital element and a large interest element at the outset with the proportions reversing in later years.

The percentage of pay method is calculated by determining the stream of payments, escalating at the rate of annual payroll inflation (7% in this example) which has a present value of the amount to be amortised (£1,400,000).

It can be seen that each of these methods results in the amortisation of a total figure which exceeds the apparent amount (£1,400,000 in this example) which was to be amortised. This is because an actuarial surplus is not an absolute amount, but rather a discounted figure because of the calculations implicit in the valuation method. It is therefore necessary to include an interest element in the amortisation calculation, as is described in each of these methods. As has been shown under 4.1 above, it is also necessary to charge or credit interest on the balance sheet figure in order to reflect fully the time value of money which is inherent in the calculation.

The three methods produce quite different profiles. The mortgage method produces a level amount, the straight line method results in a declining amount, while the percentage of pay method has the reverse effect. The effect of using these methods in the calculation of pension costs in the circumstances of Example 20.5 will be as shown in this graph:

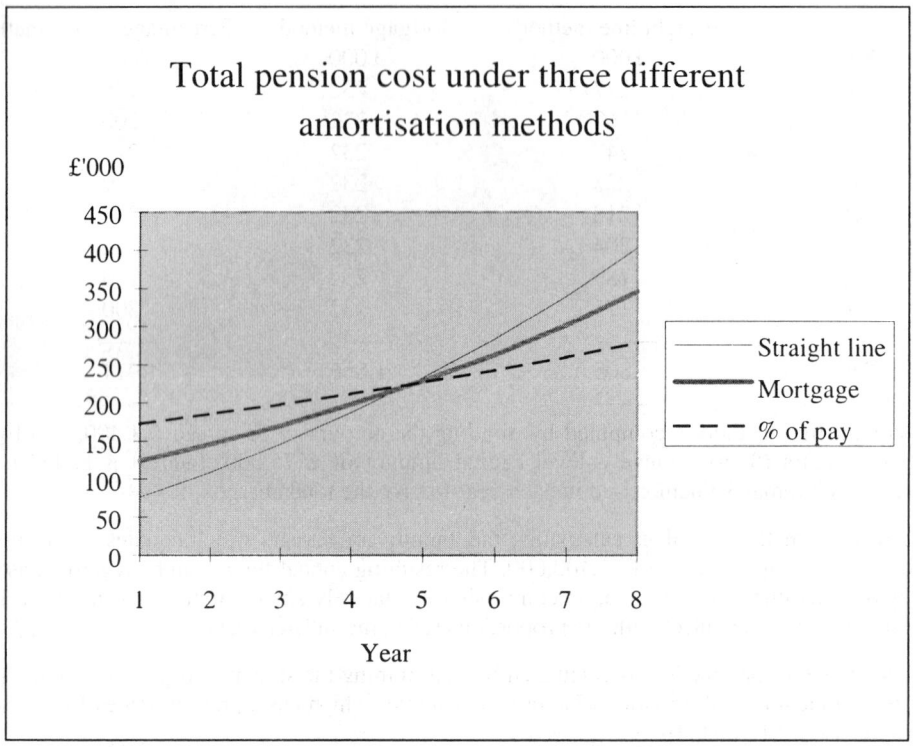

The percentage of pay method will tend to be used when the actuary expresses the variation in terms of the required change to the contribution rate rather than as a lump sum figure. It could also be argued that this is the most appropriate method because it means that the variation as well as the regular cost will be a stable proportion of the pensionable payroll. However, if the pension cost is analysed into the components shown in 4.1 above (regular cost, interest earned on the surplus in the fund and the release of variations *excluding* interest), different arguments could be summoned to support either of the other methods. The calculations of these amounts are illustrated below:

Year	Regular cost £000	Interest in fund £000	Straight line method		Mortgage method		%age of pay method	
			Release of variations £000	Total £000	Release of variations £000	Total £000	Release of variations £000	Total £000
1	360	109	175	76	127	124	78	173
2	385	101	175	109	138	146	98	186
3	412	91	175	146	151	170	123	198
4	441	79	175	187	165	198	150	212
5	472	64	175	233	179	229	181	227
6	505	46	175	284	195	263	216	243
7	540	25	175	340	213	302	255	260
8	578	0	175	403	232	346	299	279
	3,693	515	1,400	1,778	1,400	1,778	1,400	1,778

The first four columns of the table repeat the analysis shown in 4.1 above, while the remaining two pairs of columns show the effect of using the mortgage and the percentage of pay methods of spreading variations rather than the straight line method. As can be seen, the total cost shown in the last column is the same as the amount of contributions paid in Example 20.5, because the actuary had set the total contribution at the percentage of payroll which would have the effect of eliminating the surplus over eight years. The regular cost and the interest earned in the fund obviously do not change whatever amortisation method is used.

Under this analysis, it can be seen that the release of variations under the percentage of pay method is in fact heavily weighted to the end of the amortisation period, rising from only £78,000 in the first year to £299,000 in the last. The release is flexed in this way so as to offset the declining interest income earned by the fund as the surplus is reduced as a result of the lower level of contributions. However, it may be argued that pension cost *should* be proportionately lower when there is a surplus in the fund than when it has been run off, and therefore that the release of variations should not be designed to eliminate this effect. On this argument, there is more to be said for the straight line method, which releases the interest evenly over the amortisation period, or the mortgage method, which increases it only by the rate of interest used in the discounting calculation; the ASB's 1995 Discussion Paper favoured the use of the straight line method.[63] Nevertheless, since the standard does not specify the use of any particular method, it would appear that any of the above would be acceptable, and indeed there are other methods which could also be applied.

4.2.3 What is a significant reduction in employees?

As discussed at 2.5.2 D above, one of the compulsory exceptions from the normal 'spreading' rule for variations is when there has been a significant reduction in the number of employees in the scheme. However, although this exception is expressed as being mandatory, it only becomes so once it has been determined that the reduction in employees should be regarded as significant, and this term is not further defined.

The term could be thought of as meaning 'significant enough to make a measurable impact on the actuary's recommendations on funding rates', since the exception requires the accounting to follow whatever change in contributions results from the fall in the number of employees; if there is no measurable impact then clearly the provisions of this exception cannot be applied. In any event, we believe that the exception was intended to be applied relatively rarely, and should be used only where there has been a major scaling down of operations, rather than for every minor trimming exercise.

It should, however, be noted that the reduction need not result from one single closure – it could be the result of a series of redundancies over the period since the last valuation of the fund. Where it does relate to the sale or termination of an operation, the treatment will again be different, as described in 2.5.2 C above.

4.2.4 Allocation of experience differences to funding consequences

Any surplus or deficit identified by an actuarial valuation will result from a number of different causes, and it will be necessary to ask the actuary to provide an analysis in order to allow the appropriate accounting to be applied. Since there are exceptions to the normal 'spreading' rule for variations, some choices may emerge, depending on how the individual experience differences are linked with the funding consequences. An example will illustrate this:

Example 20.8: Allocation of experience differences to funding consequences

As a result of an actuarial valuation, a surplus of £5m has been identified. The actuary reports that this is mainly due to experience differences concerning investment performance of the fund, but that £1.2m of the surplus resulted from the withdrawal of a significant proportion of the workforce in the course of a redundancy programme over the last two years. The company decides that it will reduce the surplus both by suspending contributions to the fund for the next two years and also by taking a refund from the scheme of £1m, which will be subject to tax at 40%.

The standard permits taxed refunds to be taken to the profit and loss account when received, regardless of the reason for the surplus arising. It also requires variations resulting from significant reductions in the number of employees to be accounted for in line with their effect on the funding of the scheme. Accordingly the company would appear to have the following options open to it:

(a) to link the refund notionally to the reduction in the number of the employees rather than to the other experience differences. The effect of this would make it compulsory, rather than optional, to credit the refund to the profit and loss account immediately. That part of the contribution holiday which could be attributed to the remaining £0.2m surplus could also be recognised as affecting income in the year or years in which the holiday is taken. (There would appear to be a further choice between spreading it over the two years in which contributions were to be suspended and attributing it wholly to one or other of the years, although the latter would seem somewhat artificial.)

(b) to link the refund notionally to the other experience differences rather than to the reduction in the number of the employees. The effect of this would be to leave the company with the option of recognising the refund in the profit and loss account immediately, but also to require it to give full recognition to the effects of the reduction in the workforce in the year or years of the related contribution holiday. The combined effect of this notional allocation would allow the company to report higher profits in the short term than if the alternative allocation under (a) had been chosen.

No guidance can be offered on how to choose between these different approaches; either would be acceptable. This illustrates some of the anomalies which can arise because the various exceptions to the basic rule for spreading variations forward lack an adequate conceptual thread.

4.2.5 *How to account for the unamortised difference remaining in the year of the next actuarial valuation*

As mentioned at the end of 2.5.2 B above, no guidance has been given on how to account for the remaining part of previously identified variations, when a subsequent valuation is made and reveals fresh variations. Consider the situation, using the figures from Example 20.1, where a further actuarial valuation is conducted at 31 December 2001, and reveals a different surplus.

Example 20.9: Effect on unrecognised variations of subsequent valuations

The previous actuarial valuation at 31 December 1998 of the pension scheme of company B showed a surplus of £260m. The actuary recommended that B eliminate the surplus by taking a contribution holiday in 1999and 2000 and then paying contributions of £30m p.a. for 8 years. After that the standard contribution would be £50m p.a. The average remaining service life of employees in the scheme at 31 December 1998 was 10 years. As a result of the above, the accounts for the next three years showed the following:

Year	Funded	Charged	(Provision)
	£m	£m	£m
1999	–	24	(24)
2000	–	24	(48)
2001	30	24	(42)

The next actuarial valuation at 31 December 2001 showed a surplus of £80m. The actuary this time recommended that B should maintain the contribution rate at £30m p.a. until 2005 and then raise it to £50m thereafter. The average remaining service life of employees in the scheme was still 10 years. The company intends to take account of this valuation in its accounts for the year to 31 December 2002.

On the face of it, it might appear that there is a further £80m of surplus which will go to reduce the pension cost still further. However, on closer examination it is clear that there has in fact been a deterioration since the 1998 valuation, because a larger surplus would have been predicted based on that valuation. The valuation at that time showed a surplus of £260m, but contributions of only £30m have been made since then, compared with a regular cost requirement of £150m; the combination of these figures would have given rise to a predicted surplus of £140m (260+30-150), yet the surplus is now only £80m, which in fact represents a deterioration of £60m, not an improvement of £80m. There is therefore the equivalent of a new *deficit* of £60m to be accounted for over the future service lives of the employees. (NOTE: For the sake of simplicity, all these figures are presented ignoring the effects of interest and the time value of money. In practice these will form significant elements in the calculation.)

The question that then arises is how to combine the effect of this newly identified variation with the unamortised amount of the previously identified variation. Of the previously identified surplus of £260m, only 3 instalments totalling £78m have so far been recognised and the remaining £182m is still to be recognised as an adjustment of future pension costs. Either it could be combined with the newly identified variation of £60m, and the net amount of £122m could be written off over 10 years, or the original amortisation period (a further 7 years) could be retained for the original variation, and the new variation written off separately over a new period of 10 years starting from 2002. The effects of these two possibilities are shown below. Option 1 combines the elements to produce a constant charge of £37.8m (the regular cost of £50m less the amortisation of £122m over 10 years (£12.2m)), while option 2 keeps the components separate (regular cost of £50m less the amortisation of £182m over seven years (£26m) plus the amortisation of £60m over ten years (£6m)).

| | | Option 1 | | Option 2 | |
| | Funded | Charged | (Provision) | Charged | (Provision) |
Year	£m	£m	£m	£m	£m
Opening provision			(42.0)		(42)
2002	30	37.8	(49.8)	30	(42)
2003	30	37.8	(57.6)	30	(42)
2004	30	37.8	(65.4)	30	(42)
2005	30	37.8	(73.2)	30	(42)
2006	50	37.8	(61.0)	30	(22)
2007	50	37.8	(48.8)	30	2
2008	50	37.8	(36.6)	30	18
2009	50	37.8	(24.4)	56	12
2010	50	37.8	(12.2)	56	6
2011	50	37.8	–	56	–

Option 2 follows the literal requirement of the standard that variations should be spread over the remaining service lives of the employees in the scheme (i.e. without subsequent extension of that period) and may be regarded as the more appropriate method for that reason. However, option 1 can also be seen as being in line with the general philosophy of the standard that the effects of variations should be smoothed forward on a rolling basis. Nevertheless, it means that any individual variations will never be completely amortised, because the amortisation period will be continually extended, even if no significant variations arise from subsequent valuations.

In practice we believe that both methods are acceptable. Option 1 has the additional merit that it requires fewer detailed records and calculations; indeed the amount to be amortised can be identified directly following each valuation because it is the amount of the difference between the actuarial surplus or deficiency in the fund and whatever figure is in the employer's balance sheet; in the above case this works out as £122m (£80m + £42m).

Boots discloses that it applies Option 2, as shown in this extract:

Extract 20.17: The Boots Company PLC (1999)

26 Pensions [extract]

The pension charge shown in the financial statements for the year was £5m (1998 £5m). This arises as a result of the regular cost of pensions being offset by amortisation of the surpluses disclosed by the 1989, 1992 and 1998 valuations and increased by the amortisation of the deficit in respect of the 1995 valuation. The surplus disclosed at the 1998 valuation is being recognised over approximately 13 years, the expected average remaining service life of members. The remaining amortisation period of the surpluses/deficits disclosed at the 1989, 1992 and 1995 valuations are approximately three, seven and ten years respectively.

4.2.6   *How to treat a balance sheet asset which is shown to have been eroded by a subsequent valuation*

In the circumstances described in Example 20.9 in the previous section, the company was showing a liability in respect of pensions in its balance sheet. However, if it had previously incorporated the surplus as an asset in its balance sheet (on adoption of the standard for the first time), then it would be facing a different situation, as described in the following example:

Example 20.10: Effect on balance sheet figures of subsequent valuations

Company B acquires a subsidiary and in the course of the fair value exercise obtains an actuarial valuation of its pension fund which showed a surplus of £260m. Accordingly, B incorporates that amount in its consolidated balance sheet. The actuary subsequently recommends that the surplus is eliminated by a contribution holiday for the next two years and then reduced contributions of £30m p.a. for 8 years. After that the standard contribution would be £50m p.a. As a result of the above, the group accounts for the next three years included the following in respect of the acquired subsidiary:

Year	Funded £m	Charged £m	Prepayment £m
on implementation			260
1999	–	50	210
2000	–	50	160
2001	30	50	140

The next actuarial valuation at 31 December 2001 showed a surplus of £80m. The actuary this time recommended that the contribution rate at £30m p.a. should be maintained for four more years and then raised to £50m thereafter. The average working lives of the employees is ten years.

There has therefore been a deterioration of £60m (i.e. £140m - £80m) since the previous valuation and this represents the variation which has to be accounted for. Applying SSAP 24's normal approach of eliminating the variation over the average working lives of the members would add £6m to the regular cost of £50m and would produce the following results (ignoring interest etc. in order to simplify the illustration).

Year	Funded £m	Charged £m	Prepayment £m
brought forward			140
2002	30	56	114
2003	30	56	88
2004	30	56	62
2005	30	56	36
2006	50	56	30
2007	50	56	24
2008	50	56	18
2009	50	56	12
2010	50	56	6
2011	50	56	0

The only possible problem with this is that the asset in the balance sheet exceeds the surplus in the fund for the whole of the period 2002 to 2011, as shown below:

Year	Funded £m	Charged £m	Prepayment £m	Surplus £m	Difference £m
brought forward			140	80	60
2002	30	56	114	60	54
2003	30	56	88	40	48
2004	30	56	62	20	42
2005	30	56	36	0	36
2006	50	56	30	0	30
2007	50	56	24	0	24
2008	50	56	18	0	18
2009	50	56	12	0	12
2010	50	56	6	0	6
2011	50	56	0	0	0

The surplus of £80m is reduced by £20m for the first four years because the contribution is set at £30m while the regular cost remains at £50m. The difference, shown in the last column, represents the unamortised variations still to be recognised in the profit and loss account.

Normal accounting principles would dictate that, when it can be seen that an asset in the balance sheet will not be fully recoverable, it should be written down to reflect the impairment in value which has occurred. However, this would be contrary to the basic approach of the standard, which requires gradual rather than immediate recognition of experience differences, and does not discriminate between gains and losses for this purpose. Similarly, it does not require immediate recognition in the balance sheet of pension scheme deficits, whether on first application of the standard or as a result of subsequent valuations.

The ASB's 1995 Discussion Paper did propose an upper limit on the amount of any pension asset in the balance sheet, based on a recoverability test. It suggested that the asset should not exceed the capital sum that would finance the normal pension cost in perpetuity on the assumptions used in the valuation, together with the amount of any refunds that the employer is able to withdraw from the fund.[64] Such a test, however, does not really make sense in relation to the whole amount of the pension asset, but only to that component of it which represents the underlying surplus; it does not address the issue of whether it is legitimate to carry forward significant adverse variations to be written off over future years. It is also interesting that the proposed test excluded the possibility of using the surplus by increasing the benefits available under the scheme without incremental cost to the company.

We suggest, however, that if significant adverse variations do arise, companies should at least consider analysing the balance sheet figure so as to distinguish the amount which represents the surplus in the scheme from that which is simply the total of unamortised variations to be charged in the profit and loss account of subsequent years.

4.3 Negative pension cost

Where the amount of interest and/or variations credited to pension cost exceeds the regular cost, then a net negative pension cost figure will arise. Typically this will be because the surplus in the scheme is so large that it would not be eliminated even by a pension holiday for the whole of the average working lives of the employees in the scheme. However, it could also be the result of using a 'front-end' loaded amortisation method of releasing variations to the profit and loss account.

The question that then arises is whether it is legitimate in principle to recognise negative expense in respect of pensions. To some extent, this depends on a matter of perception of what SSAP 24 involves. One view would be that it is designed simply to allocate the total cost of providing pensions to the years of employment of the eventual pensioners, and since that total cost will be positive, it does not make any sense for the amount allocated to any individual year to be negative. On this interpretation, the credit arising from interest or variations should be restricted to the amount of the regular cost, so that the minimum cost is zero and no credit is taken for any negative amount. Meyer International is an example of a company that explicitly restricts credit components of pension cost so that it does not report net credits to the profit and loss account:

Extract 20.18: Meyer International PLC (1999)

1 ACCOUNTING POLICIES

(i) Pensions

The expected costs of pensions are provided on systematic and rational bases over the estimated average service lives of members of the schemes. Variations arising from actuarial surpluses are spread over the average remaining service lives of members to the extent that the resulting credit does not exceed the regular cost.

The alternative interpretation looks more deeply into the pension scheme and sees it as a store of wealth which is a source of risks and benefits to the employer. Accordingly it seeks to apply the 'half-hearted' form of equity accounting described in 2.5.4 above. On this analysis, there is no reason in principle why negative pension cost should not be recognised, and indeed this would represent a limitation on recognition of interest and variations which would in many ways be arbitrary. BOC, in Extract 20.4 above, discloses negative cost for its main schemes in 1996. We believe that this is an acceptable interpretation of the standard and therefore see no reason why negative pension cost should not be recognised. The ASB's 1995 Discussion Paper endorsed this view, although it qualified its approval by emphasising that the recognition of negative pension cost should not give rise to an asset which does not represent a source of benefits to the employer.[65]

4.4   Hybrid schemes

Although the standard lays down separate rules for defined contribution schemes and defined benefit schemes, in some cases the scheme will not fall so neatly into one or other of these classifications. There is a growing practice within pension schemes of offering elements of both kinds of arrangement; for example, a final pay scheme may give its members the option to take benefits based on an alternative money purchase-based formula, to allow them to participate to some extent in the investment performance of the fund if it proves successful. It will therefore be necessary to decide how to account for such arrangements.

The standard acknowledges that this difficulty exists. Although no easy solution can be offered, the only possible response is to try to identify the true underlying nature of the scheme as accurately as possible. Is it in essence a final pay scheme, but with some money purchase features as a theoretical extra? Alternatively, is it principally a money purchase scheme, but with some benefits linked to final pay to provide a safety net against bad fund performance? Only by assessing the basis under which benefits are likely to be paid in practice will it be possible to determine to which category the scheme can be regarded as belonging in substance. It will also be necessary to re-evaluate this regularly, since changes in economic conditions (such as inflation rates) could alter the probability that benefits will be payable on one basis rather than another. In most cases, this evaluation should be conducted with the benefit of advice from the actuary, who will advise on the most appropriate accounting treatment to be adopted.

Since the distinction between the two accounting treatments depends on whether or not the employer's obligation is limited to the contributions payable, the amount of those contributions will generally represent the minimum measure of the pension cost to be charged, and it will be necessary to consider whether the existence of the defined benefit formula means that additional costs have to be provided for in addition to those contributions. It may also be appropriate to disclose a more comprehensive description of the scheme than usual, in order to allow the reader of the accounts to appreciate the nature of the obligations to which the employer is committed.

4.5 Foreign schemes

A group which operates internationally may well have a number of local pension schemes, in some cases imposed by legal requirements of the host country, which are of quite a different nature from those of the parent company. In principle all the rules of the standard still apply, and the group accounts should contain consolidated information on these schemes which has been prepared using consistent policies and methods. However, in certain cases this may prove impracticable, and it would be unrealistic to expect quite disparate arrangements to be treated in a uniform way.

The standard acknowledges this difficulty, and broadly says that while the measurement rules should be applied so far as possible, in certain instances it will be necessary simply to take the cost as determined for local purposes as the basis of the charge. Whether or not this provides an acceptable answer will obviously also depend on the materiality of the amounts involved. Where it is not possible to apply the rules of the standard completely, it will be necessary to explain the circumstances involved, stating the amount of the charge which is affected by this difficulty, and the basis on which it has been determined.[66]

4.6 Unfunded schemes

Unfunded schemes have been relatively uncommon among private sector companies in the UK, although they have become more popular as a result of tax changes introduced in the Finance Act 1989; they may also arise in respect of foreign subsidiaries which are included within the consolidated accounts of a UK parent. In addition, where a company offers post-retirement benefits other than pensions, they are likely to be unfunded. The standard says relatively little about unfunded schemes, but the same basic accounting rules apply. In essence, an unfunded scheme can be looked upon as equivalent to a funded scheme under which no contributions have yet been paid and which accordingly has no assets.

GKN has significant unfunded obligations in respect of pensions, as shown in this extract:

Extract 20.19: GKN plc (1998)

21. Provisions for liabilities and charges [extract]

	1998 £m	1997 £m
Deferred taxation	–	2
Post-retirement and other provisions	194	174
Meineke litigation (see note 27)	–	266
	194	442

	Deferred taxation £m	Post-retirement and other provisions £m	Meineke litigation £m
At 1 January 1998	2	174	266
Charge (credit) for the year	(2)	22	(248)
Currency variations	–	11	–
Subsidiaries acquired and sold	–	2	–
Paid or accrued during the year	–	(15)	(18)
At 31 December 1998	–	194	–

... Post-retirement and other provisions include provisions relating to pension benefits of £165†million (1997 – £149 million) and provisions for other post-retirement benefits of £24†million (1997 – £213 million).

25 Post-retirement benefits [extract]

... In certain overseas companies funds are retained within the business to provide for retirement obligations. The annual charge to provide for these obligations, which is determined in accordance with actuarial advice or local statutory requirements, amounted to £19 million (1997 – £17†million).

One issue which is of particular relevance to unfunded schemes is the need to recognise interest in the measurement of the cost of providing the pension. The provision which is set up in the balance sheet will be assessed on a discounted basis. This means that the amount to be added to the provision in each year can be looked upon as having two components: an interest charge on the unfunded liability (or amortisation of the discount) together with a charge for the year which would be equivalent to the contribution which would be made if the scheme were funded. It is not clear from the above extract whether GKN's pension cost includes a specific interest component, but Extract 20.7 above shows that interest is the most significant element of the cost recognised by BOC in respect of its post-retirement health care benefits.

4.7　Deferred tax

As mentioned at 2.5.4 above, the pension prepayment or accrual appearing in the balance sheet will generally represent the cumulative timing difference in respect of pension costs which should be taken into account in the company's assessment of its deferred tax position. (Since the company will receive tax deductions in respect of contributions paid to the scheme, and since the balance sheet figure represents the amount by which the recognition of pension cost in the profit and loss account has been cumulatively more or less than the contributions paid to date, it also represents the amount of this timing difference.) It follows that any movements in the balance sheet figure, including those arising from the application of interest (see 4.1 above) should also be regarded as giving rise to timing differences.

As discussed in Chapter 21 at 1.2.6, the relevant accounting standard on deferred taxation, SSAP 15, now grants special treatment to timing differences relating to pensions and other post-retirement costs. Whereas the standard generally requires that deferred tax is recognised in relation to timing differences only to the extent that they are expected to reverse in overall terms,[67] companies are permitted (but not required) to provide deferred tax in full in relation to pensions and other similar costs.[68]

4.8 Post-retirement benefits other than pensions

In addition to pensions, some employment contracts also provide post-retirement health care or other benefits. Arrangements of this sort are not particularly significant in the UK, but they are quite frequently found in some other countries, notably the United States. UK companies with US subsidiaries may therefore have to consider how to account for them on consolidation even if they have no material obligations to account for in the UK.

SSAP 24 says that, 'although this Statement primarily addresses pensions, its principles may be equally applicable to the cost of providing other post-retirement benefits'. However, the ASC subsequently issued Technical Release 756, which said that for the time being it was not necessary to apply SSAP 24 in relation to such benefits, although companies might consider it appropriate to do so.

In November 1992 the UITF published an Abstract on the subject.[69] This said that post-retirement benefits other than pensions were liabilities, which in accordance with the accruals and prudence concepts of SSAP 2 and the Companies Act should be recognised in accounts. Since such benefits share many of the characteristics of pensions, the principles of SSAP 24 were to be applied to their measurement and disclosure. However, in recognition that these obligations were particularly difficult to measure, the requirement to apply SSAP 24 principles was not to become mandatory until periods ending on or after 23 December 1994. In the first year of implementation, the previously unrecognised obligation relating to past service was to be provided for either by means of a prior year adjustment or by spreading it forward over a period. This period was to be either the expected service lives of current employees[70] or, following the US standard SFAS 106, a period of 20 years.[71] The transitional method chosen had to be disclosed.

HSBC is spreading the obligation over 20 years, as shown in this extract:

Extract 20.20: HSBC Holdings plc (1998)

2   Principal accounting policies

h *Pension and other post-retirement benefits* [extract]

The cost of providing post-retirement health-care benefits, which is assessed in accordance with the advice of qualified actuaries, is recognised on a systematic basis over employees' service lives. At 1 January 1993, there was an accumulated obligation in respect of these benefits relating to current and retired employees. This is being charged in the profit and loss account in equal instalments over 20 years.

4   Administrative expenses

b *Retirement benefits* [extract]

The Group also provides post-retirement health care benefits under schemes, mainly in the UK and also in the United States, Canada and Brazil. The charge relating to these schemes, which are unfunded, is US$30 million for the year (1997: US$39 million). The latest actuarial review estimated the present value of the accumulated post-retirement benefit obligation at US$357 million (1997: US$280 million), of which US$240 million (1997: US$150 million) has been provided. The actuarial assumptions used to estimate this obligation vary according to the claims experience and economic conditions of the countries in which the schemes are situated. For the UK schemes, the main financial assumptions used at 31 December 1997 are price inflation at 3% per annum, health-care claims cost escalation of 8.5% per annum and a discount rate of 7% per annum.

In principle, the methods used by a company for measuring post-retirement benefits other than pensions should be the same as those already applied to pensions, but the Abstract refers to SFAS 106, as a source of guidance on the measurement bases which might be applied and says that they will be deemed to satisfy SSAP 24 principles.[72]

The Abstract also requires companies that have adopted a SSAP 24 basis of accounting for post-retirement benefits to make disclosures in relation to them equivalent to those required for pension schemes under SSAP 24, including details of any important assumptions which are specific to the measurement of such benefits, such as the assumed rate of inflation in the cost of providing the benefits. If it is material, the provision for post-retirement benefits has to be disclosed separately from other provisions in the notes to the accounts.[73]

4.9   Group schemes

Where a number of group companies participate in a common group scheme, it will be necessary to allocate the regular cost among the individual companies in order to permit them to make the necessary entries in their own accounts. In principle, there are a number of ways in which this might be done. The most rigorous approach would be to analyse the membership of the scheme into those of each of the participating companies and to make the allocations on this basis. However, this could be an onerous task and a more practical approach could be to apportion the cost to individual companies at the same percentage of pensionable pay which the total charge represents for the group as a whole.

As well as allocating the regular cost, it will be necessary to allocate variations as they arise. Where the variation arises from the enhancement of rights of members of the scheme it may in theory be possible to allocate the cost to the companies for whom they work; however, where the variation relates to the performance of the fund, no such specific allocation would be possible, and in practice some simpler form of apportionment will have to be applied such as the uniform percentage of payroll referred to in the previous paragraph.

However, the starting point for allocating both the regular cost and variations is to consider how the group intends to recover the cost from the individual subsidiary companies. The accounting in each company should then follow whatever commercial decision is made as to the allocation of the charge. For example, some groups may prefer to deal with all variations at holding company level, and therefore charge individual companies with the regular cost, in which case the accounting should reflect that decision. Whatever the basis used, it is important that the notes to the accounts of the subsidiaries should indicate that the company is a member of a group scheme and explain the basis of the charge made.

4.10   Multi-employer schemes

Where a company participates in a scheme which has been established for a number of employers (perhaps a whole industry) it is necessary to adapt the measurement and disclosure rules of the standard appropriately. Sometimes the nature of the arrangement is such that, in essence, it constitutes a defined contribution scheme and should be accounted for as such. However, where it is in the nature of a defined benefit scheme it will be necessary to determine what portion of the total fund is attributable to the reporting company.

Lookers provides an example of such an arrangement, as shown in the following extract:

Extract 20.21: Lookers plc (1998)

Principal Accounting Policies

9. Pension costs [extract]

The Group participates in the Retail Motor Industry Pension Plan which is a defined benefit scheme providing benefits based on final pensionable salary. The scheme has been registered with the Registrar of Pensions.

The assets of the scheme are held separately from those of the Group, being held in separate funds by the Trustees of the RMI plan.

Contributions to the scheme are charged to the Profit and Loss Account so as to spread the cost of pensions over employees' working lives with the Group. The contribution rate is recommended by a qualified actuary on the basis of triennial valuations, using the projected unit method.

NOTES TO THE FINANCIAL STATEMENTS

9. INFORMATION REGARDING DIRECTORS AND EMPLOYEES [extract]

The Group participates in the Retail Motor Industry Pension Plan and the most recent valuation was at 6th April 1996 using the Projected Unit Method. The assumptions which have the most significant effect on the results of the valuation are those relating to the rate of return on investments and the rate of increase in salaries. It was assumed that the investment return would be 2% p.a. higher than the increase in salaries in the period up to retirement. No allowance was made for any future discretionary increases in benefits.

The latest available actuarial valuation showed that the market value of the scheme's assets attributable to the Lookers Group was £25,940,000 and that the actuarial value of the assets represented 119% of the liabilities at the valuation date, after allowing for expected future increases in earnings. The employer's future service contribution rate has been adjusted to take into account the surplus disclosed by the valuation, spread over the average remaining service lives of the members of the scheme.

---

5   RELATED COMPANIES ACT REQUIREMENTS

5.1   Pension commitments

The Companies Act 1985 requires that particulars should be disclosed of:

(a)   any pension commitments included under any provision shown in the company's balance sheet; and

(b)   any such commitments for which no such provision has been made.[74]

The requirement goes on to say that separate disclosure should be given to any part of these commitments which relate to pensions payable to former directors of the company.

The Act offers no further interpretation of what constitutes a pension commitment for the purposes of this disclosure requirement. It could be interpreted very broadly, so that disclosure of the commitment would require a full description of the obligation which the company had accepted in making pension promises to its employees; this would involve giving details of the terms of the pension scheme, together with a description of the arrangements which had been made to meet that obligation. This broad interpretation is supported by ED 32, which proposed quite extensive disclosure requirements, and went on to say that 'the disclosures required by this proposed standard have been framed having regard to the requirements in company legislation for the disclosure of pension information. Compliance with these proposals, however, will not necessarily ensure compliance with these legal requirements which must be considered in the light of each company's individual pension arrangements.'[75]

In practice, however, the general interpretation of the requirement has been much narrower. Many companies appear to have taken the view that as long as the pension scheme is adequately funded, there is no further commitment on the part of the company itself which has to be disclosed. Companies have generally confined their disclosure to a relatively brief description of the pension arrangements in force and the fact that the schemes were fully funded. Since the introduction of SSAP 24, the disclosures given by employer companies have been much more extensive (see 2.4.2 and 2.5.5 above), and we believe that this satisfies the Companies Act requirement to disclose pension commitments.

5.2   Pension costs

The Act also requires disclosure of pension costs charged in the profit and loss account. This is one of three elements of staff costs which have to be disclosed, the other two being wages and salaries and social security costs.[76] The Act goes on to say that for this purpose pension costs 'includes any costs incurred by the company in respect of any pension scheme established for the purpose of providing pensions for persons currently or formerly employed by the company, any sums set aside for the future payment of pensions directly by the company to current or former employees and any pensions paid directly to such persons without having first been set aside'.[77]

5.3   Directors' emoluments

There are detailed requirements in the Companies Act for the disclosure of directors' emoluments, including pensions. These are discussed in detail in Chapter 29.

6   COMPARISON WITH IASC AND US PRONOUNCEMENTS

6.1   IASC

In January 1983, the International Accounting Standards Committee issued IAS 19 – *Accounting for Retirement Benefits in the Financial Statements of Employers* – which was revised ten years later in November 1993 with the shortened title of *Retirement Benefit Costs*. It was broadly similar in its approach to SSAP 24, although there were quite a number of differences of detail.

In October 1996, however, the IASC published an exposure draft proposing to make fundamental changes to IAS 19.[78] In particular, the whole focus of the standard was to be shifted from the profit and loss account to the balance sheet.

This led to the issue of a further revised version of IAS 19 in February 1998, to take effect for accounting periods beginning on or after 1 January 1999. The main features of this standard are summarised below.

6.1.1   Scope

The new version of the standard is entitled 'Employee Benefits', and as this name suggests it is not confined to pensions and other post-retirement benefits, but rather addresses all other forms of remuneration as well, including:

(a)   'short-term' benefits, including wages and salaries, holiday pay, bonuses, benefits in kind, etc. The accounting treatment of these is unsurprising; they are to be accrued as the liability to the employee is incurred and expensed as the services are provided.[79]

(b)   long term benefits, such as long service leave, long term disability benefits, long-term bonuses, etc. These are to be accounted for in a similar way to post-retirement benefits (discussed at 6.1.3 below), except that the recognition of actuarial gains and losses and past service cost is recognised immediately.[80]

(c)   redundancy pay. This is to be provided for and expensed when the employer becomes committed to the redundancy plan, on a similar basis to FRS 12 (see Chapter 25 at 4.1).[81]

(d)   equity compensation benefits, such as share option schemes, share purchase schemes at a discount, phantom share schemes etc. Here the standard ducks the difficult recognition and measurement issues that have continued to trouble other standard setters and only prescribes a set of disclosures about these arrangements.[82]

6.1.2   Defined contribution plans

IAS 19 requires defined contribution plans to be accounted for in essentially the same way as SSAP 24. Companies should recognise contributions so as to match the services rendered by the employee in exchange for these contributions. If they are not paid at the same time, the difference will be reflected as an accrual or a prepayment.[83] If any accrued amount is not wholly payable within the next financial year, it should be discounted to its present value.[84] The amount of expense recognised for defined contribution plans should be disclosed.[85]

6.1.3   Defined benefit plans

IAS 19's approach to defined benefit schemes is now quite different from that of SSAP 24, because as noted above the emphasis has switched from the profit and loss account to the balance sheet. The starting point is that the employer has to revalue its pension fund and include in its own balance sheet the resulting net surplus or deficit.[86] This is to be calculated by stating the funds' investments at fair value[87] and deducting the obligations to pay pensions (based on the Projected

Unit Credit method)[88] after discounting them at the yield obtainable on high quality corporate bonds.[89]

Any surplus resulting from this equation is subject to a ceiling test. It must not exceed 'the present value of any economic benefits available in the form of refunds from the plan or reductions in future contributions to the plan'. This limitation is in fact quite problematic. First of all, it seems to limit the recognition of the benefit of any surplus to its cash flow benefit. This would appear to mean that if the employer intends to use a surplus to improve the benefits under the plan without further contributions having to be paid, it may not recognise the surplus as an asset. Secondly, it is not clear whether the extract quoted above is referring to actual or hypothetical future cash flow benefits. If the former, the standard would only allow a surplus to be recognised to the extent that the employer intended to run it off, and this may seldom apply. Furthermore, any refunds or reductions in contributions would usually be based on a different actuarial valuation, producing a different surplus, than the one being used for accounting purposes. In the UK, the valuation for funding purposes is typically more conservative than that used for accounting purposes, so any limitation that is founded on actual or putative funding adjustments may be quite a severe one. It will therefore be interesting to see how practice develops in the interpretation of this restriction.

When benefits are improved with retrospective effect, the resulting past service cost is to be recognised on a straight line basis over the period (if any) until the benefits become vested.[90] If the improved benefits vest immediately, therefore, this will be an immediate expense, whereas SSAP 24 would spread them over the average working lives of active members of the scheme. Insofar as any of the past service cost is deferred over a vesting period, it will be added to the scheme surplus as shown on the balance sheet.

One other figure can be added to or subtracted from this balance sheet number; the amount of actuarial gains and losses that have still to be recognised in the profit and loss account. On this matter, IAS 19 offers a wide range of possibilities, which suggests that the IASC Board must have had great difficulty in reaching any consensus. Actuarial gains and losses can be deferred, so long as their cumulative amount remains within a 'corridor' (10% of the fair value of the assets or the present value of the obligations, whichever is higher). Any amount that fell outside the corridor at the previous balance sheet date must be amortised to the profit and loss account over the working lives of the employees. Alternatively, the amount outside the corridor, and optionally the amount inside the corridor, can be amortised over a shorter period, or even immediately, so long as the approach is consistently applied.[91]

When there is a curtailment (where the members of a scheme, or the future benefits they will earn, are significantly reduced) or a settlement (where a transaction eliminates a previous obligation to give benefits), a gain or loss is recognised. This gain is measured as the change in the value of the fund's assets and liabilities that results from the curtailment or settlement together with the immediate recognition of any deferred past service cost or actuarial gain or loss that had been carried forward in the balance sheet.[92]

As a result of the above rules, the profit and loss account expense for the year will be the sum of the following components:

- current service cost;
- interest cost;
- the expected return on plan assets;
- actuarial gains and losses (to the extent that they are not deferred);
- past service cost (to the extent that they are not deferred); and
- the effect of any curtailments or settlements.[93]

The standard does not specify which line(s) of the income statement these are to be shown in but requires these components to be disclosed separately. The other disclosures required by IAS 19 are:

- the accounting policy for recognising actuarial gains and losses;
- a description of the type of plan;
- a reconciliation of the assets and liabilities in the balance sheet, including:
  - the present value of defined benefit obligations that are (a) wholly unfunded and (b) wholly or partly funded;
  - the fair value of any plan assets;
  - the net actuarial gains and losses not yet recognised;
  - the past service cost not yet recognised;
  - any amount not recognised as an asset because of the ceiling test; and
  - the amounts recognised in the balance sheet;
- any amounts included in the fair value of plan assets that are invested in financial instruments of the employer, or property or other assets used by the employer;
- a reconciliation showing movements during the period in the net asset or liability in the balance sheet;
- the actual return on plan assets in the period (since the profit and loss account includes the expected return, with the difference dealt with as an actuarial gain or loss); and
- the principal actuarial assumptions made including:
  - the discount rates;
  - the expected return on plan assets;
  - the expected rates of salary increases (and of changes in any index or other variable that forms the basis for future benefit increases;

- medical cost trend rates; and

- any other material actuarial assumptions made.

These must be given in absolute terms, not as margins between one assumption and another.[94]

6.2 US

6.2.1 Background

There have been professional pronouncements in the US dealing with accounting for pension costs for many years. The subject was dealt with briefly in the compendium Accounting Research Bulletin (ARB) 43 which was issued in 1953 and subsequently in ARB 47 in 1956, but was given much more comprehensive treatment in Accounting Principles Board (APB) Opinion No. 8 – *Accounting for the Cost of Pension Plans*, issued in November 1966. The FASB first got involved with disclosure issues, publishing SFAS 36 – *Disclosure of Pension Information*, in May 1980, and later dealt with related topics in SFAS 74 – *Accounting for Special Termination Benefits Paid to Employees* – and SFAS 81 – *Disclosure of Postretirement Health Care and Life Insurance Benefits*.

The FASB's current pronouncements on pension costs are the two statements published in December 1985, SFAS 87 – *Employers' Accounting for Pensions*, and SFAS 88 – *Employers' Accounting for Settlements and Curtailments of Defined Benefit Pension Plans and for Termination Benefits*. These last two statements superseded all the earlier pronouncements on the subject. In December 1990, the Board issued SFAS 106 – *Employers' Accounting for Postretirement Benefits Other Than Pensions*, and this superseded SFAS 81. SFAS 132 was issued in February 1998 to codify the disclosure requirements of these other three standards. These four extant standards are summarised below.

6.2.2 SFAS 87

SFAS 87 requires a particular actuarial approach to be used for measuring cost, and in general prescribes tightly drawn rules as to the computation and disclosure of pension figures in the accounts. It also breaks down the cost to be charged into six components, and has detailed provisions dealing with how these are to be calculated.

Under the standard, the pension cost to be attributed to a period is that which accrues in respect of the period under the terms of the pension scheme. That is to say, it applies an accrued benefit approach to the allocation of cost to periods (as discussed in 3.1 above). This means that for final salary schemes, the statement requires that the cost be calculated using the projected unit method (as we would call it in the UK – in the US it would be described as the projected unit *credit* method).

For defined benefit schemes, the cost must be analysed into the following components:

■ service cost;

■ interest cost;

■ actual return on plan assets, if any;

■ amortisation of unrecognised prior service cost, if any;

■ gain or loss (including the effects of changes in assumptions) to the extent recognised; and

■ amortisation of the unrecognised net obligation (and loss or cost) or unrecognised net asset (and gain) existing at the date of initial application of the statement.

Each of these terms is further defined and the required accounting specified.

The standard requires that each of the significant assumptions made in valuing the scheme should be the best estimate, in relation to that individual aspect in isolation. In respect of discount rates, it departs from normal actuarial practice by requiring that these should reflect the rates at which the pension benefits could be effectively settled; this means that a market rate at each valuation date should be used, rather than a long-term rate estimated by the actuary.

Although SSAP 24 follows the same broad approach as SFAS 87 in a number of respects, the American standard is very much more tightly defined; the major difference is the specification of an accrued benefit approach to the measurement of cost, but there are several other differences of detail as well. The more significant ones are as follows:

(a) as mentioned above, SFAS 87 requires settlement rates to be used to discount the pension liability. Under SSAP 24, a long-term interest rate would be used which was compatible with the other assumptions made by the actuary in valuing the scheme;

(b) in general, SSAP 24's exceptions to the basic rule on spreading the effects of variations forward would not be permitted under SFAS 87. In particular, accounting for refunds from the scheme in the profit and loss account when the cash is received would not be allowed; and

(c) SFAS 87 treats increases in pensions as a past service cost and accordingly amortises its effects over the working lives of the members after the increase is awarded; SSAP 24 encourages expected increases to be provided for in advance by being built into the actuarial assumptions.

6.2.3 *SFAS 88*

This statement requires immediate recognition of certain previously unrecognised amounts when certain transactions or events occur. It prescribes the method for determining the amount to be recognised in the profit and loss account when a pension obligation is settled (i.e. when the employer takes action to relieve himself of responsibility for a pension obligation), or curtailed (i.e. when defined benefit accruals for the future services of present employees have been eliminated or significantly reduced). There is no direct equivalent of this standard in the UK. However, the circumstances mentioned at 2.5.2 D above, where a significant number of employees leave the scheme, would probably fall within the definition of a curtailment. Under SFAS 88, the effect of this would be recognised immediately, whereas under SSAP 24 it would be dealt with in the periods in which contributions to the scheme were adjusted as a result of the curtailment.

6.2.4 SFAS 106

Post-retirement benefits other than pensions, typically health care benefits, are a major feature of US employment contracts and often create very significant obligations for US companies. Before SFAS 106 was introduced, however, the accepted method of accounting for them was on a pay-as-you-go basis. The standard requires these obligations to be accrued, essentially on the same basis as is applied for pensions.

The standard is a complex one, running to 518 paragraphs. However, the principles it applies are familiar and conform in most respects to those which underlie SFAS 87. Estimates have to be made of the eventual obligation in respect of the benefits promised, and they have to be provided for during the employee's working life. One detailed difference from SFAS 87 is that, if the employee becomes fully eligible to receive the post-retirement benefits at some time before his retirement date, the cost of the benefit has to be provided over the period to that date, whereas the cost of an equivalent pension would be spread over the full period to retirement.

In principle, the components of cost are the same six elements as are described in relation to pensions at 6.2.2 above. However, the non-pension benefits will usually be unfunded and therefore there will be no return on plan assets to be considered. On initial application of the standard (which became mandatory for periods beginning on or after 15 December 1992, with some exemptions) companies were allowed to recognise the unprovided obligation in respect of past service either immediately as a one-off hit to the income statement, or over a period of up to 20 years as a component of the ongoing cost of the scheme.

One major difficulty in accounting for health care costs is that the eventual liability may be extremely difficult to measure. In relation to this, SFAS 106 required disclosure of the health care cost trend rate which has been assumed, and also of what the effect would be of increasing that assumption by one percentage point, and these requirements have been carried forward into SFAS 132 (see 6.2.5 below). In practice, this assumption has been found to be very sensitive, and flexing it by only 1% in this way can increase the reported cost by as much as 20%.

6.2.5   SFAS 132

In February 1998, the FASB issued SFAS 132[95] to bring together and amend the various disclosure requirements of SFAS's 87, 88 and 106. No changes to the recognition or measurement rules of these standards were made. The consolidated list of disclosures required of employers with defined benefit plans that provide pensions or other post-retirement benefits is now as follows:[96]

(a)   A reconciliation of the opening and closing balances of the benefit obligation showing the effects during the period attributable to each of the following:

- service cost;
- interest cost;
- contributions by plan participants;
- actuarial gains and losses;
- foreign currency exchange rate changes;
- benefits paid;
- plan amendments;
- business combinations;
- divestitures;
- curtailments;
- settlements; and
- special termination benefits.

(b)   A reconciliation of the opening and closing balances of the fair value of plan assets showing the effects during the period attributable to each of the following:

- actual return on plan assets;
- foreign currency exchange rate changes;
- contributions by the employer;
- contributions by plan participants;
- benefits paid;
- business combinations;
- divestitures; and
- settlements.

(c)   The funded status of the plans, the amounts not recognised in the statement of financial position, and the amounts recognised in the statement of financial position, including:

- the amount of any unamortised prior service cost;
- the amount of any unrecognised net gain or loss (including asset gains and losses not yet reflected in market-related value);

- the amount of any remaining unamortised, unrecognised net obligation or net asset existing at the initial date of application of Statement 87 or 106;

- the net pension or other post-retirement benefit prepaid assets or accrued liabilities; and

- any intangible asset and the amount of accumulated other comprehensive income recognised pursuant to paragraph 37 of Statement 87, as amended.

(d) The amount of net periodic benefit cost recognised, showing separately:

- the service cost component;

- the interest cost component;

- the expected return on plan assets for the period;

- the amortisation of the unrecognised transition obligation or transition asset;

- the amount of recognised gains and losses;

- the amount of prior service cost recognised; and

- the amount of gain or loss recognised due to a settlement or curtailment.

(e) The amount included within other comprehensive income for the period arising from a change in the additional minimum pension liability recognised pursuant to paragraph 37 of Statement 87, as amended.

(f) On a weighted-average basis, the following assumptions used in the accounting for the plans:

- assumed discount rate;

- rate of compensation increase (for pay-related plans); and

- expected long-term rate of return on plan assets.

(g) The assumed health care cost trend rate(s) for the next year used to measure the expected cost of benefits covered by the plan (gross eligible charges) and a general description of the direction and pattern of change in the assumed trend rates thereafter, together with the ultimate trend rate(s) and when that rate is expected to be achieved.

(h) The effect of a one-percentage-point increase and the effect of a one-percentage-point decrease in the assumed health care cost trend rates on:

- the aggregate of the service and interest cost components of net periodic post-retirement health care benefit cost; and

- the accumulated post-retirement benefit obligation for health care benefits.

For the purposes of this disclosure, all other assumptions are held constant, and the effects are measured based on the substantive plan that is the basis for the accounting.

(i)   If applicable, the amounts and types of securities of the employer and related parties included in plan assets, the approximate amount of future annual benefits of plan participants covered by insurance contracts issued by the employer or related parties, and any significant transactions between the employer or related parties and the plan during the period.

(j)   If applicable, any alternative amortisation method used to amortise prior service amounts or unrecognised net gains and losses pursuant to paragraphs 26 and 33 of Statement 87 or paragraphs 53 and 60 of Statement 106.

(k)   If applicable, any substantive commitment, such as past practice or a history of regular benefit increases, used as the basis for accounting for the benefit obligation.

(l)   If applicable, the cost of providing special or contractual termination benefits recognised during the period and a description of the nature of the event.

(m)   An explanation of any significant change in the benefit obligation or plan assets not otherwise apparent in the other disclosures required by SFAS 132.

7   CONCLUSION

When SSAP 24 was introduced it represented a major stride forward in the presentation of meaningful information about pension costs in the accounts of UK companies. It took the subject from a low base, where the measurement of cost could only be described as unsophisticated, to a level where serious attempts have to be made to account for that cost on a systematic basis. Companies have now gained ten years' experience of using the standard, and have a significantly greater understanding of the subject than at the outset. This puts the profession in a much better position to debate SSAP 24's successor, because we have little doubt that a revised standard is required. We are, however, not confident that the next version, if it is based on international developments, will represent an overall improvement.

We broadly agreed with the changes proposed by the majority of the Board in the ASB's 1995 Discussion Paper; indeed they largely reflected the views we expressed in the 1994 edition of this book. However, the balance of opinion among standard-setters has swung towards the balance sheet approach that was said to be favoured by the minority of the ASB in that Discussion Paper, even though it gained little support from respondents at that time. This approach makes sense in terms of the IASC Framework and the ASB's draft *Statement of Principles*, but in our view this simply illustrates the inappropriateness of these concepts.

An even more fundamental concern still remains, however. A central assumption, implicit in both SSAP 24 and any likely replacement standard, is that pension fund surpluses 'belong' to the employer company, with the result that they are included, directly or indirectly, in the employer company's balance sheet. However this remains a questionable premise, both in law and in economic reality. Before bringing forward any proposed new standard, we still believe that the ASB must assess whether it really fits the legal and economic relationships which it is intended to portray.

References

1 Christopher J. Napier, *Accounting for pension costs — An interim report*, ASC, February 1982.
2 Christopher J. Napier, *Accounting for the Cost of Pensions*, ICAEW, 1983.
3 ED 32, *The disclosure of pension information in company accounts*, May 1983.
4 *Ibid.*, para. 38.
5 *Accounting for pension costs*, ASC, November 1984.
6 ED 39, *Accounting for pension costs*, May 1986.
7 SSAP 24, *Accounting for pension costs*, May 1988.
8 *Ibid.*, para. 75.
9 TR 756, *Statement by the Accounting Standards Committee on the application of the principles of SSAP 24 'Accounting for pension costs' to other post-retirement benefits*, July 1989.
10 UITF 6, *Accounting for post-retirement benefits other than pensions*, UITF, November 1992.
11 SSAP 24, para. 16.
12 *Ibid.*, para. 12.
13 *Ibid.*, para. 78.
14 *Ibid.*, para. 87.
15 Applied either on the balance sheet figure or on the underlying surplus in the scheme, depending on how the variations are calculated — see 4.1.
16 SSAP 24, para. 20.
17 Discussion Paper, *Pension Costs in the Employer's Financial Statements*, ASB, June 1995, para. 3.3.2.
18 SSAP 24, para. 21.
19 *Pension Costs in the Employer's Financial Statements*, para. 4.6.
20 ED 39, *Accounting for pension costs*, ASC, May 1986, Appendix 2, Example 2.
21 SSAP 24, para. 81 (original version).
22 *Ibid.*, (as revised by FRS 3, para. 33(m)).
23 *Ibid.*, para. 26 (as revised by FRS 3, para. 33(k)). In fact, the words 'or the disposal of its assets' have since been deleted from FRS 3 by FRS 12, para. 100.
24 *Ibid.*, para. 81.
25 SSAP 24, para. 83.
26 *Pension Costs in the Employer's Financial Statements*, para. 5.7.3.
27 SSAP 24, para. 82.
28 *Ibid.*, para. 92.
29 As reported in the survey published in Spring 1992 by William M. Mercer Fraser Limited, entitled *SSAP 24 — Survey of company pension disclosures 1991*.
30 *Pension Costs in the Employer's Financial Statements*, para. 6.2.13.
31 UITF Abstract 4, *Presentation of long-term debtors in current assets*, July 1992.
32 SSAP 24, para. 88.
33 GN 17: *Accounting for pension costs under SSAP 24*, Institute and Faculty of Actuaries, April 1991, para. 28.
34 SSAP 24, para. 48. Arguably, this requirement, and those referred to in footnotes 36 and 39 below, are not mandatory because they appear only in the Explanatory Note of SSAP 24, and not in the Standard section itself. However, they should nonetheless be disclosed if it is sufficiently important to an understanding of the overall position.
35 *Ibid.*, para. 18.
36 The guidance issued by the actuarial profession indicates that this should be calculated using the Projected Accrued Benefit Method (GN 17, para. 30).
37 GN 17, para. 31 explains that part of this surplus or deficiency will be attributable to the use of the Projected Accrued Benefit Method for the previous disclosure unless the method used for funding is the Projected Unit method or the Attained Age method, and this fact should be explained.
38 SSAP 24, para. 49.
39 *Ibid.*, para. 92.
40 ED 32, *The disclosure of pension information in company accounts*, ASC, May 1983.
41 SSAP 24, para. 14.

42 Pension Fund Terminology — Specimen descriptions of commonly used valuation methods, The Institute of Actuaries and The Faculty of Actuaries, May 1986.

43 GN 17, para. 17.

44 Discussion Paper, *Pension Costs in the Employer's Financial Statements*, ASB, June 1995, para. 3.3.

45 GN 17, para. 18.

46 *Ibid.*, para. 20.

47 Pension Fund Terminology — Specimen descriptions of commonly used valuation methods.

48 GN 17, para. 19.

49 Pension Fund Terminology — Specimen descriptions of commonly used valuation methods.

50 GN 17, para. 16.

51 Pension Fund Terminology — Specimen descriptions of commonly used valuation methods.

52 GN 17, para. 15.

53 The UITF clarified, however, that this was not to be given any special treatment in profit and loss account recognition terms, although it might merit additional disclosure It was simply a variation to be accounted for like any other under the standard. (UITF 18, *Pension costs following the 1997 tax changes in respect of dividend income*, UITF, 2 December 1997, para. 7.)

54 SSAP 24, para. 79.

55 GN 17, para. 24

56 Auditing Practices Committee, August 1987.

57 It is, however, explicitly recognised as being the third component of cost in GN 17, para. 12. and by the ICAEW in FRAG 10/92, *Review, for major practical problems, of SSAP 24*, paras. 26 *et seq.*

58 *Pension Costs in the Employer's Financial Statements*, para. 5.3.4.

59 *Discounting in Financial Reporting*, ASB, April 1997, para. 7.3.

60 SSAP 24, para. 23.

61 *Ibid.*, para. 80.

62 FRAG 10/92, para. 42.

63 *Pension Costs in the Employer's Financial Statements*, para. 5.2.10.

64 *Ibid.*, para. 5.6.

65 *Ibid.*, para. 5.5.

66 SSAP 24, para. 91.

67 SSAP 15, *Accounting for deferred tax*, Revised 1985, paras. 24–36.

68 *Ibid.*, para. 32A, as inserted by *Amendment to SSAP 15 'Accounting for Deferred Tax'* — December 1992, ASB, para. 1.

69 UITF 6, *Accounting for post-retirement benefits other than pensions*, UITF, November 1992.

70 *Ibid.*, para. 8.

71 *Ibid.*, para. 7.

72 *Ibid.*

73 *Ibid.*, para. 9.

74 CA 85, Sch. 4, para. 50(4).

75 ED 32, para. 40.

76 CA 85, Sch. 4, para. 56(4).

77 *Ibid.*, para. 94(2).

78 E54, *Employee Benefits*, IASC, October 1996.

79 IAS 19 (Revised 1998), *Employee Benefits*, IASC, February 1998, paras. 8-23.

80 *Ibid.*, paras. 128 and 129.

81 *Ibid.*, paras. 132-143.

82 *Ibid.*, paras. 147 and 148.

83 *Ibid.*, para. 44.

84 *Ibid.*, para. 45.

85 *Ibid.*, para. 46.

86 *Ibid.*, para. 54.

87 *Ibid.*, para. 102.

88 *Ibid.*, para. 64.

89 *Ibid.*, paras. 78.

90 *Ibid.*, para. 96.

91 *Ibid.*, para. 92 and 93.

92 *Ibid.*, para. 109.
93 *Ibid.*, para. 61.
94 *Ibid.*, para. 120.
95 SFAS 132, *Employer's Disclosures about Pensions and Other Post-Retirement Benefits*, FASB, February 1998.
96 *Ibid.*, para. 5.

Chapter 21   Taxation

1   INTRODUCTION

The two accounting standards that govern tax in the UK are relatively long-established. SSAP 8 – *The treatment of taxation under the imputation system in the accounts of companies* – was issued in 1974 and SSAP 15 – *Accounting for deferred tax* – in 1978, and although there have been various amendments since then, the basic rules for accounting for tax have not changed significantly since their original publication.

However, the recent abolition of advance corporation tax (ACT) has rendered SSAP 8 more or less obsolete, and in June 1999 the ASB issued an exposure draft of a replacement standard, FRED 18 – *Current taxation*, which could well be in force for December 1999, or at the latest, March 2000 year ends. On the question of accounting for deferred tax, the significant amendments in recent years to the equivalent standards of other countries and of the IASC have left the UK and Ireland almost totally isolated in retaining the partial provision approach (see 1.2.6 below), and in August 1999 the ASB published an exposure draft, FRED 19 – *Deferred tax*, which proposes the adoption of a full provision method.

However, FRED 19's version of 'full provision' is entirely different to that of the equivalent IASC and US standards. Under these standards full provision is based on the balance sheet and 'temporary differences' (see 1.2.3 below), whereas FRED 19 is still proposing a system of deferred tax based on the income statement and 'timing differences' (see 1.2.5 below). Furthermore FRED 19 proposes such substantial exceptions to its full provision approach that it is questionable whether it is a true full provision approach at all.

1.1   The nature of taxation

A discussion of how to deal with taxation in accounts must begin with some consideration of what it is that is to be accounted for. Although it might be supposed that this is a simple question, and that taxation is a business expense to be dealt with in the same manner as any other cost, it has certain characteristics which set it apart from other costs and which might justify a different treatment. These characteristics include the fact that tax payments are not made in exchange for any goods or services and the fact that the business has no say in whether or not the payments are to be made. It is held by some that these elements mean that taxation is more in the nature of a distribution than an expense; in essence that the government is a stakeholder in the success of the business and participates in its results (generally in priority to other stakeholders).

The validity of this suggestion rather depends on what view is taken as to the purpose of accounts and the nature of the reporting entity. It is consistent with a perspective which is sometimes adopted that business entities have an existence which is independent from that of their shareholders, and should account not simply to their legal owners but to all those with an economic interest in their activities.

Adoption of the 'distribution' view of taxation would render irrelevant most of the accounting questions which follow; these are generally to do with how to allocate taxation expense to accounting periods. If taxation were regarded as a distribution, however, the question of allocation would not arise, since distributions are generally not allocated to accounting periods in the same way as is done for items of expense.

It is fair to say, however, that the 'distribution' view of taxation is not adopted in practice, although some of the accounting approaches that are sometimes proposed to deal with certain issues have their roots within it. For all practical purposes, taxation is dealt with as an expense of the business, and the accounting rules which have been developed are based on that premise.

1.2   Allocation between periods

1.2.1   Background

The most significant accounting question which arises in relation to taxation is how to allocate the tax expense between accounting periods. The recognition of trading transactions in the accounts relating to a particular year is governed primarily by the application of generally accepted accounting practice, and to a certain extent by the impact of company law. However, the timing of recognition of transactions for the purposes of measuring the taxable profit is governed by the application of tax law, which in some cases follows different rules from those under which the accounts are drawn up. It is necessary to seek some reconciliation between these different sets of rules in order to apply a matching approach to the allocation of tax expense to accounting periods, and this is where the concept of deferred taxation is brought into use.

The differences between the profit as calculated for accounting and for taxation purposes are traditionally analysed into two categories, 'permanent differences' and 'timing differences'.[1] Permanent differences comprise those items of income which are not taxable, or items of expense which are not deductible against tax, and which therefore do not appear in the tax computation of any period; they also include items which increase or decrease the liability to tax without appearing in the financial statements, an example in the UK being indexation relief which reduces gains for tax purposes.

Timing differences represent items of income or expenditure which *are* taxable or deductible, but in periods different from those in which they are dealt with in the accounts. They therefore arise when items of income and expenditure enter into the measurement of profit for both accounting and taxation purposes, but in different accounting periods. They are said to 'originate' in the first of these periods and 'reverse' in one or more subsequent periods; examples of these are given in 1.2.5 below. Deferred taxation is the taxation which relates to timing differences.

1.2.2 Conformity of UK tax legislation with accounting rules

As an aside, a recent trend in tax legislation in the UK has been to bring the tax rules more into line with accounting standards, in areas such as leasing, foreign currencies and financial instruments. This may have the benefit of removing some of the differences that cause accounting problems in accounting for tax, but the trend is not entirely welcome in other ways.

Particular areas of difficulty that arise in practice are:

- Notwithstanding group relief and similar provisions, tax in the UK is basically levied on individual companies rather than groups. By contrast accounting standards are primarily addressed, at least implicitly, at the consolidated accounts. The accounting requirements for the single entity accounts are often less clear than the tax legislation appears, from a financial accountant's perspective, to assume.

- Accounting standards (especially those issued by the ASB) often focus on the balance sheet, whereas tax is levied on profits. As a result, again from an accountant's perspective, much in the tax legislation appears to hang on the detailed journal entries affecting the profit and loss account. In practice, however, the normal accounting process is sometimes much more concerned with the final balance sheet position and is (relatively) indifferent as to the route by which it is reached.

All this tends to put a greater strain on some of the accounting rules, which were not primarily designed to provide a basis for the measurement of tax.

1.2.3   International developments - 'temporary' versus 'timing' differences

Consistent with their conceptual frameworks, both the US and the international standards now apply a balance sheet perspective rather than focusing on the allocation of tax expense between periods, and they have dropped the concept of timing differences in favour of 'temporary differences'. These are defined in the IASC standard as 'differences between the carrying amount of an asset or liability in the balance sheet and its tax base'.[2] As discussed in 5 below, we believe that this is an unhelpful change, because it inadvertently brings certain permanent differences into the scope of deferred tax. It is interesting that in FRED 19, the ASB has rejected the temporary difference approach and has proposed a modified full provision approach still based on timing differences (see 2.2.9 below).

1.2.4   Permanent differences

A permanent difference can arise in two main ways under the UK tax system:

(a)   where non-taxable income is included in the accounting profit, for example if certain government grant income is received; and

(b)   where certain types of expenditure are charged against accounting profit but not allowed as an expense against taxable profit; for example, certain entertainment expenditure, or if depreciation is charged against fixed assets for which there is no corresponding tax deduction.

It is generally accepted that there is no need to adjust the accounts for permanent differences. The transaction giving rise to the permanent difference has no tax effect. Although the tax charge for the year in which the item is reported in the accounts will deviate from the charge which would have been expected if the normal tax rate had been applied to the reported profits, this is not a distortion of the charge that needs to be corrected in any way; indeed, any 'correction' would introduce such a distortion.

1.2.5   Timing differences

A timing difference can arise in a number of ways:

(a)   income is included in the accounts but recognised in taxable profit in later years; for example, a foreign dividend receivable might be accrued in the accounts but taxed only in the period in which it was due and payable;

(b)   income may be included in taxable profit in a year earlier than it is recognised in the accounts;

(c)   expenditure or losses in the accounts might not be deductible in arriving at taxable profit until a later period; for example, a general bad debt provision could be charged in the accounts, but a tax deduction given only when the specific bad debt charge was known; or

(d)   expenditure or losses might be deducted from taxable income prior to their being charged against accounting profit; for example, research and development expenditure might be allowed as an immediate deduction against tax, but capitalised in the accounts and amortised over its useful life.

The common characteristic of all timing differences is the fact that the period in which the accounting effect of the transaction is recognised is different to the period in which the transaction falls to be taxed or deducted against taxable profit. The tax benefit or cost associated with such differences usually reverses in future periods. Situations where there might not be a complete reversal of timing differences would include the disposal of an industrial building after the expiry of its 25-year tax life.

Timing differences were traditionally split into two categories – short-term and other, terms which are still sometimes used.[3] A short-term timing difference is one which arises because an item is treated on a cash basis for tax purposes whereas the accruals concept is used in the accounts. When the term was first coined, it mainly involved such things as interest accruals, which usually reversed within a year of their origination (hence the name). More recently, however, the major timing differences of this sort have arisen on items such as pension costs, which are allowed for tax on the basis of cash contributions but accounted for on an accruals basis. Such timing differences are anything but short term, particularly for unfunded schemes, and this has shown that the category is not a very meaningful one.

The most common form of 'other' (i.e. other than 'short-term') timing difference is created by the effect of capital allowances and the charge for depreciation. Capital allowances are the amounts by which fixed assets may be written down to arrive at taxable profit, and are therefore the tax equivalent of the charge for depreciation in the accounts. Since they are deducted from profit to arrive at the taxable profit, the amount charged in the accounts for depreciation is normally disallowed in the tax computation, except in the case of some assets held under finance leases. Usually, because capital allowances might be given to provide some economic incentive for businesses to invest, the tax allowance will be given at a faster rate than the rate at which depreciation is charged in the accounts, and the timing differences created are thus sometimes referred to as 'accelerated capital allowances'.

A timing difference arises since both the charge for depreciation and the capital allowance (after an adjustment for a balancing charge or allowance) will reduce the cost of the asset to its recoverable amount at the end of its useful life, but the sums charged against accounting profit and against taxable profit, although the same in total, are likely to differ in each year. An example will illustrate the impact:

Example 21.1: Illustration of timing differences

An item of plant and machinery is purchased in 1991 for £48,000 and is estimated to have a seven year useful life, at the end of which it is estimated that it will be sold for £6,000. The depreciation charge will therefore be £6,000 p.a. (£48,000 – £6,000 over seven years).

For the purpose of this example, the rate of capital allowance for plant and machinery is assumed to be 25% p.a. on a reducing balance basis. The timing differences will arise as follows (all figures in £000s):

	1991	1992	1993	1994	1995	1996	1997
Accounts1382							
1382Carrying value of asset	48	42	36	30	24	18	12
Depreciation charge	6	6	6	6	6	6	6
Written down value	42	36	30	24	18	12	6
Tax computation							
Carrying value of asset	48	36	27	20	15	11	8
Capital allowance	12	9	7	5	4	3	2
Tax written down value	36	27	20	15	11	8	6
Timing difference arising							
Charge in accounts	6	6	6	6	6	6	6
Allowed in tax computation	12	9	7	5	4	3	2
Originating/(reversing)	6	3	1	(1)	(2)	(3)	(4)

The table shows that there are originating differences of £10,000 in the first three years, but this progressively diminishes and eventually reverses in subsequent years. For each of the first three years of the asset's life, the tax currently assessed (and hence the amount provided in the accounts as the current year tax charge for those years) is lower than the tax that will eventually fall to be paid on the profit reported in the accounts. The difference reverses from year four onwards, when the tax allowances have fallen below the level of the depreciation charge. The tax assessed (and hence the amount provided in the accounts as the current year tax charge for those years) will be higher than the sum due on the profit reported in the accounts.

The timing differences may be looked at either in terms of the profit and loss account or the balance sheet, and correspondingly computed in either of two ways. The timing difference arising in any year may be determined by comparing the depreciation provided in the accounts with the capital allowance given in the tax computation:

Computation of the timing difference	1991 £'000	1992 £'000
Depreciation per accounts	6	6
Capital allowances	12	9
Originating timing difference	6	3

Or the cumulative timing difference may be computed by comparing the net book value of the asset in the accounts with its written down value in the capital allowance computation:

Computation of the cumulative timing difference	1991	1992
	£'000	£'000
Net book value per accounts	42	36
Written down value per tax computation	36	27
	—	—
Cumulative timing difference	6	9
	—	—

The computation of the total timing differences in existence at any point in time is essentially a mathematical exercise. It is after this point that the picture becomes less clear, and different points of view arise as to:

(a) at what rate of tax the timing difference should be provided; and

(b) whether a company should account for deferred tax that it does not expect to convert into an actual liability to tax, because it can foresee that timing differences will not reverse in the future.

These questions lead us initially into the consideration of various methods of providing for deferred tax and then into the area of the 'partial provision' approach to deferred tax, all of which are discussed in 1.2.6 to 1.2.10.

1.2.6   *The deferral method*

The deferral method was for many years the required method in North America. It is an approach which places emphasis on the profit and loss account, and seeks to quantify the extent to which it has been affected by tax deferrals arising through the incidence of timing differences. When timing differences reverse, the deferral method takes the view that it is the former tax deferral which has become payable, and accordingly the deferred tax account is maintained in terms of the rates of tax which were in force when the various timing differences originated. On reversal, the amount taken out of the deferred tax account will be the amount that was accrued there when the timing difference was provided for.[4] The profit and loss account is therefore charged with a reversal which is unaffected by changes in the rates of tax in the years between origination and reversal.

By contrast, the method does not seek, as its primary purpose, to generate deferred tax figures in the balance sheet which represent accurate measurements of assets and liabilities. Where tax rates change, the balance on the deferred tax account will no longer be the amount that the company will pay or receive in future years when the timing differences reverse, because the reversal will be taxed at the rate ruling at the time of the reversal, and the rate ruling at the time that the difference originated will be of no relevance to the amount of tax paid.

Deferred tax balances under this method might be more properly thought of as deferred income and deferred expenditure, which could be said to represent the tax benefit or cost derived from the effect of timing differences quantified by reference to the rate of tax ruling at the date that the timing difference originated. This is seen as the deferral of a cost which otherwise would have arisen that year and accordingly the rate of tax applicable to that year is the one most appropriate to use in quantifying the benefit derived. On reversal the cost arising is seen as merely the amount of the earlier benefit which has now been withdrawn.

Some would argue that this method is the most conceptually pure, because the fundamental purpose of deferred tax accounting is the inter-period allocation of tax expense with taxable profits; in other words it is an application of the matching concept, which is profit and loss account driven. From this perspective, the balance sheet figures are merely the by-product of whatever amounts are passed through the profit and loss account, and it is therefore of little concern that they might not reflect current tax rates if they have changed since the timing differences originated. The liability appearing in the balance sheet is not a 'real' liability in the sense that it is not an obligation which is due to anyone; so far as tax is concerned, the only 'real' liability is that shown by the tax computation. Indeed, it can be argued that this liability is not actually *paid* in future years, it is simply released back to the profit and loss account to ensure that the reported profits are matched with an appropriate amount of tax expense. This can be shown by using the figures used in Example 21.1 above:

Example 21.2: Illustration of timing differences

A company makes annual profits before tax of £80,000 and is taxed at 25%. It experiences the following timing differences (all figures in £s):

	1991	1992	1993	1994	1995	1996	1997
Originating/(reversing)	6,000	3,000	1,000	(1,000)	(2,000)	(3,000)	(4,000)

Its tax computations for each year therefore show the following:

	1991	1992	1993	1994	1995	1996	1997
Accounting profit	80,000	80,000	80,000	80,000	80,000	80,000	80,000
Timing differences	(6,000)	(3,000)	(1,000)	1,000	2,000	3,000	4,000
Taxable profit	74,000	77,000	79,000	81,000	82,000	83,000	84,000
Tax payable @ 25%	18,500	19,250	19,750	20,250	20,500	20,750	21,000

Its accounts will show the following:

	1991	1992	1993	1994	1995	1996	1997
Profit before tax	80,000	80,000	80,000	80,000	80,000	80,000	80,000
Tax payable @ 25%	18,500	19,250	19,750	20,250	20,500	20,750	21,000
Deferred tax	1,500	750	250	(250)	(500)	(750)	(1,000)
Profit after tax	60,000	60,000	60,000	60,000	60,000	60,000	60,000

The amount shown for deferred tax in the balance sheet will be:

1,500	2,250	2,500	2,250	1,750	1,000	0

This approach looks upon deferred tax accounting in terms which might be described as 'tax equalisation' accounting. The purpose is more to do with preserving appropriate relationships for financial reporting purposes between pre- and post-tax figures, than with quantifying a liability which will have eventual cash flow consequences.

However, others will argue that the balance sheet figure should be seen as an important figure in its own right and that the deferral method is deficient because it can produce meaningless balance sheet amounts when tax rates change. Adherents to this view would favour one of the variants of the liability method of accounting for deferred tax, which are described in the next two sections.

1.2.7   The liability method (with full provision/comprehensive allocation)

In contrast to the deferral method, the liability method places emphasis on the balance sheet rather than the profit and loss account, and focuses on the future rather than on the past.[5] It treats the tax effects of timing differences as liabilities for taxes payable in the future (or as assets recoverable in the future), and the practical effect of this is that it responds to changes of tax rate by recalculating the asset or liability in the balance sheet on the basis of the new rate. This means that the charge for deferred tax in the profit and loss account will include the effects of any such change in rate which is applied to the opening balance of cumulative timing differences.

The principal objective of the liability method is to quantify the amount of tax that will become payable or receivable in the future. It follows, therefore, that the deferred tax balance is maintained at the current rate of tax since this rate is the best estimate of the rate that is likely to apply in the future when the timing differences reverse. Of course, if the future rates of tax are already set, it is necessary to examine the periods in which the timing differences will reverse, and then provide the amount of tax that is foreseen to arise as each year's reversal occurs.

The difference between the deferral method and the liability method can be illustrated as follows:

Example 21.3: Illustration of the difference between the deferral and liability methods

A company invests £48,000 in a fixed asset at the beginning of 1991, and depreciates it at £6,000 p.a. The asset attracts capital allowances of £12,000 in 1991 and £9,000 in 1992. In 1991, the tax rate is 50% and in 1992 it falls to 30%.

Under the deferral method, the calculation would be made by reference to the timing differences arising in each year in the profit and loss account, thus:

Computation of the timing difference	1991	1992
	£	£
Depreciation per accounts	6,000	6,000
Capital allowances	12,000	9,000
Originating timing difference	6,000	3,000
Deferred tax provided, at 50%/30%	3,000	900
Deferred tax balance carried forward	3,000	3,900

(Under the deferral method, it is a matter of no concern that the balance carried forward, of £3,900, has no meaning in terms of the cumulative timing difference of £9,000 and the present tax rate of 30%.)

Under the liability method, the deferred tax account would be calculated by reference to the cumulative timing difference (computed by comparing the net book value of the asset in the accounts with its written down value in the capital allowance computation, thus):

Computation of the cumulative timing difference	1991	1992
	£	£
Net book value per accounts	42,000	36,000
Written down value per tax computation	36,000	27,000
Cumulative timing difference	6,000	9,000
Deferred tax balance, at 50%/30%	3,000	2,700
Deferred tax provided/(released)	3,000	(300)

The amount of deferred tax in the profit and loss account is simply the movement between the two balance sheet figures. In this example the £300 release in 1992 is reconciled thus:

	£
Originating timing difference in 1992 – £3,000 @ 30%	900
Effect of change in rate on opening balance of cumulative timing differences – £6,000 x (50% - 30%)	(1,200)
	(300)

Where the whole amount of the cumulative timing difference is reflected in the amount provided in the balance sheet, the approach can be described as 'full provision', or 'comprehensive allocation'. This is to distinguish the method from a variant of the liability approach, 'partial provision', which is described below. The liability method with full provision has gained ascendancy internationally, although there are still a number of different variants of it.

In its 1995 Discussion Paper, the ASB tentatively concluded that the UK should move to the full provision method,[6] partly because of this growing international consensus and partly because it saw the method as the most consistent with its draft *Statement of Principles* – the amounts arising being derived from past transactions or events and taking no account of future transactions or events. However, members of the Board placed different interpretations on what the deferred tax balance signified. Some saw it straightforwardly as an asset or liability, because the incidence of timing differences had a direct incremental effect on future tax liabilities, but others saw it more as representing valuation adjustments to other assets and liabilities in the balance sheet. FRED 19 indicates that a minority of the ASB still hold this view.

1.2.8   The liability method (with partial provision)

Partial provision is the required UK method of accounting for deferred tax under the present standard, SSAP 15. Under this approach, the full amount of the deferred tax liability is calculated, but only a portion of that full liability might actually be provided in the accounts. The amount provided is based on an estimate of the liability that is expected to arise in the future, based on a projection of the extent to which the cumulative timing differences are expected to reverse in net terms. A proportion of the timing differences can be viewed as non-reversing and thus equivalent to permanent differences (on which deferred tax is not provided).

Individual timing differences (by definition) will always reverse. However, the partial provision approach permits these reversals to be offset by such new originating timing differences as can be predicted with sufficient certainty to arise in the future. This can be illustrated by an example:

Example 21.4:   Illustration of partial provision

Consider a company which commenced trade in 1991 by purchasing fixed assets for £1,000,000. It has an annual capital expenditure budget for the next four years of £400,000, £500,000, £600,000 and £700,000 respectively. Assets are depreciated over their useful lives of ten years and are expected to have a nil recoverable amount at that time. Capital allowances are 25% p.a. on a reducing balance basis, and tax is charged at a rate of 30%.

Fixed assets in accounts	1991	1992	1993	1994	1995
	£'000	£'000	£'000	£'000	£'000
Opening balance	–	900	1,160	1,470	1,820
Additions	1,000	400	500	600	700
Depreciation	(100)	(140)	(190)	(250)	(320)
Closing balance	900	1,160	1,470	1,820	2,200

Tax computation	1991	1992	1993	1994	1995
	£'000	£'000	£'000	£'000	£'000
Opening balance	–	750	862	1,022	1,216
Additions	1,000	400	500	600	700
Writing down allowance	(250)	(288)	(340)	(406)	(479)
Closing balance	750	862	1,022	1,216	1,437
Timing difference	150	298	448	604	763
Increase therein		148	150	156	159

This can be shown in the form of a graph, thus:

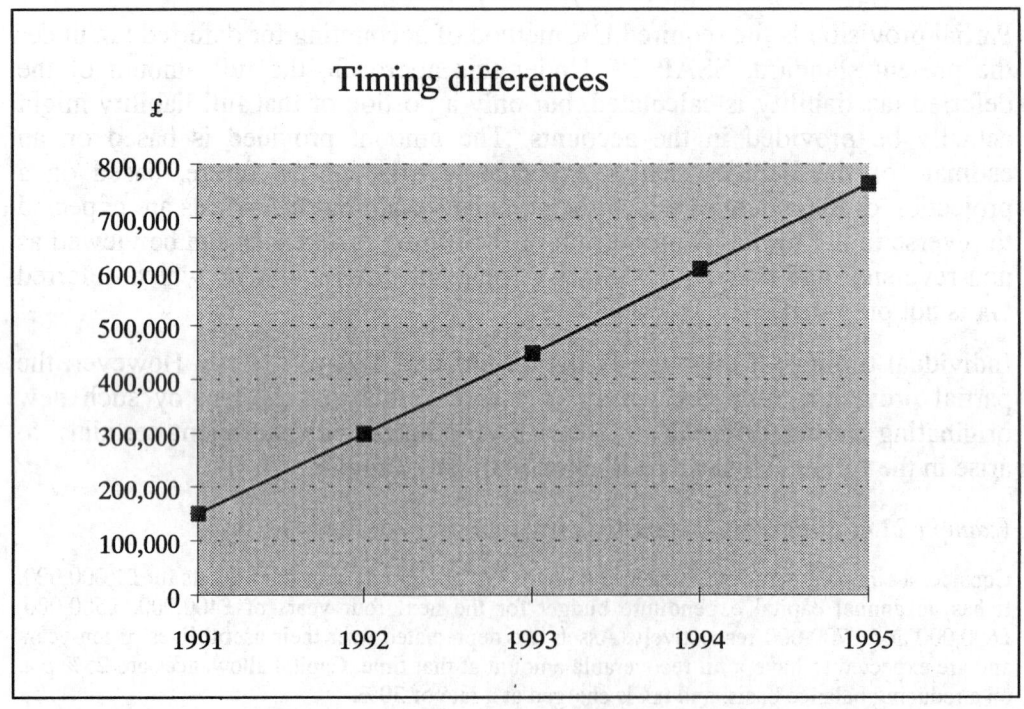

Under the full provision approach, the company would provide deferred tax at the end of 1991 of £45,000, being 30% of the timing difference of £150,000 at that time. However, the partial provision approach would consider whether any net reversal of the timing difference could be foreseen to arise in the future, and since the cumulative amount of timing differences is expected to rise, would make no provision at all in this case.

If timing differences were in fact expected to decline below the present level in the future, then provision would be made for the extent to which the timing differences were expected to reverse. Thus if the figures were the same as those above, except that the cumulative timing differences at the end of 1991 amounted to £400,000 rather than £150,000, then provision would be made for the net reversal which could be foreseen to arise when they fell to £298,000. The amount provided would be £30,600 ((£400,000 - £298,000) @ 30%). This pattern is shown in the following graph:

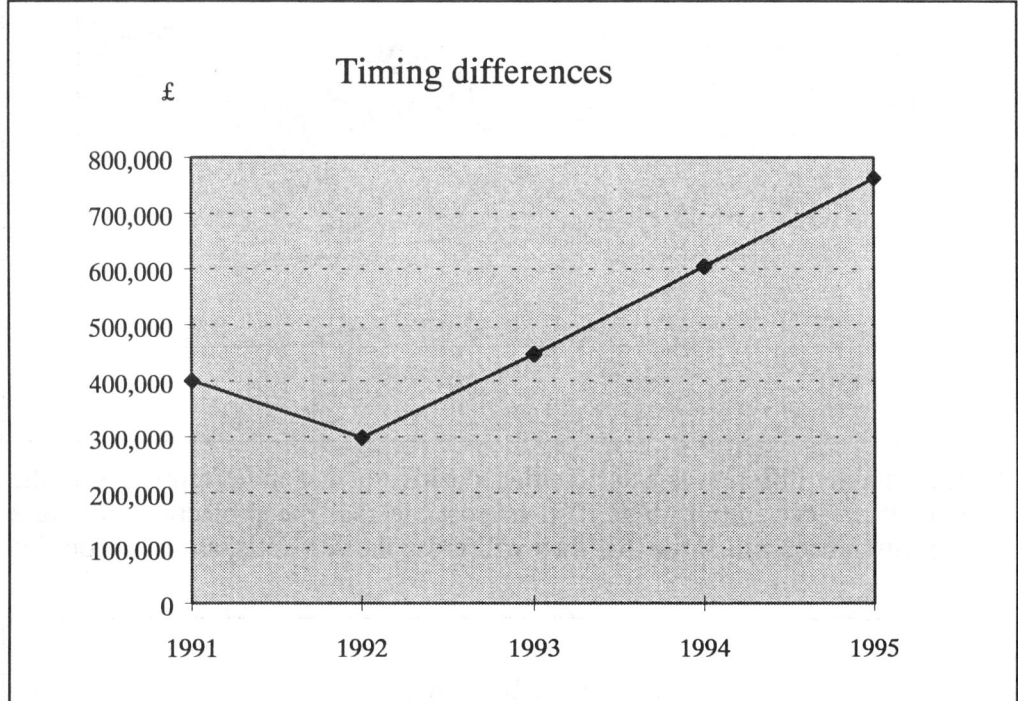

It should be noted that provision has to be made for this reversal, even though the reversal itself is expected to be temporary (in the sense that the timing differences expected to arise beyond 1992 will again lift the cumulative level above the present level). The basic rule is that provision should be made for tax on the excess of the present level of timing differences over the lowest level to which it is expected to fall at any year end in the future.

Where a converse pattern is foreseen (as shown in the next graph), the same basic rule still applies; in the following example, therefore, no provision would be needed because, although net reversals can be foreseen in years 1994 and 1995, they do not bring the cumulative level at the end of that period below its present level. However, if it were expected that this declining pattern would continue beyond 1995, it would be necessary to see to what level the timing differences could be expected to fall in the longer term, and if at any time it was expected that they would be less than the present level of £400,000, then provision would have to be made for the effect of that net reversal.

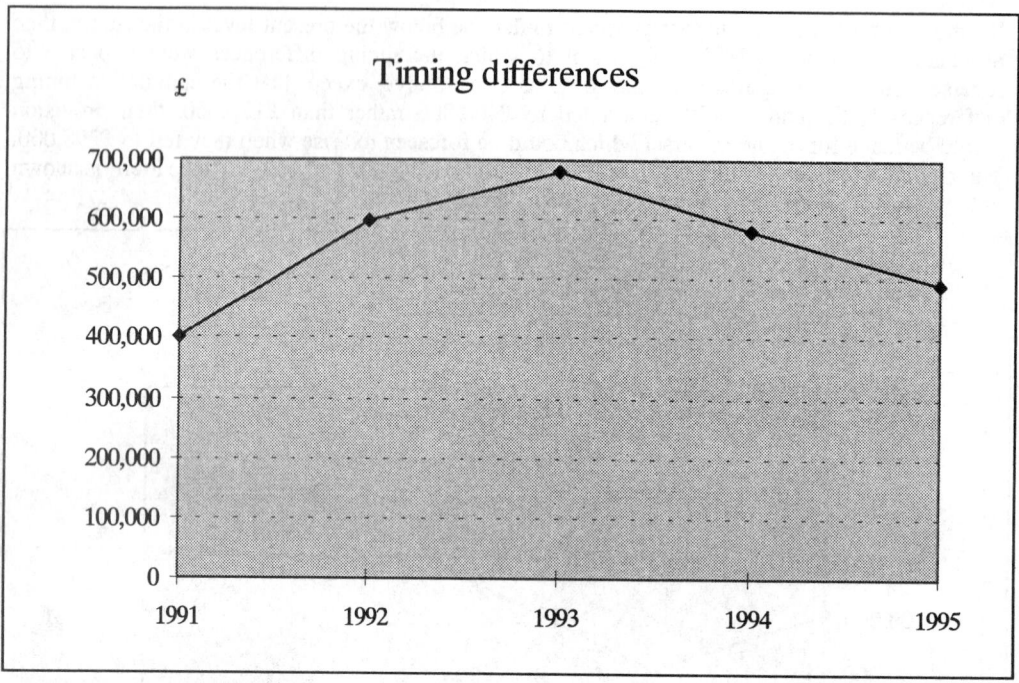

Because timing differences can be either positive or negative (representing the deferment or acceleration of tax), it is possible that the projection of future timing differences will show that they will cross the zero axis, as shown on this graph:

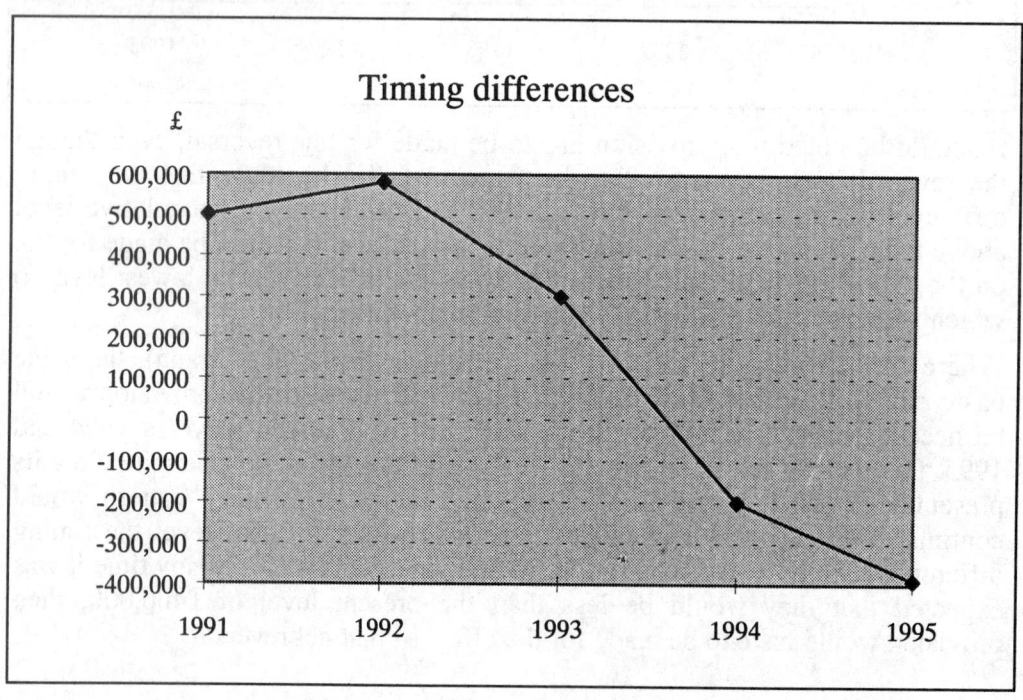

In these circumstances, the whole amount of the potential liability would be provided (£150,000 in the example – £500,000 @ 30%), but no provision would be made for the further effect of the future timing differences which went beyond the axis. The partial provision basis does not involve accounting for timing differences based on their future level; it simply seeks to identify whether a 'hard core' of timing differences exists, and if so, to avoid making provision for that amount because in substance it represents a permanent deferment of tax.

The partial provision approach arouses strong passions, both from those who support it and from those who condemn it. Most of the arguments in favour are in fact criticisms of the full provision approach on the grounds that it can lead to the provision of large sums for deferred tax which have only a remote likelihood of becoming payable. To provide for deferred tax on timing differences which are unlikely on reversal to give rise to a tax liability is said by advocates of the partial provision method to be pursuing form rather than substance and to mislead the users of accounts through the understatement of profit and capital employed. It can thereby portray companies as being more highly geared than they are in reality and give a false impression of poor creditworthiness. Further, it could affect a company's distributable reserves and borrowing powers (if they were computed by reference to reserves) because those reserves were understated because of a provision for deferred tax which might be regarded as unnecessary. In contrast, partial provision gives rise to liabilities that can be regarded as more realistic. Perhaps more importantly, the method produces an effective tax rate in the profit and loss account that reflects the company's tax planning strategies, whereas full provision simply reports a statutory tax rate which is impervious to its degree of success in managing its tax affairs more efficiently.

Critics of the partial provision approach generally say that the failure to provide for an expected reversal on the grounds that replacement will take place wrongly anticipates a future event (such as that a certain level of capital expenditure will take place). This is thought to be inappropriate partly because it may be at variance with the prudence concept, but partly also because it departs from normal accounting rules which account for the effects of transactions individually, rather than in combination with the effects of transactions which have not yet occurred. It is also argued that the method brings volatility and distortion into the profit and loss account, because earnings are affected by the incidence of transactions unrelated to trading performance, such as the acquisition of fixed assets which attract allowances for which no deferred tax provision is made.

The conceptual weakness of the partial provision approach was highlighted in 1992 when the UITF issued its sixth Abstract, relating to post-retirement health care costs (see Chapter 20 at 4.8). This requires a company to charge such costs in its profit and loss account over the working lives of its employees and set up the corresponding liability in the balance sheet; however, it does not receive any tax deduction in respect of the health care costs until the payments are eventually made. Under a comprehensive allocation approach, this would give rise to a deferred tax asset, but because such an asset will continue to grow indefinitely (because the provision for health care costs will be doing so) the partial provision approach would require that no recognition be given to the asset.

This highlighted the main conceptual inconsistency between SSAP 15 and accounting practice in all other areas; partial provision applies a principle which has no parallel in other areas of accounting, namely that assets and liabilities should not be recognised when they are expected to be replaced by equivalents in the future. If the same principle were applied to the health care costs themselves, then no provision would have to be set up so long as the existing workforce continued to earn entitlement to health care as fast as their predecessors became eligible to receive them; a 'pay-as-you-go' basis would be applied, which would not be permitted under UITF 6. Critics pointed out that the deferred tax asset was as real an asset as the pension provision was a liability.

As a result of this, in December 1992 the ASB amended SSAP 15 so as to allow (but not require) deferred tax relating to all post-retirement costs (including pensions themselves) to be accounted for on a comprehensive allocation basis, despite the fact that all other timing differences remained on a partial provision basis.[7] TI Group adopts this approach, as shown in the following extract:

Extract 21.1: TI Group plc (1998)

Accounting policies [extract]

Deferred tax

Deferred taxation relating to capital allowances and other timing differences is provided in the financial statements only in so far as a liability is expected to crystallise. Deferred taxation on pension balances and provisions for post-retirement obligations is recognised in full.

16. Debtors and prepayments [extract]

	The Group	
	1998	1997
	£m	£m
Amounts falling due after more than one year		
Prepaid pension contributions (note 32)	83.8	81.8
Other debtors	7.8	8.4
Deferred taxation	31.7	29.5
	123.3	119.7

The deferred tax asset relates to provisions for post-retirement medical and welfare benefits, principally in the USA.

This amendment to SSAP 15 has really only compounded the inconsistencies inherent in the standard. The problem was not unique to post-retirement costs, but related to all timing differences which arise from the use of the matching concept in accounts when a different basis is used in the tax computation.

Moreover, the treatment required by SSAP 15 before the Amendment was perfectly consistent with the overall rationale of partial provision. If tax relief that is effectively permanently accelerated is not a liability, tax payments above the standard rate that are effectively never recovered should not be treated as assets. As the ASB's 1995 discussion paper observed, 'the treatment required by SSAP 15, considered in terms of the underlying rationale of the standard, is entirely justifiable. In the years when the liability for pensions or OPEBs is first set up, profit before tax will include a charge for pensions or OPEBs that is not tax-deductible. In these periods the company will pay tax at more than the standard rate, in the sense that its current tax liability will be greater than the profit before tax multiplied by the tax rate.

'In the tax computations for the years in which the pensions or OPEBs are paid, tax relief for amounts paid will be offset by add-backs for amounts charged in the profit and loss account [assuming that] ... the company continues to offer such benefits as part of the remuneration package, so that the balance sheet liability for them never reduces. In other words, tax in those periods will, other things being equal, be paid at the standard rate and the effective 'overpayment' of tax in the earlier years will never be recovered. The accounting treatment required by SSAP 15 before the Amendment reflected this.'[8]

It is worth remembering that the partial provision method was introduced at a time when very substantial tax deductions were available in the form of stock appreciation relief and 100% first year allowances for capital investment, and it was much more appropriate in that context than it is now that these features have been removed from the tax system.

The ASB's 1995 Discussion Paper also criticised the partial provision approach on several conceptual grounds by reference to its own proposed framework: it used criteria for recognition that were not found elsewhere in GAAP; it inappropriately recognised the effects of future transactions; it relied on management intent; and it was internally inconsistent. The Board therefore suggested that the method should be abandoned in favour of full provision.

This has been formally proposed in FRED 19 (see 2.2.9 below), which cites as a further main reason for change the fact that the international consensus has now moved distinctly in favour of full provision. However, when one gets to the detail of FRED 19, one finds that it does not require true full provision either, since it incorporates numerous exemptions that go beyond the international consensus.

1.2.9   The hybrid method

This method seeks to combine features of the two principal methods of accounting for deferred tax (i.e. the deferral method and the liability method), by selecting the most appropriate method for the particular type of timing difference which has arisen, such that the deferred tax balance consists of elements derived under the deferral method and other elements derived under the liability method.

As discussed at 1.2.5 above, there are four basic classes of timing differences:

(a)   income can be recognised in the accounts before being taxed;

(b)   income can be taxed before being recognised in the accounts;

(c)   expenditure can be recognised in the accounts before being allowed for tax;

(d)   expenditure can be allowed for tax before being recognised in the accounts.

The hybrid method draws a distinction between those where the first leg of the timing difference passes through the accounts ('book before tax' – (a) and (c) above) and those where it passes through the tax computation ('tax before book' – (b) and (d) above).

When items of income or expenditure have been recognised in the accounts but not recognised for tax purposes, the deferred tax liability cannot be quantified with absolute certainty. It is not possible to determine the tax consequences of these transactions as they will only be apparent in the future, and the ultimate liability will be determined by the rate of tax in effect at the time of the reversal. Accordingly the best estimate of the future liability is made and tax is provided at the latest known rate. Thus deferred tax on these types of timing differences is provided using the liability method.

However, when items of income or expenditure pass through the tax computation before they are recognised in the accounts, the tax effect of those transactions is known, and the tax expense or benefit is fixed. Accordingly, deferred tax on these types of timing differences is provided using the deferral method.

If the hybrid method is used the effect of a change in the rate of tax will affect only that part of the balance computed using the principles of the liability method. That part of the deferred tax balance computed using the deferral method is not adjusted since the tax effects of these timing differences is already known.

Although there is a degree of theoretical merit in this approach, it is not adopted as standard accounting practice in any of the major developed countries of the world. This may be because it is more complicated to apply, rather than being a reflection of any lack of theoretical soundness to the approach. For example, under the current UK system, the timing differences relating to depreciation fixed assets typically change from 'tax before book' to 'book before tax' during the life of the asset.[9] The method is not considered further in this chapter.

1.2.10 Discounting the liability

Another suggestion which is sometimes made is that deferred tax should be provided on a discounted basis. This has obvious theoretical merit, because by definition deferred tax involves the postponement of the tax liability, and it is possible therefore to regard the deferred liability as equivalent to an interest-free loan from the tax authorities. An appropriate way to reflect the benefit of this postponement could be to discount the liability by reference to the period of the deferment, and accordingly to record a lower tax charge by reason of that discount. The discount would then be amortised over the period of the deferment.

Such an approach was advocated by some respondents to ASC exposure drafts on deferred tax, as well as by the ICAEW Technical Committee in a general paper on discounting.[10] It is not specifically precluded by SSAP 15, but it has seldom been adopted in practice in the UK; it is explicitly prohibited in the US and IASC standards. Discounting was considered in some detail by the ASB in its 1995 Discussion Paper, and the Board tentatively concluded that it should be adopted in conjunction with the full provision method[11].

The Discussion Paper did show that some quite complicated issues were involved. In particular, it is necessary to identify when the tax cash flow that is to be discounted is to be assumed to arise, and a choice immediately emerges which is the parallel of the basic dilemma between full provision and partial provision: are the effects of future offsetting timing differences to be assumed or not? The paper concluded that no such offsetting effect should be taken into account. The hybrid approach was also discussed, with the argument that only 'book before tax' timing differences should be discounted, since only they have a future tax cash flow effect, but this view was rejected. Even with these simplifications, however, it is clear that discounting would add substantial complexity to the method and responses to the whole idea have to date been unenthusiastic.

Another real conceptual objection to discounting of deferred tax is that it will often result in the same transaction being dealt with at historical cost at the pre-tax level, on a discounted basis at the tax level, and on a hybrid basis at the post-tax level. For example, if deferred tax relating to accelerated capital allowances on a fixed asset were discounted, the (pre-tax) depreciation charge would still remain on a historical cost basis. It is hard to reconcile such a result with the fundamental accounting concept of consistency.

Nevertheless a discounting approach is now proposed in FRED 19, published in August 1999 (see 2.2.9 H below).

1.2.11   The net of tax method

The net of tax approach is not a discrete method of measuring the tax effects of timing differences, but is concerned with the manner of its presentation in the accounts. The method recognises the tax effects of timing differences as an integral part of the asset or liability that caused the timing difference to arise. Before applying the net of tax approach the deferred tax liability is computed via the deferral method or the liability method (or conceivably the hybrid method), but then included in the carrying value of the item to which the difference relates. Thus, a deferred tax liability arising from accelerated capital allowances would be deducted from the balance sheet carrying value of the asset concerned, or the amount of a disallowable provision (such as a general bad debt provision) would be stated net of the tax effect which would arise when the provision was utilised and became tax deductible.

This method has seldom been used in practice, although there are occasions, particularly in relation to net-of-tax provisions as described above, where it has been applied. SSAP 15 dismisses it by saying that 'it fails to distinguish between a transaction and its tax consequences and therefore should not be used in financial statements'.[12] The ASB's Discussion Paper mentioned it in the context of full provision (since some Board members apparently think of deferred tax as a valuation adjustment to other items) but did not support this form of presentation.

1.2.12   The flow-through method

This theoretical approach is not really a method of accounting for deferred tax at all, but rather a justification for not accounting for it. Under the flow-through method, the tax charge is simply the amount payable based on the profits of that year, with no attempt to reallocate it between periods by reference to timing differences. The method therefore deals with tax as if it were either a period cost or a distribution (see 1.1 above). However, although it sometimes advocated, it is not presently regarded as an acceptable approach.

The ASB's Discussion Paper considered the method at some length, but ended up rejecting it,[13] partly because it is not used internationally, and partly because the Board did not consider it appropriate within its conceptual framework.

1.3   Allocation within periods

As well as allocating tax to particular accounting periods, it is also sometimes necessary to allocate it within an accounting period for presentation purposes. Normally, it will be shown in the profit and loss account under the caption of tax on profit on ordinary activities, but it may have to be allocated to the statement of total recognised gains and losses or the reconciliation of movements in shareholders' funds.

This issue is discussed in Chapter 22 at 2.10; in general the principle is that the tax effect should 'follow' (i.e. be accounted for in the same primary statement as) the item that gives rise to it. This principle was supported by the ASB's 1995 Discussion Paper,[14] subsequently reinforced in UITF Abstract 19 in relation to exchange gains and losses (see 2.3.4 below), and proposed on a more general basis in FRED 18 (see 3.2 below) and FRED 19 (see 2.2.9 below).

The windfall tax levied on privatised utilities in the July 1997 Budget gave rise to some debate as to how it should be presented. Because it is based on a formula which relies on the capitalised value of profits over a period of up to four years, it is arguably inappropriate to include it in the normal tax line in the profit and loss account, which under the Companies Act formats is captioned 'tax on profit or loss on ordinary activities'. A more appropriate alternative under these formats might be the penultimate line, 'Other taxes not shown under the above items'. The approach adopted by Thames Water in the extract below has elements of both these possible treatments, since the windfall tax is shown adjacent to, but not as part of, tax on profit on ordinary activities.

Extract 21.2: Thames Water Plc (1998)

Consolidated profit and loss account [extract]

	Note	**1998** Total **£m**	1997 Total £m
Profit on ordinary activities before taxation		**418.6**	371.8
Taxation on profit on ordinary activities		**(62.2)**	(51.4)
Windfall tax	9	**(230.7)**	–
Profit for the financial year		**125.7**	320.4
...			

9. Windfall tax

In accordance with the Finance (No 2) Act 1997 enacted on 31 July 1997, £230.7m has been charged to the profit and loss account in respect of the windfall tax of which £115.4m was paid on 1 December 1997. The balance of £115.3m will be paid on 1 December 1998.

---

2   THE DEVELOPMENT OF ACCOUNTING FOR TAXATION IN THE UK

2.1   Accounting for tax payable

2.1.1   ED 12

The introduction of the imputation system of taxation in the Finance Act 1972, which took effect from April 1973, meant that the earlier guidance on the treatment of tax in the accounts of companies, contained in the ICAEW statement N27, needed amendment. An exposure draft[15] was issued by the ASC in May 1973, entitled 'The treatment of taxation under the imputation system in the accounts of companies'. Its principal requirements were as follows:

(a) the particulars in the profit and loss account of the charge for corporation tax should show, where material, the relief for recoverable ACT and the amount of any irrecoverable ACT;

(b) appropriations for dividends payable should not include either the related ACT or the attributable tax credit;

(c) proposed dividends should be included in current liabilities without the addition of attributable ACT: the ACT on proposed dividends, whether or not recoverable, should be included as a current tax liability. Recoverable ACT on proposed dividends should be deducted from the deferred tax account if available, or otherwise shown as a deferred asset; and

(d) dividends receivable from UK resident companies could be shown either inclusive or exclusive of the related tax credit (so long as the policy was applied consistently).

2.1.2   SSAP 8

The exposure draft was converted into a Statement of Standard Accounting Practice in the following year, with comparatively little change; however, it removed the option mentioned at 2.1.1 (d) above, by requiring that dividends receivable should be included at an amount which included the associated tax credit. The requirements of SSAP 8 are dealt with in 3.1 below.

2.1.3   FRED 18

The abolition of ACT with effect from April 1999 has made much of SSAP 8 redundant. Following an aborted proposal for a limited amendment of SSAP 8 in 1997, in June 1999 the ASB issued FRED 18 which is intended, when converted into an FRS, to replace SSAP 8 completely. The development and requirements of FRED 18 are dealt with in 3.2 below.

2.2   Accounting for deferred tax

2.2.1   ED 11

The first exposure draft on deferred tax in the UK was published in May 1973.[16] Until that time, most companies had accounted for deferred tax, but it was not mandatory to do so and a variety of practices were followed. The exposure draft was controversial in that it proposed that the deferral method should be used, whereas most UK companies had up to that time been using the liability method. It also specified that revaluations of assets should be regarded as giving rise to timing differences, for which deferred tax should therefore be provided; not all companies had been taking that view.

2.2.2 SSAP 11

The exposure draft was converted into an accounting standard in 1975, to be effective for periods beginning on or after 1 January 1976.[17] However, the standard was different from the exposure draft in one fundamental respect. The requirement to use the deferral method had been relaxed, and companies were now offered the option of using the liability method as an alternative.

SSAP 11 was short lived. In many ways it was issued at precisely the wrong time. The UK was in its highest period of inflation for very many years. Capital allowances were at their most accelerated, and there was a system of 'stock appreciation relief' in force which gave businesses a tax deduction for the increase in the balance sheet value of stocks held by them. The net result was that, even though there were comparatively high nominal rates of tax in force (50–52%), a large number of companies were paying no corporation tax at all, other than ACT.

As a result of these factors many companies began to build up large deferred tax provisions in their balance sheets, when in reality they could not see that the liability was ever likely to be paid. A campaign began to gather momentum to have the subject re-examined. In the meantime, the ASC was formulating a statement on current cost accounting, which dealt with a wide range of accounting issues, and the exposure draft which was published on this subject contained the radical proposal that deferred tax should be calculated on the basis of only those timing differences which were expected to reverse without being replaced – the partial provision approach.[18] In the light of this, in October 1976 the Committee suspended indefinitely the implementation date of SSAP 11 (effectively before it came into force).

2.2.3 ED 19

A further exposure draft was issued in 1977 which was based on the approach which had been set out in ED 18.[19] This proposed that deferred tax should be provided in full, using the liability method, unless it could be demonstrated with reasonable probability that the tax reduction would continue for the foreseeable future. It also proposed that disclosure should be required of the full potential liability to deferred tax by way of note, analysed into categories of timing difference and showing how much had been provided in respect of each category.

The exposure draft differentiated short-term timing differences from others, saying that it was generally accepted that provision should be made in full for short-term differences, but that the remaining timing differences should be considered jointly to see whether it could be established that some part of the potential liability need not be provided. The reason for this distinction was not more fully explained.

2.2.4   SSAP 15

In October 1978, the ASC finally withdrew SSAP 11 and issued SSAP 15, which was based on ED 19.[20] However, there were a number of significant changes from the exposure draft, as summarised below:

(a)   the liability method was no longer mandated, and indeed the standard did not make any mention of either the liability method or the deferral method. Implicitly, therefore, the deferral method was allowed even though it did not fit naturally with the forward-looking orientation of the partial provision approach;

(b)   more specific criteria were laid down which had to be satisfied in order to justify the non-provision of deferred tax. These were that the company had to be a going concern, and that the directors had to be able to foresee, on reasonable evidence, that no liability was likely to arise as a result of reversal of timing differences for some considerable period (at least three years) ahead, and that there was no indication after that period that the situation was likely to change so as to crystallise the liabilities;

(c)   it was even more clearly stipulated that full provision was required on short-term timing differences;

(d)   a disclosure requirement was added in relation to the effect of unprovided deferred tax on the tax charge in the profit and loss account; and

(e)   the standard changed the approach to deferred tax in relation to revalued fixed assets, by stating that provision need be made in respect of a timing difference arising from a revaluation only if it had been decided in principle to dispose of the asset in question and if no rollover relief was available.

The standard took effect for accounting periods commencing on or after 1 January 1979.

2.2.5   ED 33

The ASC set up a working party to review SSAP 15 in 1982, for two principal reasons:

(a)   to incorporate the new legal requirements of the Companies Act 1981 into the standard; and

(b)   to take account of the change in the basis of stock relief in the Finance Act 1981.

The revision was also intended to take into account comments arising out of the experience gained from applying SSAP 15 in practice. On the basis of this review, a further exposure draft was issued in 1983.[21] This proposed the following main changes:

(a)   the exposure draft described the liability method as the appropriate approach to use, because the deferral method was not compatible with the partial provision concept. However, this was not stated explicitly as a requirement;

(b) the previous requirement to set up deferred tax unless it could be demonstrated that it would not be required was expressed more neutrally, by saying that deferred tax should be provided to the extent that it was probable that a liability would crystallise and not set up to the extent that it would not;

(c) there was no longer a specific reference to a period (mentioned in SSAP 15 as at least three years) for which positive evidence should be sought as to the likelihood of the liability crystallising;

(d) the distinction between short-term and other timing differences was discontinued; all timing differences were to be considered jointly when considering the need to make provision for deferred tax;

(e) more guidance was added on the criteria to be considered in deciding whether debit balances in respect of deferred tax could be regarded as recoverable. It was stated that they could be carried forward only where their recovery without replacement by equivalent debit balances was assured beyond reasonable doubt;

(f) the requirement to analyse the deferred tax which was provided into its principal categories was to be replaced by one which required disclosure of the period or periods of time in which the liability was expected to crystallise;

(g) the requirement to show the full potential liability to deferred tax, analysed into its components, was replaced by a requirement to show a similar analysis of only the unprovided amount; and

(h) a requirement was proposed that, where deferred tax was not provided in respect of overseas earnings of a subsidiary on the grounds that there was no intention to remit them to the UK, that the intention not to remit them should be disclosed.

2.2.6 SSAP 15 (Revised)

A revised version of SSAP 15[22] was issued in 1985, which was very similar to ED 33, but which included the following further changes:

(a) it was now explicitly stated that the liability method was the required method of provision for deferred tax;

(b) the proposal to require disclosure of the period or periods of time in which the liability was expected to crystallise was dropped; and

(c) the proposed requirement to state that overseas earnings were not planned to be remitted to the UK (where applicable) was replaced with one to state simply that no deferred tax had been provided in respect of these earnings.

The requirements of SSAP 15 (Revised) are set out in more detail in 3.3 below. For the remainder of this chapter, all references to SSAP 15 are to this revised version.

2.2.7   Amendment to SSAP 15 following UITF 6

As mentioned in 1.2.6 above, the ASB made a further minor amendment to SSAP 15 in December 1992. The effect of the change was to allow deferred tax relating to all post-retirement costs such as pensions and health care to be accounted for in full even though all other timing differences remained on a partial provision basis.[23]

2.2.8   The ASB's Discussion Paper

In March 1995, the ASB published a comprehensive Discussion Paper – *Accounting for tax* – which addressed the subject from first principles and put forward some tentative proposals as to how SSAP 15 might be amended. It concluded that allowing SSAP 15 to remain in force was untenable and that it should be replaced with a standard requiring some variant of full provision on a discounted basis. However, the Board was divided as to whether deferred tax should be provided on fair value adjustments following an acquisition and revaluation adjustments. The Board also recommended expanded disclosures, notably a reconciliation between the actual and the expected tax charge.

2.2.9   FRED 19

The Discussion Paper received a rather cool reception from respondents, who largely felt that partial provision, whatever its faults, was well established and understood and, in a UK context, gave intuitively right answers. However, the reality is that, with the UK's participation in the IASC's project to harmonise accounting practices internationally, the days of partial provision have been numbered for some time, since full provision is required by virtually every country in the world except the UK and Ireland (including many whose initial capital allowances are as, if not more, generous). The question has not been so much whether the ASB would propose full provision as when it would judge such a proposal politically acceptable, or at least not unacceptable, among its constituency.

During 1998 and 1999 the ASB gave a number of increasingly clear hints that it was preparing an exposure draft of a standard proposing full provision for tax, albeit with some modifications in respect of revaluation gains,[24] and this is indeed the broad approach proposed in FRED 19 – *Deferred tax*, published in August 1999, the proposed requirements of which are summarised below.

In developing FRED 19 the ASB must have found itself in an unenviable predicament. On the one hand, its commitment to the current international harmonisation project required it to move the UK on to full provision. On the other, it was clear from the 1995 Discussion Paper that several ASB members believed that full provision for deferred tax was incompatible with its draft *Statement of Principles,* and that the Board as a whole had serious reservations about the approach to accounting for tax in the US standard SFAS 109, which has been substantially replicated in the relevant international standard, IAS 12 (see 5.1 below). It is apparent from FRED 19 that these reservations remain substantially unchanged.[25]

Apart from any conceptual objections to IAS 12 and SFAS 109, the ASB will also have been well aware that, whereas it may now just be possible to gain acceptance for full provision on accelerated capital allowances in the UK, any proposal to require full provision on revaluation gains would provoke outright opposition. Moreover, if it were imposed, it could only accelerate the drift back to historical cost accounting that we already see as likely following the publication of FRS 15 – *Tangible Fixed Assets* (see Chapter 10 at 5.1.1). This would seriously undermine the ASB's long-term ambitions for the increased use of current values in financial statements.

FRED 19 has bravely tried to give some accommodation to all these views but, in our opinion, failed to do so for the simple reason that they are ultimately (and, one might add, obviously) irreconcilable. Given our own fundamental criticisms of the approach adopted by IAS 12 (see 5.1.1 and 5.1.2 below), we fully support the ASB in rejecting it. However, the result is that, in the name of international harmonisation,[26] the ASB is proposing an FRS which, if adopted, will still leave accounting for tax in the UK and Ireland significantly different from that in the rest of the world.

A   Basic approach of FRED 19

FRED 19 broadly proposes that deferred tax should be provided for in full on all timing differences except (in most circumstances) revaluation gains (see B and C below) and retained earnings of overseas investments (see D below). Under FRED 19, timing differences are defined as:

'Differences between an entity's taxable profits and its results as stated in the financial statements that arise from the inclusion of gains and losses in tax assessments in periods different from those in which they are recognised in financial statements. Timing differences originate in one period and are capable of reversal in one or more subsequent periods'.[27]

Specific examples of timing differences are given as being:

(a)   differences between accounting depreciation of fixed assets and capital allowances given for those assets for tax purposes;

(b)   pension costs that are accrued in the accounts but allowed as an expense for tax purposes only when paid or as contributions are made;

(c)   interest and development costs that have been allowed as an expense for tax purposes but capitalised in the accounts;

(d)   profit on sale of stock between group companies that has been eliminated on consolidation;

(e)   a revaluation gain that has been recognised in the accounts but which becomes taxable only when the asset is sold;

(f)   a tax loss that can be relieved only against future taxable profits; and

(g)   the unremitted earnings of overseas subsidiaries, associates and joint ventures where an additional tax liability would arise if the earnings were remitted to the UK.[28]

The ASB describes its approach to deferred tax accounting as the 'incremental liability approach'.[29] It is based on the distinction that, in the ASB's view, exists between those timing differences that, at the balance sheet date, give rise to an asset or liability as defined in the ASB's draft *Statement of Principles* and those timing differences that do not.

For example, it is argued that, if a company recognises a right to receive accrued interest that will be taxed on receipt, it cannot avoid the obligation to pay tax on that interest when it is received and a deferred tax liability should therefore be recognised. If a company has recognised an obligation to fund a pension scheme, it should recognise, as a deferred tax asset, the tax relief that it will receive when it does so. If a company claims capital allowances in advance, there is a liability to repay them if the asset is not consumed in the business, and there is therefore a liability until it has been.[30] By contrast, if a company revalues an asset, it has discretion over whether or not to sell the asset in such a way as to crystallise the tax liability on the gain; until it becomes obliged to sell the asset in these circumstances, it has no liability to tax in respect of the gain, and deferred tax should therefore not be recognised before that point.[31]

Unfortunately, in our view, the 'incremental liability' approach does not bear much scrutiny as a conceptual basis. The examples of timing differences used by FRED 19 to explain deferred tax as an asset or liability under the ASB's draft *Statement of Principles* seem to have been very carefully selected, since there are many instances of deferred tax assets and liabilities, for which FRED 19 would require provision, that cannot be rationalised in this way.

For example, if interest for which tax relief has been received is capitalised, there are no circumstances in which that tax relief will ever have to be repaid. Nevertheless, FRED 19 would require a deferred tax liability to be set up in respect of it. In our view, cases such as this demonstrate that deferred tax does not constitute an asset or liability as defined in the ASB's draft *Statement of Principles* and that the true rationale for it is the matching concept. In other words, since the gross interest cost has been deferred, the tax relief should also be deferred. We discuss this more fully at 5.1.1 below.

With regard to the treatment of deferred tax on a revaluation gain, the difficulty is more that the argument for not recognising deferred tax (essentially that the reporting entity has no plan or obligation to realise the gain through sale of the asset) seems to us an equally compelling argument for not recognising the gain in the first place, at or least for not regarding it as forming part of the reporting entity's financial performance, as is required by FRS 3 and is a recurring theme in other ASB publications.

There is a minority view on the ASB that, under the Board's draft *Statement of Principles*, deferred tax is not an asset or liability in its own right, but a value adjustment to other assets and liabilities. For example, a fixed asset for which full capital allowances are not available (e.g. a revalued tax-exhausted asset) is less valuable than one for which full allowances may be claimed and, it is argued, provision for deferred tax reflects this difference.[32]

B   Revaluations

Deferred tax should not be provided for on revaluation gains unless, at the balance sheet date, the reporting entity has:

(a)   entered into a binding sale agreement to sell the revalued assets; and

(b)   recognised the expected gain or loss on sale.[33]

In addition, deferred tax should not be provided for on revaluation gains (including those falling within (a) and (b) above), if, on the basis of all the available evidence, it is more likely than not that the taxable gain will be rolled over into replacement assets, being charged to tax only when the replacement assets are themselves sold without replacement.[34] The continued availability of relief for taxable gains rolled or held over should be reviewed in each future accounting period, and provision made for the deferred tax when it is no longer more likely than not that the gain will be rolled or held over.[35]

In practice, this means that, under FRED 19, deferred tax would not normally be provided on revaluation gains. This differs from IAS 12, which always requires tax to be provided, the only issue being the amount (see 5.1.3 B and C below).

FRED 19 does not specifically address downward revaluations of assets or revaluations of liabilities, but we assume that similar principles would apply.

C   Fair value adjustments

FRED 19 treats fair value adjustments as if they were timing differences in the acquired entity's own accounts. Where such timing differences represent revaluations (as will generally be the case), deferred tax must not be provided for in respect of them, except in those rare cases where they fall within the criteria for recognition in B above. For example, where stock held by an acquired business is revalued as part of a fair value exercise, no deferred tax is provided on the grounds that, whilst the reporting entity fully expects to realise the stock at least its revalued amount, it has no obligation to do so. Even where there is a binding contract to sell the stock at a particular amount, no deferred tax is recognised on the grounds that the contract itself is not recognised, being an executory contract as defined in FRS 12 (see Chapter 25 at 1.2.4 B).[36] This differs from IAS 12 which requires deferred tax to be provided for on fair value adjustments (see 5.1.3 G below).

D   *Retained earnings of subsidiaries, associates and joint ventures*

Tax that could be payable (taking account of double taxation relief) on future remittance of the retained earnings of subsidiaries, associates and joint ventures should be provided for only to the extent that, at the balance sheet date:

(a)   dividends have been accrued as being payable or receivable; or

(b)   there is a binding agreement to distribute the earnings at some point in the future.[37]

In practice, as FRED 19 notes, (a) is likely to be the only relevant criterion. Again this differs from IAS 12, which requires deferred tax on the distribution of retained earnings to be provided for unless the reporting entity can control their distribution (see 5.1.3 H below).

E   *Deferred tax assets*

Deferred tax assets should be recognised only to the extent that they are recoverable. They should be regarded as recoverable to the extent that, on the basis of all available evidence, it is more likely than not that there will be 'suitable taxable profits' from which the future reversal of the underlying timing differences can be deducted.[38]

'Suitable taxable profits' are those:

(a)   generated in the same taxable entity (or in an entity whose profits would be available via group relief) and assessed by the same taxation authority as the income or expenditure giving rise to the deferred tax asset;

(b)   generated in the same period as that in which the deferred tax asset is expected to reverse, or in a period in which a tax loss arising from the reversal of the deferred tax asset may be carried back or forward; and

(c)   of a type (e.g. capital or trading) from which the taxation authority allows the reversal of the timing difference to be deducted.[39]

FRED 19 clarifies that, broadly speaking, deferred tax assets may always be recognised where they may be offset against any known taxable profit of a current or previous period or taxable profit of a future period represented by a deferred tax liability that is recognised at the balance sheet date. Where, however, the recoverability of a deferred tax asset (particularly a tax loss) depends on the availability of future profits, the likelihood of recovery must be assessed in the light of all the available evidence.[40]

FRED 19 discusses at some length the conditions that must be satisfied in order for losses carried forward to be recognised as deferred tax assets. In all cases these conditions seem rather more stringent than the overall test for recognition of a tax asset (i.e. that it should simply be 'more likely than not' to be realised) would imply. In our view, the reality is the ASB felt compelled to introduce the 'more likely than not' test in the interests of consistency with IAS 12, but did not really want to change current UK practice as set out in SSAP 15, which requires the recoverability of losses to be 'assured beyond reasonable doubt' (see 3.3.3 C below). The ASB sums up this dilemma with the memorable comment that, rather than set a higher recognition test for losses, it is more appropriate to restrict their recognition by emphasising 'how unlikely it is that the 'more likely than not' threshold will be met'.[41]

F   *Recognition – allocation between profit and loss account and STRGL*

Deferred tax (and adjustments to it) should be recognised in the profit and loss account, unless it relates to an item recognised in the statement of total recognised gains and losses (STRGL), in which case the deferred tax (or adjustment) should also be recognised in the STRGL.[42] FRED 19 notes that that in exceptional circumstances it may be impossible to determine the tax relating to items in the STRGL, in which case the total tax should be allocated on either a reasonable pro-rata basis, or using another method that achieves a more appropriate allocation in the circumstances.[43] This is consistent with the approach in IAS 12, and that proposed in FRED 18 in respect of current tax (see 3.2.1 A below).

Where deferred tax has been discounted (see H below), the unwinding of the discount should always be included in the profit and loss account, even if the deferred tax was originally recognised in the STRGL or on the acquisition of a business.[44]

G   *Measurement – tax rates*

Deferred tax should be measured at the average tax rates that are expected to apply in the periods in which the timing differences are expected to reverse, based on tax rates and laws that have been enacted or 'substantively enacted' by the balance sheet date.[45] The definition of 'substantively enacted' is the same as that in FRED 18 (see 3.2.1 E below).[46]

H   *Measurement – discounting*

FRED 19 notes that the Board is split on the issue of discounting, and will therefore take particular note of comments received in reaching a final decision.[47] If it is adopted, deferred tax would be discounted where the effect of doing so is material and it does not relate to items that are themselves discounted (such as finance leases or pension assets and liabilities).[48] Deferred tax should be discounted by treating the reversal of timing differences as cash flows in the year of expected reversal. No account should be taken of the potential offsetting effects of future tax losses or of timing differences arising from future transactions.[49]

The discount rate used should be the post-tax yield to maturity that could be obtained, at the balance sheet date, on government bonds with similar maturity dates and in similar currencies to those of the deferred tax assets or liabilities.[50] FRED 19 notes that, in theory, this would require a different discount rate to be applied to each future period in each main jurisdiction, but concedes that a simpler, approximated approach may be acceptable in some cases.[51] In practice, discounting would have most impact on the deferred tax relating to capital allowances; Appendix I to the FRED gives a worked example of how the relevant calculations might be undertaken.

We have considerable doubts as to the merits of discounting from both a theoretical and practical point of view (see 1.2.10 above). Indeed, we do not think that the ASB has adequately answered some of the objections that it raised in its own 1995 discussion paper. Moreover, discounting is prohibited by IAS 12, which throws even further into question the ASB's claim that its main motive for proposing FRED 19 is international harmonisation.

I Presentation

In the balance sheet, deferred tax assets and liabilities should be offset to the extent, and only to the extent that:

(a)   the assets and liabilities relate to taxes levied by the same tax authority; and

(b)   the entity has a legal right to offset current tax assets against current tax liabilities.[52]

This requirement is proposed for consistency with IAS 12 (see 5.1.3 E below), and would represent a change to current UK practice, whereby legal offset criteria are typically taken into account in the calculation, but not the balance sheet presentation, of deferred tax.

Deferred tax liabilities should be included within 'Provisions for liabilities and charges' and deferred tax assets within debtors, as a separate subheading of debtors where material.[53] Deferred tax should be separately shown on the face of the balance sheet where it is 'so material ... that, in the absence of disclosure, readers may misinterpet the accounts'.[54]

In the profit and loss account, deferred tax should be included in 'Tax on profit or loss on ordinary activities'. However, where deferred tax has been discounted, the unwinding of the discount, and any movements due to changes in discount rates, should be included as financial items next to interest, but disclosed separately from other interest either on the face of the profit and loss account or in the notes.[55]

J Disclosure

FRED 19 reproduces many of the disclosures already required by SSAP 15 and the Companies Act. However, a number of important new disclosures are proposed, in particular:

(a) a reconciliation of the actual to the 'expected' current tax charge (i.e. that calculated by multiplying the profit before tax by the standard tax rate), or of the effective rate of tax to the standard rate.[56] This differs from the reconciliation required by IAS 12 and SFAS 109 for a reconciliation of the *total* tax charge (not just the current element). The ASB believes that its proposals better meet the needs of users;[57] and

(b) the amount, and the nature of the evidence supporting the recognition, of any deferred tax asset if its recovery depends on future taxable profits in excess of those arising from the reversal of deferred tax liabilities and the reporting entity has suffered a loss in the current or preceding period in the tax jurisdiction to which the asset relates.[58]

In addition, where deferred tax is discounted, disclosure would be required of the gross amount of deferred tax, the discount rates used and the effect of changes in those rates.[59] Examples of the disclosures required are given in Appendix II of FRED 19.

2.3 Other pronouncements

2.3.1 SSAP 5 – VAT

As well as dealing with the accounting treatment of tax on profits as described above, the ASC published SSAP 5 – *Accounting for value added tax* – in 1974,[60] based on an exposure draft which had been published in the previous year.[61] The statement is a very brief one, simply requiring that:

(a) turnover should be shown net of VAT on taxable outputs (or shown as a deduction if the gross amount is also shown);[62] and

(b) irrecoverable VAT should be included in the cost of fixed assets and any other disclosed items in the financial statements to which it relates, where it is practicable to do so and material.[63]

2.3.2 ED 28 – Petroleum revenue tax

In 1981, the ASC issued an exposure draft of a statement on Accounting for Petroleum Revenue Tax.[64] The subject was not proceeded with and the exposure draft was subsequently withdrawn. The Oil Industry Accounting Committee also studied the topic with the aim of producing a SORP, but did not continue the project. The tax is complex and presents difficult accounting problems, but its specialised nature places it beyond the scope of this chapter.

2.3.3   UITF 16

In February 1997, the UITF issued its sixteenth Abstract – *Income and expenses subject to non-standard rates of tax*. The issue was solely one of presentation; it addressed the practice that had developed, particularly in the financial services sector, of grossing-up the post-tax results of certain transactions in the profit and loss account so as to show a standardised tax rate and pre-tax result whereas the actual economics of the transaction depended on non-standard tax effects for their profitability.

A common example was so-called 'preference share lending', whereby banks, rather than making a straightforward loan, subscribed for preference shares in the borrowing company. Because dividend income was franked investment income (see 3.1.3 below), but interest income was taxed at the higher corporation tax rate, the banks required a lower pre-tax return on preference shares than on a loan to earn the same post-tax profit. If Bank A made a loan and Bank B 'lent' using preference shares and both reported the actual cashflows, Bank A would appear much more profitable at the pre-tax level than Bank B, whilst the underlying economics were the same. It was argued that the best way of adjusting for this apparent difference was to gross up Bank B's profit and loss account.

The UITF's consensus was that such practices were inappropriate, and that the profit and loss account should show the actual pre-tax and tax numbers without any such adjustment.[65] The Abstract became effective for periods ending on or after 22 June 1997.

Lloyds TSB's 1996 accounts showed the effect of this change:

Extract 21.3: Lloyds TSB Group plc (1996)

NOTES TO THE ACCOUNTS

2   Accounting policies

Accounting policies are unchanged from 1995. Abstract 16 issued by the Urgent Issues Task Force of the Accounting Standards Board, requires the gross-up calculations on certain transactions, the overall profitability of which is determined on a post-tax basis, to be made at the underlying rate of tax. In previous years, for the purposes of presentation in the profit and loss account, the income from these transactions has been grossed-up using the standard rate of tax. The 1996 accounts have been adjusted to take account of the new requirement, which has the effect of reducing total income and profit before tax by £22 million (net interest income by £12 million and other income by £10 million). The tax charge is also reduced by the same amount, so the resulting after tax figure is unaffected. No adjustment has been made to the comparative 1995 figures on the grounds of immateriality.

FRED 18 (issued in June 1999) includes the requirements of UITF 16, which will therefore be withdrawn when FRED 18 is converted into an FRS (see 3.2 below).

2.3.4 UITF 19

In 1995/6 new tax rules on the taxation of foreign exchange differences were introduced in the UK. These have the effect that in certain cases the exchange movements on borrowings taken out to hedge overseas investments are taxable. The (pre-tax) exchange gains and losses on such borrowings are taken direct to reserves in accordance with SSAP 20 and reported in the statement of total recognised gains and losses (STRGL) – see Chapter 8 at 2.3.7, 2.4.5 and 3.5. The question therefore arises as to where the tax should be shown, an issue which was discussed by the UITF in 1997.

As noted in 1.3 above, the ASB's 1995 Discussion Paper had already proposed that, in principle, the tax relating to an item should 'follow' that item in the financial statements, and this treatment was already being applied in practice to the tax on such exchange gains reported in the STRGL. The UITF confirmed this as the appropriate accounting treatment in its nineteenth Abstract – *Tax on gains and losses on foreign currency borrowings that hedge an investment in a foreign enterprise* – which was issued in February 1998, with effect for periods ending on or after 23 March 1998.

UITF 19 requires that the tax on foreign exchange differences reported in the STRGL should also be reported in the STRGL, and that the gross exchange difference and the related tax should be separately disclosed. It also states that the restriction on the amount of the exchange movements on the borrowing that can be taken to reserves under SSAP 20 (see Chapter 8 at 2.3.7 and 2.4.5) should be applied on an after-tax basis.

An example of a company complying with UITF 19 is Reckitt & Colman.

Extract 21.4: Reckitt & Colman plc (1998)

Consolidated statement of total recognised gains and losses for the 52 weeks ended 2 January 1999

	1998 £m	1997 £m
Profit for the financial year	165.3	215.8
Net exchange (loss)/gain on foreign currency borrowings*	3.7	16.9
Exchange differences arising on translation of net investments in overseas subsidiary undertakings	(17.0)	(26.7)
Total recognised gains and losses relating to the financial year	152.0	206.0

*Net exchange gain on foreign currency borrowings is stated after deducting UK corporation tax of £1.5m (1997, £8.0m) in accordance with current accounting practice.

FRED 18 (issued in June 1999) proposes that the principles of UITF 19 should apply to tax on all gains and losses recognised in the STRGL (see 3.2 below).

3   THE REQUIREMENTS OF THE RELEVANT ACCOUNTING STANDARDS AND COMPANY LAW

3.1   SSAP 8

3.1.1   *Outgoing dividends and the related ACT*

In the UK, outgoing dividends are, as a matter of practice, accounted for in the period to which they relate, which contrasts with the treatment in the United States where they are accounted for in the period in which they are declared. Accordingly, if the final dividend is expected to be declared after the year end then, even though it is subject to shareholder approval, it should be provided for in the accounts for the year just completed.

A   Dividends before 6 April 1999

A liability to ACT (advance corporation tax) arose on the payment of a dividend where the dividend was 'due and payable' before 6 April 1999. The standard considers whether ACT on outgoing dividends should be treated as part of the cost of the dividend or whether it should be treated as part of the tax on the company's profits. The amount declared as a dividend (as a sum payable per share or as a percentage) is the amount that will be received by the members. The fact that the dividend will carry a tax credit is considered to be a matter which affects the member as a recipient, rather than a matter which affects the company and the way in which it should be accounted for. It is therefore considered appropriate that outgoing dividends should be shown in the profit and loss account at the amount paid or payable to the shareholders.[66]

Prior to 6 April 1999 the ACT payable in respect of dividends will have fallen due for payment to the Inland Revenue within a period of between two weeks to three and a half months after the dividend was paid, depending on whether the date the dividend was due and payable fell at the end or the beginning, respectively, of a return period. The ACT due on any such dividend will therefore in most cases be a current liability.

ACT is generally capable of being offset only against the mainstream corporation tax liability for the period in which the liability to ACT arises. Accordingly, where a dividend is accrued in the accounts, but is not due and payable until after the year end (as is typically the case with a final dividend), the liability to ACT arises in the subsequent period and therefore will generally not rank for set off against mainstream corporation tax until the due date for payment of the mainstream liability for the *subsequent* period. This will fall due nine months and one day after that period end, i.e. (assuming that the subsequent period is a year) 21 months and one day after the current year end. Thus ACT on such dividends cannot normally be offset against the tax due on the profits for the year to which the dividend relates.

However, under the new regime requiring companies to pay their mainstream corporation tax liability in instalments, the first instalments of mainstream corporation tax for a period will now fall due during that accounting period. As the liability to corporation tax is accelerated, so is the potential recovery of ACT. This may mean that companies will have to allocate any ACT asset between amounts due within one year and amounts due after more than one year as appropriate.

The liability to ACT is strictly linked to when the dividend becomes 'due and payable' and not to the actual payment of the dividend or the ACT. Accordingly, where a dividend is payable before, but is not in fact paid until after, the year end, the ACT may be set against the mainstream corporation tax liability for that year, which becomes due nine months and one day after the year end. In this case, recoverable ACT is shown as a current asset.

B   *Dividends on or after 6 April 1999*

Where a dividend is due and payable on or after 6 April 1999, there is no longer a requirement to make a payment of ACT. Outgoing dividends should therefore continue to be shown at the amount paid or payable to shareholders.

3.1.2   *Recoverable ACT*

Recoverable ACT is defined in SSAP 8 as that amount of the ACT paid or payable on outgoing dividends paid and proposed which can be:

(a)   set off against a corporation tax liability on the profits of the period under review or of previous periods; or

(b)   properly set off against a credit balance on deferred tax account; or

(c)   expected to be recoverable taking into account expected profits and dividends – normally those of the next accounting period only.

Irrecoverable ACT is defined as ACT paid or payable on outgoing dividends paid and proposed other than recoverable ACT.[67]

The amount of ACT available under (a) above is therefore the ACT paid in respect of dividends due and payable in the accounting period together with any ACT previously paid and not yet set off.

Under (b), the ACT is set against deferred tax because it would be available to relieve tax arising from the expected reversal of timing differences at some point in the future. This is considered more fully in 4.5 below.

The amount of ACT to be carried forward under (c) is ostensibly restricted by the standard to that amount which is likely to be relieved out of the taxable profits of the next accounting period, although the inclusion of the word 'normally' leaves some apparent room for manoeuvre. In certain cases, there may be a reasonable argument for carrying the ACT forward if the company foresees with reasonable certainty that its expected profits and planned dividends will allow the ACT to be relieved outside the strict one year timescale laid down by the standard. The question of carrying forward ACT as an asset is also dealt with in SSAP 15, as discussed in 3.3.3 below.

ACT which is carried forward on the grounds that it will be recovered against future taxable profits, when not shown as a reduction of the deferred tax account, should be shown as a deferred asset, and would generally be shown under the caption of 'prepayments and accrued income'.

The availability for set off of ACT is perhaps best illustrated by examples. However, because of the new shadow ACT regime in force from 6 April 1999, it is necessary to distinguish between accounting periods ending before, and those ending on or after, that date.

A   Accounting periods ending before 6 April 1999

Example 21.5:   Set off of ACT – accounting periods ending before 6 April 1999

A company has a financial year end of 31 December 1998 in which it made a taxable profit of £500,000. An interim dividend of £50,000 was paid on 26 March 1998 and the directors recommend a final dividend of £100,000, to be paid on 15 February 1999. Last year's final dividend was £150,000, and was paid on 15 February 1998. Assume a corporation tax rate of 30%.

The corporation tax provided on the taxable profits for the year would be £150,000 (30% of £500,000). The company will have submitted a return of franked payments for the quarter ended 31 March 1998, because of the final dividend for 1997 (paid on 15 February 1998) and the interim dividend for 1998 (paid on 26 March 1998). The ACT paid amounted to 20/80ths of £200,000, or £50,000. The sum due would have been paid by 14 April 1998 (14 days after the end of the quarter).

When the final dividend is paid on 15 February 1999, the company will make a second return of franked payments in respect of the quarter ending 31 March 1999. ACT of 20/80ths of £100,000, or £25,000, is therefore provided. Both the dividend and the ACT are included in the accounts for the year ended 31 December 1998. The ACT due on the final dividend will be paid by 14 April 1999.

The mainstream corporation tax liability for the year will be due nine months and one day after the year end, i.e. on 1 October 1999. The mainstream liability arising in respect of an accounting period can be reduced only by the amount of ACT relating to dividends due and payable in that accounting period (i.e. the £50,000 accounted for in the return for the quarter ended 31 March 1998, as above).

The maximum amount of ACT that can be offset is that amount of ACT which together with the related dividend absorbs the whole of the company's taxable income for the accounting period. The taxable income for the year is £500,000, so the maximum ACT which may be set off is 20% of £500,000, or £100,000. Thus the £50,000 paid in the year can be offset in full.

This is within the maximum set off allowed. Accordingly the ACT paid in respect of the 1997 final and the 1998 interim dividend can be offset against the mainstream liability. The ACT on the 1998 final dividend cannot be offset (because the dividend is not due and payable until 15 February 1999, which is after the end of the accounting period). The mainstream liability is therefore £150,000 – £50,000, or £100,000, which is a current liability at the December 1998 year end.

The ACT relating to the final dividend to be paid on 15 February 1999 cannot be netted off against the liability to mainstream corporation tax for the accounting period ended 31 December 1998. It is therefore carried forward either as a deduction from the deferred tax account (subject to certain limitations), or if this account is insufficient, as a deferred tax asset. Unless it can be relieved in any other way, the earliest date at which it may be set against a liability to corporation tax is 14 July 1999 (if the company is within the new regime for paying corporation tax by instalments), or 1 October 2000 otherwise.

B   Accounting periods ending on or after 6 April 1999

Although ACT was abolished with effect from 6 April 1999, an arrangement known as the 'shadow ACT' regime has been put in place to allow companies to recover surplus ACT paid in previous periods. The rules for shadow ACT, which are contained in The Corporation Tax (Treatment of Unrelieved Surplus Advance Corporation Tax) Regulations 1999 (SI 1999/358), are complicated and beyond the scope of this book to discuss in detail. However, their broad intention is to allow companies with surplus ACT from previous periods to recover it as if there had been no change in the law. In other words such ACT may still be offset against future liabilities to corporation tax, but only to the extent that it would have been recoverable if ACT had continued to be accounted for on dividends paid in those later periods. As a result of these rules, surplus ACT is likely to remain a rather thorny accounting issue for some years.

The examples that follow are general in nature and are not intended to cover all possible aspects of the shadow ACT system. The basic calculation of the availability for set-off of surplus ACT is as follows:

Example 21.6:   Set off of ACT – accounting periods on or after 6 April 1999

A company has a financial year end of 30 April 2000, in which it made a taxable profit of £500,000. An interim dividend of £50,000 was paid on 26 October 1999 and the directors recommend a final dividend of £100,000 to be paid on 15 May 2000. Last year's final dividend was £150,000 and was paid on 15 May 1999. It is anticipated that taxable profits in the year to 30 April 2001 will be £300,000. The company has £100,000 of unrelieved surplus ACT as at 1 May 1999 which it has not written off in its accounts. Assume a rate of corporation tax of 30%.

The relevant dividends are:

	£
15 May 1999	150,000
26 October 1999	50,000
15 May 2000	100,000

The relevant profits chargeable to corporation tax are:

	£
30 April 2000	500,000
30 April 2001	300,000

As the dividends are due and payable after 5 April 1999, there is no requirement to pay ACT. However, the company will be treated as if it had created shadow ACT on each dividend payment in the amount of 25% of that dividend. Accordingly, shadow ACT of the following amounts arises:

	Dividend	Shadow ACT
	£	£
15 May 1999	150,000	37,500
26 October 1999	50,000	12,500
		50,000
15 May 2000	100,000	25,000

In order to determine the amount of unrelieved surplus ACT which may be set against the charge to corporation tax on profits for the year ended 30 April 2000, for a company that is not a member of a group, it is necessary to:

(a)   compute the amount of profits chargeable to corporation tax ('PCTCT'). In the absence of double tax relief, the maximum capacity to use unrelieved surplus ACT and shadow ACT will be 20% of PCTCT;

(b)   offset any shadow ACT on dividends due and payable in the year ended 30 April 2000 *before* unrelieved surplus ACT is offset; and

(c)   reduce the corporation tax payable by the maximum amount of unrelieved surplus ACT that can be offset, after first fully utilising the shadow ACT.

Applying these steps to the figures above:

	£	£
Profits chargeable to corporation tax (PCTCT)		500,000
Charge to corporation tax @ 30%		150,000
Less ACT offset:		
Maximum (20% of PCTCT)	100,000	
Less shadow ACT (25% of dividends)	(50,000)	
Utilised unrelieved ACT		(50,000)
Net corporation tax payable		100,000

It can be seen that the effect of having to take account of shadow ACT is to reduce the amount of unrelieved surplus ACT recovered. In effect, companies with unrelieved surplus ACT are being treated as if the requirement to account for ACT on outgoing dividends had not been abolished. However, before finally determining that £50,000 of unrelieved surplus ACT can be set off against the current year's corporation tax liability, as implied by Example 21.6 above, it will be important to review the company's future distribution policy (including share buy-backs) and the projected level of UK taxable profits, after allowing for any double tax relief. This is because, as illustrated by Example 21.8 below, there is a potential requirement to carry back shadow ACT arising in future periods to prior periods so as to displace real ACT that has been utilised in those periods.

Assuming, however, that the company can utilise £50,000 surplus ACT as calculated above, there is now £50,000 of unrelieved surplus ACT carried forward (being the initial unrelieved surplus ACT brought forward of £100,000 less the £50,000 set off in the current year). The question therefore arises as to whether this amount can be treated as recoverable or written off as irrecoverable. This is illustrated in Example 21.7 below.

Example 21.7:   Recoverability of surplus ACT to be carried forward

It is predicted that the company in Example 21.6 above will have taxable profits of £300,000 in its accounting period to 30 April 2001. The company will therefore have ACT capacity of £60,000 for that year (being 20% of profits chargeable to corporation tax). The final dividend on 15 May 2000 creates shadow ACT of £25,000 (being 25% of the dividend paid of £100,000).

Scenario 1: Increased dividend

Suppose that the company intends to distribute half of its anticipated profits (£150,000) as an interim dividend on 26 October 2000. This will create an additional £37,500 of shadow ACT (25% of the dividend paid), giving total shadow ACT for the year to 30 April 2001 of £62,500.

As the total shadow ACT of £62,500 will exceed the company's ACT capacity for that accounting period of £60,000, it will not be possible to recover any real ACT in that period. In addition, the £2,500 excess of shadow ACT over the ACT capacity of the company may have to be carried back and displace real ACT set off against the company's liability to corporation tax in its accounting period ended 30 April 2000 (see Example 21.8 below). In such circumstances, the company should consider whether to write off the remaining ACT asset of £50,000 in its balance sheet and to provide against the anticipated carry back of shadow ACT and displacement of real ACT.

Scenario 2: Maintained dividend

In contrast, suppose that the company maintains its previous dividend level and is therefore anticipated to pay an interim dividend of £50,000 on 26 October 2000.

In this example, total shadow ACT for the year will be £37,500 (being £25,000 on the final dividend payable on 15 May 2000 and £12,500 in respect of the interim dividend payable on 26 October 2000) as against total ACT capacity of £60,000 (as calculated above). Thus, the company should be able to utilise £22,500 of real ACT in its accounting period to 30 April 2001, being £60,000 less £37,500.

It will therefore be necessary to consider whether the full £50,000 ACT asset may be recognised at 30 April 2000 or whether it will be necessary to restrict it to £22,500, being the anticipated amount of ACT which can be set against the company's liability to corporation tax in the following accounting period. To make this assessment it may be necessary to produce forecasts of UK taxable profits (after allowing for double tax relief) and the policy on returning value to shareholders by dividends or share buy-backs, in order to demonstrate that, even after allowing for shadow ACT generated each year, it will be possible to fully utilise the unrelieved surplus ACT that is to be carried forward.

As the above example illustrates, the question of whether or not ACT is recoverable is linked inextricably to a forecast of the company's distribution policy.

A further issue that must be addressed is whether shadow ACT may arise in the subsequent year which must be carried back to displace 'real' ACT utilised in the accounting period to 30 April 2000. This is illustrated in Example 21.8 below.

Example 21.8: Displacement of 'real' ACT by surplus shadow ACT carried back

Suppose that the company in Example 21.6 above paid the final dividend on 15 May 2000, and finalised its accounts for the April 2000 year end in July 2000. Later in the year, trading conditions suddenly deteriorate such that a loss for tax and accounting purposes of £100,000 arises in the year to 30 April 2001.

Shadow ACT of £25,000 is created on the payment of the dividend on 15 May 2000. As there is no current year ACT capacity (due to the tax loss), the shadow ACT Regulations require this, in effect, surplus shadow ACT of £25,000 to be carried back against surplus ACT capacity for the previous six years under the new regime and may also displace real ACT utilised in the prior accounting period (but not so as to utilise ACT capacity, or displace real ACT utilised, prior to 6 April 1999). Accordingly, it will now be necessary to consider writing off the real ACT previously set off against the company's liability to corporation tax for 30 April 2000, but now displaced by the carry-back of shadow ACT.

Assuming that the tax losses of £100,000 will also be carried back to the company's accounting period ended 30 April 2000, this will also reduce the company's capacity to utilise ACT for that year. The revised computation for 2000 would therefore be:

	£	£
Profits for year ended 30 April 2000		500,000
Less: Losses carried back from 2001		(100,000)
Revised PCTCT		400,000
Charge to corporation tax @ 30%		120,000
Less ACT offset:		
Maximum (20% of PCTCT)	80,000	
Less shadow ACT (as in Example 21.6 above)	(50,000)	
Less shadow ACT carried back	(25,000)	
Utilised unrelieved ACT		(5,000)
Net corporation tax payable		115,000

The amount of unrelieved surplus ACT is now £95,000, being the £100,000 brought forward at 1 May 1999 less the £5,000 relieved as shown above. In this example, the effect of a loss arising in the year ended 30 April 2001 has been to require £45,000 of ACT previously set against the company's liability to corporation tax to be carried forward. This results in a net increase of £15,000 in the amount of corporation tax payable in respect of the year ended 30 April 2000 (being a £30,000 reduction in the charge to corporation tax due to the loss carry-back, but a reduction of £45,000 in the amount of 'real' ACT that may be set against the company's liability to corporation tax). This may also mean that the continued recognition of the £95,000 ACT as an asset is difficult to justify without reliable future projections showing whether or not the unrelieved ACT can be utilised.

Apart from the cash flow implications, it is important to appreciate that the effect of such a write-off can be a very high effective tax rate. For example, if the unrecovered ACT were written off in full, the tax charge in the profit and loss account for the year ended April 2001 would be £65,000 (on a *loss* of £100,000), comprising:

	£
Corporation tax for the current period	–
Prior year adjustment	(30,000)
Write-off of ACT	95,000
	65,000

C   *Accounting periods straddling 6 April 1999*

Examples 21.5 to 21.8 above consider the utilisation of shadow ACT in accounting periods ending prior to, and beginning on or after, 6 April 1999. Where an accounting period begins before, and ends after 6 April 1999 (a 'straddling accounting period') there is an interaction between the prior statutory regime set out in the Income and Corporation Taxes Act 1988 ('ICTA 1988') and the shadow ACT rules.

As discussed above, a liability to ACT arises where dividends become due and payable prior to 6 April 1999. For the purposes of the statutory regime, 6 April 1999 does not represent a termination of an accounting period. Accordingly, the provisions dealing with the set off of ACT arising on dividend payments prior to 6 April 1999 against a company's liability to corporation tax for that accounting period continue to apply in respect of the straddling accounting period. However, when considering the maximum amount of ACT which may be set against the company's liability to corporation tax for the straddling accounting period, the maximum limit set out in ICTA 1988 is restricted as if the straddling period were an accounting period beginning at the beginning of the straddling accounting period and ending on 5 April 1999 ('the notional period') and there were apportioned (on a time basis) to the notional period a proportionate amount of the profits of the company for the entire straddling accounting period. Once ACT has been set against the liability to corporation tax under the statutory regime, any unrelieved ACT is carried forward into the shadow ACT Regime as 'unrelieved surplus ACT.

The shadow ACT rules treat the straddling accounting period as if it were two separate accounting periods, the first ending on 5 April 1999 and the second commencing on 6 April 1999. The profits for the straddling accounting period are apportioned to each of these notional accounting periods. The Shadow ACT Regulations permit relief for unrelieved surplus ACT as against the liability to corporation tax arising on the profits apportioned to the accounting period deemed to commence on 6 April 1999 and ending on the last day of the straddling accounting period. Although dividends which are due and payable on or after 6 April 1999 do not give rise to a liability to ACT (and can therefore be ignored in calculating the ACT offset under the prior statutory regime), they will generate shadow ACT. Accordingly, when considering whether unrelieved surplus ACT may be set against the liability to corporation tax on profits apportioned to the notional accounting period commencing on 6 April 1999, it is necessary to take into account shadow ACT created on dividend payments on or after 6 April 1999. However, shadow ACT cannot be carried back to displace 'real' ACT utilised under the prior statutory regime for the straddling accounting period.

D   Impact of shadow ACT on groups of companies

The interaction between group relief and the recoverability of ACT under the Shadow ACT Regulations is complex. Broadly, however, where a company is within a group, shadow ACT will not normally arise where the company makes a dividend payment to its parent company. However, the payment of dividends to the ultimate investors may generate shadow ACT within the parent company. Accordingly, where profits are flowed up within a group, it will usually be the ultimate parent company which creates shadow ACT.

However, shadow ACT created in any group company must be allocated within the group; in effect, there is a forced surrender of surplus shadow ACT as between group companies. In considering the recoverability of ACT in a subsidiary company's accounts, it will therefore be necessary to review the whole group's shadow ACT position.

It is also necessary to consider whether tax losses will be surrendered to a company, as this will reduce its profits chargeable to corporation tax, and thus restrict the amount of unrelieved surplus ACT and shadow ACT that it may utilise in that accounting period.

Accordingly, where either tax losses or surplus shadow ACT are surrendered to a company, it will be important to consider whether or not the recipient will be able to obtain sufficient economic benefit from its unrelieved surplus ACT in the foreseeable future to justify its recognition as an asset.

3.1.3 Incoming dividends

A Dividends before 6 April 1999

A UK company receiving a dividend paid by another UK company before 6 April 1999 was entitled to a tax credit equal to the ACT paid by the paying company. The receiving company was treated for tax purposes as receiving 'franked investment income' equal to the dividend received plus the associated tax credit. In certain circumstances, where a subsidiary paid a dividend to a parent company, it was possible to file an election for tax purposes which removed the obligation to make a payment of ACT on dividends paid between the two group companies. In such circumstances, the recipient was not treated as receiving franked investment income.

B Dividends on or after 6 April 1999

Following the abolition of ACT, in respect of dividends paid on or after 6 April 1999 the paying company no longer makes a payment of ACT, although companies may continue to receive a notional tax credit of 1/9 of the dividend received. Given that the recipient company is unable to obtain any real economic value from the credit, it may seem at least open to debate whether it should be recognised for accounting purposes. From a practical point of view, however, the ASB, in issuing FRED 18, has effectively indicated that it believes that this credit is required to be recognised by the current accounting standard SSAP 8 (see C below).

C Requirements of SSAP 8

SSAP 8 discusses two possible ways of dealing with franked investment income in the accounts:

(a) to bring into the profit and loss account the cash received or receivable; or
(b) to bring in the full amount of the franked investment income, i.e. including the tax credit, with an equivalent amount treated as part of the tax charge.[68]

The standard requires the second option to be adopted on the basis that it allows recognition of the income at both the pre-tax and the post-tax stage in a way which is consistent with every other item of income and expenditure. Accordingly, incoming dividends from United Kingdom resident companies are included in the profit and loss account at the amount of cash received plus the related tax credit.[69]

As noted in B above, it is questionable whether this treatment makes sense in the light of all the changes to the tax system since the introduction of the imputation system in the early 1970s. In 1997, the ASB indicated that, in its view, SSAP 8 does not require the grossing up of franked investment income on shares held as trading assets by banks and others (which are in fact taxed on the net amount received). The Board also stated that tax-exempt entities such as pension schemes (which were no longer able to claim repayment of the tax credit following the July 1997 Budget) 'should consider the most appropriate presentation of dividend income in the transitional period'.[70] This was taken as a broad hint that it was acceptable for such entities not to gross up incoming UK dividends, even though a strict application of SSAP 8 would have required them to gross up dividends and show a tax charge (equal to the now irrecoverable tax credit). Charities and other bodies able to claim some repayment of tax credits should, in our view, gross up incoming dividends by the actual amount repayable.

In June 1999 the ASB issued FRED 18 (see 3.2 below), which proposes that franked investment income should no longer be grossed up. Particular issues for companies in the immediate future are:

(a)   whether they should continue to gross up franked investment income received in the light of FRED 18; and

(b)   if so, whether a distinction should be made between incoming dividends paid before 6 April 1999, and those thereafter, on the grounds that the tax credit on the latter has no real economic significance.

On the general issue of whether SSAP 8 should continue to be applied, the *Foreword to Accounting Standards* states unambiguously: 'An exposure draft is issued for comment and is subject to revision. Until it is converted into an accounting standard the requirements of any existing accounting standards that would be affected by proposals in the exposure draft remain in force.'[71] Therefore, until SSAP 8 is formally withdrawn, companies must comply with it. On the more specific question of whether incoming dividends paid before 6 April 1999 should be treated differently from others, it is, in our view, appropriate to have regard to FRED 18, under which it is clear that no distinction will be made.

SSAP 8 does not address the equivalent treatment of Foreign Income Dividends. However, they were mentioned in passing by the UITF in its sixteenth Abstract, to the effect that: 'in the case of Foreign Income Dividends, there is no tax credit and no adjustment to the amount of the dividend received is to be made'.[72] SSAP 8 also does not deal with income received subject to withholding tax, although in practice, companies have tended to gross this up in the same way as franked investment income, a treatment now formally proposed in FRED 18 (see 3.2 below).

3.1.4   *Disclosure of the tax charge in the profit and loss account*

SSAP 8 requires that the following items be included in the tax charge in the profit and loss account and, where material, be separately disclosed:

(a)   the amount of the United Kingdom corporation tax specifying:

    (i)   the charge for corporation tax on the income of the year (where such corporation tax includes transfers between the deferred tax account and the profit and loss account these should also be separately disclosed where material),

(ii)   tax attributable to franked investment income,

(iii) irrecoverable ACT,

(iv)   the relief for overseas taxation; and

(b)   the total overseas taxation, relieved and unrelieved.[73]

As general guidance, Appendix 1 to the standard gives one method of showing (by way of note) the required information, whilst acknowledging that in simple cases the information may be given entirely within the profit and loss account. Appendix 1 is as follows:

	£'000
Corporation tax on income at x per cent	
(including £b transferred to/from deferred taxation account)	a
Less relief for overseas taxation	c
	d
Overseas taxation	e
Tax credit on UK dividends received	f
Irrecoverable advance corporation tax	g
	H

In practice, most companies show corporation tax and deferred tax as separate items rather than in the above format, as will be seen from several extracts in this chapter. The analysis of the tax charge made by Barclays gives examples of most of the disclosures required by SSAP 8.

Extract 21.5: Barclays PLC (1998)

12 Tax [extract]

	1998	1997	1996
The charge for tax assumes an effective UK corporation tax rate of 31% (1997 31.5%, 1996 33%) and comprises:	**£m**	£m	£m
Current tax:			
United Kingdom	**378**	436	291
Overseas	**171**	114	151
Total current tax	**549**	550	442
Deferred tax (credit)/charge:			
United Kingdom	**(19)**	1	169
Overseas	**4**	(14)	(1)
Total deferred tax	**(15)**	(13)	168
Associated undertakings, including overseas tax of £3m (1997 and 1996 £5m)	**4**	5	10
Total charge	**538**	542	620

A   Tax rate

If the rate of corporation tax is not known for the whole or part of the period covered by the accounts, the latest known rate should be used and disclosed.[74]

If the company's accounting period is other than a year ending 31 March in a period of changing rates of corporation tax, the rate applied to the profits will need to be apportioned. For example, for a company with an accounting period ending on 31 December 1999, the first three months of the company's profit fall to be taxed at 31%, being the rate applicable up to 31 March 1999, and the remainder at the rate of 30% which applies for the following year. The following calculation gives the effective rate of tax to be disclosed in the accounts:

		%
The period January to March 1999	3/12 @ 31% =	7.75
The period April to December 1999	9/12 @ 30% =	22.50
Effective rate of corporation tax		30.25

The Companies Act used to require the corporation rate tax rate to be disclosed in all cases. Whilst this requirement no longer applies, many companies continue to give the information. As can be seen from the following extract,

BOC discloses the effective corporation tax rate not only for the UK but also for the other main jurisdictions in which the group has operations.

Extract 21.6: The BOC Group plc (1998)

4. Tax [extract]

a) Tax on profit on ordinary activities

	1998	1997	1996
	£ million	£ million	£ million
Payable in the UK			
Corporation tax at 31% (1997: 33%/31%, 1996: 33%)	**79.3**	89.8	108.9
Advance corporation tax (ACT)	**(15.6)**	(4.0)	(11.2)
Double tax relief	**(21.6)**	(30.0)	(44.1)
	42.1	55.8	53.6
Payable overseas			
US – Federal tax at 35% (1997 and 1996: Federal alternative minimum tax at 20%)	**1.1**	1.8	3.7
– State and local taxes	**1.4**	2.6	3.0
Australia at 36% (1997: 36%, 1996: 36%)	**14.4**	14.6	13.6
South Africa at 35% (1997: 35%, 1996: 35%)	**9.2**	9.2	14.8
Japan at 51% (1997: 51%, 1996: 51%)	**6.9**	10.6	6.2
Other countries	**41.8**	25.7	30.8
	74.8	64.5	72.1
Provision for deferred tax – overseas	**(12.4)**	(0.1)	1.8
Share of tax charge arising in joint ventures	**8.9**	8.0	7.7
Share of tax charge arising in associates	**0.6**	0.9	2.7
	114.0	129.1	137.9

The tax charge includes a credit of £30.8 million for the operating exceptional charges and a charge of £30.0 million for the sale of the Ohmeda health care business. The effective rate of tax excluding the operating exceptional charges and sale of the Ohmeda health care business was 29 per cent (1997: 29 per cent, 1996: 31 per cent).

The share of the tax charge of joint ventures and associates is given in compliance with FRS 9 – *Associates and joint ventures* – see Chapter 7 at 3.1.1 A (see also Extract 21.5 above). The footnote information is given in compliance with the Companies Act and FRS 3 requirements to give information on 'special circumstances' affecting the tax charge (see 3.4 below).

B   Irrecoverable ACT

As noted above, the standard requires that the amount of irrecoverable ACT should be separately disclosed if material. This is required because although the most appropriate treatment is to regard the irrecoverable amount as a charge to tax on the company's profits (the alternative view being that it is part of an appropriation), some readers or analysts may wish to regard ACT 'in some other manner',[75] and separate disclosure enables them to make any adjustment they deem necessary.

C   *Unrelieved overseas tax*

Appendix 2 to the standard considers the case of unrelieved overseas tax. If the rate of overseas tax on the company's overseas income exceeds the rate of UK tax, then the excess element of the overseas tax will be unrelieved.

3.2   FRED 18

As noted in 3.1.3 above, the requirement of SSAP 8 to gross up franked investment income is hard to reconcile with the economic reality of the abolition of ACT in April 1999. Even in the previous edition of this book, we questioned whether SSAP 8 made sense in the light of the July 1997 Budget, under which pension funds and UK companies could no longer claim a repayment of the tax credit, and banks were taxed on the (net) dividend income received on investments held as trading assets.

In October 1997 the ASB issued, at the recommendation of the UITF, a short FRED with a long title – *Amendment to SSAP 8 'The treatment of taxation under the imputation system in the accounts of companies': Presentation of dividend income*. This proposed amending SSAP 8 so as to remove the requirement to gross up the profit and loss account for the tax credit on franked investment income. The FRED expressed the hope, which then seemed almost a foregone conclusion, that this amendment would be effective for December 1997 year ends.[76]

In November 1997, however, the Chancellor of the Exchequer announced a far-reaching review of the tax system, together with an intention to abolish ACT altogether with effect from April 1999. The ASB therefore decided, on the UITF's recommendation, to defer any changes to SSAP 8, and possibly incorporate them in its scheduled FRS on deferred tax. By April 1999, however, the FRS on deferred tax had still not appeared, but the abolition of ACT made it impossible to delay revision of SSAP 8 any longer. Accordingly in June 1999 the ASB issued FRED 18 – *Current tax*; this is intended to replace SSAP 8 and UITF 16 when converted into an FRS, which we assume will occur in time for the new FRS to apply to December 1999, or at the latest March 2000, year-ends.

FRED 18 notes that, although the ASB has decided to issue a FRED dealing only with current tax at this stage, the FRSs on current and deferred tax may eventually be amalgamated.[77] This is very much to be hoped for since, as we note below (see particularly section 4.5), there are some unfortunate inconsistencies between SSAPs 8 and 15. It would be regrettable if these were perpetuated, or new ones created, which is more likely to happen if they are replaced by two standards than one.

3.2.1 Proposed requirements of FRED 18

A Allocation of current tax charge to the primary statements

Current tax should be recognised in the profit and loss account, except to the extent that it relates to items recognised in the statement of total recognised gains and losses (STRGL).[78] Tax relating to such items should also be recognised in the STRGL.[79] The FRED notes that in exceptional circumstances it may be impossible to determine the tax relating to items in the STRGL, in which case the total tax should be allocated on either a reasonable pro-rata basis, or using another method that achieves a more appropriate allocation in the circumstances.[80]

The effect of this, if read literally, is to require tax relating to items recognised in neither the profit and loss account or STRGL, but only in the reconciliation of movements in shareholders' funds, to be recognised in the profit and loss account rather than in the reconciliation of movements in shareholders' funds. It is not clear whether this reflects a definite intention or is a drafting slip. Such items do occur, albeit rarely. An example is tax relief in some jurisdictions for goodwill which has been set off against reserves in accordance with SSAP 22 and the transitional arrangements in FRS 10.

A further issue not dealt with by FRED 18, although it was addressed in the 1995 Discussion Paper, is whether tax relating to an item in the STRGL means an item in the STRGL of the current year only or also those of previous years. The problem is best explained with an example:

Example 21.9: Allocation of tax between P&L account and STRGL

A company bought a plot of land in 1986 for £2 million. In 1995 it revalued it to £4 million, but provided no deferred tax on the gain on the basis that no disposal was anticipated in the foreseeable future. In 1999 an opportunity for disposal suddenly arises and the land is sold for £5 million. Tax payable is £500,000, after allowing for indexation relief of £1.3m (these are purely notional figures and are not intended to represent the actual UK tax position).

In pre-tax terms the company will have recognised total gains of £3 million (£2 million in the STRGL in 1995 and £1 million in the profit and loss account in 1999). Should the tax of £500,000 be:

(a)   recognised entirely in the profit and loss account in 1999? This had the disadvantage that the profit and loss account is being charged with all the tax on a gain that has been recognised only partly in that statement;

(b)   allocated between the profit and loss account and the STRGL pro-rata to the pre-tax gains, such that £166,667 (£500,000 x £1,000,000/£3,000,000) is dealt with in the profit and loss account and the balance of £333,333 in the STRGL? This has the disadvantage that a tax charge appears in the 1999 STRGL without a corresponding pre-tax gain being shown (because it was included in the 1995 accounts); or

(c)   allocated between the profit and loss account and the STRGL on some basis that reflects the fact that the indexation relief (being a relief for inflation) relates more to the first £2 million of the gain recognised in the STRGL in 1995 than to the £1 million recognised in the profit and loss account in 1999? This could be done by calculating the tax that would have arisen on a disposal in 1995 and allocating this to the STRGL, with the balance of the amount actually paid being shown in the profit and loss account. This has the advantage of being arguably the most accurate method, but the disadvantage of being somewhat esoteric and complicated. It also relies on the tax system remaining substantially unchanged.

In our view, taking into account the requirements of SSAP 15 and FRS 3 and simplicity of calculation, (b) is the best answer.

B   *Transactions taxed at non-standard rates*

Income and expenses taxed at non-standard rates should be included in the pre-tax results at the actual amounts receivable and payable and not grossed up to reflect the notional amount of additional tax that would have arisen if the transaction had been taxed, or allowed for tax, on a different basis.[81] This simply repeats the requirements of UITF 16 (see 2.3.3 above), which will be withdrawn once FRED 18 becomes an FRS.[82]

C   *Withholding tax and UK tax credits*

Incoming UK dividends should be recognised net of the UK tax credit (i.e. at the amount received), irrespective of the date of receipt.[83] Incoming dividends, interest or other amounts paid subject to withholding tax should be recognised at an amount including the withholding tax, and the effect of such withholding tax taken into account as part of the tax charge.[84]

Outgoing dividends (including those proposed or declared and not yet payable) should be included net of any UK credit (i.e at the amount paid). Outgoing dividends, interest or other amounts paid subject to deduction of withholding tax should include the withholding tax deducted.[85]

The broad thrust of the proposals (to gross up income for withholding tax, but not for UK tax credits) is supported by a 'majority' of the ASB, on the grounds that franked investment income is effectively tax free, whereas income subject to withholding tax is fully taxable at the gross amount received, albeit with relief for the withholding tax paid.[86] We concur with this view.

However, the indications are that the majority on the ASB supporting this view may be very slender, since the FRED sets out at some length the arguments for the two alternative views, i.e. that income should be grossed up for both withholding tax and UK tax credits, or that it should be grossed up for neither.

The argument for grossing up income for both withholding tax and UK tax credits is that both are income on which the recipient is liable to reduced or nil tax as a result of tax already paid (either as UK corporation tax in the case of franked investment income, or withholding taxes in other cases). 'Grossing up then becomes necessary to reflect the greater value of 100 received as dividend (no tax consequences) compared with 100 earned as trading profit (taxable).'[87] The flaw in this argument, in our view, is that it implies that franked investment income should be grossed up not by the largely notional 1/9 tax credit, but rather by the marginal tax rate of the paying company, which we presume is not what those whose views it represents intended.

The argument for not grossing up for either withholding tax or UK tax credits is essentially that this is consistent with the normal requirements (see B above) for income taxed at non-standard rates. This view sees income that has suffered withholding tax as net income subject to a non-standard rate of tax rather than gross income subject to a standard rate.[88] We can see some merit in this view, although we find the position taken in the FRED much more convincing.

D   Disclosure

The following major components of current tax income (expense) for the period in the profit and loss account and statement of total recognised gains and losses should be disclosed separately:

(a)   current tax expense (income) for the current period; and

(b)   any adjustments recognised in the period for current tax of prior periods,

analysed in each case between UK and foreign taxation.[89] A suggested, but non-mandatory, presentation of a note to the profit and loss account giving this information, and that required by the Companies Act 1985, is given in Appendix I to the FRED as follows.

		£000
Current tax on income of this period		a
Of which:		
UK	b	
foreign	c	
	a	
Adjustments in the period for current tax of prior periods		d
Of which:		
UK	e	
foreign	f	
	d	
Total charge to UK and foreign corporation tax before double tax relief		a+d
Double tax relief		h
		a+d-h

The tax rate(s) used (see E below) should also be disclosed.[90]

E   *Tax rate to be used*

Where the corporation tax rate has not been enacted for the whole or part of the period covered by the accounts, the latest enacted rate should be used unless legislation setting a new rate has been 'substantively enacted' by the balance sheet date. A UK tax rate is to be taken as 'substantively enacted' if it is included in either:

(a)   a Bill that has been passed by the House of Commons and is awaiting only passage through the House of Lords and Royal Assent; or

(b)   a resolution having statutory effect that has been passed under the Provisional Collection of Taxes Act 1968.[91]

This proposed requirement has been introduced for conformity with the requirements of IAS 12 (see 5.1.3 C below). There is currently no guidance on this issue in UK standards, but current UK practice tends to be to calculate tax provisions based on what has been announced in the latest Budget before the accounts are approved, rather than on the law as 'substantially enacted' in the terms above at the balance sheet date. This issue is discussed further at 4.6 below. In our view, current practice generally gives the better estimate of the true liability to tax, particularly where deferred tax is concerned.

Whether by accident or design, FRED 18 prohibits companies from anticipating unenacted future tax rates, but not other aspects of the tax legislation. By contrast IAS 12 requires the reporting enterprise to have regard to both tax rates and laws as enacted (see 5.1.3 C below).

F   *Recoverability of ACT*

Appendix II to FRED 18 reproduces, without substantial change, the rules governing the recoverability of ACT in SSAP 8, but noting that the shadow ACT system may have some impact on whether or not ACT can be considered recoverable (see 3.1.2 above).

3.3   SSAP 15

3.3.1   *General approach*

The standard indicates that it is concerned with accounting for tax on profits and surpluses which are recognised in the accounts in one period but assessed in another. It thus relates primarily to deferred corporation tax and income tax in the United Kingdom and in the Republic of Ireland and, insofar as the principles are similar, to overseas taxes on profits payable by UK and Irish enterprises or their subsidiaries.[92]

Interestingly, the standard considers other taxes also, by providing that 'a number of other taxes, including value added tax, petroleum revenue tax and some overseas taxes, are not assessed directly on profits for an accounting period and are therefore not addressed specifically in this statement. For such taxes, enterprises should generally follow the principle underlying this statement, that deferred tax should be provided to the extent that it is probable that a liability or asset will crystallise but not to the extent that it is probable that a liability or asset will not crystallise.'[93]

The standard chooses the partial provision method as its general approach, and summarises it as follows:

'Deferred tax should be accounted for in respect of the net amount by which it is probable that any payment of tax will be temporarily deferred or accelerated by the operation of timing differences which will reverse in the foreseeable future without being replaced. Partial provision recognises that, if an enterprise is not expected to reduce the scale of its operations significantly, it will often have what amounts to a hard core of timing differences so that the payment of some tax will be permanently deferred. On this basis, deferred tax has to be provided only where it is probable that tax will become payable as a result of the reversal of timing differences.'[94]

The standard considers that there are two main methods of computation, the liability method and the deferral method. It then points out that the liability method is the method consistent with the aim of partial provision, which is to provide the deferred tax which it is probable will be payable or recoverable.[95]

3.3.2 Definitions

Part 2 of the standard contains the definitions of the terms that are used throughout its text.

Deferred tax is the tax attributable to timing differences.[96]

Timing differences are differences between profits or losses as computed for tax purposes and results as stated in financial statements, which arise from the inclusion of items of income and expenditure in tax computations in periods different from those in which they are included in financial statements. Timing differences originate in one period and are capable of reversal in one or more subsequent periods.[97]

The following definitions are given for specific timing differences:

(a) a loss for tax purposes which is available to relieve future profits from tax constitutes a timing difference;[98]

(b) the revaluation of an asset (including an investment in an associated or subsidiary company) will create a timing difference when it is incorporated into the balance sheet, insofar as the profit or loss that would result from realisation at the revalued amount is taxable, unless disposal of the revalued asset and of any subsequent replacement assets would not result in a tax liability, after taking account of any expected rollover relief;[99]

(c)   the retention of earnings overseas will create a timing difference only if:

   (i)   there is an intention or obligation to remit them; and

   (ii)   remittance would result in a tax liability after taking account of any related double tax relief.[100]

The *liability method* is a method of computing deferred tax whereby it is calculated at the rate of tax that it is estimated will be applicable when the timing differences reverse. Under the liability method deferred tax not provided is calculated at the expected long-term tax rate.[101]

3.3.3   Detailed accounting requirements

A   Method of computation

Deferred tax should be computed under the liability method. Tax deferred or accelerated by the effect of timing differences should be accounted for to the extent that it is probable that a liability or asset will crystallise. Tax deferred or accelerated by the effect of timing differences should not be accounted for to the extent that it is probable that a liability or asset will not crystallise.[102] For this purpose, the combined effect of all timing differences should be considered rather than looking at individual categories in isolation,[103] except that timing differences relating to post-retirement benefits may be considered separately and provided for in full as a result of the amendment to SSAP 15 referred to in 2.2.7 above.

B   Future projections

The assessment of whether deferred tax liabilities or assets will or will not crystallise should be based upon reasonable assumptions. The assumptions should take into account all relevant information available up to the date on which the accounts are approved by the board of directors, and also the intentions of management. Ideally this information will include financial plans or projections covering a period of years sufficient to enable an assessment to be made of the likely pattern of future tax liabilities. A prudent view should be taken in the assessment of whether a tax liability will crystallise, particularly where the financial plans or projections are susceptible to a high degree of uncertainty or are not fully developed for the appropriate period.[104]

Under the original SSAP 15, it was easy for an enterprise to ignore the partial provision approach and to remain fully provided, simply by failing to produce, or pleading an inability to produce, future plans or projections. Under the revised requirements, it is theoretically not permissible to do this, as there are two separate requirements: to provide for the tax that is expected to crystallise, and not to provide for tax that is not expected to crystallise. However, an inability to foresee the future with enough clarity may still lead to full provision in practice. Moreover, changes in the tax system since SSAP 15 was introduced mean that many companies do effectively make provision for deferred tax except in respect of such contingent liabilities as the remittance of overseas earnings and the realisation of revaluation gains. Examples are Laporte and EMI (see Extracts 21.11 and 21.12 at 3.3.4 below).

There is no longer a minimum time period which should be covered by the projections, which is a change from SSAP 15 in its original form, where 'normally three years' was quoted, although the Appendix to the standard now mentions a period of three to five years as an example of a relatively short period which might be appropriate where the pattern of timing differences is expected to be regular.[105] In practice the projection will obviously become less reliable the further into the future it goes, and the period which may be forecast with a reasonable degree of accuracy is perhaps no more than two years. Much depends on whether a pattern of originating or reversing timing differences can be discerned, which will depend on such factors as whether expansion is envisaged, and whether capital expenditure has a cyclical nature.

Each year the pattern of expected timing differences should be compared against the reversal of timing differences experienced in the past. Plans and projections require regular review; they can be influenced by many indirectly related factors, for example the reassessment of asset lives, a decision to close part of the business which renders certain assets no longer needed, or the provision of a sum in respect of the permanent diminution of an asset.

It is important that the plans and projections are based on reasonable and realistic assumptions. In particular, a planned expansion programme may allow timing differences to be projected as continuing to originate well into the future, but the working capital resources to finance the expansion need to be available to the enterprise for that expansion programme to take place.

C   *Debit balances*

(a)   General

The provision for deferred tax liabilities should be reduced by any deferred tax debit balances arising from separate categories of timing differences and any advance corporation tax which is available for offset against those liabilities.[106] This provides for the situation where there is advance corporation tax recoverable (in excess of the mainstream tax liability), which will effectively rank as a payment on account for the tax due on the future reversal of any timing differences. Further, it allows unrelieved tax losses to be netted off against deferred tax liabilities.

Deferred tax net debit balances should not be carried forward as assets, except to the extent that they are expected to be recoverable without replacement by equivalent debit balances.[107] This is simply the obverse of the same rule for liabilities. Under SSAP 15, a liability is not provided where there is a 'hard core' of timing differences which represent a perpetual postponement of tax; correspondingly, a hard core of timing differences which represents a permanent acceleration of the tax liability should not be regarded as an asset.

(b) Tax losses

Particular guidance is given in the Appendix to the standard on when it is permitted to regard tax losses as recoverable assets (which is distinguishable from when they may be set off against deferred tax liabilities). The conditions to be satisfied are as follows:

(i)   the loss has resulted from an identifiable and non-recurring cause; and

(ii) the enterprise, or predecessor enterprise, has been consistently profitable over a considerable period, with any past losses being more than offset by income in subsequent periods; and

(iii) it is assured beyond reasonable doubt that future taxable profits will be sufficient to offset the current loss during the carry-forward period prescribed by tax legislation.[108]

There are corresponding rules relating to capital losses, which prescribe the following conditions:

(i)   a potential chargeable gain not expected to be covered by rollover relief is present in assets which have not been revalued in the financial statements to reflect that gain and which are not essential to the future operations of the enterprise; and

(ii) the enterprise has decided to dispose of these assets and thus realise the potential chargeable gain; and

(iii) the unrealised chargeable gain (after allowing for any possible loss in value before disposal) is sufficient to offset the loss in question, such that it is assured beyond reasonable doubt that a tax liability on the relevant portion of the chargeable gain will not crystallise.[109]

(c) ACT

Debit balances arising in respect of advance corporation tax on dividends payable or proposed at the balance sheet date should be carried forward to the extent that it is foreseen that sufficient corporation tax will be assessed on the profits or income of the succeeding accounting period, against which the advance corporation tax is available for offset.[110] A summary of the rules for the offset of ACT is given in 3.1.2 above.

The standard requires that debit balances arising in respect of ACT other than on dividends payable or proposed at the balance sheet date should be written off unless their recovery is assured beyond reasonable doubt. It further provides that such recovery will normally be assured only where the debit balances are recoverable out of corporation tax arising on profits or income of the succeeding accounting period, without replacement by equivalent debit balances.[111]

As discussed further at 4.5.1 below, there is some tension between the requirements of SSAP 15, which appear to treat ACT recoverable as more in the nature of a timing difference, and those of SSAP 8, which treat it more as a straightforward receivable. However, the abolition of ACT means that in future ACT assets will not be replaced by equivalent debit balances as new ACT will simply not arise in future periods.

3.3.4 Disclosure

The standard requires disclosure of the following:

(a) The amount of deferred tax charged or credited in the profit and loss account for the period, split between that relating to ordinary activities and that relating to any extraordinary items.[112]

There is also a requirement within FRS 3 to disclose the amount of taxation (i.e. not just deferred taxation) attributable to extraordinary items, as well as that relating to certain exceptional items.[113]

(b) The amount of any unprovided deferred tax in respect of the period, analysed into its major components.[114] The following extract shows this disclosure:

Extract 21.7: John Lewis Partnership plc (1999)

7 TAX ON PROFIT ON ORDINARY ACTIVITIES

	1999 £m	1998 £m
Corporation tax based on the profit for the year	**46.1**	47.5
Deferred tax	**0.7**	2.4
	46.8	49.9

The tax charge is based on a corporation tax rate of 31% (31%) and has been reduced by £6.3m (£2.8m) as a result of capital allowances in excess of depreciation.

Total taxation deferred and unprovided in respect of all capital allowances in excess of depreciation amounts to £90.9m (£84.6m) based on corporation tax at 31% (31%).

No provision has been made in these accounts for the liability to taxation of £33.1m (£20.2m) on capital gains, which would arise if properties were to be sold at the amounts at which they have been revalued and included in these accounts.

The wording of the requirement in the standard presupposes that the effect to be disclosed is of new originating differences for which no provision is made. However, sometimes companies have to disclose the opposite effect – that the tax charge for the year has been increased by unanticipated reversals.

(c)   Any adjustments to deferred tax passing through the profit and loss account which relate to changes in tax rates or in tax allowances. The effect of any fundamental change in the tax system should be separately disclosed within the tax charge on the face of the profit and loss account.[115] Before FRS 3 was issued, the effect of such a change was treated as an extraordinary item if it was sufficiently material,[116] but this is no longer possible.

(d)   The deferred tax balance, analysed into its major components, and the amount of unprovided deferred tax, similarly analysed.[117] Where no information on unprovided deferred tax in respect of a revalued asset is given on the grounds that it is argued not to be a timing difference (because it will never crystallise), the fact that the potential liability has not been quantified should be stated.[118] Brunel Holdings' accounts contain the following example of this analysis:

Extract 21.8: Brunel Holdings plc (1998)

19. Deferred tax [extract]

	Provided		Unprovided	
	1998	1997	**1998**	1997
	£000	£000	**£000**	£000
Capital allowances in excess of depreciation	**424**	603	**(25)**	(15)
Other timing differences	**304**	545	**(306)**	(263)
Losses available for offset	**(335)**	(349)	**(2,999)**	(7,624)
Pension prepayment	**–**	–	**–**	6,108
	393	799	**(3,330)**	(1,794)

No deferred tax liability is expected to arise in the foreseeable future on realisation of properties, and accordingly this is not provided or quantified.

Another example of a company not quantifying the tax deferred by roll-over relief is Laporte (see Extract 21.11 below).

Rather than analysing the *unprovided* amount as required by the standard, many companies continue to follow the requirement of the original SSAP 15 (before it was amended in 1985) to show the full potential liability and the amount which has been provided, analysed by category.[119] Of course, this information allows the reader to derive the analysis of the unprovided amount, by a simple process of subtraction. An example of this form of disclosure is to be found in the accounts of The Davis Service Group:

Extract 21.9: The Davis Service Group Plc (1998)

20 Provisions for liabilities and charges

	Group 1998 £000	Group 1997 £000	Company 1998 £000	Company 1997 £000
(a) The provisions for liabilities and charges comprise deferred taxation which is attributable to:				
Excess of tax allowances over depreciation	**5,259**	4,088	–	–
Other timing differences	**(35)**	(66)	**4**	(27)
	5,224	4,022	**4**	(27)
The movement during the year in the provision for deferred tax was:				
Beginning of the year	**4,022**	5,545	**(27)**	(32)
Disposal of subsidiaries	–	26	–	–
Currency translation differences	**10**	–	–	–
Movement in respect of current and prior years	**1,192**	(1,496)	**31**	5
End of year	**5,224**	4,022	**4**	(27)
(b) The full potential amount of deferred taxation on all timing differences, including amounts provided, is as follows:				
Excess of tax allowances over depreciation	**8,294**	7,740	**(48)**	(60)
Other timing differences	**(1,802)**	(2,004)	**(69)**	(106)
Attributable to trading activities	**6,492**	5,736	**(117)**	(166)
Corporation tax on capital gains arising on the disposal of properties that have been deferred under the roll-over provisions	**1,368**	1,358	–	–
Taxes that would arise if properties were to be disposed of at their revalued amounts	**664**	775	–	–

It is arguable that the analysis of the full potential liability in fact gives much more meaningful information than can be obtained by analysing the amount which has been provided or the amount which has not been provided. Since SSAP 15 specifies that all categories of timing difference are to be considered in aggregate rather than individually for the purposes of deciding the overall net reversal which is to be provided for, it often makes little sense to try to say which particular category has been included in the provision and which has not.

Unusually, Arjo Wiggins Appleton grosses up its net deferred tax provision to show deferred tax assets and liabilities separately, as shown below. The basis of the split, however, is not made clear:

Extract 21.10: Arjo Wiggins Appleton p.l.c. (1998)

17. Provisions for liabilities and charges [extract]

	Deferred taxation
Group	£m
At 31 December 1997	12.4
Deferred taxation asset included in debtors (see note 14)	(6.6)
Net deferred taxation balance at 31 December 1997	5.8
Currency retranslation	0.2
Net charge/(release) to profit and loss account	6.3
Net deferred taxation balance at 31 December 1998	12.3
Deferred taxation asset included in debtors (see note 14)	4.8
At 31 December 1998	**17.1**

(e)   Transfers to and from the deferred tax balance.[120]

An example of this disclosure is given in the accounts of Laporte:

Extract 21.11: Laporte plc (1998)

18 Provisions for liabilities and charges [extract]

	Deferred tax (see below) £m
Balance at start of year	**32.8**
Profit and loss account	
Before exceptional items	**(10.9)**
Exceptional items – charge	**(0.9)**
Acquisition of subsidiary undertakings	**10.6**
Disposal of subsidiary undertakings	**(0.2)**
Advance corporation tax	**11.6**
Currency translation differences	**1.4**
Balance at end of year	**44.4**

	1998 £m	1997 £m
Deferred tax is represented by		
Excess of book values of fixed assets over those for taxation purposes	**35.9**	46.4
Other timing differences	**8.5**	(1.9)
Advance corporation tax	–	(11.7)
	44.4	32.8

Deferred taxation is provided in full with the exception of any further tax that would be payable on the retained profits of overseas companies where there is currently no intention to remit to the UK. Current tax is provided, if appropriate, when it is known that profits will be remitted to the UK. Deferred taxation has not been quantified on roll-over relief claims on the basis that they do not constitute timing differences.

(f)   Movements in reserves which relate to deferred tax.[121]

(g)   Where the value of an asset is disclosed by way of note and differs from its book value, the tax effect of disposing of it at that value.[122]

(h)   Any assumptions regarding the availability of group relief and the payment therefor which are relevant to an understanding of the company's deferred tax position.[123]

(i)   The fact (if applicable) that provision has not been made for tax which would become payable if retained earnings of foreign subsidiaries were remitted to the UK.[124]

EMI includes the following footnote in its accounts to explain this point:

Extract 21.12: EMI Group plc (1998)

22. DEFERRED TAXATION [extract]

No provision has been made for further taxes which could arise if subsidiary or associated undertakings are disposed of or if overseas companies were to remit dividends to the UK in excess of those anticipated in these accounts: it is considered impracticable to estimate the amount of such taxes.

...

There is no unprovided deferred tax liability as at 31 March 1998.

Cable & Wireless similarly makes no provision, but quantifies the unprovided amount:

Extract 21.13: Cable and Wireless plc (1999)

21(i) Deferred taxation [extract]

The potential deferred tax liability does not include an amount of £862m (1998 – £769m) of contingent tax liability arising on the reserves of overseas subsidiaries, associates and joint ventures which the Group does not expect to remit to the United Kingdom.

Companies sometimes disclose positively that they make provision for this liability where appropriate, an example being Laporte (see Extract 21.11 above).

3.4   FRS 2

In July 1992, the ASB published FRS 2 – *Accounting for subsidiary undertakings* – which added a further layer of complication to the rules on the disclosure of the potential tax liability on the distribution of retained earnings of overseas subsidiaries. It requires disclosure of:

(a)   the extent to which deferred tax has been accounted for in respect of future remittances of the accumulated reserves of overseas subsidiary undertakings; and

(b)   the reason for not making full provision (unless provision has been made in full).[125]

Item (a) seems redundant, because SSAP 15 already requires the deferred tax balance to be analysed into its main components. Moreover, item (b) appears to be based on the premise that full remittance of profits is the norm from which deviations must be explained, and also that there would not usually be any offsetting effects which would limit the tax payable in such an eventuality. This does not seem to be a realistic foundation on which to base the rule, and it does not seem to have resulted in the provision of much useful information. Other problems inherent in this disclosure are discussed in more detail at 4.8 below.

An example of a company giving the disclosures required by FRS 2 is Glaxo Wellcome.

Extract 21.14: Glaxo Wellcome plc (1998)

8   Taxation [extract]

Save as shown in these accounts, no provision has been made for taxation which would arise on the distribution of profits retained by overseas subsidiary and associated undertakings, on the grounds that no remittance of profit retained at 31st December 1998 is required in such a way incremental tax will arise.

...

Deferred taxation asset/(liability)

	Full potential At 31.12.98 £m	At 31.12.97 £m	Provided At 31.12.98 £m	At 31.12.97 £m
Accelerated capital allowances	**(406)**	(506)	**(16)**	(22)
Unremitted foreign investment income	**(4)**	(18)	**(4)**	(18)
Stock valuation adjustment	**(8)**	(11)	**(8)**	(11)
Intra-group profit	**116**	107	**4**	9
Pensions and other post-retirement benefits	**105**	104	**105**	104
Integration costs	**17**	49	**17**	49
Other timing differences	**144**	196	**123**	114
Advance corporation tax recoverable	**–**	37	**–**	–
	(36)	(42)	**221**	225

3.5   Companies Act 1985

The Companies Act also imposes various disclosure requirements in relation to taxation. These can be summarised as follows:

(a)   any special circumstances affecting the liability to tax on profits, income or capital gains for the current or future years.[126] (There is a similar requirement in FRS 3, which also requires the individual effects to be quantified.)[127]

A note containing examples of these disclosures can be found in the accounts of Great Universal Stores:

Extract 21.15: The Great Universal Stores P.L.C. (1999)

8.   TAX ON PROFIT ON ORDINARY ACTIVITIES [extract]

	1999 £m	1998 £m
The tax charge includes the following amounts attributable to exceptional items:		
Tax relief on closure costs of Argos Holland	(3.3)	
Tax on refund of VAT	7.3	21.8
Tax on sale of Superior Acceptance Corporation Limited		7.5
Tax relief on closure of the Canadian retail company		(5.3)
	4.0	24.0

The Group's effective rate of taxation has reduced this year from 30.2% to 28.3%. While the amortisation of goodwill on 1998/9 acquisitions does not attract tax relief, the Group has benefited from a corporate reorganisation which has enabled it to adopt a more efficient financial structure for both its recent acquisitions and existing subsidiaries.

Dawson International and Glaxo Wellcome give more detailed reconciliations, to explain the difference between the actual tax charge and notional charge which would have been derived from applying the statutory tax rate to the reported profit for the year. Dawson International reconciles the notional to the actual tax *charge*.

Extract 21.16: Dawson International PLC (1998)

9 Taxation [extract]

	52 weeks to 2 January 1999 £m	40 weeks to 3 January 1998 £m
Reconciliation of the tax charge:		
Notional (credit)/charge on (loss)/profit on ordinary activities before exceptional charges at UK corporation tax rate of 31% (1997: 31%)	**(3.4)**	4.5
Differences in effective overseas taxation rates	**0.5**	0.4
Tax losses not utilised	**0.1**	0.3
Utilisation of prior year tax losses	**(0.3)**	(4.2)
Other items	**0.3**	2.0
Adjustments in respect of earlier years	**(1.7)**	(0.7)
	(4.5)	2.3
Exceptional charges	**–**	(0.7)
	(4.5)	1.6

Tax losses carried forward at 2 January 1999 for which no benefit has been recognised are estimated be around $70 million in the US and £20 million in the UK. At current tax rates, these losses could result in future benefits of $24 million and £6 million on US and UK taxes respectively.

By contrast, Glaxo Wellcome reconciles the notional to the actual tax *rate*.

Extract 21.17: Glaxo Wellcome plc (1998)

8. Taxation [extract]

	1998	1997	1996
	%	%	%
Reconciliation of the taxation rate:			
UK statutory rate taxation	**31.0**	31.5	33.0
Deferred taxation not provided on fixed assets	**0.4**	(0.7)	(0.2)
Effect of special taxation status in Singapore	**(2.5)**	(2.4)	(3.7)
Net cost of different rates of taxation in overseas undertakings	**1.6**	1.4	1.0
ACT write-back	**(1.4)**	–	–
Other differences	**1.4**	0.7	1.4
Taxation rate in the accounts	**30.5**	30.5	31.5

Profits arising from manufacturing operations in Singapore are taxed at a reduced rate until 30th June 2002. The effect of this reduction in the taxation charge increased earnings per Ordinary share by 1.9p in 1998, by 1.8p in 1997 and by 3.1p in 1996.

Tax reconciliations are required under US GAAP and IAS 12. Often those UK companies that give a reconciliation have some form of US listing and are therefore required to report this information for US purposes anyway. As noted in 2.2.9 above, FRED 19 proposes that all UK companies should give a tax reconciliation, but only of the current tax charge.

(b)   the amount of the tax charge on ordinary activities and on extraordinary items, respectively analysed into:

    (i)   UK corporation tax, and the amount by which it has been reduced by the application of double tax relief,

    (ii)   UK income tax,

    (iii)   overseas tax;[128]

(c)   the amount of the taxation creditor balance.[129] Where there is an amount receivable in respect of tax, the Schedule 4 formats do not specify that it should be shown separately, although it is likely that it will be disclosed if material as a separate item within debtors;

(d)   movements during the year on any provision in respect of tax;[130] and

(e)   the amount of any provision for deferred taxation, shown separately from any other taxation provision.[131]

As can be seen from the above, there is substantial overlap between the disclosure requirements of accounting standards and those of the Companies Act. Illustrations of most of these disclosures have already been given (see in particular Extracts 21.5 and 21.6 at 3.1.4 above).

3.6   FRS 12

FRS 12 – *Provisions, Contingent Liabilities and Contingent Assets* – is discussed fully in Chapter 25. By virtue of the fact that FRS 12 does not apply to items dealt with in other standards (see Chapter 25 at 1.2.4), it does not apply to deferred tax, which is covered by SSAP 15. However, it does apply to other tax provisions.

Companies often include provisions for tax liabilities in the corporation tax creditor in the accounts, including those to cover potential liabilities which either are not yet the subject of an enquiry by tax authorities or are under dispute with tax authorities but where the eventual liability is uncertain. FRS 12 applies to such provisions, although companies obviously have to tread a wary course between compliance with the relevant disclosure requirements and prejudicing their tax position.

Glaxo Wellcome, whilst not purporting to comply with FRS 12 in their 1998 accounts, gives the following disclosure in respect of tax provisions.

Extract 21.18: Glaxo Wellcome plc (1998)

8.   Taxation [extract]

The integrated nature of the Group's worldwide operations, with cross-border supply routes into numerous markets, can give rise to complexity and delay in negotiations with revenue authorities as to the profits that fall to be taxed in individual territories: resolution of such transfer pricing issues is an inevitable and continuing fact of life for the Group. For a number of years the Group has had significant open issues relating to transfer pricing in the UK and the USA. In the UK the principal dispute, relating to transactions in the early 1980s, is now close to resolution. In the USA the issues date from 1989 and negotiations are less advanced; at present there is a wide variation between the claims of the authorities and the Group's estimation of its taxation liabilities. The Group uses the best local advice in seeking to manage these issues to a satisfactory conclusion and continues to believe that it has made adequate provision for all liabilities likely to arise from open assessments.

---

4   PROBLEM AREAS

4.1   Combining different categories of timing difference

SSAP 15 requires timing differences to be looked at in aggregate for the purposes of determining what net reversal need be provided for, rather than individually.[132] This is illustrated by the following example:

Example 21.10: Combination of timing differences

Assume that a company has the following projected cumulative timing differences for the next five years, and it is preparing accounts at the end of 1999:

	1999 £'000	2000 £'000	2001 £'000	2002 £'000	2003 £'000
Accelerated capital allowances	500	600	450	800	900
Other timing differences	(300)	(350)	(400)	(450)	(500)
Net position	200	250	50	350	400

The important line to focus on is the one which shows the net position, rather than either of the two which represent its components. Accordingly, the amount to be provided is determined by the extent to which the net deferral of £200,000 will fall – it can be seen that there will be a fall of £150,000 to £50,000 at the end of 2001, and accordingly the amount to be provided, at 30%, is £45,000.

Although the terms of the standard clearly state that the timing differences are to be looked at in aggregate rather than individually, it is sometimes argued that those timing differences which would give rise to debit balances may not be used to offset other timing differences if they are expected to be perpetuated. Accountants Digest No. 174 contains the following passage:

'It is important to note that, just as deferred tax liabilities should not be created unless it is probable that a liability will crystallise, so deferred tax liabilities should not be reduced by deferred tax debit balances which will not crystallise because recovery of the tax is continually deferred. For example, deferred tax liabilities should not be reduced by deferred tax debit balances arising from timing differences on recurring general bad debt provisions.'[133]

It can be argued that this approach produces anomalous results, as demonstrated by the following example:

Example 21.11: Combination of timing differences involving continuing debit balances

Assume that the same company had different expectations as to the accelerated capital allowance element of its projected cumulative timing differences, so as to give rise to the following figures for the next five years. It is still preparing accounts at the end of 1999:

	1999 £'000	2000 £'000	2001 £'000	2002 £'000	2003 £'000
Accelerated capital allowances	300	200	100	100	100
Other timing differences	(300)	(350)	(400)	(450)	(500)
Net position	–	(150)	(300)	(350)	(400)

Under the approach suggested in the Accountants Digest, the company would provide £60,000 (£200,000 @ 30%) for deferred tax in 1999, even though the incidence of timing differences experienced by it has been completely neutral in its effect, resulting in neither a postponement nor an acceleration of tax suffered. The provision would be, in effect, a provision for the effects of the acceleration of tax which was expected to occur in the future but had not yet taken place. This does not seem to produce a sensible result; it would be more appropriate to look at the effect of the timing differences in aggregate rather than individually, than to anticipate effects that will be experienced in 2000 and beyond.

4.2 Tax losses and deferred tax

4.2.1 Tax losses which have been incurred

The accounting treatment for tax losses which have been incurred is relatively straightforward, and the treatment depends upon the particular way in which the loss is to be relieved.

If the loss is to give rise to a refund of tax previously paid, then the amount of the refund is recorded in the balance sheet as a debtor (if appropriate this may be a non-current debtor).

Alternatively, the loss may be carried forward to be utilised against taxable profits which arise in the future. In such circumstances the tax loss can only be recognised in the accounts if enough taxable profit is likely to emerge in the future. It is probable that a taxable profit will emerge in the future if the company has a balance on its deferred tax account, since under the rules of partial provision, the company will have provided for deferred tax only if there is the probability of a tax liability crystallising. As the timing differences which have been identified (and provided for) reverse in future accounting periods, they will automatically give rise to taxable income against which the tax losses can be set.

Accordingly, the deferred tax account is the first point of set off for tax losses which are carried forward. An example is to be found in the accounts of Brunel Holdings (see Extract 21.8 at 3.3.4 above). The amount of deferred tax provided in the accounts should be reduced to the extent of the tax effect of the available losses. However, complications arise if the enterprise carries on a number of different trades, because a credit balance arising from one trade may not be capable of offset against a debit balance of another trade, or if the loss arises in a company which is in a different tax jurisdiction from the profitable companies, so that again no offset would be possible in practice. It will only be legitimate to make the kind of offset discussed above if the loss could in fact be applied to prevent the payment of tax having to be made if the timing differences reversed so as to crystallise a liability.

The more difficult practical problems arise when the amount of the loss is so great that the set off against deferred tax is such that the loss would be carried as an asset. This is permissible only in certain circumstances. As explained in 3.3.3 above, the tax effect of a current trading loss should only be treated as a recoverable asset when:

(a) the loss results from an identifiable and non-recurring cause; and

(b)   the enterprise, or predecessor enterprise, has been consistently profitable with any past losses being more than offset by income in subsequent periods; and

(c)   it is assured beyond reasonable doubt that future taxable profits will be sufficient to offset the current loss during the carry forward period prescribed by tax legislation.[134]

These rules are framed in an attempt to ensure that an asset is recognised only when its recoverability is assured with a very high degree of certainty and, in practice, these conditions can seldom be met.

4.2.2   Tax losses which have yet to be incurred

This is an area which causes a great deal of debate. A fundamental question emerges when looking at the foreseeable future for the purposes of assessing the deferred tax provision – if a trading loss is foreseen in the future, may it be taken into account when assessing the level of deferred tax to be provided? Take the following example:

Example 21.12: Future tax losses

A company is preparing its accounts for the year ended 31 December 1999, during which it earned a taxable profit of £100,000, on which tax of £30,000 is payable.

In considering the deferred tax provision that should be set up in its 1999 accounts, the company foresees a reversal of timing differences amounting to £150,000 in 2000, but has identified a trend from 2001 onwards of a level of capital expenditure that should give rise to originating timing differences when compared to the amount of depreciation which will be charged in the profit and loss account.

However, the company forecasts that a trading loss of £100,000 will be made in 2000 and therefore expects that the tax effect of these losses will at least partly mitigate the timing difference reversal.

The amount on which the company should base its provision is either £150,000 or £50,000, but which?

Those in favour of reducing the deferred tax liability would argue that the loss when incurred will reduce the amount of tax payable, and under the partial provision rules (which require that tax should be accounted for to the extent that it is probable that a liability will crystallise, and should not be accounted for to the extent that it is probable that a liability will not crystallise) would say that, since tax on only £50,000 will be payable, then that is all that should be provided.

The counter argument to this is that the deferred tax liability cannot be reduced by a trading loss which has not yet been incurred and which has not been accounted for. The proponents of this argument would maintain that it is only correct to recognise the tax consequences of an event when the accounting consequences have been recognised, and not before. There is no suggestion that the deferred tax provision would be *increased* if a trading *profit* were foreseen in the following year (so that in effect the originating timing differences would not offset the reversals arising in that year). It is not the function of deferred tax to anticipate the effects of future trading results, only to account for the impact of timing differences which have affected trading results reported to date.

Supporters of this view would argue that it is only possible to take account of future timing differences in assessing the deferred tax liability which is to be provided. This explains why it is considered to be legitimate to anticipate the effects of future capital expenditure but not to anticipate future trading results. Part of the confusion in this area is related to the question of whether trading losses do in fact give rise to timing differences. As mentioned at 3.3.2 above, SSAP 15 states that a loss for tax purposes which is available to relieve future profits from tax constitutes a timing difference. This is true in respect of current and past trading losses; they have been dealt with in the accounts, but not yet in arriving at the liability to tax as assessed in the tax computation. However, it is not true in respect of future trading losses, which so far have been dealt with in *neither* statement. Indeed, to recognise the tax effects of future losses, but not otherwise to provide for them in the accounts would have the effect of *creating* a timing difference where none had previously existed.

We prefer the second of these two arguments, and accordingly believe that the forecast loss should not figure in the assessment of the reversing timing differences and the deferred tax provision should be based on timing differences of £150,000 in this example. In general terms the effects of a tax loss may only be recognised if the loss has been incurred and accounted for in the accounts. Anticipated tax losses may not be used to reduce, or to avoid, a provision for deferred taxation.

4.3 Tax losses and group relief

4.3.1 *Background*

Where a member of a group has tax losses it may surrender them to another group member to be set off against their taxable profits of the same period, subject to a number of detailed provisions of the tax legislation. Such a transfer may be made with or without payment by the company receiving the group relief; this is a matter of policy for the group to decide. Where payment is made it is usually at the applicable tax rate in force, so that the profitable company is in effect paying as group relief what it would otherwise have paid in tax, and the loss-making company is having its losses relieved at the same rate.

4.3.2 *The accounts of the profitable company*

Group relief gives rise to no significant accounting implications so far as the profitable company is concerned, so long as it is being paid for at the effective rate of tax as described above; whether it pays tax to the Revenue or a payment for group relief to another company, the financial impact on it will be the same. The only difference will be that it will disclose the payments made as 'group relief' within its note analysing the tax charge, rather than as corporation tax payable.

However, where it is receiving relief without payment, different considerations apply. Where the incidence of the relief gives rise to an unusually low tax charge, it will generally be appropriate to disclose the reason for this because it constitutes 'special circumstances which affect liability in respect of taxation of profits ... for the financial year'.[135] The more significant effect, however, may be on deferred tax, because the company may be told by the holding company that there is no need to provide for the tax arising on the expected reversal of timing differences because it will be relieved without cost by losses made available to it by other group companies.

The availability of group relief without charge might strictly be thought to represent a permanent difference, because it features in the company's tax computation, and not in its accounts. In general, we believe that it is inappropriate to anticipate the effect of future permanent differences as a reason for not providing for an expected reversal of timing differences. However, even if this is true as a general rule, it is specifically contradicted in relation to group relief by SSAP 15, which states that, 'where a company is a member of a group, it should, in accounting for deferred tax, take account of any group relief which, on reasonable evidence, is expected to be available and any charge which will be made for such relief'.[136]

The standard does not explain the reasoning behind this ruling. However, it could be justified on the view that the profitable company *is* in fact providing for deferred tax, but at the rate at which it will pay for the group relief rather than at the tax rate in force. Where the group relief rate has been set at 0%, therefore, the amount of the provision will properly be calculated as being nil.

This has no overall effect on the amount of deferred tax provided by the group as a whole, because the position of the group has to be looked at as a separate exercise in any event (see 4.4 below).

4.3.3   The accounts of the loss-making company

From the point of view of the loss-making company, any losses surrendered without payment to other group companies clearly have no value to it. However, where the losses are being surrendered for consideration, the effect will be to allow the company to recoup some value from these losses sooner, and with greater certainty, than it otherwise might. In most cases, credit will be taken in the year in which the taxable loss arises, as the holding company will generally have determined the group relief situation within the group. Nevertheless, in some situations, on grounds of prudence, it may be appropriate to take no credit for this until it is certain that it will be received, which may not be until the group election has been made. Where a credit for these losses appears within the tax charge note it should be described as 'group relief receivable'.

4.4   Tax in the accounts of a group

4.4.1   Offsetting consolidated tax balances

The accounts of the group are prepared as if it were a single entity, and the question of how to portray the tax affairs of the whole group has to be considered in that light; it will not simply be a matter of aggregating the accounts of all the group companies, which have to consider their own tax position in isolation, but rather one of reassessing the position of the group as a whole. However, individual group companies may operate in different tax jurisdictions, or be subject to other constraints which keep their tax affairs separate, so it will be necessary to have regard to these factors in deciding what can be netted off for the purposes of the group accounts.

The distinction between the approach which has to be taken at group and company level is explained in this extract from the accounts of Glynwed:

> *Extract 21.19: Glynwed International plc (1998)*
>
> **1. ACCOUNTING POLICIES**
>
> **Deferred taxation**
>
> Deferred taxation is taken into account to the extent that a liability will probably arise in the foreseeable future and is calculated at taxation rates expected to apply at that time. In the holding company and its subsidiaries the liability is assessed with reference to the individual company. On consolidation the liability is assessed with reference to the Group as a whole.

Some groups simplify things by arranging that the holding company will indemnify subsidiaries against any reversal of timing differences. The effect is that the subsidiaries do not have to make any provision for deferred tax; it can all be dealt with in the accounts of the holding company. EMI is an example of such a group, as shown in this extract:

> *Extract 21.20: EMI Group plc (1998)*
>
> **22. DEFERRED TAXATION** [extract]
>
> The Company has undertaken to discharge the liability to corporation tax of the majority of its wholly-owned UK subsidiaries; their deferred tax liabilities are therefore dealt with in the accounts of the Company.

Where one company expects to have reversals of timing differences in the future, and another expects to have originating timing differences, these may in principle be looked at in aggregate to see whether any overall reversal need be provided for, subject to certain caveats. Even if one company ends up paying more tax because of the reversal, the other will pay less because of its originating differences, and the overall effect on the group will therefore be as if the timing differences had been in one company. However, this approach will have to be modified if the companies are paying tax at different rates, or if the company with originating timing differences is put into a tax loss situation which cannot be relieved, so that the group suffers a net cash outflow: in these circumstances it will be necessary to provide for the effects of that inability to treat the companies as one for tax purposes. An example will illustrate these points.

Example 21.13: Assessing the deferred tax position in a group

Company S is a wholly owned subsidiary of company H. At the end of 1991, the companies assess that their future patterns of cumulative timing differences will be as follows:

	1999	2000	2001	2002	2003
	£'000	£'000	£'000	£'000	£'000
Company H	400	500	600	650	700
Company S	500	300	250	200	200
Aggregate	900	800	850	850	900

It is expected that no reversal of timing differences will take place beyond 2003 in either company.

Taking the companies in isolation, company H would make no provision for deferred tax because it foresaw no reversal of timing differences; however, it would not be permitted to anticipate the benefit of future originating timing differences, so its balance sheet would carry neither a deferred tax asset nor a liability. Company S, on the other hand, would have to provide for tax on its anticipated reversals of £300,000 (£500,000 - £200,000).

When the group is considered as a whole, it can be seen that net reversals of only £100,000 are expected to occur (£900,000 - £800,000) so in the normal course of events, the group's deferred tax liability need be calculated only on that figure; that is the amount which would have been the basis of the provision if all the timing differences had been in a single company, and that will represent the effect of timing differences on the group as a whole.

Complications arise, however, if the companies are situated in different tax jurisdictions. If, for example, company S is in a country where tax is payable at a rate of 50%, while company H is paying tax at 35%, it is necessary to recompute the above calculation to take account of the tax rates involved. This results in the following picture:

	1999	2000	2001	2002	2003
	£'000	£'000	£'000	£'000	£'000
Company H – tax effects at 35%	140	175	210	227	245
Company S – tax effects at 50%	250	150	125	100	100
Aggregate	390	325	335	327	345

On this basis it can be seen that deferred tax of £65,000 should be provided (£390,000 - £325,000) in respect of the reversal of gross aggregate timing differences of £100,000. This is simply because the reversal in company S is taxed at a higher rate than the relief obtained in company H from its originating timing differences.

A further complication may arise if the originating timing differences anticipated by company H are likely to result in taxable losses in that company. If the two companies were in the UK, that would not make any difference, because the effect of these losses could then be transferred to S in the form of group relief. However, where the countries are in different jurisdictions, this will not be possible and the group will experience the adverse effects of company S's reversal without the benefit of any tax saving in respect of company H. In these circumstances, provision should be made in the group accounts for the deferred tax liability which relates to company S.

The implications of the above are that it is necessary to assess the deferred tax position of the group carefully to see what will be the real result, in tax terms, of future movements in timing differences. As a practical matter, it may be helpful to approach this by examining the overall position for all the group companies in each tax jurisdiction as an interim stage in the process. In general terms, the deferred tax effects of companies in different jurisdictions should not be netted off where there is a significant possibility that increased tax charges in one country might not be offset by tax savings in others.

4.4.2   Tax effects of consolidation adjustments

Another matter to be considered is how to deal with the tax effects of adjustments made when consolidating the accounts of individual companies within a group. Since members of the group will generally be assessed to tax on an individual basis, the total amount of tax borne by the group will not be affected by such adjustments. The question which then arises is whether consolidation adjustments should be treated as giving rise to timing differences and accounted for as part of the deferred tax position of the group.

Examples of such adjustments would be where inter-company profit on stock was eliminated on consolidation and recognised only when the stock was eventually sold to a third party; or where borrowing costs incurred to finance the creation of an asset were expensed by a subsidiary but capitalised on consolidation. In the first of these cases, the profit on the inter-company sale would be taxed in advance of being reported in the group accounts, while in the second case, the group would benefit from a tax deduction without having reported the associated expense in the consolidated accounts; that expense would only be reported as part of the subsequent depreciation or disposal of the asset being created.

As discussed in 3.3.2 above, SSAP 15 defines timing differences as 'differences between profits or losses as computed for tax purposes and results as stated in accounts, which arise from the inclusion of items of income and expenditure in tax computations in periods different from those in which they are included in accounts. Timing differences originate in one period and are capable of reversal in one or more subsequent periods.' While it may be argued that consolidation adjustments as such never appear in tax computations at all, and therefore do not give rise to a timing difference, they result in the acceleration or postponement of tax in relation to the consolidated results of the group, and on that basis it is customary to recognise such effects within the deferred tax account. However, this practice is not universally followed.

Similar issues arise in respect of the tax effects of fair value adjustments on the initial acquisition of a business. These are discussed in more detail in Chapter 6 at 2.4.3 E.

4.5 ACT

4.5.1 ACT carried forward as an asset

The rules regarding the carry-forward of ACT are somewhat confused. As described in 3.1.2 above, SSAP 8 says that ACT can be carried forward as an asset if it is 'expected to be recoverable taking into account expected profits and dividends – normally those of the next accounting period only'.[137] However, SSAP 15 has slightly different rules, which deal separately with ACT on dividends which are payable and proposed at the balance sheet date and ACT relating to dividends from earlier periods. The former 'should be carried forward to the extent that it is foreseen that sufficient corporation tax will be assessed on the profits or income of the succeeding accounting period, against which the advance corporation tax is available for offset'.[138] The latter 'should be written off unless their recovery is assured beyond reasonable doubt', and 'such recovery will normally be assured only where the debit balances are recoverable out of corporation tax arising on profits or income of the succeeding accounting period, *without replacement by equivalent debit balances*'[139] (emphasis added).

The application of the final part of the last rule treats ACT as if it were a timing difference, subject to the normal rules of deferred tax set out in SSAP 15, rather than a prepayment of tax, which is what it actually is. However, it is difficult to see whether this rule overrides the one set out in SSAP 8, and even if it does, whether the word 'normally' provides some latitude in its interpretation on this point. In our view, a sensible construction to be placed on these rules in combination should permit ACT to be carried forward as an asset provided it meets the basic SSAP 8 test that it is expected to be recoverable, and we do not believe that replacement by an asset of a similar amount in respect of ACT paid subsequently should inhibit this.

4.5.2 ACT set against the deferred tax liability

As stated above, ACT is a prepayment of tax, not a timing difference, but it is appropriate to deal with it as a deduction from deferred tax insofar as it would be available to offset the deferred tax liability if it became payable. There is a limit within the tax legislation on the offset of ACT against mainstream tax liabilities, and this is referred to in both SSAP 8 and SSAP 15 in terms which seek to restrict the proportion of the deferred tax account which may be offset in this way. SSAP 8 states that 'only a proportion of the balance on the account ... can be used for this purpose'.[140] SSAP 15 seems more doubtful however: 'It *may* be incorrect to carry forward an amount of ACT to offset an equal credit amount of deferred tax'[141] (emphasis added).

In practice, a variety of treatments appear to be applied, as shown in the following extracts. BICC offsets ACT against its deferred tax balances to the extent of 20/30ths (being the maximum offset expected to be available in future periods), and writes off the excess as a matter of policy; its accounting policy is shown in the extract below:

Extract 21.21: BICC plc (1998)

Principal accounting policies

10 Deferred taxation [extract]

Deferred taxation is provided using the liability method. Timing differences arising from capital allowances are fully recognised since the directors consider such differences will reverse in the foreseeable future. Unrecovered advance corporation tax on dividends paid and proposed is deducted from UK deferred taxation up to a maximum amount equivalent to 20/30ths thereof, with the balance written off.

Marks and Spencer used to offset the ACT recoverable on its proposed final dividend against deferred tax without limit – in its case this producing a net asset which was shown in debtors, as shown in Extract 21.22 below. Since the company has a March year end, no ACT was payable in respect of its final 1999 dividend, so that the current year figures do not show this treatment.

Extract 21.22: Marks and Spencer p.l.c. (1999)

13 Debtors [extract]

	THE GROUP		THE COMPANY	
	1999	1998	**1999**	1998
	£m	£m	**£m**	£m
AMOUNTS RECEIVABLE AFTER MORE THAN ONE YEAR				
Advance corporation tax recoverable on the proposed final dividend	–	76.6	–	76.6
Less amount set off against deferred tax provision (see note 21)	–	(43.0)	–	(39.0)
	–	33.6	–	37.6

21 Deferred taxation [extract]

	THE GROUP		THE COMPANY	
		1997		1997
	1998	restated	**1998**	restated
	£m	£m	**£m**	£m
Deferred taxation provision arising on short-term timing differences	**58.9**	51.6	**52.8**	47.6
Deferred tax asset arising on post-retirement health benefits	**(8.3)**	(8.6)	**(8.3)**	(8.6)
	50.6	43.0	**44.5**	39.0
Recoverable ACT offset against deferred tax provision (see note 13)	–	(43.0)	–	(39.0)
At 31 March	**50.6**	–	**44.5**	–

Some deal with all the recoverable ACT as an asset and keep the deferred tax
liability separate, such as Sears in the extract below:

Extract 21.23: Sears plc (1998)

12. Debtors [extract]

	Group		Company	
	1998	**1997**	**1998**	**1997**
	£m	**£m**	**£m**	**£m**
Due in less than one year:				
Trade debtors	393.3	358.0	0.6	–
Group undertakings	–	–	363.6	246.9
Other debtors	55.6	91.8	6.3	–
Corporation tax recoverable	–	–	52.6	44.9
Prepayments and accrued income	36.2	39.8	–	–
	485.1	489.6	423.1	291.8
Due after more than one year:				
Group undertakings	–	–	475.5	441.9
Other debtors	0.3	3.0	–	–
Prepayments	17.8	9.7	–	–
Advance corporation tax	11.1	11.1	11.1	11.1
	29.2	23.8	486.6	453.0

16. Provisions for liabilities and charges [extract]

Details of the full potential liability for deferred taxation and the extent to which provision has
been made in these accounts are set out below:

	Full potential liability		Provision made	
	1998	**1997**	**1998**	**1997**
	£m	**£m**	**£m**	**£m**
Capital allowances	4.2	17.8	(1.5)	1.4
Short term and other timing differences	9.8	19.2	9.8	19.2
	14.0	37.0	8.3	20.6

Provided the ACT can be regarded as recoverable, all the above possibilities are
simply matters of classification in the balance sheet, and any of the treatments is
probably, therefore, acceptable. In its 1995 Discussion Paper, the ASB favoured
the treatment of dividing the recoverable ACT between the amount that can be

set off against the deferred tax balance with any excess being carried as an asset.[142]

SSAP 8 also states that to the extent to which the deferred taxation account represents deferred chargeable gains, it is not available for offsetting ACT.[143] This is no longer the case; as a result of subsequent changes in the tax legislation, it is now possible to offset ACT against tax payable in respect of chargeable gains.

Where the holding company has no trade of its own to give rise to a deferred tax liability, it will generally recover its ACT by surrendering it to its subsidiaries to be offset against their tax or deferred tax liabilities. In these circumstances, it will be appropriate for it to carry forward such ACT as it expects to recover as an asset in its own balance sheet.

A   Impact of the shadow ACT regime

It is also necessary to consider the effect of the shadow ACT regime (which is discussed in more detail at 3.1.2 and 3.1.3 above) on the extent to which surplus ACT can be offset against the deferred tax balance. At first sight, it would appear reasonable to continue to permit the offset of ACT against the deferred tax liability. This is because ACT capacity is calculated by reference to (the higher) taxable profits, whilst shadow ACT is calculated by reference to dividend payments (and therefore the lower accounting profit).

However, it will still be necessary to consider all the surrounding circumstances. In particular, ACT capacity is calculated at the rate of 20% of profits chargeable to corporation tax, whilst shadow ACT is calculated at the rate of 25% of dividend payments. In addition, any surplus shadow ACT carried forward must be utilised before real ACT may be set off against the company's liability to corporation tax.

Where it is anticipated that due to timing differences, future taxable profits will be lower than accounting profits, it may be prudent, or indeed required by SSAP 15, not to recognise a deferred tax asset in the balance sheet. In such circumstances, particular attention should also be given as to whether the company can recognise an ACT asset.

In spite of the potential significance of the shadow ACT system, companies have not typically referred to it in their accounts in the 1998/9 reporting season. An exception is Inchcape:

Extract 21.24: Inchcape plc (1998)

4b   Deferred taxation liability (asset) [extract]

Advance Corporation Tax written off to date amounts to £10.9m (1997 – £25.2m) and is available for offset against future UK corporation tax liabilities subject to the restrictions of the 'shadow' ACT regulations.

4.6 Changes in tax rates

4.6.1 Corporation tax

In providing for the amount of current corporation tax that should be accrued in the accounts the best estimate of the amount payable is made. This involves a number of estimates, including the extent of disallowable expenditure (for items such as entertaining, legal fees, etc.), the amount of expenditure that will qualify for capital allowances (particularly expenditure on certain types of plant and machinery), and the standard rate of corporation tax that will apply to the taxable profits. Companies which qualify for the small companies rate or for marginal relief should make the provision in their accounts on the basis of these concessions if they estimate that the taxable profits are at the appropriate level.

Under international accounting standards, and in the US, tax rate changes cannot be recognised until they have been enacted (see 5.1 and 5.2 below). The ASB has also proposed the adoption of this treatment in the UK in FRED 18 (see 3.2 above). By contrast, current UK practice is to recognise changes in rate for accounting purposes as soon as they are announced by the Chancellor of the Exchequer in the Budget.

There is, of course, a possibility that the Budget proposals, in the form of the Finance Bill, are not successful in their passage through Parliament, and the rate suffered may therefore eventually be different to the rate used by companies in the preparation of their accounts. If this is so, then the under- or over-accrual flows through the company's profit and loss account as (a separately disclosed) part of the following year's tax charge. (Similarly if companies provided tax in their accounts using the small companies rate or marginal relief concessions, and the final agreed profits fell to be taxed at the standard rate, then a charge will arise in the following year's profit and loss account representing the under-accrual.)

4.6.2 Deferred tax

At each year end a company will provide for the appropriate level of deferred tax and will use the best estimate of the rate that will be payable on the taxable profits when the timing differences reverse. This is the fundamental approach of the liability method. Timing differences by their very nature will reverse over many years and the rate of tax will not normally be known in advance for these years. Of course, if rates were set some years in advance then those rates would be applied to the element of timing differences expected to reverse in each of the future years, and the liability computed accordingly.

Generally, the best estimate of the rate of tax that will be applied to reversing differences is the standard rate of tax currently in force, and accordingly deferred tax provisions are made on this basis. Any under or over accrual arising from a rate change will pass through the company's profit and loss account as (a separately disclosed) part of the deferred tax charge for the year, in the year in which the rate changes, or the change is announced, whichever is the earlier. Indeed, if the change of rate is announced after the year end but before the accounts are prepared, the effect will be reflected in the year which has already ended; this is given in the Appendix to SSAP 17 as an example of an adjusting event.[144] This is computed by taking the net timing differences on which deferred tax was provided in the preceding year's balance sheet and applying the difference between the old rate and the new rate.

There are exceptions to the above for those companies which qualify for the small companies rate or for marginal relief. Those companies which suffer tax at the small companies rate should generally provide for deferred tax at that rate unless they foresee that the taxable profits in the forthcoming years will rise above the small company threshold. Such taxable profits are not just the timing differences that are expected to reverse in a particular year, but must include an estimate of the taxable trading profit that will arise, since this will form part of the total taxable profits of the company. A similar estimate should be made to determine if the marginal relief provisions will apply to any of the forthcoming years, but this can be even more difficult to assess. It may in certain circumstances be impossible to determine if the marginal reliefs will apply, and in such cases the prudent view should prevail and the standard rate of tax should be used to calculate the provision.

4.7   Revaluations of fixed assets

SSAP 15 discusses the revaluation of fixed assets in relation to the tax consequences which would arise if they were disposed of at their revalued amounts. However, it contains no discussion of the effects of revaluation on the calculation of deferred tax relating to timing differences between the amounts of depreciation charged in the accounts and of capital allowances in the tax computation. Furthermore, the standard does not contain a clear statement of the concept on which it is based, from which it might be possible to infer what the treatment should be. Indeed, a large part of the problem is that the conceptual reasons for including revaluations in historical cost accounts are themselves elusive. The rules on this issue are therefore obscure; the two main possibilities are described below.

For the purposes of this discussion, it is assumed that the assets in question are depreciated and attract capital allowances, so that they will be written off over a period for both accounting and tax purposes.

The first way of looking at the revaluation of a depreciable asset is that it creates a further timing difference, because in effect it is an adjustment of depreciation, which is itself an element of a timing difference. Where, for example, an asset is purchased for £10,000, subsequently depreciated to £6,000 and then revalued to £9,000, the £3,000 revaluation surplus could be regarded as reinstating the depreciation which was previously charged, and therefore reversing the deferred tax effect of charging that depreciation. On this basis, the £9,000 would be compared with the tax written down value of the asset in order to determine the amount of the timing difference which gives a potential liability to deferred tax. This is the view taken by the Accountants Digest on SSAP 15.[145]

The alternative viewpoint sees the revaluation as giving rise to a permanent difference. This is on the basis that the revaluation, and its subsequent reversal through depreciation, has no equivalent within the tax computation and hence does not give rise to a timing difference. The revaluation is not a reversal of previous depreciation, which properly reflected the consumption of part of the asset based on its then carrying value; it simply means that the remaining part of the asset has a different value and its consumption will be measured at a different amount. The future depreciation charge will have two components; the original charge based on cost, and the further amount based on the revaluation surplus. That further amount has no tax equivalent and it would be wrong to make any tax adjustment in respect of it.

We believe that both of these arguments are coherent, and in the absence of more definitive guidance from the standard itself, we consider that they are both acceptable, so long as the approach taken is consistently applied.

Where the revaluation takes the value of the asset above its original cost, it takes the matter out of the realm of accelerated capital allowances and into that of chargeable gains. As mentioned above, SSAP 15 does deal with this issue and says that a timing difference will be created 'insofar as the profit or loss that would result from realisation at the revalued amount is taxable, unless disposal of the revalued asset and of any subsequent replacement assets would not result in a tax liability, after taking account of any expected rollover relief'.[146] Provision for this should then be considered if it is intended to dispose of the asset, unless the tax effect would be mitigated by the effects of other originating timing differences.

The reference to rollover relief in the passage quoted above adds a further element of confusion to an already confused topic. Since the effect of rollover relief is to postpone the crystallisation of a tax liability rather than to cancel it altogether, it is difficult to see whether its availability has a bearing on whether or not a timing difference has been created, although it does of course have a bearing on whether provision has to be made in respect of it. No change to a company's tax exposure is made by rolling a gain on to a replacement asset rather than keeping the old asset, and it is therefore hard to see why this should be thought to reduce any timing difference considered to have arisen as a result of the revaluation.

Rollover relief is not only relevant in the context of revalued assets. Where an asset has been sold at a profit, and tax has been deferred by the operation of rollover relief, a latent tax liability will exist quite independently of whether or not the old asset had been revalued, and arguably this should be disclosed as a potential liability. The Appendix to SSAP 15 mentions this, but in an unsatisfactory way; it says: 'Where rollover relief has been obtained on the sale of an asset, with the "base cost" of the replacement asset for tax purposes thereby being reduced, and the potential tax liability has not been disclosed, the standard requires disclosure of the fact that the revaluation does not constitute a timing difference and that tax has therefore not been quantified, as it will not otherwise be evident from the accounts.'[147] However, this mixes up two unrelated matters; as mentioned above, the tax exposure can arise without any revaluation ever having occurred, and we recommend that it should be disclosed as a potential liability.

4.8   Overseas earnings

When a UK group incorporates the earnings of a foreign subsidiary or associate in its consolidated accounts, a timing difference will arise if the earnings are to be remitted to the UK in a later period and will give rise to incremental tax payments when they are remitted. SSAP 15 requires that these timing differences should be taken into account in the calculation of deferred tax unless it is intended to retain the earnings in the foreign country indefinitely so that no further tax liability will arise.

In practice it can be extremely difficult to determine how much to provide, since this will be subject to many uncertainties; the amount of any liability will depend on factors such as the relative tax rates of the UK and the foreign country concerned, the provisions of any tax treaty between the countries, and the level of UK taxable profits at the time of the remittance. Furthermore, groups may find methods of restructuring their groups so as to minimise their tax liabilities if a major repatriation of dividends becomes necessary. Nonetheless, it is necessary that companies which expect that a liability will emerge should make the best estimate that they can in the circumstances.

As indicated in 3.4 above, it is necessary to disclose both the fact that provision has not been made, where this is the case,[148] and also now the reason for not making *full* provision.[149] However, the reasoning behind these rules is somewhat confused. The first of the two requirements was added in substitution for the proposed requirement in ED 33 to state that there were no plans to remit overseas earnings, where this applied,[150] but the two cannot be regarded as equivalent to one another. Even where earnings *will* be remitted, and where tax *will* become payable as a result, it might be concluded that no provision is needed because other originating timing differences are forecast to arise in the year of remittance. Accordingly, it is not really possible to read very much into this disclosure when it is made. Furthermore, since it will only be in rare cases that full provision will be appropriate, the thrust of the second requirement also seems rather misguided.

5   COMPARISON WITH IASC AND US PRONOUNCEMENTS

5.1   IASC

International Accounting Standard No. 12 – *Accounting for Taxes on Income* – was originally published in 1979. This was so accommodating as to hardly merit the name 'standard', since it allowed either the deferral method or the liability method to be used, and permitted both comprehensive allocation and partial provision. This was inevitable given the divergence of treatment in the countries that constituted the main members of the IASC at the time.

In January 1989, the IASC published a new exposure draft E33 – *Accounting for Taxes on Income* – which proposed that only the liability method should be permitted, and that comprehensive allocation should be the preferred method, although partial provision would remain a permitted alternative. However, this exposure draft was not taken further, largely because it was overtaken by the issue of the US standard SFAS 109, as described at 5.2.3 below.

A new exposure draft E49 – *Income Taxes* – was issued in 1994, proposing an approach to deferred tax that drew on the approach to accounting for deferred tax prescribed by SFAS 109. This was subsequently converted into a revised version of IAS 12 in October 1996 which came into force for accounting periods beginning on or after 1 January 1998.

Like FAS 109, IAS 12 requires deferred tax to be provided on 'temporary differences' (see 5.1.1 below) rather than 'timing differences'. Whilst this often leads to the same result, there are fundamental differences, from both a practical and a conceptual point of view, between the temporary difference approach and the timing difference approach as currently applied in the UK, which need to be understood before addressing the detailed requirements of IAS 12.

5.1.1   The 'temporary difference' approach – the conceptual arguments

Temporary differences are defined as 'differences between the carrying amount of an asset or liability in the balance sheet and its tax base'.[151] The 'tax base' of an asset or liability is 'the amount attributed to that asset or liability for tax purposes'.[152] In many cases, this results in no arithmetical difference between the approaches, as the following simple example illustrates.

Example 21.14 'Timing' versus 'temporary' differences

A company buys a fixed asset for £1 million, which is to be depreciated over 4 years. It attracts a 40% first year allowance for tax purposes. At the end of the year of purchase, the 'timing difference' relating to the asset would be calculated as:

	£000
Tax allowances claimed	400
Depreciation charged	250
	150

The 'temporary difference' would be calculated as follows.

	£000
Net book value of asset	750
Tax base (i.e tax written down value) of asset	(600)
	150

The essential difference between the 'timing difference' approach and the 'temporary difference' approach is that the timing difference approach provides for the reversal of cumulative differences between the (comprehensive) income statement and the tax computation, whereas the temporary difference approach effectively provides for the tax that would be payable if the balance sheet were liquidated at book value. The effect of this, discussed in 5.1.2 B below, is that all timing differences are also temporary differences, but many permanent differences are temporary differences as well.

This shift of emphasis from the income statement to the balance sheet was the result of the IASC's conceptual framework which, like that of the FASB and the ASB's draft *Statement of Principles*, requires that all items in the balance sheet, other than shareholders' equity, must be either assets or liabilities as defined in the framework. Deferred tax as traditionally calculated is not a liability, but is more in the nature of deferred income or expenditure.

However, the IASC believes that the temporary difference approach does give rise to assets and liabilities as defined in its framework. The argument for the view (which is explained more clearly in SFAS 109 than in IAS 12) is broadly as follows. If an asset is currently carried in the balance sheet at, say, £1,000 there is an implicit assumption in the accounts that the asset will ultimately be recovered or realised by a cash inflow of at least £1,000. If that inflow will enter into the determination of future taxable income, the tax (if any) on realisation of the £1,000 carrying amount of the asset should be provided for. The 'basis for conclusions' section in SFAS 109[153] puts it thus:

'A government levies taxes on net taxable income. Temporary differences will become taxable amounts in future years, thereby increasing taxable income and taxes payable, upon recovery or settlement of the recognised and reported amounts of an enterprise's assets or liabilities ... .

'A contention that those temporary differences will never result in taxable amounts ... would contradict the accounting assumption inherent in the statement of financial position that the reported amounts of assets and liabilities will be recovered and settled, respectively; thereby making that statement internally inconsistent.'

We find this argument unconvincing and suggest that it is at best a brave attempt to rationalise an already existing practice. On any natural construction of the English words in the IASC framework's definition of 'liability' (i.e. a present obligation arising from past events), the only tax liability is the amount due to the tax authorities – i.e. current tax. To put it more bluntly, if in the early 1990s deferred tax had not already been a generally accepted accounting practice, it is inconceivable to us that anyone would have been suddenly inspired with the insight that it was required by the FASB's or IASC's conceptual framework on the argument set out above! In our view, the IASC, like the FASB, has failed to confront the real issue – that it must accept either that there is no basis for deferred tax accounting in its framework or, if this is not an acceptable result, that the framework itself requires fundamental revision.

It is interesting that the ASB, whose draft *Statement of Principles* is broadly the same as the FASB's and IASC's frameworks, indicated in its 1995 discussion paper that it shares our doubts as to the validity of the arguments for the temporary difference approach. Their discussion concludes as follows:

'A further concern with regard to the temporary difference approach is that it recognises as a liability one, but only one, of the many future costs associated with the recovery of an asset. ...

'However, there are many other expenses that must be incurred in order to recover the carrying value of the [asset], such as rent, rates, power and wages. If carried to its logical conclusion, the rationale of the temporary difference approach would arguably require these other costs to be recognised as liabilities as well. These other costs are just as certain to arise as the tax, if not (given the potential for changes to the tax system) more so, but they are clearly not liabilities at the balance sheet date. This suggests that deferred tax, as rationalised under the temporary difference approach, is also not a liability.'[154]

5.1.2 *The temporary difference approach – the practical issues*

The main practical issues in applying the temporary difference approach arise in three areas:

- calculating the 'tax base' of assets and liabilities;
- non-deductible assets; and
- fair value adjustments.

These are discussed in turn below.

A   *Calculating the tax base of assets and liabilities*

As noted above, the temporary difference relating to an asset or liability is the difference between the carrying amount of that item and its 'tax base'. The 'tax base' is defined as 'the amount attributed to that item for tax purposes'. This amount is often intuitively obvious, but at other times is far less so.

For instance, Example 21.14 above deals with a tax deductible fixed asset, where it is clear that the 'amount attributed for tax purposes' is its tax written down value. Another example might be a provision of, say, £1 million for unfunded pension costs. This would appear in the accounts, but until it is actually funded it would not be of any relevance for tax purposes; in other words, the 'amount attributed for tax purposes' at the balance sheet date is nil. This would give rise to a temporary difference of £1 million (i.e. carrying amount of £1 million less tax base of nil) in respect of which a deferred tax asset would be recognised, as would be expected.

Unfortunately, this logic does not seem to apply in the case of an item neither the origination nor settlement of which has any tax consequences. Take, for example, a bank loan of £1,000. This is just as much a 'nothing' for tax purposes as the unfunded pension provision just discussed. This would suggest that the 'tax base' of the loan as defined by IAS 12 should also be nil.

However, that would give the absurd result that a deferred tax asset would be provided for on the carrying amount of the loan. The temporary difference relating to the loan must be nil which implies that its tax base must therefore be its carrying amount of £1,000.

IAS 12 addresses this problem by providing that in the case of:

(a)   an asset the recovery of which does not give rise to taxable income; and

(b)   a liability the settlement of which is not deductible for tax purposes,

the tax base is to be taken as being the carrying amount;[155] in other words, there is no temporary difference, and therefore no deferred tax. On this basis no deferred tax would be provided in respect of the loan (because its settlement will not be tax-deductible).

This is clearly the right result, but it does leave the basic definition of 'tax base' looking rather inadequate. If an item does not exist for tax purposes, the 'amount attributable to it for tax purposes' would be more obviously nil than its carrying amount! A harsher view might be that in these paragraphs IAS 12 does not so much clarify the definition of tax base as rewrite it.

In fact IAS 12 tacitly admits that there is a wider issue here, since it goes on to state that 'where the tax base of an asset or liability is not immediately apparent, it is helpful to consider the fundamental principle on which this Standard is based: that an enterprise should, with certain limited exceptions, recognise a deferred tax liability (asset) wherever recovery or settlement of the carrying amount of an asset or liability would make future tax payments larger (smaller) than they would be if such recovery or settlement were to have no tax consequences'.[156]

It is a moot point whether this tortuous sentence is a 'helpful', or even accurate, summary of the fundamental principle of IAS 12, but it comes dangerously close to saying that the tax base of an item is whatever it needs to be to generate the right deferred tax number. To put it more formally, the basic equation is:

$$\text{carrying amount} - \text{tax base} = \text{temporary difference},$$

but there is some ambiguity as to whether the true unknown is the temporary difference (as stated in paragraph 5 of the IAS) or the tax base (as implied by paragraph 10 quoted above).

In our view, this confusion arises from the fact that the temporary difference approach focuses on settlement of assets and liabilities, whereas in the real world tax is levied on gains and losses. The fundamental difference, in this context, between an unfunded pension provision and a bank loan is that the recognition of the provision gives rise to a loss whereas recognition of the loan does not.

B   *Non-deductible assets*

During the development of IAS 12 it became apparent that the temporary difference approach produced an unsatisfactory result in relation to assets that are non-deductible for tax purposes, as the following example shows.

Example 21.15: Temporary differences on non-deductible assets

A company buys a fixed asset for £1 million that will attract no tax allowances either in use or when sold or scrapped. Under the traditional timing difference approach, depreciation of the asset would be treated as a permanent difference and the lack of tax allowances would be reflected in a higher than statutory tax rate as the asset was depreciated.

Under a strict temporary difference approach, however, deferred tax would be provided on the carrying amount of the asset at the date of purchase. This is because the asset will be recovered out of future taxable income with no deductions in respect of the asset, the tax base of which is therefore nil. This would have the effect that the lack of tax allowances was provided for in full on initial recognition of the asset, with the effective tax rate in future periods being the statutory rate (as the provision was released).

IAS 12 deals with this intuitively wrong answer by simply creating an exception, whereby deferred tax is not to be provided for if it 'arises from ... the initial recognition of an asset or liability in a transaction which ..., at the time of the transaction, affects neither accounting profit nor taxable profit'.[157]

C   *Fair value adjustments*

One of the perceived weaknesses of the traditional timing difference approach is that it does not strictly allow deferred tax to be provided for on fair value adjustments. Fair value adjustments never enter into the determination of income for a period (although the goodwill generated by them may do so). This means that, under the timing difference approach, they are permanent differences and deferred tax on them should not therefore be provided for, although it is fairly common to do so (see also 4.4.2 above). The temporary difference approach requires deferred tax to be recognised on fair value adjustments because they result in assets and liabilities being recognised at amounts different from their tax base.

However, the exception discussed in B above for recognition of deferred tax on the purchase of non-deductible assets would also preclude recognition of deferred tax arising from fair value adjustments, since these result in temporary differences which, just like that on the asset in Example 21.14 above, arise 'from the initial recognition of an asset or liability in a transaction which ..., at the time of the transaction, affects neither accounting profit nor taxable profit'. IAS 12 simply provides an exception to the exception above so as to require recognition of deferred tax on fair value adjustments!

It is hard to suppress the wry observation that the overall practical result of these rules, exceptions and exceptions to exceptions is not very different from requiring deferred tax to be provided for on timing differences and fair value adjustments – a rule which would be much easier to both understand and apply!

5.1.3 Summary of IAS 12 and main differences from UK requirements

A The basic rule

IAS 12 broadly requires deferred tax to be recognised in respect of all temporary differences except those arising from:

(a) goodwill that is not deductible for tax purposes or negative goodwill; or

(b) the initial recognition of an asset or liability in a transaction which:

    (i) is not a business combination; and

    (ii) at the time of the transaction, affects neither accounting profit nor taxable profit (tax loss).[158]

Under UK GAAP, SSAP 15 requires deferred tax to be recognised on timing differences on a partial provision basis.

B Revaluations and tax rebasing of assets

The effect of the basic rule set out in A above is that deferred tax must be provided on all revaluation surpluses in a tax system, such as that in the UK, where tax deductions in respect of an asset in use are based on its historical cost. This is because the gain is considered to represent an amount that will be recovered through future taxable income that will be fully taxed, as no offsetting tax allowances will be available.

For the same reason, where a fixed asset is not depreciated (e.g. on the grounds that the annual charge would be immaterial), but capital allowances are claimed in respect of the asset, IAS 12 would require a deferred tax liability to be established. Current UK practice is to treat the allowances claimed as a permanent difference, and to take credit for them as claimed, reducing the effective tax rate.

There are also cases in the UK where the tax base of an asset may be higher than its carrying amount. For example, if a company bought freehold land for

£1 million in 1970 and has not revalued it, its base cost for tax purposes will be well in excess of £1 million due to 1982 rebasing and cumulative indexation allowances. IAS 12 would require a deferred tax asset to be recognised in respect of the land, but subject to its restrictions on the recognition of assets (see F below).

Any deferred tax on revaluation gains, and on any other items recognised directly in equity, is also recognised directly in equity.[159]

C   Measurement and presentation

Current tax should be measured by reference to tax rates and laws that have been enacted or substantively enacted by the balance sheet date.[160] Deferred tax should be measured by reference to the tax rates and laws, as enacted or substantively enacted by the balance sheet date, that are expected to apply in the periods in which the assets and liabilities to which the deferred tax relates are realised or settled.[161] Current UK practice is to have regard to changes announced in the latest Budget, even if they have not been enacted.

Deferred tax should also be measured by reference to the tax consequences that would follow from the manner in which the enterprise expects, at the balance sheet date, to recover or settle the asset or liability to which it relates.[162] This is best illustrated with a simple example.

Example 21.16: Calculation of deferred tax depending on method of realisation of gain

A building, for which full capital allowances are available, originally cost £1 million. At the balance sheet date it is carried at £750,000, but tax allowances of £400,000 have been claimed in respect of it. If the building were sold, these allowances would be clawed back, but the tax indexed cost of the building would be £1.5 million. The company revalues the building to its current market value of £1.75 million. What deferred tax liability is required to be established under IAS 12, assuming a tax rate of 30%?

If the intention is to retain the asset in the business, it will be recovered out of future income of £1.75 million, on which tax of £345,000 will be paid, calculated as:

	£000
Gross income	1,750
Future tax allowances for asset (£1m less £400,000 claimed to date)	600
	1,150
Tax at 30%	345

If, however, the intention is to sell the asset, the required deferred tax liability is only £195,000, calculated as:

	£000
Sales proceeds	1,750
Tax base cost	(1,500)
	250
Clawback of tax allowances claimed	400
	650
Tax at 30%	195

The amounts of £345,000 and £195,000 above are the total required liability. The amount charged to equity would be the difference between these amounts and the existing provision of £45,000, being 30% of (£750,000 - £600,000).

The treatment of the above revaluation under current UK GAAP could vary considerably, since SSAP 15 does not address these issues directly. If the intention were to keep the asset in the business, it is quite likely that no deferred tax would be provided on the grounds that the revaluation constituted a permanent difference (see also 4.7 above). If the intention were to dispose of the asset, SSAP 15 might require the £195,000 to be provided for, but would allow the revaluation to be treated as not giving rise to a timing difference if rollover relief were considered to be available. Under IAS 12, gains subject to UK rollover relief would be fully provided for, since the effect would be to reduce the tax base of any new asset required.

D   *Discounting*

Deferred tax may not be discounted, except to the extent that it relates to a pre-tax amount that is itself discounted (such as an unfunded pension liability).[163] Whilst there is no comparable prohibition on discounting deferred tax in the UK, it is not generally done in practice.

E   *Presentation*

Tax assets and liabilities should be shown separately from other assets and liabilities and current tax should be shown separately from deferred tax. Deferred tax should not be shown as part of current assets or liabilities.[164]

Current tax assets and liabilities should be offset if, and only if, the enterprise has a legally enforceable right to set off the recognised amounts and intends either to settle them net or simultaneously.[165]

Deferred tax assets and liabilities should be offset if, and only if:

(a)   the enterprise has a legally enforceable right to set off current tax assets and liabilities; and

(b)   the deferred tax assets and liabilities concerned relate to income taxes raised by the same taxation authority on either:

(i)   the same taxable entity; or

(ii) different taxable entities which intend, in each future period in which significant amounts of deferred tax are expected to be settled or recovered, to settle their current tax assets and liabilities either on a net basis or simultaneously.[166]

These restrictions are based on the offset criteria in IAS 32 (see Chapter 9 at 4.2.2).

In the UK, there is an argument that the offset criteria in FRS 5 (see Chapter 16 at 2.7) would (at least if deferred tax were regarded as an 'asset' or 'liability' as defined in FRS 5) strictly require grossing up of various elements of the deferred tax account of a typical multinational group. In reality, however, such an accounting treatment is very seldom, if ever, seen.

F   Deferred tax assets

All deferred tax assets arising from deductible temporary differences should initially be recognised. However, the carrying amount of deferred tax assets should be reviewed at each balance sheet date. An enterprise should reduce the carrying amount of a deferred tax asset to the extent that it is no longer probable that sufficient taxable profit will be available to enable the asset to be recovered in full. Any reduction so made should be reversed if it subsequently becomes probable that sufficient taxable profit will be available.[167]

Separate disclosure is required of the amount of any deferred tax asset that is recognised, and the nature of the evidence supporting its recognition, when:

(a)   utilisation of the deferred tax asset is dependent on future profits in excess of those arising from the reversal of deferred tax liabilities; and

(b)   the enterprise has suffered a loss in the current or preceding period in the tax jurisdiction to which the asset relates.[168]

G   Business combinations

In accordance with the basic rule in A above, deferred tax should be established in respect of the difference between the fair values assigned to acquired assets and liabilities and their tax bases. If, as a result of the acquisition, the acquiring entity is able to recognise a previously unrecognised tax asset of its own (e.g. unused tax losses), the amount of the asset should be credited to goodwill, not to income.[169]

If a deferred tax asset of the acquiree which was not recognised at the time of the acquisition is subsequently recognised, the resulting credit is taken to the profit for the period. However, the carrying amount of goodwill is reduced to the amount (net of amortisation) at which it would have been carried if the deferred tax asset had been recognised at the time of the acquisition, and the resulting write-off is charged to profit in the same period. No adjustment is made to the extent it would create or add to negative goodwill.[170]

There is no requirement to provide deferred tax on fair value adjustments as such under UK GAAP. In practice, however, companies often do provide for deferred tax on material fair value adjustments such as the recognition of a pension surplus not shown in the accounts of the acquired company.

With regard to the recognition of previously unrecognised assets such as tax losses, paragraph 22 of FRS 7 requires such assets to be recognised if they meet the criteria for recognition in SSAP 15. However, unlike IAS 12, FRS 7 is not at all specific as to whether the resulting credit forms part of goodwill or can be taken to profit. We believe that the appropriate treatment is to treat it as part of goodwill.

H   Subsidiaries, branches, associates and joint ventures

Temporary differences will almost inevitably arise, in both the single entity and group accounts of an investor, between the carrying value of its investment in, or net assets of, a subsidiary, branch associate or joint venture and its tax base. The most common cause will be undistributed profits of such entities, where distribution to the investor would trigger a tax liability. Temporary differences might also arise from exchange movements and provisions against, or revaluations of, the carrying value of investments.[171]

IAS 12 requires the deferred tax effects of such temporary differences to be recognised:

(a)   in the case of taxable temporary differences (i.e. deferred tax liabilities), unless:

   (i)   the parent, investor or venturer is able to control the timing of the reversal of the temporary difference; and

   (ii)   it is probable that the temporary difference will not reverse in the foreseeable future; or

(b)   in the case of deductible temporary differences (i.e. deferred tax assets), only to the extent that:

   (i)   the temporary difference will reverse in the foreseeable future; and

   (ii)   taxable profit will be available against which the temporary difference can be utilised.[172]

What this means in practice is best illustrated by reference to its application to the retained earnings of subsidiaries, associates and joint ventures. In the case of a subsidiary (or a branch), the parent is able to control when and whether the retained earnings are distributed. Therefore, no provision need be made for the tax consequences of distribution of profits that the parent has determined will not be distributed in the foreseeable future.[173] In the case of a joint venture, provided that the investor can control the distribution policy, similar considerations apply.[174]

In the case of an associate, however, the investor cannot control distribution policy. Therefore provision should be made for the tax consequences of the distribution of the retained earnings of an associate, except to the extent that there is a shareholders' agreement that those earnings will not be distributed.[175]

We consider this an almost perverse result. In reality, it is extremely unusual for any enterprise (other than one set up for a specific project) to pursue a policy of full distribution. To the extent that it occurs at all, it is much more likely in a wholly-owned subsidiary than in an associate; and yet IAS 12 effectively treats full distribution by associates as the norm and that by subsidiaries as the exception! Moreover, it seems to ignore the fact that the development of equity accounting in the 1960s had its origins in the perceived ability of investors in associates to exert some degree of control over the amount and timing of dividends from them. This is discussed further in the introduction to Chapter 7.

In practice, we suspect that the rules in IAS 12 have much the same effect as those in SSAP 15 (see 4.8 above), despite the apparent difference in emphasis.

I   Disclosures

IAS 12 imposes quite extensive disclosure requirements as follows.

The major components of tax expense (income) should be disclosed separately. These may include:

(a)   current tax expense (income);

(b)   any adjustments recognised in the period for current tax of prior periods;

(c)   the amount of deferred tax expense (income) relating to the origination and reversal of temporary differences;

(d)   the amount of deferred tax expense (income) relating to changes in tax rates or the imposition of new taxes;

(e)   the amount of the benefit arising from a previously unrecognised tax loss, tax credit or temporary difference of a prior period that is used to reduce current tax expense;

(f)   the amount of the benefit from a previously unrecognised tax loss, tax credit or temporary difference of a prior period that is used to reduce deferred tax expense;

(g)   deferred tax expense arising from the write-down, or reversal of a previous write-down, of a deferred tax asset; and

(h)   the amount of tax expense (income) relating to those changes in accounting policies and fundamental errors which are included in the determination of net profit or loss for the period in accordance with the allowed alternative treatment in IAS 8 – *Net Profit or Loss for the Period, Fundamental Errors and Changes in Accounting Policies* (see Chapter 22 at 4.1).[176]

The following should also be disclosed separately:

(a)   the aggregate current and deferred tax relating to items that are charged or credited to equity;

(b)   tax expense (income) relating to extraordinary items recognised during the period;

(c)   an explanation of the relationship between tax expense (income) and accounting profit in either or both of the following forms:

    (i)   a numerical reconciliation between tax expense (income) and the product of accounting profit multiplied by the applicable tax rate(s), disclosing also the basis on which the applicable tax rate(s) is (are) computed; or

    (ii) a numerical reconciliation between the average effective tax rate and the applicable tax rate, disclosing also the basis on which the applicable tax rate is computed;

(d)   an explanation of changes in the applicable tax rate(s) compared to the previous accounting period;

(e)   the amount (and expiry date, if any) of deductible temporary differences, unused tax losses, and unused tax credits for which no deferred tax asset is recognised in the balance sheet;

(f)   the aggregate amount of temporary differences associated with investments in subsidiaries, branches and associates and interests in joint ventures, for which deferred tax liabilities have not been recognised;

(g)   in respect of each type of temporary difference, and in respect of each type of unused tax losses and unused tax credits:

    (i)   the amount of the deferred tax assets and liabilities recognised in the balance sheet for each period presented;

    (ii) the amount of the deferred tax income or expense recognised in the income statement, if this is not apparent from the changes in the amounts recognised in the balance sheet; and

(h)   in respect of discontinued operations, the tax expense relating to:

    (i)   the gain or loss on discontinuance; and

    (ii) the profit or loss from the ordinary activities of the discontinued operation for the period, together with the corresponding amounts for each prior period presented.[177]

An example of some of the disclosures required under IAS 12 is given by Nokia which, like many companies complying with international accounting standards, complied with IAS 12 for the first time in its 1998 accounts.

Extract 21.25: Nokia Corporation (1998)

1. Accounting policies [extract]

Income taxes

Current taxes are based on the results of the Group companies and are calculated according to local tax rules.

Beginning January 1, 1998, deferred income tax is provided, using the liability method, for all temporary differences arising between the tax basis of assets and liabilities and their carrying values for financial reporting purposes. Currently enacted tax rates are used to determine deferred income tax.

Under this method the Group is required, in relation to an acquisition, to make provision for deferred taxes on the difference between the fair values of the net assets acquired and their tax base.

The principal temporary differences arise from intercompany profit in inventory, depreciation on property, plant and equipment, untaxed reserves and tax losses carried forward. Deferred tax assets relating to the carryforward of unused tax losses are recognized to the extent that it is probable the future taxable profit will be available against which the unused tax losses can be utilized.

9. Income taxes	**1998 MFIM**	**1997 MFIM**
Current tax	-4 473	-2 274
Deferred tax	93	–
Total	-4 380	-2 274
Finland	-2 974	-1 846
Other countries	-1 406	-428
Total	-4 380	-2 274

The differences between income tax expense computed at statutory rates (28% in Finland in 1998) and income tax expense provided on earnings are as follows at December 31:

	1998 MFIM
Income tax expense at statutory rate	4 195
Deduction for write-down of investments in subsidiaries	-73
Amortization of goodwill	33
Provisions without income tax benefit/expense	287
Taxes for prior years	42
Taxes on foreign subsidiaries' net income in excess of income taxes at statutory rates	269
Operating losses with no current tax benefit	96
Group adjustments	91
Adjustments to opening balance accruals	-428
Cumulative adjustments; change in accounting principle	-116
Other	-16
Income tax expense	4 380

Certain of the Group's subsidiaries income tax returns for periods ranging from 1992 through 1997 are under examination by tax authorities. The Group does not believe that any significant additional taxes will arise as a result of the examinations.

	1998
20. Deferred taxes	**MFIM**
In companies' balance sheet	
Tax losses carried forward	**104**
Temporary differences	**553**
	657
On consolidation	
Intercompany profit in inventory	**409**
Property, plant and equipment	**37**
Other	**15**
	461
Appropriations	
Untaxed reserves	**-477**
Net deferred tax asset	**641**

of which deferred tax assets MFIM 1 163 and deferred tax liabilities MFIM 522.

Beginning in January 1, 1998 the Group adopted revised IAS 12, Income taxes. The cumulative prior year net effect (MFIM 416) has been included in the cumulative prior year net effect of change in accounting policies in the consolidated profit and loss account for 1998. See note 1. Accounting principles.

Deferred income tax liabilities have not been established for withholding tax and other taxes that would be payable on the unremitted earnings of certain subsidiaries, as such earnings are permanently reinvested.

At December 31, 1998 the Group had loss carryforwards of MFIM 665 for which no deferred tax asset was recognised due to uncertainty of utilisation of those losses. The majority of these losses have no expiry date.

5.2   US

5.2.1   APB 11

For over 20 years, accounting for taxation in the USA was governed by an Opinion of the Accounting Principles Board issued in 1967 – APB 11.[178] This required full provision for deferred tax using the deferral method. Its objective was to match initial tax effects of timing differences with related income and expense recognised in pre-tax profits. Such an approach focused on obtaining matching in the profit and loss account, rather than on the measurement of deferred tax assets and liabilities in the balance sheet.

The computation of deferred tax on originating timing differences was conducted using the 'with-and-without' approach (i.e. with and without the inclusion of the transaction representing the timing difference). Reversals of timing differences were calculated using either the 'net change' method (i.e. at current tax rates) or the 'gross change' method (i.e. the rates at which the originating timing difference was recorded).

The tax benefit of losses carried forward could be recognised as an asset if its realisation were assured beyond reasonable doubt. In the year of realisation (if later than the year of the loss) the benefit of the loss on the tax charge would be reported as an extraordinary item. The deferred tax account was analysed and disclosed as either current or non-current in the balance sheet, depending on the classification of the asset to which it related.

5.2.2   SFAS 96

A consensus gradually emerged that a fundamental change of approach to accounting for taxation was required for several reasons. One of the most significant was that the balance sheet figures created by the deferral approach which APB 11 required were increasingly being regarded as having very little meaning. In particular, they did not conform to the definitions of assets and liabilities which the FASB had adopted in its conceptual framework study.[179]

In 1987, the FASB issued SFAS 96 – *Accounting for Income Taxes*.[180] This Statement was originally intended to become effective for accounting periods beginning on or after 15 December 1988, superseding APB 11 and other related pronouncements. However, because of the complexity and perceived artificiality of the standard, its implementation date was continually postponed to allow the FASB to give further consideration to certain aspects of the statement. They subsequently withdrew it and issued a different standard instead, SFAS 109, which is described below.

5.2.3   SFAS 109

In 1992 the FASB issued a new accounting standard on deferred tax – Statement No. 109,[181] superseding APB 11 and SFAS 96. This standard became effective for years beginning after 15 December 1992. In contrast to the deferral method required by APB 11, SFAS 109 uses the concept of 'temporary differences', which is discussed more fully in the analysis of IAS 12 in 5.1 above. The principal objective is to quantify the amount of tax that will become payable or receivable in the future due to temporary differences and tax loss carryforwards existing at the balance sheet date.[182] Changes in the amounts recognised in the balance sheet during the year represent the charge or benefit in the profit and loss account.

SFAS 109 requires deferred tax liabilities to be recognised for all taxable temporary differences, and deferred tax assets for deductible temporary differences and tax loss carryforwards if they are expected to be realised, subject to various exceptions, the more important of which are noted below. The tax effects of temporary differences and tax loss carryforwards are calculated using enacted tax rates and laws expected to apply to taxable income in future years.[183]

The rules are to be applied separately to each entity (or group of entities in cases where a consolidated tax return is submitted) in each tax jurisdiction.

Under SFAS 109, deferred tax assets should be recognised in full unless it is 'more likely than not' that some portion or all of the deferred tax assets will not be realised. A provision (or 'valuation allowance') should be made to reduce the tax asset to an amount that is 'more likely than not' (defined as a level of likelihood that is greater than 50 per cent) to be realised.[184] This test is not as prohibitive as the 'assured beyond a reasonable doubt' criterion contained in APB 11 and SSAP 15 and requires considerable judgement. In practice, companies that can demonstrate that they are likely to generate sufficient future taxable income will be able to recognise deferred tax assets in full. Evidence about such future taxable income can be obtained by considering both reversals of existing taxable temporary differences and also the results of future trading.

If consideration of taxable temporary differences and the results of future trading is not sufficient to justify full recognition of deferred tax assets (i.e. if a valuation allowance is still felt to be necessary), management is required to consider tax-planning strategies in determining the amount of the provision to be made.[185] Tax-planning strategies are defined as prudent and feasible actions that a company could undertake, if necessary, in order to realise deferred tax assets. Although they could be actions that an entity ordinarily might not take, they may provide sufficient evidence to justify reducing the amount of the provision or even eliminating the need for one.

Deferred tax balances are classified as current or non-current, depending on when the temporary difference is expected to result in a taxable or deductible amount.[186]

SFAS 109 also changed the approach to deferred tax in the context of acquisition accounting. Previously, APB 16 had required a net-of-tax approach,[187] under which the tax bases of acquired assets and liabilities were considered in establishing their fair values. SFAS 109 eliminated this and requires deferred tax assets and liabilities to be recognised in respect of differences between fair values assigned and the tax base values of the assets and liabilities acquired (except for goodwill that is not deductible for tax purposes). If any deferred tax assets of the acquired entity that were not recognised at the time of acquisition are realised later, the tax benefit is credited first to reduce any goodwill arising on the acquisition to zero, then to reduce any non-current intangibles relating to the acquisition to zero, and is only then applied to reduce income tax expense.[188]

The requirements of SFAS 109 in respect of the unremitted earnings of overseas investments are similar, but not identical, to those of IAS 12. Broadly, no provision need be made for deferred tax on retained earnings of overseas subsidiaries and corporate joint ventures, provided that the temporary differences in respect of them are 'essentially permanent in duration'. However, in respect of investments of 50 per cent or less (other than corporate joint ventures covered by the exemption in the previous sentence), provision should be made.[189]

5.2.4   *Main differences between US and UK requirements*

As explained at 5.1 above, IAS 12 is really a simplified version of SFAS 109 with very few modifications. Therefore the main differences between SFAS 109 and current UK practice are broadly the same as those between IAS 12 and UK practice, as outlined in 5.1.3 above. One significant difference between SFAS 109 and IAS 12 is that SFAS 109 has no exemption comparable to that in IAS 12 (see 5.1.2 B above) from the requirement to provide for deferred tax on initial recognition of a non-deductible asset. Rumour has it that this is not so much the result of a conscious decision as a reflection of the fact that there are no such assets in the US, so that the problem never manifested itself during the development of SFAS 109! Whatever the truth of this, in practice UK companies that are required to report their results under US GAAP tend to adopt the approach in IAS 12 rather than applying the letter of SFAS 109.

6   CONCLUSION

The most significant issue in accounting for taxation in the UK is still the application of the partial provision approach to deferred tax. As our discussion above highlights, the rules in many areas are simply not clear; the assessment of the level of provision required leaves room for significant judgement; and the method itself remains controversial, not least because of the anomalies highlighted by the interrelationship between SSAP 15 and SSAP 24 and the amendment to SSAP 15 which it provoked in 1992.

The steady fall in recent years of both the rates of taxation and the accelerated allowances available to companies in calculating their taxable profit have made these issues less important than they were when SSAP 15 was first introduced. If the major timing differences in future are going to arise because of unfunded pension schemes and similar long-term provisions, it will be necessary to reconsider whether partial provision remains a tenable approach.

Apart from these considerations, there is the international dimension. The ASB's commitment to the IASC's programme of international harmonisation of accounting standards has forced it to address the fact that the UK and Ireland are the only countries in the world now requiring the partial provision method. Unfortunately, the version of full provision that has gained international currency is not very attractive. If applied strictly, it can throw up absurd results, to which the IASC's response has been to make arbitrary exceptions to the general rules, rather than to question whether the rules themselves might not be intrinsically flawed. In our view, they are indeed flawed, since they are founded on an unconvincing attempt to rationalise as a 'liability' what is really just a balance carried over as the result of an inter-period allocation of tax expense.

We commend the ASB for having had the courage in FRED 19 to reject the methodology required by IAS 12. Whilst we do not find the conceptual basis for the methodology in FRED 19 particularly convincing in terms of the ASB's revised draft *Statement of Principles*, the ASB has at least considered the implications of the definition of 'liability'– if not, in our view, fully – at least more carefully than their international counterparts. However, the ASB may find its work cut out to make the case for a standard that is more complicated than SSAP 15, but which will probably generate much the same result once the effect of discounting is taken into account, and still leave accounting for tax in the UK and Ireland significantly different from that in the rest of the world. Putting all this together, commentators may well question the need for change.

References

1 This discussion is based on an 'income statement' approach. Some other methods of accounting for deferred tax involve a 'balance sheet' approach, notably that adopted in the US under SFAS 109, as described later in the chapter.
2 IAS 12 (Revised), *Income Taxes*, IASC, October 1996, para. 5.
3 Such a distinction was made in the original version of SSAP 15, *Accounting for deferred taxation*, ASC, October 1978 (see 2.2.4).
4 Whilst this describes the conceptually pure application of the deferral method, in practice reversals were sometimes made at the tax rate prevailing at the time of reversal (see 5.2.1).
5 Although considering the liability method, this discussion is still based on an 'income statement' approach rather than the 'balance sheet' approach adopted in the US under SFAS 109 and the IASC under IAS 12.
6 Discussion Paper, *Accounting for Tax*, ASB, March 1995, para. 4.7.1.
7 *Amendment to SSAP 15, Accounting for deferred tax*, ASB, December 1992, para. 1.
8 *Ibid.*, paras. 5.3.5, 5.3.6.
9 See *Accounting for Tax*, section 6.7, for a more detailed discussion.
10 TR 773, *The Use of Discounting in Financial Statements*, ICAEW, 1990, para. 38.
11 *Accounting for Tax*, para. 6.8.1.
12 SSAP 15, *Accounting for deferred tax*, ASC, Revised May 1985, para. 16.
13 *Accounting for Tax*, para. 3.7.1.
14 *Ibid.*, para. 11.1.4.
15 ED 12, *The treatment of taxation under the imputation system in the accounts of companies*, ASC, May 1973.
16 ED 11, *Accounting for deferred taxation*, ASC, May 1973.
17 SSAP 11, *Accounting for deferred taxation*, ASC, August 1975.
18 ED 18, *Current cost accounting*, ASC, November 1986, paras. 244–257.
19 ED 19, *Accounting for deferred taxation*, ASC, May 1977.
20 Original SSAP 15.
21 ED 33, *Accounting for deferred tax*, ASC, June 1983.
22 SSAP 15, *Accounting for deferred tax*, ASC, Revised May 1985.
23 *Ibid.*, para. 32A, as inserted by *Amendment to SSAP 15, Accounting for deferred tax*, December 1992, ASB, para. 1.
24 In particular, *Inside Track*, ASB, April 1999.
25 FRED 19, *Deferred Tax*, ASB, August 1999, Appendix V.
26 *Ibid.*, Preface.
27 *Ibid.*, para. 2.
28 *Ibid.*
29 *Ibid.*, Appendix V, paras. 31-36.
30 *Ibid.*, Appendix V, paras. 37-42.
31 *Ibid.*, Appendix V, paras. 43-52.

32 *Ibid.*, Appendix V, paras. 53-60.
33 FRED 19., para. 8.
34 *Ibid.*, para. 9.
35 *Ibid.*, paras. 13-14.
36 *Ibid.*, paras. 11-12.
37 *Ibid.*, paras. 15-16.
38 *Ibid.*, para. 17.
39 *Ibid.*, para. 18.
40 *Ibid.*, paras 18-27.
41 *Ibid.*, Appendix V, para. 71.
42 *Ibid.*, para. 28.
43 *Ibid.*, para. 29.
44 *Ibid.*, para. 30.
45 *Ibid.*, para. 31.
46 *Ibid.*, para. 34.
47 *Ibid.*, Appendix V, paras. 82-88.
48 *Ibid.*, para. 36.
49 *Ibid.*, para. 39.
50 *Ibid.*, para. 42.
51 *Ibid.*, paras 43-44.
52 *Ibid.*, para. 45.
53 *Ibid.*, para. 47.
54 *Ibid.*, para. 48.
55 *Ibid.*, paras. 50-52.
56 *Ibid.*, para. 57(a).
57 *Ibid.*, Appendix V, 118.
58 *Ibid.*, para. 55.
59 *Ibid.*, paras. 53(a), 54(b).
60 SSAP 5, *Accounting for value added tax*, ASC, April 1974.
61 ED 10, *Accounting for Value Added Tax*, ASC, May 1973.
62 SSAP 5, para. 8.
63 *Ibid.*, para. 9.
64 ED 28, *Accounting for Petroleum Revenue Tax*, ASC, March 1981.
65 UITF 16, *Income and expenses subject to non-standard rates of tax*, UITF, February 1997, para. 11.
66 SSAP 8, *The treatment of taxation under the imputation system in the accounts of companies*, August 1974, ASC, para. 24.
67 *Ibid.*, para. 20.
68 *Ibid.*, para. 13.
69 *Ibid.*, para. 25.
70 ASB PN 109, ASB, December 1997.
71 *Foreword to Accounting Standards*, ASB, June 1993, para. 31.
72 UITF 16, para. 7.
73 SSAP 8, para. 22. It should be noted that changes in tax legislation since SSAP 8 was issued have meant that unrelieved overseas taxation will not arise from the payment or proposed payment of dividends. Consequently, SSAP 8's requirement for the separate disclosure of such amounts is now redundant.
74 *Ibid.*, para. 23.
75 *Ibid.*, para. 9.
76 FRED, *Amendment to SSAP 8 'The treatment of taxation under the imputation system in the accounts of companies': Presentation of dividend income*, ASB, October 1997, Preface.
77 FRED 18, *Current taxation*, ASB, June 1999, Appendix V, para. 2.
78 *Ibid.*, para. 5.
79 *Ibid.*, para. 6.
80 *Ibid.*, para. 7.
81 *Ibid.*, para. 10.
82 *Ibid.*, para. 19.

83 *Ibid.*, para. 9. See also ASB PN 141, June 1999.
84 *Ibid.*
85 *Ibid.*, para. 8, 11.
86 *Ibid.*, Appendix V, paras. 6-7.
87 *Ibid.*, para. 8.
88 *Ibid.*, para. 9.
89 FRED 18, para. 15.
90 *Ibid.*, para. 16.
91 *Ibid.*, paras. 12-13.
92 SSAP 15, para. 1.
93 *Ibid.*, para. 2.
94 *Ibid.*, para. 12.
95 *Ibid.*, para. 14.
96 *Ibid.*, para. 17.
97 *Ibid.*, para. 18.
98 *Ibid.*, para. 19.
99 *Ibid.*, para. 20.
100 *Ibid.*, para. 21.
101 *Ibid.*, para. 23.
102 *Ibid.*, paras. 24–26.
103 *Ibid.*, Appendix, para. 4.
104 *Ibid.*, paras. 27 and 28.
105 *Ibid.*, Appendix, para. 4.
106 *Ibid.*, para. 29.
107 *Ibid.*, para. 30.
108 *Ibid.*, Appendix, para. 14.
109 *Ibid.*, Appendix, para. 15.
110 *Ibid.*, para. 31.
111 *Ibid.*, para. 32.
112 *Ibid.*, paras. 33 and 34.
113 FRS 3, paras. 22 and 20.
114 SSAP 15, para. 35.
115 FRS 3, para. 23.
116 SSAP 15, para. 36.
117 *Ibid.*, paras. 37 and 40.
118 *Ibid.*, para. 41.
119 Original SSAP 15, para. 33.
120 SSAP 15, para. 38.
121 *Ibid.*, para. 39.
122 *Ibid.*, para. 42.
123 *Ibid.*, para. 43.
124 *Ibid.*, para. 44.
125 FRS 2, *Accounting for subsidiary undertakings*, ASB, July 1992, para. 54.
126 CA 85, Sch. 4, para. 54(2).
127 FRS 3, para. 23.
128 CA 85, Sch. 4, para. 8 Profit and loss account formats and para. 54(3).
129 *Ibid.*, para. 8 Balance sheet formats.
130 *Ibid.*, para. 46.
131 *Ibid.*, para. 47.
132 SSAP 15, Appendix, para. 4.
133 Accountants Digest No. 174, ICAEW, *A Guide to Accounting Standards — Deferred Tax*, Summer 1985.
134 SSAP 15, Appendix, para. 14.
135 CA 85, Sch. 4, para. 54(2) and FRS 3, para. 23.
136 SSAP 15, para. 43.
137 SSAP 8, para. 20(c).

138 SSAP 15, para. 31.
139 *Ibid.*, para. 32.
140 SSAP 8, para. 7.
141 SSAP 15, Appendix, para. 17.
142 *Accounting for Tax*, para. 10.5.4.
143 SSAP 8, para. 7.
144 SSAP 17, *Accounting for post balance sheet events*, ASC, August 1980, Appendix, item (g) of examples of adjusting events.
145 Accountants Digest No. 174, p. 12.
146 SSAP 15, para. 20.
147 *Ibid.*, Appendix, para. 11.
148 *Ibid.*, para. 44.
149 FRS 2, para. 54.
150 ED 33, para. 35.
151 IAS 12, para. 5.
152 *Ibid.*
153 SFAS 109, *Accounting for Income Taxes*, FASB, 1992, paras. 77-78.
154 *Accounting for tax*, paras. A1.19-20.
155 IAS 12, para. 7-8.
156 *Ibid.*, para. 10.
157 *Ibid.*, paras. 15, 24.
158 *Ibid.*
159 *Ibid.*, para. 61.
160 *Ibid.*, para. 46.
161 *Ibid.*, para. 47.
162 *Ibid.*, para. 51.
163 *Ibid.*, paras. 53-5.
164 *Ibid.*, paras. 69, 70.
165 *Ibid.*, para. 71.
166 *Ibid.*, para. 74.
167 *Ibid.*, para. 56.
168 *Ibid.*, para. 82.
169 *Ibid.*, para. 67.
170 *Ibid.*, para. 68.
171 *Ibid.*, para. 38.
172 *Ibid.*, paras. 39, 44.
173 *Ibid.*, para. 40.
174 *Ibid.*, para. 43.
175 *Ibid.*, para. 42.
176 *Ibid.*, paras. 79, 80.
177 *Ibid.*, para. 81.
178 APB 11, *Accounting for Income Taxes*, AICPA, December 1967.
179 SFAC No. 6, *Elements of Financial Statements*, FASB, December 1985, paras. 25 and 35.
180 SFAS 96, *Accounting for Income Taxes*, FASB, December 1987.
181 SFAS 109, *Accounting for Income Taxes*, FASB, February 1992.
182 *Ibid.*, paras. 6–9.
183 *Ibid.*, para. 18.
184 *Ibid.*, para. 17.
185 *Ibid.*, para. 22.
186 *Ibid.*, para. 41.
187 APB 16, *Business Combinations*, Accounting Principles Board, August 1970, para. 89.
188 SFAS 109, para. 30.
189 *Ibid.* paras. 31-2.

Chapter 22   Reporting financial performance

1   THE NEED FOR A STANDARD

1.1   Income measurement

Chapter 2 of this book discusses the concept of income and outlines the emphasis placed on the transactions approach to income measurement in the development of historical cost accounting theory.   In summary, financial accounting under the historical cost system essentially involves allocating the effects of transactions between reporting periods, with the result that the balance sheet consists of the residuals of the income measurement process. Despite the conflict discussed in Chapter 2 between the asset and liability approach on the one hand, and the revenue and expense approach on the other, the importance attributed to income measurement is highlighted by the FASB's Concepts Statement No. 1. This states that 'the primary focus of financial reporting is information about an enterprise's performance provided by measures of earnings and its components. Investors, creditors, and others who are concerned with assessing the prospects for enterprise net cash inflows are especially interested in that information.'[1]   In addition, the emphasis that analysts place on companies' reported earnings as a measure of performance further illustrates the importance of income measurement.

Although the term 'income' is used to describe a concept, rather than something which is specific or precise, specific rules and procedures have been developed by accountants to measure income. These rules have been based on the concept of financial capital maintenance, which has been subscribed to by the FASB in SFAC No. 6 in terms of 'comprehensive income'. Comprehensive income is defined as 'the change in equity of a business enterprise during a period from transactions and other events and circumstances from nonowner sources'.[2] Therefore, the comprehensive income of a business enterprise over its entire lifetime will be the net of its cash receipts and cash outlays.[3] In June 1997 the

FASB issued SFAS 130 – *Reporting Comprehensive Income* – with the aim of establishing standards for the reporting and display (but not recognition and measurement) of comprehensive income and its components in a full set of general purpose financial statements.[4] SFAS 130 is discussed at 4.2.4 below. However, it is perhaps worth noting here that it is an uncharacteristically tentative standard which, despite using SFAC Nos. 5 and 6 as its *raison d'être*, does not sit very well with the FASB's conceptual framework.

In any event, the need for businesses to measure their income annually for financial reporting purposes highlighted two major accounting issues. First, there was the issue of how to allocate the effects of transactions between accounting periods for reporting purposes, instead of merely allowing them to fall in the periods in which the transactions took place. This issue is dealt with through the development of allocation rules based on the fundamental accounting concepts of matching and prudence. The second issue which arose was whether or not all recorded transactions should be included in the calculation of the figure for 'net profit/loss for the period'. Some accountants have held the view that net profit/loss should reflect the effects of all recorded transactions, whilst others have contended that net profit/loss should not be distorted by abnormal, unusual and non-recurring events and transactions. These differing viewpoints have led to two basic concepts of income: the all-inclusive concept and the current operating performance concept.[5]

1.1.1 The all-inclusive (comprehensive income) concept

Under this concept, net profit/loss would include all transactions (except dividends and capital transactions) which affect the net change in equity. Proponents of the all-inclusive concept put forward the following arguments in favour of this basis of income measurement:

(a) the annual reported net profits/losses, when aggregated over the life of the business enterprise, should be equal to the comprehensive income of the enterprise. Therefore, since charges and credits arising from extraordinary events and from corrections of prior periods are part of an enterprise's earnings history, the omission of such items from periodic income statements will result in the misstatement of the net profit/loss for a series of years;

(b) the omission of certain charges and credits from the computation of the net profit/loss for a period opens the door to possible manipulation or smoothing of results over a period;

(c) a profit and loss account which includes the effects of all transactions is more easily understood and less subject to variations resulting from the application of subjective judgements; and

(d) full disclosure in the profit and loss account of the nature of all transactions will enable users to make their own assessments of the importance of the items and derive an appropriate measurement of income based on their own specific needs.

1.1.2 The current operating performance concept

Under this concept, the emphasis is on the ordinary, normal, recurring operations of the enterprise during the accounting period. If extraordinary or prior period transactions have occurred, their inclusion in the current period's profit and loss account 'might impair the significance of net income to such an extent that misleading inferences might be drawn from the amount so designated'.[6] Advocates of the current operating performance concept put forward the following arguments in its favour:[7]

(a) users attach a particular business significance to the profit and loss account and the net profit/loss reported therein. While some users are able to analyse a profit and loss account and to eliminate from it those extraordinary and prior period transactions which may tend to impair its usefulness for their purposes, many users are not trained to do this. They believe that management (subject to the attestation of the independent auditors) is in a better position to do this and eliminate the effect of such items from the amount designated as net profit/loss for the period; and

(b) extraordinary and prior period transactions should be disclosed as direct adjustments of retained earnings, since this eliminates any distortion of reported earnings for the period, resulting in a more meaningful figure for inter-period and inter-firm comparison.

1.1.3 Which concept?

The fundamental difference in the two concepts of income discussed above lies in the perceived objectives of reporting net operating income for a particular period. The ASB's revised Draft *Statement of Principles* asserts that 'the objective of financial statements is to provide information about the reporting entity's financial performance and financial position that is useful to a wide range of users for assessing the stewardship of management and for making economic decisions.'[8]   In its Discussion Paper – *Reporting Financial Performance; Proposals for Change* – which proposes radical change to the system of performance reporting, the ASB explains further its views on the predictive role of reporting financial performance, as follows:

'Users of financial statements require information on the entity's financial performance because such information:

(a) assists users in assessing the capacity of the entity to generate cash flows from its existing resource base and in forming judgements about the effectiveness with which the entity has employed its resources and might employ additional resources; and

(b)   provides feedback to users so that they can review their previous assessments of the financial performance for past periods and can modify their assessments for, or develop expectations about, future periods."[9]

In summary, what this means is that the ASB sees the provision of information that is useful in making predictions about future cash flows as a key objective of financial reporting.

Since the current operating net income for a period emphasises an enterprise's current financial performance for each period, predictions concerning future enterprise performance might be facilitated through the elimination of non-recurring and prior period transactions. On the other hand, merely because an item is non-recurring does not mean that it is not relevant to an assessment of the past performance of management. Moreover, because of the artificial nature of the accounting period and the subjectivity necessary in the application of the current operating performance concept, the assessment of future performance can best be achieved if it is based on the *entire* historical performance of the enterprise over a series of several years. Clearly, the ASB holds this view as well, since its approach to recognition as articulated in its revised Draft *Statement of Principles* is that all gains and losses will be recognised in a single performance statement, rather than in a profit and loss account and statement of total recognised gains and losses, as required by FRS 3. This is further borne out in its Discussion Paper on performance reporting which states that 'in principle, all gains and losses ... are relevant to an understanding of financial performance', and that 'it is appropriate for all financial performance to be reported in a single expanded statement of financial performance rather than two statements'.[10]   (The ASB proposals for change to the system of reporting performance are discussed in detail at section 5 below.)

Notwithstanding the various arguments concerning the respective merits and demerits of the two basic concepts of income, there was clearly a need in the 1970s for the standardisation of accounting practice in this area of reporting. Reserve accounting, whereby companies excluded capital and non-recurring items from the profit and loss account, was prevalent. In the UK, the ASC adopted the current operating performance concept of income in SSAP 6 – *Extraordinary items and prior year adjustments*. An income statement prepared under SSAP 6 made the distinction between ordinary and extraordinary activities and excluded prior year adjustments and items accounted for directly in reserves such as goodwill and certain foreign exchange differences.

However, the publication by the ASB of the first piecemeal Discussion Draft version of its Draft *Statement of Principles* heralded a substantial change in approach to the reporting of financial performance in the UK. This is where the idea of a new statement of financial performance in addition to the profit and loss account was first mooted by the ASB, preparing the way for a balance sheet approach to income recognition. As more fully explained in section 5 of Chapter 2 and section 4.1 of Chapter 3 of this book, the three elements of the balance sheet are defined in the ASB's revised Draft *Statement of Principles* in terms of the fundamental accounting equation of assets minus liabilities equals ownership interest.

Under the ASB's revised Draft *Statement of Principles,* recognition is triggered where a past event indicates that there has been a measurable change in the assets and liabilities of an entity and, where a change in assets is not offset by an equal change in liabilities, a gain or loss will result (unless the change relates to a transaction with the entity's owners, in which case a contribution from owners or distribution to owners will be recognised). As stated above, it was in the first piecemeal Discussion Draft version of the Draft *Statement of Principles* that the ASB introduced the notion of a 'second performance statement': gains or losses should be recognised either in the profit and loss account or in the new primary financial statement, 'the statement of total recognised gains and losses'. The original omnibus version of the Draft *Statement of Principles* proposed that gains and losses on those assets and liabilities that are held on a continuing basis primarily in order to enable the entity's operations to be carried out should be reported in the statement of total recognised gains and losses, and not in the profit and loss account; all other gains and losses should be reported in the profit and loss account.[11]

The introduction of this new statement of financial performance, together with the all-inclusive concept of income, represented the most radical change brought about by FRS 3 – *Reporting financial performance* – which superseded SSAP 6. This also meant that although the ASB's views on recognition had only been issued in draft form through the Draft *Statement of Principles*, they were already being entrenched in accounting standards by means of FRS 3. Although FRS 3 is still the extant UK accounting standard on reporting financial performance, the ASB has revised its Draft *Statement of Principles* and issued proposals aimed at amending FRS 3, indicating a clear intention to merge the statement of total recognised gains and losses and the profit and loss account into a single comprehensive income statement. This is further discussed later in this Chapter.

1.2 The development of UK standards

Prior to SSAP 6, unusual or non-recurring transactions were frequently excluded from the profit and loss account for the year and accounted for as a movement on reserves so that the trend in reported results was not distorted by such transactions. However, the subjectivity inherent in determining whether an event was unusual or non-recurring would result in similar items in different companies receiving different treatments, thus rendering comparisons of the reported results of different companies relatively meaningless.

The first official guidance was given in 1958, in the form of an Accounting Recommendation issued by the ICAEW,[12] which supported the distinction between capital and revenue as a means of determining what items should be included in the profit and loss account. However, the recommendation was insubstantial as it effectively permitted capital items to be accounted for either through the profit and loss account or through reserves – depending on which treatment would facilitate the presentation of a true and fair view.

1.2.1   The original SSAP 6

The principal objects of ED 5[13] (issued in 1971), ED 7[14] (issued in 1972), and the first version of SSAP 6 (issued in 1974), were to ensure that all extraordinary or prior year items, with certain specified exceptions, should be accounted for through the profit and loss account for the period and not through reserves. In order to achieve this without losing information on the performance of the ongoing operations, SSAP 6 required the separate disclosure of profits and losses on extraordinary items after the profit or loss on ordinary activities, defining which items could be regarded as extraordinary. The standard also prescribed the only two instances where items could be retrospectively adjusted through reserves by means of a prior year adjustment.

Although SSAP 6 reduced the extent of reserve accounting, it inadvertently caused the development of a multiplicity of items classified as 'extraordinary', which would consequently be excluded from profit or loss on ordinary activities after taxation, and earnings per share. There was evidence of significant inconsistencies between the way different companies disclosed the effect of apparently similar events in their profit and loss accounts.

1.2.2   The revision of SSAP 6

The new accounts formats introduced in the Companies Act 1981[15] required separate disclosure in the profit and loss account of extraordinary items and the associated tax thereon after the profit or loss on ordinary activities, and thus standardised and gave statutory backing to the disclosure requirements of SSAP 6. This added impetus to the growing disquiet about the effectiveness of the standard, and in 1983 the ASC issued a discussion paper which identified some of the problems that had arisen since the introduction of SSAP 6 and proposed some solutions.[16] In 1985, as a result of responses to this discussion paper, the ASC issued ED 36,[17] which embodied some of the solutions originally proposed in the 1983 discussion paper. ED 36 was eventually converted to SSAP 6 (Revised) in 1986.

The revised standard attempted to reduce the problem of inconsistency in classification of items as extraordinary in three ways, by:

(a)   extending a list of examples given in the original SSAP 6 of events which were likely to be classified as extraordinary and contrasting this with a list of exceptional items;[18]

(b)   discussing the effects of terminating parts of operations and introducing a definition of a business segment to clarify when the discontinuance of part of a business could be treated as extraordinary;[19] and

(c)   defining 'ordinary activities' and 'exceptional items' in order to clarify how extraordinary items could be distinguished.[20]

There were also a number of other new ideas introduced both in the body of the standard and in the explanatory note. These included:

(a)   separate disclosure of profit before exceptional items and exceptional items on the face of the profit and loss account if necessary to show a true and fair view;[21]

(b)   disclosure of a statement of movements on reserves, or a reference to where the statement is disclosed in the notes, on the face of the profit and loss account;[22]

(c)   standardisation of the method of calculation of the tax charge or credit on extraordinary items;[23]

(d)   the recommendation that listed companies should disclose exceptional items in preliminary profit statements, half-yearly reports and historical summaries;[24] and

(e)   restatement of historical summaries retroactively in the event of a prior year adjustment or, if impracticable to do so, a statement to that effect.[25]

ED 36 had also recommended the disclosure of earnings per share both pre- and post-extraordinary items, but this idea was dropped by the ASC as it was believed that a change in disclosure requirements for earnings per share fell outside the scope of the revision of SSAP 6. However, it is noteworthy that this was one aspect which was specifically addressed by the ASB in its development of FRS 3, which superseded SSAP 6 in 1992.

1.2.3 UITF 2

In October 1991, the Urgent Issues Task Force published its second Abstract (UITF 2), clarifying the classification of restructuring costs between extraordinary and exceptional items under SSAP 6. This Abstract arose as a result of the ASB becoming concerned about the increasing number of companies which had been charging major amounts to extraordinary items for what appeared to be a general restructuring of their businesses. SSAP 6 defined extraordinary items as material items which derived from events or transactions that fell outside the ordinary activities of the entity and which were therefore not expected to occur frequently or regularly. The ASB was of the view that restructuring costs, even if they related to a fundamental restructuring of a business, were usually part of the ordinary activities of a company and should normally have been treated as charges in arriving at the profit or loss on ordinary activities.

Consequently, as an interim measure until such time as SSAP 6 was replaced, the ASB referred the matter to the UITF for consideration. The consensus reached by the UITF was that where the cost of restructuring or reorganising business activities needed to be disclosed by virtue of its size or incidence, it should be dealt with as an exceptional item, not an extraordinary item, unless it stemmed directly from a separate extraordinary event or transaction.[26]   This halted the tide of extraordinary items and gave the ASB the necessary breathing space until such time as the matter was more clearly addressed in FRS 3, which superseded both SSAP 6 and UITF 2.

1.2.4   FRED 1

The ASB issued FRED 1 – *The Structure of Financial Statements – Reporting of Financial Performance* – in December 1991 at the same time as Chapter 6 of the first piecemeal Discussion Draft version of its Draft *Statement of Principles – Presentation of financial information.*   The two documents gave the accounting world its first view of the ASB's plans to revolutionise the reporting of financial performance in general, and the profit and loss account in particular. They introduced the idea of an additional primary financial statement of performance and, although not confirmed until the publication of the third and fourth Discussion Draft chapters of the Draft *Statement of Principles* in July 1992, gave the first indication of the ASB's preference for a balance sheet approach to the recognition of comprehensive income.

Despite receiving extensive comments on FRED 1, the ASB issued FRS 3 in October 1992 with few changes in substance.

2   THE REQUIREMENTS OF FRS 3

2.1   The principal features of FRS 3

'Making Corporate Reports Valuable', a project undertaken by the Research Committee of ICAS, identified four basic shortcomings of present-day financial reporting: the adherence to legal form rather than economic substance, the use of cost rather than value, the concentration on the past rather than the future and the interest in 'profit' rather than 'wealth'.[27]   Bearing in mind that Sir David Tweedie, Chairman of the ASB, was a member of the Committee that prepared the MCRV document, it is not difficult to identify many of the ASB's initiatives as attempts to address these shortcomings. For example, the objective of FRS 5 is to ensure that the substance of an entity's transactions is reported in its financial statements; all versions of the ASB's Draft *Statement of Principles* advocate greater use of current values in financial reporting, and the Statement on the Operating and Financial Review is designed to encourage reporting entities to discuss issues which are relevant to an assessment of their future prospects.

It is not surprising, therefore, that FRS 3 was also aimed at ameliorating some of these perceived shortcomings. This was borne out by the standard's objective, which was stated as being 'to require reporting entities falling within its scope to highlight a range of important components of financial performance to aid users in understanding the performance achieved by a reporting entity in a period and to assist them in forming a basis for their assessment of future results and cash flows'.[28] Furthermore, as is more fully explained below, the new statement of financial performance introduced by FRS 3 – the statement of total recognised gains and losses – represented the ASB's first step towards requiring the reporting of changes in wealth as opposed to traditional historical cost profit and loss.

In summary, the changes to the reporting of financial performance brought about by FRS 3 were as follows:

- the profit and loss account was reshaped into a so-called 'layered format' so as to highlight a number of important components of performance:

    - the results of continuing operations (including the results of acquisitions);

    - the results of discontinued operations;

    - profits and losses on the sale or termination of an operation, costs of a fundamental reorganisation or restructuring and profits or losses on the disposal of fixed assets; and

    - extraordinary items;

- the analysis between continuing operations, acquisitions (as a component of continuing operations) and discontinued operations should be disclosed to the level of operating profit. As a minimum, the analysis of turnover and operating profit must be given on the face of the profit and loss account, with the analysis of the remaining headings allowed to be relegated to the notes.

    The question of whether the analysis of results between continuing and discontinued operations should include interest and taxation was debated extensively by the ASB. However, the ASB concluded that the analysis should only be required to the pre-interest level because interest payable is often a reflection of a reporting entity's overall financing policy, involving both equity and debt funding considerations on a group-wide basis, rather than an aggregation of the particular types of finance allocated to individual segments of the entity's operations. Consequently, any allocation of interest would involve a considerable degree of subjectivity; irrespective of the method used, assumptions would have to be made regarding such factors as the use of disposal proceeds, the appropriate interest rate to use and the reporting entity's cost of capital. However, the standard did not preclude the allocation of interest or taxation between continuing and discontinued operations, but if it is allocated, the method and underlying assumptions used in making the allocations should be disclosed;[29]

- the standard laid down strict criteria for distinguishing between continuing and discontinued operations;

■   extraordinary items were effectively eliminated, although EPS is, in any event, to be calculated *after* extraordinary items. Most (if not all) items which were previously classified as extraordinary under SSAP 6 were now to be treated as exceptional items;

■   all exceptional items (other than the three listed below) should be included in the profit and loss account under the statutory format headings to which they relate. They should be separately disclosed by way of note or, where it is necessary in order that the financial statements give a true and fair view, on the face of the profit and loss account. The following items, including provisions in respect of such items, should be shown separately on the face of the profit and loss account after operating profit and before interest, analysed between continuing and discontinued operations:

      –   profits or losses on the sale or termination of an operation;

      –   costs of a fundamental reorganisation or restructuring; and

      –   profits or losses on the disposal of fixed assets;

■   the standard introduced a new primary financial statement in the form of a 'Statement of total recognised gains and losses'. The statement would reflect the ways in which the reporting entity's net assets have increased or decreased from all sources other than investment by its owners, and represented the ASB's first step towards the reporting of changes in wealth;

■   the standard introduced a requirement to disclose a memorandum note of historical cost profits and losses immediately following the profit and loss account or statement of total recognised gains and losses. This is an abbreviated restatement of the profit and loss account which adjusts the reported profit to show that figure excluding the effects of any asset revaluations;

■   the standard required a reconciliation of the opening and closing totals of shareholders' funds for the period. The reconciliation may be presented either as a note to the financial statements or as a fifth primary statement. Where it is presented as a primary statement the FRS requires it to be shown separately from the statement of total recognised gains and losses; and

■   prior period adjustments must be accounted for by restating the comparative figures for the preceding period in the primary statements and notes and by adjusting the opening balance of reserves in the current and previous periods for the cumulative effect. The cumulative effect of the adjustments should also be noted at the foot of the statement of total recognised gains and losses of the current period.

Each of these aspects of FRS 3 is discussed in more detail in the sections which follow. Illustrative examples of the requirements of the standard are set out in an Appendix to the standard, part of which is reproduced below, showing the two alternative formats of the restyled profit and loss account:

Profit and loss account example 1

	1993	1993	1992 as restated
	£ million	£ million	£ million
Turnover			
Continuing operations	550		500
Acquisitions	50		
	600		
Discontinued operations	175		190
		775	690
Cost of sales		(620)	(555)
Gross profit		155	135
Net operating expenses		(104)	(83)
Operating profit			
Continuing operations	50		40
Acquisitions	6		
	56		
Discontinued operations	(15)		12
Less 1992 provision	10		
		51	52
Profit on sale of properties in continuing operations		9	6
Provision for loss on operations to be discontinued			(30)
Loss on disposal of discontinued operations	(17)		
Less 1992 provision	20		
		3	
Profit on ordinary activities before interest		63	28
Interest payable		(18)	(15)
Profit on ordinary activities before taxation		45	13
Tax on profit on ordinary activities		(14)	(4)
Profit on ordinary activities after taxation		31	9
Minority interests		(2)	(2)
[Profit before extraordinary items]		29	7
[Extraordinary items] (included only to show positioning)		–	–
Profit for the financial year		29	7
Dividends		(8)	(1)
Retained profit for the financial year		21	6
Earnings per share		**39p**	**10p**
Adjustments		*xp*	*xp*
[to be itemised and an adequate description to be given]			
Adjusted earnings per share		*yp*	*yp*
[Reason for calculating the adjusted earnings per share to be given]			

Profit and loss account example 2

	Continuing operations	Acquisitions	Discontinued operations	Total	Total
	1993	1993	1993	1993	1992 as restated
	£ million	£ million	£ million	£ million	£ million
Turnover	550	50	175	775	690
Cost of sales	(415)	(40)	(165)	(620)	(555)
Gross profit	135	10	10	155	135
Net operating expenses	(85)	(4)	(25)	(114)	(83)
Less 1992 provision			10	10	
Operating profit	50	6	(5)	51	52
Profit on sale of properties	9			9	6
Provision for loss on operations to be discontinued					(30)
Loss on disposal of discontinued operations			(17)	(17)	
Less 1992 provision			20	20	
Profit on ordinary activities before interest	59	6	(2)	63	28
Interest payable				(18)	(15)
Profit on ordinary activities before taxation				45	13
Tax on profit on ordinary activities				(14)	(4)
Profit on ordinary activities after taxation				31	9
Minority interests				(2)	(2)
[Profit before extraordinary items]				29	7
[Extraordinary items] (included only to show positioning)				–	–
Profit for the financial year				29	7
Dividends				(8)	(1)
Retained profit for the financial year				21	6
Earnings per share				**39p**	**10p**
Adjustments				*xp*	*xp*
[to be itemised and an adequate description to be given]					
Adjusted earnings per share				*yp*	*yp*
[Reason for calculating the adjusted earnings per share to be given]					

Notes to the financial statements

Note required in respect of profit and loss account example 1

	1993			1992 (as restated)		
	Continuing	**Discontinued**	**Total**	**Continuing**	**Discontinued**	**Total**
	£ million	*£ million*	*£ million*	*£ million*	*£ million*	*£ million*
Cost of sales	455	165	620	385	170	555
Net operating expenses						
Distribution costs	56	13	69	46	5	51
Administrative expenses	41	12	53	34	3	37
Other operating income	(8)	0	(8)	(5)	0	(5)
	89	25	114	75	8	83
Less 1992 provision	0	(10)	(10)			
	89	15	104			

The total figures for continuing operations in 1993 include the following amounts relating to acquisitions: cost of sales £40 million and net operating expenses £4 million (namely distribution costs £3 million, administrative expenses £3 million and other operating income £2 million).

Note required in respect of profit and loss account example 2

	1993			1992 (as restated)		
	Continuing	**Discontinued**	**Total**	**Continuing**	**Discontinued**	**Total**
	£ million	*£ million*	*£ million*	*£ million*	*£ million*	*£ million*
Turnover				500	190	690
Cost of sales				385	170	555
Net operating expenses						
Distribution costs	56	13	69	46	5	51
Administrative expenses	41	12	53	34	3	37
Other operating income	(8)	0	(8)	(5)	0	(5)
	89	25	114	75	8	83
Operating profit				40	12	52

The total figure of net operating expenses for continuing operations in 1993 includes £4 million in respect of acquisitions (namely distribution costs £3 million, administrative expenses £3 million and other operating income £2 million).

2.2   The scope of FRS 3

FRS 3 applies to all financial statements intended to give a true and fair view of the financial position and results of the reporting entity. The FRS states that such entities 'should apply the requirements of the FRS except to the extent that these requirements are not permitted by the statutory framework (if any) under which the entity reports'.[30]

The implication of this is that where specific industry legislation merely permits an entity not to disclose certain information, this clause within the scope section of the FRS will not be sufficient to allow the entities to depart from the requirements of the FRS. However, this is contrary to the ASB's *Foreword to Accounting Standards* which would allow a departure from the requirements of a standard in such circumstances.[31]

2.3   Continuing and discontinued operations

FRS 3 requires each of the statutory profit and loss headings between turnover and operating profit to be analysed between continuing operations, acquisitions (as a component of continuing operations) and discontinued operations. Although the term 'operating profit' is not used in the Companies Act formats, it is not defined in FRS 3 either. However, the standard does state that 'for non-financial reporting entities operating profit is normally profit before income from shares in group undertakings'.[32]

This is a somewhat curious interpretation of operating profit, since it seems to draw a distinction between operating and non-operating profit on the basis of the legal form of the income-earning vehicle, rather than on the basis of the nature of the income itself. However, this approach has now been confirmed by FRS 9 – *Associates and joint ventures* – which (a) differentiates between associates and joint ventures and (b) specifies where the income from them is to be shown in relation to operating profit in the profit and loss account.

FRS 9 states that the share of associates' operating results should be included after the group operating result and, where applicable, after and separately from the share of the operating results of joint ventures[33] (see Extract 22.1 below). We presume that this approach is to be followed at each level of the profit and loss account where the share of associates' and joint ventures' results is to be included. This is implied by the illustrative examples in Appendix IV to FRS 9, but not explicitly stated.

Extract 22.1: Cable and Wireless plc (1999)

CONSOLIDATED PROFIT AND LOSS ACCOUNT [extract]

FOR THE YEAR ENDED 31 MARCH

	Acquisitions £m	Other continuing operations £m	1999 £m	1998 £m
Turnover of the group including its share of joint ventures and associates	736	8,384	**9,120**	8,302
Share of turnover of – joint ventures	–	(1,064)	**(1,064)**	(1,141)
– associates	–	(112)	**(112)**	(160)
Group turnover	736	7,208	**7,944**	7,001
Operating costs before depreciation, amortisation and exceptional items	(596)	(4,662)	**(5,258)**	(4,517)
Exceptional items	–	46	**46**	(92)
Operating costs before depreciation and amortisation	(596)	(4,616)	**(5,212)**	(4,609)
EBITDA	140	2,592	**2,732**	2,392
Depreciation before exceptional items	(111)	(912)	**(1,023)**	(833)
Exceptional items	–	–	–	(158)
Depreciation	(111)	(912)	**(1,023)**	(991)
Amortisation of capitalised goodwill	(61)	–	**(61)**	–
Group operating profit	(32)	1,680	**1,648**	1,401
Share of operating profits in joint ventures	–	103	**103**	37
Share of operating profits/(losses) in associates	–	20	**20**	(4)
Total operating profit	(32)	1,803	**1,771**	1,434
Profits less (losses) on sale and termination of operations before exceptional items			–	6
Exceptional items			–	519
Profits less (losses) on sale and termination of operations			–	525
Exceptional costs of a fundamental reorganisation			–	(200)
Profits less (losses) on disposal of fixed assets before exceptional items			170	85
Exceptional items			198	518
Profits less (losses) on disposal of fixed assets			368	603
Net interest and other similar income – Group			(232)	(100)
– joint ventures			(85)	(78)
Profit on ordinary activities before taxation			1,822	2,184

...

2.3.1 *The definition of discontinued operations*

Under FRS 3, discontinued operations are operations of the reporting entity that
are sold or terminated and that satisfy all of the following conditions:[34]

(a)   the sale or termination is completed either in the period or before the earlier of three months after the commencement of the subsequent period and the date on which the financial statements are approved;

(b)   if a termination, the former activities have ceased permanently;

(c)   the sale or termination has a material effect on the nature and focus of the reporting entity's operations and represents a material reduction in its operating facilities resulting either from its withdrawal from a particular market (whether class of business or geographical) or from a material reduction in turnover in the reporting entity's continuing markets; and

(d)   the assets, liabilities, results of operations and activities are clearly distinguishable, physically, operationally and for financial reporting purposes.

Operations not satisfying all these conditions are classified as continuing.

Perhaps the most notable feature of this definition is the fact that 'discontinued' means what it says. The operations must have been discontinued (i.e. either sold or ceased permanently) within the financial year or shortly after the year end. Clearly, the ASB's underlying rationale for this approach was to improve the predictive value of the profit and loss account by providing users with a basis for the assessment of future income. Users now have the assurance that operations reported as discontinued in the profit and loss account will have no impact on future performance.

This differs significantly from the former rules under SSAP 6, whereby business segments could be put in the 'discontinued' category on the basis of a decision to discontinue them – even if the decision was not due to be fully implemented until several years later. Furthermore, under SSAP 6, both the results of discontinued operations from the date of implementing the disposal plan, and the gain or loss on sale or closure would commonly have been dealt with as extraordinary items. This practice is not permitted under FRS 3; the trading results of the discontinued operations are shown as a separate component of operating profit, and the gain or loss on sale or closure is shown as an exceptional item.[35]

Another clear feature of this definition is that it is not limited to business or geographical segments which are reportable under SSAP 25, which means that operations which are sold or terminated can be classified as discontinued for FRS 3 reporting purposes, even if the operations were not separately identified for segmental reporting purposes. In fact, FRS 3 specifically requires that where a sale or termination has a material impact on a major business segment this should be disclosed and explained.[36]

The standard also makes it clear that only income and costs directly related to discontinued operations should appear under the heading of discontinued operations. This means that reorganisation or restructuring of continuing operations resulting from a sale or termination should be treated as a part of continuing operations.[37]

2.3.2   The meaning of 'ceased permanently'

In the case of a termination, the operation cannot be classified as discontinued unless the 'former activities have ceased permanently'. However, FRS 3 provides no guidance about how this requirement should be applied in practice and leaves open a number of questions about when an operation can be regarded as having ceased permanently. This is because the waters are somewhat muddied by a passing reference to 'downsizing' in the explanation section of the standard, which seems to recognise that where a company takes a strategic decision 'to curtail materially its presence in a continuing market', the affected operation may be classified as discontinued.[38] Nevertheless, downsizing is not referred to at all in the standard itself and this isolated reference to the concept does not sit very comfortably with the standard's definition of discontinued operations. One possible interpretation might be that the principle of downsizing can be applied to a business which is made up of a number of distinct parts; if a significant number of the parts of the business have closed and have ceased permanently, but the other parts continue then, taken together, the business as a whole has been downsized.

In any event, whatever the term means, the standard seems to recognise downsized operations as qualifying for the discontinued classification, with the result that the phrase 'ceased permanently' presents some interpretational difficulties.

These difficulties arise most commonly in run-off situations. For example, a group might have an insurance underwriting subsidiary which has ceased business permanently, although it is possible that material unprovided claims might arise in the future. When would this business be regarded as discontinued under FRS 3? Is it when it ceases writing new business, or is it when it stops paying out claims (which might be several decades in the future)? In our view, FRS 3 does not provide a clear-cut answer to this sort of issue. However, we would suggest that since the subsidiary is in the business of underwriting, the day it ceases writing new business is the day on which the business can be regarded as discontinued. Provision would be made for future claims, which would be reassessed on an annual basis and adjusted if necessary. Similar issues would arise in the case of a group with a leasing subsidiary which ceased writing new leases.

2.3.3   The meaning of 'material effect on the nature and focus'

To be included in the category of discontinued operations, a sale or termination must have a material effect on the nature and focus of the reporting entity's operations and represent a material reduction in its operating facilities resulting either from its withdrawal from a particular market (whether class of business or geographical) or from a material reduction in turnover in the reporting entity's continuing markets. In the explanation section of FRS 3, the ASB states that the phrase 'nature and focus of the reporting entity's operations' refers to the positioning of its products or services in their markets including the aspects of both quality and location. It then cites the example of a hotel company selling a chain of hotels in the lower end of the market and replacing it with a chain in the luxury end of the market; whilst remaining in the business of operating hotels, the group would be changing the nature and focus of its operations. Similarly, if the company sold its hotels in the US and bought hotels in Europe, that sale would also be classified as discontinued. Conversely, the sale of hotels and the purchase of others within the same market sector and similar locations would be treated as wholly within continuing operations.[39]

However, these examples are simplistic and in practice the situations that arise are far less clear-cut. The issue is further confused by the reference in the discontinued operations definition to a material reduction in operating facilities. Since the fundamental concept of going concern assumes that there is no intention to 'curtail significantly the scale of operation', a strict reading of FRS 3 would imply that an entity with a discontinued operation will, by definition, no longer be a going concern. Clearly, though, this is not the intention of FRS 3, which means that a considerable amount of subjective judgement will have to be applied in determining whether or not a sale or termination should be classified as discontinued.

The matter is further obscured by the requirement that the material reduction in operating facilities must have resulted either from the withdrawal from a particular market or from a material reduction in turnover in the reporting entity's continuing markets.[40] It is in the context of this latter case that the notion of 'downsizing' is introduced in the explanation section of the standard. Downsizing is explained as being a strategic decision by the reporting entity to curtail materially its presence in a continuing market.[41]

However, the standard provides no further help about how this concept is to be applied in practice, with the result that its use merely adds to the difficulty of applying the discontinued operations definition in practice, thereby opening the door to fairly wide interpretation. In fact, the only point that is clarified is that the sale or termination of a component of a reporting entity's operations which is undertaken primarily in order to achieve productivity improvements or other cost savings is a part of the entity's continuing operations and the effects of the sale or termination should be included under that heading.[42] Nevertheless, in practice it might be difficult to determine whether or not a downsizing has been carried out with the primary objective of achieving productivity improvements and/or cost savings. What is important, though, is that a downsizing can only be classified under discontinued operations where the sale or termination also has a material effect on the nature and focus of the reporting entity's operations. So, for example, if a supermarket chain decides to close a third of its stores because they are unprofitable, then this downsizing cannot be regarded as a discontinuance as the nature and focus of the entity's operations will be unchanged. Conversely, if the supermarket chain closes the stores because it is repositioning itself in the market, and the closed stores no longer fit the chain's new market profile, then the downsizing might well fall into the discontinued category.

Amstrad presents a good example of this distinction being applied in practice. As can be seen from the following extract from its 1996 accounts, the Group's consumer electronics business (ACE) was downsized as part of a cost reduction exercise. Consequently, whilst the resulting restructuring costs were regarded as being fundamental to the Group's operations (and therefore classified in the profit and loss account as non-operating), they were nevertheless considered to be part of the Group's continuing operations:

Extract 22.2: Amstrad plc (1996)

OPERATING REVIEW [extract]

ACE has continued to experience very tough market conditions, especially in Germany, and trading losses have been incurred. The arrangements with Betacom will result in significant headcount reduction and downsizing of UK and overseas operations that will greatly reduce costs and are expected to eliminate loss making activities.

Notes to the Accounts

3 Restructuring costs

In addition to the above on 1 July 1996 the company announced a fundamental restructuring and downsizing of the Amstrad Consumer Electronics business. The costs of this restructuring (£6.7 million) have been disclosed as a non-operating exceptional item.

2.3.4 The meaning of 'clearly distinguishable'

The fourth condition which must be fulfilled for a sale or termination to be classified as discontinued is that: the assets, liabilities, results of operations and activities of the operations which are sold or terminated must be clearly distinguishable, physically, operationally and for financial reporting purposes. This means that if the financial results of a sold or terminated operation are not identifiable separately from the accounting records or to a material extent can only be derived through making allocations of income or expenses, then the operation cannot be classified as a discontinued operation.

However, the example which is given in the explanation section of the standard to illustrate the practical application of this condition seems to bear little relationship to the condition itself. The example which is cited is that of a manufacturing facility that is closed down but which lacks an external market price for its output. According to the example, this closure cannot be classified as a discontinued operation.[43] It is unclear what the link is between an operation having an external market price for its output and the requirement for the operation's assets, liabilities, results of operations and activities to be clearly distinguishable. Consequently, it again seems that the application of this condition in practice is open to considerable subjective judgement. On the other hand, it is difficult to imagine the situation of a sale or termination meeting the first three conditions for a discontinued classification but not meeting the fourth.

2.3.5 *Application of the discontinued operations definition in practice*

Although we agree that the rules on discontinued operations were in need of reform, we have reservations about the way in which the disclosure of discontinued operations has been dealt with in FRS 3. We would have preferred it if discontinued operations had been addressed as an aspect of segmental reporting, not by amendment to the presentation of the profit and loss account, for this reason: FRS 3 only considers the profit and loss account, whereas the approach to discontinued operations should be consistent throughout the accounts. Dealing with it as a segmental issue would have required the net assets of the discontinued operations to be disclosed as well (provided, of course, that they are still there), and might also have provided an opportunity to introduce segmental disclosure of cash flows (for both continuing and discontinued operations).

Hanson's demerger in 1996 of its chemicals and other businesses provides a clear-cut example of a discontinued operation under FRS 3. The discontinuance was described in the group's accounts as follows:

Extract 22.3: Hanson PLC (1996)

NOTES TO THE ACCOUNTS

21 Acquisitions, demergers and disposals [extract]

Demergers

On October 1, 1996 Hanson demerged its chemicals businesses together with its investment in Suburban Propane through Millennium and its tobacco businesses through Imperial. As a result of the demerger, approved by shareholders of Hanson at an extraordinary general meeting on September 25, 1996, each Hanson shareholder received by way of a dividend in specie one share of Millennium common stock for every 70 Hanson ordinary shares owned and one ordinary share of Imperial for every 10 Hanson ordinary shares owned. ...

The results of both Millennium and Imperial are reported within discontinued operations in the consolidated profit and loss account. The assets and liabilities of Millennium are not included in the balance sheet at October 1, 1996 whereas they are included in the balance sheet at September 30, 1995. The consolidated cash flow statement includes the cash flows of both Millennium and Imperial for the period to the date of the demergers.

As part of the demerger transactions parts of Cornerstone and Grove were demerged with Millennium on October 1, 1996 and repurchased six days after that demerger. These parts have been treated as continuing businesses in the results to October 1, 1996.

Similar examples may be found in the 1998 Report and Accounts of Arcadia Group plc, which treated the demerger of its Debenhams business as a discontinued operation, and the 1998 Report & Accounts of United News &

Media plc which accounted for the demerger of its money and securities broking and financial information businesses as discontinued operations.

In order for a discontinuance to meet FRS 3's definition of a discontinued operation, the operation must have been either sold or have ceased permanently within the financial year or the earlier of three months after the year end and when the accounts are approved. As a result, some companies find themselves in the position of having made a decision to discontinue an operation, but then not being able to disclose it as discontinued in the profit and loss account because the operation had not ceased permanently by the time the accounts are approved.

Therefore, it is increasingly becoming the practice when this situation occurs for companies to highlight the operations to be discontinued by showing them as a separate component of continuing operations. Inchcape is an example of a company that has followed this approach, distinguishing between continuing operations that are ongoing, continuing operations that are to be discontinued and discontinued operations:

Extract 22.4: Inchcape plc (1998)

Operating review [extract]

Businesses being discontinued [extract]

As part of the Group's strategy to focus on Motors the following businesses are being divested. The 1998 results arising from these businesses are included in the accounts as 'to be discontinued'. They will be treated as discontinued once the disposals are complete.

...

Consolidated profit and loss account [extract]
for the year ended 31 December 1998

	Continuing operations		Dis-		
	Ongoing	To be discontinued	continued operations	Total	
	1998	1998	1998	1998	1997 restated
	£m	£m	£m	£m	£m
Turnover including share of joint ventures and associates	**4,156.9**	**1,278.3**	**71.2**	**5,506.4**	6,650.9
Less:					
- share of joint ventures	(106.7)	(179.9)	-	(286.6)	(329.6)
- share of associates	(814.8)	(148.0)	-	(962.8)	(389.9)
Group subsidiaries' turnover	3,235.4	950.4	71.2	4,257.0	5,931.4
Cost of sales	(2,720.1)	(618.5)	(51.3)	(3,389.9)	(4,831.9)
Exceptional cost of sales	-	-	-	-	(7.7)
	(2,720.1)	(618.5)	(51.3)	(3,389.9)	(4,839.6)
Gross profit	515.3	331.9	19.9	867.1	1,091.8
Operating expenses	(456.2)	(301.4)	(41.3)	(798.9)	(974.8)
Exceptional operating expenses	(124.7)	-	(6.6)	(131.3)	(32.9)
	(580.9)	(301.4)	(47.9)	(930.2)	(1,007.7)
Utilisation of termination provisions	4.9	1.2	-	6.1	10.6
Operating (loss) profit	**(60.7)**	**31.7**	**(28.0)**	**(57.0)**	94.7
Share of profits of joint ventures	7.2	15.1	-	22.3	33.2
Share of profits of associates	29.2	9.4	-	38.6	21.1
Total operating (loss) profit	**(24.3)**	**56.2**	**(28.0)**	**3.9**	149.0
Net profit on disposal of properties and investments	2.6	1.5	-	4.1	3.8
Net (loss) including provisions on sale and termination of operations	(7.5)	(200.1)	(58.3)	(265.9)	(57.7)
Costs of fundamental reorganisation	-	(10.6)	-	(10.6)	-
(Loss) profit on ordinary activities before interest	**(29.2)**	**(153.0)**	**(86.3)**	**(268.5)**	95.1
Interest				(29.1)	(5.5)
(Loss) profit on ordinary activities before taxation				**(297.6)**	89.6
Tax on profit on ordinary activities				(61.4)	(64.8)
(Loss) profit on ordinary activities after taxation				**(359.0)**	24.8
Minority interests				(6.5)	(17.0)
(Loss) profit for the financial year				**(365.5)**	7.8
Dividends				(59.4)	(58.3)
Retained (loss) for the financial year				**(424.9)**	(50.5)

Interestingly enough, the particular disclosure route that Inchcape has chosen reflects the latest thinking of the IASC, as evidenced by one of its recent standards. IAS 35 – *Discontinuing Operations* – which was issued in 1998 addresses the presentation and disclosures relating to discontinuing (as opposed to discontinued) operations. The objectives of IAS 35 are to establish a basis for segregating information about a major operation that an enterprise is discontinuing from information about its continuing operations and to specify minimum disclosures about a discontinuing operation.

Under IAS 35, a discontinuing operation is a relatively large component of an enterprise (such as a business or geographical segment under IAS 14 – *Segment Reporting*) that the enterprise, pursuant to a single plan, either is disposing of substantially in its entirety or is terminating through abandonment or piecemeal sale.[44] The Standard uses the term 'discontinuing operation' rather than the traditional 'discontinued operation' because 'discontinued operation' implies that recognition of a discontinuance is necessary only at or near the end of the process of discontinuing the operation (as is the case under FRS 3). Instead, IAS 35 requires that disclosures about a discontinuing operation begin earlier than that, namely when a detailed formal plan for disposal has been adopted and announced or when the enterprise has already contracted for the disposal.

Consequently, there is a fairly significant difference in philosophy between the ASB's approach on 'discontinued' operations and that of the IASC on 'discontinuing' operations. Whilst FRS 3 focuses in on operations which have ceased permanently in the current financial year or shortly thereafter, the IASC calls for disclosure at an earlier point in time, namely, as soon as there is a board decision, a detailed plan and public announcement.[45] Relating this to the situation of Inchcape as illustrated in the above extract, the businesses that are in the process of divestment do not qualify as discontinued operations under FRS 3, yet it appears that they would be classified as discontinuing operations under IAS 35.

A question that sometimes arises is whether the partial disposal of a business (for example, the sale of a 70% interest in a previously wholly-owned subsidiary) meets FRS 3's definition of a discontinued operation. There is a school of thought that argues that a subsidiary becoming an associated undertaking is, ipso facto, a discontinuance. However, we consider, on balance, that for a sale to be classified as a discontinued operation it must still satisfy all the necessary conditions contained in paragraph 4 of FRS 3, set out in 2.3.1 above.

It is perhaps noteworthy that this situation has been addressed in the US in a SEC Staff Accounting Bulletin. The situation considered by the SEC staff was that of a company which disposes of a controlling interest in a business segment and either retains a minority voting interest directly in the segment or holds a minority voting interest in the buyer of the segment. This minority interest enables the company to exert significant influence over the operating and financial policies of the segment thereby requiring it to account for its residual investment using the equity method. In the view of the SEC staff, the retention of an interest sufficient to enable the company to exert significant influence was inconsistent with a discontinued operations classification.[46]

2.4 Accounting for the consequences of a decision to sell or terminate an operation

Although FRS 3 is primarily a disclosure standard, it also deals with some recognition and measurement issues. Perhaps the most controversial amongst these relates to the principle underlying the establishment of provisions as a consequence of a decision to sell or terminate an operation. This is because the principle underlying the use of provisions in FRS 3 stemmed originally from the definition of a liability in the ASB's Draft *Statement of Principles* – namely, that a provision is only raised when an obligation to transfer economic benefits arises. This principle has now been entrenched in UK GAAP by FRS 12 – *Provisions, Contingent Liabilities and Contingent Assets* – which first defines liabilities as 'obligations of an entity to transfer economic benefits as a result of past transactions or events', and then defines a provision as 'a liability of uncertain timing or amount'.[47]

FRS 3 requires that if a decision has been made to sell or terminate an operation, any consequential provisions should reflect the extent to which obligations have been incurred that are not expected to be covered by the future profits of the operation.[48] Prior to FRS 12, this requirement in FRS 3 also extended to considering the extent to which the obligations were expected to be covered by profits on the disposal of the operation's assets. However, FRS 12 made a consequential amendment to paragraph 18 of FRS 3 to the extent that expected gains from the disposal of assets should not be taken into account in determining the amount of the provision for the sale or termination of an operation. The ASB's rationale being that it believes that liabilities should be measured independently of the recognition and measurement rules for assets.

Low & Bonar presents an example where this new approach has been applied to reporting the closure of an operation, although the closure did not meet the definition of a discontinued operation:

Extract 22.5: Low & Bonar PLC (1998)

FINANCIAL REVIEW [extract]

... we have made a provision of £7.5 million to cover the costs of closure. This figure excludes an estimated gain of approximately £2 million which we anticipate on the disposal of the land, buildings and certain equipment which, due to changing accounting standards, cannot be accounted for until the assets are sold. The cash costs associated with the Irlam closure net of disposal proceeds when the land, buildings and equipment are sold, are anticipated to be between £2 million and £3 million. ...

Further, FRS 3 requires that a provision is not set up until the reporting entity is demonstrably committed to the sale or termination, arguing that it is only at this point that the obligation arises. This should be evidenced, in the case of a sale, by a binding sale agreement and, in the case of a termination, by a detailed formal plan for termination from which the reporting entity cannot realistically withdraw.[49] In the explanation section of the standard, the ASB states that evidence of such a commitment might be the public announcement of specific plans, the commencement of implementation, or other circumstances effectively obliging the reporting entity to complete the sale or termination. It then goes on to say that 'a binding contract entered into after the balance sheet date may provide additional evidence of asset values and commitments at the balance sheet date.'[50] The significance of this is that the requirement in paragraph 18 of FRS 3 for there to be a binding sale agreement does not stipulate that the binding sale agreement has to be in place at the year end. This means that, as long as the company is demonstrably committed to the sale of an operation at the year end (through, for example, public announcement or other circumstances effectively obliging the reporting entity to complete the sale, such as a sale agreement that is subject only to shareholder approval), and the sale contract becomes binding before the accounts are signed, then paragraph 18's conditions for establishing a provision to reflect the consequences of the decision to sell the operation will be met.

In the case of an intended sale for which no legally binding sale agreement exists, no obligation has been entered into by the reporting entity and accordingly no provision for the direct costs of the decision to sell and for the future operating losses should be made. However, any impairment of fixed assets should be recognised in the financial statements in accordance with FRS 11,[51] bearing in mind that an impairment loss recognised in the profit and loss account should be included within operating profit under the appropriate statutory heading, and disclosed as an exceptional item if appropriate.[52]

The provision for the sale or termination of an operation should cover only:
i)   the direct costs of the sale or termination; and
ii)   any operating losses up to the date of the sale or termination.

In both cases, the provision should be calculated after taking into account the aggregate profit, if any, to be recognised in the profit and loss account from the future profits of the operation. Again, prior to FRS 12, FRS 3 required that the provision amount should take into account profits to be recognised from the disposal of the assets of the operation, but a consequential change brought about by FRS 12 has removed this requirement.

Where the operation is classified as continuing in the period under review the write down of assets and the provision for operating losses and for the loss on sale or termination will be included in the continuing operations category. In the subsequent period the provisions will be used to offset the results of the operations. The related disclosure in that subsequent period will be to show the trading results of the operation under each of the statutory format headings with the utilisation of the provisions being separately highlighted on the face of the profit and loss account under the operating loss and, if appropriate, the loss on sale or termination of the operation. The results will be included in whichever category is appropriate, either discontinued or still under continuing. The following extract from one of FRS 3's profit and loss account examples illustrates the presentation:

	1993	1993	1992 as restated
	£ million	£ million	£ million
Operating profit			
Continuing operations	50		40
Acquisitions	6		
	56		
Discontinued operations	(15)		12
Less 1992 provision	10		
		51	52
Profit on sale of properties in continuing operations		9	6
Provision for loss on operations to be discontinued			(30)
Loss on disposal of discontinued operations	(17)		
Less 1992 provision	20		
		3	
Profit on ordinary activities before interest		63	28

FRS 3's rules on the establishment of provisions as a consequence of a decision to sell or terminate an operation reflected the ASB's underlying philosophy that costs and losses should be charged in the profit and loss account in the periods to which they relate and that future income should not be enhanced by 'buckets' of provisions being established in the current year. This was a practice which had grown from SSAP 6's somewhat liberal approach to accounting for terminated activities. Under SSAP 6, as soon as a decision had been made to discontinue a business segment, provision would be made for all anticipated future costs and losses which were expected to arise in connection with the discontinuance – even if the discontinuance was expected to take several years to complete. Since these provisions were generally charged as extraordinary items, the current and future earnings per share were protected against loss-making operations which were in the process of termination.

FRS 3 clearly took a much stricter line on the way in which discontinuing operations were to be accounted for and disclosed. Not only must the sale or termination be completed in the period to qualify for a discontinued classification in the profit and loss account, but there is also much less facility for exuberant provisioning. This is because there needs to be more than just a decision to sell or terminate: in the case of a sale, there needs to be a binding sale agreement and, in the case of a termination, a detailed formal plan for termination from which the reporting entity cannot realistically withdraw.

However, this does raise the issue of the possible conflict between SSAP 2 and FRS 3. Under the concept of prudence, provision is made for all known liabilities (expenses and losses) whether the amount of these is known with certainty or is a best estimate in the light of the information available.[53] On the other hand, FRS 3 only permits a provision to be established for known losses on sales or terminations when the reporting entity is demonstrably committed to the sale or termination.

This anomaly was illustrated by the following extract from the accounts of Coats Viyella who found that, on implementing FRS 3, provisions for losses on anticipated disposals which had been set up in prior years had to be restated under FRS 3:

Extract 22.6: Coats Viyella Plc (1992)

STATEMENT OF ACCOUNTING POLICIES

Changes in accounting policies and presentation of financial information[extract]

In addition, FRS 3 requires that provisions for losses on sale or termination of operations are only created where the Group is demonstrably committed to the sale or termination and, in the case of a sale, this should be evidenced by a binding sale agreement. Comparative figures have therefore been restated to eliminate certain provisions for losses on anticipated disposals (principally Yarns businesses) totalling £11.5m originally created in 1989 and 1990 and released in 1991.

There is clearly a fine balance between prudent accounting and over-provisioning. However, now that the ASB has issued FRS 12, it is clear that its overall mission was to ensure companies only set up provisions (particularly those in respect of future trading losses and reorganisation costs) where there exist either legal or 'constructive' obligations. (FRS 12 is discussed in detail in Chapter 25 of this book.)

2.5 The effect of acquisitions

FRS 3 requires that any material contribution to the results of a group from acquisitions made during the year should also be disclosed on the face of the profit and loss account, as a separate component of the results of continuing operations. The term 'acquisitions' is defined in the standard (somewhat circularly) as being 'operations of the reporting entity that are acquired in the period'.[54] However, the standard acknowledges that it will sometimes be impracticable to provide this disclosure – for example, if the acquired business is integrated with existing businesses in such a way that this full analysis is unobtainable. In such cases, an indication should be given in the notes to the accounts of the contribution of the acquisition to the turnover and operating profit of the continuing operations, or a statement, with reasons, that not even this information can be determined.[55]

The standard does not explain the reasoning behind this disclosure requirement, although it is presumably designed to distinguish organic growth from purchased growth and is therefore regarded as the mirror image of the requirements on discontinued operations. However, it is clear that the definition of acquisitions does not mirror that for a discontinued operation; with the latter being a lot more restrictive. For example, an operation could be classified as an acquisition even though it does not affect the nature and focus of the entity's operations, whereas the disposal of that same operation would not be classified as a discontinued operation.

The usefulness of the information presented will often be questionable. The length of the period for which the results will be analysed separately in this way will depend entirely on when the acquisition happens to fall in the financial year. For example, a company with a 31 December year end might buy a subsidiary on 2 January; if so, it would show virtually the whole of the next year's results of the subsidiary in the acquisitions column, but if it had made the acquisition two days earlier, all of the results of that same year would be presented as stemming from continuing activities. The effect of the acquisition would not be highlighted at all, and any hope of facilitating a comparison with the previous year would be frustrated. For these reasons, we believe that these disclosures are of limited value.

In addition to the above disclosure, the standard also requires that, where an acquisition has a material impact on a major business segment, this should be disclosed and explained.[56] Thomson Travel Group provides a comprehensive segmental analysis of the effect of both acquisitions and discontinued operations, as illustrated in the following extract:

Extract 22.7: Thomson Travel Group Plc (1998)

Notes to the financial statements

2 Actual group segment analysis

	Continuing operations £m	Acquisitions £m	Discontinued operations* £m	Total £m
Turnover	2,080.0	376.7	-	2,456.7
Cost of sales	(1,586.3)	(265.7)	-	(1,852.0)
Gross profit	493.7	111.0	-	604.7
Net operating expenses (note 3)	(431.4)	(80.6)	-	(512.0)
Operating profit	62.3	30.4	-	92.7
Net interest receivable/(payable)	33.9	(6.7)	(33.9)	(6.7)
Operating profit/(loss) and interest	96.2	23.7	(33.9)	86.0
Income from fixed asset investments	-	-	19.7	19.7
(Loss)/profit on disposal of fixed assets	(1.0)	0.2	-	(0.8)
Loss on disposal of subsidiaries	(0.2)	-	(24.6)	(24.8)
Profit/(loss) on ordinary activities before tax	95.0	23.9	(38.8)	80.1

* Discontinued operations relate to the sale to TTC of non travel-related companies.

Actual turnover	Continuing operations					
	Ongoing businesses £m	Thomson Sverige £m	Sub total £m	Acquisitions £m	**Total 1998 £m**	Total 1997 £m
Holiday and airline operations:						
- UK	1,770.4	-	1,770.4	40.7	**1,811.1**	1,550.8
- Nordic region	-	9.7	9.7	332.6	**342.3**	-
- Republic of Ireland	68.1	-	68.1	1.6	**69.7**	55.0
- Germany	50.1	-	50.1	-	**50.1**	2.7
Lunn Poly	144.9	-	144.9	-	**144.9**	137.3
TTG Independent Holidays Group	36.8	-	36.8	1.8	**38.6**	34.4
	2,070.3	9.7	2,080.0	376.7	**2,456.7**	1,780.2

Actual profit before tax	Continuing operations				Discontinued operations £m	**Total 1998 £m**	Total 1997 £m
	Ongoing businesses £m	Thomson Sverige £m	Sub total £m	Acquisitions £m			
Holiday and airline operations:							
- UK	72.3	-	72.3	10.0	-	**82.3**	51.3
- Nordic region	-	(7.2)	(7.2)	14.4	-	**7.2**	(0.9)
- Republic of Ireland	5.0	-	5.0	-	-	**5.0**	3.1
- Germany	0.2	-	0.2	-	-	**0.2**	(2.2)
Lunn Poly	23.8	-	23.8	-	-	**23.8**	18.1
TTG Independent Holidays Group	7.9	-	7.9	0.4	-	**8.3**	8.4
Non-travel related activities	-	-	-	-	8.0	**8.0**	9.6
Unallocated interest	(5.8)	-	(5.8)	-	-	**(5.8)**	-
Goodwill amortisation	-	-	-	(1.1)	-	**(1.1)**	-
Shareholder loan interest	-	-	-	-	(22.2)	**(22.2)**	(53.3)
(Loss/profit on disposal of fixed assets and subsidiary undertakings	(1.0)	(0.2)	(1.2)	0.2	(24.6)	**(25.6)**	1.2
	102.4	(7.4)	95.0	23.9	(38.8)	**80.1**	35.3

Net assets

The Group's net assets at 31 December 1998 are shown in note 1 to the financial statements.

It should be noted that the disclosure required by the standard in respect of acquisitions is in addition to those already required by (i) the Companies Act 1985, (for example, the requirement in paragraph 13 of Schedule 4A to disclose the profit or loss of an acquired subsidiary for the period prior to its acquisition by the group and for the previous year), and (ii) other accounting standards (for example, the FRS 6 requirements to disclose information about the results of new subsidiaries).[57]

2.6   Extraordinary and exceptional items

2.6.1   *Extraordinary items*

Extraordinary items are defined in FRS 3 in similar terms to the old SSAP 6 definition as 'material items *possessing a high degree of abnormality* which arise from events or transactions that fall outside the ordinary activities of the reporting entity and which are not expected to recur. They do not include exceptional items nor do they include prior period items merely because they relate to a prior period.'[58] (The words in italics are our emphasis, to show the main change.)   However, the standard regards extraordinary items as being 'extremely rare', so rare indeed that no examples are provided. Items which under SSAP 6 were traditionally treated as extraordinary (for example, profits or losses on the sale of fixed assets and profits or losses on the sale or termination of an operation) are now specifically listed in FRS 3 as exceptional items.[59]

In fact, Sir David Tweedie is on record as saying that the ASB has effectively succeeded in outlawing extraordinary items – despite the fact that FRS 3 provides the theoretical facility for such items to arise. Nevertheless, taking the standard's definition of extraordinary items at face value, it is still relatively easy to suggest items which fall within the extraordinary items definition (for example, costs incurred in defending a hostile take-over bid). However, the sting in the tail lies not in the standard's definition of extraordinary items, but in its definition of ordinary activities, which are stated as being 'any activities which are undertaken by a reporting entity as part of its business and such related activities in which the reporting entity engages in furtherance of, incidental to, or arising from, these activities. Ordinary activities include the effects on the reporting entity of any event in the various environments in which it operates, including the political, regulatory, economic and geographical environments, irrespective of the frequency or unusual nature of the events.'[60]

The consequence of such an all-embracing definition is that it is difficult to imagine any 'events or transactions that fall outside the ordinary activities of the reporting entity'. For example, it is difficult to argue that a hostile take-over bid is not an event of the various environments in which most, if not all, entities operate.

Fairway Group presented an example of a company which clearly did not believe that extraordinary items had been outlawed by FRS 3. In implementing FRS 3 for the first time in 1993, the company persevered with showing 'costs of aborted acquisition' as an extraordinary item in the comparative figures, and did not reclassify the item as exceptional as was done by other companies:

Extract 22.8: Fairway Group Plc (1993)

Notes to the Accounts

	1993	1992
	£'000	£'000
7. Extraordinary items		
Costs of aborted acquisition	—	(162)

The above item fell outside the ordinary activities of the Company and is not expected to recur.

It is a moot point whether the costs of an aborted acquisition incurred by an entity that has made acquisitions in the past can fall outside its ordinary activities as defined by FRS 3. Clearly, though, the directors and auditors of Fairway considered this to be the case at the time. However, this is a rare example, and the lack of any recent evidence of companies reporting extraordinary items would seem to indicate that the ASB has been successful in effectively outlawing them.

2.6.2 Exceptional items

Exceptional items are defined in FRS 3 as being 'material items which derive from events or transactions that fall within the ordinary activities of the reporting entity and which individually or, if of a similar type, in aggregate, need to be disclosed by virtue of their size or incidence if the financial statements are to give a true and fair view'.[61] Although this definition is substantially unchanged from that in SSAP 6, there has been a significant change in the way that exceptional items are disclosed in the profit and loss account and notes. Under SSAP 6 exceptional items used to be aggregated on the face of the profit and loss account under one heading; not so under FRS 3, which states that all exceptional items, other than those included in the items listed in paragraph 20 of the standard, should be credited or charged in arriving at the profit or loss on ordinary activities by inclusion under the statutory format headings to which they relate. They should be attributed to continuing or discontinued operations as appropriate. The amount of each exceptional item, either individually or as an aggregate of items of a similar type, should be disclosed separately by way of note, or on the face of the profit and loss account if that degree of prominence is necessary in order to give a true and fair view.[62]

As a definitional matter, therefore, FRS 3 recognises that there are two categories of exceptional item:

■ those listed in paragraph 20 of the standard (which must be shown on the face of the profit and loss account after operating profit and before interest); and

■ all others, which should be credited or charged in arriving at the profit or loss on ordinary activities by inclusion under the statutory format headings to which they relate, and which should be disclosed separately either by way of note, or on the face of the profit and loss account.

The disclosure of the first category of exceptional item would appear to be clear-cut: if one of the items listed in paragraph 20 arises it must be shown separately in a specific position on the face of the profit and loss account. For ease of reference we refer to this category of items as non-operating exceptional items. These are discussed at 2.6.3 below.

As far as the second category of exceptional item is concerned, attributing exceptional items to the relevant statutory format headings will, in most cases, be a straightforward exercise. However, circumstances do arise when the directors of a reporting entity reach the view that specific exceptional items are not accommodated easily within specific format headings. This eventuality is specifically provided for in Paragraph 3(2) of Schedule 4 to the Companies Act which states that a company's profit and loss account may include an item representing or covering the amount of any income or expenditure not otherwise covered by any of the items listed in the format adopted. It goes on to state in Paragraph 3(3) that, in preparing a company's profit and loss account, the directors of the company shall adapt the arrangement and headings and sub-headings otherwise required by paragraph 1 in respect of items to which an Arabic number is assigned in the format adopted.

This means that situations will arise where a new line item will have to be added to the face of the profit and loss item to accommodate an exceptional item which does not relate to any specific statutory format heading. Examples of these might include bid defence costs and abortive acquisition costs. The precise position in the profit and loss account of these items depends on the directors' view of what they consider to be most appropriate. Whether the items appear before or after the operating profit line depends entirely on the directors' definition of operating profit, since the term is not used in the statutory formats and is not formally defined in FRS 3.

We are aware that there exists a school of thought that FRS 3 precludes the disclosure of exceptional items, other than those listed in paragraph 20, after operating profit. We believe, however, that this view is mistaken and arises from the assumption that the profit or loss on ordinary activities, which is a defined term in the Companies Act, is the same thing as operating profit or loss. Of course it is not, since the term 'operating profit or loss' is defined in neither the statutory formats nor FRS 3. Indeed, the different wording highlights the anomaly of any assumption that the two terms have the same meaning. It is therefore clear that FRS 3 does permit the inclusion in the profit and loss account of non-operating exceptional items over and above those listed in paragraph 20.

2.6.3 Non-operating exceptional items

The only exception to the rule that exceptional items must be included under the statutory format headings to which they relate, applies in the case of three specific items which, if they arise, must (irrespective of the statutory formats) be shown separately on the face of the profit and loss account after operating profit and before interest, and be included under the appropriate heading of continuing or discontinued operations. The three items (including provisions in respect of such items) are as follows:

(a)   profits or losses on the sale or termination of an operation;

(b)   costs of a fundamental reorganisation or restructuring having a material effect on the nature and focus of the reporting entity's operations; and

(c)   profits or losses on the disposal of fixed assets.[63]

Only the revenue and costs directly related to the items should be taken into account in calculating the profit or loss for each of the items. This means, for example, that if a factory is sold and all the workers are made redundant, then the related redundancy costs should not be included in the profit/loss on disposal of the factory. The explanation section of FRS 3 also states that the profits or losses on the disposal of fixed assets in (c) above are not intended to include profits and losses that are in effect no more than marginal adjustments to depreciation previously charged.[64] It is not altogether clear what this means in practice, but we interpret it as meaning only that immaterial profits or losses on the disposal of depreciable fixed assets would not be disclosed as a non-operating exceptional item. Materiality should be applied to the aggregate net profits and losses for each category of fixed asset, and not to each individual asset.

The implication of this requirement is that all profits and losses on the disposal of fixed assets are excluded from the calculation of operating profit. This means that companies which are in the business of 'fixed assets trading' (i.e. have a high level of activity in buying and selling assets which are classified as fixed assets – for example, oil acreage in the case of an oil and gas company and pubs in the case of a brewer) are seemingly precluded from including the profits/losses arising on the disposal of such items within operating profit. We consider this to be a misguided requirement of FRS 3 since, in the case of companies such as these, the results of fixed assets trading are very much part of their operating performance. In any event, though, in the absence of any rules regarding the reclassification of fixed assets to current assets in anticipation of a disposal, it is quite feasible that this requirement can be circumvented in practice.

It should also be noted that provisions in respect of the three non-operating items must also be shown separately on the face of the profit and loss account after operating profit and before interest. This means, for example, that the provision for loss on disposal of a fixed asset which is expected to be sold in the future should be included in this category. This may even include goodwill that has previously been written off to reserves and, under FRS 10, is required to be charged or credited to the profit and loss account on its subsequent disposal.[65]

The standard requires further that the relevant headings for items (a) and (c) should appear on the face of the profit and loss account even where the exceptional profits and the exceptional losses within the headings net down to an immaterial amount. In such a case the standard requires that there should be a reference to a related note analysing the constituent profits and losses.

The notes to the financial statements should disclose, as a minimum, the effect on tax and on minority interest of items (a) to (c) in aggregate. However, the standard further requires that if the effect on tax and minority interests differs for the three categories further information should be given, where practicable, to assist users to assess the impact of the different items on the net profit or loss attributable to shareholders. It is not clear what the ASB had in mind in setting down this requirement. We suggest that in such a case the effect on tax and minority interests should be given for each of the categories.

Whilst the recognition and measurement of non-operating exceptional items falling within categories (a) and (c) above are reasonably clear-cut, the situation concerning item (b) is less so. This is because FRS 3 contains no additional guidance or explanation about the criteria which differentiate 'fundamental' reorganisations and restructurings from other (non-fundamental) ones – apart from the fact that they must have a material effect on the nature and focus of the reporting entity's operations. The only clue to what this means is to be found in the explanation section of the standard which deals with discontinued operations.

To be included in the category of discontinued operations, a sale or termination must, inter alia, have a material effect on the nature and focus of the reporting entity's operations. The standard explains that the phrase 'nature and focus of the reporting entity's operations' refers to the positioning of its products or services in their markets including the aspects of both quality and location.[66] However, even on the assumption that this interpretation can be applied to fundamental restructurings, it is of little additional practical value. As a result, the distinction between fundamental and non-fundamental restructurings and reorganisations becomes a highly subjective and judgmental exercise. Clearly, companies would normally prefer these provisions to be classified as non-operating, thereby protecting the operating profits line in the profit and loss account.

Even FRS 12 does not shed any further light on the distinction between fundamental and non-fundamental reorganisations and restructurings. FRS 12 defines a restructuring as 'a programme that is planned and controlled by management and materially changes either:

(a)   the scope of a business undertaken by an entity; or

(b)   the manner in which that business is conducted.'[67]

This is said to include:

(a)   sale or termination of a line of business;

(b)   the closure of business locations in a country or region or the relocation of business activities from one country or region to another;

(c)   changes in management structure, for example, eliminating a layer of management; and

(d)   fundamental reorganisations that have a material effect on the nature and focus of the entity's operations.[68]

In the absence of any requirement for companies to give details of the ways in which the nature and focus of their operations have been materially affected by the reorganisation or restructuring, the disclosure of items in this category has become fairly widespread. However, it should be noted that, just because the provision is for a large amount, it does not necessarily mean that it is a non-operating fundamental provision. It must also have a material effect on the nature and focus of the entity's operations.

It would be reasonable to expect companies that have established such provisions to give an explanation in their Operating and Financial Reviews about the fundamental nature of the reorganisation or restructuring.

The following extract from the 1998 accounts of Bass illustrates the disclosure of all three categories of the paragraph 20 non-operating exceptional items:

Extract 22.9: Bass PLC (1998)

notes to the financial statements

9 Non-operating exceptional items	Note	1998 £m	1997 £m
(Loss)/profit on disposal of fixed assets		**(10)**	3
Costs of fundamental reorganisation*	a	**(67)**	–
Loss on disposal of investment*	b	–	(35)
Loss on termination of operations*	c	–	(25)
Continuing operations		**(77)**	(57)
Loss on disposal of fixed assets		–	(3)
Profit on disposal of operations*	d	**250**	–
Provision for diminution in asset values*	e	–	(177)
Discontinued operations		**250**	(180)
		173	(237)

* Major non-operating exceptional items for the purpose of calculating adjusted earnings per ordinary share (note 13).

a   These costs arise as a result of restructuring two of the Group's three business segments.

     The restructuring of the hotels division followed its expansion further into the upscale market with the acquisition of Inter-Continental Hotels. It involves additional reorganisation designed to focus the division on separate market and geographic segments.

     The restructuring of the leisure retailing operations involved the disposal of both the leased pub business and the majority of Bass Leisure's activities as well as the merger of Bass Leisure Entertainments with the managed pub business. Bass Leisure Retail's focus has now switched from one of maximising Group benefits through operating tied beer outlets to being solely a leisure retailer.

     Further details of these reorganisations are set out in the operating and financial review on pages 2 to 11.

b   The loss relates to the disposal of a 50% investment in Carlsberg-Tetley PLC (C-T).

     No profit or loss arose on the exchange of the Group's investment in the Bristol Hotel Company (Bristol) for investments in FelCor Lodging Trust Inc. and Bristol Hotels & Resorts Inc. (see note 21), after taking account of goodwill of £98m.

c   The loss relates to the closure of two of the Group's breweries following the disposal of the investment in C-T.

d   The profit relates to the disposal of Gala, Coral, Barcrest, BLMS and the leased pub business and is shown net of goodwill of £82m and associated costs.

e   The charge relates primarily to a provision for diminution in the value of Gala as at 30 September 1997.

The profit and loss account of Inchcape (see Extract 22.4 above) presents an example of how non-operating exceptional items may be displayed on the face of the profit and loss account.

2.6.4 Disclosure of exceptional items in practice

Perhaps not unexpectedly, the disclosures in practice of exceptional items have become varied somewhat between companies. For example, one company might show abortive acquisition costs as a non-operating exceptional item, whilst another might choose to show the same costs as an exceptional item under the format heading 'Administrative expenses'. This is perhaps not surprising, given that operating profit is not defined in FRS 3, with the result that directors are required to select a definition which is most appropriate to the circumstances of their business. Consequently, the profit and loss account positioning of individual exceptional items will depend on the nature of the item, the nature of the entity's operations and the judgement of the directors.

This has become necessary largely as a result of an ill-conceived rule in FRS 3 which is based on the premise that the statutory format headings cater for all eventualities and that the objectives of FRS 3 can be achieved within the strait-jacket of the Companies Act formats. Not only do the various formats contain different headings, but a company which had adopted either Format 3 or 4 would find it virtually impossible to comply with FRS 3. Furthermore, because FRS 3 contains no additional guidance or explanation about the criteria which differentiate 'fundamental' reorganisations and restructuring from other (non-fundamental) ones, it is difficult to see any pattern of consistency in the presentation of these items.

In any event, it seems that in its proposal for a single comprehensive income statement, the ASB is seeking to remove the distinction between operating and non-operating restructuring and reorganisation provisions. This is evidenced in the ASB's Discussion Paper on performance reporting that proposes that 'entities should be permitted to disclose exceptional items on the face of the performance statement, but that these should be disclosed next to the line item to which they relate, regardless of the component of the statement of financial performance in which that line item falls, rather than aggregated under one heading of "exceptional items". For example, if an entity undertakes an internal restructuring that is regarded as exceptional, it should include the related costs (such as redundancy costs) in, say, the line item "administrative expenses" within the "operating (trading) activities" component.'[69] (The ASB proposals for change to the system of reporting performance are discussed in detail at section 5 below.)

2.6.5 The impact of the effective abolition of extraordinary items

We agree that it was appropriate for the ASB to limit the use of extraordinary items to very rare circumstances, but we consider that the standard should explain exactly what these circumstances are, and give examples. On the other hand, if FRS 3's abstruse drafting in this area reflected the ASB's intention to ensure that companies do not report extraordinary items under any circumstances, it seems to have succeeded.

However, since most items which were once shown as extraordinary are now shown as exceptional, we are concerned about the growing perception that the 'important' figure to look at in the profit and loss account is the profit from continuing operations before exceptional items, particularly as FRS 3 requires prominence to be given to certain exceptional items as a separate category on the face of the profit and loss account. Such a presentation will encourage the same misconception which was previously applied to extraordinary items under SSAP 6 – namely, that these items are something apart from the trading operations of the business and may be set on one side in any consideration of its performance. At the same time, FRS 3's definition of exceptional items is weaker even than SSAP 6's definition of extraordinary items, which can make it very easy to 'manage' the pre-exceptional figure. Apart from the three non-operating exceptional items discussed above, the exceptional item classification may now include:

■   highly unusual items which would previously have been classified as extraordinary;

■   items which quite often arise, but not in every year, which might previously have been classified as exceptional; and

■   items which arise annually, but happen to be unusually large in the current year.

In the last of these three items, the exceptional effect on the results is not the whole amount of the item, but only the excess over a 'normal' amount. Similarly, it could be misleading to show the whole amount of a charge for bad and doubtful debts as exceptional. In any event, we think it is unnecessary that exceptional items be overemphasised on the face of the profit and loss account. We would have preferred FRS 3 to have given emphasis to the overall result for the year and to have regarded the analysis of it as a secondary disclosure. As demonstrated by the current fixation on earnings per share, simplistic classifications on the face of the primary statements merely tend to encourage superficial analysis.

Carlton Communications is an example of a company that has highlighted its results and earnings per share before both exceptional items and the results of its loss-making investment in digital television. As can be seen from the following extract, the company refers to this as 'Headline Earnings per share':

Extract 22.10: Carlton Communications Plc (1998)

Profit and loss account

For the year ended 30 September 1998

	Notes	Before Digital Television £m	Digital Television (2) £m	Total £m	1997 £m
			1998		
Turnover	1	**1,861.0**	**6.7**	**1,867.7**	1,783.6
Less: share of joint ventures		**(25.6)**	-	**(25.6)**	(33.9)
Group turnover		**1,835.4**	**6.7**	**1842.1**	1,749.7
Operating costs		**1,517.4**	**16.3**	**1,533.7**	1,431.8
Group operating profit	1,3	**318.0**	**(9.6)**	**308.4**	317.9
Share of operating profit in joint ventures and associated undertakings	13	**7.5**	**(15.5)**	**(8.0)**	9.5
		325.5	**(25.1)**	**300.4**	327.4
Exceptional profit on sale of fixed asset investment	5	**9.6**	-	**9.6**	-
Exceptional provision for loss on closure of business	5	-	-	-	(6.4)
Share of associates' exceptional loss	5	-	-	-	(4.0)
Profit on ordinary activities before interest		**335.1**	**(25.1)**	**310.0**	317.0
Net interest receivable/(payable)	6	**4.9**	**(2.8)**	**2.1**	(0.7)
Profit on ordinary activities before taxation		**340.0**	**(27.9)**	**312.1**	316.3
Taxation on profit on ordinary activities	7	**(107.4)**	**7.2**	**(100.2)**	(104.1)
Profit on ordinary activities after taxation attributable to shareholders		**232.6**	**(20.7)**	**211.9**	212.2
Dividends (including non-equity) paid and proposed	8	**99.1**	-	**99.1**	91.2
Retained profit for the year		**133.5**	**(20.7)**	**112.8**	121.0
Earnings per share (pence)	9				
Basic earnings per share		**35.7p**	**(3.4)p**	**32.3p**	33.2p
Exceptional items after tax		**(1.6)p**	-	**(1.6)p**	1.6p
Headline earnings per share		**34.1p**	**(3.4)p**	**30.7p**	34.8p
Fully diluted earnings per share		**32.6p**	**(2.9)p**	**29.7p**	30.1p
Exceptional items after tax		**(1.3)p**	-	**(1.3)p**	1.3p
Headline fully diluted earnings per share		**31.3p**	**(2.9)p**	**28.4p**	31.4p

Notes to the accounts

2 Digital television

The Digital Television column of the Group's profit and loss account on page 34 comprises the 50% share of the loss before taxation of the Group's joint venture interest in ONdigital (1997 - £Nil) together with the net costs in respect of Carlton's digital channels, Carlton Online and the financing cost in the period of the investment in digital television activities, which is calculated on the project funding at the average interest rate earned on cash deposits. The tax relief in relation to Digital Television includes the Group's share of consortium relief expected to be available from ONdigital. The results of Carlton Select have been included within the Digital Television column, as its operations are now primarily concerned with Carlton's digital television channels. In the year to 30 September 1997 Carlton Select made sales of £6.3m and an operating loss of £5.5.m.

ICI provides a fairly typical example of a multi-column profit and loss account that splits its results from continuing operations into two columns ('before exceptional items' and 'exceptional items'), with 'discontinued operations' being shown in a further column. When it comes to comparative figures, ICI goes further than most by presenting its profit and loss account over two facing pages in its annual report, giving comparative figures for the previous two years, set out in four columns for each year. However, this is probably due to the fact that the company is a US SEC registrant and prepares its UK annual report and Form 20-F as a combined document. Only the figures for 1998 are included below:

Extract 22.11: Imperial Chemical Industries PLC (1998)

Group profit and loss account for the year ended 31 December 1998 [extract]

		1998 Continuing operations		Discontinued operations	Total
		Before exceptional items	Exceptional items		
	Notes	£m	£m	Total £m	1997 £m
Turnover	4,5	**9,095**		**191**	**9,286**
Operating costs	3,5	**(8,591)**	**(164)**	**(161)**	**(8,916)**
Other operating income	5	**86**	-	**7**	**93**
Trading profit (loss)	3,4,5	**590**	**(164)**	**37**	**463**
After deducting goodwill amortisation		*(23)*			*(23)*
Share of profits less losses of associated undertakings	7	**3**	-		**3**
		593	**(164)**	**37**	**466**
Profits less losses on sale or closure of operations	3		**11**	**179**	**190**
Profits less losses on disposal of fixed assets	3		**3**		**3**
Amount written off investments	3		**(34)**		**(34)**
Profit (loss) on ordinary activities before interest	4	**593**	**(184)**	**216**	**625**
Net interest payable	3,8	**(332)**			**(332)**
Profit (loss) on ordinary activities before taxation		**261**	**(184)**	**216**	**293**
Tax on profit (loss) on ordinary activities	9	**(69)**	**34**	**(77)**	**(112)**
Profit (loss) on ordinary activities after taxation		**192**	**(150)**	**139**	**181**
Attributable to minorities		**8**	**4**		**12**
Net profit (loss) for the financial year		**200**	**(146)**	**139**	**193**
Dividends	10				**(232)**
Profit (loss) retained for the year	25				**(39)**
Earnings (loss) per £1 Ordinary Share	11				
Basic		**27.6p**	**(20.1)p**	**19.2p**	**26.7p**
Diluted		**27.5p**	**(20.1)p**	**19.1p**	**26.5p**

It would seem that companies that present their profit and loss accounts in this form are perhaps wishing to focus the readers' attention on the first column, which reflects profit and earnings per share for the financial year before exceptional items and discontinued operations. It is a moot point whether or not pre-exceptional profit is the most appropriate measure of a company's underlying earning capacity; on the other hand, there is the argument that a profit and loss account presented in this way enhances the predictive value of the information. In any event, in order for the shareholders of a company to assess management performance and stewardship, they need to look at its *total* performance.

2.7   Profit or loss on the disposal of an asset

Prior to FRS 3, when an entity disposed of an asset carried at valuation, the directors had the choice of calculating the profit or loss on disposal by reference either to the depreciated historical cost or to the amount at which the asset was carried in the balance sheet. If the latter option was selected, that portion of the revaluation reserve which related to the asset would usually be transferred, as a reserve movement, to realised reserves.

FRS 3 removed this choice, requiring that the profit or loss on the disposal of an asset must be calculated as the difference between the net sale proceeds and the net carrying amount, whether carried at historical cost (less any provisions made) or at valuation.[70] A subsequent amendment to FRS 3 allowed insurance businesses limited relief from this particular requirement as it applied to the gains and losses arising on the disposal of investments. The amendment applied to insurance companies and insurance groups, both in relation to their own accounts and where these are incorporated in the consolidated accounts of a group whose main business is not insurance. These entities were thus granted an exemption from the requirement to calculate gains and losses on disposal of investments by reference to their carrying amount rather than original cost.[71] However, a further amendment to FRS 3 made in June 1999 effectively negated this exemption, by requiring insurance companies and groups to include in the profit and loss account both realised and unrealised gains and losses on investments held as part of their investment portfolios. The effect of this will be to ensure that the same amount will be accounted for on disposal of an investment held as part of the investment portfolio as would be accounted for whether or not the original exemption applied.

The reason for FRS 3's revised approach to determining the profit or loss on the disposal of an asset lies in the ASB's balance sheet approach to the recognition of gains and losses (see section 4.1 of Chapter 3 of this book). Under its revised Draft *Statement of Principles*, the ASB defines gains and losses as being increases and decreases in ownership interest, other than those relating to contributions from and distributions to owners. Recognition is triggered where a past transaction or other event indicates that there has been a measurable change in the assets and liabilities of the entity. Thus, where a change in assets is not offset by an equal change in liabilities, a gain or a loss will result (unless the change relates to a transaction with the entity's owners, in which case a contribution from owners or distribution to owners will be recognised). Consequently, once an asset has been revalued in an entity's balance sheet, any subsequent transactions must be based on the balance sheet carrying amount of that asset.

It is therefore clear why the ASB has removed the option of calculating the profit or loss on disposal of a revalued asset by reference to the asset's historical cost. Nevertheless, its removal did receive a rather mixed reaction from the business community, including the following amusing comment from the chairman of Ilex Limited, a property investment company:

Extract 22.12: Ilex Limited (1993)

CHAIRMAN'S STATEMENT

Profits after tax have risen from £564,000 to £1,698,000. These figures have been drawn up in accordance with the latest Accounting Standards and last year's figure is adjusted to make it comparable. The main change is to the manner in which capital items are taken through the Profit and Loss Account with a resulting volatility in earnings per share. We consider this a mistaken method for property investment companies which will only serve to confuse shareholders. Since it is mandatory, we accept it somewhat grumpily: the accounting profession seems to have an endemic tendency towards committees recommending changes which add to its workload and its clients' fees.

Some might argue that, so long as UK accounting is underpinned by a system of company law which recognises capital maintenance and distributable profits on an historical cost basis, companies should be able to report profits in the profit and loss account on an historical cost basis. However, there is the alternative view that income statements should be primarily concerned with the measurement of performance, and that when reported figures are not related to current values there may be over- or understatement of performance as measured by profits and return on assets. Consequently, the ASB has taken the view that, in the light of the present modified historical cost system and all its associated problems, companies that revalue assets should be required to measure future transactions by reference to the revalued amount.

2.8   Note of historical cost profits and losses

Because the profit or loss on the disposal of an asset is now to be calculated by reference to the asset's balance sheet carrying amount, FRS 3 introduced the requirement that, where there is a material difference between the result as disclosed in the profit and loss account and the result on an unmodified historical cost basis, a note of the historical cost profit or loss for the period should be presented.[72] This is a memorandum item that is an abbreviated restatement of the profit and loss account, adjusting the reported profit or loss so as to show it as if no asset revaluations had been made. Where full historical cost information is unavailable or cannot be obtained without unreasonable expense or delay, the earliest available values should be used. The note should include a reconciliation of the reported profit on ordinary activities before taxation to the equivalent historical cost amount and should also show the retained profit for the financial year reported on the historical cost basis.

Essentially, the note will incorporate adjustments for (i) the difference between the profit on the disposal of an asset calculated on depreciated historical cost and that calculated on a revalued amount, and (ii) the difference between an historical cost depreciation charge and the depreciation charge calculated on the revalued amount included in the profit and loss account of the period. The following extract from the example contained in the Appendix to FRS 3 illustrates the presentation of the note:

Note of historical cost profits and losses

	1993	1992 as restated
	£ million	£ million
Reported profit on ordinary activities before taxation	45	13
Realisation of property revaluation gains of previous years	9	10
Difference between a historical cost depreciation charge and the actual depreciation charge of the year calculated on the revalued amount	5	4
Historical cost profit on ordinary activities before taxation	59	27
Historical cost profit for the year retained after taxation, minority interests, extraordinary items and dividends	35	20

The note should be presented immediately following the profit and loss account or the statement of total recognised gains and losses. In consolidated financial statements, the profit and loss account figure for minority interests should be amended for the purposes of this note to reflect the adjustments made where they affect subsidiary companies with a minority interest.

The standard does not contain a definition of an unmodified historical cost basis. However, it is stated in the explanation section of the standard that the following are not deemed to be departures from the historical cost convention: (a) adjustments necessarily made to cope with the impact of hyper-inflation on foreign operations and (b) the practice of market makers and other dealers in investments of marking to market where this is an established industry practice.[73]

This still leaves open the position of entities marking to market where it is not industry practice. The implication from the FRS is that these other entities are deemed to have departed from the unmodified historical cost basis. However, there is an alternative view, which we support, that marking to market is not a departure from the historical cost convention, but is a method to ensure appropriate revenue recognition and as such it applies irrespective of the industry in which the entity operates. We would not therefore expect any adjustments to be included in the note of historical cost profits and losses in respect of marking current asset investments to market.

Nevertheless, in its revised Draft *Statement of Principles*, the ASB does refer to the 'mixed measurement system' where 'some categories of assets or liabilities could be measured on a historical cost basis and some on a current value basis'.[74] The ASB goes on to state that the term modified historical cost 'is something of a misnomer because it is a mixed measurement system'. This seems to suggest that all gains and loses that are recognised on the basis of current values will need to be reflected in the note of historical cost profits and losses.

It is, therefore, perhaps not surprising that when the ASB amended FRS 3 to require insurance companies to include in the profit and loss account both realised and unrealised gains and losses on investments held as part of their investment portfolios, it also exempted them from having to prepare a note of historical cost profit and losses for gains and losses arising on the holding or disposal of investments.[75]

2.9 Statement of total recognised gains and losses

2.9.1 *Primary financial statement*

FRS 3 introduced into UK GAAP a fourth primary financial statement: the statement of total recognised gains and losses. The statement has to be presented with the same prominence as the other primary statements and must show the components as well as the total of recognised gains and losses. Although there was not necessarily general agreement on the point, the statement was regarded by the ASB at least as being a statement of performance or 'comprehensive income'. It represented the ASB's first step towards requiring the reporting of changes in wealth as opposed to traditional historical cost profit and loss. The ethos of the statement lies in the ASB's Draft *Statement of Principles* and, in particular, in its balance sheet approach to the recognition of assets, liabilities, gains and losses.

According to the revised Draft *Statement of Principles*, recognition is triggered where a past transaction or event indicates that there has been a measurable change in the assets and liabilities of an entity, and where a change in assets is not offset by an equal change in liabilities a gain or loss will result (unless the change relates to a transaction with the entity's owners, in which case a contribution from owners or distribution to owners will be recognised). At the time that FRS 3 was issued, the ASB's thinking was that gains or losses should be recognised either in the profit and loss account or in the statement of total recognised gains and losses. However, as already stated, the latest proposals that the ASB has on the table are that all gains and losses should be recognised in a single statement of total financial performance. These proposals are discussed at 5 below.

Because of the company law framework that underpins UK financial reporting, it might be logical to assume that gains that are earned and realised are recognised in the profit and loss account, whilst gains that are earned (but not realised) are recognised in the statement of total recognised gains and losses – and this is more or less how things work at the moment. However, it is evident from the ASB's revised Draft *Statement of Principles* generally, and its recent Discussion Paper *Reporting Financial Performance: Proposals for Change* specifically, that it is seeking to change this approach.

Nevertheless, at the moment FRS 3 prevails, and UK GAAP still requires companies to present both a profit and loss account and a statement of total recognised gains and losses. The following extract from the example contained in the Appendix to FRS 3 illustrates the presentation of the statement:

Statement of total recognised gains and losses

	1993	1992 as restated
	£ million	£ million
Profit for the financial year	29	7
Unrealised surplus on revaluation of properties	4	6
Unrealised (loss)/gain on trade investment	(3)	7
	30	20
Currency translation differences on foreign currency net investments	(2)	5
Total recognised gains and losses relating to the year	28	25
Prior year adjustment (as explained in note x)	(10)	
Total gains and losses recognised since last annual report	18	

The £18 million net total gains represents the increase in net assets which occurred between the opening and closing balance sheet dates, and which were brought about by all transactions that the entity had entered into, other than those involving shareholders. Since the statement comprises total realised and unrealised gains and losses, the realised profit for the financial year (before dividends) is brought in as the first line of the statement. This means that the profit and loss account now provides the detailed analysis of the single line in the statement of total recognised gains and losses, whilst the unrealised gains and losses are itemised in the statement.

Where a reporting entity has no recognised gains or losses other than the profit or loss for the period, a statement to this effect immediately below the profit and loss account will suffice.

2.9.2   Share issue costs

The treatment of issue costs of both debt and equity instruments presented the ASB with an accounting dilemma. In developing FRS 4, the ASB wished to defer such costs but realised that they are not assets as defined in the Draft *Statement of Principles*. As a result, FRS 4 laid down the requirement that issue costs be accounted for as a reduction in the proceeds of a capital instrument. In the case of shares, FRS 4 states that 'issue costs are integral to a transaction with owners and for this reason the FRS requires them to be taken into account in determining the net proceeds that are reported in the reconciliation of movements in shareholders' funds. They should not be disclosed in the statement of total recognised gains and losses.'[76] However, whilst issue costs might be integral to a transaction with owners, the expenditure itself does not constitute a transaction with owners and should, therefore, be charged in the profit and loss account. Nevertheless, FRS 4 precludes this from happening.

2.9.3   *International developments*

Both the FASB and the IASC followed the ASB's lead and addressed the issue of comprehensive income in their own respective projects. This resulted, in the case of the FASB, in SFAS 130 – *Reporting Comprehensive Income* – which was issued in June 1997. The FASB attempted to develop the standard along the same lines as the ASB's statement of total recognised gains and losses, but met with strong opposition and had to back down. The result is a compromise solution with rather tentative requirements. The IASC has ended up in a similar position in its revision of IAS 1 – *Presentation of Financial Statements* – which was issued in August 1997, and was also not able to introduce the requirement for companies to present an additional statement of performance, although there is a requirement to present a form of reconciliation statement.[77] These developments are discussed in more detail at 4 below.

2.10   Taxation

If a company reports exceptional items which fall under paragraph 20 of FRS 3, the standard requires their effect on the tax charge to be disclosed in a note to the profit and loss account.[78] In addition, where (rarely) there is an extraordinary item, it is necessary to state the extraordinary item net of the tax effect, and any adjustments to the tax on extraordinary items in subsequent years also has to be shown as extraordinary.[79]

To calculate the amount to be allocated to these items, FRS 3 requires the 'with-and-without' method to be applied.[80] This means that the tax charge should be calculated as if the item(s) had not existed, then recalculated with the inclusion of the item(s); the difference between the two calculations should be attributed to the item(s) in question. Where there is more than one such item, it will be necessary to apportion the tax figure derived by this process, either pro rata or by a more appropriate method if one is available. The standard goes on to say that 'it is recognised that analysing an entity's total taxation charge between component parts of its result for a period can involve arbitrary allocations that tend to become less meaningful the more components there are. However, in respect of items such as disposal profits or losses, the tax can often be identified with the exceptional item concerned and the relationship between the profit or loss and the attributable tax may be significantly different from that in respect of operating profits or losses. In such circumstances it is relevant to identify the tax charge or credit more specifically.'[81]

There is no corresponding requirement to analyse tax between the results of continuing and discontinued operations, but where companies choose to do so they are required to explain the method and assumptions underlying the allocation.[82]

FRS 3 does not discuss the treatment of tax relating to items reported in the statement of total recognised gains and losses, but the general principle should be that the tax effect should be matched with the item to which it relates. Where deferred tax is provided in respect of the revaluation of an asset, the tax effect should follow the revaluation surplus by being taken to revaluation reserve, and therefore also dealt with in the statement of total recognised gains and losses. Similarly, where a prior year adjustment is made involving an adjustment to the opening balance on shareholders' funds, any tax effect attributable to the adjustment should be dealt with in the same way.

2.11 Earnings per share

2.11.1 EPS redefined

The ASB has long maintained that undue emphasis is placed on EPS numbers and that this leads to simplistic interpretations of financial performance.[83] In the explanation section of FRS 3, the ASB presented the view that 'it is not possible to distil the performance of a complex organisation into a single measure'. It went on to say that 'undue significance, therefore, should not be placed on any one such measure which may purport to achieve this aim. To assess the performance of a reporting entity during a period all components of its activities must be considered.'[84]

As a result, the Board attempted to de-emphasise EPS and, in so doing, laid down the requirement that EPS be calculated *after* extraordinary items. This was later reaffirmed by FRS 14 – *Earnings per share* – which stated that 'basic earnings per share should be calculated by dividing the net profit or loss for the period attributable to ordinary shareholders by the weighted average number of ordinary shares outstanding during the period.'[85] The standard went on to say that 'all items of income and expense that are recognised in a period, including tax expense, exceptional and extraordinary items and minority interests, are included in the determination of the net profit or loss for the period'.[86]

FRS 3 provided further that if an additional EPS calculated at any other level of profit is disclosed it should be presented on a consistent basis over time and, wherever disclosed, reconciled to the amount required by the FRS. Such a reconciliation should list the items for which an adjustment is being made and disclose their individual effect on the calculation. The EPS required by FRS 3 should be at least as prominent as any additional version presented and the reason for calculating the additional version should be explained. The reconciliation and explanation should appear adjacent to the EPS disclosure, or a reference should be given to where they can be found.[87]

2.11.2 *The IIMR headline EPS*

As a consequence of the virtual abolition of extraordinary items and FRS 3's amendment of the definition of EPS, considerable concern was expressed (mainly by analysts) about the inevitable volatility in reported EPS that would ensue as a result of the inclusion in the EPS calculation of both capital items and items which would formerly have been classified as extraordinary. In fact, the standard was adopted by a vote of eight of the nine members of the ASB, with Mr Robert Bradfield dissenting. In his dissenting view, Mr Bradfield expressed the fear that FRS 3 might frequently produce misleading measures of performance, in that the standard emphasises the components of pre-tax profit, which now include the results of business disposals. In Mr Bradfield's view, it is the magnitude and quality of the earnings from trading, after tax and minority interests, that are the focus of the attention for the shareholder as he uses the financial statements to assess the continuity of the source of dividends.

In a similar vein, brokers James Capel had the following to say about FRS 3 in its newsletter *Accounting Matters*, which was issued shortly after the publication of FRS 3: 'One of the principal consequences of the introduction of FRS 3 will be to render the simple reported earnings per share figure useless, thereby removing what the ASB sees as an excessive focus on earnings per share and forcing users of accounts to assess a wider range of information. In practice, we suspect the effect will be to give rise to a proliferation of "adjusted" earnings per share figures; this process may begin with EPS figures adjusted by companies themselves. In *Accounting Matters* we introduced our "James Capel" definition of Earnings per share ... . We suspect that most users of accounts will wish to re-establish a concept of "normal" or "underlying" earnings per share. In our approach we try to remain as close as possible to our existing practice.'[88]

All of this led the Institute of Investment Management and Research to issue its Statement of Investment Practice No. 1 – *The Definition of IIMR Headline Earnings* – which seeks to find an earnings figure that will reflect a company's trading performance but that will also limit the need to exercise judgement in its calculation, so that it can be used as an unambiguous reference point between users, the press and statistical companies. The IIMR headline earnings is discussed in section 5.5.1 of Chapter 23 of this book.

2.12   Reconciliation of movements in shareholders' funds

The standard requires that a note be presented reconciling the opening and closing totals of shareholders' funds of the period.[89] The rationale for this requirement was that whilst the profit and loss account and statement of total recognised gains and losses reflected the performance of a reporting entity in a period, there were other changes in shareholders' funds that could also be important in understanding the change in the financial position of the entity. The purpose of the reconciliation was to highlight those other changes.[90]

The explanation section of the standard permits the reconciliation to be presented as a 'primary statement', rather than as a note to the financial statements. However, if included as a primary statement, the reconciliation should be shown separately from the statement of total recognised gains and losses. This seems remarkable. The reconciliation is either a primary statement of financial performance, or it is not; it should not be left to the whim of preparers of accounts to make that decision.

The appendix to FRS 3 includes the following example of the reconciliation presented as a note:

Reconciliation of movements in shareholders' funds

	1993	1992 as restated
	£ million	£ million
Profit for the financial year	29	7
Dividends	(8)	(1)
	21	6
Other recognised gains and losses relating to the year (net)	(1)	18
New share capital subscribed	20	1
Goodwill written-off	(25)	
Net addition to shareholders' funds	15	25
Opening shareholders' funds (originally £375 million before deducting prior year adjustment of £10 million)	365	340
Closing shareholders' funds	380	365

The reconciliation will include the profit or loss for the period as recorded in the profit and loss account, all other recognised gains and losses for the period and all other movements to shareholders' funds. The other movements will be:

- dividends for the period; and
- capital contributed by or repaid to shareholders during the period, for example, the amount subscribed for new shares during the period.

Since FRS 10 no longer permits the direct write off of goodwill against reserves, the elimination of goodwill no longer features in the reconciliation. However, the transitional provisions of FRS 10 did not require companies to reinstate previously written off goodwill, with the result that many companies will still have cumulative amounts of goodwill previously eliminated against reserves that FRS 10 requires to be charged in the profit and loss account if and when the businesses to which it related are disposed of or closed down.[91]

When goodwill is reinstated and taken into account in calculating the profit or loss arising on disposal or closure it does not affect total shareholders' funds since it will be credited to reserves to reinstate it, and debited in the profit and loss account for the period. Since it does not affect total shareholders' funds it might be thought that it should not be included in the reconciliation. However, the profit for the period is included in the reconciliation and will be stated after the debit in respect of the goodwill. Accordingly, the reversal of the previous elimination of goodwill against reserves should also appear in the reconciliation; this will then cancel the debit that has been charged in the reconciliation through its inclusion in the profit for the year; for example:

Extract 22.13: Booker plc (1999)

Reconciliation of movements in consolidated shareholders' funds

	65 weeks ended 27 March 1999 £m	52 weeks ended 27 December 1997 £m
(Loss)/profit for the period	**(164.9)**	48.4
Dividends	**(10.4)**	(59.0)
Retained loss for the year	**(175.3)**	(10.6)
Exchange movements	**0.2**	(6.1)
New share capital issued	**0.3**	2.7
Adjustment in respect of scrip dividend	**5.9**	1.1
Amounts invested in goodwill	**-**	(3.9)
Goodwill transferred to profit and loss account in respect of disposal of businesses	**78.1**	19.0
(Decrease)/increase in shareholders' funds	**(90.8)**	2.2
Opening shareholders' funds (restated for prior year adjustments of £6.6m)	**14.6**	12.4
Closing shareholders' funds/(deficit)	**(76.2)**	14.6

Unlike its guidance on the statement of total recognised gains and losses, FRS 3 does not contain any guidance as to whether or not the note is required where the only movements in shareholders' funds are the profit for the year, other recognised gains and losses and dividends (which are required to be disclosed in the profit and loss account). The FRS similarly does not discuss whether or not the reconciliation of movements in shareholders' funds can be combined with the note, required by Schedule 4, showing the movement on reserves. The implication from the appendix to the FRS is that the two notes should be presented separately. The justification for this lies in the assertion in the explanatory section of the FRS that the purpose of the reconciliation is to highlight the changes in shareholders' funds other than the recognised gains and losses. The ASB possibly took the view that the other changes would not be sufficiently highlighted if the two notes were to be combined. Furthermore, whilst there is no requirement to give comparatives for the reserves note, the FRS requires comparatives for the reconciliation.

Nevertheless, the requirements of the standard add to the ever-increasing catalogue of unnecessary and duplicated disclosures in company accounts.

2.13 Statement of movements on reserves

It is clear that FRS 3's requirements in respect of the statement of total recognised gains and losses and the reconciliation of movements in shareholders' funds have superseded SSAP 6's former requirement that accounts should include a statement of movements on reserves. Nevertheless, the Companies Act imposes the following requirements in respect of reserve movements:

(a) any amount set aside or proposed to be set aside, or withdrawn, or proposed to be withdrawn from reserves must be separately disclosed;[92]

(b) where any amount is transferred to or from reserves, the amounts of the reserves at the beginning and end of the financial year, the amounts transferred to or from the reserves and the sources and application of these amounts must be disclosed.[93]

This means that companies will still have to prepare a conventional reserves movements note. The Appendix to FRS 3 included the following example of such a note:

Reserves

	Share premium account	Revaluation reserve	Profit and loss account	Total
	£ million	£ million	£ million	£ million
At beginning of year as previously stated	44	200	120	364
Prior year adjustment			(10)	(10)
At beginning of year as restated	44	200	110	354
Premium on issue of shares (nominal value £7 million)	13			13
Goodwill written-off			(25)	(25)
Transfer from profit and loss account of the year			21	21
Transfer of realised profits		(14)	14	0
Decrease in value of trade investment		(3)		(3)
Currency translation differences on foreign currency net investments			(2)	(2)
Surplus on property valuations		4		4
At end of year	57	187	118	362

Note: Nominal share capital at end of year £18 million (1992 £11 million).

2.14 Prior period adjustments

2.14.1 Definition

The requirements in the FRS were unaltered from those in SSAP 6, although they were extended to explain how a prior period adjustment impacts on the statement of total recognised gains and losses. The standard defines prior period adjustments as 'material adjustments applicable to prior periods arising from changes in accounting policies or from the correction of fundamental errors. They do not include normal recurring adjustments or corrections of accounting estimates made in prior periods.'[94]

2.14.2 Identification of prior year adjustments

The explanation section of the standard emphasises that 'the majority of items relating to prior periods arise mainly from the corrections and adjustments which are the natural result of estimates inherent in accounting and more particularly in the periodic preparation of financial statements'.[95] Such items are dealt with in the profit and loss account of the period in which they are identified and their effect is stated where material. They are not exceptional or extraordinary merely because they relate to a prior period; their nature will determine their classification. Prior period adjustments – that is, prior period items which should be adjusted against the opening balance of retained profits or reserves – are rare and limited to items arising from changes in accounting policies or from the correction of fundamental errors.[96]

The standard goes on to say that 'estimating future events and their effects requires the exercise of judgement and will require reappraisal as new events occur, as more experience is acquired or as additional information is obtained. Because a change in estimate arises from new information or developments, it should not be given retrospective effect by a restatement of prior periods. Sometimes a change in estimate may have the appearance of a change in accounting policy and care is necessary to avoid confusing the two.'[97]

2.14.3 Changes in accounting policy

An accounting policy should only be changed if the new policy is preferable to the policy it replaces because it will give a fairer presentation of the results and of the financial position of the business. A characteristic of a change in policy is that it is the result of a change between two accounting bases.

As stated above, a change in estimate may have the appearance of a change in accounting policy and care is necessary in order to avoid confusing the two; for example, a company may change the rate at which it depreciates a particular class of fixed asset. Such a change is not a change in accounting policy but a change in estimate of either the useful life or depreciable amount of the assets and, therefore, the effect of the change should be reflected prospectively and not as a prior year adjustment.

It is also noteworthy that a change in accounting policy which is necessitated by the adoption of a new accounting pronouncement may not necessarily result in a prior year adjustment, since the transitional or implementation provisions of the new pronouncement may override FRS 3. This was highlighted by UITF 6 – *Accounting for post-retirement benefits other than pensions* – which offered a choice between two methods of accounting for its implementation: companies could either incorporate the unprovided obligation in the balance sheet by means of a prior year adjustment accounted for in accordance with the provisions of FRS 3, or they could spread it forward over the expected remaining service lives of current employees.[98]

2.14.4 Correction of fundamental errors

The standard stresses that a fundamental error is only likely to occur in exceptional circumstances. The term 'fundamental' is implicitly defined as being of such significance as to destroy the presentation of a true and fair view and hence the validity of those financial statements.[99] The corrections of such fundamental errors and the cumulative adjustments applicable to prior periods have no bearing on the results of the current period and they are therefore not included in arriving at the profit or loss for the current period.

However, it is worth noting that when SSAP 6 was introduced there was no available procedure which allowed companies to correct and reissue accounts which are considered to be defective. Such provisions now exist in the law,[100] which means that the facility to correct fundamental errors by means of a prior year adjustment must be of less significance as a result; if the directors consider their accounts to be defective then they should avail themselves of the provisions under the Companies Act which enable them to revise the accounts; they do not have to wait to make the amendment in the accounts of the following year by means of a prior year adjustment. Nevertheless, circumstances will arise where a fundamental error is either discovered shortly before the following year's accounts are due to be issued or does not, in the opinion of the directors, warrant the preparation of revised accounts. In both instances, therefore, it would be appropriate to follow FRS 3's procedures for the correction of the error.

It is tempting to think of any adjustment which relates to an event or circumstance which arose in a prior year as a prior year item; however, if the adjustment derives from new information about that event, then it simply represents a change in the estimate of the effect of that event and is therefore a current period item. For example, if a company has to write off a debt which it previously considered to be recoverable, then the charge should be reflected in the current year's profit or loss and not accounted for by way of prior year adjustment. It is therefore appropriate to consider whether the information which indicates that a fundamental error has arisen was actually available at the time that the financial statements for the prior period were approved.

2.14.5 Accounting treatment

FRS 3 requires that prior period adjustments be accounted for by restating the comparative figures for the preceding period in the primary statements and notes and adjusting the opening balance of reserves for the cumulative effect. The cumulative effect of the adjustments should also be noted at the foot of the statement of total recognised gains and losses of the current period.[101]

This means that in the case of a change in accounting policy, the amounts for the current and corresponding periods should be restated on the basis of the new policy. The cumulative adjustments should also be noted at the foot of the statement of total recognised gains and losses of the current period and included in the reconciliation of movements in shareholders' funds of the corresponding period in order to highlight for users the effect of the adjustments. The following example illustrates the mechanics of such a process:

Example 22.1: Illustration of a change in accounting policy

Up until 31 December 2001, a company has adopted a policy of writing off its development expenditure in the year in which it was incurred. The company's financial statements for the year ended 31 December 2001 disclosed the following:

Profit and loss account	2001 £'000	2000 £'000
Profit on ordinary activities before taxation	4,200	3,800
Taxation	(1,575)	(1,400)
Profit on ordinary activities after taxation	2,625	2,400
Dividends	(600)	(500)
Retained profit for year	2,025	1,900
Balance sheet		
Tangible fixed assets	8,000	7,100
Net current assets	2,025	800
	10,025	7,900
Deferred taxation	(1,000)	(900)
	9,025	7,000
Share capital	1,000	1,000
Profit and loss account	8,025	6,000
	9,025	7,000

In preparing its financial statements for the year ended 31 December 2002 it considers that a policy of capitalising the development expenditure and amortising it over a period of four years from the date of commencing production would give a fairer presentation of the results and financial position of the company. Accordingly, it will be necessary to restate the figures for 2001 on the basis of the new policy. This initially involves computing:

(i)   the net book value of the development expenditure at 31 December 2001;

(ii)   the amortisation charge for the year ended 31 December 2001; and

(iii) the net book value of the development expenditure at 31 December 2000.

The development expenditure incurred in each of the five years ended 31 December 2001 and the calculation of the above figures are as follows (for the purposes of this example the date of commencing production is taken to be 1 January following the year in which the development expenditure was incurred):

Year	Development expenditure incurred £'000	(i) £'000	(ii) £'000	(iii) £'000
1997	260	–	65	65
1998	100	25	25	50
1999	240	120	60	180
2000	400	300	100	400
2001	40	40	–	–
	485	250	695	

Development expenditure in 2002 amounted to £800,000.

The adjustment to the pre-tax profit for 2001 will, therefore, be a reduction of £210,000 being the amortisation of £250,000 less the development expenditure of £40,000 previously charged to the profit and loss account.

Having computed these figures it is then necessary to ascertain whether any other figures in the financial statements will be affected by the change in policy; in particular, deferred taxation and stocks. For the purposes of this example the only other figures, apart from retained profits, affected by the change in policy are those relating to deferred taxation. Assuming that the development expenditure has been fully allowed as a deductible expense in arriving at the corporation tax payable in respect of the year in which it was incurred, then the new policy will give rise to timing differences for which deferred tax may have to be provided. The company considers that full provision has to be made for deferred tax and accordingly the provision at 31 December 2001, the charge for the year then ended, and the provision at 31 December 2000 have to be adjusted as follows:

	Gross timing difference £'000	Provision at 35% £'000
31 December 2001	485	170
31 December 2000	695	243
Tax charge for year		(73)

As a result of these calculations the financial statements for the year ended 31 December 2002 will therefore show the following figures in the profit and loss account, the statement of total recognised gains and losses, the balance sheet and reconciliation of movements in shareholders' funds (the 2002 figures having been prepared on the basis of the new accounting policy):

Profit and loss account

	2002 £'000	Restated 2001 £'000
Profit on ordinary activities before taxation	5,000	3,990
Taxation	(1,820)	(1,502)
Profit on ordinary activities after taxation	3,180	2,488
Dividends	(700)	(600)
Retained profit for year	2,480	1,888

Statement of total recognised gains and losses

	2002 £'000	Restated 2001 £'000
Profit for the financial year	3,180	2,488
Total recognised gains and losses relating to the year	3,180	2,488
Prior year adjustment	315	
Total gains and losses recognised since last annual report	3,495	

Balance sheet

	2002 £'000	Restated 2001 £'000
Fixed assets		
Intangible	1,090	485
Tangible fixed assets	10,000	8,000
	11,090	8,485
Net current assets	2,212	2,025
	13,302	10,510
Deferred taxation	(1,482)	(1,170)
	11,820	9,340
Share capital	1,000	1,000
Profit and loss account	10,820	8,340
	11,820	9,340

Reconciliation of movements in shareholders' funds

	2002 £'000	Restated 2001 £'000
Profit for the financial year	3,180	2,488
Dividends	(700)	(600)
Net addition to shareholders' funds	2,480	1,888
Opening shareholders' funds (originally £9,025,000 before adding prior year adjustment of £315,000)	9,340	7,452
Closing shareholders' funds	11,820	9,340

Reserves note

	Profit and loss account £'000
At 1 January 2002	
— as previously reported	8,025
Prior year adjustment	315
— as restated	8,340
Retained profit for the year	2,480
At 31 December 2002	10,820

Where prior year figures are restated it will generally be necessary (unless the effect would be immaterial) to restate the balance sheet and profit and loss account, but it should be unnecessary to amend the cash flow statement because, of course, the cash flows have not changed. However, some of the reconciling notes to the cash flow statement may be affected, particularly the calculation of operating cash flow where the indirect method has been used to generate this figure. Care should also be taken to ensure that all figures in the accounts which are affected by the change in policy are adjusted, in particular, deferred taxation.

2.14.6 *Disclosing the effect of a change in accounting policy*

One further requirement of FRS 3 in respect of prior period adjustments is that 'the effect of prior period adjustments on the results for the preceding period should be disclosed where practicable'.[102] This overlaps with the Companies Act disclosures that are required when there is a departure from the fundamental accounting principles laid down in the Act.[103] In the case of a change in accounting policy, it will be necessary for the directors to depart from the fundamental principle of consistency, in which case they are required to disclose in a note to the accounts the particulars of and reasons for the departure 'and its effect'.[104]

This gave rise to an issue of interpretation as to whether the Companies Act requirement to disclose 'its effect' related to the current period, the prior period or both. In tracing the requirement back to the EC Fourth Directive, it seems clear that the intention of the legislation was for companies to disclose the effect of the departure on the current year's financial statements as a whole, and not just on the results. The wording of the relevant Article in the Fourth Directive is as follows: 'Any such departures must be disclosed in the notes on the accounts and the reasons for them given together with an assessment of their effect on the assets, liabilities, financial position and profit or loss.'[105]

However, irrespective of what might have been the original intention of the legislation, the practice which had developed was to provide only details of the effect on the prior period's results (i.e. the information which is required by FRS 3). Apart from anything else, the principal reason for this was that it is often impracticable to provide the information in respect of the current period. For example, a company preparing its first set of accounts in compliance with FRS 4 and FRS 5 would, in order to illustrate fully the effect of the relevant changes, effectively have to present alongside the current year's accounts, a second set of accounts prepared under the old rules. Not only is this impracticable, but it is of little value to the user.

Nevertheless, this is an issue which was referred to the UITF – apparently at the insistence of the Review Panel. The UITF's deliberations resulted in UITF Abstract 14 – *Disclosure of changes in accounting policy* – which was issued in November 1995. The consensus reached by the UITF was that the disclosures necessary when a change of accounting policy is made should include, in addition to the disclosure of the effect required by FRS 3, an indication of the effect on the current year's results. In those cases where the effect on the current year was either immaterial or similar to the quantified effect on the prior year 'a simple statement saying this would suffice'. The Abstract provides further that where it is not practicable to give the effect on the current year, that fact, together with the reasons, should be stated.[106] As stated above, we believe that these are sometimes meaningless and impracticable disclosures, and companies will in such cases make use of UITF 14's get-out to avoid having to provide them.

2.15 Comparative figures

Comparative figures are required both for the figures in the primary statements and such notes thereto as are required by the standard. The comparatives in respect of the profit and loss account have to be analysed into continuing operations, acquisitions and discontinued operations to the same level as the current year's results. However, the analysis of the comparatives does not have to be on the face of the profit and loss account, but can be given in the notes.

The comparative figures will, in total, be the same as the figures reported in the previous year's profit and loss account. However, the analysis will be different;

the continuing category in the comparatives should only include results of activities that are classified as continuing in the current year. Consequently the discontinued column in the comparatives will include the results of the activities that were discontinued in both the current and the previous year. The results of the operations that were classified as acquisitions in the previous year's profit and loss account will not be presented as acquisitions in the comparative figures for the current period; they will be included in continuing activities. This is because the analysis of the comparative figures must be based on the status of an operation in the current year's profit and loss account. The only time that there will be an acquisitions category in the comparatives is when an acquisition of the current period has been accounted for as a merger; in this case the comparatives will be restated as if the companies had been combined throughout the previous period and so there will be an element in the comparatives relating to operations classified as acquisitions in the current period.

The standard provides that in some circumstances it may also be useful to disclose the results of acquisitions for the first full financial year for which they are a part of the reporting entity's activities. In this case the FRS suggests that it may be helpful also to provide the comparative figures for the acquisitions.

3 HISTORICAL SUMMARIES, HALF-YEARLY REPORTS AND PRELIMINARY PROFIT STATEMENTS

Although the London Stock Exchange published a major revision of its Listing Rules in 1993, the revised Rules take no account of the substantial changes made to the profit and loss account by FRS 3. This means that although extraordinary items remain only a theoretical possibility, the Rules specifically require that such items be disclosed in all half-yearly reports and preliminary profits statements of listed companies;[107] on the other hand, the various new components of performance which the ASB has identified as being important – notably those relating to exceptional items and discontinued operations – are not required to be identified.

Unlike SSAP 6, FRS 3 does not refer to historical summaries, half-yearly reports and preliminary profit statements. Nevertheless, there is a growing trend for companies to include comprehensive profit and loss accounts and statements of total recognised gains and losses in accordance with FRS 3 in their half-yearly reports.

Although there are no rules governing historical summaries, it is our view that they should normally be restated retrospectively for prior year adjustments. However, if this is not practicable, the part of the summary which has not been restated should be identified and the reason for not restating it explained.

In the meantime, the ASB has issued two non-mandatory statements which lay down recommended principles to be followed in the preparation of interim reports and preliminary announcements: the Statement – *Interim Reports* – was issued in September 1997 and the Statement – *Preliminary Announcements* – was issued in July 1998. Both of these documents attempt to conform the profit and loss account with the requirements of FRS 3, and both documents state that a statement of total recognised gains and losses and reconciliation of movements in shareholders' funds should be included where appropriate.

The requirements of the ASB's Statements on interim reports and preliminary announcements are covered in detail in Chapter 30 of this book.

4 COMPARISON WITH IASC AND US PRONOUNCEMENTS

4.1 IASC

4.1.1 IAS 8

The international position is set out in IAS 8 – *Net Profit or Loss for the Period, Fundamental Errors and Changes in Accounting Policies* – which was issued in revised form in December 1993 as part of the IASC's comparability/improvements project. Its main features are as follows:

■ All items of income or expense recognised in the income statement should be included in the determination of profit or loss unless an IAS permits or requires otherwise.[108]

■ The profit or loss for the period is to be split between (a) the profit and loss from ordinary activities and (b) extraordinary items, both of which are to be disclosed on the face of the income statement,[109] with the nature and amount of each extraordinary item disclosed in a note.[110] The definitions of extraordinary items and ordinary activities are less rigorous than the equivalent FRS 3 definitions, although IAS 8 states that 'only on rare occasions does an event or transaction give rise to an extraordinary item'.[111]

■ Amounts which are of such size, nature or incidence as to be relevant to an explanation of the performance for the period are to be disclosed (the term 'exceptional items' is not used).[112]

■ The standard defines a discontinued operation rather loosely as something which results from the sale or abandonment of an operation that represents a separate, major line of business of an enterprise and of which the assets, net profit or loss and activities can be distinguished physically, operationally and for financial reporting purposes.[113] Although it is not difficult to detect the influences of US GAAP on this definition, the related accounting requirements are less rigorous. Not only does the standard allow considerable flexibility in determining whether or not a disposal constitutes a discontinued operation, but it also permits the results of discontinued operations to be classified under both ordinary and extraordinary activities.[114]

However, the standard does require a number of disclosures to be given for each discontinued operation. These are the nature of the discontinued operation, the manner and effective date of the discontinuance, the gain or loss on discontinuance, and the discontinued operation's revenue and profit or loss from ordinary activities for the period and the comparative period.[115]

■   The effect of a change in an accounting estimate should be included in the determination of net profit or loss in the period of the change (if the change affects the period only), or in the period of the change and future periods (if the change affects both).[116] The effect of a change in an accounting estimate should be included in the same income statement classification as was used previously for the estimate.[117]

■   Fundamental errors and changes in accounting policy are to be dealt with either as a prior year adjustment (the 'benchmark treatment') or as a separate item in the current year's profit or loss (the 'allowed alternative treatment').[118]

4.1.2   IAS 1 (revised)

In August 1997, the IASC issued IAS 1 (revised) – *Presentation of Financial Statements* – which consolidated and replaced IAS 1 – *Disclosure of Accounting Policies*, IAS 5 – *Information to be Disclosed in Financial Statements*, and IAS 13 – *Presentation of Current Assets and Current Liabilities*. This new standard can best be described as the IASC's version of the EC Fourth Directive. It deals with the components of financial statements, fair presentation, fundamental accounting concepts, disclosure of accounting policies, the structure and content of financial statements and the statement of changes in equity. The standard can only really be termed controversial in two respects: (1) it introduced the possibility for companies reporting under IAS to apply a fair presentation override,[119] and (2) it adds the requirement for companies to present a statement of changes in equity as a fourth primary financial statement.[120]

In approving the Standard, the IASC Board agreed that, in extremely rare circumstances, enterprises may depart from a requirement if to do so is necessary in order to achieve fair presentation. (The issues of fair presentation in accordance with International Accounting Standards and the use of the override are discussed in detail in section 2.2 of Chapter 1 of this book.)

On the matter of the statement of changes in equity, the Board agreed that financial statements prepared in accordance with International Accounting Standards should include, as a separate component, a statement showing:

■   the net profit or loss for the period;

■   each item of income and expense, gain or loss which, as required by other Standards, is recognised directly in equity, and the total of these items; and

■   the cumulative effect of changes in accounting policy, and correction of fundamental errors, dealt with under the Benchmark treatment in IAS 8.

In addition, an enterprise should also present, either within this statement or in the notes:

■ capital transactions with owners and distributions to owners;

■ the balance of accumulated profit or loss at the beginning of the period and at the balance sheet date, and the movements for the period; and

■ a reconciliation between the carrying amount of each class of equity capital, share premium and each reserve at the beginning and the end of the period, separately disclosing each movement.

This is, of course, a compromise solution which is aimed at satisfying a number of different constituencies. For example, from a UK perspective the first three parts correspond to FRS 3's statement of total recognised gains and losses, with the result that the remaining three items can be disclosed in the notes thereby leaving the statement of total recognised gains and losses intact. The proposals are also compatible with SFAS 130 as a result of the flexibility on both sides. The IASC does not view the statement as a statement of performance, but it can be made into one if people so desire. Moreover, it provides a framework within which other IASC projects (such as financial instruments) can work.

However, as can be seen from section 5 below, the IASC sees IAS 1's statement of changes in equity as an interim measure, pending the development by the G4+1 (of which the IASC is a participant) of a single statement of performance that will effectively combine the profit and loss account and the first three parts of the statement of changes in equity.

4.1.3 IAS 35

The IASC issued IAS 35 – *Discontinuing Operations* – in June 1998. The standard is concerned only with the presentation and disclosures relating to discontinuing operations. It contains no recognition or measurement rules of its own, although it does require that provisions for discontinuing operations should be calculated in accordance with IAS 36 – *Impairment of assets* – and IAS 37 – *Provisions, Contingent Liabilities and Contingent Assets*. It also notes that IAS 19 – *Employee Benefits* – and IAS 16 – *Property, Plant and Equipment* – may also be relevant.

The objectives of IAS 35 are to establish a basis for segregating information about a major operation that an enterprise is discontinuing from information about its continuing operations and to specify minimum disclosures about a discontinuing operation. Distinguishing discontinuing and continuing operations improves the ability of investors, creditors, and other users of financial statements to make projections of the enterprise's cash flows, earnings-generating capacity, and financial position.

A discontinuing operation is a relatively large component of an enterprise, such as a business or geographical segment under IAS 14 – *Segment Reporting*, that the enterprise, pursuant to a single plan, either is disposing of substantially in its entirety or is terminating through abandonment or piecemeal sale. The standard defines a discontinuing operation as 'a component of an enterprise:

(a)   that the enterprise, pursuant to a single plan, is:

   (i)   disposing of substantially in its entirety, such as by selling the component in a single transaction, by demerger or spin-off of ownership of the component to the enterprise's shareholders;

   (ii)   disposing of piecemeal, such as by selling off the component's assets and settling its liabilities individually; or

   (iii) terminating through abandonment;

(b)   that represents a separate major line of business or geographical area of operations; and

(c)   that can be distinguished operationally and for financial reporting purposes.'[121]

Under criterion (a) of the above definition, a discontinuing operation may be disposed of in its entirety or piecemeal, but always pursuant to an overall plan to discontinue the entire component. If an enterprise sells a component substantially in its entirety, the result can be a net gain or net loss. For such a discontinuance, there is a single date at which a binding sale agreement is entered into, although the actual transfer of possession and control of the discontinuing operation may occur at a later date. Also, payments to the seller may occur at the time of the agreement, at the time of the transfer, or over an extended future period.

The Standard uses the term 'discontinuing operation' rather than the traditional 'discontinued operation' because 'discontinued operation' implies that recognition of a discontinuance is necessary only at or near the end of the process of discontinuing the operation (as is the case under FRS 3). Instead, IAS 35 requires that disclosures about a discontinuing operation begin earlier than that, namely when a detailed formal plan for disposal has been adopted and announced or when the enterprise has already contracted for the disposal. This is described in the standard as the 'initial disclosure event', which is defined as being 'the occurrence of one of the following, whichever occurs earlier:

(a)   the enterprise has entered into a binding sale agreement for substantially all of the assets attributable to the discontinuing operation; or

(b)   the enterprise's board of directors or similar governing body has both (i) approved a detailed, formal plan for the discontinuance and (ii) made an announcement of the plan.'[122]

The bulk of the standard's required disclosures are to be given by way of note. An enterprise should include the following information relating to a discontinuing operation in its financial statements beginning with the financial statements for the period in which the initial disclosure event (as defined above) occurs:

(a)   a description of the discontinuing operation;

(b)   the business or geographical segment(s) in which it is reported in accordance with IAS 14;

(c)   the date and nature of the initial disclosure event;

(d)   the date or period in which the discontinuance is expected to be completed if known or determinable;

(e)   the carrying amounts, as of the balance sheet date, of the total assets and the total liabilities to be disposed of;

(f)   the amounts of revenue, expenses, and pre-tax profit or loss from ordinary activities attributable to the discontinuing operation during the current financial reporting period, and the income tax expense relating thereto as required by paragraph 81(h) of IAS 12; and

(g)   the amounts of net cash flows attributable to the operating, investing, and financing activities of the discontinuing operation during the current financial reporting period.[123]

The disclosures required by IAS 35 must be presented separately for each discontinuing operation, and financial statements for periods after initial disclosure must update those disclosures, including a description of any significant changes in the amount or timing of cash flows relating to the assets and liabilities to be disposed of or settled and the causes of those changes. The disclosures would also be made if a plan for disposal is approved and publicly announced after the end of an enterprise's financial reporting period but before the financial statements for that period are approved.[124] The disclosures continue until completion of the disposal.

4.2   US

There are a number of US pronouncements which have been issued relating to this area of accounting. The main ones which are still relevant today are as follows: APB Opinion No. 20 – *Accounting Changes*; APB Opinion No. 30 – *Reporting the Results of Operations–Reporting the Effects of Disposal of a Segment of a Business, and Extraordinary, Unusual and Infrequently Occurring Events and Transactions*; AIN-APB 30 – *Reporting the Results of Operations: Accounting Interpretations of APB Opinion No. 30*; and SFAS 16 – *Prior Period Adjustments*. In addition, EITF Abstract 94–3 dealing with restructuring charges and SEC Staff Accounting Bulletin SAB No. 93 regarding discontinued operations are also relevant. More significantly, though, in June 1997 the FASB issued SFAS 130 – *Reporting Comprehensive Income*. This is discussed at 4.2.4 below.

4.2.1   Extraordinary items

Prior to FRS 3, extraordinary items were much more of a rare phenomenon in the US than in the UK. In fact, very few of the items which were being disclosed as extraordinary in financial statements in the UK would have remained so under US GAAP. However, given FRS 3's effective ban on extraordinary items, the situation has been turned on its head. Although extraordinary items are rarely found in US GAAP accounts, at least it is recognised that they can arise under certain circumstances.

The US position on extraordinary items is primarily contained within APB 30. The key issues addressed relate to the definition of an extraordinary item; the treatment of the results of discontinued activities; and the definition of a business segment. The definition of extraordinary is broadly similar to that used in FRS 3, in that it incorporates the two key elements that the event must be of an unusual nature (and possess a high degree of abnormality) and that the event would not reasonably be expected to recur in the foreseeable future.[125] However, differences in interpretation arise for two principal reasons: first, APB 30 gives a detailed interpretation of the definition of extraordinary by discussing the two key terms 'unusual nature' and 'infrequency of occurrence'.[126] Second, it lists a number of items which should not be reported as extraordinary;[127] this is complemented by AIN-APB 30 which gives specific examples of items which would be regarded as extraordinary and those which would not.[128] In contrast, FRS 3's definition of ordinary activities effectively eliminates the possibility of any item being regarded as extraordinary.

Nevertheless, APB 30's detailed discussion of the definition of extraordinary also results in a very narrow interpretation of the term. For example, it comments that an unusual event should possess a high degree of abnormality and be of a type clearly unrelated to the ordinary and typical activities of the company.[129] Furthermore, in discussing 'infrequency of occurrence' APB 30 comments that the event or transaction should be of such a type that would not be expected to occur again in the foreseeable future.[130]

The examples of items listed in APB 30 which should not be reported as extraordinary items because they are usual in nature or may be expected to recur as a consequence of customary and continuing business activities include, inter alia, the write-down or write-off of assets, e.g. debtors and stocks, and gains or losses from sale or abandonment of property, plant and equipment. Whilst such items were frequently treated as extraordinary in the financial statements of UK companies prior to FRS 3, they would now not under any circumstances be regarded as extraordinary. On the other hand, APB 30 recognises that there may be occasions when such items can be properly treated as extraordinary items, but emphasises that these will be rare; for example, as result of an earthquake or expropriation.[131] It also specifically states that gains or losses on disposal of a segment of a business should not be treated as an extraordinary item (see 4.2.2 below).

One of the examples given in AIN-APB 30 which illustrates the differences in interpretation is that of a disposal of an investment in another company held for investment purposes. If the company has never owned another investment, then clearly the disposal is of an unusual nature and could not in current circumstances ever recur and therefore the gain or loss can be regarded as extraordinary. However, if the company holds a portfolio of investments, even if their disposal is infrequent, the disposal cannot be regarded either as unusual or unlikely to recur.[132]   Under FRS 3, neither disposal would give rise to an extraordinary item.

One other particular requirement which is worthy of note is provided by SFAS 4,[133] which expressly requires the disclosure of gains or losses arising from early extinguishment of debt to be disclosed as extraordinary.

4.2.2   Discontinued operations

APB 30 deals with discontinued operations very differently from FRS 3. Whilst FRS 3 lays down four strict criteria which must be satisfied for an operation to be classified as discontinued (see 2.3.1 above), APB 30 uses the term 'segment of a business' in order to determine whether the effect of certain activities being discontinued merits separate accounting treatment.[134]

Consequently, the term discontinued operations refers to the operations of a segment of a business that has been sold, abandoned, spun off, or otherwise disposed of or, although still operating, is subject to a formal plan for disposal. In the usual circumstance, it would be expected that the plan of disposal would be carried out within a period of one year from the 'measurement date' (see below).

'Segment of a business' refers to a component of an entity whose activities represent a separate major line of business or class of customer. A segment may be in the form of a subsidiary, a division or a department and in some cases a joint venture, provided that its assets, results of operations, and activities can be clearly distinguished, physically and operationally and for financial reporting purposes, from the other assets, results of operations, and activities of the entity. The inability to identify the results of operations of the part of the business being disposed of would clearly suggest that the definition of a segment has not been met.

The SEC staff believe that there is a rebuttable presumption that the above definition of segment of a business cannot be satisfied unless the operations in question were previously disclosed as a business segment in accordance with SFAS 14, or as a separate line of business or class of customer in the segment information contained in management's discussion and analysis of financial condition and results of operations.

Furthermore, although the definition of a business segment contained in APB 30 is fairly wide, AIN–APB 30 provides illustrative examples of the application of APB 30 which assist in preventing too wide an interpretation being placed on the definition.   In particular, AIN–APB 30 provides detailed guidance with regard to the interpretation of what comprises a separate major line of business as distinct from a product line.

APB 30 requires that the income statement be completely reclassified so that the results of discontinued operations up to the measurement date are disclosed separately after the results of continuing operations.

The standard defines the measurement date as the date on which the management having authority to approve the action commits itself to a formal plan to dispose of a segment of the business. The plan of disposal should include as a minimum:

- identification of the major assets to be disposed of;
- the expected method of disposal;
- the period expected to be required for completion of the disposal;
- an active programme to find a buyer if disposal is to be by sale;
- the estimated results of operations of the segment from the measurement date to the disposal date; and
- the estimated proceeds or salvage to be realised by disposal.

The computation of the estimated gain or loss on disposal should take into account the estimated results from the discontinued operation between the measurement date and the expected disposal date. If a loss is expected from the discontinuance of a business segment, the estimated loss shall be provided for as of the measurement date. If a gain is expected, it should be recognised when realised, which ordinarily is the disposal date.

If a company expects to realise a net gain consisting of an estimated gain on disposal of the segment that will be reduced by estimated operating losses during the period between the measurement date and the expected disposal date, the estimated operating losses should be deferred until the disposal date.

The gain or loss on disposal should include such adjustments, costs, and expenses which are clearly a direct result of the decision to dispose of the segment and are clearly not the adjustments of carrying amounts or costs, or expenses that should have been recognised on a going concern basis prior to the measurement date. Results of operations after the measurement date should be included in the gain or loss on disposal.

If a large segment, a separable group of assets of an acquired company, or the entire acquired company is sold, all or a portion of the unamortised cost of the goodwill recognised in the acquisition should be included in the cost of the assets sold.

The notes to the financial statements should also disclose:

- the identity of the segment;
- the expected disposal date;
- the expected manner of disposal;

- a description of the remaining assets and liabilities of the segment at the balance sheet date; and

- the income or loss from operations and any proceeds from disposal of the segment during the period from the measurement date to the date of the balance sheet.

The above should be disclosed for periods subsequent to the measurement date and including the period of disposal. In the case of the last item above, a comparison with prior estimates should also be given.

4.2.3   *Prior year adjustments*

US accounting practice on changes in accounting policy and prior year adjustments is prescribed by APB 20 and SFAS 16 respectively.

The major difference between US GAAP and FRS 3 relates to the accounting treatment of a change in accounting policy or principle. Under US GAAP, the general rule is that where a company voluntarily changes an accounting policy, the cumulative effect of the change, i.e. the difference between retained profits at the beginning of the year as previously reported and the figure that would have been reported if the new policy had been applied retroactively for all prior periods, should be disclosed in the profit and loss account, albeit after the profit or loss on extraordinary items.[135] Consequently, comparative figures are not restated although pro forma comparatives should be disclosed for the profit or loss before extraordinary items and the net profit or loss for the year.[136] Comparatives are not adjusted, as a strict interpretation of the 'all-inclusive concept' results in the conclusion that the effect of the changes should be included in computing the net profit or loss for the period. APB 20 also comments that there could potentially be a dilution of public confidence in financial statements if prior periods were restated.[137]

However, there are certain specific exceptions, where the effect of a change in accounting policy must be accounted for retroactively as a prior period adjustment. The principal exceptions are as follows:[138]

(a)   a change from the LIFO method of stock valuation;

(b)   a change in the method of accounting for long-term construction-type contracts;

(c)   a change from the 'full cost' method in the oil and gas and similar extractive industries.

In addition, prior period adjustments are also required for correction of an error in prior periods.[139]

4.2.4   *Reporting Comprehensive Income*

The term 'comprehensive income' was first introduced in the official US literature via the FASB's conceptual framework. SFAC No. 5 concluded that comprehensive income and its components should be reported as part of a full set of financial statements. This has now come to pass through the publication of SFAS 130 – *Reporting Comprehensive Income* – which was issued by the FASB in June 1997.[140] However, a close examination of the statement soon reveals that it resembles in name only what was envisaged by the conceptual framework. This perhaps accounts for the fact that the statement was passed with two of the seven FASB members dissenting.

Some of the proposals contained in the Exposure Draft which preceded SFAS 130 met with quite strong resistance both in comment letters and at a public hearing. For example, the exposure draft proposed that comprehensive income should be seen as a performance measure and that entities should be required to disclose a per-share amount for comprehensive income. As a result of the not inconsiderable opposition to many of its proposals, the FASB decided to limit the project's scope to issues or presentation and disclosure 'so that it could complete the project in a timely manner'.[141] As a result, the statement does not address issues of recognition or measurement of comprehensive income and its components.

Consequently, the statement is unusually tentative for the FASB. It uses the SFAC No. 6 definition of comprehensive income, namely the change in equity of a business enterprise during a period from transactions and other events and circumstances from non-owner sources. It includes all changes in equity during a period except those resulting from investments by owners and distributions to owners. The statement uses the term 'comprehensive income' to describe the total of all components of comprehensive income, including net income. It then uses the term 'other comprehensive income' to refer to revenue, expenses, gains and losses that are included in comprehensive income but excluded from net income.

However, having set down these basic concepts, the statement then, in effect, gives preparers *carte blanche* to report comprehensive income in virtually whatever manner they choose, provided that all components of comprehensive income are reported in the financial statements in the period in which they are recognised, and the total amount of comprehensive income is disclosed in the financial statement where the components of other comprehensive income are reported.[142]

Appendix B to SFAS 130 contains four different formats for reporting comprehensive income. These comprise a single statement approach, a two statement approach, and two alternative ways of displaying comprehensive income as part of the statement of changes in equity. But even then, other formats are possible: the statement states that 'other formats or levels of detail may be appropriate for certain circumstances'.[143] An observer may be forgiven for thinking that this seems to be a bit of a free-for-all. In fact, this was the root of the concern of the two FASB members who voted against the statement. In their dissenting opinion, they expressed the concern that 'it is likely that most enterprises will meet the requirements of this Statement by providing the required information in a statement of changes in equity, and that displaying items of other comprehensive income solely in that statement as opposed to reporting them in a statement of financial performance will do little to enhance their visibility and will diminish their perceived importance'.[144]

Perhaps the most interesting aspect of the statement is that it contains requirements relating to 'reclassification adjustments' (otherwise known as recycling). The statement states that these adjustments need to be made in order to avoid double counting in comprehensive income items that are displayed as part of net income for a period that also had been displayed as part of other comprehensive income in that period or earlier periods.[145] The reclassification being required as a result of a previously reported unrealised gain being realised. This is where SFAS 130 is fundamentally different from FRS 3. Under FRS 3, once an item has been reported in either the profit and loss account or the statement of total recognised gains and losses, it is not reported again in either of the statements. So for example, if an investment is revalued, the revaluation is reported in the statement of total recognised gains and losses, and if it is later sold for its revalued amount (i.e. the gain is realised), no further amount is reported in either statement. Not so with SFAS 130. In this example, the gain would again be reported, this time in the income statement and, to avoid double counting, a deduction would be made at the same time through other comprehensive income for the period. This requirement to record reclassification adjustments does, indeed, mean that the statement of comprehensive income is not a measure of performance. Consequently, the term 'comprehensive income' is somewhat of a misnomer.

5 THE ASB'S PROPOSALS FOR CHANGE TO REPORTING FINANCIAL PERFORMANCE

In June 1999 the ASB published a discussion paper – *Reporting Financial Performance: Proposals for Change*. This had been developed in association with other members of the G4+1 group and followed an earlier paper published by that group in 1998.[146]

The crux of the proposal is that the profit and loss account and the statement of total recognised gains and losses should be combined into a single performance statement divided into three sections: operating (or trading) activities; financing and other treasury activities; and other gains and losses (comprising some of those shown as non-operating exceptional items under FRS 3 together with those formerly shown in the statement of total recognised gains and losses). In total, this statement would include all movements between one balance sheet and the next, other than transactions with shareholders such as dividends or changes in share capital.

The paper includes this example to illustrate the intended format.[147]

STATEMENT OF FINANCIAL PERFORMANCE		
OPERATING (TRADING) ACTIVITIES		
Revenues		775
Cost of sales		(620)
Other expenses		(104)
Operating income		**51**
FINANCING AND OTHER TREASURY ACTIVITIES		
Interest on debt	(26)	
Gains and losses on financial instruments	8	
Financing income		**(18)**
Operating and financing income before taxation		**33**
Taxation on income		(12)
Operating and financing income after taxation		**21**
OTHER GAINS AND LOSSES		
Profit on disposal of discontinued operations	3	
Profit on sale of properties in continuing operations	6	
Revaluation of long-term assets	4	
Exchange translation differences on foreign currency net investments	(2)	
Other gains and losses before taxation	11	
Taxation on other gains and losses	(4)	
Other gains and losses after taxation		**7**
Total		**28**

One of the key issues under this proposal is exactly how items should be allocated among the three categories. The paper is surprisingly tentative and unconvincing on this matter. The closest it comes to any principle is to suggest that the following matrix be used to guide allocations between the first and third categories; that is, between operating items and other gains and losses.[148] No similar demarcation is suggested for financing items on the basis that this is likely to be determined in the course of the financial instruments project that the G4+1 is engaged in along with other members of the IASC Board.[149]

Characteristics more typical of operating items	Characteristics more typical of other gains and losses
Operating activities	Non-operating activities
Recurring	Non-recurring
Non-holding items	Holding items
Internal events (e.g. value adding activities)	External events (e.g. price changes)

The paper goes on to say that no one line of the matrix is proposed to be used to the exclusion of the others, but rather that items that predominantly have the characteristics in the left-hand column should be in the operating section and those with characteristics mainly on the right would be reported as other gains and losses.[150] The overall intention is that 'items actively managed to add value to the entity should be shown in the operating or financing activities, while the economic impact of changes affecting peripheral aspects of an activity should be shown in "other gains and losses".'[151] This sounds a superficially attractive ambition, but in fact the polarities set out in the matrix do not really bear much scrutiny.

First of all, no definition of either 'operating activities' or 'non-operating activities' is offered. This is an existing failing of FRS 3, and one which would be perpetuated under this proposal. In fact the paper acknowledges that there is a view that *all* activities undertaken by a company must by definition be part of its operations, which would make this distinction redundant, and in the absence of any convincing definitions of the categories, we share that view.

Secondly, any distinction between recurring and non-recurring items, even if it could be reliably made, does not seem to warrant reporting the results in a different part of the statement. This is redolent of the extraordinary item problem that the ASB was proud to abolish when it issued FRS 3. In our view, the non-recurring nature of a gain or loss may require its separate disclosure, but does not justify its exclusion from the operating section of the statement if it otherwise belongs there.

The third category is the only one where any kind of definition is offered. No attempt is made to define the hollow concept of a 'non-holding item', but holding gains and losses are said to be those that 'arise from price changes during the time that an asset or liability is held by the reporting entity. They do not include profits and losses arising from the use of that asset or liability.'[152] This at least provides the foundation of a fathomable distinction, but it is clear from the rest of the paper that it is not intended to apply it with any rigour. To do so would require a current cost basis of measurement to be applied to all items – such as depreciation and cost of sales – in the operating section, but this is not proposed. And, of course, if a current cost perspective were to be invoked then it would be wrong to regard these holding gains and losses as elements of performance at all; they would simply be capital maintenance adjustments that had to be eliminated from historical cost results in order to measure performance on a current cost basis.

The final polarity – internal versus external events – also lacks any clear definition, and since external events are explained as embracing such things as price changes, this seems to be simply another version of the third category.

It is interesting to compare this matrix with the rationale that has been applied in the past in determining that certain items were to be reported in the statement of total recognised gains and losses rather than the profit and loss account. The ASB acknowledges that FRS 3 did not 'explicitly' state the conceptual basis for the distinction, but implies that the Board nonetheless had a reason in mind at that time: such items 'were in the nature of "holding" gains and losses relating to items of a capital nature'.[153] If this has indeed always been the Board's unstated view, it is not evident from some of its subsequent proposals. For example:

■	FRS 4 requires the proceeds of issuing a warrant that has subsequently lapsed unexercised to be reported in the STRGL.[154] This may have 'capital' overtones, but it is not a holding gain as the Board now defines the term;

■	The alternative approach proposed in the ASB's 1995 Discussion Paper on pension cost accounting suggested that actuarial gains and losses should be taken to the statement of total recognised gains and losses, in order that the amounts remaining in the profit and loss account would show 'a stable charge that would have the predictive characteristics expected of items in that performance statement.'[155] This seems more like a desire to eliminate volatility from the profit and loss account than anything more principled.

■	The ASB's 1996 Discussion Paper on financial instruments proposed that the change in value of various items should be taken to the statement of total recognised gains and losses: those arising on the revaluation of fixed rate debt and non-equity shares; changes in the value of derivatives that hedge the interest basis of debt, and of investments in debt instruments that 'match-fund' a borrowing; and changes in the value of strategic investments.[156] The reason given was that they were 'gains and losses on those assets and liabilities that are held on a continuing basis in order to enable the entity's operations to be carried out'.[157]

■	Although it was not carried through into FRS 10, the ASB's proposal in the exposure draft that preceded it was that negative goodwill should be amortised through the statement of total recognised gains and losses rather than the profit and loss account on the basis that it was an unrealised gain.[158]

It is hard to detect any real thread of consistency in these various proposals, which reinforces our concern that the new proposals in the latest discussion paper do not lend themselves to any consistent application either.

We are certainly dubious about any attempt to report the results of 'items actively managed to add value to the entity' separately from 'the economic impact of changes affecting peripheral aspects of an activity'. The detailed implementation of such a woolly idea could lead to a number of quite unsatisfactory proposals such as these.

■	Pension cost reported in the top half of the performance statement would comprise the regular cost of pensions, the expected return on fund assets and the unwinding of the discount on the obligation to pay pensions, with all actuarial gains and losses in the bottom half. But this would mean that the top half would only ever report whatever numbers had been assumed in advance, with the variances permanently consigned to the bottom half. Thus, a company could take credit for a projected 10% return on the assets in its pension fund in the top half, and if it only achieved a 7% return, the resulting minus 3% difference would be lost in the bottom half. This is tantamount to reporting budgeted earnings rather than actual results.

■ Interest expense shown in the top half would always reflect current interest rates, regardless of what actual rate of interest the company had contracted to pay; the difference would be shown as a gain or loss on revaluation of the loan in the bottom half. Since an increasing number of items in the accounts are now measured on a discounted basis (leasing payables and receivables, provisions, impaired assets, etc.) this approach might be extended over a large part of the company's activities.

■ Similarly, all operating charges in the top half would be reported on a current cost basis with the difference reported as revaluation differences in the bottom half.

Trying to distinguish the results of actively managed activities from peripheral economic effects fosters a false view of the business environment and the role of management within it. 'We would have been really profitable if only these unfortunate economic events had not occurred.' The reality is that management must take economic conditions as they find them, and although they may wish to explain how their results have been influenced by external factors, they should not think of these as extraneous to the operating results that have been achieved.

This paper is founded on the preconception that all the non-owner movements from one balance sheet to the next represent 'performance', and this is the fundamental problem. Although the ASB may regard the statement of total recognised gains and losses as a performance statement, this is not a view that is widely shared; this statement is rarely even discussed by either preparers or users of accounts. Revaluations that reflect changes in the replacement cost of operational fixed assets, or the effects of retranslating the opening balance sheets of foreign subsidiaries, are more in the nature of capital maintenance adjustments than performance measures.

Rather than assuming that all its balance sheet-orientated measurement rules contribute inexorably to an assessment of performance, we think the ASB needs to start at the other end. It should first consider what deserves to be regarded as performance and then devise a framework of accounting rules to fit that definition. It comes as no surprise that the Board has had difficulty in devising a statement that sensibly explains the other side of the journal entries that its balance sheet approach has spawned, and has resorted to this 'other' category as a result. However, in our view that category must be eliminated. The items in it either belong in the operational part of the statement or should not be reported as performance at all.

6 CONCLUSION

When it was issued in 1992, FRS 3 represented a radical new approach to the reporting of financial performance. Contrary to first appearances, it was much more than a mere exercise in the reformatting of the profit and loss account and the introduction of additional analyses of reserve movements. It significantly changed the rules of recognition and measurement governing many aspects of a company's performance, including discontinued operations, extraordinary and exceptional items and provisions.

More importantly, though, FRS 3 was the first manifestation of the ASB's balance sheet approach to income recognition as outlined in the Board's Draft *Statement of Principles*. This was highlighted through the introduction into UK GAAP of an additional primary statement of financial performance – the statement of total recognised gains and losses – which focused on changes in wealth as the means of performance measurement, rather than traditional historical cost profit and loss.

However, it has now become clear that the statement of total recognised gains and losses represented the ASB's first step along a road of performance reporting that will eventually lead to a single statement of total financial performance. The latest initiative to emerge from the G4+1 – that the profit and loss account and the statement of total recognised gains and losses should be combined into a single performance statement divided into three sections – represents a radical change in approach and underlying philosophy. In particular, the proposals articulate the principle that once items of financial performance can be measured reliably, they should be recognised, and once recognised in the appropriate component of financial performance, should not be recognised again. This means that when an unrealised gain is subsequently realised, the gain will not be recycled within the statement of performance. This heralds the abandonment of the realisation principle, which for many may well be a bridge too far.

References

1 SFAC No. 1, *Objectives of Financial Reporting by Business Enterprises*, FASB, November 1978, para. 43.

2 SFAC No. 6, *Elements of Financial Statements*, FASB, December 1985, para. 70.

3 *Ibid.*, para. 73.

4 SFAS 130, *Reporting Comprehensive Income*, FASB, June 1997, para. 1.

5 For a full discussion of these two concepts of income, see ARB No. 43, *Restatement and Revision of Accounting Research Bulletins*, AICPA, June 1953, Chapter 8, or APB 9, *Reporting the Results of Operations*, AICPA, December 1966, paras. 9–14.

6 APB 9, para. 10.

7 *Ibid.*, para. 11.

8 Statement of Principles Revised Exposure Draft, *Statement of Principles for Financial Reporting*, ASB, March 1999, Chapter 1, Principles.

9 Discussion paper, *Reporting Financial Performance: Proposals for Change*, ASB, June 1999, para. 1.5.

10 *Ibid.*, paras. 1.10 and 2.5.

11 Statement of Principles Exposure Draft, *Statement of Principles for Financial Reporting*, ASB, November 1995, paras. 6.27 and 6.28.

12 ICAEW, Accounting Recommendation N18, *Presentation of balance sheet and profit and loss account*, October 1958.

13 ED 5, *Extraordinary items and prior year adjustments*, August 1971.

14 ED 7, *Accounting for extraordinary items*, July 1972.

15 CA 81, Sch. 1, Part. 1, Section B; now CA 85, Sch. 4, Part. 1, Section B.

16 ASC Discussion Paper, *A review of SSAP 6*, 1983.

17 ED 36, *Extraordinary items and prior year adjustments*, January 1985.

18 SSAP 6 (Revised), paras. 2 and 4.

19 *Ibid.*, paras. 11–14 and 32.

20 *Ibid.*, paras. 28–30.

21 *Ibid.*, paras. 3 and 34.

22 *Ibid.*, paras. 25 and 35.

23 *Ibid.*, paras 8–10 and 38.

24 *Ibid.*, para. 26.

25 *Ibid.*, para. 18.

26 UITF 2, *Restructuring costs*, ASB, October 1991, para. 2.

27 The Institute of Chartered Accountants of Scotland, *Making Corporate Reports Valuable*, ICAS, 1988, para. 1.18.

28 FRS 3, *Reporting financial performance*, ASB, October 1992, para. 1.

29 *Ibid.*, para. 14.

30 *Ibid.*, para. 12.

31 *Foreword to Accounting Standards*, ASB, June 1993, para. 15

32 FRS 3, para. 14.

33 FRS 9, *Associates and joint ventures*, ASB, November 1997, para. 27.

34 FRS 3, para. 4.

35 *Ibid.*, para. 14.

36 *Ibid.*, para. 15.

37 *Ibid.*, para. 17.

38 *Ibid.*, para. 43.

39 *Ibid.*, para. 42.

40 *Ibid.*, para. 4(c).

41 *Ibid.*, para. 43.

42 *Ibid.*, para. 43.

43 *Ibid.*, para. 44.

44 IAS 35, *Discontinuing Operations*, IASC, 1998, para. 2.

45 *Ibid.*, para., 16.

46 SAB No. 93, *Accounting and Disclosure Regarding Discontinued Operations*, SEC, 11-4-93, Question 4.

47 FRS 12, *Provisions, Contingent Liabilities and Contingent Assets*, ASB, September 1998, para. 2.

48 FRS 3, para. 18.

49 *Ibid.*

50 *Ibid.*, para. 45.

51 *Ibid.*

52 FRS 11, *Impairment of Fixed Assets and Goodwill*, ASB, July 1998, para. 67.

53 SSAP 2, para. 14(d).

54 FRS 3, para. 3.

55 *Ibid.*, para. 16.

56 *Ibid.*, para. 15.

57 FRS 6, *Acquisitions and Mergers*, ASB, September 1994, para. 36.

58 FRS 3, para. 6.

59 *Ibid.*, para. 20.

60 *Ibid.*, para. 2.

61 *Ibid.*, para. 5.

62 *Ibid.*, para. 19.

63 *Ibid.*, para. 20.

64 *Ibid.*, para. 46.

65 FRS 10, *Goodwill and Intangible Assets*, ASB, December 1997, para. 71(a)(iii).

66 FRS 3, para. 42.

67 FRS 12, para. 2.

68 *Ibid.*, para. 75.

69 Discussion paper, *Reporting Financial Performance: Proposals for Change*, para. 5.10.

70 FRS 3, para. 21.

71 *Ibid.*, para. 31A.

72 *Ibid.*, para. 26.

73 *Ibid.*, para. 55.

74 Statement of Principles Revised Exposure Draft, *Statement of Principles for Financial Reporting*, para. 6.2(c).

75 FRS 3, para. 31A.

76 FRS 4, *Capital Instruments*, para. 93.

77 IAS 1 (revised), *Presentation of Financial Statements*, IASC, August 1997, paras. 86 to 89.

78 FRS 3, para. 20.

79 *Ibid.*, para. 22.

80 *Ibid.*, para. 24.

81 *Ibid.*, para. 50.

82 *Ibid.*, para. 14.

83 See, for example, Preface to FRED 1, para. iv.

84 FRS 3, para. 52.

85 FRS 14, *Earnings per share*, ASB, October 1998, para. 9.

86 *Ibid.*, para. 11,

87 FRS 3. para. 25.

88 James Capel & Co., U.K. Equity Research, *Accounting Matters – Update on 1992, Potential Developments in 1993*, January 1993, p. 17.

89 FRS 3, para. 28.

90 *Ibid.*, para. 59.

91 FRS 10, paras. 69 and 71(a)(iii).

92 CA 85, Sch. 4, para. 3(7).

93 *Ibid.*, para. 46.

94 FRS 3, para. 7.

95 *Ibid.*, para. 60.

96 *Ibid.*

97 *Ibid.*, para. 61.

98 UITF 6, *Accounting for post-retirement benefits other than pensions*, ASB, November 1992, para. 8.

 99 FRS 3, para. 63.
100 CA 85, ss 245–245B.
101 FRS 3, para. 29.
102 *Ibid.*
103 CA 85, Sch. 4, para. 15.
104 *Ibid.*
105 EC Fourth Company Law Directive (78/660/EEC), Article 31(2).
106 UITF 14, *Disclosure of changes in accounting policy*, UITF, 21 November 1995, para. 3.
107 London Stock Exchange, *The Listing Rules*, Chapter 12, para. 12.52.
108 IAS 8, *Net Profit or Loss for the Period, Fundamental Errors and Changes in Accounting Policies*, IASC, Revised December 1993, para. 7.
109 *Ibid.*, para. 10.
110 *Ibid.*, para. 11.
111 *Ibid.*, para. 12.
112 *Ibid.*, para. 16.
113 *Ibid.*, para. 6.
114 *Ibid.*, para. 21.
115 *Ibid.*, para. 20.
116 *Ibid.*, para. 26.
117 *Ibid.*, para. 28.
118 *Ibid.*, paras. 34–57.
119 IAS 1, *Presentation of Financial Statements*, IASC, August 1997, para. 13.
120 *Ibid.*, paras. 7 and 86 to 89.
121 IAS 35, para. 2.
122 *Ibid.*, para. 16.
123 *Ibid.*, para. 27.
124 *Ibid.*, para. 29.
125 APB 30, *Reporting the Results of Operations–Reporting the Effects of Disposal of a Segment of a Business, and Extraordinary, Unusual and Infrequently Occurring Events and Transactions*, AICPA, June 1973, para. 20.
126 *Ibid.*, paras. 21 and 22.
127 *Ibid.*, para. 23.
128 AIN-APB 30, *Reporting the Results of Operations: Accounting Interpretations of APB Opinion No. 30*, AICPA, November 1973, Examples 10–17.
129 APB 30, para. 20.
130 *Ibid.*, para. 20.
131 *Ibid.*, para. 23.
132 AIN-APB 30, Examples 12 and 16.
133 SFAS 4, *Reporting Gains and Losses from Extinguishment of Debt, an amendment of APB Opinion No. 30*, FASB, March 1975.
134 APB 30, para. 8.
135 APB 20, *Accounting Changes*, AICPA, July 1971, para. 20.
136 *Ibid.*, para. 21.
137 *Ibid.*, para. 18.
138 *Ibid.*, para. 27.
139 SFAS 16, *Prior Period Adjustments*, FASB, June 1977, para. 11.
140 SFAS 130, *Reporting Comprehensive Income*, FASB, June 1997.
141 *Ibid.*, para. 53.
142 *Ibid.*, para. 14.
143 *Ibid.*, para. 129.
144 *Ibid.*, Messrs. Cope and Foster's dissenting opinion.
145 *Ibid.*, para. 18.
146 *Reporting Financial Performance: Current Practice and Future Developments*, G4+1, January 1998.
147 Discussion Paper, *Reporting Financial Performance: Proposals for Change*, para. 2.7.
148 *Ibid.*, para. 2.12.
149 *Ibid.*, para. 2.16.

150 *Ibid.*, para. 2.13.
151 *Ibid.*, para. 2.15.
152 *Ibid.*, para. 2.12, footnote.
153 *Ibid.*, Appendix A, para. A5.
154 FRS 4, *Capital instruments*, ASB, December 1993, para. 47.
155 *Pension costs in the employer's financial statements*, ASB, June 1995, para. 7.4.1.
156 *Derivatives and other financial instruments*, ASB, July 1996, para. 3.3
157 *Ibid.*, para. 3.3.2.
158 FRED 12, *Goodwill and intangible assets*, ASB, June 1996, para. 39 and Appendix III para. 45.

Chapter 23   Earnings per share

1   INTRODUCTION

Earnings per share (EPS) is one of the most widely quoted statistics in financial analysis. It came into great prominence in the US during the late 1950s and early 1960s due to the widespread use of the price earnings ratio (PE) as a yardstick for investment decisions. By the late 1960s, its popularity had switched across the Atlantic and for the purposes of consistency and comparability, it became important that an agreed method of computing EPS was established.

In March 1971, the Accounting Standards Steering Committee issued an exposure draft, ED 4 – *Earnings per share*. The exposure draft represented a departure by UK accounting bodies into the area of financial ratios and financial analysis. ED 4 was, in general, favourably received and in February 1972, SSAP 3 – *Earnings per share* – was issued with the objective of providing a minimum standard for disclosure of EPS in financial statements and the basis of its calculation.

EPS has also served as a means of assessing the stewardship and management role performed by company directors and managers; by linking remuneration packages to EPS growth performance, some companies deliberately increase the pressure on management to improve EPS. Not surprisingly, such powerful factors and incentives have all contributed to the growth of attempts to distort EPS.

The ASB has stated its belief that undue emphasis is placed on EPS numbers and that this leads to simplistic interpretations of financial performance. As a result in October 1992 when it issued FRS 3 – *Reporting of financial performance* – the ASB attempted to de-emphasise EPS by requiring it to be calculated *after* extraordinary items. In view of this change and the other requirements of FRS 3 (see Chapter 22) the EPS number which companies were required to disclose became much more volatile and was really only a starting point for further analysis. The ASB recognised that companies would therefore be likely to provide additional EPS numbers prepared on what they saw as a more meaningful basis and therefore introduced rules dealing with the disclosure of such additional numbers.

SSAP 3 had operated fairly satisfactorily for over 20 years and, without the impulse of international harmonisation, it is unlikely that the ASB would have sought to change it. Indeed, the Board has hinted that earnings per share is perhaps not an appropriate subject for an accounting standard at all, since it concerns financial analysis more than financial reporting. Nevertheless in May 1996 the ASB issued a Discussion Paper – *Earnings Per Share*, in order to solicit comments on proposals put forward by the IASC in its exposure draft (E52) on the topic. In the US, the FASB had also issued a similar exposure draft to E52. Both of these bodies subsequently published new standards based on those proposals. In the interests of international harmonisation the ASB therefore issued FRED 16 in June 1997 containing proposals for a revised standard which, with minimal exceptions, followed the international standard, IAS 33. In March 1998 the ASB issued a supplement to FRED 16, dealing with three issues: contingently issuable shares, employee share schemes and the coupling of a special dividend with a share consolidation. FRS 14 – *Earnings per share* was published on 1 October 1998 and superseded SSAP 3 for periods ending on or after 23 December 1998. FRS 14 is based on its international equivalent, and adopts a similar structure and wording. It also includes detailed interpretative guidance and illustrative examples which draw heavily on the US standard.

2   OBJECTIVE AND SCOPE OF FRS 14

2.1   Objective

The objective of the standard is:

'to improve the comparison of the performance of different entities in the same period and of the same entity in different accounting periods by prescribing methods for determining the number of shares to be included in the calculation of earnings per share and other amounts per share and by specifying their presentation.'[1]

The underlying logic here is that EPS, including diluted EPS, should be an historical performance measure. This impacts particularly on diluted EPS, in steering it away from an alternative purpose: to warn of potential future dilution. Indeed the tension between these differing objectives is evident in the standard. As discussed more fully at 6.5.5 below, FRS 14 sets out a very restrictive regime for including certain potentially dilutive shares in the diluted EPS calculation. Yet diluted EPS is only to take account of those potential shares that would dilute earnings from *continuing* operations which seems to have more of a forward looking 'warning signal' flavour.

Also noteworthy is the strong emphasis in the objective on the denominator of the calculation, effectively making it a 'per share' standard, whilst avoiding reference to the provisions the standard actually contains relating to the numerator.

2.2   Scope

FRS 14 applies to all entities whose ordinary shares (or potential ordinary shares) are publicly traded and to entities that are in the process of issuing ordinary shares (or potential ordinary shares) in public securities markets.[2] Thus companies whose shares are traded on the Alternative Investment Market (AIM) are required to follow the standard. SSAP 3 did not apply to AIM listed companies, but a number disclosed earnings per share figures. FRS 14 also applies to any other entity which discloses earnings per share. Where both the parent's and consolidated accounts are presented, the standard only requires consolidated earnings per share to be given.[3]

The detailed wording of the standard is phrased in terms of *earnings* per share, whether those specifically required or other elements of earnings. The scope section of the standard, in a change from FRED 16 and IAS 33, makes it clear that the rules in FRS 14 should be used in determining the number of shares to be used, as far as appropriate, in any per share disclosures, such as net assets per share.[4]

The customary exclusion for entities adopting the financial reporting standard for smaller entities (FRSSE) is not included in FRS 14, presumably on the grounds that no listed companies can adopt the FRSSE.

3   THE BASIC EPS

FRS 14 defines, or rather describes, basic earnings per share as follows:

'Basic earnings per share should be calculated by dividing the net profit attributable to ordinary shareholders by the weighted average number of ordinary shares outstanding during the period.'[5]

The earnings figure to be used in the basic EPS calculation is the net profit or loss for the period attributable to ordinary shareholders after deducting preference dividends and other appropriations in respect of non-equity shares.[6]

Ordinary shares are defined as 'an instrument falling within the definition of equity shares as defined in FRS 4' (see Chapter 15 at 2.2.2). Whilst it may seem strange that one defined term should be referred to by two different names in two different standards, the reason for this is that IAS 33 uses the term 'ordinary share' rather than 'equity share'. Where there is more than one class of ordinary shares, earnings should be apportioned between them based on their respective rights to dividends or other profit participation and separate EPS figures given for each class.[7]

Under FRS 14 all ordinary shares are to be included in the calculation of the weighted average number of shares, whereas under SSAP 3 it was only equity shares which ranked for dividend in the period which were included. How shares rank for dividend, however, still has some impact on the calculation. Under FRS 14, shares that are issued as partly paid are included in the weighted average as a fraction of a share based on dividend participation relative to fully paid shares.[8]

There is an exception to the above rule that all ordinary shares should be included in the calculation, which relates to shares held by a group member. Any non-cancelled ordinary shares held by an entity within the group should be excluded from the calculation. In particular, shares held by an employee share ownership (ESOP) trust shown as assets in the balance sheet should be treated as if they were cancelled for EPS purposes until they vest unconditionally in the employees.[9]

The standard contains some specific guidance on when newly issued ordinary shares should be brought into the calculation. In general shares are to be included from the date consideration is receivable, for example:[10]

- shares issued in exchange for cash are included when cash is receivable;

- shares issued on the voluntary reinvestment of dividends on ordinary or preference shares are included at the dividend payment date;

- shares issued as a result of the conversion of a debt instrument to ordinary shares are included as of the date interest ceases accruing;

- shares issued in place of interest or principal on other financial instruments are included as of the date interest ceases accruing;

- shares issued in exchange for the settlement of a liability of the entity are included as of the settlement date; and

- shares issued as consideration for the acquisition of an asset other than cash are included as of the date on which the acquisition is recognised.

More generally, the standard goes on to say that due consideration should be given to the substance of any contract associated with the issue.[11] No illustrations are given of such associated contracts, but one example could be convertible unsecured loan stock (CULS). Although less fashionable in recent years, these were a not uncommon mechanism allowing companies to finance potential acquisitions by the issue of shares, while retaining the flexibility to return funds not subsequently needed.

Tomkins, for example, issued CULS to finance an acquisition and converted it into shares a short time later. The loan stock carried no interest and was simply an intermediate step in the share issue. The practical impact was that 60% of the consideration for the shares was received over a month before they were actually issued.

Extract 23.1: Tomkins PLC (1993)

18 SHARE CAPITAL [extract]

The Company financed the purchase of RHM by way of a rights issue which took the form of 5p nominal non-interest bearing convertible unsecured loan stock (loan stock) which was payable in two instalments of 120p and 80p on 30 November 1992 and 4 January 1993 respectively. ... The 335,784,658 units of loan stock, which were issued under the rights issue at 200p per unit, were converted into fully paid ordinary shares of 5p each, on a one for one basis, on 5 January 1993.

One question that arises is when should the new shares be brought into the calculation of the weighted average in such circumstances? Given the examples in the standard which focus on the date consideration is received, and the requirement to consider the substance of associated contracts, it seems such shares should be deemed to be issued in partly paid form on 30 November.

Ordinary shares that are issuable on the satisfaction of certain conditions (contingently issuable shares) are to be included in the calculation of basic EPS only from the date when all necessary conditions have been satisfied; in effect when they are no longer contingent.[12] This provision is interpreted strictly, as illustrated in example 6 of the standard. In that example earnings in a period, by exceeding a given threshold, trigger the issue of shares. Because this condition was not satisfied until the end of the year the new shares are excluded from basic EPS until the following year.

The calculation of the basic EPS is often simple but a number of problems can arise; these may be considered under the following two headings:

(a) changes in equity share capital; and

(b) matters affecting the numerator.

These are discussed in the next two sections.

4 CHANGES IN EQUITY SHARE CAPITAL

Changes in equity share capital can occur under a variety of circumstances, the most common of which are dealt with below. Whenever such a change occurs during the accounting period, an adjustment is required to the number of shares in the EPS calculation for that period; furthermore, in certain situations the EPS for previous periods will also have to be recalculated.

4.1 Issue for cash at full market price

If new ordinary shares have been issued for cash at full market price the earnings should be divided by the average number of shares outstanding during the period weighted on a time basis.[13]

Example 23.1: Weighted average calculation

At 1 January, 3,000,000 ordinary shares were in issue. On 30 September, 1,000,000 further shares were issued for cash at full market price.

The number of shares to be used in the calculation of EPS will be:

	m
For 9/12 (of the year) x 3m (shares in issue)	2.25
For 3/12 (of the year) x 4m (shares in issue)	1.00
Number of shares to be used in the calculation	3.25

The use of a weighted average number of shares is necessary because the increase in the share capital would have affected earnings only for that portion of the year during which the issue proceeds were available to management for use in the business.

It is possible that shares could be allotted as a result of open offers, placings and other offerings of equity shares not made to existing shareholders, at a discount to the market price. In such cases it would be necessary to consider whether the issue contained a bonus element, akin to a rights issue (see 4.3.3 below), or rather simply reflected differing views on the fair value of the shares. In our opinion the latter seems a far more realistic alternative. Accordingly the shares should be dealt with on a weighted average basis without calculating any bonus element when computing the EPS.

4.2   Purchase and redemption of own shares

A company may, if it is authorised to do so by its articles and it complies with the related provisions of the Companies Act, purchase/redeem its own shares (see Chapter 15 at 3.3). Assuming this is done at fair value, then the earnings should be apportioned over the weighted average share capital in issue for the year. If, on the other hand, the repurchase is at significantly more than market value then FRS 14 requires adjustments to be made to EPS for periods before buy-back. This is discussed at 4.3.5 below.

4.3   Changes in ordinary shares without corresponding changes in resources

FRS 14 requires the number of shares used in the calculation to be adjusted (for all periods presented) for any transaction (other than the conversion of potential ordinary shares) which changes the number of shares outstanding without a corresponding change in resources.[14] This is also to apply where such changes have happened after the year end but before the approval of the accounts.[15]

Unlike its predecessor SSAP 3, FRS 14 requires that adjustments are made for *all* events which change the number of shares outstanding without a corresponding change in resources. In contrast, the equivalent SSAP 3 provisions were limited to specified types of transaction.

The standard gives the following as examples of such changes in the number of ordinary shares without a corresponding change in resources:

' (a) a bonus issue;

(b) a bonus element in any other issue or buy-back, for example a bonus element in a rights issue to existing shareholders or a put warrant, involving the repurchase of shares at significantly more than their fair value;

(c) a share split; and

(d) a share consolidation.'[16]

The adjustments required to EPS for each of these is discussed below.

The standard requires that other per share disclosures for earlier periods, notably dividends per share, are similarly adjusted for such changes.[17]

4.3.1 *Bonus issue, share split and share consolidation*

A bonus issue has the effect of increasing the number of shares in issue without any inflow of funds to the company. Consequently, no additional earnings will accrue as a result of the issue. The bonus shares should be treated as having been in issue for the whole year and also included in the previous year's EPS calculation to give a comparable result. The EPS for the earlier period should therefore be adjusted by the following fraction:

$$\frac{\text{Number of shares before the bonus issue}}{\text{Number of shares after the bonus issue}}$$

Similar considerations apply where equity shares are split into shares of smaller nominal value. Financial ratios for earlier periods, which are based on the number of equity shares at a year end (e.g. dividend per share) should also be adjusted by the above factor.[18]

The notes to the financial statements should refer to the adjustments made,[19] as illustrated in the following extract:

Extract 23.2: Sema Group plc (1998)

EARNINGS PER SHARE [extract]

The comparative weighted average number of shares in issue has been adjusted to reflect the issue of three bonus shares for every one held during the year ended 31 December 1998.

Scrip dividends refer to the case where a company offers its shareholders the choice of receiving further fully paid up shares in the company as an alternative to receiving a cash dividend. The accounting entries for scrip dividends are discussed in Chapter 15 at 4.6. As regards EPS, practice in this area has varied in the past. Some companies have taken the view that shares issued are in substance bonus issues which require the EPS for the earlier period to be adjusted. Others have considered that the dividend foregone represents payment for the shares, usually at fair value, and hence no restatement is appropriate. In our view the more general approach in FRS 14 to corresponding changes in resources seems to support the latter view, as illustrated in the following extract:

Extract 23.3: Lloyds TSB Group plc (1998)

11   Ordinary dividends [extract]

During 1998, £139 million (1997: £63 million) was transferred to reserves in respect of shares issued instead of cash, in respect of the 1997 final dividend.

12   Earnings per share [extract]

	1998	1997
Profit attributable to shareholders	**£2,120m**	£2,335m
Weighted average number of ordinary shares in issue during the year **	**5,400m**	5,341m

---

The weighted average number of ordinary shares for 1997 of 5,341 million remains unchanged from that used in the 1997 accounts, indicating that no adjustment has been made to earlier EPS figures to reflect a bonus issue.

This view is not, however, universally held. As illustrated in the following example BAA considers its scrip dividend as being a change in ordinary shares without corresponding changes in resources, and adjusts earlier EPS accordingly.

Extract 23.4: BAA plc (1999)

Consolidated profit and loss account [extract]

		1999			1998		
	Note	Before exceptional items	Exceptional items	Total	Before exceptional items	Exceptional items	Total
*Earnings per share	9	**36.7p**	**0.9p**	**37.6p**	35.2p	(8.9p)	26.3p

*The comparative figures have been restated to adjust for shares issued in lieu of dividends.

9   Earnings per share [extract]

The number of shares in issue for 1999 and 1998 has been adjusted so as to treat the shares issued under the scrip dividend scheme as though they were a bonus issue. This resulted in the earnings per share for 1998 being restated at 26.3p per share from 26.4p per share.

In practice the fair value of shares received as a scrip alternative may exceed the cash alternative; this is often referred to as an enhanced scrip dividend. In these cases FRS 14 will require a bonus element to be identified, and prior EPS figures restated accordingly. This is essentially the same as adjustments for the bonus element in a rights issue, discussed at 4.3.3 below.

Occasionally, companies will consolidate their equity share capital into a smaller number of shares of a greater nominal value. Again in such situations the EPS for the earlier period should be adjusted for by the following fraction:

$$\frac{\text{Number of shares before the share consolidation}}{\text{Number of shares after the share consolidation}}$$

An example of a company making such an adjustment is shown in the following extract, although it predates FRS 14 the adjustment under current guidance would be the same:

Extract 23.5: Berisford International plc (1993)

9   Loss per ordinary share

The calculation of loss per ordinary share is based on the loss of £5.6m and on 99.4m ordinary shares, being the weighted average number of ordinary shares in issue throughout the year (1992 494.1m weighted average). On 20 January 1993 shareholders approved a 1 for 5 share consolidation. Thus the loss per share for the year ended 30 September 1992 has been restated from 4.9p to 24.5p as a consequence of the share consolidation and then restated again to 67.9p as a consequence of the implementation of FRS 3 referred to in the Accounting policies, under which the loss for 1992 was £67.1m.

4.3.2   Share consolidation with a special dividend

Share consolidations as discussed at 4.3.1 above normally do not involve any outflow of funds from the company. However, a number of companies have been returning surplus cash to their shareholders by paying special dividends accompanied by a share consolidation, the purpose of which is to maintain the value of each share following the payment of the dividend. This issue is specifically addressed by FRS 14, presumably as such schemes were quite common when it was first being drafted. The normal rule of restating all periods' EPS for a share consolidation is not applied when 'a share consolidation is combined with a special dividend where the overall commercial effect in terms of net assets, earnings and number of shares is of a repurchase at fair value'.[20] In such cases the weighted average number of shares is adjusted for the consolidation from the date the special dividend is paid. As discussed at 4.3 above, the initial need to restate EPS for a share consolidation stems from the requirement that prior periods' EPS should be adjusted for events which change the number of shares outstanding without a corresponding change in resources. So what the standard is saying here is that a special dividend can be such a corresponding change in resources.

There is undoubtedly a conceptual attraction in trying to standardise adjustments made to prior years' EPS figures. Indeed even before FRS 14 came into force some companies had already taken this approach to special dividends, for example as shown in the 1996 accounts of both Argos and Reckitt & Colman below.

Extract 23.6: Argos plc (1996)

9   Earnings per share [extract]

Following approval at the annual general meeting the Company paid a special dividend of £126.8 million and at the same time carried out a share consolidation of 14 shares for every 15 held. The consolidation was carried out so as to reflect in the capital structure the effect of the special dividend in order to achieve the same overall effect as a buyback of shares. Accordingly, the directors consider it appropriate to present the Company's earnings per share as if a buyback of shares had taken place.

Extract 23.7: Reckitt & Colman plc (1996)

8.   Earnings per ordinary share [extract]

As described in Note 7, during the year the company paid an exceptional dividend of £151.9m and at the same time carried out a consolidation of its share capital. These transactions were conditional on each other. They were specifically designed to achieve the same overall effect on the company's capital structure as a buy back of shares in a way in which all shareholders could participate. Accordingly, earnings per share is presented on the basis that in substance a share buy-back has occurred.

In our view the approach taken by the standard is rather piecemeal, in that restatement is only ever triggered by a change in the number of shares, and it will not necessarily achieve the objective of standardising the restatement of EPS. Companies may return capital to their shareholders in various different ways, including demergers and group reconstructions, as well as share buybacks and special dividends. In many such cases the number of shares in issue is only reduced if the company opts to consolidate its shares. The natural consequence of returning capital is that earnings will fall, so it is debatable whether a fall in EPS in these circumstances should be regarded as a distortion that needs to be corrected at all. Of course, if a company buys back its shares, the number of shares will automatically be reduced and therefore affect the EPS calculation in a way that other returns of capital do not, but this does not necessarily mean that a special dividend should be treated as if it were a share buyback. However, the standard is now extant, so companies must apply these new provisions so that this specific type of return of capital will fall to be treated as a share repurchase, but only when the company also chooses to consolidate its shares.

4.3.3 Rights issue

A rights issue is a popular method through which public companies are able to access the stock market for further capital. Under the terms of such an issue, existing shareholders are given the opportunity to acquire further shares in the company on a pro-rata basis to their existing shareholdings.

The 'rights' shares will usually be offered either at the current market price or at a price below that. In the former case, the treatment of the issue for EPS purposes is as discussed in 4.1 above. However, where the rights price is at a discount to market it is not quite as straightforward, since the issue is equivalent to a bonus issue combined with an issue at full market price (see Example 23.2B). In such cases, FRS 14 states that it is necessary to adjust the number of shares in issue before the rights issue to reflect the bonus element inherent in the issue.[21] The notes to the financial statements should state that such adjustments have been made.[22]

The bonus element of the rights issue is given by the following fraction, sometimes referred to as the bonus fraction:[23]

$$\frac{\text{Fair value per share immediately before the exercise of rights}}{\text{Theoretical ex-rights fair value per share}}$$

The fair value per share immediately before the exercise of rights is the *actual* price at which the shares are quoted inclusive of the right to take up the future shares under the rights issue. Where the rights are to be traded separately from the shares the fair value used is the closing price on the last day on which the shares are traded inclusive of the right.[24]

The 'ex-rights fair value' is the *theoretical* price at which the shares would be expected to be quoted, other stock market factors apart, after the rights issue shares have been issued.

Example 23.2: Illustration of calculation of EPS following a rights issue at less than full market price

Capital structure

Issued share capital at 31 December 1998
24m Ordinary shares of 50p each, fully paid.

Trading results

	1999	1998
	£	£
Profit on ordinary activities after taxation	1.2m	1.0m

A rights issue took place on 31 August 1999 on a 1 for 4 basis at 80p. The fair value per share immediately before the exercise of rights was £1 per share.

The calculation of EPS can be tackled in the following manner:

A   What is the theoretical ex-rights fair value per share?

The theoretical ex-rights fair value per share is calculated as follows:

	No		p
Initial holding of	4	shares, market value	400
Rights taken up	1	share, at a cost of	80
New holding	5	shares, theoretical value	480

$$\text{Theoretical ex-rights fair value} = \frac{480}{5} = 96 \text{ pence}$$

which is the average price per share of the final holding.

B   What is the bonus element inherent in this issue?

The *bonus element* of the rights issue is given by the fraction:

$$\frac{\text{Fair value per share immediately before the exercise of rights}}{\text{Theoretical ex-rights fair value per share}} = \frac{100}{96} = \frac{25}{24}$$

This corresponds to a bonus issue of 1 for 24. Circumstances may arise where fair value per share immediately before the exercise of rights is less than the theoretical ex-rights fair value per share giving a bonus fraction of less than 1, in which case the rights issue should be treated as an issue for cash at full market price for EPS purposes (see 4.1 above). This may be the case where, for example, the market has suffered a significant downturn during the rights period which was not anticipated when the rights issue was announced.

Hence, the rights issue can be split into a bonus issue of 1 for 24, which will reduce the theoretical price per share to 96 pence, combined with an issue of the residue of the shares at the new theoretical price per share of 96 pence. This can be illustrated by considering the position of a shareholder who holds 360 shares before the rights issue takes place.

	No		£
Initial holding of	360	shares, valued at	360
Bonus issue (1 for 24)	15	shares,	–
	375	shares, (theoretical price per share : 96p)	360
Issue at full market	75	shares, at a cost of	72
New holding	450	shares, cost	432

The shareholder is indifferent as to whether he is offered a 1 for 4 rights issue at 80 pence a share *or* a combination of a 1 for 24 bonus issue (bringing the market price down from £1 to 96p) and a 1 for 5 rights issue at full market price (i.e. 96p). Consequently, it is appropriate to treat the rights issue as a combination of a bonus issue and a rights issue at full market price.

C   Weighted average share capital

In order to calculate the earnings per share for the year in which a rights issue is made, it will be necessary to calculate the weighted average share capital for the year after adjusting the capital in issue before the rights issue for that part which represents the bonus element. The number of shares in issue before the rights issue, adjusted for the bonus element would be:

$$24m \times \frac{25}{24} = 25m$$

The number of shares after the rights issue would be:

$$24m \times \frac{5}{4} = 30m$$

The share issue may be summarised as follows:

		m
1.1.X2	Opening number of shares	24
31.8.X2	Bonus issue (1 for 24)	1
	Adjusted opening number of shares	25
31.8.X2	Full market price issue (1 for 5)	5
31.12.X2	Closing number of shares	30

Therefore the weighted average number of shares during the year will be:

For 8/12 (of the year) x 25m	16,666,667
For 4/12 (of the year) x 30m	10,000,000
Weighted average number of shares	26,666,667

D   EPS calculation

To make the previous year's EPS comparable, the number of shares used in the recalculation has to increase to take into account the bonus element. Thus:

Current year's EPS:	*Previous year's EPS was:*	*Previous year's EPS now is:*
$\dfrac{£1.2m}{26.67m} = 4.50p$	$\dfrac{£1m}{24m} = 4.17p$	$\dfrac{£1m}{24m \times 25/24} = 4.00p$

Rather than multiplying the denominator by 25/24ths, the previous year's EPS (and any EPS disclosures in a historical summary) could alternatively be arrived at by multiplying the original EPS by 24/25ths. One company which gave very full disclosure about the restatement of comparative EPS amounts as a result of a rights issue during the year was Rolls-Royce, as shown below; although it predates FRS 14 the adjustment under current guidance would be the same:

Extract 23.8: Rolls-Royce plc (1993)

11   Earnings/(loss) per share [extract]

Earnings/(loss) per ordinary share on the net basis are calculated by dividing the profit attributable to the shareholders of Rolls-Royce plc of £63m (1992 loss £202m) by 1,058 million (1992 966†million) ordinary shares, being the average number of shares in issue during the year.

Prior year restatement

On September 2, 1993 the Company announced a rights issue to raise approximately £307m, net of expenses. Under the terms of the rights issue 242,736,773 new ordinary shares were issued in September 1993 at 130p per share on the basis of one new ordinary share for every four existing ordinary shares.

The actual cum rights price on September 6, 1993, the last day of quotation cum rights, was 148.5p and the theoretical ex rights price for an ordinary share was therefore 144.8p per share. The comparative earnings per share are shown after applying the factor 144.8/148.5 to the published figures for 1992 in order to adjust for the bonus element in the rights issue.

Many companies, however, only include a statement that the comparative EPS amounts have been restated as a result of a rights issue, along the lines of that shown below:

Extract 23.9: Bodycote International PLC (1998)

9   Earnings per share [extract]

The figures for 1997 have been adjusted to take into account the rights issue completed in January 1998.

4.3.4   B share schemes

One method by which some companies have returned capital to shareholders is the so called B share scheme. These schemes involve issuing 'B shares' (usually undated preference shares with low or zero coupons) to existing shareholders, either as a bonus issue or via a share split. These are then repurchased for cash and cancelled, following which the ordinary shares are consolidated. The overall effect is intended to be the same as a repurchase of ordinary shares at fair value. A typical example is Severn Trent. Although this pre-dates FRS 14 it illustrates the required treatment.

Extract 23.10: Severn Trent Plc (1998)

Directors' report [extract]

Capital reorganisation

On 8 August 1997 the company effected a capital reorganisation under which each Ordinary Share of £1 was divided into one ordinary share of 62p and one B share of 38p. Following this sub-division every 20 ordinary shares of 62p each were consolidated into 19 Ordinary Shares of 65 5/19p each. Schroders acting as agents for the company offered to purchase from shareholders all their B Shares at their nominal value on 11 August 1997. A second repurchase offer was made in September 1997. ...

8 Earnings per share [extract]

Earnings per share is calculated on the net basis on earnings of £14.7 million being profit for the financial year of £14.9 million (1997: £316.7 million), less £0.2 million B share dividend (1997: nil), divided by 343.6 million shares, being the weighted average number of Ordinary Shares in issue during the year (1997: 363.3 million), excluding those held in the Severn Trent Employee Share Ownership Trust on which dividends have been waived. ...

18 Called up share capital [extract]

b) Capital reorganisation

As a result of the 19 for 20 consolidation and issue of B shares on 8 August 1997, 356,623,364 ordinary shares of £1 became 338,792,195 ordinary shares of 65 5/19p and 356,623,364 B Shares of 38p. ...

c) Shares purchased during the year

In August 1997 and September 1997, the company purchased for cancellation 297,054,463 and 35,723,317 B Shares of 38p ...

The number of shares used in the EPS calculation for the comparative year of 363.3 million is unchanged from the 1997 annual accounts. This indicates that the prior periods' EPS figures have not been restated for the share consolidation, which would have been required under a strict reading of SSAP 3. Instead Severn Trent, in common with other companies who had returned capital in this way, took the view that the substance of the combined transaction is a buy-back at fair value, and hence no restatement is needed. Before FRS 14, the only authoritative rationale for such a treatment would have been paragraph 14 of FRS 5 *Reporting the substance of transactions* which includes the requirement that 'A group or series of transactions that achieves or is designed to achieve an overall commercial effect should be viewed as a whole.'[25]

FRS 14 seems to remove the doubt over which treatment is appropriate by requiring companies to adjust prior periods' EPS only when the change in shares happens without a corresponding change in resources. However, some room for doubt remains, as it is not entirely clear in FRS 14 when a change in resources and a change in the number of shares should be viewed as corresponding to one another. On the one hand a quite wide interpretation of this correspondence is required; as discussed at 4.3.2 above, when a special dividend is combined with a share consolidation it *is* treated as a corresponding change in resource. This is the case notwithstanding the fact that the change in resources does not take the legal form of consideration for the reduction in shares. On the other hand, Appendix II to the standard, which sets out the development of the FRS, indicates that treating transactions that replicate repurchases, but do not take their legal form, *as* repurchases was intended to be limited to the case of special dividends.

One further subtlety relates to how closely the ratio of share consolidation succeeds in mirroring the commercial effect of a fair value repurchase. In the Severn Trent example above, of the potential repurchase of 356,623,364 B shares only 332,777,780 were in fact bought back. It seems likely that the consolidation of 19 for 20 would have been calculated so as to reproduce the effects of a fair value repurchase assuming *all* the B shares were redeemed. If so then the share consolidation is *more* than adjusting for the resources that have left the group. FRS 14 would strictly require that some element of the consolidation should be viewed as happening without a corresponding change in resource, and hence prior periods' EPS adjusted accordingly.

4.3.5   Put warrants priced above market value

The reference to put warrants at significantly more than fair value is a change from FRED 16 and its supplement, and it is not mentioned in Appendix II to the standard dealing with the development of the FRS. It may have been added because such a scheme came to the attention of the ASB whilst it was finalising the standard, for example the scheme proposed by GEC in its accounts to 31 March 1998.

Extract 23.11: The General Electric Company plc (1998)

Finance Director's review [extract]

To manage the balance sheet structure of the Group and ensure all shareholders participate equitably, the Board also proposes to make a bonus issue of Put Warrants to shareholders, pro rata to their shareholdings. The Put Warrants will entitle each shareholder to sell to the Company one share for every 50 shares they hold, at a price that is 150 pence higher than the market price, subject to a maximum of 650 pence per share. This enables shareholders either to maintain their percentage shareholding and receive a distribution of cash of up to 13 pence per share held on 4th September, 1998 which will provide a total cash distribution (including the dividend) of 24.43 pence per share; or shareholders can retain all their shares and will still benefit from these proposals by increasing their percentage ownership and selling the warrants for up to 150 pence each (3 pence per share).

If shareholders wish to sell their entitlement to Put Warrants they need take no action and will bear no expense; the Company will automatically organise the sale.

GEC's proposed scheme was effected in the year to 31 March 1999. The 1999 accounts disclose adjustments to prior period EPS as follows:

Extract 23.12: The General Electric Company plc (1999)

8   Earnings per share [extract]

Earnings per share are calculated by reference to a weighted average of 2,711.6 million ordinary shares (1998 restated 2,793.4 million ordinary shares) in issue during the year, which have been adjusted following the exercise of the put warrants on 6th October, 1998, as required by FRS 14.

Unfortunately the standard does not give an illustrative calculation for a put warrant at significantly more than fair value, but it does for the familiar rights issue[26] (rights issues are discussed at 4.3.3 above). In a rights issue new shares are issued at a discount to market value, whereas with put warrants shares are bought back at a premium to market value. In both cases the remaining shares are viewed as being devalued for the purposes of comparing EPS over time. Applying the logic of adjusting EPS when there is a change in the number of shares without a corresponding change in resources seems to require that put warrants are treated as a reverse rights issue. This would mean calculating a similar 'adjustment factor', and applying it to the number of shares outstanding before the transaction. The difference in the calculation would be that the number of shares issued and the consideration received for them would be replaced by negative amounts representing the number of shares put back to the company and the amount paid for them.

An illustration of what this might entail is as follows:

Example 23.3:   Put warrants priced above market value

The following example takes the same scenario as Example 23.2 above (a rights issue), altered to illustrate a put warrant scheme. In that example the shares are issued at a discount of 20p to the £1 market price on a one for four basis 8 months into the year. Reversing this would give a put warrant to sell shares back to the company at a 20p premium, again on a one for four basis. All other details have been left the same for comparability, although in reality the rising earnings following a rights issue may well become falling earnings after a buy-back. The calculation would then become:

Computation of theoretical ex-warrant value per share

fair value of all outstanding shares	-	total amount paid on exercise of warrants
shares outstanding before exercise	-	shares cancelled in the exercise

$$\frac{(£1.00 \times 24{,}000{,}000) \quad - \quad (£1.20 \times 6{,}000{,}000)}{24{,}000{,}000 \quad - \quad 6{,}000{,}000} = £0.93$$

Computation of adjustment factor

Fair value per share before exercise of warrants

$$\frac{\text{Fair value per share before exercise of warrants}}{\text{Theoretical ex-warrant value per share}} = \frac{£1.00}{£0.93} = 1.075$$

Theoretical ex-warrant value per share

Computation of earnings per share

	1998	1999
1998 EPS as originally reported: £1m / 24m shares	4.17p	
1998 EPS restated for warrants: £1 / (24m shares x 1.075)	3.88p	
1999 EPS including effects of warrants: £1.2m		5.17p

(24m x 1.075 x 8/12) + (18m x 4/12)

Whilst the above seems a sensible interpretation of the requirements, as the procedure is not specified there may be scope for other interpretations. It remains to be seen how any companies affected will apply these new rules. Furthermore the standard refers to put warrants at *significantly* more than their fair value. In practice a lot may turn on the interpretation of when 'more than fair' value becomes 'significantly more'.

4.4   Options exercised during the year

Shares allotted as a result of options being exercised should be dealt with on a weighted average basis in the basic EPS.[27] Furthermore, options which have been exercised during the year will also affect diluted EPS calculations. If the options in question would have had a diluting effect on the basic EPS had they been exercised at the beginning of the year, then they should be considered in the diluted EPS calculation as explained in 6.5.2 below, but on a weighted average basis for the period up to the date of exercise. The exercise of options is a 'conversion of potential ordinary shares'. The standard excludes such conversions from the general requirement (see 4.3 above) to adjust prior periods' EPS when a change in the number of shares happens without a corresponding change in resources.[28]

4.5   Post balance sheet changes in capital

The EPS shown in the profit and loss account should not reflect any change in the capital structure occurring after the accounting date, but before the accounts are approved, which was effected for fair value. This is because any proceeds received from the issue were not available for use during the period. However, EPS for all periods presented should be adjusted for any bonus element in post year end changes in the number of shares. When this is done that fact should be stated.[29]

An example of such disclosure is shown in the following extract from the accounts of Calluna for the year ended 31 March 1999:

Extract 23.13: Calluna plc (1999)

7   Loss per share [extract]

The above calculations of basic and diluted loss per share for both 1999 and 1998 have been retrospectively adjusted to take account of the bonus element of the April 1999, 33 for 100 rights issue at 12.5p per ordinary share.

4.6   Issue to acquire another business

As a result of a share issue to acquire another business, funds or other assets will flow into the business and extra profits will be generated. When calculating EPS, it should be assumed that the shares were issued on the first day that profits of the newly acquired business are recognised in the profit and loss account (even if the actual date of issue is later).[30] Under FRS 2, this will be the date on which control of a subsidiary undertaking passes to its new parent undertaking.[31]

If the business combination is accounted for as an acquisition, this means that when calculating EPS, the period for which earnings of the acquired company are consolidated should be the same as the period for which the shares are weighted, thus achieving comparability within the EPS calculation.

Where a business combination has been accounted for as a merger, the number of shares taken as being in issue for all periods should be the aggregate of the weighted average number of shares of the merged companies, adjusted to equivalent shares of the post merger holding company.[32] This treatment reflects the fact that earnings are combined for both years and is appropriate even where not all of the consideration given for the equity share capital in the 'offeree' company is in the form of equity share capital.

4.7   Group reconstructions

In the case where a new holding company is established by means of a share for share exchange and merger accounting principles have been adopted, the number of shares taken as being in issue for both the current and preceding periods should be the number of shares issued by the new holding company in the reconstruction. However, EPS calculations for previous periods in the new holding company's financial statements would have to reflect any issues for cash by the former holding company that may have occurred in those periods, as illustrated in the example below:

Example 23.4:   Calculation of EPS where a new holding company is established

Company A has acquired Company B in a one for one share exchange on 30 June 1999. At that date, Company B has 1,000,000 £1 ordinary shares in issue. Previously, on 30 June 1998 Company B had issued 200,000 £1 ordinary shares for cash at full market price. Both companies have a 31 December year end and the trading results of Company B are as follows:

	1999 £	1998 £
Profit for equity shareholders after taxation	500,000	300,000

The earnings per share calculation of Company A is shown below:

	1999	1998
Number of equity shares	$800,000 \times \dfrac{6}{12} = 400,000$	
	$1,000,000 \times \dfrac{6}{12} = 500,000$	
	1,000,000	900,000
EPS	$\dfrac{500,000}{1,000,000} = 50\text{p}$	$\dfrac{300,000}{900,000} = 33.33\text{p}$

If, in the above example, the share exchange did not take place on a one for one basis, but Company A issued three shares for every one share held in Company B, then the number of shares issued by Company B in 1998 would have to be apportioned accordingly before carrying out the weighted average calculation. The earnings per share calculation would, therefore, have been as follows:

	1999	1998
Number of equity shares	$2,400,000 \times \dfrac{6}{12} = 1,200,000$	
	$3,000,000 \times \dfrac{6}{12} = 1,500,000$	
	3,000,000	2,700,000
EPS	$\dfrac{500,000}{3,000,000} = 16.67\text{p}$	$\dfrac{300,000}{2,700,000} = 11.11\text{p}$

4.8   Adjustments to EPS in five year summaries

In order to ensure comparability of EPS figures quoted in a five year summary, the previously published EPS figures should be adjusted for subsequent changes in capital not involving full consideration at fair value in the manner described in 4.3 above; they should also be adjusted for merger accounting. The resultant figures should be described as restated and should be clearly distinguished from other financial data which is not so adjusted.[33] Where there is more than one such change, these factors will operate cumulatively.

5 MATTERS AFFECTING THE NUMERATOR

5.1 Earnings

The earnings figure on which the EPS calculation is based should be the consolidated net profit or loss for the year after tax, exceptional and extraordinary (if any) items, minority interests and after deducting preference dividends and other appropriations in respect of non-equity shares.[34]

5.2 Preference dividends

If a company has preference shares, the amount of preference dividends that is deducted from the net profit for the period is:

(a) the amount of any preference dividends on non-cumulative preference shares declared in respect of the period; and

(b) the full amount of the required preference dividends for cumulative preference shares for the period, whether or not the dividends have been declared, as the undeclared amount is still deductible as an appropriation. The amount of preference dividends for the period does not include the amount of any preference dividends for cumulative preference shares paid or declared during the current period in respect of previous periods.[35]

As indicated at 4.4.1 of Chapter 15, FRS 4 requires such dividends to be accounted for on an accruals basis, except in those circumstances where ultimate payment is remote. Accordingly, the amount to be taken into account will normally be that accounted for as the appropriation for the year.

As indicated at 5.1 above, any other appropriations in respect of the preference shares should also be deducted in arriving at the earnings figure.

5.3 Prior year adjustments

Where comparative figures have been restated (for example, to correct a fundamental error or as a result of a change in accounting policy), earnings per share for the corresponding previous period should also be restated.

5.4 Different classes of ordinary shares

If there is more than one class of ordinary shares, earnings should be apportioned over the different classes of shares in accordance with their dividend rights or other rights to participate in profits.[36]

5.5   Other bases

As indicated at 1 above, the ASB when issuing FRS 3 attempted to de-emphasise EPS by requiring it to be calculated *after* extraordinary items. In view of this change and the other requirements of FRS 3 (see Chapter 22) the EPS number which companies are required to disclose has become much more volatile, and really only a starting point for further analysis. The ASB recognised that companies would therefore be likely to provide additional EPS numbers prepared on what they saw as a more meaningful basis and therefore the ASB introduced rules dealing with such additional EPS disclosures. [37]

These disclosure requirements are repeated in FRS 14 as follows: 'Such additional earnings per share computations should be presented on a consistent basis over time and, wherever disclosed, reconciled to the amount required by the FRS. The reconciliation should list the items for which an adjustment is being made and disclose their individual effect on the calculation. The earnings per share required by the FRS should be at least as prominent as any additional version presented and the reason for calculating the additional version should be explained. The reconciliation and explanation should appear adjacent to the earnings per share disclosure, or a reference should be given to where they can be found. Where both additional basic and diluted amounts per share are presented, they should be disclosed with equal prominence.' [38]

The standard also makes clear that the number of shares used in the denominator for additional EPS disclosures should be the same as that used for the required EPS figures. [39]

Since the issue of FRS 3, many companies have been providing additional EPS numbers; however, it is clear that there is no universal view as to the basis of such a number. Indeed, as can be seen from some of the extracts below some companies give a number of additional EPS figures.

5.5.1   IIMR headline earnings

In view of the volatility of 'earnings' numbers of companies following the issue of FRS 3, the Institute of Investment Management and Research ('IIMR') sought to find an earnings figure that would reflect a company's trading performance but that would limit the need to exercise judgement in its calculation so that it could be used as an unambiguous reference point between users, the press and statistical companies. Accordingly, in September 1993 the IIMR issued Statement of Investment Practice No. 1 in which it sets out a definition of 'headline' earnings. The statement is not mandatory. However, the IIMR does suggest that companies themselves may wish to adopt the IIMR calculation of headline earnings in presenting an additional EPS in their accounts.

The IIMR discusses both maintainable and headline earnings. Maintainable earnings is the level of earnings that is expected to be earned in future years. The

IIMR argues that, although it is maintainable earnings that should ideally be used in a price-earnings ratio computation, its calculation is too subjective to be calculated on a standardised basis. Headline earnings is a measure of the company's trading performance in the year and is calculated by adjusting a company's profit for certain specific items. The need for judgement in the calculation, while not completely eliminated, is reduced. The IIMR therefore concluded that headline earnings should be the benchmark measure.

Headline earnings is the trading results, after interest and taxation, for the year. It is the result actually achieved and contains no 'as if' adjustments; for example, where a subsidiary is acquired part way through a year it does not require adjustments to reflect the earnings that would have been achieved if the subsidiary had been part of the group all along.

To arrive at headline earnings, the profit for the financial year is adjusted for the after tax and minority interest effect of, amongst other things, the following:

(a)   profits/losses on sale/termination of an operation. However, the trading results of the discontinued operation remain in the calculation;

(b)   profits/losses on disposal of, and permanent diminutions in, fixed assets, irrespective of whether such amounts are included in arriving at operating profit or not;

(c)   the reversal of provisions in respect of FRS 3's paragraph 20 items (see Chapter 22 at 2.6.3); and

(d)   any goodwill charged in the profit and loss account.

Reorganisation provisions, fundamental or otherwise, are not excluded. Exceptional trading items are also to be included in the calculation of headline earnings.

A number of companies have disclosed an additional EPS number based on IIMR headline earnings, as illustrated in the following extracts:

Extract 23.14: Sema Group plc (1998)

EARNINGS PER SHARE [extract]

	1998	1997
Earnings per share	**14.9p**	9.8p
Adjustments for non-operating items:		
Profit on disposal of discontinued operations	**(2.6)p**	–
Earnings per share on ordinary activities	**12.3p**	9.8p
Goodwill amortisation	**0.1p**	–
Adjusted earnings per share	**12.4p**	9.8p

An adjusted earnings per share has been provided in order to eliminate the distortions caused by certain non-trading items. The items eliminated are profits after tax and minority interests on disposals of discontinued activities, and the amortisation of goodwill. Such adjustments have been made in accordance with the guidelines laid down by the Institute of Investment Management and Research (IIMR).

The above extract illustrates the requirement under FRS 3 and FRS 14 to provide a reconciliation between the additional EPS and that required under the standard, showing the individual effect of each item.[40] This can be contrasted with the following extract which illustrates a treatment adopted by a number of companies whereby the reconciliation is of the amount of earnings used in the calculation:

Extract 23.15: Bodycote International PLC (1998)

9   Earnings per share [extract]

| | **1998** | 1997 |
	£000	£000
Profit for the financial year	**53,475**	35,583
Goodwill amortisation charge	**1,166**	–
Exceptional items after tax	**(366)**	(571)
Headline earnings	**54,275**	35,012

It could be argued that users of accounts find such a reconciliation easier to follow as the numbers can normally be seen elsewhere in the accounts; however, it is not what the standard requires. Some companies, therefore, provide both types of reconciliation, as illustrated below:

Extract 23.16: Coats Viyella Plc (1998)

Consolidated profit and loss account [extract]

	Notes		**1998**	1997
Basic (loss)/earnings per ordinary share of 20p	11		**(3.8)p**	Nil
Diluted (loss)/earnings per ordinary share of 20p	11		**(3.8)p**	Nil
Headline (loss)/earnings per ordinary share of 20p	11		**(1.4)p**	2.8p

11 (Loss) / earnings per share	**1998**	1997	**1998 £m**	1997 £m
(Loss)/earnings per share are based on (loss)/profit available for ordinary shareholders of:			**(26.6)**	Nil
and on average number of shares of:	**702.6m**	701.9m		
resulting in basic and diluted (loss)/earnings per share of:	**(3.8)p**	Nilp		
Less:				
operating loss charged to provisions	**(0.2)p**	–p	**(1.6)**	–
profit on sale of fixed assets	**(0.5)p**	(0.4)p	**(3.2)**	(2.9)
losses/(gains) on sale or termination of operations	**3.0p**	3.2p	**21.3**	22.5
impairment of goodwill	**0.1p**	–p	**0.8**	–
taxation relating to these items	**–p**	–p	**(0.2)**	(0.3)
minority interests relating to these items	**–p**	–p	**(0.3)**	0.2
Headline (loss)/earnings per share	**(1.4)p**	2.8p	**(9.8)**	19.5

Headline earnings per share have been calculated in accordance with Statement of Investment Practice Number 1 issued by The Institute of Investment Management and Research and are provided in order to assist users of accounts to identify earnings derived from trading activities.

Exercise of outstanding share options and conversion of all the £65.229m 6.25% Senior Convertible Bonds of Coats Viyella Plc would not result in any dilution of earnings per share.

5.5.2 *Excluding exceptional items*

As mentioned above, in calculating headline earnings all reorganisation costs and exceptional trading items are to be included. Clearly, some companies believe it is more meaningful to provide an alternative EPS excluding the effects of all exceptional items, as shown in the following extracts:

Extract 23.17: Transport Development Group PLC (1998)

consolidated profit and loss account [extract]

	Notes	1998	1997
Earnings per Ordinary Share	13	**(4.06)p**	15.73p
Earnings per Ordinary Share before exceptional items	13	**23.94p**	17.67p

13   Earnings per Ordinary Share [extract]

Earnings before exceptional items is calculated as follows:

	1998	1997
	£'000	£,000
(Loss)/profit for the financial year	**(3,950)**	21,569
Preference and B Share dividends	**(95)**	(66)
Earnings attributable to Ordinary Shares	**(4,045)**	21,503
Capital reorganisation, restructuring and systems implementation costs (net of tax)	**3,186**	–
Exceptional losses	**25,314**	4,161
Prior year tax credits	**(2,485)**	–
Tax on exceptional items	**361**	(1,513)
ACT write off	**1,500**	–
	23,831	24,151

Extract 23.18: Inchcape plc (1998)

Consolidated profit and loss account [extract]

Notes		**1998**	1997 restated
	Headline profit before tax (£m)	**106.1**	184.1
2e	Headline earnings per share (pence)	**8.4p**	19.3p
	FRS 3 (loss) profit before tax (£m)	**(297.6)**	89.6
2e	Basic and diluted (loss) earnings per share (pence)	**(69.1)p**	1.5p

2   Profit and loss [extract]

			Headline		FRS 3
		1998	1997	**1998**	1997
e	**Earnings per ordinary share**	**£m**	£m	**£m**	£m
	Headline profit before tax	**106.1**	184.1	**106.1**	184.1
	Exceptional items – note 2d	–	–	**(403.7)**	(94.5)
	Profit (loss) before tax	**106.1**	184.1	**(297.6)**	89.6
	Taxation – note 4a	**(55.2)**	(63.1)	**(61.4)**	(64.8)
	Minority interests	**(6.6)**	(18.7)	**(6.5)**	(17.0)
	Earnings (loss)	**44.3**	102.3	**(365.5)**	7.8
	Headline earnings per share	**8.4p**	19.3p		
	Basic and diluted (loss) earnings per share			**(69.1)p**	1.5p

The weighted average number of fully paid shares in issue during the year, excluding those held by the Inchcape Employee Trust (note 8a), was 529,306,833 (1997 restated – 528,805,341).

Options have no dilutive effect on basic earnings per share as the exercise price of all outstanding options are greater than the average share price during the period of 171p.

Headline profits and earnings (before total exceptional items and after the utilisation of termination provisions) are adopted in that they provide a representation of underlying performance.

It can be seen that Inchcape although calculating EPS before all exceptional items has somewhat confusingly used the term 'headline earnings' which is defined differently from that used by the IIMR. Indeed, in its 1995 accounts in addition to disclosing EPS numbers on the bases used in the 1998 accounts Inchcape had also disclosed an IIMR headline earnings EPS but evidently decided to drop this in favour of its own definition (in its 1996 and subsequent accounts).

Some companies, rather than disclosing an additional EPS which excludes the effects of all exceptional items, only exclude certain exceptional items in providing an alternative EPS number. For example, T&N only excluded its exceptional asbestos-related costs:

Extract 23.19: T&N plc (1997)

Group profit and loss account [extract]

	Notes	**1996**	1995
Earnings/(loss) per share	8	**22.9p**	(75.4)p
Earnings per share pre asbestos-related costs	8	**20.4p**	14.8p

---

In addition to the exceptional asbestos-related costs, T&N also had some non-operating exceptional items.

5.5.3 Excluding discontinued operations

One of the main impacts of FRS 3 has been for companies to analyse their results between continuing and discontinued operations (see Chapter 22 at 2.3). Accordingly, a number of companies have provided an additional EPS by excluding the amounts relating to the discontinued operations, thereby disclosing a figure related purely to the continuing operations, as illustrated in the following extracts:

Extract 23.20: Delta plc (1998)

GROUP PROFIT AND LOSS ACCOUNT [extract]

	Notes					1998
		Continuing				
		Pre-exceptional £ million	Exceptional items (note 5) £ million	Sub total £ million	Discontinued operations £ million	Total £ million
Profit (loss) for the financial year		20.6	(4.2)	16.4	3.3	19.7
Dividends	9	(12.1)	–	(12.1)	–	(12.1)
Transfer to (from) reserves	25	8.5	(4.2)	4.3	3.3	7.6
Earnings per 25p ordinary share:						
Basic	10	13.8p		10.8p		13.1p
Diluted	10	13.7p		10.8p		13.1p
Earnings per 25p ordinary share before goodwill amortisation						
Basic	10	15.7p		12.8p		15.1p
Diluted	10	15.7p		12.8p		15.1p

	Notes				1997 (as restated)	
			Continuing			
			Exceptional			
		Pre-	items	Sub	Discontinued	
		exceptional	(note 5)	total	operations	Total
		£ million	£ million	£ million	£ million	£ million
Profit (loss) for the financial year		30.6	–	30.6	(74.5)	(43.9)
Dividends	9	(24.1)	–	(24.1)	–	(24.1)
Transfer to (from) reserves	25	6.5	–	6.5	(74.5)	(68.0)
Earnings per 25p ordinary share:						
Basic	10	20.5p		20.5p		(29.5)p
Diluted	10	20.5p		20.5p		(29.5)p
Earnings per 25p ordinary share						
before goodwill amortisation						
Basic	10	20.5p		20.5p		(29.5)p
Diluted	10	20.5p		20.5p		(29.5)p

10 Earnings per Share

Basic earnings per share (EPS) is calculated in accordance with FRS 14, by dividing the earnings attributable to ordinary shareholders by the weighted average number of ordinary shares in issue during the year. For diluted earnings per share, the weighted average number of ordinary shares in issue is adjusted to assume conversion of all dilutive potential ordinary shares. The Group has only one category of dilutive potential ordinary shares: those granted to employees where the exercise price is less than the average market price of the Company's ordinary shares during the year. Adjustments to comparative figures have been made to reflect the requirements of FRS 14. Reconciliations of the earnings and weighted average number of shares used in the calculations are set out below:

	1998			1997		
	Total earnings £ million	weighted average no. of shares	Per-share amount pence	Total earnings £ million	weighted average no. of shares	Per-share amount pence
Profit attributable to shareholders	19.7	148,945,244		(43.9)	149,214,879	
Less: preference dividends	(0.1)			(0.1)		
Basic EPS earnings attributable to ordinary shareholders	19.6	148,945,244	13.1	(44.0)	149,214,879	(29.5)
Effect of dilutive securities: Options		425,549	–		54,466	–
Diluted EPS adjusted earnings	19.6	149,370,793	13.1	(44.0)	149,269,345	(29.5)
EPS excluding goodwill amortisation:						
Basic EPS	19.6	148,945,244	13.1	(44.0)	149,214,879	(29.5)
Effect of goodwill amortisation: Subsidiaries	3.0		2.0	–		–
Basic EPS excluding goodwill amortisation	22.6	148,945,244	15.1	(44.0)	149,214,879	(29.5)
Diluted EPS	19.6	149,370,793	13.1	(44.0)	149,269,345	(29.5)
Effect of goodwill amortisation: Subsidiaries	3.0		2.0	–		–
Diluted EPS excluding goodwill amortisation	22.6	149,370,793	15.1	(44.0)	149,269,345	(29.5)

To give a better understanding of the underlying results of the year, additional earnings per share figures are given on the face of the profit and loss account for continuing activities (both pre and post-exceptional items). The earnings are based on the attributable profit (pre and post-exceptional items) less preference dividends and goodwill amortisation (where applicable) as shown above. The weighted average number of shares used in the calculations are those shown in the above table.

Since the implementation of FRS 10 increasing numbers of companies have chosen to present an EPS figure excluding goodwill amortisation, as illustrated by Delta above.

Extract 23.21: Imperial Chemical Industries PLC (1998)

Group profit and loss account for the year ended 31 December 1998 [extract]

	Notes	Continuing operations Before exceptional items £m	Continuing operations Exceptional items £m	Discontinued operations £m	Total £m
Net profit (loss) for the financial year		200	(146)	139	193
Dividends	10				(232)
Profit (loss) retained for the year	25				(39)
Earnings (loss) per £1 Ordinary Share Basic	11	27.6p	(20.1)p	19.2p	26.7p
Diluted		27.5p	(20.1)p	19.1p	26.5p

5.5.4   Other amounts per share

For some companies, the conventional method of assessing performance by reference to reported earnings is not entirely satisfactory; for example, many property companies consider the 'net assets per ordinary share' to be a more appropriate performance indicator. In such circumstances, in addition to the requirements of FRS 14, we believe that it is desirable to present other statistics that are appropriate to assessing the company's performance, including an adequate explanation of the basis of calculation.

There is some ambiguity in FRS 14 as to what number of shares to include in the denominator for per share figures other than earnings. The scope section of the standard contains the following 'The provisions of the FRS are drafted principally in terms of amounts per share as components of net profit; however, the requirements also apply, as far as appropriate, to other amounts per share, eg net assets per share.'[41] Whilst the specific mention of net assets per share could be read as a requirement to base such disclosure on the weighted average number of shares, the inclusion of 'as far as appropriate' seems to leave room for other interpretations. One quite persuasive argument is that, as net assets represent a snap-shot of the entity at its balance sheet date, it is more appropriate to base net assets per share on the number of shares as at that date. This was the approach taken by Slough Estates, which also discloses a number of performance indicators, as illustrated below:

Extract 23.22: Slough Estates plc (1998)

9 Earnings, capital surplus and net assets per ordinary share [extract]

			Basic		Fully diluted	
			1998	1997 Restated	**1998**	1997 Restated
The earnings, capital surplus and net assets per ordinary share have been calculated as follows:						
Profit attributable to ordinary shareholders	(a)	£m	**69.2**	61.3	**69.2**	61.3
Profit attributable to ordinary shareholders excluding profits and losses on sale of investment properties	(b)	£m	**71.3**	58.0	**71.3**	58.0
Capital surplus	(c)	£m	**196.9**	222.4	**196.9**	222.4
Average of shares in issue during the year	(d)	shares m	**395.5**	391.8	**396.3**	393.1
Earnings per share (a) ÷ (d)		pence	**17.5**	15.7	**17.5**	15.6
Earnings per share excluding profits and losses on sale of investment properties (b) ÷ (d)		pence	**18.0**	14.9	**18.0**	14.8
Capital surplus per share		pence	**49.8**	56.8	**43.9**	49.9
Equity attributable to ordinary shareholders	(e)	£m	**1,653.3**	1,376.5	**1,794.4**	1,517.6
Shares in issue at the end of the year	(f)	shares m	**410.9**	392.8	**464.0**	446.4
Net assets per share (e) ÷ (f)		pence	**402**	350	**387**	340

	1998 m	1997 m
Average of shares in issue during the year	**395.5**	391.8
Adjustment for the dilutive effect of employee share options and save as you earn schemes	**0.8**	1.3
Average of shares in issue during the year diluted	**396.3**	393.1

The earnings per share and fully diluted earnings per share excluding profits and losses (net of tax and minority) on the sale of investment properties have been calculated in addition to the disclosures required by FRS 3, since in the opinion of the directors this gives shareholders a more meaningful measure of performance.

The question of whether the weighted average or year end number of shares is a more appropriate basis applies also to dividends per share, which companies sometimes present on the face of the profit and loss account. In our view the ambiguity in the standard allows companies the discretion to base such a figure on the basis they consider most appropriate.

6   DILUTED EARNINGS PER SHARE

6.1   The need for diluted EPS

The presentation of basic EPS seeks to show a performance measure, by computing how much profit a company has earned for each of the shares in issue for the period. Companies often enter into commitments to issue shares in the future which would result in a change in basic EPS. FRS 14 refers to such commitments as potential ordinary shares, which it defines as follows:

'A financial instrument or a right that may entitle its holder to ordinary shares.

Examples of potential ordinary shares are:

(a)   debt or equity instruments, including preference shares, that are convertible into ordinary shares;

(b)   share warrants and options;

(c)   rights granted under employee share plans that may entitle employees to receive ordinary shares as part of their remuneration and similar rights granted under other share purchase plans; and

(d)   rights to ordinary shares that are contingent upon the satisfaction of certain conditions resulting from contractual arrangements, such as the purchase of a business or other assets, i.e. contingently issuable shares.'[42]

When potential shares are actually issued, the impact on basic EPS will be two-fold. Firstly the number of shares in issue will change, secondly profits could be affected, for example by lower interest charges or the return made on cash inflows. This potential change in EPS is quantified by computing diluted EPS.

SSAP 3 only required the disclosure of fully diluted EPS in certain circumstances, so as to act as a warning signal for possible future falls in EPS. FRS 14, however, requires disclosure of diluted EPS in all circumstances as a more sophisticated measure of past performance.[43] Accordingly, it gives more specific guidance on the calculation than SSAP 3 did, including the sequence in which potential shares should be considered when calculating the diluted EPS.

The rationale that a *future* dilution is relevant for measuring *past* performance is this. Companies can use potential ordinary shares to achieve illusory growth in basic EPS. Consider, for example, a company that has used convertible loan stock or convertible preference shares to finance an acquisition or expansion. These securities usually carry a low fixed interest or dividend coupon due to the presence of a compensatory factor, the conversion privilege. It is therefore possible to boost basic EPS so long as the incremental post-tax finance cost is covered and current performance is sustained. However, examination of the underlying trend in the diluted EPS figures will reveal a more 'real' growth in earnings so far as concerns existing equity shareholders, since an attempt is made to reflect the ultimate 'cost' of using convertible securities to finance growth in earnings. Convertible securities are discussed in more detail at 4.2 in Chapter 15.

6.2 Calculation of diluted EPS

In calculating diluted EPS, the number of shares should be that used in calculating basic EPS, plus the weighted average number of shares that would be issued on the conversion of all the dilutive potential ordinary shares into ordinary shares. Potential ordinary shares should be deemed to have been converted into ordinary shares at the beginning of the period or, if not in existence at the beginning of the period, the date of the issue of the financial instrument or the granting of the rights by which they are generated.[44]

6.2.1 Earnings

The earnings figure should be adjusted to reflect any changes in profit that would arise when the potential shares outstanding in the period are actually issued. Adjustment is to be made for the post-tax effects of:

(a) any dividends on potential shares, for example on convertible preference shares, that have been deducted in calculating the earnings for basic EPS;

(b) interest recognised in the period on the potential shares such as convertible loan stock; and

(c) any other changes in income or expense that would result from the conversion of the potential shares.[45]

These adjustments will also include any amounts charged in the profit and loss account under FRS 4 as a result of allocating fees, premiums or discounts over the term of the instrument.

An example of an adjustment covered by (b) above is as follows:

Extract 23.23: BAA plc (1999)		
9 Earnings per share [extract]		
	1999	1998
	£m	£m
Profit attributable to shareholders	**398**	277
Interest on convertible bonds	**17**	15
Diluted profit	**415**	292

The standard notes that certain earnings adjustments directly attributable to the instrument could have a knock on impact on other profit and loss items which will need to be accounted for. For example, the lower interest charge on conversion of convertible debt could lead to higher charges under profit sharing schemes.[46]

Unlike SSAP 3, however, no imputed earnings are taken into account in respect of share options or warrants. The effect of such potential ordinary shares on the diluted EPS is reflected in the computation of the denominator. This is discussed at 6.5.2 below.

In the vast majority of cases the earnings impact will be covered by the first two points above, or be nil. One unusual example of other earnings effects is BPP, as follows:

Extract 23.24: BPP Holdings plc (1998)

13.   *Earnings per share* [extract]

(b)   *Diluted earnings per share*

Diluted earnings per share is calculated by adjusting profit, after tax and minority interest, and the weighted average number of shares for the effects of all dilutive potential shares. Options granted under Employee Share Schemes dilute the earnings per share by increasing the weighted average number of shares without changing net profit. Shares potentially issuable as consideration for the purchase of minority interests will change net profit. Net profit attributable increases because of the elimination of the profit attributable to minority shareholders but is reduced by the charge to the profit and loss, from 1998 onwards under FRS 10, for goodwill amortisation.

	Attributable profit		Weighted no. of shares	
	1998	1997	**1998**	1997
	£'000	£'000	**No.**	No.
Basic earnings per share	**8,185**	4,507	**26,649,310**	26,444,217
Dilutive potential ordinary shares:				
Employee share schemes	–	–	**683,369**	550,484
Purchase minority interests	**174**	–	**916,709**	–
	8,359	4,507	**28,249,388**	26,994,701

The dilutive impact of Employee Share Schemes is to reduce earnings per share to 30.0p (1997 – 16.7p).

For the purposes of calculating diluted eps, the goodwill arising has been assumed to be amortised over twenty years. If goodwill was not written off, the purchase of minority interests would be earnings enhancing as the p/e ratio applied for the purchase of minority interests is a proportion of BPP's p/e ratio. The dilutive impact of this is to reduce earnings per share to 29.6p (1997 – 16.7p).

A subsequent note further describes the details of these contingent purchase arrangements, which subsist for a number of subsidiaries. An example of one is as follows:

Extract 23.25: BPP Holdings plc (1998)

25.   *Minority interests and deferred consideration* [extract]

(b)   *Further consideration payable in respect of the acquisition of minority interests* [extract]

The consideration for the acquisition of minority interests in subsidiary undertakings which may be payable has not yet been determined. As a result, additional goodwill may arise in the future in relation to the following subsidiary undertakings:

The group owns 77.5% of the issued share capital of BPP Manchester Limited and has entered into put and call options with the shareholders of the balance of BPP Manchester Limited's issued share capital. The put and call options are exercisable within 30 days of the group announcing its preliminary results for the year just ended in any of the years 1997 to 2000 inclusive. The amount payable is based on the earnings of BPP Manchester Limited for the three years ended prior to the exercise of the option and will be satisfied, in whole or in part, by the issue of shares or cash at the company's option.

6.2.2   *Number of shares*

FRS 14 discusses a number of specific types of potential ordinary shares, and how they should be brought into the calculation, which are discussed later. More generally, the standard first discusses, in two explanatory paragraphs,[47] the impact on the basic requirement that *all* dilutive potential ordinary shares are included of situations where an entity may be entitled or required to fulfil its obligations either in shares or cash. The general tenor of these two paragraphs seems to be that if the outcome is uncertain, then the more dilutive outcome should be assumed. However, the wording of these paragraphs and how they interact is far from clear, and is discussed in more detail below.

(a)   The standard notes that the number of shares issued on the conversion of an instrument will be governed by the terms of the instrument, and concludes by saying 'The computation assumes the most advantageous conversion rate or exercise price from the stand point of the holder'.[48] Whilst the meaning of this is fairly obscure, the fact that it envisages more than one outcome presumably encompasses scenarios where the holder has a choice whether to accept cash or shares.

(b)   Contracts which can be settled either in shares or cash are specifically covered. The standard indicates that where 'past experience or a stated policy provides a reasonable basis for concluding how the contract will be satisfied, that policy or experience is followed'. In the absence of any such past experience or stated policy it should be presumed that the contract will be settled by the more dilutive method.[49]

A possible question that arises is what happens if these two requirements are in conflict with each other? An example would be a contract providing for the issue of a fixed quantity of shares or a fixed monetary sum at the option of the holder. If the value of the shares were less than the cash option then (a) above seems to be saying that, for diluted EPS purposes, it should be assumed that cash will be paid (most advantageous for the holder). However, (b) above appears to require either 'past experience or a stated policy' or, in the absence of such, that the cash route were more dilutive. The standard does not elaborate on how to compare, in these circumstances, a cash payment with a share issue to decide which is more dilutive. At first sight a cash payment (say to buy an asset), would have no dilutive impact, whereas a share issue clearly would. It is possible that the standard is trying to allude to a wider interpretation of dilutive, and that some notional interest cost associated with a cash payment should be considered.

Given that the overall tenor of the FRS is to arrive at the most fully diluted EPS it seems the most likely interpretation would be to include such potential shares. However the lack of clarity surrounding the issue will require detailed consideration of each specific case.

6.3   Dilutive potential ordinary shares

Only those potential shares whose issue would have a dilutive effect on EPS are brought into the calculation. The standard gives detailed guidance for determining which potential shares are deemed to be dilutive, and hence brought into the diluted EPS calculation. This guidance covers: the sequence in which potential shares are tested to establish cumulative dilution, and the element of profit which needs to be diluted to trigger inclusion. Each is discussed below.

6.3.1   *Dilution judged by the cumulative impact of potential shares*

Where a company has a number of different potential ordinary shares, in deciding whether they are dilutive (and hence reflected in the calculation), each type is to be considered in sequence from the most to the least dilutive. Only those potential shares which produce a cumulative dilution are to be included.[50] This means that some potential shares which would dilute basic EPS if viewed on their own may need to be excluded. This results in a diluted EPS showing the maximum overall dilution of basic EPS. The way this is to be done is illustrated in the following example.

Example 23.5: Determining whether potential ordinary shares are dilutive or antidilutive

Capital structure

Issued share capital as at 31 December 1998 and 31 December 1999:
2,000,000 ordinary shares of 10p each
The average market price of the shares during the year was 75p.

Options have been granted to the directors and certain senior executives giving them the right to subscribe for 100,000 ordinary shares between 2003 and 2005 at 60 pence per share.

800,000 8% convertible cumulative preference shares of £1 each
Each preference share is convertible into 2 ordinary shares.

£1,000,000 of 5% Convertible bonds
Each bond is convertible into 2 ordinary shares.

Trading results

Net profit attributable to ordinary shareholders for the year ended 31 December 1999 is £100,000, all of which relates to continuing operations.

Assume corporation tax at 30%.*Increase in earnings attributable to ordinary shareholders on conversion of potential ordinary shares*

	Increase in earnings £	Increase in number of ordinary shares No	Earnings per incremental share Pence
(a) Options	–	20,000	–
(b) Convertible cumulative preference shares	64,000	1,600,000	4.00
(c) 5% Convertible bonds	35,000	2,000,000	1.75

(a) As discussed at 6.5.2 below, under FRS 14 conversion of options is treated as not giving rise to any increase in earnings, but the dilution is calculated as if the proceeds on conversion had been received for issuing a certain number of shares at fair value and the excess for zero consideration. It is only the excess which is taken into account in calculating diluted EPS (see Example 23.9 below). In this example the number can be computed as being 100,000 x (75-60)/75.

(b) Increase in earnings represents the dividends on the shares being 8% x £800,000. The increase in shares resulting from conversion would be 800,000 x 2.

(c) Increase in earnings represents interest saved of £50,000 being 5% x £1,000,000 less taxation thereon at 30% (£15,000). The increase in shares resulting from conversion would be 1,000,000 x 2.

These are therefore taken into account in computing whether they are dilutive or antidilutive in the order of (a), (c) and (b) as follows:

Computation of whether potential ordinary shares are dilutive or antidilutive

	Net profit from continuing operations £	Ordinary shares No	Per share Pence	
Basic net profit from continuing operations per share	100,000	2,000,000	5.00	
Options	–	20,000		
	100,000	2,020,000	4.95	Dilutive
5% Convertible bonds	35,000	2,000,000		
	135,000	4,020,000	3.36	Dilutive
Convertible cumulative preference shares	64,000	1,600,000		
	199,000	5,620,000	3.54	Antidilutive

Notwithstanding the fact that the convertible cumulative preference shares would be dilutive on their own (basic EPS of 5.00p would be diluted to 4.56p), since the effect of the convertible cumulative preference shares increases the pence per share from 3.36p (after taking account of the more dilutive items) to 3.54p, then these are regarded as antidilutive and are to be ignored in the calculation of diluted earnings per share. Therefore, in this example, the diluted EPS to be disclosed would be 3.36p.

One company which discloses a diluted EPS, excluding items which have no dilutive effect, is Tarmac, as illustrated below:

Extract 23.26: Tarmac plc (1998)

9   Earnings per ordinary share [extract]

The diluted earnings per ordinary share figure, on both bases above, has been calculated, using the same earnings numerators as set out above, by reference to an adjusted average number of shares, as follows:

	1998 **Millions**	1997 Millions
Weighted average, per basic calculation	**947.7**	928.5
Adjustment to reflect dilutive shares under option	**2.7**	8.4
Adjustment to reflect dilutive shares held by Employee Ownership Plan	**1.0**	0.3
	951.4	937.2

Convertible capital bonds are at present anti-dilutive.

6.3.2   *Dilution judged by effect on profits from continuing operations*

Potential ordinary shares are only to be treated as dilutive if their conversion to ordinary shares would dilute net profit per share from *continuing* operations.[51] The 'control number' that this focuses on is therefore the net profit from continuing operations, which is the net profit from ordinary activities after deducting preference dividends and after excluding items relating to discontinued operations. This number will not always be evident from the profit and loss account as FRS 3 requires the profit from continuing and discontinued operations to be analysed before tax and interest. An allocation of interest and tax will therefore be necessary; this is permitted to be done on a pro-rata basis at the operating profit level in the absence of a 'practical, more reliable method'.[52] The standard states that such an allocation will often be possible for post operating exceptionals presented in accordance with FRS 3.[53]

This means that the EPS to be disclosed will not necessarily be the same as that computed in testing whether the potential ordinary shares were dilutive, because the starting point is the earnings used in computing the basic EPS. This can lead to some strange results. As illustrated in the following example (which is based on Example 23.5 above) it is possible to exclude instruments which would dilute basic EPS (but not continuing EPS), and even show a diluted EPS that exceeds basic EPS.

Example 23.6: *Computation of diluted EPS where the control number for computing*
dilutive effects is different from profits used in computing basic EPS

In Example 23.5, the net profit attributable to ordinary shareholders used in the calculation of basic EPS all related to continuing operations. If, however, there were also profits of £150,000 attributable to discontinued operations then the diluted EPS to be disclosed would be 7.09p computed as follows:

	Net profit attributable to ordinary shareholders £	Ordinary shares No	Per share Pence
Basic EPS	250,000	2,000,000	12.50
Options	–	20,000	
5% Convertible bonds	35,000	2,000,000	
Diluted EPS	285,000	4,020,000	7.09

However, if the convertible cumulative preference shares were taken into account then the diluted EPS would have been 6.21p computed as follows:

	Net profit attributable to ordinary shareholders £	Ordinary shares No	Per share Pence
Basic net profit from continuing operations per share	250,000	2,000,000	12.50
Options	–	20,000	
5% Convertible bonds	35,000	2,000,000	
Convertible cumulative preference shares	64,000	1,600,000	
	349,000	5,620,000	6.21

If, however, instead of profits of £150,000 attributable to discontinued operations there were losses of £75,000 attributable to discontinued operations then the diluted EPS to be disclosed would be 1.49p computed as follows:

	Net profit attributable to ordinary shareholders £	Ordinary shares No	Per share Pence
Basic EPS	25,000	2,000,000	1.25
Options	–	20,000	
5% Convertible bonds	35,000	2,000,000	
Diluted EPS	60,000	4,020,000	1.49

In our view it is a mistake to use net profit per share from continuing ordinary operations as the control number for the purpose of determining the items to be included in the calculation of diluted EPS, when this is not the focus of the earnings per share disclosure nor a required disclosure in the accounts. There is clearly a tension between this requirement and the idea of EPS as a past performance measure rather than a warning signal for future dilution. This conflict is acknowledged in FRS 14,[54] and the treatment is justified because profit from continuing operation is expected to be more stable over time and 'stability was of primary importance to the function of the control number'.[55] However there is nothing to prevent companies from presenting additional figures which they believe to be more meaningful.

6.4   Dilution in the context of a loss per share

In a change from SSAP 3, FRS 14 requires basic and diluted EPS to be presented in all circumstances, even if the amounts disclosed are negative (i.e. a loss per share).[56]

In the vast majority of cases, if basic EPS is a loss, then diluted EPS will be exactly the same number. The reason for this is that potential shares are only considered dilutive, and hence included in the calculation, when their conversion would decrease a net profit or *increase a net loss per share*.[57] The impact on the calculation (if any) of all potential shares is to increase the denominator, hence (in the absence of any adverse earnings impact) making a loss per share smaller not larger, meaning that the instrument is antidilutive and therefore excluded. An example of a company specifically referring to this is Liberty, as follows:

Extract 23.27: Liberty Public Limited Company (1999)

11   Loss per ordinary share

The earnings per ordinary share is calculated by reference to the loss attributable to ordinary shareholders, after deducting dividends on preference shares. This calculation was; in 1998/99 a loss of £314,000 *(1997/98 – £12,579,000 loss)* on a weighted average number of ordinary shares in issue during the year of 22,665,421 *(1997/98 – 22,636,588)*.

The loss attributable to ordinary shareholders and weighted average number of ordinary shares for the purpose of calculating the diluted earnings per ordinary share are identical to those used for basic earnings per ordinary share. This is because the exercise of share options would have the effect of reducing the loss per ordinary share and is therefore not dilutive under the terms of FRS 14.

In order to increase a loss per share there would need to be a *negative* earnings impact resulting from conversion sufficient to increase the loss by proportionately more than the rise in the number of shares. In our view such potential ordinary shares are unlikely to be seen in practice.

It would seem that the stress the standard lays on always presenting diluted EPS, even if the amounts are negative, has led some loss making companies to bring anti-dilutive instruments into the diluted EPS calculation. An example is PPL Therapeutics, as follows:

Extract 23.28: PPL Therapeutics plc (1998)

Consolidated Profit and Loss Account [extract]

	Note	**1998**	1997
Loss per share			
Basic	10	**(51)p**	(37)p
Diluted		**(50)p**	(36)p

10 Loss per share

The basic loss per ordinary share is based on the loss before and after taxation of £14,245,000 (1997: £10,209,000) and on the weighted average number of ordinary shares in issue during the year of 28,164,628 (1997: 27,622,040). The diluted loss per ordinary share is based on a diluted weighted average number of shares of 28,273,606 (1997: 28,208,465). The dilutive effect of the Company share option schemes was 9,202 (1997: 566,316) and of the SAYE scheme was 99,776 (1997: 20,109). Comparative figures have been restated to take account of the 6 for 5 Rights Issue.

The results of PPL Therapeutics arise entirely on continuing operations, and as can be seen the only dilutive instruments are options which leads to the diluted loss per share being a lower loss than the basic one.

There is, rather counter-intuitively, one situation when a diluted loss per share could be different from the basic loss per share. It arises from the requirement to test for the dilutive impact of potential shares by reference to their effect on profits from *continuing* operations. If an overall net loss (and hence loss per share) comprised a profit on continuing activities and a larger loss on discontinued activities then potential ordinary shares could be brought into the calculation, resulting in the actual diluted loss per share that is disclosed being a smaller loss than the basic one. An illustration of how this might happen is given as follows:

Example 23.7: Computation of diluted EPS where there are overall net losses, yet profits from continuing operations

Capital structure

Issued share capital as at 31 December 1998 and 31 December 1999:
2,000,000 ordinary shares of 10p each

£1,000,000 of 5% Convertible bonds
Each £1 nominal value of bond is convertible into 2 ordinary shares.

Trading results

Net loss attributable to ordinary shareholders for the year ended 31 December 1999 is £50,000, comprising £100,000 profit from continuing operations and a loss of £150,000 from discontinued activities.

Assume corporation tax at 30%.

Computation of whether potential ordinary shares are dilutive or antidilutive

	Net profit from continuing operations £	Ordinary shares No	Per share Pence
Profit from continuing operations	100,000	2,000,000	5.000
5% Convertible bonds (1)	35,000	2,000,000	
Diluted EPS	135,000	4,000,000	3.375

(1)   Increase in earnings represents interest saved of £50,000 being 5% x £1,000,000 less taxation thereon at 30% (£15,000). The increase in shares resulting from conversion would be 1,000,000 x 2.

Hence the convertible bonds are dilutive, and are used in the diluted EPS calculation as follows.

Computation of basic and diluted EPS to be disclosed on the P&L account

	Net profit attributable to ordinary shareholders £	Ordinary shares No	Per share Pence
Basic loss per share	(50,000)	2,000,000	(2.5)
5% Convertible bonds	35,000	2,000,000	
Diluted loss per share	(15,000)	4,000,000	(0.4)

An example of a company in this situation is Delta, as shown in Extract 23.20 at 5.5.3 above. The comparative period shows continuing profits of £30.6 million and discontinued losses of £74.5 million. Notwithstanding this overall loss per share, note 10 indicates that the dilutive impact of options has been factored in, presumably on the grounds that they do have a dilutive effect on continuing operations.

6.5   Particular types of dilutive instruments

6.5.1   *Convertible securities*

In order to secure a lower rate of interest, companies sometimes attach benefits to loan stock or debentures in the form of conversion rights. These permit the stockholder to convert his holding in whole or part into equity capital. The right is normally exercisable between specified dates. The ultimate conversion of the loan stock will have the following effects:

(a)   there will be an increase in earnings by the amount of the loan stock interest no longer payable. Because this interest is allowable for corporation tax purposes, the effect on earnings will be net of corporation tax relief; and

(b)   the number of ordinary shares in issue will increase. The diluted EPS should be calculated assuming that the loan stock is converted into the maximum possible number of shares.

Example 23.8:   Treatment of convertible loan stock in diluted EPS calculations

Net profit	£1,000
Ordinary shares outstanding	10,000
Basic earnings per share	10p
Convertible 10% bonds	1,000

Each block of 10 bonds is convertible into 15 ordinary shares

Interest expense for the current year relating to the liability component of the convertible bond	£100
Current and deferred tax relating to that interest expense	£30
Adjusted net profit	£1,000 + £100 - £30 = £1,070
Number of ordinary shares resulting from conversion of bond	1,500
Number of ordinary shares used to compute diluted earnings per share	10,000 + 1,500 = 11,500
Diluted earnings per share	$\frac{£1,070}{11,500} = 9.3p$

The rules for convertible preference shares are very similar to those detailed above in the case of loan stock, i.e. the dividend is added back to earnings and the maximum number of ordinary shares that could be issued on conversion should be used in the calculation.

6.5.2   *Options or warrants to subscribe for ordinary shares*

Companies may grant options to directors and employees or issue warrants which give holders (not usually employees) the right to subscribe for shares at fixed prices on specified future dates. If the options or warrants are exercised then:

(a)   the number of shares in issue will be increased; and

(b)   funds will flow into the company and these will produce income.

Under FRS 14 no imputed income is taken into account in respect of share options or warrants; rather the effects of such potential ordinary shares on the diluted EPS are reflected in the computation of the denominator.

For this purpose, the weighted average number of shares used in calculating the basic EPS is still increased, but not by the full number of shares that would be issued on exercise of the instruments. To work out how many additional shares to include in the denominator, the assumed proceeds from these issues are to be treated as having been received in exchange for:

■   a certain number of shares at fair value (i.e. no EPS impact); and

■   the remainder for no consideration (i.e. full dilution with no earnings enhancement).[58]

This means that the excess of the total number of potential shares over the number that could be issued at fair value out of the issue proceeds is included within the denominator; the calculation is illustrated as follows:

Example 23.9:   Effects of share options on diluted earnings per share

Capital structure

Issued share capital for both years ending 31 December 1998 and 1999:
400,000 ordinary shares of 25p each.

Options have been granted to the directors and certain senior executives giving them the right to subscribe for ordinary shares between 2003 and 2005 at 90 pence per share.

Options outstanding at	31 December 1998	40,000
	31 December 1999	50,000

(The additional 10,000 options were granted on 1 January 1999.)

Average market value of ordinary shares:

Year ending 31 December 1998	£1.50
Year ending 31 December 1999	£1.80

Trading results

Profit for equity shareholders after taxation:

Year ending 31 December 1998	£60,000
Year ending 31 December 1999	£70,000

Calculation of diluted EPS

	1999 £	1998 £
Profit for basic EPS	70,000	60,000

The profit is not increased for any notional income on proceeds of options issuable.

Number of equity shares after exercise of options:

	1999 No	1998 No
Number of equity shares for basic EPS	400,000	400,000
Number of shares under option	50,000	40,000
Number of shares that would have been issued at fair value:		
(50,000 x £0.90)/£1.80	(25,000)	
(40,000 x £0.90/£1.50		(24,000)
Adjusted capital	425,000	416,000

Diluted EPS	1999	1998
	£70,000	£60,000
=	425,000	416,000
=	16.47p	14.42p

As can be seen the profit used in the calculation is not increased, but the number of shares has been increased by 25,000 (19X1 16,000) shares which are deemed to have been issued for no consideration.

Fair value for this purpose is calculated on the basis of the average price of the ordinary shares during the reporting period.[59] These would be deemed to have been issued at the beginning of the period or, if later, the date of issue of the warrants or options. Options which are exercised or lapse in the period are included for the portion of the period during which they were outstanding.[60]

It is not immediately obvious why the fair value used should be the average for the reporting period rather than, for example, the value at balance sheet date or that on the date the instruments were issued, or the average for the period they were outstanding (if issued or lapsed in the period). The reason given is contained in paragraph 15 of Appendix II to FRS 14 – the development of the standard. This says, without further elaboration, that a period average best fits the objective of EPS as a past performance measure. That explanation seems quite clearly to rule out a year end or issue date price. However, in our view, a credible case could be made that an average price over the life of the instrument would be more relevant for instruments issued or lapsed in the year.

One practical problem of this requirement is that the average market price of ordinary shares for the reporting period may not be available. Examples would include a company only listed for part of the period, or an unlisted company giving voluntary disclosures. In such cases estimates of the market price would need to be made.

A further possible anomaly resulting from this approach surrounds partly paid shares, and is discussed below.

6.5.3 Partly paid shares

As noted at 3 above, shares issued in partly paid form are to be included in the *basic* EPS as a fraction of a share, based on dividend participation. As regards *diluted* EPS they are to be treated, to the extent that they are not entitled to participate in dividends, as the equivalent of options or warrants.[61] The mechanics of this treatment are not spelt out in the standard, but curiously the phrase 'treated as a fraction of an ordinary share' is not repeated. Whilst this could be read to mean that the remaining unpaid consideration is to be treated as the exercise price for options over *all* of the shares, the results would make little sense. The more sensible interpretation is that the unpaid capital should be viewed as the exercise price for options over the proportion of the shares *not* reflected in the basic EPS. This would mean that if the average share price for the period was the same as the total issue price, then no dilution would be reported. This gives rise to the somewhat counter-intuitive result that the additional number of shares (if any) to be included for diluted EPS will not just be a function of dividend participation, but also of the average share price for the period. An illustration of what the calculation would look like is as follows:

Example 23.10: Partly paid shares

Capital structure

Issued share capital as at 31 December 1998:
2,000,000 ordinary shares of 10p each

Issued on 1 January 1999:
500,000 part paid ordinary shares of 10p each. Full consideration of 50p per share (being fair value at 1 January 1999) paid up 50% on issue. Dividend participation 50% until fully paid. New shares remain part paid at 31 December 1999.

Average fair value of one ordinary share for the period 60p.

Trading results

Net profit attributable to ordinary shareholders for the year ended 31 December 1999: £100,000.

Computation of basic and diluted EPS

	Net profit attributable to ordinary shareholders £	Ordinary shares No	Per share Pence
Fully paid shares	100,000	2,000,000	
Partly paid shares (1)		250,000	
Basic EPS	100,000	2,250,000	4.44
Dilutive effect of partly paid shares (2)		41,667	
Diluted EPS	100,000	2,291,667	4.36

(1) 50% dividend rights for 500,000 shares.

(2) Outstanding consideration of £125,000 (500,000 x 25p), using fair value of 60p this equates to 208,333 shares, hence the number of dilutive shares deemed issued for free is 41,667 (250,000-208,333).

The example assumes the fair value of the shares over the year is higher than the issue price, which explains why some extra shares fall to be included in the diluted EPS. If the average fair value remained at the issue price of 50p then no additional shares would be included for diluted EPS.

6.5.4 Employee share incentive plans

The standard comments that share option and other incentive schemes are an increasingly common feature of employee remuneration, and acknowledges that they come in many forms.[62] However, for diluted EPS purposes employee share schemes are divided into two categories:

- long-term incentive schemes – where awards are based on performance criteria; and

- any other schemes.

Schemes in the first category are to be treated as contingently issuable shares (see 6.5.5 below). This gives rise to an apparent paradox relating to shares held by an employee share ownership plan (ESOP) trust. The rules for, and indeed the title, 'contingently issuable shares' clearly refers to shares which do not exist at the balance sheet date, but may be issued subsequently.[63] Shares held by an ESOP to satisfy employee options are obviously already in issue, so a strict reading of the standard would imply that these have no dilutive impact. In our view this makes little sense, and does not seem to be what the standard setters intended. A sensible interpretation would be to consider the vesting of ESOP shares (and hence ceasing to be treated as cancelled for EPS purposes[64]) as an issue for calculating diluted EPS.

Those in the second category are to be treated as options (see 6.5.2 above). They should be regarded as outstanding from the grant date, even if they vest, and hence can be realised by the employees, at some later date.[65] An example would be an unexpired loyalty period. This means that some shares may be included in diluted EPS which never, in fact, get issued to employees because they fail to remain with the company for this period. Whilst this requirement is clear, it sits rather awkwardly with the rules for contingently issuable shares which, as discussed at 6.5.5 below, tend to restrict the number of potential shares accounted for. Furthermore the proceeds figure to be used in calculating the dilution under such schemes should be increased by any UITF 17 cost which has yet to be charged to the profit and loss account. The standard provides an example of this latter point (Example 5), as follows:

Example 23.11: Share option scheme not related to performance

Company A has in place an employee share option scheme that awards share options to employees and their dependants on the basis of period of service with the company.

The provisions of the scheme are as follows at the 20X0 year-end.

Date of grant	1 January 20X0
Market price at grant date	£4.00
Exercise price of option	£2.50
Date of vesting	31 December 20X2
Number of shares under option	1 million

Applying UITF 17, the profit and loss account is charged with 50p per option in each of the three years 20X0-20X2.

Net profit for year 20X0	£1,200,000
Weighted average number of ordinary shares outstanding	5 million
Average fair value of an ordinary share during the year	£5.00
Assumed proceeds per option	£3.50 (exercise price of £2.50 and compensation cost attributable to future service, not yet recognised, of £1.00). Next year £3.00 (ie £2.50 plus 50p).

Computation of earnings per share

	per share	earnings	shares
Net profit for year 20X0		£1,200,000	
Weighted average shares outstanding for 20X0			5m
Basic earnings per share	24p		
Number of shares under option			1m
Number of shares that would have been issued at fair value: (1 million x £3.50) / £5.00			(0.7m)
Diluted earnings per share	22.6p	£1,200,000	5.3m

This example alludes to the fact that the dilutive effect of the options increases over the three years as the deemed proceeds on exercise of the options reduces. The computational impact of this increasing dilution can be illustrated as follows. Assuming the average share price remained constant for the remaining two years, the number of shares used in the diluted EPS calculation would increase as thus:

	20X1	20X2
Weighted average shares outstanding	5m	5m
Number of shares under option	1m	1m
Number of shares that would have been issued at fair value:		
20X1: (1 million x £3.00) / £5.00	(0.6m)	
20X2: (1 million x £2.50) / £5.00		(0.5m)
Number of shares for diluted EPS	5.4m	5.5m

Assuming constant net profit of £1.2m for these years, diluted EPS would fall to 22.2p in 20X1 and 21.8p in 20X2.

FRS 14 rationalises this escalating dilution as follows: 'Initially, dilution is less because part of the consideration consists of future services not yet received. It becomes greater, over time, as the entity's earnings reflect the benefits of having received those services.'[66] Given that this provision only applies to non-performance based share schemes, then any UITF 17 cost that is spread forward (rather than expensed immediately) must presumably relate to a loyalty period. In our view such a treatment under UITF 17 would be rare, as that abstract says, 'Where a further period of continued employment is required before the participants become unconditionally entitled to the shares, the period over which the cost is recognised should not normally include that period unless it is clear that the effect of the scheme is to reward services over the longer period.'[67]

6.5.5   *Contingently issuable shares*

Whereas SSAP 3 gave no guidance on contingently issuable shares, FRS 14 contains eight detailed paragraphs and a numerical worked example. The basic rule is that the number of contingently issuable shares to be included in the diluted EPS calculation is 'based on the number of shares that would be issuable if the end of the reporting period was the end of the contingency period'.[68] This requirement to look at the status of the contingency at the balance sheet date, rather than to consider the most likely outcome, seems to have the overall result of *reducing* the amount of dilution disclosed. Furthermore, these detailed rules on contingently issuable shares (which are contained in explanatory sections of the standard) are at odds with the more general requirement to 'give effect to *all* dilutive potential ordinary shares outstanding during the period'.[69]

Having introduced the basic rule for contingently issuable shares the standard goes on to explore it in more detail, and includes some briefly sketched narrative examples and one numerical worked example. The discussions cover three broad categories: earnings-based contingencies, share-price-based contingencies, and other contingencies. These are discussed in turn below.

A   *Earnings-based contingencies*

When the number of shares that could be issued depends on earnings, the basic rule above (i.e. how many shares would be issued if the reporting date was the end of the contingency period) is applied very strictly. In deciding how many shares should be included it is assumed that no more profits will be earned after the balance sheet date. This is a reversal of the line taken in FRED 14, which required a steady state extrapolation of earnings.[70] The narrative example given is 'if the number of shares to be issued depends on whether profits average £100,000 over a three-year period, the condition is expressed as in terms of a cumulative target of £300,000 over the three-year period. If, at the end of the first year, profits are £150,000, no additional shares are brought into the calculation.'[71] This example illustrates the new principle that a contingency which is expressed in terms of an average over a number of reporting periods should be treated as if it were a cumulative target over the entire period.

We do not agree that such a methodology gives the most meaningful EPS figure. A better approach, in our view, would have been to base the dilution on a reasonable assessment of the outcome of the contingency; this would also be more consistent with the treatment of other contingent forms of finance. For example if contingent consideration under an earn-out clause is payable in cash, FRS 7 requires the best estimate of the amount payable to be provided at its present value, with the result that EPS will bear interest on this amount as the discount unwinds. It would seem appropriate for diluted EPS similarly to reflect the likely dilution when the consideration is in the form of shares. Notwithstanding this, the rule for contingencies determined solely by an entity's earnings is now clear. However, the treatment of contingencies which are partly determined by earnings and partly by other criteria is less clear.

The standard only discusses earnings criteria based on *absolute* measures; in the example above a cumulative profit of £300,000. In our experience such criteria are rare. In practice criteria are often phrased in terms of *relative* performance against an external benchmark. Examples would be earnings growth targets of RPI plus 2% or EPS growth being in the top quartile of a group of competitors. For contingencies such as these it is impossible to establish an absolute target in order to ask whether it is met at the year end. For example, consider the earnings contingency in FRS 14, discussed above, to average profits of £100,000 over a three-year period. If this instead required the profits to be £100,000 rising in line with RPI, it would be impossible to express it as a cumulative hurdle. Until the end of the three year period the absolute level of profit required would be unknown; it would be more or less than £300,000 depending on the level of inflation or deflation over the period.

There would seem to be (at least) two different ways of interpreting the requirements of FRS 14 in such a scenario, each resulting in a different diluted EPS figure. One approach would be to consider such criteria as being 'based on a condition other than earnings or market price'. That would mean (as discussed under C below) that the number of shares brought into diluted EPS would be based on the status of the condition at the balance sheet date.[72] So, if the target was earnings growth of RPI plus 2% over three years and at the end of year one earnings growth had been RPI plus 3%, then all the shares would be included for diluted EPS. An alternative approach would be to regard it as an earnings-based contingency and make an assumption as to future RPI movements over the contingency period. This would allow a cumulative hurdle to be calculated and compared with actual earnings to date. Given the lack of clarity in the standard, it seems likely that either of the above approaches may be selected in practice.

B   Share-price-based contingencies

The provisions here are more straightforward. The share price used to compute how many, if any, shares to bring in to the calculation is 'the current market price at the end of the current reporting period or the average over a specified period, depending on the terms of the underlying contract'.[73] However, in cases where the quantity of shares is derived from a period average share price, it is not clear how 'the average over a specified period' should be interpreted. At any time within the contingency period the choice would be between average to date and final average if the share price remained at its current level. Consistency with the rules for earnings-based contingencies would imply that the former is required by the standard.

There is a specific rule for deferred consideration agreements, where a fixed monetary sum is to be satisfied by a variable quantity of shares. In such cases the market price at the balance sheet date is to be used.[74]

C   *Other contingencies*

The requirement regarding contingencies not driven by earnings or share price is 'shares are included on the assumption that the current status of the condition at the end of the reporting period will remain unchanged until the end of the contingency period.'[75]

The standard illustrates the 'other contingency' rules as follows: 'if a further issue of shares is generated on the opening of the tenth new retail outlet and at the year end only five have been opened, no contingently issuable shares are included in the diluted earnings per share computation.'[76] As is specifically required for earnings-based contingencies discussed above, it would seem that such conditions are always deemed to be expressed as a cumulative hurdle which may or may not be met by the balance sheet date. Accordingly, the required treatment would be the same if the condition had been expressed in terms of achieving a certain average annual level of shop openings. Once again it seems inappropriate to us that management plans for a shop opening programme would be disregarded for EPS purposes when such estimates would be essential in other accounting areas, for example to determine the reasonable estimates required by FRS 7 or UITF 17, or to support any deferred tax computations.

7   PRESENTATION, RESTATEMENT AND DISCLOSURE

7.1   Presentation

Disclosure of basic and diluted EPS is required on the face of the profit and loss account, with equal prominence, for each class of ordinary shares that has a different right to share in the profit for the period.[77] In practice however, more than one class of ordinary share is rarely seen. Diluted EPS must always be disclosed, even when the basic EPS is a loss per share, although as discussed at 6.4 above in most cases these will be the same.[78] The specific exemption in SSAP 3 on grounds of materiality (dilution less than 5%) has been dropped in FRS 14. Comparative figures are to be given in all cases. Appendix II to the standard reveals the reason for removing the 5% test, by reiterating that EPS under FRS 14 is a past performance measure rather than a warning signal for future dilution.[79] This logic also explains the requirement to give basic and diluted EPS for all periods presented, hence showing trends over time. An example of profit and loss account presentation is as follows:

Extract 23.29: Hammerson plc (1998)

Consolidated Profit and Loss Account [extract]

	Notes	**1998**	*1997*
Earnings per share	*10*	**23.1p**	15.8p
Diluted earnings per share	*10*	**23.1p**	15.8p

10   EARNINGS PER SHARE [extract]

In accordance with Financial Reporting Standard 14 Earnings per Share, earnings per share have been calculated on the profit for the financial year of £66.4m (1997: £45.0) and the weighted average number of shares in issue during the year ended 31 December 1998 of 287.2m (1997: 284.4m). Fully diluted earnings per share reflect the exercise of conversion rights relating to the convertible bonds and of options relating to shares.

The above illustrates a literal reading of the standard by presenting a separate line for each of basic and diluted EPS, even though the amounts are identical. Other companies have chosen to present one line in the profit and loss account, and amend the title accordingly.

Extract 23.30: Raglan Properties plc (1999)

Consolidated profit and loss account [extract]

	Note	**1999** **£000**	1998 £000
Retained profit for the year	20	**4,610**	3,390
Basic and diluted earnings per ordinary share	9	**4.05p**	3.27p

---

7.2   Restatement

FRS 14 contains requirements to restate prior periods' EPS for events that change the number of shares outstanding without a corresponding change in resources. Additionally it specifies circumstances when EPS should not be restated.

Basic and diluted EPS for all periods presented should be adjusted for:[80]

- events (other than the conversion of potential ordinary shares) which change the number of ordinary or potential ordinary shares without a corresponding change in resources (discussed at 4.3 above); and

■ the effects of business combinations that are accounted for as a merger under FRS 6 (discussed at 4.6 above).

No adjustment should be made:

■ to basic or diluted EPS when a share consolidation is combined with a special dividend where the overall commercial effect is that of a share repurchase at fair value[81] (discussed at 4.3.2 above);

■ to prior period diluted EPS for changes in the assumptions used or for the conversion of potential ordinary shares into ordinary shares;[82] and

■ to prior period diluted EPS as a result of a contingency period coming to an end without the conditions attaching to contingently issuable shares being met.[83]

FRS 14 also contains some rules for figures in any historical summary, which are the same as those previously contained in SSAP 3.

■ any restatement required by the rules noted above should be applied retrospectively to all figures in the historical summary, with the cumulative effect on EPS taken into account;[84]

■ restated figures are described as such and clearly distinguished from non-adjusted data;[85]

■ the same requirements for restatement and description should be applied to any dividend per share figures included in the summary;[86] and

■ any dividend cover figures presented should be based on the theoretical maximum dividend (i.e. after allowing for any further tax triggered by a distribution) rather than simply total earnings.[87]

It is not clear however, given that such summaries are voluntary and usually presented outside the accounts, what authority an accounting standard has regarding them.

7.3   Disclosure

7.3.1   *Components of the calculation*

For each class of ordinary share, disclosure is required, for both the basic and diluted EPS, of the numerators and denominators used in the calculations. The numerators are to be reconciled to the net profit or loss for the period (see, for example, Extract 23.23 at 6.2.1 above) and the denominators are to be reconciled to each other (see, for example, Extract 23.26 at 6.3.1 above).[88] Companies choosing to present additional EPS figures are required to reconcile these to those required by the standard and explain why the additional version is given. The reconciliation should list the items for which adjustment is being made, and disclose their individual effect on the calculation.[89] Presentation of additional EPS is discussed at 5.5 above.

7.3.2   Post year end share transactions

Changes in share capital which happen after the year end will fall into two categories, similar to adjusting and non-adjusting events under SSAP 17 *Accounting for post balance sheet events*. The first category comprises those transactions which change the number of shares outstanding without a corresponding change in resources (bonus issues, share consolidations etc). As described at 4.5 above such transactions occurring before the issue of the accounts will be incorporated in the EPS calculations for all periods presented. When the EPS calculations reflect such changes in the number of shares, that fact should be disclosed.[90] The second category will comprise any other transactions in ordinary shares or potential ordinary shares. Disclosure is required of a description of any such transactions when 'they are of such importance that non-disclosure would affect the ability of users of the financial statements to make proper evaluations and decisions.'[91] The standard gives the following examples of the types of transactions involved:[92]

(a)   the issue of shares for cash;

(b)   the issue of shares when the proceeds are used to repay debt or preference shares outstanding at the balance sheet date;

(c)   the redemption of ordinary shares;

(d)   the issue of potential ordinary shares;

(e)   the buy back of ordinary shares outstanding;

(f)   the conversion of potential ordinary shares, outstanding at the balance sheet date, into ordinary shares; and

(g)   the achievement of conditions that would result in the issue of contingently issuable shares.

It is not clear how these latter disclosures, which were not included in the exposure draft, help achieve the objective of a consistently calculated EPS as a measure of past performance. Furthermore, we are not sure that this requirement adds any more disclosure to that which would be required under SSAP 17. It seems the ASB must have in contemplation some post balance sheet events which do not affect users' ability to 'reach a proper understanding of the financial position' (the test in SSAP 17), but which do affect their ability to 'make proper evaluations and decisions'. Unfortunately the standard does not give any examples to illustrate the subtlety of this distinction.

7.3.3   Share consolidation with a special dividend

As discussed at 4.3.2 above, in certain circumstances no adjustment is made to prior periods' EPS when a share consolidation is combined with a special dividend. Where that is the case disclosure should be made of that fact.[93]

7.3.4 Potential ordinary shares

The standard notes that the terms and conditions of potential ordinary shares may determine whether they are dilutive, and if so the effect they will have on the figures used in the diluted EPS calculation. In such cases it encourages, but does not require, disclosure of those terms and conditions.[94]

8 COMPARISON WITH IASC AND US PRONOUNCEMENTS

8.1 IASC

In early 1990 a Steering Committee was set up by the IASC to begin work on developing an international standard on earnings per share. This project was then put on the back burner while the IASC was progressing its comparability/improvements project relating to its existing standards on other topics. However, while that latter project was coming to a close, the Steering Committee recommenced its business and produced a Statement of Principles which was approved by the IASC's Board in June 1994. In January 1996 an exposure draft, E52, was issued and the resulting standard IAS 33 – *Earnings Per Share* – was published in June 1997. IAS 33 is applicable for accounting periods beginning on or after 1 January 1998, with earlier application encouraged.

As indicated at 1 above, the requirements of FRS 14 are the same as those of IAS 33, with the following minor exceptions:

- IAS 33 limits its scope to earnings per share, whereas FRS 14 extends to other amounts per share (see 5.5.4 above).

- If additional EPS numbers are presented for components of profit which are not reported as line items in the profit and loss account, then IAS 33 requires a reconciliation between the component used and a line item which is reported. FRS 14 retains the pre-existing disclosure requirements regarding additional EPS numbers as required by FRS 3 (see 5.5 above);

- FRS 14 gives additional guidance in computing 'net profit from continuing operations' which is used as the control number for establishing whether potential ordinary shares are dilutive or not. IAS 33 does not need such guidance as that number can be computed from information disclosed in the profit and loss account under IAS 8;

- Under FRS 14 the normal requirement to restate prior periods' EPS following a share consolidation is not applied when the consolidation is combined with a special dividend. IAS 33 does not address the issue of such 'in substance share buy-backs';

- FRS 14 contains more detailed guidance on contingently issuable shares and employee share schemes. In particular the requirement to increase the proceeds on the exercise of employee options by any unamortised UITF 17 charge is not mentioned in IAS 33 (see 6.5.4 above); and

■   FRS 14 gives additional guidance in respect of historical summaries and the calculation of dividend cover.

8.2   US

Until recently the disclosure of earnings per share in the US was based on several statements issued by the American Institute of Certified Public Accountants (AICPA). The principal statement, APB Opinion No. 15 – *Earnings per Share* – was published in May 1969 and required the calculation of two earnings per share figures, the primary EPS and the fully diluted EPS.

In view of the work being carried out by the IASC, the FASB pursued a project concurrently with the IASC to help achieve international harmonisation in this area. As a result, the FASB issued SFAS 128 – *Earnings per Share* – in February 1997. SFAS 128 is applicable for interim and annual accounting periods ending after 15 December 1997. Its requirements are discussed below.

As the FASB had been working closely with the IASC, the requirements of SFAS 128 are similar to those in the international equivalent, IAS 33 (see 8.1 above) and are therefore similar to the requirements of FRS 14. There are, however, the following differences:

■   Basic EPS and diluted EPS are to be given, based not only on net income but also on income from continuing operations.[95]

■   The effect that has been given to preferred dividends in arriving at income available to common stockholders is to be disclosed.[96]

■   Securities that could potentially dilute basic EPS in the future that were not included in the computation of diluted EPS because to do so would be antidilutive are to be disclosed.[97]

■   Companies that report a discontinued operation, an extraordinary item, or the cumulative effect of an accounting change in the period have to disclose the basic EPS and fully diluted EPS amounts for those line items either on the face of the income statement or in the notes to the accounts.[98]

■   More detailed requirements are given in respect of certain securities for the purposes of computing diluted EPS, such as stock-based compensation arrangements, written put options and purchased options relating to the company's own stock, and contracts that may be settled in stock or cash.[99]

■   General guidelines are included in respect of contingently issuable shares, with an example given in Illustration 3 in Appendix C to the standard.[100]

■   Greater computational guidance is given in Appendix A, which is to be regarded as an integral part of the standard. This is supplemented by a number of illustrations, some of which are effectively reproduced in FRS 14. In addition to Illustration 3 referred to above, there are also illustrations on the 'two class method' of computing basic EPS where an entity has more than one class of nonconvertible securities, the effect on diluted EPS of securities of a subsidiary, and the application of the treasury stock method for stock appreciation rights and other variable stock option award plans.[101]

9   CONCLUSION

In our view ratios for financial analysis, like EPS, do not properly fall within the remit of accounting standard setters. Companies use their annual report and accounts to communicate with shareholders on a variety of issues, many of which are supplementary to giving a true and fair view of profit for the period and the state of affairs at the balance sheet date. A widespread practice of giving information is not, of itself, sufficient grounds for regulators to start specifying computational methods. Many companies frequently disclose other financial analysis statistics, such as return on capital and gearing, yet (thankfully) there seems no impetus for accounting standards on these. Indeed the stated view of the ASB that 'it is not possible to distil the performance of a complex organisation into a single measure'[102] sits rather uneasily with an accounting standard requiring companies to do just that (or two such measures if one counts the diluted EPS).

The case for international harmonisation is similarly a nebulous one. It is true that FRS 14 and IAS 33 prescribe virtually identical denominators for the EPS calculation. However, given the potentially wide ranging GAAP differences affecting the numerator it is hard to see what is achieved by such harmonisation.

As regards the content of FRS 14, most of its provisions are not unreasonable and should prove workable for companies. It is a shame, however, that some of the more complex issues (particularly contingently issuable shares) were not more thoroughly field tested in a UK context, which may have helped remove some of the difficulties discussed earlier.

References

1 FRS 14, *Earnings per share*, ASB, October 1998, para. 1.
2 *Ibid.*, para 3.
3 *Ibid.*, para 4.
4 *Ibid.*, para 8.
5 *Ibid.*, para 9.
6 *Ibid.*, para 10.
7 *Ibid.*, para 13.
8 *Ibid.*, para 19.
9 *Ibid.*, para 16.
10 *Ibid.*, para 17.
11 *Ibid.*, para 17.
12 *Ibid.*, para 20.
13 *Ibid.*, para 14.
14 *Ibid.*, para. 21.
15 *Ibid.*, para. 63.
16 *Ibid.*, para. 22.
17 *Ibid.*, para. 77.
18 *Ibid.*, para. 76.
19 *Ibid.*, para. 63.
20 *Ibid.*, para. 26.
21 *Ibid.*, para. 24.
22 *Ibid.*, para. 63.
23 *Ibid.*, para. 24.
24 *Ibid.*, para. 24.
25 FRS 5, *Reporting the substance of transactions*, ASB, April 1994, para. 14.
26 FRS 14, para. 24.
27 *Ibid.*, para. 62.
28 *Ibid.*, para. 21.
29 *Ibid.*, para. 63.
30 *Ibid.*, para. 18.
31 FRS 2, *Accounting for subsidiary undertakings*, ASB, July 1992, para. 45.
32 FRS 14, para. 18.
33 *Ibid.*, para. 76.
34 *Ibid.*, paras. 10 and 11.
35 *Ibid.*, para. 12.
36 *Ibid.*, para. 13.
37 FRS 3, para. 25.
38 FRS 14, para. 74.
39 *Ibid.*, para. 73.
40 *Ibid.*, para. 74.
41 *Ibid.*, para. 8.
42 *Ibid.*, para. 2.
43 *Ibid.*, para. 69.
44 *Ibid.*, para. 29.
45 *Ibid.*, para. 53.
46 *Ibid.*, para. 55.
47 *Ibid.*, para. 31 and 32.
48 *Ibid.*, para. 31.
49 *Ibid.*, para. 32.
50 *Ibid.*, para. 61.
51 *Ibid.*, para. 56.
52 *Ibid.*, para. 60.
53 *Ibid.*, para. 59.
54 *Ibid.*, Appendix 1, para. 17.

55 *Ibid.*, Appendix 1, para. 19.
56 FRS 14, para. 70.
57 *Ibid.*, para. 56.
58 *Ibid.*, para. 35.
59 *Ibid.*, para. 36.
60 *Ibid.*, para. 62.
61 *Ibid.*, para. 34.
62 *Ibid.*, para. 39.
63 *Ibid.*, para. 46.
64 *Ibid.*, para. 16.
65 *Ibid.*, para. 41.
66 *Ibid.*, para. 42.
67 UITF 17, para 13(d).
68 FRS 14, para. 46.
69 *Ibid.*, para. 29.
70 FRED 16 Supplement, para. 41D
71 FRS 14, para. 46.
72 *Ibid.*, para. 49.
73 *Ibid.*, para. 47.
74 *Ibid.*, para. 48.
75 *Ibid.*, para. 49.
76 *Ibid.*, para. 49.
77 *Ibid.*, para. 69.
78 *Ibid.*, para. 70.
79 *Ibid.*, Appendix 1, para. 24.
80 FRS 14, para. 63.
81 *Ibid.*, para. 64.
82 *Ibid.*, para. 65.
83 *Ibid.*, para. 52.
84 *Ibid.*, para. 76.
85 *Ibid.*, para. 76.
86 *Ibid.*, para. 77.
87 *Ibid.*, para. 78.
88 *Ibid.*, para. 71.
89 *Ibid.*, para. 74.
90 *Ibid.*, para. 63.
91 *Ibid.*, para. 66.
92 *Ibid.*, para. 67.
93 *Ibid.*, para. 64.
94 *Ibid.*, para. 72.
95 SFAS 128, *Earnings per share*, FASB, February 1997, para. 36.
96 *Ibid.*, para. 40.
97 *Ibid.*
98 *Ibid.*, para. 37.
99 *Ibid.*, paras. 20-25 and 29.
100 *Ibid.*, paras. 31-34.
101 *Ibid.*, Appendix C, Illustrations 6-8.
102 FRS 3, para. 52.

Chapter 24   Post balance sheet events

1 THE DEVELOPMENT OF ACCOUNTING FOR POST BALANCE SHEET EVENTS

1.1 Introduction

A 'post balance sheet event' is defined by SSAP 17 – *Accounting for post balance sheet events* – as 'those events, both favourable and unfavourable, which occur between the balance sheet date and the date on which the financial statements are approved by the board of directors'.[1] This definition, therefore, incorporates all events occurring between those dates – irrespective of whether or not they relate to conditions which existed at the balance sheet date. Consequently, the principal issue to be resolved is which post balance sheet events should be reflected in the financial statements?

Since the financial statements of an entity purport to present, inter alia, its financial position at the balance sheet date, it is clear that the statements should be adjusted for all post balance sheet events which offer greater clarity of conditions that existed at the balance sheet date. However, the application of the prudence concept might take this further and suggest that *all* post balance sheet events which adversely affect the value of assets and liabilities should be reflected in financial statements – even if they relate to conditions which arise subsequent to the balance sheet date. Whether provisions should be made will depend on the particular circumstances and the requirements of more relevant accounting standards; in particular, the recently issued FRS 11 – *Impairment of Fixed Assets and Goodwill* – and FRS 12 – *Provisions, Contingent Assets and Contingent Liabilities*. These standards are discussed in Chapters 10 and 25 respectively.

In addition to the above, there has sometimes been a practice of manipulating the balance sheet by going outside the normal trading pattern of the business on a short-term basis in order to display a more favourable financial position. This has been done by either delaying or bringing forward specific transactions or by entering into transactions which are reversed shortly after the balance sheet date. The term used to cover such practices is 'window dressing'.

1.2   ICAEW Recommendation N17

In October 1957, the ICAEW issued Recommendation N17 'Events occurring after the balance sheet date'. This discussed the treatment of post balance sheet events and gave examples of how specific items should be treated.

N17 stated that events which are known to have occurred after the balance sheet date should not be reflected in the financial statements unless either:

(a)   they assist in forming an opinion as to the amount properly attributable, in the conditions on the balance sheet date, to any item the amount of which was subject to uncertainty on that date; or

(b)   they arise from legislation affecting items in the accounts, for example changes in taxation, or are required by law to be shown in the accounts, for example appropriations and proposed appropriations of profit.[2]

The Recommendation[3] discussed the realisation of certain assets and liabilities subsequent to the balance sheet and how consideration should be given to additional evidence received upon realisation of those assets and liabilities.

It also stated that there may be events occurring after the balance sheet date which should be excluded from the financial statements but may be of such importance to shareholders that they would need to be disclosed in some other way. Examples given of such events were the disposal of a significant part of a business or a profit or loss, either capital or revenue, which would have a considerable influence on 'the financial resources of the business'.[4]

1.3   ED 22

Despite the recommendations in N17, a variety of disclosures continued to be adopted by businesses and some confusion remained as to what represented events that required disclosure to shareholders and how events that had a significant effect on a business's continuing existence should be reflected. This led to the ASC issuing ED 22 – *Accounting for post balance sheet events* – in February 1978.

ED 22 differentiated between 'adjusting events' and 'non-adjusting events' and gave examples of each.[5] It explained that no separate disclosure was required for adjusting events as they merely gave additional evidence in support of items in financial statements, but non-adjusting events needed to be disclosed where their materiality would mean that not to do so would result in the financial statements presenting a misleading financial position. ED 22 stated that disclosure should be made of non-adjusting events which:

'(a) do not affect the condition of assets or liabilities at the balance sheet date, but do represent abnormal changes to them since that date; or

(b) do not relate to the financial position at the balance sheet date, but are of such importance that their non-disclosure would affect the ability of the users of the financial statements to make proper evaluations.'[6]

ED 22 clarified the date up to which post balance sheet events should be taken into account for inclusion in the financial statements.[7]

1.4 SSAP 17

In general the contents of ED 22 were supported by those who commented on it. However, concern was expressed that no guidance was given on what to do when the going concern concept was questioned by a post balance sheet event, which was defined as a non-adjusting event in the ED. In addition, the ASC was forced to react to increasing adverse opinion about the practice of window dressing, including pressure from the government of the day.

These problems were therefore dealt with when SSAP 17 – *Accounting for post balance sheet events* – was issued in August 1980. The detailed provisions of the standard are discussed at 2 below.

2 REQUIREMENTS OF SSAP 17

2.1 Definitions

As stated in 1.1 above, SSAP 17 defines post balance sheet events as 'those events, both favourable and unfavourable, which occur between the balance sheet date and the date on which the financial statements are approved by the board of directors'.[8]

This therefore includes events that provide additional evidence as to conditions which existed at the balance sheet date and those that do not.

Adjusting events are 'post balance sheet events which provide additional evidence of conditions existing at the balance sheet date. They include events which because of statutory or conventional requirements are reflected in the financial statements.'[9]

Examples given of events normally classified as adjusting are as follows:[10]

(a) the subsequent determination of the purchase price or the sales proceeds of fixed assets purchased or sold before the year end;

(b) a valuation of property which indicates a permanent diminution in value of the asset at the balance sheet date;

(c) the receipt of information, such as financial statements of an unlisted company, which provides evidence of a permanent diminution in value of a long-term investment;

(d)   the sale of stock after the balance sheet date showing that the estimate of net realisable value was incorrect;

(e)   the discovery of evidence showing that estimates of accrued profit on a long-term contract were inaccurate;

(f)   a trade debtor going into liquidation or receivership;

(g)   the declaration of dividends by subsidiaries and associated companies for periods prior to the balance sheet date;

(h)   a change in taxation rates applicable to periods before the balance sheet date;

(i)   the receipt of insurance claims which were in the process of negotiation at the balance sheet date; and

(j)   the discovery of significant errors or frauds which show that the financial statements were misstated.

The standard states that non-adjusting events are 'post balance sheet events which concern conditions which did not exist at the balance sheet date'.[11]

The appendix to the standard gives examples of items which would usually be classified as non-adjusting events.[12] These include:

(a)   mergers and acquisitions;

(b)   reconstructions and proposed reconstructions;

(c)   the issue of shares and debentures;

(d)   the purchase or disposal of fixed assets and investments;

(e)   the loss of fixed assets or stocks due to a catastrophe such as a fire or a flood;

(f)   the opening of new trading activities or extension of existing trading activities;

(g)   the closing of a significant part of trading activities if this was not foreseen at the balance sheet date;

(h)   a decrease in the value of property and investments held as fixed assets, if it can be shown that the decline took place subsequent to the balance sheet date;

(i)   changes in foreign currency exchange rates;

(j)   government action, such as nationalisation;

(k)   strikes and other labour disputes; and

(l)   the augmentation of pension benefits.

2.2   Events requiring adjustment

SSAP 17 requires that the financial statements be adjusted to take account of:

(a)   an adjusting event; or

(b)   a post balance sheet event which indicates that the application of the going concern concept to the whole or a material part of the company is no longer appropriate.[13] This could include a deterioration of trading results and the financial position, or the refusal of the bank to continue overdraft facilities.

2.3   Events not requiring adjustment but requiring disclosure

The standard states that an event of this type should be disclosed where:

'(a)   it is a non-adjusting event of such materiality that its non-disclosure would affect the ability of the users of financial statements to reach a proper understanding of the financial position; or

(b)   it is the reversal or maturity after the year end of a transaction entered into before the year end, the substance of which was primarily to alter the appearance of the company's balance sheet.'[14] Such alterations include those commonly known as 'window dressing' (see 3.5 below).

The ambiguity which renders SSAP 17 relatively meaningless in the case of (a) above is the *date* as at which the financial position is to be understood by the users. If it is the balance sheet date (which is what the law requires), then non-adjusting events need never be disclosed, since it is difficult to see how the financial statements could ever fail to give a true and fair view of the year end position because of the absence of such disclosure. What the standard's requirements in this area boil down to, therefore, is to highlight those major non-adjusting post balance sheet events which have resulted in the financial position at the date of approval being significantly different from that portrayed by the balance sheet.

The non-adjusting events which appear most regularly in financial statements are possibly the acquisition/disposal of a fixed asset, normally an investment in a subsidiary or a business, subsequent to the balance sheet date. Examples of disclosure in such situations are shown in the following extracts:

Extract 24.1: British American Tobacco p.l.c. (1998)

25   Post balance sheet event - proposed merger with Rothmans International

On 11 January 1999 it was announced that British American Tobacco, Richemont and Rembrandt had reached agreement on the terms of a proposed merger of British American Tobacco and Rothmans International. Under the terms of the agreement, British American Tobacco will issue ordinary shares and convertible redeemable preference shares to a company jointly owned by Richemont and Rembrandt. On a fully diluted basis, the new shares will account for approximately 35 per cent of the enlarged British American Tobacco Group, 25 per cent in ordinary shares and 10 per cent in convertible preference shares. Richemont and Rembrandt have agreed to restrict their voting rights to a maximum 25 per cent.

Based on British American Tobacco's share price of 541 pence per share at the close of business on 8 January 1999, and before taking account of the value attributable to the fact that the convertible preference shares can be redeemed for cash at a premium in due course, the new shares have a value of £4.6 billion. The transaction will be accounted for as an acquisition giving rise to goodwill of approximately £5 billion.

The proposed merger is subject to relevant regulatory consents and shareholder approvals. A circular containing notice convening an Extraordinary General Meeting and giving further information on the merger, is being sent to shareholders during March 1999.

Extract 24.2: Friends' Provident Life Office (1998)

33.   Post Balance Sheet Event - Friends Ivory & Sime plc

On 12 February 1999 Friends Ivory & Sime plc purchased the entire issued share capital of each of London and Manchester (Portfolio Management) Limited and London and Manchester Property Asset Management Limited, the two wholly owned subsidiaries of London and Manchester Group plc which undertake the asset management activities for that Group.

The initial consideration for the sale amounted to £35m which was satisfied by the issue to London and Manchester Group plc of 12,631,579 ordinary shares in Friends Ivory & Sime plc with a market value of £18m and subordinated loan totalling £17m. The subordinated loan carries interest at 2% over 6 month libor and is repayable not later than 31 December 2006.

In addition, deferred consideration of up to £5m is payable dependent on the extent to which the revenues attributable to the businesses sold exceed £6.5m in the year to 31 December 1999. For the maximum deferred consideration of £5m to become payable, revenues of at least £7m will need to be generated.

Extract 24.3: Hepworth PLC (1998)

27   Subsequent events

Hepworth Building Products has signed a conditional contract to acquire Naylor Drainage Limited and Naylor Plastics Limited ("the Naylor companies"). The acquisition is conditional, inter alia, on obtaining clearance from the Office of Fair Trading, which is in progress. £1.5m cash is payable on completion and the Naylor companies are expected to have net debt of £13.5m and net assets of £2.7m before applying Group policies. In 1998 the reported turnover and operating profit of the Naylor companies were £16.7m and £1.6m respectively.

On 11th March 1999 Hepworth Home Products sold the business and certain assets of Henderson Hardware Limited for £4.2m cash. The turnover and operating profit from this business in 1998 were £7.3m and £0.6m respectively. After charging goodwill, previously written off to reserves, neither profit nor loss is expected as a result of this sale.

Extract 24.4: Scapa Group plc (1999)

24 Post balance sheet event

In a circular to shareholders dated 14 April 1999 Scapa Group announced the disposal of the paper machine clothing, paper rolls and industrial businesses to J M Voith AG for £329m payable on completion. The sales price is based on the purchaser acquiring a debt and cash free business. The deal, approved by shareholders at an Extraordinary General Meeting on 5 May 1999, is conditional on completion approvals and is expected to be completed at the end of June.

The proceeds of £329m will be increased or reduced by the net amount of cash and borrowings left within the businesses at the date of completion. Goodwill totalling £37.9m previously written off to reserves will be reflected in the profit and loss account following completion. Taxation and other costs relating to the disposal are estimated by the Directors at £55m.

In order to facilitate the overall transaction, Scapa Dryer Fabrics Inc (which is a party to a number of asbestos litigation claims in the US, see note 23) has given certain undertakings regarding the use of the proceeds of sale of its businesses (estimated to be in the region of £25m), including not to distribute the proceeds for two years. The Board believes that the likelihood of any significant liabilities accruing to the Group from this litigation is remote.

The combined profit and loss accounts of the businesses being sold for the years ended 31 March, 1998 and 1999 are as follows:

	1999 £m	1998 £m
Turnover	**248.3**	263.3
Operating costs	**(211.3)**	(217.9)
Operating profit before exceptional items and allocated head office costs	**37.0**	45.4
Allocated head office costs	**(4.2)**	(4.4)
Operating profit	**32.8**	41.0

The combined net assets of the businesses as at 31 March 1998 and 1999 are as follows:

	31 March 1999 £m	31 March 1998 £m
Tangible fixed assets	169.2	164.9
Current assets		
Stocks	70.8	69.3
Debtors	73.6	71.9
Cash	12.9	7.7
	157.3	148.9
Creditors: amounts falling due within one year		
Borrowings	(10.3)	(2.5)
Creditors	(37.3)	(38.2)
	(47.6)	(40.7)
Net current assets	109.7	108.2
Total current assets less current liabilities	278.9	273.1
Creditors: amounts falling due after more than one year		
Borrowings	(45.5)	(50.1)
Creditors	(1.0)	(1.0)
	(46.5)	(51.1)
Provisions for liabilities and charges	(2.7)	(11.0)
Deferred income		
Government grants	(0.6)	(0.7)
Net assets before minority interests	229.1	210.3
Minority interests	(2.2)	(2.1)
Net assets	226.9	208.2
Net assets excluding debt and cash	269.8	253.1

Extract 24.5: The Greenalls Group plc (1998)

25   PROPOSED SALE OF INN PARTNERSHIP

The Group has announced the proposed disposal of Inn Partnership, subject to Shareholders' approval, for a cash consideration of £370m. The approval of Shareholders will be sought at an Extraordinary General Meeting of the Company on 11 January 1999.

The profit on disposal, based on the net book amount of assets being sold as at 25 September 1998, is £48.5m after disposal costs and before adjusting for goodwill previously written off. The disposal will also give rise to a corresponding increase in Shareholders' funds before payment of the special dividend. The loss on disposal, net of goodwill previously written off, will be approximately £1.3m. This will be accounted for as an exceptional item. In addition, the Directors expect to make a provision for reorganisation costs directly attributable to the disposal of £11.0m net of tax.

It is intended that £100m would be distributed to Shareholders by way of special dividend payable after 6 April 1999, subject to completion of the proposed disposal. It is also proposed that in connection with the payment of the special dividend, a subdivision and consolidation of the Ordinary share capital will be carried out, primarily to maintain comparability of future and historical earnings per share, dividends per share and share price.

This transaction will be accounted for in the Accounts for the year ending 24 September 1999.

Extract 24.6: Cookson Group plc (1998)

34   Post balance sheet events

In February 1999, the Group disposed of Cookson Fibres, Inc. for a cash consideration of £93.0m ($153m). Cookson Fibres achieved operating profits of £10.3m in 1998. The disposal resulted in a loss of £61.3m, including £58.3m in respect of goodwill.

The sale of the Group's 45% interest in Zimco, a South African-based industrial group, was completed in February 1999 for a consideration of £3.4m. Zimco contributed £2.2m to the Group's operating profit in 1998. The transaction resulted in a loss of £9.0m, including £2.1m in respect of goodwill.

Information in respect of these disposals has been included in the notes to the accounts as discontinued operations both for 1998 and 1997. Information relating to 1997 for these two businesses, together with those sold or terminated in 1997 is shown as discontinued operations for that year.

It can be seen from the last two extracts that both companies expect to make a loss on disposal, after taking account of goodwill written off to reserves. An issue therefore arises as to whether provision should be made for such a loss. This is discussed at 3.4 below.

In disclosing information about such post balance sheet events some companies do so by providing proforma information, as illustrated below:

Extract 24.7: Amersham International plc (1997)

34   Post balance sheet event

Merger of Amersham Life Science and Pharmacia Biotech Subsequent to the balance sheet date, Amersham has entered into a conditional agreement with Pharmacia & Upjohn Inc. ('P&U') to merge Amersham Life Science with Pharmacia Biotech, the biotechnology supply business of P&U, forming a new Company, proposed to be named Amersham Pharmacia Biotech Limited ('Amersham Pharmacia Biotech').

Under the terms of the merger, Amersham and P&U will transfer their respective life science businesses to Amersham Pharmacia Biotech, of which Amersham will own 56% of the issued ordinary share capital and P&U will hold the remaining 45%. In addition, Amersham and P&U will receive US$61m (£37m) and US$50m (£31m) respectively of preference shares. Amersham and P&U will also, in effect, contribute US$89m (£55m) and US$52m (£32m) respectively of debt to the combined entity.

The merger of the two businesses will, for accounting purposes, be treated by Amersham as a disposal of a 45% minority interest in Amersham Life Science and an acquisition of a 55% controlling interest in Pharmacia Biotech.

The following unaudited *pro forma* statement of net assets of the enlarged Amersham Group is provided for illustrative purposes only. Its purpose is to illustrate the effect on the net assets and equity shareholders' funds of the Amersham Group of the merger of the two life science businesses.

	Amersham Group as at 31 March 1997 (audited) £m	Pharmacia Biotech as at 31 December 1996 (unaudited) £m	Adjustments £m	Pro forma £m
Fixed assets				
Intangible assets	1.3	–	–	1.3
Tangible assets	120.9	84.6	–	205.5
Investments	34.5	1.1	–	35.6
	156.7	85.7	–	242.4
Current assets				
Stocks	41.3	48.8	–	90.1
Debtors	100.5	75.3	–	175.8
Short term deposits and interest bearing investments	16.8	–	–	16.8
Cash at bank and in hand	9.5	12.4	(12.4)	9.5
	168.1	136.5	(12.4)	292.2
Creditors: amounts due within one year				
Loans	(16.4)	(61.7)	61.7	(16.4)
Other creditors	(83.5)	(86.8)	27.9	(142.4)
	(99.9)	(148.5)	89.6	(158.8)
Net current assets/(liabilities)	68.2	(12.0)	77.2	133.4
Total assets less current liabilities	224.9	73.7	77.2	375.8

Creditors: amounts falling due after more than one year				
Loans	(73.6)	(7.3)	(30.9)	(111.8)
Other creditors	(3.7)	(1.0)	–	(4.7)
	(77.3)	(8.3)	(30.9)	(116.5)
Provisions for liabilities and charges	(38.3)	(32.2)	–	(70.5)
Accruals and deferred income				
Investment grants	(4.8)	–	–	(4.8)
Total net assets	104.5	33.2	46.3	184.0
Minority interest	(1.8)	–	(42.6)	(44.4)
Equity shareholders' funds	102.7	33.2	3.7	139.6

Notes

1 The Pharmacia Biotech figures have been extracted from unaudited financial information for the year ended 31 December 1996 adjusted for UK GAAP and are stated before any fair value adjustments.

2 The adjustments represent certain assets and liabilities of Pharmacia Biotech retained by P&U, additional debt injected into Pharmacia Biotech prior to completion and the increase in minority interest.

3 Pharmacia Biotech's financial information has been translated into sterling at a rate of £1:SEK11.685, being the rate of exchange as at the close of business on 31 December 1996.

4 The *pro forma* balance sheet excludes any trading results or cash flows by Pharmacia Biotech after 31 December 1996 and Amersham Group after 31 March 1997 and is stated before transaction costs.

Extract 24.8: Guinness Peat Group plc (1998)

27 Subsequent event

On 17 February 1999, the Company announced the conditional sale by Kuvondo Limited, a wholly owned subsidiary, of 25,100,000 Tyndall Shares (then amounting to 9.9 per cent. of Tyndall's issued share capital) to RSA Overseas Holdings B.V. at a price of A$2.80 per share pursuant to a sale agreement ("the Kuvondo Sale Agreement"). That day Royal & Sun Alliance Australia Holdings also announced a cash offer for Tyndall at a price of A$2.80 per share, which values Tyndall's issued share capital at A$716 million (equivalent to £279 million) and the Group's aggregate shareholding in Tyndall at A$357 million (equivalent to £139 million) (the "RSA Offer"). The offer is conditional on a minimum acceptance level of 90 per cent (which Royal & Sun Alliance Australia Holdings may waive). Under the RSA Offer, Tyndall shareholders will retain the dividend for the year ended 31 December 1998 of A3.5 cents per Tyndall Share. GPG will also retain this dividend in respect of the Tyndall Shares to be sold under the Kuvondo Sale Agreement. The Kuvondo Sale Agreement will terminate if the RSA Offer has not become unconditional by 17 May 1999.

The Group has indicated that, in the absence of a higher offer and subject to the consent of Shareholders, it intends to accept the RSA Offer for its remaining 102,234,717 Tyndall Shares (amounting to 40.0 per cent of Tyndall's issued share capital). The directors estimate that the gain on the disposal of the Group's entire investment in Tyndall, after expenses, will be in excess of £90 million.

Owing to its size, the above proposed combined disposal is conditional upon the approval of Shareholders and an Extraordinary General Meeting will be held on 19 April to approve the proposal.

The statement below is intended to show the effect of the proposed disposal of Tyndall Shares on the net assets of the Group as if the disposal had been completed as at 31 December 1998. The statement is prepared for illustrative purposes only.

Pro forma statement of net assets showing effect of the proposed disposal of shares in Tyndall

	Group net assets at 31 December 1998 £000	Adjustments net assets of Tyndall Group £000	other (see note 2) £000	**Adjusted** **group** **net assets** **£000**
Fixed assets				
Tangible fixed assets	**3,266**	(2,596)	–	**670**
Land for development	**2,755**	–	–	**2,755**
Intangible assets	**612**	(238)	(374)(a)	**–**
Investments	**82,505**	(13,044)	–	**69,461**
Net assets of the Life assurance business	**56,099**	(56,099)	–	**–**
	145,237	(71,977)	(374)	**72,886**
Current assets				
Debtors: amounts falling due within one year	**16,269**	(6,977)	1,643(c)	**10,935**
Development work-in-progress	**2,981**	–	–	**2,981**
Investments	**10,341**	(541)	–	**9,800**
Cash at bank and in hand	**72,854**	(24,206)	138,408(b)	**187,056**
	102,445	(31,724)	140,051	**210,772**
Creditors: amounts falling due within one year				
Trade and other creditors	**(19,635)**	11,057	(1,643)(c)	**(10,221)**
Borrowings	**(2,931)**	1,106	–	**(1,825)**
Net current assets	**79,879**	(19,561)	138,408	**198,726**
Total assets less current liabilities	**225,116**	(91,538)	138,034	**271,612**

Creditors: amounts falling due after one year				
Trade and other creditors	**(891)**	783	–	**(108)**
Borrowings	**(11,263)**	9,954	–	**(1,309)**
	(12,154)	10,737	–	**(1,417)**
Provisions for liabilities and charges	**(3,221)**	800		**(2,421)**
Net assets	**209,741**	(80,001)	138,034	**267,774**
Minority interests	**(42,689)**	39,923	–	**(2,766)**
Shareholders' funds	**167,052**	(40,078)	138,034	**265,008**

Notes:

1. The figures for the net assets of the Tyndall Group have been derived from the consolidated balance sheet as at 31 December 1998.

2. The other adjustments comprise:

   (a) the elimination of capitalised goodwill arising from the acquisition of Tyndall Shares in 1998 (£0.4 million);

   (b) the estimated cash proceeds from the proposed disposal and the Kuvondo Sale Agreement of £138.4 million, based on a sale price of A$2.80 per share translated at £1:A$2.5694 (being the exchange rate on 22 March 1999), less estimated expenses; and

   (c) recognition of the dividend payable by Tyndall to GPG which had previously been eliminated on consolidation.

3. No account has been taken of trading or other transactions by the Group since 31 December 1998.

4. The expenses of the proposed disposal are estimated to be £355,000. No tax is expected to be payable by the Group in respect of the proposed disposal.

5. Goodwill previously written off to reserves in respect of the Tyndall Group amounts to £2,492,000. This goodwill will be charged to the profit and loss account following completion of the proposed disposal.

Extract 24.9: The McKechnie Group plc (1998)

26   Post balance sheet event

On 6 August 1998 the Group sold substantially all of its Australian and New Zealand interests for a cash consideration of £63.5m. The results of these businesses have been disclosed as Discontinued in the Consolidated profit and loss account.

The Pro-forma Group balance sheet as at 31 July 1998 adjusted to reflect the effect of the disposal had it occurred at that date is:

	Reported £m	Adjustments £m	Pro-forma £m
Fixed assets			
Tangible assets	165.8	(21.3)	144.5
Investments	4.0	–	4.0
	169.8	(21.3)	148.5
Current assets			
Stocks	75.9	(21.8)	54.1
Debtors	122.0	(24.2)	97.8
Cash at bank and in hand	28.0	49.9	77.9
	225.9	3.9	229.8
Creditors: amounts falling due within one year			
Short term borrowings	(38.8)	0.8	(38.0)
Other creditors	(163.1)	20.0	(143.1)
Net current assets	24.0	24.7	48.7
Total assets less current liabilities	193.8	3.4	197.2
Creditors: amounts falling due after more than one year			
Loans and other borrowings	(69.3)	9.8	(59.5)
Other creditors	(0.2)	–	(0.2)
Provisions for liabilities and charges	(0.2)	–	(0.2)
Net assets	124.1	13.2	137.3
Net borrowings	(80.1)	60.5	(19.6)
Gearing %	64.5		14.3

The disposal of these businesses has resulted in a profit on disposal of £13.2m before goodwill adjustment of £22.7m. A provision of £9.5m has been made in the accounts in respect of this transaction.

Examples of disclosures in respect of other types of non-adjusting events are shown in the following extracts:

Extract 24.10: British Airways Plc (1998)

40   Post balance sheet event

On May 12, 1999 euro 300 million (£196 million) 6.75 per cent guaranteed Non-voting Cumulative Preferred securities guaranteed by British Airways Plc were issued by British Airways Finance (Jersey) L.P., in which the general partner is British Airways Holdings Limited, a wholly owned subsidiary of British Airways Plc. The guarantee in relation to these securities places holders of these securities in an equivalent position to senior preference shareholders of British Airways Plc.

Extract 24.11: Premier Oil plc (1998)

25   **Post Balance Sheet Events**

Since the year end there have been three significant transactions:

a)   Arrangements for the funding of the Company's development commitments in Myanmar were concluded in March 1999. This financing will provide all of Premier's share of the estimated costs of the development which is expected to be finished in early 2000. Completion results in Premier receiving £77 million, of which £56 million relates to expenditure incurred prior to 31 December 1998. This expenditure was classified as fixed assets at 31 December 1998. The remaining estimated development expenditure will be financed by additional drawings under the facility. The financing is secured on the assets of Premier Petroleum Myanmar Limited (PPML), the Company's subsidiary in Myanmar, and on the shares of PPML and will be repaid out of the proceeds of gas sales. The lender's recourse is limited to the extent of a parent company guarantee of $10 million covering cost overruns prior to the completion of the development stage. The funding is by way of discounted zero coupon bonds with an interest accrual rate equivalent to LIBOR plus 550 basis points and has been raised by a joint venture company. In addition, the Company has agreed to the covenants and to the terms of the Senior Notes and the Corporate Credit Facility which are likely to increase net interest cost by around £1.2 million in a full year.

b)   On 31 January 1999 the Myanmar Oil and Gas Enterprise exercised its right to acquire a 15% share in the Yetagun development. This resulted in a cash receipt by Premier of £17.3 million, being a reimbursement of costs already incurred since the beginning of the development phase.

c)   Following completion of the joint venture with Shell in Pakistan, £11.3 million is receivable in 1999 in respect of working capital movements and capital expenditure in the period 1 January 1998 to 31 December 1998.

Extract 24.12: MDIS Group plc (1998)

27.   POST BALANCE SHEET EVENT

On 4 March 1999, the Group issued 19,780,220 ordinary shares and £6.0 million of loan notes in consideration for the termination of the existing lease and a subsequent new lease on the Group's UK headquarters building in Hemel Hempstead, reducing annual lease costs from £3.8 million to £1.4 million.

No account has been taken of this transaction in the 1998 results; net of provisions established in 1996, a book write-off of approximately £2.0 million will be reported as an exceptional item in 1999.

Extract 24.13: Town Centre Securities PLC (1998)

2.   Transfer of investment and reorganisation of share capital

In order to provide information to the shareholders the following note sets out certain supplemental proforma information, summarising the effects of the reorganisation. This information does not form part of the statutory accounts of the group or company and has not been audited.

On 3 September 1998 the company transferred its shareholding in Stylo plc to the shareholders of the company resulting in a reduction of £1,707,000 in share capital and £1,544,000 in share premium. The company's remaining share capital was then consolidated and subdivided into 123,404,369 ordinary shares of 25 pence each.

The company has transferred £3,251,000 to a special reserve account from its realised capital account and share premium account. This account shall be treated as representing an undistributable reserve of the company and may be used for the same purposes as if it were share premium account.

The investment in Stylo plc has been revalued at 30 June 1998 to reflect the market value at which it was subsequently transferred to shareholders. This has resulted in an exceptional loss of £2,592,000 arising during the year, which has been transferred to realised capital reserves.

Set out on page 25 are proforma balance sheets of the group at 30 June 1998 and 30 June 1997 to reflect the following adjustments:

   (i)   the transfer of the group's investment in Stylo plc to shareholders at a value of £3,151,000 based on the middle market price of a Stylo plc share of 35 pence on 1 September 1998 and the consequential reduction in share capital of £1,707,000 (1997 £1,794,000) and share premium account of £1,444,000 (1997 £1,357,000).

   (ii)   the reduction in share premium account of £100,000 in 1997 and 1998 in respect of the payment of estimated fees in connection with the transaction.

   (iii) the transfer of £3,251,000 to a special reserve comprising £3,151,000 from realised capital reserves and £100,000 from share premium account in the year ended 30 June 1998. For the year ended 30 June 1997 the transfer to special reserve of £3,251,000 comprises £1,186,000 from realised capital reserves, £1,965,000 from profit and loss account and £100,000 from share premium account.

   (iv)   the provision for and assumed write off of £158,000 in each year in respect of Advance Corporation Tax arising as a consequence of the transaction.

   (v)   the elimination of net dividends receivable from Stylo plc of £419,000 and £315,000 for the years ended 30 June 1998 and 30 June 1997 respectively.

   (vi)   the number of Town Centre Securities PLC shares in issue and net assets per share have been adjusted for the effect of the consolidation and subdivision of the company's share capital into new 25p ordinary shares.

Consolidated Proforma Balance Sheet

	Notes	1998 (Unaudited) (Restated)		1997 (Unaudited) (Restated)	
		£000	£000	£000	£000
Fixed assets					
Tangible assets		307,234		284,576	
Investments	(i)	927		1,012	
			308,161		285,588
Current assets					
Trading properties		291		5,467	
Listed investments		–		90	
Debtors		7,299		7,156	
		7,590		12,713	
Creditors (due within one year)					
Bank overdraft (secured)	(iv), (v)	10,912		6,045	
Loan capital (secured)		18		17	
Other creditors		21,213		18,477	
		32,143		24,539	
Net current liabilities			(24,553)		(11,826)
Total assets less current liabilities			283,608		273,762
Creditors (amounts due after more than one year)					
Loan capital (secured)			(111,845)		(112,935)
			171,763		160,827
Capital and reserves - equity interests					
Called up share capital	(i)		30,851		30,963
Share premium account	(i), (ii), (iii)		–		–
Special reserve	(iii)		3,251		3,251
Property revaluation surplus			101,895		97,502
Other reserves			395		358
Realised capital reserves	(iii)		1,512		–
Profit and loss account	(iv), (v)		33,859		29,023
Shareholders' funds			171,763		160,827
Number of shares in issue restated (000)	(vi)		123,404		123,138
Net asset per share restated	(vi)		139.2p		130.6p

Extract 24.14: Medeva plc (1998)

27   POST BALANCE SHEET EVENTS [extract]

On the 11th January 1999 Medeva signed an agreement with Connetics Corporation ("Connetics") to license *ConXn®* (recombinant human relaxin), a treatment for scleroderma, for development and exclusive marketing in Europe, and to provide Medeva with co-promotion rights to *ConXn®*, once developed by Connetics and approved, for a limited period in the USA. Under the terms of the agreement Medeva paid to Connetics an upfront payment of $4 million in cash in January 1999 and invested $4 million in Connetics' equity. Under the agreement Medeva will pay Connetics up to $17 million of staged payments linked to development and regulatory milestones. Medeva will also share Connetics' development costs, up to a capped limit estimated at $10m. The agreement makes provision for the approval of additional indications for the product in Europe. One-off payments of $5 million will be payable by Medeva to Connetics for each additional indication.

Extract 24.15: Marks and Spencer p.l.c. (1999)

31.   Post balance sheet events

On 28 April, the Group announced the closure of its Canadian operations. As a consequence, its subsidiary, Marks & Spencer Canada Inc, will cease to operate during the financial year ending 31 March 2000. The total cost of closure is estimated to be £25m, excluding goodwill of £24.4m previously written off to reserves.

On 10 May, the Group announced the rationalisation of its UK store management. The cost of this rationalisation is estimated to be £14m.

Extract 24.16: Pilkington plc (1999)

43   Post-balance sheet event

On 26th May 1999 the Group announced its plans to reorganise and streamline its automotive manufacturing operations in North America. This will involve the closure of a plant and the transfer of its production to two other existing facilities in North America. The programme is expected to involve exceptional restructuring costs of approximately £30 million, of which half are expected to be cash costs. No adjustment for this has been made in the financial statements.

The last two extracts illustrate examples of situations which in the past would normally have been dealt with as adjusting events on the basis that the directors had taken the decisions before the balance sheet date. However, as a result of the recognition rules contained in FRS 12, provision can no longer be made for such costs where the announcements are made post year-end. This issue is discussed in 4.1.2 of Chapter 25.

All of the above extracts disclose the information about the post balance sheet event in a note to the financial statements. Other companies have gone further by including a pro-forma column on the face of the balance sheet to illustrate the impact of the post balance sheet event as shown in the extracts below:

Extract 24.17: Geest PLC (1995)

Balance sheets
As at 30 December 1995

		Group		Company	
£millions	Pro forma (note 25) 1995	1995	1994	1995	1994
Fixed assets					
Tangible assets	**69.9**	**179.6**	183.5	**1.2**	1.5
Investments	**3.3**	**3.5**	2.4	**72.0**	41.0
	73.2	**183.1**	185.9	**73.2**	42.5
Current assets					
Stocks	**10.3**	**14.5**	16.6	**0.1**	0.1
Debtors	**45.5**	**69.9**	72.4	**49.2**	62.7
Cash at bank and short term deposits	**42.0**	**25.0**	33.5	**28.0**	29.6
	97.8	**109.4**	122.5	**77.3**	92.4
Creditors: due within one year					
Borrowings	–	**(18.8)**	(22.8)	**(15.7)**	(27.3)
Other creditors	**(75.7)**	**(98.7)**	(114.6)	**(30.9)**	(27.7)
Net current assets/(liabilities)	**22.1**	**(8.1)**	(14.9)	**30.7**	37.4
Total assets less current liabilities	**95.3**	**175.0**	171.0	**103.9**	79.9
Creditors: due after one year					
Borrowings	–	**(96.6)**	(87.7)	**(42.4)**	(12.8)
Other creditors	–	**(1.8)**	–	–	–
Provisions for liabilities and charges	**(9.2)**	**(9.5)**	(11.5)	**(0.1)**	(0.1)
Net assets	**86.1**	**67.1**	71.8	**61.4**	67.0
Capital and reserves					
Called up share capital	**3.6**	**3.6**	3.6	**3.6**	3.6
Share premium account	**12.6**	**12.6**	12.6	**12.6**	12.6
Revaluation reserve	**0.2**	**0.2**	0.2	–	–
Merger reserve	–	–	–	**14.5**	14.5
Profit and loss account	**68.9**	**49.9**	54.3	**30.7**	36.3
Equity shareholders' funds	**85.3**	**66.3**	70.7	**61.4**	67.0
Equity minority interests	**0.8**	**0.8**	1.1	–	–
	86.1	**67.1**	71.8	**61.4**	67.0

Statement of accounting policies [extract]

2   **Pro forma information** - On 9 January 1996 the disposal of the Group's Banana Sector was completed. In order to provide shareholders with additional information as to the financial impact of the disposal, the directors have included a pro forma consolidated balance sheet as at 30 December 1995. This has been prepared on the basis that both proceeds and costs were paid out on 30 December 1995. More information on the disposal is given in the financial review on page 14.

25   **Post balance sheet events**

On 9 January 1996, the sale of the Banana Sector was completed for a cash consideration of £92.3 million and the assumption of financing obligations attaching to Geest's two Island Class vessels, which amounted to £54.8 million as at 30 December 1995. In addition the consideration is to be increased (or decreased) by the amount of the adjusted net working capital of the Banana Sector at completion. The disposal is estimated to give rise to a £19.0 million increase in the Group's pro forma net assets as at 30 December 1995 to £86.1 million and is shown on page 26. After estimated disposal costs of £7.7 million, including those related to overhead reduction, this generates a pro forma exceptional profit of £18.2 million, the remaining £0.8 million being attributable to goodwill. The basis of preparation is detailed in the accounting policies note 2 on page 23.

Of the purchase consideration £5.0 million has been paid into an escrow account, amounts will only be released, to Geest, on registration of certain Costa Rican property.

Geest will continue to be the guarantor of the obligations under the two Island Class Charters whilst this guarantee remains outstanding. The Buyer has agreed to indemnify Geest against any liabilities in respect of the guarantee.

Extract 24.18: Costain Group plc (1995)

CONSOLIDATED BALANCE SHEET

As at 31 December

	Notes	1995 £m	1994 £m	Pro forma 1995 (unaudited) (note 30) £m
Fixed assets				
Tangible assets	13	94.0	192.4	94.0
Investments	14	30.1	74.6	30.1
		124.1	267.0	124.1
Current assets				
Stocks	15	34.7	42.7	34.7
Debtors				
– pension fund prepayment	16	55.5	60.0	55.5
– other	16	202.1	235.6	202.1
Cash at bank, monies on deposit and in hand	17	58.7	63.0	96.1
		351.0	401.3	388.4
Less Creditors: amounts falling due within one year				
Borrowings	18	124.3	36.4	30.1
Other creditors	19	265.9	300.3	265.9
		390.2	336.7	296.0
Net current (liabilities)/assets				
Due within one year		(108.9)	(14.3)	22.7
Due after one year		69.7	78.9	69.7
		(39.2)	64.6	92.4
Total assets less current liabilities		84.9	331.6	216.5
Less Creditors: amounts falling due after more than one year				
Borrowings	18	10.8	123.5	68.8
Other creditors	19	34.4	51.7	34.4
		45.2	175.2	103.2
Less provisions for liabilities and charges	20	70.5	54.7	70.5
Net (liabilities)/assets		(30.8)	101.7	42.8
Share capital and reserves				
Called up ordinary share capital	21	5.2	129.5	20.7
Share premium account	22	27.3	141.0	85.4
Revaluation reserve	22	–	22.7	–
Profit and loss account	22	(62.4)	(193.0)	(62.4)
Ordinary shareholders' funds		(29.9)	100.2	43.7
Equity minority interests		(0.9)	1.5	(0.9)
		(30.8)	101.7	42.8

30   Note to pro forma unaudited consolidated balance sheet

The proforma balance sheet of the Group is based on the audited consolidated balance sheet of the Group as at 31 December, 1995 adjusted in accordance with the notes set out below.

Since the balance sheet date, as detailed in note 27, the Group has completed an open offer to raise £73.6m (net of expenses). The directors consider the commercial impact significant enough to justify separate identification on a proforma basis as at 31 December 1995.

NOTE	Costain Group as at 31 December, 1995 £m	Net proceeds of the open offer £m (i)	New banking arrange- ments £m (ii)	Proforma Group (unaudited) £m
Fixed assets				
Tangible assets	94.0			94.0
Investments	30.1			30.1
	124.1			124.1
Current assets				
Stocks	34.7			34.7
Debtors				
– pension fund prepayment	55.5			55.5
– other	202.1			202.1
Cash at bank, monies on deposit and in hand	58.7	37.4		96.1
	351.0	37.4		388.4
Less Creditors: amounts falling due within one year				
Borrowings	124.3	(36.2)	(58.0)	30.1
Other creditors	265.9			265.9
	390.2	(36.2)	(58.0)	296.0
Net current (liabilities)/assets				
Due within one year	(108.9)	73.6	58.0	22.7
Due after one year	69.7			69.7
	(39.2)	73.6	58.0	92.4
Total assets less current liabilities	84.9	73.6	58.0	216.5
Less Creditors: amounts falling due after more than one year				
Borrowings	10.8		58.0	68.8
Other creditors	34.4			34.4
	45.2		58.0	103.2
Less provisions for liabilities and charges	70.5			70.5
Net (liabilities)/assets	(30.8)	73.6		42.8
Ordinary shareholders' funds	(29.9)	73.6		43.7
Equity minority interests	(0.9)			(0.9)
	(30.8)	73.6		42.8

NOTES:
(i)   The proceeds of the open offer are derived from gross proceeds of £77.6m less £4.0m of expenses.

(ii) £58.0m of short term borrowings have been converted into long term borrowings as part of the new banking arrangements.

(iii) The proforma takes no account of trading results since 1 January 1996.

27 Post balance sheet events

On 4 July 1996 the Group announced an underwritten open offer of ordinary shares, on the basis of 3 new shares for each existing share, to raise £73.6m (net of expenses). The open offer was approved by shareholders on 22 July 1996 and was completed on 31 July 1996.

On 1 July 1996, the Group completed the sale of Costain Industrial Services for £2.0m, paid in cash.

2.4   Disclosure requirements

As SSAP 17 requires consideration to be given to events which occur up to the date on which the financial statements are approved by the board of directors, then the standard requires that date to be disclosed.[15] This is normally done by dating the signature of the directors signing the balance sheet.

SSAP 17 states that for each post balance sheet event for which disclosure is required as per 2.3 above, the nature of the event and an estimate of its financial effect should be stated by way of note in financial statements. Where it is not practicable to estimate the financial effect, then a statement should be made explaining this fact.[16]

In addition, the Companies Act 1985 states that the directors' report must include 'particulars of any important events affecting the company or any of its subsidiary undertakings which have occurred since the end of the financial year'.[17] This links in with another Companies Act requirement to give an indication of likely future developments in the business of the company and of its subsidiary undertakings, i.e. the requirement to discuss the period after the balance sheet date falls under two headings. It is not primarily intended as an equivalent to the requirement of SSAP 17. The Companies Act requirement would seem to imply that both adjusting and non-adjusting events should be disclosed; however, in practice, only non-adjusting events will normally be included.

There is considerable diversity in the financial statement disclosure of post balance sheet events. Some companies disclose these events in both the directors' report and notes to the financial statements, whilst others provide disclosure in either the directors' report or notes.

The following extracts are examples of companies which have discussed post balance sheet events in the directors' report, but not in the notes to the financial statements:

Extract 24.19: Headlam Group plc (1998)

Report of the directors [extract]

Post balance sheet events

On 27 February 1999, the company acquired Tayrich Limited and its wholly owned subsidiary company, Joseph, Hamilton & Seaton Limited, from Interface Europe Limited for a cash consideration of £7.0 million funded from internal resources. Tayrich Limited, through its subsidiary, Joseph, Hamilton & Seaton Limited, is a contract floorcovering supplier based in Tamworth, Staffordshire. As at 3 January 1999, these companies had net assets of £1.9 million and, for the twelve month-period ended 3 January 1999, recorded a profit before taxation of £1.1 million on sales of £12.8 million.

Extract 24.20: Powell Duffryn plc (1997)

Directors' Report [extract]

Business development [extract]

Following the year end, Andrews Weatherfoil Ltd. was sold in May 1997. In the same month the Group entered into an agreement for the sale of its remaining terminal at Lemont, Chicago for US$8.0m, and the Group's 50% interest in Corrall-Montenay Ltd was sold for £9.6m. In June 1997 the Group acquired the business of Air Compressor Products USA Inc. for US$1.5m.

It would appear that these companies have taken the view that SSAP 17 does not require disclosure of these events as 'non-adjusting events', but that the Companies Act does. This highlights an important difference between a non-adjusting post balance sheet event under SSAP 17 (requiring disclosure in the notes), and a post balance sheet event under the Companies Act (requiring disclosure in the directors' report). Whilst SSAP 17 requires disclosure of non-adjusting events which are of such materiality that their non-disclosure 'would affect the ability of the users of financial statements to reach a proper understanding of the financial position'[18] of the company, the Companies Act has the much wider requirement for disclosure of 'any important events affecting the company or any of its subsidiaries which have occurred since the end of the financial year'.[19] One unusual example of such disclosure is shown in the following extract:

Extract 24.21: De La Rue plc (1999)

Directors' Report [extract]

Post balance sheet events

Mr Michael Pugh, managing director, Security Paper and Printing Division, retired from the Board on 6 April 1999. The Company announced on 13 April 1999 that Mr Richard Laing, finance director, had decided to leave the Company. Mr Laing will continue in his role until the end of August when he will resign as a director.

Although most companies would note changes to the directorate after the year end, this would not normally be done under the heading of 'post balance sheet events' but as part of the section of the directors' report dealing with directors and their interests.

Where it is considered that a post balance sheet event requires disclosure under both SSAP 17 and the Companies Act, then theoretically disclosure should be made both in the notes to the financial statements and in the directors' report. However, in our view it would suffice if disclosure is made in either the notes or the directors' report, with an appropriate cross reference in the other as illustrated in the following extract:

Extract 24.22: Daily Mail and General Trust plc (1998)

Directors' Report [extract]

Post Balance Sheet Events

On 30th September, 1998, the Group purchased Landmark Information Group which produces property related information for a payment of £7.2 million, together with deferred consideration, capped at £10 million.

Further details are given in the Review of Operations on page 24.

Notes to the Balance Sheet [extract]

38   Post Balance Sheet Events

    Details of material post balance sheet events are given in the Directors' Report on page 29.

---

3   PROBLEM AREAS

3.1   Reclassification of a non-adjusting event as adjusting in exceptional circumstances

The general guidance given in the Appendix to SSAP 17, states that 'in exceptional circumstances, to accord with the prudence concept, an adverse event which would normally be classified as non-adjusting may need to be reclassified as adjusting. In such circumstances, full disclosure of the adjustment would be required.'[20]

Whilst this may appear to be a concession by the ASC, following the comments raised during the exposure period of ED 22 that the definition of adjusting events was too narrow, it should be emphasised that the issue has been dealt with in the Appendix to SSAP 17, rather than in the main body of the standard. Consequently, three issues arise in the application of this provision: first, it has limited status, and therefore may result in inconsistency in its application; second, its application will negate the fundamental distinction between an adjusting and non-adjusting event; and, third, what is meant by the phrase 'in exceptional circumstances', as the Appendix fails to provide any guidance as to the circumstances under which the provision should be applied?

The argument always exists that if full details of the non-adjusting event are disclosed in the directors' report and/or notes to the financial statements, users will be able to make their own adjustments and evaluate the impact of the event for themselves. However, it is our view that this application of the prudence override should only be used when the loss due to the post balance sheet event is of such magnitude that its exclusion from the financial statements would render them completely misleading.

In the US, it has been long established practice that events which provide evidence with respect to conditions that did not exist at the balance sheet date, but arose subsequent to that date, should not result in adjustment of the financial statements. This is referred to in the above terms in SAS 1 – *Codification of Auditing Standards and Procedures*.[21] However, SAS 1 goes on to say that some of these events 'may be of such a nature that disclosure of them is required to keep the financial statements from being misleading. Occasionally such an event may be so significant that disclosure can best be made by supplementing the historical financial statements with pro forma financial data giving effect to the event as if it had occurred on the date of the balance sheet. It may be desirable to present pro forma statements, usually a balance sheet only, in columnar form on the face of the historical statements.'[22]

In the UK, companies seem to prefer to follow the US approach of presenting pro-forma financial statements, rather than adopt the more drastic step of reflecting the non-adjusting event in the financial statements. Extracts 24.7, 24.8, 24.9, 24.13, 24.17 and 24.18 at 2.3 above illustrate examples of companies which have produced pro-forma information.

3.2   The valuation of stock realised after the balance sheet date

The sale of stock after the balance sheet date is normally a good indicator of the realisable value at that date. However, there will be circumstances where there is evidence which suggests that a fall in realisable value took place because of conditions which did not exist at the balance sheet date.

The problem, therefore, is determining when the fall in realisable value occurred; did the fall in value occur as a result of circumstances which existed at the balance sheet date, or did it occur as a result of circumstances which arose subsequently? A decrease in price is merely a response to changing conditions, and so it is important that the reasons behind these changes are fully assessed.

This can be seen by reviewing some examples of changing conditions:

(a)   Price reductions due to a sudden increase in cheap imports

Whilst it could be argued that the 'dumping' of cheap imports after the balance sheet date is a condition that has arisen subsequent to that date, it is more likely to be the case that this will be a reaction to a condition which already existed, such as overproduction in other parts of the world. Thus, it might be appropriate in such a situation to be prudent and adjust the value of stock to its subsequent net realisable value.

(b)   Price reductions due to increased competition

It is common for companies to adjust the valuation of stocks when their fall in value is due to price reductions of competitors. This is because the reasons for price reductions will not have arisen overnight, but will normally have occurred over a period of time. For example, a competitor may have built up a comparative advantage because of investment in more efficient machinery in the past. Thus, it is usually appropriate for a company to adjust its valuation in stocks, as its past investment in technology will have been inferior to its competitors, and will not have arisen subsequent to the balance sheet date.

(c)   Price reductions due to the introduction of an improved competitive product

As an improved product introduced by competitors is unlikely to have been developed overnight it is correct to adjust the valuation of stock to its net realisable value following that introduction. This is because it reflects the company's failure to maintain its position in relation to technological improvements.

It can be seen in these cases that when a company is forced to reduce its prices after the balance sheet date, the fall provides additional evidence of conditions which existed at the balance sheet date. The reason for this is that, in general, the post balance sheet reduction in the realisable value of stock represents the culmination of conditions which existed over a relatively long period of time, with the result that the effects thereof would normally require adjustment in the financial statements. However, there will be certain types of stock for which there is clear evidence of a higher price available at the year end, when it would be inappropriate to write down the stock to reflect a subsequent decline. An example of this would be stocks for which there was a price on the international commodities market.

3.3   Long-term contracts

It is not uncommon for events to take place after the balance sheet date which provide further evidence as to the profitability of long-term work in progress. It is our view that *all* further evidence of eventual profit should be taken into account in determining the valuation of long-term contract balances.

3.4   Acquisitions and disposals of fixed assets

If at the balance sheet date there are fixed assets in the process of being bought or sold, where there has been a contract signed before the year end, but there is uncertainty as to the amounts involved, the subsequent realisation of those amounts should be treated as an adjusting event.

Clearly, it is appropriate to make provision for known losses on the disposal of fixed assets which were in the process of being sold at the year end; and this will normally be the case whether or not a contract had been signed before the balance sheet date. However, a difficulty arises in the case where the assets are sold at a profit. Should the gain on disposal be recognised in the profit and loss account as an adjusting event? The answer lies in determining whether or not the sale had been completed at the year end. It is unlikely that a sale would be complete if the sale price had yet to be determined; however, if this were the case then the sale should be recognised in the financial statements.

Disposals of fixed assets after the balance sheet date, but which were not contemplated at that date, are generally non-adjusting events. However, if a large loss results this might provide evidence of impairment, and so an adjustment to the net book value may be appropriate. Whether an impairment loss is recognised will depend on the application of the impairment review under FRS 11. Such reviews are generally carried out at the level of income-generating units, rather than individual assets. It may therefore be the case that no impairment loss needs to be recognised because the recoverable amount of the income generating unit is greater than the carrying value of the overall net assets attributable to the income generating unit. However, FRS 11 also states that 'the income stream of a fixed asset to be disposed of will be largely independent of the income stream of other assets. Such an asset therefore forms an income-generating unit of its own and does not belong to any other income-generating unit.'[23] As most of the income that the asset will be generating is its disposal proceeds, then this would suggest that if such proceeds are lower than the net book value then an impairment loss should be recognised. This issue is discussed more fully at 4.4 of Chapter 10.

Similar issues also arise where subsidiaries or businesses are in the course of being sold or terminated and companies expect to make a loss on disposal or termination. Whether or not companies should provide for such losses will depend on the particular circumstances and the requirements of other accounting standards.

As discussed further at 2.4 of Chapter 22, FRS 3 – *Reporting Financial Performance* – requires that if a decision has been made to sell an operation, any consequential provisions should reflect the extent to which obligations have been incurred that are not expected to be covered by the future profits of the operation. Such a provision is not to be set up until the reporting entity is demonstrably committed to the sale; this should be evidenced by a binding sale agreement. This suggests that unless the binding sale agreement has been entered into by the balance sheet date no provision can be made. However, FRS 3 contains an additional suggestion in its explanatory section that a binding contract entered into after the balance sheet date may provide additional evidence of commitments at the balance sheet date. This implies that the binding sale agreement does not have to be in place at the balance sheet date, as long as there is demonstrable commitment to sell by the balance sheet date, and the binding sale agreement is entered into before the accounts are signed. Where there is only an intention to sell, but there is no legally binding contract, FRS 3 does not allow a provision to be made for the consequences of the sale; however, it does emphasise that asset values need to be considered.

FRS 12 is now also relevant. This standard only allows provisions to be made where an entity has a present obligation (i.e. at the balance sheet date) as a result of a past event and it states that no obligation arises for the sale of an operation until the entity is committed to the sale, i.e. there is a binding sale agreement.[24] Although this is similar to FRS 3, FRS 12 does not repeat the explanatory wording that is contained in FRS 3. As discussed further at 4.1.2 of Chapter 25, it could be argued that if the explanatory paragraph in FRS 3 has previously been used to justify setting up provision for the disposal of an operation where the binding sale agreement was entered into after the balance sheet date but before the accounts were signed, this interpretation is no longer allowable under FRS 12. However, this is unclear, given that the relevant paragraph in FRS 3 itself has not been deleted or amended. If the sale of an operation is envisaged as part of a larger restructuring, FRS 12 notes that the assets of the operation must be reviewed for impairment under FRS 11 (see 4.4 of Chapter 10).

Extracts 24.5, 24.6 and 24.9 at 2.3 above illustrate examples of companies in the process of selling off businesses and which are expected to make a loss on disposal, after taking account of goodwill written off to reserves. It can be seen from Extract 24.9 that McKechnie has made a provision for the loss on disposal. Similarly, Cookson Group (Extract 24.6) also provided for the losses on disposal. In both these cases the companies had binding sale agreements after the year end so it appears that provision has been made using the explanatory paragraph of FRS 3. On the other hand, Greenalls (Extract 24.5) still had to obtain shareholders' approval to the sale. It therefore did not have a binding sale agreement and accordingly could not provide for the expected loss on sale. It would have had to consider whether the assets had been impaired, but such an exercise need not be extended to include goodwill written off to reserves.

3.5 Window dressing

SSAP 17 requires the disclosure of the reversal or maturity after the year end of transactions entered into before the year end, the substance of which was primarily to alter the appearance of the company's balance sheet.[25] Such alterations include those commonly referred to as 'window dressing'.

The difficulty that arises is that there is no clear view of what 'window dressing' is; this fact was conceded by the ASC in their Technical Release issued on the publication of SSAP 17.[26] The term can encompass both:

(a)   the fraudulent falsification of accounts to make things look better than they really are; and

(b)   the lawful arrangement of affairs over the year end to make things look different from the way they usually are.[27]

Nevertheless, the ASC indicated that as the 'fraudulent falsification of accounts is clearly unacceptable and unlawful and is not a subject for an accounting standard',[28] the term 'window dressing' as used in SSAP 17 is confined to the meaning in (b) above.[29] However, this interpretation raises the question as to whether or not it is the function of the balance sheet to reflect the company's typical financial position throughout the year. For example, should the balance sheet illustrate the typical gearing throughout the year, or only at the year end? Companies quite legitimately select the year end as being the time when stocks are lowest, their monthly creditors have been paid etc. Therefore, in order to develop any rule which requires disclosure or restatement of disclosure from the norm, we need to understand what the norm actually is. Furthermore, if what are regarded as artificial transactions are discovered, should they not be restated, rather than merely disclosed?

The end result is that the SSAP 17 definition of these so called window dressing transactions is inadequate. Consequently, SSAP 17 is inevitably ineffectual in this regard, and this is possibly supported by the fact that there is no significant evidence of such disclosure in practice.

3.6   Valuations of property

If an asset is revalued after the balance sheet date and a significant fall in the value of that asset is revealed, there are two matters which need to be considered.

The first matter to be considered is the determination of the period in which the decline in value took place. If there is sufficient evidence to show that the asset had fallen in value after the year end, then no adjustment should be made but full disclosure should be made of the subsequent fall in value. However, in many situations this will not be the case; the valuation is likely to indicate that the decline in value had already taken place prior to the balance sheet date.

If that is the case, then the second matter to be considered is whether an adjustment should be made to the carrying value of the asset. If the fall in value is deemed to have taken place before the balance sheet date then, as such a fall in value is one of the examples contained within FRS 11 which indicate the possible impairment of the asset, an impairment review will need to be carried out. If, having carried out the review, the recoverable amount is less than the carrying amount, an adjustment would have to be made because FRS 11 requires the impairment loss to be recognised. The treatment of impairment losses is discussed more fully at 4.4 of Chapter 10.

3.7   Insolvency of a debtor

The insolvency of a debtor and his inability to pay his debts usually builds over a period of time which would commence long before the balance sheet date. Consequently, if a debtor has an amount outstanding at the year end, and this amount has to be written off due to information received subsequent to the period end, it is normal to classify the event as adjusting. If, however, there is evidence to suggest that the insolvency of the debtor has been determined solely by an event occurring after the balance sheet date, then the event should be treated as non-adjusting.

4 COMPARISON WITH IASC AND US PRONOUNCEMENTS

4.1 IASC

The relevant international standard is IAS 10 – *Events After the Balance Sheet Date*. The original standard – *Contingencies and Events Occurring After the Balance Sheet Date* – was issued in October 1978. However, in 1998 the portion of that standard dealing with contingencies was replaced by IAS 37 – *Provisions, Contingent Liabilities and Contingent Assets* – and IAS 10 was revised in May 1999 so as to deal only with events after the balance sheet date. The revised standard becomes operative for annual accounts covering periods beginning on or after 1 January 2000. Most of IAS 10's accounting and disclosure requirements are essentially the same as those of SSAP 17 – any differences are noted in the discussion below.

Like SSAP 17, IAS 10 defines events after the balance sheet date as 'those events, both favourable and unfavourable, that occur between the balance sheet date and the date when the financial statements are authorised for issue'.[30] Where an enterprise is required to submit its accounts to its shareholders, or a supervisory board, for approval, IAS 10 regards the financial statements as having been authorised for issue on the date of original issuance, not when approved by the shareholders or the supervisory board.[31]

An enterprise should adjust the amounts recognised in its financial statements to reflect adjusting events after the balance sheet date,[32] i.e. those that provide evidence of conditions that existed at the balance sheet date.[33]

An enterprise should not adjust the amounts recognised in its financial statements to reflect non-adjusting events after the balance sheet date,[34] i.e. those that are indicative of conditions that arose after the balance sheet date.[35] Where such events are of such importance that non-disclosure would affect the ability of the users of the financial statements to make proper evaluations and decisions, an enterprise should disclose the following information for each significant category of non-adjusting event after the balance sheet date:

(a) the nature of the event; and

(b) an estimate of its financial effect, or a statement that such an estimate cannot be made.[36]

IAS 10 therefore does not allow adjustments for non-adjusting events, whereas the Appendix to SSAP 17 theoretically allows for the reclassification of a non-adjusting event as adjusting in exceptional circumstances (see 3.1 above). Instead it would appear that the US approach of providing pro-forma financial information would be more appropriate (see 4.2 below).

Where management determines after the balance sheet date either that it intends to liquidate the enterprise or to cease trading, or that it has no realistic alternative but to do so, an enterprise should not prepare its financial statements on a going concern basis.[37] Deterioration in operating results and financial position after the balance sheet date may indicate a need to consider whether the going concern assumption is still appropriate. Although this seems like adjusting for a non-adjusting event, because the effect is pervasive the IASC sees this as a fundamental change in the basis of accounting, rather than an adjustment to the amounts recognised within the original basis of accounting.[38] Although this requirement is similar to SSAP 17, it does not allow adjustment where the going concern basis is not appropriate for only part of the enterprise (which was the case under the original IAS 10).

The main area of difference between IAS 10 and the UK is in the accounting treatment of dividends. The original IAS 10 provided that 'dividends stated to be in respect of the period covered by the financial statements that are proposed or declared after the balance sheet date but before approval of the financial statements should be either adjusted or disclosed'.[39] This provision was presumably intended to allow flexibility as between, for example, the US and UK, since dividends are accounted for in the US when they are declared, whereas in the UK they are accounted for in the period to which they relate. However, IAS 10 now specifically states that 'if dividends to holders of equity instruments ... are proposed or declared after the balance sheet date, an enterprise should not recognise those dividends as a liability at the balance sheet date.'[40] The disclosure of such dividends is required by IAS 1 – *Presentation of Financial Statements*. IAS 1 permits an enterprise to make this disclosure either:[41]

(a)   on the face of the balance sheet as a separate component of equity; or

(b)   in the notes to the financial statements.

Like SSAP 17, IAS 10 requires disclosure of the date when the financial statements were authorised for issue. However, it also requires disclosure of who gave that authorisation, and if the enterprise's owners or other parties have the power to amend the financial statements after issuance, the enterprise should disclose that fact.[42]

If an enterprise receives information after the balance sheet date about conditions that existed at the balance sheet date, IAS 10 requires the enterprise to update the disclosures that relate to these conditions, in the light of the new information.[43] There is no such equivalent requirement in SSAP 17, but in practice this will generally be done.

4.2   US

The accounting treatment and disclosure of post balance events in financial statements is referred to in SAS 1 – *Codification of Auditing Standards and Procedures* – issued in November 1972. However, guidance on accounting for subsequent events appears in several accounting standards, including SFAS 12, SFAS 52 and SFAS 96.

SAS 1 follows a similar line to that of SSAP 17, in that it recognises two categories of 'subsequent events' which require consideration by management. The first category consists of those events which provide additional evidence with respect to conditions that existed at the balance sheet date and affect the estimates inherent in the process of preparing financial statements. The statement requires that all information that becomes available prior to the issuance of the financial statements should be used by management in its evaluation of the conditions on which the estimates were based, and the financial statements should be adjusted for any changes in estimates resulting from the use of such evidence.[44]

The second category of subsequent events consists of those events which provide evidence with respect to conditions that did not exist at the date of the balance sheet, but arose subsequent to that date. SAS 1 states that these events should not result in adjustment of the financial statements.[45] However, provision is made for the presentation of additional pro-forma information where 'such an event may be so significant that disclosure can best be made by supplementing the historical financial statements'[46] (see 3.1 above).

5   CONCLUSION

SSAP 17 essentially deals with three principal issues: adjusting events (including the appropriateness of the continued application of the going concern concept), non-adjusting events and window dressing. The standard is generally useful in respect of adjusting events, and it is normally clear as to which events should be adjusted in financial statements. In the case of non-adjusting events, a preferable requirement might be that companies should be required to present supplementary pro-forma financial statements (made up to the date on which the financial statements are approved by the board of directors) which reflect these events.

In the case of window dressing, not only is it unclear as to what the term actually means, but it appears strange that the statement calls for the disclosure, rather than restatement, of what are regarded as artificial transactions. In any event, SSAP 17 does not seem to deal adequately with those artificial transactions which it suggests should be disclosed.

References

1   SSAP 17, *Accounting for post balance sheet events*, ASC, August 1980, para. 18.
2   N17, *Events occurring after the balance sheet date*, ICAEW, October 1957, para. 16.
3   *Ibid.*, paras. 3–12.
4   *Ibid.*, para. 13.
5   ED 22, *Accounting for post balance sheet events*, ASC, February 1978, para. 6.
6   *Ibid.*, para. 18.
7   *Ibid.*, para. 14.
8   SSAP 17, para. 18.
9   *Ibid.*, para. 19.
10 *Ibid.*, Appendix.
11 *Ibid.*, para. 20.
12 *Ibid.*, Appendix.
13 *Ibid.*, para. 22.
14 *Ibid.*, para. 23.
15 *Ibid.*, para. 26.
16 *Ibid.*, para. 24.
17 CA 85, Sch. 7, para. 6(a).
18 SSAP 17, para. 23(a).
19 CA 85, Sch. 7, para. 6(a).
20 SSAP 17, Appendix.
21 AICPA, *Codification of Statements on Auditing Standards*, AU § 560.05.
22 *Ibid.*, AU § 560.05.
23 FRS 11, *Impairment of Fixed Assets and Goodwill*, ASB, July 1998, para. 31.
24 FRS 12, *Provisions, Contingent Liabilities and Contingent Assets*, ASB, September 1998, para. 83.
25 SSAP 17, para. 23(b).
26 TR 398, *Statement by the Accounting Standards Committee on the publication of SSAP 17: Accounting for post balance sheet events*, para. 14.
27 *Ibid.*, para. 14.
28 *Ibid.*, para. 14.
29 *Ibid.*, para. 14.
30 IAS 10, *Events After the Balance Sheet Date*, IASC, Revised 1999, para. 2.
31 *Ibid.*, paras. 4 and 5.
32 *Ibid.*, para. 7.
33 *Ibid.*, para. 2.
34 *Ibid.*, para. 9.
35 *Ibid.*, para. 2.
36 *Ibid.*, para. 20.
37 *Ibid.*, para. 13.
38 *Ibid.*, para. 14.
39 IAS 10, *Contingencies and Events Occurring After the Balance Sheet Date*, IASC, Reformatted 1994, para. 31.
40 IAS 10, Revised 1999, para. 11.
41 IAS 1, *Presentation of Financial Statements*, IASC, Revised 1997, para. 74.
42 IAS 10, Revised 1999, para. 16.
43 *Ibid.*, para. 18.
44 AICPA, *Codification of Statements on Auditing Standards*, AU § 560.03.
45 *Ibid.*, AU § 560.05.
46 *Ibid.*

Chapter 25

Provisions and contingencies

1 INTRODUCTION

1.1 Background

A provision is defined in the Companies Act as 'any amount retained as reasonably necessary for the purposes of providing for any liability or loss which is either likely to be incurred, or certain to be incurred but uncertain as to amount or as to the date on which it will arise.'[1] This definition applies only to 'provisions for liabilities or charges', in other words those that appear in the liabilities section of the balance sheet, and not to provisions for depreciation or diminution in value of assets, which are separately defined in the Act.[2] Similarly, this chapter focuses only on provisions that are shown as liabilities, and does not deal with amounts written off against assets.

FRS 12's definition of a provision is much shorter: 'a liability of uncertain timing or amount'.[3] The ASB says that it believes that 'although the Act and the FRS define provisions in different terms, when taken in their respective contexts, FRS 12 is consistent with the requirements of the Schedule 4.'[4] This form of words is subtle, because it is clear that the Board's wording has deliberately excluded some aspects of the Act's definition that it has found troublesome. In particular, the reference in the Act to *retaining* amounts carries connotations of appropriations, and sounds altogether too discretionary for the Board's taste. Consistent with its proposed *Statement of Principles*, the Board is anxious to ensure that only those amounts that meet its definition of liabilities end up being reported as such in the balance sheet. Liabilities are defined as 'obligations of an entity to transfer economic benefits as a result of past transactions or events'.[5]

A similar line is taken by the IASC in its standard IAS 37 – *Provisions, Contingent Liabilities and Contingent Assets.* Both FRS 12 and IAS 37 appear to contradict the requirements of European Accounting Directives: the Fourth Directive Article 31.1(c)(bb) requires businesses to take account of 'all foreseeable liabilities and potential losses arising in the course of the financial year concerned or of a previous one even if such liabilities or losses become apparent only between the date of the balance sheet and the date on which it is drawn up'. This conflict has been noted by the European Commission in a document published by the Contact Committee on the Accounting Directives, stating that 'IAS 37's definition of a provision as it is applied to the specific case of restructuring provisions is inconsistent with the Fourth Directive because it will prevent provision being made for items for which provision is required by Articles 31.1(c)(bb) and 31(d) of the Directive.'[6]

The Act's reference to 'providing for any ... loss that is ... likely to be incurred' also seems to open up a possibility that the ASB wished to close down; the Board was anxious to prevent companies from providing for future operating losses, because they properly belong in the future. However, as discussed later in this chapter, this distinction is sometimes less easy to make than it might appear.

There is clearly an area of overlap between provisions and contingent liabilities, and indeed the ASB has addressed them in a single standard. Contingent liabilities are clearly not certain to give rise to outflows, but provision may nonetheless be required for them if they are sufficiently likely to do so. Accordingly, both the ASB and the IASC have addressed provisions and contingent liabilities in the same standard, and thrown in contingent assets for good measure. Previously, contingent assets and liabilities were governed by SSAP 18[7] (see 1.2.1 below), and the Companies Act also imposes rules for the disclosure of contingent liabilities (see 5.2.1 below).

A further demarcation line has to be drawn between provisions and other liabilities, such as trade creditors and accruals. The ASB differentiates provisions on the basis that 'there is uncertainty about the timing or amount of the future expenditure required in settlement. By contrast:

(a) trade creditors are liabilities to pay for goods or services that have been received or supplied and have been invoiced or formally agreed with the supplier; and

(b) accruals are liabilities to pay for goods or services that have been received or supplied but have not been paid, invoiced or formally agreed with the supplier, including amounts due to employees (for example amounts relating to accrued holiday pay). Although it is sometimes necessary to estimate the amount or timing of accruals, the uncertainty is generally much less than is the case for provisions.

Accruals are often reported as part of trade and other creditors whereas provisions are reported separately.'[8]

This is true, but by concentrating on trade creditors and their associated accruals the Board has cited only the most straightforward case. In practice the difference between provisions and liabilities is often far from clear-cut, and reclassification from one category to the other is not uncommon. TI Group provides an example:

Extract 25.1: TI Group plc (1998)

22 PROVISIONS FOR LIABILITIES AND CHARGES [extract]

	Pensions and Other Post-Retirement Obligations £m	Product Warranty and Onerous Contracts £m	Deferred Taxation £m	Other Liabilities £m	Group Total £m
At 31st December 1997	112.2	–	30.4	–	142.6
Exchange rate adjustments	1.0	0.3	0.1	–	1.4
Transferred from creditors	6.7	11.6	–	0.9	19.2
Transferred to debtors falling due within one year	–	–	21.9		21.9
New subsidiaries	27.7	14.6	(6.7)	15.7	51.3
Utilised	(6.9)	(3.5)	–.	(7.9)	(18.3)
Profit and loss account	9.6	3.5	(3.3)	5.5	15.3
At 31st December 1998	**150.3**	**26.5**	**42.4**	**14.2**	**233.4**

Provisions for liabilities and charges include provisions for

- Unfunded post-retirement medical and welfare benefit schemes, unfunded pension arrangements, principally overseas, and the actuarially estimated deficit in the EIS Group UK pension schemes (see note 32);

- Future product warranty costs arising in the normal course of business from prior period sales, and onerous contract liabilities;

- Deferred taxation;

- Other liabilities, which include actual and potential legal claims where resolution is anticipated during 1999 and committed reorganisation expenditure.

Following the adoption of FRS 12 'Provisions, Contingent Liabilities and Contingent Assets', certain balances relating to the above items, previously reported within Creditors, have been reclassified as Provisions with effect from 1st January 1998. 1997 comparatives have not been restated.

One reason why this distinction matters is that provisions are subject to disclosure requirements that do not apply to other creditors, as discussed at 5 below. In fact, although questions of recognition and measurement are important, transparency of disclosure is also a very significant issue in relation to accounting for provisions. The problem is that, once a provision has been established, expenditure that is charged to it bypasses the profit and loss account and to some extent therefore disappears from view. The original charge may well have been dealt with as an exceptional item and glossed over by management in any discussion of their performance, and the subsequent application of the provision has no further impact on earnings – giving rise to a kind of 'off profit and loss account' treatment. And in recent years, some of the provisions that have been set up have been extremely large and wide-ranging. An example is to be found in the 1993 accounts of what was then British Gas:

Extract 25.2: British Gas plc (1993)

Review of operating results

Operating costs [extract]

The results for 1993 include an exceptional charge of £1,650 million for the major restructuring of the UK Gas Business. This restructuring into five separate business streams will ensure that the Company's UK Gas Business will be leaner, more competitive and more commercially focused at a time when the gas market in Great Britain is undergoing radical change. The exceptional charge comprises severance and pension costs associated with the reduction in approximately 25,000 people and the related costs of restructuring the integrated UK Gas Business. The cash effect of this restructuring will be borne largely over the next three years.

The corresponding note to the profit and loss account contained substantially the same information but added that the amount also included 'other incremental costs that will be required to implement the restructuring, such as training, property related costs and information technology costs'. The effect of this charge was to convert a pre-tax profit of approximately £1 billion into a loss of £613 million.

The need to restrict the creation of such 'big bath' provisions provided much of the impetus for the ASB's project on provisions, although the Board addressed some other important issues as well, notably on how provisions should be measured. The development of FRS 12 is discussed in the next section.

1.2   The development of FRS 12

1.2.1   SSAP 18

The first standard to address matters now covered by FRS 12 was SSAP 18 – *Accounting for contingencies* – issued by the ASC in August 1980. This closely followed an exposure draft that had been published in November 1978.[9]

SSAP 18 defined a contingency as a 'condition which exists at the balance sheet date, where the outcome will be confirmed only on the occurrence or non-occurrence of one or more uncertain future events'.[10] It said that contingencies could result in both gains and losses, the treatment of which was to be determined by the likelihood of their expected outcome.

A contingent gain was defined by SSAP 18 as a gain dependent on a contingency.[11] It said that contingent gains should not be credited to income, since to do so would mean the recognition of income prior to realisation. Consequently, SSAP 18 did not permit such gains to be accrued, and only allowed their disclosure if realisation was probable.[12] This meant that a contingent gain was not to be disclosed if it was only possible that it would be realised. The standard, therefore, restricted the amount of disclosure in a company's financial statements in this respect, as it was considered misleading to disclose the existence of future gains where the likelihood of realisation was less than probable. However, when the realisation of the gain became 'reasonably certain', then the gain was no longer a contingency and accrual was to be made.[13]

SSAP 18 similarly defined a contingent loss as a loss dependent on a contingency.[14] Where it was probable that a loss would be confirmed by future events in the future, it was to be accrued in the accounts provided it could be estimated with reasonable accuracy and otherwise it had to be disclosed by way of note. If it was not probable that a loss would occur then again it was not accrued but only disclosed by way of note, unless the chances of a loss being confirmed were remote; in which case no disclosure was required.

SSAP 18 was superseded by FRS 12, as discussed below, but the requirements set out above are still very similar in effect, even though the approach and the definitions used by FRS 12 are rather different. In particular, FRS 12 approaches the subject from a balance sheet perspective, setting rules for the recognition of assets and liabilities, whereas SSAP 18 focused on the recognition of gains and losses.

1.2.2 The ASB Discussion Paper

The ASB published a Discussion Paper – *Provisions* – in November 1995. This proposed the general principles that should govern the recognition, measurement and disclosure of provisions; these were derived from the Board's *Statement of Principles*, which was published in draft on the same day. It devoted much of its content to the consideration of three particular kinds of provision: those for future operating losses, reorganisation costs and environmental liabilities, and these topics continued to feature prominently in the project as it progressed towards an accounting standard. However, the paper did not deal with contingencies at all, and at that stage it was intended that SSAP 18 should be left in force.

1.2.3 FRED 14

FRED 14 was issued in June 1997. The exposure draft closely followed the philosophy of the Discussion Paper, but it had now been expanded to embrace contingencies as well as provisions and accordingly was intended to supersede SSAP 18.

1.2.4 FRS 12

The ASB published FRS 12 in September 1998. Its stated objective is 'to ensure that appropriate recognition criteria and measurement bases are applied to provisions, contingent liabilities and contingent assets and that sufficient information is disclosed in the notes to the financial statements to enable users to understand their nature, timing and amount'.[15]

The only entities specifically exempt from FRS 12 are those applying the ASB's Financial Reporting Standard for Smaller Entities (FRSSE).[16] This was really only a procedural exemption, because the essence of the standard was to be incorporated in a revised version of the FRSSE. In addition, certain specific provisions, contingent liabilities and contingent assets are exempt,[17] namely those:

A   *resulting from financial instruments carried at fair value*

The standard emphasises, on the other hand, that it does apply to financial instruments (including guarantees) that are *not* carried at fair value.[18] This is somewhat confusing. It is understandable that items such as guarantees, which give rise to contingent liabilities, fall within the scope of the standard. However, if the scope of the standard were extended to other financial instruments, some surprising results would be achieved.

For example, consider a forward foreign currency contract taken out to hedge future contracted purchases of goods from an overseas supplier, which is to be settled after the balance sheet date. Such derivatives would currently be accounted for as hedges, fixing the rate at which the purchases are recorded next year. However, applying FRS 12 could give rise to the requirement for a provision to be made for any loss subsisting on the contract at the balance sheet date.

We do not believe that the ASB intended this standard to change current accounting for financial instruments such as derivatives, given that it is currently reviewing the accounting for financial instruments in a separate project. This view is supported by the fact that FRS 13 – *Derivatives and Other Financial Instruments: Disclosures* – came into effect at the same time as FRS 12 and contains disclosure requirements for financial instruments which are consistent with the view that the accounting requirements have not changed.

B   *resulting from executory contracts, except where the contract is onerous*

The standard uses the term executory contracts to mean 'contracts under which neither party has performed any of its obligations or both parties have partially performed their obligations to an equal extent'.[19] This means that contracts such as supplier purchase contracts and capital commitments, which would otherwise fall within the scope of the standard, are exempt.

This exemption prevents the balance sheet from being grossed up by all sorts of commitments that an entity has entered into, and is to be welcomed as a pragmatic measure. However, there is little theoretical justification for the exemption, in that such items meet the definition of liabilities used by the standard. The need for this exemption arises because the liability framework on which this standard is based would otherwise give rise to unwelcome effects.

An executory contract will still require provision if the contract becomes onerous. Onerous contracts are dealt with in 4.3 below.

C   *arising in insurance entities from contracts with policy-holders*

The ASB refers to the special regulatory position of insurance companies and the review of the accounting framework for insurance companies as reasons for this exemption. However, the standard requires insurance entities to apply the standard to other (non-insurance) provisions and contingencies.

D   *covered by another FRS or a SSAP*

Where there is a more relevant standard, it should be applied to the provision or contingency it addresses instead of FRS 12. Examples given in the standard are:

■   long term contracts (dealt with in SSAP 9 – *Stocks and long-term contracts*)

■   deferred tax (dealt with in SSAP 15 – *Accounting for deferred tax*)

■   leases (dealt with in SSAP 21 – *Accounting for leases and hire purchase contracts*). However, the standard argues that if operating leases become onerous, there are no specific requirements within SSAP 21 to address the issue and thus FRS 12 applies to such leases.

■   pension costs (dealt with in SSAP 24 – *Accounting for pension costs*). Although not specifically mentioned, it would be reasonable to assume that the exemption also extends to other post retirement benefits, which are addressed in UITF 6 – *Accounting for post-retirement benefits other than pensions*.

The standard does not give provisions for discontinued operations (which are dealt with in FRS 3 – *Reporting Financial Performance*) as an example of an item which is exempt from FRS 12. Instead, it specifically requires that where a restructuring meets the definition of a discontinued operation, the additional FRS 3 disclosures are given in addition to complying with FRS 12.[20] Presumably, this is because the standard does not consider that such provisions are more specifically dealt with in FRS 3.

FRS 12 came into effect for financial statements relating to accounting periods ending on or after 23 March 1999. Since it embraces contingencies, SSAP 18 was withdrawn. FRS 3 – *Reporting Financial Performance* was also amended to bring it in line with the FRS 12 measurement rules for gains on disposals of assets, as explained in 3.5 below.

There are no specific transitional provisions in the standard. This means that any previously existing provisions must be adjusted on to an FRS 12 basis. The question then arises as to whether such adjustments should be regarded as changes of policy and treated as prior year adjustments, or as changes in accounting estimate to be dealt with in the profit and loss account of the year of implementation. The standard is not very helpful in distinguishing between these cases.

It seems reasonably clear that changes in recognition – such as making provisions for onerous contracts for the first time, and reversing out restructuring costs that do not meet the recognition criteria – represent changes in policy. However, the standard is unclear about how to treat changes in the measurement of an existing provision. It cites the case where an entity has previously provided for warranty costs but FRS 12 requires the provision to be measured at a different amount, and says that this should be treated as a change in estimate.[21] This could be read to imply that any changes in the basis of measuring an existing provision should be treated as changes in estimate, but we would tend to doubt that this can be a general rule. For example, many would argue that the introduction of discounting is a change in accounting policy and should be treated as a prior year adjustment; as shown in Extract 25.18 below, this is the view that BP Amoco took when it implemented the standard. However, in the absence of more specific guidance, each case will have to be judged on its merits.

2   RECOGNITION

2.1   Provisions

FRS 12 requires that a provision should be recognised when, and only when, three conditions are all satisfied:

(a)   an entity has a present obligation (legal or constructive) as a result of a past event;

(b)   it is probable that a transfer of economic benefits will be required to settle the obligation; and

(c)   a reliable estimate can be made of the amount of the obligation.[22]

Each of these three conditions is discussed separately below.

2.1.1   *'An entity has a present obligation (legal or constructive) as a result of a past event.'*

The standard defines both legal and constructive obligations. The definition of a legal obligation is fairly straightforward and uncontroversial; it refers to an obligation that derives from a contract (through its explicit or implicit terms), legislation or other operation of law.[23]

Constructive obligations, on the other hand, may give rise to more problems of interpretation. A constructive obligation is defined as 'an obligation that derives from an entity's actions where:

(a)   by an established pattern of past practice, published policies or a sufficiently specific current statement, the entity has indicated to other parties that it will accept certain responsibilities; and

(b) as a result, the entity has created a valid expectation on the part of those other parties that it will discharge those responsibilities.'[24]

The essence of the idea is that the entity may be committed to certain expenditure because any alternative would be too unattractive to contemplate. The standard cites habitual refunds made to customers, and contamination clean-ups as examples of this.[25]

The second half of this condition uses the phrase 'as a result of a past event'. This is based on the concept of an obligating event, which the standard defines as 'an event that creates a legal or constructive obligation and that results in an entity having no realistic alternative to settling that obligation.'[26] The standard uses this concept when discussing specific examples of recognition, which we discuss further in 4 below. However, it is worth mentioning here that this concept, like that of a constructive obligation, is open to interpretation, as the obligating event is not always easy to identify.

FRS 12 disallows certain provisions that might otherwise qualify to be recognised by stating that 'It is only those obligations arising from past events existing independently of an entity's future actions (i.e. the future conduct of its business) that are recognised as provisions'.[27] It illustrates this restriction with an example of an entity required, because of commercial pressures or legal requirements, to fit smoke filters in a factory. It argues that the entity can avoid the expenditure by its future actions, for example by changing its method of operation, so there is no present obligation for the future expenditure. Other kinds of provisions disallowed because the entity can avoid the future expenditure are repairs and maintenance of assets, and future staff training, both of which are illustrated in the examples.[28]

There is no requirement for an entity to know to whom an obligation is owed. The obligation may be to the public at large. It follows that the obligation could be to one party, but the amount ultimately payable will be to another party. For example, in the case of a constructive obligation for an environmental clean-up, the obligation is to the public, but the liability will be settled by making payment to the contractors engaged to carry out the clean-up. However, the principle is that there must be another party for the obligation to exist. It follows from this that a board decision will not give rise to a constructive obligation unless it is communicated in sufficient detail to those affected by it before the balance sheet date. The most significant application of this requirement relates to restructuring provisions, which is discussed further in 4.1 below.

The standard discusses the possibility that an event that does not give rise to an obligation immediately may do so at a later date, because of changes in the law or an act by the entity which gives rise to a constructive obligation. Changes in the law will be relatively straightforward to identify. The only issue that arises will be exactly when that change in the law should be recognised. FRS 12 states that an obligation arises only when the legislation is virtually certain to be enacted as drafted, and suggests that in many cases, this will not be until it is enacted.[29]

The more subjective area is the possibility that an act by the entity will give rise to a constructive obligation. The example given is of an entity publicly accepting responsibility for rectification of previous environmental damage in a way that creates a constructive obligation. This seems to introduce a certain amount of flexibility to management in reporting results. By bringing forward or delaying a public announcement of a commitment that management had always intended to honour, it can affect the period in which a provision is charged.

As the FASB has also commented,[30] the critical event that creates a constructive obligation tends to be elusive, and this is demonstrated by the discussion of some of the examples in 4 below. That is not to say that we believe that only legal obligations deserve to be in the balance sheet, but we doubt if this particular approach is the best way of determining which additional items deserve to be there. As with other aspects of the ASB's framework and its recognition criteria in particular, we think that the question is in reality one of expense recognition – in what period should the cost be charged to the profit and loss account – not liability recognition at all.

2.1.2   'It is probable that a transfer of economic benefits will be required to settle the obligation.'

This requirement has been included as a result of the standard's attempt to incorporate contingent liabilities within the definition of provisions. This is discussed in detail in 2.2 below.

The interpretation of *probable* in these circumstances is that the transfer of economic benefits is more likely than not to occur; that is, it has a probability greater than 50%. The standard also makes it clear that where there are a number of similar obligations, the probability that a transfer will occur is based on the class of obligations as a whole. This is because in the case of certain obligations such as warranties, the possibility of a transfer for an individual item is very small (likely to be much less than 50%) whereas the possibility of at least some transfer of economic benefits for the population as a whole will be much greater (almost certainly greater than 50%).

2.1.3   'A reliable estimate can be made of the amount of the obligation.'

The standard takes the view that a reasonable estimate can always be made for a provision where an entity can determine a range of possible outcomes. Hence, it will only be in extremely rare cases that a range of outcomes cannot be determined and so no provision is recognised. In these circumstances, the liability should be disclosed as a contingent liability (see disclosure requirements in 5.2).

2.2   Contingencies

FRS 12 says that contingent assets and liabilities should not be recognised,[31] but only disclosed. At least for contingent liabilities, this may seem a surprising position to take and one which is different from the previous regime under SSAP 18. However, the explanation lies in the peculiar way in which a contingent liability has been defined. It is:

(a)   a possible obligation that arises from past events and whose existence will be confirmed only by the occurrence of one or more uncertain future events not wholly within the entity's control; or

(b)   a present obligation that arises from past events but is not recognised because:

    (i)   it is not probable that a transfer of economic benefits will be required to settle the obligation; or

    (ii)   the amount of the obligation cannot be measured with sufficient reliability.[32]

This approach is very different from that used in SSAP 18. What the ASB has done is to define the category in a back to front way that depends on the recognition rule that it wants to apply. Contingent liabilities as defined are now meant to be those that the Board does not think deserve recognition.

Even with that explanation, the above definition is not easy to understand. One problem with (a) is that the term 'possible' is not defined. Literally, it could mean any probability greater than 0% and less than 100%. However, in the context of the standard, a more sensible assumption is that since 'probable' is used within the standard as meaning 'more likely than not to occur', i.e. a probability of greater than 50%, then 'possible' means a probability of 50% or less. Assuming that this is what is meant, the definition restricts contingent liabilities to those where either the existence of the liability or the transfer of economic benefits arising is less than 50% probable (or where the obligation cannot be measured at all, but as noted in 2.1 above, this would be very rare).

The ASB's definition of a contingent liability is therefore tortuous and counter intuitive. To say that a contingent liability is no longer contingent if it becomes more than 50% probable is likely to cause a great deal of confusion. It is contrary to the natural meaning of the words, whereby a contingent liability is a liability that is contingent on a future event.

If the meaning of contingent liabilities is restricted in this way, the question obviously arises as to what happens to items that would previously have been classified as contingent liabilities, where the existence of the liability and the resulting transfer of economic benefits are greater than 50% probable. The answer is that the standard has attempted to catch these within provisions. As noted in 2.1 above, the recognition criteria for provisions include the requirement that it is probable that a transfer of economic benefits will be required to settle the obligation. Hence an item that would previously have been regarded as a contingent liability under SSAP 18, for which a cash outflow is probable, would now be classified as a provision under FRS 12.

However, the uncertainty surrounding a liability is not always related only to whether a cash outflow will arise, but may also relate to whether the liability exists at all. For example, take the case of litigation against a company. The facts may suggest that the company will probably be found negligent and required to pay appropriate damages, but it is still contesting the action and may win the case. In these circumstances, as well as uncertainty over any level of damages, there is currently uncertainty over whether the company has a liability at all.

The standard has attempted to deal with these circumstances by stating that 'in rare cases it is not clear whether there is a present obligation. In these cases, a past event is deemed to give rise to a present obligation if, taking account of all available evidence, it is more likely than not that a present obligation exists at the balance sheet date'.[33] Accordingly, if it is concluded that a present obligation is more likely than not to exist, a provision will be required (assuming that the other recognition criteria are met). Unfortunately, this is a direct contradiction of the standard's condition (a) for the recognition of a provision, which requires there to be a definite obligation, not just a probable one.

A contingent asset is defined in a more normal way. It is 'a possible asset that arises from past events and whose existence will be confirmed only by the occurrence of one or more uncertain future events not wholly within the entity's control'.[34] In this case, the word 'possible' is *not* confined to a level of probability of 50% or less, which may further increase the confusion over the different meaning of the word in the definition of contingent liabilities.

The standard states that a contingent asset should not be recognised, as this could give rise to recognition of profit that may never be realised.[35] However, when the realisation of profit is virtually certain, then the related asset is no longer regarded as contingent and recognition is appropriate. SSAP 18 had a similar criterion, but used the phrase 'reasonably certain' rather than 'virtually certain'. It is not clear whether the ASB intended there to be a different level of certainty required by using the phrase 'virtually certain', but in practice the level of certainty required was already high (a suggested interpretation being between 95% and 100% probable) so it is unlikely that the wording change has altered previous practice.

The standard requires disclosure of the contingent asset when the inflow of economic benefits is probable.[36] The disclosure requirements are detailed in 5.3 below.

Despite the changes in terminology that FRS 12 introduced, therefore, in practice contingencies continue to be dealt with on a similar basis to the regime established by SSAP 18.

The following matrix summarises the treatment of contingencies under FRS 12:

Likelihood of outcome	Accounting treatment: contingent liability	Accounting treatment: contingent asset
Virtually certain (say, >95% probable)	Not a contingent liability, therefore provide	Not a contingent asset, therefore accrue
Probable (say, 50 - 95% probable)	Not a contingent liability, therefore provide	Disclose
Possible but not probable (say, 5 - 50% probable)	Disclose	No disclosure permitted
Remote (say, <5% probable)	No disclosure required under FRS 12, but consider disclosure under CA 85, Sch. 4, para. 50	No disclosure permitted

The standard does not put a numerical measure of probability on either 'virtually certain' or 'remote', which lie at the outer ends of the range, but we think it reasonable to regard them as falling above the 95th percentile and below the fifth percentile respectively. However, these are not definitive guides and each case must be decided on its merits. In any event, it is usually possible to assess the probability of the outcome of a particular event only very approximately.

3 MEASUREMENT

3.1 Best estimate of provision

FRS 12 says that the amount provided should be the best estimate of the expenditure required to settle the present obligation at the balance sheet date.[37] The standard equates this estimate with 'the amount that an entity would rationally pay to settle the obligation at the balance sheet date or to transfer it to a third party at that time'.[38] It is interesting that a hypothetical transaction of this kind should be proposed as the conceptual basis of the measurement required, rather than putting the main emphasis upon the actual expenditure that is expected to be incurred in the future. This represents 'relief value' as it is described in the 1995 draft of the ASB's *Statement of Principles*,[39] and belongs in a current value system rather than one founded on historical cost.

The standard does acknowledge that it would often be impossible or prohibitively expensive to settle or transfer the obligation at the balance sheet date. However, it goes on to state that 'the estimate of the amount that an entity would rationally pay to settle or transfer the obligation gives the best estimate of the expenditure required to settle the present obligation at the balance sheet date'.[40]

Different methods of dealing with the uncertainties surrounding the amount to be recognised as a provision are detailed in the standard. Where a large population of items is being measured, such as warranty costs, the standard advances the use of 'expected values'.[41] This is a statistical computation which weights the cost of all the various possible outcomes according to their probabilities.

Another measurement approach described in the standard covers the situation where there is a continuous range of possible outcomes and each point in that range is as likely as any other. FRS 12 requires that, in this case, the mid-point of the range should be used.[42] This is not a particularly helpful example. It does not make it clear what the principle is meant to be, since the mid-point in this case represents the median as well as the expected value. The latter may have been what the Board had in mind, but the median could be equally well justified on the basis that it is 50% probable that at least this amount will be payable, while anything in excess of that constitutes a possible but not a probable liability, that should be disclosed rather than accrued. Interestingly, US GAAP has a different approach to this issue in relation to contingencies. FASB Interpretation No. 14 states that where a contingent loss could fall within a range of amounts then, if there is a best estimate within the range, it should be accrued, with the remainder noted as a contingent liability. However, if there is no best estimate then the *lowest* figure within the range should be accrued, with the remainder up to the maximum potential loss noted as a contingent liability.[43]

Where the obligation being measured relates to a single item, the standard suggests that the best estimate of the liability may be the most likely outcome.[44] However, it notes that regard should be had to other possible outcomes. It gives an example of an entity that has to rectify a fault in a major plant that it has constructed. The most likely outcome is that the repair will succeed at the first attempt. However, a provision should be made for a larger amount if there is a significant chance that further attempts will be necessary.[45] This again sounds like a vague leaning towards an expected value approach.

This example illustrates an inconsistency between these measurement rules and the recognition rules for contingent liabilities. Compare the above example with a case where the most likely outcome is that no repair will be required at all, but there is still a significant chance that a repair will be needed. In this scenario, there is a less than 50% probability that a cash outflow will arise, and so the item will fall within the definition of a contingent liability and no provision will be required. No account will have been taken of any other possible outcomes, unlike the first scenario.

It is also interesting to consider how the measurement rules detailed above fit in with the concept of prudence. It is worth noting that FRED 14 required the provision to be a 'realistic and prudent estimate',[46] but this was altered to refer to 'best estimate' in the final standard, with references to prudence being dropped.

The standard does however discuss the concept of risk. It refers to risk as being variability of outcome, and states that 'the risks and uncertainties that inevitably surround many events and circumstances should be taken into account in reaching the best estimate of a provision'. It suggests that a risk adjustment may increase the amount at which a liability is measured, but gives no indication of how this may be done. The paragraph goes on to warn against duplicating adjustments for risk, for example by estimating costs of an adverse outcome on a prudent basis and then overestimating its probability.[47]

The overall result of all this is somewhat confusing. The measurement rules no longer appear to take account of prudence. Certainly, using a best estimate based on the expected value concept or the mid-point of a range cannot be building in prudence to the estimate. However, the discussion on risk gives the impression that some sort of adjustment should be made which builds prudence into the estimate, but quite how this might be done is unclear.

This rather vague drafting leaves a certain amount of scope in the estimation of provisions. It seems likely that in practice prudence will continue to be applied in the way it always has been in the estimation process.

3.2 Discounting

The standard requires that where the effect of the time value of money is material, the provision should be discounted to its net present value.[48] The discount rate used is to be 'a pre-tax rate that reflects current market assessments of the time value of money and the risk specific to the liability'.[49] However, it is worth noting that for many provisions, no discounting will be required as the cash flows will not be far enough into the future for discounting to have a material impact. A number of problems arise on the issue of discounting which are discussed below.

3.2.1 *Real v nominal rate*

The discount rate used depends on whether:

(a)   the future cash flows are expressed in current prices, in which case a real discount rate (which excludes the effects of general inflation) should be used; or

(b)   the future cash flows are expressed in expected future prices, in which case a nominal discount rate (which includes a return to cover expected inflation) should be used.

The standard allows either method to be used, and both these methods may produce the same figure for the initial present value of the provision. However, the effect of the unwinding of the discount will be different in each case.

3.2.2   Adjusting for risk

As noted above, FRS 12 also requires that risk is taken into account in the calculation of a provision, but gives little guidance as to how this should be done. Within the discounting section, it goes on to suggest that using a discount rate that reflects the risk associated with the liability (a risk-adjusted rate) may be the easiest method of reflecting risk. It gives no indication of how to calculate such a risk adjusted rate, but a little more information can be obtained from the ASB's earlier Working Paper – *Discounting in Financial Reporting*,[50] which included this example.

Example 25.1: Calculation of a risk-adjusted rate

A company has a provision for which the expected value of the cash outflow in three years' time is £150, and the risk-free rate is 5%. The company is risk averse and would settle instead for a certain payment of £160 in three years' time. The effect of risk in calculating the present value is that either:

(a) the 'certainty equivalent' of £160 is discounted at the risk-free rate of 5%, giving a present value of £138; or

(b) the expected cash flow of £150 is discounted at a risk-adjusted rate that will give the present value of £138, i.e. a rate of 2.8%.

As can be seen from this example, the risk-adjusted rate is a *lower* rate than the risk-free rate. The problem with this approach is that this risk-adjusted rate is a theoretical rate (which may even be negative) and has no obvious meaning in real life. It is also difficult to see how a risk-adjusted rate could be obtained in practice. In this example, it was obtained only by working backwards; it was already known that the net present value that we wanted to obtain was £138, so the risk-adjusted rate was just the discount rate applied to £150 to give that result.

The standard does offer an alternative approach – instead of using a risk-adjusted discount rate, the cash flows themselves can be adjusted for risk and then discounted using a risk-free rate.[51] This does of course give the problem of how to adjust the cash flows for risk. However, this may be easier than attempting to risk-adjust the discount rate.

The standard suggests that an example of a risk-free rate would be a government bond rate.[52] Presumably, this government bond rate should strictly have a similar remaining term to the liability, although this is not specified in the standard.

3.2.3 Pre-tax discount rate

Since FRS 12 requires provisions to be measured before tax, it follows that cash flows should be discounted at a pre-tax discount rate. No further explanation of this is given in the body of the standard. However, paragraph 27 in the Appendix on the *Development of the FRS* states that 'the discount rate should be the rate of return that will, after tax has been deducted, give the required post-tax rate of return'. The paragraph goes on to explain that because the tax consequence of different cash flows may be different, the pre-tax rate of return is not always the post-tax rate of return grossed up by the standard rate of tax.

In practice, it is unlikely that companies need be too concerned about this paragraph. This is because, in reality, the discount rate will be calculated directly as a pre-tax discount rate, as the required post-tax rate of return will not be known. Supposing for example, the risk-free rate of return is being used, then the discount rate used will be a government bond rate. This rate will be obtained gross. Thus, the idea of obtaining a required post-tax rate of return and adjusting it for the tax consequences of different cash flows will seldom be relevant.

The calculation is illustrated in the following example.

Example 25.2: Use of discounting and tax effect

It is estimated that the settlement of an environmental provision will give rise to a gross cash outflow of £500,000 in three years time. The gross interest rate on a government bond maturing in three years time is 6%. The tax rate is 30%.

The net present value of the provision is £419,810 (£500,000 x $1/(1 + 0.06)^3$). Hence, a provision of £419,810 should be booked in the balance sheet. A corresponding deferred tax asset of £125,943 (30% of £419,810) would be set up if it met the SSAP 15 criteria for recognition.

3.2.4 Unwinding of the discount

The standard requires that 'the unwinding of the discount should be included as a financial item adjacent to interest, but should be shown separately from other interest either on the face of the profit and loss account or in a note'.[53]

This is the only guidance that the standard gives on the unwinding of the discount. There is no discussion of the impact that the original selection of discount rate can have on its unwinding, that is the selection of real versus nominal rates, and risk-free versus risk-adjusted rates. The ASB appears to have overlooked the fact that these different discount rates will unwind differently. This is best illustrated by way of an example.

Example 25.3 Effect of different bases of interest

A provision is required to be set up for an estimated cash outflow of £100,000 (estimated at current prices), payable in three years' time. The real discount rate is 2.5%, and inflation is estimated at 5%.

The net present value of £100,000, discounted at 2.5%, is £92,860. This is the provision that should be booked in the balance sheet in year 0. The same balance sheet provision would also be arrived at if the cash outflow was adjusted to reflect future prices, and then discounted at 7.5%.

In year 1, if a real discount rate is used and all assumptions remain valid, the effect of unwinding the discount gives rise to an interest charge of £2,322.

However, if a nominal rate is used, the result in year 1 is an interest charge of £6,965.

Obviously, using the real discount rate will give rise to a much lower interest charge. This leads to the question of whether it also leads to a lower provision in the balance sheet at the end of year 1. Provisions have to be revised annually to reflect the current best estimate of the obligation. Thus, the provision in the above example will be adjusted to reflect current prices at the end of year 1 and any other adjustments that arise from changes in estimate of the provision, as well as being adjusted for the unwinding of the discount. If prices do increase at the rate of inflation assumed (5% in this example), then the balance sheet provision at the end of year 1 will be £99,825 under both methods. What will be different under the two methods, however, is the allocation of the change in provision between operating costs and interest. If the real discount rate is used, the interest charge each year will be lower and the operating costs higher than if the nominal rate is used.

A similar issue arises with the option of using the risk-free or the risk-adjusted discount rate. However, this is a more complex problem, because it is not clear what to do with the risk-adjustment built into the provision. This is illustrated in the following example, using the same facts as in Example 25.1 above:

Example 25.4: Use of risk-free and risk-adjusted figures

As before, a company requires to make a provision for which the expected value of the cash outflow in three years' time is £150, when the risk-free rate is 5%. The reporting entity is risk averse and would settle instead for a certain payment of £160 in three years' time. The discounting options are:

(a) the 'certainty equivalent' of £160 is discounted at the risk-free rate of 5%, giving a present value of £138; or

(b) the expected cash flow of £150 is discounted at a risk-adjusted rate that will give the present value of £138, i.e. a rate of 2.8%.

Assuming that there are no changes in estimate required to be made to the provision during the three year period, alternative (a) will unwind to give an overall interest charge of £22 and a final provision of £160. Alternative (b) will unwind to give an overall interest charge of £12 and a final provision of £150.

In this example, the unwinding of different discount rates gives rise to different provisions. The difference of £10 relates to the risk adjustment that has been made to the provision. The standard gives no guidance as to how to treat this £10 if the provision is unwound at the risk-free rate. Given that the expected cash outflow is only £150, this additional £10 is likely to have to be released at some point, but it is unclear how to do this. Two alternatives are that it could be done gradually over the period in which the provision is unwound (perhaps as a reassessment of the required provision as it becomes less risky), or could be taken in total once the provision has been settled. The lack of guidance in the standard appears to give companies flexibility on this point.

3.2.5 Change in interest rates

The standard requires the discount rate to reflect current market assessments of the time value of money.[54] This appears to mean that where interest rates change, the provision should be recalculated on the basis of revised interest rates. This interpretation is reinforced by the disclosure requirement in the standard that entities should disclose the effect of any change in discount rate.[55] As with the equivalent proposals in relation to financial instruments and the requirements of FRS 11 in respect of impaired assets (see Chapters 9 and 10 respectively) this implicitly introduces a new capital maintenance concept into accounting, based on the ability of the entity to earn a current market rate of return.

This will give rise to an adjustment charged within the interest line in the year of change, which may be either a debit or a credit depending on which way interest rates move. It does, however, seem fairly alarming that companies may be able to report a substantial profit in a year purely as a result of increasing its discount rate.

Calculating this adjustment is not straightforward either, because the standard gives no guidance on how it should be done. For example, it is unclear whether the new interest rate should be applied during the year or just at year end, and whether the rate should be applied to the new estimate of the provision or the old estimate. This again appears to give companies flexibility in the approach that they adopt, although once a particular approach is adopted, it should be applied consistently.

3.2.6 Conclusions on discounting

The ASB has introduced the concept of discounting into FRS 12, with almost no guidance on the related implementation issues that arise, resulting in all sorts of ambiguities in the requirements.

However, the considerations detailed above lead us to suggest that for practical purposes, cash flows are assessed prudently and then discounted using the gross rate on a government bond (taking either a real rate or a nominal rate depending on whether the future cash flows are being estimated using current or future prices). On unwinding the discount, a number of options appear to be acceptable, so long as they are consistently applied.

3.3 Future events

The standard states that 'future events that may affect the amount required to settle an obligation should be reflected in the amount of a provision where there is sufficient objective evidence that they will occur'.[56] The types of future events that the standard has in mind are advances in technology and changes in legislation.

This is intended to mean that a provision cannot be reduced simply on the basis that new technology is likely to be developed in the intervening period before the liability is settled. There will need to be sufficient objective evidence of this new technology. Similarly, if new legislation is to be anticipated, there will need to be evidence of what the legislation will demand, and whether it is virtually certain to be enacted and implemented in due course.

These requirements are most likely to impact provisions for liabilities that will be settled some distance in the future, such as decommissioning costs (see 4.5 below).

3.4   Recoveries from third parties

In some circumstances an entity is able to look to a third party to reimburse part of the costs required to settle a provision. Examples are insurance contracts, indemnity clauses and suppliers' warranties. In the majority of cases where a recovery is expected, the entity would remain liable for the whole costs if the third party failed to pay for any reason, for example as a result of the third party's insolvency.

If the entity would not be liable for these costs even if the third party failed to pay, the amount should not be included within the provision. However, if the entity remains liable for the whole amount, the provision should be made gross and any such reimbursement should be treated as a separate asset (provided it is virtually certain that the reimbursement will be received if the entity settles the obligation). The amount recognised for the reimbursement should not exceed the amount of the provision.[57] This is different from the previous rule under SSAP 18, where such provisions were made net of expected recoveries, although FRS 12 still allows the amounts to be netted off in the profit and loss account.[58]

This change has caused Hanson to reinstate insured environmental liabilities on its balance sheet, as shown in this extract from its interim accounts to June 1999.

Extract 25.3: Hanson PLC (1999)

Interim Results for 6 months ended June 30, 1999

Accounting Issues

Hanson is required to adopt Financial Reporting Standard 12 'Provisions, Contingent Liabilities and Contingent Assets' (FRS12) for this accounting period including the restatement of comparative figures. A profit and loss effect of the standard is the requirement to unwind the discounting of our reclamation provisions which is shown as a separate financing charge on the profit and loss account.

The adoption of the standard also requires Hanson to reinstate on the balance sheet the pre-funded and insured Koppers environmental liabilities. At the same time, the company recognises as an asset in the balance sheet the equivalent amount that will be due from its insurers, Centre

Solutions, a member of the Zurich Group, and Swiss Re. The net effect of this is zero, reflecting the effective transfer of risk with the asset offsetting the liability. This recognises the commercial reality that expenditure under the provision will be reimbursed by the insurance companies.

CONSOLIDATED BALANCE SHEET
at June 30, 1999 and at December 31, 1998 [extract]

	June 30 1999 Unaudited £million	December 31 1998 £million
Fixed assets		
Intangible assets	154.3	70.6
Tangible assets	2,132.7	1,997.8
Investments	68.4	132.0
	2,355.4	2,200.4
Other assets		
Amounts due from insurers for Koppers liabilities (see below)	173.1	164.3
Current assets		
...		
Provisions for liabilities and charges		
Provisions for liabilities	626.2	629.2
Koppers liabilities transferred to insurers (see above)	173.1	164.3
...		

Notes

6. Restatement of comparatives [extract]

The adoption of Financial Reporting Standard 12 'Provisions, Contingent Liabilities and Contingent Assets' (FRS 12) has necessitated an adjustment to certain provisions made in prior years. FRS 12 has required changes in the method of accounting for reclamation costs, health care obligations in respect of US employees, environmental obligations, decommissioning costs and other liabilities. Provisions have been discounted at a rate of 2.5% on current prices, except where more appropriate discounting rates have been used having regard to information provided by actuaries or other independent advisers.

As a result of these changes in accounting policy the comparatives have been restated as follows:

a) Consolidated balance sheet

	Tangible fixed assets £million	Other assets £million	Koppers liabilities transferred to insurers £million	Other provisions for liabilities and charges £million	Shareholders Funds £million
1998 reported	2,000.3	–	–	(684.6)	(1,539.4)
Adoption of FRS 12	(2.5)	164.3	(164.3)	55.4	(52.9)
1998 restated	1,997.8	164.3	(164.3)	(629.2)	(1,592.3)

The principal changes arise from the elimination, increase and reclassification of provisions for liabilities and charges. In the case of Koppers environmental liabilities the obligation is recognised in provisions with a corresponding asset representing the amounts receivable under the insurance arrangements entered into in 1998. Under these arrangements the funding and risk of the environmental liabilities relating to the former Koppers company operations of Beazer PLC have been transferred to and underwritten by subsidiaries of two of the world's largest reinsurance companies, Centre Solutions (a member of the Zurich Group) and Swiss Re.

We are not convinced that the standard's requirement to gross up in such circumstances is an improvement on the previous rules. Again, it is a consequence of approaching the subject from a balance sheet perspective rather than as an expense recognition issue, but it has the effect of including assets in the balance sheet that do not meet the usual recognition criteria. Furthermore, it is inconsistent with existing practice under a number of other standards. For example, under FRS 3, provisions for the sale or termination of an operation have to be calculated 'after taking into account the aggregate profit ... from the future profits of the operation'.[59] Under SSAP 9 provision has to be made for long-term contracts which are projected to make a loss, but there is no suggestion that the remaining revenue and costs would have to be recorded in the balance sheet in full even though the contract had not been completed.[60] And even the ASB's earlier Discussion Paper said that provisions for vacant leasehold properties should be net of expected recoveries from subletting the property (which we still believe to be the appropriate treatment), and did not suggest that all future rental income and expenditure should be brought on to the balance sheet.[61]

In an attempt to rationalise the inconsistency, FRED 14 acknowledged the FRS 3 case cited above but said that 'the Board is of the view that it is appropriate to calculate closure provisions on a net basis because a unit that is not a going concern is most usefully represented to users in one line, separately from continuing operations'.[62] This did nothing to justify the inconsistency, but it does at least open up a new possibility: perhaps it would be equally 'useful' simply to abandon the supposed sanctity of the offsetting rule in relation to provisions of other kinds as well.

It is difficult to predict how much impact this requirement will have in practice. Certainly, if interpreted strictly, a number of items which were previously netted off in the balance sheet may now have to be shown gross. Even so, it is possible that the overall effect on the balance sheet will often not be material, so entities may avoid the requirement on this basis. We expect that certain major items will be grossed up, such as those illustrated by the Hanson extract above, but do not consider that it would be appropriate to gross up such things as vacant leasehold property provisions.

The issue that may give more concern is whether the strict criteria that need to be applied to the corresponding asset might mean that some reimbursements will not now be able to be recognised at all. For items such as insurance contracts, this may not be a concern, as entities will probably be able to argue that a recovery on an insurance contract is virtually certain if the entity is required to settle the obligation. For other types of reimbursement, however, recovery may be less certain. It remains to be seen how practice develops in this area.

It is interesting to contrast this approach with the case where an entity is jointly and severally liable for an obligation. In that case, the company provides only for its own share and the remainder that is expected to be met by other parties is treated only as a contingent liability.[63] This means that a similar economic position is not always portrayed in the same way. If it were, then a liability would have to be set up for the whole amount for which the entity is jointly and severally liable, with a corresponding asset being recognised for the amount expected to be met by other parties.

3.5 Gains on disposals of related assets

One refinement to the measurement rules was only introduced after the exposure draft stage – that gains from the expected disposal of assets should not be taken into account in measuring a provision.[64] The rationale behind this is that the ASB believes that liabilities should be measured independently of the recognition and measurement rules for assets. The area where this requirement is likely to have most impact is in the measurement of restructuring provisions. Low & Bonar refers to this in relation to a provision in its 1998 accounts:

Extract 25.4: Low & Bonar PLC (1998)

FINANCIAL REVIEW [extract]

... we have made a provision of £7.5 million to cover the costs of closure. This figure excludes an estimated gain of approximately £2 million which we anticipate on the disposal of the land, buildings and certain equipment which, due to changing accounting standards, cannot be accounted for until the assets are sold. The cash costs associated with the Irlam closure net of disposal proceeds when the land, buildings and equipment are sold, are anticipated to be between £2 million and £3 million. ...

Rather more spectacularly, this change has led British Aerospace to write off the remarkable sum of £267 million, as shown in this extract:

Extract 25.5: British Aerospace Public Limited Company (1998)

24 Reserves [extract]

FRS 12 – Provisions, contingent liabilities and contingent assets

In previous years, expenditure on rationalisation schemes initiated before 1991 was included within development properties to the extent that it was recoverable from the estimated disposal proceeds. FRS 12 does not permit such expected gains to be taken into account when assessing the level of provision relating to such schemes. These rationalisation costs which amounted to £267 million at 31 December 1997 are now no longer included.

FRS 3 *Reporting Financial Performance* has been amended to bring it in line with this requirement in FRS 12. A provision made for the sale or termination of an operation under FRS 3 will no longer be able to take into account gains from expected disposals of assets, although it will still be able to take into account future profits of the operation (see Chapter 22 at 2.4).

3.6   Changes and uses of provisions

The standard requires provisions to be revised annually to reflect the current best estimate of the obligation.[65] This seems uncontroversial, other than in relation to changes in discount rates, which are discussed in 3.2.5 above.

The standard emphasises that provisions should be used only for expenditures for which the provision was originally recognised.[66] This means that the questionable practice of charging costs against a provision that was set up for a different purpose is specifically prohibited and the profit and loss account will have to charge the new expenses separately from any release of an unused provision.

4   EXAMPLES OF PROVISIONS IN PRACTICE

4.1   Restructuring provisions

4.1.1   *Definition*

FRS 12 defines a restructuring as 'a programme that is planned and controlled by management and materially changes either:

(a)   the scope of a business undertaken by an entity; or

(b)   the manner in which that business is conducted.'[67]

This is said to include:

(a)   sale or termination of a line of business;

(b)   the closure of business locations in a country or region or the relocation of business activities from one country or region to another;

(c)   changes in management structure, for example, eliminating a layer of management; and

(d)   fundamental reorganisations that have a material effect on the nature and focus of the entity's operations.[68]

This definition is very wide, and could encourage companies to classify all kinds of operating costs as restructuring costs, and thereby invite the reader to perceive them in a different light from the 'normal' costs of operating in a dynamic business environment. Even though FRS 12 prevents such costs being expensed too early (see recognition rules below), and FRS 3 might stop them being charged outside the operating profit section of the profit and loss account, their separate disclosure as restructuring costs may nonetheless cause users of accounts to misinterpret the business's performance. 'Restructuring' is a term of art which can be, and is, used to cover a multitude of sins, and there is a risk that the standard will perpetuate this. The reality is that change has become a perennial feature of business and it is potentially misleading to afford it any special status in accounting terms.

4.1.2   Recognition

FRS 12 requires that restructuring costs are recognised only when the general recognition criteria in the standard are met. The interpretation of these criteria give rise to further specific requirements that 'a constructive obligation to restructure arises only when an entity:

(a)   has a detailed formal plan for the restructuring identifying at least:

   (i)   the business or part of a business concerned;

   (ii)   the principal locations affected;

   (iii)   the location, function, and approximate number of employees who will be compensated for terminating their services;

   (iv)   the expenditures that will be undertaken; and

   (v)   when the plan will be implemented; and

(b)   has raised a valid expectation in those affected that it will carry out the restructuring by starting to implement that plan or announcing its main features to those affected by it.'[69]

The standard gives examples of the entity's actions that may provide evidence that the entity has started to implement a plan, quoting the dismantling of plant or selling of assets, or the public announcement of the main features of the plan. However, it also emphasises that the public announcement of a detailed plan to restructure will not automatically create an obligation; the important principle is that the entity's actions give rise to valid expectations in other parties such as customers, suppliers and employees.[70]

The standard also suggests that any extended period before commencement of implementation will mean that a provision is premature, because the entity is still likely to have a chance of changing the plan.[71] In summary, these conditions require the plan to be detailed and specific, to have gone beyond the directors' powers of recall and to be put into operation without delay or significant alteration.

The criteria set out above for the recognition of provisions mean that a board decision, if it is the only relevant event arising before the balance sheet date, will no longer suffice. This message is reinforced specifically in the standard, the argument being made that a constructive obligation is not created by a management decision. The standard acknowledges that there will be examples where a board decision does trigger recognition, but this would only be if earlier events such as negotiations with employee representatives for termination payments, or with purchasers for the sale of an operation, have been concluded subject only to board approval. In such circumstances, it is reasoned that when board approval has been obtained and communicated to the other parties, the entity is committed to restructure, assuming all other conditions are met.[72]

There is also discussion in the standard of the situation that may arise in some countries where, for example, employee representatives may sit on the board, so that a board decision effectively communicates the decision to them, which may result in a constructive obligation to restructure.[73]

These recognition rules are substantially different from those that most companies have applied in the past. De La Rue provides an example of a group that has had to restate the accounts of earlier years to alter the timing of recognition of such costs.

Extract 25.6: De La Rue plc (1999)

29 Prior year adjustments [extract]

The implementation of new accounting standards has resulted in a number of prior year adjustments. These can be summarised as follows:

(a) The reorganisation cost of £14.8m in respect of Security Paper and Print which was previously charged in 1996/97 has been recharged in 1997/98.

(b) Camelot has also restated its results on the implementation of FRS 12, the net impact of which has been to increase our equity accounted share of its profits by £1.2m in 1997/98 and £1.2m prior to 1997/98.

...

The dismissal of the significance of board decisions was not well supported when the ASB proposed it in FRED 14. A large number of commentators suggested that board decisions should act as a trigger for recognition of provisions, particularly if supported by subsequent events between the year end and approval of the accounts which indicate that the board decision was a meaningful one. However, the ASB made no concessions to this view, and has merely added a paragraph in the final standard which suggests that where events after the balance sheet date indicate the existence of a constructive obligation to restructure that did not exist at the balance sheet date, this may require disclosure as a non-adjusting event under SSAP 17[74] (see Chapter 24).

The 1999 accounts of both Pilkington and Marks and Spencer disclose the costs of restructurings that were announced after the year end and hence were not provided for.

Extract 25.7: Pilkington plc (1999)

43 Post-balance sheet event

On 26th May 1999 the Group announced its plans to reorganise and streamline its automotive manufacturing operations in North America. This will involve the closure of a plant and the transfer of its production to two other existing facilities in North America. The programme is expected to involve exceptional restructuring costs of approximately £30 million, of which half are expected to be cash costs. No adjustment has been made for this in the financial statements.

Extract 25.8: Marks and Spencer p.l.c. (1999)

31 Post-balance sheet events

On 28 April, the Group announced the closure of its Canadian operations. As a consequence, its subsidiary Marks & Spencer Canada Inc. will cease to operate during the financial year ending 31 March 2000. The total cost of closure is estimated to be £25m, excluding goodwill of £24.4m previously written off to reserves.

On 10 May, the Group announced the rationalisation of its UK store management. The total cost of this rationalisation is estimated to be £14m.

De La Rue has given supplementary disclosure in its financial review of its future expected reorganisation costs, which contrast with the provisions it is now able to make under FRS 12, as shown in this extract.

Extract 25.9: De La Rue plc (1999)

Financial Review

Analysis of reorganisation costs

During the last year, we have announced major reorganisations within Cash Systems and Security Paper and Print, together with the relocation of our head office. In line with current accounting practice, costs are written off against profits as committed. A significant element of these costs will not be committed until our financial year ending in March 2000. Set out in Table 1 is a summary which shows the charge in 1999 and the expected charge in our current year's accounts and corresponding cash outflows.

Table 1 – Reorganisation costs

	1999 £m	Expected 2000 £m	2001 £m
Cash Systems	25.9	20.0	–
Security Paper and Print	18.7	5.0	–
Head Office relocation	3.9	–	–
Total profit and loss cost	48.5	25.0	–
Cash outflow	26.2	28.0	5.0

17 Provisions for liabilities and charges [extract]

The reorganisation within Security Paper and Print utilised £3.7m of the provision created in 1996/97, leaving a total of £0.2m carried forward within other provisions. Further reorganisation provisions were established during the current year of which £1.4m remains within other provisions.

With regard to the Cash Systems reorganisation, £2.9m is carried forward within other provisions.

A total of £2.8m is carried forward in other provisions in respect of the relocation of Head Office from London to Basingstoke.

Disclosure of this kind adds to the transparency of such costs and can be very helpful to the reader. Nevertheless, we are not convinced that the change in recognition of reorganisation costs that FRS 12 has brought about is a beneficial one. We believe that it is misguided to ignore the effect of management intentions in portraying the financial performance and position of an entity, as this can often be highly relevant to an understanding of the entity's affairs. Although board decisions are capable of being reversed, this does not happen as a general rule.

Furthermore, the exclusion of the effect of management decisions is not a principle that has been applied consistently by the ASB. Take the example of a restructuring which is announced shortly after the balance sheet date involving the closure of plants and large scale redundancies. The reporting entity will be precluded from recognising the direct costs of the restructuring, as it does not have a constructive obligation at the balance sheet date. However, the entity will be required to make provision for impairment in the carrying value of plant and other assets at the affected sites under FRS 11 (see Chapter 10 at 4.4). Hence, board decisions would appear to be relevant when assessing impairment of assets but not when determining the reporting entity's liabilities, with the result that only some of the costs that result from the closure decision are recognised.

It is also the case that the apparently robust tests of a constructive obligation set out in the standard are weaker than they seem. The interpretation of the concept of actions that 'raise a valid expectation in third parties' is likely to be extremely difficult and subjective. Even if a trigger point is easily identifiable, such as when an entity makes a detailed public announcement which meets all the specified criteria, it does not necessarily commit management to the 'restructuring' as such, but only to specific items of expenditure such as redundancy costs. Nevertheless, in practice, once a trigger point has been identified, an entity will presumably provide for all the costs of the reorganisation, assuming that they meet the measurement criteria set out in 4.1.3 below.

Furthermore, the test is at least as manipulable as board decisions. Companies anxious to accelerate or postpone recognition of a liability could readily do so by advancing or deferring an event that signals such a commitment, such as a public announcement, without any change to the substance of their position.

FRS 12 has some further specific rules governing when to recognise the loss arising on the sale of an operation. It requires there to be a binding sale agreement before a provision can be made for such a loss.[75] This requirement is similar to one already contained in FRS 3 (see Chapter 22 at 2.4). However, FRS 3 contains an additional suggestion in its explanatory section that a binding contract entered into after the balance sheet date may provide additional evidence of commitments at the balance sheet date.[76] The meaning of this explanatory paragraph has never been clarified, and similar wording is not included within FRS 12. Hence, it could be argued that if the explanatory paragraph in FRS 3 has previously been used to justify setting up provision for the disposal of an operation where the binding sale agreement was entered into after the balance sheet date but before the accounts were signed, this interpretation is no longer allowable under FRS 12. However, this is unclear, given that the relevant paragraph in FRS 3 itself has not been deleted or amended.

If the sale of an operation is envisaged as part of a larger restructuring, the standard notes that the assets of the operation must be reviewed for impairment. The standard also recognises that where a sale is part of a larger restructuring, the entity could be committed to the other parts of restructuring before the binding sale agreement is in place.[77] Hence, the costs of the restructuring will be spread over different accounting periods.

4.1.3 Costs that can be recognised within a restructuring provision

The recognition tests for reorganisation costs that are set out above are designed to establish whether or not there is a liability at the balance sheet date, which is consistent with the conceptual approach of the standard and indeed with the ASB's draft *Statement of Principles*. It is therefore rather surprising to find an additional paragraph in the standard that further limits the costs that can be provided for and which is founded on quite a different conceptual approach. It states that 'provision should include only the direct expenditures arising from the restructuring, which are those that are both:

(a)   necessarily entailed by a restructuring; and

(b)   not associated with the ongoing activities of the entity'.[78]

While (a) is perhaps a further elaboration of the rules for defining the extent of the company's obligations, the rationale for (b) is not so straightforward. The justification given for it ties in with the more general requirement in the standard that 'it is only those obligations arising from past events existing independently of an entity's future actions that should be recognised'.[79] Hence, these costs are recognised on the same basis as if they arose independently of the restructuring.

In reality, this is an approach based on expense recognition, in that the costs associated with ongoing activities will produce future benefits, and thus should not be anticipated, whether or not a liability for them exists. Expense recognition is a concept not adequately acknowledged by the ASB's draft *Statement of Principles*, but one which the Board seems unable to do without.

The standard gives specific examples of those costs that may not be included within the provision. Such costs include:

(a)   retraining or relocating continuing staff;

(b)   marketing; or

(c)   investment in new systems and distribution networks.[80]

United Utilities disclosed a restructuring provision in its 1998 accounts:

Extract 25.10: United Utilities PLC (1998)

20 Provisions for liabilities and charges [extract]

						Group	Company
	Restructuring £m	Onerous contracts £m	Bangkok £m	Retail divestment £m	Other £m	Total £m	Other £m
At 31 March 1997	127.7	166.6	42.0	41.8	51.2	429.3	12.3
Utilised	(49.0)	(5.7)	(21.2)	(20.6)	(39.8)	(136.3)	(3.9)
Profit and loss account	(6.5)	–	–	–	(4.7)	(11.2)	–
At 31 March 1998	72.2	160.9	20.8	21.2	6.7	281.8	8.4

Restructuring

The restructuring provisions relate primarily to:

- the cost of completing the reorganisation of North West Water operations;
- the cost of completing the voluntary redundancy programme established by NORWEB plc prior to the acquisition; and
- the cost of reorganising the Group following the acquisition of NORWEB plc (including an expansion of the Norweb voluntary redundancy programme outlined above).

The above costs primarily relate to terminations, training, relocation of employees and systems improvements.

The description of the costs in the last sentence of this extract shows that some of the items provided for appear to be associated with ongoing activities, which meant that they would be unlikely to be permitted in the future under FRS 12. Accordingly. in its 1999 accounts United Utilities amended its provisions as shown in this extract.

Extract 25.11: United Utilities PLC (1999)

1 Accounting policies

(a) Basis of preparation of financial statements [extract]

– restatement of provisions to comply with Financial Reporting Standard 12. The effect of this standard is to change the allocation of restructuring costs between previous reporting periods. Costs previously provided for did not meet the stringent criteria for recording a liability now embodied in Financial Reporting Standard 12. Consequently, the results of previous periods have been amended to reflect the requirements of the new standard and the results for the year ended 31 March 1998 have been reduced by £55.6 million and for the year ended 31 March 1997 have been reduced by £46.5 million. These adjustments reflect the profile of the utilisation of the original provisions. There has been no material impact on the results for the year ended 31 March 1999 in respect of these adjustments.

19 Provisions for liabilities and charges [extract]

						Group	Company
	Restructuring Restated £m	Onerous contracts Restated £m	Bangkok £m	Retail divestment £m	Other £m	Total Restated £m	Other £m
At 1 April 1998	38.8	192.9	20.8	21.2	6.7	280.4	8.4
Utilised	(23.5)	(8.0)	(2.2)	(0.7)	(3.9)	(38.3)	(1.8)
At 31 March 1998	**15.3**	**184.9**	**18.6**	**20.5**	**2.8**	**242.1**	**6.6**

Restructuring

The restructuring provisions relate primarily to:

– the cost of completing the reorganisation of North West Water operations;

– the cost of completing the voluntary redundancy programme established by NORWEB plc prior to the acquisition; and

– the cost of reorganising the Group following the acquisition of NORWEB plc (including an expansion of the Norweb voluntary redundancy programme outlined above).

No examples of allowable costs are given within the standard. However, FRED 14 gave certain examples. These were the costs of:

(a) making employees redundant;

(b) terminating leases and other contracts whose termination results directly from the reorganisation; and

(c) expenditures to be made in the course of the reorganisation, such as employees' remuneration while they are engaged in such tasks as dismantling plant, disposing of surplus stocks and fulfilling contractual obligations.[81]

Examples (a) and (b) would certainly be permitted under the rules in FRS 12. Example (c) is slightly more contentious in relation to employee remuneration, in that unless an employee is being retained solely for the purpose of dismantling plant, etc, before being made redundant, it is questionable whether the remuneration costs meet the definition of being 'necessarily entailed by a restructuring'.

A further rule in FRS 12 is that the provision should not include identifiable future operating losses up to the date of the restructuring, unless they relate to an onerous contract.[82] This is consistent with the more general requirement in the standard that provision should not be made for future operating losses, discussed in 4.2 below. However, it may lead to a certain amount of confusion in relation to discontinued operations. This is because they fall within the definition of a restructuring as defined in FRS 12, and provisions for discontinued operations are also dealt with in FRS 3 where they are required to include any operating losses of the operation up to the date of sale or termination.[83] Given that no amendment has been made to FRS 3, it seems reasonable to assume that entities will be able to continue to make provision for future operating losses in these circumstances.

The general rule noted in 3.5 above that gains on the expected disposal of assets cannot be taken into account in the measurement of provisions will be particularly relevant to the measurement of restructuring provisions. This might suggest that larger restructuring provisions than before will be required as any corresponding expected gains on assets will no longer be available for set off, as was the case with British Aerospace as shown in Extract 25.5 above. However, sometimes the impact of this rule will be mitigated by the fact that fewer costs will also be recognised within a provision, as some will not meet the criteria set out above. Hence, both restructuring costs and revenues on asset disposals will often be recognised in later accounting periods than was normal practice before FRS 12.

4.2   Operating losses

The standard explicitly states that 'Provisions should not be recognised for future operating losses'.[84] Such costs should be left to be reported in the future in the same way as future profits are.

However, it would be wrong to assume that this requirement has effectively prevented any future operating losses from being anticipated, because they are sometimes recognised as a result of requirements in another standard. For example:

- under SSAP 9, stocks are written down to the extent that they will not be recovered from future revenues, rather than leaving the non-recovery to show up as future operating losses (see Chapter 14 at 6.2.2);

- under FRS 11, fixed asset impairment is measured on the basis of the present value of future operating cash flows, meaning that provision will be made not simply for future operating losses but for sub-standard operating profits as well (see Chapter 10 at 4.4). FRS 12 specifically makes reference to the fact that an expectation of future operating losses may be an indication that certain assets are impaired;[85]

■ provision is made for future operating losses of operations that are committed to be sold or terminated under FRS 3 (see Chapter 22 at 2.4); and

■ provision is made for losses expected on long-term construction contracts under SSAP 9. Indeed, this sometimes extends even to provision for future administration costs where existing unprofitable contracts will absorb a large part of the company's future capacity.[86]

This is therefore a rather more complex issue than FRS 12 acknowledges.

4.3 Onerous contracts

Although future operating losses in general cannot be provided for, FRS 12 requires that 'If an entity has a contract that is onerous, the present obligation under the contract should be recognised and measured as a provision'.[87] It defines an onerous contract as 'a contract in which the unavoidable costs of meeting the obligations under it exceed the economic benefits expected to be received under it'.[88] This seems to require that the contract is onerous to the point of being directly loss-making, not simply uneconomic by reference to current prices. In this respect the definition is narrower than should be applied in the context of acquisition accounting, where the task is to put a fair value on identifiable assets and liabilities. Occasionally, similar considerations apply in the context of disposals, where a fair value has to be put on residual obligations that are part of the bargained transactions. Allied Domecq disclosed this provision in respect of an uneconomic contract in its 1996 accounts, relating to the disposal of Carlsberg-Tetley:

Extract 25.12: Allied Domecq PLC (1996)

7. SALE OR TERMINATION OF BUSINESSES [extract]

The brewing operation sold in the year to 31 August 1996 was Carlsberg-Tetley and a provision of £63m was set up to cover the uneconomic supply of beer to Allied Domecq Retailing from the date of disposal in August 1996 until the end of the supply agreement with Carlsberg-Tetley in December 1997.

In the context of ongoing operations, however, FRS 12 considers that 'the unavoidable costs under a contract reflect the least net cost of exiting from the contract ie the lower of the cost of fulfilling it and any compensation or penalties arising from failure to fulfil it'.[89] An example of such a provision is BG's gas contract loss provisions, which stood at £222 million at 31 December 1998, and are described in this extract.

Extract 25.13: BG plc (1998)

20 Provisions for liabilities and charges [extract]

Long term gas sales contract provisions

These represent forecast future losses under certain gas purchase and supply sales contracts assigned to BG on demerger in 1997. The contracts terminate in years 2001 and 2008. The estimated net losses have been discounted and are dependent upon factors such as prices, which vary with a basket of indices, and supply and demand volumes.

The most common example of an onerous contract in practice probably relates to leasehold property. From time to time entities may hold vacant leasehold property (or property which is only partly occupied) which they have substantially ceased to use for the purpose of their business and where sub-letting is either unlikely, or would be at a significantly reduced rental.

This issue was addressed previously in 1993, when the UITF proposed to introduce an abstract to require provision to be made, but as a result of the large amount of opposition that it received to its draft did not proceed with the abstract. Until FRS 12 clarified the matter, this meant that various treatments continued in practice, as shown in these extracts from accounts that predated the standard.

Extract 25.14: Cordiant Communications Group plc (1998)

PRINCIPAL ACCOUNTING POLICIES

Property provisions

Provision is made on an undiscounted basis for the future rent expense and related costs of leasehold property (net of estimated sublease income) where the space is vacant or currently not planned to be used for ongoing operations.

Extract 25.15: The Rank Group Plc (1998)

Accounting policies

8 Leased assets [extract]

... Operating lease payments are charged to the profit and loss account as incurred. No provision is made for future costs on vacant leasehold properties. Such costs are expensed as incurred.

Now that this issue has been addressed by the standard, and reinforced by the inclusion of a specific example of a provision for a vacant leasehold property, companies will have to make systematic provision when properties become vacant, and on a discounted basis where the effect is sufficiently material.

However, a number of difficulties remain. The first is how the provision should be calculated. It is unlikely that the provision will simply be the net present value of the future rental obligation, because if a substantial period of the lease remains, the entity will probably be able either to agree a negotiated sum with the landlord to terminate the lease early, or to sub-lease the building at some point in the future. Hence, the entity will have to make a best estimate of its future cash flows taking all these factors into account.

Another issue that arises from this is whether the provision can be shown net of any cash flows that may arise from sub-leasing the property, or whether the provision must be shown gross, with a corresponding asset set up for expected cash flows from sub-leasing only if they meet the recognition criteria of being 'virtually certain' to be received. The strict offset criteria in the standard would suggest the latter to be required, as the entity would normally retain liability for the full lease payments if the sub-lessor defaulted. It is unlikely that this is really the result that the ASB intended, particularly as the Board's earlier Discussion Paper anticipated that a net provision should be made.

In the past, some companies have maintained that no provision is required for vacant properties, because if the property leases are looked at on a portfolio basis, the overall economic benefits from properties exceed the overall costs. However, this argument does not appear to be sustainable under FRS 12, as the definition of an onerous contract refers specifically to costs and economic benefits *under the contract.*

It is more difficult to apply the definition of onerous contracts to the lease on a head office which is not generating revenue specifically. If the definition were applied too literally, one may end up concluding that all head office leases should be provided against because no specific economic benefits are expected under them. It would be more sensible to conclude that the entity as a whole obtains economic benefits from its head office, which was presumably the reason for entering in to the lease to start with. However, this does not alter the fact that if circumstances alter and the head office becomes vacant, a provision should then be made against the lease.

The standard also requires that any assets dedicated to an onerous contract should be written down before a provision is made.[90] For example, any leasehold improvements that have been capitalised should be written off before provision is made for excess future rental costs.

4.4   Environmental provisions

FRED 14 proposed specific recognition rules in relation to environmental liabilities. It said that 'provisions for environmental liabilities should be recognised at the time and to the extent that the entity becomes obliged, legally or constructively, to rectify environmental damage or to perform restorative work on the environment.'[91] The further discussion in the draft focused on the idea of 'constructive obligations', making it clear that provision was possible only if the company had no real option but to carry out the remedial work.[92]

These specific rules are not included in the final standard, but the general recognition rules which apply have the same impact. These requirements are not particularly controversial and, apart from the general difficulty in knowing exactly when a constructive obligation comes into existence, are unlikely to change prevailing practice.

The standard illustrates two examples of circumstances where environmental provisions would be required. The first deals with the situation where it is virtually certain that legislation will be enacted which will require the clean up of land already contaminated.[93] In these circumstances, a provision would obviously be required. The second example deals with the situation where an entity has contaminated land, but is not legally required to clean it up.[94] In these circumstances, a provision is required if the entity has a constructive obligation to clean up the land. In the example given, a constructive obligation is said to exist because the entity has a widely publicised environmental policy undertaking to clean up all contamination that it causes, and has a record of honouring this policy.

ICI and BP Amoco disclosed these respective policies on environmental liabilities, in accounts that predated FRS 12:

Extract 25.16: Imperial Chemical Industries PLC (1998)

Accounting policies
Environmental liabilities

The Group is exposed to environmental liabilities relating to its past operations, principally in respect of soil and groundwater remediation costs. Provisions for these costs are made when expenditure on remedial work is probable and the cost can be estimated within a reasonable range of possible outcomes.

Extract 25.17: BP Amoco p.l.c. (1998)

Accounting policies
Environmental liabilities

Environmental expenditures that relate to current or future revenues are expensed or capitalized as appropriate. Expenditures that relate to an existing condition caused by past operations and that do not contribute to current or future earnings are expensed.

Liabilities for environmental costs are recognized when environmental assessments or clean-ups are probable and the associated costs can be reasonably estimated. Generally, the timing of these provisions coincides with the commitment to a formal plan of action or, if earlier, on divestment or on closure of inactive sites.

The more significant effect of the standard may be its requirement that provisions should be discounted, which will have a material impact if the expenditure is not expected to be incurred for some time. As shown in Extract 25.20 below, BP Amoco has since adopted FRS 12; this change had the effect of reducing its environmental provision by £350 million because of the discount factor.

4.5   Decommissioning provisions

Decommissioning costs are those that arise, for example, when an oil rig or nuclear power station has to be dismantled at the end of its life. The impact of the standard on such costs is profound. Previous practice in line with the SORP of the Oil Industry Accounting Committee (OIAC) was to build up the required provision over the life of the facility by appropriate charges against revenues. BP Amoco described the process in this policy note:

Extract 25.18: BP Amoco p.l.c. (1998)

Accounting policies

Decommissioning

Provision is made for the decommissioning of production facilities in accordance with local conditions and requirements on the basis of costs estimated as at the balance sheet date. The provision is allocated over accounting periods using a unit-of-production method based on estimated proved reserves.

The scale of this obligation is evident from its provisions note:

Extract 25.19: BP Amoco p.l.c. (1998)

23 Other provisions [extract]	**$ million**
	Decommissioning
At 1 January 1998	3,201
Exchange adjustments	10
Charged to income	130
Utilized/deleted	(31)
At 31 December 1998	**3,310**

FRS 12, on the other hand, now requires that the liability is recognised as soon as the obligation exists, which will normally be at commencement of operations. The example in the standard discusses the situation where ninety per cent of the damage is done by building the rig, and ten per cent through the extraction of oil.[95] In these circumstances, a provision for ninety per cent of the total costs will be set up when the rig has been constructed, with the balance being recognised as the oil is extracted.

FRS 12 also says that provisions should be capitalised if the expenditure provides access to future economic benefits.[96] Hence, in the case of decommissioning costs, the oil rig provides access to oil reserves over the years of its operation, so the balance sheet will be grossed up to show this corresponding asset representing access to future oil reserves.

Although we understand why the Board's conceptual framework pushes it towards recognition of the full liability, it seems that this can only be achieved by including a spurious asset on the other side of the balance sheet. In any case, if the principle that a liability should be recognised once costs have become unavoidable were really to be applied on a consistent basis, various other commitments (for example, expenditure commitments under licence agreements) would also be caught and there would be considerable grossing up of balance sheets. We therefore question whether this change has much merit.

This form of presentation had been considered but rejected by the Oil Industry Accounting Committee when it produced its earlier SORP on the subject. Although acknowledging the conceptual arguments that now lie behind FRS 12, it said that 'the OIAC has no doubt that the gradual build-up of the provision is the appropriate method of recognising this obligation because of the fact that changes in the scope of work, technology and prices are likely to result in great subsequent changes, downwards as well as upwards, in the amounts originally recognised. Whilst changes in estimates of liabilities are an unavoidable and therefore accepted feature of historical cost accounting, these changes would also affect the recorded amounts of assets. The OIAC believes that the resulting changes to the structure of oil company balance sheets would be unlikely to enhance their usefulness.'[97]

The more significant change for most companies, however, will involve the use of discounting for the measurement of the liability. Although it has been used for some time in the nuclear industry, discounting is not consistent with previous accounting practice for oil companies. The effect of discounting on the profit and loss account will be to split the cost of the eventual decommissioning into two components: an operating cost based on the discounted amount of the provision; and an interest element representing the unwinding of the discount. The overall effect will be to produce a rising pattern of cost over the life of the facility, often with most of the total cost of the decommissioning recognised in the interest line. In contrast, previous practice for oil companies was to show the whole amount in arriving at their operating results, and to aim to charge a level amount for each barrel of oil extracted, although the effects of changing estimates of costs, particularly inflation (which was not factored into the original estimates made), was likely to mean that this is not precisely achieved.

As a result of FRS 12, BP Amoco has changed its policy, as shown below in this extract from Listing Particulars issued in July 1999.

Extract 25.20: BP Amoco p.l.c. (1998 restated)

Statement of Accounting Policies

Decommissioning

Provision for decommissioning is recognised in full at the commencement of oil and natural gas production. The amount recognised is the present value of the estimated future expenditure determined in accordance with local conditions and requirements. A corresponding tangible fixed asset is also created of an amount equal to the provision. This is subsequently depreciated as part of the capital costs of the production and transportation facilities. Any change in the present value of the estimated expenditure is reflected as an adjustment to the provision and the fixed asset.

46 New accounting standard for provisions

The BP Amoco Group has adopted Financial Reporting Standard No. 12 'Provisions, Contingent Liabilities and Contingent Assets' ("FRS 12") with effect from 1 January 1999. The standard changes the criteria for recognising provisions for such costs as decommissioning, environmental liabilities and restructuring charges. It also requires provisions for liabilities which may not be settled for a number of years to be discounted to their net present value. The adoption of this standard has been treated as a change in accounting policy. Comparative figures have been restated to reflect the change in accounting policy.

The principal effects of the adoption of FRS 12 are as follows:

(a) Provisions for environmental liabilities are determined on a discounted basis as the effect of the time value of money is material. Previously these liabilities were on an undiscounted basis.

(b) Provisions for decommissioning are recognised in full, on a discounted basis at the commencement of oil and natural gas production. The BP Amoco Group's prior practice was to accrue the expected cost of decommissioning oil and natural gas production facilities on a unit-of-production basis over the life of the field. FRS 12 also requires the BP Amoco Group to capitalise an amount equivalent to the provision as a tangible fixed asset and to amortise this amount over the life of the field on a unit-of-production basis.

(c) The unwinding of the discount, which represents a period-by-period cost, is included within interest expense.

(d) Certain restructuring costs associated with refinery network rationalisation and European refining and marketing joint venture implementation are recognised in a later period than originally charged.

One question on which FRS 12 gives no guidance is how to treat changes in the estimate of the decommissioning provision which arise over the life time of the oil rig. Where the estimate of the expenditure changes from the amount originally provided for, is the difference added to or deducted from the asset and dealt with in the future as an adjustment to amortisation, or is it taken immediately to the profit and loss account? In our view the former is the sensible treatment, and this is what BP Amoco have chosen to do, as shown in the policy quoted above.

4.6 Cyclical repairs

Before FRS 12 came into force, it was common for some companies to account for the costs of major periodic repair to large assets by making regular provisions against which the repairs were then charged when incurred. Examples are to be found in the (pre-FRS 12) accounts of St Ives, Rugby Group and Pilkington:

Extract 25.21: St Ives plc (1998)

1. Accounting policies

(h) Provisions for repairs

Provision is made for repairs to major items of plant and machinery and freehold and leasehold premises based on estimates of expenditure required to sustain the operating capacity of the assets at present levels over their estimated useful lives.

18. Provisions for liabilities and charges [extract]

	The Group Provision for repairs £'000	The Company Provision for repairs £'000
Balance at 1 August 1997	4,205	350
Charged to profit and loss account	622	50
On acquisition of subsidiary undertaking	1,152	–
Applied	(1,215)	(301)
Exchange differences	8	–
	4,772	99

Extract 25.22: The Rugby Group plc (1998)

1. Accounting policies

DEFERRED REPAIRS

Provision is made for future repairs to major items of plant by spreading the expected cost over the appropriate period of production.

15. Provisions for Liabilities and Charges [extract]

GROUP	Other £ million
At 1st January 1998	44.1
Utilised	(11.3)
Charge to profit and loss account	10.3
Impact of exchange rate changes	(0.1)
At 31st December 1998	43.0

Other provisions include... provisions for deferred repairs of **£5.0 million** (1997: £8.1 million) ...

Extract 25.23: Pilkington plc (1998)

ACCOUNTING POLICIES

8 Glass tank repairs

A charge is made annually against profits to provide for the accrued proportion of the estimated revenue cost of major glass tank repairs which are carried out periodically.

The actual revenue cost of such repairs, when incurred, is charged against the provision.

NOTES ON THE FINANCIAL STATEMENTS

27 Provisions for liabilities and charges [extract]

Group	Other provisions £m
At beginning of year	114
Exchange rate adjustments	(8)
Provided during year	53
Utilised during year	(27)
Changes in composition of the Group	1
At end of year	133

Other provisions at 31st March 1998 include £10 million (1997 £17 million) for tank repairs, ...

Provisions of this kind are specifically disallowed under the standard. The examples it gives are of a furnace that has a lining that needs replacing every five years, and an aircraft that needs overhauling every three years.[98] Neither of these provisions is allowed to be set up on the basis that there is no obligation to carry out the expenditure independently of the company's future actions. This argument is used even in the circumstances where there is a legal requirement for the asset in question to be repaired, since it is asserted that, even then, the entity could avoid the expenditure by, for example, selling the asset.

As a result, Pilkington has amended its practice as shown in this extract.

Extract 25.24: Pilkington plc (1999)

7   Changes in accounting policies

(c) FRS 12 (Provisions, Contingent Liabilities and Contingent Assets)

The previous policy of providing for the accrued proportion of the future estimated revenue costs of major glass tank repairs, carried out periodically, has changed in accordance with the new standard and the balance has been released to this year's profit and loss account ((note 30(e)). All such revenue costs are now charged in the period in which the float tanks are repaired.

30   Provisions for liabilities and charges

	1999 Group £m
(e) Other provisions [extract]	
At beginning of the year	80
Exchange rate adjustments	1
Charged to profit and loss account during the year	21
Released to profit and loss account during the year	(10)
Utilised during year	(22)
At end of the year	70

As a result of the introduction of FRS 12, the tank repair provision at 31st March 1998 has been released to the profit and loss account during the year.

This change was made as a current year credit to the profit and loss account rather than as a change of policy requiring a prior year adjustment, but perhaps the £10 million release was regarded as insufficiently material to warrant restatement.

It is interesting to note that Railtrack did not reverse its 'property maintenance backlog provision' on implementing FRS 12. This stood at £259 million at 31 March 1999 (£92 million having been utilised in the year) and was described in the following words in the accounts drawn up to that date.

Extract 25.25: Railtrack Group PLC (1999)

22 PROVISIONS FOR LIABILITIES AND CHARGES [extract]

The Group, as publicly stated in its Share Offer Prospectus dated 1 May 1996, has implemented a programme of repairs in respect of the property maintenance backlog at stations and depots which is due to be completed by 31 March 2001.

There can be no doubt about Railtrack's need or commitment to carry out this work; however, it is difficult to see exactly why this qualifies as a liability under FRS 12 whereas, for example, an airline company is considered not to have any obligation to continue to overhaul its planes. If there is a distinction, it is perhaps to do with the 'backlog' feature of the maintenance work – Railtrack had this inheritance when it was floated – but it is hard to see this as a relevant distinction. This again illustrates the rather nebulous nature of the concept of a 'constructive obligation'.

The effect of this prohibition on setting up provisions for repairs will obviously impact balance sheet presentation. It may not always, however, have as much impact on the profit and loss account. This is because it is suggested that depreciation might be adjusted to take account of the repairs. For example, in the case of the furnace lining, the lining should be depreciated over five years in advance of its expected repair. Similarly, in the case of the aircraft overhaul, the example in the standard suggests that an amount equivalent to the expected maintenance costs is depreciated over three years. The result of this is that the overall charge to the profit and loss account that will now arise from depreciation may be equivalent to that which would previously have arisen from the combination of depreciation and provision for repair. However, it may give rise to some very odd depreciation policies, with different parts of assets which are not separately distinguishable being depreciated over different lives.

Water utility companies used to follow a similar policy of provisioning in relation to the maintenance of their infrastructure assets. In this case there were slightly different arguments because external regulation on both pricing structures and service standards had a bearing on the maintenance required. Maintenance expenditure in any particular year could vary significantly from the long term norm that had been agreed with the regulator, but the charge against profits was a normalised amount, with the difference taken up in a rolling provision (or a prepayment, if actual expenditure exceeded the norm). Despite the influence of the regulator, the ASB still does not believe that such a provision qualifies as an obligation under FRS 12, but the Board has again permitted the same profit and loss account effect to be preserved by flexing the asset accounting to fit, using 'renewals accounting' as it is described in FRS 15 (see Chapter 10 at 3.3.2).

Scottish Power's accounts show the effect of this change.

Extract 25.26: Scottish Power plc (1999)

Accounting Policies and Definitions

Infrastructure accounting

Water infrastructure assets, being mains and sewers, reservoirs, dams, sludge pipelines and sea outfalls comprise a network of systems. Expenditure on water infrastructure assets relating to increases in capacity or enhancement of the network and on maintaining the operating capability of the network in accordance with defined standards of service is treated as an addition to fixed assets.

The depreciation charge for water infrastructure assets is the estimated level of annualised expenditure required to maintain the operating capability of the network and is based on the asset management plan agreed with the water industry regulator as part of the price regulation process.

The asset management plan is developed from historical experience combined with a rolling programme of reviews of the condition of infrastructure assets.

The method of accounting for water infrastructure renewals has been revised following the introduction of FRS 12 'Provisions, contingent liabilities and contingent assets' and the infrastructure renewals accounting basis as set out in FRS 15 'Tangible fixed assets'. As a consequence the balance sheet has been restated to take account of the necessary changes since the date of acquisition of Southern Water in August 1996. Further information is given in Note 16. The change of accounting policy has no effect on the profit and loss account other than to reclassify the renewals charge on depreciation.

Notes to the Balance Sheets

16 Tangible fixed assets

(iv) The opening balances in respect of cost or valuation and depreciation of water infrastructure assets have been restated as a result of implementing the infrastructure renewals accounting basis as set out in FRS 15 'Tangible fixed assets'. The effect of the adjustment has been to increase tangible fixed assets and reduce prepayments and accrued income by £15.7 million (1998 £5.4 million). There is no effect on the profit and loss account other than to reclassify the renewals charge as depreciation.

It is difficult to see this as a beneficial change. The previous approach had the benefit of transparency, whereas now the maintenance expenditure is mingled with genuine additions to fixed assets. The profit and loss account effect is unaltered, so it appears that the ASB's only reason for requiring the reclassification has been to preserve the supposed purity of its conception of a liability. And even that is somewhat debatable; many would think that agreeing a maintenance programme with the industry regulator would have been enough to create at least a constructive obligation.

4.7   Year 2000 costs

A particular form of 'repair' cost that has preoccupied the management of many companies over the last few years has been the need to rectify inadequate computer systems for their inability to cope with the change of dates entailed by the new millennium. Many computers had been programmed to record only the last two digits of the year, and would be unable to cope with the implications of a change in the first two.

The UITF issued an abstract in March 1998, addressing accounting issues relating to Year 2000 costs.[99] The abstract avoided giving a specific ruling on whether provisions for Year 2000 costs could be set up. It did, however, note that if a standard was issued based on what were then the proposals in FRED 14, then Year 2000 costs should be recognised in the accounting period in which modification work is carried out and no provision should be made for future estimated costs.[100] The arguments used were similar to those set out above for other repairs.

Despite this, the issue is not at all clear cut. If an entity had made a public announcement of its policy of updating its computer systems and so created a valid expectation in third parties – particularly its customers and suppliers – that its computer systems are expected to be year 2000 compliant, it would appear that it had thereby established a constructive obligation to carry out the work. But this was clearly not the ASB's view; although FRS 12 does not mention the issue specifically, the press notice that accompanied its publication cited Year

2000 costs as an example of costs that could be avoided by the entity's future actions and accordingly should not be provided for.

4.8 Dilapidation provisions

Operating leases often contain clauses which specify that the tenant should incur periodic charges for maintenance or make good dilapidations or other damage occurring during the rental period. Hence, some entities in the past have built up a provision over the life of the lease for costs of repair and renovation of the property.

The question arises as to whether such a provision meets the recognition criteria in the standard. The issue, whilst not addressed in FRS 12 itself, is mentioned briefly in the appendix discussing the development of the standard. This notes that 'the principle illustrated in [the example on repairs] does not preclude the recognition of such liabilities once the event giving rise to the obligation under the lease has occurred'.[101]

This means that a provision for specific damage done to the property would meet the criteria, as the event giving rise to the obligation under the lease has certainly occurred. What is less clear is whether a more general provision can be built up over time for maintenance charges and dilapidation costs. It could be argued that in this case, the event giving rise to the obligation under the lease is simply the passage of time, and so a provision can be built up over time. However, a stricter interpretation of the phrase 'the event giving rise to the obligation under the lease' may lead one to conclude that a more specific event has to occur; there has to be specific evidence of dilapidation etc before any provision can be made.

The fact that provision for repairs can be made at all in these circumstances might appear inconsistent with the circumstances where the asset is owned by the entity. In these circumstances, as discussed in 4.6 above, no provision for repairs could be made. There is, however, a difference between the two cases. Where the entity owns the asset, it has the choice of selling it rather than repairing it, and so the obligation is not independent of the entity's future actions. However, in the case of an entity leasing the asset, it has a legal obligation to repair any damage from which it cannot walk away.

4.9 Warranty provisions

Warranty provisions are specifically addressed in one of the examples appended to FRS 12, which concludes that such provisions are appropriate.[102] The obligating event giving rise to the legal obligation is the sale of the product on which the warranty is given. We concur with this view, although in practice considerations of materiality may sometimes permit it to be treated on a pay-as-you-go basis.

As noted in 3.1 above, the standard makes it clear that where there are a number of similar obligations, the probability that an economic outflow will occur is based on the class of obligations as a whole. Hence, the probability of an economic outflow occurring for warranties as a whole will need to be evaluated. If this probability exceeds 50% (which seems very likely), then the expected value of the estimated warranty costs should be calculated and provided for.

Vosper Thornycroft is an example of a company that provides for such costs, as described in this note.

Extract 25.27: Vosper Thornycroft Holdings plc (1999)

18 Provisions for liabilities and charges [extract]

	Contract and warranty provisions £000
Group	
At 1 April 1998	6,869
Exchange differences	32
Created during the year	7,973
Unused amounts reversed	(3,605)
Utilised	(2,668)
At 31 March 1999	**8,601**

Contract and warranty provisions

Provisions are made when contracts are put to sales to cover expected warranty claims. Provisions are based on an assessment of future claims with reference to past experience. Such costs are generally incurred within one to five years post delivery.

4.10   Self insurance

One of the examples in FRS 12 deals with the practice of self insurance,[103] which arises when an entity decides not to take out external insurance in respect of a certain category of risk because it would be uneconomic to do so. The same position may arise when a group insures its risks with a captive insurance subsidiary, the effects of which have to be eliminated on consolidation. The standard's example considers the question of whether provision can be made for the amount expected to arise in a normal year. The conclusion reached is that no such provision can be made, as the entity does not have a present obligation for this amount. Instead, it should recognise the reality of the situation – that it is uninsured – and report losses based on their actual incidence, rather than smoothing them from period to period by reference to a simulated insurance premium that it has not in fact paid. As a result, any provisions that appear in the balance sheet should reflect only the amounts expected to be paid in respect of those losses that have occurred by the balance sheet date.

In fact, however, the example is somewhat misleading, since it deals with a very basic case where it is known with certainty at the time of preparing the accounts that no losses have arisen in the period. In real life, a provision will often be needed not simply for known incidents, but also for those which insurance companies call IBNR – Incurred But Not Reported – representing an estimate of the latent liabilities at the year end that experience shows will come to the surface only gradually.

Severn Trent discloses this policy on the subject in relation to a £13 million insurance provision:

Extract 25.28: Severn Trent Plc (1999)

1 Accounting policies

k) Insurance

Provision is made for claims notified and for claims incurred but which have not yet been notified based on advice from the group's external insurance advisers.

17 Provisions for liabilities and charges [extract]

Derwent Insurance Limited, a captive insurance company, is a wholly owned subsidiary of the group. Provisions for insurance claims are made as set out in note 1k). The associated outflows are estimated to arise over a period of up to five years from the balance sheet date.

It is entirely appropriate that provision for expected claims is made. However, it might be questioned whether this should properly be described as a provision for *insurance* claims; from a group perspective, there is no insurance, and the provision is simply for legal claims from third parties.

4.11 Litigation and other legal claims

Assessing the need to provide for legal claims is one of the most difficult tasks in the field of provisioning. This is due mainly to the inherent uncertainty in the judicial process itself, which may be very long and drawn out. Furthermore, this is an area where either provision or disclosure might risk prejudicing the outcome of the case, because they give an insight into the company's own view on the strength of its defence that can assist the claimant. Similar considerations apply in other related areas, such as tax disputes.

In principle, however, provision is required when the company believes that there is a probability of having to make payments either to settle the case or to meet any award given by the court. In the US, Appendix A to SFAS 5 lists the following three factors which should be considered in determining whether accrual and/or disclosure is required with respect to pending or threatened litigation:

(a)   the period in which the underlying cause for action of the pending or threatened litigation occurred;

(b)   the degree of probability of an unfavourable outcome; and

(c)   the ability to make a reasonable estimate of the amount of loss.[104]

Powerscreen discloses that it has provided for certain litigation losses, as shown in this extract.

Extract 25.29: Powerscreen International PLC (1999)

25 Contingent liabilities

a. Legal contingencies

A number of claims have been made against the group, the most significant of which related to:

i)   alleged patent infringements. The directors have received expert opinion that no infringement of valid patents has taken place.

ii) product liability claims involving personal injuries allegedly sustained from the use of the products manufactured by certain group companies.

iii) general commercial disputes.

Notwithstanding the intention of the directors to defend vigorously these claims, some of which are substantial, a provision of £10,279,000 has been made in respect of these claims and associated costs. Having obtained legal advice and on the basis of the information available, the directors believe that the provision made represents their best estimate of the outcome of the claims and associated costs.

P&O, on the other hand, has made no provision for a fine that has been levied on one of its joint ventures, on the grounds that it believes that the fine will be reversed on appeal and thus still does not represent a probable liability.

Extract 25.30: The Peninsular and Oriental Steam Navigation Company (1998)

28 Contingent liabilities [extract]

Other contingent liabilities in the Group and the Company include £14.0m, being the Group's share of fines imposed by the European Union on P&O Nedlloyd for anti-competitive practices on the North Atlantic trade. Together with other members of the Trans Atlantic Conference Agreement, P&O Nedlloyd has appealed against the fine and, on the basis of legal advice, is confident the appeal will succeed and the fine would in any event be severely reduced or quashed. Accordingly no provision has been made in these accounts.

4.12   Refunds policy

An example is given within FRS 12 of a retail store that has a policy of refunding goods returned by dissatisfied customers. There is no legal obligation to do so, but the company's policy of making refunds is generally known.[105]

The example argues that the conduct of the store has created a valid expectation on the part of its customers that the store will refund purchases. The obligating event is the original sale of the item, and the probability of some economic outflow is greater than 50%, as there will nearly always be some customers demanding refunds. Hence, a provision should be made, presumably calculated again on the 'expected value' basis (see 3.1 above).

This example is straightforward when the store has a very specific and highly publicised policy on refunds. However, some stores' policies on refunds might not be so clear cut. A store may offer refunds under certain circumstances, but not widely publicise its policy. In these circumstances, it is likely to be open to interpretation as to whether the store has created a valid expectation on the part of its customers that the store will refund purchases. Notwithstanding this, it would seem sensible to make provision for whatever refunds are expected to be made.

4.13 Staff training costs

FRS 12 gives an example of the government introducing changes to the income tax system, such that an entity in the financial services sector needs to retrain a large proportion of its administrative and sales workforce in order to ensure continued compliance with financial services regulation. At the balance sheet date no retraining has taken place.[106]

The standard argues that the obligating event is the staff retraining, and since at the year end no training has taken place, there is no obligating event, and so no provision should be made. We agree with this outcome, but the reasoning behind it seems fragile. This example again seems to illustrate the subjectivity of the concepts of 'constructive obligations' and 'obligating events'. Another interpretation of the position could be that the entity has a constructive obligation to retrain its sales force, as it has built up a valid expectation in its employees and customers that the sales force will be up to date on changes to the income tax system which affect the products it sells, to enable it to adequately meet the needs of its customers. If this approach were taken, a provision would be required. The argument could be strengthened if the entity had published some sort of policy statement reassuring employees and customers that the sales force would receive adequate training on the income tax changes.

A counter argument might be that the standard states that an entity can only provide for obligations which are independent of the entity's future actions. Hence, in this case, the entity can avoid the costs of staff training by changing its method of operation and no longer selling certain products to customers. However, this argument does not help in distinguishing staff training costs from provisions for refunds, which are required to be made. After all, the customer in the example on refunds has no legal right to a refund. The entity could refuse, but presumably would not because of the bad publicity and loss of goodwill that would be suffered. Similarly, in this example, the sales force could cease selling certain financial products, but would not do so because it would lose customers.

In reality, the distinction between the two examples comes down to when the benefits are obtained in each case, not whether the entity has a liability at the year end. In the case of the refund policy, the revenue from the sale has already been booked, so any reversal of it should be recognised. However, in the case of staff training, the benefits of the training will be the impact on future sales, so it is not appropriate to provide for the costs of training in advance. This dimension of revenue and expense recognition is not acknowledged in the standard, but it does seem to underlie a number of the conclusions that are reached.

5   DISCLOSURE REQUIREMENTS

5.1   Provisions

5.1.1   *Companies Act*

The Companies Act requires disclosure of the amount of provisions at the beginning and the end of the year and movements during the year saying where they have come from and gone to, except for those amounts which have been applied for the purpose for which the provision was established.[107]

5.1.2   *FRS 12*

The standard requires disclosure of the following information:

(a)   For each class of provision:
   (i)   the carrying amount at the beginning and end of the period;
   (ii)   additional provisions made in the period, including increases to existing provisions;
   (iii) amounts used (i.e. incurred and charged against the provision) during the period;
   (iv)   unused amounts reversed during the period; and
   (v)   the increase during the period in the discounted amount arising from the passage of time and the effect of any change in the discount rate.
   Comparative information is not required.[108]

Disclosure (v) effectively requires the charge that is recognised in the profit and loss account for discounting to be split between the element that relates to the straightforward unwinding of the discount, and any further charge or credit that arises if discount rates have changed during the period. It is interesting that there is no specific requirement to disclose the discount rate used, although this information is given in one of the illustrative examples in Appendix IV to the standard, where discounting has been applied.

These disclosures build on the Companies Act requirements to show movements on provisions. One of the important disclosures which is reinforced here is the requirement to disclose the release of provisions found to be unnecessary. This disclosure, along with the requirement in the standard that provisions should be used only for the purpose for which the provision was originally recognised, is designed to prevent entities from concealing expenditure by charging it against a provision that was set up for another purpose.

(b) For each class of provision:

    (i) a brief description of the nature of the obligation, and the expected timing of any resulting transfers of economic benefits;

    (ii) an indication of the uncertainties about the amount or timing of those transfers of economic benefits. Where necessary to provide adequate information, an entity should disclose the major assumptions concerning future events, as addressed in paragraph 51 [of FRS 12. This refers to future developments in technology and legislation and is of particular relevance to environmental liabilities.]; and

    (iii) the amount of any expected reimbursement, stating the amount of any asset that has been recognised for that expected reimbursement.[109]

These disclosures mean that entities are required to give more narrative disclosure in connection with their provisions than previously. Appendix IV to the standard provides examples of suitable disclosures in relation to warranties and decommissioning costs.

Cable and Wireless gives this note on its provisions, which illustrates most of FRS 12's disclosure requirements described above.

Extract 25.31: Cable and Wireless plc (1999)

21 Provisions for liabilities and charges [extract]

	Note	At 1 April 1998 £m	Additions £m	Amounts used £m	Unused amounts reversed £m	Other movements £m	At 31 March 1999 £m
Group							
Deferred tax – amount provided	(i)	84	29	–	–	76	**189**
Pension, redundancy payments							
and unfunded gratuities	(ii)	6	10	–	–	–	**16**
Onerous contracts	(iii)	–	59	–	–	–	**59**
Litigation claims	(iv)	88	5	(37)	(46)	(6)	**4**
Reorganisation	(v)	141	10	(105)	(14)	(4)	**28**
Other	(vi)	5	12	–	–	–	**17**
		324	125	(142)	(60)	66	**313**

Other movements in litigation claims and reorganisation provisions relate to liabilities for which the timing and amount of the expected payments became certain during the year. The provisions for these have been transferred to creditors.

(ii) Pension, redundancy payments and unfunded gratuities
The group operates various unfunded pension plans and has a provision of £15m to cover the expected cost. These provisions are long term and the timing of their utilisation is unknown. The Group holds a provision for approximately £1m to cover the expected cost of redundancy resulting from the planned closure of a business in the UK. This is to be utilised within the next financial year.

(iii) Onerous contracts
Cable & Wireless Optus is party to a number of contracts for pay television programming including agreements with various television programme providers. The terms of most of these contracts include "minimum subscriber guarantees" where Cable & Wireless Optus is required to pay predetermined amounts to the programme providers when subscriber numbers fail to reach a minimum guaranteed level. These minimum guarantees are in some instances significantly in excess of current, and in certain future periods, anticipated subscriber numbers. At the time Cable & Wireless Optus acquired control of Optus Vision, Cable & Wireless provided for the onerous element of these contracts. In previous periods the provision was shown as a reduction in the carrying value of the Group's share of Cable & Wireless Optus. The utilisation of the provision is expected over the next seven years.

(iv) Litigation claims
At 31 March 1998 Cable & Wireless, USA were in dispute with a telecommunications carrier over surcharges invoiced above the original contracted price for carriage of traffic over the carrier's network. This case has been heard in court and the court found against Cable & Wireless USA. The dispute has since been resolved satisfactorily. During they year the Group has written back £46m of the original provision and utilised £37m. The balance at the year end relates to actual and threatened legal claims against Optus Vision.

(v) Reorganisation
This provision principally relates to costs associated with the fundamental reorganisation of Cable & Wireless Communications plc in the previous period. Included in the closing balance is a £16m provision for property costs relating to property which became surplus to requirements as a result of the fundamental reorganisation. This is to be utilised within the next four years.

(vi) Other
The Group includes a captive insurance company. The provision of £17m relates to specific non re-insured claims to this company of which £15m relates to claims made in the two years ending 31 March 1999. It is expected that this provision will be utilised within two years.

The standard states that in determining which provisions may be aggregated to form a class, it is necessary to consider whether the nature of the items is sufficiently similar for a single statement about them to fulfil the requirements of (b)(i) and (ii) above.[110] An example is given of warranties: it is suggested that, while it may be appropriate to treat warranties of different products as a single class of provision, it would not be appropriate to aggregate normal warranties with amounts that are subject to legal proceedings. This could be interpreted to mean that in disclosing restructuring costs, the different components of the costs, such as redundancies, termination of leases, etc, should be disclosed separately. However, materiality will be an important consideration in judging how much analysis is required.

Companies are quite often reluctant to show litigation provisions separately because they fear that the information might be used against them by the other litigating parties. Pilkington has aggregated its warranty and litigation provisions, as shown below. It may be that the litigation element is not very material; certainly the description of it (in the last sentence of the extract) can hardly be described as informative.

Extract 25.32: Pilkington plc (1999)

30 Provisions for liabilities and charges

	1999 Group £m
(c) Warranty and litigation [extract]	
At beginning of the year	51
Exchange rate adjustments	1
Charged to profit and loss account during the year	16
Released to profit and loss account during the year	(4)
Utilised during year	(4)
Changes in composition of the Group	(3)
At end of the year	57
Maturity profile:	
Within one year	34
Between one and two years	17
Between two and five years	5
Over five years	1
At end of the year	57

Warranty provisions are created where the company has given a guarantee to cover the reliability and performance of products over an extended period. Litigation provisions principally include various legal actions.

5.2 Contingent liabilities

5.2.1 *Companies Act*

The Companies Act requires disclosure of the following information in respect of any material contingent liability not provided for:

(a)   the amount or estimated amount of the liability;

(b)   its legal nature; and

(c)   whether any valuable security has been provided by the company in connection with that liability and if so, what.[111]

5.2.2 *FRS 12*

FRS 12 requires the following disclosure for each class of contingent liability at the balance sheet date unless the possibility of any transfer in settlement is remote:

(a)   a brief description of the nature of the contingent liability, and where practicable:

(b)   an estimate of its financial effect, measured in accordance with paragraphs 36-55 [of FRS 12];

(c)   an indication of the uncertainties relating to the amount or timing of any outflow; and

(d)   the possibility of any reimbursement.[112]

Where any of the information above is not disclosed because it is not practicable to do so, that fact should be stated.[113]

The only change from the disclosure requirements previously required by SSAP 18 is that separate disclosure is required in FRS 12 of the possibility of reimbursement. This presumably arises because FRS 12 does not allow the netting off of reimbursements that would have been made under SSAP 18.

The guidance given in the standard on determining which provisions may be aggregated to form a class referred to in 5.2.1 above also applies to contingent liabilities.

A further point noted in the standard is that where a provision and a contingent liability arise from the same circumstances, an entity should ensure that the link between the provision and the contingent liability is clear.[114] This may arise, for instance, where there is a range of possible losses under a claim, for which part of the potential maximum has been provided. A further example of when this may arise would be where an entity is jointly and severally liable for an obligation. As noted in 3.4 above, in these circumstances the part that is expected to be met by other parties is treated as a contingent liability.

It is not absolutely clear what is meant by 'financial effect' in (b) above. Is it the *potential* amount of the loss or is it the *expected* amount of the loss? The explicit cross-reference to the measurement principles in paragraphs 36-55 might imply the latter, but in our view the former would be preferable. A number of companies adopt this approach and disclose the potential amounts involved, as illustrated in the following extracts (which predate FRS 12):

Extract 25.33: Brammer plc (1996)

21   Contingencies

In the ordinary course of business certain leasehold properties which the group no longer requires have been assigned to third parties. The ultimate responsibility for the lease payments relating to some of the properties remains with the group. In the event of the assignees defaulting, the maximum annual liability of the group (ignoring the effects of possible future rent reviews) is £257,000 (1997 £285,000).

Extract 25.34: Wace Group PLC (1998)

21 PROVISIONS FOR LIABILITIES AND CHARGES [Extract]

Contingent liabilities

Taxation

The Group's liability to corporation tax for the year ended 31 December 1994 was reduced by tax losses arising on properties transferred intra Group. The Inland Revenue are challenging these losses. The directors are advised that the Group should succeed in its argument and accordingly no provision has been made for the tax or the interest thereon. In the event that the Inland Revenue were to be successful the Group would have liabilities at 31 December 1998 of £5,389,000 for tax and £1,276,000 for interest (see note 18).

21 CASH AT BANK AND IN HAND

Pursuant to an agreement dated 15 April 1998 for the sale of the UK specialist printing businesses, an amount of £3.3m was paid into escrow on 11 January 1999 pending the resolution of the contingent liability referred to in note 21. The directors do not consider that placing these funds into escrow reflects any change in the nature of the contingent liability.

However, some other companies tend not to disclose the potential amounts involved where claims have been made against them or they are involved in litigation, but rather comment that once resolved there is unlikely to be any significant effect, as illustrated in the following extracts:

Extract 25.35: Charter plc (1998)

22 COMMITMENTS AND CONTINGENCIES [extract]

Charter, together with certain of its wholly-owned subsidiaries, has been named as defendant in a number of asbestos-related actions in the United States on the basis that it is allegedly liable for the acts of a former subsidiary Cape PLC. Charter contests the existence of any such liability. The issue went to trial in three cases involving the Company's principal subsidiary, Charter Consolidated P.L.C., and other wholly-owned subsidiaries, between 1985 and 1987. In the first of these cases, tried in Pennsylvania, after an adverse lower court decision the appeal court gave judgement in the Charter defendants' favour. In the second case, in New Jersey, judgement was also given for the Charter defendants. The third case in South Carolina, was dismissed for lack of subject matter jurisdiction, without a decision having been rendered on the issue. During recent years, Charter and/or certain of its subsidiaries have been served in a number of cases in Mississippi and a few other states. Charter is seeking dismissals in these pending cases. Upon advice of counsel, Charter has settled the majority of the cases brought in Mississippi and will continue to pursue dismissals in the remaining cases. The directors have received legal advice that Charter and its wholly-owned subsidiaries should be able to continue to defend successfully the actions brought against them, but that uncertainty must exist as to the eventual outcome of the trial of any particular action. It is not practicable to estimate in any particular case the amount of damages which might ensue if liability were imposed on Charter or any of its wholly-owned subsidiaries. The litigation is reviewed each year and, based on that review and legal advice, the directors believe that the aggregate of any such liability is unlikely to have a material effect on Charter's financial position. In these circumstances, the directors have concluded that it is not appropriate to make any provision in respect of such actions.

Extract 25.36: British American Tobacco p.l.c. (1998)

Other financial information

22 Contingent liabilities and financial commitments

There are contingent liabilities in respect of litigation, overseas taxes and guarantees in various countries.

Group companies, notably Brown & Williamson Tobacco Corporation ('B&W') as well as other leading cigarette manufacturers, are defendants, principally in the United States, in a number of product liability cases, including a substantial number of new cases filed in 1998. Significant compensatory and punitive damages are being sought by a number of plaintiffs.

US Litigation

The total number of US product liability cases pending at year end involving Group companies was 678 (31 December 1997 547 cases). The Company and other UK Group companies were named as co-defendants in 238 of those cases (1997 143 cases). Since many of these pending cases seek unspecified damages, it is not possible to determine the total amount of claims pending, but the aggregate amounts involved in such litigation are significant. The cases fall into four broad categories:

(1) Medical reimbursement cases. These civil actions seek to recover amounts spent by US government entities and other third party providers on health care and welfare costs claimed to result from illnesses associated with smoking. The leading US cigarette manufacturers including B&W ('the US industry') have settled all these suits at the state level, but the settlement has yet to be approved by the supervising courts of one state. Similar reimbursement suits have been filed by nine Indian tribes and by eight county or other political subdivisions of certain states. The settlement of the states' suits includes a credit for any amounts paid in suits which may be brought by the states' political subdivisions; nevertheless, the Company and its subsidiaries intend to defend these cases vigorously.

President Clinton has requested the Department of Justice to develop plans to bring a suit against the US industry seeking reimbursement for Medicare and other healthcare expenses incurred by the US federal government. The amounts being sought in such a suit would be significant.

B&W is named as a defendant in six cases brought by non-US governments in courts in the US seeking reimbursement of medical costs which they incurred for treatment of persons in their own countries who are alleged to have smoked imported cigarettes including those manufactured by B&W. Group UK companies are named as co-defendants in four of these cases.

Based on somewhat different theories of claim are some 80 non-governmental medical reimbursement cases and health insurers claims, the majority of which were filed by labour union health and welfare funds on behalf of their members. Of these, 14 have already been dismissed in whole or in part, one is currently in trial and another is scheduled for trial in 1999.

(2) Class actions. As at 31 December 1998, B&W was named as a defendant in some 55 separate actions attempting to assert claims on behalf of classes of persons allegedly injured by smoking. While nine courts refused to do so, eight courts have certified classes of tobacco claimants in cases involving B&W but four of these classes have subsequently been decertified. Even if the classes remain certified and the possibility of class-based liability is eventually established, it is likely that individual trials will still be necessary to resolve any actual claims. If this happens, certain of the defences that have contributed to more than 500 individual cases being successfully disposed of over the years by the US industry without, to date, monetary loss, will be available.

One case (Engle) is presently in the first phase of a trifurcated trial in Florida. Two further claimed class actions against B&W are currently scheduled for trial in 1999. The Court in the Broin case approved a settlement which provides for payment to the plaintiffs' lawyers and for the creation of a research fund but for no payments to any plaintiff.

(3) Individual cases. Approximately 497 cases were pending against B&W at 31 December 1998 filed by or on behalf of individuals in which it is contended that diseases or deaths have been caused by cigarette smoking or by exposure to environmental tobacco smoke. One case (Dunn) was tried to conclusion in 1998 resulting in a verdict for the defendants, and the time to appeal that case has expired. A second case (Widdick) was tried in 1998 resulting in a verdict for the plaintiff of $1,000,000 (including $450,000 punitive damages) against B&W. The Florida Court of Appeals for the First District has ruled subsequently that the case should not have been tried in its current venue, vacated the verdict and ordered that, if the case is retried, the trial be in a different county. Philip Morris Inc. has lost a case (Henley) at first instance in California and is appealing the decision. The US industry has not paid any damages in any smoking and health case which has gone to verdict. It is not likely that all of the 19 individual cases against B&W currently scheduled for 1999 will actually go to trial in the year.

(4) Other claims. Seven cases are pending on behalf of asbestos companies. Those companies seek reimbursement from the US industry for costs and judgements paid in litigation brought by third parties against them. These companies claim that but for the smoking of the successful third parties the damages awarded against them would have been lower.

The Company (or its then publicly quoted predecessor) has been named as a co-defendant in the US in most of the medical reimbursement cases, in 33 of the class actions and in 64 of the individual cases. They are contesting the jurisdiction of the US courts since they are 'holding' companies not transacting business in the United States. In the 36 cases that have decided this issue to date, 23 courts have dismissed them prior to trial. In the balance of 13 cases, there has been no adverse ruling on the issue of jurisdiction affirmed through appeal: merely, the courts involved have said that the issue is, in their court system, not sufficiently beyond doubt to prevent the question even coming into a trial. Some 70 plaintiffs have voluntarily agreed to drop them and substitute the Company's indirectly held subsidiary British American Tobacco (Investments) Limited (formerly called British-American Tobacco Company Ltd.), as a co-defendant.

Legal Matters Outside the United States

There are no active claims against Group companies in respect of health-related claims outside Argentina, Brazil, Canada, Chile, Israel, Nigeria, the Philippines and Sri Lanka. A representative action has been threatened in Australia and actions have been brought in Canada against an associated company, Imperial Tobacco Company Ltd. of Canada and others.

Conclusion

While it is impossible to be certain of the outcome of any particular case or of the amount of any possible adverse verdict, the Company believes that the defences of the Group companies to all these various claims are meritorious both on the law and the facts, and a vigorous defence is being made everywhere. If an adverse judgement were entered against any of the Group companies in any case, an appeal would be made. Such appeals could require the posting of appeal bonds or substitute security by the appellants for the amounts of such adverse judgements: at least in the aggregate and despite the quality of defences available to the Group, it is not impossible that the results of operations or cash flows of the Group in particular quarterly or annual periods could be materially affected by this and by the final outcome of the larger litigation.

Having regard to all these matters, the Directors (i) do not consider it appropriate to make any provision in respect of any pending litigation and (ii) do not believe that the ultimate outcome of all this litigation will significantly impair the financial condition of the Group.

As indicated above, where it is not practicable to make an estimate of the financial effect, FRS 12 requires a statement explaining this fact. Mirror Group provides an example of this disclosure, although it again predates FRS 12:

Extract 25.37: Mirror Group PLC (1998)

23   Contingent liabilities [extract]

INVESTIGATION UNDER SECTIONS 432 AND 442 OF THE COMPANIES ACT 1985

On 8 June 1992 the President of the Board of Trade appointed inspectors under Sections 432 and 442 of the Companies Act 1985 to examine the affairs of the Group, particularly the circumstances surrounding its flotation in April 1991. The directors have been advised that it is possible that the circumstances surrounding the flotation, and the conduct of its affairs between its flotation in April 1991 and December 1991, may give rise to claims against the Company. However, it is not at this stage possible to identify specific claims against the Company nor to quantify either the prospect of

> success of such claims or the magnitude of any potential liability. Moreover, if such claims were successfully established the Company might have claims against certain of its professional advisers who acted at that time. After discussing all circumstances known to the Company with its legal advisers, no provision has been made in the financial statements for any such claims.
>
> UNUSUAL RECEIPTS AND PAYMENTS DURING 1991
>
> During 1991 the Group recorded substantial payments to and receipts from financial institutions and payments from Maxwell controlled companies outside the ordinary course of business. The directors are unaware of any unprovided claims against the Group arising from these transactions and, other than where the receipt of cash is certain, no benefit has been taken for potential recoveries.

FRS 12, like SSAP 18 before it, does not require the disclosure of remote contingencies, as discussed above. An Accountants Digest published soon after the issue of SSAP 18 stated that 'the application of this concession is, however, limited by the over-riding requirements of the 1948 and 1967 Companies Acts which require disclosure of the "general nature of any contingent liabilities not provided for and, where practicable, the aggregate amount or estimated amount of those liabilities, if it is material".'[115] (Since that time, the Companies Act provisions have been amended so as to require the disclosures described in 5.2.1 above.)

Possibly because of this apparent overriding Companies Act requirement to disclose *all* material contingent liabilities not provided for, companies sometimes include information in their financial statements on contingencies which could be considered to be remote. Some examples of such disclosures are shown below.

A   Guarantees of subsidiary company liabilities

Where companies are disclosing the fact that they have guaranteed the liabilities of another party, consideration has to be given as to what amount should be disclosed in respect of the guarantee. The amount given is often merely the year end liability guaranteed, whilst in other cases it is not stated whether the amount given is the year end liability or the maximum liability guaranteed. It could be argued that both amounts require disclosure, as the maximum amount is part of the 'nature' of the guarantee and the year end amount is the 'estimate' of the financial effect. We therefore believe that best practice is to disclose both the year end liability and the maximum amount guaranteed, as shown in the following extracts:

Extract 25.38: Inchcape plc (1998)

12   Guarantees and contingent liabilities [extract]

	Company	
	1998	1997
	£m	£m
Guarantees of various subsidiaries' borrowings (against which £13.8m has been drawn, 1997 – £47.4m).	**531.8**	373.5

> *Extract 25.39: Anglian Water Plc (1999)*
>
> **30. contingent liabilities** [extract]
>
> ... In addition, the company has guaranteed the overdrafts of a number of subsidiaries amounting to £4.6 million (utilised), £27.3 million (unutilised) at 31 March 1999 (1998 – £13.8 million (utilised), £23.3 million (unutilised)).

> *Extract 25.40: British American Tobacco p.l.c. (1998)*
>
> **61   Contingent liabilities and financial commitments**[extract]
>
> British American Tobacco p.l.c. has guaranteed borrowings by subsidiary undertakings of **£3,089 million** and total borrowing facilities of **£10,748 million**, although the total borrowings restriction contained in the US$8 billion facility would limit the total amount Group companies could draw under these facilities to US$11 billion (£6,611 million)
>
> Performance guarantees given to third parties in respect of Group companies were **£21 million**.

In contrast, Silentnight Holdings discloses only the year end liability, as shown below:

> *Extract 25.41: Silentnight Holdings Plc (1999)*
>
> **27.   Contingent liabilities** [extract]
>
> **Bank guarantees**
>
> The Company has provided cross guarantees in respect of certain bank loans and overdrafts of its subsidiary undertakings, the amount outstanding at 30 January 1999 being £12,953,000 (1998: £9,375,000).

Where the amount of the liability at the year end varies significantly from the amount at the date on which the accounts are approved by the directors, consideration should be given to disclosing both amounts.

On the other hand, certain guarantees are sometimes disclosed without any amounts at all being given. For example:

> *Extract 25.42: Tesco PLC (1999)*
>
> **29   Contingent liabilities** [extract]
>
> The company has irrevocably guaranteed the liabilities as defined in Section 5(c) of the Republic of Ireland (Amendment Act) 1986 of various undertakings incorporated in the Republic of Ireland.

B   Bills discounted with recourse

Clearly, where a company discounts bills without recourse in the event of the bills being dishonoured on maturity, no contingent liability exists and, therefore, no disclosure is required. Also under FRS 5, where bills have been discounted with recourse, it will in most circumstances be necessary to account for such liabilities on the balance sheet, not simply as a disclosed contingency – see Chapter 16.

However, where bills are discounted with recourse and a liability does not need to be recognised under FRS 5, the question arises as to what amount should be disclosed in the financial statements as the contingent liability. Is it the amount which relates to all such bills discounted at the balance sheet date, or is it the amount which relates to those bills which have yet to mature at the date of approval of the financial statements? It could be argued that it is the latter and, therefore, if all the bills have matured by that date no disclosure is required. However, if the company is continually discounting bills of exchange then at the date of approval the company will have a contingent liability in respect of bills discounted since the year end. Consequently, we believe that in order to provide information relevant to the financial position of the company, the amount of bills outstanding at the balance sheet date should be disclosed.

C   *Membership of VAT groups*

Companies may be part of a VAT group and as such have joint and several liability for the whole of the group VAT liability. Again, similar considerations apply as to the amount to be disclosed as were discussed above in relation to discounted bills. Consequently, we believe that the amount of this contingent liability at the balance sheet date should be disclosed in each group member's financial statements. For example:

Extract 25.43: British Polythene Industries plc (1998)

23.   Contingent Liabilities [extract]

The company also has an obligation under the Group VAT registration amounting at 31 December 1998 to £4,001,000 (1997 – £4,733,000) .

D   *Performance bonds*

It is common practice in some industries for companies to procure that a third party guarantees to their customers that they will carry out their contracts to a specific standard. The question then arises as to whether the existence of such a performance bond means that the company has a contingent liability which has to be disclosed. The granting of the performance bond does not normally impose any greater liability on the company than does the contract itself. If a company regularly fulfils its obligations on time and up to the required standard and there is nothing to suggest that there are any unusual circumstances which might affect this, then there is justification in deciding that there is no contingency which needs to be disclosed.

In addition to performance bonds, companies may also arrange tender bonds (i.e. a guarantee against the company withdrawing from the contract after having submitted a tender for the contract which has been accepted) and advance payment bonds (i.e. a guarantee to reimburse advance payments made by the customer if the company cannot fulfil the contract).

In most cases the above bonds or guarantees will be given by the company's bankers and the company will indemnify the bank. Again, this does not normally impose any greater liability on the company than that under the contract with the customer.

Although it could be argued that in most cases above no contingent liability arises and therefore no disclosure is necessary, it would appear that many companies do give some disclosure in respect of such bonds. In practice, many companies merely note the existence of the bonds. For example:

Extract 25.44: BICC plc (1998)

24   Contingent liabilities [extract]

BICC plc and certain subsidiary undertakings have, in the normal course of business, given guarantees and entered into counter indemnities in respect of bonds relating to the Group's own contracts and given guarantees in respect of the Group's share of certain contractual obligations of joint ventures and associates. ...

Extract 25.45: Vosper Thornycroft Holdings plc (1999)

28   Contingent liabilities

In the ordinary course of business, group companies from time to time enter into contracts which can account for a substantial part of the consolidated turnover.

In connection with these contracts, particularly with overseas customers, group companies are required to undertake significant obligations in relation to the performance and financing of the contracts.

In the opinion of the directors no further provision is required in respect of these obligations.

Some other companies do, however, quantify the amount of the bonds or guarantees. For example:

Extract 25.46: Hepworth PLC (1998)

28. Contingent liabilities [extract]

As part of its normal trading, the Group had issued guarantees and performance bonds as at 31 December 1998 amounting to £1.6m (1997, £1.0m)

In our view, given the fact that the company in most cases will incur no extra liability as a result of the performance bond, it is sufficient just to disclose the existence of the bonds without quantification. Where, however, a parent company or other group company guarantees or counter-indemnifies a bank for the performance of another group company then it would be preferable if the amount were quantified as this would be consistent with the approach generally taken in respect of guarantees of group borrowings.

5.3   Contingent assets

FRS 12 requires disclosure of contingent assets where an inflow of economic benefits is probable. The disclosures required are:

(a)   a brief description of the nature of the contingent assets at the balance sheet date; and

(b)   where practicable, an estimate of their financial effect, measured using the principles set out for provisions in paragraphs 36-55 [of FRS 12].[116]

Where any of the information above is not disclosed because it is not practicable to do so, that fact should be stated.[117] The standard goes on to emphasise that the disclosure must avoid giving misleading indications of the likelihood of a profit arising.[118]

In practice, disclosures of contingent assets are relatively rare. One example can be seen in the 1996 accounts of Graseby:

Extract 25.47: Graseby plc (1996)

28   Contingent items [extract]

(d)   The group has a claim for compensation against a customer for cancellation of long term contracts in 1995. Compensation received in 1996 of £384,000 (1995 £240,000) has been recognised in the profit and loss account as a contribution towards overheads incurred. The final outcome of the claim cannot be determined with any certainty at present. However, the directors continue to expect that further appropriate compensation will be received.

The disclosure requirements of FRS 12 are similar to those previously required by SSAP 18. However, one problem that arises with FRS 12 is that it requires the disclosure of an estimate of the potential financial effect for contingent assets to be measured in accordance with the measurement principles in the standard. Unfortunately, the measurement principles in the standard are all set out in terms of the measurement of provisions, and these principles cannot readily be applied to the measurement of contingent assets. Hence, judgement will have to be used as to how rigorously these principles should be applied.

5.4   Exemption from disclosure when seriously prejudicial

FRS 12 contains an exemption from disclosure of information in the following circumstances. It says that, 'in extremely rare cases, disclosure of some or all of the information required by [the disclosure requirements in 5.1.2, 5.2.2 and 5.3 above] can be expected to prejudice seriously the position of the entity in a dispute with other parties on the subject matter of the provision, contingent liability or contingent asset.'[119]

In such circumstances, the information need not be disclosed unless it is required by law. However, disclosure will still need to be made of the general nature of the dispute, together with the fact that, and the reason why, the required information has not been disclosed.[120]

This exemption applies to provisions, contingent liabilities and contingent assets. It is unclear, however, as to whether it can actually be used in practice for contingent liabilities. This is because the Companies Act requires disclosure of contingent liabilities including the estimated amount of each contingent liability and contains no exemption for information that is seriously prejudicial to the entity. Therefore, a strict interpretation of this exemption would suggest that it will never be available for contingent liabilities. Unfortunately, no clarification of the position is given in the appendix to the standard that discusses the corresponding legal requirements, so the issue remains unclear.

6   COMPARISON WITH IASC AND US PRONOUNCEMENTS

6.1   IASC

The first IASC standard in this field was IAS 10 – *Contingencies and Events Occurring After the Balance Sheet Date*, and its requirements on contingencies were in essence the same as those of SSAP 18. In November 1996, the IASC issued a Draft Statement of Principles – *Provisions and Contingencies*, proposing to take contingencies out of IAS 10 and to deal with them in the same standard as provisions, using the same recognition and measurement rules.[121] In July 1997, the IASC published an exposure draft on this basis, which was converted into a standard – IAS 37 – in September 1998. This standard applies to accounting periods beginning on or after 1 July 1999.

IAS 37 was developed in parallel with FRS 12 under a joint project between the ASB and the IASC and the two standards were published on the same day. There are no differences of substance between the requirements of the two standards – indeed the text is mostly identical – but FRS 12 touches on two additional areas – recognition of an asset when a provision is recognised, and slightly more guidance on the discount rate to be used in the net present value calculation, together with the profit and loss account classification of the discount as it unwinds.

6.2   US

The US does not have an accounting standard on the general issue of provisions, but does have detailed rules in relation to some of the specific issues covered by FRS 12, as set out below.

6.2.1 Restructuring costs

In January 1995, the Emerging Issues Task Force of the FASB issued Abstract 94-3 which was the forerunner of FRS 12's rules on reorganisation costs.[122] This considered, but did not adopt, the approach of trying to define restructuring costs and instead simply laid down rules for certain kinds of costs that typically arise in a restructuring.

The conditions set for the recognition of redundancy costs were these:

(a) Prior to the date of the financial statements, management having the appropriate level of authority to involuntarily terminate employees approves and commits the enterprise to the plan of termination and establishes the benefits that current employees will receive upon termination.

(b) Prior to the date of the financial statements, the benefit arrangement is communicated to employees. The communication of the benefit arrangement includes sufficient detail to enable employees to determine the type and amount of benefits they will receive if they are terminated.

(c) The plan of termination specifically identifies the number of employees to be terminated, their job classifications or functions, and their locations.

(d) The period of time to complete the plan of termination indicated that significant changes to the plan of termination are not likely.

In relation to other costs to exit an activity, the EITF decided that liabilities for such costs could be recognised if they met the following conditions:

(a) Prior to the date of the financial statements, management having the appropriate level of authority approves and commits the enterprise to an exit plan.

(b) The exit plan specifically identifies all significant actions to be taken to complete the exit plan, activities that will not be continued, including the method of disposition and location of these activities, and the expected date of completion.

(c) Actions required by the exit plan will begin as soon as possible after the commitment date, and the period of time to complete the exit plan indicates that significant changes to the exit plan are not likely.

The only costs that qualify to be accrued even if they meet the above conditions are those that are not associated with or do not benefit activities that will be continued, and that meet either criterion (a) or (b) below:

(a) The cost is incremental to other costs incurred by the enterprise in the conduct of its activities prior to the commitment date and will be incurred as a direct result of the exit plan. The notion of incremental does not contemplate a diminished future economic benefit to be derived from the cost but rather the absence of the cost in the enterprise's activities immediately prior to the commitment date.

(b)   The cost represents amounts to be incurred by the enterprise under a contractual obligation that existed prior to the commitment date and will either continue after the exit plan is completed with no economic benefit to the enterprise or be a penalty incurred by the enterprise to cancel the contractual obligation.

These conditions are rather more detailed than those in FRS 12, but are similar in their general approach. However, it is noteworthy that the EITF's rules permit a liability to be set up on the basis of a management commitment, even if they have not yet put the decision beyond their powers of recall.

6.2.2   Environmental costs

In October 1996, the Accounting Standards Executive Committee of the AICPA issued Statement of Position (SOP) 96-1 – *Environmental Remediation Liabilities*. This interprets SFAS 5 – *Accounting for Contingencies* – which requires provision for environmental liabilities if it is probable that a liability has been incurred and the amount of the loss can be reasonably estimated. It says that the 'probable liability' test is met for environmental liabilities if, by the time the accounts are issued:

(a)   Litigation, a claim, or an assessment can be asserted, or is probable of being asserted; and

(b)   It is probable that the outcome of such litigation, claim, or assessment will be unfavourable.[123]

Given the US climate on environmental litigation, there is a presumption that (b) will be established if the reporting entity is associated with a contaminated site in respect of which litigation has commenced or a claim or assessment has been asserted (or if such actions are probable).[124]

Measurement of the liability will often be difficult, but at least the minimum amount in the range of possible loss should be accrued. This should be based on both the direct incremental costs of the remediation effort and the payroll cost of those employees who are expected to spend a significant amount of time on it.[125] Where the entity is one of a number of parties against whom the claim is made, it should accrue its share of the costs after taking account of the possible effect of other responsible parties failing to meet their share.[126] The costs accrued should be based on present legislation and technology,[127] and may be discounted only if the amount and timing of the expenditure that is provided for are reasonably estimable.[128]

6.2.3   Decommissioning costs

Present accounting practice in the US is similar to that previously used by oil companies in the UK under the OIAC SORP mentioned at 4.5 above. However, the FASB is presently developing an accounting standard which seeks to change it in a similar way to FRS 12. An exposure draft was issued in February 1996 – *Accounting for Certain Liabilities Related to Closure or Removal of Long-Lived*

Assets – proposing that such obligations should be recognised as a liability when the obligation is incurred, with a corresponding increase in the cost of the related asset. The draft said that the liability was to be discounted at a risk-free rate of interest, and changes in the estimated cost were to be recognised as an adjustment to the cost of the asset, with depreciation revised prospectively. The last point is more explicit than FRS 12, which is far from clear on this issue. A further exposure draft is planned.

6.2.4   Vacant leasehold property

In 1988 the EITF considered the question of how to deal with the remaining rental payments on leased property when the entity moved to a replacement property. It concluded that if the leased property had no substantive future use of benefit to the entity these rentals, together with any other associated costs, should be expensed, net of any actual or probable sublease income. The amount provided could be measured on either a discounted or an undiscounted basis.[129]

6.2.5   Year 2000 costs

The EITF issued an Abstract on this subject in 1996.[130] The consensus of the Task Force was that external and internal costs specifically associated with modifying internal-use software for the year 2000 should be charged to expense as incurred.

6.2.6   Contingencies

In March 1975, the FASB published SFAS 5 – *Accounting for Contingencies* – which superseded ARB No. 50 – *Contingencies*. The requirements within the statement are broadly similar in effect to those adopted by FRS 12.

A contingency is defined in SFAS 5 as 'an existing condition, situation, or set of circumstances involving uncertainty as to possible gain ... or loss ... to an enterprise that will ultimately be resolved when one or more future events occur or fail to occur'.[131] This is more in tune with the definitions in SSAP 18 than those now in FRS 12. The statement requires that the estimated loss from a loss contingency should be accrued if both the following conditions are met:

'a.   Information available prior to issuance of the financial statements indicates that it is probable that an asset had been impaired or a liability had been incurred at the date of the financial statements. It is implicit in this condition that it must be probable that one or more future events will occur confirming the fact of the loss.

b.   The amount of loss can be reasonably estimated.'[132]

The principal difference from FRS 12 is that SFAS 5 requires disclosure of certain loss contingencies even though the possibility of loss may be remote. The standard states that the common characteristic of such a contingency is a 'guarantee'. Examples given include:

(a) guarantees of indebtedness to others;

(b) guarantees to repurchase receivables that have been sold in certain situations;

(c) obligations of banks under 'standby letters of credit'.[133]

In September 1976, the FASB published FASB Interpretation No. 14 – *Reasonable Estimation of the Amount of a Loss* – to give guidance on the treatment to be adopted where a loss is probable, and the amount lies within a range of figures (see 3.2 above).

7 CONCLUSION

The subject of provisions and contingencies is a wide ranging one, but at its heart lie fundamental questions concerning the recognition and measurement of items in the accounts. The ASB sees these issues straightforwardly in terms of balance sheet recognition, and has sought to apply its draft *Statement of Principles* as a means of resolving them, but in many cases we think this does not work well and that it is more fruitful to address the question from the point of view of expense recognition. In particular, we think the concepts of 'obligating events' and 'constructive obligations' are rather more nebulous than they are represented to be, and not always useful in identifying reliably when to include certain items in the accounts. We would not be as dismissive about the relevance of management intent, since accounts necessarily represent the report of management and it is futile to try to divorce them from that context. We are also concerned that the Board's approach means that the balance sheet will be inappropriately grossed up in some cases so as to include dubious assets.

The measurement requirements also have their difficulties. We are concerned that they seem to be seeking to derive some form of theoretical market value for the obligations reported whereas we would prefer to focus more directly on the actual expenditure that the company is likely to make. We also think that the rules on discounting should have been given much deeper consideration.

As a result, we do not think that FRS 12 is a very satisfactory standard. While the answers it gives rise to are usually acceptable, the reasoning that lies behind them is frequently suspect and is more likely to puzzle readers than enlighten them. We think that there are likely to be many problems of interpretation in practice as a result.

References

1   CA 85, Sch. 4, para. 89.
2   *Ibid.*, para. 88.
3   FRS 12, *Provisions and Contingencies*, ASB, September 1998, para. 2.
4   *Ibid.*, Appendix V, para. 5.
5   FRS 12, para. 2.
6   *Examination of the conformity between IAS 37 and the European Accounting Directives*, XV/6010/99 EN, Brussels, 27 April 1999.
7   SSAP 18, *Accounting for contingencies*, ASC, August 1980.
8   *Ibid.*, para. 11.
9   ED 23, *Accounting for contingencies*, ASC, November 1978.
10 SSAP 18, para. 14.
11 *Ibid.*
12 *Ibid.*, para. 17.
13 *Ibid.*, para. 4.
14 *Ibid.*, para. 14.
15 FRS 12, para 1.
16 *Ibid.*, para. 4.
17 *Ibid.*, para. 3.
18 *Ibid.*, para. 5.
19 *Ibid.*, para. 6.
20 *Ibid.*, para. 10.
21 *Ibid.*, para. 101-102.
22 *Ibid.*, para. 14.
23 *Ibid.*, para. 2.
24 *Ibid.*, para. 2.
25 *Ibid.*, Appendix III, Examples 2B and 4.
26 FRS 12, para. 2.
27 *Ibid.*, para. 19.
28 *Ibid.*, Appendix III, Examples 11A and 7.
29 FRS 12, para. 22.
30 FASB Newsletter No. 310, 25 February 1999, p. 5.
31 FRS 12, paras. 27 and 31.
32 *Ibid.*, para. 2.
33 *Ibid.*, para 15.
34 *Ibid.*, para. 2.
35 *Ibid.*, para. 33.
36 *Ibid.*, para. 94.
37 *Ibid.*, para. 36.
38 *Ibid.*, para. 37.
39 Exposure draft of *Statement of Principles*, ASB, November 1995, para. 5.27.
40 FRS 12, para. 37.
41 *Ibid.*, para. 39.
42 *Ibid.*
43 FASB Interpretation No. 14, *Reasonable Estimation of the Amount of a Loss*, FASB, September 1976, para. 3.
44 FRS 12, para. 40.
45 *Ibid.*
46 FRED 14, para. 7.
47 FRS 12, Appendix III, Examples 2B and 4.3.
48 FRS 12, para. 45.
49 *Ibid.*, para. 47.
50 *Discounting in Financial Reporting*, ASB, April 1997.
51 FRS 12, para. 49.
52 *Ibid.*
53 *Ibid.*, para. 48.

54 *Ibid.*, para. 47.
55 *Ibid.*, para. 89(e).
56 *Ibid.*, para. 51.
57 *Ibid.*, para. 56.
58 *Ibid.*, para. 57.
59 FRS 3, *Reporting financial performance*, ASB, October 1992, para. 18.
60 SSAP 9, *Stocks and long-term contracts*, ASC, revised September 1988, para. 11.
61 Discussion Paper – *Provisions*, ASB, November 1995, para. 2.6.
62 FRED 14, Appendix III, para. 21.
63 FRS 12, para. 29.
64 *Ibid.*, para. 54.
65 *Ibid.*, para. 62.
66 *Ibid.*, para. 64.
67 *Ibid.*, para. 2.
68 *Ibid.*, para. 75.
69 *Ibid.*, para. 77.
70 *Ibid.*, para. 78.
71 *Ibid.*, para. 79.
72 *Ibid.*, para. 81.
73 *Ibid.*, para. 82.
74 *Ibid.*, para. 80.
75 *Ibid.*, para. 83.
76 FRS 3, para. 45.
77 FRS 12, para. 84.
78 *Ibid.*, para. 85.
79 *Ibid.*, para. 19.
80 *Ibid.*, para. 86.
81 FRED 14, para. 61.
82 FRS 12, para. 87.
83 FRS 3, para. 18.
84 FRS 12, para. 68.
85 *Ibid.*, para. 84.
86 SSAP 9, para. 11.
87 FRS 12, para. 71.
88 *Ibid.*, para. 2.
89 *Ibid.*, para. 73.
90 *Ibid.*, para. 74.
91 FRED 14, para. 5(c).
92 *Ibid.*, para. 48.
93 FRS 12, Appendix III, Example 2A.
94 *Ibid.*, Example 2B.
95 *Ibid.*, Example 3.
96 FRS 12, para. 66.
97 *Accounting for abandonment costs*, OIAC, June 1988, para. 10.
98 FRS 12, Appendix III, Examples 11A and 11B.
99 UITF 20, *Year 2000 issues: accounting and disclosures*, ASB, March 1998.
100 *Ibid.*, para. 5.
101 FRS 12, Appendix VII, para. 39.
102 *Ibid.*, Appendix III, Example 1.
103 *Ibid.*, Example 12.
104 SFAS 5, Appendix A, para. 33.
105 FRS 12, Appendix III, Example 4.
106 *Ibid.*, Example 7.
107 CA 85, Sch. 4, para. 46(1) and (2).
108 FRS 12, para. 89.
109 *Ibid.*, para. 90.

110   *Ibid.*, para. 92.
111   CA 85, Sch. 4, para. 50(2).
112   FRS 12, para. 91.
113   *Ibid.*, para. 96.
114   *Ibid.*, para. 93.
115   Accountants Digest No. 113, *Accountants Digest Guide to Accounting Standards – Accounting for Contingencies*, Winter 1981/82, p. 5.
116   FRS 12, para. 94.
117   *Ibid.*, para. 96.
118   *Ibid.*, para. 95.
119   *Ibid.*, para. 97.
120   *Ibid.*
121   Draft Statement of Principles, *Provisions and Contingencies*, IASC, November 1996, paras. 89 - 95.
122   EITF 94-3, *Liability Recognition for Certain Employee Termination Benefits and Other Costs to Exit an Activity (including Certain Costs Incurred in a Restructuring)*, EITF, January 1995.
123   SOP 96-1, *Environmental Remediation Liabilities*, AICPA, October 1996.
124   *Ibid.*, para. 5.6.
125   *Ibid.*, para. 6.5.
126   *Ibid.*, para. 6.14.
127   *Ibid.*, paras. 6.10 and 6.11.
128   *Ibid.*, para. 6.13.
129   EITF 88-10, *Costs Associated with Lease Modification or Termination*, EITF, April 1988.
130   EITF 96-14, *Accounting for the Costs Associated with Modifying Computer Software for the Year 2000*, EITF, July 1996.
131   SFAS 5, *Accounting for Contingencies*, FASB, March 1975, para. 1.
132   *Ibid.*, para. 8.
133   *Ibid.*, para. 12.

Chapter 26   Cash flow statements

1   EVOLUTION OF THE CASH FLOW STATEMENT

1.1   Statements of source and application of funds

The inclusion of statements of source and application of funds in annual reports can probably be attributed to a desire to provide users with a more complete picture of resource flows than that provided by the profit and loss account.[1] Because the latter is concerned with resource flows that are part of the earnings activity, it does not report changes resulting from investing or financing activities nor does it distinguish between the different types of resources consumed in the earnings activity.[2]

By the 1950s there was widespread experimentation by US companies with the inclusion of various forms of 'funds statement'[3] in annual reports.[4] This became a source of concern for the AICPA which commissioned a research study on cash flow analysis and the funds statement.[5] It is clear from the director's preface that the AICPA saw 'the increased use of the statement of source and application of funds and the recent emergence of an amorphous concept known as "cash flow" ' as a threat to the perfection of the accrual basis of accounting.[6]

In 1963, following the publication of the study, the Accounting Principles Board issued Opinion No. 3 – *The Statement of Source and Application of Funds* – which encouraged (but did not require) the presentation of a funds statement. This was the first official pronouncement on funds statements to be issued by a major accounting body. It received wide support from the principal stock exchanges and the business community in the US and resulted in a significant increase in the inclusion of such statements in US company annual reports. In 1970 the SEC made the funds statement an obligatory element of financial statement filing.

In 1971 APB Opinion No. 3 was superseded by APB Opinion No. 19, which required a 'statement summarizing changes in financial position [to] be presented as a basic financial statement for each period for which an income statement is presented'.[7]

In contrast to the US, there was a much slower acceptance in the UK of the view that the funds statement should be a complementary statement to the balance sheet and profit and loss account. Prior to the 1970s, few British companies published funds statements. Whereas in the US and Canada the emphasis was on achieving the most useful form and content of the funds statement, UK companies were still trying to decide whether the statement should be included in their annual reports at all. It was not until ED 13[8] was issued in April 1974 that the ASC offered any guidance on the subject. ED 13 led ultimately to the publication in July 1975 of SSAP 10,[9] which had the objective of establishing 'the practice of providing source and application of funds statements as a part of audited accounts and to lay down a minimum standard of disclosure in such statements'.[10]

1.2   The SSAP 10 funds statement

The form and content of the SSAP 10 funds statements were governed by two principal factors: the objective of the statement and the interpretation of the concept of 'funds'. However, there was widespread dissatisfaction with SSAP 10 in that it failed either to establish the objective of the funds statement or to define 'funds' adequately. Furthermore, the standard did not prescribe a specific format designed to provide useful and meaningful information in a consistent manner. A common criticism of the funds statement was that it was a repetitive and unnecessary rearrangement of figures already appearing in the financial statements. In fact, paragraph 4 of SSAP 10 bears out this charge, confirming that the funds statement was effectively a reconciliation of the information already provided in the accounts, providing the user with virtually no new information:

> 'The funds statement will provide a link between the balance sheet at the beginning of the period, the profit and loss account for the period and the balance sheet at the end of the period. ... The figures from which a funds statement is constructed should generally be identifiable in the profit and loss account, balance sheet and related notes.'

This contrasted significantly with the purpose of the funds statement as set out in a study on the subject by the Accountants International Study Group:

> 'The objective of the funds statement is to provide information as to how the activities of the enterprise have been financed and how its financial resources have been used during the period covered by the statement. It is not intended to, nor can it, supplant the balance sheet, income statement and retained earnings statement; neither is it a supporting schedule to these statements. The funds statement is, rather, a complementary statement which is important

in its own right and which is designed to present information that the other financial statements either do not provide or provide only indirectly.'[11]

It is indeed difficult to determine precisely what the drafters of SSAP 10 saw as the objective of the funds statement.[12] The following extracts from the standard illustrate conflicting views (emphases added):

> 'The objective of such a statement is to show the manner in which the operations of a company have been financed and in which its *financial resources* have been used and the format selected should be designed to achieve this objective.'[13]

> '... it is necessary also to identify the movements in net assets, liabilities and capital which have taken place during the year and the resultant effect on *net liquid funds.*'[14]

> 'It should show clearly the funds generated or absorbed by the operations of the business and the manner in which any resulting surplus of *liquid assets* has been applied or any deficiency of such assets has been financed, distinguishing the long term from the short term.'[15]

> 'The statement should distinguish the use of funds for the purchase of new fixed assets from funds used in increasing the *working capital* of the company.'[16]

It was not surprising that a statement purporting to accommodate all of the above turned out to be largely meaningless. SSAP 10 certainly did not promote uniformity in reporting practice, evidenced by the varying ways in which it was interpreted by companies in practice. The principal shortcoming was the focus on balance sheet classifications. The statement analysed the sources and applications of funds (however defined) in terms of movements within individual categories and groupings of assets and equities, rather than in terms of how the various activities of the business had either generated or absorbed funds. A funds statement prepared under SSAP 10 was largely a reconciliation of balance sheet changes, rather than a statement which provided additional information useful to the user.

Meanwhile, US companies were also encountering difficulties with the form and content of the funds statement presented under APB Opinion No. 19. The FASB had identified certain practical problems, 'including the ambiguity of terms such as *funds*, lack of comparability arising from diversity in the focus of the statement (cash, cash and short-term investments, quick assets, or working capital) and the resulting differences in definitions of funds flows from operating activities (cash or working capital), differences in the format of the statement (sources and uses format or activity format), variations in classifications of specific items in an activity format, and the reporting of net changes in amounts of assets and liabilities rather than gross inflows and outflows'.[17] This diversity in reporting practice was seen to be caused mainly by the lack of clear objectives for the funds statement.[18]

1.3   The move towards cash flow information

There was an increasing acknowledgement through the 1980s of the critical role played by cash in the operation of any economic entity. Hendriksen states that 'in the final analysis, cash flows into and out of a business enterprise are the most fundamental events upon which accounting measurements are based and upon which investors and creditors are assumed to base their decisions'.[19]

The importance of providing cash flow information was reinforced by the FASB through its concepts statements. SFAC No. 1 states that 'financial reporting should provide information to help present and potential investors and creditors and other users in assessing the amounts, timing, and uncertainty of prospective cash receipts from dividends or interest and the proceeds from the sale, redemption, or maturity of securities or loans. The prospects for those cash receipts are affected by an enterprise's ability to generate enough cash to meet its obligations when due and its other cash operating needs, to reinvest in operations, and to pay cash dividends ... . Thus, financial reporting should provide information to help investors, creditors, and others assess the amounts, timing, and uncertainty of prospective net inflows to the related enterprise.'[20]

Further recognition of the need for business enterprises to provide cash flow information in their external reporting was given by SFAC No. 5, which states that 'a full set of financial statements for a period should show: ... cash flows during the period'.[21] It then goes on to say that 'a statement of cash flows directly or indirectly reflects an entity's cash receipts classified by major sources and its cash payments classified by major uses during a period. It provides useful information about an entity's activities in generating cash through operations to repay debt, distribute dividends, or reinvest to maintain or expand operating capacity; about its financing activities, both debt and equity; and about its investing or spending of cash. Important uses of information about an entity's current cash receipts and payments include helping to assess factors such as the entity's liquidity, financial flexibility, profitability, and risk.'[22]

Liquidity reflects an asset's or liability's nearness to cash; whilst financial flexibility is the ability of an entity to raise cash at short notice so that it can meet unforeseen contingencies or take advantage of favourable opportunities that may arise. Although the balance sheet includes information that is often used in assessing an entity's liquidity and financial flexibility, it only provides an incomplete picture of these factors, unless it is used in conjunction with at least a cash flow statement.[23]

As a result of the increasing recognition of the significance of cash flow information, coupled with the diversity in the formats caused by the lack of a clear objective for the funds statement, the FASB issued SFAS 95 – *Statement of Cash Flows* – in November 1987. This superseded APB Opinion No. 19 and requires that 'a business enterprise that provides a set of financial statements that reports both financial position and results of operations shall also provide a statement of cash flows for each period for which results of operations are provided'.[24]

The US requirement to present a statement of cash flows started a worldwide trend in financial reporting, with several standard-setting bodies re-examining the nature and objectives of the funds statement, and concluding that the statement should focus on flows of cash rather than flows of working capital, or some other concept of funds.[25] In September 1991, the ASB published FRS 1 – *Cash flow statements* – which superseded SSAP 10 and required reporting entities to prepare a modified US-style cash flow statement instead of a SSAP 10 funds statement. In 1992, the IASC revised IAS 7, which now requires enterprises to prepare a cash flow statement instead of a statement of changes in financial position.

1.4   The distinction between 'funds flow' and 'cash flow'

Although the examples given in the Appendix to SSAP 10 seemed to emphasise a 'working capital' interpretation of funds, the funds statement was required to include all movements in financial resources. The 'all financial resources' concept, which originated from APB Opinion No. 3, sought to include in the funds statement all additions to, distributions of, and changes in composition of the financial resources of the entity. Accordingly, transactions such as the issue of shares for non-cash consideration or the conversion of loans to share capital were reflected in the funds statement, even though they did not affect working capital.

In contrast to the funds statement, a cash flow statement reflects only those transactions which result in an increase or decrease in cash. Thus, the initial purchase of a fixed asset under a finance lease will not appear in the cash flow statement (except to the extent that lease premiums are paid in cash), whereas the gross amount capitalised as an asset would have been shown as an application of funds and the assumption of the lease obligation as a source of funds in the funds statement. Similarly, neither the conversion of debt to equity nor the acquisition of a subsidiary settled by the issue of shares will feature in a cash flow statement.

The publication of FRS 1 also had the effect of dispelling the frequently held notion that profit after tax plus depreciation equated to operating cash flow. This misconception was, to a certain extent, reinforced by the accounts of some major companies. For example, the 1990 group flow of funds statement of Reckitt & Colman described funds from ordinary operations after tax as being 'net cash generation':

Extract 26.1: Reckitt & Colman plc (1990)

Group flow of funds statement

for the financial year ended 29 December 1990 [extract]

	1990 £m	1989 £m
Generation of funds from ordinary operations:		
Profit before tax	235·17	217·40
Depreciation	47·08	40·15
Disposal of fixed assets	16·04	10·67
	298·29	268·22
Tax paid	(56·33)	(54·06)
Net cash generation	241·96	214·16

In 1991, Reckitt & Colman opted for early implementation of FRS 1 and presented a cash flow statement. It is interesting to contrast the 'net cash generation' of £241.96m for 1990 shown in the funds statement above with the pre-dividend net cash inflow before investing and financing of £201.74m (i.e. £158.49m + £43.25m) for that year shown in the cash flow statement below:

Extract 26.2: Reckitt & Colman plc (1991)

Group cash flow statement

for the fifty-three weeks ended 4 January 1992 [extract]

	£m	1991 £m	£m	1990 £m
Net cash inflow from trading activities		329·97		276·07
Returns on investments and servicing of finance				
Interest received	20·57		39·44	
Interest paid	(63·02)		(55·40)	
Coupon on convertible capital bonds	(19·08)		(2·04)	
Dividends paid (including minorities)	(50·57)		(43·25)	
Net cash outflow from returns on investments and servicing of finance		(112·10)		(61·25)
Taxation		(50·25)		(56·33)
Net cash inflow before investing and financing		167·62		158·49

Clearly, FRS 1 enabled Reckitt & Colman to define its operating cash flows more precisely than it was able to under the SSAP 10 funds statement. At the same time, the two extracts illustrate one of the fundamental differences between funds flow and cash flow.

Since the Companies Act distribution rules allow the payment of dividends on the strength of net profit after tax and extraordinary items, a company is permitted to pay cash dividends on accrual based profits, even though it may not have generated sufficient cash flow from operations to cover such dividends. Whilst it was not always easy to determine from the funds statement whether the company had generated sufficient cash to cover its dividend payment, this will be evident from the cash flow statement. The importance of this information has been highlighted by corporate failures where the companies concerned had been unable to convert profits into cash and yet had maintained or even increased the payment of cash dividends.

1.5 The original FRS 1

FRS 1 was loosely based on ED 54 – *Cash flow statements* – the second to last exposure draft issued by the ASC before it was disbanded in July 1990. In fact, what ED 54 proposed was essentially a reformatted source and application of funds statement which used the 'cash and cash equivalents' definition of funds. Consequently, although ED 54 served as the catalyst in introducing the cash flow statement as the third primary financial statement, the requirements of FRS 1 were substantially different to those proposed in ED 54.

The statement required by FRS 1 was in many respects a modified US-style cash flow statement. Cash flows (defined as increases or decreases in 'cash and cash equivalents') were to be analysed under five standard headings:

- operating activities;
- returns on investments and servicing of finance;
- taxation;
- investing activities; and
- financing.

Presentation was required to follow the above sequence with a total being shown for the net cash flow for each standard heading. In addition, the total net cash inflow or outflow before financing was required to be disclosed.[26] This was intended to focus the statement on the effect of cash flows on the debt financing needs of the reporting entity, rather than on the balances held in cash and cash equivalents (these often being insignificant in size in relation to the level of debt).

Cash and cash equivalents were defined in FRS 1 as follows:[27]

Cash – Cash in hand and deposits repayable on demand with any bank or other financial institution. Cash includes cash in hand and deposits denominated in foreign currencies.

Cash equivalents – Short-term, highly liquid investments which are readily convertible into known amounts of cash without notice and which were within three months of maturity when acquired; less advances from banks repayable within three months from the date of the advance. Cash equivalents include investments and advances denominated in foreign currencies provided that they fulfil the above criteria.

Although the focus of the statement was on cash rather than on funds, restricting the definition to cash in hand or at the bank would not have reflected the reality of the cash management policies employed by reporting entities. Cash in excess of immediate needs is often invested in short-term investments. So long as these investments are highly liquid, are convertible into known amounts of cash without notice and are not subject to any significant changes in value because of changes in interest rates, they are virtually equivalent to cash. The statement therefore focused not just on flows of cash, but on flows of cash and cash equivalents.

Highly liquid investments realisable at any point for a known amount of cash did not qualify as cash equivalents where the term to maturity was long, for example Treasury Stock 9% 2008. This was because a change in interest rates would significantly affect the value of the stock. For this reason, the FRS restricted the definition of cash equivalents to those investments having a maturity of three months or less at the date of acquisition.

Negative balances had to be set off against the positive balances in computing the net holding of, and movement in, cash and cash equivalents. The FRS required short term advances to be treated as negative cash equivalents. However, only overdrafts and short-term bank advances were to be treated in this manner. Other short-term advances and loans constituted financing flows. In deciding whether a short-term bank loan could be included within cash and cash equivalents, a cut-off period of three months was adopted, consistent with the approach for short-term investments.

1.6   The need for revision

Without doubt the publication of FRS 1 was a quantum leap in the ASB's financial reporting reform process. It generally worked well in practice and enhanced the quality of financial reporting considerably. However, it was felt that the standard fell short in a number of respects from what could be achieved.[28] Consequently, the decision by the ASB to call for comments on the functioning of the standard in March 1994 (as part of the Board's policy for reviewing the effectiveness of major new standards) was well received.

The most common complaint concerned the definition of cash equivalents. In practice, companies' treasury operations did not draw the distinction between investment and cash management in the way that the original standard seemed to imply, since the three month cut-off for cash equivalents bore little relationship to companies' treasury maturity horizons. Normal treasury management meant investing in instruments which, as far as the company was concerned, were cash equivalents, but which were not treated as such for FRS 1 purposes. Cash flows related to these instruments had to be included under the investing activities heading. This resulted in a meaningless sub-total (struck after investing activities) which purported to show the cash inflow or outflow before financing. Bass dealt with the offending sub-total by providing additional detail within the investing activities section and by adding a new caption 'Net cash flow' at the foot of the statement:

Extract 26.3: Bass PLC (1995)

GROUP CASH FLOW STATEMENT[extract]

For the year ended 30 September 1995	1995 52 weeks £m	1995 52 weeks £m	1994 53 weeks £m	1994 53 weeks £m
Investing activities				
Capital expenditure				
Tangible fixed assets	**(372)**		(356)	
Trade loans advanced and other investments	**(133)**		(116)	
Cost of acquisitions	**(306)**		(10)	
	(811)		(482)	
Capital disposals				
Tangible fixed assets	**97**		98	
Trade loans and other investments	**124**		93	
	221		191	
Short-term investments				
Acquired	**(799)**		(628)	
Sold	**1,015**		452	
	216		(176)	
Investing activities		**(374)**		(467)
Net cash flow before financing		**96**		(185)
...				
Net cash flow*		**(120)**		(9)

* Net cash flow is net cash flow before financing, excluding the movement in short-term investments (highly liquid marketable securities and deposits maturing between 91 and 365 days from the date of acquisition).

Marks and Spencer adopted a more adventurous approach to solving essentially the same problem. Instead of showing non-cash equivalent deposits and short-term investments under investing activities, the company changed the next section from 'Financing' to 'Financing and treasury activities' so as to include these deposits and investments under that heading. The movement in short-term funds (£109.1m in 1996 and £140.6m in 1995) was therefore excluded from the sub-total required by FRS 1, with the caption being amended to 'Net cash (outflow)/inflow before financing *and treasury activities*' (emphasis added):

Extract 26.4: Marks and Spencer p.l.c. (1996)

Consolidated cash flow statement

FOR THE YEAR ENDED 31 MARCH 1996 [extract]

	1996	1995
	£m	£m
NET CASH (OUTFLOW)/INFLOW BEFORE FINANCING AND TREASURY ACTIVITIES	**(29.0)**	19.7
FINANCING AND TREASURY ACTIVITIES		
Shares issued under employees' share schemes	**36.2**	32.0
Redemption of cumulative preference shares	–	(1.4)
Repayment of long-term borrowing	–	(15.0)
Increase in non-cash equivalent bank loans and overdrafts	**96.2**	16.8
Increase in non-cash equivalent deposits and short-term investments	**(109.1)**	(140.6)
Net cash inflow/(outflow) from financing and treasury activities	**23.3**	(108.2)

Not surprisingly, dissatisfaction with the arbitrary cut-off in the definition of 'cash equivalents' featured prominently in the replies to the ASB's call for comments on FRS 1. Other matters raised by respondents included the exemptions from the scope of the standard; when net presentation of cash flows was appropriate; the implications of the changes to the profit and loss account brought about by FRS 3 and the need generally for further guidance on the classification of cash flows under the standard headings; the treatment of intragroup cash flows involving foreign currency; the presentation of cash flows resulting from hedging transactions and the treatment of cash subject to restriction.[29]

1.7   FRS 1 (Revised 1996)

The revised version of FRS 1 was published in October 1996, more than two years after the ASB's call for comments on the functioning of the existing standard. The ASB had warned that any changes were unlikely to come into effect before 1995. In the event, the process took longer than envisaged and FRED 10, the exposure draft of the revised standard, was published only in December 1995. The revised standard became mandatory for accounting periods ending on or after 23 March 1997.[30]

2 THE REQUIREMENTS OF FRS 1 (REVISED 1996)

2.1 Scope and exemptions

Like its predecessor, the revised FRS 1 applies to accounts intended to give a true and fair view of the reporting entity's financial position and profit or loss (or income and expenditure).[31] Although the relevance of a statement of cash flows to the truth and fairness of the financial position or the profit or loss for the period has never been entirely clear, the press release which accompanied the original FRS 1 stressed that the cash flow statement formed 'an essential element of the information required for accounts to give a true and fair view of the state of affairs of [large] companies at the end of the financial year, and of the profit or loss for the year. Accordingly, non-compliance with the standard may be a matter to be taken into account by the Financial Reporting Review Panel or the court in any consideration of whether or not accounts comply with the Companies Act.'[32] The Auditing Practices Board seems to have adopted a similar line of reasoning because its example of a qualified audit report in circumstances where a cash flow statement has been omitted explains that 'information about the company's cash flows is necessary for a proper understanding of the company's state of affairs and profit [loss].'[33]

Notwithstanding the apparent importance of cash flow information to the truth and fairness of the accounts, the revised standard exempts certain entities from the requirement to prepare a cash flow statement:[34]

(a) *Subsidiary undertakings where 90% or more of the voting rights are controlled within the group, provided that group accounts which include the subsidiary are publicly available*

This exemption is similar to the one in FRS 8 (see Chapter 27 at 2.3.5 C) and it applies regardless of the country of incorporation of the parent. The choice of a 90% threshold would seem to be a pragmatic compromise designed to deal with subsidiaries with small amounts of voting preference shares, or small numbers of shares held by employees. Neither FRS gives any guidance as to what is meant by 'publicly available'. The rationale behind this stipulation is a little puzzling since there is no requirement for the publicly available group accounts to contain a cash flow statement, or for that matter to be in English.

The reason given by the ASB for exempting subsidiaries where 90% of the votes are held by the group is that the solvency, liquidity and financial adaptability of these entities will essentially depend on the group rather than their own cash flows.[35]

Because the exemption applies to subsidiaries where 90% or more of the votes are *held by the group*, the effective interest held by the parent whose group accounts are publicly available is irrelevant, as illustrated below:

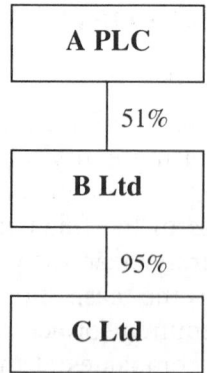

C Ltd is entitled to the exemption regardless of whether B Ltd prepares group accounts because more than 90% of C Ltd's voting rights are controlled within the group (comprising itself, B Ltd and A PLC).

(b) *Mutual life assurance companies*

The ASB is of the view that insurance companies should include the cash flows of their long-term business only to the extent of cash transferred and available to meet the obligations of the company or group as a whole.[36] This is because the shareholders of an insurance company generally have restricted rights to the profits and associated cash surpluses made by their long-term business. Mutual life assurance companies, which are owned by policy holders, are accordingly exempt from the requirements of the FRS.

(c) *Pension funds*

Pension funds are exempt because a cash flow statement would add little information to that already available from the rest of the accounts.

(d) *Open-ended investment funds substantially all of whose investments are highly liquid and carried at market value, on condition that a statement of changes in net assets is provided*

This exemption is similar to that for pension funds, recognising that a cash flow statement would be of limited additional use. The definition of an 'investment fund' in the standard is based on that used in companies legislation, but with the notable exception that there is no restriction on the distribution of capital profits.[37]

(e) *Building societies that prepare a statement of source and application of funds in a prescribed format as required by law*

This exemption was available for two years from the effective date of the revised FRS 1, but has now ceased to exist. For accounting periods ending on or after 23 March 1999, building societies are no longer obliged by law to prepare a statement of source and application of funds and will instead be subject to the requirements of FRS 1.[38] This reflects the ASB's view that the similarity and competition between banks and building societies is such that both should prepare cash flow statements.[39]

(f)   Small (but not medium-sized) companies entitled to the filing exemptions under sections 246 and 247 of the Companies Act 1985

As at August 1999, these are, broadly speaking, companies which satisfy two of the following criteria:

- turnover not more than £2.8 million;
- balance sheet total not more than £1.4 million; and
- not more than 50 employees.[40]

PLCs, banks, insurance companies and companies authorised under the Financial Services Act 1986 do not qualify for the exemption, nor do members of a group which contains any of these entities.

This exemption was re-visited as part of the wider examination of the reporting requirements for small entities. The majority of respondents to the December 1996 exposure draft of the FRSSE supported the exemption and the ASB acknowledged that the format prescribed by FRS 1 was not necessarily suitable or appropriate for smaller businesses. However, the Board agreed with the minority of respondents that a cash flow statement was important, given that the management of cash was fundamental to the success of small businesses.[41] Accordingly, the FRSSE encourages, but does not require, reporting entities to provide a cash flow statement using the indirect method.[42]

(g)   Small entities which would have qualified under the previous category had they been companies

This exemption is a natural consequence of the exemption for small companies referred to above.

2.2   The definition of cash

Since the objective of a cash flow statement is to provide an analysis of the reporting entity's inflows and outflows of cash, the definition of cash is crucial to its presentation:[43]

Cash – Cash in hand and deposits repayable on demand with any qualifying financial institution, less overdrafts from any qualifying financial institution repayable on demand. Deposits are repayable on demand if they can be withdrawn at any time without notice and without penalty or if a maturity or period of notice of not more than 24 hours or one working day has been agreed. Cash includes cash in hand and deposits denominated in foreign currencies.

Overdrafts ('a borrowing facility repayable on demand that is used by drawing on a current account with a qualifying financial institution')[44] are often a source of finance that extends for a significant period of time. Nevertheless, the revised standard is clear that they should be treated as negative cash balances. Pragmatically, this is the only possible treatment, since otherwise all cheques written on an overdrawn account would have to be shown under the financing heading of the cash flow statement as new borrowings and payments in to the account would have to be separately shown as repayments of those borrowings.

It is sometimes argued that certain deposits with notice or maturity periods in excess of 24 hours should be treated as cash. This is because these funds will often be available on demand, albeit that interest is then recalculated as if the deposit were a current account. However, the standard makes it clear that deposits qualify as cash only if the money is available within 24 hours *without penalty*.

A more restrictive definition of cash was the most important change made to the original FRS 1, where the focus was on inflows and outflows of cash and cash equivalents.

It is clear that the amount shown alongside 'cash at bank and in hand' in the balance sheet will rarely be a reliable guide to 'cash' for FRS 1 purposes. Apart from the need to include overdrafts for cash flow purposes, the balance sheet caption will often include bank deposits with notice or maturity periods in excess of 24 hours, as illustrated in the following extract:

Extract 26.5: Rio Tinto plc and Rio Tinto Limited (1998)

Notes to the 1998 accounts

14 CURRENT ASSET INVESTMENTS, CASH AND LIQUID RESOURCES [extract]

	1998 US$m	1997 US$m
Cash		
Cash as defined in FRS 1 Revised ("FRS 1 cash")	381	295
Deposits with an original maturity of over 24 hours	395	1,080
Exclude: bank overdrafts and notes	127	145
Cash at bank and in hand per balance sheet	**903**	1,520

Because the standard requires the amount of cash and other components of net debt to be traced back to the equivalent captions in the balance sheet,[45] any difference between 'cash' for FRS 1 purposes and 'cash' for balance sheet purposes will be evident from the notes to the accounts.

2.3   Format of the cash flow statement

The format of the cash flow statement is tightly prescribed. Cash flows are required to be presented under a series of standard headings:[46]

- operating activities;
- dividends from joint ventures and associates;
- returns on investments and servicing of finance;
- taxation;
- capital expenditure and financial investment;
- acquisitions and disposals;
- equity dividends paid;
- management of liquid resources; and
- financing.

The first seven headings (but not necessarily the last two – see Extract 26.6 below) should follow the sequence shown above.[47] Cash flows relating to the management of liquid resources and financing can be combined under a single heading provided that the cash flows relating to each are shown separately and that separate sub-totals are given.[48]

The requirement to include dividends from joint ventures and associates under a separate heading was brought about by the publication of FRS 9 – *Associates and joint ventures* – in November 1997. The new rule became effective for accounting periods ending on or after 23 June 1998.[49]

Within each standard heading, the FRS identifies certain categories of cash inflows and outflows which are to be separately identified, where they are material. This can be done either on the face of the statement or in a note.[50]

The cash flow statement in the 1998 accounts of BP Amoco is of particular interest – see Extract 26.6 below. As permitted by the FRS, the last two headings have been reversed. Another feature is that the statement does not focus on the net decrease or increase in cash. Instead, the last two headings and the movement in cash have been combined to produce a sub-total which equates to the 'net cash inflow (outflow)' for the year. The ASB considered prescribing a format which results in the increase or decrease in cash being shown as the residual amount. This approach had a number of supporters but the respondents to FRED 10 did not want it to be mandatory. Preparers have accordingly been allowed to choose the format of their cash flow statements 'provided that these comply with the requirements for classification and order'.[51]

In BP Amoco's cash flow statement, the individual cash flows required to be shown under returns on investments and servicing of finance, taxation, capital expenditure and financial investment, and acquisitions and disposals are shown on the face of the cash flow statement. As permitted by the FRS, the individual cash flows under the financing and management of liquid resources headings appear in a separate note to the accounts, which is reproduced in Extract 26.7:

Extract 26.6: BP Amoco p.l.c. (1998)

Group cash flow statement [extract]

	$ million	
For the year ended 31 December	**1998**	1997
Net cash inflow from operating activities	**9,586**	15,558
Dividends from joint ventures	**544**	190
Dividends from associated undertakings	**422**	551
Servicing of finance and returns on investments		
Interest received	**223**	243
Interest paid	**(961)**	(911)
Dividends received	**43**	13
Dividends paid to minority shareholders	**(130)**	–
Net cash outflow from servicing of finance and returns on investments	**(825)**	(655)
Taxation		
UK corporation tax	**(391)**	(500)
Overseas tax	**(1,314)**	(1,773)
Tax paid	**(1,705)**	(2,273)
Capital expenditure and financial investment		
Payments for fixed assets	**(8,431)**	(8,600)
Purchase of shares for employee share schemes	**(254)**	(300)
Proceeds from the sale of fixed assets	**1,387**	1,468
Net cash outflow for capital expenditure and financial investment	**(7,298)**	(7,432)
Acquisitions and disposals		
Investments in associated undertakings	**(396)**	(1,021)
Acquisitions	**(314)**	–
Net investment in joint ventures	**708**	(1,967)
Proceeds from the sale of businesses	**780**	364
Net cash inflow (outflow) for acquisitions and disposals	**778**	(2,624)
Equity dividends paid	**(2,408)**	(2,437)
Net cash inflow (outflow)	**(906)**	878
Financing	**(377)**	1,012
Management of liquid resources	**(596)**	(167)
Increase (decrease) in cash	**67**	33
	(906)	878

Extract 26.7: BP Amoco p.l.c. (1998)

30 Group cash flow statement analysis [extract]

	$ million	
(c) Financing	**1998**	1997
Long-term borrowing	**(2,196)**	(1,179)
Repayments of long-term borrowing	**1,217**	884
Short-term borrowing	**(513)**	(1,285)
Repayments of short-term borrowing	**692**	1,342
	(800)	(238)
Issue of share capital	**(161)**	(172)
Repurchase of share capital	**584**	1,422
Net cash (inflow) outflow	**(377)**	1,012

(d) Management of liquid resources

Liquid resources comprise current asset investments which are principally commercial paper issued by other companies. The net cash inflow from the management of liquid resources was $596 million ($167 million).

Irrespective of whether the individual categories of inflows and outflows under the standard headings are shown on the face of the statement or in a note, they must be shown gross. This rule does not apply to cash flows relating to operating activities and certain cash flows under the management of liquid resources and financing headings.[52] To qualify for net presentation, the cash flows within management of liquid resources and financing must *either*:

■ be related in substance to a single financing transaction as defined by FRS 4 (one where the debt and the facility are under a single agreement with the same lender, the finance costs for the new debt are not significantly higher than the existing debt, the obligations of the lender are firm and the lender is expected to be able to fulfil its obligations);[53] *or*

■ be due to short maturities and high turnover occurring from rollover or reissue (for example, short-term deposits or a commercial paper programme).[54] Extract 26.7 above is an example of net presentation using this dispensation.

It should be noted that the financing cash flows arising under a commercial paper programme do not qualify as a single financing transaction as defined in FRS 4. This is because the debt and the back-up facility are not under a single agreement with the same lender.[55] Although net presentation is not sanctioned by the first dispensation referred to above, it is permitted under the second.

Notwithstanding the dispensations referred to above, gross presentation will still be required for many of the cash flows under the management of liquid resources heading. For example, the placing of surplus cash on short-term deposit from time to time followed by the subsequent withdrawal of these funds when needed gives rise to two cash flows, one out and the other in. However, in many instances it will not be possible to extract this information from the books and records without expending considerable time and effort. This might explain why net presentation of the movement in term deposits is a common feature under the management of liquid resources heading:

Extract 26.8: The British Land Company PLC (1999)		
Group Cash Flow Statement for the year ended 31st March, 1999 [extract]		
	1999 **£m**	1998 £m
Management of Liquid Resources and Financing		
Decrease (increase) in term deposits	**27.7**	(47.6)

Whether disclosure of the gross outflows and inflows in term deposits would provide useful additional information must be doubtful.

2.4 Classification of cash flows by standard heading

2.4.1 General principle

The standard requires each cash flow to be classified according to the substance of the transaction or event giving rise to it.[56] Because the other primary statements are based on accounting standards which, in theory, use the same substance principle, the end result should be consistent treatment across all the primary statements. In essence, this means that capitalised development costs should appear under capital expenditure and financial investment. Finance lease rentals should be split into their interest and capital elements, with the former appearing under returns on investments and servicing of finance and the latter under financing. Operating lease rentals should appear under operating activities. Classification in the cash flow statement effectively becomes a function of the accounting policies adopted by the reporting entity. Some might regard this as counter-intuitive, but it is designed to achieve the ASB's objective of consistent treatment in all the primary statements.

An unexpected consequence of the requirement for consistent treatment across the primary statements is the impact of FRS 12 on the cash flow statements of certain public utilities. The following extracts compare the 1998 and 1999 cash flow statements for Severn Trent. Up to and including 1998, a provision for planned infrastructure maintenance expenditure was charged in arriving at operating profit. In accordance with paragraph 11 of FRS 1, the cash outflow for maintenance expenditure was shown as part of the cash inflow from operating activities, which totalled £549.0m in 1998. Following the implementation of FRS 12 in 1999, this inflow was restated and increased by £79.2m to £628.2m:

Extract 26.9: Severn Trent Plc (1998)

Group cash flow statement year ended 31 March 1998 [extract]

	1998 **£m**	1997 £m
Net cash inflow from operating activities	**549.0**	505.9
Dividends received from associated undertakings	**1.7**	2.0
Returns on investments and servicing of finance	**(54.5)**	(39.1)
Tax paid	**(194.8)**	(39.1)
Capital expenditure and financial investment	**(347.0)**	(355.2)
Acquisitions	**(31.9)**	(10.7)
Equity dividends paid	**(91.4)**	(108.3)
Net cash outflow before use of liquid resources and financing	**(168.9)**	(44.5)

The impact of the FRS 12 restatement on the figures for 1998 can be seen in Extract 26.10 below. The net cash outflow before use of liquid resources (£168.9m) is unchanged but the cash inflow from operating activities and the outflow for capital expenditure and financial investment are both adjusted by £79.2m.

Extract 26.10: Severn Trent Plc (1999)

Group cash flow statement

Year ended 31 March 1999 [extract]

	1999 **£m**	1998 £m
Net cash inflow from operating activities	**628.0**	628.2
Dividends received from associated undertakings	**1.6**	1.7
Returns on investments and servicing of finance	**(79.1)**	(54.5)
Taxation	**(209.6)**	(194.8)
Capital expenditure and financial investment	**(609.7)**	(426.2)
Acquisitions	**(81.3)**	(31.9)
Equity dividends paid	**(35.7)**	(91.4)
Net cash outflow before use of liquid resources and financing	**(385.8)**	(168.9)

1998 comparative figures in the group cash flow statement for cash inflow from operating activities, and capital expenditure and financial investment have been restated following the adoption of Financial Reporting Standard 12 'Provisions, Contingent Liabilities and Contingent Assets' (Note 1(d)i)).

The background to the £79.2m restatement is explained in more detail in the relevant note:

Extract 26.11: Severn Trent Plc (1999)

Notes to the financial statements

Accounting policies [extract]

Tangible fixed assets and depreciation

Tangible fixed assets comprise:

i) *Infrastructure assets*

Infrastructure assets comprise a network of systems being mains and sewers, impounding and pumped raw water storage reservoirs, dams and sludge pipelines.

Expenditure on infrastructure assets relating to increases in capacity or enhancements of the network and on maintaining the operating capability of the network in accordance with the defined standards of service is treated as an addition and included at cost after deducting grants and contributions.

The depreciation charged for infrastructure assets is the estimated level of annual expenditure required to maintain the operating capability of the network, based on the company's independently certified asset management plan.

It has been necessary to change the method of accounting for infrastructure maintenance expenditure following the introduction of FRS 12, as it is no longer permissible to account for the difference between planned and actual expenditure on infrastructure renewals as a provision or prepayment. As a consequence, the balance sheet and cash flow statement have been restated to take account of necessary changes since the year ended 31 March 1989, when renewals accounting was first adopted, and any previous provisions or prepayments have been subsumed into fixed assets. Further information is given in note 10. This change of accounting has no effect on the profit and loss account other than to reclassify the renewals charge as depreciation.

Because the maintenance expenditure is being capitalised (and subsequently depreciated), the related cash outflow falls to be included under capital expenditure and financial investment (see 2.4.6 below).

2.4.2   Operating activities

Somewhat tentatively, the standard explains that cash flows from operating activities are *in general* those related to operating or trading activities, *normally* shown in the profit and loss account in arriving at operating profit (emphases added).[57]

'Operating or trading activities' are not defined which leaves the definition dangerously close to being circular: operating cash flows are operating cash flows. However, the standard does contain some examples of operating or trading activities (receipts from customers, payments to suppliers and payments to employees, including redundancy) which should mitigate the problem.[58]

The presentation of cash flows related to the (sometimes fundamental) reorganisation and restructuring of businesses, both existing and acquired, has proved to be controversial. Inclusion of these cash flows under operating activities is illustrated below:

Extract 26.12: Zeneca Group PLC (1998)

Statement of Group Cash Flow [extract]

For the year ended 31 December	Notes	**1998** **£m**	1997 £m	1996 £m
Cash flow from operating activities				
Net cash inflow from trading operations		**1,263**	1,235	1,155
Outflow related to exceptional items	24	**(46)**	(66)	(76)
Net cash inflow from operating activities		**1,217**	1,169	1,079

24 Cash flows related to exceptional items [extract]
The cash outflow relating to exceptional items includes expenditure charged to exceptional provisions raised in prior years relating to business rationalisation and restructuring including severance and other employee costs. It also includes £4m of expenditure relating to the closure of the Organophosphate Intermediates business (Note 5).

The above presentation of restructuring costs can be contrasted with that used by Cadbury Schweppes:

Extract 26.13: Cadbury Schweppes p.l.c. (1998)

Group Cash Flow Statement for the 52 weeks ended 2 January 1999 [extract]

	1998 **£m**	1997 £m	1996 £m
Acquisitions and disposals			
Acquisitions of businesses	**(96)**	(95)	(135)
Expenditure on post-acquisition restructuring	**(4)**	(15)	(18)

In Cadbury Schweppes' profit and loss account, the cost of restructuring acquired subsidiaries is charged in arriving at operating profit. However, in preparing the cash flow statement, the company was presumably of the view that the related cash outflows were not related to operating items.

Prior to FRS 7, the cost of restructuring acquired subsidiaries was often not charged in the profit and loss account at all. This was sometimes cited as a reason for excluding the related cash flows from operating activities heading. A similar argument existed in connection with the costs of a fundamental restructuring which (if certain conditions are met) FRS 3 requires to be excluded from the operating profit total.[59] In order to standardise practice in this area, FRS 1 states that 'operating item cash outflows relating to provisions' should appear under operating activities *regardless* of whether the provision was deducted in arriving at operating profit.[60] As examples of such cash flows, the standard[61] cites operating item cash flows provided for on an acquisition and redundancy payments provided for on the termination of an operation or for a fundamental reorganisation or restructuring, the last two under paragraphs 20a and 20b of FRS 3.[62] In Extract 26.12 above, the £4m of expenditure relating to the closure of the Organophosphate Intermediates business is an example of a paragraph 20a 'non-operating' cost being shown under operating activities.

FRS 1 allows a choice between the direct and indirect methods of presenting operating cash flows. The direct method is essentially based on an analysis of the cash book. It shows operating cash receipts and payments, including cash receipts from customers, cash payments to suppliers and cash payments to and on behalf of employees which, when added to the other operating cash payments, aggregate to the net cash flow from operating activities.

A   *The indirect method*

The indirect method arrives at the same net cash flow from operating activities, but does so by working back from operating profit in the form of a reconciliation.

To obtain the cash flow information, the balance sheet figures have to be analysed according to the various standard headings in the cash flow statement. Thus the reconciliation of operating profit to cash flow from operating activities will include, not the increase or decrease in all debtors or creditors, but only those elements which relate to operating activities. Accordingly, accrued interest or amounts payable in respect of the acquisition of fixed assets or investments will be excluded from the movement in creditors included in this reconciliation. Although this may not present practical difficulties in the preparation of single company cash flow statements, it is necessary to ensure that sufficient information is collected from subsidiaries for purposes of preparing the group cash flow statement. Where a group has made an acquisition of a subsidiary during the year, the change in working capital has to be split between the increase due to the acquisition (which will be shown under acquisitions and disposals to the extent that the purchase consideration is settled in cash) and the element related to operating activities which will appear in the operating profit reconciliation.

The reconciliation of operating profit to cash inflow from operating activities is required to be disclosed, either adjoining the cash flow statement itself (provided it is clearly labelled), or as a note.[63] Two of the four illustrative examples in Appendix I to the standard show the cash flow statement wedged in between two reconciliations – one to operating profit and the other to net debt (or its equivalent). To comply with the labelling requirement, the heading 'Cash Flow Statement' has to be duplicated – an untidy outcome. Not surprisingly, the great majority of companies have elected to show the reconciliation of operating profit to cash inflow from operating activities in a note, as illustrated in the following extract:

Extract 26.14: United News & Media plc (1998)

Notes to the financial statements

26. RECONCILIATION OF OPERATING PROFIT TO CASH INFLOW FROM OPERATING ACTIVITIES [extract]	Continuing 1998 £m	Discontinued 1998 £m	Total 1998 £m
Operating profit	117.8	45.7	163.5
Depreciation charges	42.1	9.9	52.0
Amortisation of goodwill on subsidiaries	153.3	–	153.3
Share of results of joint ventures	(4.8)	(0.1)	(4.9)
Share of results of associates	3.5	(0.7)	2.8
Loss/(profit) on sale of tangible fixed assets	1.1	–	1.1
Profit on sale of businesses	(0.4)	–	(0.4)
Payments against provisions	(34.4)	(0.9)	(35.3)
Decrease/(increase) in stocks	2.6	–	2.6
(Increase)/decrease in debtors	(4.0)	5.5	1.5
Increase/(decrease) in creditors	1.4	(18.0)	(16.6)
Other non-cash items including movements on provisions	(6.4)	(0.8)	(7.2)
Cash inflow from operating activities	271.8	40.6	312.4

The extract above illustrates the requirement to disclose separately the movements in stocks, debtors and creditors related to operating activities and other differences between cash flows and profits.[64] The inclusion of reconciling items for the share of results of joint ventures and associates is a consequence of the operating profit above being the total operating profit (inclusive of joint ventures and associates), not that of the group. The dividends received from joint ventures and associates appear under their own heading (see section 2.4.3 below).

United News & Media has analysed the cash inflow from operating activities between continuing and discontinued operations. Reporting entities are encouraged, but not required, to disclose additional information like this.[65] Other suggestions put forward by the ASB include the provision of segmental information[66] and the division of cash flows in a way that highlights different degrees of access to the underlying cash balances which might be of special relevance to regulated industries like insurance.[67]

B   The direct method

The ASB encourages disclosure of the information provided by the direct method where it is not too costly to obtain.[68] However, the information provided by the indirect method is required even where the direct method has been adopted[69] so there is little incentive to adopt the direct method. This, coupled with the additional burden involved, means that it is rarely used in practice. It is sometimes found in the accounts of property companies, as shown in the next extract:

Extract 26.15: Greycoat PLC (1999)

21. Notes to the cash flow statement [extract]

Analysis of cash flows by headings for amounts netted in the cash flow statement:

	1999 £m	1998 £m
Operating activities		
Net rental income	20.9	17.1
Fee income	0.4	0.4
Administration and other expenses	(3.7)	(3.3)
Cash flow from operating activities	17.6	14.2
Reconciliation of operating profit to net inflow from operating activities:		
Operating profit	17.8	15.8
Depreciation charge	0.1	0.1
(Increase) decrease in debtors	(0.5)	1.9
Increase (decrease) in creditors	0.2	(3.6)
Net cash inflow from operating activities	17.6	14.2

2.4.3   Dividends from joint ventures and associates

The requirement to show dividends received from joint ventures and associates under a separate heading below operating activities was brought about by the publication of FRS 9 in November 1997.[70] The change is a consequence of the requirement in FRS 9 to exclude the results of these entities from group operating profit. It reflects the ASB's view that dividends from joint ventures and associates are not on a comparable basis to the cash flows arising from the group's operating activities and have a different significance from its returns on investments.[71] Although the drafting of the amendment to FRS 1 is not entirely clear, it would seem that 'Dividends from joint ventures and associates' is intended to be a single main heading[72] which is required to be analysed further:[73]

Extract 26.16: TI Group plc (1998)

CASH FLOW STATEMENT
FOR THE YEAR ENDED 31ST DECEMBER 1998 [extract]

	Notes	1998 £m	1997 £m
Dividends received from joint venture and associates	25	**7.3**	10.6
25 NET CASH INFLOW FROM OPERATING ACTIVITIES [extract]			
Dividends received from joint venture		**7.1**	10.4
Dividends received from associates		**0.2**	0.2
Dividends received from joint venture and associates		**7.3**	10.6

Separate disclosure of the dividends from joint ventures and those from associates is consistent with the approach adopted throughout FRS 9.

Other cash flows from associates and joint ventures – those arising from trading, or loan interest, for example – should be included under the appropriate heading.

2.4.4   *Returns on investments and servicing of finance*

Returns on investments and servicing of finance are receipts resulting from the ownership of investments and payments to providers of finance, non-equity shareholders and minority interests, excluding those items (like dividends from joint ventures and associates) which are specifically required by the standard to be classified under another heading.[74] The following extract illustrates many of the items which are required to be separately disclosed under this heading:[75]

Extract 26.17: Daily Mail and General Trust plc (1998)

Notes to the Cash Flow Statement

15 Analysis of Cash Flows given in the Cash Flow Statement [extract]

	1998 **£m**	1997 £m
Returns on investments and servicing of finance		
Interest received	**5.3**	3.6
Interest paid	**(45.0)**	(36.3)
Interest element of finance lease rental payments	**(1.3)**	(1.6)
Issue costs of Eurobond	**–**	(1.7)
Premium paid on repurchase of Exchangeable Bonds	**(1.1)**	(15.2)
Premium on repurchase of US $ Loan Notes	**(2.6)**	–
Dividends received from other investments	**2.9**	3.1
Dividends paid to minority shareholders	**(5.5)**	(4.5)
	(47.3)	(52.6)

Because FRS 1 requires cash flows that are treated as finance costs under FRS 4 to be shown under returns on investments and servicing of finance,[76] debt and non-equity share issue costs appear under this heading. The link with FRS 4 also explains why the premiums paid by the Daily Mail and General Trust on repurchasing the Exchangeable Bonds and US $ Loan Notes are included here. The same principle means that the redemption of deep discount bonds is required to be split between interest and principal, with the former being shown under returns on investments and servicing of finance and the latter under financing (see Extract 26.28 at 2.4.10 below).

Not illustrated above is the requirement to show dividends paid on the entity's non-equity shares (as defined in FRS 4) under this heading.[77] Dividends paid on equity shares appear lower down the statement (see 2.4.8 below).

Although the cash flows to be included under this heading are essentially interest and dividends received and paid, there are some complications in the identification of the relevant amounts. With respect to interest, deduction of tax at source means that amounts received may be net of tax. The amount of cash actually received should be shown as a cash inflow but if any tax withheld is subsequently recovered, this should also be included as part of interest received. Similarly, where tax is withheld when interest is paid, the interest actually paid should be included as a cash outflow together with the tax paid to the relevant tax authority. Dividends received and paid should be shown at the amount of cash actually received and paid.

In a departure from the general principle outlined under 2.4.1 above, the standard requires all interest paid (even if capitalised) to appear under this heading. This is because the Board wants the cash flow statement to 'give a complete picture' of the interest cash flows.[78] This is a difference in treatment between SFAS 95 and FRS 1. Under SFAS 95 the payment of capitalised interest is reported as part of the cost of the asset, and therefore as part of investing activities. The approach adopted by SFAS 95 presumably reflects the philosophy that interest is an intrinsic part of the historical cost of an asset.

2.4.5   *Taxation*

Cash flows included under the taxation heading are those to or from taxation authorities in respect of the reporting entity's revenue and capital profits.[79] Inclusion of these cash flows under a separate section in the cash flow statement reflects the Board's view that 'it is not useful to divide taxation cash flows into constituent parts relating to the activities that gave rise to them because the apportionment will, in many cases, have to be made on an arbitrary basis.'[80] A further complication is that taxation cash flows generally arise from activities in an earlier period. This makes it difficult to report taxation cash flows along with the transactions that gave rise to them.

VAT, other sales taxes, property taxes and any other taxes not assessed on the revenue and capital profits of the reporting entity should not be included under the taxation heading.

Cash flows associated with VAT and other sales taxes should normally be dealt with as a single net cash flow in the operating activities section of the statement. Thus, all cash flows should be shown net of any attributable VAT or other sales tax. Although the actual cash flows will include VAT where appropriate, the taxation element has only a short-term effect on the entity's overall cash position. Although the practice of collapsing these tax flows into a net payment to or from the tax authorities should usually be adopted, a different treatment may be applied if it is more appropriate. In particular, where VAT or other sales tax paid by a business is irrecoverable, cash flows should include the associated tax. If this is impracticable, the irrecoverable tax should be included under the most appropriate standard heading. This will be the case for businesses which are exempt or partially exempt, for example charities.

Taxation cash flows, other than those in respect of the reporting entity's profits and VAT or other sales taxes, should be included under the same standard heading as the cash flow that gave rise to the taxation cash flow, unless a different treatment is more appropriate.[81]

Although there is no requirement to split UK and overseas tax paid, this is sometimes done in practice:

Extract 26.18: Bass PLC (1998)

group cash flow statement

for the year ended 30 September 1998 [extract]

	1998 £m	1998 £m	1997 £m	1997 £m
UK corporation tax paid	**(128)**		(151)	
Overseas corporate tax paid	**(24)**		(14)	
Taxation		**(152)**		(165)

The standard includes guidance for subsidiaries on cash flows relating to group relief. These should be included under 'taxation' even though they are not paid to a taxation authority.

2.4.6 *Capital expenditure and financial investment*

This section has its origin in what might be described as the ASB's pursuit of the 'free cash flow' Holy Grail. When the investing activities caption was scrapped pursuant to the introduction of an eight-heading format for the cash flow statement, FRED 10 raised the possibility of striking a sub-total after capital expenditure but before acquisitions and disposals.[82] However, responses to the exposure draft persuaded the ASB to abandon this proposal. The explanation given was that 'there were several interpretations of the exact composition of "free cash flows" – indeed the commentators themselves suggested several different definitions – but a key issue was to distinguish cash flows for investing to maintain the business from cash flows for investing to expand the business'.[83] One company regularly making such a distinction is Whitbread:

Extract 26.19: Whitbread PLC (1999)

FINANCE REVIEW

Cash flow [extract]

The cash outflow before financing was £78 million. In order to assess the underlying cash flow performance, it is necessary to eliminate the cash flows relating to the acquisition and disposal of businesses (net outflow of £10 million) and the investment in new retail outlets (outflow of £247 million included within 'property and plant purchased'). Underlying cash inflow, after making these adjustments, was £179 million. The equivalent figure for 1997/8 was £191 million.

Although Whitbread identified £247m of the £443m cash outflow for property and plant purchased as being in respect of investment to expand the business, the ASB decided it was not feasible for an accounting standard 'to set out how to distinguish expenditure for expansion from expenditure for maintenance'.[84] This was the same conclusion the Board reached in 1991 prior to issuing the original FRS 1 when it commented that 'criteria for distinguishing expenditure to expand the level of operations would vary from reporting entity to reporting entity and would distort the comparability provided by the standard headings. Similar problems arise in analysing changes in working capital'.[85]

However, in revising FRS 1 in 1996, the ASB nevertheless decided that cash flows relating to capital expenditure should be shown separately from acquisitions and disposals. The reason for this is hard to fathom, given the Board's warning that 'this distinction should not be interpreted as reflecting on the one hand maintenance expenditure and on the other expenditure for expansion because these may both fall under either heading depending on the circumstances'.[86]

Although the sub-total (after the capital expenditure and financial investment heading) proposed in FRED 10 was not incorporated into the revised FRS 1, there is nothing to prevent companies from including free cash flow (or indeed any other sub-total) in their cash flow statements, as illustrated in the following extract:

Extract 26.20: Cadbury Schweppes p.l.c. (1998)

Group Cash Flow Statement for the 52 weeks ended 2 January 1999 [extract]

	1998 **£m**	1997 £m	1996 £m
Free cash flow			
Cash inflow/(outflow) before use of liquid resources and financing	**78**	193	(16)
Add back:			
Cash flows from acquisitions and disposals	**79**	(36)	153
	157	157	137

Cash flows required to be included under capital expenditure and financial investment are those related to the acquisition or disposal of fixed assets (including investments).[87] In addition, current asset investments that do not qualify as 'liquid resources' (see 2.4.9 below) effectively default to this section. Cash flows related to the acquisition or disposal of investments in associates and joint ventures should be excluded because they are required to be shown under acquisitions and disposals.[88]

The capital expenditure and financial investment heading will usually include the following cash flows, which should be separately disclosed:[89]

(a)   receipts from sales of, and payments made to acquire, property, plant and equipment;

(b)   receipts from the repayment of, and loans made to, other entities (other than payments forming part of an acquisition or disposal or a movement in liquid resources – see 2.4.7 and 2.4.9 below); and

(c)   receipts from the sale of, and payments to acquire, debt instruments of other entities (other than payments forming part of an acquisition or disposal or a movement in liquid resources – see 2.4.7 and 2.4.9 below).

Where there are no cash flows relating to financial investment (i.e. those under (b) and (c) above), the section heading may be reduced to capital expenditure.[90]

The treatment of loans to associates (and the repayment thereof) is not entirely clear and has given rise to some inconsistency. For example, Vodafone has included these loans under capital expenditure and financial investment whereas the Daily Mail and General Trust appears to have adopted a different approach:

Extract 26.21: Vodafone Group Plc (1999)

25 Analysis of cash flows [extract]

	1999 £m	1998 £m
Net cash outflow for capital expenditure and financial investment		
Purchase of intangible fixed assets	**(17.6)**	(24.9)
Purchase of tangible fixed assets	**(736.8)**	(491.5)
Purchase of trade investments	**(4.2)**	–
Disposal of trade investments	**53.6**	–
Disposal of tangible fixed assets	**14.0**	6.7
Loans to associated undertakings	–	(1.3)
Loans repaid by associated undertakings	**2.6**	1.4
	(688.4)	(509.6)

Extract 26.22: Daily Mail and General Trust plc (1998)

Notes to the Cash Flow Statement

15 Analysis of Cash Flows given in the Cash Flow Statement [extract]

	1998 £m	1997 £m
Acquisitions and disposals		
Purchase of businesses	**(151.5)**	(169.8)
Cash acquired with subsidiaries	**9.9**	2.8
Investments in associates	**(4.9)**	(12.3)
Disposal of businesses	**2.5**	2.3
Disposal of associates	**3.0**	14.2
	(141.0)	(162.8)

Investments in associates of £4.9m shown in the cash flow statement above can be traced to 'additions' of the same amount shown in the investment in associates' note. That note splits the £4.9m between cost of shares (£1.9m) and loans (£3.0m).

Uncertainty about the treatment of loans to associates stems from whether they constitute an 'investment in' the associate concerned or whether they are loans made to another entity (which clearly belong under the capital expenditure and financial investment heading). A similar approach to that adopted by the Daily Mail and General Trust can be found in Extract 26.23 at 2.4.7 below.

The outflow shown in the cash flow statement in respect of the acquisition of property, plant or equipment is unlikely to be the same as 'additions' as reported in the fixed assets note. Whilst this is usually a function of movements in creditors relating to fixed assets and the inception of finance leases, it may also be due to exchange rate differences on foreign currency liabilities incurred on the purchase of fixed assets. The amount paid might be different to that used to record the increase in fixed assets, with the difference taken to the profit and loss account as an exchange gain or loss.

The purchase of fixed assets on credit is a complicated area because the associated cash flows may sometimes not be capital expenditure. In the US, SFAS 95 takes the line that only advance payments, the down payment or other amounts paid at or near to the time of purchase of fixed assets are investing cash flows.[91] This treatment also appears to be implicit in FRS 1. The most common example of this (although the payments are strictly not made to purchase the asset) is where a reporting entity makes payments in respect of assets obtained under a finance lease. In this case, the payments of principal are classified as financing rather than capital expenditure. The interest element of the lease payments would be shown under returns on investments and servicing of finance. The acquisition of assets under hire purchase contracts would be dealt with in a similar way. On the other hand, short-term differences between acquisition and payment should not be interpreted as changing the nature of the cash flow from capital expenditure to financing.

2.4.7   Acquisitions and disposals

Included under this heading are cash flows related to the acquisition or disposal of any trade or business, or of an investment in an entity that is or, as a result of the transaction, becomes or ceases to be either an associate, a joint venture or a subsidiary.[92]

In addition to the payments made on the purchase of subsidiaries, FRS 1 requires any balances of cash and overdrafts acquired to be shown separately.[93] The same rule applies to any balances of cash and overdrafts transferred as part of the sale of subsidiaries.[94] It is not entirely clear whether the separate disclosure of these cash balances and overdrafts should be part of the cash flow statement itself or whether it could be relegated to another note. The former interpretation, which is consistent with the illustrative example in Appendix I to the standard,[95] is illustrated in the following extract:

Extract 26.23: RMC Group p.l.c. (1998)

GROUP CASH FLOW STATEMENT

For the Year Ended 31st December 1998 [extract]

	1998		1997	
	£m	£m	£m	£m
Acquisitions and disposals				
Deferred cash payment	**(11.1)**		(0.6)	
Purchase of subsidiaries	**(226.5)**		(74.4)	
Net cash acquired with subsidiaries	**3.8**		16.3	
Purchase of minority interests in subsidiaries	**(12.1)**		–	
Sale of subsidiaries	**210.3**		–	
Net cash disposed of with subsidiaries	**(19.4)**		–	
Purchase of and loans to joint ventures and associated undertakings	**(5.8)**		(7.2)	
Sale of and loans from joint ventures and associated undertakings	**55.3**	**(5.5)**	1.2	(64.7)

The above presentation of net cash acquired and disposed of can be contrasted with that in GKN's cash flow statement:

Extract 26.24: GKN plc (1998)

Consolidated cash flow statement

For the year ended 31 December 1998 [extract]

	1998		1997	
	£m	£m	£m	£m
Acquisitions and disposals				
Purchase of subsidiaries	**(129)**		(294)	
Purchase of joint ventures	**(54)**		(20)	
Sale of subsidiaries	**17**		7	
		(166)		(307)

Cash acquired and cash transferred as part of GKN's purchase and sale of subsidiaries is disclosed in a separate note (see Extract 26.32 at 2.7.1 below).

The principle discussed at 2.4.6 above regarding the acquisition of fixed assets on credit also applies to deferred consideration on the acquisition of a subsidiary. No cash flows arise at the time that the liability is set up. When the deferred consideration is ultimately paid, the resulting cash flow should arguably be shown under financing. However, practice under the original FRS 1 had been to include these payments under investing activities (now acquisitions and disposals) rather than financing.[96] Extracts 26.23 and 26.32 reveal that this approach has continued under the revised FRS. However, where the deferred consideration takes the form of loan notes, the cash outflows on redemption of the notes are more clearly in the nature of financing. Cadbury Schweppes adopted this approach, but from a vendor's perspective, in connection with the disposal of a subsidiary for loan notes:

Extract 26.25: Cadbury Schweppes p.l.c. (1998)

Group Cash Flow Statement for the 52 weeks ended 2 January 1999 [extract]

	1998 £m	1997 £m	1996 £m
Management of liquid resources			
Net change in commercial paper investments	24	(235)	–
Redemption of loan notes*	278	180	–
Net change in bank deposits	(45)	(80)	(24)
Net change in bond investments	11	(14)	(5)
Sale of money market fund	–	–	13
Net change in equity investments	(4)	–	–

*£458m of the proceeds on the disposal of CCSB in 1997 (Note 2) were initially received as loan notes and £15m of borrowings were left in CCSB on disposal; these items are shown in the movement in net borrowings (Note 19) rather than as sale proceeds in the Group Cash Flow Statement. All of the loan notes have now been realised as cash.

A question that sometimes arises is how to treat a payment made to the vendor of a new subsidiary to take over a loan that is owed to the vendor by that subsidiary. Payments made to acquire debt instruments of other entities are normally included under capital expenditure and financial investment. However, the FRS states that this is not appropriate for payments 'forming part of' an acquisition or disposal[97] because the cash flows 'related to' such transactions are required to be shown under acquisitions and disposals.[98] This presentation can be contrasted with the repayment of external debt in the new subsidiary, using funds provided by the parent, which falls to be included as an outflow under the financing heading.

A similarly fine distinction might apply on the demerger of subsidiaries. These sometimes involve the repayment of intra-group indebtedness out of external finance raised by the demerged subsidiary. If the money is raised immediately prior to the demerger, it is strictly a financing inflow in the parent company's consolidated cash flow statement. If raised and repaid after the demerger, there would be an argument for showing the inflow under capital expenditure and financial investment, being the repayment of a loan to another entity. Alternatively, it could conceivably be shown under acquisitions and disposals, being a cash inflow 'related to' to an entity that has ceased to be a subsidiary undertaking. The five year financial record (restated for the revised FRS 1) in ICI's 1998 annual report shows 'Zeneca debt repayment', a cash inflow in 1994 relating to the former subsidiary demerged in 1993, as a separate caption after acquisitions and disposals.[99]

Although FRS 1 does not seem to have been written with demergers in mind, practice has been to show the cash and overdrafts in the demerged entity under the acquisitions and disposals heading. This is on the basis that they are 'related to … an investment in an entity that … as a result of the transaction … ceases to be … a subsidiary undertaking.'[100] Arcadia Group did, however, make a slight alteration to the standard heading:

Extract 26.26: Arcadia Group plc (1998)

Consolidated cash flow statement [extract]

For the financial year ended 29th August 1998	1998 £m	1998 £m	1997 £m	1997 £m
Acquisitions/disposals and demerger of Debenhams				
Bank overdraft acquired with acquisitions	**(2.7)**		(2.5)	
Purchase of Innovations Group	–		(23.1)	
Purchase of Racing Green	–		(18.9)	
Purchase of Wade Smith	**(8.8)**		–	
Sale of Innovations non-fashion brands	**20.0**		–	
Cash less overdrafts of Debenhams at demerger	**(55.4)**		–	
Proceeds on establishment of joint venture	**15.0**		–	
		(31.9)		(44.5)

2.4.8 Equity dividends paid

Included under this heading are dividends paid on the reporting entity's equity shares (as defined in FRS 4).[101] As noted at 2.4.4 above, the amount shown should exclude any related tax credit.

The ASB originally intended to include all dividends, including those paid to preference shareholders and minorities, under this heading.[102] However, the proposal was amended in the light of comments made in response to FRED 10.[103]

2.4.9 Management of liquid resources

This heading was introduced in response to the most common complaint about the usefulness of the old FRS 1: the three month cut-off in the definition of cash equivalents. By creating a new format heading, the ASB effectively separated treasury management cash flows from the purchase and sale of fixed assets and new businesses. Although it might have been possible to solve the problem by adopting a more flexible definition for cash equivalents (similar to those in IAS 7 and SFAS 95, which are arguably more likely to include the instruments used by a typical treasury department) this would not have provided additional information about treasury activities.

Cash flows required to be classified under management of liquid resources are those related to 'current asset investments held as readily disposable stores of value'.[104] The key to this definition is 'readily disposable', by which is meant that the investment 'is disposable by the reporting entity without curtailing or disrupting its business; and is *either*:

■   readily convertible into known amounts of cash at or close to its carrying amount, or

■   traded in an active market'.[105]

In the ASB's view, the first bullet point above would tend to exclude short-term deposits with a maturity of more than one year, measured from the date the deposit was made.[106] That aside, the definition deliberately allows the inclusion of a wide range of investments in order to recognise the different ways in which reporting entities manage their resources to ensure the availability of cash to carry on or expand the business. Reporting entities must explain their policy for determining liquid resources and any changes to it.[107]

Cash inflows from the management of liquid resources will include the following, which should be separately disclosed:

(a)   withdrawals from short-term deposits not qualifying as cash; and

(b)   inflows from the disposal or redemption of any other investments (such as government securities, loan stock, equities and derivatives) held as liquid resources.[108]

Cash outflows will include the following separately disclosable items:

(a)   payments into short-term deposits not qualifying as cash; and

(b)   outflows to acquire any other investments (such as government securities, loan stock, equities and derivatives) held as liquid resources.[109]

The following extract is an example of the cash flows required to be shown under this heading. It includes unlisted securities (which may not be readily convertible into known amounts of cash) which is a little unusual:

Extract 26.27: Reuters Group PLC (1998)

Notes on the consolidated cash flow statement *continued*

11. Analysis of cash flows for headings netted in the cash flow statement [extract]

	1998	1997	1996
	£M	£M	£M
Management of liquid resources			
Increase in term deposits	(7,145)	(5,826)	(6,110)
Decrease in term deposits	7,250	5,739	5,982
Purchase of certificates of deposit	(580)	(842)	(433)
Sale of certificates of deposit	597	940	432
Purchase of listed/unlisted securities	(465)	(771)	(74)
Sale of listed/unlisted securities	656	505	31
	313	(255)	(172)

As discussed in 2.3 above, net presentation is allowed under this heading where the cash inflows and outflows are due to short maturities and high turnover occurring from rollover or reissue. However, the placing of surplus cash on term deposit followed by the subsequent withdrawal of these funds gives rise to two cash flows, one out and the other in. These gross cash flows do not qualify for net presentation because there is no rollover or reissue.

2.4.10 Financing

Financing cash flows are receipts from, and repayments to, external providers of finance.[110] However, as discussed at 2.4.4 above, only cash flows relating to *principal* amounts of finance are dealt with here, since those relating to interest and other finance costs are dealt with under returns on investments and servicing of finance.

Financing cash flows include the following separately disclosable items:

(a)   receipts from the issue of shares and other equity instruments;

(b)   receipts from the issue of debentures, loans, notes and bonds and from other long-term and short-term borrowing (other than overdrafts);

(c)   repayments of amounts borrowed (other than overdrafts);

(d)   the capital element of finance lease rental repayments;

(e)   payments to reacquire or redeem the entity's shares; and

(f)   payments of expenses or commissions on any issue of equity shares.[111]

In addition, any financing cash flows received from or paid to equity accounted entities should be disclosed separately.[112]

The following extract illustrates the items commonly found under this heading:

Extract 26.28: Arcadia Group plc (1998)

Consolidated cash flow statement [extract]

For the financial year ended 29th August 1998	1998 £m	1998 £m	1997 £m	1997 £m
Financing				
Issue of ordinary shares	**32.5**		6.0	
Redemption of loan stocks	**(0.1)**		(2.2)	
Repayment of Zero Coupon Secured Bonds	–		(61.0)	
Repayment of bank and term loans	**(8.0)**		(10.6)	
Repayment of property lease obligations	**(37.7)**		–	
New bank and term loans	**15.0**		16.5	
Capital element of finance lease rental payments	**(0.4)**		(0.4)	
		1.3		(51.7)

In June 1997, Arcadia Group redeemed the £100m Zero Coupon Secured Bonds originally issued at 60.98 per cent in June 1992. Because the premium paid on redemption (£39.0m) is treated as a finance cost under FRS 4, it appears under returns on investments and servicing of finance (see 2.4.4 above).

2.4.11 *Exceptional and extraordinary items*

To allow users to understand the effect on cash flows of items shown as exceptional or extraordinary in the profit and loss account, there is a requirement to identify the related cash flows and to explain their relationship with the originating item in profit and loss account.[113] ICI dealt with this as follows:

Extract 26.29: Imperial Chemical Industries PLC (1998)

Notes relating to the accounts [extract]

26 Net cash inflow from operating activities

	1998 £m	1997 £m	1996 £m
Trading profit	463	418	528
Exceptional charges within trading profit	164	202	137
Trading profit before exceptional items	627	620	665
Depreciation and amortisation of goodwill	350	434	402
Stocks decrease	40	18	62
Debtors decrease/(increase)	168	(31)	(86)
Creditors (decrease)/increase	(148)	(42)	93
Other movements, including exchange	(76)	(83)	(7)
	961	916	1,129
Outflow related to exceptional items	(105)	(159)	(123)
	856	757	1,006

Outflow related to exceptional items includes expenditure charged to exceptional provisions relating to business rationalisation and restructuring and for sale or closure of operations, including severance and other employee costs, plant demolition and site clearance. The major part of the 1998 expenditure relates to provisions raised in prior years.

Cash flows related to exceptional items should appear under the format heading which best reflects the nature of the item.[114] Many exceptional items will not entail any cash flow – provisions for impairment of fixed assets and exceptional stock provisions clearly have no consequences for the cash flow statement. For exceptional items like the profit or loss on disposal of fixed assets, the inclusion of the cash proceeds from the sale under capital expenditure and financial investment is uncontroversial and hardly needs to be spelt out as exceptional.

The standard recognises that some cash flows might be exceptional of themselves, such as the advance payment of utility bills which the electricity companies received in 1994. Users would undoubtedly like exceptional non-recurring cash flows to be highlighted but drafting guidance for preparers of accounts is far from straightforward. FRS 1 is not very forthcoming on this point, but says simply that 'for a cash flow to be exceptional on the grounds of its size alone, it must be exceptional in relation to cash flows of a similar nature'. An example provided by the ASB is a large prepayment against a pension liability.[115]

The publication of FRS 3, which effectively outlawed extraordinary items, made the requirement to disclose the cash flows related to these items redundant.

2.5 Reconciliations

In addition to the reconciliation to operating profit discussed at 2.4.2 above, FRS 1 requires two additional reconciliations to be given.

The first is a requirement to reconcile the increase or decrease in cash to the movement in net debt in the period.[116] The revised standard explains that movements in net debt are widely used as indicators of changes in liquidity and in assessing the financial strength of the reporting entity. The reconciliation to net debt is accordingly intended to provide information that assists in the assessment of liquidity, solvency and financial adaptability,[117] a key objective of the standard.[118]

'Net debt' is defined as borrowings (being capital instruments that are classified as liabilities under FRS 4) together with related derivatives and obligations under finance leases, less cash and liquid resources.[119] As explained at 2.4.9 above, liquid resources are essentially current asset investments held as readily disposable stores of value. The reference to FRS 4 means that redeemable preference shares issued by the reporting entity are excluded from net debt whereas the same shares issued by a subsidiary, but guaranteed by the parent, would be included. Where cash and liquid resources exceed debt, the surplus should be described as 'net funds'.[120]

To reconcile the movement of cash in the period to the movement in net debt, it is necessary first to adjust the change in cash shown at the foot of the cash flow statement to arrive at the change in net debt resulting from cash flows. This entails adding back the cash flows related to borrowings and finance leases shown under financing as well as the cash flows shown under management of liquid resources. The second stage is to include the changes in net debt which have been excluded from the cash flow statement altogether, i.e. those that do not involve cash flows, such as:

- liquid resources and borrowings in entities acquired or disposed of during the period;
- debt instruments issued as consideration for acquisitions;
- new finance leases;
- the conversion of debt into equity;
- exchange adjustments to cash, borrowings and liquid resources; and
- other adjustments such as the amortisation of debt issue costs, the accretion of redemption premiums, changes in market value and the profit or loss on the sale of current asset investments qualifying as liquid resources.

Most of the reconciling items listed above are included in the following example:

Extract 26.30: Cable and Wireless plc (1999)		
NOTES TO THE ACCOUNTS CONTINUED		
28 Reconciliation of net cash flow to movement in net debt [extract]		
	1999	1998
	£m	£m
(Decrease)/increase in cash in the period	**(94)**	256
Cash outflow/(inflow) resulting from decrease/(increase) in debt and		
lease financing	**215**	(168)
Cash outflow/(inflow) resulting from increase/(decrease) in liquid resources	**131**	(299)
Changes in net debt resulting from cash flows	**252**	(211)
Amortisation of bond issue costs	–	(1)
Conversion of Unsecured Loan Stock	**23**	40
Borrowings of businesses acquired and disposed	**(1,348)**	(2,216)
Inception of finance lease contracts	–	(30)
Translation and other differences	**49**	(13)
Movement in net debt in the period	**(1,024)**	(2,431)
Net debt at 1 April	**(2,960)**	(529)
Net debt at 31 March	**(3,984)**	(2,960)

The reconciliation to net debt should be given either adjoining the cash flow statement or in a note.[121]

Because 'net debt' will not be readily apparent from the accounts, the standard requires a second reconciliation whereby the component parts are traced back to the equivalent captions in the opening and closing balance sheets. In addition, this reconciliation is required to show the changes in the component parts of net debt, analysed between:

(a)   the cash flows of the entity;

(b)   the acquisition or disposal of subsidiaries;

(c)   other non-cash changes; and

(d)   the recognition of changes in market value and exchange rate movements.[122]

A number of companies have elected to combine the two reconciliations required by the FRS into one enlarged note. In doing this, it should be borne in mind that comparative figures are required for the former (Extract 26.30 above) but not the latter[123] (Extract 26.31 below). Combining the two has the disadvantage of having to present comparative figures for the changes in the component parts of net debt.

Extract 26.31: Daily Mail and General Trust plc (1998)

Notes to the Cash Flow Statement continued
16 Analysis of Net Debt [extract]

	At beginning of year £m	Cash Flow £m	Acquisition (excluding cash and overdrafts) £m	Other non-cash changes £m	At end of year £m
Cash	29.9	5.5	–	(0.3)	35.1
Bank overdrafts	(1.7)	(1.6)	–	–	(3.3)
	28.2	3.9	–	(0.3)	31.8
Debt due within one year	(44.0)	12.7	(5.1)	0.4	(36.0)
Debt due after one year					
Eurobonds	(273.3)	2.4	–	1.2	(269.7)
Loans	(229.5)	51.5	(5.6)	15.2	(168.4)
	(502.8)	53.9	(5.6)	16.4	(438.1)
Finance lease obligations	(22.3)	4.6	–	–	(17.7)
	(569.1)	71.2	(10.7)	16.8	(491.8)
Short-term investments	21.8	20.8	1.7	–	44.3
Net debt	(519.1)	95.9	(9.0)	16.5	(415.7)

(i) The increase in debt of £9.0 million (excluding cash and overdrafts) arising from acquisitions was due to the assumption of loans of £10.7 million in SGI, offset by liquid resources of RMS of £1.7 million.

(ii) The non-cash movements of £16.5 million include foreign exchange movements of £15.3 million on loans and cash and exchanges of Eurobonds of £3.6 million. These were offset by the accretion of £1.8 million to the principal of the 2.5% deep discount Eurobond and by amortisation of issue costs of Eurobonds of £0.6 million.

2.6   Comparative figures

Comparative figures are required for all items in the cash flow statement and the related notes. The only exceptions are the note analysing changes in the balance sheet amounts making up net debt (Extract 26.31 above) and the note showing the material effects of acquisitions and disposals on the standard headings (see 2.7.1 below).[124]

2.7   Groups

The cash flow statement presented with group accounts should reflect the external cash flows of the group. Cash flows that are internal to the group (such as payments and receipts for intra-group sales, management charges, dividends, interest and financing arrangements) should be eliminated.[125] However, dividends paid to minority shareholders in subsidiaries represent an outflow of cash from the perspective of the shareholders in the parent company. They should accordingly be included under returns on investments and servicing of finance.[126]

2.7.1 Acquisition and disposal of subsidiaries

When a subsidiary joins or leaves the group, it should be included in the group cash flow statement for the same period as its results are reported in the group profit and loss account.[127]

As noted at 2.4.7 above, the consideration shown under acquisitions and disposals should be the cash paid or received, together with any cash balances (including overdrafts) obtained or surrendered as part of the purchase or sale.

Although the impact on the cash flow statement itself might be limited, a note is required of the effects of the acquisition or disposal, indicating how much of the consideration comprised cash:[128]

Extract 26.32: GKN plc (1998)

Notes on the cash flow statement [extract]

PURCHASE AND SALE OF SUBSIDIARIES	Acquisitions		Sales	
	1998 £m	1997 £m	1998 £m	1997 £m
Fixed assets	(48)	(115)	22	–
Working capital and provisions	(6)	6	12	2
Taxation payable	–	1	(4)	–
Cash	(2)	(3)	1	–
Loans and finance leases	2	112	(1)	–
Minority interests	(1)	(7)	(23)	–
	(55)	(6)	7	2
Change from/(to) joint venture/associate status	1	2	(2)	–
Surplus on sales	–	–	2	2
Goodwill	(39)	(328)	11	–
Total consideration	(93)	(332)	18	4
Deferred consideration	(38)	35	–	3
Consideration (paid)/received	(131)	(297)	18	7
Less: cash	2	3	(1)	–
Net cash (outflow)/inflow	(129)	(294)	17	7

GKN has followed the illustrative example in the FRS and provided a full breakdown of the assets and liabilities acquired and disposed of, together with an analysis of the consideration paid and received. Comparative figures have also been given. However, it is not entirely clear whether 'a summary of the effects of acquisitions and disposals of subsidiary undertakings indicating how much of the consideration comprised cash'[129] requires this extent of detail. Some companies have read it as requiring only disclosure of the more limited information about the cash consideration paid and any cash balances acquired.

The FRS also requires disclosure of the effect (where material) on the standard headings in the cash flow statement of the cash flows of subsidiaries acquired or disposed of in the period.[130] Comparative figures are not required.[131] GKN dealt with this requirement as follows:

Extract 26.33: GKN plc (1998)

Notes on the Accounts (continued)

24 Acquisitions [extract]

> The post-acquisition contribution of subsidiary acquisitions to Group cash flow was a net cash outflow of £5 million from operating activities, payments of nil in respect of interest and taxation and payments of £5 million in respect of capital expenditure and financial investment.

2.7.2 *Preparation of the group cash flow statement*

In principle, the group cash flow statement should be built up from the cash flow statements prepared by individual subsidiaries with intra-group cash flows being eliminated as part of the aggregation process.

In practice, however, it may be possible to work at a more consolidated level, using the adjustments performed as part of the accounts consolidation process together with external cash flow information provided by individual subsidiaries. Thus, the group's cash flow from operating activities could be calculated using the indirect method based on operating profit in the consolidated profit and loss account. The cash flows under the other standard headings could similarly be derived from a reconciliation of profit and loss account entries to balance sheet movements. In all cases, however, subsidiaries would have to provide supplementary information to prevent gross cash flows from being netted off and to ensure that the cash flows are shown under the correct headings. In particular, detailed information about debtors and creditors is essential to ensure that the movements included in the reconciliation of operating profit to cash inflow from operating activities relate only to operating debtors and creditors.

The 'consolidated level' approach described above becomes unduly complicated when there are overseas subsidiaries accounted for under the closing rate/net investment method. The movement in stocks, debtors and creditors between the opening and closing group balance sheets will include changes in exchange rates. For example, an increase in stocks held by a US subsidiary from $240 to $270 during the year will be reported as an unchanged amount of £150 if the opening exchange rate of £1=$1.60 becomes £1=$1.80 by the year-end. In these circumstances it is usually easier to take the financial statements of the foreign subsidiary as the starting point. The $30 increase in stocks can then be translated using either the closing or average exchange rate, as discussed at 2.8.2 below.

2.7.3 *Associates, joint ventures and joint arrangements*

The cash flow statements of associates and joint ventures have a limited impact on the group cash flow statement, which will reflect only the cash actually transferred between the group and the associate or joint venture. Examples include cash dividends received and loans made or repaid. The amounts of any financing cash flows received from, or paid to, equity accounted entities should be disclosed separately (see 2.4.10 above), as should any cash dividends received (2.4.3 above).

Participants in a joint arrangement that is not an entity should account for their own cash flows, measured according to the terms of the agreement.[132] This is because each participant is deemed to be, in effect, operating its own business independently of the others.

2.8   Foreign currency

2.8.1   Individual entities

When an entity enters into a transaction denominated in a foreign currency, there are no consequences for the cash flow statement until payments are received or made. The receipts and payments will be recorded in the accounts at the exchange rate ruling at the date of payment (or at the contracted rate if applicable) and these amounts should be reflected in the cash flow statement.

Exchange differences will appear in the profit and loss account when the settled amount differs from the amount recorded at the date of the transaction. Alternatively, if the transaction remains unsettled, exchange differences will also be taken to the profit and loss account on the retranslation of the unsettled monetary balances at year-end rates.

Where the exchange differences relate to operating items such as sales or purchases of stock, no further adjustments need be made when the indirect method of calculating the cash flow from operating activities is used. Thus, if a sale transaction and cash settlement take place in the same period, the operating profit will include both the amount of the sale and the amount of the exchange difference, the combined effect being the amount of the cash flow. No reconciling item would therefore be needed in the reconciliation of operating profit to cash flow from operating activities. Similarly, where an exchange difference has been recognised on an unsettled balance no reconciling item is needed. This is because the movement in the related debtor or creditor included in the reconciliation to operating profit will incorporate the exchange gain or loss, effectively reversing the amount taken to the profit and loss account.

However, where an exchange difference on a non-operating item such as the purchase of plant has been accounted for in arriving at operating profit, this should appear as a reconciling item between operating profit and the cash flow from operating activities. The difference needs to be taken into account in calculating the cash flow to be shown under the relevant standard heading, in this case capital expenditure and financial investment, which would otherwise be recorded at the amount shown in the fixed assets note.

Exchange differences arising on foreign currency denominated cash balances, borrowings and liquid resources which have been taken to the profit and loss account should be extracted and shown as part of the reconciliation to net debt. These exchange differences do not represent cash flows and have no place in the cash flow statement.

2.8.2   Groups

Where the temporal method is used to account for an overseas operation, the issues that arise are no different to those for foreign currency denominated transactions discussed at 2.8.1 above. Use of the closing rate/net investment method, by contrast, requires the application of very different principles which are discussed below.

The standard requires the cash flow statements of foreign subsidiaries to be translated on the same basis used for their profit and loss accounts (which under the closing rate method will be either the year-end exchange rate or an average for the reporting period).[133] Where the year-end exchange rate is used, this rate must be applied to *all* the foreign entity's cash flows, not just those from operating activities. Thus, a cash inflow from an external loan raised on the first day of the financial period would be translated into sterling at the closing rate rather than the rate prevailing at the date of the transaction.

When the indirect method is used to calculate the cash inflow from operating activities, the movement in stocks, debtors and creditors shown in the reconciliation to operating profit should be arrived at by converting the foreign currency movement into sterling at the same exchange rate used for the profit and loss account.[134] For example, an increase in stocks held by a US subsidiary from $240 to $270 during the year will be translated into sterling at either the year-end exchange rate or the average for the period, depending on which rate is used to translate the subsidiary's operating profit. The reconciliation of operating profit to operating cash inflow should show an increase in stocks regardless of the movement in the sterling balance sheet. The latter may, for example, show an unchanged amount of £150 if the opening exchange rate of £1 = $1.60 becomes £1 = $1.80 by the year-end. Using the same exchange rate to translate operating profit and the movement in stocks, debtors and creditors ensures that the cash inflow from operating activities under the indirect method is the same as the sterling equivalent of subsidiary's cash inflow from operating activities calculated under the direct method.

The anomaly highlighted in the previous paragraph of an increase in stocks for FRS 1 purposes when the balance sheet amount is unchanged, could apply equally to the items making up net debt. In the latter case, the impact needs to be quantified and disclosed in the reconciliation to net debt. Using the figures in the previous example, the change in cash reported in the cash flow statement would be the sterling equivalent of the increase from $240 to $270. This should be reconciled to the unchanged balance sheet movement in net funds of £150.

Where the closing rate (£1 = $1.80) is used to translate the increase of $30 into £17, the only exchange difference will be that arising on the retranslation of the opening net funds of $240 from opening rate of £1 = $1.60 to the closing rate (a loss of £17). When the average rate is used, two elements have to be recorded. These are the retranslation of the opening balances from opening rate to closing rate and the difference arising on translating the cash flows in the period at an average rate rather than the closing rate.

Translating a foreign subsidiary's cash flows at the same exchange rate used for that entity's profit and loss account is problematic when there are intra-group cash flows. This is because there will invariably be a residual exchange difference, as illustrated in the following simplified example:

Example 26.1: Non-elimination of intra-group cash flows

A UK holding company takes out a 3-year loan of £30m and advances the proceeds interest-free to its German subsidiary. Repayment is to be in euros (€42m) in 3 years' time. On receipt, the German subsidiary converts the £30m into €42m. The fate of the €42m is unknown because it is merged with other cash resources raised by the subsidiary from trading and other external sources later in the year. The cash flow statements for the two companies are as follows:

	Parent £m	Subsidiary €m
Cash inflow from operating activities	–	6
Returns on investments and servicing of finance	–	(3)
Capital expenditure	–	(60)
Financing:		
-loan to subsidiary	(30)	
-loan from parent	–	42
-external bank loans	30	30
Increase in cash	–	15

The year-end exchange rate (£1=€1.50) is used to translate the results of the subsidiary.

Under FRS 1, the group cash flow statement is required to be drawn up as follows:

	Subsidiary €m	Parent £	Group £	Group £
Cash inflow from operating activities	6	4	–	4
Returns on investments and servicing of finance	(3)	(2)	–	(2)
Capital expenditure	(60)	(40)	–	(40)
Financing				
-loan to subsidiary	–	–	(30)	(2)
-loan from parent	42	28	–	–
-external bank loans	30	20	30	50
Increase in cash	15	10	–	10

In this example, the intra-group cash flows fail to eliminate on consolidation. To balance the group cash flow statement, it is necessary to allocate the £2m difference (which represents the exchange loss in the accounts of both the parent and the group) to one of the format headings.

Although this situation is not uncommon, published accounts provide very few clues as to how companies are dealing with the non-elimination of their intra-group cash flows. A pragmatic approach would be to net the difference off against the movement in debtors or creditors in the reconciliation of operating profit to cash inflow from operating activities, effectively including it under the operating activities heading. However, in the example above it might be more appropriate to include it under capital expenditure if the cash was spent immediately after the transfer of the £30m from the UK. The €60m outflow would become €42m (or £30m) from the UK parent and €18m (or £12m) from cash raised in Germany, giving rise to a total of £42m in the group cash flow statement. The US and international accounting standards effectively require an approach similar to this because they use the actual exchange rates prevailing at the dates of the cash flows.

FRS 1 contains some (less than helpful) guidance on this point. It proposes that 'where intragroup cash flows are separately identifiable and the actual rate of exchange at which they took place is known, that rate, or an approximation thereto, may be used to translate the cash flows in order to ensure that they cancel on consolidation'.[135] In the example above, the subsidiary should translate the loan from its parent at £1=€1.40. This converts into £30m and ensures that the intra-group cash flows eliminate. The snag is that the subsidiary's cash flow statement (in £) still fails to balance by £2m! The revised standard is silent on what should be done with this difference (even though this is the problem the guidance is attempting to solve).

The alternative approach proposed in the standard is equally unsatisfactory: 'If the rate used to translate intragroup cash flows is not the actual rate, any exchange rate differences arising should be included in the effect of exchange rate movements shown as part of the reconciliation to net debt.'[136] This appears to be saying that the £2m difference should not be adjusted against any of the standard headings in the cash flow statement. The statement will only balance if the residual increase in cash is increased by £2m to £12m. This is, of course, £2m higher than cash in the closing balance sheet. It would seem that the difference is then required to appear in the reconciliation to net debt as an exchange rate movement.

A better approach would be to require all cash flows to be translated using the exchange rates prevailing at the time of the transaction, as done in the international and US standards. This ensures not only that the intra-group cash flows eliminate but also that the statement balances. In practice, UK companies will probably be able to continue using the pragmatic approach of including the difference on intra-group cash flows as part of the cash flow from operating activities. This is unlikely to produce a material distortion.

2.8.3   Hedging transactions

Where an entity enters into one transaction to hedge another, the underlying nature of the two transactions could be different. For example, a foreign currency loan taken out to hedge an equity investment denominated in the same currency would normally appear under the financing heading in the cash flow statement. Perhaps inadvertently, the original standard required the cash flows under the hedging transaction (the loan in this example) to appear under the same heading as the transaction that is the subject of the hedge (investing activities under that standard).[137]

The revised standard clarifies that the loan should not be accounted for in the manner described above. It is only cash flows from futures contracts, forward contracts, option contracts or swap contracts that should be accounted for under the same heading as the transaction that is the subject of the hedge.[138] Loans should be accounted for as loans.

An example of an item falling under the hedging requirement is an interest rate swap. An entity wishing to convert an existing fixed rate borrowing into a floating rate equivalent could enter into an interest rate swap under which it receives fixed rates and pays floating rates. All the cash flows under the swap should be reported under returns on investments and servicing of finance because they are equivalent to interest or are hedges of interest payments.

The requirements in the revised standard are described by the ASB as a pragmatic position that follows the US cash flow standard while awaiting the outcome to the Board's Discussion Paper on derivatives and other financial instruments.[139] The terminology in SFAS 95 has been updated (see 4.2.4 below) following the publication of SFAS 133 – *Accounting for Derivative Instruments and Hedging* – but the requirements in the revised FRS 1 described above remain unchanged pending the development of a UK standard on the measurement of derivatives and other financial instruments.

2.9   Notes to the cash flow statement

There are several requirements for the cash flow statement to be supplemented by the disclosure of additional information in a note. Those discussed in earlier sections of this Chapter are summarised below for ease of reference:

- a reconciliation of operating profit to cash flow from operating activities (see 2.4.2 above);

- the reporting entity's policy for determining liquid resources and any changes to it (2.4.9);

- cash flows related to exceptional or extraordinary items and cash flows that are exceptional in their own right because of their size or incidence (2.4.11);

- a reconciliation of the change in cash to the movement in net debt (2.5);

■ an analysis of the changes in the opening and closing component amounts of net debt (2.5);

■ a summary of the effects of acquisitions and disposals of subsidiary undertakings (2.7.1); and

■ a note of the material effects of acquisitions and disposals of subsidiary undertakings on each of the standard headings (2.7.1).

In addition to the above, there are two other disclosure requirements. These are illustrated in the next extract and discussed below:

Extract 26.34: The Go-Ahead Group plc (1998)

Notes to the Cash Flow Statement [extract]

5 RESTRICTED CASH
Included in cash at bank and cash on short term deposit are balances amounting to £38,900,000 (1997: £29,400,000) held by the train companies which cannot be distributed by means of a dividend, of which £16,018,000 (1997: £14,291,000) is cash collateral for Railway season ticket bonds.

6 MAJOR NON-CASH TRANSACTION
A proportion of the consideration for the sale of tangible assets comprised the exchange of a property at a value of £1,449,000.

2.9.1 Restrictions on remittability

Where restrictions (like exchange control) prevent the transfer of cash from one part of the business to another, there should be disclosure of the amounts involved and an explanation of the circumstances.[140] It would seem that this requirement is referring to the balance sheet amounts, not the cash flows during the period.

The ASB is keen to stress that note disclosure is required only where external factors have a severe effect in practice, rather than where the sole constraint is a special purpose designated by the entity itself. Examples of the former could include cash balances in escrow, deposited with a regulator or held within an employee share ownership trust.[141] The implication is that, whilst these balances still fall within the definition of 'cash', additional disclosure is necessary to provide meaningful information about liquidity, solvency and financial adaptability.

2.9.2 Material non-cash transactions

The move away from the 'all financial resources' concept in the old funds flow statement means that the cash flow statement reflects fewer transactions, and more limited consequences of those transactions. In order to provide a better understanding of the underlying transactions and a full picture of the change in financial position, FRS 1 requires material non-cash transactions to be disclosed in the notes.[142] Examples include shares issued for the acquisition of a subsidiary, the exchange of major assets or the inception of finance lease contracts.

3   BANKS AND INSURANCE COMPANIES

FRS 1 contains a number of specific provisions affecting the preparation of cash flow statements by banks and insurance companies. These are covered in broad outline below.

3.1   Banks

It has been argued that a cash flow statement is not particularly relevant to a bank because cash is its stock in trade. Measures like regulatory capital ratios derived from statements of capital resources may therefore give a better indication of a bank's solvency and financial adaptability. Although the ASB shares this view, banks are not exempted from preparing cash flow statements because the Board believes that the statement contains useful information about the generation and utilisation of cash.[143] However, the special nature of banking and its regulation are recognised in certain aspects of the detailed requirements. These apply to 'any entity whose business is to receive deposits or other repayable funds from the public and to grant credits for its own account'.[144]

- definition of cash – because banks do not usually have borrowings with the characteristics of an overdraft, cash for their purposes should normally include only cash and balances at central banks, together with loans and advances to other banks repayable on demand;[145]

- presentation of interest – to the extent that interest received or paid (and dividends received) are included as part of operating profit, the related cash flows should appear under operating activities. Where interest clearly relates to financing, the cash flows should be included under returns on investments and servicing of finance. Examples include loan capital and other subordinated liabilities;[146]

- investments held for trading – the related cash flows should be included under operating activities;[147]

- management of liquid resources – this heading is not required because meaningful identification of cash flows relating to the management of liquid resources is not possible;[148]

- reconciliation to net debt – this is not required because the change in net debt has very little (if any) meaning in the context of a bank;[149] and

- notes to the cash flow statement – in the absence of the reconciliation to net debt it would seem that the note which reconciles all items shown under financing to the opening and closing balance sheets (for both years) might still be required.[150] This interpretation is supported by current practice.[151]

3.2   Insurance companies

Since insurance premiums are received in advance of the related cash outflows, sometimes long in advance, it has been argued that an insurance company's cash flow statement provides little information about liquidity, viability and financial adaptability, a key objective of the FRS. In its response to FRED 10, the Association of British Insurers pointed out that an insurance transaction reverses the normal sequence of cash flow. The receipt of cash is the commencement of the transaction rather than its completion. The Association proposed that it would accordingly be more appropriate to include a discussion of liquidity, solvency and financial adaptability in the Operating and Financial Review.

Presumably because the provision of information about liquidity, solvency and financial adaptability is not the sole objective of the FRS (the other is the standardised reporting of cash generation and absorption), insurance companies (other than mutual life assurers) have not been exempted. However, the special nature of their business is recognised in certain departures from the presentation used by other entities:

- cash flows relating to long-term business (long-term life, pensions and annuity businesses) should be included only to the extent of cash transferred and available to meet the obligations of the company or group as a whole.[152] This is because the shareholders of an insurance company generally have restricted rights to the profits and associated cash surpluses made by their long-term business. Mutual life assurance companies, which are owned by policy holders, are therefore exempt from the requirements of the FRS;[153]

- internal cash flows of the long-term business may be shown as supplementary information in a note to the cash flow statement;[154]

- an analysis of portfolio investment should replace management of liquid resources and explain how the cash inflow for the period has been invested (including the movement in cash holdings);[155]

- portfolio investment for the period (as shown in the cash flow statement) should be reconciled to the balance sheet movement in portfolio investments less financing;[156]

- the note analysing the balance sheet movements in portfolio investment less financing should show the component parts and highlight the movements in long-term business to the extent that these are consolidated in the accounts;[157] and

- the reconciliation of operating profit to cash flow from operating activities should normally start with profit before tax because returns on investments form part of operating activities.[158]

The FRS encourages the use of segmentation to reflect the different degrees of access to cash balances.[159]

Appendix I to the FRS contains an example of a cash flow statement for an insurance company. This reveals a very different statement to that required of other entities in that it shows the net investment of cash flows rather than the net change in cash.

4   COMPARISON WITH IASC AND US PRONOUNCEMENTS

4.1   IASC

4.1.1   *Introduction*

In October 1977, the IASC issued IAS 7 – *Statement of Changes in Financial Position* – which required the presentation of a statement of sources and uses of funds. However, the standard was even less prescriptive than SSAP 10, and contained virtually no requirements as to the form or content of the funds statement.

Although the IASC did not deal with IAS 7 in its comparability/improvements project, a separate project on cash flow statements was started in April 1989. This culminated in the publication in 1992 of a revised version of IAS 7 – *Cash Flow Statements*.

4.1.2   *Objective and scope of IAS 7 (revised 1992)*

The stated objective of IAS 7 is 'to require the provision of information about the historical changes in cash and cash equivalents of an enterprise by means of a cash flow statement which classifies cash flows during the period from operating, investing and financing activities'.[160]

IAS 7 applies to all enterprises including banks, insurance companies and other financial institutions. The reason for this is explained as follows: 'Users of an enterprise's financial statements are interested in how the enterprise generates and uses cash and cash equivalents. This is the case regardless of the nature of the enterprise's activities and irrespective of whether cash can be viewed as the product of the enterprise, as may be the case with a financial institution. Enterprises need cash for essentially the same reasons however different their principal revenue-producing activities might be. They need cash to conduct their operations, to pay their obligations, and to provide returns to their investors. Accordingly, this Standard requires all enterprises to present a cash flow statement.'[161]

4.1.3   *Cash equivalents*

IAS 7 defines cash equivalents as short-term, highly liquid investments that are readily convertible to known amounts of cash and which are subject to an insignificant risk of changes in value.[162]

Normally, only an investment with an original maturity of three months or less qualifies under the above definition.[163] Equity shares are excluded unless they are cash equivalents in substance, an example being redeemable preference shares acquired within a short period of their maturity.[164]

Although bank borrowings are generally considered to be financing activities, bank overdrafts repayable on demand are included as a component of cash and cash equivalents. This is because, under this kind of banking arrangement, the bank balance often fluctuates from being positive to overdrawn.[165]

There is a requirement to disclose both the policy adopted in determining the composition of cash and cash equivalents and the component parts (which should be reconciled to the equivalent items reported in the balance sheet).[166]

Significant cash and cash equivalent balances that are not available for use by the group should be disclosed, together with a commentary by management.[167]

4.1.4 *Presentation of the cash flow statement*

IAS 7 requires cash flows (inflows and outflows of cash and cash equivalents) to be classified by operating, investing and financing activities, in a manner which is most appropriate to the business of the enterprise.[168] This is intended to allow users to assess the impact of these three types of activity on the financial position of the enterprise and the amount of its cash and cash equivalents.

Provided that a consistent approach is adopted and that they are disclosed separately, cash flows from interest and dividends received and paid can be classified as either operating, investing or financing activities.[169]

Cash flows arising from futures contracts, forward contracts, option contracts and swap contracts which are accounted for as hedges of an identifiable position should be classified in the same manner as the cash flows of the position being hedged.[170] The terminology used in IAS 7 has not been updated to reflect IAS 39 – *Financial Instruments: Recognition and Measurement* – but this should not change the treatment of these contracts in the cash flow statement when they are accounted for as fair value hedges or cash flow hedges under IAS 39.

4.1.5 *Operating activities*

Operating activities are defined as the principal revenue-producing activities of the enterprise and other activities that are not investing or financing activities.[171] Cash flows from operating activities generally result from transactions and other events that enter into the determination of net profit or loss.[172] Examples include:

(a) cash receipts from the sale of goods and the rendering of services;

(b) cash receipts from royalties, fees, commissions and other revenue;

(c) cash payments to suppliers for goods and services;

(d) cash payments to and on behalf of employees; and

(e) cash payments or refunds of income taxes unless they can be specifically identified with financing and investing activities.[173]

Cash flows arising from taxes on income should be separately disclosed and classified under this heading unless they can be specifically identified with financing and investing activities.[174]

Interest (paid and received) and dividends received may be classified as operating cash flows because they are included in arriving at net profit.[175] Dividends paid may be classified as a component of operating cash flow in order to assist users in determining the ability of the enterprise to pay dividends out of operating cash flows.[176]

Where securities and loans are held for dealing or trading purposes, the related cash flows are classified as operating activities.[177]

4.1.6   Investing activities

Investing activities are defined as the acquisition and disposal of long-term assets and other investments not included in cash equivalents.[178] Cash flows required to be shown under this heading include:

(a)   payments to acquire, and receipts from the sale of, property, plant and equipment, intangibles and other long-term assets;

(b)   payments to acquire, and receipts from the sale of, equity or debt instruments of other enterprises and interests in joint ventures (other than payments for those instruments considered to be cash equivalents or those held for dealing or trading purposes); and

(c)   advances and loans made to, and repaid by, other parties (other than advances and loans made by a financial institution).[179]

Interest and dividends received may be classified as investing cash flows because they represent returns on investments.[180]

For acquisitions and disposals of subsidiaries and businesses, there is a requirement to disclose, in aggregate, the purchase or disposal consideration (including the portion thereof discharged by means of cash and cash equivalents) and a summary by major category of the assets and liabilities, including the cash and cash equivalents, in the unit acquired or sold.[181]

4.1.7   Financing activities

Financing activities are defined as those that result in changes in the size and composition of the equity capital and borrowings of the enterprise.[182] Cash flows from financing activities include:

(a)   proceeds from issuing shares or other equity instruments;

(b)   payments to owners to acquire or redeem the enterprise's shares;

(c)   proceeds from issuing, and outflows to repay, debentures, loans, notes, bonds, mortgages and other short- or long-term borrowings; and

(d)   payments by a lessee for the reduction of the outstanding liability relating to a finance lease.[183]

Interest and dividends paid may be treated as financing cash flows because they are a cost of obtaining financial resources.[184]

4.1.8   *Cash flows from investing and financing activities are presented gross*

Major classes of gross receipts and gross payments should be reported separately[185] unless the cash flows reflect the activities of the customer rather than those of the enterprise[186] or the cash flows relate to items in which the turnover is quick, the amounts are large, and the maturities are short.[187]

4.1.9   *Non-cash transactions*

Investing and financing transactions that do not involve cash or cash equivalents should be excluded from the cash flow statement but disclosed elsewhere in the accounts in order to provide all relevant information about these activities. Examples listed include converting debt to equity, acquiring assets by assuming directly related liabilities or by means of a finance lease and the acquisition of another enterprise via an equity issue.[188]

4.1.10   *Use of the direct or indirect methods*

Although enterprises are encouraged to use the direct method whereby major classes of gross cash receipts and gross cash payments are disclosed, the indirect method of presentation is also available for reporting the net cash flow from operating activities.[189]

4.1.11   *Foreign currency cash flows*

Transactions in a foreign currency should be reported in the cash flow statement by applying the exchange rate ruling on the date of the cash flow.[190] Similarly, the cash flows of a foreign subsidiary should be converted using the exchange rates prevailing at the dates of the cash flows.[191] An approximation of the actual rates (like a weighted average for the period) is permitted.[192]

Although the effect of exchange rate movements on foreign currency cash and cash equivalents is not a cash flow, it is necessary to include these exchange differences at the foot of the statement in order to reconcile the movement in cash and cash equivalents to the equivalent amounts shown in the balance sheet at the beginning and end of the period.[193]

4.1.12   *Summary of principal differences between FRS 1 and IAS 7*

It is clear from the stated objective of IAS 7 that the key differences between the international and UK standards are to be found in the definition of cash flows and their categorisation in the cash flow statement. Whereas IAS 7 is concerned with reporting inflows and outflows of cash and cash equivalents, FRS 1 concentrates on changes in cash. Cash flows related to cash equivalents are included under the management of liquid resources section in the UK. The IAS 7 cash flow statement is illustrated below, followed by a summary of the principal differences:

Extract 26.35: Nestlé S.A. (1998)

Consolidated cash flow statement
for the year ended 31st December 1998 [extract]

In millions of Swiss francs	1998	1997
Operating activities		
Net profit of consolidated companies	**4,119**	4,096
Depreciation of tangible fixed assets	**2,609**	2,677
Amortisation of intangible assets	**301**	140
Increase/(decrease) in provisions and deferred taxes	**(41)**	84
Decrease/(increase) in working capital	**(506)**	328
Other movements	**(110)**	76
Operating cash flow[(a)]	**6,372**	7,401
Investing activities		
Expenditure on tangible fixed assets	**(3,061)**	(3,261)
Sale of tangible fixed assets	**487**	289
Acquisitions	**(4,031)**	(903)
Disposals	**236**	332
Income from associated companies	**75**	68
Other movements	**117**	(168)
Cash flow from investing activities	**(6,177)**	(3,643)
Financing activities		
Dividend for the previous year	**(1,376)**	(1,180)
Purchase of treasury shares (net)	**(306)**	(14)
Movements with minority interests	**(167)**	(107)
Bonds issued	**1,009**	738
Bonds repaid	**(1,238)**	(1,404)
Increase/(decrease) in other medium/ long term financial liabilities	**230**	(22)
Increase/(decrease) in short term financial liabilities	**1,659**	501
Decrease/(increase) in marketable securities	**1,258**	(677)
Decrease/(increase) in short term investments	**418**	(918)
Cash flow from financing activities	**1,487**	(3,083)
Translation differences on flows	**(23)**	(14)
Increase/(decrease) in cash and cash equivalents	**1,659**	661
Cash and cash equivalents at beginning of year	**3,412**	2,786
Effects of exchange rate changes on opening balance	**(87)**	(35)
Cash and cash equivalents retranslated at beginning of year	**3,325**	2,751
Cash and cash equivalents at end of year	**4,984**	3,412

[(a)] Taxes paid amount to Fr. 1,932 million (1997: Fr. 1,893 million). Interest received/paid does not differ materially from interest shown under note 2 "Net financing costs".

Because IAS 7 does not have separate headings for dividends from joint ventures and associates, returns on investments and servicing of finance, taxation, capital expenditure and financial investment, acquisitions and disposals and equity dividends paid:

- interest and dividends can be classified as either operating, investing or financing activities provided this is done in a consistent manner from period to period.[194] As shown in Extract 26.35 above, Nestlé has included interest received and paid under operating activities, dividends received from associates under investing activities and dividends paid under financing activities;

- cash flows arising from taxes on income are classified as operating activities (as done by Nestlé) unless they can be specifically identified with financing and investing activities;[195] and

- cash flows arising from the acquisition and disposal of long-term assets and other investments (other than those included in cash equivalents) as well as those arising from the acquisition and disposal of subsidiaries and business units should be classified as investing activities.[196] It is not clear why Nestlé has included the cash flows related to marketable securities and other short term investments as part of financing activities rather than investing activities.

Other significant differences between the two standards are that:

- IAS 7 permits both the direct and indirect methods to be used for reporting the net cash flow from operating activities but does not require the reconciliation to operating profit when the direct method is used. Where the indirect method is used, the reconciliation may be shown as part of the cash flow statement itself (as done by Nestlé);

- IAS 7 does not require a reconciliation to the movement in net debt;

- IAS 7 requires foreign subsidiary cash flows to be translated at the exchange rates prevailing at the dates of the cash flows. A suitable weighted average may be used as an approximation.[197] It would seem that Nestlé has included exchange differences under a separate caption rather than adjusting the amounts shown under the standard headings, possibly because the amounts are immaterial.

4.2   US

4.2.1   Introduction

In 1980, as part of its conceptual framework project, the FASB issued a Discussion Memorandum – *Reporting Funds Flows, Liquidity, and Financial Flexibility*. The major issues raised in the Memorandum relating to funds flow reporting included (a) the concept of funds that should be adopted as the focus of the funds flow statement, (b) the reporting of transactions that have no direct impact on funds, (c) the approaches for presenting information about funds flows, (d) the presentation of information about funds flows from operations, and (e) the separation of funds flow information about investing activities into outflows for maintenance of operating capacity, expansion of operating capacity, or non-operating purposes.

Although this Discussion Memorandum was followed by an Exposure Draft of a proposed concepts statement – *Reporting Income, Cash Flows, and Financial Position of Business Enterprises* – which suggested that funds flow reporting should focus on cash rather than working capital, the FASB decided not to issue a final statement on the subject. Instead, the FASB chose to consider the subject in connection with its study of recognition and measurement concepts. The outcome was that Concepts Statement No. 5 – *Recognition and Measurement in Financial Statements of Business Enterprises* – concluded that a full set of financial statements should include a statement of cash flows. This led to the FASB setting up a Task Force on Cash Flow Reporting, and ultimately to the publication in November 1987 of SFAS 95 – *Statement of Cash Flows*. In February 1989, SFAS 102 – *Statement of Cash Flows – Exemption of Certain Enterprises and Classification of Cash Flows from Certain Securities Acquired for Resale*, and in December 1989, SFAS 104 – *Statement of Cash Flows–Net Reporting of Certain Cash Receipts and Cash Payments and Classification of Cash Flows from Hedging Transactions* – were issued as amendments to SFAS 95; these amendments have been incorporated in the discussion of SFAS 95 below. The changes brought about by SFAS 133 – *Accounting for Derivative Instruments and Hedging Activities* – have also been taken into account.

4.2.2   Focus of SFAS 95

SFAS 95 concluded that the primary purpose of a statement of cash flows is to provide relevant information about the cash receipts and cash payments of an enterprise during a period.[198] The information provided by the statement, if used in conjunction with related disclosures in the other financial statements, should assist users to:

(a)   assess the enterprise's ability to generate positive future net cash flows;

(b)   assess the enterprise's ability to meet its obligations, pay dividends and meet its needs for external financing;

(c)   assess the reasons for differences between net income and related cash receipts and payments; and

(d)   assess the effects on the enterprise's financial position of both cash and non-cash investing and financing transactions during the period.[199]

In order to achieve these objectives, the statement focuses on the change during the period in *cash* and *cash equivalents*, rather than working capital; ambiguous terms such as 'funds' are not to be used. The total amounts of cash and cash equivalents at the beginning and end of the period shown in the statement of cash flows will be the same amounts as presented in the balance sheets as of those dates. A statement of cash flows is not required for defined benefit pension plans and certain other employee benefit plans or for certain investment companies.[200]

4.2.3   Cash equivalents

SFAS 95 defines cash equivalents as short-term, highly liquid investments that are both:

(a)   readily convertible to known amounts of cash; and

(b)   so near their maturity that they present insignificant risk of changes in value because of changes in interest rates.[201]

Generally, only an investment with an original maturity (i.e. original maturity to the entity holding the investment) of three months or less qualifies under the above definition.[202]

It is noteworthy that not all investments that qualify are required to be treated as cash equivalents; for example, an enterprise may classify short-term, highly liquid investments as investments rather than cash equivalents. However, a company must disclose its policy for determining cash equivalents, and any change to that policy is considered to be a change in accounting principle, requiring restatement of comparative financial statements.

4.2.4   *Form and content of the statement of cash flows*

SFAS 95 requires cash receipts and cash payments to be classified as resulting from investing, financing or operating activities.[203] Generally, each receipt or payment is to be classified according to its nature without regard to whether it stems from an item intended as a hedge of another item. For example, the proceeds of a borrowing are a financing cash inflow even though the debt is intended as a hedge of an investment, and the purchase or sale of a futures contract is an investing activity even though the contract is intended as a hedge of a firm commitment to purchase inventory.[204]

However, cash flows from derivative instruments that are accounted for as fair value hedges or cash flow hedges under SFAS 133 may be classified in the same category as the cash flows from the items being hedged provided that the accounting policy is disclosed. If for any reason hedge accounting for an instrument that hedges an asset, liability, firm commitment or forecasted transaction is discontinued, then any cash flows subsequent to the date of discontinuance are classified consistent with the nature of the instrument.[205]

4.2.5   *Investing activities*

Investing activities include:

(a)   making and collecting loans; and

(b)   acquiring and disposing of

(i)   securities that are not cash equivalents;

(ii)   property, plant and equipment; and

(iii) other productive assets, other than inventory materials.[206]

Investing activities exclude acquiring and disposing of certain loans or other debt or equity instruments that are acquired specifically for resale.[207]

Cash inflows from investing activities are:

(a)   receipts from collections or sales of loans made by the enterprise and of other entities' debt instruments (other than cash equivalents and certain debt instruments that are acquired specifically for resale) that were purchased by the enterprise;

(b)   receipts from sales of equity instruments of other enterprises (other than certain equity instruments carried in a trading account), and from returns of investment in those instruments; and

(c)   receipts from sales of property, plant and equipment and other productive assets.[208]

Cash outflows for investing activities are:

(a)   disbursements for loans made by the enterprise, and payments made to acquire debt instruments of other entities (other than cash equivalents and certain debt instruments that are acquired specifically for resale);

(b)   payments to acquire equity instruments of other enterprises (other than certain equity instruments carried in a trading account); and

(c)   payments to acquire property, plant and equipment and other productive assets (including interest capitalised as part of the cost of those assets).[209]

4.2.6   Financing activities

Financing activities include obtaining resources from owners and providing them with a return on, and a return of, their investment; borrowing money and repaying amounts borrowed, or otherwise settling the obligation; and obtaining and paying for other resources obtained from creditors on long-term credit.[210]

Cash inflows from financing activities are:

(a)   proceeds from issuance of equity securities; and

(b)   proceeds from issuing bonds, mortgages, notes and from other short- or long-term borrowing.[211]

Cash outflows for financing activities are:

(a)   payments of dividends to owners;

(b)   cash outlays to repurchase the enterprise's shares;

(c)   repayments of amounts borrowed; and

(d)   other principal payments to creditors who have extended long-term credit.[212]

4.2.7   Operating activities

Operating activities include:

(a)   all transactions and other events not defined as investing or financing activities; and

(b)   delivering or producing goods for sale and providing services.

Cash flows from operating activities are, generally, the cash effects of transactions and other events that enter into the determination of income.[213]

Cash inflows from operating activities are:

(a)   cash receipts from sales of goods or services (the term 'goods' includes certain loans and other debt and equity instruments of other enterprises that are acquired specifically for resale);

(b)   cash receipts from returns on loans (interest) and on equity securities (dividends); and

(c)   all other cash receipts that do not stem from transactions defined as investing or financing activities, for example amounts received in settlement of lawsuits.[214]

Cash outflows for operating activities are:

(a)   cash payments to acquire materials for manufacture or goods for resale (the term 'goods' includes certain loans and other debt and equity instruments of other enterprises that are acquired specifically for resale);

(b)   cash payments to other suppliers and employees for other goods or services;

(c)   cash payments to governments for taxes, duties, fines etc.;

(d)   cash payments to lenders and other creditors for interest; and

(e)   all other cash payments that do not stem from transactions defined as investing or financing activities.[215]

4.2.8   Receipts and payments are presented gross

In general, a greater and more meaningful assessment of cash flows can be derived from reporting cash receipts and cash payments gross, rather than net. Nevertheless, SFAS 95 takes the view that, where the turnover is quick, the amounts are large and the maturities are short, the item may be reported net. Examples include receipts and payments relating to investments (other than cash equivalents), loans receivable and debt, provided that the original maturity of the asset or liability is three months or less.[216] SFAS 95 argues that items with these characteristics may be reported net, since knowledge of the related gross receipts and payments is not necessary to understand the enterprise's operating, investing and financing activities.

Banks, savings institutions and credit unions are not required to report gross amounts of cash receipts and cash payments for:

(a)   deposits placed with other financial institutions and withdrawals of deposits;

(b)   time deposits accepted and repayments of deposits; and

(c)   loans made to customers and principal collections of loans.

When these enterprises constitute part of a consolidated enterprise, the net amounts of receipts and payments for deposit or lending activities of these enterprises must be reported separately from the gross amounts of receipts and payments for other investing and financing activities of the consolidated enterprise, including those of a subsidiary of a bank, savings institution or credit union that is not itself a bank, savings institution or credit union.[217]

4.2.9   Non-cash activities are disclosed separately

Information about investing and financing activities that affect recognised assets or liabilities, but that do not result in cash receipts or payments in the period should be disclosed. This disclosure may be in narrative form or summarised in a schedule. Examples include converting debt to equity, acquiring assets by assuming directly related liabilities (e.g. purchasing a building by incurring a mortgage to the seller), or obtaining an asset by entering into a capital lease.[218]

4.2.10   Use of the direct or indirect methods

As is the case under FRS 1 and IAS 7, both the direct and indirect methods of presentation are available for reporting the net cash flow from operating activities. However, regardless of which method is used, SFAS 95 (like FRS 1) requires a reconciliation of net income to net cash flow from operating activities to be presented. In addition, the amounts of interest paid (net of capitalised interest) and income tax paid should be separately disclosed.[219]

4.2.11   Summary of principal differences between FRS 1 and SFAS 95

The most important difference between the US and UK standards is that the former focuses on the change during the period in cash and cash equivalents, whereas the latter highlights the movement in cash. Cash flows related to cash equivalents are shown under the management of liquid resources heading in the UK.

The categorisation of cash flows under nine headings in the UK compared with three under SFAS 95 naturally results in a number of presentational differences. In the UK, there are separate headings for dividends from joint ventures and associates, returns on investments and servicing of finance, taxation, capital expenditure and financial investment, acquisitions and disposals and equity dividends paid, whereas under SFAS 95:

■ interest received and paid as well as dividends received are included in operating activities. Capitalised interest, however, is treated as part of the cost of the asset into which it is capitalised and thus appears in investing activities;

■ taxation cash flows are included in operating activities;

■ cash flows related to capital expenditure and financial investment and acquisitions and disposals are shown in investing activities; and

■ dividends paid are included in financing activities.

Other significant differences between the two standards include the following:

■ SFAS 95 does not require a reconciliation to the movement in net debt;

■ SFAS 95 requires the cash flows of foreign operations to be translated using the exchange rate in effect at the time of the cash flow. FRS 1 generally requires the same rate used in translating the results of the foreign operations to be used in translating their cash flows;

■ SFAS 95 requires information about non-cash investing and financing activities only. FRS 1 requires all material non-cash transactions to be disclosed;

■ where the indirect method of presenting the cash flow from operating activities is used, SFAS 95 allows the reconciliation to operating profit to be shown as part of the cash flow statement itself. FRS 1 stipulates that the reconciliation should be given either adjoining the statement or as a note;

■ SFAS 95 does not require note disclosures dealing with exceptional and extraordinary cash flows or the acquisition or disposal of subsidiaries; and

■ SFAS 95 permits but (unlike FRS 1) does not require cash flows relating to futures contracts, forward contracts, option contracts and swap contracts to be classified along with the cash flows from the item being hedged.

5   CONCLUSION

The publication of FRS 1 in 1991 was undoubtedly a quantum leap in the ASB's financial reporting reform process. It generally worked well in practice and enhanced the quality of financial reporting considerably. It was clear, though, that certain aspects of the original standard needed re-examining and most of these were addressed in the 1996 revision.

However, in deciding to withdraw the original standard the ASB arguably used a sledgehammer to crack a nut. The three month cut-off in the old definition of cash equivalents was clearly unsatisfactory but it might have been possible to adopt a more flexible definition, similar to that used in IAS 7 and SFAS 95. International harmonisation was also not helped by converting three standard headings into eight, subsequently increased to nine by the later FRS 9 amendment. It is debatable whether the extra headings required in the UK have had the effect in practice of portraying increasing degrees of discretion in cash flows or indeed anything else. Also, there is no convincing evidence that the layout has enabled meaningful sub-totals to be given.

Nevertheless there are areas where the UK standard is arguably superior. In particular, the reconciliation to net debt has worked well in practice and helped to place the cash flow statement in its proper context. Also, the requirement to identify and explain the cash flows related to exceptional items provides valuable additional information about the link between operating profit and the cash inflow from operating activities. With a few exceptions (one being the tendency to use management of liquid resources as a repository for the net difference between two balance sheet amounts), the standard is achieving its objective of facilitating a meaningful comparison of the cash flow performance of different businesses in the UK.[220]

References

1 There is evidence of companies publishing funds statements as far back as 1862 in the UK and 1863 in the US – see L. S. Rosen and Don T. DeCoster, ' "Funds" Statements: A Historical Perspective'. *The Accounting Review*, January 1969, pp. 124–136. However, it was not until the 1950s (in the US) and the early 1970s (in the UK) that the funds statement was commonly presented in one form or another in annual reports.

2 See Ross M. Skinner, *Accounting Standards in Evolution*, Canada: Holt, Rinehart and Winston of Canada, Limited, 1987, p. 397.

3 The term 'funds statement' has been used throughout this Chapter in preference to the alternatives of 'statement of source and application of funds' or 'statement of changes in financial position'.

4 A review of the 1959 annual reports of the 600 US industrial companies included in the AICPA's publication *Accounting Trends and Techniques* revealed that in 190 cases some form of funds statement was presented.

5 AICPA Accounting Research Study No. 2, *"Cash Flow" Analysis and The Funds Statement*, New York: AICPA, 1963.

6 *Ibid.*, p. xi.

7 APB 19, *Reporting Changes in Financial Position*, AICPA, 1971, para. 7.

8 ED 13, *Statements of Source and Application of Funds*, ASC, April 1974.

9 SSAP 10, *Statements of source and application of funds*, ASC, July 1975.

10 See the foreword to SSAP 10.

11 Accountants International Study Group, *The Funds Statement: Current Practices in Canada, the United Kingdom and the United States*, 1973, para. 8.

12 For a full discussion of the detailed requirements and practical application of SSAP 10, readers should refer to the 2nd Edition of this book which was published by Longman in August 1990.

13 SSAP 10, para. 2.

14 *Ibid.*, para. 1.

15 *Ibid.*, para. 3.

16 *Ibid.*

17 SFAS 95, *Statement of Cash Flows*, FASB, November 1987, para. 2.

18 *Ibid.*

19 Eldon S. Hendriksen, *Accounting Theory*, Fourth Edition, Illinois: Richard D. Irwin, Inc., 1982, p. 236.
20 SFAC No. 1, *Objectives of Financial Reporting by Business Enterprises*, FASB, November 1978, para. 37.
21 SFAC No. 5, *Recognition and Measurement in Financial Statements of Business Enterprises*, FASB, December 1984, para. 13.
22 *Ibid.*, para. 52.
23 See SFAC No. 5, at para. 24.
24 SFAS 95, para. 3.
25 For example, the US, Canada, New Zealand and South Africa.
26 FRS 1 (Original), *Cash flow statements*, ASB, September 1991, para. 12.
27 *Ibid.*, paras. 2 and 3.
28 FRS 1, *Cash Flow Statements*, ASB, October 1996, Appendix III, para. 6.
29 For a full discussion of the criticisms surrounding the original FRS 1, readers should refer to the 4th Edition of this book which was published by Macmillan in September 1994.
30 FRS 1, para. 49.
31 *Ibid.,* para. 5.
32 ASB, Press Notice PN 6, 26 September 1991.
33 SAS 600, *Auditors' Reports on Financial Statements*, APB, May 1993, Appendix 2, Example 12.
34 FRS 1, para. 5.
35 *Ibid.*, Appendix III, para. 12.
36 FRS 1, para. 36.
37 *Ibid.*, Appendix III, para. 12.
38 The Building Societies (Contents of Accounts) Regulations 1999 (SI 1999 No. 248), Regulation 3.
39 FRS 1, Appendix III, para. 22.
40 In March 1999, the DTI issued a Consultative Document, *Raising the Threshold Levels for SMEs*, outlining proposals to raise the financial limits up to the level permitted by EC law. There is also a proposal that the limits under the EC Accounting Directives should be increased by 25%. If that is adopted the new UK financial limits would be increased to those higher levels. This would mean that the limits under FRS 1 would be, for turnover, £4.8m and balance sheet total, £2.4m.
41 Financial Reporting Standard for Smaller Entities (Effective March 1999), ASB, December 1998, Appendix IV, para. 11.
42 Financial Reporting Standard for Smaller Entities (Effective March 1999), Part D, para 1.
43 FRS 1, para. 2.
44 *Ibid.*
45 *Ibid.*, para. 33.
46 *Ibid.,* para. 7.
47 *Ibid.*
48 *Ibid.*
49 FRS 9, *Associates and Joint Ventures*, ASB, November 1997, para. 61.
50 FRS 1, para. 8.
51 *Ibid.*, Appendix III, para. 13.
52 FRS 1, para. 9
53 FRS 4, *Capital Instruments*, ASB, December 1993, para. 35.
54 FRS 1, para. 9.
55 FRS 4, para. 35.
56 FRS 1, para. 10.
57 *Ibid.*, para. 11.
58 *Ibid.*, para. 58.
59 FRS 3, *Reporting financial performance*, ASB, October 1992, para. 20.
60 FRS 1, para. 11.
61 *Ibid.*, para. 58.
62 FRS 3, *Reporting financial performance*, ASB, October 1992, para. 20.
63 FRS 1, para. 12.
64 *Ibid.,* para. 12.
65 *Ibid.,* para. 56.

66 *Ibid.*, para. 8.
67 *Ibid.*, para. 56.
68 *Ibid.*, Appendix III, para. 18.
69 FRS 1, para. 58.
70 FRS 9, para. 61.
71 *Ibid.*, Appendix III, para. 22.
72 FRS 9, para. 61(a).
73 *Ibid.*, para. 61(d).
74 FRS 1, para. 13.
75 *Ibid.*, paras. 8, 14, 15.
76 *Ibid.*, para. 15.
77 *Ibid.*, paras. 8 and 15.
78 *Ibid.*, Appendix III, para. 17.
79 FRS 1, para. 16.
80 *Ibid.*, para. 61.
81 *Ibid.*, para. 40.
82 FRED 10, Appendix III, para. 15.
83 FRS 1, Appendix III, para. 14.
84 *Ibid.*
85 FRS 1 (Original), para. 81.
86 FRS 1, Appendix III, para. 14.
87 FRS 1, para. 19.
88 *Ibid.*, para. 22.
89 *Ibid.*, paras. 8, 20, 21.
90 *Ibid.*, para. 19.
91 SFAS 95, para. 17.
92 FRS 1, para. 22.
93 *Ibid.*, para. 24.
94 *Ibid.*, para. 23.
95 *Ibid.*, Appendix I, Example 2.
96 See, for example, the 1996 Annual Report of Emap plc, p. 48.
97 FRS 1, para. 21(b).
98 *Ibid.*, para. 22.
99 Imperial Chemical Industries PLC, Annual report and accounts and Form 20-F, 1998, p. 5.
100 FRS 1, para. 22.
101 *Ibid.*, para. 25.
102 FRED 10, para. 25.
103 FRS 1, Appendix III, para. 13.
104 FRS 1, para. 2.
105 *Ibid.*
106 *Ibid.*, para. 52.
107 *Ibid.*, para. 26.
108 *Ibid.*, paras. 8 and 27.
109 *Ibid.*, paras. 8 and 28.
110 *Ibid.*, para. 29.
111 *Ibid.*, paras. 8, 30, 31.
112 *Ibid.*, para. 32.
113 *Ibid.*, para. 37.
114 *Ibid.*
115 *Ibid.*, para. 63.
116 *Ibid.*, para. 33.
117 *Ibid.*, para. 53.
118 *Ibid.*, para. 1.
119 *Ibid.*, para. 2.
120 *Ibid.*
121 *Ibid.*, para. 33.

122 *Ibid.*
123 *Ibid.*, para. 48.
124 *Ibid.*
125 *Ibid.*, para. 43.
126 *Ibid.*, para. 15.
127 *Ibid.*, para. 43.
128 *Ibid.*, para. 45.
129 *Ibid.*
130 *Ibid.*
131 *Ibid.*, para. 48.
132 FRS 9, para. 18.
133 FRS 1, para. 41.
134 *Ibid.*
135 *Ibid.*
136 *Ibid.*
137 FRS 1 (Original), para. 37.
138 FRS 1, para. 42.
139 *Ibid.*, Appendix III, para. 30.
140 FRS 1, para. 47.
141 *Ibid.*, para. 68.
142 *Ibid.*, para. 46.
143 FRS 1, Appendix III, para. 20.
144 FRS 1, para. 2.
145 *Ibid.*, para. 34.
146 *Ibid.*, para. 60.
147 *Ibid.*, para. 34.
148 *Ibid.*, Appendix III, para. 21.
149 *Ibid.*
150 *Ibid.*, Appendix I, Example 3, Note 3.
151 See, for example, the Barclays PLC Annual Report 1998, p. 133 and the Bank of Scotland Report and Accounts 1999, p. 87.
152 FRS 1, para. 36.
153 *Ibid.*, para. 5.
154 *Ibid.*, Appendix III, para. 24.
155 FRS 1, para. 35.
156 *Ibid.*
157 *Ibid.*, para. 36.
158 *Ibid.*, para. 35.
159 *Ibid.*, Appendix III, para. 23.
160 IAS 7, *Cash Flow Statements*, IASC, Revised 1992, Objective.
161 *Ibid.*, para. 3.
162 *Ibid.*, para. 6.
163 *Ibid.*, para. 7.
164 *Ibid.*
165 *Ibid.*, para. 8.
166 *Ibid.*, paras. 45-6.
167 *Ibid.*, para. 48.
168 *Ibid.*, para. 11.
169 *Ibid.*, para. 31.
170 *Ibid.*, para. 16.
171 *Ibid.*, para. 6.
172 *Ibid.*, para. 14.
173 *Ibid.*
174 *Ibid.*, para. 35.
175 *Ibid.*, para. 33.
176 *Ibid.*

177 *Ibid.,* para. 15.
178 *Ibid.,* para. 6.
179 *Ibid.,* para. 16.
180 *Ibid.,* para. 33.
181 *Ibid.,* para. 40.
182 *Ibid.,* para. 6.
183 *Ibid.,* para. 17.
184 *Ibid.,* paras. 33-4.
185 *Ibid.,* para. 21.
186 *Ibid.,* para. 22(a).
187 *Ibid.,* para. 22(b).
188 *Ibid.,* paras. 43-4.
189 *Ibid.,* paras. 18-9.
190 *Ibid.,* para. 25.
191 *Ibid.,* para. 26.
192 *Ibid.,* para. 27.
193 *Ibid.,* para. 28.
194 *Ibid.,* para. 31.
195 *Ibid.,* para. 35.
196 *Ibid.,* paras. 6 and 39.
197 *Ibid.,* paras. 26–27.
198 SFAS 95, para. 4.
199 *Ibid.,* para. 5.
200 SFAS 102, *Statement of Cash Flows–Exemption of Certain Enterprises and Classification of Cash Flows from Certain Securities Acquired for Resale*, FASB, February 1989, para. 10.
201 SFAS 95, para. 8.
202 *Ibid.*
203 *Ibid.,* para. 14.
204 SFAS 104, *Statement of Cash Flows–Net Reporting of Certain Cash Receipts and Cash Payments and Classification of Cash Flows from Hedging Transactions*, FASB, December 1989, para. 7b.
205 SFAS 133, *Accounting for Derivative Instruments and Hedging Activities*, FASB, June 1998, para. 530.
206 SFAS 95, para. 15.
207 SFAS 102, para. 10.
208 SFAS 95, para. 16.
209 *Ibid.,* para. 17.
210 *Ibid.,* para. 18.
211 *Ibid.,* para. 19.
212 *Ibid.,* para. 20.
213 *Ibid.,* para. 21.
214 *Ibid.,* para. 22.
215 *Ibid.,* para. 23.
216 *Ibid.,* para. 13.
217 SFAS 104, para. 7a.
218 SFAS 95, para. 32.
219 *Ibid.,* para. 29.
220 FRS 1, para. 1.

Chapter 27   Related parties

1 INTRODUCTION

Related party relationships and transactions between related parties are a normal feature of business. Many enterprises carry on their business activities through subsidiaries and associates and there will inevitably be transactions between the parties comprising the group. It is also common for companies under common control, but not comprising a legal group, to transact with each other. However, experience shows that the existence of related party relationships brings with it the scope for abuse, most recently illustrated in the UK by the Robert Maxwell affair, where it was alleged that both the MGN Group and Maxwell Communications and their pension funds had suffered serious losses as a result of a number of related party transactions.

Whilst a number of other countries (including the US, Canada, Australia and New Zealand) have had accounting standards on related party transactions for some time, the relevant UK standard, FRS 8 – *Related Party Disclosures*, was not issued until 1995. The ASC had issued ED 46 – *Disclosure of related party transactions* – in April 1989. Nothing ever came from ED 46, however, and the ASB regarded the topic as a relatively low priority when it inherited the ASC's work programme on its formation in 1990. However, in the light of the Maxwell affair, the ASB revived the related party project, issuing FRED 8 – *Related Party Disclosures* – in March 1994, which was converted into FRS 8 in October 1995.

1.1 The related party issue

The problem with related party relationships and transactions is expressed in FRS 8 as follows:

'In the absence of information to the contrary, it is assumed that a reporting entity has independent discretionary power over its resources and transactions and pursues its activities independently of the interests of its individual owners, managers and others. Transactions are presumed to have been undertaken on an arm's length basis, ie on terms such as could have been obtained in a transaction with an external party, in which each side bargained knowledgeably and freely, unaffected by any relationship between them.

'These assumptions may not be justified when related party relationships exist, because the requisite conditions for competitive, free market dealings may not be present. Whilst the parties may endeavour to achieve arm's length bargaining the very nature of the relationship may preclude this occurring. ...

'Even when terms are at arm's length, the reporting of material related party transactions is useful information, because the terms of future transactions are more susceptible to alteration as a result of the nature of the relationship than they would be in transactions with an unrelated party.'[1]

A related party relationship can affect the financial position and operating results of an enterprise in a number of ways:

- Transactions may be entered into with a related party which would not occur if the relationship did not exist. For example, a company may sell a large proportion of its production to its parent company, where it might not have found an alternative customer if the parent company had not purchased the goods.

- Transactions may be entered into with a related party on terms different from those applicable to an unrelated party. For example, a subsidiary may lease equipment to a fellow subsidiary on terms imposed by the common parent entirely unrelated to market prices for similar leases; indeed, the terms may be such that no financial consideration passes between the parties.

- Transactions with third parties may be affected by the existence of the relationship; for example, two enterprises in the same line of business may be controlled by a common party that has the ability to increase the volume of business done by each.

1.2   Possible solutions

1.2.1   *Remeasurement of transactions at fair values*

One solution would be to try to adjust the financial statements to reflect the transaction as if it had occurred with an independent third party and record the transaction at the corresponding arm's length price. However, as a study by the Accountants International Study Group stated, it often is impossible to establish what would have been the terms of any non-arm's length transaction had it been bargained on an arm's length basis, because no comparable transactions may have taken place and, in any event, the transaction might never have taken place at all if it had been bargained using different values.[2]

1.2.2 Disclosure of transactions

As a result of the above difficulty, accounting standards internationally have required disclosure of related party transactions and relationships, rather than adjustment of the financial statements. This is the approach adopted by the IASC in its standard on related parties, IAS 24, and by the FASB in its standard, SFAS 57. The ASB has adopted a similar approach in FRS 8 (see 2 below).

The main issues which have to be considered in determining the disclosures to be made are as follows:

- identification of related parties;

- types of transactions and arrangements; and

- information to be disclosed.

1.3   Position in the UK

It was not until the publication of FRS 8 in 1995 that there was a UK accounting standard requiring general related party disclosures in financial statements. Before then, companies legislation introduced disclosures on a piecemeal basis, which are largely restricted to transactions with directors and balances with group companies.

The legal disclosure requirements relating to loans and other transactions with directors, which are now incorporated in the Companies Act 1985, are discussed briefly in 3.1 below and more fully in Chapter 28. They were originally introduced in the Companies Act 1980, largely as a result of reports by DTI Inspectors on their investigations into the affairs of various companies, in which related party matters, particularly transactions with directors, featured prominently. Ironically, one of the earliest examples was the 1969 report on the affairs of Pergamon Press Limited, whose chairman was one Robert Maxwell.

There is also an overriding obligation, under sections 226 and 227 of the Companies Act 1985, for the accounts of the reporting entity to give a true and fair view of the state of affairs and the profit or loss. If the financial statements drawn up in compliance with the detailed requirements of the Act do not contain sufficient information, any necessary additional information must be provided in the balance sheet, or profit and loss account, or in a note to the financial statements.[3] Therefore, if a related party disclosure is necessary to give a true and fair view, it ought to be made, whether or not specifically required by FRS 8 or the law.

In addition to the requirements of FRS 8 and the Companies Act, the Stock Exchange imposes additional disclosures on listed and AIM companies which impinge on related party issues. These are discussed at 3.3 below.

2   FRS 8

2.1   Contrasted with ED 46 and FRED 8

The objective of FRS 8 is 'to ensure that financial statements contain the disclosures necessary to draw attention to the possibility that the reported financial position and results may have been affected by the existence of related parties and by material transactions with them'.[4]

In FRS 8 the ASB opted for a more conventional approach than that originally advocated by the ASC in ED 46, which had proposed the disclosure of only 'abnormal' related party transactions, which it defined and illustrated. The logic behind the ASC's suggested approach was to attempt to avoid the plethora of disclosures that would inevitably arise if all transactions were to be disclosed. However, not only was this approach contrary to generally accepted international practice, but also it was seen by most commentators to be unworkable. Moreover, as noted above, there is a view that the existence of a related party relationship brings with it the possibility that future transactions may be undertaken on a non-arm's length basis and, accordingly, all material transactions with such parties should be disclosed, whatever their terms.

Accordingly, in FRED 8 the ASB proposed the approach now required in FRS 8 of disclosing all material related party transactions, with the result that there were no differences of substance between FRED and the final FRS. However, there were some major differences of detail, which are noted in the commentary below.

FRS 8 became mandatory for related party transactions first accounted for in accounting periods beginning on or after 23 December 1995.[5] It is a short standard and its basic requirements are deceptively simple. However, FRS 8 has often proved to be far from easy to apply in practice. We address the more common questions of interpretation in the following discussion.

2.2   Identification of related parties

FRS 8 sets out four general definitions of 'related party', two of which are based on the concept of 'control', and two on that of 'influence'; these are discussed in 2.2.1 below. These general definitions are supplemented by two lists of specific examples. One (in paragraph 2.5(b) of the FRS) gives types of entities and individuals that are always to be regarded as related parties; the other (in paragraph 2.5(c)) lists entities and individuals that are normally, in the absence of evidence to the contrary, to be so regarded. As a shorthand, the following discussion refers to parties named in paragraph 2.5(b) as 'deemed related parties' and those in paragraph 2.5(c) as 'presumed related parties'.

In many instances it is possible to decide whether or not an entity or individual is a related party purely by reference to the lists of deemed and presumed related parties, which are discussed in 2.2.2 and 2.2.3 below. However, the standard indicates that these examples are not intended to be exhaustive.[6] It will therefore be necessary to refer to the general definitions in other cases.

The explanation section of the FRS clarifies that, where relevant, the definitions are intended to include both natural and legal persons. For example, the party that 'controls' the reporting entity could be either a company (or other vehicle) or an individual. The standard also states that, while all the definitions and examples are framed in terms of single entities or individuals, they are to be read as including entities and/or individuals acting in concert.[7]

2.2.1   General definitions of related party

FRS 8 defines two or more parties as related parties when at any time during the financial period:

(a)   one party has direct or indirect control of the other party; or

(b)   the parties are subject to common control from the same source; or

(c)   one party has influence over the financial and operating policies of the other party to an extent that that other party might be inhibited from pursuing at all times its own separate interests; or

(d)   the parties, in entering a transaction, are subject to influence from the same source to such an extent that one of the parties to the transaction has subordinated its own separate interests.[8]

The wording of these general definitions clearly envisages reciprocity – in other words, if A is a related party of B, B is a related party of A. Somewhat inconsistently, however, this is not always the case with the more specific definitions of deemed and presumed related parties. Instances of this are noted in the discussion in 2.2.2 and 2.2.3 below.

A   Definitions based on control

The definitions based on 'control' (Definition (a) and Definition (b) above) are relatively easy to understand. Control is defined as 'the ability to direct the financial and operating policies of an undertaking with a view to gaining economic benefits from its activities'.[9] The same definition is used in FRS 5 – *Reporting the substance of transactions* – in respect of 'control of another entity'.[10] It is thus not restricted to voting (i.e. ownership) control, but includes economic control as well.

Definition (a) will most obviously include the reporting entity's parent and subsidiary undertakings and any individuals controlling the entity or its ultimate parent undertaking. However, it can include other relationships, for example those between the reporting entity and its directors or other key management, or its shareholders. Indirect control is simply control exercised through another vehicle (e.g. an intermediate holding company).

Definition (b) has the effect that fellow subsidiary undertakings of the same parent are related parties of each other. It also means that members of so-called 'horizontal' groups (i.e. entities controlled by the same non-corporate shareholders such as individuals, partnerships or trusts) are related parties of each other, even though under UK company law they are not members of the same group.

The explanation section of the standard clarifies that common control is also deemed to exist where two or more parties are subject to control from boards having a 'controlling nucleus' of directors in common.[11] It is thus not open to a reporting entity to argue that common directorships can never give rise to related parties by virtue of the directors' common law duty (in the UK at least) to act in the best interests of each individual company. 'Controlling nucleus' is not defined, but the intention seems reasonably clear.

B   Definitions based on 'influence'

The definitions of related party based on 'influence' (Definition (c) and Definition (d) above) are far less straightforward than those based on 'control', partly because there is no specific definition of 'influence'. However, the explanation section of the FRS contrasts influence with control on the criterion that the outcome (or potential outcome) of a relationship based on influence is less certain than one based on control.[12]

For example, a company can effectively compel a subsidiary to enter into a particular transaction (control). However, it cannot ensure that a 30%-owned associated undertaking enters into the same transaction, although it may well be able to persuade it to do so (influence). The practical implication of this is that, whereas the existence of a relationship based on control will generally be clear cut, the existence of one based on influence will be open to debate. This is most easily illustrated by considering the definitions themselves.

Definition (c) is similar, but not identical, to the concept of 'significant influence' used in the definition of 'associate' in FRS 9 – *Associates and Joint Ventures* – and the Companies Act. Thus, it will clearly capture the relationship between investors and their associates. However, it also covers situations where one entity influences another without having any ownership interest (e.g. through a 'friendly' director on the other entity's board).

Significantly, Definition (c) requires that the party subject to influence '*might* be' (rather than has *actually* been) inhibited from pursuing its own interests. It does not therefore seem possible to contend that Definition (c) does not apply in a particular case by arguing that, although one party (A) is subject to the influence of another (B), A *has not* failed to pursue its own interests. Rather, it would appear to be necessary to argue that A *could never* fail to pursue its own interests as the result of B's influence – a much heavier burden of proof. In this respect, the threshold at which influence is seen to exist by FRS 8 is somewhat lower than that for determining whether an investee is an associated undertaking under FRS 9, which requires the investor actually to exercise significant influence (see Chapter 7).

There is also the question of what is meant by a party's being 'inhibited from pursuing ... its separate interests'. A narrow view would be that it implies that the party has entered into a transaction on unfavourable terms. A broader view would be that it means simply that the party has entered into a transaction that it would not have undertaken otherwise, whatever its terms. This is not specifically addressed, although it seems clear that the broader view should be taken, since, as noted in 1.1 above, FRS 8 states that related party transactions can occur on arm's length terms. In other words, it is not a necessary condition of a related party transaction that one party has apparently been financially disadvantaged.

Definition (d) above is fundamentally different from all the others, in that its focus is the circumstances of individual transactions rather than the overall relationship between the parties. In contrast to Definition (c), which refers merely to the possibility that one party might influence the other, Definition (d) also requires the transacting parties actually to have been subject to common influence. Furthermore, a much stronger degree of influence is implied by Definition (d) (which requires that one party *'has subordinated* its own ... interests') than by Definition (c) (which merely requires that the party subject to influence *'might be inhibited* from pursuing ... its own ... interests'). Somewhat confusingly, Definition (d), which refers to the concept of 'influence' uses the same wording ('subordinated its separate interests') as is used in the explanation section of the FRS to describe the concept of 'control' and contrast it with that of 'influence'![13]

In our view, the intention of Definition (d) can be explained only when one understands how it evolved. Originally, FRED 8 proposed that a party subject to control and another subject to influence from the same source would be related parties of each other.[14] This would have had the effect, for example, that a subsidiary and an associated undertaking of the same investor were treated as related parties. In developing FRS 8, the ASB took the view that this was both too wide and too narrow a definition of a related party. On the one hand, a subsidiary and associate of the same investor may happen to transact with each other without any interference from their common shareholder. On the other hand, a common shareholder is clearly in a position to engineer transactions not only between its subsidiaries and associates but also between different associates or joint ventures.

The final version of Definition (d) is intended to resolve this dilemma by requiring the circumstances of each case to be examined. The explanation section of the FRS reinforces this point by stating that the effect of Definition (d) is that two parties are not 'necessarily' related purely because:

(a)   they are both associates (or one is an associate and another a subsidiary) of the same investor; or

(b)   they have a director in common.[15]

Nevertheless, and somewhat confusingly, the great majority of parties related by virtue of Definition (d) will probably fall into one or other of these categories.

Whilst we understand the difficulty facing the ASB in drafting Definition (d), we believe that the final wording is unsatisfactory, since it is clear that in practice it leads to different views being taken of similar situations, as the following example illustrates:

Example 27.1

Mr X is a director of A plc, a listed company, and the owner of B Limited. Both companies are supplied by S Limited. Mr X has negotiated a deal with S Limited to supply goods to B Limited at a discount that would not normally be available to a company of the size of B Limited.

In discussing a virtually identical situation, Wild and Creighton conclude that B Limited and S Limited are related parties under Definition (d) because they have transacted at the instigation of Mr X, who has influenced S Limited 'to subordinate its own separate interests and offer discounts that it would otherwise not have given.'[16] In our view, however, the opposite conclusion is equally valid, on the basis that S's purpose in offering discounts to B is presumably to retain and, possibly expand, its relationship with A. On this construction of the facts, S is promoting, rather than subordinating, its own interests, and therefore Definition (d) does not apply. We also question whether, given the history of Definition (d), it was ever really intended to apply to this type of situation at all.

As noted above, Definition (d) focuses on an individual transaction rather than an ongoing relationship. It would therefore seem logical that, where a party is related to the reporting entity by virtue of a transaction of a type described by Definition (d), it is only that transaction that is disclosable and not, for example, routine sales and purchases of goods. However, the FRS makes it clear that two parties are related when the circumstances giving rise to the relationship exist 'at any time during the financial period'.[17] In other words, even if only one transaction of this type occurs during a financial period, all other transactions with the relevant party in that period are deemed to be related party transactions. This can lead to the slightly strange result that two parties are treated as related in one year but not the next, even though they have transacted a similar amount of business, as the following example shows:

Example 27.2

S is a subsidiary undertaking, and A an associated undertaking, of H. In both 1998 and 1999 S makes sales of £1 million of finished goods to A which, for the purposes of this example, do not fall within Definition (d). However, in 1998 A also bought a freehold property from S for £100,000 at the instigation of H, a transaction that therefore does fall within Definition (d). Thus S and A are related parties in 1998, but not in 1999. Their 1998 accounts (subject to the availability of any exemptions, discussed in 2.3.5 below) will therefore disclose related party transactions of £1.1 million (with a comparative of nil), whilst those for 1999 will show related party transactions of nil, with a comparative of £1.1 million. This verges on the misleading, since it confuses the true related party transaction with the ongoing trading relationship.

In our view, the above discussion indicates that reconsideration of Definition (d) should be a high priority for the ASB in any future review of FRS 8.

2.2.2   Deemed related parties

FRS 8 states that 'for the avoidance of doubt, the following are related parties of the reporting entity':

(a)   its ultimate and intermediate parent undertakings, subsidiary undertakings, and fellow subsidiary undertakings;

(b)   its associates and joint ventures;

(c)   the investor or venturer in respect of which the reporting entity is an associate or a joint venture;

(d)   directors of the reporting entity and the directors of its ultimate and intermediate parent undertakings; and

(e)   pension funds for the benefit of employees of the reporting entity or of any entity that is a related party of the reporting entity.[18]

Entities falling within (a) above have not, in our experience, given rise to any difficulties of interpretation or identification in practice. Issues raised by the other categories are discussed below.

A   Associates and joint ventures and their investors

As noted in 2.2.1 above, it is slightly curious that certain of the deemed and presumed related party relationships are not reciprocal. In other words, it may be the case that A and B are deemed or presumed to be related parties when A is the reporting entity, but not when B is the reporting entity. This contradicts the general definitions of related party, which explicitly assume that relationships are reciprocal in all cases. The deemed relationships between associates and their investors are a common case in point, as the following example illustrates:

Example 27.3

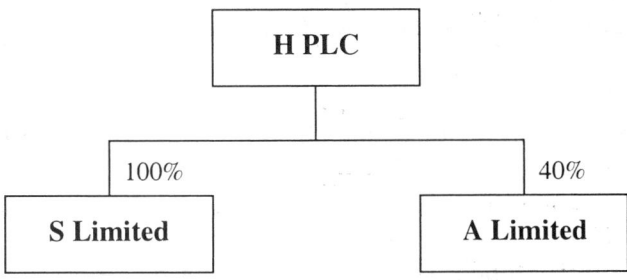

If H is the reporting entity, A is deemed to be a related party of both H and the H group (because it is an associate of both). Thus any transactions between A and either H or S will automatically be disclosed in H's accounts. If, however, A is the reporting entity, H is deemed to be a related party (because it is the investor of which A is an associated undertaking), but S is not. This has the effect that, if A transacts directly with H, those transactions will be disclosed in A's accounts, but, if it undertakes identical transactions with S, disclosure is not *automatically* required. It would be necessary to show that the relationship fell within one of the general definitions based on 'influence' discussed in 2.2.1 above, the more likely being Definition (d).

Another possible issue is that an investor and investee may have a different perception of the relationship between them. It has not been unknown for an investor to equity account for an investee which does not regard itself as being subject to significant influence from the investor, although this is now unlikely to happen following the implementation of FRS 9. In such cases, it would appear sensible to have regard to the perception of the reporting entity. However, there may still be a related party relationship by virtue of the presumption (discussed at 2.2.3 B below) that investors owning 20% or more of the reporting entity are related parties.

B   *Directors of the reporting entity and its parent undertakings*

In treating directors of the reporting entity and its parent undertakings (but not those of its subsidiary undertakings) as related parties, FRS 8 has taken its lead from the Companies Act 1985, rather than the Stock Exchange, which also treats directors of subsidiaries as related parties – see 3.3.3. Again echoing the Companies Act, FRS 8 states that 'directors' for this purpose include shadow directors as defined in the Act[19] (see Chapter 28 at 2.2). However, because the definition of 'materiality' used by FRS 8 is different from that used by the Companies Act, FRS 8 may well require disclosure of some transactions with directors that escape disclosure under the Companies Act. This is discussed more fully in 2.3.2 below.

A final point of detail is that, for many companies the only related party transactions are with directors and, accordingly, they are disclosed within the directors' report or the remuneration report. However, the Financial Reporting Review Panel has indicated, in its ruling on the 1997 accounts of H & C Furnishings (now Harveys Furnishings), that it interprets strictly the requirement of FRS 8 that the disclosures should be given in the 'financial statements'.[20] Thus it is not sufficient to give such disclosures in the directors' report only and there should be at least a cross-reference thereto in the main accounts.

C   *Pension funds*

Given the alleged transactions between companies controlled by Robert Maxwell and their pension funds, it was inevitable that FRS 8 would treat pension funds as deemed related parties. However, the ASB was clearly concerned that this might offend the sensitivities of some pension fund trustees. Accordingly, the FRS emphasises that the fact that pension funds are treated as related parties 'is not intended to call into question the independence of trustees with regard to their fiduciary obligations to members of the scheme'. The FRS goes on to say, although without explaining why, that 'transactions between the reporting entity and the pension fund may be in the interest of members but nevertheless need to be reported in the accounts of the reporting entity.'[21]

In any event, as discussed in 2.3.5 D, contributions paid to the scheme are exempt from disclosure. It is only other transactions with the reporting entity (e.g. loans, sales of fixed assets) that must be disclosed. A more common transaction in practice is the recharge of administrative costs by the sponsoring company, an example being Rank:

Extract 27.1: The Rank Group Plc (1998)

34   Related party transactions [extract]

The Group recharges The Rank Group UK Pension Schemes with the costs of administration and independent pension advisers borne by the Group. The total recharged in the year ended 31 December 1998 was £1,506,285 (1997 £1,168,000).

It is curious that a pension fund and the sponsoring employer are deemed to be related parties when the employer is the reporting entity, but not when the fund is the reporting entity. This is another example of the non-reciprocal nature of some of the deemed and presumed related party relationships referred to above. However, the SORP on accounting for pension schemes requires the sponsoring employer to be treated as a related party.[22]

2.2.3   Presumed related parties

FRS 8 requires that the following should be presumed to be related parties of the reporting entity:

(a)   the key management of the reporting entity and the key management of its parent undertaking or undertakings;

(b)   a person owning or able to exercise control over 20% or more of the voting rights of the reporting entity, whether directly or through nominees;

(c)   each person acting in concert in such a way as to be able to exercise control or influence over the reporting entity; and

(d)   an entity managing or managed by the reporting entity under a management contract.[23]

The presumption that the above are related parties of the reporting entity can be rebutted in a particular case only if 'it can be demonstrated that neither party has influenced the financial and operating policies of the other in such a way as to inhibit the pursuit of separate interests.'[24]   .

It is far from clear by virtue of which of the general definitions of related party (Definitions (a) to (d), discussed in 2.2.1) these parties are presumed to be related. In particular, the fact that it is possible to rebut the presumption that these parties are related if neither party *'has influenced'* the other contradicts

Definition (c), which defines a relationship as created by the mere ability to exercise, rather than the actual exercise of, influence.

The FRS gives no guidance as to what is meant by the words 'inhibit the pursuit of separate interests'. One interpretation would be that one of the parties has been disadvantaged, financially or otherwise. However, this seems inconsistent with the ASB's view that a related party transaction can be undertaken on an arm's length basis. We therefore interpret this phrase as meaning that one of the parties has entered into a transaction that it would not have undertaken in the absence of the relationship, rather than that it has been disadvantaged. On this view, a heavy burden of proof is needed to rebut the presumption that the parties listed above are related parties if they have transacted with the reporting entity. Against that, however, as the following discussion shows, parties falling under most of these headings will be relatively rare.

A   Key management

The FRS defines 'key management' as 'those persons in senior positions having authority or responsibility for directing or controlling the major activities and resources of the reporting entity'.[25]   This clearly cannot include directors or shadow directors, since these are treated as related parties in all circumstances, as set out in 2.2.2 above.

The main intention of the definition is presumably to ensure that transactions with persons with responsibilities similar to those of directors do not escape disclosure simply because they are not directors. This would otherwise have provided an obvious loophole in the FRS. However, it is not clear whether many individuals will fall within this heading. It seems, for example, to be restricted to even fewer persons than the term 'officer' used by the Companies Act to refer to senior persons other than directors.

In the first place, the individual concerned must apparently be in a position to direct or control 'the major activities and resources' of the entity – i.e. all of them, not just one or some of them. It is doubtful whether most board directors would have such power, let alone other staff. It may be that this is a drafting slip and that the ASB's intention was that a member of key management should control '*a* major activity or resource'. This semantic quibble aside, it is still doubtful whether many persons will fall into this category. For example, a purchasing manager may have wide discretion to choose suppliers and negotiate prices, but he will generally be subject to various constraints imposed by the board, so that his authority falls short of an ability to 'direct and control' the purchasing function.

In our view, the type of person most likely to be a 'key manager' is a director of a subsidiary undertaking, but not of the holding company, who nevertheless participates in the management of the group. Companies may argue that, if the individual concerned were truly part of the 'key management' of the group, he would be on the parent company board. However, this would be inconsistent with the view taken by the ASB at the individual company level that 'key management' may be found outside the boardroom. Moreover, a review of the chairman's statement (and the photographs!) in the published accounts of certain groups makes it fairly clear that such individuals do exist.

While 'key management' would normally be employees of the reporting entity (or of a company in the same group), seconded staff and persons engaged under management or outsourcing contracts may well have a level of authority or responsibility such that they should be regarded as 'key management'. However, the wording of the definition of 'key management' appears to restrict its application to natural persons. It is hard to see how corporate entities could be regarded as 'persons in a senior position'.

Perhaps for the various reasons set out above, disclosures relating to key managers (at least, explicitly described as such) are relatively rare. An example is given by Friends' Provident, although the disclosure indicates that this effectively aggregates transactions with key management and those with directors:

Extract 27.2: Friends' Provident Life Office (1998)

32.   Related party transactions [extract]

Key management, which includes their close family and undertakings controlled by them, had various transactions with the Group during the year. Key management consists of all directors and executive management of the Group

In aggregate these were as set out below:

	£000
Payments during the year by key management in respect of policies and investments issued or managed by the Group:	
Periodic payments	91
Single payments	106
Payments during the year by the Group to key management in respect of such policies and contracts	201

B   Shareholders owning 20% or more

There will not normally be any difficulty identifying such persons. The debate will be whether it is possible to rebut the presumption that such persons are related parties. Where the party holding 20% or more is itself a minority shareholder this may be relatively easy. In other cases, however, the issue will not be so clear cut, as the following example shows:

Example 27.4

Company A holds 25% of Company B as the result of a failed takeover bid. It has no representation on the board of Company B and does not account for it as an associated undertaking. On the face of it, it might seem possible to rebut the presumption that A exercises sufficient influence over B to require them to be treated as related parties. On the other hand, if A and B are transacting with each other, the question must be asked as to why those transactions are occurring, and this may lead to the conclusion that they are indeed related parties.

If the transactions are occurring at non-arm's length prices, the presumption must be that A and B are related parties. Even if B is purchasing goods from A on arm's length terms, it begs the question as to why B is choosing to put business in the direction of an unwelcome predator. It may be that B is anxious to maintain a good relationship with A, which could (for example) crash B's share price by suddenly offloading a large part of its shareholding on to the market. In this case B could clearly be construed as acting under the influence (albeit passive) of A. On the other hand if A were a long-standing trading partner, particularly if it were the only available supplier of a particular product, it could be reasonable to rebut the presumption that A and B are related. It would also be possible to rebut the presumption if the transactions arose from contracts entered into before the bid.

A rather curious, and we suspect unintended, side-effect of the presumption that major shareholders are related parties is that participation by those shareholders in share issues and dividends should technically be disclosed as related party transactions. In practice, however, this requirement does not generally appear to be followed strictly, presumably on the view that if both major shareholders and total transactions with shareholders are disclosed, the portion relating to individual shareholders can be readily derived. However, some companies do disclose this information, an example being Associated British Foods (see Extract 27.9 at 2.3.3 below).

C   *Each person acting in concert so as to be able to control or influence the reporting entity*

'Control' and 'influence' mean the same here as in the context of the general definitions of related party discussed in 2.2.1 above.[26] Persons acting in concert 'comprise persons who, pursuant to an agreement or understanding (whether formal or informal), actively co-operate, whether through the ownership by any of them of shares in an undertaking or otherwise, to exercise control or influence over that undertaking'.[27]

The concept is clear enough. An individual who is not able to control or influence the reporting entity on his own may be able to do so by acting with others. The practical difficulty is how to identify concert parties, particularly as the FRS creates a presumed related party relationship where a concert party 'is able to' (rather than actually does) control or influence the reporting entity.

It is very unlikely that a concert party would be constituted under a formal agreement, and in any event such an agreement would be a private matter between the members of the concert party. The fact that a group of shareholders consistently vote together at meetings of the company might be evidence of a concert party; on the other hand, it could simply be coincidental. As is often the case when applying FRS 8, it would be necessary to look behind the position 'on paper' to the actual circumstances of the case. For example, a group of shareholders who regularly force through controversial resolutions at extraordinary general meetings will probably comprise a concert party, whereas a group who simply vote the same way on routine matters will probably not.

D   Entities managing or managed by the reporting entity

The relationship between an entity and one managed by it is not dissimilar to that between a company and its directors and key management. However, related parties falling under this heading may be less common than might appear at first sight, since the requirement, at least if read literally, is that one entity must manage another (i.e. as a whole). In practice, however, many management contracts cover specific assets and functions of an entity, not the entity as a whole.

Suppose that A is a property company that owns a block of flats. Under a management contract, company B manages the flats on a day-to-day basis. B is managing an asset (in fact the sole asset) of A, but is not managing A as a whole, and therefore does not apparently fall within this definition. One would therefore have to consider whether A and B fell within one of the general definitions of related party discussed above. In practice, it is very unlikely that there would be any transactions between A and B, other than the payment of the management fee. The issue would rather be whether B used its influence to initiate transactions between A and another party connected in some way with B.

A rare example of disclosure under this requirement is given by Associated Nursing Services:

Extract 27.3: Associated Nursing Services plc (1999)

28.   Related Party Transactions [extract]

The following companies are deemed to be related parties by virtue of the fact that Associated Nursing Services plc manages their day to day operations and has influence over their financial and operating policies.

…

Grosvenor Care plc
Associated Nursing Services plc has a management contract to manage The Haven Nursing Home.

Nightingale Nursing Homes plc
Associated Nursing Services plc has a management contract to manage the Nightingale Nursing Home.

Summerville Nursing Homes plc
Associated Nursing Services plc has a management contract to manage the Summerville Nursing Home.

…

During the year the following amounts were charged to related parties for the following services:
Year ended 31 March 1999

	Management fees £000's	Construction fees £000's	Other £000's	Total £000's
...				
Grosvenor Care plc	23	–	5	28
Nightingale Nursing Homes plc	20	–	5	25
Summerville Nursing Homes plc	28	–	5	33
...				

As at 31 March 1999 the following amounts were outstanding:
Year ended 31 March 1999

	Management fees £000's	Construction fees £000's	Other £000's	Total £000's
Grosvenor Care plc	27	122	3	152
Nightingale Nursing Homes plc	3	25	2	30
Summerville Nursing Homes plc	141	14	2	157
	171	161	7	339

2.2.4   Close family and controlled entities

Where an individual is identified as a related party of the reporting entity, there is a presumption that the following are also related parties:

(a)   the 'close family' of that individual; and

(b)   any partnerships, companies, trusts or other entities controlled by that individual or his 'close family'.[28]

A   Close family

'Close family' of an individual is defined as 'those family members, or members of the same household, who may be expected to influence, or be influenced by, that person in their dealings with the reporting entity'.[29]   FRED 8 referred to 'immediate' rather than 'close' family and listed the relatives who would normally fall under this heading. FRS 8 abandoned this approach, on the basis that the degree of influence arising from the relationship is more important than its immediacy. However, we assume that 'close family' in FRS 8 is normally intended to include at least those relatives identified as 'immediate family' in FRED 8, i.e. a spouse, parent, child (adult or minor), brother, sister and the spouses of any of these.[30]

The definition refers to the person's 'dealings' with the reporting entity, but it does not make it clear whether the FRS is concerned with dealings in a business capacity only, or also those in a private capacity. We presume that the former only are intended. Otherwise it would, for example, be necessary (subject to considerations of materiality) for a food retailer to disclose details of each director's household shopping at its supermarkets!

An example of a disclosure made as a result of this requirement (and, to some extent, possibly Part II of Schedule 6 to the Companies Act as well) is given by Kwik-Fit (Sir Tom Farmer being the chairman and chief executive):

Extract 27.4: Kwik-Fit Holdings plc (1999)

Note 9(d) DIRECTORS' REMUNERATION AND INTERESTS [extract]

Sir Tom and Lady Farmer and family lease certain properties to the Group. The rentals payable on these properties were £348,837 (1998 – £341,000) and the balance owing by the Group at 28 February 1999 was Nil (1998 – Nil).

B   Controlled entities

Although the FRS does not specify whether legal or de facto control is intended in this context, we believe that the broad definition of control used elsewhere in the standard is meant to apply. In other words, controlled entities are not restricted to those subject to legal control. Kwik-Fit provides examples of disclosure that may have been given in pursuance of this provision of FRS 8, although they could equally have been given in order to comply with one or more requirements of Schedule 6 to the Companies Act:

Extract 27.5: Kwik-Fit Holdings plc (1999)

Note 9(d) DIRECTORS' REMUNERATION AND INTERESTS [extract]

E. Landau is a partner in Landau Nock who received professional fees and reimbursement of expenses of £476,933 (1998 – £479,578) in relation to services provided to the Group during the year. The balance owing to Landau Nock at 28 February 1999 was Nil (1998 – Nil).

J. Padget is a Principal of Padget Associates B.V. who received fees of £65,623 (1998 – £107,446) and reimbursement of expenses of £10,562 (1998 – £16,002) in relation to services provided to the Group during the year in addition to the Director's fees shown in (a) above. The balance owing to Padget Associates B.V. at 28 February 1999 was Nil (1996 – £53,439).

Entities controlled by an individual related party are a further example of a presumed related party relationship that is not reciprocal, as the following example illustrates. Suppose that Mr X is a director of A plc and the owner of B Limited. If A is the reporting entity, B is presumed to be a related party (because it is an entity controlled by Mr X, who, being a director of A, is a deemed related party of A). However, if B is the reporting entity, A is not presumed to be a related party (because FRS 8 does not presume that a company, a director of which controls the reporting entity, is a related party of the reporting entity).

This seems slightly counter-intuitive, since, if A (a listed company) and B (a small private company) are transacting, the chances are that those transactions are in fact more significant to B than to A. However, this is not the end of the matter, since it could be that A and B are related parties by virtue of one of the general definitions discussed in 2.2.1 above.

C   Rebutting the presumption

We assume that the presumption that close family and controlled entities are related parties is rebuttable, although the FRS provides no guidance as to whether, or on what basis, it may be rebutted. In general, though, it seems very difficult to rebut the presumption where transactions are occurring.

Suppose, for example, that the reporting entity X buys widely available raw materials from Y, a company controlled by Mrs A, the sister of Mr B, a director of X. The transactions are on normal commercial terms, but as has been emphasised elsewhere, the FRS takes the view that this is not relevant. Rather, the basic question that must be addressed is why, out of all of the suppliers in the country, the reporting entity chose Y. Is it really credible that it had nothing to do with the family connection between Mrs A and Mr B?

2.2.5   *Parties presumed not to be related parties*

FRS 8 does not require the following entities to be treated as related parties:

(a)   providers of finance in the ordinary course of business;

(b)   utility companies;

(c)   government departments and their sponsored bodies; or

(d)   parties with whom the reporting entity transacts a significant volume of business.[31]

The reason for this exemption is that, without it, many entities that would not normally be regarded as related parties could fall within the general definitions of related party. For example, a small clothing manufacturer selling 90% of its output to a high street chain could be under the effective control of that customer. The ASB has already (and more appropriately) addressed the issue in its Statement on the *Operating and Financial Review* (OFR), under the heading of 'Dynamics of the business'. Here it is suggested that the OFR should discuss the main factors and influences that may have a major effect on future results, whether or not they were significant in the period under review; for example, dependence on major suppliers or customers.[32]

The exemption is effective only where these parties would be considered as related to the reporting entity 'simply as a result of their role' as providers of finance etc. If there are other reasons why a party would be considered a related party, the exemption does not apply.[33] For example, the water company that supplies the reporting entity is not considered a related party if the only link between the two is the supply of water. If, however, the water company is also an associated undertaking of the reporting entity, the exemption does not apply and the two are considered related parties, in which case transactions relating to the supply of water must be disclosed if material.

2.3 Disclosure of related party transactions

FRS 8 requires disclosure of material related party transactions in the 'financial statements'.[34] Where disclosure is made in another part of the annual report (e.g. the directors' report, remuneration report, or OFR), it is important that there is a cross-reference to it in the main body of the accounts, particularly in view of the Review Panel's ruling on the 1997 accounts of H & C Furnishings (see 2.2.2 B above).

A transaction is defined as 'the transfer of assets or liabilities or the performance of services by, to or for a related party irrespective of whether a price is charged'.[35] Read literally, this definition requires many transactions to be disclosed more than once. For example, if a company buys goods on credit from a related party and pays for them 30 days later, both the original sale and the final payment represent a 'transfer of assets ... by [or] to ... a related party' and should therefore on the face of it be separately disclosed. However, we doubt that this was the ASB's intention, and the nature of the disclosures required by FRS 8 seems to support this view.

2.3.1 Disclosable transactions

The FRS provides a list, not intended to be exhaustive, of the types of transaction which should be disclosed:

(a)   purchases or sales of goods (finished or unfinished);

(b)   purchases or sales of property and other assets;

(c)   rendering or receiving of services;

(d)   agency arrangements;

(e)   leasing arrangements;

(f)   transfer of research and development;

(g)   licence agreements;

(h)   provision of finance (including loans and equity contributions in cash or in kind);

(i)   guarantees and the provision of collateral security; and

(j)   management contracts.[36]

The FRS emphasises that disclosure is required irrespective of whether or not a price is charged.[37] This means that the standard applies to gifts of assets or services and to asset swaps. Common examples of such transactions include:

- administration by a company of the company pension scheme free of charge;

- transfer of group relief from one member of a group to another without payment;

- guarantees by directors of bank loans to the company.

2.3.2 Materiality

FRS 8, like all accounting standards, applies only to material items. However, the FRS contains a definition of materiality that goes well beyond the undefined concept in general use, which focuses more on the financial effect on the company's accounts, and is often thought of as a percentage of turnover, profit or net assets.

For the purposes of FRS 8, 'transactions are material when their disclosure might reasonably be expected to influence decisions made by the users of general purpose financial statements'.[38] This has the effect that virtually any related party transaction whose disclosure is sensitive (for tax reasons perhaps) is by definition material, because it is expected by the reporting entity to influence a user of the accounts. It is therefore not possible to avoid disclosing such items on the grounds that they are financially immaterial.

FRS 8 does not clarify whether the materiality of transactions is to be considered individually or in aggregate. Whilst a literal reading of the FRS suggests that they should be considered individually, such an interpretation cannot, in our view, be correct, since it would effectively frustrate the intentions of the FRS, as the following example shows:

Example 27.5

H plc is a small listed company for which transactions of £1 million or more are regarded as material. Each month it makes sales of £90,000 to its associated undertaking A. If each transaction is considered in isolation no disclosure would be made. If, however, the total transactions for the year (i.e. £1,080,000) are considered together disclosure would be made. In this case, we believe that the latter interpretation is correct.

The situation becomes less clear, however, if for example H had made sales of £90,000 to each of twelve different associates, or to an assortment of associates, joint venture partners and its pension fund. In such cases, it seems more important to focus on the likelihood that disclosure of the transactions will influence a reader of the accounts than on their purely financial materiality.

In addition, where the related party is:

(a)   a director, key manager, or other individual in a position to influence, or accountable for stewardship of, the reporting entity;

(b)   a member of the close family of any individual within (a) above; or

(c)   an entity controlled by any individual within (a) or (b) above, the FRS requires the materiality of related party transactions with such individuals and entities to be judged 'not only in terms of their significance to the reporting entity, but also in relation to the other related party'.[39] The intention is clearly to ensure that transactions that could be beneficial to individuals do not escape disclosure on the basis that they are immaterial to the reporting entity.

This requirement impacts mainly on disclosure of transactions with directors and persons or companies connected with them. Such transactions are prima facie disclosable under Part II of Schedule 6 to the Companies Act, except when the interest of the director concerned is not considered material. Prior to FRS 8, there was some debate as to whether materiality should be judged by reference to the circumstances of the company or those of the director (see Chapter 28 at 3.5). FRS 8 now requires materiality to be judged by reference to the circumstances of both parties. We have considerable doubts as to the wisdom of this aspect of FRS 8. As a matter of principle, it seems wrong that an accounting standard should require disclosure of transactions that are not material to the truth and fairness of the accounts. If it is thought desirable to make such disclosures for other reasons, the proper place to make them is in the report on corporate governance matters, not the financial statements. In addition, strict application of the requirement could lead to anomalies, as the following example shows:

Example 27.6

X PLC sells two company cars to two retiring directors, Mr A and Mr B, for £10,000 and £15,000 respectively, which are their fair market values. Neither transaction is material to the company. Mr A earns £40,000 and Mr B £400,000 a year. The effect of FRS 8 could be that the (lower) £10,000 transaction is disclosed (because it is material to Mr A, but not the company), but that the (higher) £15,000 transaction is not (because it is not material either to the company or to Mr B).

In practice, many companies, perhaps mindful of the spirit of the Combined Code and its predecessors, the Cadbury and Greenbury codes, seem to prefer to disclose details of all transactions with which a director is associated, whether they are material or not and even where the third party would not strictly be regarded as a related party by either FRS 8 or the Companies Act. An example of this was given in the 1996 accounts of Redland PLC (the 'Braas group companies' referred to then being subsidiaries of Redland):

Extract 27.6: Redland PLC (1996)

19   Related Party Transactions [extract]

Mrs H Bruhn-Braas, a non-executive director of Redland PLC, has a controlling interest in BTI. During the year ended 31st December 1996, Braas group companies paid to BTI a total of £16.2 million for transportation services on an arm's length basis. At 31st December 1996, the Braas group owed BTI £0.8 million

Mr DRW Young, an executive director of Redland PLC, is Chairman and a director of Young Samuel Chambers (YSC) Limited, a management consultancy company, which provided Redland companies with services invoiced at a cost of £17,131 during the year ended 31st December 1996. The amount involved is not considered material to either party. Mr Young has no financial interest in, nor received any director's fees from, YSC in 1996.

Whilst we are obviously not privy to the full facts, it is our view that, on the basis of the above descriptions, the transaction involving Mrs Bruhn-Braas did require disclosure, but that involving Mr Young strictly did not and appears to have been given more for the sake of completeness.

Some companies disclose that immaterial transactions have taken place with directors, but do not quantify them. An example is Royal Sun Alliance:

Extract 27.7: Royal & Sun Alliance Insurance Group plc (1998)

40.   TRANSACTIONS WITH RELATED PARTIES [extract]

A number of the directors, other key managers, their close families and entities under their control have general and/or long term insurance policies with subsidiary companies of the Group. Such policies are on normal commercial terms except that executive directors and key managers are entitled to special rates which are also available to other members of staff. The Board has considered the financial effect of such insurance policies and other transactions with Group companies and has concluded that they are not material to the Group and, if disclosed, would not influence decisions made by users of these financial statements.

FRS 8 also requires the materiality of any such transactions to be considered in the context of a director's or key manager's own financial affairs. In that context, the Group acts as an insurer for Grosvenor Estate Holdings, a company in which the Duke of Westminster has an interest. All transactions are conducted on normal commercial terms. The directors have reviewed the related financial information and have determined that the amounts involved are not material to the Group or to the director concerned.

The Board also concluded that there are no transactions with other directors or key managers that are material to their own financial affairs.

This represents quite extensive disclosure in respect of items that do not require disclosure! Perhaps this indicates that the company shares our doubts as to whether FRS 8 really intended to capture transactions such as this, but is concerned not to be seen as ignoring the prima facie requirement for disclosure.

An example of a company which actually quantifies what it regards as a material transaction for its directors is Norwich Union.

Extract 27.8: Norwich Union plc (1998)

Remuneration report of the Board [extract]

10. ...

For the purpose of reporting related party transactions with directors, as required by FRS 8, materiality of transactions has to be considered in the context of the financial affairs of each director. The directors consider that transactions with individual directors which total less than £10,000 are immaterial. ...

In our view, there is a clear case in any future revision of FRS 8 to exempt from disclosure transactions undertaken on non-preferential terms by individuals in a private (as opposed to a business) capacity with companies whose normal business is trading directly with the general public (e.g. high street banks, certain insurance companies, and retailers).

2.3.3 *Disclosures required*

FRS 8 requires the following details to be given in respect of related party transactions:

(a) the names of the related parties;

(b) a description of the relationship between the parties;

(c) a description of the transactions;

(d) the amounts involved;

(e) any other elements of the transactions necessary for an understanding of the financial statements;

(f) the amounts due to or from related parties at the balance sheet date and provisions for doubtful debts due from such parties at that date; and

(g) amounts written off in the period in respect of debts due to or from related parties.[40]

A comprehensive example of the required disclosures, covering various categories of related party, is given by Associated British Foods.

Extract 27.9: Associated British Foods plc (1998)

30.   RELATED PARTY TRANSACTIONS

The Associated British Foods group's ("ABF") related parties, as defined by Financial Reporting Standard 8, the nature of the relationship and the extent of the transactions with them are summarised below:

	Sub note	1998 £'000	1997 £'000
Management charge from Wittington Investments Limited, principally in respect of directors and staff paid by them	1	450	450
Charges to Wittington Investments Limited in respect of services provided by ABF and its subsidiaries	1	(44)	(46)
Dividends paid by ABF and received in a beneficial capacity by:			
(i) Trustees of The Garfield Weston Foundation	2	4,926	3,176
(ii) Directors of Wittington Investments Limited who are not Trustees of The Foundation		892	565
(iii) Directors of ABF who are not Trustees of The Foundation and are not directors of Wittington Investments Limited	3	18	11
(iv) a member of the Weston family employed within the ABF group	4	496	308

		£m	£m
Sales to fellow subsidiary on normal trading terms	5	6	6
Amounts due from fellow subsidiary undertaking	5	1	1
Sales to associates and joint ventures on normal trading terms	6	21	62
Purchases from associates and joint ventures on normal trading terms	6	16	3
Amounts due from associates and joint ventures	6	5	9
Amounts due to associates and joint ventures	6	2	1

Sub notes

1.   At 12 September 1998 Wittington Investments Limited held 458,342,290 ordinary shares (1997 – 458,342,290) representing in aggregate 50.9% (1997 – 50.9%) of the total issued ordinary share capital of ABF.

2.   The Garfield Weston Foundation ("The Foundation") is an English charitable trust which was established in 1958 by the late Mr W Garfield Weston. The Foundation has no direct interest in ABF but as at 12 September 1998 held 683,073 shares in Wittington Investments Limited representing 79.2% of that company's issued share capital and is, therefore, ABF's ultimate controlling party. The Trustees of the Foundation comprise six of the late Mr W Garfield Weston's children, including Garry H Weston who acts as Chairman of the Board of Trustees, and four of Garry H Weston's children.

3.   Details of the directors of ABF are given on page 20. Their beneficial interests, including family interests, in ABF and its subsidiaries are given on page 49. ...

4.   A member of the Weston family who is employed by the group and is not a director of ABF or Wittington Investments and is not a Trustee of the Foundation.

5.   The fellow subsidiary company is Fortnum and Mason plc.

6.   Details of the group's principal associated undertakings and joint ventures are set out on page 48.

None of the disclosures appears to present much practical difficulty, other than, in some cases, sensitivity. In Extract 27.9 above, for instance, the name of the 'member of the Weston family employed within the ABF group' has not been given as strictly required by the FRS (although, in our view, and presumably that of the company, it would add no useful additional information).

One possible problem area is the need to give 'any other elements of the transactions necessary for an understanding of the financial statements'. This is one of the less clear requirements of the FRS. It was proposed in FRED 8, which noted in the explanatory section that 'an example falling within this requirement would be a material difference between the fair value and the transacted amount where material transfers of assets, liabilities or services have taken place'.[41] This provoked some adverse comment, largely because of the difficulties in calculating it.

There was also some concern that the proposals in FRED 8 would have required commercially sensitive transfer pricing information to be given. In fact, such concern was misplaced since nearly all such transactions would have been exempt from disclosure as being between members of the same group (see 2.3.5 below). Be that as it may, the ASB attempted to address these concerns by modifying the final wording in FRS 8 to say that an example of a disclosure falling within this requirement 'would be the need to give an indication that the transfer of a major asset had taken place at an amount materially different from that obtainable on normal commercial terms'.[42]

We consider this somewhat confusing. Either fair value disclosures are required or they are not; and if they are, the requirement should be in the main body of the proposed standard, rather than dealt with almost in passing in the explanation section. Our strong view is that FRS 8 should not require disclosure of the fair value of transactions, since it is often impossible to calculate them meaningfully. We suspect that the underlying objective is to indicate the entity's true economic performance, as if it were unaffected by the influence of related parties. But this may not reflect the reality of the reporting entity's position, since many transactions with related parties would simply not occur at all if the parties were unrelated and it would be misleading to disclose the terms on which they might have been undertaken with third parties.

Example 27.7

A company sells a surplus property whose fair value is said to be £2 million to a related party for £1.5 million. If the financial statements were to disclose the transaction in these bald terms, users would inevitably infer that the company's interests had been prejudiced to the tune of £500,000. However, it may be the case that, in the market conditions at the time, the chances of making any sale were unlikely, and the company is better off with £1.5 million now than the off-chance of £2 million in several months' time. In these circumstances, a case could be made that the property's fair value, on the basis of an immediate sale to a third party, was nearer zero than £2 million, although few would regard a disclosure to this effect as acceptable either.

Perhaps, given the history of this paragraph, there is room to argue that the example in the FRS is a hint that fair value information is required for 'one-off' capital transactions but not for ongoing revenue items. However, this is a frankly unsatisfactory distinction, for which there can be no conceptual justification. On the other hand, from a pragmatic point of view, it would deal with preparers' concerns about giving sensitive pricing information, which is generally more of an issue when the transfer of goods or services is involved.

A further complication arises where assets, liabilities or services are transferred without charge. Where an asset or liability is transferred free of charge, its carrying amount prior to transfer gives at least a starting point for disclosing the value of the transaction. Problems may arise, however, with such items as ceded tax losses which may arguably have markedly different values to the transferor and transferee (e.g. because they can be used by the transferee sooner than by the transferor, or because there is a tax rate difference).

The FRS discourages companies from making 'boiler plate' disclosures to the effect that transactions have been undertaken on normal commercial terms. Such assertions should not be made 'unless the parties have conducted the transactions in an independent manner'. The standard clearly implies that the ASB believes this will rarely be the case, although it gives as a possible example the situation where two fellow subsidiary undertakings deal with each other without interference from their parent.[43] Notwithstanding this hint in the FRS, however, disclosures that transactions have been undertaken on an arm's length basis are very common, as shown by the extracts from Redland (Extract 27.6 at 2.3.2 above), Royal Sun Alliance (Extract 27.7 at 2.3.2 above) and Associated British Foods (Extract 27.9 above).

2.3.4 Aggregation

Because of the voluminous disclosures that could result if each related party transaction were shown separately, the FRS permits aggregation of similar transactions with similar parties. However, this should not be done in a way that obscures the importance of significant transactions. For example, purchases or sales of goods with group companies could be aggregated, but any purchases or sales of fixed assets with such companies should be shown as a separate category. Equally, it would not be acceptable to aggregate sales of fixed assets to group companies with sales of fixed assets to key management.[44]

Most companies have taken advantage of the opportunity to aggregate disclosures in this way, very often in relation to transactions with associated undertakings. In its 1999 accounts BPB adopts the aggregated approach in respect of trading transactions, but gives separate disclosure of what it presumably regards as a significant loan transaction with an individual joint venture.

Extract 27.10: BPB plc (1999)

28. Related party transactions

During the year the group purchased goods from, and sold goods to, its associated companies and joint ventures for £5.2 million and £2.0 million respectively *(1998 £7.6 million and £5.0 million)*. The amounts outstanding at the year end on these purchases and sales were £0.2 million and £0.5 million respectively *(1998 £0.6 million and £0.5 million)*.

The group received royalties from associated companies of £0.8 million *(1998 £0.6 million)*, of which £0.2 million was outstanding at the year end *(1998 £0.2 million)*. In addition the group recharged £1.4 million *(1998 £1.2 million)* to its associated companies in respect of administrative costs incurred on their behalf; the amount outstanding at the year end was £0.2 million *(1998 £0.2 million)*.

At the year end, a loan from BPB United Kingdom Ltd to a joint venture, British Gypsum-Isover Ltd, of £10.7 million (including £0.2 million interest) was outstanding *(1998 £9.2 million, including £0.2 million interest)*.

However, British Aerospace discloses trading transactions with each of its main joint ventures separately, presumably because these transactions form such a significant part of its business:

Extract 27.11: British Aerospace Public Limited Company (1998)

31 Related party transactions

The Group has an interest in a number of joint ventures as disclosed in note 12. Transactions occur with these joint ventures in the normal course of business. The more significant transactions are disclosed below.

Related party	Sales to related party £m	Purchases from related party £m	Amounts owed by related party £m	Amounts owed to related party £m
Airbus Industrie GIE	1,088	3	–	–
Eurofighter Jagdflugzeug GmbH	657	–	3	10
Matra BAe Dynamics SAS	40	–	30	–
Panavia Aircraft GmbH	79	–	32	–
Saab AB	2	–	1	–

FRS 8 additionally requires that any material transactions with an individual should be shown separately and not aggregated with others.[45] Thus, if a company sells two assets to two different directors, and the transactions are both material, they cannot be grouped as 'Sales to directors' but must be disclosed individually.

A Transactions with directors and officers of banking companies

As discussed more fully in section 4.1 of Chapter 28, the Companies Act permits banking companies to disclose in aggregate certain types of transactions with directors which other (non-banking) companies would be required to disclose for each individual director. Banking companies that take advantage of this exemption are also exempt from the requirement of FRS 8 to give individual disclosure of these transactions, by virtue of the *Foreword to Accounting Standards*; this states that 'where accounting standards prescribe information to be contained in financial statements, such requirements do not override exemptions from disclosure given by law to, and utilised by, certain types of entity'.[46]

2.3.5   *Exemptions from disclosure*

FRS 8 does not require disclosure:

(a)   in consolidated financial statements, of any transactions or balances between group entities that have been eliminated on consolidation;

(b)   in a parent's own financial statements when those statements are presented together with its consolidated financial statements;

(c)   in financial statements of subsidiary undertakings, 90 per cent or more of whose voting rights are controlled within the group, of transactions with entities that are part of the group or investees of the group qualifying as related parties, provided that the consolidated financial statements in which that subsidiary is included are publicly available;

(d)   of contributions paid to a pension fund; or

(e)   of emoluments in respect of services as an employee of the reporting entity.

Reporting entities that take advantage of exemption (c) are required to state that fact.[47]   Although these exemptions appear quite extensive, in many cases they are effectively over-ridden by other requirements, as explained in the following discussion.

A   *Transactions eliminated on consolidation*

This is not so much an exemption as a statement of the obvious since, so far as the group accounts are concerned, such items do not exist. The effect is that no related party disclosures relating to subsidiary undertakings are required in group accounts. However, disclosure is still required in respect of transactions or balances with associates or joint ventures since these are not 'eliminated' on consolidation, although they may be subject to consolidation adjustments.

Where a subsidiary joins or leaves the group during the period, it is treated as a related party for the whole period, not just for the period when it is a subsidiary, because the FRS makes it clear that two parties are related when the circumstances giving rise to the relationship exist 'at any time during the financial period'.[48]   Where the reporting entity has transacted with such a company during the part of the period when it was not a member of the group, the transactions during that time will not have been eliminated on consolidation and, accordingly, must be disclosed. An example of such disclosure was given in the 1996 accounts of Thomas Cook:

Extract 27.12: Thomas Cook Limited (1996)

27. Related party disclosures [extract]

On 28 June 1996, Sunworld Limited and its subsidiaries were acquired. Trading between this entity and the Thomas Cook Group post acquisition has been eliminated upon consolidation. However, from 1 January 1996 to the point of acquisition, it is classed as a related party under FRS 8. Sales to the Thomas Cook Group during this period were £23.2 million.

Kwik-Fit discloses transactions with a company that was an associate for part of the accounting period, before becoming a wholly-owned subsidiary.

Extract 27.13: Kwik-Fit Holdings plc (1999)

32(c) Transactions with associated undertakings [extract]

Up to the date of its acquisition by the Company, Apples Limited had rent of £924,306 (1998 – £1,238,962) and invoice collection fees of £115,232 (1998 – £97,890) payable to the Group. During that period, the Group purchased servicing costs for resale of £1,150,480 (1998 – £1,215,795) from Apples Limited.

This extract highlights an inevitable anomaly arising from the disclosures required by FRS 8 in that the comparative figures represent amounts for the whole prior period, and the current year figures cover only the nine-month period when Apples Limited was an associate (since transactions after that period will have been eliminated on consolidation and are therefore exempt from disclosure). However, it may well have been the case that the actual transactions between the two entities in each period were not significantly different.

An example of disclosure of the converse situation of a company leaving a group is given by Debenhams.

Extract 27.14: Debenhams plc (1998)

32 RELATED PARTY TRANSACTIONS [extract]

...

On 26 January 1998, Debenhams demerged from Burton Group (now known as Arcadia Group plc). Prior to that date Burton Group exercised control over all of the operations of Debenhams and provided a number of group services to those operations. All transactions since 26 January 1998 have been on an arms length basis on normal commercial terms.

In 1998, Arcadia raised management charges of £nil (1997: £32.2 million) in respect of the continuing operations and recharged Debenhams for central service costs of £nil in 1998 (1997: £15.6 million). It has not been practicable to quantify all other, and less material, services arising between the Arcadia Group and Debenhams.

...

B   *Parent company financial statements when group accounts presented*

This exemption is largely a logical extension of the last. However, this is a case where the requirements of other pronouncements largely negate the FRS 8 exemption. For example:

■   the statutory accounts formats in Schedules 4, 9 and 9A to the Companies Act require separate disclosure in the parent company balance sheet of balances with subsidiary and associated undertakings (see 3 below); and

■   Part II of Schedule 6 to the Companies Act requires disclosure of certain transactions between directors of the parent company and group companies (see Chapter 28 at 3.5).

Also, all related party transactions of the company (other than those eliminated on consolidation) will in any event be disclosed in the group accounts. Parent companies that do not prepare group accounts (e.g. those heading small or medium-sized groups, or subsidiaries of parents complying with the EU Seventh Directive) have to comply with FRS 8 in full in their own accounts, subject to the '90% subsidiary' exemption (see C below).

C   *Transactions with group investees in accounts of 90% (or more) owned subsidiaries*

This exemption covers only transactions with members, or investees (such as associates and joint ventures), of the group. Transactions with other types of related party (e.g. directors or major shareholders) must still be disclosed. In our view, this exemption is unsatisfactory for a number of reasons and should be carefully re-examined by the ASB in any future review of FRS 8.

The choice of 90%-owned subsidiaries as a threshold is odd, since it is unclear whose interest it serves. If the general public is regarded as the main user, it is sufficient for them to be aware that the reporting entity is a subsidiary undertaking, whatever the level of ownership. If, however, the intention is to protect the interests of minority shareholders, a 100% threshold would have been more appropriate. The FRS suggests that the choice of 90% is a pragmatic compromise to deal with subsidiaries with small amounts of voting preference shares, or small numbers of shares held by employees.[49]

Be that as it may, the following examples show how the exemption can lead to plainly anomalous results:

Example 27.8

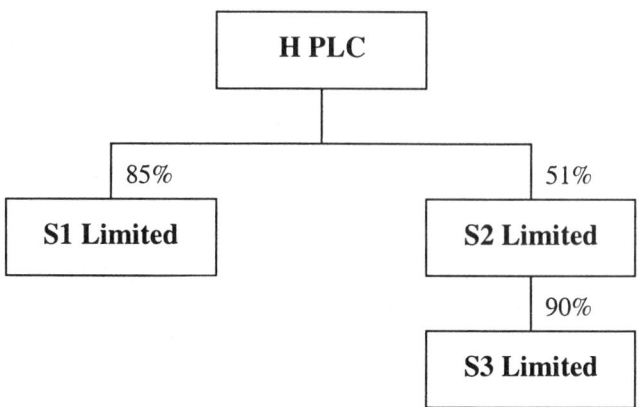

The minority shareholding in S1 Limited is owned by the controlling shareholder of H, whereas those of S2 and S3 are held by completely independent third parties. S1 is not eligible to claim the exemption because only 85% of its voting rights are controlled within the H group. However, S3 can claim the exemption because 90% of its voting rights are controlled by the H group, even though H's effective interest in S3 is only 46%. This means that, if S1 transacts with S3, details of the transactions must, somewhat perversely, be given in the accounts of S1 (whose minority shareholder is presumably fully aware of the transactions), but not those of S3 (whose minority shareholders may not be).

Example 27.9

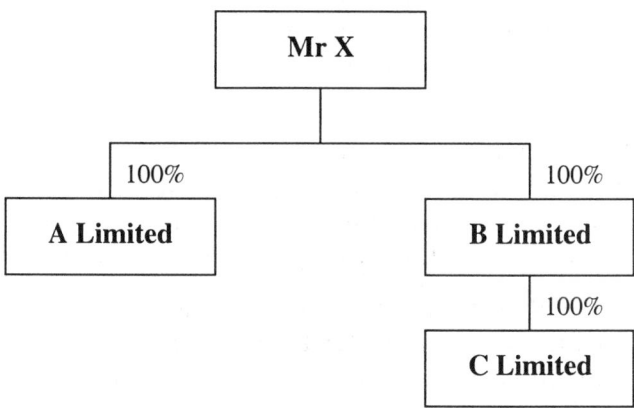

C derives 50% of its profit from transactions with A and 50% from transactions with B. Assuming that B Limited prepares group accounts, C will not have to disclose details of its transactions with B, but will have to disclose details of those with A, even though in substance there is little difference between them. This is because A is a related party of C (both are under the common control of Mr X), but not an investee of the B group.

It should be emphasised, however, that the over-riding requirement for accounts to give a true and fair view may still require disclosure of transactions covered by an exemption under FRS 8.

The FRS does not provide explicit guidance on the situation where the reporting entity seeking to claim the exemption is not a 90% (or more) owned subsidiary for the whole period. However, we interpret the phrase 'in the financial statements of subsidiary undertakings' as indicating that it is the status of the reporting entity at the balance sheet date that is relevant.

The exemption is simply conditional upon group accounts including the reporting entity being 'publicly available', without any further requirement for the group accounts concerned to give related party disclosures comparable to those required by FRS 8 (or, for that matter, to be in English or even the Western alphabet!). A further issue is that, even if the group accounts comply with FRS 8, many of the transactions exempt from disclosure at the subsidiary level will be eliminated on consolidation and will therefore not be disclosed at the group level either.

If the group accounts on which the exemption depends will not provide users with the information omitted from the subsidiary's accounts, it is in practice irrelevant whether or not they are publicly available. Perhaps it is for this reason that the FRS requires companies taking advantage of this exemption to disclose that they have done so.

In our view, for the exemption to be available it is not necessary for the group accounts concerned to be deposited in some central bureau comparable to Companies House in the UK. They could equally be 'publicly available' on request, from the offices of an overseas parent for example. However, companies taking advantage of the exemption will be subject to the Companies Act requirement to disclose the address from which group accounts can be obtained (see 3.1.3 A below).[50]

In any event, this exemption is largely negated by other requirements. For example, the accounts formats in the Companies Act and FRS 9 – *Associates and Joint Ventures* – require some information, particularly year-end balances, to be given in respect of transactions with group companies and investees.

All in all, we consider this exemption ill-thought out and urge the ASB to reconsider it in any future review of FRS 8. We much prefer the approach of the equivalent exemption in the international standard IAS 24 (see 4.1.3 below).

D   *Pension contributions to a pension fund*

This seems a reasonable exemption and, as noted above, may have been granted in order to mitigate the requirement to treat pension funds as related parties in all circumstances. However, the information may well be given more or less directly in the disclosures required by SSAP 24 – *Accounting for pension costs*. Certainly, if the proposed disclosures in the ASB's Discussion Paper *Pension costs in the employer's financial statements* are given effect in a future FRS, the information will be given explicitly as part of the reconciliation of the movement in the balance sheet figure for pension costs.[51] The exemption covers only contributions paid to the scheme and not, for example, refunds of surpluses and other transactions with the scheme.

E   Emoluments in respect of services as an employee of the reporting entity

In many cases, this will be over-ridden by the disclosure requirements in respect of directors' emoluments contained in Part I of Schedule 6 to the Companies Act and, for listed companies, the Stock Exchange requirements. It does, however, mean that salaries of key management other than directors do not need to be disclosed. There is no requirement that such amounts must be paid under a contract of employment, so that ex gratia bonuses and similar payments are exempt from disclosure.

Fees paid to directors (particularly non-executive directors) in their capacity as such may not be exempt from disclosure under FRS 8, since they are not 'emoluments is respect of services as an *employee*'. However, this is unlikely to have much practical significance. So far as listed companies are concerned, fees for each director will be disclosed under the Stock Exchange requirements. For other companies, if they have non-executive directors at all, the materiality of the amounts involved will mean that disclosure of fees by individual director will rarely be required.

2.3.6   Transactions subject to a duty of confidentiality

In addition to the types of transaction discussed in 2.3.5 above, FRS 8 does not require any related party transaction to be disclosed where this would involve the reporting entity's breaching a legal duty of confidentiality. It is clear from the explanatory section of the FRS that this concession is aimed principally at banks and similar institutions and covers only those obligations imposed by a generally applicable statute or common law. It does not include the effects of terms in a private contract, for the obvious reason that compliance with the standard would otherwise be voluntary, because companies could insert a confidentiality clause in all related party contracts.[52]

2.4   Disclosure of control

FRS 8 asserts that where a reporting entity is controlled by another party, that fact is relevant information, irrespective of whether transactions have taken place with that party. This is because the control relationship prevents the reporting entity from having independent discretionary power over its resources and transactions. The FRS goes on to suggest that the existence and identity of the controlling party may sometimes be at least as relevant in appraising an entity's prospects as are the performance and financial position presented in its accounts. The reason is that the controlling party may establish the entity's credit standing, determine the source and price of its raw materials, determine the products it sells, to whom and at what price, and may affect the source, calibre and allegiance of its management.[53]

Where the reporting entity is controlled by another party, the FRS requires it to disclose the identity of that controlling party and, if different, of the ultimate controlling party. This disclosure is required irrespective of whether or not the entity has entered into any transactions with the controlling party or parties. If the ultimate controlling party is not known, that fact should be disclosed.[54] The controlling party simply means, in the context of a company, the entity or individual that directly controls the company. The ultimate controlling party means the entity or individual at the top of any 'chain' that controls the immediate controlling party.

For many companies this requirement will be satisfied by disclosing the names of the immediate and ultimate parent companies, the latter being required already by the Companies Act. However, the FRS also requires the identification of non-corporate controlling persons such as trusts, partnerships or individuals. Hitherto these tended to escape disclosure under the Companies Act, although they were highlighted in the accounts of listed companies by the Stock Exchange requirement to disclose major shareholdings. An example of disclosure of control by a trust is given by Associated British Foods (see Extract 27.9 in 2.3.3 above).

Control by directors is disclosed in the directors' report by virtue of the Companies Act requirement to give certain details of directors' interests in the shares of the company and other group companies.[55] However, FRS 8 requires disclosure of the controlling party to be made in the 'financial statements' (rather than the directors' report). In the light of the ruling of the Financial Reporting Review Panel on the 1997 accounts of H & C Furnishings referred to at 2.2.2 B above, it would be advisable for there to be at least a note within the accounts cross-referred to the directors' report.

The FRS, obviously, does not supersede the Companies Act requirements to disclose the ultimate parent company and the parent undertaking(s) of the largest and, if different, smallest groups of which the company is a member and for which group accounts are prepared. This means that, potentially, a company may have to disclose as many as five parties further up the 'chain':

(a)   the immediate parent undertaking;[56]

(b)   the parent undertaking of the smallest group for which group accounts are prepared;[57]

(c)   the parent undertaking of the largest group for which group accounts are prepared;[58]

(d)   the ultimate parent company;[59] and;

(e)   the ultimate controlling party (where this is not a company).[60]

Incidentally, this provides a vivid illustration of the somewhat absurd over-disclosure that can arise when rules are made piecemeal by different sources of regulation (in this case UK law, the EC Seventh Directive and UK accounting standards) without regard to their overall context and pre-existing requirements.

2.5   Small companies

When it was originally issued, FRS 8 gave no exemptions for disclosure for small companies. The ASB had specifically sought commentators' views on this issue in FRED 8, whilst indicating its own preference for granting no exemption. Among the possible reasons for exempting small companies, the FRED highlighted the following:

(a)   the external shareholders of all companies already have some protection in the requirements of companies legislation that deal with disclosure of directors' and other officers' transactions; and

(b)   other users of small companies' accounts may have to rely on an abbreviated balance sheet and notes, which are all that need be filed by small companies and which would not include related party disclosures.

FRED 8 gave the following arguments against granting any exemptions:

(a)   the disclosure of information about related party transactions is no less important to the user of the accounts of small companies than it is to the user of those of larger entities. Indeed, certain kinds of related party transaction (e.g. those involving individuals) may be more prevalent and of greater significance for the financial statements when the company is small than when it is large; and

(b)   the confidential nature of such disclosures need not be a cause for concern, since they would be excluded from the abbreviated accounts available to the public.[61]

In the event, the ASB's view prevailed, supported by a majority of commentators, including ourselves. The development section of FRS 8 indicates that there was more than one round of consultation on this issue, the overall effect, if anything, being to harden the ASB's stance. As the FRS puts it: 'Representations from those auditing and using the accounts of small companies reinforced the view that appropriate related party disclosure is particularly important and relevant information in their financial statements, since transactions with related parties are more likely to be material in small companies.'[62]

This position is reinforced in the *Financial Reporting Standard for Smaller Entities (effective March 1999)* (FRSSE), which requires related party disclosures very similar to those laid down by FRS 8. However, there are some striking differences of detail, which may indicate that the ASB has had second thoughts on some aspects of FRS 8. In particular, there is only a single definition of related party arising from 'influence'. This states that two parties are related if 'one party has significant influence over the operating and financial policies of the other party. Significant influence would occur if that other party is inhibited from pursuing its own separate interests.'[63]

In contrast to FRS 8 (see 2.2.1 above), this refers to 'significant influence' rather than 'influence', and states that this will apply when the party subject to influence 'is' (as opposed to be 'might be') inhibited from pursuing its own interests. We assume that this change of emphasis was made to make the FRSSE more consistent with the definition of associate in FRS 9 – *Associates and Joint ventures* – which was issued at the same time as the first (November 1997) version of the FRSSE (see Chapter 7). It is not clear why FRS 8 was not similarly amended.

There is no equivalent in the FRSSE of the definition of related party in paragraph 2.5(a)(iv) of FRS 8 (entities transacting on terms such that one has subordinated its own interests). It would be interesting to know whether this was omitted because it was thought to be unnecessarily complicated for smaller entities, or because the ASB now shares some of our own reservations on this aspect of FRS 8 (see 2.2.1 B above).

The other main respects in which the FRSSE differs from FRS 8 are:

(a)　there is a list of deemed related parties broadly corresponding to that in FRS 8 (see 2.2.2 above), but no list of presumed related parties;

(b)　there is a specific requirement to disclose guarantees by directors in respect of borrowings of the reporting entity; and

(c)　the materiality of transactions with individuals is to be judged by reference to the reporting entity only, rather than by reference to both the entity and the individual, as required by FRS 8 (see 2.3.2 above).[64]

3　OTHER REQUIREMENTS IN THE UK

In addition to the requirements of FRS 8, the disclosure of some related party matters is dealt with in the Companies Act 1985, existing standards and, for listed and AIM companies, Stock Exchange requirements.

3.1　Legislative requirements

The Companies Act 1985 requires the financial statements (or directors' report) to contain what might be considered as related party disclosures in relation to:

(a)　directors;

(b)　non-director officers or senior employees; and

(c)　group companies (including associates and other major investments).

The disclosures for other related party matters are only regulated by the overriding requirement for the financial statements to give a true and fair view.

The disclosure requirements relating to each of the above categories of related parties are outlined below.

3.1.1 Directors

In general, the Companies Act requires the following information to be disclosed in respect of directors of a company:

(a)   names of directors who have served during the year;[65]

(b)   interests of each director in the share capital or debentures of the company or of any other group company;[66]

(c)   information about directors' emoluments (see Chapter 29); and

(d)   loans and other transactions with directors or persons connected with the directors (see Chapter 28).

3.1.2 Non-director officers

The Companies Act also requires disclosure of information relating to loans and other transactions with officers of the company other than directors; these requirements are discussed in Chapter 28 at 6.

3.1.3 Subsidiary, associated and other related undertakings

Schedules 4 and 5 to the Companies Act set out detailed disclosure requirements in respect of group companies (including undertakings in which the company has a participating interest),[67] many of which were added by the Companies Act 1989 when the EU Seventh Company Law Directive was incorporated into UK companies legislation. Certain of these disclosures apply to companies which are not required to prepare group accounts and subsidiary undertakings which have been excluded from the consolidated accounts.

A   *Ultimate parent company and parent undertaking(s) drawing up accounts for larger group*

Where a company or parent company is itself a subsidiary undertaking, it must give the name and, if known to the directors, the country of incorporation (if outside Great Britain[68]) of the company (if any) regarded by the directors as the company's ultimate parent company. For this purpose, the term 'company' includes any body corporate (i.e. a UK corporate entity not registered under the Companies Act or an overseas corporate entity).[69]

The Companies Act also requires additional disclosures in relation to the parent undertaking(s) (which need not be a corporate entity) of the largest and smallest group of undertakings for which group accounts are drawn up and of which the reporting company is a member.

The information to be given about each such parent undertaking is:

(a)   its name;

(b)   (i)   its country of incorporation (if outside Great Britain)

    (ii)   if unincorporated, the address of its principal place of business; and

(c)   if copies of its group accounts are available to the public, the address from which they may be obtained.[70]

B   *Subsidiary undertakings*

A parent company, whether or not it is preparing group accounts, must give the following information about each of its subsidiary undertakings:

(a)   its name;

(b)   its country of incorporation (if outside Great Britain);

(c)   if it is unincorporated, the address of its principal place of business;[71] and

(d)   the identity of each class of shares held and the proportion of the nominal value of the shares of that class represented by those shares. If applicable, the holdings should be split between those held directly by the parent company, and those held indirectly via other group companies.[72]

A parent company that does not prepare group accounts must disclose, for each subsidiary undertaking, its profit or loss for, and capital and reserves at the end of, its 'relevant financial year' – i.e. its latest financial year coterminous with, or ending before, that of the parent. In a case where a subsidiary's relevant financial year ends before that of the parent, the year-end date must given.

However, this information need not be given if the parent is exempt from preparing accounts under section 228 of the Companies Act 1985 (subsidiary of EU parent – see Chapter 5, at 4.1), or if the group's investment in the undertaking is included in the accounts by way of the equity method of valuation, or if:

(a)   the undertaking is not required by any provision of the Companies Act to deliver a copy of its balance sheet for its relevant financial year and does not otherwise publish its balance sheet in Great Britain or elsewhere; and

(b)   the holding of the group is less than 50% of the nominal value of the shares in the undertaking.[73]

Where a parent company does prepare group accounts it must disclose why each subsidiary is a subsidiary undertaking, unless the reason is (as it typically will be) that the subsidiary's immediate parent holds a majority of voting rights, and the same proportion of the shares, in the subsidiary undertaking.[74] It must also state whether each subsidiary undertaking is included in the consolidation, and give the reason for non-consolidation in any particular case.[75]

In respect of each unconsolidated subsidiary, the parent must disclose its profit or loss for its 'relevant financial year' (see above) and its total capital and reserves at the end that year. However, this information need not be given in respect of any subsidiary undertaking if the group's investment in the undertaking is included in the accounts by way of the equity method of valuation or if:

(a) the undertaking is not required by any provision of the Companies Act to deliver a copy of its balance sheet for its relevant financial year and does not otherwise publish its balance sheet in Great Britain or elsewhere; and

(b) the holding of the group is less than 50% of the nominal value of the shares in the undertaking.[76]

For each subsidiary undertaking whose financial year did not end with that of the company, the parent must explain why the directors of the parent consider this appropriate, and give the date of its last year-end before that of the reporting company. Alternatively, where there are a number of subsidiary undertakings, the earliest and latest of those dates may be given.[77]

C Associated undertakings

The following information must be given in group accounts in respect of each associated undertaking:

(a) its name;

(b) its country of incorporation (if outside Great Britain);

(c) if it is unincorporated, the address of its principal place of business; and

(d) the identity of each class of shares held and the proportion of the nominal value of the shares of that class represented by those shares. If applicable, the holdings should be split between those held directly by the parent company, and those held indirectly via other group companies.[78]

D Joint ventures

Where an undertaking is accounted for in group accounts using proportional consolidation, the following information must be disclosed:

(a) its name;

(b) its principal place of business;

(c) the factors on which joint management is based;

(d) the proportion of the capital of the joint venture held by the group; and

(e) where the financial year end of the joint venture did not coincide with that of the parent company of the reporting group, the date of its last year-end ending before that of the parent.[79]

In practice, this requirement has been rendered redundant by the prohibition of proportional consolidation by FRS 9 – *Associates and Joint Ventures* (see Chapter 7).

E Investments in 'qualifying undertakings'

Where a company or group has an investment in a 'qualifying undertaking' (i.e. a partnership or unlimited company each of whose members is either a limited company or an unlimited company (or Scottish firm), each of whose members is a limited company),[80] it must state the name and legal form of the qualifying undertaking together with its address or that of its head office. This information need not be given if it is not material.

There must also be stated either:

(a) that a copy of the latest accounts of the undertaking has been, or is to be, appended to the copy of the company's accounts filed with the Registrar of Companies; or

(b) the name of at least one body corporate (which can be the reporting company) in whose consolidated accounts the qualifying undertaking has been included. This information need not be given if the qualifying undertaking is exempt from preparing accounts.[81] (Somewhat contrarily, the key condition for obtaining such an exemption is that the undertaking has been included in the consolidated accounts of one of its members!)[82]

F   *Other significant holdings of the parent company or group*

Schedule 5 to the Companies Act also requires certain disclosures to be given where a parent company has a significant investment in an undertaking which is not a subsidiary or associated undertaking or joint venture.[83]

A holding is 'significant' for the purposes of these disclosures if either:

(a) it amounts to 20% or more of the nominal value of any class of shares in the undertaking; or

(b) the book value of the holding exceeds one-fifth of the company's (or group's) assets as stated in its accounts.

For companies required to prepare group accounts, the disclosures must be given both for investments of the parent company of the reporting group and investments of the group as a whole.

In relation to holdings which amount to 20% or more of the nominal value of the shares in the investee, companies must also disclose (if material):

(a) the aggregate amount of its capital and reserves of the undertaking at the end of its relevant financial year; and

(b) its profit or loss for that year.

However, this information need not be given if:

(a) the undertaking is not required by any provision of the Companies Act to deliver a copy of its balance sheet for its relevant financial year and does not otherwise publish its balance sheet in Great Britain or elsewhere, and the holding of the group is less than 50% of the nominal value of the shares in the undertaking; or

(b) the company is not required to prepare group accounts because it is an intermediate holding company, and the company's investment in all undertakings in which it has such a holding is shown, in aggregate, in the notes to the accounts by way of the equity method of valuation.

G   *Transactions with group undertakings and undertakings in which the company has a participating interest*

In addition to requiring the amounts in respect of shares in group undertakings and participating interests to be separately disclosed, the balance sheet formats also require separate disclosure of the following inter-company balances involving (i) group undertakings and (ii) undertakings in which the company has a participating interest:

(a)   loans to (under the heading of fixed asset investments);

(b)   amounts owed by (under the heading of current assets, debtors);

(c)   amounts owed to (under both headings for creditors).[84]

The profit and loss account formats contained in the Companies Act require separate disclosure of:

(a)   income from shares in group undertakings;

(b)   income from participating interests;

(c)   income and interest derived from group undertakings; and

(d)   interest and similar charges payable to group undertakings.[85]

In group accounts, amounts relating to participating interests must be analysed between those relating to associated undertakings and those relating to other participating interests.[86]

The Companies Act requires companies to disclose details of any guarantees and other financial commitments.[87] Where such guarantees or commitments are undertaken on behalf of or for the benefit of:

(a)   any parent undertaking or fellow subsidiary undertaking; or

(b)   any subsidiary undertaking of the company,

they are required to be disclosed separately from any other guarantees and financial commitments; furthermore, guarantees and commitments within (a) above should be disclosed separately from those within (b).[88]

3.2   UK accounting standards other than FRS 8

The main UK accounting standards other than FRS 8 which impinge on the issue of related parties are FRS 2 – *Accounting for Subsidiary Undertakings* and FRS 9 – *Associates and Joint Ventures*, which require certain disclosures to be made in the financial statements of the investing company in addition to those required by the Companies Act as described in 3.1 above. These are discussed in detail in Chapters 5 and 7 respectively.

3.3   Stock Exchange requirements

The Stock Exchange requires fully listed and, to a lesser extent, AIM companies to disclose, in their annual reports and accounts, various information relevant to related parties, or which indicate the existence of related parties, in addition to that required by the Companies Act. The specific disclosures relevant to related parties concern either the directors or the shareholders of the company.

3.3.1 Directors

A   Emoluments and other benefits

There are extensive requirements for the disclosure of individual directors' emoluments and other benefits, introduced in response to the Cadbury and Greenbury codes. These are discussed in Chapter 29 at 4.

B   Directors' interests in share capital

The requirements extend beyond those contained in the Companies Act 1985 in that they require disclosure of:

(a)   beneficial and non-beneficial interests, separately distinguished. For this purpose a holding is non-beneficial only if neither the director, nor his spouse, nor any of his children under 18 has any beneficial interest; and

(b)   changes in interests between the balance sheet date and a date not more than one month before the date of the notice of the annual general meeting. If there has been no change, then that fact should be disclosed.[89]

C   Contracts of significance with directors

Particulars of any contract of significance subsisting during the financial year, to which the company or one of its subsidiary undertakings is a party, and in which a director of the company is or was materially interested are required to be disclosed by listed companies. If there has been no such contract, a statement of that fact is required.[90]

A 'contract of significance' is defined as one which represents in amount or value, a sum equal to 1% or more, calculated on a group basis where relevant, of:

(a)   in the case of a capital transaction or a transaction of which the principal purpose or effect is the granting of credit, the aggregate of the group's share capital and reserves; or

(b)   in other cases, the total annual purchases, sales, payments or receipts, as the case may be, of the group.[91]

(See Chapter 28 at 5 for further discussion of these requirements.)

3.3.2 Shareholders

A   Substantial holdings of the company's shares

A statement is required to be given showing particulars, as at a date not more than one month prior to the date of the notice of the annual general meeting, of an interest of any person (other than a director), in any substantial part of the share capital of the company. A substantial holding is one which amounts to 3%

or more of the nominal value of any class of capital carrying rights to vote in all circumstances at general meetings of the company. If there is no such interest, a statement of that fact is required to be made.[92]

B   *Contracts of significance*

Particulars of any contract of significance between the company, or one of its subsidiaries, and a controlling shareholder are required to be disclosed by listed companies.[93]

A controlling shareholder is one who is entitled to exercise, or control the exercise of, 30% or more of the rights to vote at general meetings, or is able to control the appointment of directors who are able to exercise a majority of votes at board meetings.[94]

In addition, particulars of any contract for the provision of services to the company or any of its subsidiaries by a controlling shareholder are also required to be disclosed. Such a contract need not be disclosed, if it is a contract for the provision of services which it is the principal business of the shareholder to provide and it is not a contract of significance.[95]

C   *Waived dividends*

Particulars of any arrangement under which a shareholder has waived or agreed to waive any dividends are required to be disclosed. Where a director has agreed to waive future dividends, details should be given of such waiver together with those relating to dividends which are payable during the period under review. Waivers of less than 1% of the total value of any dividend may be disregarded provided that some payment has been made on each share of the relevant class during the relevant calendar year.[96]

In practice, waivers are likely to arise only where the shareholder is a director or has some influence over the company.

D   *Purchase by the company of its own shares*

The Companies Act contains provisions requiring disclosures of certain information where a company has purchased some of its own shares.[97] The Stock Exchange extends these for listed companies by requiring disclosure of, in the case of purchases made otherwise than through the market or by tender or partial offer to all shareholders, the names of the sellers of such shares purchased.[98]   Again, in most cases, this is likely to arise only where the shareholder is a director or has some influence over the company.

3.3.3   *Smaller related party transactions*

Under the Listing Rules of the Stock Exchange, listed companies are normally required to issue a circular to shareholders where a related party transaction is contemplated.[99]   In the case of some smaller transactions, however, companies are able instead, subject to various conditions, to disclose details of the transactions in their accounts. The transactions concerned are those where one or more of the following ratios is between 0.25% and 5%:

(a)   net assets the subject of the transaction, to those of listed company;

(b)   profits attributable to net assets the subject of the transaction, to those of listed company;

(c)   consideration, to net assets of listed company;

(d)   consideration, to market capitalisation of equity shares of listed company; and;

(e)   where a business is being acquired, its gross capital, to that of listed company. [100]

'Related party transactions' are defined for this purpose as transactions (other than revenue transactions in the ordinary course of business) between a related party and the company or any company in the same group.[101]

'Related parties' are defined for this purpose as:

(a)   a 'substantial shareholder' (broadly a person able to control, now or at any time during the previous 12 months, 10% of the votes of the company or any other group company);

(b)   any person who is (or was during the previous 12 months) a director or shadow director of the company or any other group company; or

(c)   an associate of any person falling within (a) or (b). An 'associate' is broadly:

    (i)   with respect to an individual: his immediate family; a trust for the benefit of him or his immediate family; or a company in which he and/or his immediate family can either control 30% of the votes or appoint a majority of the board; and

    (ii)   with respect to a company: any company in the same group; any company whose directors are accustomed to act in accordance with its instructions; or any company in which it and/or its other associates can either control 30% of the votes or appoint a majority of the board.[102]

In order to qualify for this exemption a company must, prior to completing the transaction:

(a)   inform the Stock Exchange in writing of the details of the proposed transaction;

(b)   provide the Stock Exchange with written confirmation from an independent adviser acceptable to the Stock Exchange that the terms of the proposed transaction with the related party are fair and reasonable so far as the shareholders of the company are concerned; and

(c) undertake in writing to the Stock Exchange to include details of the transaction in the company's next published annual accounts, including the identity of the related party, the value of the consideration for the transaction and all other relevant circumstances.[103]

The requirement to include details of small related party transactions in the annual report and accounts of companies which have taken advantage of the facility of not having to issue a circular to shareholders is listed as one of the continuing obligations of the Listing Rules.[104] The following are examples of disclosures which appear to have been made in pursuance of this requirement:

Extract 27.15: EMI Group plc (1997)

32. RELATED PARTY TRANSACTIONS [extract]

EMI Music Publishing acquired the music publishing catalogues of The Entertainment Group of Companies on 31 March 1997 for a total consideration of US$7.8m (£4.8m). These companies were owned by Charles Koppelman and Martin Bandier, directors of certain Group companies.

Extract 27.16: TI Group plc (1996)

31. RELATED PARTY TRANSACTIONS [extract]

On 30th December 1996 Bundy Corporation sold its 20% investment in Usui Bundy Tubing Ltd ('Usui') to Usui Kokusai Sangyo Kaisha Ltd, which already held 60% of Usui, for ¥1,077m (£6m). TI Group retained the rights to use the name 'Bundy' in Japan.

3.3.4 AIM companies

AIM companies are required to disclose in their accounts details of any related party transaction (defined as for listed companies in 3.3.3 above)[105] where any one of the following ratios exceeds 0.25%:

(a) net assets the subject of the transaction, to those of AIM company;

(b) profits attributable to net assets the subject of the transaction, to those of AIM company;

(c) consideration, to net assets of AIM company; and

(d) consideration, to market capitalisation of equity shares of AIM company.

The details given must include the identity of the related party, the value of the consideration and all other relevant circumstances.[106]

4 COMPARISON WITH IASC AND US PRONOUNCEMENTS

4.1 IASC

The relevant international standard which deals with the disclosure of related parties and transactions between a reporting enterprise and its related parties is

IAS 24 – *Related Party Disclosures* – which was originally issued in July 1984 and issued in a revised format in 1994.

4.1.1   Definition of related party

IAS 24 considers two parties as related 'if one party has the ability to control the other party or to exercise significant influence over the other party in making financial and operating decisions'.[107] For the purposes of IAS 24, 'control' is defined as 'ownership, directly, or indirectly through subsidiaries, of more than one half of the voting power of an enterprise, or a substantial interest in voting power and the power to direct, by statute or agreement, the financial and operating policies of the management of the enterprise'.[108] This is somewhat wordier that the equivalent definition in FRS 8, but has much the same result.

'Significant influence' is defined as 'participation in the financial and operating policy decisions of an enterprise, but not control of those policies'. IAS 24 goes on to say that whilst significant influence will normally be exercised through board representation, it may also arise through 'participation in the policy making process, material intercompany transactions, interchange of managerial personnel or dependence on technical information.' Whether significant influence arises as a result of share ownership is to be determined in accordance with IAS 28 – *Accounting for Investments in Associates* (see Chapter 7 at 6.1).[109] Taken at face value, therefore, IAS 24's definition of 'significant influence' is more restrictive than that of 'influence' in FRS 8 (see 2.2.1 B above). In practice, however, we see their effect as essentially the same.

Notwithstanding the broad definition of related party, however, IAS 24 requires disclosure only in respect of the following types of related party that meet the general definition:

(a)   enterprises controlling, controlled by, or under common control with, the reporting enterprise;

(b)   associates;

(c)   individuals owning, directly or indirectly, an interest in the voting power of the reporting enterprise that gives them significant influence over the enterprise, and close members of the family of any such individual;

(d)   key management personnel, that is, those persons having authority and responsibility for planning, directing and controlling the activities of the reporting enterprise, including directors and officers of companies and close members of the families of such individuals; and

(e)   enterprises in which a substantial interest in the voting power is owned, directly or indirectly, by any person described in (c) or (d) or over which such a person is able to exercise significant influence. This includes enterprises owned by directors or major shareholders of the reporting enterprise and enterprises that have a member of key management in common with the reporting enterprise.[110]

For the purposes of (c) and (d) above 'close members of the family' are defined as 'those that may be expected to influence, or be influenced by, that person in their dealings with the enterprise'.[111]

Moreover, the standard deems the following not to be related parties:

(a)   two companies 'simply' because they have a director in common, although 'it is necessary to consider the possibility, and to assess the likelihood, that the director would be able to affect the policies of both companies in their mutual dealings';

(b)   providers of finance, trade unions, public utilities and government departments and agencies, in each case in the course of their normal dealings with the enterprise by virtue only of those dealings;

(c)   a single customer, supplier, franchisor, distributor or general agent with whom the enterprise conducts a significant volume of business merely by virtue of the resulting economic dependence.[112]

This is broadly similar to, but somewhat more extensive than, the list of such parties in FRS 8 (see 2.2.5 above).

4.1.2   Disclosures required

As under FRS 8, related party relationships where control exists should be disclosed irrespective of whether there have been transactions between the related parties.[113] Where transactions have taken place between related parties, the reporting enterprise should disclose the nature of the related party relationships as well as the types of transactions and the elements of the transactions necessary for an understanding of the financial statements.[114] Items of a similar nature may be disclosed in aggregate, except when separate disclosure is necessary for an understanding of the effects on the financial statements.[115] The standard points out that certain other IASs call for disclosures which may also be relevant in respect of related parties.[116]

The disclosure requirements of IAS 24 are, however, considerably less rigorous than those of FRS 8. IAS 24 does not specifically require disclosure of either the name of the related party or the amounts involved in the transactions.

IAS 24 gives an indicative list of transactions that 'may lead to disclosures' of related party transactions, which is identical to that in FRS 8 (see 2.3.1 above).

4.1.3   Exemptions from disclosure

IAS 24 does not require disclosure of related party transactions:

(a)   in consolidated financial statements in respect of intra-group transactions;

(b)   in parent company financial statements when they are made available or published with the consolidated financial statements;

(c)　in financial statements of a wholly-owned subsidiary if its parent is incorporated in the same country and provides consolidated financial statements in that country; and

(d)　in financial statements of state-controlled enterprises of transactions with other state-controlled enterprises.[117]

(a) and (b) mirror the similar exemptions in FRS 8 (see 2.3.5 above). There is no equivalent of (d) in FRS 8, and conversely IAS 24 contains no exemptions for contributions to pension funds or employees' emoluments comparable to those in FRS 8. The lack of this exemption has the effect that IAS 24 requires disclosure of directors' emoluments, although many accounts purporting to comply with IASs do not give this information. An example of a company that does disclose details of directors' remuneration and loans is Nokia.

Extract 27.17: Nokia Corporation (1998)

4. Personnel expenses [extract]

	1998 **MFIM**	1997 MFIM
Remuneration of the members of the Boards of Directors, Group Executive Board, President and Chief Executive Officer, and President and Managing Directors*	**67**	64
* Salaries include incentives	**15**	5

Pension commitments for the management:

　　The retirement age of the management of the Group companies is between 60–65 years.
　　For the Chief Executive Officer of the Parent Company the retirement age is 60 years.

26. Loans granted to top management

	1998 **MFIM**	1997 MFIM
Loans granted to top management	**3**	3

The loan period is generally between 5 and 10 years. The interest rates vary between 3–8% depending on the level of interest rate in the respective country.

It will be seen that the information given here is far less than would be required for a listed UK company (see Chapters 28 and 29).

The exemption for subsidiaries (item (c) above) is superficially similar to the equivalent in FRS 8, but differs in all key respects as the following matrix illustrates.

	IAS 24	FRS 8
Qualifying entities	wholly-owned subsidiaries	90% or more owned subsidiaries
Exempt transactions	all related party transaction	transactions with other members of the group, or investees of the group qualifying as related parties
Group accounts required to be prepared	by parent in same country and publicly available in that country	by parent in any country and publicly available anywhere
Disclosure required	none	that exemption has been taken, and where group accounts can be obtained

As noted in 2.3.5 C above, we consider the exemption in IAS 24 preferable to that in FRS 8. Interestingly, this is the only major difference between FRS 8 and IAS 24 highlighted in FRS 8 itself,[118] although, as the discussion above indicates, there are numerous other differences of detail.

Given that, barring matters of relative detail, FRS 8 and IAS 24 have much the same requirements, the expectation would be that accounts prepared under the two standards would have similar levels of disclosure of related party transactions. However, this is not the case. Broadly speaking, whilst it is now the exception for a UK listed company not to have a related party disclosures note, accounts prepared under IAS 24 almost invariably have no related party disclosures other than directors' emoluments and those required by other IASs. Whilst this may, of course, simply reflect the facts of the particular cases, it is hard to resist the conclusion that on the whole IAS 24 is applied with much less rigour than FRS 8.

4.2 US

The main accounting standard in the US dealing with this issue is SFAS 57 – *Related Party Disclosures* – which was issued in March 1982, as a codification into GAAP of SAS 6. While SFAS 57 outlines general US GAAP in this area, there are a number of other pronouncements in the US which impact on the reporting of certain related party transactions. These include SFAS 68 – *Research and Development Arrangements* – and SFAS 13 – *Accounting for Leases* – as well as various Staff Accounting Bulletins issued by the SEC.

The requirements of SFAS 57 are such that related parties under FRS 8 are effectively related parties under SFAS 57[119] and, apart from the following minor differences, FRS 8 is effectively an elaboration of SFAS 57:

- SFAS 57 requires disclosure of all material related party transactions in the financial statements of wholly owned subsidiaries if these are produced,[120] whereas FRS 8 exempts 90% (or more) owned subsidiaries from having to disclose transactions with group companies;

- like IAS 24, SFAS 57 does not specifically require disclosure of the names of the related parties as required by FRS 8; it only requires the nature of the relationship to be disclosed, although it does state that the name should be disclosed if necessary to the understanding of the relationship;[121]

- in addition to requiring disclosure of amounts due to/from the related party, SFAS 57 requires the terms and manner of settlement to be disclosed if not otherwise apparent;[122]

- SFAS 57 does not specifically require disclosure of any material difference between the fair value and the transacted amount of related party transactions as is suggested in certain circumstances by FRS 8. However, SFAS 57 does require 'such other information deemed necessary to an understanding of the effects of the transactions on the financial statements'[123] (much like FRS 8) and 'the effects of any change in the method of establishing the terms from that used in the preceding period' to be disclosed.[124]

5   CONCLUSION

In drafting ED 46, the ASC attempted to break away from international practice by proposing that only abnormal transactions be disclosed. This was done so that companies could avoid having to provide over-lengthy disclosures which it was assumed arose under SFAS 57 and IAS 24. However, given the anticipated difficulties that would arise in practice in applying the definitions of normal and abnormal transactions, the ASB decided to abandon the distinction and adopt the more conventional approach.

FRS 8, though brief, is a much more complex standard than it appears at a first reading. In the light of our experience in dealing with it in the last few reporting seasons, we would urge the ASB to re-address certain aspects of it, in particular:

- the inconsistency between the treatment of the concept of 'significant influence' in FRS 8 on the one hand and in FRS 9 and the FRSSE on the other (see 2.5 above);

- the definition of related party in paragraph 2.5(a)(iv) of the FRS based on entities transacting on terms such that one has subordinated its own interests (see 2.2.1 above);

- the requirement, in certain cases, to judge materiality by reference to the circumstances of the related party rather than those of the reporting entity (see 2.3.2 above); and

■   the exemptions from disclosure for 90% (or more) owned subsidiaries (see 2.3.5 C above).

In addition, whilst we would not advocate a return to a general 'abnormal transaction' approach such as that proposed in ED 46, we are concerned that FRS 8 unintentionally embraces certain types of transactions, disclosure of which distracts readers from those related party transactions that are more truly worthy of their attention. We believe that, where possible, such transactions should be removed from the scope of the FRS. Obvious examples include:

■   participation by major shareholders in transactions with shareholders as a whole (e.g. dividends, rights issues); and

■   where companies trade with the public (e.g. retailers, certain banks and insurance companies), transactions with directors and key managers (and their close family and entities controlled by them) as members of the public on non-preferential terms. However, transactions with such individuals (and persons and entities connected with them) in a business capacity should, in our view, always be disclosed whatever their terms.

Some form of related party disclosure standard was long overdue in the UK. However, users of accounts should be under no illusion that FRS 8 will act as more than a mild deterrent to those intent on corporate fraud on the scale that allegedly occurred in companies connected with Robert Maxwell.

References

1 FRS 8, *Related Party Disclosures*, ASB, November 1995, paras. 8-10.
2 Accountants International Study Group, *Related Party Transactions*, para. 15.
3 CA 85, ss 226(4) and 227(5).
4 FRS 8, para. 1.
5 *Ibid.*, para. 7.
6 *Ibid.*, para. 2.5.
7 *Ibid.*, para. 11.
8 *Ibid.*, para. 2.5(a).
9 *Ibid.*, para. 2.2.
10 FRS 5, *Reporting the substance of transactions*, ASB, April 1994, para. 8.
11 FRS 8, para. 13.
12 *Ibid.*, para. 14.
13 *Ibid.*
14 FRED 8, *Related party disclosures*, ASB, March 1994, para. 2(a)(iv).
15 FRS 8, para. 14.
16 *Implementing FRS 8: Some practical aspects*, Ken Wild and Brian Creighton, Accountancy, October 1996, page 128.
17 FRS 8, para. 2.5(a).
18 *Ibid.*, para. 2.5(b).
19 *Ibid.*, para. 2.5(b)(iv), footnote.
20 FRRP PN 53, Financial Reporting Review Panel, August 1998.
21 FRS 8, para. 15.
22 Statement of Recommended Practice, *Financial Reports of Pension Schemes*, Pensions Research Accountants Group, July 1996, para. 2.65.
23 FRS 8, para. 2.5(c).
24 *Ibid.*
25 *Ibid.*, para. 2.3.
26 *Ibid.*, paras. 2.2 and 2.5(c)(iii) (footnote).
27 *Ibid.*, para. 2.4.
28 *Ibid.*, para. 2.5.
29 *Ibid.*, para. 2.1.
30 FRED 8, para. 2(d)(iii).
31 FRS 8, para. 4.
32 ASB Statement, *Operating and Financial Review*, ASB, July 1993, para. 12.
33 FRS 8, para. 4.
34 *Ibid.*, para. 6.
35 *Ibid.*, para. 2.6.
36 *Ibid.*, para. 19.
37 *Ibid.*, paras. 2.6 and 19.
38 *Ibid.*, para. 20.
39 *Ibid.*
40 *Ibid.*, para. 6.
41 FRED 8, paras. 8(f) and 23.
42 FRS 8, para. 22.
43 *Ibid.*, para. 10.
44 *Ibid.*, paras. 6 and 21.
45 *Ibid.*, para. 21.
46 Foreword to Accounting Standards, ASB, June 1993, para. 15.
47 FRS 8, para. 3.
48 *Ibid.*, para 2.5(a).
49 *Ibid.*, Appendix IV, para 12.
50 CA 85, Sch. 5, paras. 11 and 30.
51 Discussion Paper, *Pension Costs in the Employer's Financial Statements*, ASB, June 1995, para. 6.2.13.
52 FRS 8, para.16.

53 *Ibid.*, para. 18.
54 *Ibid.*, para. 5.
55 CA 85, Sch. 7, paras. 2-2B.
56 FRS 8., para. 5.
57 CA 85, Sch. 5, paras. 11 and 30.
58 *Ibid.*
59 *Ibid.*, paras. 12 and 31.
60 FRS 8, para. 5.
61 FRED 8, Preface.
62 FRS 8, Appendix IV, para. 14.
63 *Financial Reporting Standard for Smaller Entities (effective March 1999)* ('FRSSE'), ASB, December 1998, section C.
64 *Ibid.* para. 15.
65 CA 85, s 234(2).
66 *Ibid.*, Sch. 7, para. 2A.
67 Under the Companies Act and FRS 9, an undertaking in which a participating interest is held and over which significant influence is exercised is an 'associated undertaking'.
68 Throughout section 3.1, references to 'Great Britain' should, where the reporting entity is a company incorporated in Northern Ireland, be read as references to 'Northern Ireland'. The relevant legislation for such companies is the Companies (Northern Ireland) Order 1986, the provisions of which are in substance identical to those of the Companies Act 1985.
69 CA 85, Sch. 5, paras. 12 and 31, section 740.
70 *Ibid.*, paras. 11 and 30.
71 *Ibid.*, para. 15(2) and (3).
72 *Ibid.*, paras. 2(2) and 16(1).
73 *Ibid.*, para.4.
74 *Ibid.*, para. 15(5).
75 *Ibid.*, para. 15(4).
76 *Ibid.*, para. 17.
77 *Ibid.*, para. 19.
78 *Ibid.*, para. 22.
79 *Ibid.*, para. 21.
80 SI 1993/1820, *The Partnerships and Unlimited Companies (Accounts) Regulations 1993*, Regulation 3.
81 CA 1985, Sch. 5, paras. 9A and 28A.
82 SI 1993/1820, Regulation 7.
83 CA 85, Sch. 5, paras. 7–9 and 23–28.
84 *Ibid.*, Schs. 4, 9 and 9A, balance sheet formats.
85 *Ibid.*, profit and loss account formats.
86 CA 85, Sch. 4A, para. 21.
87 *Ibid.*, Sch 4, para. 50.
88 *Ibid.*, para. 59A.
89 *The Listing Rules*, London Stock Exchange, Chapter 12, para. 12.43(k).
90 *Ibid.*, Chapter 12, para. 12.43(q).
91 *Ibid.*, para. 12.44.
92 *Ibid.*, para. 12.43(l); CA 85, s 199(2).
93 *Ibid.*, para. 12.43(r).
94 *Ibid.*, Chapter 3, para. 3.12.
95 *Ibid.*, Chapter 12, para. 12.43(s).
96 *Ibid.*, para. 12.43(e).
97 CA 85, Sch. 7, para. 8.
98 *The Listing Rules*, London Stock Exchange, Chapter 12, para. 12.43(n).
99 *Ibid.*, Chapter 11.
100 *Ibid.*, Chapter 10, para. 10.5 and Chapter 11, para. 11.8.
101 *Ibid.*, Chapter 11, para. 11.1.
102 *Ibid.*

103 *Ibid.*, para. 11.8.
104 *Ibid.*, Chapter 12, para. 12.43(t).
105 Rules of the London Stock Exchange, Definitions
106 *Ibid.*, Chapter 16, para. 16.24 (for ratios, see para. 16.23(b))
107 IAS 24, *Related Party Disclosures*, IASC, 1984 (reformatted 1994), para. 5
108 *Ibid.*
109 *Ibid*
110 *Ibid.*, para. 3.
111 *Ibid.*, footnote.
112 *Ibid.*, para. 6.
113 *Ibid.*, para. 20.
114 *Ibid.*, para. 22.
115 *Ibid.*, para. 24.
116 *Ibid.*, para. 18.
117 *Ibid.*, para. 4.
118 FRS 8, Appendix III.
119 SFAS 57, *Related Party Disclosures*, FASB, March 1982, para. 24f.
120 *Ibid.*, para. 2, footnote 2.
121 *Ibid.*, footnote 3.
122 *Ibid.*, para. 2(d).
123 *Ibid.*, para. 2(b).
124 *Ibid.*, para. 2(c).

Chapter 28   Directors' and officers' loans and transactions

1   INTRODUCTION

Company directors are treated as fiduciaries[1] and as such must not permit their personal interests and their duty to the company to conflict. In order to avoid such conflicts or potential conflicts arising, transactions between a company and its directors are restricted. Such transactions are regulated in a number of ways, in particular, by means of statutory prohibition, corporate approval and disclosure in the statutory accounts. In this chapter, attention is focused on the Companies Act requirements for disclosure in a company's financial statements of transactions involving directors (except for those relating to directors' remuneration, including share options, which are dealt with in Chapter 29). The provisions determining the legality or otherwise of such transactions are discussed in outline in the Appendix to this chapter.

In considering the disclosures to be made in respect of transactions involving directors (and persons connected with them) it will also be necessary to consider the requirements of FRS 8 – *Related Party Disclosures*, an accounting standard issued by the ASB in November 1995. These are only referred to in passing in this chapter; they are dealt with in their entirety in Chapter 27.

1.1   Outline of historical development in the UK

The Companies Act 1948 provided that a public company could not make a loan to any of its directors or directors of its holding company.[2] Loans to directors of exempt private companies (in essence, companies where the number of members was restricted) were permitted.[3] However, it became apparent over the years that directors could circumvent the restrictions on loans by carefully structuring transactions with their company. Thus, a company could make payments in respect of a director's personal expenditure and seek reimbursement from him without contravening the statutory prohibitions. In such cases, the director would be in substantially the same position as if he had been lent funds to pay off his debts. In an effort to close these loopholes, more extensive requirements were enacted by the Companies Act 1980;[4] for example, the types of unlawful transaction were extended to encompass quasi-loans and credit transactions (see respectively 2.7 and 2.8 below). The relevant legislation is now consolidated in the Companies Act 1985.[5]

2   DEFINITIONS

In order to promote a fuller understanding of this chapter, the following definitions have been included:

2.1   Director

This term includes any person occupying the position of director, by whatever name called;[6] i.e. it is a person's role and duties and not his title which determines whether or not he is a director. Thus, for example, a director's appointment may be defective because the procedure prescribed in the company's articles has not been followed; however, if he performs the functions associated with a person in such a position, he will be regarded as a director for the purposes of the legislation. Conversely, a person may be designated a director yet not be regarded as a director for statutory purposes; for example, it is common for companies to recognise senior managers by conferring titles such as divisional director[7] on them. These persons usually only exercise limited managerial power and hence are unlikely to be subject to the restrictions on directors' transactions, although the disclosure requirements relating to officers may be of relevance (see 2.5 and 6 below).

2.2   Shadow director

This is a person in accordance with whose directions or instructions the directors of the company as a whole (i.e. the board as a collective unit) are accustomed to act. However, if the directors' reason for following a person's advice is that it is given in a professional capacity, that person is not regarded as a shadow director.[8] Clearly, a professional adviser might fall to be treated as a shadow director if the advice which he gives to the board is not given in a professional capacity.

A holding company is not deemed to be a shadow director of a subsidiary even though the directors of the subsidiary act as the holding company directs.[9]

2.3   Alternate director

Broadly, an alternate director is a person who is nominated by another director to act in that director's place during his absence from the company.[10] Alternate directors may only be appointed if the company's articles expressly so provide; for example, Table A[11] provides that: 'any director (other than an alternate director) may appoint any other director or any other person approved by resolution of the directors and willing to act, to be an alternate director and may remove from office an alternate director so appointed by him'.

2.4   Connected person

If the restrictions on directors' transactions extended solely to directors, they could easily be circumvented by the company making, say, a loan to the director's spouse or a company controlled by him. The concept of the connected person seeks to close this loophole.

A person is connected with a director if (not being a director himself) he is:

(a)   that director's spouse, child or step-child (legitimate or otherwise) under the age of 18; or

(b)   a body corporate with which the director is associated.

Broadly speaking, a company is associated with a director if the director and his connected persons are either interested in at least 20% of the company's equity share capital or are entitled to exercise or control more than 20% of the voting power in general meeting.

The director's interest may be direct (i.e. he personally owns the shares or controls the votes) or indirect (i.e. a company that he controls owns the shares or controls the votes). In this latter context, a director will have control of a company (X Co.) if:

(i)   he and his connected persons are interested in X Co.'s equity share capital or are entitled to exercise voting power at a general meeting of X Co.; and

(ii)   he, his connected persons and fellow directors are together interested in more than 50% of X Co.'s share capital or are entitled to exercise more than 50% of the voting power in general meeting.

In order to determine whether or not a company is associated with or controlled by a director, another company with which the director is associated is only deemed to be connected with him if connected by virtue of (c) or (d) below; similarly for these purposes, a trustee of a trust, the beneficiaries of which include another company with which the director is associated, is not thereby deemed to be connected with the director;

(c)   a person acting as trustee of any trust, the beneficiaries of which include the director or his family or a company with which the director is associated. In addition, where the director or his family or an associated company is the object of a discretionary trust, the trustee thereof is also deemed to be a connected person. Trustees of employee share or pension schemes are excluded;

(d)   a partner of the director or any person connected with him by virtue of (a) to (c) above;

(e)   a Scottish firm in which the director or a connected person is a partner, or in which a partner is a Scottish firm in which the director or a connected person is a partner.[12]

These provisions are complex and may be illustrated in the following example:

Example 28.1

Mr A owns 40% of the equity capital of Company X, and his wife and his daughter, aged 17, each hold 6% of the company's equity capital. Company X holds 12% of the equity capital of Company Y. Mr A's partner, Mr B, holds 13% of Company Y's equity capital.

Company X is clearly a connected person of Mr A; he and members of his family are interested in more than 20% of the company's equity capital.

The position of Company Y is more difficult. In order to determine whether Company Y is connected with Mr A, Company X's interest in Company Y's equity capital must initially be disregarded.[13] However, Mr A, by virtue of his family's holdings in Company X, is deemed to control the company (i.e. the total holding of Mr A and his connected persons is 52% of Company X's equity capital).[14] Company Y therefore, is connected with Mr A because he is deemed to have an interest in 25% of the company's equity capital (since Mr B's 13% stake in Company Y is added to Company X's holding of 12%).[15]

It should be noted that FRS 8 presumes that 'close family' members of a director are related parties for the purposes of that standard (see Chapter 27 at 2.2.4 A). The definition of 'close family' is likely to encompass more than just the family members mentioned in (a) above. Thus transactions which may escape disclosure under the Companies Act may need to be disclosed under FRS 8.

2.5   Officer

The statutory definition of officer encompasses directors, managers and company secretaries.[16] This definition is not, however, exhaustive and it would appear that the term extends to any person who exercises a significant degree of managerial power; for example, a financial controller of a company is likely to be an officer, whereas a branch manager of a bank is not.

2.6   Loan

There is no statutory definition of a loan for the purpose of the legislation. However, the term has been judicially defined as 'a sum of money lent for a time, to be returned in money or money's worth'.[17] It is crucial to this definition that the parties to the agreement intend that the amount will be repaid. Recurring problems in this context arise where a director draws remuneration on account or expense advances. Such drawings may constitute a loan depending on the particular circumstances. There is no litmus test which can be applied in determining whether, say, a salary advance is in fact a loan; it is necessary to examine each transaction to decide whether in light of all the facts the director is really receiving an interest free loan. The example below illustrates this problem:

Example 28.2

Mr A, a director of Company Y, draws an expense advance of £9,000, on 1 January 1999. By the end of the financial year (31 December 1999), the director has only incurred business expenditure of £2,500 and the outstanding sum is then repaid. Ordinary expense advances would not normally fall within the scope of the legislation because such advances are made on the understanding that the director will apply the funds in performance of his duties to the company. However, in these circumstances the funds have remained outstanding for an unusually long period and, prima facie, the advance appears to have taken on the nature of a loan.

2.7   Quasi-loan

This is a transaction under which one party (the creditor) pays a sum on behalf of another (the borrower) or reimburses expenditure incurred by a third party for the borrower, in circumstances:

(a)   where the borrower (or a person on his behalf) will reimburse the creditor; or

(b)   which gives rise to a liability on the borrower to reimburse the creditor.[18]

A quasi-loan will only arise where the borrower is under an obligation to reimburse the expenditure incurred by the company. Quasi-loans commonly arise where a director is permitted to use a company credit card to pay for private and business expenditure and he undertakes to reimburse the company in respect of personal expenses charged to the card. Likewise, if a company pays a director's household bills on the understanding that the expenses will be recouped by making a deduction from his monthly salary, a quasi-loan will arise.

The following example shows the distinction between a loan and a quasi-loan:

Example 28.3

A director of Company X wishes to buy a painting for £2,000 which is coming up for sale, but will not have the money at that time. If he draws a cheque for £2,000 from the company made payable to himself so that he can buy the painting then, assuming he intends to repay this sum, this will constitute a loan as it is 'a sum of money lent for a time, to be returned in money or money's worth'. If, however, he arranges for the company to pay for the painting on his behalf in the meantime, with the intention that he will repay the company at a later date, then this will be a quasi-loan.

2.8   Credit transaction

This is a transaction whereby a person either:

(a)   supplies any goods or sells any land under a hire-purchase agreement or a conditional sale agreement; or

(b)   leases or hires any land or goods in return for periodical payments; or

(c)   otherwise disposes of land or supplies goods or services on the understanding that payment (whatever form it may take) is to be deferred;

i.e. repayment need not be made by means of instalment but could be made by means of a single lump sum.[19]

In this context, services are defined as anything other than goods or land.[20]

The examples below indicate two of the many forms which a credit transaction may assume:

Example 28.4

A property company leases a residence to a director in return for monthly rental payments. This constitutes a credit transaction under (b) above, irrespective of whether the rental payments are made in advance or arrears. Consideration should also be given to whether this arrangement gives rise to a benefit-in-kind which requires disclosure (see 2.3.2 of Chapter 29).

If, however, the lease was rent-free then it would not be a credit transaction as there are no periodical payments.

Alternatively, if the company had granted the director a one year lease but he had made a lump sum payment covering the term of the lease at the outset, then again the transaction would not have constituted a credit transaction, as there would have been no periodical payments.

Example 28.5

A director of a company which repairs motor vehicles has his motor car serviced by the company and payment is to be effected by a single deduction from his following month's salary. The company normally requires payment immediately after the work has been done. This constitutes a credit transaction under (c) above, as payment has been deferred.

However, what if the company's normal procedure was to invoice customers for work done and request payment 30 days after the date of invoice, and the date the amount is to be deducted from the director's salary falls before the date the invoice would be due for payment?

It is unclear whether or not this would constitute a credit transaction, since the legislation does not define what is meant by 'deferred'. It could be argued that this is not a credit transaction as payment is not deferred beyond normal credit terms. However, the legislation makes no reference to normal credit terms and the service would thus appear to require disclosure as a credit transaction.

There is, however, a degree of overlap between credit and material interest transactions and, therefore, those transactions referred to in the above examples which are not credit transactions might require disclosure as material interest transactions (see 3.5 below) or under the requirements of FRS 8 (see generally Chapter 27).

3 DISCLOSURE REQUIREMENTS

3.1 Introduction

A director (including a shadow director) of a company who is interested in a contract with the company must declare the nature of that interest to the board.[21] In this context, transactions include loans, quasi-loans and credit transactions[22] (see E of the Appendix below).

A considerable level of disclosure is required in the notes to both group and individual company financial statements in respect of transactions with directors (including shadow directors).[23] Even where the holding company is not required to produce group accounts by virtue of one of the statutory exemptions (for example, because it is itself a wholly owned subsidiary or the group qualifies as a small or medium-sized group), these requirements still apply in full,[24] and therefore, for example, require disclosure of transactions between the directors and subsidiaries.

If the notes to the financial statements do not disclose the required details of directors' transactions, it is the auditors' duty to include the relevant information in their audit report 'so far as they are reasonably able to do so'.[25]

3.2 Scope

A company's financial statements must disclose transactions between the following:[26]

(a) the company and its directors and their connected persons;

(b) the company's subsidiaries (including non-UK subsidiaries) and its directors and connected persons thereof;

(c) the company, its subsidiaries and the directors (and their connected persons) of any holding company of the company.

A company need not disclose details of transactions entered into between the company or its subsidiaries and directors (and their connected persons) of the subsidiaries (provided the director is not also a director of the company or its holding company).

It should be noted that the term 'subsidiary undertaking' (see Chapter 5 at 1.2.2) does not apply in this context and therefore transactions entered into by such entities, which are not also 'subsidiaries', with a director of the company or any holding company, will not require to be disclosed.

The multiplicity of disclosures which may ensue from a single transaction are detailed below:

Example 28.6

Assume the following group structure:

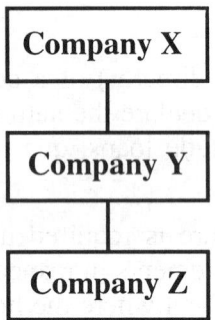

Companies Y and Z are both wholly owned subsidiaries of Company X. Company Z undertakes to guarantee a loan made by a bank to Mr A, a director of company X. The guarantee will be disclosed as follows:

(a)   in the financial statements of Company Z as a guarantee of a loan to a director of its holding company;

(b)   in the financial statements of Company Y as a guarantee of a loan by a subsidiary to a director of its holding company;

(c)   in the financial statements of Company X as a guarantee of a loan by a subsidiary to a director.

These requirements do not apply to banking companies under the Banking Act 1987, which are subject to separate disclosure provisions (see 4 below).[27]

3.3   Transactions requiring disclosure

Broadly, the legislation[28] requires disclosure of two types of transaction involving directors, namely:

(a)   loans, quasi-loans, credit transactions, related guarantees,[29] assignments and arrangements (section 330 type transactions); and

(b)   transactions (other than section 330 type transactions) in which a director has a material interest.

The disclosure provisions apply irrespective of whether:

(a)   the transaction was lawful;

(b)   the person for whom the transaction was made was at the time of its execution a director or a connected person; or

(c)   the company was a subsidiary at the time the transaction was executed.[30]

For example, details of the following transactions would need to be disclosed in a company's financial statements:

(a)   a loan made to an employee who later becomes a director; for example:

Extract 28.1: BAA plc (1999)

3   Directors' remuneration [extract]

At 31 March 1999 the company had outstanding an £18,958 interest free loan to Mr Collie. The loan was made on 1 August 1992, prior to his appointment to the BAA board, for relocation purposes. At 1 April 1998 the loan was £21,458, its maximum for the year.

(b)   a contract entered into with a director who retired during the financial year; for example:

Extract 28.2: Cable and Wireless plc (1999)

DIRECTORS' REPORT [extract]

Directors' remuneration

After his resignation as a Director [on 26 June 1998] payments of £122,500 were made to Sir Brian Smith for consultancy services and his continuing Non-executive Directorship of Hong Kong Telecommunications Limited.

(c)   a credit transaction entered into with a director of another company which then becomes the reporting company's parent.

3.4   Section 330 transactions

3.4.1   *Introduction*

Details of these transactions must be disclosed in both group and individual company financial statements (subject to various exemptions: see 3.6 below).[31]

Thus, disclosure must be made where any company:

(a)   makes a loan or a quasi-loan to, or enters into a credit transaction with, or enters into a guarantee or provides any security in connection therewith for one of its directors, a director of its holding company or a connected person thereof;

(b)   arranges for the assignment to it, or the assumption by it, of any rights or obligations or liabilities under a transaction that would have contravened section 330 if the company had originally entered into it (see B.3 of the Appendix below);

(c)   takes part in any arrangement such that another person enters into a transaction that would have contravened section 330 had the company entered into it (see B.4 of the Appendix below);

(d)   agrees to enter into any of the above transactions or arrangements.

3.4.2   *Disclosure requirements*

The particulars to be disclosed are the principal terms of the transaction, arrangement or agreement.[32] The principal terms must include, as a minimum:[33]

(a) a statement of the fact that the transaction was made or existed during the financial year;

(b) the name of the person for whom it was made and, if this person is connected with a director, that director's name;

(c) for loans (including agreements and arrangements relating thereto):

(i) the principal and interest at the beginning and the end of the financial year,

(ii) the maximum amount outstanding during the year,

(iii) the amount of any interest due but unpaid,

(iv) the amount of any provision in respect of non-payment of the loan;

(d) for guarantees and security:

(i) the potential liability of the company (or its subsidiary) at the beginning and the end of the financial year,

(ii) the maximum potential liability of the company (or its subsidiary),

(iii) any amount paid and any liability incurred by the company in fulfilling the security or discharging the security;

(e) for quasi-loans and credit transactions, it is necessary to disclose the value of the transaction. The value of a quasi-loan is defined as the maximum amount which the person to whom the quasi-loan is made is liable to reimburse the creditor. In the case of a credit transaction, value is defined as the price which it is reasonable to expect could be obtained for the goods, land or services to which the transaction or arrangement relates if they had been supplied in the ordinary course of business and on the same terms (apart from price) as they have been supplied, under the transaction or arrangement in question.[34] Although the legislation does not specify the extent of disclosures, given that details of any transaction subsisting during the year must be disclosed, it would be relevant for the disclosures to be similar to those for loans (see (c) above).

In addition to the above, it may be necessary to disclose other principal terms of the transaction; for example, the repayment term in the case of a loan or the credit limit for credit transactions and quasi-loans.

The following extracts illustrate a variety of section 330 type transactions:

A   Loans

Extract 28.3: Friends' Provident Life Office (1996)

10.   LOANS TO DIRECTORS [extract]

	Amount outstanding 1 January 1996 £	31 December 1996 £	Maximum outstanding during the year £
K. Satchell House purchase loan (repaid during year)	30,000	-	30,000

The loan was secured by mortgage on the property and by a life assurance policy on the life of the borrower. The rate of interest payable was 4% p.a. on the first £15,000 and 8% p.a. on the remainder. The loan was made by the Office on the same terms as were available to other employees.

Extract 28.4: Cordiant plc (1996)

Remuneration and Nominations Committee report[extract]

On appointment to the Board on 9 January 1995, Mr Bungey already had a loan from the Company which totalled US$261,699 including interest charged at US prime rate. At 31 December 1995, he owed US$79,400 (which included interest of US$4,400) which was repaid in full in April 1996. During 1996, the maximum amount outstanding was US$81,144. There are no outstanding loans granted by any member of the Group to any of the Directors or guarantees provided by any member of the Group for their benefit.

It can be seen from the above extracts that, even though there are no amounts outstanding at the year end, disclosure is required; this is because the transactions *existed* during the period. This would also be the case where there are no amounts outstanding at either the beginning or the end of the year. (An example of this is shown in Extract 28.8 below in respect of a quasi-loan.)

Similarly, even if the individual concerned is no longer a director at the year end, disclosure would be required; this is because the loan was in respect of someone who was a director at some time during the financial year.

B   Guarantees and security

Extract 28.5: The Body Shop International PLC (1996)

7   Directors [extract]

Transactions involving Directors

Prior to her appointment as a Director on 25 July 1994, the Company provided a bank guarantee in respect of J Reid. This guarantee had been cleared to nil by 2 March 1996 (1995: £73,750).

C   *Credit transactions*

Extract 28.6: First Leisure Corporation PLC (1998)

23   Transactions with related parties [extract]

(ii) Directors

Mr Bollom, through a company controlled by him, had an interest in a lease of property owned by the Group in Blackpool. Payments under this lease in the year ended 31st October 1998 amounted to £0.4m (1997: £0.4m). The property was disposed of in September 1998.

Extract 28.7: The Body Shop International PLC (1996)

7   Directors [extract]

Transactions involving Directors

M J Ross owns jointly with his wife all the shares in Craigross Holdings Limited ("Craigross"), subsidiaries of which hold six franchises with the Company.

...

In common with the arrangements with other UK franchisees, the Company has leased the premises relating to three of the franchised outlets to Craigross and has guaranteed the lease commitments on the three other shops. The annual rentals payable in respect of the premises leased to Craigross by the Company were £0.267 million (1995: £0.227 million). ...

D   *Quasi-loans*

Extract 28.8: Chrysalis Group PLC (1998)

26   Related party transactions [extract]

c   During the year a quasi loan was made to C N Wright. The highest amount outstanding in the year was £15,522. The amount outstanding at 31st August 1998 was £nil (1997: £nil).

3.5   Material interest transactions

3.5.1   Introduction

The group and individual company financial statements must disclose details of transactions or arrangements in which any person who was a director of the company, its holding company or a connected person thereof had a material interest (subject to various exemptions: see 3.6 below).[35] Section 330 type transactions are excluded from this category.[36]

It is for the directors to determine whether a transaction is material.[37] For these purposes, a transaction is not material if the directors of the reporting company (or at least a majority of them), excluding the director whose interest is under review, decide that it is not.[38] However, if the directors do not consider the question of materiality, it cannot be presumed that the interest was immaterial.[39]

In these circumstances, the question of the materiality of the transaction will be regarded as a matter of fact.

3.5.2   *Definition of material interest*

The definition of 'material' has proved to be one of the more problematic issues in this area of the law. There are two widely accepted interpretations; namely, that 'material':

(a)   should be judged by what is relevant to the users of the financial statements (the relevant view). Rumbelow[40] suggests that the rationale for this disclosure requirement is to ensure that shareholders are better informed about their directors and better able to take any decisions they may have to take as shareholders (particularly as regards those directors). Consequently, he reasons that to decide what is material, one must look to see if the interest is such that its disclosure would be likely to influence a reasonable shareholder in making those decisions;

(b)   means substantial in relation to the individual transaction in which the director is interested (the 'Mars Bar' view). Proponents of this view claim that the wording of the provision points to this interpretation.

However, as the following example illustrates, the 'Mars Bar' view may give rise to curious results:

Example 28.7

A director arranges a £50m contract on behalf of his company; the agreement provides for an arrangement fee of ½% of the value of the contract (i.e. commission of £250,000). The director will not need to disclose his interest if the 'Mars Bar' approach is adopted because his interest in the transaction is insignificant in relation to that transaction. However, if a director purchases a bar of chocolate for himself in the staff restaurant, the 'Mars Bar' view would demand disclosure of this transaction (subject to the de minimis exceptions: see 3.6.3 below); in this instance, he has a 100% interest in the transaction.

There is a third possible interpretation; namely, that material must be determined by reference to the director's financial position. Proponents of this view argue that if a transaction is not material vis-à-vis the director's personal position, there will be no conflict of duty and interest. However, the jurisprudence in this area makes it clear that the courts will not look into the merits of a transaction but adhere strictly to the rule that the possible conflict of interest and duty must not be allowed to arise, hence this rationale is somewhat spurious. On a practical note, if this view were adopted curious results could arise, as shown in the following example:

Example 28.8

Mr M, a director of ABC plc, has amassed a personal fortune of £10m. The latest audited accounts of ABC plc show net assets of £50,000 and turnover of £200,000. XYZ plc, a company of which Mr M is the majority shareholder, enters into a contract to buy goods worth £20,000 from ABC plc. Arguably, if the foregoing basis of assessing materiality is used, the transaction would not require disclosure.

On balance, we prefer the relevant view since its application is most likely to satisfy the needs of the users (or potential users) of the accounts, by keeping them informed of the types of dealing between a company and its directors which impact upon investment, credit and other decisions which they may be required to take. Clearly, this test involves the making of a qualitative judgement, that is, whether disclosure of the transaction might make a difference to a business decision. In practice, as Swinson argues,[41] this qualitative assessment may often be answered by establishing whether a director's interest is material in quantitative terms. If an interest is immaterial in quantitative terms, it may be irrelevant to the users of the accounts and vice-versa.

It should be emphasised that the above discussion of 'material' is only in the context of whether the transaction requires disclosure as a result of the Companies Act. However, this will not be the end of the matter in determining whether disclosure is necessary in the accounts because the requirements of FRS 8 also apply. As discussed at 2.3.2 in Chapter 27, FRS 8 requires that in considering whether transactions with individuals (such as directors) need to be disclosed, materiality has to be judged not only in terms of their significance to the reporting entity but also in relation to the other party, which in this case is the director.

The effect of FRS 8 has been that more transactions with directors are now disclosed than hitherto under the Companies Act requirements.

3.5.3 *Disclosure requirements*

The principal terms of material interest transactions must be disclosed;[42] in particular:

(a) the name of the director who has the material interest and the nature thereof;[43]

(b) the value of the transaction.[44]

The types of transaction in which a director may have an interest are diverse: the purchase or disposal of residential properties, other arrangements in respect of such property which arise due to the relocation of the directors, purchase or disposal of investments or businesses, provision of professional services and transactions in the ordinary course of business. Some of these are illustrated in the following extracts:

Extract 28.9: The Royal Bank of Scotland Group plc (1998)

50 Transactions with directors, officers and others [extract]

(b) Dr G. R. Mathewson, a director and chief executive of the company and the Bank, has a right to repurchase from the Bank his former dwellinghouse which the Bank purchased from him and his wife in May 1988 at a price of £125,000. The right will become exercisable (1) in the event that Dr Mathewson ceases to be an executive director of the company or its subsidiaries; or (2) on 31st May 2008 in the event that he remains an executive director at that date; or (3) on such earlier date as the directors of the company may allow. Any repurchase is to be at the higher of the purchase price paid by the Bank or a price determined by independent professional valuation at the time of repurchase. The dwellinghouse is at present let by the Bank on commercial basis, with any rentals being received wholly by the Bank.

Extract 28.10: Coats Viyella Plc (1998)

Report by the Board on Directors' Remuneration [extract]

In 1992 the Company, through a subsidiary, acquired a joint interest in a property with Mr Flower on his taking permanent residence in England. The subsidiary's investment was £180,000. Under the agreement Mr Flower has the option to purchase the Group's interest at market value. The Group's investment was reduced to £75,000 in January 1994 following partial exercise of Mr Flower's option.

Extract 28.11: Alfred McAlpine PLC (1996)

14. Fixed Assets – Investments [extract]

During 1996, the Group completed the deferred consideration payments to the Grove family in respect of the acquisition of the minority holding of Alfred McAlpine Homes Holdings Limited (formerly Alfred McAlpine Developments Limited). Mr E W Grove is a former director of both the Company and Alfred McAlpine Homes Holdings Limited. The final element of the deferred consideration was agreed at £15,242,000 and was settled during the year by cash payments of £7,621,000, plus interest of £99,000, and the issue of ordinary shares in the Company to the Grove family to the value of £7,621,000.

(Mr Grove resigned as a non-executive director during the year, on 22 July 1996.)

Extract 28.12: Rio Tinto plc and Rio Tinto Limited (1998)

36 RELATED PARTY TRANSACTIONS [extract]

Mr L A Davis occupied, without payment of rent, accommodation in central London under a licence agreement granted by a subsidiary company. The value based on the estimated market rent was £201,504.

This extract highlights the fact that the value of the transaction is not necessarily the amount at which the transaction is transacted, but is the amount which could have been obtained in the ordinary course of business.[45]

Where the value of the transaction cannot be expressed as a specific amount of money, then it is deemed to exceed £100,000,[46] as the following extract shows:

Extract 28.13: British Gas plc (1991)

3. Directors and employees [extract]

Norman Blacker was required to relocate during the year ended 31 March 1990 and Cedric Brown during the year ended 31 March 1991. Norman Blacker participated in the Company's relocation scheme throughout the period to December 1991 and Cedric Brown until May 1991. The value of these arrangements cannot be expressed as a specific sum of money and in these circumstances the Companies Act 1985 provides that the value is individually deemed to exceed £100 000. During 1991 approximately 570 employees participated in this scheme, which complies with Inland Revenue guidelines.

Extract 28.14: Kwik-Fit Holdings plc (1999)

9.   DIRECTORS' REMUNERATION AND INTERESTS [extract]

(d)   Transactions

Sir Tom and Lady Farmer and family lease certain properties to the Group. The rentals payable on these properties were £348,837 (1998 – £341,000) and the balance owing by the Group at 28 February 1999 was Nil (1998 – Nil).

E. Landau is a partner in Landau Nock who received professional fees and reimbursement of expenses of £476,933 (1998 – £479,578) in relation to services provided to the Group during the year. The balance owing to Landau Nock at 28 February 1999 was Nil (1998 – Nil).

J. Padget is a Principal of Padget Associates B.V. who received fees of £65,623 (1998 – £107,446) and reimbursement of expenses of £10,562 (1998 – £16,002) in relation to services provided to the Group during the year in addition to the Director's fees shown in (a) above. The balance owing to Padget Associates B.V. at 28 February was Nil (1998 – £53,439).

The above extract illustrates the situation where a professional firm, such as solicitors, in which one of the directors is a partner, provide services to the company in the ordinary course of business.

Disclosure of such transactions is not required where the firm, or company, providing the services is not a connected person as defined by the Act (see 2.4 above); for example, where the director concerned is not a partner in the firm providing the services, but is merely a consultant. Nevertheless some companies disclose information about such transactions within the directors' report, presumably to meet the requirements of the Stock Exchange (see 5 below). One company which disclosed such a transaction, but within the notes to the accounts, as well as numerous other directors' interests in transactions is Chrysalis Group, as shown below:

Extract 28.15: Chrysalis Group PLC (1998)

26   Related party transactions [extract]

a   Sir George Martin has an interest in certain subsidiary undertaking's agreements with Airborn Productions Limited and Airborn Production (Overseas) Limited by virtue of his share interests in those companies. The producer royalties payable to these companies in respect of the year were £121,949 (1997: £115,362). The amount accrued (but not due) at the balance sheet date was £12,161 (1997: £14,010).

b   Sir George Martin was paid a contractual royalty advance of £32,500 (1997: £nil) by Echo Label Limited in connection with an album released during the year.

...

d   S G Lewis has an interest in a subsidiary company The Echo Label Limited by virtue of his interest in the share capital of Armourvale Limited ('Armourvale') and Lapishaven Limited ('Lapishaven'), two companies which together hold 75% of the share capital of The Echo Label Limited. Mr Lewis' interest in The Echo Label Limited amounts to 18.75% of its capital. Certain put and call option agreements exist between the Group and Mr Lewis in respect of his shares in Armourvale and Lapishaven other than his B shares in Lapishaven, as referred to in note 25a [below].

e   C J C Levison has, since 1st August 1994, been a consultant with one of the Group's solicitors, Harbottle & Lewis. Mr Levison received fees from Harbottle & Lewis through his company, Clarion Media Europe Limited. All fees paid to Harbottle & Lewis are on ordinary commercial terms incurred in the normal course of the Group's business. Neither Mr Levison nor Clarion Media Europe Limited participate in any fees or profits of Harbottle & Lewis relating to the Group, or any of its subsidiary or joint venture companies.

f   From 1st September 1996 the services of C N Wright provided to Loftus Road plc (a company in which Mr Wright has a beneficial interest of 30% of the issued share capital and of which he, Mr Butterfield and Mr Levison are all non-executive directors) are being reimbursed to Chrysalis Group PLC at a rate of £8,000 per month. The amount outstanding at 31st August 1998 was £28,000. Notice was serviced by Loftus Road plc on 28th September 1998 of its intention to terminate these arrangements from 28th September 1999.

There are no provisions for doubtful debts or amounts written off during the year in respect of any of the above transactions.

25   Capital commitments [extract]

a   Under the terms of the Option Agreement dated 29th November 1993 between the Group and Mr S G Lewis, set out in the circular to shareholders dated 30th November 1993, the Group may be required to purchase certain of Mr Lewis' shares in Armourvale Limited and Lapishaven Limited (which holds the Group's interest in The Echo Label Limited. Mr Lewis may exercise this put option at any time after 1st September 1998 whilst he is still employed by the Company, or within 30 days of the subsequent termination of his employment, for a consideration based upon the fair market value of the shares, and capped at £10 million.

3.6   Exemptions from disclosure

The following transactions involving directors do not require disclosure:

3.6.1   *General*

(a)   Transactions between companies in which a director is interested only by virtue of his being a director of both companies;[47]

(b) directors' service contracts.[48] However, details of service contracts of directors of listed companies may require disclosure (see 4.4.10 of Chapter 29);

(c) transactions which were not entered into or which did not subsist during the year.[49] However, transactions which were entered into after the year end will require disclosure if at the year end there was an agreement between the parties to enter into the transaction.[50] In addition, material transactions involving directors post year-end may fall to be disclosed as post balance sheet events in accordance with the provisions of SSAP 17 (see Chapter 24).

3.6.2 Section 330 transactions

(a) Credit transactions and related guarantees, arrangements and agreements where the aggregate amount outstanding for the director and his connected persons did not at any time during the financial year exceed £5,000;[51]

(b) there is a reduced level of disclosure for intra-group loans and quasi-loans,[52] although relief has not been granted for guarantees, credit transactions etc. The only details to be disclosed in respect of such transactions are:

   (i)   a statement that the transaction etc. was made or subsisted during the financial year;

   (ii) the name of the person for whom it was made and in the case of a loan or quasi-loan to a connected person, the name of the director.

This exemption only applies if there are no minority interests involved.

3.6.3 Material interest transactions

(a) Transactions in which the director's interest is not material (as decided by a majority of his fellow directors);[53]

(b) transactions in which a director has a material interest which are entered into at arm's length in the ordinary course of business.[54] This exemption has given rise to particular difficulty. It is sometimes argued that the exemption, as presently drafted, only applies if each party to the transaction is a member of the same group. The explanatory note to the statutory instrument[55] which introduced the exemption indicates that there is no need for the counterparties to the transaction to be group companies. Given that one of the aims of introducing the exemption was to reduce the level of disclosure, it seems logical to interpret the provision as exempting all arm's length material interest transactions involving directors. This view, however, is not universally held.[56]

(c) any material interest transaction between members of a group of companies which would have been disclosable only because of a director being associated (see 2.4 above) with the contracting companies, provided that no minority interests in the reporting company are affected.[57] A higher level of disclosure is required where there are minority interests since minorities can be affected by transfers of value within a group. The wording of this exemption is arcane and the drafting is considered to be defective;

(d)   transactions in which a director had a material interest where the value of each transaction (with no reduction in the amount outstanding) in the financial year and the value of transactions in preceding financial years (less the amount by which the director's liabilities have been reduced) did not at any time during the financial year exceed £1,000 or, if more than £1,000, did not exceed £5,000 or 1% of the value of the net assets of the reporting company. Net assets is defined as the aggregate of the company's assets, less the aggregate of its liabilities.[58] It is not clear how this provision interacts with the other exemptions for material interest transactions (see (b) and (c) above). Unless these provisions are discrete, the exemptions are likely to be rendered ineffective.

Whether the effect of any of these exemptions will result in non-disclosure of the relevant transactions in the accounts will depend on whether or not FRS 8 requires disclosure of the transactions. As noted at 3.5.2 above, FRS 8 has a different concept of materiality; it also requires transactions to be disclosed even when the terms are at arm's length. Companies should therefore ensure that, before relying on any of the exemptions above, they have considered the requirements of FRS 8 (see generally Chapter 27).

4   BANKING COMPANIES UNDER THE BANKING ACT 1987

A banking company under the Banking Act 1987 is subject to different disclosure requirements in respect of section 330 type transactions to which the company is a party.[59] Material interest transactions involving directors of banking companies must be disclosed as for other companies (see 3.5 above).[60] Similar requirements apply to a company which is the holding company of a credit institution. References to banking companies below should be read as including such companies.

In brief,[61] banking companies must maintain a register of section 330 type transactions for the current and preceding ten financial years.[62] A statement of such transactions must be:[63]

(a)   made available for members to inspect; and

(b)   examined and reported on by the company's auditor.

4.1   Disclosure of transactions by banking companies

The financial statements must disclose:

(a)   the aggregate amounts of loans, quasi-loans, credit transactions and related transactions outstanding at the end of the financial year; and

(b)   the number of persons for whom the transactions were made.[64]

In this context,[65] amount outstanding means the outstanding liabilities of the person for whom the transaction was made and as respects a guarantee or security, the amount guaranteed or secured.

The following extract provides an illustration of the disclosures of transactions between a banking company and its directors:

Extract 28.16: National Westminster Bank Plc (1998)

49   Transactions with related parties [extract]

i   The aggregate amounts outstanding at 31 December 1998 under transactions, arrangements and agreements made by institutions authorised under the Banking Act 1987 within the Group for persons who are, or were, directors of the Bank during the year and their connected persons, and with executive officers listed on page 60 and their connected persons comprised the following:–

	Number of directors/ officers	Number of connected persons	Aggregate amount £000
Directors and their connected persons			
Loans and credit card transactions	5	8	61
Other executive officers			
Loans and credit card transactions	19	5	904

It must be emphasised that these disclosures only apply to section 330 type transactions with the banking company. The disclosure requirements outlined in 3.4.2 above still apply to any such transaction with other companies within the group.

5   STOCK EXCHANGE REQUIREMENTS

In addition to the disclosure provisions imposed by the Companies Act 1985 (and those of FRS 8 – see Chapter 27), the Stock Exchange imposes additional requirements in respect of transactions involving directors of listed companies.[66]

Transactions (other than those of a revenue nature in the ordinary course of business) involving directors, shadow directors, past directors of the company (or other member of the group) and their associates (similar to connected persons) constitute transactions with related parties (formerly known as Class 4 transactions).[67] Generally, full particulars of the transaction must be given in a circular including the name of the related party concerned and of the nature and extent of the interest of such party in the transaction.[68]

Normally these particulars should be circulated to the company's shareholders prior to obtaining their approval[69] and the Stock Exchange must also be notified of the proposed transaction.[70] A number of exceptions from the requirements are made, one of which is for small transactions provided that an independent adviser expresses the opinion that the terms of the transaction are fair and reasonable. Where this exception applies, the company must also disclose details of the transaction in the next published annual accounts, including the identity of the related party, the value of the consideration for the transaction and all other relevant circumstances.[71]

The annual report and accounts of listed companies must also disclose particulars of any contract of significance to which the company, or one of its subsidiary undertakings, is a party and in which a director of the company is or was materially interested.[72] A contract of significance is defined as one which represents in amount or value, a sum equal to 1% or more, calculated on a group basis where relevant, of:

(a)   in the case of a capital transaction or a transaction the principal purpose of which is the granting of credit, the aggregate of the group's share capital and reserves; or

(b)   in other cases, the total annual purchases, sales, payments or receipts, as the case may be, of the group.[73]

As a result of a change made to the requirements in June 1996, there is now no need to make a statement if there has been no such contract.

The Stock Exchange also imposes additional requirements on companies quoted on the Alternative Investment Market.

Where an AIM company proposes to enter into related party transactions (similar to those for listed companies) which result in specified percentage ratios being 5% or more then it must give particulars to the Stock Exchange and send a copy of the announcement to the shareholders.[74] Where any of the percentage ratios exceed 0.25%, then disclosure of the transaction must be made in the next set of published accounts, including the identity of the related party, the value of the consideration for the transaction and all other relevant circumstances.[75]

6   TRANSACTIONS INVOLVING OFFICERS

6.1   Introduction

The Act requires certain details of transactions between a company and its officers to be disclosed.[76] To this end, group and individual company financial statements must contain particulars in the notes of transactions entered into by officers. A holding company's financial statements must take into account transactions between the company and its subsidiaries with officers of the company; however, transactions between the subsidiaries and their officers do not need to be included in the holding company's financial statements. If a company does not produce group financial statements by virtue of one of the statutory exemptions, these requirements still apply in full.[77]

6.2   Disclosure requirements

The financial statements must disclose the following details in respect of transactions with officers (which, for these purposes, in order to avoid duplication of disclosure excludes directors):[78]

(a)   the aggregate amounts of loans, quasi-loans, credit transactions, guarantees and arrangements outstanding at the end of the financial year; and

(b)   the number of officers for whom the transactions were made.[79]

For these purposes, the amount outstanding is defined as the outstanding liabilities of the person for whom the transaction was made and in the case of a guarantee or security, the amount guaranteed or secured.[80]

Disclosure of such transactions is not, however, necessary for a particular officer if the aggregate amount outstanding under the transactions at the end of the financial year for that officer does not exceed £2,500.[81]

The following extracts illustrate the disclosure of transactions involving officers:

Extract 28.17: British Aerospace Public Limited Company (1998)

5   Employees and directors [extract]

Transactions

At 31 December, 1998 there was an aggregate balance of £695,601 (1997 £794,420) outstanding on house purchase loans made to or arranged for 10 officers (1997 11 officers) to assist with their relocation at the Company's request.

Extract 28.18: Imperial Chemical Industries PLC (1998)

41   Statutory and other information [extract]

Included in debtors is an interest-free loan of £8,000 (1997 £30,000) to an officer (1997 two officers) of the Company.

6.3   Banking companies under the Banking Act 1987

Financial statements of banking companies (or companies which are holding companies of credit institutions) do not generally require disclosure of transactions between officers (who were not also directors) and the banking company. However, the information described at 6.2 above is required to be disclosed in respect of transactions between the banking company (or as the case may be the credit institution) and a chief executive or manager of the company or its holding company.[82]

A 'chief executive' means a person who, either alone or jointly with one or more other persons, is responsible under the immediate authority of the directors for the conduct of the business of the company and a 'manager' means a person (other than a chief executive) who, under the immediate authority of a director or chief executive of the financial institution, exercises managerial functions or is responsible for maintaining accounts or other records of the financial institution.[83]

7   CONCLUSION

The provisions of the Companies Act governing the disclosure of transactions between a company and its directors and officers are generally regarded as unsatisfactory. They do not appear to form a coherent whole whereby a director's contractual freedom can be meaningfully regulated; for example, there are de minimis exemptions from disclosure of credit and material interest transactions yet no parallel provisions for loans and quasi-loans. In addition, aspects of the legislation are difficult to comprehend, for example, the material interest transaction exemptions.

Over the years various professional bodies have made representations to the DTI suggesting that the legislation be clarified and simplified. The Companies Act 1989 did make some minor amendments relating to this area, although it was indicated while the Bill was going through the parliamentary process that further changes would be made by Statutory Instrument.[84]

The DTI had indicated that it was the intention to review the legislation in this area, but that it was a long-term task. It did publish in 1991 a consultative document in which it proposed to simplify the rules contained in Schedule 6 to the Act, dealing with the information required to be disclosed in companies' financial statements, but nothing has ever come of it.[85]

In September 1998, the Law Commission and the Scottish Law Commission published a joint Consultation/Discussion Paper – *Company Directors: Regulating Conflicts of Interest and Formulating a Statement of Duties* – which considered this whole area. However, earlier in 1998 the Government had announced the launch of a fundamental review of the framework of core company law, and the Law Commissions' work covers ground which is part of the area in which that review will be making integrated proposals, principally in relation to corporate governance. It is therefore likely to be quite a while before there is any change to the legislation.

APPENDIX: LEGAL REQUIREMENTS

A   INTRODUCTION

Although the primary objective of this chapter is to discuss how transactions with directors should be disclosed in a company's financial statements, a brief exposition of the statutory provisions determining the legality of such transactions is considered necessary in order to place the disclosure requirements in context.

B   PROHIBITED TRANSACTIONS

The Companies Act 1985 contains complex provisions[86] which prohibit or restrict many transactions involving directors (and shadow directors).[87] The legality of a transaction is determined at the time of its execution. Therefore, a loan to a person who subsequently becomes a director is legal because the recipient was not a director at the time of its making.

The basic prohibitions are dealt with in B.1 to B.4 below and the exemptions therefrom are dealt with in C below.

B.1   Loans

A company may not make a loan to its directors or those of its holding company.[88] In addition, a relevant company[89] (i.e. a public company or a company which is part of a group which includes a public company) may not make a loan to a connected person thereof.[90] Likewise, a company may not enter into a guarantee[91] or provide any security in connection with a loan made by another person to its directors or those of its holding company[92] and, in the case of a relevant company, a connected person thereof.[93]

B.2   Quasi-loans and credit transactions

A relevant company may not make a quasi-loan nor enter into a credit transaction with its directors, the directors of its holding company or a connected person thereof. There is a similar restriction on the provision of guarantees or security in connection with such transactions.[94]

B.3   Assignment/assumption of rights, obligations or liabilities

A company may not arrange for the assignment to, or the assumption by it, of any rights, obligations or liabilities in respect of transactions which, if undertaken by the company in the first place, would have been unlawful;[95] for example:

Example 28.9

A bank makes a loan to a director of Company X and thereafter assigns its rights to Company X. The company will have entered into an unlawful assignment.

Example 28.10

The facts are as above, but the loan from the bank is guaranteed by a friend of the director. Subsequently, Company X becomes the guarantor of the loan releasing the director's friend from his obligations. The assumption of the guarantee by Company X is unlawful.

B.4 Arrangements

Schemes whereby a third party enters into an arrangement which if entered into by the company would have been unlawful, in circumstances where the company (or a fellow group company) provides a benefit to the third party, are not permitted;[96] for example:

Example 28.11

Company X arranges for a bank to make a loan to one of its directors on favourable terms in return for which the company places business with the bank. This series of transactions constitutes an unlawful arrangement whereby the bank enters into an arrangement forbidden to Company X and receives a benefit for so doing.

C EXEMPTED TRANSACTIONS

C.1 Loans of small amounts

A loan to a director of a company or its holding company is not illegal if the aggregate of the sums advanced to the director does not exceed £5,000; in computing the sum of £5,000, amounts already advanced to the director must be taken into account.[97] It should be noted that this exemption does not extend to loans of small amounts to connected persons of directors of a relevant company.

C.2 Short-term quasi-loans

Quasi-loans by a relevant company are permitted if made on the condition that the director reimburses the company within two months and where the aggregate of the sums outstanding under quasi-loans does not exceed £5,000.[98] Again, this exemption does not extend to quasi-loans made to connected persons of directors of a relevant company.

C.3 Minor or business credit transactions

A relevant company may enter in a credit transaction for a person if:

(a)   the aggregate of such amounts does not exceed £10,000;[99] or

(b)   the transaction is entered into by the company in the ordinary course of its business on terms which the company would have extended to a person of the same financial standing unconnected with the company.[100]

It should be noted that this exemption extends to credit transactions for connected persons of directors of a relevant company.

C.4   Inter-company transactions

A relevant company is not prohibited from making loans and quasi-loans to a group company where a director of one company is associated with another.[101] Likewise, a company may make a loan or quasi-loan to or enter into a credit transaction as creditor for its holding company.[102]

Furthermore, a holding company may make a loan to a director of its subsidiary or a connected person thereof; similarly, a subsidiary may make a loan to a director of a fellow subsidiary (provided in both cases that the director is not on the board of the company or the holding company and that the other group company does not thereby obtain some benefit: see B.4 above).

C.5   Directors' business expenditure

A director can be placed in funds to enable him properly to perform his duties as a corporate officer. However, funds may only be advanced:

(a)   if prior approval of the company in general meeting has been obtained; or

(b)   where approval is not obtained at or before the next annual general meeting, the loan is to be repaid within six months of the conclusion of that meeting.[103]

Furthermore, relevant companies may only advance an aggregate of £20,000 to the director for these purposes.[104]

C.6   Money-lending companies

A money-lending company (namely one whose ordinary business includes the making of loans or quasi-loans) may make loans or quasi-loans or enter into related guarantees to its directors, directors of its holding company and connected persons. However, such transactions are only permitted if made by the company in the ordinary course of its business on terms which are no more preferential than are available to persons who have no connection with the company. In addition, relevant companies (excluding banking companies: see 4 above) may make loans or quasi-loans only up to a £100,000 limit.[105]

Loans made for the purpose of facilitating the purchase of or improving a director's house may also be made by money-lending companies if the facility is ordinarily available to employees of the company on equally favourable terms; this exemption is again subject to a £100,000 limit for all companies.[106]

There is some doubt as to the interaction between the monetary limit on housing and 'other' loans to directors of relevant money-lending companies (which are not banking companies under the Banking Act 1987: see 4 above). This problem is compounded by what appears to be a drafting error[107] in references in section 339(1) which impacts upon how previous loans etc. made by money-lending companies are to be aggregated with amounts already advanced to directors and their connected persons. On balance, we believe that the intention of the legislation is that the aggregate value of all loans, whatever their nature, made by money-lending companies to any given director and his connected persons, must not exceed £100,000.

C.7   Companies registered overseas[108]

The following transactions entered into by an overseas company are not subject to the statutory restrictions; transactions entered into by an overseas incorporated subsidiary:

(a)   with a director of its UK incorporated parent; and

(b)   of a UK incorporated parent with a director of the UK parent's overseas incorporated holding company.

D   SANCTIONS

D.1   Civil remedies

A prohibited transaction is voidable at the company's option unless:

(a)   restitution is impossible, for example, where the proceeds of an illegal loan have been used to build an extension to the director's house; or

(b)   the company has been indemnified for the loss suffered by it; or

(c)   rights have been acquired by a bona fide purchaser for value who does not have notice of the contravention.[109]

The director, any connected person for whom the transaction was made and any director who authorised the transaction is liable:

(a)   to account for any gain which he has made; and

(b)   to make good any loss made by the company.[110]

However, where the transaction is made for a person connected with a director, then that director will not be liable if he can demonstrate that he took all reasonable steps to secure the company's compliance with the legislation.[111]

The person connected with the director and any other director who authorised the transaction will not be liable if he can demonstrate that at the time the transaction was entered into he did not know the circumstances constituting the contravention.[112]

D.2   Criminal penalties

A director of a relevant company who authorises or permits the company to enter into a transaction knowing or believing that the transaction was illegal is guilty of an offence and is liable to imprisonment and/or a fine. A relevant company entering into an illegal transaction is also guilty of an offence unless it did not know the circumstances at the time of the transaction. A person who knowingly procures the transaction or arrangement is also guilty of an offence.[113]

E   INTERESTS IN CONTRACTS

A director must, upon pain of a fine,[114] declare any interest (direct or indirect) in a contract with the company at a board meeting.[115] In this context, an interest in a section 330 type transaction requires disclosure[116] (see generally 3 above). If the contract is merely proposed, the director must declare his interest at the board meeting at which the contract is under consideration.[117] The Court of Appeal held in *Guinness plc v Saunders & Ward* [118] that this duty cannot be fulfilled by disclosure to a sub-committee of the board; only disclosure to a properly convened meeting of the full board will suffice. If the director was not interested in the contract at the time it was made, disclosure should be made at the first board meeting after the director becomes interested.[119] For these purposes, a general notice of interest in specific types of contracts given to the board suffices.[120]

Example 28.12

Mr A, a director of Company X is the majority shareholder in Company Y. Company X purchases quantities of stock from Company Y. Mr A must disclose his interest in such contracts to the board of Company X.

These requirements also apply to shadow directors who are required to make disclosure of interests in contracts by means of a written notice addressed to the board.[121]

In addition to the statutory restrictions, the company's articles may amplify the director's ability to enter into contracts. Thus, Table A provides that: 'Subject to the provisions of the Act, and provided that he has disclosed to the directors the nature and extent of any material interest of his, a director notwithstanding his office

(a)   may be a party to, or otherwise interested in, any transaction or arrangement with the company or in which the company is otherwise interested;

(b)   may be a director or other officer of, or employed by, a party to any transaction or arrangement with, or otherwise interested in, any body corporate promoted by the company or in which the company is otherwise interested; and

(c)   shall not, by reason of his office, be accountable to the company for any benefit which he derives from any such office or employment or from any such transaction or arrangement or from any interest in any such body corporate and no such transaction or arrangement shall be liable to be avoided on the ground of any such interest or benefit.'[122]

F   SUBSTANTIAL PROPERTY TRANSACTIONS

A director or connected person may not acquire from or sell to the company a non-cash asset[123] above the requisite value unless the transaction has been approved by the company in general meeting. If the transaction occurs between the company and a director or connected person of its holding company, the holding company's approval is also required.[124]

In this context, the requisite value of transactions is the lower of 10% of the company's net asset value or £100,000. This is subject to a de minimis threshold of £2,000, below which property transactions do not require approval.[125]

There are a number of exemptions from the requirement to obtain approval; for example, an acquisition of an asset of the requisite value:

(a)   by a director from a company which is a wholly owned subsidiary of another company, and

(b)   by a person from a company of which he is a member (i.e. a shareholder acting in his capacity as member), and

(c)   by one group company from another, provided there are no minority interests involved,

do not require approval. In addition, no approval is required for transactions entered into through an independent broker.[126]

A transaction entered into without the necessary approval is voidable at the company's option unless:

(a)   restitution of the property is impossible; or

(b)   rights to the property have been acquired by a bona fide purchaser for value who does not know that approval has not been obtained; or

(c)   the arrangement has been affirmed by the company (and if appropriate its holding company) in general meeting within a reasonable period.[127]

The director, any connected person for whom the transaction was made and any director who authorised the transaction is liable:

(a)   to account for any gain which he has made; and

(b)   to make good any loss made by the company.[128]

However, where the transaction is made for a person connected with a director, and that director can demonstrate that he took all reasonable steps to secure the company's compliance with these provisions,[129] he will escape liability.

The person connected with the director and any other director who authorised the transaction will not be liable if he can demonstrate that at the time the transaction was entered into he did not know the circumstances constituting the contravention.[130]

G   TRANSACTIONS INVOLVING OFFICERS

Officers, other than directors, are not subject to any statutory restrictions on their ability to transact with their company. A company's articles may address the contractual position of its officers, although Table A[131] is silent on this issue.

References

1 A person who holds anything in trust. A fiduciary relationship arises where a person has rights and powers which he is bound to exercise for the benefit of another. Hence he is not allowed to derive any profit or advantage from the relationship between them, except with the knowledge and consent of the other person: J. Burke, *Jowitt's Dictionary of English Law, Volume 1 A–K*, p. 788. If a director breaches this duty, a range of remedies is available to the company. The company may, inter alia, seek an injunction, claim damages or compensation, require the director to account for profits made or rescind contracts entered into with him.

2 CA 48, s 190(1).

3 *Ibid.*, s 190(1)(a).

4 CA 80, ss 49–50.

5 CA 85, ss 330–346, Sch. 6, Parts II and III.

6 *Ibid.*, s 741(1).

7 Companies should ensure that they do not allow persons described as divisional directors to hold themselves out as being members of the board. Otherwise there is a danger that contracts entered into by such persons, in excess of their managerial authority, may be binding on the company.

8 CA 85, s 741(2).

9 *Ibid.*, s 741(3).

10 The position of the alternate director is discussed in more detail in R. Pennington, *Company Law*, p. 628, and C. M. Schmithoff (ed.), *Palmer's Company Law Volume 1*, p. 879.

11 The Companies (Tables A–F) Regulations 1985 (SI 1985 No. 85), Table A, Article 65.

12 CA 85, s 346.

13 *Ibid.*, s 346(6)(a).

14 *Ibid.*, s 346(7) and Sch. 13, para. 5.

15 *Ibid.*, s 346(8).

16 *Ibid.*, s 744.

17 *Champagne Perrier–Jouet SA v H.H. Finch Ltd* [1982] 1 WLR 1359.

18 CA 85, s 331(3).

19 *Ibid.*, s 331(7).

20 *Ibid.*, 331(8).

21 *Ibid.*, ss 317(1), (8).

22 *Ibid.*, s 317(6).

23 *Ibid.*, ss 232(1)–(2) and Sch. 6, Part II.

24 *Ibid.*, Sch. 6, para. 15.

25 *Ibid.*, s 237(4).

26 *Ibid.*, s 232(1)–(2) and Sch. 6, paras. 15–16.

27 *Ibid.*, Sch. 9, Part IV.

28 *Ibid.*, s 232(1)–(2), and Sch. 6, paras. 15–16.

29 This includes indemnities: *ibid.*, s 331(2).

30 *Ibid.*, Sch. 6, para. 19.

31 *Ibid.*, ss 232(1)–(2) and Sch. 6, paras. 15(a)–(b) and 16(a)–(b).

32 *Ibid.*, Sch. 6, para. 22(1).

33 *Ibid.*, para. 22(2).

34 *Ibid.*, para. 27(c).

35 *Ibid.*, ss 232(1)–(2) and Sch. 6, paras. 15(c) and 16(c).

36 *Ibid.*, Sch. 6, paras. 15(c) and 16(c) refer to any 'other transaction or arrangement'.

37 *Ibid.*, para. 17(2). Materiality for these purposes should not be confused with the materiality level calculated for the purposes of the audit of the financial statements.

38 *Ibid.*, Assuming the directors' opinion is formed in good faith and is not perverse, their view should prevail. However, in extreme circumstances the directors' opinion may need to be overridden in order for the accounts to give a true and fair view.

39 *Ibid.*,

40 C. Rumbelow, 'When Directors Must Tell', *The Law Society's Gazette*, Wednesday 3 November 1982, pp. 1390–1392.

41　C. Swinson, 'Director's "Material interest" – just how do you measure it', *Accountancy*, October 1983, p. 110.
42　CA 85, Sch. 6, para. 22(1).
43　*Ibid.*, para. 22(2)(c).
44　*Ibid.*, para 22(2)(f).
45　*Ibid.*, s 340(6).
46　*Ibid.*, s 340(7).
47　*Ibid.*, Sch. 6, para. 18(a).
48　*Ibid.*, para. 18(b).
49　*Ibid.*, para. 18(c).
50　*Ibid.*, paras. 15(b) and 16(b).
51　*Ibid.*, para. 24.
52　*Ibid.*, para. 23.
53　*Ibid.*, para. 17(2).
54　*Ibid.*, para. 20.
55　SI 1984 No. 1860.
56　B. Johnson and M. Patient, *Accounting Provisions of the Companies Act 1985*, p. 270.
57　CA 85, Sch. 6, para. 21.
58　*Ibid.*, para. 25.
59　*Ibid.*, Sch. 9, Part IV, para. 2.
60　*Ibid.*, para. 3.
61　See generally *Ibid.*, ss 343–344.
62　*Ibid.*, s 343(2).
63　*Ibid.*, ss 343(5)–(6).
64　*Ibid.*, Sch. 9, Part IV, para. 3 and Sch. 6, Part III.
65　*Ibid.*, Sch. 6, para. 30.
66　*The Listing Rules*, London Stock Exchange, Chapter 11.
67　*Ibid.*, para. 11.1.
68　*Ibid.*, para. 11.10(c).
69　*Ibid.*, para. 11.4(c).
70　*Ibid.*, para. 11.3.
71　*Ibid.*, paras. 11.7 and 11.8.
72　*Ibid.*, Chapter 12, para. 12.43(q).
73　*Ibid.*, para. 12.44.
74　*Rules of the London Stock Exchange*, London Stock Exchange, Chapter 16: The Alternative Investment Market Admission Rules, rules 16.22–16.24. The percentage ratios are based on assets, profits, consideration to assets and consideration to market capitalisation.
75　*Ibid.*, rule 16.25.
76　CA 85, ss 232(1)–(2) and Sch. 6, Part III.
77　*Ibid.*, ss 232(1)–(2) and Sch. 6, para. 29.
78　*Ibid.*, Sch. 6, para. 29.
79　*Ibid.*, paras. 28 and 29(1).
80　*Ibid.*, para. 30.
81　*Ibid.*, para. 29(2).
82　*Ibid.*, Sch. 9, Part IV, para. 3(1).
83　Banking Act 1987, ss 105(6)–(7).
84　Hansard, *Parliamentary Debates*, 22 June 1989, Column 507.
85　DTI, *Consultative Document on Amendments to Schedule 6 to the Companies Act 1985: Disclosure by Companies of Dealings in favour of Directors*, October 1991.

Appendix

86　CA 85, ss 317, 320, 330–346.
87　*Ibid.*, ss 317(8), 320(3), 330(5).
88　*Ibid.*, s 330(2).
89　*Ibid.*, s 331(6).

90 *Ibid.*, s 330(2)(b).
91 This includes indemnities: *Ibid.*, s 331(2).
92 *Ibid.*, s 330(2)(b).
93 *Ibid.*, s 330(3)(c).
94 *Ibid.*, ss 330(3)–(4).
95 *Ibid.*, s 330(6).
96 *Ibid.*, s 330(7).
97 *Ibid.*, s 334. S 339 determines how the threshold is to be calculated.
98 *Ibid.*, s 332.
99 *Ibid.*, s 335(1). See also s 339.
100 *Ibid.*, s 335(2).
101 *Ibid.*, s 333.
102 *Ibid.*, s 336.
103 *Ibid.*, ss 337(1)–(3).
104 *Ibid.*, s 337(3). See also s 339.
105 *Ibid.*, ss 338(1)–(4). See also s 339.
106 *Ibid.*, s 338(6).
107 If the pre-consolidation legislation is to be reproduced accurately, the reference in s 339(1) to s 338(4) should actually be a reference to s 338(1).
108 The legislation applies to companies; that is, an entity formed and registered under the various Companies Acts: *Ibid.*, s 735. This definition applies unless the contrary intention appears: *Ibid.*, s 735(4). Since no contrary intention is expressed, a body incorporated overseas is not a company for the purposes of the directors' transactions provisions.
109 *Ibid.*, s 341(1).
110 *Ibid.*, s 341(2).
111 *Ibid.*, s 341(4).
112 *Ibid.*, s 341(5).
113 *Ibid.*, s 342.
114 *Ibid.*, 317(7).
115 *Ibid.*, s 317(1).
116 *Ibid.*, s 317(6).
117 *Ibid.*, s 317(2).
118 [1988] 1 WLR 863.
119 CA 85, s 317(2).
120 *Ibid.*, s 317(3).
121 *Ibid.*, s 317(8).
122 The Companies (Tables A–F) Regulations 1985, *op. cit*, Article 85.
123 CA 85, s 739(1).
124 *Ibid.*, s 320(1).
125 *Ibid.*, s 320(2).
126 *Ibid.*, s 321.
127 *Ibid.*, ss 322(1)–(2).
128 *Ibid.*, s 322(2).
129 *Ibid.*, s 322(5).
130 *Ibid.*, s 322(6).
131 The Companies (Tables A–F) Regulations 1985, *op. cit.*

Chapter 29 — Directors' remuneration

1 INTRODUCTION

This chapter focuses primarily on the disclosure requirements in respect of directors' remuneration. However, preparers of company financial statements should possess an awareness of the law governing the remuneration of directors and their service contracts. Accordingly, a brief exposition of these requirements has been included (see 1.1 to 1.4 below).[1]

Professor Gower reasoned that the need to disclose directors' remuneration was because 'it is too obvious that the system [of remunerating directors] lends itself to abuse, since directors will be encouraged to bleed the company by voting themselves excessive salaries and expense allowances. The latest Act [the Companies Act 1948] attempts to minimise these dangers by providing for full disclosure of the total emoluments received by directors ... '.[2] This requirement is simply a feature of the principle that a fiduciary should not allow his personal interests and duty to the company to conflict.[3]

These original requirements for aggregate information were added to in 1967 by the introduction of a requirement for individual information by the disclosure of the emoluments of the chairman, and of the highest paid director where this was not the chairman, together with the number of directors whose remuneration fell within specified bandings.[4] Although there had been a number of amendments over the years since then (principally revising the amounts of the bandings and when such individual information is required, as well as tightening up some of the potential loopholes), these basic requirements had until recently been in place for 30 years. As a result, they failed to keep up with recent developments in remuneration packages and accounting practice. This had been most evident in the case of listed companies.

In recent years executive remuneration has become a focus of public attention. Controversy surrounding the salaries and benefits of directors of British Gas and some other privatised utility companies in 1995 was simply the most well-publicised expression of public concern as to both the level and the structure of boardroom pay.

This concern was first addressed in 1992 by the Cadbury Committee, which was set up in May 1991 by the Financial Reporting Council, the London Stock Exchange and the accountancy profession, when it issued its report on 'corporate governance'.[5] At the heart of the Committee's recommendations was its Code of Best Practice for the boards of listed companies, paragraph 3.2 of which stated that 'there should be full and clear disclosure of directors' total emoluments and those of the chairman and highest paid UK director, including pension contributions and stock options. Separate figures should be given for salary and performance-related elements and the basis on which performance is measured to be explained.'

In view of increasing debate about share options granted to directors, in September 1994 the UITF issued Abstract 10 – *Disclosure of Directors' Share Options*. This recommends that further information concerning the option prices applicable to individual directors, together with market price information at the year end and at the date of exercise, should be disclosed (see 4.4.9 A below). However, the UITF had received legal advice that the recommended disclosures could not all be construed as being necessary to meet the legal requirements. Consequently, the disclosures are only recommendations and are not mandatory, although as a result of later developments discussed below they are effectively mandatory for listed companies.

The remit of the Cadbury Committee had been corporate governance as a whole, of which executive remuneration was only a part. The comprehensive review of directors' pay as a single issue fell to the Study Group on Directors' Remuneration, commonly known as the Greenbury Committee after its chairman Sir Richard Greenbury, chairman of Marks and Spencer. This Committee was established in January 1995 at the initiative of (but independent from) the CBI, with the remit of identifying good practice in determining directors' remuneration and preparing a Code of such practice for use by UK PLCs.

The Greenbury Committee issued its report in July 1995.[6] This contained a Code of Best Practice, summarised briefly at 4.2 below. In October 1995 and June 1996 the London Stock Exchange gave effect to certain of these recommendations by amending its *Listing Rules* and in May 1997 completed the jigsaw by introducing its requirements on the disclosure of directors' pension entitlements. These required listed companies to produce a report to the shareholders on behalf of the board by the remuneration committee (remuneration committee report), which included, inter alia, a statement of remuneration policy and for each director an analysis of remuneration, details of share options (in accordance with the recommendations of UITF 10), long-term incentive schemes and pension benefits.

In the light of these detailed disclosures required by listed companies, the Greenbury Committee recommended that the Companies Act requirements should be amended by removing the obligation to give banding information and to change the requirements in respect of disclosure of directors' pensions. Accordingly, the DTI issued a consultative document in January 1996 which aimed to implement the recommendations of the Greenbury Committee, align the Companies Act with the revised *Listing Rules* and, where possible, reduce disclosure requirements for unlisted companies.

Thus in February 1997 the DTI issued The Company Accounts (Disclosure of Directors' Emoluments) Regulations 1997 (SI 1997/570), which changed the requirements for directors' emolument disclosures for accounting periods ending on or after 31 March 1997. The main changes were as follows:

■   In addition to total emoluments, listed companies (including companies quoted on the Alternative Investment Market) must disclose total gains on share options and all companies must disclose benefits (in cash or in kind) under long-term incentive schemes.

■   Pension contributions are to be given for defined contribution schemes only, but the number of directors qualifying for defined contribution and defined benefit schemes respectively must be given.

■   The requirements to give £5,000 bandings and the emoluments of the chairman were abolished.

■   The emoluments of the highest paid director need be given only where total emoluments are £200,000 or more (formerly £60,000 and the company must not be member of a group). However, where the highest paid director is a member of a defined contribution pension scheme, the contributions paid must be shown. Where he is a member of a defined benefit pension scheme, his accrued pension and (where applicable) accrued lump sum at the end of the financial year must also be given.

■   The exemption for emoluments earned overseas was abolished.

■   The requirement to disclose the number of directors who have waived their rights to emoluments, and the amount of such emoluments, was abolished.

The Stock Exchange requirements have since been amended as a result of the work of the successor body to the Cadbury Committee, under the chairmanship of Sir Ronald Hampel, Chairman of ICI. In January 1998 the final report of the Committee on Corporate Governance (the Hampel Committee) was issued[7] and in June 1998, the Stock Exchange published the final version of the Principles of Good Governance and Code of Best Practice (the Combined Code), together with revised *Listing Rules*.

The Combined Code deals with corporate governance as a whole and has been derived from the Hampel Committee's final report and from the Cadbury and Greenbury Reports. It contains both principles and detailed Code provisions. Under the revised *Listing Rules*, companies are required to disclose how they have applied the principles and the extent to which they have complied with the detailed provisions of the Combined Code in their annual report in respect of periods ending on or after 31 December 1998 (see 2 of Chapter 4). Part B of Section 1 of the Combined Code deals with directors' remuneration (see 4.3 below). However, the changes made to the *Listing Rules* in respect of directors' remuneration are relatively minor. The report to shareholders is now to be made by the board (rather than by the remuneration committee on its behalf) but the information to be included within the report is virtually the same as before. There is also no longer any specific compliance statement to be made in respect of directors' remuneration as it is encompassed by the statement on compliance with the Combined Code.

The current Companies Act and Stock Exchange requirements are dealt with at 2 and 4 below.

1.1   Remuneration

Remuneration paid to directors may assume any form and its amount will depend on the terms of the directors' service contracts (if any) and the company's articles of association; for example, Table A[8] provides that 'the directors shall be entitled to such remuneration as the company may by ordinary resolution determine ... '. Accordingly, if the directors do not have service contracts and the articles are silent on this issue, the directors are not *entitled* to receive anything.[9]

Remuneration may not be paid to a director (in whatever capacity he acts) free of income tax nor may a company pay him remuneration of an amount such that, after paying income tax, it will leave a specified sum in his hands.[10] Any provision in a company's articles, or in any contract, or in any resolution for payment to a director of remuneration free of income tax takes effect as if it provided for payment of the gross amount subject to income tax payable by the director.[11]

1.2   Pensions

Pensions are only payable to former directors if the company is authorised to do so by its memorandum or articles of association. Table A[12] contains an express power to provide benefits to former directors and for any member of his family or any dependant and to make contributions to secure such benefits.

1.3   Compensation for loss of office

Payments to a director for loss of office, or as consideration for or in connection with his retirement from office, must be disclosed to and approved by the company in general meeting.[13] It is unclear whether payments to directors in respect of compensation for loss of other offices, for example, the company secretaryship, require approval. Pennington[14] believes that this rule applies irrespective of the office lost, although this view is not universally held. This requirement does not apply to 'any bona fide payment by way of damages for breach of contract or by way of pension in respect of past services'.[15] Thus, for approval purposes, a payment is only treated as compensation for loss of office if the company is under no legal obligation to make it.

1.4 Service contracts

In outline, the provisions of the Companies Act 1985 relating to service contracts are as follows:

(a) a copy or memorandum of the terms of directors' service contracts must be kept at an appropriate place, e.g. the company's registered office, and be available for inspection. The level of information required for directors who discharge their duties wholly or mainly outside the UK is reduced. These requirements do not apply where the unexpired portion of the contract is less than 12 months or where the company is able to terminate within the ensuing 12 months the director's contract without payment of compensation;[16]

(b) terms incorporated into a director's service contract for a period of more than five years during which time his employment either cannot be terminated or can only be terminated in special circumstances are void unless approved by the company in general meeting. The resolution is only valid if a written memorandum setting out the proposed agreement is available for inspection for 15 days before and at the meeting itself.[17]

The Stock Exchange imposes additional requirements in relation to service contracts of directors of listed companies. These are discussed at 4.4.10 below.

2 DISCLOSURE OF REMUNERATION UNDER THE COMPANIES ACT 1985

2.1 Introduction

The Companies Act 1985 requires the following information in respect of directors to be disclosed in aggregate by way of note to the company's financial statements:[18]

(a) emoluments (see 2.2 to 2.4 below);

(b) gains made on exercise of share options (see 2.5 below);

(c) cash and/or value of other assets (excluding share options) receivable under long-term incentive schemes (see 2.6 below);

(d)   pension contributions in respect of money purchase benefits (see 2.7 below);

(e)   excess retirement benefits (see 2.8 below);

(f)   compensation for loss of office (see 2.9 below); and

(g)   sums paid to third parties in respect of directors' services (see 2.10 below).

There are exceptions to the requirements under (b) and (c) above for companies which are not listed on the Stock Exchange or quoted on the Alternative Investment Market. Information is also required in respect of the number of directors to whom retirement benefits are accruing (see 2.7 below). In certain circumstances, individual information is required to be given in respect of the highest paid director (see 2.11 below). Comparative figures are required for all disclosures.[19]

In group financial statements, the above requirements only extend to directors of the holding company. It is the duty of each director to give notice to the company of such matters relating to himself as may be necessary for the purposes of these disclosures.[20] If these disclosures are not made in the financial statements, it is the auditors' duty to include in their report, so far as they are 'reasonably able to do so', a statement giving the required particulars.[21]

In view of the fact that companies listed on the Stock Exchange will be giving information in respect of each director, the Companies Act has granted dispensation from providing some of the above information which is to be given on aggregate basis. Accordingly, the Act states that 'any information, other than the aggregate amount of gains made by directors on the exercise of share options [(b) above], shall be treated as shown if it is capable of being readily ascertained from other information which is shown'. Apart from (b) above, this dispensation applies to all of the other disclosures noted above, other than (e) and (g) above. It also extends to the disclosures in respect of the highest paid director (from the information given for each director, users will be able to determine who it is). Accordingly, aggregate information should always be given for gains made on exercise of share options, excess retirement benefits and sums paid to third parties in respect of directors' services. In using this dispensation, listed companies should ensure that all comparative figures can also be ascertained.

2.2   Disclosure of aggregate emoluments

2.2.1   *Legal requirements*

The aggregate amount of emoluments paid to or receivable by directors in respect of qualifying services must be disclosed.[22] Qualifying services mean services:

(a)   as director of the company;

(b)   as director of any of the company's subsidiary undertakings (whilst a director of the company);

(c) in connection with the management of the affairs of the company or any of its subsidiary undertakings (whilst a director of the company).[23]

In this context, the definition of a subsidiary undertaking is extended to include the situation where the director of the reporting company is nominated by that company to act as its representative on the board of another undertaking (whether or not it is actually a subsidiary undertaking of the reporting company).[24] This extended definition applies for the purposes of all the disclosures discussed in 2.3 to 2.9 below, and is illustrated in Examples 29.1 and 29.2 below:

Example 29.1

Company X has an investment in Company Y. Company X appoints one of its directors, Mr A, to the board of Company Y. Mr A receives fees of £10,000 in respect of this appointment. The financial statements of Company X must include the fees receivable by Mr A in respect of his services as director of Company Y, in the relevant disclosures.

Example 29.2

Company A is a debenture holder of a non-group company, Company B. The trust deed entitles Company A to appoint one of its directors to the board of Company B. The emoluments of the appointee from Company B must be included in the relevant disclosures in Company A's financial statements.

The definition of emoluments and the computation thereof are dealt with at 2.3 and 2.4 below.

Examples of disclosure of aggregate emoluments are shown in Extracts 29.4 and 29.5 at 2.3 below.

2.2.2 Problem areas

A Other services

The disclosures in respect of directors' remuneration relate to a person's services as director of a company and management services (see 2.2.1 above). In some companies, particularly small private companies, directors may also perform services unrelated to the above and for which they receive remuneration. Such remuneration should be excluded from the directors' emoluments disclosures, as illustrated in the example below:

Example 29.3

A journalist director of a small provincial newspaper is paid a fee for writing a weekly column. Since this fee is quite distinct from his directors' fees or management remuneration, it should be excluded from the remuneration disclosures. However, consideration should be given to disclosing this arrangement as a transaction in which a director has a material interest (see 3.5 of Chapter 28) or as a related party transaction under FRS 8 (see generally Chapter 27).

In practice however, it is often difficult to determine whether or not such services are, in fact, unrelated, since directors are often appointed as a result of the other services which they perform. In such cases where doubt exists, the remuneration for other services is often included with directors' remuneration.

One company which has excluded fees received for services from the aggregate amount of emoluments is Volex Group, as shown below:

Extract 29.1: Volex Group p.l.c. (1999)

10   Directors' remuneration, interests and transactions[extract]

*   Total aggregate emoluments for directors during the year comprised £785,531 (1998 – £740,729).

In addition to the emoluments shown above:

(i)   Mr. Kennedy received fees of £10,320 (1998 – £10,320) during the year in respect of services provided under a consultancy agreement.

These fees are in addition to fees received as a non-executive director. In many other cases 'consultancy fees' are paid in respect of the person's services as director and management services and are therefore included as part of the emoluments.

B   'Golden hellos'

A number of companies offer payments (of varying kinds) as incentives for particular staff to join them (so-called 'golden hellos'). These payments made to directors do not relate to a person's services as director of the company; nor do they pertain to management services and thus, until the Companies Act 1989, were not required to be disclosed as part of directors' remuneration. Previously, such payments were only required to be disclosed as a transaction in which a director has a material interest (see 3.5 of Chapter 28).

However, the Companies Act is now clear that such 'golden hellos' paid to or receivable by a director are to be treated as 'emoluments paid or receivable ... in respect of his services as director'; consequently, such payments have to be included within emoluments disclosed in financial statements.[25]

Examples of golden hellos are shown below:

Extract 29.2: WH Smith Group PLC (1998)

Report of the Remuneration Committee[extract]

(i)   As part of the recruitment arrangements for Beverley Hodson the Company has made payments to her totalling £80,000 to cover relocation expenses. These payments are included in the table under Benefits and other payments.

(j)   As part of the recruitment arrangements for Lloyd Wigglesworth the Company has made a payment to him of £40,000 as compensation for loss of benefits under his previous employment and £87,000 to cover relocation expenses. These payments are included in the table under Benefits and other payments.

> *Extract 29.3: The Royal Bank of Scotland Group plc (1998)*
>
> **Remuneration Committee Report**[extract]
>
> Mr F. A. Goodwin received a payment of £90,000 on the commencement of his employment with the Group on 1st August 1998.

The £90,000 was included as part of 'Other' within the remuneration table.

There is no specific requirement to disclose the fact that 'golden hellos' are included within the figures or to disclose any details. However, consideration may need to be given as to whether disclosure is still required as a transaction in which a director has a material interest (see 3.5 of Chapter 28). In any event, companies may wish to give disclosure in order to explain any distorting effect of including such payments within emoluments in view of their 'one-off' nature.

2.3   Definition of emoluments

2.3.1   Legal requirements

Emoluments are defined as including:[26]

- salary;
- fees;
- bonuses;
- any sums paid by way of expenses allowance (insofar as those sums are charged to UK income tax); and
- the estimated money value of any other benefits received by the director otherwise than in cash (this will include, in particular, company cars, cheap loans (including mortgage subsidies) and cheap accommodation).

However, emoluments are not to include any of the following:[27]

- the value of any share options granted to a director or the amount of any gains made on the exercise of such options;
- any contributions paid, or treated as paid, in respect of the director under any pension scheme or any benefits to which he is entitled under any such scheme. For these purposes, a pension scheme has the meaning assigned to 'retirement benefit scheme' by section 611 of the Income and Corporation Taxes Act 1988;[28] or
- any money or other assets paid to or received or receivable by a director under any long-term incentive scheme.

These have been excluded as there are separate requirements for such items.

The aggregate emoluments disclosure should exclude employers' national insurance contributions as such sums are not paid to or receivable by the director. However, these contributions will need to be disclosed in the wages and salaries note as part of social security costs (see 3.1 below).

Although there are various items to be included within aggregate emoluments, there is no need under the Companies Act to give separate disclosure in respect of them as the requirement is merely to disclose the aggregate amount, as illustrated below:

Extract 29.4: Premier Farnell plc (1999)

4.   **Employees and Directors** [extract]

	1999 £m	1998 £m
Aggregate emoluments	**0.8**	1.1
Termination payment	–	0.5

Nevertheless a number of companies do give separate disclosure of the amounts included within aggregate emoluments, as shown below:

Extract 29.5: Caledonia Investments plc (1999)

35   **DIRECTORS' REMUNERATION AND INTERESTS** [extract]

Directors' remuneration

Total emoluments were as follows:

	1999 £'000	1998 £'000
Fees	**67**	63
Salaries	**900**	845
Benefits	**83**	71
Performance related bonuses	**153**	327
	1,203	1,306
Gains made on exercise of share options	**890**	–
	2,093	1,306

2.3.2   *Problem areas*

A   *Benefits-in-kind*

(a)   General

There is no universally accepted basis upon which the estimated money value of benefits received by directors is assessed; consequently, the valuation of such benefits is problematic. There are a number of possible methods whereby such benefits may be determined, in particular:

(i)   market value of the facility provided for the private benefit of the director (less any personal contribution paid by him);

(ii)   taxable values. Tax scale rates are often used as a yardstick whereby the values of benefits-in-kind can be readily determined. Indeed, in practice, this method is the most widely used thereby ensuring some degree of comparability between the relevant disclosure in the financial statements of different companies (see (f) below).

(iii) cost to the company. Proponents of this method argue that since the directors are appointed by the shareholders of a company to run the company on their behalf, they are entitled to be informed as to how much it is costing the company, and therefore ultimately themselves, for the directors to perform this stewardship function. However, this interpretation does not appear to be supported by the wording of the legislation, which refers to the *money value* of benefits received;

(iv) perceived benefit to the director. It is sometimes argued that companies expect their directors to maintain certain appearances and thus provide them with, say, a particular motor car which they would not drive if they had to finance the transaction personally. In this particular example, the benefit to the director would be the cost of the make of car which he himself would have purchased, had he not been provided with a company car. This argument assumes that the company restricts the director's freedom of choice by imposing the particular benefit on him which, in practice, is unlikely.

We believe that given the wording of the legislation, the most appropriate basis for determining the money value of benefits-in-kind received by the director is by reference to the market value of the facility provided for his benefit, (i) above, notwithstanding computational difficulties inherent in using this basis. Where it is not practicable to use the market value basis, taxable values, (ii) above, should be used.

Based on our preferred approach, the method of determining the more common benefits might be as follows:

(b) Motor cars

Where a company provides a director with a leased motor car, the market value of this facility could be calculated with reference to the lease payments and any additional running costs borne by the company. Likewise, if the company purchases a car for the use of the director, then the sum disclosed could be calculated by reference to the annual running costs, including depreciation, and associated interest costs. This may involve distinguishing between private and business mileage.

(c) Cheap loans

The benefit derived by a director on a cheap loan (including a subsidised mortgage) could be assessed as the difference between the interest payable on the loan and the market interest payable on a like loan, calculated in accordance with a weighted average rate for the financial year.

Companies should ensure that any loans made to directors do not contravene the prohibitions on transactions with directors (see generally Chapter 28).

(d)   Cheap accommodation

Directors of companies are frequently permitted to reside in property owned or leased by the company. Where the company owns the property, the benefit derived by the director is the difference between the rent he pays and the estimated market rent for that property which the company would receive if it were to lease the premises on a commercial basis. If the company merely leases the property, the benefit could be assessed as the difference between the rent and other expenses paid by the company and that paid by the director.

Companies should ensure that any such arrangements do not contravene the restrictions on transactions with directors (see generally Chapter 28).

(e)   Indemnity insurance

Companies may purchase and maintain for any officer, including directors, insurance against any liability he may incur for negligence, default, breach of duty, or breach of trust.[29] Where such insurance is purchased or maintained, it is arguable that the premiums incurred should be regarded as being the value of the benefit to be included within the figure for directors' emoluments.

(f)   Disclosure in practice

Although our preferred treatment is to include benefits-in-kind based on their market value, it would seem that in practice a number of companies use taxable values, as indicated by the following extracts:

Extract 29.6: Carclo Engineering Group PLC (1999)

Remuneration report [extract]

(iii)   Benefits comprise taxable non cash emoluments, mainly in respect of the provision of a company car and medical insurance, which are provided as part of the directors' service contracts.

Extract 29.7: Land Securities PLC (1999)

7   Directors' Emoluments, Share Options and Interests in Ordinary Shares[extract]

Benefits include all assessable tax benefits arising from employment within the group comprising the provision of a company car, private medical facilities, the value of shares allocated under the 1989 Profit Sharing Scheme, payments under the profit related pay scheme and a bonus of 5 per cent of salary payable under the annual bonus scheme.

It can be seen from the above extracts that the nature of the benefits has been disclosed. There is no requirement under the Companies Act for such disclosure but the Greenbury Report recommended that the nature of benefits should be disclosed and it is now arguably required by listed companies under Schedule B to the Combined Code (see 4.4.3 below). The benefits identified in the above extracts are probably the more common types of benefits receivable by directors. Other examples are illustrated below:

Extract 29.8: Marks and Spencer p.l.c. (1999)

REMUNERATION REPORT [extract]

1   DIRECTORS' EMOLUMENTS

(6)   Benefits for UK directors relate mainly to the provision of cars, fuel and travel. For expatriate directors see footnote (8).

(8)   Expatriate directors carrying out their duties overseas have their remuneration adjusted to take account of local living costs. This adjustment is to put them in a position, after taking into account taxation differentials, where they are no better or worse off as a result of carrying out their duties overseas. Payments made to them, or on their behalf, such as allowances for working overseas and the provision of accommodation, are treated as benefits for the purposes of the above table and are non-pensionable.

Extract 29.9: Cable and Wireless plc (1999)

DIRECTORS' REPORT [extract]

Directors' remuneration

Allowances and benefits include such items as fuel and medical insurance. Linus W L Cheung's allowances and benefits include housing and related benefits, which it is common practice to pay on behalf of senior executive officers in Hong Kong.

Extract 29.10: Chloride Group PLC (1998)

9   *Directors' emoluments and pension entitlements* [extract]

Certain directors and officers of the Group's subsidiary undertakings in the USA, including Mr Vass, were indemnified by US subsidiaries against personal liability which they might incur in their capacity as directors and/or officers of relevant subsidiary undertakings and remained covered by those indemnities in 1997/98. The value attributable to the indemnities granted to Mr Vass is unascertainable as at 23 July 1997, the date Mr Vass ceased to be a director, since the indemnities are of a contingent nature and no claims were outstanding in connection with them.

It can be seen that in this case no value has been placed on the benefit as the value is unascertainable.

2.4   Computing aggregate emoluments

2.4.1   *Legal requirements*

A   Bonuses

The amounts to be disclosed are the sums receivable in respect of a financial year irrespective of when paid.[30] Thus, a director's service contract may provide that he is to receive a bonus for the financial year of X% of the company's profits as disclosed in the statutory financial statements duly presented to the members in general meeting. This bonus should be accrued and included in the financial statements for the relevant financial year, notwithstanding that it is not payable until the financial statements are laid in general meeting.

An example of a company including bonuses on this basis is Chloride Group, as indicated below:

Extract 29.11: Chloride Group PLC (1999)

9   Directors' emoluments and pension entitlements[extract]

Performance related bonuses are earned in respect of the year under which they are shown but are not paid until the following year.

It would appear, however, that not all companies deal with annual bonuses in such a manner. For example:

Extract 29.12: Fine Art Developments p.l.c. (1999)

11   DIRECTORS' REMUNERATION AND INTERESTS IN SHARES [extract]

The bonuses of £63,000 relate to the year ended 31 March 1998.

However, it is fair to say that a number of companies in recent years have changed their practice so that they include annual bonuses in the year earned rather than in the year of payment.

Some bonuses given in respect of services or performance for the financial year may be subject to the condition that the director has to remain in employment until the bonus is paid. Should this be disclosed in the year to which it relates or in the year in which this further condition is satisfied?

Example 29.4

A company with a 30 June year end has a bonus scheme whereby bonuses will be payable based on the EPS performance for each financial year. Payments are to be made to participating employees on 31 March the following year, subject to them remaining in employment until then. For the year ended 30 June 1999 a director is due to receive £20,000 based on the performance for that year. Should this be disclosed as part of the director's emoluments in the 1999 or the 2000 accounts?

Although this bonus is clearly in respect of the year ended 30 June 1999, it is only to be disclosed in that year's accounts if it is *receivable* by the director. It could be argued that the director is entitled to the bonus at the year end, subject to the fulfilment of a condition which is not that onerous and therefore it should be regarded as being receivable and disclosed in the 1999 accounts. Alternatively, the fact that there is this condition means that the director is only entitled to the bonus if he is still employed by the company on 31 March 2000 and it is at that date the amount is receivable by the director. On this basis, disclosure would therefore be made in the 2000 accounts.

On balance, we believe that the bonus should be disclosed in the 1999 accounts as this is when it was earned by the director.

For companies listed on the Stock Exchange, such a bonus falls within the definition of a 'deferred bonus' which has to be separately disclosed in the remuneration table for the period under review (see 4.4.5 below).

A number of companies listed on the Stock Exchange have introduced bonus schemes whereby the director may apply a proportion of his annual bonus for the purchase of shares in the company with an equivalent value which, generally, will be matched by an equivalent number of shares at nil cost. This raises further issues and these are discussed at 4.4.5 below.

As noted at 2.1 above, bonuses which are to be included within 'emoluments' do not include any bonuses which are receivable under a long-term incentive scheme.

B   Amounts repayable by directors

If a director is liable to repay the company for any amount paid to him (for example, a season-ticket advance) such payments do not require disclosure as emoluments.[31] However, if the director is subsequently released from the liability or any expense allowance is charged to tax after the end of the financial year, these sums must be:[32]

(a)   disclosed in the first financial statements in which it is practicable to show them; and

(b)   distinguished from other remuneration.

In order to prevent companies making indefinite loans to directors, any such amount which a director is liable to repay which remains unpaid for two years or more after the due date, will require disclosure as above.[33]

C   Payments by other persons

The sums disclosed must include all sums paid by or receivable from the company, its subsidiary undertakings or any other person.[34] Indeed, in group situations, where directors of the holding company also act as directors of subsidiary companies, it is common for the holding company to remunerate the directors in respect of their services to the subsidiary companies. The notes to the financial statements of those subsidiaries must include details of the emoluments paid by the holding company in respect of the directors' services. Where this is the case, we consider that the notes to the subsidiaries' financial statements should explain that the charge for directors' remuneration has been borne by the holding company. Similarly, a blanket management charge may be made by a holding company to its subsidiaries in respect of a variety of expenditure incurred by it on the subsidiaries' behalf including the emoluments of the subsidiaries' directors. The reporting company should seek to analyse the expenditure between types and thereby arrive at a figure for directors' emoluments. If such an exercise is not practicable, the notes to the reporting company's financial statements should state this fact; for example:

> A management charge of £100,000 in respect of administration costs has been made by Y Co. the company's holding company, which includes the directors' emoluments which it is not possible to identify separately.

In some groups, all contracts of employment and/or directors' service contracts are vested in one company. The company will provide the personnel requirements (including directors) of other group companies and in return will levy a management charge. In these situations, the considerations outlined above are equally applicable.

If it is necessary to apportion the emoluments received by a director (for example, where he acted as director for a number of group companies and was remunerated by a single composite sum from the holding company which requires analysis between the group companies), the directors may apportion these payments in such manner as they deem appropriate.[35] However, where the directors consider that they are unable to make an appropriate apportionment, the note to the subsidiaries' financial statements should reflect this fact. For example:

> The directors of the company are also directors of the holding company and fellow subsidiaries. The directors received total remuneration for the year of £120,000 (1998: £105,000), all of which was paid by the holding company. The directors do not believe that it is practicable to apportion this amount between their services as directors of the company and their services as directors of the holding and fellow subsidiary companies.

D   Payments to connected persons

Payments made to persons connected with the director or persons connected with a body corporate 'controlled' by a director are required to be included in the aggregate emoluments to be disclosed.[36] 'Connected persons' and 'controlled bodies corporate' are as defined for directors' loans and transactions (see Chapter 28 at 2.4). An example of such payments are shown below:

> *Extract 29.13: Kwik-Fit Holdings plc (1999)*
>
> **9.   DIRECTORS' REMUNERATION AND INTERESTS [extract]**
>
> Fees, including expenses, for N. Hood and I McIntosh are paid to Neil Hood Associates and Ian McIntosh Limited respectively. Fees, including expenses, for J. Padget are paid to Padget Associates B.V. in addition to consultancy payments and expenses disclosed in Note 9(d).

The fees are included within aggregate emoluments.

2.4.2 Problem areas

A Payments to consultancy companies/partnerships

It is not uncommon for a director's emoluments to be paid to a consultancy company/partnership of which the director and/or members of his family are shareholders/partners. In such situations the consultancy company/partnership levies a charge to the company preparing the financial statements for the services of the director. Such payments are required to be included in aggregate emoluments if the consultancy company/partnership is a person connected with the director. Clearly, if it is a consultancy partnership then this will be the case; however, if it is a consultancy company this may not always be so. If the consultancy company is not a person connected with the director then, even though payments need not be included in aggregate emoluments, separate disclosure will be required as a payment to a third party for the services of a director (see 2.10 below).

These arrangements may also require disclosure as transactions in which a director has a material interest (see 3.5 of Chapter 28) or as related party transactions under FRS 8 (see generally Chapter 27).

B Payments to other connected persons

In some companies, particularly in family held companies, payments and/or benefits in kind are paid to a director's spouse. Where the spouse is unconnected with the company, then any such payments made should be included as part of the director's emoluments. Difficulties may arise, however, where the spouse either is employed by, or provides a service to, the company. Where the amounts paid to the spouse are commensurate with the services rendered then these should not be included within the directors' emoluments disclosures. However, where the amounts paid are excessive, then it is likely that a proportion of the payment effectively relates to the director's services and therefore should be included in the director's emoluments. Again, these arrangements may also require disclosure as transactions in which a director has a material interest (see 3.5 of Chapter 28) or as related party transactions under FRS 8 (see generally Chapter 27).

C Services to holding company

Complications may also arise if the reporting company considers that emoluments paid by its holding company are purely in respect of a director's services to the holding company and not for services as director of the reporting company. It is sometimes argued that the emoluments do not need to be disclosed in the subsidiary's financial statements but should simply be disclosed in the financial statements of its holding company, assuming that:

(a) the director is also a director of that company; and

(b) the holding company is incorporated in the UK.

However, it is our view that if the director's services to the subsidiary company occupy a significant amount of time, an appropriate apportionment should be made and the relevant disclosures given. If the directors consider that they are unable to make an appropriate apportionment, the note to the subsidiary's financial statements should reflect this fact (see 2.4.1 C above). If the director's services to the subsidiary company do not occupy a significant amount of time, it may be concluded that the director is not remunerated for them and that, therefore, the subsidiary's financial statements should reflect the director as not having received any remuneration. It will be necessary to review the particular facts in each case to ascertain whether disclosure is necessary.

However, in the case of a foreign holding company where the director works full-time in managing its UK subsidiary, disclosure of the emoluments for such work should be made in the subsidiary's financial statements as the director is clearly providing full-time management services to that company.

2.5   Gains made on exercise of share options

As noted at 4.4.9 A below, the UITF believed that under the old legislation the grant of an option should be treated as giving rise to a benefit and should be included in the aggregate of directors' emoluments. However, the UITF recognised the practical difficulties of attributing a meaningful estimated money value to the option at the date of grant, particularly where the rights under the option are contingent on future performance or other factors, and also given the differing views on whether to apportion any benefit over time. Accordingly, the UITF concluded that it was not practicable at that time for it to specify an appropriate valuation method for options as a benefit in kind and therefore recommended detailed disclosures in respect of directors' options as a surrogate for any value.

The current legislation has dispensed with these problems of valuing any benefit at the time of granting the option by requiring the disclosure of the aggregate amount of gains made by directors on the exercise of share options,[37] an example of which is shown below:

Extract 29.14: Gerrard Group plc (1999)

4   Directors' emoluments [extract]

Total emoluments of all directors are as follows:

	1999 £	1998 £
Aggregate emoluments	3,633,120	2,715,834
Gains made on exercise of share options	175,175	66,378
Company pension contributions to money purchase schemes	95,475	78,825

Retirement benefits are accruing to three directors under money purchase arrangements and to four directors under a defined benefit scheme.

The amount of the gain is calculated as being the difference between:

(a) the market price of the shares on the day on which the option was exercised, and

(b) the price actually paid for the shares.[38]

The figure to be disclosed is therefore unaffected by whether a director immediately sells the shares after exercising the option or retains them. (This is highlighted in Extract 29.15 below.) Where they are retained then no disclosure is required of any subsequent gain (or loss) when the shares are eventually sold.

'Share option' means a right to acquire shares which in turn means shares (whether allotted or not) in the company, or any undertaking which is a group undertaking in relation to the company, and includes a share warrant as defined by section 188(1) of the Act.[39] This means that it will encompass options to subscribe for new shares and options to acquire shares from, say, an ESOP trust, not only in respect of shares of the reporting company, but also, say, in respect of shares of a subsidiary or a holding company.

By omitting the words 'in respect of qualifying services' in the requirement, this means that the amount of the gains will also include gains made on the exercise of options which had been granted prior to the director's appointment as a director. However, this has also meant that where a director has ceased to be a director during the year and has subsequently exercised options then it would appear that any gains made on the exercise of such options are not to be included in the aggregate amount to be disclosed. For companies listed on the Stock Exchange such amounts may be apparent from their disclosures under the requirements of the Stock Exchange (see 4.4.9 A below). If in such circumstances the former director is allowed to exercise options earlier than would otherwise have been the case, then any gains should probably be disclosed as part of compensation for loss of office (see 2.9 below).

This requirement is only to apply to listed companies. However, this term is wider than its normal usage, because the Act defines a listed company as being 'a company –

(a) whose securities have been admitted to the Official List of the Stock Exchange in accordance with the provisions of Part IV of the Financial Services Act 1986; or

(b) dealings in whose securities are permitted on any exchange which is an approved exchange for the purposes of that Part'.[40]

The inclusion of (b) means that companies quoted on the Alternative Investment Market are to be treated as listed for this purpose and will therefore have to comply with this requirement.

As noted earlier, although companies listed on the Stock Exchange (and any other companies which choose to do so) give disclosure of individual directors' options, including information under UITF 10 which would allow the calculation of gains made on exercise of options, they need to give the aggregate information which is required by the Act (including comparatives). Indeed, Marks and Spencer has made such disclosure even although the amount of gains are quantified for each director, as shown below:

Extract 29.15: Marks and Spencer p.l.c. (1999)

REMUNERATION REPORT [extract]

2   GAINS MADE ON DIRECTORS' SHARE OPTIONS

	1999 £000	1998 £000		1999 £000	1998 £000
Sir Richard Greenbury	–	242	J T Rowe	–	66
P L Salsbury	4	30	D K Hayes	10	0
P G McCracken	7	49	C Littmoden	–	9
Lord Stone of Blackheath	11	152	S J Sacher	–	201
R Aldridge	7	309	P P D Smith	56	188
J R Benfield	7	470	J K Oates[3]	–	747
R W C Colvill	–	375	D G Trangmar	n/a	172
Mrs C E M Freeman	14	240	The Hon David Sieff	n/a	84
B S Morris	–	68			

(1)   The total gain made by the directors on their exercise of their share options was £116,000 (last year £3.4m).

(2)   Details of options giving rise to these gains can be found on pages 13 to 15. The gains are calculated as at the date of exercise although the shares may have been retained. (Directors' interests in shares are shown on page 16.)

(3)   J K Oates resigned from the Board and took early retirement on 31 January 1999. His details are calculated to this date.

This requirement to disclose the aggregate gains on share options exercised by the directors, notwithstanding the fact that information is disclosed which allows the amounts to be calculated, was highlighted in the Review Panel's ruling on the 1997 accounts of H & C Furnishings.[41]

The original Consultative Document issued by the DTI had proposed that the requirement should apply to all companies, but they recognised that for unlisted companies there may not be a readily available market value to use as a basis for calculating the gain when the option is taken up. Accordingly, companies which are not listed (as defined by the Act) are not required to give this disclosure. This will even apply in situations where the gains are easily quantified such as where a director of an unlisted subsidiary exercises options over shares in a listed parent. As a quid pro quo for not disclosing the amount of any gains made by directors on the exercise of options, unlisted companies are required to state the number of directors who exercised share options (including share options granted prior to a director's appointment as director).[42]

2.6   Long-term incentive schemes

In recent years there has been a move, principally by companies listed on the Stock Exchange, to provide a greater proportion of a director's remuneration by way of rewarding long-term performance. This was further encouraged by the Greenbury Committee recommending that in general there should be a move away from short-term cash-based schemes to longer-term share-based schemes (see 4.4.9 B below).

The old legislation did not specifically deal with such long-term incentive schemes; they were merely covered by the general disclosure requirement that the amounts to be disclosed as emoluments were the sums receivable in respect of a financial year irrespective of when paid and that any remuneration which was not receivable in respect of a period was to be disclosed in the financial statements when actually paid. Bonuses which were based on the company's results or the market performance of its shares over several years were arguably not receivable in respect of any given period, and thus were to be disclosed when paid.

Disclosure about long-term incentive schemes has become more of a feature in the disclosures of directors' emoluments by listed companies initially as a result of the recommendations of Cadbury (see 4.1 below) and Greenbury (see 4.2 below) and now as required by the Stock Exchange (see 4.4 below).

In view of the Stock Exchange requirements, the Companies Act now requires disclosure of the aggregate of:

(a)   the amount of money paid to or receivable by directors under long-term incentive schemes in respect of qualifying services; and

(b)   the net value of assets (other than money and share options) received or receivable by directors under such schemes in respect of such services.[43]

A 'long-term incentive scheme' is defined as being 'any agreement or arrangement under which money or other assets may become receivable by a director and which includes one or more qualifying conditions with respect to service or performance which cannot be fulfilled within a single financial year; and for this purpose the following shall be disregarded:

(a)   bonuses, the amount of which falls to be determined by reference to service or performance within a single financial year;

(b)   compensation for loss of office, payments for breach of contract and other termination payments; and

(c)   retirement benefits'.[44]

This is similar to the definition contained in the *Listing Rules* (see 4.4.9 B below).

In this context, 'net value' in relation to assets received or receivable by a director means value after deducting any money paid or other value given by the director in respect of those assets and 'value' in relation to shares received or receivable by a director on any day means the market price of the shares on that day.[45]

This requirement applies to all companies. However, for companies which are not listed (as defined in the Act – see 2.5 above), the net value of assets received or receivable excludes the value of shares received or receivable by directors.[46] However, in that case, the number of directors (if any) in respect of whose qualifying services shares were received or receivable has to be disclosed.[47]

As with gains made on share options (see 2.5 above), the original Consultative Document issued by the DTI had proposed that the requirement should apply to all companies, but the exclusion of share awards for unlisted companies was included for the same reasons as for share options. Again this will apply in situations where the share awards are easily quantified such as where a director of an unlisted subsidiary is awarded shares in a listed parent.

Unlike the requirement in respect of share options the words 'in respect of qualifying services' are included in this requirement. This would appear to mean that any amount which relates to the period prior to the director's appointment as a director is not to be included in the disclosure. However, it can be seen from Extract 29.16 below that such amounts are included. Where a director has ceased to be a director during the year, then any amount that he is entitled to under the scheme should be included in the amount to be disclosed. If in such circumstances the former director is given an amount to which he was not entitled then it should be disclosed as part of compensation for loss of office (see 2.9 below).

An example of a company disclosing the aggregate amount of cash receivable by directors is Boots, as illustrated below:

Extract 29.16: The Boots Company PLC (1999)

Board Remuneration Report [extract]

Long term bonus scheme This scheme provides a direct link between the pay of executive directors and the creation of value for shareholders. Company performance is measured over rolling, four year cycles, in terms of total shareholder return relative to a peer group of ten other leading companies. Transitional performance cycles began on 1st April 1995, a three year performance cycle ended on 31st March 1998 and the first four year cycle ended on 31st March 1999.

During the cycle ended 31st March 1999, the chosen peer group was:

Great Universal Stores	Sears
Kingfisher	Smith & Nephew
Marks & Spencer	SmithKline Beecham
Reckitt & Colman	Tesco
J Sainsbury	W H Smith

The peer group is reviewed before each performance cycle to maintain its relevance.

The amount of bonus depends upon the company's comparative performance against its peer group on the following scale:

Comparative position in peer group league table	1	2	3	4	5	6	7	8	9	10	11
Bonus % of average annual salary	90	90	90	65	55	45	35	25	Nil	Nil	Nil

For the cycle which commenced in April 1997 and April 1998 there will be nil bonus if the position in the above league table is eighth or lower.

Approval for a revision to the long term scheme for the cycle which commenced in April 1999 is being sought at the annual general meeting.

After the end of each performance cycle, one half of any bonus earned is paid in cash. The value of the remaining half is converted into an equivalent number of shares in the company in respect of which the executive director will have conditional rights. The number of shares will be calculated by dividing half of the value of the long term bonus by the quotation for a share as derived from the official daily list of the London Stock Exchange on the date for payment of the cash proportion (in 1999, being 21st June). The executive director will normally become entitled to receive those shares only after remaining employed for a further three years. If a director leaves the company during the three-year period (except in the case of normal retirement, disability or death), his conditional entitlement to those shares will lapse.

In respect of the four year period to 31st March 1999, the company achieved position four in the league table referred to above.

Accordingly the long term bonus amounts earned in respect of that period by executive directors, including amounts relating to periods of service before appointment to the board, were as follows:

£000	Cash	Value of vested shares	Total 1997	Total 1998
Lord Blyth	170	–	170	162
M F Ruddell	74	–	74	71
S G Russell	87	–	87	77
D A R Thompson	93	–	93	87
J J H Watson	49	–	49	30
B E Whalan (to 31st July 1997)	–	–	–	94
	473	–	473	521

Each executive director will also be awarded conditional rights to receive ordinary shares in the company having a market value on 21st June 1999 equivalent to the cash bonus shown above. The director will normally become entitled to receive those shares in June 2002 if the conditions are satisfied.

Details of the numbers of shares which have been conditionally awarded during the year under the long term bonus scheme for the cycle which was completed at the end of the previous financial year and the cumulative entitlement are shown below:

	Conditional entitlement 1999	Conditional entitlement 1998	Cumulative total
Lord Blyth	15,956	22,263	38,219
M F Ruddell	6,991	9,525	16,516
S G Russell	7,652	9,570	17,222
D A R Thompson	8,538	11,475	20,013
J J H Watson	4,242	4,876	9,118
	43,379	57,709	101,088

It can be seen from the above example Boots has gone further than the Companies Act requires, by disclosing the amounts for each director. However, this will have been given so as to meet the requirements of the Stock Exchange (see 4.4.9 B below).

Such long-term bonuses are to be disclosed in the year in which they become receivable and therefore a similar question arises as with annual bonuses when some or all of the bonus is conditional on the director remaining in employment with the company for a future period (see Example 29.4 at 2.4.1 A above).

In Extract 29.16 above, Boots has clearly regarded the cash element as receivable. However, this only represents half of the bonus. The remainder is to be converted into a certain number of shares with an equivalent value and the director will normally become entitled to these shares only after remaining employed for a further three years. If a director leaves the company during that period then (except in specified circumstances), his conditional entitlement will lapse. Whether such amounts should be included or not will for companies listed on the Stock Exchange normally be of academic interest only, because sufficient information will generally be disclosed to meet the Stock Exchange requirements (see 4.4.9 B below). If that is the case, then the Companies Act requirement (whatever it may be) will have been deemed to have been met under the dispensation that 'information shall be treated as shown if it is capable of being readily ascertained from other information which is shown' (see 2.1 above).

It should be emphasised that the disclosure of the amounts receivable under long-term incentive schemes is completely independent of the charge recognised in the profit and loss account for such schemes. In April 1997, the UITF published its seventeenth Abstract, *Employee share schemes*.[48] This addresses the relatively narrow issue of how companies should recognise and measure the cost of new shares issued as part of an employee share scheme. This is discussed further at 4.7.2 of Chapter 15.

2.7   Pension contributions in respect of money purchase schemes

Under the old legislation, all pension contributions were required to be included within the computation of 'emoluments'. Whilst this gave an accurate indication of the cost of a defined contribution scheme, it was common ground that it inadequately measured the cost of a defined benefit scheme relative to any individual (particularly where companies may have been taking pension holidays). However, given the rest of the requirements for directors' remuneration which were based more on valuing the benefits receivable by the directors, such an approach, particularly in relation to pension rights under defined benefit schemes, clearly did not represent the value of the benefit receivable by the director.

As discussed at 4.4.8 below, the Greenbury Report had recommended that the benefit should be measured as the present value of pension entitlement earned during the year resulting from additional length of service, increases in salary or changes in the terms of the scheme, less any contributions made by the director during the year. In the light of this, the DTI proposed in its Consultative Document that there should be disclosure of the aggregate value of directors' pension entitlements and that this would apply to all companies. However, following comments received on the Consultative Document, this proposal was dropped, although there is a requirement for such information in respect of the highest paid director (see 2.11 below).

Accordingly, all that the Companies Act now requires is disclosure of the aggregate value of any company contributions paid, or treated as paid, to a pension scheme in respect of directors' qualifying services, being contributions by reference to which the rate or amount of any money purchase benefits that may become payable will be calculated.[49] An example of such disclosure is shown in Extract 29.14 at 2.5 above.

For this purpose, the following definitions apply:

- 'Company contributions' mean 'any payments (including insurance premiums) made, or treated to be made, to the scheme in respect of the director by a person other than the director'.[50] The words 'treated to be made' are to cater for disclosure of notional contributions under underpinned schemes (see below).

- 'Pension scheme' has the meaning assigned to 'retirement benefits scheme' by section 611 of the Income and Corporation Taxes Act 1988.[51] This latter definition is generally interpreted as extending to unfunded pension arrangements.

- 'Money purchase benefits' are defined as 'retirement benefits payable under a pension scheme the rate or amount of which is calculated by reference to payments made, or treated as made, by the director or by any other person in respect of the director and which are not average salary benefits'.[52]

- 'Retirement benefits' has the meaning assigned to 'relevant benefits' by section 612(1) of the Income and Corporation Taxes Act 1988.[53]

In most cases the amount to be disclosed will be the contributions to a money purchase scheme (defined contribution scheme) but it will also include contributions to a defined benefit scheme, to the extent that the contributions go to entitling directors to money purchase benefits under that scheme.

The legislation also provides for disclosure of information relating to a pension scheme with an underpin. Such a scheme, although primarily a defined benefit scheme or a money purchase scheme, has a shadow scheme underpinning it with notional contributions and rates. Accordingly the Act states that 'where a pension scheme provides for any benefits that may become payable to or in respect of any director to be whichever are the greater of:

(a) money purchased benefits as determined under the scheme; and

(b) defined benefits as so determined,

the company may assume that those benefits will be money purchased benefits, or defined benefits, according to whichever appears more likely at the end of the financial year'.[54]

It should be emphasised that comparative figures are required for such aggregate pension contributions. For companies listed on the Stock Exchange who rely on the dispensation allowed under the Companies Act referred to at 2.1 above, it is important that where such pension contributions are given for each individual director within the remuneration table, then unless comparative figures are also given for the pension contributions (see Extract 29.33 at 4.4.3 A below), disclosure of the comparative aggregate amount needs to be made.

As a quid pro quo for not requiring disclosures in respect of the value of pension entitlements under defined benefit schemes (other than in respect of the highest paid director, where applicable – see 2.11 below), the Act also requires disclosure of the number of directors (if any) to whom retirement benefits are accruing in respect of qualifying services under:

(a)   money purchase schemes; and

(b)   defined benefit schemes.[55]

A 'money purchase scheme' is defined as being a pension scheme under which *all* benefits that may become payable to a director are money purchase benefits.[56] The Act has not used the term 'defined contribution scheme' in order to align the terminology with the definition of money purchase benefits (see above).

A 'defined benefit scheme' means a pension scheme which is not a money purchase scheme.[57] The most obvious example is a final salary scheme. However, any scheme which is not classified as a money purchase scheme will fall to be regarded as defined benefit scheme. Therefore if a director is a member of a hybrid pension scheme under which both money purchase and defined benefits are payable then it is to be classified as a defined benefit scheme.

For the purpose of determining whether a pension scheme is a money purchase or defined benefit scheme, any death in service benefits provided for by the scheme are disregarded.[58] Thus a scheme in which the only defined benefit element relates to death in service benefits should be classified as a money purchase scheme.

One company which has disclosed this information on the number of directors is Gerrard Group, as shown in Extract 29.14 at 2.5 above.

In our view such information on the number of directors is virtually worthless and should never have been introduced. We would recommend that where companies listed on the Stock Exchange are disclosing information for individual directors (see 4.4.8 below), then they should use the dispensation allowed under the Companies Act referred to at 2.1 above.

2.8   Excess retirement benefits of directors and past directors

The old legislation used to require disclosure of pensions paid by the company to directors or former directors, but this did not include pensions paid by a pension scheme since the company's contributions thereto had already been disclosed as emoluments.

This has now been replaced by a requirement whereby disclosure should be given of the aggregate amount of retirement benefits paid to or receivable by directors and past directors under pension schemes in excess of the retirement benefits to which they were respectively entitled on the date on which the benefits first became payable or 31 March 1997, whichever is the later.[59]

Amounts paid or receivable under the pension scheme need not be included in the aggregate amount if:

(a)   the funding of the scheme was such that the amounts were or, as the case may be, could have been paid without recourse to additional contributions; and

(b)   amounts were paid to or receivable by all pensioner members of the scheme on the same basis.[60]

For this purpose, 'pension scheme' and 'retirement benefits' have the same meaning as discussed at 2.7 above and 'pensioner member' means any person who is entitled to the present payment of retirement benefits under the scheme.[61]

The intention of this requirement is to ensure that companies disclose any discretionary increases in pensions of directors or former directors. However, if a former director receives, say, a 3% inflationary increase in his pension and this is given to all pensioner members then this amount, although in excess of his entitlement when benefits first became payable, is not to be disclosed under this provision.

The inclusion of the reference to 31 March 1997 in the requirement provides the baseline for disclosures in respect of pensions in payment at the commencement of the first financial year to which the legislation applied.

The amounts to be disclosed in respect of retirement benefits include any benefits in kind given in respect of retirement benefits at the estimated money value of the benefit. In such a case, the nature of the benefit is also required to be disclosed.[62]

2.9   Compensation for loss of office

2.9.1   *Legal requirements*

The aggregate amount of any compensation payable to directors or past directors in respect of loss of office must be disclosed.[63]

In this context, compensation for loss of office includes compensation in consideration for, or in connection with, a person's retirement from office.[64]

The changes made to the legislation by SI 1997/570 also clarified that it is to include payments made by way of damages for breach of the person's contract with the company or with a subsidiary undertaking of the company or payments made by way of settlement or compromise of any claim in respect of the breach.[65]

These are illustrated in the following extracts:

Extract 29.17: Meyer International PLC (1999)

Report on Directors' remuneration [extract]

Following Mr J G R Perry's resignation as a Director of the Company on 27th May 1998, it was agreed that he would continue to receive basic salary and certain benefits until the earlier of 30th November 1999 or the date he commences comparable permanent full-time employment. In the event of the latter occurring, he would then be entitled to receive 50% of the balance of the emoluments which he would have received under these arrangements had he continued to be employed by the Company until 30th November 1999.

The payments made to Mr Perry in accordance with these arrangements are as follows:

	1999	1998
	£000	£000
Payment to former Director	129	–
Pension contributions for former Director	43	–

In accordance with the arrangements disclosed in the 1997/98 Report of the Compensation and Appointments Committee, payments made to Mr B Wright who resigned as a Director of the Company in January 1997 are as follows:

	1999	1998
	£000	£000
Payment to former Director	58	178
Pension contributions for former Director	19	57

Extract 29.18: Volex Group p.l.c. (1997)

9   Directors' remuneration, interests and transactions [extract]

§   Total aggregate emoluments for directors during the year comprised £921,072.

In addition to the emoluments shown above:

(i)   Mr Chapple received payments under the terms of a compromise agreement made upon his resignation from the Board on 21 May 1996 comprising cash payments of £131,429 and contributions to a funded unapproved retirement benefit scheme of £12,850: a further contribution of £17,176 was outstanding at the end of the year. The compromise agreement provides for payments to Mr Chapple throughout the unexpired portion of his service agreement (i.e. to 20 May 1998) net of all income earned by Mr. Chapple from other sources during that period.

(ii)   Mr. Davies received an ex gratia payment of £28,333 upon his retirement on 31 March 1997.

Contributions to a pension scheme made in connection with a director's loss of, or retirement from, office should be included within the aggregate amount of compensation to be disclosed, as illustrated below:

Extract 29.19: Norcros p.l.c. (1997)

REPORT OF THE REMUNERATION COMMITTEE [extract]

Compensation for loss of office and pension rights of Mr M E Doherty and Mr R H Alcock

Mr M E Doherty received compensation for his change of status in May 1996 from executive to non-executive Chairman, as a consequence of the termination with effect from 4 April 1996 of his previous executive employment agreement (which had a two year notice period). A sum of £234,000 was paid into the Norcros Security Plan to augment his pension by £21,781 per annum to give a total of £147,972 per annum payable from his normal retirement age of 60. In addition, an amount of £6,000 was paid to the Norcros Security Plan to provide a lump sum death benefit.

A sum of £250,000 was paid to Mr R H Alcock as compensation for loss of office. In addition he received fees of £102,570 plus VAT under the terms of a consultancy agreement dated 6 May which expired on 31 October 1996.

Although no aggregate amount for compensation for loss of office is disclosed in the above extracts they are deemed to have been disclosed in view of the dispensation mentioned at 2.1 above.

Another company which has disclosed such pension contributions is Sainsbury, as shown below:

Extract 29.20: J Sainsbury plc (1997)

Report of the Remuneration Committee [extract]

4. Retired as a Director on 26th April 1996. 1997 pension contributions included £556,000 in respect of compensation for loss of office.

Elsewhere in the report, the amount of compensation for loss of office for 1997 is disclosed as £336,000. Although this method of presentation might not be ideal, it does comply with the requirement for the reason mentioned above in respect of the other extracts.

These requirements extend to the loss of any office or otherwise in connection with the management of the affairs of the company or any of its subsidiary undertakings[66] and apply whether or not the compensation requires company approval (see 1.3 above). For example, if the managing director of a subsidiary company ceases to act in that capacity but remains on the boards of both that company and its parent, any compensation paid by the subsidiary in respect of this loss of office should be disclosed in both the holding company's and subsidiary's financial statements.

The amounts to be disclosed in respect of compensation include any benefits received, or receivable, otherwise than in cash, at the estimated money value of the benefit.[67] In such a case, the nature of the benefit is also required to be disclosed.[68] One company which has made such disclosure is PIC, as shown below:

Extract 29.21: PIC International Group PLC (1998)

REPORT OF THE REMUNERATION COMMITTEE [extract]

DIRECTORS' REMUNERATION

R J Clothier resigned as a director on 12 September 1997 and left the Group's employment on 30 September 1997. He received compensation for loss of office of £505,345, subject to deduction of tax, which included non-cash compensation for the use of a motor car, and medical, personal accident and life assurance cover to 31 March 1999. He receives a pension of £145,848 per annum which commenced on 1 October 1997 and has retained rights to exercise his outstanding executive share options in the period up to 26 September 2000.

R N Harris retired as a director on 30 September 1997 and received compensation for loss of office of £105,135, subject to deduction of tax, and which included non-cash compensation for the provision of medical insurance cover to January 1999. He receives a pension of £120,000 per annum which commenced on 1 October 1997, and he retained the right to exercise his outstanding share options in the period up to 16 March 2001.

P Kirk, who resigned as a director on 1 May 1998, was paid £320,221 in compensation for loss of office and which included non-cash compensation for the loss of medical, personal accident and life insurance cover. He also received cash compensation of £67,821 in lieu of an annual bonus for the year, and entitlements under the Dalgety Long Term Incentive Plan. Mr Kirk receives a pension of £93,537 per annum which commenced 23 May 1998, and he retained the right to exercise his outstanding executive share options in the period up to 13 November 2001.

K G Hanna is to relinquish his position as Group Chief Executive on 30 September 1998. He will receive compensation for loss of office of £794,722, subject to deduction of tax, together with an additional deferred pension of £15,500 per annum payable at normal retirement age, in 2013. Mr Hanna remains entitled to a proportionate payment of any bonus payable in 1999 under the Long Term Incentive Plan, the amount of which will depend on the results achieved in the three years ending 30 June 1999. His compensation includes an amount payable for relinquishing his right under the Long Term Incentive Plan to a bonus prospectively payable in June 2000, and also includes compensation for the loss of use of a motor car, medical, personal accident and life insurance cover to 30 September 2000. Mr Hanna has retained rights to exercise his outstanding share options. The majority must be exercised by 30 September 1999 and 25,677 by 7 November 2000. Mr Hanna is to serve as a non-executive director of the Company from 1 October 1998.

A particular problem associated with non-cash compensation relates to the valuation of such benefits. Ordinarily, the market value of any asset transferred should be disclosed; however, if the book value of the asset is used, an explanatory note should indicate the asset's market value. For example:

Example 29.5

A director is given a motor car upon retirement from the company and the book value of the car is £2,000 and its market value is £3,000. The company should either disclose the market value of the car in the compensation for loss of office disclosure or use the book value of the asset and append an explanatory note to the directors' remuneration note to the following effect: 'the amount for compensation for loss of office includes the written down value of a [description of vehicle] the market value of which was £3,000'.

2.9.2 Problem areas

A   Ex-gratia payments

Ex-gratia payments which do not constitute compensation for loss of office and which are not in connection with a person's retirement need not be disclosed. In order to decide whether a payment is ex-gratia, regard should be had to the nature of and all the circumstances surrounding the payment. The donor company's classification of the payment is irrelevant. The following examples distinguish a disguised retirement payment from an ex-gratia payment:

Example 29.6

Mr A retires from the board of Company X. The following week, Company X makes Mr A an ex-gratia payment of £25,000. In these circumstances, the payment, albeit described as ex-gratia, should be disclosed as compensation for loss of office for it would appear to be connected with the director's retirement from the board.

Example 29.7

Mr A is a former director of Company X. After leaving Company X, Mr A sets up his own business, which through no fault of his own, goes into liquidation. Company A learns of Mr A's plight and gifts him the sum of £20,000. In these circumstances, the payment is unrelated to Mr A's retirement from the board of Company X and need not be disclosed in its financial statements as compensation for loss of office.

Where an ex-gratia payment requires to be disclosed as a compensation payment, the note will generally indicate the 'ex-gratia' nature of the payment, as seen in Extract 29.18 above.

Companies listed on the Stock Exchange would require to disclose the payment in Example 29.7 if it was considered significant (see 4.4.7 below).

B   *Augmentation of pension rights*

As discussed above, contributions to a pension scheme made in connection with a director's loss of, or retirement from, office should be included within the aggregate amount of compensation to be disclosed. However, it may be that in certain situations where there is a surplus on the company's pension scheme, it is agreed with the trustees of the scheme that the augmentation of the pension rights of the retiring director is to be met out of the surplus of the pension scheme, with no specific contribution being made by the company. In these circumstances, we believe that the capital cost of the augmentation of the pension rights should still be disclosed as part of the compensation for loss of office. This is because the amounts to be included within compensation for loss of office are to include non-cash benefits and are also to include payments made not only by the company and its subsidiary undertakings, but any other person (i.e. the pension scheme). One company which appears to have adopted this view was APV in its 1993 accounts, as illustrated below:

Extract 29.22: APV plc (1993)

4   DIRECTORS [extract]

	1993	1992
	£'000	£'000
Compensation for loss of office	**332**	–

(iv) Compensation of £216,042 was paid in respect of loss of office of a former director, together with an additional deferred pension of £9,875 per annum payable at normal retirement date. The actuarial valuation of this deferred pension has been calculated as £116,400.

However, such an approach is not always followed, as illustrated in Gerrard Group's 1997 accounts below:

Extract 29.23: Gerrard Group plc (1997)

Report of the Remuneration Committee[extract]

d)   Termination payments

Arrangements for the early termination of contracts are carefully considered by the Committee. When calculating termination payments, the Committee takes into account a variety of factors including age, years of service and the individual director's obligation to mitigate his own loss by seeking new employment.

D A Brayshaw retired from the Board on 31st March 1996. At that date he had a two year rolling contract. The Committee agreed to make a termination payment of £139,000 and not to apply any additional actuarial discount to his pension when he draws it early at age 50 in 1998. R B Williamson retired as executive chairman in December 1996. He received a termination payment of £100,000 and was granted a full pension even although he had not reached the Normal Retirement Age. T W Fellows retired in November 1996 and was granted a full pension even although he had not reached the Normal Retirement Age.

C   Consultancy agreements

Over the years, a number of ex-directors have entered into consultancy agreements with the companies on whose boards they have ceased to serve. Typically, these grant the ex-directors a guaranteed fee for a period of time. Whether payments to be made under such agreements should be disclosed as compensation for loss of office will depend on the particular circumstances and the extent to which it is envisaged that consultancy services will be provided by the former director. Where it is unlikely that the director will provide any consultancy service we believe that the amount should be disclosed as compensation for loss of office. However, where it is considered that the ex-director will provide services commensurate with the level of fees which are to be made then it may be appropriate not to include the fees as compensation for loss of office. Nevertheless, in such a situation consideration would need to be given as to whether such a consultancy agreement was a transaction in which the director had a material interest. An example of a company disclosing consultancy fees is Gerrard Group as shown below.

Extract 29.24: Gerrard Group plc (1999)

Report of the Remuneration Committee[extract]

N F Andrews retired on 30th June 1998. The remuneration shown is that paid during the year. In addition, a consultancy payment of £75,000 was paid to N F Andrews. Greig Middleton has entered into an arrangement with N F Andrews for five years, during which the Company will be entitled to call upon his services for a specified number of days each year in return for a consultancy payment of £100,000.

Another example is that of Norcros (see Extract 29.19 at 2.9.1 above).

However, companies listed on the Stock Exchange would require to disclose the payments in respect of consultancy agreements if they were considered significant (see 4.4.7 below).

2.10 Payments to third parties

As a result of the Companies Act 1989, financial statements are required to disclose amounts payable to or receivable by third parties for making available the services of any person:

(a) as director of the company; or

(b) as director of any of the company's subsidiary undertakings (whilst a director of the company); or

(c) in connection with the management of the affairs of the company or any of its subsidiary undertakings (whilst a director of the company).[69]

'Third parties' means persons other than:

(a) the director himself; or

(b) persons connected with the director or connected with bodies corporate controlled by the director; or

(c) the company and any of its subsidiary undertakings.[70]

Consequently, payments made to an unconnected organisation, such as a bank, for persons on secondment as a director will have to be disclosed; payments made to a holding company, or fellow subsidiary, for the services of a director will also have to be disclosed. Examples of disclosures in these circumstances are shown in the following extracts:

Extract 29.25: Powell Duffryn plc (1999)

2   Directors and employees [extract]

The aggregate remuneration of all directors during the year was as follows:

	1999 £000	1998 £000
Emoluments	1,166	1,048
Gains on share option exercise	57	8
Amounts receivable under long-term incentive schemes	–	54
Company pension contributions to money purchase schemes	–	–
Sums paid to third parties for directors' services	19	9

£19,000 was paid to Smith & Nephew plc for the services of Mr Hooley as a non-executive director during the year. No sums were paid to former directors during the year in respect of consultancy services (1998 £2,000). Retirement benefits are accruing to five directors under the defined benefit scheme.

The above disclosure in respect of payments to third parties is what is strictly required to comply with the requirement. However, many other companies include such payments within aggregate emoluments, but as long as the amounts paid to third parties are separately identified then they are deemed to meet the requirements under the dispensation noted at 2.1 above. One company which adopts such a treatment is Pilkington, as illustrated below:

Extract 29.26: Pilkington plc (1999)

Report on directors' remuneration [extract]

Non-executive directors' remuneration

    Sir Nigel Rudd's remuneration amounted to £200,000 (1998 £153,000), of which £nil (1998 £90,000) was paid to Williams PLC, his employer.

The amounts disclosed have to include any benefits in kind given to a third party for the services of a director at the estimated money value of the benefit. In such a case, the nature of the benefit is also required to be disclosed.[71]

2.11   Highest paid director

Where the aggregate amounts shown under 2.2 (emoluments), 2.5 (gains on exercise of share options, where applicable) and 2.6 (long-term incentive schemes) total £200,000 or more, the following shall be shown in respect of the highest paid director:

(a)   the total of such aggregate amounts (there is no need to disclose the separate amounts);[72]

(b)   the value of any pension contributions shown under 2.7 above;[73] and

(c)   where he/she has performed qualifying services during the financial year
       by reference to which the rate or amount of any defined benefits that may
       become payable will be calculated;

    (i)   the amount at the end of the year of his/her accrued pension; and

    (ii)   where applicable, the amount at the end of the year of his/her accrued
        lump sum.[74]

Examples of such disclosures are shown below:

Extract 29.27: John Lewis Partnership plc (1999)

10   DIRECTORS' EMOLUMENTS [extract]

The emoluments of the Chairman, who is also the highest paid director, were £466,000
(£435,000), including Partnership bonus of £72,000 (£76,000). The Chairman's aggregate pension
entitlement from the age of 60 accrued at the end of the year was £199,000 per annum (£168,000
per annum), with a further temporary pension, payable from the age of 60 until the State pension
starts, of £1,000 per annum (£1,000 per annum). The transfer value of the increase in accrued
entitlement, including temporary pension, during the year was £372,000 (£315,000).

The transfer value is not required to be disclosed by the Companies Act, but
companies listed on the Stock Exchange are required to disclose such
information for all directors (see 4.4.8 C below).

Extract 29.28: Scottish Power plc (1999)

33   Directors emoluments and interests [extract]

(b)   Total emoluments

The emoluments of the highest paid director (Mr Robinson) excluding pension contributions were
£515,293 (1998 £487,345). In addition, gains on exercise of share options during the year by Mr
Robinson amounted to £592,966 (1998 £nil). Pension contributions made by the company under
approved pension arrangements for Mr Robinson amounted to £nil (1998 £nil). Mr Robinson also
has an entitlement under the unapproved pension benefits described further in Note c(iii) below.

(c)   Directors' pension benefits

(i)   The accrued entitlement of the highest paid director (Mr Robinson) was £180,080 (1998
£141,348).

(iii)   Executives who joined the company on or after 1 June 1989 are subject to the earnings cap
introduced in the Finance Act 1989. Pension entitlements which cannot be provided through the
company's approved schemes due to the earnings cap are provided through unapproved pension
arrangements. Full details are included in the Remuneration Report. The pension benefits disclosed
above include approved and unapproved pension arrangements.

As with many of the disclosure requirements, the Act will regard such
information as having been disclosed if it can be determined from other
information which is shown (see 2.1 above). As companies listed on the Stock
Exchange are required to provide information for each director, then they will
generally have complied with this requirement. It is important, however, if listed
companies are to rely on this dispensation that sufficient information is given,
particularly about gains on exercise of share options and accrued pension

benefits, so that the details for the highest paid director for *both* years can be determined.

The determination of whether disclosure of information in respect of the highest paid director is required excludes the following amounts:

■   pension contributions in respect of money purchase benefits (see 2.7 above);

■   excess retirement benefits (see 2.8 above);

■   compensation for loss of office (see 2.9 above); and

■   sums paid to third parties in respect of directors' services (see 2.10 above).

However, 'Golden hellos' (see 2.2.2 B above) and payments made to persons connected with a director have to be taken into account.

Once it is determined that disclosure of information about the highest paid director is required, the next step is to identify which director this is.

The 'highest paid director' for this purpose means the director to whom is attributable the greatest part of the total of the aggregates under 2.2 (emoluments), 2.5 (gains on exercise of share options, where applicable) and 2.6 (long-term incentive schemes). This therefore excludes the value of any pension contributions shown under 2.7 above (even though such amounts are to be disclosed for whoever is determined to be the highest paid director).

In view of the fact that gains on exercise of share options and amounts receivable under long-term incentive schemes are included in this determination, some companies which are listed on the Stock Exchange may wish to identify the highest paid director and highlight such amounts that are applicable to that director, as it may appear from the remuneration table provided (see 4.4.3 below) that another director is the highest paid director. An example of such disclosure is given by BAA, as shown below:

Extract 29.29: BAA plc (1999)

3   Directors' emoluments [extract]

	Salary/fees		Bonus		Benefits		Total	
	1999	1998	**1999**	1998	**1999**	1998	**1999**	1998
(a) Emoluments	**£000**	£000	**£000**	£000	**£000**	£000	**£000**	£000
Executive directors								
Sir John Egan	**494**	475	**160**	92	**28**	25	**682**	592
J R F Walls	**285**	274	**91**	53	**22**	21	**398**	348

The highest paid director was Sir John Egan whose emoluments are shown above, but when emoluments and gains on the exercise of share options are aggregated, the highest paid director in 1999 was Mr Walls (emoluments: £398,000, gains on options: £322,000 and, in 1998, was Sir John Egan (emoluments: £592,000, gains on options: £697,000).

As indicated earlier, comparative information is required to be given for the highest paid director. However, this does not mean that the comparatives to be disclosed are for the individual director who is identified as being the highest paid director for the current year. The information to be disclosed is in respect of the individual who was identified in the previous year as being the highest paid director for that year. This is illustrated in the extract above.

For the purposes of the disclosure of (c) above, 'accrued pension' and 'accrued lump sum' mean respectively the amount of the annual pension, and the amount of the lump sum, which would be payable under the scheme on his/her attaining normal pension age if:

(a)   he/she had left the company's service at the end of the financial year;

(b)   there were no increase in the general level of prices in Great Britain during the period beginning with the end of that year and ending with his/her attaining that age;

(c)   no question arose of any commutation of the pension or inverse commutation of the lump sum; and

(d)   any amounts attributable to voluntary contributions paid by the director to the scheme, and any money purchase benefits which would be payable under the scheme, were disregarded.[75]

'Normal pension age' means the age at which the director will first become entitled to receive a full pension on retirement of an amount determined without reduction to take account of its payment before a later age (but disregarding any entitlement to pension upon retirement in the event of illness, incapacity or redundancy).[76]

Most defined benefit schemes entitle employees to a pension, some of which can be commuted for a lump sum. As a result of (c) above, there is therefore only a need to disclose the accrued pension as done by John Lewis and Scottish Power in Extracts 29.27 and 29.28 above. Both amounts should only be disclosed if the pension scheme benefits are such that the director receives a pension *and* a lump sum. Although the director may be able to commute either some of the pension for an extra lump sum or vice versa, the effect of paragraph (c) is that such a choice should be ignored.

Example 29.8 at 4.4.8 C below illustrates how the accrued pension is calculated.

For unlisted companies (as defined – see 2.5 above) which have not disclosed amounts in respect of gains made on the exercise of options or share awards under long-term incentive schemes, then there is no requirement to disclose any such amounts in respect of the highest paid director. However, such companies are required to state whether the highest paid director exercised any share options and whether any shares were receivable by that director under a long-term incentive scheme.[77] If the highest paid director has not been involved in any such transactions then that fact need not be stated.[78]

3   EMPLOYEE DISCLOSURES

The Companies Act contains disclosure requirements relating to employees' remuneration which may also impact upon directors.

3.1   Director as an employee

Directors may have a contract of service with the company, in which case they should be included in the detailed employee disclosures. Accordingly, certain of their costs will require disclosure in the wages and salaries note[79] (in addition to the disclosures in the directors' remuneration note), as is illustrated below:

Extract 29.30: John Mowlem & Company PLC (1998)

7   Employees

	1998 **Number**	1997 Number
The average weekly number of persons employed by the Group including Directors during the year was:		
Access Products and Services	**4,304**	4,200
Construction Activities and Services	**7,133**	7,198
Facilities Services	**946**	932
Environmental Services	**713**	443
Project Investment and Property and Corporate activities	**186**	191
	13,282	12,964
	1998 **£m**	1997 £m
The aggregate payroll cost was:		
Wages and salaries	**261.0**	238.9
Social security costs	**23.4**	21.8
Other pension costs	**12.1**	11.0
	296.5	271.7

In this context, the employer's national insurance contributions should be included as part of social security costs (that is, any contributions by the company to any state social security or pension scheme, fund or arrangement);[80] however, the value of benefits-in-kind must be excluded.

The emoluments of directors who have a contract only for services as director (i.e. most non-executive directors) should not be included in the wages and salaries note, since such persons are not employees of the company. However, their emoluments will be included in the information disclosed in respect of directors' remuneration.

4   STOCK EXCHANGE REQUIREMENTS

As discussed earlier, in recent years executive remuneration of companies listed on the Stock Exchange has become a focus of public attention with regard to both the level and the structure of boardroom pay.

This concern was first addressed in 1992 by the Cadbury Committee which made various recommendations in respect of directors' remuneration. These are outlined at 4.1 below.

Also in September 1994 the UITF issued an Abstract which recommended various disclosures in respect of directors' share options (see 4.4.9 A below)

The remit of the Cadbury Committee had been corporate governance as a whole, of which executive remuneration was only a part. The comprehensive review of directors' pay as a single issue fell to the Study Group on Directors' Remuneration, commonly known as the Greenbury Committee after its chairman Sir Richard Greenbury, chairman of Marks and Spencer. This Committee was established in January 1995 at the initiative of (but independent from) the CBI, with the remit of identifying good practice in determining directors' remuneration and preparing a Code of such practice for use by UK PLCs.

The Greenbury Committee issued its report in July 1995. This contained a Code of Best Practice, summarised briefly at 4.2 below. In October 1995 and June 1996 the London Stock Exchange gave effect to certain of these recommendations by amending its *Listing Rules* and in May 1997 completed the jigsaw by introducing its requirements on the disclosure of directors' pension entitlements.

The Stock Exchange requirements have since been amended as a result of the work of the successor body to the Cadbury Committee, under the chairmanship of Sir Ronald Hampel, Chairman of ICI. In January 1998 the final report of the Committee on Corporate Governance (the Hampel Committee) was issued[81] and in June 1998, the Stock Exchange published the final version of the Principles of Good Governance and Code of Best Practice (the Combined Code), together with revised *Listing Rules*.

The Combined Code deals with corporate governance as a whole and has been derived from the Hampel Committee's final report and from the Cadbury and Greenbury Reports. It contains both principles and detailed Code provisions. Under the revised *Listing Rules*, companies are required to disclose how they have applied the principles and the extent to which they have complied with the detailed provisions of the Combined Code in their annual report in respect of periods ending on or after 31 December 1998. The principles and detailed provisions of the Code relating to directors' remuneration are outlined at 4.3 below.

The current requirements of the Stock Exchange are described at 4.4 below.

4.1   Cadbury Code

In December 1992, the Cadbury Committee, which was set up in May 1991 by the Financial Reporting Council, the London Stock Exchange and the accountancy profession, issued its report on 'corporate governance'.[82] The Committee's purpose was to review those aspects of corporate governance specifically related to financial reporting and accountability, in the light of concern at the perceived low level of confidence both in financial reporting and in the ability of auditors to provide the safeguards which the users of company reports sought and expected.

At the heart of the Committee's recommendations is its Code of Best Practice for the boards of listed companies. Paragraph 3.2 of the Code stated that 'there should be full and clear disclosure of directors' total emoluments and those of the chairman and highest paid UK director, including pension contributions and stock options. Separate figures should be given for salary and performance-related elements and the basis on which performance is measured should be explained.'

This certainly extended the Companies Act disclosures which were required at that time, so as to require further analysis of total emoluments and those of the chairman and the highest paid director. However, there were always going to be differing views as to exactly what disclosures would be required in order to comply with the requirement for 'full and clear disclosure'.

4.2   Greenbury Code

As mentioned above, the comprehensive review of directors' pay as a single issue fell to the Greenbury Committee. Like the Cadbury Committee before it, the Report that it issued contained a Code of Best Practice containing a number of recommendations split into four sections, A to D, which are summarised below.

4.2.1   Section A – The remuneration committee

The remuneration of executive directors should be determined by a remuneration committee consisting entirely of non-executive directors, with no personal financial interest (other than as shareholders) or other potential conflicts of interest. The members of the committee should be named in their annual report to shareholders (see Section B below). They should consult the chairman and/or chief executive on their proposals and should also have access to other advice from inside and outside the company.

4.2.2   Section B – Disclosure and approval provisions

The remuneration committee should make an annual report to shareholders to be included in, or annexed to, the annual report and accounts. This should set out the policies and criteria for determining directors' pay and an analysis of the remuneration of each director by name, together with information on pension entitlements and share options, all of these figures being subject to audit. There should also be a statement that the committee has given full consideration to the recommendations of Sections C and D, as described below. Departures from certain of these recommendations (in particular those relating to length of service contracts and pensionable bonuses) should be explained.

4.2.3   Section C – Remuneration policy

Remuneration packages should pay the rate for the job, but no more. Performance-related pay should be based on genuinely demanding criteria, and in general there should be a move away from short-term cash-based schemes to longer-term share-based schemes. Share-based schemes should be designed to encourage the holding of shares for the longer term rather than realising them for cash. Share-based schemes should aim to measure the company's performance against that of comparator companies using measures such as total shareholder return. The consequences of pay increases on pension entitlements should be carefully considered, and in general annual bonuses should not be pensionable.

4.2.4   Section D – Service contracts and compensation

Companies should generally aim to reduce the notice period of directors' service contracts to one year or less, although in some cases periods of up to two years may be acceptable. Any provision for compensation payments in the event of early termination should not appear to reward failure and should have regard to an outgoing director's obligation to mitigate damages by seeking new employment.

4.3   Combined Code

As indicated earlier, the Combined Code contains principles and detailed provisions of the Code relating to directors' remuneration. Companies therefore need to disclose how they have applied these principles and the extent to which they have complied with the detailed provisions. These deal with the level and make-up of remuneration, procedure and disclosure and are set out below.

4.3.1   Principle B.1   The Level and Make-up of Remuneration

Levels of remuneration should be sufficient to attract and retain the directors needed to run the company successfully, but companies should avoid paying more than is necessary for this purpose. A proportion of executive directors' remuneration should be structured so as to link rewards to corporate and individual performance.

Code Provisions - Remuneration policy

- The remuneration committee should provide the packages needed to attract, retain and motivate executive directors of the quality required but should avoid paying more than is necessary for this purpose. (B.1.1)

■ Remuneration committees should judge where to position their company relative to other companies. They should be aware what comparable companies are paying and should take account of relative performance. But they should use such comparisons with caution, in view of the risk that they can result in an upward ratchet of remuneration levels with no corresponding improvement in performance. (B.1.2)

■ Remuneration committees should be sensitive to the wider scene, including pay and employment conditions elsewhere in the group, especially when determining annual salary increases. (B.1.3)

■ The performance-related elements of remuneration should form a significant proportion of the total remuneration package of executive directors and should be designed to align their interests with those of shareholders and to give these directors keen incentives to perform at the highest levels. (B.1.4)

■ Executive share options should not be offered at a discount save as permitted by paragraphs 13.30 and 13.31 of the Listing Rules. (B.1.5)

■ In designing schemes of performance related remuneration, remuneration committees should follow the provisions in Schedule A to this code. (B.1.6)

Code Provisions - Service Contracts and Compensation

■ There is a strong case for setting notice or contract periods at, or reducing them to, one year or less. Boards should set this as an objective; but they should recognise that it may not be possible to achieve it immediately. (B.1.7)

■ If it is necessary to offer longer notice or contract periods to new directors recruited from outside, such periods should reduce after the initial period. (B.1.8)

■ Remuneration committees should consider what compensation commitments (including pension contributions) their directors' contracts of service, if any, would entail in the event of early termination. They should in particular consider the advantages of providing explicitly in the initial contract for such compensation commitments except in the case of removal for misconduct. (B.1.9)

■ Where the initial contract does not explicitly provide for compensation commitments, remuneration committees should, within legal constraints, tailor their approach in individual early termination cases to the wide variety of circumstances. The broad aim should be to avoid rewarding poor performance while dealing fairly with cases where departure is not due to poor performance and to take a robust line on reducing compensation to reflect departing directors' obligations to mitigate loss. (B.1.10)

4.3.2   Principle B.2   Procedure

Companies should establish a formal and transparent procedure for developing policy on executive remuneration and for fixing the remuneration packages of individual directors. No director should be involved in deciding his or her own remuneration.

Code Provisions

■   To avoid potential conflicts of interest, boards of directors should set up remuneration committees of independent non-executive directors to make recommendations to the Board, within agreed terms of reference, on the company's framework of executive remuneration and its cost; and to determine on their behalf specific remuneration packages for each of the executive directors, including pension rights and any compensation payments. (B.2.1)

■   Remuneration committees should consist exclusively of non-executive directors who are independent of management and free from any business or other relationship which could materially interfere with the exercise of their independent judgement. (B.2.2)

■   The members of the remuneration committee should be listed each year in the board's remuneration report to shareholders [B.3.1 below]. (B.2.3)

■   The Board itself or, where required by the Articles of Association, the shareholders should determine the remuneration of the non-executive directors, including members of the remuneration committee, within the limits set in the Articles of Association. Where permitted by the Articles, the Board may however delegate this responsibility to a small sub-committee, which might include the chief executive officer. (B.2.4)

■   Remuneration committees should consult the chairman and/or chief executive officer about their proposals relating to the remuneration of other executive directors and have access to professional advice inside and outside the company. (B.2.5)

■   The chairman of the Board should ensure that the company maintains contact as required with its principal shareholders about remuneration in the same way as for other matters. (B.2.6)

4.3.3   Principle B.3   Disclosure

The company's annual report should contain a statement of remuneration policy and details of the remuneration of each director.

Code Provisions

■   The board should report to the shareholders each year on remuneration. The report should form part of, or be annexed to, the company's annual report and accounts. It should be the main vehicle through which the company reports to shareholders on directors' remuneration. (B.3.1)

- The report should set out the company's policy on executive directors' remuneration. It should draw attention to factors specific to the company. (B.3.2)

- In preparing the remuneration report, the board should follow the provisions in Schedule B to this code. (B.3.3)

- Shareholders should be invited specifically to approve all new long term incentive schemes (as defined in the Listing Rules) save in the circumstances permitted by paragraph 13.13A of the Listing Rules. (B.3.4)

- The board's annual remuneration report to shareholders need not be a standard item of agenda for AGMs. But the board should consider each year whether the circumstances are such that the AGM should be invited to approve the policy set out in the report and should minute their conclusions. (B.3.5)

The main impact of these provisions is that the remuneration report is to be given by the board rather than by the remuneration committee on its behalf. As far as the content of the remuneration report is concerned, Schedule B to the Combined Code requires the following to be included:

- Full details of all elements in the remuneration package of each individual director by name, such as basic salary, benefits in kind, annual bonuses and long term incentive schemes including share options.

- Information on share options, including SAYE options, should be given for each director in accordance with the recommendations of UITF 10.

- If grants under executive share option or other long-term incentive schemes are awarded in one large block rather than phased, the report should explain and justify.

- Also included in the report should be pension entitlements earned by each individual director during the year, disclosed on one of the alternative bases recommended by the Faculty of Actuaries and the Institute of Actuaries and included in the *Listing Rules*. Companies may wish to make clear that the transfer value represents a liability of the company, not a sum paid or due to the individual.

- If annual bonuses or benefits in kind are pensionable the report should explain and justify.

- Any service contracts which provide for, or imply, notice periods in excess of one year (or any provisions for predetermined compensation on termination which exceed one year's salary and benefits) should be disclosed and the reasons for the longer notice periods explained.

The amounts received by, and commitments made to, each director under the first, second and fourth bullet points above should be subject to audit.

These broadly repeat what was already required by the Stock Exchange, although Schedule B incorporates the Hampel Committee's suggestion that companies might spell out that the transfer value of a director's increase in accrued pension is not a sum paid or due to the individual. Interestingly, it doesn't repeat the Committee's suggestion that it cannot meaningfully be added to annual remuneration.

4.4 Stock Exchange requirements following the Combined Code

To give effect to the Greenbury recommendations, in October 1995 the Stock Exchange amended the *Listing Rules* by adding a non-mandatory annexe – *Best Practice Provisions: Directors' Remuneration* – and some new mandatory disclosures. These disclosures can be summarised as follows.

- A statement that the company has complied with Section A of the Best Practice Provisions (broadly corresponding to Section A of the Greenbury Code).

- A statement of the company's remuneration policy and a confirmation that, in framing this policy, the remuneration committee has 'given full consideration to' Section B of the Best Practice Provisions (broadly corresponding to Sections C and D of the Greenbury Code).

- An analysis of the remuneration of each director by name, together with information on share options and long-term incentive schemes other than share options, all of these figures being subject to audit.

- The unexpired term of the service contract of any director proposed for re-election at the annual general meeting.

The first two items were mandatory for accounting periods beginning, and the other two items for periods ending, on or after 31 December 1995.

These disclosures essentially mirrored those proposed in Section B of the Greenbury Code, with the important exception that the *Listing Rules* did not yet require disclosure of individual directors' pension benefits.

A further aspect of the Greenbury Code not specifically dealt with by the October 1995 amendment to the *Listing Rules* was the recommendation that share options should be phased rather than awarded in a large block. In June 1996, however, the Stock Exchange issued a further amendment implementing this recommendation requiring companies to disclose their policy on the granting of options. This was effective for accounting periods ending on or after 30 September 1996.

As mentioned above, the one aspect which was outstanding was the disclosure of individual directors' pension benefits. The Institute of Actuaries and the Faculty of Actuaries published a joint consultation paper on this issue in January 1996, followed in April 1996 by a second paper summarising the comments received on the first and making recommendations on the basis of those comments (see 4.4.8 B below for a discussion of these papers). In May 1996 the Stock Exchange issued a consultative document setting out proposed changes to its requirements so as to give effect to these recommendations. A year later in May 1997 it finally issued its requirements in this regard. These were effective for accounting periods ending on or after 1 July 1997.

Following the publication of the Combined Code in June 1999 some minor amendments were made to the *Listing Rules*. The specific statements required in the first two items above were dispensed with and replaced by the all-embracing statement on compliance with the Combined Code; and the remuneration report is to be given by the board rather than by the remuneration committee on its behalf.

Accordingly the Stock Exchange now requires all listed companies (other than investment companies, investment trusts, investment property companies and venture capital trusts with no executive directors) to include within their annual report and accounts:

(a)   a report to the shareholders by the board containing:[83]

    (i)   a statement of the company's policy on executive directors' remuneration;

    (ii)   the amount of each element in the remuneration package for the period under review of each director by name, including, but not restricted to:

- basic salary and fees;
- the estimated money value of benefits in kind;
- annual bonuses;
- deferred bonuses;
- compensation for loss of office and payments for breach of contract or other termination payments;

together with the total for each director for the period under review and for the corresponding prior period, and any significant payments made to former directors during the period under review.

Such details are to be presented in tabular form, unless inappropriate, together with explanatory notes as necessary;

    (iii)   information on share options, including SAYE options, for each director by name in accordance with the recommendations of UITF 10. Such information is to be presented in tabular form together with explanatory notes as necessary;

    (iv)   details of any long-term incentive schemes, other than share options details of which have been disclosed under (iii) above, including:

- the interests of each director by name in the long-term incentive schemes at the start of the period under review;

- entitlements or awards granted and commitments made to each director under such schemes during the period, showing which crystallise either in the same year or subsequent years;

- the money value and number of shares, cash payments or other benefits received by each director under such schemes during the period; and

- the interests of each director in the long-term incentive schemes at the end of the period;

(v) explanation and justification of any element of remuneration, other than basic salary, which is pensionable;

(vi) details of any directors' service contract with a notice period in excess of one year or with provisions for predetermined compensation on termination which exceeds one year's salary and benefits in kind, giving the reasons for such notice period;

(vii) the unexpired term of any directors' service contract of a director proposed for election or re-election at the forthcoming AGM and, if any director proposed for election or re-election does not have a service contract, a statement to that effect;

(viii) a statement of the company's policy on the granting of options or awards under its employees' share schemes and other long-term incentive schemes, explaining and justifying any departure from that policy in the period under review and any change in the policy from the preceding year;

(ix) for defined benefit schemes (as defined in the Companies Act – see 2.7 above):

- details of the amount of the increase during the period under review (excluding inflation) and of the accumulated total amount at the end of the period in respect of the accrued benefit to which each director would be entitled on leaving service or is entitled having left service during the period under review;

- and either:

  (a) the transfer value (less director's contributions) of the relevant increase in accrued benefit (to be calculated in accordance with Actuarial Guidance Note GN11 but making no deduction for any underfunding) as at the end of the period; or

  (b) so much of the following information as is necessary to make a reasonable assessment of the transfer value in respect of each director:

    - current age;

    - normal retirement age;

- the amount of any contributions paid or payable by the director under the terms of the scheme during the period under review;

- details of spouse's and dependants' benefits;

- early retirement rights and options, expectations of pension increases after retirement (whether guaranteed or discretionary); and

- discretionary benefits for which allowance is made in transfer values on leaving and any other relevant information which will significantly affect the value of the benefits.

Voluntary contributions and benefits should not be disclosed; and

(x) for money purchase schemes (as defined in the Companies Act – see 2.7 above): details of the contribution or allowance payable or made by the company in respect of each director during the period of review.

Whilst these requirements are closely based on the Greenbury Code, there are some differences of emphasis and detail, which are noted in the relevant sections below.

In June 1996 the Stock Exchange also introduced a requirement that where a company (unusually) sets up a long-term incentive scheme for an individual director then certain detailed disclosures about such a scheme have to be disclosed in the next annual report.[84]

In addition to the above disclosure requirements the Stock Exchange has another long-standing requirement relating to directors' remuneration which is to disclose particulars of arrangements under which a director has either waived or agreed to waive any current or future emoluments (this applies in respect of emoluments from the company or any of its subsidiaries).[85] As noted at 1 above, the Companies Act no longer requires information about emoluments which have been waived.

4.4.1 Positioning of Remuneration Report

Item (a) at 4.4 above requires the detailed disclosures to be given in 'a report to the shareholders by the Board', although it is silent as to where this report should appear in the annual report and accounts. As might therefore be expected, there is some variety of treatment among companies. Most companies give all the required information in a separate remuneration report presented alongside (or as part of) the directors' report, the chairman's statement and similar sections of the annual report. Where this is done, many such companies do not include any of the information required by the Companies Act in the main body of the accounts, but merely make a statement along the lines of 'Details, for each director, of remuneration, compensation for loss of office, pension entitlements and interests in share options are set out on pages ...'.

Another treatment is for the remuneration report to consist of the narrative disclosures only, with the figures being included in the main body of the accounts.

4.4.2   Statement of remuneration policy

Item (a) (i) at 4.4 above requires the remuneration committee report to include a 'a statement of the company's policy on executive directors' remuneration'. Combined Code Provision B.3.2 adds that 'it should draw attention to factors specific to the company'.

This is a considerably less detailed requirement than that of the corresponding paragraph (B2) of the Greenbury Code, which recommended disclosure of 'the company's policy on executive Directors' remuneration, including levels, comparator groups of companies, individual components, performance criteria and measurement, pension provision, contracts of service and compensation commitments on early termination'.

The Greenbury Report expanded on this recommendation by suggesting that the section on general policy should set out the company's policy on major issues such as:

■ the total level of remuneration;

■ the main components and the arrangements for determining them, including the division between basic and performance-related components;

■ the comparator groups of companies considered;

■ the main parameters and rationale for any annual bonus schemes, including caps;

■ how performance is measured, how rewards are related to it, how the performance measures relate to longer-term objectives and how the company has performed over time relative to comparator companies;

■ the company's policy on allowing executive directors to accept appointments and retain payments from sources outside the company;

■ the company's policy on contracts of service and early termination;

■ the pension and retirement benefit schemes for directors, including the main types of scheme, the main terms and parameters, what elements of remuneration are pensionable, how the Inland Revenue pensions cap has been accommodated and whether the scheme is part of, or separate from, the main company scheme.[86]

The Greenbury Report also recommended that the provisions should also apply to non-executive directors and that the report should state how, and by whom, the fees and other benefits of the non-executive directors are determined.[87]

General practice among companies is to give only factual details rather than policies in respect of all these items and to give only a general policy on remuneration, as required by the Stock Exchange. Examples of statements made about particular elements, such as bonuses, share options and long-term incentive schemes, are illustrated in the extracts in the relevant sections below.

This was an issue considered by the Hampel Committee which stated that 'a number of companies have met the letter of [the Stock Exchange] requirement with anodyne references to the need to "recruit, retain and motivate" or to pay "market rates".' By including within Combined Code Provision B.3.2 that the report 'should draw attention to factors specific to the company' the Committee hopes that companies will provide more informative statements.[88]

4.4.3 *Individual directors' emoluments*

The remuneration report is to include the amount of each element in the remuneration package for the period under review of each director by name 'including, but not restricted to, basic salary and fees, the estimated money value of benefits in kind, annual bonuses, deferred bonuses, compensation for loss of office and payments for breach of contract or other termination payments, together with the total for each director for the period under review and for the corresponding prior period ...'.

Disclosure of annual bonuses, deferred bonuses and compensation payments is discussed in more detail at 4.4.4, 4.4.5 and 4.4.6 below.

This requirement for a detailed breakdown of each director's remuneration is probably the most sensitive incremental disclosure arising from the implementation of the Greenbury Code. Previously, such analyses had been required (by virtue of the Cadbury Code) in respect only of the pay packages of the chairman and highest paid director (normally the chief executive); the other directors being anonymously included within the bandings formerly required by the Companies Act.

An illustration of the required disclosure is given in the following extract:

Extract 29.31: Christian Salvesen PLC (1999)

Remuneration Report [extract]

DIRECTORS' EMOLUMENTS EXCLUDING PENSION CONTRIBUTIONS

	Note	Salary £'000	Fees £'000	Taxable Benefits £'000	Cash Bonus £'000	Other Taxable Pay £'000	Compen- sation payments £'000	1999 Total £'000	1998 Total £'000
Chairman									
J M Fry		88	–	–	–	–	22	**88**	58†
Former director									
Sir Alick Rankin		–	–	–	–	–	–	**–**	26
Executive directors									
E J Roderick		219	–	8	–	1	–	**228**	135*
P G Aspden	(i)	130	–	10	–	–	–	**140**	–
A M Callaghan	(ii)	76	–	4	–	–	–	**80**	–
Former directors									
I C Adam	(iii)	41	–	–	–	41	398	**480**	198
D J Bristow	(iv)	126	–	6	–	1	52	**185**	121*
P I Redfern	(v)	53	–	3	–	–	290	**346**	81*
Dr C Masters		–	–	–	–	–	–	**–**	228
Non-executive directors									
P E B Cawdron		–	20	–	–	–	–	**20**	10*
Dr A Edelman		–	20	–	–	–	–	**20**	3#
R S Salvesen		–	20	–	–	–	–	**20**	18
J M Fry		–	–	–	–	–	–	**–**	4•
Other former directors									
Sir Ronald Miller		–	–	–	–	–	–	**–**	8
A C Salvesen		–	–	–	–	–	–	**–**	8
B H Fidler		–	–	–	–	–	–	**–**	6
		733	60	31	–	43	740	**1,607**	904

Notes:
Emoluments in respect of the period:
(i) from 7 May 1998, the date of appointment   from 10 July 1997†
(ii) from 3 September 1998, the date of appointment   from 29 September 1997*
(iii) to 9 July 1998, the date of resignation   from 5 February 1998#
(iv) to 12 February 1999, the date of resignation   to 10 July 1997•
(v) to 18 August 1998, the date of resignation

The amounts shown as emoluments for Mr A M Callaghan, Mr D J Bristow and Mr P I Redfern
include amounts paid by a subsidiary company.

It can be seen from the above extract that not only is information given for the executive directors but information is also included in respect of the non-executive directors. However, this is what is required even although the policy statement discussed at 4.4.2 above is only required by the Stock Exchange to be in respect of the executive directors.

It can also be seen that the table excludes pension contributions as disclosures about the pension benefits of directors are covered by a separate requirement (see 4.4.8 below). Nevertheless some companies include pension contributions as part of the remuneration table as illustrated below:

Extract 29.32: Land Securities PLC (1999)

7   Directors' Emoluments, Share Options and Interests in Ordinary Shares[extract]

EMOLUMENTS

The emoluments of the directors including pension contributions and **£178,500** receivable (1998 £Nil) under the long term incentive plan amounted to **£1,891,000** (1998 £1,620,000).

£'000	Basic Salary	Profit Sharing & Bonuses	Benefits Car & Medical	Fees	Total Emoluments excluding Pensions 1999	1998	Pension Contributions 1999	1998
EXECUTIVE:								
I J Henderson	**300**	**36**	**11**	–	**347**	282	**126**	84
M R Griffiths	**205**	**27**	**12**	–	**244**	228	**83**	57
K Redshaw	**205**	**27**	**6**	–	**238**	223	**83**	57
J I K Murray	**212**	**28**	**7**	–	**247**	234	**86**	59
Sir Peter Hunt (Chairman – to 8.12.97)	–	–	–	–	–	250	–	–
NON-EXECUTIVE:								
P G Birch (Chairman – appointed 1.7.98)	–	–	**14**	**100**	**114**	23	–	–
John Hull (Chairman – to 30.6.98)	–	–	**9**	**80**	**89**	54	–	–
H I Connick (Retired 1.7.98)	–	–	–	**6**	**6**	23	–	–
P B Hardy	–	–	–	**26**	**26**	23	–	–
Sir Alistair Grant	–	–	–	**24**	**24**	23	–	–
Total 1999	**922**	**118**	**59**	**236**	**1,335**		**378**	
Total 1998	1,024	160	33	146		1,363		257

Although the pension contributions are included in the remuneration table, it can be seen from the above extract that a sub-total excluding the pension contributions is also given, not only for the current year but also for the comparative year. This will generally be necessary to comply with the Stock Exchange requirement and enable sufficient information to be disclosed so that the aggregate amounts of emoluments and pension contributions in respect of money purchase schemes required by the Companies Act can be determined. Some companies include the pension contributions in arriving at a total figure for each director and give a comparative total. Although this allows the current emoluments excluding pension contributions to be computed for each director, it does not allow the comparative figures excluding pension contributions to be determined as required (see A below).

The Greenbury Report also recommended that the nature of benefits in kind should be disclosed.[89] Although not required by the Stock Exchange many companies give such disclosure (see extracts at 2.3.2 A above). Arguably, Schedule B to the Combined Code could be interpreted to require such information as it says that 'full details of all elements in the remuneration package ... such as ... benefits in kind' should be included within the remuneration report.

A   Comparative figures

The above extracts do not include comparatives for each element of the total remuneration package. However, this is all that is necessary as the requirement is just to provide comparatives in respect of the total emoluments for each director; this is the approach followed by many companies. However, other companies disclose comparative amounts for each element, as shown below:

Extract 29.33: Storehouse plc (1999)

Remuneration Report [extract]
Directors' emoluments

		Salary fees £000s	Benefits £000s	Total remuneration ex. pension contributions £000s	Pension contributions £000s
Executive directors					
Keith Edelman	**1999**	**400**	**16**	**416**	**80**
	1998	369	15	384	74
Steve Bedford	**1999**	**221**	**23**	**244**	**–**
	1998	218	24	242	–
Chris Martin	**1999**	**210**	**11**	**221**	**8**
	1998	175	12	187	5
Non-executive directors					
Alan Smith	**1999**	**150**	**15**	**165**	**–**
	1998	150	14	164	–
Brian Hardy	**1999**	**25**	**–**	**25**	**–**
	1998	25	–	25	–
Angela Heylin	**1999**	**23**	**–**	**23**	**–**
	1998	23	–	23	–
David Tagg	**1999**	**25**	**–**	**25**	**–**
	1998	25	–	25	–
Martin Sorrel	1998	6	–	6	–

Another company that discloses the comparative elements but in columnar fashion is United Utilities, as shown below:

Extract 29.34: United Utilities PLC (1999)

Remuneration report [extract]

Directors' emoluments

Emoluments comprise salaries, fees, taxable benefits and the value of short term incentive awards. The aggregate emoluments of directors in the year ended 31 March 1999 amounted to £1.548 million (1998 – £2.079 million). Individual directors' emoluments for the financial year were:

	Salary/ Fees		Short term incentive award		Taxable benefits		Total	
	1999 £'000	1998 £'000	**1999 £'000**	1998 £'000	**1999 £'000**	1998 £'000	**1999 £'000**	1998 £'000
Derek Green	**311.7**	272.7	**128.0**	120.0	**21.5**	18.1	**461.2**	410.8
John Beckitt	**178.8**	167.7	**74.0**	68.0	**17.9**	12.0	**270.7**	247.9
Bob Ferguson	**202.8**	191.0	**82.3**	79.4	**15.5**	14.0	**300.6**	284.4
Gordon Waters	**170.6**	134.6	**56.8**	55.7	**12.6**	9.0	**240.0**	199.3
Sir Christopher Harding	**100.0**	20.8	–	–	**0.4**	–	**100.4**	20.8
Eric Clark	**23.0**	25.7	–	–	–	0.9	**23.0**	26.6
Sir Richard Evans	**20.0**	11.7	–	–	–	–	**20.0**	11.7
Robin Leach	**27.0**	26.7	–	–	–	1.2	**27.0**	27.9
Sir Peter Middleton	**41.0**	40.7	–	–	–	–	**41.0**	40.7
Jane Newell	**37.0**	25.2	–	–	–	–	**37.0**	25.2
John Seed	**27.0**	24.5	–	–	–	0.5	**27.0**	25.0

A related issue is whether the disclosure of comparative amounts should identify the names of former directors who received remuneration in the previous year but did not receive any remuneration in the current year or indeed whether such payments need to be disclosed at all. The requirement seems to be only in respect of the directors in the period under review, i.e. the current year; this suggests that the amounts in respect of such former directors are not required. However, although the totals of such amounts are not required by the Stock Exchange they will still have to be given, thereby providing sufficient information to enable the company to comply with the requirement of the Companies Act of disclosing comparative figures for aggregate emoluments (unless such an amount is separately disclosed for Companies Act purposes).

Notwithstanding the fact that it is unnecessary to name such former directors and quantify their individual emoluments in the previous year, as can be seen from the above extracts a number of companies do disclose such information.

B   Companies Act information

As noted at 2.1 above, the Companies Act deems that the information that it specifies for disclosure is treated as having been given if it can be ascertained from information disclosed elsewhere. Many listed companies appear to take advantage of this dispensation as they do not disclose all of the Companies Act information together as a separately identifiable section of the remuneration report or within a note to the accounts.

4.4.4   Annual bonuses

A   Performance criteria

Item (a) (ii) at 4.4 above requires the amount of the annual bonus payment made to each director to be disclosed. This falls a little short of what was apparently envisaged by the Greenbury Report, which also recommended that 'the extent to which any performance criteria have been met should be explained, as should any particular performance criteria on which individual Directors' entitlements depend and any special arrangements for them'.[90]

In practice, however, many companies attempt to comply with the spirit of Greenbury rather than just the letter of the *Listing Rules*. This is hardly surprising given that an explanation of the operation of bonus schemes had been recommended by the Cadbury Code in 1992. Such disclosure is generally given in the policy statement dealing with the annual bonus element of the remuneration package.

Where a bonus scheme is linked to a relatively straightforward accounting measure, it can be clearly summarised in a few lines, as illustrated below:

Extract 29.35: Carclo Engineering Group PLC (1999)

Remuneration report [extract]

Remuneration policy

(ii) **Performance related bonus** – executive directors participate in an annual non pensionable performance related cash bonus scheme known as the Short Term Incentive (STI) Scheme to encourage operating efficiency and earnings growth. The STI Scheme for executive directors is restricted to a maximum of 30% of basic salary and is based on the growth in pre tax earnings per share before exceptional items ("pre tax earnings") above a minimum performance target, the basis of which is annually determined by the committee taking into account inflation and prevailing market conditions. For 1998/99 and 1999/2000 the minimum performance targets have been set at a level of 3% above the previous year's pre tax earnings. The bonus is calculated as follows:

1998/1999

An increase of 0.1% in pre tax earnings beyond the minimum performance target is rewarded by a bonus equivalent to 0.2% on salary up to a total maximum bonus equivalent to 30% of salary. The effect of the arrangement is for a maximum bonus of 30% of salary to be earned when the pre tax earnings increases by 18.0% over the previous year.

No bonus is payable in respect of 1998/99.

1999/2000

An increase of 0.1% in pre tax earnings beyond the minimum performance target is rewarded by a bonus equivalent to 0.1% on salary up to a total maximum bonus equivalent to 30% of salary. The effect of the arrangement is for a maximum bonus of 30% of salary to be earned when the pre tax earnings increases by 33.9% over the previous year.

> *Extract 29.36: The Boots Company PLC (1999)*
>
> **Board Remuneration Report** [extract]
>
> **Components of emoluments**
>
> **Short term executive bonus scheme** This scheme rewards executive directors for achieving operating efficiencies and profitable growth in the relevant year by reference to challenging but achievable forecasts derived at the beginning of the year from strategic plans.
>
> During 1998/99, the performance criterion was profit after tax. A bonus of 10% of base salary was payable for performance at 95% of profit after tax target rising to 25% of salary for performance at target level and to a maximum of 35% when profit after tax was 110% of target. Performance against target during the year was such that no bonus was earned by executive directors.

However, there remains the basic problem that very few companies state exactly what the relevant performance criteria are and even fewer explain how achievement of those criteria translates into payments to directors. This is not necessarily a criticism of the companies concerned, but in many cases simply reflects the fact that criteria for short-term bonus schemes tend to be more complicated than the more objective yardsticks (such as earnings per share or total shareholder return) used for longer-term schemes.

Performance may be linked to a number of financial measures, some of which may not be apparent from the published accounts (e.g. average daily cash balances), production targets, comparison with peer groups and personal performance; it is therefore more difficult to meet what Greenbury recommended.

In such situations, we would recommend that companies give a general description of the factors that are taken into account in determining the annual bonuses, the maximum bonus which may be payable and the extent to which a bonus has been paid. For example:

> *Extract 29.37: BAA plc (1999)*
>
> **REPORT ON DIRECTORS' REMUNERATION** [extract]
>
> **Annual bonuses**
>
> A proportion of the executive directors' remuneration is structured so as to link rewards to corporate and individual performance. The annual bonus is subject to performance conditions which are considered to be relevant, stretching and are designed to enhance the business.
>
> The 1998/99 bonus payable to the executive directors was subject to the achievement of an EPS improvement threshold and limited to a maximum potential of 50% of salary (1998: 40%).
>
> The annual bonus scheme was revised for 1998/99 to provide an incentive for improved performance at individual, team, business and Group level.
>
> It included individual business operating profit targets and key performance indicators such as safety performance, customer service and construction costs. The 1998/99 performance resulted in bonuses averaging 30% of salary being achieved. The 1999/2000 annual bonus scheme is similar to that for 1998/99.

B   Caps

The Greenbury Report expressed the view that 'bonuses should not be allowed to become, in effect, another guaranteed element of remuneration. They should normally be subject to an upper limit or cap, such as a specified percentage of basic pay'.[91] Each of the extracts shown above discloses the existence of caps. As noted previously, we recommend that disclosure of any such caps should be given as part of the details in respect of the annual bonus scheme.

C   Incentives to take shares

The Greenbury Report suggested that 'some proportion at least of any bonuses paid to Directors should take the form of shares to be held for a minimum period rather than cash'.[92] One company which has such a bonus scheme is TI Group, as shown below:

Extract 29.38: TI Group plc (1998)

REMUNERATION REPORT [extract]

Remuneration package

ii Annual bonus

For headquarters staff executive Directors the annual bonus is based partly on Group performance against plan, and partly on achievement of individual objectives. The annual bonus for executive Directors with line responsibility for operations is based partly on a combination of Group performance and business area performance against annual plan and partly on achievement of individual objectives. The annual plan includes specific cash targets. In 1998 the maximum potential cash bonus for members of the Chairman's Committee was 80% of basic salary, and for the other executive Directors 60% of basic salary, with the maximum amount normally achievable only if performance exceeds plan by a clear margin. The Committee retains the right to exercise an overview with regard to the quality of achievement. For 1999 a similar scheme is in force.

Payments in respect of 1998, comprising shares and/or cash, are shown in the table on page 47. The share element reflects Directors' individual elections to be paid annual bonus in TI shares rather than cash.

SUMMARY REMUNERATION TABLE

Executive Directors

– Salary, Annual Bonus and Benefits

As in prior years the annual performance-related bonus is an amount determined in cash. Executive directors may elect to receive a proportion of this bonus in the form of TI shares. Details of such elections appear in the table below.

	1997 Basic Salary £'000	1998 Basic Salary £'000	Benefits (Note 1) £'000	Annual Bonus — Cash £'000	Annual Bonus — Elected Share Allocation (Note 2) £'000	Compensation for loss of office £'000	1998 Total £'000	1997 Total £'000
Sir Christopher Lewinton	675	725	46	0	577	–	**1,348**	1,157
W J Laule	294	431	156	0	338	–	**925**	500
M D Angle (appointed 19th February 1997)	259	350	67	121	139	–	**677**	467
J Langston (appointed 20th October 1998)	–	44	8	11	13	–	**76**	–
D P Lillycrop (appointed 24th June 1998)	–	103	9	27	32	–	**171**	–
J L Roe	210	225	13	75	50	–	**363**	299
Former Directors:								
G O Aronson (resigned 28th May 1998)	174	90	16	–	–	307	**413**	262
L A Edwards (resigned 10th November 1998)	315	284	16	99	0	–	**399**	489
R J M Fisher (resigned 2nd December 1998)	300	284	29	110	0	–	**423**	474
J W Potter (resigned 2nd December 1998)	330	302	18	37	0	216	**573**	402

Notes:

2. Where the Directors have elected to receive an element of annual bonus in TI shares from the TI Group Employee Share Ownership Trust, the numbers of shares thus acquired are included in the holdings as at 5th March 1999 shown in the summary of Directors' share interests on page 64.

Some companies have introduced schemes whereby a director may receive free shares if he uses some of his annual bonus to purchase shares. The receipt of the extra shares are normally conditional upon the director remaining in employment with the company. Such schemes are discussed at 4.4.5 below.

D   Pensionable bonuses etc.

The Greenbury Report stated that 'Annual bonuses are a management instrument designed to promote and reward short-term performance. In general neither they nor payments under long-term incentive schemes nor benefits in kind should be pensionable. If such elements are pensionable, the remuneration committee report should explain and justify why.'[93] This has been implemented by the Stock Exchange requirement set out at (a) (v) at 4.4 above. Schedule B to the

Combined Code also requires an explanation and justification to be given where annual bonuses or benefits in kind are pensionable (see 4.3.3 above).

4.4.5   *Deferred bonuses*

The Stock Exchange defines a deferred bonus as 'any arrangement pursuant to the terms of which the participant(s) may receive an award of any asset (including cash or any security) in respect of service and/or performance in a period not exceeding the length of the relevant financial year notwithstanding that any such asset may, subject only to the participant(s) remaining a director or employee of the group, be receivable by the participant(s) after the end of the period to which the award relates'.[94]

Such bonuses are identified as one of the elements to be included within the remuneration table under (a) (ii) at 4.4 above. However, it is fair to say that it is unusual to see a heading of 'deferred bonuses' as part of the table; it may be that companies consider it inappropriate to include them, particularly as they generally involve shares, and therefore provide explanatory notes as necessary.

It is unclear from the requirement as to whether the deferred bonuses to be included for the period under review are those bonuses in respect of the current period but which are deferred or whether it is bonuses which relate to previous years, the conditions of which have been fulfilled during the period under review and the award finally given to the director.

A number of companies have introduced bonus schemes whereby the director may apply a proportion of his annual bonus for the purchase of shares in the company with an equivalent value which, generally, will be matched by an equivalent number of shares at nil cost. Such schemes normally involve a condition whereby the director must remain in employment with the company and are therefore 'deferred bonuses'.

Perhaps as a result of differing views of the interpretation of the disclosure requirement, or it may be because of differences between the various schemes, the treatment of such 'deferred bonus plans' varies. One company which has such a scheme is Booker:

Extract 29.39: Booker plc (1996)

Report of the Remuneration Committee[extract]

- **Share based incentives**

In addition to the all-employee SAYE share option scheme, the company has a deferred bonus plan (open to all senior managers on invitation) in order to encourage over the longer term identification with the success of Booker. For those electing to participate in this plan, part (currently one-third) of any performance-related bonus is put into a discretionary employee benefit trust, together with a further payment by the company. The trustees of the plan use the funds to purchase Booker shares in the market. After three years the bonus shares plus an equal number of matching shares become distributable, alternatively participants (who remain in the company's employment) can elect to leave them in the plan for a further two years, after which they will receive twice the bonus shares. The company's current policy is to offer executive share options once only when executives join the company.

Directors' remuneration

	Salary (incl. fees) £000	Benefits £000	Annual Bonus £000	1996 Total £000	1995 Total £000	Pension entitlement accrued in:	
						1996 £000	1995 £000
Chairman							
J F Taylor	122	7	–	129	213	–	2
Executive Directors							
C J Bowen	313	2	–	315	343	11	11
A J Busby	147	3	18 [2]	168	–	10	6
J E Kitson	158	11	–	169	187	2	3
J D Nelson	220	4	18 [2]	242	277	7	7
E C Robinson	151	10	11	172	171	10	12

Notes:

[2] These executive directors have elected to participate in the deferred bonus plan described on page 30 whereby part (currently one-third) of the bonus is put into a discretionary trust. The bonus payments shown above therefore relate solely to the cash element.

It can be seen that Booker has only included the cash element of the bonus. Therefore the one-third of the bonus which the directors are putting into the plan is excluded as well as any of the matching shares to be provided by the company.

Another treatment that is adopted by some companies is to include all of the annual bonus (including that proportion that the director will effectively take in shares by putting them into the plan), but not the matching shares. For example:

Extract 29.40: Laporte plc (1998)

25   Directors remuneration [extract]

Table 1   Executive directors

Remuneration excluding pensions

	Basic Salary 1998 £'000	Basic Salary 1997 £'000	Bonus 1998 £'000	Bonus (a) 1997 £'000	Benefits and other payments 1998 £'000	Benefits and other payments 1997 £'000	Total 1998 £'000	Total 1997 £'000
J W Leng	**400**	385	**158**	223	**27**	38	**595** (e)	646 (e)
P H Fearn	**211**	203	**83**	118	**15**	15	**309**	336
M A Kayser	**200**	187	**79**	108	**13**	13	**292**	308
M J Kenny (b)	**214**	209	**84**	121	**71**	16	**369**	346
R Parrot (c)	**211**	203	**83**	118	**13**	12	**307**	333

Notes

a   Annual bonus amounts are stated at their cash amounts. In 1997, half of these awards were taken in cash and the balance in shares.

The following executive directors have been awarded shares under the Company's bonus and long-term incentive plans.

Director	Balance at 1.1.98	Shares awarded	Shares waived	Shares taken up Number	Shares taken up Market value	Balance at 31.12.98	Earliest vesting date
J W Leng							
Annual bonus plan							
1996 bonus shares	10,000					10,000	9.7.97
1996 incentive shares	5,000					5,000	9.7.98
1997 bonus shares	–	14,788				14,788	27.3.98
1997 incentive shares	–	14,788				14,788	28.3.01
Deferred bonus	–	39,939				39,939	31.12.99
Long-term incentive plan	66,042	31,870	66,042			31,870	28.3.01
P H Fearn							
Annual bonus plan							
1997 bonus shares	–	7,797				7,797	27.3.98
1997 incentive shares	–	7,797				7,797	28.3.01
Deferred bonus	–	21,058				21,058	31.12.99
Long-term incentive plan	35,142	16,804	35,142			16,804	28.3.01
M A Kayser							
Annual bonus plan							
1997 bonus shares	–	7,182				7,182	27.3.98
1997 incentive shares	–	7,182				7,182	28.3.01
Deferred bonus	–	19,399				19,399	31.12.99
Long-term incentive plan	32,370	15,480	32,370			15,480	28.3.01
M J Kenny							
Annual bonus plan							
1996 bonus shares	5,573					5,573	9.7.97
1996 incentive shares	2,786					2,786	9.7.98
1997 bonus shares	–	7,859				7,859	27.3.98
1997 incentive shares	–	7,859				7,859	28.3.01
Deferred bonus	–	21,767				21,767	31.12.99
Long-term incentive plan	35,940	17,089	35,940			17,089	28.3.01

R Parrot (e)

Annual bonus plan					
1997 bonus shares	–	7,797		7,182	27.3.98
1997 incentive shares	–	7,797		7,182	1.1.99
Deferred bonus	–	21,058		19,399	1.1.99
Long-term incentive plan	35,142	16,804	35,142	16,804	1.1.99

Notes

a   The 1996 and 1997 annual bonus plans provide for an initial award of bonus shares plus an entitlement to receive additional incentive shares which vest at a later date, provided that the relevant bonus shares have not previously been sold.

b   Shares awarded under the deferred bonus scheme were given in respect of the successful achievement of the Group's restructuring and will vest subject to continuous employment with the Group until the vesting date.

c   The 1996 and 1997 awards under the long-term incentive plan were waived by all directors and lapsed on 8 January 1998. The shares awarded in 1998 will vest subject to the performance criteria set out on page 27.

d   Awards are made in the form of market price options or nil paid options as appropriate.

e   Mr Parrott retired on 31 December 1998. His annual bonus plan shares will lapse if not taken up by 30 June 1999 and his deferred bonus shares will lapse if not taken up by 31 December 1999. He will retain 11,203 of the 16,804 long-term incentive plan shares which must be taken up by 31 December 1999.

35   Employee share schemes [extract]

b   The 1997 Laporte Deferred Bonus Scheme

The awards under this plan have been made to the executive directors and other key executives who were fundamental to the successful achievement of the Group's restructuring. The award of shares will vest on 1 January 2000 subject to continuous employment with the Group until that date.

c   The Laporte plc Annual Bonus Scheme

Share awards under this plan consist of a bonus share option and an incentive share option. As an incentive to defer the receipt of the bonus shares for up to seven years from the date of grant, the executive is entitled to receive additional shares, the right to which lapses if the relevant bonus shares are taken up before a specified date. For the 1996 bonus, executives were able to take their award in cash or shares or a combination of both. Those who elected to receive their bonus as shares were entitled to receive additional incentive shares which vested in equal annual instalments, commencing on the first anniversary of the award. In 1997, half of the awards could be taken in the form of shares, deferral of which for at least three years would attract the right to receive additional incentive shares.

By disclosing that half of the 1997 bonus was taken in shares Laporte has effectively identified the share element of the 'deferred bonus'. Although the additional shares have been excluded, the footnote discloses the bonus and the incentive shares separately and therefore the value of the additional shares, at the date of the award, can be computed. It can be seen from the above extract that Laporte also has another deferred bonus scheme. The value of this bonus in 1997 has been excluded from the remuneration table, but the number of shares awarded are disclosed.

One company which goes further and includes the additional shares in quantifying the bonus is Prudential, as shown below:

Extract 29.41: Prudential Corporation plc (1998)

Remuneration Report [extract]

Executive Directors' Remuneration

Annual bonus

This element of the directors' remuneration package is designed to encourage directors to achieve the highest levels of annual corporate performance.

During 1998, executive directors other than Derek Higgs qualified for awards under the Group's short-term deferred bonus plan, known as the Share Participation Plan. Awards were determined by the Remuneration Committee based on the performance of the Group against quantitative financial and business targets, as well as specific personal objectives, up to a maximum total award of 45 per cent of salary at the time of the award.

Under the Plan executive directors received an initial cash award. Either the net amount of this award had to be used to buy shares or an equivalent number of shares had to be lodged with the Trustees of the Plan. The Company then lodged additional shares with the Trustees equivalent to the gross value of the cash award. Both sets of shares are held in trust for five years. If a director leaves prior to this, the additional shares may be released in certain circumstances.

During 1998, Derek Higgs was eligible to be awarded a bonus, up to a maximum of 100 per cent of salary at the time of the award. Half of the net amount of the bonus was used to buy Prudential shares. The bonus was based on the overall performance of Prudential Portfolio Managers, his performance as an executive director of the Company and performance against personal objectives.

For 1999, both the above arrangements will be replaced by a short-term incentive plan in which awards will be made in cash with no deferral period. These awards will continue to be based on the performance of the Group against quantitative financial and business targets, and to take account of an element of personal performance. The maximum awards under this plan will remain as at present. Awards under this plan will not be pensionable.

Directors' Remuneration	Salary /Fees £000	Annual Bonus £000	Benefits £000	Total 1998 £000	Total 1997 £000
Executive directors					
Keith Bedell-Pearce	275	75	27	377	336
Jonathan Bloomer	347	99	30	476	457
Sir Peter Davis	513	148	28	689	655
Derek Higgs	347	172	19	538	486
Jim Sutcliffe (resigned 30/9/97, note 2)					359
Total executive directors	1,482	494	104	2,080	2,293

Notes:

4.   The annual bonus reflects the total award under the Share Participation Plan, including the cost of the shares lodged by the Company with the Plan Trustees.

On balance we believe that where the only condition is that the director has to remain in employment for a future period, then as the bonus has been earned for the year in question the total value (including that relating to the additional shares) should be disclosed. However, other treatments such as that adopted by Laporte are acceptable. The important issue is that all of the relevant details are disclosed whereby the full value of the bonus can be determined. Such an approach will also meet the Companies Act requirements given that as long as information is disclosed it is deemed to have been disclosed under the Act (see 2.1 above).

To the extent that bonus schemes involve awards which are conditional upon future performance over a longer period than the financial year, then such a scheme is a long-term incentive scheme (see 4.4.9 B below).

4.4.6 Compensation payments

The Greenbury Committee took the view that 'compensation payments to Directors on loss of office have been a cause of public and shareholder concern in recent times'.[95] It is therefore rather surprising that the Greenbury Code contained no recommendation for disclosure of such payments. However, as noted in item (a) (ii) at 4.4 above, the Stock Exchange requires such payments to be disclosed for each director. The Companies Act requires only an aggregate figure for all directors (see 2.9 above).

An example of a company giving the disclosure required by the Stock Exchange within its remuneration table is Christian Salvesen, as illustrated in Extract 29.31 at 4.4.3 above.

However, it could be regarded that this is the minimum to be disclosed because the relevant requirement also says that 'such details are to be presented in tabular form, unless inappropriate, together with explanatory notes as necessary'.

Possibly as a result of this, a number of companies go further than just disclosing the amounts by disclosing details of the compensation arrangement. Extracts 29.18 and 29.19 at 2.9 above illustrate such extra disclosures. We believe it is good practice for such disclosures to be made and we would recommend that companies in this situation should provide this extra information.

4.4.7 Payments to former directors

The Greenbury Report recommended disclosure of 'any payments and benefits not previously disclosed, including any additional pension provisions, receivable by Directors who have retired during the accounting period or the previous accounting period'.[96] The intention of this recommendation was that amounts that are in substance compensation payments do not escape disclosure by being dressed up as something else. However, this has been translated into a Stock Exchange requirement to disclose 'any significant payments made to former directors during the period under review', which is a little curious in two respects.

First, whereas the other amounts (e.g. basic salary, benefits, annual bonus etc.) disclosed under item (a) (ii) at 4.4 above must be given for each director by name, payments to former directors can apparently be given in aggregate and without naming the directors concerned (although each of the extracts noted below identifies the former directors concerned). Second, unlike the original Greenbury recommendation, the Stock Exchange requirement applies to all former directors, not just those who have retired in the current or previous period.

The reason for this change is clear. Had the original Greenbury recommendation been retained, disclosure could easily have been avoided by deferring such payments until the second accounting period after retirement.

Examples of the type of payments which will need to be disclosed under this requirement will be payments under consultancy arrangements, as illustrated in the following extracts:

Extract 29.42: Scapa Group plc (1999)

Report of the Board on Directors' Remuneration[extract]

Directors' emoluments

Payments were made to Mr A. J. Ainsworth, a former director in a consultancy capacity amounting to £148,413.

Extract 29.43: The Body Shop International PLC (1999)

REMUNERATION REPORT [extract]

DIRECTORS' EMOLUMENTS

The Company has a three year consultancy agreement with EG Helyer, a former Director, who received £78,000 (not included in the amounts above) in 1999.

Another example of the type of payment which could be caught by this requirement is the payment of pensions by the company to former directors. One company which has disclosed this information is Marks and Spencer, as shown below:

Extract 29.44: Marks and Spencer p.l.c. (1999)

REMUNERATION REPORT [extract]

4   PAYMENTS TO FORMER DIRECTORS

In relation to three former directors, their Pension Scheme entitlement is supplemented by an additional, unfunded, pension paid by the Company. Pensions paid by the Company to former directors were:

	1999	1998
	£000	£000
Lord Sieff of Brimpton	**63**	61
The Lord Rayner[1]	**21**	83
C V Silver	**82**	79
	166	223

(1) Payments were made until The Lord Rayner's death on 29 June 1998.

Due to the continuing ill health of Lord Sieff the Company no longer incurs the cost of providing administrative support for the position of Honorary President but has instead met costs relating to his necessary care assistant. Payments of this nature in the period under review amount to £73,000 (last year £69,000).

Additional payments amounting to £70,000 (last year £70,000) have been made to C V Silver in respect of consultancy services provided to the Company.

Although such payments are strictly required to be disclosed when significant, we do not believe that such pension payments should be disclosed in all circumstances. Where such unfunded entitlements have been taken into account when giving the disclosures discussed at 4.4.8 C below in respect of the former directors whilst they were directors then this would effectively be disclosing the benefit twice. Also, the Companies Act only requires disclosure of the pension payments which are in excess of their original entitlement (see 2.8 above).

Another situation which would be covered by this requirement is when a dispute over a former director's termination of employment is finally settled as illustrated below.

Extract 29.45: United Utilities PLC (1999)

Remuneration report [extract]

Directors' emoluments

During the year, the company settled its dispute with Brian Staples, the previous Chief Executive, whose employment with the company terminated on 31 July 1997. The company paid £60,000 (plus VAT) towards Mr Staples' legal fees. Mr Staples was allowed to exercise options granted on 18 September 1995 to subscribe for 124,435 ordinary shares at an exercise price of 530.12p per ordinary share. All other options to subscribe for ordinary shares granted to him subsequently under the executive share option scheme, and options granted to him under the employee sharesave scheme, lapsed. The mid market price of a share on the day of exercise was 895 pence. Mr Staples was reimbursed for previously incurred relocation expenses of £34,142 (inclusive of VAT) in accordance with the company's relocation policy. Pursuant to that policy, that amount was grossed up to take account of higher rate income tax payable by Mr Staples on receipt of that payment.

A possible unwelcome side-effect of the *Listing Rules* wording is that, if a person who ceases to be a main board director continues to work for the group, amounts paid to that person would appear, in principle, to be required to be disclosed until ceasing to be an employee.

A company which faced this dilemma was National Westminster Bank. In its 1995 accounts the company disclosed the following:

Extract 29.46: National Westminster Bank Plc (1995)

Remuneration committee's annual report to shareholders to shareholders[extract]

Mr J Tugwell

Mr Tugwell resigned as a director of the Bank in December 1995, although he continues to be employed as Chairman and Chief Executive of Bancorp. He is resident in the US and does not receive benefits under the remuneration schemes applicable to UK-based directors. His contract of employment is with Bancorp. He has a rolling three-year service agreement and, in accordance with US practice, his agreement excludes mitigation in the event of early termination. His emoluments are reviewed annually by Bancorp's board, with assistance from independent consultants, and referred to the Committee.

...

There then followed a further 30 lines of detailed disclosure of Mr Tugwell's remuneration package. Arguably, a literal interpretation of the requirement would mean that any payments (including his emoluments as an employee) made to Mr Tugwell should be disclosed in the report every year until he retired from the group altogether. However, it would appear that National Westminster Bank thought otherwise as there was no disclosure in its 1996 remuneration committee report of any payments made to Mr Tugwell during 1996 up until the time Bancorp was sold.

4.4.8 Pension benefits

As noted at 4.4 above, this was the last remaining aspect of the Greenbury recommendations to be given effect by the Stock Exchange in its requirements.

A The issue

Under the old legislation, all pension contributions were required to be included within the computation of 'emoluments'. Whilst this gave an accurate indication of the cost of a defined contribution scheme, it was common ground that it inadequately measured the cost of a defined benefit scheme relative to any individual. However, given the rest of the requirements for directors' remuneration which were based more on valuing the benefits receivable by the directors, such an approach, particularly in relation to pension rights under defined benefit schemes, clearly did not represent the value of the benefit receivable by any one individual director.

The basic difficulty was that it is not readily possible to calculate the amount relating to an individual who is a member of a larger scheme. The common practice of applying the standard employer's contribution rate to each director's pensionable salary is no more than an arbitrary allocation which in most cases understates the real cost very considerably, since directors are typically nearer retirement age than the average member of the scheme. The cost of providing an additional year's service benefit increases with each year of a working life, because contributions have less time to accumulate investment income to provide funds out of which pensions will be paid.

Particular problems noted by the Greenbury Report were:

- Where the company is taking a contribution holiday, there are no contributions to be disclosed in the accounts, although application of the surplus in the pension fund to 'pay up' directors' pension rights clearly represents a real cost to the company.

- In a final salary scheme, increases in pensionable pay towards the end of a director's working life can increase the cost of his pension much more than would appear to be the case simply by looking at the increased contributions in those years.[97]

The Greenbury Report therefore recommended that the cost of defined benefit pension schemes should be measured as 'the present value of pension entitlement earned during the year resulting from additional length of service, increases in salary or changes in the terms of the scheme, less any contributions made by the Director during the year'. However, it conceded that there was a 'technical issue' as to how such benefits should be valued and noted that the actuarial profession had agreed to advise on the issue.[98]

B Actuaries' joint consultation papers

In response to this request, in January 1996 the Institute of Actuaries and the Faculty of Actuaries issued a joint consultation paper – *Disclosure of directors' pensions: Possible methods of calculation of entitlements*. They discussed, and sought comments on, five possible methods of calculating the pension benefit for disclosure purposes, which can be summarised as follows:

Method 1:   Cash contribution (the method then currently required by the Companies Act 1985, as discussed above).

Method 2:   Accrued benefit (the change in the director's accrued pension entitlement over the period).

Method 3:   Transfer value (the change in the transfer value of the director's accrued pension entitlement over the period).

Method 4:   SSAP 24 (the amount that would be accounted for under SSAP 24 if the director had an individual pension scheme).

Method 5:   Notional funding (the amount that would have to be paid to fund an individual pension for the director on the basis of a fixed percentage of pensionable pay over the rest of the director's working life).

In April 1996, a second paper was published summarising the comments received. Broadly, these indicated no consensus in favour of a single method, but showed strong support for Method 2 from industry and for Method 3 from advisers and investors. In the absence of consensus, the paper recommended disclosure combining aspects of both Methods.

C   *Stock Exchange requirements*

In May 1996 the Stock Exchange responded by issuing a consultative document seeking comments on its proposals to amend its *Listing Rules* so as to require disclosure of individual directors' pension benefits. As a result of responses received, a number of minor changes were made to clarify the requirements and also to reflect the fact that the Institute of Actuaries and the Faculty of Actuaries had revised their Guidance Note, *GN11 – Retirement Benefit Schemes – Transfer Values,* when the final requirements were published a year later in May 1997. Illustrative examples of the disclosures and how to calculate the year's increase in, and the accumulated total of, the accrued pension were given in an accompanying note.[99] These new requirements (see item (a) (ix) and (x) at 4.4 above) were mandatory for accounting periods ending in or after 1 July 1997.

The required disclosures for defined benefit schemes are illustrated in the following extract:

Extract 29.47: Caledonia Investments plc (1999)

35   DIRECTORS' REMUNERATION AND INTERESTS [extract]

Directors' pensions

Pension benefits earned by directors during the year and the accumulated total accrued pension at 31 March 1999 were as follows:

	Increase in accrued pension £'000	Transfer value of increase £'000	Total accrued pension at year end £'000
P N Buckley	7	110	153
M G Wyatt	6	99	42
Sir David Kinloch	14	210	127
J H Cartwright	8	67	42
Hon C W Cayzer	4	39	38

The pension entitlement shown is that which would be paid annually on retirement based on service to the end of the year. The increase in accrued pension during the year excludes any increase in inflation.

The transfer value has been calculated on the basis of actuarial advice in accordance with Actuarial Guidance Note GN11 less directors' contributions. This value represents a liability of the Company – not a sum paid or due to the individual director – and cannot therefore be added meaningfully to annual remuneration.

This disclosure follows closely the wording recommended by the Stock Exchange in its illustrative disclosures.

The calculation of the accrued pension benefit information is relatively straightforward, as illustrated in the following example:

Example 29.8

Mr A, a director, is a member of the company's defined benefit pension scheme which provides for a pension of one-sixtieth of final pensionable salary for each year of pensionable service. At the start of the year Mr A had 10 years' service and a salary of £120,000 p.a. During the year his salary was increased to £150,000 p.a. Inflation during the year was 5%.

The accumulated total and the increase in the year are as follows:

		£
Accumulated total at end of year: 11/60 x £150,000	=	27,500
Accumulated total at beginning of year: 10/60 x £120,000	=	20,000
Increase in accrued pension during the year	=	7,500
Less effect of inflation on total accrued pension: £20,000 x 5%	=	1,000
Increase in accrued pension during the year excluding inflation		6,500

The amounts to be disclosed under the Stock Exchange requirements are the £6,500 and the £27,500.

It should be emphasised, however, that if Mr A is the highest paid director then under the Companies Act (see 2.11 above), the comparative figure of £20,000 would also need to be disclosed or else sufficient information to allow it to be calculated, for example, by disclosing either the inflation rate or the inflationary increase. The inflation rate to be used in the calculation should be that rate published by the Secretary of State for Social Security each year in accordance with Schedule 3 to the Pension Schemes Act 1993.[100]

The omission of such comparative information appears to be a common error in annual accounts. This may be due to the fact that when the requirement first came the Stock Exchange's illustrative example reflected the then current exemption in the Companies Act from such disclosure. Extract 29.28 at 2.11 above provides an example of a company disclosing the comparative information for the highest paid director. Other companies go further by disclosing the comparative accrued benefit for all of the directors (see Extract 29.50 below). Cable & Wireless not only discloses the comparative accrued pension but also gives a full analysis of the increase in the accrued benefit over the year as illustrated below.

Extract 29.48: _Cable and Wireless plc (1999)_

Directors' Report [extract]

Directors' pension entitlement per annum

	Richard H Brown £	Robert E Lerwill £	Rodney J Olsen £	Stephen R Petit £	Graham M Wallace £
Accrued pension at 1 April 1998 or date of appointment if later	72,239	12,030	197,498	26,002	21,000
Increase/(decrease) in accrued pension during year as a result of inflation	1,483	247	4,053	534	(38)
Adjustment to accrued pension as a result of salary increase, other than for inflation	842	789	31,158	3,261	2,493
Increase in accrued pension as a result of additional period's service	29,639	10,453	10,951	7,297	8,225
Accrued pension at 31 March 1999 or earlier date of resignation	**104,203**	**23,519**	**243,660**	**37,094**	**31,680**

Great Portland in addition to disclosing the accrued pension benefit as required also discloses the current pension entitlement of the directors at the year end as shown below.

Extract 29.49: _Great Portland Estates plc (1999)_

Report of the Remuneration Committee [extract]

Pension benefits earned by the directors who are members of the Group Pension Plan are set out below:

	AGE AT 31ST MARCH 1999	YEARS OF PENSIONABLE SERVICE	INCREASE IN ACCRUED PENSION IN THE YEAR	ACCUMULATED TOTAL ACCRUED PENSION AT 31ST MARCH 1999	CURRENT PENSION ENTITLEMENT AT 31ST MARCH 1999
Richard Peskin	54	32	–	250	185
Paul Gittens	52	28	7	64	40

The accumulated total accrued pension is that which would be paid annually to Mr Peskin and Mr Gittens from the age of 62 and 64 respectively, if they retired on 31st March 1999 and did not claim a pension until reaching that age, and is based on service to 31st March 1999. The current pension entitlement is the annual pension which the directors could have received from 1st April 1999 had they retired on 31st March 1999.

Although the calculation of the accrued pension benefit information is relatively straightforward, this is not the case with respect to the calculation of the transfer value of the increase in the accrued benefit. This will require to be calculated by an actuary in accordance with the Actuarial Guidance Note GN11.

It can be seen that Caledonia chose the option of disclosing the transfer value of the increase in the accrued benefits. Another example is Marks and Spencer, as shown below:

Extract 29.50: Marks and Spencer p.l.c. (1999)

REMUNERATION REPORT [extract]

3 DIRECTORS' PENSION INFORMATION

(i) Pension Scheme

The executive directors, management and staff all participate in the Company's Pension Scheme. The Scheme is non-contributory, fully funded and the subject of an Independent Trust. With effect from 1 January 1997, the normal retirement age under the Pension Scheme for all staff below age 60 (including executive directors) engaged on or before 31 December 1995 was changed from 60 to 65. Accrued rights of these staff were not affected by the change. For staff engaged on or after 1 January 1996 the normal retirement age is 65.

The Pension Scheme enables members to achieve the maximum pension of two-thirds of their salary in the twelve months ending at normal retirement age after 30 years' service. For staff who joined the Scheme prior to 1 January 1996 no actuarial reduction is applied to pensions payable from the age of 58. Staff who joined the Scheme on or after 1 January 1996 are subject to an actuarial reduction in their pension if payment starts prior to age 65.

In the case of earnings over £100,000 per annum, the pensionable salary is based on an average of the earnings over the last three years to retirement.

Pension commutation to enable participants to receive a lump sum on retirement is permitted within Inland Revenue limits.

For death before retirement, a capital sum equal to four times salary is payable, together with a spouse's pension of two-thirds of the member's prospective pension at the age of 65. For death in retirement, a spouse's pension is paid equal to the member's current pension. In the event of death after leaving service but prior to commencement of pension, a spouse's pension of two-thirds of the accrued preserved pension is payable. In all circumstances, children's allowances are also payable, usually up to the age of 16. Substantial protection is also offered in the event of serious ill health.

Post-retirement pension increases for pension earned before 6 April 1997 are purely discretionary, but the practice has been to award annual increases in line with inflation.

	Age at 31 March 1999	Years of service at 31 March 1999	Increase in transfer value in excess of inflation[1] during the year ended 31 March 1999 £000	Increase in pension earned in excess of inflation[1] during the year ended 31 March 1999 £000	Accrued entitlement at year end 31 March 1999 £000	31 March 1998 £000
Sir Richard Greenbury[3]	62	45	n/a	n/a	465	415
P L Salsbury	49	28	421	31	227	189
P G McCracken	50	23	274	21	183	157
Lord Stone of Blackheath	56	31	333	20	230	204
R Aldridge	52	25	315	22	137	111
J R Benfield	49	28	259	19	138	115
R W C Colvill	58	14	247	14	89	73
Mrs C E M Freeman	46	24	205	17	97	78
B S Morris	51	28	130	9	69	59
J T Rowe	51	24	318	22	123	98
D K Hayes	50	29	271	20	135	111
S J Sacher	58	31	34	2	166	159
P P D Smith	58	33	460 [5]	15	153	135
J K Oates[4]	56	15	444	27	302	268

(1)   Inflation has been assumed to be equivalent to the actual rate of price inflation which was 3.2% for the year to 30 September 1998. This measurement date accords with the Stock Exchange Listing Rules.

(2)   The pension entitlement shown above is that which would be paid on retirement based on service to 31 March 1999, except for J K Oates who retired on 31 January 1999 and service is calculated to this date. At State Pension Age this will be reduced by a proportion of the Basic State Pension.

(3)   Sir Richard Greenbury has accrued no further benefit in the scheme since taking a lump sum in July 1997. This year's accrued entitlement has increased over last year due to two factors (i) the pension, having been deferred has, in line with normal practice, been increased by a late retirement factor, (ii) a notional increase has been applied in line with the pension increase for all current pensions.

(4)   Although J K Oates retired on 31 January 1999, he has yet to elect to commence drawing a pension. Therefore the amounts shown above are calculated on the assumption that payment of his pension is deferred until aged 60.

(5)   The greater part of the actuarial increase in the transfer value in respect of P P D Smith relates to the effect, on the year, of his full pension being paid immediately following his retirement at 31 March 1999. For the directors retiring on 31 May 1999, a similar effect is likely to be shown next year should they choose to draw their pension immediately.

(6)   C Littmoden is not shown in the above table because he has ceased to accrue benefits in the UK Scheme during his time in North America. His accrued entitlement at the time of his transfer to North America was £64,000.

(7)   The pension entitlement shown excludes any additional pension purchased by the member's Additional Voluntary Contributions.

(ii)   Early Retirement Plan

The Board recognises the need to maintain a proper flow of succession to senior management positions. It has therefore decided that although the Company's Pension Scheme is administered assuming a normal retirement age of 65 for all staff, senior management should have a contractual retirement age of 60. To meet the same successional needs, it may be appropriate to ask a member of senior management to retire before the age of 60. To facilitate the smooth implementation of this process the Company established an Early Retirement Plan for senior management. Where such a request is made by the Company the Remuneration Committee may, at its discretion, offer an unfunded Early Retirement Pension, separate from the Company pension, which will be payable from the date of retirement to age 60. To ensure that early retirement does not confer an advantage over continued employment the value of the Early Retirement Pension may not exceed the value of the individual's total net salary less net Company pension from actual date of retirement to age 60. Each Early Retirement Pension must be approved individually by the Remuneration Committee. The Early Retirement Pension is fully taxable; it is normally fully commutable at the election of the recipient.

It can be seen that Marks and Spencer has shown more information in the table than is required by the Stock Exchange (it is only the amounts shown in bold that are actually required). It has also felt it necessary to explain some of the figures.

As indicated at 4.3.3 above, Schedule B to the Combined Code suggests that companies may wish to make it clear that the transfer value represents a liability of the company, not a sum paid or due to the individual. Such a statement is illustrated in Extract 29.47 above.

Clearly not all companies will wish to disclose the transfer values, particularly as it can be a sizeable number compared to the increase in the accrued benefit for the year and it will be necessary for it to be calculated by an actuary. However, in that case it will be necessary to give the alternative information required by the Stock Exchange. One company which does this is Boots, as shown below:

Extract 29.51: The Boots Company PLC (1999)

Board Remuneration Report [extract]

Pension entitlement

All executive directors in office at 31st March 1999 receive pension entitlements from the company's principal UK defined benefit pension scheme, referred to in note 26, and supplementary pension arrangements which provide additional benefits aimed at producing a pension of two-thirds final base salary at normal retirement age. Executive directors are members of the pension scheme and non-executive directors do not participate. There are no money purchase schemes. Pension entitlement is calculated only on the salary element of remuneration. The chairman is entitled to the same level of pension benefits enjoyed by other executive directors despite his shorter service but after adjusting for pensions arising from earlier employment.

Details of pensions earned by the executive directors in office at 31st March 1999 are shown below.

	Age at 31st March 1999	Directors' contributions during the year £000	Increase in accrued pension entitlement during the year £000	Total accrued pension entitlement at 31st March 1999 £000
Lord Blyth (chairman and highest paid director)	58	29	44	330
M F Ruddell	55	12	9	147
S G Russell	54	17	28	191
D A R Thompson	56	17	31	208
J J H Watson	57	10	16	128

The pension entitlement shown is that which would be paid annually on retirement based on service to the end of the year. No account is taken of any retained benefits from previous employments which will act to reduce the benefits shown. The increase in accrued pension during the year excludes any increase for inflation. Members of the scheme have the option to pay additional voluntary contributions; neither the contributions nor the resulting benefits are included in the above table.

The normal retirement age is 60. Early retirement is available subject to Trustee consent and a reduction in the accrued pension. Under the current early retirement terms the pension can be drawn from age 59 without reduction.

On death after retirement spouses' pensions of two-thirds of members' pensions and children's pensions of two-ninths of members' pensions for up to three dependant children are payable (subject to Inland Revenue limits).

Pensions in payment are guaranteed to be increased annually by 5% or the increase in the Index of Retail Prices (RPI) if less. Additional increases may be granted at the discretion of the Trustees and subject to the consent of the company.

Any transfer value calculations would make allowance for discretionary benefits including pension increases and early retirement.

We have to say that such a compromise treatment is less than ideal. Although this alternative information is intended to be a surrogate for the transfer value, it is incomprehensible to the non-actuary and, even for an actuary, is likely to be less than sufficient to allow the transfer value to be calculated. It is interesting to note that Marks and Spencer adopted this latter treatment in its 1996 accounts but now discloses the transfer value information as seen in Extract 29.50 above.

For companies with defined contribution schemes the requirements are less onerous. An example of such disclosure is illustrated below:

Extract 29.52: Halma p.l.c. (1999)

Report on Remuneration [extract]

Money Purchase Arrangements

Mr J C Conacher has a money purchase arrangement in an overseas pension plan established under a trust into which he pays 5% of his salary. The Company also pays into his plan an additional amount equal to 24.4% of salary each year. In the financial year this amount was £48,000 (1998: £42,000).

The Finance Act 1989 introduced a restriction for employees joining a company after 31 May 1989 on the amount of earnings that could be pensioned through an Inland Revenue approved pension scheme (earnings cap). Accordingly, many companies have put in place additional arrangements to compensate those directors affected by the earnings cap. The disclosures that need to be given for these additional arrangements will depend on their exact nature. It may be that companies will provide a top-up arrangement such that the directors are put in the same position as directors whose pensions are unaffected by the earnings cap. If that is the case then the defined benefit disclosures should be made taking account of the top-up arrangement. This is done by Scottish Power as illustrated in Extract 29.28 at 2.11 above. If the arrangement is akin to a defined contribution scheme then disclosure as such should be made as shown below:

Extract 29.53: Safeway plc (1999)

Report of the directors [extract]

Pensions

All executive directors are members of the Safeway Pension Scheme which is a funded, Inland Revenue approved, final salary, occupational pension scheme (Note 24.3 on page 50).

The Finance Act 1989 introduced a restriction ("Cap") for employees joining the Company after 31 May 1989, on earnings that could be pensioned through an Inland Revenue approved pension scheme. The limit is based on a maximum annual pensionable salary (currently £90,600). Accordingly, the Company has established a Funded Unapproved Retirement Benefits Plan ("Furb") for executive directors (currently two) subject to the Cap and pays a defined annual contribution to this Plan which is based on a percentage of their basic salary over the Cap. The Company also makes a discretionary annual pension related payment to executive directors subject to the Cap. This payment is sufficient to meet the income tax liability that executive directors suffer on the Company's contribution to the FURB, and is fixed such that the contribution of the FURB contributions and this payment is 24% of pensionable salary over the Cap.

For the directors who held office during the year, pension benefits earned in the Safeway Pension Scheme and the Company's contributions to the FURB (and related payments) were as follows:

| | Age at year end | Years of service | Directors' contributions in the year (Note 1) £'000 | Safeway Pension Scheme | | FURB |
				Increase in accrued pension during the year (Note 2) £'000	Accumulated total pension at year end (Note 3) £'000	Company contribution including related payment £'000
D G C Webster	54	22	29	18	281	–
C D Smith	51	20	32	41	274	–
S T Laffin	39	9	4	2	18	36
R E Partington	42	5	4	2	10	37
G Wotherspoon	51	29	16	17	153	–

It was seen from the above extract that the top-up arrangements were provided by means of a Funded Unapproved Retirement Benefit Scheme (FURB). Another company that used this means was British Land, but as can be seen from the following extract, the benefit to be received by the directors are defined lump sums.

Extract 29.54: The British Land Company PLC (1999)

Remuneration Report [extract]

Pensions

The Company sponsors a tax approved non-contributory defined benefit pension scheme. The scheme generally aims to provide executives with at least 20 years service to age 60 with a pension at that age of two-thirds of basic salary, less the single person's basic state pension. Four executive directors, Mr. Kalman, Mr N. Ritblat, Mr. Bowden and Mr. Adam earned pension benefits in the scheme during the year.

Mr. Bowden's and Mr. Adam's benefits from the tax approved scheme are restricted by the earnings cap. They are, therefore, entitled to benefit from the Company's Funded Unapproved Retirement Benefit Scheme (FURBS). The benefits provided by the FURBS are defined lump sums. Mr. Bowden and Mr. Adam are liable to income tax, which the Company has agreed to pay on their behalf, (known as pension related payments) on Company contributions paid into the FURBS. The Company has not paid any contributions to the FURBS to date. However, the notional pension related payments accrued in the year 1998/99 were £14,000 and £9,000 for Mr. Bowden and Mr. Adam respectively.

Non-executive directors do not participate in any Company sponsored pension arrangement.

The pension benefits earned during the year by Mr. Kalman, Mr. N. Ritblat, Mr. Bowden and Mr. Adam were as follows:

Name	Age at year end	Increase in accrued pension during the year £	Total accrued pension entitlement at year end £	Increase in accrued FURBS lump sum entitlement during the year £	Total accrued FURBS lump sum entitlement at year end £
S. L. Kalman	59	8,000	112,000		
N. S. J. Ritblat	37	6,000	36,000		
R. E. Bowden	55	2,000	13,000	24,000	105,000
S. Adam	52	2,000	7,000	17,000	48,000

FURBS

(a) Normal retirement age for arrangement is age 60.

(b) Retirement may take place at any age after 50 subject to the Company's consent. Benefits are reduced to allow for their early retirement.

(c) On death in service top up lump sums are provided so that, in aggregate, the payee receives broadly the same value of benefits (net of tax) as if the earnings cap did not apply. On death, in deferment if a spouse's or dependant's pension is payable from the main scheme a lump sum of two-thirds of the member's accrued lump sum is also payable.

(d) In deferment accrued lump sums are increased in line with statutory increases on pensions in deferment.

Alternatively, companies may just make additional payments to the directors affected by the earnings cap. In this case, these could be disclosed as other benefits although it may be that companies would wish to disclose them separately as done by Christian Salvesen as shown below.

Extract 29.55: Christian Salvesen PLC (1999)

Remuneration Report [extract]

PENSIONS

The pension arrangements of Mr Roderick, Mr Aspden, Mr Callaghan and Mr Bristow were based upon membership of the Scheme. However, they were all subject to the earnings cap and received payments equivalent to the amount that it would otherwise have cost the company to fund their pension benefits. Death in service cover was also provided, outside the Scheme arrangements, on earnings above the cap. In addition to the emoluments shown below in respect of the period they were directors of the company during the year they received the following payments/benefits:

	PAYMENT IN LIEU OF PENSION BENEFITS		COST OF DEATH IN SERVICE COVER	
	1999 £	1998 £	1999 £	1998 £
E J Roderick	39,014	19,289	2,610	1,110
P G Aspden	16,839	–	1,030	–
A M Callaghan	9,786	–	780	–
D J Bristow	19,639	16,209	1,320	720

4.4.9   *Share options and other long-term schemes*

The Greenbury Report took the view that in general there should be a move away from short-term cash-based bonus schemes to longer-term share-based bonus schemes.[101] However, such schemes should be based on genuinely demanding criteria, rather than simply vesting after a given time period. For example, they should aim to measure the company's performance against that of comparator companies using measures such as total shareholder return. Share-based schemes should also be designed to encourage the holding of shares for the longer term rather than realising them for cash.

The disclosures required by the Stock Exchange to reinforce these recommendations are, briefly:

- in respect of share options, the information required by UITF 10;

- various details of other long-term incentive schemes; and

- statement of policy in granting options or awards under such long-term incentive schemes.

A   *Share options – UITF 10*

The Stock Exchange had for some years required companies to disclose in respect of each director the number of options outstanding at the beginning and end of the year, together with material changes since the year end.[102] The Companies Act 1989 added to this a requirement to disclose the number of options granted and exercised during the year. Companies typically dealt with these two requirements by giving a reconciliation between the numbers of options outstanding at the beginning and end of the financial year, together with any material changes after the end of the year.

In 1992, the Cadbury Committee recommended that 'relevant information about stock options [and] stock appreciation rights ... should also be given'. In response, in September 1994 the UITF issued Abstract 10 – *Disclosure of Directors' Share Options*.

The UITF believed that the grant of an option should be treated as giving rise to a benefit and should be included in the aggregate of directors' emoluments under the old Companies Act requirements. However, the UITF recognised the practical difficulties of attributing a meaningful estimated money value to the option at the date of grant, particularly where the rights under the option are contingent on future performance or other factors, and also the differing views on whether, and if so how, to apportion any benefit over time. Accordingly, the UITF concluded that it was not presently practicable for it to specify an appropriate valuation method for options as a benefit in kind.

Nevertheless, the UITF considered that further information concerning the option prices applicable to individual directors, together with market price information at the year end and at the date of exercise, should be disclosed. In an appendix to the Abstract it also states that for each director, the following information for options exercisable at different prices and/or dates should be disclosed:

(a)   the number of shares under option at the end of the year and at the beginning of the year (or date of appointment if later);

(b)   the number of options (i) granted, (ii) exercised and (iii) lapsed unexercised during the year;

(c)   the exercise prices;

(d)   the dates from which the options may be exercised;

(e)   the expiry dates;

(f)   the costs of the options (if any);

(g)   for any options exercised during the year, the market price of the shares at the date of exercise; and

(h)   a concise summary of any performance criteria conditional upon which the options are exercisable.

In addition, the market price of the shares at the end of the year, together with the range during the year (high and low) is to be disclosed.

Where the information disclosed would be excessive in length, a more concise disclosure using weighted average exercise prices for each director may be given. Where this is done then:

(a)   disclose total shares under option at the beginning and end of the year for each director, with appropriate weighted average prices applicable to shares under option at the end of the year;

(b)   disclose full details of any movements during the year (covering options granted and lapsed during the year with disclosure of the exercise price and options exercised in the year disclosing the exercise price and the share price at date of exercise);

(c)   'out of the money' options should be distinguished from 'in the money' options;

(d)   unusually large individual items may need to be noted to prevent misleading conclusions being drawn from an average; and

(e)   a reference should be made to the fact that the company's register of directors' interests (which is open to inspection) contains full details of directors' shareholdings and options to subscribe.

Such disclosures did not have mandatory status because the UITF had received legal advice that the recommended disclosures, other than the number of options granted or exercised during the year which were specifically required by the Companies Act, could not be construed as being necessary to meet the legal requirements. Consequently, the disclosures were only recommendations and were not mandatory. Notwithstanding the fact that they were not mandatory most listed companies gave the disclosures suggested.

However, the impact of the Stock Exchange requirement set out in item (a) (iii) at 4.4 above is that it has effectively made UITF 10 mandatory for listed companies.

The following extract illustrates one way of giving these disclosures:

Extract 29.56: Allied Domecq PLC (1998)

Report of the Remuneration Committee [extract]

The following movements in options over the ordinary share capital of the company (excluding options granted under the long term incentive scheme) took place during the period:

		Number of options at 1 September 1997	Options granted during period	Options exercised during period	Number of options at 31 August 1998	Exercise Price	Market Price at date of exercise	Gain made on exercise £'000	Date from which exercisable	Expiry Date
S H Alexander	(a)	2,084	–	2,084	–	383p	540p	3	14.09.91	14.09.98
	(a)	1,395	–	–	1,395	475p	–	–	08.12.92	08.12.99
	(c)	43,262	–	–	43,262	570p	–	–	08.08.94	08.08.01
	(c)	11,194	–	–	11,194	609p	–	–	08.01.96	08.01.03
	(b)	715	– (lapsed)715	–	524p	–	–	01.08.97	31.01.98
	(b)	822	–	822	–	419p	540p	1	01.08.98	31.01.99
	(c)	3,491	–	–	3,491	631p	–	–	20.12.96	20.12.03
	(d)	21,739	–	–	21,739	552p	–	–	19.12.97	19.12.04
	(b)	806	–	–	806	428p	–	–	01.08.00	31.01.01
	(d)	30,807	–	–	30,807	516p	–	–	18.12.98	18.12.02
	(b)	1,778	–	–	1,778	388p	–	–	01.08.01	31.01.03
	(d)	52,812	–	–	52,812	427.5p	–	–	10.12.99	10.12.03
	(b)	953	–	–	953	362p	–	–	01.08.02	31.01.03
	(d)	–	49,671	–	49,671	533.5p	–	–	01.12.00	01.12.04
	(b)	–	688	–	688	501p	–	–	01.08.03	31.01.04
Total		**171,138**	**50,359**	**3,621**	**217,876**					
A J Hales	(a)	1,395	–	–	1,395	475p	–	–	08.12.92	08.12.99
	(c)	139,207	–	–	139,207	570p	–	–	08.08.94	08.08.01
	(c)	29,401	–	–	29,401	609p	–	–	08.01.96	08.01.03
	(b)	2,798	–	2,798		419p	555.5p	4	01.08.98	31.01.99
	(c)	43,427	–	–	43,427	569p	–	–	17.06.97	17.06.04
	(c)	29,419	–	–	29,419	552p	–	–	19.12.97	19.12.04
	(d)	33,986	–	–	33,986	552p	–	–	19.12.97	19.12.01
	(b)	1,289	–	–	1,289	428p	–	–	01.08.00	31.01.01
	(d)	68,062		–	68,062	516p	–	–	18.12.98	18.12.02
	(d)	93,848	–	–	93,848	427.5p	–	–	10.12.99	10.12.03
	(d)	–	82,474	–	82,474	533.5p	–	–	01.12.00	01.12.04
	(b)	–	2,341	–	2,341	501p	–	–	01.08.03	31.01.04
Total		**442,832**	**84,815**	**2,798**	**524,849**					

Name										
P F Macfarlane	(c)	125,802	–	–	125,802	572p	–	–	09.12.94	20.09.98
	(c)	4,871	–	–	4,871	609p	–	–	08.01.96	20.09.98
	(b)	3,785	–	–	3,785	419p	–	–	01.08.98	20.09.98
	(c)	7,158	–	–	7,158	569p	–	–	17.06.97	20.09.98
	(c)	37,568	–	–	37,568	552p	–	–	19.12.97	20.09.98
	(d)	44,360	–	–	44,360	516p	–	–	18.12.98	18.06.99
Total		**223,544**	**–**		**– 223,544**					
G F McCarthy	(d)	57,264	–	–	57,264	569p	–	–	17.06.97	17.06.04
	(d)	21,376	–	–	21,376	552p	–	–	19.12.97	19.12.04
	(d)	30,087	–	–	30,087	516p	–	–	18.12.98	18.12.05
	(d)	52,812	–	–	52,812	427.5p	–	–	10.12.99	10.12.06
	(d)	–	46,860	–	46,860	533.5p	–	–	01.12.00	01.12.07
Total		**161,539**	**46,860**		**– 208,399**					
D Scotland	(c)	49,210	–	–	49,210	609p	–	–	08.01.96	08.01.03
	(c)	2,295	–	–	2,295	569p	–	–	17.06.97	17.06.04
	(c)	20,516	–	–	20,516	552p	–	–	19.12.97	19.12.04
	(d)	30,087	–	–	30,087	516p	–	–	18.12.98	18.12.02
	(d)	52,812	–	–	52,812	427.5p	–	–	10.12.99	10.12.03
	(b)	538	–	–	538	362p	–	–	01.08.00	31.01.01
	(d)	–	46,860	–	46,860	533.5p	–	–	01.12.00	01.12.04
Total		**155,458**	**46,860**		**– 202,318**					
J A F Trigg	(a)	1,395	–	–	1,395	475p	–		08.12.92	08.12.99
	(c)	63,117	–	–	63,117	570p	–		08.08.94	08.08.01
	(c)	33 46)	–	–	33,462	609p	–		08.01.96	08.01.03
	(b)	3,291	–	3,291	–	419p	555.5p	4	01.08.98	31.01.99
	(c)	16,037	–	–	16,037	569p	–		17.06.97	17.06.04
	(c)	16,627	–	–	16,627	552p	–		19.12.97	19.12.04
	(d)	15,995	–	–	15,995	552p	–		19.12.97	19.12.01
	(b)	806	–	–	806	428p	–		01.08.00	31.01.01
	(d)	48,449	–	–	48,449	516p	–		18.12.98	18.12.02
	(d)	61,988	–	–	61,988	427.5p	–	–	10.12.99	10.12.03
	(d)	–	52,483	–	52,483	533.5p	–	–	01.12.00	01.12.04
Total		**261,167**	**52,483**	**3,291**	**310,359**					

(a) Employee Share Option (No. 2) Scheme

(b) 1991 Share Savings Scheme

(c) 1991 Executive Share Option Scheme

(d) 1991 International Executive Share Option Scheme

The aggregate value of the gain made on the exercise of share options by all directors was £12,000.

R Mora-Figueroa and all non-executive directors do not hold options over the ordinary share capital of the company.

The middle market price of the ordinary shares at 31 August 1998 was 506.0p and the range during the year to 31 August 1998 was 460.5p to 635.5p.

(Options granted under the long-term incentive scheme are disclosed elsewhere in the report.)

It can be seen from the above extract that such disclosure can be quite voluminous and indeed a common practical problem for companies in complying with UITF 10 is the need to condense details of several option schemes into a digestible note.

Accordingly a number of companies adopt the alternative treatment of providing the information on a weighted average basis, as illustrated below:

Extract 29.57: Smiths Industries plc (1998)

14   Directors' emoluments and interests [extract]

Directors' share options

Scheme	Options held on 1 August 1998 Number	Options held on 2 August 1997 Number	Weighted average Exercise price	Options exercised				Options granted			
				Date exercised	Number	Exercise price	Market price†	Date of grant	Number	Exercise price	Expiry date
Sir Roger Hurn A		173,582		21/10/97	173,582	451.00p	903.00p				
B	138,062	138,062	728.66p								
C	3,654	3,654	389.88p								
D	49,683	49,683	0.10p								
K O Butler											
-Wheelhouse B	151,583	68,043	884.17p					17/10/97	83,540	934.00p	17/10/2007
C	2,578		669.00p					14/5/98	2,578	669.00p	1/1/2004
D	9,429		0.10p					28/10/97	9,429	0.10p	28/9/2004
N V Barber A		108,189		24/10/97	108,189	451.00p	913.00p				
B	63,623	63,623	721.04p								
C	2,729	10,289	632.00p	15/10/97	7,560	248.00p	940.00p				
D	19,476	20,539	0.10p	28/10/97	6,989	0.10p	840.25p	28/10/97	5,926	0.10p	28/9/2004
G M Kennedy A		62,661		21/10/97	62,661	451.00p	909.00p				
B	86,061	86,061	786.33p								
C	6,941	6,941	334.94p								
D	16,931	19,792	0.10p	18/11/97	5,824	0.10p	787.75p	28/10/97	2,963	0.10p	28/9/2004
E Lindh A	16,851	51,939	701.16p	17/10/97	16,416	347.00p	915.00p				
				17/10/97	8,000	395.00	915.00p				
				11/5/98	10,672	395.00p	975.00p				
B	43,030	23,719	851.04p					17/10/97	19,311	934.00p	17/10/2007
C	3,409	3,409	572.00p								
D	15,140	10,830	0.10p					28/10/97	4,310	0.10p	28/9/2004
A M Thomson A	62,500	62,500	480.00p								
B	65,148	43,558	799.48p					17/10/97	21,590	934.00p	17/10/2007
C	3,015	3,015	572.00p								
D	12,245	7,396	0.10p					28/10/97	4,849	0.10p	28/9/2004

Key:

A.   The Smiths Industries (1984) Executive Share Option Scheme

B.   The Smiths Industries 1995 Executive Share Option Scheme

C.   The Smiths Industries 1982 SAYE Share Option Scheme

D.   The Smiths Industries Senior Executive Deferred Share Scheme

†   Mid-market quotation from the London Stock Exchange Daily Official List or actual sale price is shares sold on date of acquisition.

Notes:

The high and low market prices of the ordinary shares during the period 2 August 1997 to 1 August 1998 were 997p and 702p respectively.

The market price on 2 August 1997 was 796p and on 1 August 1998 was 711p.

All options held on 1 August 1998 were granted at exercise prices less than the market price on that date, except for options granted under the Smiths Industries 1995 Executive Share Option Scheme on 25 October 1996 (exercise price 823p per share) and on 17 October 1997 (exercise price 934p per share).

No options lapsed during the period 2 August 1997 to 1 August 1998.

On 5 August 1998 1,241 shares were allotted to Sir Roger Hurn, following the exercise of an option under the Smiths Industries 1982 SAYE Share Option Scheme at an exercise price of 278p per share (market price 726.75p); otherwise no options have been granted or exercised or have lapsed between 1 August and 13 October 1998.

There are no performance criteria for The Smiths Industries (1984) Executive Share Option Scheme or The Smiths Industries Senior Executive Deferred Share Scheme apart from market price. The Smiths Industries 1995 Executive Share Option Scheme is subject to a performance criterion based on total shareholder return of the Company versus the total return of the Engineering Sector of the FTSE Actuaries Index.

Deferred Share Scheme options were granted on 28 October 1997 at an exercise price of 0.1p per share and match shares purchased in the market by the grantee on that day. At 1 August 1998, the deferred share scheme held 215,976 shares for the benefit of senior executives (including the directors as disclosed above). The market value of these shares at that date was £1.54m and dividends of approximately £39,009 were waived in the year in respect of the shares.

Special provisions permit the early exercise of SAYE Options in the event of retirement; redundancy; death; etc.

No other director held any options over the Company's shares during the period 2 August 1997 to 1 August 1998.

Full details of the directors' shareholdings and options are contained in the Registrar of Directors' Interests in Shares (which is open to inspection).

As discussed earlier, the Companies Act now requires the aggregate gains made by directors on the exercise of options to be disclosed by listed companies (see 2.5 above) and also such gains made by the highest paid director (see 2.11 above). This information must be disclosed notwithstanding the fact that the information enabling such amounts to be calculated is disclosed under UITF 10. Indeed, some companies in addition to giving the information required under UITF 10 are disclosing the gains made on the exercise of options by each director (see Extract 29.56 above).

One particular issue which is not clear in either the Stock Exchange requirement, Schedule B to the Combined Code or in UITF 10 is whether such information is required in respect of all persons who served as directors during the period or only in respect of directors at the year end (as is the case for interests in shares disclosed under the Companies Act). Some companies do not provide the information for those directors who retired or resigned during the year, presumably on the basis that the information is similar to that required for interests in shares. However, as this information is being given as part of directors' remuneration information, it would seem more in line with the rest of the requirements if the information was given for all directors who served during the year.

B   Long-term incentive schemes

The Stock Exchange defines a 'long-term incentive scheme' as 'any arrangement (other than a retirement benefit plan, a deferred bonus or any other arrangement specified by paragraph 12.43A(c)(ii) as an element of a remuneration package) which may involve receipt of any asset (including cash or any security) by a director or employee of the group:

(a)   which includes one or more conditions in respect of service and/or performance to be satisfied over more than one financial year; and

(b)   pursuant to which the group may incur (other than in relation to the establishment and administration of the arrangement) either cost or a liability, whether actual or contingent'.

This is similar to the definition incorporated in the Companies Act (see 2.6 above). It can be seen that the definition excludes retirement benefit plans (for disclosure purposes these are subject to separate requirements – see 4.4.8 above). A distinction is also made between a long-term incentive scheme and a deferred bonus. The definition of this latter item is discussed at 4.4.5 above. The distinguishing feature of a long-term incentive scheme is that the conditions as to service and/or performance is to satisfied over more than one financial period.

The requirements for long-term incentive schemes are set out at (a) (iv) at 4.4 above. It can be seen that the details do not specifically include performance criteria – rather surprisingly perhaps, in view of the importance that the Greenbury Committee attached to them and the fact that such information is required by UITF 10 for option schemes within its scope. However, in most cases such information will generally be given in a discussion of the scheme as part of the remuneration policy disclosures.

Since the Greenbury Report a number of companies have been introducing long-term incentive schemes (or L-tips as they are commonly called), although the names and the form of the schemes may be different. Accordingly, many of the companies have only recently given conditional awards and have not had to consider the disclosures necessary once the awards have crystallised. One company which has introduced such a scheme, whereby conditional allocations of shares have been awarded is United Assurance Group:

Extract 29.58: United Assurance Group plc (1998)

REPORT ON DIRECTORS' REMUNERATION [extract]

The committee believes that share ownership, particularly if it is deferred, facilitates the alignment of employee aspirations with those of the shareholders. Accordingly, the Company encourages staff to participate in the Company sharesave scheme.

Following shareholder approval at the last annual general meeting, a new performance share plan and a discretionary executive share option plan were introduced to replace the previous executive share option plan which had become time-expired. These plans were designed to enhance the link between the remuneration of executives and the Company's medium and long term performance by incorporating challenging performance targets, based on total shareholder return (TSR) represented by dividends paid and the change in the share price relative to, in the case of the performance share plan, specifed United Kingdom quoted life assurance companies and, in the case of the discretionary executive share option plan, the FTSE 250 index (excluding investment trusts). Executive directors may only participate up to the Inland Revenue approved limit of £30,000 in respect of the discretionary executive share option plan.

Under the performance share plan, executive directors are conditionally allocated shares up to a maximum value of 80% of their basic salary. The shares are held in trust and the number that are eventually awarded to them depends on the extent to which the performance conditions are met. No awards will be made unless the Company's TSR performance is at least equal to the average TSR of the comparator group. (Threshold). If the Threshold is achieved, awards may be made over an amount of up to 30% of the value of the shares conditionally allocated. For the 1998 conditional share allocation, the number of shares over which awards may be made rises on a straight line basis from the Threshold to a TSR performance equal to or above the average TSR of the top two companies in the comparator group, when awards of the total value of allocations may be made. The remuneration committee retains a discretion to withhold or reduce awards under the plan to any extent it considers appropriate, having regard to the Company's underlying financial performance and irrespective of the level of attainment of the TSR performance targets.

Because of the importance of the performance share plan in facilitating senior executive focus on shareholder returns, the remuneration committee will monitor the results of the plan's operation, and the scheme's parameters, such as the comparator group, the performance targets and the size of the awards will be adjusted, if necessary, to ensure the scheme's efficacy.

Details of conditional share allocations and share option grants to directors are set out in the tables on pages 24 and 25.

PERFORMANCE SHARE PLAN

Details of the Company's ordinary shares provisionally allocated to directors under the performance share plan are as follows:

	Shares held under the plan at 1 January 1998	Rights granted during the year	Shares held under the plan at 31 December 1998
F A Crayton	–	19,607	19,607
A J Frost	–	35,014	35,014
W M McDonald	–	19,607	19,607
J J McLachlan	–	22,408	22,408

Shares provisionally allocated under the performance plan to A J Frost will be provided from the United Friendly Group plc Employee Share Trust. Shares provisionally allocated to the other directors will be brought to the market and be held by the United Assurance Group plc Employee Share Trust. At 31 December 1998, no acquisition of shares for this purpose had been made. The cost of conditional awards is being charged to the profit and loss account over the three-year performance period to which they relate. In 1998, an appropriate amount was charged to the profit and loss account.

Subject to performance and other criteria being satisfied, awards will be granted during the six-week period following the announcement of the preliminary financial results for the year ended 31 December 2000. The awards will be included in directors' emoluments in the year in which they are granted.

The aggregate maximum value of the provisional allocations shown above, based on the maximum number of shares which would be transferred to the directors if the Company's total shareholder return (TSR) is equal to or above the average TSR of the top two companies in the comparator group, and on the market price of the Company's shares at 31 December 1998 of £5.475 per share, would have been £529,082.

By virtue of being a potential beneficiary of the United Friendly Group plc Employee Share Trust (Trust), A J Frost is deemed, for the purpose of the Companies Act 1985, to have an interest in the shares held in the Trust. At 31 December 1998, the Trust held 3,244,431 ordinary shares (31 December 1997 – 4,347,474) for the benefit of certain Group employees.

A variant on such schemes is where a conditional allocation of shares is made, but the director will receive cash at the end of the day rather than receiving the shares. One company which has introduced such a scheme is Powerscreen International, as illustrated below:

Extract 29.59: Powerscreen International PLC (1999)

REMUNERATION REPORT [extract]

Executive long term incentive arrangements

A.   Share Value Plan As reported in our 1997 Annual Report and Accounts, on May 28 1996 a new Share Value Plan ("the plan") was adopted by the Remuneration Committee. The plan is a cash bonus scheme based on increases in the value of shares in the Company. Under it, a participant in the plan may be awarded a right to receive a cash bonus calculated by reference to a specified number of ordinary shares multiplied by the result obtained by subtracting the initial market values of those shares from the market value per share as at the date the bonus is exercised. The committee believes a significant advantage of the plan therefore to be that it provides a similar incentive to that provided by share options without causing any dilution of existing holdings. All executive directors and employees are eligible to participate.

The initial market value of a share by reference to which an award is made may not be less than the market value per share on the date of award. The plan gives an absolute discretion in determining when to make awards under it although no award can be made in breach of the Model Code on Directors' Dealings in Securities.

The receipt of a bonus under the plan may be made conditional upon the achievement of an objective performance target determined by the committee when the original award is made. The minimum performance target which the committee intends to impose on the making of awards under the plan will be that in normal circumstances a bonus may only be paid if, during a period of three consecutive years (commencing no earlier than the year in which the award is made) the growth in earnings per share of the Company is at least 2% per annum in excess of the growth in the retail prices index (as published by the Central Statistical Office) over the same three year period.

Awards under the plan will not be transferable and bonuses may normally only be paid between the third and tenth anniversaries of the date of award to a person who remains a director or employee. Bonuses may, however, be paid during a limited period at other times in certain special circumstances including death, retirement, redundancy, ill-health, injury or disability of the award holder or where the award holder's employing company or business is disposed of outside the group, or upon a change in control of the Company, or, at the discretion of the committee, if the award holder ceases to be employed within the group in any other circumstances. Within these limits the timing of the calculation and payment of the bonus will be determined by the award holder. In the event of any rights issues, rights offers, capitalisation issues or other variation of or increase in the share capital of the Company, the number and/or nominal value of shares the subject of awards and/or the relevant share values may be adjusted by the committee in such manner as it deems appropriate.

The criteria on which performance related awards will be based under the Share Value Plan are determined by the Remuneration Committee from time to time with due regard to Association of British Insurers guidelines and industry practice.

The Remuneration Committee put into effect during the year its proposals set out in last year's Report and Accounts to make awards under the Share Value Plan. The awards made to the directors and company secretary are set out on page 28 and in addition, awards in respect of a further 575,000 shares were made to management and key employees during the year. The exercise criteria for these awards were that during a period of three consecutive years (commencing no earlier than the year in which the award was made) the growth in the Company's earnings per share exceed by at least 6% the growth in the retail prices index over the same three year period.

C. Cash bonus arrangement for Mr Kennerley

As permitted under the Listing Rules, Mr Kennerley is the sole participant in a cash bonus arrangement which was put in place in order to recruit him in July 1998. The full text of the arrangement is set out in Schedule 2 of Mr Kennerley's 23 July 1998 service agreement with the Company (a copy of which is available for inspection at the Company's registered office during normal business hours). Mr Kennerley's participation in the arrangements was effective on the date of his service agreement. The principal terms of the arrangement are as follows:

i)   Mr Kennerley has been awarded the right to receive a cash bonus calculated by reference to the amount by which the market value of 250,000 shares in the Company, on the date the bonus is exercised, exceeds 100p per share and also the amount by which the market value of a further 250,000 shares in the Company on the date the bonus is exercised, exceeds 150p per share. These share prices are higher than the market value of a company share on the date at which the arrangement took effect.

ii)   The receipt of the cash bonus is subject to the condition that during the three consecutive years prior to the date such award is exercised, the growth in the Company's earnings per share must have been at least 2% per annum in excess of the growth in the retail prices index over the same three year period.

iii) The right to receive the cash bonus is exercisable by Mr Kennerley in whole or in part during the period commencing after the third anniversary of the date of this service agreement and the day immediately before the tenth anniversary.

iv) The right is personal and not transferable. The bonus may, however, be paid during a limited period at other times in special circumstances including death, retirement, redundancy, ill health or disability, or a change in control of the Company.

v)   In the event of any re-organisation for any reason of the Company's issued share capital, the remuneration committee can make the appropriate adjustment to Mr Kennerley's rights.

Table 4 – **Awards under the Share Value Plan for directors and company secretary**

Director	At 31.3.98 (or date of appointment if later)	Granted	Exercised	Lapsed	At 31.3.99 (or date of departure if earlier)	Exercise price	Exercise period
J E Craig	–	250,000	–	–	250,000	78.5p	2001/2008
W M Caldwell	–	–	–	–	–	–	–
A D Harris*	–	100,000	–	–	100,000	78.5p	2001/2008
P A Perry	–	–	–	–	–	–	–
H J Watson	–	250,000	–	–	250,000	78.5p	2001/2008
J F W Kennerley**	–	200,000	–	–	200,000	92.0p	2001/2008
B J Kearney	–	250,000	–	–	250,000	100.0p	2001/2008
	–	250,000	–	–	250,000	150.0p	2001/2008
	–	300,000	–	–	300,000	92.0p	2001/2008

* Upon his appointment to the Board on 1 April 1999, Mr Harris was granted a further award in respect of 150,000 shares at 112.4p exercisable 2002/2009.

** Mr Kennerley is also entitled to a bonus linked to increases in the company's share price as set out in more detail on page 30.

Some companies have introduced schemes which combine aspects of both deferred bonuses and long-term incentive schemes, an example of which is shown below:

Extract 29.60: Rebus Group plc (1997)

Report of the Remuneration Committee[extract]

The Rebus Group 1996 Restricted Share Plan ("the Plan")

The principal objectives of the Plan, which was adopted by the Board on 20 March 1996, are to encourage a community of interest between the participants in the Plan and the shareholders and to establish a clear link between the rewards of the participants and the Group's performance. The Plan uses existing shares in the Company rather than newly issued shares.

The Plan was operated for the first time immediately following the demerger of the Company from its former parent company in April 1996. The current participants in the Plan are the four executive directors of the Company, although it may ultimately be extended to other senior executives of the Group. The principal terms of the Plan are summarised below.

For each year in which the Plan is operated, the Remuneration Committee, acting on recommendations of the Board, will decide which senior executives should be granted awards ("Awards") under the Plan for that year. The Committee will notify the participants selected that they have been granted Awards and will inform them of the value of the ordinary shares subject to their Awards, the periods over which the ordinary shares subject to the Awards are capable of vesting and the performance criteria applicable to the vesting of the ordinary shares.

As the Plan is currently operated, Awards have an initial five year life (extending to a maximum of eight years in the event that any ordinary shares subject to the Award remain unvested at the fifth anniversary). In addition, each Award is split into three equal parts and different performance criteria and periods of vesting are applicable to those parts.

The performance criteria applicable to the first part of the Award are linked to the Company's performance against annual budgets set each year by the Remuneration Committee. In each year, a maximum of one fifth of the ordinary shares subject to this part of the Award can vest and, therefore, ultimately be capable of transfer to the participant.

The performance criteria for the other two parts of the Award are the Company's performance measured against an index of the companies in the FTSE 350 as at the date of grant of the Award. One part of the Award is subject to the Company's comparative performance by reference to the increase in its share price over the five year life of the Award and the second part is subject to the Company's comparative performance by reference to the increase in its earnings per share over the same period. After the fifth anniversary of the grant of an Award, any ordinary shares remaining unvested can vest and be transferred to the participant at any time until the eighth anniversary of the grant of the Award, provided that the performance criteria are met.

The number of ordinary shares subject to parts two and three of the Award that vest and which will, therefore, be capable of transfer to the participant subject to the Plan rules and the time at which vesting will occur is determined by reference to the Company's ranking in the relevant index.

While shares can vest under the respective parts of the Award over the life of the Award, a participant will have no entitlement to receive any ordinary shares subject to his Award unless either he remains in employment until the fifth anniversary of the date when the Award was made to him or his employment is terminated prior to that time in certain circumstances. Vested ordinary shares may be transferred earlier in the event of the termination of the participant's employment by reason of injury, disability, illness or redundancy or for any other reason at the discretion of the Remuneration Committee prior to the date on which vested ordinary shares would otherwise have qualified for transfer.

In the event of a reorganisation of the share capital of the Company, the ordinary shares subject to Awards will be adjusted on a basis approved as appropriate by the Remuneration Committee.

Any dividends paid on any ordinary shares subject to Awards that have vested will accrue to the relevant participant and will be reinvested in further ordinary shares in the Company. Any such further ordinary shares will be held subject to such of the terms of the Plan as are applicable to the ordinary shares from which they derive.

The rules of the Plan may be amended by the Remuneration Committee, where necessary with the consent of the trustee of The Rebus Group Employee Share Trust. The Plan cannot be amended to the advantage of participants without the prior approval of shareholders in general meeting, except for minor amendments to benefit its administration or to take account of any changes in legislation or to obtain or maintain favourable taxation, exchange control or regulatory treatment for the Company or a participating company or an associated company of the Company or any participant in the Plan.

Details of directors' remuneration

Awards have been granted to the executive directors, and restricted shares have vested in respect of performance during the year, under the Plan described above as follows:

	Date of Award	Number of restricted shares subject to Award	Number of restricted shares vested	Number of restricted shares lapsed	Number of restricted shares still capable of vesting
D A Laking	17 April 1996	252,551	5,000	11837	235,714
N J Loney	17 April 1996	229,591	3,500	11,806	214,285
P E Presland	17 April 1996	378,826	7,000	18,255	353,571
R D Summers	17 April 1996	252,551	5,000	11,837	235,714

The restricted shares that have vested will in due course be transferred to the directors only in accordance with the rules of the Plan described above. The amount charged against profits by the Group in the year ended 31 March 1997 in respect of the Plan was £173,000.

The restricted shares that have vested are presumably those shares relating to the first part of the award which is linked to annual performance and therefore represent the 'deferred bonus' element of the scheme.

One company which has had long-term incentive schemes for a number of years is Safeway. It has therefore had to consider the disclosures required when the awards crystallise:

Extract 29.61: Safeway plc (1997)

Report of the remuneration committee [extract]

Long term incentive plan

The Company has operated a long term incentive plan since 1988. The plan is designed to align the efforts of key executives with the Company's objective of creating shareholder value in the longer term. Executives are selected to participate on the basis that they are in a position to influence significantly the performance of the Company.

The plan is a performance share plan. Under the terms of the plan, executives receive a conditional award of shares at the beginning of a three year period. The actual number of shares to which executives obtain vested rights depends on the Company's performance over that same period. Executives have no rights or entitlements to an award of shares and no awards are made if a participant has left the Company's employment prior to the end of the performance period.

Shares for use in the plan are ordinary shares in the Company which are transferred out of the Safeway plc Employee Share Ownership Plan ("ESOP"), a discretionary trust, set up to administer the plan (Note 13.1 on page 52). In order to hedge the Company's liability to payments under the plan, the Company funds the anticipated payout over each three year cycle by ensuring that the Trustee has sufficient funds to purchase the Company's ordinary shares through the ESOP.

Cycles:

1992 cycle – The performance objectives under the 1992 cycle, which covered the three financial years ended 1 April 1995, were not achieved and accordingly no awards were made in the year or in previous financial years.

1994 cycle – Awards due under the 1994 cycle, covering the three financial years ended 29 March 1997, are determined by comparing the Company's Total Shareholder Return to that of a weighted, by market capitalisation, basket of competitor companies (comprising Asda, Budgens, Iceland, Kwik Save, Wm. Morrison, J. Sainsbury and Tesco) based on the average three month period up to both the 1994 and 1997 year ends. Actual awards to be made to executive directors and other senior executives under the 1994 cycle will vest in the two financial years immediately following the end of the performance period, ie. in the 1998 and 1999 financial years.

Over the three year period from April 1994 to March 1997, the Company's Total Shareholder Return increased on average by 17.77% per annum compared to the basket of competitor companies which increased by 9.41% per annum. Over the same period, the FTSE 100 Index increased by 13.5% per annum and the FTSE All Share Index by 12.3% per annum. Accordingly, the Company out-performed the index of competitor companies by 8.36% per annum which, dependent on the discretion of the Committee and the Trustee, could give rise to the following awards to executive directors:

	Vesting in 1998	Vesting in 1999	Total Shares (if awarded)
Sir Alistair Grant	382,860	127,620	510,480
D G C Webster	239,287	79,763	319,050
C D Smith	233,970	155,980	389,950
R G B Charters	53,175	17,725	70,900
S T Laffin	74,445	24,815	99,260
G Wotherspoon	132,937	44,313	177,250
Total	1,116,674	450,216	1,566,890

Mr D G C Webster and Mr C D Smith have confirmed that any shares vested in them in 1998 will be retained in full (net of any sales necessary to pay the income tax liability) for a minimum period of three years.

In addition, Mr R G B Charters and Mr S T Laffin have confirmed that they will retain all and Mr G Wotherspoon half, the number of shares that may be awarded to them in 1998 (net of any sales necessary to pay the income tax liability).

The charges made in the profit and loss account in respect of the 1994 cycle and included in staff costs (Note 8.2 on page 48) totalled £8.9 million (executive directors £4.9 million and senior executives £4.0 million). In addition, £1.1 million has been provided in respect of estimated National Insurance payable. Of this, £5.7 million (including National Insurance) was charged in the year ended 29 March 1997 (1996 – £1.4 million; earlier years – £2.9 million).

1996 and 1997 cycles – In July 1996, the Company sought and obtained the approval of shareholders to its long term incentive plan as explained more fully above. Cycles of the plan are now annual and the Remuneration Committee believes that the plan has served the Company well. Accordingly, the Remuneration Committee initiated a 1996 and a 1997 cycle with effect from the beginning of the 1997 and 1998 financial years.

The 1996 and 1997 cycles cover the three financial years ending in 1999 and in 2000. Awards will be determined after measuring the Company's performance according to:

    (a) the Company's Total Shareholder Return compared to that of a basket of competitor companies; and

    (b) the increase in the Earnings per share of the Company.

Both measures are determined independently and each may provide up to 50% of an individual's personal maximum award. The maximum award that any executive director could receive under these cycles is:

	Maximum share award	
	1996 cycle	1997 cycle
D G C Webster	120,000	138,000
C D Smith	140,000	140,000
R G B Charters	80,000	78,000
S T Laffin	57,500	58,000
G Wotherspoon	65,000	63,000
	462,500	477,000

The actual position will not be known until the end of the 1999 and 2000 financial years and could, dependent upon performance, be a nil award or up to a maximum of the number of shares shown in the table above. Details of the actual awards will be reported in future Remuneration Committee Reports.

A provisional amount of £1.1 million (including £0.1 million of estimated National Insurance payable) has been charged this year in respect of the 1996 cycle and is included in staff costs (Note 8.2 on page 48).

In this case, disclosure has been given of the number of shares which are likely to be awarded to the directors based on the three-year performance up to the year end, with an indication of when they will ultimately vest, but no value has been disclosed.

This highlights one of the problems with the requirements. The third bullet point of the requirement set out in (a) (iv) at 4.4 above is that it is 'the money value and number of shares, cash payments or other benefits received by each director under such schemes during the period' which are to be disclosed. As in this case the shares have not yet been 'received' then arguably there is no need for any disclosure. A similar issue arises in respect of the Companies Act requirement in respect of long-term incentive schemes as to when such amounts are 'receivable'. This is discussed at 2.6 above.

However, as with the Boots example illustrated in Extract 29.16 at 2.6 above, sufficient information is likely to have been given to satisfy the interpretation that such an amount was receivable in the year the performance period ended as this will usually be the year end and the company's share price at that date will have been disclosed under UITF 10 (see A above).

Another company which has long-term incentive schemes, for one of which the performance period ended with the current year, was WPP:

Extract 29.62: WPP Group plc (1998)

Directors' remuneration and interests [extract]

Remuneration of the directors was as follows:

Executive directors	Location	Salary and fees £000	Other benefits £000	Short-term incentive plans (annual bonus) £000	1998 Total £000	1997 Total £000	Long-term incentive plans 1998 Total £000	Long-term incentive plans 1997 Total £000
M S Sorrell	UK	712	23	605	1,340	1,349	–	1,219 [8]
B J Brooks	USA	172	2	95	269	240	188 [4]	831
P W G Richardson	UK	180	22	99	301	291	107 [5]	87
F R Salama	UK	150	19	90	259	235	126 [5]	47
G C Sampson	UK	70	7	5	82	76	–	–

Notes

3   The amount in respect of 1997 of £1,219 million was in respect of phantom options granted in relation to 1993. No amount was received in 1998. The performance conditions for the final tranches of the Capital Investment Plan and the Notional Share Award Plan respectively met on 4 June 1998. This value of these Plans is not shown in the above table as the ultimate value will depend on the share price in September 1999 and beyond.

---

4   This amount in 1998 represents a payment under the Performance Share Plan and in 1997 represented a payment under the Performance Share Plan and a gain realised on the exercise of share options.

5   This amount represents a payment under the Performance Share Plan.

Other long-term incentive plan awards

Long-term Incentive Plan awards granted to directors are as follows:

	At 1 Jan 1998 Number	Granted/ (lapsed) 1998 Number	Vested 1998 Number	At 31 Dec 1998 Number	Granted 1999 Number	Vested 1999 Number	At 6 May 1999 Number	Performance period	Price per share of vested units on valuation date[2]
B J Brooks	48,869	–	48,869	–	–	–	48,869	1 Jan 1995 – 31 Dec 1997	269.5p
	73,933	–	–	73,933	–	36,966	36,966	1 Jan 1996 – 31 Dec 1998	365.8p
	60,864	–	–	60,864	–	–	60,864	1 Jan 1997 – 31 Dec 1999	n/a
	–	46,728	–	46,728	–	–	46,728	1 Jan 1998 – 31 Dec 2000	n/a
P W G Richardson	32,265	–	32,265	–	–	–	–	1 Jan 1995 – 31 Dec 1997	269.5p
	42,172	–	–	42,172	–	21,086	21,086	1 Jan 1996 – 31 Dec 1998	365.8p
	67,925	–	–	67,925	–	–	67,925	1 Jan 1997 – 31 Dec 1999	n/a
	–	55,513	–	55,513	–	–	55,513	1 Jan 1998 – 31 Dec 2000	n/a
F R Salama	17,559	–	17,559	–	–	–	–	1 Jan 1995 – 31 Dec 1997	269.5p
	49,438	–	–	49,438	–	24,719	24,719	1 Jan 1996 – 31 Dec 1998	365.8p
	67,925	–	–	–	56,604	–	56,604	1 Jan 1997 – 31 Dec 1999	n/a
	–	46,261	–	46,261	–	–	46,261	1 Jan 1998 – 31 Dec 2000	n/a
M S Sorrell[3]	6,445,912	–	–	6,445,912	–	–	6,445,912	4 Sep 1994 – 4 Sep 1999	n/a

Notes

1   All awards shown on this table, except the 6,445,912 shares referred to in note 3, were made under the performance share plan, details of which can be found on page 87.

2   Valuation date is 31 December at the end of the relevant performance period.

3   The 6,445,912 shares represent the maximum number of shares, or cash equivalent of shares which could vest under the Capital Investment Plan and the Notional Share Award Plan. Details of these two Plans which expire in September 1999 are set out on page 88. All shares and awards must be retained until September 1999 and consequently their value cannot be established until that time. As of 6 May 1999, the performance conditions in respect of all four tranches of the Capital Investment Plan and all three tranches of the Notional Share Award Plan had been satisfied. Under arrangements made with Mr M S Sorrell relating to the payment on his behalf of US withholding tax under the Capital Investment Plan and pension payments made under the US Agreement, WPP Group USA Inc. has made payments of which the maximum amount outstanding during the year was $500,967 and which remained outstanding at 31 December 1998.

In this case, the shares under the performance share plan relating to the performance period ended at the year end have vested in 1999, but the value using the year end share price is included within the remuneration table under 1998. This would therefore satisfy the Companies Act requirement. However, disclosure is also given of the number of shares which vested during 1998, the value of which is shown under the 1996 column of the remuneration table. This therefore satisfies the Stock Exchange requirement to disclose the amounts 'received' during the year. Further details about the various plans are disclosed elsewhere in the Compensation Committee Report.

It should be emphasised that the disclosures in respect of long-term incentive schemes are completely independent of the charge recognised in the profit and loss account for such schemes, although some companies disclose the annual charge and the cumulative provision (see Extracts 29.60 and 29.61 above). In April 1997, the UITF published its seventeenth Abstract, *Employee share schemes*.[103] This addresses the relatively narrow issue of how companies should recognise and measure the cost of new shares issued as part of an employee share scheme. This is discussed further at 4.7.2 of Chapter 15.

Where a company (unusually) sets up a long-term incentive scheme for an individual director then certain detailed disclosures about such a scheme have to be disclosed in the next annual report (see 4.4 above).

C   *Policy in granting options or awards under such long-term incentive schemes*

The Greenbury Report stated that 'to reduce freak results from share price fluctuations, grants of share options should normally be phased over time rather than made as one large block. Executive options should never be issued at a discount.'[104] Paragraph B6 of the Code recommended that 'if grants under executive share option or other long-term incentive schemes are awarded in one large block rather than phased, the report should explain and justify'. This has been repeated in Schedule B to the Combined Code (see 4.3.3 above).

The requirement introduced by the Stock Exchange set out in (a) (viii) at 4.4 above to effect the latter recommendation, however, goes further than the Code because it requires a company to give a statement of the policy, whatever it might be, not just where such items are awarded in a large block. At the same time as introducing this disclosure requirement, the Stock Exchange also changed its *Listing Rules* such that options could not be issued at a discount to the prevailing market price without being first approved by the shareholders (although exceptions to this rule are allowed in specific circumstances, such as for employee share schemes which are available to substantially all the employees).[105]

Examples of such policies in respect of long-term incentive schemes are illustrated in the extracts shown at B above.

As far as policies in respect of the granting of options are concerned, many of them do no more than give a description of the option schemes that are in place. In our view a statement of policy should deal with whether options are phased or granted in blocks, whether there are annual or overall caps in the number of shares which can be under option and whether there are any performance criteria to be satisfied. This last item is required, in any case, in respect of options which have already been granted (see A above). Examples of policies in respect of options are illustrated below:

Extract 29.63: Zeneca Group PLC (1998)

Report of the Board on Remuneration of Directors[extract]

Components of the remuneration package

Longer term performance incentive: Directors are also rewarded for improvement in the performance of the Group sustained over a period of years in the form of share options and the policy is that these are granted incrementally to the value of four times each Director's salary. The exercise of options granted under the 1994 Executive Share Option Scheme is currently subject to the performance condition that before any exercise, earnings per share must grow by at least the increase in the UK retail price index over three years plus 3% per annum. This is a strengthened version of the performance condition approved by shareholders at the 1998 AGM. There is a policy, subject to the discretion of the Committee, of phasing the grant of replacement options following any exercise.

Extract 29.64: Allied Domecq PLC (1998)

Report of the Remuneration Committee[extract]

8.   Share options

Directors are eligible for grants of options to acquire shares under the terms of the following schemes:

(a)   The Allied Domecq 1991 Share Savings Scheme – this scheme is based on a three or five year savings contract and is open to all UK employees. Options are granted at an exercise price of not less than 80 per cent of the market price on the last dealing day prior to the date of the invitation.

(b)   The Allied Domecq 1991 Executive Share Option Scheme – options up to a value of £30,000 may be granted at an exercise price not less than the market price on the last dealing day prior to the date of grant and under normal circumstances remain exercisable between the third and tenth anniversaries of the date of grant.

(c)   The Allied Domecq 1991 International Executive Share Option Scheme – options are granted at an exercise price not less than the market price on the last dealing day prior to the date of grant and under normal circumstances remain exercisable between the third and tenth anniversaries of the date of grant (though shorter life options may be granted).

Options under the executive schemes are generally granted to directors annually to a value equivalent to 100 per cent of salary subject to individual subscription limits in accordance with institutional guidelines. Grants of options since 1995 will become exercisable only if the total shareholder return (change in value of the shares plus gross dividends paid, treated as invested) on Allied Domecq shares exceeds that of the FTSE 100 Index Total Share Return over any consecutive three year period between the dates of grant and exercise.

4.4.10 Directors' service contracts

The Greenbury Report took the view that 'there is a strong case for setting [directors'] notice or contract periods at, or reducing them to, one year or less'.[106] Accordingly paragraph B10 of the Greenbury Code recommended that companies should disclose contracts with notice periods in excess of one year, and explain why such periods are considered appropriate. This recommendation has been incorporated in the Stock Exchange requirements (see (a) (vi) at 4.4 above). Schedule B to the Combined Code has a similar requirement (see 4.3.3 above).

The Stock Exchange already had an existing rule that the directors' report must state the unexpired portion of any service contract of any director proposed for re-election at the forthcoming AGM (where details are required to be available for inspection) or that there are no such contracts. Given the requirement for companies to have a remuneration report, the opportunity was taken to modify this rule by requiring the information to be given in the remuneration report (see (a) (vii) at 4.4 above). A 'directors' service contract' is defined by the Stock Exchange as 'a service contract with a notice period of one year or more or with provisions for predetermined compensation on termination of an amount which equals or exceeds one year's salary and benefits in kind'.[107] The revised requirement also no longer requires a statement to be made where there are no such contracts.

An example of such disclosures is given by United Utilities, as shown below:

Extract 29.65: United Utilities PLC (1999)

Remuneration report [extract]

Contracts of service

The review of remuneration policies conducted during the year included the issue of notice periods. A change was made to comply with the combined code and, in future, new executive directors joining the board will normally be offered one year notice periods. An initial longer notice period may be offered where it is considered necessary to recruit an appropriate individual. Where an initial notice period of more than one year is offered, the company would normally look to reduce that period to one year after the initial period.

All the current executive directors serve under contracts which are terminable by the company giving two years' notice. As those periods have previously been reduced from three years by agreement with each of the executive directors concerned and without compensation, it is not intended to seek a further reduction in the case of the current executive directors.

The Committee's policy on termination of contracts is to apply mitigation as far as is fair and reasonable in each circumstance. In so doing, it will have due regard to the best practice provisions of the combined code and the company's legal liability in each instance.

Directors standing for re-election

Norman Broadhurst and John Seed are standing, and are recommended by the board, for re-election at the 1999 annual general meeting. As non-executive directors, Norman and John do not have contracts of service.

Like many other companies United Utilities continues to disclose the fact that non-executive directors standing for re-election do not have service contracts and have also made a statement about mitigation in the event of the termination of a director's contract.

In addition to the above disclosure requirements in respect of directors' service contracts, the Stock Exchange also requires that such contracts or written memoranda of the terms of all directors' service contracts must be available for inspection at the registered office during normal business hours on each business day and at the place of the annual general meeting for at least 15 minutes prior to and during the meeting.[108]

5   CONCLUSION

The disclosure of directors' remuneration remains a bit of a nightmare. Over the past few years there has been a dramatic increase in the volume of disclosure given by listed companies on directors' pay and benefits, as companies have implemented the new disclosure requirements imposed by the Stock Exchange as a result of the Greenbury Report. Almost as much time nowadays is spent discussing the directors' remuneration disclosures as the rest of the report and accounts. In some cases the sheer volume of information has become a barrier to effective communication.

The rationalisation of the Companies Act requirements is welcomed in this regard. This has gone some way to reduce the volume of disclosures given by listed companies and has also been beneficial to companies which are not governed by the Stock Exchange requirements, but some of the requirements are still too complicated and confusing.

Although pleased when the Stock Exchange had finally decided upon its rules on pension disclosures, we were sorry that they felt it necessary not only to require both accrued benefit and transfer value information, but also to allow alternative information as a surrogate for transfer values, thereby adding further incomprehensible information to that already disclosed. Too much of a company's annual report has to be devoted to directors' emoluments nowadays, and we would like to see the rules substantially simplified.

References

1 A more detailed exposition of the law governing directors' remuneration can be found in R. Pennington, *Company Law*, pp. 634–641 and C.M. Schmitthoff (ed.), *Palmer's Company Law (Volume 1)*, pp. 902–907.
2 L. C. B. Gower, *The Principles of Modern Company Law*, p. x.
3 See Chapter 28, footnote 1.
4 CA 67, s 6.
5 The Committee on the Financial Aspects of Corporate Governance, *The Financial Aspects of Corporate Governance*, (The Cadbury Report), December 1992.
6 The Study Group on Directors' Remuneration, *Directors' Remuneration: Report of a Study Group chaired by Sir Richard Greenbury*, (The Greenbury Report), July 1995.
7 Committee on Corporate Governance, *Final Report*, January 1998.
8 The Companies (Tables A–F) Regulations 1985 (SI 1985 No. 805), Table A, Article 82.

9 *Hutton v West Cork Railway* (1883) 23 Ch.D. 654. For a discussion of the extent to which company law is able to control the level of directors' remuneration, see J. E. Parkinson, *Directors' Remuneration,* pp. 130–132, 142–143.

10 CA 85, s 311(1).

11 *Ibid.*, s 311(2).

12 The Companies (Tables A–F) Regulations 1985 (SI 1985 No. 805), Table A, Article 87.

13 CA 85, s 312.

14 Pennington, *op. cit.*, p. 639.

15 CA 85, s 316(3).

16 *Ibid.*, s 318.

17 *Ibid.*, s 319.

18 *Ibid.*, ss 232(1)–(2), Sch. 6, Part I. If the directors are entitled to deliver accounts to the registrar modified as for small companies, the modified accounts may omit these details. In the annual accounts for shareholders, small companies need only disclose the aggregate amount of directors' emoluments (being emoluments, amounts under long-term incentive schemes and pension contributions in respect of money purchase benefits), the numbers of directors who are members of money purchase and defined benefit schemes, compensation for loss of office and sums paid to third parties in respect of directors' services.

19 CA 85, Sch. 4, para. 58.

20 *Ibid.*, s 232(3). This duty also extends to anyone who is, or has within the last five years been, an officer of the company.

21 *Ibid.*, s 237(4). A discussion of the procedures which the auditor should adopt in relation to directors' emoluments can be found in A. Brown and D. Foster, *Directors' loans, other transactions and remuneration,* pp. 25–27.

22 CA 85, Sch. 6, para. 1(1)(a).

23 *Ibid.*, para. 1(5).

24 *Ibid.*, para. 13(2)(a).

25 *Ibid.*, para. 1(6)(b).

26 *Ibid.*, para. 1(3)(a).

27 *Ibid.*, para. 1(3)(b).

28 *Ibid.*, para. 13(3)(a).

29 CA 85, s 310(3)(a).

30 *Ibid.*, Sch. 6, para. 11(1).

31 *Ibid.*, para. 10(2).

32 *Ibid.*, para. 11(2).

33 *Ibid.*

34 *Ibid.*, para. 10(2).

35 *Ibid.*, para. 12.

36 *Ibid.*, para. 10(4).

37 *Ibid.*, para. 1(1)(b).

38 *Ibid.*, para. 1(5).

39 *Ibid.*

40 *Ibid.*

41 FRRP PN 53, 7 August 1998.

42 CA 85, Sch. 6, para. 1(2).

43 *Ibid.*, para. 1(1)(c).

44 *Ibid.*, para. 1(4).

45 *Ibid.*, para. 1(5).

46 *Ibid.*, para. 2(a).

47 *Ibid.*, para. 2(b).

48 UITF 17, *Employee share schemes,* UITF, April 1997.

49 CA 85, Sch. 6, para. 1(1)(d).

50 *Ibid.*, para. 1(5).

51 *Ibid.*, para. 13(3).

52 *Ibid.*, para. 1(5).

53 *Ibid.*, para. 13(3).

54 *Ibid.*, para. 1(7).
55 *Ibid.*, para. 1(1)(e).
56 *Ibid.*, para. 1(5).
57 *Ibid.*
58 *Ibid.*, para. 1(8).
59 *Ibid.*, para. 7(1).
60 *Ibid.*, para. 7(2).
61 *Ibid.*
62 *Ibid.*, para. 7(4).
63 *Ibid.*, para. 8(1).
64 *Ibid.*, para. 8(4).
65 *Ibid.*
66 *Ibid.*, para. 8(2)(b).
67 *Ibid.*, para. 8(3).
68 *Ibid.*
69 *Ibid.*, para. 9(1).
70 *Ibid.*, para. 9(3).
71 *Ibid.*, para. 9(2).
72 *Ibid.*, para. 2(1)(a).
73 *Ibid.*, para. 2(1)(b).
74 *Ibid.*, para. 2(2).
75 *Ibid.*, para. 2(5).
76 *Ibid.*
77 *Ibid.*, para. 2(3).
78 *Ibid.*, para. 2(4).
79 *Ibid.*, Sch. 4, paras. 56(4), 94.
80 *Ibid.*, para. 94(1).
81 Committee on Corporate Governance, *Final Report*, (The Hampel Report), January 1998.
82 The Committee on the Financial Aspects of Corporate Governance, *The Financial Aspects of Corporate Governance*, (The Cadbury Report), December 1992.
83 *The Listing Rules*, London Stock Exchange, Chapter 12, para. 12.43(x).
84 *Ibid.*, para. 12.43(u). The detailed requirements are set out in Chapter 13, paras. 13.13A and 13.14.
85 *Ibid.*, para. 12.43(d).
86 The Greenbury Report, para. 5.5.
87 *Ibid.*, para. 5.7.
88 The Hampel Report, para. 4.15.
89 The Greenbury Report, para. 5.8.
90 *Ibid.*, para. 5.9.
91 *Ibid.*, para. 6.21.
92 *Ibid.*, para. 6.22.
93 *Ibid.*, para. 6.44.
94 *The Listing Rules*, Definitions.
95 The Greenbury Report, para. 7.2
96 *Ibid.*, para. 5.10.
97 *Ibid.*, para. 5.18.
98 *Ibid.*, para. 5.19.
99 *Note to subscribers to the Listing Rules Amendment No. 10*, London Stock Exchange, May 1997.
100 *Ibid.*
101 The Greenbury Report, paras. 6.23–40.
102 *The Listing Rules*, Chapter 12, para. 12.43(k).
103 UITF 17, *Employee share schemes*, UITF, April 1997.
104 The Greenbury Report, para. 6.29.
105 *The Listing Rules*, Chapter 13, paras. 13.30–31.
106 The Greenbury Report, para. 7.13.
107 *The Listing Rules*, Definitions.
108 *The Listing Rules*, Chapter 16, para. 16.9.

Chapter 30   Interim reports and preliminary announcements

1   INTRODUCTION

The publication of interim financial reports and preliminary announcements have been requirements for listed companies for many years, although the Stock Exchange's rules governing their form and content remain sketchy. However, in 1997 the Accounting Standards Board issued a non-mandatory Statement on interim reports,[1] based on work undertaken by the Financial Reporting Committee of the ICAEW, and in 1998 followed this up with a similar non-mandatory Statement on preliminary announcements.[2]

The most frequently debated issue relating to interim financial reporting is whether the interim period should be regarded as a discrete period in its own right, or whether it should be seen primarily as a mere instalment of the financial year. Under the first perspective, it would be appropriate to apply the same accounting policies and principles as are used for the annual accounts, treating the interim period in just the same way as the full financial year. Under the second, some modifications to these policies and principles are made to allow the interim report to give a better guide to the outcome of the year as a whole. The former approach is generally referred to as the 'discrete' approach, and the latter as the 'integral' approach. In practice, however, these categories are less clear-cut than the above description might suggest, and companies generally follow an approach which is a hybrid of these two theoretical extremes.

The integral approach has no clear definition. It implies some pragmatic modification of the inter-period allocation of transactions, so as to match costs more evenly with revenues in the different halves (or quarters) of the year. Critics would say that this is not matching, but smoothing, and that it obscures the results of the interim period rather than presents them more fairly. On the other hand, supporters would say that such modifications are necessary to prevent meaningless distortions arising; an interim period is an even more artificial interval than a financial year, and that to report transactions without trying to relate them to the annual cycle of activity for which they have been incurred would not make sense. Moreover, it can be argued that similar allocations are often necessary in annual accounts. For example, depreciating fixed assets (particularly on a usage basis) necessarily involves deciding how much of the cost of the asset should be related to this year's revenues and how much to those of future years. The debate on this subject is therefore less straightforward than it appears at first sight.

The extent of disclosure in interim reports raises similar issues. If interim reporting is no different in concept from annual reporting, but is simply a more frequent version of the same thing, then one might suppose that the form and content of the report should also be the same. If, however, it is seen as a subsidiary form of reporting which only deals with an instalment of a longer period, then it is easier to justify a different reporting package. Present practice undoubtedly reflects the latter view, although probably more as an expedient compromise than as the result of an attempt to meet a carefully researched need.

In the UK, the normal frequency of reporting is biannual. Relatively few British companies follow the North American practice of reporting every quarter. In this chapter, reference is often made to 'half-yearly' reports, but the discussion applies to interim reports of any duration.

It should be explained that the term 'interim accounts' also appears in the Companies Act, but with quite a different meaning. This refers to the accounts which public companies have to draw up to justify paying a dividend if their last annual accounts show that their distributable reserves were insufficient for this purpose.[3] Such requirements are beyond the scope of this book and are not discussed further in this chapter.

Preliminary announcements are regarded as very important by the stock market because they are the first formal release of annual results and are highly price-sensitive. In contrast, when the full annual report is subsequently released it rarely triggers any share price reaction or receives much attention from analysts. It is therefore paradoxical that, until the ASB's recent Statement, so little guidance on preliminary announcements had been developed in the past compared to the extensive regulation of the full annual report. Alternatively, the paradox could be more tellingly expressed the other way round – it is anomalous that the annual report has been the focus of so much attention by regulators, since the stock market appears to care so little about it!

The ASB, having finalised its Statement on preliminary announcements, asked its working party to review the year-end financial reporting structure as a whole, and to develop ideas and proposals for consideration by the Board.

2 REQUIREMENTS FOR INTERIM REPORTS

2.1 The Stock Exchange Listing Rules

The Stock Exchange requires listed companies to publish a half-yearly report on their activities and profit and loss account information covering the first six months of their financial year. These rules embody the requirements of the EU Interim Reports Directive, which were enacted in UK law in 1984.[4]

The Listing Rules are not demanding. They require only a minimal profit and loss account to be presented, and in a slightly archaic form. They also contain some general injunctions, borrowed from the Directive, concerning the quality of the information presented. In practice, companies tend to go beyond these requirements so as to present a more informative report.

The profit and loss account information which the Stock Exchange requires is as follows:

(a)   net turnover;*

(b)   profit or loss before taxation and extraordinary items;*

(c)   taxation on profits (UK taxation and, if material, overseas and share of associated undertakings' taxation to be shown separately);

(d)   minority interests;

(e)   profit or loss attributable to shareholders, before extraordinary items;

(f)   extraordinary items, net of taxation;

(g)   profit or loss attributable to shareholders;

(h)   rates of dividend(s) paid and proposed and amount absorbed thereby;* and

(i)   earnings per share expressed as pence per share.[5]

These figures are to be on a consolidated basis and comparative figures also have to be given.[6] They have to use the same policies and form of presentation as were used in the previous annual accounts, unless these are to be changed in the next annual accounts (e.g. to conform with a new standard or piece of legislation) which must be explained, or if the Exchange otherwise agrees.[7]

The asterisked items in the above list may be omitted if the Stock Exchange agrees that their disclosure would be seriously detrimental to the company, so long as 'such an omission would not be likely to mislead the public with regard to facts and circumstances, knowledge of which is essential for the assessment of the shares in question'.[8] This can only be described as a nonsensical proposition, but it comes straight from the European Directive. The Stock Exchange can also authorise omission of these figures on public interest grounds,[9] and indeed has discretion to authorise any other omissions if it believes it necessary or appropriate to do so.[10] Companies should also modify the items disclosed if they are not suited to their particular activities.[11]

Although this version of the Listing Rules was published in 1993, it reflects a rather out of date view of the profit and loss account. In particular, it clings to a pre-1981 Companies Act approach, which does not seek to explain the link between turnover and pre-tax profit, and it takes no account of the substantial changes made to the profit and loss account by FRS 3,[12] which was issued in 1992. Following FRS 3, extraordinary items remain only a theoretical possibility but various new components of performance have to be identified, notably those relating to exceptional items and discontinued operations, as discussed in Chapter 22.

Other aspects of the requirements are strange as well. For example, they require the tax charge to be analysed to show that which relates to associates, but do not require the associates' results themselves to be disclosed. Similarly, overseas tax is to be shown separately, but no such analysis of the profit figure is required. The rules also say that in exceptional circumstances the Stock Exchange may allow 'estimated figures for profit and loss' to be given so long as this is explained.[13] Again, this comes from the Directive and suggests a rather limited understanding of the nature of financial reporting; *all* profit figures should be seen as 'estimates' rather than as precise and objective statements of fact.

As well as the numerical information described above, the Listing Rules require the half-yearly report to contain the following:

(a) an explanatory statement including any significant information enabling investors to make an informed assessment of the trend of the group's activities and profit or loss;

(b) an indication of any special factor which has influenced those activities and the profit or loss during the period in question;

(c) enough information to enable a comparison to be made with the corresponding period of the preceding financial year; and

(d) so far as possible, a reference to the group's prospects in the current financial year.[14]

The report must be published within four months of the half-year to which it relates.[15] It may be either sent to the shareholders, or inserted as an advertisement in a national newspaper,[16] and it must also be communicated to the Stock Exchange.[17] If the company extends its accounting period to more than 14 months, it must publish a further interim report covering the second six months up to its old year end, or another period that ends not more than six months before the new year end.[18]

2.2   The Cadbury Committee

The Cadbury Report made some passing comments on interim reporting, but did not get into the subject in any detail. Its main recommendation was that companies should supplement the profit and loss account information required by the Stock Exchange with balance sheet information, and that an amendment to the Listing Rules to this effect should be considered.[19] In addition, the Committee said that its own successor body should consider whether information on cash flows should have to be included as well.[20]

Although these suggestions had no mandatory force, they helped to encourage the presentation of fuller interim reports, and the Committee's successor did not need to consider the subject any further because the ASB then picked up the issue, as discussed in 2.4 below.

2.3   The ICAEW Consultative Paper

In September 1993, the Financial Reporting Committee of the ICAEW published a consultative paper on Interim Financial Reporting, with the aim of converting the rather loose requirements of the Stock Exchange into a more comprehensive reporting framework. This was the UK profession's first attempt to develop authoritative guidance on the subject, and after responses were received the project was passed to the ASB as the basis for a Statement on the subject.

2.4   The ASB's Statement

In November 1996, the Accounting Standards Board published an exposure draft of a non-mandatory Statement – *Interim Reports* – and converted it into a final document with little change in September 1997. Its main recommendations are as follows:

2.4.1   *Statements to be included*

The ASB calls for interim reports to include summarised versions of all the four primary statements that are required in annual accounts – profit and loss account, balance sheet, cash flow statement and (where relevant) a statement of total recognised gains and losses – together with a narrative management commentary.[21] Two sets of comparative figures (for the previous interim period, and the whole of the previous financial year) are recommended, although the Statement is rather tentative about the need for a comparative balance sheet for the previous interim period.[22] Since the comparative figures for the full year will not constitute full statutory accounts, they will have to be accompanied by a statement explaining that these are not the statutory accounts for that year, and that the statutory accounts have been delivered to the Registrar of Companies and have been the subject of an auditors' report which was unqualified (assuming that to be the case).[23]

A   *Profit and loss account*

The Statement seeks to improve the Stock Exchange rules for the profit and loss account by adding various items and bringing it more in line with FRS 3. It suggests that the following items should be disclosed:

- Turnover
- Operating profit or loss
- Exceptional items (individually), both those included in operating profit and the three specified by paragraph 20 of FRS 3 to come after operating profit and before interest, namely
  - (a) profits and losses on the sale or termination of an operation;
  - (b) costs of a fundamental reorganisation or restructuring having a material effect on the nature and focus of the reporting entity's operations; and
  - (c) profits and losses on the disposal of fixed assets.
- Interest payable less interest receivable (net)
- Profit and loss on ordinary activities before tax
- Tax on profit and loss on ordinary activities (with separate disclosure of the tax effects of exceptional items that have been shown on the face of the profit and loss account)
- Profit and loss on ordinary activities after tax
- Minority interests
- Profit or loss for the period
- Dividends paid and proposed.[24]

The Statement calls for any of the above amounts that relate to associates and joint ventures to be disclosed separately, and also for segmental analyses of turnover and profit to be given on the same basis as is used in the annual accounts.[25]

The Statement also asks that the turnover and operating profit relating to acquisitions and discontinued operations should be disclosed separately. For this purpose, the exposure draft had proposed that discontinued operations should be those that were expected to be classified as such in the accounts for the full year. In terms of FRS 3, this would have included not only those that had been discontinued during the interim period, but also those that were expected to be discontinued in the remaining part of the year and even in the first three months of the following year. However, the final version has reverted to a more normal definition that restricts the classification to those activities that were discontinued before the interim report was issued with an overall limit of three months after the end of the interim period.[26] Nevertheless, the ASB has suggested that extra disclosure could be given of activities that are in the process of being terminated or are likely to be shown as discontinued in the full year accounts.[27]

The ASB notes that the Stock Exchange requires earnings per share to be disclosed, and says that it should be calculated and disclosed in the same manner as is used in the annual accounts. This means that both basic and diluted figures should be given, and companies who give additional versions of earnings per share for the full year should also do so in their interim reports.[28]

B   *Balance sheet*

In respect of the balance sheet, the Statement says that a similar classification to that used in the full year accounts should be used, and recommends that the following information should be presented:

- Fixed assets
- Current assets
  - Stocks
  - Debtors
  - Cash at bank and in hand
  - Other current assets
- Creditors: amounts falling due within one year
- Net current assets/(liabilities)
- Total assets less current liabilities
- Creditors: amounts falling due after more than one year
- Provisions for liabilities and charges
- Capital and reserves
- Minority interests[29]

The Statement says that the balance sheet should highlight significant movements in key indicators of the company's financial position,[30] and this may require some further analysis; a frequent example of this would be to show the components of net debt, which is not necessarily available from the above headings.

C   *Cash flow statement*

The Statement suggests that companies should use the main headings specified for the cash flow statement by FRS 1, namely:

- Net cash inflow/outflow from operating activities
- Returns on investments and servicing of finance
- Taxation
- Capital expenditure and financial investment
- Acquisitions and disposals
- Equity dividends paid
- Management of liquid resources
- Financing
- Increase/decrease in cash[31]

However, this list predates FRS 9, which amended FRS 1 to require extra lines to be included on the face of the cash flow statement for dividends received from associates and joint ventures. We recommend that these should be given where they are material.

The two main reconciliations required by FRS 1 are also to be given; operating profit is to be reconciled to operating cash flow, at least in outline, and the movement in cash is to be reconciled to the movement in net debt and its various components.[32]

D   Statement of total recognised gains and losses

The Statement calls for a statement of total recognised gains and losses to be presented where there have been any material gains and losses other than profit or loss for the interim period.[33] International groups will require such a statement if there are material foreign currency differences to be recognised, but there may be little else to report. The ASB acknowledges that companies will seldom revalue their properties in the middle of the year, although investment companies with a portfolio of quoted securities at market value will revalue them for interim reporting purposes.

E   Management commentary

The Statement emphasises the importance of a narrative commentary in which management discusses and analyses the interim performance being reported. This may be regarded as a cut-down version of the Operating and Financial Review (see Chapter 4), which aims to explain movements in key indicators and trends affecting the business. Among the more specific matters that the Board recommends be discussed are:

■   The effects of seasonality on the business, with an explanation of the principles that have been used to reflect seasonal results in the interim report

■   Material changes in the business's capital structure or financing

■   Changes in contingencies, commitments and off balance sheet financial instruments since the previous year end

■   The effect of major acquisitions and disposals during the period

■   Post balance sheet events (since the end of the interim period)[34]

2.4.2   Accounting policies and measurement principles

Except in relation to taxation, the ASB espouses the discrete approach, and it calls for disclosure where the integral approach has been used for any other item.[35] It does not really explain its reasoning, beyond saying that the discrete approach has the advantage that the elements of financial statements are defined in the same way as for the annual accounts.

The Statement says that 'items of income and expense are measured and recognised on a basis consistent with that used in the preparation of annual financial statements. ... Depending on the item, this might be for example, on the basis of time expired, the benefit received, or the activity associated with the period.'[36] Interestingly, the wording of the last sentence is borrowed from the relevant US standard, APB 28[37] (see 5.2.2 below), but in fact that standard endorses the integral approach! This underlines the difficulty in distinguishing the two methods, and the ambiguity of the extract quoted above. Allocating costs on the basis of time expired suggests the discrete approach, whereas matching it with benefits received or activity associated with the period moves towards the integral method.

Some discussion of how to apply these approaches to specific items, including the ASB's recommendations, is contained in 3 below.

As explained at 2.1 above, the Stock Exchange requires the accounting policies used to be the same as those used in the last annual accounts unless there are good reasons to the contrary. Accordingly, the interim accounts need only say that they have used the policies disclosed in the last accounts, rather than disclosing the policies themselves. However, where there has been a change of policy, this should be stated and explained.[38] The ASB Statement says that it is preferable that any change that is to be made in the accounts for the full year (perhaps because of the introduction of a new accounting standard) should first be made at the interim reporting date, rather than letting the two be prepared on different bases.[39]

Because of the large number of new accounting standards introduced in 1997 and 1998, many companies have recently disclosed changes in policy in their interim accounts. Whitbread provides one example.

Extract 30.1: Whitbread PLC (1998)

1 BASIS OF PREPARATION OF ACCOUNTS [extract]

With the following exceptions the interim accounts, which are abridged and unaudited, have been prepared on the basis of the accounting policies set out in the 1997/8 group accounts:

- Following the adoption of FRS 9 (Associates and joint ventures), further disclosures have been provided in respect of the results, assets, liabilities and cash flows of the group's interests in joint ventures and associates. The comparative figures for 1997/8 have been restated accordingly, resulting in an increase in both operating profit and the interest charge of £2.7m for the full year and £1.6m for the first half.

- Following the adoption of FRS 10 (Goodwill and intangible fixed assets), goodwill arising on acquisitions will be capitalised and depreciated over its estimated useful economic life. In addition the net balance in respect of payments made in previous years for distribution rights has been transferred to intangible fixed assets. Goodwill previously eliminated against reserves has not been reinstated.

- FRS 11 (Impairment of fixed assets and goodwill) has been adopted, although it has had no effect on the period being reported on.

- FRS 14 (Earnings per share) has been adopted, although it has had no effect on the period being reported on, other than the disclosure of fully diluted earnings per share. This has not previously been published as it is not materially different from basic earnings per share.

If it is not practicable to implement a known future change, an estimate of its effect should be given or an explanation where it is not possible to give such an estimate.[40] Premier Oil provides an example of this.

Extract 30.2: Premier Oil plc (1998)

New Accounting Standard

Premier Oil will apply the new Financial Reporting Standard (FRS) 11 in the annual accounts for the year ended 31 December 1998 as required by the Accounting Standards Board. In the results for the six months ended 30 June 1998 the Company has continued to apply the accounting policies followed in the preparation of the accounts for the year ended 31 December 1997. Specifically, the full cost accounting method has been followed using a single worldwide cost pool for the purposes of capitalisation, amortisation and the assessment of any permanent diminution of value occurring in the carrying amount of fixed assets. FRS 11 requires these calculations to be made on a much more restrictive regional or territorial basis. Any write down of the carrying amount of fixed assets arising from the application of FRS 11 will be charged to the profit and loss account in the annual accounts for the year ended 31 December 1998. These changes will have no impact whatsoever on our cash generation ability.

The consistency of measurement principle applies also to the use of foreign currency translation rates. The Statement says that the profit and loss account of foreign entities should be translated at the average rate for the interim period or the closing rate at the end of that period, whichever is the normal policy.[41] This may seem straightforward, but in fact there can be difficulties for companies who report quarterly rather than half-yearly, as discussed more fully in Chapter 8 at 3.4.11. (The basic problem is that the results of later interim periods can be distorted by the catch-up effect of updating the exchange rates that were used to translate the results of earlier interim periods.)

Unilever employs an unusual approach that uses the exchange rates of the *previous* year for all the detailed analysis of its interim profit and loss accounts, restating only the bottom line on the basis of current exchange rates. It is not uncommon for companies to use constant exchange rates when making inter-period comparisons in narrative statements such as the OFR, but it is rare to see this approach applied in the primary report itself, as in this case.[42] Moreover, whether the result is really meaningful seems questionable, as this extract from the group's interim statement for the third quarter of 1998 demonstrates.

Extract 30.3: Unilever PLC (1998)

Unilever results

Business performance [extract]

In Asia & Pacific, sales increased by 13%, largely reflecting price increases to recover higher costs in South East Asia following currency devaluations ...

Consolidated profit and loss account

Constant exchange rates

In the profit and loss account given below, the results in both years have been translated at constant exchange rates, being the annual average exchange rates for 1997. This reporting convention facilitates comparisons since the impact of exchange fluctuations is eliminated.

Geographical analysis [extract]

Third quarter		£ millions	Nine months	
1998	**1997**	**Operating profit – before exceptional items**	**1998**	**1997**
536	522	Europe	**1 242**	1 214
174	193	North America	**367**	341
57	43	Africa and Middle East	**141**	103
131	106	Asia and Pacific**	**363**	281
74	83	Latin America	**257**	227
972	947	Sub-total	**2 370**	2 166

**Note: At current rates of exchange for the first nine months, 1998 operating profit for those countries in South East Asia which have experienced significant currency devaluation, reduces by approximately £82 million.

The footnote appears to say that the entire reported growth of £82 million in the profit of Unilever's Asia & Pacific region (from £281 million in 1997 to £363 million in 1998), is due to its use of out-of-date exchange rates. As the commentary on Business performance quoted in the extract explains, the currency devaluation in that region made it necessary to increase prices, but if that is the case it does not seem appropriate to use *pre-devaluation* exchange rates to translate results that have benefited from the *post-devaluation* price increases; far from removing a distorting effect, this approach seems positively to introduce one. It was for this reason that the FASB rejected the idea of requiring such an analysis under its standard on foreign currency translation, as discussed at 3.4.11 in Chapter 8.

2.4.3   Timescale

The Statement calls for the interim report to be published within sixty days of the end of the interim period.[43] This is a rather more demanding schedule than the four months allowed by the Stock Exchange (see 2.1 above).

3   PROBLEM AREAS IN INTERIM REPORTING

3.1   Seasonal businesses

Some companies operate in businesses which are heavily seasonal; examples include agricultural businesses with seasonal crops, holiday companies, domestic fuel suppliers, retailers who depend on Christmas sales, and so on. Their financial year is often chosen to fit their annual operating cycle, but this may equally mean that their first six months gives little indication of their likely annual results. In some cases, they may have negligible sales in the first half of the year.

An extreme application of the integral approach in theory might suggest that they should try to predict their annual results and contrive to report half of that in the interim accounts. However, this would be a pointless exercise, and would bear little relation to the reality of their business in the first six months. In practice, seasonal companies report their actual sales (if any) for the first six months, and those which espouse the integral approach may then seek to flex their costs to some degree to match their sales.

So far as direct costs are concerned, this is entirely appropriate. The more controversial area concerns indirect costs which would normally be accounted for on a time basis. Recognising these in the normal way could easily result in a loss being reported in the first half of the year because there are insufficient revenues to cover them. This would be the result of applying the discrete approach in its pure form; it would reflect the reality of that period's performance, but it would also emphasise the limited usefulness of the interim report, because it would show that the results of that period really have little meaning in isolation. Allocating them in proportion to expected activity levels for the two halves of the year would be an attempt to show the results in their proper context, but it involves a higher degree of uncertainty and it becomes at least partly an exercise in forecasting rather than a report on the results of an expired period.

The ASB's Statement says that 'fluctuating revenues of seasonal businesses are generally understood by the marketplace and it is appropriate to report them as they arise'.[44] This rather misses the point, because it could not be seriously suggested that revenues should be transferred from one interim period to another. The real issue concerns the possible flexing of associated costs, but the Statement is silent on this matter apart from the general statement quoted at 2.4.2 above that expenses should be recognised on the basis of time expired, the benefit received, or the activity associated with the period. As already noted, this ambiguous statement might either support some flexing of costs to match seasonal revenues (on the basis of activity associated with the period) or forbid such a practice (on the basis of time expired).

The Statement's recommendations on the management commentary relating to seasonal businesses are more constructive. It says that 'the commentary should describe the nature of any seasonal activity and, together with other disclosures, provide adequate information for the performance of the business and its financial position at the end of the period to be understood in the context of the annual cycle. The principles by which seasonal results are reflected in the interim report should be stated, particularly where there are any expected changes in the effects of seasonality.'[45]

Such a discussion provides the essential context for the reader to interpret the information presented. In addition, of course, the relationship between first half and full year results can already be seen from the comparative figures when both of these are shown for the previous period. However, the reality is that interim reports are necessarily of lesser value for seasonal businesses because they focus on only part (and a potentially misleading part) of the story.

Scottish Power included this note in its interim report for the six months to 30 September 1998 to describe a change to its policy on seasonal adjustments.

Extract 30.4: Scottish Power plc (1998)

1 Basis of preparation [extract]

(c) To comply with the recommendation of the Accounting Standards Board's Statement on Interim Reports, comparative figures have been restated to eliminate seasonal adjustments in relation to accounting for the cost of electricity sales. This statement recommends that revenues and costs, wherever possible, should be recognised on a discrete basis for the purposes of the interim Accounts and not treated as a component of the full year's results, as was previously the policy adopted. The adjustments relate to the interim figures only and do not affect the full year results.

The effect on the comparative figures for the half-year ended 30 September 1997 is as follows:

	Cost of sales £m	Ordinary taxation £m	Loss retained £m	Net assets £m
As previously reported	(803.5)	(56.9)	(214.0)	1,537.5
Effect of implementing new accounting policy	4.7	(1.2)	3.5	3.5
As restated	**(798.8)**	**(58.1)**	**(210.5)**	**1,541.0**

3.2   Taxation

Taxation is problematical because it is assessed on an annual basis, which would make the discrete approach particularly difficult to apply. This is especially so in the UK, where the partial provision approach to deferred tax means that tax is not accounted for on all timing differences. A rigorous application of the discrete approach would therefore require a detailed examination of the timing differences which arose in the six months under review, without regard to what might happen in the remainder of the year. This could give rise to some very strange results, particularly for companies whose capital investment programme was weighted towards one end of the year or the other.

For these reasons, the approach generally adopted in practice is to predict what the effective tax rate is likely to be for the year and then to apply it to whatever results are reported for the interim period. This is an application of the integral approach, and it is one which is endorsed by the ASB's Statement, despite its general stated preference for the discrete approach.[46] Coats Viyella provides an example of this approach:

Extract 30.5: Coats Viyella Plc (1998)

3 Taxation [extract]

The taxation charge for the six months ended 30 June 1998 is based on the estimated effective tax rate for the full year, including the effect of prior period tax adjustments and the foreign income dividend basis for the 1998 interim dividend. ...

The Statement says that 'events and expenditure that are expected to fall in the second part of the year and would affect the annual tax rate should be brought into the estimate on a prudent basis. Capital expenditure is usually planned in advance; it is, therefore, usually possible to take account of the expected capital allowances in calculating the effective tax rate for the year. It would not normally be appropriate, however, to take account of the tax effects of other significant events that, although expected to arise in the second part of the year, are subject to considerable uncertainty.'[47]

It goes on, 'In determining the amount of tax losses and recoverable advance corporation tax to recognise in the interim period, an estimate should be made of the utilisation expected over the whole tax year. The amount recognised in the interim period should be proportional to the profit before tax of the interim period and the estimated annual profit before tax, but limited to the amount recoverable for the year as a whole.'[48] It illustrates this with the following example:

Example 30.1 Treatment of tax losses brought forward

Company A has losses brought forward of £75,000. It has earned taxable profits of £100,000 in the interim period, but expects to record taxable losses of £40,000 in the remaining part of the year. How should the effect of the opening tax losses be taken into account in the interim period, assuming an effective tax rate of 30%?

The Statement notes that in these circumstances the tax charge for the year will be nil, with £60,000 of the losses being utilised in the full year to relieve an equal amount of profits. But the passage quoted above also says that the amount of losses recognised in the interim period should be limited to the amount recoverable for the year as a whole (£60,000), which means that tax on profits of £40,000 have to be provided in the interim accounts, giving rise to a tax charge of £12,000 for the half year. In the second half of the year, the losses of £40,000 will be relieved by a tax credit of £12,000 that brings the tax charge for the year back to nil.

Unusually, Marks and Spencer discloses that it restates its previous year's interim report to reflect the actual effective tax rate experienced, as shown below. However, the great majority of companies make no such adjustment.

Extract 30.6: Marks and Spencer p.l.c. (1998)

9)   The taxation charge for the 26 weeks ended 26 September 1998 is based on an estimated effective tax rate of 30% for the full year. This rate excludes the effect of exceptional items.

Consistent with the treatment adopted in prior years, the taxation charge for the first half of last year has been decreased by £4.5m to reflect the actual rate of taxation on that full year's profit. Creditors falling due after more than one year and shareholders' funds for last half year have also been adjusted to reflect this change.

3.3   Other items determined on an annual basis

Like tax, a number of other items are also determined only at the end of a year (which is not necessarily always the financial year) or sometimes even a longer period. These include staff bonuses or profit sharing, sales commissions, volume discounts on both purchases and sales, and so on. It will again be necessary to try to predict the outcome for the whole year in order to determine the effective rate to apply in measuring the results for the interim period. While this smacks of the integral approach, in reality it is no different from the estimates which have to be made in annual accounts whenever the base period for measuring a variable amount of this kind is different from the financial year.

This issue is acknowledged by the ASB Statement, but it seeks to distinguish between those where there is a recognisable obligation at the period end and those where there is not, using the same approach as FRS 12 on provisions (see Chapter 25). Thus, the Statement would support provision for an estimated liability under a contractual supplier volume discount, or for a profit-related bonus where the staff's expectations give rise to a constructive obligation, but not for a 'genuinely discretionary one-off bonus given at the end of the year'.[49]

Railtrack discloses in its interim accounts that certain items have been included by reference to estimates relating to the full year.

Extract 30.7: Railtrack Group PLC (1998)

1   BASIS OF PREPARATION

(i)   **Performance regimes**

       Bonuses and penalties are included on the basis of an estimate of the amounts receivable and
       payable for the financial year as a whole.

       ...

(iii) **Property clawback**

       Train operating companies are entitled to a share of any property gains (above certain
       thresholds). The total clawback is allocated between the Profit and Loss Account and the
       Statement of Total Recognised Gains and Losses according to the treatment of the excess
       gains.

       The profit and loss account charge in the interim results is one half of the forecast charge for
       the year.

Bank of Scotland's interim report includes a charge in respect of staff profit
sharing schemes, which is explained in this note:

Extract 30.8: Bank of Scotland (1998)

3.   Provision has been made in the Interim Accounts towards the end of year allocation of profit to
      the Staff Profit Sharing Schemes. This provision is calculated on the results for the six months
      to 31st August 1998 alone. The bases used, therefore, relate only to that period, whereas the
      actual allocation will be calculated by reference to the results for the full year.

3.4   Non-recurring items

When major items of expenditure arise in the first half of the year which will not
be repeated in the second (or vice versa), the question arises of whether these
should be spread over the whole year or dealt with in the period in which they
fall. Such items may be genuinely one-off, such as reorganisation costs or a loss
on repurchasing debt, or they may be cyclical expenditures such as major repairs
during an annual shutdown of a plant.

The discrete approach would obviously let all such costs lie in whatever period
they are incurred, and the ASB supports this view in relation to exceptional
items.[50] Proponents of the integral approach, on the other hand, might wish to
spread them over the year, particularly if they are of a regular but cyclical
nature.

Again, this issue can be defused to some extent by disclosure. The desire to
spread these costs springs from a concern that false conclusions will be drawn
about the sustainable profitability of the business and in particular the likely
result for the full year. But so long as such costs are disclosed and appropriately
explained, the reader will not be likely to jump to the wrong conclusion about
the company's underlying profitability.

3.5   Asset values

UK GAAP requires current assets to be carried at the lower of cost and net realisable value and fixed assets to be written down to their recoverable amount if they are impaired. The question which arises is whether such assessments have to be made at the date of the interim balance sheet in just the same way as they are made at the end of the year. The ASB's support for the discrete approach would suggest that they should.

We are not convinced that this will always make sense. In the case of stocks, for example, there may be a fall in value at the half-year which simply reflects the seasonality of the product, but which will be restored by the year end. Also, some accounting routines are governed by accounting standards which were written with annual accounts in mind. For example, SSAP 13 permits development expenditure to be capitalised only when the profitable outcome of the project can be foreseen (see Chapter 12). Having to make this assessment more frequently because of shorter reporting periods would result in less being capitalised, because it would curtail the time available for the expenditure to prove its worth. Again, we think this would be inappropriate, and that an annual perspective should be retained. In general, we do not believe that the needs of interim reporting should affect the application of accounting standards in this way.

The ASB's Statement does modify its approach for certain assets. It says that it would be in order to leave revalued properties at the amounts shown at the previous year end (but would like this fact disclosed),[51] and also that new actuarial valuations of the pension scheme would only be required if a significant event rendered the previous estimate misleading.[52] However, it says that quoted stocks carried at market value should be updated to values ruling at the end of the interim period.[53]

Unusually, Liberty has a practice of valuing properties at the half-year, as disclosed in this extract.

Extract 30.9: Liberty International Holdings PLC (1998)

Chairman's statement

Net asset value [extract]

Continuing the practice started last year of conducting property revaluations at the interim stage, revaluations of all the group's completed investment property portfolio have been undertaken as at 30 June 1998 ...

Notes to the accounts

Investment properties

Completed investment properties are professionally valued on an open market basis by external valuers at the end of each financial year. Surpluses and deficits arising during the year are reflected in the revaluation reserve. Permanent diminutions in value of an investment property are charged in the profit and loss account. A full valuation of completed investment properties was carried out at 30 June 1998 and these valuations have been incorporated in the balance sheet as at 30 June 1998. In the case of UK shopping centres of Capital Shopping Centres PLC, these valuations were carried out by external professional valuers; in the case of other investment properties, on the grounds of cost and lower risk exposure, by professionally qualified directors of Capital & Counties plc on a basis consistent with the external valuation.

---

4   REQUIREMENTS FOR PRELIMINARY ANNOUNCEMENTS

4.1   Introduction

The preliminary announcement is an important factor in the market's evaluation of a company's performance. Under the Listing Rules of the London Stock Exchange, listed companies are required to notify the Exchange of their preliminary statement of annual results and dividends (known as the preliminary announcement) without delay after board approval. There is a widely held view that the preliminary announcement is more price-influential than the subsequent publication of a company's full annual report and accounts. Consequently there has been a tendency for companies to publish more information in their preliminary announcements than is strictly required by the Stock Exchange. These developments clearly influenced the ASB to publish in July 1998 its non-mandatory Statement – *Preliminary Announcements* – which is intended to provide 'valuable guidance for directors wishing to embrace best practice when preparing their preliminary announcements'.[54] The Statement provides voluntary guidance which is intended to supplement the requirements of the Stock Exchange.[55]

The Statement intends to 'improve the timeliness, quality, relevance and consistency of preliminary announcements within the constraints of reliability'.[56] The Statement refers to the similarity between interim reports and preliminary announcements and states that their contents are likely to be similar.[57] However in the introduction it warns that the interaction of the preliminary announcement with the other year end financial reports and the year end financial reporting structure as a whole are being 'explored further by the Board ... . This is intended to be a relatively long-term project to allow time for debate and future consultations ... and for changes in practice to become accepted'.[58]

4.2   The Stock Exchange Listing Rules

The Stock Exchange requires listed companies to make a preliminary announcement by notifying the Company Announcements Office of its annual results immediately after board approval has been obtained.[59] In turn, the Stock Exchange disseminates the information given to it by electronic means using its Regulatory News Service. It is not mandatory for preliminary announcements to be sent to shareholders; in practice, often only financial analysts and institutional shareholders receive them. The Listing Rules contain no time limit for the issue of the preliminary announcement; the only constraint is that the annual report should be published within six months after the financial period to which they relate (unless in exceptional circumstances the Exchange grants an extension).[60]

The preliminary announcement must have been agreed with the auditors and must show at least the items required to be shown in a half yearly report (see 2.1 above). These figures should be shown in the form of a table, consistent with the presentation to be adopted in the full annual accounts. The announcement must also show any significant additional information necessary for the purpose of assessing the results.[61]

The preliminary announcement must also contain details of any decision to pay or make any dividend or other distribution on the listed shares or to withhold any dividend or interest payment on listed securities, giving details of:

(a)   the exact net amount payable per share;

(b)   the payment date;

(c)   the record date (where applicable); and

(d)   any foreign income dividend election, together with any income tax treated as paid at the lower rate and not repayable.[62]

If the audit report is likely to be qualified, details of the nature of the qualification need to be given.[63]

As indicated at 2.1 above in relation to interim reports, these Listing Rules are not demanding. However, in practice, companies tend to go beyond these requirements to present a more informative announcement.

Although the Stock Exchange requires the preliminary announcement to have been 'agreed' with the company's auditors, it does not define what is meant by the term. There is clearly an expectation that the information will be consistent with that in the audited financial statements, which at that stage may not be complete. However, guidance for auditors was issued in July 1998 by the

Auditing Practices Board in Bulletin 1998/7 – *The auditors' association with preliminary announcements.* The Bulletin includes guidance on:

■   audit procedures to be completed before agreeing an 'unaudited' announcement;

■   communication of the auditors' agreement to the directors; and

■   actions to be taken when directors make an announcement without agreement.

4.3   The ASB's Statement

4.3.1   Overview of the Statement

In October 1997, the Accounting Standards Board published an exposure draft of a non-mandatory Statement – *Preliminary Announcements* – and converted it into a final document with little change in July 1998. It follows the same approach adopted in the Statement on Interim Reports (see 2.4 above).

The Statement is non-mandatory and has been issued as a result of companies frequently producing far more comprehensive and detailed preliminary announcements than the Stock Exchange Listing Rules actually require. The ASB therefore took the view, as with its interim reporting statement, that guidance about best practice would be valuable, thereby promoting increased comparability between preliminary announcements and previously published accounts, while also being consistent with the subsequently published full annual report and accounts. The content and presentation recommended for preliminary announcements are in line with current reporting practice, but there is considerable scope for the individual company to exercise judgement over exactly what degree of detail is included. The Statement is full of phrases, relating to what should be disclosed, such as: 'significant movements', 'sufficient information should be given to understand', and 'should explain any other matter that the directors think would help users'. Therefore much of what is recommended is of a generalised rather than specific nature.

However, most intriguing is the reference in the Statement to the Board's project exploring the year end financial reporting structure as a whole, referred to above. As the preliminary announcement becomes more comprehensive, it may possibly become more important in the formal company financial reporting structure.

4.3.2   Statements to be included

As for interim reports, the ASB calls for preliminary announcements to contain:

■   a narrative commentary, along similar lines to the operating and financial review, although not as lengthy and with greater focus on areas of change;[64]

- a summarised profit and loss account, based on the presentation used in the full accounts;[65]

- a statement of total recognised gains and losses;[66]

- a summarised balance sheet, using similar presentation to that in the full accounts;[67] and

- a summarised cash flow statement, using the headings stipulated in FRS 1.[68]

The Statement also recommends that segmental information should be given for turnover and profit on the same basis as in the full annual report[69] and that the turnover and operating profit relating to acquisitions and discontinued operations be presented on the face of the summarised profit and loss account.[70]

The ASB also notes that the Stock Exchange requires earnings per share to be disclosed, and says that it should be calculated and disclosed in the same manner as is used in the annual accounts. This means that both basic and diluted figures should be given, and companies who give additional versions of earnings per share in their annual accounts should also do so in their preliminary announcement.[71]

The above information to be included is essentially the same as that recommended for interim reports as discussed at 2.4.1 above.

The ASB notes that the 'market normally tends to react only to new information arising from the final interim period (ie the second half, or if quarterly reporting is adopted, the fourth quarter of the year) that has not been previously reported upon. However, the preliminary announcement and the annual results have traditionally focused on the results for the year, generally without presenting or discussing the results for the final interim period of the year. This means that the results for this period are subsumed within those for the year and not generally reported to shareholders.'[72] Accordingly, the Statement calls for the salient events and features of the final interim period to be referred to and explained as part of the management commentary.[73] It also encourages companies to give separate presentation of the final interim period figures, together with corresponding amounts, although in some cases it suggests that a reference to the key figures in the narrative commentary will suffice.[74]

4.3.3   Accounting policies and prior year adjustments

The accounting policies and presentation of figures in the preliminary announcement should be consistent with those in the full accounts, that have yet to be published.[75] The ASB recommends that the preliminary announcement should include a statement that they are prepared on the basis of the accounting policies as set out in the most recently published set of annual accounts. Accounting policies need to be stated and explained only where they differ from those adopted in the previous year.[76] Following a change in accounting policy, the amounts for the current and prior years should be restated on the basis of the new policy, consistent with the annual accounts. The cumulative effect on opening reserves should be disclosed at the foot of the statement of total recognised gains and losses of the year. Similar disclosures are recommended in respect of other prior year adjustments.[77]

4.3.4 Distribution

The Statement notes that although it is not mandatory for preliminary announcements to be sent to shareholders, all shareholders should be entitled, on request, to have access to the preliminary announcement as soon as it becomes available,[78] and provides the following examples of how this can be achieved:[79]

■ press advertisements containing the essential details of the preliminary announcement;

■ pre-registration schemes (e.g. with reply cards that could be sent out with interim reports);

■ publicising an address or telephone number by which shareholders can obtain copies of the announcement; and

■ notifying shareholders (e.g. with the last interim report of the period) of the exact date that the announcement is expected to be issued, so that they can take appropriate action.

It also recommends that companies explore the use of electronic means, e.g. the Internet, as a way of disseminating financial information, and in particular the preliminary announcement, to a wider audience.[80]

4.3.5 Reliability

As noted at 4.2 above, the Stock Exchange requires the preliminary announcement to be agreed by the auditors before publication. The Statement indicates that there is an expectation that the information in the preliminary announcement will be consistent with that in the audited accounts and to achieve this:

(a) the audit should be complete or at least at an advanced stage at the date of the preliminary announcement;

(b) all the figures in the preliminary announcement should agree with the figures in the audited accounts or in the draft accounts; and

(c) the other information and commentary in the preliminary announcement should be consistent with the figures in the preliminary announcement and with the audited or draft accounts.[81]

The ASB emphasises that the overriding consideration is that the information in the preliminary announcement should be reliable and not subject to later alterations. The risk of later changes to figures can only be extinguished if the preliminary announcement is issued at the same time as the full accounts are approved by the directors and the auditors have signed their opinion on them.

However, against this, the ASB notes that there is the need for timely publication of price-sensitive information and that the Stock Exchange requires the preliminary announcement to be notified to the Exchange without delay after board approval.[82] The Statement goes on to say 'It is accepted practice, therefore, that, where the reliability of the information in the announcement is not compromised, the main figures and highlights from the financial statements are issued as the preliminary announcement when the audit is at an advanced stage (ie when any outstanding audit matters are unlikely to have a material impact on the financial statements or disclosures in the preliminary announcement), but before the audit report on the financial statements has been signed.'[83]

4.3.6 Timescale

The Statement notes that the benefits of providing the market with early notification of the annual results needs to be balanced against the practical problems of producing the information at an acceptable cost, and with the same reliability as is required of the full annual accounts. With this in mind, the ASB suggests that companies should consider ways of accelerating their year-end timetable, so that they can issue their preliminary announcement as soon as possible after the year-end. Within the bounds of practicality, it encourages companies to issue their preliminary announcements within 60 days of the year end.[84] This is a far more demanding schedule than the six months effectively allowed by the Stock Exchange (see 4.2 above).

4.3.7 Companies Act

The Companies Act does not contain any specific provisions relating to preliminary announcements. However, for the purpose of section 240 of the Act, preliminary announcements constitute non-statutory accounts and, therefore, they must include a statement indicating:

(a)   that they are not the statutory accounts;

(b)   whether statutory accounts dealing with any financial year covered by the announcement have been delivered to the Registrar of Companies;

(c)   whether the auditors have reported on the statutory accounts for any such financial year; and

(d)   if so, whether any auditors' report so made was qualified or contained a statement under section 237(2) or (3) (accounting records or returns inadequate, accounts not agreeing with records and returns or failure to obtain necessary information and explanations).[85]

As the preliminary announcement will normally include comparative figures, the statement will need to refer not only to the position for the current financial period, but also for the comparative period.

5 COMPARISON WITH IASC AND US PRONOUNCEMENTS

5.1 IASC

5.1.1 E 57

The IASC published an exposure draft on Interim Reporting in August 1997.[86] In many respects, this was similar to the ASB's contemporaneous proposals. The main difference from the ASB's approach, however, was that the IASC was proposing a normal accounting standard on interim reporting, whereas the ASB's Statement is only a non-mandatory recommendation. E 57 was converted into a standard only six months later, without significant alteration.

5.1.2 IAS 34

In February 1998, the IASC issued the resulting standard,[87] and it came into force for (interim) periods beginning on or after 1 January 1999. It does not dictate who should prepare interim reports, but it sets rules for the form and content of such reports for enterprises that are required or elect to produce them in accordance with international accounting standards.[88]

The standard requires interim reports to include the following:

- A condensed balance sheet
- A condensed income statement, including disclosure of basic and diluted earnings per share
- A condensed statement showing either (a) all changes in equity or (b) changes in equity other than those arising from capital transactions with owners and distributions to owners (equivalent to the STRGL in the UK)
- A condensed cash flow statement
- Certain notes[89]

The format of these condensed statements should include at least all of the headings and subtotals that were included in the equivalent primary statements in the enterprise's last annual accounts.[90]

The approach to comparative figures is somewhat different from that taken in the UK. The only statement that is required to be repeated from the last full year accounts is the balance sheet; no full year comparatives need be given for the other three statements. Instead, these other three statements must be for the cumulative position for the year to date, with comparatives for the same period in the previous year. Where the enterprise reports quarterly, the income statement must show the results of the most recent quarter (again with comparatives) as well as its cumulative results to date. Also in contrast to UK practice, no balance sheet need be presented as at the end of the equivalent interim period last year.[91]

The notes specified for inclusion are more extensive than is required in the UK, although in practice UK companies will tend to deal with most of the issues covered either in notes to the interim accounts or in the accompanying narrative statement. One specific requirement of IAS 34 which is not common in the UK, however, is to disclose the nature and effect of changes made in the current interim period to estimates made in earlier periods.[92] There is also a requirement to make equivalent disclosure in the full year accounts of adjustments to estimates made in interim accounts of the period under review, unless such disclosure has already been made in subsequent interim accounts.[93]

These requirements to disclose the effects of changes in estimates have a particular significance because of IAS 34's rules on measurement. Like other standard setters, the IASC's approach reflects something of a hybrid between the discrete and the integral methods; however, there is an additional principle in IAS 34 to say that 'the frequency of an enterprise's reporting (annual, half-yearly or quarterly) should not affect the measurement of its annual results'.[94] The effect of this is that certain measurement adjustments which would be regarded as irreversible if made at the year end can be revisited if they were made in the first interim period and circumstances justify a different answer by the end of the year (or by the end of a subsequent interim period). An example would be where development expenditure was expensed in the first interim period because the ultimate success of the project that would justify its capitalisation could not be foreseen at that stage, but by the year end the criteria for capitalisation are met, so that the expenditure can be reinstated as an asset. This is therefore a rather more subtle approach than the discrete method, because each quarter (say) is evaluated not as an isolated period but as part of a cumulative period that builds up to a full year whose results are not to be influenced by the operation of interim reporting practices.

5.2   US

5.2.1   SEC requirements

In the US, SEC registrant companies are required to report quarterly, using Form 10-Q. This comprises a set of condensed financial statements including balance sheets, income statements and cash flow statements together with Management's Discussion and Analysis (MD&A) of the company's financial condition and results of operations, and a number of other mandatory disclosures.

Balance sheets have to be given as at the end of both the quarter and the previous financial year. They should also be given at the end of the corresponding quarter of the previous year if management believes that this is necessary to explain the impact of seasonal fluctuations on the company's financial condition. Income statements are to be given for the quarter, for the year to date, and for the corresponding periods of the previous year. Cash flow statements are needed only for the year to date and the corresponding period of the previous year. It is also permitted to give both income statements and cash flow statements for the twelve months ending at the end of the quarter, again with comparatives.

5.2.2   APB 28

The main source of measurement principles for interim reporting in the US is APB 28, which was issued in 1973. This establishes the overall presumption that each interim period should be seen primarily as an integral part of an annual period,[95] and hence allows some modification of annual reporting practices where appropriate to that objective. However, a minority of the Board dissented from this conclusion, preferring the discrete approach instead. Three of the dissenters made the observation 'that any interim period is both a discrete accounting period and a fraction of an annual period in the same manner that an annual report is both a discrete accounting period and a segment of the period representing the life of the enterprise; ... it is unnecessary to characterise an interim period as either of these things to the exclusion of the other for purposes of establishing appropriate accounting principles.'[96]

APB 28 requires revenues and costs directly associated with revenues to be accounted for in the same way as for annual reporting periods. The modifications come in relation to other costs. In respect of these, the standard says that:

'(a)   Costs and expenses other than product costs should be charged to income in interim periods as incurred, or be allocated among interim periods based on an estimate of time expired, benefit received or activity associated with the periods. Procedures adopted for assigning specific cost and expense items to an interim period should be consistent with the bases followed by the company in reporting results of operations at annual reporting dates. However, when a specific cost or expense item charged to expense for annual reporting purposes benefits more than one interim period, the cost or expense item may be allocated to those interim periods.

(b)   Some costs and expenses incurred in an interim period, however, cannot be readily identified with the activities or benefits of other interim periods and should be charged to the interim period as incurred. Disclosure should be made as to the nature and amount of such costs unless items of a comparable nature are included in both the current interim period and in the corresponding interim period of the preceding year.

(c)   Arbitrary assignment of the amount of such costs to an interim period should not be made.

(d)   Gains and losses that arise in any interim period similar to those that would not be deferred at year end should not be deferred to later interim periods within the fiscal year.'[97]

APB 28 goes on to illustrate the application of this approach with these examples:

(a) When a cost that is expensed for annual reporting purposes clearly benefits two or more interim periods (e.g. annual major repairs), each interim period should be charged for an appropriate portion of the annual cost by the use of accruals or deferrals.

(b) When quantity discounts are allowed customers based upon annual sales volume, the amount of such discounts charged to each interim period should be based on the sales to customers during the period in relation to estimated annual sales.

(c) Property taxes (and similar costs such as interest and rent) may be accrued or deferred at annual reporting date, to achieve a full year's charge of taxes to costs and expenses. Similar procedures should be adopted at each interim reporting date to provide an appropriate cost in each period.

(d) Advertising costs may be deferred within a fiscal year if the benefits of the expenditure made clearly extend beyond the interim period in which the expenditure is made. Advertising costs may be accrued and assigned to interim periods in relation to sales prior to the time the service is received if the advertising program is clearly implicit in the sales arrangement.[98]

However, a number of the members of the Board, who either dissented or gave only qualified approval to the issue of APB 28, clearly regarded this guidance as equivocal. Several of them commented that these paragraphs 'provide inadequate and inherently contradictory guidelines for the determination of income and expenses appropriate for interim reporting'.[99]

In relation to taxation, APB 28 says that provision should be made at the best estimate of the effective rate expected to apply to the full fiscal year.[100]

5.2.3 SFAS 131

The requirement to give segmental disclosures in interim accounts was added by SFAS 131, issued in June 1997. This requires companies to include in their interim accounts the following information about each reportable segment:

- Revenues from external customers
- Intersegment revenues
- A measure of segment profit or loss
- Total assets for which there has been a material change from the amount disclosed in the last annual report
- A description of differences from the last annual report in the basis of segmentation or in the basis of measurement of segment profit or loss
- A reconciliation of the total of the reportable segment's measures of profit or loss to the enterprise's consolidated income before tax, extraordinary

items, discontinued operations, and the cumulative effect of changes in accounting principles.[101]

6   CONCLUSION

Interim reports and preliminary announcements were for many years neglected subjects in the UK. Practice had grown up around the minimal reporting requirements of the Stock Exchange, although major companies tended to go considerably beyond that minimum. The ASB's Statements have codified these better practices by prescribing more comprehensive reporting packages and has also addressed the issues of accounting measurement that interim reporting throws up.

It has to be said, however, that the Board's discussion of measurement issues is not wholly convincing. The theoretical debate between the discrete approach and the integral approach remains a sterile one, because the distinctions between the methods are more than a little blurred in practice. Furthermore, the actual recommendations made by the ASB and other standard setters who have addressed these issues still involve a number of pragmatic compromises.

The underlying issue that has been inadequately discussed concerns the essential purpose of interim reporting. The ASB's Statement asserts that 'interim reports, like annual financial statements, are presented in respect of a distinct reporting period. A fair assessment of the progress of the business can be made only if the interim accounts are presented on a consistent and comparable basis taking one reporting period with another.'[102] Starting from that presumption, it is no surprise that the discrete approach is favoured, particularly as this is such a tidy answer for a standard setter to adopt. But is interim reporting *really* only a more frequent version of annual reporting, but with fewer disclosures? This is probably not how it is perceived by preparers and users, who see it much more as a signalling device as to the outcome of the real period they are interested in, the financial year. It would be fruitful to give deeper consideration to the essential purpose of the exercise before the next revision of the rules on interim reporting is undertaken.

References

1 Statement, *Interim Reports*, ASB, September 1997.
2 Statement, *Preliminary Announcements*, ASB, July 1998.
3 CA 85, s 270(4).
4 SI 1984 No. 716.
5 *The Listing Rules*, London Stock Exchange, Chapter 12, paras. 12.46 and 12.52.
6 *Ibid.*, para. 12.52.
7 *Ibid.*, para. 12.47.
8 *Ibid.*, para. 12.58.
9 *Ibid.*
10 *Ibid.*, para. 12.59.
11 *Ibid.*, para. 12.53.
12 FRS 3, *Reporting Financial Performance*, ASB, December 1992.
13 *The Listing Rules*, para. 12.55.
14 *Ibid.*, para. 12.56.
15 *Ibid.*, para. 12.48.
16 *Ibid.*, para. 12.50.
17 *Ibid.*, para. 12.49.
18 *Ibid.*, para. 12.60.
19 Report of the Committee on the Financial Aspects of Corporate Governance, para. 4.56(a) and (b).
20 *Ibid.*, para. 4.56(d).
21 *Interim Reports*, para. 17.
22 *Ibid.*, paras. 48 and 49.
23 CA 85, s 240(3).
24 *Interim Reports*, paras. 40 and 45-47.
25 *Ibid.*, paras. 43-44.
26 *Ibid.*, para. 41.
27 *Ibid.*, para. 42.
28 *Ibid.*, para. 48.
29 *Ibid.*, para. 52.
30 *Ibid.*
31 *Ibid.*, para. 53.
32 *Ibid.*, para. 54.
33 *Ibid.*, para. 49.
34 *Ibid.*, paras. 34-39.
35 *Ibid.*, para. 8.
36 *Ibid.*
37 APB 28, *Interim Financial Reporting*, Accounting Principles Board, May 1973.
38 *Interim Reports*, para. 9.
39 *Ibid.*, para. 11.
40 *Ibid.*
41 *Ibid.*, para 25.
42 Unilever's treatment is not unique, however. For example, British American Tobacco uses a similar approach in its interim reports.
43 *Ibid.*, para. 3.
44 *Ibid.*, para. 16.
45 *Ibid.*, para. 37.
46 *Ibid.*, para. 30.
47 *Ibid.*, para. 21.
48 *Ibid.*, para. 24.
49 *Ibid.,* para. 15.
50 *Ibid.*, para. 45.
51 *Ibid.*, para. 26.
52 *Ibid.*, para. 27.
53 *Ibid.*, para. 26.

54 *Preliminary Announcements*, ASB, July 1998, Foreword.
55 *Ibid.*, Introduction.
56 *Ibid.*, Introduction.
57 *Ibid.*, Introduction.
58 *Ibid.*, Introduction.
59 *The Listing Rules*, para. 12.40.
60 *Ibid.*, para. 12.42(e).
61 *Ibid.*, para. 12.40(a).
62 *Ibid.*, para. 12.40(c).
63 *Ibid.*, para. 12.40(a)(iii).
64 *Preliminary announcements*, paras. 27–32.
65 *Ibid.*, paras. 36–41.
66 *Ibid.*, paras. 42 and 43.
67 *Ibid.*, para. 44.
68 *Ibid.*, paras. 45 and 46.
69 *Ibid.*, para. 38.
70 *Ibid.*, para. 37.
71 *Ibid.*, para. 41.
72 *Ibid.*, para. 33.
73 *Ibid.*, para. 34.
74 *Ibid.*, para. 35.
75 *Ibid.*, para. 16.
76 *Ibid.*, para. 17.
77 *Ibid.*, para. 18.
78 *Ibid.*, para. 6.
79 *Ibid.*, para. 8.
80 *Ibid.*, para. 7.
81 *Ibid.*, para. 12.
82 *Ibid.*, para. 13.
83 *Ibid.*, para. 14.
84 *Ibid.*, para. 9.
85 CA 85, s240(3).
86 E57, *Interim Reporting*, IASC, August 1997.
87 IAS 34, *Interim Financial Reporting*, IASC, February 1998.
88 *Ibid.*, para. 1.
89 *Ibid.*, para. 8.
90 *Ibid.*, para. 10.
91 *Ibid.*, para. 20.
92 *Ibid.*, para. 16(d).
93 *Ibid.*, para 26.
94 *Ibid.*, para. 28.
95 APB 28, para. 9.
96 IAS 34, Appendix of dissenting views.
97 *Ibid.*, para. 15.
98 *Ibid.*, para. 16.
99 *Ibid.*, Appendix of dissenting views.
100 *Ibid.*, para. 19.
101 SFAS 131, *Disclosures about Segments of an Enterprise and Related Information*, para. 33.
102 *Interim Reports*, para. 4.

Appendix   Specimen financial statements

This appendix contains the annual report and accounts of a mythical UK company – *Good Group P.L.C.*, a listed public company with subsidiaries. The report and accounts are only illustrative and do not attempt to show all possible disclosure requirements. In any case of doubt as to the legal or other requirements, it is essential to refer to the relevant source and, where necessary, to seek appropriate professional advice. Although the specimen accounts attempt to illustrate the most likely disclosure requirements of a manufacturing company, they should not be regarded as a comprehensive checklist of statutory and accounting requirements. They comply with the Companies Act 1985, as amended (the Companies Act), with other requirements in force at 31 July 1999, together with FRS 15 *Tangible Fixed Assets* and are drawn up in accordance with current best practice at the date of issue. The requirements of exposure drafts are not dealt with in these specimen accounts.

The formats used in the specimen accounts are consolidated accounts with the profit and loss account in format 1 and the balance sheet in format 1 taken from Schedule 4 to the Companies Act. The marginal annotations accompanying the accounts contain source references to the Companies Act, Statements of Standard Accounting Practice, Financial Reporting Standards and Urgent Issues Task Force abstracts, together with the requirements of the London Stock Exchange for listed companies.

The recommendations of the Committee on Corporate Governance (the 'Hampel Committee') have been reflected in the accounts for Good Group P.L.C.

Northern Ireland

The specimen accounts are based on the statutory requirements for Great Britain. For companies incorporated in Northern Ireland the equivalent, and in substance identical, legislation is contained in the Companies (Northern Ireland) Order 1986, as amended.

Abbreviations

The following abbreviations are used in this appendix:

The Companies Act	The Companies Act 1985, as amended
s 238(1)	Section 238(1) of the Companies Act
4 Sch 58(1)	Paragraph 58(1) of Schedule 4 to the Companies Act
4 Sch Formats	Statutory formats contained in Schedule 4 to the Companies Act
SI 85/802	Statutory Instrument No. 802 issued in 1985
SSAP 9(25)	Paragraph 25 of Statement of Standard Accounting Practice No. 9
FRS 1(12)	Paragraph 12 of Financial Reporting Standard No. 1
YB 12.43(e)	London Stock Exchange *The Listing Rules* (Yellow Book) Chapter 12 Paragraph 43(e)
CA89	The Companies Act 1989
OFR (2)	Paragraph 2 of the Best Practice Statement *Operating and Financial Review* issued by the Accounting Standards Board
Hampel Committee	The Committee on Corporate Governance
The Combined Code	Principles of good governance and the Code of Best Practice derived by the Committee on Corporate Governance from the Committee's Final Report and from the Cadbury and Greenbury Reports
Code D.2.1	Provision D.2.1 of the Combined Code
SAS 600(20)	Paragraph 20 of the Statement of Auditing Standards No. 600 issued by the Auditing Practices Board
ICAEW CP	Consultative Paper issued by the Institute of Chartered Accountants in England and Wales in September 1993 on interim reports
APB	The Auditing Practices Board
UITF 7(4)	Paragraph 4 of the seventh abstract of the Urgent Issues Task Force.

REPORT AND ACCOUNTS

Good Group P.L.C.

30 JUNE 1999

REGISTERED NUMBER: 1591134   s706

DIRECTORS
Sir Joshua Barraclough (Chairman)
J N Smith (Chief Executive)
J Archer
H C Black
J Corless
N O Evans
Mrs L B Green
M C Holman
P A MacBryde

SECRETARY
J Harris

AUDITORS
Chartered Accountants & Co.
7 Christian Street
London EC2 1VQ

BANKERS
Bank P.L.C.
George Street
London EC3 4AB

SOLICITORS
Solicitors & Co.
7 Scott Street
London WC3 4AB

REGISTRARS
Registration Services
45 Market Street
London W2 7JA

REGISTERED OFFICE
Homefire House
Ashdown Square
London EC2 3AS

Good Group P.L.C.

CHAIRMAN'S STATEMENT

The year was one when, having successfully defended the takeover offer made by Fire Products P.L.C. for the company at the start of the year, strong foundations were laid for the future growth of Good Group.

As in the three previous years, the results showed the increased importance of the fire-prevention division, and your directors have continued to make decisions which will further develop this sector.

The group has sold its loss-making subsidiary, Hose Limited, and this has led to an exceptional charge for the year of £2,437,000, although £400,000 of this relates to the goodwill previously set off against reserves.

The group has continued to extend its North American activities and to this end has set up a new company, Sprinklers Incorporated, in Chicago. It is expected that, by the Spring of 2000, Sprinklers will be manufacturing the group's newest fire-prevention products in the United States.

The acquisition, on 1 October 1998, of Extinguishers Limited, a company which has been established in Lincoln for many years, has further strengthened the fire-prevention division. This company has a well established research and development department, and will help ensure that the group's products remain 'state of the art'.

The electronics division has shown only a small increase in sales during the year ended 30 June 1999, up by 3% to £59,150,000, although profit margins have held up well. Your directors believe that the group's research and development activities will ultimately lead to a resurgence of sales in this sector, but 2000 sales are expected to continue at 1999 levels.

This year we have further strengthened the board with the appointment of a fourth non-executive director and I welcome Laura Green. I have included a separate report on the company's corporate governance. This is set out on pages 2018 to 2021.

The year's results would not have been possible without the enthusiastic participation of all our employees and I thank them all sincerely for their efforts.

Robert Jones retired during the year after a long career with the group.

We now look forward with confidence to a very busy and productive period for the group.

Joshua Barraclough
Chairman

27 September 1999

Good Group P.L.C.

DIRECTORS   Code A.6.2

Non-executive directors

Sir Joshua Barraclough, 64, joined the board of Good Group P.L.C. in 1991 and was   Code A.2.1
appointed chairman in 1995. He is Lord Lieutenant of Borsetshire, non-executive
chairman of the Pole Star Building Society and a director of Antimony Holdings Plc,
Northland Bank plc and Wessex TV PLC. Between 1988 and 1992, he was chairman
of the Board of Governors of Wessex College of Management Science.

H C Black, 52, joined the board of Good Group P.L.C. as a non-executive director on 1
July 1997 upon his return to the United Kingdom after spending 10 years working in
North America for EFG Incorporated.

Mrs L B Green, 48, joined the board of Good Group P.L.C. on 1 September 1998. She
was previously a partner with a firm of accountants, Alpha and Beta. In addition to her
role as finance director of South Supermarkets plc, she is non-executive director of a
number of companies, including Midclays plc.

M C Holman, 61, considered by the board to be the senior independent non-executive   Code A.2.1
director, has been a non-executive director of Good Group P.L.C. since 1992. As well
as being Professor of Business Studies at Wessex College of Management Science, he
is a director of St. James' Bank PLC and Sheen Palace Estates P.L.C. Until 1985, he
was a director of Ulster Extinguishers plc.

Executive directors

J N Smith, 50, joined Good Group P.L.C. in 1993 as finance director and was   Code A.2.1
appointed chief executive in 1996. Previously he held a number of senior finance
positions. He is a non-executive director of N&T Engineering plc and Bridge
Construction plc.

J Archer, 51, has spent 15 years working in the group. He is sales director and his
other responsibilities include research and development.

J Corless, 43, joined the board of Good Group P.L.C. following its acquisition of
Bright Sparks Limited in 1996. He currently heads up the fire prevention division. He
is a non-executive director of C&J Chemicals plc.

N O Evans, 40, took over responsibility of the electronics division this year from R P
Jones. He was appointed to the board two years ago.

P A MacBryde, 45, was appointed finance director in 1996 having previously been
group financial controller and, latterly, finance director at Good Company Limited.
Prior to that he worked for Gamma and Co., Chartered Accountants.

Good Group P.L.C.
OPERATING AND FINANCIAL REVIEW

OFR (2)

Code D.1.2

INTRODUCTION
This review has been prepared in accordance with the Accounting Standards Board's   OFR (38)
statement, issued in July 1993, on the operating and financial review.

OPERATING REVIEW
OFR (8) - (22)

The group's turnover has shown an overall increase of 18.3%. However, this includes
the activities of Hose Limited, which manufactures rubber hosepipes, for the eleven
months up to its disposal on 28 May 1999. Hose Limited had been loss-making for a
number of years; in the current year it generated an operating loss of £563,000 on
turnover of £42,196,000. Consequently, although its disposal may lead to a reduction
in the overall level of future turnover in the short term, it should nevertheless result in
increased profit figures. Group turnover from the remaining activities increased by
28.0% which is made up of a 46.6% increase in sales of fire prevention equipment
(excluding the results of Hose Limited) and a 3.2% increase in sales in the electronics
division. The group's share of turnover from its joint venture, Showers Limited,
increased by 31.5% to £30,438,000.

The increase in sales of fire prevention equipment is made up of two elements: a
growth of 17.7% in our original operations (excluding the results of Hose Limited)
together with the introduction of the results of Extinguishers, which contributed sales
of £21,979,000 in the nine months since its acquisition on 1 October 1998.

The growth of 17.7% in the fire prevention operations before the acquisition of
Extinguishers was particularly pleasing; the year has been yet another difficult one in
which to operate. The property market both here and in the United States, despite
small signs of recovery periodically being reported, has continued to be depressed.
Opportunities for the installation of fire-prevention equipment in new buildings have
therefore continued to be low. Nevertheless, the activity in other markets has held up
well, safety being an area where cut-backs are more difficult to achieve. With this
background it was therefore inevitable that profit margins would be further squeezed
despite the cost efficiencies introduced at the start of the year. The margins on
Extinguishers' sales were this year lower than those achieved by the rest of the
operations. We are looking at ways of improving the margin in future.

Extinguishers is best known for its fire-retardant fabrics, which are currently sold
mainly for commercial use. The company is looking into expanding production to
supply manufacturers of domestic products.

Sales in the electronics division have shown only a slight increase this year, although
profit margins have held up well. The activity to date has been mainly on defence
projects and for the aviation industry.

Expenditure on defence is being cut and the group is moving its focus and reducing
work in this area.

The group has made a small move into the electrical safety market and is looking to
expand this by means of acquisition. The directors believe that this would be
compatible with the fire prevention equipment division and would be part of an overall
move to enhance our reputation in the safety market.

Looking at the geographical split of sales, the increases were all generated in the
United Kingdom; although sales to the United States showed an increase, sales
generated in the United States fell slightly in sterling terms. The US results are even
more disappointing given the favourable dollar exchange rates ruling this year.

Good Group P.L.C.

OPERATING AND FINANCIAL REVIEW   OFR (2)

Code D.1.2

OPERATING REVIEW (continued)

Action is already being taken to improve the performance in the United States. A new company, Sprinklers Incorporated, has been set up to manufacture the group's new fire-prevention system in the United States. Manufacturing is scheduled to start this Summer.

During the year the signs of recovery in the UK economy were more positive. The directors are hopeful that the construction industry will continue its recent improvements, particularly in the commercial sector. The recovery in the United States was initially a little ahead of that here. The directors consider that if the construction industry maintains its recent improvements, the current year will see an increase in sales of new fire-protection products in the United Kingdom.

Extinguishers has a strong research and development department, with a long history of introducing new products. With the acquisition, the number of staff employed by the group on research and development has more than doubled. Today's research and development forms the basis of future years' business and therefore is an area in which we place extreme significance. This year we have increased expenditure on research and development by 135% even though the department was not enlarged until three months into the year. We will be increasing the expenditure further in the next few years to enhance further the prospects for the future

There are two main fire-prevention research and development activities: improved fire detection and sprinkler systems; and fire-retardant fabrics.

Research and development in the electronics business is concentrated on the development of new products capable of generating greater turnover.

Exceptional items totalling £2,192,000 were charged in the accounts this year, compared with £850,000 last year. This year's charge includes a loss on disposal of Hose Limited of £2,437,000 (£400,000 of which represents goodwill previously written off against reserves), a loss on disposal of fixed asset investments of £350,000 and a profit on disposal of fixed tangible assets of £1,250,000. These were all charged below operating profit. The balance of this year's charge was professional expenses of £655,000 incurred in the successful defence of the bid from Fire Products P.L.C.; these were charged in arriving at operating profit.

Capital expenditure on land, buildings, plant and machinery of £12,815,000 was higher than usual. The expenditure on plant and machinery included the initial purchases of equipment for Sprinklers Incorporated.

Good Group P.L.C.

OPERATING AND FINANCIAL REVIEW

OFR (2)

Code D.1.2

OPERATING REVIEW (continued)

Earnings per share are based on the results recognised in the profit and loss account. In addition to these profits there have been a number of other gains and losses, primarily movements in the value of the group's properties and exchange differences, which the group is precluded from recognising in the profit and loss account. These, together with the profit for the year, are included in the statement of total recognised gains and losses. In both 1999 and 1998, the property market in general has fallen and we have recognised a revaluation deficit in each of the two years following the revaluation of the investment properties. This year showed an overall exchange gain net of attributable tax, although it was less than the downward movement in property, and 1997/98 showed an exchange loss.

At the start of the year the property market had started to show a slight upward movement. However, this has since been eroded. The directors are hopeful that the properties might show a small increase in value during 2000.

This year the directors changed the dividend policy. In the past the total dividend has been paid out in two equal halves. Under the new policy the company will pay, at the interim stage, a smaller percentage of the expected total dividend with the balance as the final dividend.

The company's share price reflects many factors other than reported results and balance sheet net assets. One of the factors influencing the share price is the market's expectations of the group's future performance in relation to its competitors and this, in part, is linked with the research and development into new and improved products. The group's commitment to stronger research and development was discussed above. Uncertainty about interest rates both here and in the United States has had an unsettling effect on equity prices during the year and the company's share price has at times been trading at a discount to the net asset value per share.

As from 1 July 1999 the performance-related bonus scheme for executive directors and senior employees was replaced with a long-term incentive plan based on total return to shareholders over a four year period relative to that of the company's top ten competitors. This scheme will help to ensure that the directors' and employees' goals will echo those of the shareholders.

Good Group P.L.C.

OPERATING AND FINANCIAL REVIEW

OFR (2)

Code D.1.2

FINANCIAL REVIEW

The group's capital structure is as follows:

OFR (23) - (37)

	£000	£000
Net debt		
Loans		13,182
Finance leases and hire purchase contracts		1,045
Cash and short-term deposits		(7,964)
		6,263
Shareholders' funds		
Equity	53,937	
Non-equity	2,813	
		56,750
		63,013

The acquisition of Extinguishers Limited was funded by the issue of 2.5 million shares at £3.50 per share. Accordingly, although it has widened the share ownership of the company, it did not cause any funds to leave the group other than to the extent that the legal and professional expenses incurred exceeded the cash balance in Extinguishers Limited at the date of its acquisition.

Derivatives and other financial instruments

The group's principal financial instruments, other than derivatives, comprise bank loans, debentures, preference shares, finance leases and hire purchase contracts, cash and short-term deposits. The main purpose of these financial instruments is to raise finance for the group's operations. The group has various other financial instruments such as trade debtors and trade creditors, that arise directly from its operations.

FRS 13(6), (8), (13), (14), (15), (23)

The group also enters into derivative transactions (principally interest rate swaps and forward currency contracts). The purpose is to manage the interest rate and currency risks arising from the group's operations and its sources of finance.

It is, and has been throughout the period under review, the group's policy that no trading in financial instruments shall be undertaken.

The main risks arising from the group's financial instruments are interest rate risk, liquidity risk and foreign currency risk. The board reviews and agrees policies for managing each of these risks and they are summarised below. These policies have remained unchanged since the beginning of 1997. The group also monitors the market price risk arising from all financial instruments. The magnitude of this risk that has arisen over the period is detailed in note 22.

Interest rate risk

The group borrows in desired currencies at both fixed and floating rates of interest and then uses interest rate swaps to generate the desired interest profile and to manage the group's exposure to interest fluctuations. The group's policy is to keep between 30% and 60% of its borrowings at fixed rates of interest. At the year end, 37% of the group's borrowings were at fixed rates after taking account of interest rate swaps.

FRS 13(20)

Good Group P.L.C.

OPERATING AND FINANCIAL REVIEW   OFR (2)

                                                           Code D.1.2

FINANCIAL REVIEW (continued)

Liquidity risk

The group's objective is to maintain a balance between continuity of funding and flexibility through the use of overdrafts, bank loans, debentures, finance leases and hire purchase contracts. The group's policy is that not more than 30% of borrowings should mature in any 12 month period. In addition, to preserve continuity of funding, at least 70% of borrowings should mature in more than two years and at least 50% in more than five years. 77% of the group's total borrowings at the year end will mature in more than two years and over 55% will mature in more than five years.   FRS 13(20)

Short term flexibility is achieved by overdraft facilities. In addition this year the group has arranged a six year multi-option facility (MOF). Under the MOF, the bank has guaranteed that over a period to 31 January 2005 the group can draw up to an additional £7,500,000. At 30 June 1999 the group had drawn down £2,500,000 under this facility.

Foreign currency risk

As a result of the significant investment in operations in the United States, the group's balance sheet can be significantly affected by movements in the US dollar/sterling exchange rates. The group seeks to mitigate the effect of this structural currency exposure by borrowing in US currency. Between 20% and 50% of the group's investment in non-sterling operations will be hedged in this way, with the exact percentage varying depending on the group's transactional currency exposures. In managing its structural currency exposures, the group's objectives are to maintain a low cost of borrowings and to retain some potential for currency-related appreciation while partially hedging against currency depreciation.   FRS 13(20) - (22)

The group also has transactional currency exposures. Such exposures arise from sales or purchases by an operating unit in currencies other than the unit's functional currency. The group requires all its operating units to use forward currency contracts to eliminate the currency exposures on any balance that is not expected to mature within 30 days of its arising. The forward currency contracts must be in the same currency as the hedged item.

The group also hedges foreign currency sales that are expected to occur in future periods. Over 30% of the group's sales are denominated in currencies other than the functional currency of the operating unit making the sale, whilst almost 95% of costs are denominated in the unit's functional currency. The group's policy is to actively manage the resulting currency risk within overall limits. Expected future net cash flows are covered on a rolling basis at levels from 40% to 90% for sales expected in the next year and 20% to 50% for sales expected in one to two years. Cover takes the form of forward currency contracts. At 30 June 1999, the group had hedged 75% of the foreign currency sales expected in 1999 and 43% of those expected in 2000.

Good Group P.L.C.

OPERATING AND FINANCIAL REVIEW   OFR (2)

Code D.1.2

FINANCIAL REVIEW (continued)

Year 2000 compliance

As is well known, many computer and digital storage systems express dates using only   UITF 20(11), (12)
the last two digits of the year and will thus require modification or replacement to
accommodate the year 2000 and beyond in order to avoid malfunctions and resulting
widespread commercial disruption. This is a complex and pervasive issue. The
operation of our business depends not only on our own computer systems, but also to
some degree on those of our suppliers and customers. This could expose us to further
risk in the event that there is a failure by other parties to remedy their own year 2000
issues.

A significant risk analysis was performed in 1998 to determine the impact of the issue
on all our activities. From this, prioritised action plans were developed which
addressed the key risks. Priority was given to those systems which could cause a
significant financial or legal impact on the group's business if they were to fail. The
modification of systems is now almost complete. The focus of the group's IT resource
is now on testing system changes which involves the participation of users.

The risk analysis also considered the impact on our business of year 2000 related
failures by our significant suppliers (including computer bureaux) and customers. In
appropriate cases we have initiated formal communication with these other parties.

Given the complexity of the problem, it is not possible for any organisation to
guarantee that no year 2000 problems will remain, because at least some level of failure
may still occur. However, the board believes that it will achieve an acceptable state of
readiness and has also provided resources to deal promptly with significant subsequent
failures that might arise.

Much of the cost of implementing the action plans has been subsumed into the
recurring activities of the departments involved. The total cost of modifications to our
computer hardware and software is estimated at £1.5 million, of which about half is
new equipment that has been capitalised and the remainder will be expensed as
incurred. Of this £1.5 million total, expenditure of £1.2 million has been incurred to
date.

Economic monetary union

During the year the board has appointed a project manager and undertaken a high level   UITF 21(18)
analysis of the impact of the introduction of the euro. We do not expect costs to be
exceptional in the context of the group, and systems related issues are being dealt with
as part of an overall systems review.

Taxation

An analysis of the taxation charge is set out in note 8 to the accounts. The taxation
charge as a percentage of profit before taxation was 32.0% in the current year and
31.0% in the previous year. The effective tax rate for the current is higher than a
standard rate as a result of disallowable entertaining expenditure which has been partly
offset by accelerated capital allowances.

Good Group P.L.C.

OPERATING AND FINANCIAL REVIEW   OFR (2)

Code D.1.2

FINANCIAL REVIEW (continued)

Liquidity

The statement of cash flows illustrates that there was an increase in cash in the year ended 30 June 1999 of £695,000 (1998 – £4,611,000). The sharp reduction in cash inflow for the year is caused by a number of factors; the two main changes within the total are with respect to operating cash flows and with respect to capital expenditure. Operating activities generated £1,215,000 (1998 – £4,719,000) of cash. The decrease was due largely to a significant increase in stocks and debtors and a decrease in creditors. Dividends of £700,000 and £135,000 were received from the group's joint venture and associates respectively compared with £545,000 and £105,000 in 1998. The outflow of cash from capital expenditure and financial investment was £3,713,000 compared with an outflow of £385,000 in 1998. Within this, increased activity in purchases and sales of tangible fixed assets accounted for an outflow of £4,190,000 this year. The group's cash position was improved by £2,172,000 upon the sale of Hose Limited (see note 14 to the accounts).

Going concern

After making enquiries, the directors have a reasonable expectation that the group has adequate resources to continue in operational existence for the foreseeable future. For this reason, they continue to adopt the going concern basis in preparing the accounts.

Code D.1.3

YB 12.43(v)

Good Group P.L.C.

CORPORATE GOVERNANCE   YB 12.43A(a)

The company is committed to high standards of corporate governance. The board is accountable to the company's shareholders for good corporate governance. This statement describes how the principles of corporate governance are applied to the company and the company's compliance with the Code provisions set out in Section 1 of the Combined Code prepared by the Committee on Corporate Governance chaired by Sir Ronald Hampel.

STATEMENT BY THE DIRECTORS ON COMPLIANCE WITH THE PROVISIONS OF THE COMBINED CODE

The company has been in full compliance with the provisions set out in Section 1 of YB 12.43A(b) the Combined Code throughout the year with the exception of provision C.2.3. Due to unforeseen circumstances the chairman of the remuneration committee was not available to attend and answer questions from shareholders at the Annual General Meeting of the company held on 26 November 1998. The chairmen of the audit, remuneration and nomination committees will be available to answer questions at this year's AGM to be held on 15 November 1999.

As guidance is not yet available for directors on reviewing and reporting on the wider aspects of internal control relating to operational and compliance controls and risk management as required by provision D.2.1, the board has continued to review and report on the effectiveness of the group's system of internal financial controls.

THE WORKINGS OF THE BOARD AND ITS COMMITTEES

The Board

The board currently comprises the independent non-executive chairman, the chief Code A.2.1 executive, four other executive directors and three other independent non-executive Code A.3.2 directors. The biographies appear on page 2010. These demonstrate a range of experience and sufficient calibre to bring independent judgement on issues of strategy, performance, resources and standards of conduct which is vital to the success of the group. The board is responsible to shareholders for the proper management of the group. A statement of the directors' responsibilities in respect of the accounts is set out on page 2032 and a statement on going concern is given on page 2017.

The board has a formal schedule of matters specifically reserved to it for decision. All directors have access to the advice and services of the company secretary, J Harris, who is responsible to the board for ensuring that board procedures are followed and that applicable rules and regulations are complied with. In addition, the company secretary ensures that the directors receive appropriate training as necessary. The appointment and removal of the company secretary is a matter for the board as a whole.

The board meets every month, reviewing trading performance, ensuring adequate funding, setting and monitoring strategy and examining major acquisition possibilities. The non-executive directors have a particular responsibility to ensure that the strategies proposed by the executive directors are fully considered. To enable the board to discharge its duties, all directors receive appropriate and timely information. Briefing papers are distributed by the company secretary to all directors in advance of board meetings. The chairman ensures that the directors take independent professional advice as required.

The following committees deal with the specific aspects of the group's affairs.

Good Group P.L.C.

CORPORATE GOVERNANCE   YB 12.43A(a)

Nomination committee

During the year the nomination committee comprised the non-executive directors.   Code A.5.1
With effect from 1 July 1999, Sir Joshua Barraclough stepped down from this
committee and Mrs L B Green was appointed as its chairman. The committee is
responsible for proposing candidates for appointment to the board, having regard to the
balance and structure of the board. In appropriate cases, recruitment consultants are
used to assist the process. All directors are subject to re-election at least every three
years.

Remuneration committee

The group's remuneration committee which is chaired by M C Holman, comprises all   Code B.2.1
the non-executive directors. It is responsible for making recommendations to the   Code B.2.2
board, within agreed terms of reference, on the company's framework of executive
remuneration and its cost. The committee determines the contract terms, remuneration
and other benefits for each of the executive directors, including performance related
bonus schemes, pension rights and compensation payments. The board itself
determines the remuneration of the non-executive directors. The committee is advised
by a leading firm of remuneration consultants.

Further details of the company's policies on remuneration, service contracts and
compensation payments are given in the report on directors' remuneration on pages
2022 to 2027. The report has been prepared by the board following the provisions in
Schedule B to the Combined Code.

Audit committee

The audit committee is chaired by Sir Joshua Barraclough, and its other members are   Code D.3.1
H C Black, Mrs L B Green and M C Holman. The committee meets not less than three
times annually. The committee provides a forum for reporting by the group's external
and internal auditors. Meetings are also attended, by invitation, by the chief executive
and the finance director.

The audit committee is responsible for reviewing a wide range of matters including the
half year and annual accounts before their submission to the board and monitoring the
controls which are in force to ensure the integrity of the information reported to the
shareholders. The audit committee advises the board on the appointment of external
auditors and on their remuneration both for audit and non-audit work, and discusses the
nature, scope and results of the audit with external auditors. The audit committee
keeps under review the cost effectiveness and the independence and objectivity of the
external and internal auditors.

RELATIONS WITH SHAREHOLDERS

The board recognises the importance of communications with shareholders. The   Code C.1
operating and financial review on pages 2011 to 2017 includes a detailed review of the
business and future developments. There is regular dialogue with institutional
shareholders including presentations after the company's preliminary announcement of
the year end results and at the half year.

The board uses the Annual General Meeting to communicate with private and   Code C.2
institutional investors and welcomes their participation. The chairman aims to ensure   Code C.3
that the chairmen of the audit, remuneration and nomination committees are available
at Annual General Meetings to answer questions.   Details of resolutions to be
proposed at the Annual General Meeting on 15 November 1999 can be found in the
Notice of the meeting on page 2096.

Good Group P.L.C.

CORPORATE GOVERNANCE   YB 12.43A(a)

INTERNAL FINANCIAL CONTROL   Code D.2.1
The board is responsible for establishing and maintaining the group's system of   Guidance for
internal financial control. Internal control systems are designed to meet the particular   directors reporting
needs of the group concerned and the risks to which it is exposed, and by their nature   on internal control
can provide reasonable but not absolute assurance against material misstatement or
loss. The key procedures which the directors have established with a view to providing
effective internal financial control are as follows:

■ **Management structure**

The board has overall responsibility for the group and there is a formal schedule
of matters specifically reserved for decision by the board. Each executive
director has been given responsibility for specific aspects of the group's affairs.
The executive directors together with key senior executives constitute the
management committee, which meets fortnightly, to discuss day-to-day
operational matters.

■ **Corporate accounting and procedures manual**

Responsibility levels are communicated throughout the group as part of the
corporate accounting and procedures manual which sets out, inter-alia, the general
ethos of the group, delegation of authority and authorisation levels, segregation of
duties and other control procedures together with accounting policies and
procedures. The manual is updated regularly.

■ **Quality and integrity of personnel**

The integrity and competence of personnel is ensured through high recruitment
standards and subsequent training courses. High quality personnel are seen as an
essential part of the control environment and the ethical standards expected are
communicated through the corporate accounting and procedures manual.

■ **Identification of business risks**

The board is responsible for identifying the major business risks faced by the
group and for determining the appropriate course of action to manage those risks.
The internal audit department focuses on these areas.

■ **Budgetary process**

Each year the board approves the annual budget and rolling three-year strategic
plan. Key risk areas are identified. Performance is monitored and relevant action
taken throughout the year through the monthly reporting to the board of variances
from the budget, updated forecasts for the year together with information on the
key risk areas.

Good Group P.L.C.

CORPORATE GOVERNANCE　　　　　　　　　　　　　　　　YB 12.43A(a)

■ **Investment appraisal**

Capital expenditure is regulated by a budgetary process and authorisation levels. For expenditure beyond specified levels, detailed written proposals have to be submitted to the board. Reviews are carried out after the acquisition is complete, and for some projects, during the acquisition period, to monitor expenditure; major overruns are investigated.

Proposals for research and development programmes are considered by a team led by J Archer and proposals beyond specified limits are considered by the board. Regular progress reports are submitted to J Archer's team and to the board.

Due diligence work is carried out if a business is to be acquired.

■ **Internal audit**

The group has an internal audit department. Its responsibilities include ensuring that the controls stipulated in the corporate accounting and procedures manual are being adhered to. It reports to management and to the audit committee.

■ **Audit committee**

The audit committee monitors, through reports to it by the internal audit department, the controls which are in force and any perceived gaps in the control environment. The audit committee also considers and determines relevant action in respect of any control issues raised by the internal or external auditors.

The audit committee has reviewed the effectiveness of the system of internal financial control as it operated during the year and reported its conclusions to the board.

Good Group P.L.C.

REPORT ON DIRECTORS' REMUNERATION

YB 12.43A(c)

Code B.3.1, B.3.2, B.3.3

The group's remuneration committee is chaired by M C Holman and its other members are Sir Joshua Barraclough, H C Black and Mrs L B Green. The committee makes recommendations to the board, within agreed terms of reference, on an overall remuneration package for executive directors and other senior executives in order to attract, retain and motivate high quality executives capable of achieving the group's objectives. The package consists of basic salary, benefits, share options, performance related bonuses and pensions, with a significant proportion based on performance and dependent upon the achievement of demanding targets. Consideration is given to pay and employment policies elsewhere in the group, especially when determining annual salary increases. In addition, the remuneration committee is advised by a leading firm of executive remuneration consultants to maximise comparability within the marketplace and pays particular attention to the remuneration levels of the company's ten closest competitors.

Code B.2.3, B.3.3

YB 12.43A(c)(i)

Although the executive directors are encouraged to accept appointments as non-executive directors, if they accept more than two such appointments they are required to pass their fees for those appointments to the company.

The details of individual components of the remuneration package and service contracts are discussed below.

Basic salary and benefits: The salary and benefits are reviewed annually. No director has received an increase in basic salary for the next financial year, although the maximum amount due under the new bonus scheme has increased. The increase in basic salary from 1997/98 to 1998/99, the maximum of which was 5.7%, is in line with the increase for all employees throughout the group. Benefits principally comprise a car and private healthcare.

Share options: The share options are awarded by the remuneration committee based on the movement in the company's share price relative to that of the company's ten closest competitors. Since 1 July 1998 the maximum number of options that can be awarded in a year is the number that when multiplied by the then current share price equates to half of the director's basic salary. The maximum number that may be awarded in a 10 year period is an amount equating to 30% of the basic salary in that period. The exercise price of options granted is the higher of the nominal value of the shares and the average market price over the 10 business days prior to the date of grant. No value is included in directors' emoluments in respect of share options granted during the year because in the absence of a readily available market value for options over the company's shares we are unable to arrive at an accurate assessment of the value of the options granted. Share options issued during the year are detailed below; they are exercisable, at a price of £3.85 per share, between 1 July 2002 and 30 June 2010.

YB 12.43 A(c)(viii)

The directors may only exercise the options granted to them if the company's earnings per share has increased by 10% more than the increase in the RPI over the period from the date of grant of the options up to the date they first become exercisable and dividends per share have similarly increased by at least the same amount.

Performance related bonuses: These are calculated based on fixed formulae which are determined in advance of each year by the remuneration committee. The formulae for J N Smith and P A MacBryde measure the group's performance against specified targets, principally relating to sales, profit after tax but excluding non-operating exceptional items and their tax effect, gearing and net assets. The formulae for J Archer, J Corless, N O Evans and R P Jones measure performance against targets, principally financial, in individual divisions.

Good Group P.L.C.

REPORT ON DIRECTORS' REMUNERATION

YB 12.43 A(c)
Code B.3.1, B.3.2, B.3.3

On 1 July 1999 the company replaced the above scheme with a long-term incentive plan which was approved at last year's AGM. In designing the new scheme the remuneration committee followed the provisions in Schedule A of the Combined Code. The bonus payable under this scheme is payable in shares at the end of four years and is based on the total return to shareholders (measured using share price and dividends) over that period relative to that of the company's top ten competitors. The Good Group Employee Share Trust will purchase shares each year in the market to cover the anticipated entitlement, the funds being provided to it by the company. The directors may choose not to take any of the shares immediately upon vesting, but to leave them within the trust; the company will increase their entitlement by 5% if they leave them in the trust for an additional two years after vesting.

YB 12.43A(c)(viii)
Code B.1.6

Under both the old and new schemes the amount of the bonus increases in accordance with the level of performance achieved, with the maximum bonus being 10 - 14% of basic salary for the old scheme and 17% of basic salary in the first of the four years under the new scheme.

Pensions: The executive directors are members of the Good Group Employee Pension Scheme (see note 29) which pays an annual pension of 1/60th of final pensionable pay (which consists solely of basic salary) for each year of service. For the last two years the company's contributions have been 17% of total pensionable earnings, which is higher than usual as the company is eliminating the deficit indicated at the last valuation.

Fees: The fees for non-executive directors are determined by the board within the limits stipulated in the Articles of Association. The non-executive directors are not involved in any discussions or decision about their own remuneration.

Service contracts: The service contracts of all the executive directors, expire on 30 June 2000, being for one year's duration commencing on 1 July 1999. None of the non-executive directors have service contracts. There are no special provisions for compensation in the event of loss of office. The remuneration committee considers the circumstances of individual cases of early termination and determines compensation payments accordingly.

YB 12.43A(c)(vii)

Mrs L B Green, who was appointed a director on 1 September 1998, retires from the board at the Annual General Meeting and, being eligible, offers herself for re-election. J N Smith, M C Holman and P A MacBryde retire by rotation and, being eligible, offer themselves for re-election. Biographical details of all directors can be found on page 2010.

Code A.6.2

Good Group P.L.C.

REPORT ON DIRECTORS' REMUNERATION

YB 12.43 A(c)

Code B.3.1, B.3.3

Directors' remuneration

The remuneration of the directors is as follows:

YB 12.43A(c)(ii)

6 Sch 1, 2

	Basic salary and fees £	Benefits £	Performance related bonuses £	Compensation for loss of office £	Total 1998 £	Total 1997 £
Executive directors:						
J N Smith	77,700	7,173	10,256		95,129	88,997
J Archer	51,800	4,981	5,400		62,181	59,972
J Corless	53,700	5,235	6,000		64,935	62,323
N O Evans	50,300	4,981	5,500		60,781	57,960
R P Jones (1)	19,750	1,905		16,150	37,805	55,860
P A MacBryde	59,700	6,150	7,700		73,550	70,740
Non-executive directors:						
Sir Joshua Barraclough	20,000				20,000	17,000
H C Black	7,500				7,500	3,750
L B Green (2)	6,250				6,250	–
M C Holman	7,500				7,500	7,500
	354,200	30,425	34,856	16,150	435,631	424,102

(1)   Resigned 30 November 1998. Compensation for loss of office represents the market value of a car given by the company to R P Jones upon his retirement from executive office.   6 Sch 8

(2)   Appointed 1 September 1998.

Good Group P.L.C.

REPORT ON DIRECTORS' REMUNERATION   YB 12.43 A(c)

Code B.3.1, B.3.3

Pension entitlements   YB 12.43 A(c) (ix)

The pension entitlements of the directors are as follows:

	Increase, excluding inflation, in accrued pension during the year	*Transfer value of increase**	*Accumulated total accrued pension at*	6 Sch 1, 2
			30 June 1999	*30 June 1998*
	£	£	£	£
J N Smith	1,530	10,494	20,785	18,338
J Archer	898	2,880	14,117	12,590
J Corless	545	1,503	14,201	13,006
N O Evans	622	1,929	12,227	11,052
R P Jones	576	2,013	12,535 †	11,675
P A MacBryde	357	1,239	15,245	14,179

*   Transfer values represent a liability of the company, not a sum paid or due to the individual.

†   Accumulated total pension at date of retirement.

In addition to the amounts disclosed above, during 1997/98 an additional pension payment of £40,000 was made to S B Clark who retired as an executive director in 1996.   6 Sch 7

Good Group P.L.C.

REPORT ON DIRECTORS' REMUNERATION   YB 12.43 A(c)

                                                                     Code B.3.1, B.3.3

Interests in options

The company has two share option schemes by which executive directors and other senior executives are able to subscribe for ordinary shares in the company and acquire shares in the company from Good Group Employee Trust. The interests of the directors were as follows:

     YB 12.43(k)
     YB 12.43A(c)(iii)
     UITF 10
     7 Sch 2A, 2B

	Exercise price	At 1 July 1998 No.	Granted during the year No.	Exercised during the year No.	Lapsed during the year No.	At 30 June 1999 No.
J N Smith	(a) £2.31	10,000	–	–	–	10,000
	(b) £2.33	10,000	–	(10,000) †	–	–
	(c) £3.80	35,000	–	–	–	35,000
	(d) £3.85	–	10,000	–	–	10,000
		55,000	10,000	(10,000)	–	55,000
J Archer	(a) £2.31	5,000	–	–	–	5,000
	(c) £3.80	35,000	–	–	–	35,000
	(d) £3.85	–	6,500	–	–	6,500
		40,000	6,500	–	–	46,500
J Corless	(a) £2.31	5,000	–	–	–	5,000
	(d) £3.85	–	6,500	–	–	6,500
		5,000	6,500	–	–	11,500
N O Evans	(d) £3.85	–	6,500	–	–	6,500
R P Jones	(c) £3.80	8,000	–	–	(8,000)	–
P A MacBryde	(c) £3.80	5,000	–	–	–	5,000
	(d) £3.85	–	7,500	–	–	7,500
		5,000	7,500	–	–	12,500

† At the date of exercise, the company's share price was £4.10 per share. 6 Sch 1
Accordingly, J N Smith was able to realise a gain of £17,700. The aggregate amount of gains made by directors on the exercise of share options in 1997/98 was £5,500.

The options are exercisable between the following dates:

     (a)   1 January 2000 and 31 December 2002;
     (c)   1 July 2000 and 30 June 2004;
     (d)   1 July 2002 and 30 June 2010.

Good Group P.L.C.

REPORT ON DIRECTORS' REMUNERATION   YB 12.43 A(c)

Code B.3.1, B.3.3

The directors may only exercise any of the above options if the group's earnings per share has increased by 10% more than the increase in the RPI over the period from the date of grant of the options up to the date they first become exercisable and dividends per share have similarly increased by at least the same amount.

The market price of the company's shares on 30 June 1999 was £4.43 per share and   UITF 10 the high and low share prices during the year were £4.43 and £3.42 respectively. The company's average share price over the 10 business days prior to the date of grant of options during the year was £3.85.

The interests of the directors to subscribe for or acquire ordinary shares have not   YB 12.43(k) changed since the year end.

Good Group P.L.C.

DIRECTORS' REPORT   s234

The directors present their report and the group accounts for the year ended 30 June 1999.

RESULTS AND DIVIDENDS
The group profit for the year, after taxation and minority interests, amounted to £7,406,000, an increase of 22.3% from the previous year.

The directors recommend a final ordinary dividend of 8.67 pence per share, amounting   s234(1)(b) to £1,061,000, making totals of 15.23 pence and £1,859,000 for the year respectively after taking account of the dividends waived by the Good Group Employee Share Trust (see note 10). Preference dividends of £175,000 were also paid during the year.

The final ordinary dividend, if approved, will be paid on 3 January 2000 to ordinary shareholders whose names were on the register on 13 December 1999.

PRINCIPAL ACTIVITIES
The group's principal activities during the year continued to be electronics and the   s234(2) manufacture and installation of fire-prevention equipment.

REVIEW OF THE BUSINESS
The group has had a satisfactory year with an overall increase in sales. There has been   s234(1)(a) a substantial increase in sales of fire-prevention equipment, which have grown in total by 25.3% during the year. However, this included the results of Hose Limited which was sold during the year (see below); when the results of Hose Limited have been eliminated, the sales of the continuing operations of this segment grew by 46.6%. The growth has been most marked in the home market. Although sales to the United States have shown an increase from the year ended 30 June 1998 levels, the increase was well below that achieved in the home market and the sales generated in the United States fell slightly. However, a new company, Sprinklers Incorporated, has been set up to manufacture the group's new fire-prevention system in the United States.

During the year the group acquired all of the issued share capital of Extinguishers Limited, a company which is best known for its fire-retardant fabrics.

The directors decided that the group should withdraw from the manufacture of rubber hosepipes, an activity which had been loss-making for some years. To this end the directors were successful in completing a sale of the subsidiary, Hose Limited, on 28 May 1999. The loss on disposal of the subsidiary amounted to £2,437,000, of which £400,000 represents goodwill previously set off against reserves.

The group's electronics activities have shown only slight growth during the year although profit margins in this area generally remain good.

FUTURE DEVELOPMENTS
The directors are hopeful that the current year will see an increase in sales of new fire-   7 Sch 6(b) protection products in the United Kingdom. Sprinklers Incorporated is expected to commence production in December 1999 and this will lead to an expansion in sales in the United States. The group is looking for ways of making the electronics business more profitable by way of acquisitions and new product lines.

Good Group P.L.C.

DIRECTORS' REPORT   s234

RESEARCH AND DEVELOPMENT

With the acquisition of Extinguishers Limited, the number of staff employed by the   7 Sch 6(c)
group on research and development has more than doubled.

There are two main fire-prevention research and development projects: improved fire
detection and sprinkler systems and fire-retardant fabrics for vehicles and aircraft.

Research and development in the electronics business is concentrated on the
development of new products capable of generating greater turnover.

EVENTS SINCE THE BALANCE SHEET DATE

On 14 August 1999 a short leasehold building, with a net book value of £1,695,000,   7 Sch 6(a)
was severely damaged by flooding. It is expected that insurance proceeds will fall
short of the costs of rebuilding and loss of stocks by some £750,000. No provision has
been made in these accounts for this loss.

POLITICAL AND CHARITABLE CONTRIBUTIONS

During the year, the group made a political contribution of £5,500 to the United Party   7 Sch 3-5
and various charitable contributions totalling £10,000.

DISABLED EMPLOYEES

The group gives full consideration to applications for employment from disabled   7 Sch 9
persons where the requirements of the job can be adequately fulfilled by a handicapped
or disabled person.

Where existing employees become disabled, it is the group's policy wherever
practicable to provide continuing employment under normal terms and conditions and
to provide training and career development and promotion to disabled employees
wherever appropriate.

Good Group P.L.C.

DIRECTORS' REPORT s234

EMPLOYEE INVOLVEMENT

During the year, the policy of providing employees with information about the group   7 Sch 11
has been continued through the newsletter 'Good Group News' in which employees
have also been encouraged to present their suggestions and views on the group's
performance. Regular meetings are held between local management and employees to
allow a free flow of information and ideas. Employees participate directly in the
success of the business through the group's profit sharing schemes and are encouraged
to invest in the group through participation in share option schemes.

DIRECTORS AND THEIR INTERESTS

The directors at 30 June 1999 and their interests in the share capital of the company (all   s234(2)
beneficially held except those marked with an asterisk which are held as trustee), other   7 Sch 2A, 2B
than with respect to options to acquire ordinary shares (which are detailed in the   YB 12.43(k)
analysis of options included in the report on directors' remuneration), were as follows:

	At 30 June 1999 Ordinary shares	At 1 July 1998 or subsequent date of appointment Ordinary shares
Sir Joshua Barraclough	15,000	15,000
J N Smith	105,000	95,000
J Archer	–	–
H C Black	1,500	1,500
J Corless	55,000	55,000
	19,000*	19,000*
N O Evans	15,000	15,000
Mrs L B Green	1,000	–
M C Holman	1,000	1,000
P A MacBryde	40,000	40,000

No director was interested in the preference shares or debentures of the company, or in
the shares or loan stock of any subsidiary company.

During the period from the end of the financial year to 18 September 1999,   YB 12.43(k)
P A MacBryde acquired a beneficial interest in 1,000 ordinary shares in the company,
increasing his total beneficial holding to 56,000 ordinary shares. In all other respects
the interests of the directors were unchanged.

The executive directors, along with other employees, have been granted options over
the shares held by the Good Group Employee Trust. Details of these interests, along
with options to subscribe for shares in the company, are disclosed in the report on
directors' remuneration.

In addition to the directors listed above, R P Jones served as a director until   s234(2)
30 November 1998 when he resigned.

Good Group P.L.C.

DIRECTORS' REPORT   s234

MAJOR INTERESTS IN SHARES

On 18 September 1999, International Fires P.L.C. held 3,958,350 ordinary shares of £1   YB 12.43(1)
each (31.48% of the ordinary share capital) in the company. Details of transactions   s199(2)
between the group and International Fires P.L.C. are given in note 33 to the accounts.
No other person has notified an interest in the ordinary shares of the company required
to be disclosed to the company in accordance with sections 198 to 208 of the
Companies Act 1985.

CREDITOR PAYMENT POLICY AND PRACTICE

It is the company's policy that payments to suppliers are made in accordance with   7 Sch 12(2)
those terms and conditions agreed between the company and its suppliers, provided
that all trading terms and conditions have been complied with.

At 30 June 1999, the company had an average of 23 days purchases outstanding in   7 Sch 12(3)
trade creditors.

SPECIAL BUSINESS AT THE ANNUAL GENERAL MEETING

At the Annual General Meeting on 15 November 1999 resolutions 1 to 7 are termed   YB 14.17
ordinary business, while resolutions 8(A) and 8(B) will be special business. The
special business covers the directors' authority to allot shares and the partial
disapplication of pre-emption rights as explained below. The resolutions are set out in
the Notice of Annual General Meeting on page 2096.

Resolution 8(A) gives authority to the directors to allot shares up to a total nominal
amount of £4,925,000 being the nominal value of the authorised ordinary share capital
less the nominal value of the issued share capital at 1 July 1999 and representing 39%
of the equity share capital in issue on 1 July 1999 and at the date of the notice of
Annual General Meeting. The authority will expire at the conclusion of the Annual
General Meeting to be held in 2000 and replaces a similar authority granted on 26
November 1998, which expires at the conclusion of the forthcoming Annual General
Meeting. Save for any options granted under the share option scheme, the directors
have no present intention of exercising the authority conferred by this resolution.

The passing of resolution 8(B), a special resolution, will permit the directors, until the
conclusion of the Annual General Meeting of the company to be held in 2000, to make
issues of equity securities for cash either by way of rights issue or in any other way up
to a total nominal amount of £4,925,000, provided the shares issued other than by way
of rights issue be limited to shares with a nominal value of £628,750, being the
equivalent of 5% of the equity share capital in issue on the date of the notice of Annual
General Meeting. The power will, if granted, replace the similar power conferred on
the directors on 26 November 1998 and which lapses on 15 November 1999.

In the opinion of the directors, the passing of these resolutions is in the best interests of
the shareholders.

AUDITORS

A resolution to reappoint Chartered Accountants & Co. as auditors will be put to the   s384(1)
members at the Annual General Meeting.

By order of the board

J Harris   Secretary   s234A

27 September 1999

Good Group P.L.C.

STATEMENT OF DIRECTORS' RESPONSIBILITIES IN RESPECT OF THE
ACCOUNTS

Company law requires the directors to prepare accounts for each financial year which give a true and fair view of the state of affairs of the company and of the group and of the profit or loss of the group for that period. In preparing those accounts, the directors are required to: *(right margin: Code D.1.1 SAS 600 (20), (21) (App.3))*

- select suitable accounting policies and then apply them consistently;

- make judgements and estimates that are reasonable and prudent; and

- state whether applicable accounting standards have been followed, subject to any material departures disclosed and explained in the accounts.

The directors are responsible for keeping proper accounting records which disclose with reasonable accuracy at any time the financial position of the group and to enable them to ensure that the accounts comply with the Companies Act 1985. They are also responsible for safeguarding the assets of the group and hence for taking reasonable steps for the prevention and detection of fraud and other irregularities.

REPORT OF THE AUDITORS
to the members of Good Group P.L.C.

s235(1), (2)
SAS 600 (14)

We have audited the accounts on pages 2034 to 2093, which have been prepared under the historical cost convention as modified by the revaluation of investment properties and on the basis of the accounting policies set out on pages 2042 to 2048.

Respective responsibilities of directors and auditors

The directors are responsible for preparing the annual report including, as described on page 2032, the accounts. Our responsibilities, as independent auditors, are established by statute, the Auditing Practices Board, the Listing Rules of the London Stock Exchange and by our profession's ethical guidance. SAS 600 (20)
APB Bulletin
1998/10

We report to you our opinion as to whether the accounts give a true and fair view and are properly prepared in accordance with the Companies Act. We also report to you if, in our opinion, the directors' report is not consistent with the accounts, if the company has not kept proper accounting records, if we have not received all the information and explanations we require for our audit, or if the information specified by law or the Listing Rules regarding directors' remuneration and transactions with the company is not disclosed.

We read the other information contained in the annual report and consider whether it is consistent with the audited accounts. We consider the implications for our report if we become aware of any apparent misstatements or material inconsistencies with the accounts.

We review whether the statement on page 2018 reflects the company's compliance with those provisions of the Combined Code specified for our review by the Stock Exchange, and we report if it does not. We are not required to form an opinion on the effectiveness of either the company's corporate governance procedures or the group's internal controls.

Basis of audit opinion

We conducted our audit in accordance with Auditing Standards issued by the Auditing Practices Board. An audit includes examination, on a test basis, of evidence relevant to the amounts and disclosures in the accounts. It also includes an assessment of the significant estimates and judgements made by the directors in the preparation of the accounts, and of whether the accounting policies are appropriate to the group's circumstances, consistently applied and adequately disclosed. SAS 600 (24)

We planned and performed our audit so as to obtain all the information and explanations which we considered necessary in order to provide us with sufficient evidence to give reasonable assurance that the accounts are free from material misstatement, whether caused by fraud or other irregularity or error. In forming our opinion we also evaluated the overall adequacy of the presentation of information in the accounts.

Opinion

In our opinion the accounts give a true and fair view of the state of affairs of the company and of the group as at 30 June 1999 and of the profit of the group for the year then ended and have been properly prepared in accordance with the Companies Act 1985. SAS 600 (30)

Chartered Accountants & Co.
Registered Auditor
London

SAS 600 (14)

27 September 1999

SAS 600 (76)

Good Group P.L.C.

GROUP PROFIT AND LOSS ACCOUNT   s227(2)
for the year ended 30 June 1999   4A Sch 17, 21

TURNOVER	Notes	1999 £000	1999 £000	1998 £000	
Turnover: group and share of joint venture's turnover			243,288	203,145	
Less: share of joint venture's turnover			30,438	23,145	FRS 9(21)
Continuing operations:					FRS 3(14)
ongoing			148,675	133,372	
acquisitions - Extinguishers Limited			21,979	–	FRS 6(28)
			170,654	133,372	
Discontinued operations			42,196	46,628	FRS 3(14)
GROUP TURNOVER	2		212,850	180,000	
Cost of sales	3		169,537	144,500	
Gross profit			43,313	35,500	
Distribution costs	3	16,836		14,330	
Administrative expenses	3	16,458		12,925	
			33,294	27,255	
			10,019	8,245	
Other operating income	3		688	650	
			10,707	8,895	
Bid defence costs	3,5		655	–	
OPERATING PROFIT					
Continuing operations:					FRS 3(14)
ongoing			9,377	9,415	
acquisitions - Extinguishers Limited			1,238	–	FRS 6(28)
			10,615	9,415	
Discontinued operations			(563)	(520)	FRS 3(14)
GROUP OPERATING PROFIT	4		10,052	8,895	
Share of operating profit in joint venture			2,435	1,007	FRS 9(21)
Share of operating profit in associate			425	325	FRS 9(27), 4A Sch 21
Amortisation of goodwill arising on acquisition of associate			(70)	(70)	FRS 9(21), (27), (38)
			2,790	1,262	
TOTAL OPERATING PROFIT: GROUP AND SHARE OF JOINT VENTURE AND ASSOCIATE			12,842	10,157	

Good Group P.L.C.

GROUP PROFIT AND LOSS ACCOUNT   s227(2)

for the year ended 30 June 1999 (continued)   4A Sch 17, 21

	Notes	1999 £000	1999 £000	1998 £000	
TOTAL OPERATING PROFIT: GROUP AND SHARE OF JOINT VENTURE AND ASSOCIATE			12,842	10,157	
Continuing operations:					
Profit/(loss) on disposal of tangible fixed assets		1,250		(850)	FRS 3(20)
(Loss) on disposal of fixed asset investments		(350)		–	FRS 3(20)
		900		(850)	
Discontinued operations					
(Loss) on sale of operations		(2,437)		–	FRS 3(20)
	5		(1,537)	(850)	
PROFIT ON ORDINARY ACTIVITIES BEFORE INVESTMENT INCOME, INTEREST AND TAXATION			11,305	9,307	
Income from investments		250		200	
Bank interest receivable		1,018		395	
Interest payable and similar charges	7	(1,204)		(1,041)	
			64	(446)	
PROFIT ON ORDINARY ACTIVITIES BEFORE TAXATION	2		11,369	8,861	4 Sch 3(6)
Tax on profit on ordinary activities	8		3,652	2,749	
PROFIT ON ORDINARY ACTIVITIES AFTER TAXATION			7,717	6,112	
Minority interests:					
Equity			296	40	FRS 4(60)
Non-equity			15	15	FRS 4(60)
			311	55	4A Sch 17(3) FRS 2(36)
PROFIT FOR THE FINANCIAL YEAR ATTRIBUTABLE TO MEMBERS OF THE PARENT COMPANY			7,406	6,057	
DIVIDENDS:					
Ordinary dividend on equity shares			1,859	1,266	FRS 4(59)
Preference dividends on non-equity shares			175	175	FRS 4(59)
	10		2,034	1,441	4 Sch 3 (7)(b)
OTHER APPROPRIATIONS:					
Non-equity shares	10		81	74	FRS 4(59)
RETAINED PROFIT FOR THE YEAR	24		5,291	4,542	4 Sch 3(7)(a)
Earnings per share – basic	11		61.9p	60.1p	FRS 14(69)
– diluted	11		59.7p	57.6p	FRS 14(69)

Good Group P.L.C.

GROUP STATEMENT OF TOTAL RECOGNISED GAINS AND LOSSES   FRS 3(27)
for the year ended 30 June 1999

	1999 £000	1998 £000	
Profit for the financial year excluding share of profits of joint venture and associate	5,634	5,377	
Share of joint venture's profit for the year	1,557	555	FRS 9(21)
Share of associate's profit for the year	215	125	FRS 9(28)
Profit for the financial year attributable to members of the parent company	7,406	6,057	
Deficit on revaluation of investment properties	(350)	(474)	
Exchange difference on retranslation of net assets of subsidiary undertaking	460	(147)	
Exchange difference on loan	(179)	–	SSAP 20(60)
Tax on exchange difference on loan	34	–	UITF 19(9)
Total recognised gains and losses relating to the year	7,371	5,436	

RECONCILIATION OF SHAREHOLDERS' FUNDS   FRS 3(28)
for the year ended 30 June 1999

	1999 £000	1998 £000	
Total recognised gains and losses	7,371	5,436	
Dividends	(2,034)	(1,441)	
Other movements:			
New shares issued	8,825	–	FRS 4(93)
Goodwill reinstated on sale of subsidiary	400	–	
	9,225	–	
Total movements during the year	14,562	3,995	
Shareholders' funds at 1 July	42,188	38,193	
Shareholders' funds at 30 June	56,750	42,188	

NOTE OF HISTORICAL COST PROFITS
 AND LOSSES   FRS 3(26)
for the year ended 30 June 1999

	1999 £000	1998 £000
Reported profit on ordinary activities before taxation	11,369	8,861
Realisation of property revaluation gains of previous years	235	–
Historical cost profit on ordinary activities before taxation	11,604	8,861
Historical cost profit for the year retained after taxation, minority interests, dividends and other appropriations	5,456	4,542

Good Group P.L.C.

GROUP BALANCE SHEET s227(2)
at 30 June 1999 4A Sch 17, 21

	Notes	1999 £000	1999 £000	1998 £000	1998 £000	
FIXED ASSETS						4 Sch 17-19
Intangible assets	12		3,510		1,685	
Tangible assets	13		33,801		30,055	
Investments	14					
Investment in joint venture:						FRS 9(21)
Share of gross assets		2,886		1,435		
Share of gross liabilities		(1,051)		(457)		
		1,835		978		
Investment in associate		1,257		1,177		FRS 9(29)
Other investments		2,040		2,050		
			5,132		4,205	
			42,443		35,945	
CURRENT ASSETS						4 Sch 22, 23
Stocks	15	26,125		20,100		
Debtors	16	20,203		11,957		
Cash at bank and in hand		8,724		11,330		
		55,052		43,387		
CREDITORS: amounts falling due within one year	17	24,734		25,263		
NET CURRENT ASSETS			30,318		18,124	
TOTAL ASSETS LESS CURRENT LIABILITIES			72,761		54,069	
CREDITORS: amounts falling due after more than one year	18		12,563		9,465	
PROVISIONS FOR LIABILITIES AND CHARGES	21		752		381	
ACCRUALS AND DEFERRED INCOME						
Deferred government grants			2,070		1,690	
			15,385		11,536	
			57,376		42,533	
MINORITY INTERESTS						
Equity		416		135		FRS 4(50)
Non-equity	34	210		210		FRS 4(50)
						4A Sch 17(2)
			626		345	FRS 2(35)
			56,750		42,188	

Good Group P.L.C.

GROUP BALANCE SHEET   s227(2)
at 30 June 1999 (continued)   4A Sch 17, 21

	Notes	1999 £000	1998 £000	
CAPITAL AND RESERVES				
Called up share capital	23	15,075	12,500	
Share premium account	24	494	500	
Revaluation reserve	24	5,039	5,554	
Other reserves	24	6,250	–	
Profit and loss account	24	29,892	23,634	
Shareholders' funds:				
Equity		53,937	39,456	FRS 4(40)
Non-equity		2,813	2,732	FRS 4(40)
		56,750	42,188	FRS 4(38)

Sir Joshua Barraclough   Chairman   s233

27 September 1999   SSAP 17(26)

Good Group P.L.C.

BALANCE SHEET				s226(1)
at 30 June 1999				4 Sch Formats

	Notes	1999 £000	1998 £000	
FIXED ASSETS				4 Sch 17, 19
Tangible assets	13	16,440	14,504	
Investments	14	17,110	9,145	
		33,550	23,649	
CURRENT ASSETS				4 Sch 22, 23
Stocks	15	11,570	7,125	
Debtors:	16			
amounts falling due after one year		9,215	6,680	UITF 4(3)
amounts falling due within one year		6,173	4,622	
		15,388	11,302	
Cash at bank and in hand		4,030	6,555	
		30,988	24,982	
CREDITORS: amounts falling due within one year	17	11,784	8,784	
NET CURRENT ASSETS		19,204	16,198	
TOTAL ASSETS LESS CURRENT LIABILITIES		52,754	39,847	
CREDITORS: amounts falling due after more than one year	18	10,063	9,465	
PROVISION FOR LIABILITIES AND CHARGES	21	70	141	
ACCRUALS AND DEFERRED INCOME				
Deferred government grants		1,230	925	
		11,363	10,531	
		41,391	29,316	
CAPITAL AND RESERVES				
Called up share capital	23	15,075	12,500	
Share premium account	24	494	500	
Revaluation reserve	24	2,765	3,084	
Other reserves	24	6,250	–	
Profit and loss account	24	16,807	13,232	
Shareholders' funds:				
Equity		38,578	26,584	FRS 4(40)
Non-equity		2,813	2,732	FRS 4(40)
		41,391	29,316	FRS 4(38)

Sir Joshua Barraclough	Chairman	s233
27 September 1999		SSAP 17(26)

Good Group P.L.C.

GROUP STATEMENT OF CASH FLOWS   FRS 1(4), (7), (48)
for the year ended 30 June 1999

	Notes	1999 £000	1998 £000	
NET CASH INFLOW FROM OPERATING ACTIVITIES	25(a)	1,215	4,719	FRS 1(11)
DIVIDENDS FROM JOINT VENTURE AND ASSOCIATE				FRS 1(12A)
Dividends from joint venture		700	545	
Dividends from associate		135	105	
		835	650	
RETURNS ON INVESTMENTS AND SERVICING OF FINANCE				FRS 1 (13)-(15)
Interest received		993	345	
Interest paid		(973)	(1,090)	
Interest element of finance lease rental payments		(40)	(35)	
Issue costs of new long-term loans		(50)	(56)	
Dividends received		200	160	
Dividends paid to minority interests		(30)	(30)	
Dividends paid to preference shareholders		(175)	(175)	
		(75)	(881)	
TAXATION				FRS 1(16)-(18)
Corporation tax paid (including advance corporation tax)		(1,356)	(550)	
Overseas tax paid		(1,075)	(980)	
		(2,431)	(1,530)	
CAPITAL EXPENDITURE AND FINANCIAL INVESTMENT				FRS 1(19)-(21)
Payments to acquire intangible fixed assets		(575)	(1,010)	
Payments to acquire tangible fixed assets		(12,815)	(3,875)	
Receipts from sales of tangible fixed assets		8,625	3,965	
Payments to acquire investments		(465)	(230)	
Receipts from sales of investments		125	–	
Receipt of government grants		1,392	765	
		(3,713)	(385)	
ACQUISITIONS AND DISPOSALS				FRS 1 (22)-(24)
Sale of subsidiary undertaking	14	55	–	
Net overdrafts disposed of with subsidiary undertaking	14	2,117	–	
Purchase of subsidiary undertaking	14	(500)	–	FRS 6(33)
Net cash acquired with subsidiary undertakings	14	230	–	FRS 6(33)
		1,902	–	
EQUITY DIVIDENDS PAID		(1,431)	(1,170)	FRS 1(25)
NET CASH (OUTFLOW)/INFLOW BEFORE USE OF MANAGEMENT OF LIQUID RESOURCES AND FINANCING		(3,698)	1,403	

Good Group P.L.C.

GROUP STATEMENT OF CASH FLOWS   FRS 1(4), (7), (48)
for the year ended 30 June 1999

	Notes	1999 £000	1998 £000	
NET CASH (OUTFOW)/INFLOW BEFORE USE OF MANAGEMENT OF LIQUID RESOURCES AND FINANCING		(3,698)	1,403	
MANAGEMENT OF LIQUID RESOURCES				FRS 1(26)-(28)
Decrease/(increase) in short term deposits	25(b)	528	(907)	
FINANCING				FRS 1(29)-(31)
Issue of ordinary share capital		175	–	
Share issue costs		(100)	–	
New long-term loans	25(b)	4,660	4,500	
Repayment of long-term loans	25(b)	(500)	–	
Repayments of capital element of finance leases and hire purchase contracts	25(b)	(370)	(385)	
		3,865	4,115	
INCREASE IN CASH	25(b)	695	4,611	

RECONCILIATION OF NET CASH FLOW TO MOVEMENT IN NET DEBT   FRS 1(33)

	Notes	1998 £000	1997 £000
Increase in cash		695	4,611
Cash inflow from increase in loans		(4,660)	(4,500)
Repayment of long term loans		500	–
Issue costs of new long-term loans		50	56
Repayments of capital elements of finance leases and hire purchase contracts		370	385
Cash inflow from short term deposits		(528)	907
Change in net debt resulting from cash flows	25(b)	(3,573)	1,459
Exchange differences		92	102
Other		(27)	(14)
MOVEMENT IN NET DEBT		(3,508)	1,547
NET DEBT AT 1 JULY	25(b)	(2,755)	(4,302)
NET DEBT AT 30 JUNE	25(b)	(6,263)	(2,755)

Good Group P.L.C.

NOTES TO THE ACCOUNTS
at 30 June 1999

1. **ACCOUNTING POLICIES**	4 Sch 36 SSAP 2(17), (18)

Basis of preparation

The accounts are prepared under the historical cost convention modified to include the revaluation of investment properties.	
The accounts are prepared in accordance with applicable accounting standards. The true and fair override provisions of the Companies Act 1985 have been invoked, see 'investment properties' below.	4 Sch 36A UITF 7(7)

Basis of consolidation

The group accounts consolidate the accounts of Good Group P.L.C. and all its subsidiary undertakings drawn to 30 June each year. No profit and loss account is presented for Good Group P.L.C. as permitted by section 230 of the Companies Act 1985.	s227(2), s230 4A Sch 2(1) 5 Sch 15(4) FRS 2(23)
Extinguishers Limited has been included in the group accounts using the acquisition method of accounting. Accordingly, the group profit and loss account and statement of cash flows include the results and cash flows of Extinguishers Limited for the nine month period from its acquisition on 1 October 1998. The purchase consideration has been allocated to assets and liabilities on the basis of fair value at the date of acquisition.	4A Sch 13(2)(a) 4A Sch 9 FRS 6(20), (21) FRS 2(23)
The group profit and loss account and statement of cash flows also include the results and cash flows of Sprinklers Incorporated for the seven-month period from its incorporation on 5 December 1998 and includes the results and cash flows of Hose Limited for the eleven month period to 28 May 1999, the date of its sale outside the group.	4A Sch 15(a) FRS 2(23)
Entities in which the group holds an interest on a long term basis and are jointly controlled by the group and one or more other venturers under a contractual arrangement are treated as joint ventures. In the group accounts, joint ventures are accounted for using the gross equity method.	4A Sch 22 FRS 9 (31)
Entities, other than subsidiary undertakings or joint ventures, in which the group has a participating interest and over whose operating and financial policies the group exercises a significant influence are treated as associates. In the group accounts, associates are accounted for using the equity method.	4A Sch 22 FRS 9(31)

Good Group P.L.C.

NOTES TO THE ACCOUNTS
at 30 June 1999

1.   ACCOUNTING POLICIES (continued)

Goodwill

Depending on the circumstances of each acquisition, goodwill arising on acquisitions FRS 10(71)
prior to 30 June 1998 was either set off directly against reserves or amortised through
the profit and loss account over the directors' estimate of its useful life. Goodwill
previously eliminated against reserves has not been reinstated on implementation of
Financial Reporting Standard No. 10 *Goodwill and Intangible Assets.*

Positive goodwill arising on acquisitions since 1 July 1998 is capitalised, classified as FRS 10(7), (8),
an asset on the balance sheet and amortised on a straight line basis over its useful (15), (34), (55)
economic life up to a presumed maximum of 20 years. It is reviewed for impairment at 4 Sch 21
the end of the first full financial year following the acquisition and in other periods if
events or changes in circumstances indicate that the carrying value may not be
recoverable.

If a subsidiary, associate or business is subsequently sold or closed, any goodwill FRS 2(52)
arising on acquisition that was written off directly to reserves or that has not been FRS 10(71)
amortised through the profit and loss account is taken into account in determining the
profit or loss on sale or closure.

Intangible assets

Intangible assets acquired separately from a business are capitalised at cost. Intangible FRS 10(9), (10),
assets acquired as part of an acquisition of a business are capitalised separately from (13), (14), (52)
goodwill if the fair value can be measured reliably on initial recognition, subject to the
constraint that, unless the asset has a readily ascertainable market value, the fair value
is limited to an amount that does not create or increase any negative goodwill arising
on the acquisition. Intangible assets, excluding development costs, created within the
business are not capitalised and expenditure is charged against profits in the year in
which it is incurred.

Intangible assets are amortised on a straight line basis over their estimated useful lives FRS 10(15), (28),
up to a maximum of 20 years. The carrying value of intangible assets is reviewed for (34), (55)
impairment at the end of the first full year following acquisition and in other periods if
events or changes in circumstances indicate the carrying value may not be recoverable.

Good Group P.L.C.

NOTES TO THE ACCOUNTS
at 30 June 1999

1.   ACCOUNTING POLICIES (continued)

Investment properties
Certain of the group's properties are held for long-term investment. Investment
properties are accounted for in accordance with SSAP 19, as follows:

(i)   investment properties are revalued annually.   The surplus or deficit on   SSAP 19(11), (13)
        revaluation is transferred to the revaluation reserve unless a deficit below
        original cost, or its reversal, on an individual investment property is expected to
        be permanent, in which case it is recognised in the profit and loss account for
        the year; and

(ii)   no depreciation is provided in respect of leasehold investment properties where   SSAP 19(10)
        the lease has over 20 years to run.

Although the Companies Act would normally require the systematic annual   s226(5)
depreciation of fixed assets, the directors believe that the policy of not providing   s227(6)
depreciation is necessary in order for the accounts to give a true and fair view, since the   UITF 7(4)-(7)
current value of investment properties, and changes to that current value, are of prime
importance rather than a calculation of systematic annual depreciation. Depreciation is
only one of the many factors reflected in the annual valuation, and the amount which
might otherwise have been included cannot be separately identified or quantified.

Depreciation
Depreciation is provided on all tangible fixed assets, other than leasehold investment   FRS 15(100)
properties where the lease has 20 years or more to run, at rates calculated to write off
the cost or valuation, less estimated residual value based on prices prevailing at the
date of acquisition or revaluation, of each asset evenly over its expected useful life as
follows:

Leasehold land and buildings   —   over the shorter of the lease term and 20 years
Plant and machinery   —   over 5 to 15 years

The carrying values of tangible fixed assets are reviewed for impairment in periods if   FRS 11(8)
events or changes in circumstances indicate the carrying value may not be recoverable.

Government grants
Government grants in respect of capital expenditure are credited to a deferred income   SSAP 4(23)-(25),
account and are released to profit over the expected useful lives of the relevant assets   (28)
by equal annual instalments. Grants of a revenue nature are credited to income so as to
match them with the expenditure to which they relate.

Stocks
Stocks are stated at the lower of cost and net realisable value. Cost includes all costs   SSAP 9(26), (32)
incurred in bringing each product to its present location and condition, as follows:

Raw materials, consumables and goods for resale   —   purchase cost on a first-in,
                                                          first-out basis.
Work in progress and finished goods   —   cost of direct materials and
                                                          labour plus attributable
                                                          overheads based on
                                                          a normal level of activity.

Net realisable value is based on estimated selling price less any further costs expected
to be incurred to completion and disposal.

Good Group P.L.C.

NOTES TO THE ACCOUNTS
at 30 June 1999

1.   ACCOUNTING POLICIES (continued)

Research and development
Research and development expenditure is written off as incurred, except that   4 Sch 20(2)
development expenditure incurred on an individual project is carried forward when its   SSAP13(30)
future recoverability can reasonably be regarded as assured. Any expenditure carried
forward is amortised in line with the expected future sales from the related project.

Provisions for maintenance warranties
Provisions for the expected costs of maintenance under guarantees are charged against
profits when products have been invoiced. The effect of the time value of money is not
material and therefore the provisions are not discounted.

Deferred taxation
Deferred taxation is provided using the liability method on all timing differences,   SSAP 15(24)-(32)
including those relating to pensions and other post-retirement benefits, to the extent
that they are expected to reverse in the future without being replaced, calculated at the
rate at which it is anticipated the timing differences will reverse. Advance corporation
tax which is expected to be recoverable in the future is deducted from the deferred
taxation balance.

Deferred taxation assets are only recognised if recovery without replacement by
equivalent debit balances is reasonably certain.

Good Group P.L.C.

NOTES TO THE ACCOUNTS
at 30 June 1999

1.   **ACCOUNTING POLICIES** (continued)

Foreign currencies

Company

Transactions in foreign currencies are recorded at the rate ruling at the date of the transaction or at the contracted rate if the transaction is covered by a forward foreign currency contract.   Monetary assets and liabilities denominated in foreign currencies are retranslated at the rate of exchange ruling at the balance sheet date or if appropriate at the forward contract rate.   All differences are taken to the profit and loss account with the exception of differences on foreign currency borrowings, to the extent that they are used to finance or provide a hedge against foreign equity investments, which are taken directly to reserves together with the exchange difference on the carrying amount of the related investments.   Tax charges and credits attributable to exchange differences on those borrowings are also dealt with in reserves.

4 Sch 58(1)
SSAP 20(46)-(51), (59)

Group

The accounts of overseas subsidiary undertakings are translated at the rate of exchange ruling at the balance sheet date.   The exchange difference arising on the retranslation of opening net assets is taken directly to reserves.   All other translation differences are taken to the profit and loss account with the exception of differences on foreign currency borrowings to the extent that they are used to finance or provide a hedge against group equity investments in foreign enterprises, which are taken directly to reserves together with the exchange difference on the net investment in these enterprises.   Tax charges and credits attributable to exchange differences on those borrowings are also dealt with in reserves.

4 Sch 58(1)
SSAP 20(52)-(59)

Good Group P.L.C.

NOTES TO THE ACCOUNTS
at 30 June 1999

1. ACCOUNTING POLICIES (continued)

Derivative instruments

The group uses forward foreign currency contracts to reduce exposure to foreign exchange rates. The group also uses interest rate swaps to adjust interest rate exposures. FRS 13(74)-(76)

The group considers its derivative instruments qualify for hedge accounting when certain criteria are met.

Forward foreign currency contracts

The criteria for forward foreign currency contracts are:

- the instrument must be related to a foreign currency asset or liability that is probable and whose characteristics have been identified;

- it must involve the same currency as the hedged item; and

- it must reduce the risk of foreign currency exchange movements on the group's operations.

The rates under such contracts are used to record the hedged item. As a result, gains and losses are offset against the foreign exchange gains and losses on the related financial assets and liabilities, or where the instrument is used to hedge a committed, or probable, future transaction, are deferred until the transaction occurs.

Interest rate swaps

The group's criteria for interest rate swaps are:

- the instrument must be related to an asset or a liability; and

- it must change the character of the interest rate by converting a variable rate to a fixed rate or vice versa.

Interest differentials are recognised by accruing with net interest payable. Interest rate swaps are not revalued to fair value or shown on the group balance sheet at the year end. If they are terminated early, the gain/ loss is spread over the remaining maturity of the original instrument.

Good Group P.L.C.
NOTES TO THE ACCOUNTS
at 30 June 1999

1.   ACCOUNTING POLICIES (continued)

Leasing and hire purchase commitments   SSAP 21(32)-(36), (57)
Assets held under finance leases, which are leases where substantially all the risks and
rewards of ownership of the asset have passed to the group, and hire purchase contracts
are capitalised in the balance sheet and are depreciated over their useful lives. The
capital elements of future obligations under leases and hire purchase contracts are
included as liabilities in the balance sheet. The interest elements of the rental
obligations are charged in the profit and loss account over the periods of the leases and
hire purchase contracts and represent a constant proportion of the balance of capital
repayments outstanding.

Rentals payable under operating leases are charged in the profit and loss account on a   SSAP 21(37)
straight line basis over the lease term.

Pensions
The group operates two defined benefit pension schemes, both of which require   SSAP 24(79), (80),
contributions to be made to separately administered funds. Contributions to these   (86), (88)
funds are charged in the profit and loss account so as to spread the cost of pensions
over the employees' working lives within the group. The regular cost is attributed to
individual years using the projected unit credit method. Variations in pension cost,
which are identified as a result of actuarial valuations, are amortised over the average
expected remaining working lives of employees in proportion to their expected payroll
costs. Differences between the amounts funded and the amounts charged in the profit
and loss account are treated as either provisions or prepayments in the balance sheet.

Post-retirement benefits other than pensions
The group has agreed to provide certain additional post-retirement benefits to senior   UITF 6(5)-(11)
employees in the United States. The estimated cost of providing such benefits is
charged against profits on a systematic basis over the employees' working lives within
the group.

Capital instruments
Shares are included in shareholders' funds. Other instruments are classified as   FRS 4(24), (28),
liabilities if they contain an obligation to transfer economic benefits and if not they are   (37), (42)
included in shareholders' funds. The finance cost recognised in the profit and loss
account in respect of capital instruments other than equity shares is allocated to periods
over the term of the instrument at a constant rate on the carrying amount.

2.   TURNOVER AND SEGMENTAL ANALYSIS
Turnover represents the amounts derived from the provision of goods and services   s262(1)
which fall within the group's ordinary activities, stated net of value added tax.   SSAP 5(8)

The group operates in two principal areas of activity, that of electronics and the   SSAP 25(34)
manufacture and installation of fire-prevention equipment. It also operates within two
geographical markets, the United Kingdom and the United States.

The discontinued operations comprise Hose Limited, the subsidiary that manufactured
rubber hosepipes.

The results of Extinguishers Limited, which was acquired on 1 October 1998, all relate   FRS 3(15)
to fire-prevention activity. Its turnover, both by source and destination, all relates to   FRS 6(28)
the United Kingdom.

Turnover, group profit on ordinary activities before tax and net assets are analysed as
follows:

Good Group P.L.C.

NOTES TO THE ACCOUNTS
at 30 June 1999

2. **TURNOVER AND SEGMENTAL ANALYSIS** (continued)

Area of activity

	Electronics 1999 £000	Electronics 1998 £000	Fire-prevention equipment 1999 £000	Fire-prevention equipment 1998 £000	Total 1999 £000	Total 1998 £000	
GROUP TURNOVER							SSAP 25(34)-(38)
Continuing operations:							
Total sales	66,325	61,595	111,504	76,077	177,829	137,672	
Inter-segment sales	(7,175)	(4,300)	–	–	(7,175)	(4,300)	
Sales to third parties	59,150	57,295	111,504	76,077	170,654	133,372	FRS 3(15)
Discontinued operations:							
Sales to third parties	–	–	42,196	46,628	42,196	46,628	FRS 3(15)
	59,150	57,295	153,700	122,705	212,850	180,000	4 Sch 55(1)
Turnover of Extinguishers Limited included in the above	–	–	21,979	–	21,979	–	FRS 3(15) FRS 6(28)
PROFIT							
Segment profit:							
Continuing operations	4,529	4,394	8,194	6,456	12,723	10,850	FRS 3(15)
Discontinued operations	–	–	(563)	(520)	(563)	(520)	FRS 3(15)
	4,529	4,394	7,631	5,936	12,160	10,330	
Common costs					(2,108)	(1,435)	
Group operating profit					10,052	8,895	
Share of operating profit of joint venture and associate and amortisation of associate goodwill					2,790	1,262	FRS 9(21), (27)
Non-operating exceptional items					(1,537)	(850)	
Net interest and income from investments					64	(446)	
Profit on ordinary activities before taxation					11,369	8,861	
Operating profit of Extinguishers Limited included in the above	–	–	1,238	–	1,238	–	FRS 3(15) FRS 6(28)

Good Group P.L.C.

NOTES TO THE ACCOUNTS
at 30 June 1999

2.   TURNOVER AND SEGMENTAL ANALYSIS (continued)
Area of activity

	Electronics		Fire-prevention equipment		Total		
	1999	*1998*	*1999*	*1998*	*1999*	*1998*	
	£000	*£000*	*£000*	*£000*	*£000*	*£000*	SSAP 25(34)-(38)
NET ASSETS							
Net assets by segment:							
Continuing operations	16,416	10,874	31,676	15,136	48,092	26,010	
Discontinued operations	–	–	–	8,872	–	8,872	
	16,416	10,874	31,676	24,008	48,092	34,882	
Unallocated net assets					6,192	5,496	
					54,284	40,378	
Share of net assets of joint venture and associate					3,092	2,155	FRS 9(21), (27)
					57,376	42,533	
Minority interest					(626)	(345)	
Total net assets					56,750	42,188	
Net assets of Extinguishers Limited included in the above	–	–	10,098	–	8,648	–	FRS 3(15) FRS 6(28)

Unallocated net assets comprise certain fixed assets, loan notes, net debt, taxation and   SSAP 25(37)
dividends.

Good Group P.L.C.
NOTES TO THE ACCOUNTS
at 30 June 1999

2. TURNOVER AND SEGMENTAL ANALYSIS (continued)

Geographical area

	United Kingdom		United States		Total		
	1999	*1998*	*1999*	*1998*	*1999*	*1998*	
	£000	*£000*	*£000*	*£000*	*£000*	*£000*	SSAP 25(34)-(38)
TURNOVER							
Turnover by destination:							
Sales to third parties							
Continuing	129,835	96,672	40,819	36,700	170,654	133,372	
Discontinued	42,196	46,628	–	–	42,196	46,628	
	172,031	143,300	40,819	36,700	212,850	180,000	4 Sch 55(2)
Turnover by origin:							
Continuing operations:							
Total sales	120,777	85,557	62,567	62,440	183,344	147,997	
Inter-segment sales	(8,235)	(11,385)	(4,455)	(3,240)	(12,690)	(14,625)	
Sales to third parties	112,542	74,172	58,112	59,200	170,654	133,372	
Discontinued operations	42,196	46,628	–	–	42,196	46,628	
	154,738	120,800	58,112	59,200	212,850	180,000	
Turnover of Extinguishers Limited included in the above	21,979	–	–	–	21,979	–	
PROFIT							
Segment profit:							
Continuing operations	9,460	7,438	3,008	3,137	12,468	10,645	
Discontinued operations	(563)	(520)	–	–	(563)	(520)	
	8,897	6,918	3,008	3,137	11,905	10,125	
Common costs						(1,853)	(1,230)	
Group operating profit					10,052	8,895	
Share of operating profit of joint venture and associate and amortisation of goodwill					2,790	1,262	FRS 9(21), (27)
Non-operating exceptional items					(1,537)	(850)	
Net interest and income from investments					64	(446)	
Profit on ordinary activities before taxation					11,369	8,861	
Operating profit of Extinguishers Limited included in the above	1,238	–	–	–	1,238	–	

Good Group P.L.C.

NOTES TO THE ACCOUNTS
at 30 June 1999

2.   TURNOVER AND SEGMENTAL ANALYSIS (continued)

Geographical area

	United Kingdom		United States		Total		
	1999	1998	1999	1998	1999	1998	
	£000	£000	£000	£000	£000	£000	SSAP 25(34)-(38)
NET ASSETS							
Net assets by segment:							
Continuing operations	40,918	23,331	17,883	12,199	58,801	35,530	
Discontinued operations	–	8,872	–	–	–	8,872	
	40,918	32,203	17,883	12,199	58,801	44,402	
Unallocated net liabilities					(4,517)	(4,024)	
					54,284	40,378	
Share of net assets of joint venture and associate					3,092	2,155	FRS 9(21), (27)
					57,376	42,533	
Minority interest					(626)	(345)	
Total net assets					56,750	42,188	
Net assets of Extinguishers Limited included in the above	8,648	–	–	–	8,648	–	

Unallocated net liabilities comprise certain fixed assets, loan notes, net debt, taxation and dividends.   SSAP 25(37)

Segmental analysis of joint venture and associate

	Electronics		Fire-prevention equipment		Total		
	1999	1998	1999	1998	1999	1998	
	£000	£000	£000	£000	£000	£000	SSAP 25(36) FRS 9(21), (27)
Turnover	8,500	7,235	30,438	23,145	38,938	30,380	
Profit before tax, including goodwill amortisation	345	240	2,335	1,074	2,680	1,314	
Net assets	1,257	1,177	1,835	978	3,092	2,155	

The group's joint venture and associate operate in the United Kingdom.

Good Group P.L.C.

NOTES TO THE ACCOUNTS
at 30 June 1999

3. COST OF SALES AND OPERATING EXPENSES

	Contin-uing £000	*Discon-tinued* £000	*Total* £000	*Contin-uing* £000	*Discon-tinued* £000	*Total* £000	
			1999			*1998*	
Cost of sales	131,391	38,146	169,537	105,051	39,449	144,500	FRS 3(14)
Distribution costs	14,449	2,387	16,836	10,134	4,196	14,330	
Administrative expenses	14,232	2,226	16,458	9,422	3,503	12,925	
Other operating income	688	–	688	650	–	650	
Bid defence costs	655	–	655	–	–	–	

The total figures for continuing operations in 1998/99 include the following amounts relating to the acquisition of Extinguishers Limited: cost of sales £17,978,000; distribution costs £1,415,000; administrative expenses £1,396,000 and other operating income £48,000.   FRS 6(28)

Good Group P.L.C.

NOTES TO THE ACCOUNTS
at 30 June 1999

4.   OPERATING PROFIT

This is stated after charging/(crediting):

	1999 £000	1998 £000	
Auditors' remuneration – audit services *	467	385	s390A
– non-audit services - UK	92	59	s390B SI 91/2128 s390A

* £147,000 (1997 - £121,000) of this relates to the company.

	1999	1998	
Research and development expenditure written off	2,140	910	SSAP 13(31)
Amortisation of deferred development expenditure	125	40	4 Sch Formats SSAP 13(31)
Total research and development	2,265	950	SSAP 13(31)
Depreciation of owned assets	3,127	2,347	4 Sch Formats
Depreciation of assets held under finance leases and hire purchase contracts	263	263	4 Sch Formats SSAP 21 (49), (50)
Total depreciation charge	3,390	2,610	4 Sch 42 FRS 15(100)
Amortisation of patents	50	10	
Amortisation of goodwill	75	25	4 Sch Formats
Provision for maintenance warranties	200	50	
Operating lease rentals – land and buildings	55	50	SSAP 21(55)
– plant and machinery	192	130	SSAP 21(55)
Government grants	(1,012)	(530)	SSAP 4(28)

Good Group P.L.C.

NOTES TO THE ACCOUNTS
at 30 June 1999

5. **EXCEPTIONAL ITEMS**

	1999	*1999*	*1998*	
	£000	*£000*	*£000*	FRS 3(19), (20)
				4 Sch 57(3)
Recognised in arriving at operating profit:				
Professional expenses incurred in respect of bid defence		655	–	
Recognised below operating profit:				
Profit on disposal of land and buildings	(863)		(110)	
(Profit)/loss on disposal of plant and machinery	(387)		960	
	(1,250)		850	
Loss on disposal of fixed asset investments	350		–	
	(900)		850	
Loss on sale of operations (including goodwill of £400,000)	2,437		–	FRS 2(47)
				FRS 10(71)
		1,537	850	
		2,192	850	
Minority interests' share of profit on disposal of plant and machinery		(32)	–	FRS 3(20)

The effect on the taxation charge for the year of the exceptional items recognised below FRS 3(20)
operating profit is disclosed in note 8.

Good Group P.L.C.

NOTES TO THE ACCOUNTS
at 30 June 1999

6.   STAFF COSTS

	1999 £000	1998 £000	
			4 Sch 56
Wages and salaries	8,376	7,188	
Social security costs	821	702	
Other pension costs (note 29)	1,290	1,093	
Post retirement benefits other than pensions (note 30)	20	19	UITF 6(9)
	10,507	9,002	

Other pension costs include £200,000 (1998 – £175,000) arising from variations in SSAP 24(88) pension cost which were identified by the most recent actuarial valuation. These are being written off over 11 years, the average remaining service lives of employees.

The average monthly number of employees during the year was made up as follows:

	1999 No.	1998 No.	
			4 Sch 56
Electronics	156	146	
Manufacturing and installation of fire-prevention equipment	359	323	
Research and development	60	32	
Administration	43	38	
	618	539	

Details, for each director, of remuneration, compensation for loss of office, pension APB Bulletin entitlements and interests in share options are set out on pages 2024 to 2027. 1997/2

7.   INTEREST PAYABLE AND SIMILAR CHARGES

	1999 £000	1998 £000	
Bank loans and overdrafts	643	559	4 Sch 53(2)
Other loans	411	365	4 Sch 53(2)
Finance charges payable under finance leases and hire purchase contracts	40	35	SSAP 21(53)
Group interest payable and similar charges	1,094	959	
Share of joint venture's interest	100	67	FRS 9(21)
Share of associate's interest	10	15	FRS 9(27)
			4A Sch 21
	1,204	1,041	

Good Group P.L.C.
NOTES TO THE ACCOUNTS
at 30 June 1999

8.   TAX ON PROFIT ON ORDINARY ACTIVITIES

The taxation charge is made up as follows:

	1999	*1998*	4 Sch 54
	£000	*£000*	SSAP 8(22), (23)
Corporation tax	3,089	2,234	
Tax credits attributable to dividends received	50	40	
Deferred taxation (note 21)	(340)	100	SSAP 15(33), (38)
	2,799	2,374	
Double taxation relief	(1,075)	(935)	
	1,724	1,439	
Overseas taxation	1,075	980	
	2,799	2,419	
Corporation tax overprovided in previous years	(55)	(170)	4 Sch 57
	2,744	2,249	
Share of joint venture's tax	778	385	FRS 9(21)
Share of associate's tax	130	115	FRS 9(27)
	3,652	2,749	

The effective tax rate for the current year is higher than standard as a result of   4 Sch 54(2)
disallowable entertaining expenditure. The tax year effect in the profit and loss   FRS 3(20), (23)
account relating to the exceptional items recognised below operating profit is a credit
of £623,000 (1998 – £216,000 credit).

If full provision had been made for deferred tax for the year, the tax charge would have
been increased by £419,000 (1998 – £147,000), as follows:

	1999	*1998*	
	£000	*£000*	SSAP 15(35)
Capital allowances in advance of depreciation	385	91	
Other timing differences	34	56	
	419	147	

9.   PROFIT ATTRIBUTABLE TO MEMBERS OF THE PARENT COMPANY

The profit dealt with in the accounts of the parent company was £5,383,000   s230(1)(b)
(1998 – £4,285,000).

Good Group P.L.C.

NOTES TO THE ACCOUNTS
at 30 June 1999

10.   DIVIDENDS AND OTHER APPROPRIATIONS

	1999 £000	1998 £000	
Dividends:			4 Sch 3(7)
Equity dividends on ordinary shares*:			
interim paid 6.56p (1997 – 6.55p)	798	633	
final proposed 8.67p (1997 – 6.55p)	1,061	633	
	1,859	1,266	FRS 4(59)
Non-equity dividends on preference shares:			
31 December paid	88	88	
30 June paid	87	87	
	175	175	
	2,034	1,441	FRS 4(59)
Other appropriations:			
Non-equity:			
Amortisation of redemption premium and issue costs			
on preference shares	81	74	FRS 4(59)

* Good Group Employee Share Trust has waived the dividends payable on the 335,000 (1997 – 335,000) shares that it owns. See note 14 for further details about the shares. The trust has agreed to waive future dividends on these shares, which are under option to employees exercisable between 1 January 2000 and 31 December 2002.   UITF 13(9)   YB 12.43(e)

Good Group P.L.C.

NOTES TO THE ACCOUNTS
at 30 June 1999

11. EARNINGS PER ORDINARY SHARE

The calculation of basic earnings per ordinary share is based on earnings of £7,150,000   FRS 14(9), (71)
(1998 – £5,808,000), being profit for the year of £7,406,000 (1998 – £6,057,000) less
preference dividends and other appropriations in respect of preference shares of
£256,000 (1998 – £249,000), and on 11,552,000 (1998 – 9,665,000) ordinary shares,
being the weighted average number of ordinary shares in issue during the year after
excluding the shares owned by the Good Group Employee Share Trust.

The diluted earnings per share is based on profit for the year of £7,406,000 (1998 –   FRS 14(27), (71)
£6,057,000), and on 12,395,000 (1998 – 10,519,000) ordinary shares, calculated as
follows:

	1999 *thousands*	1998 *thousands*
Basic weighted average number of shares	11,552	9,665
Dilutive potential ordinary shares:		
Employee share options	10	21
Convertible preference shares	833	833
	12,395	10,519

Good Group P.L.C.

NOTES TO THE ACCOUNTS
at 30 June 1999

12. INTANGIBLE FIXED ASSETS

	Development expenditure £000	Patents £000	Goodwill £000	Total £000	
					4 Sch Formats
					4 Sch 42
					FRS 10(53)
Cost:					SSAP 13(32)
At 1 July 1998	1,010	500	250	1,760	
Increase during the year	575	–	–	575	
Acquisition of subsidiary undertaking	–	–	1,500	1,500	
At 30 June 1999	1,585	500	1,750	3,835	
Amortisation:					
At 1 July 1998	40	10	25	75	
Provided during the year	125	50	75	250	
At 30 June 1999	165	60	100	325	
Net book value at 30 June 1999	1,420	440	1,650	3,510	
Net book value at 1 July 1998	970	490	225	1,685	

Goodwill is being amortised as follows:

4 Sch 21(4)
FRS 10(55)

■   Goodwill arising on the acquisition of Bright Sparks Limited is being amortised evenly over the directors' estimate of its useful economic life of 10 years.

■   Goodwill arising on the acquisition of Extinguishers Limited is being amortised evenly over its presumed useful economic life of 20 years.

4 Sch 21(4)
FRS 10(55)

Patents are being amortised evenly over their useful economic life of 10 years.

Good Group P.L.C.

NOTES TO THE ACCOUNTS
at 30 June 1999

13.   TANGIBLE FIXED ASSETS

Group	*Land and buildings £000*	*Plant and machinery £000*	*Total £000*	
				4 Sch Formats
				4 Sch 42
Cost or valuation:				FRS 15(100)
At 1 July 1998	20,405	19,850	40,255	
Exchange adjustment	50	775	825	
Additions	2,723	10,092	12,815	
Acquisition of subsidiary undertaking	2,897	4,145	7,042	
Deficit on revaluation	(350)	–	(350)	
Disposals	(3,625)	(7,250)	(10,875)	
Disposal of subsidiary undertaking	(3,108)	(2,701)	(5,809)	
At 30 June 1999	18,992	24,911	43,903	
Depreciation:				
At 1 July 1998	1,675	8,525	10,200	
Exchange adjustment	–	550	550	
Provided during the year	425	2,965	3,390	
Disposals	(600)	(2,700)	(3,300)	
Disposal of subsidiary undertaking	(521)	(217)	(738)	
At 30 June 1999	979	9,123	10,102	
Net book value at 30 June 1999	18,013	15,788	33,801	
Net book value at 1 July 1998	18,730	11,325	30,055	
Company				
Cost or valuation:				
At 1 July 1998	8,754	9,450	18,204	
Additions	2,275	3,475	5,750	
Deficit on revaluation	(154)	–	(154)	
Disposals	(625)	(4,000)	(4,625)	
At 30 June 1999	10,250	8,925	19,175	
Depreciation:				
At 1 July 1998	950	2,750	3,700	
Provided during the year	250	1,035	1,285	
Disposals	–	(2,250)	(2,250)	
At 30 June 1999	1,200	1,535	2,735	
Net book value at 30 June 1999	9,050	7,390	16,440	
Net book value at 1 July 1998	7,804	6,700	14,504	

Good Group P.L.C.

NOTES TO THE ACCOUNTS
at 30 June 1999

13.   TANGIBLE FIXED ASSETS (continued)

The net book value of land and buildings comprises:

	Group		Company		
	1999	*1998*	*1999*	*1998*	
	£000	*£000*	*£000*	*£000*	4 Sch 44
Investment properties at valuation:					
Long leasehold	7,163	7,003	4,184	3,900	SSAP 19(15)
Other properties at cost:					
Long leasehold	6,841	6,198	3,952	2,902	
Short leasehold	4,009	5,529	914	1,002	
	18,013	18,730	9,050	7,804	

The long leasehold investment properties were valued by Chartered Surveyors & Co., 4 Sch 33, 43
as at 30 June 1999, on the basis of open market value in accordance with the Appraisal SSAP 19(12)
and Valuation Manual of The Royal Institution of Chartered Surveyors. The historical
cost of investment properties included at valuation is as follows:

	Group *£000*	Company *£000*
At 30 June 1999	2,124	1,419
At 1 July 1998	1,379	746

Included in the amounts for plant and machinery above are the following amounts SSAP 21(49), (50)
relating to leased assets and assets acquired under hire purchase contracts:

	Group and Company *£000*
Cost:	
At 1 July 1998 and 30 June 1999	2,102
Depreciation:	
At 1 July 1998	1,051
Depreciation provided during the year	263
At 30 June 1999	1,314
Net book value:	
At 30 June 1999	788
At 1 July 1998	1,051

Good Group P.L.C.

NOTES TO THE ACCOUNTS
at 30 June 1999

14.   INVESTMENTS

Group	1999 £000	1998 £000	
Joint venture (a)	1,835	978	FRS 9(21)
Associate (b)	1,257	1,177	FRS 9(29)
Own shares (c)	774	774	UITF 13(8)
Other fixed asset investments (c)	1,266	1,276	
	5,132	4,205	

4 Sch 42
4A Sch 22

(a) *Joint venture*	£000
At 1 July 1998	978
Share of profit retained by joint venture	857
At 30 June 1999	1,835

Additional disclosures are given in respect of Showers Limited, which exceeds certain   FRS 9(58)
thresholds under Financial Reporting Standard No. 9 *Associates and Joint Ventures,* as
follows:

	1999 £000	1998 £000
Fixed assets	1,482	1,225
Current assets	1,404	210
Share of gross assets	2,886	1,435
Liabilities due within one year	551	57
Liabilities due after more than one year	500	400
Share of gross liabilities	1,051	457
Share of net assets	1,835	978

	1999 £000	1998 £000
Turnover	30,438	23,145
Profit before tax	2,335	940
Taxation	778	385
Profit after tax	1,557	555

Good Group P.L.C.

NOTES TO THE ACCOUNTS
at 30 June 1999

14.   INVESTMENTS (continued)

(b)   *Associate*

	Share of net tangible assets £000	Goodwill £000	Total £000	
At 1 July 1998	897	280	1,177	
Share of profit retained by associate	150	–	150	
Amortisation of goodwill	–	(70)	(70)	
At 30 June 1999	1,047	210	1,257	

Goodwill is being amortised over the directors' estimate of its useful economic life of six years.

4 Sch 42
4A Sch 22
FRS 9(29)

4 Sch 21(4)
FRS 9(31)
FRS 10(55)

Good Group P.L.C.

NOTES TO THE ACCOUNTS
at 30 June 1999

14.   **INVESTMENTS** (continued)

(c)   *Own shares and other fixed investments*

	Listed £000	Unlisted £000	Total £000	
Cost:				4 Sch Formats
At 1 July 1998	774	2,101	2,875	4 Sch 42
Additions	465	–	465	4 Sch 45
Disposals	–	(475)	(475)	
At 30 June 1999	1,239	1,626	2,865	
Amounts provided:				
At 1 July 1998 and 30 June 1999	–	825	825	
Net book value at 30 June 1999	1,239	801	2,040	
Net book value at 1 July 1998	774	1,276	2,050	

The market value of the listed investments at 30 June 1999 was £2,105,000 (1998 –   4 Sch 45
£1,307,000); if they had been sold at this value there would have been a liability to tax   SSAP 15(42)
of £260,000 (1998 – £160,000) on the capital gain arising from the sale. £1,484,000   UITF 13(9)
(1998 – £1,307,000) of the market value relates to own shares, being 335,000 shares
with a nominal value of £1 each, acquired at a cost of £2.31 each (1998 – 335,000
shares at £2.31 each) held by Good Group Employee Share Trust. Options over these
shares have been granted to senior employees, exercisable at £2.31 per share between
1 December 2000 and 30 December 2002. The options may not be exercised unless
the company's earnings per share has increased by 10% more than the increase in the
retail price index over the period from the date of grant of the options up to the date
they first become exercisable and dividends per share have similarly increased by at
least the same amount.

Dividends on the shares owned by the trust, the purchase of which was funded by an   UITF 13(9)
interest free loan to the trust from Good Group P.L.C., are waived. All expenses
incurred by the trust are settled directly by Good Group P.L.C. and charged in the
accounts as incurred.

Good Group P.L.C.

NOTES TO THE ACCOUNTS
at 30 June 1999

14.   INVESTMENTS (continued)

Company

	Subsidiary undertakings £000	*Joint ventures & associates* £000	*Own shares* £000	*Other investments* £000	*Total* £000	
Cost:						4 Sch 42
At 1 July 1998	6,420	675	774	2,101	9,970	
Exchange adjustment	200	–	–	–	200	
Additions	10,910	–	–	–	10,910	
Disposals	(2,670)	–	–	(475)	(3,145)	
At 30 June 1999	14,860	675	774	1,626	17,935	
Amounts provided:						
At 1 July 1998 and 30 June 1999	–	–	–	825	825	
Net book value at 30 June 1999	14,860	675	774	801	17,110	
Net book value at 1 July 1998	6,420	675	774	1,276	9,145	

The market value of the investment in the company's own shares at 30 June 1999 was £1,484,000 (1998 – £1,307,000); if they had been sold at this value there would have been a liability to tax of £213,000 (1998 – £150,000) on the capital gain arising from the sale. The shares are held by Good Group Employee Share Trust. See above for details.   4 Sch 45   SSAP 15(42)   UITF 13(9)

No other investments are listed.

Good Group P.L.C.

NOTES TO THE ACCOUNTS
at 30 June 1999

14. INVESTMENTS (continued)

Details of the investments in which the group and the company (unless indicated) holds 20% or more of the nominal value of any class of share capital are as follows:

Name of company	Holding	Proportion of voting rights and shares held	Nature of business	5 Sch 15, 16, 22 FRS 2(33)
Subsidiary undertakings				
Extinguishers Limited	Ordinary shares	100%	Fire-prevention equipment	
Bright Sparks Limited	Ordinary shares	85%	Electronics	
	Preferred shares	45%*		
Wireworks Incorporated †	Common stock	90%	Electronics	
Sprinklers Incorporated †	Common stock	100%	Fire-prevention equipment	
Lightbulbs Limited	Ordinary shares	100%	Dormant	

* Held by a subsidiary undertaking.
† Incorporated in the United States.

Joint venture				
Showers Limited	Ordinary shares	50%	Fire-prevention equipment	FRS 9(52)

All held by the company unless indicated.

Associate				
Power Works Limited	Ordinary shares	25%†	Electronics	FRS 9(52)

† 7% held by a subsidiary undertaking.

Good Group P.L.C.

NOTES TO THE ACCOUNTS
at 30 June 1999

14.   INVESTMENTS (continued)

On 1 October 1998 the group acquired Extinguishers Limited for a consideration of £8,750,000 satisfied by the issue of 2,500,000 ordinary shares of £1 at £3.50 each. Goodwill arising on the acquisition of Extinguishers Limited has been set off against other reserves. The investment in Extinguishers Limited has been included in the company's balance sheet at its fair value at the date of acquisition. *FRS 6(21), (24) 4A Sch 13(2)*

Analysis of the acquisition of Extinguishers Limited:

Net assets at date of acquisition:

	Book value £000	Adjustments Revaluation £000	Other £000	Fair value to group £000	
Tangible fixed assets	5,684	1,358 (a)	–	7,042	*4A Sch 13(5)*
Stocks	3,804	540 (b)	–	4,344	*FRS 6(25)*
Debtors	2,170	(434)(c)	–	1,736	
Cash	230	–	–	230	
Creditors due within one year	(5,077)	–	–	(5,077)	
Provisions for maintenance warranties	(300)	(100)(d)	–	(400)	
Deferred taxation	(167)	–	42(e)	(125)	
Net assets	6,344	1,364	42	7,750	
Goodwill arising on acquisition				1,500	
				9,250	

Discharged by:		
Fair value of shares issued (note 23)	8,750	
Costs associated with the acquisition	500	
	9,250	*4A Sch 13(3)*
		FRS 6(24)
		4A Sch 13(3)

Adjustments: *4A Sch 13(5)* *FRS 6(25)*

(a)   Increase in value of long leasehold properties since last revaluation in 1989 and increase in value of plant and machinery to its depreciated replacement cost.

(b)   Increase in value of stock to its current cost.

(c)   Write-down of debtors following reassessment of realisable value of aged debtors listing.

(d)   Reassessment of the provision for maintenance warranties on Extinguishers Limited's products.

(e)   Adjustment to provision for deferred tax.

Good Group P.L.C.

NOTES TO THE ACCOUNTS
at 30 June 1999

14.   INVESTMENTS (continued)

Extinguishers Limited contributed £265,000 to the group's net operating cash flows,   FRS 1(45)
paid £85,000 in respect of net returns on investments and servicing of finance, paid   FRS 6(34)
£180,000 in respect of taxation and utilised £225,000 for capital expenditure and
financial investment.

Extinguishers Limited earned a profit after tax of £1,128,000 in the year ended   4A Sch 13(4)
30 June 1999 (1998 - £974,000), of which £230,000 arose in the period from   FRS 6(35), (36)
1 July 1998 to 1 October 1998. The summarised profit and loss account for the period
from 1 July 1998 to the effective date of acquisition is as follows:

	£000
Turnover	7,258
Operating profit	398
Loss on fixed asset disposals	(61)
Profit before tax	337
Taxation	(107)
Profit for the three months ended 30 September 1998	230

There were no recognised gains or losses in the three months ended   FRS 6(36)
30 September 1998 other than the profit of £230,000 above.

Good Group P.L.C.

NOTES TO THE ACCOUNTS
at 30 June 1999

14.   INVESTMENTS (continued)

On 30 May 1999, the group completed the sale of Hose Limited. The disposal is   4A Sch 15
analysed as follows: FRS 2(46)-(48)

	£000	
Net assets disposed of:		
Fixed assets	5,071	
Stocks	3,315	
Debtors	1,916	
Bank overdraft	(2,117)	
Other creditors	(2,093)	
Goodwill	400	
	6,492	
Loss on disposal (including goodwill of £400,000)	(2,437)	FRS 10(54), (71)
	4,055	
Satisfied by:		
Loan notes	4,000	
Cash	55	FRS 1(45)
	4,055	

The profit attributable to members of the parent company includes losses of £538,000   4A Sch 15
incurred by Hose Limited up to its date of disposal on 30 May 1999.

During the year, Hose Limited utilised £385,000 of the group's net operating cash   FRS 1(45)
flows, paid £96,000 in respect of net returns on investments and servicing of finance,
paid £176,000 in respect of taxation and utilised £487,000 for capital expenditure and
financial investment.

Good Group P.L.C.

NOTES TO THE ACCOUNTS
at 30 June 1999

15. STOCKS

	Group 1999 £000	Group 1998 £000	Company 1999 £000	Company 1998 £000	
					4 Sch Formats
					SSAP 9(27)
Raw materials and consumables	7,565	6,375	3,155	2,300	
Work in progress	10,840	8,425	4,715	3,125	
Finished goods and goods for resale	7,720	5,300	3,700	1,700	
	26,125	20,100	11,570	7,125	

The difference between purchase price or production cost of stocks and their replacement cost is not material.   4 Sch 27(3)

16. DEBTORS

	Group 1999 £000	Group 1998 £000	Company 1999 £000	Company 1998 £000	
					4 Sch Formats
Loan notes	4,000	–	4,000	–	
Trade debtors	14,260	10,452	4,085	3,100	
Amounts owed by group undertakings	–	–	6,900	6,350	
Amounts owed by associate	230	145	–	–	FRS 9(55)
Other debtors	1,159	930	33	1,507	
Prepayments and accrued income	554	430	370	345	
	20,203	11,957	15,388	11,302	

Included within prepayments and accrued income for the group is £370,000 (1998 – £320,000) in respect of pension contribution payments made in advance of their recognition in the profit and loss account (company – £315,000 (1998 – £275,000)).   SSAP 24(88)

Amounts falling due after more than one year included above are: 4 Sch Formats (Note 5)

	Group 1999 £000	Group 1998 £000	Company 1999 £000	Company 1998 £000
Loan notes	2,000	–	2,000	–
Amounts owed by group undertakings	–	–	6,900	6,350
Included in other debtors:				
Advance corporation tax recoverable	–	–	–	55
Other	1,000	855	–	–
Included in prepayments and accrued income:				
Pension prepayments	370	320	315	275
	3,370	1,175	9,215	6,680

Good Group P.L.C.

NOTES TO THE ACCOUNTS
at 30 June 1999

17. CREDITORS: amounts falling due within one year

	Group		Company		
	1999	1998	1999	1998	
	£000	£000	£000	£000	4 Sch Formats
Current instalments due on loans	1,485	480	1,485	480	
Bank overdraft	760	3,770	–	–	
Obligations under finance leases and hire purchase contracts	179	370	179	370	SSAP 21(51)
Trade creditors	15,660	13,843	5,169	2,906	
Amounts owed to joint venture	30	12	–	–	FRS 9(55)
Corporation tax	2,899	2,280	1,495	1,280	4 Sch Formats
Advance corporation tax	–	180	–	180	(Note 9)
Other taxes and social security costs	150	420	60	95	4 Sch Formats
Other creditors	2,510	3,275	2,335	2,840	(Note 9)
Proposed dividend	1,061	633	1,061	633	4 Sch 51(3)
	24,734	25,263	11,784	8,784	

The bank overdraft is secured by a floating charge over certain of the group's assets.

4 Sch 48(4)

18. CREDITORS: amounts falling due after more than one year

	Group		Company		
	1999	1998	1999	1998	
	£000	£000	£000	£000	4 Sch Formats
Loans	11,697	8,420	9,197	8,420	
Obligations under finance leases and hire purchase contracts	866	1,045	866	1,045	SSAP 21(51)
	12,563	9,465	10,063	9,465	

Good Group P.L.C.

NOTES TO THE ACCOUNTS
at 30 June 1999

19. LOANS

	Group 1999	Group 1998	Company 1999	Company 1998	
	£000	£000	£000	£000	FRS 4(33)
Amounts falling due:					
In one year or less or on demand	1,500	500	1,500	500	
In more than one year but not more than two years	1,500	1,500	1,500	1,500	
In more than two years but not more than five years	2,350	3,400	2,350	3,400	
In more than five years	7,955	3,600	5,455	3,600	
	13,305	9,000	10,805	9,000	
Less: issue costs	123	100	123	100	
	13,182	8,900	10,682	8,900	
Less: included in creditors: amounts falling due within one year	1,485	480	1,485	480	
	11,697	8,420	9,197	8,420	

Good Group P.L.C.

NOTES TO THE ACCOUNTS
at 30 June 1999

19.   LOANS (continued)

Details of loans not wholly repayable within five years are as follows: 4 Sch 48

	Group		*Company*	
	1999	*1998*	*1999*	*1998*
	£000	*£000*	*£000*	*£000*
8.25% secured loan of US$3,600,000 repayable on 30 November 2004	2,305	–	2,305	–
Secured loan repayable on 31 January 2005*	2,500	–	–	–
	4,805	–	2,305	–
8% debentures repayable in annual instalments of £450,000 commencing 1 July 2001	4,500	4,500	4,500	4,500
	9,305	4,500	6,805	4,500
Less issue costs	96	53	96	53
	9,209	4,447	6,709	4,447

*   This loan has been drawn down under a six year multi-option facility (MOF).   FRS 4(36)
    The loan is repayable within twelve months of the balance sheet date, but has
    been classified as long-term because under the MOF immediate replacement
    funding is available through to 31 January 2005. The rate of interest payable on
    the loan is 2.0% above LIBOR.

The long-term loans are secured by fixed charges over various of the group's   4 Sch 48(4)
properties. Company and group loans wholly repayable within five years include
£1,500,000 (1998 – £1,500,000) secured by a floating charge over the company's
assets.

Good Group P.L.C.

NOTES TO THE ACCOUNTS
at 30 June 1999

20. OBLIGATIONS UNDER LEASES AND HIRE PURCHASE CONTRACTS

Amounts due under finance leases and hire purchase contracts:

Group and company	*1999*	*1998*	
	£000	*£000*	SSAP 21(51), (52)
Amounts payable:			
Within one year	214	410	
In two to five years	1,029	1,243	
	1,243	1,653	
Less: finance charges allocated to future periods	198	238	
	1,045	1,415	

Annual commitments under non-cancellable operating leases are as follows:

	Land and buildings		*Other*		
	1999	*1998*	*1999*	*1998*	4 Sch 50(5)
Group	*£000*	*£000*	*£000*	*£000*	SSAP 21(56)
Operating leases which expire:					
Within one year	–	–	50	30	
In two to five years	–	–	100	75	
In over five years	60	50	40	70	
	60	50	190	175	
Company					
Operating leases which expire:					
Within one year	–	–	20	15	
In two to five years	–	–	90	45	
In over five years	60	50	10	40	
	60	50	120	100	

Good Group P.L.C.

NOTES TO THE ACCOUNTS
at 30 June 1999

21.   PROVISIONS FOR LIABILITIES AND CHARGES

	Post-retirement benefits £000	Provision for maintenance warranties £000	Deferred taxation £000	Group Total £000	Company Deferred taxation £000	
At 1 July 1998	95	60	226	381	141	4 Sch 46
Exchange adjustment	2	–	–	2	–	UITF 6(9)
Arising on the acquisition of subsidiary undertaking	–	400	125	525	–	FRS 12(89)
ACT movement	–	–	164	164	109	
Arising during the year	20	200	(340)	(120)	(180)	
Utilised	–	(200)	–	(200)	–	
At 30 June 1999	117	460	175	752	70	

Maintenance warranties

A provision is recognised for expected warranty claims on products sold during the last FRS 12(90)
2 years. It is expected that most of these costs will be incurred in the next financial
year and all will have been incurred within two years of the balance sheet date.

Deferred taxation

Deferred taxation provided in the accounts and the amounts not provided are as
follows:

Group	Provided 1999 £000	Provided 1998 £000	Not provided 1999 £000	Not provided 1998 £000	
					4 Sch 47
					SSAP 15(37), (40)
Capital allowances in advance of depreciation	175	320	1,270	885	
Other timing differences	–	–	80	46	
	175	320	1,350	931	
Less: advance corporation tax	–	164	–	–	
	175	156	1,350	931	
Taxation on valuation surplus	–	70	530	180	
	175	226	1,880	1,111	

No provision has been made for deferred taxation in respect of earnings which are SSAP 15(44)
retained overseas because the availability of double tax relief will ensure that no tax FRS 2(54)
will be payable on any earnings remitted to the United Kingdom.

The deficit arising on the valuation of investment properties at the end of the year SSAP 15(41)
reverses, in part, previous surpluses. No deferred tax has been provided on the 4 Sch 34
previous revaluation surpluses as there is no present intention to dispose of the
properties. Accordingly there are no deferred tax implications of the deficit recognised
this year.

Good Group P.L.C.

NOTES TO THE ACCOUNTS
at 30 June 1999

21. PROVISIONS FOR LIABILITIES AND CHARGES (continued)

Deferred taxation provided in the accounts and the amounts not provided are as follows:

Company	*Provided*		*Not provided*		
	1999	*1998*	*1999*	*1998*	4 Sch 47
	£000	*£000*	*£000*	*£000*	SSAP 15(37), (40)
Capital allowances in advance of depreciation	70	180	635	645	
Other timing differences	–	–	70	55	
	70	180	705	700	
Less: advance corporation tax	–	109	–	–	
	70	71	705	700	
Taxation on valuation surplus	–	70	365	150	
	70	141	1,070	850	

Good Group P.L.C.

NOTES TO THE ACCOUNTS
at 30 June 1999

22.   DERIVATIVES AND OTHER FINANCIAL INSTRUMENTS

An explanation of the group's objectives, policies and strategies for the role of   FRS 13(23)
derivatives and other financial instruments in creating and changing the risks of the   FRS 13(6)
group in its activities can be found on pages 2014 and 2015. The disclosures below
include amounts relating to short term debtors and creditors.

Interest rate risk profile of financial liabilities

The interest rate profile of the financial liabilities of the group as at 30 June was as   FRS 13(26), (27)
follows:

	Total £000	Fixed rate financial liabilities £000	Floating rate financial liabilities £000	Financial liabilities on which no interest is paid £000
1999				
Sterling	26,110	5,495	7,211	13,404
US dollar	7,843	–	2,281	5,562
Other	295	–	–	295
	34,248	5.495	9,492	19,261
1998				
Sterling	26,411	5,862	8,223	12,326
US dollar	4,737	–	–	4,737
Other	700	–	–	700
	31,848	5,862	8,223	17,763

Good Group P.L.C.

NOTES TO THE ACCOUNTS
at 30 June 1999

22.   **DERIVATIVES AND OTHER FINANCIAL INSTRUMENTS** (continued)

Interest rate risk profile of financial liabilities (continued)

Currency	*Fixed rate financial liabilities*		*Financial liabilities on which no interest is paid* FRS 13(30)
	Weighted average interest rate %	*Weighted average period for which rate is fixed years*	*Weighted average period until maturity years*
1999			
Sterling	7.6	8.8	0.4
US dollar	–	–	0.5
Other	–	–	0.2
	7.6	8.8	0.4
1998			
Sterling	7.6	9.8	0.3
US dollar	–	–	0.5
Other	–	–	0.2
	7.6	9.8	0.3

The amounts shown in the tables above take into account various interest rate swaps used to manage the interest rate profile of financial liabilities.

The floating rate financial liabilities comprise:

- sterling denominated bank loans and overdrafts that bear interest at rates based on the six month LIBOR; and

- US dollar bank loan that, after taking account of interest rate swaps, bears interest at rates based on the US Prime rate.

Interest rate risk profile of non-equity shares   FRS 13(8)

The company has in issue £2,500,000 of convertible cumulative redeemable preference shares with a fixed coupon rate of 7% and an effective rate of 10%. The shares are denominated in sterling and have an average period until conversion or redemption of 3 years.

Good Group P.L.C.

NOTES TO THE ACCOUNTS
at 30 June 1999

22.   DERIVATIVES AND OTHER FINANCIAL INSTRUMENTS (continued)

Interest rate risk profile of financial assets

The interest rate profile of the financial assets of the group as at 30 June was as   FRS 13(32), (33)
follows:

	Total £000	Fixed rate financial assets £000	Floating rate financial assets £000	Financial assets on which no interest is earned £000
1999				
Sterling	21,409	4,000	6,551	10,858
US dollar	8,414	–	2,173	6,241
	29,823	4,000	8,724	17,099
1998				
Sterling	15,575	–	6,684	8,891
US dollar	8,668	–	4,646	4,022
	24,243	–	11,330	12,913

Floating rate financial assets comprise cash deposits on money market deposit at call, 7
day and monthly rates. The interest on the fixed rate financial asset is 4.3% which is
fixed until maturity in 1.5 years. The weighted average period for financial assets on
which no interest is paid is 0.3 years (1998 – 0.3 years).

Good Group P.L.C.

NOTES TO THE ACCOUNTS
at 30 June 1999

22. DERIVATIVES AND OTHER FINANCIAL INSTRUMENTS (continued)

Currency exposures

As explained on page 2015, the group's objectives in managing the currency exposures   FRS 13(34)
arising from its net investment overseas (in other words, its structural currency
exposures) are to maintain a low cost of borrowings and to retain some potential for
currency-related appreciation while partially hedging against currency depreciation.
Gains and losses arising from these structural currency exposures are recognised in the
statement of total recognised gains and losses.

The table below shows the group's currency exposures; in other words, those
transactional (or non-structural) exposures that give rise to the net currency gains and
losses recognised in the profit and loss account. Such exposures comprise the
monetary assets and monetary liabilities of the group that are not denominated in the
operating (or 'functional') currency of the operating unit involved, other than certain
non-sterling borrowings treated as hedges of net investments in overseas operations.
As at 30 June, these currency exposures were as follows:

Functional currency of group operations	*Net foreign currency monetary assets (liabilities)*			
	Sterling £000	*US dollar* £000	*Other* £000	*Total* £000
1999				
Sterling	–	(845)	(295)	(1,140)
US dollar	436	–	–	436
	436	(845)	(295)	(704)
1998				
Sterling	–	(236)	(700)	(936)
US dollar	50	–	–	50
	50	(236)	(700)	(886)

The amounts shown in the table above take into account the effect of forward foreign
currency contracts entered into to manage these currency exposures.

As at 30 June, the group also held open various forward foreign currency contracts
taken out to hedge expected future foreign currency sales.

Good Group P.L.C.

NOTES TO THE ACCOUNTS
at 30 June 1999

22.   DERIVATIVES AND OTHER FINANCIAL INSTRUMENTS (continued)

Maturity of financial liabilities

The maturity profile of the group's financial liabilities at 30 June was as follows: FRS 13(38)

	1999 £000	1998 £000
In one year or less, or on demand	21,685	22,383
In more than one year but not more than two	1,669	1,664
In more than two years, but not more than five	3,010	4,234
In more than five years	7,884	3,567
	34,248	31,848

Borrowing facilities

The group has various borrowing facilities available to it. The undrawn committed   FRS 13(40)
facilities available at 30 June in respect of which all conditions precedent had been
met at that date are as follows:

	1998 £000	1997 £000
Expiring in one year or less	740	1,230
Expiring in more than one year but not more than two years	–	–
Expiring in more than two years	5,000	–
	5,740	1,230

Good Group P.L.C.

NOTES TO THE ACCOUNTS
at 30 June 1999

22.   DERIVATIVES AND OTHER FINANCIAL INSTRUMENTS (continued)

Fair value of financial assets and financial liabilities

Set out below is a comparison by category of book values and fair values of all the   FRS 13(44), (45)
group's financial assets, financial liabilities and non-equity shares as at 30 June:

	Book value 1999 £000	Fair value 1999 £000	Book value 1998 £000	Fair value 1998 £000
Primary financial instruments				
Short term borrowings and current portion of long term borrowings	(2,424)	(2,565)	(4,620)	(4,550)
Short term creditors	(19,261)	(19,185)	(17,763)	(17,834)
Long term borrowings	(12,563)	(12,845)	(9,465)	(9,326)
Non-equity shares	(2,813)	(2,623)	(2,732)	(2,485)
Fixed asset investments (other than joint ventures, associates and own shares)	1,266	1,435	1,276	1,135
Short term debtors	19,833	19,925	11,637	11,492
Cash and short term deposits	8,724	8,724	11,330	11,330
Derivative financial instruments held to manage the interest rate profile				
Interest rate swaps	–	(35)	–	–
Derivative financial instruments held to hedge the currency exposure on expected future sales				
Forward foreign currency contracts	–	(104)	–	(134)

Market values have been used to determine the fair value of interest rate swaps,   FRS 13(51)
forward foreign currency contracts, listed non-equity shares and listed fixed asset
investments. The fair value of all other items have been calculated by discounting the
expected future cash flows at prevailing interest rates.

Good Group P.L.C.

NOTES TO THE ACCOUNTS
at 30 June 1999

22.   DERIVATIVES AND OTHER FINANCIAL INSTRUMENTS (continued)

Hedges   FRS 13(59), (60)

The group's policy is to hedge the following exposures:

■   interest rate risk; and

■   structural and transactional currency exposures and currency exposures on
     future expected sales.

Gains and losses on instruments used for hedging are not recognised until the exposure
that is being hedged is itself recognised. Unrecognised gains and losses and deferred
gains and losses on financial instruments used for hedging are as follows:

	Gains *£000*	*Losses* *£000*	*Total* *£000*
1999			
Gains and losses unrecognised at 30 June 1999	45	(184)	(139)
Gains and losses deferred at 30 June 1999	107	(21)	86
	152	(205)	(53)
Of which:			
Gains and losses expected to be recognised in the profit and loss account in 1999/2000	146	(167)	(21)
Gains and losses included in the profit and loss account that arose in previous years	137	(220)	(83)
1998			
Gains and losses unrecognised at 30 June 1998	108	(242)	(134)
Gains and losses deferred at 30 June 1998	45	(21)	24
	153	(263)	(110)
Of which:			
Gains and losses expected to be recognised in the profit and loss account in 1998/99	125	(232)	(107)
Gains and losses included in the profit and loss account that arose in previous years	43	(123)	(80)

Good Group P.L.C.

NOTES TO THE ACCOUNTS
at 30 June 1999

22.   DERIVATIVES AND OTHER FINANCIAL INSTRUMENTS (continued)

Market price risk

The group's exposure to market price risk comprises interest rate and currency risk exposures. It monitors those risks through a process known as 'sensitivity analysis'. This involves estimating the effect on profit before tax over various periods of a range of possible changes in interest rates and exchange rates.

FRS 13(66), (67), (69), (71)

The model used for this purpose makes no assumptions about the interrelationships between movements in interest rates and exchange rates or about the way in which such movements may impact on the economies involved. As a result, figures derived from the group's sensitivity analysis model should be used in conjunction with other information about the group's risk profile.

The group accepts a degree of interest rate risk and currency risk as long as the effects of various changes in rates, as calculated using its sensitivity analysis model, remain within certain prescribed ranges. The figures disclosed below are within those ranges.

On the basis of the group's analysis, it is estimated that a rise of up to three percentage points in the principal interest rates to which the group is exposed would have a minimal effect on profit before tax for the year ended 30 June 1999. However, it is estimated that a strengthening of sterling by 10 per cent against all the currencies in which the group does business would generate currency losses equal to about 4% of profit before tax for the year ended 30 June 1999.

Good Group P.L.C.

NOTES TO THE ACCOUNTS
at 30 June 1999

23. SHARE CAPITAL

Authorised	1999	1998	
	£000	*£000*	4 Sch 38(1)
Ordinary shares of £1 each	17,500	15,000	
7% convertible cumulative redeemable preference shares of £1 each	2,500	2,500	
	20,000	17,500	

Allotted, called up and fully paid	1999	1998	1999	1998	4 Sch Formats
	thousands	*thousands*	*£000*	*£000*	(Note 12)
					4 Sch 38(1)
Ordinary shares of £1 each	12,575	10,000	12,575	10,000	
7% convertible cumulative redeemable preference shares of £1 each	2,500	2,500	2,500	2,500	
			15,075	12,500	

During the year the authorised share capital was increased by £2,500,000 by the creation of 2,500,000 ordinary shares of £1 each.

On 1 October 1998, 2,500,000 ordinary shares were issued at £3.50 each. In addition, during the year 75,000 ordinary shares were allotted at £2.33 each.   FRS 6(24)

The company has a share option scheme under which options to subscribe for the company's shares have been granted to certain executives. At 1 July 1998 options under this scheme were outstanding over (a) 75,000 ordinary shares at £2.33 each, exercisable between 1 May 1999 and 30 April 2000, and (b) 500,000 ordinary shares at £3.80 each, exercisable between 1 July 2000 and 30 June 2008. During the year options were granted over 250,000 ordinary shares at £3.85 each, exercisable between 1 July 2002 and 30 June 2010. All the options under (a) above were exercised during the year.   4 Sch 40

The 7% convertible cumulative redeemable preference shares, which were issued at par on 1 July 1992, are convertible at the option of the company or the shareholder into ordinary shares on 1 July 2001, 2002 or 2003 on the basis of one ordinary share for every three preference shares. They are redeemable at the option of the shareholder on 1 July 2001, 2002 and 2003 at £1.20 per share. Any preference shares not converted are redeemable at £1.20 per share on 30 June 2008.   4 Sch 38(2), 40   FRS 4(56)

The preference shares carry a dividend of 7% per annum, payable half-yearly in arrears on 31 December and 30 June. The dividend rights are cumulative.

Good Group P.L.C.

NOTES TO THE ACCOUNTS
at 30 June 1999

23.   SHARE CAPITAL (continued)

The preference shares carry no votes at meetings unless the dividend thereon is six months or more in arrears or the company fails to redeem the shares on the redemption date or the business of the meeting includes a resolution for the winding up of the company or reducing its share capital, in which event each holder will be entitled to one vote on a show of hands or one vote per share on a poll.

On a winding up of the company the preference shareholders have a right to receive, in preference to payments to ordinary shareholders, £1 per share plus any accrued dividend.

24.   RESERVES

Group	Share premium account £000	Revaluation reserve £000	Other reserves £000	Profit and loss account £000	
At 1 July 1998	500	5,554	–	23,634	
Exchange differences on retranslation of net assets of subsidiary undertakings	–	–	–	460	SSAP 20(60)
Exchange difference on loan	–	–	–	(179)	SSAP 20(60)
Tax on exchange difference on loan	–	–	–	34	UITF 19(9)
Deficit on revaluation of investment properties	–	(350)	–	–	
Realised revaluation surplus on sale of investment property	–	(235)	–	235	
Deferred tax released on sale of investment property	–	70	–	(70)	
Arising on share issues	100	–	6,250	–	
Goodwill reinstated on disposal of Hose Limited	–	–	–	400	
Share issue costs	(100)	–	–	–	
Retained profit for the year	–	–	–	5,291	
Other appropriations added back	17	–	–	64	
Transfer in respect of issue costs on debentures and preference shares	(23)	–	–	23	
At 30 June 1999	494	5,039	6,250	29,892	

(Marginal references: 4 Sch 46, SSAP 19(15))

The cumulative amount of goodwill written off at 30 June 1999, net of goodwill relating to undertakings disposed of, is £1,320,000 (1998 – £1,720,000).   FRS 10(71) 4A Sch 14

Good Group P.L.C.

NOTES TO THE ACCOUNTS
at 30 June 1999

23.   RESERVES (continued)

Company	*Share premium account £000*	*Revaluation reserve £000*	*Other reserves £000*	*Profit and loss account £000*	
					4 Sch 46 SSAP 19(15)
At 1 July 1998	500	3,084	–	13,232	
Exchange difference on investment in subsidiary undertaking	–	–	–	200	SSAP 20(60)
Exchange difference on loan	–	–	–	(179)	SSAP 20(60)
Tax on exchange difference on loan	–	–	–	34	UITF 19(9)
Deficit on revaluation of investment properties	–	(154)	–	–	
Realised revaluation surplus on sale of investment property	–	(235)	–	235	
Deferred tax released on sale of investment property	–	70	–	(70)	
Arising on share issues	100	–	6,250	–	
Share issue costs	(100)	–	–	–	
Retained profit for the year	–	–	–	3,268	
Transfers in respect of other appropriations	17	–	–	64	
Transfer in respect of debenture and preference share issue costs	(23)	–	–	23	
At 30 June 1999	494	2,765	6,250	16,807	

Good Group P.L.C.

NOTES TO THE ACCOUNTS
at 30 June 1999

25.   NOTES TO THE STATEMENT OF CASH FLOWS

(a)   Reconciliation of operating profit to net cash inflow from operating activities

	1999	*1998*	FRS 1(12)
	£000	*£000*	
Operating profit	10,052	8,895	
Depreciation	3,390	2,610	
Amortisation of development expenditure	125	40	
Amortisation of patents	50	10	
Amortisation of goodwill	75	25	
Provision for maintenance warranties utilised	(200)	(25)	
Deferred government grants released	(1,012)	(530)	
Increase in debtors	(4,181)	(2,745)	
Increase in stocks	(4,976)	(2,585)	
Decrease in creditors	(2,328)	(1,045)	
Increase in provision for maintenance warranties	200	50	
Increase in provision for post-retirement benefits other than pensions	20	19	
Net cash inflow from operating activities	1,215	4,719	

Good Group P.L.C.

NOTES TO THE ACCOUNTS
at 30 June 1999

25.   NOTES TO THE STATEMENT OF CASH FLOWS (continued)

(b)   Analysis of net debt

	At 1 July 1998 £000	*Cash flow £000*	*Exchange differences £000*	*Other non-cash movements £000*	*At 30 June 1999 £000*	
						FRS 1(33), (48)
Cash at bank and in hand	9,291				7,241	
Bank overdrafts	(3,770)				(760)	
Cash	5,521	695	265	–	6,481	
Short term deposits*	2,039	(528)	(28)	–	1,483	
Loans	(8,900)	(4,110)	(145)	(27)	(13,182)	
Finance leases	(1,415)	370	–	–	(1,045)	
	(2,755)	(3,573)	92	(27)	(6,263)	

* Short term deposits are treated as liquid resources in the statement of cash flows   FRS 1(26)
and are included within cash at bank and in hand in the balance sheet.

(c)   Major non-cash transactions   FRS 1(46)

See note 14 for an analysis of the acquisition of Extinguishers Limited and the
disposal of Hose Limited.

(d)   Exceptional items   FRS 1(37)

Cash flows relating to operating exceptional items

Net cash inflow from operating activities in 1998 includes cash outflows of £630,000
in respect of professional expenses incurred in respect of the bid defence.

Cash flows relating to non-operating exceptional items

Capital expenditure and financial investment cash flows include £8,625,000 from the
sale of tangible fixed assets (1998 – £3,965,000) and £125,000 from the sale of fixed
asset investments (1998 – £ nil).

26.   POST BALANCE SHEET EVENT

On 14 August 1999 a short leasehold building with a net book value of £1,695,000 was   SSAP 17(23)-(25)
severely damaged by flooding. It is expected that insurance proceeds will fall short of
the costs of rebuilding and loss of stocks by some £750,000. No provision has been
made in these accounts for this loss.

Good Group P.L.C.

NOTES TO THE ACCOUNTS
at 30 June 1999

27.   CAPITAL COMMITMENTS

Amounts contracted for but not provided in the accounts amounted to £4,500,000 for the group and £1,750,000 for the company (1998 – £4,250,000 and £950,000 respectively).

4 Sch 50(3)

28.   CONTINGENT LIABILITY

The company has guaranteed the bank overdraft of a subsidiary undertaking to the extent of £1,500,000 (1998 – £1,000,000), of which £760,000 was utilised at 30 June 1999 (1998 – £375,000).

4 Sch 50(2), 59A
FRS 12(91)

29.   PENSION COMMITMENTS

The group operates two defined benefit pension schemes, one in the United Kingdom, the Good Group Employee Pension Scheme, and one in the United States, the Good Group Employee Pension Plan. Both schemes are funded by the payment of contributions to separately administered trust funds.

4 Sch 50(4)
SSAP 24(88)

The pension costs are determined with the advice of independent qualified actuaries on the basis of triennial valuations using the projected unit credit method. The results of the most recent valuations, which were conducted as at 30 June 1996, were as follows:

	United Kingdom	United States
Main assumptions:		
Rate of return on investments (% per annum)	10.0	10.0
Rate of salary increases (% per annum)	8.0	7.0
Rate of pension increases (% per annum)	6.0	Nil
Market value of scheme's assets (£000)	4,550	1,450
Level of funding being the actuarial value of assets expressed as a percentage of the benefits accrued to members, after allowing for future salary increases	90%	106%

Further contributions, in addition to the employer's current contribution of 12% of pensionable earnings, are being made in order to eliminate the deficiency in the UK scheme by 2003. The deficit in the UK scheme and the surplus in the US scheme are being recognised as variations from regular cost over 11 years, the average expected remaining service lives of both the UK and the US employees.

Since the date of these valuations, the group has acquired Extinguishers Limited and sold Hose Limited. The group's actuarial advisers have confirmed that these events are unlikely to have had a significant effect on the position of the UK fund. A revised valuation as at 30 June 1999 is currently being undertaken.

Good Group P.L.C.

NOTES TO THE ACCOUNTS
at 30 June 1999

30.   POST-RETIREMENT BENEFITS OTHER THAN PENSIONS

The group also operates a plan in the United States which provides employees with   4 Sch 50(5)
certain post-retirement benefits other than pensions. The liabilities in respect of these   UITF 6(9)
benefits are assessed by qualified independent actuaries, applying the projected unit
credit method. The charge for the year is £20,000 (1998 – £19,000). The main
assumptions used in the calculation were:

Rate of inflation in the cost of providing benefits (% per annum)   9.0

Discount rate for obligations (% per annum)   7.0

31.   DIRECTORS' LOAN

At the Annual General Meeting held on 26 November 1998 approval was given for an   6 Sch Part II
interest-free loan up to a maximum of £10,000 to be made as necessary to J Archer to
enable him to meet expenditure to be incurred in his capacity as sales director at
marketing exhibitions and tours in the United States. During the year £6,500 was
advanced to him for this purpose and at 30 June 1999 £2,432 was outstanding and is
included in debtors.

32.   OTHER DIRECTORS' INTERESTS

During the year, purchases totalling £510,000 (1998 – £490,000), at normal market   6 Sch Part II
prices have been made by group companies from UK Gnome Industries Limited, of   FRS 8(6)
which P A MacBryde's wife is a director and controlling shareholder. £10,000 was
outstanding at 30 June 1999 (1998 – £9,000).

J Corless was interested throughout the year, through his 25% equity interest in Home
Fires Limited, in a contract for the supply of fire extinguishers to that company.
During the year the company supplied extinguishers to Home Fires Limited to a value
of £225,000 at normal market prices. At 30 June 1999, Home Fires Limited owed
£20,000 to the company.

Good Group P.L.C.
NOTES TO THE ACCOUNTS
at 30 June 1999

33.   OTHER RELATED PARTY TRANSACTIONS

During the year the group entered into transactions, in the ordinary course of business, with other related parties. Transactions entered into, and trading balances outstanding at 30 June, are as follows:

Related party	Sales to related party £000	Purchases from related party £000	Amounts owed from related party £000	Amounts owed to related party £000	
					FRS 8(6)
					YB 12.43(r)
International Fires PLC					
1999	6,975	–	600	–	
1998	6,410	–	550	–	
Power Works Limited					
1999	2,800	–	230	–	
1998	2,300	–	145	–	
Showers Limited					
1999	–	580	–	30	
1998	–	430	–	12	

International Fires P.L.C.
International Fire P.L.C. owns 31.48% of the ordinary shares in the company.

Power Works Limited
The group has a 25% interest in Power Works Limited.

Showers Limited
The group has a 50% interest in Showers Limited.

34.   MINORITY INTERESTS

The non-equity minority interests represent a holding of 55% of the preferred shares in Bright Sparks Limited (see note 14). The holders of those shares have no rights against any other group company.   FRS 4(61)

Good Group P.L.C.

FIVE YEAR SUMMARY

Years ended 30 June	1999 £000	1998 £000	1997 £000	1996 £000	1995 £000	
						1964 letter from Stock Exchange
TURNOVER:						
Continuing	170,654	133,372	126,704	97,913	107,696	
Discontinued	42,196	46,628	44,296	31,587	38,104	
	212,850	180,000	171,000	129,500	145,800	
GROUP OPERATING PROFIT:						
Continuing	10,615	9,415	8,431	5,915	7,645	
Discontinued	(563)	(520)	(500)	(475)	(497)	
	10,052	8,895	7,931	5,440	7,148	
Share of operating profit in joint ventures and associates, including goodwill amortisation	2,790	1,262	1,504	798	–	
NON-OPERATING EXCEPTIONAL ITEMS:						
Continuing:						
profit/(loss) on fixed asset disposals	900	(850)	(258)	(328)	26	
loss on sale/ termination of operations	–	–	–	–	(412)	
Discontinued:						
loss on fixed asset disposals	–	–	(387)	(213)	(97)	
loss on sale/ termination of operations	(2,437)	–	–	–	–	
	(1,537)	(850)	(645)	(541)	(483)	
Net interest and income from investments	64	(446)	(262)	(593)	(345)	
PROFIT ON ORDINARY ACTIVITIES BEFORE TAXATION	11,369	8,861	8,528	5,104	6,320	
Tax on profit on ordinary activities	(3,652)	(2,749)	(2,875)	(2,030)	(2,455)	
Minority interests	(311)	(55)	–	–	–	
Dividends and other appropriations	(2,115)	(1,515)	(1,316)	(1,182)	(1,031)	
RETAINED PROFIT	5,291	4,542	4,337	1,892	2,834	
STATISTICS						
Earnings per share - basic	61.9p	60.1p	55.9p	28.4p	36.3p	
Earnings per share - diluted	59.7p	57.6p	54.9p	28.1p	35.2p	
Dividends per ordinary share	15.23p	13.10p	11.10p	9.45p	8.00p	
Dividend cover (times)	4.1	4.6	5.0	3.0	4.5	
Group operating margin (%)	4.7	4.9	4.6	4.2	4.9	

Good Group P.L.C.

FIVE YEAR SUMMARY

1964 letter from Stock Exchange

At 30 June	*1999*	*1998*	*1997*	*1996*	*1995*
	£000	*£000*	*£000*	*£000*	*£000*
EMPLOYMENT OF GROUP CAPITAL					
Fixed assets	42,443	35,945	32,871	29,650	24,500
Net current assets (less provisions and deferred government grants)	27,496	16,053	11,217	12,154	13,724
	69,939	51,998	44,088	41,804	38,224
GROUP CAPITAL EMPLOYED					
Creditors falling due after more than one year	12,563	9,465	5,895	6,780	7,430
Minority interests	626	345	–	–	–
Capital and reserves	56,750	42,188	38,193	35,024	30,794
	69,939	51,998	44,088	41,804	38,224
SHAREHOLDERS' FUNDS					
Equity	53,937	39,456	35,535	32,434	28,266
Non-equity	2,813	2,732	2,658	2,590	2,528
	56,750	42,188	38,193	35,024	30,794
NET DEBT					
Cash at bank and in hand	7,241	9,291	5,233	4,489	3,808
Bank overdraft	(760)	(3,770)	(4,425)	(3,185)	(1,025)
Short term deposits	1,483	2,039	1,132	1,456	1,222
Loans	(13,182)	(8,900)	(4,442)	(4,884)	(5,383)
Finance leases	(1,045)	(1,415)	(1,800)	–	–
	(6,263)	(2,755)	(4,302)	(2,124)	(1,378)
Net gearing (%)†	10.9	6.5	11.3	6.1	4.5

$$\dagger \ \frac{\text{Net borrowings}}{\text{Shareholders' funds + minority interests}}$$

Good Group P.L.C.

NOTICE OF ANNUAL GENERAL MEETING

NOTICE IS HEREBY GIVEN that the Annual General Meeting of the company will   Code C.2.2
be held at Homefire House, Ashdown Square, London EC2 3AS on 15 November
1999 at 11.00 a.m. for the following purposes:

1.   To receive the directors' report and accounts for the year ended 30 June 1999
      and the auditors' report thereon.

2.   To re-elect Mrs L B Green as a director following her appointment as a director
      during the year.

3.   To re-elect J N Smith, who is retiring by rotation, as a director.

4.   To re-elect J Archer, who is retiring by rotation, as a director.

5.   To re-elect P A MacBryde, who is retiring by rotation, as a director.

6.   To reappoint Chartered Accountants & Co. as auditors.

7.   To authorise the directors to fix the remuneration of the auditors.   s385(2)

8.   As special business to consider and, if thought fit, to pass resolutions (A) and   s390A
      (B) of which resolution (A) will be proposed as an ordinary resolution and
      resolution (B) will be proposed as a special resolution:

(A)   To authorise the directors to allot relevant securities in accordance with section
      80 of the Companies Act 1985 subject to the following restrictions and
      provisions:

      (i)   this authority shall be limited to the allotment of relevant securities up to
             an aggregate nominal value of £4,925,000;

      (ii)   this authority shall expire at the conclusion of the next Annual General
             Meeting, save that the company may before such expiry make an offer or
             agreement which would or might require relevant securities to be allotted
             after such expiry and the directors may allot relevant securities in
             pursuance of such offer or agreement as if the authority conferred hereby
             had not expired.

(B)   Subject to the passing of resolution (A) as an ordinary resolution, to empower
      the directors in terms of section 95 of the Companies Act 1985 to allot equity
      securities (as defined by section 94 of the said Act) for cash as if section 89(1)
      of the said Act did not apply to such allotment, provided that such powers shall
      be limited to:

      (i)   the allotment of such equity securities in connection with a rights issue in
             favour of ordinary shareholders where the equity securities allotted are in
             proportion (as nearly as may be) to the respective number of ordinary
             shares held by such ordinary shareholders subject to such exclusions and
             other arrangements as the directors may deem necessary or expedient;
             and

      (ii)   the allotment (otherwise than pursuant to paragraph (i) above) of such
             equity securities up to an aggregate nominal value of £628,750;

      and provided that this power shall expire at the conclusion of the next Annual   YB 9.20
      General Meeting of the company.

By order of the board,

J Harris   Registered office: Homefire House
Secretary   Ashdown Square
14 October 1999   London EC2 3AS   Code C.2.4

Good Group P.L.C.

NOTICE OF ANNUAL GENERAL MEETING

A member entitled to attend and vote at the above meeting is entitled to appoint one or more proxies to attend and vote instead of him. A proxy need not also be a member of the company.

s372(1)

Forms of proxy must be deposited at the company's registrars, Registration Services Limited, 45 Market Street, London W2 7JA, not less than 48 hours before the time fixed for the meeting.

A statement or summary of transactions of directors (and their family interests) in the share capital of the company and copies of their service contracts will be available for inspection at the company's registered office during normal business hours on each business day from the date of this notice up to the close of the Annual General Meeting on 15 November 1999 and will be available for inspection at the place of the Annual General Meeting for at least 15 minutes prior to and during the meeting.

13 Sch 29
YB 16.9, 14.20

Index of extracts from accounts

Index of Statutes and Standards

This index refers to places in the text where individual paragraphs of accounting standards, exposure drafts, the Companies Act 1985 and the Stock Exchange Listing Rules are discussed.

Keep up to date with **GAAP** by joining the

GAAP *Club*

Purchasers of **UK GAAP** can receive FREE updates on major developments in UK financial reporting by joining our free **GAAP** *Club*. As well as receiving our **UK GAAP News** newsletter, members of the **GAAP** *Club* will receive other supporting literature on the likely impact of changes in current accounting practice.

UK GAAP News, the newsletter supplement to **UK GAAP**, brings you up-to-date information on:

- developments in financial reporting
- implementation issues
- new and revised rules

Also provided as part of the **GAAP** *Club* service are regular commentaries on developments of particular importance, both how they will work in practice and their wider implications.

If you would like to receive this free service, please complete the order form below and send to our FREEPOST address or fax it to us at 0181 662 2012.

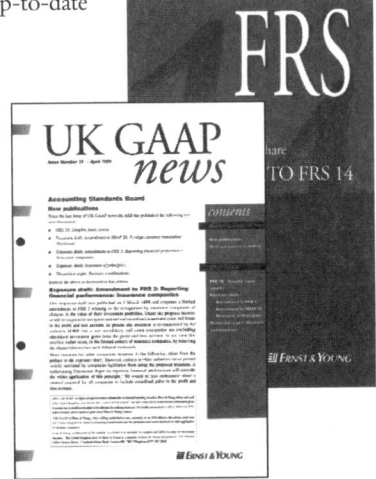

UK GAAP*plus*

UK GAAP*plus* is the CD-ROM edition of **UK GAAP**.
The ideal companion to **UK GAAP** 6th Edition, **UK GAAP***plus* includes the complete text of **UK GAAP** as well as all UK and International Accounting Standards, the Companies Act and 50 other, fully annotated, relevant Acts, and more than 30 full sets of annual reports and accounts and Ernst & Young's model accounts. Fully searchable and interactively linked for the most comprehensive research, the single user price for **UK GAAP***plus* is just £245.

How you can benefit from the updating service offered FREE by **UK GAAP**

☐ Please add me to the circulation list for other materials produced by the Ernst & Young **UK GAAP** team
☐ Please send me order details for **UK GAAP***plus* CD-ROM

Name:...

Position:...

Company/Organisation:..

Address:..

....Postcode:...

Telephone No: ....Fax No: ....Email:...

GAAP *Club* registration
Tracy Eagles
Butterworths Tolley
FREEPOST 6983
London WC2A 1BR

Index